India

Sarina Singh
Joe Bindloss
Teresa Cannon
Joyce Connolly
Peter Davis
Paul Greenway
Anthony Ham
Paul Harding
Alan Murphy
Richard Plunkett

LONELY PLANET PUBLICATIONS
Melbourne • Oakland • London • Paris

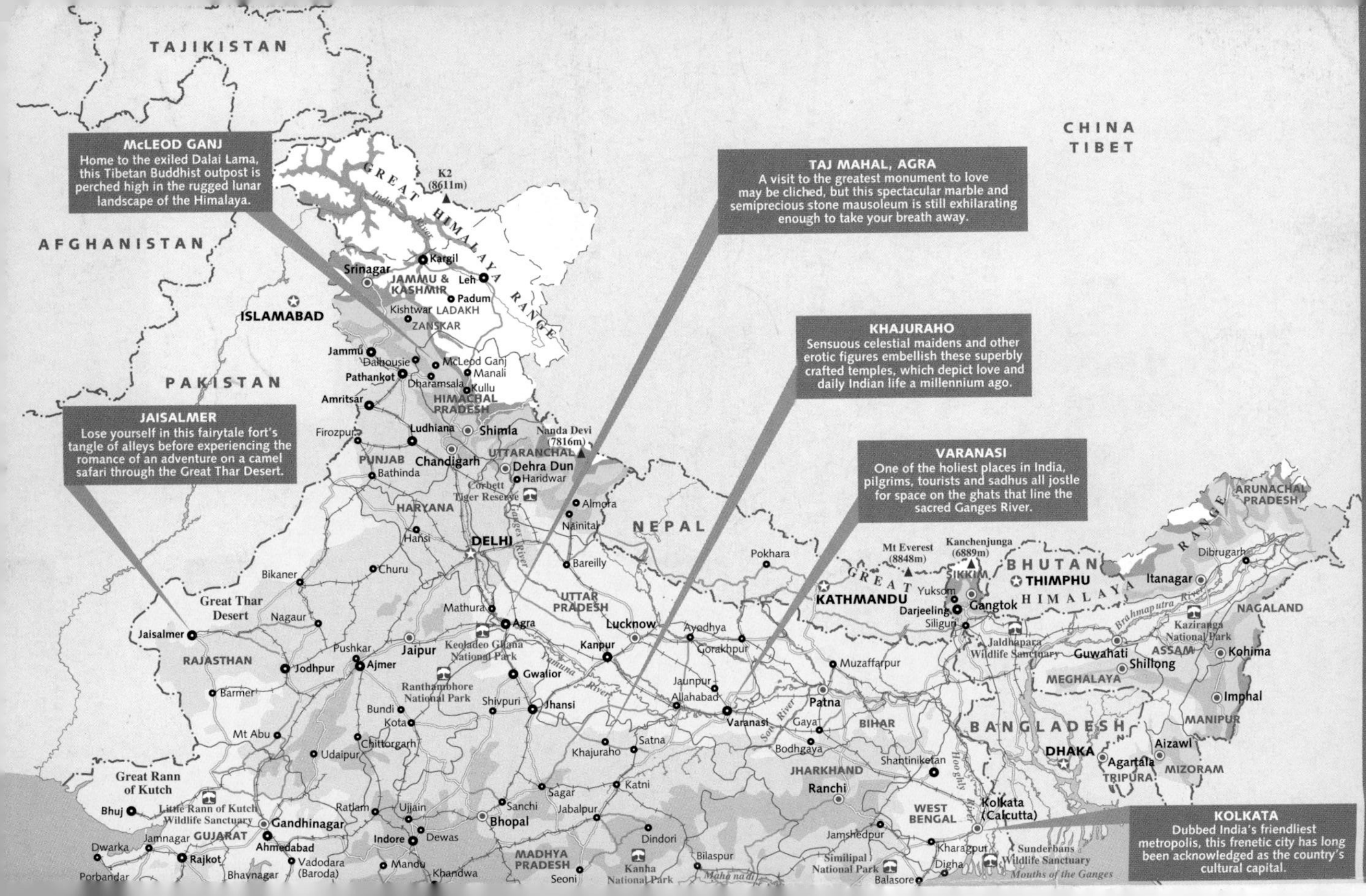
McLEOD GANJ
Home to the exiled Dalai Lama, this Tibetan Buddhist outpost is perched high in the rugged lunar landscape of the Himalaya.
JAISALMER
Lose yourself in this fairytale fort's tangle of alleys before experiencing the romance of an adventure on a camel safari through the Great Thar Desert.
TAJ MAHAL, AGRA
A visit to the greatest monument to love may be cliched, but this spectacular marble and semiprecious stone mausoleum is still exhilarating enough to take your breath away.
KHAJURAHO
Sensuous celestial maidens and other erotic figures embellish these superbly crafted temples, which depict love and daily Indian life a millennium ago.
VARANASI
One of the holiest places in India, pilgrims, tourists and sadhus all jostle for space on the ghats that line the sacred Ganges River.
KOLKATA
Dubbed India's friendliest metropolis, this frenetic city has long been acknowledged as the country's cultural capital.
TAJIKISTAN
AFGHANISTAN
PAKISTAN
ISLAMABAD
CHINA
TIBET
NEPAL
KATHMANDU
BHUTAN
THIMPHU
BANGLADESH
DHAKA
GREAT HIMALAYA RANGE
K2 (8611m)
Mt Everest (8848m)
Kanchenjunga (6889m)
Nanda Devi (7816m)
DELHI
JAMMU & KASHMIR
HIMACHAL PRADESH
PUNJAB
HARYANA
UTTARANCHAL
UTTAR PRADESH
RAJASTHAN
GUJARAT
MADHYA PRADESH
BIHAR
JHARKHAND
WEST BENGAL
SIKKIM
ARUNACHAL PRADESH
ASSAM
NAGALAND
MEGHALAYA
MANIPUR
MIZORAM
TRIPURA
Great Thar Desert
Great Rann of Kutch
Srinagar
Kargil
Leh
Padum
Agra
Jaipur
Jaisalmer
Jodhpur
Lucknow
Kanpur
Varanasi
Khajuraho
Patna
Kolkata (Calcutta)
Darjeeling
Gangtok
Bhopal
Indore
Ahmedabad
Gandhinagar

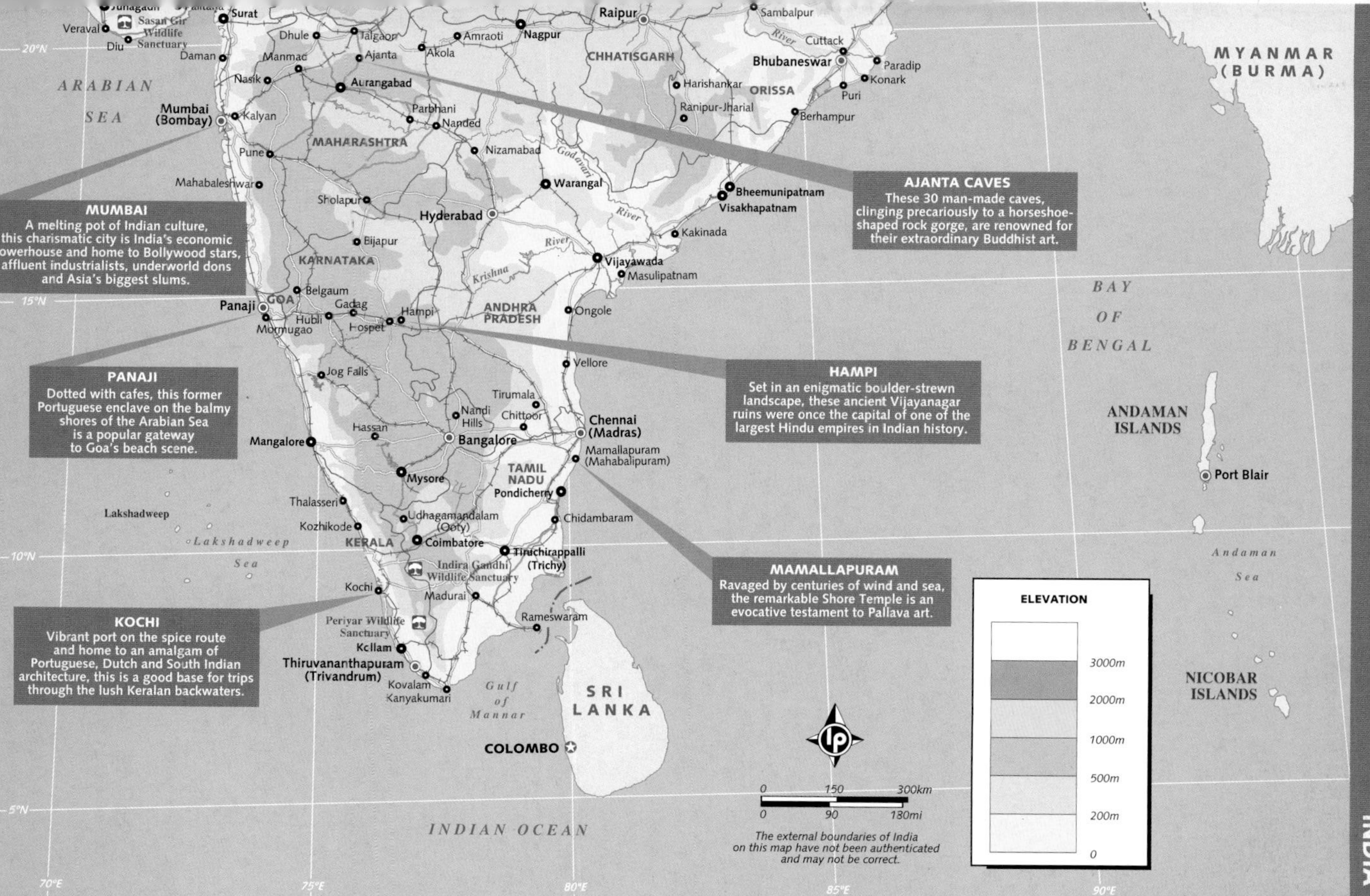
MUMBAI
A melting pot of Indian culture, this charismatic city is India's economic powerhouse and home to Bollywood stars, affluent industrialists, underworld dons and Asia's biggest slums.
PANAJI
Dotted with cafes, this former Portuguese enclave on the balmy shores of the Arabian Sea is a popular gateway to Goa's beach scene.
KOCHI
Vibrant port on the spice route and home to an amalgam of Portuguese, Dutch and South Indian architecture, this is a good base for trips through the lush Keralan backwaters.
AJANTA CAVES
These 30 man-made caves, clinging precariously to a horseshoe-shaped rock gorge, are renowned for their extraordinary Buddhist art.
HAMPI
Set in an enigmatic boulder-strewn landscape, these ancient Vijayanagar ruins were once the capital of one of the largest Hindu empires in Indian history.
MAMALLAPURAM
Ravaged by centuries of wind and sea, the remarkable Shore Temple is an evocative testament to Pallava art.
ELEVATION
3000m
2000m
1000m
500m
200m
0
0 150 300km
0 90 180mi
The external boundaries of India on this map have not been authenticated and may not be correct.
ARABIAN SEA
BAY OF BENGAL
INDIAN OCEAN
MYANMAR (BURMA)
SRI LANKA
ANDAMAN ISLANDS
NICOBAR ISLANDS

India
9th edition – August 2001
First published – October 1981

6-monthly upgrades of this title are available free from
www.lonelyplanet.com/upgrades

Published by
Lonely Planet Publications Pty Ltd ABN 36 005 607 983
90 Maribyrnong St, Footscray, Victoria 3011, Australia

Lonely Planet Offices
Australia Locked Bag 1, Footscray, Victoria 3011
USA 150 Linden St, Oakland, CA 94607
UK 10a Spring Place, London NW5 3BH
France 1 rue du Dahomey, 75011 Paris

Photographs
Many of the images in this guide are available for licensing from Lonely Planet Images.
email: lpi@lonelyplanet.com.au

Front Cover Photograph
Crowd at a religious festival, Rajasthan (Greg Elms)

India at a Glance Title Page Photograph
Procession on main bathing day, Mauni Amavasya (New Moon for the Saints) at the Maha Kumbh Mela (Richard I'Anson)

Arts & Crafts Title Page Photograph
Embroidery, an art practised throughout India (Pramod Mistry)

ISBN 1 86450 246 0

Printed by The Bookmaker International Ltd
Printed in China

Contents – Text

HIMACHAL PRADESH 229

JAMMU & KASHMIR 286

LADAKH & ZANSKAR 290

UTTAR PRADESH & UTTARANCHAL 323

BIHAR & JHARKHAND 410

Contents – Maps

CHENNAI

TAMIL NADU

ANDAMAN & NICOBAR ISLANDS

MAP LEGEND

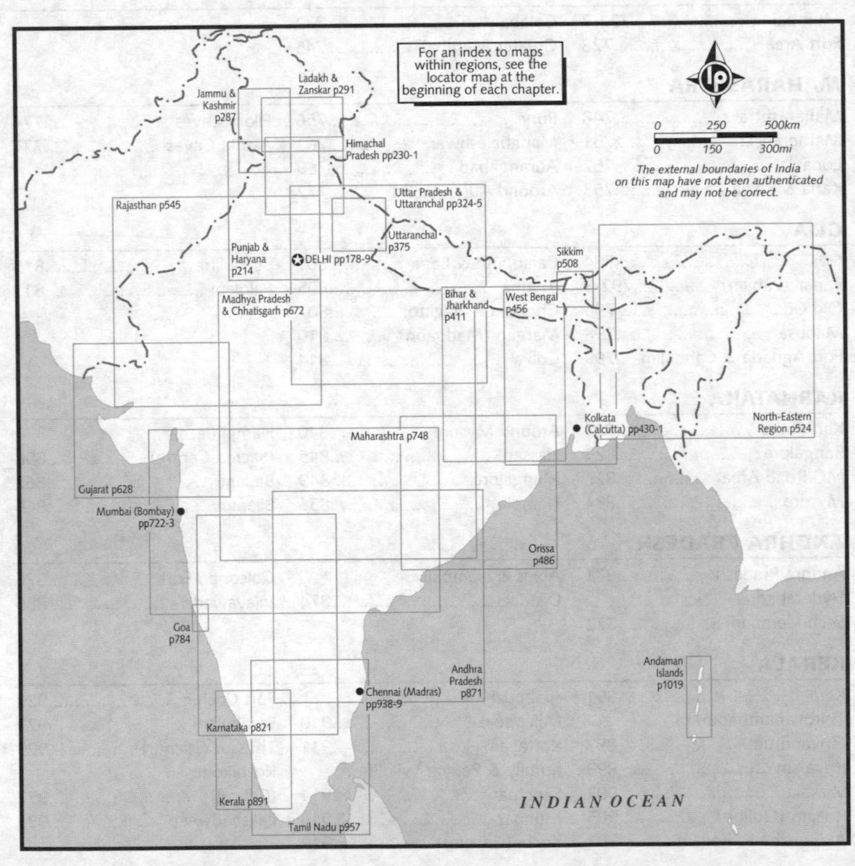

The Authors

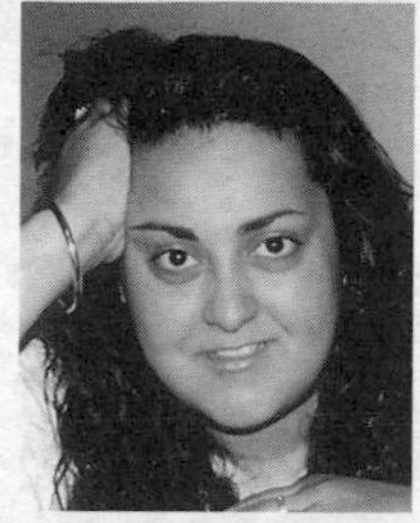

Sarina Singh

Sarina was the coordinating author of this book. A passionate traveller ever since she can remember, Sarina bought a one-way ticket to Delhi after finishing a business degree in Melbourne. In India she completed a corporate traineeship with the Sheraton but later ditched hotels for newspapers, working as a freelance journalist and foreign correspondent. After four years in the subcontinent she returned to Australia, pursued postgraduate journalism qualifications and wrote two television documentary scripts. Other Lonely Planet books Sarina has worked on include *Aboriginal Australia & the Torres Strait Islands, North India, Mauritius, Réunion & Seychelles, Africa on a shoestring, Sacred India*, two editions of *Rajasthan* and the *Out to Eat* restaurant guides to Melbourne and Sydney. She is also the author of *Polo in India* and has contributed to various international publications, including the *Sunday Times* and *National Geographic Traveler*.

Joe Bindloss

Joe was born in Cyprus, grew up in England and has since lived and worked in several other countries. He currently calls London home. Joe gravitated towards journalism after a degree in biology eliminated science from his choice of future careers; he has also worked as a mural painter, book-maker and sculptor. Joe first developed wanderlust on family trips through the Mediterranean in an old VW Kombi. He has also worked on LP guides to *Australia*, the *Philippines* and the *Indian Ocean* islands.

Teresa Cannon & Peter Davis

After too many years in a suffocating bureaucracy, Teresa escaped to the rarefied environment of the Himalaya. Her love of travel led her back to Asia several times where she gathered material and co-authored a book on Asian elephants (published in 1995). This is her fifth project for Lonely Planet.

Following a brief stint as a cadet photographer on the Melbourne *Herald*, Peter studied economics and politics followed by graduate studies in media. He then drifted into freelance journalism and photography. He is co-author and photographer of the book *Aliya – Stories of the Elephants of Sri Lanka*. Peter has contributed to Lonely Planet's *South India*, *Kerala* and *Sacred India*. He lectures in professional writing at Deakin University and in photojournalism at Melbourne's Photography Studies College.

Joyce Connolly

Born in Scotland, Joyce has been on the road since an early age, including six years in Germany and the Netherlands where she developed a deep appreciation of beer. Fuelled by the travel bug, she studied to become a professional tourist but instead stumbled into publishing. In 1995 she set off for Australia in pursuit of Jason Donovan, who obligingly moved house to become her neighbour. Having satisfied that urge she turned her attention to Lonely Planet; she updated part of the *Victoria* guide and has subsequently researched *Zimbabwe*, *Morocco* and *India*. Joyce has recently traded her *salwar kameez* for a bikini and was last spotted chasing cyclones in Western Australia.

Paul Greenway

Paul caught his first tropical disease in 1985 and has had the travel bug ever since. Gratefully plucked from the blandness and security of the Australian Public Service, he is now a full-time traveller and writer. Paul has contributed to several Lonely Planet guides, including *South India* and *Indonesia*, and has written guides to countries such as *Mongolia*, *Iran* and *Bali & Lombok*. During the rare times he is not travelling (or writing, reading or dreaming about it), Paul writes and records tuneless ditties, eats and breathes Australian Rules Football, and does anything else necessary to avoid settling down.

Anthony Ham

Anthony worked as a refugee lawyer for three years, during which time the people of the world visited him in his office. After tiring of daily battles with a mean-spirited Australian government, he set out to see the world and restore his faith in humanity. He has been travelling ever since, throughout Asia and Africa, all the while discovering unimagined uses for his masters degree in Middle Eastern politics. He is now based in Melbourne and works as a freelance writer and photographer. During his travels for Lonely Planet, Anthony has eaten rat in West Africa, been arrested in Iran and found himself constantly overwhelmed by the many kindnesses from anything-but-ordinary people wherever he's travelled.

Paul Harding

Born in Melbourne, Paul grew up mostly in country Victoria and started working life as a reporter on a local newspaper. He spent three years backpacking in Europe and Asia, stopping briefly to work as editor of a London travel magazine – among assorted low-paying jobs – before landing at Lonely Planet's Melbourne office as an editor in 1996. Reading guidebook manuscripts only made his itchy feet worse, so he swapped his red pen for a blue one and now works as a full-time writer and researcher. This was Paul's third trip to India for Lonely Planet. He has also worked on Lonely Planet's *Istanbul to Kathmandu*, *South-East Asia*, *South India*, *Australia*, *New South Wales* and *Read this First: Europe*.

Alan Murphy

Born in Melbourne, Alan took off for a six-month stint around Europe and the Middle East in 1992. Four years later, after dipping his toes into the world of marketing and banking in between travel stints, he was back on home soil. Convinced of the need to avoid the 'corporate ladder' and peak hour traffic, he returned to studies in 1997. After completing a journalism course at Murdoch University he offered his services to Lonely Planet. Alan currently lives in Melbourne. He enjoys working strange hours and sniffing out new watering holes, and hopes one day to write a good pub guide. Alan has previously worked on Lonely Planet's *Southern Africa* and *Africa* titles.

Richard Plunkett

Richard grew up near Avenel, central Victoria. Before joining Lonely Planet he worked on the *Age* newspaper in Melbourne, played a small part in getting the Australian *Big Issue* on its feet and worked on the family farm during bouts of unemployment. He first visited India solo as an 18-year-old and has worked on various Lonely Planet guidebooks to the subcontinent, as well as guides to *Central Asia* and *Turkey*.

FROM THE AUTHORS

Sarina Singh

In India I'm very grateful to the following people for so generously offering me their time and insights: to the remarkably knowledgeable Bhaichand Patel for his perpetual assistance; to Mr and Mrs Neeraj Padhi for their help and wonderful company in Kolkata; to Arati Oberoi for her constant updates; to Tilottama Das (West Bengal Tourism Centre, Kolkata) and Satarupa Das and Ashok Banerjie (Government of India tourist office, Kolkata). For precious tips, thanks to Abisheik Khan, Priya Sharma, Rahul Bhatia, Ashok Roy, Shalini and Anand Krishnan and Arvind Narayan. Special thanks to Patrick Moffat for casting an expert eye over the motorbike information and to Amit, Swati and Parth Jhaveri in Mumbai for their ongoing support and friendship.

To all the authors who worked on this edition, thank you for your tremendous enthusiasm and hard work. Many thanks also to the South and North India coordinating authors – Richard Plunkett and Mark Honan. At Lonely Planet thanks to everyone who worked on this book, in particular to Brigitte Ellemor for efforts well beyond the call of duty; to Leonie Mugavin for taking time out to help with the Getting There & Away chapter; and to Geoff Stringer, Adriana Mammarella, Julia Taylor, Shahara Ahmed and Sharan Kaur. Thanks also to Gabrielle Knight (Lonely Planet USA) for casting light on visa information. Last, thanks to Hilary Ericksen for being such an encouraging senior editor, especially during those many solitary weeks back home tapping away at the keyboard.

Joe Bindloss

Thanks firstly to Rajinder Budhraja in Delhi for making the impossible possible. Thanks also to Ramesh Wadhwa in Agra for keeping me abreast of the Taj fee crisis. In Uttaranchal, thanks to the helpful staff of the GMVN and KMVN. This project could not have been completed without the help of the Tibetan Government in Exile in Dharamsala. And thanks to all the travellers who wrote in with advice, warnings and tips.

Teresa Cannon & Peter Davis

We wish to thank Mr Shankaran for his ever generous assistance. Ms Nalini Chettur continued her skilful detection of yet more useful tomes. Members of the Railway Ticket Collectors' Union gave us a delightful and unexpected insider's guide to journeying on, and off, the tracks. Mr JR Moses provided insight into environmental issues, while Professor CT Indra was generous with her knowledge on matters literary. We also extend thanks to Mrs Eugenie Pinto and Mrs Mridula Syed and all the staff of the Australian Studies Centre, Madras University, for their generosity. Thanks to our fellow travellers, especially Bette and Beck, who shared their ideas and experiences. And, finally, thanks to our in-house and out-house colleagues who, like the globe-trotting, glove-puppeted guru, continue to remind us of life's absurdities.

Joyce Connolly

Thanks to my mum and Reem Mina. Cheers to Rujendra Kumar, and also to Martin Hughes, Louari Ramouch and Isla James for a few unravelling sessions. Helpful people in Ladakh include: Tsering Dolang at LEDeG; Rebecca Norman, Aachan Dolma and Roxanna at Secmol; Dawa at Oriental Guest House; and Unchuck, the best driver in Ladakh. In Punjab, Prince Manyot Bubber made Amritsar fun, Manoj Sharma showed me Jalandhar and RC Yadar from the Punjab Department of Tourism helped me get there. Finally, I'd like to dedicate my contribution to Molly Blackford-Jennings; I'm doing it for you from now on.

Paul Greenway

Special plaudits to: Pema Gyaltsen Bhutia of the Khangchendzonga Conservation Committee in Yuksom; Bubu from Heritage Tours in Puri; and Amy Smith for being my drinking and travelling companion in Sikkim. At Lonely Planet, thanks to Geoff Stringer for sending me to all these weird and wonderful places; and apologies to all the long-suffering and unsung editors, cartographers and designers.

Anthony Ham

Special thanks must go to Ron, Jan, Lisa, Greg, Alex, Thomas, Tanya, Samantha and Damien for accepting my absences. Thanks also to Alan Paruit at STA Travel. Thanks in particular to Pankaj Shah of the KMVS in Bhuj; the staff at the SEWA Reception Centre in Ahmedabad; Mr Sorathia in Junagadh; Vinod Bhojak in Bikaner; Mukesh Mehta in Bundi; JD Khan at the Tourist Reception Centre in Ranthambore; Digvijay Singh Patan and his family; and Viro in Bharatpur. Special mention must be made of Shabir Ali Lalah – watch out for him at the Jaipur railway station (rickshaw registration RN 1406). Bhuwneshwari and Vishwa Vijay Singh taught me anew the magic of Udaipur and the hospitality of the Rajputs. Also in Udaipur, thank you to Meenu for her dignity and selflessness. Thank you to the travellers: Hamish and Anna, Matt and Bel, Laurent, Alpa and especially Carinae.

Paul Harding

Thanks to everyone and anyone who helped during this research trip. In Mumbai, big thanks to David Collins and Kamlesh for sharing their knowledge, and to the staff at Bentley's Hotel. In Maharashtra, thank you, as always, to Mr Yadav at the Government of India tourist office in Aurangabad (I'll be back for the *paan*); and Mr Lord in Matheran, and the helpful staff at Nasik's town council. In Goa, thanks to the folks at Afonso Guest House and to everyone at Goacom – a fantastic resource. Also thanks to Sarina for encouragement, and the editing and design team at Lonely Planet Melbourne.

Richard Plunkett

A special thanks to Santosh Kumar for risking a drive during a *hartal*. In Bangalore, thanks to Alice Malpass, Ravi, Tony Scully and Karin. Thanks to Richard Tricot, Emmanuelle Boue, Nathan Barley and friends in Varkala. Thanks also to Ganesh Aiyappa and Ravi Ananth Giri for their help in Kodagu, and to Lidy van den Berg and Hanneke Sletering for a free ride from Madikeri to Bylakuppe. Raoul Butler has my eternal admiration for driving a scooter from Chennai to Karnataka via Kerala. Raghu Kumar and Mohammed Hossein may have failed to sell me a necklace, but were great company in Sravanabelgola. And thank you to Sarina Singh.

This Book

When the first edition of this book emerged in 1981 it was the biggest, most complicated and most expensive project we'd tackled at Lonely Planet. It began with an exploratory trip to South India by Tony and Maureen Wheeler – they returned the following year with Geoff Crowther and Prakash Raj. Following editions included research by Teresa Cannon, Geert Cole, David Collins, Michelle Coxall, Peter Davis, Hugh Finlay, Rob Flynn, Paul Harding, Mark Honan, Leanne Logan, Bradley Mayhew, Christine Niven, Richard Plunkett, Phillipa Saxton, Sarina Singh, Bryn Thomas and Dani Valent.

For this ninth edition of *India*, Sarina Singh coordinated the project. She also updated the introductory chapters, Kolkata (Calcutta) and most of West Bengal. Joe Bindloss updated Himachal Pradesh, Uttaranchal and the Agra region of Uttar Pradesh. Teresa Cannon and Peter Davis updated Andhra Pradesh, Chennai (Madras), Tamil Nadu and the Andaman & Nicobar Islands. Joyce Connolly updated Delhi, Haryana, Punjab and Jammu & Kashmir. Paul Greenway updated Orissa, North-Eastern Region, Sikkim, and Darjeeling and Kalimpong in West Bengal. Anthony Ham updated Rajasthan and Gujarat. Paul Harding updated Mumbai (Bombay), Maharashtra and Goa. Alan Murphy updated central Uttar Pradesh and the Varanasi region, Bihar, Jharkhand and Madhya Pradesh. Richard Plunkett updated Karnataka and Kerala, and supplied Sarina with information for the Getting Around chapter.

Bhaichand Patel wrote the boxed text 'Behind the Scenes of Indian Cinema', Martin Hughes wrote the 'Indian Cuisine' special section and Michael Sklovsky wrote the 'Arts & Crafts' special section.

From the Publisher

Brigitte Ellemor was the coordinating editor of this edition, while Shahara Ahmed and Anna Judd coordinated the mapping and design. Julia Taylor, Justin Flynn, Bethune Carmichael, John Hinman, Thalia Kalkipsakis, Evan Jones, Bruce Evans, Kim Hutchins, Hilary Rogers, Susannah Farfor, Sam Carew, Melanie Dunkel and Jenny Mullaly all helped with editing and proofreading. Julia Taylor steered the book through proofing when Brigitte moved across to the Eastern Europe unit, and Bethune Carmichael joined Julia to take the book through layout. Isabelle Young and Shelley Muir assisted with the index. Quentin Frayne compiled the language chapter with help from Vivek Wagle.

Assisting Shahara and Anna in mapping were Sarah Sloane, Jody Whiteoak, Amanda Sierp, Birgit Jordan, Hunor Csutoros, Pablo Gastar, Heath Comrie, Csanad Csutoros, Huw Fowles and Rodney Zandbergs. Maree Styles assisted during layout, while Mark Germanchis gave invaluable Quark support. The climate chart was compiled by Hunor Csutoros. Matt King liaised with the book's illustrators while Annie Horner from LPI coordinated the photographic images. The cover was designed by Margaret Jung.

Thanks also to Bruce Evans for supplying specialist Buddhist advice and Simon Tillema for making urgent deliveries. Thanks to Hilary Ericksen, senior editor, and Adriana Mammarella, senior designer for expertly overseeing the project.

THANKS
Many thanks to the travellers who used the last edition and wrote to us with helpful hints, advice and interesting anecdotes. Your names appear in the back of this book.

Foreword

ABOUT LONELY PLANET GUIDEBOOKS

The story begins with a classic travel adventure: Tony and Maureen Wheeler's 1972 journey across Europe and Asia to Australia. Useful information about the overland trail did not exist at that time, so Tony and Maureen published the first Lonely Planet guidebook to meet a growing need.

From a kitchen table, then from a tiny office in Melbourne (Australia), Lonely Planet has become the largest independent travel publisher in the world, an international company with offices in Melbourne, Oakland (USA), London (UK) and Paris (France).

Today Lonely Planet guidebooks cover the globe. There is an ever-growing list of books and there's information in a variety of forms and media. Some things haven't changed. The main aim is still to help make it possible for adventurous travellers to get out there – to explore and better understand the world.

At Lonely Planet we believe travellers can make a positive contribution to the countries they visit – if they respect their host communities and spend their money wisely. Since 1986 a percentage of the income from each book has been donated to aid projects and human rights campaigns.

Updates Lonely Planet thoroughly updates each guidebook as often as possible. This usually means there are around two years between editions, although for more unusual or more stable destinations the gap can be longer. Check the imprint page (following the colour map at the beginning of the book) for publication dates.

Between editions up-to-date information is available in two free newsletters – the paper *Planet Talk* and email *Comet* (to subscribe, contact any Lonely Planet office) – and on our Web site at www.lonelyplanet.com. The *Upgrades* section of the Web site covers a number of important and volatile destinations and is regularly updated by Lonely Planet authors. *Scoop* covers news and current affairs relevant to travellers. And, lastly, the *Thorn Tree* bulletin board and *Postcards* section of the site carry unverified, but fascinating, reports from travellers.

Correspondence The process of creating new editions begins with the letters, postcards and emails received from travellers. This correspondence often includes suggestions, criticisms and comments about the current editions. Interesting excerpts are immediately passed on via newsletters and the Web site, and everything goes to our authors to be verified when they're researching on the road. We're keen to get more feedback from organisations or individuals who represent communities visited by travellers.

Lonely Planet gathers information for everyone who's curious about the planet – and especially for those who explore it first-hand. Through guidebooks, phrasebooks, activity guides, maps, literature, newsletters, image library, TV series and Web site we act as an information exchange for a worldwide community of travellers.

Research Authors aim to gather sufficient practical information to enable travellers to make informed choices and to make the mechanics of a journey run smoothly. They also research historical and cultural background to help enrich the travel experience and allow travellers to understand and respond appropriately to cultural and environmental issues.

Authors don't stay in every hotel because that would mean spending a couple of months in each medium-sized city and, no, they don't eat at every restaurant because that would mean stretching belts beyond capacity. They do visit hotels and restaurants to check standards and prices, but feedback based on readers' direct experiences can be very helpful.

Many of our authors work undercover, others aren't so secretive. None of them accept freebies in exchange for positive write-ups. And none of our guidebooks contain any advertising.

Production Authors submit their raw manuscripts and maps to offices in Australia, USA, UK or France. Editors and cartographers – all experienced travellers themselves – then begin the process of assembling the pieces. When the book finally hits the shops, some things are already out of date, we start getting feedback from readers and the process begins again…

WARNING & REQUEST

Things change – prices go up, schedules change, good places go bad and bad places go bankrupt – nothing stays the same. So, if you find things better or worse, recently opened or long since closed, please tell us and help make the next edition even more accurate and useful. We genuinely value all the feedback we receive. Julie Young coordinates a well-travelled team that reads and acknowledges every letter, postcard and email and ensures that every morsel of information finds its way to the appropriate authors, editors and cartographers for verification.

Everyone who writes to us will find their name in the next edition of the appropriate guidebook. They will also receive the latest issue of *Planet Talk*, our quarterly printed newsletter, or *Comet*, our monthly email newsletter. Subscriptions to both newsletters are free. The very best contributions will be rewarded with a free guidebook.

Excerpts from your correspondence may appear in new editions of Lonely Planet guidebooks, the Lonely Planet Web site, *Planet Talk* or *Comet*, so please let us know if you *don't* want your letter published or your name acknowledged.

Send all correspondence to the Lonely Planet office closest to you:

Australia: Locked Bag 1, Footscray, Victoria 3011
USA: 150 Linden St, Oakland, CA 94607
UK: 10A Spring Place, London NW5 3BH
France: 1 rue du Dahomey, 75011 Paris

Or email us at: talk2us@lonelyplanet.com.au

For news, views and updates see our Web site: www.lonelyplanet.com

HOW TO USE A LONELY PLANET GUIDEBOOK

The best way to use a Lonely Planet guidebook is any way you choose. At Lonely Planet we believe the most memorable travel experiences are often those that are unexpected, and the finest discoveries are those you make yourself. Guidebooks are not intended to be used as if they provide a detailed set of infallible instructions!

Contents All Lonely Planet guidebooks follow roughly the same format. The Facts about the Destination chapters or sections give background information ranging from history to weather. Facts for the Visitor gives practical information on issues like visas and health. Getting There & Away gives a brief starting point for researching travel to and from the destination. Getting Around gives an overview of the transport options when you arrive.

The peculiar demands of each destination determine how subsequent chapters are broken up, but some things remain constant. We always start with background, then proceed to sights, places to stay, places to eat, entertainment, getting there and away, and getting around information – in that order.

Heading Hierarchy Lonely Planet headings are used in a strict hierarchical structure that can be visualised as a set of Russian dolls. Each heading (and its following text) is encompassed by any preceding heading that is higher on the hierarchical ladder.

Entry Points We do not assume guidebooks will be read from beginning to end, but that people will dip into them. The traditional entry points are the list of contents and the index. In addition, however, some books have a complete list of maps and an index map illustrating map coverage.

There may also be a colour map that shows highlights. These highlights are dealt with in greater detail in the Facts for the Visitor chapter, along with planning questions and suggested itineraries. Each chapter covering a geographical region usually begins with a locator map and another list of highlights. Once you find something of interest in a list of highlights, turn to the index.

Maps Maps play a crucial role in Lonely Planet guidebooks and include a huge amount of information. A legend is printed on the back page. We seek to have complete consistency between maps and text, and to have every important place in the text captured on a map. Map key numbers usually start in the top left corner.

Although inclusion in a guidebook usually implies a recommendation we cannot list every good place. Exclusion does not necessarily imply criticism. In fact there are a number of reasons why we might exclude a place – sometimes it is simply inappropriate to encourage an influx of travellers.

Introduction

With one foot swathed in ancient traditions and the other striding into the entrepreneurial e-age, few countries on earth embrace diversity as passionately as India.

With a population of one billion people and growing, India is as vast as it is crowded and as sublime as it is squalid. The plains are as flat and featureless as the Himalaya are towering and spectacular, the religious texts as perplexing as their underlying message is simple, and the people as easy-going as they are tenacious.

Perhaps the one thing that encapsulates India is that it is a place to expect the unexpected. Indeed that's what often makes travelling in the subcontinent so frustratingly draining, yet also so inimitably inspirational. Love it or hate it, India gets into your blood and, while more than a few travellers are only too happy to get on their flight home, most will later find themselves hankering to get back.

Undoubtedly India can be hard going – the poverty is confronting, Indian bureaucracy would test the patience of a saint, bus trips on pothole-riddled roads can zap your energy in a flash, and even the most experienced travellers find their tempers frayed at some point. Yet it's all worth it (though often only realised in hindsight).

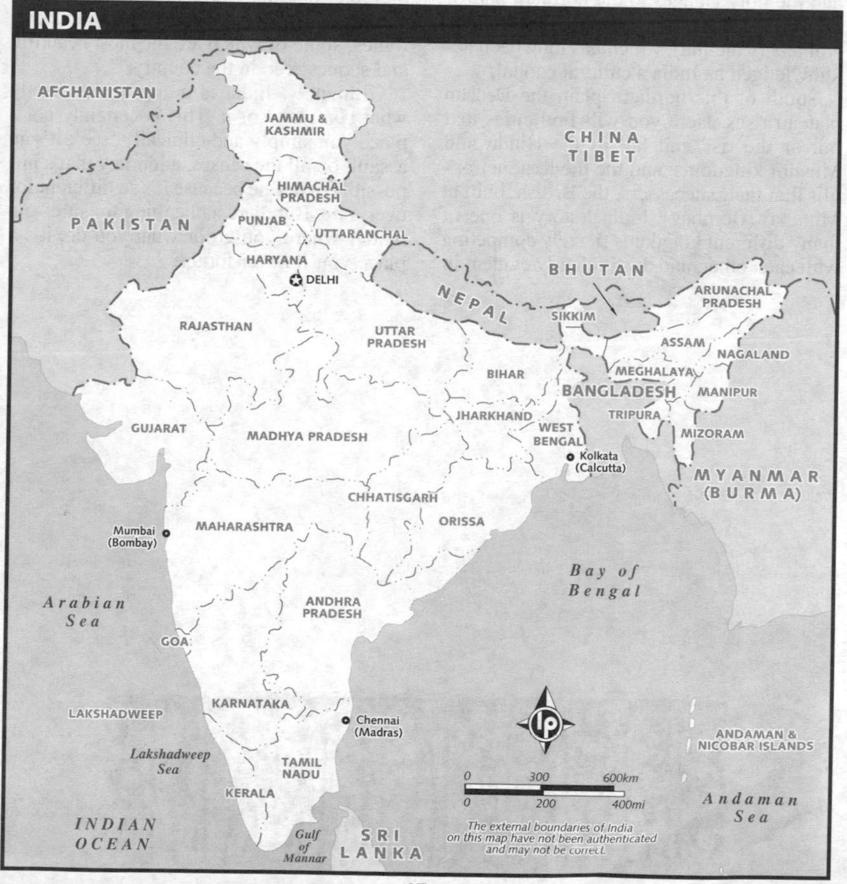

India, it is often said, is not a country but a continent. From north to south and east to west, the people are different, the languages are different, the customs are different, the country is different.

In a nutshell, India's landmass is roughly an upside-down triangle with the top formed by the mighty Himalayan mountain chain. Here you will find the intriguing Tibetan-influenced region of Ladakh and the awesome mountainous areas of Himachal Pradesh, Garhwal and the Darjeeling and Sikkim regions. South of this is the flat Ganges plain, crossing east from the colourful and comparatively affluent Punjab in the north-west, past the capital city Delhi and buzzing tourist attractions such as Agra (with the Taj Mahal), Khajuraho, Varanasi and the holy Ganges to the northern part of the Bay of Bengal, where you find frenetic Kolkata (Calcutta), which has long been acknowledged as India's cultural capital.

South of this northern plain the Deccan plateau rises. Here you will find cities that mirror the rise and fall of the Hindu and Muslim kingdoms, and the modern metropolis that their successors, the British, built at Mumbai (Bombay). India's story is one of many different kingdoms fiercely competing with each other, and this is clearly evident in places such as Bijapur, Mandu, Golconda and other central Indian centres. Finally, there is the steamy south, India's Dravidian heartland, which is just as extraordinarily diverse in terms of its landscapes, people, arts, traditions and culture as is North India.

India's glorious diversity can make it a veritable quagmire when planning itineraries. If you want to see places of worship, there is an astonishing array of sacred sites, from immaculately kept Jain temples to weathered Buddhist stupas. If it's history you're after, India is bursting with it; the battle-scarred forts, breathtaking palaces, abandoned cities, ancient ruins and monuments all have their tales to tell. If you want some time out to simply splash around, there are beaches to satiate the most avid sun worshipper. Lovers of the great outdoors have no dearth of scenic walks; these include the Himalayan trekking routes, some of which are the most beautiful and sequestered in the country.

Ultimately, India is going to be exactly what *you* make of it. This is certainly not a place you simply and clinically 'see'; it's an assault on all the senses, a journey that's impossible to define because it's so different for everyone. But there's one thing for sure – no matter where you go or what you do, it's a place you'll never forget.

Facts about India

For many thousands of years, India's social and religious structures have withstood invasions, famines, religious persecutions, political upheavals and many other cataclysms. Few other countries could claim to have a national identity with such a long and vibrant history. To describe India as a land of incredible contrasts is to state the obvious. Although there are many countries which would qualify for such a description in terms of their different ethnic groups, languages, religions, geography and traditions, few can match the vast scale and diversity found in India.

But India is just as dynamic as it is enduring and change is inevitably taking place as modern technology is woven into the fabric of society. Yet essentially rural India remains much the same as it has been for thousands of years. Even in the modern cities such as Delhi, Kolkata (Calcutta), Mumbai (Bombay) and Bangalore, what appears to be a complete swing of attitude and lifestyle is largely surface gloss. Underneath, the age-old verities, loyalties and obligations still flourish.

Possibly no other country has its religions so intertwined with every aspect of life. Coming to understand it can be a long process, particularly for those educated in the Western liberal tradition with its basis in cut and dried logic. For those people, 'Indian logic' can often seem bizarre, convoluted and even exasperating. Yet it encompasses a unique cosmology that is holistic and coherent as well as fascinating.

India was the birthplace of two of the world's great religions (Hinduism and Buddhism) and one of its smallest (Jainism). It's also home to one of the world's few remaining communities of Parsis, adherents of the Zoroastrian faith (see Religion later in this chapter).

The modern state itself is a relatively recent creation born out of a people's zeal to throw off the yoke of colonialism. Even the mightiest of India's ancient civilisations could not encompass all of modern India, and today it is still as much a country of diversities as of unities. Although there are many different Indias, sometimes hindering the development of a national conscience, it's worth remembering that India has remained the world's largest democracy for more than 50 years.

HISTORY

Indus Valley Civilisation

India's first major civilisation flourished around 2500 BC in the Indus river valley, much of which lies within present-day Pakistan. This civilisation, which continued for 1000 years and is known as the Harappan culture, appears to have been the culmination of thousands of years of settlement. Excavation of different strata of Neolithic sites shows that the earliest inhabitants were nomadic tribesmen who began to cultivate the land and keep domestic animals. Considerable trade grew up, and by around 3500 BC an urban culture began to emerge. By 2500 BC the large cities of the Mature Harappa period were established.

The major cities such as Mohenjodaro and Harappa (discovered in the 1920s) in Pakistan, and Lothal near Ahmedabad in India, were carefully laid out with precise street plans. Several sites had a separate acropolis pointing to a clear religious function, and the great tank at Mohenjodaro may well have been used for ritual bathing purposes. The major cities were sizable – estimates of the population of Mohenjodaro are as high as 30,000 to 40,000.

By the middle of the 3rd millennium BC the Indus Valley culture was the equal of other great cultures emerging at the time. The Harappans traded with Mesopotamia, and developed a system of weights and measures, a script (which remains undeciphered), and a developed art in the form of terracotta and bronze figurines. Recovered relics include models of bullock carts and jewellery, demonstrating an already distinctively Indian culture. Clay figurines found at these sites suggest a Mother goddess (later personified as Kali) and a male three-faced god sitting in the attitude of a yogi attended by four animals (the prehistoric Shiva) were worshipped. Black stone pillars (associated with phallic worship of Shiva) and animal figures (the most prominent being the humped bull; later Shiva's mount) have also been discovered.

MOMENTS IN INDIAN HISTORY

PETER DAVIS

TONY WHEELER

BILL WASSMAN

BILL WASSMAN

RICHARD I'ANSON

CIRCA 2200 BC

INDUS VALLEY CIVILISATION

Also known as the Harappan culture, this advanced civilisation developed trading networks, planned gridded cities, built sewerage systems, advanced the arts and laid the foundations of the religions that predominate today. Centred at Mohenjodaro and Harappa, on the fertile plains of the Indus Valley in present-day Pakistan, Harappan influence in India can be seen in archaeological finds of pottery, statues, walls and drains at Kalibangan and Lothal.

CIRCA 1500 BC

VEDIC–ARYAN PERIOD

As the Aryans rose to power they introduced the caste system and created sacred Sanskrit texts known as the Vedas. Together with later texts, such as the Brahmanas and the Upanishads, the concepts of karma, samsara and nirvana were expounded. These philosophical teachings were fundamental to the development of Buddhism and Hinduism, which in turn have shaped the consciousness of India.

CIRCA 326 BC

ALEXANDER THE GREAT

Although Alexander's troops refused to march any farther east than Himachal Pradesh, Alexander and his successors left their cultural mark on north-west India. This Hellenising influence was evident for hundreds of years, especially in the arts and sculpture of Gandhara (present-day Pakistan).

CIRCA 321 BC

THE MAURYAN EMPIRE

Founded by Chandragupta Maurya, this was the first great Indian empire and it controlled much of central, eastern and western India. Reaching its peak under the charismatic emperor Ashoka, the empire was converted to Buddhism after the Battle of Kalinga (260 BC). This heralded a long period of political stability, and architecture and the arts flourished under the great Buddhist patron. The Mauryan empire introduced new political and social systems, while consolidating the caste system. The power of the empire was vast – ambassadors were sent to Sri Lanka and Nepal to propagate Buddhism, and records exist from Greek envoy Megasthenes describing the wealth of Pataliputra (the Mauryan capital). Stupas, pillars and edicts on stone remain today at Sanchi, Sarnath and Mathura, indicating the extent of the empire.

PATRICK HORTON

CIRCA 321 AD

GUPTA EMPIRE

Although mainly Buddhist, the Gupta empire spread Hinduism throughout central India. The stability of the empire fostered institutions such as universities and monasteries and promoted a grand period of art and architecture, known as the classic period.

RICHARD I'ANSON

RICHARD I'ANSON

CIRCA 800 AD

CHOLA EMPIRE

This empire of great builders and traders was responsible for the introduction of Hinduism to other parts of Asia. The Cholas controlled much of South India and left some of their most remarkable monuments at Thanjavur and Kumbakonam.

LEANNE LOGAN

EDDIE GERALD

EDDIE GERALD

TERESA CANNON

CIRCA 700 AD

THE ARRIVAL OF ISLAM

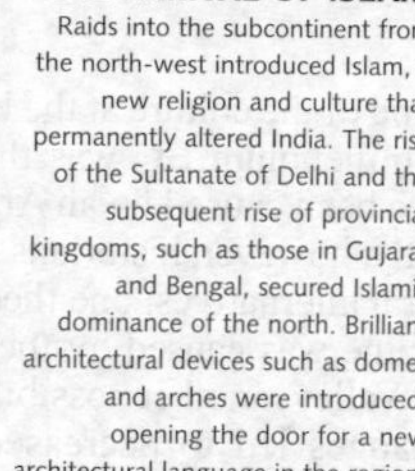

Raids into the subcontinent from the north-west introduced Islam, a new religion and culture that permanently altered India. The rise of the Sultanate of Delhi and the subsequent rise of provincial kingdoms, such as those in Gujarat and Bengal, secured Islamic dominance of the north. Brilliant architectural devices such as domes and arches were introduced, opening the door for a new architectural language in the region.

CIRCA 1336 AD

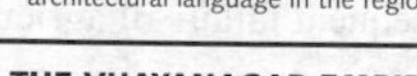

THE VIJAYANAGAR EMPIRE

MARK DAFFEY

This extensive Hindu empire controlled nearly all of South India by the 16th century. The capital at Vijayanagar (Hampi) was a place of bloody slaughter and atrocities until the Vijayanagars' eventual defeat by the Muslim coalition at the Battle of Talikota (1565). The fascinating architectural heritage of the empire encompasses Hindu and Islamic themes due to its location in the Deccan region between the Muslim-dominated north and the Hindu south.

CIRCA 1526 AD

THE MUGHAL EMPIRE

CHRIS MELLOR

RICHARD I'ANSON

Six great Mughal emperors (from Babur to Aurangzeb) oversaw a golden age of arts and military advancement. Under the Mughals, Hindu and Muslim integration was encouraged until a period of religious intolerance and harsh taxes weakened their power. Fine examples of Mughal power and culture remain today in structures such as the Taj Mahal and the Red Fort.

CIRCA 1690 AD

EUROPEAN COLONISATION

GREG ELMS

NEIL SETCHFIELD

Many European powers flocked to India, but it was the Portugese (who used Goa to gain a monopoly on trade in the Far East) and the British (who, under the guise of the East India Trading Company, 'ruled' India for 250 years) that had the greatest impact. Both powers have left a legacy of grandiose buildings.

CIRCA 1947 TO PRESENT DAY

INDEPENDENCE

MARK HONAN

Although India is now the world's largest democracy, the road to Independence was long. Despite Gandhi's campaign of passive resistance, the partition of 1947 was bloody. The country split along religious lines, creating the predominantly Muslim states of West and East Pakistan (the latter now known as Bangladesh). Post-Independence saw rapid industrialisation and population growth, with many people moving from rural to urban areas. Cultural and artistic traditions have developed further through large civic projects, such as the construction of Chandigarh and other projects in Mumbai and Ahmedabad, and through the growth of the prolific film industry in the south. But political instability has always plagued India, evidenced by the political assassinations of Mahatma, Indira and Rajiv Gandhi and by continual border tensions. In recent years India has restructured industrially and economically, positioning itself as a base for e-technologies of the future.

The decline of the culture at the beginning of the 2nd millennium BC was thought by some to have been caused by an Aryan invasion. Recently, however, historians have suggested several alternatives, one theory being that the decline was caused by the flooding of the Indus Valley; another possibility is that climatic changes led to decreased rainfall and the subsequent failure of agriculture.

Early Invasions & the Rise of Religions

It is important to note that some academics ardently dispute the 'colonial-missionary' Aryan invasion theory, claiming that there is no archaeological proof or evidence of an invasion in the ancient Indian texts. Some argue that the Aryans were in fact the original inhabitants of India and the invasion theory was actually devised by self-serving foreign conquerors. Others say that the arrival of Aryans was more of a gentle migration than an invasion.

Those who defend the invasion theory believe that from around 1500 BC, Aryan (from a Sanskrit word meaning noble) tribes from Afghanistan and Central Asia began to filter into north-west India. Despite their military superiority, their progress was gradual, with successive tribes fighting over territory and new arrivals pushing farther east into the Ganges plain. Eventually these tribes controlled northern India as far as the Vindhya Hills, and many of the original inhabitants, the Dravidians, were pushed south.

The invaders brought with them their nature gods, among whom the gods of fire (Agni) and battle (Indra) were predominant, as well as cattle-raising and meat-eating traditions. It was during this period of transition (1500–1200 BC) that the Hindu sacred scriptures, the Vedas, were written, and that the caste system became formalised. The Vedas justify caste (see Society & Conduct later in this chapter) by describing the natural creation of the system when the universe was formed:

> When they divided Purusha, how many portions did they make?
> What do they call his mouth, his arms? What do they call his thighs and feet?
> The Brahmin was his mouth, of both arms was the Rajanya Kshatriya made.
> His thighs became the Vaishya, from his feet the Shudra was produced.

As the Aryan tribes spread out across the Ganges plain in the late 7th century BC many of them became grouped together into 16 major kingdoms. The *asvamedha* (horse sacrifice) was one aspect of an increasingly formal system of rule that prevailed. In this ritual a horse was allowed to roam freely, followed by a band of soldiers. If the horse's progress was impeded the king would fight for the land in question. At the end of the prescribed period, the entire area over which the horse had wandered was taken to be the king's unchallenged territory, and the horse was sacrificed. This ritual was still being performed centuries later by dynasties such as the Chalukyas of Badami to assert their unchallenged right to territory, and to demonstrate the ruler's complete control of his kingdom.

Gradually the 16 major kingdoms were amalgamated into four large states, with Kosala and Magadha emerging to be the most powerful during the 5th century BC. After a series of dynastic changes, the Nanda dynasty came to power in 364 BC, ruling over a huge area of North India.

During this period, the heartland narrowly avoided two other invasions from the west. The first was by the Persian king, Darius (521–486 BC), who annexed Punjab and Sind (on either side of the modern India-Pakistan border). Alexander the Great marched to India from Greece in 326 BC, but his troops refused to go beyond the Beas river, in Himachal Pradesh. It was the easternmost extent of the Persian empire he conquered, and he turned back without extending his power into India itself. His most lasting reminder in the east was the development of Gandharan art, an intriguing mix of Grecian artistic ideals and the new religious beliefs of Buddhism.

Buddhism and Jainism arose around 500 BC. Both questioned the Vedas and condemned the caste system, though, unlike the Buddhists, the Jains never denied their Hindu heritage and their faith never extended beyond India.

Buddhism, on the other hand, drove a radical swathe through the spiritual and social body of Hinduism and experienced some spectacular growth after emperor Ashoka embraced it in 262 BC and declared it the state religion. Nevertheless, it gradually lost touch with the masses and faded as

Hinduism underwent a revival between AD 200 and 800. Yet such was the appeal of Buddha that it could not be sidelined and forgotten. Buddha was therefore incorporated into the Hindu pantheon as yet another of the avatars (manifestations) of Vishnu; a prime example of the way in which Hinduism has absorbed spiritual competitors and heretical ideologies.

The Mauryas & Emperor Ashoka

Chandragupta Maurya, the founder of the first great Indian empire, came to power in 321 BC, having seized the Magadha throne from the Nandas. He soon expanded the empire to include a huge area of the Indus Valley previously conquered by Alexander. According to an eyewitness account by an ambassador to the Mauryan court, Megasthenes, Chandragupta's capital at Pataliputra (modern-day Patna) was of an awesome size – 33.8km in circumference. If this is true, it would have been the largest city in the world at the time.

The Mauryan empire eventually spread across North India and as far south as modern day Karnataka. The Mauryas set up a well-organised kingdom with an efficient bureaucracy, organised tiers of local government and a well-defined social order consisting of a rigid caste system. Security was maintained by a huge standing army consisting, according to one account, of 9000 elephants, 30,000 cavalry and 600,000 infantry.

The empire reached its peak under Ashoka, who left pillars and rock-carved edicts that delineate the enormous span of his territory; these can be seen in Delhi, Gujarat, Orissa, Sarnath in Uttar Pradesh (on the spot where Buddha delivered his first sermon expounding the Noble Eightfold Path, or middle way to enlightenment) and Sanchi in Madhya Pradesh.

Ashoka also sent missions abroad, and he is revered in Sri Lanka because he sent his son and daughter to carry Buddhism to the island. The development of art and sculpture also flourished during his rule, and his standard, which topped many pillars, is now the seal of modern-day India (four lions sitting back to back atop an abacus decorated with a frieze and the inscription 'truth alone triumphs'). The Republic of India, established on 26 January 1950, chose emperor Ashoka's standard as its national emblem to reaffirm the ancient commitment to peace and goodwill. Under Ashoka, the Mauryan empire probably controlled more of India than any subsequent ruler prior to the Mughals or the British. Following Ashoka's death, in 232 BC, the empire rapidly disintegrated, finally collapsing in 184 BC.

An Interlude, then the Guptas

A number of empires rose and fell following the collapse of the Mauryas. The Sungas ruled from 184 to 70 BC before being overcome by the short-lived Kanvas. In the north-west, the successors to Alexander's kingdoms expanded their power into Punjab, before being overrun by a new wave of invaders from Central Asia, including the Shakas. The Shakas were later relieved of power in North India (but not in the north-west and south) by the Kushanas, who briefly ruled over a massive area of North India and Central Asia. In central India the powerful Shatavahanas ruled the roost, and throughout the subcontinent small tribes and kingdoms held varying amounts of territory and influence.

Despite the lack of a central power, this was a period of intense development. Trade with the Roman Empire (both overland and by sea through the southern ports) became substantial during the 1st century AD, and there was also overland trade with China. Buddhism flourished, despite experiencing a doctrinal split. Jainism's doctrine underwent a similar division, giving rise to the Digambara (sky clad) and Svetambara (white clad) sects.

In AD 319, Chandragupta I, the third king of the little-known Gupta tribe, came to prominence by a fortuitous marriage to the daughter of one of the most powerful tribes in the north, the Licchavis. The Gupta empire grew rapidly and under Chandragupta II (r. AD 375–413) it achieved its greatest extent. The Chinese pilgrim Fa-hsien, visiting India at the time, described what he found:

> The people are rich and contented, the kings govern without recourse to capital punishment, but offenders are fined lightly or heavily according to the nature of their crime.

The arts flourished during this period, and some of the finest work was done at Ajanta,

Ellora, Sanchi and Sarnath. Poetry and literature also experienced a golden age. Towards the end of the Gupta period, however, Buddhism and Jainism both began to decline and Hinduism began to rise in popularity once more.

The invasions of the Huns at the beginning of the 6th century signalled the end of this era of history, and in AD 510 the Gupta army was defeated by the Hun leader Toramana. Subsequently, North India broke up into a number of separate Hindu kingdoms and was not really unified again until the arrival of the Muslims.

Meanwhile in the South

Following the decline of the Mauryan empire in the early 2nd century BC, a number of powerful kingdoms arose in central and South India, among them the Shatavahanas, Kalingas and Vakatakas. In the far south, despite slight influence from the Mauryas, the political developments of the north had little direct impact, and a completely separate set of kingdoms emerged, developing mainly from tribal territories on the fertile coastal plains. These subsequently grew into the great empires of the Cholas, Pandyas, Cheras, Chalukyas and Pallavas. The Chalukyas ruled mainly over the Deccan region of central India, although their power occasionally extended farther north. With a capital at Badami in Karnataka, they ruled from AD 550 to 753 before falling to the Rashtrakutas. An eastern branch of the Chalukyas, with their capital at Kalyani (now in modern-day Karnataka), rose and ruled again from 972 to 1190.

In the far south, the Pallavas pioneered Dravidian architecture with its exuberant, almost baroque, style. In 850, the Cholas rose to power and gradually superseded the Pallavas. They, too, were great builders who carried their power overseas and, under the reign of Raja Raja (985–1014), controlled almost the whole of South India, the Deccan plateau, Sri Lanka, and parts of the Malay peninsula and Sumatran-based Srivijaya kingdom.

The south's prosperity was based upon its long-established trading links with other civilisations. The Egyptians, and later the Romans, traded by sea with South India. In return for spices, pearls, ivory and silk, the Indians received Roman gold. Indian merchants also extended their influence to South-East Asia.

While Buddhism and, to a lesser extent, Jainism were displacing Hinduism in central and northern India, Hinduism continued to flourish in the south. For a time Buddhism, and later Hinduism, flourished in Indonesia, and the people of the region looked towards India as their cultural mentor. The Ramayana, that most famous of Hindu epics, is today told and retold in various forms in many South-East Asian countries. Another possible outside influence to South India during this period was St Thomas the Apostle, who is said to have arrived in Kerala in AD 52. To this day, there is a strong Christian influence in the region.

First Muslim Invasions

During the period following the demise of the Guptas, North India, like the south, was controlled by a number of regional powers. Despite constant competition between the states, a power balance was maintained. At the very beginning of the 11th century, however, a new enemy threatened India from the north-west.

Muslim power first made itself strongly felt on the subcontinent with the raids of Mahmud of Ghazni. Today, Ghazni is just a nondescript little town between Kabul and Kandahar in Afghanistan, but in the early years of the 2nd millennium, Mahmud turned it into one of the world's most glorious capital cities. The funds for this development were plundered from his neighbours' territories; from 1001 to 1025 Mahmud conducted 17 raids into India, including one on the famous Shiva temple at Somnath (Gujarat). A Hindu force of 70,000 died in fierce fighting trying to defend the temple, which eventually fell in early 1026. In the aftermath of his victory Mahmud, not particularly intent on acquiring new territory at this stage, successfully transported a massive haul of gold and other booty back across the desert to his capital. These raids effectively shattered the balance of power in North India, allowing subsequent invaders to claim the territory for themselves.

Following Mahmud's death in 1033, Ghazni was seized by the Seljuqs and subsequently fell to the Ghurs, who originated in western Afghanistan. Their style of warfare was brutal – having taken Ghazni in

1150, they are reported to have spent seven days sacking the city, a feat which they achieved so thoroughly that the Ghur general, Ala-ud-din was subsequently titled 'Burner of the World'.

In 1191, Mohammed of Ghur, who had been expanding his powers across Punjab, advanced into India and fought a major battle against a confederacy of Hindu rulers. He was defeated, but returned the following year and routed his enemies. One of his generals, Qutb-ud-din, captured Delhi and was appointed governor, while another continued east carving out a separate empire in Bengal. Within a short time almost the whole of North India was under Ghur control and, following Mohammed's death in 1206, Qutb-ud-din became the first of the sultans of Delhi. His successor, Iltutmish, brought Bengal back under central control and defended the empire from an attempted invasion by the Mongols.

After a brief interlude in which his succession was fought over, Ala-ud-din Khilji came to power in 1296. Through a series of phenomenal campaigns, he pushed the borders of the empire south, while simultaneously fending off further attacks by the Mongols.

After Ala-ud-din's death in 1320, Mohammed Tughlaq, having murdered his father, ascended the throne in 1324. During Mohammed's reign the empire achieved its greatest extent and also, due to Mohammed's overreaching ambition, began to disintegrate. Unlike his forebears (including great rulers such as Ashoka), Mohammed dreamed not only of extending his indirect influence over South India, but of controlling it directly as part of his empire. After a series of successful campaigns he decided to move the capital from Delhi to a more central location. The new capital was called Daulatabad and was near Aurangabad in Maharashtra. In order to populate the city he forced every single inhabitant out of Delhi and marched them southwards, with great loss of life. After only a short period, however, he realised that this left the north undefended and so the entire capital was moved north again. Raising revenue to finance his huge armies was another problem; an attempt to introduce copper coinage had disastrous results and wide counterfeiting soon buried the plan.

With the withdrawal from the south, several splinter kingdoms arose, including, in the Deccan, the Bahmani sultanate and the Hindu Vijayanagar empire. The last of the great sultans of Delhi, Firoz Shah, died in 1388 and the fate of the sultanate was sealed when Tamerlane (Timur) made a devastating raid from Samarkand (in Central Asia) into India in 1398. Tamerlane's sacking of Delhi is supposed to have been truly merciless; some accounts say his soldiers slaughtered every Hindu inhabitant.

Meanwhile in the Centre & South (Again)

Once again, events in South India took a different path to those in the north, with the peninsula having largely escaped central rule from Delhi. Between 1000 and 1300, the Hoysala empire, which had centres at Belur, Halebid and Somnathpur, was at its peak (see Belur and Halebid in the Karnataka chapter). It eventually fell to a predatory raid by Mohammed Tughlaq in 1328, followed by the combined opposition of other Hindu states.

Two great kingdoms developed in the wake of Mohammed Tughlaq's withdrawal from central and South India. The Vijayanagar empire, with its capital at Hampi, was founded in 1336. In the following two centuries it became the strongest Hindu kingdom in India. The other, Vijayanagar's great rival to the north, the Muslim Bahmani sultanate, emerged in 1345 with its capital at Gulbarga and then Bidar. At the end of the 15th century, however, following much intrigue and plotting in the royal court, the sultanate disintegrated. As a result, five separate kingdoms, based on the major cities, were formed: Berar, Ahmednagar, Bijapur, Golconda and Ahmedabad.

While the five northern powers fought among themselves, Vijayanagar enjoyed a golden age of almost supreme power in the south and in 1520 the Hindu king Krishnadevaraya even took Bijapur. In 1565, however, the northern Muslim states combined to destroy Vijayanagar power in the epic Battle of Talikota. Later, the Bahmani kingdoms were to fall to the Mughals.

The Mughals

Back in the north, even as Vijayanagar was experiencing its last days, the next great

The Rise & Fall of the Vijayanagar Empire

Founded as an alliance of Hindu kingdoms banding together to counter the threat from the Muslims, the Vijayanagar empire rapidly grew into one of India's wealthiest and greatest Hindu empires. Under the rule of Bukka I (c. 1343–79) the majority of South India was brought under its control. Its wealth, accrued through trade, began to flood in.

The kingdom and the Bahmani sultanate, which controlled much of the Deccan, had a fairly even balance of power, creating an almost constant struggle and numerous bloody wars. The Vijayanagar armies occasionally got the upper hand, but generally the Bahmanis inflicted the worst defeats. The atrocities committed almost defy belief. In 1366, Bukka I responded to a perceived sleight by capturing the Muslim stronghold of Mudkal and slaughtering every inhabitant bar one, who managed to escape and carry news of the attack to Mohammad Shah, the sultan. Mohammad swore that he would not rest until he had killed 100,000 Hindus, but he far exceeded even his own predictions. The Muslim historian Firishtah estimates that half a million infidels were killed in the ensuing campaign.

Vijayanagar's fortunes improved considerably after 1482 when the Bahmani kingdom disintegrated. With little realistic opposition from the north, the Hindu empire reached its peak over the following years. The empire's heyday was also, however, the start of its decline. A series of uprisings divided the kingdom fatally, just at a time when the Muslim sultanates were beginning to form a new alliance. In 1565 a Muslim coalition engaged the Hindu armies at the Battle of Talikota. The result was a complete rout of the Vijayanagar forces, and the devastation of Hampi. The last of the Vijayanagar line escaped, and the dynasty limped on for several years. In reality, however, power in the region passed either to Muslim rulers or local chiefs who had come to power as loyal followers of the Vijayanagar kings.

Indian empire was being founded. Although the Mughals' heyday was relatively brief, their empire was massive and covered, at its height, almost the entire subcontinent. Its significance was not only in its size, however. The Mughal emperors presided over a golden age of arts and literature and had a passion for building that resulted in some of the finest architecture in India. In particular, Shah Jahan's magnificent Taj Mahal ranks as one of the wonders of the world. The six great Mughals and their reigns were:

Babur	1526–30
Humayun	1530–56
Akbar	1556–1605
Jehangir	1605–27
Shah Jahan	1627–58
Aurangzeb	1658–1707

The founder of the Mughal line, Babur, was a descendant of both Genghis Khan and Tamerlane. In 1525 he marched into Punjab from his capital at Kabul in Afghanistan. With revolutionary new knowledge of firearms, and consummate skill in simultaneously employing artillery and cavalry, Babur defeated the numerically superior armies of the sultan of Delhi at the Battle of Panipat in 1526.

Despite this initial success, Babur's son, Humayun was defeated by a powerful ruler of eastern India, Sher Shah, in 1539 and forced to withdraw to Iran. Following Sher Shah's death in 1545, Humayun returned to claim his kingdom, eventually conquering Delhi in 1555. He died the following year and was succeeded by his young son Akbar who, during his 49-year reign, managed to extend and consolidate the empire until he ruled over a mammoth area.

Akbar was probably the greatest of the Mughals, for he not only had the military ability required of a ruler at that time, but was also a man of culture and wisdom with a sense of fairness. He saw, as previous Muslim rulers had not, that the number of Hindus in India was too great to subjugate. Instead, he integrated them into his empire and used them as advisers, generals and administrators. Akbar also had a deep interest in religious matters, and spent many hours in discussion with religious experts of all persuasions, including Christians and Parsis. He eventually formulated a religion, Deen Ilahi, which combined the favoured parts of all of those he had studied.

Jehangir ascended to the throne following Akbar's death in 1605. Despite several challenges to the authority of Jehangir himself, the empire remained in more or less the same form as Akbar had left it. In periods of stability Jehangir took the opportunity to spend time in his beloved Kashmir, eventually dying en route there in 1627. He was succeeded by his son, Shah Jahan, who secured his position as emperor by executing all male collateral relatives. During his reign, some of the most vivid and permanent reminders of the Mughals' glory were constructed.

The last of the great Mughals, Aurangzeb, came to the throne in 1658 after a two-year struggle against his brothers and having imprisoned his father (Shah Jahan). Aurangzeb devoted his resources to extending the empire's boundaries, and fell into much the same trap that Mohammed Tughlaq had some 300 years earlier. He, too, tried moving his capital south (to Aurangabad) and imposed heavy taxes to fund his military. A combination of decaying court life and dissatisfaction among the Hindu population at inflated taxes and religious intolerance, weakened the Mughal grip.

The empire was also facing serious challenges from the Marathas in central India and, more significantly, the British in Bengal (see Expansion of British & European Power later in this section). With Aurangzeb's death in 1707, the empire's fortunes rapidly declined, and the sack of Delhi by Persia's Nadir Shah in 1739 served to confirm the lack of real power. Mughal 'emperors' continued to rule right up to the Indian Uprising in 1857, but they were emperors without an empire. In sharp contrast to the magnificent tombs of his Mughal predecessors, Aurangzeb's tomb is a simple affair at Rauza, near Aurangabad.

The Rajputs & the Marathas

Throughout the Mughal period, there were still strong Hindu powers, most notably the Rajputs. Centred in Rajasthan, the Rajputs were a proud warrior caste with a passionate belief in the dictates of chivalry, both in battle and in the conduct of state affairs. Their place in Indian history is much like that of the knights of medieval Europe. The Rajputs opposed every foreign incursion into their territory, but were never united or adequately organised to deal with superior forces on a long-term basis. Not only that, but when they weren't battling foreign oppression, they squandered their energies fighting each other. This eventually led to them becoming vassal states of the Mughal empire, but their prowess in battle was acknowledged, and some of the best military men in the emperors' armies were Rajputs.

The Marathas first rose to prominence under their great leader Shivaji, who gathered popular support by championing the Hindu cause against the Muslim rulers. Between 1646 and 1680 Shivaji performed heroism across most of central India, and tales of his larger-than-life exploits are still popular with wandering storytellers today. He is a particular hero in Maharashtra, where many of his wildest adventures took place, but he is also revered for two other things: as a lower-caste Shudra, he showed that great leaders do not have to be of the Kshatriya (soldier or administrator) caste; and he demonstrated great abilities in confronting the Mughals. At one time, Shivaji was captured by the Mughals and taken to Agra but, naturally, he managed to escape and continued his adventures.

Shivaji's son was captured, blinded and executed by Aurangzeb. His grandson was not made of the same sturdy stuff so the Maratha empire continued under the Peshwas, hereditary government ministers who became the real rulers. They gradually took over more and more of the weakening Mughal empire's powers, first by supplying troops and then actually taking control of Mughal land.

When Nadir Shah sacked Delhi in 1739, the declining Mughals were weakened further. But the expansion of Maratha power came to an abrupt halt in 1761 at Panipat. There, where Babur had won the battle that established the Mughal empire more than 200 years earlier, the Marathas were defeated by Ahmad Shah Durani from Afghanistan. Their expansion to the west was halted, but the Marathas consolidated their control over central India and the region known as Malwa. Soon, however, they were to fall to India's final imperial power, the British.

Expansion of British & European Power

The British were not the first European power to arrive in India, nor were they the last to leave – both those honours go to the Portuguese. In 1498, Vasco da Gama arrived on the coast of modern-day Kerala, having sailed around the Cape of Good Hope. Pioneering this route gave the Portuguese a century of uninterrupted monopoly over Indian and far-eastern trade with Europe. In 1510 they captured Goa, the Indian enclave they controlled until 1961. In its heyday, the trade flowing through 'Golden Goa' was said to rival that passing through Lisbon. In the long term, however, the Portuguese did not have the resources to maintain a worldwide empire and they were quickly eclipsed after the arrival of the British, French and Dutch.

In 1600 Queen Elizabeth I granted a charter to a London trading company giving it a monopoly on British trade with India. In 1612, representatives of the East India Company (which was actually known by several other names until the 1830s, including the 'Company of Merchants') established their first trading post at Surat in Gujarat. Further British trading posts, administered and governed by representatives of the company, were established at Madras (now called Chennai) in 1640, Bengal in 1651 and Bombay (Mumbai) in 1668. Strange as it seems now, for nearly 250 years a commercial trading company and not the British government 'ruled' British India.

The British and Portuguese were not the only Europeans in India. The Danes and Dutch also had trading posts, and in 1672 the French established themselves at Pondicherry, an enclave that they would hold even after the British had departed. The stage was set for more than a century of rivalry between the British and French for control of Indian trade. At one stage, under the guidance of a handful of talented and experienced commanders, the French appeared to hold the upper hand. In 1746, they took Madras (only to hand it back in 1749) and their success in placing their favoured candidate on the throne as Nizam of Hyderabad augured well for the future. Serious French aspirations effectively ended, however, in 1750 when the directors of the French East India Company decided their representatives were playing too much politics and doing too little trading. The key representatives were sacked and a settlement designed to end all ongoing political disputes was made with the British. Although the French company's profits may have risen in the short term, the decision effectively removed France as a serious competitor for influence on the subcontinent. French interests remained strong enough, however, for them to continue supporting various local rulers in their struggles against the British.

The transformation of the British from traders to governors began almost by accident. Having been granted a licence to trade in Bengal by the Great Mughal, and following the establishment of a new trading post (Calcutta, now called Kolkata) in 1690, business began to expand rapidly. Under the apprehensive gaze of the nawab (local ruler), British trading activities became extensive, and the 'factories' took on an increasingly permanent (and fortified) appearance.

Eventually the nawab decided that British power had grown far enough. In June 1756 he attacked Calcutta and, having taken the city, locked his British prisoners in a tiny cell. The space was so cramped and airless that many were dead by the following morning, and the cell infamously became known as the 'Black Hole of Calcutta'.

Six months later, Robert Clive led a relief expedition to retake Calcutta and entered into an agreement with one of the nawab's generals to overthrow the nawab himself. This he did in June 1757 at the Battle of Plassey (now called Palashi), and the general who had assisted him was placed on the throne. During the period that followed, with the British effectively in control of Bengal, the company's agents engaged in a period of unbridled profiteering. When a subsequent nawab finally took up arms to protect his own interests, he was defeated at the Battle of Baksar in 1764. This victory confirmed the British as the paramount power in east India. The following year, Clive returned to Calcutta to sort out the administrative chaos and profiteering that was prevailing.

In 1771 one of the greatest figures of the time, Warren Hastings, was made governor in Bengal and during his tenure the company greatly expanded its control. His astute statesmanship was aided by the fact that India at this time was in a state of flux – a power vacuum had been created by the disintegration of the Mughal empire. The Marathas were the only real Indian power to step into this gap and they themselves were divided. Hastings concluded a series of treaties with local rulers, including one with the main Maratha leader, thus removing a major threat (at least for the time being).

In the south, where Mughal influence had never been great, the picture was confused by the strong British-French rivalry, as one ruler was played off against another. This was never clearer than in the series of Mysore wars where Hyder Ali and his son, Tipu Sultan, waged a brave and determined campaign against the British. In the Fourth Mysore War (1789–99), Tipu Sultan was killed at Srirangapatnam and British power took another step forward. The long-running struggle with the Marathas was finally concluded in 1803, leaving only Punjab outside British control; it too finally fell in 1849 after the two Sikh wars.

It was during this time, following a brief series of battles between the British and the Gurkhas in 1814, that the borders of Nepal were delineated. The Gurkhas were initially victorious but, two years later, were forced to sue for peace as the British marched on Kathmandu. As part of the price for peace, the Nepalese were forced to cede the provinces of Kumaon and Shimla, but mutual respect for each other's military prowess prevented Nepal's incorporation into the Indian empire and led to the establishment of the Gurkha regiments that still exist in the British army today.

British India

By the early 19th century, India was effectively under British control. The country remained a patchwork of states, many nominally independent, and governed by their own rulers, the maharajas and nawabs. While these 'princely states' administered their own territories, a system of central government was developed. British organisation was replicated in the Indian government and civil service – a legacy that still exists today. From 1784 onwards, the British government in London began to take a more direct role in supervising affairs in India, although the territory was still notionally administered by the East India Company until 1858.

An overwhelming interest in trade and profit resulted in far-reaching changes. Iron and coal mining were developed and tea, coffee and cotton became key crops. A start was made on the vast rail network still in use today, irrigation projects were undertaken and the zamindar (landowner) system was encouraged. These absentee landlords eased the burden of administration and tax collection for the British, but contributed to an impoverished and landless peasantry.

The British also imposed English as the local language of administration. While this may have been useful in a country with so many different languages, and even today fulfils an important function in nationwide and international communication, it did keep the new rulers at arm's length from the Indians.

The Indian Uprising

In 1857, half a century after having established firm control of India, the British suffered a serious setback. To this day, the causes of the Uprising (known at the time as the 'Indian Mutiny' and subsequently labelled by nationalist historians a 'War of Independence') are the subject of debate. The key factors included the influx of cheap goods, such as textiles, from Britain that destroyed many livelihoods, the dispossession of many rulers of their territories, and taxes imposed on landowners.

The incident that is popularly held to have sparked the Uprising, however, took place at an army barracks in Meerut in Uttar Pradesh on 10 May 1857. A rumour leaked out that a new type of bullet was greased with animal fat. In Hindu circles the rumour held that it was cow fat, in Muslim company the grease came from pigs. Pigs, of course, are unclean to Muslims, and cows are sacred to Hindus. Since the procedure for loading a rifle involved biting the end off the waxed cartridge, there was considerable unrest.

In Meerut, the situation was handled with a singular lack of judgment. The commanding officer lined up his soldiers and ordered them to bite off the ends of their issued bullets. Those who refused were immediately marched off to prison. The following morning the soldiers of the garrison rebelled, shot their officers and marched to Delhi. Of the 74 Indian battalions of the Bengal Army, seven (one of them Gurkhas) remained loyal, 20 were disarmed and the other 47 mutinied. The soldiers and peasants rallied around the ageing Great Mughal in Delhi, but there was never any clear idea of what they hoped to achieve. They held Delhi for four months and besieged the British Residency in Lucknow for five months before they were finally suppressed. The incident left deep scars on both sides.

Almost immediately the East India Company was wound up and direct control of the country was assumed by the British government. The government announced its support for the existing rulers of the princely states, claiming they would not interfere in local matters as long as the states remained loyal to the British. A decision was also wisely taken that there should be no public search for scapegoats.

Road to Independence

Opposition to British rule began to increase at the turn of the 20th century, spearheaded by the Indian National Congress, the country's oldest political party, also known as the Congress Party and Congress (I).

It met for the first time in 1885 and soon began to push for a measure of participation in the government of the country. Progress was painfully slow, although there was movement after 1906 towards enfranchising a small proportion of Indian society. A highly unpopular attempt to partition Bengal in 1905 resulted in mass demonstrations and brought to light Hindu opposition to the division; the Muslim community formed its own league and campaigned for protected rights in any future political settlement. As pressure rose, a split emerged in Hindu circles between moderates and radicals, the latter resorting to violence to publicise their aims.

With the outbreak of WWI, the political situation eased. India contributed hugely to the war (over one million Indian volunteers were enlisted and sent overseas, suffering more than 100,000 casualties). The contribution was sanctioned by congress leaders, largely on the expectation that it would be rewarded after the war was over. Despite a number of hints and promises, no such rewards emerged and disillusion was soon to follow. Disturbances were particularly noticeable in Punjab and, in April 1919, following riots in Amritsar, a British army contingent was sent to quell the unrest. Under direct orders of the officer in charge they fired into a crowd of unarmed protesters attending a meeting. Firing continued for some 15 minutes, until there were well over 1000 casualties. News of the massacre spread rapidly throughout India and turned huge numbers of otherwise apolitical Indians into congress supporters.

At this time, the congress movement also found a new leader in Mohandas Gandhi. Gandhi, who subsequently became known as the Mahatma, or Great Soul, adopted a policy of passive resistance, known as satyagraha, to British rule. Not everyone involved in the struggle agreed with or followed Gandhi's policy of noncooperation and nonviolence, yet the Congress Party and Gandhi remained at the forefront of the push for Independence.

As political power sharing began to look increasingly likely, and the mass movement led by Gandhi gained momentum, the Muslim reaction was to look to their own interests. The large Muslim minority had realised that an independent India would also be a Hindu-dominated India, and despite Gandhi's fair-minded approach, others in the Congress Party would not be so willing to share power. By the 1930s Muslims were raising the possibility of a separate Muslim state.

Political events were partially disrupted by WWII when large numbers of Congress supporters were jailed to prevent disruption to the war effort. During this time, support grew among Muslims for an independent state of their own.

Independence

The Labour Party victory in the British elections in July 1945 brought a new breed of political leaders to power. They realised that a solution to the Indian problem was imperative. Despite their willingness to grant Independence, there appeared to be no way to resolve the divergent wishes of the two major Indian parties. Mohammed Ali Jinnah, the leader of the Muslim League, declared that he wished to have 'India divided or India destroyed'. Meanwhile the Congress Party, led by Jawaharlal Nehru, campaigned for an independent greater India. Gandhi, the father figure of Congress, urged reconciliation, but his voice was drowned out by others.

Each passing day increased the risks of intercommunity strife and bloodshed. In early 1946 a British mission failed to bring the two sides together and the country slid closer towards civil war. A 'Direct Action Day', called by the Muslim League in August 1946, led to the slaughter of Hindus in

Calcutta, followed by reprisals against Muslims. Faced by a crisis, in February 1947 the British government made a momentous decision. The viceroy, Lord Wavell, would be replaced by Lord Louis Mountbatten and Independence would come by June 1948.

The new viceroy made a last-ditch attempt to convince the rival factions that a united India was a more sensible proposition, but they – Jinnah in particular – remained intransigent. The reluctant decision was then made to divide the country. Only Gandhi stood firmly against the division, preferring the possibility of a civil war to the chaos he so rightly expected. Faced with increasing civil violence, Mountbatten decided to follow a breakneck pace to Independence and announced that it would come on 14 August 1947. Once the decision had been made to divide the country with one section for Hindus and the other for Muslims, there were countless administrative decisions to be made, the most important being the actual location of the dividing line.

Neatly slicing the country in two proved to be an impossible task. Although some areas were clearly Hindu or Muslim, others had evenly mixed populations, and there were isolated 'islands' of communities in areas predominantly settled by other religions. Moreover, the two overwhelmingly Muslim regions were on opposite sides of the country and, therefore, Pakistan would inevitably have an eastern and western half divided by a hostile India. The instability of this arrangement was self-evident, but it was 25 years before the predestined split finally came and East Pakistan became Bangladesh.

Since a locally adjudicated dividing line was certain to bring recriminations from either side, an independent British referee was given the odious task of drawing the borders, knowing that the effects would be disastrous for countless people. The decisions were fraught with impossible dilemmas. In Bengal, Calcutta, with its Hindu majority, port facilities and jute mills, was divided from East Bengal, which had a Muslim majority, large-scale jute production, no mills and no port facilities. It has been estimated that one million Bengalis became refugees in the mass movement across the new border.

The problem was far worse in Punjab, where intercommunity antagonisms were already running at fever pitch. Punjab was one of the most fertile and affluent regions of the country, and had large Muslim, Hindu and Sikh communities. The Sikhs had already campaigned unsuccessfully for their own state and now saw their homeland divided down the middle. The new border ran straight between Punjab's two major cities – Lahore and Amritsar. Prior to Independence, Lahore's total population of 1.2 million included approximately 500,000 Hindus and 100,000 Sikhs. When the dust had finally settled, Lahore had a Hindu and Sikh population of only 1000.

It was clear that Punjab contained all the ingredients for an epic disaster, but the resulting bloodshed was even worse than expected. Huge exchanges of population took place. Trains full of Muslims, fleeing westward, were held up and slaughtered by Hindu and Sikh mobs. Hindus and Sikhs fleeing to the east suffered the same fate. The army that was sent to maintain order proved totally inadequate and, at times, all too ready to join the partisan carnage. By the time the Punjab chaos had run its course, more than 10 million people had changed sides and even the most conservative estimates calculate that 250,000 people had been slaughtered. The true figure may well have been more than half a million.

The provision of an independently adjudicated border between the two nations failed to prevent disputes. The issue was complicated largely by the fact that the 'princely states' in British India were nominally independent. As part of the settlement process, local rulers were asked which country they wished to belong to – in almost all cases the matter was solved relatively simply. Kashmir, however, was a predominantly Muslim state with a Hindu maharaja who, by October 1948, had still not opted for India or Pakistan when a rag-tag Pathan (Pakistani) army crossed the border, intent on racing to Srinagar and annexing Kashmir without provoking a real India-Pakistan conflict. Unfortunately for the Pakistanis, the Pathans, inspired to mount their invasion by the promise of plunder, did so much plundering en route that India had time to rush troops to Srinagar and prevent the town's capture. The indecisive maharaja finally opted for India, provoking the first, albeit brief, India-Pakistan war.

Mahatma Gandhi

Mohandas Karamchand Gandhi was born on 2 October 1869 in Porbandar in Gujarat where his father was chief minister. He was married at the age of 13. In 1888 he left India to train as a barrister in London. On his return to India in 1891 he found the legal profession oversubscribed and accepted a contract to work in South Africa. On arrival there he experienced the discrimination directed at the Indian community and others and soon became the spokesman for the Indian community and championed equality for all.

Gandhi returned to India in 1915 with many of his policies and beliefs in place. The doctrine of *ahimsa* (nonviolence) was central to his beliefs, as was his devotion to a simple and disciplined lifestyle. He set up an ashram in Ahmedabad (Gujarat) which was innovative for its admission of Untouchables, and for its economic and social activities, such as community spinning and weaving.

Gandhi initially felt his way cautiously around the Indian political scene, but within a year he had his first victory, defending farmers in Bihar from exploitation. This was when he first received the title 'Mahatma' (Great Soul) from an admirer. The passage of the discriminatory Rowlatt Acts in 1919 spurred him to further action and he organised a national protest. In the days that followed this hartal (strike), feelings ran high throughout the country. In Amritsar, protesters at a peaceful meeting were massacred by soldiers and Gandhi, deeply shocked, called the movement off immediately.

By 1920 Gandhi was a key figure in the Indian National Congress, and he coordinated a national campaign of noncooperation. The effort was hugely successful in raising nationalist feelings, but once again led to violence. Throughout the mid-1920s Gandhi kept a relatively low profile. He returned to the struggle in 1927 and three years later captured the imagination of the country, and the world, with his most successful act of defiance against the British government. In early 1930 he led a march of several thousand followers from Ahmedabad to Dandi on the coast of Gujarat. On arrival, Gandhi ceremoniously made salt by evaporating sea water, thus publicly defying the hated salt tax; once again he was imprisoned. He was released in 1931 in order to represent the Indian National Congress at the second Round Table Conference in London where, despite winning over the hearts of the British people, he failed to gain many real concessions from the government.

Jailed again on his return to India, Gandhi immediately began a hunger strike, aimed at forcing his fellow Indians to accept the rights of the Untouchables. The country was seized with apprehension and, as Gandhi grew weaker, pressure on politicians mounted. Finally, just as it seemed that Gandhi was on the verge of death, an agreement was reached.

Emerging from jail, Gandhi found himself disillusioned with politics, believing the Congress leaders were ignoring his guidance. In 1934 he resigned his seat in congress and began to follow a personal policy of rural education. He returned to the fray very publicly in 1942 with the Quit India campaign, in which he urged the British to leave India immediately. During the tension of WWII his actions were deemed subversive and he and most of the Congress leadership were imprisoned.

In the frantic bargaining that followed the end of the war, Gandhi was largely excluded, and watched helplessly as plans were made to partition the country – a tragedy in his eyes. He toured the trouble spots, using his own influence to calm intercommunity tensions and promote peace.

His work on behalf of members of all communities inevitably drew resentment from Hindu hardliners. It was this that led to his death when, on his way to an evening prayer meeting on 30 January 1948, he was assassinated by a Hindu fanatic.

The UN eventually stepped in to keep the two sides apart, but the issue of Kashmir has remained a central cause for intense disagreement and conflict between the two countries ever since. With its overwhelming Muslim majority and its geographic links to Pakistan, many people were inclined to support Pakistan's claims to the region. To this day, India and Pakistan are divided in this region by a demarcation line (known as the Line of Actual Control), yet neither side agrees that this constitutes the official border.

The final stages of Independence had one last tragedy to be played out. On 30 January 1948, Mohandas Gandhi, deeply disheartened by Partition and the subsequent bloodshed, was assassinated by a Hindu zealot. Throughout the events leading up to Independence, he had stood almost alone in urging tolerance and the preservation of a single India. He argued that Jinnah should be given the leadership of a united India, if that was what it would take to prevent Partition. To some, whipped up by the events of the preceding months, this appeared to be tantamount to colluding with the enemy.

Independent India

Since Independence, India has faced many problems and made considerable progress. The fact that it has not, like so many developing countries, succumbed to dictatorships, military rule or wholesale foreign invasion, is a testament to the basic strength of the country's government and institutions. Economically, it has made major steps in improving agricultural output and is one of the world's top 10 industrial powers.

Jawaharlal Nehru, India's first prime minister, tried to follow a strict policy of nonalignment. Yet, despite maintaining generally cordial relations with Britain and electing to join the Commonwealth, India moved towards the former USSR – partly because of conflicts with China and US support for its arch enemy Pakistan.

There were further clashes with Pakistan in 1965 and 1971, one over the intractable Kashmir dispute and another over Bangladesh. A border war with China in 1962 in what was then known as the North-East Frontier Area (NEFA; now the north-eastern region) and Ladakh resulted in the loss of Aksai Chin (in Ladakh) and smaller NEFA areas. India continues to dispute sovereignty.

These outside events drew attention away from India's often serious internal problems, especially the failure to address rapid population growth.

Indira's India

Politically, India's major problem since Independence has been the personality cult that has developed around its leaders. There have only been three real prime ministers of stature – Nehru, his daughter Indira Gandhi (no relation to Mahatma Gandhi) and her son Rajiv Gandhi. Nehru personally led a series of five-year plans to improve output and managed to keep India nonaligned, thereby receiving aid from the then USSR, USA and Europe. He died in 1964 and in 1966 Indira was elected as prime minister. In 1975 she faced serious opposition and unrest which she countered by declaring a state of emergency (which became known as the Emergency) – a situation that in many other countries might have become a dictatorship.

During the Emergency, a mixed bag of good and bad policies were followed. Freed of many parliamentary constraints, Gandhi was able to control inflation remarkably well, boost the economy and decisively increase efficiency. On the negative side, political opponents often found themselves behind bars, India's judicial system was turned into a puppet theatre, the press was fettered and there was more than a hint of nepotism, particularly with her son, Sanjay. His disastrous program of forced sterilisations, in particular, caused much anger.

Despite murmurings of discontent, Gandhi decided the people were behind her and in 1977 called a general election. Things did not go her way and her partially renamed Congress Party (Indira) was bundled out of power in favour of the Janata People's Party, a coalition formed with the sole purpose of defeating her. This party was founded by Jaya Prakash Narayan, 'JP', an ageing Gandhian socialist who established the party to fight against corruption and Indira's increasingly authoritarian rule. He was jailed for five months in 1975 and this took a terrible toll on his health. When Narayan died in 1977 the Janata party had defeated Indira at the polls. Many believe that without Narayan's moral stature and courage to stand up to Congress' monolithic rule, democracy might not have survived.

Once victorious, it quickly became obvious that Janata had no other cohesive policies. Its leader, Morarji Desai, seemed more interested in protecting cows, banning alcohol and getting his daily glass of urine (high in vitamins and minerals) than coming to grips with the country's problems. With inflation soaring, unrest rising and the economy faltering, nobody was surprised when Janata fell apart in late 1979. The 1980 election brought Indira Gandhi back to power with a larger majority than ever before.

India in the 1980s & 1990s

Indira Gandhi's political touch seemed to have faded as she grappled unsuccessfully with communal unrest in several areas, violent attacks on Dalits (the Scheduled Caste or Untouchables), numerous cases of police brutality and corruption, and the upheavals in the north-east and Punjab. Then her son and political heir, the unpopular Sanjay, was killed in a light-aircraft accident in June 1980. In 1984, following an ill-considered decision to send in the Indian army to flush out armed Sikh separatists (demanding a separate Sikh state, to be called Khalistan) from Amritsar's Golden Temple, Mrs Gandhi was assassinated by her Sikh bodyguards. Her highly controversial decision to desecrate the Sikhs' holiest temple was catastrophic and sparked Hindu-Sikh riots that left more than 3000 people dead (mostly Sikhs who had been lynched). The quest for Khalistan has since been quashed.

Mrs Gandhi's son, Rajiv, a former Indian Airlines pilot, became the next prime minister. However, after a brief golden reign, which included breaking India's protectionist stance to world trade, he was dogged with corruption scandals (most notably the notorious Bofors scandal) and also failed to quell unrest in Punjab, Kashmir and elsewhere. In 1991, during an election campaign tour in Tamil Nadu, Rajiv and others were killed by a bomb carried by a supporter of the Liberation Tigers of Tamil Eelam (LTTE; a Sri Lankan armed separatist group).

Narasimha Rao assumed the leadership of the Congress Party and led it to victory at the polls in 1991. Rao shared Rajiv's determination to shove India into the economic realities of the 1990s. In 1992 the economy was given an enormous boost after the finance minister, Manmohan Singh, made the momentous step of partially floating the rupee against a basket of 'hard' currencies.

However, Rao inherited a number of intractable problems that tested the mettle of his government. His biggest headache, though, was the festering issue of communalism, particularly between Hindus and Muslims, for which Ayodhya (revered by Hindus as the birthplace of Rama) in Uttar Pradesh became a hotbed. In December 1992 Hindu zealots, egged on by the staunchly Hindu revivalist Bharatiya Janata Party (BJP), decimated a mosque, the Babri Masjid, which they claimed stood on the site of what was formerly the Rama Temple. Rioting flared across the north; more than 250 people were killed and 1100 wounded following a series of bomb blasts in Mumbai.

The simmering unrest between India and neighbouring Pakistan took centre stage during the 1990s, with an alarming increase in guerrilla activities. India accused Pakistan of training and arming Kashmiri insurgents – of course Islamabad denied such claims, instead placing blame on the antagonistic Indian army. Foreign and Indian tourists were targeted by Kashmiri terrorists; a number of them were murdered. See the Jammu & Kashmir chapter for more information.

A rise in Hindu nationalism, along with various corruption scandals plaguing the Rao Government (see India Beyond 2000), spelt disaster for the Congress Party, which was defeated by the BJP in the 1996 general election. The government formed by the BJP lasted less than two weeks, and was replaced by a coalition of 13 parties called the United Front – this didn't last either. Just nine months later, in April 1997, it was voted out of office after Congress withdrew its support. Then, in 1998, the BJP and its allies emerged with the most seats of any single party causing Congress president Sitaram Kesri to step aside to make way for Sonia Gandhi (Rajiv Gandhi's widow). This move was vociferously condemned by some within the party (and beyond) who believed high positions (and the possibility of becoming prime minister) should go to Indian-born members. Some party members were so disgusted they resigned in protest, creating turmoil in the party. But Sonia Gandhi stayed on; many believe she is keeping the political seat warm for her daughter, Priyanka, cited as a future leader.

In 1998 the BJP, led by Prime Minister Atal Behari Vajpayee, assumed power and promptly blasted its way into world headlines by defiantly detonating five nuclear devices in the deserts of Rajasthan. This shattered any hopes of a peaceful resolution to the Kashmir crisis. Pakistan furiously responded to India by testing its own nuclear devices, igniting global concern about a nuclear arms race in south Asia. Despite international condemnation (translating to punitive economic sanctions by many nations), Vajpayee bagged the top job again after the BJP won elections in October 1999. In these elections, only 43 women were elected (a bill to boost the number of women in key positions has been pledged by the government, but this is yet to be passed).

Although Vajpayee and his party are dubbed by many as intolerant Hindu chauvinists, they have so far proved to be more judicious administrators than the Congress Party, despite the March 2001 arms scandal allegations.

India Beyond 2000

Over recent decades Indian politics has been plagued with corruption scandals. This very publicly came to the fore in October 2000, when one of the nation's most senior political figures, former Prime Minister Narasimha Rao, was sentenced to three years imprisonment. Rao, who held office from 21 June 1991 to 16 May 1996, was found guilty of paying bribes to garner support during a vital 1993 parliamentary vote. He is on bail and is appealing the decision.

In March 2001 dirty deals at high levels hit world headlines yet again when senior Indian government officials were implicated in an alleged arms bribery scandal that was first revealed via an Indian news Web site. To restore public confidence in the Vajpayee Government, India's Defence Minister George Fernandes resigned soon after the scandal emerged, even though he claimed to have had no involvement. Despite vehement calls by opposition parties for the entire BJP-led coalition to resign, Prime Minister Vajpayee refused to step down. Instead, he promptly pledged to 'get to the bottom of the allegations' by ordering a high level judicial inquiry. The inquiry findings are scheduled to be released by the end of July 2001.

The beginning of the new millennium has centered on the interminable dissension between India and Pakistan over the disputed territory of Kashmir. Despite continuing vows by both countries to resume constructive dialogue, tensions between the South Asian neighbours remain volatile.

GEOGRAPHY & GEOLOGY

India covers a total area of 3,287,263 sq km. This is divided into 29 states and six directly administered union territories. The states are further subdivided into districts.

The Himalaya

The north of the country is decisively bordered by the long sweep of the Himalaya, the world's highest mountains. They run from south-east to north-west, separating India from China, and form one of the youngest mountain ranges on earth. The Himalaya evolution can be traced to the Jurassic era (80 million years ago) when the world's land masses were split into two: Laurasia in the northern hemisphere and Gondwanaland in the southern hemisphere. The land mass that is now India broke away from Gondwanaland and floated across the earth's surface, eventually colliding with Laurasia. The hard volcanic rocks of India were thrust against the soft sedimentary crust of Laurasia, forcing it upwards to create the Himalaya. This continental collision still continues and the mountains rise by up to 8mm each year.

The Himalaya are not a single mountain range but a series of ranges with beautiful valleys wedged between them. The Kullu Valley in Himachal Pradesh and the Vale of Kashmir in Jammu and Kashmir are both Himalayan valleys, as is the Kathmandu Valley in Nepal. Kanchenjunga (8598m) is the highest mountain in India, although until Sikkim (and Kanchenjunga) were absorbed into India that honour went to Nanda Devi (7817m). Beyond the Himalaya stretches the high, dry and barren Tibetan plateau; Ladakh is a small part of this plateau actually lying within India's boundaries.

The final southern range of the Himalaya, the Siwalik Hills, ends abruptly in the great northern plain in the north-west.

The Northern Plain

In complete contrast to the soaring mountain peaks, the northern plain is flat and

Gujarat's Devastating Earthquake

On 26 January 2001, India's Republic Day, a massive earthquake hit the western state of Gujarat causing massive loss of life and widespread damage (see also the boxed text 'The Day the Earth Shook' in the Gujarat chapter). Centred on the isolated region of Kutch and measuring 7.9 on the Richter scale, the tremors were felt as far away as Chennai in the south and Nepal to the north-east.

The official death toll was close to 17,000 (including 15,000 in the Kutch district). Although some government ministers speculated that the number killed could reach as high as 100,000 people, the most likely figure is closer to 30,000. The exact figure will never be known, in part because the devastation was so widespread. Emergency relief efforts were so stretched and the potential for disease from unburied bodies was such that hundreds, if not thousands of buildings had to be bulldozed without ever accounting for the bodies inside.

It's now up to the survivors to rebuild their devastated lives and there is no doubt that this will happen, but the enduring human suffering cannot be measured. However, in economic terms, the damage could have been much worse. Gujarat is one of India's most industrialised and hitherto wealthiest states, accounting for 13% of the country's industrial output and 11% of its income. Although there was much damage in Gujarat's economic capital of Ahmedabad, the state's industrial infrastructure remained largely intact. Of greater concern for Gujarat's, and hence India's, economic recovery was the significant damage suffered by Kandla Port which handles 17% of India's seagoing traffic. Not to mention the staggering social and economic cost for the reconstruction of shattered towns and communities.

slopes so gradually that as it stretches east from Delhi to the Bay of Bengal it only drops a total of 200m. The mighty, sacred Ganges River rises in Gangotri and drains a large part of the northern plain before merging with the Brahmaputra river. In the north-west, the Indus river starts flowing through Ladakh in India but soon diverts into Pakistan to become that country's most important river.

The North-East

The north-east boundary of India is defined by the foothills of the Himalaya, separating it from Myanmar (Burma). It's here that India bends around Bangladesh, nearly meeting the sea on its eastern side.

Centre & South

South of the northern plains, the land rises up into the high plateau of the Deccan. The plateau is bordered on both sides by ranges of hills that parallel the coast to the east and west. Of these, the Western Ghats are higher and have a wider coastal strip than the eastern; the two ranges meet in the extreme south in the Nilgiri Hills. The major rivers of the south are the Godavari and the Krishna. Both rise on the eastern slope of the Western Ghats and flow across the Deccan into the sea on the eastern coast.

The West

On the western side, India is separated from Pakistan by three distinct regions. In the north, in the disputed area of Kashmir, the boundary is formed by the Himalaya which drop down to the plains of Punjab, merging into the Great Thar Desert in the western part of Rajasthan. This is an area of great natural beauty and is extremely barren. It's hard to imagine that it was once covered by thick forests. Discoveries made by palaeontologists in 1996 suggest that the area was inhabited by dinosaurs and their ancestors as long as 300 million years ago.

Finally, the Indian state of Gujarat is separated from the Sind in Pakistan by the unusual marshland known as the Rann of Kutch. In the dry season (November to April), this marshland dries out, leaving many isolated salt islands perched on an expansive plain. In the wet season (June to August), the marshland floods to become a vast inland sea.

The Islands

Although politically part of India, the Andaman and Nicobar Islands, scattered along the eastern extremity of the Bay of Bengal, are in fact closer both physically and geographically to Myanmar and Indonesia respectively. The coral atolls, which are known as Lakshadweep, some 300km west of the Malabar coast, are in effect a northern extension of the Maldives.

There are 300 Andaman Islands in total and the dense forests that once covered their hilly interiors are unfortunately now much sparser due to rampant logging. The coasts are fringed with coral and are deeply indented, providing natural harbours and tidal creeks. The 19 Nicobar Islands are largely flat and coral-covered. An exception is Great Nicobar, which reaches 642m and has numerous streams making it the only island in the group with plentiful fresh water.

Lakshadweep consists of some two dozen islands covering a total land area of 22 sq km. All of the islands are coral atolls (theoretically formed around a submerged volcano) that slope towards the west, where low-lying lagoons protect the islands' inhabitants from the worst effects of the south-west monsoon.

CLIMATE

India is so vast that the climatic conditions in the far north have little relation to those of the extreme south. While the heat is building up to breaking point on the plains, the people of Ladakh, high in the Himalaya, will still be waiting for the snow to melt on the high passes.

India has a three-season year – the hot, the wet and the cool. Generally, the best time to visit is during winter (November to February) although there are regional variations (see the 'At a Glance' boxes at the start of each chapter for the best times to go to each area).

The Hot

The heat starts to build up on the northern plains of India from around February, and by April or May it becomes unbearable. In central India temperatures of 45°C and above are commonplace. It's dry and dusty and everything is seen through a haze.

Later in May, the first signs of the monsoon are visible – high humidity, violent electrical storms, short rainstorms and dust storms that turn day into night. The hot and humid weather towards the end of the hot season can leave you frazzled.

The hot season is the time to leave the plains and retreat into the hills, and this is when Himalayan hill stations and states such as Sikkim are at their best (and busiest). By early June, the snow on the passes into Ladakh melts and the roads reopen.

The Wet

When the monsoon finally arrives, it does not just suddenly appear. After some advance warning, the rain comes in steadily, starting around 1 June in the extreme south and sweeping north to cover the whole country by early July. The monsoon doesn't really cool things off; at first hot, dry, dusty weather is simply traded for hot, humid, muddy conditions. Even so, it's a great relief, not least for farmers who face their busiest time of year as they prepare fields for planting. It doesn't rain solidly all day during the monsoon, but it certainly rains every day; the water tends to come down in buckets for a while followed by the sun, which can be quite pleasant.

The main monsoon comes from the south-west, but the south-eastern coast is affected by the short and surprisingly wet north-east monsoon, which brings rain from mid-October to the end of December.

Although the monsoon brings life to India, it also brings its share of death. Almost every year there are destructive floods and thousands of people are made homeless. Rivers rise and sweep away road and railway lines and many flight schedules are disrupted, making travel during this period uncertain.

The Cool

Finally, around October, the monsoon ends for most of the country, and this is when most tourists visit. However, this is already too late to visit Ladakh and Zanskar – May to October is the optimum period. Generally, it's not too hot and not too cool (although in October it can still be humid in some regions). The air is clear in the Himalaya, and the mountains are clearly visible, at least early in the day. Delhi and other northern cities become quite crisp at night in December and January. It becomes downright cold in the far north, but snow brings India's small skiing industry into action so a few places, such as the Kullu Valley, have a winter season too.

In the far south, where it never gets cool, the temperatures become comfortably warm rather than hot. Then, around February, the temperatures start to climb again

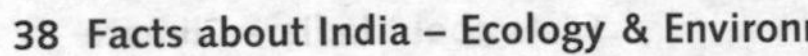

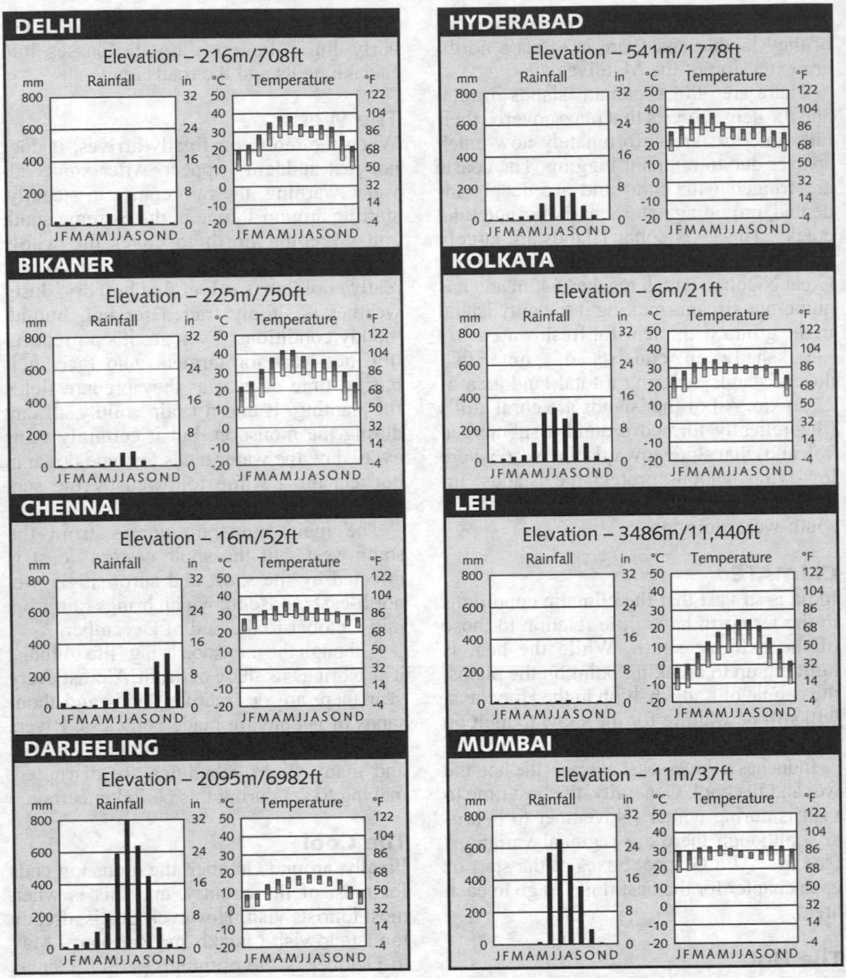

DELHI
Elevation – 216m/708ft

BIKANER
Elevation – 225m/750ft

CHENNAI
Elevation – 16m/52ft

DARJEELING
Elevation – 2095m/6982ft

HYDERABAD
Elevation – 541m/1778ft

KOLKATA
Elevation – 6m/21ft

LEH
Elevation – 3486m/11,440ft

MUMBAI
Elevation – 11m/37ft

and, before you know it, you're back in the sweltering hot weather.

ECOLOGY & ENVIRONMENT

With more than one billion people, rapid industrialisation, poor infrastructure, ongoing deforestation and heavy reliance on chemical fertilisers, pesticides and herbicides, India's environment is under immense pressure. While there is no shortage of legislation designed to protect the environment, corruption and flagrant abuses of power are exacerbating India's environmental degradation. Another growing problem is the use of outdated factory equipment that does not meet new pollution control guidelines, resulting in serious cases of ongoing air and water pollution.

Some of the most positive and tenacious conservation efforts have emerged from within grassroots communities intent on saving their homes, livelihoods and traditions. For example, in environmentally fragile Ladakh the locals are undertaking several initiatives, including energy-saving power and environmentally friendly tourism.

Of escalating concern nationwide is the level of discarded plastic (see Plastic Waste).

Conservation Contacts

The following organisations are working towards environmental protection and conservation in India and can offer information on conservation efforts nationwide. They may also be able to offer volunteer work.

Bombay Natural History Society (☎ 022-2821811, fax 2837615, ⓔ bnhs@bom4.vsnl.net.in) Hornbill House, Shahid Bhagat Singh Rd, Mumbai 400023. One of the more renowned environmental groups in India and the largest nongovernmental organisation (NGO) on the subcontinent, it publishes an impressive list of books on India's flora, fauna and conservation issues.

Equations (ⓔ admin@equation.ilban.ernet.in) 198 2nd Cross, Church Rd, New Thippasandra, Bangalore, Karnataka 560075. This tourism pressure group helps indigenous people.

Global Village Development Trust (☎ 07686-74237, 72250) Chandra Prabha Gardens, Rajnagan Rd, Khajuraho, Madhya Pradesh. Launched by residents of Khajuraho in 2000 with the aim of empowering the local community to combat ecological devastation, major issues include tackling polythene bags and other plastic waste, diminishing water sources, vehicle pollution and unhygienic garbage disposal practices. For more details contact Ajay Awasthi or Shailesh Singh.

Goa Desc Resource Centre (☎ 0832-252660) No 11 Liberty Apartments, Feira Alta, Mapusa, Goa 403507. The centre hosts a fortnightly discussion group on issues affecting Goa's environment.

Goa Foundation (☎ 0832-263305) c/o Other India Bookstore, Mapusa, Goa 403507. Goa's main environmental group publishes the monthly paper *Green Goa* and administers projects such as ridding Goa's beaches of plastic bottles.

Himalayan Environment Trust (☎ 011-6215635, fax 6862374) Legend Inn E-4 East of Kailash, New Delhi. This nonprofit trust raises public awareness about increasing ecological threats to the Himalaya.

Himalayan Foundation (☎ 0137-251268, fax 252367, ⓔ happrc@vsnl.com) Sartoli Village, PO Bagna, Nandprayag, Uttaranchal. The foundation is involved in large-scale afforestation in the Himalaya. The foundation has conservation projects covering 26,864 hectares in the Garhwal Himalaya.

Himalaya Trust (☎ 0135-773081, fax 620334, ⓔ ubcentre@del2.vsnl.net.in) 274/2 Vasant Vihar, Dehra Dun, Uttaranchal. The trust promotes the sustainable development of isolated mountain communities while safeguarding their environmental, cultural and spiritual heritage.

Madras Naturalists' Society (☎ 044-4997614) 8 Janaki Ave, Abhiramapuram, Chennai 600018. This is a good contact for environmental matters in this part of Tamil Nadu.

Mysore Amateur Naturalists (☎ 0821-541744) 571 9th Cross, Anikethana Rd, Kuvempu Nagar, Mysore, Karnataka. The naturalists are involved in Project Pelican, a local project to protect pelicans.

Sankat Mochan Foundation (☎ 0542-313884, fax 314278, ⓔ vbmganga@satyam.net.in) Tulsi Ghat, Varanasi. This foundation established the Swatcha Ganga Environmental Education Centre, which runs environmental education courses with schools, villages, Brahmin priests, pilgrims and boatmen regarding pollution problems in the Ganges river at Varanasi. Contact Professor Veer Bhadra Mishra.

Society for the Prevention of Cruelty to Animals
Bangalore: (SPCA; ☎ 080-5540205) Kasturba Rd, near Queen's Circle, Karnataka 560001
Kolkata: (☎ 033-2370520, ☎/fax 2365592, ⓔ bdhar@caltiger.com) 276BB Ganguly St, 700012
Both of these branches are deeply involved in animal cruelty issues.

Traffic India (☎ 011-4698578, fax 4626837, ⓔ traffic@wwfind.ernet.in) 172B Lodi Estate, New Delhi 110003. Active in campaigns against illegal wildlife trade.

Wildlife Institute of India (☎ 0135-620910, ⓔ wii.isnet@axcess.net.in) PO Box 18, Chandrabani, Dehra Dun, Uttaranchal. A leading authority on Indian fauna, it is involved in monitoring populations of Indian species.

Wildlife Preservation Society of India (no phone) 7 Astley Hall, Dehra Dun, Garhwal, Uttar Pradesh. The society promotes conservation awareness.

Wildlife Protection Society of India (☎ 011-6213864, fax 3368729, ⓔ blue@giasdlol.vsnl.net.in) Thapara House, 124 Janpath, Delhi. This society runs wildlife projects throughout the country.

World Wide Fund for Nature
Headquarters: (WWF; ☎ 011-4627586, fax 4626837) 172B Lodi Estate, Max Mueller Marg, New Delhi 110003
Mumbai: (☎ 022-2078105, fax 2076037) National Insurance Bldg
Goa: (☎ 0832-226020) Hill Side Apartments, Block B, Flat B2, Ground Floor, Fontainhas, Panaji, 403001
Kerala: (☎/fax 0471-325183) A/10 Tagore Nagar, TC No 15/989, Vazhutacaud, Thiruvananthapuram, 695014
Bangalore: (☎ 080-2863206, fax 2866685) Kamala Mansion, 143 Infantry Rd, 560001
Tamil Nadu: (☎ 044-4348064, fax 4347967) 28, 4th Main Road, CIT Nagar, Chennai, 600035
Hyderabad: (☎ 040-3327246) 38/A New Shanthi Nagar, 500057

Deforestation

India has a long tradition of venerating forests, and trees have always had their defenders. In the 18th century hundreds of men and women from the Bishnoi cult in Rajasthan risked their lives to save the sacred khejri trees – which the authorities wanted in order to burn lime – and this resulted in a ban on cutting any trees near a Bishnoi village. When the British commercialised forestry, protesters turned to the Gandhian protest form, satyagraha, to get their message across. In more recent times the Chipko Movement has taken up the cause. Begun as a localised protest in Uttarakhand (now Uttaranchal) in the mid-1970s, it has evolved into a much larger and more powerful force with women playing a leading role. When the authorities closed in to clear the protesters, women embraced the trees and refused to move. 'Soil, water and oxygen – not timber' is the Chipko catch cry, and this has echoed the length and breadth of India as communities fight to save their forest.

India's first Five Year Plan in 1951 recognised the importance of forest cover for soil conservation, and the national forest policy supported the idea of increasing forest cover to at least 33%. But today about a third of dense forest cover remains and, despite laws to protect it, more is lost every year.

There are many reasons why this has happened. Fuel wood, upon which millions of people depend, is being removed from forests at a rate of about 250 million tonnes a year – only a quarter of this can be extracted without permanent damage. As grazing lands shrink, domestic animals increasingly move into the forests causing damage. Denotification, a process whereby states may relax the ban on commercial exploitation of protected areas, is another factor. States are supposed to earmark an equivalent area for reafforestation, but conservationists say this isn't always happening or the land set aside often isn't suitable. Smuggling is another problem in some areas; the Western Ghats are regularly plundered for valuable sandalwood and rosewood. Forest rangers are ill-equipped to deal with armed-to-the-teeth tree poachers. Natural disasters such as a series of landslides in northern Uttar Pradesh (now Uttaranchal) in 1998 (which killed 400 people and destroyed 12 villages) also contribute to deforestation. While plantation forest has increased in relative terms, critics point out that eucalyptus and other similarly exotic strands are no substitute for native forest.

In the late 1990s the government took steps to increase reafforestation, calling for action at village level and more vigilant antipoaching measures. It is yet to be seen whether there will be marked improvements.

Many of the organisations mentioned under Conservation Contacts are involved in afforestation campaigns. The Web site www.greencleanindia.com is dedicated to planting more trees, ecological protection and increased public awareness of environmental issues.

Soil Degradation

An estimated 65% of India's land is degraded in some way, causing a rethink in the heavy use of chemicals encouraged during the Green Revolution of the 1960s when a quantum leap in agricultural output was achieved. India is the world's fourth largest consumer of fertilisers, but with some 20 million more mouths to feed every year, fertiliser will continue to be dumped on agricultural land. Much of this runs off into surface water and leaches into ground water. The insecticides DDT and Benzene Hexachloride (BHC) were outlawed in 1992 and 1996 respectively. (Since Independence more than one million tonnes of DDT and BHC have been dumped on the land.)

Yet the demand for other chemicals seems unlikely to decline. Between 10 and 25% of annual produce is damaged by pests. Most of the damage, however, is caused by water erosion, which accounts for around 80% of degraded land. Water and wind erosion are largely caused by the loss of tree cover. Unfortunately, policies aimed at helping agriculturalists, such as providing subsidies on irrigation and pesticides and bringing village water resources under government control, have added to the problem. Constant cropping also creates problems. Recent reports indicate that constant cropping has caused severe mineral depletion from soils. This, coupled with the dumping of industrial effluents, explains the rise in various diseases in humans, ranging from goitre to respiratory ailments.

But, at a local level, some people are trying to turn the tide. In October 1997, for example, farmers in the orchard-rich area of Dahanu near Mumbai, disillusioned with conventional techniques, welcomed a visit from Masanobu Fukuoka, Japanese natural-farming guru and author of the *One Straw Revolution.*

Water Resources

Arguably the biggest threat to public health in India is inadequate access to clean drinking water and proper sanitation. Agriculture, which uses 85% of water consumed in India, is expected to double its demand by 2025. Industry is similarly expected to double the amount it uses, and domestic use will triple. Already some parts of India, eg, northern Gujarat, are suffering serious shortages. More than 40% of Gujarat's electricity is expended on powering bore wells. And big cities such as Chennai and Delhi cannot supply all their citizens' water needs; water tankers are a frequent sight in the suburbs that can afford to truck in water from other areas. Ground water (the source of 85% of rural drinking water and 55% of urban drinking water) is suffering from uncontrolled extraction and is extremely vulnerable to contamination from leaching. In West Bengal (and Bangladesh) ever-deeper tube wells contaminated with arsenic (which occurs naturally in pyrite bedrock) are poisoning tens of thousands of villagers. In Tamil Nadu the water table is falling by more than 1m every year. Much pumped water trickles away from leaky pipes (some estimate that nationwide the loss amounts to at least half of all water piped). India's rivers, too, suffer from run off, industrial pollution and sewage contamination – the Sabarmati and Ganges are the most polluted rivers in India.

The Dam Debate

Few projects highlight so tragically the dilemmas of development as the Narmada Valley Development Project. The ambitious and highly controversial US$6 billion project seeks to harness the waters of the river systems of the Narmada Valley and create 30 major, 135 medium and 3000 small dams. Anyone who spends any time in the states of Gujarat, Madhya Pradesh and Rajasthan will understand the region's critical need for water. During the crippling drought of 1999–2000, some towns received piped water supplies only every three days and the failure of monsoonal rains ensured that the agricultural sector was decimated. The Gujarat government has also claimed that all available surface waters have been tapped, ground water aquifers have contributed to a falling water table leading to problems with fluoride, nitrate and salinity, and 43% of Gujarat's energy is consumed by power bore-wells that go deeper every year. In contrast, exploiting the waters of the Narmada is said to provide reliable drinking water to 8215 villages and 135 urban centres, not to mention the flow-on effects of stemming urban migration and slowing the process of desertification.

The human and environmental consequences of the project, however, are similarly compelling. Critics of the project – the most prominent among them being Booker Prize-winning Indian author Arundhati Roy and the Narmada Bachao Andolan (Save the Narmada Movement) – vehemently oppose the project on the grounds that it will displace tens of thousands of Adivasi villagers who have lived along and worshipped the waters of the Narmada river for generations and will significantly alter the ecology of an entire river basin. Such concerns were sufficient for the World Bank to withdraw its support for the project in 1993.

For now, the argument seems to have been won by the government and developers. On 18 December 2000 the Indian Supreme Court gave permission for the project to proceed and even allowed the dam to be raised to a height of 90m, above the minimum height supporters of the project were willing to accept. A minority judgment called for an environmental impact statement before proceeding.

The Gujarat government hailed the decision as ushering in 'a golden age in the history of Gujarat' and pointed to overwhelming popular support from the population because it will alleviate critical water shortages. The project's critics decried the decision as 'antipeople' and vowed to fight on to protect the rights of the soon-to-be-displaced villagers to gain recognition for alternatives such as biomass and solar energy systems and rain-fed irrigation systems. In the meantime, the dam walls (and river levels) are slowly rising.

Less than 20% of the newly formed Chhatisgarh state is irrigated and the region experiences frequent droughts. In 2000 more than 50% of landless labourers and farmers migrated from the region because of droughts, which had the domino effect of preventing production from more than half of the rice mills, Chhatisgarh's main crop.

Air Pollution

There are approximately 45 million vehicles plying Indian roads. About 60% of them are two-stroke vehicles such as autorickshaws which, though economical to run and despite attempts to control their emissions, spew out pollutants. There's little incentive to move away from diesel, which is subsidised and relatively cheap.

Over the past decade, Delhi's vehicles have been a major source of air pollutants (see the boxed text 'Kicking the Habit' in the Delhi chapter). However, in recent years there has been a push to improve the situation: Taxis, rickshaws and buses that are more than eight years old are now banned from Delhi and all taxis now use gas instead of diesel. In addition, the completion of the metro (currently under way) should further improve the situation. There are also plans to clean the Yamuna and move all industry out of the city.

Meanwhile in Agra, the 4km area surrounding the Taj Mahal was designated as a traffic-free zone in 1994. This was followed in 1999 by a Supreme Court ruling that ordered the closure of various polluting factories in the area. Illegal buildings within 500m of the Taj were also torn down under the ruling. Unfortunately, the legislature was sanctioned without any provision for the people affected by it. Many factories were forced to close without compensation, and others signed up to government relocation schemes only to find that the sites set aside for relocation were little more than plots in the desert, without water, power or roads. However, there have been positive developments in Agra, most notably the introduction of nonpolluting electric vehicles (many of which featured in the entourage during former US President Bill Clinton's visit to the Taj in 2000), and even cycle-rickshaws have been designed to lighten the load on the driver. Most of these schemes have been funded by American and European NGOs in collaboration with local hotels and Uttar Pradesh Tourism.

Despite ongoing government pledges and laws aimed at curtailing toxic emissions, industry accounts for significant levels of pollution around the nation, especially in the major cities. In fact, the worst disaster in India, indeed one of the worst industrial disasters in the world, was Bhopal (see boxed text 'The Bhopal Disaster – Curing an Outrage with Neglect' in the Madhya Pradesh & Chhatisgarh chapter).

Plastic Waste

Almost everywhere in India plastic bags and bottles clog drains, litter city streets, deserts and beaches and even stunt grass growth in the parks. Of growing concern are the number of cows, elephants and other creatures that consume plastic waste, resulting in a slow and painful death. The antiplastic lobby estimates that about 72% of the plastics used are discarded within a week and only 15% are recycled. It's up to individuals (including travellers) to restrict their use of plastic, and responsibly recycle bottles and bags. Fortunately there are more and more local initiatives to combat the plastic peril. For instance, shopping bags in Kodaikanal are now made from paper instead of plastic. For more information see Responsible Tourism in the Facts for the Visitor chapter.

Energy

Thermal plants account for about 75% of India's total power generation. Coal is the primary source of this energy, accounting for 67% of the nation's commercial requirement. In 1976 oil was discovered off the shores of Maharashtra. Crude production grew at about 10% a year until the mid-1980s when it declined due to ageing fields and delays in finding new sources. The government has been forced to turn to imports to meet domestic demand.

Far less important, but much more controversial, is the use of hydro and nuclear power. The benefits of hydro dams have been offset by environmental and social costs that critics claim cannot be justified in many cases (see the boxed text 'The Dam Debate'). Himachal Pradesh has recently begun a vast campaign to harness the hydroelectric potential of the state's major rivers. Construction is under way on a series of huge dams and power plants on the Sutlej, Baspa, Ravi and Parbati rivers, all of which pass through areas of great natural beauty. The projects were conceived as a way to open up the rugged mountain country to economic development, but threaten both the local environment and the traditional mountain way of life.

The installed power generation capacity in India has escalated from just 1400MW in 1947 to 92,864MW at the close of 1999. Nuclear power contributes less than 2000 MW, and the share of electricity produced is usually about 1%.

Biomass (cow dung, agricultural residues, wood) is important in the noncommercial sector, especially for cooking. About three-quarters is consumed as firewood.

Renewable energy installations include wind energy, solar and mini/micro hydro. India is the fourth largest producer of wind energy (Germany, the USA and Denmark are the leaders).

FLORA & FAUNA

There's a certain place on the Gulf of Kutch in Gujarat where the desert merges with the sea. It's here that the flamingos with brilliant, pink plumage come in their thousands to build nest mounds from the salty mud, and then raise their young. It's just one among many extraordinary sights in a country that can claim one of the world's richest natural heritages: 65,000 species of fauna including 350 of mammals (7.6% of the world's total), 408 of reptiles (6.2%), 197 of amphibians (4.4%), 1244 of birds (12.6%), 2546 of fish (11.7%) as well as 15,000 of flowering plants (6%).

Out of this huge number, the nation has chosen the tiger as its national animal, the peacock as its national bird and the lotus as the national flower.

Flora

The country has some 16 major forest types which can be further subdivided into 221 minor types. Tropical forests are found in the Andaman and Nicobar Islands, the Western Ghats and the greater Assam region. There are a few patches left in Orissa. The commercial value of the trees within these forests have opened them to exploitation; in the Western Ghats, for example, Indian rosewood *(Dalbergia latifolia)*, Malabar kino *(Pterocarpus marsupium)* and teak have been virtually cleared from some areas.

In the Himalaya alpine, temperate and subtropical vegetation can be found. Above the snowline hardy little plants like anemones, edelweiss and gentian grow. Farther down, in the monsoon-soaked foothills, are mossy evergreen forests with cinnamon, chestnut, birch and plum. On the terai (plain), the

Mother Nature's Healing Touch

When Rama's brother lay mortally wounded in Lanka, home of the evil king Ravana, Rama's loyal deputy Hanuman (the monkey god) flew to a sacred mountain in the Himalaya for lifesaving herbs. But when Hanuman got there he couldn't decide which plants to pick. Instead, he lifted up the entire mountain and carried it back to Lanka. On the way there, and during the return journey, bits and pieces of earth dropped off, scattering plants all over the Western Ghats in South India. This, or so the story goes, is how plants used in traditional Ayurvedic medicine came to grow in southern India.

Ayurveda is the ancient and complex science of Indian herbal medicine/healing. Some 2000 plant species are described in Ayurveda and at least 550 are in regular use. More than 85% are gathered from the wild, but many are now under threat. The *Rauwolfia serpentina*, for example, used to treat blood pressure, is found only in India. It is in worldwide demand but the supply cannot meet the demand, with worrying consequences for the future of the species. In addition, there are questions arising over intellectual property rights to medicinal plants and the equitable distribution of the benefits of their commercial development.

In present-day medicine, many doctors in India are looking to the past to treat the diseases of today. In Mumbai a group of Indian doctors and herbalists is currently investigating whether Ayurvedic medicine can cure AIDS (see also the boxed text 'AIDS in India' under Health in the Facts for the Visitor chapter). Meanwhile at Delhi's All India Institute of Medical Sciences, doctors are combining *pranayama*, the traditional science of breath control, with chemotherapy.

dominant vegetation is usually sal *(Shorea robusta)*, a hardwood tree. The Indian banyan (fig) tree is dotted throughout India.

In the harsh extremes of India's hot deserts the khejri tree *(Prosopis cineraria)* and various strains of acacia (scrubby, thorny plants well adapted to the conditions) flourish. Any plant here needs to withstand temperatures of 50°C plus. Many have roots that can snake down deep into the soil to find water, and the leaves on most are small to minimise evaporation.

Fauna

The Himalaya harbour a hardy range of creatures. Ladakh's freezing, high altitudes are home to the yak, a shaggy, horned wild ox weighing around one tonne; the two-humped Bactrian camel, which inhabits high-altitude dunes; a wild sheep called the Ladakh urial; the Tibetan antelope; the bharal (blue sheep); the kiang (Tibetan wild ass); the Himalayan ibex; and the Himalayan tahr. Other Himalayan inhabitants include black and brown bears (found in Kashmir), marmot, mouse-hare and musk deer. The musk deer are delicate creatures lacking antlers, but with hare-like ears and canines that in males look like tusks. This animal, not a true deer at all, has been hunted mercilessly for its musk, which is used in perfume.

When it comes to mystique, none of these animals matches the snow leopard. It's so elusive that many myths have grown up around it; some believe it can appear and disappear at will. There are fewer than 5000 snow leopards left in the world, and the number is dropping. They can still be found in Sikkim and Arunachal Pradesh.

The endearing but very rare red panda inhabits the bamboo thickets of the eastern Himalaya where it feeds on bamboo shoots, fruit, leaves and insects. The lakes and marshes of Kashmir provide temporary homes to migrating waterbirds, geese and ducks, many of which fly all the way from Siberia to winter here. Some species exhibit an extraordinary affinity with high altitude travel; the red and yellow-billed crow-like choughs are capable of flying well above 5000m.

Down on the lowlands India teems with life. It is here that nature and humanity are locked in the most intense competition for land and livelihood. Nature is on the run in many places; animals are losing their habitat as poverty and population pressure drives people beyond their cities and villages, and possibly into poaching and hunting.

The Ganges and Yamuna merge on the northern plain before twisting and turning their way for thousands of kilometres to empty into the Bay of Bengal, creating a delta of some 80,000 sq km. Within this delta are the swampy Sunderbans, home to a large population of tigers (estimated to number just under 300 in 2000), aquatic reptiles, fish, crabs, wild boars, visiting sea turtles, snakes and chital. The chitals have adapted to the environment's saltiness by acquiring the ability to secrete salt from glands. In the freshwater reaches of the Ganges River (Ganga) live Gangetic dolphins, Shiva's mythical messengers; crocodiles (mugger or marsh crocs, plus the narrow-snouted antediluvian-looking gharial), scavenger crabs and many species of fish.

The one-horned rhino and elephant can still (only just) be found in the northern grasslands (see Endangered Species later in this section).

The harsh deserts of Rajasthan and Gujarat are surprisingly well populated. The chinkara (Indian gazelle), the wild ass, the Indian wolf and the black buck have all adapted to the heat, salty soils, and limited water resources of the region. The 1400 sq km Sasan Gir Wildlife Sanctuary in Gujarat is the last refuge of the Asiatic lion; in May 2000 these were an estimated 325. These lions lack the impressive shaggy mane of their African relatives and they have an extra fold of skin on their bellies.

India's primates range from the extremely rare golden langur, found near the Bhutanese border, to more common species such as the

The one-horned rhino struggles for survival in India.

bonnet macaque and its northern cousin, the rhesus macaque. The rainforests of the south also have rare lion-tailed macaques, glossy black Nilgiri langurs and the endangered slender loris (the slow loris is found in eastern India).

Distributed reasonably widely in peninsular India are dhole (wild dogs), jackals, and several species of deer and gazelle, including the relatively common sambar. Barking deer and mouse deer are now quite rare. The snake-killing mongoose, immortalised by Kipling, is still hale and hearty.

Those averse to slithering creatures may prefer to ignore the fact that India has 238 species of snakes, 50 of them (including 20 species of sea snakes) being poisonous. Found widely in India, the cobra, king of the snakes (at least mythologically), is the world's largest venomous snake – it grows up to 5m long. Its characteristic pose of arousal, hood spread, is an enduring image for anyone who's seen a snake charmer at work. Other poisonous snakes include the krait, Russel's viper and the saw-scaled viper. These four snakes together account for some 10,000 deaths each year, but on the whole it's rare for snakes and humans to come in contact. Harmless snakes include the rat snake, which looks disturbingly like a cobra, the bright green vine snake, the dark brown bronze-back tree snake and the rock python.

The forests of the Western Ghats, which stretch all the way south from Mumbai to the tip of the peninsula, harbour a wealth of wildlife and plant life. Within their wet, relatively undisturbed confines can be found one of the rarest bats in the world, the small fruit-eating *Latidens salimalii*, flying lizards that can glide for up to 12m, sloth bears, leopards, jungle cats, hornbills and many other species of bird. Here, too, on the mountains' rocky, misty slopes is the last remaining stronghold of the endangered Nilgiri tahr, or cloud goat.

Beyond the mainland, in the waters of the Bay of Bengal to the east and the Indian Ocean to the west, lie the Andaman and Nicobar Islands and Lakshadweep, respectively. Marine turtles, bottle-nosed dolphins, a hugely rich bird population (225 species and subspecies in the Andaman and Nicobar Islands alone), reptiles, amphibians, butterflies (hundreds of species), fish and coral are all found here. Also in the Andamans is a small population of elephants (some of which roam wild) brought over from the mainland by logging companies. These elephants are capable of swimming up to 3km between islands. Another oddity found in this part of the world is the coconut or robber crab, which (despite weighing up to 5kg) scuttles up coconut trees and tears open the fruit with its strong claws.

Endangered Species

Large animals such as elephants, tigers and rhinos are often early and highly noticeable indicators of things going wrong with the ecosystem. By that measure, India's natural world is looking less than robust. All three species are in danger of extinction.

Wildlife sanctuaries have existed since ancient times, but after Independence many more were created. In 1972 the Wildlife Protection Act was introduced to stem the abuse of wildlife, followed by other conservation-oriented legislation such as the Forest Conservation Act and the Environment Protection Act. India is one of 143 signatories to the Convention on International Trade in Endangered Species of Fauna and Flora (Cites) brought into force in 1975 to regulate the trade in endangered wildlife. But huge pressure from a growing population hungry for land, a massive demand for animal body parts from the insatiable Chinese medicine market and an international market for skins and fur are proving to be a virtually insurmountable force.

There are an estimated 65,000 animals belonging to about 645 different species in India's 230 zoos, most of which are run by state governments. The recent death of a dozen tigers (including eight rare white tigers) in Orissa's Nandankanan zoo, highlighted the dire need to review its (and other zoos') shoestring budgets, cramped cages and overall tardy management of animals in captivity. Authorities claim the tigers at Nandankanan died from an insect-transmitted disease, which could have been avoided if detected earlier. Some vets advocate that over-population (56 tigers were confined to a limited area) triggered the deadly disease.

India is one of 12 so-called megadiversity countries which together account for up to 70% of the world's biodiversity. It's the only country in the world that is home

Major National Parks & Wildlife Sanctuaries

national park/ wildlife sanctuary	location	features	best time to visit
Valley of Flowers National Park	25km from Badrinath, Uttaranchal	3500m above sea level: wildflowers & butterflies	June–Nov
Corbett Tiger Reserve	50km from Ramnagar, Uttaranchal	sal forest & river plains: tigers, chitals, deers, elephants, leopards & sloth bears	Nov–June
Rajaji National Park	13km from Haridwar, Uttaranchal	forested hills: elephants, tigers, leopards, deer & sloth bears	Nov–June
Govind Wildlife Sanctuary & National Park	Saur-Sanki, Uttaranchal	mountain scenery: black & brown bears, snow leopards, deer, birdlife	June–Nov
Pin Valley National Park	Dhankar, Himachal Pradesh	pristine mountains: snow leopards, ibex, black bears, deer	June–Nov
Sunderbans Wildlife Sanctuary	southern West Bengal	mangrove forests: tigers, deer, monkeys & birdlife	Jan–Mar
Jaldhapara Wildlife Sanctuary	northern West Bengal	forest & grasslands: Indian rhinos, deer & elephants	Oct–May
Kaziranga National Park	Assam, North-Eastern Region	tall grasslands & swamp: rhinos, elephants, tigers & birdlife	Feb–Mar
Sariska National Park	Sariska, Rajasthan	plains: tigers, chinkaras, sambars, nilgais & wild boars	Nov–June
Ranthambhore National Park	south of Jaipur, Rajasthan	around crocodile-filled lake: crocodiles & tigers	Oct–Apr
Keoladeo Ghana National Park	Bharatpur, Rajasthan	plains: Siberian cranes, herons, storks, geese & deer	Oct–late Feb
Sasan Gir Wildlife Sanctuary	Sasan Gir, Gujarat	oasis in desert: Asian lions, chowsinghas leopards & crocodiles	Dec–Apr
Velavadar National Park	near Bhavnagar, Gujarat	grasslands in delta region: blackbucks	Oct–June
Little Rann of Kutch Wildlife Sanctuary	north-western Gujarat	desert region: Indian wild ass (khurs), wolves & caracals	Oct–June

to both lions and tigers. But all across India a great many species are facing a perilous future. The tiger, India's national animal, seems to personify the situation. In 2000 the Environmental Investigation Agency (EIA) believed that at least 100 tigers had been slaughtered by poachers in that year. With skins used as trophies and bones ground into virility potions (like rhinos' horns), a whole tiger can fetch at least US$10,000. With over half the world's remaining tiger population in India, environmentalists are calling for the creation of a government agency to deal specifically with tiger poaching. While the statistics for the tiger population are unclear, it is clear that as long as its natural habitats are decreasing and there is no government protection agency, the tiger's days are numbered.

The one-horned rhinoceros' position is equally tenuous as it loses its natural grasslands habitat to sugar cane plantations and other cultivation. It's now found only in small pockets near the Nepalese border. Its horn, actually matted hair, is sought for its supposed medicinal properties, as are its urine, flesh and blood.

The snow leopard, which is found in Sikkim and Arunachal Pradesh, is recognised internationally as endangered. Its fur obtains high prices, so it continues to be a prime target.

Major National Parks & Wildlife Sanctuaries

national park/ wildlife sanctuary	location	features	best time to visit
Kanha National Park	Jabalpur, Madhya Pradesh	swamp: deer, tigers, chitals, gaurs, blackbucks, leopards & hyenas	Mar–June
Bandhavgarh National Park	Jabalpur, Madhya Pradesh	old fort on cliffs above plains: tigers	Nov–Apr
Navagaon National Park	135km east of Nagpur, Maharashtra	hilly forest & bamboo groves around a man-made lake: leopards, sloth bears, deer & migratory birds	Oct–June
Similipal National Park	Balasore, Orissa	forest: tigers, leopards, elephants, crocodiles & birdlife	Nov–June
Sanjay Gandhi National Park	near Mumbai, Maharashtra	scenic area: waterbirds, butterflies	Oct–Apr & Aug–Nov
Periyar Wildlife Sanctuary	Kumily, Kerala	highland deciduous forest & grasslands: langurs, elephants, gaurs, otters, wild dogs, tortoises kingfishers & fishing owls	Nov–Apr
Nilgiri Biosphere Reserve (Bandipur, Nagarhole, Wayanad & Mudumulai)	Karnataka, Tamil Nadu & Kerala	forest: elephants, gaurs, sambars, muntjacs, chevrotains, chitals, bonnet macaques, leopards, giant squirrels & birds	Jan–June
Vedantangal Bird Sanctuary	near Chengalpattu, Tamil Nadu	lake & island: cormorants, egrets, herons, stork ibis, spoonbills, grebes & pelicans	Nov–Jan
Calimere Wildlife & Bird Sanctuary	near Thanjavur, Tamil Nadu	coastal wetland: blackbucks, flamingos, water fowls, wild pigs & deer	Nov–Jan
Indira Gandhi Wildlife Sanctuary	near Pollachi, Tamil Nadu	forested mountains: elephants, gaurs, tigers, panthers, boars, bears, deer, porcupines & civet cats	Nov–Dec
Mahatma Gandhi National Marine Park	Andaman & Nicobar Islands	mangrove, rainforest & coral: diving & snorkelling	year-round

Meanwhile, in December 2000 Indian police seized 809 tortoises from smugglers, estimated to be worth around US$30,000 on the international market. The tortoise has recently been declared an endangered species and its future also looks bleak unless adequate protection measures are implemented.

At present there are about 2500 Indian elephants in the wild and, inspired by efforts to save the tiger, conservationists have launched a major effort to ensure their numbers stay relatively stable. Project Elephant began in 1992 under the auspices of the Ministry of Environment & Forests, but with individual states contributing towards field costs and salaries. Eleven elephant reserves have been established, encompassing the four main elephant populations. These are in the north-west (Uttar Pradesh and Uttaranchal); central and east (Bihar and Jharkhand, Orissa, West Bengal); north-east (Arunachal Pradesh, Assam, Meghalaya, Nagaland); and south (Karnataka, Kerala, Tamil Nadu, Andhra Pradesh). Overall, the project aims to protect elephants and elephant habitats. Although the project has achieved marked results, poaching and elephant deaths in captivity continues to pose a real threat to the existing elephant population.

Trade in plants, animals and insects, both dead and alive, is monitored by a WWF

SIMON BORG

The tiger, India's national animal, is now an endangered species.

division called Traffic India (see Conservation Contacts earlier in this chapter). It targeted domestic consumers and overseas travellers in the hope of making them more aware of India's role in the insidious US$20 billion global wildlife market. Of particular concern is the trade in tiger bones, rhino horns, reptile skins, live mammals and reptiles, turtle shells and birds. A Delhi-based NGO called Friends of Butterflies has been instrumental in raising awareness of the trade in rare species, especially from the north-east (the 1972 Wildlife Protection Act specifically bans the trade in butterflies). The global butterfly trade is worth some US$200 million and rising, and the Himalaya mountains and foothills are the source of many rare species. Butterfly conservationists point out that the Atlas moth of the Khasi Hills is almost extinct due to poaching – this is an environmental catastrophe because it cross-pollinates many plants.

National Parks & Sanctuaries

India has 84 national parks and 447 wildlife sanctuaries which constitute about 4.5% of the entire country. India currently has 11 biosphere reserves. These biosphere reserves have been established to conserve the diversity of various ecosystems and to promote research into ecological conservation.

Parks and sanctuaries are a major tourist drawcard. Whenever possible, book in advance for transport and accommodation and check whether a permit is required (see individual chapters for details). Various fees are charged for your visit (entrance, photography etc) and these are often included in advance arrangements.

Most parks offer jeep or van tours and some offer boat trips or elephant safaris to approach wildlife more discreetly. Watchtowers and hides are also sometimes available – they're great for observing wildlife close up.

GOVERNMENT & POLITICS

India is a constitutional democracy. There are 29 states and six union territories (which are administered by the President in Delhi, through an appointed administrator) and the constitution (which came into force on 26 January 1950) details the powers of the central and state governments as well as those powers that are shared. If the situation in a particular state is deemed to be unmanageable, the central government has the controversial right to assume power there. Known as President's Rule, this has been enforced in recent years, either because the law and order situation has got out of hand – notably in Punjab from 1985 to 1992, Kashmir in 1990 and in Assam in 1991 – or because there is a political stalemate, such as occurred in Goa, Tamil Nadu, Pondicherry, Haryana and Meghalaya in the early 1990s.

Parliament is bicameral; the lower house is known as the Lok Sabha (House of the People) and the upper house is known as the Rajya Sabha (Council of States).

The Lok Sabha has 545 members, and elections (using the first past the post system) are held every five years, unless the government calls an election earlier. All Indians over the age of 18 have the right to vote. Of the 545 seats, 125 are reserved for the Scheduled Castes (official term for Dalits or Untouchables) and Tribes.

The upper house consists of 245 members; members are elected for six-year terms and a third of the house is elected every two years. The president appoints 12 members and the rest are elected by state assemblies using a regional quota system. The president, whose duties are largely ceremonial, is elected by both houses and the state legislatures (the election is held once every five years). The president must act on the advice of a council of ministers, chosen by the prime minister. The president may dissolve the lower house but not the upper.

At state level some legislatures are bicameral, and are run along the lines of the two houses of the national parliament. The chief minister is responsible to the legislature in the same way as the prime minister is responsible to parliament. Each state has a governor, who is appointed by the president and who may assume wide powers in times of crisis. At village level (where 75% of the population lives) there has been renewed interest in reviving the panchayat system of village councils, from where a number of volunteers are elected to represent the local people's interests.

After years of lobbying for autonomy, in November 2000 India gained three new states. Chhatisgarh has been carved out of Madhya Pradesh, Uttaranchal out of Uttar Pradesh and Jharkhand out of Bihar. Many analysts say that the creation of these new states will intensify campaigning by other secessionist groups seeking autonomy within India.

ECONOMY

In June 1991 India ended 40 years of central planning. Since Independence it had been so highly protectionist that its share of world trade had declined from 2% in the 1950s to less than 0.5% in the 1980s. The reforms generated a huge increase in private investment, boosting exports and reducing the role of the public sector in many areas including heavy manufacturing, banking, telecommunications, power generation and distribution, ports and roads.

In 1999 export growth was pegged at 6.1%. The 1999 budget concluded that the only way India could sustain and accelerate economic growth was by combining fiscal discipline with robust economic reforms. Time will only tell if the government puts this into action.

India's exports comprise some 7500 commodities to almost 200 countries. Imports come from more than 140 countries and cover around 6000 types of products. The country's main exports are gems and jewellery, cotton yarn and fabrics, handicrafts, cereals, marine products, ready-made garments and transport equipment. India's burgeoning software industry has recently emerged as a major foreign exchange earner (see Information Technology).

The Indian government is facing rapidly escalating pressure to further deregulate (a condition of World Bank and International Monetary Fund monies) which has fuelled certain anxieties. In particular, inexpensive Chinese imports have begun to flood local markets and while Indian politicians promote this as an indication that India is indeed a truly free market, there are some concerns as to whether Indian producers are adequately geared up to face such stiff competition.

India's current account deficit increased from US$4.04 billion in 1998–99 to US$4.16 billion in 1999–2000. Economic growth in 1999 was a healthy 6.8%, however economists say that policies need further restructuring to achieve the 8% growth rate of the mid-1990s. Although the Vajpayee government vows to improve the economic climate through greater privatisation, a substantial proportion of potential foreign investors claim that there is still far too much red tape involved, making India a 'too hard' option.

While Vajpayee may publicly champion growth, a recent Indian magazine reported that he is particularly worried about the digital divide 'between the IT haves and have-nots' and the ramifications it could have on societal inequalities. Nonetheless, India is striding ahead. In the late 1990s, for instance, the government of Andhra Pradesh in collaboration with leading private enterprises, established 'Hitec City' (Hyderabad Information Technology Engineering Consulting), 20km from Hyderabad. Offering generous tax breaks and other attractive subsidies, this is one of many mushrooming developments aimed at luring international software development corporations to India. Already more than 45 companies have set up shop at Hitec City and many more are expected to follow. So significant is this place that it was on President Clinton's schedule when he visited the region in 2000.

Agriculture

Agriculture contributes 27% of India's gross domestic product (GDP) and employs some 64% of the workforce. It is highly protected and subsidised. Less than 1% of the raw commodities produced (India is one of the world's most prolific producers of fruit, vegetables, milk, wheat, rice and sugar) is processed and there are heavy restrictions on the import of processed foods. Foodgrains make up 63% of India's agricultural output (203 million tonnes in 1998–99), with the government expecting to produce 234 million tonnes in 2001–02.

Punjab, the 'breadbasket of India', is one of the country's leading food producers (about 85% of the total land area is covered in crops, mainly wheat and rice). In fact, India is the world's second largest producer of paddy rice and the fourth largest wheat producer. It is the world's number one tea producer – the main growing regions are Assam, West Bengal, Kerala and Tamil Nadu – most is exported. Coffee is a smaller plantation crop; Karnataka is the major centre. Rubber is an important crop domestically (India only imports about 5% of its needs). Kerala leads the country in rubber production, and together with Tamil Nadu accounts for 86% of the area given over to rubber plantation. India leads the world in the production of bananas, mangoes, coconuts and cashews, as well as potatoes, tomatoes, onions and green peas. It is among the top 10 producers of citrus, pineapples and apples. India has the world's biggest livestock population; 57% of the world's buffalo population and 15% of cattle. It is the largest milk producer on earth, producing 73.5 million tonnes in 1998–99.

Industry

The state and central governments own and operate many of the enterprises that supply other producers, eg, fertiliser, machinery and chemicals. The private sector is made up of thousands of producers as well as a few large conglomerates (eg, the Tata Iron and Steel Company).

Of the big industry sectors, it's textile manufacturing – jute, cotton, wool, silk and synthetics – that employs the largest workforce (64.2 million in the mid-1990s as opposed to 39 million at the beginning of that decade). Textile exports currently account for more than one-third of India's total earnings. But by far the biggest employers in the manufacturing sector are the millions of small handicraft businesses, some of which service only their own village.

Manufacturing growth in the textile industry in 1999 was pegged at 6.7%, as compared to 3.9% in the previous year. The rise is partly due to improved electricity infrastructure. The textile industry in India is a well-established one, with the first mill being opened back in 1854 in Mumbai.

In 1993–96 growth in India's industrial sector touched 9% per annum, but slowed in the late 1990s and was 6.2% in the latter half of 1999, a result, it's claimed, of the high cost of credit and infrastructure impediments. In its latest budget, the BJP-led government remained committed to privatisation in certain public sector industries and pledged a 35% increase in outlay for power, communications and energy.

Information Technology

In 1999–2000 Indian software exports earned about US$4 billion. By 2002 earnings are expected to touch US$6 billion, with the number of companies exporting software tipped to exceed 1000. Tamil Nadu, Karnataka and Andhra Pradesh currently account for 60% of India's software exports. Bangalore is the industry's centre with exports of US$1.2 billion in 1998–99 (see the boxed text 'India's Silicon Valley' in the Karnataka chapter), while Tamil Nadu's software exports trebled between 1996 and 1999 to US$270 million, and Andhra Pradesh's exports grew even faster. Bangalore boasts the headquarters of one of India's software giants Infosys, while the other, Satyam Infoway, calls Chennai home.

Interestingly, India's software industry actually started in Mumbai during the early 1980s, but the high cost of living and inadequate infrastructure forced IT developers and overseas companies to look elsewhere – chiefly to Bangalore, but also to Hyderabad and Chennai. Nonetheless, Mumbai has maintained a firm grip on software production, particularly in the film and television industries. Since 1998 an estimated 122 software companies have set up in Mumbai. However, during recent years, Pune (Maharashtra) has made enormous strides, with its cheaper property costs and more agreeable climate than the capital, Mumbai. Pune has attracted software giants to a handful of IT parks, including Pune Infotech Park, Software Tech Park Pune and Kharadi Knowledge Park. The success of these ventures has sparked increased investment, resulting in a flow-on effect to Mumbai (now that the six-lane expressway between the two cities is functional). This so-called 'knowledge corridor' between Mumbai and Pune now has a dozen IT parks housing various companies such as IBM and AT&T. Analysts predict that Mumbai and Pune will eventually overtake Bangalore as the top producer of software in India, although the majority of the companies are domestic.

India's pool of highly skilled (and relatively inexpensive) labour has been attracting a proliferating number of multinationals in recent years, which has prompted more Indian states to set up software development cities. But the information superhighway within India is still surprisingly limited considering the one billion plus population. By mid-2001 the number of Indian Internet subscribers is expected to only number around 1.5 million.

Mining

Coal is India's main source of energy, accounting for around 67% of the nation's commercial requirements. In 1998–99, 290 million tonnes of coal was produced. Since about the 1970s Indian coal production has grown at about 4% per annum. There are more than 500 coal mines (mostly state-owned) and India produces a small surplus. However, the quality is low. India also has rich reserves of limestone, iron ore, bauxite and manganese.

Fishing & Forestry

Fishing takes place all along India's coastline and in the rivers and waterways of the interior. This is a growing industry in India; the commercial catch was 5.3 million tonnes in 1997–98 (marine and inland sources), compared to 4.6 million tonnes earlier that decade. Most boats are nonmechanised, although mechanisation is increasing, causing a detrimental effect on local fishing communities and on the marine environment. Commercial forestry, though not a large industry in India, is found in the Western Ghats, the western Himalaya and hilly areas of central India.

Tourism

In 1999 there were an estimated 2.4 million visitors to India and this was expected to rise to 2.6 million in 2000–01. Tourism is a crucial foreign-exchange earner for the country and it also stimulates the economy by boosting employment. Tourism officials claim that the lack of adequate flights to India coupled with lacklustre marketing policies is severely hindering tourism growth. Poor infrastructure within the country is another significant impediment.

In the late 1990s, most tourists to India come from the UK, followed by Germany, the USA and then (interestingly) Sri Lanka.

Although not a foreign exchange earner, domestic tourism still has a positive effect on the economy. In 1999 approximately 160 million Indian people travelled within India; some 100 million for religious reasons.

POPULATION & PEOPLE

India has the world's second-largest population exceeded only by that of China. India crossed the billion mark in May 2000 and is tipped to be the planet's most populous nation in the next couple of decades. However, the people of India are not homogenous; various groups look different and there is a plethora of customs, religions and languages.

A population census is held once every 10 years – most recently in 2001. According to this census India's population is now 1,027,015,247. Check out the Census of India Web site at www.censusindia.net.

According to the 1991 census (the 2001 census results were incomplete as we went to press and the most recent city populations were unavailable) Mumbai is India's most populated city, with an urban population of 16 million; Kolkata ranks second with 14 million and Delhi and Chennai third and fourth with 13.8 and 5.9 million respectively.

The bias against India's female population continues (see Society & Conduct later in this chapter); more women die before the age of 35 than men and maternal mortality rates are high (forming 25% of the world's childbirth related deaths). The proportion of females to males has declined over the years (it was 972:1000 in 1901; the 2001 census figure was 933). Kerala is the only state where women outnumber men. Here there are 1058 females for every 1000 males.

Adivasis

At least 55 million people belong to tribal communities. Adivasis, as they are known in India, have origins that precede the Vedic Aryans and the Dravidians of the south. For thousands of years they have lived more or less undisturbed in the hills and densely wooded regions regarded as unattractive by agriculturists. Many still speak tribal languages not understood by the politically dominant Hindus, and follow customs foreign to both Hindus and Muslims.

Although there has obviously been some contact between the Adivasis and the Hindu villagers on the plains, this has rarely led to friction since there was little or no competition for resources and land. All this has changed. In the past 50 years the majority of Adivasis have been dispossessed of their ancestral land and turned into impoverished labourers. However, some argue that Adivasis still have more political representation in India than the indigenous people of countries such as Australia and Canada because of a quota system for parliamentary representation.

In parts of India, especially in Madhya Pradesh, Andhra Pradesh, Bihar and the Andaman and Nicobar Islands, a shocking tale of exploitation, dispossession and widespread hunger has unfolded with the connivance and encouragement of officialdom. It's a record the government would prefer to forget and one it vehemently denies. Instead it points to the millions of rupees said to have been sunk into schemes to improve the conditions of Adivasis. Although some of this has got through, corruption has gobbled a substantial portion.

It's unlikely that much genuine effort will be made to improve the lot of Adivasis in India, given the pressure for land. What is far more likely is that the erosion of the cultures and traditions will continue until they are close to being wiped out.

Improving the living standards of the poor has been a priority for governments since Independence. However, poverty remains widespread. The GNP per capita is just US$360 per year. Of India's children, half are undernourished. Preventable diseases such as TB, malaria, blindness and leprosy account for half of all reported illnesses. HIV/AIDS is a major cause for concern (see the boxed text 'AIDS in India' under Health in the Facts for the Visitor chapter).

Despite India's many large cities, the nation is still overwhelmingly rural. It is estimated that close to 75% of the population lives in the countryside.

EDUCATION

Under the Indian constitution, education is compulsory and free for all up to the age of 14. There are 688,000 primary schools and 110,000 secondary schools. In terms of tertiary institutions, there are 10,555 colleges and 221 universities (with 7,078,000 students currently enrolled). For the socially disadvantaged Scheduled Castes, government subsidised tuition is offered to those wishing to take university entry exams. This scheme is currently implemented at 22 universities and 57 colleges. However, in addition to state schools, there are many private (usually English-language) schools, very often run by church organisations. Places in these exclusive institutions are highly coveted among those who can afford them.

Two-thirds of India's children are enrolled in school, including most children of primary-school age. However, many don't attend regularly and at least 33 million aren't enrolled at all. Girls are under-represented, especially in higher education. At least half of all students from rural areas drop out before completing school. In 1997–98 the national drop-out rate for secondary school students was 69%. There is an estimated 20 million disabled children attending primary and secondary schools, however this only represents a fraction of India's total number. On top of that, the drop-out rate is high. Attempts to boost literacy among adults (especially women) have met with mixed success.

Much investment has gone into higher education, although critics say the quality has declined, with many liberal arts graduates unable to find work. India's brightest students frequently go abroad to undertake their higher degrees and many never return.

The state and union governments share responsibility for education, although the union government has been more active in promoting education for girls and other disadvantaged groups. At 65.38% in the 2001 census, the literacy rate is a 13.75% improvement on the 1991 census figures; with a 76% literacy rate for males and a 54% rate for females there is also heightened gender equality. Kerala recorded the highest literacy rate (91%) and Bihar the lowest (48%), with the new state of Jharkhand just ahead (54%).

SCIENCE & PHILOSOPHY

Religion & Philosophy

In ancient India the Vedic religion permeated every aspect of the culture, including philosophy and the sciences. Through the Brahmin or priestly caste, Vedic knowledge has remained the central feature of Indian thought throughout its long history. Religion and philosophy don't compete; philosophical wisdom has the status of religious truth. Students had to gain a deep knowledge of the Vedic mantras and the correct Sanskrit phonetics before going on to participate in philosophical discussions at a *parisad* or academy. Orthodox schools of Hindu philosophy hold that the Vedic texts are the ultimate authority.

One of the great wellsprings of mystic philosophy is the Upanishads, the oldest of which are deemed to be Vedic. They promote the notion of an all-pervading, universal One, in which there is no split between matter and spirit (nondualism). But the Vedic texts and the Upanishads themselves offer more than one path; basically between striving to make this life better, or renouncing society to seek enlightenment.

But unorthodox ideas developed as well. Buddhism rejected the concept of atman (soul), although retained the notions of karma (justice for past deeds) and the goal of moksha (liberation from endless

Only in India

India – with its 330 million Hindu gods and goddesses – is a land of inimitable records. While you're probably aware that India has the planet's biggest film industry, did you know that the 1982 epic, *Gandhi*, has the world record for the most film extras (300,000 people)? When it comes to epics, India also bags the world record for the longest will (104,567 words) and the shortest one (two words: *sub beta* – everything to son).

Among India's luscious mix of other world records are the following: Indians are credited with many mathematical records, including the invention of trigonometry (2 BC) and the earliest recorded decimal system (AD 6). The world's highest nonmilitary airport is at Leh in Ladakh (3256m); the highest cricket pitch at Chail, near Shimla (2250m); and the world's longest train platform (833m) at Kharagpur in West Bengal.

India shows the rest of the world that anything is possible when you put your mind to it: A Rajasthani septuagenarian wears the world's longest moustache (3.39m) – unless of course he incurs the wrath of scissor-happy Ramzan Ali of Delhi, who holds the record for uninterrupted hairdressing (1200 customers in 102 hours). A Maharashtran man has the world's longest fingernails (totalling 6.15m on one hand); a farming family in Karnataka accommodates the largest extended family (170 people); and a fellow in Kerala has the world beat when it comes to dehusking a coconut...with his bare teeth (an unbelievable 25 seconds)! But it doesn't stop there! Some other world records held by Indians include nonstop crawling (1400km), balancing on one foot (65 hours 50 minutes), handshaking (31,118 people in eight hours), belching (92 burps per minute), vegetable chopping (964kg in 130 hours), and the list goes on.

With ebullient talk of *more* records on the horizon, who better to document them all than India's Dinesh Pathak, the world-record holder for continuous typing (210 hours).

reincarnations). Jainism holds to the concept of *naya*, the idea that there are many perspectives of reality, all of which are partially valid.

The challenges from Buddhism, and later from Islam, spurred a shift in Hindu thought. The Keralan-born Hindu saint, theologian and philosopher, Shankaracharya (AD 788– 820), looking to turn the tide, promoted nondualism and *jnana* (the importance of knowledge) as a means to salvation. He argued that you should be free to pursue your own reasoning, as long as it doesn't contradict the Vedic scriptures. His view was challenged by the Tamil Brahmin Ramanuja who, influenced by the southern bhakti cult (devotion to a personal god and the rejection of Brahminic ritual), promoted the idea that while knowledge was one path to salvation, it wasn't the only path or even the most effective one.

While Islam and Hinduism are very different religions, Sufi mystics were important missionaries for Islam and used indigenous ideas such as yoga and fasting to spread the word.

In the 19th century the Bengali Ramakrishna and his disciple Vivekananda started a reform movement in Hinduism that acknowledged that other religions were striving towards the same goal as Hinduism.

Leading philosophers of the 20th century include Sri Aurobindo, who moved from political activism to the study of yoga and, of course, Mahatma Gandhi, who took traditional ideas such as ahimsa (nonviolence) and remoulded them as weapons in the struggle against British rule.

Indian philosophy and science in the ancient era cross paths frequently. In about 600 BC the philosopher Kanada proposed the existence of an indivisible unit of matter he called *parmanu* (atoms). He believed that different states of matter (fire, water, earth) had different parmanu, and that parmanu join to become a *dwinka* (molecule) with some of the properties of each.

Science

The history of sciences such as mathematics, medicine and linguistics stretches back to Vedic times when the Aryan rituals were anthologised. The study of linguistics by the 4th century BC Sanskrit grammarian Panini claims to be the first scientific analysis of an alphabet. Indian mathematics emerges from the 5th century *Shulvasutras*, which examined geometry and algorithms. A theory of numbers also developed about this time, and included the concepts of zero and negative numbers and the use of simple algorithms using place-value notations. The concept of zero is in fact India's contribution to the world of mathematics and arrived in Europe via Arab traders.

About the same time as the *Shulvasutras* were being penned, the great Keralan mathematician Aryabhara also concluded that the earth's shadow was responsible for the waxing and waning of the moon and that the earth rotated on its own axis, while the moon rotated around earth. Aryabhara also came up with a value for pi. Brahmagupta, born in Gujarat in AD 598, collected and edited a work on astronomy and mathematics that was used for centuries. He also helped refine the concept of zero.

The classic works on Ayurvedic medicine, the *Charak Samhita* and the *Sushrita*, were written in the 6th century BC. Surgeons such as Susruta were even experimenting with plastic surgery in this age.

In 1930 Sir Chandrasekhar Venkata Raman won the Nobel Prize for Physics for his work on how light changes when passing through transparent bodies (the Raman effect). Since Independence the government's emphasis has been on space technology, nuclear power and electronics. The latter sowed the seeds for India's increasingly important software industry. But some argue that there has not been enough emphasis on 'social' sciences, a point reinforced when, in 1998, Amartya Sen won the Nobel Prize for Economics for his contribution to the field of welfare economics. Sen lives and works in the UK but was born in India, where few of his ideas have been effectively put into practice.

ARTS

Dance

Dance is an ancient art form in India and is inextricably linked to mythology and classical literature. Dance can be divided into two main forms: classical and folk.

Classical dance is essentially based on well-defined traditional disciplines. They include Bharata Natyam, Kathakali, Kathak, Manipuri, Kuchipudi and Odissi.

Bharata Natyam originated from the southern state of Tamil Nadu but has been widely embraced throughout India. **Kathakali**, which has its roots in Kerala, is often referred to as dance but essentially is not. It's actually a play (or drama) performed with words and gestures. While the script is vocalised by singers, the performers actually 'narrate' the drama through precise movements and gestures. Kathakali dancers are traditionally male, and stories are usually based on the great Hindu epics. The dancers' striking make-up and costumes leave a lasting impression.

Kathak, which has Hindu and Islamic influences, was particularly popular with the Mughals and dancers still wear costumes that hark back to the 17th century. Kathak suffered a period of notoriety when it moved from the courts into houses where *nautch* (dancing) girls tantalised audiences with renditions of the Krishna and Radha love story. It was restored as a serious art form in the early 20th century.

Manipuri, which has a delicate, lyrical flavour, hails from Manipur. It attracted a wider audience in the 1920s when the Bengali poet Rabindranath Tagore invited one of its most revered exponents to teach at Shantiniketan, near Kolkata.

Kuchipudi is a 17th-century dance-drama which originated in an Andhra Pradesh village from which it takes its name. The story centres on the envious wife of Krishna.

Odissi, claimed to be India's oldest classical dance form, was originally a temple art, and was later also performed at royal courts.

India's second major dance form, **folk**, is widespread and varied. It ranges from the high-spirited Bhangra dance of Punjab, to the theatrical dummy horse dances of Karnataka and Tamil Nadu and the graceful fishers' dance of Orissa.

Pioneers of modern dance forms in India include Uday Shankar (older brother of sitar master Ravi) who once partnered Anna Pavlova, the Russian ballerina. Tagore was another innovator and in 1901 he set up a school at Shantiniketan (near Kolkata) that promoted the arts. A poet, playwright, philosopher, actor, painter and novelist, Tagore brought gurus from all over India to Shantiniketan, where a distinctive dance style evolved. Although this style was eventually criticised for its lack of technical precision, it is claimed the real achievement of the experiment lay in stimulating interest in dance within the wider public.

Music

Classical music in India traces its roots back to Vedic times, when religious poems chanted by priests were first collated in an anthology called the Rig-Veda. Over the millennia classical music has been shaped by many influences, and the legacy today is Carnatic (characteristic of South India) and Hindustani (the classical style of North India). With common origins, both share a number of features. Both use the raga (the melodic shape of the music) and *tala* (the rhythmic meter characterised by the number of beats). *Tintal* for example, has a tala of 16 beats. The audience follows the tala by clapping at the appropriate beat, which in tintal is at one, five and 13. There is no clap at the beat of nine since that is the *khali* (empty section), indicated by a wave of the hand. Both the raga and the tala are used as a basis for composition and improvisation.

Both Carnatic and Hindustani music are performed by small ensembles comprising about six musicians and both have many instruments in common. Neither style uses a change of key or harmonies. There is no fixed pitch, but there are differences. Hindustani has been more heavily influenced by Persian musical conventions (a result of Mughal rule); Carnatic music, as it developed in South India, cleaves more closely to theory. The most striking difference, at least for those unfamiliar with India's classical forms, is Carnatic's greater use of voice. All composed pieces are mainly for the voice and possess lyrics; the most popular of these (devotional songs called *kriti*) having been created less than 200 years ago. Hindustani music has more purely instrumental compositions. The most common vocal forms in Hindustani music today are the *khyal* and the *thumri;* the latter is a light classical style based on devotional literature centred around the Krishna and Radha love story.

Classical music, however, is enjoyed by a relatively small section of society. Most people are more familiar with their own local, folk forms, popular during festivities and ceremonies – or with popular music.

[Continued on Page 57]

Classical Musical Instruments

Hindustani (Classical North Indian) Instruments

Instrumental music has gained increasing prominence in performances, with secondary melody instruments being employed during vocal music.

Stringed Prominent among the melody instruments is the sitar, the rather larger *surbahar*, the shorter-necked, fretless sarod, and the bowed sarangi. The *santoor* is of Persian origin and has more than 100 strings divided into pairs and is struck with two wooden sticks. The violin and a plucked board zither called a *surmandal* may be used as secondary melody instruments when there is a singer. The *tambura* (see Carnatic Instruments) remains the main drone instrument.

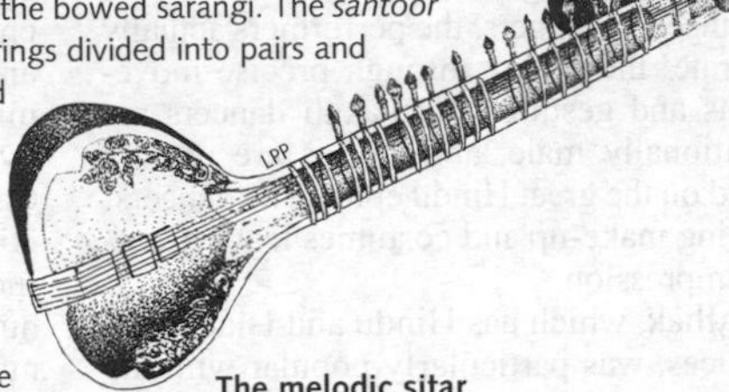

The melodic sitar

Wind Prominent melody instruments are the *bansuri*, a side-blown bamboo flute and the *shehnai*, which resembles an oboe.

The tabla is used to keep the beat.

Percussion The tabla, like the sitar, is well known to Western audiences and is the most popular percussive instrument. Others include the *bayan* and *pakhavaj*; the latter is similar to a large *mridangam* (see Carnatic Instruments).

Keyboard The hand-pumped keyboard harmonium is used as a secondary melody instrument for vocal music.

Carnatic (Classical South Indian) Instruments

A typical South Indian concert employs either a singer or a main melody instrument (usually a violin), a secondary melody instrument, a drone (eg, the tambura – a four-stringed instrument that provides the tonic note and a constant reference point) and one or two percussion instruments.

Stringed The vina and the *chitravina* are arguably the most popular plucked instruments. The vina has 24 frets and seven strings. It's held like a sitar, the left hand pressing between the frets or pulling on the strings to produce ornamentations. The chitravina is fretless, has 21 strings and is played like a slide guitar. The guitar, the mandolin and the violin, adopted from the West, are also used, although tuning and playing techniques have been adapted to suit the Indian musical style. The most commonly used drone in Carnatic music is the tambura, which is plucked throughout the concert.

Wind The *nagaswaram* (double-reed flute) and the *venu* (side-blown flute) are used but Western instruments such as the clarinet and saxophone sometimes make an appearance.

Percussion Perhaps the most popular, the mridangam is a double-sided drum that produces tones of definite pitch. The more characteristically northern dual drum, the tabla, is sometimes used. Other instruments are the *ghatam* (clay pot with no covering), *thavil* (barrel-shaped double-ended drum) and *timila* (long, thin hour-glass shaped drum).

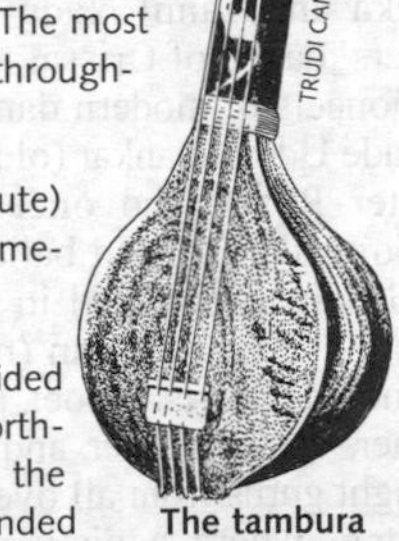

The tambura provides the drone.

Arts & Crafts

2 Arts & Crafts

Travelling anywhere in India is a visually rich experience. Over centuries innumerable ethnic groups have produced an exuberant artistic heritage, rich in spirit, inventiveness and significance. Arts and crafts are more than just the self-expression of an artisan or the product of a religion – they are the deepest representation of a culture and are accessible at different levels.

When hassled by a tout trying to drag you to yet another workshop owned by his brother, it's possible to regard 'arts and crafts' as a device used by locals to fleece tourists. However, like food and music, craft is a fundamental part of the culture. Every view seems to contain a truck or bus decorated with folk craft, a casually worn yet stunning textile or an intricately crafted piece of jewellery. Every village has its craftspeople and artists, and houses, rickshaws and most everyday objects are adorned using various decorative techniques. All natural materials, including wood, leather, bone, metal, stone, grass, papier-mache (a Kashmir speciality), cotton and wool can be found in a range of exciting forms.

PRAMOD MISTRY

Left: The elaborate handiwork of *mehndi* (henna) artists

PAUL BEINSSEN

ANTHONY HAM

BRYN THOMAS

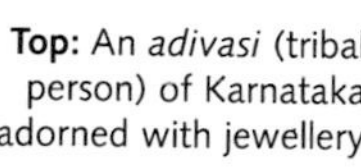

Top: An *adivasi* (tribal person) of Karnataka adorned with jewellery

Middle: Miniature dolls are a familiar sight in Rajasthan's bazaars.

Bottom: Throughout India, everyday objects are lavishly embellished with decorative artwork.

Crafts are not always confined to the region of origin: people migrate, creative people are influenced by the ideas of other regions, and business will move to where the market is. For these and other reasons you can come across a speciality Kashmir handicraft emporium or Tibetan shop anywhere. See Shopping in the Facts for the Visitor chapter for a detailed listing of products, where they are available and how much you should pay, as well as information on ethical shopping, buying at government emporiums and bargaining.

CERAMICS

The potter's craft is steeped in mythology. The first humans are said to have been shaped from clay by Brahma, the Creator, and indeed the name with which potters are most closely identified, *prajapati*, is one of Brahma's titles. But potters claim another link to the divine. When Shiva wished to marry Parvati it is said they lacked a necessary water pot, so Shiva created a man and a woman from two beads plucked from his necklace – the man created the pot and together the man and woman created a lineage of potters. Today potters are also known as *kumbhar* or *kumbar*, a name shared with the ubiquitous water pot *(kumbh)*.

Despite the intrusion of plastic into the marketplace, the potter's craft is evident in every household and at shrines throughout the country. Smooth, round terracotta water pots are arguably the most commonly used household utensils in India; the narrow neck prevents spillage as women carry the pots on their heads. Although plastic pots are also used these days, baked clay keeps the water pleasantly cool in a country where many households have no access to refrigeration. Potters also make a variety of cooking utensils; some say traditional dishes just don't taste the same when prepared in metal pots and pans. Travellers will invariably come across these terracotta pots when they buy curd or when they buy *chai* (tea) in cups from vendors at train stations. Once emptied, these cups are smashed on the tracks. In Tamil Nadu, it's traditional to smash one's old pots on the eve of the Pongal (harvest) festival, and replace them with new ones.

Pots and storage jars of various kinds are created on the wheel (only men may use the wheel, although women may decorate the pot after it has been removed); sometimes they are built up using slabs or coils. Plaster moulds are occasionally used.

The potter is also skilful in making *chillums* (clay smoking pipes), hookahs, beads and *jhanvan* (serrated palm-sized slabs) that can be

EDDIE GERALD

Left: Clay is moulded into shape and intricate[ly] decorated in the age-o[ld] art of pottery.

used like pumice stone for smoothing rough skin on the feet.

Votive offerings, including terracotta horses and other creatures, idols of various descriptions, and even replicas of parts of the human body (these are placed before a shrine by those hoping for a miraculous recovery), also have a place in the potter's repertoire. Occasionally the potter acts as an intermediary between the worshipper and the divine. For example, in Tamil Nadu terracotta horses are made in honour of the protective deity Ayannar. The potter, requested to make the horses by villagers in times of dire need, also attends the associated ceremony and, in a trance-like state, intercedes between the god and the community.

RICHARD I'ANSON

Top: Statue makers at work in Kumartali, Kolkata

Bottom: Water pots are carried with amazing balance and grace.

The Mughals manufactured coloured and patterned glazed tiles with which they decorated their mosques, forts and palaces.

Blue pottery (such as vases, plates, tiles and doorknobs), now largely produced for export, is made in various places around India, but the major centre is Jaipur. Modern science has revealed high levels of lead in these pieces, making plates and bowls unsuitable for using with food. This revelation has had a significant impact on a traditional craft that supported around 15,000 potters. The few remaining potters now make decorative items such as vases, planters, jewellery boxes and ashtrays. This range is distinctive for its hand-painted artwork and is low-fired to retain the brilliant colours (750°C).

Most village-produced work is low-fired and fragile. All glazed ceramicwares have been fired twice: an initial bisque firing and a subsequent glaze firing. An easy way to tell if a piece is high- or low-fired is to tap the item – the higher the firing the higher the pitch. A cracked item can also be detected by this method. Both earthenware and stoneware are nonporous, however some Indian earthenware is slightly under-fired and not always fabulously glazed, so it is still a little porous.

PETER DAVIS

INCENSE

The smell of incense is common throughout India and its production is an ancient craft. It is associated with meditation and devotion, and there are thousands of makers in India. Indian incense is exported throughout the world and Bangalore and Mysore are major centres for its production.

Incense is commonly used in religious ceremonies. Taxi, bus and truck drivers often burn incense in their vehicles before they set out on a journey. The incense is part of a *puja* (offering to the gods) to the driver's chosen deity to implore the god or goddess to protect the vehicle and all who travel in it. Similarly, many shopkeepers light incense and play *bhajans* (devotional songs) in the morning in the hope their shop will be blessed with a good day's business.

Incense from Auroville, an ashram near Pondicherry, is of high quality. Nag Champa is another very popular incense and is produced by devotees of Sai Baba. It has a sandalwood base yet has a distinctive fragrant scent drawing from a variety of sources. It is great when used as meditation incense! But beware: due to lack of copyright enforcement there are many counterfeit copies of the famous brands.

SARA-JANE CLELAND

KOLAMS

The rice-flour designs or *kolams* (also called *rangoli*) that adorn thresholds throughout the state of Tamil Nadu are much more than mere decorations. Kolams (meaning play, form or beauty in the Tamil language) are most auspicious and symbolic. Traditionally they are drawn at sunrise and are made of rice-flour paste, which may be eaten by small creatures – thus symbolising a reverence for all life, even the most apparently insignificant.

This gesture is doubly blessed; giving as one's first act of the day is viewed as extremely auspicious. Beneficial deities are deemed to be attracted to a beautiful kolam; the goddess Lakshmi, representing wealth, may thus be tempted to symbolically cross the threshold and bestow her beneficence on those who dwell within.

Kolams transmit all sorts of information to those who understand their nuances. They may signal to sadhus that they can expect food at a particular house or they may be a sign of the family's prosperity and

Left: Commonly used in religious ceremonies, incense here forms part of an offering to Buddha in Bodhgaya.

LEANNE LOGAN

hospitality generally. The absence of a kolam might signal ill fortune or a death in the household, or it might simply mean that the household has no women or that they are too busy working in the fields to make a kolam. Some believe kolams protect against the evil eye, acting as a sort of deflector of ill intentions, envy and greed.

White and red are favoured colours in kolam design, although others, such as blue, may be used. Black is never used because of its association with dark and evil forces. Motifs vary. Some feature complex geometric shapes, others depict lotus flowers and sundry bird and animal creations. These days it is possible to buy bamboo or plastic tubes with holes punched into them. The tube is filled with chalk dust and rolled over a piece of moistened, hard-packed ground to make an attractive kolam design.

Right: Auspicious in intent and beautiful in design, Tamil Nadu's *kolams* signal a dawn offering to the gods.

THOMAS BOEHM

JEWELLERY

The wearing of jewellery is a sign of status and wealth, and a form of investment. Jewellery is made from gold, silver and white metal. It can be found in many forms and it is bought and sold by weight. Sometimes a lower-quality piece masquerades as something more precious.

Gold is very expensive in India as demand is high and the material scarce. Until recently, people smuggled gold from elsewhere because it was so much cheaper. It is, therefore, not really worth buying unless you find something with special Indian characteristics. Gold plating, with few exceptions, is done with little technology and is usually of a low standard.

Traditional silver comes in many grades (including 0% white metal) and is rarely found to be above 84%, despite much information to the contrary. Sterling silver (92.5%) is sold by reputable jewellers, although you should request to see a comparison with lower grades and you will soon be able recognise the difference.

Top: The wearing of jewellery is an integral part of any special occasion, even for young girls.

Bottom: This prize camel from Pushkar displays his finest attire

Many precious and semiprecious stones are mined and cut in India. The Kohinoor (Mountain of Light) diamond, now part of the British royal family's crown jewels and set in the Queen Mother's crown, was handed down from ruler to ruler in India until it was presented to Queen Victoria in 1849. The well-recognised *pietra dura* work, prevalent during the Mughal empire, used semiprecious stones to decorate monumental buildings and household items. Today, you can buy your own piece of Taj Mahal–style work, particularly around Agra.

It takes much knowledge to enter the gemstone field. Stone colour can be falsely heightened, raising an ordinary specimen to a rich, more-prized hue, and many synthetic imitations can be found. Nail polish remover, or a vigorous rub with a white cloth, will often reveal the deception. However, colours of stones are often heightened by heating processes and cannot be 'rubbed off'. Enjoy the learning experience by asking questions and you'll likely find that the jeweller will enjoy this as well.

Some palace museums have displays of marvellous royal or state collections of all items, including jewellery.

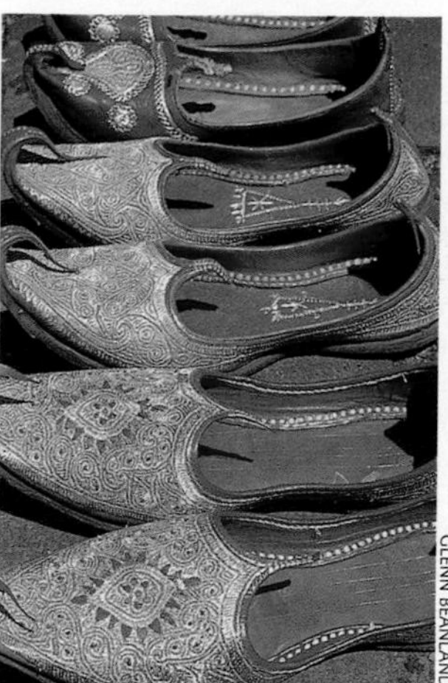

GLENN BEANLAND

RICHARD I'ANSON

LEATHER

Sheep, goat and camel skin are used to make various qualities of leather. Cowhide is generally not used because of the animal's religious significance. In a country where the cow is both common and sacred to the Hindu majority, it is the job of low-caste people to work with the skin of a fallen beast. Tanning styles vary from simple village preparation to sophisticated factory methods producing for the Italian market.

Traditional shoes are usually made from leather and are a slip-on style. Called *jootis*, they are highly decorative, and often feature a curled front and colourful embroidery which varies from region to region. Left and right shoes are the same and it is best to mark the inside so that you wear them on the same foot each time and they mould to your foot shape.

METAL

The versatility of metal craft can be seen in fine *qandeels* (hanging lamps with cut-out patterns), jewellery and the traditional water pipes used for smoking. Two important centres of production are Moradabad in Uttar Pradesh, where there is large-scale commercial production, and Bidar in Karnataka, which produces *bidri* work (fine, silvery inlay on metal).

Objects of devotion are traditionally made by the lost-wax method. The image is first made in wax. This model is dipped in clay, forming a mould. Molten metal is then poured in, melting and replacing the wax. It is then a huge job to remove the clay

RICHARD I'ANSON

Top left: *Jootis*, or traditional shoes, highlight the fine workmanship of local craftspeople.

Top right: A door from Jaipur's City Palace displays skilful metalwork

Bottom right: An artist involved in the upkeep of Hari Mandir (Golden Temple) in Amritsar, Punjab

DAVID TIPLING

and polish the metal. This is a time-consuming process, requiring much skill, and each mould is only used once. Consequently, ornaments or images made in this manner are often expensive. A machine-made, multi-use mould is a much simpler and cheaper production method.

Metalwork is one medium that has been influenced by migrant communities. Since China took control of Tibet, Tibetan communities have moved to numerous locations in India, including Dharamsala and McLeod Ganj, Darjeeling, Kodaikanal, Bodhgaya, Jabalpur and Gwalior, and there they produce distinctive metal crafts. Tibetan singing bowls, made from a secret mix of seven different metals, are a meditation device originating from the Bon religion of pre-Buddhist Tibet. These produce the 'disassociated' mystic hum when a playing stick is rotated around the outer edge of the bowl. Healing bowls should be partially filled with water and struck on the outer edge using a playing stick. Enlightenment may not always follow! Yak butter lamps, horns and ornate teapots are other popular items.

TEXTILES

In India, textiles have always played an important role in society and trade – it was the land in which the Romans chose to have their textiles made to order. This fabulous tradition includes brocade wedding saris, handloom rugs, block-print bedspreads, embroidered cushions,

RICHARD I'ANSON

Top: A villager from Bharatpur, Rajasthan, with a metal-crafted vessel

Bottom: Intricate brocades and richly coloured fabrics swathe the bodies of women throughout India.

zaris (metal thread brocade) and festival tents (a reminder of the days when maharajas and Mughals used tents for special occasions).

India is rightfully famous for *khadi*, hand-spun silk and cottons, including cheesecloth and voile. In fact, the promotion of khadi by Mahatma Gandhi was an important aspect of the struggle for Indian independence. The replacement of cotton from Manchester's mills with the home-made product was such an important political event that the spinning wheel still represents freedom and is the symbol on India's national flag.

Although the use of chemical dyes has been widespread for almost a century, there is also much use of natural products: blue from the indigo plant; red from the madder root, poppy, tulip petals, rhubarb, rose roots, cherry skins and bark of the jujube tree; yellow from camomile and turmeric; orange from the red/yellow combination, as well as from henna and plum bark; black from pomegranate peel and oak apples; tan and brown from acorn cups, walnut husks and from natural brown wool; purple and violet from the red/blue combination as well as from grape skin and cochineal.

Great textiles of wonderful variety are seen throughout India, although some particularly distinctive styles can be found in Chennai (Madras), Gujarat, Rajasthan and Kashmir.

PRAMOD MISTRY

Rugs

Kashmir has a rich tradition of textiles that includes fine shawls, chain stitching and the embroidered felt rugs known as *numda*. When the felt for numdas has been made with 50% or more wool it is more durable. Nearly all styles of rug are made from mostly wool, including some in the Persian tradition, with a blend of other fibres such as cotton and silk.

There are huge factories, or workshops, producing copies of Persian rugs. The use of child and bonded (some would say slave) labour is an ugly

RICHARD I'ANSON

Middle: A fine example of geometric patterns on a woollen carpet from Gujarat

Bottom: A Keralan craftsman hard at work making floor coverings

MICHELLE COXALL

reality associated with some of these workshops and you should think twice before buying (see Be Shop Smart under Responsible Tourism in the Facts for the Visitor chapter).

Wherever you go in India you will find dealers in pile rugs and kilims (flat-weave tribal carpets). A myth of the rug world is that the durability of rugs depends on the number of knots per square inch. Although this is a factor, the type of wool used is more important. The wiry wool from local sheep makes an uncomfortably itchy jumper, but wonderful, long-lasting carpets.

Dhurries are flat-weave rugs made from cotton or wool and are chemically dyed. They are often striped, but come in an extensive range of motifs and colours. Dhurries are produced throughout India, but the main centre for commercial export is in the country's north-west.

Applique & Embroidery

Applique (decoration or trimming made of one material attached by sewing to another) is particularly widespread in Rajāsthani and Gujarati textile work. The motifs used in these pieces include colourful animals and tree-shaped patches sewn onto cotton cloth. Applique is often made into wall and door hangings and windsocks. Another style of door and wall hanging is called *toran* and features hand-embroidered cross-stitch patterns. Traditionally, a bridegroom would pierce a toran over the doorway of his bride's house with his sword, symbolically 'winning' his bride and having the right to enter the family home and claim her. This practice is still prevalent among the Rajputs and other Hindu clans. Decorative crewel work (chain stitch) is used to make many wall hangings. Some pieces also have small mirrors and these are very popular

Left: Textile merchants sell their wares to passers-by

PAUL BEINSSEN

with travellers. Beautiful embroidery, sometimes incorporating mirrors, is used on caps, shawls and other clothing in an endless variety of styles, and in every marketplace you will find specialist traders.

Shawls, often embroidered, are varied throughout the country and are particularly striking. They are light to carry, may be worn in numerous ways and are used as throws over furniture, as well as for curtains and wall hangings. See Shopping in the Facts for the Visitor chapter for more information on shawls.

In Tamil Nadu, shawls have assumed a significant role in the culture of the Toda people of the Nilgiri Hills. Embroidered exclusively by women, the shawls are made of thick white cotton material, about 2m by 1.5m. A large pocket is stitched into each shawl. According to anthropologists, Todas have never weaved their own cloth, instead they purchase plain cloth from the market and dedicate many hours to embroidering the distinctive black and red designs onto it. Although many Todas are now completely integrated into mainstream Indian society, this tradition of embroidering the cloth continues in Toda villages.

RICHARD I'ANSON

MICHELLE COXALL

Top: Beautiful fabrics featuring small mirrors are a feature of Rajasthani embroidery.

Bottom left: Shawls come in a range of colours, designs and textures and are worn mainly in the north of India.

Bottom right: Splashed by the waters of Holi, the colours that mark the end of winter reflect the colours of craft.

The shawls, worn by both women and, less commonly, by men, serve many purposes. A basic shawl is for everyday use. The thickness of the cloth shields the wearer from the morning and evening chill in the mountains. On formal occasions, the shawl covers the head as well as the body. More intricate shawls are stitched for significant occasions such as weddings and births. However, the best-quality shawls are reserved for funerals. During the complex rituals of a traditional Toda funeral the finest shawl is hung outside the hut where the corpse lies. Mourners touch the shawl with their forehead as they enter. At a certain point in the ceremony the shawl is taken inside the hut and a handful of leaves is placed into the pocket. The shawl is then wrapped carefully around the corpse, offering protection and security in the next life.

Saris

Saris are worn by women all over India, many working women prefer the practicality of a *salwar kameez* or Punjabi suit (a two-piece outfit consisting of a long kurta-style top with drawstring pantaloons and a flowing scarf called a *dupatta*). This is not to undermine the importance of a sari, which is still the preferred choice by most women for special occasions such as weddings. Much time, effort and expense is put into selecting the base fabric, the style of embroidery used to decorate it, the

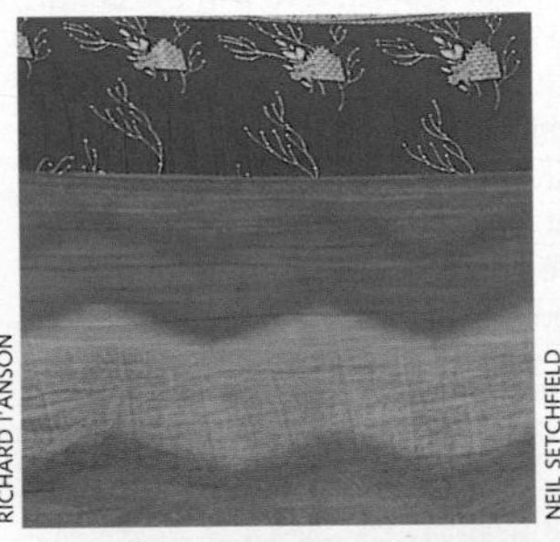

RICHARD I'ANSON

NEIL SETCHFIELD

RICHARD I'ANSON

This page: The eye-catching colours of saris saturate the streets and markets of India.

colour and the thread. Adornments range from synthetic materials right through to silver or gold, beads, sequins, tassels and mirrors. The intricacies of the work all contribute to the final cost of the garment.

All sequined, beaded and *salma* (continuous spring thread) saris are hand-worked. The fabric is generally rayon, cotton, georgette, satin or silk and, being about 6m x 1m, can be used for other purposes such as in cushions, curtains and fashion clothing.

Recycled saris are made into fashion garments for export as well as for street sale to tourists in places such as Rajasthan (especially Udaipur, Jaipur and Pushkar) and Delhi.

WOODWORK

Wood is used to great effect in all regions of India. In Kashmir, where wood has been plentiful, large slabs have been beautifully utilised in the local architecture and craftwork for many centuries. Throughout India, many types of wood are used in carving, including teak, aromatic sandalwood, sheesham, walnut and other fruit trees and, in the north, Himalayan cedar. However, the most common is sheesham plantation wood grown in North India, which has a dark stain. Mango wood is becoming a preferred alternative because of its affordability and quality. It is also a valuable re-use of natural resources given that the wood comes from old, less productive mango trees. (Forest conservation is a major issue in India as it is all over the world; see Ecology & Environment in the Facts about India chapter.)

South India offers a very different style of the craft. Because the wood is more dense, it can be carved in more detail.

The skill of many woodwork artisans is extraordinary. They effortlessly carve detailed works with great precision, while steadying the block with their feet. *Jali* work is a term referring to the holes or spaces produced through carving.

Furniture made for export often has ironwork features such as studs, grilles and decorative edge-work. Coffee and dining tables, bedside cabinets, chairs, CD racks, cupboards (known as *almirahs*) and chests of drawers are all produced.

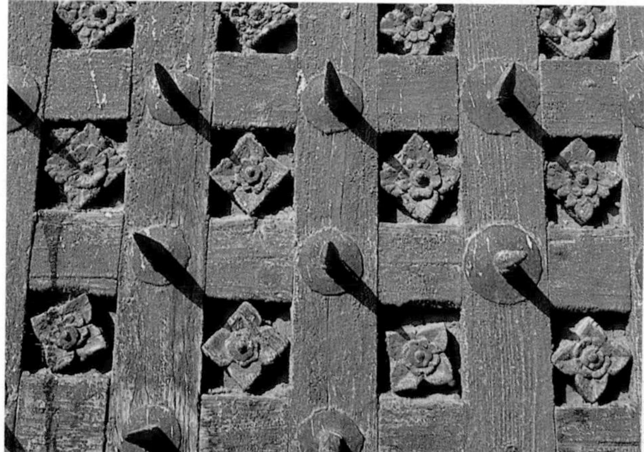

GREG ELMS

Bottom: Throughout he ages artisans have created magnificent ɔrks from wood, such .s this carved Mughul gate at Lal Ghat, Udaipur, Rajasthan.

PAUL BEINSSEN

The *pitara*, a traditional piece of furniture, is a carved wooden chest on legs. These pieces are generally quite old and rustic in appearance, with some having a distressed painted finish. They have small doors on the front of the chest which, according to folk stories, deter thieves from stealing too many items from the chest at one time (the hand in the cookie jar theory!).

Traditional doors are magnificent examples of wood artistry as most have intricate geometric designs. Unfortunately, most new housing has moved away from using this fixture. Common household items made out of wood include boxes with brass, ironwork or hand-carvings, storage containers, chapati boards, bowls and platters, rectangular-shaped chests with iron latches, jewellery boxes, cooking utensils such as rolling pins and spoons, as well as hand-carved ornamental pieces (figurines, masks and block-print blocks).

Michael Sklovsky

Michael Sklovsky is a designer and craftsman. He founded the Ishka shops in Melbourne, Australia.

Left: Traditional stringed instruments are crafted by hand throughout India.

[Continued from page 55]

Wandering magicians, snake charmers and storytellers may also use song to entertain their audiences; the storyteller often sings the tales from the great epics. Radio, TV and cinema have played a major role in broadcasting popular music to the remote corners of India. Bollywood's latest musical offerings are never far away, thanks to the proliferation of cassette players throughout the country.

Fusion music – an innovative blend of Eastern and Western influences – has become increasingly popular around the world. This style of music has featured on a number of Western blockbusters, including *Dead Man Walking*, which included some evocative fusion compilations by the renowned Nusrat Fateh Ali Khan.

Literature

India has a long tradition of Sanskrit literature, although works in the vernacular have contributed to a particularly rich legacy. In fact, it's claimed that there are as many literary traditions as there are written languages. For most visitors, only those written in (or translated into) English are accessible (see also Books in the Facts for the Visitor chapter).

Poets include AK Ramanujan *(The Striders, Relations)* and Arun Kolatkar, the latter winning the Commonwealth poetry prize in 1977 for *Jejuri*, a collection of 31 poems in English. Kamala Das is one of the best-known women poets.

Prominent authors include Mulk Raj Anand whose work focuses on the downtrodden (*Cooli*, *Untouchable* was hailed as the first Dalit novel), novelist Raja Rao *(Kanthapura, The Serpent and the Rope, The Cat and Shakespeare)* and Nissam Ezekiel, an Indian Jew whose poetry largely explores aspects of Jewish identity in India. Shashi Tharoor's work *The Great Indian Novel* won the Commonwealth Writer's Prize and he has also written *India: From Midnight to the Millennium*, which examines the successes and failures of independent India. Rohinton Mistry's *A Fine Balance* is a harrowing tale of the fate of two tailors and an insight into India's caste system. The widely translated novelist Amitav Ghosh, won the Prix Medici Estranger, one of France's top literary awards, with his work *The Circle of Reason* in 1990. And, of course, there is the renowned Rabindranath Tagore, who was awarded the Nobel Prize for Literature in 1913.

One of India's best-known writers, RK Narayan, hails from Mysore and many of his stories centre on the fictitious South Indian town of Malgudi. His most well-known works include: *Swami And Friends*, *The Financial Expert*, *The Guide*, *Waiting for the Mahatma* and *Malgudi Days*. His most recent book, *The World of Nagaraj*, offers a unique flavour of the language and ambience of South India.

Khushwant Singh is certainly one of India's most published contemporary authors and journalists, although this prolific Sikh writer seems to have as many detractors as fans. His books include writing on the holocaust of Partition in the harrowing *Train to Pakistan*; the Sikh campaign for a separate homeland in *My Bleeding Punjab*; and the history of Delhi from the first Mughal invasions to the fall of the British empire, as seen through the eyes of series of poets, soldiers, sultans and ordinary people in *Delhi*.

Salman Rushdie's *Midnight's Children*, which won the Booker Prize in 1981, tells of the children who were born, like modern India itself, at the stroke of midnight on that August night in 1947 and how the life of one particular midnight child is inextricably intertwined with events in India itself. Rushdie's follow-up, *Shame*, was set in modern Pakistan. *The Moor's Last Sigh* centres on a political party called Mumbai Axis.

Keralan-born Arundhati Roy grabbed the headlines in 1997 by winning the Booker Prize for her novel *The God of Small Things*. The story, centring on the fate of seven-year-old twins, is set in Kerala, which is evoked in deliciously, sensuous language. In recent times Roy has been actively campaigning against the Narmada Dam project (see the boxed text 'The Dam Debate' earlier in this chapter).

Kolkata-born Vikram Seth's epic novel about post-Independence India, *A Suitable Boy*, centres on a Hindu mother's search for a suitable husband for her daughter.

Anita Desai has written widely on India, including *Cry*, *The Peacock*, *Fire on the Mountain*, and *In Custody* – which was filmed by Merchant-Ivory.

A Matter of Time by Shashi Deshpande centres on the problems a middle-class family faces when the husband walks out. Deshpande (from Bangalore) writes powerful narratives on the relationships between men and women. *The Dark Holds No Terror* and *That Long Silence* are two of her most recent works.

Sharanpanjara, or Cage of Arrows, by a Karnatakan author who simply calls herself Triveni, is hailed as one of the great novels in the Kannada language (it's now available in English translation). The story centres on an upper-class Mysore woman facing the stigma of mental illness.

Kaveri Nambisan from Karnataka writes eloquent historical novels that shed light on the colonial period. *The Scent of Peppers* and *Mango Coloured Fish* are worth reading.

Ruskin Bond, a respected and widely published author in India, has written a number of terrific books, including *Delhi is Not Far*, *An Island of Trees* and a compilation of short stories called *Collected Fiction*.

Upamanyu Chatterjee has written two books well worth reading. *English, August* is the cynical, funny tale of a dope-smoking civil servant sent to Madna, one of India's dreariest towns. The darkly humorous *The Last Burden* is an examination of a dysfunctional family.

Firdaus Kanga's *Trying to Grow* is the story of a crippled homosexual Parsi boy growing up in Colaba, Mumbai.

Hullabaloo in the Guava Orchard by Kiran Desai follows a bored post office clerk and dreamer who takes to the branches of a secluded guava tree in search of the contemplative life, only to be pursued by crowds of people seeking enlightenment.

Shobha De's raunchy (Jackie Collins–style) novels have been heralded by some critics as being extremely significant in their representation of Indian female sexuality, although others have condemned them as shameful trash. Nonetheless, she is the largest-selling Indian English-language author in India.

The Indian bookshop Crossword has instigated a literary prize for the best English-language novel by an Indian writer. In 1999 two prizes were given: The prize for a novel translated into English was awarded to Mukundan (a writer from Kerala) for *On the Banks of the Mayyazhi*, while Vikram Seth was awarded for his English-language novel, *An Equal Music*.

Architecture

In ancient times Indian builders used wood (sometimes brick) to construct their temples. None has survived the vagaries of climate and today all that remain are Buddhist stupas (monument of a solid hemisphere topped by spire). By the advent of the Guptas (4th to 6th centuries AD) of North India, sacred structures of a new type were being built, and these set the standard for temples for several hundred years (see Religion, later in this chapter). One of the main distinguishing features between temples in the north and south is the sikara or vimana. In the north, the sikara is curvilinear and topped with a grooved disk, on which sits a pot-shaped finial, and in the south the *vimana* is stepped with the grooved disk being replaced with a solid dome.

Kerala's temple styles vary in deference to its climate – marked by heavy rainfall – and typically have steeply sloping roofs of stone that effectively drain the water away. The *gopuram* is a soaring pyramidal gateway tower of a Dravidian temple.

The Muslim invaders contributed their own architectural conventions; arched cloisters and domes were among them. The Golgumbaz tomb in Bijapur, Karnataka, is one of the largest domes in existence. Under the Mughals, Persian, Indian and provincial styles were successfully melded to create works of great refinement and quality. They include the Persian influenced tomb of Humayun in Delhi, the great fort at Agra and the city of Fatehpur Sikri. But it's Shah Jahan (r. 1627–58) who has made the most enduring mark on architectural history. He built the Red Fort in Delhi, but is better remembered for the Taj Mahal, the tomb for his queen Mumtaz Mahal.

Europeans left their mark in the churches of Goa (eg, the Basilica of Bom Jesus, completed in 1605), in the neoclassical style buildings built by the British in the 18th and 19th centuries (and of course the parliament complex of New Delhi), and in attempts to meld neo-Gothic and neo-Saracenic (Muslim) styles with local architectural traditions. Swiss architect Le Corbusier designed the entire city of Chandigarh in the capital of Punjab and Haryana in the early 1950s.

Painting

Some 1500 years ago artists covered the walls and ceilings of the Ajanta caves in western India with scenes from Buddha's life, lotus flowers, animals and birds. The figures are endowed with an unusual freedom and grace and contrast with the next major style that emerged from this part of India in the 11th century. To attain spiritual merit, the Jain lay community – which flourished thanks to its stake in trade and local rulers being sympathetic to the large community of Svetambara monks living in Gujarat – poured their money into lavish displays of temple building. However, after the Muslim conquest of Gujarat in 1299 they turned their attention to illustrated manuscripts, which could be hidden away and preserved. These manuscripts are the only form of Indian painting that survived the Muslim conquest of North India. At first artists painted on palm leaves, but the availability of paper from the late 14th century allowed larger and more elaborate works, with gold-leaf script and lavish borders in blue, gold and red (complex designs and luxurious materials testified to the wealth of the patron). Unlike the flowing Ajanta paintings, the Jain style is angular, with deities and mortals depicted in profile, the eye projecting beyond the face.

The Indo-Persian style developed from Muslim royals, although the depiction of the elongated eye is one convention that seems to have been retained from indigenous sources. The Persian influence flourished when artisans fled to India following the 1507 Uzbek attack on Heart (in present-day Afghanistan), and with trade and gift-swapping between the Persian city of Shiraz, an established centre for miniature production, and Indian provincial sultans.

The 1526 victory by Babur at the Battle of Panipat ushered in the era of the Mughals in India. Although Babur and his son Humayun were both patrons of the arts, it was Humayun's son Akbar who is generally credited with developing the characteristically Mughal style. Akbar recruited artists from far and wide to create an *atelier* (studio or workshop) that was, initially anyway, under the control of Persian artists. Artistic endeavour at first centred on the production of illustrated manuscripts (topics varied from history and romance to myth and legend), but later broadened into portraiture and the glorification of everyday events.

Akbar took a personal interest in the artists' work and rewarded those who pleased him. Within the atelier there emerged a high division of labour, which meant more work could be turned out in less time. Skilled designers sketched the outlines of the work. Colourists applied layer upon layer of pigment, burnishing each to achieve an enamel-like finish. Painters used squirrel or camel-hair brushes to create the finest of lines. Artists of extraordinary talent, however, were allowed to do their own paintings and so display their mastery. European paintings influenced the artists, and occasionally reveal themselves in experiments with motifs and perspective.

Akbar's son, Jehangir, also patronised painting, but his tastes and interests were different. He preferred portraiture and his fascination with natural science resulted in a rich legacy of paintings of birds, flowers and animals. Style also took a distinctive turn under Jehangir. Despite its richness, there is nothing frivolous or wasteful about the paintings turned out by his atelier. The more formal ordering of figures reflects a penchant for strict etiquette in court life. Jehangir also saw portraiture as a useful tool for sizing up foreign rivals; he desired such paintings to reveal personality and requested them so that he might judge the subject's characteristics. Under Jehangir's son Shah Jahan, the Mughal style became less fluid, and although the colouring was bright and eye-catching, the paintings lacked the life and vigour of before. It was a trend that continued, hastened by the disintegration of the Mughal court in the 18th century. Mughal painting as such ended with the reign of Shah Alam II (1759–1806).

By the 19th century, painting in North India was heavily influenced by Western styles (especially English watercolours), giving rise to what's been dubbed the Company School, which had its centre in Delhi.

In Rajasthan distinctive styles developed that were influenced by Mughal tastes and conventions, in part because local Rajput rulers were required to spend time at the Mughal court. But Rajasthani painting had its own characteristics, marked by a poetic imagery evident in such popular themes as the *ragamala*, a depiction of musical modes, and the *nayakanayikabheda*, a classification of ideal types of lovers. The romanticism and eroticism they depict are in stark contrast to the strict morality that pervaded Rajput society. Portraiture was influenced by Mughal trained artists recruited by Rajput rulers. But rather than the revealing pictures favoured by Jehangir, these portraits lean more towards ideal representations of individuals, whose weaknesses are well and truly disguised.

In the Himalayan foothills of north-west India a distinctive style of painting, dubbed Pahari, developed during the 17th and 18th centuries. This relatively small area (roughly between Jammu and Garhwal) was divided into 35 kingdoms. Pahari painting can be divided into two main schools: The Basholi school preceded the Kangra, which eclipsed it in the late 18th century. Basholi art is robust, bold and colourful. Kangra art is more subdued and fluid, probably testament to the influence of Mughal court painters migrating into the area at the time. The Kangra school survived until the late 19th century, but its best works are usually dated to around the late 18th and early 19th centuries.

Sculpture

For about 1500 years after the demise of the Indus Valley civilisation, sculpture in India seems to have vanished as an art form. Then suddenly, in the 3rd century BC, it reappeared in a new, technically accomplished style that flourished under the Maurya rulers of central India.

It's a phenomenon that still puzzles scholars and art historians; some say Mauryan sculpture must have had its genesis abroad, possibly in Persia. But this has never been proven. The legacy of the Mauryan artists includes the burnished, sandstone columns

Behind the Scenes of Indian Cinema

India's incredibly popular and successful film industry was born in 1897, when the first Indian-made motion picture, *Panorama of Calcutta*, was screened in the Star theatre in Kolkata. It was made with foreign technicians and didn't have a story line. India's first feature film, *Raja Harishchandra*, was made in the silent era in 1913. It is from this film that Indian cinema traces its lineage. Between 1931 (when the talkies began) and 1999 India produced over 30,000 feature films, a world record by a long stretch.

India's film industry is the largest in the world, larger than Hollywood. And Mumbai, the film capital, has earned itself the nickname 'Bollywood'. Other main film-producing centres are Chennai and Hyderabad. In 1999, 764 feature films were produced in 12 languages. Over 2.5 million people are employed in the film industry and India has around 13,000 theatres, including touring cinemas that go from village to village. For the poor, movies are the cheapest and most popular form of entertainment.

A visit to an Indian cinema can be quite rewarding if you don't mind the hustle and bustle. If the film has just opened and is a hit, filmgoers will probably have to buy the ticket at a premium price from a tout hanging in the alleys around the theatre. The transaction will be totally illegal, but the police will look the other way because they are in cahoots. Still, this method of purchase is not recommended.

There are two categories of Indian films. For a cultural experience or, more likely, a culture shock, you should try what is known as the mainstream movie. You probably haven't seen anything quite like it. Three hours and still running, the blockbusters are 'multistarrers' with up to three starring couples. You'll find rape, violence, a dream sequence, up to a dozen songs, an honest policeman with an evil brother who was probably lost in childhood, or a car chase that doesn't take the plot anywhere.

It is all done with such verve, exuberance and sheer vitality that it carries the local audience along and leaves the foreigner dumbfounded. On the surface it may be Rambo, Romeo or Dirty Harry, but the subtext is likely to be the Mahabharata, dharma and social justice. These movies are heady, spicy stuff. Not for nothing do the locals call them *masala* (mixed spice) movies. They are pure fantasies. What the audience sees on the screen does not happen in the mundane day-to-day lives of ordinary Indians. Technically, these days the films are as slick as anything made anywhere.

There is also a sub-genre, the C-grade movie. These are truly awful. The story would have the heroine 'lose her honour' to the local feudal land owner. She becomes a vengeance-seeking dacoit (outlaw). There are variations of this theme and a rape scene is obligatory. Not much acting skill is erected by the Buddhist emperor Ashoka, the most famous of which, the lion-topped column at Sanchi (Madhya Pradesh), has become the state emblem of modern India.

Midway through the 2nd century BC a new format emerged, evident in the stupa railing of Bharut, Madhya Pradesh. Here can be seen the style and motifs that have since become an integral part of Indian sculpture. The ornamentation is symbolic of abundance (beauty and abundance are closely linked in Indian sculpture); the pot overflowing with flowers, the lotus, the trees, the elephants and the mythical *makara* (a protective crocodile-like creature). Here, too, are the *yakshas* and *yakshis*, male and female deities associated with ancient fertility cults and whose images provided the basis for Buddhist, Jain and Hindu iconography.

While there was an early reluctance to represent Buddha in more than symbolic form, yaksha figures gradually became Buddha-like in the succeeding centuries, albeit devoid of their elaborate dress and ornamentation (deemed inappropriate in the light of Buddhism's monastic traditions). The Sarnath Buddha, for example, has a robe characteristically thrown over the left shoulder, the right hand raised in a *mudra* (gesture) signifying freedom from fear, the left resting on the waist, but empty handed. By the Gupta period in North India (4th to 6th centuries AD) the rather earthy and robust yaksha-style Buddha icons had been transformed into models of serene contemplation, eyes lowered, as befitting the compassionate Master of the Law.

Hindu and Jain iconography also began to evolve their distinctive forms at this time. Images sprouted multiple arms and heads (distinguishing them from mere mortals), and eventually adopted the serene expressions

Behind the Scenes of Indian Cinema

required, but the heroine must have an ample bosom and know how to ride a horse. These films cater to a male crowd that wants action and has no time for the love angle. Made on a shoestring, they head straight for the flea-infested halls of smaller towns.

There are no explicit sex scenes in Indian films made for the local market. The censors are rigid on this score. Kissing has recently crept in, but established actresses still refuse to be kissed on screen. The camera discreetly moves away at the crucial moment. However, lack of nudity is more than compensated for by heroines writhing to music in the rain with clinging wet saris. The front-benchers are delirious with contentment.

The big budget films are often shot abroad. Switzerland is very popular – alpine peaks and lakes pass off as the Himalaya. The biggest box office hit of 2000, *Kaho Na Pyar Hai* (Say You Love Me), was largely shot in New Zealand. Australia and Eastern Europe are also becoming popular locations, the latter because it's cheaper.

The art or 'parallel' cinema, on the other hand, takes Indian reality as its base. The images are a faithful reproduction of what we see around us and the idiom in which it is presented is a Western one. They are, or at least supposed to be, socially and politically relevant. Made on infinitely smaller budgets than their commercial cousins, these films win awards at film festivals abroad. Most of them make little money or sink without trace in the home market. If the film is any good, you can probably catch it back home at your local cinema.

Some of the better-known films in this category are the works of directors like Satyajit Ray *(The Apu Trilogy, Charulata)*, Mira Nair *(Salaam Bombay, Mississippi Masala, Kama Sutra)* and Deepa Mehta *(Earth, Fire)*. Mehta was to complete a trilogy with her third film, *Water,* but a few days into the shoot in Varanasi the unit was forced to pack up and leave. The script concerned the sorry plight of Hindu widows and the theme and treatment did not go down well with right-wing Hindu zealots. (See the boxed text 'Drowning in Conservatism' in the Uttar Pradesh & Uttaranchal chapter.)

Bhaichand Patel

Bhaichand Patel was formerly the Director of the UN Information Centre for India. He now divides his time between Delhi and New York and writes a column about the art scene for the *Hindustan Times* (Delhi) and *Mid-Day* (Mumbai).

which have become associated with calm contemplation.

From the 10th century, sculpture and architecture were generally inseparable; temples were lavishly decorated with religious sculpture designed to impress and instruct. The fantastic animal forms and towering gopurams of the great temple complexes of South India (eg, Meenakshi in Madurai, Tamil Nadu) took ornamentation and monumentalism to new levels.

Most, but not all, sculpture has left its legacy in stone. From South India comes a brilliant series of bronzes, created during the Chola dynasty of the 9th and 10th centuries. The lost-wax technique artisans used to produce images of the most popular deities are still found in Tamil Nadu, but the brilliance of the Chola period has never quite been recaptured.

Theatre

The oldest form of classical theatre in India, Sanskrit theatre, shares a common ancestry with dance. Details on both were laid down in the *Natya Shastra* in ancient times. Sanskrit theatre, like dance, was divided into performances for the gods and those rendered for people's pleasure, and was further classified into naturalistic and stylised productions, notions reflected in the folk traditions of later times. This type of theatre thrived until about AD 1000 when it was eclipsed by folk theatre. Today it lives only in the *kudiyattam* Sanskrit theatrical style of Kerala.

The many regions and languages of India provided fertile ground for folk theatre, which employs a few Sanskrit theatrical conventions such as the opening prayer and the *vidushaka* (clown) – the hero's comic alter ego and the audience's ally. Folk theatre draws heavily from the Vedic epics (see Religion later) but will also canvass current political and social issues. Performances always take place outdoors and actors are invariably from castes where the art is passed from father to son; in rare cases women may also act. Troupes may tour for several months at a time and the more popular theatrical forms (secular rather than religious in nature) have a very healthy following.

Puppetry has also enjoyed a good following in India, although most people are only familiar with Rajasthani puppets *(kathputlis)*; wooden creations, dressed in colourful costumes and manipulated by the puppeteers (always male) using strings. Less well known are the leather stick puppets of Andhra Pradesh (similar to the *wayang kulit* puppets of Indonesia) and the glove puppets of Kerala. Puppetry is losing its audience to competing attractions such as cinema and television and because puppeteers are reluctant to challenge the epic-based repertoire.

Modern theatre had its inception in Bengal in the 18th century. Exposed to Western theatrical and literary conventions earlier than most, Bengali artists combined Western staging techniques with folk and Sanskrit conventions. Their plays soon became vehicles for social and political comment and opposition to British rule. The touring Bombay Parsi theatre companies that developed in the north and west of India in the 19th century also used Western, classical and folk conventions to bring dramatic, lively entertainment in Hindi and Urdu to a wide audience.

SOCIETY & CONDUCT

Marriage, Birth & Death

Ceremonies for important occasions, such as marriages, vary in the many religions found in the subcontinent (see Religion later in this chapter) and each would need at least several pages to describe.

In Hindu-dominated India, although *samskaras* (rites of passage ceremonies) have been simplified over the centuries, they still hold great importance. One highly auspicious event is the marriage ceremony, which is an elaborate and expensive affair. Although 'love marriages' have risen in recent years (mostly in urban centres), most Hindu marriages are arranged (see also Women in Society later in this section). Discreet inquiries are made within the community, or, where the community isn't very close-knit, such as in big cities, advertisements may be placed in the local newspapers or on the Internet. Many nonresident Indians (NRIs) also advertise via newspapers or the Internet. They will make a special trip to India to meet prospective applicants who have made it to the short list.

Horoscopes are checked, and if they match, a meeting between the two families usually takes place. Many potential matches are rejected purely on the basis that the astrological signs are not propitious. An astrologer is consulted again when it comes to fixing a wedding date. Dowry, although illegal, is still a key issue in many arranged marriages. In theory, the larger the dowry, the greater the chances of the bride's family securing a good match for their daughter. Families will often go into horrendous debt to raise the required cash and merchandise.

On the day of the wedding the bridegroom is escorted to his future in-law's home (usually accompanied by an exuberant brass band and plenty of friends and well-wishers) where offerings of roasted grain are tossed into the hearth fire. The ceremonies are officiated by a priest and the marriage is formalised when the bridegroom holds his bride's hand and they walk around the fire seven times.

The birth of a child is another momentous event, replete with its own set of special ceremonies. These rituals centre on the casting of the child's first horoscope, name giving, feeding the first solid food and hair cutting (performed on boys once they are about five years of age).

Divorce and remarriage are still generally frowned upon in India. Among the higher castes, widows are not expected to remarry, but are admonished to wear white and live pious, celibate lives. Traditionally, widows have been excluded from religious ceremonies and festivals, and they are generally regarded as harbingers of bad luck.

Hindus cremate their dead, and funeral ceremonies are designed to purify and console both the living and the deceased. An important aspect of the proceedings is the *sharadda*, or paying respect to one's ancestors by offering water and rice cakes. It's an observance that's repeated at each anniversary of the death. After the cremation the ashes are collected and 13 days after the death (when blood relatives are deemed ritually pure) a member of the family will usually scatter them in a holy river such as the Ganges, or in the ocean.

Pilgrimage

Devout Hindus are expected to go on *yatra* (pilgrimage); at least once a year is considered desirable. Pilgrimages are undertaken for various reasons: to implore the gods to grant a wish, to take the ashes of a cremated relative to a holy river, to seek good health and fortune, or to gain spiritual merit. There are many thousands of holy sites in India to which pilgrims travel (the elderly often make Varanasi their final goal, as many believe that dying here releases them from the cycle of rebirth). Despite the carnival-like atmosphere of some fairs (such as the Pushkar Camel Fair in Rajasthan), most festivals in India are rooted in religion and are thus a magnet for pilgrims.

The Caste System

Caste is the basic social structure of Hindu society. Living a righteous life and fulfilling your dharma (duty) will augment your chances of being born into a higher caste and thus better circumstances (see Religion later in this chapter). Hindus are born into one of four varnas (castes): Brahmin (priests), Kshatriya (warriors), Vaishya (merchants) and Shudra (peasants). The Brahmins were said to have emerged from the mouth of Lord Brahma at the moment of creation, Kshatriyas were said to have come from his arms, the Vaishyas from his thighs and Shudras from his feet. Beneath the four main castes are the Dalits (formerly known as Untouchables and officially known as the Scheduled Castes). Their lives were the most menial of all, and even today sweepers and latrine cleaners are invariably drawn from their ranks. Within the varnas are thousands of *jati*, or groups of 'families'.

Today the caste system, although weakened, still wields considerable power. The relationship between caste and politics is quite potent; those seeking power may look to certain jatis as potential vote banks. Tensions between the upper castes and the Dalits often turn violent. In an effort to improve the position of the Dalits, the government reserves significant numbers of public sector jobs, parliamentary seats and university places for them. This has angered many well-educated people who miss out on jobs they would otherwise get on merit. In 1994 some state governments (such as Karnataka) boldly raised the number of places in an attempt to win mass support from Dalits. In 1991 and again in 1994, there were serious protests against the raising of the quotas, and in 1991 at least 100 protesters immolated themselves. The situation remains prickly. In 1999 the Indian government admitted 242 castes to the 'Other Backwards

Classes' list. Castes on this list are eligible for special quotas representing 27% of positions in government employment. But this is still far less than the number recommended by the National Commission for Backward Classes (a body established by the Supreme Court), which states that an additional 110 castes be added.

Women in Society

Although the professions are still very much male dominated, women are making inroads – in 1993 the first women were inducted into the armed forces, and they currently account for around 10% of all parliamentarians. Less visible to the public is the woman's influence in family affairs, especially when it comes to ceremonies.

However, for village women, it's much more difficult to get ahead, but groups such as Self-Employed Women's Association (SEWA) in Ahmedabad (Gujarat) have shown what's possible. Here, poor and low-caste women, many of whom work on the fringes of the economy, have been organised into unions, offering at least some lobbying power against discriminatory and exploitative work practices (for details see the boxed text 'SEWA' in the Gujarat chapter).

Traditionally, especially in the less affluent stratas of Indian society, the desire to have male children is so strong that the government has had to pass legislation to prohibit the abortion of healthy foetuses, the modern equivalent of the age-old practice of female infanticide. 'Sex determination' clinics are also banned, but abortions, following examinations in illegal ultrasound clinics, continue. In poorer families girls are often regarded as a liability on the family, not only because they leave the family when married (traditionally boys remain in their parents' home even after marriage), but also because an adequate dowry must be supplied – an immense financial drain for many families.

Arranged marriages are still the norm rather than the exception. A village girl may well find herself married off while still in her early teens to a man she has never met. She then goes to live in his village, where she is expected not only to do manual labour (at perhaps half the wages that a man would receive for the same work), but also to raise children and keep house. This might

Glorifying the Burning Widow

In September 1987 India was plunged into controversy when an 18-year-old recently widowed woman, Roop Kanwar, burned to death on her husband's funeral pyre at the village of Deorala in Rajasthan. According to the dead girl's family and the entire village of Deorala, Roop Kanwar voluntarily ascended the funeral pyre and calmly recited prayers while she was consumed by flames. Sceptics have alleged that the young woman, who had only been married seven months, was drugged and forcibly thrown on the fire.

What is equally as shocking as the fact that a young woman should needlessly perish by fire, whether voluntarily or not, is that in the late 20th century the act of *sati* (a widow's act of suicide on her husband's funeral pyre) was glorified and the victim deified, not just by superstitious rural folk, but by hundreds of thousands of people around the country. Within one week of Roop Kanwar's death, Deorala had become a major pilgrimage site, attracting *half a million* pilgrims, most of whom left substantial donations for a temple to be built in her honour. Among the pilgrims who visited the site of the calamity were several members of both the state and central governments.

On 27 September Prime Minister Rajiv Gandhi issued a statement declaring the circumstances of the death of Roop Kanwar 'utterly reprehensible and barbaric'. In December 1987 a law was passed by the central government banning sati, with family members of persons committing sati to be divested of their right to inherit her property. Persons charged with 'glorifying' sati would be prohibited from contesting elections. In addition, sati *melas* (fairs), were banned.

Despite these measures, the incontestable power of the sati still holds sway over the population, both educated and uneducated. Women reverently pay homage at shrines erected in honour of satis, believing that they have the power to make barren women fertile, or cure terminal illnesses.

So sati continues to occur. In November 1999 a 55-year-old Dalit village woman in Satpurva (Uttar Pradesh) committed sati after her husband died from tuberculosis. Thousands of villagers gathered to glorify the suicide.

involve a daily trek of several kilometres to fetch water, as much again to gather firewood, and a similar amount again to gather fodder for domestic animals. She has no property rights if her husband owns land, and domestic violence is not uncommon.

For the urban, middle-class woman, life is materially much more comfortable, but pressures still exist. She is much more likely to be given an education, but only because this will improve her marriage prospects. Once married, she is still expected to 'fit in' with her new in-laws, and to be homemaker above all else. Like her village counterpart, if she fails to live up to expectations – even if it is just not being able to give her in-laws a grandson – the consequences can be dire, as demonstrated in the practice of 'bride burning'. It's claimed that for every reported case, some 320 go unreported and that less than 8% of the reported cases are actually pursued through the legal system.

A married woman faces even greater pressure if she wants to divorce her husband. Although the constitution allows for divorcees (and widows) to remarry, few are in a position to do so simply because they are considered outcasts from society – even a woman's own family will usually turn its back on a woman who seeks divorce, and there is no social security net to provide for her. For many, another marriage also means another dowry has to be paid. A marriage in India is not so much a union based on love between two individuals, as a social contract joining two people and their families. It is then the responsibility of the couple to make the marriage work, whatever the obstacles; if the marriage fails, both husband and wife are tainted, but the fall-out for the woman is far worse. Divorce rates are, not surprisingly, low. The majority are in the larger cities, such as Mumbai and Delhi, where it is also generally more acceptable (although not particularly socially desirable) for women to pursue careers and independent lives.

Regarding contemporary urban male attitudes, a recent survey conducted in Delhi, Mumbai, Chennai and Bangalore by an Indian magazine indicated that the most important quality unmarried men sought in a spouse was self-confidence. Intellectual compatibility rated low but, ironically, as many as 65% of participants said that a willingness to adjust was very important (old traditions die hard it seems).

Birth Control

With a population tipped to exceed China's in the coming decades, birth control is a perennial concern. Moves to introduce birth control gained notoriety in the 1970s especially during the Emergency when sterilisation squads moved around the countryside and terrorised villagers. In the 1980s Prime Minister Rajiv Gandhi instituted an ambitious sterilisation target of 1.3 billion Indians by 2050. It met with mixed success, especially in rural areas where children (especially male children) are regarded as security for one's old age. Widespread media coverage in support of birth control has promoted the ideal of the two-child family, as has the use of contraceptives, especially condoms. However, families with more than two children are still common in rural India.

Indian Clothing

These days, in the larger cities (especially Mumbai and Delhi) it's not unusual to see young Indian women wearing jeans and T-shirts. However, the sari, which would have to be the world's most graceful attire, is still worn by most Indian women. In the upper echelons of society (among resident and nonresident Indians), the sari has become even more of a fashion statement, largely thanks to innovative, contemporary designs by leading Indian fashion designers.

Buying a sari is an experience in itself. Invited to sit, shoeless, on a spotless, white, cotton-covered mattress, you watch as the sari seller pulls out bolster after bolster of shiny fabrics, tossing them on the mattress where they roll out to reveal brilliant colours and patterns. It's hard to say no. Many travellers use the fabric to make garments or to use as home decorations.

The sari comes in a single piece (between 5m and 9m long and 1m wide) and is ingeniously tucked and pleated into place without the need for pins or buttons. Worn with the sari is a choli (tight-fitting blouse) and a cotton draw-string petticoat. The *palloo* is that part of the sari draped over the shoulder.

Young Indian women in particular tend to wear the *salwar kameez*, a loose tunic top over drawstring trousers. This outfit is also popular with travellers (see also Women

Travellers in the Facts for the Visitor chapter). The salwar kameez is accompanied by a scarf-like length of matching fabric called a dupatta, which is usually draped across the neck at the front so that the two ends cascade down the back. The dupatta is also used to cover the head in temples, or in front of elders (especially in-laws) as a mark of respect.

Of course there are regional and religious variations in costume. For instance, you may see some Muslim women wearing the all-enveloping tent-like burkha.

Indian men generally wear Western-style trousers and shirts, although the dhoti and (in the south) the lungi and the *mundu* are also commonly worn. The dhoti is a loose white garment pulled up between the legs like a long loincloth. The lungi is more like a sarong, and is always coloured. Its end is usually sewn up like a tube; the wearer merely pleats it at the waist so that it fits snugly. The mundu, worn in Kerala, is like a lungi but is always white. Men frequently tuck the hems into the waist giving the garment a skirt-like appearance; a lungi or mundu should always be lowered when sitting down or entering someone's house.

Dos & Don'ts

India is a country of time-honoured traditions and customs. While you are obviously not expected to get everything right, common sense and courtesy will take you a long way. If in doubt about how you should behave, watch what the locals do (eg, at a temple), or simply ask; people are generally happy to point you in the right direction and appreciate your sensitivity.

Kissing and hugging in public is not on, and neither is full nudity; even if you're getting changed at a swimming pool. Before throwing something away to lighten your backpack, think about donating it to a local charity. Lastly, watch where you're walking at night – any undefined, decent-sized shape is likely to be a sleeping human (especially in Mumbai and other large cities).

Bathing Public nudity is completely taboo so if you fancy a cool dip, make sure you cover up (even in remote locations). Indian women invariably wear saris when bathing in a river or any place where they are in public view. For female travellers, a sarong is a great alternative for bathing – unless at a hotel swimming pool, when a swimsuit is acceptable. See also Women Travellers in the Facts for the Visitor chapter.

Eating & Visiting Etiquette It's customary to use your right hand for eating and other social acts such as shaking hands; the left hand is used for less delicious matters like wiping your backside and removing grotty shoes. If you are drinking from a shared water container, hold the container a little above your mouth and pour (thus avoiding contact between lips and the mouth of the container).

If you are invited to dine with a family, it's polite to take off your shoes if they do and wash your hands before taking your meal. The hearth is traditionally the sacred centre of the home, so it's best to approach it only if invited to do so. The same often applies for the kitchen (remove shoes). It's inappropriate to touch food or cooking utensils. At a meal, the etiquette is not to help yourself to food – wait to be served or invited to help yourself. If you are unsure about protocol, simply wait for your host to direct you.

Photography Etiquette Exercise sensitivity when taking photos of people, especially women, who may find it embarrassing and offensive – always ask first. Taking photos inside a shrine, at a funeral, a religious ceremony or of people bathing in public baths or rivers may cause offence (see Photography & Video in the Facts for the Visitor chapter). Flash photography should not be used in prayer rooms in *gompas* (monasteries) or to take pictures of murals (if in doubt, ask).

Religious Etiquette With so many spectacular and ancient religious shrines, most travellers to India will visit at least one. These places hold enormous spiritual significance, so please be respectful in your conduct and the way you dress. Do not wear shorts or sleeveless tops (this applies to men and women) and don't smoke. Loud and intrusive behaviour isn't appreciated, and neither are public displays of affection, or kidding around.

Before entering a holy place, remove your shoes (remember to tip the shoe minder a couple of rupees when you retrieve them). Photography is usually prohibited – check before taking photos. Never touch a carving or statue of a deity. In some places, such as mosques and some Hindu temples, you will be required to cover your head. For women, a dupatta is ideal. Many mosques do not admit non-Muslims, and some don't admit women. Always inquire to see if you are allowed into a particular mosque. Women are required to sit apart from the men. Some Jain temples request the removal of leather items you may be wearing. They may also stipulate that menstruating women should not enter.

Religious etiquette advises against touching locals on the head, nor directing the soles of your feet at a person, religious shrine, or image of a deity, as this may cause offence. It is also offensive to touch someone with your feet (see also Religion later in this chapter).

Taxi & Rickshaw Drivers & Hotels

If you hire a car and driver, keep in mind that many hotels (especially in tourist magnets like Rajasthan and Agra) do not permit taxi or rickshaw drivers onto their premises to dine, even if you are paying. That's because the commission racket has created all sorts of problems for many hotels and while your intentions may be warm-hearted, the hotel owners are the ones who may face problems with demanding drivers long after you have departed India.

Although some places don't mind drivers joining guests at hotel restaurants, respect those that refuse entry – if in doubt, ask. If you want to shout your driver a meal, there are plenty of good, independent restaurants not attached to hotels that welcome one and all. And, of course, if you are happy with your driver's services, a tip at the end of your trip goes down well. See also Car in the Getting Around chapter.

Treatment of Animals

India's ancient reverence for the natural world manifests itself in numerous ways; in myths, beliefs and cults that are an intrinsic part of the cultural fabric. But in a country where millions live below the poverty line, survival often comes before sentiment. In addition, big money is involved in the trade of animal parts for Chinese medicine, which has been a major factor in bringing India's national animal, the tiger, to the brink of extinction.

The World Society for the Protection of Animals (WSPA) is working to raise awareness of cases of cruelty and exploitation, with one recent campaign focusing on dancing bears. Endangered sloth bear cubs are captured from the wild, their muzzles are pierced so lead rope can be threaded through the hole, and their teeth are pulled out. The bears' nomadic handlers ply tourist traps in Karnataka, and more usually in Agra and Jaipur. WSPA strongly urges visitors not to photograph the performances or give money, which is what leads to this cruelty in the first place.

A WSPA report on the conditions of domestic elephants was completed in 1999. Most domestic elephants are caught from the wild and the breaking-in process is extremely cruel. But elephants sometimes get their own back. In 1998 a court in Kerala ordered an elephant to appear before it after its keeper was accused of mistreating the animal!

In 2000 captive snakes were the focus of animal rights activists, who claimed that their treatment in captivity was extremely cruel. According to the WWF, around 70,000 snakes (including the endangered king cobra) perish annually due to dreadful living conditions in captivity. There has recently been a crackdown on the vicious fights staged between snakes and mongooses; a snake charmer was recently arrested by police in Mumbai and his three snakes (including a black cobra) and one mongoose were set free in the nearby Sanjay Gandhi National Park. Snake charmers fear that the crackdown will end an ancient and time-honoured tradition in India and rob them of their livelihood.

RELIGION

From a postal worker performing puja (prayers) for the safe passage of a parcel, to a former car salesman who has renounced his material life and set off on the path to self-realisation, religion suffuses every aspect of life in India.

India's major religion, Hinduism, is practised by approximately 82% of the population and has the largest number of adherents of any religion in Asia. It is also (along with Buddhism, Jainism and Zoroastrianism) one of the oldest extant religions and has firm roots extending back beyond 1000 BC. The Indus Valley civilisation seems to have developed a religion closely related to Hinduism, but it was the Veda scriptures that gave Hinduism its framework.

Buddhism and Jainism arose contemporaneously in the 6th century BC at a time of social and religious ferment. Both were reactions against the strictures of Brahminical Hinduism. Although more recent, Sikhism too has its roots in a protest movement, the bhakti (devotional) tradition of southern India. Islam swept into India from the north and was introduced to the south by Arab traders. Today it's the largest minority religion in the land. Christianity arrived in southern India with Syrian immigrants long before the first European ever dropped anchor in that part of the world. India is also home to one of the world's oldest Jewish communities.

For information on appropriate behaviour at temples and other places of worship, see Religious Etiquette under Society & Conduct earlier in this chapter.

Hinduism

Hinduism defies attempts to define it. It has no founder, central authority nor hierarchy. It is not a proselytising religion.

Essentially, Hindus believe in Brahman. Brahman is eternal, uncreated and infinite; everything that exists emanates from Brahman and will ultimately return to it. The multitude of gods and goddesses are merely manifestations – knowable aspects of this formless phenomenon – and one devotee may freely pick and choose among them.

Although beliefs and practices vary widely from region to region, there are several unifying factors. These include samsara (common beliefs in reincarnation), karma (conduct or action) and dharma (appropriate behaviour for one's station in life), as well as the caste system.

Hindus believe that earthly life is cyclical; you are born again and again (a process known as samsara), the quality of these rebirths being dependent upon your karma in previous lives. Living a righteous life and fulfilling your dharma will enhance your chances of being born into a higher caste and better circumstances. Alternatively, if enough bad karma has accumulated, rebirth may take animal form. But it's only as a human that you can gain sufficient self-knowledge to escape the cycle of reincarnation and achieve moksha (liberation). Traditionally, women are unable to attain moksha. The best they can do is fulfil their dharma and hope for a male incarnation next time round.

Essentially there are three stages in life recognised under this ashrama system: *brahmachari* (chaste student); *grihastha* (householder who discharges their duty to their ancestors by having sons and making sacrifices to the gods); and *sanyasin* (wandering ascetic who has renounced worldly things). The disinterested discharge of your ritual and social obligations is known as *karma-marga* and is one path to liberation. But there are others, including *jnana-marga*, or the way of knowledge (the study and practice of yoga and meditation) and *bhakti-marga*, devotion to a personal god. The latter path is open to women and Shudras (caste of labourers).

While in India, you'll notice many sadhus. A sadhu is someone who has surrendered all family and social responsibilities and material possessions in order to totally pursue a spiritual search by meditation, devotion, the study of sacred texts, self-mortification and pilgrimage.

Gods & Goddesses

According to the scriptures there are around 330 million deities in the Hindu pantheon. All are regarded as a manifestation of Brahman, and the particular object of veneration and supplication is often a matter of personal choice or tradition at a local or caste level. Brahman is often described as having three main representations, the Trimurti: Brahma, Vishnu and Shiva.

Brahman The One; the ultimate reality. Brahman is formless, eternal and the source of all existence. Brahman is *nirguna* (without attributes), as opposed to all the other gods which are manifestations of Brahman and therefore *saguna* (with attributes).

Brahma He only plays an active role during the creation of the universe. The rest of the time he is in meditation and is therefore regarded as an aloof figure, unlike the two other members of the Trimurti, Shiva and Vishnu. His consort is Saraswati, goddess of learning, and his vehicle is a swan. He is sometimes shown sitting on a lotus which rises from Vishnu's navel, symbolising the

OM

One of Hinduism's most venerated signs is 'om'. Pronounced 'aum', it is an important mantra (sacred word or syllable). The 'three' shape symbolises the creation, maintenance and destruction of the universe (and thus the Trimurti). The inverted *chandra* (crescent or half moon) represents the discursive mind and the *bindu* (dot) within it, Brahman.

For Buddhists, if repeated often enough with complete concentration, it is believed to lead to a state of emptiness.

interdependence of the gods. He is generally depicted with four (crowned and bearded) heads, each turned towards the four points of the compass.

Vishnu The preserver or sustainer, Vishnu is associated with 'right action' and behaves as a lawful, devout Hindu. He protects and sustains all that is good in the world. He is usually depicted with four arms, each respectively holding: a lotus (the petals are symbolic of the unfolding of the universe); a conch shell (as it can be blown like a trumpet it symbolises the cosmic vibration from which all existence emanates); a discus; and a mace (a reward for conquering Indra – the god of battle). His consort is Lakshmi, the goddess of wealth. His vehicle is Garuda, a half bird-half beast creature, and he dwells in a heaven called Vaikuntha. The Ganges is said to flow from his feet. Vishnu has 22 incarnations including Rama, Krishna and Buddha. He is alternatively known as Narayan and Lakshmi is known as Mohini.

Shiva He is the destroyer, but without whom creation could not occur. Shiva's creative role is phallically symbolised by his representation as the frequently worshipped lingam. With 1008 names, Shiva takes many forms including Pashupati, champion of the animals, and Nataraja, lord of the *tandava* (cosmic dance), who paces out the cosmos' creation and destruction.

Shiva is also characterised as the lord of yoga, a Himalaya-dwelling ascetic with matted hair and a naked, ash-smeared body; a third eye in his forehead symbolises wisdom. Sometimes Shiva has snakes draped around his neck and is shown holding a trident (representative of the Trimurti) as a weapon while riding Nandi, his bull. Nandi (literally, enjoyment) symbolises power and potency, justice and moral order. Shiva's consort, Parvati, is capable of taking many forms. Because of his generosity and reverence towards Parvati, women consider Shiva to be an ideal role model for a husband.

Other Gods The jolly, pot-bellied elephant-headed **Ganesh** is held in great affection and is especially popular in Mumbai. He is the god of good fortune and patron of scribes (the broken tusk he holds is the very one he used to write down later sections of the Mahabharata). His animal mount is a rat-like creature. How Ganesh came to have the head of an elephant is a story with many variations. One legend says that Ganesh was born to Parvati in Shiva's absence – Ganesh grew up without knowing his father. One day as Ganesh stood guard while his mother bathed, Shiva returned and asked to be let into Parvati's presence. Ganesh refused him entry. Enraged, Shiva lopped off Ganesh's head, only to later discover that he had slaughtered his own son! He resolved to replace Ganesh's head with the head of the first live creature that he came across. This happened to be an elephant, so that's how Ganesh came to have an elephant's head.

Krishna is an incarnation of Vishnu sent to earth to fight for good and combat evil. Krishna is tremendously popular. His alliances with the *gopis* (milkmaids) and his love for Radha (a married woman) have inspired countless paintings and songs. Krishna is depicted as being dark blue in colour and usually carries a flute.

Hanuman is the hero of the Ramayana and loyal ally of Rama; he embodies the concept of bhakti (devotion). Images of Rama and Sita are said to be emblazoned upon his heart. He is king of the monkeys, therefore assuring them refuge at temples across the country, but he is capable of taking on any form he chooses.

Murugan is the son of Shiva and brother of Skanda. God of war, Murugan is extremely popular in South India, especially

Tamil Nadu. Some say Murugan and Skanda are one and the same. He is usually shown carrying a spear or trident.

Goddesses Within the Shaivite (followers of the Shiva movement), Shakti – the goddess as mother and creator – is worshipped as a force in her own right. Those who follow her are known as shaktis.

The concept of shakti is embodied in the ancient goddess Devi (mother and fierce destroyer). In West Bengal she is known as Durga (a manifestation of Devi) and the Durga puja (commemorating Parvati's return to Shiva, Parvati being the benign aspect of Devi) is popular there. Durga's slaughter of the buffalo demon Mahishasura is a well-known Hindu myth and is frequently depicted in Hindu art as well as being the focus of the Dussehra festival held across India (see Public Holidays & Special Events in the Facts for the Visitor chapter).

Kali, the 'Black One' with the red tongue, is the most fearsome of the Hindu deities. She is often depicted dancing on Shiva's 'corpse' garlanded with human heads. She is bloodthirsty, hankering after battle and carnage and, until its outlaw in the early 19th century, was appeased with human sacrifice.

Saraswati, goddess of learning, is the porcelain skinned consort of Brahma, widely considered to be the most beautiful goddess.

Sacred Texts Hindu sacred texts fall into two categories: those believed to be the word of god (*shruti* meaning heard) and those produced by people (*smriti*; remembered).

The Vedas, introduced to the subcontinent by the Aryans, are regarded as shruti knowledge and are considered the authoritative basis for Hinduism. The oldest of the Vedic texts, the Rig-Veda, was compiled more than 3000 years ago. Within its 1028 verses are prayers for prosperity and longevity as well as an explanation of the origins of the universe. The Upanishads, the last parts of the Vedas, reflect on the mystery of death and emphasise the oneness of the universe.

The oldest of the Vedic texts were written in Vedic Sanskrit, which is related to Old Persian. Later texts were composed in classical Sanskrit, but many have been translated into the vernacular.

The smriti texts comprise a large collection of literature spanning many centuries and include expositions on the proper performance of domestic ceremonies as well as proper pursuit of government, economics and religious law. Among the better known works contained within this body of literature are the Kamasutra, Ramayana, Mahabharata and Puranas, which expand on the epics and promote the notion of the Trimurti. Unlike the Vedas, the Puranas are not limited to initiated males of the higher castes and therefore have wider popular appeal. Also highly popular today are the Mahabharata and Ramayana, which drew an estimated audience of 80 million when they were serialised by Indian state television in the 1980s.

The Mahabharata The Mahabharata is thought to have been composed some time around the 1st millennium BC and to have been the prerogative of the ruling and warrior classes, focusing as it did then on the exploits of their favourite deity, Krishna. By about 500 BC the Mahabharata had evolved into a far more complex creation, with substantial additions, including the Bhagavad Gita (where Krishna gives advice to Arjuna before a great battle). It is in fact the world's longest work of literature; eight times longer than the Greek epics the *Iliad* and the *Odyssey* combined.

The story centres on conflict between the gods – the heroes (Pandavas) and the demons (Kauravas). Overseeing events is Krishna (an incarnation of Vishnu) who has taken on human form. Krishna acts as charioteer for the Pandava hero, Arjuna, who eventually triumphs in a great battle with the Kauravas.

The Ramayana The Ramayana was composed around the 3rd or 2nd century BC and is believed to be largely the work of one person, the poet Valmiki. Like the Mahabharata, it centres on conflict between the gods and demons.

Basically, the story goes that the childless king of Ayodhya called upon the gods to provide him with a son. His wife duly gave birth to a boy. But this child, named Rama, was in fact an incarnation of Vishnu who had assumed human form to overthrow the demon king of Lanka, Ravana. The adult Rama, who won the hand of the princess Sita in a competition, was chosen by his father to inherit his kingdom. But at the last minute Rama's stepmother intervened and demanded her son take Rama's place. Rama, Sita and Rama's brother, Lakshmana, were duly exiled and went off to the forests where Rama and Lakshmana battled demons and dark forces. Ravana's sister attempted to seduce Rama. She was rejected and in revenge, Ravana captured Sita and spirited her away to his palace in Lanka. Rama, assisted by an army of monkeys led by the loyal monkey god, Hanuman, eventually found the palace, killed Ravana and rescued Sita. All returned victorious to Ayodhya where Rama was crowned king.

Sacred Places The number seven has special significance in Hinduism. There are seven especially sacred cities that are major pilgrimage centres: Varanasi (associated with Shiva); Haridwar (where the Ganges enters the plains from the Himalaya); Ayodhya (birthplace of Rama); Mathura (birthplace of Krishna); Dwarka (legendary capital of Krishna thought to be off the Gujarat coast); Kanchipuram (the great Shiva temple); and Ujjain (site every 12 years of the Kumbh Mela). There are also seven sacred rivers: Ganges (Ganga); Saraswati (thought to be underground); Yamuna; Indus; Narmada; Godavari; and Cauvery.

Of course there are thousands more sacred sites that can include groves, caves, mountains and other natural phenomena, or anything associated with the epics.

Temples There is a saying that if the measurement of the temple is perfect, then there will be perfection in the universe. For Hindus the square is the perfect shape and complex rules govern the location, design and building of each temple, based on numerology, astrology, astronomy and religious law. These are so complicated and important that it's customary for each temple to harbour its own particular set of calculations as though they were religious texts.

Essentially, a temple is a map of the universe. At the centre there is an unadorned space, the *garbhagriha* (inner shrine), which is symbolic of the 'womb-cave' from which the universe emerged. This provides a residence for the deity to which the temple is dedicated. Above the shrine rises a superstructure known as a vimana in South India and a sikara in North India, which is representative of Mt Meru, the cosmic mountain that supports the heavens. Cave and mountain are linked by an axis that rises vertically from the shrine's icon to the finial atop the towering vimana.

Because a temple provides a shelter for a deity it is sacred. Devotees acknowledge this by performing a *parkrama* (clockwise circumambulation) of it, a ritual that finds architectural expression in the passageways that track round the main shrine. Some temples also have a *mandapa* (forechamber of a temple) connected to the sanctum by vestibules. These mandapas may also contain vimanas or sikaras. Devotees ring brass bells upon entering the temple to attract the deity's attention.

Holy Creatures & Plants

Animals, particularly snakes and cows, have been worshipped since ancient times in India. The cow represents fertility and nurturing. The bull is more aggressive but its association with Shiva (as his mount, Nandi) accords it enormous respect. Cows and large white bulls roam freely in India, even in cities where they repose beside busy roads (sometimes on traffic islands) seemingly unperturbed by the noisy, fume-belching vehicles surging around them.

Snakes, especially cobras, are also considered sacred. Naga stones (snake stones) serve the dual purpose of protecting humans from snakes and propitiating snake gods. Snakes are associated with fertility and welfare.

Some plants also have strong spiritual significance. The banyan tree *(Ficus benghalensis)* is so sacred that only in times of dire need would people pick its leaves or otherwise interfere with it. It symbolises the Trimurti and a pilgrimage to a sacred banyan is equal to 12 years of sacrifice. Its ashes are said to have the power to eradicate sin. Mango trees *(Mangifera indica)* are symbolic of love; Shiva is believed to have married Parvati under a mango tree and so mango leaves are often used to decorate marriage *pandals* (marquees).

Islam

Islam is the country's largest minority religion (around 12%). It was introduced to the north by invading armies (in the 16th century the Mughal empire controlled much of North India) and to the south by Arab traders.

Islam as a religion was founded in Arabia by the Prophet Mohammed in the 7th century AD. The Arabic term *islam* means to surrender and believers (Muslims) undertake to surrender to the will of Allah (God). The will of Allah is revealed in the scriptures, the Quran (sometimes spelt Koran). God revealed his will to Mohammed, who acted as his messenger.

Islam is monotheistic; God is unique and has no equal or partner. Everything is believed to be created by God and is deemed to have its own place and purpose within the universe. Only God is unlimited and self-sufficient. The purpose of all living things is submission to the divine will. Although God never speaks to humans directly, his word is conveyed through messengers called prophets, who are charged with calling people back to God. Prophets are never themselves divine. Mohammed is the most recent prophet.

In the years after Mohammed's death a succession dispute split the movement and the legacy today is the Sunnis and the Shi'ias. The Sunnis, the majority, emphasise the 'well-trodden' path or the orthodox way. They look to tradition and the customs and views of the greater community. Shi'ias believe that only imams (exemplary leaders) are able to reveal the hidden and true meaning of the Quran. The orthodox view is that there have been 12 imams, the last of them being Mohammed. However, since then *mujtahids* (divines) have interpreted law and doctrine under the guidance of the imam, who will return at the end of time to spread truth and justice throughout the world. Most Muslims in India are Sunnis.

All Muslims, however, share a belief in the Five Pillars of Islam: the shahada or declaration of faith ('there is no God but Allah; Mohammed is his prophet'), which must be recited aloud with conviction and true understanding at least once in a believer's lifetime; prayer (ideally five times a day and on one's own if one can't make it to a mosque); the zakat (tax) which today is usually a voluntary donation in the form of charity; fasting (during the month of Ramadan) for all except the sick, the very young, the elderly and those undertaking arduous journeys; the haj (pilgrimage) to Mecca, which every Muslim aspires to do at least once.

One of the most striking differences between Hinduism and Islam is religious imagery. While Islamic art eschews any hint of idolatry or portrayal of god, it has evolved a rich heritage of calligraphic and decorative designs.

The basic elements of a typical mosque are essentially the same worldwide. A large space or hall is dedicated to communal prayer. In the hall is a mihrab (niche), which indicates the direction of Mecca. Outside the hall there is usually some sort of courtyard that has places where devotees may wash their feet and hands before prayers. Minarets are placed at the cardinal points and it's from here that the faithful are called to prayer.

Sikhism

There are some 18 million Sikhs in India, mostly from Punjab, where the Sikh religion was founded by Guru Nanak in the late 15th century. Sikhism began as a reaction against the caste system and the Brahmin domination of ritual. It was aimed at fusing the best of Islam and Hinduism. The Sikh's holy text, the Guru Granth Sahib, contains the teachings of the 10 Sikh gurus, among others.

Sikhs believe in one god and reject the worship of idols. Although Sikhs do not believe in idol worship, some have pictures of the 10 gurus in their homes as a point of focus. Like Hindus and Buddhists, they accept the cycle of birth, death and rebirth and karma, as well as the notion that only a human birth offers the chance for salvation. There is no ascetic or monastic tradition ending the eternal cycles of death and rebirth in Sikhism.

Fundamental to Sikhs is the concept of *khalsa*, or belief in a chosen race of soldier-saints who abide by strict codes of moral conduct (abstaining from alcohol, tobacco and drugs) and engage in a crusade for *dharmayudha* (righteousness). There are five *kakkars* (emblems) denoting the Khalsa brotherhood: *kesh* (the unshaven beard and uncut hair that symbolises saintliness); *kangha* (comb to maintain the ritually uncut hair); *kaccha* (loose underpants that symbolise modesty); *kirpan* (sabre or sword which symbolises power and dignity); *karra* (steel bangle usually worn on the right wrist which symbolises fearlessness and strength). Singh, literally 'lion', is the name adopted by Rajputs and Sikhs.

Gurdwaras (Sikh temples) usually have a *nishan sahib* (flagpole) flying a triangular flag with the Sikh insignia. The Golden Temple in Amritsar (Punjab) is Sikhism's holiest shrine.

Buddhism

Some seven million people practise Buddhism in India, fewer than either Christianity or Sikhism. Buddha (Awakened One) was a historical figure who is generally believed to have lived from about 563 to 483 BC. Formerly a prince (Siddhartha Gautama), Buddha, at the age of 29, embarked on a quest for enlightenment and relief from the world of suffering. He finally achieved nirvana (the state of full awareness) at Bodhgaya (Bihar), aged 35. Critical of the caste system, dependence upon Brahmin priests and the unthinking worship of gods, Buddha urged his disciples to seek truth within their own experiences. His teachings were oral, but were eventually recorded by his disciples.

Buddha taught that existence is based on Four Noble Truths: life is rooted in suffering; suffering is caused by craving for worldly things; one can find release from suffering by eliminating craving; and the way to eliminate craving is by following the Noble Eightfold Path. This path consists of: right understanding; right intention; right speech; right action; right livelihood; right effort; right awareness; and right concentration. By successfully complying with these things one can attain nirvana.

Buddhism had virtually died out in most of India by the turn of the 20th century. However, it enjoyed something of a revival from the 1950s onward among intellectuals and Dalits, who were disillusioned with the caste system. The number of followers has been further boosted with the influx of Tibetan refugees and the 1975 annexation of the previously independent kingdom of Sikkim. Ladakhi Buddhists follow traditions similar to those found in Tibet.

Stupas, which characterise Buddhist places of worship, essentially evolved from burial mounds. They were never designed to hold congregations, but were to serve as repositories for relics of Buddha and, later, other venerated souls. A relatively recent innovation is the addition of a *chaitya* (hall) leading up to the stupa itself. Devotees walk clockwise around the stupa. Bodhgaya in Bihar, where Buddha attained enlightenment, is an important centre of pilgrimage.

The Tibetan gompas found in Ladakh and Dharamsala are quite unlike anything else found on the subcontinent, embellished as they are with colourful, distinctly Tibetan motifs dedicated to the propagation of Mahayana Buddhist beliefs. See the boxed text 'Visiting Gompas' in the Ladakh & Zanskar chapter for information on etiquette.

Jainism

Jainism, which today has at least four million followers in India, was founded in the 6th century BC by Mahavira, a contemporary of Buddha. Jains believe that only by achieving complete purity of the soul can one attain liberation. Purity means shedding all *karman*, matter generated by one's actions that binds itself to the soul. By following various austerities (eg, fasting, meditation, retreating to lonely places) one can shed karman and purify the soul. Right conduct is essential, and can really only be fully realised by monks as opposed to the ordinary person. Fundamental to the right mode of conduct is ahimsa (nonviolence) in thought and in deed.

The religious disciplines of the laity are less severe than for monks. Some Jain monks go naked and use the palms of their hands as begging bowls. The slightly less ascetic maintain a bare minimum of possessions including a broom, with which they sweep the path before them to avoid stepping on any living thing, and a piece of cloth that is tied over their mouth to prevent the accidental inhalation of insects.

From the outside Jain temples resemble Hindu temples. But inside, Jain temples are a riot of sculptural ornamentation, the very opposite of ascetic austerity. This is partly explained by the Jain notion that beauty is found within. The Jain community is a wealthy one and believes in spending money to keep temples in immaculate condition.

Christianity

When the Portuguese explorer Vasco da Gama dropped anchor at Calicut (in present-day Kerala) in 1498 he claimed to be seeking Christians and spices. He found both.

Christianity is said to have arrived in South India (specifically the Malabar Coast) with St Thomas the Apostle in AD 52. However, scholars say that it's more likely Christianity arrived around the 4th century with a Syrian merchant, Thomas Cana, who set out for Kerala with 400 families. Catholicism established a strong presence in South India in the wake of Vasco da Gama's visit and sects that have been active in the region include the Dominicans, Franciscans and Jesuits. Protestantism arrived with the English, Dutch and Danish.

Today India has about 19 million Christians, around three-quarters of whom live in South India.

Churches in India reflect the fashions and trends of typically European ecclesiastical architecture. Gothic arches and flying buttresses, baroque ornamentation and elegant classical lines can all be found, many with Hindu decorative qualities added by local artisans.

The Portuguese and others far from home made impressive attempts to replicate the great churches and cathedrals of their day. The St Francis Church at Fort Cochin was built in 1503 by Portuguese Franciscan friars and for 14 years housed the remains of Vasco da Gama, the first recorded European to traverse the Indian Ocean.

Judaism

There are fewer than 17,000 Jews left in India, but the community is an ancient one. Jews arrived in Kochi (Kerala) in the 6th century BC and flourished (see the boxed text 'The Jews of Kochi' in the Kerala chapter). However, over the years, more and more Jews emigrated to Israel and other countries.

Zoroastrianism

Zoroastrianism had its inception in Persia and was certainly known to the ancient Greeks. It influenced the evolution of Judaism and Christianity. Founder Zoroaster (Zarathustra) was a priest about whom little is known except that he lived in eastern Persia. The religion that bears his name, however, became the state religion of the region now known as Iran and remained so for some 1200 years.

Zoroastrianism has a dualistic nature whereby good and evil are locked in continuous battle, with good always triumphing. While Zoroastrianism leans towards monotheism, it isn't quite: good and evil entities coexist, although believers are enjoined to honour only the good. Humanity therefore has a choice; purity is achieved by avoiding contamination with dead matter and things pertaining to death. Unlike Christianity, there is no conflict between body and soul; both are united in the good versus evil struggle. Zoroastrianism therefore rejects such practices as fasting and celibacy except in purely ritualistic circumstances. Humanity, although mortal, has components such as the soul, which are timeless. One's prospects for a pleasant afterlife depend on one's deeds, words, and thoughts during one's earthly existence. But not every lapse is entered on the balance sheet and the errant soul is not called to account on the day of judgment for each and every misdemeanour.

Zoroastrianism was eclipsed in Persia by the rise of Islam in the 7th century and its followers, many of whom openly resisted this, suffered persecution. In the 10th century some emigrated to India, where they became known as Parsis (Persians). These Parsis settled in Gujarat, becoming farmers and adopting the Gujarati language. When the British ruled India the Parsis moved into commerce and industry, forming a prosperous community in Mumbai (the Tata family is one example). They adopted many British customs and banned child marriages.

Sacred fire and sacrifice still play a fundamental role in Zoroastrian ritual. But perhaps the most famous practice involves the 'Towers of Silence'. The tower plays an important role in the rituals surrounding death. It is composed of three concentric circles (one each for men, women and children). The corpse is placed within, naked, and exposed to vultures, who pick the bones clean. The bones, once they have been dried by the sun, are swept into a central well. The fourth day of the death rites is the most important for it is on this day that the deceased's soul reaches the next world and presents itself before the deities for judgment.

Parsis only marry other Parsis; there are an estimated 90,000 or so left in India today. They remain economically and politically influential.

Tribal Religions

Tribal religions have so merged with Hinduism and other mainstream religions that very few are now clearly identifiable. It is believed that some basic tenets of Hinduism possibly originated in tribal culture.

In the Nilgiri Hills of South India, the Toda people cling to their own beliefs even though they have adopted some Hindu and Christian customs. The vegetarian Toda venerate the buffalo upon which they depend for milk, butter and ghee. This relationship extends to the afterlife. When a Toda dies, a buffalo is killed to accompany them into the next world where it will continue to provide milk and its by-products for sustenance and for ritual purposes.

LANGUAGE

Although Hindi is India's national language, there are 18 official languages and more than one thousand dialects. English is widely spoken, but attempting to speak a local language will be greatly appreciated. See the Language chapter at the end of the book for lists of useful words and phrases in Hindi and Tamil.

Facts for the Visitor

HIGHLIGHTS

India has so much to see and do that it would take several lifetimes to experience everything. The following is just a sprinkling of possibilities for this lifetime.

Temples & Tombs

India has some of the most historic and breathtaking shrines on earth – living legacies of the country's charismatic religious heritage and former rulers. Tamil Nadu has some particularly fine temples – including Sri Meenakshi at Madurai and Nataraja in Chidambaram – although no part of India is without some focus for worshippers. Other notable places are the rock-cut temples on Elephanta Island near Mumbai, the stunning Golden Temple at Amritsar in Punjab, the Sun Temple at Konark in Orissa and the exquisite Dilwara at Mt Abu and Ranakpur Jain temples of Rajasthan.

The Mughal rulers left a legacy of tombs in the north; these are beautifully carved and embellished in marble. Most famous of all is the Taj Mahal (Agra), a mausoleum built by Emperor Shah Jahan for his favourite wife, Mumtaz. Also impressive are Humayun's tomb and Nizam-ud-din's Shrine in Delhi.

Phenomenal Forts

India's scores of mighty forts serve as stark reminders of the country's tumultuous history. The Red Fort in Delhi is one of the most striking, but Agra Fort is an equally massive reminder of Mughal power at its height. A short distance south is the huge, impregnable-looking Gwalior Fort.

The chivalrous Rajputs were masters when it came to forts and they've got them in all shapes and sizes and with every imaginable tale to tell. Chittorgarh is tragic, Bundi and Kota forts are whimsical, Jodhpur's fort is massive, Amber Fort is simply beautiful and Jaisalmer's is the essence of romance. Way out west in Gujarat are the impressive forts of Junagadh built by the princely rulers of Saurashtra.

Farther south there's Mandu, another grand fort with a tragic tale to tell. Farther south again at Daulatabad, where the immense fort was built and soon deserted, it's a tale of power, ambition and not all that

Fit for a King

If it's palaces and forts you want to see, India is going to tickle your fancy big time. It boasts some of the world's most spectacular palaces and forts, some of which are still inhabited by the sons and daughters of former rulers. Rajasthan undoubtedly has the most diverse and breathtaking range. Indeed, it was a Rajput ruler, Maharana Bhagwat Singh of Udaipur, who was largely responsible for putting Rajasthan (if not India) on the international tourist map, after he converted his summer abode (the Lake Palace) into an upmarket hotel in the 1960s. Nowadays most palace owners have a finger in the tourism pie, whether it be a palace hotel or restaurant or a palace museum. After all, they don't enjoy the financial privileges that their ancestors did (see History in the Facts about India chapter).

Palaces traditionally had separate sections, with women generally having their own quarters (often known as a zenana), connected to the royal chambers by discreet tunnels. An interesting exception is Padmanabhapuram, palace of the maharajas of Tranvancore (now in Kerala). In this matrilineal society, the maharaja was expected to remain celibate so you'll find no secret tunnels here. In fact, although the maharaja's quarters are elevated above those of the other palace dwellers, they are smaller than those belonging to the matriarch.

Wherever possible, India's fort builders exploited natural barriers (to make invasion more difficult): water, such as lakes and the ocean; mountains and hills; forests and desert. Deforestation has robbed some forts of their once notable impregnability, but some clearly reflect the strategic positioning, such as the mighty Meherangarh (fort) at Jodhpur, which looms high above the city on an unassailable rocky base. In the south, Vellore remains one of the best examples of a water fort. And, of course, there was the man behind the Taj Mahal, Shah Jahan, who is also responsible for the Red Fort in Delhi – which demonstrates a marriage of practical considerations with aesthetic appeal.

much sense. Significant forts in the south include Bijapur and Golconda.

Naturally the European invaders had their forts, too. You can see Portuguese forts in Goa, Bassein, Daman and Diu. The British also built their share including Fort St George in Chennai. Those built by the French, Dutch and Danes are, regrettably, largely in ruins, although the ruins also have a certain appeal.

Deserted Cities

There is a handful of spots in crowded India where once-great cities have been deserted. Fatehpur Sikri, near Agra, is the most famous. Akbar founded, built and left this impressive centre in less than 20 years. Hampi, the centre of the Vijayanagar empire, is equally evocative. Not too far from there are the ancient centres of Aihole and Badami. Some of the forts mentioned earlier were also former centres.

Beaching It Up

Few travellers come to India purely to laze on a beach – but for those who do, there are some tempting options. In Kerala there's Varkala; farther north, Goa has a bounty of fine beaches replete with swaying palms. For less tourist hype, there's always the tiny ex-Portuguese island of Diu off the southern coast of Saurashtra (Gujarat), or Gokarna in Karnataka, where many ex-Goa fans are now sunning themselves.

Over on the east coast you could try the beach at Mamallapuram in Tamil Nadu. In Orissa the beach at Gopalpur-on-Sea is clean and peaceful. And then, of course, there are the beaches of the Andamans with white sand, gin-clear water and funky-coloured fish and coral. Also gorgeous are the beaches of Lakshadweep, a sublime series of coral atolls off the west coast – alas, they're only accessible to those with plump wallets.

Festivals & Other Special Events

The bounty of festivals and fairs of India, most of which have religious roots, are celebrated with inimitable zeal (see Public Holidays & Special Events later in this chapter). They kick off with the Republic Day Festival in Delhi each January – a procession and military might are the order of the day. Also early in the year are the Bikaner Camel Festival, the Nagaur Fair and the rather contrived Jaisalmer Desert Festival, all in festival-laden Rajasthan. Holi, the festival of colour marked by the exuberant throwing of coloured water and *gulal* (powder), heralds the onset of Spring and takes place in February/March. In June/July the great Car Festival (Rath Yatra) in Puri is another superb spectacle as the gigantic temple car of Jagannath makes its annual journey, pulled by thousands of eager devotees. In Kerala, one of the big events of the year is the Nehru Cup Snake Boat Races on the backwaters at Alappuzha (Alleppey). September/October is the time to head for the hills to see the delightful Festival of the Gods in Kullu. This is part of the Dussehra Festival, which is at its most spectacular in Mysore. In November it's time for the famous Camel Festival at Pushkar in Rajasthan. Finally, at Christmas where else is there to be in India than Goa?

Kicking Back

Craving some time out from the rigours of travelling? Well, you're in luck. India has plenty of places where you can chill out with like-minded souls. Goa's beaches are perennially popular for this purpose, but Hampi, nearby, has become a magnet for those who find Goa's beach life too much of a scene. Pushkar in Rajasthan has a semi-permanent traveller population drawn by the enchanting (if somewhat commercial) atmosphere of this holy town. If you'd prefer more solitude, Rajasthan also has plenty of small royal abodes off the beaten track, which are now atmospheric hotels. The technicolour Tibetan outlook on life works well in Kathmandu, so why not in India – you'll find Dharamsala and Manali, both in Himachal Pradesh, also have longer-term visitors. Finally, Puri (Orissa) and Mamallapuram (Tamil Nadu) both have temples and beaches, a sure-fire attraction.

SUGGESTED ITINERARIES

India offers such a tantalising smorgasbord of things to do and places to see that it can be difficult making choices about what to do in the time you have available.

Keep in mind that travelling in India can be exhausting – some travellers squeeze too much into a day, leaving them completely frazzled at the end of their trip and in desperate need of a holiday when returning home! Take some time to simply chill out.

The following itineraries assume you have a month to spend in India. They take in the highlights of a region and hopefully will help you make the most of your time. They also assume that you don't want to spend the greater part of your time actually travelling between places. For details about travel options, see the regional chapters. If you have limited time, you may like to consider 'air packages' – see Air Passes in the Getting Around chapter.

Rajasthani Colour

Delhi – Agra – Bharatpur – Jaipur – Shekhawati – Bikaner – Jaisalmer – Jodhpur – Pushkar – Bundi – Chittorgarh – Udaipur – Mumbai

This route gives you a taste of Mughal architecture, including, of course, the Taj Mahal; wildlife; the desert; Hindu temples; hippie hang-outs; Rajput exuberance; unusual Islamic architecture; and a taste of two very different major cities, Delhi and Mumbai.

Mughals, Jains & the Portuguese

Delhi – Agra – Jaipur – Pushkar – Jodhpur – Ranakpur – Udaipur – Rajkot – Junagadh – Sasan Gir – Diu – Palitana – Ahmedabad – Mumbai

This route takes in not only Rajasthan but also the best of what Gujarat has to offer – the tribal cultures of the Rann of Kutch in the far west of the state; the fortified town of Junagadh with some fine buildings; the magnificent Jain temples atop Girnar Hill; Sasan Gir Wildlife Sanctuary – the last home of the Asiatic lion; Diu – the old Portuguese enclave with its beaches; Palitana – another town with hilltop Jain temples; and Ahmedabad – the busy city with its array of Indo-Saracenic architecture.

Hindu & Mughal Heartlands

Delhi – Jaipur – Agra – Varanasi – Khajuraho – Jhansi – Sanchi – Mandu – Aurangabad – Mumbai

Madhya Pradesh is another state that is visited by few tourists but has enough places of interest to make a visit worthwhile. The erotic temples at Khajuraho are the big attraction, but Sanchi and Mandu between them have fine examples of Buddhist, Hindu and Afghan architecture.

Varanasi, one of the holiest places in the country; Agra, with the incomparable Taj Mahal; and the caves of Ajanta and Ellora are other attractions on this route.

Hill Stations & the Himalaya

Delhi – Dalhousie – Dharamsala – Shimla – Manali – Leh – Delhi

This is a good route to follow if you're in India during the summer, when the heat on the plains becomes unbearable – in fact, the road from Manali to Leh is only open for a couple of months a year after the snow melts.

The hill stations of Shimla and Dalhousie hark back to an era that is rapidly being consigned to history; Dharamsala is a fascinating cultural centre, being the home of the exiled Dalai Lama; Manali in the Kullu Valley is simply one of the most beautiful places in the country; while Leh, high on the Tibetan plateau, is the capital of Ladakh and centre for another unique Himalayan culture.

Trekkers and adventure seekers are well catered for at various places on this route. From Manali there are literally dozens of treks, ranging from a couple of days to a couple of weeks, into places such as the remote Zanskar Valley. Leh, too, is a centre for trekkers.

Palaces, Temples & Holy Cities

Delhi – Jaipur – Agra – Jhansi – Khajuraho – Jabalpur – Kanha – Varanasi – Kolkata

This route gives you a taste of Rajasthan and includes the Taj Mahal. Jhansi is the station for the bus journey to the famous temples of Khajuraho, but it's worth stopping at Orchha, 18km from Jhansi, to see this well-preserved old city of palaces and temples. From Khajuraho, a three-hour bus journey brings you to Satna for trains to Jabalpur where a boat trip through the Marble Rocks is the main attraction. Next stop is Kanha National Park for tiger spotting, and then it's back to Jabalpur to catch a train to the holy city of Varanasi. The last stop is Kolkata, one of the most fascinating cities in the country.

Temples & Ancient Monuments

Chennai – Kanchipuram – Mamallapuram (Mahabalipuram) – Pondicherry – Kumbakonam – Thanjavur – Tiruchirappalli – Madurai – Kodaikanal – Udhagamandalam (Ooty) – Mysore – Bangalore – Belur/Halebid/Sravanabelagola – Hampi – Badami – Bijapur – Mumbai

This route takes in a small wedge of modern India, a popular travellers' beach resort, a glimpse of ex-French India, the experimental international community settlement of Auroville, the temple towns of Belur, Halebid and Sravanabelagola, and several days in the mountains of the Western Ghats bordering Tamil Nadu and Kerala.

Temples & Beaches

Chennai – Mamallapuram – Pondicherry – Thanjavur – Tiruchirappalli – Madurai – Kanyakumari – Thiruvananthapuram (Trivandrum) – Kovalam Beach – Kollam – Alappuzha – Kochi – Bangalore – Mysore – Hampi – Bijapur – Mumbai

This route, a variation of Temples & Ancient Monuments, gives you a much broader perspective of southern India and takes you through the tropical paradise of Kerala with its beaches, backwaters, Kathakali dance-dramas and historical Indo-European associations. It also includes some of the major temple complexes of Tamil Nadu, the palaces of Mysore, the Vijayanagar ruins of Hampi and the Muslim splendour of Bijapur.

PLANNING

When to Go

Most foreign travellers visit India in the cooler months from around November to March. For the Himalaya, it's too cold in winter – April to September is the season here, although there are regional variations according to the onset and departure of the monsoon. For more information about when to go where, see Climate in the Facts about India chapter.

The timing of certain festivals and other special occasions may also influence when you want to go (see Public Holidays & Special Events later in this chapter). Incidentally, if your visit coincides with an election campaign, be prepared for transport delays, large crowds and other possible disruptions.

Upgrade This Book

The world can change a lot in a day. Borders may open, hotels close or currencies crash. So before you leave home, check out Upgrades on the LP Web site (www.lonelyplanet.com/upgrades) for significant changes that might have occurred since this book went to press. View or download them, print them and fold them to fit inside the guidebook.

Upgrades are available for over 60 guidebooks, including our most popular titles and those covering countries or regions that are changing rapidly. They are revised every six months until the new, thoroughly updated edition of the book is published.

Maps

Lonely Planet's *India & Bangladesh Road Atlas* breaks the country down into more than 100 pages of maps, and gives unequalled coverage at a scale of 1:1,250,000. It includes city maps, distance charts, climate info, trip maps and a complete index. Its handy size and hinged spine also make it easy to refer to, even on jam-packed buses.

There is a dearth of reliable (and easily accessible) maps available on India – the Lascelles 1:4,000,000 map of *India, Pakistan, Nepal, Bangladesh & Sri Lanka* is probably the most useful general map of India. The Bartholomews map is similar.

When it comes to regional maps, be prepared to be disappointed. Probably the best (and most easily found in India) is the Discover India series, which has some useful state and city maps; prices range from Rs 35 to 50. The Indian Map Service (☎ 0291-740874), Sector G, Shastri Nagar, Jodhpur, Rajasthan 342003, produces a decent series of state road atlases based on Survey of India maps. They include Rajasthan, Gujarat, Tamil Nadu, Maharashtra, Andhra Pradesh, Kerala, Karnataka and India.

Throughout India, state government tourist offices stock local maps, which may at first glance appear pretty snazzy, but are usually dated and lacking essential detail.

What to Bring

If you are only travelling to a single destination, a suitcase is a good option. It's lockable, keeps your clothes flat and is less likely to get damaged by careless luggage handlers at the airport. Heavy luggage presents few problems if all you've got to do is get it into the taxi and to a hotel.

For others, a backpack is still the best carrying container. It's worth paying the money for a strong, good-quality pack, complete with lock, as it's much more likely to withstand the rigours of Indian travel.

If you're not a fan of backpacks, an alternative is a large, soft, zip bag with a wide, securely fastened shoulder strap. This is not an option if you plan to do any trekking.

If you are spending time in the hill stations, especially during the cool season, bring along

The Art of Not Getting Lost

Watching foreigners scramble around like headless chickens (in all the wrong directions) before asking for help can be a great source of curiosity and entertainment to the locals.

To save precious time, don't be shy about asking people on the street, who are usually happy to point you in the right direction. Having said that, there is an art to asking directions in India: You may well receive a fabricated answer (usually 'yes') if the person can't quite decipher your weird accent or simply didn't hear you properly. There is no malicious intent in this misinformation – they're just trying to be polite – after all, 'no' sounds so unsympathetic.

The key to getting as close to accurate directions as possible lies in the phrasing of your question. For instance, it's best to ask 'Which way to the zoo?' rather than pointing and asking 'Is this the way to the zoo?' It's also worth asking several people en route, just to ensure you're not going astray.

Finally, always remember that a casual sideways shake of the head does not always mean no. It can also translate to: yes, maybe, or I don't have a clue, buddy.

warm clothing for chilly nights. During winter, other regions, particularly in North India, can also get surprisingly cold at night.

No matter what kind of trip you're doing, the usual travellers' rule applies – bring as little as possible.

It's important to bring clothing that is culturally appropriate (see Society & Conduct in the Facts about India chapter). A reasonable list would include:

- Underwear and swimming gear.
- One pair of cotton trousers.
- One pair of shorts (men only).
- One long cotton skirt (women).
- A few T-shirts or lightweight shirts.
- Sweater or lightweight jacket for cool nights in the hills or North Indian winters.
- One pair of sneakers or shoes.
- Sandals.
- Flip-flops (thongs) – handy when showering in shared bathrooms.
- Raincoat if you're visiting during the monsoon.
- A set of 'dress up' clothes for that splurge on a meal or night at the disco.
- Wide-brimmed hat – for protection from the sun.

If you are going camping or trekking you will need to take:

- Walking boots – these must give good ankle support and have a sole flexible enough to meet the anticipated walking conditions. Ensure your boots are well broken in beforehand.
- Warm jacket (for cold conditions).
- Wool shirt or pullover (for cold conditions).
- Trousers or shorts – shorts are ideal in hot conditions but should not be worn in places (eg, temples) where they may cause offence.
- Shirts – T-shirts are OK, but shirts with collars and sleeves will give added protection against the sun.
- Socks – a sufficient supply of thick and thin pairs.
- A sun hat.
- Warm gloves (for cold conditions).
- Thermal underwear (for cold conditions).
- A multifuel stove (optional).

Bedding A sleeping bag, although a bit of a bother to carry, can really come in handy. You can use it to spread over unsavoury-looking hotel bedding (especially at some budget places), as a cushion on hard train seats, and as a seat for long waits on railway platforms. If you are planning on spending time in the hills, or going on an overnight camel safari in Rajasthan during winter, a sleeping bag is essential. An inflatable pillow is also worth considering, especially if you are camping or staying in rock-bottom hotels, which usually have rock-hard pillows to match.

Toiletries Soap, toothpaste, shampoo and other toiletries are readily available in India, although hair conditioner often comes in the 'shampoo and conditioner in one' format, so if you don't use this stuff, bring along your own. Astringent is useful for wiping away the grime at the end of the day and is available at most pharmacies. A nail brush and moisture-impregnated disposable tissues are also useful.

Tampons are not easily found (even in the larger cities), so it's certainly worth bringing your own stock. No need to bring sanitary pads – you'll find them in pharmacies at even the smallest towns. It's wise to bring your own condoms, as the quality of local brands is variable. Shower caps can be hard to find (unless you're staying at a five-star hotel), so bring your own. A universal sink plug is useful, as few of the cheaper hotels have plugs. Women should consider bringing a lingerie bag to prevent delicate (and expensive) underwear from being battered or completed ruined by dhobi-wallahs (washer-people) and even hotel laundries (see also Laundry later in this chapter).

Men can safely leave shaving gear at home, as there are plenty of barber shops where you'll get the works for a nominal price. With India's HIV/AIDS problem, however, only choose those barber shops that look clean, and ensure that a fresh blade is used (you may like to bring your own).

Miscellaneous Items See Health later in this chapter for a medical kit check list. Some items to stow away in your pack could include:

- A padlock, especially for budget travellers – most lower-priced hotels have doors locked by a flimsy latch and padlock. You'll find having your own sturdy lock on the door does wonders for your peace of mind. Some travellers bring a heavy-duty chain to secure their pack to the luggage racks of trains and buses.
- A knife (preferably Swiss Army) – it has a whole range of uses, such as peeling fruit.
- A sarong – can be used as a bed sheet, an item of clothing (recommended for bathing in public places), an emergency towel and a pillow.
- Insect repellent, a box of mosquito coils or an electric mosquito zapper – you can buy them in India (electric stuff is useless during power cuts, however). A mosquito net can be very useful – bring tape with you if it doesn't come with a portable frame.
- A torch (flashlight) and/or candles – power cuts (euphemistically known as 'load shedding') are not uncommon and there's little street lighting at night.
- A voltage stabiliser – for those travellers who may be bringing sensitive electronic equipment.
- A spare set of glasses (although several travellers say good-quality glasses are cheaply available in India) and your spectacle prescription. If you wear contact lenses, bring enough solution to last your trip.
- Earplugs (to shut out the din in some hotels as well as outside traffic noise and barking dogs) and a sleeping mask.
- A sun hat and sunglasses – if you dislike sweaty hats, buy an umbrella in India (it provides shade plus air circulation).
- A water bottle – it should always be by your side. It's highly recommended that you use water purification tablets or filters to avoid adding to India's alarming plastic waste problem (see Water Purification under Health later in this chapter).
- High-factor sunscreen and lip balm – though becoming more widely available in India it's *expensive*!
- String – useful as a makeshift clothes line (double-strand nylon is good to secure your clothes if you have no pegs). You can buy small, inexpensive sachets of washing powder almost everywhere in India.
- Women should consider bringing a sports bra if they intend doing a camel safari, as the trotting momentum can cause discomfort, even for just a few hours.
- Binoculars – if you plan to do bird-watching and wildlife-spotting.
- A high-pitched whistle – some women carry these as a possible deterrent to would-be assailants.

If you are motorcycling, bring a good helmet from home, as the quality in India can be variable. You should also bring wet-weather gear, strong waterproof boots and thermal underwear if you plan to ride the Himalaya (even in summer). For more details see Motorcycle in the Getting Around chapter.

RESPONSIBLE TOURISM

Responsible tourism doesn't simply mean behaving in an appropriate manner when you are in another country, although of course common sense and courtesy go a long way when you are travelling (see Dos & Don'ts under Society & Conduct in the Facts about India chapter). Being a responsible tourist also means taking the time to understand as much about a region as possible before travelling there, and being aware of the implications of your presence in that region. You can do this by contacting relevant organisations in your own country – for example, Oxfam in the UK and Community Aid Abroad in Australia are good information sources about various matters such as fair trade, child labour and economically sustainable tourism. Various magazines, such as *The New Internationalist*, are other useful sources of information. For information on environmental organisations working in India, see Conservation Contacts under Ecology & Environment in the Facts about India chapter.

There are a number of monuments in India that are suffering irreparable damage from tourism and government indifference. Arguably one of the most threatened is the Jaisalmer Fort in Rajasthan, which has been listed in the New York-based World Monuments Watch list of 100 endangered sites worldwide. Over the years, as tourism numbers have risen, so too have the number of shops, hotels and restaurants within the fort walls – this has had a detrimental impact on the historic fort.

Tourism growth has also had negative environmental repercussions elsewhere. In Udaipur (Rajasthan), the large number of hotels around Lake Pichola has contributed to widespread pollution within and around the lake. Travellers can help the situation by encouraging hotel management to dispose of rubbish in an environmentally friendly manner. Goa's environment has also suffered simply from the sheer number of tourists. For instance, there is concern that the sewage from a number of hotels is polluting village well water, and that bores sunk by larger hotels (to fill their swimming pools and provide constant running water) is lowering the water table. In Agra, continuing efforts are being made to reduce the impact of tourism on the Taj Mahal. In addition to the introduction of electric buses and autorickshaws and the creation of a traffic exclusion zone, the recent hike in the admission fee to the Taj was partly devised to raise revenue for conservation purposes and also to limit visitor numbers to more manageable levels.

Responsible tourism also extends to the people you interact with during your travels. For example, if you happen to be invited to stay with an Indian family, despite all good intentions, the cost of housing and feeding you can be a considerable financial drain to those families on small incomes. That's not to suggest you shouldn't stay – just exercise judgment and help out by contributing to daily living expenses. Also, if you agree to post someone a copy of a photograph, it's considerate to follow through on this (or else don't make promises in the first place). Many Indians urge tourists not to hand out sweets, pens or money to children since it is positive reinforcement to beg. A donation to a charitable organisation (see Volunteer Work later in this chapter), health centre or school is a more constructive way to help in the long term.

Responsible Diving

Diving in the Andaman Islands, Lakshadweep and elsewhere is putting pressure on sites. To help preserve the ecology and beauty of reefs, consider the following when diving:

- Avoid touching or disturbing living marine organisms. They can be damaged by even the gentlest contact. Never stand on coral, even if it looks solid.
- Be conscious of your fins. Even without contact the surge from heavy fin strokes near the reef can harm delicate organisms.
- Practise proper buoyancy control. Major damage can be done by divers descending too fast and colliding with the reef.
- Dispose of rubbish sensibly, including litter you find.
- Don't collect or buy corals or shells.
- Choose a dive company with appropriate environmental policies and practices.

Say No to Plastic

Many parts of once pristine regions of India are vanishing under a sea of abandoned plastic mineral-water bottles (see also Ecology & Environment in the Facts about India chapter). Travellers are largely responsible for plastic waste and can make a real difference by only purchasing products that use environmentally friendly packaging. Please avoid buying anything in plastic bags and bottles and if you must buy plastic, reuse it. Other ways of reducing India's plastic peril include: buying tea in terracotta cups at train stations rather than plastic; bringing along your own canteen and purifying your water rather than buying water in plastic bottles (see Water Purification under Health later in this chapter); and buying soft drinks in (recyclable) glass bottles rather than in plastic bottles.

The refusal of many travellers to buy plastic products has already sent a powerful

Responsible Trekking

Consider the following tips when trekking to help preserve the ecology of the Himalaya and elsewhere:

Rubbish

- Always carry out all your rubbish (including cigarette butts, sanitary napkins, tampons and condoms) and any rubbish you find.
- Never bury rubbish: digging encourages erosion and buried rubbish may be dug up and consumed by animals (which can kill them).
- Take reusable containers or stuff sacks. Please don't buy plastic bottles.

Human Waste Disposal

- To prevent the spread of disease, use toilets where provided. If there aren't any, bury your waste. Dig a small hole at least 100m from any watercourse (bring a lightweight trowel) and adequately cover it with soil and a rock. Use minimal toilet paper (preferably none). In snow, make sure you dig the hole in the soil so your waste isn't exposed when the snow melts.
- If the area is inhabited, ask locals if they have any concerns about your chosen toilet site.
- Ensure that these guidelines are applied to a portable toilet tent if one is being used by a trekking party. All members (including porters) should use it.

Washing

- Don't use detergents or toothpaste in or near watercourses, even if these products are biodegradable.
- For personal washing, use biodegradable soap and a water container at least 100m away from the watercourse. Disperse the waste water widely so the soil can adequately filter it.
- Wash cooking utensils 100m from watercourses using a scourer, sand or snow instead of detergent.

Appropriate Clothing, Fires & Low-Impact Cooking

- Many travellers aren't well prepared for the extreme cold of the mountains – comprehensively research the weather conditions in advance and seek professional advice on appropriate clothing. This will also reduce the need for fires for warmth.
- Cutting wood causes deforestation – a major problem in India – so avoid open fires and only stay at lodgings that don't use wood to cook or heat water.
- Use a lightweight kerosene, alcohol or Shellite (white gas) stove and avoid those powered by disposable butane gas canisters.
- If you must light an open fire, use any existing fireplaces and only use dead, fallen wood. Always fully extinguish a fire; it's only truly safe to leave when you can comfortably place your hand in it.

Other

- Respect local cultural practices when interacting with communities. Observe any regulations in areas you visit and always seek permission from landowners if you intend entering private property.
- Always stick to existing tracks. Blazing new trails on slopes may turn them into watercourses, causing erosion. If an established track passes through a mud patch, walk in it: walking around the edge increases the patch size.
- Hunting is illegal in India and even if locals encourage it, *never* agree.
- Refrain from feeding wildlife (don't leave food scraps behind either); this can lead to animals becoming dependent on hand-outs and increases their risk of disease. Place gear out of reach (possibly tie packs to rafters or trees).

message to tourism officials, but few are making efforts beyond politically correct statements to actually implement environmental protective measures. On the other hand, some communities are independently taking action to fight plastic pollution. For instance, Leh (Ladakh) is a plastic-bag-free zone and all shops now use paper. In Delhi there are 'say no to plastic' signs all around the city (although shopkeepers still largely use plastic bags). In Tamil Nadu, the Palani Hills Conservation Council has been successful in banning plastic from the Kodaikanal area, and bags are made of newspaper instead of plastic. In the same vein, the Sikkim government has banned the sale and use of plastic bags in that state. Many of Goa's beaches have also been severely affected by prolific plastic waste, which prompted the Goa Foundation to start a 'Clean up Calangute' project in 2000.

Be Shop Smart

Tourists can put their money to excellent use by shopping at cooperatives. These have been set up to protect and promote the income of day labourers and handicraft producers at the grass roots level. For the customer, the quality and price of products on sale is superior to other shops and the prices are fixed so you don't have to haggle. Gujarat has a number of cooperatives, the most prominent being the Self-Employed Women's Association (SEWA) – see the Gujarat chapter for details. In the neighbouring state of Rajasthan, the Urmul Trust supports and promotes handicrafts produced by rural artisans. Profits go directly back to these artisans.

In Himachal Pradesh, the Bhuttico program (Bhutti Weavers' Cooperative) is a huge enterprise that employs village women to make shawls and caps that are sold at fair prices with little sales pressure at the organisation's many shops statewide.

In the same state, at McLeod Ganj, the Tibetan Office of Handicrafts and the Tibetan Handicrafts Cooperative employs newly arrived refugees who produce high-quality items at reasonable prices. Similarly, in Bodhgaya, Jabalpur and Gwalior, Tibetan refugee markets are a splendid opportunity for tourists to purchase woollen handicrafts, thereby supporting Tibetans in exile.

If you're on the hunt for a carpet, look out for the Smiling Carpet label; this is a United Nations and nongovernmental organisation (NGO) initiative to try to discourage the use of child labour in carpet manufacture.

As exotic as they may be, do not buy products that further endanger threatened species and habitats (see also the boxed text 'Responsible Diving' earlier in this chapter and Endangered Species under Flora & Fauna in the Facts about India chapter).

Be Vigilant on Tour

Many travellers take an organised tour of some sort when in India. Some, such as camel safaris in Rajasthan, have been especially guilty of leaving rubbish behind. On any tour, always pay particular care to how you dispose of your rubbish and encourage tour operators to do the same. The same applies when trekking and mountaineering. Always discourage the use of plastic.

Other ways of minimising your impact while on tour are to refrain from picking any flowers or plants, discouraging wood fires, and always closing any gates you may open.

If you intend hiring a guide, it's wise to use only authorised guides (ask for their identification), especially in Varanasi, where some travellers have been robbed (or worse) by bogus guides (see Varanasi in the Uttar Pradesh & Uttaranchal chapter).

Child Prostitution

Since 'Anglo India' Freddy Peat was convicted in 1996 of a number of horrific sex crimes against children in Goa, there has been increasing acceptance in that state that child prostitution is a problem that needs to be tackled. There is now greater vigilance by police and locals and a legal procedure is now in place to deal with paedophiles. Offenders face life imprisonment in an Indian jail if convicted. International watchdog organisation End Child Prostitution, Pornography and Trafficking (Ecpat) included Goa in a series of research papers produced for the 1996 World Congress Against the Commercial Sexual Exploitation of Children.

The Indian Penal Code and India's Immoral Traffic Act impose penalties for kidnapping and prostitution. In addition, the international community has responded to what is a global problem with laws that allow their nationals to be prosecuted for child sex offences upon their return home.

If you know, witness or suspect that anyone is engaged in these activities you should report it to police in the country you're in and again to the police when you get home.

TOURIST OFFICES

Local Tourist Offices

In addition to the national (Government of India) tourist office, each state also maintains its own tourist office. These state tourist offices vary widely in their efficiency and usefulness. While some are run by enthusiastic souls, others have grumpy staff who can be abrupt to the point of rudeness. At 90% of offices you'll be lucky to get more than 'yes, no' responses – just persist. Many state governments also operate a chain of tourist bungalows, a number of which house state tourism offices.

The overlap between national and state tourist offices often causes wasteful duplication. Both might produce a terrific brochure on place A, while neither has anything on place B. To add to the confusion, in addition to the Government of India tourist office, in many places there is also an office of the Indian Tourism Development Corporation (ITDC). The latter (which also operates hotels) is more an actual 'doing' organisation than a 'telling' one. For example, the ITDC will actually operate the tour bus for which the tourist office sells tickets.

For more details about tourist offices, see individual regional chapters.

Tourist Offices Abroad

The Government of India Department of Tourism (www.tourismindia.com and www.tourismofindia.com) operates tourist offices, which include the following:

Australia
(☎ 02-9264 4855, fax 9264 4860, ⓔ indtour@ozemail.com.au) Level 2, Piccadilly, 210 Pitt St, Sydney NSW 2000

Canada
(☎ 416-962 3787, fax 962 6279, ⓔ india@istar.ca) 60 Bloor St West, Suite 1003, Toronto, Ontario M4N 3N6

France
(☎ 01 45 23 30 45, fax 01 23 33 45, ⓔ goitotar@aol.com) 1113 Blvd Haussmann, F-76009, Paris

Germany
(☎ 069-2429490, fax 2429497, ⓔ info@india-tourism.com) Baseler Strasse 48, D-60329, Frankfurt am-Main 1

Italy
(☎ 02-8053505, fax 72021681) Via Albricci 9, Milan 21022

UK
(☎ 171-4373677, fax 4941048, ⓔ info@indiatouristoffice.org) 7 Cork St, London W1X 2AB

USA
New York: (☎ 212-586 4901, fax 582 3274) 30 Rockefeller Plaza, Suite 15, North Mezzanine, New York
Los Angeles: 10020 (☎ 213-390 8855, fax 380 6111) 3550 Wiltshire Blvd, Suite 204, Los Angeles, CA 90010

Digging up Your Roots

Tourism officials in Uttar Pradesh have come up with a novel way of increasing its visitor numbers while assisting millions of people of Indian origin to trace their family roots.

Officials say that of the estimated 10 million ethnic Indians living overseas, the majority were born to migrant indentured labourers from eastern Uttar Pradesh who left in the 18th and 19th centuries for different parts of the planet. They are targeting groups in Mauritius, Fiji, Trinidad and Surinam, as well as in Europe, Canada and the USA. A substantial number of Indians living abroad have high disposable incomes, and a desired spin-off of the 'Discover Your Roots' scheme is to attract financial investment to the state.

Interested nonresident Indians should forward as much information as possible about their ancestry to Uttar Pradesh (UP) Tourism so officials can try to track down their ancestor's birthplace and possible relatives. The UP Tourism Web site (www.up-tourism.com) has more information, an application form and contact details. Good luck!

VISAS & DOCUMENTS

Passport

You must have a passport with you all the time; it is the most basic travel document. Ensure that it will be valid for the entire period you intend to remain overseas. If your passport is lost or stolen, immediately contact your country's representative (see Embassies & Consulates later in this chapter).

Visas

Six month multiple-entry visas (valid from the date of issue) are issued to most nationals (check visa options with the Indian embassy in your country) regardless of whether you intend staying that long or re-entering the country. Visas cost A$75 (an extra A$10 service fee applies at consulates) for Australians, US$65 for US citizens, UK£30 for Britons and 320FF for French passport holders.

A special People of Indian Origin (PIO) card is available only to people of Indian descent (excluding those in Pakistan and Bangladesh) who hold a non-Indian passport and live abroad (maximum fourth generation). This card costs US$1000 and offers multiple-entry for 20 years. People of Indian origin can also apply for a five-year multiple entry visa, which is about a quarter of the cost of the PIO card. Both are valid from the date of issue.

Visa Extensions Fifteen-day extensions may be possible (only under exceptional circumstances, not as a matter of routine) from Foreigners' Registration Offices in the main Indian cities. You can only get another six-month visa by leaving the country.

Restricted Area Permits

Even with a visa you are not allowed everywhere in India. Certain places require special additional permits. The permit requirements mentioned below are covered in detail in the respective regional chapters.

Andaman Islands Foreigners require permits to visit the Andaman Islands; thankfully the procedures are much easier than in recent years, and the fees have been waived. Additional permits are also required for many of the outlying islands.

Himachal Pradesh & Uttaranchal Permits are required to enter some regions close to the India-Tibet border in Himachal Pradesh and Uttaranchal. For the crossing from Kinnaur to Spiti in Himachal Pradesh, tourists must obtain a free inner-line permit (see the Himachal Pradesh chapter for details).

The Milam glacier in northern Kumaon in Uttaranchal, which also falls under Indo-Tibetan Border Authority jurisdiction, is currently open to visitors at the discretion of the local police. Other areas around Nanda Devi are officially off-limits, but groups may succeed in getting the relevant inner line permits from the district magistrate in Pithoragarh (☎ 05964-22202).

Ladakh You don't require a permit for most of Ladakh, however, you must fill out a Foreigners' Registration Form upon arrival at Leh airport or at a road checkpoint en route, and again at each hotel you stay in. Once in Leh you can apply for permits to the newly opened regions of Ladakh – you can either pay around Rs 100 for a travel agent to handle the bureaucratic formalities, or battle the red tape yourself.

Lakshadweep This southern archipelago is opening up. Five islands (Agatti, Bangaram, Kadmat, Kalpeni and Minicoy) are currently open to foreigners, while two others (Andrott and Kavaratti) can be visited by Indian citizens. In the future, foreigners might be allowed to take the boat cruises currently now only available to Indians. For bookings and permits for Lakshadweep contact the Society for the Promotion of Recreational Tourism & Sports in Lakshadweep (Sports), part of the main Lakshadweep Tourism organisation. Its office (☎ 0484-668387, fax 668647) is on IG Rd, Willingdon Island, Kochi, Kerala 682003.

North-Eastern Region There are a number of permit regulations for this part of India. Permits are no longer required for Assam, Meghalaya or Tripura, though you should check to see if it's safe to go. Permits are required for Mizoram and Manipur. Foreigners may be issued a permit allowing independent travel in Arunachal Pradesh and Nagaland, but most visitors go on an organised tour. (See the North-Eastern Region chapter for comprehensive details.)

Sikkim A 15-day permit is required to enter Sikkim. These are free and easy to obtain (see the Sikkim chapter for details).

West Bengal Foreigners need a permit (no charge) for the Sunderbans Wildlife Sanctuary and these are issued on the spot (on presentation of your passport) at the West Bengal Tourism Centre in Kolkata.

Onward Tickets

Many Indian embassies and consulates will not issue a visa to enter India unless you hold an onward ticket, which is taken as sufficient evidence that you intend to leave the country.

Travel Insurance

A travel insurance policy to cover theft, loss and medical problems is a good idea. Some policies offer lower and higher medical expense options; the higher ones are chiefly for countries such as the USA, which have high medical costs. There is a wide variety of policies available, so check the small print.

Some policies specifically exclude 'dangerous activities', which can include scuba diving, motorcycling, or even trekking. A locally acquired motorcycle licence is not valid under some policies.

You may prefer a policy that pays doctors or hospitals directly rather than you having to pay on the spot and claim later. If you have to claim later make sure you keep all documentation. Some policies ask you to call back (reverse charges) to a centre in your home country where an immediate assessment of your problem is made.

Check that the policy covers ambulances or an emergency flight home.

Driving Licence

If you are planning to drive in India, get an International Driving Licence from your national motoring organisation. In some cities, such as Delhi, it's possible to hire or purchase motorcycles, and you'll often need to produce a drivers licence of some sort (see Motorcycle in the Getting Around chapter). An International Driving Licence can also come in handy for other identification purposes, such as plain old bicycle hire.

Other Documents

A health certificate, while not necessary in India, may well be required for onward travel. Student cards are virtually useless these days – many student concessions have either been eliminated or replaced by 'youth fares' or similar age concessions. Similarly, a Youth Hostel (Hostelling International – HI) card is not generally required for India's many hostels, but you do pay slightly less at official youth hostels if you have one.

It's worth having a batch of passport photos for visa applications and for obtaining permits to remote regions. If you run out, Indian photo studios will do snappy portraits at pleasantly low prices.

Copies

All important documents (passport data page and visa page, credit cards, travel insurance policy, air/bus/train tickets, driving licence etc) should be photocopied before you leave home. Leave one copy with someone at home and keep another with you, separate from the originals.

It's also a good idea to store details of your vital travel documents in Lonely Planet's free online Travel Vault. Your password-protected Travel Vault is available online anywhere in the world. Create it at www.ekno.lonelyplanet.com.

EMBASSIES & CONSULATES

Indian Embassies & High Commissions

There are numerous Indian missions worldwide – the following list contains just some of them (apart from an embassy, many countries also have consulates – inquire locally for details):

Australia (☎ 02-6273 3999, fax 6273 3328) 3/5 Moonah Place, Yarralumla, ACT 2600

Bangladesh (☎ 02-603717, fax 863662) 120 Road No 2, Dhanmondi Residential Area, Dhaka

Bhutan (☎ 09752-22162, fax 23195) India House Estate, Thimphu

Canada (☎ 613-744 3751, fax 744 0913) 10 Springfield Rd, Ottawa, Ontario K1M 1C9

France (☎ 01 40 50 70 70, fax 01 40 50 09 96) 15 Rue Alfred Dehodencq, 75016 Paris

Germany (☎ 0228-540500, fax 5405154) Adenauerallee 262–264, 53113 Bonn

Ireland (☎ 01-497 0843, fax 497 8074) 6 Leeson Park, Dublin 6

Israel (☎ 03-510 1431, fax 510 1434) 4 Kaufman St, Sharbat House, Tel Aviv 68012

Italy (☎ 06-488 4642, fax 481 9539) Via XX Settembre 5, 00187 Rome

Japan (☎ 03-3262 2391, fax 3234 4866) 2-2-11 Kudan Minami, Chiyoda-ku, Tokyo 102

Myanmar (Burma; ☎ 01-282550, fax 254086) 545–547 Merchant St, Yangon

Nepal (☎ 071-414940, fax 413132) Lain Chaur, PO Box 292, Kathmandu

The Netherlands (☎ 070-346 9771, fax 361 7072) Buitenrustweg 2, 2517 KD, The Hague

New Zealand (☎ 04-473 6390, fax 499 0665) 180 Molesworth St, Wellington

Pakistan (☎ 051-814371, fax 820742) G-5, Diplomatic Enclave, Islamabad

Sri Lanka (☎ 01-421605, fax 446403) 36–38 Galle Rd, Colombo 3

Thailand (☎ 02-258 0300, fax 258 4627) 46 Soi 23 (Prasarnmitr), Sukhumvit Rd, Bangkok 10110

UK (☎ 071-836 8484, fax 836 4331) India House, Aldwych, London WC2B 4NA

USA (☎ 202-939 9839, 939 9806, fax 265 7532) 2536 Massachusetts Ave NW, Washington, DC 20008
Web site: www.indianembassy.org

Embassies, High Commissions & Consulates in India

Most foreign diplomatic missions are based in the nation's capital, Delhi, but there are also quite a few consulates in the other major cities of Mumbai, Kolkata and Chennai.

If your country's mission is not listed below, that doesn't necessarily mean it is not represented in India – see the Indian phone directory to locate it, or call one of the listed missions to find out contact details.

Australia
High Commission: (☎ 011-6888223, fax 6885199) 1/50G Shantipath, Chanakyapuri, Delhi
Consulate: (☎ 022-2181071, fax 2188189, ⓔ mumbai.immi@dfat.gov.au) 16th floor, Maker Tower, E Block, Cuffe Parade, Colaba, Mumbai

Bangladesh
High Commission: (☎ 011-6834065, fax 6839237) 56 Ring Rd, Lajpat Nagar III, Delhi
Consulate: (☎ 033-2475208) 9 Circus Ave, Kolkata
Consulate: (☎ 0381-225260) Palace Compound Rd, Agartala, Tripura

Bhutan
Embassy: (☎ 011-6889807, fax 6876710) Chandragupta Marg, Chanakyapuri, Delhi

Canada
High Commission: (☎ 011-6876500, fax 6876579) 7/8 Shantipath, Chanakyapuri, Delhi

China
Embassy: (☎ 011-6871585, fax 6885486) 50D Shantipath, Chanakyapuri, Delhi

France
Embassy: (☎ 011-6118790, fax 6872305) 2/50E Shantipath, Chanakyapuri, Delhi
Consulate: (☎ 022-4950918, fax 4950312, ⓔ consufra@bom3.vsnl.net.in) 2nd floor, Datta Prasad Bldg, 10 NG Cross Rd, off N Gamadia Marg, Cumballa Hill, Mumbai
Consulate: (☎ 0413-334058, fax 335594) Rue de la Marine, Pondicherry, Tamil Nadu

Germany
Embassy: (☎ 011-6871831, fax 6873117) 6/50G Shantipath, Chanakyapuri, Delhi
Consulate: (☎ 022-2832422, fax 2025493) 10th floor, Hoechst House, Vinayak K Shah Rd, Nariman Point, Mumbai
Consulate: (☎ 033-4792150, fax 4793029) 1 Hastings Park Rd, Kolkata
Consulate: (☎ 044-8271747) 49 Ethiraj Rd, Chennai
Consulate: (☎ 0832-235526, fax 223441) c/o Cosme Matias Menezes Group, Rua de Ourem, Panaji, Goa

Ireland
Embassy: (☎ 011-4626733, fax 4697053) 230 Jor Bagh Rd, Delhi
Consulate: (☎ 022-2024607, fax 2871087) 2nd floor, Royal Bombay Yacht Club, Shivaji Marg, Colaba, Mumbai

Israel
Embassy: (☎ 011-3013238, fax 3014298) 3 Aurangzeb Rd, Delhi
Consulate: (☎ 022-2819993, fax 2824676) 16th floor, Earnest House, Nariman Point, Mumbai
Consulate: (☎ 033-2800040, fax 2470561) 86C Topsia Rd (south), Kolkata

Italy
Embassy: (☎ 011-6114355, fax 6873889) 50E Chandragupta Marg, Chanakyapuri, Delhi
Consulate: (☎ 033-4792426, fax 4793892) 3 Raja Santosh Rd, Kolkata

Japan
Embassy: (☎ 011-6876581, fax 6885587) 4–5/50G Shantipath, Chanakyapuri, Delhi
Consulate: (☎ 022-4933843, fax 4932146) 1 ML Dahanukar Rd, Mumbai
Consulate: (☎ 033-4211970, fax 4211971) 55 MN Sen Lane, Tollygunge, Kolkata
Consulate: (☎ 044-8265594, fax 8278853) 60 Spur Tank Rd, Chetput, Chennai

Malaysia
Embassy: (☎ 011-6111291, fax 6881538) 50M Satya Marg, Chanyakyapuri, Delhi
Consulate: (☎ 044-4343048, fax 4343049) 6 Sri Ramnagar Nth St, Alwarpet, Chennai

Maldives
Embassy: (☎ 033-2485400, fax 2485750) 7C Kiron Shankar Roy Rd, Kolkata

Myanmar (Burma)
Embassy: (☎ 011-6889007, fax 6877942) 3/50F Nyaya Marg, Chanakyapuri, Delhi

Nepal
Embassy: (☎ 011-3328191, fax 3326857) Barakhamba Rd, Delhi
Consulate: (☎ 033-4791224, fax 4791410) 1 National Library Ave, Kolkata

The Netherlands
Embassy: (☎ 011-6884951, fax 6884956) 6/50F Shantipath, Chanakyapuri, Delhi

New Zealand
Embassy: (☎ 011-6883170, fax 6872317) 50N Nyaya Marg, Chanakyapuri, Delhi

Pakistan
Embassy: (☎ 011-4676004, fax 6872339) 2/50G Shantipath, Chanakyapuri, Delhi

Singapore
Embassy: (☎ 011-6877939, fax 6886798) E6 Chandragupta Marg, Chanakyapuri, Delhi
Consulate: (☎ 044-8415541, fax 8415544) West Minster, 108 Dr Radhakrishnan Salai, Chennai

South Africa
Embassy: (☎ 011-6149411, 6143605) B18 Vasant Marg, Vasant Vihar, Delhi

Sri Lanka
High Commission: (☎ 011-3010201, fax 3015295) 27 Kautilya Marg, Delhi
Consulate: (☎ 022-2045861, fax 2876132) 34 Homi Modi St, Fort, Mumbai
Consulate: (☎ 033-2485102, fax 2486414) Nicco House, 2 Hare St, Kolkata
Consulate: (☎ 044-4987896, fax 4987612) 196 TTK Rd Alwarpet, Chennai

Switzerland
Embassy: (☎ 011-6878372, fax 6873093) Nyaya Marg, Chanakyapuri, Delhi
Consulate: (☎ 033-2265557) 113 Park St, Kolkata

Thailand
Embassy: (☎ 011-6118103, fax 6872029) 56N Nyaya Marg, Chanakyapuri, Delhi
High Commission: (☎ 033-4407836, fax 4406251) 18B Mandeville Gardens, Kolkata

UAE
Embassy: (☎ 011-6872937, fax 6873272) EP-12 Chandragupta Mary, Chanakyapuri, Delhi
Consulate: (☎ 022-2183021, fax 2181162) Jolly Makers Apartment, No 1, Bungalow 7, Cuffe Parade, Colaba, Mumbai

UK
High Commission: (☎ 011-6872161, fax 6872882) 50 Shantipath, Chanakyapuri, Delhi
Consulate: (☎ 022-2830517, fax 2027940) 2nd floor, Maker Chambers IV, J Bajaj Marg, Nariman Point, Mumbai
Consulate: (☎ 033-2885171, fax 2883435) 1 Ho Chi Minh Sarani, Kolkata
Consulate: (☎ 044-8273136, 8273137, fax 8269004) 24 Anderson Rd, Chennai
Consulate: (☎ 0832-228571, fax 232828) Manguirish Bldg, 3rd floor, 18th June Rd, Panaji, Goa

USA
Embassy: (☎ 011-6889033) Shantipath, Chanakyapuri, Delhi
Consulate: (022-3633611, fax 3630350) Lincoln House, 78 Bhulabai Desai Rd, Cumballa Hill, Mumbai
Consulate: (☎ 033-2823611, fax 2822335) 5/1 Ho Chi Minh Sarani, Kolkata
Consulate: (☎ 044-8112000) Gemini Circle, 220 Anna Salai, Chennai

CUSTOMS

The usual duty-free regulations apply for India; that is, 1L of alcohol and 200 cigarettes or 50 cigars or 250g of tobacco.

You're allowed to bring in all sorts of Western technological wonders, but expensive items, such as video cameras and laptop computers, may be entered on a 'Tourist Baggage Re-export' form to ensure you take them out with you when you go (although this is not always policed).

Technically you are supposed to declare any amount of cash or travellers cheques over US$10,000 on arrival. Regarding Indian currency, officially you are not supposed to take any into or out of India, however a number of travellers have been told that they can import a maximum of Rs 5000.

Your Own Embassy

It's important to realise what your own embassy – the embassy of the country of which you are a citizen – can and can't do to help you if you get into trouble.

Generally speaking, it won't be much help in emergencies if the trouble you're in is remotely your own fault. Remember that you are bound by the laws of India. Your embassy will not be sympathetic if you end up in jail after committing a crime locally, even if such actions are legal in your own country.

In real emergencies you might get some assistance, but only as a last resort. For example, if you need to get home urgently, a free ticket is exceedingly unlikely – the embassy would expect you to have insurance. If all your money and documents are stolen, it might assist you to get a new passport, but a loan for onward travel is out of the question.

Note that if you are entering India from Nepal you are not entitled to import anything free of duty.

There are certain restrictions in what you can take out of India – see Antiques & Wildlife Restrictions under Shopping later in this chapter.

MONEY

Currency

The rupee (Rs) is divided into 100 paise (p). There are coins of five, 10, 20, 25 and 50 paise, and Rs 1, 2 and 5, and notes of Rs 10, 20, 50, 100 and 500. In 1996 the Reserve Bank of India decided to stop printing Rs 1, 2 and 5 notes, but there may still be a sprinkling of these in circulation. At the time of writing a new Rs 1000 note had been issued, but was in limited circulation.

Whenever you change money, take your time and check each note even if the wad appears to have been stapled together. Don't accept any utterly filthy, ripped or disintegrating notes, as you'll have difficulty in getting people to accept these (you can change them at the Reserve Bank of India as a last resort). As well, some bills look quite similar, so check them carefully.

It is difficult to use large denomination notes because of a perpetual lack of change in shops, taxis etc, so it's a good idea to maintain a constant stock of smaller notes.

Exchange Rates

To find out the latest exchange rates, visit the Web site www.oanda.com or ask at a bank. At the time of going to press, the exchange rates were:

country	unit		rupee
Australia	A$1	=	Rs 23.06
Canada	C$1	=	Rs 29.82
euro	€1	=	Rs 42.13
France	10FF	=	Rs 64.21
Germany	DM1	=	Rs 21.54
Israel	1NIS	=	Rs 11.16
Japan	¥100	=	Rs 37.71
Nepal	NepRs 100	=	Rs 62.64
New Zealand	NZ$1	=	Rs 19.00
Pakistan	PakRs 100	=	Rs 75.74
Singapore	S$1	=	Rs 25.73
UK	UK£1	=	Rs 67.14
USA	US$1	=	Rs 46.64

Exchanging Money

Cash It's usually no problem changing money in capital cities and tourist hotbeds. However, it's advisable to have some US dollars or UK pounds sterling in cash in case you are unable to change travellers cheques or use a credit card, especially in smaller towns. Many off-the-beaten-track places may not offer any money-changing facilities at all, so take along an adequate stock of rupees.

Travellers Cheques All major brands are accepted in India, with American Express (AmEx) and Thomas Cook being the most widely traded. Pounds sterling and US dollars are the safest bet; Yen, Deutschmarks and Australian dollars can be changed in the larger cities, but usually not at out-of-the-way places. Not all places take all brands – which means it pays to carry more than one flavour. Charges for changing travellers cheques vary from place to place and bank to bank.

ATMs Mumbai, Kolkata, Bangalore, Chennai and Delhi, plus a few (but slowly growing number of) larger towns, including Jaipur and Ahmedabad, have ATMs (many 24 hour) that accept Cirrus, Maestro, MasterCard and Visa (but not always all cards). However, you should definitely not rely on them as your sole source of cash, especially if you're planning to travel beyond the big cities. Ladakh, for instance, does not currently have any ATMs, nor do many of the smaller towns or less touristy destinations throughout India. Note that some ATMs in smaller towns don't accept foreign cards. Check with your local bank before departing to confirm that your card can access international banking networks.

Credit Cards Most major cities and tourist centres accept credit cards, with MasterCard and Visa being the most widely accepted. Cash advances on major credit cards can be made at various banks (although not always in smaller towns). For details about whether you can access home accounts in India, inquire at your home bank before leaving.

Credit cards are accepted at most top-end hotels and a rapidly growing number of mid-range ones, however very few budget hotels/restaurants/shops accept them. In the Andaman Islands, major credit cards are only accepted at the upmarket hotels; on the outlying islands, only cash is accepted.

International Transfers It's best not to run out of money in India, but if you do, you can have money transferred in no time at all via Thomas Cook's Moneygram service (charges are relatively high as it's only considered an emergency service), or the more competitively priced Western Union (via Sita World Travels, ☎ 011-3311122, 12 F-Block, Connaught Circus, Delhi, or DHL agencies). Western Union also has other agencies including Nucleus Forex, which has branches in Delhi, Bangalore, Chennai, Mumbai and Hyderabad. Some private moneychangers, such as the Travellers Express Club in Kolkata, also offer money transfer facilities (see regional chapters for details). You need to bring along your passport when picking up money.

Black Market The rupee is a convertible currency, which means the exchange rate is set by the market not the government. For this reason there's not much of a black market, although you can get a couple of rupees more for your dollars or pounds cash. There's little risk involved (provided you check on the spot that you have received the agreed amount), although it's still officially illegal.

Moneychangers Usually open for longer hours than the banks, moneychangers are a convenient option and they are everywhere. It pays to check the bank rates first, and as with anywhere, check the money you are given (see Currency earlier in this section).

Re-Exchange Before leaving India you'll probably want to change any leftover rupees back into foreign currency. To do so, you must produce encashment certificates (see Encashment Certificates later in this section) that cover the rupee amount and are less than three months old. You'll also have to show your passport and airline ticket.

You can convert rupees back to major currencies at some city banks and moneychangers and at international airports, although if you want US dollars cash, some places will only allow you to re-exchange up to US$500 worth of rupees, and only within 48 hours of leaving the country.

Security

The safest place for your money and your passport is next to your skin, either in a moneybelt around your waist or in a pouch under your shirt or T-shirt. Never, ever carry these things in your luggage. You are also asking for trouble if you walk around with your valuables in a shoulder bag. Bum bags are not recommended as they virtually advertise that you have a stash of goodies; this could make you a target for a mugging. Never leave your valuable documents and travellers cheques in your hotel room. If the hotel is a reputable one, you should be able to use the hotel safe. It is wise to peel off at least US$50 and keep it stashed away separately from your main horde, just in case. Finally, try to separate your big notes from your small ones so you don't publicly display large wads of cash when paying for minor services such as shoe polishing and tipping.

Costs

Costs tend to vary depending on whether or not it's the tourist season. They also shoot up during festivals or other special events when it's not unusual for hotel rates to double. In addition, be prepared to pay more at the larger cities (such as Mumbai, Delhi and Kolkata), as well as at popular tourist destinations.

Costs also vary depending on whether you are travelling solo or in a group. It's more economical travelling with one or more people, as you can save money by sharing hotel rooms, taxis or rickshaws and car hire.

Although it's cheaper to stay in some places than others, at rock bottom you can generally live on about US$8 per person; you should expect to pay around US$10 to 17 in larger cities such as Mumbai, as well as at hill stations and tourist hot spots (note that some regions, such as the Andamans, are more expensive). This means serious scrimping – dormitories, travel in public buses and the cheaper classes on trains, and basic meals (eg, dhal and rice). The sky's the limit at the other extreme. In Rajasthan you can easily blow upwards of US$200 a night in a swanky palace hotel, and of course there are plenty of things to buy and tours to take that will set you back even more.

Most people will, of course, fall somewhere in the middle. If you want to stay in decent mid-range hotels, eat at regular restaurants, occasionally splurge on a meal at a fancy restaurant and largely travel by autorickshaw or taxi, you're looking at an average of between US$18 and 35 a day (including the taxes that mid-range accommodation attracts). Again, the upper end of this scale pertains to the larger cities and tourist hot spots. Of course, you may manage to subsist on just under US$18 at some smaller towns which lack 'splurge-type' restaurants.

Entry Charges Most tourist sites have an entry fee and most levy a charge for cameras and videos. Many sites have a lower charge for Indian residents than for foreigners. In case you're wondering, if you're of Indian descent (but not an Indian resident), the 'foreigners' rate officially applies – although you may escape detection or even be knowingly offered the lower local rate.

Tipping, Baksheesh & Bargaining

In tourist restaurants or hotels, where a service fee (amounts vary regionally) is usually already added on to your bill, tipping is optional. In smaller places, where there is no service fee, a tip is greatly appreciated (even if it's just a few rupees). Hotel and train porters expect about Rs 10 to carry

Cashing in on Foreign Tourists

In late 2000 the Archaeological Survey of India (ASI) announced new entry fees for non-Indian tourists at 72 of India's national monuments. Entry fees to all World Heritage monuments – including the Taj Mahal, Agra Fort and Fatehpur Sikri – were set to be cranked up by a steep Rs 450 (US$10, payable in the rupee equivalent). Entry to non-World Heritage monuments were pegged to increase by Rs 220 (US$5). The ASI has come under attack from the National Chamber of Commerce & Industries for the hard-hitting hike. Tourism officials have grave concerns that the sharp increase may result in a marked drop in visitor numbers.

In this book we have included the new beefed-up charges where available; however ,as not all price changes had been implemented at the time of writing, some of the prices in this book may have changed by the time you read this. Conversely, there were rumours that the price hikes may actually be reversed because of the vehement protests by tourism operators, so it's best check the situation locally. See also the boxed text 'Price Hikes at the Taj' in the Uttar Pradesh & Uttaranchal

bags, and hotel staff also expect around the same to provide services above and beyond the call of duty. It's not mandatory to tip taxi or autorickshaw drivers.

Baksheesh can be defined as a 'tip' and if you're going to be using a service repeatedly, an initial tip will ensure that standards are kept up. Baksheesh also refers to giving alms to beggars. Giving money to beggars is a matter of personal choice – but please don't hand out sweets, pens or money to children since it encourages begging. Instead you may like to donate to a school or charitable organisation (see also Volunteer Work later in this chapter).

While there are fixed-price stores in major cities, in bazaars and at markets specifically geared to tourists, you are generally expected to bargain. The trick with bargaining is that you should have some idea of what you should be paying for any given article. You can find out by checking prices at fixed-priced stores (although these are often on the high side), asking other travellers what they have paid and shopping around before settling on a particular vendor. If all else fails, a general rule of thumb is to take the plunge and halve the original asking price. The shopkeeper will know that you are not going to be taken for a ride and you now begin negotiations. You'll often find that the price drops if you proceed to head out of the shop saying you'll 'think about it'. Always keep in mind that haggling is a form of social interaction, not a vicious contest. It's worth remembering exactly how much a rupee is worth in your home currency, so you don't lose perspective and raise your blood pressure.

Taxes

A tax or two (or even more) is usually whacked onto accommodation at mid-range and top-end hotels in India, as well as on food and beverages at the more upmarket restaurants. It usually starts at around 10%, but can be much more for air-con rooms and top-end hotels. It's not a bad idea to inquire whether you will be taxed and by how much before you check in, just to save yourself from a nasty surprise when you get the bill.

The prices quoted in the Places to Stay sections of this book are *without* tax, unless otherwise indicated. For more information on which taxes apply in which states, see the regional chapters.

If you've got a visa enabling you to stay in India for more than 180 days, you must technically get a tax clearance certificate to leave the country. This certificate supposedly proves that your time in India was financed with your own money, not by working in India or by selling things (contact one of India's Foreigners' Registration Offices located in the major cities). You'll need to show your passport, visa extension form, any other appropriate paperwork and a handful of bank encashment certificates.

Encashment Certificates

By law, all money must be changed at official banks or moneychangers, and you are supposed to be given an encashment certificate (money-exchange receipt) for each transaction – ask for it if you don't receive one. It is definitely worth getting them, especially if you want to re-exchange excess rupees for hard currency when you depart India (see Re-Exchange earlier in this section).

The other reason for saving encashment certificates is that if you stay in India longer than 180 days, you have to get a tax clearance certificate. Some shipping agents may also request these certificates.

POST & COMMUNICATIONS

Post

Indian postal and poste restante services are generally very good. Expected letters are almost always there and letters you send reach their destination, although they may take up to three weeks. Although the Indian postal system is fairly reliable, don't count on a letter or package getting to you if there's anything of market value inside it. AmEx in major city locations offers an alternative to the poste restante system. Some cities also offer courier services (such as DHL Worldwide Express) that can arrange speedy and safe air freight around the world (at a higher cost).

Sending Mail Posting aerograms and postcards costs Rs 8.50 and airmail letters are Rs 15.

Posting parcels is straightforward if you go about it as described here. Prices are reasonable and vary depending on the weight.

- Take the parcel to a tailor, or to a parcel-stitching wallah (occasionally just outside post offices) and ask for your parcel to be stitched up in cheap linen. Negotiate the price and expect to pay upwards of Rs 50 per package, depending on size.
- At the post office, ask for the necessary customs declaration forms. Fill them in and glue one to the parcel. The other will be stitched onto it. To avoid duty at the delivery end it's best to specify that the contents are a 'gift'.
- Be careful how much you declare the contents to be worth. If you specify over Rs 1000, your parcel will not be accepted without a bank clearance certificate, which is a hassle to get.
- Have the parcel weighed and franked at the parcel counter.

Books or printed matter can go by bookpost, which is considerably cheaper than parcel post, but the package must be wrapped a certain way: make sure that the package can either be opened for inspection along the way, or that it is wrapped in brown paper or cardboard and tied with string, with the two ends exposed so that the contents are visible. To protect the books, wrap them in clear plastic first. No customs declaration form is necessary. Bookpost rates are about Rs 230 for 500g, Rs 455 for 1kg and Rs 1010 for 2kg.

Be cautious with places that offer to mail things to your home address after you have bought them. Government emporiums are usually OK but in most other places it pays to do the posting yourself.

Receiving Mail Ask senders to address letters to you with your surname in capital letters and underlined, followed by poste restante, GPO (main post office), and the city or town in question. Many 'lost' letters are simply misfiled under given (first) names, so always check under both your names. Ask senders to provide a return address, just in case you don't collect your mail. Letters sent via poste restante are generally held for one month before being returned. You'll need to show your passport to claim mail.

Telephone

Even in the smallest towns, you'll find private PCO/STD/ISD call booths with direct local, interstate and international dialling. These are invariably cheaper than direct dialling from hotel rooms. Usually found in shops or other businesses, they are easy to spot because of the large PCO/STD/ISD signs advertising the service. Many are open 24 hours. A nifty digital meter lets you keep an eye on what the call is costing and gives you a printout at the end.

Throughout most of India, interstate calls from booths (not hotels) charge the full rate from around 9 am to 8 pm. After 8 pm the cost slides, with the cheapest time to call being between 11 pm and 6 am.

Direct international calls from call booths (not hotels) cost an average of Rs 100 per minute, depending on the country you are calling. There are often cheaper rates at certain times of the day – the cheapest times to make calls at the time of writing were: Europe (10 pm to 11 am), USA (11 am to 6 pm and midnight to 6 am), Australia (7 pm to 8 am). Some places also offer cheaper rates on Indian national holidays. To make an international call, you will need to dial the following:

00 (international access code from India) + country code (of the country you are calling) + area code + local number

In some centres PCO/STD/ISD booths may offer a 'call back' service – you ring your folks or friends, give them the phone number of the booth and wait for them to call you back. The booth operator will charge about Rs 5 per minute for this service, in addition to the cost of the preliminary call. Advise your caller how long you intend to wait at the booth in the event that they have trouble getting back to you. The number your caller dials will be as follows:

(caller's country international access code) + 91 (international country code for India) + area code + local number (booth number)

The central telegraph offices in major towns are usually reasonably efficient and some remain open 24 hours. Prices are comparable with PCO/STD/ISD booths.

Also available is the Home Country Direct service, which gives you access to the international operator in your home country. For the price of a local call, you can then make reverse-charge (collect) or phonecard calls, although you may have trouble convincing the owner of the telephone you are using that they are not going to get charged for the call. The countries and numbers to dial are:

country	number
Australia	☎ 0006117
Canada	☎ 000167
Germany	☎ 0004917
Italy	☎ 0003917
Japan	☎ 0008117
The Netherlands	☎ 0003117
New Zealand	☎ 0006417
Singapore	☎ 0006517
Spain	☎ 0003417
Taiwan	☎ 00088617
Thailand	☎ 0006617
UK	☎ 0004417
USA	☎ 000117

India's Yellow Pages can be found at www.indiayellowpages.com. For those who may be trying to locate a long-lost friend, you could try your luck at the Welcome to 1 Billion Indians site (www.1billionindians.com), affectionately dubbed as 'India's People Finder'.

Fax

Many of the PCO/STD/ISD booths also have a fax machine for public use. The going rate for international faxes ranges from Rs 125 to 155 per A4 page. Receiving faxes can range from Rs 10 to 30 per page.

Email & Internet Access

Internet outlets in India are spreading faster than rumours. Be warned that some bureaus have poor connections and can be excruciatingly slow. Connections and speed are usually superior in the morning and early afternoon (peak demand seems to fall between 5 pm and 9 pm, making this a slow period). Places to surf the Internet are widespread in the larger cities, but a growing number of smaller places (all travellers haunts such as Dharamsala and Pushkar) have email facilities, too, even if it's just one computer in a cramped little back office.

Costs range anywhere from Rs 30 to 100 per hour (see regional chapters for specific costs – Bangalore for instance is significantly cheaper), but as more and more bureaus mushroom throughout India, charges should tumble.

INTERNET RESOURCES

The World Wide Web is a rich resource for travellers. You can research your trip, hunt down bargain air fares, book hotels, check on weather conditions or chat with locals and other travellers about the best places to visit (or avoid!).

There's no better place to start your Web explorations than the Lonely Planet Web site (www.lonelyplanet.com). Here you'll find succinct summaries on travelling to most places on earth, postcards from other travellers and the Thorn Tree bulletin board, where you can ask questions before you go or dispense advice when you get back. You can also find travel news and updates to many of our most popular guidebooks, and the subWWWay section links you to the most useful travel resources elsewhere on the Web.

There are many Web sites relating to India, but they come and go with some frequency. You'll find that more than a few sites are nothing more than glossy (often inaccurate) PR puff. On the plus side, many newspapers and magazines have useful sites and these include:

Hindu National newspaper.
www.the-Hindu.com

Hindustan Times National newspaper. www.hindustantimes.com
Indian Express 'India's first e-biz paper.' www.indian-express.com
India Today Weekly magazine covering everything from Bollywood gossip to politics. www.india-today.com
Times of India National newspaper. www.timesofindia.com

Good portals and search engines include:

Khoj www.khoj.com
Rediff On The Net www.rediff.com
123 India www.123india.com

And for those of you seeking the perfect Indian name for your unborn child, you may be interested in checking out www.indiaexpress.com/special/babynames – good luck!

BOOKS

India is one of the world's largest publishers of books in English. You'll find a treasure trove of interesting, affordable books about India by Indian publishers, which are generally not available in the West. Recently published Western books also reach Indian bookshops remarkably fast and with very low mark-ups. If a bestseller in Europe or America has major appeal for India, the publisher will often rush out a paperback in India to forestall possible pirates.

See Literature under Arts in the Facts about India chapter for details about prominent Indian authors and their works.

Most books are published in different editions by different publishers in different countries. As a result, a book might be a hardcover rarity in one country while it's readily available in paperback in another. Fortunately, bookshops and libraries search by title or author, so your local bookshop or library is best placed to advise you on the availability of the following recommendations. Please note that the following list is not exhaustive and that there are other excellent books – far too many to be included here.

Lonely Planet

Lonely Planet publishes a wide range of detailed guides to India's regions and cities: there's *Delhi, Mumbai (Bombay), Rajasthan, Kerala, Goa, South India, North India, Indian Himalaya* and *Trekking in the Indian Himalaya*. We also cover the region with the following guides: *Pakistan*, *Nepal*, *Bangladesh*, *Sri Lanka*, *Bhutan* and *The Maldives*, as well as the route guide *Istanbul to Kathmandu*. Lonely Planet also publishes a handy *Hindi/Urdu phrasebook, Healthy Travel Asia & India* and *Read This First: Asia & India.*

World Food India will take you on a mouth-watering tour through Indian cuisine, exploring its cultural significance and many regional specialities.

Travel Photography: A Guide to Taking Better Pictures is written by internationally renowned travel photographer, Richard I'Anson. It's full colour throughout and designed to take on the road.

In Rajasthan by Royina Grewal is an insider's view of this enthralling state, and is one of many titles in Lonely Planet's travel literature series, Journeys. Another is *Hello Goodnight: A Life in Goa* by David Tomory, which explores what Goa has meant to travellers over history. Tomory has also written *A Season in Heaven: True Tales from the Road to Kathmandu,* also available in Journeys (see under Travel on the next page.)

Lonely Planet also has some lavishly illustrated offerings, including *Chasing Rickshaws*, a tribute to cycle-powered vehicles and their drivers by Tony Wheeler and photographer Richard I'Anson (see the Kolkata chapter for an excerpt). There's also *Sacred India*, another full-colour book with stunning images of India's diverse religious culture written by Lonely Planet staff and authors. *Buddhist Stupas in Asia: The Shape of Perfection* is a full colour hardback pictorial that explores the spread of Buddhism and stupa-building across India and Asia.

Specialist Guidebooks

There are a number of general guidebooks about India, many with an emphasis on colourful pictorial content – you'll find them at most bookshops in India.

When it comes to specialist titles, some recommended reading includes *From Here to Nirvana* by Anne Cushman & Jerry Jones, which is a popular guide to India's many and varied ashrams and gurus. It provides useful practical information that will help you figure out which place suits your particular needs and aspirations. It also provides useful tips on how to spot dodgy operators.

Window on Goa by Maurice Hall took nearly 10 years to complete. The author writes authoritatively about the churches, forts, villages and other aspects of Goa. Another excellent specialist guide about the painted *havelis* (ornately decorated traditional mansions) in Rajasthan is *The Guide to the Painted Towns of Shekhawati* by Ilay Cooper, which provides information about the buildings accompanied by some fine sketch maps.

For relatively cheap but brilliantly produced photo-essays of the subcontinent, try Insight Guides' *Rajasthan* and *India*.

Travel

Karma Cola by Gita Mehta. Amusingly and cynically describes the collision between India looking to the West for technology and modern methods, and the West descending upon India in search of wisdom and enlightenment.

Walking the Indian Streets by Ved Mehta. Mehta has written a number of interesting personal views of India and this is a slim and highly readable account of the culture shock he went through on returning to India after a long period abroad. *Portrait of India* is by the same author.

The Crisis of India by Ronald Segal. Written by a South African Indian on the premise that spirituality is not always more important than a full stomach.

The Gunny Sack by MG Vasanji. Explores a similar theme, this time from the point of view of a group of Gujarati families that migrated to East Africa in Raj times but retained their connections with India.

City of Djinns by William Dalrymple. Delves into Delhi's fascinating history.

The Age of Kali also by William Dalrymple. A compilation of insights gleaned from 10 years of travelling the subcontinent.

Slowly Down the Ganges by Eric Newby. An entertaining boat-trip tale, bordering, at times, on sheer masochism.

A Season in Heaven: True Tales from the Road to Kathmandu by David Tomory. An enticing and historic narrative from travellers who took the 'hippie trail' to India and Nepal in the 1960s and 1970s.

Chasing the Monsoon by Alexander Frater. An Englishman's account of a journey panning out around the monsoon as it moves north across the country.

Desert Places by Robyn Davidson. About the author's journey, as a solo woman, by camel with the nomadic Rabari of Rajasthan.

An Area of Darkness by VS Naipaul. No survey of personal insights into India can ignore VS Naipaul's two controversial books, *An Area of Darkness* and *India – A Wounded Civilisation*. Born in Trinidad of Indian descent, Naipaul tells in the first book of how India, unseen and unvisited, haunted him and of the impact upon him when he eventually made the pilgrimage to his motherland. In the second book he writes of India's unsuccessful search for a new purpose and meaning for its civilisation. His *A Million Mutinies Now* is also evocative reading.

History & Politics

A History of India If you want a general but thorough introduction to Indian history then look for this two-volume title. In volume one Romila Thapar follows Indian history from 1000 BC to the coming of the Mughals in the 16th century. Volume two by Percival Spear follows the rise and fall of the Mughals and the period to independent India.

Oxford History of India by Vincent Smith. More cumbersome, but offering more detail than *A History of India*.

The Wonder That Was India by AL Basham. Has detailed descriptions of the Indian civilisations, major religions, origins of the caste system and social customs.

A History of South India From Prehistoric Times to the Fall of Vijayanagar by Nilakanta Sastri. Arguably the most comprehensive (sometimes heavy going) history of this region.

The Career and Legend of Vasco da Gama by Sanjay Subrahmanyam. One of the best recent investigations of the person who is credited with 'discovering' the sea route from Europe to India.

The Nehrus and the Gandhis by Tariq Ali. A very readable account of the history of these families and, subsequently, of India in this century.

Plain Tales from the Raj by Charles Allen (ed). Consists of a series of interviews with people who played a role in British India on both sides of the table.

Freedom at Midnight by Larry Collins & Dominique Lapierre. An enthralling account of the events that led up to Independence in 1947.

No Full Stops in India by Mark Tully. This title explores life in the subcontinent via a collection of short stories, ranging from communism in Kolkata to the Kumbh Mela. *From Raj to Rajiv* traces India's first 40 years of independence. And *Amritsar* explores the events leading up to (and beyond) Indira Gandhi's highly controversial decision to have soldiers storm the sacred Golden Temple in Punjab's Amritsar. The former BBC correspondent has written very widely on India.

Prison and Chocolate Cake by Nayantara Sahgal. The author's account of growing up in Allahabad when Mahatma Gandhi was campaigning for an independent India.

The Proudest Day – India's Long Road to Independence by Anthony Read & David Fisher. An engaging account of India's pre-independence period.

The Great Indian Middle Class by Pavan K Varma. A powerful and often cutting social history of India's most influential socio-economic group and its descent into cynicism and materialism.

The Marathas – 1600–1818 by Stewart Gordon. A somewhat academic but easy-to-follow account of the rise of Shivaji and the Maratha dynasty.

Women

A Princess Remembers by Gayatri Devi & Santha Rama Rau. Contains the memoirs of the maharani of Jaipur, Gayatri Devi, glamorous wife of the last maharaja, Man Singh II. It provides a vivid insight into the bygone days of India's royalty.

India's Bandit Queen by Mala Sen. The biography of the remarkable Phoolan Devi (now a politician). It portrays her struggle with the caste system in rural India and the atrocities she endured as a consequence. The book also describes her life as a bandit and her eventual surrender to the authorities.

May You Be the Mother of One Hundred Sons by Elisabeth Bumiller. Offers some interesting insights into the plight of women, especially with regard to arranged marriages, dowry deaths, *sati* (woman's suicide on husband's funeral pyre) and female infanticide.

Unveiling India by Anees Jung. The author was born in Hyderabad and brought up in purdah. Her book touches on her own experiences and those of other women, both rural and urban, and explores various issues that affect women all over India today.

Difficult Daughters by Manju Kapor. Set at the time of Partition, this provides an insight into the conflict between love and duty from the point of view of a young woman from Amritsar.

Caste as Woman by Vrinda Nabar. Looks at what feminism really means in India in a variety of contexts.

Mother Teresa by Navin Chawla. One of a plethora of books on the life of Mother Teresa. Others include *The Joy In Loving* complied by Jaya Chaliha & Edward Le Joly, *Mother Teresa: A Life For God* by Lavonne Neff and *Mother Teresa: Beyond the Image* by Anne Sebba.

Adivasis

The Todas of South India – A New Look by Anthony R Walker. A comprehensive study of the Toda people of South India. It's an accessible read on one of the most documented Indian tribal groups.

Tribes of India – the Struggle for Survival by Christoph von Fürer-Haimendorf. A scholarly title that documents the sometimes shocking treatment of India's tribal peoples.

Blue Mountains Revisited – Cultural Studies on the Nilgiri Hills by Paul Hockings (ed). A collection of essays on culture, language and anthropology in South India.

The Tribal World of Verrier Elwin by Verrier Elwin. The autobiography of an Oxford graduate who became a follower of Gandhi, adopted Indian citizenship and later rose to become an influential force in tribal affairs.

Religion & Spirituality

There are often booklets available at temples and other shrines throughout India that provide excellent religious insights.

If you want to read the Hindu holy books these are available in translations: The Upanishads and The Bhagavad Gita. The Ramayana is easily digestible in DS Sarma's summary written for children.

Hindu Mythology by Wendy O'Flaherty (ed). An interesting annotated collection of extracts from the Hindu holy books.

Am I a Hindu? by Viswanathan (ed). A Hinduism primer that attempts to explore and explain the fundamental tenets of Hinduism through a discourse of questions and answers.

Why I am not a Hindu by Kancha Ilaiah. An insightful and provocative analysis of the caste system in modern India.

The Riddle of Ganesha by Rankorath Karunakaran. A beautifully illustrated and informative book that explains some of the nuances and complexities of the many sides of this popular elephant-headed god.

Hinduism, an Introduction by Shakunthala Jagannathan. Seeks to explain what Hinduism is all about – if you have no prior knowledge of the subject matter, this book is a good starting point.

A Classical Dictionary of Hindu Mythology & Religion by John Dowson. In dictionary format, this can help unravel who's who in Hinduism.

A Handbook of Living Religions by John R Hinnewls (ed). Provides a succinct and readable summary of India's religions, including Judaism.

The Marriage of East and West by Bede Griffiths. An attempt by the author (a monk who has lived in Tamil Nadu for many years) to distil the essence of Eastern and Western spiritual thought.

The Way to Enlightenment and ***Transforming the Mind*** by His Holiness the 14th Dalai Lama. The first title, a personal discourse on the nature of Buddhism, and the commentary on the *lojong* texts written by the 11th century Buddhist philosopher Langri Thangpa, provide an excellent starting point for anyone interested in Tibetan Buddhism. Also fascinating is the Dalai Lama's autobiography *Freedom in Exile*.

Cave in the Snow by Vicki MacKenzie. The autobiography of a British woman who converted to Buddhism and spent 12 years meditating in a cave above Keylong in Himachal Pradesh.

Environment & Wildlife

The World Wide Fund for Nature (WWF) in Delhi and other cities usually has a bookshop that stocks a decent collection of books about wildlife and the environment.

There are numerous glossy coffee-table books on Indian wildlife. Among the best are: *In Danger: Indian Wildlife & Habitat* by Paola Mandredi; *India's Wild Wonders* by Rajesh Bedi; *Through the Tiger's Eyes: A Chronicle of India's Wildlife* by Stanley Breeden & Belinda Wright; *In Search of Wild India* by Charlie Pye-Smith; and *Wild India: The Wildlife & Scenery of India and Nepal* by Cubitt & Mountfire and the WWF. The book from the BBC series of the same name, *Land of the Tiger*, by one of India's foremost wildlife experts, Valmik Thapar, is beautifully illustrated with plenty of interesting facts, figures and background.

The Book of Indian Animals by SH Prater. First written in 1948 but remains one of the best overviews of wildlife in India and includes colour illustrations.

Indian Wildlife published by Insight Guides. Provides solid background and plenty of colour illustrations.

Cheetal Walk: Living in the Wilderness by ERC Davidar. Describes the author's life among the elephants of the Nilgiri Hills and looks at how they can be saved from extinction.

This Fissured Land – An Ecological History of India by Madhav Gadgil & Ramachandra Guha. Provides a good overview of ecological issues.

Architecture, Arts & Crafts

The Archaeological Survey of India (www.asi.nic.in) publishes a series of booklets on major sites and works (eg, *Chola Temples*) which are inexpensive and available in India.

The History of Architecture in India: From the Dawn of Civilisation to the End of the Raj by Christopher Tadgell. Provides a good overview, including important sites in South India, and has plenty of illustrations.

The Royal Palaces of India by George Michell with photography by Antonio Martinelli. A comprehensive guide to the forts and palaces of India. In addition to the photographs, there are some excellent archaeological maps.

Arts and Crafts of India by Ilay Cooper & John Gillow. Examines India's wealth of handicrafts and their manufacture and significance.

The Arts and Crafts of Tamil Nadu by Nanitha Krishna with photography by VK Rajamani. A beautifully crafted volume with detailed information on a wide range of crafts including textiles, terracotta, woodcraft, stone carving, basketry and painting.

Woodcut Prints of Nineteenth Century Calcutta by Ashit Paul (ed). A collection of woodcut prints covering mythology, social scenes, book illustrations and advertising from 1816 to the early 20th century. Four essays focus on this short-lived but vital urban art form.

Novels

The golden oldies, such as Rudyard Kipling's *Kim*; *A Passage to India* by EM Forster; *Heat & Dust* by Ruth Prawer Jhabwala; and the *Far Pavilions* by MM Kaye focus on colonial perspectives of India.

The Storyteller by Adib Khan. Set in the backstreets of Delhi, this novel centres around an outcast dwarf with a skill for storytelling who shares Delhi's darker side with pimps, pickpockets and *hijras* (eunuchs).

Are You Experienced? by William Sutcliffe. A hilarious tale of a first-time backpacker who accompanies his best friend's girlfriend to India in an attempt to seduce her. The story follows him as he gets the girl, suffers Delhi-belly and 'experiences' India.

General

Autobiography of an Unknown Indian and ***Thy Hand, Great Anarch!: India 1921–1952*** by Nirad Chaudhuri. Two autobiographical books by one of India's most prominent contemporary writers. They are a superb account of the history and culture of modern India.

Everybody Loves a Good Drought by Palagummi Sainath. A collection of reports on the living conditions of the rural poor by this Mumbai-based journalist.

The Idea of India by Sunil Khilnani. A perceptive examination of India as it is today.

The Vintage Book of Indian Writing 1947–97 by Salman Rushdie and Elizabeth West (eds). A collection of essays and short stories. It's one of the many books published in celebration of India's 50 years of independence and contains some brilliant writing by such acclaimed authors as Jawaharlal Nehru, Nayantara Sahgal, Anita Desai, Vikram Seth and Arundhati Roy.

The Garden of Life – An Introduction to the Healing Plants of India by Naveen Patnaik. A magnificently illustrated book on an intriguing subject. The text is interspersed with fine drawings and some glorious poetry.

The Anger of Aubergines: Stories of Women and Food by Bubul Sharma. An amusing and unique culinary analysis of social relationships, interspersed with mouthwatering recipes.

Religion and Society Among the Coorgs of South India, ***The Remembered Village*** and ***Social Change in Modern India*** by MN Srinivas. Books by one of India's most distinguished sociologists.

The Namaste Book of Indian Short Stories by Monisha Mukunda (ed). Provides a delightful cross-section of voices and styles from contemporary Indian writing.

NEWSPAPERS & MAGAZINES

English-language dailies include the *Times of India*, the *Hindustan Times*, *The Statesman*, *The Pioneer*, the *Asian Age*, *The Hindu* and the *Indian Express*; many rate the *Express* as the pick of the bunch. The *Economic Times* is for those interested in business and economic analysis. There are also various city and regional English-language dailies such as *Mid-Day* in Mumbai, the *Bihar Times* and Goa's *Herald* and *Navhind Times*.

Popular news magazines include *Frontline*, *India Today*, *Sunday*, *Rashtriya Sahara*, *Outlook*, *The Week* and the *Illustrated Weekly*. They're widely available at bookshops and newspaper stands.

Major city bookshops and top-end hotels usually stock a healthy collection of international fare (although they can be dated and are pricey by local standards). These include *The Economist*, *Time*, *Newsweek*, *The International Herald-Tribune* and *Der Spiegel*.

Popular women's magazines include *Femina*, *Savvy* and *Gladrags*, as well as Indian versions of *Elle* and *Cosmopolitan*. To get the lowdown on who's who and who's doing what to whom in Bollywood, grab a copy of *Stardust*, *Cineblitz* or *Filmfare*.

There are also other English-language magazines, specialising in everything from sports to information technology.

TV & RADIO

Television viewing was once dominated by the rather dreary national broadcaster, Doordarshan. However, since the arrival of satellite and cable TV (starting in the early 1990s) India fast became one of the world's most avid channel-surfing nations. Cable is available at all top-end hotels, most mid-range ones and a handful of budget places. Check local newspapers for the program details.

Running 24 hours, cable offers some 50 plus channels with plenty of Hindi-language ones, including the immensely popular Zee TV. Bollywood buffs are well catered for with multiple movie channels churning out blockbuster after blockbuster. Meanwhile, those in need of spiritual sustenance can switch to the Maharishi Mahesh Yogi's channel, which offers a devout diet of holy images, bhajans (devotional songs) and overall positive vibes. There are also some Indian regional channels that broadcast in local languages.

English-language channels include the BBC (has anyone told them about the Bombay, Madras, Calcutta name changes?!), CNN, Discovery and National Geographic channels. There are also the Star TV offerings, which include Star Movies (for Hollywood blockbusters), Star Plus (for American sitcoms, soapies and more), Star Sports and Star News; the latter two broadcast in Hindi and English. Also in English, Nickelodeon rolls out various sitcoms, while AXN and HBO screen movies (including some great golden oldies). MTV and Channel 5 are the premier music channels, with everything from *bhangra* (Punjabi disco) to American rap.

Radio programs on All India Radio (AIR; www.air.kode.net) include various interviews, music, sports and news features. In 1999 the government announced that FM broadcasting licences would be opened up to private operators (via a bidding process). Mumbai has been allocated 10 slots on the FM band (more than any other city). Frequency allocation had not been completed at the time of writing, so check local newspapers and magazines for the latest offerings. Several that were up-and-running during our research include 102.6FM (Delhi) and FM107 (Kolkata), which both broadcast local event information, news and classical Indian and regional music. In Chennai, contemporary and classical Indian music can be heard on 102FM and 108FM. AIR Panaji (105.4FM) is the first FM station in Goa and is aimed at younger listeners, hence its emphasis on music. Details on programs and frequencies are provided in all the major English-language dailies.

Some radio stations broadcast late night talkback in English and this can be highly amusing and enlightening. However, you need to scan the dial to find these programs as they tend to jump about.

VIDEO SYSTEMS

Video in India uses the VHS format, although it is possible to convert to and from PAL and NTSC in the larger cities.

PHOTOGRAPHY & VIDEO

Film & Cartridges

Colour print film processing facilities are readily available in major cities and larger towns. Film is relatively cheap and the quality is usually (but not always) good. Same-day processing is often available. Colour slide film is less widely available than print film. You'll generally only find it in the major cities and tourist traps. Colour slides can be processed (usually in two to three days; specify if you want them mounted or not) in major cities including Delhi, Kolkata, Mumbai, Chennai, Hyderabad and Jaipur, but most travellers prefer to get them developed back home. On average, to develop 36 colour prints costs around Rs 18 plus Rs 3.50 per print. To develop slide film, you'll pay around Rs 120 (cardboard mounts) or Rs 160 (plastic mounts) for 36 shots.

Always check the use-by date on local film or slide stock. Make sure you get a sealed packet and ensure you're not handed a roll that's been sitting in a glass cabinet in the sunshine for the last few months: heat and humidity can play havoc with film, even if the use-by date hasn't been exceeded. A tip: Be wary of street hawkers in India. Some travellers report that old, useless film is loaded into new-looking canisters. The hapless tourist only discovers the trick when the film is developed back home. The best advice is to avoid street vendors and only buy film from reputable stores – and preferably film that's been refrigerated.

Video users can get cartridges (including VHS, Super 8 and Betacam) in major cities such as Delhi, Mumbai, Bangalore, Hyderabad, Kolkata and Chennai. Cartridges cost from Rs 220 to 450.

Technical Tips

Lonely Planet's *Travel Photography: A Guide to Taking Better Pictures*, written by internationally renowned travel photographer, Richard I'Anson, will give you comprehensive advice on photographing while travelling.

The following are some handy hints for taking better photos:

- The quality of your photos depends on the quality of light you shoot under. Light is best when the sun is low in the sky – around sunrise and sunset.
- Don't buy cheap equipment, but don't load yourself down with expensive equipment you don't know how to use properly either.
- A good SLR camera is advisable, but be aware that the quality of your lenses is the most important thing. Zoom lenses are heavier than fixed focal length lenses and the quality isn't as good. An alternative to the zoom is a teleconverter that fits over your lens and doubles the focal length.
- Always carry a skylight or UV filter. A polarising filter can create dramatic effects and cut glare, but don't fit it over a UV filter.
- Take a tripod and faster film (at least 400ASA) rather than a flash. Flash creates harsh shadows. A cable release is useful for shooting with a tripod.
- Settle on a brand of film and know how it works *before* you head off.
- Keep your film in a cool dark place if possible, before and after exposure. However, in practice, film seems to last, even in India's summer heat. Silica gel sachets distributed around your gear will help absorb moisture.
- Bring a camera cleaning kit.
- Expose for the main component of a scene and fill the frame with what you are taking.
- Previsualise – it's one of the most important elements in photographic vision. You must 'see' your picture clearly before you take it.

Restrictions

Be careful what you photograph. India is touchy about places of military importance – this can include train stations, bridges, airports, military installations and sensitive border regions. Temples may prohibit photography in the *mandapam* (forechamber of a temple) and inner sanctum. If in doubt, ask. Some temples, and numerous sites such as museums and forts, levy a camera and video fee that you must pay upfront (see regional chapters for exact costs).

Photographing People

Some people are more than happy to be photographed, but care should be taken in pointing cameras, especially at women. Again, if in doubt, ask. A zoom is a less intrusive means of taking portraits – even when you've obtained permission to take a portrait, shoving a lens in your subject's face can be disconcerting. A reasonable distance between you and your subject will help reduce your subject's discomfort, and will result in more natural shots.

Airport Security

Some travellers invest in a lead-lined bag, as repeated exposure to X-ray (even so-called 'film proof' X-ray) can damage film. Never put your film in baggage that will be placed in the cargo holds of aeroplanes, as it may be subjected to large doses of X-ray which will ruin it. Some professional photographers never take film through any X-ray machine, but prefer to pack it in see-through plastic containers and carry them by hand through customs. Just be aware that some customs officers may wish to open every single canister before you're allowed through.

TIME

India is 5½ hours ahead of GMT/UTC, 4½ hours behind Australian Eastern Standard Time (EST) and 10½ hours ahead of American EST. The local standard time is known as IST (Indian Standard Time), although many fondly dub it as 'Indian Stretchable Time'.

ELECTRICITY

The electric current is 230–240V AC, 50 Hz. Electricity is widely available, but power cuts are not uncommon – keep a torch (flashlight) or candle handy. Breakdowns and blackouts ('load shedding') lasting from several minutes to several hours are common, especially in the hotter months when demand outstrips supply. If you are bringing any sensitive electrical equipment (eg, laptop computer), you'll require a voltage stabiliser to safeguard it from the power fluctuations.

Sockets are the three round-pin variety, similar (but not identical) to European sockets. European round-pin plugs will go into the sockets, but as the pins on Indian plugs are somewhat thicker, the fit is loose and connection is not always guaranteed.

You can purchase small immersion elements, perfect for boiling water for tea or coffee, for around Rs 55. For about Rs 75 you can buy electric mosquito zappers. These take chemical tablets that melt and emit deadly vapours (deadly for the mozzie, that is). They're widely available in various brands, with delightful names such as Good Knight.

WEIGHTS & MEASURES

Although India is officially metricated, imperial weights and measures are still used in some areas of commerce. You will often hear people referring to lakhs (one lakh = 100,000) and crore (one crore = 10 million) of people, camels, money or whatever. A metric conversion chart is included on the inside back cover of this book.

LAUNDRY

Getting your sweaty, crumpled clothes washed and ironed in India is a breeze. Unless the hotel has its own in-house laundry your clothes will be washed by a dhobi-wallah at the dhobi ghats (see the boxed text 'India's Washing Wizards' below). If you don't think they will stand up to being beaten clean, then hand wash them yourself. Washing powder can be bought very cheaply in small sachets almost anywhere

India's Washing Wizards

Thanks to India's *dhobi-wallahs* (washerpeople) you hardly need more than one change of clothes. You simply give them your dirty clothes in the morning and hey presto, they come back freshly washed and crisply ironed later that very day. And all for a ridiculously low price. But what happened to your clothes between their departure and return?

Well, they certainly did not get anywhere near a washing machine. First of all they're taken to the dhobi ghat – a series of steps near a lake or river where the dhobi-wallahs ply their trade. Upon arrival at the ghat the clothes are separated – all the white T-shirts are washed together, all the burgundy socks, all the blue jeans. Your clothes are soaked in soapy water for a few hours, following which the dirt is literally belted out of them. No newfangled washing machine can wash as clean as a determined dhobi, although admittedly after a few visits to the Indian laundry your clothes do look distinctly thinner and faded. Buttons also tend to get shattered, so bring some spares. Zips, lace, bras and flimsy panties sometimes fare likewise. Once clean, the clothes are dried in the glorious Indian sun, then they're pressed with primitive-looking irons – even your underwear will come back with knife-edge creases.

Even though hundreds, even thousands, of items are washed at the same place each day, the deft dhobi-wallah's secret system of marking means your clothes won't get mistakenly bundled into another dhobi's load. Apparently criminals have even been tracked down by these tell-tale 'dhobi marks'.

in India, and hotels are usually happy to lend you a bucket.

At budget and mid-range hotels clothes are usually washed by a dhobi (inquire at reception). You simply hand over your dirty clothes in the morning and you'll usually get them back washed and pressed that same evening for a minimal cost (around Rs 10 per item; often a little more in touristy places). Most, if not all, upmarket hotels have an in-house laundry with upmarket charges to match. Many crank up the price for same-day service.

Women should consider bringing a lingerie bag to protect delicate bras and undies if they intend handing them over to either a dhobi-wallah or a hotel laundry. A tip: make sure you explain *how* the bag is actually used or else your precious lingerie will promptly be taken out and thrashed like regular clothes.

TOILETS

All top-end and most mid-range hotels have sit-down flush toilets with toilet paper supplied. Some mid-range and most budget hotels usually have a choice of squat and sit-down toilets (see also the boxed text 'Get To Know Your Bathroom' under Accommodation later in this chapter). In the real rock-bottom category and in places well off the tourist circuit, squat toilets are the norm (and are actually a more hygienic option than the sit-down variety) and toilet paper is rarely provided.

Most upmarket restaurants have sit-down flush toilets, while most budget eateries will make you work those thigh muscles.

When it comes to effluent etiquette, it's customary to use your left hand and water, not toilet paper. A strategically placed tap, usually with a little plastic jug nearby, is available in most bathrooms. If you can't get used to the Indian method, bring your own paper (widely available in cities and towns). However, stuffing paper, sanitary napkins and tampons down the toilet is going to further clog an already overloaded sewerage system. Often a bin is provided for used toilet paper and other items – please use it.

HEALTH

Travel health depends on your predeparture preparations, your daily health care while travelling and how you handle any medical problem that does develop. While the potential dangers can seem quite frightening, in reality few travellers experience anything more than an upset stomach.

In even the smallest Indian town you'll find at least one well-stocked pharmacy (selling everything from malaria medication to nail polish remover). Many are open until late, or even around-the-clock. Many

Medical Kit Check List

Following is a list of items you should consider including in your medical kit – consult your pharmacist for brands available in your country.

- ☐ **Aspirin or paracetamol (acetaminophen in the USA)** – for pain or fever
- ☐ **Antihistamine** – for allergies, eg, hay fever; to ease the itch from insect bites or stings; and to prevent motion sickness
- ☐ **Cold and flu tablets, throat lozenges and nasal decongestant**
- ☐ **Multivitamins** – consider for long trips, when dietary vitamin intake may be inadequate
- ☐ **Antibiotics** – consider including these if you're travelling well off the beaten track; see your doctor, as they must be prescribed, and carry the prescription with you
- ☐ **Loperamide or diphenoxylate** – 'blockers' for diarrhoea
- ☐ **Prochlorperazine or metaclopramide** – for nausea and vomiting
- ☐ **Rehydration mixture** – to prevent dehydration, which may occur, for example, during bouts of diarrhoea; particularly important when travelling with children
- ☐ **Insect repellent, sunscreen, lip balm and eye drops**
- ☐ **Calamine lotion, sting relief spray or aloe vera** – to ease irritation from sunburn and insect bites or stings
- ☐ **Antifungal cream or powder** – for fungal skin infections and thrush
- ☐ **Antiseptic (such as povidone-iodine)** – for cuts and grazes
- ☐ **Bandages, Band-Aids (plasters) and other wound dressings**
- ☐ **Water purification tablets or iodine**
- ☐ **Scissors, tweezers and a thermometer** – note that mercury thermometers are prohibited by airlines
- ☐ **Sterile kit** – in case you need injections in a country with medical hygiene problems; discuss with your doctor

pharmaceuticals sold in India are manufactured under licence from multinational companies, so you'll probably be familiar with many brand names. Always check expiry dates.

There are plenty of English-speaking doctors and pharmacists in urban centres, but fewer in rural areas. Most hotels have a doctor on call (see regional chapters for details) – if you're staying at a budget hotel and it can't help you, try contacting an upmarket hotel to find out which doctor they use. If you're seriously ill, contact your country's embassy (see Embassies & Consulates earlier in this chapter); it will usually have a list of recommended doctors and dentists.

There have been reports that some private clinics have bumped up the level of treatment to higher than is necessary in order to procure larger medical insurance claims (see Dangers & Annoyances later in this chapter).

Accidents are a major cause of injury and death among visitors to India, in particular vehicle crashes (see the boxed text 'Surviving the Roads' in the Getting Around chapter). In the Himalaya, using coal heaters in unventilated hotel rooms may cause death by carbon monoxide poisoning (see the boxed text 'Carbon Monoxide Poisoning' under Dangers & Annoyances later in this chapter). Consider taking a smoke detector as these are quite cheap and light to carry.

Predeparture Planning

Immunisations Plan ahead for getting your vaccinations: some of them require more than one injection, while some vaccinations should not be given together. Note that some vaccinations should not be given during pregnancy or to people with allergies – discuss with your doctor.

It is recommended that you seek medical advice at least six weeks before travel. Be aware that there is often a greater risk of disease with children and during pregnancy.

Discuss your requirements with your doctor, but vaccinations you should consider for this trip include the following (for more details about the diseases see Infectious Diseases later in this section). Carry proof of your vaccinations, especially yellow fever, as this proof is sometimes needed to enter some countries.

Everyday Health

Normal body temperature is up to 37°C (98.6°F); more than 2°C (4°F) higher indicates a high fever. The normal adult pulse rate is 60 to 100 per minute (children 80 to 100, babies 100 to 140). As a general rule the pulse increases about 20 beats per minute for each 1°C (2°F) rise in fever.

Respiration (breathing) rate is also an indicator of illness. Count the number of breaths per minute: Between 12 and 20 is normal for adults and older children (up to 30 for younger children, 40 for babies). People with a high fever or serious respiratory illness breathe more quickly than normal. More than 40 shallow breaths a minute may indicate pneumonia.

Diphtheria & Tetanus Vaccinations for these two diseases are usually combined and are recommended for everyone. After an initial course of three injections (usually given in childhood), boosters are necessary every 10 years.

Polio Everyone should keep up to date with this vaccination, which is normally given in childhood. A booster every 10 years maintains immunity. India accounts for four out of 10 polio cases worldwide, with most occurring in Uttar Pradesh and Bihar.

Hepatitis A This vaccine (eg, Avaxim, Havrix 1440 or VAQTA) provides long-term immunity (possibly more than 10 years) after an initial injection and a booster at six to 12 months. Alternatively, an injection of gamma globulin can provide short-term protection against hepatitis A – two to six months, depending on the dose given. It is not a vaccine, but is a ready-made antibody collected from blood donations. It is reasonably effective and, unlike the vaccine, it is protective immediately, but because it is a blood product there are current concerns about its long-term safety. Hepatitis A vaccine is also available in a combined form, Twinrix, with the hepatitis B vaccine. Three injections over a six-month period are required, with the first two providing substantial protection against hepatitis A.

Typhoid Vaccination against typhoid may be required if you are travelling for more than a couple of weeks in India. It is now available either as an injection or as capsules to be taken orally. A combined hepatitis A/typhoid vaccine was launched recently but its availability is still limited – check with your doctor to find out its status in your country.

Meningococcal Meningitis Vaccination is recommended for travellers to certain parts of India. A single injection gives good protection against the major epidemic forms of the disease for three years. Protection may be less effective in children under two years.

Hepatitis B Travellers who should consider vaccination against hepatitis B include those on a long trip, as well as those visiting countries (including India) where there are high levels of hepatitis B infection, where blood transfusions may not be adequately screened or where sexual contact or needle sharing is a possibility. Vaccination involves three injections, with a booster at 12 months. More rapid courses are available if necessary.

Rabies Vaccination should be considered by those who will spend a month or longer in India (where rabies is common), especially if they are cycling, handling animals, caving or travelling to remote areas, and for children (who may not report a bite). Pretravel rabies vaccination involves having three injections over 21 to 28 days. If someone who has been vaccinated is bitten or scratched by an animal, they will require two booster injections of vaccine; those not vaccinated require more.

Japanese B Encephalitis Consider vaccination against this disease if spending a month or longer in high-risk areas in India, making repeated trips to a risk area or visiting during an epidemic. It involves three injections over 30 days.

Tuberculosis The risk of TB to travellers is usually very low, unless you will be living with or closely associated with local people in high risk areas (including India). Vaccination against TB (BCG) is recommended for children and young adults living in these areas for three months or more.

Yellow Fever Travellers arriving within six days of departure from an infected area, such as Central Africa and northern parts of South America, are required to have yellow fever vaccination certificate for entry into India.

Malaria Medication Malaria occurs in most parts of India. Antimalarial drugs do not prevent you from being infected but they kill the malaria parasites during a stage in their development and significantly reduce the risk of becoming very ill or dying. Expert advice on medication should be sought, as there are many factors to consider, including the area to be visited, the risk of exposure to malaria-carrying mosquitoes, the side effects of medication, your medical history and whether you are a child or an adult or pregnant. Travellers to isolated areas in high-risk countries may like to carry a treatment dose of medication for use if symptoms occur.

Health Insurance Make sure that you have adequate health insurance (see Travel Insurance earlier in this chapter).

Travel Health Guides Lonely Planet's *Travel with Children* includes advice on travel health for younger children.

There are also a number of excellent travel health sites on the Internet. From the Lonely Planet home page there are links at www.lonelyplanet.com/weblinks/wlheal.htm to the World Health Organization and the US Centers for Disease Control & Prevention.

Other Preparations Make sure you're healthy before you start travelling. If you are going on a long trip make sure your teeth are OK. If you wear glasses take a spare pair and your prescription.

If you require a particular medication take an adequate supply, as it may not be available locally. Take part of the packaging showing the generic name rather than the brand, which will make getting replacements easier. It's a good idea to have a legible prescription or letter from your doctor to show that you legally use the medication in order to avoid any problems.

Basic Rules

Food Although you should be careful about what you eat and drink, don't become paranoid – sampling the local cuisine is a highlight of travel and India. It's sensible to modify your diet gradually, so resist that urge to feast on deep-fried brain pakoras the moment you arrive.

Vegetables and fruit should be washed with purified water or peeled where possible. Beware of ice cream that is sold in the street or anywhere it might have been melted and refrozen; if there's any doubt (eg, a power cut in the last day or two), steer well clear. Shellfish such as mussels, oysters and clams should be avoided as should undercooked meat, particularly in the form of mince. Steaming does not make shellfish safe to eat.

If a place looks clean and well run and the vendor also looks clean and healthy, then the food is probably safe. In general, places that are packed with travellers or locals will be fine, while empty restaurants are questionable. The food in busy restaurants is cooked and eaten quite quickly with little standing around and is probably not reheated. Although street stalls may look unappetising, the big plus is that you can usually see your food being freshly cooked in front of your eyes.

Nutrition

If your diet is poor or limited in variety, if you're travelling hard and fast and therefore missing meals or if you simply lose your appetite, you can soon start to lose weight and place your health at risk.

Make sure your diet is well balanced. Cooked eggs, tofu, beans, dhal and nuts are all safe ways to get protein. Fruit you can peel is usually safe and a good source of vitamins. Melons can harbour bacteria in their flesh and are best avoided. Try to eat plenty of grains (including rice) and bread. Remember that although food is generally safer if it is cooked well, overcooked food loses much of its nutritional value. If your diet isn't well balanced or if your food intake is insufficient, it's a good idea to take multivitamin tablets.

In hot climates make sure you drink enough – don't rely on feeling thirsty to indicate when you should drink. Not needing to urinate or voiding small amounts of very dark yellow urine is a danger sign. Always carry a water bottle on long trips. Excessive sweating can lead to loss of salt and therefore muscle cramping. Salt tablets are not a good idea as a preventative, but in places where salt is not used much, adding salt to food can help. Most Indian food is cooked with salt.

Water The number one rule is *be careful of the water* and especially ice. If you don't know for certain that the water is safe, assume the worst. Reputable brands of bottled water or soft drinks are generally fine, although in some places bottles may be refilled with tap water. Only use water from containers with a serrated seal – not tops or corks. Take care with fruit juice, particularly if water may have been added. Milk should be treated with suspicion as it is often unpasteurised, though boiled milk is fine if it is kept hygienically. Tea or coffee should also be OK, since the water should have been boiled.

Water Purification The simplest way of purifying water is to boil it thoroughly. Vigorous boiling should be satisfactory; however, at high altitude water boils at a lower temperature, so germs are less likely to be killed. Boil it for longer in these environments.

Consider purchasing a water filter for a long trip. There are two main kinds of filter. Total filters take out all parasites, bacteria and viruses and make water safe to drink. They are often expensive, but they can be more cost-effective than buying bottled water. Simple filters (which can even be a nylon mesh bag) take out dirt and larger foreign bodies from the water so that chemical solutions work much more effectively; if water is dirty, chemical solutions may not work at all. It's very important when buying a filter to read the specifications so that you know exactly what it removes from the water and what it doesn't. Simple filtering will not remove all dangerous organisms, so if you cannot boil water it should be treated chemically. Chlorine tablets will kill many pathogens, but not parasites such as giardia and amoebic cysts. Iodine is more effective in purifying water and is available in tablet form. Follow the directions carefully and remember that too much iodine can be harmful.

Discarded plastic mineral water bottles are causing environmental havoc in India (see Responsible Tourism earlier in this chapter).

Medical Problems & Treatment

Self-diagnosis and treatment can be risky, so you should always seek medical help. An embassy, consulate or five-star hotel can usually recommend a local doctor or clinic. Although we do give drug dosages in this section, they are for emergency use only. Correct diagnosis is vital. In this section we have used the generic names for medications – check with a pharmacist for brands available locally.

Note that antibiotics should ideally be administered only under medical supervision. Take only the recommended dose at the prescribed intervals and use the whole course, even if the illness seems to be cured earlier. Stop immediately if there are any serious reactions and don't use the antibiotic at all if you are unsure that you have the correct one. Some people are allergic to commonly prescribed antibiotics such as penicillin; carry this information (eg, on a bracelet).

Environmental Hazards

Air Pollution This is something you'll become very aware of in India if you are travelling in urban environments, especially in Delhi and Kolkata. Air pollution can be a health hazard, particularly if you suffer from a lung disease such as asthma. It can also aggravate coughs, colds and sinus problems and cause eye irritation. Consider avoiding badly polluted areas, especially if you have asthma, or you could invest in a surgical mask.

Altitude Sickness Parts of North India form the southern Himalaya so lack of oxygen at high altitudes (over 2500m) affects most people to some extent. The effect may be mild or severe and occurs because less oxygen reaches the muscles and the brain, requiring the heart and lungs to compensate by working harder. Symptoms of acute mountain sickness (AMS) usually develop during the first 24 hours but may be delayed by up to three weeks. Mild symptoms include headache, lethargy, dizziness, difficulty sleeping and loss of appetite. AMS may become more severe without warning and can be fatal. Severe symptoms include breathlessness, a dry and irritative cough (which may progress to the production of pink, frothy sputum), severe headache, lack of coordination and balance, confusion, irrational behaviour, vomiting, drowsiness and unconsciousness. There is no hard-and-fast rule as to what is too high – AMS has been fatal at 3000m, although 3500m to 4500m is the usual range.

Treat mild symptoms by resting at the same altitude until recovery, usually for a day or two. Paracetamol or aspirin can be taken for headaches. If symptoms persist or become worse, however, *immediate descent is necessary*; even 500m can help. Drug treatments should never be used to avoid descent or to enable further ascent.

The drugs acetazolamide and dexamethasone are recommended by some doctors for the prevention of AMS; however, their use is controversial. They can reduce the symptoms, but they may also mask warning signs; severe and fatal AMS has occurred in people taking these drugs. In general we do not recommend them for travellers. To prevent acute mountain sickness:

- Ascend slowly – have frequent rest days and spend two to three nights at each rise of 1000m. If you reach a high altitude by trekking, acclimatisation takes place gradually and you are less likely to be affected than if you fly directly to high altitude.
- If possible, it is always wise to sleep at a lower altitude than the greatest height reached during the day. Also, once above 3000m, care should be taken not to increase the sleeping altitude by more than 300m per day.
- Drink extra fluids. The mountain air is dry and cold and moisture is lost as you breathe. Evaporation of sweat may occur unnoticed and result in dehydration.
- Eat light, high-carbohydrate meals for more energy.
- Avoid alcohol as it may increase the risk of dehydration.
- Avoid sedatives.

The Himalayan First Aid & Survival Manual by Jim Duff & Peter Gormly has practical advice treat ailments associated with high altitudes. All profits go to the Kathmandu Environmental Education Project. It's available from both Dr J Duff, PO Box 53, Repton, NSW 2454, Australia and KEEP, PO Box 9178, Jyathu, Kathmandu, Nepal.

Heat Exhaustion Dehydration and salt deficiency can cause heat exhaustion. Take time to acclimatise to high temperatures, drink sufficient liquids and do not do anything too physically demanding.

Salt deficiency is characterised by fatigue, lethargy, headaches, giddiness and muscle cramps; salt tablets may help, but adding extra salt to your food is better.

Anhidrotic heat exhaustion is a rare form of heat exhaustion that is caused by an inability to sweat. It tends to affect people who have been in a hot climate for some time, rather than newcomers. It can progress to heatstroke. Treatment involves removal to a cooler climate.

Heatstroke This serious, occasionally fatal, condition can occur if the body's heat-regulating mechanism breaks down and the body temperature rises to dangerous levels. Long, continuous periods of exposure to high temperatures and insufficient fluids can leave you vulnerable to heatstroke.

The symptoms are feeling unwell, not sweating very much (or at all) and a high body temperature (39° to 41°C or 102° to 106°F). Where sweating has ceased, the skin becomes flushed and red. Severe, throbbing headaches and lack of coordination will also occur, and the sufferer may be confused or aggressive. Eventually the victim will become delirious or convulse. Hospitalisation is essential, but in the interim get victims out of the sun, remove their clothing, cover them with a wet sheet or towel and then fan continually. Give fluids if they are conscious.

Hypothermia Too much cold can be just as dangerous as too much heat. If you are trekking at high altitudes or simply taking a long bus trip over mountains, particularly at night, be prepared.

Hypothermia occurs when the body loses heat faster than it can produce it and the core temperature of the body falls. It is surprisingly easy to progress from very cold to dangerously cold due to a combination of wind, wet clothing, fatigue and hunger even if the air temperature is above freezing. It is best to dress in layers; silk, wool and some of the new artificial fibres are all good insulating materials. A hat is important, as a lot of heat is lost through the head. A strong, waterproof outer layer (and a 'space' blanket for emergencies) is essential. Carry basic supplies, including food containing simple sugars to generate heat quickly, and fluid to drink.

Symptoms of hypothermia are exhaustion, numb skin (particularly toes and fingers), shivering, slurred speech, irrational or violent behaviour, lethargy, stumbling, dizzy spells, muscle cramps and violent bursts of energy. Irrationality may take the form of sufferers claiming they are warm and trying to take off their clothes.

To treat mild hypothermia, first get the person out of the wind and/or rain, remove their clothing if it's wet and replace it with dry, warm clothing. Give them hot liquids – not alcohol – and some high-kilojoule, easily digestible food. Do not rub victims: instead, allow them to slowly warm themselves. This should be enough to treat the early stages of hypothermia. The early recognition and treatment of mild hypothermia is the only way to prevent severe hypothermia, which is a critical condition.

Jet Lag This is experienced when a person travels by air across more than three time zones (each time zone usually represents a one-hour time difference). It occurs because many of the functions of the human body (such as temperature, pulse rate and emptying of the bladder and bowels) are regulated by internal 24-hour cycles. When we travel long distances rapidly, our bodies take time to adjust to the 'new time' of our destination and we may experience fatigue, disorientation, insomnia, anxiety, impaired concentration and loss of appetite. These effects will usually be gone within three days of arrival, but to minimise the impact of jet lag:

- Rest for a couple of days prior to departure.
- Try to select flight schedules that minimise sleep deprivation; arriving late in the day means you can go to sleep soon after you arrive. For very long flights, try to organise a stopover.
- Avoid excessive eating (which bloats the stomach) and alcohol (which causes dehydration) during the flight. Instead, drink plenty of noncarbonated, nonalcoholic drinks.
- Avoid smoking.
- Make yourself comfortable by wearing loose-fitting clothes and perhaps bringing an eye mask and ear plugs to help you sleep.
- Try to sleep at the appropriate time for the time zone you are travelling to.

Motion Sickness Eating lightly before and during a trip will reduce the chances of motion sickness. If you are prone to motion sickness try to find a place that minimises movement – near the wing on aircraft, close to midships on boats, near the centre on buses. Fresh air usually helps; reading and cigarette smoke don't. Commercial motion-sickness preparations, which can cause drowsiness, have to be taken before the trip commences. Ginger (available in capsule form) and peppermint (including mint-flavoured sweets) are natural preventatives.

Prickly Heat This is an itchy rash caused by excessive perspiration trapped under the skin. It usually strikes people who have just arrived in a hot climate. Keeping cool, bathing often, drying the skin and using a mild talcum or prickly heat powder, or resorting to air-conditioning may help.

Sunburn In the tropics, the desert or at high altitude you can get sunburnt surprisingly quickly, even through cloud. Use a sunscreen, a hat, and a barrier cream for your nose and lips. Calamine lotion or a commercial after-sun preparation are good for mild sunburn. Protect your eyes with good quality sunglasses, particularly if you will be near water, sand or snow.

Infectious Diseases

Diarrhoea Simple things like a change of water, food or climate can all cause a mild bout of diarrhoea, but a few rushed toilet trips with no other symptoms is not indicative of a major problem.

Dehydration is the main danger with any diarrhoea, particularly in children or the elderly, as dehydration can occur quite quickly. Under all circumstances *fluid replacement* (at least equal to the volume being lost) is the most important thing to remember. Weak black tea with a little sugar, soda water, or soft drinks allowed to go flat and diluted 50% with clean water are all good. With severe diarrhoea a rehydrating solution is preferable to replace minerals and salts lost. Commercially available oral rehydration salts (ORS) are very useful; add them to boiled or bottled water. In an emergency you can make up a solution of six teaspoons of sugar and a half teaspoon of salt to a litre of boiled or bottled water. You need to drink at least the same volume of fluid that you are losing in bowel movements and vomiting. Urine is the best guide to the adequacy of replacement – if you have small amounts of concentrated urine, you need to drink more. Keep drinking small amounts often. Stick to a bland diet while you recover.

Gut-paralysing drugs such as loperamide or diphenoxylate can be used to bring relief from the symptoms, although they do not actually cure the problem. Only use these drugs if you do not have access to toilets, eg, if you *must* travel. Note that these drugs are not recommended for children under 12 years.

In certain situations antibiotics may be required: diarrhoea with blood or mucus (dysentery), any diarrhoea with fever, profuse watery diarrhoea, persistent diarrhoea not improving after 48 hours and severe diarrhoea. These suggest a more serious cause of diarrhoea and in these situations gut-paralysing drugs should be avoided.

In these situations, a stool test may be necessary to diagnose what bug is causing your diarrhoea, so you should seek medical help urgently. Where this is not possible the recommended drugs for bacterial diarrhoea (the most likely cause of severe diarrhoea in travellers) are norfloxacin 400mg twice daily for three days or ciprofloxacin 500mg twice daily for five days. These are not recommended for children or pregnant women. The drug of choice for children would be co-trimoxazole with dosage dependent on weight. A five-day course is given. Ampicillin or amoxycillin may be given in pregnancy, but medical care is necessary.

Two other causes of persistent diarrhoea in travellers are giardiasis and amoebic dysentery.

Giardiasis is caused by a common parasite, *Giardia lamblia*. Symptoms include stomach cramps, nausea, a bloated stomach, watery, foul-smelling diarrhoea and frequent gas. Giardiasis can appear several weeks after you have been exposed to the parasite. The symptoms may disappear for a few days and then return; this can go on for several weeks.

Amoebic dysentery, caused by the protozoan *Entamoeba histolytica*, is characterised by a gradual onset of low-grade diarrhoea, often with blood and mucus. Cramping abdominal pain and vomiting are less likely than in other types of diarrhoea, and fever may not be present. It will persist until treated and can recur and cause other health problems.

You should seek medical advice if you think you have giardiasis or amoebic dysentery, but where this is not possible, tinidazole or metronidazole are the recommended drugs. Treatment is a 2g single dose of tinidazole or 250mg of metronidazole three times daily for five to 10 days.

Fungal Infections These occur more commonly in hot weather and are usually found on the scalp, between the toes (athlete's foot) or fingers, in the groin and on the body (ringworm). You get ringworm (which is a fungal infection, not a worm) from infected animals or other people. Moisture encourages these infections.

To prevent fungal infections wear loose, comfortable clothes, avoid artificial fibres, wash frequently and dry yourself carefully. If you do get an infection, wash the infected area at least daily with a disinfectant or medicated soap and water, and rinse and dry well. Apply an antifungal cream or powder such as tolnaftate. Try to expose the infected area to air or sunlight as much as possible and wash all towels and underwear in hot water, change them often and let them dry in the sun.

Hepatitis This is a general term for inflammation of the liver. It is a common disease in India and worldwide. There are several different viruses that cause hepatitis, and they differ in the way that they are transmitted. The symptoms are similar in all forms of the illness, and include fever, chills, headache, fatigue, feelings of weakness and aches and pains, followed by loss of appetite, nausea, vomiting, abdominal pain, dark urine, light-coloured faeces, jaundiced (yellow) skin and yellowing of the whites of the eyes. People who have had hepatitis should avoid alcohol for some time after the illness, as the liver needs time to recover.

Hepatitis A is transmitted by contaminated food and drinking water. You should seek medical advice, but there is not much you can do apart from resting, drinking lots of fluids, eating lightly and avoiding fatty foods. **Hepatitis E** is transmitted in the same way as hepatitis A; it can be particularly serious in pregnant women.

There are almost 300 million chronic carriers of **hepatitis B** in the world. It is spread through contact with infected blood, blood products or body fluids, for example through sexual contact, unsterilised needles and blood transfusions, or contact with blood via small breaks in the skin. Other risk situations include having a shave, tattoo or body piercing with contaminated equipment. The symptoms of hepatitis B may be more severe than those of type A and the disease can lead to long-term problems such as chronic liver damage, liver cancer or a long-term carrier state. **Hepatitis C and D** are spread in the same way as hepatitis B and can also lead to long-term complications.

There are vaccines against hepatitis A and B, but there are currently no vaccines against the other types of hepatitis. Following the basic rules about food and water (hepatitis A and E) and avoiding risk situations (hepatitis B, C and D) are important preventative measures.

HIV & AIDS Infection with the human immunodeficiency virus (HIV) may lead to acquired immune deficiency syndrome (AIDS), which is a fatal disease. Any exposure to blood, blood products or body fluids may put the individual at risk. The disease is often transmitted through sexual contact or dirty needles – vaccinations, acupuncture, tattooing and body piercing can be potentially as dangerous as intravenous drug use. HIV/AIDS can also be spread through infected blood transfusions. Although India does have the resources to screen blood donations, extreme care should still be taken, as not all laboratories have adequate controls implemented to ensure this is done thoroughly. If you do need an injection, ask to see the syringe unwrapped in front of you, or take a needle and syringe pack with you.

Fear of HIV infection should never preclude treatment for serious conditions.

AIDS in India

In 2000 India recorded the highest number of HIV infections on the planet, with 3.7 million reported cases of HIV – a figure believed to be artificially low as most AIDS cases and deaths go unreported. Mumbai has the highest rate of infection in India. In this city an estimated 72% of sex workers (who service an average of 50 clients each per day) are believed to be HIV-positive. Apart from sex workers, truck drivers (nationwide) also fall into the high-risk category.

In a country of more than one billion people, some health officials warn that unless there are dedicated educational programs and increased condom use throughout India, the number of HIV-positive cases could swell to a staggering 31 million by 2010.

Intestinal Worms These parasites are most common in rural, tropical areas. The different worms have different ways of infecting people. Some may be ingested on food such as undercooked meat (eg, tapeworms) and some enter through your skin (eg, hookworms). Infestations may not show up for some time, and although they are generally not serious, if left untreated some can cause severe health problems later. Consider having a stool test when you return home to check for these and to determine the appropriate treatment.

Meningococcal Meningitis This serious disease can be fatal. There are recurring epidemics in northern India and Nepal.

A fever, severe headache, sensitivity to light and neck stiffness that prevents forward bending of the head are the first symptoms. There may also be purple patches on the skin. Death can occur within a few hours, so urgent medical treatment is required.

The disease is spread by close contact with people who carry it in their throats and noses and spread it through coughs and sneezes; they may not be aware that they are carriers. Lodges in the hills where travellers spend the night are prime spots for the spread of infection.

Treatment is large doses of penicillin given intravenously, or chloramphenicol injections.

Sexually Transmitted Infections HIV/AIDS and hepatitis B can be transmitted through sexual contact – see Infectious Diseases earlier in this section for more details. Other STIs include gonorrhoea, herpes and syphilis. Sores, blisters or rashes around the genitals and discharges or pain when urinating are common symptoms. In some STIs, such as wart virus or chlamydia, symptoms may be less marked or not observed at all, especially in women. Chlamydia infection can cause infertility in men and women before any symptoms have been noticed. Syphilis symptoms eventually disappear completely but the disease continues and can cause severe problems in later years. While abstinence from sexual contact is the only 100% effective prevention, using condoms is also effective. The treatment of gonorrhoea and syphilis is with antibiotics. The different sexually transmitted infections each require specific antibiotics.

Travellers to India should consider bringing condoms from their home country – these may be more reliable than local brands.

Typhoid This fever is a dangerous gut infection caused by contaminated water and food. Medical help must be sought.

In its early stages sufferers may feel they have a bad cold or flu on the way, as early symptoms are a headache, body aches and a fever that rises a little each day until it is around 40°C (104°F) or more. The victim's pulse is often slow relative to the degree of fever present – unlike a normal fever where the pulse increases. There may also be vomiting, abdominal pain and diarrhoea.

In the second week the high fever and slow pulse continue and a few pink spots may appear on the body; trembling, delirium, weakness, weight loss and dehydration may occur. Possible complications are pneumonia, perforated bowel or meningitis.

Insect-Borne Diseases

Filariasis, leishmaniasis, Lyme disease and typhus are all insect-borne diseases, but they do not pose a great risk to travellers. For more information on them see Less Common Diseases later in this section.

Travellers are advised to prevent mosquito bites at all times. The main messages are:

- Wear light-coloured clothing.
- Wear long trousers and long-sleeved shirts.
- Use mosquito repellents containing the compound DEET on exposed areas (prolonged overuse of DEET may be harmful, especially to children, but its use is considered preferable to being bitten by disease-transmitting mosquitoes).
- Avoid perfumes or aftershave.
- During the night, use a mosquito net impregnated with mosquito repellent (permethrin) – it may be worth taking your own.
- Impregnating clothes with permethrin effectively deters mosquitoes and other insects.

Malaria This serious and potentially fatal disease is spread by mosquito bites. If you are travelling in endemic areas it is extremely important to avoid mosquito bites and to take tablets to prevent this disease. Symptoms range from fever, chills and sweating, headache, diarrhoea and abdominal pains to a vague feeling of ill-health. Seek medical help immediately if malaria is suspected. Without treatment malaria can rapidly become more serious and can be fatal.

If medical care is not available, malaria tablets can be used for treatment. You need to use a malaria tablet that is different from the one you were taking when you contracted malaria. The standard treatment dose of mefloquine is two 250mg tablets and a further two six hours later. For Fansidar, it's a single dose of three tablets. If you were previously taking mefloquine and cannot obtain Fansidar, then other alternatives are Malarone (atovaquone-proguanil; four tablets once daily for three days), halofantrine (three doses of two 250mg tablets every six hours) or quinine sulphate (600mg every six hours). There is a greater risk of side effects with these dosages than in normal use if used with mefloquine, so medical advice is preferable. Be aware also that halofantrine is no longer recommended by the World Health Organisation (WHO) as an emergency standby treatment because of side effects and should only be used if no other drugs are available.

Dengue Fever This viral disease is transmitted by mosquitoes and is fast becoming one of the top public health problems in the tropical world, including India. Unlike the malaria mosquito, the *Aedes aegypti* mosquito, which transmits the dengue virus, is most active during the day, and is found mainly in urban areas, in and around human dwellings.

Signs and symptoms of dengue fever include a sudden onset of high fever, headache, joint and muscle pains (hence its old name, 'breakbone fever') and nausea and vomiting. A rash of small red spots sometimes appears three to four days after the onset of fever. In the early phase of illness, dengue may be mistaken for other infectious diseases, including malaria and influenza. Minor bleeding such as nose bleeds may occur in the course of the illness, but this does not necessarily mean that you have progressed to the potentially fatal dengue haemorrhagic fever (DHF). This is a severe illness, characterised by heavy bleeding, which is thought to be a result of second infection due to a different strain (there are four major strains) and usually affects residents of the country rather than travellers. Recovery, even from simple dengue fever, may be prolonged, with tiredness lasting for several weeks.

You should seek medical attention as soon as possible if you think you may be infected. A blood test can exclude malaria and indicate the possibility of dengue fever. There is no specific treatment for dengue. Aspirin should be avoided as it increases the risk of haemorrhaging. There is no vaccine against dengue fever. The best prevention is to avoid mosquito bites at all times.

Japanese B Encephalitis This viral infection of the brain is transmitted by mosquitoes. Most cases occur in rural areas as the virus exists in pigs and wading birds. Symptoms include fever, headache and alteration in consciousness. Hospitalisation is needed for correct diagnosis and treatment. There is a high mortality rate among those who have symptoms and many of those who survive -are intellectually disabled.

Cuts, Bites & Stings

See Less Common Diseases later in this section for details of rabies, which is passed through animal bites.

Cuts & Scratches Wash well and treat any cut with an antiseptic such as povidone-iodine. Where possible avoid bandages and Band-Aids, which can keep wounds wet. Coral cuts are notoriously slow to heal and if they are not adequately cleaned small pieces of coral can become embedded in the wound.

Bedbugs & Lice Bedbugs live in various places, but particularly in dirty mattresses and bedding, evidenced by spots of blood on bedclothes or on the wall. Bedbugs can be a real problem at rock-bottom hotels in India. Bedbugs leave itchy bites in neat rows. Calamine lotion or a sting relief spray may help.

All lice cause itching and discomfort. They make themselves at home in your hair (head lice), your clothing (body lice) or in your pubic hair (crabs). You catch lice through direct contact with infected people or by sharing combs, clothing and the like. Powder or shampoo treatment will kill the lice and infected clothing should then be washed in very hot, soapy water and left in the sun to dry.

Bites & Stings Bee and wasp stings are usually painful rather than dangerous. However, in people who are allergic to them, severe breathing difficulties may occur and will require urgent medical care. Calamine lotion or a sting relief spray will give relief and ice packs will reduce the pain and swelling. There are some spiders with dangerous bites but antivenenes are usually available. Scorpion stings are notoriously painful and can actually be fatal. Scorpions often shelter in shoes or clothing.

There are various fish and other sea creatures that can sting or bite dangerously or that are dangerous to eat – seek local advice.

Jellyfish Avoid contact with these sea creatures, which have stinging tentacles – seek local advice. Dousing in vinegar will deactivate any stingers that have not 'fired'. Calamine lotion, antihistamines and analgesics may reduce the reaction and relieve the pain.

Leeches & Ticks Leeches may be present in damp rainforest conditions; they attach themselves to your skin to suck your blood. Trekkers often get them on their legs or in their boots. Salt or a lighted cigarette end will make them fall off. Do not pull them off as the bite is then more likely to become infected. Clean and apply pressure if the point of attachment is bleeding. An insect repellent may keep them away.

You should always check all over your body if you have been walking through a potentially tick-infested area as ticks can cause skin infections and other more serious diseases. If a tick is found attached, press down around the tick's head with tweezers, grab the head and gently pull upwards. Avoid pulling the rear of the body as this may squeeze the tick's gut contents through the attached mouth parts into the skin, increasing the risk of infection and disease. Smearing chemicals on the tick will not make it let go and this is not recommended.

Snakes To minimise your chances of being bitten always wear boots, socks and long trousers when walking through undergrowth where snakes may be present. Don't put your hands into holes and crevices and be careful when collecting firewood.

Snake bites do not cause instantaneous death and antivenenes are usually available. Immediately wrap the bitten limb tightly, as you would for a sprained ankle, and then attach a splint to immobilise it. Keep the victim still and seek medical help, if possible with the dead snake for identification. Don't attempt to catch the snake if there is a possibility of being bitten again. Tourniquets and sucking out the poison are now comprehensively discredited treatments.

Women's Health

Gynaecological Problems Antibiotic use, synthetic underwear, sweating and contraceptive pills can lead to fungal vaginal infections, especially when travelling in hot climates. Thrush or vaginal candidiasis is characterised by a rash, itch and discharge. Nystatin, miconazole or clotrimazole pessaries are the usual treatment, but some people use a more traditional remedy involving vinegar or lemon juice douches, or yogurt. Maintaining good personal hygiene and wearing loose-fitting clothes and cotton underwear may help prevent these infections.

Sexually transmitted infections are a major cause of vaginal problems. Symptoms include a smelly discharge, painful intercourse and sometimes a burning sensation when urinating. Medical attention should be sought and male sexual partners must also be treated. For more details see Sexually Transmitted Infections earlier in this section. Besides abstinence, the best thing is to practise safer sex using condoms.

Pregnancy It is not advisable to travel to some places while pregnant as a number of vaccinations normally used to prevent serious diseases are not advisable during pregnancy (eg, yellow fever). In addition, some diseases are much more serious for the mother (and may increase the risk of a stillborn child) in pregnancy (eg, malaria).

Most miscarriages occur during the first three months of pregnancy. Miscarriage is not uncommon and can occasionally lead to severe bleeding. The last three months should also be spent within reasonable distance of good medical care. A baby born as early as 24 weeks stands a chance of survival, but only in a good modern hospital. Pregnant women should avoid all unnecessary medication, although vaccinations and malarial prophylactics should still be taken where needed. Additional care should be taken to prevent illness and particular attention should be paid to diet and nutrition. Alcohol and nicotine, for example, should be avoided.

Less Common Diseases

The following diseases pose a small risk to travellers, and so are only mentioned in passing. Seek medical advice if you think you may have any of these diseases.

Cholera This is the worst of the watery diarrhoeas and medical help should be sought. Outbreaks of cholera are generally widely reported, so you can avoid such problem areas. *Fluid replacement is the most vital treatment* – the risk of dehydration is severe as you may lose up to 20L a day. If there is a delay in getting to hospital, then begin taking tetracycline. The adult dose is 250mg four times daily. It is not recommended for children under nine years or for pregnant women. Tetracycline may help shorten the illness, but adequate fluids are required to save lives.

Filariasis This is a mosquito-transmitted parasitic infection found in various countries including India. Possible symptoms include fever, pain and swelling of the lymph glands; inflammation of lymph drainage areas; swelling of a limb or the scrotum; skin rashes; and blindness. Treatment is available to eliminate the parasites from the body, but some of the damage already caused may not be reversible. Medical advice should be obtained promptly if the infection is suspected.

Leishmaniasis This is a group of parasitic diseases transmitted by sandflies, which are found in India and other parts of the world. Cutaneous leishmaniasis affects the skin tissue causing ulceration and disfigurement, and visceral leishmaniasis affects the internal organs. Seek medical advice, as laboratory testing is required for diagnosis and correct treatment. Avoiding sandfly bites is the best precaution. Bites are usually painless, itchy and yet another reason to cover up and apply repellent.

Lyme Disease This is a tick-transmitted infection that may be acquired in India. The illness usually begins with a spreading rash at the site of the tick bite and is accompanied by fever, headache, extreme fatigue, aching joints and muscles and mild neck stiffness. If untreated, these symptoms usually resolve over several weeks but over subsequent weeks or months disorders of the nervous system, heart and joints may develop. Treatment works best early in the illness. Medical help should be sought.

Rabies This fatal viral infection is found in many countries, including India. Many animals can be infected (such as dogs, cats, bats and monkeys) and it is their saliva that is infectious. Any bite, scratch or even lick from an animal should be cleaned immediately and thoroughly. Scrub with soap and running water, and then apply alcohol or iodine solution. Medical help should be sought promptly to receive a course of injections to prevent the onset of symptoms and death.

Tetanus This disease is caused by a germ that lives in soil and in the faeces of horses and other animals. It enters the body via breaks in the skin. The first symptom may be discomfort in swallowing, or stiffening of the jaw and neck; this is followed by painful convulsions of the jaw and whole body. It can be prevented by vaccination.

Tuberculosis TB is a bacterial infection usually transmitted from person to person by coughing, but that may be transmitted through consumption of unpasteurised milk. Milk that has been boiled is safe to drink, and the souring of milk to make yogurt or cheese also kills the bacilli. Travellers are usually not at great risk as close household contact with the infected person is usually required before the disease is passed on. You may need to have a TB test before you travel as this can help diagnose the disease later if you become ill.

Typhus This disease is spread by ticks, mites or lice. It begins with fever, chills, headache and muscle pains followed a few days later by a body rash. There is often a large painful sore at the site of the bite and nearby lymph nodes are swollen and painful. Typhus can be treated under medical supervision. Seek local advice on areas where ticks pose a danger and always check your skin carefully for ticks after walking in a danger area such as a tropical forest. An insect repellent can help, and walkers in tick-infested areas should consider having their boots and trousers impregnated with benzyl benzoate and dibutylphthalate.

WOMEN TRAVELLERS

India is generally perfectly safe for women travellers, including those travelling alone. Although foreign women (including those of Indian descent) have been hassled, you can rest assured that India is much safer for women travellers than many other countries and getting ogled (incessantly) is the most you'll probably encounter. The tips provided in this section are intended to reduce the problems, not to alarm you. (See also Women in Society under Society & Conduct in the Facts about India chapter).

Women travelling with a male partner are less likely to be harassed. However, a foreign woman of Indian descent travelling with a non-Indian male should be prepared to cop disapproving stares; having a non-Indian partner is still not condoned in many parts of India.

Being a woman has some advantages. Women can usually queue-jump without consequence, use ladies-only carriages on trains, and sometimes get free entry into nightclubs. There are even special ladies' sections in some cinemas, restaurants and other public places.

For information on what to take, see Planning earlier in this chapter.

What to Wear

Staying safe is a matter of common sense and culturally appropriate behaviour. Close attention to standards of dress will go a long way towards minimising problems for female travellers. Refrain from wearing sleeveless blouses, shorts, skimpy or tight-fitting clothing and, of course, the bra-less look. Women who publicly flash ample flesh are not only making themselves an easy target for sexual harassment, they're also making it hard for fellow travellers by painting a poor image of foreign women in general.

Wearing Indian dress, when done properly, makes a positive impression.

Going into public wearing a choli (small tight blouse worn under a sari) or a sari petticoat (which many foreign women mistake for a skirt) is rather like strutting around half dressed – don't do it. On the other hand, the *salwar kameez* (traditional Punjabi long tunic and trouser combination) is considered to be respectable attire and has become increasingly popular among female travellers. It's practical, comfortable, attractive and comes in a range of prices. A cotton salwar kameez is also surprisingly cool in the hot weather and keeps the burning sun off your skin. The dupatta (long scarf) that is worn with this outfit is handy if you visit a shrine that requires your head to be covered.

Safety Precautions

Getting constantly stared at is something you'll simply have to get used to. Don't allow it to get the better of you. Just walk confidently and refrain from returning male stares, as this may be considered a come-on; dark glasses can help. A good way to block out stares in restaurants is to take along a book or letters to write home.

Whenever you wish to keep conversations short, get to the point as quickly and politely as possible. Getting involved in inane conversations with men can be considered a turn-on. Questions like 'has anyone ever told you that your eyes are like the sunset?' or 'do you have a boyfriend?' are strong indicators that the conversation may be taking a steamy tangent. Some women prepare in advance by wearing a pseudo wedding ring, or by announcing early on in the conversation that they are married or engaged (regardless of whether they are or not). This is a highly effective way of keeping interactions 'lust-free'. If you still get the uncomfortable feeling that he's encroaching on your space, the chances are that he is. A firm request to keep away is usually enough to take control of the situation – especially if it's loud enough to draw the attention of passers-by. If this request is ignored, the silent treatment (not responding to questions at all) is an effective way of getting rid of unwanted male company.

On trains and buses, don't hesitate to return any errant limbs, put some item of lug-

Sexual Harassment

Foreign women are not alone when it comes to unwanted male attention. In recent years there have been more and more reports of Indian women being subjected to what is locally dubbed as 'Eve-teasing' (a euphemistic term for what is invariably sexual harassment, often verbal). One recent newspaper report went so far to say that up to 80% of city women are subjected to 'this disgusting experience once in awhile', predominantly at college campuses and bazaars. According to authorities, most Eve-teasers are groups of teenagers and university students, many the sons of wealthy families.

Good-intentioned authorities have made laudable attempts to deal with the problem. For instance, in Indore (Madhya Pradesh) police launched 'Operation Rangeen' aimed at stamping out Eve-teasing; regrettably the campaign failed to yield adequate results and was promptly shelved. Meanwhile, in some Indian police stations, special 'We Care for You' units have been set up with the sole intent of encouraging women to report sexual harassment. However, the response to this has also been disappointing. Many women have said they're too ashamed to file reports. Some have openly declared that they have no faith in the system because they've been harassed by men of the law in the past. Other women have simply been too afraid to lodge complaints after receiving brutal threats from their perpetrators if they 'blab to the cops'.

gage in between you and, if all else fails, find a new spot. You're also within your rights to tell him to shove off! It's wise to arrive in towns before it gets dark and, of course, avoid walking alone at night, especially in isolated areas.

Other harassment women travellers have encountered includes lewd comments, provocative gestures, jeering, getting 'accidentally' bumped into on the street, and being groped. There have been several reported cases of rape among foreign women. Exuberant special events (such as the Holi festival) can pose problems for women (see Dangers & Annoyances later in this section).

GAY & LESBIAN TRAVELLERS

Although the more liberal sections of certain cities (predominantly the larger centres such as Mumbai, Delhi, Kolkata and Bangalore) are becoming more tolerant of homosexuality, generally gay life is still largely suppressed in India. You may see Indian men holding hands with each other or engaged in other public affectionate behaviour, but don't instantly assume they are gay; this is an accepted expression of nonsexual friendship.

Since marriage is still very highly regarded in India, most gay people stay in the closet or risk being disowned by their families and society.

As with relations between heterosexual Western couples travelling in India – both married and unmarried – gay and lesbian travellers should exercise discretion and refrain from displaying overt affection towards each other in public.

India's most visible nonheterosexual group are the hijras – a caste of transvestites and eunuchs who dress in women's clothing. Some are gay, some are hermaphrodites, and some were unfortunate enough to be kidnapped and castrated. As it is traditionally unacceptable to live openly as a gay man, hijras get around this by becoming, in effect, a sort of third sex. They work mainly as uninvited entertainers at weddings and celebrations of the birth of male children, and as prostitutes.

Legal Status

Homosexual relations for men are illegal in India. Section 377 of the national legislation forbids 'carnal intercourse against the order of nature' (that is, anal intercourse). The penalties for transgression can be up to life imprisonment. There is no law against lesbian relations.

Publications & Web Sites

The Mumbai publication, *Bombay Dost*, is a popular gay and lesbian magazine available from 105 Veena-Beena Shopping Centre, Bandra West, Mumbai, as well as at a number of bookshops and newsstands in various Indian cities.

Delhi's own gay magazine, *Darpan*, is published by the gay group Humrahi. It can also be found at city bookshops and pavement stalls.

For further information about India's gay scene, there are some excellent Web sites including:

Bombay Dost Gay and lesbian newspaper. www.bombay-dost.com

Gay Bombay Events, legal issues, arts and entertainment in Mumbai. www.gaybombay.com

Gay Delhi Horoscopes, events, news and reviews in Delhi. www.members.tripod.com/gaydelhi

Humrahi Forum for gay men in Delhi. www.geocities.com/WestHollywood/Heights/7258

Humsafar Support group in Mumbai with a focus on health issues. www.humsafar.org

Sahodaran Social groups and discussions, yoga and entertainment in Chennai. www.sahodaran.faithweb.com

DISABLED TRAVELLERS

Travelling in India can entail some fairly rigorous challenges, even for the able-bodied traveller – long bus trips in crowded vehicles between remote villages, the crush of people in larger towns and the steep staircases in some budget and mid-range hotels can test even the hardiest traveller. If you can't walk, these challenges are increased many-fold. Very few buildings have wheelchair access; toilets have certainly not been designed to accommodate wheelchairs; footpaths, where they exist (only in larger towns), are generally riddled with holes, littered with debris and packed with pedestrians, severely restricting mobility. However, seeing the way the mobility-impaired locals whizz through city traffic at breakneck speed in modified bicycles might even serve as inspiration! If your mobility is restricted you will need a strong, able-bodied companion to accompany you, and it would be well worth considering hiring a private vehicle and driver.

Organisations that may be able to assist with information on travel practicalities in India for disabled people include:

The Royal Association for Disability and Rehabilitation (RADAR; ☎ 020-7250 3222, fax 250 0212, ⓔ radar@radar.org.uk) 12 City Forum, 250 City Rd, London EC1V 8AF, UK
Web site: www.radar.org.uk

Wheelchair Travel (☎ 1800-674 468, ⓔ sales@travelability.com), 29 Ranelagh Dr, Mount Eliza, VIC 3930, Australia
Web site: www.travelability.com

SENIOR TRAVELLERS

Unless your mobility or vision is severely impaired or you're seriously incapacitated in any other way, there is absolutely no reason why your age should prevent you from considering India as a potential holiday destination.

It's worth keeping in mind that travelling in India can be downright exhausting (even for the most effervescent young traveller), so try not to cram too much sightseeing into a day. In fact, it's not a bad idea to set aside several intermittent days devoted purely to doing absolutely nothing – a tremendous way to recharge your batteries.

If you like your creature comforts, opt for top-end or mid-range hotels (although some mid-range places are far from luxurious) and consider incorporating some organised tours into your trip (see regional chapters for details). Many senior travellers hire a car and driver, which allows greater flexibility (and comfort) in moving around than does public transport (see Car in the Getting Around chapter).

No matter what you plan to do in India, discuss your proposed trip with your local GP (see also Health earlier in this chapter).

TRAVEL WITH CHILDREN

India is a very child-friendly destination – not so much because of the facilities available for kids, but rather in the way children are accepted. Indeed, children can often enhance your encounters with local people, as they possess little of the self-consciousness and sense of the cultural differences that can inhibit interaction between adults.

Being a family-oriented society, children are heartily welcomed at most hotels and restaurants. A number of hotels have 'family rooms' or will happily provide an extra bed. Some upmarket hotels also offer babysitting services.

When it comes to meals, although few restaurants offer a special children's menu, many will happily whip up simple requests. Staff don't usually get snooty if your little angels treat the dining area a bit like a playroom (please take the initiative to ensure they don't ruin it for other diners, though).

It's worth bringing along some favourite books, toys and hand-held video games to keep the children occupied when you need some quiet time. If you're staying in a hotel with cable TV, there are several English-language children's channels, including the Cartoon Network.

Despite the acceptance of children, travelling with kids in India can be hard work and, ideally, the burden needs to be shared between two adults. Although caution should be exercised at all times, be especially careful near roads, as Indian traffic can be erratic, even in smaller towns. Any long-distance road travel undertaken should include adequate stops, as rough road conditions can make travel more tiring than usual, especially for little ones. Train is usually a more comfortable mode of travel, especially for long trips. Remember to bring enough sunscreen and a wide-brimmed hat, as the midday sun can really pack a punch (even during winter). Always carry sufficient drinking water.

Standard baby products such as nappies (diapers) are available in big cities and even in smaller towns; the larger cities often stock some Western brands too, but they can be expensive. To give you an idea of costs, Nestlé baby food costs Rs 77 (400g), locally made nappies are Rs 160 (pack of 10), and Lactogen milk powder is Rs 236 (1kg tin). It's wise to bring from home any special items such as medication and baby food if your child is fussy, just in case you can't locate them in India or are visiting islands like Lakshadweep, where few baby products are for sale. Travellers have also recommended that parents bring a washable changing mat, which comes in handy for covering dirty surfaces.

For details about attractions that may appeal to children (such as zoos, amusement parks and sound-and-light shows) see the regional chapters.

See Health earlier in this chapter for important tips, and get hold of a copy of Lonely Planet's *Travel with Children* by Maureen Wheeler. A good Web site for a personal account of travelling in India with children is www.southwest.com.au/~lockley. Lonely Planet's Thorn Tree Web site (www.lonelyplanet.com.au) has a subdirectory on travelling with children.

DANGERS & ANNOYANCES

Although we provide warnings about current scams and other potential dangers in this section, there's no need to be suspicious to the point of paranoia. We certainly don't intend to paint a negative picture of India or its people. Like anywhere else, common sense and reasonable caution are your best weapons against theft or worse. The tips we offer are intended to alert you to possible risks in India, most of which are based on travellers' reports. During your trip, it's worth taking the time to chat with other travellers, hotel staff and tour operators in order to stay abreast of the latest potential hazards.

Theft

Never leave those most important valuables (passport, tickets, money) in your room; they should be with you at all times (see Security under Money earlier in this chapter). On trains, keep your gear near you; padlocking a bag to a luggage rack can be useful, and some of the newer trains have loops under the seats that you can chain things to. Never walk around with valuables casually slung over your shoulder. Take extra care on crowded public transport.

Thieves are particularly prevalent on train routes where there are lots of tourists. The Delhi to Agra *Shatabdi Express* service is particularly notorious; no matter which train you are travelling on exercise caution at all times. Train departure time, when the confusion and crowds are at their worst, is the time to be most careful. In one ploy, just as the train is about to leave, you are distracted by someone while their accomplice is stealing your bag from by your feet. Airports are another place to be careful, especially if arriving in the middle of the night when you are unlikely to be at your most alert.

Be Cautious, Not Paranoid

Although this book alerts you to the latest scams experienced by fellow travellers, it would be a real shame if an overriding preoccupation with the potential problems prevented you from participating in activities and meeting Indian people.

A regrettable consequence of touts and others who pester tourists is that many paranoid foreigners are getting a reputation for rudeness towards genuinely friendly Indian people, especially in places like Delhi and parts of Rajasthan.

Remember, India is renowned for its hospitality to visitors, so don't go jeopardising potential friendships by prematurely jumping to the conclusion that *everyone* is out to get you. They're not.

From time to time there are also drugging episodes. Travellers meet somebody on a train or bus or in a town, start talking and are then offered a chai or something similar. Hours later the traveller wakes up with a headache and all their gear gone, the tea having been full of sleeping pills. Be cautious about accepting any drinks or food from strangers, particularly if you're on your own.

Beware, also, of your fellow travellers. Unhappily, there are more than a few backpackers who make their money go a little bit further by helping themselves to other people's.

Keep in mind that backpacks are very easy to rifle through. Never leave valuables in them, especially during flights. Remember also that something may be of little or no value to a thief (eg, film), but to lose it would be a real heartbreak to you.

A good travel insurance policy is essential. If you do have something stolen, you're going to have to report it to the police. You'll also need a statement proving you have done so if you want to make an insurance claim. Insurance companies, despite their rosy promises of full protection and speedy settlement of claims, are just as disbelieving as the Indian police and will often try to avoid paying out on a baggage claim. Note that some policies specify that you must report an item stolen to the police within a certain amount of time after you observe that it is missing.

Travellers Cheques If you're unlucky enough to have things stolen, some precautions can ease the pain. All travellers cheques are replaceable, although this does you little immediate good if you have to go home and apply to your bank. What you want is instant replacement. Furthermore, what do you do if you lose your cheques and money and have a day or more to travel to the replacement office? The answer is to keep an emergency cash stash in a totally separate place. In that same place you should keep a record of the cheque's serial numbers, proof of purchase slips, encashment vouchers and your passport number.

AmEx and others tend to make considerable noise about 'instant replacement' of their cheques but a lot of people find out, to their cost, that without a number of precautions 'instantly' can take longer than you think. If you don't have the receipt you were given when you bought the cheques, rapid replacement will be difficult. Obviously the receipt should be kept separate from the cheques, and a photocopy in yet another location doesn't hurt either.

To replace lost AmEx travellers cheques you need a photocopy of the police report and one photo, as well as the proof-of-purchase slip and the numbers of the missing cheques. If you don't have the latter they will contact the place where you bought them. If you've had the lot stolen, AmEx is empowered to give you limited funds while all this is going on. For lost or stolen cheques, it has a 24-hour number in Delhi (☎ 011-6145151) which you must ring within 24 hours of the theft.

Holi Festival

The Hindu festival of Holi (see Public Holidays & Special Events later in this chapter) isn't dubbed the 'Festival of Colours' for nothing. Merrymakers stock up on water and coloured *gulal* (powder) and proceed to douse anything that moves (pedestrians, buses, rickshaws…good god, even the holy cow gets walloped!). This is your golden opportunity to wear that putrid shirt grandma gave you last Christmas and watch it blossom into a psychedelic fashion statement with every successful gulal missile.

Although it's mostly good fun, unfortunately some revellers can go too far. Some travellers have been hit with toxic substances mixed in water, leaving them with painful and disfiguring scars. There is also an unwritten tradition of guzzling alcohol and consuming cannabis-derived bhang in the form of lassis, pakoras and cookies during Holi. Female travellers have reported being groped by spaced out blokes – particularly in the tourist traps such as Rajasthan. It's highly advisable for women to avoid venturing onto the streets alone.

Contaminated Food & Drink

Sometimes microbes aren't the sole risk: in Rajasthan and other places bhang lassis can pack more of a punch than the hapless traveller would expect.

There have been reports that some private clinics have provided more treatment than is necessary for stomach upsets in order to procure larger medical insurance claims – get several opinions where possible. Worse still, a serious food scare broke out in northern India in 1998, principally in Agra and Varanasi, when numerous travellers became sick and two died after eating at local establishments (see the boxed text 'Diarrhoea with Your Meal, Sir?' under Agra in the Uttar Pradesh & Uttaranchal chapter).

Water can also be a potential problem. Always ensure the seal is intact on bought mineral water and also check that the bottom of the bottle has not been tampered with. A traveller has reported that he was sold drugged mineral water. Crush plastic bottles after use to eradicate the possibility of them being resold with contaminated water. Better still, bring along water-purification tablets to avoid adding to India's alarming waste plastic problem (see Responsible Tourism and Health earlier in this chapter).

Beware of Those Bhang Lassis!

Although rarely printed in menus, some restaurants in certain parts of India (predominantly the tourist hot spots such as Rajasthan) clandestinely whip up bhang lassi, a yogurt and iced-water beverage laced with bhang, a derivative of marijuana. Usually called 'special lassi', this often potent concoction does not agree with everyone. Some travellers have been stuck in bed for several miserable days after drinking it; others have been robbed while lying in a state of delirium.

Risky Regions

In the past few years 17 foreigners have vanished or been murdered in the Kullu region. You're advised to trek in an organised group and steer clear of drugs (see Legal Matters later in this chapter). Trekkers should also make a point of telling people where they are going and when they will be back (see the boxed text 'Warning – Fatal Vacations' in the Himachal Pradesh chapter).

Some sensitive border areas, particularly strife-torn Jammu and Kashmir, are subject to terrorist activities including kidnappings. Although you may be cajoled by smooth-talking touts trying to get you to these areas (especially in Delhi), seek the latest advice from your embassy.

Racism

It's not unusual for black travellers to encounter outright racism in India. Speak to African students in India and you'll often hear about racist attitudes towards them, ranging from name-calling to being refused admission to certain restaurants and nightclubs.

Although skin colour is not always related to caste in India, lighter shades of brown are considered more attractive than dark skin – just have a look at the matrimonial pages in Indian newspapers and you'll see that being 'fair' is often a prerequisite for a potential spouse.

Although not all black travellers encounter racism during their time in India, at the very least they should be prepared for even more incessant (often disapproving) stares than lighter-skinned travellers.

Other Important Warnings

Several women have reported being molested by masseurs and other therapists in McLeod Ganj (Himachal Pradesh). No matter where you are, it's always wise to check the reputation of any teacher or therapist before going along to a solo session. If at any time you feel uneasy, simply leave.

Many travellers have reported being hoodwinked by fake gurus, sometimes resulting in theft, injury or worse (see the boxed text 'Gurus, Ashrams & Your Spiritual Journey' under Courses later in this chapter).

For important information about current cons, including notorious gem rackets, see the boxed text 'Travellers Beware!' under Shopping later in this chapter. The boxed text 'Choose Carefully' under Activities later in this chapter has tips on assessing adventure activity operators. Meanwhile, Touts under Accommodation later in this chapter has details about the hotel commission racket.

Indian beaches can have dangerous rips and currents and many people drown on them each year. Some of the more popular beach destinations may have lifeguards or signs warning of dangers, but many do not. Exercise caution and always check locally before swimming anywhere in the sea. Remember, no matter what you do, if in doubt, ask. If swimming in Puri, currents can be treacherous, so ask a lifeguard for help (see Puri in the Orissa chapter).

For information about rebel movements and bandhs (strikes) in the north-eastern region, see that chapter.

If you're travelling in cool, mountainous areas, be aware of carbon monoxide poisoning (see the boxed text below).

In Varanasi you'll notice 'missing persons' posters around town; see Dangers & Annoyances under Varanasi.

EMERGENCIES

Throughout many parts of India, local emergency numbers are as follows. However, if you are in a major predicament it's wise to contact your country's embassy (see Legal Matters).

Ambulance	☎ 102
Fire	☎ 101
Police	☎ 100

Carbon Monoxide Poisoning

Fires – charcoal burners in particular – are not recommended as a means of heating in hotel rooms because a number of deaths from carbon monoxide poisoning occur each year.

If you're cold, and unsure of the ventilation in the room, take a tip from trekkers who fill their drinking bottles with boiling water at night to use as a hot-water bottle (covered with a sock to prevent burning). In the morning, the water can be drunk because it's been purified. Some hotels even provide hot-water bottles. At all costs, *never* use a charcoal burner.

LEGAL MATTERS

If you find yourself in a sticky legal predicament, immediately contact your embassy (see Embassies & Consulates earlier in this chapter). Foreign travellers are subject to Indian laws and in the Indian justice system it can often seem that the burden of proof is on the accused.

You should carry your passport at all times and the less you have to do with local police the better.

Drugs

India has long been known for its smorgasbord of illegal drugs (mostly grass and hashish), but would-be users should be aware of the severe risks. Apart from opening yourself up to being taken advantage of, the penalties for possession, use and trafficking in illegal drugs are enforced and Westerners have been jailed. If convicted on a drugs-related charge, sentences are a *minimum* of 10 years for trafficking and at least a year for possession. In addition, there's usually a hefty monetary fine.

In Goa the police have taken a tough anti-drugs line. A special court, the Narcotic Drugs and Psychotropic Substances Court, with its own judge, has been established expressly to try drug offences. It seems as though the prevailing attitude is 'if in doubt convict' on the basis that the accused can always appeal to a higher court if they wish to do so. Court appearances can be slow – in early 2000 there were an estimated 25 million cases waiting to be heard in courts around India!

Smoking

In February 2001 the Indian government decided it would ban smoking in public places and prohibit all forms of tobacco advertising. The ban will not cover snuff and chewing tobacco, which account for the bulk of tobacco consumption in India. However, it's hard to see how they're going to enforce this law – first-time transgressors face a Rs 100 fine.

BUSINESS HOURS

Official business hours are generally 9.30 am to 5.30 pm Monday to Friday. Unofficially they tend to be more like 10 am to 5 pm. Government offices in particular seem to have lengthy lunch hours, which are sacrosanct and can last from noon to late into the afternoon.

Most banks are open 10 am to 2 pm on weekdays, and 10 am to noon on Saturday – there are variations, so it pays to check. Travellers cheque transactions usually cease 30 minutes before the official bank closing time. In some tourist centres there may be foreign exchange offices that stay open longer (eg, Thomas Cook is open 9.30 am to 6 pm Monday to Saturday).

In the state capitals, the main post office is generally open from 10 am to 5 pm weekdays and on Saturday morning. Many public institutions such as museums and galleries close at least one day during the week (see regional chapters for details).

Shop hours vary from state to state, but most tend to open from around 10 am to late afternoon daily except Sunday. It's wise to check locally so you don't leave all your shopping to the last day of your stay only to find that's the day they're closed!

PUBLIC HOLIDAYS & SPECIAL EVENTS

Rich in religions and traditions, India has scores of vibrant holidays and festivals. Many festivals occur during *purnima* (full moon), which is considered to be traditionally auspicious. Some Web sites pertaining to festivals in India include: www.hindunet.org/festivals and www.indiatimes.com (go to festivals under arts).

The 'wedding season' generally falls between the cooler months of November and March (although dates still revolve around auspicious dates set by astrologers). If you visit during this period, you're likely to see at least one wedding procession on the street – a merry mix of singing, dancing and a loud brass band.

Most holidays and festivals follow either the Indian lunar calendar (a complex system determined chiefly by astrologers) or the Islamic calendar (which falls about 11 days earlier each year; 12 days earlier in leap years), and therefore changes from year to year according to the Gregorian calendar.

The India-wide holidays and festivals listed below are arranged according to the Indian lunar (and Gregorian) calendar which starts in Chaitra (March or April) – contact local tourist offices for the exact dates (especially for Muslim festivals, which have particularly variable dates). Regional festivals are marked on the map at the start of each regional chapter.

Chaitra (Mar/Apr)

Mahavir Jayanti This Jain festival commemorates the birth of Mahavira, the founder of Jainism.

Ramanavami Hindu temples all over India celebrate the birth of Rama. In the week leading up to Ramanavami, the Ramayana is widely read and performed.

Easter This Christian holiday marks the crucifixion and resurrection of Christ.

Vaisakha (Apr/May)

Muharram This 10-day Muslim festival commemorates the martyrdom of Mohammed's grandson, Imam Hussain.

Buddha Jayanti This 'triple blessed festival' falls on the full moon (usually in May, sometimes in late April or early June) and celebrates Buddha's birth, enlightenment and attainment of nirvana. Processions of monks carrying sacred scriptures pass through the streets of Gangtok (Sikkim) and other towns.

Jyaistha (May/June)

Milad-un-Nabi This Muslim festival celebrates the birth of Mohammed.

Asadha (June/July)

Rath Yatra (Car Festival) Hindu Lord Jagannath's great temple chariot makes its stately journey from his temple in Puri, Orissa, during this festival. Similar festivals take place in other locations, particularly in the Dravidian south.

Sravana (July/Aug)

Naag Panchami This Hindu festival is dedicated to Ananta, the serpent upon whose coils Vishnu rested between universes. Offerings are made to snake images and snake charmers do a roaring trade. Snakes are supposed to have power over the monsoon rainfall and keep evil from homes.

Raksha Bandhan (Narial Purnima) On the full-moon day girls fix amulets known as *rakhis* to their brothers' (not necessarily blood related) wrists to protect them in the coming year. The brothers reciprocate with gifts. Some people also worship the Vedic sea-god deity Varuna.

Bhadra (Aug/Sept)

Independence Day This public holiday on 15 August celebrates the anniversary of India's independence from Britain in 1947. The prime minister delivers an address from the ramparts of Delhi's Red Fort.

Drukpa Teshi This festival celebrates the first teaching given by Buddha.

Ganesh Chaturthi This joyful festival celebrates the birth of the popular elephant-headed god, Ganesh. It is widely celebrated across India, but with particular verve in Mumbai. Firecrackers explode at all hours and families buy clay idols of Ganesh, the god of good fortune. On the last day of the festival the idols are paraded through the streets before being ceremoniously dunked in a river, sea or tank.

Janmashthami The anniversary of Krishna's birth is celebrated with happy abandon – in tune with Krishna's own mischievous moods. Devotees fast all day until midnight and in Mathura (Krishna's birthplace) the festivities last for an entire month.

Shravan Purnima On this day of fasting, high-caste Hindus replace the sacred thread which they always wear looped over their left shoulder.

Pateti Parsis celebrate their new year at this time.

Asvina (Sept/Oct)

Dussehra This popular festival celebrates Durga's victory over the buffalo-headed demon Mahishasura. In many places it culminates with the burning of huge images of the demon king Ravana and his accomplices, symbolic of the triumph of good over evil. In Delhi it is known as Ram Lila (life story of Rama), with fireworks and re-enactments of the Ramayana, while in Mysore and Ahmedabad there are processions. In West Bengal the festival is known as Durga Puja and in Gujarat it's Navratri (Festival of Nine Nights).

Gandhi Jayanti This public holiday is a solemn celebration of Mohandas Gandhi's birth anniversary on 2 October with prayer meetings at the Raj Ghat in Delhi where he was cremated.

Kartika (Oct/Nov)

Diwali (Deepavali) This is the happiest (and noisiest) festival of the Hindu calendar, celebrated on the 15th day of Kartika. At night decorative oil lamps are lit to show Rama the way home from his period of exile. The festival is also dedicated to Lakshmi (particularly in Mumbai) and to Kali (Kolkata). In all, the festival lasts five days. On the first day, houses are thoroughly cleaned and doorsteps are decorated with intricate *rangolis* (chalk designs). Day two is dedicated to Krishna's victory over Narakasura, a legendary tyrant. In the south on this day, a pre-dawn oil bath is followed by the donning of new clothes. Day three is spent worshipping Lakshmi, the goddess of wealth. Traditionally, this is the beginning of the new financial year for companies. Day four commemorates the visit of the friendly demon Bali whom Vishnu put in his place. On the fifth day men visit their sisters to have a tikka put on their forehead. Diwali has also become the 'festival of sweets'. Giving sweets has become as much a part of the tradition as the lighting of oil lamps and firecrackers.

Govardhana Puja A Hindu festival dedicated to that holiest of animals, the cow.

Aghan (Nov/Dec)

Nanak Jayanti The birthday of Guru Nanak, the founder of Sikhism, is celebrated with prayer readings and processions.

Ramadan This 30-day dawn-to-dusk fast is the most auspicious Muslim festival. It was during this month that the Prophet Mohammed had the Quran revealed to him in Mecca. This festival generally occurs between November and December, but can also fall in early January.

Eid al-Fitr This is a day of feasting to celebrate the end of Ramadan.

Pausa (Dec/Jan)

Christmas Day Christians celebrate the anniversary of the birth of Christ on 25 December.

Magha (Jan/Feb)

Republic Day This public holiday on 26 January celebrates the anniversary of India's establishment as a republic in 1950; there are activities in all state capitals but most spectacularly in Delhi, where there is a colourful military parade along Rajpath. As part of the same celebration, three days later a Beating of the Retreat ceremony takes place near Delhi's Rashtrapati Bhavan, the residence of the Indian president.

Pongal This Tamil festival marks the end of the harvest season. It is observed on the first day of the Tamil month of Thai, which is in the middle of January. The festivities last four days and include such activities as the boiling-over of a pot of *pongal* (a mixture of rice, sugar, dhal and milk), symbolic of prosperity and abundance. On the third day, cattle are washed, decorated and even painted, and then fed the pongal.

Vasant Panchami It is traditional to dress in yellow to celebrate this Hindu festival, held on the 5th day of Magha. In some places, especially West Bengal, Saraswati, the goddess of learning, is honoured. Books, musical instruments and other related objects are placed in front of the goddess to receive her blessing.

Phalguna (Feb/Mar)

Holi This is one of the most exuberant Hindu festivals, when people celebrate the end of winter by throwing coloured water and *gulal* (powder) at one another. In tourist places it might be seen as an opportunity to take liberties with foreigners, especially women (see Dangers & Annoyances earlier in this chapter); don't wear good clothes on this day and be ready to duck. On the night before Holi, bonfires are built to symbolise the destruction of the evil demon Holika. It's mainly a northern festival; there is no real winter to end in the south so it is as not widespread there. In Barsana near Mathura, women not only douse men in coloured powder, they also get the pleasure of beating them with sticks, reliving the routing of the *gopas* by the *gopis* (milkmaids).

Shivaratri This day of Hindu fasting is dedicated to Shiva, who danced the *tandava* (cosmic dance) on this day. Temple processions are followed by the chanting of mantras and anointing of lingams.

Eid al-Zuhara This Muslim festival commemorates Abraham's attempt to sacrifice his son.

Losar Tibetan new year is a great time to be in McLeod Ganj in Himachal Pradesh – the Dalai Lama gives week-long teachings.

ACTIVITIES

Whether it's plodding through the desert atop a sleepy-eyed camel or swooshing down snowy mountains, India has no shortage of activities for both the adventurous and the not-so-adventurous. The following offers a sample of possibilities – see the regional chapters for more details (and for more gentle pastimes such as ten-pin bowling, billiards and boating).

Camel, Horse & Jeep Safaris

Camel safaris have taken off big time in Rajasthan, especially around Jaisalmer. You can opt for an afternoon trot or take longer jaunts lasting a few days or longer. If Jaisalmer is too much of a scene, you could try Bikaner or Shekhawati. Camel safaris are also possible through the dunes at Hunder (Ladakh) on native double-humped Bactrian camels.

Short or long horse safaris are offered in many tourist tramping grounds, particularly Rajasthan, the hill stations and the Himalaya. You may be required to bring your own riding boots (inquire when booking).

There are plenty of jeep safaris around, especially in tourist-laden Rajasthan; one-day jeep village safaris to the Bishnoi villages around Jodhpur are especially popular.

Cycling & Motorcycling

There are some excellent organised bicycle or motorcycle tours, or you can arrange your own rental (usually available on an hourly, daily or weekly basis). For more details, see Bicycle and Motorcycle in the Getting Around chapter.

Diving & Water Sports

There are dive schools in Goa, Lakshadweep and the Andaman Islands (see the boxed text 'Responsible Diving' under Responsible Tourism earlier in this chapter).

In Goa there are several beach operators offering water sports such as waterskiing, parasailing, windsurfing and jet-skiing.

Looking for Mr Good Guide

If you fancy a ramble around the hills or elsewhere, strolls lasting a couple of hours can usually be completed without a guide. Other walks can be more challenging and may take a full day or even longer – these walks require local experience and knowledge and are best undertaken with the help of a professional guide. The problem is, how do you know a good guide when you see one? Well, there is no sure-fire answer. Some places in India have a flood of touts claiming to be professional guides. Certainly some guides who offer their services are highly professional and will probably make your outing far more rewarding than if you did it independently. Others may have little knowledge and will take you for a ride rather than a walk.

The first thing to do is ascertain exactly what type of walk you wish to do as well as your capability. Are you looking for something leisurely or strenuous? Do you want to return before nightfall or are you keen to get out there for a few days?

Seek specific recommendations from other travellers, and if you are engaged in negotiations with a potential guide, the following questions are worth asking:

- Do you have any written testimonials? (These, of course, are easy to fabricate but they can give you a sense of who you may be talking with.)
- Can you give us an idea of the route we'll take, including the distances, grades and the type of terrain involved?
- Can you identify any potential obstacles we may encounter: river crossings, wild animals etc?
- If we are walking for more than a day, how many hours a day will we need to walk to complete the trek?
- If we are trekking into tribal areas do you speak the language? Know the customs?
- What time can we expect to return?
- Do you have a torch (flashlight) and first-aid equipment? (Trekkers should always have their own, but a good guide will also have some.)
- If the guide (or the booking company) is going to supply camping equipment, can we inspect the equipment before we agree to the deal?
- If the trek includes a cook, what's on the menu and who supplies the food?
- Will there be places along the way to replenish water?
- Is the price quoted per person, group, day, hour or some combination of these? Does it include meals?

It is preferable to travel with even a small group rather than setting out alone with a guide, and of course you should ensure that you have adequate clothing (including footwear) for variable weather. It's also wise to let someone know where you will be and when you expect to return. See also the boxed text 'Responsible Trekking' earlier in this chapter.

Always thoroughly question your potential guide.

Kayaking & River Rafting

India's mountain rivers are ideal for rafting, with grades of white-water to suit all levels of experience. In Himachal Pradesh, rafting is possible on the Beas, Ganges, Indus, Spiti and Kanskar Rivers, all of which are accessible from Manali. In Uttaranchal, Rishikesh is the starting point for one-day river rafting trips on the Ganges. River rafting expeditions are also possible in other regions, including the Indus and Zanskar Rivers in Ladakh and Zanskar, on the Teesta River in the West Bengal hills and Sikkim and in the national parks of the north-eastern region.

Mountaineering

Mountaineering expeditions interested in climbing peaks over 6000m need to obtain clearance from the International Mountaineering Foundation (IMF; ☎ 011-4677935, fax 6883412), Benito Juarez Marg, Anand Niketan, New Delhi 110021.

For information on mountaineering expeditions to less lofty heights in Uttaranchal, contact the Trekking & Mountaineering division of the Garhwal Mandal Vikas Nigam (GMVN), Kailash Gate, Muni-ki-Reti, Rishikesh (☎ 0135-431793, fax 430372). It offers an extensive range of organised trips and can also arrange guides, porters and equipment for independent groups.

In Himachal Pradesh, mountaineering trips can be organised by tour operators in Manali or through the Institute of Mountaineering and Allied Sports in Manali (☎ 01902-52342) or Bharmour (☎ 01090-25036). Also useful is the Regional Mountaineering Centre in McLeod Ganj (☎ 01892-21787).

Travel agencies in Gangtok (Sikkim) can help with mountaineering expeditions to Kanchenjunga.

See the boxed text 'Responsible Trekking' earlier in this chapter for advice.

Paragliding, Hang-Gliding & Joy Rides

To get a bird's-eye view of Udhagamandalam (Ooty), you could go paragliding (using a parachute instead of a hang-glider) or take a joy ride in a microlight.

Paragliding is also available from several sites in Maharashtra and Goa, including near Lonavla, between Mumbai and Pune. There is also tandem paragliding and courses from the cliff-top at Arambol Beach in Goa.

For a breathtaking view of the Himalaya, tandem hang-gliding and paragliding is possible at Solang Nullah, just north of Manali, and at Billing, in the hills north-east of Mandi. Himachal Tourism conducts the Himalayan Hang-Gliding Rally in Billing every May.

Excursion flights usually operate from February to June and September to November. Unfortunately, safety standards are variable (see the boxed text 'Choose Carefully' on the next page). Reliable organisations include North Face Adventure Tours (☎ 01902-52441) and Himalayan Journeys (☎ 01902-52365) in Manali. Based in Delhi, Himalayan Adventure Club International (☎ 011-7178870) E15, Plot No 144–145, Sector 8, Rohini, offers excursion flights and training courses at various locations throughout the Himalaya. Nainital in Uttaranchal is also emerging as a future paragliding destination.

Sikkim offers all sorts of adventures, ranging from a yak ride around Tsomgo (Changu) Lake to a helicopter joy ride over West Sikkim.

Skiing

India's premier ski resort is at Auli, near Joshimath in Uttaranchal. The GMVN, 74/1 Rajpur Rd, Dehra Dun (☎ 0135-46817, fax 744408) runs very competitively priced ski packages that include ski hire, tows, lessons and accommodation. The Auli season runs from early January to late March.

There are less-developed resorts in Himachal Pradesh at Solang Nullah, north of Manali, and Kufri and Narkanda, near Shimla. Skiing packages at both resorts are run by Himachal Tourism, which has conveniently located offices in Shimla (☎ 0177-214311, fax 212591) and Manali (☎ 01902-52175). Most travellers report that the residential skiing packages to Solang Nullah offered by private tour operators in Manali are superior.

Trekking

With some of the highest mountains in the world, it's hardly surprising that India has some breathtaking trekking regions, although the trekking industry is not as developed as it is in Nepal. The main areas are Uttaranchal, Himachal Pradesh, Ladakh, the Darjeeling area (West Bengal) and Sikkim and the north-eastern region.

Trekking advice and organised trekking packages in Uttaranchal are provided by the GMVN (☎ 0135-431793, fax 430372) in Rishikesh and the Kumaon Mandal Vikas Nigam (KMVN; ☎ 05942-36209) in Nainital. In Himachal Pradesh, try the Institute of Mountaineering & Allied Sports in Manali (☎ 01902-52342) or contact the Regional Mountaineering Centre in McLeod Ganj (☎ 01892-21787). For extra detail, see Lonely Planet's *Trekking in the Indian Himalaya*, and the boxed text 'Responsible Trekking' earlier in this chapter.

Wildlife Safaris

Various major wildlife sanctuaries, including Rajaji National Park and Corbett Tiger

Reserve in Uttaranchal, offer sensational elephant-back safaris, which are generally a better way of getting closer to wildlife than passenger jeeps. Other places where short elephant safaris are possible include the Jaldhapara Wildlife Sanctuary in West Bengal, as well as at some of Madhya Pradesh's national parks.

Wildlife safaris by jeep are more widely available and although not as romantic as those on a pachyderm, are still worthwhile. Options include Rajasthan's Sariska and Ranthambhore National Parks, Gujarat's Sasan Gir Wildlife Sanctuary, the Kanha and Bandhavgarh National Parks in Madhya Pradesh and Kaziranga National Park in Assam.

Adventure Tour Operators

Local tour operators are listed in regional chapters. The following trek and tour outfits are all based in Delhi:

Amber Tours Pty Ltd (☎ 011-3312773, fax 3312984) Flat 2, Dwarka Sadan, 42 C-Block, Connaught Place. Offers yoga and mystic tours, river rafting, trekking, fishing for mahseer, and private jet or helicopter flights over the Himalaya.

Himalayan River Runners (☎ 011-615736) 188A Jor Bagh. Has a range of rafting expeditions in the western Himalaya.

Mercury Himalayan Explorations (☎ 011-312008) Jeevan Tara Bldg, Parliament St. Specialises in organised treks in the western Himalaya.

Shikhar Travels (☎ 011-3312444, fax 3323660) S209 Competent House, 14 Middle Circle, Connaught Circus. Specialises in trekking and mountaineering tours and can also organise mountaineering expeditions for beginners.

World Expeditions (☎ 011-6983358, fax 698 3357) ground floor, MG Bhawan-1, 7 Local Shopping Centre, Madangir. Has operated world-class Himalayan tours and treks since 1975.

COURSES

You may like to combine your holiday with a course – the following are a smattering of possibilities offering a brief overview (see the regional chapters for more details).

Language

From February to December, the Landour Language School, near Mussoorie in Uttaranchal, offers three-month beginners' courses in Hindi, as well as more advanced courses. In Varanasi, Hindi courses are available at Bhasha Bharati (the length is flexible). At McLeod Ganj (Himachal Pradesh) it's possible to learn Tibetan either at the Library of Tibetan Works & Archives or from private teachers. Private Hindi lessons are also available. In Darjeeling, beginners' courses in Tibetan are available at the Manjushree Centre of Tibetan Culture. Davar's College in Mumbai offers courses in Hindi and Marathi.

Choose Carefully

While India has some world-class adventure activities on offer – and there are plenty of good, reputable and trustworthy operators around – it's worth noting that the level of experience and equipment available is not always up to scratch. When undertaking potentially dangerous sports and activities in India, whether it be paragliding in Himachal Pradesh or diving in Lakshadweep, you should always exercise good judgment (much the same as you would at home) and carefully scrutinise operators before committing yourself to their operation.

Over the years Lonely Planet has received numerous reports of dodgy operators taking naive tourists into dangerous situations, often resulting in serious injury and sometimes even in death. Always check safety equipment before you set out and make sure it is included in the price quoted. If you're not comfortable with the operator's standards, inform them; if they refuse to replace equipment or improve their standards refuse to use them and file a report with the local tourism authorities.

Once you have found an operator you are satisfied with, ensure you have adequate insurance should something go wrong; many travel insurance policies won't cover dangerous activities, including trekking!

Music & Dance

In Pushkar (Rajasthan) the Saraswati Music School offers lessons in classical tabla (drums) and singing. In the same state, at Udaipur, you can take sitar, tabla and flute lessons at Prem Musical Instruments.

In Varanasi, the Triveni Music Centre provides lessons for most classical Indian instruments including the tabla and sitar.

Lessons in traditional Indian musical instruments are also available in Tamil Nadu, at a site just 3km from Mamallapuram. In the same state, the Kuchipudi Art Academy in Chennai offers free lessons and accommodation to serious students of the traditional Kuchipudi dance form. Classical dance courses may also be available at Kalakshetra, also in Chennai (inquire in advance).

Cooking

Kali Travel Home conducts a two-week food and cultural tour in Kolkata, during which you see the city, dine at various restaurants and learn to cook Bengali food under the tutelage of local Bengali women. Shorter cooking courses are also possible.

In McLeod Ganj (Himachal Pradesh), Tibetan refugees offer private classes in Tibetan cooking, including lessons on how to make the perfect *momo* (dumpling).

Meditation, Reiki, Yoga & Philosophy

Most Indian cities and towns have at least one place where you can pursue courses in meditation, yoga and philosophy. Ask at the tourist office or your hotel or keep an eye on the local newspapers.

Courses in aspects of Tibetan Buddhism and culture, including meditation and Buddhist philosophy, are offered in McLeod Ganj, Darjeeling, Choglamsar (near Leh) and Leh. McLeod Ganj (Himachal Pradesh) also has a formal study centre for Indian Early Buddhism and there are various private centres for yoga, reiki and other alternative therapies.

Rishikesh in Uttaranchal is the undisputed yoga capital of India with literally dozens of ashrams and yoga centres offering courses in hatha and other disciplines of yoga. Many of the more reputable centres only accept long-term students and have strict rituals of daily prayer and meditation.

Yoga courses are also prolific in Varanasi. The Malaviya Bhavan at Benares Hindu University offers courses in yoga and Hindu philosophy. The International Yoga Clinic & Meditation Centre has also been strongly recommended. For the less committed, various places in the old city (including hotels) run yoga classes.

In Maharasthra, there are yoga courses in Mumbai and Lonavla, as well as a Vipassana meditation course in Igatpuri.

Dozens of yoga, meditation and massage courses are available in Goa. In Bodhgaya (Bihar) you can also learn Vipassana meditation or go on a retreat. The Burmese Monastery here is also worth an inquiry, as its courses are popular with Westerners.

Arts & Crafts

There are scores of centres nationwide where you can learn everything from miniature

Gurus, Ashrams & Your Spiritual Journey

India has long attracted travellers from around the globe in search of spiritual guidance, including some who weren't actually aware that they were looking for it when they arrived. Travellers who come to India on a spiritual quest are many and varied and India offers an equally varied array of gurus and ashrams.

A guru is a spiritual guide. The word guru means 'the dispeller of darkness' or 'heavy with wisdom'. Most gurus live in an ashram, a 'place of striving', which is usually established when gurus stay in one place and disciples congregate around them. Many ashrams are the legacies of deceased gurus. The atmosphere surrounding the ashram can have a profound and deeply moving effect on visitors; however, some ashrams are more reputable than others.

Lonely Planet has received numerous reports from travellers who have been conned, drugged (then robbed) or worse by people falsely claiming to be gurus. While there are plenty of genuine gurus and ashrams, sadly, some self-styled spiritual impersonators are not as sincere in their motives: always exercise common sense and talk to locals and other travellers before rushing into a decision as to which guru and ashram is likely to best suit you. If you don't feel comfortable with a guru or ashram, don't stay. See also the boxed text 'Wolves in Sadhu's Clothing' in the Uttar Pradesh & Uttaranchal chapter.

Many ashrams have codes of conduct; most are vegetarian and you may also be asked to abstain from eggs, tobacco and alcohol. Some ashrams may request that you wear white; others aren't so specific. Many ashrams don't require notice of your arrival, but you should check in advance. Keep in mind that some gurus move from place to place without notice, so check to avoid disappointment.

painting to pottery. Ask at the tourist office or your hotel, and look in local newspapers and magazines. For traditional Tibetan woodcarving, there's the Tibetan Refugee Self-Help Centre in Darjeeling (West Bengal).

VOLUNTEER WORK

Numerous charities and international aid agencies have branches in India and, although they're mostly staffed by locals, there are some opportunities for foreigners. Don't assume it's your right to volunteer your services at any place. You are more use to the charity concerned if you write in advance and, if you're needed, if you stay for long enough to be of help. A week on a hospital ward may go a little way towards salving your own conscience, but you may actually do not much more than get in the way of the people who work there long term.

Flexibility in what you are prepared to do is also vital. Some charities are inundated with foreign volunteers to help babies in an orphanage for instance, but few are willing to work with adults with physical or mental disabilities.

If you want to help clean up India and meet local volunteers as part of the Clean Up the World program (an annual litter clearing project), keep your eye on its Web site (www.cleanuptheworld.org.au).

Overseas Volunteer Placement Agencies

For long-term posts, the following organisations may be able to help or offer advice and further contacts:

Australian Volunteers International (☎ 03-9279 1788, fax 9419 4280, ⓔ ozvol@ozvol.org.au) PO Box 350, Fitzroy VIC 3065, Australia
Web site: www.ozvol.org.au

Co-ordinating Committee for International Voluntary Service (☎ 01 45 68 49 36, fax 01 42 73 05 21, ⓔ ccivs@zcc.net) Unesco House, 1 Rue Miollis, 75732 Paris Cedex 15, France
Web site: www.unesco.org/ccivs

Global Volunteers (☎ 800-487 1073, fax 651-482 0915, ⓔ info@globalvolunteers.org) 375 East Little Canada Rd, St Paul, MN 55117-1627, USA
Web site: www.globalvolunteers.org

Voluntary Service Overseas (VSO; ☎ 020-8780 7200, fax 8780 7300, ⓔ enquiry@vso.org.uk) 317 Putney Bridge Rd, London SW15 2PN, UK
Web site: www.vso.org.uk

Volunteer Work Information Service (VWIS; ☎/fax 1273 470015, ⓔ info@workingabroad.com) PO Box 2759, Lewes, BN7 1WU, East Sussex, UK
Web site: www.workingabroad.com

Aid Programs in India

Following are some of the programs operating in India that may have opportunities for volunteers. It's best to contact them in advance and discuss volunteer possibilities, rather than just turning up on their doorstep expecting to be automatically offered work.

Bihar In Bodhgaya, the Sujata Charitable Society (☎ 0631-400463) runs a school that provides free education to illiterate children and adults. There are also plans to make free medical services available for people in Bihar. In Bodhgaya, the Samanway Ashram may offer voluntary work on social development projects in the area.

Goa The Goa Foundation (☎ 0832-263305) c/o Other India Bookstore, Mapusa, Goa 403507, is Goa's main environmental group. It runs some voluntary programs such as clean-ups – inquire for further details.

Himachal Pradesh Long-term visitors at McLeod Ganj are always welcome to teach English and computer skills to newly arrived Tibetan refugees. Ask at the Library of Tibetan Works and Archives in Gangchen Kyishong or check out local noticeboards and the classified section of *Contact* magazine. Volunteers are also considered at the Tibetan Youth Congress, Tibetan Welfare Office, Tibetan Children's Village, Tibetan Women's Association and Refugee Reception Centre. Medical practitioners may be able to volunteer at the Delek Hospital (☎ 01892-22053).

Ladakh Mahabodhi International Meditation Centre (PO Box 22, Leh, Ladakh, 194101, Jammu and Kashmir) operates a residential school for poor children and accepts volunteers to assist with teaching and secretarial work. Contact the centre at the above address, or through its head office (☎ 0812-260684, fax 260292) at 14 Kalidas Rd, Gandhinagar, Bangalore 560009.

Organisations in Leh that are involved in educational and environmental aid are the Ladakh Ecological Development Group (LEDeG), the Child Welfare Society and the Student's Educational & Cultural Movement of Ladakh (Secmol).

Madhya Pradesh Voluntary work may be possible at the Global Village Development Trust in Khajuraho (see Conservation Contacts under Ecology & Environment in the Facts about India chapter).

Mumbai The Concern India Foundation (☎ 022-2029707, fax 2043625, e concern@vsnl.com), Ador House 6K Dubash Marg, Mumbai 400001, is a charitable trust that supports development-oriented organisations working with vulnerable members of the community. It doesn't engage in fieldwork; its speciality is networking. It is happy to field requests from travellers who wish to offer their time and will try to match your skills or interests with particular projects. Web site: www.concernindia.org

Child Relief and You (CRY; ☎ 022-306651, e crymum@bom3.vsnl.net.in), 189A Anand Estate, Sane Guruji Marg, is an independent trust organising fundraising for more than 300 projects India-wide, including a dozen projects in Mumbai helping deprived children.

The Vatsalya Foundation, Anand Niketan, King George V Memorial, Dr E Moses Rd, Mahalaxmi, Mumbai 400011, works with Mumbai's street children, focusing on rehabilitation and reintroducing them to mainstream society. For quicker communication, it can be contacted through the Concern India Foundation.

Rajasthan SOS Worldwide runs more than 30 programs across India. The society looks after orphaned, destitute and abandoned children, who are cared for by unmarried women, abandoned wives and widows. In Jaipur, SOS has a fine property surrounded by gardens and cares for more than 150 children and young adults. Volunteers are welcome at the centre to teach English, help the children with their homework and simply to join in their games. For more information contact SOS Children's Village (☎ 0141-202393, fax 200140), opposite Pital Factory, Jhotwara Rd, Jaipur 302016.

The Urmul Trust provides primary health care and education to the people of remote villages in Rajasthan; raises awareness among the women of the desert of their rights and privileges in society; and promotes the handicrafts of rural artisans with its profits going directly back to them. There is volunteer work available in social welfare, teaching English, health care, and other projects. Even if you don't have skills in these areas, Urmul may have positions in implementation and overseeing of projects. Contact the secretary at the Urmul Trust (☎/fax 0151-523093), inside Urmul Dairy, Ganganagar Rd, Bikaner (next to the bus terminal).

Les Amis du Shekhawati is one of a number of charities whose aim is to safeguard and preserve India's crumbling architectural heritage – in this case the havelis and paintings of the Shekhawati region in Rajasthan. Ramesh Jangid, the president of the association, welcomes volunteers keen to preserve the paintings of Shekhawati and can be contacted at Ramesh Jangid's Tourist Pension (☎ 01594-24060, fax 24061) in Nawalgarh.

Help in Suffering (☎ 0141-760803, fax 761544, e hisjpr@datainfosys.net), an animal hospital based in Jaipur, is doing excellent work. It's funded by the World Society for the Protection of Animals (WSPA) and Animaux Secours, Arthaz, France. Qualified vets interested in volunteering should write to: Help in Suffering, Maharani Farm, Durgapura, Jaipur, 302018 Rajasthan.

Uttaranchal In the Garwhal region, the International Society For Alternative Medicine (ISAM; ☎ 0135-653709, e arawal@nde.vsnl.net.in), Rawal Nursing Home, 35/1 East Canal Rd, Dehra Dun, is a charitable organisation providing health care to disabled and impoverished local people, using alternative and traditional medicines. ISAM welcomes volunteers and can help arrange accommodation.

West Bengal & Kolkata Mother Teresa's Missionaries of Charity headquarters, the 'Motherhouse' (☎ 033-2447115), is at 54 AJC Bose Rd, Kolkata 700016. Volunteers can work in a number of homes including Nirmal Hriday (Home for the Dying), Prem Dan (for the sick and mentally ill) and Shishu Bhavan (the children's orphanage). There are also opportunities to work with the sisters in rural areas. If you're in Kolkata, you can visit the Motherhouse for placement information on Monday, Wednesday and Friday at 3 pm (double check in case these timings change). See the Kolkata chapter for background information about the late Mother Teresa.

For those with the time to give a medium to long-term commitment, especially if you have any medical background, there's Calcutta Rescue. Started in 1979 by Dr J Preger, and now encompassing several different clinics, Dr Jack's, as it affectionately known, caters to the medical, nutritional and educational needs of the destitute and socially disadvantaged of Kolkata and rural West Bengal. Postal inquiries should be directed to Calcutta Rescue, PO Box 9253, Middleton Row PO, Kolkata 700071. In Kolkata, you can visit the administrative office at 85 Collins St (☎/fax 033-2175675, 2461520, ⓔ calres@cal.vsnl.net.in).

The Calcutta Society for the Prevention of Cruelty to Animals (CSPCA) is doing a truly admirable job to help the animals of this city. Established in 1861, this organisation helps the many street dogs and other sick and injured animals of Kolkata. It desperately needs volunteers and donations. Anyone who loves animals is welcome to volunteer, but qualified vets are especially needed (a minimum of one month is requested). Donations can be forwarded to the CSPCA, 276BB Ganguly St, Kolkata 700012. Signing up as a life member costs Rs 1000. To arrange volunteer work, contact the president of the CSPCA (☎ 033-2370520 or ☎/fax 2365592, ⓔ bdhar@caltiger.com).

Volunteer work may be available at the following places in Darjeeling. The Nepali Girls' Social Service Centre (☎ 0354-2985), Gandhi Rd, undertakes projects to protect the environment, and to promote the empowerment of women, child survival and development. Volunteers are welcome on an informal basis to teach English, art or music.

Hayden Hall is a Christian-based organisation that can arrange volunteer work in medicine, teaching, handicrafts and counselling, but volunteers must be prepared to commit themselves for six months. For more information contact the staff (ⓔ hayden@cal.vsnl.net.in) at 42 Laden La Rd.

The Tibetan Refugee Self-Help Centre has openings for volunteer teachers (of children and adults), medical staff and geriatric and child-care workers. For more information, contact its head office (☎ 0354-52346) at 65 Gandhi Rd.

Film Studios

Although film studios are not officially open to volunteers, a couple of travellers have reported being 'spotted' while visiting and subsequently asked to play a small role in a Bollywood film. The following are contacts for some of the major film studios in Mumbai, but official permission *must* be obtained before you can even set foot in one, let alone hope to score a part as an extra (don't set your heart on getting a part as an extra, though, as opportunities are few and far between).

Film City (☎ 022-8401755, fax 8400734 ⓔ filmcityfilmcity@hotmail.com) Goregaon (East), Mumbai 400065

Kamal Amrohi Studio (☎ 022-8371160, fax 8371170, ⓔ mahal_pictures@hotmail.com) Mahal Pictures Pty Ltd, 6 Jogeshwari Vikhroli Link Road, Andheri (East), Mumbai 400093.

RK Studio (☎ 022-5580234, fax 5563533) Sion Trombay Rd, Chembur, Mumbai 400071

ACCOMMODATION

India has a mixed bag of places to stay, ranging from remarkably cheap (but very basic) guesthouses for shoestringers, to incredibly ritzy top-end hotels for those with cash to flash. Some hotels operate on a 24-hour system (ie, your time starts when you check in). Others have fixed check-out times (from an ungenerous 9 am to a more civilised 1 pm) – it pays to ask before checking in. Some hotels even offer a handy half-day rate – ideal for breaking long journeys.

Credit cards are accepted at most top-end hotels and a rapidly growing number of mid-range ones; however, very few budget hotels will take them. Some hotels may request an upfront payment based on your estimated length of stay. If your expenses don't match the prepaid amount you'll receive a refund at the time of check-out. You may be asked to sign a blank impression of your credit card, which will be reportedly destroyed when you pay your bill at the end of your stay. This should be avoided. If a hotel does demand an impression of your card you should refuse to sign it. If they still insist, then write in an amount that will be less than your estimated expenditure.

Although rare, some of the ultra-cheap, under-staffed lodgings refuse to accept foreigners because of the hassle of the foreign registration 'C forms' (these must be

Get to Know Your Bathroom

Certain terminology is commonly used in the places-to-stay sections throughout this book; private bathroom and shared bathroom. However, several other terms may be used throughout the country. 'Common bath', 'without bath' or 'shared bath' means communal bathroom facilities. 'Attached bath', 'private bath' or 'with bath' indicates that the room has its very own bathroom, which means you can belt out your favourite tune in the shower without being snickered at over the breakfast table.

'Running' or 'constant' water indicates that there is water available around the clock (although this is not always the case in reality). 'Bucket water' means that water is, as the name suggests, available in buckets. Many hotels only have running cold water in guest bathrooms but can provide hot water in buckets (sometimes only between certain hours and sometimes at a small charge).

Hotels that advertise 'room with shower' can sometimes be misleading. Even if a bathroom does indeed have a shower, it's a good idea to actually check that it works before accepting the room. Some hotels surreptitiously disconnect showers to save costs, while the showers at other places render a mere trickle of water.

A geyser is a small hot water tank, usually found in cheaper hotels. Some geysers need to be switched on an hour or so before use.

Regarding toilets, unless squat toilets are specifically mentioned in this book, bathrooms have sit-down flush toilets. Keep in mind that in North India some hoteliers refer to squat toilets as 'Indian-style' and sit-down flush toilets as 'Western-style'. In South India, squat toilets are often referred to as 'Indian' or 'floor' toilets, while the sit-down variety is commonly known as 'Western' or 'commode'. In some places you may come across the curious hybrid toilet, which is basically a sit-down flush toilet with footpads on the edge of the bowl! (See also Toilets earlier in this chapter.)

submitted to the local police station within 24 hours of a foreigner checking in).

During the peak tourist season and during some festivals, hotel tariffs can really shoot up and it can be difficult finding a bed, especially in tourist hot spots. Advance reservations are advisable. Although most prices quoted in this book are for single and double rooms, many hotels will put an extra bed in a room to make a triple for an extra 25%.

Cheap Hotels

India has no shortage of cheap hotels, ranging from squalid dives (but at rock-bottom prices), to well-kept mid-range places at pleasantly moderate charges. Many cheap hotels come with mosquito zappers or possibly even nets. Most rooms have ceiling fans but be careful when adjusting mosquito nets on your bed, as low ceilings mean low ceiling fans – a dangerous combination if the fan is spinning at full speed! Some mid-range hotels have 'air-cooled' rooms that are one step up from a ceiling fan and one step below air-con. An air-cooler is a large (usually notoriously noisy) fan built into a frame within a wall. However, as this is a water-filled cooling system, air-cooling is pretty ineffective in humid conditions, making air-con the best option for keeping cool.

Don't expect cheap hotels to be completely flawless – even if budget or mid-range hotels in this book are described as 'clean', they're unlikely to be absolutely spotless. Indeed, even in some respectable mid-range hotels, it's usual for rooms to have minor imperfections and in some places you may even find yourself sharing the room with cockroaches or other creepy crawlies.

Throughout India, you may hear locals categorise hotels as 'Western' or 'Indian'. The 'Indian' hotels are usually more modestly furnished and thus cheaper. Most also have squat toilets (not only because they are cost-effective, but also because they are generally considered to be more hygienic). 'Western' hotels invariably have a sit-down flush toilet and may be more fancy inside. However, don't instantly assume that the 'Western' hotels are necessarily superior; you can often find modern, well-maintained 'Indian' hotels and dishevelled, poorly run 'Western' hotels.

Some cheap hotels (particularly in parts of Rajasthan) allow guests to sleep on the rooftop (which resembles a large flat balcony) for a nominal charge. This should include a pillow, sheet or blanket, and use of a shared bathroom.

Some of the cheaper hotels in India lock their gates at night and remain unmanned on the outside, so let the appropriate staff member know if you intend coming back late.

It's worth making a mental note that some hotel rooms have a master switch on the *outside* of each room (usually near the door). If you return to your room to find that the lights, TV and geyser don't work, check that your master switch has not been turned off. If you make a hasty assumption that there's a general power cut, you'll be waiting an awfully long time to see the light.

Expensive Hotels

India boasts some exquisite hotels, from world-renowned hotel chains such as the Oberoi, Taj and Welcomgroup (affiliated to Sheraton); to lusciously romantic palace hotels in exotic settings. You'll generally only find top-end hotels in the bigger cities and major tourist centres.

The government-operated ITDC hotels can be found nationwide and often fall into the top-end price category. Although they're often cheaper than other upmarket hotels, most lack attention to detail and get poor reports from travellers.

If you're interested in staying at a top-end hotel, it's sometimes cheaper to book them through a travel agent at home.

Government Accommodation & Tourist Bungalows

Back in the days of the British Raj, a string of government-run accommodation units were set up with labels like Rest Houses, Dak Bungalows, Circuit Houses, PWD (Public Works Department) Bungalows, Forest Rest Houses and so on. Today, most of these are reserved for government officials, although in some places they may still be available for tourists (except Circuit Houses which are strictly for travelling VIPS).

'Tourist Bungalows' are usually run by the state government and often serve as replacements for the older (often decrepit) government-run accommodation. Their facilities and level of service vary enormously; the majority are below average. For shoestringers, some offer cheap dorm beds. Most have a restaurant (commonly called the 'dining hall') that generally has good food at reasonable prices. Some also have a nondescript bar. The local branch of the state government tourist office is often on the premises of these Tourist Bungalows.

Home-stays & Paying Guesthouse Scheme

Staying with an Indian family can be an enriching experience and a refreshing change from dealing strictly with tourist-oriented people. This Paying Guest House Scheme is particularly popular in tourist-laden Rajasthan, but is also available elsewhere in India (see regional chapters).

If you're interested, state tourist offices have details about the scheme. Expect to pay upwards of Rs 100.

Railway Retiring Rooms

These are just like regular hotels or dormitories except they are at train stations. To stay here you are technically supposed to have a train ticket or Indrail Pass. The rooms are handy if you have an early train departure, although they can be noisy if it is a busy station. Nonetheless, in some places they're the most convenient option and can be super value. Most are let on a 24-hour basis.

Other Possibilities

There are YMCAs and YWCAs in many of the big cities – the quality varies, but some are in good shape and cost about the same as a mid-range hotel. There are a few camping places around India, but travellers with their own vehicles can almost always find hotels with gardens where they can park and camp (sometimes for a nominal charge which includes communal bathroom facilities).

Indian youth hostels (HI – Hostelling International) can be very cheap but the quality of the building, rooms and service is variable. You are not usually required to be a HI member (as in other countries) to use the hostels, although your HI card will generally get you a lower rate.

Accommodation (for a donation) is available at some gurdwaras (Sikh temples) and *dharamsalas* (pilgrims' guesthouses). These simple places are essentially designed to cater for pilgrims so please exercise judgment about the appropriateness of staying. If you are welcome, abide by any protocols (eg, Jain places usually don't allow leather articles inside) and behave with respect.

[Continued on Page 142]

INDIAN CUISINE

Perhaps the best way of cutting to the heart of this extraordinary culture is by exploring its protean gastronomy. Dining in Indian restaurants abroad cannot prepare you for the experience of eating Indian food in India as the food is inextricably particular to place and is not easily exported. It reflects the multilayered culture that fascinates every visitor, and it changes shape as you move between each neighbourhood, town and state.

Amazingly, many travellers 'do' India *despite* the food, treating the cuisine as something suspect, to be tolerated or even avoided. Do this and you'll be like a pebble skimming across the cultural surface. You might get splashed every now and then but you'll never be immersed in it. Yes, you stand a good chance of getting a dose of the runs at some stage, but – with equal measures of good sense and adventure – a few desperate dashes to the toilet will seem like a trifling inconvenience compared with the culinary rewards and cultural insight you will glean.

The basis of any Indian meal is a grain – rice in the south, and wheat in the form of **roti** (bread) in the north. These are generally eaten with **dhal** (lentils), **sabzi** (vegetables) and **chatni** (chutney). Depending on circumstances, fish and meat may be added. Beyond these familiar staples, the diversity and potential of Indian food knows no bounds and is limited only by the geography of the region and the imagination of each cook.

Staples & Specialities

Spices

Walk into any Indian home at meal time and you will be enveloped in a waft of exotic aromas that will make your taste buds stand to attention.

> **Indian Food Fallacies**
>
> What most of us know as Indian cuisine – think dhal, tandoori chicken, naan, aloo gobi, lassi, chicken tikka etc – can all be found in one of India's states, Punjab. When the state was carved up during Partition, millions of displaced Punjabis scattered around India and beyond. Some opened restaurants that popularised their favourite dishes and Punjabi fare came to represent Indian cuisine the world over.
>
> There is no such thing as a 'curry' in India, and the word – an Anglicised derivative of the Tamil word **kari** (black pepper) – was used by gentlemen of the British empire as an all-encompassing term for any dish that included spices. Similarly, curry powder was invented purely for export to the nostalgic former residents of the Raj in Britain, and no self-respecting Indian cook would dream of using the same **masala** (combination of spices) in multiple dishes. Similarly the word balti, which is used in balti houses all over England, was created as a marketing ploy by entrepreneurial restaurateurs. Balti is a north-western name for the common Indian wok, better known as a *kadhai*. In the better balti houses of Birmingham, the term generally refers to dishes of Punjab and north-western frontier.

Top: Rice is South India's staple food. Phot by Paul Beinssen & illustrations throughout by Mick Weldon

Christopher Columbus was actually looking for the **black pepper** of Kerala's Malabar Coast when he stumbled upon America. The region still grows the finest quality of the world's favourite spice, and it is integral to most savoury dishes. **Turmeric** is the essence of every Indian curry but **coriander seeds** are the most widely used spice and lend flavour and body to just about every savoury dish, while most Indian 'wet' dishes – curries as they're known in the West – begin with the crackle of **cumin seeds** in hot oil. **Tamarind** is sometimes known as the 'Indian date' and is a popular souring agent in the south. The green **cardamom** of Kerala's Western Ghats is regarded as the world's best, and you'll find it in savouries, desserts, warming winter **chai** (tea). It is also a mouth-refreshing digestive.

Saffron evokes images of wealth and rarity unparalleled in the culinary lexicon. It is the dried stigmas of a crocus grown in Kashmir, and is made up of fine, orange-red threads that are so light that it takes more than 1500 hand-plucked flowers to yield just 1g of saffron. It is worth its weight in gold and makes a wonderful gift to bring home. Because of the prices it can fetch, it is frequently adulterated, usually with safflower, dubbed – no doubt by disgruntled tourists – as 'bastard saffron'.

Rice

Rice is the most important staple and, in a place where food and spirituality are inseparable, it is commonly used as a symbol of purity and fertility. It turns up in virtually every meal in the south, east and west, and the average Indian eats 2kg of it each week. Long-grain white rices are the most common but, between Assam's sticky rice and Kerala's red grains, you will find innumerable local varieties. Many are indistinguishable to the visiting palate, although one stands out above all. **Basmati** gets its name from the Hindi 'queen of fragrance', and its scent is well known around the world. The grains are white, long and silky and its aroma is reminiscent of the uncluttered freshness of the Himalayan foothills from where the best variety comes.

Roti (Bread)

A meal is not a meal in North India unless it comes with **roti**. The most common is the irresistible **chapati**, made with whole wheat flour and water, and cooked on a concave hot plate known as a *tawa*. **Puris** are wholewheat discs of stiff dough that, when deep-fried, puff up into soft crispy balloons and are eaten with various stewed meats and vegetables. **Kachoris** are similar only the dough is pepped up with lentils, corn or split peas. Flaky **parathas**, combined with any typical north Indian sauce, make for a delicious snack and nothing beats a **naan** fresh from the tandoor (clay oven).

Dhal (Lentils)

While the staples divide north and south, the whole of India goes doolally for dhal, a dish of stewed pulses and spices. Where we refer to our basic living as our 'bread and butter', Indians refer to **dhal roti** (dhal and bread) as all they need to survive. From the thin sambars of the south to the thick mung (pronounced moong) dhals of the north, you may encounter up to 60 different pulses including lentils, dried beans and peas, which are eaten with most meals.

Street Food

It's on the streets where you'll find India at its vital best and revolting worst – at its most colourful and drab, and its most joyful and depressing. India is laid bare in the theatre of its thoroughfares and the streets are a banquet for the senses. You won't like some of the courses, but the tastes, smells, sights, rhythm and atmosphere of street cooking will be an experience you will never forget.

Whatever the time of day, people are boiling, frying, roasting, peeling, juicing, simmering, mixing or baking some class of food and drink to lure passers-by. It can be as simple as puffed rice or peanuts roasted in hot sand, as unexpected as a fried-egg sandwich, or as complex as the riot of different flavours known as **chaat** (any snack seasoned with the popular spice blend chaat masala – the closest approximation in the West would be salad). It will be served in biodegradable bowls made of roughly stitched sal leaves or yesterday's newspaper. Deep-fried fare is the staple of the boulevards, and you'll find samosas, **aloo tikkis** and **bondas** (both mashed potato patties), **pakora** and **bhaji** (vegetable fritters) in varying degrees of spiciness. In season, cobs of roasted corn are hard to resist and you can't visit Mumbai without sampling **pao-bhaji** (spiced vegetables with bread) and **bhelpuri** on Chowpatty Beach. Popular 'modern' items include omelettes, hard-boiled eggs, and even regular old sandwiches (tomato, cucumber and green chutney).

PAUL BEINSSEN

Meat

While India probably has more vegetarians than the rest of the world put together, it still has an extensive repertoire of carnivorous fare largely lapped up by the Muslim and Christian communities. Goat (known as 'mutton' since the days of the Raj), lamb and chicken are the mainstays because religious taboos forbid Hindus from eating beef and Muslims from pigging out on pork. Even in the predominantly vegetarian inland south, you'll have little difficulty finding meat as long as you look for the crescent or the cross.

Papadams, here for sale in a busy Jaipur street, are crispy, deep fried lentil-flour wafers eaten as a snack or served with a meal such as a thali.

Fish & Seafood

Blessed with rich waters surrounding three sides of the subcontinent, fish and seafood are important staples. India's west coast – from Mumbai (Bombay) down to Kerala – is famous for its seafood dishes that showcase the treasures of the Arabian Sea, and many of the most popular restaurants in cosmopolitan Mumbai specialise in these regional seafood cuisines. Freshwater fish is the mainstay in West Bengal, where it is commonly curried in nose-tingling mustard.

Fruit & Vegetables

Indian fruit and vegetable markets are mesmerising, a feast for the eyes and foreplay for the touring taste buds. With its climatic range, India grows more fruit and vegetables than most countries. You'll find different species of familiar vegetables as well as truly exotic ones, like gourds that look more like props from the *X-Files* than edibles. Visit the market to get your culinary bearings. Indians are also fond of **saag** (leafy greens), which include mustard, spinach, fenugreek and white radish.

From the exotic delights of the balmy south to the temperate favourites of the north, India is a paradise for those who like fruit. Whatever time of year, there's always something to entice you, set your heart racing, and make your vitamin count surge. If you're mad about mango you might consider migrating here; Indians enjoy more than 500 varieties of what they regard as the king of fruit. The most exquisite is the **alphonso**, the first of which you'll find in Mumbai's Crawford Market from November.

Citrus fruits (oranges that are actually yellow-green, tangerines, pink and white grapefruits, kumquats, and sweet limes) grow throughout the country. Himachal Pradesh produces delicious apples in autumn. Juicy and flavoursome strawberries abound in Kashmir during summer. Labour intensive pomegranates, with their leathery jackets and sweet seeds encased in an inedible membrane, are winter favourites. Reach for a gorgeous guava to slake your thirst or, if you're game, have a juice made from sweet lime from the ubiquitous juice cart.

Dairy

The cow wasn't deemed sacred because of its grace, athleticism and good looks; it was protected because to the Indian diet it is worth a lot more alive than dangling from a hook. For Hindus the cow is also venerated because it represents fertility and nurturing. Milk and milk products make a staggering contribution to Indian cuisine: **dahi** (curds) are served with most meals and are handy for countering heat; **paneer** (unfermented cheese) is a godsend for the vegetarian majority; popular **lassi** (yogurt drink) is just one in a host of nourishing sweet and savoury drinks; **ghee** (clarified butter) is the traditional and pure cooking medium (although not used nearly as much in India as in Indian restaurants abroad); and the best sweets are made with milk.

Oils

Just as each state uses different ingredients, different cooking mediums are used to give dishes their characteristic regional flavours. Peanut (groundnut) oil is the most common, and is especially important around

Platform Food

One of the thrills of travelling by rail is the culinary circus that greets you at every station. As the train arrives the platform springs into a frenzy. Roving vendors accost the trains yelling and scampering up and down the carriages; bananas, omelettes and nuts are offered through the grilles on the windows; and platform chefs try to lure you from the train with the sizzle of fresh samosas. Frequent rail travellers know which station is famous for which food item, and plan their appetites accordingly. Lonavla station in Maharashtra is famous for **chikki** (nut and jaggery toffee), Agra for **peitha** (crystallised gourd), and Dhaund near Delhi for its biryani.

Maharashtra and Gujarat. It is high in protein and has a neutral flavour and taste. Strong, pungent mustard oil is the preferred medium along the east coast, particularly West Bengal and Bihar as well as in parts of Punjab and in Jammu and Kashmir. Discerning cooks in the south use light sesame oil, which imparts a nutty nuance to the food and has a high boiling point, making it ideal for frying. In the south and west, where coconuts grow so abundantly, coconut oil is widely used. To the uninitiated, the flavour coconut oil imparts in many dishes can be strong and unpleasant. If, while in Kerala, you're unable to work out which ingredient is offending your taste buds, it's probably the coconut oil. Many out-of-state Indians don't dig coconut oil either, and there's no problem asking the cook to use something else. On your travels, you may also find rapeseed oil – the poor man's oil – but never olive oil.

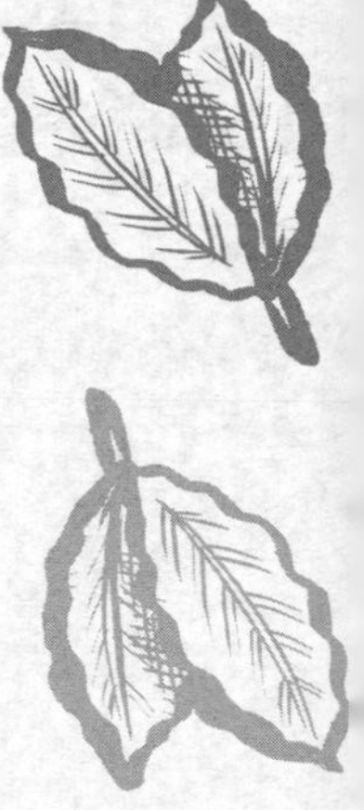

Thali

Don't be disappointed if the waiter tells you there is no menu, 'only meals'. In this case you'll have the choice of veg or nonveg thalis, delicious and inexpensive all-you-can-eat lunches. The thali is named after the dish in which it is traditionally served, usually a plate with bowl-shaped indentations known as **katori.** It is a wonderful way to explore regional variations and always features dry and wet vegetable preparations, chapati, pappadam, rice, pickle, curd, a sweet and a meat if that's what you're after. As soon as you've put a dent in any of the dishes, the waiter will come around and top you up (usually when you've got your mouth full).

In South India, and for communal feasts, thalis are usually served on banana leaves. The form originated in Gujarat and although a thali provides a great opportunity to explore regional differences, don't leave India until you've sampled a lightly spiced and sweet Gujarati one. Even if you can't make it to Gandhi's original stomping ground, you'll find Gujarati thalis in neighbouring states and major towns.

Pickles, Chutneys & Relishes

No Indian meal is complete without one, and often all, of the above. The most well known relish is **raita** (plain yogurt combined with vegetables or fruit, and served chilled), which makes a delicious and refreshing counter to even the most fiery meal. There is a litany of 'little bits' that can go a long way to changing the flavour of your meal, but

Celebrating with Sweets

Food is a medium for joy and celebration and you could hardly make it through a week here without getting caught up in the excitement of some looming festival, which will be marked with special feasts and specific dishes.

Mithai (sweets) are the most luxurious foods and vast quantities are made, exchanged and consumed during festivals. Most are sickeningly sweet to Western tastes although the milk-based concoctions of West Bengal, particularly **rasgullas** (balls of soft, unfermented cheese in syrup), are a glorious exception. Visit during a festival and you'll be smothered with sweet offerings. The main categories are **barfi** (a fudge-like sweet made from milk), **halwa** (soft sweetmeats which can be made with vegetables, cereals, lentils, nuts or fruit) and **ladoo** (sweetmeat balls made with gram flour, semolina and umpteen other ingredients). Many sweets come shimmering in a foil you might presume to discard; this is actually edible silver.

proceed with caution before polishing off that pickled speck on your thali; it'll quite possibly be the hottest thing you've ever tasted and usually the smaller the speck, the bigger the smash.

Desserts

Kheer – called **payasam** in the south – is a rice pudding and India's favourite dessert. It might be flavoured with cardamom, saffron, pistachios, flaked almonds, cashews or dried fruit. You can bet your sweet tooth that all communal gatherings will conclude with delicious, creamy payasam served in earthenware cups or bowls. **Vermicelli** – yes, the Italian pasta – is another common dessert, popularly made into a milk pudding or fried in ghee with raisins, flaked almonds and sugar in a sweet, dry treat. **Gulab jamun** are deep-fried balls of **khoya** (reduced milk) dough soaked in rose-flavoured syrup, and are eaten both as a snack and at the end of a meal. **Kulfi** is a delicious firm-textured Indian ice cream made with reduced milk and flavoured with any number of nuts, fruits and berries.

Paan

Meals are polished off with **paan**, a sweet, spicy and fragrant mixture of betel nut, also called areca nut, lime paste, spices and condiments wrapped up in an edible betel leaf (a different plant) and eaten as a digestive and mouth freshener. The betel nut is mildly narcotic and some aficionados eat them the same way heavy smokers consume cigarettes. If you chew a lot of paan, over many years the betel nut will rot your teeth red and black, which accounts for the number of people you'll encounter who look like they had their faces kicked in the night before.

There are two basic types; **mitha** (sweet) and **saadha** (with tobacco). Avoid the foul tobacco version, but a parcel of mitha paan is an excellent way to finish a satisfying meal without any harm. You'll soon find yourself walking out of restaurants and immediately heading for the nearest paan-wallah, whom you'll find in a jiffy, for they are as common as bumpy roads. Pop the whole parcel in your mouth and chew slowly, letting the juices secrete around your gob. When you've chewed the flavour out, spit the remains out onto the street (there really is no point in trying to be discreet).

To give somebody paan is a mark of great respect. Shah Jahan, he who built the Taj Mahal, once caught his daughter with a man he didn't care for. He smiled and offered the unapproved beau a betel leaf. The betel leaf was packed with poisonous ingredients but the beau could not risk offending the emperor, thanked him, started to chew and commenced dying.

Regional Dishes

The cauldron of Indian cuisine overflows with dishes that vary so immensely, that no Indian would be able to taste them all in a lifetime. It is a fascinating kaleidoscope of different regional influences, as varied as those of Europe, and you should seek out the regional specialities wherever you go.

Northern Specialities

Mughlai cuisine is popular in the north, particularly in the cities of Delhi and Lucknow where you'll find rich **pulous**, known as pilaus in the West, and **biryanis** infused with nuts, dried fruits, spices and meat. **Kebabs** are another popular Muslim staple and come in two basic varieties; **sheekh** (skewered) and **shami** (wrapped). **Kakori kebabs** are a delicacy named after the town near Lucknow. The meat is pounded into a fine paste, which is then spiced, wrapped around a skewer and quickly charred until crispy on the outside and almost creamy within. Speciality Muslim breakfasts include **nihari** (a rich broth made by simmering goat trotters overnight on low embers and eaten with warm bread) and **harissa** (wheat porridge with lamb also slowly cooked over embers).

From Punjab's tandoors emerge **tangri** (plump chicken drumsticks), **boti** (spicy bits of bite-sized boneless lamb), **chicken tikka** (succulent pieces of marinated chicken on a skewer) and, of course, the ubiquitous tandoori chicken. Tandoori dishes get their characteristic flavour from the charcoal used in the oven and from the blend of spices used in the marinade, known as tandoori masala. It consists of cumin, coriander seeds, chilli, ginger, turmeric and a flavourless red colouring that gives the food its distinctive red tinge. **Palak paneer** (soft, unfermented cheese in a spicy gravy of pureed spinach) is a popular Punjabi vegetarian alternative.

The Meaning of Vegetarian

There are now multitudes of restaurants – or 'hotels' – all over India and their signage will identify them as either 'veg', 'pure veg' or 'nonveg'. Pure veg indicates that no eggs are used and that there is no risk of the food being contaminated with meat. Most mid-range restaurants serve one of two basic genres; **South Indian** (which in restaurants means the vegetarian food of Tamil Nadu and Karnataka) and **North Indian** (which comprises Punjabi food with Mughlai touches). You will also find the cuisines of neighbouring regions and states. Indians frequently migrate in search of work and these restaurants cater to the large communities seeking the familiar tastes of home, as well as locals.

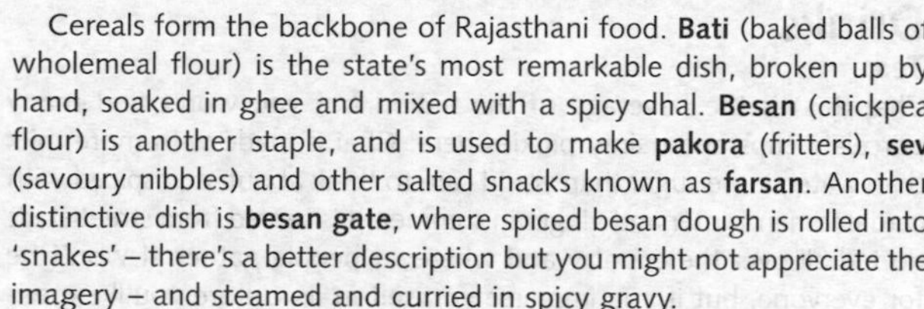

Cereals form the backbone of Rajasthani food. **Bati** (baked balls of wholemeal flour) is the state's most remarkable dish, broken up by hand, soaked in ghee and mixed with a spicy dhal. **Besan** (chickpea flour) is another staple, and is used to make **pakora** (fritters), **sev** (savoury nibbles) and other salted snacks known as **farsan**. Another distinctive dish is **besan gate**, where spiced besan dough is rolled into 'snakes' – there's a better description but you might not appreciate the imagery – and steamed and curried in spicy gravy.

Freshwater fish is the food closest to the heart of Bengalis. Hilsa, a relative of the herring, is the most popular and is made into a spicy **jhaal** (a curry made with ground mustard seeds and chillies).

No occasion passes in Orissa without **ghanto tarkari** (a mix of colocasia – leaves of the taro plant – yams, peas, potatoes, cauliflowers and brinjals, spiced up with horse gram and slivers of coconut). **Sattu** (roasted yellow gram, ground to a fine flour) is the unifying theme in Bihar and is enjoyed by all classes. There are few more tempting smells than sattu being roasted in earthenware pots over coals.

Tenga, the favourite Assamese fish stew, is made of pieces of sweet-tasting **rohu** (a type of carp), lightly sauteed with onions and simmered in a watery gravy, zested with lots of lemon juice. And if you venture as far as Kashmir you can taste an authentic **rogan josh**, the fiery lamb curry.

Southern Specialities

Sambar (a dhal with cubed vegetables and vegetable puree) and **rasam** (a thin tamarind-flavoured vegetable broth) are staples in the vegetarian cuisines of Tamil Nadu and Karnataka, as are the family of mouth-watering dosas. Our favourite is the **masala dosa** (a large lentil-flour crepe stuffed with a delicious yellow-coloured filling of potatoes cooked with onions and curry leaves). **Idlis** (spongy, round, fermented rice cakes) are often made with the same batter as dosas. These highly nutritional and easily digested snacks provide an alternative to oil, spice and chilli.

Khichdi (a kind of risotto sometimes made with lentils, potatoes and peanuts) is a forerunner to the British kedgeree and is popular in Maharashtra. However, **bhelpuri**, a riotious mix of sweet, sour, hot, soft and crunchy sensations tossed up in a leaf plate, is the dish most synonymous with the state – it's popularly eaten along Mumbai's Chowpatty Beach. **Bombay duck** is a pungent salty fish. In Mumbai you can also sample the Parsis' signature dish **dhansak** (a one-pot wonder consisting of meat, usually chicken, and vegetables in a spicy puree of several dhals).

Goa is famous for its fish curries, **chicken cafreal** (pieces of fried chicken coated in a mildly spicy green paste), and **fish caldeen** (simmered in coconut milk, ginger and cumin). Goan Christians will giddily prepare their famous tongue-searing **vindaloo** (pork curry made in a marinade of vinegar and garlic), one of the dishes the Portuguese brought to soften the blow of their colonisation. Save some room for the wonderful **bebinca** (a layered 40-egg sweetmeat, rich with ghee and coconut milk).

You'll find **toran** (a stir-fried green vegetable dish), **appam** (a rice pancake) and a plethora of fish dishes in Kerala. Fish and prawns are relished and fiery red **meen** (fish curry) is cooked in earthenware pots and kept to mellow in flavour before it is served with rice. Fish **molee** (fish pieces poached in coconut milk and spices) is another favourite considered by many Malayali Christians as their 'special'.

Drinks

Tea

Chai (tea) is the beverage of the nation but you won't find many porcelain cups and dainty pinkies here. Chai is made with more milk than water, more sugar than you'd care to think about, and spiced with cardamom in winter and ginger in summer. It is served from street stalls dotted all over the country and wherever people gather. It won't be for everyone, but if you immerse yourself in its culture you'll experience the very essence of this mad and magical country.

A glass of steaming sweet milky and frothy chai is the perfect antidote to the heat and stress of Indian travel and is a tonic for body and soul. The disembodied voice droning 'chai, chai garam' (hot tea) down the carriageway of your train will become one of the most familiar and welcome sounds of your trip. You can have a 'boy' bring it to even the most basic hotel room – whether he's 10 or 80, if he fetches tea or carries your bag, he's the boy.

If chai's not your cuppa, you'll be able to find the familiar formula of black tea, milk and lumps of sugar in multistarred hotels and in the planters clubs of tea-growing regions. You can order 'tray' or 'separate' tea just about anywhere, but if it's not the establishment's usual offering, you'll wish you hadn't.

The fragrant, light and sweet tea produced in Darjeeling will be familiar to even amateur connoisseurs. However, how many of us have actually tasted it before? While there are 12 million kilograms of tea produced in Darjeeling per annum, more than 60 million kilograms of 'Darjeeling Tea' are sold around the world each year! (See Darjeeling in the West Bengal chapter). Assam and Nilgiri Hills are India's other tea-growing regions.

Coffee

While chai is the choice of the nation, South Indians share their loyalty with coffee, although it's sometimes made with so much milk and sugar that you couldn't tell them apart. In the more discerning establishments, you'll be pleasantly surprised with Indian coffee, most notably beans like Mysore Nuggets and the enchantingly named Monsooned Malabar.

Other Non-Alcoholic Drinks

Coca-Cola and Pepsi are bombarding India with advertising and young 'hip' locals are lapping up their sickly sweet concoctions. These – and local brands such as Thums Up and Campa Cola – are generally safe to drink as long as you're not diabetic. '**Masala soda**' is the quintessentially Indian soft drink available at all drinks stalls. It is a freshly opened bottle of soda pepped up with a lime, spices, salt and sugar.

There's a mind-boggling range of fruit, most of which is blended into juice at some stage. Restaurants think nothing of adding salt and sugar to intensify the flavours but if you just want vitamins, tell the waiter to leave the additives out. The most popular street juices are made from sweet lemon, and sugar cane, which is pressed in front of you by a mechanised wheel complete with jingling bells.

Jal Jeera is the most therapeutic and refreshing indigenous drink. It's made with lime juice, cumin, mint and rock salt. It is sold in large earthenware pots by street vendors as well as in restaurants. The juice from the **green tender coconut** is safe and refreshing, and you'll find it sold from carts all over the country, particularly in the south. Watching the machete-wielding wallah whop the coconut into a drink is half the fun. After you've drunk the juice, he'll whop the coconut some more and give the remains back to you as chunks of tasty coconut meat.

Sweet and savoury **lassis** (yogurt drinks) are popular throughout, although the best are in Varanasai and Punjab. **Faluda** is a rose-flavoured Muslim speciality made with milk, cream, nuts and strands of vermicelli. Hot or cold **milk badam**, flavoured with saffron and almonds, is an invigorating morning drink.

Beer

Most travellers look forward to a beer at the end of a hot, dusty day, although the quality generally isn't worthy of your thirst. Most brands are straightforward pilsners around the 5% alcohol mark, and have glycerine as an emulsifier. Outside the cities and tourist centres, you'll struggle to find a beer cold enough to quench your thirst. Make sure you feel the bottle first before letting the waiter open it; beer is expensive and the only thing worse than drinking lukewarm Indian beer is blowing your budget in the process.

Most travellers champion Kingfisher, which is available nationwide. Royal Challenge, Dansberg, Golden Eagle, London Pilsner and Sandpiper are our favourite brands. Solan, from Himachal Pradesh and the highest brewery in the world at 2400m, is also a reasonable choice.

Other Alcoholic Drinks

Indian drinkers come in two categories; the hoi polloi who drink to get blotto and the hoity-toity who sip Indian and imported spirits. The common man quaffs 'country liquor' such as the notorious arrack of the south, which comes with quaint names like Amanush (Inhuman) and Asha (Hope) in the north. It is cheap, gives an instant high and taste ghastly. If you feel compelled to sample some, make sure you drink the government-distilled variety. Each year, hundreds of people are killed and blinded by the methyl (wood) alcohol in illegal arak.

Most Indian spirits are made of rectified spirit and flavouring, and taste vaguely familiar yet unpleasant. Peter Scott, Antiquity and Solan No 1 – in that order – are the best legal whiskies.

The best-known drink is a clear spirit with a heady pungent flavour called **mahua** and distilled from the flower of the mahua tree. It is brewed in makeshift village stalls all over central India during March and April, when these trees bloom. It's safe to drink as long as it comes from a trustworthy source.

Toddy, the sap from the palm tree, is drunk in coastal areas, especially Kerala. Wherever you hear the rhythmic tapping of buffalo bone against the palm bud (in the morning and evening), look for the toddy tapper and beg him for a sample of this mildly alcoholic natural wonder.

Feni is the primo Indian spirit, and the preserve of laid-back Goa. Coconut and cashew are the two main varieties. Coconut feni is light and unexceptional but the much more popular cashew feni – made from the fruit of the cashew tree – is worth taking home.

Martin Hughes

Martin is one of the authors of Lonely Planet's World Food India

[Continued from page 131]

Taxes & Service Charges

Most state governments slap a variety of taxes on hotel accommodation (and restaurants). At most rock-bottom budget places you won't have to pay any taxes. Once you get into the topend of budget places, and certainly for mid-range accommodation, you will have to pay something (usually 10%), and top end places can really stack on all sorts of taxes. Taxes vary from state to state.

Another common tax, in addition to the basic tax, is a service charge that's usually pegged at 10%. In some hotels this is only levied on room service and telephone use, not on the accommodation costs. At others, it's levied on the total bill.

Many hotels raise their tariffs on an annual basis, so expect increments on the room rates quoted in this book. Rates quoted in the regional chapters of this book exclude tax unless otherwise indicated.

Seasonal Variations

In popular tourist hang-outs (hill stations, beaches and the Delhi-Agra-Rajasthan triangle), most hoteliers crank up their high-season prices by two to three times the low-season price.

The definition of the high and low seasons obviously varies depending on location. For the beaches and the Delhi-Agra-Rajasthan triangle it's basically a month before and two months after Christmas. In the hill stations it's usually April to July when the lowlands are unbearably hot. In some locations and at some hotels there are even higher rates for the brief Christmas and New Year period, or over major festivals such as Diwali, Dussehra and the Pushkar Camel Fair. Conversely, in the low season, prices at even normally expensive hotels can be surprisingly affordable.

Touts

Hordes of accommodation touts operate in many Indian towns – Agra, Rajasthan and Varanasi in particular. They're usually most prevalent at airport terminals and bus and train stations. Often they are the rickshaw-wallahs. Their technique is simple – they take you to hotel A and pocket a commission for taking you there rather than to hotel B. The problem with this procedure is that you may well end up not at the place you want to go to but at the place that pays the best commission. Some very good cheap hotels simply refuse to pay the touts and you'll then hear lots of stories about the hotel you want being 'full', 'closed for repairs', 'no good any more' or even 'burnt down'. Nine times out of 10 they will be just that – stories.

Think twice before agreeing to stay in a hotel recommended by touts or rickshaw-wallahs, as some travellers have warned that they stayed in such hotels only to be subsequently badgered to take part in rip-off insurance and import schemes or to accept the sightseeing services of a particular taxi or rickshaw driver.

Touts do have a use, though – if you arrive in a town when some big festival is on, or during peak season, finding a place to stay can be almost impossible. Hop into a rickshaw, tell the driver in what price range you want a hotel, and off you go. The driver will know which places have rooms available and, unless the search is a long one, you shouldn't have to pay the driver too much. But he will be getting a commission from the hotel, too.

ENTERTAINMENT

If you confine your expectations of entertainment to bars, nightclubs and other activities you may take for granted at home, you're going to miss out on an awful lot. Entertainment in India is everywhere – the opportunities are limited only by your imagination.

Although many of the bigger cities do have independent bars and nightclubs, the majority of upmarket ones tend to be found in top-end hotels. Here you'll get the chance to rub shoulders with the local Indian yuppies (if that's your thing). However, many hotel discos restrict admission to members and hotel guests; couples have a better chance of being admitted. Plus, they're *expensive* – once you've shelled out the hefty door charge, a pricey drinks menu awaits inside.

Unlike discos and pubs, one thing you're likely to find in most towns is a cinema. There are many thousands of cinemas all over the country and entry is nominal. If you're passing through Jaipur (Rajasthan) catch a Bollywood blockbuster at the beautiful Raj Mandir cinema (see Jaipur in the Rajasthan chapter). No matter where you see a flick, never make the mistake of shushing people once the film begins – Indian cinema is just as much about audience participation as it is about the movie itself. So don't be a prude – clear your throat and join fellow viewers in booing the conniving villain and cheering the hunky 'hero' as he saves the damsel in distress (usually just after a monsoonal downpour or near-drowning scene when the vulnerable damsel, wrapped in a figure-clinging wet sari, is ripe to be ravished). With so much action – plus the obligatory medley of song and dance routines – where's the time for a meaty plot anyway?

Vibrant traditional regional music and dance performances are usually held at major hotels and other venues (see regional chapters for details). At some festivals, such as Pushkar's Camel Fair in Rajasthan, you may be treated to impromptu performances by livestock traders around a campfire. *Kathputlis* (traditional puppeteers) are another attraction of Rajasthan. Many major cities, such as Delhi, Khajuraho and Kolkata, have a spectacular sound-and-light show that is an atmospheric way of absorbing culture and history.

Finally, India is a glorious place to simply sit back and watch the day unfold. 'People watching' arguably rivals any form of contrived entertainment. Not only is it a veritable feast for the eyes and mind, it's also absolutely free! Simply sitting in the lobby of a five-star hotel, for instance, can be an incredibly fascinating way of 'accessing' the local high society. You'll see a cross section of people, from elegant Indian women decked out in stunning saris, to glam young things sporting the latest Western designer labels. At the other end of the social spectrum, there's the inimitable (and highly inspirational) scene of everyday life on the streets – from the indefatigable traffic police zealously trying to tame the wild traffic, to mobile street vendors selling everything from bulky plastic rubbish bins to dainty plastic bangles.

SPECTATOR SPORTS

India's national sport (obsession almost) is cricket. During the cricket season, if an international side is touring India and there is a test match on, you'll see crowds outside the many shops that have a TV, and people walking down the street with a pocket radio pressed to their ear. Test matches with Pakistan have a particularly strong following as the rivalry is intense. One thing you can count on is that most Indians will know the names of the entire touring cricket team and, if you come from the same country but don't know their names, then you may well be regarded as somewhat of a loony. If you do have an interest in cricket, the atmosphere in India is phenomenal and always a sure-fire way of igniting passionate conversations.

World cricket has recently been plagued with match-fixing scandals involving Indian bookmakers and various international teams. Indian cricketers have also been embroiled. When former Indian captain, Mohammed Azharuddin, was first accused of match-fixing, infuriated Indian cricket fans publicly burnt effigies of him, and the others who had been accused, as they were considered to be traitors to their nation. Azharuddin and ex-Test player, Ajay Sharma were found guilty of match fixing in late 2000 and banned for life. Manoj Prabhakar and Ajay Jadeja have been punished with a five-year ban for their involvement with Indian bookmakers. Allegations that Indian icon, Kapil Dev, was also involved in wrongdoing have still not been proven.

International cricket matches are played at several major centres in India (mainly during winter) including Mumbai's Wankhede

Playing with Tradition

Board games have a long tradition in India. Chess, for example, is thought to have originated in India in the 6th century AD. Carrom, although its origins are obscure, is a traditional game that has survived over time and has its fans to this very day. It is not only played in India, but also in Sri Lanka. Carrom centres on a square wooden board and allows a maximum of four players. In the centre of the board are nine black and nine white tokens plus one token coin called a queen. On each corner of the board are pockets and the goal is to use a striker to send the tokens (black or white depending on which you have drawn) into one of the pockets.

Traditional sports that still enjoy a healthy following in India include *kho-kho* and *kabaddi*, both of which are essentially elaborate games of tag, but which require great skill and stamina.

The King of Games & Game of Kings

Horse polo has always been immensely popular among Indian royalty, especially during the British Raj period. Wealthy Indian kings would pump huge sums of money into facilities, training and polo ponies. Indeed, some erstwhile Indian rulers themselves were among the top players in the world, including Marahaja Man Singh II of Jaipur, whose polo team was champion on the European polo circuit in the 1930s. This charismatic maharaja had a stable of some 40 ponies, which were shipped over to England when required. The team was even accompanied by a carpenter (to keep them supplied with high-quality polo sticks). Man Singh actually died playing the game he adored at a polo match in England in 1970. His widow, Rajmata Gayatri Devi, still lives in Jaipur (Rajasthan) and continues to be a polo aficionado.

Emperor Akbar was believed to have been the first person to introduce rules to the game, but polo, as it is played today, was largely influenced by a British cavalry regiment stationed in India during the 1870s. A set of international rules was implemented after WWI. One of the world's oldest polo clubs, established back in 1862, is in Kolkata.

Polo flourished in India until Independence, when patronage sharply declined (the game requires great sums of money) and it became less popular. However, today there is a renewed interest in the game, largely due to beefed-up sponsorship. One major patron is the current Maharana of Udaipur, who has injected copious capital into keeping this traditional game alive in India. His efforts have

Stadium, just off Marine Drive. The best (if not the only) way to get a ticket here is to apply in advance in writing to the secretary, Wankhede Stadium, D Rd, Churchgate 400020 (fax 022-2817851) well in advance. Tickets for one-day matches here start at Rs 150. For a Test match you'll have to pay for the full five days – Rs 500 for general admission, or Rs 3000 if you want to do it in style in the members stand, replete with lunch and afternoon tea. For state matches at Wankhede you can just turn up and get tickets (Rs 25) at the gate. Other renowned cricket centres in India include those at Ahmedabad (Sardar Patel Stadium & Modhara Stadium), Bangalore (M Chinnaswamy Stadium), Kolkata (Ranji Stadium, Eden Gardens), Delhi (Firoz Shah Kotla Stadium), Chennai (MA Chidambaram – Chepauk – Stadium), Mohali (PCA Stadium) and Nagpur (VCA Stadium). The Ranji Stadium in Kolkata holds more than 100,000 people and has one of the best atmospheres of any cricket ground in the world.

Tickets for cricket matches are usually advertised in the press a few weeks in advance; it's obviously preferable to buy a ticket well ahead, although some travellers claim they have been able to get tickets from the stadium on the same day a match is being played.

India is also one of the world leaders in hockey and has several Olympic gold medals to its credit – although none since 1980. At the 2000 Olympics at Sydney, the one billion-strong nation only bagged one medal: a bronze for weightlifting, won by Karnam Malleswari. India's dismal performance at the Olympics sparked heated debate in India, with bitter accusations of corruption and mismanagement aimed at Indian officials. Many argue that if India's Olympic team got the same financial backing as its cricket team, the country would be in an exceedingly better position to excel.

When it comes to tennis, India traces its links to Wimbledon right back to 1908 when Sadar Nihal Singh was the first Indian to ever compete there. However, the first Indian to bag a major award was Ramanathan Krishnan, who became the junior Wimbledon champion in 1954. In the 1970s India's Vijay Amritraj reached the quarterfinals at both Wimbledon and the US Open. However, the biggest success stories are Leander Paes and Mahesh Bhupathi, who won Wimbledon's prestigious men's doubles title in 1999 – the first Indians to ever do so.

Polo is particularly popular among elite circles. You can see it being played during the winter months at various centres including Delhi, Jaipur, Kolkata and Mumbai – check local newspapers for current venues and events.

SHOPPING

India is bursting with beautiful things to buy. The cardinal rule when purchasing handicrafts is to bargain and bargain hard. You can get a good idea of what is reasonable (in terms of quality and price) by visiting the various state emporiums and the Central Cottage Industries Emporiums, which can be found in major cities. At these places you can inspect items from all over the country. Because prices are fixed (albeit often quite high), you can get an idea of how hard to bargain when you purchase similar items from regular vendors. In the tourist traps, the offerings at craft emporiums is almost identical – expect to find Kashmiri carpets and papier-mache, sandalwood elephants, Rajasthani textiles, Tibetan trinkets, imitation Mughal miniature paintings and Benares (Varanasi) silk. For information about cooperatives see Responsible Tourism earlier in this chapter.

Be careful when buying items that include delivery to your home country. You may be told that the price includes home delivery and all customs and handling charges. Inevitably this is not the case, and you may find yourself having to collect the item yourself from your country's main port or airport, pay customs charges (which could be as much as 20% of the item's value) as well as handling charges levied by the airline or shipping company (up to 10% of the value). If you can't collect the item promptly, or get someone to do it on your behalf, exorbitant storage charges may also apply.

Opening hours for shops differ (Sunday seems to be a holiday for most), so check this out locally to ensure you don't leave all your shopping to your last day in India only to discover that all shops are shut!

See the colour section 'Arts & Crafts' for more background information.

Carpets

In Kashmir, where India's finest carpets are produced, the carpet-making techniques and styles were brought from Persia even before the Mughal era. The art flourished under the Mughals and today Kashmir is packed with small carpet producers. Persian motifs have been much embellished on Kashmiri carpets, which come in a variety of sizes: 3ft x 5ft, 4ft x 6ft and so on. They are either made of pure wool, wool with a small percentage of silk to give a sheen (known as 'silk touch') or pure silk. The latter are more for decoration than hard wear. Expect to pay at least Rs 7000 for a good-quality 4ft x 6ft carpet and don't be surprised if the price is more than twice as high.

Other carpet-making areas include Badhoi and Mirzapur in Uttar Pradesh and Warangal and Eluru in Andhra Pradesh.

In Kashmir and Rajasthan, coarsely woven woollen *numdas* are produced. These are more primitive and folksy, and consequently cheaper, than the fine carpets. Around the Himalaya and Uttar Pradesh *dhurries*, flat-weave cotton warp-and-weft rugs are woven. In Kashmir, *gabbas* are applique-like rugs. The numerous Tibetan refugees in India have brought their craft of making superbly colourful Tibetan rugs with them. A Tibetan rug with 48 knots per square inch will cost around Rs 2300 per square metre. Good places to buy Tibetan rugs are Darjeeling, Gangtok and McLeod Ganj, which is also a good place to pick up Kashmiri souvenirs.

Unless you're an expert it's best to get advice or buy from a reputable dealer if you're spending large amounts of money on carpets. Check prices back home too; many Western carpet dealers sell at prices you would have difficulty matching even at the source. Also look out for the Smiling Carpet label; this is a UN and NGO initiative to try to discourage the use of child labour in carpet manufacture.

Textiles

This is still India's major industry and 40% of the total production is at the village level, where it is known as *khadi*. There are government khadi emporiums (known as Khadi Gramodyog) around the country, and these are good places to buy handmade items of home-spun cloth, such as the popular 'Nehru jackets' and the kurta pyjama. Bedspreads, tablecloths, cushion covers or material for clothes are other popular khadi purchases.

There is an amazing variety of cloth styles, types and techniques around the country, including mirrorwork in Rajasthan and Gujarat and tie-dye work in Rajasthan and Kerala. In Sualkuchi (Assam) a speciality is the *muga* silk, while Orissa has a reputation for bright applique and handmade silk and cotton fabrics.

Punjab is known for its *phulkari* (flower work embroidery with stitches in diagonal, vertical and horizontal directions on cotton cloth) bedspreads or wall hangings, while

Barmer (Rajasthan) is famous for its embroidery. Indeed Rajasthan is noted for its wonderfully vibrant textiles – Jaipur probably has the widest range.

Batik (with an emphasis on Indian motifs and usually executed on cotton) can be found throughout India, but is particularly popular in the larger cities such as Mumbai and Delhi. You can pick up some nice batik Western-style clothing in city markets at reasonable prices. Stunning batik work can also be found on saris and salwar kameez in trendy city boutiques. *Kaalamkari* cloth from Andhra Pradesh and Gujarat is an associated but far older craft. It traditionally emerged around South Indian temples – the designs reflect elements of temple murals and are largely used as decorative cloths during devotional ceremonies and festivals. Also in Gujarat is the mirrored embroidery of Kutch, which usually sports geometric designs.

Markets in some of the larger cities, especially Delhi and Mumbai, stock decent Western fashions at competitive prices.

Shawls, Silk & Saris

Traditional wool shawls from the Kullu Valley are one of the most popular souvenirs from the Himalaya and are excellent value for money. Most are produced on traditional wooden handlooms by cooperatives of village weavers. Prices range from about Rs 200 for a simple wool shawl to Rs 6000 for a stylish pashmina or angora shawl. The heavy, embroidered shawls worn by many women in the mountain villages can cost as much as Rs 10,000. One excellent organisation is Bhuttico (the Bhutti Weavers Cooperative), which has fixed-price shops in many towns in Himachal Pradesh. Also popular are the traditional caps worn by men and women from the mountain tribes. These range from Rs 30 for a thin but colourful Kullu cap, to Rs 200 for a warm woollen Kinnaur cap. Ladakh is also known for its beautiful pashmina shawls.

Aurangabad in Maharashtra is the traditional centre for the production of Himroo shawls, sheets and saris. A blend of cotton, silk and silver thread, these garments cost from Rs 500 and are often decorated with motifs from the Ajanta Cave paintings. The exquisite silk and gold thread saris produced at Paithan are more exclusive – they range from Rs 6000 to a mind-blowing 300,000.

The 'silk capital' of India is Kanchipuram in Tamil Nadu, although Varanasi is also popular, especially for silk saris. In Varanasi expect to pay at least Rs 150 per metre of silk. It costs about Rs 125 to 140 for a tailor to make you a long-sleeve shirt or knee-length dress. Kolkata is also known for its fine, handwoven cotton and silk saris, which are widely displayed in city shops and markets.

Jewellery

Many Indian women put a large chunk of their wealth into jewellery, so it is no wonder that the range is so great. However, for Western tastes it's the heavy folk-art jewellery that has particular appeal – you'll find it all over the country, but particularly in Rajasthan. In the north you'll also find Tibetan jewellery, which is even chunkier and more folk-like.

If you're looking for fine jewellery as opposed to folk jewellery, you may well feel that much of what is produced in India is too ornate for your liking.

In Rajasthan, Jaipur is most especially renowned for its precious and semiprecious gems (see the boxed text 'Travellers Beware!' later in this chapter).

Some of the jewellery pieces on offer in Tibetan centres such as McLeod Ganj and Darjeeling are genuine antiques carried in by refugees, but most are actually reproductions made locally and artificially 'aged'. Loose beads of agate, turquoise, carnelian and silver are also available if you feel like stringing your own necklace. Buddhist meditation beads made of gems, wood or inlaid bone make great souvenirs; prices range from around Rs 20 for wooden beads to Rs 500 for an amber string. Pearls are a speciality of Hyderabad.

Leatherwork

Of course Indian leatherwork is not made from cow-hide but from buffalo-hide, camel, goat or some other substitute. Kanpur in Uttar Pradesh is the country's major centre for leatherwork.

Chappals, those basic leather sandals found all over India, are a particularly popular purchase. In southern Maharashtra, the town of Kolhapur is famous throughout India for its chappals. They can be purchased from Kolhapur, Pune and in the hill

Travellers Beware!

In popular travellers hang-outs, particularly Agra, Jaipur (and other parts of Rajasthan), Varanasi, Delhi and Kolkata, take extreme care with the commission merchants. These incredibly tenacious fellows hang around waiting to pick you up and cart you off to their favourite dealers where whatever you pay will have a hefty margin built into it to pay their commission. Stories about 'my family's place', 'my brother's shop' and 'special deal at my friend's place' are just stories and nothing more.

Whatever you might be told, if you are taken by a rickshaw driver or tout to a place, be it a hotel, craft shop, market or even restaurant, the price you pay will be inflated. This can be by as much as 50% (even more), so try to visit these places independently – no matter how persistent the touts are.

Another trap that many travellers fall into occurs when using a credit card. You may well be told that if you buy the goods, the merchant won't forward the credit slip for payment until you have received the goods, even if it is in three months' time – this is total rubbish. No trader will be sending you as much as a postcard until they have received the money, in full, for the goods you are buying. What you'll find in fact is that within 48 hours of you signing the credit slip, the merchant has contacted the bank in Delhi and the money will have been credited to their account.

Also beware of any shop that takes your credit card out the back and comes back with the slip for you to sign. Sometimes, while out of sight, the vendor will imprint a few more forms, forge your signature, and you'll be billed for items you haven't purchased. Have the slip filled out right in front of you.

If you believe any stories about buying anything in India to sell at a profit elsewhere, you'll simply be proving (once again) that old adage about separating fools from their money. Precious stones and carpets are favourites for this game, particularly in Jaipur and Agra. Operators who practise such schemes are very good at luring trusting souls – they are invariably very friendly – often taking travellers to their homes and insisting on paying for meals. They'll often tell you hard-luck stories about an inability to obtain an export licence, hoping to garner your sympathy. It's all part of the con – do *not* fall for it. Merchants will tell you that you can sell the items in Australia, Europe or the USA for several times the purchase price, and will even give you the (often imaginary) addresses of dealers who will buy them. You'll also be shown written statements, supposedly from other travellers, documenting the money they have supposedly made – it's all a sophisticated scam. The stones or carpets you buy will be worth only a fraction of what you pay (or if you agreed to have them sent, they probably won't even arrive). Don't let your desire for a quick buck cloud your judgment. Despite our warnings over many editions, we inevitably receive at least a handful of reports from distressed travellers with tales of woe about the scams we warn of.

While it is certainly a minority of traders who are actually involved in dishonest schemes, virtually all are involved in the commission racket, so you need to shop with care – take your time, be firm, bargain hard and don't hesitate to say no. (See also the boxed text 'Agra-phobia' in the Uttar Pradesh & Uttaranchal chapter.)

station of Matheran, priced from Rs 150. In Rajasthan you can buy the delightful traditional leather shoes – *jootis*; those for men often have curled-up toes.

At craft shops in Delhi you'll find well-made leather bags, handbags and other items. Kashmiri leather shoes and boots, often of reasonably good quality, are widely found, along with coats and jackets of often abysmally low quality.

Paintings

Reproductions of the beautiful old miniatures are painted in many places, but beware of paintings purported to be antique – it's highly unlikely that they are. Also note that quality can vary widely; low prices often mean low quality, and if you buy before you've had a chance to look at a lot of miniatures (thus developing some knowledge about them) you'll inevitably find you bought unwisely. Udaipur (Rajasthan) has some good shops specialising in modern reproductions on silk and paper. In the same state, Jaipur has several shops with brilliant contemporary paintings by local artists (prices range from Rs 200 to 50,000).

In Kerala and, to a lesser extent, Tamil Nadu, you'll come across vibrant miniature paintings on leaf skeletons enclosed on a printed card depicting domestic and rural scenes, as well as gods and goddesses. In Andhra Pradesh you can buy paintings on cloth called kalamkari.

The murals of Shantiniketan (West Bengal) hail from the town that they are named after, which also happens to be famous for its association with Nobel Prize winning author, Rabindranath Tagore.

Bihar's unique folk art is the sublime Mithila or Madhubani paintings, created by the women of Madhubani (see the boxed text 'Mithila Paintings' in the Bihar & Jharkhand chapter). They're most easily found in Patna.

In Mumbai, contemporary original paintings or sculptures can be bought at various outlets including the Jehangir Art Gallery. Expect to pay well over Rs 1000, even for a small painting.

Papier-Mache

This is probably the most characteristic Kashmiri craft. The basic papier-mache article is made in a mould, then painted and polished in successive layers until the final intricate design is produced. Prices depend upon the complexity and quality of the painted design and the amount of gold leaf used. Items include bowls, cups, containers, jewellery boxes, letter holders, tables, lamps, coasters and trays. A small bowl might cost only Rs 40, whereas a large, well-made item might approach Rs 1000.

Rajasthan (especially Jaipur and Jaisalmer) is *the* place to buy colourful papier-mache puppets – they make wonderful gifts (prices range from around Rs 100 to 1000).

Bronze Figures, Pottery & Terracotta

In the south, delightful small images of the gods are made by the age-old lost-wax process. A wax figure is made, a mould is formed around it and the wax is melted and poured out. The molten metal is poured in and when it's solidified the mould is broken open. Figures of Shiva as dancing Nataraja are among the most popular.

Jaipur (Rajasthan) specialises in blue-glazed pottery which usually features floral and geometric motifs.

Kolkata is known for its terracotta ware, from simple little bowls to large decorative figurines. Terracotta images of gods and children's toys are also made in Bihar.

Woodcarving

In the south, images of the gods are carved out of sandalwood. Rosewood is used to carve animals – elephants in particular. Carved wooden furniture and other household items, either with a natural finish or lacquered, are also made. In Kashmir, intricately carved wooden screens, tables, jewellery boxes and trays have a similar pattern to the decorative trim of houseboats. Sandalwood carving is one of Karnataka's specialities, while Kerala is noted for its rosewood carving.

Wood-inlay work is one of Bihar's oldest craft industries and you'll find wooden wall hangings, tabletops, trays and boxes decorated with inlaid metals and ivory.

The carved wooden massage wheels and rollers available at many Hindu pilgrimage sites make great gifts – they're cheap and light to carry.

Metalwork & Marble

Copper and brass items are popular throughout India. Candle-holders, trays, bowls, tankards and ashtrays are made in Mumbai and other centres. In Rajasthan and Uttar Pradesh the brass is inlaid with exquisite designs in red, green and blue enamel. *Bidri* (a form of damascening) comes from the medieval Muslim city of Bidar in northern Karnataka, where silver is inlaid into gunmetal (see the boxed text 'The *Bidriware* of Bidar' in the Karnataka chapter). Hookah pipes, lamp bases and jewellery boxes are made in this manner. Many Tibetan religious objects are made using a similar technique, inlaying silver into copper. Prayer wheels, ceremonial horns and document cases are all popular and inexpensive purchases. Painted cast-metal statues of Tibetan deities are heavier but will look stunning back home. Prices start at Rs 350 for small figurines.

A sizable cottage industry has sprung up in Agra – marble souvenirs inlaid with semi-precious stones. The inspiration for most pieces comes from the *pietra dura* inlays found on the Taj Mahal and other monuments. Expect to pay about Rs 200 for a jewellery box and Rs 1000 upwards for a detailed wall plaque.

Musical Instruments

Indian musical instruments have long been an attraction for travellers and are mainly available in the larger towns (including Delhi, Kolkata and Jaipur), some with beautiful inlay work. Make sure you shop around to find the highest quality items at the most competitive prices.

In Delhi the best place to buy instruments is Netaji Suhash Marg. The cost of a tabla and *doogi* (drums are traditionally paired – the tabla is the long drum with tuning blocks and the doogi is the broader metal drum) is upwards of Rs 950. Ornamental souvenir drums cost as little as Rs 100, but the quality of fabric and sound are inferior. Good-quality sitars range from Rs 3000 to 16,000. Kolkata also offers some fine Indian instruments at competitive prices.

In Varanasi you can buy musical instruments at the Triveni Music Centre; depending on the quality, a sitar can cost anything from Rs 5000 to 30,000.

Note that certain types of wood with which some sitars are made may warp in certain climates, adversely affecting the sound of the instrument.

Other Buys

Throughout India, books are a brilliant buy. There's a wide range of titles at prices likely to be far cheaper than you'd pay back home. You can easily while away several hours simply browsing through bookshops and it's a perfect way to spend a lazy afternoon.

Islamic attar (essential oil) perfume shops can be found in Mumbai. These sell arguably India's largest range of perfumes (upwards of Rs 150 a bottle).

Specialities of Goa include cashew and coconut feni. This head-spinning spirit, which often comes in decorative souvenir bottles, cost from Rs 30 to more than 1000. Another speciality of this area is the traditional clay pipe chillums and hookah pipes (smoking and possessing drugs is illegal but buying the paraphernalia is not!). Darjeeling and Kalimpong (West Bengal), and parts of South India are splendid places to pick up aromatic tea. Also in West Bengal, but this time in Siliguri, caneware does a roaring trade. You can get everything from small letter racks to bulky lounge furniture.

An interesting speciality of Bihar is the tapper mats of the Palamau district. Tapper is a durable material derived from the sun hemp plant – bags made from the fibre were once used to transport grains and other heavy loads. Nowadays, tapper yarn is dyed in various colours and available in various forms, such as handbags.

Meanwhile, in Bhopal, *jari* shoulder bags are a specialty. Made of cotton, they sport colourful designs and can be purchased for as little as Rs 35. Meghalaya, over in India's north-eastern region, is particularly noted for its beautiful hand-woven baskets.

Antiques & Wildlife Restrictions

Articles over 100 years old cannot be exported from India without an export clearance certificate (which is not easy to obtain anyway). If you have doubts about any item and think it could be defined as an antique, you can check with regional branches of the Archaeological Survey of India (☎ 011-3019451, 3017220 in Delhi).

The Indian Wildlife Protection Act bans any form of wildlife trade. Don't buy any products that further endanger threatened species and habitats – the consequences of doing so may result in heavy fines and even imprisonment.

Getting There & Away

Warning

The information in this chapter is particularly vulnerable to change: Prices for international travel are volatile, routes are introduced and cancelled, schedules change, special deals come and go, and rules and visa requirements are amended. Airlines and governments seem to take pleasure in making price structures and regulations as complicated as possible. You should check directly with the airline or a travel agent to make sure you understand how a fare (and the ticket you may buy) works. In addition, the travel industry is highly competitive and there are many lurks and perks.

The upshot of this is that you should always get opinions, quotes and advice from as many airlines and travel agencies as possible before parting with your hard-earned cash. The details in this chapter should be regarded as pointers. They are not a substitute for your own careful, up-to-date research.

AIR

Airports & Airlines

Mumbai (Bombay), Delhi, Kolkata (Calcutta) and Chennai (Madras) are the main gateways for international flights. Ahmedabad (Gujarat) has a more limited international service (see Tickets in India). The proposed international airport at Hyderabad was not operational at the time of writing.

India's national carrier is Air India (www.airindia.com), which also carries passengers on some domestic sectors of international routes (see also Air in the Getting Around chapter). Indian Airlines, the country's major domestic carrier, offers flights to some 16 neighbouring countries (for specific destinations see the Web site at www.indian-airlines.nic.in).

Buying Tickets

World aviation has never been so competitive, making air travel better value than ever. But you have to research the options carefully to make sure you get the best deal. The Internet is an increasingly useful resource for checking air fares.

Full-time students and people aged under 26 years (under 30 in some countries) have access to better deals than other travellers. You have to show a document proving your date of birth or a valid International Student Identity Card (ISIC) when buying your ticket and possibly also when boarding the plane.

Generally, there is nothing to be gained by buying a ticket direct from the airline. Discounted tickets are released to selected travel agents and also specialist discount agencies. These are usually the cheapest deals going.

One exception to this rule is the expanding number of 'no-frills' carriers, which mostly only sell direct to travellers. Another exception is booking on the Internet. Many airlines offer some excellent fares to Web surfers. They may sell seats by auction or simply cut prices to reflect the reduced cost of electronic selling.

Many travel agencies around the world have Web sites, which can make the Internet a quick and easy way to compare prices. There is also an increasing number of on-line agencies that operate only on the Internet.

Online ticket sales work well if you are doing a simple one-way or return trip on specified dates. However, online super-fast fare generators are no substitute for a travel agent who knows all about special deals, has strategies for avoiding layovers and can offer advice on everything from which airline has the best vegetarian food to the best travel insurance to bundle with your ticket.

You may find the cheapest flights are advertised by obscure agencies. Most such firms are honest and solvent, but there are some rogue fly-by-night outfits around. Paying by credit card generally offers protection, as most card issuers provide refunds if you can prove you didn't get what you paid for. Similar protection can be obtained by buying a ticket from a bonded agent, such as one covered by the Air Travel Organiser's Licence (ATOL) scheme in the UK (more details available at www.atol.org.uk). Agents who only accept cash should hand over the tickets straight away and not tell you to 'come back tomorrow'. After you've made a booking or paid your deposit, call the airline and confirm that the booking was made. It's generally not advisable to send money (even cheques) through the post unless the agent is very well established – some travellers have

Air Travel Glossary

Alliances Many of the world's leading airlines are now intimately involved with each other, sharing everything from reservations systems and check-in to aircraft and frequent-flyer schemes. Opponents say that alliances restrict competition. Whatever the arguments, there is no doubt that big alliances are the way of the future.

Courier Fares Businesses often need to send urgent documents or freight securely and quickly. Courier companies hire people to accompany the package through customs and, in return, offer a discount ticket which is sometimes a bargain. However, you may have to surrender all your baggage allowance and take only carry-on luggage.

Fares Airlines traditionally offer 1st-class (coded F), business-class (coded J) and economy-class (coded Y) tickets. These days there are so many promotional and discounted fares available that few passengers pay full fare.

Lost Tickets If you lose your airline ticket, an airline will usually treat it like a travellers cheque and, after inquiries, issue you with another one. Legally, however, an airline is entitled to treat it like cash and if you lose it then it's gone forever. Take very good care of your tickets.

Onward Tickets An entry requirement for many countries is that you have a ticket out of the country. If you're unsure of your next move, the easiest solution is to buy the cheapest onward ticket to a neighbouring country or a ticket from a reliable airline which can later be refunded if you do not use it.

Open-Jaw Tickets These are return tickets where you fly out to one place but return from another. If available, this can save you backtracking to your arrival point.

Overbooking Since every flight has some passengers who fail to show up, airlines often book more passengers than they have seats. Usually excess passengers make up for the no-shows, but occasionally somebody gets 'bumped' onto the next available flight. Guess who it is most likely to be? The passengers who check in late. If you do get 'bumped', you are normally offered some form of compensation.

Reconfirmation Some airlines require you to reconfirm your flight at least 72 hours prior to departure. Check your travel documents to see if this is the case

Restrictions Discounted tickets often have various restrictions on them – such as needing to be paid for in advance and incurring a penalty to be altered or cancelled. Others are restrictions on the minimum and maximum period you must be away.

Round-the-World Tickets RTW tickets give you a limited period (usually a year) in which to circumnavigate the globe. You can go anywhere the carrying airlines go, as long as you stay within the set mileage/number of stops and, with some tickets, don't backtrack. The number of stopovers or total number of separate flights is decided before you set off and they usually cost a bit more than a basic return flight.

Ticketless Travel Airlines are gradually waking up to the realisation that paper tickets are unnecessary encumbrances. On simple one-way or return trips, reservations details can be held on computer and the passenger merely shows ID to claim their seat.

Transferred Tickets Airline tickets cannot be transferred. Travellers sometimes try to sell the return half of their ticket, but officials can ask you to prove that you are the person named on the ticket. On an international flight, tickets are compared with passports.

reported being ripped off by fly-by-night mail-order ticket agents.

If you purchase a ticket and later want to make changes to your route or get a refund, you need to contact the original travel agent. Airlines only issue refunds to the purchaser of a ticket – usually the travel agent who bought the ticket on your behalf. Think carefully before you buy a ticket that is not easily refunded.

Travellers with Special Needs

If they are warned early enough, airlines can usually make special arrangements for travellers such as wheelchair assistance at airports or vegetarian meals on the flight. Children under two years travel for 10% of the standard fare (or free on some airlines) as long as they don't occupy a seat. They don't get a baggage allowance. 'Skycots', baby food and nappies (diapers) should be provided by the airline if requested in advance. Children aged between two and 12 can usually occupy a seat for half to two-thirds of the full fare, and they do get a baggage allowance.

The Web site, www.everybody.co.uk has a useful airline directory that provides information on the facilities offered by the various airlines.

Departing India

It's important to reconfirm international tickets at least 72 hours before departure; some travellers have reported having their seat cancelled for not doing so.

Airlines recommend travellers check in three hours prior to international flight departures; allow time for getting stuck in India's often congested traffic, especially during peak hours. Most Indian airports have free luggage trolleys, but you'll probably be accosted by porters eagerly offering to lug your load for a tip (Rs 10 is fine). Once inside the airport, you'll be required to have your check-in baggage screened and sealed by security tape before proceeding to check-in. Don't forget to fill out an embarkation card before heading for the customs gate.

Departure Tax The departure tax of Rs 500 (Rs 150 for Bangladesh, Bhutan, Nepal, Sri Lanka, Pakistan and Maldives) is included in the price of virtually all airline tickets – check with your travel agent.

Tickets in India

Although you can get international tickets in Mumbai and Kolkata, it is in Delhi where the real wheeling and dealing goes on. There are a number of bucket shops (unbonded travel agencies that specialise in discounted airline tickets) around Connaught Place, but inquire with other travellers about their current trustworthiness. And if you use a bucket shop, double check with the airline itself that the booking has been made.

To give you an idea of costs, the table 'Fares from India' presents a selection of fares from international departure points in India (flights from other countries to India are provided under country headings later in this section). The list is not exhaustive –

Fares from India

from	to	one-way fare
Delhi	Auckland	Rs 26,800
	Bangkok	Rs 11,000
	Dubai	Rs 7700
	Kathmandu	US$142
	Kuala Lumpur	Rs 18,000
	Lahore	Rs 5880
	Singapore	Rs 18,000
	Sydney	Rs 20,280
	Toronto	Rs 29,500
	Vancouver	Rs 36,000
Mumbai	Bangkok	Rs 15,000
	Colombo	Rs 13,350
	Dhaka	Rs 9975
	Hong Kong	Rs 24,000
	Kathmandu	US$217
	London	Rs 26,500
	Nairobi	Rs 19,300
	New York	Rs 31,000
	Paris	Rs 25,700
	Singapore	Rs 21,550
	Sydney	Rs 29,000
Kolkata	Bangkok	Rs 7300
	Dhaka	Rs 2560
	Geneva	Rs 21,000
	Hong Kong	Rs 11,800
	Kathmandu	US$96
	London	Rs 18,000
	Los Angeles	Rs 32,000
	New York	Rs 23,700
	Paris	Rs 21,000
	Rome	Rs 19,000
	Singapore	Rs 7100
	Toronto	Rs 33,300
	Yangon	Rs 5775
Chennai	Bangkok	Rs 12,800
	Colombo	Rs 3765
	Hong Kong	Rs 18,500
	London	Rs 18,250
	Nairobi	Rs 16,180
	New York	Rs 25,000
	Paris	Rs 18,250
	Sydney	Rs 23,000
Ahmedabad	Chicago	Rs 27,000
	London	Rs 22,000
	Muscat	Rs 10,300
	New York	Rs 27,000
	Sharjah	Rs 10,300

many more international destinations are serviced from India (check with travel agents). Note that fares here are one way and given in the currency in which they are quoted in India. Fares vary considerably according to peak and low seasons, so it's best to consult a travel agent for the latest deals.

The USA

Discount travel agents in the USA are known as consolidators (although you won't see a sign on the door saying Consolidator). San Francisco is the ticket consolidator capital of America, although good deals can be found in Los Angeles, New York and other big cities. Consolidators can be found through the *Yellow Pages*, the Internet or the major daily newspapers.

For students or travellers under 26 years, popular travel agencies in the USA include Council Travel (☎ 800-226 8624), which has a Web site at www.ciee.org and its head office is at 205 E 42 St, New York, NY 10017; and STA Travel (☎ 800-777 0112), which has offices in Boston, Chicago, Miami, New York, Philadelphia, San Francisco and other major cities. STA's Web site is at www.statravel.com. Ticket Planet is a leading ticket consolidator in the USA. Visit its Web site at www.ticketplanet.com.

The high season for flights from the USA to India is June to August and from December to January. Low season runs from March to around mid-May and from September to November.

From the US east coast most flights to India are via Europe. Low-season return fares to Mumbai start at around US$1480 with Air India via London and American Airlines via Zurich. Fares to Delhi start at around US$1270 with Singapore Airlines via Frankfurt or Air India via London. To Chennai, fares start at US$1460 with KLM-Royal Dutch Airlines via Amsterdam.

From the US west coast to Mumbai or Delhi, Aeroflot has the best bargain fares. Expect to pay around US$1000 for a low-season fare via Moscow. Another good deal to Delhi is with Korean Air or Asiania Airlines, both via Seoul; return fares start at around US$1200.

Other fares include Cathay Pacific Airways to Mumbai via Hong Kong from around US$1396, and US$1581 with El Al Israel Airlines via Tel Aviv.

To Chennai, return low-season fares are around US$1400 with Air India via Taipei and Singapore or KLM-Royal Dutch Airlines via Amsterdam.

Canada

Fares from Canada are similar to fares from the USA. Travel CUTS (☎ 800-667 2887) is Canada's national student travel agency and has offices in all major cities. Its Web address is www.travelcuts.com.

From Canada, most flights to India are via Europe but there are options for travel via the USA or Asia.

Low-season return fares from Vancouver to Delhi or Mumbai start at around C$2500 flying Northwest Airlines via Hong Kong or Singapore, or Air France via Paris.

Return fares from Montreal or Toronto to Mumbai or Delhi in the low season start at C$2117 with Air France via Paris, or C$2340 via Frankfurt with Lufthansa Airlines.

Australia

Two well-known agencies for cheap fares are STA Travel and Flight Centre. STA Travel (☎ 03-9349 2411) has its main office in Melbourne at 224 Faraday St, Carlton 3053, and offices in all major cities and on many university campuses. Call ☎ 131 776 Australiawide for the location of your nearest branch or visit its Web site at www.statravel.com.au. Flight Centre (☎ 131 600 Australiawide) has a central office at 82 Elizabeth St, Sydney, and there are dozens of offices throughout Australia. Its Web address is www.flightcentre.com.au.

From Australia, low-season return fares to Delhi start at A$1290 with SriLankan Airlines, Air India and Qantas via Singapore. Malaysia Airlines, Air Lanka and Gulf Air all have return fares starting from around A$1345 to Mumbai, Chennai and Delhi. Low-season return fares to Kolkata start at around A$1500.

New Zealand

As in Australia, STA Travel and Flight Centre are popular travel agencies. Flight Centre (☎ 09-309 6171) has a large central office in Auckland at National Bank Towers (corner Queen and Darby Sts) and many branches throughout the country. Its Web site is at www.flightcentre.com/nz. STA Travel (☎ 09-309 0458) has its main office at 10 High St,

Auckland, and has other offices in Auckland as well as in Hamilton, Palmerston North, Wellington, Christchurch and Dunedin. The Web address is www.statravel.com.

There are no direct flights between India and New Zealand so airlines offer Asian stopovers. Low-season return fares to Delhi from Auckland start at NZ$1799 with Malaysia Airlines via Kuala Lumpur, or NZ$1940 with Air New Zealand via Singapore.

The UK & Ireland

Discount air travel is big business in London. Advertisements for many travel agencies appear in the travel pages of the weekend broadsheet newspapers, in *Time Out*, the *Evening Standard* and in the free magazine *TNT*.

For students or travellers under 26 years, popular travel agencies in the UK include STA Travel (☎ 020-7361 6262), which has an office at 86 Old Brompton Rd, London SW7, and branches across the country (Web site: www.statravel.co.uk); and Usit Campus (☎ 0870-240 1010), which has an office at 52 Grosvenor Gardens, London SW1 and branches throughout the UK (Web site: www.usitcampus.co.uk). Both these agencies sell tickets to all travellers but cater especially to young people and students.

Other recommended travel agencies for all age groups include:

Bridge the World (☎ 020-734 7447) 4 Regent Place, London W1
Web site: www.b-t-w.co.uk

Flightbookers (☎ 020-7757 2000) 177–178 Tottenham Court Rd, London W1
Web site: www.ebookers.com

Quest Travel (☎ 020-8547 3123) 10 Richmond Rd, Kingston-upon-Thames, Surrey KT2 5HL
www.questtravel.co.uk

Trailfinders (☎ 020-7938 3939) 194 Kensington High St, London W8
Web site: www.trailfinders.co.uk

From London to Delhi, Aeroflot has low-season return fares starting from £380 via Moscow. British Airways' direct flights to Delhi start at £580, direct Virgin Atlantic flights are around £481 in the low season. London-Kolkata fares start at £430, London-Mumbai from £348 and London-Chennai from £420.

Some companies offer packages to Goa and Kerala at competitive rates. These packages include accommodation, breakfast and transfers. Charter flights are also available to Goa – prices depend on availability and season. Check with travel agencies and travel page ads in newspapers and magazines.

Return fares from Belfast to Mumbai or Delhi start from £694 with British Airways.

Europe

In the Netherlands, recommended agencies include NBBS Reizen (☎ 020-620 50 71) at 66 Rokin, Amsterdam, plus branches in most cities and a Web site at www.nbbs.nl, and Budget Air (☎ 020-627 12 51) at 34 Rokin, Amsterdam.

Travel agencies in Germany include STA Travel (☎ 030-311 09 50) at Goethesttrasse 73, 10625 Berlin, which has a Web site at www.statravel.com/de, and Usit Campus (☎ 01805-788336) with its Web site at www.usitcampus.de. Both these very popular agencies have a number of branches throughout Germany.

Agencies in France include Usit Connect Voyages (☎ 01 42 44 14 00) 14 rue de Vaugirard, 75006 Paris, with a Web site at www.usitconnect.fr/newsite/index.asp, and OTU Voyages (☎ 01 40 29 12 12) 39 Ave Georges-Bernanos, 75005 (www.otu.fr). Like Usit, this is a student and young person specialist agency. Nouvelles Frontières (☎ 01 45 68 70 00) 87 Blvd de Grenelle, 75015 Paris (www.nouvelles-frontieres.fr) also has many branches throughout France.

The return fare from Frankfurt to Delhi is DM1758, from Amsterdam to Delhi is f1350 and from Paris to Delhi is 4040FF.

Africa

There are plenty of flights between East Africa and Mumbai due to the large Indian population in Kenya. A typical one-way fare from Nairobi to Mumbai is US$399.

Bangladesh

There are Indian Airlines flights between several Bangladeshi centres and Kolkata, including Dhaka for US$52 and Chittagong for US$67.

Malaysia

As Thailand has more flight options, most travellers in South-East Asia choose to depart for India from Bangkok, rather than Kuala Lumpur. The one-way economy fare from Kuala Lumpur to Delhi is US$230.

Maldives

Indian Airlines flights from Thiruvananthapuram (Trivandrum) to Malé cost US$68 one way.

Myanmar (Burma)

There are no land crossing points between Myanmar and India (or between Myanmar and any other country), so your only choice from India is to fly there. Indian Airlines flies Yangon (Rangoon) to Kolkata for US$152 one way.

Nepal

Royal Nepal Airlines Corporation (RNAC) and Indian Airlines share routes between India and Kathmandu. Druk Air also has flights. RNAC and Indian Airlines have one-way flights from Kathmandu to Delhi for US$102, to Mumbai for US$151 and to Kolkata for US$96.

Pakistan

Pakistan International Airlines (PIA) has one-way flights from Karachi to Delhi via Lahore for US$107 and from Lahore to Delhi for US$70.

Singapore

The one-way economy fare from Singapore to Delhi is US$670 with Singapore Airlines or Thai Airways International.

Sri Lanka

There are flights between Colombo and Mumbai, Delhi, Chennai, Tiruchirappalli (Trichy) or Thiruvananthapuram. Fares from Colombo to Mumbai start at US$210 with SriLankan Airlines or Indian Airlines.

Thailand

Bangkok is the most popular departure point from South-East Asia into India. Flights are available from Bangkok to major Indian cities, including Kolkata for US$159 and Delhi for US$203, both one way. Thai International and Indian Airlines also fly via Yangon in Myanmar to Kolkata for around US$410 return.

LAND

The following section explains where you can cross borders into India. For more specific details and information, see the regional chapters.

Bangladesh

To the immense delight of locals and travellers alike, a direct bus service between Kolkata (India) and Dhaka (Bangladesh) was introduced in 1999, making the once complex task of crossing the border far more straightforward. Although there are also minor crossing points from India, the new bus service between Kolkata and Dhaka is by far the most convenient option, as access via lesser-used routes is variable and thus uncertain.

If you're travelling from Bangladesh to India, no exit permit is required to leave Bangladesh, but if you enter Bangladesh by air and leave via a land crossing, a road permit is officially required. This can be obtained in Dhaka at the Immigration & Passport office (☎ 02-9556020), 127 New Eskaton Rd, Mogh Bazar. It's open from 10 am to noon Saturday to Thursday.

Kolkata to Dhaka The direct bus to Dhaka departs Kolkata daily at 7 am, arriving in Dhaka at about 8 am the next morning. A return ticket costs Rs 1000.

You can purchase the Kolkata-Dhaka bus ticket from Shyamoli Paribahan (☎ 033-2290345, fax 2293715) at 51 Mirza Ghalib St (Free School St; near the Hotel VIP International) in Kolkata. At the time of writing, buses departed from the International Bus Depot out at Salt Lake (double check in case a more convenient departure point has since commenced). A taxi from the Sudder Street area (where most tourists stay) to Salt Lake should cost around Rs 40.

You need a visa for Bangladesh and these are available at the Bangladesh foreign missions (see Embassies & Consulates in the Facts for the Visitor chapter). In Kolkata, the Bangladesh consulate processes visa applications from 9 am to noon on weekdays and these are ready for collection on the same afternoon between 3 and 5 pm. You'll need to supply your passport and three passport photos (for places to have these taken see Photography in the Kolkata chapter). Visas are for a maximum of one month but you can extend these at the Immigration & Passport office in Dhaka (see Bangladesh earlier in this section). Visa costs vary depending on one's nationality: US$21 for Australians, Rs 2900 for Britons and US$45 for Americans.

Siliguri to Bhurungamari This northern border crossing is rarely used by travellers. Getting to the Indian border town of Chengrabandha from Siliguri in West Bengal is relatively straightforward. There are buses every hour between 6 am and 1 pm. The 70km trip costs Rs 35 and takes about 3½ hours. The Indian immigration office opens at 9 am daily (except Sunday). You can take buses direct to Rangpur (5½ hours), Bogra (eight hours) or Dhaka (15 hours).

New Jalpaiguri to Chilahati Take a train from New Jalpaiguri (northern West Bengal) to Haldibari, the Indian border checkpoint (Rs 20, two hours). From here it's a 7km walk along a disused railway line to the Bangladesh border point at Chilahati, where there's a train station.

Shillong to Sylhet The border post is at Dawki in Meghalaya, 70km from Shillong and accessible by daily buses from Shillong. From Dawki, it's a 1.5km walk to Tamabil, from where it's a 15-minute walk to the bus station and about 2½ hours by bus to Sylhet.

Agartala to Dhaka This border is close to Dhaka, along Akhaura Rd, 4km west of Agartala in Tripura. From the Bangladeshi side, plenty of transport goes to Akhaura, 5km away.

From Akhaura, a train to Dhaka (2½ hours) leaves at 12.15 pm Bangladeshi time. Alternatively, more uncomfortable buses (four hours) leave when there's enough demand. The border is open from 8 am to 6 pm daily.

Nepal

Political and weather conditions permitting, there are three main land entry points into Nepal. The most popular crossing points from India are Sunauli in Uttar Pradesh to Bhairawa (south of Pokhara), Raxaul in Bihar to Birganj (south of Kathmandu) and Kakarbhitta in West Bengal (near Siliguri in the far east). If you are travelling to or from Delhi or elsewhere in western India the route through Sunauli/Bhairawa is the most convenient. An ordinary bus to Sunauli from Varanasi costs Rs 140 (10 hours).

From Delhi, private buses to Kathmandu leave at 1.30 pm on Monday and Thursday, arriving around 6 or 7 am two days later. The journey requires a six-hour wait at the border where you must change buses. The fare is Rs 800. Most travellers seem to find that it's a lot more comfortable and better value to do the trip by train to Gorakhpur (Uttar Pradesh), and then take a bus from there.

You can also enter via the little-used border crossing from Banbassa in Uttaranchal to Mahendrenagar in western Nepal. Despite its proximity to Delhi, this is probably the slowest route to Kathmandu or Pokhara, but it does provide a chance to explore western Nepal en route. Buses to Banbassa leave Delhi's Anand Vihar bus stand hourly from 7 am to 9 pm (Rs 138, 10 hours). Visas are available at the border (US$30, two passport photos required), but only from 9 am to 4 pm. The border post itself is open from 7 am to 7 pm. It's a short rickshaw ride to the border. Buses wait on the far side to transfer you to the old bus stand in Mahendrenagar, from where there are daily buses to Kathmandu at around 2 pm which take a bum-numbing 24 hours. Alternatively, you can take a bus from Mahendrenagar's new bus stand to Nepalganj (nine hours) and pick up a bus to Kathmandu or Pokhara from there (15 hours). You can forget about rail connections to Banbassa; this is really a dry-season only route as the road on from Mahendrenagar is prone to flooding in the monsoon.

From Kolkata, Patna or most of eastern India, Raxaul Bazaar to Birganj is the best entry point. From Kolkata to Raxaul, catch the *Mithilla Express* which departs Kolkata at 4 pm daily and arrives the next morning at 7.30 am (be warned that it's notorious for arriving at least two to three hours late). The ticket costs Rs 245 (second class) or Rs 1085 (air-con two-tier). From Raxaul, get an autorickshaw to Birganj for about Rs 10. From Birganj to Kathmandu it's about 350km and there are frequent buses (Rs 156, about

Warning

Many travellers have complained about scams involving ticket packages to India, especially out of Pokhara – bookings fail to materialise or are for lower quality services than were paid for. The package usually involves coordination between at least three different companies so the potential for an honest cock-up is at least as high as the potential for a deliberate rip-off.

eight hours). To Pokhara, it's about 255km and there are hourly buses (Rs 125, about 5½ hours).

A visa is required to enter Nepal (see Embassies & Consulates in the Facts for the Visitor chapter for embassy addresses). You'll need a passport photo and visas are usually ready in 24 hours (except Friday when you should apply in the morning and your visa will be ready later that afternoon). In Delhi, the embassy is open for visa processing from 9 am to noon Tuesday to Friday. A multiple-entry 60-day visa costs Rs 1410. It's also possible to get a visa at the airport or at the border (US$30).

Pakistan

Currently, due to the continuing unstable political situation between India and Pakistan, there's only one border crossing open and that remains hostage to the volatility with Pakistan-India relations.

A visa is required for Pakistan. One- and two-month single-entry visas are available from the Pakistan embassy in Delhi (see Embassies & Consulates in the Facts for the Visitor chapter for addresses). Applications are accepted between 8.30 and 11.30 am on weekdays and visas are issued the next working day. The cost depends on your nationality, ranging from Rs 120 for Swiss nationals to Rs 2975 for Canadians.

Delhi to Lahore There is a direct bus linking Delhi with Lahore, crossing the border at Wagah. Buses leave the Dr Ambedkar Bus Terminal near Delhi Gate at 6 am each Tuesday, Wednesday, Friday and Saturday. The journey takes 12 hours and costs Rs 800 (including meals).

Amritsar to Lahore The only legal overland crossing between India and Pakistan is at Wagah, just east of Lahore (Attari on the India side), by rail and road; you can also drive your own vehicle across here. On each side you clear immigration, customs and further security checks. The border is open from 9 am to 3 pm (9.30 am to 3.30 pm India time) daily. Daily express trains link Lahore with Amritsar. There are also slower daily trains between Lahore and Wagah. Buses are quicker and more frequent, though the trip still takes nearly half a day. Ultimately, the most convenient and straightforward option is the direct bus between Delhi and Lahore.

Bhutan

Siliguri to Phuentsholing It's a 169km trip between Siliguri (West Bengal) and Phuentsholing (Bhutan). From Siliguri, buses from the Bhutan bus stand on Burdwan Rd leave daily at 8 and 11 am, and 2 and 3 pm (Rs 60, 3½ hours). There are various bus options from Phuentsholing to Thimphu costing from Rs 107 to 149. The trip takes around six to seven hours.

Although no permits are currently required for Phuentsholing, you *must* get a visa at least 15 days before your trip from a registered travel agent listed under the Tourism Authority of Bhutan (TAB).

Europe

A trickle of people drive their own motorcycles or vehicles overland from Europe. There are some interesting, if difficult, routes to the subcontinent through Eastern Europe and the republics that were once part of the USSR. An international carnet is required. Many people combine travel to the subcontinent with the Middle East by flying from India or Pakistan to Amman in Jordan or one of the Gulf States. A number of the London-based overland companies operate bus or truck trips across Asia (see Organised Tours later in this chapter for some possibilities).

South-East Asia

In contrast to the difficulties of travelling overland in Central Asia, the South-East Asian overland trip is still wide open. From Australia the first step is to Indonesia – Timor, Bali or Jakarta. Most people fly from an east coast city or Perth to Bali, but there are also other options such as Darwin (inquire at local travel agencies).

From Bali head north through Java to Jakarta, from where you either travel by ship or fly to Singapore or continue north through Sumatra and then cross to Penang in Malaysia. After travelling around Malaysia you can fly from Penang to Chennai or, more popularly, continue north to Thailand and then fly out from Bangkok to India, perhaps with a stopover in Myanmar. Unfortunately, crossing by land from Myanmar to India (or indeed to any other country) is not posible as it is forbidden by the Myanmar government.

An interesting alternative route is to travel from Australia to Papua New Guinea and from there cross to Irian Jaya; then to Sulawesi in Indonesia. There are all sorts of travel variations possible in South-East Asia; the region is quite a delight to travel through and heartily recommended.

SEA

The only sea crossing from Chennai is to the Andaman Islands (see the Andaman & Nicobar Islands chapter for information). The shipping services between Africa and India only carry freight (including vehicles), not passengers.

ORGANISED TOURS

In addition to the companies that provide more standard tours, there are numerous foreign eco, leisure and adventure-travel companies that can provide unusual, exotic and interesting trips. There are far too many to include them all here – the following list supplies just a sample of the companies that organise tours to India.

Australasia

Community Aid Abroad Tours (☎ 08-8232 2727) PO Box 34, Rundle Mall, SA 5000
Web site: www.caa.org.au

Peregrine Adventures (☎ 03-9663 8611) 258 Lonsdale St, Melbourne, Vic 3000; plus offices in Sydney, Brisbane, Adelaide, Perth and Hobart
Web site: www.peregrine.net.au

World Expeditions (☎ 02-9264 3366) 3rd floor, 441 Kent St, Sydney, NSW 2000
New Zealand: (☎ 09-522 9161) 21 Reumera Rd, New Market, Auckland
Web site: www.worldexpeditions.com.au

UK

Encounter Overland (☎ 020-7370 6845) 67 Old Brompton Rd, London SW5 9JA
Web site: www.encounter-overland.com

Essential India (☎ 01225-868544) Upper Westwood Bradford on Avon, Wiltshire, BA15 2DS
Web site: www.essential-india.co.uk

Exodus Expeditions (☎ 020-8673 0859) 9 Weir Rd, London SW12 OLT
Web site: www.exodustravels.co.uk

Imaginative Traveller (☎ 020-8742 3113) 14 Barley Mow Passage, Chiswick, London W4 4PH
Web site: www.imaginative-traveller.com

Indian Encounters (☎ 01929-481421) Creech Barrow, East Creech, Wareham, Dorset, BH20 5AP
Web site: www.indianencounters.com

USA

Adventure Center (☎ 800-227 8747) 1311 63rd St, Suite 200, Emeryville, CA 94608
Web site: www.adventure-center.com

Asian Pacific Adventures (☎ 800-825 1680) 826 Sierra Bonita Ave, Los Angeles, CA 90036
Web site: www.asianpacificadventures.com

Geographic Expeditions (☎ 415-922 0448, fax 346 5535) 2627 Lombard St, San Francisco, CA 94123
Web site: www.geoex.com

Nature Exhibitions International (☎ 800-869 0639) 7860 Peters Rd, Plantation, FL 33324
Web site: www.naturexp.com

Sacred India Tours (☎ 310-834 9843) 350 West Pacific Coast Highway, Wilmington, CA 70744
Web site: www.sacredindia.com

Getting Around

AIR

Domestic Air Services

India's aviation industry is booming, with services to more than 70 airports. Indian Airlines (www.indian-airlines.nic.in) and its subsidiary, Alliance Air, fly to practically every corner of the country (59 destinations), as well as to neighbouring countries from the Gulf States to Thailand. Some of its fleet is ageing and it has a reputation for being unreliable. However, Indian Airlines is being partially privatised and will not be under government management after 2001, which will hopefully lead to some major improvements.

The international carrier, Air India, also flies on several domestic routes. Note that most of these flights leave from international terminals (check ahead).

Jet Airways (www.jetairways.com) flies to 38 cities and is rated as the country's best airline, with efficient staff and a modern fleet. The third biggest carrier is Sahara Airlines (www.saharaairline.com), which flies to 14 major destinations.

Fares are practically identical between the major carriers.

There is also a handful of small regional airlines, but services can be erratic so it's best to check the current situation with a travel agent.

Reservations

The main airlines have computerised booking services and there are thousands of computerised travel agencies. Phone numbers for city offices are given in the regional chapters. All the airlines require you to give a telephone number and address when booking. The major airlines don't require reconfirmation unless your ticket was bought outside India, in which case the usual 72-hour rule applies.

Tickets can be paid for with rupees, foreign currency and in most cases with credit cards. Change is given in rupees. A lost ticket is very bad news – airlines may issue a replacement ticket at their discretion, but a refund is almost impossible.

Indian Airlines offers a 25% discount for students as well as for those aged between 12 and 30.

Air Passes

Indian Airlines' 'Discover India' pass costs US$500/700 for 15/21 days. It allows unlimited travel with one restriction – you can't go to the same place twice unless to take a connecting flight. Visiting the four biggest cities with individual tickets costs about US$750, so if you want to do that and more it's good value.

Jet Airways' 'Visit India' pass costs US$300/550/800 for 7/15/21 days, 50% less for children aged under 12. Jet also offers discounts in luxury hotels, mostly in North India. The same restriction applies on visiting a city twice.

There's also Indian Airlines 'India Wonder' fare, which costs US$300 for one week's unlimited travel within any of four regions. Note that Port Blair in the Andaman Islands is not included in this scheme.

Eastern Agartala, Bhubaneswar, Kolkata (Calcutta), Dibrugarh, Guwahati, Imphal, Jorhat, Lucknow, Patna, Ranchi, Silchar, Tezpur, Vadodara, Varanasi, Visakhapatnam

Northern Agra, Amritsar, Bhopal, Delhi, Chandigarh, Gwalior, Indore, Jaipur, Jammu, Jodhpur, Khajuraho, Leh, Lucknow, Raipur, Srinagar, Udaipur, Varanasi

Southern Bangalore, Chennai (Madras), Coimbatore, Goa, Hyderabad, Kochi, Kozhikode, Madurai, Nagpur, Pune, Thiruvananthapuram (Trivandrum), Tiruchirappalli (Trichy), Visakhapatnam

Western Ahmedabad, Aurangabad, Bhavnagar, Bhuj, Goa, Indore, Jamnagar, Jodhpur, Kozhikode, Mangalore, Mumbai (Bombay), Nagpur, Rajkot, Udaipur, Vadodara (Baroda)

Check-In

Check-in is an hour before departure. An extra 15 minutes is needed for flights to and from Leh, Jammu and Srinagar.

The baggage allowance is 20kg in economy class, 30kg in business. Some flights have security measures such as having to identify your baggage on the tarmac just before boarding (ask if this is required when checking in), and comprehensive clothing and baggage searches. You have to take out all batteries, even cells used for camera flashguns, and put them into checked luggage. Any batteries discovered by security personnel on your person or in cabin luggage

Air Routes

from	to	approx duration (hrs)	flights per day	one-way (US$)
Delhi	Mumbai	2	20	175
	Chennai	1½	6	260
	Kolkata	2	4	200
	Leh	1¼	1	105
	Khajuraho	1¾	1	100
	Varanasi	1¼	1	125
Kolkata	Chennai	2	2	220
	Bangalore	2¼	2	265
	Hyderabad	2	2	210
	Guwahati	1¼	4	70
	Agartala	¾	2	50
Mumbai	Aurangabad	¾	2	75
	Bangalore	1¾	14	140
	Chennai	1¾	9	160
	Kolkata	2¼	7	230
	Goa	1	6	93
	Jaipur	1½	3	155
Chennai	Hyderabad	1½	3	105
	Thiruvananthapuram	1¼	2	105
	Kochi	1	2	120
	Port Blair	2	2	195
Bangalore	Delhi	2¾	7	255
	Thiruvananthapuram	1	2	120
	Goa	1	3	105
	Kochi	1¼	2	80

will be confiscated. This is so no-one detonates anything once aboard.

If you've got some hand luggage, remember to get a tag for it when you check-in, or you may later be sent back to the check-in counter to get one (as the tag must be stamped when you clear security).

BUS

Although India has a comprehensive bus network, most travellers prefer to travel by train, as it's generally more comfortable and lacks the nerve-wracking zigzagging of road travel. Nonetheless, bus travel can make a refreshing change from trains, even though the journey can be a lot slower (involving frequent stops to pick up or drop off passengers), or alternatively, frighteningly fast. On top of that, many buses are in an advanced state of decrepitude.

The big advantage of buses over trains is that they travel more frequently and getting one involves generally less predeparture hassle. They're best suited to short journeys; if you've got a long trip, particularly overnight, opt for a train if there's a choice.

Finally, it's worth taking earplugs (or a walkman) on bus trips, as some drivers love their Hindi pop and have no qualms about pumping up the volume. Some of the more expensive bus services have videos, which are also usually turned up at full volume for hours on end. If you're travelling overnight by bus and hope to get some shut-eye, avoid video coaches.

Classes

The quality and choice of buses can vary wildly from state to state. In some states there is a choice of state-run buses plying the main routes, including ordinary, express and deluxe. Additionally, private buses operate in some regions, and apart from often being a quicker and more comfortable option (some have 'luxuries' like tinted windows and reclining seats), the booking procedure is usually much simpler than for state-run buses. However, unlike state-operated bus

India's Mechanical Monsters

Local city buses in India, particularly in the big cities such as Kolkata and Delhi, are generally fume-belching human-stuffed mechanical rattletraps which travel at breakneck speed; except when they are stuck in traffic. Little time is given for disembarkation and there are daily reports of injury and death caused by buses. This is largely due to the immense pressure placed on bus drivers to rake in as much cash as possible.

Bus drivers are often paid by the number of passengers they carry, and may even be fined for each minute they are late. Naturally, this leads to dangerous and cut-throat competition among bus drivers. Those drivers who are caught for dangerous driving are given bail and immediately return to work, content in the knowledge that their case won't come to court for years; by that time any witnesses have disappeared or have little memory of the incident. According to newspaper reports, four out of five drivers are simply fined, never tried.

Many drivers openly admit they are 'forced' to adopt 'techniques' such as intentionally blocking the way of rival buses, or taking risky measures to overtake them, all at the peril of innocent pedestrians and fellow road users. According to drivers, in off-peak times they initially drive slowly to scoop up the maximum number of passengers, then wildly accelerate towards the end of the journey to make up time.

The moral is, when crossing a road don't even entertain the notion of stepping out in front of an oncoming bus. Moreover, don't even weave through a group of buses at a stop, as another, faster moving bus may be obscured by the first one!

companies, private operators are exceptionally eager to maximise their profits and, unfortunately, this can mean maintenance is less and speed more – a dangerous combination. Another downside of some private companies is that they will change schedules at the last minute to get as many bums on seats as possible. As the standard of private operators is so variable, it's best to seek advice from fellow travellers, tour operators etc to ascertain which companies have a good reputation at the time of your visit.

Two common bus types are: 'ordinary' and 'express.' 'Ordinary' buses generally have five seats across – three on one side of the aisle, two on the other – although if there are only five people sitting in them consider yourself lucky! Aisles are often crammed with baggage and in some more remote places there will be people travelling 'upper class' (ie, on the roof).

'Express' buses are a big improvement in that they make fewer stops – they're still usually crowded, but at least you feel like you're getting somewhere. The fare is usually a bit more than on an ordinary bus – well worth the extra. Most states also offer some more upmarket services which go by various names – inquire locally.

Reservations

For the cheaper bus services it pays to have a strategy; if there are two of you, one of you can guard luggage while the other storms the bus in search of a seat. The other accepted method is to pass a book or article of clothing through the open window and place it on an empty seat, or ask a passenger to do it for you. Having made your 'reservation' you can then board the bus after things have simmered down. This method rarely fails.

You can, however, often make advance reservations (sometimes for a small additional fee), but this usually only applies to the more upmarket services such as express and deluxe. Private buses should always be booked in advance.

Many bus stations have a separate women's queue, although this is not always obvious because the relevant sign (where it exists at all) is not often in English and there may not be women queuing. More often than not, the same ticket window will handle the male and the female queue (don't be surprised if you get stories to the contrary from men!). Despite the glares (or even men's refusals to shift in the queue), female travellers should simply sharpen their elbows and confidently make their way to the front, where they will get almost immediate service.

Baggage

Some companies charge a few rupees to store your luggage in an enclosed compartment at the back of the bus. Alternatively, baggage is sometimes carried for free on the roof and if this is the case, it's worthwhile taking some precautions. Make sure it's tied on securely and that nobody dumps a heavy tin trunk on top of your gear. If someone lugs your bag onto the roof, make sure you pay a few rupees for their service. Theft can be a problem so keep an eye on your bags during any stops en route (which are an ideal time to stretch your legs anyway).

Toilet Stops

On long-distance bus trips, chai stops can be far too frequent or, conversely, agonisingly infrequent. Long-distance trips can be a real hassle for women travellers as toilet facilities are generally inadequate, to say the least. For stops in the middle of nowhere, forget about modesty and do what the local women do – wander a few yards off to find a convenient bush.

TRAIN

India has the world's biggest network under one management; over 60,000km of track. Indian Railways (www.indianrailway.com) also has 1.6 million staff, which makes it the world's biggest employer. Moving 11 million passengers daily to any of 7085 stations, it's a ride in India's mainstream. At first the railways can seem as complicated as India – trains range from intercity Shatabdi ('arrow') expresses to country passenger services on narrow gauge tracks with 10 classes, from air-conditioned executive chair to ordinary wooden bench, and separate reservation offices or chaotic queues. It's simple enough once you get used to it. While sometimes slower than buses, train journeys can be relaxing, fascinating and even a little romantic. And for overnight journeys they are much preferred to buses.

There are tourist quotas for many express trains, and special offices or counters for foreigners in major cities and destinations (you must bring a money-changing receipt or ATM slip when paying with rupees). We've listed important trains but there are many, many more. The national *Trains at a Glance* (Rs 25) has 200 pages of trains, and there are timetables covering each regional zone. Check at station newsstands.

Despite a seemingly alarming rate of accidents it's a secure way to travel, though not always fast. Mumbai to Chennai takes around 30 hours by train, or 1¾ hours if you fly. In the monsoon, floods and high rivers cause havoc with tracks and bridges, particularly in North India's Ganges basin and coastal deltas.

Several cities have suburban train networks, which are usually comfortable during the day, but overcrowded in peak hours. These trains might stop only briefly at a station; if its crowded, you have to edge your way to the door in preparation.

Classes

Shatabdi express trains are same-day services between major and regional cities of between three and eight hours distance. These are the fastest and most expensive trains, with only two classes; air-con executive chair and air-con chair. Shatabdis are comfortable, but the glass windows cut the views considerably compared to nonair-con classes on slower trains, which have barred windows and fresh air.

Rajdhani express trains are long-distance express services between Delhi and state capitals, and offer air-conditioned 1st class (1A), two-tier air-con (2A), three-tier air-con (3A) and 2nd class. Two-tier means there are two levels of bunks in each compartment, which are a little wider and longer than their counterparts in three-tier. Two- and three-tier air-con cost respectively a half and a third as much as air-con 1st class, and are perfectly adequate for an overnight trip.

Other express trains and mail trains have two-tier air-con coaches, chair car (if it runs only during the day), nonair-con sleeper (bring your own bedding), nonair-con 2nd class, and finally there's unreserved tickets. A sleeper costs only a quarter as much as two-tier air-con. Some trains also have three-tier air-con and nonair-con 1st class, but the

Express Train Fares in Rupees

distance (km)	1st-class air-con (1A)	2-tier air-con (2A)	3-tier air-con (3A)	chair car (CC)	sleeper (SL)	second (II)
100	542	322	158	114	84	32
200	778	430	243	171	84	54
300	1052	543	329	231	114	73
400	1296	653	405	277	140	90
500	1541	771	482	323	166	107
1000	2506	1253	783	522	270	174
1500	3154	1577	986	658	340	219
2000	3644	1841	1139	800	393	253

latter is being phased out. Mail and express trains carry some fine titles (the *Flying Mail*, *Himalayan Queen* or *Black Diamond Express*) which don't necessarily tell you the destination. You can search through *Trains at a Glance*, or big stations often have English-speaking staff at inquiry counters, who can be helpful with picking the best train. At a smaller station mid-level officials such as the deputy station master usually speak English.

Aficionados of 2nd class can seek out the one-class-only *Janata* (People) express trains, which cost as little as Rs 174 (US$4) to go 1000km. Second-class travel on passenger trains is even cheaper, about 60% less than 2nd class on express trains. In the cheaper classes the squat toilet is usually cleaner than the sit-down flush toilet. Passenger trains do slow local routes, stopping at each tiny country station. These are best on a quiet day, when you can feel the breeze through the windows and listen to local itinerant singers at an unthreatening pace.

Reservations

To make a reservation you must fill out a form stating which class you need and the train's name and number. For overnight journeys it's best to reserve your place a couple of days in advance, particularly if it's a holiday period. If there is no special counter or office for foreigners at the station (sometimes classed with other minorities such as 'Freedom Fighters'), you have to adopt local queuing practices. These range from reasonably orderly lines to mosh pits. There are sometimes separate Ladies' Queues, but usually the same window handles men and women each at a time. So women can go to the front of the queue, next to the first male at the window, and get served.

If the latter is too much, many travel agencies and hotels are in the business of purchasing train tickets for a small commission. But watch out for small-fry travel agents who promise express train tickets and deliver tickets for obscure mail or passenger trains. Only leave a small deposit, if any, and check the tickets before paying.

Reserved tickets show your berth and carriage number. Efficient railway staff also stick lists of names and berths on each reserved carriage, as well as the carriage number in chalk. Air-con carriages tend to be towards the front of trains.

If you can't buy a reserved seat you can ask if there is a waiting list, or try your luck by getting on anyway. Unless it's a popular express train or it's a busy holiday it usually works out. You can get on without a ticket but it is more polite to buy an unreserved ticket, which go on sale an hour before departure, and try to upgrade it. Find a reserved-class carriage and a spare seat, and wait for the conductor (officially the TTE or Travelling Ticket Examiner) to find you. Explain you could only buy an unreserved ticket and ask about vacancies. With luck, the conductor is happy to oblige. You pay the difference between the ordinary fare and the fare of whichever class you're in, plus a small excess charge of around Rs 25. It's a hassle if you don't have enough change, as conductors usually don't either. You might have to wait until he can collect it.

Costs

Fares are calculated by distance. To go between Delhi and Mumbai on the fastest train in the most expensive class costs Rs 4180, while a three-tier air-con berth costs Rs 1485 and the nonair-conditioned sleeper

'Bringing People Together'

Indian Railway sees itself not just as a train operator but as a force for national unity, where people of all communities and castes meet as equals. But more than this, it reaches out to many groups with discounts for both the worthy and the unfortunate. These include a 50% discount for cadets of marine engineering, senior citizens, amateur performers, professional circus parties, unemployed youth and deaf people, and a 75% cut for leprosy patients (non-infectious at least), blind people, war widows and cancer sufferers. Freedom fighters, a range of award winners and parents accompanying child winners of the National Bravery Award are also honoured with concessions. Unfortunately, even if you should be a deaf amateur acrobat studying marine engineering, foreigners are not eligible.

class Rs 431. Reserved tickets attract extra fees of around Rs 50. If your journey is longer than 500km, you can take a day's break en route but you must have your ticket endorsed by the station master or ticket collector at the station you stop at.

Bedding is free in air-con classes, and costs Rs 20 in nonair-con 1st class. Meals are free on Rajdhani and Shatabdi trains, and cheap meals are available on other trains.

Important stations have retiring rooms, which are available if you have a valid ticket. They vary in quality, but at best they're very cheap and can even be ruthlessly clean, with either dormitories or private rooms (see also Accommodation in the Facts for the Visitor chapter).

Refunds Tickets are refundable but fees apply. If you present at least two days in advance, a fee of up to Rs 50 applies. Steeper charges apply with less than four hours to departure, but you can get some sort of refund as late as 12 hours afterwards.

When refunding your ticket you officially have a magic pass to go to the front of the queue, as the next person might require the spot you're surrendering. We've never seen if this actually works.

Indrail Passes

Indrail passes permit unlimited travel for the period of their validity, but they are both expensive and don't get you to the front of the queue. To get full value out of them you'd need to travel about 300km every single day. However, some people find them useful for journeys soon after they arrive in India. Most Western countries have travel agencies that arrange or sell Indrail passes, and they're sold at railway offices in 20 Indian cities.

Children aged between five and 12 pay half fare. There is no refund for either lost or partially used tickets.

Special Trains

The *Palace on Wheels* makes an eight-day circuit of Rajasthan, and you stay in the 'fit for a maharaja' carriages (see the Rajasthan chapter for details). In the opulent saloon cars of *The Royal Orient*, you travel predominantly through Gujarat, but it also takes in some of Rajasthan (see the Gujarat chapter).

Left Luggage

Most stations have left-luggage rooms which cost a couple of rupees per day for one bag. It's useful if you want to visit but not stay in a town, or to hunt for accommodation unencumbered.

CAR

Few people bring their own vehicles to India. If you do decide to bring a car or motorcycle it must be brought in under a carnet, a customs document guaranteeing its removal at the end of your stay. Failing to do so will be very expensive.

Rental

Self-Drive In India self-drive car rental is a possibility. By Western standards the cost is quite low, but given India's hair-raising driving conditions it's much better and

Indrail Pass Prices (US Dollars)

days	1st-class air-con	2-tier air-con	nonair-con
1	57	26	11
2	95	47	19
7	270	135	80
15	370	185	90
30	495	248	125
60	800	400	185
90	1060	530	235

more economical to hire a car and driver (described later).

If you're still interested in self-drive, expect to pay around Rs 1500 per day (with a two-day minimum). Insurance is extra and you usually have to leave a deposit (refundable) of Rs 10,000. Budget, Euro Car, Hertz and several other companies maintain offices in the major cities. You officially need either a valid international driving licence or a regular licence from your home country.

Private Car & Driver Hire Long-distance car hire with driver is becoming an increasingly popular way to get around parts of India. Spread among say, four people, it's not overly expensive and you have the flexibility to go where you want when you want. Rental rates increase in line with hikes in petrol prices.

Almost any local taxi will quite happily set off on a long-distance trip in India. Inquiring at a taxi rank is the easiest way to find a car – you can also ask your hotel to book one for you, although this will usually cost more.

Most trips are officially based on a minimum of 250km a day (about Rs 4 per kilometre) but if you're hiring for at least several days, try to negotiate a daily rate, as this works out cheaper. If you're only taking a day trip, remember that a one-way fare is more expensive per kilometre because it is based on the assumption that the driver will return empty to the starting point. An air-con car will cost almost twice as much as a nonair-con vehicle. Note that there is sometimes an entry fee into other states.

The usual quote for a nonair-con Ambassador car and driver in Delhi is around Rs 1300 per day, but you should be able to barter this down if you intend to hire for a few days. In the hills, the charge starts at Rs 800 per day, however, journeys are usually priced by the farthest point reached. If you want to detour off the most direct route to

Tips for Hiring a Car & Driver

If you hire a car and driver for an extended period of time, try to get a driver who speaks at least some English and who is knowledgeable about the region(s) you intend visiting. It's wise to shop around before deciding so that you have a fair idea of costs and won't be easily hoodwinked.

More than a few travellers have shelled out much more money than is reasonable, paying for the driver's accommodation and meals (even booze!), completely unaware that his lodging/meal cost has already been factored into the fee. Make sure you understand the accommodation/meal arrangement for the driver *before* paying the car hire company and ensure this is made clear to the driver before you set off. In most cases, the charge that is quoted includes an allowance for the driver's daily living expenses (ie, food and lodging).

When it comes to where the driver stays overnight, this is for him to decide and should never be your headache (many choose to sleep in the back seat of the car thus pocketing their accommodation allowance). Some hotels (especially in remote areas) will provide free (or minimal cost) accommodation for drivers, as there is nowhere else to stay.

In the cities and towns, many hotels (especially in tourist hot spots such as Rajasthan) do not permit drivers to stay or eat in guest areas, even if you insist on paying – for more details, see Taxi & Rickshaw Drivers & Hotels in the Society & Conduct section of the Facts about India chapter.

When it comes to safety, given India's often hazardous driving conditions, night travel is best avoided (see the boxed text 'Surviving the Roads' later in this chapter).

Finally, and very importantly, it is imperative to set the ground rules from day one. Many travellers have complained of having their holiday completely dictated by their driver – one couple were bullied into having meals only when it suited the driver. Another set of travellers could only stay at hotels decided by their driver (see also Touts in the Accommodation section of the Facts for the Visitor chapter). Your holiday is going to be much more pleasant if you don't have prickly relations with your driver. The way to achieve this is by politely, but firmly, letting him know from day one that you are the boss. That way, he'll know that you won't put up with any bullying.

At the end of your trip, a tip is the best way of showing your appreciation. So how much should you tip? Well, Rs 50 per day is considered fair, but if you are really chuffed with your driver's service, anything above that is going to get a bigger smile.

this farthest point, the side trips will be priced as extra journeys and added to the total cost for the trip.

Share-Jeeps In many parts of the Himalaya (and elsewhere) share-jeeps supplement the bus service and are particularly useful for getting to the trail-heads for trekking routes, as few buses run out to the smaller villages.

Jeeps generally run between transport hubs, which are usually the junctions of major roads, with connections to local towns and villages. For many destinations in the Himalaya there is often only one bus a day, but you can almost always complete the same route in several stages by share-jeep. Jeeps leave when full from well-established 'passenger stations' on the outskirts of towns and villages; locals should be able to point you in the right direction. The average fare for a one-hour trip is about Rs 50.

Some share-jeeps can really pack in the passengers so as to make as much money as possible (despite maximum passenger regulations) – some travellers may find them too claustrophobic for longer trips.

Beep or Be Beeped

Bald tyres and dodgy brakes hardly raise an eyebrow in India, but a vehicle without a horn is considered almost as absurd as chai without sugar. Surveys by Lonely Planet authors have revealed that the average driver uses the horn 10 to 20 times per kilometre, so a 100km trip can involve a mind-blowing 2000 blasts of the trusty beeper! An unwritten road rule seems to be that the horn should be checked for its continued loud operation at least every 100m. Needless to say, signs prohibiting use of horns are not taken seriously.

Purchase

Buying a car is expensive and not worth the effort unless you intend to stay in India for many months.

On the Road

Because of the extreme congestion in the cities and the narrow, bumpy roads in the country, driving is often a slow, stop-start process – hard on you, the car and fuel economy. Service is so-so in India, parts and tyres are not always easy to obtain, though there are plenty of puncture-repair places. All in all, driving is not all that pleasurable (especially for longer trips) except in rural areas where there's little traffic.

MOTORCYCLE

Travelling by motorcycle is exhilarating and offers the freedom to go when and where you like. Sure you'll probably get a sore backside and receive misleading directions on the way (see the boxed text 'The Art of Not Getting Lost' in the Facts for the Visitor chapter), but you'll also have priceless experiences not available to travellers who rely on public transport. These days, there are a number of excellent motorcycle tours on offer (see Organised Motorcycle Tours, following) which take the hassle out of doing it solo.

There is an array of books about motorcycle travel in India including *Bullet up the Grand Trunk Road* by Jonathan Gregson, which is the author's account of his journey through northern India on a classic Enfield motorcycle. Bill Aitken's *Divining the Deccan* and *Riding the Ranges* are also accounts of motorcycle journeys across some interesting parts of India.

Equipment

You must have either an International Driving Licence or a regular licence from your home country to motorcycle in India.

It's definitely worth bringing your own helmet. Even though Indian helmets may be cheaper, it can be tough finding one that fits well, and the quality is variable. Leathers, gloves, boots, driving goggles, waterproofs and other protective gear should also be brought from your home country.

Organised tours often have a vehicle which transports luggage, but if you're travelling independently, make sure you have a pack that is easy to carry.

Rental

Organised tours provide motorcycles, but if you are planning an independent trip, bikes can be rented in several places in India, such as Delhi and Goa, at negotiable prices. Expect to pay upwards of Rs 400/10,000 per day/month for a 500cc bike (including insurance). You'll probably have to leave a cash deposit (returnable) and/or your return air ticket.

Purchase

To purchase a second-hand machine is a matter of asking around and a perfect place to start is with mechanics, who can usually also offer advice about insurance options.

In Delhi the area around Hari Singh Nalwa St in Karol Bagh is full of places buying, selling and renting motorcycles. Two places recommended by travellers are:

Inder Motors (☎ 011-572 8579, fax 5781052) 1744/55 Hari Singh Nalwa St, Karol Bagh
Madaan Motors (☎ 011-573 5801, fax 7235684, ⓔ madaanmotors@yahoo.com) 1767/53 Naiwala St, Karol Bagh

To buy a new bike, you officially have to have a local address and be a resident foreign national. When buying second-hand, all you need to do is give an address.

Prices for new motorcycles at the time of research were:

Enfield 500cc	Rs 69,000
Enfield 350cc	Rs 54,000 (standard)
	Rs 58,000 (deluxe)
Rajdoot 175cc	US$800

Inder Motors and Madaan Motors can ship a bike for around Rs 13,500 including the crate, packing and insurance. Second-hand bikes (two to three years old) cost about US$1000 for a 500cc. Transferring ownership costs Rs 1000 to 1500.

When the time comes to sell the bike, try not to appear too anxious to get rid of it. But if you get a reasonable offer, grab it.

Ownership Papers An obvious tip perhaps, but do not part with your money until you have the ownership papers, receipt and affidavit signed by a magistrate authorising the owner (as recorded in the ownership papers) to sell the machine – not to mention the keys to the bike and the bike itself!

Each state often has a different set of ownership transfer formalities – inquire locally to find out the latest requirements.

Which Bike? The big decision to make is whether to buy new or second hand. Obviously, cost is the main factor, but remember that with a new bike you are less likely to get hoodwinked (as the price is fixed). Old bikes are obviously cheaper and you don't have to be a registered resident foreign national, but you are far more open to getting gypped, either by paying too much or by being sold a dud bike.

The best advice is to do your homework thoroughly and shop around to get an idea of the latest machines on the market and their costs. It also pays to speak to people who have travelled around India by motorcycle – they're a gold mine of information.

On the Road

It must be said that, given the general road conditions, motorcycling is a reasonably hazardous endeavour, and one ideally undertaken by experienced riders. Hazards range from goats crossing the road to defunct trucks which have been abandoned in the middle of the road. And of course there are the perpetual potholes and unmarked speed humps to contend with. Rural roads sometimes have various grain crops laid out on roads to be threshed by passing vehicles – it can be a real hazard for bikers.

The risk of bike theft is minimal. The worst you're likely to experience is the way people seem to treat parked motorcycles as public utilities – handy for sitting on, using the mirror to comb their hair, fiddling with the switches – none of which is usually intended to do any damage. You'll just have to turn all the switches off and readjust the mirrors when you get back on.

Avoid covering too much territory in one day. A lot of energy is spent simply concentrating on the road, making long days exhausting and potentially dangerous. On the busy national highways expect to average 50km/h without stops; on smaller roads, where driving conditions are worse, 10km/h is not an unrealistic average. On the whole, on good roads you can easily expect to cover a minimum of 100km a day (up to 300km with minimal stops).

Night driving should be avoided at all costs. If you think driving in daylight is difficult, imagine what it's like at night when there's the added hazard of half the vehicles being inadequately lit (or without headlights on at all), not to mention other hindrances such as animals crossing and broken-down vehicles.

For really long hauls, putting the bike on a train can be a convenient option. You'll generally pay about as much as the 2nd-class passenger fare for the bike. The petrol tank must be empty, and there should be a tag in an obvious place detailing name, destination, passport number and train details. When you pack the bike, it's wise to remove the mirrors and loosen the handlebars to prevent damage.

Repairs & Maintenance

Original spare parts bought from an 'authorised dealer' can be expensive compared to copies available from your spare-parts wallah. Delhi's Karol Bagh is a good place to go for spare parts for all Indian and imported bikes. If you're going to remote regions, take basic spares with you (valves, piston rings etc) as they may not be readily available.

For all machines (particularly older ones), make sure you regularly check and tighten all nuts and bolts, as Indian roads and engine vibration tend to work things loose quite quickly. Check the engine and gearbox oil level regularly – with the quality of oil it is advisable to change it and clean the oil filter every couple of thousand kilometres.

Punctures Given the condition of many Indian roads, the chances are you'll make constant visits to a puncture-wallah. These phenomenal fix-it men are found almost everywhere, but it's obviously good to have the tools to at least remove your own wheel. Indeed, given the hassles of constant flat tyres, it's worth lashing out on new tyres if you buy a second-hand bike with worn tyres. A new rear tyre for an Enfield costs around Rs 600 to 700.

Organised Motorcycle Tours

Motorcycle tours are a superb, no-hassles way of seeing India. They usually operate with a minimum number of people and some can even be tailor-made. Contact operators directly for prices and other details:

Asia Safari (☎/fax 011-613 6752) 491 Sector A, Pocket C, Vasant Kunj, New Delhi. This company offers tours of Kumaon, Garwhal, Lahaul, Spiti and Kinnaur.
Web site: www.asiasafari.com

Classic Bike Adventure (☎ 0832-262076, fax 276124, 277343, ⓔ info@classic-bike-india.de) Casa Tres Amigos, Socol Vado No 425, Assagao, Bardez, Goa. This is a German company that organises bike tours to various destinations lasting several weeks.
Web site: www.classic-bike-india.de

Ferris Wheels (☎/fax 61-2-9904 7419, ⓔ safari@ferriswheels.com.au) Box 743, Crows Nest, NSW 2065, Australia. This company organises tours through the Himalaya and Rajasthan on classic Enfields.
Web site: www.ferriswheels.com.au

Himalayan Motorcycle Tours (☎/fax 44-1256-771773, ⓔ patrickmoffat@yahoo.com) 16 High St, Overton, Hants R625 3HA, UK. This is run by an easy-going American expat, Patrick Moffat. Patrick conducts upmarket tours of Himachal Pradesh, Sikkim, Rajasthan and Ladakh, as well as Tibet, Bhutan and Nepal.
Web site: www.himalayanmotorcycles.com

Indian Motorcycle Adventures (☎ 64-9-372 7550, ⓔ gumby@ihug.co.nz) 40 O'Brien Rd, Rocky Bay, Waiheke Island, New Zealand. This company offers 20-day tours of Rajasthan.

BICYCLE

India offers an immense array of experiences and challenges for a long-distance cyclist: there are high-altitude passes and rocky dirt tracks; smooth-surfaced highways; coastal routes through lush coconut palms; and meandering country roads through picturesque tea plantations. Hills, plains, plateaus, deserts – you name it, India's got it!

Nevertheless, long-distance cycling is not for the faint of heart or weak of knee. You'll need physical endurance to cope with the roads, traffic and the climate.

Before you set out, read some books on bicycle touring such as the Sierra Club's *The Bike Touring Manual* by Rob van de Plas (Bicycle Books, 1993). Cycling magazines provide useful information including listings for bicycle tour operators and the addresses of spare-parts suppliers. Their classifieds sections are also good places to look for a riding companion.

For a real feel for the adventure of touring by bicycle in strange places, read Dervla

Murphy's *Full Tilt – From Dunkirk to Delhi on a Bicycle*, Lloyd Sumner's *The Long Ride* and Bettina Selby's *Riding the Mountains Down* (subtitled *A Journey by Bicycle to Kathmandu*).

Your local cycling club may also be able to help with information and advice. In the UK, the Cyclists Touring Club (☎ 01483-417217, fax 426994, ⓔ cycling@ctc.org.uk), 69 Meadrow, Godalming, Surrey GU7 3HS, has country touring sheets that are free to members and a Web site at www.ctc.org.uk. The International Bicycle Fund (☎ 206-767 0848), 4887 Columbia Drive South, Seattle, WA 98108-1919, USA, has a Web site at www.ibike.org and two useful publications: *Selecting and Preparing a Bike for Travel in Remote Areas* and *Bikes Can Fly* (about flying with your bike).

If you're a serious cyclist or amateur racer and want to contact counterparts while in India, there's the Cycle Federation of India; contact the Secretary, Yamun Velodrome, New Delhi. If you're after anything bike related in Delhi head for Jhandwalan market, near Karol Bagh, which has imported and domestic new and second-hand bikes and spare parts.

Using Your Own Bike

It may be hard to find parts, especially wheels, for touring bikes with 700cc wheels. Parts for bicycles with 26-inch wheels and parts (of variable standards) are available.

Carry a good lock and use it. Consider wrapping your bicycle frame in used inner tubes – this not only hides fancy paint jobs, but protects them from knocks and scrapes. If planning to buy a bike in India, consider bringing you own saddle, rack and good-quality panniers.

Rental & Purchase

Even in the smallest towns there is usually at least one outlet that rents bikes. In tourist areas (eg, hill stations, Goa and Rajasthan) there are a handful of places, but the rates are cranked up.

You may like to buy a bike in India and your best bet is to shop around to get a feel for brands and prices. There are many brands of Indian clunkers, including Hero, Atlas, BSA and Raleigh. Raleigh is considered the finest quality, followed by BSA, which has a big line of models including some sporty jobs. Hero mountain-style bicycles are on sale in the larger towns.

Once you've decided on a bike you have a choice of luggage carriers – mostly the rat-trap type varying only in size, price and strength. There's a plethora of saddles available but all are equally bum-breaking. Get a machine fitted with a stand and bell.

Reselling is usually a breeze. Count on getting about 60% to 70% of what you originally paid, if it was a new bike. A local cycle-hire shop will probably be interested, or simply ask around to find potential buyers.

Most travellers prefer to buy a bike in India, but by all means consider bringing your own. Mountain bikes are especially suited to India – their sturdier construction makes them more manoeuvrable, less prone to damage, and allows you to tackle rocky, muddy roads unsuitable for lighter machines. Inquire in your home country about air transport and custom formalities.

Transporting Your Bike

Remove pedals, all luggage and accessories, turn the handlebars, cover the chain and let the tyres down a bit.

On the Road

It's obviously more pleasurable to ride on quieter roads – avoid big cities where the chaotic traffic can be a real hazard for bikers. National highways can also be a nightmare with speeding trucks and buses. Always make inquiries before venturing off road.

If you've never cycled long distances, start with 20km to 40km a day and increase this as you gain stamina and confidence.

Be warned that asking directions can send you on a wild goose chase (see the boxed text 'The Art of Not Getting Lost' in the Facts for the Visitor chapter).

Avoid leaving anything on your bike that can easily be removed when it's unattended. You may like to bring along a padlock and chain. However, don't be paranoid – your bike is probably safer in India than in many Western cities.

Distances

For an eight-hour pedal an experienced cycle tourist will average 70km to 100km a day on undulating plains, or 50km to 70km in mountainous areas on sealed roads; cut this by at least one-third for unsealed roads.

The distance you cycle can be dictated by available accommodation; not all villages have a place to stay. If you're cycling in a hot climate, try to get your cycling done by noon as the sun may be too strong in the afternoon. Hotels also fill up in the afternoon and it's usually dark by 6 pm, so these are additional reasons to get an early start.

Repairs & Maintenance

For Indian bikes, there are plenty of repair 'shops' (some consist only of a puncture-wallah with his box of tools under a tree), which makes maintenance delightfully straightforward. Puncture-wallahs will patch tubes for a nominal cost. Check the tyres regularly for bits of glass or other sharp objects and dig them out before they make it through to the tube.

If you bring your own bicycle to India, you'll need to be prepared for the contingencies of part replacement or repair. Several travellers warn that it is not at all easy locating foreign parts. Ensure you have a working knowledge of your machine. Bring all necessary tools with you as well as a compact bike manual with diagrams – Indian mechanics can work wonders and illustrations help overcome the language barrier. Roads don't often have paved shoulders and are very dusty, so keep your chain lubricated, and bring a spare.

HITCHING

Hitching is never entirely safe in any country in the world, and we don't recommend it. Travellers who decide to hitch should understand that they are taking a small but potentially serious risk. People who do choose to hitch will be safer if they travel in pairs and let someone know where they are planning to go.

Surviving the Roads

In 1951 the number of motorised vehicles on India's roads totalled 300,000. The figure had climbed to 5.4 million by 1981 and swelled to an estimated 45 million by 2001. Road deaths have risen in line with vehicle numbers and are in fact the highest in the world – an estimated 80,000 people each year! According to the Central Road Research Institute, about 10% of road fatalities are pedestrians and cyclists in the major cities. The pavements are a big problem; they are often in a state of severe disrepair, tiny or nonexistent, therefore tempting pedestrians to jaywalk – with deadly results.

The reasons for the high road toll in India are numerous, and many of them fairly obvious. Firstly, there's road congestion and vehicle overcrowding – when a bus runs off the road there are plenty of people stuffed inside to get injured, and it's unlikely too many of them will be able to escape in a hurry.

Secondly, there is India's unwritten 'might is right' road rule, which means that vehicles always have the right of way over pedestrians and bigger vehicles always have the right of way over smaller ones. It's not surprising that so many pedestrians are killed in hit-and-run accidents. (The propensity to disappear after the incident is not wholly surprising since lynch mobs can assemble remarkably quickly, even when the driver is not at fault.)

A substantial number of accidents involve trucks. Being the biggest, heaviest and mightiest vehicles on the road, you either get out of their way or get mowed down. Also, as with so many Indian vehicles, they're likely to be grossly overloaded and not in the best condition. Trucks invariably carry considerably more than the maximum recommended by the manufacturer. It's a real eye-opener to see the number of trucks crumpled by the sides of the national highways, and these aren't old accidents, but ones that have obviously happened in the last 24 hours or so.

If you are driving, you need to be alert at all times. At night there are unilluminated cars and ox carts, and in the daytime there are zigzagging bicycle riders and hordes of pedestrians. Day and night there are the fearless truck drivers to contend with. The other thing you have to endure at night is the eccentric way in which headlights are used – a combination of full beam and totally off (dipped beams are virtually unheard of). A loud horn definitely helps since the normal driving technique is to put your hand firmly on the horn, close your eyes and plough through regardless. Considering the hazards of night driving, it's best to avoid it altogether.

Even though the Indian roads can be a nail-biting experience, it may help if you take solace in the Indian karma theory – it's not so much the vehicle that collides with you as the events of your previous life that caused the accident.

Hitching in India is not a realistic option. There are not that many private cars whizzing by so you are likely to be on board trucks. You are then stuck with the old quandaries of: 'Do they understand what I am doing?', 'Should I be paying for this?', 'Will the driver expect to be paid?', 'Will they be unhappy if I don't offer to pay?', 'Will they be unhappy if I offer or will they simply want too much?'.

It is a very bad idea for women to hitch. A woman in the cabin of a truck on a lonely road is perhaps tempting fate.

BOAT

Apart from ferries across rivers (of which there are many), the only *real* boating possibility is through the beautiful backwaters of Kerala – not to be missed.

The only other ferries connecting coastal ports are those from Kolkata and Chennai to the Andaman Islands.

LOCAL TRANSPORT

Although there are comprehensive local bus networks in most major towns, unless you have time to familiarise yourself with the routes you're better off sticking to taxis, autorickshaws, cycle-rickshaws and hiring bicycles. The buses are often so hopelessly overcrowded that you can only really use them if you get on at the starting point and get off at the terminus.

A basic ground rule applies to any form of transport where the fare is not ticketed or fixed (unlike a bus or train), or calculated by a meter – agree on the fare beforehand. If you fail to do that you can expect enormous arguments and hassles when you get to your destination. And agree on the fare clearly – if there is more than one of you make sure it covers all of you. If you have baggage make sure there are no extra charges, or you may be asked for more at the end of the trip. If a driver refuses to use the meter, or insists on an extortionate rate, simply walk away – if he really wants the job the price will drop. If you can't agree on a reasonable fare, find another driver.

Other useful tips when catching taxis/rickshaws include: always have enough small change, as drivers rarely do, which can be a real hassle especially at night when shops/banks (where you can get change) are closed; if you are staying, or dining at a top-end venue and you need to catch a rickshaw, try walking a few hundred metres down the road to avoid the drivers who hang outside assuming you're a cash cow. Finally, it's a good idea to carry around a business card of the hotel in which you are staying, as your pronunciation of streets, hotel names etc may be incomprehensible to drivers. Some hotel cards even have a nifty little sketch map clearly indicating their location.

Fares are often steeper (as much as double the day fare) at night and some drivers charge a few rupees extra for luggage.

Many autorickshaw drivers are right into the commission racket – see Touts in the Accommodation section of the Facts for the Visitor chapter.

To/From the Airport

There are official buses, operated by the government, Indian Airlines or some local cooperative, to a number of airports in India. Where there aren't any, there will be taxis or autorickshaws. There are some airports close enough to town to get to by cycle-rickshaw.

When arriving at an airport anywhere in India, the first thing to do is find out if there's a prepaid taxi booth inside the arrivals hall. If there is, pay for one there. If you don't do this and simply walk outside to negotiate your own price, you'll invariably pay more and also have to go through the hassle of negotiating. Taxi drivers are notorious for refusing to use the meter outside airport terminals. Obviously some taxi drivers don't like the pre-paid system (as there's no scope for rip-offs), so it's a good idea not to present the voucher until you have arrived at your destination.

Taxi

There are taxis in most towns in India, and most of them (certainly in the major cities) are metered. Getting a metered fare is rather a different situation. First of all the meter may be 'broken'. Threatening to get another taxi will usually fix it immediately, except during rush hours. It's best to get a pre-paid taxi if it's available.

Secondly, the meter will almost certainly be out of date. Fares are adjusted upwards so much faster and more frequently than meters are recalibrated that drivers almost always have 'fare adjustment cards' indicating what you should pay compared to what the meter indicates. This is, of course, wide open to abuse. You have no idea if you're being shown the right card or if the taxi's meter has actually been recalibrated and you're being shown the card anyway. In states where the numbers are written differently (such as Gujarat) it's not much use asking for the chart if you can't read it!

The only answer to all this is to try to get an idea of what the fare should be before departure (ask information desks at the airport or at your hotel). You'll soon begin to develop a feel for what the meter says, what the cards say and what the two together should indicate.

In various regions, particularly in the hills of Himachal Pradesh and Uttaranchal, taxi operators have organised themselves into unions and offer fixed rates to common destinations, often with some local sightseeing tours thrown in. Generally these rates cannot be bargained down, although drivers may approach you away from the union office and offer lower fares. Taxi union offices can be found at the bus stands in major towns

Autorickshaw

An autorickshaw is a noisy three-wheel device powered by a two-stroke motorcycle engine with a driver up front and seats for two (or sometimes more) passengers behind. They don't have doors (except in Goa) and have just a canvas top. They are also known as scooters or autos. Although they are all made by Bajaj, it's amazing how the decor can differ. Many display artistic devotional images, while others are almost completely covered with glossy pictures of the driver's favourite Bollywood stars.

They're generally about half the price of a taxi, usually metered and follow the same ground rules as taxis.

Because of their size, autorickshaws are often faster than taxis for short trips and their drivers are decidedly nuttier – hair-raising near-misses are guaranteed and glancing-blow collisions are not infrequent; thrillseekers will love it!

In busy towns you'll find that, when stopped at traffic lights, the height you are sitting at is the same as most bus and truck exhaust pipes – copping dirty great lungfuls of diesel fumes is part of the autorickshaw experience. Also, their small wheel size and rock-hard suspension makes them supremely uncomfortable; even the slightest bump will have you instantly airborne.

Tempo

Somewhat like a large autorickshaw, these ungainly looking three-wheel devices operate rather like minibuses or share-taxis along fixed routes. Unless you are spending large amounts of time in one city, it is generally impractical to try to find out what the routes are. You'll find it much easier and more convenient to go by autorickshaw.

Cycle-Rickshaw

This is effectively a three-wheeler bicycle with a seat for two passengers behind the rider. Although they no longer operate in most of the big cities, except in the old part of Delhi and parts of Kolkata, you will find them in all the smaller cities and towns, where they're the basic means of transport.

As with taxis and autorickshaws, fares must always be agreed on in advance. Avoid situations where the driver says something like: 'As you like'. He's hoping you are not well acquainted with the correct fares and will overpay. But more importantly, invariably, no matter what you pay in situations like this, it will be deemed too little and a very unpleasant situation can quickly develop. This is especially the case in heavily touristed places, such as Agra and Jaipur – simply settle on the price before you get moving to avoid prickly arguments. A typical ride in a cycle-rickshaw is generally between one and three kilometres and will cost between Rs 15 and 30. The ride is extremely strenuous work for the driver, so a tip is much appreciated.

It's also quite feasible to hire a rickshaw-wallah by time, not just for a trip. Hiring one for a day or several days can make good financial sense for both you as well as the rickshaw-wallah.

Other Transport

In some places, tongas (horse-drawn two-wheelers) and victorias (horse-drawn carriages) still run. Kolkata has a large tram network and India's first underground. Mumbai, Delhi and Chennai have suburban trains. People-drawn rickshaws still operate in parts of Kolkata – see the Kolkata chapter for more information.

ORGANISED TOURS

At almost any place which is of tourist interest in India, and quite a few places which aren't, there will be tours operated either by the Government of India tourist office, the state tourist office or the local transport company – sometimes all three. There are also a growing number of private operators. Tours are usually very good value, particularly in places where the sights are spread out. You probably couldn't get around Delhi on public transport as cheaply as you can on a tour, for instance. However, admission fees and camera and video charges are usually not included in the tour fees.

These tours are not purely aimed at foreign tourists; you will almost always find yourself outnumbered by local tourists. Despite this, the tours are usually in English (ask when booking). One major drawback of many tours is that they try to cram too much into a short a period. If a tour looks too hectic, do it yourself at a more appropriate pace – or you could go on it with the intention of finding out which places you'd like to visit on your own at a later time.

DELHI

Delhi

Delhi is the capital of India, its third-largest city and North India's industrial hub. Old Delhi was the capital of Muslim India between the 17th and 19th centuries and a legacy of mosques, monuments and forts testify to this. New Delhi was built as the imperial capital of India by the British. It is a spacious, open city and contains embassies and government buildings. The newer, wealthy suburbs are mostly to the south of New Delhi, and an ever-growing belt of poorer suburbs and *jhuggies* (slums) stretches in all directions.

In addition to its historic interest and role as the government centre, Delhi is a major travel gateway. It is one of India's busiest entrance points for overseas airlines, the hub of the North Indian travel network, and a stop on the overland route across Asia. The city of Delhi covers most of Delhi state.

Few travellers have anything good to say about Delhi; the intense air pollution and persistent touts often make it an unsettling experience for newcomers. It does, however, have a long and fascinating history and there is plenty to see and do.

Deli at a Glance

Population: 13.8 million
Area: 1483 sq km
Main Languages: Hindi, Urdu, English & Punjabi
Telephone Area Code: 011
When to Go: Oct to Mar

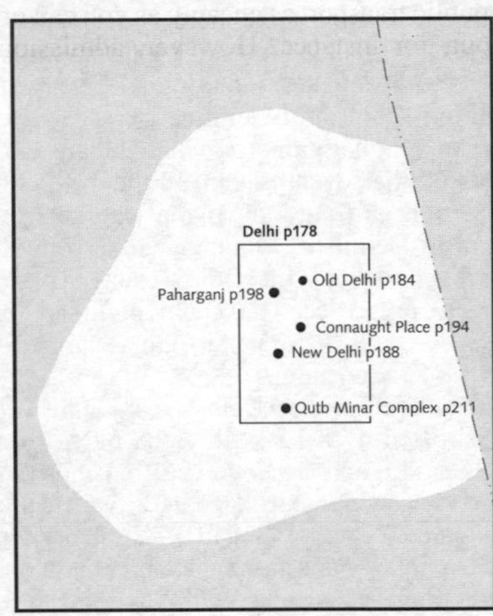

- Wander at leisure around the Red Fort, Delhi's massive Mughal-era fort
- See Qutb Minar, a massive tower built to proclaim the arrival of Islam in India
- Discover Jama Masjid, the largest mosque in India and built by Shah Jahan of Taj Mahal fame
- Explore Connaught Place, the thriving heart of New Delhi
- Visit Humayun's tomb, a fine example of early Mughal architecture
- Peruse and purchase arts and crafts at Janpath's Central Cottage Industries Emporium or Dilli Haat

HISTORY

Delhi hasn't always been the capital of India, but it has played an important role in Indian history. The settlement of Indraprastha, which featured in the epic Mahabharata over 3000 years ago, was approximately on the site of present-day Delhi. Over 2000 years ago, Pataliputra (near modern-day Patna) was the capital of Ashoka's empire. The Mughal emperors made Agra the capital through the 16th and 17th centuries. Under the British, Kolkata (Calcutta) was the capital until the inauguration of New Delhi in 1931.

There have been at least eight cities around modern Delhi, and the old saying that whoever founds a new city at Delhi will lose it has come true every time – most recently for the British who lasted only 16 years. The first four cities were to the south around the area where the Qutb Minar stands.

Indraprastha, the earliest known Delhi, was centred near present-day Purana Qila. At the beginning of the 12th century the last Hindu kingdom of Delhi was ruled by the Tomara and Chauthan dynasties and was also near the Qutb Minar and Surajkund, now in Haryana.

This city was followed by Siri, built by Ala-ud-din near present-day Hauz Khas in the 12th century. The third Delhi was Tughlaqabad, now entirely in ruins, which stood

10km south-east of the Qutb Minar. The fourth Delhi dates from the 14th century and was also a creation of the Tughlaqs. Known as Jahanpanah, it also stood near the Qutb Minar.

The fifth Delhi, Firozabad, was at Firoz Shah Kotla in present-day New Delhi. Its ruins include an Ashoka pillar, moved from elsewhere, and traces of a mosque where Tamerlane prayed during his attack on India.

Emperor Sher Shar created the sixth Delhi at Purana Qila, near India Gate in New Delhi today. Sher Shar was an Afghan ruler who defeated the Mughal Humayun and took control of Delhi.

The Mughal emperor, Shah Jahan, constructed the seventh Delhi in the 17th century, thus shifting the Mughal capital from Agra to Delhi; his Shahjahanabad roughly corresponds to Old Delhi today and is largely preserved. His Delhi included the Red Fort and the majestic Jama Masjid (a *masjid* is a mosque).

Finally, the eighth Delhi, New Delhi, was constructed by the British – the move from Kolkata was announced in 1911 but construction was not completed, and the city officially inaugurated, until 1931. In 1947, it became the capital of truncated India, and Hindu and Sikh refugees poured in from Pakistan.

SIMON BORG

India's national bird, the magnificent peacock, is featured in many artworks

Many have invaded Delhi through the ages. Tamerlane plundered it in the 14th century; the Afghan Babur occupied it in the 16th century, and in 1739 the Persian emperor, Nadir Shah, sacked the city and carted the Kohinoor Diamond (now part of the British royal family's crown jewels) and the famous Peacock Throne off to Iran. The British captured Delhi in 1803, but during the Indian Uprising of 1857 it was a centre of resistance against the British. Prior to Partition, Delhi had a very large Muslim population and Urdu was the main language. Now Hindu Punjabis have replaced many of the Muslims, and Hindi predominates.

William Dalrymple's excellent *City of Djinns* is a wonderfully entertaining introduction to Delhi's past and present.

ORIENTATION

Delhi is a relatively easy city to find your way around although it is very spread out. The section of interest to visitors is on the west bank of the Yamuna River and is divided basically into two parts – the tightly packed streets of Old Delhi and the spacious, planned areas of New Delhi.

Old Delhi is the 17th-century walled city of Shahjahanabad, with city gates, narrow alleys, constant traffic jams and terrible air pollution, the enormous Red Fort and Jama Masjid, temples, mosques, bazaars and the famous street known as Chandni Chowk. Here you will find the New Delhi train station and, a little farther north, the main Inter State Bus Terminal (ISBT) near Kashmiri Gate. Near New Delhi train station, and acting as a sort of buffer zone between the old and new cities, is the crowded market area of Paharganj. This has become the budget travellers' hang-out, and there are many popular cheap hotels and restaurants in this area.

New Delhi is a planned city of wide, tree-lined streets, parks and fountains, but it retains Indian touches of doe-eyed cows calmly ignoring the traffic and squatter hovels on waste land. It can be further subdivided into the business and residential areas around Connaught Place and the government areas around Rajpath to the south. At the eastern end of Rajpath is the India Gate memorial and at the west end is Rashtrapati Bhavan, the residence of the Indian president.

The hub of New Delhi is the great circle of Connaught Place and the streets that

Dodgy Delhi

Delhi is an assault on all the senses that daunts most new arrivals to both the city and India. Frazzled from a long journey, most find the hounding of the beggars and touts too much, especially as they're often trying to manoeuvre past cows and rickshaws and deal with the myriad smells, noise and pollution at the same time.

This is compounded by many international flights arriving and departing Delhi airport at terrible hours of the morning. Fortunately most airport facilities are open 24 hours, so it's possible to change cash and make travel arrangements before you brave the onslaught. No matter the time of arrival, it's advisable to book a decent hotel room in advance and notify it if you're arriving late or early. Many places have 24-hour receptions; those that don't will have a staff member sleeping nearby to check you in. It's also possible to sleep or hang out at the airport until morning but this is only putting off the inevitable and, anyway, it's a much quicker and easier drive into the city at night.

Even with a hotel booking, getting from the airport can be tricky. The EATS bus stops at large hotels, the Kashmiri Gate Inter State Bus Terminal (ISBT), New Delhi train station and Connaught Place. A taxi is a better option especially at night – if you're on your own, look for others to share with. Get a receipt with the taxi number and destination from the traffic police prepaid taxi booth; the others overcharge. Despite the taxi registration number and destination being written down, airport taxi drivers are notorious for scams to get tourists into expensive and commission-paying hotels. Be firm and confident – don't let on if this is your first visit; if the driver is not prepared to go where *you* want, find another taxi. You can make complaints about drivers on ☎ 6101197.

Most effective during the wee hours, popular stories to get you to another hotel include the hotel 'full', 'burnt down' and 'closed' lines as well as a few more:

Riots-in-Delhi syndrome Your driver claims there are riots in Delhi and as you're insisting you still want to be dropped at your chosen hotel the taxi is flagged down by a man in uniform – the police, you assume. There's a heated exchange in Hindi and you're informed the rioting is very bad and many people have been killed. You end up in an expensive hotel in a 'safe' area.

Lost-driver syndrome Your driver doesn't know where your hotel is (everyone knows where Main Bazaar and Connaught Place are), so stops at a travel agency to get directions. The agent offers a free phone call to check your hotel reservation as it's a busy holiday or festival that day. They dial the number and you talk to the 'receptionist' who apologises but your room is double-booked and your reservation is cancelled. Fortunately you're in a travel agency and they can get you into a much better (commission-paying) place.

radiate from it, which are divided into blocks from A to N. Signs indicate where you are. Here you will find most of the airline offices, banks, travel agents, state and national tourist offices, more budget accommodation and several of the big hotels. The Regal Cinema, at the south side of the circle, and the Plaza Cinema, at the north, are two important landmarks and are useful for telling taxi or autorickshaw drivers where you want to go.

Janpath, running off Connaught Place to the south, has the Government of India tourist office, hotels, airlines and a number of other useful addresses. South of the New Delhi government areas are Delhi's more expensive residential areas, with names like Defence Colony, South Extension, Lodi Colony, Greater Kailash and Vasant Vihar. Many of the better (and more expensive) cinemas and shopping centres are found here. Indira Gandhi international airport is about 17km to the south-west of the city, and about halfway between the airport and Connaught Place is Chanakyapuri, the diplomatic enclave. Most of Delhi's embassies (and the prime minister's house) are concentrated in this strikingly tidy area and there are several major hotels here. (For details on foreign embassies and consulates in Delhi see Embassies & Consulates in the Facts for the Visitor chapter.)

Across the Yamuna River (heavily polluted for the nine months of the year when the monsoon is not flushing it) are many new industrial and residential areas, as well as some of the grimmest slum areas.

Dodgy Delhi

Many decide that Delhi (and therefore India) is just too much and book the next flight home. Hang in there if you start feeling this way, it's really not that bad. Take a few days to chill out and acclimatise to the Indian surroundings. Don't hide away in the tourist ghettoes – explore some of Delhi's more relaxed sights such as the gardens, the Red Fort, Humayun's tomb, the National Museum and Raj Ghat. If you're really suffering, head for Connaught Place where air-con and familiar brands of beer and pizza can help transport you home for a while. Avoid chaotic Old Delhi until you're more relaxed and are ready to appreciate the city's colourful history and vibrant personality – who knows, you may even start to like the place. If you're still determined to leave, there are plenty of calmer places easily accessible from Delhi (see also Getting There & Away in this chapter and individual entries):

Train One of the easiest and most comfortable ways out, there are special foreigner railway reservation offices at central locations. Beware of touts outside New Delhi train station who redirect travellers to their travel agencies (generally across the road) on the pretext that the reservation office is closed, has moved or spontaneously combusted the day before.

Bus Public and private buses ply popular routes. Private buses, booked through accommodation and travel agencies, are generally the more comfortable and direct option.

Tours If you prefer minimum hassle then tours are good, the Delhi-Jaipur-Agra triangle is popular. Tourist offices and accommodation have details. Beware of travel agents and touts dedicated to helping confused tourists – we get hundreds of complaints about these guys (see Travel Agencies later in this chapter for recommended operators). Kashmiris around Connaught Place and Paharganj in particular do the hard sell on their economically crippled yet beautiful homeland. There's a good reason they tout so hard – it's a war zone.

Taxi It's possible to hire the use of a taxi and driver for around US$30 per day (based on two sharing an all-inclusive tour around North India) through accommodation and travel agencies. Airport transfers and Delhi sightseeing tours are usually 'thrown-in' on longer trips.

The 250-page *Eicher City Map* (Rs 270) includes 174 area maps, and is a good reference if you are venturing further into the Delhi environs. It's available at most larger bookshops and modern fuel stations.

INFORMATION

Tourist Offices

The Government of India tourist office (☎ 3320005) at 88 Janpath is open 9 am to 6 pm Monday to Friday and 9 am to 2 pm Saturday. The office has a lot of information and brochures on destinations from all over India, but you have to ask for it. It has a good giveaway map of the city, and can also help with accommodation. Some of the staff have been known to try to sell overpriced taxi tours.

There are tourist offices in the arrivals halls of the international (☎ 5694229) and domestic (☎ 5665296) airports, which are open around the clock. Here, too, they can help you find accommodation although, like many other Indian tourist offices, they may tell you the hotel you choose is 'full'.

There are two Delhi Tourism Corporation offices in Connaught Place: in N-Block (☎ 3313637), open 7 am to 9 pm Monday to Friday, and near the state emporiums on Baba Kharak Singh Marg (with a pleasant coffee shop and garden). It also has counters at New Delhi, Old Delhi, and Nizamuddin train stations, as well as at the Kashmiri Gate ISBT.

There are several guides available from newsstands – *Delhi City Guide* and *Delhi*

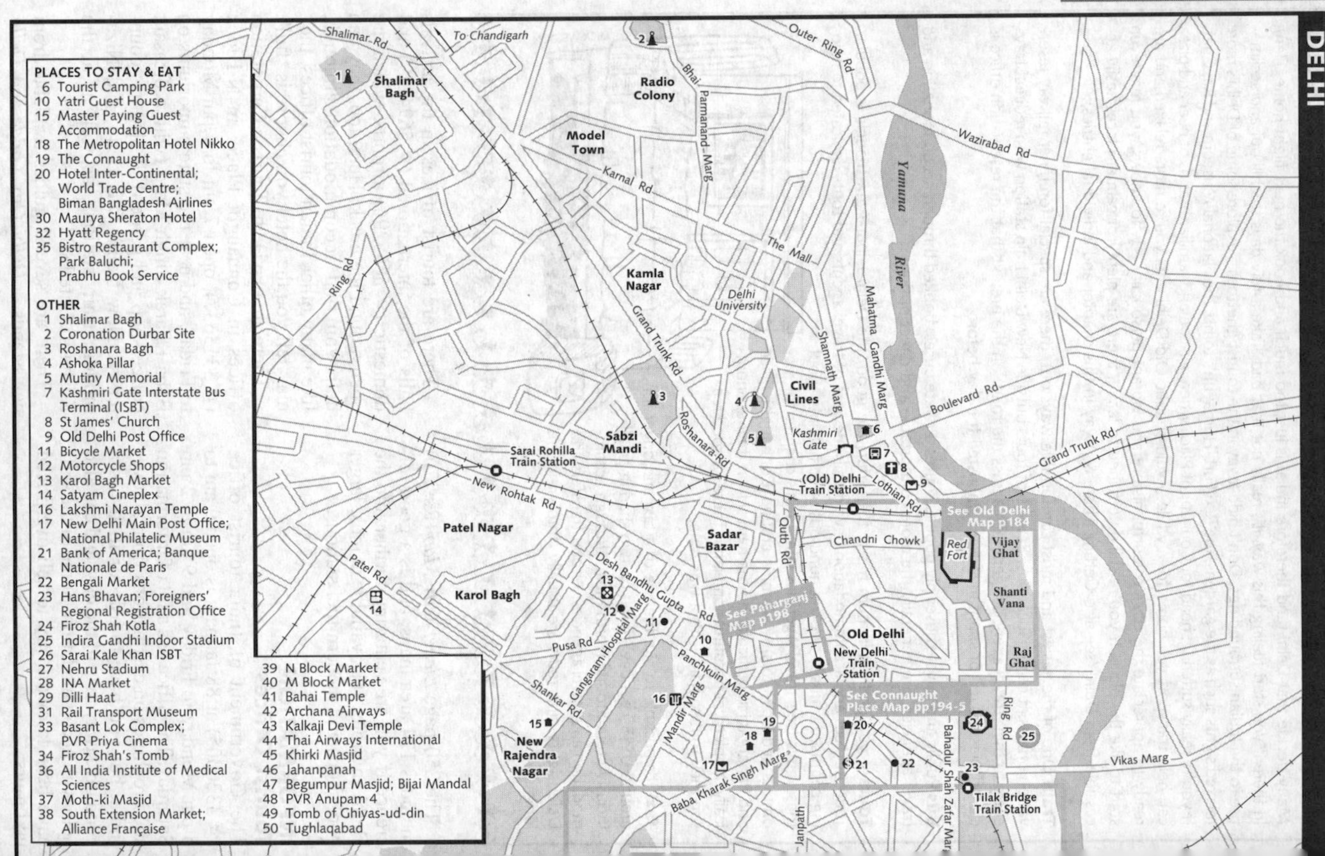
DELHI
PLACES TO STAY & EAT
6 Tourist Camping Park
10 Yatri Guest House
15 Master Paying Guest Accommodation
18 The Metropolitan Hotel Nikko
19 The Connaught
20 Hotel Inter-Continental; World Trade Centre; Biman Bangladesh Airlines
30 Maurya Sheraton Hotel
32 Hyatt Regency
35 Bistro Restaurant Complex; Park Baluchi; Prabhu Book Service
OTHER
1 Shalimar Bagh
2 Coronation Durbar Site
3 Roshanara Bagh
4 Ashoka Pillar
5 Mutiny Memorial
7 Kashmiri Gate Interstate Bus Terminal (ISBT)
8 St James' Church
9 Old Delhi Post Office
11 Bicycle Market
12 Motorcycle Shops
13 Karol Bagh Market
14 Satyam Cineplex
16 Lakshmi Narayan Temple
17 New Delhi Main Post Office; National Philatelic Museum
21 Bank of America; Banque Nationale de Paris
22 Bengali Market
23 Hans Bhavan; Foreigners' Regional Registration Office
24 Firoz Shah Kotla
25 Indira Gandhi Indoor Stadium
26 Sarai Kale Khan ISBT
27 Nehru Stadium
28 INA Market
29 Dilli Haat
31 Rail Transport Museum
33 Basant Lok Complex; PVR Priya Cinema
34 Firoz Shah's Tomb
36 All India Institute of Medical Sciences
37 Moth-ki Masjid
38 South Extension Market; Alliance Française
39 N Block Market
40 M Block Market
41 Bahai Temple
42 Archana Airways
43 Kalkaji Devi Temple
44 Thai Airways International
45 Khirki Masjid
46 Jahanpanah
47 Begumpur Masjid; Bijai Mandal
48 PVR Anupam 4
49 Tomb of Ghiyas-ud-din
50 Tughlaqabad
Shalimar Rd
To Chandigarh
Shalimar Bagh
Radio Colony
Bhai Parmanand Marg
Outer Ring Rd
Model Town
Karnal Rd
Wazirabad Rd
Yamuna River
The Mall
Ring Rd
Kamla Nagar
Delhi University
Grand Trunk Rd
Shamnath Marg
Mahatma Gandhi Marg
Civil Lines
Boulevard Rd
Sabzi Mandi
Roshanara Rd
Kashmiri Gate
Sarai Rohilla Train Station
(Old) Delhi Train Station
Lothian Rd
Grand Trunk Rd
New Rohtak Rd
See Old Delhi Map p184
Patel Nagar
Sadar Bazar
Qutb Rd
Chandni Chowk
Red Fort
Vijay Ghat
Patel Rd
Desh Bandhu Gupta Rd
Shanti Vana
Karol Bagh
Hospital Marg
See Paharganj Map p198
Pusa Rd
Gangaram
Old Delhi
New Delhi Train Station
Raj Ghat
Panchkuin Marg
Shankar Rd
Mandir Marg
See Connaught Place Map pp194-5
Ring Rd
New Rajendra Nagar
Bahadur Shah Zafar Marg
Vikas Marg
Baba Kharak Singh Marg
Janpath
Tilak Bridge Train Station

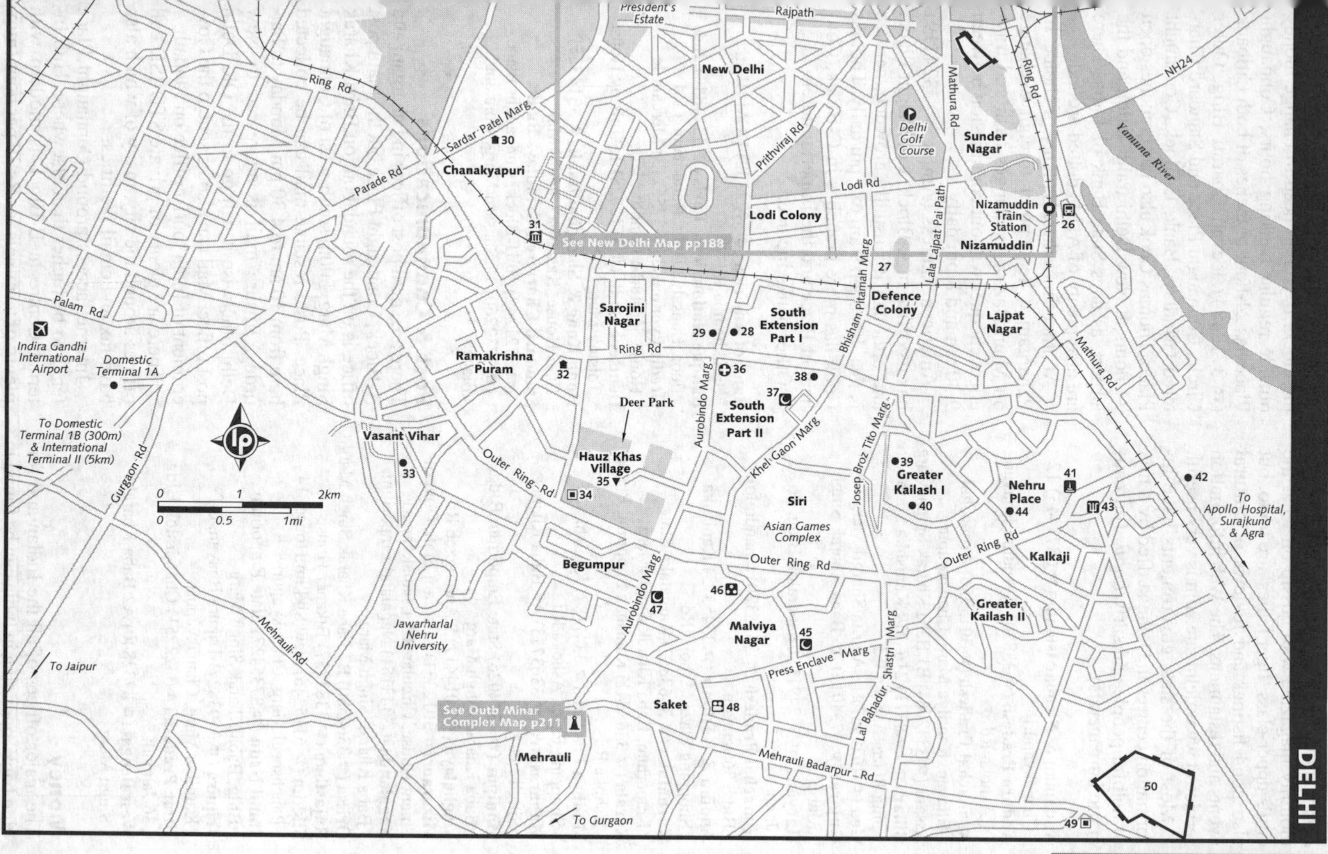
DELHI
President's Estate
Rajpath
New Delhi
Ring Rd
Sardar Patel Marg
30
Chanakyapuri
Parade Rd
Prithviraj Rd
Delhi Golf Course
Mathura Rd
Ring Rd
NH24
Yamuna River
Sunder Nagar
Lodi Rd
Lodi Colony
Lala Lajpat Rai Path
Nizamuddin Train Station
26
Nizamuddin
31
See New Delhi Map pp188
Bhisham Pitamah Marg
27
Defence Colony
Lajpat Nagar
Palam Rd
Indira Gandhi International Airport
Domestic Terminal 1A
Sarojini Nagar
29
28
South Extension Part I
Ring Rd
Ramakrishna Puram
32
36
38
Mathura Rd
37
Deer Park
Aurobindo Marg
South Extension Part II
Khel Gaon Marg
Josep Broz Tito Marg
To Domestic Terminal 1B (300m) & International Terminal II (5km)
Vasant Vihar
33
Hauz Khas Village
35
Outer Ring Rd
34
39
Greater Kailash I
40
Nehru Place
41
44
43
42
To Apollo Hospital, Surajkund & Agra
Gurgaon Rd
0 1 2km
0 0.5 1mi
Siri
Asian Games Complex
Outer Ring Rd
Outer Ring Rd
Kalkaji
Begumpur
Aurobindo Marg
47
46
Greater Kailash II
Mehrauli Rd
Jawaharlal Nehru University
Malviya Nagar
45
To Jaipur
Press Enclave Marg
Lal Bahadur Shastri Marg
Saket
48
See Qutb Minar Complex Map p211
Mehrauli
Mehrauli Badarpur Rd
50
49
To Gurgaon

Diary among them. *First City* (Rs 30) is a monthly magazine with gossip on what the city's upper-class 'tiger ladies' are up to, but also good listings and reviews of cultural events and restaurants. The Web information service at www.delhigate.com is very useful.

Most of the state governments have information centres in Delhi, staffed by a mix of helpful people and surly *babus* (bureaucratic bureaucrats).

Andaman & Nicobar Islands (☎ 6871443) 12 Chanakyapuri
Andhra Pradesh (☎ 3382031) Andhra Bhavan, 1 Ashoka Rd
Arunachal Pradesh (☎ 3013956) Arunachal Bhavan, Kautilya Marg, Chanakyapuri
Assam (☎ 3342064) B1 Baba Kharak Singh Marg
Bihar (☎ 3368371) 216–217 Kanishka Shopping Plaza, Ashoka Rd
Goa (☎ 4629967) 18 Amrita Shergil Marg
Gujarat (☎ 3734015) A6 Baba Kharak Singh Marg
Haryana (☎ 3324911) Chandralok Bldg, 36 Janpath
Himachal Pradesh (☎ 3325320) Chandralok Bldg, 36 Janpath
Jammu & Kashmir (☎ 3345373) Kanishka Shopping Plaza, Ashoka Rd
Karnataka (☎ 3363862) Karnataka State Emporium, Baba Kharak Singh Marg
Kerala (☎ 3368541) Kanishka Shopping Plaza, Ashoka Rd
Madhya Pradesh (☎ 3341187) Kanishka Shopping Plaza, Ashoka Rd
Maharashtra (☎ 3363773) A8 Baba Kharak Singh Marg
Manipur (☎ 3344026) State Emporium Bldg, Baba Kharak Singh Marg
Meghalaya (☎ 3014417) 9 Aurangzeb Rd
Mizoram (☎ 3012331) Mizoram State Government House, Circular Rd, Chanakyapuri
Nagaland (☎ 3343161) Nagaland Emporium, Baba Kharak Singh Marg
Orissa (☎ 3364580) B4 Baba Kharak Singh Marg
Rajasthan (☎ 3383837) Bikaner House
Sikkim (☎ 6115346) New Sikkim House, 14 Panchsheel Marg, Chanakyapuri
Tamil Nadu (☎ 3735427) State Emporium Bldg, Baba Kharak Singh Marg
Tripura (☎ 3793827) Tripura Bhavan, off Kautilya Marg, Chanakyapuri
Uttar Pradesh (☎ 3322251) Chandralok Bldg, 36 Janpath
West Bengal (☎ 3732840) A2 Baba Kharak Singh Marg

Money

The major offices of all the Indian and foreign banks operating in India can be found in Delhi, where it's possible to get cash around the clock. If you do need to change money outside regular banking hours, Connaught Place has 24-hour branches of both Citibank (☎ 3712484) Jeevan Bharati Bldg, Outer Circle, Connaught Place and Standard Chartered Grindlays Bank, E-Block, Connaught Place. Thomas Cook also has branches open 24 hours at New Delhi train station and the airport, as does State Bank of India. There are also plenty of ATMs dotted around.

At other times there's plenty of choice. In Paharganj, Chequepoint foreign exchange on Main Bazaar exchanges cash and travellers cheques without commission between 9.30 am and 8 pm daily.

American Express (AmEx; ☎ 3324119) has its office in A-Block, Connaught Place, and although it's usually crowded, service is fast. It's open 9 am to 7 pm daily. Thomas Cook has more branches in C-Block, Connaught Place and the Imperial hotel.

Other banks include:

Bank of America (☎ 3722332) DCM Bldg, Barakhamba Rd
Banque Nationale de Paris (☎ 3314848) 2nd floor, Hansalya Bldg, Barakhamba Rd
Crediţ Lyonnaise (☎ 3755213) Mercantile House, Kasturba Gandhi Marg
Deutsche Bank (☎ 3712028) 15 Tolstoy House, Tolstoy Marg
Hong Kong & Shanghai Bank (☎ 3314355) ECE House, Kasturba Gandhi Marg
Standard Chartered Grindlays Bank (☎ 3721242) 10 H-Block, Connaught Place; (☎ 3732260) 17 Sansard Marg, Connaught Place

Post & Communications

There are small post offices in Paharganj and A-Block, Connaught Place but the main post office is on the roundabout on Baba Kharak Singh Marg, 500m south-west of Connaught Place. Poste restante mail can be collected here from 10 am to 4.30 pm Monday to Saturday. Ensure mail is addressed to New Delhi otherwise it will go to the Old Delhi post office. Mail can also be sent to the Government of India tourist office on Janpath.

There are plenty of private STD/ISD call offices around the city, many of which also have fax and email facilities.

Internet access around Connaught Place tends to be higher than elsewhere. Hub Internet Centre in B-Block is modern with plenty of terminals for Rs 30 per hour (minimum time). DSIDC Cyber Cafe next to Delhi Tourism in N-Block is smaller and more expensive, charging Rs 30/50 per 30 minutes/hour, but you get a free drink. It's open 9 am to 8 pm. There are a couple of smaller places around Ringo Guest House with similar charges.

In Paharganj a few guesthouses have 24-hour Internet access at around Rs 20 per hour and there are many Internet centres in the lanes running off Main Bazaar. If your guesthouse doesn't have access, you can enjoy a beer while you surf the Internet at Hotel Gold Regency. Internet access here costs Rs 20 per hour but it's electronically timed and can cut off halfway through sending a message. A really good 24-hour Internet centre is down the small lane east of Khosla Cafe. It's a bit pricier at Rs 30 per hour but access is fast. There's another fast-access Internet centre opposite Malhotra Restaurant which is open to 9 pm.

Visa Extensions & Other Permits

Hans Bhavan, near the Tilak Bridge train station, is where you will find the Foreigners' Regional Registration Office (FRRO; ☎ 3319489). Come here to get permits for restricted areas such as Mizoram. The office is open 9.30 am to 1.30 pm and 2 to 4 pm Monday to Friday.

The FRRO can issue 15-day visa extensions free if you just need a few extra days before you leave the country. To apply for a maximum one-month extension on a six-month visa is more complicated. First you need a very good reason, then you must collect the long-term visa extension form from the Ministry of Home Affairs at Lok Nayak Bhavan near Khan Market (☎ 4693334), open 10 am to noon Monday to Friday. It's a typical Indian government office, so be prepared to wait. Then take the form and four photos to the FRRO (about a Rs 20 rickshaw ride away). A one-month extension costs US$30. When (or if) the extension is authorised, the authorisation has to be taken *back* to the Ministry of Home Affairs, where the actual visa extension is issued.

Since it's difficult to get an extension on a six-month visa, you may be approached by people offering to forge your visa for a longer stay. Don't fall for this one, as the authorities will check your details carefully against their computer records when you leave India. There are heavy fines and you won't be allowed to visit India again.

If you need a tax clearance certificate before departure, the Foreign Section of the Income Tax Department (☎ 3317826) is at Indraprastha Estate. Bring exchange certificates with you, though it's entirely likely nobody will ask for your clearance certificate when you leave the country. The office is closed 1 to 2 pm.

Export of any object more than 100 years old requires a permit. If in doubt, contact the Director (☎ 3017220), Antiquities, Archaeological Survey of India, Janpath, next to the National Museum.

Travel Agencies

At Hotel Janpath, the Student Travel Information Centre (☎ 3327582) is used by many travellers and is the place to renew or obtain student cards; its tickets are not usually as cheap as elsewhere.

Some of the ticket discounters around Paharganj and Connaught Place are real fly-by-night operations, so take care. Those that have been recommended by readers include:

Aa Bee Travels (☎ 7520117) Hare Rama Guest House, Paharganj
Cozy Travels (☎ 3312873) BMC House, 1 N-Block, Connaught Place
Don't Pass Me By Travels (☎ 3352942) Upstairs in the cafe of the same name, Ringo Guest House Bldg
VINstring Holidays (☎ 3368717) YWCA International Guest House, Sansad Marg
Vin Tours (☎ 3348571) YWCA Blue Triangle Family Hostel, Ashoka Rd
Y Tours & Travel (☎ 3711662) YMCA, Ashoka Rd

Hotel Namaskar (☎ 3621234), just off Main Bazaar, Paharganj, and the travel agency at Hotel Ajanta (☎ 7520925), Arakashan Rd have also been recommended. (See Places to Stay – Mid-Range later in this chapter.)

For more upmarket travel arrangements, both within India and for foreign destinations, there are a number of places, mostly around Connaught Place. These include: Cox & Kings (☎ 3320067) and Sita World Travels (☎ 3311133).

Bookshops

Connaught Place and Khan Market are the main places to look for interesting Indian books or to stock up with hefty paperbacks to while away those long train rides. Some of the better shops include:

Bahri & Sons Khan Market, Subramania Bharati Rd, New Delhi
Bookworm 29 B-Block, Radial Rd 4, Connaught Place
English Book Store 17 L-Block, Radial Rd 5, Connaught Place
New Book Depot 18 B-Block, Connaught Place
The Bookshop Khan Market, Subramania Bharati Rd, New Delhi

There are plenty of footpath stalls at various places around Connaught Place, on Sansad Marg, near Kwality Restaurant, and in Paharganj. They have a good range of cheap paperbacks and will often buy them back from you if they' re still in reasonable condition. Almost next door to Kwality Restaurant is People Tree, which sells books about the environment, and ecofriendly crafts.

Prabhu Book Service in Hauz Khas Village has an interesting selection of second-hand and rare books. Bookshops in deluxe hotels are more expensive but have a good selection of novels, glossy art books and historical works.

Libraries & Cultural Centres

Delhi has a fair selection of libraries and cultural centres, including Delhi Public Library, opposite the (Old) Delhi Train Station on SP Mukherjee Marg, open 8.30 am to 8.30 pm daily, except Sunday. Others include:

Alliance Française (☎ 6258128) D-13 South Extension Part II
American Center (☎ 3316841) 24 Kasturba Gandhi Marg, Connaught Place. Open 10 am to 6 pm Thursday to Saturday and Monday to Tuesday.
British Council Library (☎ 3711401) 17 Kasturba Gandhi Marg, Connaught Place. Open 10 am to 6 pm Tuesday to Saturday. It's better than the US equivalent, but officially you have to join to get in.
India International Centre (☎ 4619431) Near the Lodi tombs. Has weekly lectures on art, economics and other contemporary issues by Indian and foreign experts.
Sangeet Natak Akademi (☎ 3387248) 35 Firoz Shah Rd, Rabindra Bhavan. A major performing arts centre with substantial archive material. The academy of fine arts and sculpture, Lalit Kala Akademi, and the literature academy, Sahitya Akademi, are also here in separate wings. All have galleries and there are souvenirs on sale.
World Wide Fund for Nature India (☎ 469 3744) 172-B Lodi Estate. Has excellent computerised environmental records, a good library, and an ecoshop selling handicrafts and books. It's open from 9.30 am to 5.30 pm Monday to Friday.

Laundry

Most hotels and guesthouses have a laundry service. You'll save a bit of cash by taking it yourself to the parcel office next door to Hare Rama Guest House where T-shirts/trousers are machine washed for around Rs 5/10 each.

Left Luggage

Most hotels will store baggage for free or for a nominal fee. Otherwise gear can be safely stored at the Luggage Room (☎ 3618971), in a lane east of Hare Rama Guest House in Paharganj, for Rs 4 per day. It won't accept cash, cameras or Walkmans and you'll need your passport for both deposit and collection, which is available between 8 am and 8 pm daily. Shota Tours & Travel above Diamond Cafe charges a rupee or two more for the same service.

Photography

There are lots of places around Connaught Place to buy and process film. The Delhi Photo Company, at 78 Janpath, close to the Government of India tourist office, processes both print and slide film competently. Kinsey Bros in A-Block, Connaught Place is a bit quicker but also a bit more expensive.

Motorcycle Shops

If you are in the market for a new Enfield motorcycle or anything else bike related, Karol Bagh is the place to look. There are many to choose from, try Madaan Motors at 1770/53 Naiwala Gali, Har Kishan Das Rd, and Inder Motors (☎ 5728579, fax 5781052) 1744/55 Hari Singh Nalwa St.

Medical Services & Emergency

If you need an ambulance call ☎ 102. Embassies have lists of recommended doctors and dentists. The following is a selection of medical services in Delhi:

All India Institute of Medical Sciences (AIIMS; ☎ 6561123) Ansari Nagar. A government hospital.
Apollo Hospital (☎ 6925858) Sarita Vihar, Mathura Rd. Has a good reputation.

Dr Ram Manohar Lohia Hospital (☎ 3365525) Baba Kharak Singh Marg. A government hospital.

East West Medical Centre (☎ 4623738/ 4699229) 38 Golf Links Rd. Recommended by many travellers, diplomats and expats. Near Delhi Golf Course – all rickshaw-wallahs know where it is.

Pharmacy (☎ 3310163 ext 180) Super Bazaar, Connaught Place. A 24-hour chemist.

OLD DELHI

The old walled city of Shahjahanabad spreads west from the Red Fort and was at one time surrounded by a sturdy defensive wall, only fragments of which now exist. The **Kashmiri Gate**, at the northern end of the walled city, was the scene of desperate fighting when the British retook Delhi during the 1857 Uprising. West of here, near Sabzi Mandi, is the British-erected **Mutiny Memorial** to the soldiers who lost their lives during the Uprising. Near the monument is an **Ashoka pillar**; like the one in Firoz Shah Kotla, it was brought here by Firoz Shah.

Red Fort

The red sandstone walls of Lal Qila, the Red Fort, extend for 2km and vary in height from 18m on the river side to 33m on the city side. Shah Jahan started construction of the massive fort in 1638 and it was completed in 1648. He never completely moved his capital from Agra to his new city of Shahjahanabad in Delhi because he was deposed and imprisoned in Agra Fort by his son Aurangzeb.

The Red Fort dates from the very peak of Mughal power. When the emperor rode out on an elephant into the streets of Old Delhi it was a display of pomp and power at its most magnificent. The Mughal reign from Delhi was a short one, however: Aurangzeb was the first and last great Mughal emperor to rule from here.

Today, the fort is typically Indian, with would-be guides leaping forth to offer their services as soon as you enter, but it's still a calm haven of peace if you've just left the frantic streets of Old Delhi. The city noise and confusion are light years away from the fort gardens and pavilions.

The Yamuna River used to flow right by the eastern edge of the fort, and filled the 10m deep moat. These days the river is more than 1km to the east and the moat remains empty. Entry to the fort is US$10 and tickets are available from the kiosk opposite the main gate. The fort is closed Monday.

Lahore Gate The main gate to the fort takes its name from the fact that it faces towards Lahore, now in Pakistan. If one spot could be said to be the emotional and symbolic heart of the modern Indian nation, the Lahore Gate of the Red Fort is probably it. During the struggle for Independence, one of the nationalists' declarations was that they would see the Indian flag flying over the Red Fort in Delhi. After Independence, many important political speeches were given by Nehru and Indira Gandhi to the crowds amassed on the *maidan* (open place or square) outside, and on Independence Day (15 August) each year, the prime minister addresses a huge crowd from the gate.

You enter the fort here and immediately find yourself in a vaulted arcade, the **Chatta Chowk** (Covered Bazaar). The shops in this arcade used to sell the upmarket items that the royal household might fancy – silks, jewellery and gold. These days they cater to the tourist trade and the quality of the goods is certainly a little lower, although some still carry a royal price tag! This arcade of shops was also known as the Meena Bazaar, the shopping centre for ladies of the court. On Thursday the gates of the fort were closed to men; only women were allowed inside the citadel.

The arcade leads to the **Naubat Khana,** or Drum House, where musicians used to play for the emperor, and the arrival of princes and royalty was heralded from here. There is a dusty **Indian War Memorial museum** (Rs 2) upstairs. The open courtyard beyond the Drum House formerly had galleries along either side, but these were removed by the British army when the fort was used as its headquarters. Other reminders of the British presence are the monumentally ugly, three-storey barrack blocks that are situated to the north of this courtyard.

Diwan-i-Am The Hall of Public Audiences was where the emperor would sit to hear complaints or disputes from his subjects. His alcove in the wall was marble panelled and set with precious stones, many of which were looted following the 1857 Indian Uprising. This elegant hall was restored as a

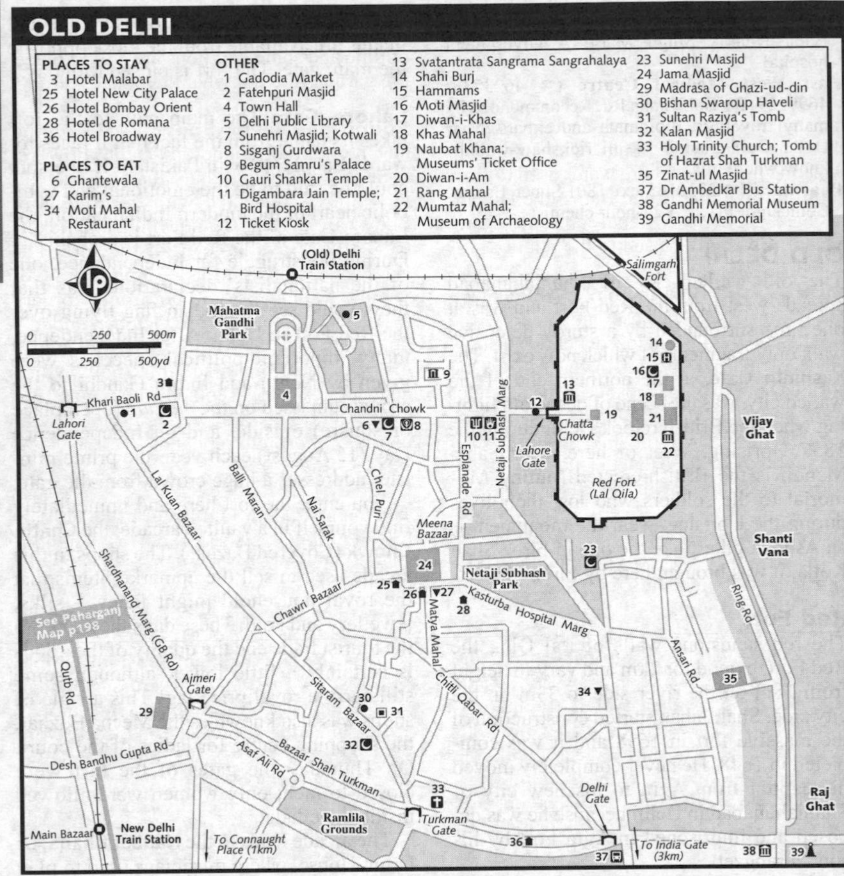

result of a directive by Lord Curzon, the viceroy of India between 1898 and 1905.

Diwan-i-Khas The Hall of Private Audiences, constructed of white marble, was the luxurious chamber where the emperor would hold private meetings. The centrepiece (until Nadir Shah carted it off to Iran in 1739) was the magnificent Peacock Throne. The solid-gold throne had figures of peacocks standing behind it, their beautiful colours achieved with countless inlaid precious stones. Between them was a parrot carved out of a single emerald.

A masterpiece in precious metals, sapphires, rubies, emeralds and pearls was broken up, and the so-called Peacock Throne, now displayed in Tehran, simply utilises various bits of the original. The marble pedestal on which the throne used to sit remains in place.

In 1760, the Marathas also removed the silver ceiling from the hall, so today it is a pale shadow of its former glory. Inscribed on the walls of the Diwan-i-Khas is that famous Persian couplet:

> If there is a paradise on earth it is this, it is this, it is this.

Royal Baths Next to the Diwan-i-Khas are the *hammams* or baths – three large rooms surmounted by domes, with a fountain in the centre – one of which was set up as a sauna. The floors used to be inlaid with *pietra dura* (marble inlay) work, and the rooms were illuminated through panels of coloured glass in the roof. The baths are closed to the public.

Shahi Burj This modest, three-storey octagonal tower at the north-eastern edge of the fort was once Shah Jahan's private working area. From here water used to flow south through the Royal Baths, the Diwan-i-Khas, the Khas Mahal and the Rang Mahal. Currently closed to the public.

Moti Masjid Built in 1659 by Aurangzeb for his own personal use and security, the small and totally enclosed Pearl Mosque, made of marble, is next to the baths. One curious feature of the mosque is that its outer walls are oriented exactly to be in symmetry with the rest of the fort, while the inner walls are slightly askew, so that the mosque has the correct orientation with Mecca.

Other Features The **Khas Mahal**, south of the Diwan-i-Khas, was the emperor's private palace, divided into rooms for worship, sleeping and living.

The **Rang Mahal** or Palace of Colour, farther south again, took its name from the painted interior, which is now gone. This was once the residence of the emperor's chief wife, and is where he ate. On the floor in the centre is a beautifully carved marble lotus, and the water flowing along the channel from the Shahi Burj used to end up here. Originally there was a fountain made of ivory in the centre.

There is a small Museum of Archaeology in the **Mumtaz Mahal**, still farther south along the eastern wall. It's well worth a look, although most visitors seem to rush through the Red Fort, bypassing the museum.

Another museum worth seeing is the **Svatantrata Sangrama Sangrahalaya** (Museum of the Independence Movement), to the left before the Naubat Khana, among the army buildings. The Independence movement is charted with newspaper cuttings, letters, photos and several impressive dioramas. Did the Rani of Jhansi really ride into battle with a baby strapped to her back? Tickets to all three museums (Rs 2 each) are available from the booth by the Naubat Khana.

Gardens Between these exquisite buildings were highly formal *charbaghs* (gardens in four sections), complete with fountains, pools and small pavilions. While the general outline and some pavilions are still in place, the gardens are not what they once were.

Sound-and-Light Show Each evening an entertaining sound-and-light show recreates events of India's history, particularly those connected with the Red Fort. Shows are in English and Hindi, and tickets (Rs 30) are available from the fort. The English sessions start at 7.30 pm from November to January, 8.30 pm from February to April and September to October, and at 9 pm from May to August. It's well worth making the effort to see this show, which degenerates into a comedy at stages, but make sure you are well equipped with plenty of mosquito repellent.

Chandni Chowk

The main street of Old Delhi is the colourful shopping bazaar known as Chandni Chowk. It's hopelessly congested (and polluted) day and night, a very sharp contrast to the open, spacious streets of New Delhi. At the eastern (Red Fort) end of Chandni Chowk, there is a **Digambara Jain** temple with a small marble courtyard surrounded by a colonnade. Traditionally, Jain monks of the Digambara, or Sky Clad, sect, wore no garments. There's an interesting **bird hospital** here, run by the Jains; entry is free but donations are gratefully accepted.

Next to the *kotwali* (old police station) is the **Sunehri Masjid**. In 1739, Nadir Shah, the Persian invader who carried off the Peacock Throne, stood on the roof of this mosque and watched while his soldiers conducted a bloody massacre of Delhi's inhabitants.

The western end of Chandni Chowk is marked by the **Fatehpuri Masjid**, which was erected in 1650 by one of Shah Jahan's wives.

Jama Masjid

The great mosque of Old Delhi is both the largest in India and the final architectural extravagance of Shah Jahan. Begun in 1644, the mosque was not completed until 1658. It has three great gateways, four angle towers and two minarets standing 40m high and is constructed of alternating vertical strips of red sandstone and white marble.

Broad flights of steps lead up to the imposing gateways. The eastern gateway was

RICHARD I'ANSON

The Jama Masjid, along with the Red Ford, dominates Old Delhi and is one of the city's major tourist attractions.

originally only opened for the emperor, and is now only open on Friday and Muslim festival days. The general public can enter by either the north or south gate (Rs 10). Shoes must be removed, and those people considered unsuitably dressed (bare legs for either men or women) can hire robes at the northern gate.

The courtyard of the mosque can hold 25,000 people. For Rs 5 (Rs 10 with a camera) it's possible to climb the southern minaret – although women shouldn't do this unaccompanied as molestations have been reported. The views in all directions are superb – Old Delhi, the Red Fort and the polluting factories beyond it across the river, and New Delhi to the south. You can also see one of the features that the architect Edwin Lutyens incorporated into his design of New Delhi – the Jama Masjid, Connaught Place and Sansad Bhavan (Parliament House) are in a direct line. There's also a fine view of the Red Fort from the east side of the mosque.

Raj Ghat

North-east of Firoz Shah Kotla, on the banks of the Yamuna, a simple square platform of black marble marks the spot where Mahatma Gandhi was cremated following his assassination in 1948. A commemorative ceremony takes place each Friday, the day he was killed.

Jawaharlal Nehru, the first Indian prime minister, was cremated just to the north at Shanti Vana (Forest of Peace) in 1964. His daughter, Indira Gandhi, who was killed in 1984, and grandsons Sanjay (1980) and Rajiv (1991) were also cremated in this vicinity.

The Raj Ghat area is now a beautiful park. The **Gandhi Memorial Museum** here is well worth a visit; a macabre relic is the pistol with which Gandhi was assassinated. Entry is free; it's open 9.30 am to 5.30 pm Tuesday to Sunday.

NEW DELHI

Connaught Place

At the northern end of New Delhi, Connaught Place is the business and tourist centre. It's a vast traffic circle with an architecturally uniform series of colonnaded buildings around the edge, devoted to shops, banks, restaurants and airline offices. It's spacious but busy, and you're continually approached by people willing to provide you with anything from an airline ticket for Timbuktu to your fortune read.

In 1995 the inner and outer circle were renamed Rajiv Chowk and Indira Chowk respectively (the son within the mother), but everyone still calls it CP (Connaught Place) despite the signs. The outer circle is known as Connaught Circus.

Jantar Mantar

Only a short stroll down Sansad Marg from Connaught Place, this strange collection of salmon-coloured structures is one of Maharaja Jai Singh II's observatories. The ruler from Jaipur constructed this observatory in

1725 and it is dominated by a huge sundial known as the Prince of Dials. Other instruments plot the course of heavenly bodies and predict eclipses. The US$5 entry fee is not really worth it as you can see most of the instruments from outside.

Rajpath

The Rajpath (Kingsway) is another focus of Lutyens' New Delhi. It is immensely broad and is flanked on either side by ornamental ponds. The Republic Day parade is held here every 26 January, and millions gather to enjoy the spectacle.

At the eastern end of Rajpath is India Gate, while at the western end is Rashtrapati Bhavan, now the president's residence, but built originally for the viceroy. It is flanked by the two large Secretariat buildings, and these three buildings sit upon a small rise, known as Raisina Hill.

India Gate This 42m-high stone arch of triumph stands at the eastern end of the Rajpath. It bears the names of 85,000 Indian army soldiers who died in the campaigns of WWI, the North-West Frontier operations of the same time and the 1919 Afghan fiasco.

Rashtrapati Bhavan The official residence of the president of India stands at the opposite end of the Rajpath from India Gate. Completed in 1929, the palace-like building is an interesting blend of Mughal and Western architectural styles, the most obvious Indian feature being the huge copper dome. To the west of the building is a Mughal garden that occupies 130 hectares. This garden is only open to the public in February and early March; book through the Government of India tourist office on Janpath.

Prior to Independence this was the viceroy's residence. At the time of Mountbatten, India's last viceroy, the number of servants needed to maintain the 340 rooms and its extensive gardens was enormous. There were 418 gardeners alone, 50 of them boys whose sole job was to chase away birds.

Secretariat Buildings The north and south Secretariat buildings are on either side of Rajpath on Raisina Hill. These imposing buildings, topped with *chhatris* (small domes), now house the ministries of finance and external affairs respectively.

Sansad Bhavan Although another large and imposing building, Sansad Bhavan, the Indian parliament building, stands hidden and virtually unnoticed at the end of Sansad Marg, just north of Rajpath. The building is a circular colonnaded structure 171m in diameter. Its relative physical insignificance in the grand scheme of New Delhi shows how the focus of power has shifted from the viceroy's residence, which was given pride of place during the time of the British Raj when New Delhi was conceived.

Permits to visit the parliament and sit in the public gallery are available from the reception office on Raisina Rd, but you'll need a letter of introduction from your embassy.

Purana Qila

Just south-east of India Gate and north of Humayun's tomb and Nizamuddin train station is the Purana Qila (Old Fort). This is the supposed site of Indraprastha, the original city of Delhi. The Afghan ruler, Sher Shar, who briefly interrupted the Mughal sovereignty by defeating Humayun, completed the fort during his reign from 1538 to 1545, before Humayun regained control of India. The fort has massive walls and three large gateways.

Entering from the south gate you'll see the small octagonal red sandstone tower, the Sher Mandal, later used by Humayun as a library. It was while descending the stairs of this tower in 1556 that he slipped, fell and received injuries from which he later died. Just beyond it is the **Qila-i-Kuhran** Mosque, or Mosque of Sher Shar, which, unlike the fort itself, is in a reasonable condition.

There's a small **archaeological museum** just inside the main gate, and there are good views of New Delhi from atop the gate. Entry is US$5.

A **sound-and-light show** (through poor-quality loudspeakers) is held each evening (Rs 25). English sessions start at 7.30 pm from November to January, 8.30 pm from February to April and September to October and 9 pm from May to August. Tickets are available on site or from the tourist office.

An autorickshaw ride from Connaught Place should cost about Rs 30 one way.

Humayun's Tomb

Built in the mid-16th century by Haji Begum, the Persian-born senior wife of

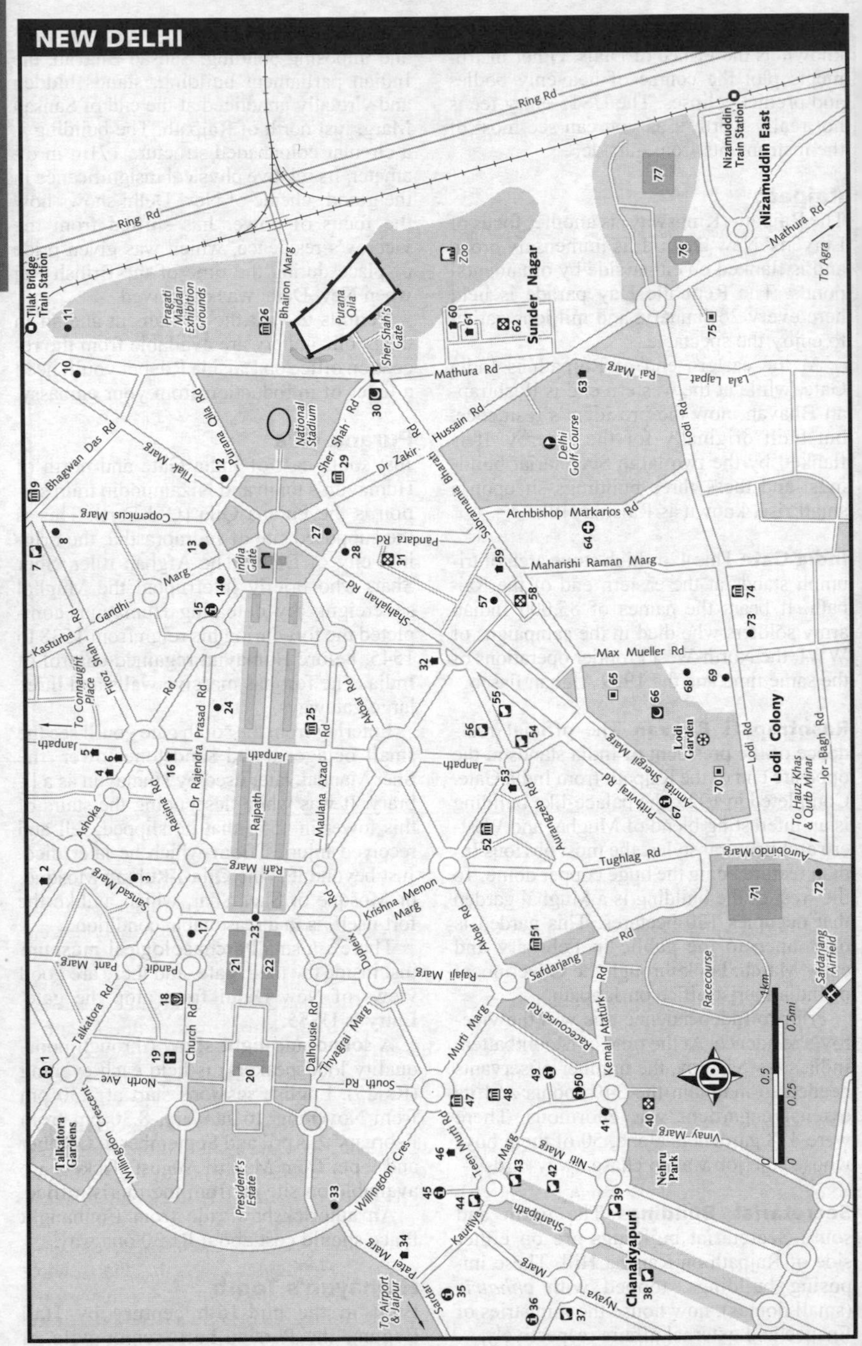
NEW DELHI
Ring Rd
Nizamuddin Train Station
Nizamuddin East
Mathura Rd
To Agra
Tilak Bridge Train Station
Pragati Maidan Exhibition Grounds
Bhairon Marg
Purana Qila
Sher Shah's Gate
Zoo
Sunder Nagar
Lala Lajpat Rai Marg
National Stadium
Dr Zakir Hussain Rd
Delhi Golf Course
Lodi Rd
Tilak Marg
Purana Qila Rd
Bhagwan Das Rd
Sher Shah Rd
Subramania Bharati Marg
Archbishop Markarios Rd
Copernicus Marg
Pandara Rd
India Gate
Maharishi Raman Marg
Shahjahan Rd
Max Mueller Rd
Kasturba Gandhi Marg
Firoz Shah Rd
To Connaught Place
Janpath
Dr Rajendra Prasad Rd
Akbar Rd
Lodi Colony
Lodi Garden
Amrita Shergil Marg
Prithviraj Rd
Aurangzeb Rd
Ashoka Rd
Raisina Rd
Rajpath
Maulana Azad Rd
Tughlag Rd
Aurobindo Marg
To Hauz Khas & Qutb Minar
Jor Bagh Rd
Sansad Marg
Rafi Marg
Krishna Menon Marg
Pandit Pant Marg
Talkatora Rd
Church Rd
Dalhousie Rd
Duplex Rd
Thyagraj Marg
Rajaji Marg
Safdarjang Rd
Racecourse Rd
Kemal Atatürk Rd
Racecourse
Safdarjang Airfield
North Ave
South Rd
Murti Marg
Teen Murti Rd
Talkatora Gardens
Willingdon Crescent
President's Estate
Willingdon Cres
Niti Marg
Vinay Marg
Nehru Park
Kautilya Marg
Shantipath
Chanakyapuri
Nyaya Marg
Sardar Patel Marg
To Airport & Jaipur
0 0.25 0.5 1km
0 0.5mi

NEW DELHI

PLACES TO STAY
- 2 YWCA Blue Triangle Family Hostel
- 4 ITDC Hotel Indraprastha
- 5 ITDC Hotel Janpath; SriLankan Airlines; Virgin Airways; STIC; Kazakhstan Airlines
- 6 ITDC Hotel Kanishka; Kanishka Shopping Plaza; Bihar Tourist Office; Jammu & Kashmir Tourist Office; Kerala Tourist Office; Madhya Pradesh Tourist Office
- 16 Hotel Le Meridien
- 32 Taj Mahal Hotel
- 34 Hotel Diplomat
- 46 Youth Hostel
- 53 Claridges Hotel
- 59 Ambassador Hotel
- 60 Kailash Inn; La Sagrita Tourist Home
- 61 Jukaso Inn
- 63 The Oberoi

OTHER
- 1 Dr Ram Manohar Lohia Hospital
- 3 Indian Airlines
- 7 Nepalese Embassy
- 8 Rabindra Bhavan; Sangeet Natak Akademi; Lalit Kala Akademi; Shahitya Akademi
- 9 National Museum of Natural History
- 10 Supreme Court
- 11 Appu Ghar
- 12 Patiala House
- 13 Baroda House
- 14 Hyderabad House
- 15 Andhra Pradesh Tourist Office
- 17 Sansad Bhavan
- 18 Gurdwara Rakab Ganj
- 19 Cathedral Church of the Redemption
- 20 Rashtrapati Bhavan
- 21 Secretariat (North Block)
- 22 Secretariat (South Block)
- 23 Vijay Chowk
- 24 Indira Gandhi National Centre for the Arts
- 25 National Museum; Archaeological Survey of India
- 26 Crafts Museum
- 27 Children's Park
- 28 Bikaner House; Rajasthan Tourist Office
- 29 National Gallery of Modern Art
- 30 Khairul Manzil Masjid
- 31 Pandara Market; Ichiban; Pindi; Chicken Inn
- 33 Gandhi Salt March Sculpture
- 35 Andaman & Nicobar Tourist Office
- 36 Sikkim Tourist Office
- 37 US Embassy
- 38 French Embassy
- 39 Australian Embassy
- 40 Santushti Shopping Centre; Basil & Thyme
- 41 Ashok Hotel; Iran Air
- 42 UK Embassy
- 43 Norwegian Embassy
- 44 Sri Lankan High Commission
- 45 Mizoram Tourist Office
- 47 Nehru Planetarium
- 48 Nehru Memorial Museum
- 49 Tripura Tourist Office
- 50 Arunachal Pradesh Tourist Office
- 51 Indira Gandhi Memorial Museum
- 52 Gandhi Smriti
- 54 Danish Embassy; Meghalaya Tourist Board
- 55 Israeli Embassy
- 56 Brazilian Embassy
- 57 Lok Nayak Bhavan; Ministry of Home Affairs
- 58 Khan Market; The Bookshop; Bahri & Sons; China Garden; China Fare
- 62 Sunder Nagar Market
- 64 East West Medical Centre
- 65 Sikander Lodi's Tomb
- 66 Bara Gumbad Masjid
- 67 Goa Tourist Office
- 68 India International Centre
- 69 World Wide Fund for Nature India
- 70 Mohammed Shah's Tomb
- 71 Safdarjang's Tomb
- 72 Indian Airlines (24 Hours)
- 73 Indian Habitat Centre; Habitat World
- 74 Tibet House
- 75 Nizam-ud-din's Shrine
- 76 Isa Khan's Tomb
- 77 Humayun's Tomb

Humayun, the second Mughal emperor, this is a wonderful early example of Mughal architecture. The elements in its design – a squat building, high arched entrances that let in light, topped by a bulbous dome and surrounded by formal gardens – were to be refined over the years to the magnificence of the Taj Mahal in Agra. This earlier tomb is thus of great interest for its relation to the later Taj. Haji Begum is also buried in the red-and-white sandstone and black-and-yellow marble tomb.

Other tombs in the classic Persian charbagh include that of Humayun's barber. The octagonal tomb of Isa Khan is through a gate to the left of the entrance (which you don't have to pay to enter), and is a good example of Lodi architecture. Entry to Humayun's tomb is US$10 (and Rs 25 for video cameras). An excellent view can be obtained over the surrounding area from the terraces of the tomb. Humayun's tomb is down near Nizamuddin train station, off Mathura Rd. An autorickshaw should cost about Rs 50 one way from Connaught Place.

Nizam-ud-din's Shrine

Across the road from Humayun's tomb is the shrine of the Muslim Sufi saint, Nizam-ud-din Chishti, who died in 1325 aged 92. His shrine, with its large tank, is one of several interesting tombs here. The construction of Nizam-ud-din's tank caused a dispute between the saint and the constructor of Tughlaqabad, farther to the south of Delhi (see Tughlaqabad in the Greater Delhi section later in this chapter).

Other tombs include the later grave of Jahanara, the daughter of Shah Jahan, who stayed with her father during his imprisonment by Aurangzeb in Agra's Red Fort. Amir Khusru, a renowned Urdu poet, also has his tomb here, as does Atgah Khan, a friend of Humayun and his son Akbar. Atgah Khan was murdered by Adham Khan in Agra. In turn Akbar had Adham Khan terminated and his grave is near the Qutb Minar.

To get there, walk through the alleys from Mathura Rd; you'll know when you're getting close as beggars will start pestering you and others will be hassling to look after shoes which must be removed before entering the shrine complex. Always a hive of activity, it's particularly worth visiting around sunset on Thursday, a popular time for worship when *qawwali* (Sufi devotional singing) follow evening prayers. This is one of Delhi's most important pilgrimage sites, so dress conservatively.

Lodi Garden

About 3km to the west of Humayun's tomb and adjoining the India International Centre is Lodi Garden. In this well-kept garden are the **tombs** of the Sayyid and Lodi rulers. Mohammed Shah's tomb (1450) was a prototype for the later Mughal-style tomb of Humayun, a design that would eventually develop into the Taj Mahal. Other tombs include those of his predecessor, Mubarak Shah (1433), Ibrahim Lodi (1526) and Sikander Lodi (1517). The Bara Gumbad Masjid is a fine example of its type of plaster decoration. An autorickshaw should cost about Rs 30 from Connaught Place one way.

Safdarjang's Tomb

Beside the small Safdarjang airfield, this tomb was built in 1753–54 by the Nawab of Avadh for his father, Safdarjang, and is one of the last examples of Mughal architecture before the final remnants of the great empire collapsed. The tomb stands on a high terrace surrounded by an extensive walled garden. It makes a pleasant retreat from the urban bustle. Entry is US$5. It's a short walk from Lodi Garden.

Museums & Galleries

National Museum On Janpath and just south of Rajpath, the National Museum (☎ 3019272) has a pretty good collection of Indian bronze, terracotta and wood sculptures dating back to the Mauryan period (2nd to 3rd century BC), exhibits from the Vijayanagar period in South India, miniature and mural paintings, and costumes of the various Adivasis (tribal peoples). The museum, open 10 am to 5 pm Tuesday to Sunday, with free guided tours at 10.30 and 11.30 am, noon and 2 pm, is definitely worth visiting. Admission is Rs 150. There are film shows on weekends.

Next door is the **Archaeological Survey of India** office. Publications available here cover all the main sites in India. Many of these are not available at the particular sites themselves. The office is open 9 am to 1 pm and 3.30 to 5 pm Monday to Friday.

National Gallery of Modern Art This gallery (☎ 3382835) stands near India Gate at the eastern end of Rajpath, and was formerly the Delhi residence of the Maharaja of Jaipur. It houses an excellent collection of works by both Indian and colonial artists.

It is open 10 am to 5 pm Tuesday to Sunday. Admission is Rs 150, although you can wander the sculpture garden for free.

Nehru Memorial Museum & Planetarium On Teen Murti Rd near Chanakyapuri, the residence of Jawaharlal Nehru, Teen Murti Bhavan, has been converted into a museum. Photographs and newspaper clippings on display give a fascinating insight into the history of the Independence movement. The museum is open 10 am to 5 pm Tuesday to Sunday. Admission is free.

There's also a **planetarium** in the grounds (40-minute shows at 11.30 am and 3 pm, Rs 10), above which is a small cafe.

Tibet House A small museum (☎ 4611515) is found within Tibet House where you will find a fascinating collection of ceremonial items brought out of Tibet when the Dalai Lama fled following the Chinese occupation. Downstairs is a shop selling a wide range of Tibetan handicrafts. There are often lecture and discussion sessions. On Lodi Rd, Tibet House is open 10 am to 1 pm and 2 to 5.30 pm Monday to Friday. Admission to the museum is Rs 5.

Crafts Museum In the Aditi Pavilion at the Pragati Maidan Exhibition Grounds, Mathura Rd, this museum (☎ 3371817) contains a collection of traditional Indian crafts in textiles, metal, wood and ceramics. The museum is part of a 'village life' complex where you can visit rural India without leaving

Delhi. Opening hours are 9.30 am to 4.30 pm Tuesday to Sunday. Admission is free.

Indira Gandhi Memorial Museum The former residence of Indira Gandhi at 1 Safdarjang Rd has also been converted into a museum (☎ 3010094). On show are some of her personal effects, including the sari (complete with blood stains) she was wearing at the time of her assassination. The crystal plaque in the garden, flanked constantly by two soldiers, protects a few brown spots of Mrs Gandhi's blood where she fell after being shot by two of her Sikh bodyguards in December 1984. Opening hours are 9.30 am to 4.45 pm Tuesday to Sunday, but it's a good idea to avoid weekends when hordes of Indian tourists are herded through. Admission is free and you're not allowed to take food or water in.

National Museum of Natural History This museum (☎ 3314849) is opposite the Nepalese embassy on Barakhamba Rd. Fronted by a large model dinosaur, it has a collection of fossils, stuffed animals and birds, and a 'hands-on' discovery room for children. It's open 10 am to 5 pm Tuesday to Sunday.

OTHER ATTRACTIONS

Coronation Durbar Site

This is a sobering sight for people interested in the Raj. It's north of Old Delhi and is best reached by autorickshaw (about Rs 120 return from Paharganj) or taxi. In a desolate field stands a lone obelisk – this is where, in 1877 and 1903, the great theatrical durbars featuring the full set of Indian rulers paid homage to the British monarch.

It was also here in 1911 that King George V was declared emperor of India. If you look closely you can still see the old boy – a statue of him rises nearby in an unkempt walled park, where it was unceremoniously dumped after being removed from the canopy midway along Rajpath, between India Gate and Rashtrapati Bhavan. Further inspection reveals other imperial dignitaries in the scrub, though mysteriously there are many more plinths these days than statues.

Firoz Shah Kotla

Erected by Firoz Shah in 1354, the ruins of Firozabad, the fifth city of Delhi, can be found at Firoz Shah Kotla, just off Bahadur Shah Zafar Marg between the old and new Delhis. In the fortress-palace is a 13m-high sandstone **Ashoka pillar** inscribed with Ashoka's edicts (and a later inscription). The remains of an old mosque and a fine well can also be seen in the area, but most of the ruins of Firozabad were used for the construction of later cities. Entry to the fort costs US$5.

National Philatelic Museum

This museum (☎ 3710154), hidden in the post office at Dak Bhavan, Sardar Patel Chowk on Sansad Marg, has an extensive collection. It's open Monday to Friday.

Lakshmi Narayan Temple

Due west of Connaught Place, this Orissan-styled temple was erected by the industrialist BD Birla in 1938. Dedicated to Lakshmi, the goddess of prosperity and good fortune, it's commonly known as Birla Mandir (*mandir* means temple). It's a great place for kids of any age with man-made caves and creatures in large gardens. You can even get a novelty souvenir photo taken.

Rail Transport Museum

This museum (☎ 6881816) at Chanakyapuri will be of great interest to anyone fascinated by India's exotic collection of railway engines. The exhibit includes an 1855 steam engine, still in working order, and a large number of oddities such as the skull of an elephant that charged a mail train in 1894, and lost. A toy train chugs around the grounds throughout the day according to demand (Rs 10). The museum is open between 9.30 am and 5.30 pm Tuesday to Sunday (to 7.30 pm from April to September); admission costs Rs 5.

Hauz Khas Village

Midway between Safdarjang's tomb and the Qutb Minar, this urban village surrounded by parkland was once the reservoir for the second city of Delhi – Siri – which is situated slightly to the east. Interesting sights here include **Firoz Shah's tomb** and the remains of an ancient college. It was around here that Tamerlane was victorious in 1398. Hauz Khas is now one of the more chic places in Delhi; there are some excellent (if pricey) restaurants and shops here. Also part of the old city of Siri is the **Moth-ki Masjid**,

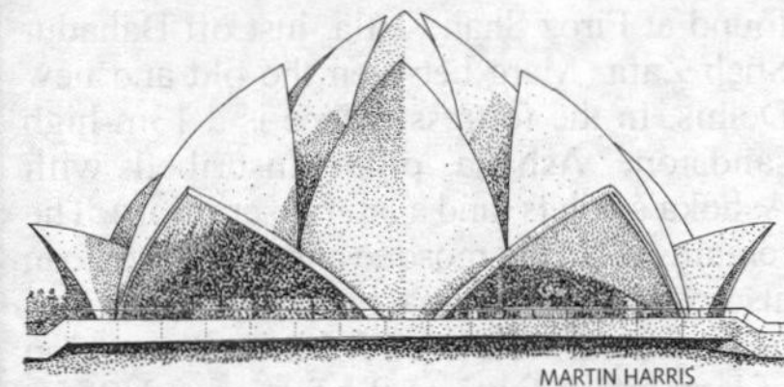

Delhi's Bahai Temple is shaped like a lotus flower and made of white marble.

which is some distance to the east of Hauz Khas. It is said to be the finest mosque in the Lodi style. Count on a fare of about Rs 70 for an autorickshaw from Connaught Place.

Bahai Temple

Lying to the east of Siri is this building shaped like a lotus flower. Completed in 1986, it is set among pools and gardens, and adherents of any faith are free to visit the temple and pray or meditate silently according to their own religion. It looks spectacular at dusk, particularly from the air, when it is floodlit, but is rather disappointing close up. The temple is just inside the Outer Ring Road, 12km south-east of the city centre. A one-way autorickshaw fare should be around Rs 70.

ORGANISED TOURS

Delhi is very spread out, so taking a city tour makes a lot of sense. Two major organisations arrange Delhi tours – beware of agents offering cut-price tours. The Indian Tourism Development Corporation (ITDC), operating under the name Ashok Travels & Tours (☎ 3322336), has tours that include guides and a luxury coach. Its office is in L-Block, Connaught Place, near Nirula's Hotel, but you can book at the Government of India tourist office on Janpath or at the major hotels. Delhi Tourism Corporation (☎ 3313637), a branch of the city government, arranges similar tours and its office is in N-Block, Middle Circle.

A five-hour morning tour of New Delhi costs Rs 147 with Delhi Tourism. Starting at 8 am, the tour includes the Lotus Temple, Qutb Minar, Humayun's tomb, India Gate, the Jantar Mantar and the Lakshmi Narayan Temple. The afternoon Old Delhi tour for Rs 126 starts at 2.15 pm and covers the Red Fort, Jama Masjid, Raj Ghat, Shanti Vana and Firoz Shah Kotla finishing at 5 pm. If you take both tours on the same day it costs Rs 231. These tours don't include entry fees which on a full-day tour would total US$35.

Hotel Broadway, near Delhi Gate, has gastronomic walking tours of Old Delhi (Rs 450). Following a guided wander through historical bazaars and alleys, participants get to digest it all over a meal at the hotel's excellent restaurant.

Taxis also offer guided tours, and will wait for you outside main attractions.

SPECIAL EVENTS

Delhi hosts a number of festivals.

Lori Citywide, January. Features bonfires, singing and dancing
Delhi Horse Show Below Red Fort, January
Delhi Flower Show Citywide, January
Republic Day Rajpath, 26 January. Features a military parade
Beating Retreat Vijay, 29 January. Features a ceremony near Delhi's Rashtrapati Bhavan, the president's residence
Independence Day Red Fort, 15 August. Prime minister addresses the nation
Dusshera Sudhash Maidan and Ramlila Grounds, October. Features fireworks and fair
Indian Trade Fare Pragati Maidan, Mathura Rd, November

PLACES TO STAY

If Delhi is your first stop in India it's probably a good idea to book a room in advance from home – reasonable places fill up quickly, leaving new arrivals easy prey for the commission sharks. This is especially true if you're arriving in the middle of the night. Fortunately many places, including budget hotels, have 24-hour receptions allowing for late arrivals. See the boxed text 'Dodgy Delhi' earlier in this chapter.

Prices given here don't include luxury tax which reaches up to 22.5% in mid-range to top-end places; budget places generally don't charge tax. During summer (May to August) discounts of up to 50% are often available and it's always worth asking for one if you're staying more than a couple of days.

Unless stated otherwise checkout is noon, although if you check in between 6 am and noon most will apply a 24-hour checkout and rooms have fans and/or air-coolers. There is little need for an air-con room out of the hot sticky summer months especially as Delhi central government forbids the use

RICHARD I'ANSON

GREG ELMS

RICHARD I'ANSON

CHRIS MELLOR

A minaret of the beautiful Jama Masjid towers above Old Delhi **(top right)**, while Humayun's tomb sits in splendid isolation **(bottom)** south of the hustle and bustle of Old Delhi's crowded Chandni Chowk **(middle & top left)**

PATRICK HORTON

RICHARD I'ANSON

RICHARD I'ANSON

RICHARD I'ANSON

The serene side of Delhi is captured in the lotus-flower-shaped Bahai Temple **(top)**; in the graceful forms and quiet prayers of Jama Masjid, India's largest mosque **(bottom right & left)**; and in a decorative detail from Nizam-ud-Din's Shrine **(middle left)**.

of air-conditioners between 6.30 and 9.30 pm. Unless stated otherwise, toilets are sit-down flush toilets and hot water is available 24 hours.

PLACES TO STAY – BUDGET

While most budget rooms may not be much to write home about, facilities such as 24-hour room service, TV, baggage storage, travel arrangements, airport pick-ups and laundry services make them good value and pleasant places to stay.

Camping

The main camping ground in Delhi closed in 2000 after some drug-related problems with the police. It may open in the future, but in the meantime it is possible to pitch a tent at ***Tourist Camping Park*** *(☎ 3973121)* opposite the ISBT in Old Delhi. You can camp in the small lawned area next to the very busy main road for Rs 30 per person. It also has some very basic rooms for Rs 140/175 a single/double and a few with private bathroom for Rs 250. The toilet and shower blocks are reasonably clean with hot water.

Hostel

Youth Hostel *(☎ 6116285, fax 6113469, ⓔ yhoste@del2.vsnl.net.in, 5 Nyaya Marg)* is in serene Chanakyapuri, but you have to be a member to stay (available for Rs 250). Beds in single-sex nonair-con/air-con dorms cost Rs 50/250 and doubles with shared bathroom start at Rs 300/650 – prices go up after five days and there's no smoking or alcohol allowed. Open 24 hours (although check-in/checkout is 11 am/noon) it has a cafe, bank, garden and recreation centre.

Connaught Place

Ringo Guest House *(☎ 3310605)*, down a side street near the tourist office, is an ageing travellers' institution with its fair share of detractors as well as fans. Small, basic and gloomy rooms around a central courtyard restaurant are Rs 125/250 a single/double with shared bathroom and Rs 350 and Rs 400 for a double with private bathroom (squat toilet and 24-hour hot water). Dorm beds are Rs 90.

Sunny Guest House *(☎ 3312909)* is nearby and marginally better then Ringo. Not quite so dark rooms with shared bathroom are Rs 125/250 or Rs 350 and Rs 450 for doubles with private bathroom, again around a central courtyard restaurant. Dorm beds are available for Rs 90. Both places are reasonably clean and friendly albeit with a shabby charm and are good for swapping travellers' tales and storing luggage (Rs 8 per day). However, it can be pretty awful when it's very hot (ie, July) or very cold (rainy February nights) and unless you specifically want to be near Connaught Circus you can find much better deals in Paharganj.

Hotel Blue *(☎ 3322222, ⓔ hotel-blue@yahoo.com, M-Block)* is an older 3rd-floor place with a fair amount of character. There are decent-sized rooms with phone, TV and shared bathroom for Rs 300/500; those with private bathroom are Rs 500/800. Tax is added. There's a large balcony terrace and small open courtyard.

Hotel Bright *(☎ 3323456, fax 3736049)*, directly below, is of a similar style without the terrace and therefore not quite as nice. Rooms with shared bathroom cost Rs 350/550; Rs 575/1100 with private bathroom.

Central Court Hotel *(☎ 3315013, N-Block)* has a bit of character with old-style rooms with bath, fireplace and separate lounge area going for Rs 800/1150; the fact they're accessed from the terrace almost makes up for them having no windows. Rooms with shared bathroom cost Rs 600/800 and all rooms have air-con, TV, fridge and phone. The hotel has a coffee shop and two restaurants.

Paharganj

Hotel Navrang *(☎ 521965)* on Baoli Chowk is popular with the grungy crowd and even serves a selection of Japanese dishes in its secluded terrace cafe. Rooms with private bathroom (squat toilet and bucket hot water – Rs 10) are Rs 80/100/150 – the more you pay the bigger they get. Try for one on the block overlooking the cafe as these get more light and have small terrace areas outside.

Ajay Guest House *(☎ 35431253, fax 3540656, ⓔ sent@ndf.vsnl.net.in)* has average doubles without/with windows onto the stairwell, phone and private bathroom with geyser hot water for Rs 260/270; a couple of larger air-con rooms (Rs 400) have small balconies. There is a rooftop cafe (with great views), a travel agency and an Internet centre. The best thing about this place is the bakery on the ground floor which has

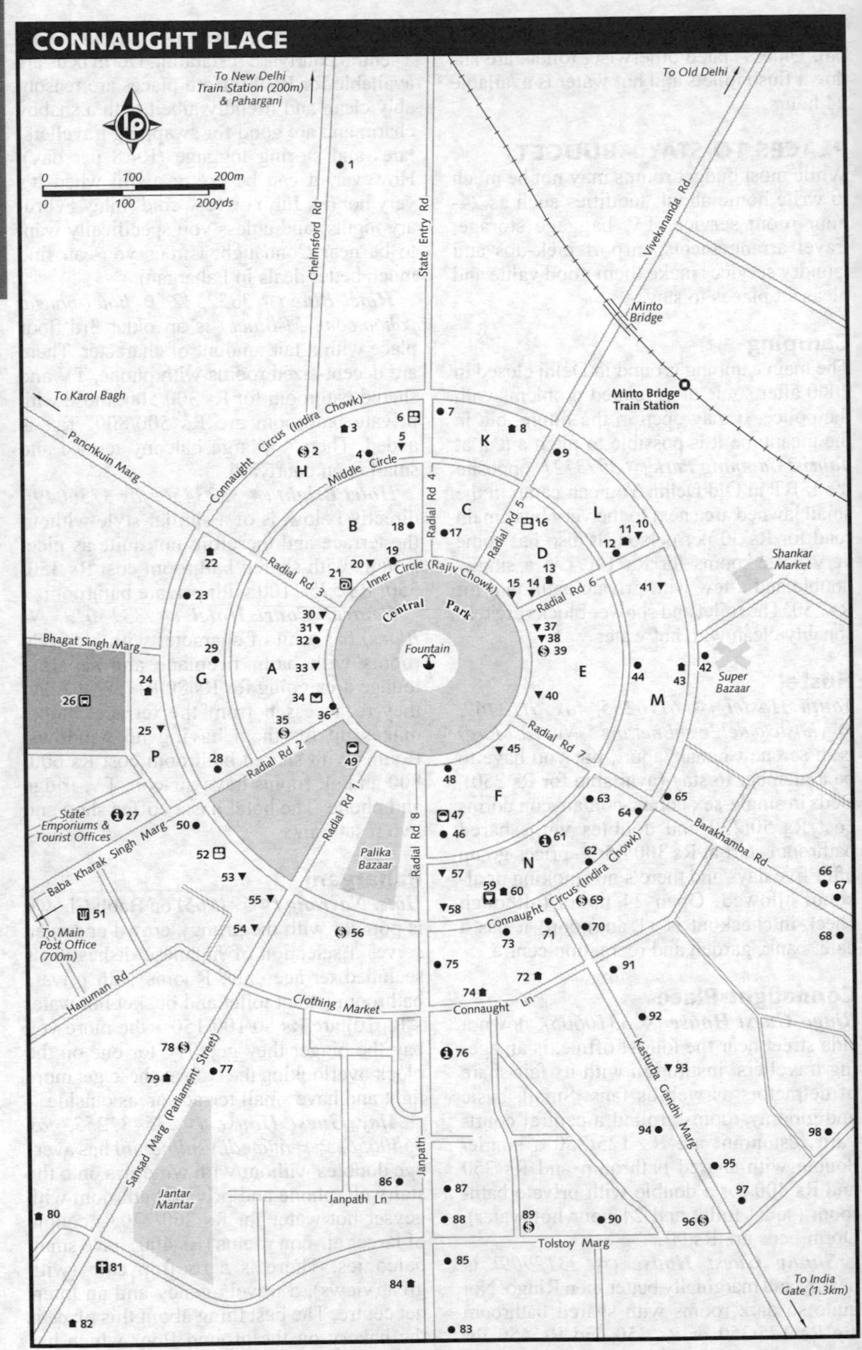
CONNAUGHT PLACE
To New Delhi Train Station (200m) & Paharganj
0 100 200m
0 100 200yds
To Old Delhi
Vivekananda Rd
Minto Bridge
Minto Bridge Train Station
To Karol Bagh
Panchkuin Marg
Chelmsford Rd
State Entry Rd
Connaught Circus (Indira Chowk)
Middle Circle
Radial Rd 4
Radial Rd 5
Radial Rd 6
Radial Rd 3
Radial Rd 2
Radial Rd 1
Radial Rd 8
Radial Rd 7
Inner Circle (Rajiv Chowk)
Central Park
Fountain
Shankar Market
Super Bazaar
Bhagat Singh Marg
State Emporiums & Tourist Offices
Baba Kharak Singh Marg
Palika Bazaar
Barakhamba Rd
To Main Post Office (700m)
Hanuman Rd
Clothing Market
Connaught Ln
Kasturba Gandhi Marg
Sansad Marg (Parliament Street)
Jantar Mantar
Janpath
Janpath Ln
Tolstoy Marg
To India Gate (1.3km)
A
B
C
D
E
F
G
H
K
L
M
N
P

CONNAUGHT PLACE

PLACES TO STAY
- 3 Hotel 55
- 8 York Hotel
- 11 Nirula's Hotel
- 13 Hotel Palace Heights
- 22 Hotel Marina
- 24 Hotel Alka; Vega
- 43 Hotel Blue; Hotel Bright
- 60 Central Court Hotel
- 72 Sunny Guest House
- 74 Ringo Guest House; Don't Pass Me By Cafe; Don't Pass Me By Travels
- 79 The Park
- 80 YMCA Tourist Hotel; Y Tours & Travels
- 82 YWCA International Guest House; VINstring Holidays
- 84 The Imperial; Thomas Cook

PLACES TO EAT
- 5 Katri Kebab
- 10 Nirula's Complex; Pegasus
- 14 The Embassy
- 15 Pizza Pizza Express
- 20 Cafe 100
- 25 McDonald's
- 30 Keventer's
- 31 Wenger's
- 33 Rodeo
- 37 Kovil; Pizza Hut
- 38 Berco's
- 40 United Coffee House
- 41 Domino's Pizza
- 45 The Host
- 53 Gaylord
- 54 Kwality Restaurant; People Tree
- 55 DV8
- 57 Nirula's (Branch)
- 58 Wimpy
- 93 Parikrama; Tarom

OTHER
- 1 Railway Booking Office
- 2 Standard Chartered Grindlays Bank
- 4 Cox & Kings
- 6 Plaza Cinema
- 7 Alcohol Shop
- 9 English Book Store
- 12 Ashok Travels & Tours
- 16 Odeon Cinema
- 17 Thomas Cook
- 18 Bookworm
- 19 New Book Depot
- 21 Hub Internet Centre
- 23 Gulf Air
- 26 Local Bus Station
- 27 Delhi Tourism Corporation; Indian Coffee House
- 28 Royal Jordanian
- 29 Alcohol Shop
- 32 American Express
- 34 Post Office
- 35 American Express Bank (ATM)
- 36 Kinsey Bros
- 39 24-Hour Standard Chartered Grindlays Bank (ATM)
- 42 24-Hour Pharmacy
- 44 Singapore Airlines
- 46 Indian Airlines
- 47 EATS Airport Bus
- 48 Sita World Travels
- 49 Prepaid Autorickshaw Kiosk
- 50 Khadi Gramodyog Bhavan
- 51 Hanuman Mandir
- 52 Regal Cinema
- 56 24-Hour Citibank (ATM); Air India
- 59 Blues Bar
- 61 Delhi Tourism Corporation; DSIDC Cyber Cafe
- 62 Jet Airways
- 63 Aeroflot
- 64 Cozy Travels
- 65 British Airways; Qantas Airways
- 66 Emirates
- 67 Kuwait Airways
- 68 Saudi Arabian Airlines
- 69 Hong Kong & Shanghai Bank (ATM)
- 70 Air Canada
- 71 Air France
- 73 Delhi Transport Corporation
- 75 Air India; Budget Car Rental
- 76 Government of India Tourist Office; Delhi Photo Company
- 77 Swissair
- 78 Standard Chartered Grindlays Bank (ATM)
- 81 Free Church
- 83 Chandralok Building; Haryana, Himachal Pradesh & Uttar Pradesh Tourist Offices; Delta Air Lines; Druk Air; Japan Airlines
- 85 Central Cottage Industries Emporium
- 86 Map Sales Office
- 87 Lufthansa Airlines; Budget Car Rental
- 88 Royal Nepal Airlines Corporation (RNAC)
- 89 Deutsche Bank (ATM)
- 90 Jagson Airlines
- 91 Pakistan International Airlines
- 92 American Center
- 94 British Council
- 95 Asiana Airlines; Ethiopian Airlines; Kuwait Airways
- 96 Credit Lyonnaise
- 97 United Airlines; Sahara Airlines; Scandinavian Airlines
- 98 KLM; Northwest Airlines; El Al Israel Airlines; Uzbekistan Airways

good coffee and tasty cakes, pizzas and rolls as well as a couple of pool tables.

Hare Rama Guest House *(☎ 3521413, fax 7532795, ⓔ harerama@ndf.vsnl.net.in)*, opposite, has similar rooms around a covered courtyard, with a mix of sit-down flush and squat toilets and the addition of a fridge and TV, for Rs 250/320. It, too, has a 24-hour rooftop restaurant on its treetop-flanked terrace with TV. Catering to a large Israeli clientele it also has a travel agency, Internet centre, art shop and luggage storage. Checkout for Hare Rama and Ajay, both of which attract louder late-night crowds, is 24 hours.

Hare Krishna Guest House *(☎ 3521467, ⓔ anoophotel@hotmail.com)*, on Main Bazaar and under the same management as Hare Rama, has rooms with phone for Rs 220 with shared bathroom, and Rs 230 and Rs 250 with private bathroom (geyser hot water).

Anoop Hotel *(☎ 3521451, fax 7532942, ⓔ anoophotel@hotmail.com)* is almost next door to Hare Krishna and has marble-lined singles/doubles with phone and private bathroom (geyser hot water) for Rs 220/280, and Rs 150/220 with shared bathroom. These two places share a good 24-hour Thai restaurant on their large rooftops and Internet facilities on the ground floor of the Anoop. Checkout for both is 24 hours.

Major's Den *(☎ 3629599)*, in a lane by the Imperial Cinema, has few of the facilities of its competitors (ie, no restaurant or Internet) but remains a popular and safe haven for those looking for respite from Main Bazaar. It has a terrace, travel agency and clean rooms with private bathroom and windows from Rs 250/300. The major, who lives downstairs with his wife and daughter, is both a businessman and a pukkah chap who can help in times of need. The doors close at midnight.

Hotel Victoria *(☎ 3524413)* is a very friendly place in a quiet area, east of Rajguru Rd. The large rooms with TV and private bathroom (both sit-down flush and squat toilet) have equally as large windows covered in plastic which gives everything a lovely pink hue. They start at Rs 222/250.

Vivek Hotel *(☎ 3512900, fax 7537103, ⓔ vivekhotel@mailcity.com)* has bright rooms with a few windows around an open courtyard for Rs 200/250 with private bathroom or Rs 150/200 with shared bathroom. Leema Restaurant is on the 1st floor but it's worth risking the elevator to get up to the much nicer rooftop terrace restaurant complete with a tiny lawned area.

Hotel Satyam *(☎ 3525200)* has rooms with TV, phone, private bathroom (both sit-down flush and squat toilet and geyser hot water) and grubby sheets for Rs 250/300. There's a long rooftop terrace and balconies overlooking Rajguru Rd.

Hotel Star View *(☎ 3556300, fax 3554220, ⓔ starview@vsnl.com)*, next door, has the same views down Rajguru Rd from its terrace, the back section of which is a restaurant. Comfortable doubles with TV, phone, velour covered furniture and private bathroom (geyser hot water) cost Rs 300 (with air-con it's Rs 500).

Hotel Bajrang *(☎ 3551730)*, in a lane north of Main Bazaar, is a basic but friendly place with doubles around an open courtyard for Rs 100/150 without/with private bathroom (geyser hot water). There's a very cheap canteen for food and drink in the courtyard and Internet access is available for Rs 12 per hour.

Shivlok Palace *(☎ 3511270)*, opposite, has a bit of character with sofas on its rooftop terrace and circular beds. Rooms with phone, TV and private bathroom start at a negotiable Rs 350/400 (plus 10% service charge).

Hotel Sweet Dream *(☎ 3629801)*, in a lane off Main Bazaar, has rooms with private bathroom (and some with balcony) for Rs 175/200 plus 10% service charge.

Smyle Inn *(☎ 3559107, ⓔ smyleinn@hotmail.com)*, around the corner, has rooms with private bathroom, TV and phone for Rs 150/200.

Camran Lodge *(☎ 3526053, fax 3621030, ⓔ camranlodge@id.eth.net)* is basic but has a fair amount of funky character. It's the unmissable old red building on Main Bazaar with onion domes and a disused mosque on the roof – a great place to catch the sunset. Blue and green rooms have windows onto Main Bazaar, although those on the 2nd floor created by metal partitions could get a bit hot. Rooms with shared bathroom are Rs 80/160 or Rs 100/180 with private bathroom (squat toilet and bucket hot water). Doors close at midnight.

Hotel Namaskar *(☎ 3621234, fax 3622233, ⓔ namaskarhotel@yahoo.com)*, in a lane north of Main Bazaar, gets good reports and the brothers who own it thrive on helping out travellers. Airy pink and green rooms, most with windows, are Rs 200/250 with shared bathroom, Rs 300 and Rs 400 with private bathroom (both sit-down flush and squat toilet and hot water); air-con rooms cost Rs 450. One of the few where the owners also manage the hotel, it is a good source of information and offers free luggage store.

Hotel Payal *(☎ 3520867)* is a place where you forfeit facilities such as room service for cleanliness. Good-sized rooms with private bathroom (geyser hot water) and window cost Rs 200/250; they start at Rs 150 with shared bathroom. Doors close at midnight.

Hotel Vishal *(☎ 3526314)* has a couple of good restaurants downstairs but the rooms are a bit cell-like and most lack windows. With private bathroom and phone they cost Rs 200/250.

Hotel Fortuna *(☎ 3614211)*, with an arcade on the ground floor, is recently painted and has rooms with TV, phone and private bathroom for Rs 200/250. Those at the front have balconies.

Hotel Rak International *(☎ 3550478, ⓔ hotelrak@yahoo.com)* on Baoli Chowk has rooms with TV, phone, sofa and private bathroom (both sit-down flush and squat toilet and geyser hot water) for Rs 250/350. A 24-hour terrace restaurant, with a waterfall feature, overlooks the square and temple below.

Old Delhi Staying in Old Delhi bases you right in the thick of things with a hugely colourful atmosphere and not too many other tourists – the clientele is predominantly Indian males.

Rail Yatri Niwas *(☎ 3313484)*, at the high-rise on the eastern side of New Delhi train station, has railway retiring rooms available for those in transit. Bona fide rail travellers with tickets for distances over 500km can stay in singles/doubles with shared bathroom for Rs 150/210 or Rs 250/500 with private bathroom and air con. There are also dorm beds for Rs 70. Check-in is from 9 am and the maximum stay is three days.

Hotel New City Palace *(☎ 3279548, fax 3289923)* makes the most of its position overlooking the Jama Masjid with plenty of balconies and a roof terrace with restaurant. The rooms with phone and private bathroom (squat toilet and 24-hour hot water) for Rs 450 are less impressive and somewhat contradict the hotel's self-promotion as a 'home for palatial comfort' – try to get one at the front. Checkout is 24 hours.

Hotel de Romana *(☎ 3266031, fax 3286635, ⓔ de-romana@hotmail.com)*, in a lane behind the Jagat Cinema, is a better deal with 'every damn thing' (except the view) including OK rooms with TV, phone, private bathroom and air-con for Rs 330/400. Checkout is noon.

Hotel Bombay Orient *(☎ 3286253)* on a main lane leading away from Jama Masjid is another reasonable choice. Rooms with private bathroom cost Rs 250/350.

Hotel Malabar *(☎ 3956669)* at the end of Chandni Chowk has basic rooms with private bathroom are Rs 150/250.

PLACES TO STAY – MID-RANGE

The Ys

The YMCA/YWCA has a large complex, about a 10-minute walk south-west of Connaught Place, with three accommodation options. They all have a religious institution air and aren't that great a deal, although they are clean and central and good places to meet other travellers. Check-in and checkout for all is noon and rates, which are subject to tax and service charge, (except dorms) include breakfast.

YMCA Tourist Hostel *(☎ 3361915, fax 3746032, ⓔ ymcath@ndf.vsnl.net.in, Jai Singh Rd)* is closest to Connaught Circle and the largest of the bunch with a laundry, swimming pool (April to October), fitness centre, restaurant, travel agency and Internet access. Rooms with shared bathroom cost Rs 415/725 rising to Rs 800/1350 with air-con, TV, phone and private bathroom, plus a Rs 30 temporary membership fee. It's open 24 hours and accepts credit cards.

YWCA International Guest House *(☎ 3361561, fax 3341765, ⓔ ywcaind@del3.vsnl.net.in, 10 Sansad Marg)* is surrounded by a small garden and has a 24-hour cafe and a travel agency. Rooms cost Rs 800/1000 and it accepts AmEx cards.

YWCA Blue Triangle Family Hostel *(☎ 3360133, fax 3360202, ⓔ ywcadel@vsnl.net, Ashoka Rd)* has a restaurant, TV lounge and Internet facilities. Rooms with phone start at Rs 575/1035 ranging to Rs 2875 for a two-bedroom suite with kitchen/lounge room. There are also dorm beds for Rs 185 (Rs 275 with air-con). All accommodation requires becoming a temporary member for Rs 20. Children under five free.

Connaught Place

ITDC Hotel Indraprastha *(☎ 3344511, fax 3368153, 19 Ashok Rd)* is a high-rise popular with Indian holidaymakers. It has a very institutionalised atmosphere; rooms are a reasonable size but you might want to have a look at a few. They cost Rs 600/750/1000 for one/two/three people in a standard room or Rs 750/850/1100 in a deluxe (plus 12.5% tax for both). There's a bar and a characterless 24-hour self-service restaurant and cafe.

Places directly on Connaught Circus are housed in colonial-era buildings and therefore have a modicum of character.

Hotel Alka *(☎ 3344328, fax 3732796, ⓔ hotelalka@vsnl.com, P-Block, Connaught Circus)* has a mad mirrored corridor, good vegetarian restaurant and bar, and a terrace overlooking the local bus station. Rooms start at Rs 1800/2900 and the hotel accepts credit cards.

Hotel Marina *(☎ 3324658, fax 3328609, ⓔ marina@nde.vsnl.net.in)* is quite swish with a bar, restaurant, 24-hour coffee shop and resident dentist. Its rooms start from Rs 2600/3200, including breakfast, and credit cards are accepted. Incidentally, this is the place where Gandhi's assassin stayed the night before the horrific act.

Nirula's Hotel *(☎ 3322419, fax 3353957, L-Block)*, next to the restaurant of the same name, has rooms with phone, fridge and TV for Rs 1995/3500. Free for children under 12.

Paharganj

Prince Polonia *(☎ 3511930, fax 3557646)*, near the Imperial Cinema, has a small clean pool, the only one in the area, on its rooftop terrace (nonguests can use it for two hours for Rs 100). Double deluxe rooms/super deluxe rooms/suites, most with balcony and all with TV, fridge, solar heated hot water and air-con cost Rs 935/1155/1320. There are also another couple of terraces to relax on and a lift to get you up to them.

Metropolis Tourist Home *(☎ 7531782, e metravel@bom9.vsnl.net.in)* has basic but clean air-con rooms with phone, TV and private bathroom (with geyser hot water) for Rs 600/675. There's a cheerless ground floor (licensed) restaurant and a pleasant roof terrace restaurant with tablecloths and atmosphere, foreign exchange and a travel agency.

Hotel Relax *(☎ 3681030, e vidur109@hotmail.com)* is a shiny new place on Nehru Bazaar. The management is very enthusiastic and clean rooms come with phone, TV, fridge and air-con for Rs 800/1000. There's a good balcony from where you can watch the masses below while eating.

Vinn Inn *(☎ 3677705, fax 3621398)* is a modern and nicely furnished place away from the madness of Main Bazaar, off Rajguru Rd. Cleanish rooms with windows are Rs 500/700.

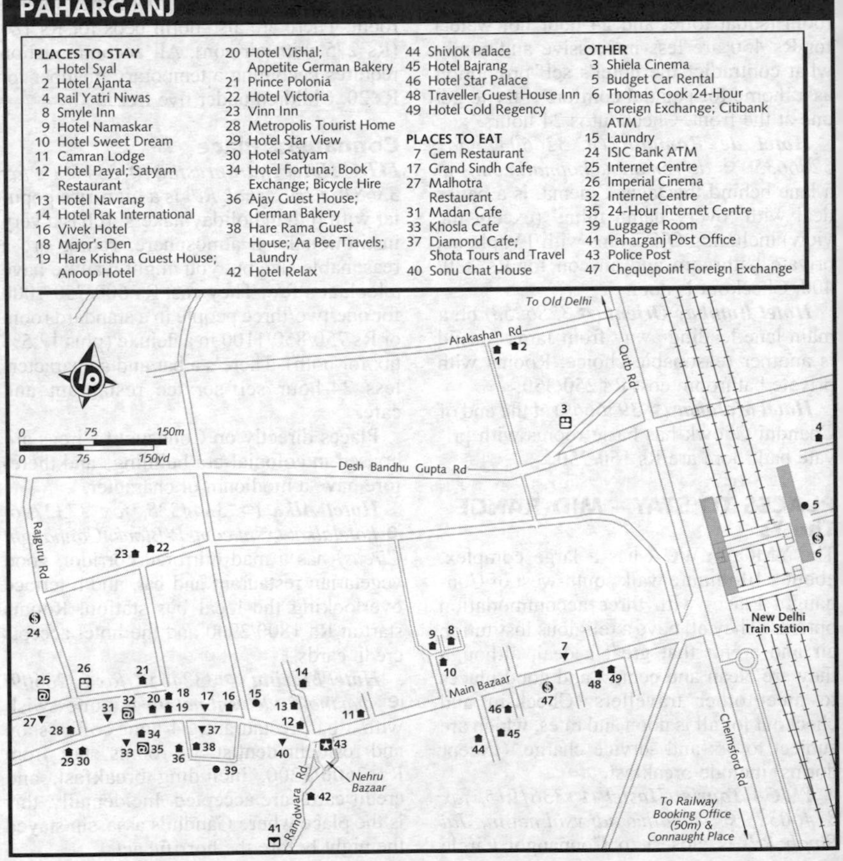

Yatri Guest House *(☎ 3625563, ⓔ yatri@nde.vsnl.net.in, 3/4 Punchkuin Marg)* is actually in a small lane off Punchkuin Marg, opposite the junction with Mandir Marg. It's small, calm and secure with a lawn out front and a couple of open courtyards at the back. Spotless, fan-cooled doubles with big beds and private bathrooms (geyser hot water), cost Rs 1100/1250, including tax. There are meals and snacks as well as all-inclusive taxi tours from US$28 per day.

Hotel Ajanta *(☎ 3620927, fax 3620228, ⓔ ccity@nda.vsnl.net.in)*, north of Paharganj on Arakashan Rd, is one of the best hotels providing a good service to travellers with a restaurant, Internet access and a reputable travel agency. Rooms are on the small side but are very clean and those at the front have balconies. They cost from Rs 425/525. There is a 10% service charge.

Hotel Syal *(☎ 3610091, fax 3514290, ⓔ nomex@vsnl.com)*, nearby, is a centrally air-conditioned place used by tour groups. Rooms, some with balcony, start at Rs 450 and there's a nice terrace and good restaurant.

Other Areas

Master Paying Guest Accommodation *(☎ 5741089, R-500 New Rajinder Nagar)*, en route to the airport, is a cool little place in a residential area away from the action. Rooms with classic furniture and French windows – full of character – cost Rs 500/600 with shared bathroom (including tax). Breakfast, drinks and snacks are served in the homey lounge or shady roof terrace.

Hotel Broadway *(☎ 3273821, fax 3269966, ⓔ broadway@oldworldhospitality.com, 4/15 Asaf Ali Rd)*, near Delhi Gate in Old Delhi, is a classy place with attentive staff, a very good restaurant, busy bar and informative and gastronomical walking tours of Old Delhi. Rooms start at Rs 1195/1495, those at the rear have Jama Masjid views.

There are a few places in the Sunder Nagar, conveniently located between Purana Qila and Humayun's tomb, which has antique shops, a couple of reasonable restaurants and lots of greenery. The air-con hotels are all set within lawned gardens offering clean comfort in relative tranquillity.

La Sagrita Tourist Home *(☎ 4694541, fax 4636956, ⓔ lasagrit@del3.vsnl.net.in)*, the pick of the bunch, has very comfortable rooms from Rs 1490/2090.

Kailash Inn *(☎ 4623634, fax 4617401)*, a few doors down, has rooms for Rs 1500/1900; children under six stay free.

Jukaso Inn *(☎ 4692137, fax 4694402, ⓔ jukaso@hotmail.com)* attracts business travellers. Rooms start at Rs 1650/2400 and it has a pool table and restaurant with buffet breakfast/dinner for Rs 150/250.

PLACES TO STAY – TOP END

Four-Star Hotels

ITDC Hotel Kanishka *(☎ 3344422, fax 3368242, 19 Ashoka Rd)* is next to Janpath and not great but it does have a small swimming pool. Rooms cost Rs 4000/4500 plus 22.5% tax.

ITDC Hotel Janpath *(☎ 3340070, fax 3347083)* is next to Kanishka, but is better value with rooms for Rs 1999/2900. There are restaurants, bars and travel services but no pool.

The Connaught *(☎ 3364225, fax 3340757, ⓔ prominent.hotels@gems.vsnl.net.in, 37 Shahhed Bhagat Singh Marg)* is a modern place with restaurants, a travel agency, 24-hour coffee shop, boutiques and an astro-palmist. Rooms cost US$120/130 with breakfast.

Hotel Diplomat *(☎ 3010204, fax 3018605, 9 Sardar Patel Marg)*, within a manicured garden in Chanakyapuri, is a bit of a showpiece for its associate, an obviously Indian interior design company. There are 25 individually styled rooms with minibar at US$100/110 each and there is a bar and restaurant.

Five-Star Hotels

The Claridges *(☎ 3010211, fax 3010625, ⓔ Claridges.hotel@gems.vsnl.net.in, 12 Aurangzeb Rd)* has a European package holiday look from the outside with an Art Deco-esque marbled interior. It also has four restaurants (see Places to Eat – International Hotels), a bakery, a bar overlooking the lawn, swimming pool, health club and car parking. It's a good choice in this category with rooms for a negotiable US$175/200.

The Imperial *(☎ 3341234, fax 3342255, ⓔ luxury@theimperialindia.com)* on Janpath, designed in a mix of Victorian and Art Deco styles, has cool green lawns and an avenue of palms. With marbled halls and colonially furnished rooms it's a good place to step back in time to the days of the Raj.

Rooms start at US$200 with the royal suite costing US$1000.

The Oberoi *(☎ 4363030, fax 4360484, ⓔ reservationsoberoidel.com, Dr Zakir Hussain Marg)*, on the edge of Delhi Golf Course, is a member of the World's Leading Hotels. A very swish place it has a tempting pool, bars, and restaurants with renowned chefs. Rooms start at US$295/320.

Le Meridien *(☎ 370101, fax 3714545, ⓔ info@lemeridien-newdelhi.com)* is a modern and fairly characterless place on Janpath. Inside the atrium is very opulent and the usual five-star facilities, including a health club, are provided. Rooms are less opulent but do have good views; they start at US$220/240.

The Park *(☎ 3733737, fax 3732025, 15 Sansad Marg)* is central and overlooks the Jantar Mantar. With the usual assortment of coffee shops and restaurants it has a particularly good Spanish restaurant and a bar-cum-nightclub for guests only. Rooms start at US$225/250.

Maurya Sheraton Hotel *(☎ 6112233, fax 6113333, ⓔ maurya@cyber-club.com, Sardar Patel Marg)* is very plush with a whole eight floors designed to cater to every good businessperson's whim. It also has a few renowned restaurants, the usual bar, nightclub, swimming pool etc, and the not so usual Internet cafe and indoor golf. Rooms start at Rs 7000/7500.

The Ambassador Hotel *(☎ 4632600, fax 4632252, ⓔ ambassador.delhi@tajhotels.com, Cornwallis Rd)* is a recently renovated Raj-era place. Rooms start at US$135/145 and there's a 'trying to be trendy' bar.

Five-Star Deluxe

Hotel Inter-Continental *(☎ 3320101, fax 3325335, ⓔ newdelhi@interconti.com, Barakhamba Ave)* is a large modern place with a marbled foyer combining Indian and colonial styles. With all you would expect, including a 3rd-floor outdoor swimming pool and business lounges (including one catering specifically to legal executives) rooms start at US$220/245 – nonsmoking rooms are available.

The Metropolitan Hotel Nikko *(☎ 3342000, fax 3343000, ⓔ reservations@hotelnikko delhi.com)* is a swish new place with some good dining options with a more intimate feel than some of its competitors. Rooms start at US$210/240, which includes perks such as a welcome drink, mineral water, use of the health spa and special souvenir on departure. Executive rooms at US$330/360 also include transfers, access to an exclusive lounge and use of a car, butler and boardroom, plus more. Nonsmoking rooms are available.

PLACES TO EAT

Delhi has an excellent array of places to eat – from *dhabas* (snack bars) with dishes from Rs 15 to top-of-the-range restaurants where a meal for two can top Rs 3500.

Connaught Place

There are many fast-food places – Western and Indian – around Connaught Place. You'll find ***McDonald's*** here along with ***Wimpy***, ***Kwality***, ***Pizza Hut*** and ***Domino's***. ***Nirula's***, a Delhi-based chain, is very good with Indian, burgers, pizzas and ice cream (the best in Delhi that you can try before you buy). Their plus point is that they have good food at reasonable prices and are clean and healthy. A minus point for some of them is they have no place to sit – it's stand, eat and run. More upmarket chains such as ***TGI Friday's*** and ***Pizza Pizza Express*** are also appearing.

Cafe 100 *(B-Block, Connaught Place)* is a very popular semi self-service place that's giving Nirula's a run for its money. There are Indian snacks, burgers, a wide range of ice creams, and an excellent buffet upstairs (open noon to 3 pm and 7 to 11 pm).

Berco's *(☎ 3323757, E-Block, Connaught Place)* is one of Delhi's most popular places serving Chinese and Japanese for about Rs 150 per dish. Don't be surprised if you have to queue.

DV8 *(☎ 3361444)*, on the corner of Connaught Circus and Sansad Marg, is a place that keeps re-creating itself to attract the 'in-crowd'. The scene of Delhi's first disco (now closed) back in the 1960s, today it is a welcome place to chill out while enjoying a drink or some pretty good fusion food. Upstairs you have the opportunity for fine dining while downstairs the mood is more relaxed with leather couches, a library and pool table (Rs 125 per 30 minutes). The menu, with a large and varied choice, is the same in both and a meal for two will cost around Rs 800. If that's beyond your budget, but you can afford Rs 70/150 for a coffee/pitcher of beer, take the time to linger and enjoy some cool tunes while reading the paper. It's open 11 am to late and sometimes has live music (cover charge).

Rodeo *(A-Block, Connaught Place)* is a lively restaurant serving good Tex-Mex and Indian food; it's worth visiting just for the sight of waiters in cowboy suits. Dinner for two will set you back about Rs 400. After 8.30 pm a Rs 175 cover charge is applied, unless you are dining, and there's a singing and organ playing duo to entertain.

Gaylord *(Connaught Circus)* is one of the priciest, plushest restaurants on Connaught Place, with big mirrors, chandeliers and excellent Indian food. Main dishes are around Rs 200, but the high quality of the ingredients makes this a worthwhile splurge.

Parikrama *(Kasturba Gandhi Marg)*, a revolving restaurant, is an interesting place to eat. Unlike many places of this ilk where the 1st-class views are supposed to distract you from decidedly 2nd-class food, the fare here is excellent but pricey. Main dishes are around Rs 150. It's open daily for lunch and dinner, and for drinks from 3 to 7 pm.

The Embassy *(D-Block, Connaught Place)* has excellent veg and nonveg food. It is popular among office workers; meals for two cost about Rs 350.

Kovil *(E-Block, Connaught Place)* is one of the best places for south Indian vegetarian food, costing about Rs 150 per person.

Vega, at Hotel Alka, specialises in vegetarian food cooked Delhi style (in pure ghee but without onion and garlic) for about Rs 200 per person.

United Coffee House *(E-Block, Connaught Place)* is quite plush with a very pleasantly relaxed atmosphere, good food and some of the best coffee in Delhi for about Rs 100.

The Host *(F-Block, Connaught Place)* serves excellent Indian and Chinese food. It's extremely popular with well-heeled Indians, but it isn't cheap.

Nizam Katri Kabab in H-Block is the place to head if you fancy a quick and cheap meat-on-a-stick fix for about Rs 30 to 40.

Keventers on the corner of Connaught Place and Radial Rd 3 is a small milk bar around the corner from AmEx that has good fresh milk.

Wenger's *(A-Block, Connaught Place)* is a cake shop with a range of little cakes for about Rs 20 each that they'll put in a cardboard box and tie up with a bow so you can self-consciously carry them back to your hotel room for private consumption.

Yamu's Panchayat is where the wealthy go to round off their meal with some of the most pricey paan in the city. They range from Rs 5 to 50 and some contain edible silver leaf.

Paharganj

There is a whole band of similarly styled restaurants catering to the hungry traveller along Main Bazaar. The menus are a fairly standard mix of Indian, Chinese and continental fare with the odd Israeli, Japanese and Korean specialty thrown in. Service is conducive to lingering and you can eat pretty well for around Rs 50 to 100. Most travellers' cafes have at least one other service such as travel agency, bookshop, clothing shop and/or baggage store attached.

Diamond Cafe and ***Grand Sindh Cafe*** have cassettes and CDs for sale – great places to relax and sip coffee while picking out some souvenir tunes.

Khosla Cafe and ***Madan Cafe*** have footpath seating which can be pleasant or a nightmare depending on the time of day you're there. Sitting there mid-morning or late afternoon you're going to be pestered by beggars, hawkers, dogs and who knows what else. If you want the fresh air but not the hassle try ***Satyam***, next to Hotel Payal, which has a terrace overlooking the vegetable market.

The place for a dosa, ***Sonu Chat House*** is popular with locals but also caters to travellers' tastes with banana chocolate dosas.

If you want a really good feed and don't mind paying an extra few rupees, ***Malhotra Restaurant***, behind Metropolis Tourist Home, is the place to go. Popular with tourists and locals alike, it never disappoints.

Appetite German Bakery, next to Hotel Vishal, has a small selection of tempting cakes accompanied by new-age music, chess and a small library.

Gem Restaurant is a new, and therefore clean, place with fluorescent lighting and large 1st-floor windows – goldfish would feel at home here.

Those in need of a vitamin C burst should stop at one of the ***juice shops*** dotted around; those close to Diamond Cafe are popular.

Many guesthouses and hotels have their own restaurants, some of which are on rooftop terraces (see Places to Stay for details).

Old Delhi

ISBT Workers' Canteen, in the Kashmiri Gate ISBT, has good food at good prices.

Karim's, down a lane across from the south gate of the Jama Masjid, is very well known among Delhi-wallahs for its excellent nonveg food. In this large restaurant there's everything from kebabs to the richest Mughlai dishes, and prices are reasonable.

Moti Mahal Restaurant *(Netaji Subhash Marg, Daryaganj)* is an open-air place with live qawwali nightly. It's particularly noted for its tandoori dishes.

Chor Bizarre at Hotel Broadway serves tasty Kashmiri and Indian fare in quirky surrounds. Bizarre features include a vintage car, still in working condition, that serves as a salad bar and, for those planning a romantic liaison, there's a four-poster bed table. The menu makes great reading and not just for the excellent dishes; it recommends you go for a thali which gives you a good range of tasty dishes for Rs 225/295 (veg/nonveg). If you can get eight people together take advantage of the Kashmiri feast eaten on the floor around a large platter (Rs 585 each).

Hotel Inter-Continental has a range of restaurants such as the Indian ***Baluchi***, offering a biryani buffet on Sunday for Rs 500 including beer, and the Thai ***Blue Elephant*** with buffet lunches on Wednesday, Thursday and Sunday for Rs 550 including sparkling wine and soft drinks (sodas).

Ghantewala *(Chandni Chowk)*, near the Sisganj Gurdwara (Sikh temple), is reputed to have some of the best Indian sweets in Delhi. The stalls along the road in front of the Jama Masjid are very cheap.

New Delhi

There are some excellent eating options in the area south of Connaught Place, but you'll need a taxi or transport to get to most of them.

At Pandara Market, which is a shopping centre near Bikaner House, are some good-value mid-range places such as ***Ichiban***, ***Pindi*** and ***Chicken Inn***, plus several others popular with middle-class Delhiites. They all cost around Rs 300 to 400 for two.

Khan Market also has some good restaurants, including ***China Garden*** and ***China Fare***, for a little less than the Pandara Market places.

Basil & Thyme *(Chanakyapuri)*, in the swish Santushti Shopping Centre, is still quite hip. The continental food is good and the service excellent. Meals for two cost about Rs 500 and it opens for lunch Monday to Saturday only.

Dilli Haat *(Aurobindo Marg)*, opposite the INA Market, is a great place to sample food from all over India – many of the stalls devoted to particular states have restaurants and for around Rs 50 per person they offer good value. This may be your one chance to try Naga or Mizo food. There is a Rs 7 entrance fee.

There are lots of restaurants in Hauz Khas Village, nearly all of them mid-range places that charge around Rs 250 per person. ***Bistro Restaurant Complex*** includes ***Kowloon*** (Chinese restaurant), ***Mohalla*** (curries in gravy) and ***The Roof-top*** (Indian barbecue plus live music) and is very popular. ***Park Baluchi***, within the nearby Deer Park, specialises in Afghan cuisine such as tandoori chicken wrapped around a sword.

International Hotels

Many Delhi residents reckon the best food is at the major hotels.

Ambassador Hotel There are upmarket thalis at ***Dasaprakash*** vegetarian restaurant, and ***Larry's China***.

The Claridges The restaurants at this hotel are very good value and they're interesting places to eat. ***Dhaba*** offers 'rugged roadside' cuisine, and is set up like a typical roadside cafe; ***Jade Garden*** serves Chinese food in a bamboo grove setting; ***Pickwicks*** offers Western food, and the decor is 19th-century England; while outdoor ***Corbetts*** gets its inspiration from Jim Corbett of tiger hunting fame, complete with recorded jungle sounds. As might be expected, meat features prominently on the menu. All restaurants are moderately priced – most main dishes are under Rs 200.

Hyatt Regency ***Delhi Ka Angan*** specialises in very rich Punjabi and Mughlai food; ***La Piazza*** has Italian food and possibly Delhi's best Italian wine list. Both restaurants charge about Rs 1000 for two.

The Imperial is a great place for an alfresco breakfast in the pleasant garden. ***Spice Route*** offers mainly Thai and Keralan dishes; it's very popular and very expensive (Rs 1800 for two).

At ***Tavern Restaurant*** main dishes are around Rs 200. Prices at the less formal ***Garden Party*** are 10% lower.

Maurya Sheraton Hotel One of the best restaurants in the city is ***Bukhara***. It has many central Asian specialities, including tandoori cooking and dishes from the Peshawar region in northwest Pakistan. The dhal here is so popular they've started selling it in cans for Rs 150. ***Bali Hi*** is its Chinese restaurant, and ***West View*** its European one. All these restaurants cost around Rs 1000 per person. Another restaurant here is ***Dum Pukht***, named after the cuisine championed by the Nawabs of Avadh (Lucknow) around 300 years ago. The dishes are covered by a pastry cap while cooking, so the food is steamed as much as anything else. It's quite distinctive and absolutely superb, and a little cheaper than the others at Rs 1200 for two.

The Oberoi Probably the best Thai restaurant in Delhi is ***Baan Thai***. Count on Rs 1000 for two.

ENTERTAINMENT

Cultural Programs

Delhi is renowned for its dance and visual arts scene; check out *First City* magazine for what's going on. Major dance and live music venues include:

Habitat World (☎ 4691920) Lodi Rd, Indian Habitat Centre

India International Centre (☎ 4619431) near Habitat World

Kamani Auditorium (☎ 3388084) Copernicus Marg, near Rabindra Bhavan

Triveni Chamber Theatre (205 Tansen Marg) Triveni Kala Sangam, near Rabindra Bhavan

Cinemas

In 2000, following some tragic cinema fires, Delhi police reported that only six of Delhi's cinemas were safe – they wouldn't name which these were.

If you're willing to risk it, a number of cinemas around Connaught Place screen typically Hindi mass-appeal movies; seats range from Rs 25 to 50. For something a little more cerebral, the ***British Council*** *(☎ 3710111, Kasturba Gandhi Marg)* often screens good foreign films.

The better cinemas are mostly in the southern suburbs, including ***PVR Priya Cinema*** *(☎ 6140048, 61 Basant Lok, Vasant Vihar)* in the Basant Lok Complex and ***PVR Anupam 4*** *(☎ 6865999)*, in the Saket Community Centre, Saket. ***Satyam Cineplex*** *(☎ 5797387, Patel Nagar)* is on Patel Rd, west of Karol Bagh. These cinemas regularly show Hollywood blockbusters tame enough to sneak past the Indian censors. Habitat World also has a cinema featuring Indian documentaries and art-house films.

Bars & Nightclubs

Most bars and discos are at the five-star hotels and are wildly expensive. The discos especially are quite exclusive and entry is usually restricted to members and hotel guests; couples and women stand a better chance of being admitted than unaccompanied men. Alcohol is served in some restaurants (where they usually have no problem with you drinking only) and the more expensive hotel bars, pretty pricey to start with it's then taxed another 30% – expect to pay between Rs 75 to 200 per beer before tax. Fortunately many places have happy hours although these are mainly from mid-afternoon to early evening. You don't have to worry too much about completely breaking the bank though as most places stop the alcohol flowing at 10.30 pm curtailing serious drinking sessions.

There are a few options for a beer in Paharganj. Some backpacker restaurants will serve you beer in a teacup if you're discreet about it, otherwise ***Hotel Gold Regency*** is very sociable. Its licensed restaurant has a bit of a beer hall feel and is usually full of Indians and foreigners in equal numbers swapping info and stories and no doubt a few dodgy deals. It also has a bar area which sometimes doubles as a dance and gay venue, although it's had problems with Russian prostitutes in the past. Buy two beers or whisky, get one free until 10 pm.

In Connaught Place, ***The Blues Bar***, ***DV8***, ***Pizza Express*** and ***Rodeo*** are good for drinks while listening to live or recorded music, although the latter applies a Rs 175 cover charge after 8.30 pm if you're not dining (see also Places to Eat earlier). ***Pegasus*** bar at Nirula's complex tries hard to re-create an English pub but doesn't quite pull it off. There are also plenty of other restaurants to choose from, look for their happy hours/offers on their windows.

If you feel like a bit of a sing-song, ***Ruby Tuesday's*** has karaoke on a Tuesday night. It also has stuff for the kids on a Sunday lunch time and a ventriloquist and magician the same evening for the adults. It's a licensed restaurant that serves up burgers, grills, baked spuds and salads and attracts a wacky, fun-seeking crowd.

Sound-and-Light Shows

These light-hearted introductions to the history of Delhi take place in the atmospheric surrounds of the Red Fort and Purana Qila (see those individual entries). They have the added bonus of offering a reasonable opportunity to get into these particular sights without paying the inflated day-time tourist prices.

SHOPPING

Good buys include silk products, precious stones, leather and woodwork, but the most important thing about Delhi is that you can find almost anything from anywhere in the whole country. If this is your first stop in India, and you intend to buy something while you are here, then it's a chance to compare what is available from all over the country. If this is your last stop and there was something you missed elsewhere in your travels, Delhi provides a chance to find it.

Two good places to start are in New Delhi, near Connaught Place. The **Central Cottage Industries Emporium** is on Janpath. In this building you will find items from all over India, generally of good quality and reasonably priced. Whether it's woodcarvings, brassware, paintings, clothes, textiles or furniture, you'll find it here. Along Baba Kharak Singh Marg, two streets around (clockwise) from Janpath, are the **state emporiums** run by the state governments. Each of them displays and sells handicrafts from their state.

There are many other shops around **Connaught Place** and **Janpath**. By The Imperial hotel are a number of stalls and small shops run by Tibetan refugees and rapacious Kashmiris selling carpets, jewellery and many (often instant) antiques.

In Old Delhi, **Chandni Chowk** is the famous shopping street. Here you will find carpets and jewellery, but you have to search the convoluted back alleys. Perfumes are made in the narrow street called Kariba Kalan.

Main Bazaar in Paharganj has a good range. You can find an interesting variety of perfumes, oils, soaps and incense at two places (both signposted), one near Vivek Hotel and another near Camran Lodge. Take advantage of all the free testers. Monday is the official weekly holiday for the shops in Main Bazaar, and many are closed on that day, although a surprising number remain open seven days a week.

In recent years, the **Karol Bagh Market**, 3km west of Connaught Place along Panchkuin Marg (Radial Rd 3), has become even more popular than Connaught Place or Main Bazaar.

Just south of the Purana Qila, beside Dr Zakir Hussain Rd, across from the Oberoi and the Delhi Golf Course, is the **Sunder Nagar Market**, a collection of shops selling antiques and brassware. The prices may be high but you'll find fascinating and high-quality artefacts. Shops in the major international hotels often have high-quality items, at equally high prices.

Opposite Ashok Hotel in Chanakyapuri is the **Santushti Shopping Centre**. There's a string of small upmarket boutiques here with a good range of crafts and high prices to match.

The **M-Block Market** in Greater Kailash I is one of the biggest upper- and middle-class shopping centres. The **N-Block Market** in Greater Kailash I has a similar collection of upmarket stores, including the famous clothing, fabric and furnishings store Fab India (younger Indian parliamentarians are sometimes referred to as the Fab India gang).

Hauz Khas Village in south Delhi has become a very interesting little shopping enclave, with an ever-changing collection of art galleries and boutiques catering for the upper end of the market.

GETTING THERE & AWAY

Delhi is a major international gateway to India; for details on arriving from overseas see the introductory Getting There & Away chapter. At certain times of the year international flights out of Delhi can be heavily booked so it's wise to make reservations as early as possible. This particularly applies to some of the heavily discounted airlines out of Europe – check and double-check your reservations and make sure you reconfirm your flight.

Delhi is also a major centre for domestic travel, with extensive bus, rail and air connections. Delhi airport is prone to fog in December and January when flights in and out can be severely delayed.

Air

The domestic terminals (Terminals IA and IB of the Indira Gandhi International Airport) are 12km from the centre, and the international terminal (Terminal II) is a farther 5km. There's a free IAAI bus between the two terminals, or you can use the Ex-Servicemen's Air Link Transport Service (EATS; see Getting Around later in this chapter).

If you're arriving at the airport from overseas, there's 24-hour State Bank of India and Thomas Cook foreign exchange counters in the arrivals hall, after customs and immigration. Once you've left the arrivals hall you won't be allowed back in.

Several airlines now require you have your baggage X-rayed and sealed; do this at the machines just inside the departure hall before you queue to check in. Nearly all airline tickets include the departure tax in the price; if not included, you must pay at the State Bank counter in the departures hall.

Facilities at the international terminal include a snack bar, bookshop and banks. Once inside the departure lounge there are a few duty-free shops with the usual inflated prices, and another snack bar.

Indian Airlines The Malhotra Building office (☎ 3310517) in F-Block, Connaught

Domestic Flights from Delhi

destination	duration (hrs)	airline	freq	fare (US$)
Ahmedabad	1¼	IC	2d	135
		9W	1d	
Amritsar	1	IC	5w	100
Aurangabad	3½	IC	1d	175
Bagdogra	1½	IC	3w	185
		9W	1d	
Bangalore	2½	S2	2d	255
		IC	3d	
Bhopal	½	CD	1d	120
Bhubaneswar	2	CD	1d	215
Chandigarh	¾	CD	2w	75
		9W	1d	
Chennai	2½	S2	1d	260
	1½	IC	2d	
Cochin	4	IC	1d	330
Coimbatore	4½	IC	1d	285
Dehra Dun	1	IC	3w	100
Dharamsala	1½	IC	3w	145
Dibrugarh	3½	S2	1d	254
Goa	2½	S2	2d	235
		IC	4w	
Guwahati	3¼	S2	1d	210
	2¼	IC	1d	
		9W	1d	
Gwalior	¾	IC	5w	70
Hyderabad	2	IC	2d	205
Imphal	3¾	IC	2w	240
Indore	2¼	CD	1d	135
		9W	1d	
Jaipur	¾	CD	1d	55
		9W	1d	
Jammu	1¼	CD	1d	105
		9W	1d	
Jodhpur	1½	CD	1d	105
Kolkata	3½	S2	4w	200
	2	IC	3d	
Kozhikode	5¾	IC	1d	315
Kullu	1¾	IC	3w	145
Leh	1¼	CD	4w	105
Lucknow	1	S2	1d	90
		IC	17w	
		9W	1d	
Mumbai	2	S2	2d	175
		IC	7d	
		CD	5w	
		9W	8d	131
Nagpur	2¾	CD	1d	150
Patna	1½	S2	1d	145
	2¼	IC	2d	
Pune	2	IC	1d	205
		9W	1d	
Shimla	1	IC	3w	110
Srinagar	2½	IC	1d	115
		9W	1d	
Thiruvananthapuram	4½	IC	2d	360
Udaipur	3	CD	1d	105
		9W	1d	
Varanasi	2½	S2	1d	125
		IC	1d	
		9W	1d	
Visakhapatnam	3½	CD	4w	285

Airline codes:

CD	Alliance Air (Indian Airlines)
IC	Indian Airlines
S2	Sahara Airlines
9W	Jet Airways

Frequency abbreviations:

d	daily
w	weekly

Place, is probably the most convenient of the Indian Airlines offices, though busy at most times. It's open 10 am to 5 pm daily except Sunday.

There's another office in the PTI Building (☎ 3719168) on Sansad Marg, open 10 am to 5 pm daily except Sunday.

At Safdarjang airfield on Aurobindo Marg there's a 24-hour office (☎ 141), and this can be a quick place to make bookings.

Business-class passengers can check in by telephone (☎ 5665166) and prerecorded flight departure information is available (☎ 142).

Indian Airlines flights depart from Delhi to all the major Indian centres – see the boxed text 'Domestic Flights from Delhi' on the previous page. Check-in at the airport is 1¼ hours before departure. Note that if you have just arrived and have an onward connection to another city in India, it may be with Air India, the country's international carrier, rather than the domestic carrier, Indian Airlines. If that is the case, you must check in at the international terminal (Terminal II) rather than the domestic terminal.

Other Domestic Airlines As well as the offices listed following, private airlines have offices at the airport's domestic terminal.

Archana Airways (☎ 6842001, 5665768) 41A Friends Colony East, Mathura Rd
Jagson Airlines (☎ 3721594) 12E Vandana Bldg, 11 Tolstoy Marg
Jet Airways (☎ 6853700) 40 N-Block, Connaught Circus
Sahara Airlines (☎ 3326851) Ambadeep Bldg, Kasturba Gandhi Marg

International Airlines Offices in Delhi include the following:

Aeroflot (☎ 3312843) BMC House, 1st floor, 1 N-Block, Connaught Place
Air Canada (☎ 3720014) ALPs Bldg, 56 Janpath
Air France (☎ 3738004) 7 Atma Ram Mansion, Connaught Circus
Air India (☎ 3311225) 2nd floor, Jeevan Bharati Bldg, Sansad Marg
Asiana Airlines (Korea; ☎ 3315631) Ansal Bhavan, 16 Kasturba Gandhi Marg
Biman Bangladesh Airlines (☎ 3354401) World Trade Centre, Babar Rd, Connaught Place
British Airways (☎ 5652077) 11th floor, Gopal Das Bhawan, Barakhamba Rd
Delta Airlines (☎ 3325222) Chandralok Bldg, 36 Janpath
Druk Air (Bhutan; ☎ 3310990) Chandralok Bldg, 36 Janpath
El Al Israel Airlines (☎ 3357965) Prakash Deep Bldg, 7 Tolstoy Marg
Emirates (☎ 3324665) Kanchenjunga Bldg, 18 Barakhamba Rd
Ethiopian Airlines (☎ 3312302) Ansal Bhavan, Kasturba Gandhi Marg
Gulf Air (☎ 3324922) 12 G-Block, Connaught Circus
Japan Airlines (☎ 3324922) Chandralok Bldg, 36 Janpath
Kazakhstan Airlines (☎ 3367889) ITDC Hotel Janpath
KLM-Royal Dutch Airlines (☎ 3721141) Prakash Deep Bldg, 7 Tolstoy Marg
Kuwait Airways (☎ 3359711) 16 Kasturba Gandhi Marg
Lufthansa Airlines (☎ 3323310) 56 Janpath
Northwest Airlines (☎ 3721141) Prakash Deep Bldg, 7 Tolstoy Marg
Pakistan International Airlines (PIA; ☎ 3313161) Kailash Bldg, Kasturba Gandhi Marg
Qantas Airways (☎ 3329027) Barakhamba Rd
Royal Jordanian (☎ 3320635) 56 G-Block, Connaught Place
Royal Nepal Airlines Corporation (RNAC; ☎ 3321164) 44 Janpath
Saudi Arabian Airlines (☎ 3310466) DCM Bldg, 16 Barakhamba Rd
Scandinavian Airlines (SAS; ☎ 3352299) Ambadeep Bldg, Kasturba Gandhi Marg
Singapore Airlines (☎ 3329036) Ashoka Estate Bldg, Barakhamba Rd
SriLankan Airlines (☎ 3731473) 55 G-Block, Connaught Circus
Swissair (☎ 3325511) DLF Bldg, Sansad Marg
Thai Airways International (THAI; ☎ 6239988) Park Royal Hotel, America Plaza, Nehru Place
United Airlines (☎ 3353377) Ambadeep Bldg, Kasturba Gandhi Marg
Virgin Atlantic (☎ 33699663) ITDC Hotel Janpath

Bus

All the main roads leading out of Delhi are heavily congested and more than a little scary. It's best to leave early in the morning. The main bus station is the ISBT at Kashmiri Gate, north of the (Old) Delhi train station. It has 24-hour left-luggage facilities, a State Bank of India branch, post office, pharmacy and restaurant. City buses depart from here to locations all around Delhi. State government bus companies (and the counter they operate from) are:

Delhi Transport Corporation (☎ 3354518) Counter 34

Haryana Roadways (☎ 2961262) Counter 35
Himachal Roadways (☎ 2968694) Counter 40
Punjab Roadways (☎ 2967842) Counter 37
Rajasthan Roadways (☎ 2961246) Central block; bookings can also be made at Bikaner House, south of Rajpath
Uttar Pradesh Roadways (☎ 2968709) Central block

Rajasthan Bikaner House, near India Gate, is the place to head for more comfortable state-operated buses to Rajasthan. Daily buses leave for Ajmer (Rs 269, nine hours, 7, 10 and 11.40 pm), Jaipur (Rs 206/331 deluxe/air-con, six hours, between 6 am and 12.30 am), Jodhpur (Rs 364, 14 hours, 10 pm) and Udaipur (Rs 404, 15 hours, 7 pm). There are more buses from the ISBT to Ajmer (Rs 174) at 11 pm, Jaipur (Rs 113) between 6 am and 5 pm, Jodhpur (Rs 364) and Udaipur (Rs 404) at 6.15 pm.

North of Delhi For Himalayan destinations it's a much better option to take a train as far as Pathankot or Shimla then transfer to a bus. Should you prefer to take the bus the whole way you can opt for the public buses that leave the ISBT in Old Delhi or a private bus from Paharganj or Connaught Place. The public buses are generally operated by the state that your destination is in.

Private buses usually leave in the evening and prices fluctuate according to the season and price wars; the fares given here are the average cost.

Private Buses

destination	fare (Rs)
Agra (tour coach)	200
Ajmer (for Pushkar)	250
Amritsar	250
Dehra Dun	200/300*
Dharamsala	300
Haridwar	200/300*
Jaipur	200
Jammu	250
Jodhpur	250
Manali	300
Mussoorie	200/300*
Nainital	200/300*
Rishikesh	200/300*
Shimla	350
Udaipur	275

* ordinary/air-con

South of Delhi From the Sarai Kale Khan ISBT, close to Nizamuddin train station, there are frequent departures for Agra (Rs 75 to 100 depending on class, five hours), Mathura and Gwalior. It's generally quicker to go by train to all these places, though. There's a city bus link between this station and Kashmiri Gate ISBT.

Nepal & Pakistan For information about land crossings to Kathmandu and Lahore, see the Land section in the introductory Getting There & Away chapter.

Public Buses

destination	duration (hrs)	departures	fare (Rs)
Amritsar	11	6.30 pm	430
Chandigarh	5	half-hourly	205/215∗
Dehra Dun	7	7.15 am – 9.30 pm ◆	120/163∗
Dharamsala	13	6.30 am – 11 pm	240/340∗
Haridwar	6	5.45 am – 5 pm ◆	95/129∗
Jammu	12	1 am – 2.15 pm ◆	242
Kullu	13	6.40 am – 8 pm ◆	266/452∗
Manali	16	11.30 am – 10.15 pm ◆	322
Mandi	16	5.40 am	222
McLeod Ganj	14	5.30 pm	246
Rekong Peo	20	8 pm	351
Rishikesh	7	8 am; 8 – 10 pm	96/108∗
Shimla	10	5 am – 10 pm	182/360∗

∗ ordinary/deluxe ◆ six departures

DELHI

Major Trains from Delhi

destination	train No & name	departures	distance (km)	approx duration (hrs)	fare (Rs) (2nd/1st)
Agra	2180 *Taj Exp*	7.15 am HN	199	2½	53/279
	2002 *Shatabdi Exp*	6 am ND		2	390/760 *
Amritsar	2013 *Shatabdi Exp*	4.30 pm ND	447	5½	610/1220 *
Bangalore	2430 *Rajdhani Exp*	8.50 pm HN	2444	34	2205/3470/6385 ◆
	2628 *Karnataka Exp*	9.15 pm ND	2434	41	278/1659
Chennai	2434 *Rajdhani Exp*	3.30 pm HN	2194	28	2045/3335/5965 ◆
	2622 *Tamil Nadu Exp*	10.30 pm ND		33	1524/2664
Haridwar	2017 *Shatabdi Exp*	7 am ND	320	4½	60/910 *
Jaipur	2413 *Delhi Jaipur Intercity Exp*	5.15 am OD	308	5¾	77/405
	2015 *Shatabdi Exp*	6.15 am ND		4½	495/985 *
Kolkata	2302 *Rajdhani Exp*	5.15 pm ND	1441	17½	1500/2470/4270 ◆
	2304 *Poorva Exp*	4.15 pm ND		24	213/1119
Lucknow	4230 *Lucknow Mail*	2.20 pm ND	487	17½	105/552
	2004 *Shatabdi Exp*	6.20 am ND		6	640/1320 *
Mumbai	2952 *Rajdhani Exp*	4 pm ND	1388	16½	485/2405/4180 ◆
	2926 *Paschim Exp*	4.30 pm ND		23	210/1103
Shimla	4095 *Himalayan Queen*	6 am ND	364	4	84/441
Udaipur	9615 *Chetak Exp*	8.35 am SR	739	21	145/762
Varanasi	2382 *Poorva Exp*	4.15 pm ND	764	12½	149/783

Abbreviations for train stations: ND – New Delhi, OD – Old Delhi, HN – Hazrat Nizamuddin, SR – Sarai Rohilla

* Air-con chair/Air-con executive class – fare includes meals and drinks

◆ Air-con 3-tier sleeper/Air-con 2-tier sleeper/Air-con 1st class – fare includes meals and drinks

Train

Delhi is an important rail centre and an excellent place to make bookings. The best place is the special foreign tourist booking office upstairs in New Delhi train station, open 7.30 am to 5 pm Monday to Saturday and 8 am to 2 pm Sunday. This is the place to go if you want a tourist-quota allocation, are the holder of an Indrail Pass or want to buy an Indrail Pass. If you make bookings here tickets must be paid with rupees backed up by bank exchange certificates, or in US dollars and pounds sterling with any change given in rupees.

Other foreigner reservation offices include one at the airport open 24 hours and another at the Delhi Tourism Corporation in N-Block, Connaught Place open 7.30 am to 5 pm Monday to Saturday.

The main ticket office is on Chelmsford Rd, between New Delhi train station and Connaught Place. This place is well organised, but can get chaotic – the women-only queues are much shorter.

It's best to arrive first thing in the morning, or when it reopens after lunch. The office is open 8 am to 8 pm Monday to Saturday and 8 am to 2pm Sunday.

Remember that there are two main stations in Delhi – Delhi train station in Old Delhi, and New Delhi train station at Paharganj. New Delhi is much closer to Connaught Place, and if you're departing from the Old Delhi train station you should allow adequate time (up to an hour in peak times) to wind your way through the traffic snarls of Old Delhi. Between the Old Delhi and New Delhi stations you can take the No 6 bus.

There's also the Nizamuddin train station south of the New Delhi area where some trains start or finish. It's worth getting off here if you are staying in Chanakyapuri or anywhere else south of Connaught Place.

Some trains between Delhi and Jaipur, Jodhpur and Udaipur operate to and from Sarai Rohilla train station rather than Old Delhi – it's about 3.5km north-west of Connaught Place on Guru Govind Singh Marg.

GETTING AROUND

Delhi is large, congested, and the buses get hopelessly crowded. The alternative is a taxi, an autorickshaw, or for the truly brave, a bicycle. At the time of research the first phase of construction of a metro system had commenced; it's due for completion in 2005.

To/From the Airport

Although there are a number of options, airport-to-city transport is not as straightforward as it should be, due to predatory taxi and autorickshaw drivers who target unwary first-time visitors. See the boxed text 'Dodgy Delhi' earlier in this chapter.

Bus The Ex-Servicemen's Air Link Transport Service (EATS; ☎ 3316530) has a regular bus service between the airport (both terminals) and its office near Indian Airlines in F-Block, Connaught Place, between 4 am and 11 pm. The fare is Rs 50 plus Rs 5 per large piece of luggage, and it will drop you off at most of the major hotels, and the Ajmeri Gate entrance to New Delhi train station (for Paharganj) en route.

When leaving the international terminal, the counter for the EATS bus is just to the right as you exit the building. This is probably the best, although not the quickest, way into the city if you arrive late at night (see the boxed text 'Dodgy Delhi' earlier in this chapter).

Taxi What you want from the airport is not just a prepaid taxi, but the right prepaid taxi. Look for the Delhi Traffic Police Prepaid Taxi Booth just to the right outside the terminal entrance, where you'll get the lowest prices (Rs 170 to Paharganj). The others will try for much more. You'll be given a voucher that you should give to the driver at your destination.

At the domestic terminal, the taxi booking desk is just inside the terminal and charges Rs 120 to Paharganj, plus Rs 5 per bag. The taxi-wallahs outside will try for much more.

Bus

Avoid buses during the rush hours. Whenever possible try to board (and leave) at a starting or finishing point, such as the Regal and Plaza cinemas in Connaught Place, as there is more chance of a seat. There are some seats reserved for women on the left-hand side of the bus. The Delhi Transport Corporation runs some buses, others are privately owned, but they all operate along the same set routes. Western embassies generally advise their staff not to take buses, but if you want to, the White Line and Green Line buses are slightly more expensive and thus a little less crowded. Private buses and minibuses also run on these routes. A short bus ride (like Connaught Place to Red Fort) is only about Rs 2.

Useful buses include the following:

Bus No 505 Super Bazaar or Janpath (from opposite The Imperial hotel) to the Qutb Minar
Bus No 101 Kashmiri Gate Inter State Bus Terminal to Connaught Place
Bus Nos 620 & 630 Connaught Place (from outside the Jantar Mantar) to Chanakyapuri
Bus Nos 101, 104 & 139 Regal Cinema bus stand to the Red Fort

Car

Given Delhi's chaotic traffic (six road deaths per day on average), it's better not to drive. If you must rent a self-drive car Budget has offices on Janpath (☎ 3318600, fax 3739182, ⓔ bracindia@hotmail.com) and at New Delhi train station (☎ 3232725).

Taxi & Autorickshaw

All taxis and autorickshaws are metered but the meters are invariably out of date, allegedly 'not working' or the drivers will simply refuse to use them.

If you're anywhere near Connaught Place and need an autorickshaw, pick one up from the very useful prepaid booth near Palika Bazaar. Otherwise, you'll need to negotiate a price before you set out and this will always be more than it should be.

At the end of a metered journey you will have to pay according to a perversely complicated scale of revised charges (there are separate charts for recalibrated and unrecalibrated meters). Drivers are supposed to carry conversion cards but if you demand to see one, strangely enough they won't be able to find it. The fare charts are, however, also printed in the *Delhi City Guide* (Rs 15, available from newsagents). If you have a chart, pay what you think is the right price and leave it at that. Rest assured that no one is going to be out of pocket, except yourself, despite hurt or angry protestations to the contrary.

Connaught Place to the Red Fort should cost around Rs 60 by taxi or Rs 30 by

Kicking the Habit

During the 1990s the number of vehicles whizzing around Delhi's roads tripled. Their uncontrolled emissions together with foul smoke belching forth from factories was poisoning the air. Vehicles standing at traffic intersections, carbon monoxide pouring out of exhaust pipes which bore stickers reading 'Pollution Under Control', contributed to emissions as high as 5000mg per cubic metre – 50 times the WHO standard. On windless days a dark veil hung over the city.

In 1997 Delhi council took the dramatic step of banning smoking in public places. Given that simply to breathe Delhi's foul air was equivalent to smoking 20 cigarettes a day (40 a day in traffic) it seemed a small step. Pressure to improve on this, including a supreme court directive to clean up Delhi, led to on-the-spot fines for littering and spitting, the banning of commercial vehicles over eight years old, the conversion of all taxis to gas instead of diesel, improvements in public transport and the banning of trucks from the city during peak hours (24 hours in Connaught Place).

Proposals for further improvements, such as moving all industry outside of the city limits (helping the Yamuna River which is estimated to receive more than two billion litres of waste per day), continue to be acted upon. At the same time many slums are being bulldozed and one has to wonder where the current 320,000 slum dwellers are going to live, especially as Delhi's homeless already numbers 23,000.

While there has been a noticeable improvement, Delhi remains heavily polluted, especially during the humid summer months, and you're still likely to be on a pack a day. If you're asthmatic don't stay too long.

autorickshaw, although the traffic jams can make this a long trip. From Connaught Place to Paharganj should cost about Rs 15 according to the meter system, but Rs 30 seems to be the standard minimum fare for foreigners. About Rs 30 is fair for an autorickshaw from Connaught Place to Humayun's tomb.

From 11 pm to 5 am there is a 20% surcharge for autorickshaws and 25% for taxis. If you're on your own at night make a show of writing down the licence plate number before setting off.

You will no doubt be asked if you want to go shopping (the driver will insist that 'just looking' is OK), as drivers get paid (Rs 200 is standard) just for taking foreigners to stores – even if you don't purchase anything. You could arrange with your driver to make a show of looking around a few shops and in return get your sightseeing for free, although the hard-sell tactics at the shops can wear you down. To hire a taxi for eight hours should cost around Rs 450, though the driver will expect a tip (around Rs 100).

Bicycle & Cycle-Rickshaw

Although traffic is dreadful in Old Delhi and around Connaught Place, the bicycle is one way of getting around the sights to the south, though cyclists are an oppressed caste on Delhi's roads. There are very few places to hire bikes, however. In Paharganj, there's a small cycle hire shop near Rajguru Rd.

Cycle-rickshaws are banned from the Connaught Place area and New Delhi itself, but they can be handy for travelling between Connaught Circus and Paharganj, for around Rs 10, and around Old Delhi.

Greater Delhi

KHIRKI MASJID & JAHANPANAH

About 12km south of the city, this interesting mosque with its four open courts dates from 1380. The nearby village of Khirki also takes its name from the mosque.

Close to the mosque are remains of the fourth city of Delhi, Jahanpanah, including the Bijai Mandal platform and the Begumpur Masjid with its multiplicity of domes.

TUGHLAQABAD

The massively strong walls of Tughlaqabad, the third city of Delhi, are east of the Qutb Minar. The walled city and fort with its 13 gateways was built by Ghiyas-ud-din Tughlaq. Its construction involved a legendary quarrel with the saint Nizam-ud-din – when the Tughlaq ruler took the workers whom Nizam-ud-din wanted for work on his shrine, the saint cursed the king, warning that his city would be inhabited only by shepherds. Today that is indeed the situation.

The dispute between king and saint did not end with curse and counter-curse. When the king prepared to take vengeance on the saint, Nizam-ud-din calmly told his followers (in a saying that is just as current in India today): 'Delhi is a long way off'. Indeed it was, for the king was murdered on his way from Delhi in 1325.

The fort walls are constructed of massive blocks and outside the south wall of the city is an artificial lake with the king's tomb in its centre. A long causeway connects the tomb to the fort, both of which have walls that slope inward.

Getting There & Away

The easiest way to visit Tughlaqabad is to combine it with a visit to the Qutb Minar. It is a long trip by autorickshaw so a taxi is preferable. It will cost about Rs 150.

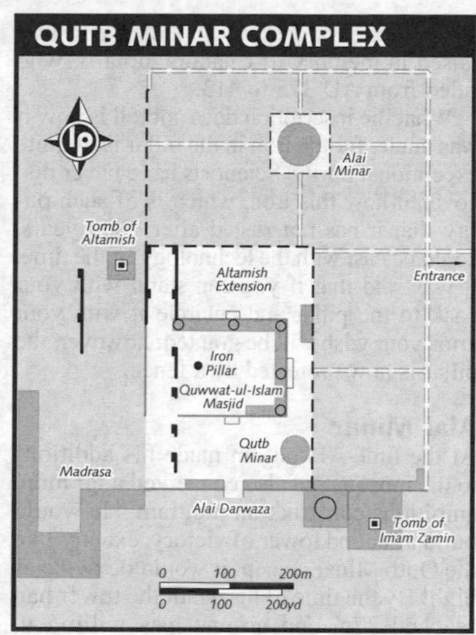

QUTB MINAR COMPLEX

The buildings in this complex, 15km south of Connaught Place, date from the onset of Muslim rule in India and are fine examples of early-Afghan architecture. It's open from sunrise to sunset; entry is US$5.

The Qutb Minar itself is a soaring tower of victory that was started in 1193, immediately after the defeat of the last Hindu kingdom in Delhi. It is nearly 73m high and tapers from a 15m diameter base to just 2.5m at the top.

The tower has five distinct storeys, each marked by a projecting balcony. The first three storeys are made of red sandstone, the fourth and fifth of marble and sandstone. Although Qutb-ud-din began construction of the tower, he only got to the first storey. His successors completed it and, in 1368, Firoz Shah rebuilt the top storeys and added a cupola. An earthquake brought the cupola down in 1803 and an Englishman replaced it with another in 1829. However, that dome was deemed inappropriate and was removed some years later.

Today, this impressively ornate tower has a slight tilt, but otherwise has worn the centuries remarkably well. It is no longer possible to climb the tower.

Quwwat-ul-Islam Masjid

At the foot of the Qutb Minar stands the first mosque to be built in India, the Might of Islam Mosque. Qutb-ud-din began construction of the mosque in 1193, but it has had a number of additions and extensions over the centuries. The original mosque was built on the foundations of a Hindu temple, and an inscription over the east gate states that it was built with materials obtained from demolishing '27 idolatrous temples'. Many of the elements in the mosque's construction indicate their Hindu or Jain origins.

Altamish, Qutb-ud-din's son-in-law, surrounded the original mosque with a cloistered court built between 1210 and 1220. Ala-ud-din added a court to the east and the magnificent Alai Darwaza gateway in 1300.

Iron Pillar This 7m-high pillar stands in the courtyard of the mosque and has been there since long before the mosque's construction. A six-line Sanskrit inscription indicates that it was initially erected outside a

Vishnu temple, possibly in Bihar, and was raised in memory of Chandragupta II, who ruled from AD 375 to 413.

What the inscription does not tell is how it was made, for the iron in the pillar is of quite exceptional purity. Scientists have never discovered how this iron, which is of such purity that it has not rusted after 2000 years, could be cast with the technology of the time. It was said that if you can stand with your back to the pillar and encircle it with your arms your wish will be granted; however, the pillar is now protected by a fence.

Alai Minar

At the time Ala-ud-din made his additions to the mosque, he also conceived a far more ambitious construction program. He would build a second tower of victory, exactly like the Qutb Minar, except it would be twice as high! By the time of his death the tower had reached 27m and no-one was willing to continue his overambitious project. The incomplete tower stands to the north of the Qutb Minar and the mosque.

Other Features

Ala-ud-din's **Alai Darwaza** gateway is the main entrance to the whole complex. It was built of red sandstone in 1310 and stands just south-west of the Qutb Minar. The **tomb of Imam Zamin** stands beside the gateway, while the **tomb of Altamish**, who died in 1235, is by the north-western corner of the mosque. The largely ruined **madrasa of Ala-ud-din** stands at the rear of the complex.

A short distance west of the enclosure, in Mehrauli Village, is the **tomb of Adham Khan** (see Nizam-ud-din's Shrine in the New Dehli section). Also in Mehrauli, a large new Shakti Pitha temple complex is under construction. South of the enclosure is the Jain Ahimsa Sthal, and an impressive 4m statue in pink granite of Mahavir.

There are some summer palaces in the area and also the tombs of the last kings of Delhi, who succeeded the last Mughals. An empty space between two of the tombs was intended for the last king of Delhi, who died in exile in Yangon, Burma (Myanmar), in 1862, following his implication in the 1857 Indian Uprising.

Getting There & Away

You can get out to the Qutb Minar on a No 505 bus from the Ajmeri Gate side of New Delhi train station, or from Janpath, opposite the Imperial hotel. A taxi is more convenient.

Punjab & Haryana

Punjab was probably the part of India that suffered the most destruction and damage at the time of Partition, yet today it is far and away the most affluent state in India. No natural resource or advantage gave Punjabis this enviable position; it was sheer hard work.

Although Punjab is mainly an agricultural state, supplying a large proportion of India's rice and wheat, it also has a number of thriving industries, including Hero Bicycles – the world's biggest bicycle manufacturer.

Traditionally, each state has just one main attraction for travellers – Amritsar in Punjab and Chandigarh in Haryana. However, Punjab in particular has a number of impressive gurdwaras (Sikh temples). Grand Trunk Rd (GT Rd), one of the busiest in India, has many serais (travellers' accommodation) and Moghul monuments straddling it as it cuts across to Lahore in Pakistan.

Punjab & Harayana at a Glance

PUNJAB

Population: 24.3 million
Area: 50,362 sq km
Capital: Chandigarh
Main Language: Punjabi
When to Go: Oct to Mar

HARYANA

Population: 21.1 million
Area: 44,212 sq km
Capital: Chandigarh
Main Language: Hindi
When to Go: Oct to Mar

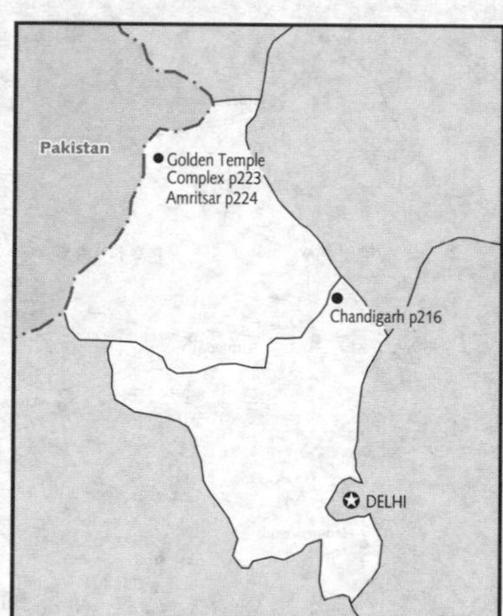

- Admire Amritsar's Golden Temple, Sikhism's most sacred site
- Visit Le Corbusier's planned city of Chandigarh; see the Rock Garden, where the city's discarded junk has been recycled into bizarre human and animal sculptures

History

Prior to Partition, Punjab extended across both sides of what is now the India-Pakistan border, and what was its capital, Lahore, is now the capital of the Pakistani state of Punjab. The grim logic of Partition sliced the population of Punjab into a Muslim region and a Sikh and Hindu region. As millions of Sikhs and Hindus fled eastward and equal numbers of Muslims fled west, there were innumerable atrocities on both sides.

Punjab's major city is Amritsar, the holy city of the Sikhs, but it is so close to the Pakistani border that it was thought wise to build a safer capital farther within India. At first Shimla, the old imperial summer capital, was chosen, but Chandigarh, a new planned city, was conceived and built in the 1950s to serve as capital of the new state.

Following Sikh demands for the creation of an independent Sikh state, to be called Khalistan (Land of the Pure), Punjab underwent another split in 1966. This time it was divided along predominantly linguistic lines: the mostly Sikh, Punjabi-speaking state of Punjab and the majority Hindi-speaking state of Haryana.

But this further partition did not have the desired effect of appeasing the Sikh separatists. At the same time, some of the northern parts of the Punjab were hived off to Himachal Pradesh. Chandigarh, on the border of Punjab and Haryana, remained the capital of both of the states. The separatist movement gained ground in 1973 when Sikh leaders listed their religious, political and economic demands in the Anandpur Sahib resolution. In 1984 when extremists

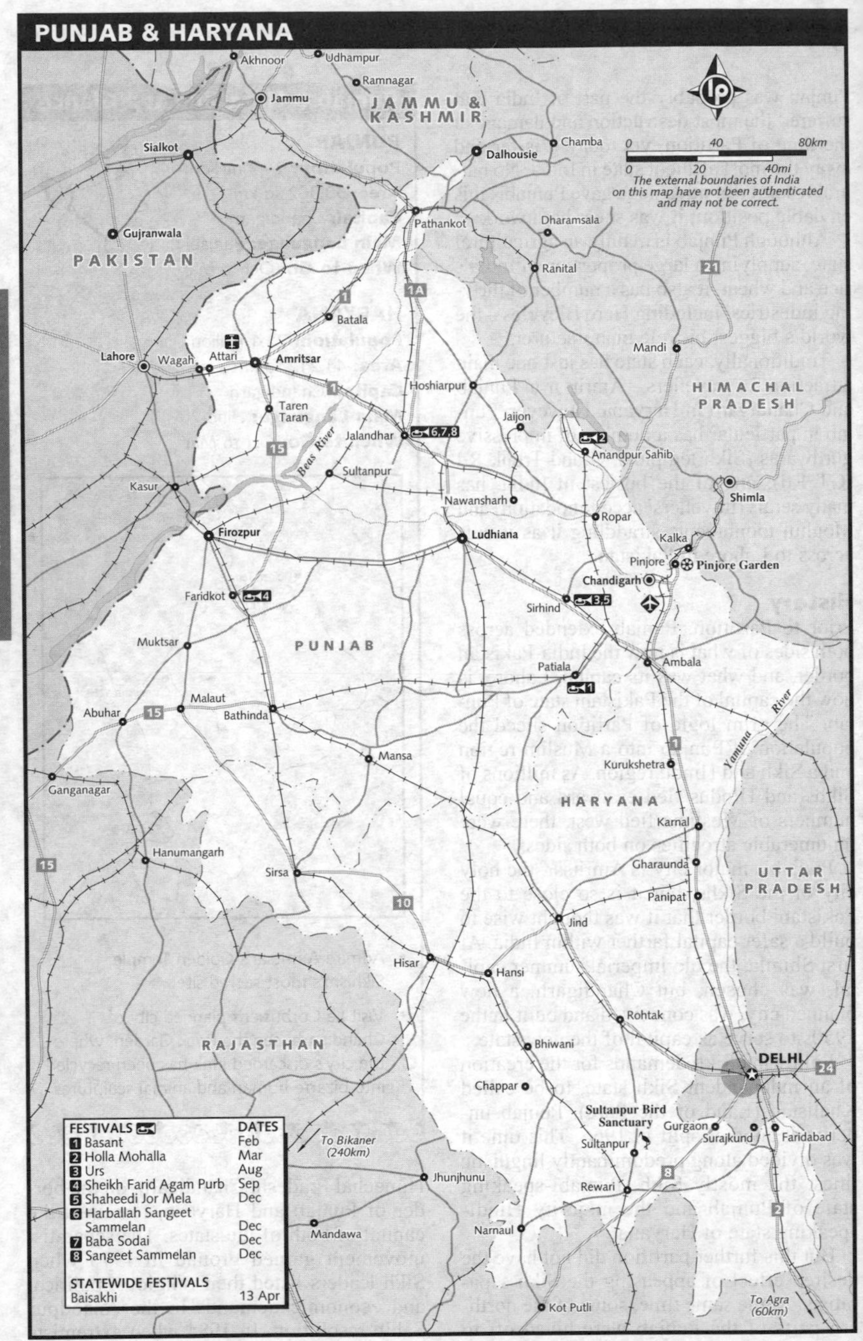

FESTIVALS	DATES
1 Basant	Feb
2 Holla Mohalla	Mar
3 Urs	Aug
4 Sheikh Farid Agam Purb	Sep
5 Shaheedi Jor Mela	Dec
6 Harballah Sangeet Sammelan	Dec
7 Baba Sodai	Dec
8 Sangeet Sammelan	Dec
STATEWIDE FESTIVALS	
Baisakhi	13 Apr

occupied the Golden Temple in Amritsar, a bloody battle ensued.

Punjab was considered by the central government to be in a state of emergency and was placed under President's Rule from 1985 to 1992. 'Supercop', KPS Gill, was sent in to stamp out militancy in the state. He did this very effectively and by 1992 most militants were either dead or in prison. Gill left behind a legacy of police brutality and human rights issues which are still being contested today. For more information on the events of the 1980s, Sikh demands and the response of the Indian state, the following books are good options: *My Bleeding Punjab* by Khushwant Singh and *Amritsar: Mrs Gandhi's last battle* by Mark Tully and Satish Jacob.

In 1986 the government announced that Chandigarh would be handed over to Punjab in an attempt to placate the Sikhs. However, with the continued violence in Punjab this didn't take place, although eventually it will. In the meantime, Chandigarh remains the capital of the two states, yet is itself administered as a Union Territory from Delhi.

The Sikhs still dream of Khalistan but the memories of the past violence are still raw enough for them to seek a peaceful resolution. In the meantime, the state prospers economically and is a calm, friendly and peaceful place to visit.

Haryana

If you're travelling from Delhi to almost any major attraction in the north of India – Jaipur, Agra, Amritsar – you will need to go through Haryana.

Shah Jahan built *kos minars* (milestones) along the road from Delhi to Lahore and serais (caravanserais) at longer intervals. Most kos minars still stand but there is little left of the various serais. The Haryanans have, however, built a series of 'service centres' along the main roads – motel-restaurant-service station complexes named after birds found in the state – that can make travelling through the area more enjoyable. The complexes have a camping ground, camper huts (usually for around Rs 350) and rooms (in the Rs 450 to 650 range if they have air-con, and cheaper without). Some places also have dorms. All have restaurants, and some serve fast food. For details pick up a pamphlet from the Haryana Government Tourist Bureau (☎ 332 4910), at the Chandralok Building, 36 Janpath, Delhi, or from the tourist office in Chandigarh (Sector 17B).

Places of interest along the route between Delhi and Chandigarh include Surajkund, only 10km from Delhi, where the **Surajkund Crafts Mela**, one of Haryana's highlights, takes place in the first two weeks of February. Showcasing crafts from a different state each year, you can buy direct from the craftspeople, quality is very high and prices lower than in the state emporiums.

There are many birds, including flamingos, at Sultanpur bird sanctuary, 46km south-west of Delhi. September to March is the best time to visit, and you can stay at Haryana Tourism's ***Rosy Pelican*** complex. At the time of research, public transport to the lake from Delhi didn't really justify a trip out here, although Haryana Tourism is planning a rail link in the very near future. To get there by bus, take a blue Haryana bus from Delhi's Sarai Kale Khan ISBT to Gurgaon, and then a Chandu bus to Sultanpur.

Panipat, 92km north of Delhi, is reputed to be one of the most fly-infested places in India – due, it is said, to a Muslim saint buried here. He is supposed to have totally rid Panipat of flies, but when the people complained that he had done too good a job he gave them all the flies back, multiplied by a thousand.

The gateways of an old Mughal serai stand to the west of **Gharaunda**, 102km north of Delhi.

Karnal, mentioned in the Mahabharata, is the place from where in 1739 Nadir Shah, the Persian who took the Peacock Throne from Delhi, defeated the Mughal emperor Mohammed Shah. Continuing north, the **Kurukshetra tank** has attracted as many as one million pilgrims during eclipses, when the water is believed to be especially purifying.

There are other minor, interesting towns in Haryana on the alternative train route to Amritsar. See the introduction to the Punjab section later in this chapter.

CHANDIGARH

☎ 0172 • pop 750,000

Chandigarh was conceived and born in the 1950s and was the masterplan of the European modernist architect Le Corbusier. No other Indian city feels quite like this one.

Indians are very proud of it and it would have to be one of the cleanest and healthiest cities in the country.

Orientation

Chandigarh is on the edge of the Siwalik Hills, the outermost edge of the Himalaya. Divided into 61 sectors, it's separated by broad avenues. Each sector is quartered into four zones, A-D, and each building within them has a unique number.

Despite this logical breakdown, orientation can be tricky without a map, as only the broad separating avenues have street names. 'SCO' in business addresses, stands for 'shop-cum-office'. The bus station, modern shopping centre, and many of the restaurants are in Sector 17. As the train station is 8km out of Chandigarh, buses are a much more convenient mode of transport.

Information

Tourist Offices The Chandigarh tourist office (☎ 703839), upstairs at the bus station, is open 9 am to 5 pm Monday to Friday and to 1 pm Saturday. Open roughly the same hours, next door is Himachal Tourism (☎ 708 569) and one floor up are Punjab Tourism (☎ 711878) and Uttar Pradesh (UP) Tourism (☎ 707649). Haryana Tourism (☎ 702955), in Sector 17B, SCO 17–19, is open 9 am to 5pm weekdays only.

Money The major institutions for foreign exchange are in Sector 9. Here you'll find branches of Punjab National Bank, with an

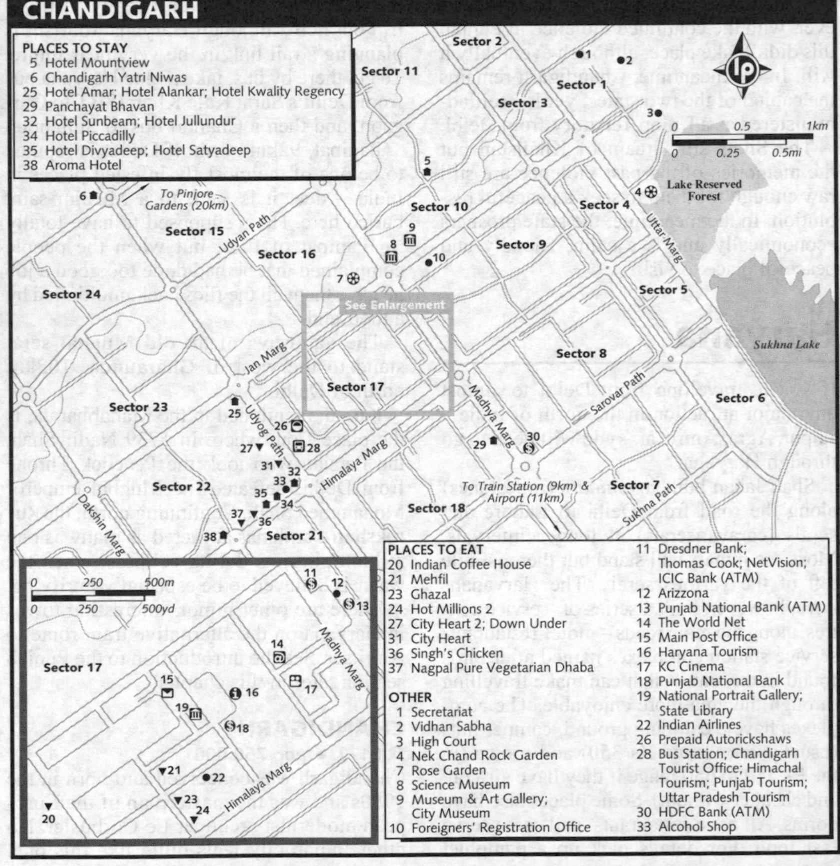

Chandigarh – a Living City

Chandigarh is unlike any other city in India. On the positive side, it is orderly and regulated. It has a wonderful feeling of space, with modern concrete buildings broken up by broad boulevards and many open, green parks and lawns. It has an air of prosperity; footpath dwellers, streetside cobblers and vendors, bedraggled beggars – all are mostly absent. Also – almost unique in India – there are no cows or other livestock roaming the streets. On the negative side, it is *too* spread out; some of the open stretches are rather barren, and it takes a long time to get anywhere, especially by cycle-rickshaw. The town seems to lack the life and colour of other Indian cities.

Most of these differences stem from the fact that it is a planned city. The government of Punjab appointed American town planner Albert Mayer and Polish architect Matthew Nowicki to create their new capital. But in the early days of the project Nowicki died in a plane crash (in 1950), prompting Mayer to withdraw.

The Swiss-born architect Le Corbusier was appointed to take over the project. Le Corbusier was known for his functional, concrete-and-steel buildings and he completely revised Nowicki and Mayer's plans. Le Corbusier wanted Chandigarh to fulfil four basic functions: living, working, circulation and care of body and spirit. He conceived of the city as a unified entity, like a living organism, with the administrative buildings in Sector 1 forming the head, the city centre (Sector 17) the heart, cultural institutions the intellect and the roads the circulatory system.

Had Nowicki survived to complete his commission Chandigarh would undoubtedly have looked very different. Nowicki commented that the 'dream of some modern planners depends entirely on a way of life alien to that of India'. Did Le Corbusier take notice of these sentiments? Judge for yourself.

ATM that accepts MasterCard, Maestro and Cirrus cards, and ICIC Bank with an ATM accepting Visa cards. There is also a Dresdner Bank behind them, as well as a branch of Thomas Cook that is open 9.30 am to 6 pm Monday to Saturday.

Post & Communications The main post and 24-hour phone office is in Sector 17.

For Internet and email access try The World Net in Sector 17 which charges Rs 35 per hour or NetVision near the banks in Sector 9.

Film & Photography There are camera and film shops along Udyog Path opposite the bus station.

Government Buildings

The Secretariat and the Vidhan Sabha (Legislative Assembly) buildings are in Sector 1. The roof garden at the top of the Secretariat yields an excellent view over Chandigarh, but the building is less accessible since the chief minister of Punjab was assassinated here in 1995. Nearby is a huge, revolving open-hand sculpture, conceived as a symbol of unity, and the colourful High Court with its double roof.

It's possible to visit some of the government buildings, including the industrial-looking Vidhan Sabha, with prior permission from the friendly Architect Department on the 2nd floor of the UD Secretariat in Sector 9 – the tourist office can help arrange this.

Nek Chand Rock Garden

The highlight of a trip to Chandigarh has to be a visit to this whimsical and inspirational garden. A Disneyworld without the rides, it is a series of interconnected rocky grottoes, walkways and water features overlooked by turrets, miniature houses and thousands of animal and humanoid figures assembled in silent armies. A path through the gardens takes you through squat archways (specifically designed to make visitors bow to the 'gods') opening up into the different areas.

Incredibly popular with Indian tourists it is open 9 am to 6 pm daily (7 pm between 1 April and 30 September); entry costs Rs 3/5 for children/adults. (See the boxed text 'Rock Garden – the Evolution of a Fantasy Land'). To the south-east is the artificial **Sukhna Lake**, where you can rent rowboats or stroll around its 2km perimeter.

Rose Garden

The rose garden in Sector 16 is claimed to be the biggest in Asia and contains more than one thousand varieties of roses. It's open daily and entry is free.

Rock Garden – the Evolution of a Fantasy Land

The Nek Chand Rock Garden is named after a former roads inspector for Chandigarh's engineering department. In 1958, while working for the department, Chand began collecting and using discarded objects – broken ceramics, electrical wires and sockets, *lac* (plastic) bangles and bits of machinery – to create an array of fantastic figures.

Fearing ridicule he set up his studio in a small hut set in a forest far away from the prying eyes of the embryonic city – even his wife initially had no idea what he was up to. So began a routine of scouring the city for materials by day and transforming them into art under the light of burning tyres by night.

In 1972 disaster loomed when workmen clearing space for the expanding city stumbled upon Chand's secret. Occupying government land, it was immediately slated for destruction. But the garden's discovery soon became the talk of the town and the authorities relented. In fact they went one step further and Chand was given a salary and workforce to continue and extend his garden. Soon the work was acclaimed internationally and Chand was lauded as a key exponent of non-mainstream 'outsider' art and invitations to exhibit abroad started arriving.

Chand is often to be found in the garden which now covers 10 acres and is still growing. Already some 5000 sculptures populate the garden, which is visited by a similar number of visitors daily. A self-effacing chap, he is generally happy to speak to visitors and modestly describes his work as 'engineering rather than art'.

Museums

Three museums are clustered in Sector 10C. The **Museum & Art Gallery** contains a modest collection of Indian stone sculptures dating back to the Gandhara period, together with some miniature paintings and modern art (entry Rs 1). The adjacent **City Museum** gives an excellent rundown of the planning, development and architecture of Chandigarh. The nearby **Science Museum** covers the evolution of life on earth, and displays fossils and implements of prehistoric humans found in India. The city and science museums are both free. All three museums are open around 10 am to 4.30 or 5 pm Tuesday to Sunday.

The National Portrait Gallery, behind the State Library in Sector 17, is open 9 am to 1 pm and 1.30 to 5 pm Monday to Friday.

Organised Tours

As Chandigarh is so spread out it may be good to take a city tour (Rs 50, minimum of four required). Organised through the tourist office it departs at 11.30 am daily and visits the Rose Garden, Rock Garden, Punjab University, the museums, the Capitol and Sukhna Lake. A tour to Pinjore Gardens, just outside Chandigarh, will cost Rs 80.

Places to Stay

Chandigarh has scant budget accommodation, and hotels are often full. There are some cheap guesthouses but the government is trying to close these and you will be told that they 'aren't registered to take foreigners'. It's still worth checking them out to see if the situation has changed, there are a couple on the street behind Hotel Jullundur.

Many places add a 10% luxury tax, all rooms listed have private bathrooms (sit-down flush toilets and hot water) and check out is noon.

Places to Stay – Budget

Panchayat Bhavan *(☎ 780701, Sector 18)* has the least-expensive options. However, it's an institutional block with a youth hostel atmosphere. Dorm beds cost Rs 24 or there are large, bare doubles with TV for Rs 200/500 without/with air-con.

Hotel Divyadeep *(☎ 705191, Sector 22B)* has simple single/double rooms with fan for Rs 250/300, Rs 450/500 with air-con.

Hotel Satyadeep *(☎ 703103)* is just along the road and gives an almost identical deal, except rooms are Rs 50 cheaper and it only has singles at the lowest price. Divyadeep has a good vegetarian restaurant below it and Satyadeep has a sweet shop. Check out for both hotels is 24 hours.

Chandigarh Yatri Niwas *(☎ 706038, Sector 24B)* is a bit far out but has clean rooms with TV and phone for Rs 500/750 with air-cooler/air-con. It also has dorms for eight people for Rs 800. There is a cheap restaurant here and free bicycle hire.

Places to Stay – Mid-Range

Hotel Jullundur *(☎ 706777, ⓔ info@jullundurhotel.com, Sector 22)* is opposite the bus station. Standard rooms with TV and air-con start at Rs 300/550; the single is really small. It has a licensed restaurant.

About 500m north-west of the bus station there are a few hotels with ground floor restaurants and bars side by side on Udyog Path in Sector 22.

Hotel Amar *(☎ 704638)* charges Rs 300/400 for small and plain rooms with TV and bath; air-con rooms start at Rs 600.

Hotel Alankar *(☎ 708802)* has air-cooled rooms with TV for Rs 500/600 and air-con rooms cost Rs 800.

Hotel Kwality Regency *(☎ 720205, fax 720206)* is nearly top-end quality with 12 stylish, air-con 'designer rooms' from Rs 1295/1425. It also has business facilities.

Aroma Hotel *(☎ 700045, fax 700051, ⓔ hotelaroma@glide.net.in, Sector 22)* on Himalaya Marg is similarly swish but on a slightly larger scale. Rooms start at Rs 1145/1395. It has business facilities, a courtyard restaurant with waterfall feature, bar and 24-hour coffee shop and bakery.

Places to Stay – Top End

Hotel Sunbeam *(☎ 708101, fax 708900, Udyog Path, Sector 22)* is opposite the bus station. Pleasant air-con rooms with fridge start at Rs 1095/1495. It has a restaurant, 24-hour coffee shop and bar with live music.

Hotel Piccadilly *(☎ 707571, fax 705692, Sector 22)* is popular with businesspeople. It charges Rs 1838/2165 and has a restaurant and bar.

Hotel Mountview *(☎ 740544, fax 742220, ⓔ citci10@ch1.dot.net.in, Sector 10)* is set in peaceful gardens. It has air-con rooms with balcony for Rs 1950/2450, a restaurant and 24-hour coffee shop, swimming pool, health club and bar with live music. It also has free bicycle hire.

Places to Eat

Chandigarh has many modern places to eat offering a variety of Western-style fast food, Chinese and Indian regional dishes, usually found within the same venue.

City Heart *(Udyog Path)*, near the bus station, serves cheap Indian veg food. Nearby, ***City Heart 2*** is more expensive, nonveg, and serves beer.

Singh's Chicken *(Sector 22, Himalaya Marg)* has a good range of chicken dishes for about Rs 25 to 50. Its sign makes the erroneous claim that it's the 'Winner of Lonely Planet Book of UK World Tourism Guide'.

Along the road, ***Nagpal Pure Vegetarian Dhaba*** is popular for Indian veg food dishes for less than Rs 40.

There are lots of places to eat in the Sector 17 shopping district. ***Hot Millions 2*** *(SCO 74–75, Sector 17)* serves fast food (pizzas, Tex-Mex and Indian) on three different and loud levels and is very popular with families.

Around the corner, ***Indian Coffee House*** is much more subdued serving cheap Indian fare until 9.30 pm.

Mehfil *(SCO 185, Sector 17)* and, across the road, ***Ghazal*** *(SCO 189–91)* are Chandigarh's top restaurants. Their menus are the standard mix of continental, Chinese and Indian, with main courses around Rs 100 (half portions are available). Mehfil has live music nightly, except Monday, and both have bars.

The open-air restaurant attached to the ***rock garden*** is a good place to stop before or after visiting the main attraction; it serves meals, snacks and beer.

A couple of the hotels have 24-hour coffee shops which, should you have the midnight munchies, also serve food. ***The Eating House*** at Hotel Aroma is one with particularly good cakes and ice cream.

Food stalls are set up along Udyog Path each evening where, along with Himalaya Marg, there are cheap alcohol shops.

Entertainment

Down Under, in the basement of Hot Millions 2, is an Aussie-themed pub with pool table, very loud music and food.

Arizzona is a dance venue that is open from 1 to 6 pm on Saturday and Thursday. Popular with a younger crowd, it's dark and loud.

KC Cinema, near Haryana Tourism, shows the latest USA and Bollywood movie releases.

Shopping

Woollen sweaters and shawls from Punjab are good buys, especially in the government emporiums. Most of these are in Sector 17, which probably has the most extensive range of shops in India.

Buses from Chandigarh

destination	fare (Rs) ordinary/deluxe	approx duration (hrs)	platform No	departures
Anandpur Sahib	50/–	2½	29 ◆	hourly
Amritsar	196/–	6	29 & 34	hourly
Delhi	108/215	5½	12 & 13/11	½ hourly/every 5 mins
Dharamsala	140/–	10	9	1.30 pm
Haridwar/Rishikesh	95/–	6	16	½ hourly
Manali	155/–	10	–	5.50, 6.40 & 7.30 pm
Pinjore	15/–	1	7 *	every 10 mins
Sirhind	29/–	2	26	two hourly

* from local bus stand
◆ between 10 am and 4 pm buses depart from the bus station in Sector 43

Getting There & Away

Air Indian Airlines (☎ 704539), SCO 170, Sector 17, is open 10 am to 5 pm Monday to Saturday. It has flights on Wednesday and Saturday to both Delhi (US$65) and Amritsar (US$55) and one flight on Wednesday to Leh (US$70).

Bus Chandigarh's noisy bus station is in Sector 17, alongside the local bus terminal. There is a post office, luggage store, phone offices and prepaid rickshaw booth. Buses depart between 7 am and midnight.

Train The train station is most inconveniently located 8km south-east of the centre; however, reservations can be made at the office (☎ 708573) upstairs in the bus station, open 8 am to 8 pm (2 pm Sunday). Local bus No 37 runs between the bus and train stations to coincide with train arrivals/departures.

It is 245km from Delhi to Chandigarh, which the twice-daily *Shatabdi Express* covers in three hours. The fare is Rs 400/790 in an air-con chair car/executive class. There is also a slower overnight train (Rs 97/489 in normal/air-con sleeper, six hours).

There are daily trains to Kalka (Rs 5, one hour), just 24km up the line, from where four daily trains rattle up the narrow-gauge mountain railway to Shimla (Rs 31, five hours).

Getting Around

To/From the Airport The airport is 11km south of Sector 17. Fares are Rs 250 by taxi or Rs 57 by autorickshaw.

Local Transport Chandigarh is far too spread out to walk around. The extensive bus network is the cheapest option. Bus No 13 runs by the Aroma Hotel as far as the government buildings in Sector 1, and bus No 37 connects the train and bus stations.

If you're planning a longer trip across the city consider taking a blue autorickshaw. There is a prepaid autorickshaw stand behind the bus station. Rickshaw-wallahs may offer lower rates when business is slack. From the bus station it should cost Rs 34 to the train station or Rs 20 to the Rock Garden.

Bicycle is the best form of transport and a couple of the hotels have free bike hire. Alternatively the tourist office can help out with rentals.

There are 24-hour taxi stands near the larger hotels; return fares are Rs 250 for local runs lasting up to two hours, Rs 400 for Pinjore and Rs 800 for Anandpur Sahib.

AROUND CHANDIGARH

Pinjore

The **Yadavindra Gardens** at Pinjore were designed by Fidai Khan, Mughal ruler Aurangzeb's foster brother, who also designed the Badshahi Mosque in Lahore, Pakistan. Situated 20km from Chandigarh, near Kalka, the terraced gardens feature the Rajasthani Mughal-style Shish Mahal, the Rang Mahal, the cubical Jal Mahal and a series of fountains and waterfalls. The gardens (Rs 5), open 7 am to 10 pm daily, are illuminated at night. There is also a small zoo, with an otter house and animals, near the gardens.

The restaurant and accommodation within the gardens make a lovely venue, rooms cost

Rs 400/600 for nonair-con/air-con. There are many more hotels and restaurants in town.

Buses from Chandigarh (Rs 15, one hour) stop at the entrance to the gardens every 10 minutes or so (see the 'Buses from Chandigarh' table).

Punjab

There are many sights of interest along the main routes from Delhi to Amritsar which until now have been largely overlooked by most travellers. Punjab Tourism has recently started promoting them and it's possible to overnight at any of the following as they either have ***Tourist Complexes*** or gurdwaras.

Sirhind, 72km south-east of Ludhiana, was once a very important town and the capital of the Pathan Sur dynasty. Today it is an important site of pilgrimage for both Sikhs and Sunni Muslims. The main gurdwara commemorates the martyrdom in 1708 of the two young sons of the tenth Sikh guru, who were completely sealed within a brick chamber as punishment for not converting to Islam. The two-day fair, Shaheedi Jor Mela, takes place here in December.

About 500m beyond the gurdwara is a small mausoleum, Rauza Sharif, venerated as a second Mecca by Sunni Muslims who flock here to pay homage every August for the Urs festival.

Just off Surhind's GT Road is Aam Khas Bagh, a large Mughal serai constructed for the use of both royalty and the riff-raff. Started by Babar it was completed by Emperor Shah Jahan and today the gardens and tank continue to make a good stopover. At one end of the garden is the Shish Mahal and tank within a walled enclosure, and at the other is a *hammam* (Turkish bath) and Jahan's private quarters. It's possible to stay next to the monument at ***Red Rose Tourist Complex*** for Rs 500 per room. It also has a restaurant.

About 35km south of Sirhind is **Patiala**, which was once the capital of an independent Sikh state. There is a fort with a museum of chandeliers and weapons, and the Motibagh Palace which has been declared a national monument on account of its well-preserved frescoes – more than 75% of the originals remain. The National Institute of Sports is also based here. Patiala is the site of the Basant festival in February.

The textile centre of India, **Ludhiana** was the site of a great battle in the First Sikh War in 1845–46. The world's largest bicycle manufacturer, Hero Bicycles, which produces nearly three million bikes annually, is based here. There's little to see in Ludhiana, though the archaic, bureaucratic muddle of the offices of the old law courts (the Purana Karcharia) is worth a look.

Once the capital of an ancient Hindu kingdom, **Jalandhar** survived a sacking by Mahmud of Ghazni nearly 1000 years ago and later became an important Mughal city. Nowadays it is both a major crossroads and an important commercial centre famous for the production of sporting goods and handtools. Jalandhar is the site of three main festivals all held in December – Sangeet Sammelan, Harballah Sangeet Sammelan and Baba Sodai.

An alternative railway route to Amritsar runs 70km north-west of Delhi to **Rohtak**, which was once a border town between the Sikhs' and Marathas' regions, and was the subject of frequent clashes. **Hansi**, north-west of Rohtak, was where Colonel Skinner died. (Skinner's Horse, the private cavalry regiment he founded in the 1790s, was responsible for the conquest of large areas of northern India for the East India Company.) **Sirsa**, 90km farther north-west, is an ancient city but little remains apart from the city walls.

The railway line continues to **Bathinda**, which was an important town of the Pathan Sur dynasty. **Faridkot**, 350km north-west of Delhi and close to the Pakistan border, was once the capital of a Sikh state of the same name and has a 700-year-old fort. It is the site of the Sheikh Farid Agam Purb festival in September.

Firozpur is almost on the border, 382km north-west of Delhi, but is not really worth a visit; before Partition the railway line continued to Lahore, now in Pakistan.

AMRITSAR

☎ 0183 • pop 1 million

Founded in 1577 by Ram Das, the fourth guru of the Sikhs, Amritsar is both the centre of the Sikh religion and the major city of Punjab state. The name means Pool of Nectar, referring to the sacred tank around which the Sikhs' Golden Temple is built. Although Amritsar is just another dusty Indian city, the

Golden Temple is an exceptionally beautiful and peaceful place.

The original site for the city was granted by the Mughal emperor, Akbar, but in 1761 Ahmad Shah Durani sacked the town and destroyed the temple. The temple was rebuilt in 1764, and in 1802 was roofed over with copper-gilded plates by Ranjit Singh and became known as the Golden Temple. During the turmoil of the partition of India in 1948, Amritsar was a flash point for the terrible events that shook Punjab.

During unrest in Punjab in the early 1980s the Golden Temple was occupied by Sikh extremists who were intent on expelling non-Sikhs from the state and creating a Sikh homeland. They were finally evicted, under the orders of Indira Gandhi, by the Indian army in 1984 in a military action that resulted in hundreds of Sikh deaths. Later that year Indira Gandhi was assassinated by her Sikh bodyguards. The temple was again occupied by extremists in 1986. The damage wrought on the Golden Temple by the tanks of the Indian army has now been repaired, and following a few years of unrest things are quiet.

Sikhs are justifiably proud of their capital city and Golden Temple and they are known for their friendliness and helpfulness.

Orientation

The old city is south-east of the main train station, surrounded by a circular road that once contained massive city walls. There are 18 gates still in existence but only the north gate, facing the Ram Bagh gardens, is original. The Golden Temple and the narrow alleys of the bazaar area are in the old city.

The more modern part of Amritsar is north of the train station, where you will find most of the hotels. The bus station is 2km east of the train station on GT Rd.

Information

Tourist Offices In the former youth hostel, 1km east of the bus station, the tourist office (☎ 231452) is fairly helpful. It's open 9 am to 5 pm Monday to Saturday. The information office at the Golden Temple is open 8 am to 1 pm and 2.30 to 8 pm daily; and staff who offer free guided tours are very helpful.

Money There are numerous moneychangers on Link Rd, opposite the train station and near the Golden Temple; rates are marginally worse than at banks. There is a Bank of Punjab at the Golden Temple that changes US dollars only and has an ATM which accepts MasterCard. State Bank of India in the old city changes US dollars and pounds sterling.

Post & Communications A post office at the Golden Temple sells stamps (open 9 am to 6.30 pm Monday to Saturday). The main post office is on Court Rd, north-west of the train station (open 9 am to 5 pm Monday to Saturday).

There are quite a few Internet places around town charging Rs 30 per hour. Cybercity at Nehru Shopping Centre is open 24 hours, @Internet near the train station is open from 8.30 am to 10 pm as is Cyberhut near the Golden Temple.

Golden Temple Complex

The holiest shrine of the Sikh religion is in the centre of the old part of Amritsar. The temple itself, known as the Hari Mandir (or Darbar Sahib), is surrounded by the pool Amrit Sarovar, which gave the town its name, and is reached by a causeway. Open to all, it's a beautiful place, especially early in the morning; weekends can get crowded.

Pilgrims and visitors must remove their shoes, wash their feet and cover their heads before entering the precincts. No smoking is allowed; photography is only permitted from the Parkarma, the marble walkway that surrounds the sacred pool. An English-speaking guide is available at the information office near the clock tower that marks the temple's main entrance; the office also has a number of interesting free publications.

The two-storey marble temple, which stands in the middle of the sacred pool, is reached by a causeway known as the Gurus' Bridge. The lower parts of the marble walls are decorated with inlaid flower and animal motifs in the *pietra dura* (marble inlay) style of the Taj Mahal. Once inside the temple, pilgrims offer sweet doughy *prasad* (food offering) to the attendants, who take half to distribute to everyone as they leave.

The temple's architecture is a blend of Hindu and Muslim styles. The golden dome (said to be gilded with 100kg of pure gold) is supposed to represent an inverted lotus flower. It is inverted, turning back to the earth, to symbolise the Sikhs' concern with the problems of this world.

Guru Granth Sahib Four priests at key positions around the temple keep up a continuous reading in Punjabi from the Sikhs' holy book. The reading is broadcast by loudspeaker. The original copy of the Guru Granth Sahib is kept under a pink shroud in the Hari Mandir during the day; at around 10 pm each day it is ceremoniously returned to the Akal Takht (Sikh Parliament) building. The morning processional ceremony takes place at 4 am in summer and 5 am in winter.

Sikh Museum Upstairs in the clock tower this museum comprises a gallery of often gruesome paintings telling the story of the Sikhs and their martyrs. It's open 7 am to 7 pm daily.

Akal Takht The Shiromani Gurdwara Parbandhak Committee, or Sikh Parliament, traditionally meets in this building, which is why it was a target for the Indian army in 1984. It has since been completely rebuilt.

Guru-ka-Langar & Gurdwaras All Sikh temples have a community kitchen, and in this one volunteers prepare free meals for around 30,000 people every day – you can see them busy just outside the main hall. The food is very basic – chapatis and lentils – and is prepared and dished out daily in an orderly fashion. Grab a plate, sit on the rush matting and wait for the prayers to be completed before tucking in. Nearby are the gurdwaras, offering free accommodation to all. Pilgrims are well provided for and there's a good library, a post office, bank and railway booking agency.

Other Buildings To the south-east of the temple enclosure is the nine-storey (30m) **Baba Atal Tower**, built in 1784. The tall **Ramgarhia Minars**, scarred by tank fire, stand outside the temple enclosure.

The Old City

A 15-minute walk from the Golden Temple through the narrow alleys of the old city brings you to the Hindu **Durgiana Temple**. This temple, dedicated to the goddess Durga, dates back to the 16th century. A larger temple, built like the Golden Temple in the centre of a tank, is dedicated to the Hindu deities, Lakshmi and Narayan (Vishnu).

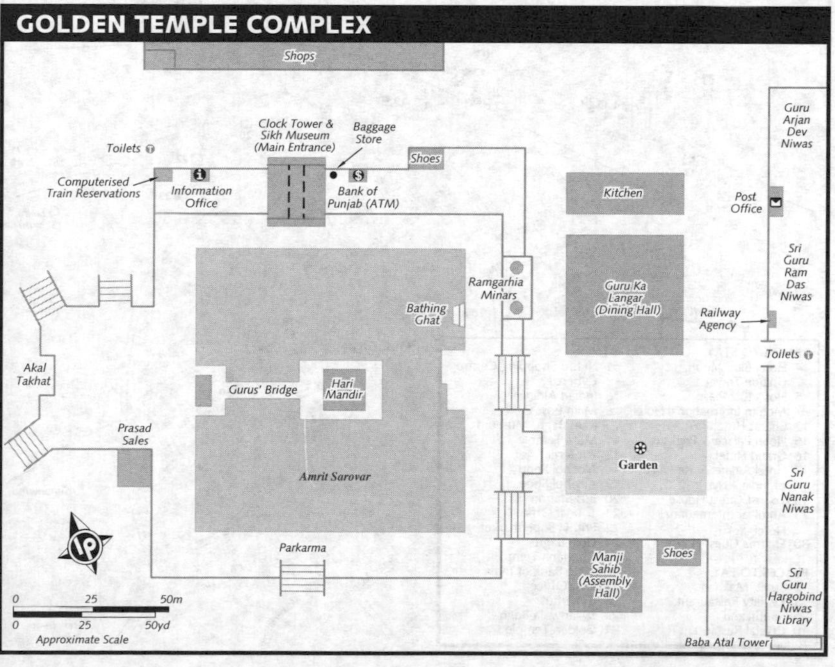

There are a number of mosques in the old city, including the mosque of **Mohammed Jan**, with three white domes and slender minarets.

Mata Temple

North-west of the train station, this Hindu temple commemorates a bespectacled 20th-century female saint, Lal Devi, and is a scaled down version of the Vaishno Devi cave temple found near Jammu. Women who wish to become pregnant come here to pray. It's notable for a striking Disney-esque series of grottoes and shrines featuring Hindu deities (take the stairs on the left) and a circumnavigation involves crawling through a tunnel and wading through a stream.

Jallianwala Bagh

This tree- and flower-filled park commemorates the 2000 Indians who were killed or wounded here, shot indiscriminately by the British in 1919. This appalling massacre was one of the major events in India's struggle for Independence movingly re-created in the film *Gandhi*.

The park is a five-minute walk from the Golden Temple Complex and is open 6 am to 7 pm in summer and 7 am to 6 pm in winter. A section of wall with visible bullet marks is preserved, as is the well that some people jumped into in an attempt to escape; 120 bodies were recovered from the well. Portraits and potted histories of some appear in the **Martyrs' Gallery**, open 9 am to 5 pm in summer and 10 am to 4 pm in winter.

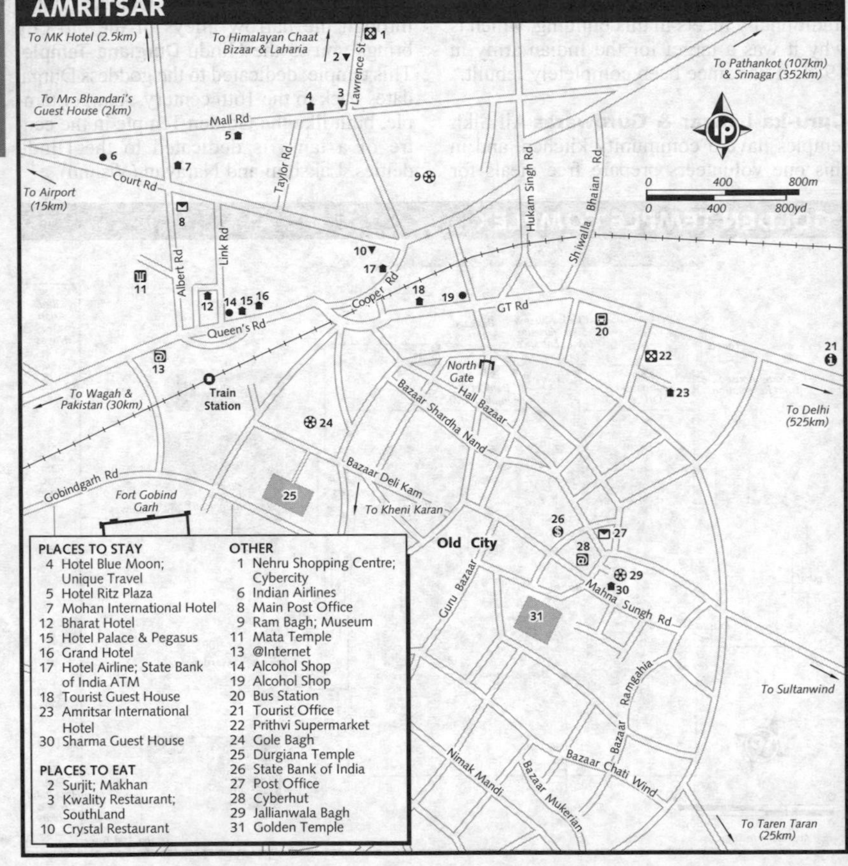

RICHARD I'ANSON

PATRICK HORTON

GARRY WEARE

Cultural contrasts and dramatic scenery summarise India's north-west: a mother and child from the mainly Muslim Kashmir **(top left)**; Buddhist prayer flags fly over the 15th-century Spituk Gompa, near Leh **(top right)**; and Hindu settlements dominate the Garhwal foothills in Uttaranchal **(bottom)**

PATRICK HORTON

PATRICK HORTON

RICHARD I'ANSON

SARA-JANE CLELAND

India's north-west is a remote and beautiful mountainous region where you'll find hairpin bends ascending to Lamayuru from Leh **(top left)**, bathing buffalos **(top right)**, traditional peoples **(middle right)** and the official residence of the Dalai Lama in McLeod Ganj **(bottom)**.

Carnage at Jallianwala Bagh

Unrest in Amritsar was sparked by the *Rowlatt Act* (1919), which gave the British authorities emergency powers to imprison without trial Indians suspected of sedition. Hartals (one-day strikes) were organised in protest. The Lieutenant Governor of Punjab, Sir Michael O'Dwyer ('a reactionary with contempt for educated Indians', according to text in the Martyrs' Gallery) adopted a hard line, and an Indian leader was arrested. Further Indian protests escalated into rioting and looting after the British fired upon the protesters.

General Dyer was called upon to return order to the city. He and 150 troops arrived at a peaceful demonstration on 13 April 1919 in Jallianwala Bagh, attended by 20,000 Indians. Dyer ordered the crowd to disperse – tricky seeing that the meeting space was surrounded by high walls, and he and his men were ranged in front of the main entrance. Without further warning the British opened fire. Some six minutes later the toll of Indian deaths numbered 337 men, 41 boys and one baby. A further 1500 men and boys lay wounded. Some were shot as they tried to escape over the wall.

Although there was an international outcry over this massacre, O'Dwyer and Dyer were not considered culpable by the British; on the contrary, some thought them heroes. Meantime, in response, Gandhi instigated his program of civil disobedience and announced that 'co-operation in any shape or form with this satanic government is sinful'.

Dyer died in 1927 from a fall. O'Dwyer met his end in London in 1940, assassinated by a Sikh volunteer who had been serving water at the 1919 meeting.

Ram Bagh
This park in the new part of town has a **museum** in the small palace built by the Sikh maharaja Ranjit Singh. The museum contains weapons dating back to Mughal times and some portraits of the ruling houses of Punjab (entry Rs 5). It's open 10 am to 4.45 pm Tuesday to Sunday.

Taren Taran
This is an important Sikh tank about 25km south of Amritsar. There's a temple, which predates Amritsar, and a tower on the eastern side of the tank, which was constructed by Ranjit Singh. It's said that any leper who can swim across the tank will be miraculously cured. Buses run every five minutes from Amritsar bus station (Rs 9, one hour).

Places to Stay – Budget
Tourist Guest House *(☎ 553830, 1355 Grand Trunk Rd)* has some clean and lovely old rooms with lots of character. With private bathroom (geyser hot water) they cost Rs 150 and Rs 200, without bathroom Rs 100. There is a nice small lawn and a good terrace, the only drawback comes from the smell of animal hides from the nearby market. It also has evening Internet access and reception is manned 24 hours.

Bharat Hotel *(☎ 227536)* near the train station, off Link Rd, is a friendly place with reasonable, clean rooms with TV, phone and private bathroom (geyser hot water) for Rs 150 to 250.

Hotel Palace & Pegasus *(☎ 565111, Queen's Rd)* is more basic but closer to the station. Single/double rooms with private bathroom (squat toilets and bucket hot water) cost from Rs 150/250.

There are a few cheapies around the Golden Temple, ***Sharma Guest House*** *(☎ 551657)* is very friendly and has a restaurant. Rooms with shared bathroom are Rs 150/200 and Rs 250 with private bathroom.

Many enjoy the camaraderie at the pilgrim accommodation at the ***Golden Temple***. It's open 24 hours, although checkout is noon. If you want to stay more than one night you will need to get special permission. A Rs 50 refundable deposit is required and a donation is expected.

Places to Stay – Mid-Range
Mrs Bhandari's Guest House *(☎ 228509, fax 222390, e payal@mol.net.in, 10 Cantonment)* is set in a large peaceful garden with a swimming pool. Clean rooms with fireplaces vary in size and cost from Rs 750/950 for a single/double; camping in the garden costs Rs 150 per person. Meals are available to residents (Rs 250) who are also welcome to have a nose around Mrs Bhandari's house which has a fantastic Art Deco interior.

Grand Hotel *(☎ 562424, fax 229677, e grand@jla.vsnl.net.in)*, opposite the train station, is a good choice with rooms around a grassy, flowered (no plucking) garden. With

PUNJAB & HARYANA

TV, phone and private bathroom (geyser hot water) they cost Rs 395/500, or Rs 675/775 with air-con; it takes credit cards. There's also a good bar and restaurant here and a pool table (Rs 100 per hour) on the patio.

Hotel Airline *(☎ 564848)* has rooms with interesting features such as cushioned swings and bathtubs and a central courtyard patio. Rooms also have TV and phone and cost Rs 350/450 or Rs 600/750 with air-con. At the time of research a new restaurant was being built.

Run by Punjab Tourism, ***Amritsar International Hotel*** *(☎ 555991, fax 556234)*, near the bus station, is a typical high-rise government hotel with a small lawn area, restaurant and parking. Rooms with private bathroom start at Rs 475/550 and the staff are uncharacteristically helpful.

Hotel Blue Moon *(☎ 220416, ⓔ bluemoon@jla.vsnl.net.in)* on The Mall is a reasonable place surrounded by lawns. Rooms with TV, phone and private bathroom cost Rs 695 to 745. The more-expensive rooms (Rs 990/1080) are modern and brighter.

Places to Stay – Top End

Mohan International Hotel *(☎ 227801, fax 226520, Albert Rd)* is the most central top-end hotel with swimming pool and the Unique Travel agency. Rooms cost from Rs 1500/2500.

Amritsar's newest hotel, ***MK Hotel*** *(☎ 504610, fax 507910, ⓔ mkhotel@mol.net.in, Ranjit Ave)* is a sparkling place quite a way out of town. It has a 1st-floor terrace courtyard pool and restaurant with ghazal music. Rooms start at Rs 1600/2500.

Hotel Ritz Plaza *(☎ 562836, 226657, ⓔ litz@del3.vsnl.net.in, 45 The Mall)* is another posh place with good service. It too has a pool, a sophisticated lounge bar and a restaurant. Rooms with balconies start at Rs 1650/2200 and meals cost Rs 275.

Places to Eat

Lawrence St is the place to head for excellent, cheap food with lots of interesting *dhabas* (snack bars). These include ***Surjit***, the most famous tandoori chicken shop in Punjab, and ***Makhan***, an open-air tandoori fish place which always sells out within a couple of hours but refuses to cook more food. Other good spots along this street include ***Himalyan Chaat Bizaar*** and ***Lahoria*** sweet shop.

The popular and licensed ***Crystal Restaurant*** *(☎ 225555)* serves a tasty range of Indian, Chinese and continental cuisine in swish air-con surrounds for around Rs 60 to 120 per dish. Another of Amritsar's better restaurants is ***Napoli*** at Hotel Blue Moon which is also licensed.

Amritsar is renowned for lassis and you can buy them all over the old town. There are ***alcohol shops*** around the train station. ***Prithvi supermarket*** near the bus stand is the place to stock up on food and toiletries.

Shopping

Woollen blankets, shawls and sweaters are supposed to be cheaper in Amritsar than in other places in India, as they are locally manufactured – look around Guru Bazaar near the Golden Temple. Tea and silver are other good buys and Katra Jaimal Singh, near the telephone exchange in the old city, has good shopping.

Getting There & Away

Air Air India (☎ 546122) operates international flights to and from Amritsar airport mainly to the Middle East.

The Indian Airlines office (☎ 503780) is at 39A Court Rd. Amritsar is linked to Delhi (US$90, one hour) five times a week, Chandigarh (US$55) twice weekly and Lucknow (Rs 4565, 1½ hours) twice weekly.

Bus Local buses leave frequently for Delhi (Rs 160, 10 hours), Chandigarh (Rs 90, five hours, counter 15), Jammu (Rs 70, five hours, counter 15), Taren Taran (Rs 9, one hour, counters 1 and 4) and Wagah (Rs 13, one hour, counters 2 and 3). There is a bus to Dehra Dun at 7 am (Rs 167, 10 hours, counters 13 and 14), Dalhousie at 9.20 am (Rs 90, 10 hours, counter 8) and Dharamsala at 11 am (Rs 93, 10 hours, counters 13 and 14); it's easier to get a train as far as Pathankot then change to a bus there. For bus inquiries call ☎ 551734.

Private buses leave from in front of the train station and tickets are available at agencies there.

Train In addition to reservations at the train station there is a train reservation service at the Golden Temple which is open from 8 am to 2 pm and 2.15 to 8 pm Monday to Saturday and 8 am to 2 pm Sunday.

There are direct rail links to Delhi (Rs 99/520 in 2nd/1st class, eight to 10 hours, 447km) but the daily *Shatabdi Express* does the journey in only 5½ hours (Rs 610/1220 in chair car/executive class). The *Amritsar-Howrah Mail* links Amritsar with Lucknow (Rs 158/830, 17 hours, 850km), Varanasi (Rs 201/1056, 23 hours, 1251km) and Kolkata (Calcutta; Rs 245/1336, 38 hours, 1829km).

The rail crossing point to Pakistan is at Attari, 26km from Amritsar, and the *4607 Indo-Pak Express* leaves Amritsar at 7 am, reaching Lahore in Pakistan at 4.15 pm. However, it only goes on Monday and Thursday (returning Tuesday and Friday) and spends hours at the border.

The road crossing at Wagah, about 4km beyond Attari, is quicker. The border is open from 9 am to 3.30 pm (winter) or 4 pm (summer) daily, and most people walk across as vehicles are delayed. There are hourly buses until about 3 pm from Amritsar to Attari (Rs 13, one hour), but not all continue on to Wagah. It's easy to get a rickshaw between Attari and Wagah. Taxis from Amritsar cost Rs 300 to 400, or look for minibuses by the train station (Rs 60).

Neem Chameli Tourist Complex *(☎ 231452)*, operated by Punjab Tourism at Wagah, has dorm beds and cheap doubles, and there are cafes where you can eat or change money.

See the Getting There & Away chapter for further details on this border crossing.

Border Displays

Relations between India and Pakistan are rarely tranquil – each country seems determined to outdo the other at every opportunity, whether on the cricket pitch or, more worryingly, in the field of nuclear armaments. A harmless but entertaining manifestation of this long-standing rivalry can be witnessed daily at the Wagah border, the only road crossing between the two countries.

About 30 minutes before sunrise and sunset, the guards on each side of the border assemble to parade and preen themselves in an immaculately turned out display of synchronised marching and bellowed military commands. The flag of each country is then carefully raised or lowered and the gates are opened or slammed shut.

Crowds congregate on both sides of the border, but the Indians seem to have the upper hand with a concrete stand which has been specially built for this event, and guards with whistles ensure everyone gets a good view. The total number of spectators is amazing, around 5000 each evening, all of whom are there to cheer on the efforts of their own guards and deride those of the opposition. At the end of the ceremony the crowds are encouraged to surge forward to the gates for some serious fist-shaking – don't get caught waving or being friendly to the opposition or you'll be severely whistled at by an irate border guard.

Getting Around

The airport is 15km from the city centre, a Rs 100/400 autorickshaw/taxi ride away.

Cycle and autorickshaws run all over town; from the train station to the Golden Temple they should cost Rs 15 and Rs 30 respectively.

PATHANKOT

☎ 0186 • pop 150,000

Pathankot (pronounced Pattan-cot), in the extreme north of Punjab is an important railhead for those travelling to Dharamsala and Dalhousie. (There is a helpful Himachal Pradesh tourist office, open from 10 am to 5 pm Monday to Saturday, opposite the main train station entrance.) Regular buses mean you won't have to stay in this uninspiring town too long; should you find yourself here for a while you can spend time chatting to the locals at a dhaba, wandering the bazaar or exploring the nearby Beas River.

Bank of India and the main post office are along the left fork in Gurdaspur Rd – the main road in from Delhi. There's also an Internet cafe here.

Places to Stay

Most hotels are along Gurdaspur Rd which makes front facing rooms noisy, and unless stated otherwise all have noon checkout, sit-down flush toilets and geyser hot water. Closest to the train station is ***Green Hotel*** with rooms off a side balcony with TV, phone and bathroom for Rs 250. There's a 1st-floor restaurant and ground floor bar.

Near the fork in Gurdaspur Rd, ***Hotel Tourist*** is the best of the cheapies with rooms around an open courtyard. Single/double rooms on the terrace with squat toilets are bright and Rs 90/100, those on the first two floors with private bathroom (squat toilets) are Rs 220/225. There are plenty of rooms, all of which have TV and phone, and there's even a 'sex, VD and skin' doctor on the 1st floor should you need him.

North-east of the post office, ***Hotel Airlines*** *(☎ 20505)* is a bit quieter than those on Gurdaspur Rd and has a licensed restaurant. Rooms around a covered courtyard cost Rs 150 with squat toilet, Rs 250 with private bathroom and balcony.

About 100m beyond the bus station towards Delhi, ***Hotel Parag*** *(☎ 25672)* has large rooms with TV, phone and private bathroom for Rs 250 to 350 if air-cooled, and Rs 500 if air-con, plus 10% service charge.

Places to Eat

There are heaps of ***dhabas*** along Gurdaspur Rd and the hotels all have their own reasonable restaurants, the best of which is ***Vitaka*** at Hotel Parag.

Kalotra Coffee House, east of the post office, has good coffee and mango shakes but unmarried couples are only allowed a maximum of 20 minutes to enjoy them.

Getting There & Away

Gurdaspur Rd is where you'll find the bus station and, about 400m farther towards town, Pathankot train station – if arriving at Chowkibank train station you can cover the 3km between the two by cycle-rickshaw for Rs 25.

Several daily trains leave for Delhi (Rs 105/552 in 2nd/1st class). There are also trains to Amritsar (Rs 20/173, 2½ hours) and Jammu (Rs 32/173, three hours). The station has a computer reservation office open daily.

Buses to Dalhousie (Rs 45, three hours), Chamba (Rs 70, five hours), Dharamsala (Rs 60, four hours) and McLeod Ganj (Rs 90, 4½ hours) leave every hour or so between 5 am and 5 pm. Buses to Manali leave between 4.30 and 8 am and 5 and 8 pm (Rs 225, 13 hours) and every five minutes or so to Chandigarh (Rs 48, three hours).

You can do the same journeys by taxi slightly quicker for much more cash – around Rs 800 to Dalhousie or Dharamsala. The 24-hour taxi stand is next to the Himachal Pradesh tourist office.

ANANDPUR SAHIB

☎ 01881

One of the Sikh's holiest sites with a number of historical gurdwaras, this expanding town has been a pilgrimage site for over 300 years. Backed by the Naina Devi Hills it's the birthplace of the Khalsa (Sikh brotherhood), the tricentenary was celebrated in 1999. To cater to the influx of pilgrims and to assist the tourist authorities in their drive to attract visitors, new infrastructure was put in place. There's a tourist information office as you enter town and facilities such as foreign exchange, restaurants and top-end accommodation should soon be in place. The bus and train stations are about 200m apart on the main road through town.

Gurdwara Kesgarh Sahib is the largest gurdwara and this is where the Khalsa was born. Inside the shrine devotees sing devotional songs and weapons are displayed. There is an information office, accommodation and a kitchen. In March every year the birth of the movement is commemorated with the festival of Holla Mohalla. Hordes of pilgrims gather on the ground below the gurdwara to watch armies of colourful Sikh warriors re-enact the bloody scenes from the religion's history.

Back on the hill and facing Kesgarh Sahib is **Gurdwara Anandgarh Sahib**. Distinguishable by its small fort, below which a series of steps lead to a well, it is the scene for a nightly sound-and-light show.

At the time of research accommodation in Anandpur Sahib was limited to the gurdwaras and a government tourist complex. There are snack stands, and of course you can always get a meal at the gurdwaras.

Anandpur Sahib, 75km north-west of Chandigarh in Haryana, can be reached by bus or train. Buses leave for Sector 43 in Chandigarh (Rs 29, 2½ hours) hourly but it's probably easier to get a more regular bus to Ropar and change for Chandigarh (or elsewhere) there.

Trains to Ambala (Rs 25) leave four times daily. A return taxi for a day trip from Chandigarh should cost around Rs 800.

Himachal Pradesh

Himachal Pradesh at a Glance

Population: 6.1 million
Area: 55,673 sq km
Capital: Shimla
Main Languages: Hindi & Pahari
When to Go: mid-May to mid-Oct (trekking); late-Dec to Mar (winter sports)

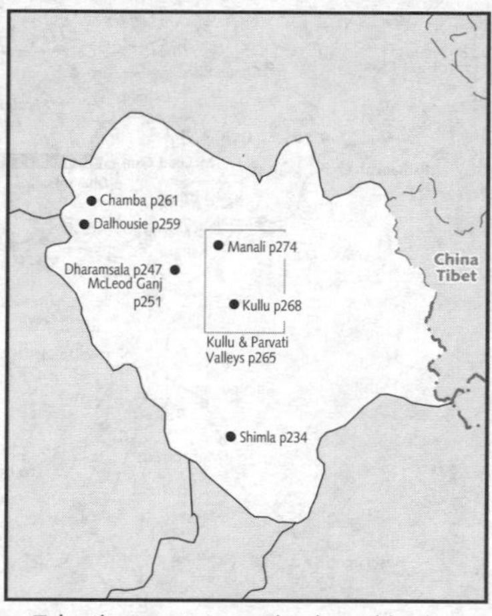

- Take the toy train to Shimla and bask in the faded grandeur of the Raj
- Study Buddhism or volunteer to help Tibetan refugees at McLeod Ganj
- Explore the wild frontier of Kinnaur in the far north
- Take in the ancient temples and mountain scenery in the Chamba Valley
- Go skiing, rafting or paragliding at Manali, Himachal's adventure playground

Himachal Pradesh – the land of eternal snow peaks – takes in the transition zone from the plains to the high Himalaya and, in the trans-Himalayan region of Lahaul and Spiti, actually crosses that mighty barrier to the Tibetan plateau.

The Kullu Valley, with its developed and tourist-oriented economy, can be considered the backbone of the state, though commercialism has eroded some of the charm that first drew travellers here back in the 1960s. Off to the east is the Parvati Valley, popular with long-stay visitors. Few make it farther north to the splendid Chamba Valley, with its rugged scenery, hill stations and beautiful temple complexes. The Kangra Valley is best known as the home of the Tibetan Government in Exile, with its headquarters, including the residence of the Dalai Lama, in Upper Dharamsala (McLeod Ganj).

For untouched mountain scenery, head for the bleak, high-altitude regions of Lahaul, Spiti and Kinnaur. Closed to foreigners until 1992, the region is situated in the rain shadow of the Himalaya and has more in common with nearby Tibet than the rest of India. Permits (easily obtained) are necessary to visit the sensitive area that links Spiti and Kinnaur.

See Lonely Planet's *Trekking in the Indian Himalaya* and *Indian Himalaya* for details on trekking in this region.

History

The regions that today comprise Himachal were, in ancient times, crossed by trade routes to Tibet (over the Shipki La) and Central Asia (via the Baralacha La and Leh) and also commanded the Sach Pass that led to Kashmir. Rajas, Ranas and Thakurs ran their rival *rahuns* and *thakurais*, making Himachal a patchwork quilt of tiny states. Only Kangra and Kullu (and later Chamba) had the power to break out of the petty feuding system.

Several Himachal states had kings from Bengal; the best known of these is Mandi, which was founded in 1527. With the exception of the bigger states, most of the later hill states were founded by Rajput adventurers from the plains in the early medieval period. During the colonial period, many Rajas cast in their lot with the British, only to lose their kingdoms and titles when India became independent.

The first Westerners to visit the region were Jesuit missionaries in search of the legendary kingdom of Prester John. The British 'discovered' Himachal after their wars with the Sikhs and the Gurkhas, and little bits of England were created at Shimla, Dalhousie

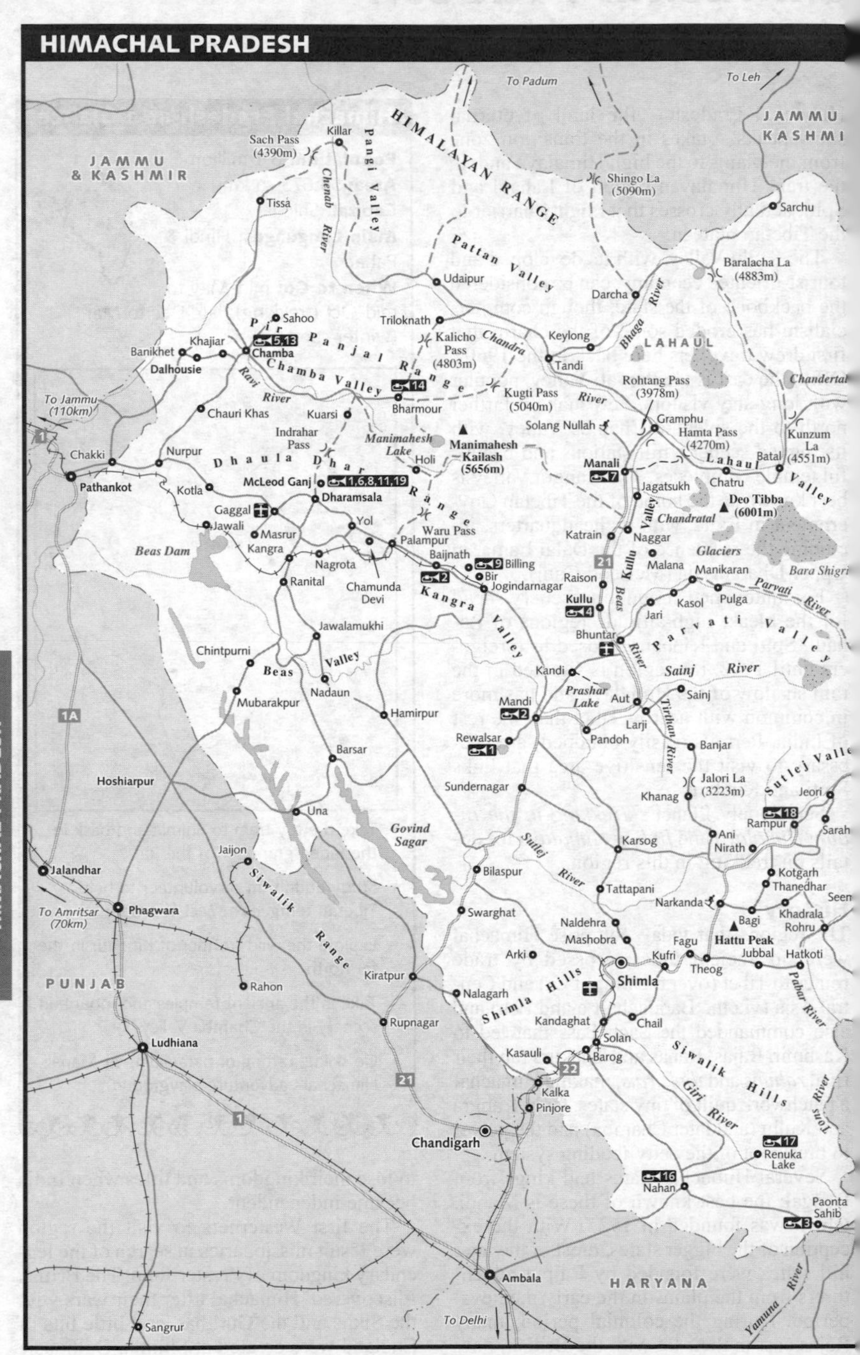
HIMACHAL PRADESH
To Padum
To Leh
JAMMU & KASHMIR
HIMALAYAN RANGE
Killar
Sach Pass (4390m)
Pangi Valley
Chenab River
Tissa
Shingo La (5090m)
Sarchu
Pattan Valley
Baralacha La (4883m)
Udaipur
Darcha
Bhaga River
LAHAUL
Sahoo
Triloknath
Kalicho Pass (4803m)
Chandra
Keylong
Tandi
Pir Panjal Range
Banikhet
Khajiar
Chamba
Dalhousie
Chamba Valley
Ravi River
Bharmour
Kugti Pass (5040m)
River
Rohtang Pass (3978m)
Chandertal
To Jammu (110km)
Chauri Khas
Kuarsi
Indrahar Pass
Manimahesh Lake
Manimahesh Kailash (5656m)
Solang Nullah
Gramphu
Hamta Pass (4270m)
Kunzum La (4551m)
Chakki
Nurpur
Holi
Dhaula Dhar Range
Manali
Lahaul Valley
Batal
Pathankot
Kotla
McLeod Ganj
Dharamsala
Jagatsukh
Chatru
Deo Tibba (6001m)
Gaggal
Jawali
Masrur
Kangra
Yol
Waru Pass
Palampur
Chandratal
Katrain
Naggar
Glaciers
Beas Dam
Nagrota
Baijnath
Billing
Bir
Kullu Valley
Malana
Manikaran
Bara Shigri
Ranital
Chamunda Devi
Jogindarnagar
Kangra Valley
Raison
Beas
Parvati River
Pulga
Kullu
Kasol
Jari
Jawalamukhi
Bhuntar
Parvati Valley
Chintpurni
Beas Valley
River
Kandi
Sainj River
Nadaun
Mubarakpur
Prashar Lake
Aut
Sainj
Mandi
Hamirpur
Larji
Tirthan River
Pandoh
Rewalsar
Banjar
Barsar
Jalori La (3223m)
Sutlej Valley
Hoshiarpur
Sundernagar
Khanag
Jeori
Rampur
Una
Sarah
Govind Sagar
Ani
Nirath
Jaijon
Sutlej River
Karsog
Jalandhar
Bilaspur
Kotgarh
Siwalik Range
Tattapani
Thanedhar
To Amritsar (70km)
Phagwara
Swarghat
Narkanda
Seen
Khadrala
Naldehra
Bagi
Rohru
Mashobra
Hattu Peak
Arki
Fagu
Kufri
Jubbal
Hatkoti
Theog
Shimla
Shimla Hills
Pabar River
PUNJAB
Rahon
Kiratpur
Nalagarh
Chail
Kandaghat
Rupnagar
Solan
Ludhiana
Kasauli
Barog
Siwalik Hills
Kalka
Pinjore
Giri River
Tons River
Chandigarh
Renuka Lake
Nahan
Paonta Sahib
Ambala
HARYANA
Yamuna River
Sangrur
To Delhi

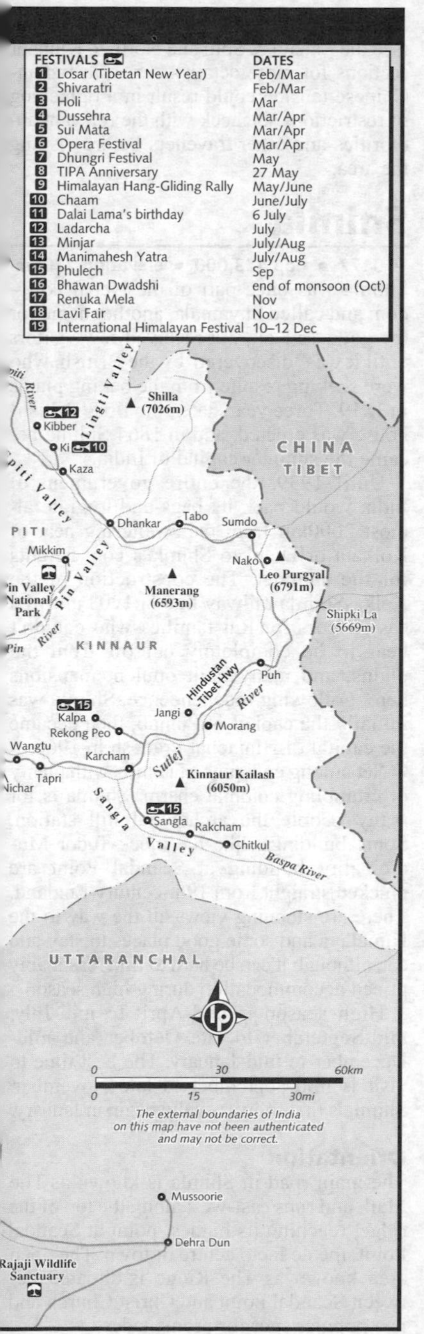

FESTIVALS	DATES
1 Losar (Tibetan New Year)	Feb/Mar
2 Shivaratri	Feb/Mar
3 Holi	Mar
4 Dussehra	Mar/Apr
5 Sui Mata	Mar/Apr
6 Opera Festival	Mar/Apr
7 Dhungri Festival	May
8 TIPA Anniversary	27 May
9 Himalayan Hang-Gliding Rally	May/June
10 Chaam	June/July
11 Dalai Lama's birthday	6 July
12 Ladarcha	July
13 Minjar	July/Aug
14 Manimahesh Yatra	July/Aug
15 Phulech	Sep
16 Bhawan Dwadshi	end of monsoon (Oct)
17 Renuka Mela	Nov
18 Lavi Fair	Nov
19 International Himalayan Festival	10–12 Dec

and Dharamsala during the late 19th century. Early in the 20th century a railway was built to Shimla and another was laid through the Kangra Valley.

The state of Himachal Pradesh was formed in 1948, liberating many villages from the feudal system. By 1966, the Pahari-speaking parts under Punjab administration – including Kangra, Kullu, Lahaul and Spiti – were added. Full statehood was achieved in 1971.

Much of Himachal's income comes from tourism, agriculture and the textile industry. The Himachal government is now hoping to add hydroelectric power to that list with the construction of huge dams across many of the state's rivers, which are believed to hold 25% of India's hydroelectric potential.

A large part of the revenue from tourism is generated by the 10% luxury tax, which all but the cheapest hotels slap onto the bill. Rates quoted for accommodation in this chapter do not include tax.

Geography

Himachal Pradesh is dominated by mountains, which rise steeply from the Punjabi plains, and their associated rivers and valleys. The tallest peaks here are Leo Purgyal (6791m), near Nako in Kinnaur; Kinnaur Kailash (6050m), which dominates the views from Rekong Peo and Kalpa in Kinnaur; and Deo Tibba (6001m), not far from Manali.

Himachal is formed of several culturally distinct regions which are isolated by mountain ridges. To this day, the only links to some parts of the state are high mountain passes, eg, Baralacha La (4950m), Kunzum La (4551m) and Rohtang La (3978m) – 'la' is a Tibetan word meaning pass – .which are frequently blocked by snow in winter.

The Chandra and Bhaga Valleys of Lahaul were formed by the Chandra River, which turns into the Chenab River, before flowing west into Kashmir. Farther east, the Spiti River joins the Sutlej River in Kinnaur and flows all the way to Punjab. The Kullu Valley is drained by the Beas River (pronounced '**bee**-ahs') and stretches from Mandi to Manali. The Parvati River flows down the valley of the same name to the east, joining the Beas near Bhuntar.

In the west of the state is the peaceful Kangra Valley and the wonderfully rugged Chamba Valley (Ravi River valley), separated by the snowcapped Dhaula Dhar Range.

The Pir Panjal Range separates the Chamba Valley from the remote Pattan Valley (upper Chenab River valley) in the far north.

Information

Tourist Offices The Himachal Pradesh Tourist Development Corporation (HPTDC) offers local information and maps, runs local tours and manages a number of mid-range hotels in the state, which provide reliable, if slightly institutional, accommodation and often dorm beds. HPTDC hotels often act as informal tourist centres in areas without a tourist office, and can book HPTDC tours and other hotels run by the group.

In season, HPTDC organises 'deluxe' buses for tourists between Shimla, Kullu and Manali, and links these places with Delhi and Chandigarh. HPTDC buses are more expensive than public buses but are quicker and far more comfortable, offering the much-desired two by two seating configuration. HPTDC also organises daily sightseeing tours out of Shimla and Manali, which can be a useful way of visiting local areas.

HPTDC offices elsewhere in India can also provide worthwhile information:

Ahemdabad (☎ 079-7544800) B/163/8 Navdeep House, Ashram Rd
Bangalore (☎ 080-2876591) Ganesh Complex, No 13 SC Rd
Chandigarh (☎ 0172-707267) Inter State Bus Terminal, Sector 17
Chennai (☎ 044-8272966) 28 Commander-in-Chief Rd
Delhi (☎ 011-3325320) Chandralok Bldg, 36 Janpath
Kolkata (Calcutta; ☎ 033-2219072) 2H, 2nd floor, Electronic Centre, 1-1A, BAC St
Mumbai (Bombay; ☎ 022-2181123) 36 World Trade Centre, Cuffe Parade

Internet Resources For good tourist info on the Himachal Pradesh area, the official Himachal Tourism Web site is at www.himachaltourism.com (mirrored at www.himachaltourism.nic.in). The HPTDC Web site at www.hptdc.com exists to promote HPTDC hotels and tours, and www.himachalguide.com is a useful independent site.

Permits The region surrounding the Tibetan border is politically sensitive and foreigners currently require a permit to cross from Kinnaur to Spiti via Tabo (or vice versa). The easiest places to obtain an inner line permit are Kaza in Spiti and Rekong Peo in Kinnaur (see the Lahaul & Spiti and North to Kinnaur sections for more details). A rise in Indian-Chinese tension could result in a tightening of restrictions so check with the relevant authorities and other travellers before visiting the area.

Shimla

☎ 0177 • pop 123,000 • elevation 2205m

Shimla was once part of the Nepali kingdom and called Shyamala, another name for the goddess Kali, but received few visitors until it was 'discovered' by the British, who were seeking respite from the baking plains in 1819. Three years later, the first 'British' house was erected, and in 1864 Shimla became the summer capital of India.

Until 1939, the entire government of India would pack its bags and migrate almost 2000km from the sweltering heat of Kolkata or Delhi to Shimla's cool heights for the summer. The construction of the Kalka-Shimla railway line in 1903 allowed easy access for Raj families who couldn't bear to be completely cut off from the plains, and many built opulent mansions here. Following Independence, Shimla was initially the capital of Punjab, then became the capital of Himachal Pradesh in 1966.

Set among cool pine-clad hills with plenty of crumbling colonial charm, Shimla is for many people the archetypal hill station. Some buildings, like the mock-Tudor Municipality building at Scandal Point are plucked straight from 19th-century England. There are stunning views all the way to the Himalaya and some good places to stay and eat, although it can be hard to find reasonably priced accommodation during high season.

High season is mid-April to mid-July, mid-September to late October and mid-December to mid-January. The best time to visit is mid-September to late November. Shimla's first snows usually begin in January.

Orientation

The main road in Shimla is known as The Mall, and runs east-west along the top of the ridge, reaching its highest point at Scandal Point, the de facto centre of town. The open area known as The Ridge is situated between Scandal Point and Christ Church and is a popular spot for promenades.

Downhill, Cart Rd circles the southern part of Shimla, and is where you'll find the bus and taxi stands and train station. It's a steep hike uphill from here to almost everywhere. Numerous alleyways and lively bazaars zigzag up and down between Cart Rd and the pedestrian-only Mall. There is also a passenger lift connecting Cart Rd to The Mall, emerging near Solitaire Restaurant.

At the bus or train stations you will be besieged by porters offering to carry your luggage for Rs 10 to 30, depending on weight and distance. Many double as hotel touts, and hotels will double your room tariff to cover their commission; ask to be taken to a prominent landmark on The Mall such as Christ Church and walk from there.

Information

Tourist Offices The HPTDC tourist office (☎ 252561) at Scandal Point primarily exists to take bookings for HPTDC buses, hotels and local tours, but has a small amount of information on the local area. It's open 9 am to 8 pm daily in high season and 9 am to 6 pm in low season. There's a small satellite office by the Victory Tunnel, 1km west of Scandal Point.

Money State Bank of India, at the western end of The Mall can only exchange Thomas Cook or American Express (AmEx) cheques in US dollars and pounds sterling. Visa and AmEx cheques in US dollars or pounds sterling are accepted at Punjab and Sind Bank on The Mall. UCO Bank only changes cash in US dollars or pounds sterling.

ANZ Grindlays Bank, at Scandal Point, charges an outrageous Rs 200 to change travellers cheques but accepts most major cheques. Cash advances on Visa and MasterCard cost Rs 100. Bank of Baroda, down on Cart Rd, also gives cash advances on Visa and MasterCard. If you are headed to Kinnaur it's worth changing extra money in Shimla as there are no exchange facilities at all in Kinnaur, Spiti or Lahaul.

Post & Communications The main post office is housed in a mock-Tudor building not far from Scandal Point, open 10 am to 5 pm Monday to Saturday. There's a reliable poste restante service here. The central telegraph office (fax 202598), west of Scandal Point, is open 24 hours and is the cheapest place to make telephone calls and to send and receive faxes. There's also a small, unreliable, Internet cafe (Rs 65 per hour). Slightly more reliable Internet access is available at the Elegance Internet cafe, just off The Mall below Scandal Point (Rs 60 per hour).

Bookshops The well-stocked bookshop Maria Brothers and Minerva Bookshop have good stocks of novels, plus maps and glossy books on Himachal.

Film & Photography If you're heading farther north, Shimla is your last chance to stock up on slide film. Processing of print film is also available for Rs 20 plus Rs 3.50 per print. Try Sohans Studios on The Mall.

Himachal State Museum & Library

About 2.5km west of Scandal Point, near the communications mast, the state museum has a good collection of statues, miniatures, coins, photos and other items from around Himachal Pradesh and is worth a visit. Entry is free and the museum is open 10 am to 5 pm daily (closed Monday and public holidays). Photography is strictly prohibited.

Viceregal Lodge & Botanical Gardens

The Viceregal Lodge, also known as Rashtrapati Niwas, was formerly the residence of the British Viceroy Lord Dufferin, and is now the home of the Indian Institute of Advanced Study. This appealing colonial structure was where many decisions affecting the destiny of the subcontinent were made. Incredibly, every brick of the six-storey building was transported by mule (the railway wasn't built at that stage). The lodge was eventually finished in 1888.

You can take a guided tour of the lodge from 9 am to 5.30 pm daily (except Monday) for only Rs 10. While you're here, take time to explore the lawns and botanical gardens. The lodge is a pleasant 2km walk west of the museum – about 4.5km from Scandal Point – and there's a small cafe where you can get a well-earned cup of hot coffee.

Next to the lodge is a small **aviary** featuring, among other birds, the Monal pheasant (Himachal's state bird). The aviary is open 10 am to 5 pm daily (closed Monday). Entry is Rs 5, but use of a camera/video costs an extra Rs 25/100.

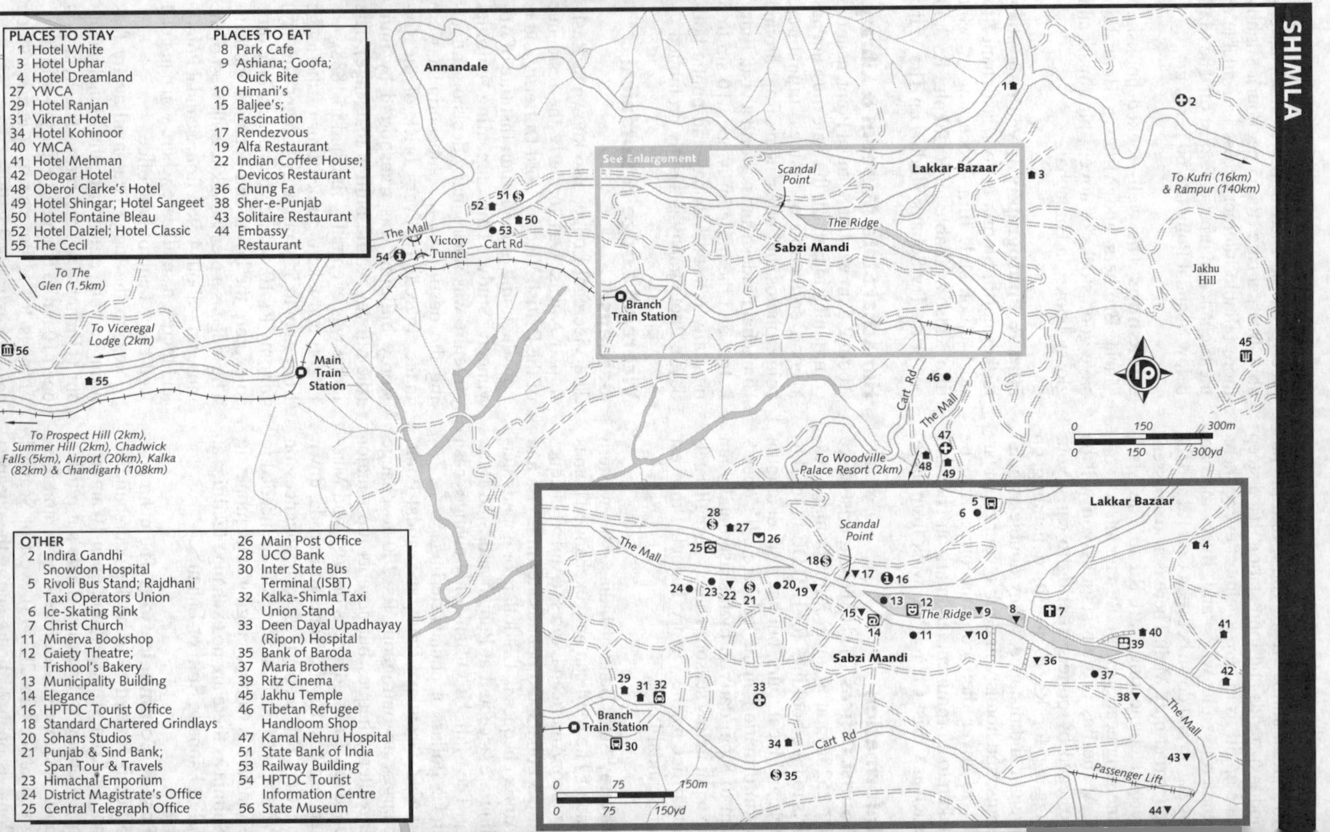
SHIMLA
PLACES TO STAY
1 Hotel White
3 Hotel Uphar
4 Hotel Dreamland
27 YWCA
29 Hotel Ranjan
31 Vikrant Hotel
34 Hotel Kohinoor
40 YMCA
41 Hotel Mehman
42 Deogar Hotel
48 Oberoi Clarke's Hotel
49 Hotel Shingar; Hotel Sangeet
50 Hotel Fontaine Bleau
52 Hotel Dalziel; Hotel Classic
55 The Cecil
PLACES TO EAT
8 Park Cafe
9 Ashiana; Goofa; Quick Bite
10 Himani's
15 Baljee's; Fascination
17 Rendezvous
19 Alfa Restaurant
22 Indian Coffee House; Devicos Restaurant
36 Chung Fa
38 Sher-e-Punjab
43 Solitaire Restaurant
44 Embassy Restaurant
OTHER
2 Indira Gandhi Snowdon Hospital
5 Rivoli Bus Stand; Rajdhani Taxi Operators Union
6 Ice-Skating Rink
7 Christ Church
11 Minerva Bookshop
12 Gaiety Theatre; Trishool's Bakery
13 Municipality Building
14 Elegance
16 HPTDC Tourist Office
18 Standard Chartered Grindlays
20 Sohans Studios
21 Punjab & Sind Bank; Span Tour & Travels
23 Himachal Emporium
24 District Magistrate's Office
25 Central Telegraph Office
26 Main Post Office
28 UCO Bank
30 Inter State Bus Terminal (ISBT)
32 Kalka-Shimla Taxi Union Stand
33 Deen Dayal Upadhayay (Ripon) Hospital
35 Bank of Baroda
37 Maria Brothers
39 Ritz Cinema
45 Jakhu Temple
46 Tibetan Refugee Handloom Shop
47 Kamal Nehru Hospital
51 State Bank of India
53 Railway Building
54 HPTDC Tourist Information Centre
56 State Museum
Annandale
See Enlargement
Scandal Point
Lakkar Bazaar
The Ridge
Sabzi Mandi
Branch Train Station
Main Train Station
The Mall
Victory Tunnel
Cart Rd
To The Glen (1.5km)
To Viceregal Lodge (2km)
To Prospect Hill (2km), Summer Hill (2km), Chadwick Falls (5km), Airport (20km), Kalka (82km) & Chandigarh (108km)
To Woodville Palace Resort (2km)
To Kufri (16km) & Rampur (140km)
Jakhu Hill
Passenger Lift
0 150 300m
0 150 300yd
0 75 150m
0 75 150yd

Christ Church & St Michael's Cathedral

The second-oldest church in northern India (the oldest is in Ambala), Christ Church was built between 1846 and 1857. The church is one of Shimla's major landmarks and is renowned for its stained-glass windows. You can discreetly have a look inside the church, or attend English-language services every Sunday morning during the tourist season.

Jakhu Temple

Dedicated to the monkey god, Hanuman, Jakhu Temple is east of the town centre near the highest point of the Shimla ridge (2455m). It offers a fine view over the surrounding valleys out to the snowcapped peaks, and over Shimla itself. Appropriately, there are many monkeys around the temple. It's a steep 45-minute walk from Scandal Point. Take the footpath that heads east past Hotel Dreamland. Sunrise is a good time to be there.

Hikes

There are a number of interesting short hikes from Shimla.

The Glen, about 4km west of Scandal Point, is one of the former playgrounds of rich British colonialists. The turn-off is on the way to the state museum and goes through **Annandale**, another lovely area. This was the site of a famous racecourse, and cricket and polo are still played there.

Summer Hill is 5km away, on the Shimla-Kalka railway line, and has pleasant, shady walks. It's also famous because Mahatma Gandhi once stayed at the Raj Kumari Amrit Kaur mansion here. In the same direction, **Chadwick Falls** (67m high) are 2km farther west, but only really worth visiting during or just after the monsoons (July to October).

There's a Kamna Devi Temple and excellent views at **Prospect Hill**, about 5km west of Shimla, and a 15-minute climb from Boileauganj.

Organised Tours

HPTDC organises the following daily sightseeing tours in high season, which leave from the Rivoli bus stand between 10.30 and 11 am, and drop off at the end of the day at the bottom of the passenger lift on Cart Rd:

- Chail via Kufri (Rs 172)
- Fagu and Theog & Narkanda (Rs 168)
- Kufri, Fagu, Mashobra & Naldehra (Rs 151)

The Kalka-Shimla Taxi Union (☎ 258225) on Cart Rd and the Rajdhani Taxi Operators Union (☎ 208654) at the Rivoli bus stand both offer one-day sightseeing tours to:

- Chail/Kufri (Rs 810)
- Narkanda via Fagu and Theog (Rs 810)

In season the HPTDC also offers a heritage walk, which takes in many of the historic buildings around town, including the Viceregal Lodge (Rs 50).

Places to Stay

Accommodation in Shimla is expensive, particularly during the high season. But in low season, or when business is quiet, prices drop substantially, sometimes by as much as 50%. Prices given here are for the high season, but don't include the 10% luxury tax.

Places to Stay – Budget

The cheapest areas are around the Inter State Bus Terminal and along Cart Rd heading east.

YMCA *(☎ 250021, fax 211016)* accepts men and women and is probably the best budget choice in high season, when it can be booked out (reservations are accepted by phone). It's a big old institutional place, with singles/doubles for Rs 133/173 with breakfast and shared hot-water bathroom (7 pm to 9 am). Nonmembers will need to pay Rs 40 for a seven-day temporary membership. Doubles with hot water cost Rs 250 with breakfast. It's not far behind the Christ Church, up the lane beside the Ritz cinema.

YWCA *(☎ 203081)*, also for men and women, above the main post office, isn't quite as good value but it's a convenient, friendly old place, with great views. Small rooms with private bathroom cost Rs 150/200 in low/high season. There is a Rs 20 temporary membership charge.

Near the Inter State Bus Terminal (ISBT), but a hike from The Mall, the ***Hotel Ranjan*** *(☎ 252818)* and ***Vikrant Hotel*** *(☎ 253602)*, offer doubles with private bath from Rs 300 (Rs 150 in low season).

Hotel Kohinoor *(☎ 202008)*, farther east along Cart Rd, has nice rooms with private

A Home in the Hills

Whether it was homesickness or the heat of the plains that drove the British to the hills, they certainly made their presence felt. Miniature versions of Britain were re-created at Shimla, Dalhousie, Mussoorie and Nainital (to name just a few locations), complete with quaint stone churches, ballrooms, cricket pitches, summer houses and tea parties on the lawn.

Most of the hill stations owe their existence to British explorers who built holiday homes in scenic spots that reminded them of Britain. As the hill station phenomenon took off, whole towns of summer houses sprung up in the hills, attracting vast crowds of homesick Brits every summer.

At the height of the Raj, even the colonial government in Delhi and Kolkata packed up its bags and retreated to Shimla, which was declared the 'summer capital' of India. A special railway line was constructed to help move all the documents and officials required to run the nation from the hills. In fact, the British were continuing a centuries-old tradition; the ancient rulers of Himachal Pradesh and Uttaranchal also headed for the hills in the summer, creating their own summer capitals such as Almora in the Kumaon highlands.

Many maharajas built opulent summer palaces in the British hill stations to hob-nob with the cream of colonial society; the Maharaja of Patiala was exiled from Shimla for taking this familiarity too far and having an affair with the daughter of the British commander in chief! However, the experience of most Indians was less glamorous. Every summer, hundreds of coolies and porters had to physically haul the British and their belongings up into the hills.

After Independence, the hill stations were finally reclaimed by ordinary Indians, the region finding a new role as the honeymoon capital of India. These days, tens of thousands of newlyweds flock to the hills every summer to have honeymoon portraits taken among the crumbling British houses and Himalayan backdrops.

HIMACHAL PRADESH

bathroom and running hot water for Rs 200 to 350.

Around the Lakkar Bazaar area, a steep climb past The Ridge, are several reasonably priced places. ***Hotel Dreamland*** *(☎ 206897)* has rooms ranging from Rs 250/400 for a single/double to Rs 650 for a deluxe double. Credit cards are accepted.

The nearby ***Hotel Uphar*** *(☎ 257670)* is used to backpackers and has adequate doubles with hot shower and TV for Rs 275, or Rs 400 with a view and minibalcony.

Those in search of old-world charm should head for the quaint, family-run ***Hotel Fontaine Bleau*** *(☎ 253549)*, just downhill from State Bank of India, at the western end of The Mall. Large doubles in this old house start at Rs 250, with hot shower.

Places to Stay – Mid-Range

The majority of rooms in this range will usually include cable TV and private bathroom with hot water. They are particularly good value in low season; at most hotels the rate for a double drops to about Rs 200.

Just off The Mall, a short walk up from the main train station, is the friendly and comfortable ***Hotel Classic*** *(☎ 253078)*, with tacky singles for Rs 300 and decent doubles from Rs 400 to 500 with good views. A few doors down, ***Hotel Dalziel*** *(☎ 252691)* is also good value, with rooms from Rs 350 to 600, all with carpets and hot-water geyser. All rates drop by 50% in the winter.

North of The Ridge in the Lakkar Bazaar is the good-value ***Hotel White*** *(☎ 255276)*, with comfortable doubles for Rs 425, and Rs 500 with good views; superior rooms with superior views cost Rs 700 upwards.

A few minutes' walk east of Christ Church, ***Deogar Hotel*** *(☎ 208527)* is a good choice, with comfortable doubles from Rs 650 to 950 (Rs 250 to 300 in low season). The pricier rooms have great views over Shimla.

Just uphill, the modern ***Hotel Mehman*** *(☎ 213692)* has spotlessly clean carpeted rooms with private bathroom. Comfortable rooms range from Rs 550 to 1000, depending on the views, with a 50% discount in the low season.

Across from Oberoi Clarke's Hotel, at the south-east end of The Mall. ***Hotel Shingar*** *(☎ 252881, fax 252998)* has rooms for Rs 900, or Rs 1100 with a view (30% less in low season). Nearby, ***Hotel Sangeet*** *(☎ 202506, fax 255823)* has good-value rooms from Rs 700 to 900, which are discounted in low season.

Places to Stay – Top End

***Woodville Palace Resort** (☎ 223919, fax 223098)*, 2km south of Oberoi Clarke's Hotel on The Mall, is an ivy-covered building constructed in 1938 by Raja Rana Sir Bhagat Chandra, the ruler of the former princely state of Jubbal. It's a small place, set among very pleasant gardens. Doubles are Rs 2000, and suites start at Rs 3000 – bookings are recommended.

***Oberoi Clarke's Hotel** (☎ 251010, fax 211321)*, at the south-east end of The Mall, is one of Shimla's earliest hotels. The luxurious rooms start at US$70/125 a single/double (plus 10% tax), including the compulsory three-meal 'American Plan'.

The spectacular ***The Cecil** (☎ 204848)*, at the western end of The Mall, is easily the classiest place in town. The hotel is part of the Oberoi Group and rooms arranged around a central atrium start at Rs 6075/7875 for a single/double in low season.

Places to Eat

Indian Shimla has many places serving Indian food, primarily South Indian.

On The Mall close to the tourist office, are ***Baljee's*** and ***Fascination***, offering delicious Indian and Western food and have some of the best ambience in Shimla. Prices start at Rs 100 for a meat dish. ***Alfa Restaurant***, near Scandal Point, is about the same standard, price and popularity.

Himani's, just downhill from the Municipality Building on The Mall, does tasty South Indian snacks and meals ranging from Rs 70 to 150, and has a popular and relaxed bar.

The dingy ***Rendezvous***, on Scandal Point, offers Indian and Thai food from Rs 65 and has a bar but the service is slow.

Sher-e-Punjab, along The Mall just east of Scandal Point, is an excellent cheap option, offering Indian fast-food standards like *channa* (curried chickpeas) starting at Rs 50.

Farther downhill, ***Solitaire Restaurant*** serves a good selection of Indian dishes from Rs 70, in a big dining room overlooking the valley. The absurdly popular ***Indian Coffee House***, along The Mall, near Punjab & Sind Bank, is an India-wide institution, run by a cooperate of workers in the coffee industry. Above average India coffee and South Indian snacks are served up by waiters in cummerbunds.

Western & Chinese The nonsmoking ***Embassy Restaurant***, not far from the top of the lift on The Mall, is a canteen-style place with great pizzas and hamburgers, as well as Indian and Chinese food for around Rs 40.

Devicos Restaurant, on The Mall near Scandal Point, is a clean, trendy place that does good, but a little overpriced, fast food.

The cosy ***Park Cafe***, below Scandal Point and up some steps from The Mall is popular with backpackers and local students. It's a bohemian spot with good pizza (Rs 60 to 80), milkshakes, breakfasts and laid-back late-evening music.

HPTDC has a building on The Ridge with three places to eat but extremely slow service. ***Ashiana*** is about the best (and most expensive) for decor and speed. Expect to pay around Rs 150 for a meal here. ***Goofa*** downstairs is nowhere near as classy, but serves a reasonable (and early) breakfast. In the same complex, ***Quick Bite*** has cheap pizzas and Indian food.

Chung Fa, down some steps just off The Mall, is the best place for cheap Chinese food. There is a good range of noodles, dumplings and main dishes, all for less than Rs 40 a dish.

Oberoi Clarke's Hotel is good for a splurge in some luxurious surroundings; expect to pay around Rs 250 for a meal.

For a quick snack, ***Trishool's***, next to the Gaiety Theatre, is recommended for its cakes and pastries.

Baljee's has a bakery counter at the front, and is a great place for morning tea.

Entertainment

Probably the most popular, and best, entertainment is to stroll along The Mall and The Ridge (vehicle-free!) and watch everyone else watch everyone else. The ice-skating rink by the Rivoli bus stand is open in winter – follow the signs from Scandal Point.

The lovely old ***Gaiety Theatre** (☎ 205639)* occasionally has shows or recitals. ***Ritz*** cinema near Christ Church screens all-singing, all-dancing Indian blockbusters. The bar at ***Himani's*** is popular and upbeat. ***Rendezvous*** on Scandal Point also has a bar, albeit dingy.

Shopping

The Himachal Emporium on The Mall near The Ridge has a reasonable collection of local handicrafts and, inexplicably, pottery dogs. The Tibetan Refugee Handloom Shop, at the other end of The Mall, is the showroom for a local development project and sells carpets, clothes and other Tibetan crafts.

North of The Ridge is the small, bustling Lakkar Bazaar, Shimla's main souvenir market, though most of the offerings are firmly aimed at Indian tourists. Wooden massage wheels and rollers make cheap and lightweight mementos.

For fruit, vegetables and just about anything else, head for the bustling Sabzi Mandi (Vegetable Market), between The Ridge and Cart Rd. The kinetic chaos of the streets is a refreshing contrast to the genteel, British-influenced Mall.

Getting There & Away

Air Shimla airport is about 23km south at Jubbarhatti and is served by small aircraft from Delhi. Indian Airlines flies from Delhi to Shimla (US$110, one hour) at 9 am on Monday, Wednesday and Friday, continuing on to Kullu/Manali airport at Bhuntar (US$100, 30 minutes) at 10.20 am. From Kullu, the plane returns directly to Delhi.

Jagson Airlines has a flight from Delhi to Shimla (US$100) at 8 am daily, except Sunday, continuing on to Kullu at 9.20 am (US$85). To get to Delhi from Shimla, you'll have to fly via Kullu.

Airline bookings can be made with travel agencies on The Mall – Span Tour & Travels (☎ 260850) is reliable. There is no bus to the airport, so you'll have to take a taxi for a flat rate of Rs 410.

Bus The large and chaotic Inter State Bus Terminal (ISBT) on Cart Rd has a computer booking booth (Counter 9), where the employees speak English; you can book a ticket on any public bus up to a month ahead.

Buses to destinations east of Shimla depart from the Rivoli bus station, on the northern side of the main ridge, below the HPTDC office. For Tattapani, Kasauli and local destinations en route to Kalka or Narkanda, catch one of the regular local buses along Cart Rd.

To Manali (11 hours) there are buses at 4.40, 8 and 9.15 am (Rs 160) and a night bus at 7 pm (Rs 207). All Manali buses stop in Kullu. There are buses to Dharamsala every few hours until 10.30 pm (Rs 152 day, Rs 190 night, 10 hours). Buses leave frequently until late in the evening for Mandi (Rs 90, six hours) and Chandigarh (Rs 70, four hours).

Deluxe buses to Delhi leave every few hours from 8.25 am through to 9.45 pm and offer your best chance of sleeping en route (Rs 360). Ordinary buses leave every hour and cost Rs 182. Buses depart at 5.10 am and 5.40 and 6.30 pm for Haridwar (Rs 171, 10 hours), via Paonta Sahib (Rs 110) and Dehra Dun (Rs 137, nine hours).

From the Rivoli bus station, there are hourly buses all morning going to Narkanda (Rs 38, three hours) and Rampur (Rs 78, six hours) continuing on to Rekong Peo in Kinnaur (Rs 143, 10 hours). Depending on the status of the road, you may have to get out at Karcham and walk around several damaged sections of highway. There is one bus at 7.30 am direct to Sangla (Rs 143), or you can change to a local bus or jeep at Karcham. For Sarahan, buses leave at 3.30, 9.45 and 10.10 am (Rs 104, 7½ hours).

Travel agencies along The Mall offer private overnight 'deluxe' buses (two by two seating) to Manali (Rs 275) and to Delhi (Rs 300). Prices and timings change according to demand and the season.

In high season, HPTDC offers daily buses to Manali at 8.30 am and 8 pm (Rs 338, 10 hours) and a night bus to Delhi at 8 pm (Rs 339, 10 hours) via Chandigarh. You can book these buses at the tourist office at Scandal Point; the buses leave from the satellite office at Victory Tunnel. All buses have a two by two seating arrangement, offering your best chance of sleeping on night trips.

Train There are two train stations in Shimla, but most trains arrive and depart from the main train station on the western edge of town. The train reservation office (☎ 252915) at the main station can arrange bookings for the Kalka and Delhi line and, in theory, for other trips in northern India. It's open 10 am to 1.30 pm and 2 to 5 pm Monday to Saturday and 10 am to 2 pm Sunday.

The train journey from Delhi to Shimla involves a change from broad to narrow gauge at Kalka, a little north of Chandigarh, where the Shimla toy train begins its tortuous ascent into the hills. The tiny railway was built to ferry the colonial government into the hills in 1903 and passes through a staggering 103 tunnels as it snakes its way up to Shimla. Unsurprisingly, it's a scenic trip, and even more so if you can afford the special Rail Car service (Rs 340) which runs during the high season and offers luxury seats in a special glass-sided carriage. For lesser mortals, there are three more conventional classes; 2nd class (Rs 16), chair car (Rs 140) and 1st class (Rs 170). Trains run uphill from Kalka at 4, 5.30, 6.30 and 11.55 am, heading back down to Kalka from the main station in Shimla at 10.35 am and 2.25, 5.30 and 5.45 pm. In high season, there are three extra trains in each direction. Ask at the station for details.

To travel from Delhi to Shimla by train without too much delay en route, the best and most reliable way is to catch the *Himalayan Queen* from New Delhi station at 6 am, arriving in Kalka at 11.40 am to connect with the 11.55 am toy train to Shimla (Rs 400 from Delhi to Shimla in air-con chair class). In the reverse direction, the 10.35 am train from Shimla connects with the *Himalayan Queen* at Kalka and arrives in New Delhi at 10.30 pm. The best overnight connection is the *Shivalik Express*, which leaves Shimla at 5.30 pm to connect with the *Kalka-Howrah Mail*, arriving in Delhi at 6.25 am. (Fares are Rs 140/589 in sleeper/two-tier).

From Kalka there is a train to Amritsar at 4.15 pm (Rs 151 sleeper) and several trains daily to Chandigarh (Rs 104/347 sleeper/two-tier).

Taxi There are taxi unions at both the ISBT and Rivoli bus stands, and the set rates are almost impossible to bargain down, even in low season. The Kalka-Shimla Taxi Union (☎ 258225) is on Cart Rd, just east of the ISBT bus station. At the Rivoli bus stand, talk to the Rajdhani Taxi Operators Union (☎ 208654). The cheapest taxis are 'multivans'; Sumo or Maruti jeeps and Ambassador taxis charge 10% more than the prices that follow.

Examples of one-way taxi fares from Shimla are: Chandigarh (Rs 910), Dehra Dun (Rs 2550), Delhi (Rs 2850), Dharamsala (Rs 2450), Kalka (Rs 610), Kullu (Rs 1850), Manali (Rs 2450), Rampur (Rs 1450) and Kalpa/Rekong Peo (Rs 2650).

Getting Around

To/From the Airport A fixed-price taxi costs Rs 410 from the airport to Shimla, but if you are staying anywhere along or near The Mall, you may have to walk the last bit yourself anyway. Local buses headed to Nalagarh go past the airport but they're hopelessly crowded.

Passenger Lift To save you lugging your bags uphill there is a lift that goes up to the eastern end of The Mall (Rs 5) from Cart Rd, a short walk east from the bus station. It runs 8 am to 9 pm.

Around Shimla

There are several interesting villages and towns in the area that can be visited as day or overnight trips from Shimla.

About 11km from Shimla, the small village of **Mashobra** has some pleasant walks, including one to Sipi, where there is a fair every May and a wooden **temple** dedicated to Shiva. The only place to stay in Mashobra is ***Gables Resorts*** *(☎ 0177-480169)*, which offers rural luxury from Rs 2200 upwards, and a dining rooms with views of the mountains. The village has one or two ***dhabas*** (snack bars).

About 3km from Mashobra, along a lovely trail, is the resort of **Craignano** – the path leads downhill from the temple in the middle of Mashobra. You can book a room at ***Municipal Rest House*** *(☎ 224850)* in Craignano through HPTDC in Shimla.

NALDEHRA

At an altitude of 2050m, 15km north of Mashobra, the village of Naldehra is known mostly for its golf course, which is one of the oldest and highest in the world. The park (Rs 5 entry) surrounding the course is a popular picnic spot, with the inevitable horse rides on offer. Most popular is the trip up to the **Mahunag Mandir** temple in the middle of the golf course (Rs 250).

The golf course is only open from March to November and green fees are US$10 (Rs 100 for Indians) for 18 holes (twice around the course), plus US$5 for club hire and Rs 60 for a caddy. During the season, the course is open 7 am to 7 pm daily.

HPTDC runs ***Hotel Golf Glade*** *(☎ 0177-487739)*, with six luxurious log cabins from Rs 1100 to 4000, and better-value rooms from Rs 800 to 1000, plus a restaurant that functions as an informal clubhouse.

Occasional buses run here for Rs 31, or it's a Rs 700 return taxi ride from Shimla.

TATTAPANI

About 30km north of Naldehra, this peaceful village was known for its hot sulphurous springs, but the Sutlej River burst its banks in August 2000 and washed away the baths as well as half the village. The ruins are an impressive testament to the power of the river, but in its current state, Tattapani isn't really worth the long journey out here.

There are a few places to stay, including ***HPTDC Tourist Inn***, uphill from the bridge, with reasonable rooms from Rs 250. You can get here by bus or taxi.

CHAIL

☎ 01792 • elevation 2250m

The hilltop village of Chail, 65km south of Shimla, was created by the Maharaja of Patiala as a summer capital after he was expelled from Shimla, following an illicit encounter with the daughter of the British commander in chief! The town is built on three hills – one is topped by the Chail Palace, one by the village itself and the other by the Snowview mansion.

About 3km from the village is the world's highest **cricket ground** (2444m), built in 1893. There is also a **wildlife sanctuary** 3km from Chail with a limited number of deer and birds. There are plenty of interesting hikes in the surrounding hills.

Places to Stay & Eat

HPTDC Palace Hotel *(☎ 48141, fax 48142)* has a range of suites, cottages, log huts and rooms set among 28 hectares of lawns. Modest luxury starts at Rs 1000 for a log hut or Rs 1200 for a regular room, and moves up to Rs 6000 for the four-bed 'maharaja suite'.

HPTDC Hotel Himneel *(☎ 48337)* has more-modest rooms for Rs 600 a double with private bathroom.

Hotel Deodar *(☎ 48318)* has doubles with TV and private bathroom from Rs 250 to 350 and ***Pine View Tourist Lodge*** *(☎ 48349)* has rooms from Rs 150 with shared bathroom and Rs 200 to 500 with private bathroom.

Getting There & Away

Chail can be reached from the Shimla-Kalka road via Kandaghat or, more commonly, via the turn-off at Kufri. A one-way/return taxi from Shimla, via Kufri, costs Rs 600/800. There are occasional buses (more in high season) to Chail from Shimla and Chandigarh.

KASAULI

☎ 01792 • elevation 1850m

About 75km from Shimla and 12km from Kalka road, Kasauli is a charming village surrounded by pines, and makes a popular day trip from Shimla. There several Raj-era buildings in town, and numerous peaceful walks around Kasauli, including one to **Sanawar**, another picturesque hill town, and the location of a famous colonial college.

The upmarket ***Alasia Hotel*** *(☎ 72008)* has rooms with private bathroom from Rs 1500 with good views. More humble accommodation is available at ***Anchal Guest House*** *(☎ 72052)* from Rs 350 a double with private bathroom. ***HPTDC Hotel Ros Common*** *(☎ 72005)* has rooms with TV and private bathroom from Rs 800 to 1300 and a pleasant location.

Local buses run between Shimla and Kausali. A one-way/return taxi from Shimla to Kasauli costs about Rs 750/1000.

NAHAN

The historical town of Nahan, founded in 1621, has an interesting bazaar, packed with crumbling temples, but most tourists just pass through on the bus between Shimla and Dehra Dun. Nahan hosts a festival called **Bhawan Dwadshi** at the end of the monsoon, when over 50 idols of Hindu gods are led through the streets and ceremonially bathed in Ranital (Rani Lake) in the town centre. The most appealing structure here is the old **Raja Mahal** palace (closed to visitors).

There are several cheap and cheerful hotels in Nahan, including ***Hotel Hill View*** *(☎ 01702-22338)* by the bus station, which has decent rooms for Rs 200/450 a single/double, and ***Hotel Regency*** *(☎ 01702-23302)* with good-value rooms from Rs 275 to 495 with balcony and private bathroom with hot water. The pleasant ***Milan Restaurant*** here serves the best food in town.

Nahan is served by regular buses from Shimla (Rs 85) and Dehra Dun (Rs 52). For Renuka Lake, there are hourly buses to Dadahu (Rs 20).

RENUKA LAKE

About an hour by bus from Nahan is lovely Renuka Lake (Renukaji), the largest natural lake in Himachal Pradesh. It's a growing centre for water sports, but unless you come on an organised tour, you'll probably be restricted to hiring a pedal boat from Hotel Renuka. There are several temples here and a small **wildlife park**, which has Asiatic lions, barking deer and Himalayan black bears. The week-long **Renuka Mela** is held in November to honour the goddess Renukaji. It attracts thousands of pilgrims who ritually bathe in the lake.

HPTDC Hotel Renuka *(☎ 67339)* has spacious rooms in secluded gardens from Rs 450 to 900, all with water. There are also dorm beds for Rs 75, and a good restaurant.

A bus from Nahan goes to Dadahu roughly every hour, from where you can walk 40 minutes to the lake (though some buses do continue on to the lake). There are private buses from the lake direct to Paonta Sahib (Rs 30, two hours) every few hours.

PAONTA SAHIB

On the Uttaranchal border is the town of Paonta Sahib, which is home to an impressive **gurdwara** (Sikh temple) dedicated to the 10th Sikh guru, Gobind Singh, who lived there between the ages of 16 and 20. The gurdwara has an attractive location on the banks of the holy Yamuna River and overflows with pilgrims during the **Holi festivals** in March. Inside the temple is a small **museum** housing the personal weapons and other relics of Gobind Singh.

HPTDC Hotel Yamuna *(☎ 01704-22341)*, on the riverside, about 100m from the entrance to the temple, is the best option. Nice doubles with private bathroom cost from Rs 450 to 1200, the latter with air-con, and there's a good restaurant and bar. It's worth the splurge as the alternatives are fairly poor.

Hourly buses go to Shimla (Rs 110; until 1 pm), Dehra Dun (Rs 27, 1½ hours) and Nahan (Rs 25, two hours). There are three morning buses to Delhi (Rs 110, seven hours).

SHIMLA TO THE SUTLEJ VALLEY

The Sutlej River runs through a narrow gorge providing the southern access to Kinnaur. The road that runs along the gorge was constructed by Lord Dalhousie in 1850, and originally ran to Tibet, but foreigners are only allowed as far north as Sumdo in Kinnaur, where the road to Spiti and Lahaul branches off. The string of resorts established by the British finishes at Narkanda and settlements farther north owe their existence to the Bushahr maharajas who once ruled over all of Kinnaur. Perhaps the most interesting is Sarahan, home to the famous Bhimkali Temple, which once played host to human sacrifices.

Kufri

☎ 0177 • elevation 2510m

Kufri is a fairly nondescript little highway village. On the road to Chail, the **Himalayan Nature Park** (Rs 10, open 10 am to 5 pm daily) has a collection of animals and birds unique to Himachal Pradesh. On the road up to the park, you can take a horse ride to Mahashu Peak, for good forest views (Rs 160).

Places to Stay & Eat On the main road in the village, ***Hotel Snow Shelter*** *(☎ 480135)* has cosy rooms, great views and hot water at a reasonable Rs 275/440 a single/double.

Kufri Holiday Inns *(☎ 480341)*, next door, has upmarket rooms from Rs 400 to 1250 (the pricier rooms have great views) and ***Honey Dew***, the best restaurant in town.

Uphill on the way to the nature park, the ***Kufri Holiday Resort*** *(☎ 480300)* is a posh place with luxurious rooms for Rs 2550 upwards, two restaurants and a bar.

Near the nature park is the HPTDC run **Indira Tourist Park** (Rs 5 entry), which has the friendly ***Cafe Lalit***, serving good veg and nonveg food for Rs 40 upwards.

Getting There & Away Kufri is a stop on any of the regular bus routes between Shimla, Narkanda, Chail and Rampur. A one-way taxi from Shimla to Kufri costs Rs 350.

Narkanda

☎ 01782 • elevation 2708m

Halfway between Shimla and Rampur, Narkanda is basically a truck stop town, but the surrounding hills are popular place for **skiing** in winter. The ski season lasts from January to mid-April, but Narkanda is not as well set up for skiing as Solang Nullah, north of Manali, and nowhere near the standard of Auli in Uttaranchal. The HPTDC offers seven-day skiing packages for Rs 3900 including board, lodging, equipment and tuition. You may also be able to ski here with the Institute of Mountaineering & Allied Sports in Manali; both organisations offer mainly fixed-date packages. Locally, Highland Travel and Adventures (☎ 8444) can organise ski-hire and trekking.

Places to Stay & Eat On the main road, ***Hotel Mahamaya Palace*** *(☎ 8448)* has lovely large rooms with hot water, balcony and views for Rs 400 to 800. There's a good restaurant and discounts in low season.

Perched above the village, ***Himalayan Hotel*** *(☎ 8440)* has slightly ramshackle doubles with private bathroom for Rs 250 to 300; amazing views and friendly staff make the place tolerable. Take the steps up behind the bus stand (the hotel is the big white building on top of the hill).

HPTDC's secluded ***Hotel Hatu*** *(☎ 8430)* is 250m up a track east of the main road (look for the sign). Good doubles with private bathroom cost Rs 600 to 900 in high season (reductions are possible at other times).

There are many basic, friendly ***dhabas*** in the town centre. If you prefer eating with cutlery try the restaurants at ***Hotel Hatu*** or ***Hotel Mahamaya Palace*** with staples like tandoori chicken for around Rs 75.

Getting There & Away Narkanda is served by regular buses on the Shimla to Rampur route – you shouldn't have to wait more than 30 minutes in either direction. A taxi from Shimla will cost about Rs 700.

HIMACHAL PRADESH

Rampur

☎ 01782 • elevation 924m

Rampur was once on the ancient trade route between India and Tibet, and was centre of the mighty Bushahr empire, but these days it's a fairly typical hill town. The **Padam Palace**, built in 1925, is along the main road, and belonged to the Maharaja of Bushahr. You can't go inside, but there are lovely gardens, which you can wander around. There are several interesting old temples, including the ancient stone **Raghunath Temple**, in a compound opposite the bus stand. Also worth a look are the old stone **Purohit Mandir** and the colourful stucco **Sri Sat Narain Temple**, built in 1926, both down by the river on the main bazaar. The ancient **Lavi Fair** is held in Rampur every year in the second week of November. People from the remote regions of Lahaul, Spiti and Kinnaur congregate in the town to trade local produce and horses. If you are heading on to Kinnaur, you should ask about the current condition of the road here.

Orientation & Information Rampur consists of a network of narrow lanes, squeezed between the highway and the river. All the places to stay are downhill from the highway. For the main bazaar and most of the temples, follow the steps down across from the bus stand.

Places to Stay & Eat Rampur is a popular liquor stop for truck drivers so the hotels here can be a little rowdy.

One of the best options is the popular ***Hotel Bhagwati*** *(☎ 33117)*, just off the main bazaar at the bottom of town (follow the signs from the bus stand). Comfortable doubles with private bathroom start at Rs 110 (Rs 165 with TV); deluxe rooms cost Rs 385.

A short walk uphill from the bus station, ***Narindera Hotel*** *(☎ 33155)* has decent doubles with private bathroom and hot water from Rs 150 to 275. Air-con rooms are Rs 500. There is a good restaurant here.

There are dozens of cheap dosshouses (flophouses) in Rampur. Most have noisy bars and spartan rooms from Rs 75 to 200. Perhaps the best is ***Highway Home*** *(☎ 33063)*, downhill from the bus stand along the highway.

The HPTDC-run ***Cafe Sutlej*** is worth the 1km walk from the palace towards Shimla for views and good food. The old town has plenty of ***dhabas*** – the best is just down the steps opposite the bus stand on the right-hand side.

Getting There & Away Rampur is a major transport hub, so is well connected by (crowded) buses. There are buses every 30 minutes (4.30 am to 6.30 pm) to Narkanda (Rs 38, two hours) and then on to Shimla (Rs 78, six hours). The road to Rekong Peo was destroyed in August 2000; at the time of writing buses only ran as far as Karcham (Rs 45, 3½ hours), the junction to the Sangla Valley, from where it's a 5km hike and 20-minute jeep or bus ride on to Rekong Peo. Buses to Sarahan depart every two hours or so from 7.30 am to 4.30 pm (Rs 25, one hour).

Sarahan

☎ 01782

The former summer capital of the Bushahr empire, Sarahan is a wonderful little village set high above the valley floor. Sarahan is best known for the ancient Bhimkali Temple, but it's also a good base for hikes to nearby villages such as Ranwin and the towering Bashal peak. The flamboyant palace of the last Maharaja of Bushahr is just behind the Bhimakali Temple (the other mansion belongs to the temple guardian). There are spectacular views of Srikhand Mahadev (5227m) from almost everywhere in the village.

Bhimakali Temple This ancient temple complex is regarded as one of the finest examples of Himachal architecture. The two main temples are built in the form of towers with elaborately carved overhanging upper storeys. As with many Himachal buildings, alternating layers of timber and stone were used to enable the temples to withstand earthquakes.

The right-hand temple is around 800 years old but is no longer structurally sound. Visitors can climb the newer left-hand temple, which dates from the 1920s. Stairs ascend to the 2nd floor where the main statue of Bhimakali (a local version of the bloodthirsty goddess Kali) is housed, surrounded by images of Parvati, Buddha and Annapurna, among others, all under a beautiful filigree silver canopy. Stairs descend to the 1st floor where there is a statue of Parvati, wife of Shiva.

The temple is open 9 am to 7 pm daily and there are some strict entry rules. Visitors must wear a cap (which can be borrowed from inside the temple), leather goods like belts and wallets must be left with the guards, photography is only allowed outside the two main temples, and shoes must be removed.

In the far right of the courtyard is a small display of ancient ceremonial lamps and weapons. Also in the compound is the squat **Lankra Vir Temple** where, up until the 19th century, human sacrifices were performed to appease Bhimakali. The tradition lives on in the bizarre Astomi ritual during **Dussehra**, in which various animals are sacrificed to Bhimkali, including goats, chickens, buffaloes, and (rumour has it) a spider!

Places to Stay & Eat The excellent ***temple guesthouse*** *(☎ 74248)*, inside the temple complex, is the best budget bet. It offers a handful of clean, quiet rooms with private bathroom for Rs 150, Rs 200 or Rs 300, plus some extremely basic dorms for Rs 25.

Close to the temple gates, ***Bushahr Guest House*** *(☎ 74238)* charges Rs 150 for clean, cosy doubles with hot water.

Beside the bus stand, ***Snow View Hotel*** *(☎ 74383)* has seen better days. Ramshackle doubles with private bathroom cost Rs 100 or Rs 200 with a view.

Nearby, the distinctive ***Hotel Srikhand*** *(☎ 74234)* is run by the HPTDC and offers large, comfortable rooms with TV, hot water and views over the valley from Rs 600 to 1100. Dorm beds cost Rs 75 when available. The restaurant here is excellent.

Better restaurants in Sarahan include ***Ribal***, for Chinese food, and ***Ajay*** for Tibetan and Indian offerings.

Getting There & Away There are three direct buses daily from Shimla to Sarahan (Rs 105) but it's easier to get a through bus to the junction at Jeori and wait for a local bus (every hour or two) up the steep 17km road to Sarahan. Buses run between Rampur and Sarahan every few hours for Rs 25. A taxi from Rampur to Sarahan is pricey at around Rs 500 but will save a lot of time; from Jeori to Sarahan costs about Rs 200.

North to Kinnaur

Kinnaur is a remote mountainous district between Shimla and the Tibetan border. The region was de-restricted in 1991 and travel to and around Kinnaur is now possible with easy-to-obtain permits.

Kinnaur is drained by the Sutlej River, which flows from close to Mt Kailash in Tibet. The region is flanked by the central Himalaya to the east. To the north is the formidable Zanskar Range, dividing Jammu & Kashmir, Himachal and Tibet. The most spectacular peak here is Kinnaur Kailash (6050m), which lords over the beautiful Sangla Valley.

The region is home to the Kinnauri tribal group, an Aryan people who have always regarded themselves as distinct from other Indians. Most Kinnauris follow a mixture of

Hinduism and Tibetan Buddhism and villages often have both Hindu and Buddhist temples. Probably the most distinctive part of the Kinnauris' dress is the grey woollen cap worn by men and women, called a *thepang*. Kinnauri (often called Homskad) is the major indigenous language and it has about 12 different dialects. The Kinnauris are traditionally farmers, growing wheat, barley and apples, but the area has been placed on a fast track to development by the huge dams that have been constructed on the Sutlej and Baspa Rivers as part of the Himachal government's hydroelectric program.

The roads in upper Kinnaur rank as some of the most spectacular in the Himalaya. An epic all-weather highway – the Hindustan-Tibet Highway – links upper Kinnaur and Spiti, passing through some of the most breathtaking scenery in the region. The road celebrated its 150th anniversary in June 2000 (construction began in 1850 under Lord Dalhousie) and was promptly washed away in August 2000 by the flooding Sutlej River. At the time of writing, engineers were struggling to rebuild the road.

Permits

For travel to northern Kinnaur, past Jangi to Tabo in Spiti, you currently need an inner line permit, which will satisfy the India-Tibet border police that you aren't going to make a run for the border. The policy is a hangover from the 1962 conflict between India and China, but it is still strictly enforced, so you'll need to visit the subdivisional magistrate's (SDM) office in Rekong Peo before you go any farther.

Fortunately, getting hold of a permit is relatively easy, providing the SDM in Rekong Peo is 'in station' (call ahead on ☎ 01786-22252 to make sure). Officially tourists must be in a group of four and be booked on an official tour to get a permit, but this is rarely enforced. The permit is valid for seven days and is normally issued the same day on production of three passport photos and photocopies of the identity pages and Indian visa from your passport. In theory, permits are also available from the SDM in Rampur and the divisional magistrate in Shimla. If you come here on a tour, the travel agent will usually arrange the permit for you.

Despite what may be written on the permit, you can stay in any village and camp anywhere along the main road between Rekong Peo and Kaza; you can travel on any form of public or private transport, and you can travel alone or in a group of any size. The form states you 'shall not resort to photography' but you should be fine as long as you avoid military areas or bridges. It also states that you cannot carry any 'maps' – you are allowed to do this, but most maps aren't very good anyway.

Coming from Lahaul and Spiti, permits are best obtained from the SDM office in Kaza (☎ 01906-22302), though the magistrates' offices in Manali, Kullu and Keylong may also be willing to fill in the paperwork. The rule about groups of four is much more likely to be enforced at these offices. At the time of writing there were rumours of a US$30 fee being introduced for this permit.

REKONG PEO

☎ 01786 • elevation 2290m

The modern settlement of Rekong Peo is an important transport and administrative hub and has good views of Kinnaur Kailash, but it lacks the charm of nearby Kalpa. You'll need to come here to apply for an inner line permit if you're heading north to Spiti; the SDM office (☎ 22252) is in the administrative complex at the bottom of town (look for the red roof). Across the road are several places to make photocopies of permits and passports, and stock up on some necessities (mineral water is hard to find outside of Rekong Peo). There is nowhere to change money in Rekong Peo.

A lovely, brightly coloured *gompa* (Tibetan Buddhist monastery), the **Kinnaur Kalachakra Celestial Palace**, or Mahabodhi Gompa, is a 20-minute steep walk above the village, just behind the radio station.

Places to Stay & Eat

Most places to stay are grouped around the intersection of the road to Kalpa and the pedestrian main bazaar, which also provides a handy shortcut to the bus stand at the top of the hill.

Fairyland Guest House *(☎ 22477)*, 200m from the bus stop, has a restaurant and decent rooms with hot water from Rs 200.

Shivling View Hotel & Restaurant *(☎ 22421)* is a short walk downhill from the bus stand. Pleasant doubles with hot water cost Rs 300 to 500.

In the centre of town, ***Hotel Snow View*** *(☎ 22048)* has Rs 220 doubles with private bathroom and an OK restaurant. Similar rooms at similar prices can be found at ***Hotel Rangin*** *(☎ 22246)* in the main bazaar and ***Shambhala Hotel*** *(☎ 22852)*, a 10-minute walk uphill from the bus station.

Manish Bhojnayla restaurant, in the centre of town, serves excellent Tibetan *thugpa* (Tibetan noodle soup) and *momos* (dumplings). ***Vijay Bhojnayla*** next door is good for Indian food.

Getting There & Away

Most arriving buses let passengers off in the centre of town but officially depart from the new bus station, a five-minute walk uphill from the centre (follow the bazaar opposite Hotel Snow View and bear right at the police station – it's farther along the highway). Most buses are through buses, so departure times and seat bookings are a little unpredictable.

There are buses uphill to Kalpa (via Pangi) at 7.30 and 9 am and 1, 3.30 and 5 pm, for Rs 5. The last trip downhill is at 6 pm. Taxis to Kalpa charge a steep Rs 250 one way.

There are daily buses to Kaza (Rs 120, 12 hours) at 7.30 am, returning from Kaza at the same time. To Sangla, you'll have to take a jeep downhill and walk back to Karcham, where there are several buses daily to Sangla village and Chitkul (unless the road has been repaired, in which case there may be direct buses). Buses to Shimla (Rs 45) leave from Karcham every hour or so, or there numerous public and private buses to Rampur.

KALPA

☎ 01786

This spectacular mountain village is the legendary winter home of Shiva, who is said to retire here each winter for some hashish-inspired meditation. Known as Chini back in the days when it was the regional capital, Kalpa has changed little in the last 500 years, and is a far nicer place to stay than Rekong Peo.

The views across to Kinnaur Kailash are some of the most spectacular in the Himalaya. You can get a full panorama from behind the *chorten* (Tibetan pagoda) at the top of the hill. Also interesting is the **Narayan-Nagini** temple complex, which includes shrines to Hindu, Buddhist and local deities. In September, villagers offer wildflowers here as part of the colourful **Phulech festival**.

Places to Stay & Eat

In the centre of town is the modern and bland ***Hotel Blue Lotus*** *(☎ 26001)*, with expensive rooms for Rs 500 upwards, and a decent restaurant. On the road above the village, ***HPTDC Kinner Kailash Cottage*** *(☎ 26159)* was being redeveloped at the time of writing, but should be open by the time you read this.

Across the road is the modern but friendly ***Shivalik Guest House*** *(☎ 26158)*, which has good doubles with hot shower for Rs 300 to 500 (Rs 200 in winter).

A five-minute walk north-east along the same road will bring you to the homey ***Auktong Guest House*** *(☎ 26019)*, set in a pleasant apple orchard overlooking the valley. The simple but comfortable rooms have lovely views across to the mountains and cost Rs 100 with shared bathroom.

Timberline Trekking Camps, on the outskirts of the village, offers luxury tents (with hot water) in a pleasant location for Rs 1250 a double. The whole place packs up and goes back to Delhi from October to May (☎ 011-6984049 for details).

Getting There & Away

There are somewhat unreliable buses from Kalpa to Rekong Peo (Rs 5, one hour), at 8.30 and 10 am and 2, 4.30 and 6 pm. Most buses continue on from Rekong Peo to other destinations farther south. Taxis to Rekong Peo cost a steep Rs 250/400 one way/return.

It's a pleasant 45-minute walk downhill from Kalpa to Rekong Peo – follow the short cuts rather than the winding road.

SANGLA VALLEY

The Sangla, or Baspa, Valley has been called 'the most beautiful valley in the Himalaya' and for once this is more than just marketing jargon. Strung along the valley floor are a number of ancient villages with traditional stone and timber architecture, friendly people and magnificent mountain scenery on all sides. The mouth of the valley is marred somewhat by the construction of yet another hydroelectric plant, but it soon vanishes out of sight as you climb up the gorge.

The Sangla Valley is best visited in spring (April to May) or autumn (September to early November). In the summer the monsoon makes for long damp days, and roads are regularly blocked by snow in winter. The road into the valley must be one of the most hair-raising in the Himalaya.

Sangla

☎ 01786 • elevation 2680m

This wonderful village is the largest in the valley. Traditional slate-roofed houses are seemingly stacked on top of each other and there are awe-inspiring views of Kinnaur Kailash (6050m). The town has several ancient Hindu and Buddhist temples, including the **Bering Nag Temple**, which forms the centrepiece of the annual September **Phulech flower festival**.

It's a short walk through orchards to nearby Kamru, with its old fort – follow the road behind the Department of Public Works.

Places to Stay & Eat A short walk down the highway from the bus stand, ***Baspa Guesthouse*** *(☎ 42206)* has rooms going for Rs 165, or Rs 275 with private bathroom.

Farther downhill and up a road to the right is ***Mount Kailash Guest House*** *(☎ 42527)*, with good doubles with private bathroom upstairs for Rs 380 (Rs 300 downstairs), and a dorm for Rs 75 per person.

On the next corner is ***Highland Guest House*** *(☎ 42285)* with basic rooms going for Rs 150 to 200.

In the summer ***Banjara Camps*** offers accommodation in luxury tents on the far side of the river at Batseri. Call the Delhi office for more details (☎ 011-6855153). The lovely old ***Forest Rest House*** nearby must be reserved with the District Forest Officer *(☎ 01786-22252, 25207)* in Kalpa.

Monal Reception restaurant in the centre of town is a good place for Indian and Chinese food, and breakfast.

Getting There & Away There are buses uphill to Chitkul at noon and 4 pm (Rs 15), but both return at 6 am the next morning. For a day trip, you'll have to take one of the infrequent share-jeeps (Rs 50) or a taxi (Rs 600 return). Buses head downhill to Rampur (Rs 12) at 7, 8 and 10 am and 3 pm. If the road is repaired there may also be buses to Rekong Peo. Share-jeeps run down to Karcham at the mouth of the valley, where you can pick up frequent buses to Shimla and Rampur.

Around Sangla

Clinging to a narrow rocky spur 2km above Sangla, the village of **Kamru** was the former capital of the Bushahr empire which once ruled Kinnaur. Kamru is dominated by the fort-like **Kamakhya Devi Temple**, which can be visited from 8 to 9 am and 7 to 8 pm only (a hat is required and shoes must be removed). There are several wooden Buddhist and Hindu temples just downhill.

A sealed road runs through apple orchards from Sangla to a stone gateway, from where it's a steep climb to the village proper. By the gate is a cairn of carved *mani* stones (stones carved with the Tibetan Buddhist mantra 'Om mani padme hum' or 'Hail to the jewel in the lotus') and a Buddha image said to prevent people smuggling in ghosts and other evil spirits.

High above Sangla are the remote villages of **Rakcham** (3050mm), 14km from Sangla, and **Chitkul** (3450m), which have stunning views and traditional architecture.

REKONG PEO TO TABO

Inner line permits are required for this section of the road from Kinnaur to Spiti. The only private accommodation between Rekong Peo and Tabo is in the village of **Nako**, 7km uphill from Yangthang (share-jeeps cost Rs 40). This remote village has a beautiful setting around a lovely small lake. There is an 11th-century **gompa** here, with four temples, and you can hike from here to the peak of Leo Purgyal and the ancient gompas at Tashigang (five hours) and Somang (seven hours).

The yellow ***guesthouse*** by the bus stop is one of several places offering rooms for around Rs 100 (ask for directions). It's an easy downhill walk.

Other sights include small **gompas** at Khanum, near Spillo, and at Morang.

Kangra Valley

The beautiful Kangra Valley starts near Mandi, runs north, then bends west and extends to Shahpur near Pathankot. To the north the valley is flanked by the Dhaula Dhar Range, to the side of which clings Dharamsala. There are a number of places of interest along the valley, including McLeod Ganj, home of the Dalai Lama and headquarters of the Tibetan Government in Exile.

The main Pathankot to Mandi road runs through the valley, and there is a narrow-gauge railway line from Pathankot as far as Jogindarnagar. The Kangra school of painting developed in this valley.

DHARAMSALA

☎ 01892 • pop 19,200

While Dharamsala is synonymous with the Tibetan Government in Exile, the actual headquarters is about 4km above Dharamsala at Gangchen Kyishong, and most travellers hang out at McLeod Ganj, strung along a high ridge 10km above Dharamsala.

Dharamsala itself is of little interest to travellers, although Kotwali Bazaar, at the foot of the roads leading up to McLeod Ganj, is an interesting and colourful market, and you can visit the Kangra Art Museum.

Information

HPTDC's tourist office (☎ 24212) is friendly and provides better than average information as it doesn't offer its own tours. The office is open 10 am to 5 pm Monday to Saturday.

The computerised branch of State Bank of India accepts most travellers cheques in US dollars and pounds sterling, and cash; Punjab National Bank just accepts travellers cheques. Bank of Baroda, nearby, can give cash advances on Visa cards within 24 hours (you can call ahead to reserve on ☎ 23175 and pick up your money the next day).

The Divisional Forest Office (☎ 24887) opposite the post office is the place to book Forest Rest Houses on the trekking routes above McLeod Ganj.

Kangra Art Museum

This museum, a few minutes' walk south of the tourist office, has miniature paintings from the Kangra school of art, which flourished in the Kangra Valley during the 17th century, it also has elaborately embroidered costumes of Kangra people, woodcarvings and tribal jewellery. It's open 10 am to 5 pm Tuesday to Sunday. Entry is free.

Places to Stay & Eat

Sood Guest House *(☎ 24269)* on Cantt Rd, Kotwali Bazaar, has OK rooms with private bathroom that can function as singles/doubles/triples for Rs 75/100/125.

B Mehra Hotel *(☎ 23582)*, a few doors up on the opposite side of the road, has

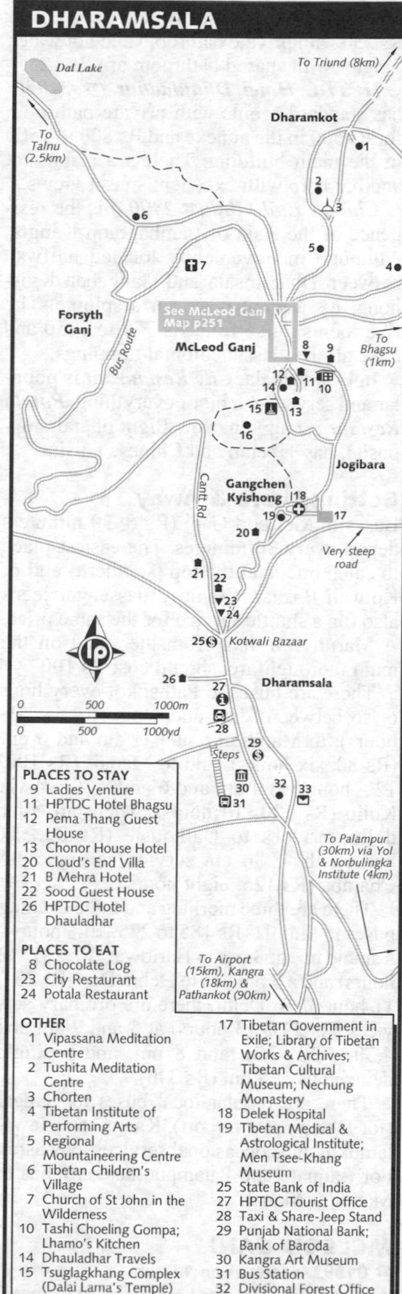

scruffy doubles (with brilliant views!) for Rs 250 with private bathroom and hot water. Singles with shared bathroom are Rs 125.

HPTDC Hotel Dhauladhar *(☎ 24926)* has standard rooms with private bathroom for Rs 500 in the annexe and Rs 800 to 1500 in the main building. There's a restaurant and bar here with excellent sunset views.

Cloud's End Villa *(☎ 24904)* is the residence of the Raja of Lambagraon-Kangra. Although inconveniently located halfway between Dharamsala and Gangchen Kyishong, it's a great place for a splurge. The five rooms range from Rs 770 to 1250 and have all the classic colonial trappings.

In Dharamsala, ***City Restaurant*** is popular and serves up a bit of everything. ***Potala Restaurant***, up a narrow flight of stairs opposite, has Tibetan and Chinese cuisine.

Getting There & Away

Buses to McLeod Ganj (Rs 6, 30 minutes) depart every 30 minutes. The easiest place to catch one is at the top (southern) end of Kotwali Bazaar. Cramped passenger jeeps also run a shuttle service for the same price. A Maruti van taxi, from the stand on the main thoroughfare, should cost Rs 100.

There are buses to Pathankot every hour or so between 5 am and 5 pm (Rs 55, 3½ hours); to Mandi at 5 and 11 am and 6 pm (Rs 80, six hours); and to Manali (Rs 190, 12½ hours) at 4 am and 6 and 8.30 pm via Kullu (Rs 120, 10 hours). There are four daily services to Dalhousie (Rs 85, six hours); the 8.30 am service continues to Chamba (Rs 125, eight hours).

There are three morning and three evening buses to Shimla (Rs 185 to 225, 10½ hours), a single bus at 3 pm to Haridwar (Rs 237, 12 hours) and a 9 pm bus to Dehra Dun (Rs 231, 11 hours). To Delhi, there are ordinary services (Rs 237, 13 hours) at 5 and 7 am and 4.30, 5.30, 7.30 and 8 pm, and a single deluxe bus at 8 pm (Rs 340).

There are regular local buses to Gaggal (for Dharamsala airport), Kangra and Jawalamukhi, plus occasional services to Masrur. For Baijnath and Palampur, take any bus to Mandi or Manali.

MCLEOD GANJ

☎ 01892 • elevation 1770m

About 4km by foot above Dharamsala (10km by road), McLeod Ganj is the headquarters of the Tibetan Government in Exile and the home of His Holiness the 14th Dalai Lama, as well as being the main traveller hang-out in the Kangra Valley. Here you'll find friendly Tibetan monks, budget hotels, trekking companies, Western food, video movies and wall to wall shops selling Tibetan souvenirs.

The town was established in the mid-1850s as a British garrison and became an important administrative centre for the Kangra region until a disastrous earthquake in 1905 forced the British to move down into the valley. Things were fairly quiet until 1960 when the Dalai Lama and his entourage claimed asylum here following the Chinese invasion of Tibet (see the boxed text 'Exiles').

The curious name comes from the Lieutenant Governor of Punjab, David McLeod and the Hindi word for market *(ganj)*. Before the arrival of the British, Upper Dharamsala was home to the seminomadic Gaddi people and there is still a sizable Gaddi population in the surrounding villages.

Orientation

The heart of McLeod Ganj is the bus stand. From here roads radiate to various points around the township, including the main road back down to Dharamsala, which passes en route the Church of St John in the Wilderness and the cantonment area of Forsyth Ganj. Other roads lead to the villages of Dharamkot and Bhagsu.

To the south, Temple Rd proceeds to the Tsuglagkhang Temple, about 800m to the south. From there it's possible to take a short cut down to the administrative area of Gangchen Kyishong, where you'll find the Library of Tibetan Works & Archives. The other road through the bazaar, Jogibara Rd, also winds its way down to Gangchen Kyishong via the village of Jogibara.

Information

Tourist Offices The new HPTDC office, opposite Bookworm, is open 10 am to 1.30 pm and 2 to 5 pm daily, and sells maps and guides to the area, as well as providing train information.

Money Punjab National Bank on Temple Road can change US dollars and pounds sterling travellers cheques but not cash. Fortunately most travel agencies in Dharamsala

Exiles

In May 1949, the newly established communist government of China signed a treaty extending Chinese sovereignty to Tibet, based on the premise that both nations were once part of the Mongol empire. The Chinese People's Army marched into Lhasa the same year, beginning a brutal regime which has left some 1.2 million Tibetans dead and countless others imprisoned in forced labour camps.

Since 1949, some 90% of the nation's religious institutions have been destroyed in the name of the Cultural Revolution. Fearing for his life and the lives of his people, the spiritual leader of Tibet, His Holiness the 14th Dalai Lama, Tenzin Gyatso made the difficult decision to lead his people into exile in 1959.

Accompanied by a small entourage, the Dalai Lama arrived in India, on foot, after trekking for weeks across the Himalaya. Since then, some 292,000 Tibetans have followed in his footsteps, settling in Dharamsala, Darjeeling and other mountain communities. The exiled Tibetan government was granted political asylum in Gangchen Kyishong below McLeod Ganj, which has become the headquarters for a 40-year struggle for liberation. Tenzin Gytaso was awarded the Nobel Peace Prize in 1989 for his efforts to find a peaceful solution for the liberation of Tibet.

China has continued to resist all attempts at dialogue over the Tibet issue. With Western nations relaxing their restrictions on China, many now fear for the future of the Free Tibet Movement. The Tibet Museum at Namgyal Gompa in the Tsuglagkhang Complex has extensive displays telling the tragic story of the Chinese occupation.

The Dalai Lama, Tibet's spiritual leader, lives in exile in India.

can change both cash and travellers cheques. Summit Adventures is reliable and displays a noticeboard with the daily exchange rates. Several places offer Western Union money transfers; try Paul Merchants Ltd in the arcade opposite the bus stand.

Post The post office is on Jogibara Rd, just past State Bank of India. To post parcels you need to complete a customs form (in triplicate!), which you can get for Rs 3 at the Office of Tibetan Handicrafts north of State Bank of India. Several places offer a parcel packing service, including a couple on Jogibara Rd. Letters sent 'c/o poste restante, GPO McLeod Ganj' are held for one month.

Telephone & Fax The telecom office (fax 21528) is up a flight of stairs behind the bus stand and charges government rates for faxes and calls. Most hotels charge around Rs 3 per minute to receive incoming international calls.

Email & Internet Access McLeod Ganj has the best Internet facilities in the Himalaya with fast connections and reasonable prices (Rs 60 per hour is the going rate). Probably the most popular place is the Green Cyber Cafe at the Green Hotel, which has loads of PCs and funky mandala screen savers. The nearby Himalaya Bamboo Hut Cafe, and Aroma Cybercafe on Jogibara Rd, also charge Rs 60 per hour.

Travel Agencies There are numerous travel agencies in McLeod Ganj that can book air, train and bus tickets, as well as arrange tours. The following travel agencies are reliable:

Himachal Travels (☎ 21428, fax 21528, ⓔ himachaltravels@vsnl.com) Jogibara Rd
Potala Tours & Travels (☎ 21378, fax 21427, ⓔ potaa@vsnl.net.in) Bhagsu Rd
Summit Adventures (☎ 21679, fax 21681, ⓔ summit65@yahoo.com) Jogibara Rd
Tibet Tours & Travels (☎ 21966, fax 21528) Temple Rd

Trekking Companies Close to the taxi stand on Mall Rd, Eagle Height Trekkers (in the Occidental Bookshop; ☎ 21330) can

HIMACHAL PRADESH

organise trekking for US$40 per day including porters and guides. It's possible to trek from here to the Kullu, Chamba, Lahaul and Spiti Valleys and Ladakh.

Yeti Trekking (☎ 21060) also arranges tailor-made treks to most areas, with accommodation en route in huts and houses. They can be found in a fine old building, reached through a gate off the Dharamkot road. Rates start at around Rs 800 per day.

A steep 15-minute walk above McLeod on the road to Dharamkot, is the Regional Mountaineering Centre (☎ 21787). You can get advice here on treks and mountaineering in the Chamba and Kangra Valleys, and there's a useful list of registered local guides and porters. It's a good idea to advise the centre if you are planning an independent trek.

Bookshops McLeod has numerous bookshops specialising in Buddhist literature, usually with an excellent range of novels thrown in. The Diir Bookshop on Jogibara Rd is run by the Tibetan Government in Exile and has an excellent range of books on Tibetan history and Buddhism. The nearby Charitable Trust Bookshop also has an excellent selection.

For novels, try Bookworm, opposite the tourist information centre. Youtse Bookshop, on Temple Rd, and Hills Bookshop, on Bhagsu Rd, are also worth a look.

Tibetan Organisations McLeod Ganj has numerous offices and organisations concerned with Tibetan affairs and the welfare of the refugee community. These include the Tibetan Welfare Office, the Refugee Reception Centre (part of the government compound at Gangchen Kyishong), Tibetan Youth Congress, Tibetan Children's Village (TCV) and the Tibetan Women's Association. Interested visitors are welcome at all of these.

All offices and institutions are open 9 am to 5 pm (closed for lunch 1 to 2 pm in summer and noon to 1 pm in winter) weekdays; all are closed on Tibetan holidays and three Indian national holidays (26 January, 15 August and 2 October).

Tibetan Publications *Contact* is a free local magazine with a useful 'what's on' listing, plus information on local courses and volunteer work. Other journals published in McLeod include the *Tibetan Bulletin* and *Rangzen* (Freedom), published by the Tibetan Youth Congress.

Laundry The two best laundries in McLeod are Premier (at Hotel Tibet) and the slightly cheaper RK Laundry down the road. Expect to pay Rs 10 to 20 for each pair of trousers, shirt or T-shirt. Same-day service may be available if you can drop off before 10 am.

Medical Services The Delek Hospital (☎ 22053) in Gangchen Kyishong is a charitable hospital for refugees that has open consultation sessions on weekday mornings. The official charge is Rs 5, but any donation you make over this will go towards the treatment of refugees.

In McLeod Ganj, try the Civil Dispensary on Jogibara Rd.

Alternative Therapies For traditional Tibetan medicine, try Dr Yeshi Dhonden's clinic or the Dr Lobsang Dolma Khangsar Clinic, both near the Office of Tibetan Handicrafts. Consultation is free and herbal cures are used to treat the disharmony between body and mind believed to cause illness.

Various other alternative treatments are available, including massage, reflexology and Reiki but several women travellers have been molested by so-called 'therapists' – check your practitioner's reputation before agreeing to a solo session. Practitioners advertise in *Contact* magazine, or on the noticeboards in guesthouses and restaurants.

Tsuglagkhang Complex

This complex, a five-minute walk south of McLeod Ganj, comprises the official residence of the Dalai Lama, as well as the Namgyal Gompa, bookshop and cafe and the Tsuglagkhang itself.

The **Tsuglagkhang**, or Central Chapel, is the exiled government's equivalent of the Jokhang Temple in Lhasa and as such is the most important Buddhist monument in McLeod Ganj. Although a relatively modest structure, it enshrines three magnificent images, including an enormous 3m-high gilt statue of Sakyamuni Buddha. To the left of this (and facing Tibet) are statues of Avalokitesvara (Tibetan: Chenrezig), the Tibetan deity of compassion, of whom the Dalai Lama is considered an incarnation, and Padmasambhava (Tibetan: Guru Rinpoche), the

MCLEOD GANJ

PLACES TO STAY
3 Loling Guest House
4 Kalsang Guest House
5 Tashi Khansar Guest House
6 Green Hotel
13 Hotel India House
15 Hotel Tibet; Take Out Bakery; Premier Laundry
27 Shangrila Guest House; Snow Lion Guest House
30 Om Guest House
32 Drepung Loseling Guest House; Sangye's Kitchen
33 Tibetan Ashoka Guest House
50 Surya Resorts
51 Hotel Him Queen

PLACES TO EAT
7 Himalaya Bamboo Hut Cafe
8 Nick's Italian Kitchen
22 McLlo Restaurant
23 Friend's Corner
25 Malabar Cafe
34 Snowland Restaurant; Civil Dispensary
36 Gakyi Restaurant

OTHER
1 Private Bus Stand
2 Yeti Trekking
9 RK Laundry
10 Tibetan Youth Congress
11 Hills Bookshop
12 Tibetan Welfare Office
14 Potala Tours & Travels
16 Eagle Height Trekkers; Occidental Bookshop
17 Paul Merchants Ltd
18 Telecom Office
19 Taxi Stand
20 Nowrojee & Son Store
21 Bus Stand
24 Punjab National Bank
26 Video Hall
28 Diir Bookshop; Tibetan Information Centre
29 Chorten & Prayer Wheels
31 Charitable Trust Bookshop
35 Himachal Travels
37 Video Hall
38 Office of Tibetan Handicrafts
39 Aroma Cybercafe
40 Tibetan Handicrafts Cooperative; Ashoka Restaurant
41 Dr Yeshi Dhonden's Clinic
42 Summit Adventures
43 State Bank of India
44 Dr Lobsang Dolma Khangsar Clinic
45 Bookworm
46 HPTDC Tourist Office
47 Post Office
48 Tibet Tours & Travels
49 Youtse Bookshop

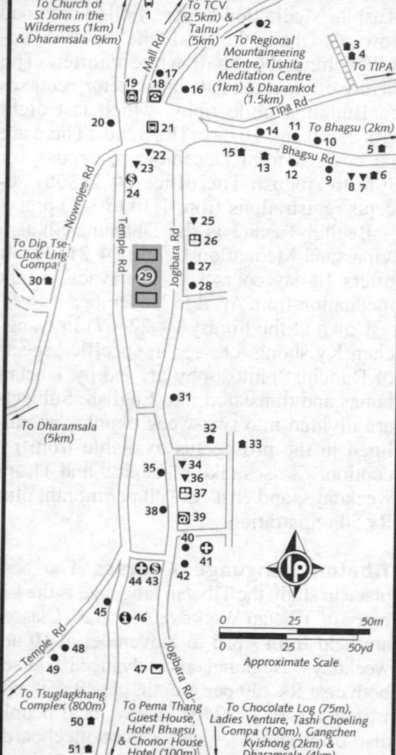

Indian scholar who introduced Buddhism to Tibet in the 8th century. Inside the Avalokitesvara statue are several relics rescued from the Jokhang Temple during the Cultural Revolution.

Next to the Tsuglagkhang is the **Kalachakra Temple**, built in 1992, which houses a stunning mural of the Kalachakra (Wheel of Time) mandala (circle symbolising the universe). Sand mandalas are created here annually on the 5th day of the third Tibetan month. Photography is allowed in the Tsuglagkhang, but not the Kalachakra Temple.

The remaining buildings form the **Namgyal Gompa**, where it is possible to watch monks debate most afternoons, sealing points of debate with a great flourish and a clap of the hands. The bookshop at the monastery has a good selection of Buddhist texts. Nearby is the excellent **Tibet Museum**, open 10 am to 6 pm daily, except Monday, which uses photos and video clips to tell the tragic story of the Tibetan struggle (Rs 5 entry).

Most Tibetan pilgrims make a *kora* (ritual circuit) of the Tsuglagkhang complex. Take the road to the left, past the entrance to the temple, and after a few minutes a small path leads off to the right, eventually looping all the way around the Dalai Lama's residence back to the entrance to the temple. The kora should be made in a clockwise direction only.

It may be possible to meet the Dalai Lama (albeit briefly) at one of the occasional public audiences held in Dharamsala. Contact the Office of His Holiness the Dalai Lama (☎ 01892-21343) for details. Requests for private audiences should be made in writing four months in advance to: the Office of His Holiness the Dalai Lama, Thekchen Choeling, PO McLeod Ganj, Dharamsala 176219, India.

Dip Tse-Chok Ling Gompa

This beautiful little gompa is at the bottom of a steep track, which leads off the lane past Om Guest House. The main *dukhang* (prayer hall) houses an image of Sakyamuni, and two enormous goat-skin drums made by monks at the gompa. Also here are some superb butter sculptures, made during Losar and destroyed the following year. Fine and detailed sand mandalas are also made here.

Tibetan Institute of Performing Arts (TIPA)

This institute promotes the study and performance of the Tibetan performing arts to ensure the preservation of Tibet's traditional cultural heritage. The most important of the arts taught and practised at the institute is traditional *lhamo* (Tibetan opera), which can be seen at the annual festivals organised by TIPA (see Special Events later).

Library of Tibetan Works & Archives

Many of Tibet's ancient texts were destroyed when the Cultural Revolution came to Tibet, but what was saved (representing some 40% of the nation's sacred literature) was brought here. The library is housed in the government compound at Gangchen Kyishong and includes translations of many Buddhist texts into English and other European languages.

To access the collection you must become a temporary member (Rs 15 per month; bring your passport as ID when you apply). The library is open 9 am to 5.30 pm weekdays only (5 pm in winter).

There's also a **Tibetan Cultural Museum** on the 1st floor, with some excellent exhibits including fine statues, rare Tibetan stamps and a medal from the Younghusband mission to Lhasa. Entry costs Rs 10.

Also worth a visit near the library complex is the **Nechung Monastery**, home to the Tibetan state oracle. Taxis run up to McLeod Ganj for Rs 50.

Tibetan Medical & Astrological Institute

This institute is at Gangchen Kyishong, about a five-minute walk below the main entrance to the library area. There's a museum, library, research unit and a college at which Tibetan medicine and astrology is taught. It's possible to have a life horoscope prepared for US$30.

Also here is the fascinating **Men Tsee-Khang Museum** devoted to traditional Tibetan medicine. The well-labelled exhibits cover all manner of plants and minerals used in Tibetan medicine, including such oddities as the mysterious 'Great Precious Hot Compound'. The museum is open from 9 am to 1 pm and from 2 to 5 pm daily (Rs 5 entry).

Walks

Interesting short walks around McLeod include the 2km stroll east to **Bhagsu**, where there is a temple and waterfall, and the 3km walk north-east to the little village of **Dharamkot**, where there are fine views. From Dharamkot, you can continue east down to Bhagsu and walk back to McLeod along the main Bhagsu road.

An interesting longer trek from McLeod is the 8km to **Triund** (2827m), a flat green area at the foot of the Dhaula Dhar with magnificent views. The path veers off to the right across scree just beyond Dharamkot. From Triund it's another 5km to the snow line at **Ilaqa** where there's a ***forest rest house***. In summer, it's possible to trek from Ilaqa all the way to Bharmour in the Chamba Valley over the Indrahar Pass (4300m).

Courses

Buddhist Philosophy Courses About a 20-minute walk above McLeod is the Tushita Meditation Centre. Follow the road towards Dharamkot and take the steps uphill behind the small white chorten. The centre offers fixed date introductory courses in Buddhist philosophy, which last eight (Rs 2560) and 10 days (Rs 3200). There are no courses from December to January or July to August. The office (☎ 21866) accepts registrations from 1.30 to 3.30 pm.

Behind Tushita is the Dhamma Sikhara Vipassana Meditation Centre (☎ 21309). It offers 10-day courses in Theravada insight meditation from April to November.

Down at the library (☎ 22467) in Gangchen Kyishong, classes in specific aspects of Buddhist philosophy are led by Tibetan lamas and translated into English. Subjects are divided into two-week chunks, as outlined in the prospectus available from reception. Classes take place at 9 and 11 am weekdays, and cost Rs 100 per month, plus Rs 50 registration.

Tibetan Language Courses The best place to study the Tibetan language is the Library of Tibetan Works & Archives. Classes are held from April to November at 10 am weekdays. Beginner and advanced courses both cost Rs 200 per month, plus Rs 50 registration. Call ☎ 22467. Many local people also offer lessons – check the noticeboards in town or *Contact* magazine for details.

Tibetan Cooking Courses Several refugees have started up Tibetan cooking courses. Options include Sangye's Kitchen near Drepung Loesling Guest House and Lhamo's Kitchen at the Tashi Choeling Gompa on Jogibara Rd. Classes for both courses run three times a week at 11 am and 5 pm and cost Rs 100 per day.

Volunteer Work

If you're interested in teaching English or computer skills to newly arrived refugees, check notice boards at the Library of Tibetan Works & Archives, as well as looking in *Contact* magazine, or offer your services in person at any of the Tibetan organisations listed under Information, earlier.

Special Events

From 27 March to 4 April, TIPA runs an **opera festival**, which includes folk dancing and performances of traditional folk operas (lhamo). There is also a three-day **TIPA Anniversary Festival** from 27 May, celebrating the foundation of TIPA.

Losar (Tibetan New Year, February/March) is a great time to be in McLeod Ganj, when the Dalai Lama gives week-long teachings. From 10 to 12 December, McLeod Ganj is home to the **International Himalayan Festival**, featuring cultural events from all the Himalayan nations.

Another great time to be in McLeod Ganj is 6 July, when Buddhists celebrate the Dalai Lama's birthday.

Organised Tours

The following fixed-rate taxi tours to points of interest around McLeod Ganj and in the Kangra Valley have been devised:

- Bhagsunath Temple, Tsuglagkhang, Dal Lake, St John's Church & Talnu (Rs 300, three hours)
- Norbulingka, Chinmaya ashram at Tapovan, Chamunda Devi, Kangra & Jawalamukhi temple (Rs 1600, eight hours)
- Norbulingka, Tapovan, Chamunda Devi, Palampur & Baijnath (Rs 1000, eight hours)

Places to Stay – Budget

There are dozens of budget options in McLeod Ganj but accommodation can be tight during Losar (Tibetan New Year, in February/March), the Dalai Lama's birthday (6 July) and other Tibetan festivals.

Kalsang Guest House (☎ *21709*) is the first of several places up some steep steps above the TIPA road. It's cheap and deservedly popular, with tiny singles with shared bathroom for Rs 50 and doubles with private bathroom for Rs 150 to 275 (the more-expensive rooms have great views).

Farther up the same set of stairs ***Loling Guest House*** (☎ *21072*) is run by the Drepung Gompa and offers clean singles/doubles for Rs 50/75 with shared bathroom and Rs 150 with private bathroom.

Green Hotel (☎ *21200*), on Bhagsu Rd, is a long-time favourite with travellers. Small spartan rooms with shared bathroom cost Rs 80, or Rs 175/250 with private bathroom and cold/hot water. Some rooms have great valley views, and there's a good restaurant here.

Tashi Khansar Guest House, opposite Green Hotel, has basic singles with shared bathroom for Rs 70, and doubles with private hot shower for Rs 165, some with excellent views.

Om Guest House (☎ *24313*), on a path leading down from the bus stand, is a very good choice. Pleasant rooms with shared bathroom cost Rs 160/180 a single/double and nicer upper floor rooms with private bathroom cost Rs 225 or Rs 250. The views from the restaurant terrace are marvellous.

Shangrila Guest House (☎ *21661*), on the other side of the chorten, has doubles with shared bathroom (bucket hot water) for Rs 70.

Snow Lion Guest House (☎ *21289*), next door, is friendly and has clean and well-maintained rooms with private bathroom and hot water for Rs 175, or Rs 200 with private balcony and good views.

Drepung Loseling Guest House (☎ *23187*), down an alley off Jogibara Rd, is popular with volunteers. Singles with shared bathroom cost Rs 75, while doubles with private bathroom range from Rs 125 to 200.

Tibetan Ashoka Guest House (☎ *21763*), opposite, is similar but plainer, with doubles with shared bathroom for Rs 90, and brighter rooms with private bathroom for Rs 275 and Rs 330.

Ladies Venture (☎ *21559*), opposite the Geden Choeling nunnery down Jogibara Rd, is a very quiet and friendly place. Singles/doubles with private bathroom are Rs 100/250 or big doubles cost Rs 150 with shared bathroom. Popular dorms cost Rs 40.

Places to Stay – Mid-Range & Top End

Hotel Tibet (*☎ 21587, fax 21327*), a few steps from the bus stand on Bhagsu Rd, has standard doubles for Rs 500, semideluxe doubles for Rs 600, and deluxe rooms for Rs 900. All rooms are carpeted and have cable TV and private bathroom. There's a very good restaurant and bar here.

Hotel India House (*☎ 21144*), nearby, is bright, comfortable and a good option, though it lacks the Tibetan touch. Rooms cost Rs 600/800 a single/double (Rs 1100/1500 for deluxe rooms) and most have a balcony with excellent views.

There are a few other large Indian-run hotels on the road past the tourist office but the service in some of these places leaves a little to be desired. Better places include ***Surya Resorts*** (*☎ 21418*), which has smart rooms from Rs 1400 to 2200, and ***Hotel Him Queen*** (*☎ 21861*) with good doubles from Rs 750 to 1600.

Farther along is the pleasant ***Pema Thang Guest House*** (*☎ 21871*), which has tasteful rooms with wooden trim for Rs 600 downstairs and Rs 700 upstairs.

Opposite is ***HPTDC Hotel Bhagsu*** (*☎ 21091*), which has good doubles from Rs 700 to 1500 (half this in low season).

The most stylish place to stay in McLeod Ganj is the splendid ***Chonor House Hotel*** (*☎ 21006, fax 21468*), which is owned by the Norbulingka Institute. Doubles range from Rs 1900 to 2800 (with Rs 300 discount for singles) and are beautifully decorated with traditional Tibetan artefacts. There's also a good Tibetan restaurant and bakery here. Bookings are recommended.

Places to Eat

Green Hotel has a very popular restaurant, with a range of excellent home-made cakes, as well as vegetarian dishes like spinach quiche. Most meals cost around Rs 50. It's also a good place for breakfast.

The nearby ***Himalayan Bamboo Hut Cafe*** also has good food and a wonderful rooftop balcony with views over the plains, though the service is very slow.

Nick's Italian Kitchen, nearby, is renowned for it's vegetarian Italian food, including excellent home-made spinach and cheese ravioli. Meals cost around Rs 40 to 50 and there are also great cakes and coffee.

Hotel Tibet has probably the best restaurant in town and features Tibetan, Chines and Indian cuisine. There's also a convivia bar here. Prices reflect the classier surroundings. The attached ***Take Out Baker*** serves up great cakes and bread.

McLlo Restaurant, right above the bu stand, has an extensive menu, good foo and a bar, though it's a little overpricec Dishes like chilli chicken cost around R 90. The kitchen is open until 10.30 pm.

Friend's Corner, nearby, serves excellent Chinese food and prices are reasonab for the large portions.

Malabar Cafe, north of the chorten, is pleasant little place serving good India Chinese and continental cuisine.

Also on Jogibara Rd are ***Gakyi Restaura*** and ***Snowland Restaurant***, which both serv cheap and tasty vegetarian Tibetan food.

For nonveg Tibetan food, you can't be ***Snow Lion Restaurant*** at the guesthouse c same name. Their mutton momos a strongly recommended and they also serv real coffee.

Ashoka Restaurant, on Jogibara Rd, ha the best Indian food in town. The tandoo chicken (Rs 70 for a half portion) ar chicken Mughlai (Rs 100) are excellent ar there are also continental dishes such pizza and spaghetti.

Another popular place is the restaurant ***Om Guest House***. The vegie burger here served with salad, a banana and chips, ar is quite good. There's also a good soun system, plus spectacular sunset views.

The restaurant at ***Hotel Bhagsu*** is prici but has very good food and cold beers. C sunny days, tables are set up in the garder and you can eat outside.

Pema Thang Guest House has a ni restaurant – the Sunday vegetarian buff lunch is good value.

Chocolate Log, a few minutes' wa down past the post office on Jogibara Rd, an old favourite serving various types cakes and snacks on its sunny veran (closed Tuesday).

Entertainment

There are several ***video halls*** in the tov centre on Jogibara Rd. They show new leases and documentaries on Tibet all d and evening, with the program posted c the front. Tickets are Rs 10.

At the end of an evening most visitors end up in the bar at ***McLlo Restaurant***.

Shopping

Tibetan textiles such as bags, *chubas* (dresses worn by Tibetan women), hats and trousers can be found at the Office of Tibetan Handicrafts, just north of State Bank of India, and Stitches of Time, farther downhill on Temple Rd. Here you can have a chuba made to order with your own fabric (Rs 100) or some of theirs (Rs 650).

Near the Aroma Cybercafe is the Tibetan Handicrafts Cooperative, which employs about 145 people, many of them newly arrived refugees, in the weaving of Tibetan carpets. Fine New Zealand wool carpets, with 48 knots per sq inch are Rs 2603 per sq metre. The society can pack and post purchases home, and visitors are welcome to watch the carpet makers at work on traditional looms.

There are dozens of other shops selling Tibetan artefacts. Interesting purchases include inlaid prayer wheels, prayer flags (a bargain at Rs 20 a bundle), gem-stone rosary beads, traditional silver jewellery and figurines of Tibetan gods.

Getting There & Away

Air Kangra airport is 15km south-west of Dharamsala at Gaggal (it used to be called Gaggal airport). Indian Airlines flies from Delhi to Kangra on Monday, Wednesday and Friday at 1.15 pm (US$145, 1½ hours), returning to Delhi at 3 pm the same day. Competition for the 18 seats on each flight is fierce so book *well* ahead. Dhalaudhar Travels (☎ 21158, fax 21246) on Temple Rd is the agent for Indian Airlines in Dharamsala.

Bus All the roads in McLeod radiate out from the bus stand, where you'll find the Himachal Roadways Transport Corporation (HRTC) booking office. Here you can book seats on the daily buses to Delhi, Dehra Dun and Pathankot.

Ordinary Delhi buses leave at 4.30, 6.15 and 7.30 pm (Rs 247, 12 hours), but you're better off taking the super deluxe bus at 7 pm (Rs 346). Buses leave for Pathankot at 10, 11.20 and 11.50 am and at 3 and 4 pm (Rs 60, four hours). There's also a daily bus to Dehra Dun at 8 pm (Rs 260, 12 hours). For other services you'll have to head down to Dharamsala.

Various travel agencies in town offer deluxe (two by two) buses to Delhi, which leave at around 6 pm just downhill from McLeod Ganj on the Dharamsala road. Other destinations include Dehra Dun (Rs 280, 7 pm) and Manali (Rs 250, 9 am).

There are also buses for the 40-minute trip down to Dharamsala (Rs 6), departing every 30 minutes between 4.15 am and 8.30 pm. Cramped passenger jeeps also run when full for the same price.

Train Many travel agencies will book train tickets for services out of Pathankot, down on the plains in Punjab (see Pathankot in the Punjab & Haryana chapter). It's worth booking as early as possible, preferably a week in advance. Generally, a Rs 75 to 100 booking fee is levied.

The most convenient train station for McLeod is at Kangra (Kangra Mandir station), about 20km south of Dharamsala, which sits on the narrow-gauge line from Pathankot to Jogindarnagar. The best train on the line is the *Kangra Queen*, which leaves Pathankot at 8.20 am, arriving in Kangra around 11 am (Rs 155/245 sleeper/chair-class). There are at least four other daily trains which take five hours to reach Kangra (Rs 20 a seat). All trains continue to Palampur.

Taxi McLeod's taxi stand (☎ 21034) is next to the bus station. A taxi to Pathankot is around Rs 900. To hire a taxi for the day, covering less than 80km, costs Rs 800.

Short hops include Gangchen Kyishong (Rs 70), Dharamsala's Kotwali Bazaar (Rs 90) and Dharamsala bus station (Rs 100).

Autorickshaw Because of the steep roads, autorickshaws are only really useful for getting to Bhagsu (Rs 30) and Gangchen Kyishong (Rs 70).

AROUND MCLEOD GANJ

Bhagsu

If you find McLeod too much of a scene, there is quieter accommodation available in the village of Bhagsu, 2km east. Also known as Bhagsunag, the village has a cold spring with **baths** and a small **Shiva temple** built by the Raja of Kangra in the 16th century. There's an attractive **waterfall** a short walk beyond the temple.

At the far end of the village, ***Hotel Meghavan*** *(☎ 21277)* is a big hotel catering largely to Indian tourists; rooms cost from Rs 750 to 950.

Opposite, ***Pink White Guest House*** *(☎ 21917)* has good singles/doubles with private bathroom, balcony and views for Rs 150/200 upwards.

If you take the path leading uphill from the main bus stop you come to three guesthouses aimed squarely at Western backpackers. ***Samgyal Guest House*** has rooms with shared/private bathroom for Rs 150/250 and ***Seven Seas Lodge*** *(☎ 23359)* has clean and spacious marble-clad rooms for Rs 150 (ground floor) and Rs 200 (1st floor). Farther uphill is ***Omni Guest House*** *(☎ 21576)* with lots of murals, a decent restaurant and basic rooms with shared hot shower for Rs 80.

Trimurti Restaurant has good, cheap veg food like *aloo gobi* (potato and cauliflower) for around Rs 40 and there's a notice board detailing local yoga and massage courses.

HPTDC Cafe Jaldhara nearby offers south Indian dishes like dosa for about Rs 50. ***Shiva Cafe***, above the waterfall in Bhagsu, is a good spot for a chai (tea).

HIMACHAL PRADESH

SOUTH & WEST OF DHARAMSALA

Kangra

☎ 01892

Kangra was once the capital of the princely state of Kangra, part of the Chand dynasty, but few traces of this golden period survive today. The famous **Temple of Bajreshwari Devi** was of such legendary wealth that every invader worth their salt took time to sack it, including Mahmud of Ghazni in 1009 and Tughlaq in 1360. Each time the temple bounced back and in Jehangir's reign, was paved in plates of pure silver. These days, it's worth visiting more for the atmosphere than the building. The temple is reached through a labyrinth of alleyways flanked with stalls selling *prasad* (food offering used in religious ceremonies).

The British took possession of the ancient fort of **Nagar Kot**, 2.5km south of modern Kangra, and established a garrison, but abandoned it after the disastrous earthquake of 1905. The ruins are perched high on a windswept ridge overlooking the confluence of the Manjhi and Baner Rivers, and can be reached from Kangra by autorickshaw (Rs 40). The Archaeological Survey of India has imposed a US$5 entry fee for foreign tourists.

Places to Stay Close to the centre on Dharamsala Rd, ***Hotel Royal*** *(☎ 65013)* has spotless doubles with hot shower for Rs 300 and Rs 350. Farther down Dharamsala Rd, ***Hotel Maurya*** *(☎ 65875)* has singles for Rs 150, and doubles for Rs 250 and Rs 350, all with private bathroom.

Standing out among the cheap hotels near the bus stand, ***Hotel Raj*** *(☎ 64478)* has good rooms with hot shower from Rs 300/400 a single/double. Of the cheapies, ***Jai Hotel*** *(☎ 65568)* isn't bad, with doubles for Rs 100.

There are several ***dhabas*** by the taxi stand in the centre of town and along the bazaar that runs up to Bajreshwari Devi.

Getting There & Away Kangra's bus stand is 1.5km north of the bazaar along Dharamsala Rd, a Rs 20 autorickshaw-ride from the centre. There are buses to Dharamsala every 15 minutes (Rs 12, 45 minutes) and to Palampur (Rs 25, two hours) every 20 minutes. Local buses run to Masrur at 10 am and 3 pm (Rs 20). It's Rs 7 to Gaggal (for Kangra airport).

By rail, it's easier to get off at Kangra Mandir station, 3km east of town, rather than Kangra station, 5km south. Rickshaws and taxis wait at the crossroads in the centre of town and charge about Rs 60 to the station. A taxi from McLeod Ganj to Kangra will cost Rs 400 (Rs 600 return).

Masrur

South-west of Dharamsala, Masrur has 15 badly damaged Indo-Aryan style rock-cut temples, which date from the 10th century. The temples were ruined by the earthquake of 1905 (which also put paid to McLeod Ganj) but it's still possible to see the resemblance between these temples and those at Ellora in Maharashtra. Masrur is really only worth a visit for hardcore temple buffs as the Archaeological Survey of India has introduced a whopping US$5 entry fee.

There are buses to Masrur from Kangra, but from Dharamsala you'll probably have to change at Gaggal. A taxi from McLeod Ganj will charge around Rs 800 one way (Rs 1200 return).

Jawalamukhi

About 34km south of Kangra is the temple of Jawalamukhi, the goddess of light. Pilgrims descend into a tiny square chamber where a priest, while intoning a blessing on their behalf, ignites natural gas emanating from a copper pipe, from which a blue flame, worshipped as the manifestation of the goddess, briefly flares. The temple is one of the most sacred sites in the Kangra Valley, and is topped by a golden dome and spire, the legacies of Ranjit Singh and the Mughal emperor Akbar.

HPTDC Hotel Jawalaji *(☎ 01970-22280)* has doubles with private bathroom from Rs 450 to 1000. Dorm beds are Rs 75. There's a 30% low-season discount.

Buses to Dharamsala (Rs 35) leave all day from the stand below the road leading up to the temple. Taxis charge Rs 700/1000 one way/return from McLeod Ganj.

EAST OF DHARAMSALA

Norbulingka Institute

This educational complex, 14km from McLeod Ganj and 4km from Dharamsala, was established to teach and preserve traditional Tibetan art, such as woodcarving, *thangka* painting (rectangular painting on cloth), goldsmithing and embroidery. Norbulingka is set amid Japanese-influenced gardens with shady paths, wooden bridges across small streams and tiny waterfalls.

Nearby is the **Dolmaling Nunnery**, site of the Women's Higher Studies Institute, offering courses at advanced levels in Buddhist philosophy to nuns.

The friendly ***Norling Guest House*** *(☎ 01892-22664)* in the institute gardens has good singles/doubles from Rs 1000/1150. Meals can be ordered or you can eat at the nearby ***Norling Cafe***.

To get here, catch a Yol-bound bus from Dharamsala and ask to be let off at Sidhpur, near the Sacred Heart School, from where it's a 20-minute walk. A taxi from McLeod will cost Rs 200.

Palampur

About 30km south-east of Dharamsala, Palampur is a pleasant little junction town surrounded by tea plantations, but there isn't a great deal to see. A short trek takes you to **Bundla chasm**, just outside of town, where a waterfall drops into the Bundla stream.

HPTDC Hotel T-Bud *(☎ 01894-31298)*, 1km north of Main Bazaar, has doubles with private bathroom from Rs 550 to 800 (Rs 330 to 450 in low season). Next to the old bus stand, ***Pine's Hotel*** *(☎ 01894-32633)* has singles from Rs 110 to 140, and doubles from Rs 175 to 250.

Probably the best dining options are the restaurant at ***Hotel T-Bud*** and ***Joy Restaurant*** uphill from old bus stand.

The new bus station is 1km south of Main Bazaar; a taxi from the centre costs a steep Rs 50. Buses leave all day for Dharamsala (Rs 20, two hours); Mandi (Rs 57, four hours) and Pathankot (Rs 70, four hours; last bus at 2.15 pm). A taxi from Dharamsala costs Rs 500 (Rs 700 return).

Tashijong Gompa

This friendly gompa, 5km north-west of Baijnath, is the focus of a small Drukpa Kagyud community of 150 Tibetan monks and 400 refugees. The monastery complex has several halls you can visit and there's a carpet-making, thangka-painting and woodcarving cooperative here. Tashijong village is a 2km walk north from the main Palampur-Baijnath road. Ask the bus to let you off near the Tashijong turn-off. Alternatively, you can take a taxi for Rs 600/750 one way/return.

About 2km south of Tashijong, at Taragarh, is the extraordinary ***Palace Hotel*** *(☎ 01894-63034)*, the summer palace of the last Maharaja of Jammu & Kashmir, now run as a hotel by his son, Dr Karan Singh. Portraits of the royal family are displayed throughout the hotel, which has the usual assortment of tiger skins and colonial furnishings. Doubles range from Rs 950 to 2000; the beautifully furnished suites cost up to 2500.

Baijnath

☎ 01894 • elevation 1010m

The small town of Baijnath, 46km south-east of Dharamsala, is an important pilgrimage place due to its ancient stone **Baidyanath Temple**, sacred to Shiva in his incarnation as Vaidyanath, Lord of the Physicians. Said to date from AD 804, the temple features intricate carvings on the exterior walls, and the inner sanctum enshrines one of India's 12 *jyoti linga* (linga of light). Large numbers of pilgrims make their way here for the **Shivaratri Festival** in late February/early March.

Baijnath itself is a chaotic and ramshackle town, although the Dhaula Dhar Range provides a fine backdrop. ***Hotel Shanker View*** *(☎ 63036)*, 300m out of town on the road to Mandi, has rooms from Rs 150/250; bucket hot water is Rs 10.

The best place to eat here is ***HPTDC Cafe Bhairav***, back down the hill towards Palampur, with great views over the river.

Most buses between Mandi and Dharamsala stop in Baijnath. The narrow-gauge railway passes through Paprola, 1km west of the main bus stand. A taxi from Dharamsala costs Rs 700 (Rs 1000 return).

BIR & BILLING

About 9km south-east of Baijnath is the little Tibetan settlement of Bir, perched at 2080m, where there's a beautiful **gompa** belonging to the Tibetan Nyingmapa order. Far above Bir at 2600m, Billing is the setting for the **Himalayan Hang-Gliding Rally** every May/June, which attracts participants from all over the world. Contact the HPTDC in Shimla (☎ 0177-252561) or Delhi (☎ 011-3325320) for more information.

There is one daily bus from Jogindarnagar to Bir, or you can catch any bus between Baijnath and Jogindarnagar and walk the 4km up from the junction.

Chamba Valley

Separated from the Kangra Valley to the south by the high Dhaula Dhar Range and the remote Pattan Valley to the north by the Pir Panjal Range is the beautiful Chamba Valley, through which flows the Ravi River. For over 1000 years this region formed the princely state of Chamba, the most ancient state in North India.

Few travellers come here and even fewer continue down the valley beyond the hill station of Dalhousie. The valley is renowned for its fine shikara temples, with excellent examples in the beautiful town of Chamba, 56km from Dalhousie, and at the ancient capital of Bharmour, 65km farther down the valley to the south-east.

DALHOUSIE

☎ 01899 • pop 10,100 • elevation 2036m

Sprawling over five hills at around 2000m, Dalhousie was, in the British era, a sort of 'second string' hill station, mainly used by people who lived in Lahore. It was acquired from the Raja of Chamba by the British and was named after Lord Dalhousie, then viceroy of India, by David McLeod (after whom McLeod Ganj was named). These days, Dalhousie is best known for its public schools.

Dalhousie is home to quite a large refugee Tibetan community. Midway along Garam Sarak, between Gandhi and Subhash Chowks (intersections), you'll pass brightly painted low-relief **pictures of Tibetan deities**, including Padmasambhava and Avalokitesvara. There's also a small **Tibetan market**.

The main reason to come to Dalhousie is for the **views** (which are stupendous) or to stay in one of the old Raj-era hotels. The high season (when it can be hard to find a room) runs from mid-April to mid-July, mid-September to mid-November and mid-December to early January.

Orientation

The British managed to built a number of fairly level roads linking the various parts of town, so getting around is relatively easy. The bus stand and several of the poshest hotels are about 1km downhill from the rest of town. The settlements of Subhash Chowk and Gandhi Chowk up on the ridge are linked by Garam Sarak (Hot Rd) – which receives more sunshine – and Thandi Sarak (Cold Rd), collectively known as The Mall.

From the bus stand to Gandhi Chowk or Subhash Chowk is Rs 50 by taxi, or you can hire a porter for about Rs 20.

Information

The tourist office (☎ 42136) is on the top floor of the telegraph office, just below the bus stand. It's open 10 am to 5 pm Monday to Saturday; and Sunday during the tourist season.

State Bank of India, near the bus stand, changes US dollar travellers cheques issued by AmEx, Thomas Cook or Citicorp. Punjab National Bank, a five-minute walk south of the St Francis church, can exchange cash and travellers cheques in US dollars and pounds sterling weekdays, except Wednesday.

Trek-n-Travels (☎ 40277, fax 40476) near the bus stand can arrange treks in the local area for Rs 300 to 600 per day, depending on the duration and route of the

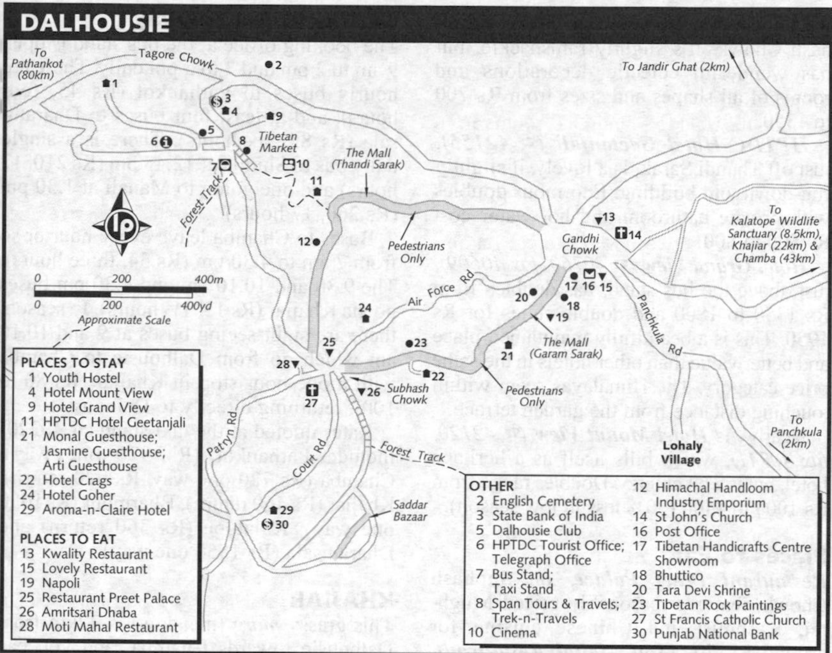

trek. Span Tours & Travels (☎ 40281, fax 40341), nearby, can book luxury coaches to Delhi, Manali and Dharamsala.

Kalatope Wildlife Sanctuary

This pleasant reserve is 8.5km from Gandhi Chowk. The sanctuary is home to a variety of species including black bear and barking deer. There's a checkpoint at **Lakkar Mandi**, on the perimeter of the sanctuary, which has fine mountain views. It's possible to get a taxi here (Rs 200 return), and walk 3km into the sanctuary. To take a vehicle into the sanctuary, you require a permit from the District Forest Officer (DFO) in Chamba (☎ 01899-22239).

Places to Stay

Dalhousie has over 50 hotels, although a fair number of them have a run-down, left-by-the-Raj feel to them. Rates quoted are for high season; at other times expect to pay half or even one-third of these rates.

Places to Stay – Budget

The ***youth hostel*** *(☎ 42189)*, is a five-minute walk from the bus stand. Rates remain constant all year, at Rs 20 (Rs 40 for nonmembers). This doesn't get you bedding, but pillows, sheets and blankets can be hired for Rs 2 (quilts are Rs 6). The hostel is closed between 10 am and 5 pm.

Hotel Goher *(☎ 42253)*, just off Subhash Chowk, is the most reasonably priced of the hotels on Air Force Rd. Doubles cost from Rs 600 in high season; at other times they drop to Rs 200.

Hotel Crags *(☎ 42124)* is a five-minute walk along Garam Sarak, just below the road. It has various doubles for Rs 350 to 550, but rarely charges the full rate. All rooms have private bathroom and hot water. It's a somewhat dilapidated place, but the peaceful location and the spectacular terrace overlooking the valley more than make up for it.

Farther around Garam Sarak, near Gandhi Chowk, is a cluster of guesthouses including ***Arti***, ***Jasmine*** and ***Monal*** where you can get a comfortable room with good views for Rs 400 in high season and Rs 150 in low season.

Places to Stay – Mid-Range

Aroma-n-Claire Hotel *(☎ 42199, fax 42639)* is an atmospheric hotel on Court

HIMACHAL PRADESH

Rd, about a five-minute walk south of Subhash Chowk. It's slightly ramshackle, but has wonderful eclectic decorations and rooms of all shapes and sizes from Rs 700 to 1350.

HPTDC Hotel Geetanjali *(☎ 42155)*, just off Thandi Sarak, is a lovely, if slightly run-down, old building. Enormous doubles with private bathroom and hot water cost Rs 500 to 800.

Hotel Grand View *(☎ 40760, fax 40609)*, just above the bus stand, has doubles from Rs 1350 to 1800 and double suites for Rs 1950. This is a beautifully maintained place and better value than other hotels in the same price category. The Himalayas seem within touching distance from the garden terrace.

Nearby, is ***Hotel Mount View*** *(☎ 42120, fax 40741)*, which bills itself as a heritage hotel, but is a bit chintzy. Doubles range from Rs 1000 to 1400 (30% less in low season).

Places to Eat

Restaurant Preet Palace, on Subhash Chowk, features reasonably priced Mughlai, Kashmiri and Chinese cuisine for around Rs 70. ***Moti Mahal Restaurant***, nearby, serves Southern Indian food from Rs 55, and also has a bar.

Better value are the dhabas just off Subhash Chowk. Best of the lot is probably ***Amritsari Dhaba*** with good Punjabi offerings from Rs 50. Dalhousie's dhabas are a cut above the usual Indian dhaba.

Lovely Restaurant, at Gandhi Chowk, has a sun terrace with outdoor seating and serves South Indian and Chinese cuisine from Rs 45 and upwards. Also at Gandhi Chowk is the popular ***Kwality Restaurant*** with an extensive menu.

In the bazaar at the western end of Garam Sarak, ***Napoli*** is a posh sit-down place that serves no Italian food, but lots of Indian and Chinese choices for around Rs 100.

Shopping

The Himachal Handloom Industry Emporium on Thandi Sarak has a good selection of Kullu shawls. Bhuttico has a branch on the bazaar on Garam Sarak with a wide selection of shawls and fair prices. You can buy carpets, bags and purses from the Tibetan Handicrafts Centre Showroom, on Garam Sarak. The shops nearby sell a range of goods, including Kashmiri shawls.

Getting There & Away

The booking office at the bus stand is open 9 am to 2 pm and 3 to 5 pm daily. There are hourly buses to Pathankot (Rs 45, four hours), and at least four buses to Dharamsala (Rs 85, six hours). There is a single daily bus to Shimla at 12.45 pm (Rs 210, 12 hours) and one going to Manali at 1.30 pm (Rs 260, 17 hours).

Buses to Chamba leave every hour or so from 7 am to 4.30 pm (Rs 34, three hours). The 9.30 and 10.10 am and 4.30 pm buses go via Khajiar (Rs 15, 1½ hours). In season, there are sight-seeing buses at 9 and 10.10 am which go from Dalhousie to Chamba with a one-hour stop in Khajiar (Rs 80 to 100), returning directly to Dalhousie.

Rates quoted at the taxi stand (☎ 40220) include Pathankot (Rs 920 one way), Chamba (Rs 720 one way, Rs 920 return), Khajiar (Rs 460 return), Bharmour (Rs 1650 one way), Kalatope (Rs 360 return) and Dharamsala (Rs 1550 one way).

KHAJIAR

This grassy *marg* (meadow) is 22km from Dalhousie towards Chamba, and you can get here by bus (1½ hours) or on foot (a day's walk). Over 1km long and nearly 1km wide, it is ringed by pine trees with a pond in the middle. The 12th-century **Khajjinag Temple** has fine woodcarving on the cornices, and some crude carvings of the five Pandavas, the heroes of the Mahabharata, which were installed in the temple by the Raja of Chamba in the 16th century.

Places to Stay & Eat

HPTDC Hotel Devdar *(☎ 01899-36333)* has cottages on the edge of the marg for Rs 750 to 1100 a double, plus dorm beds for Rs 75. There are more dorm beds for Rs 75 in HPTDC's basic ***Khajiar Cottage*** on the north side of the marg.

Gautam Guest House *(☎ 01899-36355)*, a two-minute walk east of the marg, is the best budget choice. Clean, bright rooms with private bathroom and hot water cost Rs 250 and there's a nice sitting area. There are several ***restaurants*** on the marg.

Getting There & Away

Buses from Dalhousie to Khajiar (Rs 13, 1½ hours) leave at 9.30 and 10.10 am and 4.30 pm. In the reverse direction most buses skip Khajiar; the only reliable service leaves Khajiar at 3.30 pm. To Chamba, they should depart at 11 am and 12.30 and 5.30 pm (Rs 15, 1½ hours). Tourist buses to Chamba stop at Khajiar for an hour. A taxi from Khajiar to Chamba is around Rs 400.

CHAMBA

☎ 01899 • pop 19,000 • elevation 996m

It's a beautiful, if somewhat hair-raising 56km trip from Dalhousie to Chamba (43km via Khajiar). The views down over the terraced fields are spectacular, with tiny villages clinging to the sheer slopes of the valley.

Chamba sits an altitude of 926m, perched on a ledge flanking the Ravi River. It has often been compared to a medieval Italian village, with its narrow streets and ancient temples.

For 1000 years prior to Independence, Chamba was the headquarters of a district of the same name, and was ruled by a single dynasty of maharajas. The town was founded by Raja Sahil Varman, who shifted the capital here from Bharmour and named it after his daughter Champavati.

Chamba has a grassy promenade known as the Chowgan, which is the focus for the Minjar and Sui Mata Festivals (see Special Events on the next page).

Information

The tourist office (☎ 24002) is in the interesting beige building next to Hotel Iravati on Court Rd. It's open 10 am to 5 pm daily, except Sunday.

The only place currently changing money is Punjab National Bank on Hospital Rd, which will fortunately change all travellers cheques in US dollars or pounds sterling.

Organised Tours

The very friendly and helpful family-run Mani Mahesh Travels (☎ 22507), close to the Lakshmi Narayan temple complex, can arrange treks with guides and porters for Rs 700 to 900 per day (although this rises to Rs 1400 over the high mountain passes). The owner's son can provide a commentary on Chamba's beautiful temples (Rs 300) and his daughter acts as a guide for female trekkers when required.

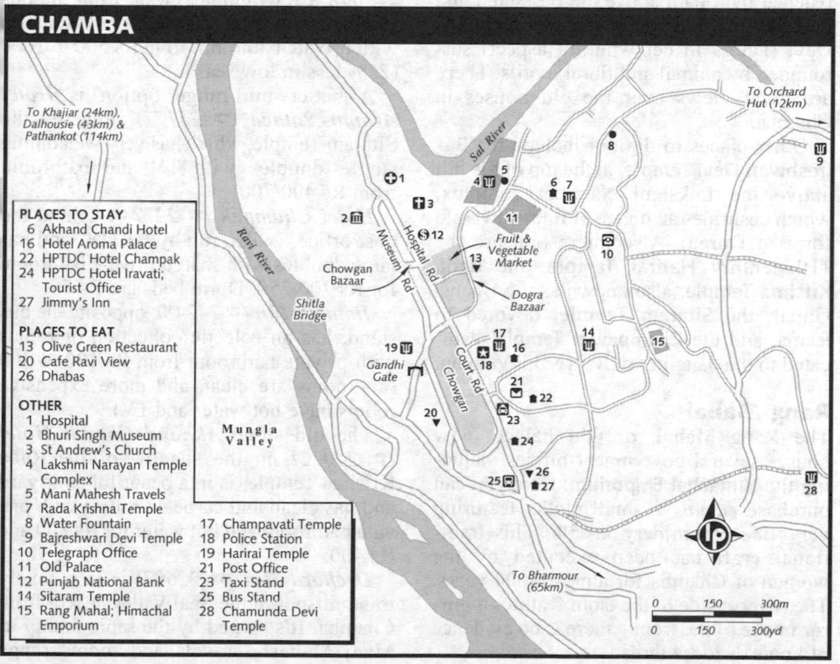

HIMACHAL PRADESH

Lakshmi Narayan Temple Complex

The six sikhara-style temples in this complex all feature exquisite sculpture and date from the 10th century all the way up to the 19th century. The largest (and oldest) temple in the group is that of Lakshmi Narayan (Vishnu) which was built during the reign of the founder of Chamba, Raja Sahil Varman, in the 10th century AD. It was extensively renovated in the 16th century by Raja Partap Singh Varna.

Set into alcoves around the exterior of the temple are fine sculptures of Narsingh (Vishnu in his lion form), and Krishna with the *gopis* (milkmaids). The fourth temple on the right, the Gauri Shankar Temple, is the most interesting of the other shrines here. It's dedicated to Shiva and features fine stone carvings of the Ganges and Yamuna Rivers personified as goddesses on either side of the door frame.

Other Temples

Numerous other temples lay hidden within Chamba's maze of backstreets. Up on the hilltop, the **Chamunda Devi Temple** is reached by a path above the bus stand and features impressive carvings of Chamunda Devi (Durga in her wrathful aspect) surrounded by animal and floral motifs. There are great views over the old houses in Chamba.

Other places to dig out include the **Bajreshwari Devi Temple**, at the top of the hill above the Lakshmi Narayan complex, which enshrines an image of Bajreshwari (a form of Durga). Also interesting are the 11th-century **Harirai Temple**, the **Rada Krishna Temple**, also known as the Bhansi Gopal, the **Sitaram Temple**, devoted to Rama, and the **Champavati Temple**, dedicated to the daughter of Raja Sahil Varman.

Rang Mahal

The Rang Mahal, or Old Palace, now houses several government offices including the **Himachal Emporium**. Here you can purchase *rumals* – small cloths featuring very fine embroidery in silk. This traditional craft has been executed by the women of Chamba for almost 1000 years. The reverse side of the cloth features a mirror image of the front – there is no evidence of knots or loose threads.

Bhuri Singh Museum

This museum has an interesting collection representing the art and culture of this region – particularly the miniature paintings of the Basohli and Kangra schools. It also houses some of the murals that were recovered from the Rang Mahal after it was damaged by fire. The museum is open 10 am to 5 pm daily, except Monday; entry is free.

Special Events

The four-day **Sui Mata Festival** is held in March/April on the Chowgan. Sui Mata, the daughter of an ancient raja, gave her life to save the inhabitants of her father's kingdom. She is particularly revered by Chamba women, who carry her image from the Old Palace up to her small shrine, accompanied by singing and dancing.

The **Minjar Festival** has been celebrated in late July/early August since AD 935 and culminates with a colourful procession headed by a palanquin bearing an image of Raghuvira, who is an incarnation of Rama.

Places to Stay

HPTDC Hotel Iravati *(☎ 22671, fax 22565)*, a few minutes' walk from the bus stand on Court Rd, has slightly old doubles with private bathroom from Rs 500 to 1000 (25% less in low season).

A better mid-range option is ***Hotel Aroma Palace*** *(☎ 25177)*, towards the Sitaram Temple, which has very welcoming singles/doubles with TV and bathroom from Rs 400/700.

Hotel Champak *(☎ 22774)*, behind the post office, is also run by HPTDC and has large doubles with shared/private bathroom for Rs 200/250. Dorm beds are Rs 75.

Jimmy's Inn *(☎ 24748)*, opposite the bus stand, has an eclectic collection of rooms with private bathroom from Rs 100 to 300 (all rooms are clean and more expensive rooms have hot water and TV).

The old stone ***Akhand Chandi Hotel*** *(☎ 24072)*, in the shadow of the Rada Krishna Temple, is in a beautiful courtyard and has clean and carpeted rooms with private bathroom and hot water for Rs 300 and Rs 400.

Orchard Hut *(☎ 22607)* is in a lovely tranquil spot in the Saal Valley, 12km from Chamba. It's owned by the same family as Mani Mahesh Travels and rooms range from Rs 350 with breakfast and dinner, to Rs 650 for three superior meals. When you arrive in Chamba, go to Mani Mahesh Travels first, and they'll arrange transfers.

Places to Eat

Chamba is known for its *chukh* – a chilli sauce consisting of red and green peppers, lemon juice, mustard oil and salt – but sadly not its restaurants.

HPTDC runs the little ***Cafe Ravi View*** on the edge of the Chowgan area, which serves the standard HPTDC range of Indian and Chinese dishes from around Rs 50. A better choice is the restaurant at ***Hotel Iravati***, also run by the HPTDC, with good veg and nonveg options for about Rs 75.

Also worth a visit is ***Olive Green Restaurant***, upstairs on Temple Rd. There is a good range of reasonably priced veg and nonveg dishes, including the local dish *chamba madhra* (kidney beans with curd and ghee).

There are a few basic ***dhabas*** by the bus station.

Getting There & Away

There are six buses daily for the somewhat nerve-shattering trip to Bharmour (Rs 38, 3½ hours). To Dharamsala (Rs 100 to 135, 10 hours) there are buses at 6 and 11.30 am and 4 and 9.30 pm. To Khajiar (Rs 15, 1½ hours), buses leave at 7.30 am and 2 and 5 pm. Buses to Dalhousie depart every few hours from 6 am to 6 pm (Rs 34, three hours). There are hourly services to Pathankot (Rs 67, six hours). From Dharamsala, the best bus is probably the 8.30 am service (Rs 125).

One way/return taxi fares include Rs 400/600 to Khajiar, Rs 800/1000 to Bharmour and 800/1050 to Dalhousie.

BHARMOUR

☎ 01090 • elevation 2195m

About 64km south-east of Chamba is the ancient slate-roofed village of Bharmour. The trip follows a precarious road along the Ravi River valley, offering spectacular views, though the lower stretches are marred by yet another hydroelectric project.

Bharmour was the ancient capital of the princely state of Chamba for over 400 years, until Raja Sahil Varman moved the capital to Chamba in AD 920. Bharmour is a centre for the seminomadic Gaddis, pastoralists who move their flocks up to alpine pastures during the summer, and descend to Kangra, Mandi and Bilaspur in winter.

Things to See & Do

The **Chaurasi temples** are mainly devoted to Shiva and there are dozens of Shiva lingam shrines dotted around the courtyard. The largest temple in the group is the central shikara-style **Manimahesh Temple**, faced by a huge bronze Nandi statue. Farther back is the smaller sikhara-style **Narsingh Temple** dedicated to Vishnu in his lion form. Next to the Manimahesh temple is the older **Laskna Devi** temple from AD 700, featuring a truly wonderful carved doorway, topped by a 12-armed Vishnu riding Garuda.

There are some fine **treks** that commence from Bharmour; see Lonely Planet's *Trekking in the Indian Himalaya* for details. The Mountaineering & Allied Sports Sub-Centre (☎ 25036) can arrange guides and porters.

In July/August pilgrims from all over northern India converge on Bharmour for **Manimahesh Yatra** to commence the pilgrimage to the sacred lake of Manimahesh, 28km away and below the peak of Manimahesh Kailash (5656m). By the lake is an ancient and very beautiful **temple** dedicated to Lakshmi Devi in her form as slayer of the buffalo demon (Mahishasuramardini), dating to the 7th century AD.

Places to Stay

On the road up to the temple compound, ***Amit Guest House*** *(☎ 25104)* has overpriced doubles with private bathroom and hot water for a pricey Rs 350.

Better value is the Public Works Department ***rest house*** on the lower of the two roads leading up from the bus stand, which charges Rs 250 per night for doubles with bath.

Just downhill is the friendly ***Chamunda Guest House*** *(☎ 25056)*. Simple rooms with shared bathroom cost Rs 150 (Rs 100 at quiet times).

There are several ***dhabas*** just downhill from the Chaurasi temples.

Getting There & Away

There are buses to Chamba every two hours from 6.30 am to 5.30 pm (Rs 38, 3½ hours). Taxis charge Rs 800/1000 one way/return from Chamba. The road here is particularly prone to landslides.

Kullu & Parvati Valleys

The Kullu Valley and, to a lesser extent, the Parvati Valley have always been popular places to hang out and take in some mountain scenery. Recent tourist spillover from the political violence in Kashmir, however, has had a profound effect on the valley and Manali, in particular, has developed rapidly, threatening the valley's peaceful and unhurried atmosphere.

Originally known as Kulanthapitha (End of the Habitable World), the first recorded inhabitants of the Kullu Valley date back to the 1st century AD. The capital was first at Jagatsukh, then moved to Naggar before the British moved it to Kullu town. The Kullu Valley, about 80km long and often less than 2km wide, rises northward from Mandi at 760m to the Rohtang La at 3978m, the gateway to Lahaul and Spiti.

Shopping for Shawls

The Kullu Valley is known as the Valley of Apples, but a more appropriate name might be the Valley of Shawls. From Bhuntar to Manali, the road is lined with literally hundreds of shops selling traditional Kullu shawls. Woven on wooden handlooms, Kullu shawls are light and remarkably warm, and make great souvenirs.

Originally a cottage industry, the shawl business now employs hundreds of village women. As well as countless emporiums, there are dozens of places where you can see weaving in action. You can even visit the farms where the pashmina goats and angora rabbits are raised. With this much competition, the sales pressure in most places can be fairly overbearing, though prices are often surprisingly low.

For high quality without the hard sell, head for Bhuttico, the Bhutti Weavers' Cooperative. Established in 1944 by a group of village women, Bhuttico has outlets in major towns throughout Himachal Pradesh. The cheapest shawls are made of lambswool but for a good-quality shawl made of angora or pashmina wool, you should be prepared to pay at least Rs 1000. The embroidered shawls worn by village women take months to produce and cost upwards of Rs 6000.

The Kullu and Parvati Valleys, from Mandi to Manali, are serviced by the Kullu/Manali airport at Bhuntar, 10km south of Kullu town.

The high season is mid-April to mid-June, mid-September to early November, Christmas and New Year.

MANDI

☎ 01905 • pop 26,000

Formerly an important junction on the salt route to Tibet, Mandi is the gateway to the Kullu Valley, and the junction of roads from the Kullu Valley, the Kangra Valley and Shimla. The town is more Punjabi than Himalayan in atmosphere, with a large Sikh community and around 81 temples of varying ages dotted around the hillside. It's a pleasant place to break the journey between Shimla and the Kullu Valley and there are some interesting detours into the surrounding hills, including the holy lakes at Rewalsar and Prashar.

Orientation & Information

The centre of Mandi is the town square, dominated by a sunken multistorey shopping complex called the Indira Market. Most of the hotels and places to eat are around or very near the square. Over the river, to the east, is the bus station, a 15-minute walk away.

The only place to change money is Evening Plaza Hotel in the main square, which also changes AmEx travellers cheques for a 1% commission. Below the town on the way to Rewalsar, Bank of Baroda gives cash advances on Visa and MasterCard.

Things to See & Do

Perched at the top of Tarna Hill is the **Rani Amrit Kaur Park** with superb views and a nice cafe. In the park, the 17th-century Hindu **Syamakali Temple**, also called the Tarna Devi Temple, is worth a look. You can walk the 5km from town or take an autorickshaw (Rs 30).

From the Bhutnath Temple you could head north into the cloth bazaar, down to the Beas River and its collection of riverside temples and ghats, including the impressive **Triloknath** and **Panjvaktra Temples**.

Mandi's **Shivaratri Festival** is one of the most interesting held in Himachal Pradesh. Much of the lively activity takes place at the

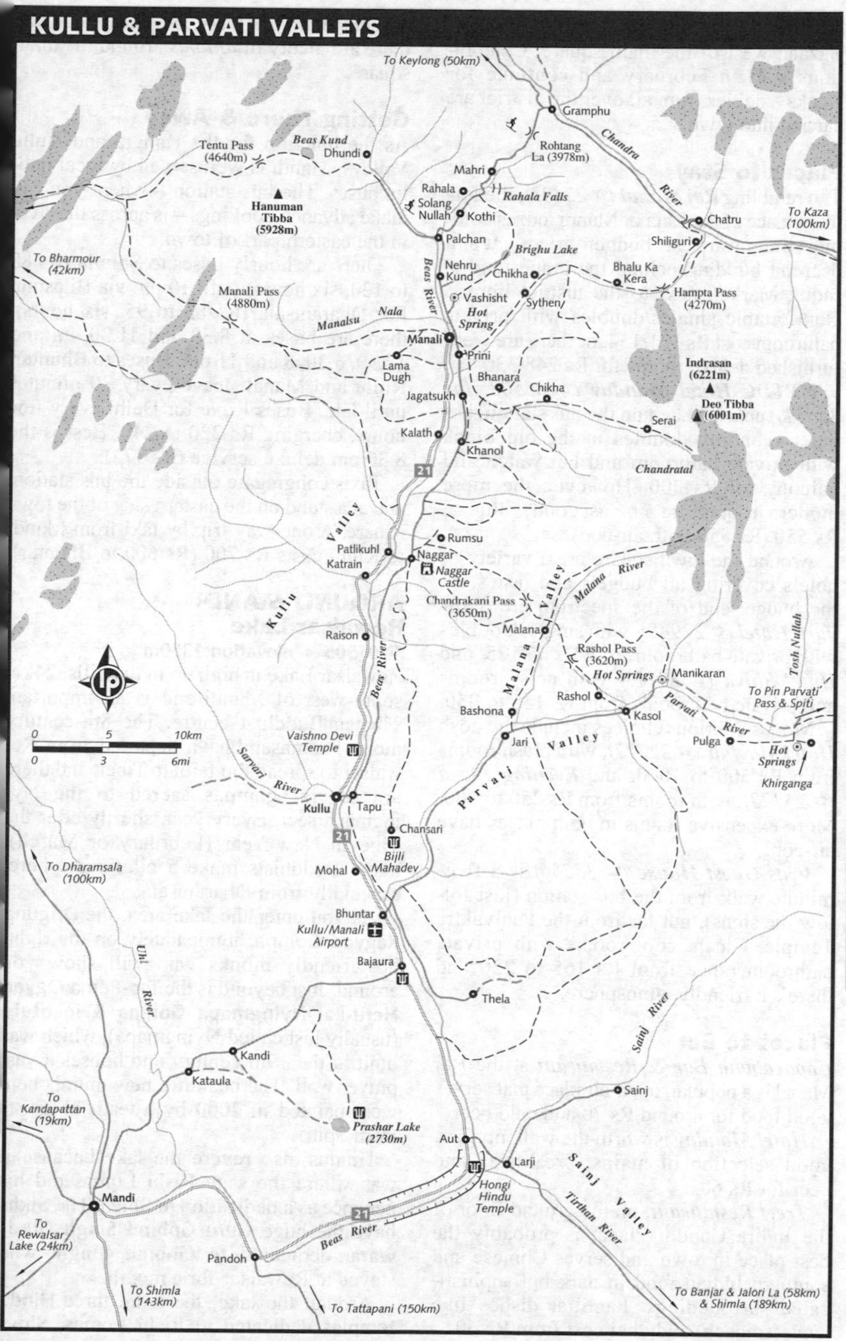
KULLU & PARVATI VALLEYS
To Keylong (50km)
Gramphu
Rohtang La (3978m)
Chandra River
Tentu Pass (4640m)
Beas Kund
Dhundi
Hanuman Tibba (5928m)
Mahri
Rahala
Rahala Falls
Solang Nullah
Kothi
To Kaza (100km)
Chatru
Shiliguri
Palchan
Brighu Lake
To Bharmour (42km)
Nehru Kund
Chikha
Bhalu Ka Kera
Vashisht
Hampta Pass (4270m)
Sythen
Manali Pass (4880m)
Manalsu Nala
Hot Spring
Beas River
Manali
Prini
Lama Dugh
Bhanara
Indrasan (6221m)
Jagatsukh
Chikha
Deo Tibba (6001m)
Serai
Kalath
Khanol
Chandratal
21
Kullu Valley
Rumsu
Patlikuhl
Naggar
Katrain
Naggar Castle
Malana River
Chandrakani Pass (3650m)
Malana
Malana Valley
Raison
Rashol Pass (3620m)
Tosh Nullah
Hot Springs
Manikaran
Rashol
To Pin Parvati Pass & Spiti
Kasol
Parvati River
Bashona
Pulga
Jari
Hot Springs
Khirganga
Parvati Valley
Vaishno Devi Temple
0 5 10km
0 3 6mi
Sarvari River
Kullu
Tapu
Chansari
Bijli Mahadev
To Dharamsala (100km)
Mohal
Bhuntar
Kullu/Manali Airport
Uhl River
Bajaura
Thela
Sainj River
Kandi
Kataula
Sainj
To Kandapattan (19km)
Prashar Lake (2730m)
Aut
Larji
Sainj Valley
Hongi Hindu Temple
Mandi
Tirthan River
To Rewalsar Lake (24km)
Beas River
Pandoh
To Shimla (143km)
To Tattapani (150km)
To Banjar & Jalori La (58km) & Shimla (189km)
HIMACHAL PRADESH

16th-century **Bhutnath Temple** in Moti Bazaar, west of the main square. Celebrations start in February and continue for weeks – deities from all over the district are carried into town.

Places to Stay

The rambling ***Raj Mahal*** *(☎ 22401)*, the former palace of the Raja of Mandi, oozes colonial time warp at budget prices. It's a decrepit building behind the grandstand at Indira Market, next to the district library. Comfortable singles/doubles with private bathroom cost Rs 121/154, or there are well-furnished deluxe rooms for Rs 248/330.

HPTDC Hotel Mandav *(☎ 35503, fax 35551)*, up a lane behind the bus station, has quiet economy doubles in the old block with private bathroom and hot water, and balcony for Rs 300. However, the more modern rooms are not as good value at Rs 550 (Rs 850 with air-con).

Around the town square are a variety of hotels covering all budgets and tastes. At the budget end of the spectrum are ***Standard Hotel*** *(☎ 22948)*, with singles/doubles with private bathroom from Rs 65/125, and ***Hotel Shiva*** *(☎ 24211)* with noisy rooms and private bathrooms from Rs 135 to 350.

More salubrious choices include the posh ***Hotel Mayfair*** *(☎ 22777)*, with plush rooms from Rs 500 to 1000, and ***Evening Plaza*** *(☎ 25123)*, with rooms from Rs 250 to 800. More-expensive rooms in both places have air-con.

Vyas Guest House *(☎ 35556)* is a five-minute walk from the bus station (just follow the signs), not far from the Panjvaktra Temple. Clean, cool rooms with private bathroom range from Rs 165 to 220 and there's a friendly atmosphere.

Places to Eat

Copacabana Bar & Restaurant at the Raj Mahal is a popular, open-air place that serves good food for around Rs 70 and cold beer.

Hotel Mandav is worth the walk up for a good selection of mains, breakfasts and beer for Rs 60.

Treet Restaurant, on the ground floor of the Indira Gandhi Plaza, is probably the best place in town and serves Chinese and southern Indian food in dark but sophisticated surroundings. Familiar dishes like *saag* (spinach) and dhal cost from Rs 60.

Hotel Standard has good, cheap food and there are plenty of ***dhabas*** around the main square.

Getting There & Away

As the junction for the Kangra and Kullu Valleys, Mandi is well served by local public buses. The bus station – where you can make advance bookings – is across the river in the eastern part of town.

There are hourly buses to Shimla (Rs 88 to 120, six hours) until 10 pm via Bilaspur. For Dharamsala (Rs 85 to 95, six hours), there are buses at 8.30 and 11.30 am and 12.30, 6.30, 8 and 11 pm. Buses to Bhuntar, Kullu and Manali leave every 30 minutes until late. Buses leave for Delhi every few hours, charging Rs 220 to 240. Best is the 8.30 pm deluxe service (Rs 372).

Taxis congregate outside the bus station, and at a stand on the eastern side of the town square. A one-way trip by taxi from Mandi to Kullu costs Rs 700 (Rs 600 to Bhuntar).

AROUND MANDI

Rewalsar Lake

☎ 01905 • elevation 1350m

Rewalsar Lake is high up in the hills, 24km south-west of Mandi and is an important Tibetan Buddhist centre. The 8th-century monk Padmasambhava departed from Rewalsar to spread the faith to Tibet, and there are several gompas sacred to the Nyingmapa sect. Every year, shortly after the Tibetan New Year (February or March), many Buddhists make a pilgrimage here, especially from Dharamsala.

As you enter the lake area, the **Drigung Kagyud Gompa**, immediately on the right, has friendly monks who will show you around. Just beyond is the **Tso-Pema Ogyen Heru-kai Nyingmapa Gompa & Institute** (usually just called Nyingmapa), which was built in the 19th century and houses a vast prayer wall. The beautiful new murals here were painted in 2000 by a team of artists from Spiti.

Hindus also revere the lake because it was where the sage Rishi Lomas did his penance as a dedication to Shiva. The Sikhs have the huge **Guru Gobind Singh Gurdwara**, dedicated to Gobind Singh, who stayed at Rewalsar for a month.

Around the lake, there are three **Hindu temples** dedicated to Rishi Lomas, Shiva and Krishna. A steep 30-minute hike above the lake is a huge Buddha image in a cave; head for the prayer flags at the top of the hill.

Places to Stay & Eat The ***HPTDC Tourist Inn*** *(☎ 80252)* has dorm beds for Rs 75, and nice doubles/triples for Rs 200/300 in the old building and Rs 300/350 in the new building. The restaurant here serves a good mix of Indian and Chinese food.

The Drigung Kagyud Gompa offers cosy rooms in its ***Peace Memorial Inn*** for Rs 65/150 with shared/private bathroom.

The ***guesthouse*** at the Nyingmapa Gompa has basic rooms on the lakeside for Rs 25/50 and deluxe rooms for Rs 100/150 with hot-water bath. It's popular with Western Buddhists.

The Zigar Gompa ***guesthouse*** has rooms with private bathroom for Rs 50 and the friendly ***Tibetan Food Corner*** restaurant. Nearby are ***Mentok*** and ***Choesang*** restaurants, which serve good momos and thugpa for around Rs 35.

Getting There & Away Buses from Mandi go to Rewalsar village every few hours (Rs 14, 1½ hours), making it an easy day trip along a pretty, but fairly rough, road. A taxi from Mandi costs about Rs 300/450 one way/return.

MANDI TO KULLU

About 15km south of Kullu in the village of Bajaura is the **Basheshar Mahadev**, the largest stone temple in the Kullu Valley. Built in the 8th century from carved stone blocks, the temple has fine carvings and sculptures. It's at the end of a 200m trail leading from the main road with a sign reading 'Indo Italian Fruit Dev'.

Hidden away in the hills between Mandi and Bajaura is spectacular **Prashar Lake** set at 2730m. There's an ancient temple beside the lake with wonderful Himalayan views. Prashar is an 8km walk from the village of Kandi on the Mandi-Bajaura road. Buses leave Mandi at 6.30 am and 2 pm for Kandi for Rs 20.

Bhuntar

☎ 01902

This unremarkable junction town only warrants a mention for its airport, which serves all of the Kullu Valley, and its position as the turn-off to the Parvati Valley on the other side of the Beas. Bhuntar is only 10km from Kullu but if you have an early departure or a late arrival, it might be handy to stay here.

Jagson Airlines (☎ 65222) has an office next to the airport and there are several travel agencies across the road.

Places to Stay & Eat Best of a bad bunch near the airport/bus station is ***Hotel Airport-End***, with clean but noisy rooms for a negotiable Rs 250 to 350 with private bathroom.

About 500m north of the airport, towards Kullu, are some mid-range places. All give a 50% discount in low season. ***Hotel Sunbeam*** *(☎ 65790)* has reasonable rooms with hot shower for Rs 200 to 550. ***Hotel Amit*** *(☎ 65123)*, next door, has doubles for Rs 450 to 850.

Around the bus station, several ***dhabas*** serve basic Indian and Chinese food; ***Malabar Restaurant*** opposite the airport entrance is probably the best of the lot.

Getting There & Away Bhuntar is well served by buses, which leave from the bus stand outside the airport entrance. Most buses go to Kullu (Rs 5), where you may have to change for destinations farther north. All buses between Manali and anywhere south of Kullu stop at, or very near, Bhuntar. Regular buses run to Manikaran (Rs 20) via Jari (Rs 17) and Kasol (Rs 17).

Taxis charge Rs 125 to Kullu, Rs 650 to Manali, Rs 500 to Manikaran and Rs 700 to Mandi.

For details of flights from Bhuntar see Getting There & Away in the Kullu section.

KULLU

☎ 01902 • pop 16,000 • elevation 1200m

The busy town of Kullu is the district headquarters of the valley but there isn't a great deal to see. Kullu is reasonably set up with hotels and other facilities, and is not a bad place (especially around Dhalpur), but most visitors head straight for the travellers centres dotted around the valleys.

Orientation & Information

Kullu is divided in two by the Sarvari River. The maidan (parade ground) area at Dhalpur (the setting for Kullu's festivals) is on the south bank, where you'll find the taxi stand and the tourist office. The bus station and

Raghunath Temple are both on the north bank; it's quicker to take the footpath next to Hotel Shobla than the road.

The HPTDC tourist office (☎ 22349) is by the maidan at Dhalpur. It's open 10 am to 7 pm daily in summer (10 am to 5 pm in winter), useful for booking HPTDC buses, which leave from outside the office.

State Bank of Patiala, at the northern end of Akhara Bazaar, accepts most travellers cheques (except Citicorp) but doesn't change cash.

The main post office is uphill from the taxi stand but service is a bit slow. The Madhu Chandrika Guest House offers Internet access for Rs 100 per hour.

The best places to buy Kullu Shawls are Bhuttico and the Himachal Emporium on the highway in Akhara Bazaar (you may pass the huge Bhuttico headquarters on the bus south to Mandi). See the boxed text 'Shopping for Shawls' earlier in this chapter.

KULLU

PLACES TO STAY & EAT
2 Central Hotel
7 Madhu Chandrika Guest House
8 Aaditya Guest House
11 New Vikrant
12 Hotel Ramneek
13 Dhabas
14 Hotel Shobla
17 Hotstuff
18 Hotel Bijleshwar View
19 Hotel Aroma Classic
20 HPTDC Hotel Sarvari

OTHER
1 Bhuttico
3 Telegraph Office
4 Himachal Emporium
5 Raghunath Temple
6 Palace
9 Main Bus Station
10 Main Post Office
15 Taxi Stand
16 HPTDC Tourist Office; HPTDC Monal Cafe

To Bhekhli (3km)
To State Bank of Patiala (800m), Bijli Mahadev Temple (14km) & Manali (40km)
Akhara Bazaar
National Hwy 21
Sultanpur
Sarvari
Beas River
Sarvari River
Dhalpur
Dhalpur Maidan
0 150 300m
0 150 300yd
To Kullu/Manali Airport (10km), Parvati Valley & Mandi (69km)

Temples

The **Raghunath Temple** (1660), in the north of town, is dedicated to the principal god in the valley. Although it's the most important temple in the area, it's not terribly interesting and is only open before 9 am and after 5 pm.

About 3km from Kullu, in the village of Bhekhli, is the **Jagannathi Devi Temple** (also known as the Bhekhli Temple). It's a stiff 1½-hour climb, but from the temple there are great views over Kullu. Take the main road to Akhara Bazaar then follow the path to Bhekhli after crossing the bridge. A taxi will charge Rs 200/300 one way/return, or there are public buses at 9 am and 2.30 and 5.30 pm (Rs 7, 45 minutes)

Special Events

Kullu holds one of the most colourful **Dussehra** festivals in India (March/April). During the festival, Rama is worshipped in his form as Raghunath, whose image is borne through the streets on a wheeled *rath* (palanquin) pulled by pilgrims. Following the procession, villagers dance in traditional dress. The festival is quite spectacular, but it is becoming increasingly commercialised and finding transport and accommodation in the Kullu area at this time can be a real problem.

Organised Tours

The Kullu Taxi Operators' Union (☎ 22332), just north of the Dhalpur maidan, offers a variety of sightseeing tours. Options include:

- Bhekhli Temple, Vaishno Devi Temple, Raghunath Temple, shawl factory & Bajaura (Rs 550, five hours)
- Kasol & Manikaran (Rs 700, six hours)
- Larji, Banjar & Jalori La (Rs 1500, 10 hours)
- Rewalsar Lake (Rs 1300, eight hours)
- Vaishno Devi Temple, Naggar Castle & Roerich Castle (Rs 550, five hours)

Places to Stay – Budget

In Dhalpur, the popular ***Hotel Bijleshwar View*** *(☎ 22677)*, behind the tourist office, has quiet rooms with private bathroom and hot water from Rs 350 to 500 (less in low season). ***New Vikrant*** *(☎ 22756)*, is on an alley behind the taxi stand and has a great range of rooms from Rs 150 to 375 and some nice communal sitting areas. Nearby is the large ***Hotel Ramneek*** *(☎ 25588)*, which offers good rooms with hot showers, TV and carpets from Rs 350.

In the Akhara Bazaar Area, ***Aaditya Guest House*** *(☎ 24263)*, beside the river, has bright doubles with shared/hot-water bathroom for Rs 100/200. The nearby ***Madhu Chandrika Guest House*** *(☎ 24395)* charges Rs 100/150 with/without bathroom, and has a small dorm for Rs 40. There's also an Internet cafe (Rs 100 per hour).

The friendly ***Central Hotel*** *(☎ 22482)* is the oldest in Kullu, with an infinite range of threadbare rooms from Rs 50 to 200.

Places to Stay – Mid-Range

Hotel Shobla *(☎ 22800)*, in the centre of town, has luxury rooms for Rs 550 to 950. Packages that include meals are available.

HPTDC Hotel Sarvari *(☎ 22471)* is a little south of the maidan, and a short walk off the main road. It's a well-run place with clean, bright doubles in the old block for Rs 450, rooms in the new block for Rs 800 upwards, and dorm beds for Rs 75.

Hotel Aroma Classic *(☎ 23075)*, just past Hotel Bijleshwar, also well run, has rooms from Rs 500 to 750 and a good restaurant.

Places to Eat

HPTDC Monal Cafe, by the tourist office, serves good meals and snacks. ***Hotstuff***, just opposite, is a good fast-food place that serves up pizzas, soup and more.

There are numerous ***dhabas*** north of the taxi stand and around the bus stand.

Alternatively, try the restaurants at ***Hotel Aroma Classic*** and ***Hotel Shobla***, which both serve good food at fair prices.

Getting There & Away

Air Jagson Airlines flies between Delhi and Kullu/Manali airport (Bhuntar) daily for US$145, with a stop in Shimla. The flight leaves Delhi at 8 am, returning directly to Delhi at 10.10 am. Indian Airlines flies the same route on Monday, Wednesday and Friday at 9 am (US$145), returning directly to Delhi at 11.10 am.

Jagson Airlines has an office (☎ 65222) opposite the airport in Bhuntar; Indian Airlines can be booked through Ambassador Travels in Kullu (☎ 25286).

Bus Kullu has a large, busy bus station; timetables are displayed in English, and there's an advance booking system.

Buses pass through Kullu on their way to Mandi (Rs 44, two hours) every 30 minutes from 4 am to 8.15 pm, also stopping in Bhuntar (Rs 5, 15 minutes). There are buses to Shimla every three hours from 4.30 am to 7.45 pm (Rs 132, eight hours). Buses leave for Manikaran hourly (Rs 27); alternatively, change at Bhuntar. There is a bus every 15 or 20 minutes between Kullu and Manali (Rs 24, two hours).

There are public buses to Dharamsala at 9.50 am and 5 and 8 pm (Rs 135 to 160, eight hours). Buses to Delhi leave every hour in the afternoon (Rs 270 to 290, 14 hours). Buses to Kandi (for Prashar Lake) leave at 6.30 am and 2 pm (Rs 21).

HPTDC buses from Manali stop at the tourist office in Kullu and bookings can be made in advance there. Buses run daily in season to Shimla (Rs 337, 9.15 am), Delhi (Rs 521, 6.30 pm) and Chandigarh (Rs 312, 8.15 am).

Travel agencies in Kullu sell tickets for deluxe private buses 'from Kullu', but these are just part of the trips from Manali organised by bus companies. In season, overnight buses to Delhi cost Rs 350; to Dharamsala, Rs 250; to Leh, with a connection in Manali, Rs 1000; and to Shimla, Rs 250.

Taxi From Kullu to Manali costs Rs 550 via National Highway 21 (on the western side of the river), or Rs 700 if you take the slower, but more scenic route via Naggar.

Fixed taxi fares include Katrain (Rs 225/325), Naggar (Rs 400/550 one way/return), Manikaran (Rs 450/600), Mandi (Rs 800 one way), Dharamsala (Rs 1900) and Shimla (Rs 1900). To Bhuntar airport, the set price is Rs 125.

Getting Around

An autorickshaw is handy to get around, particularly if you have heavy gear, or want to visit the nearby temples. From Dhalpur to the bus station should cost about Rs 15, or to the airport at Bhuntar, Rs 60.

JARI

☎ 01902

Jari is halfway along the Parvati Valley – about 19km from Bhuntar. Like Kasol, it has become something of a traveller resort, though on a much smaller scale. Several of the best places to stay are located in the hamlets above Jari. The views and tranquillity of Jari have been marred slightly by the new Parvati River hydroelectric project.

Just above the bus stand, the huge white ***Dharma Family Guest House*** has OK rooms for Rs 60. Along the main road are the pleasant ***Om Shiva Guest House*** (*☎ 73202)* with singles/doubles for Rs 50/100 and a rooftop cafe, and ***Roman Guest House*** (*☎ 73461)* with rooms from Rs 100.

Golden Rays Hotel (*☎ 73210)* is the best bet on the main road, with clean, spacious doubles with shared/private bathroom for Rs 100/165.

Village Guest House (*☎ 73570)*, a 10-minute uphill hike from the village centre, is a peaceful, well-run place with decent rooms for Rs 50 or Rs 75.

Deepak Restaurant on the main road is the best and most popular place for food.

Parvati Valley buses charge Rs 7 to Manikaran, Rs 12 to Bhuntar and Rs 20 to Kullu. A one-way taxi from Kullu to Jari is around Rs 350.

HIMACHAL PRADESH

MALANA

Across the river from Jari is the interesting Malana Valley. The town of Malana (2652m) can be reached in a full day trek from Jari. It's an isolated village with its own system of government and a caste structure so rigid that it's forbidden for visitors to touch either the people or any of their possessions. It's very important to respect this custom; wait at the edge of the village for an invitation to enter. Organised treks are the way to go; talk to Negi's Himalayan Adventures (☎ 01902-73619) in Jari.

KASOL

☎ 01902

Kasol is another tiny village that has developed (some would say overdeveloped) into a travellers' centre. The village has a lovely setting among pines and streams, but has seen a spate of guesthouse building in recent years. The prettier part of the village, known as 'Old Kasol', is on the Bhuntar side of the bridge. Charmless 'New Kasol' is on the Manikaran side.

In a modern building in the centre of New Kasol are ***Rainbow Cafe & Guest House*** (*☎ 73714)* and ***Parvati River View Guest House*** (*☎ 73716)*, which both cater to the dope crowd and offer reasonable rooms from Rs 100 to 150 with shared bathroom (Rainbow also has doubles with private bathroom for Rs 200).

Two of the nicest places to stay in Old Kasol are ***Yerpa's Guest House*** (*☎ 73763)* on the main drag, and ***Alpine Guest House***, which is tucked away in the woods. Both offer clean rooms with shared bathroom and hot water for Rs 100 to 150 as well as more expensive deluxe rooms, and they both have pleasant restaurants.

Near the bridge are ***Deep Forest Cafe*** and ***Moon Dance***; both offer Western food and groovy tunes.

High above Old Kasol in an old village house is the friendly ***White House Guest House***, which has great views from its restaurant and spartan but spotless rooms with shared bathroom. Follow the signs from the village.

Warning – Fatal Vacations

! Between 1996 and 2000 more than 17 foreign tourists have disappeared or been murdered in the Kullu Valley. Most were reported missing from the travellers centres of Naggar, Malana, Manali, Manikaran and Kasol after setting off on unaccompanied treks into the Kullu hills. Until recently, Indian police put most of the disappearances down to accidents while trekking, but following the brutal murders of a German tourist in July 2000 and a Spanish woman and her child in August 2000, it seems likely that many of the others who have disappeared have met a similar fate.

The area is a major centre for *charas* (marijuana) production – many travellers come here for just this reason – and drugs are believed to have played a part in some of the disappearances. If you go to the area we recommend that you avoid trekking alone, stay clear of drugs and tell your hotel where you are going before you set out on any walk. Be extremely cautious of befriending *sadhus* (spiritual men) and other people wandering in the hills.

If you have any information about any of the disappeared, a Foreign Missing Persons Bureau has been set up in Delhi and can be contacted through the British high commission (☎ 011-6872161).

MANIKARAN

☎ 01902 • elevation 1737m

Famous for its hot springs, which are hot enough to boil rice and apparently cure anything from rheumatism to bronchitis, Manikaran is another place from which many foreigners have forgotten to leave.

Manikaran means 'jewel from the ear' in Sanskrit. According to the local legend, a giant snake took earrings from Parvati while she was bathing and then snorted them through its nose to create spaces where the hot springs spewed forth.

The clouds of steam spewing out from the baths and temples make Manikaran quite atmospheric, but once the sun leaves the valley (early in the afternoon), it can be cold and gloomy. The town is revered by both Hindus and Sikhs and is chock-a-block with sadhus, pilgrims and religious souvenir shops.

At the start of the village is the monumental but not hugely appealing **Sri Guru Nanak Dev Ji** Sikh gurdwara. Diluted to a bearable heat, there are **baths** where you can sample the beneficial effects of the waters at the Sikh temple beneath the gurdwara (separate facilities for men and women). Alternatively there is a fairly unhygienic public bathroom in the town square. For a more private bath, Hotel Parvati charges Rs 25 for one person, or Rs 40 for two, for a 20-minute bath; or there are baths in most local guesthouses.

Access to Manikaran from the bus stand is via the pedestrian-only suspension bridge at the end of the Parvati Valley road. Moneychangers at the bus stand can exchange cash only. In the light of the murders of foreigners in the surrounding countryside, this is not the place to befriend chillum smokers or go off wandering by yourself in the hills.

Places to Stay

Like the rest of the region, prices vary according to demand. Most of the guesthouses are on the north bank of the Parvati River.

Sharma Guest House (*☎ 73742*) is the first place you come to after crossing the foot bridge. It has decent doubles for Rs 75 to 125.

Sharma Sadan (*☎ 73703*) has a fine location next to the Rama Temple on the main square and has nice rooms from Rs 125 (low season) to 400 (June/July).

Just off the square are ***Padha Family Guest House*** (*☎ 73728*) and ***Kailash Guest House*** (*☎ 73717*), which both offer naturally hot spa-baths and courtyard rooms from Rs 75 to 300.

HPTDC Hotel Parvati (*☎ 73735*) has clean doubles at Rs 450 (Rs 200 in low season), which is not particularly good value around here.

By the bus stand are the dingy ***Hotel Amar Palace*** (*☎ 73740*) and better ***Hotel Sharda Classic*** (*☎ 73851*), with OK rooms for around Rs 500 (Rs 200 in low season).

Places to Eat

At the east end of the village, the ***Hot Springs Restaurant*** serves delicious pizzas. ***Holy Palace*** has an impressive carved wooden frontage and reasonable Italian and Israeli food for around Rs 40 a dish.

Nearby, overlooking the river, is the similar ***O-Rest*** with international dishes for around Rs 45.

Shiva Restaurant, near the gurdwara, caters to pilgrims as well as travellers with a menu of thalis and Italian standards.

Getting There & Away

Buses between Kullu and Manikaran leave Kullu every 30 minutes or so until 1.15 pm (Rs 27, 2½ hours). For Manali, take any of the Kullu or Bhuntar buses headed downhill (Rs 20, two hours). The last trip to Bhuntar leaves Manikaran at 5.45 pm. Another option is a day trip from Manali on a tourist bus for Rs 197, which stops at Kasol for a quick look on the way.

A return taxi from Manali to Manikaran will cost Rs 1100. A fixed-price taxi from the stand at the bus station in Manikaran will cost Rs 500 to Bhuntar (one way), and Rs 600 to Kullu.

NAGGAR

☎ 01902 • elevation 1760m

The lovely little village of Naggar is known for its castle, its ancient temples and its Russian art gallery. There are also pleasant treks in the surrounding forests (arrangements can be made at the Ragini, Snow View and Poonam Lodge hotels for around US$30 per day).

The main settlement of Naggar lies on the eastern Kullu to Manali road, but the hotels, temples and gallery are grouped around the castle at the top of a steep 2km road. To get here get off the bus at the village on the main road, Patlikuhl, and walk up, or take one of the taxis or autorickshaws milling around.

Naggar Castle

Naggar was capital of the Kullu Valley for nearly 1500 years and the castle was built by the Raja Sidh Singh about 500 years ago. The castle is built around a courtyard, containing the tiny **Jagtipath Temple**, which houses a slab of stone said to have been carried there by wild bees, and a small **museum**. Surrounding the castle is a fortified veranda offering stupendous views of the Beas Valley. The living quarters were converted into a hotel in 1978 when the raja fell on hard times. The castle is open 7 am to 10 pm daily for a Rs 10 entry fee, but it's free if you're staying here or dining at the restaurant.

Temples

The grey sandstone Shiva **Temple of Gauri Shankar** is at the foot of the small bazaar below the castle and dates from the 11th or 12th century. Almost opposite the front of the castle is the curious little **Chatar Bhuj Temple** dedicated to Vishnu. Near Snow View Guest House is the pagoda-like **Tripura Sundari Devi Temple**, with some ornate wooden carvings. High up on the ridge above Naggar, near the village of Thawa, is the **Murlidhar Krishna Temple**, reached by a woodland path beyond the Roerich Gallery.

Roerich Gallery

About 1km past the castle is the interesting Roerich Gallery, a fine old house displaying the artwork of the eccentric Russian painter Professor Nikolai Roerich, who died in Naggar in 1947, and his son, Svetoslav Roerich, who died in Bangalore in 1993. The Roerich style falls somewhere between surrealism and Russian icon painting and is quite distinctive. It's open 9 am to 5 pm daily (10 am to 5 pm in winter); entry is Rs 10. Leave your shoes at the front door.

A five-minute walk uphill from the gallery is the **Urusvati Himalayan Folk & Art Museum**, which houses a collection of embroidery and folk art. Upstairs is a modern art gallery, which sells postcards and copies of Roerich's paintings.

Places to Stay

Housed in the castle, the ***HPTDC Castle Hotel*** *(☎ 47816)* is reputedly haunted and is certainly one of the more interesting heritage places. Basic rooms with shared bathroom cost Rs 250 and much better doubles with private bathroom range from Rs 600 to 1500. Dorm beds cost Rs 75, but are often full.

Poonam Mountain Lodge & Restaurant *(☎ 47747)* is down the alley behind the castle. Good singles/doubles with hot water cost Rs 150/200 and you can rent trekking gear.

Hotel Ragini *(☎ 47855)* is a mid-range place with wooden decor and excellent rooms from Rs 350 to 500 with TV, hot shower and balcony (heaters are an extra Rs 50).

Closer to the Roerich Gallery, ***Snow View Guest House*** *(☎ 47325)*, has dark but OK doubles from Rs 100 to 200 and small singles for Rs 50 and Rs 70.

Alliance Guest House *(☎ 47763)* is simple but clean, friendly and comfortable. It's run by an expat Frenchman and offers rooms with shared bathroom and hot water for Rs 100 and a few doubles with private bathroom for Rs 200 to 300. In winter, you'll want to avail yourself of a heater for Rs 50.

Places to Eat

Castle Hotel provides the best views, certainly the best atmosphere in the village, and the food is pretty good, too with nonveg dishes like tandoori chicken around Rs 75. The pleasant ***Kailash Rooftop Restaurant*** at Hotel Ragini is worth a try.

Poonam Restaurant has vegetarian food and a great location in the shadow of the Vishnu Temple. Next door, ***Rollick Restaurant*** is a tiny pure-veg place.

La Purezza Italian Restaurant, in the village on the main road, at the start of the road up to the castle, serves authentic pasta dishes for around Rs 70.

Getting There & Away

Buses go directly between the village of Naggar (on the main road) and Manali six times a day (Rs 11, one hour). Another option is to get the bus to Patlikuhl (there are more buses along the western side of the river) from either Manali or Kullu, then take a taxi (Rs 100) from Patlikuhl to Naggar Castle (you could walk, but it's a steep 7km).

A one-way/return taxi from Manali to Naggar Castle will cost Rs 300/400; a return taxi from Kullu is Rs 400. A Kullu to Manali taxi (Rs 550) will probably charge an extra Rs 150 for a quick stopover in Naggar.

Manali

☎ 01902 • pop 4200 • elevation 2050m

At the northern end of the Kullu Valley, the popular resort of Manali is the last major settlement in the Kullu Valley. When it was first discovered by travellers during the 1960s, Manali was a peaceful mountain Shangri-La, with old stone houses and tranquil alpine scenery. The last of the views vanished behind hotel buildings sometime in the 1980s and today Manali looks like any other modern resort, with wall-to-wall souvenir shops, travel agencies and dozens of hotels.

During the 1970s and 1980s, Manali picked up a reputation as a kind of Amsterdam of the Himalaya because of the charas (marijuana) produced in the local area. These days, the dope scene has died down considerably and most tourists come here mainly to take advantage of the good skiing and other adventure sports on offer in the surrounding hills.

Legend has it that Manu, the Noah of Hinduism, stepped off a boat in Manali to re-create human life after floods had devastated the world – Manali means 'Home of Manu'. From mid-April to late June, mid-September to early November, Christmas and New Year it can seem like all of humanity has descended on Manali. The outlying settlements of Old Manali, Dhungri and Vashisht attract large numbers of travellers in the summer, but close down almost entirely in the winter.

Orientation

Manali is based around one street, The Mall, which is effectively a continuation of the highway that runs into town. North of the main town and across the Manalsu River is Old Manali, which has much more character, while the pretty village of Vashisht is due east, high above the Beas on the east side of the valley.

Information

Tourist Offices For tourist information go to the Himachal Pradesh Tourism Reception Centre (☎ 52175), the small white hut under Hotel Kunzam. It's open 10 am to 5 pm daily, except Sunday (open seven days in summer). Don't confuse this place with the far larger HPTDC Tourism Marketing Office (☎ 52116) next door, which sells bus tickets for HPTDC buses and makes reservations for HPTDC skiing courses and hotels, but doesn't have local information. It's open 8 am to 7 pm daily.

Money UCO Bank opposite the tourist offices can change most travellers cheques in US dollars and pounds sterling but not cash, and is open seven days a week (only to noon Saturday). State Bank of India is south of Ibex Hotel on The Mall and changes cash and most travellers cheques. Numerous moneychangers and travel agencies also offer exchange facilities.

Bear in mind that if you are heading north of Manali then you should change some extra money here as there are no exchange facilities available in Lahaul, Spiti or Kinnaur.

Post & Communications The main post office, in Model Town, is open 9 am to 5 pm Monday to Saturday. The poste restante here is reliable. The central telegraph office (fax 52404), a block north, is the cheapest place to receive/send faxes (Rs 10/100 per page).

There are several good Internet cafes. In the centre, try Himalayan Quest, above Chopsticks restaurant, or Himalaya Internet, next to the post office, which both charge Rs 60 per hour. Just below Old Manali, Nirvana Travels has lots of PCs and charges Rs 60 per hour.

Adventure Tour Operators The following locally run places are reliable and long established. They also organise their own tours and activities, which means safety standards are high.

Antrek Tours (☎ 52292, fax 52786, ⓔ naushad_kaludi@yahoo.com) Manu Market
Himalayan Adventures (☎ 52750, fax 52182, ⓔ roopu@nde.vsnl.net.in) The Mall (next to UCO Bank)
Himalayan Journeys (☎ 52365, fax 53065, ⓔ himjourn@del3.vsnl.net.in) The Mall (opposite Nehru Park)
Institute of Mountaineering & Allied Sports (☎ 52342) opposite Ram Regency Honeymoon Hotel (3km from the centre)
North Face Adventure Tours (☎ 52441, fax 52694, ⓔ northface_adventures@usa.net) The Mall (near Mount View Restaurant)

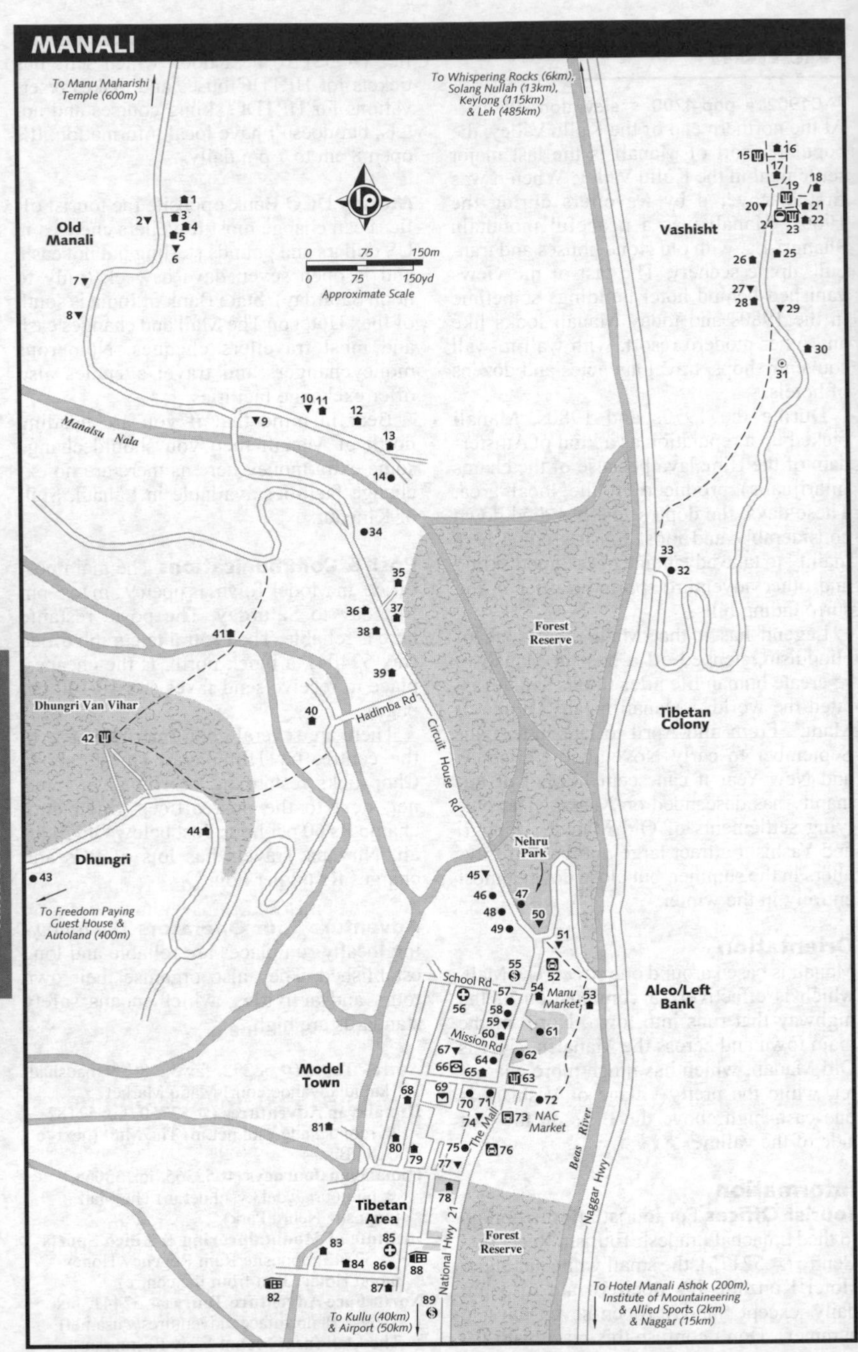
MANALI
To Manu Maharishi Temple (600m)
To Whispering Rocks (6km), Solang Nullah (13km), Keylong (115km) & Leh (485km)
Old Manali
Vashisht
0 75 150m
0 75 150yd
Approximate Scale
Manalsu Nala
Forest Reserve
Dhungri Van Vihar
Hadimba Rd
Circuit House Rd
Tibetan Colony
Dhungri
To Freedom Paying Guest House & Autoland (400m)
Nehru Park
School Rd
Manu Market
Aleo/Left Bank
Mission Rd
Model Town
NAC Market
The Mall
Beas River
Naggar Hwy
Tibetan Area
National Hwy 21
Forest Reserve
To Kullu (40km) & Airport (50km)
To Hotel Manali Ashok (200m), Institute of Mountaineering & Allied Sports (2km) & Naggar (15km)
HIMACHAL PRADESH

MANALI

PLACES TO STAY
1 Dragon Guest House
3 Tourist Nest
4 Veer Paying Guest House
5 Kishoor Guest House
11 Hotel Riverbank; Hotel Him View
12 Rising Moon; Riverside; Hema Guest House; Mamta Paying Guest House
13 Jungle Bungalow
16 Bodh Guest House
17 Dolath Guest House
18 Dharma Guest House; Amrit Guest House
21 Kalptaru Guest House
22 New Dharma Guest House
25 Anand Hotel
26 Surabhi Guest House; World Peace Cafe
28 Hotel Valley View
30 Sita Cottage
35 Pinewood Hotel
36 Sunshine Guest House
37 Hotel Mayflower
38 Banon Resorts
39 John Banon's Hotel
40 HPTDC Hotel Rohtang Manalsu
41 Hotel Chetna
44 Hotel Shrinagar Regency
53 HPTDC Hotel Beas
54 HPTDC Hotel Kunzam; Himachal Pradesh Tourism Reception Centre; HPTDC Tourism Marketing Office
60 Hotel Renuka; Verma Newsagency
65 Su-Khiran Guest House
68 Mona Lisa
78 Hotel Ibex; Ibex Travels; Underground Market
79 Premier Hotel
80 Hotel Shishar; Lhasa Hotel
81 Mount View Hotel
83 Potala Hotel
84 Sunflower
87 Hotel Snow Drop

PLACES TO EAT
2 Mount View Cafe
6 Little Tibet Cafe; Shiva Garden Cafe
7 Ish Cafe
8 Moon Dance Garden
9 River Music Cafe
10 Tibet Kitchen
20 Super Bake; Zodiac Cafe; Ranu Rooftop Cafe
27 Freedom Cafe
29 Rose Garden Inn
33 Phuntsok Coffee House
45 Johnson's Cafe
50 Sa-Ba Restaurant
51 HPTDC Juniper; HPTDC Chandertal
59 Sher-e-Punjab
67 Swamiji's Madras Cafe
74 Mount View Restaurant; Chopsticks; Himalayan Quest
77 Gozy Restaurant

OTHER
14 HPTDC Club House
15 Two-storey Temple
19 Vashisht Temple
23 Rama Temple; Public Baths
24 Bus & Taxi Stand
31 HPTDC Hot Baths Complex
32 The Enfield Club
34 Nirvana Travels
42 Dhungri Temple
43 Utopia Complex
46 Ambassador Travels (Indian Airlines)
47 Himachal Emporium
48 Himalayan Journeys
49 Jagson Airlines
52 Him-Aanchal Taxi Stand
55 UCO Bank
56 Mission Hospital
57 Himalayan Adventures; Bhuttico
58 Charitrust Tibetan Handicraft Emporium
61 Antrek Tours
62 Bhuttico
63 Temple
64 Swagtam Tours
66 Central Telegraph Office
69 Main Post Office; Himalaya Internet
70 Delightful Things
71 Harison Travels
72 Bookworm
73 Bus Station
75 North Face Adventure Tours
76 Him-Aanchal Taxi Stand
82 Gadhan Thekchokling Gompa
85 Mentsikhang Clinic
86 Inder Motors
88 Himalayan Nyingmapa Gompa
89 State Bank of India

Bookshops The best choice in town is at Bookworm, 16 NAC Markets, behind the bus station. It has a great selection of imported novels and books on India.

Dangers & Annoyances Travellers should remember that drugs are still illegal in Manali. Over the last decade, 140 foreigners have been arrested for drug-related offences and drugs are believed to have played a part in many of the disappearances and murders of foreigners in the Kullu Valley.

Dhungri Temple

The Dhungri or Hadimba Temple is a four-storey wooden building in the middle of a lovely forested park, known as the Dhungri Van Vihar. Erected in 1553, the temple is dedicated to the goddess Hadimba and features intricate wooden carvings of dancers and characters from various Hindu stories; horns of bulls and other animals decorate the walls. Every May, there is a major **festival** at the temple, when sacrifices are carried out in honour of Hadimba.

A road goes all the way to the entrance of the park. It's a 20-minute walk or take a taxi or autorickshaw (Rs 20).

Gadhan Thekchokling Gompa

Built by Tibetan refugees in the late 1960s, the gompa has some brightly coloured frescoes and a central statue of Sakyamuni Buddha and dominates the Tibetan area at the bottom of The Mall. It's open 6 am to 7 pm and there's a Rs 2 charge for photography.

Old Manali

The original settlement of Manali is about 2.5km north-west of 'new' Manali. It's a

Outdoor Activities in Manali

Fishing

The Himachal Pradesh Tourism Reception Office (☎ 52175) in Manali issues one-day fishing permits for Rs 100. The season runs from March to June and July to November. You can also get permits at the fisheries office in Patlikuhl. The best angling in the Kullu Valley is at Larji, Katrain and Kasol.

Rafting

Basic rafting is available along the Beas River from April to July and, depending on the monsoon, from mid-September to mid-October. Trips generally start at Pirdi and continue 16km down to Jhiri. Prices depend on the number of passengers and your bargaining power but are around Rs 900 for the day, including transport, equipment, lunch and a guide. Contact Himalayan Adventures or Himalayan Journeys for more details.

Paragliding

In summer, several travel agencies organise paragliding on the slopes of Solang Nullah, north of Manali. Himalayan Journeys and North Face Adventure Tours both offer two-minute tandem 'joy rides' for Rs 400, or 10- to 15-minute 'high rides' for Rs 1500. For more extensive flights, you'll have to head up to Gullubah on the way to the Rhotang La (Rs 2500, 30 minutes to one-hour flight).

Skiing

Skiing for beginners is possible at Solang Nullah from January to March. For details, see Solang Nullah in the Around Manali section later in this chapter. Skiing in summer (April to June) is possible on virgin snow (experienced skiers only) at Rohtang La, north of Manali (Rs 100 per day).

Mountaineering

The Institute of Mountaineering & Allied Sports offers fixed date basic and advanced mountaineering courses lasting 25 days, with food, gear, training and (dormitory) accommodation included, but not transport (Rs 700 to 1000 per day). Himalayan Journeys offers weekly courses for beginners for Rs 7000 (you'll need your own boots).

Hiking

There are several good day hikes from Manali. The 12km hike up the western side of the Beas River to the Solang Valley is a nice alternative to the bus. Lama Dugh meadow is a 6km hike up the Manalsu Nala, west of Manali town and makes a nice day trip. For longer expeditions, book onto an organised trip; there are other less risky, more beautiful areas for hiking by yourself. See the boxed text 'Warning – Fatal Vacations' earlier in this chapter.

Popular options include Beas Kund (three days), Hamta Pass (4270m, five days) and the village of Malana in the Parvati Valley (five days). Rates with Himalayan Journeys start at around US$45 a day, including guides, porters, meals and good camping gear.

pleasant (but rapidly developing) area of old guesthouses and orchards. The modern but tasteful **Manu Maharishi Temple** is built on the site where Manu meditated after he arrived in the area. Old Manali is uphill from The Mall on the far side of the Beas. Follow the road to the left at the top of The Mall.

Clubs

The HPTDC Club House, over the bridge to Old Manali, offers one day temporary membership (Rs 5), allowing access to the bar and restaurant, and a library where you can read (but not borrow) English-language books. Table tennis and snooker can be played for a few extra rupees.

Near the Dhungri Temple, the Utopia Complex (☎ 53846) offers a fairly pedestrian vision of utopia in the form of snooker tables, steam baths and a gymnasium (Rs 25 per session), as well as a restaurant and small museum of handicrafts (Rs 5 entry).

Organised Tours

The HPTDC offers a tour of the Rohtang La (3978m), Nehru Kund (lake), Kothi, Rahala

Falls and Marrhi for Rs 172 and a tour of the Parvati Valley, Vaishno Temple and Manikaran for Rs 197. In season only, there's a tour to Solang Nullah and Naggar Castle for Rs 146. Private travel agencies and taxis offer the same tours plus a trip to Naggar Castle, Roerich Gallery & the Jagatsukh temples for Rs 400.

Places to Stay

Prices listed in hotel receptions are the authorised *maximum* price and most places will quickly offer a 'low-season discount' of up to 50%, even during high season if things are quiet. The high season is from May to July and mid-December to mid-January, though some places also up their rates in October. Prices quoted are for high season.

Note that few hotels in Manali have heating or insulation. Even in some mid-range places, be prepared to dive under four or five blankets to stay warm.

Places to Stay – Budget

Budget accommodation can be easily found in Manali, especially the nearby villages of Old Manali, Vashisht (see Around Manali) and Dhungri. All places in this section have shared bathroom unless otherwise stated.

Manali Behind The Mall, ***Su-Khiran Guest House*** *(☎ 52178)* is one of the best-value places in Manali. Basic doubles are Rs 125 and dorms are Rs 25.

Hotel Renuka *(☎ 53294)* is central but can be noisy and rooms are a little pricey at Rs 450 with hot water and balcony.

Mount View Hotel *(☎ 52465)*, in Model Town, has decent doubles with TV for around Rs 450, plus good low-season discounts and recommended food.

Hotel Snow Drop *(☎ 52883)* in the Tibetan area offers clean, airy rooms from Rs 150 to 350, depending on the season.

Potala Hotel *(☎ 52950)*, nearby, has clean and comfortable rooms for Rs 425 to 625 (Rs 250 to 300 in low season).

Sunflower *(☎ 52419)* is cheaper, with doubles for Rs 275 and Rs 450, and big triples from Rs 325. All rooms have TV. Low-season rates drop to Rs 100.

Uphill from the turn-off to Old Manali, ***Hotel Chetna*** *(☎ 52245)* has lovely views of the pine forest and rooms from Rs 450 (Rs 200 in low season).

Old Manali This overgrown village offers numerous hotels firmly aimed at backpackers, but it's not as atmospheric as nearby Vashisht. Most places are downhill from the old village on the road to new Manali. Most of Old Manali closes down for the winter.

Tourist Nest *(☎ 56520)*, in the village itself, is new with clean bright doubles with private bathroom and hot water for Rs 200 to 300. There's a travel agency and the new wing should be finished by the time you read this.

The family-run ***Dragon Guest House*** *(☎ 52790)*, opposite, is a thriving concern with big, modern rooms for Rs 250 and Rs 300 fronting onto an orchard.

Down a path behind the Tourist Nest, the old wooden ***Veer Paying Guest House*** and the concrete ***Kishoor Guest House*** have nice settings and charge about Rs 150 for clean rooms with private bathroom.

Downhill, in a less-appealing area by the bridge and the HPTDC Club House are several basic guesthouses including ***Rising Moon*** *(☎ 52731)*, ***Riverside***, ***Mamta Paying Guest House*** and ***Jungle Bungalow***, all of which have doubles for about Rs 150 and fairly poor traveller-cafes. Slightly posher places include ***Hotel Riverbank*** *(☎ 53004)*, ***Hotel Him View*** *(☎ 53074)* and ***Hema Guest House*** *(☎ 52285)*, with rooms from around Rs 200 to 400.

Dhungri The village of Dhungri attracts a certain kind of traveller, but there's not much reason to be here unless you have a special herbal interest in the area. Old village family homes have been converted to guesthouses with cheap ultra-basic rooms and the owners walk around the place soliciting for guests.

Places include ***Freedom Paying Guest House*** *(☎ 53673)* with rooms for Rs 50 and ***Autoland*** *(☎ 53673)* with OK rooms for Rs 150. Villagers offer rooms for Rs 50.

Places to Stay – Mid-Range

A lot of the mid-range places are new concrete hotels all lined up in the charmless, uninspiring 'suburb' called Model Town, one block west of The Mall. Each hotel offers almost identical facilities – usually including TV and hot water – for an almost identical price of around Rs 450 for a double (high season) or Rs 250 (low season). Good choices include: ***Mona Lisa*** *(☎ 52447)*, ***Hotel Shishar*** *(☎ 52745)*, ***Lhasa Hotel*** *(☎ 52134)* and ***Premier Hotel*** *(☎ 52473)*.

There are some much more attractive options on the main road between Manali and Old Manali, catering mainly for the Indian family and honeymoon market. Quite a few are housed in old colonial houses and offer TV, hot showers, gardens and (a rare luxury!) fireplaces.

John Banon's Hotel *(☎ 52335)* is an old Raj-era building offering clean, large old-fashioned rooms for Rs 550 a double.

Just uphill, ***Pinewood Hotel*** *(☎ 52118)* is another old colonial-style place run by the Banon family. Rooms in this rambling building cost Rs 650 a double.

Across the road, ***Sunshine Guest House*** *(☎ 52320)* is yet another old-style place with a nice lawn and good rooms with fireplace from Rs 350 to 600.

Farther uphill is the excellent ***Hotel Mayflower*** *(☎ 52104, fax 53923)*, a brand-new hotel with lovely pine-furnished rooms for Rs 600 to 700, and great suites for Rs 1400.

HPTDC runs several places. Bookings can be arranged at the HPTDC Tourism Marketing Office on The Mall. ***Hotel Beas*** *(☎ 52832)*, on the eastern side of The Mall, has great views of the river, and rooms from Rs 250 to 650. ***Hotel Rohtang Manalsu*** *(☎ 52332)*, on the road to the Dhungri Temple, is a pleasant place with good views across the valley. Doubles cost Rs 500 or Rs 700 in the new block.

At the upper end of this price bracket are ***Hotel Ibex*** *(☎ 52480)* with good rooms for Rs 900 in season, or Rs 450 at other times.

Places to Stay – Top End

Top-end prices in Manali won't necessarily get you top-end service, but it will guarantee you central heating and working geysers.

HPTDC Hotel Kunzam *(☎ 53197)*, at the top of The Mall, has good rooms from Rs 1000 to 1600 (30% less in low season).

Hotel Shrinagar Regency *(☎ 52251)*, en route to Dhungri village, is more central and has doubles from Rs 1650.

On the road to Old Manali is the splendid ***Banon Resorts*** *(☎ 53026, fax 52378)* with luxurious rooms, a plush restaurant, a terrace cafe and a bar. Rates start at Rs 1400 (Rs 900 low season).

Hotel Manali Ashok *(☎ 52331, fax 53108)* is just south of Manali on the left bank of the Beas and offers luxurious rooms with views from Rs 1700 to 2150.

Halfway to Solang Nullah, the excellent ***Whispering Rocks*** *(☎ 56680, fax 56622)* has a splendidly isolated location, attractive gardens, a restaurant and an outdoor swimming pool. Well-appointed rooms range from Rs 1200 to 2000.

Places to Eat

Manali The ***Sa-Ba Restaurant*** in Nehru Park, at the top of The Mall, has good Western food such as hamburgers, pizzas and milkshakes from Rs 35.

HPTDC has a complex containing ***Juniper*** and ***Chandertal*** restaurants, near the bridge, which offers a selection in a good setting, but with higher prices at around Rs 65.

Sher-e-Punjab, on The Mall, has a sterile setting, but its Indian food is recommended. There's another (unassociated) restaurant with the same name just down the road, but it's often empty.

Gozy Restaurant, at the southern end of The Mall, is where many people end up of an evening. There's a great selection of authentic Punjabi and Gujarati food at reasonable prices and good service. A meal here shouldn't cost more than Rs 120.

Swamiji's Madras Cafe, farther along The Mall, has large thalis for Rs 35.

Mount View Restaurant and ***Chopsticks***, next door, are cosy, friendly places where you can order authentic Chinese food, Tibetan momos or Japanese sukiyaki (thinly sliced meat) from Rs 45.

Johnson's Cafe is farther uphill and a bit more upmarket. This is a pleasant open-air garden cafe serving good pasta and pizza (Rs 100), excellent desserts (creme caramel!) and cold beer.

Phuntsok Coffee House, at the junction of the Naggar Highway and the road to Vashisht, is a Tibetan-run place that serves up great traveller-oriented breakfasts and the standard Tibetan fare.

Old Manali There are various traveller-oriented options up in the old village of Old Manali. Most food is tempered to the visiting crowds, so there's plenty of Italian and Israeli food, but not much Indian fare. Few places charge more than Rs 65 for a dish.

Moon Dance Garden, just over the bridge, is a typical laid-back, outdoor place with one of the many local 'German bakeries'.

Ish Cafe, farther up, is deservedly popular for its laid-back atmosphere and good if Westernised food. Nearby, ***Little Tibet Cafe*** serves wholesome, cheap Tibetan food.

Also nearby, ***Shiva Garden Cafe*** has good Italian food, and also serves Israeli cuisine.

Back by the bridge, ***Tibet Kitchen*** is the best bet, with an excellent range of hearty Tibetan noodles and Western delicacies. The funky ***River Music Cafe*** has good music and traveller-friendly food.

Up a small path above Old Manali, ***Mount View Cafe*** has great views and the usual travellers' cuisine.

Shopping

The shawl industry that has been building up all along the Kullu Valley comes to a head in Manali, with dozens of shawl emporiums vying for trade. A good place to start is Bhuttico, which has two branches, on The Mall and near Himalayan Adventures. It charges fair, fixed prices and won't try to sell you wool as pashmina. The Himachal Emporium farther north offers high quality at reasonable prices. The main market areas are the **Underground Market** under Hotel Ibex and the **NAC market** behind the bus stand. See the boxed text 'Shopping for Shawls' in the Kullu & Parvati Valleys section for more information on what to look for in a shawl.

There are also a few Tibetan refugee shops selling jewellery and other Tibetan handicrafts. The Charitrust Tibetan Handicraft Emporium on The Mall, and Delightful Things on the road behind the post office both sell good-quality thangkas and other crafts.

Getting There & Away

Air See Getting There & Away under Kullu, earlier, for details on flights into Kullu/Manali airport (Bhuntar). You can book at the Jagson Airlines office (☎ 52843) in the north of Manali town (Visa cards accepted), and at most travel agencies. Ambassador Travels (☎ 52110), at the north end of The Mall, is the agent for Indian Airlines.

Bus At the main bus stand are two booths, open 9 am to noon and 2 to 5 pm, which provide computerised booking services. You can book a ticket up to a month in advance, which is a good idea on the popular routes to Leh, Dharamsala and Delhi.

Long-distance bus companies from Manali (and local sightseeing tour operators) are:

Harison Travels (☎ 53319) The Mall
Ibex Travels (☎ 53180) Hotel Ibex, The Mall
Swagtam Tours (☎ 52390) Mission Rd

Leh Several daily deluxe and public buses connect Manali with Leh from about June to mid-September. This long, truly spectacular ride takes two days, with a stopover in a tent.

HPTDC runs a daily bus (originating in Delhi) for Rs 1100, including an overnight camp at Sarchu, dinner and breakfast. Private agencies charge around Rs 1000 without food or accommodation. Buses depart at 5 am. The daily public bus leaves Manali at noon and costs Rs 405, with an overnight stop at Keylong. Take some food, water and warm clothes and try not to sit at the back of the bus.

For details about the route, see Leh to Manali in the Ladakh & Zanskar chapter.

Spiti, Lahaul & Kinnaur All roads between Manali and Spiti cross over high mountain passes and are only open from April to October. In season, there are regular buses to Keylong between 4.30 am and 3 pm (Rs 72, six hours). For Spiti catch the 4.30 am departure to Tabo (Rs 160, 15 hours) or the 6 am bus to Kaza (Rs 135, 12 hours).

Kullu & Parvati Valleys Public buses shuttle between Manali and Kullu town every 30 minutes (Rs 24, 1½ hours), continuing on to Mandi (Rs 71, four hours). All these buses pass close to the airport in Bhuntar (Rs 31). To Naggar (Rs 11, one hour) there are six daily buses from Manali between 7 am and 5.30 pm.

For the Parvati Valley, you'll have to take a bus to Bhuntar (Kullu buses leave Manali every 15 minutes and pass through Bhuntar), from where there are frequent connections uphill until 6 pm.

Other Destinations To Delhi (16 hours), there is one public 'deluxe' bus at 5 pm (Rs 492) and at least six ordinary buses (Rs 305). Considering the length of the journey, it's probably worth splashing out for a private '2x2' bus on this route. HPTDC have one overnight bus at 5 pm (Rs 521) or you can book a trip with any of the private bus companies in town for Rs 350 to 450. All buses leave around 3.30 pm and pass through Chandigarh (Rs 300, 10 hours). The same luxury buses can be booked through travel agencies in Paharganj in Delhi, but make sure you are getting a 2x2 bus when you book; more than a few travellers have paid luxury prices only to be dumped on a very ordinary village bus.

In season, there are also private and HPTDC buses to Shimla (Rs 250 to 275, 10 hours) and Dharamsala (Rs 250 to 275, 10 hours) at around 7 pm.

Public buses to Dharamsala leave at 8 and 9 am and 6 pm (Rs 157 day, Rs 190 night). There are also five daily buses to Shimla (Rs 160). For Uttar Pradesh, there are buses to Haridwar at 10 am and 12.40 pm (Rs 280, 16 hours) and Dehra Dun at 5.15 pm (Rs 305, 15 hours).

Taxi Long-distance taxis are available from the two Him-Aanchal Taxi Operators' Union stands (☎ 52120) on The Mall. A one-way/return taxi from Manali to Kullu is Rs 550/700 (Rs 800 returning via Naggar). One way/return to Naggar is Rs 300/400. Some other one-way fares include Bhuntar (Rs 650), Dharamsala (Rs 2500) and Leh (Rs 13,000, for three days, two nights).

HIMACHAL PRADESH

Getting Around

Autorickshaw Known locally as three-wheelers, these can take you, and your heavy luggage, to Dhungri, Old Manali and Vashisht, but not much farther, for a negotiable Rs 30 to 60.

Motorcycle Nirvana Travels (☎ 53222), in north Manali, hires Enfields and smaller Japanese bikes for Rs 300 per 24 hours, including third-party insurance. For bike repairs or a tune-up before heading up to Leh, try Inder Motors in Manali's Tibetan area or The Enfield Club by the turn-off to Vashisht.

Around Manali

VASHISHT

Vashisht is a lovely little village, about 4km by road up the hillside from The Mall, with hot springs, plenty of old stone houses and some ancient temples, but it's definitely a 'scene'. The village was founded by the sage Vashisht Muni and there are several old temples in the village dedicated to the sage and the god Rama.

The footpath and road to Vashisht go straight past the HPTDC **Vashisht Hot Baths Complex**, open 8 am to 8 pm daily (but often closed for industrial action). A 30-minute soak in the regular baths costs Rs 40 for one person, Rs 60 for two; a splash-out in the deluxe baths costs Rs 80/100 for one/two people. The public baths (separate areas for men and women) in Vashisht village are free, but don't look very hygienic (open 9 am to 5 pm).

Travellers should note that many places to stay and eat are closed in winter.

Orientation & Information

Buses and taxis stop in the centre of the village near Superbake; pedestrian-only footpaths radiate from here through the village. The path uphill to the right leads to the Vashisht temple and the public baths. Most guesthouses are tucked away in the alleys north of the taxi stand.

Try the World Peace Cafe, near Surabhi Guest House, for Internet access. Travel agencies by the bus stand can book places on luxury buses out of Manali. Several video houses screen foreign movies for about Rs 10.

Places to Stay

Vashisht remains a very popular place for long-term budget travellers who are attracted by its cheap facilities, great setting and herbal attractions.

Budget places include ***Dharma Guest House*** *(☎ 52354)*, ***Amrit Guest House*** and ***Kalptaru Guest House*** *(☎ 53443)*, behind the Vashisht temple, and ***Bodh Guest House*** and ***Dolath Guest House***, downhill from the bus stand, which all offer very similar, no-frills rooms with shared bathrooms. Rates vary from Rs 50 to 100.

New Dharma Guest House *(☎ 52354)* has the same owners as Dharma Guest House and is in a big white building on the hilltop, behind Kalptaru Guest House; it charges Rs 200 for a double with private bathroom.

Downhill, ***Anand Hotel*** *(☎ 54153)* has cleaner, spacious rooms with private bathroom for Rs 100 to 150.

Nearby, ***Surabhi Guest House*** *(☎ 52796)* is a well-maintained modern building overlooking the valley with rooms for Rs 200 to 350 with private bathroom (hot shower). There's also an Internet cafe and a good restaurant.

Farther towards Manali, ***Hotel Valley View*** *(☎ 53420)* offers good rooms and great views from Rs 200 to 500.

Vashisht's best option is the lovely ***Sita Cottage*** *(☎ 52164)*, near the HPTDC baths, with rooms with all mod-cons for Rs 500 upwards, and a very stylish restaurant.

Places to Eat

The ***cafe*** at the HPTDC Hot Baths Complex serves hot and cold drinks, and a selection of good Chinese and Indian and Israeli food, though it's a little pricey compared to other options in town.

Rose Garden Inn, next door, has pricey but delicious Italian and other 'continental' food. Just uphill the restaurant at Sita Cottage has the best ambience in town.

Freedom Cafe, just up the road, has a great outdoor setting and serves good Western breakfasts and Israeli food, though it's becoming a little more expensive than it used to be.

Super Bake, in the village centre, serves wonderful baked goodies. At the bus stand, ***Ranu Rooftop Cafe*** and ***Zodiac Cafe*** are both good places to hang out.

Getting There & Away

From Manali, a three-wheeler will charge about Rs 60. If you are on foot, it's quicker to take the unmarked trail that begins about 200m past the turn-off to Vashisht and goes all the way to Hotel Valley View via the HPTDC Hot Baths Complex.

SOLANG NULLAH

Some of Himachal Pradesh's best ski slopes are at Solang Nullah, about 13km north of Manali. There is 2.5km of runs, with black, red and blue routes mainly for beginners, but only one 300m ski lift – a longer lift is still in the planning stages. February and March are the best months to ski.

Several options for skiing courses exist. The HPTDC (☎ 01902-52116) in Manali organises seven-day skiing packages, including accommodation in Manali, food, lessons and some sightseeing for Rs 3900 per person. Some travellers have written complaining about poor tuition and service. The Institute of Mountaineering & Allied Sports (☎ 01902-52342), also in Manali, runs basic, intermediate and advanced all-inclusive 15-day courses for US$220. These include all equipment, food and dorm accommodation near the slopes, but not transport.

Private courses vary from Rs 6000 to 8000 for a week's skiing, including accommodation in one of the lodges in Solang Nullah, tuition, meals and ski hire. Reliable operators include Antrek Tours, North Face Adventure Tours, Himalayan Journeys and Himalayan Adventures (see Adventure Tour Operators in the Manali section earlier for contact details).

Places to Stay & Eat

All the hotels in Solang Nullah have dining rooms with lovely cosy fireplaces where you can warm yourself with nutritious veg meals and hot cups of chai.

By the bus stop, the ***Friendship Guest House*** *(☎ 56510)* has large rooms going for Rs 300 and smaller rooms with shared bathroom for Rs 250. ***Friendship Fastfood Corner*** serves good food.

Raju Paying Guest House *(☎ 56575)* has large doubles with attractive wood paneling and private bathroom for Rs 200, or four-bed rooms for Rs 300.

Downhill is the grey-stone ***Hotel Patalsu Heights*** *(☎ 56509)* with simple rooms for Rs 100/200 (shared/private bathroom). However, this is also home to the ***North Face Ski School*** and is usually booked up with skiers on courses.

Getting There & Away

Buses leave Manali at 8 am and 2 and 4 pm every day for Solang Nullah (Rs 8). Another option is to take the bus to Palchan, the turn-off to Solang Nullah from the main road, and then walk for about an hour to Solang through gorgeous countryside. Taxis from Manali cost Rs 300 one way. Roads may be blocked by snow in January and February.

Getting Around

The slopes are a steep climb above the village. There is a single ski-lift which covers only 300m of the most basic slope. The rest of it is on foot though you may be able to hire a porter through your hotel.

Lahaul & Spiti

Lahaul and Spiti, the largest district in Himachal Pradesh, is an area of high mountains and narrow valleys bounded by Ladakh to the north, Tibet to the east, Kinnaur to the south-east and the Kullu Valley to the south. Lahaul and Spiti fall in the rain-shadow of the Himalaya, creating a bleak high-altitude desert that inspired Rudyard Kipling to proclaim, 'Surely the gods live here; this is no place for men'.

Centred on Keylong, Lahaul is often regarded as a midway point en route to Leh and the Indus Valley, but there are several ancient gompas in the surrounding hills. To the east, linking Lahaul to Kinnaur, Spiti was only opened to foreign tourists in 1991, and is still regarded as a frontier territory, with basic facilities and limited transport links.

Most people in Spiti are Buddhists, and colourful gompas dominate the villages and village life. In Lahaul, about half of the population is Buddhist, while the other half is Hindu, but as in Kinnaur, it's not unusual to see idols from both religions side by side in temples and homes.

The main crops are barley and wheat, though hops (for beer-making) and *kuth*, a herb reputedly endowed with medicinal powers, are also grown. The indigenous language of the area is Bhoti, which is very similar to Tibetan; there are several distinct, but mutually comprehensible, dialects. The very handy word *jule* (pronounced **joo**-lay) – which in Ladakh means hello, goodbye, please and thank you – is also used in Lahaul and Spiti.

Both Lahaul and Spiti are cut off from the Kullu Valley by heavy snow for up to eight months of the year. The Rohtang La to Lahaul is normally closed between mid-November and mid-June and the Kunzum La to Spiti is normally closed from mid-October to mid-July.

In theory, the road from the Sutlej Valley to Kaza is open year-round, but landslides and flooding frequently block the route, requiring travellers to hike some of the way. At the time of writing, the road had been severely damaged south of Rekong Peo and north of Kharu, requiring travellers to trek 7km in total (until the road is repaired, there is no access to Lahaul and Spiti for motorcycles via this route).

History

In the 10th century, upper Lahaul was united with Spiti and Zanskar as part of the vast Guge kingdom of western Tibet. After Ladakh's defeat by the Mongol-Tibetan armies in the 18th century, Lahaul was split into two regions. Upper Lahaul came under the influence of the Kullu raja, while lower Lahaul, across to the district of Pangi, came under the influence of the courts of Chamba. The more geographically isolated Spiti remained part of Ladakh.

In 1847, Kullu and Lahaul came under British administration as a division of the Kangra state; Spiti was added two years later. In reality power rested with the Nonos, hereditary rulers of Spiti.

With the Chinese occupation of Tibet in 1949, the region's cultural links were severed but there has been a resurgence in the cultural and religious life of Spiti following the creation of the Tibetan Government in Exile by the Dalai Lama. Much work has been done recently to preserve the ancient Buddhist art in the region's gompas.

Permits

Inner line permits are not necessary for travel from Lahaul to Spiti and you are now permitted to go as far down valley as Tabo. A permit is only necessary if you're travelling between Tabo and Rekong Peo, the capital of Kinnaur. For more information, see Permits under North to Kinnaur earlier in this chapter.

KAZA

☎ 01906 • elevation 3640m

The low-rise mountain town of Kaza is the administrative centre and transport hub of Spiti subdistrict, and is surrounded by inspirational scenery. Kaza's 'old town', around the new bus stand, is a maze of little shops, hotels and whitewashed houses. The 'new town', across the creek, is a collection of tin-roofed government buildings, including the subdivisional magistrate's office (look for the Indian flag). State Bank of India doesn't change money, though some shopkeepers might exchange small US dollar notes.

It's an easy-going place to spend a few days – to rest from the arduous bus trips, to visit some stunning monasteries or to apply for an inner line permit if you're heading on to Kinnaur.

Places to Stay & Eat

Mahabauda Guest House, on the main road at the top end of the old town, is a family-run place offering cosy rooms with shared bathroom for Rs 150. ***Snow Lion Hotel and Restaurant***, next door, is also friendly and good value.

Travellers have recommended ***Hotel Snow View*** and ***Hotel Moonlight***, which both offer doubles from Rs 100 to 250.

The accommodating ***Milaraepa Guesthouse***, across the creek, has good-value rooms for Rs 175.

Sakya's Abode *(☎ 22254)*, next door, is a favourite of tour groups in a lovely garden. Good rooms cost from Rs 250 to 500, while gloomy singles cost Rs 100. It has a dining hall serving good Spitian food.

HPTDC Tourist Lodge, in the new town, isn't a bad choice, with five comfortable rooms with private bathroom and hot water for Rs 400.

Layul Cafe serves huge bowls of excellent *kiyu* (square noodles, potato, tomato and onion stew). Other places for food include the Tibetan-style ***Himalaya Hotel*** and ***Il Pomo d'Oro***, run by an Italian expat and serving good, but pricey Italian food.

Getting There & Away

The new bus stand is on the southern edge of town. A bus to Rekong Peo (Rs 105, 12 hours) leaves Kaza at 7 am. There are one or two daily buses to/from Manali (Rs 100, 12 hours) at around 6 am and one to Kullu (Rs 145) at about 4.30 am. There are also irregular buses between Kaza and Keylong (Rs 115, eight hours); otherwise take a Manali-bound bus to Gramphu (Rs 85) and change there. For Tabo (Rs 30, two hours) take any east-bound bus.

There's an informal taxi stand in front of Zambala Guest House, but minivans also hang around the old town centre. Fares are high because of the lack of competition and petrol transportation costs. A taxi to Manali costs a pricey Rs 4000.

AROUND KAZA

Ki Gompa & Kibber

Ki (pronounced 'key'), the oldest and largest gompa in Spiti, has a spectacular location (4116m), 14km from Kaza and surrounded by high-altitude desert. It was built by the famous Tibetan translator Ringchen Zangpo and belongs to the Gelukpa order. The gompa was invaded three times in the 19th century by Ladakhis, Dogras and Sikhs, and later partially destroyed by an earthquake in 1975, but a priceless collection of ancient thangkas has survived these various assaults. No photos are allowed inside the gompa.

Repairing the damage done by the 1975 earthquake, the restoration of the gompa was completed in 2000, just in time for the visit of the Dalai Lama, who performed an auspicious *kalachakra* ritual here, intended to promote harmony throughout the world. Ki has a **chaam festival** in June or July, and one of the most popular **Losar festivals** in February or March.

About 11km from Ki village is the small village of **Kibber**, also known as Khyipur. Kibber was once part of the overland salt trade, and has a dramatic, if desolate location. At 4205m, it used to claim to be the highest village in the world, but now only claims to be the highest village in the world with a 'motorable' road and electricity. The **Ladarcha Festival**, held near Kibber each July, attracts Buddhists from all over.

Places to Stay & Eat It is normally possible to stay at Ki Gompa for a donation, otherwise the friendly ***Samdup Tashi Khangsar Hotel & Restaurant*** in Ki village has nice rooms for around Rs 50.

Kibber has three small guesthouses. ***Sargaung Guest House*** and ***Hotel Rainbow*** rent out no-frills rooms for Rs 50 and offer basic food. ***Resang Hotel & Restaurant***, at the entrance to the village, has carpeted rooms with private bathroom for Rs 150.

Getting There & Away In summer, a bus leaves Kaza every day at 2 pm for Ki and Kibber (Rs 10). This will allow you time to see Ki Gompa while the bus continues on to Kibber, but you won't be able to see both Ki and Kibber in one day. A return taxi from Kaza to Ki will cost about Rs 350. Combining both Ki and Kibber will cost about Rs 400/500 one way/return in a taxi.

Dhankar Gompa

Built nearly 1000 years ago, Dhankar Gompa has a spectacular rocky setting. Once the site of the capital of Spiti, and then a jail, the gompa still has some interesting sculptures and frescoes. A new monastery is being constructed 1km from the site and this is the place to look for a guide to show you around. Herbs growing here are claimed to cure lung and heart complaints.

From Kaza to Dhankar, take any bus headed down the valley and get off just before the village of Sichling, from where there is a steep 8km walk (including an altitude increase of about 600m). Jeeps may occasionally run up here from Sichling. A return taxi from Kaza to Dhankar Gompa costs Rs 800.

Pin Valley National Park

The Pin Valley, south of Dhankar, has been declared a national park and is famous for its wildlife – tourist agencies refer to it as the 'land of ibex and snow leopard' – but the wildlife is elusive. Also here is the 600-year-old **Kungri Gompa**, 2km off the main road near Gulling and is part of the Nyingmapa sect. With a guide and a vast amount of energy, it's possible to hike from the Pin Valley all the way to the Parvati Valley via the Pin Parvati Pass (5319m).

This is trekking and camping country. Accommodation is limited to ***Hotel Himalaya*** at Gulling (Rs 120) and ***Ibex*** and ***Narzang*** guesthouses at Sagnam (Rs 50).

Public transport goes only to Mikkim, though a road is currently being built as far as Mud. There's a single morning bus from Kaza to Mikkim (Rs 25). If you're coming from the east, wait for it at Attargo, at the junction with the main road. A one-way taxi from Kaza to Mikkim costs Rs 800.

Tabo Gompa

Tabo Gompa is one of the most important monasteries in the Tibetan Buddhist world, and is planned as the place where the current Dalai Lama will retire. It was built in AD 996 by The Great Translator, Ringchen Zangpo, who brought artists from Kashmir to decorate the gompa. Along with Alchi in Ladakh and Thöling in western Tibet, Tabo Gompa has some of the best-preserved Indo-Tibetan art remaining in the world (the Cultural Revolution destroyed most of the examples in Tibet).

There are nine temples in the complex (collectively known as the *choskhor*), all at ground level and dating from the 10th to the 16th century. The main assembly hall of the **Tsuglhakhang** is surrounded by 33 raised Bodhisattva statues and houses a four-sided statue of Sarvarvid Vairocana, one of the five Dhyani Buddhas.

To the left of the Tsuglhakhang is the **Lhakang Chenmo**, featuring a central Sakyamuni Buddha and eight Medicine Buddhas. Farther left is the **Serkhang** (Golden Chapel). The statue of Tara is particularly beautiful, showing the same fluid lines and coloured dhoti (long loincloth) as seen in Ladakh's Alchi Gompa.

Around the back of the main complex is the **Kyil Khor** (Mystic Mandala Temple), with some beautiful but faded mandalas. On the other side of the road, opposite Tabo village, there are some **caves** known locally as Pho Gompa, with some faded ancient murals – bring a torch. Photography is prohibited inside the temples.

The excellent **library** in the monastery guesthouse is open to all and is an excellent place to learn about Tibetan Buddhism. There is also a **thangka painting school** nearby, founded by the Dalai Lama.

Places to Stay & Eat The ***gompa guesthouse*** has good rooms with private bathrooms around a central atrium for Rs 200. If they aren't being used by monks, dorms may be available for around Rs 50.

Himalayan Ajanta Hotel has peaceful, carpeted rooms for Rs 100 to 150. Another possibility is ***Forest Rest House***, which must be reserved at the District Forest Office in Keylong (☎ 019002-22235).

The best food is at ***Tenzin Restaurant*** and ***Millennium Monastery Restaurant*** at the back of the gompa guesthouse.

Getting There & Away From Kaza to Tabo (Rs 35, two hours), take the 7 am bus, which goes on to Rekong Peo. Buses returning to Kaza pass through Tabo in the afternoon. A bus from Tabo to Kullu departs around 5.30 am daily. A taxi from Kaza costs Rs 1200.

KAZA TO KEYLONG

From Kaza, the first main village is Losar, about 60km away. It is a beautiful place with a couple of cheap ***guesthouses***. A little farther on is the Kunzum La (4551m). From the pass, a 9km trail goes to the lovely **Chandratal** (Moon Lake), at about 4250m.

Batal is the starting point for treks to nearby **Bara Shigri** (Big Glacier), one of the longest glaciers in the Himalaya. There are a couple of ***dhabas*** at Batal offering basic food.

The road continues on to Gondhla, site of the seven-storey **castle** of the Thakur of Gondhla and the starting point for a visit to the **Guru Ghantal Gompa** at the village of Tupchiling, a steep 4km away.

KEYLONG

☎ 019002 • pop 1797 • elevation 3350m

In the fertile Bhaga Valley, Keylong, the capital of Lahaul and Spiti, is a reasonable place to break up the journey from Leh to Manali (although you're almost there) or to base yourself. The bus station is on the main Manali to Leh road, from where it's a short walk down a series of steps to the town itself. There's a telegraph office in the north of town but nowhere to change money. Drilbu Adventures (☎ 22207), next to Gyespa Hotel, is a new travel agency and can help arrange porters and transport.

Places to Stay & Eat

Lamayuru Hotel *(☎ 22279)* is a good budget bet; spacious, but damp rooms with private bathroom and hot water are Rs 100.

Hotel Dubchen Keylong is better, with doubles from Rs 200.

Hotel Snowland *(☎ 22219)*, a two-minute walk uphill from the Lamayuru, has comfortable rooms with nice bathrooms from Rs 300 to 500.

HPTDC Tourist Bungalow *(☎ 22247)* has a few overpriced doubles at Rs 350, and some dorm beds (six in a room) for Rs 50.

Hotel Dekyid *(☎ 22217)* and ***Tashi Deleg*** *(☎ 22450)* are mid-range places, with clean rooms with private bathroom for around Rs 300. Tashi Deleg has a good restaurant.

About 18km north of Keylong in the village of Jispa is the posh ***Hotel Ibex-Jispa*** *(☎ 019003-33204)* with luxury rooms from Rs 800 to 1200, plus a dorm for Rs 100.

Getting There & Away

Six daily buses travel between Keylong and Manali (Rs 72, six hours); book your ticket in advance at the ticket office. To Kaza there's a direct bus at 6 am (Rs 115); otherwise change at Gramphu (Rs 30).

From 15 July to 15 September the daily long-distance deluxe HPTDC buses between Leh and Manali stop in Keylong but it's very hard to get a confirmed seat. You may have to book the ticket from Manali to Leh, paying the full whack (about Rs 1000). The public bus leaves Keylong at 4 am. Plenty of trucks ply the busy road and are a good alternative. (See the Leh to Manali section in the Ladakh & Zanskar chapter for more details.)

AROUND KEYLONG

Khardong Gompa

The 900-year-old gompa at Khardong, formerly a capital of Lahaul, is situated directly across the Bhaga Valley from Keylong. This Drukpa Kagyud monastery is the largest in the area with about 30 lamas and *chomos* (nuns). There are excellent frescoes but you'll have to track down a nun to open the doors for you. The prayer wheel here is reputed to contain one million strips of paper bearing the mantra 'Om mani padme hum'.

To get to the monastery, head through the bazaar, follow the stepped path down to the hospital and take the bridge over the Bhaga River, from where it's 4km up to Khardong.

Shashur Gompa

About 3km from Keylong is the Shashur Gompa. Dedicated to the Zanskari lama Deva Gyatsho, it was built in the 16th century and is of the Gelukpa order. The annual **Chaam Festival**, held every June or July (depending on the Tibetan calendar) is renowned for the mask dances performed by the lamas.

Jammu & Kashmir

The state known in India as Jammu & Kashmir (J&K) incorporates the regions of Ladakh and Zanskar which are covered in the Ladakh & Zanskar chapter. Srinagar is J&K's summer capital, while the city of Jammu, farther south on the plains, is the winter capital. The regions of Jammu and Kashmir (as distinct from Ladakh) have been subject to political unrest since the late 1980s and the following information is intended for background only.

There are strong cultural and geographical contrasts in J&K. The Kashmir Valley, or Vale of Kashmir, is a fertile, verdant region enclosed by the high snow-capped ridges of the Pir Panjal range to the west and south, and the main Himalaya range to the east. Its population is over 60% Muslim (the only Indian state with a Muslim majority), with a rich Islamic history that can be traced back to the 14th century. South of the Kashmir Valley is the region of Jammu. It includes the city of Jammu, situated on the north Indian plains, a short distance from the rolling Siwalik Hills. North of the Siwaliks, the rest of the Jammu region is drained by the Chenab River whose vast catchment area includes several narrow valleys that extend deep into the high Himalaya. The region of Jammu is predominantly Hindu, although there are small Muslim communities in the vicinity of Banihal and Kishtwar immediately south of the Kashmir Valley.

The political violence in the Kashmir Valley since the late 1980s has discouraged most travellers from visiting the region. Until 1989, a stay on the famous houseboats

Warning

! Lonely Planet strongly advises against travelling to Jammu and Kashmir. While the Indian government has not placed restrictions on visitors, it is foolhardy to go. There are hundreds of militant groups in the state and the risk of being kidnapped is very real – four of the six Westerners taken hostage in the Lidder Valley near Pahalgam in 1995 have never been accounted for. Bomb blasts and shootings are common on the streets of Jammu and Srinagar (curfews are occasionally enforced), and foreigners have been robbed at gunpoint. Buses and trains en route to Jammu have also come under attack and areas near the Pakistani border (eg, near Drass heading towards Kargil) are often shelled.

Ignore the Kashmiri touts in Delhi who will very convincingly tell you that it's perfectly safe to visit. They will have photos and reports from other travellers who have had a 'fantastic' time. Some who have fallen for this (and have usually paid well over the odds for it, too) have found that once in Kashmir the conflict is used to hold them a virtual prisoner with little opportunity to explore independently.

Peace talks continue, but tensions, especially since the nuclear tests of 1998, are still running high. The Indian army's Web site (armyinkashmir.org) gives their perspective on the conflict with biased details of the latest violence; www.kashmirnews.com gives a slightly more balanced view. If you are determined to go, personally check the latest information with your embassy in Delhi beforehand.

Jammu & Kashmir at a Glance

Population: 10.1 million
Area: 222,236 sq km
Capital: Srinagar (summer), Jammu (winter)
Main Languages: Kashmiri, Dogri, Urdu & Ladakhi
When to Go: May to Sept

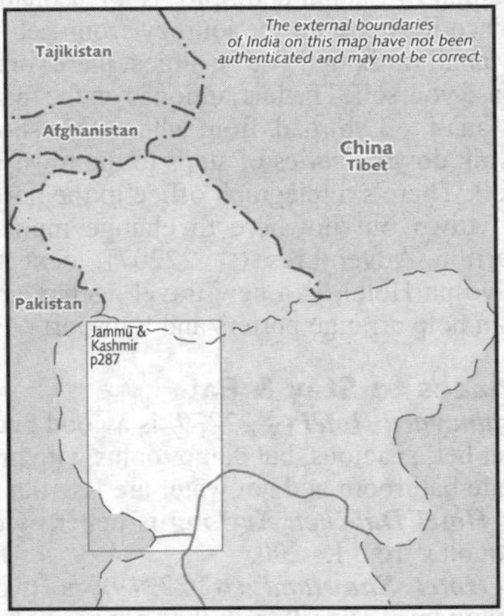

The external boundaries of India on this map have not been authenticated and may not be correct.

Tajikistan
Afghanistan
China
Tibet
Pakistan
Jammu & Kashmir p287

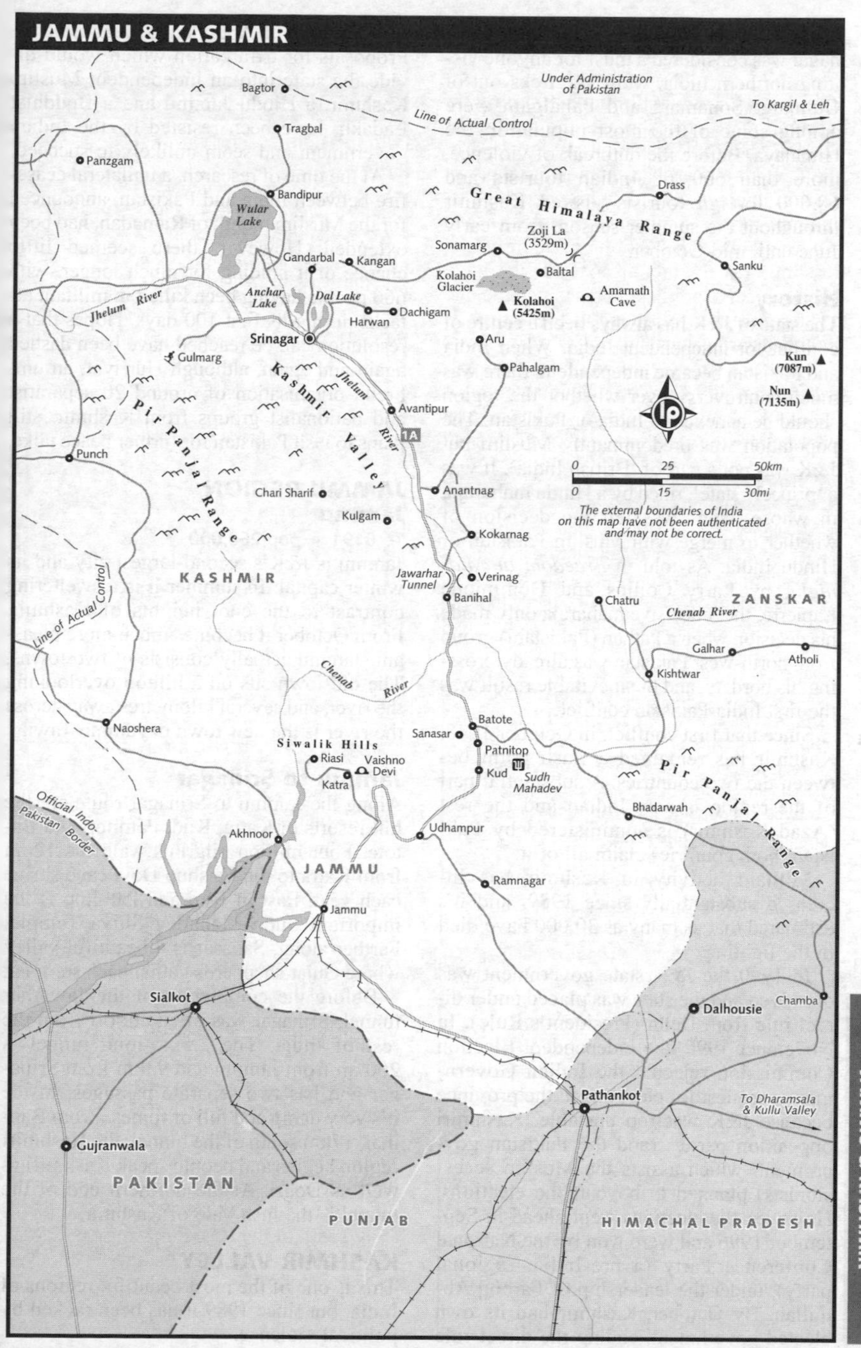

JAMMU & KASHMIR

of Dal Lake close to the city centre of Srinagar was considered a must for anyone visiting northern India, while the treks out of Gulmarg, Sonamarg and Pahalgam were among some of the most popular in the Himalaya. Before the outbreak of violence, more than 600,000 Indian tourists and 60,000 foreign tourists visited Kashmir throughout the summer season, from early June until mid-October.

History

The state of J&K has always been a centre of conflict for independent India. When India and Pakistan became independent, there was much controversy over whether the region should be annexed to India or Pakistan. The population was predominantly Muslim but J&K was not a part of 'British India'. It was a 'princely state', ruled by a Hindu maharaja, in whose hands was left the decision of whether to merge with Muslim Pakistan or Hindu India. As told in *Freedom at Midnight*, by Larry Collins and Dominique Lapierre, the indecisive maharaja only made his decision when a Pathan (Pakistani) group from north-west Pakistan was already crossing his borders, and the inevitable result was the first India-Pakistan conflict.

Since that first conflict, in October 1948, Kashmir has remained a flash point between the two countries. A substantial part of the region is now Indian and the rest (Azad Kashmir) is administered by Pakistan; both countries claim all of it.

Militant activity in Kashmir has increased substantially since 1989, and it's estimated that as many as 30,000 have died in the fighting.

In 1990 the J&K state government was dissolved and the state was placed under direct rule from Delhi (President's Rule). In November 1995, the independent Election Commission rejected the Indian Government's request for elections in the province because J&K was too unstable. Kashmiri opposition parties (and the Pakistan government, which assists the Muslim secessionists) planned to boycott the elections. However, the elections went ahead in September 1996 and were won by the National Conference Party (a pro-India, regional party), under the leadership of Farooq Abdullah. By October, Kashmir had its own elected government, ending the direct rule from Delhi, with Abdullah as chief minister. Proposals for trifurcation which would divide the state into an independent Muslim Kashmir, a Hindu Jammu and a Buddhist Ladakh, have been resisted by the Indian government and seem unlikely to succeed.

At the time of research, a unilateral ceasefire between India and Pakistan, announced for the Muslim month of Ramadan, had been extended. However, there seemed little chance of it holding for much longer, with 666 people having been killed in militant attacks during its first 100 days. Hopes that a resolution can be reached have been dashed again and again, although Hurriyat, an umbrella organisation of around 20 separatist and nationalist groups from Kashmir, still plans to visit Pakistan for further peace talks.

JAMMU REGION

Jammu

☎ 0191 • pop 260,000

Jammu is J&K's second-largest city and its winter capital. In summer it is a sweltering contrast to the cool heights of Kashmir. From October it becomes much more pleasant. Jammu actually consists of two towns. The old town sits on a hilltop overlooking the river, and several kilometres away across the river is the new town of Jammu Tawi.

Jammu to Srinagar

Along the Jammu to Srinagar route are the hill resorts of Katra, Kud, Patnitop and Batote. Four million pilgrims walk the 12km from Katra to the Vaishno Devi cave shrine each year. East of Kud and Patnitop is the important Sudh Mahadev Shiva Temple. Farther along, Sanasar is a beautiful valley where Gujar shepherds gather each summer.

Before the completion of the Jawarhar tunnel, Srinagar was often cut off from the rest of India. The 2.5km-long tunnel is 200km from Jammu and 93km from Srinagar and has two separate passages; inside it's very damp and full of fumes. From Banihal, 17km south of the tunnel, the Kashmiri region begins and people speak Kashmiri as well as Dogri. At the northern end of the tunnel is the lush Vale of Kashmir.

KASHMIR VALLEY

This is one of the most beautiful regions of India, but since 1989 it has been racked by political violence.

The Mughal rulers of India were always happy to retreat from the heat of the plains to the cool green heights of Kashmir, and indeed Jehangir's last words, when he died in 1627 en route to the 'happy valley', were a simple request for 'only Kashmir'. The Mughals developed their art of formal gardens to its greatest heights in Kashmir.

Among Kashmir's greatest attractions were the Dal Lake **houseboats**. During the Raj period Kashmir's ruler would not permit the British (who were as fond of Kashmir's cool climate as the Mughals) to own land here. So they adopted the solution of building houseboats – each one a little bit of England afloat on Dal Lake. A visit to Kashmir, it was often said, was not complete until you had stayed on a houseboat.

Srinagar

☎ 0194 • pop 725,000

Srinagar, the summer capital of Kashmir, stands on Dal Lake and the picturesque Jhelum River.

It is a city with a distinctly Central Asian flavour; when you head south from Srinagar it is always referred to as 'returning to India'.

The old city is in the vicinity of Hari Parbat Hill and includes the labyrinth of alleyways, mosques and houses that constitute the commercial heart of the city. The more modern part of the city is farther up the Jhelum River (above its famous seven bridges), which sweeps through Srinagar.

East of the city is Dal Lake, much of it a maze of intricate waterways. Dal comprises a series of lakes, including Nagin Lake some 8km from the city centre. Most of the more modern houseboats are on these lakes. The famous Mughal gardens, including the Shalimar Bagh and Nishat Bagh, are on the far (east) side of Dal Lake.

Pahalgam

Pahalgam is about 95km east of Srinagar, at an altitude of 2130m. At the junction of the East and West Lidder Rivers, Pahalgam was a popular trekking base before the present troubles. Each year in July/August the Sri Amarnath *yatra* (pilgrimage) attracts thousands of Hindu pilgrims, who approach the Amarnath cave from this area.

Gulmarg

The large meadow of Gulmarg is 52km south-west of Srinagar at 2730m. The name means Meadow of Flowers and in spring it's just that. Also once a popular trekking base, Gulmarg used to be India's premier skiing resort.

Srinagar to Kargil

At 2740m, **Sonamarg** is the last major town before Ladakh and, until the terrorist activity began, it was an excellent base for trekking. Its name means Meadow of Gold.

Baltal, an army camp, is right at the foot of the Zoji La (3529m). **Zoji La** is the watershed between Kashmir and Ladakh: – on one side you have the green, lush scenery of Kashmir while on the other side everything is barren and dry. **Drass** is the first main village after the pass. From here it's another 56km to Kargil (see the Ladakh & Zanskar chapter).

Ladakh & Zanskar

Ladakh – the land of high passes – marks the boundary between the peaks of the western Himalaya and the vast Tibetan plateau. Opened up to tourism in 1974, Ladakh has been variously described as 'the Moonland', 'Little Tibet' and even 'the last Shangri La'. Whatever the description, it's one of the most remote regions of India. As Ladakh has always had close cultural and trading connections with Tibet, its predominant culture stems from Buddhism. This is particularly evident in the most populated region of Leh and the Indus Valley, with its many whitewashed *gompas* (monasteries) and forts perched on top of sugarloaf mountains. Padum, the capital of the more remote Zanskar, shares this Buddhist heritage. Kargil and the Suru Valley, the third main region of Ladakh, is predominantly Shi'ia Muslim and shares a cultural affinity with Baltistan (in Pakistan since Indian Partition in 1947). You do not need a permit to travel to Zanskar, Leh, or anywhere along the major routes to Srinagar and Manali. However, they're required for other remote areas and no-one should ever stray too close to sensitive border areas. The Kargil to Srinagar road can be closed to foreigners when things with Pakistan get heated.

Money-changing facilities are poor, to say the least – Leh is the only place to change

Warning

! Ladakh is a sensitive area; its borders with both Pakistan and China have been disputed. India's war with China in 1962 exacerbated the problem and was the main reason for Ladakh being closed to outsiders until 1974. While China and India are approaching accord on the border dispute, fighting continues between India and Pakistan on the Siachen Glacier (above 6000m in the eastern Karakoram region). This costly warfare – US$1 million a day since 1988 – ensures a significant military presence in Ladakh. Travellers are forbidden to go near the border areas.

The Kargil to Srinagar road was closed to foreigners for a time in 1998 and again in 1999 as Pakistan shelled Kargil and the surrounding area. Always check the latest before approaching Ladakh along this route.

Ladakh & Zanskar at a Glance

Population: 140,000
Area: approx 96,701 sq km
Capitals: Leh & Kargil
Main Languages: Ladakhi, Purig, Tibetan & English
When to Go: May to Oct
Trekking Areas: Padum to Darcha, Lamayuru & Leh; Spituk to Markha Valley & Hemis; Lamayuru to Chiling; Likir to Temisgam

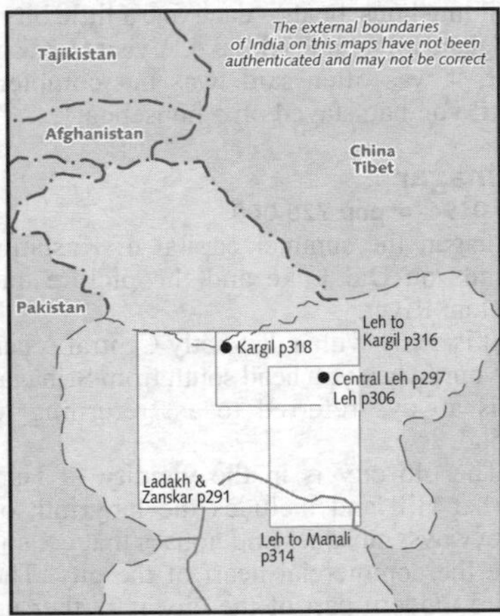

- Explore the labyrinthine alleyways of Leh's old town and wander up to Leh Palace, Ladakh's 'mini Potala'
- Witness the extraordinary austerities performed by the monks at Matho Gompa's annual festival
- Follow the Nubra Valley's old trading route that once connected Tibet with Turkistan, and traverse the world's highest motorable mountain pass
- Explore one of Ladakh's finest and most stunningly set gompas, Lamayuru
- Trek across the high mountain passes of the isolated region of Zanskar
- Stand in awe before some of the finest artwork in the Buddhist world at Alchi, Hemis and Tikse
- Visit the region of the nomadic Khampa people, Tso Moriri, and take in a diverse range of wildlife

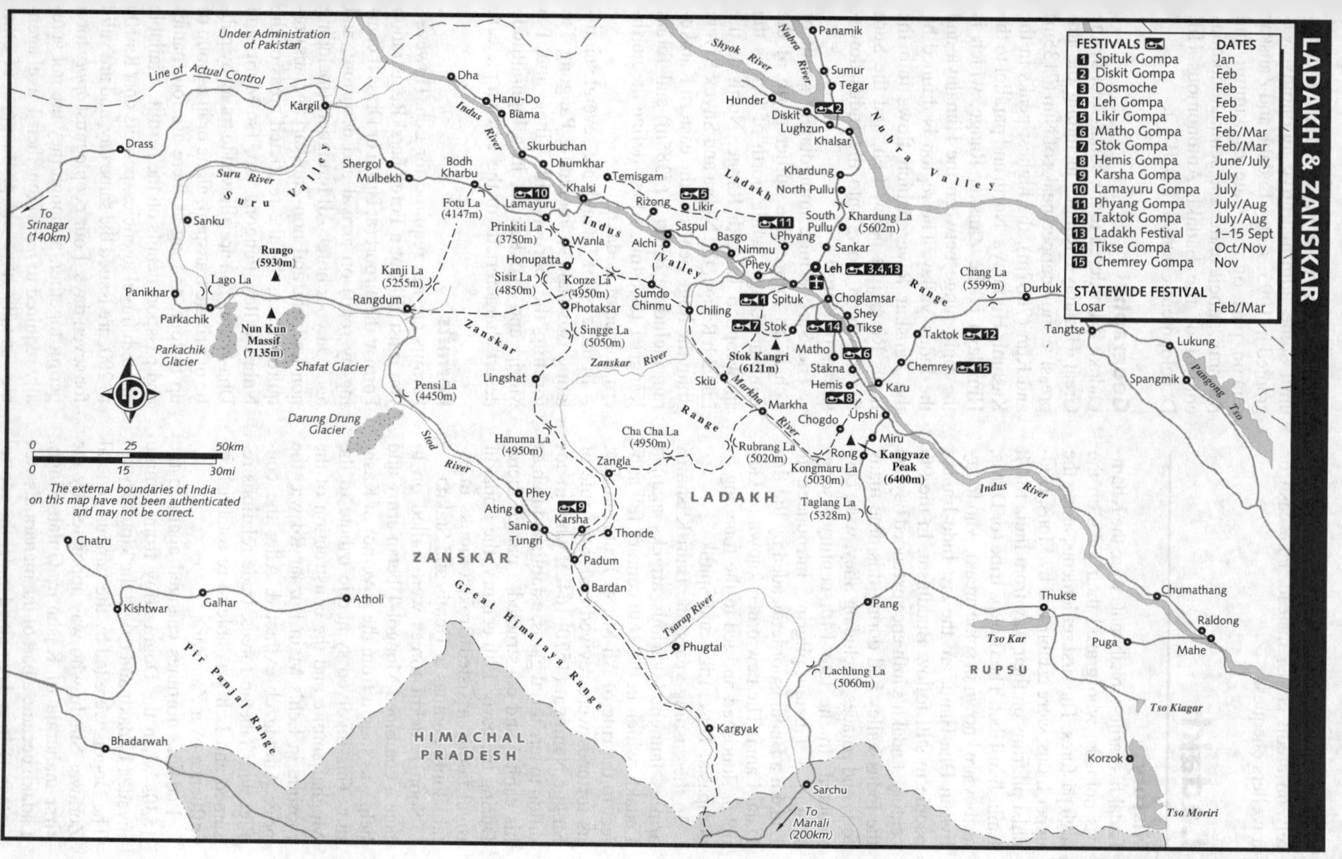
LADAKH & ZANSKAR
FESTIVALS
1 Spituk Gompa Jan
2 Diskit Gompa Feb
3 Dosmoche Feb
4 Leh Gompa Feb
5 Likir Gompa Feb
6 Matho Gompa Feb/Mar
7 Stok Gompa Feb/Mar
8 Hemis Gompa June/July
9 Karsha Gompa July
10 Lamayuru Gompa July
11 Phyang Gompa July/Aug
12 Taktok Gompa July/Aug
13 Ladakh Festival 1–15 Sept
14 Tikse Gompa Oct/Nov
15 Chemrey Gompa Nov
DATES
STATEWIDE FESTIVAL
Losar Feb/Mar
Under Administration of Pakistan
Line of Actual Control
To Srinagar (140km)
Drass
Kargil
Dha
Hanu-Do
Biama
Indus River
Skurbuchan
Dhumkhar
Shergol
Mulbekh
Bodh Kharbu
Suru River
Suru Valley
Sanku
Rungo (5930m)
Lago La
Panikhar
Parkachik
Parkachik Glacier
Nun Kun Massif (7135m)
Shafat Glacier
Rangdum
Kanji La (5255m)
Fotu La (4147m)
Lamayuru
Khalsi
Temisgam
Rizong
Likir
Prinkiti La (3750m)
Wanla
Honupatta
Sisir La (4850m)
Konze La (4950m)
Photaksar
Singge La (5050m)
Sumdo
Chinmu
Chiling
Alchi
Saspul
Basgo
Nimmu
Indus Valley
Ladakh
Phyang
Phey
North Pullu
South Pullu
Khardung
Khardung La (5602m)
Sankar
Leh
Spituk
Choglamsar
Shey
Tikse
Stok
Matho
Stok Kangri (6121m)
Stakna
Hemis
Karu
Chemrey
Taktok
Chang La (5599m)
Durbuk
Tangtse
Lukung
Spangmik
Pangong Tso
Panamik
Sumur
Tegar
Hunder
Diskit
Lughzun
Khalsar
Shyok River
Nubra River
Nubra Valley
Ladakh Range
Zanskar Range
Zanskar River
Lingshat
Pensi La (4450m)
Darung Drung Glacier
Stod River
Skiu
Markha
Markha River
Chogdo
Upshi
Miru
Rong
Kangyaze Peak (6400m)
Rubrang La (5020m)
Kongmaru La (5030m)
Taglang La (5328m)
Cha Cha La (4950m)
Hanuma La (4950m)
Zangla
LADAKH
Phey
Ating
Karsha
Sani
Tungri
Thonde
Padum
Bardan
ZANSKAR
Great Himalaya Range
Tsarap River
Phugtal
Kargyak
Chatru
Kishtwar
Galhar
Atholi
Bhadarwah
Pir Panjal Range
HIMACHAL PRADESH
Sarchu
To Manali (200km)
Lachlung La (5060m)
Pang
Indus River
Thukse
Tso Kar
RUPSU
Puga
Chumathang
Raldong
Mahe
Tso Kiagar
Korzok
Tso Moriri
0 25 50km
0 15 30mi
The external boundaries of India on this map have not been authenticated and may not be correct.

money between Manali and Kargil. Don't rely on credit cards. Instead, take cash or travellers cheques.

Ladakh

History

Ladakh's earliest inhabitants were the Khampas nomads, who grazed their yaks on the high pastures. The first settlements, along the upper Indus, were established by Mons, Buddhist pilgrims on their way from India to Mt Kailash in Tibet. The Brokpa tribe (or Dards, as they are known in some areas), who today live in Dha-Hanu, are the last Indo-Iranian people to still follow Buddhism. In the 9th century, Ladakh's influence extended beyond the Indus Valley and during this time many forts and palaces, including Shey, were constructed. In the late 14th century Tsongkhapa, a Tibetan pilgrim, introduced to Ladakh a Buddhist order headed by the first Dalai Lama. The new order, known as Gelupka, flourished and led to the founding of gompas at Tikse, Likir and Spituk.

In the ensuing years, the Balti-Kashmiri armies launched various attacks against Ladakh, which in the 16th century fell subject to the rule of Ali Mir of Baltistan. But its fortunes were revived under the rule of Singge Namgyal (1570–1642), who, in addition to territorial gains, established Leh as his capital and constructed a palace there. During the early 17th century, the Ladakhi royal family assisted Brokpa monks in establishing gompas at Hemis and Stakna.

Soon Ladakhi forces were called on to face a combined Mongol-Tibetan army and help was sought from the governor of Kashmir. This involved symbolic tribute to the Mughal empire and the construction of the mosque in Leh's Main Bazaar Rd was the price Aurangzeb extracted. After the conflict with Tibetan forces, trade relations resumed and Leh was able to re-establish its influence over Zanskar.

Ladakh's fortunes changed again in the 1830s when the Dogra army from Jammu invaded Ladakh and exiled the king to Stok. The Dogras were led by the famous general Zorawar Singh, who was appointed by the first maharaja of Kashmir, Gulab Singh. Ladakh became a part of the maharaja's vast state in 1846 and remained under the control of Jammu and Kashmir after Independence until some administrative autonomy was granted in 1995. Today Ladakh and Zanskar remain part of the state of Jammu and Kashmir, albeit under the semiautonomous control of the Ladakh Autonomous Hill Development Council (LAHDC).

Geography

Ladakh is bordered to the south-west by the Great Himalaya Range, including the impressive snowcapped peaks of Nun (7135m) and Kun (7087m), the highest peaks in the Kashmir Himalaya. North and parallel to the Himalaya is the Zanskar Range, which is the main range between the Himalaya and the Indus Valley. The region is drained by the Zanskar River, which flows into the Indus River just below Leh, and the Suru River, which flows into the Indus downstream of Kargil.

The Stok Range immediately south of Leh is an impressive outlier north of the Zanskar Range, while north of Leh is the snowcapped Ladakh Range. North of the Ladakh Range, the Nubra and Shyok Rivers drain the huge peaks of the eastern Karakoram including Rimo 1 (7385m) and Teram Kangri 1 (7464m), which define the northern border of Ladakh.

In the east of Ladakh are several scintillating *tsos* (lakes), including Pangong Tso forming the border with Tibet, and Tso Moriri and Tso Kar set in a high-altitude desert characteristic of the Tibetan plateau.

Permits

Permits are not required for Leh. However, you must fill out a Foreigners' Registration Form at the airport (at Upshi or Drass if coming by road) on arrival and departure, and again at your hotel. All foreigners (including non-Ladakhi and non-Zanskari Indians) require permits for the restricted areas of the Nubra Valley, Pangong Tso, Tso Moriri and Dha-Hanu. You are allowed to travel by public or private transport, alone or in a group of up to four, as long as there are four names and passport details on the permit. Available through travel agencies, permits cost Rs 100 to 200, are issued the same day, and are valid for seven days. Four people must *apply* for a permit together, although they are not actually required to *travel* together. Travel agencies usually have old photocopies of other passports to help 'fill up' the required numbers for 'groups'. List every place you may visit and carry the original and photocopies of the permit – there are several checkpoints to pass, all of which require a copy of the permit. Don't even think about setting off without a permit, going to forbidden areas or overstaying your allotted seven days. If you get caught breaking the rules, a visit to an Indian jail is not unlikely, and your travel agency will be severely penalised.

Climate

The temperatures in Ladakh are extreme; some people claim it's the only place where it's possible to sit in the sun with your feet in the shade and catch sunstroke and frostbite at the same time. The sun, which shines, on average, for 300 days of the year, is deceptively strong at this high altitude – bring sunscreen.

Over the past few years the climate has been changing, with more rain and snow, creating problems for inhabitants of a traditionally desert region. Average summer (June to September) and winter (October to May) temperatures are:

region	summer	winter
Dha-Hanu region	-3–29°C	-15–15°C
Leh	-9–30°C	-20–17°C
Nubra Valley	-3–28°C	-15–15°C
Pangong Tso	-12–18°C	-25–18°C
Tso Moriri	-10–17°C	-22– 6°C

What to Bring

Even at the height of summer, temperatures in some valleys can be extremely cold. A sleeping bag and warm clothes are vital in all areas. The days can be hot, causing dry skin and sunburn, so a hat and sunscreen are important, as are paracetamol for acute mountain sickness (AMS). Other items worth considering are torches (flashlights) and candles, as electricity, if there is any, is unreliable, with an official cut-off time of 10 pm. Binoculars might be handy for admiring wildlife, which is guaranteed to disappear as soon as you get close.

Dangers & Annoyances

Over the past few years Pakistan has sporadically shelled the area in and around Kargil (see the boxed text 'Warning' at the start of this chapter). Then in 2000, further violence erupted when Buddhist monks clashed with the police in Leh, causing shops and businesses to close. The Buddhists feel they are being increasingly persecuted by the government in an attempt to eradicate their culture and they continue campaigning for full autonomy. The area was relatively quiet at the time of research but it's always prudent to check locally before visiting this potentially volatile area. At an altitude of 3505m, visitors to Leh invariably suffer some symptoms of AMS (see Environmental Hazards under Health in the Facts for the Visitor chapter). Always allow for this; enjoy full rest in the first 24 hours

Winter in Ladakh

To visit Ladakh in winter you either have to be a bit mad or seriously tough. Although it's sunny during the day, night temperatures drop drastically and you'll find yourself wrapping up as soon as the sun goes down. Hot water is supplied in buckets, but getting your clothes off to have a wash is torturous. Many guesthouses and restaurants close, tourist attractions and services all but disappear and home comforts such as heating become a distant and longed-for luxury.

Despite all the hardship, this is still a great time to visit. Tourist numbers are low and you feel a certain satisfaction to hear just how crowded Ladakh becomes during summer when Western faces far outnumber the locals. This is most apparent during festivals, which have traditionally been held in winter but are increasingly being moved to the summer tourist season. Winter festivals offer a much greater opportunity to participate in and appreciate the centuries-old rituals being re-enacted without having to wrestle with busloads of tourists.

Perhaps the best thing is the opportunity to interact more with the hardy Ladakhis. It's impossible not to respect those who endure this hardship year after year with their ever-smiling faces and unfaltering generous disposition.

The isolation provides another buzz – you feel truly intrepid knowing that the road routes are cut off. For those flying out it's easy to worry about being stranded here for longer than planned and many travellers spend their last few days nervously scanning the skies for the dreaded clouds that will lock them in here.

after arrival and drink plenty of water. If you plan to fly one way, fly into Leh and take the bus out – the effects of the altitude on the Leh to Manali journey will not be so great as doing the journey in the other direction. Many people coming from Manali spend an uncomfortable night at Sarchu, where the altitude is around 4100m.

Travellers have reported that when using a non-Ladakhi vehicle to visit gompas on the tourist circuit from Leh, they've been fined Rs 500 for not having a 'gompa ticket' (Rs 20), supposedly available from the taxi union in Leh. No-one there knows anything about it, which suggests it's yet another scam.

Visiting Gompas

Mahayana Buddhist Tibetan *gompas* (monasteries) dominate the Ladakhi landscape; they are still active places of worship and teaching. Colourfully clad with flags and wheels relaying prayers through the breeze, they've become popular tourist attractions with their shrines and stupas embellished with superb ancient frescoes. Gompas usually have a caretaker monk on site who finds visitors and shows them around for an expected donation of Rs 10 to 20. Some gompas provide cheap accommodation for serious students of Buddhism. Always show respect by adhering to these guidelines when visiting a gompa:

- Your arms and legs should be covered.
- Remove your shoes before entering a shrine.
- Don't drink, smoke or spit.
- Never touch religious objects.
- Don't disturb monks during prayers, including festival ceremonies.
- Never use a camera flash – the frescoes are very fragile.
- Always pass *chortens* (Tibetan for stupa), *mani* walls (Tibetan stone walls with sacred inscriptions) and prayer wheels in a clockwise direction, keeping them to your right.

Special Events

Now that tourism is flourishing in the region, the annual **Ladakh Festival** has been extended and, in a blatant attempt to prolong the tourist season, is now held in the first two weeks of September. Nevertheless, the festival should not be missed. Regular large, colourful displays of dancing, sports, ceremonies and exhibitions are held throughout Ladakh. Leh is the main venue, with other smaller, associated festivals in Tangtse, near Pangong Tso; Shey; Basgo; Korzok, on Tso Moriri; and Biama, in Dha-Hanu. The festival starts with a spectacular march through Leh's main streets. People from all over Ladakh, monks in yellow and orange robes, polo and archery troupes and Tibetan refugees from Choglamsar, walk proudly in traditional costume, wearing *perak* (tall, bright hats) and *papu* (curled shoes). The march culminates in a day-long cultural display at Leh polo ground. (For the best view of the opening ceremonies, ignore the march and get to the polo ground early.)

Other activities during the two weeks include mask dances, which are serious and hypnotic when performed by monks, and cheeky and frivolous when performed by small children. There are also archery and polo competitions, concerts and other cultural programs throughout Ladakh.

The Nubra Valley isn't as crowded with gompas as the area around Leh, so festivals there tend to be less religious and more sports-oriented. During the Ladakh Festival, activities not to be missed include a camel safari between Diskit and Hunder, 'warfare demonstrations' (not quite as violent as they sound), ibex and peacock dances, traditional marriage ceremonies, sword dancing from Baltistan, flower displays and archery competitions. Activities are generally centred in the main villages of Diskit and Sumur.

Festivals still held in winter include the New Year festivals: **Dosmoche**, also known as the Festival of the Scapegoat, and **Losar**. For the first, a large wooden mast is erected outside Leh and dough figures are cast into the desert or burnt, thus carrying away the evil spirits of old year. The second concentrates on offerings to the gods. There are individual festivals held at Ladakh's gompas throughout the year which feature religious ceremonies, music and dance.

Volunteer Work

Nongovernmental organisations (NGOs) are constantly attracted to Ladakh, perhaps because it is so active itself in retaining Tibetan Buddhist culture and the delicate balance of its fragile ecosystem. One target has been the poor education record; 90% of Ladakhi year 10 students fail their exams, with only 1200 per year (85% of whom are female) advancing to further education in Jammu, Chandigarh or Delhi. The main problem has been language. Until Year 8, lessons are in Urdu, followed by two years of lessons in English, in which the exams are set.

Various groups have campaigned to change lessons to English from the start and to produce locally relevant books (ie, picture books with yaks instead of elephants). These organisations run summer and winter schools, pay and train teachers and provide medicine and materials. They are very keen for volunteers to help students with English and provide a cross-cultural experience while helping to preserve Ladakhi culture.

Volunteers with teaching or trade skills are most useful but almost anyone who simply wants to interact with and help local kids is welcome. Work is generally only available in summer, but those with specialised skills can get work through winter too. It's easiest to arrange work through Leh offices upon arrival.

Ecologists, permaculturists and engineers should have no problem finding voluntary work. All organisations listed below would welcome assistance with construction and research into new technologies for preserving the region's environment and natural resources.

Child Welfare Society of Ladakh (☎/fax 53308) Fort Rd, Leh. This society provides aid to students in remote areas of Ladakh and Zanskar. Held in Leh, it takes volunteers during winter school, December to February, to teach English, provide administration and generally hang out with the students. Its office is open 10 am to 1 pm and 2 to 5 pm Monday to Saturday and they always have a cuppa for visitors.

Ladakh Ecological Development Group (LEDeG; ☎ 52646) Karzoo. This group initiates and promotes ecological and sustainable development in accordance with traditional culture. (See Ecology Centre later in this section.) With an emphasis on training, LEDeG accepts skilled volunteers for research and development and teaching.

The Students Educational and Cultural Movement of Ladakh (Secmol; ☎ 53012, fax 53561) Founded by returning Ladakhi graduates, this organisation runs courses for students and teachers. It also produces teaching aids, encourages the arts and is working as part of Operation New Hope to overhaul the education system in Ladakh. Based at Phey, 18km from Leh, a maximum of eight volunteers pay Rs 100 day for a bed in a solar-heated dorm (own sleeping bag required), and veg food. Your English doesn't need to be perfect and illustrators are needed year-round. Drop into the Leh office, on the road to the polo ground.

Language

Ladakhi is the most common language used in Ladakh and Zanskar. Once similar to Tibetan, Ladakhi has now changed considerably. If you only remember one word, it should be the all-purpose *'jule'* (pronounced **joo**-lay), which means 'hello', 'goodbye', 'please' and 'thank you'.

Activities

Ladakh is an adventure playground, with an increasing number of adrenaline-pumping activities on offer. Safety standards are reasonable and in the case of an emergency, the omnipresent Indian army will helicopter casualties out – make sure you have adequate insurance. There are a heap of agencies in Leh and Delhi that organise trips. Ensure your choice has environmentally friendly policies in place (see Responsible Tourism in the Facts for the Visitor chapter).

White-Water Rafting Several agencies offer white-water rafting trips on the Indus and Zanskar Rivers. Rafting is not especially popular, as the rivers aren't particularly reliable, and the season only lasts from about early July to mid-September. A three-hour, calm trip from Hemis to Choglamsar or Phey to Nimmu costs Rs 1000 per person. Nimmu to Alchi costs Rs 2000 and full-moon overnight trips cost Rs 5000. Longer, customised rafting trips for the adventurous cost about US$70 per day, including all transport, gear, food and a guide.

Two of the better travel agencies in Leh which handle rafting trips are Indus Himalayan Explorers (☎ 52788), opposite the taxi stand on Fort Rd, and Rimo Expeditions (☎ 53257) at Hotel Kamglachan.

Camel Safaris Just to prove Ladakh is a desert, it has camels. It's possible to trek 8km across the sand dunes at Hunder on one of these shaggy double-humped beasts. One-day, all-inclusive jeep trips from Leh cost around Rs 1000, or you can organise it yourself through your guesthouse in Hunder and Diskit.

Mountaineering Unsurprisingly, Ladakh is a mountaineering and climbing paradise. Popular climbs include Stok Kangri (6121m) in the Zanskar Mountains south of Leh, Kangyaze Peak (6400m) south-east of Leh and the Nun Kun Massif accessible from the Kargil-Padum road.

Groups wishing to climb in the region should first obtain permission from the International Mountaineering Foundation in Delhi (see Mountaineering under Activities in the Facts for the Visitor chapter). Agencies in Leh also arrange expeditions for around US$60 per day (based on a four- to five-day expedition).

Trekking Trips cost US$30 to US$40 per day all inclusive (minimum of four people required). See Trekking in Ladakh later in this chapter.

LEH

☎ 01982 • pop 15,000

Leh is nestled in a side valley just to the north of the Indus Valley. Until 1947 it had close trading relations with Central Asia; yak trains would set off from the Leh Bazaar to complete the stages over the Karakoram Pass to Yarkand and Kashgar. Today Leh is an important strategic centre for the military, which has a large presence here and is a reminder that the region is along India's sensitive borders with Pakistan and China.

Leh's character changed when Ladakh was opened to foreign tourists in 1974. Since then, more than 100 hotels have been established and many of the shops in the main bazaar have been converted to sell arts and crafts. Leh is dominated by the dilapidated nine-storey Leh Palace, home of the Ladakhi royal family before it was exiled to Stok in the 1830s. Above the palace at the top of Namgyal Hill is the Victory Fort, built to commemorate Ladakh's victory over the Balti-Kashmir armies in the 16th century.

The old town of Leh, situated at the base of Namgyal Hill, is a labyrinth of alleyways and houses stacked with dry wood and dung, which is collected to use as fuel to withstand the long winter months. To the south of the old town is the polo ground (see Spectator Sports later in this chapter). The mosque at the head of Main Bazaar Rd was commissioned by the Mughal emperor Aurangzeb.

In Changspa, an outlying village of Leh, there are important Buddhist carvings dating back to the 8th and 9th centuries, when Ladakh was converted to Buddhism. Close by is the village of Sankar, the site of a modern gompa which serves much of the Leh Valley. The gompa is attended by some 15 to 20 monks from the gompa at Spituk. Leh's main Buddhist place of worship is the Soma Gompa, close to the mosque.

Recently the mood in Leh has become heated, as Buddhists and Muslims, feeling their culture is under threat, have taken to the streets. Buddhists are worried about Muslim backing from Pakistan and the increasing number of Buddhist girls converting to Islam for marriage. They also feel the distribution of government jobs to non-Buddhists is part of a government ethnic-cleansing conspiracy.

Orientation

Leh is small enough to find your way around easily. The road from the airport goes past the new and old bus stands, then turns into the main street, Main Bazaar Rd, where there are plenty of shops and restaurants. South-west of Leh Palace, around Fort Rd, is the most popular area for places to eat, sleep and spend money. About 2km north-west of town and out of Leh is the village of Changspa, with its many guesthouses and long-term visitors. A similar distance north-east, Sankar also has many family-run guesthouses.

Information

Tourist Offices The Tourist Reception Centre (☎ 52297) is 3km south of the town centre, on the road to the airport. For general inquiries the small office on Fort Rd is far handier. Both tourist offices are open 10 am to 4 pm Monday to Saturday. There is a small tourist information counter at the airport open for flight arrivals to handle Foreigners' Registration Forms and distribute maps.

Money Both money and travellers cheques can be exchanged at the State Bank of India and Jammu & Kashmir Bank foreign-exchange offices around Main Bazaar Rd. The former is open 10.30 am to 4 pm, and the latter from 10.30 am to 2.30 pm Monday to Friday; both open 10.30 am to noon on Saturday. Expect long queues in high season.

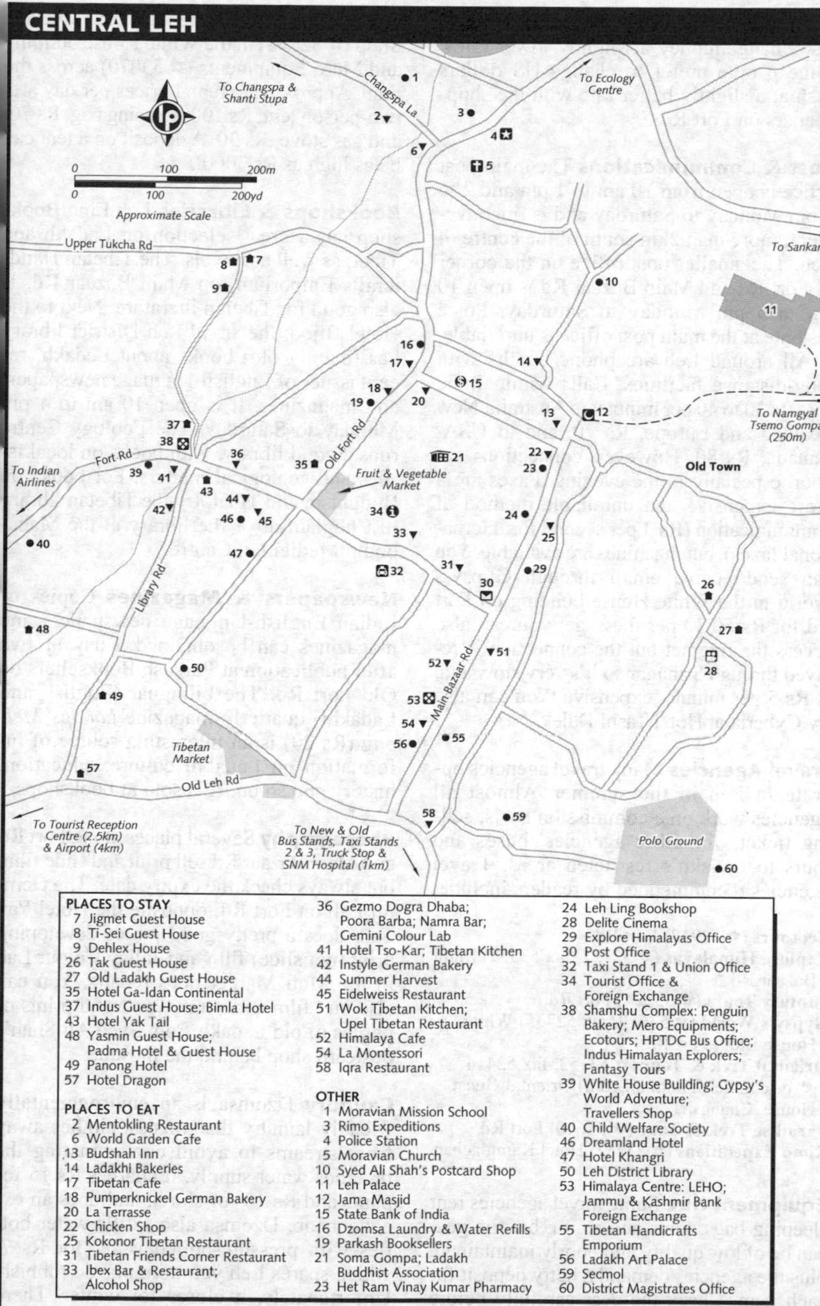
CENTRAL LEH
To Changspa & Shanti Stupa
Changspa La
To Ecology Centre
0 100 200m
0 100 200yd
Approximate Scale
Upper Tukcha Rd
To Sankar
To Namgyal Tsemo Gompa (250m)
Old Town
Fort Rd
Old Fort Rd
To Indian Airlines
Fruit & Vegetable Market
Library Rd
Main Bazaar Rd
Tibetan Market
Old Leh Rd
To Tourist Reception Centre (2.5km) & Airport (4km)
To New & Old Bus Stands, Taxi Stands 2 & 3, Truck Stop & SNM Hospital (1km)
Polo Ground
PLACES TO STAY
7 Jigmet Guest House
8 Ti-Sei Guest House
9 Dehlex House
26 Tak Guest House
27 Old Ladakh Guest House
35 Hotel Ga-Idan Continental
37 Indus Guest House; Bimla Hotel
43 Hotel Yak Tail
48 Yasmin Guest House; Padma Hotel & Guest House
49 Panong Hotel
57 Hotel Dragon
PLACES TO EAT
2 Mentokling Restaurant
6 World Garden Cafe
13 Budshah Inn
14 Ladakhi Bakeries
17 Tibetan Cafe
18 Pumperknickel German Bakery
20 La Terrasse
22 Chicken Shop
25 Kokonor Tibetan Restaurant
31 Tibetan Friends Corner Restaurant
33 Ibex Bar & Restaurant; Alcohol Shop
36 Gezmo Dogra Dhaba; Poora Barba; Namra Bar; Gemini Colour Lab
41 Hotel Tso-Kar; Tibetan Kitchen
42 Instyle German Bakery
44 Summer Harvest
45 Eidelweiss Restaurant
51 Wok Tibetan Kitchen; Upel Tibetan Restaurant
52 Himalaya Cafe
54 La Montessori
58 Iqra Restaurant
OTHER
1 Moravian Mission School
3 Rimo Expeditions
4 Police Station
5 Moravian Church
10 Syed Ali Shah's Postcard Shop
11 Leh Palace
12 Jama Masjid
15 State Bank of India
16 Dzomsa Laundry & Water Refills
19 Parkash Booksellers
21 Soma Gompa; Ladakh Buddhist Association
23 Het Ram Vinay Kumar Pharmacy
24 Leh Ling Bookshop
28 Delite Cinema
29 Explore Himalayas Office
30 Post Office
32 Taxi Stand 1 & Union Office
34 Tourist Office & Foreign Exchange
38 Shamshu Complex: Penguin Bakery; Mero Equipments; Ecotours; HPTDC Bus Office; Indus Himalayan Explorers; Fantasy Tours
39 White House Building; Gypsy's World Adventure; Travellers Shop
40 Child Welfare Society
46 Dreamland Hotel
47 Hotel Khangri
50 Leh District Library
53 Himalaya Centre: LEHO; Jammu & Kashmir Bank Foreign Exchange
55 Tibetan Handicrafts Emporium
56 Ladakh Art Palace
59 Secmol
60 District Magistrates Office

The Khangri, Yasmin and Paradise hotels also change money at slightly lower rates; some people prefer to change US dollars cash at a slightly better rate with the shopkeepers on Fort Rd.

Post & Communications The main post office is open from 10 am to 1 pm and 2 to 5 pm Monday to Saturday and is inconvenient, more than 2km south of the centre of Leh. The smaller post office on the corner of Fort Rd and Main Bazaar Rd is open 10 am to 5 pm Monday to Saturday. Poste restante at the main post office is unreliable.

All around Leh are phone booths with long-distance facilities. Calls within India cost Rs 30 to 40 per minute; to Australia/New Zealand and Europe, Rs 70; and to USA/Canada, Rs 80. However, connections are poor, especially in the evening. Faxes are a more expensive and unreliable method of communication (Rs 3 per second for international faxes), but machines are available. You can send/receive email through Gypsy's World in the White House building on Fort Rd for Rs 50/30 per message; you can also access the Internet but the connection is relayed through Srinagar so it's very slow and, at Rs 5 per minute, expensive. You can also try Cyberia at Hotel Tashi Dalek.

Travel Agencies Many travel agencies operate in Leh in the summer. Almost all agencies work on a commission basis, selling tickets for other agencies' buses and tours to Ladakh's restricted areas. Travel agencies recommended by readers include:

Ecotours (☎ 52918) Fort Rd
Explore Himalayas (☎ 52727, fax 53354) Main Bazaar Rd
Fantasy Tours (☎ 53124) Fort Rd
Gypsy's World (☎ 53659, fax 52735) White House Bldg, Fort Rd
Oriental Trek & Tour (☎ 53153, fax 52414, e orientalleh@hotmail.com) Oriental Guest House, Changspa
Paradise Trek & Tour (☎ 52640) Fort Rd
Rimo Expeditions (☎ 53257) Hotel Kamglachan

Equipment Hire Some travel agencies rent sleeping bags, tents and so on, but the gear can be of low quality and poorly maintained, plus the agencies demand a hefty deposit for each item. Check the gear carefully before you take it. Places that rent gear including mountaineering equipment are the Travellers Shop (☎ 52248) in the White House building and Mero Equipments (☎ 53070) across the road. Approximate rental prices per day are: two-person tent, Rs 100; sleeping bag, Rs 70; and gas stove, Rs 30. A deposit on a tent can be as high as Rs 3000.

Bookshops & Libraries Leh Ling Bookshop has a great selection on Ladakh and Tibet, as well as novels. The Tibetan Handicrafts Emporium, on Main Bazaar Rd, is also good for Tibetan literature. Next to the Hotel Bijoo, the small Leh District library has (mainly old) books about Ladakh, recent issues of English-language newspapers and magazines. It is open 10 am to 4 pm Monday to Saturday. The Ecology Centre runs a good library, with books on local issues and ecological matters. For books on Buddhism and Tibet, try the Tibetan library in Choglamsar or the library at the Mahabodhi Meditation Centre.

Newspapers & Magazines Copies of Indian English-language newspapers and magazines can be obtained a day or two after publication at Parkash Booksellers on Old Fort Rd. The bilingual (English and Ladakhi) quarterly magazine *Ladags Melong* (Rs 20) is an interesting source of information on Ladakhi culture, education, history and so on. It is sold at bookshops.

Photography Several places along Fort Rd and Main Bazaar Rd sell print and slide film, but always check the expiry date. The Gemini Lab on Fort Rd, opposite the Hotel Yak Tail, does a pretty good job of developing print (not slide) film and Jullay Colour Lab in the Moti Market does repairs. You can also buy film and some wonderful prints of photos of old Ladakh from Syed Ali Shah's postcard shop behind the mosque.

Laundry Dzomsa is an environmentally friendly laundry that washes clothes away from streams to avoid contaminating the precious water supply. It charges Rs 15 for pants and Rs 10 for shirts, and does an excellent job. Dzomsa also refills water bottles with pressure-boiled water for Rs 7, which spares Leh yet more plastic rubbish. Unfortunately, it closes for winter. There are plenty of other laundries.

Medical Services & Emergency If you suspect you are suffering from the symptoms of AMS, medical advice is available (☎ 52014 from 10 am to 4 pm, ☎ 52360 from 4 pm to 10 am). For more information on AMS, see Environmental Hazards under Health in the Facts for the Visitor chapter. Leh has several clinics and pharmacies that can dispense advice and medicines for low-level complaints. For anything serious, the public Sonam Norbu Memorial (SNM) Hospital (☎ 52360) is about 3km south of town. There are also a few *amchi* (traditional Tibetan medicine) clinics around town, including one with English-speaking doctors between 9 am and 3 pm on Sunday at the Ecology Centre (all proceeds go towards developing the practice further) – make an appointment one day in advance. Lectures on amchi are held the same day at 10 am. The Het Ram Vinay Kumar near the mosque on Main Bazaar Rd sells medicines and Western toiletries such as tampons.

The number for the police is ☎ 52018; if you need an ambulance call ☎ 53629.

Leh Palace

Looking for all the world like a miniature version of the Potala in Lhasa, Tibet, Leh Palace was built in the 17th century but is now deserted. It's open 7 am to 9 pm. Entry is Rs 10, including a look at the central prayer room. Watch out for holes in the floor.

Namgyal Tsemo Gompa

This gompa built in 1430, contains a fine three-storey-high Buddha image, and ancient manuscripts and frescoes. It's usually open 7 to 9 am. The fort above the Tsemo Gompa is ruined, but the views of Leh from here are superb. The steep path starts from the road to the Leh Palace; a taxi costs Rs 150 return.

Soma Gompa

Leh's modern centre of Buddhism and headquarters of the Ladakh Buddhist Association has the usual gompa features, including a library and notice board displaying articles on Buddhist 'persecution'. This is the place from which the chanting, which competes with the mosque's call to prayer, comes.

Sankar Gompa

The Sankar Gompa is an easy 2km walk north of the town centre. The upstairs part of this interesting little gompa belonging to the Gelukpa order has an impressive representation of the Buddhist deity of compassion, Avalokitesvara (or Chenresig), complete with 1000 arms and 1000 heads. The gompa is only open between 7 and 10 am and 5 and 7 pm. A return taxi from Leh costs Rs 135.

Shanti Stupa

Looming impressively, especially at night when it is lit up, this stupa was built by a Japanese order with the intention of spreading the word of Buddhism by building temples throughout the world. With some financial assistance from the Japanese government, it was opened by the Dalai Lama in 1985.

The stupa is at the end of the road through Changspa, about 3km from Fort Rd. If you're on foot, be warned that there is a very steep set of steps – not to be attempted if you have just arrived in Leh. By taxi (Rs 135 return) or with your own transport, a longish, winding (but less steep) road goes straight to the top, from where there are great views.

Ecology Centre

Known as the Ecology Centre, Ladakh Ecological Development Group (LEDeG, founded 1983) initiates and promotes 'ecological and sustainable development which harmonises with and builds on the traditional culture'. This includes environmental and health education, strengthening the tradition of organic farming, and publishing local-language books. LEDeG accepts volunteer workers.

The small library is very good; the handicraft shop has a good, if a little pricey (it is nonprofit) selection of locally made goods and there's an amchi clinic each Sunday. The centre is open 10 am to 4.30 pm from 1 April to 30 October and 10.30 am to 1.30 pm and 2 to 4 pm the rest of the year.

Sauna & Massage

To help unwind after a trek, Ladakh Sauna and Massage in Changspa offers a sauna for Rs 100 and a massage for Rs 300 with one day's advance notice.

Courses

Buddhist study centres have been set up in both Leh and nearby Choglamsar. In summer, the Mahabodhi Meditation Centre

(☎ 44025) on Changspa Lane has yoga between 3.15 and 4.45 pm and one-hour group meditation sessions at 5 pm Monday to Friday. The centre also holds study camps taking upwards of five days and has a bookshop and library.

Organised Tours

Jeep and taxi trips to the sights around Leh can be organised through travel agencies. The quality of vehicle, tent accommodation, food, destination and guide, and demand, all affect the price, but expect to pay around Rs 5985 for a three-day trip to Diskit and Panamik and US$140 for four days including Stok. Ensure you don't just get a local taxi-driver-cum-guide, which can be organised for far less at the taxi stand. Unionised fares are listed in Getting Around later in this chapter.

Places to Stay

Unless stated otherwise, the hotels and guesthouses listed here close down during winter. The exact time of closure depends on demand, but generally they start shutting shop any time from 15 September, reopening from March onwards. Within this time it's still worth checking out your first choice, but be aware that many places will have turned off their hot and cold water supplies to avoid broken pipes. At these times hot and cold water is available in buckets and the rates given here become highly negotiable. Many mid-range to top-end places will also charge an arbitrary 'service tax' of about 10%.

Although very few places have heating, most rooms are designed with large windows, which allows them to be heated from the daytime sun. Their biggest bonus, when it's warm enough, comes with leaving the curtains open at night to enjoy the luxury of sunrise over the mountains from the comfort of bed. At any time of the year, inquire how regular hot water is before paying extra for it. Leh's electricity supply is spasmodic, so torches (flashlights) may be needed.

There are literally hundreds of guesthouses in and around Leh. The following is only a small selection.

Places to Stay – Budget

Leh The ***Old Ladakh Guest House*** *(☎ 52951)*, which has remained open every single day from 1974, is a wonderful place and full of character, north of the polo ground. It has cosy, individually styled rooms from Rs 180/250 without/with bathroom, and creaky wooden stairs rising from its small tree-filled courtyard up to its terrace. Almost directly opposite, ***Tak Guest House*** is much simpler, with shared squat toilets and bathrooms. Dark rooms downstairs are Rs 100, but the upstairs rooms for Rs 150 are brighter.

North of Fort Rd is a cluster of reasonable places. ***Jigmet Guest House*** *(☎ 53563)* has large rooms, one of which doubles as a library, for Rs 150/300 without/with bathroom. ***Ti-Sei Guest House*** *(☎ 52404)* has a nice garden and Ladakhi kitchen. Rooms cost Rs 150/200. ***Dehlex Guest House*** has a large garden and singles/doubles with shared bathroom cost Rs 100/200.

Changspa ***Oriental Guest House*** *(☎ 53153, fax 52414, ⓔ orientalleh@hotmail.com)*, in a garden below Shanti Stupa, is a friendly, family-run place that has good local information. Singles/doubles with shared bathroom in the old section are Rs 80/120, while those in the new section with private bathroom and heating are Rs 250/300. There is solar-heated water year-round and a large, sociable, cushioned dining area where breakfast (Rs 35) and dinner (Rs 45) are served. It stays open in winter and organises eco-friendly tours in collaboration with an NGO.

Goba Guest House is similar, but surrounded by more fields. Simple rooms with shared bathroom are Rs 80/150 and meals can be enjoyed with the family in the kitchen. One traveller likes it so much they've been here for the last three years, ensuring it stays open during winter.

Shanti Guest House *(☎ 53084)* is another popular farmhouse. Below the Shanti Stupa, it too has been recommended as friendly. Rooms cost Rs 100/200. It stays open for winter. Behind it, ***LEDeG Hostel*** *(☎ 52918)* is a nonsmoking eco-friendly hostel with rooms for those with a particular interest in LEDeG projects. Solar-heated rooms with hot water cost Rs 100/160.

Asia Guest House *(☎ 53403)* is an old favourite, with a terrace restaurant overlooking a large garden. Rooms cost Rs 150.

Eagle Guest House *(☎ 53074, fax 52107)* has rooms for Rs 100/250 and a terrace overlooking the surrounding fields.

Stumpa Guest House is a family home with rustic rooms from Rs 60/160. ***Greenland Guest House*** *(☎ 53156)* is similar, with a small garden and large rooms for Rs 100/160.

Places to Stay – Mid-Range

Bimla Hotel *(☎ 52754)*, just off Fort Rd and surrounded by trees, has singles/doubles with big windows and private bathroom for Rs 200/300. Some rooms have verandas and there are views from the roof over to the palace and fort as well as a downstairs lounge. Next door, ***Indus Guest House*** *(☎ 52502)* is similar but the views can be enjoyed from its rooms, which cost Rs 250/350 with private bathroom. Both stay open during winter.

Padma Hotel & Guest House *(☎ 52630, fax 51019)* offers the best of both worlds, with rooms in the original farmhouse and in a modern block. Large, cosy rooms in the old section cost Rs 150/300 and those in the spotless new section cost Rs 900/1500 with meals. Meals can be taken on the roof terrace, garden or kitchen, and it remains open during winter.

Yasmin Guest House *(☎ 52405)* is a two-storey modern place with a sunny courtyard garden. Good doubles with hot water cost Rs 400/500. ***Panong*** *(☎ 52300)* is a modern place used by Indian Airlines to accommodate passengers when flights are delayed because of bad weather, so it remains open in winter, when rooms cost from Rs 200 to 500.

Hotel Saser *(☎ 52654, fax 52575)*, near the Ecology Centre, is modern with traditional features and has rooms around a garden courtyard for Rs 800/900.

Silver Cloud Guest House *(☎ 53128, fax 52659)*, away from the crowds in Sankar, has been repeatedly recommended by travellers. Rooms, some with balcony, cost from Rs 300/400 with private bathroom and Rs 150/300 without.

Places to Stay – Top End

Places in this category generally don't offer much more comfort than the cheapies, although hot water will generally be running when the others have resorted to sloshing it into buckets. ***Hotel Yak Tail*** *(☎/fax 52118, Fort Rd)* is a large central place with a pleasant courtyard, restaurant and money exchange. The largish rooms with bathroom also have B&W TVs and some even have an attached loungeroom. Full-board rates are Rs 1600/2070 and room only is Rs 1000/1300. This place has nightly entertainment during summer (see Entertainment later).

One of the few actually worthy of being in this range is ***Hotel Dragon*** *(☎ 52139, fax 52720, ⓔ advnorth@vsnl.com)*. Bright and nicely decorated rooms cost from Rs 850/1200. There are a few balcony terraces around the central courtyard and plenty of traditional woodcarvings to admire. It also has a large dining room and travel agency.

Hotel Ga-Idan Continental *(☎ 52173, fax 52414, Old Fort Rd)* is central. Rooms cost Rs 1595/1895 and some have TV. ***Hotel Lasermo*** *(☎ 52313)* has rooms for Rs 1890/2270, including meals in its Ladakhi-style dining room. It remains open during winter.

Gypsy's Panorama Hotel *(☎ 52660, fax 52735, ⓔ matin@vsnl.com)* in Changspa has central heating and so remains open year-round. Rooms are still quite basic, but when freezing, the heating and meals are well worth the Rs 1800/2277 charged. Rooms without heating are available for Rs 800.

Places to Eat

Most hotels have restaurants offering a good enough range of dishes, although these are likely to be closed during winter unless they consider their guest register to be full enough to justify staying open. Bakeries are usually restaurants, so there are licensed bakeries, too. Guesthouses with their cosy Ladakhi kitchens, with warm stoves and shelves of copper pots, are still likely to offer wholesome meals (usually made from organically home-grown vegies) regardless of the number of guests. Leh has a sizable Tibetan refugee population, which naturally has influenced the cuisine and increased the number of Tibetan (and therefore vegetarian) restaurants. There are plenty to choose from, a handful of which remain open during winter to cater to hardy tourists and locals. Unless stated otherwise the following are open year-round serving a range of Tibetan, Chinese and Western-oriented dishes. You'll need to be seated before 8.30/7.30 pm in summer/winter to guarantee a feed.

Main Bazaar Area Along Main Bazaar Rd, mostly on buildings' 2nd or 3rd floors, are several good, cheap (and well-signed) places with large windows looking onto the activity below. Popular choices for Tibetan fare include ***Himalaya Cafe***, which has Leh's most ambient lighting and music, ***Kokonor Tibetan Restaurant***, ***Wok Tibetan Kitchen***, ***La Montessori*** and ***Upel Tibetan Restaurant***. Near the Soma Gompa, ***La Terrasse*** has a pleasant upstairs terrace with umbrellas, although it is better for breakfast and snacks than main meals. It closes during winter.

Budshah Inn, close to the mosque, has pretty good Kashmiri dishes for about Rs 100 per person – a good place if you're craving meat. ***Iqra Restaurant***, at the other end of Main Bazaar Rd, serves a much more limited range of basic Kashmiri meat dishes, but has good views.

Tibetan Cafe on Old Fort Rd is good for tea and snacks.

There's a ***spit-roasted-chicken shop*** on Main Bazaar Rd. A full chicken – great for a picnic – costs Rs 100.

Hot, fresh Indian- and Tibetan-style bread can be bought from the ***Ladakhi bakeries*** in the street just behind the mosque. They bake throughout the day and you can watch them make your loaf – it's great with locally made jam.

Fort Road Opposite the Hotel Yak Tail, ***Gezmo Dogra Dhaba*** is the place for cheap Indian food, such as filling vegetable curries and rice, and it has a useful notice board. Nearby, ***Poora Barba*** is good for tea.

Tibetan Kitchen, in Hotel Tso-Kar, is the best restaurant in town and charges accordingly – around Rs 250 for dinner. For the uninitiated, the varieties of Tibetan cuisine are explained on the menus. It will do a famous *gyarhcee* (Tibetan hotpot) for at least four people with a day's notice. Unfortunately, it closes for winter.

Tibetan Friends Corner Restaurant, lacking views as it's down a side entrance opposite the taxi stand, is an established favourite with the locals who love *thugpa* (Tibetan noodle soup).

Summer Harvest, upstairs on Fort Rd near the Hotel Yak Tail, is very popular, and deservedly so. It closes for winter.

Instyle German Bakery, just off Fort Rd, is a great place for a cup of coffee and a cake, sandwiches and breakfast, including piping-hot porridge. ***Pumperknickel German Bakery***, at the top of Old Fort Rd, is very popular; specialities include lasagne and a big set-price breakfast (Rs 40).

If you fancy a beer with your meal, try ***Eidelweiss***, down a driveway next to Summer Harvest, ***Penguin*** or ***Ibex Bar & Restaurant***. The first two close for winter. There is a ***fruit and vegetable market*** on the corner of Fort and Old Fort Rds.

Changspa The places to eat here are open during summer only. If you're based here you'll be restricted to your own guesthouse's fare unless you fancy a dark and cold walk or can arrange a taxi into Leh.

Shelden Green Restaurant serves beer rather more quickly than it serves the usual mix of Western, Chinese and Indian meals, but the shady garden is pleasant. ***Mentokling Restaurant*** near the Moravian Mission School is another open-air place selling beer. The ***World Garden Cafe***, in pleasant gardens, is good for chilling out.

The open-air ***Mona Lisa Bar & Restaurant***, near the Ecology Centre, is very relaxing and serves beer, pizzas and Ladakhi bread with falafel for about Rs 60, and it has Western popular music.

If you run out of wind on the walk into town, ***Rainbow Cafe*** makes a good drink stop and it's open during winter.

Entertainment

Bars If you're desperate for a bottle of Turbo Extra Strong Lager, there are a couple of bars and licensed restaurants (see Places to Eat). It should cost around Rs 60. *Chang* (Tibetan rice or millet beer) is hard to find; ask your hotel if it can acquire some for you. ***Namra Bar***, opposite Hotel Yak Tail, is Leh's best bar, with dark lighting and music. It also serves food, but is more of a drinking venue.

There is a ***shop*** selling bottles of Indian beer and whiskey at the Hotel Ibex complex, slightly ominously situated just across from where the taxi-stand drivers are. Another can be found at the Moti Market.

Cultural Performances In summer only, the ***Cultural & Traditional Society*** puts on a cultural show behind the Shamshu Complex at 6 pm; tickets cost Rs 50. In competition with this, the ***Ladakh Artists' Society of Leh*** also puts on a show of Ladakhi songs and dances at 5.30 pm daily outside the Leh Palace, costing Rs 70. It's an entertaining show, at a great location. Bring a torch (flashlight) for the walk back. While they *are* set up for tourists, these shows are likely to be the closest you'll get to traditional singing and dancing, and to try (if you dare) some Ladakhi *gur-gur* (butter tea). It's a good idea to avoid the front rows unless you want to become part of the spectacle at the end of the show.

Cinemas Fans of old Hindi musicals with gory fight scenes can get their fix at the ***Delite Cinema*** in the old town. The video *Ancient Futures – Learning from Ladakh* is shown at the Ecology Centre, usually at 4.30 pm Monday to Saturday, depending on demand. It's worth seeing for an insight into Ladakh, and the problems associated with tourism. An earnest discussion group follows the video. The Tibetan Environment Network in Choglamsar also screens movies with a Tibetan theme at 4.30 pm Monday and Friday.

Spectator Sports

Weekly polo matches are contested between Leh and the outlying villages of the Indus Valley at the polo ground south of the old town. During winter the locals play ice hockey in the pond outside the Ecology Centre. See also the boxed text 'Polo & Archery'.

Shopping

Local specialities include Tibetan handicrafts, *pashminas* (wool shawls), woolly socks and organic apricots. Prices can be high; you may find exactly the same item on sale for less in Delhi, Dharamsala or Nepal. The Tibetan Market, off Old Leh Rd, sells Western products and is a good place to look for coats, bags and sunglasses for trekking trips. Moti Market, en route to the bus stands, has a more interesting selection, with local crafts and jewellery. Other reasonable places are the shops in the old town behind Main Bazaar Rd, including Ladakh Art Palace and the Tibetan Handicrafts Emporium, the Ecology Centre and the Cottage Industries Exposition in Changspa. If you are around Leh at the time of the Ladakh Festival, it has good exhibitions and stalls selling local handicrafts and clothes.

Ladakh Environment & Health Organisation (LEHO; ☎ 53691) is training local women in the traditional production of pashminas. It organises for shoppers to visit its village cooperative 20km outside Leh, where they can watch the women at work before making a purchase. Shawls range from Rs 50 to 4500.

Polo & Archery

During the last century, polo games were played in the bazaar and main street of Leh. Nowadays, on Tuesday and Saturday in summer, they are often held at the Leh polo ground (although on Thursday the ground is reserved for a serious football game), with regular matches and competitions during the Ladakh Festival.

Historically, the game has always been more popular in the Muslim regions near Kargil than in Buddhist areas. In Leh, the two goals are placed about 100m apart, although in some villages more than a dozen players in both teams may use fields more than 350m long. Normally, a team consists of six men on horses (normally tough little Zanskari ponies), with one player defending the goal. One local rule stipulates that the team changes ends after each goal, so when a goal is scored defenders make an immediate dash to the opposite goal. The game is played at a frantic pace in 20-minute halves. (Beware, it can be hazardous sitting in the first row at the Leh polo ground!)

Archery competitions are usually held between two teams in the villages, or more often at the National Archery Stadium in Leh. The team with the most arrows closest to the target – often just a lump of sand with a painted round symbol – wins. Archery is not particularly exciting to watch, but it's a great excuse for local people to dress up in their finest traditional clothing. During a match, there is plenty of dancing, singing and drinking of *chang* (Tibetan rice or millet beer) – and some archery in between it all. Not surprisingly, the standard of archery is much higher in Kargil, where Islam forbids drinking.

Getting There & Away

Air Indian Airlines is currently the only airline flying to Leh, as compensation for the loss-making flights it must maintain during the winter. It warns passengers it cannot depart Leh with more than 60 to 75 passengers because of the altitude, climatic conditions and short runway. So, at peak periods, flights can be heavily overbooked. To avoid this, book well ahead and be prepared for disappointment. If you can't get a booking in economy class, it's worth trying for 1st class. Another option is to go on the wait list – even if you're number 100, there is still a good chance you will get on a flight, especially as an improvement in conditions can increase the passenger load. Don't book your Delhi flight and flight home for the same day; always allow a couple of days for bad weather. If flights from Leh are delayed, Indian Airlines will pay for passengers' overnight accommodation.

When flying into the world's highest commercial airport (☎ 52255) at Leh it is important to be aware that the altitude is likely to have a severe effect – allow at least two days for your body to adjust before setting out on proper exploration of the area. It's a great excuse to spend at least the first 24 hours doing absolutely nothing.

The Indian Airlines office (☎ 52076) is on the extension of Fort Rd, in a small white building, and is open 10 am to 1 pm and 2 to 5 pm Monday to Saturday and 10 am to noon Sunday. The competition for seats is savage during high season – some desperate people even resort to bribery. It is worth getting to the office early.

From June to September, Indian Airlines has daily flights between Leh and Delhi (US$105), via Chandigarh (US$70) on Wednesday. From October to May the Delhi-Leh flight goes four times weekly, but this depends greatly on weather conditions. There are year-round direct flights on Sunday from Leh to Srinagar (US$55), and twice a week to Jammu (US$65). They can be a useful, indirect, way of getting out of Leh if the Delhi flights are overbooked.

Bus There is a good local bus and minibus network to take visitors to the main sights and farther afield (see individual entries). Buses leave from the new bus stand, south of town. There are only two overland routes across the Himalaya to Leh: the road from Srinagar, and the road from Manali in Himachal Pradesh. A complication when trying to leave Leh for Srinagar or Manali is that you may not be able to buy tickets on the local buses (or private buses at the end of the high season) until the evening before departure, because buses may not turn up from either of these places. Thus you can't be certain you will be leaving until the last moment. Try to book ahead, if possible, especially in the high season, at the new bus stand in Leh, from where the public buses leave.

To/From Srinagar The Leh to Srinagar road is usually open from the beginning of June to October, but in practice the opening date can be variable. In recent years the road from Kargil to Srinagar has been closed to foreigners because of Pakistani shelling; check at the tourist office for more information. The trip takes two days (about 12 hours travel each day), with an overnight halt at Kargil. There are two classes of public bus, but you may not get the class you want on the day you want. Jammu & Kashmir State Transport Corporation (J&KSTC) buses to Kargil/Srinagar cost: air-con Rs 145/285; general Rs 110/220. Deluxe buses to Srinagar cost Rs 460. They all leave from the new bus stand in Leh at 3.30 am daily in high season.

To/From Manali The Leh to Manali road is open for a shorter period, usually from mid-July and never after 15 October; again, the opening and closing dates can be variable depending on climatic conditions. There is a good selection of private and public buses for this route. As the road goes up to 5328m at its highest point, most people suffer the effects of altitude (headaches, nausea), unless they have spent time acclimatising elsewhere. There are three types of buses which travel between Leh and Manali, all of which generally run daily during the high season, more often if there is demand. Late in the high season, the availability of buses from Leh depends on the demand for passengers travelling from Manali to Leh.

The most comfortable HPTDC (Himachal Pradesh Tourist Development Corporation) bus departs at 6 am from the Shamshu Complex on Fort Rd in Leh, and the HPTDC Marketing Office (☎ 01902-2116) on The Mall, Manali. Tickets, available from travel agencies and at the new bus stand, cost Rs 750, and Rs 1000 including a tent, dinner and breakfast in Sarchu. You can stay in the same tent and order the same meals yourself in Sarchu for less.

Privately owned (mostly by Manali travel agencies) buses offer an alternative. They all leave around 3.30 am and cost about Rs 800, plus accommodation and food in Sarchu or Darcha – the price is subject to change according to demand. In Leh, you can buy your tickets from any travel agency, which means you probably won't know what bus you have a ticket for until you get on. In Manali, bookings can be made directly with the bus agencies or travel agencies. See Getting There & Away under Manali in the Himachal Pradesh chapter for details.

The third alternative is the less comfortable and generally slower, but certainly cheaper, public bus. These buses leave from Leh at about 5 am daily. Tickets, which should be bought at least one day in advance from the new bus stand, cost Rs 400.

Truck These are a worthy, and acceptable, method of travelling to, or to places on the way to, Manali or Srinagar. However, trucks may not stop overnight, but instead drive through – not a great idea; or they may stop anywhere alongside the road – not much fun. They can be more comfortable if there are only a couple of people in the cabin and are faster and cheaper (around Rs 300) than the bus. Plenty of trucks travel this route in season. Talk to drivers at the old bus stand in Leh the day before you want to travel.

Jeep & Taxi These are an expensive, but useful alternative to the bus, and they allow for stops to take photos and visit villages. 'Indian jeeps' take five passengers, while 'Japanese jeeps' and Ambassador taxis take four. Taxis can be hired through accommodation, or at three designated stands. Taxi stand No 1 (☎ 52723) on Fort Rd is open 7 am to 7 pm. Additional taxis hang around Fort Rd very early in the morning. Stand No 2 is at the old bus stand, where a few old taxis loiter, and No 3 is at the new bus stand, but fewer taxis hang around here. If planning a long trip or tour, try to get a driver who speaks English and knows the area – you can arrange this the day beforehand.

Unionised fares are listed at the stands (discounts of up to 40% are negotiable in low season). Return trips to nearby gompas cost:

Sankar, Spituk and Phyang	Rs 580
Shey, Tikse and Stok	Rs 685
Stakna and Matho	Rs 785
Two-day trip from Leh to Manali (including an overnight stop)	Rs 10,130

Extra charges are Rs 250 if staying overnight and waiting time for the second and third hours (the first is free) is Rs 115 per hour.

Motorcycle Riding a motorcycle is just about the perfect way of getting to and travelling around Ladakh. It is worth remembering that there are no villages between Keylong and Leh, so you will have to take all your spare parts, particularly spare chains and tubes. There are petrol stations at Tandi and Keylong, and tent sites may sell limited (and sometimes diluted) petrol at twice the Leh or Manali price. At all times, it is advisable to wear cold- and wet-weather gear, including boots, because the road is always substandard, muddy, wet and/or dusty.

For local exploration, World Adventure (☎ 53373), on Main Bazaar Rd, and Peaks and Lamas, on Fort Rd, hire bikes for about Rs 500 per day, plus petrol. Ensure that you have comprehensive insurance that covers you in an accident in which either yourself or a local person is injured.

Getting Around

To/From the Airport There is an erratic bus service from the airport but it's much easier to take a taxi to Leh/Changspa for Rs 80/125. Some of the 'taxi drivers' awaiting flight arrivals are actually hotel touts, but they don't pressure you too much if you insist on being taken to your chosen hotel.

Bicycle There are many sights within cycling distance of Leh. Dreamland Hotel and Wisdom Travels, both on Fort Rd, hire out mountain bikes for around Rs 250 per day.

AROUND LEH

Making good day trips from Leh are many beautiful gompas and villages, as well as areas which have recently been opened to travellers (with permits) by the Indian authorities. In some, such as Pangong Tso and Tso Moriri, there are no guesthouses or shops to buy supplies (although this is likely to change soon). You must take all your own food, as well as sleeping and cooking equipment (which can be hired in Leh). In the more populated areas with guesthouses and shops you still might want to bring some canned meat and fresh vegetables from Leh to liven up a boring plate of dhal and rice or to share with the locals.

Spituk Gompa

On a hilltop above the Indus river and only 8km from Leh, the Spituk Gompa was built in the 15th century under the Gelukpa order. It is next to the airport, so it has an ugly view at the front, but the back looks onto the pretty local village. The two prayer rooms have some nice Buddha statues, only unveiled once a year during the January festival.

Spituk has nowhere to stay or eat. From Leh to Spituk is a long, hot walk. Alternatively, take one of the minibuses (Rs 4.50), which leave Leh every 30 minutes. Taxis from Leh cost Rs 225 return.

Phyang

Not far past Spituk, a long, roughish track off the main road leads to the pretty village of Phyang. **Mani walls** lead to the little-visited gompa, which was built around the 16th century by King Tashi Namgyal and is today home to about 45 monks of the Kagyupa order. An elaborate *thangka* (Tibetan religious cloth painting) is unveiled at the annual festival in July/August.

Minibuses leave Leh for Phyang (Rs 9) at 8 am, returning 10 am. Buses from Leh leave daily at 7.30 am and 1.30 and 4.30 pm (Rs 11.50). Taxis from Leh cost Rs 495 return.

Nimmu

Nimmu is a pleasant place to stop for tea. About 8km east, towards Leh and easily seen from the road, is the junction of the differently coloured Indus and Zanskar Rivers. If you can, get out and admire this

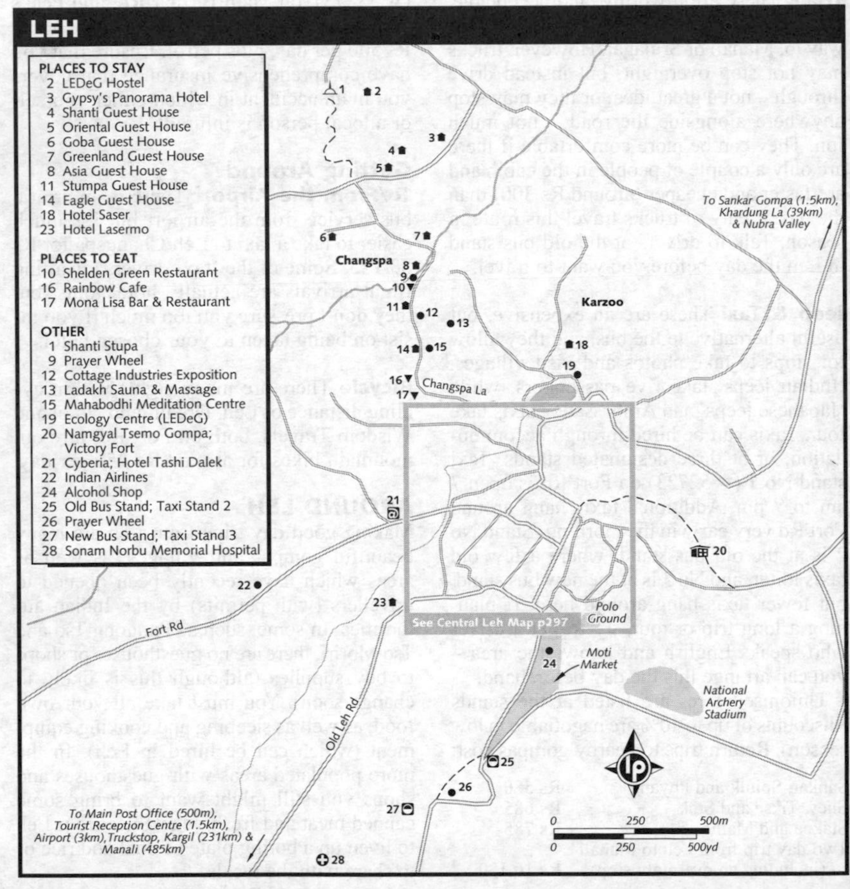

really spectacular sight. A direct minibus leaves Leh for Nimmu (Rs 16) at 3.30 pm, returning at 7 am; a one-way/return taxi from Leh costs Rs 577/715.

Basgo

Basgo was the capital of lower Ladakh before the Ladakh kingdom was united at Leh. Listed as one of the top 100 endangered World Heritage Sites in 2000, the 400-year-old mud-brick **gompa** is up winding, steep tracks. The prayer room in the **Ser Zung Temple** has great frescoes; another temple has an enormous gold-and-copper statue of the Maitreya Buddha (the future Buddha), and some elaborate roof and wall frescoes. The Basgo Welfare Committee of Volunteers is working to restore the gompa as best it can. In 2000, after three months of hard work, a wall that the volunteers had just completed promptly fell down. There are a couple of options for staying in ***family homes*** just below the gompa. Daily buses from Leh to Alchi pass Basgo. A one-way/return taxi from Leh costs Rs 660/825.

Likir

The magnificent gompa at Likir, known as the **Klu-kkhyil Gompa** (Klu-kkhyil means water spirits), was founded in the 14th century, and was the first in Ladakh known to have been built under the direction of Tibetan monks. The present gompa was rebuilt in the 18th century, rededicated to the Gelukpa order, and is now inhabited by almost 150 monks, who offer free tea and guided tours to visitors.

To stay in Likir, return to the village, about a 30-minute walk across the fields. The pleasant ***Norboo Guest House*** has a large, authentic Ladakhi kitchen and a thangka studio. Rooms here, including all meals, are good value at Rs 150 per person. ***Gaph-Chow Guest House and Camping*** has rooms for Rs 200, and a big kitchen. Camping costs Rs 60. Further accommodation and refreshments are available at the gompa.

A minibus from Leh to Likir (Rs 26.50) leaves at 3.30 pm daily, returning at 7 am. A one-way/return taxi from Leh costs Rs 795/890.

Saspul

Saspul is a village on the main road, over the river from Alchi. There is a small white-and-red **cave temple** to the left of the gompa. ***Chakzoth Guest House***, on the main road in Saspul, has small rooms for Rs 50. ***Hotel Duke*** (☎ *194106-27021*) is a decent mid-range place, with Ladakhi murals and carved doors; it has comfortable doubles for Rs 500, and dinner for Rs 120.

Minibuses to Saspul (Rs 27.50) leave Leh at 3.30 pm, returning at 7 am.

Alchi

Alchi Gompa is the only one in Ladakh on flat ground, so no knee-breaking climb is involved. The gompa was founded in the 11th century by The Great Translator, Ringchen Zangpo, on his return from India, which accounts for the Indian, and particularly Kashmiri, influences.

The three-storey **Dharma Wheel Gompa** (actually run by the gompa in Likir) is noted for its massive Buddha statues. Within the complex, there are other statues made of clay, lavish woodcarvings, Kashmiri-style wall paintings, and the village is dotted with chortens. Unfortunately, some of the frescoes showing the life of Buddha have been rather badly restored. But thanks to some help from German experts, all may not be lost and restoration continues.

Places to Stay & Eat Alchi's accommodation is mainly grouped around the gompa and car park (with a tea stand and small grocery shop), both of which are at the end of the road into the village. As this is primarily a summer tourist resort virtually everything here closes in winter. During the rest of the year, guesthouses operate restaurants.

Choskor Guest House, to the left as you enter Alchi, is a cosy traditional house with singles/doubles for Rs 80/100.

Lotsava has basic but clean and comfortable rooms for Rs 100/150. Most of the bathrooms are outside, within the small garden.

Samdup Ling Guest House has rooms with private bathroom for Rs 150 and a garden restaurant.

Alchi Resort, in a fairly ugly compound, has two-room huts with bath and solar-heated hot water for Rs 500. There is a bit of a courtyard, which helps the ambience a little.

Getting There & Away There is one daily minibus to Alchi (Rs 32), leaving Leh at 3.30 pm, returning at 7 am. Otherwise, take a bus to Khalsi or beyond and walk the fairly easy 3km from the bridge about 2km past Saspul. A one-way/return taxi from Leh costs Rs 935/1155.

Rizong

About 6km along a steep, rocky track north of the main road is the start of the isolated area containing **Julichen Nunnery** and **Rizong Gompa**. There is no village at Rizong, but you may be able to stay at the gompa (men only) or the nunnery (women only); bring your own supplies. Alternatively, near the turn-off to Rizong, about 200m towards Alchi on the main road, is the pricey ***Uley Tokpo Camping Ground*** *(☎ 53640, fax 52735)*, with mildly luxurious tents set among apricot trees for Rs 2280 a double including meals. There is no direct bus to Rizong from Leh, so it is a matter of getting a bus bound for Kargil. If coming from Alchi, it is not difficult to hitch a ride on a truck or bus between the turn-offs for Alchi and Rizong. As an alternative, a taxi one way from Leh to the bottom of the walk up to the gompa will set you back Rs 1330.

Khalsi

There has been a bridge over the Indus River, at the turn-off to Dha-Hanu, at Khalsi for many centuries, the latest of which was being constructed at the time of research. This is a major military area, where your passport will be checked regardless of where you are going, and your permit checked if you're going to Dha-Hanu. There are food stalls and unsavoury accommodation options on the road through town.

Choglamsar

This is an important centre for Tibetan Buddhism and the study of Tibetan culture and history. Around the refugee camp, off the main road from Leh, is a Tibetan library, medical centre, handicraft shops, study centre, bookshops, plenty of restaurants, and the Central Institute of Buddhist Studies.

Choglamsar buses leave the new bus stand in Leh every 15 minutes (Rs 4); a one-way taxi costs Rs 130. There are a couple of crummy guesthouses along the main road.

Shey Gompa

Shey, 15km south of Leh, was the former summer palace of the kings of Ladakh. The gompa, still partially used, is being restored. There's a small library, a collection of thangkas, and some stupas and **mani walls** (stone walls with sacred inscriptions) nearby. The 12m **Sakyamuni Buddha statue**, made of copper but gold-plated, is the largest in the region, built by King Singge Namgyal's son. More crumbling **chortens** are scattered around the nearby fields.

Shey is easy to reach and can be combined with a visit to Tikse. Minibuses to Shey (Rs 8) leave every 30 minutes; by taxi, it will cost Rs 265 return. The only place to stay is the pleasant and large ***Shilkhar Hotel & Restaurant***, near the road up to the gompa. Rooms with private bathroom cost Rs 150/200.

Tikse Gompa

About 17km south of Leh, this beautiful gompa, part of the Gelukpa order, has an important collection of Tibetan books in its library, some excellent artwork and a new Maitreya temple. It's a busy place, with almost incessant chanting and music, and there is a good chance to witness a puja (ritual offerings or prayers). Go to the roof for great views of the valleys and villages. There is even a small (and welcome) cafe and shop. The gompa is open 7.30 am to 6 pm daily. Permission is required to use video cameras.

The only place to stay in Tikse is ***Skalzang Chamba Hotel*** *(☎ 47004)*, at the start of the road leading to the gompa. It is a well-run, pleasant place, with a small garden. It costs Rs 200 per room and there is a restaurant. A bus from Leh to Tikse (Rs 8) leaves every 15 minutes. From the bus stop, it is, as usual, a fair walk up to the gompa. A return taxi from Leh will cost Rs 400.

Matho Gompa

Built in the 16th century under the Sasakya order, Matho holds an annual festival during February and March during which the monks and novices go into trances and self-inflict wounds which appear to leave no marks. A 5km walking trail links Matho and Stakna Gompa. The minibus from Leh to Matho (Rs 12) leaves Leh at 7.30 am and 4.30 pm; returning at 6.30 am. A taxi to Stakna and Matho from Leh costs about Rs 785. There is no accommodation in Matho, but it's possible to camp.

Stakna Gompa

The gompa at Stakna – meaning Tiger's Nose – is another set spectacularly on the Hemis side of the Indus river. Built by King Singge Namgyal's stepbrother, as part of the Brokpa order, it is accessible from, and can be combined with a trip to, Matho.

To get there, take the 7.30 am minibus from Leh (Rs 12) and get off at the sign by the road to the gompa. Cross the bridge and walk for 30 minutes across the shadeless fields and up the steep path. A return taxi from Leh costs Rs 630. There is no guesthouse in the village, but it should be possible to camp near the Indus.

Hemis Gompa

Also known as Chang-Chub-Sam-Ling (or the Lone Place of the Compassionate Person), Hemis Gompa, 45km south of Leh, belongs to the Brokpa order and was founded in the early 17th century. Now it is one of the most accessible, famous and, therefore, most visited gompas. The gompa has an excellent library, well-preserved frescoes showing some Kashmiri influence, and good Buddha figures and the largest thangka in Ladakh, over 12m long. The famous annual festival commemorating the birth of the renowned Indian sage Padmasambhava is held on the ninth to 11th days of the fifth Tibetan month, in June/July. Every 12 years, during the Year of the Monkey, the festival is the scene for the unfurling of the thangka. It's next on display in 2004.

There are no guesthouses near the gompa, but the ***East West Guesthouse*** in the village, a long walk away, has doubles for Rs 150. Several places near the gompa allow camping; you can set up your own tent next to the gompa for Rs 35, or rent a preset two-person tent for Rs 50. Book at the nice ***outdoor restaurant*** next to the gompa entrance, which serves unexciting but welcome Chinese food, tea and beer. A daily minibus (Rs 20) leaves Leh for Hemis at 9.45 am and 4 pm, returning to Leh at 7 am and noon. A bus also leaves Leh at 1.30 pm, returning at 9 am. Return taxis from Leh cost Rs 860.

Stok Gompa & Museum

Over the bridge from Choglamsar, the Stok Gompa is where the last king of Ladakh died in 1974. Built in 1814, it is popular because it is so easy to get to. There are more than 80 rooms, only a few of which are open to the public.

The museum has a unique display of rare ornaments from the royal family, plus thangkas, traditional clothing and jewellery. It's open in summer from 8 am to 7 pm; entry is Rs 20. Photography is not permitted. The gompa, which has some fine masks and frescoes, is behind the museum.

The only nearby place to stay is the elegant ***Hotel Highland*** (☎ *3783)*, just under the museum, with doubles for Rs 600. There are other smaller places to stay towards the main road. Direct buses (Rs 7) leave Leh at 1, 4 and 4.30 pm, returning at 8 and 8.30 am and 2 pm. A return taxi from Leh will cost Rs 370.

NUBRA VALLEY

☎ 01982

The Nubra Valley – nubra means green – used to be on the trading route connecting Tibet with Turkistan, and was the envy of Turkistan, which invaded it several times. Also known as the Valley of Flowers, Nubra has always been well cultivated and fertile, with the best climate in Ladakh, so grains and fruits, such as apples and apricots, have always been plentiful. Ninety per cent of Nubra's population is Buddhist.

The valley is a wonderful area to visit, dominated by an incredible broad, empty flood plain through which the Nubra and Shyok Rivers pass. There are pretty, small villages, dense forests and some wildlife – camels are common on the sand dunes near Hunder – but, inevitably, the area is slowly becoming more affected by the increasing number of travellers who make the effort to visit. Your permit only allows you to travel as far as Hunder along the southern valley, and to Panamik in the northern valley.

All places in the valley provide meals and electricity until 10 pm but are very basic. Most close in winter and the only place where you will find accommodation at this time is in Diskit, during which time hot water is provided in buckets. Unless stated otherwise, toilets are sit-down flush style.

Getting There & Away

The road to the Nubra Valley, along the highest motorable road in the world, is officially open year-round. Trucks and buses are only allowed across the pass in each direction between 10 am and noon on alternate days: Tuesday, Thursday and Saturday towards Nubra, and Monday, Wednesday, Friday and Sunday towards Leh. Taxis, private vehicles and the military can travel at any time.

Bus Buses travel to both sides of the Nubra Valley from Leh every few days. The buses are slow and crowded, as to be expected in this region, but fun. Buses between Leh and Diskit travel on Thursday (Rs 57.50, six hours); they leave Leh at 5.30 am. A bus to Sumur and Panamik (Rs 79, 10 hours) leaves Leh at 5.30 am Tuesday and Saturday.

Truck Lifts on trucks, even military ones – in fact, anything travelling along the roads to and around the Nubra Valley – is quite acceptable for tourists and locals alike. As usual, negotiate a fare (around the cost of the bus fare) the day before, and prepare yourself for a rough old ride.

Taxi Hiring jeeps or taxis may be the only alternative, and with a group it is often a good option. A one-way/return taxi to Diskit from Leh will cost Rs 3355/4425. A taxi from Leh to Panamik will cost Rs 3520 one way, and Rs 4700 return. A return trip from Leh visiting Diskit, Hunder, Sumur and Panamik for three days will cost about Rs 8000 per taxi.

Getting Around

In the valley there is a limited public bus service which you can use for exploration. From Diskit, buses to Panamik (Rs 28, two hours) via Sumur (Rs 16, one hour) leave at 4 pm Monday and Wednesday, returning the next day at 8.30 am. If there are taxis around Diskit, they will offer full-day tours around the southern side of the valley for Rs 950; Rs 1250 including both sides. From Diskit to Panamik, one-way/return fares are Rs 1155/1490; from Diskit to Sumur it's Rs 770/970.

Khardung La

The road to the Nubra Valley goes through the highest motorable pass in the world at Khardung La (5602m). The pass is almost permanently covered in fog and snow, and is likely to be bitterly cold at the top regardless of the time of year. The pass is occupied by a grubby military camp, the highest temple in the world, a free tea stand and stacks of oil drums. In summer, you may see one of the world's highest traffic jams of trucks and buses. The road between Leh and Khalsar is reasonable, except between the miserable road-building camps of South Pullu and North Pullu, just before and after Khardung La, where the road is atrocious. The camps have toilets, tea shops and food, and there are many places to stop for views near the pass, such as India Gate.

Beyond the pass is Khardung village, with one very basic shop, and an unused Government Rest House. A small office may collect Rs 40 for 'wildlife' – perhaps to buy some.

Khalsar The Nubra Valley really starts at the village of Khalsar (3018m), where there are several teahouses and huge amounts of discarded army equipment. The road then divides just before the village of Lughzun – the left fork going to Hunder and beyond following the Shyok River, and the right heading north to Panamik and beyond, following the Nubra River.

Diskit The turn-off to Diskit (3144m) stretches about 3km along an awesome, wide and dry riverbed before climbing, and clinging to the hillside for another 13km.

Diskit Gompa, with about 100 monks, is the oldest – more than 500 years old – and biggest of its kind in the Nubra Valley. If you want to see the heads of the statues uncovered you'll have to visit at festival time (February).

Between Diskit and Hunder is an area of **sand dunes**, not unlike the Sahara (if you can ignore the snowcapped mountains in the background!).

Places to Stay & Eat The guesthouses in Diskit almost run in a line from below the gompa to the village centre.

The first you'll spot is ***Olthang Guest House*** *(☎ 20025)*, which has nicely furnished singles/doubles with private bathroom (squat toilets) for Rs 150/200. At the time of research a couple of other rooms with sit-down flush toilets were being built next to the main building. There's a comfortable lounge area, a sun room and a large garden with car parking, and it's open in winter. On the opposite side of the road as you head down to the right of Olthang is ***Sunrise Guest House*** *(☎ 20011)*. In a nice garden, it has sunny rooms with good views and bathrooms (sit-down flush and squat toilets) for Rs 100/200, and a cosy Ladakhi kitchen.

On the same side of the road, through an archway with a stupa on top, is ***Karakuram Guest House*** *(☎ 20024)*. Quite basic singles/doubles around a 1st-floor terrace with the choice of private or shared squat toilets are Rs 50/100. It's also possible to camp here for Rs 25 per tent and it's open in winter.

Next up, and open year-round, is ***Khangsar Guest House*** *(☎ 20014)*, a farmhouse which you enter through a yard full of cows. It has even more basic rooms, again around a 1st-floor terrace, but it's homey, with rooms with shared squat toilets for Rs 50/100.

Opposite the hospital in an overgrown garden is ***Sangum Guest House*** *(☎ 20016)*, which is made of concrete but has an Australian weatherboard house appearance. Clean rooms with private bathroom (squat and sit-down flush toilets), homey furniture and good views are Rs 200/300, Sangum is open year-round.

In the centre near a couple of roadside ***restaurants*** and the bus stand, and set within a scruffy garden, is ***Sand Dune Guest House***. Spacious rooms are Rs 150/200 with private bathroom (sit-down flush toilets).

Hunder

Hunder is a pretty village, set among lots of trees and gurgling streams. It is nicer than Diskit, but Diskit, the bigger village of the two, has slightly better facilities. From Diskit, it's about 7km to Hunder; some visitors enjoy the 8km walk between the villages, either along the main road or across the sand dunes (watch out for wild camels!). Alternatively, you can ride a tame camel across for around Rs 200 – guesthouses can organise this.

The **gompa** at Hunder is about a 2km walk above the village, including a short, steep, rocky climb. It is completely deserted and quite eerie. There is only a small Buddha statue and some damaged frescoes, but the climb is worth it for the views and atmosphere. Don't wander too far up the road – there's a heavy military presence.

Places to Stay Hunder is quite a sprawl, so you'll probably need to ask directions to the following places, which are both central but a bit of a trek north of the dunes. They offer the same facilities as those in Diskit.

Moon Land Guest House is a big, signposted, brick place in a pleasant and large garden, with a nice Ladakhi kitchen. Large rooms with private bathroom (sit-down flush toilets) are Rs 100/150 a single/double and it stays open in winter.

Snow Leopard Guest House, also in a nice garden, has biggish rooms with bathroom (sit-down flush toilets) for Rs 200.

At the time of research a new place was being built opposite Moon Land.

Sumur

Sumur (3096m), a major village along the Nubra River side of the valley, is a pretty place worth exploring.

The **Samstemling Gompa** at Sumur, over 150 years old, is a large complex with seven temples. Inaugurated by the Dalai Lama in 1962, it is a busy, friendly place with about 45 children busy chanting, or cultivating apples and apricots. The prayer rooms that are open to the public house an impressive collection of thangkas and excellently restored frescoes. Strict rules apply here, including one that forbids females entry to the gompa between sunset and sunrise.

By road, it is a fair distance from Sumur village to the gompa: about 3km south towards the village of Tegar, from where a 3km road to the gompa starts. It's far quicker on foot, as you can go up the hill from the village and avoid the road, but you will have to ask directions. It can be confusing because the gompa near the start of the road to the Samstemling Gompa is actually the Tegar Gompa. The Samstemling Gompa is the more colourful one closer to Sumur.

On the opposite side of the river to Sumur is Charasa, easily identifiable atop a hillock. Facing Samstemling, the valley's most important gompa, it served as the palace of Nubra's royalty until the region came under the direct control of Leh.

Places to Stay Just by the turn-off into the centre and close to the shops, ***Twesang Jorgais Guest House***, in a big garden, has rooms on the 1st floor of the family house for Rs 100/150 a single/double.

Farther down the same road, ***Tashi Khangsar Guest House*** is a concrete-block place, but the rooms, for Rs 100/150, are comfortable enough.

Continuing farther down the lane, ***LP Guest House*** has rooms within a farmyard for Rs 100/150. Although the toilets are sit-down flush style, you have to go outside to get to them.

Probably the nicest place, with basic rooms within a traditional farmhouse for Rs 100/200, is ***Largyal Guest House***. Prices include meals served in the Ladakhi kitchen. Camping is also available here.

There are a couple of upmarket options. ***Hotel Yarabtso*** (☎ *20008)* is a big place in Tegar village just north of Sumur. Rooms with private bathroom are Rs 1200/1750, including all meals.

Back in Sumur, down by the river, ***Lharimo North Camp*** (☎ *52177)* charges Rs 1650/200, including all meals.

Panamik

Panamik (3183m) is another small village, famous for centuries for its **hot springs**, and as the first or last stop along the ancient trade route between Ladakh and Central Asia. Don't come specifically for the springs – you'll be disappointed. Do come for the satisfaction of reaching the end of the road and to appreciate the natural beauty of this isolated spot.

The spring water, rumoured to cure rheumatism and other ailments, is pumped in from the Nubra River, about 2km away. There is a dark, double-chambered hut for bathing, but it's male-dominated and none too clean. The 250-year-old **Ensa Gompa** is a fair trek from the village – a couple of hours at least. It is farther than it seems. If you do want to get there, walk about 5km to Hargam, then cross the bridge for some more walking. Some have tried to cross the river by swimming or wading, and many have nearly come to a tragic end. Be sensible and take the bridge.

Overlooking the river and Ensa Gompa, ***Silk Route Guest House*** is in a large garden, and has big, well-furnished rooms with squat toilets for Rs 100/200. Although it's open during summer only, one room and the dining room have heaters.

RUPSU VALLEY

Known as 'mountain lake', Tso Moriri is in the Rupsu Valley, about 140km (but a rough-and-tumble six or so hours by jeep) from Leh. The saltwater lake is about 28km long, 8km at its widest and at an elevation of more than 4000m. Surrounded by barren hills, which are backed by snow-covered mountains, Tso Moriri is a good place to relax, visit nearby **gompas** and do some walking. On the way from Leh to Tso Moriri is another brackish lake, the smaller Tso Kar, or 'White Lake'. This is an area of nomadic people, known as Khampas, who can often be seen taking advantage of the summer and moving herds of goats, cows and yaks from one grazing spot to another. Khampas live in large, movable family tents or in solid winter-proof brick huts, and are referred to as Chinese cowboys. Another great aspect of this region is the amount of wildlife – the best (accessible) place in Ladakh for it. Commonly seen are wild asses (known as *kiangs*), foxes and cuddly marmots busy waking up from their last hibernation, or preparing for the next. On the lakes, you may see large flocks of black-necked geese; the best times for spotting birds are July and August.

There is nowhere to stay in the region at all – though this may change as demand increases. You must bring your own tent and all equipment. There are preset tents at the astronomical price of Rs 800 per two-person tent at Tso Moriri village; these are set up for upmarket, organised tour groups. There is no place to eat in the region so, again, bring your own food and cooking equipment. This is a very fragile environment, so take out everything you bring in – cans, bottles, papers, *everything*.

Getting There & Away

There are two ways that your 4WD jeep is physically able, and permitted, to enter or leave the region. The first route takes you over the Mahe bridge (near Raldong, at the eastern end of the Indus Valley road) through Puga, and then to one or both lakes. The other route is the road south from Upshi, over the Taglang La, then a detour off the road – look out for the yellow sign. No public transport goes even remotely near the lakes. The area has no signposts, and quality maps of the area are nonexistent, so motorcycles are not recommended unless you have a guide (you could easily burn out the clutch in the sand drifts as well). There will be very few people around to give you directions – the marmots around here outnumber humans by about 50 to one!

A return taxi trip from Leh to Tso Moriri over three days will cost about Rs 9000 via Tso Kar and Taglang La, or the shorter, more direct way is Rs 7500. From Leh, a two-day return trip just to Tso Kar will be Rs 6500. Travel agencies in Leh can organise a three-day 'jeep safari' from Rs 7500 to 10,000 per vehicle, including meals and tent accommodation, depending on which way you go.

Tso Moriri

The small collection of huts on the shore of Tso Moriri is also called Tso Moriri. Here you must register and show your permit. You can pitch your tent here (there's a toilet), but there is nothing stopping you from camping anywhere else.

Korzok

A path at the back of the huts leads for 1km or so to the delightful village of Korzok. The **gompa** here is quite unusual because it is inhabited predominantly by women, who often spend their days making beautiful garments for themselves, but which are not for sale (or, at least, not yet). The gompa was built in about 1850, replacing one destroyed during a Dogra invasion.

Tso Kar

On Tso Kar, 6km from Tso Moriri, there is a small **gompa** at the village of Thukse, a collection of solid brick huts set up for the dramatic winters. You will have to find the monk to let you in. On a slight – and legal – detour off the track linking Tso Kar and Tso Moriri is the smaller lake of **Tso Kiagar**.

DHA-HANU

Dha-Hanu consists of a handful of villages along the road leading north-west from Khalsi. The steep bare walls of the Indus give the terraced fields more light and heat than other parts of Ladakh, which, combined with the lower altitude, enables rich crops of vegetables and fruits (especially apricots) to grow here. The area is probably most famous for its inhabitants, known as Dards or Brokpas, 'people of the land', an ancient Indo-Iranian people. Despite their proximity to Pakistan and other Islamic regions, they are traditionally not Muslims (although there are a few mosques in the area) but retain their own Buddhist traditions and beliefs.

Places to Stay & Eat There are a handful of basic guesthouses in the village of Dha; ***Skyababa Guesthouse*** at the Leh end of the village has basic doubles for Rs 100, and the family is friendly. In the heart of the village, ***Chunu Guesthouse*** has very rustic double rooms for Rs 60. Nearby, ***Lhariemo Shamo Guesthouse*** is similar, but charges RS 100 a double.

There are recognised camp sites at the villages of Dhumkhar, Skurbuchan, Hanu-Do, Biama and Dha, and plenty of other legal, but unofficial, places along the way. The one or two shops at Dha and Skurbuchan offer little in the way of food, but guesthouses usually provide basic meals.

Getting There & Away Daily buses between Leh and Dha (Rs 72) leave in each direction at 9 am; another daily bus from Leh to Skurbuchan leaves at 10 am, returning at 9 am. A taxi to Dha from Leh will cost Rs 2486/3393 one way/return over two days.

LEH TO MANALI

Since opening to foreigners in 1989, this road has become a popular way into and out of Leh. (The only other road to Leh goes through Kashmir and along a stretch between Drass and Kargil made hazardous by Pakistani artillery. There is often difficulty in getting flights into and out of Leh.) There is nothing to see along the road in the way of villages or gompas; it is the raw high-altitude scenery that will certainly impress, and is reason enough for travelling this way.

The road to Manali is the world's second-highest motorable road, reaching 5328m at Taglang La. As only about half of the total distance of 485km between Leh and Manali is paved, it can be a rough journey. For much of the way the only inhabitants of the high plateaus are Khampa nomads, soldiers and teams of tar-covered workers from Bihar and Nepal struggling to keep this strategic road open. Whatever form of transport, it will take at least two days, with an overnight stop at a tent camp, probably in Sarchu.

Sudden changes in weather are common, even in the mid-summer month of August, and can cause delays of several days. It is worth having some cold- and wet-weather gear with you in the bus because the weather, especially around the highest passes, can be very cold and/or wet. The road is usually open between early June and mid-October.

Leh to Upshi

Leaving Leh, from the main road you will get your last glimpse (or your first, of course, if coming from Manali) of the magnificent gompas at Tikse, Shey and Stok. For an hour or so before Upshi, along a paved but dusty road, there are plenty of ugly military sites, such as at Karu, where there is the turn-off to the Pangong Tso area, and to the gompas at Taktok and Chemrey. For a description of the villages and places of interest between Leh and Upshi, see Around Leh earlier in this chapter.

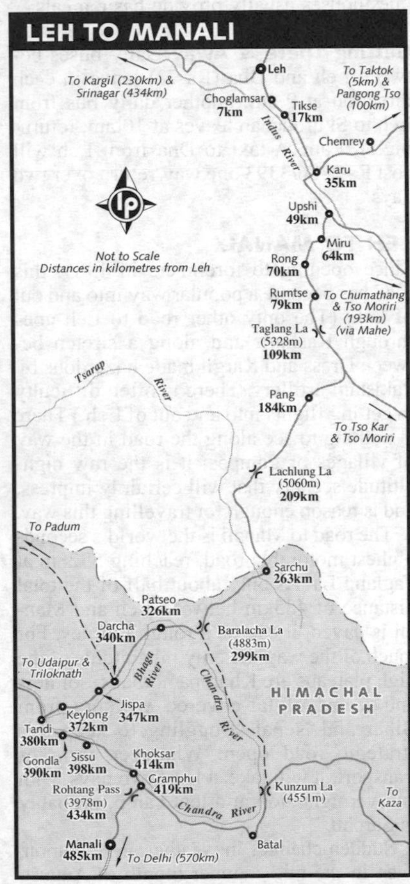

The first checkpoint of Upshi is the turn-off south to Manali. Although permits are not needed for this trip, foreigners have to register at the police hut. If travelling on a bus with plenty of other foreigners, there is lots of time for tea, a greasy 'omlate', or to stock up on supplies of chocolate and other goodies.

Upshi to Taglang La

At Miru, there is a crumbling little **gompa** (worth a look) on the nearby hill and surrounded by chortens. There is nowhere to stay or eat, but plenty of camping sites. Lato has a huge **chorten** on the side of the road, but there is no village to speak of. From here the road starts to climb for about three hours to Taglang La (5328m), where there's a little shrine, and possibly the world's highest 'Gents Urinal' and 'Ladies Urinal'. The bus will stop to give passengers a rest and a look around. If you are coming from Manali and haven't acclimatised to the altitude, take it easy.

Taglang La to Lachlung La

Not long after Taglang La, the road flattens out along the Morey plain, and becomes paved. This area is occasionally inhabited by Khampa nomads. The road to Pang is good, through a windswept valley, then becomes hopelessly potholed. About 5km before Pang, the road descends through a dramatic series of **gorges** before reaching the teahouse settlement. **Pang**, at the bottom of these gorges, has several ***restaurants*** in tents by the river, where most buses stop for lunch. A plate of rice, dhal and vegetables costs about Rs 30, and you may be able to stock up on mineral water and biscuits. Most tents have a mattress where you can unroll your sleeping bag for around Rs 50 per night. There are some grim toilets.

At 5060m, Lachlung La is the second-highest pass on the Leh to Manali road. Nearby, there is an incredible 20km of switchback roads, which includes the spine-tingling 21 Gata Loops, or hairpin bends, on one side of one mountain.

Sarchu

Sarchu is just inside Himachal Pradesh, and is where most buses stop overnight. It is just a collection of tents, dotted over a length of 15km or so, which are all packed up for eight months of the year (ie, October to May). Just opposite the striped HPTDC tent camps, you must register, again, with the police. Your bus driver may collect passports and do it himself, but it still involves a lot of waiting.

HPTDC buses stop at HPTDC's own ***tent camps***. They are the best of the lot; clean two-person tents with camp beds and lots of blankets are Rs 115 per person. A ***tent kitchen*** does passable dhal and rice for dinner, and omelettes for breakfast, for about Rs 40.

Public and other private bus drivers seem to have some sort of 'arrangement' with other tent-site owners, so you may have little choice but to stay in a tent camp not even remotely as good as the HPTDC site, but for around the same price. Travellers on buses arriving late at the camps suffer the most. Although the driver may try to dissuade you, you can sleep on the bus for free, where it will be warmer. There are plenty of places to put your own tent.

Just over the bridge from the HPTDC camp are several ***tent restaurants*** which serve dhal and rice, tea, omelettes, curried noodles, and, for those long cold evenings, a shot of whiskey or chang (take it easy, though; alcohol is more powerful at high altitude).

Baralacha La

It's only a short climb to this 4883m pass; Baralacha La means 'crossroads pass' – it is a double pass linking both the upper Chandra and Bhaga Valleys with the Lingti Valley and vast Lingti plains around Sarchu. About an hour farther on is the police checkpoint at Patseo. Here the road begins to hug the Bhaga River to Tandi, where it meets the Chandra River.

Darcha

Darcha is the other major tent site on this road. Faster buses from Leh, or slower ones from Manali, may stay here, depending on the time and the state of the road around Baralacha La. Like Sarchu, Darcha is just a temporary place, with some crummy tents for hire (Rs 50) and a few ***tent restaurants***. Shortly after Darcha, you pass through Jispa, where there is yet another large army camp.

Darcha is the start of a popular trekking option to get into Padum, and in winter it is the only way. From here, you can also trek into places such as Hemis (about 11 days). If you have your own transport, try to get to the little lake of **Deepak Tal**, about 16km from Darcha. It is a great spot for camping and exploring.

Keylong to Manali

Keylong is the first town of any size on the journey from Leh to Manali, and the administrative centre of Lahaul and Spiti. From Keylong, it isn't far to the T-junction at Tandi. From here there is a road that goes sharply to the north-west along the Chenab River to the little-visited parts of Himachal Pradesh towards Udaipur and the famous temple site of Triloknath. The road to Manali heads south-east, and climbs steadily past Gondla, Sissu and Khoksar. There are ***Public Works Department (PWD) rest-houses*** which you may be able to use, in all three places, but nothing much else. At Sissu, there is a nice **waterfall** nearby, set under spectacular peaks. Farther on, at Gramphu, the road continues to climb along Lahaul and Spiti – get off at Gramphu or at Keylong if you want to continue to Kaza – or heads south to Manali. Rohtang Pass (3978m) – not high, but treacherous all the same – marks the start of the descent into Manali. See the Himachal Pradesh chapter for more details on Keylong and Manali.

LEH TO KARGIL

This section refers to places on, or near, the main road from Leh to Kargil. A number of buses ply the 231km road to Kargil. Trucks are also a good option for a lift between villages. Taxi fares may seem outragcous, but with a group sharing the cost you can visit several gompas on the way. For a description of the villages and places of interest between Leh and Khalsi, see Around Leh earlier in this chapter.

Lamayuru

After you've explored other villages in the area, Lamayuru (3390m) will seem a relatively scruffy little place. But it is completely overshadowed by one of the most famous and spectacularly set gompas in Ladakh.

The **gompa**, part of the Kagyupa order, is not as interesting as others; the location –

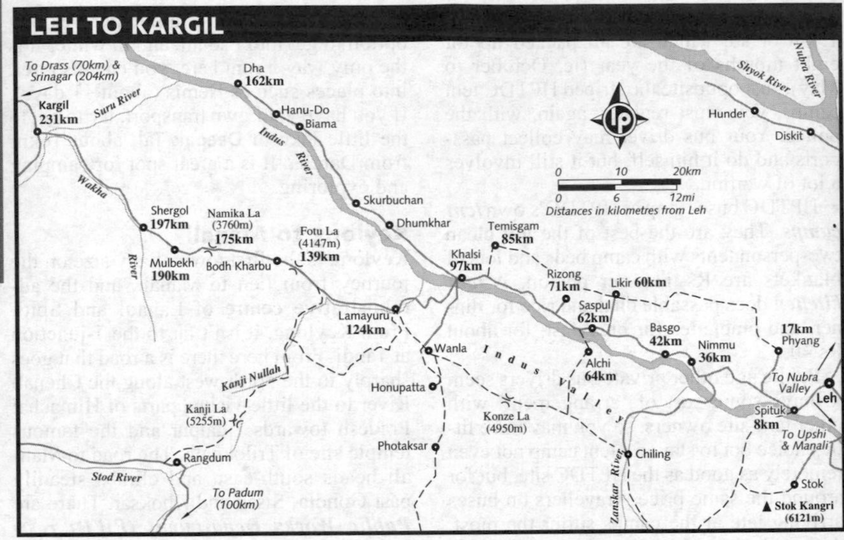

perched above a drained lake on an eroded crag overlooked by massive mountains – makes it special. The oldest known gompa in Ladakh, dating back beyond the 10th century, it has been destroyed and restored several times over the centuries. There are renowned collections of carpets, thangkas and frescoes. Criminals were once granted asylum here (not any more, you'll be glad to know!), which explains one previous name for the gompa: Tharpa Ling, or 'Place of Freedom'. Get there early to witness a mesmerising puja.

Several kilometres south of Lamayuru is the small **Wanla Gompa**, set on the popular trekking route to Padum in Zanskar.

Places to Stay & Eat There are a few choices in Lamayuru, although bathrooms are shared and hot water comes in a bucket. ***Hotel Shangri-La***, on the main road through the village, is a bit run-down, but the views from its Rs 150 rooms are good. It also has a restaurant, but the whole place closes down for winter.

In the village, and signposted from the tracks up to the gompa, are two family-run places with a bit more character that are more likely to be open during the colder months. ***Hotel Dragon*** has pleasantly decorated rooms for Rs 100, and prepares meals on request. ***Hotel Moonland*** is also good, and has the bonus of a restaurant. At the time of research, the ***gompa*** accommodation was a dubious choice, but a new building which promises to be much more salubrious was being constructed.

Getting There & Away There are no buses from Leh or Kargil directly to Lamayuru, so take the Leh to Kargil/Srinagar bus and get off at the truck stop at the top of the village. A better option is a ride on one of the many trucks that stop overnight, leaving Lamayuru early in the morning. A one-way taxi from Leh costs Rs 1952.

Mulbekh

From Lamayuru the road passes Fotu La (4147m), the highest pass on the route, then Namika La (3760m), before turning into a fertile valley. Mulbekh is the last sign of Buddhism before you head into the Muslim-dominated regions near Kargil and beyond.

Mulbekh's main claim to fame is the impressive 8m-high **Maitreya statue**, an image of a future Buddha, cut into the rock face and dating back to about AD 700. Unfortunately, all buses stop for food and a rest at the village of Wakha, 2km from Mulbekh, so this gives you no opportunity to inspect the statue on the way, but you can see it from the bus window. There are also two gompas, **Serdung** and **Gandentse**, offering great views of the valley. As in other smaller villages, it is wise to inquire if the gompa is open before making the ascent.

Paradise Hotel and Restaurant, directly opposite the Chamba statue, costs Rs 80 per room. ***Namchung Hotel*** is similar. Another option is ***Jammu & Kashmir Tourism Development Corporation (J&KTDC) Tourist Bungalow***, on the Leh side of the statue, with rooms for Rs 40 per person.

From Leh, take the Kargil/Srinagar bus. Mulbekh makes a decent day trip from Kargil. A couple of buses leave Kargil for Mulbekh daily. A return taxi from Kargil plus an hour or so in Mulbekh will cost Rs 800.

KARGIL

☎ 01985

Administering the valleys of Suru, Drass, Wakha and Bodkarbu, Kargil lies midway between the alpine valleys of Kashmir and the fertile reaches of the Indus Valley and Ladakh. The region is politically part of India, ethnically part of Baltistan and geographically an integral part of Ladakh.

Until 1947, Kargil (2817m) was an important trading centre linking Ladakh with Gilgit (Pakistan) and the lower Indus Valley. There were also important trading links between the villages of the Suru Valley and the Zanskar Valley, and even 20 years ago it was not uncommon to see yak trains making their way from Padum all the way into Kargil Bazaar.

Continuing political problems in Kashmir have seriously affected the number of visitors to Kargil and the hotels survive at present from the handful of visitors making their way from Leh to Padum and the Zanskar Valley.

The people of Kargil are mostly Shi'ia Muslims: Arabic script is found everywhere and men and mosques dominate the town, which has been shelled by the Pakistani army several times. When artillery duels flare up, the town is declared off-limits.

Orientation & Information

Kargil, next to the roaring Suru River, is the second-largest town in Ladakh, but is really little more than one long main road called Main Bazaar, with lots of little lanes jutting off (watch out for wide trucks!). Along Main Bazaar are plenty of places with long-distance/international telephone facilities, the post office and State Bank of India, open 10 am to 2 pm weekdays.

If you have enough time, walk up Hospital Rd for some decent views of the area. There are also nice fields and villages across the Qatilgah Bridge, at the end of Balti Bazaar Rd.

The Tourist Reception Centre (☎ 2228) is next to the taxi stand, just off the main road. Open 10 am to 4 pm on normal working days, it has no great information on local areas, or on Zanskar. It does, however, rent out trekking gear: tents Rs 40 per day, sleeping bags Rs 16 per day. The best place to arrange trekking and travel is through the Siachen and Greenland hotels.

The phone number for the police is ☎ 2210 and the hospital is ☎ 2216.

Places to Stay

Catering mainly for those on an overnight stop en route between Leh and Srinagar, Kargil has a few good choices close to the transport hubs. Hotel staff are generally helpful and friendly, and where hot water is limited they will provide you with bucket hot water. There are two ***J&KTDC Tourist Bungalows*** *(☎ 2328)* in town. The first, up the hill behind the hospital, has a variety of singles/doubles/triples for Rs 200/300/400, but they really don't warrant the climb. Much more convenient and cheaper, the second, next to the bus station, has rooms for Rs 45 per person.

Hotel Tourist Marjina *(☎ 33085)* has basic rooms with private bathroom for Rs 150/200/250 on the ground/1st/2nd floor. They are set around a garden and you enter the hotel through the (decent) restaurant.

Hotel Kargil Continental *(☎ 2304)* has large rooms with private bathroom and warm bedding for a negotiable Rs 200/400. The rooms at the back look onto the river and there is parking and a restaurant.

If everything else in the budget range is full you could try ***Hotel Greenland*** *(☎ 2324)*, which has grubby ground-floor rooms with private bathroom for Rs 50/100. Try for the upper floors, which have verandas and cost Rs 150/300.

Hotel Siachen *(☎ 2221)* has excellent rooms with verandas and hot water for Rs 350/500. They are on three floors set around a garden and there's a travel agency, restaurant and parking.

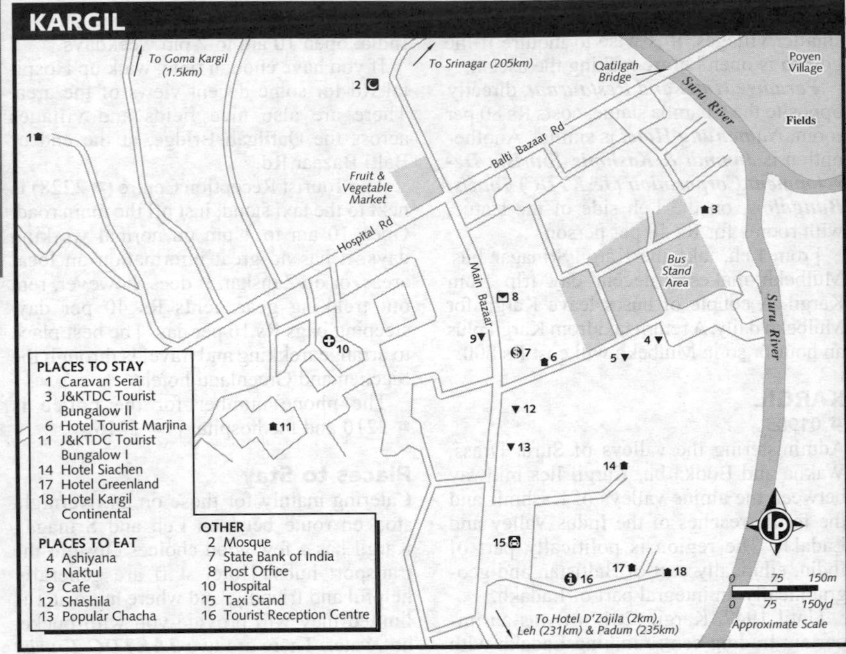

The classiest place in town, ***Caravan Serai*** *(☎ 2278)* is on a hill overlooking town. It has good rooms with hot water and views for Rs 1500/2000, including breakfast. Catering primarily for upmarket trekking parties, it closes during winter. About 2km out of town on the Padum road, the ***Hotel D'Zojila*** *(☎/fax 2227)* is not really worth the effort unless you specifically want river views and running hot water. The rooms with private bathroom are large, basic and overpriced at Rs 1200/1500. They would rather you take an all-inclusive package with meals in the restaurant for Rs 2064/2484.

Places to Eat

There is not much to recommend the restaurants in Kargil. The choice is limited to Kashmiri and Chinese food and hotels usually do omelettes and bread for breakfast. On and near Main Bazaar are some bearable small restaurants: ***Ashiyana***, ***Naktul***, ***Shashila*** and ***Popular Chacha***. One of a few open for breakfast is the ***cafe*** across the road from the bank.

The ***restaurants*** at the Siachen and Greenland hotels are quite adequate and they'll discreetly serve a bottle of beer for Rs 125 in the evening (alcohol is prohibited in Kargil, hence the price). There is a ***fruit and vegetable market*** on the corner of Hospital Rd and Main Bazaar and plenty of shops to pick up other picnic supplies.

Getting There & Away

Bus Daily buses leave for Leh at 5.30 am (Rs 140/200 ordinary/air-con, 12 hours) and Srinagar at 4.30 am (Rs 160/200 ordinary/air-con, 12 hours). The road to Srinagar has been closed to foreigners in the past during periods of Pakistani shelling – check locally for the latest information. Towards Leh, there are also two daily buses to Mulbekh and one to Shergol; towards Srinagar, there are regular daily buses to Drass.

There are at least two daily buses to nearby Panikhar and Parkachik. To Padum, in Zanskar, there is a 4.30 am bus on alternate days (Rs 150/220 B/A Class, 15 hours).

The Kargil bus stand is just off the main road. Book tickets one day ahead.

Taxi In one day, a taxi from Leh can get you to Kargil for Rs 3355, or from Kargil to Srinagar for Rs 3100. A taxi from Kargil to Padum is not a bad alternative to the bus, but the trip will cost a hefty Rs 7000 one way and Rs 12,000 return. The Kargil taxi stand is on Main Bazaar.

KARGIL TO PADUM

Sanku

The road from Kargil heads south-west, away from Padum, following the Suru Valley. It's still predominantly inhabited by Muslims, who converted to Islam in the 15th century; a **Muslim shrine**, dedicated to Sayed Mir Hashim, is located in Karpo-Khar near Sanku. Sanku can also be reached from Drass, west of Kargil on the road to Srinagar, on a two- to three-day trek.

There's a daily bus from Kargil to Sanku at 3 pm (Rs 18). Sanku accommodation is limited to the ***Government Rest House*** and ***J&KTDC Tourist Bungalow***, which at the time of research was barely operational but charged only Rs 40 per person. One-way/return taxis from Kargil cost Rs 700/1050.

Panikhar

Farther down the Suru Valley, Panikhar and Parkachik are the places to get off and admire, or even get closer to, the twin mountains of **Nun** (7135m) and **Kun** (7087m). It is a lovely area in summer, often full of flowers. In Panikhar, the best accommodation option is a room at the comfortable ***J&KTDC Tourist Bungalow*** for Rs 150 per person.

Between Panikhar and Kargil, buses cost Rs 35, and leave twice daily in the morning; or take the Kargil to Padum bus, which leaves at 5.30 am on alternate days. One-way/return taxis cost Rs 1200/1800.

Rangdum

About halfway in time, but not distance, between Kargil and Padum, is Rangdum, where taxis and trucks (but not buses) may stop for the night. You can visit the 18th-century **Rangdum Gompa**, which serves as a base for about 35 monks and many novices. ***J&KTDC Tourist Complex*** has basic facilities for Rs 40 per person. Several village ***teahouses*** offer unexciting food. From Rangdum, there is another good trek, east through the Kanji La (5255m), which links up to the Leh-Kargil road at Lamayuru.

The road from Rangdum heads in a more southerly direction and crosses Pensi La (4450m). Farther on is Ating, from where you can visit the **Zongkul Gompa**. As you approach Padum, the valley becomes more populous, with plenty of small villages such as Tungri, Phey and Sani.

TREKKING IN LADAKH

The following information is an overview for travellers wishing to experience a trek. Serious trekkers might consider buying Lonely Planet's *Trekking in the Indian Himalaya*. See Books in the Facts for the Visitor chapter for details. Treks out of Leh and the Indus Valley include the popular trek from Spituk just below Leh to the Markha Valley and Hemis Gompa, and the trek from Lamayuru Gompa to Chiling village alongside the Zanskar River. Treks can be completed from the end of June until the middle of October, when the first of the winter snow settles on the high passes. Proper acclimatisation is also necessary as many of the passes are in the vicinity of 5000m. A few days resting in Leh (3505m) is recommended before commencing your trek.

There are many trekking agencies in Leh offering inclusive treks with a guide, packhorses, food and supplies. You should allow a minimum of US$40 per day for an all-inclusive trek. If you are making your own arrangements, packhorses can be hired from Spituk or Lamayuru for around Rs 250 to 300 per horse per day. It is recommended that all camping gear, including a sleeping bag and tent, are brought with you even on *inclusive* treks, as the gear provided may not be adequate. Food supplies should also be carried with you from Leh, as village lodges and teahouses are not available on all stages of the treks.

Spituk to Markha Valley & Hemis via Kongmaru La

The trek from Spituk Gompa follows the Jingchen Valley to Ganda La (4920m). At least one rest day should be included before crossing the pass. Thereon, it is a steady descent to the Markha Valley and the village of Skiu. It is a further stage to Markha village, before ascending to the yak-grazing pastures at Nimaling. Above the camp is the impressive peak of Kangyaze (6400m). Kongmaru La (5030m) is the highest pass on the trek and affords great views, south to the Zanskar Range and north to the Ladakh Range. After crossing the pass there is one further camp site at the village of Chogdo before reaching Hemis Gompa. From Hemis there is a daily bus back to Leh.

stage	route	duration (hrs)
1	Spituk to Rumbak	6–7
2	Rumbak to Yurutse and camp	4–5
3	Yurutse to Skiu via Ganda La	6–7
4	Skiu to Markha	7–8
5	Markha to Nimaling	7–8
6	Nimaling to Chogdo via Kongmaru La	6
7	Chogdo to Hemis	4–5

Lamayuru to Chiling via Konze La & Dung Dung La

From Lamayuru the trek crosses Prinkiti La (3750m) to the ancient gompa and village at Wanla. It is a further stage to the village of Hinju at the base of Konze La (4950m), where an additional day is recommended for acclimatisation before crossing the pass. From Konze La there are impressive views of the East Karakoram Range before a short descent to the village of Sumdo Chinmu. The following day's climb to Dung Dung La (4820m) is rewarded with views of the Zanskar Range and a bird's-eye view of the swirling Zanskar River before a long and tiring descent to the village of Chiling.

From Chiling you can either return to Leh or continue to the Markha Valley. The stage from Chiling to the village of Skiu in the Markha Valley can be completed in three hours. It's an interesting stage that includes crossing the Zanskar River by a pulley bridge; the bridge is maintained and operated by villagers from Chiling, who charge Rs 100 per crossing.

stage	route	duration (hrs)
1	Lamayuru to Wanla via Prinkiti La	3–4
2	Wanla to Hinju	4–5
3	Hinju to Sumdo Chinmu via Konze La	6
4	Sumdo Chinmu to Dung Dung La base camp	3
5	Base camp to Chiling via Dung Dung La	6

Likir to Temisgam

This trek can be completed in a day if you are fit! From Likir Gompa the trail crosses a small pass to the village of Yantang a short distance from Rizong Gompa. Stage 2 leads to the village of Hemis-Shukpachu. It is a further short stage over two minor passes to the roadhead at Temisgam. The trek can be completed throughout the year. Horses can be hired from Likir, while supplies and a tent must be brought from Leh. Road-building will eventually render this trek obsolete. Until then there is a daily bus service to Likir and another from Temisgam back to Leh.

stage	route	duration (hrs)
1	Likir to Yangtang	4–5
2	Yangtang to Hemis-Shukpachu	3
3	Hemis-Shukpachu to Temisgam	3–4

Zanskar

The isolated region of Zanskar is composed of a number of small mountain-locked valleys to the south of Ladakh. The valleys are bounded to the north by the Zanskar Range, and to the south by the main Himalaya. To the east and west, high ridges linking the Himalaya and Zanskar mountains ensure that there is no easy connection between Zanskar and the outside world.

Zanskar essentially comprises the Stod Valley in the west and the Lunak Valley in the east, which converge at Padum, the administrative centre of the region. The fertile region of Padum and its outlying villages and gompas form the nucleus of Zanskar. The area's uninterrupted Buddhist heritage has been principally due to its isolation.

PADUM

Padum is the administrative headquarters of the Zanskar region but was once an ancient capital. It is not an attractive place, with incongruous government buildings that were constructed when the road from Kargil was completed in 1981. This has resulted in the town gaining a character similar to roadheads everywhere; much that is not used is disposed of here. The main camp site and the small hotel area is close to the newly constructed mosque (the only one in the Zanskar region) which serves the Sunni Muslim community. The only telephone office is at the Hotel Ibex.

Padum is also the starting point for a number of demanding treks.

Places to Stay & Eat

There's a limited choice of basic guesthouses and one more comfortable option.

Hotel Shapodok-la, in the centre of town, has cheap dorm beds. ***Hotel Haftal View***, by the bus stand, is a bit grubby, with rooms for Rs 100/150. ***Hotel Chorala*** nearby is somewhat better, also with doubles for Rs 150.

Hotel Snowland is one of the better choices, with a nice garden and singles/doubles for Rs 100/150. It is set in the fields about 100m behind the Hotel Chorala.

J&KTDC Tourist Bungalow has fairly big rooms with bath (cold water only) for Rs 50 per person. ***Hotel Ibex*** *(☎ 01983-45012)* is the best in town, with decent doubles set around a sheltered courtyard for Rs 300 (no discount for singles).

There isn't much to report on eating in Padum. The least worst place is the ***restaurant*** at Hotel Ibex. The ***Lhasa Tibetan restaurant*** across the road from the Ibex is OK, as is ***Hotel Chorala*** and the ***Tibetan restaurant*** at the bus stand under the Campa Cola sign.

Getting There & Away

The trip between Kargil and Padum is spectacular, even impressing those jaded travellers who thought that they had seen it all along the Leh to Kargil road. But as usual in this part of the world, the road is also narrow, winding and slow. It is only open from July to early October and is completely impassable the rest of the year, effectively isolating the Zanskari people.

Bus In season, a bus runs between Padum and Kargil every alternate day (check with local bus stations for up-to-date information), departing at about 4.30 am. The cost of the bus between Kargil and Padum is Rs 150/220 for B/A Class (it depends which bus shows up), and the trip usually takes about 15 hours, but can take a lot longer.

You can and should book your ticket the day before in Padum or Kargil. You can get off anywhere you want on the road between Kargil and Padum, but you may have to then wait a day or so for another bus, or rely on hitching a lift on an infrequent truck.

Taxi By taxi, it costs Rs 7000 one way and Rs 12,000 return from Kargil to Padum, but with a group to cut costs, this is a great way to really admire the amazing scenery. This trip can be done in one long day with about 12 hours driving, or you can stop at Rangdum, Parkachik or Panikhar.

Truck Trucks go along this route, but not nearly as often as the Kargil to Leh road, because so few people live in and around Zanskar. Nevertheless, hitching a ride on a truck, if you can find one, is normal practice, and most drivers will take you for a negotiable fee, maybe about the same as the bus fare.

Getting Around

Jeep & Taxi The Padum Taxi Union office across from the Hotel Haftal View charges exorbitant rates: Rs 650 return to Sani Gompa, Rs 800 return to Karsha Gompa, and Rs 5500/7000 to Rangdum. Not surprisingly, few visitors get around by taxi; most choose to trek.

TREKS IN ZANSKAR

Treks in the Zanskar area include the popular treks from Padum over Shingo La (5090m) to Darcha and Manali, and over Singge La (5050m) to Lamayuru and Leh. There is also a remote trek north over Cha Cha La (4950m) and Rubrang La (5020m) to the Markha Valley and Leh.

These treks can be undertaken from the end of June, when the snows begin to melt on the high passes, to the middle of October, before the first of the winter snows. There are of course exceptions to this as heavy storms blowing up from the Indian plains occasionally interrupt itineraries in August and September. River crossings are also a problem, particularly on the trek from Padum to the Markha Valley; it is advisable not to undertake this trek until the middle of August, when waters subside. It is also important to note that all of these treks involve high-pass crossings of around 5000m so proper acclimatisation is essential.

If making your own arrangements, packhorses can be hired from Padum or Karsha for around Rs 200 a day, although this can increase during the harvest period in late August to early September. A local guide is also a valuable asset, particularly on the trek from Padum to the Markha Valley.

Camping gear including a tent and sleeping bag must be brought with you, as there are a number of stages on these treks where there are no villages to stay. Food supplies must also be brought from Leh.

Padum to Darcha via Shingo La

This trek follows the well-defined route up the Tsarap Valley for the first three stages before diverting to Phugtal Monastery, one of the oldest monasteries in Zanskar. The trek continues through a number of villages to the highest settlement at Kargyak. From here it is a further stage to the base of Shingo La (5090m) before traversing the Great Himalaya Range. A final stage brings you to the roadhead at Darcha and your onward arrangements to Leh or Manali.

stage	route	duration (hrs)
1	Padum to Mune	6
2	Mune to Purne	8
3	Purne to Phugtal Monastery and Tetha	6
4	Tetha to Kargyak	7
5	Kargyak to Lakong	6–7
6	Lakong to Rumjak via the Shingo La	6–7
7	Rumjak to Darcha	6–7

Padum to Lamayuru via Singge La

This trek may commence from either Padum or from Karsha Monastery, the largest in the Zanskar region. The trek follows the true left bank of the Zanskar River for two stages before diverting towards the Hanuma La (4950m) and Lingshat Monastery. It is a further stage to the base of the Singge La (5050m) before crossing the Zanskar Range. From the pass there are dramatic views of the Zanskar gorges while to the south are the snowcapped peaks of the Great Himalaya Range. Singge La is not a particularly demanding pass crossing and the gradual descent to the village of Photaksar can be completed in one stage.

From Photaksar the trail crosses Sisir La (4850m) to the village of Honupatta. It is a further stage to the ancient monastery at Wanla before finally crossing Prinkiti La (3750m) to Lamayuru Gompa and onward transport by bus or truck to Leh.

stage	route	duration (hrs)
1	Padum to Karsha	2
2	Karsha to Pishu	4–5
3	Pishu to Hanumil	4–5
4	Hanumil to Snertse	5
5	Snertse to Lingshet via Hanuma La	5–6
6	Lingshet to Singge La base camp	5–6
7	Singge La base camp to Photaksar via Singge La	5–6
8	Photaksar to Honupatta via Sisir La	6
9	Honupatta to Wanla	5
10	Wanla to Lamayuru via Prinkiti La	3–4

Padum to Leh via Cha Cha La, Rubrang La & the Markha Valley

This challenging trek is followed by only a handful of trekkers each season. From Padum the trail heads north to the village of Zangla before diverting from the Zanskar Valley to Cha Cha La (4950m).

From the pass there are uninterrupted views south towards the Great Himalaya Range. Heading north, the trail enters a series of dramatic gorges that support rare wildlife including brown bears, bharal and snow leopards. It takes a minimum of two stages to reach Rubrang La (5020m) and the crest of the Zanskar Range before a steady descent to the villages of the Markha Valley. From Markha Village it takes a further three stages to cross Kongmaru La (5030m) to Hemis Gompa and the Indus Valley.

stage	route	duration (hrs)
1	Padum to Zangla	7
2	Zangla to Cha Cha La base camp	3
3	Base camp to Gorge camp via Cha Cha La	6
4	Gorge camp to Tilat Sumdo	6
5	Tilat Sumdo to Rubrang La base camp	5–6
6	Base camp to Markha via Rubrang La	6
7	Markha to Nimaling	7–8
8	Nimaling to Chogdo via Kongmaru La	6
9	Chogdo to Hemis	4–5

Uttar Pradesh & Uttaranchal

Uttar Pradesh used to stretch from the Ganges plain all the way up to the Tibetan border, but the vast territory was chopped down to size with the creation of the new state of Uttaranchal in November 2000. Uttar Pradesh still includes Agra, Varanasi and Lucknow.

Uttar Pradesh & Uttaranchal at a Glance

Population: 166.1 million (Uttar Pradesh), 8.5 million (Uttaranchal)
Area: 231,254 sq km (Uttar Pradesh), 63,157 sq km (Uttaranchal)
Capital: Lucknow (Uttar Pradesh), Dehra Dun (Uttaranchal)
Main Language: Hindi
When to Go: Oct to Mar

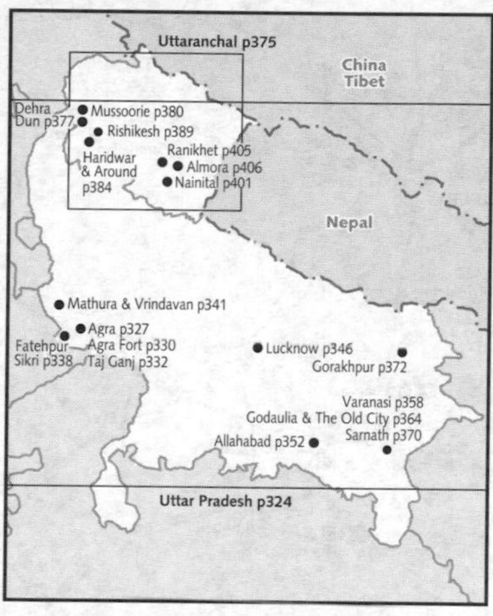

- Visit the Taj Mahal at sunrise and deserted Fatehpur Sikri at sunset
- Follow in the footsteps of Krishna in Mathura and Vrindavan
- Take a dawn boat ride on the Ganges at Varanasi
- Meditate at the ancient Buddhist shrine of Sarnath
- Practise yoga on the banks of the Ganges in Rishikesh
- Tour the sacred Char Dham in the high Himalaya
- Trek to remote lakes and glaciers in Garhwal and Kumaon
- Scout for tigers in Corbett Tiger Reserve

Uttar Pradesh

Often referred to as the cow belt or Hindi belt, Uttar Pradesh has been the most dominant state in Indian politics and culture since Independence, producing over half of India's prime ministers. This is partly because it's the nation's most populous state and partly because of the central role the region plays in the religious landscape of Hinduism. The Ganges River, the backbone of Uttar Pradesh, is the sacred river of Hinduism, reaching its most significant point at Varanasi, the holiest pilgrimage centre in India. Sarnath, just outside Varanasi, was where Buddha first preached his message of the middle way.

The people of Uttar Pradesh are predominantly poorly educated farmers who stand in stark contrast to the wealthy urbanites who control the state's political and economic destiny. Aside from its religious centres, Uttar Pradesh is best known as the home of India's most famous monument, the Taj Mahal. Fans of Mughal architecture can find numerous other fine examples of this effusive style dotted around the state.

Except in the very cheapest hotels, you can expect a 5% luxury tax to be added to your hotel bill in Uttar Pradesh. Rates quoted for accommodation in this chapter do not include tax.

History

Over 2000 years ago the area that became Uttar Pradesh was part of Ashoka's great Buddhist empire. Muslim raids from the north-west began in the 11th century, and by the 16th century the region was part of the famed Mughal empire whose capital was for some time at Agra and Fatehpur Sikri.

Following the decline of the Mughal empire, Persian invaders stepped in briefly before the nawabs of Avadh rose to prominence in the central part of the region. The

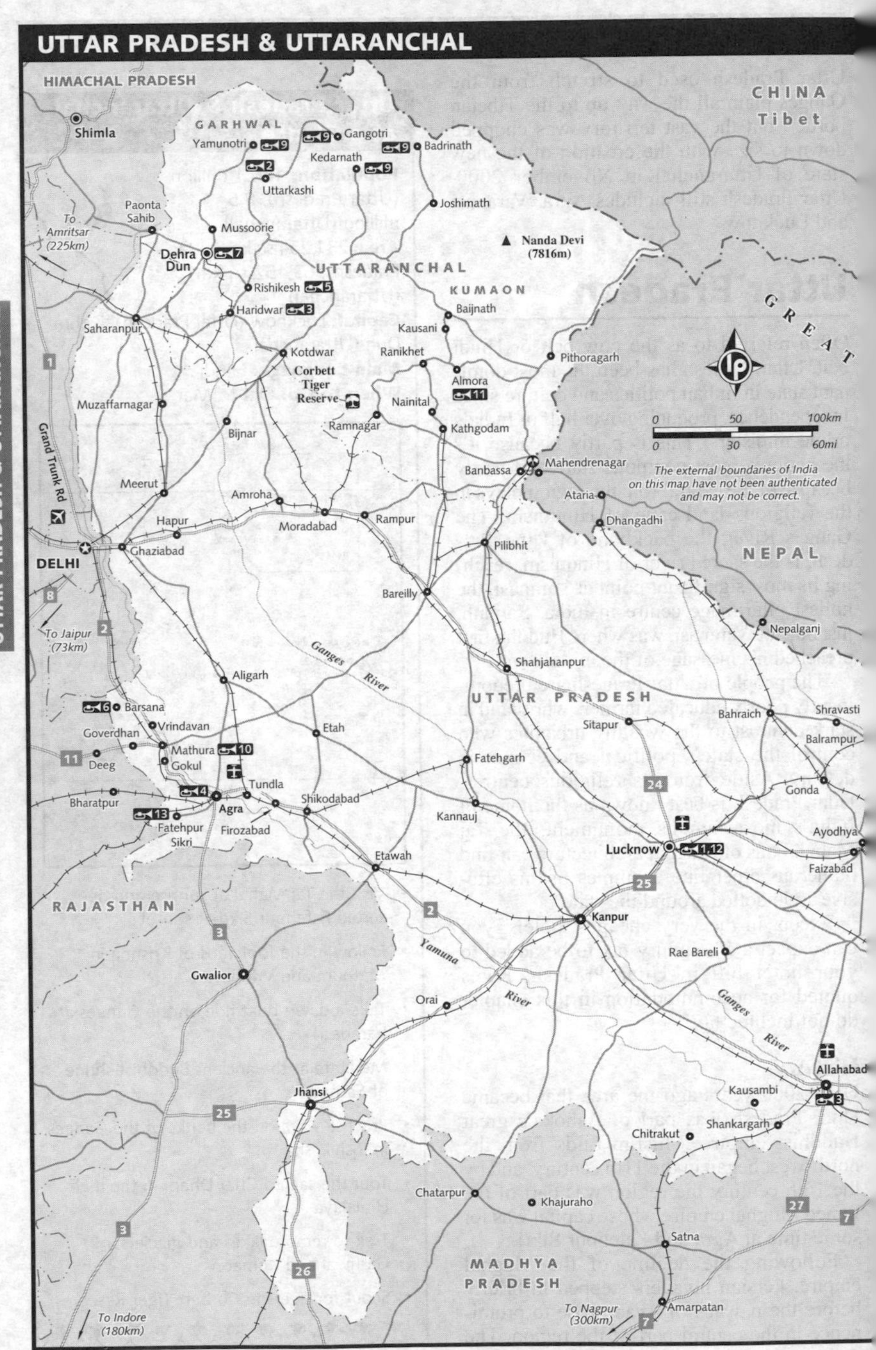
UTTAR PRADESH & UTTARANCHAL
HIMACHAL PRADESH
Shimla
GARHWAL
Yamunotri
Gangotri
Badrinath
Kedarnath
Uttarkashi
Joshimath
CHINA
Tibet
Paonta Sahib
To Amritsar (225km)
Mussoorie
Dehra Dun
Nanda Devi (7816m)
UTTARANCHAL
Rishikesh
KUMAON
Haridwar
Baijnath
Saharanpur
Kausani
Kotdwar
Ranikhet
Pithoragarh
Corbett Tiger Reserve
Almora
Nainital
Muzaffarnagar
Ramnagar
Kathgodam
0 50 100km
0 30 60mi
GREAT
Bijnar
Mahendrenagar
Banbassa
The external boundaries of India on this map have not been authenticated and may not be correct.
Grand Trunk Rd
Meerut
Ataria
Amroha
Dhangadhi
Hapur
Moradabad
Rampur
DELHI
Ghaziabad
Pilibhit
NEPAL
Bareilly
To Jaipur (73km)
Nepalganj
Ganges River
Shahjahanpur
Aligarh
UTTAR PRADESH
Barsana
Bahraich
Shravasti
Vrindavan
Sitapur
Balrampur
Goverdhan
Etah
Mathura
Deeg
Gokul
Fatehgarh
Gonda
Tundla
Shikodabad
Kannauj
Ayodhya
Bharatpur
Agra
Fatehpur Sikri
Firozabad
Lucknow
Faizabad
Etawah
RAJASTHAN
Kanpur
Yamuna River
Rae Bareli
Gwalior
Orai
Ganges River
Allahabad
Jhansi
Kausambi
Shankargarh
Chitrakut
Chatarpur
Khajuraho
Satna
MADHYA PRADESH
To Nagpur (300km)
Amarpatan
To Indore (180km)

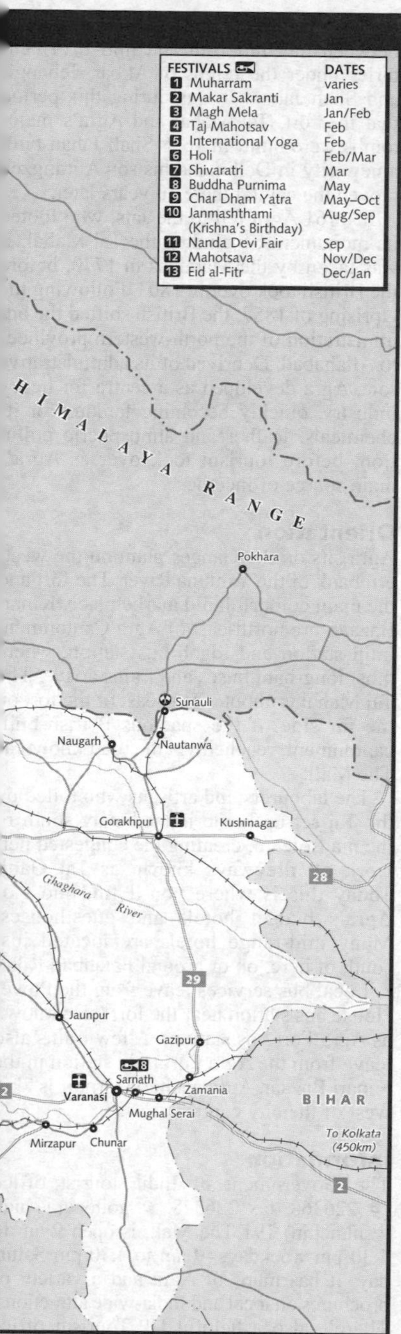

nawabs were responsible for turning Lucknow into a flourishing centre for the arts but their empire came to a dramatic end when the British East India Company deposed the last nawab, triggering the Uprising of 1857. Agra was later merged with Avadh and the state became known as United Province. It was renamed Uttar Pradesh (Northern State) after Independence, and is often known simply as UP.

In recent times Uttar Pradesh has become the main support base for the ruling Hindu fundamentalist Bharatiya Janata Party (BJP). The desecration of Hindu temples by Mughal invaders was used as a rallying cry by the BJP, leading to tension between Hindus and Muslims in many key cities. Things came to a flash point in 1992 in the town of Ayodhya, when rioting Hindus tore down a mosque built by the Mughals over the temple of Rama. The recent discovery of Jain ruins under the Mughal city of Fatehpur Sikri, near Agra, has caused some ominous rumblings.

In late 1996 the state was placed under direct rule from Delhi when elections resulted in a hung assembly. After five months of political stalemate the BJP, which won the most seats, formed a coalition government with the BSP, an anticaste, secular party at the opposite end of the political spectrum. The Congress Party was also briefly included, before both it and the BSP were replaced by the UP Loktrantrik Congress and JBS parties. Currently, the BJP is facing struggles from within and several party members have resigned in protest at the 'autocratic' political style of UP Chief Minister Kalyan Singh.

Tourist Offices

UP Tourism offices can be found in the following major Indian cities, as well as in cities throughout Uttar Pradesh and Uttaranchal.

Ahmedabad (☎ 079-6560752) 303 Ashwamedh House, 5 Smriti Kunj, Navrangpura
Chandigarh (☎ 0172-707649) SCO 1046–1047, 1st floor, Sector 22B
Chennai (Madras; ☎ 044-8283276) 28 Commander-in-Chief Rd
Delhi (☎ 011-3322251, fax 3711296) Chandralok Bldg, 36 Janpath, Delhi
Kolkata (Calcutta; ☎ 033-2207855) 12A Netaji Subashi Rd
Mumbai (Bombay; ☎ 022-2185458) 38 World Trade Centre, Cuffe Parade, Colaba

Internet Resources

The best sites relating to Uttar Pradesh are the UP Tourism Web site at www.up-tourism.com and the thorough, independent site www.upportal.com, which has hotel listings and also covers Uttaranchal.

AGRA

☎ 0562 • pop 1,118,800

This sprawling industrial town, 204km from Delhi, is synonymous with the Taj Mahal, India's most famous building, which sits on the banks of the Yamuna River in the east of town. The Mughal emperor Babur established his capital here in 1526 and for the next hundred years Agra witnessed a remarkable spate of architectural activity as each monarch tried to outdo the grandiose monuments built by his predecessor.

Choking these ancient monuments is the hectic and polluted modern city of Agra. There is a lively *chowk* (market) and a wide range of places to stay and eat, but for most visitors Agra is more a place to endure than enjoy. Much of the blame falls on the local rickshaw-wallahs, touts and souvenir vendors, who seem to stop at nothing in their efforts to separate tourists from their money. The polluted atmosphere further reduces Agra's charm. Former US president Bill Clinton used his visit to Agra in 2000 to highlight the damage that air pollution is causing to Agra's ancient monuments.

Following the controversial price hikes at the Taj Mahal and other Mughal sites, many tourists are choosing to visit Agra on a whistle-stop day trip from Delhi and there's an excellent train service making this eminently practicable. However, it would be a shame to miss Agra's other attractions if you can afford the entry fees. Agra Fort, the tombs of Itimad-ud-Daulah and Akbar (Sikandra), and the nearby deserted city of Fatehpur Sikri make for several days of sightseeing.

History

Agra is believed to have been founded on the site of an ancient Hindu kingdom, but the city was destroyed by the Afghan king Mahmud of Ghazni in about AD 1022. Agra did not come into its own until 1501, when sultan Sikander Lodi established his capital here. The city fell into Mughal hands in 1526, when the emperor Babur defeated the last Lodi sultan at Panipat, 80km north of Delhi.

Agra reached the peak of its magnificence between the mid-16th and mid-17th centuries under the reigns of Akbar, Jehangir and Shah Jahan. It was during this period that the fort, Taj Mahal and Agra's major tombs were built. In 1638 Shah Jahan built a new city in Delhi, and his son Aurangzeb moved the capital there 10 years later.

In 1761 Agra fell to the Jats, who looted its monuments, including the Taj Mahal. It was taken by the Marathas in 1770, before the British took over in 1803. Following the Uprising of 1857, the British shifted the administration of the north-western provinces to Allahabad. Deprived of its administrative role, Agra developed as a centre for heavy industry, quickly becoming famous for its chemicals, leather and atmospheric pollution, before tourism took over as Agra's main source of income.

Orientation

Agra sits on the Ganges plain on the western bank of the Yamuna River. The fort and the main colourful, old marketplace, Kinari Bazaar, are north-east of Agra Cantonment train station and Idgah bus station, where most long-haul buses and trains arrive. The Taj Mahal is about 1.5km east of the fort on the far side of the spacious British-built cantonment, reached via the road known as The Mall.

The labourers and artisans who toiled on the Taj set up home immediately south of the mausoleum, creating the congested network of alleyways known as Taj Ganj. Today this is where you'll find most of Agra's budget hotels and guesthouses. Many mid-range hotels are located just south of here, on or around Fatehbad Rd.

Local bus services leave from the Power House bus station near the fort (also known as Agra Fort bus station). A few trains also leave from the Agra Fort train station in the Kinari Bazaar. Agra's Kheria airport is 7km west of the city centre.

Information

The Government of India tourist office (☎ 226368, fax 226378, ⓔ goitoagra@nde.vsnl.net.in) 191 The Mall, is open 9 am to 5.30 pm weekdays, 9 am to 4.30 pm Saturday. It has maps of Agra and a variety of brochures on local and India-wide attractions. There's also a helpful UP Tourism office

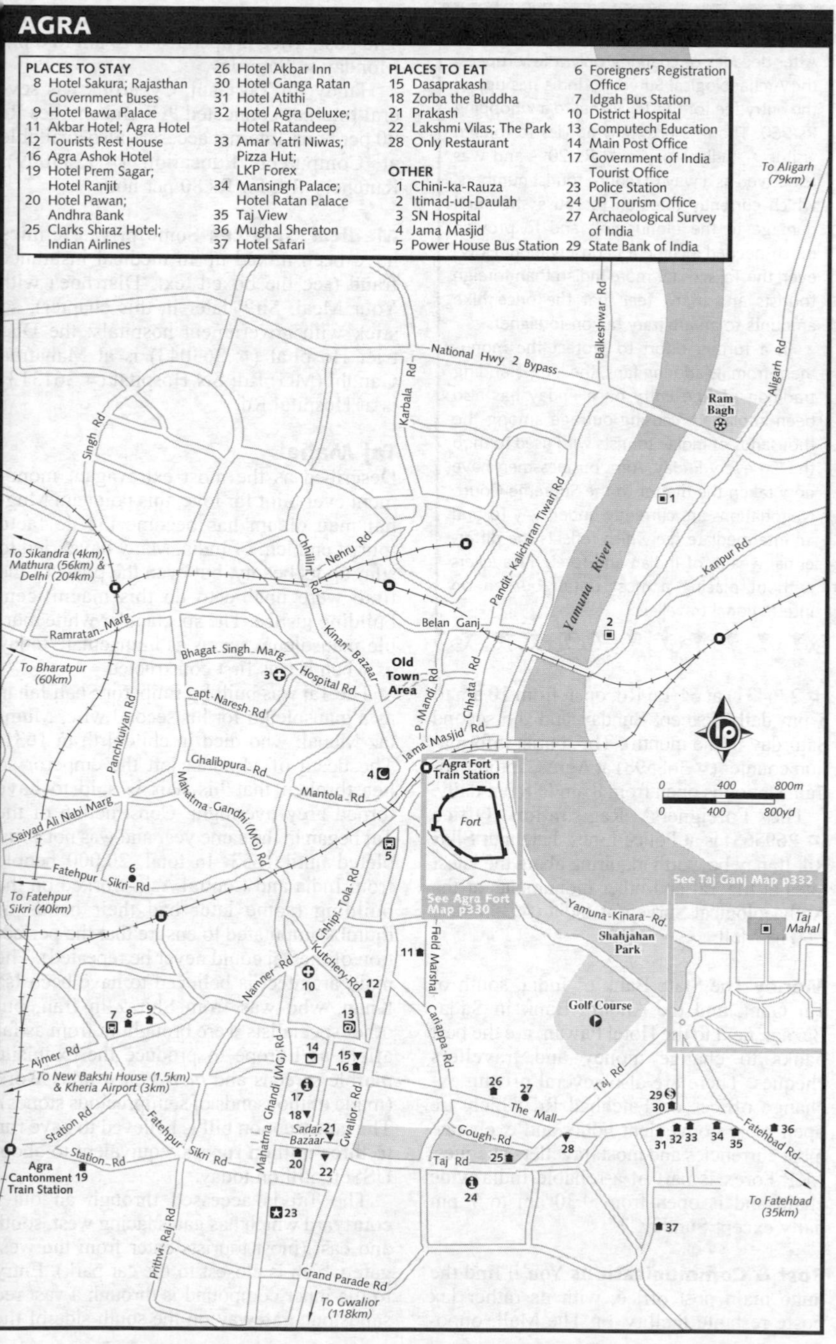

AGRA
PLACES TO STAY
8 Hotel Sakura; Rajasthan Government Buses
9 Hotel Bawa Palace
11 Akbar Hotel; Agra Hotel
12 Tourists Rest House
16 Agra Ashok Hotel
19 Hotel Prem Sagar; Hotel Ranjit
20 Hotel Pawan; Andhra Bank
25 Clarks Shiraz Hotel; Indian Airlines
26 Hotel Akbar Inn
30 Hotel Ganga Ratan
31 Hotel Atithi
32 Hotel Agra Deluxe; Hotel Ratandeep
33 Amar Yatri Niwas; Pizza Hut; LKP Forex
34 Mansingh Palace; Hotel Ratan Palace
35 Taj View
36 Mughal Sheraton
37 Hotel Safari
PLACES TO EAT
15 Dasaprakash
18 Zorba the Buddha
21 Prakash
22 Lakshmi Vilas; The Park
28 Only Restaurant
OTHER
1 Chini-ka-Rauza
2 Itimad-ud-Daulah
3 SN Hospital
4 Jama Masjid
5 Power House Bus Station
6 Foreigners' Registration Office
7 Idgah Bus Station
10 District Hospital
13 Computech Education
14 Main Post Office
17 Government of India Tourist Office
23 Police Station
24 UP Tourism Office
27 Archaeological Survey of India
29 State Bank of India
To Aligarh (79km)
National Hwy 2 Bypass
Balkeshwar Rd
Aligarh Rd
Karbala Rd
Ram Bagh
Singh Rd
Pandit-Kalicharan Tiwari Rd
Yamuna River
Kanpur Rd
Nehru Rd
Chhilli Rd
To Sikandra (4km), Mathura (56km) & Delhi (204km)
Ramratan Marg
Belan Ganj
To Bharatpur (60km)
Bhagat Singh Marg
Kinari Bazaar
Hospital Rd
Old Town Area
Capt Naresh Rd
P Mandi Rd
Chhata Rd
Panchkuiyan Rd
Jama Masjid Rd
Ghalibpura Rd
Agra Fort Train Station
Mantola Rd
Saiyad Ali Nabi Marg
Mahatma Gandhi (MG) Rd
Fort
0 400 800m
0 400 800yd
Fatehpur Sikri Rd
To Fatehpur Sikri (40km)
Chhipi Tola Rd
See Agra Fort Map p330
See Taj Ganj Map p332
Yamuna Kinara Rd
Taj Mahal
Shahjahan Park
Field Marshal Cariappa Rd
Kutchery Rd
Namner Rd
Golf Course
Ajmer Rd
To New Bakshi House (1.5km) & Kheria Airport (3km)
Mahatma Ghandi (MG) Rd
Taj Rd
The Mall
Station Rd
Fatehpur Sikri Rd
Sadar Bazaar
Gwalior Rd
Gough Rd
Fatehbad Rd
Agra Cantonment Train Station
Taj Rd
To Fatehbad (35km)
Prithvi Raj Rd
Grand Parade Rd
To Gwalior (118km)

Price Hikes at the Taj

After decades of charging only a few rupees, the Archaeological Survey of India has upped the entry fee for the Taj Mahal to a whopping Rs 960. The rate hike only applies to foreign visitors – Indians pay only Rs 20 – and was conceived as a way to reduce tourist numbers, which currently threaten to cause structural damage to the monument, and to provide much-needed income for conservation. However, the Taj sees far more Indian than foreign tourists and many feel that the price hike amounts to an arbitrary tax on foreigners.

In a further effort to protect the monument from its adoring fans, the long-standing tradition of free entry on a Friday has also been abolished, causing outrage among the thousands of Indian tourists who used to mob the Taj every Friday. Agra businessmen have now taken the matter to the Supreme Court. Negotiations are currently under way to find an intermediate fee which reflects the differential wealth of Indian and foreign travellers without placing a most unfair burden on international travellers.

(☎ 226431) at 64 Taj Rd, open from 10 am to 5 pm daily (except Sunday and the second Saturday in the month). The tourist information counter (☎ 368598) at Agra Cantonment train station is open from 8 am to 8 pm daily.

The Foreigners' Registration Office (☎ 269563) is at Police Lines, Fatehpur Sikri Rd. It may be worth inquiring about the latest rates at the Taj and other monuments at the Archaeological Survey of India (☎ 363506), 22 The Mall.

Money The State Bank of India, south of Taj Ganj, and the Andhra Bank in Sadar Bazaar, next to the Hotel Pawan, are the best banks to change money and travellers cheques. There are also several private exchange offices on Fatehbad Rd which are open more convenient hours and exchange most currencies and most travellers cheques. LKP Forex is part of a reliable India-wide chain and is open from 9.30 am to 7 pm daily except Sunday.

Post & Communications You'll find the huge main post office, with its rather lax poste restante facility, on The Mall, opposite the Government of India tourist office. The post office is open from 10 am to 6 pm Monday to Saturday.

Handy for Taj Ganj, Cyberlink has several Internet-connected PCs and charges Rs 90 per hour. Internet access is also available at Computech Education (☎ 253059), Kutchery Rd, for Rs 80 per hour.

Medical Services Some private clinics have been mixed up in medical insurance fraud (see the boxed text 'Diarrhoea with Your Meal, Sir?' later in this chapter), so stick with government hospitals: the District Hospital (☎ 363043) is at Mahatma Gandhi (MG) Rd; SN Hospital (☎ 361313) is at Hospital Rd.

Taj Mahal

Described as the most extravagant monument ever built for love, this poignant Mughal mausoleum has become the de facto tourist emblem of India. Many have tried to sum up its beauty, but even the poets of the time were unable to do this magnificent building justice. The spectacular white marble mausoleum seems as immaculate today as when it was first constructed.

The Taj was built by Emperor Shah Jahan as a mausoleum for his second wife, Mumtaz Mahal, who died in childbirth in 1631. The death of Mumtaz left the emperor so heartbroken that his hair is said to have turned grey overnight. Construction of the Taj began in the same year and was not completed until 1653. In total, 20,000 people from India and Central Asia worked on the building (some later had their hands or thumbs amputated to ensure that the perfection of the Taj could never be repeated). The main architect is believed to have been Isa Khan, who was from Shiraz in Iran, but other specialists were brought in from as far afield as Europe to produce the exquisite marble screens and *pietra dura* inlay work (made of thousands of semiprecious stones). The construction bill is believed to have run to three million rupees, equivalent to about US$60 million today.

The Taj is accessed through an outer courtyard which has gates facing west, south and east (most tourists enter from the west gate which is closest to the car park). Entry to the inner compound is through a vast red sandstone **gateway** on the south side of the forecourt, inscribed with verses from the Quran in Arabic. Beside the gateway is the ticket office and a small **cloakroom** where prohibited items must be deposited, including food, tobacco, matches, mobile phones, camera tripods, and *paan* (betel nut), introduced to keep the Taj free of unsightly red blotches. Anything you don't feel comfortable leaving in the cloakroom should be left at your hotel.

Cameras are permitted, and there's no problem taking photos of the outside of the Taj, though guards will prevent you from taking photographs inside the mausoleum. You probably won't immediately be able to see the Taj through the crowds of tourists taking *the* shot of the Taj reflected in the watercourse that runs through the gardens. You can bring in your video camera for Rs 25, but the guards won't let you take it beyond the gateway steps (thereafter it must be left in a locker until you return).

The ornamental gardens are set out along classical Mughal *charbagh* (formal Persian garden) lines – a square quartered by watercourses, with an ornamental marble plinth at the centre. To the west is a very small **museum**, open 10 am to 5 pm daily except Monday and Friday (free entry). It houses original architectural drawings of the Taj and some nifty celadon plates, said to split into pieces or change colour if the food served on them contains poison (handy for those dodgy Taj Ganj meals!).

The Taj Mahal itself stands on a raised marble platform at the northern end of the ornamental gardens. Purely decorative white **minarets** grace each corner of the platform. The red sandstone mosque to the west of the main structure is an important gathering place for Agra Muslims. The identical building to the east is purely for symmetry (it can't be used as a mosque because it faces in the wrong direction).

The central Taj structure is constructed of semitranslucent white marble, carved with flowers and inlaid with thousands of semiprecious stones in beautiful patterns. A perfect exercise in symmetry, the four identical faces of the Taj feature vast vaulted arches embellished with pietra dura scrollwork and quotations from the Quran. The whole structure is topped off by four small domes surrounding the famous bulbous central dome.

Despite the effects of pollution and overexposure, a visit to the Taj Mahal is still an overwhelming experience.

Below the main dome is the **Cenotaph of Mumtaz Mahal**, an elaborate false tomb surrounded by an exquisite perforated screen inlaid with some 43 different types of semiprecious stones. Beside it, offsetting the symmetry of the Taj, is the **Cenotaph of Shah Jahan**, who was interred here with little ceremony by Aurangzeb in 1666. Light is admitted into the central chamber by finely cut marble screens. The physical **tombs** of Mumtaz Mahal and Shah Jahan are in a locked basement room below the main chamber.

In recent years, there has been growing concern about the damage that atmospheric pollution is causing to the Taj. Acid rain, produced by sulphur dioxide from vehicle emissions, is discolouring the famous white marble and eroding the fine carving and inlays. In an attempt to reduce pollution, new industrial developments were banned from a 10,400 sq km exclusion zone around the Taj Mahal in 1994, and motor vehicles are now prohibited from the 4km area surrounding the monument.

As of October 2000, the entry fee was raised to a staggering Rs 960 for foreigners, while Indians continue to pay Rs 20, or Rs 110 before 7 am or after 5 pm. Free entry on Friday has also been abandoned; the Taj is now open daily except Friday from sunrise to 7 pm. However, the charges at the Taj are currently being reviewed by the Indian Supreme Court; ask about the current situation when you arrive in Agra. For more information on the rate hike controversy, see the boxed text 'Price Hikes at the Taj' earlier in this chapter.

Sunset is an extremely impressive time to see the Taj as the white marble first takes on a rich golden sheen, then slowly turns pink, red and finally blue with the changing light. In winter, it's not really worth getting up early for the sunrise as it's invariably foggy.

Agra Fort

Construction of the massive red sandstone Agra Fort on the bank of the Yamuna River was begun by Emperor Akbar in 1565, though additions were made up until the rule of his grandson, Shah Jahan. The fort was built primarily as a military structure, but during Shah Jahan's reign it was upgraded to a palace, and finally became a prison (albeit a gilded one) for Shah Jahan after Aurangzeb seized power in 1658.

The auricular fort's colossal double wall rise over 20m in height and measure 2.5km in circumference. They contain a maze of buildings that form a small city within a city. Unfortunately many of the structures here were severely damaged over the years by Nadir Shah, the Marathas, the Jats and finally the British during the Uprising of 1857. The most impressive building to survive is the legendary white marble Moti Masjid (Pearl Mosque), regarded by some as the most beautiful mosque in India. Sadly it's not open to visitors.

The Amar Singh Gate to the south is the sole entry point to the fort, and is open from sunrise to sunset daily; admission is Rs 51(for foreigners and Rs 20 for Indians (free on Friday). Having paid the steep entry fee, it's worth hiring a guide to get the most out of your visit.

Diwan-i-Am & Diwan-i-Khas The Hall of Public Audiences (Diwan-i-Am) was used by Shah Jahan for domestic government business and features a marble throne room where the emperor listened to petitioners. Nearby are the tiny **Nagina Masjid** or Gem Mosque and **Ladies' Bazaar**, where female merchants came to sell goods to the ladies of the Mughal court.

The Hall of Private Audiences (Diwan-i-Khas) was reserved for important digni-

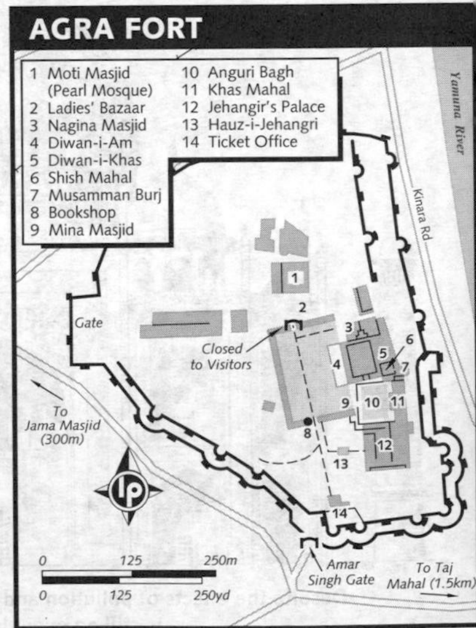

taries or foreign ambassadors and consists of two rooms connected by three arches. The famous Peacock Throne was housed here until Aurangzeb moved it to Delhi. It was later carted off to Iran and its remains are now in Tehran.

Musamman Burj The exquisite Musamman Burj (Octagonal Tower) stands close to the Diwan-i-Khas and looks towards the Taj. It was here that Shah Jahan was imprisoned by Aurangzeb, ending his days gazing over the Yamuna towards the mausoleum of his wife.

Jehangir's Palace Akbar is believed to have built this palace for his son. It was the largest private residence in the fort and displays an interesting blend of Hindu and Central Asian architectural styles – a contrast to the unique Mughal style which had developed by the time of Shah Jahan.

In front of Jehangir's Palace is the **Hauz-i-Jehangri**, a huge bowl beautifully carved out of a single block of stone. According to one traditional story, Jehangir's wife, Nur Jahan, made *attar* (perfumed essential oil) of roses in the bowl.

Other Buildings Shah Jahan's **Khas Mahal** is a beautiful white marble structure used as a private palace. The rooms underneath it were intended as a cool retreat. The **Shish Mahal** (Mirror Palace) is reputed to have been the harem dressing room and its walls are inlaid with tiny mirrors.

The **Amar Singh Gate** takes its name from a maharaja of Jodhpur who slew the imperial treasurer in the Diwan-i-Am in 1644 and, in a bid to escape, reputedly rode his horse over the fort wall near here. Amar Singh survived the fall but not Shah Jahan's wrath, and was hurled from the walls a second time, this time fatally.

Itimad-ud-Daulah

On the opposite bank of the Yamuna, north of the fort, is the exquisite Itimad-ud-Daulah – the tomb of Mirza Ghiyas Beg. This Persian gentleman was Jehangir's *wazir*, or chief minister, and his beautiful daughter, Nur Jahan, later married the emperor. Nur Jahan constructed the tomb between 1622 and 1628 in a style similar to the tomb she built for Jehangir near Lahore in Pakistan.

Although much less elaborate, many of the Itimad-ud-Daulah's design elements foreshadow the Taj, earning it the nickname 'Baby Taj'. The Itimad-ud-Daulah was the first Mughal structure totally built from marble and the first to make extensive use of pietra dura. Though small and squat, the mausoleum features extremely fine marble latticework passages, admitting decorative shafts of light to the interior, and the surface of the tomb is exquisitely patterned.

The Itimad-ud-Daulah is open from sunrise to sunset daily and carries the usual royal price tag of Rs 235 for foreigners and Rs 15 for Indians (free on Friday). Video cameras require a Rs 25 permit.

Akbar's Mausoleum

The sandstone and marble tomb of Akbar, the greatest of the Mughal emperors, lies in the centre of a peaceful garden grazed by deer at Sikandra, 4km north-west of Agra. Akbar started its construction himself, blending Islamic, Hindu, Buddhist, Jain and Christian motifs and styles, much like the syncretic religious philosophy he developed called Din-i-Ilahi (see the boxed text 'Akbar the Great' later in this chapter). When Akbar died, the mausoleum was completed by his son, Jehangir, who significantly modified the original plans.

The stunning southern gateway is the most impressive part of the complex. It has three-storey minarets at each corner and is built of red sandstone strikingly inlaid with white marble abstract patterns. The ticket office is located here, to the left of the arched entrance. The mausoleum is open from sunrise to sunset and entry is Rs 235 for foreigners, Rs 15 for Indians and free on Friday. A video camera permit costs Rs 25.

Sikandra is named after Sikander Lodi, the Delhi sultan who ruled from 1488 to 1517, before the rise of Mughal power on the subcontinent. He built the **Baradi Palace**, in the mausoleum gardens. Across the road from the mausoleum is the **Delhi Gate**.

Local buses for Sikandra run along MG Rd from the Power House bus station (Rs 4). Autorickshaws charge around Rs 80 for the return trip with an hour's waiting time.

Other Attractions

Across the train tracks from the Delhi Gate of Agra Fort is the **Jama Masjid**, built by

Shah Jahan in 1648, which has no minarets but features striking marble patterning on its domes. The mosque is reached though the alleyways of the colourful **Kinari Bazaar**, or old marketplace.

Within the market are several distinct areas whose names are relics of the Mughal period, although they don't always bear relation to what is sold there today. The **Loha Mandi** (Iron Market) and **Sabji Mandi** (Vegetable Market) are still operational, but the **Nai-ki-Mandi** (Barber's Market) is now famous for textiles.

The squat **Chini-ka-Rauza** (China Tomb), 1km north of the Itimad-ud-Daulah, is the mausoleum of Afzal Khan, a poet and high official in the court of Shah Jahan. Over the centuries the mausoleum has lost most of its brightly coloured enamelled tiles, but you can still get an impression of the building's former glory.

About 500m north, **Ram Bagh**, the earliest of India's Mughal gardens, were built by Babur in 1528, but are pretty forlorn these days. The gardens are open from sunrise to sunset daily, but they don't really warrant the Rs 225 entry fee (Rs 5 for Indians). Entry is free on Friday.

Swimming

The following hotels allow nonguests to use their pools for a fee: Agra Ashok Hotel (Rs 200), Hotel Atithi (Rs 250) and the Clarks Shiraz Hotel (Rs 300). Ashok has the best pool.

Organised Tours

Guided tours depart from the Government of India tourist office at 9.30 am and proceed to Agra Cantonment train station to pick up passengers arriving from Delhi on the *Taj Express*, which pulls in at 9.47 am. The tours include the Taj Mahal, Agra Fort and a rather hasty visit to Fatehpur Sikri, returning to the station by 6 pm so day-trippers can catch the *Taj Express* back to Delhi at 6.35 pm.

With the new entry fees, the tours cost Rs 2100 for foreigners and Rs 250 for Indians. You can just take the Fatehpur Sikri part of the tour for Rs 650 (Rs 175 Indians) and finish up at the eastern gate to the Taj Mahal at 1.30 pm. Tickets must be bought from the tourist information counter at the train station (you can board the bus at the Government of India tourist office before buying).

Special Events

From 18–27 February every year, the **Taj Mahotsav Festival** is held in Shilpgram, a crafts village and open-air emporium about a kilometre along the road running from the eastern gate of the Taj. The festival features live performances of music and dance.

Places to Stay – Budget

The cheapest rooms can be found in Taj Ganj, but there are better options which only cost a little more in the Sadar Bazaar and Fatehbad Rd areas. Unless stated otherwise, rooms mentioned have private bathroom and checkout is 10 am. Expect to pay double the quoted rates if you arrive with a rickshaw-wallah in tow.

Taj Ganj Area There are plenty of remarkably cheap hotels immediately south of the Taj, all of which claim to offer rooftop views of the Taj and promise 'cheap and best' rooms. Usually this translates to an interrupted view of the famous onion dome and basic rooms with thin mattresses and leaky plumbing. But they're cheap and you'll bump into plenty of other travellers

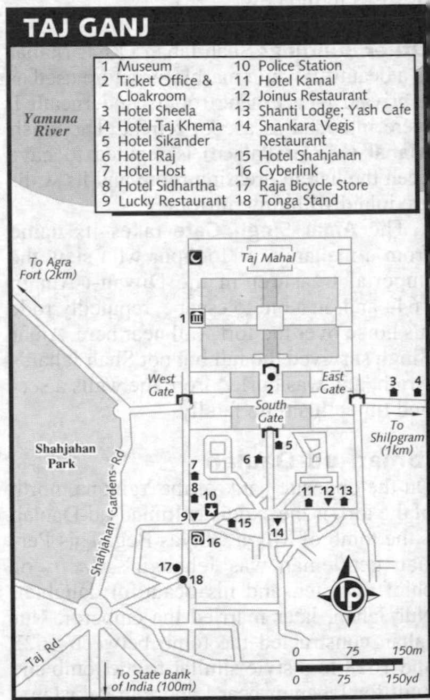

who are scrimping and saving in order to cover the hefty entrance fee at the Taj.

Hotel Kamal *(☎ 330126, ⓔ hotelkamal@hotmail.com)*, right in the middle of things, gets consistently good reports from travellers and boasts a clear view of the Taj from the eating area on the roof. The staff are helpful, and OK singles/doubles cost Rs 120/150 (Rs 150/200 with private bathroom).

Shanti Lodge *(☎ 330900)*, a few doors down, gets mixed reviews, but it has a decent view of the Taj from its rooftop. Slightly cramped rooms cost from Rs 80/100, or Rs 150 for doubles with reasonable views. Some rooms are definitely better than others.

Hotel Host *(☎ 331010)*, not far from the Taj's western gate, has rather plain little singles/doubles at Rs 100/150 and better doubles with balcony for Rs 200. All rooms have private bathroom and there's an OK view from the roof.

Hotel Sidhartha *(☎ 331238)*, close by, is a clean, spacious place built motel-style around a garden courtyard and the rooms benefit from decent-sized windows. Singles/doubles with bucket hot water cost Rs 100/150, or it's Rs 200/300 for big rooms with hot water on tap.

Hotel Raj *(☎ 331314)*, by the south gate to the Taj, is large and was once quite upmarket for the area, but has fallen in line with everyone else over the years. Clean rooms with hot water start at Rs 100/150 a single/double.

Hotel Sikander *(☎ 330279)*, across the road, is more basic and offers simple rooms with hot water for Rs 80/100.

Hotel Shahjahan *(☎ 331159)*, near the police station, has rather ordinary rooms with shared bathroom for Rs 60/100 and nicer rooms with private bathrooms and hot water for Rs 150. There's a free luggage room for guests.

Hotel Sheela *(☎ 331194)*, near the Taj's eastern gate, is a good choice. The hotel lies within the nontraffic zone close to the eastern gate, and has a variety of rooms set around a peaceful garden. Smaller doubles cost Rs 200, while the larger rooms cost Rs 300 or Rs 350 (the latter have cavernous bathrooms). This place is often full so it's wise to book ahead.

Sadar Bazaar The ***Tourists Rest House*** *(☎ 363961, ⓔ trh@vsnl.com, Kutchery Rd)* is one of the best options in Agra. Set in a quiet location with a peaceful garden dining area, this homely guesthouse gets good reports from travellers year after year. The approachable owners can make train/air reservations, arrange tours and provide unbiased local information. Comfortable, spotless, air-cooled singles/doubles are Rs 75/120 with shared hot shower and Rs 150/200 with hot water on tap; toiletries and towels are provided. Decent vegetarian food is served in the candle-lit courtyard or in the rooftop restaurant. Rickshaw-wallahs may try to steer you away because the guesthouse doesn't give commissions.

Hotel Akbar Inn *(☎ 226836, 21 The Mall)* is midway between Sadar and Taj Ganj. It is quiet and has a peaceful lawn and relaxed atmosphere, which makes up somewhat for the ageing facilities. Simple rooms with shared bathroom are a bargain at Rs 60, while fan-cooled doubles cost from Rs 150 to 200.

Agra Hotel *(☎ 363331, Field Marshal Cariappa Rd)* is housed in an ageing cantonment building and is a popular wedding venue so it is often booked out. The rooms are OK though, and cost Rs 150 for a single with fan and bathroom and Rs 250 to 450 for doubles with hot shower.

Akbar Hotel *(☎ 363312, 196 Field Marshal Cariappa Rd)*, next door to the Agra, but quieter, offers doubles with cold shower for Rs 150 and rooms with hot shower for Rs 300 to 450. A new block of ultra-basic 'student' rooms is under construction, tipped to cost Rs 50.

Hotel Pawan *(☎ 225506, fax 225604, 3 Taj Rd)* is well located for the restaurants at Sadar Bazaar. It's a passable mid-range hotel with hot water in all the rooms. Those with fan start at Rs 240/350 a single/double while much better air-con rooms with phone and TV start at Rs 500/600. Checkout is noon.

West of Sadar Bazaar There are several hotels located right by the Idgah bus station, though the noise levels here are correspondingly high.

Hotel Sakura *(☎ 369961, Ajmer Rd)* is the pick of the bunch and is also the departure point for deluxe buses to Jaipur. Clean fan-cooled rooms with hot shower are Rs 200/250. Slightly chintzy air-con rooms with TV cost Rs 450/600.

Hotel Bawa Palace *(☎ 265681, Ajmer Rd)* is more upmarket, with carpets, TV and hot water throughout. Singles/doubles cost Rs 550/700 with fan and Rs 800/1000 with air-con.

Hotel Prem Sagar *(☎ 267408, 264 Station Rd)* is one of the better mid-range places with friendly staff and a bright, airy building. Spacious and clean doubles/triples with fan and hot water cost Rs 275/325.

Hotel Ranjit *(☎ 364446, 263 Station Rd)* isn't bad for the money. Fan-cooled rooms with hot shower cost Rs 250/400 a single/double, or Rs 330/480 with TV, phone and air-con.

Fatehbad Road Area Set back from Fatehbad Rd, the ***Hotel Ratan Palace*** *(☎ 333 400)* is OK for the money. Adequate rooms with bathroom cost Rs 250/300 with fan and Rs 500 for doubles with air-con.

Hotel Safari *(☎ 333029, Shamsabad Rd)*, south of Fatehbad Rd, is a friendly hotel run by the same owners as the Tourists Rest House. It's popular and clean. Air-cooled singles/doubles with hot water and bathtub cost Rs 175/250 (plus Rs 100 for air-con). Rooms with shower only cost Rs120/200. All come with towel, soap and toilet roll.

Places to Stay – Mid-Range

Most places in this price bracket are around Fatehbad Rd and you can expect hot water, TV, phone and air-con.

Hotel Taj Khema *(☎ 330140)*, close to the eastern gate to the Taj, is a ramshackle UP Tourism hotel. Its main claim to fame is that former US president Bill Clinton delivered his environmental address from the hummock in the garden. There are good views of the Taj from this point, but the rooms are expensive for what you get. Fan-cooled singles/doubles start at Rs 600/700, while air-con rooms are Rs 800/900. From April to September, rates drop by 20%.

Hotel Agra Deluxe *(☎ 330110, fax 331330, Fatehbad Rd)* is one of several OK mid-range places along Fatehbad Rd offering passable carpeted rooms with TV. Rates start at Rs 400 with fan and Rs 500 with air-con.

Hotel Ratandeep *(☎ 331074, fax 334 920)* is another good option with prices and amenities similar to Agra Deluxe.

Amar Yatri Niwas *(☎ 333800, fax 333 805, Fatehbad Rd)*, by the Pizza Hut, isn't much to look at from the outside, but the rooms are definitely above average. Tidy and well-maintained singles/doubles with air-con, TV and phone start at Rs 900/1100.

Hotel Ganga Ratan *(☎ 330329, fax 330193, Fatehbad Rd)*, near the State Bank of India, is a no-nonsense hotel with good facilities and a professional attitude. All rooms have air-con and singles/doubles with TV and hot showers start at Rs 900/1020.

New Bakshi House *(☎ 302176, fax 301 448, 5 Laxman Nagar)* is between the train station and the airport. It's effectively a private home, and you can use the family's lounge. Comfortable doubles in this clean place range from Rs 850 to 1250, some with air-con.

Hotel Atithi *(☎ 330879, fax 330878, Fatehbad Rd)* has good-sized, well-equipped air-con rooms from Rs 1175/1425, plus a swimming pool and restaurants.

Places to Stay – Top End

All the top-end hotels are air-conditioned and have pools. Except for Agra Ashok and Clarks Shiraz Hotel, all are on Fatehbad Rd.

Agra Ashok Hotel *(☎ 361223, fax 361 620, 6B The Mall)*, midway between Agra Cantonment and the Taj, is a well-managed, pleasant place to stay; doubles cost Rs 2000 from April to September and Rs 2500 from October to March (inexplicably, singles cost Rs 1995 year round).

Clarks Shiraz Hotel *(☎ 226121, fax 282001, ⓔ clarkraz@nde.vsnl.net.in)* is a long-standing, if curiously named, Agra landmark (Shiraz was the home of one of Agra's Persian conquerors). Rooms for US$45/90 have the expected comforts, including a fridge.

Mansingh Palace *(☎ 331771, fax 330202, Fatehbad Rd)* was built using local red sandstone. Splendid and stylishly themed, it has lots of Mughal details and attentive staff. Such luxury doesn't come cheap: sophisticated rooms start at Rs 1995/3000 a single/double.

Taj View *(☎ 331841, fax 331860)* is a five-star member of the Taj Group of hotels and has all the usual luxury trimmings. You'll pay US$105/115 a single/double for the view of the Taj; similar rooms without the view cost US$90/95.

Mughal Sheraton *(☎ 331701, fax 331 730)*, far from the centre, is arguably Agra's top hotel. The award-winning red-brick building fails to win over all visitors, but the hotel boasts an impressive range of luxury facilities and has standard rooms from US$110/120, or US$175/185 with a medium-range view of the Taj Mahal.

Places to Eat

Agra offers a wide range of prices and standards of dining. If you're walking around the Kinari Bazaar, don't forget to try the local speciality, ultra-sweet candied pumpkin *peitha*.

Diarrhoea with Your *Meal*, Sir?

During the late 1990s, Agra became the centre for a food-poisoning scam of monstrous proportions. Over several years, hundreds of travellers were given adulterated food by restaurants in Taj Ganj and taken to private clinics where doctors treated them for severe food poisoning. In the process foreign insurance companies were billed for thousands of dollars worth of phoney treatments.

Mercifully, there were no fatalities in Agra, but two Irish backpackers died in 1998, apparently due to a similar scam in Varanasi. The insurance companies soon got wise and sent in their own investigators, leading to the arrest of several doctors and restaurant staff. There were no new cases at the time of writing, but many of the clinics and restaurants involved are still in business, so the scheme could resurface at any time. In this edition, we haven't recommended any establishment known to be linked to the scam.

Taj Ganj Area In the Taj Ganj area there are a huge number of rooftop eateries catering to budget travellers. All offer almost identical menus of Indian and international favourites, and these days most will refrain from adding bacteria to your meal (see the boxed text 'Diarrhoea with Your Meal, Sir?'), though you should still be wary of eating in empty restaurants. None are licensed but beer can usually be 'arranged' if you ask. Take a stroll around to see which places are currently drawing a crowd.

Joinus Restaurant, close to the Hotel Kamal, is situated on the highest rooftop and turns out a passable range of curries, Western dishes and breakfasts for less than Rs 50, accompanied by good music. On clear days, there are good views of the Taj.

Shankara Vegis Restaurant, across the road, is another rooftop place which tries its hand at everything from *murg masala* (chicken curry) to beef schnitzel. Meals cost roughly Rs 30 to 55.

Yash Cafe, close to the Shanti Lodge, is on a terrace rather than a rooftop. It's a good place to unwind, with Western music, games and comfy chairs. There is a wide range of Western food, but usually not beer.

Lucky Restaurant, back at street level, has the usual have-a-go-at-everything menu but it's one of the more convivial places to hang out. There are a also a few tables on the roof with views of the Taj.

Elsewhere Although Agra has a fine tradition of Mughlai food, you wouldn't know it from most of the offerings served up in Taj Ganj. For quality Mughlai cuisine, you need to dip deeper into your wallet and head for Sadar Bazaar or the big hotels.

Zorba the Buddha *(☎225055)* in Sadar Bazaar is run by devotees of the late guru Osho (Bhagwan Shree Rajneesh) and offers truly excellent vegetarian food in a pleasant nonsmoking environment. The naan bread made from yogurt dough is magnificent; main dishes cost from Rs 70 to 80. It's wise to book in the evening. (The restaurant is closed each May and June.)

Lakshmi Vilas *(Taj Rd)*, around the corner, is a cheap south Indian veg restaurant serving 23 varieties of *dosa* (lentil pancakes) for around Rs 30.

Prakash is dingy but popular, with great value vegetarian thalis for Rs 38.

The Park, nearby, is an upmarket restaurant serving Indian and Chinese food in stylish surroundings. Dishes cost from Rs 70 to 130.

Dasaprakash, upstairs in the Meher Cinema complex near the Agra Ashok Hotel, serves tasty and highly regarded South Indian food in the Rs 45 to 100 range and is open late into the evening.

Only Restaurant, at the Taj Ganj end of The Mall, is highly rated by locals, though the food is fairly bland. There's often live Indian music in the evening.

Pizza Hut *(Fatehbad Rd)*, for those craving Western familiarity, is next to Hotel Atithi, but it's rather pricey.

There is top-end dining at top-end prices at the restaurants in most of the luxury hotels. Try the ***Clarks Shiraz Hotel*** and the ***Mughal Sheraton*** for a splurge.

Shopping

Agra is well known for marble items inlaid with coloured stones, similar to the pietra dura work on the Taj. Sadar Bazaar and the area south of Taj Ganj are full of emporiums of one kind or another, but prices here are more expensive than in the bazaars of the old part of the city. Expect to pay around Rs 200 for an inlaid jewellery box and Rs 1000 for a richly inlaid wall plaque.

Other popular buys include rugs, leather, and gemstones, though the latter are imported from Rajasthan and can be brought much more cheaply in Jaipur. Gem shops are also some of the worst offenders when it comes to credit card fraud and other scams (see the boxed text 'Agra-phobia').

About a kilometre along the road running from the eastern gate of the Taj is Shilpgram, a crafts village and open-air emporium. Electric shuttle buses run here from both Agra Fort and the eastern gate, and you can pick up good-quality crafts from all over the country, though prices are aimed at the package-tour bracket.

Getting There & Away

Air Agra's Kheria airport, 7km from town, is a stop on the extremely popular tourist shuttle route from Delhi to Agra, Khajuraho and Varanasi with Indian Airlines. The 40-minute flight leaves Delhi at 11.30 am, continuing on from Agra to Khajuraho and Varanasi at

Agra-phobia

With its many and varied scams and persistent touts and rickshaw-wallahs, Agra can leave many travellers on the verge of hysteria. The many pitfalls can be negotiated, but you'll need to be on your toes. Be wary of anyone who offers to make things easier for you. A cheap or free ride will inevitably lead you straight to a craft shop. If you accept assistance with train bookings, don't be surprised if the service you want suddenly turns out to be full in all classes, necessitating an expensive private bus or taxi ride. Anyone turning up to the steps of a hotel with a rickshaw-wallah in tow is likely to pay a 100% mark-up on the rate for their room.

If you accept any of the detours to gem and souvenir shops offered by rickshaw drivers, you will inevitably pay elevated prices to cover the drivers' commission. Some shops may take advantage of the fact that you will be unable to find them again and will pull a variety of stunts, from substituting marble souvenirs for soapstone to the grandmaster of all Agra scams, the 'gem import scam'.

In this neat bit of credit-card fraud, travellers are invited to help a shop avoid import duty by carrying gems back to their home country (for a small expenditure by credit card), where a company representative will reimburse them for their costs plus a tidy profit. Without exception, the gems are worthless, the representative never materialises and travellers are lumped with a credit card bill of around US$1000. Keep your credit card firmly sheathed!

12.35 pm. The return flight to Delhi leaves at 5.20 pm. Fares from Agra are U$55 to Delhi, US$80 to Khajuraho and US$160 to Varanasi. Indian Airlines has an office (☎ 360948) at the Clarks Shiraz Hotel, open 10 am to 1.15 pm and 2 to 5 pm daily.

Bus Most long-haul buses leave from the Idgah bus station (☎ 363588) near the train station. Buses to Delhi's Sarai Kale Khan bus station leave hourly from 4 am to 11.30 pm (Rs 92, five hours). There are also hourly services to Jaipur (Rs 103, six hours) and Mathura (Rs 28, 1½ hours). Buses to Fatehpur Sikri (Rs 17, 1½ hours) leave every 30 minutes from 6.30 am to 7 pm. There is one bus to Khajuraho (Rs 140, 10 hours) at 5 am.

The smaller Power House/Agra Fort bus station in the old city has regular slow buses to Mathura (Rs 23, two hours) and other local destinations.

Rajasthan government buses depart from a small booth outside the Hotel Sakura, close to the Idgah bus station. There are departures every hour for Jaipur (Rs 201, air-con, six hours) from 6.30 am to midnight, but you should book a day in advance.

Train Agra Cantonment train station is an important stop on the main Delhi-Mumbai (Bombay) train line with several trains daily from both New Delhi train station and Nizamuddin. The fastest train to Delhi is the daily air-con *Shatabdi Express* (Rs 390, air-con, chair class; Rs 125, sleeper class; two hours). It leaves New Delhi at 6 am and departs from Agra for the return trip at 8.18 pm, making it ideal for day-tripping.

A much cheaper alternative is the daily *Taj Express* (2½ hours). It leaves Delhi's Nizamuddin train station at 7.15 am and departs from Agra for the return trip at 6.35 pm. This gives you less time in Agra but it conveniently connects with the organised tour (see Organised Tours earlier). There are at least four other express trains from New Delhi train station daily. Be doubly cautious with your baggage on this route; a chain and padlock (obtainable from vendors on the platform) isn't a bad idea.

Agra has several daily trains to Howrah in Kolkata (Rs 337 in sleeper class) but none of these pass via Varanasi. The best option is the daily *Marudhar Express* which leaves Agra Cantonment train station at 8.45 pm, reaching Varanasi between 8 and 9.30 am the next morning (Rs 208).

If you're bound for Rajasthan, the daily *Marudhar Express* leaves Agra Cantonment train station at 7.15 am, reaching Jaipur at 2 pm (Rs 123) and Jodhpur at 8.50 pm (Rs 205). For Khajuraho, take any train to Jhansi (Rs 95, three hours), and change to a bus.

There are also trains to Mumbai, Pune (Goa), Chennai and Thiruvananthapuram (Trivandrum).

Getting Around

To/From the Airport Agra's Kheria airport is 7km from the centre of town and 3km west of Idgah bus station. From Taj Ganj, taxis charge around Rs 100 and autorickshaws Rs 60, but try to bargain.

Taxis & Autorickshaws Although they are some of the biggest creators of atmospheric pollution, taxis and autorickshaws are useful for longer trips such as to Sikandra and Fatehpur Sikri. They are both unmetered so be prepared to haggle if you pick up a lift in the street.

Prepaid taxis and autorickshaws can be booked at a booth in Agra Cantonment train station. From the station to Taj Ganj costs Rs 40/150 by rickshaw/taxi. A four-hour sightseeing trip by taxi to the Taj Mahal and Agra Fort costs Rs 250/350. An eight-hour trip costs Rs 500 (Rs 650 if you include Fatehpur Sikri). Expect to pay 25% more for air-conditioning. If there's no-one in the booth, you'll have to haggle with the drivers in front of the station.

Cycle-Rickshaw This nonpolluting form of transport is probably the best way to get around Agra, if you can handle the endless offers of lifts from cycle-rickshaw wallahs. Try to keep your patience, agree a price before setting out and don't take any nonsense from rickshaw-wallahs who offer to take you from A to B via a few marble or jewellery shops.

From Taj Ganj to Sadar Bazaar should be Rs 15 or less, and all other trips in Agra shouldn't cost more than Rs 20. Few drivers will accept less than Rs 30 from Taj Ganj to Agra Cantonment train station.

Bicycle The simple solution to Agra's transport problem is to hire a bicycle, though most of the bikes on offer are of the Indian bone-shaker variety. Try Raja Bicycle Store, on the way out of Taj Ganj towards the cantonment; bicycles cost Rs 50 for a full day. If you get a puncture, there will usually be a puncture-wallah within a few blocks. Several budget hotels can also arrange bike hire.

Environmentally Friendly Transport

As part of the government's anti-pollution drive, electric buses and tempos (large three-wheelers) operate from the Taj Mahal to Agra Fort and Shilpgram craft village (Rs 4). Several big hotels, including the Sheraton, Taj View and Ashok, offer specially designed cycle-rickshaws, which are more comfortable for passengers and drivers.

FATEHPUR SIKRI

☎ 05619 • pop 29,280

This magnificent fortified ghost city was the capital of the Mughal empire between 1571 and 1585, during the reign of Emperor Akbar. Although brilliant from an architectural point of view, Akbar's city was erected in an area that was plagued by water shortages and it was abandoned shortly after Akbar's death because of this. The main palace compound and the magnificent Jama Masjid have been brilliantly restored by the Archaeological Survey of India, but perhaps the most interesting part of Fatehpur is the ruined city which spreads out as far as the eye can see across the surrounding country.

Most people visit Fatehpur Sikri as a day trip from Agra, but there are several places to stay, and the ruined city is at its most atmospheric at sunset or first thing in the morning. The best viewpoint is from the top of the city walls, a 2km walk to the south. The town which has grown up around Fatehpur has a lively little bazaar and comes alive every year for Eid al-Fitr, the festival celebrating the end of Ramadan.

Orientation & Information

The deserted city lies along the top of a ridge, 40km west of Agra. The village of Fatehpur Sikri, where you'll find the train and bus stations, is just south of the ridge. If you come by taxi, a Rs 5 fee per car is payable at Agra Gate, the eastern entrance to the village.

The historic enclosure is open from sunrise to sunset and the entry fee is a steep Rs

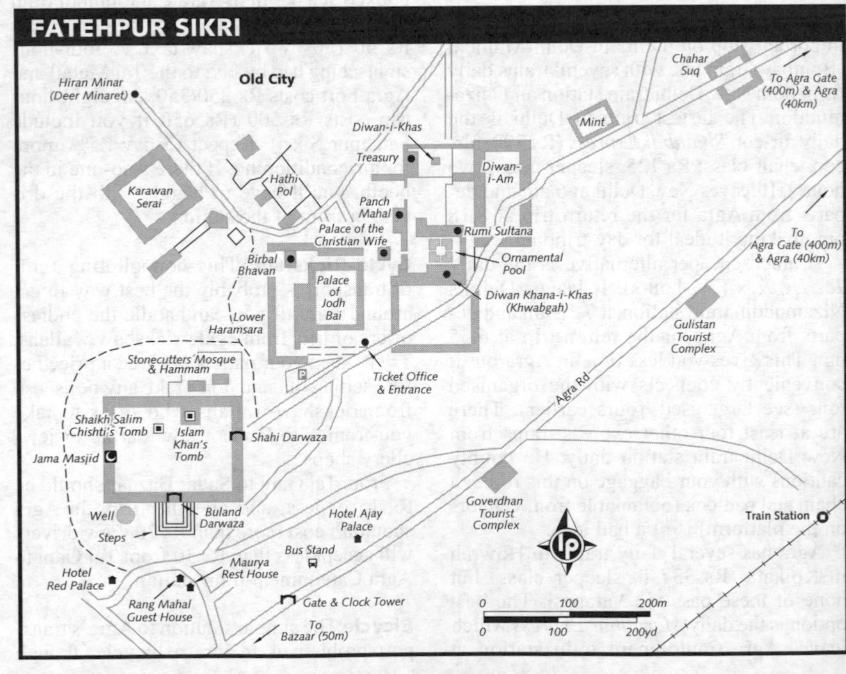

Akbar the Great

Regarded as the greatest of the Mughals, Akbar was thrust into power at the tender age of 13 and expanded the Mughal empire to cover most of northern India. A wise and just ruler, Akbar believed in the principle of Sulh-i-Kul (peace for all) and abolished many of the restrictions placed on infidels (nonbelievers), including the vastly unpopular 'pilgrimage tax' on Hindus.

Although Akbar's military campaigns were as bloody as any in the Mughal era – following his victory at Panipat, he is said to have built a tower of Hindu heads – the great Mughal is best remembered for his tolerance of other religions. Akbar counted Christians and Hindus among his 5000 wives and went on to invent a philosophy known as Din-i-Ilahi (Faith of God), asserting the common truth in all religions.

MARTIN HARRIS

Honouring the Sufi mystic Shaikh Salim Chishti, who Akbar credited with bringing him an heir, a 'perfect city' was constructed in the desert at Fatehpur Sikri, designed as a physical expression of Din-i-Ilahi. A community of intellectuals from many different religions was created to fulfil the emperor's love of debate.

In fact, the perfect city was Akbar's only folly. Built far from the nearest river, Fatehpur was plagued by water shortages and all the ingenious irrigation systems developed by Akbar's engineers were unable to solve the problem. Fatehpur was abandoned shortly after Akbar's death, along with most of his liberal attitudes. In a final twist to the Akbar story, ancient Jain statues have been found under Fatehpur, suggesting that Akbar may have demolished a Jain settlement to build his tolerant kingdom!

475 for foreigners and Rs 24.50 for Indians (free on Friday). A video camera permit is Rs 25. As yet, there is no charge to visit the spectacular Jama Masjid and the ruined city surrounding the Archaeological Survey area. The function and even the names of many buildings at Fatehpur remain contentious so you may find it useful to hire a guide. Licensed guides cost around Rs 85 and loiter near the ticket office; unlicensed guides solicit tourists outside the Jama Masjid.

Jama Masjid

Fatehpur Sikri's beautiful mosque, known as Dargah Mosque, contains elements of Persian and Hindu design and is said to be a copy of the mosque at Mecca. The main entrance is through the impressive 54m-high **Buland Darwaza** (Victory Gate), constructed to commemorate Akbar's victory in Gujarat. A Quran inscription inside the archway quotes Jesus saying: 'The world is a bridge, pass over it but build no house upon it. He who hopes for an hour may hope for eternity', which seems highly appropriate considering the fate of the city.

In the northern part of the courtyard is the superb white marble *dargah* or **tomb of Shaikh Salim Chishti**, built in 1570. Just as Akbar came to the saint four centuries ago looking for a son, childless women visit his tomb today. The carved marble lattice screens *(jalis)* are probably the finest examples of such work you'll see anywhere in the country. The saint's grandson, Islam Khan, also has his tomb within the courtyard. The persistence of would-be guides in the mosque can be tiresome.

Palace of Jodh Bai

North-east of the mosque is the ticket office and entrance to the old city. The first building inside the gate is a palace, commonly but wrongly ascribed to Jodh Bai, Jehangir's Hindu mother and the daughter of the maharaja of Amber. The architecture is a blend of styles with Hindu columns and Muslim cupolas.

The **Hawa Mahal** (Palace of the Winds) is a projecting room whose walls are made entirely of stone latticework. The ladies of the court may have sat inside to keep an unobtrusive eye on events below.

Close to the Jodh Bai Palace, the **Palace of the Christian Wife** was used by Akbar's Goan Christian wife, Maryam, and at one time was gilded throughout – giving it the name the Golden House.

Birbal Bhavan

This elegant building blends Hindu and Mughal features and is thought to have been built either by or for Akbar's favourite Hindu courtier, Raja Birbal. The palace fronts onto the **Lower Haramsara**, which was once believed to be an enormous stable, with nearly 200 enclosures for elephants, horses and camels. This is now thought to be where the palace maids lived. The stone rings still in evidence were more likely to have been used to secure curtains than to fetter pachyderms.

Panch Mahal

This whimsical five-storey palace was probably once used by the ladies of the court and originally had stone screens on the sides. These have now been removed, making the open colonnades inside visible. Like a house of cards, each of the five storeys is stepped back from the previous one until the top floor consists of only a tiny kiosk. The lower floor has 84 columns, no two of which are exactly alike.

Treasury

For a long time this building was known as Ankh Micholi, which translates roughly as 'hide and seek' – a game the emperor is supposed to have played here with ladies of the harem. However, current thinking suggests that the building was the imperial treasury – an idea supported by the curious struts carved with sea monsters who are believed to protect the treasures of the deep.

Diwan-i-Khas

The Hall of Private Audiences, known as the Jewel House, has a fairly plain exterior, but the interior is dominated by a magnificently carved stone column in the centre of the building. The pillar flares to create a flat-topped plinth linked to the four corners of the room by narrow stone bridges, from where Akbar is believed to have debated with scholars of different religious persuasions who stood at the ends of the four bridges.

Diwan-i-Am

Just inside the north-eastern gates of the deserted city is the Hall of Public Audiences, a large open courtyard surrounded by cloisters. Beside the Diwan-i-Am is the **Pachisi Courtyard**, set out like a gigantic game board. It is said that Akbar played the game pachisi here, using slave girls as the pieces.

The Ruined City

Surrounding the restored palaces and stretching to the horizon are the ruins of Akbar's city. Among the recognisable structures are the **Karawan Serai**, or Caravanserai, a vast courtyard surrounded by the hostels used by visiting merchants, and the distinctive 21m **Hiran Minar** (Deer Minaret) decorated with hundreds of stone representations of elephant tusks.

Near the Karawan Serai, badly defaced elephants still guard the **Hathi Pol**, or Elephant Gate, to the palace. Immediately behind the Jama Masjid are the remains of the small stonecutters' mosque which was supposedly erected on the site of Shaikh Salim Chishti's cave and predates Akbar's city. There's also a fine **hammam**, or Turkish bath, here. Other impressive ruins can be found around Agra Gate, to the east of modern Fatehpur Sikri.

Places to Stay & Eat

Fatehpur has no shortage of cheap, basic guesthouses.

Maurya Rest House *(☎ 882348)* is closest to the Buland Gate. There are basic singles/doubles with shared bathroom for Rs 60/90 or Rs 120/150 with private bathroom (free bucket of hot water). It's well run by a friendly family, and food is available in the small, shady courtyard or the rooftop restaurant.

Rang Mahal Guest House *(☎ 883020)* and ***Hotel Red Palace*** *(☎ 882637)*, both nearby, offer rooms of a similar standard and price.

The other offerings in town are all near the bus stand.

Hotel Ajay Palace *(☎ 882950)* is run by the amiable and friendly Ajay family and offers just four clean rooms with fan and private bathroom for Rs 100 for a single or double. The ***restaurant*** here is excellent.

Goverdhan Tourist Complex *(☎ 882643)*, farther from the centre, is more family oriented, with a large garden and a variety of clean airy rooms. Beds in the dorm cost Rs 50, while large rooms with fan and private bathroom cost Rs 100/150 a single/double or a flat Rs 300 with hot water and TV.

Gulistan Tourist Complex *(☎ 882490)*, about 300m towards Agra Gate, is run by UP Tourism, which explains the slightly institutional feel. Large rooms with fan and private bathroom cost Rs 525/575 a single/double, while similar air-con rooms with phone, TV and fridge cost Rs 775/900.

There are plenty of snack and soft-drink vendors around all the entrances to the enclosures. Fatehpur Sikri's speciality is *khataie*, the shortbread biscuits you'll see piled high in the bazaar.

Getting There & Away

Tour buses only stop for an hour or so at Fatehpur Sikri, but it's worth making a day of it and catching a bus from Agra's Idgah bus station (Rs 17, 1½ hours). Buses depart every 30 minutes between 6.30 am and 7 pm. There are also eight trains a day to Fatehpur Sikri from Agra Fort (Rs 8, one hour).

You can spend a day in Fatehpur Sikri and continue on to the world-renowned bird sanctuary at Bharatpur in the evening. Buses depart from Fatehpur Sikri's bus station every hour until 5 pm (Rs 10).

Don't encourage the villagers along the Agra road who force dancing bears to stop the passing traffic. Animal welfare groups are making concerted efforts to save India's bears from this miserable life, which only survives because tourists pay to watch the bears perform.

MATHURA

☎ 0565 • pop 272,500

Although identified with Lord Krishna today, Mathura was originally a Buddhist monastic centre. At one time, Mathura had 20 Buddhist monasteries attended by some 3000 monks, but the town began to decline in the 8th century as Buddhism gave way to Hinduism throughout the north. The Afghan warlord Mahmud of Ghazni finished off the job in 1017, levelling most of the Buddhist and Hindu shrines.

In the 16th century, Hindu scholars identified the town as the birthplace of Krishna and the town's renaissance began, only to be nipped in the bud when the fanatical Aurangzeb flattened the Kesava Deo Temple, which marked the exact spot Krishna was born, and built a mosque in its place. The Afghan Ahmad Shah Abdali finished off what the others began by torching Mathura in 1757.

With such an important religious pedigree, Mathura bounced back, and is today a bustling religious centre. The most interesting part of town lies along the Yamuna River, where there are numerous bathing

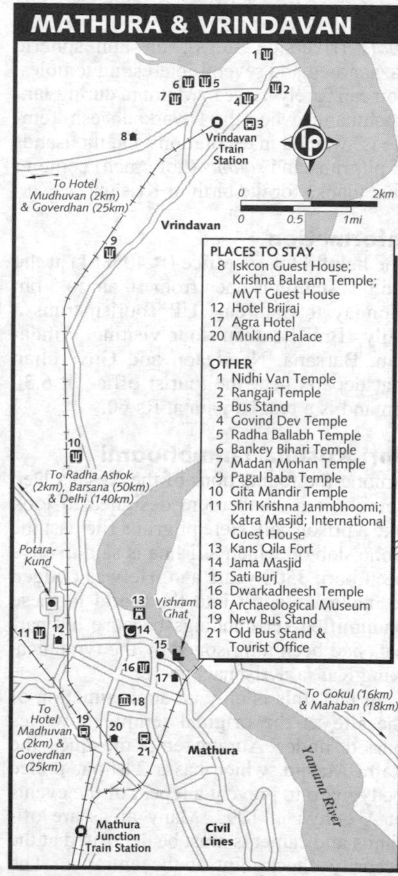

Braj Bhoomi

Braj Bhoomi, the 'Land of Eternal Love', existed only in the collective consciousness of Hindus until it was rediscovered in the physical world in the area around Mathura, 58km north-west of Agra. Identified in the 16th century from references in early Hindu texts, Mathura (Muttra) is believed to be the birthplace of Krishna, who later revealed himself to be an incarnation of Vishnu.

Many formative events in Krishna's life have been mapped to the surrounding countryside. Krishna was raised by cowherders in nearby Gokul and Mahaban. As an adolescent, he 'sported' with his *gopis* (milkmaids) in the forest of Vrindavan (Vrindaban). Goverdhan is the site of the hill which Krishna raised on one finger to shelter the people of Braj from Indra's wrath.

Today these towns are important pilgrimage sites for devotees of Krishna and are home to hundreds of temples, bathing ghats and ashrams. The whole area comes alive every year for Holi, the festival of colours (February/March), and more significantly at Janmashthami (August/September), the celebration of the birth of Lord Krishna.

HIRA LAL DANGOL

ghats (riverside steps), an atmospheric bazaar area and several interesting temples. You can barely move in Mathura during Janmashthami, when the Dwarkadheesh Temple is swathed in decorations and thousands of pilgrims and *sadhus* (holy men) come to give thanks for the birth of Krishna.

Information

The helpful tourist office (☎ 405351) at the old bus station is open from 10 am to 5 pm Monday to Saturday. UP Tourism runs a daily 'Braj Brashan' tour visiting Vrindavan, Barsana, Nandgaon and Goverdhan that departs near the tourist office at 6.30 am and is a real bargain at Rs 60.

Shri Krishna Janmbhoomi

Among the foundations of the Kesava Deo Temple is a small room designed to look like a prison cell. Here pilgrims file past the stone slab on which Krishna is said to have been born 3500 years ago. He was obliged to make his entry into the world in these undignified surroundings because his parents had been imprisoned by the tyrannical King Kansa, Krishna's uncle.

In fact, this is only an approximation of the site as the original temple now lies buried under Aurangzeb's mosque, the **Katra Masjid**, which has a 24-hour police bodyguard to prevent a repeat of the events at Ayodhya in 1992. Many areas are off-limits and cameras must be deposited at the security checkpoint at the entrance. The temple is open 5 am to noon and 4 to 9 pm (3 to 8 pm in winter).

About 200m from the Shri Krishna Janmbhoomi there's an alternative Krishna birthplace, and nearby is the **Potara-Kund**, a tank where baby Krishna's nappies (diapers) are supposed to have been washed.

Things to See

The Yamuna River, which flows through Mathura, is lined with ghats. **Vishram Ghat** is the most important bathing ghat and is where Krishna is said to have rested after killing King Kansa. Shoes must be removed and a donation is expected. You can hire a boat for a spell on the river for Rs 30 for half an hour.

The **Sati Burj**, beside Vishram Ghat, is a four-storey tower built by the son of Behari Mal of Jaipur in 1570 to commemorate his mother's *sati* (her self-immolation on her husband's funeral pyre). Aurangzeb knocked down the upper storeys, but they have since been rebuilt.

The surrounding **bazaar** is full of colourful little shops selling items of religious devotion. Along the narrow alleys which lead up towards Shri Krishna Janmbhoomi, an ornate gateway leads into the **Dwarkadheesh Temple**, built in 1814 by Seth Gokuldass in honour of who else but Lord Krishna. Nearby in a predominantly Muslim area is the ancient **Jama Masjid**, built by Abo-in Nabir Khan in 1661.

The ruined fort, **Kans Qila**, on the riverbank, was built by Raja Man Singh of Amber.

The **Archaeological Museum** is well worth visiting to see its superb collection of 1st to 6th century Jain and Buddhist sculptures from the Mathura school, including a famous and immaculately preserved 5th-century standing Buddha, attributed to the monk Dinna. The museum is open from 10.30 am to 4.30 pm daily except Monday. Admission is free.

Places to Stay & Eat

International Guest House *(☎ 423888)*, next to Shri Krishna Janmbhoomi, is excellent value with singles/doubles with shared bathroom for Rs 35/50 and doubles with private bathroom from Rs 85, but it also serves as a barracks for soldiers protecting the nearby mosque and is often full. There is a pleasant garden and a cheap vegetarian restaurant.

Hotel Brijraj *(☎ 424172)* is a simple but comfortable place nearby offering clean rooms with private bathroom from Rs 175/ 200.

Agra Hotel *(☎ 403318, Bengali Ghat)*, tucked away beside the Yamuna River, gets mixed reports, but the rooms are OK. Fan-rooms with private bathroom (hot water) cost Rs 250 to 400, while air-con will set you back Rs 600.

Mukund Palace *(☎ 410316, Junction Rd)*, closer to the train station, is a new and stylish red sandstone building with superior fan-rooms for Rs 500/600 and air-con rooms for Rs 700/800.

Hotel Madhuvan *(☎ 420064, fax 420 684)* is a three-star establishment which is a Rs 20 cycle-rickshaw ride north-west from the new bus stand. Rooms start at Rs 1000/1200, and there's a swimming pool, restaurant and bar.

Radha Ashok *(☎ 405557, fax 409557)* is the top hotel in the area. This Best Western is 3km from town on the Delhi road. Rooms cost a hefty US$140/160 and there's the obligatory restaurant and swimming pool.

Getting There & Away

Mathura is 47km north-west of Agra and 141km south of Delhi. From the new bus station there are half-hourly buses to Delhi's Sarai Kale Khan bus stand (Rs 69, 3½ hours) until 1.45 pm and to Agra (Rs 28, 1½ hours) until 10.30 pm. The old bus station serves local destinations, including Goverdhan and Barsana, but also has two daily buses to Agra.

The fastest train to Delhi's Nizamuddin station is the *Taj Express*, which departs Mathura at 7.30 pm (Rs 42/213 in seat/ sleeper class, 2¼ hours). Mathura also has direct trains to Agra (Rs 43, one hour), Bharatpur, Sawai Madhopur (for Ranthambhore) and Kota.

VRINDAVAN

Vrindavan is where Krishna indulged in adolescent pranks such as stealing the gopis' clothes while they bathed in the river. Little now remains of the legendary forests and the river has meandered away from most of Vrindavan's bathing ghats, but pilgrims still flock here in droves from all over India, and in the case of the Hare Krishna community, from all over the world.

There are dozens of temples here, from garish modern shrines to more refined ancient temples. The bulky red sandstone **Govind Dev Temple** is the most impressive building in Vrindavan and architecturally one of the most advanced Hindu temples in northern India. The temple was built in 1590 by Raja Man Singh of Amber in honour of the Divine Cowherd (Krishna) but Aurangzeb lopped off the top four floors during one of his demolition sprees.

The **Rangaji Temple** dates from 1851 and is a bizarre mixture of architectural styles, including a Rajput entrance gate, a soaring south Indian *gopuram* (intricate gateway tower) and an Italianate colonnade. At the entrance are two amusing electronic puppet shows telling the stories of the Ramayana and the Mahabharata. Non-Hindus are not allowed in the middle enclosure of the temple where there's a 15m gold-plated pillar. There are said to be 4000 other temples in Vrindavan, including the truly massive 10-storey **Pagal Baba**, the popular **Bankey Bihari**, and the **Radha Ballabh**, built in 1626.

The International Society for Krishna Consciousness (Iskcon; ☎ 446053) is based at the incredible white marble **Krishna Balaram Temple** complex. Also known as the Hare Krishnas, the organisation was founded in New York in the 1960s by Swami Prabhupada, who died in 1977, and several hundred Westerners attend courses and seminars here every year (call the centre for more details). The Hare Krishna organisation has faced some controversy in recent years; see the boxed text 'The Rochford Files'.

The Rochford Files

Long regarded as a benign institution, the International Society for Krishna Consciousness (Iskcon) stunned the world in 1999 by admitting the existence of widespread child-abuse at its boarding schools during the 1970s and 1980s. In a damning report commissioned by the organisation, the American sociologist E Burke Rochford exposed a culture of abuse, linked to the society's stance on celibacy, marriage and the value of the family unit.

In response to the report, Iskcon has radically shifted its emphasis away from residential centres and revised its policies to ensure better protection for the children in its care. However, the report highlights a growing concern about New Age religious sects. The Indian guru Sai Baba, who has an estimated 25 million followers worldwide, has recently faced a string of sexual abuse allegations. See the boxed text 'The God of Big Things' in the Andhra Pradesh chapter.

Places to Stay & Eat

Iskcon Guest House** (☎ 442478)*, at the Iskcon complex, has clean doubles with private bathroom, bucket hot water and very hard beds for Rs 200. Iskcon can also arrange accommodation in some of Vrindavan's ashrams, such as ***Chitrakoot** (☎ 442729)* and ***Sadhna Kunj (no phone), which both charge Rs 100 per night.

***MVT Guest House** (☎ 443400)*, next door to Iskcon, has a decent restaurant and some well-equipped rooms with private bathroom for Rs 600 (with fan) and Rs 850 (with air-con).

The ***restaurant*** at the Iskcon Guest House is the best place to eat in this veg-only town. It serves thalis for Rs 40 and other meals for less than Rs 25.

Getting There & Away

Tempos travel the 10km stretch between Mathura and Vrindavan and charge Rs 5 for the 25-minute journey. You can pick them up at Mathura's new bus station or on the main road near the Shri Krishna Janmbhoomi temple. These vehicles are packed to capacity so be prepared to carry your luggage on your lap. Autorickshaws are more comfortable, but they charge around Rs 60 one way.

AROUND MATHURA & VRINDAVAN

Krishna's consort Radha was from **Barsana**, 50km north-west of Mathura. The village is dominated by the huge Ladli-ji temple, sacred to Radha, which sprawls along the ridge. Barsana is an interesting place to be during the festival of Holi when local women attack the men of nearby Nandgaon with sticks and coloured water.

Goverdhan is 25km west of Mathura, on the road to Deeg, and is said to be where Krishna protected the inhabitants of Goverdhan from Indra's wrath (rain) by holding a hilltop, neatly balanced on top of his finger, over the town for seven days and nights. There are numerous temples around the sacred hill, including the Har Deva Ji temple founded during the reign of Akbar. Buses to Barsana (Rs 16) and Goverdhan (Rs 11) leave from Mathura's new bus station.

Gokul, where Krishna was secretly raised, is 16km south of Mathura. Hordes of pilgrims flock here during his birthday festival, Janmashthami, each August/September. It's best to get to Gokul by autorickshaw. It costs around Rs 160 return, with bargaining, which should include waiting time.

Mahaban, 18km south-east of Mathura, is another location from Krishna's idyllic childhood, though it's just a dusty village today. The ancient Mathura Nath temple is worth a look. You can get here by bus or rickshaw.

MEERUT

☎ 0121 • pop 980,000

Only 70km north-east of Delhi, this is where the 1857 Uprising broke out, when the British unwisely deposed the last nawab of Lucknow. There's little to remember that event by today – just the cemetery near St John's Church, which also has the grave of General Ochterlony, whose monument dominates the Maidan in Kolkata (Calcutta). The **Suraj Khund** is the most interesting Hindu temple in Meerut and there's also a **Mughal mausoleum**, the Shahpir, near the old Shahpir Gate.

There are several hotels in Meerut. The best is the ***Hotel Shaleen*** and there's also the cheaper ***Anand Hotel*** – both in the Begum Bridge area.

Meerut can be reached by bus from the Kashmiri Gate Interstate Bus Terminal in Delhi (Rs 36, two hours).

KANPUR

☎ 0512 • pop 2,470,000

Although Lucknow is the capital of Uttar Pradesh, Kanpur is the state's largest city. and has the unfortunate distinction of being one of the most polluted cities in the world.

Things to See

There's not much to see in Kanpur, though you can visit the site of **General Sir Hugh Wheeler's entrenchment**, just over 1km from Kanpur Central train station. General Wheeler was massacred with most of his party at Sati Chaura Ghat during the 1857 Uprising. Nearby is **All Souls' Memorial Church**, which has poignant reminders of the tragedy of the Uprising. There's a large **zoo** at Allen Park, a few kilometres northwest of The Mall.

The main shopping centre, **Navin Market**, is famous for its locally produced cotton goods. Kanpur is a good place to find cheap leather shoes and bags.

Places to Stay & Eat

Kanpur has a string of overpriced hotels along The Mall, which is where you'll probably have to stay since the city's budget hotels, located around the train station, do not accept non-Indians. All the hotels listed here provide room service.

The ***retiring rooms*** at Kanpur Central train station are a useful, cheap option and have certainly improved since travel writers Eric and Wanda Newby spent a sleepless night here on their way down the Ganges in 1963. Dorm beds cost Rs 100, doubles Rs 250 and air-con doubles Rs 450 for 24 hours.

Meera Inn *(☎ 319972, 37/19 The Mall)* has good air-cooled singles/doubles with private bathroom and hot water geyser from Rs 375/475 or air-con for Rs 600/700.

The Attic *(☎ 311691, 15/198 Vikramajit Singh Rd)*, just north of The Mall, is a Raj-era bungalow in a pleasant garden with a good restaurant. Air-con rooms cost Rs 550/650 which, for Kanpur, is good value. Both places add a 10% 'amenities' charge.

Hotel Landmark *(☎ 317601, fax 315 291)* is farther up the luxury scale and has been recommended by travellers.

Getting There & Away

The Chunniganj bus stand, 3km west of The Mall, services destinations to the west. The Collectorganj bus stand, 300m from the train station, covers points east, and has plenty of buses to Lucknow (Rs 39, two hours).

Kanpur has plenty of train connections to Delhi (Rs 99/520 in 2nd/1st class, around six hours) and Kolkata (Rs 284/961 in sleeper/ 1st class, 16 to 25 hours). There are also trains to Mumbai (Rs 326/1103, around 24 hours), Allahabad (Rs 53/279, 2nd/1st class, three hours), Varanasi (Rs 77/441, seven hours) and Lucknow (Rs 28/173, 1½ hours).

LUCKNOW

☎ 0522 • pop 1,917,000

The capital of Uttar Pradesh rose to prominence as the centre of the nawabs of Avadh. These decadent Muslim rulers, also known as the nawabs of Oudh, controlled a region of north-central India for about a century after the decline of the Mughal empire. Most of the interesting monuments in Lucknow date from this period.

The capital of Avadh was moved from Faizabad to Lucknow during the reign of Asaf-ud-Daula (1775–97). After Sa'adat Ali Khan (1798–1814), the rest of the Avadh nawabs were uniformly hopeless at running affairs of state. Wajid Ali Shah (1847–56) was so extravagant and indolent that to this day his name is regarded by many in India as synonymous with lavishness. However, the nawabs were great patrons of the arts, especially dance and music, and Lucknow's reputation as a city of culture and gracious living stems from this time.

In 1856 the British annexed Avadh, exiling the incompetent Wajid Ali Shah to a palace in Kolkata with an annual pension of UK£120,000. The annexation was one of the sparks that ignited the Indian Uprising in 1857.

Despite its rich cultural associations, Lucknow is not a particularly attractive city and it suffers from high levels of pollution. However, the huge crumbling mausoleums of the nawabs and the pock-marked ruins of the Residency, in particular, make it an interesting place to visit.

Orientation

Lucknow is very spread out. The historic monuments are mainly in the north-western part of the old city, near the Gomti River. The narrow alleys of Aminabad are the

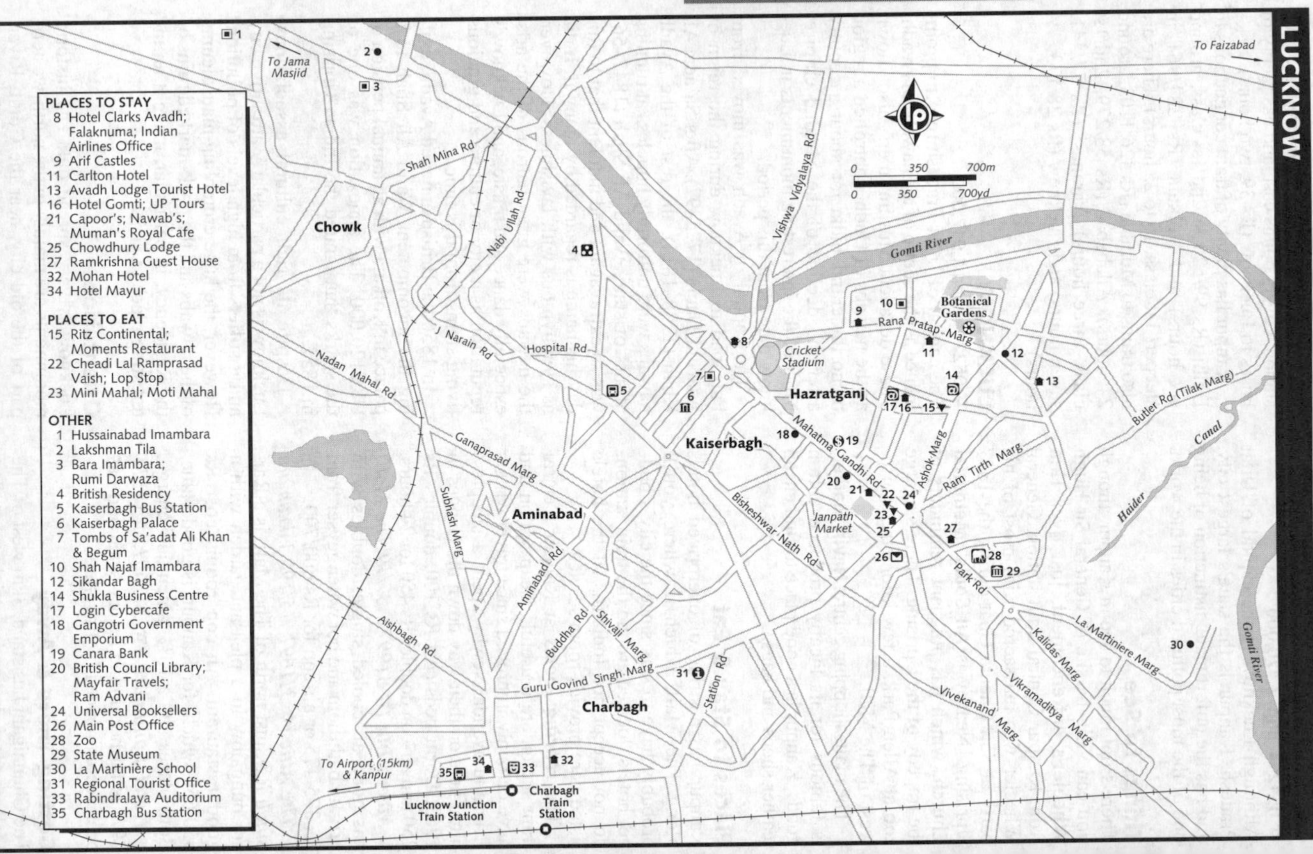
LUCKNOW
Gomti River
Canal
Haider
To Faizabad
Butler Rd (Tilak Marg)
La Martiniere Marg
Kalidas Marg
Vikramaditya Marg
Vivekanand Marg
Park Rd
Ram Tirth Marg
Ashok Marg
Rana Pratap Marg
Botanical Gardens
Cricket Stadium
Hazratganj
Mahatma Gandhi Rd
Janpath Market
Bisheshwar Nath Rd
Station Rd
Vishwa Vidyalaya Rd
Kaiserbagh
Hospital Rd
Nabi Ullah Rd
Shah Mina Rd
J Narain Rd
Ganaprasad Marg
Aminabad
Aminabad Rd
Buddha Rd
Shivaji Marg
Guru Govind Singh Marg
Charbagh
Charbagh Train Station
Lucknow Junction Train Station
Subhash Marg
Nadan Mahal Rd
Aishbagh Rd
To Airport (15km) & Kanpur
Chowk
To Jama Masjid
0 350 700m
0 350 700yd
PLACES TO STAY
8 Hotel Clarks Avadh; Falaknuma; Indian Airlines Office
9 Arif Castles
11 Carlton Hotel
13 Avadh Lodge Tourist Hotel
16 Hotel Gomti; UP Tours
21 Capoor's; Nawab's; Muman's Royal Cafe
25 Chowdhury Lodge
27 Ramkrishna Guest House
32 Mohan Hotel
34 Hotel Mayur
PLACES TO EAT
15 Ritz Continental; Moments Restaurant
22 Cheadi Lal Ramprasad Vaish; Lop Stop
23 Mini Mahal; Moti Mahal
OTHER
1 Hussainabad Imambara
2 Lakshman Tila
3 Bara Imambara; Rumi Darwaza
4 British Residency
5 Kaiserbagh Bus Station
6 Kaiserbagh Palace
7 Tombs of Sa'adat Ali Khan & Begum
10 Shah Najaf Imambara
12 Sikandar Bagh
14 Shukla Business Centre
17 Login Cybercafe
18 Gangotri Government Emporium
19 Canara Bank
20 British Council Library; Mayfair Travels; Ram Advani
24 Universal Booksellers
26 Main Post Office
28 Zoo
29 State Museum
30 La Martinière School
31 Regional Tourist Office
33 Rabindralaya Auditorium
35 Charbagh Bus Station

main shopping area. Hazratganj is the modern part with most of the cheaper hotels.

Information

Tourist information is available at the Hotel Gomti from UP Tours (☎ 212659), a branch of UP Tourism. The regional tourist office (☎ 226205) is hidden down an alley off Station Rd, but it's hopeless. There's a useful information booth at Lucknow Junction train station, open daily. The Garhwal Mandal Vikas Nigam (GMVN; ☎ 207844, Flats 4 to 7, RF Bahadur Marg) has a regional office here, as does the Kumaon Mandal Vikas Nigam (KMVN; ☎ 239434, 2 Gopai Khera, Sarojini Marg).

Changing money can be a real hassle – although there are a lot of banks in the city, few seem interested in converting travellers cheques. Don't even bother trying on Saturday morning. The Canara Bank in Hazratganj should be able to help, alternatively try a branch of the State Bank of India in the same area. The jewellery shop at the Carlton Hotel changes money.

Login Cybercafe, 1A Sapru Marg, upstairs next to Hotel Gomti, has very quick Internet connections for Rs 50 per hour.

There's a British Council library in Hazratganj, open 10.30 am to 6.30 pm Tuesday to Saturday. Next door on one side is Mayfair Travels, the AmEx representative; on the other side is Ram Advani, an excellent bookshop. Universal Booksellers on Mahatma Gandhi Rd has a vast selection of books and sells a superior street map of Lucknow for Rs 35.

Bara Imambara

The Bara or Great Imambara (an *imambara* is the tomb of a Shi'ia Muslim holy man) was built in 1784 by Asaf-ud-Daula as a famine relief project. The central hall, at 50m long and 15m high, is one of the largest vaulted galleries in the world. An external stairway leads to an upper floor laid out as an amazing labyrinth known as the **bhulbhulaiya**; a guide may be useful since the dark passages stop abruptly at openings which drop straight to the courtyard below. Guides claim that tunnels extend as far as Jaipur, Delhi and Mumbai! The labyrinth entry fee of Rs 12 includes entry to a picture gallery.

There's a mosque with two tall minarets in the courtyard complex but non-Muslims are not allowed in. To the right of this is a 'bottomless' well. The Imambara complex is open from sunrise to sunset.

Beside the Bara Imambara, and also built by Asaf-ud-Daula, is the imposing **Rumi Darwaza**, a replica of an entrance gate built in Istanbul. 'Rumi' (relating to Rome) is the term Muslims applied to Istanbul when it was still Byzantium, the capital of the Eastern Roman Empire.

Lakshman Tila, the high ground on the southern bank of the Gomti River nearby, was the original site of the town which became known as Lucknau in the 15th century. Aurangzeb's mosque now stands on this site.

Hussainabad Imambara

Also known as the Chhota, or Small Imambara, this was built by Mohammed Ali Shah in 1837 as his own mausoleum. The large courtyard encloses a raised rectangular tank with small imitations of the Taj Mahal on each side. One of them is the tomb of Mohammed Ali Shah's daughter, the other that of her husband. The main building, topped by a golden dome, contains the tombs of Ali Shah and his mother. The nawab's silver-covered throne, other paraphernalia of state and lots of tacky chandeliers are stored here. It's open from sunrise to sunset.

The decaying **watchtower** opposite the Hussainabad Imambara is known as Satkhanda, or the Seven Storey Tower, but it actually has four storeys because construction was abandoned when Ali Shah died in 1840. A 67m-high defunct **clock tower**, reputedly the tallest in the country, overlooks the Hussainabad Tank nearby. A *baradari*, or **summer house**, built by Ali Shah, fronts onto the tank. It houses portraits of the nawabs of Avadh.

West of the Hussainabad Imambara is the **Jama Masjid**, started by Mohammed Ali Shah and completed after his death.

Residency

Built in 1800 for the British Resident, this group of buildings became the stage for the most dramatic events of the 1857 Uprising – the Siege of Lucknow. The red-brick ruins are peaceful nowadays, surrounded by lawns and flowerbeds, but thousands died during the months-long siege.

The Residency has been maintained as it was at the time of the final relief, and the shattered walls are still scarred by cannon

The Siege of Lucknow

The Uprising of 1857 is known to some as the 1857 Mutiny and to others as the First War of Independence, or the First Freedom Struggle.

Upon the outbreak of the Uprising the British inhabitants of the city all took refuge with Sir Henry Lawrence in the Residency. In total there were 2994 people crammed into the Residency's grounds, including soldiers, officers, women and children. The Residency was technically indefensible, but those seeking shelter expected relief to arrive in a matter of days.

In fact it was 87 days before a small force under Sir Henry Havelock broke through the besiegers to the remaining half-starved defenders. But once Havelock and his troops were within the Residency, the siege immediately recommenced. It continued unabated from 25 September to 17 November, when relief finally arrived with Sir Colin Campbell. Only 980 of the original inhabitants survived the ordeal. Many who did not die from bullet wounds succumbed to cholera, typhoid or smallpox.

The published accounts of the siege of Lucknow combine tales of derring-do with traces of domestic comedy wrung from the British contingent's struggle to maintain a stiff upper lip in the face of adversity.

Several accounts were written by women, some of whom at first seemed more troubled by the shortage of good domestic help than by being surrounded by tens of thousands of bloodthirsty mutineers. This changed during the drawn-out months of the siege, by the end of which they were said to be able to judge the weight of shot being fired into the compound better than the men.

In *The Siege of Lucknow*, Julia Inglis (whose husband took command on the death of Sir Henry Lawrence) flatly records the day-to-day horrors of life in the Residency: 'July 8th – Mr Polehampton, one of our chaplains, was shot through the body to-day whilst shaving...'.

shot. Even since Independence, little has changed. The only major work done on the place was the unveiling of an **Indian Martyrs' Memorial** directly opposite.

There's a **model room** in the main Residency building which is worth visiting to get your bearings from the rather tatty model. Downstairs you can see the cellars where many of the women and children lived throughout the siege. The **cemetery** at the nearby ruined church has the graves of 2000 men, women and children, including that of Sir Henry Lawrence, 'who tried to do his duty' according to the famous inscription on his weathered gravestone.

The Residency is open from sunrise to sunset, but the model room is open only 10 am to 5 pm; Rs 250 for foreigners.

Other Attractions

The plain **Shah Najaf Imambara**, opposite the Carlton Hotel, is the tomb of Ghazi-ud-din Haidar, who died in 1827.

Sikandar Bagh, the scene of pitched battles in 1857, is a partially fortified garden with a modest gateway bearing the nawabs' fish emblem.

The stately **tombs** of Sa'adat Ali Khan and his wife (the begum) are close to the remnants of **Kaiserbagh Palace** on the south-eastern edge of the large double roundabout near the cricket stadium.

The dusty Lucknow **zoo** in the Banarsi Bagh (Park) is open 8 am to 5 pm (6.30 pm in summer) daily except Monday; entry costs Rs 10. Within the zoo is the **state museum**, which contains an impressive collection of stone sculptures, especially from the Mathura school (1st to 6th centuries). Don't miss the British-era statues (of Queen Victoria and others) that have been dumped in a garden round the back. It's open 10.30 am to 4.30 pm daily except Monday, and entry is Rs 2.

La Martinière School on the eastern edge of the city was designed by the Frenchman Major-General Claude Martin as a palatial home. His architectural abilities were, to say the least, a little confused – Gothic gargoyles were piled merrily atop Corinthian columns to produce a finished product which a British marquess sarcastically pronounced to be inspired by a wedding cake. The school can be visited with permission from the principal (☎ 223863).

Organised Tours

UP Tours (☎ 212659) runs worthwhile half-day sightseeing tours of Lucknow (Rs 75, reserve ahead). Tours pick up people from the train station (8.30 am) and various hotels, including Hotel Gomti next door.

Special Events

The spirit of the nawabs returns during the **Lucknow Mahotsava** between late November and early December. During the 10-day festival of nostalgia there are processions, plays, *kathak* dancing (an energetic style of traditional dancing, performed in striking costumes), *ghazal* (Urdu songs) and sitar recitals, kite flying and tonga races.

Lucknow is a good place to see the **Shi'ia Muharram** celebrations (dates vary from year to year) as it has been the principal Indian Shi'ia city since the nawabs arrived. The activity during Muharram, which centres on the Bara Imambara, can get intense as penitents scourge themselves with whips; keep a low profile.

Places to Stay – Budget

Most travellers head for the Hazratganj area. Rooms mentioned here have private bathroom.

Chowdhury Lodge (☎ *221911, 273135, 3 Vidhan Sabha Marg*), down an alley opposite the main post office near the Capitol Cinema, has singles/doubles, some without windows, from Rs 125/170 and air-cooled rooms for Rs 200/250. The lodge has 24-hour checkout and charges extra for bedding and buckets of hot water.

Ramkrishna Guest House (☎ *238363, 4A Park Rd*) has fairly good air-cooled doubles for Rs 340 and air-con doubles with TV for Rs 575. The rooms are on the small side, and those at the front are pretty noisy. The guesthouse is handy for the zoo.

Avadh Lodge Tourist Hotel (☎ *282861, 1 Ram Mohan Rai Marg*), near Sikandar Bagh, was closed for repairs at the time of research so expect prices to have increased. Varied singles/doubles/triples with hot water were Rs 200/300/375.

Hotel Mayur (☎ *451824, Subhash Marg*) is the best option in the noisy area near the train stations. It has rooms with TV, hot water geyser and squat toilet for Rs 275/350.

The Lucknow Junction ***retiring rooms*** offer dorm beds (Rs 50), doubles (Rs 250) and air-con rooms (Rs 450) for a 24-hour period.

Mohan Hotel (☎ *635642/635797, Buddha Rd*) is fine but generally overpriced. Rooms with air-con start at Rs 450/600. It's better value for three people in a double room – Rs 150 per extra person.

Places to Stay – Mid-Range & Top End

Carlton Hotel (☎ *224021, fax 229793*) was once a palace and is still an impressive building with a musty air of decaying elegance. Large rooms with character cost Rs 600/700, or Rs 900/1200 with air-con and TV. Extensive gardens make it a relaxing place to stay.

Capoor's (☎ *223958, Mahatma Gandhi Rd*) is a long-established hotel in the heart of Hazratganj. The hotel was closed at the time of research due to the death of the owner; however, it should have reopened by the time you read this.

Hotel Gomti (☎ *220624, 6 Sapru Marg*) is a UP Tourism operation with overpriced but good air-cooled rooms with TV for Rs 550/650 and air-con rooms for Rs 875/975. The hotel has a restaurant, coffee shop and a popular bar.

Arif Castles (☎ *211313,* ⓔ *arifind@lw1.vsnl.net.in, 4 Rana Pratap Marg*) is a modern hotel with small but pleasant rooms starting from Rs 900/1000.

Hotel Clarks Avadh (☎ *216500, fax 216507, 8 MG Rd*) has rooms with good views and the expected luxury fittings from Rs 3700/4000. There's a restaurant, coffee shop and bar.

Places to Eat

The refined palates of the nawabs have left Lucknow with a reputation for rich Mughlai cuisine. The city is famous for its wide range of kebabs and for *dum pukht* – the 'art' of steam pressure cooking, in which meat and vegetables are cooked in a sealed clay pot. Huge paper-thin *rumali roti* (chapatis) are served in many small Muslim restaurants in the old city. They arrive folded up and should be eaten with a goat or lamb curry like *bhuna ghosht* or *rogan josh*. The popular dessert *kulfi faluda* (ice cream with cornflour noodles) is served in several places in Aminabad. The sweet orange-coloured rice dish known as *zarda* is also popular.

Hazratganj's Mahatma Gandhi (MG) Rd is lined with restaurants, snack bars and Western-style fast-food joints.

Nawab's, in Capoor's hotel, serves decent veg/nonveg fare from Rs 45, and has live Indian music in the evenings. Nawab's *khas* dishes have a good, rich sauce.

Muman's Royal Cafe, next to Capoor's, is also good and has live music. It offers both veg and nonveg Indian and Chinese food, prompt service, and a civilised ambience. Snacks start at Rs 25, and nonvegetarian mains are around Rs 65. The excellent *chaat* (snack) ***stall*** outside does a roaring trade in tasty snacks costing only Rs 15.

Cheadi Lal Ramprasad Vaish *(MG Rd)* has great coffee, juices and ice cream. It's poorly marked, but next to the Lop Stop fast-food joint.

Mini Mahal nearby has a good selection of Indian sweets and pastries, and Chinese fast food. ***Moti Mahal*** next door is similar, but has Indian food.

Ritz Continental *(Sapru Marg)* is a fairly upmarket vegetarian restaurant serving good snacks (from Rs 16), Indian (mains around Rs 40) and Chinese food, and pizzas (Rs 38 to 50). The restaurant has diner-like booths.

Next door, ***Moments Restaurant*** is inexpensive, and good for kebabs and chicken.

Falaknuma, in Hotel Clarks Avadh, is one of the best places to try Lucknow cuisine. Main courses are expensive but the food is good and the restaurant has great views across the city.

Entertainment

Lucknow has a strong tradition in the performing arts. The Rabindralaya Auditorium (☎ 455670), opposite the train stations, hosts classical music, dance and theatrical performances.

Some restaurants have live Indian music in the evening.

Shopping

In the narrow lanes of Aminabad you can buy *attar* – pure essential oils extracted from flowers in the traditional manner. In the chowk, you'll find a bird-sellers' district known as Nakkhas – pigeon-keeping and cockfighting have been popular in Lucknow since the time of the nawabs.

The Gangotri Government Emporium in Hazratganj sells local handicrafts, including the hand-woven embroidered cloth known as *chikan* for which Lucknow is famous.

Getting There & Away

Air Amausi Airport is 15km south-west of Lucknow. The Indian Airlines office (☎ 220927) is at the Hotel Clarks Avadh. Indian Airlines operates daily flights to Delhi (US$90), and flights to Patna (US$100) and Kolkata (US$155) four times weekly.

Sahara India Airlines (☎ 377675) has daily flights to Delhi (US$90) and Mumbai (US$250). Jet Airways (☎ 202026) also has flights to Delhi and Mumbai.

Bus There are two bus stations: Charbagh, near the train stations, and Kaiserbagh. From Charbagh there are regular departures to Kanpur (Rs 39, two hours) and Allahabad (Rs 86, five hours), and early-morning and evening buses to Varanasi (Rs 120, 8½ hours) and Agra (Rs 105, 10 hours). From Kaiserbagh there are buses to Delhi (Rs 207, 12 hours), Gorakhpur (Rs 112, 7½ hours) and Faizabad (Rs 55, three hours).

Train The two main stations, Charbagh and Lucknow Junction, are side by side; Northern Railway trains run to both, North Eastern Railway trains only to the latter. Essentially, Charbagh handles all trains between New Delhi and Kolkata, while Lucknow Junction handles many of the trains heading to cities in the south.

The *Shatabdi Express* runs between Lucknow and Delhi (Rs 640 in chair class, 6½ hours) via Kanpur (Rs 210, 1½ hours). There are also regular expresses to Delhi (Rs 107/588 in 2nd/1st class, eight to nine hours) and Kolkata (Rs 270/914 in sleeper/1st class, around 23 hours). Other express trains (2nd/1st class) from Lucknow are:

destination	duration	cost
Allahabad	4 hours	Rs 36/321
Faizabad	3 hours	Rs 43/226
Gorakhpur	5–6 hours	Rs 70/368
Varanasi	5–6 hours	Rs 73/384

The train to Mumbai costs Rs 331/1119 in sleeper/1st class (27 hours) and to Agra Rs 143/222/751 in 2nd/sleeper/1st class (five to six hours).

Getting Around

To/From the Airport Taxis charge around Rs 220 for the trip; if you don't have much baggage catch a tempo from Charbagh train station for Rs 8.

Local Transport There are autorickshaws at the train station – to Hazratganj will cost about Rs 35. Tempos run along fixed routes, connecting Charbagh train station with the main post office (Hazratganj), Sikandar Bagh, Kaiserbagh (for the bus terminal) and the chowk (for the imambaras). Most journeys cost around Rs 4.

The best way to get around is on the back of a cycle-rickshaw, a pleasant way to cruise the manic streets around the centre. A cycle-rickshaw between the train stations and Hazratganj costs locals Rs 5 but foreigners can expect to pay Rs 10 to 15. From Hazratganj to the imambaras costs Rs 20; sightseeing is around Rs 25 per hour but you'll need to bargain.

ALLAHABAD

☎ 0532 • pop 2 million

The city of Allahabad is 135km west of Varanasi at the confluence of two of India's most important rivers – the Ganges and the Yamuna (Jumna). The mythical Saraswati River, the River of Enlightenment, is also believed to join them here. The confluence, known as the *sangam*, is considered to have great soul-cleansing powers and all pious Hindus hope to bathe here at least once in their lifetime.

Not many foreign travellers pause in this friendly city but it's an interesting, worthwhile stop, especially if you're partial to Indian-style espressos and sidewalk cafes.

History

Built on a very ancient site, Allahabad was known in Aryan times as Prayag, and it is said that Brahma himself performed a sacrifice here. The Chinese pilgrim Xuan Zhang described visiting the city in AD 634, and it acquired its present name in 1584, under Akbar. Later Allahabad was taken by the Marathas, sacked by the Pathans and finally ceded to the British in 1801 by the nawabs of Avadh.

The city was a centre of the Indian National Congress and at the conference here in 1920, Mahatma Gandhi proposed his program of nonviolent resistance to achieve independence.

Orientation & Information

Allahabad's Civil Lines is an area of broad avenues, Raj-era bungalows, modern shops and some outdoor eating stalls. The main bus terminal, the Civil Lines bus stand, is also here. It's divided from the dense, older part of town, known as Chowk, by Allahabad Junction train station.

There's a UP Tourism office (☎ 601873) in the Tourist Bungalow–Hotel Ilawart on Mahatma Gandhi (MG) Marg. It's open 10 am to 5 pm daily except Sunday.

The main branch of the State Bank of India in Police Lines is the place to change money. SAS Travels (☎ 623598) is an agent for Sahara, Jet and Indian Airlines.

For Internet access, try the STD booth on MG Marg, next to the tandoor restaurant. It's open 9 am to 9.30 pm daily; browsing costs Rs 60 per hour.

Sangam

At this point the shallow, muddy Ganges meets the clearer, deeper, green Yamuna. During the month of Magha (mid-January to mid-February) pilgrims come to bathe at this holy confluence for the festival known as the **Magh Mela**. Astrologers calculate the holiest time to enter the water and draw up a 'Holy Dip Schedule'. The most propitious time of all happens only every 12 years when the massive **Kumbh Mela** takes place. There's a half-mela (Ardh Mela) every six years. See the boxed text 'Kumbh Mela' in the Maharashtra chapter for more information.

During Kumbh Mela, a huge temporary township springs up on the vacant land on the Allahabad side of the river and elaborate precautions have to be taken for the pilgrims' safety – in the early 1950s, 350 people were killed in a stampede to the water (an incident recreated in Vikram Seth's novel, *A Suitable Boy*).

Sunrise and sunset can be spectacular here. Boats out to the confluence are a bit of a tourist trap and what you pay very much depends on how many other people are around. Next to the fort you should be able to hire a whole boat for Rs 50 to 60, though you'll probably be asked Rs 200 initially. It's more interesting sharing with Indians on a pilgrimage since you'll then appreciate the spot's religious significance.

Fort

Built by Akbar in 1583, the fort stands on the northern bank of the Yamuna, near the confluence with the Ganges. It has massive

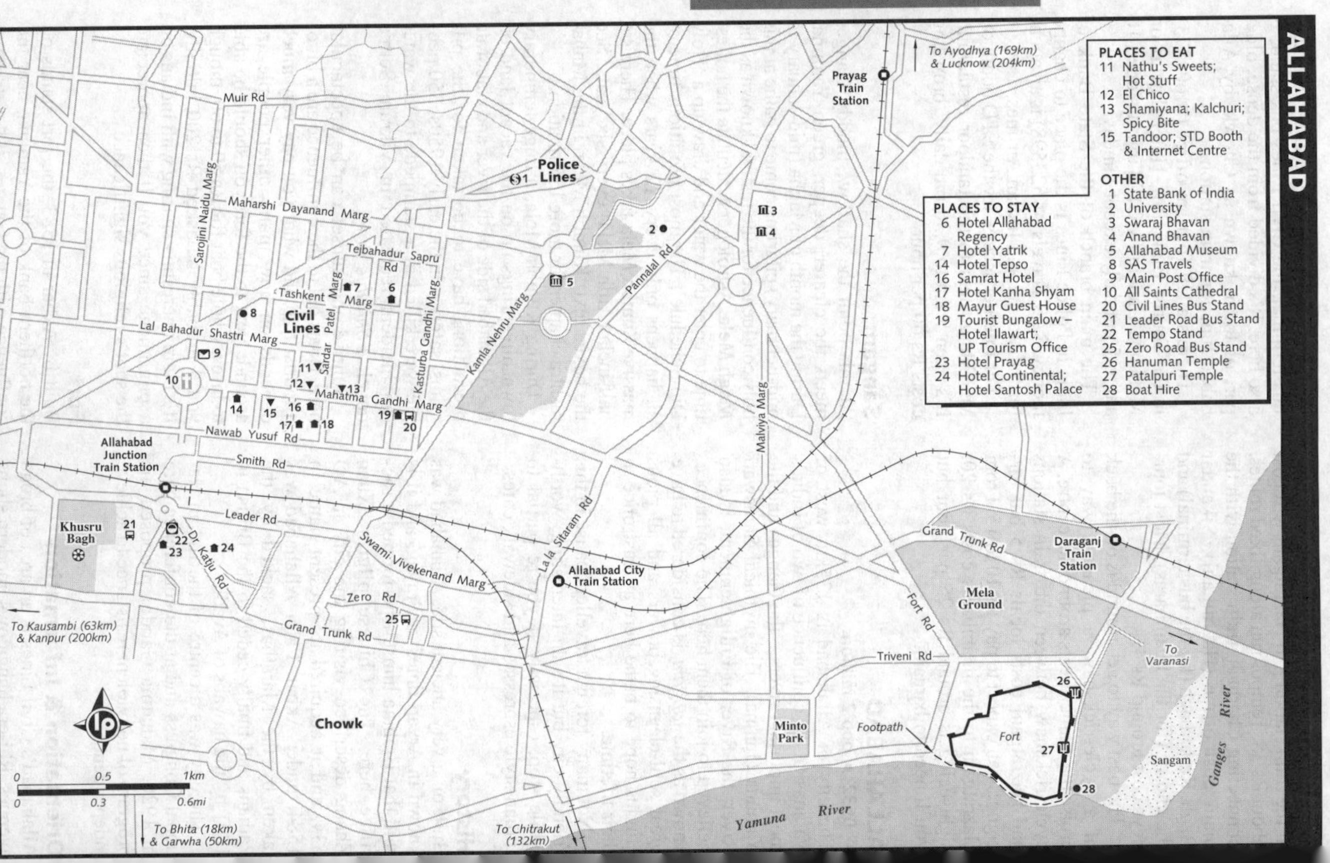
ALLAHABAD
PLACES TO STAY
6 Hotel Allahabad Regency
7 Hotel Yatrik
14 Hotel Tepso
16 Samrat Hotel
17 Hotel Kanha Shyam
18 Mayur Guest House
19 Tourist Bungalow – Hotel Ilawart; UP Tourism Office
23 Hotel Prayag
24 Hotel Continental; Hotel Santosh Palace
PLACES TO EAT
11 Nathu's Sweets; Hot Stuff
12 El Chico
13 Shamiyana; Kalchuri; Spicy Bite
15 Tandoor; STD Booth & Internet Centre
OTHER
1 State Bank of India
2 University
3 Swaraj Bhavan
4 Anand Bhavan
5 Allahabad Museum
8 SAS Travels
9 Main Post Office
10 All Saints Cathedral
20 Civil Lines Bus Stand
21 Leader Road Bus Stand
22 Tempo Stand
25 Zero Road Bus Stand
26 Hanuman Temple
27 Patalpuri Temple
28 Boat Hire
To Ayodhya (169km) & Lucknow (204km)
Prayag Train Station
Muir Rd
Police Lines
Sarojini Naidu Marg
Maharshi Dayanand Marg
Tejbahadur Sapru Rd
Tashkent Marg
Civil Lines
Lal Bahadur Shastri Marg
Sardar Patel Marg
Mahatma Gandhi Marg
Kasturba Gandhi Marg
Kamla Nehru Marg
Pannalal Rd
Malviya Marg
Nawab Yusuf Rd
Allahabad Junction Train Station
Smith Rd
Leader Rd
Khusru Bagh
Dr Katju Rd
Swami Vivekenand Marg
Lala Sitaram Rd
Allahabad City Train Station
Zero Rd
Grand Trunk Rd
To Kausambi (63km) & Kanpur (200km)
Chowk
Minto Park
Grand Trunk Rd
Daraganj Train Station
Mela Ground
Fort Rd
Triveni Rd
To Varanasi
Footpath
Fort
Sangam
Ganges River
Yamuna River
0 0.5 1km
0 0.3 0.6mi
To Bhita (18km) & Garwha (50km)
To Chitrakut (132km)

walls and three gateways flanked by high towers. It's most impressive when viewed from the river, so if you don't catch a boat out to the sangam it's worth walking along the riverbank footpath which skirts the fort's southern wall. The fort is in the hands of the army so prior permission is required for a visit. Passes can be obtained from the Defence Ministry Security Officer, though these are only usually granted to VIPs – in any case, there's nothing very much to see.

Patalpuri Temple & Undying Tree A small door in the fort's eastern wall leads to the one portion of the fort you can visit without permission – the underground Patalpuri Temple which is home to the 'Undying Banyan Tree'. Also known as Akshai Veta, this tree is mentioned by Xuan Zhang, who tells of pilgrims sacrificing their lives by leaping to their deaths from it in order to seek salvation. This would be difficult now as there's not much of it left.

Hanuman Temple This popular temple, open to non-Hindus, is unusual because the Hanuman idol is reclining rather than upright. It's said that each year during the floods the Ganges rises to touch the feet of the sleeping Hanuman before receding.

Anand Bhavan

This shrine to the Nehru family must be the best-kept museum in the country, indicating the high regard in which this famous dynasty is held in India. The exhibits in the house show how this well-off family became involved in the struggle for Indian independence and produced four generations of astute politicians – Motilal Nehru, Jawaharlal Nehru, Indira Gandhi and Rajiv Gandhi.

Visitors walk around the verandas of the two-storey mansion looking through glass panels into the rooms. A quick look at the extensive bookshelves (full of Marx and Lenin) indicates where India's post-Independence faith in socialism sprang from. The house is open between 9.30 am and 5 pm daily except holidays and Monday. It's free to see the ground floor but costs Rs 5 to go upstairs. Last entry is at 4.30 pm, and no tickets are sold from 12.45 to 1.30 pm.

In the manicured garden is an outbuilding housing a pictorial display of Jawaharlal Nehru's life. A **planetarium**, built in the grounds in 1979, has hourly shows between 11 am and 4 pm; tickets cost Rs 10.

Next door is **Swaraj Bhavan**, where Motilal Nehru lived until 1930 and where Indira Gandhi was born. It houses a museum featuring dimly lit rooms and is open from 11 am to 1 pm and 2 to 5 pm daily except Monday; entry is Rs 5.

Other Attractions

All Saints Cathedral was designed by Sir William Emerson, the architect of the Victoria Memorial in Kolkata. Its brass memorial plaques show that even for the sons and daughters of the Raj, life was not all high teas and pink gins. The inscriptions morbidly record the causes of death: 'died of blood poisoning', 'died in a polo accident' and, probably even more likely today, 'died in a motor accident on the road to Nainital'. It is open 8 to 10 am and has services in English on Sunday.

Allahabad Museum has galleries devoted to local archaeological finds, including terracotta figurines from Kausambi. It also has a large room of artefacts donated by the Nehru family, including all sorts of wonderful and ridiculous items presented to Nehru while he was prime minister. The museum is open 10.15 am to 4.30 pm daily except Monday. Admission is a hefty Rs 100.

The **Nag Basuki Temple** is mentioned in the *Puranas* and is on the bank of the Ganges, north of the railway bridge.

Places to Stay – Budget

Budget hotels can be found in the peaceful Civil Lines area though many are immediately south of Allahabad Junction train station. All rooms have private bathroom.

The ***Tourist Bungalow–Hotel Ilawart*** *(☎ 601440, fax 611374, 35 MG Marg)* is a clean UP Tourism operation set back from the road in a well-tended garden, with a restaurant. Dorm beds are overpriced at Rs 100 and spacious air-cooled rooms are Rs 300/400; air-con rooms go for Rs 650/800. The rooms are not bad value if you can put up with the noise that filters through from the adjacent bus stand.

Mayur Guest House *(☎ 420250, 10 Sardar Patel Marg)*, just off MG Marg, is friendly and pokey with smallish air-cooled rooms with hot water geyser and TV from Rs 265/345 and air-con rooms for Rs 475/600.

Hotel Tepso *(☎ 623635, MG Marg)* has a dilapidated reception area but the rooms are very clean and reasonably quiet. Singles/doubles are Rs 275/400.

Hotel Prayag *(☎ 656416, fax 655596, 73 Noorullah Rd)*, south of Allahabad Junction train station, is a typically good budget hotel. It has rooms (most with TV) from Rs 150/185 to Rs 475/525 with air-con.

Hotel Continental *(☎ 652629)* is one of many in a similar price bracket along Dr Katju Rd. Rooms start at Rs 140/260 and checkout is 24 hours.

Hotel Santosh Palace *(☎ 654773, fax 609791, 100 Dr Katju Rd)* offers a generally higher standard. Modern spacious rooms with TV and air-cooling start from Rs 220/300, or from Rs 600/700 with air-con. The cheaper rooms have squat toilets.

Places to Stay – Mid-Range & Top End

All the mid-range and top-end hotels are in the Civil Lines area.

Samrat Hotel *(☎ 420780, fax 420785)*, in an alley off MG Marg, has clean rooms with TV for Rs 500/700 with air-cooling and Rs 900/1000 with air-con. Samrat is looking pretty tired these days and although the rooms have a certain charm, they're a bit overpriced.

Hotel Allahabad Regency *(☎ 601519, e tglalld@hotmail.com, 16 Tashkent Marg)* is a tranquil two-star place with air-con rooms from Rs 1050/1250, including breakfast. It has a nice pool (open April to September), a garden and a gym.

Hotel Yatrik *(☎ 601713, fax 601434, 33 Sardar Patel Marg)* is a smart, modern establishment. Air-con rooms are a slightly higher standard and cost Rs 1100/1300. It has a lovely garden and a good pool (open late April to September). Checkout is 24 hours.

Hotel Kanha Shyam *(☎ 420281, fax 622164, e info@kanhashyam.com)*, just off MG Marg, is a modern, four-star high-rise and the classiest hotel in Allahabad. Prices start at Rs 1550/1750 and there's a health club, coffee shop, restaurant and bar.

Places to Eat

Outdoor eating is all the rage in Allahabad. Many semipermanent stalls set up tables and chairs on the footpath of MG Marg in the evening, making it a popular, atmospheric and cheap area to eat.

Shamiyana is one of the few established food stalls on MG Marg that is open all day. It dishes up excellent chow mein for Rs 18/32 a half/full plate and OK masala dosa for Rs 16. A little farther east, ***Kalchuri*** and neighbouring ***Spicy Bite*** are stalls serving cheap and tasty Chinese food.

El Chico is arguably the best of Allahabad's handful of proper restaurants, although meals are not cheap at Rs 60 to 130. At the time of research it was being renovated. The ***potato chaat stand*** directly in front of El Chico serves fantastic snacks for Rs 5.

Tandoor, also on MG Marg, focuses more closely on Indian food, although it does pizzas as well; half a tandoori chicken is Rs 70 and a veg pizza is Rs 60. ***Nathu's Sweets*** *(18B Sardar Patel Marg)* is a vegetarian place with pizza, South Indian dishes and a wide selection of sweets downstairs. A few doors along is ***Hot Stuff***, a Western-style fast-food joint with pizzas from Rs 55, burgers, Indian and Chinese food, and a good range of ice cream.

There are many basic restaurants in the old town, plus several ***dhaba*** places close to the train station along Dr Katju Rd.

Getting There & Away

At the time of research there were no flights to Allahabad, though some services may operate during the Kumbh Mela.

Bus From the Civil Lines bus stand, beside the Tourist Bungalow, there are regular buses to Varanasi (Rs 55, three hours), Lucknow (Rs 74 ordinary, Rs 105 deluxe, five hours), Faizabad (Rs 72, five hours) and Gorakhpur (Rs 119, 9½ hours), via Jaunpur. There are four buses to Sunauli (Rs 158, 13 hours) if you're heading to Nepal.

Train The main train station is Allahabad Junction, in the centre of the city. There are connections to Varanasi (Rs 41/365 in 2nd/2nd air-con class, three hours) and Lucknow (Rs 61/321, in 2nd/1st class, four hours). There are also expresses to Delhi (Rs 204/688 in sleeper/1st class, 10 hours), Kolkata (Rs 242/819, 15 hours) and Mumbai (Rs 326/1512, sleeper/2nd air-con class, 24 hours).

Allahabad is a good place from which to travel to Khajuraho, since there are numerous express trains to Satna (Rs 104/448/784, sleeper/2nd/1st class, 3½ hours). The *Patna-Kurla Express* leaves at 8.30 am, leaving plenty of time to catch a bus from Satna to Khajuraho (four hours).

Getting Around

There are plenty of cycle-rickshaws for hire but few autorickshaws. Use the back exit at Allahabad Junction train station to reach Civil Lines. A cycle-rickshaw from the train station to the Civil Lines bus stand costs no more than Rs 5. It's a Rs 20 cycle-rickshaw ride from the train station to the fort and Rs 10 from MG Marg to Anand Bhavan. Tempos go from Allahabad Junction train station to Daraganj train station, which is 800m north of the fort.

AROUND ALLAHABAD

Excavations at **Bhita** on the Yamuna River, 18km south of Allahabad, have revealed the remains of an ancient fortified city. There's a museum with stone and metal seals, coins and terracotta statues.

The ruined temples in the walled enclosure of **Garwha** are about 50km south-west of Allahabad. The major temple has 16 beautifully carved stone pillars.

The best way to get to Bhita and Garwha is by taxi from Allahabad.

Kausambi, once known as Kosam, is an ancient Buddhist centre 63km south-west of Allahabad. There's a huge fortress near the village which contains the broken remains of an Ashoka pillar. Buses depart irregularly from Allahabad's Leader Rd bus stand.

It was in **Chitrakut**, 132km from Allahabad, that Brahma, Vishnu and Shiva are believed to have been 'born' and taken on their incarnations, which makes this town a very popular Hindu pilgrimage place. UP Tourism has a ***Tourist Bungalow*** (*☎ 22219*) here, with ordinary singles/doubles Rs 150/175. Buses depart from Allahabad's Zero Rd bus stand.

FAIZABAD

☎ 05278 • pop 350,000

Faizabad was once the capital of Avadh but rapidly declined after the death of Bahu Begum, the wife of Nawab Shuja-ud-Daula. Most of the Islamic buildings in Faizabad were built at her behest, and her mausoleum is said to be the finest of its type in Uttar Pradesh. Her husband also has an impressive mausoleum. There are three large mosques in the chowk area and pleasant gardens in Gupta Park, where the temple from which Rama is supposed to have disappeared stands. The town makes a convenient base for visiting nearby Ayodhya.

There is an Internet cafe just up the road from the Hotel Krishna Palace.

Places to Stay & Eat

If your pack isn't too heavy you can walk to the hotels from the bus stand, which is on the same road; the train station is a Rs 5 cycle-rickshaw ride away.

Hotel Shane-Avadh (*☎ 23586*) is a clean, efficiently run place with a lift. Singles/doubles with private bathroom and hot water cost from Rs 150/175 and air-con rooms with TV are Rs 550/650. Its ***Mezban*** restaurant turns out decent veg/nonveg and Chinese fare in big portions.

Hotel Tirupati (*☎ 23231*) next door is also good value and has helpful staff. Rooms with private bathroom, hot water and TV cost from Rs 135/175, or Rs 550/650 with air-con. It has a rather small, but very grand, restaurant, with a similar range to the Mezban. Snacks start from about Rs 20 and vegetarian mains are around Rs 40.

Abha Hotel (*☎ 22550*) is the best of several places on a side street near the Majestic Cinema in the chowk area. It has good-size rooms with TV and large, clean, private bathrooms from Rs 160/200, and a veg/nonveg restaurant. There were renovations going on at the time of research.

Hotel Krishna Palace (*☎ 21367, fax 21371*), a short walk from the train station, is Faizabad's top hotel, though there's no lift. It has a range of modern, comfortable rooms starting at Rs 550/650 with fan.

Getting There & Away

Faizabad has fairly good train connections, including expresses to Lucknow (Rs 39/205 in 2nd/1st class, three hours) and Varanasi (Rs 54/284, four to six hours).

There are numerous buses from the quiet bus stand on the Lucknow-Gorakhpur Rd, 750m west of Hotel Shane-Avadh. Connections include Gorakhpur (Rs 62, four hours), Lucknow (Rs 55, three hours), Allahabad

(Rs 71, five hours), Sunauli (Rs 94) and Ayodhya (Rs 10). Tempos to Ayodhya (Rs 8) depart from the main road, about 80m north of the clock tower in the chowk area.

AYODHYA

☎ 05278 • pop 75,000

Ayodhya, 6km from Faizabad, is one of Hinduism's seven holy cities. It's a major pilgrimage centre since it is not only the birthplace of Rama, but is also connected with many events in the Ramayana. Unfortunately, its name has become synonymous with rising Hindu fanaticism since the fateful day on 6 December 1992 when a Hindu mob destroyed a mosque they believed had been built on the site of a temple marking Rama's birthplace. The event sent shock waves throughout India and threatened the nation's secular framework.

The Atharvaveda described Ayodhya as 'a city built by gods and being as prosperous as paradise itself' although today it's just a small, dusty town with an amazing abundance of temples and monkeys. It sees few foreigners, and anyone intending to visit should keep an eye on the latest developments in the temple-mosque saga. Give the town a wide berth during festivals. Be particularly careful on the 6 December.

Babri Masjid – Ram Janam Bhumi

The **Babri Masjid** was constructed by the Mughals in the 15th century on what was reputed to be the site of Rama's birth. The mosque was little used and was eventually closed to Muslims by the civil authorities and limited Hindu *puja* was permitted inside.

By 1990, Rama had been appropriated by Hindu fundamentalists to justify their calls for a Hindu India. Their plans to build a temple to Rama (the Ram Mandir) in place of the mosque led to outbreaks of violence between local Hindus and Muslims. A fragile court order called for the maintenance of the status quo and armed guards surrounded the mosque and attempted to keep the two communities apart.

In late 1992, a Hindu mob stormed the site and destroyed the Babri Masjid, erecting a small Hindu shrine known as **Ram Janam Bhumi** (also known as Ram Janmabhoomi) in its place. The destruction sparked riots across India and caused unrest in neighbouring Muslim countries.

The government, which owns the site, has promised to build a temple here if it is decided a temple was here before the mosque. In late 1994 the Indian High Court wisely refused to adjudicate on the issue, after which the matter moved on to the Allahabad High Court. In 2001 a final resolution had yet to be reached, though orders were still in force which required the union government to maintain the status quo as it existed on 7 January 1993.

There is a massive security presence at the temple/mosque site, since it's the country's most volatile flash point. You will be thoroughly (and rather over-zealously) searched. Cameras are prohibited, and you cannot safely deposit them. In fact you can't take any bags in with you – even pens are taken away. Make sure you carry your passport.

Although the palpable tension in the air makes a visit memorable, as a tourist spectacle it's eminently forgettable; all you see is a small shrine protected by a tent-like structure. The site is open daily. The exact hours change periodically; at the time of research they were 8 am to 1 pm and 3 to 5 pm.

If you arrive by tempo from Faizabad, ask the driver to drop you at the Hanuman Temple, from where it's about a 10-minute walk.

Places to Stay

The ***UP Tourist Bungalow*** *(☎ 32435)*, also known locally as the Saket Hotel, is near the train station and is the only acceptable place to stay in Ayodhya. It's a peaceful place and some rooms have good balconies. Clean singles/doubles with private bathroom cost from Rs 175/200, air-con rooms are Rs 450/500 and a bed in the dorm costs Rs 60. There's a lacklustre veg restaurant and a tourist office.

Getting There & Away

There are regular tempos shuttling along the main road between Ayodhya and Faizabad for Rs 8, or you can take a bus for Rs 4. Ayodhya bus station is about 300m from the Hanumangadhi temple in the direction of Faizabad.

SHRAVASTI

The extensive ruins of this ancient city and Jetavana Monastery are near the villages of Saheth-Maheth. Here, Buddha performed the miracle of sitting on a 1000-petalled lotus and multiplying himself a million times while fire and water came from his body. Ashoka was an early pilgrim and left a couple of pillars to commemorate his visit.

The site can be reached from Gonda, 50km north-west of Ayodhya. The nearest train station is Gainjahwa, on the Gonda-Naugarh-Gorakhpur loop. The nearest large town is 20km away at Balrampur.

VARANASI

☎ 0542 • pop 2 million

Varanasi, the city of Shiva, on the bank of the sacred Ganges is one of the holiest places in India. Hindu pilgrims come to bathe in the waters of the Ganges, a ritual which washes away all sins. The city is an auspicious place to die, since expiring here offers *moksha* – liberation from the cycle of birth and death. It's a magical city where the most intimate rituals of life and death take place in public on the city's famous ghats. It's this accessibility to the practices of an ancient religious tradition that captivates so many visitors.

In the past, the city has been known as Kashi and Benares, but its present name is a restoration of an ancient name meaning the city between two rivers – the Varuna and Assi.

History

Varanasi has been a centre of learning and civilisation for over 2000 years, and claims to be one of the oldest living cities in the world. Mark Twain obviously thought it looked the part when he dropped by on a lecture tour, since he told the world that 'Benares is older than history, older than tradition, older even than legend, and looks twice as old as all of them put together'.

The first historical event known about Varanasi occurred between 1400 and 1000 BC when the Kasis (an Aryan tribe in northern India) settled in the Ganges valley, near present-day Varanasi. Before this time there is speculation that Varanasi could have been a place of primitive sun worship.

The city became a great Hindu centre and the Kasis were eventually absorbed into the Kosala kingdom, which was in turn incorporated into the great empire of Magadha, ruled from modern-day Patna.

Around the 8th century AD, Varanasi went through a revival period with the appearance of Shankaracharya, a reformer of Hinduism who established Shiva worship as the principal sect in the Hindu religion.

From the 11th century Varanasi was looted by Muslim invaders. It is believed the Afghans destroyed Varanasi around AD 1300, after laying waste to nearby Sarnath. The Mughal emperor Aurangzeb was the most destructive, looting and destroying almost all of the temples.

Today the old city of Varanasi does have an antique feel, but few buildings are more than a couple of hundred years old.

Orientation

The old city of Varanasi is situated along the western bank of the Ganges and extends back from the riverbank ghats in a labyrinth of alleyways that are too narrow for traffic. Godaulia is just outside the old city, and

Drowning in Conservatism

Given Varanasi's importance to Hinduism, it's no surprise to learn that the city has an element of entrenched religious conservatism. In January 2000 Canadian-Indian film director, Deepa Mehta, and her crew discovered the ferocity of this conservatism when violated.

They were in town shooting a film called *Water*. The third piece in a trilogy that includes the equally controversial films *Fire* and *Earth*, *Water* is the story about the predicament of Indian widows (there are over 30 million in India today); many turn to prostitution in order to survive.

After shooting one scene, director and crew were practically run out of the city by enraged crowds who believed the subject of the film was the product of Western decadence.

In fact it appears that the volatile reaction to the film was a carefully orchestrated political stunt. A distorted copy of the script was leaked to journalists to stir up trouble – and it worked. Blazing headlines followed around the country and the film was condemned. Local politicians jumping on the conservative bandwagon were quick to denounce the film and support the backlash from hard-liners.

Filming continued in the state of Madhya Pradesh where Mehta was offered sanctuary by the chief minister, who was happy to admit that his invitation was motivated politically and not because of his interest in film making.

VARANASI

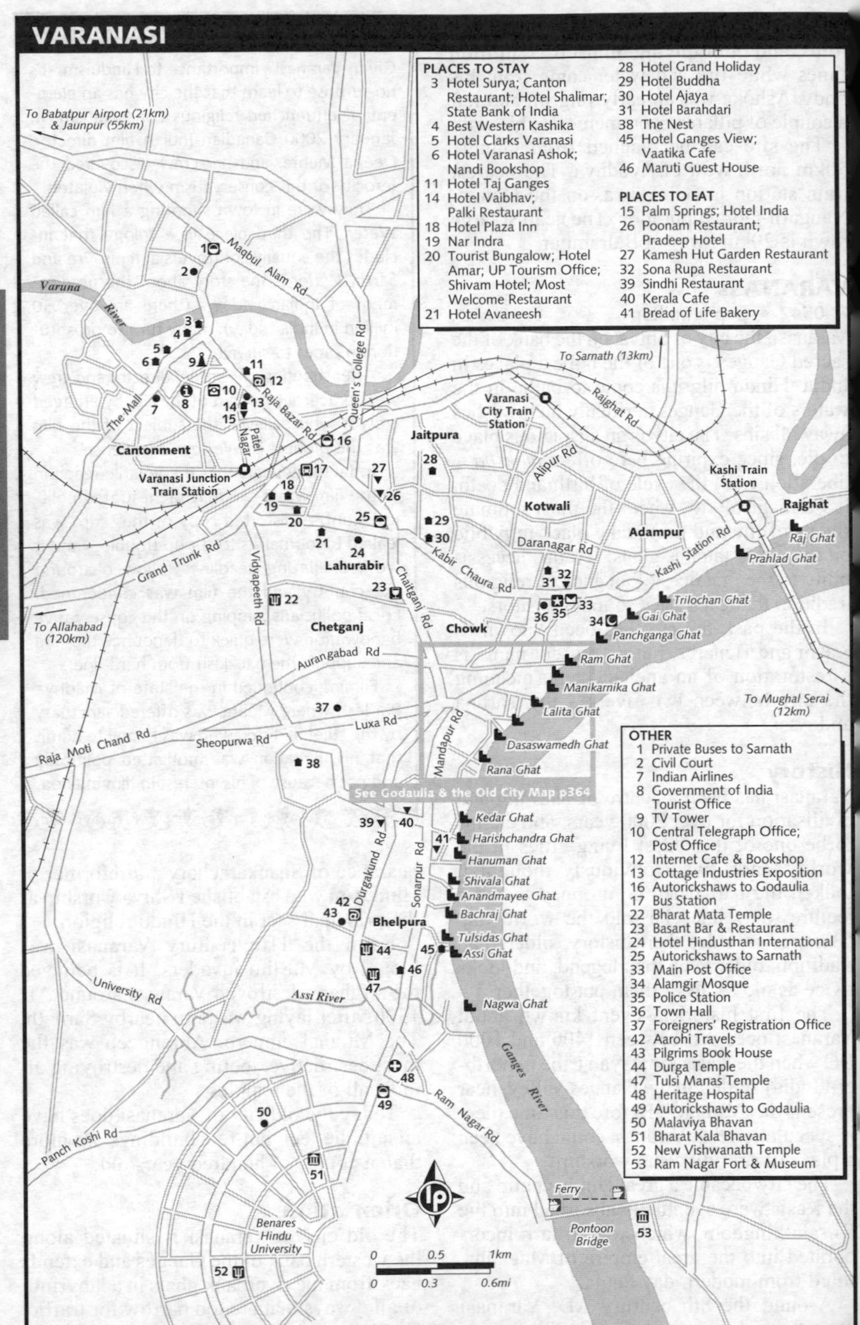
PLACES TO STAY
3 Hotel Surya; Canton Restaurant; Hotel Shalimar; State Bank of India
4 Best Western Kashika
5 Hotel Clarks Varanasi
6 Hotel Varanasi Ashok; Nandi Bookshop
11 Hotel Taj Ganges
14 Hotel Vaibhav; Palki Restaurant
18 Hotel Plaza Inn
19 Nar Indra
20 Tourist Bungalow; Hotel Amar; UP Tourism Office; Shivam Hotel; Most Welcome Restaurant
21 Hotel Avaneesh
28 Hotel Grand Holiday
29 Hotel Buddha
30 Hotel Ajaya
31 Hotel Barahdari
38 The Nest
45 Hotel Ganges View; Vaatika Cafe
46 Maruti Guest House
PLACES TO EAT
15 Palm Springs; Hotel India
26 Poonam Restaurant; Pradeep Hotel
27 Kamesh Hut Garden Restaurant
32 Sona Rupa Restaurant
39 Sindhi Restaurant
40 Kerala Cafe
41 Bread of Life Bakery
OTHER
1 Private Buses to Sarnath
2 Civil Court
7 Indian Airlines
8 Government of India Tourist Office
9 TV Tower
10 Central Telegraph Office; Post Office
12 Internet Cafe & Bookshop
13 Cottage Industries Exposition
16 Autorickshaws to Godaulia
17 Bus Station
22 Bharat Mata Temple
23 Basant Bar & Restaurant
24 Hotel Hindusthan International
25 Autorickshaws to Sarnath
33 Main Post Office
34 Alamgir Mosque
35 Police Station
36 Town Hall
37 Foreigners' Registration Office
42 Aarohi Travels
43 Pilgrims Book House
44 Durga Temple
47 Tulsi Manas Temple
48 Heritage Hospital
49 Autorickshaws to Godaulia
50 Malaviya Bhavan
51 Bharat Kala Bhavan
52 New Vishwanath Temple
53 Ram Nagar Fort & Museum
To Babatpur Airport (21km) & Jaunpur (55km)
To Sarnath (13km)
To Allahabad (120km)
To Mughal Serai (12km)
Varuna River
Ganges River
Assi River
Maqbul Alam Rd
Queen's College Rd
The Mall
Raja Bazar Rd
Patel Nagar
Cantonment
Varanasi Junction Train Station
Varanasi City Train Station
Kashi Train Station
Rajghat Rd
Alipur Rd
Jaitpura
Kotwali
Adampur
Rajghat
Daranagar Rd
Kashi Station Rd
Kabir Chaura Rd
Lahurabir
Chetganj
Chowk
Grand Trunk Rd
Vidyapeeth Rd
Chaitganj Rd
Aurangabad Rd
Luxa Rd
Sheopurwa Rd
Raja Moti Chand Rd
Mandapur Rd
Durgakund Rd
Sonarpur Rd
Bhelpura
University Rd
Ram Nagar Rd
Panch Koshi Rd
Benares Hindu University
Raj Ghat
Prahlad Ghat
Trilochan Ghat
Gai Ghat
Panchganga Ghat
Ram Ghat
Manikarnika Ghat
Lalita Ghat
Dasaswamedh Ghat
Rana Ghat
Kedar Ghat
Harishchandra Ghat
Hanuman Ghat
Shivala Ghat
Anandmayee Ghat
Bachraj Ghat
Tulsidas Ghat
Assi Ghat
Nagwa Ghat
Ferry
Pontoon Bridge
See Godaulia & the Old City Map p364
0 0.5 1km
0 0.3 0.6mi

Lahurabir is to the north-east, separated from the cantonment by the train line.

One of the best ways to get your bearings in Varanasi is to remember the positions of the ghats, particularly important ones like Dasaswamedh Ghat. The alleyways of the old city can be disorienting, but the hotels here are well signposted. The big international hotels and the Government of India tourist office are in the cantonment north of Varanasi Junction train station. The TV tower is the most obvious landmark in this area.

Information

Tourist Offices There's a UP Tourism information booth (☎ 346370) at Varanasi Junction train station. If you've just come into town it's a good place for directions, beyond that they're pretty useless. Another UP Tourism office (☎ 341162) is in the Tourist Bungalow hotel, open daily except Sunday.

The friendly and helpful Government of India tourist office (☎ 343744, ⓔ goitovns@satyam.net.in) at 15B The Mall in the cantonment is the best place for information about Varanasi. It's open from 9 am to 6 pm weekdays, and until 4 pm Saturday.

Visa Extensions The Foreigners' Registration Office (☎ 351968) is in Srinagar Colony, Siddgiri Bagh, Sigra. Head west along Luxa Rd away from the river and turn right just before the Theosophical Society on the left. Follow this road until it ends at a T-junction; the office is 50m to the right.

Money In the cantonment area, the State Bank of India near the Hotel Surya changes cash and US dollar travellers cheques, but won't accept travellers cheques in pounds sterling. There are also exchange facilities in several upmarket cantonment hotels. The State Bank of India near Dasaswamedh Ghat changes only Thomas Cook travellers cheques (US dollar or pounds sterling) and won't touch other currencies.

The most convenient place to change money is Radiant Services, on the Luxa Rd, Godaulia. Rates are slightly lower than in the banks but it is quick, open from around 9 am to 8 pm daily, and changes all travellers cheques and 36 currencies. Branches are also at Shanti Guest House, Radiant YMCA Tourist Hostel, and above the Union Bank of India in The Mall, Cantonment. The Bank of Baroda (near the Hotel Ganges) and the Andhra Bank on Dasaswamedh Ghat Rd, next to Yelchiko restaurant, provide cash advances on major credit cards.

The black market is a possibility, mainly in the form of silk shops, where you can usually change cash and sometimes travellers cheques.

Post & Communications The main post office is a short cycle-rickshaw ride north of the old city. The poste restante here is open 10 am to 6 pm Monday to Saturday. In the cantonment there's a post office at the central telegraph office (CTO). You can make international and STD calls from the CTO 24 hours a day.

Lots of places have Internet access, but only a few use service providers based in Varanasi, so it can be costly. The rate will be around Rs 50 to 70 per hour outside the old city in a place that uses a local service provider and Rs 2 per minute if the service provider is based in Lucknow. Rates can drop after 7 pm. Two places to try are a bookshop (which has four terminals) near Hotel Vaibhav on Raja Bazar Rd and Aarohi Travels, on Durgakund Rd, if you're farther south. The old city is a different story and rates can be as low as Rs 30 per hour. A good place is a private call booth, just near Dasaswamedh Ghat. There are six terminals and connections are quick. Another good place is Fontac Computer, behind the Garden Restaurant in Godaulia.

Bookshops The Universal Book Company in Godaulia is an excellent bookshop. Pilgrims Book House, just off Durgakund Rd, is great for books on Buddhism and Hinduism; it's open daily. The Nandi Bookshop in the Hotel Varanasi Ashok has lots of unusual titles. *Benares: City of Light* by Diana Eck (Princeton University Press) has information on each ghat and temple, and a good introduction to Hinduism.

Medical Services The Heritage Hospital (☎ 313977) is close to the main gate of Benares Hindu University. Medical supplies are available all over the city through pharmacies. There is a group of small pharmacies just before the entrance to Benares Hindu University.

Emergency The closest police station (☎ 330653) to the old city is between the town hall and the main post office.

Dangers & Annoyances Predatory rickshaw-wallahs and persistent touts are the main hassles for most travellers.

Unfortunately Varanasi does have a darker side. There is a very small criminal element operating mainly at the major entry points to the city, ie, airport, train station and bus station. They offer information to tourists about hotels, taxis etc. When you arrive in Varanasi catch a taxi/rickshaw to the hotel of your choice, on your own. Don't listen to people who try to lead you to a different hotel or offer you services as a 'guide'. (Especially ignore nonsense from autorickshaw drivers about 'your hotel' being closed, full, burnt down etc. Be firm.)

It has been unofficially estimated that two or three travellers go missing in the city every three or four months. Three Japanese tourists disappeared in November 2000. Only do boat trips in groups and ignore any other services offered by boatmen. Use authorised guides from the Government of India tourist office or the bigger hotels.

The old city is also said to be potentially dangerous after dark, and many hotels in this area lock their doors at 10 or 11 pm.

Ghats

Varanasi's principal attraction is the long string of ghats that line the western bank of the Ganges. Most are used for bathing but there are also several 'burning ghats' where bodies are cremated. The best time to visit the ghats is at dawn when the river is bathed in a magical light and pilgrims come to perform puja to the rising sun.

There are around 100 ghats in Varanasi, but Dasaswamedh Ghat is probably the most convenient starting point. A short boat trip from Dasaswamedh to Manikarnika Ghat can be an interesting introduction to the river (see Activities later in this chapter). Alternatively, if the water level is low, you can walk from one ghat to the next. This way you're among the people who come to the edge of the Ganges not only for a ritual bath, but to do yoga, offer blessings, buy paan, sell flowers, get a massage, play cricket, get a shave, and improve their karma by giving money to beggars.

The city extends from Raj Ghat, near the major road and rail bridge, to Assi Ghat, near the university. The **Assi Ghat** is one of the five special ghats which pilgrims are supposed to bathe at in sequence during the ritual route called Panchatirthi Yatra. The order is Assi, Dasaswamedh, Adi Keshava, Panchganga and finally Manikarnika.

Much of the **Tulsi Ghat** has fallen down towards the river. The **Bachraj Ghat** is Jain and there are three riverbank Jain temples. Many of the ghats are owned by maharajas or other princely rulers, such as the very fine **Shivala Ghat** owned by the maharaja of Varanasi. The **Dandi Ghat** is the ghat of ascetics known as Dandi Panths, and nearby is the very popular **Hanuman Ghat**.

The **Harishchandra**, or Smashan Ghat, is a secondary burning ghat. It's one of the oldest ghats in the city. Above it, the crowded **Kedar Ghat** is a shrine popular with Bengalis and South Indians. **Mansarowar Ghat** was built by Raja Man Singh of Amber and named after the Tibetan lake at the foot of Mt Kailash, Shiva's Himalayan home. **Someswar**, or Lord of the Moon Ghat, is said to be able to heal diseases. The **Munshi Ghat** is very picturesque, while **Ahalya Bai's Ghat** is named after the female Maratha ruler of Indore.

The name of **Dasaswamedh Ghat** indicates that Brahma sacrificed (*medh*) 10 (*das*) horses (*aswa*) here. Conveniently central, it's one of the most important and busiest ghats and therefore is a good place to linger and soak up the atmosphere, as long as you don't mind being pestered by people wanting to read your palm. Note its statues and the shrine of Sitala, goddess of smallpox.

Raja Man Singh's **Man Mandir Ghat** was built in 1600 but was poorly restored in the 19th century. The northern corner of the ghat has a fine stone balcony and Raja Jai Singh of Jaipur erected one of his unusual observatories on this ghat in 1710.

The **Meer Ghat** leads to the Nepalese Temple, which has erotic sculptures. The **Jalsain Ghat**, where cremations take place, virtually adjoins **Manikarnika Ghat**, one of the oldest and most sacred in Varanasi. Manikarnika is the main burning ghat and one of the most auspicious places that a Hindu can be cremated. Bodies are handled by outcasts known as *doms*, and they are carried through the alleyways of the old city to the holy Ganges on a bamboo stretcher swathed in cloth. The corpse is doused in the Ganges prior to cremation. You'll see huge piles of firewood stacked along the top of the ghat, each log carefully weighed on giant scales so that the price of cremation can be calculated. There are no problems watching cremations, since at Manikarnika death is simply business as usual, but don't take photos and keep your camera well hidden.

Above the steps here is a tank known as the **Manikarnika Well**; Parvati is said to have dropped her earring here and Shiva dug the tank to recover it, filling the depression with his sweat. The **Charanpaduka**, a slab of stone between the well and the ghat, bears footprints made by Vishnu. Privileged VIPs are cremated at the Charanpaduka. There is also a temple dedicated to Ganesh on the ghat.

Dattatreya Ghat bears the footprint of the Brahmin saint of that name in a small temple nearby. **Scindia Ghat** was originally built in 1830 but was so huge and magnificent that it collapsed into the river and had to be rebuilt. The **Ram Ghat** was built by the maharaja of Jaipur. The **Panchganga Ghat**, as its name indicates, is where five rivers are supposed to meet. Dominating the ghat is Aurangzeb's smaller mosque, also known as the **Alamgir Mosque**, which he built on the site of a large Vishnu temple erected by the Maratha chieftain Beni Madhav Rao Scindia. The **Gai Ghat** has a figure of a cow made of stone upon it. The **Trilochan Ghat** has two turrets emerging from the river, and the water between them is especially holy. **Raj Ghat** was the ferry pier until the road and rail bridge was completed here.

Vishwanath Temple

The Vishwanath Temple, or Golden Temple, is the most sacred temple in Varanasi and is dedicated to Vishveswara – Shiva as lord of

Helping the Great Mother to Breathe Again

The Ganges River, or Great Mother as it is known to Hindus, provides millions of Indians with an important link to their spirituality. Around 60,000 people go down to the ghats to take a holy dip every day along a 7km area of the river. Along this same stretch, 30 sewers are continuously discharging into the river.

The Ganges River is so heavily polluted at the end of Varanasi that the water is septic – no dissolved oxygen exists. The statistics get worse. Samples from the river show the water has 1.5 million faecal coliform bacteria per 100mL of water. In water that is safe for bathing this figure should be less than 500!

The problem extends much farther beyond Varanasi – 400 million people live along the basin of the Ganges River. The pollution levels mean that waterborne diseases run rampant among many villages using water from the river.

The battle to clean up the Ganges River has intensified in recent years. A nonprofit initiative, the Sankat Mochan Foundation, is dedicated to cleaning it up. Between 1986 and 1993 there was enough lobbying to see the government invest about US$25 million to set up three sewage treatment plants and an electric crematorium.

Unfortunately there have been many problems with the plants, which are very power intensive; Varanasi regularly has long blackout periods. In addition, their operation causes a build up of pollution in nearby villages and is also the cause of sewage backing up throughout Varanasi; this in turn flows out into bathing areas, out through manhole covers and into the streets.

A plan for a better sewage treatment system, which has lower costs and is far more effective than the current system, has been developed by the foundation. The plan has not yet been accepted by the government, but the signs are good.

In 1998 the Swatcha Ganga Environmental Education Centre was established at Tulsi Ghat. The centre runs environmental education courses with schools, local villages, pilgrims and boatmen. Changes have started to creep in, albeit slowly – in some cases Brahmin priests have persuaded pilgrims to bury their relatives by the side of the river instead of cremating them.

Visitors who wish to make a contribution, financially or through voluntary work efforts, should contact Professor Veer Bhadra Mishra at the Sankat Mochan Foundation (☎ 313884, fax 314278, ⓔ vbmganga@satyam.net.in), Tulsi Ghat, Varanasi.

the universe. The current temple was built in 1776 by Ahalya Bai of Indore, and the 800kg of gold plating on the towers, which gives the temple its colloquial name, was provided by Maharaja Ranjit Singh of Lahore some 50 years later. It's located in the narrow alleys of the old city. Non-Hindus are not allowed into the temple but can view it from the upper floor of a silk shop across the street.

There has been a succession of Shiva temples in the vicinity for at least the past 1500 years, but they were routinely destroyed by Muslim invaders. Aurangzeb continued this tradition, knocking down the previous temple and building his **Great Mosque** over it. Armed guards protect the mosque since the BJP has declared that, after Ayodhya, the mosques at Varanasi and Mathura are its next targets. Be discreet if taking photographs in this area.

Next to the Vishwanath Temple is the **Gyan Kupor Well** (Well of Knowledge). The faithful believe drinking its water leads to a higher spiritual plane, though they are prevented from doing so by both tradition and a strong security screen. The well is said to contain the Shiva lingam removed from the previous temple and hidden to protect it from Aurangzeb.

Durga Temple

The Durga Temple is commonly known as the Monkey Temple due to the many frisky monkeys that have made it their home. Located about 2km south of the old city, this small temple was built in the 18th century by a Bengali maharani and is stained red with ochre. It's in North Indian Nagara style with a multitiered *sikhara* (spire). Durga is the 'terrible' form of Shiva's consort Parvati, so at festivals there are often sacrifices of goats. Non-Hindus can enter the courtyard but not the inner sanctum.

Tulsi Manas Temple

Only 150m south of the Durga Temple is the modern marble sikhara-style Tulsi Manas Temple, built in 1964. Its two-tier walls are engraved with verses and scenes from the *Ram Charit Manas*, the Hindi version of the Ramayana. Its author, poet Tulsi Das, lived here while writing it. Watch figures performing scenes from Hindu mythology on the 2nd floor for Rs 1. The temple is open 6 to 11.30 am and 3 to 9 pm.

Benares Hindu University

Varanasi has long been a centre of learning and that tradition is continued today at the Benares Hindu University (BHU), built in 1917. It was founded by the great nationalist Pandit Malaviya as a centre for education in Indian art, music, culture and philosophy, and for the study of Sanskrit.

The lovely, green 5 sq km campus houses the **Bharat Kala Bhavan**, which has a fine collection of miniature paintings, sculptures from the 1st to 15th centuries and old photographs of Varanasi. It's open 11 am to 4 pm Monday to Saturday (7.30 am to 12.30 pm May/June). To visit all sections costs Rs 40, or Rs 10 for Indian nationals. BHU is a 20-minute walk or a short rickshaw ride from the Durga Temple.

You can walk from the gates of the university to the **New Vishwanath Temple** in about 30 minutes. Planned by Pandit Malaviya and built by the wealthy Birla family of industrialists, this temple, unlike most in Varanasi, is open to all, irrespective of caste or religion. It's open 4 am to noon and 1 to 9 pm. From Godaulia it costs around Rs 20 by cycle-rickshaw or Rs 35 by autorickshaw to reach the temple.

Ram Nagar Fort & Museum

On the opposite bank of the river, this 17th-century fort is the home of the former maharaja of Benares. It looks impressive from the river, though the decrepit planking of the pontoon bridge you cross to reach it is something of a distraction. During the monsoon, access is by ferry. The interesting museum here contains old silver and brocade palanquins for the ladies of the court, gold-plated elephant *howdahs* (seats for carrying people on an elephant's back), an astrological clock, macabre elephant traps and an armoury of swords and old guns. The fort is open 9 am to noon and 2 to 5 pm daily; entry is Rs 7.

River Trips

A boat ride on the Ganges has become one of the must-dos of a visit to Varanasi, but be prepared to see the odd corpse floating down the river. It's customary to do the trip early in the morning when the light is particularly inspiring. Even if you're not staying near the river, it is easy to organise a boat for sunrise as most rickshaw-wallahs are keen to get a pre-dawn rendezvous arranged. Get the rickshaw-wallah to take you to a large ghat such as Dasaswamedh, where there will be a number of boats.

The government rate for hiring a boat capable of holding up to four people is supposedly set at Rs 50 per hour; for a boat that can seat up to 15 people it's Rs 75 per hour. You'll undoubtedly have to remind boatmen of these rates since tourists frequently pay much more. Be sure to agree on a price before getting into a boat.

Steam Baths & Massage

The Hotel Surya offers steam baths for just Rs 50, and body massages for Rs 150. You can get a vigorous head, neck and back massage at Dasaswamedh Ghat from about Rs 10.

Swimming

If the sight of pilgrims bathing in the Ganges makes you want to have a splash yourself, the following hotels permit nonguests to use their pools: Hotel Varanasi Ashok (Rs 150), Hotel Hindusthan International (Rs 200), and Hotel Clarks Varanasi (Rs 200). Clarks has the best pool.

Courses

Language Bhasha Bharati (☎ 320447, ⓔ bhasha_bharati@hotmail.com), Ck 19/8 Thatheri Bazar, has language courses for those interested in learning Hindi. Basic courses are 30 hours and these are designed for travellers – the emphasis is on speaking and listening, not reading and writing. The course can be done in a week or it can be done over a longer period (you can have a one-hour lesson every day for a month).

Music Triveni Music Centre (☎ 452266), D24/38 Panday Ghat, Dasaswamedh Ghat Rd, has been recommended for tuition in classical Indian music. It teaches a range of instruments including the sitar and tabla. Lessons by professionals such as Sri Monilal Hazra and Sri Nandlal Mishra are one to 1½ hours and cost about Rs 50. It's also possible to buy a sitar here.

Aarohi Travels (☎ 312729, ⓔ arohivns@satyam.net.in), 74–75, 2nd floor, Dharm Sangh Complex, Durkakund Rd, can organise music tuition in Indian classical and folk music. Lessons are generally between Rs 50 and Rs 100 for 1 to 1½ hours.

Yoga & Hindu Philosophy We've heard good things from travellers about the International Yoga Clinic & Meditation Centre (☎ 327139), D16/19 Man-Mandir, Dasaswa medh, near Meer Ghat. Yoga classes are for one hour and cost Rs 100 per person, less if you are in a group.

The Malaviya Bhavan (☎ 310291, fax 312059) at Benares Hindu University offers courses in yoga and Hindu philosophy, such as a four-week certificate course or a four-month part-time diploma.

Organised Tours

Government guides hired via the Government of India tourist office cost Rs 255/380 for a half/full day, or you can pay more to include road and/or boat transport. Three-hour tours of the old city by foot, Sarnath by rickshaw or the river by boat cost Rs 300 each. (Note that the entry fee to the ruins at Sarnath is extra.) You can choose from their set itineraries or construct your own.

Places to Stay

There are three main accommodation areas in Varanasi: the old city, Lahurabir and the cantonment. Wherever you intend to stay in Varanasi, be firm when giving instructions to your rickshaw-wallah when you first arrive. See Dangers & Annoyances earlier. For places in the old city, it's better to just ask the rickshaw-wallah for Dasaswamedh Ghat and walk to the hotel from there, since rickshaws won't be able to negotiate the alleyways anyway.

Contact the Government of India tourist office or the UP Tourism office about Varanasi's paying guest accommodation, which enables you to stay with a local family. ***The Nest*** *(☎ 360137, ⓔ goitovns@satyam.net.in, B21/122 A2, Kamachha)*, near Baijnath Mandir (an old Shiva temple), is one of the cheapest of such places and charges Rs 60/125 for singles/doubles. If you have your own bed roll it's only Rs 15 per night.

Note that most hotels drop their rates by up to 50% in the low season (April to July).

Places to Stay – Budget & Mid-Range

Old City & Ghats Area The old city is the place to look for budget hotels if you don't mind living in cramped conditions. The area is certainly the city's most atmospheric and

UTTAR PRADESH & UTTARANCHAL

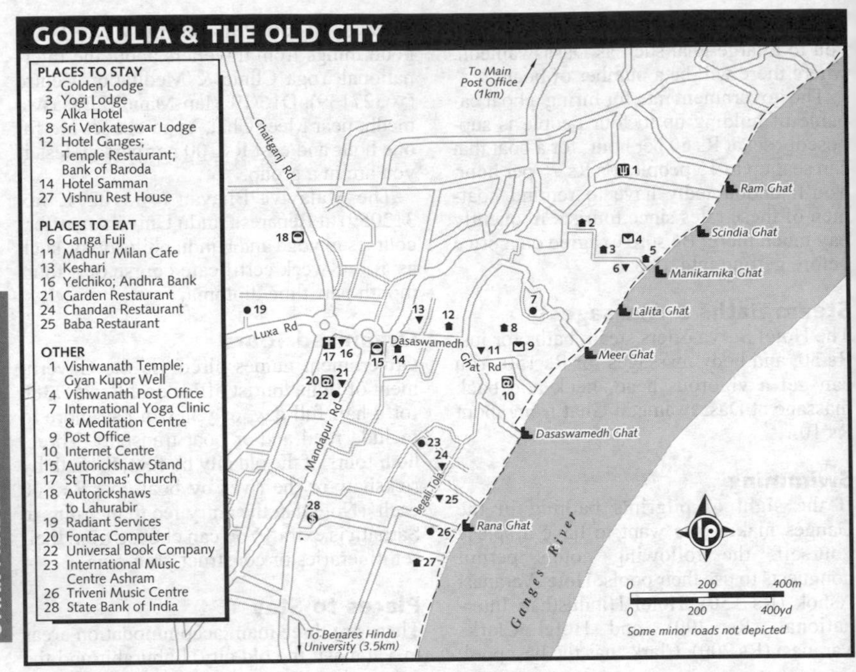

there are several good lodges right on the river with superb views along the ghats. Nearly all the hotels have rooftop terraces to relax on.

Vishnu Rest House *(☎ 450206, Panday Ghat)* is a popular riverside place with terraces offering great views. Fine singles without/with bathroom start at Rs 60/70 and dorm beds are Rs 40. Doubles start at Rs 120. Bucket hot water is free. Don't confuse it with the Real Vishnu Guest House or various other similarly named lodges which deliberately try to feed off its success. Phone ahead as it's generally full.

Alka Hotel *(☎ 328445, ⓔ hotelalka@hotmail.com, Meer Ghat)* is slightly more upmarket than other riverside places in the area. There's constant hot water, a pleasant terrace restaurant, and some rooms have TV. Prices range from Rs 120/200 with shared bathroom up to Rs 750 for air-con rooms with a balcony.

Scindia Guest House *(☎ 320319, Scindia Ghat)*, a little way north, has clean rooms, some with superb river views. It charges Rs 100/150 with shared bathroom; doubles with private bathroom and hot water, a balcony and air-cooling go for Rs 350. The management is not keen on drug use.

You don't need a river view to enjoy the old city and many travellers prefer the places in the alleys set back from the ghats.

Yogi Lodge *(☎ 392588, ⓔ yogilodge@yahoo.com, Kalika Gali)* has long been a favourite with budget travellers and is run by a friendly family. Dorm beds cost from Rs 50, and small rooms with shared bathroom cost from Rs 80/100. Sheets and blankets are Rs 5 extra. Like many other popular hotels in the old city, its success has spawned countless similarly named, inferior places.

Golden Lodge *(☎ 328788)*, close by, is a quiet place with basic rooms for Rs 50/100 with shared bathroom (hot water) or Rs 80/120 with private bathroom. It sells a good selection of ice cream.

The ***Sri Venkateswar Lodge*** *(☎ 392357, ⓔ venlodge@satyam.net.in)*, behind the Shiva temple on Dasaswamedh Ghat Rd, is a quiet place with hot water and rooms round a courtyard. It charges Rs 70/110 with shared bathroom and from Rs 175 for doubles with private bathroom. Rooms are clean and air cooled and the management is helpful.

***Shanti Guest House** (☎ 392568, ⓔ info@visitvaranasi.com)* is just off an alleyway leading to Manikarnika Ghat. It's very popular and has a 24-hour rooftop restaurant that has great views of the old city and the river. Spartan rooms with shared bathroom start from a mere Rs 40/60. Rooms with private bathroom and lukewarm water start from Rs 100/125. Unfortunately, the place has few outward facing windows and the slightest noise reverberates through the building.

There are a couple of decent choices on Dasaswamedh Ghat Rd in Godaulia. They are a bit more spacious than those in the alleyways of the old city but try to avoid rooms that front onto the noisy main road.

***Hotel Samman** (☎ 392241)* is good value and often full. Basic but fine rooms with private bathroom start from Rs 100/150. Bucket hot water is free and checkout is 24 hours.

***Hotel Ganges** (☎ 321097, ⓔ bhataksun@yahoo.com)* has variable rooms with private bathroom from Rs 175/225, to Rs 400/500 with air-con. Add 5% service charge. There are pool tables and table tennis.

Bhelpura This area is by the river, midway between the old town and the university.

***Maruti Guest House** (☎ 312261, Assi Rd)* is a friendly, family-run place with singles/doubles from just Rs 50/80, or from Rs 200 with private bathroom. Interesting conversation is provided by the doctor-owner, who gives free yoga and meditation lessons. It can be hard to spot – it's upstairs next to the 'Dr Maruti, Yoga & Meditation' sign.

***Hotel Ganges View** (☎ 313218, fax 367 495)* is a stylish, cultured place overlooking Assi Ghat. There are lots of paintings and ornaments on display, and excellent vegetarian meals are available in the evening. Double rooms start at Rs 450.

Lahurabir & Chetganj While these areas offer nothing of particular interest, they may be to your liking if you want to keep out of the crush of the old city, or need to be close to transport options.

***Hotel Ajaya** (☎ 207763, Kabir Chaura Rd)* is good value. It has clean, pleasant rooms with private bathroom and colour TV for Rs 150/250 and air-con rooms for Rs 450/500. Checkout is 24 hours.

***Hotel Buddha** (☎ 343686, ⓔ hotel_buddha@satyam.net.in)* is one of the best low-budget hotels in the area. It's behind the Hotel Ajaya, off the main street, so it's quieter. The rooms are a little plain, but they're mostly spacious with high ceilings. Singles/doubles with private bathroom and hot water cost from Rs 170/250. There are also a few tiny rooms with shared bathroom for Rs 90/130.

***Hotel Grand Holiday** (☎ 203792, Narain Villa)* is in a quiet residential street, and has variable rooms with private bathroom and hot water from Rs 250, or Rs 500 with air-con. There are also dorms for Rs 75. The best thing about this place is the garden and the friendly, family atmosphere. Checkout is 24 hours. Call ahead for free pick-up.

***Hotel Barahdari** (☎ 330040, ⓔ baradari@lw1.vsnl.net.in)* is east of Lahurabir, not far from the main post office and within walking distance of the ghats. It's a bit overpriced but well run by a friendly Jain family and has a vegetarian restaurant and a peaceful garden. Comfortable, smallish, air-cooled rooms with private bathroom and hot water and TV cost Rs 425/475, or Rs 625/700 with air-con.

***Hotel Avaneesh** (☎ 350730, Station Rd)* is a modern place offering small but comfortable air-con rooms with private bathroom, balconies and TV from Rs 450/550.

Train Station Area There are lots of cheap hotels close to Varanasi Junction train station if you need to be close to transport options. Most supply bucket hot water during the cool season.

***Nar Indra** (☎ 343586)* is one of several hotels lining the noisy Grand Trunk Rd, right outside the train station. Clean, simple rooms with TV cost Rs 200/250 with shared bathroom, Rs 225/275 with private bathroom and Rs 325/375 with air-con. It has 24-hour checkout.

***Tourist Bungalow** (☎ 343413, Parade Kothi)*, just off Grand Trunk Rd, is quite popular since it has a pleasant garden. Dorm beds cost Rs 75, singles/doubles with private bathroom go for Rs 200/250 and air-con rooms are Rs 550/650. Some cheaper rooms have squat toilets.

***Shivam Hotel** (☎ 348412)*, next to the Tourist Bungalow, is an excellent new place with squeaky-clean rooms, smiling staff and modern facilities. Singles/doubles start at Rs 275/375 and air-con rooms are Rs 500/650.

Across the road is ***Hotel Plaza Inn*** *(☎ 348210, fax 340504)*, with comfortable good-value rooms that have all the amenities. Prices start at Rs 500/600 for rooms with a fan.

The other places in this street are very basic, but at least at ***Hotel Amar*** *(☎ 343509)* there's hot water (Rs 5 a bucket) and all rooms have a TV, although they are rather dark and smelly. Singles are Rs 100 to 200 and doubles are Rs 175 to 300, the more expensive rooms have private bathroom and are air-cooled.

Cantonment Area This area, on the northern side of Varanasi Junction station, contains a sprinkling of budget hotels and most of the city's upmarket accommodation. It's the place to retreat to when the claustrophobia of the old city gets to you.

Hotel Surya *(☎ 343014, fax 348330, ⓔ Suria@lw1.vsnl.net.in, The Mall)* is a great place to stay if you need to wind down from the rigours of being on the road. The hotel is set around a pleasant garden and has singles/doubles with private bathroom and constant hot water for Rs 250/350, or Rs 500/650 with air-con.

Hotel Shalimar *(☎ 346227)* is next door; it's a similar standard but lacks the garden. The rooms for Rs 250/350 are fine, but the air-con rooms for Rs 600/700 aren't such good value, despite having colour TV.

There's a group of hotels on Patel Nagar, the street that runs north from the train station into the cantonment.

Hotel Vaibhav *(☎ 345056, fax 346466, 56 Patel Nagar)* is clean, well run and has a bar and a good restaurant. Comfortable rooms with private bathroom, constant hot water and TV cost Rs 400/500 and air-con rooms are Rs 600/700. Rooms in the new wing (from Rs 750/850) are very pleasant.

Places to Stay – Top End

Nearly all the top-end hotels are in the cantonment.

Hotel Clarks Varanasi *(☎ 348501, fax 348186, The Mall)* is the oldest hotel in the city. It dates back to the British era, though it now has a large modern extension and a good swimming pool. Air-con singles/doubles cost US$80/90.

Hotel Taj Ganges *(☎ 345100, fax 348067, Nadesar Palace)* is equally upmarket and has the most luxurious double rooms in town, costing from US$125. It has a swimming pool, tennis court, jogging track and other amenities.

Best Western Kashika *(☎ 348091, fax 348685, The Mall)*, formerly Hotel Ideal Tops, near Clarks, is a modern hotel with well-appointed air-con rooms for US$45/70.

Hotel Varanasi Ashok *(☎ 346020, fax 348089, The Mall)*, on the other side of Clarks, is a four-star establishment with air-con rooms with balconies for Rs 1600/2500 (Rs 1400/2000 April to September). It has a swimming pool, restaurant, a bar and a quiet atmosphere.

Places to Eat

Godaulia & the Old City The food in the old city is pretty uninspiring and standards of hygiene are not all that they might be. On the other hand, Varanasi is well known for its sweets and high-quality paan. The alleyways of the old city are full of shops offering ample opportunity to indulge in either. Places in the old city are not supposed to serve alcohol, though in one or two places you can get beer: it's served discreetly in a teapot! If you arrive during mango season, try the locally grown variety known as Langda Aam.

Ganga Fuji, not far from the Vishwanath Temple, is a snug place offering Western breakfasts and Indian, Chinese and Japanese meals for between Rs 25 and Rs 40, including nonveg. There's live classical Indian music in the evenings, starting at 7 pm.

Garden Restaurant is a relaxing little rooftop eatery with the usual travellers' menu. It also has veg/nonveg Indian food for between Rs 25 and Rs 60, though portions are quite small. Breakfast starts at Rs 15.

There are a number of eateries along Dasaswamedh Ghat Rd offering Indian food.

Yelchiko, by the main roundabout in Godaulia, is a basement restaurant serving standard Indian-Chinese-continental fare for between Rs 25 and Rs 55. The food is merely adequate, but you can get special 'tea' here for Rs 75.

Keshari, down a small alley opposite, is a clean, popular veg restaurant providing an extensive menu of meals and snacks. Main dishes are around Rs 35 to 60.

Temple Restaurant in the Hotel Ganges offers a fine 1st-floor view of the hustle and bustle of Dasaswamedh Ghat Rd. It serves good veg/nonveg Indian fare, Chinese food and Western breakfasts. Main dishes (which are 'very pleasing' according to the menu) are between Rs 30 and Rs 70.

A little way east is ***Madhur Milan Cafe***, a small but busy vegetarian restaurant with cheap dosas, samosas and thalis.

Traveller-style restaurants on Begali Tola, an alley south of Dasaswamedh Ghat Rd, include ***Chandan Restaurant***, a small eatery with an extensive menu (meals Rs 35 and under), and ***Baba Restaurant***, where you can really chow down on delicious veg/nonveg thalis for Rs 25/75.

Bhelpura ***Sindhi Restaurant***, by the Lalita Cinema, prepares a range of good Indian vegetarian food for less than Rs 40.

Even more popular is the ***Kerala Cafe*** *(Mandapur Rd)*, across the junction, which mostly specialises in dosas for only Rs 12 to 18. Their masala dosa is apparently the best in the city.

Bread of Life Bakery *(Sonarpur Rd)* is heaven for lovers of Western-style breads and biscuits. It also has a restaurant section with tuna burgers for Rs 65, plus breakfasts and baked potatoes. It's open 8 am to 9 pm (the restaurant is closed from 3 to 6 pm).

Vaatika Cafe, next to the Hotel Ganges View and overlooking Assi Ghat, serves reasonable versions of pizza and spaghetti dishes for Rs 35 to 50.

Train Station & Lahurabir There are several places to choose from in these areas. In addition to the places listed here, the ***restaurants*** in the Hotels Buddha, Shivam and Plaza Inn are worth visiting.

Most Welcome Restaurant, a cute little eatery near the Tourist Bungalow, has cheap veg/nonveg fare and Western breakfasts (between Rs 15 and Rs 40). It's a great spot – the service is attentive and lashings of food are served with a smile.

Poonam Restaurant, which is inside the Pradeep Hotel, Jagatganj, has good service and decent Indian, Chinese and continental dishes. There is also a very pleasant rooftop restaurant for hotel guests. Mains start from Rs 75/100 for veg/nonveg.

Kamesh Hut Garden Restaurant is around the corner. It has a pleasant garden setting and excellent food for the price. Indian, Chinese and continental dishes start at Rs 25 for veg and Rs 45 for nonveg.

Sona Rupa Restaurant, opposite the main post office, serves Indian vegetarian dishes. The dosas for around Rs 20 are popular. There's also a bakery on site. It can be hard to spot – it's downstairs and has a green door.

Cantonment Area Hotel restaurants are the best bet in this area. ***Canton Restaurant*** at the Hotel Surya serves good veg/nonveg fare, Western stand-bys and, despite its name, more Indian than Chinese dishes. The restaurant overlooks the hotel garden and a lazy breakfast on the lawn makes a great start to the day. Mains cost between Rs 40 and Rs 80; beer is a tad pricey at Rs 80.

Palm Springs in the Hotel India has excellent Indian cuisine. Dishes cost around Rs 100 but they're worth it. If you can order the Huggy Buggy without laughing you should win a prize. ***Palki Restaurant*** in the next-door Hotel Vaibhav is equally good.

Hotel Clarks Varanasi and the ***Hotel Taj Ganges*** are the places to go if you want to dine in style. Each has a choice of restaurants.

Entertainment

Varanasi is not renowned for its nightlife. About the only choice, other than the cinemas showing Bollywood fare, are the Indian classical music recitals. These are mostly held at music teaching centres (and cost about Rs 50), such as at the International Music Centre Ashram, south of Dasaswamedh Ghat Rd (between 7 and 9 pm on Wednesday and Saturday) and the Triveni Music Centre, near Panday Ghat (between 8 and 10.30 pm on Monday and Thursday). Major classical concerts are also occasionally held at Nagari Natak Mandali. Check the *Pioneer* newspaper for details.

Ganga Fuji restaurant also has music in the evenings.

Bars are few and far between in Varanasi. You could try the ***Basant Bar & Restaurant*** *(Chaitganj Rd)*. A bottle of beer starts at about Rs 65. Otherwise you're better off at one of the big hotels.

Shopping

Varanasi is famous throughout India for silk brocades and beautiful Benares saris. However, there are lots of rip-off merchants and commission people at work. Invitations to 'come to my home for tea' will inevitably mean to somebody's silk showroom, where you will be pressured into buying things. See the UP Tourism city map (free from the tourist offices) for addresses of government emporiums and 'recognised' souvenir shops.

There's a market west of the main post office called Golghar where the makers of silk brocades sell directly to local shops. You can get cheaper silk brocade in this area than in the big stores in the chowk area, but you must be careful about the quality. Mixtures of silk and cotton can look very like pure silk to the untrained eye. Pilikothi, a Muslim area north-east of the main post office, also has good silk.

It's difficult to give an idea of price as silk is worth whatever the shopkeeper can get for it, but as a rough guide, silk may cost from Rs 150 to 600 per metre; you can expect a discount of at least 20% off this if you are making multiple purchases. It costs about Rs 125 to 140 for a tailor to whip you up a long sleeve shirt or knee-length dress.

You can buy musical instruments at the Triveni Music Centre – see Courses earlier in this chapter. A sitar can cost from Rs 5000 to 30,000. Be careful of the type of wood the sitar is made from as it may change shape in a different climate, destroying the sound of the instrument.

Varanasi is also renowned for its ingenious toys and expensive Bhadohi carpets. There's a range of local and national products in the fixed-price Cottage Industries Exposition in the cantonment, opposite the Hotel Taj Ganges. The prices are high, but a visit will give you an idea of the relative costs of various items.

Getting There & Away

Air Varanasi is on the popular daily tourist shuttle route linking Khajuraho (US$80), Agra (US$105) and Delhi (US$125). There are also daily Indian Airlines flights to Mumbai (US$235). The Indian Airlines office (☎ 345959) is in the cantonment near the Hotel de Paris. Office hours are 10 am to 1 pm and 2 to 5 pm.

Sahara India Airlines (☎ 343094) has four flights a week to Mumbai and Lucknow and three flights a week to Delhi.

Bus Varanasi's bus station is a few hundred metres east of Varanasi Junction train station. It's a fairly sleepy depot and there's no timetable information in English. Buses lined up on the street out front are mostly faster, private buses. There are frequent express buses to Jaunpur (Rs 26, 1½ hours), Allahabad (Rs 54, three hours), Lucknow (Rs 120, 8½ hours), Faizabad (Rs 94, seven hours) and Gorakhpur (Rs 95, seven hours).

Buses to Khajuraho leave from the other side of the terminal and cost Rs 165. Buses also leave from here to Bodhgaya (Rs 91).

Buses to Sarnath (Rs 4) leave from just north of the Cantonment.

Train Varanasi Junction (also known as Varanasi Cantonment) is the main station. There is a separate reservation centre building on the left as you approach the station, but foreign tourist quota tickets must be purchased at the Foreign Tourist Assistance Bureau by the UP Tourism information booth in the main station building. This office is open between 8 am and 8 pm daily except Sunday.

Not all trains between Delhi and Kolkata stop at Varanasi Junction but most halt at Mughal Serai, 12km south of Varanasi. This is a 45-minute ride by bus (Rs 5), tempo (Rs 10) or autorickshaw (Rs 70) along a congested stretch of the Grand Trunk Rd. You can make reservations at Varanasi Junction train station for trains leaving from Mughal Serai.

Travellers should keep a close eye on their baggage while on trains heading to Varanasi. The tourist information booth at Varanasi Junction reckons hardly a day goes by without a traveller arriving on the platform without their backpack.

Nepal There are regular ordinary buses from Varanasi's bus stand to Sunauli (Rs 120, 10 hours). Plenty of travel agents and lodges offer 'through' tickets to Kathmandu and Pokhara (Rs 400). The bus leaves Varanasi at 8.30 am and includes breakfast and spending a night in spartan accommodation in Sunauli, and a change of buses at the border. Doing it yourself is not only cheaper but gives you a choice of accommodation and buses at the border.

It's not worth catching a train to the border since the line from Gorakhpur to Sunauli is metre gauge, though you could catch an express train to Gorakhpur and pick up a bus to Sunauli from there.

Major Trains from Varanasi

destination	train No & name	departures	distance (km)	duration (hrs)	fare (Rs)
Chennai	6040 *Ganga Kaveri Exp*	5.45 pm V	2144	41	262/1913 *
Delhi	2301 or 2305 *Rajdhani Exp*	2.35 am MS	764	9	–/1073 *
	2381 *Poorva Exp*	8.00 pm V	792	12	151/1088 *
	4257 *Kashi Vishwanath Exp*	2.10 pm V	792	17	151/1088 *
Gwalior	1108 *Bundelkhand Exp*	1.30 pm V	679	9	135/972 *
Gorakhpur	5003 *Chauri Exp*	12.00 am V	231	5	61/470 *
Kolkata	2382 *Poorva Exp*	5.00 am V	678	11	135/972 *
	3010 *Doon Exp*	4.15 pm V	678	15	135/972 *
Lucknow	4227 *Varuna Exp*	5.10 am V	302	5	77/– *
Mumbai	1094 *Mahanagri Exp*	11.30 am V	1509	22	221/1592 *
New Jalpaiguri	5622 *NE Exp*	6.35 pm MS	848	16	158/1138 *
Patna	3484 *Farrakka Exp*	3.20 pm V	228	6	61/470 *
Puri	8476 *Neelachal Exp*	8.10 pm V	1061	23	186/1340 *
Satna	5218 *Tilak Exp*	11.30 pm V	236	7	62/477 *

All trains run daily except:
Ganga Kaveri 6040 only Mon/Wed
Poorva 2382 only Mon/Tue/Fri
Poorva 2381 only Wed/Thu/Sun
Rajdhani 2301 only Mon/Tue/Thu/Fri/Sat
Rajdhani 2305 only Wed/Sun
Neelachal 8476 only Mon/Wed/Sat

Station abbreviations: V – Varanasi Junction, MS – Mughal Serai
* 2nd class/2-tier air-con

Indian Airlines has a daily flight to Kathmandu (US$72 plus US$4 tax), but it can be difficult getting a seat. If you're under 30, you'll get 20% off this price. If you can't get on the plane and don't want to experience the long bus journey, travel agents can arrange a car for about Rs 4.25 per kilometre; the 620km route to Kathmandu should take about 12 hours.

Getting Around

To/From the Airport Babatpur Airport is 22km north-west of the city. A bus runs from the Hotel Vaibhav in the cantonment at 10.30 am and 2.30 pm, going via the Government of India tourist office and the Indian Airlines office. The fare is Rs 30 and it takes around 45 minutes. If you bargain hard you should get an autorickshaw to the airport for around Rs 120 to 150. In the opposite direction, rickshaw-wallahs may charge much less since they assume they'll pick up a commission at the hotel where they drop you. Taxis will try to charge well over Rs 200 to the airport; from the airport to the city will cost from Rs 210, depending on your destination.

Bus Local buses are very crowded unless you can get on at the starting point. They cost Rs 2 to 5, but they're irregular and you need to be aware of pickpockets. A useful bus goes from Varanasi Junction train station to Lanka, which is close to Benares Hindu University.

Taxis & Autorickshaws For 'private' trips by taxi or autorickshaw you'll have to agree on a price since they do not have meters. You'll have a hard time trying to get a decent rate, but there are prepaid booths on the south side of Varanasi Junction train station. In theory, the booths should be staffed 24 hours. Some of the displayed prepaid taxi rates from there are: Dasaswamedh Ghat Rs 50, Assi Ghat Rs 64, Benares Hindu University or Sarnath Rs 78, Mughal Serai Rs 136. Some prepaid autorickshaw rates are: Godaulia Rs 25, Benares Hindu University Rs 30, Sarnath Rs 40 and Mughal Serai Rs 70.

Note that since the introduction of the booths several years ago they have not been overly successful and are rarely staffed, so expect to pay over and above these prices.

Shared Autorickshaw & Tempo These operate along set routes with fixed prices (Rs 3 to 5). They can be the best way to get around the city cheaply, although not when you have hefty baggage. From the stand outside the northern entrance of Varanasi Junction train station it's Rs 5 to the cantonment TV tower. You will find a stand outside the southern entrance for destinations including Lahurabir (Rs 5). Be warned, they may try to charge tourists at least double these rates.

Cycle-Rickshaw & Bicycle It won't take long walking the streets before you start perceiving yourself as transport bait for cycle-rickshaw-wallahs. Figures quoted for trips usually start five times the price instead of just double, and some rickshaw-wallahs in the cantonment are cheeky enough to quote prices in US dollars. In theory, a trip between the train station and Godaulia should cost about Rs 10; from the cantonment hotels to Godaulia should be around Rs 15 and to Lahurabir around Rs 10. However, these prices are what Indians would pay, and it is generally accepted locally that foreigners should pay more: expect to pay double.

SARNATH

☎ 0542

Buddha came to this hamlet, 10km northeast of Varanasi, to preach his message of the middle way to nirvana after he achieved enlightenment at Bodhgaya. Later, the great Buddhist emperor Ashoka erected magnificent stupas and monasteries here.

Sarnath was at its peak when the indefatigable Chinese traveller Fahsien visited the site early in the 5th century AD. When Xuan Zhang, another Chinese traveller, dropped by in AD 640, Sarnath had 1500 priests, a stupa nearly 100m high, Ashoka's mighty stone pillar and many other wonders. The city was known as the Deer Park, after Buddha's famous first sermon, *The Sermon in the Deer Park*.

Soon after, Buddhism went into decline and when Muslim invaders destroyed and desecrated the city's buildings, Sarnath became little more than a shell. It was not until 1835 when British archaeologists started excavations that Sarnath regained some of its past glory. It's now a major Buddhist centre.

Most of Sarnath's monuments are set in landscaped gardens, making it a pleasant place to spend half a day. The entry fee is US$5 (Rs 230) and you must pay an extra Rs 25 if you want to use your video camera. During the **Buddha Purnima Festival** in May, Sarnath celebrates the birth of Buddha with a big fair and a procession.

Dhamekh Stupa

This 34m stupa dominates the site and is believed to mark the spot where Buddha preached his famous sermon. In its present form it dates from around AD 500 but was probably rebuilt a number of times. The geometrical and floral patterns on the stupa are typical of the Gupta period, but excavations have revealed brickwork from the Mauryan period – around 200 BC. Originally there was a second stupa, Dharmarajika Stupa, but this was reduced to rubble by 19th-century treasure seekers.

The nearby **Jain Temple**, built in 1824, is thought to mark the birthplace of the 11th Jain tirthankar, Shreyanshnath.

Main Shrine & Ashoka Pillar

Ashoka is said to have meditated in the building known as the 'main shrine'. The

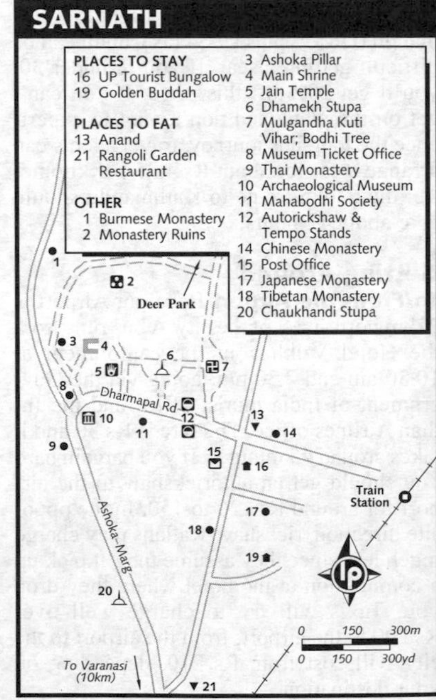

foundations are all that can now be seen, and to its north are the extensive ruins of the monasteries.

Standing in front of the main shrine are the remains of Ashoka's Pillar. At one time this stood over 20m high, but the capital is now in the Archaeological Museum, significantly shortening the column. An edict issued by Ashoka is engraved on the remaining portion of the column.

Archaeological Museum

The main attraction at this excellent museum is the superb capital from the Ashokan pillar. It has the Ashokan symbol of four back-to-back lions which has been adopted as the state emblem of modern India. Below this are representations of a lion, elephant, horse and bull. The lion represents bravery, the elephant symbolises the dream Buddha's mother had before his birth, and the horse recalls that Buddha left his home on horseback in search of enlightenment.

Other finds from the site include figures and sculptures from Sarnath's Mauryan, Kushana and Gupta periods. Among them is the (very fine) earliest Buddha image found at Sarnath, and many images of Hindu gods dating from the 9th to 12th centuries. The museum is open 10 am to 5 pm daily except Friday; entry is Rs 2. Buy tickets from the booth across the road.

Mulgandha Kuti Vihar

This modern Mahabodhi Society temple has a series of frescoes by the Japanese artist Kosetsu Nosi in the interior. A bodhi tree growing here was transplanted in 1931 from the tree in Anuradhapura, Sri Lanka, which in turn is said to be an offspring of the original tree under which Buddha attained enlightenment. There's a group of statues here showing Buddha giving his first sermon to his five disciples. The temple is closed between 11.30 am and 1.30 pm.

Organised Tours

The UP Tourist Bungalow runs six-day 'Buddhist Circuit' tours of important Buddhist sites in Uttar Pradesh and Nepal. Tours include Varanasi, Kushinagar, Lumbini, Shravasti, Allahabad and Sarnath. The cost is Rs 9000, including meals and accommodation, and there is a minimum requirement of two people.

In summer they also offer a range of one-day sightseeing tours, including Varanasi or Lucknow for Rs 400, which include one meal, a guide and transport.

Places to Stay & Eat

The ***UP Tourist Bungalow*** (☎ *586965*) has rooms with private bathroom for Rs 250/300, or Rs 450/550 with air-con. The bathrooms are clean (some have bucket hot water) and there's also a basic dorm costing Rs 70 per bed, and a restaurant serving the standard tourist bungalow fare.

Golden Buddah (☎ *587933*) has a beautiful garden and well-kept rooms. Doubles/triples with private bathroom and hot water geyser are Rs 350/450. There are also some dorm beds available.

Anand is a small, inexpensive restaurant serving Indian and Chinese food.

Rangoli Garden Restaurant is a larger place with inside and garden seating. Indian meals start at Rs 45 for veg and Rs 100 for nonveg.

Getting There & Away

Most visitors day-trip from Varanasi. An autorickshaw for the 20-minute journey costs Rs 40 (prepaid rate). Local buses depart frequently from the south side of Varanasi Junction train station (Rs 4, 45 minutes); they call at the Civil Court (Rs 3) in the **cantonment**, but they'll be full by then. Only a few local trains stop at Sarnath.

JAUNPUR

☎ 05452 • pop 160,000

This bustling town, 58km north-west of Varanasi, sees very few travellers but it is of interest to architectural historians for its mosques, which are built in a fascinating style that is part Islamic, part Hindu and part Jain.

The few travellers who come here tend to day-trip from Varanasi. If you want to stay, ***Hotel Amber*** (☎ *63201*), near the fort, has basic but acceptable singles/doubles with private bathroom for Rs 100/200. Checkout is 24 hours.

There are regular buses to and from Varanasi (Rs 26, 1½ hours). A few express trains connect Jaunpur Junction with Varanasi (Rs 25/173 in 2nd/1st class, 1½ hours), Faizabad (Rs 42/221, three hours) and Lucknow (Rs 61/321, six hours).

GORAKHPUR

☎ 0551 • pop 575,000

Most travellers happily pass straight through Gorakhpur on their way to or from Nepal. This is hardly surprising since the city is infamous for its annual plagues of flies and mosquitoes and even the local tourist office candidly tells visitors 'there are no sights in Gorakhpur'. The city is, however, the headquarters of the North Eastern Railway and is a useful train junction.

Gorakhpur is home to well-known Hindu religious publishers Geeta Press. A visit to their office will result in a pile of invaluable English-language books being offered to you with titles like *How to Lead a Household Life*. These make excellent presents to friends back home with a sense of humour.

Information

Tourist offices are at the train station and on Park Rd (☎ 335450). They're open 10 am to 5 pm Monday to Saturday and have a useful map of Gorakhpur and Kushinagar. The State Bank of India on Bank Rd exchanges only cash and American Express travellers cheques (US dollars or UK pounds).

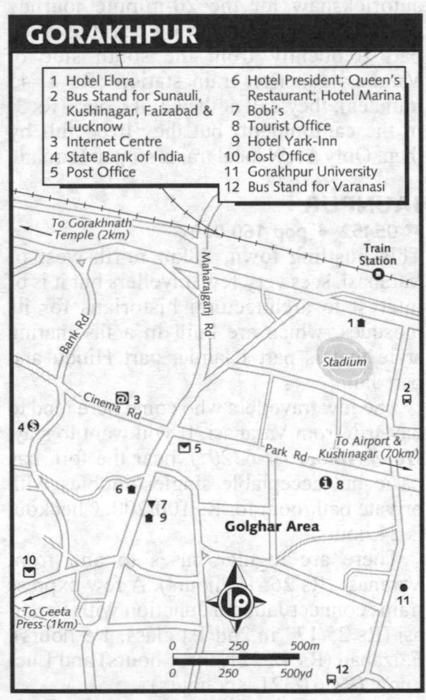

There is a group of Internet centres down an alley off Cinema Rd, around the corner from Hotel President. Among them, the Internet Club is the best. Connections are fast and cost Rs 35 per hour.

Places to Stay

The best places to stay in Gorakhpur are in the central Golghar area close to the few decent restaurants in the city, but none are particularly inspiring and all have bucket hot water. Checkout is typically 24 hours. It costs about Rs 10 to reach them by cycle-rickshaw from the train station.

Hotel Yark-Inn *(☎ 338233)* has a range of rooms with private bathroom and (usually) TV. Prices go from Rs 120/200 a single/double up to Rs 500 for a large air-con double.

Hotel Marina *(☎ 337630)* has clean rooms from Rs 170/195 with private bathroom and B&W TV, and air-con doubles from Rs 500. The cheaper rooms tend to be on the small, dark side and have squat toilets.

Hotel President *(☎ 337654)*, in front of Hotel Marina, has a lift but is a bit on the expensive side. It has clean, tiled double rooms only at Rs 350 with fan, private bathroom and TV or Rs 550 with air-con.

The hotels opposite the train station are the closest to the bus stand – handy for those early buses to Sunauli. Unfortunately, the area can be so noisy that you may not need to set your alarm.

Hotel Elora *(☎ 200647)* is friendly and the best of this bunch. Rooms at the back have balconies overlooking a large playing field and are sheltered from the worst of the noise. Singles/doubles cost from Rs 110/150 with private bathroom and TV and Rs 300/400 for air-con.

Places to Eat

There aren't many places in Gorakhpur so you could do worse than try the small ***outdoor eateries*** near the train station.

Bobi's at the Ambar Hotel in the city centre is busy and has decent veg/nonveg fare, including vegetarian pizzas (Rs 40), pastries and ice cream.

Queen's Restaurant in the Hotel President is also good. It's inexpensive, and has the added advantage of staying open until 11 pm – long after the rest of the city is safely tucked up in bed. Like Bobi's, it serves Indian and Chinese food.

Getting There & Away

Bus There are frequent buses from the bus stand just south of the train station to Lucknow (Rs 113, 7½ hours) and Faizabad (Rs 62, four hours). Buses to Kushinagar (Rs 24, 1½ hours) depart every 30 minutes.

Buses to Varanasi (Rs 95, seven hours) depart regularly from the Katchari bus stand, a Rs 5 cycle-rickshaw ride south-east of the city centre.

Nepal There are regular departures for the border at Sunauli (Rs 33, three hours) from 5.30 am onwards from the bus stand just south of the train station. You'll need to be on the 5.30 am bus from Gorakhpur to be sure of catching a day bus from the border to Kathmandu or Pokhara. Travel agents offer 'through' tickets (Rs 265) to Kathmandu or Pokhara, though you still have to change buses at the border. Doing it yourself is cheaper and gives you a choice of buses at the border.

Train Gorakhpur has direct train connections with Varanasi (Rs 62/326 in 2nd/1st class, five hours), Lucknow (Rs 70/368, five to six hours), Delhi (Rs 231/793 in sleeper/1st class, 15 hours), Kolkata (Rs 248/840, 18 to 22 hours) and Mumbai (Rs 366/1278, 30 to 34 hours, 1690km).

There are also metre-gauge trains to Nautanwa, which is 8km short of the border at Sunauli. It's much faster and more convenient to get to Sunauli by bus.

KUSHINAGAR

☎ 05564

Kushinagar is a peaceful, green town and makes a great respite from the chaotic larger towns in north-east Uttar Pradesh. It's a good place to kick back and take a break from the road for a day or two.

Buddha is reputed to have breathed his last words, 'Decay is inherent in all component things', and expired at Kushinagar. Now pilgrims come in large numbers to see the remains of his brick **cremation stupa**, the reclining Buddha figure in the **Mahaparinirvana Temple**, the modern **IndoJapan-Sri Lanka Buddhist Centre** and the numerous Buddhist monasteries here.

The tourist office opposite the Myanmar monastery is helpful and open 10 am to 5 pm Monday to Saturday, and some Sundays.

Places to Stay & Eat

Budget accommodation, either by donation or for a set fee, is provided at the Chinese, Myanmar, Thai and Tibetan monasteries.

International Cultural Guest House *(☎ 72164)*, opposite the Buddhist Centre, is simple, has 18 rooms and charges Rs 100 for bare, clean doubles.

Pathik Nivas *(☎ 71038)*, the UP tourist bungalow, is in a quiet, spacious garden setting and has good but overpriced singles/doubles with private bathroom and hot water from Rs 500/600 to Rs 1100/1400 (with aircon). Its pricey restaurant charges Rs 30 for a bottle of water.

Lotus Nikko Hotel *(☎/fax 71139)* is a three-star establishment popular with Japanese visitors touring India's Buddhist sites. It costs US$90 per person, including three meals a day, in the huge rooms, or Rs 4500 (including one meal) in the cheaper annexe which has simple four-bed rooms.

Yama Kwality Cafe, by the Chinese temple, provides inexpensive veg/nonveg fare.

Getting There & Away

Kushinagar is 55km east of Gorakhpur and there are frequent buses (Rs 24, 1½ hours) between the two towns (the last at around 6 pm). The Kushinagar bus stand is several kilometres from the temples and monasteries, so get off by the Kushinagar Police Post, and walk down the southwards turn-off for the temples.

SUNAULI

☎ 05522

This sleepy village straddling the Nepali border is little more than a bus stop, a couple of hotels, a few shops and a 24-hour border post. There's a much greater range of facilities on the Nepali side, where the atmosphere is decidedly more upbeat. Local Indians and Nepalese are free to wander back and forth between the two parts of Sunauli (without going through any formalities), others need a passport. Foreigners, however, must officially exit one country and acquire the requisite visa for the other.

The Nepali border post is actually called Belhiya but everyone refers to it as Sunauli. Nepali visas are available 24 hours (so they claim!) from the immigration office in 10 minutes. Visas cost US$30 for 60 days, payable in US dollars, not travellers cheques.

The easy-to-miss Indian immigration checkpoint is on the right-hand side of the road heading towards Nepal, about 200m from the border post.

The State Bank of India in Sunauli does not change money, but there are numerous foreign exchange offices on the Nepali side offering competitive rates. Note that you can pay for bus tickets and just about anything else in Indian rupees on the Nepali side of the border.

Places to Stay & Eat

Hotel Niranjana *(☎ 38201)*, one of UP Tourism's establishments, is a clean and friendly place with a garden, 600m from the border. It has air-cooled singles/doubles with private bathroom and hot water for Rs 275/350, some air-con rooms with TV for Rs 450/500 and a dorm for Rs 50. The restaurant serves unexciting but acceptable fare.

Baba Lodge & Restaurant *(☎ 38366)*, by the bus stand, is very friendly and has double rooms for Rs 150/250 without/with private bathroom. Dorm beds cost Rs 40. Prices are negotiable so try bargaining. The restaurant serves cheap veg/nonveg food.

Sanju Lodge *(☎ 38355)* is around the corner from the Indian immigration post. It's fairly rudimentary, but has pleasant common areas and a hard bed in a clean but crowded dorm costs only Rs 30. Rooms cost Rs 60/90 with shared bathroom and Rs 140/170 with private bathroom and hot water.

There are several good, cheap hotels, plenty of open-air restaurants and a sudden blitz of beer advertisements on the Nepali side of the border, where most travellers prefer to stay.

Getting There & Away

Bus Buses to Indian cities depart from the Sunauli bus stand on the edge of town, about 800m from the border post. There are plenty of buses to and from Gorakhpur (Rs 33, three hours) and direct buses to Varanasi (Rs 140, 10 hours) and Delhi (Rs 358, 24 hours), via Lucknow (12 hours).

If you're entering India at Sunauli, be wary of touts offering onward combined bus/rail tickets, since these are not 100% reliable. It's easy enough to arrange onward train travel yourself at the Gorakhpur or Varanasi train stations.

Nepal Private buses leave from the Nepali side of the border for Kathmandu (Nep Rs 240, nine hours) or Pokhara (Nep Rs 230, nine hours), roughly every hour between 6 am and 1 pm and between 4 and 8 pm. Travelling during the day is preferable – at night it not only takes longer, you also miss the great views on the journey. You should get a ticket in advance; there's a booking office at the Nepali bus stand. Travel agents on either side of the border also sell bus tickets, or can arrange a taxi (about Nep Rs 850, six hours).

Government 'Sajha' buses leave for Kathmandu from Bhairawa, 4km north of Sunauli, at 6.45 and 8 am, and at 6.30 and 7 pm. They're very popular as they're cheaper (around Nep Rs 185) and bookings should be made a day in advance. Tickets are sold from a kiosk near the Hotel Yeti in Bhairawa, on the main road from Sunauli. Catching a cycle-rickshaw from the border to Bhairawa costs only Nep Rs 3. There are no government buses to Pokhara.

Numerous buses ply the 22km stretch between Bhairawa and Lumbini, the birthplace of Buddha. They depart from the bus stand, which is about 1km north of the Hotel Yeti.

Uttaranchal

Formerly northern Uttar Pradesh, the new state of Uttaranchal came into being on 9 November 2000. Forged from the regions of Garhwal and Kumaon – known collectively as Uttarakhand, the Land of the North – Uttaranchal is a region of rolling hills and snow-covered mountains, divided by some of Hinduism's most sacred rivers. Most significant is the Ganges, which rises at Gaumukh in the far north of the state, and winds its way down to the plains via the pilgrimage centres of Rishikesh and Haridwar.

As in nearby Himachal Pradesh, the Himalaya is surrounded by extensive foothills, which are home to many popular hill stations, including Nainital and Mussoorie. Farther north, the high Himalaya beckons to trekkers and mountaineers. Garhwal, the western portion of the state, is more visited than Kumaon to the east, but both regions see more Indian pilgrims than foreign visitors, and most of these stick to strictly defined *yatra* (pilgrimage) trails.

Most important among the many pilgrimage routes which wind through the Uttaranchal Himalaya are the Char Dham, which mark the spiritual sources of the Yamuna, Bhagirathi (Ganges), Mandakini and Alaknanda Rivers. Closer to the plains, many visitors head for Corbett Tiger Reserve and Rajaji National Park, which are home to some of India's rare wild tigers and elephants. Yoga fans have been coming to Rishikesh to attend meditation classes since the 1960s. A few visitors also pass through en route to Nepal, via the little-used border crossing at Banbassa.

Except in budget hotels, you can expect a 10% tax to be added to your bill throughout Uttaranchal. Most hotels drop their rates by up to a third from August to March.

History

The idea of carving a new state out of overpopulated Uttar Pradesh had existed almost since Partition, but it wasn't until the election of a Hindu-nationalist BJP government in Delhi that the movement began to gain ground. The main factor that tipped the balance in Uttaranchal's favour was the allocation of government jobs and places in educational institutions to members of backward castes in the 1990s. Recognising a political opportunity, the BJP championed the cause of the impoverished but predominantly high-caste Hindu population of Uttaranchal, promising to create a new state and a whole new set of government jobs in the process.

After years of negotiations, the state was formally declared on 9 November 2000,

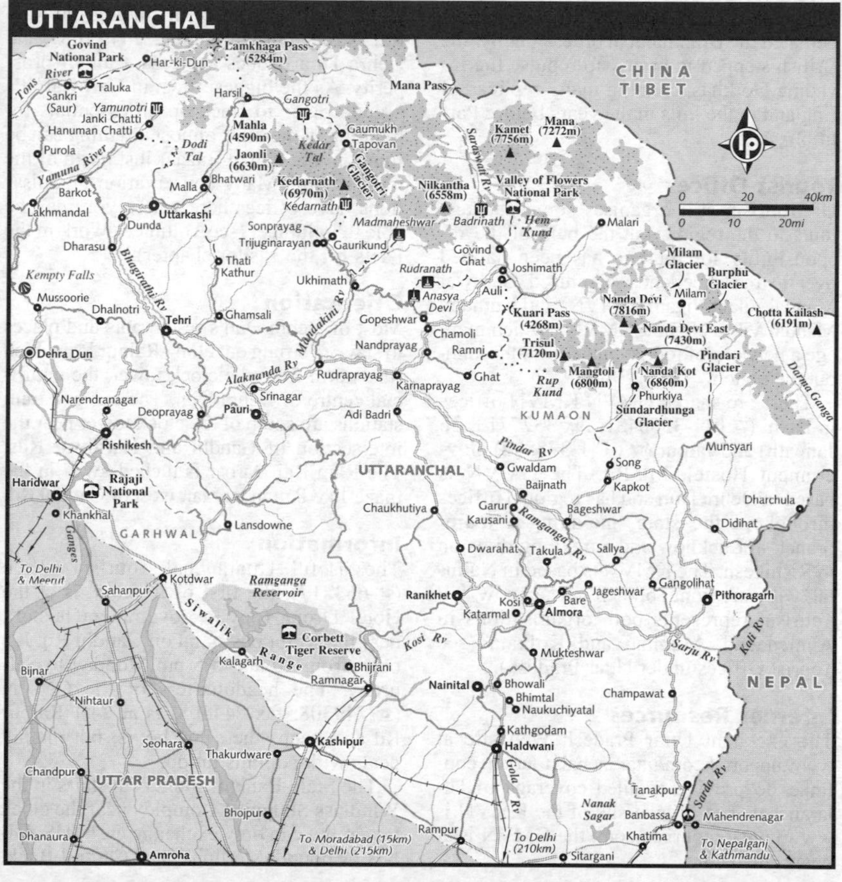

with its capital in Dehra Dun. However, the transfer of power to the new state government is likely to take several years. For now, some roles will continue to be governed from Lucknow until the relevant departments are established in Uttaranchal. From a tourist perspective, the most disruptive event is likely to be the creation of a new state bus company, scheduled for 2001.

The region of Uttarakhand was originally home to the Kuninda people, an Aryan group who practised a primitive version of Shaivism and lived a seminomadic existence, herding livestock and trading salt across the Himalaya to neighbouring Tibet. Many of their shrines have been incorporated in modern Hindu mythology.

Over the centuries, various dynasties dominated the area, including the Guptas, Katuryi and Chand rajas, all of whom perpetuated the Brahmanical order. Finally, the British stepped in briefly to repulse the invading Gorkhas, creating many replicas of England in the hills in the years before Partition.

Tourist Offices

UP Tourism still organises some package tours to the region, but the bulk of the responsibility for tourism has been handed over to the excellently organised Garhwal Mandal Vikas Nigam (GMVN) and Kumaon Mandal Vikas Nigam (KMVN), which manage a network of tourist bungalows throughout the region.

There are shared GMVN/KMVN offices in Delhi (☎ 011-3350481, fax 3327713, 36 Janpath) and Jaipur (☎ 0141-378892) Government Hostel, MI Rd. The GMVN is based in Dehra Dun and has regional offices throughout the state, including a major branch in Lucknow and a trekking division in Rishikesh. The KMVN is based in Nainital, with a regional branch in Lucknow. UP Tourism represents both organisations in Ahmedabad, Mumbai and Kolkata (see Tourist Offices under Uttar Pradesh).

Internet Resources

The excellent Uttar Pradesh Web site at www.upportal.com/uttaranchal/ tourism continues to provide detailed coverage of Uttaranchal. The official site of the KMVN is www.kumaontourism.com; the GMVN is at www.gmvn.com.

DEHRA DUN

☎ 0135 • pop 424,500

Now the capital of Uttaranchal, this old centre of the Raj is situated in the broad Doon Valley between the Siwaliks and the front range of the Himalaya. Although it's a historic town, Dehra Dun is probably best known for the institutions the British left behind, most notably the huge Forest Research Institute in the north of town. Other important institutions include the Indian Military Academy, the Wildlife Institute of India and the Survey of India. The prestigious Doon School, where Rajiv Gandhi was educated, is India's most exclusive private school.

The town is well served by buses and trains and many tourists just whistle through on their way to Mussoorie, Haridwar or Rishikesh. However, there are several things to see here, including the Ram Rai Darbar, built by Aurangzeb in 1687, and Dehra Dun exudes a pleasant air of prosperity. As the biggest town in Garhwal, it's a good place to stock up on essentials for trekking in the hills; almost anything can be found in the Paltan Bazaar just north of the train station. Many conservation organisations have offices here where you may be able to volunteer (see Volunteer Work in the Facts for the Visitor chapter).

Orientation

Most of Dehra Dun's restaurants and places to stay are strung out along Rajpur Rd, which runs north from the clock tower, the unofficial centre of Dehra Dun. The bus and train stations are south of the clock tower near the intersection of Gandhi and Haridwar Rds. The Ram Rai Darbar is tucked away in the maze-like Paltan Bazaar, west of Gandhi Rd.

Information

The useful Uttaranchal Tourism office (☎ 653217), the first of its kind, is at the Hotel Drona (now a government hostel), near the Delhi bus stand on Gandhi Rd. It's open from 10 am to 5 pm Monday to Saturday. The headquarters of the GMVN (☎ 749308, fax 744408) is at 74/1 Rajpur Rd and keeps the same hours, but mainly deals with administration.

The State Bank of India is upstairs in the Windlass Shopping Complex near the clock tower, but can only exchange cash (US dollars or pounds sterling). The Central Bank,

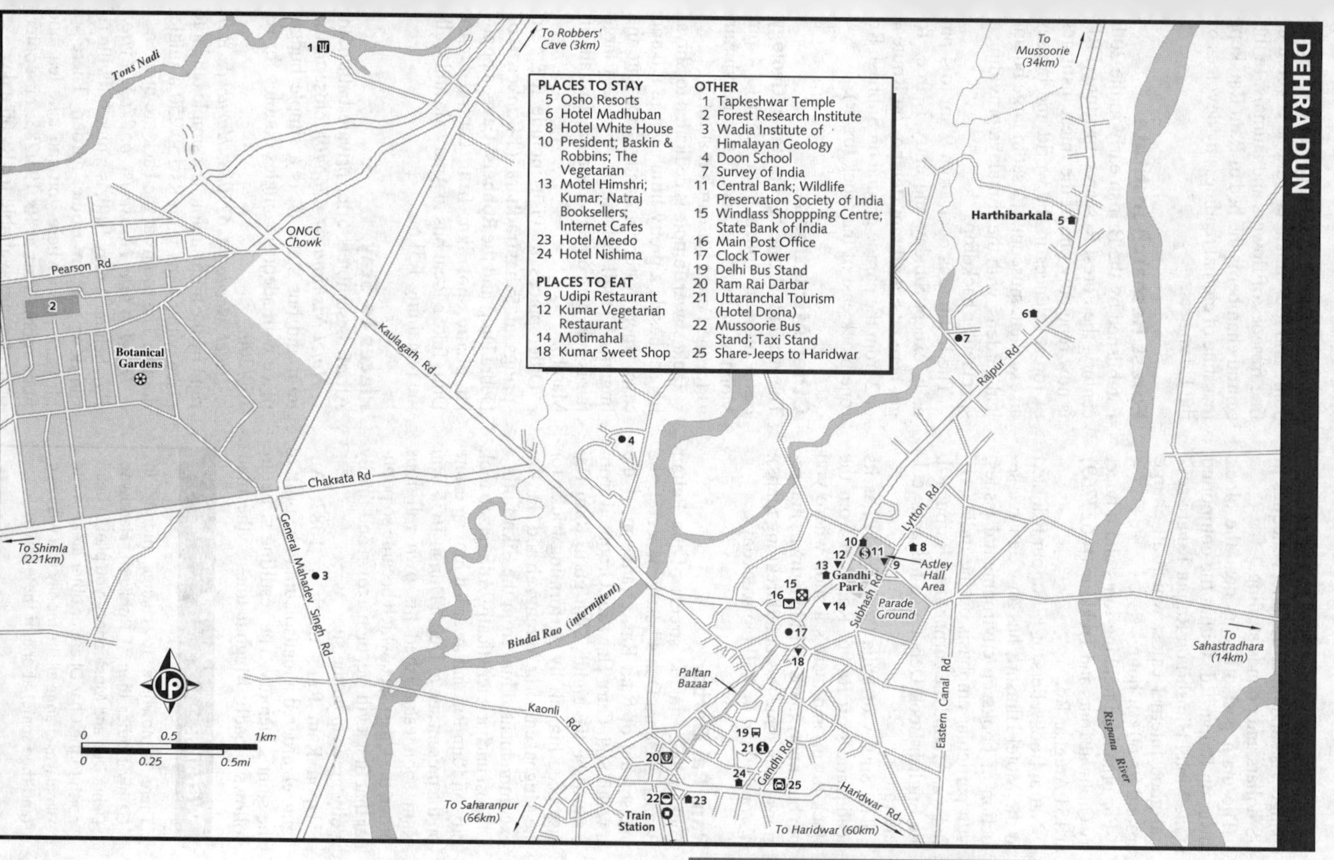
DEHRA DUN
PLACES TO STAY
5 Osho Resorts
6 Hotel Madhuban
8 Hotel White House
10 President; Baskin & Robbins; The Vegetarian
13 Motel Himshri; Kumar; Natraj Booksellers; Internet Cafes
23 Hotel Meedo
24 Hotel Nishima
PLACES TO EAT
9 Udipi Restaurant
12 Kumar Vegetarian Restaurant
14 Motimahal
18 Kumar Sweet Shop
OTHER
1 Tapkeshwar Temple
2 Forest Research Institute
3 Wadia Institute of Himalayan Geology
4 Doon School
7 Survey of India
11 Central Bank; Wildlife Preservation Society of India
15 Windlass Shoppping Centre; State Bank of India
16 Main Post Office
17 Clock Tower
19 Delhi Bus Stand
20 Ram Rai Darbar
21 Uttaranchal Tourism (Hotel Drona)
22 Mussoorie Bus Stand; Taxi Stand
25 Share-Jeeps to Haridwar
Tons Nadi
To Robbers' Cave (3km)
To Mussoorie (34km)
Harthibarkala
ONGC Chowk
Pearson Rd
Botanical Gardens
Kaulagarh Rd
Chakrata Rd
Rajpur Rd
Lytton Rd
Astley Hall Area
Gandhi Park
Subhash Rd
Parade Ground
To Shimla (221km)
General Mahadev Singh Rd
Bindal Rao (intermittent)
Paltan Bazaar
Kaonli Rd
Gandhi Rd
Haridwar Rd
Eastern Canal Rd
Rispana River
To Sahastradhara (14km)
To Saharanpur (66km)
Train Station
To Haridwar (60km)
0 0.5 1km
0 0.25 0.5mi

Astley Hall area, on Rajpur Rd, can exchange Visa and other travellers cheques in US dollars and pounds sterling.

The main post office is near the clock tower on Rajpur Rd. Within the compound at the Motel Himshri on Rajpur Rd are several good Internet cafes, which all charge around Rs 60 per hour.

For organised trekking tours and advice, try Garhwal Tours and Trekking (☎ 627769) at 151 Araghar Rd.

Natraj Booksellers, at 17 Rajpur Rd, next to the Motel Himshri, has an extensive selection of books on environmental issues, with particular emphasis on the Indian Himalaya. Around the corner at 15 Rajpur Rd, the English Book Depot also has an excellent range.

The Survey of India (☎ 747051) has its headquarters off Rajpur Rd, 4km from the clock tower, and there's a shop where you can buy many maps of Indian towns and regions (plus some low detail trekking maps). It's open 9 am to 4.30 pm weekdays.

Ram Rai Darbar

Tucked away in the streets of the Paltan Bazaar is Dehra Dun's best-kept secret, the mausoleum of Ram Rai, errant son of the seventh Sikh Guru Har Rai. Groomed from birth to be the eighth Sikh guru, Ram Rai disgraced himself by performing tricks for the Mughal emperor Aurangzeb and Har Rai excommunicated him from the Sikh faith.

Most uncharacteristically, Aurangzeb took pity on Ram Rai and awarded him an estate on the present site of Dehra Dun in 1675. Rai Ram soon established his own religious order, the Udasi sect, which became so popular that first a village, then a town and finally a city grew up on the site.

Upon Ram Rai's death in 1687, Aurangzeb ordered a mausoleum to be built to the saint's memory. The resulting structure follows broadly Mughal lines – the mausoleum is in the centre, topped by an onion dome and four minarets – and is covered in fine frescoes of flowers and animals. In the central chamber is the bed of Ram Rai, kept in a state of eternal readiness by devotees of the Udasi sect.

Warning

There is nowhere to change money in Garhwal other than at Rishikesh, Haridwar, Dehra Dun and Mussoorie. If you plan to head north to the Char Dham or other areas in the Himalaya, change all the money you will need (and then some) at one of these towns!

Forest Research Institute

Established by the British early in the 20th century, the Forest Research Institute (FRI) is now reputedly one of the finest institutes of forest sciences in the world and houses an excellent museum. It's set in large botanical gardens, with the Himalaya providing a spectacular backdrop.

The institute is open from 9 am to 4 pm daily except Sunday and entry is free. To get here take a vikram (tempo) on Route 1 or 2 from the parade ground on Subhash Rd (one block east of the clock tower).

Other Attractions

The **Wadia Institute of Himalayan Geology** has a museum (open from 9 am to 4 pm Monday to Friday). Take the same vikram as for the Forest Research Institute.

Tapkeshwar Temple is dedicated to Shiva. It's set beside a pretty little river in a damp cave, where water constantly drips onto the lingam. A small donation is asked. A large fair is held here on Shivaratri day (usually in March).

Other places to visit include the cold springs at **Sahastradhara** (14km east of Dehra Dun) and the **Robbers' Cave**, a popular picnic spot 8km from central Dehra Dun. Take a local bus to Anarwala and walk the remaining 1.5km.

Places to Stay

All of these hotels offer private bathroom.

Hotel Nishima *(☎ 626640)*, close to the train and bus stations, is a simple budget place with adequate singles/doubles for Rs 150/200.

Hotel Meedo *(☎ 627088, Haridwar Rd)*, right by the train station, is a simple but large place with rooms from Rs 150/250 a single/double. The rooms at the back are quieter.

Hotel White House *(☎ 652765, Lytton Rd)*, behind Astley Hall, is a nice old villa (if run down) set in a quiet garden. There's a pleasant patio where you can take tea, and huge rooms start at Rs 195/285; air-coolers or heaters are available for Rs 60 a day.

Motel Himshri *(☎ 653880, fax 650177, 17 Rajpur Rd)* is well located with ordinary rooms from Rs 325/395. Larger deluxe rooms cost Rs 525/625 (with air-con).

President *(☎ 657082, fax 658883)* at Astley Hall is a charming and tastefully decorated establishment. All rooms have air-con and TV and rates start at Rs 1100/1300. The hotel has a restaurant, bar and coffee shop.

Osho Resorts *(☎ 749544, fax 748535, 111 Rajpur Rd)* is a curious retreat belonging to the organisation of the late guru Osho. There's a good veg restaurant and free videos of Osho lectures. Fan rooms start from Rs 390/490 (Rs 790/990 with air-con).

Hotel Madhuban *(☎ 749990, fax 746496, 97 Rajpur Rd)*, the most lavish hotel in town, is on the way out of town. There's a minigolf course and a very good (and very expensive) restaurant. Air-con rooms start at Rs 1700/2500, with all the creature comforts.

Places to Eat

Kumar, an upmarket place near the Motel Himshri on Rajpur Rd, serves excellent chicken and mutton dishes for around Rs 75, and gives huge portions.

Kumar Vegetarian Restaurant, a few doors down, is the place for vegetarians.

Motimahal, one of the best in a string of eateries on the opposite side of Rajpur Rd, serves good veg and nonveg dishes in a pleasant environment.

Udipi Restaurant on Lytton Rd is a good South Indian place with air-con; *masala dosas* (stuffed lentil pancakes) cost Rs 80.

The Vegetarian by the President hotel dishes up inexpensive (Rs 30 and under) but tasty meals.

Dehra Dun is known for its excellent sweet shops. Probably the most popular is the ***Kumar Sweet Shop*** near the clock tower, which has a huge range of sticky sweet things for only a few rupees and great *kulfi* (Indian ice cream).

For 21 flavours of ice cream, the American chain ***Baskin & Robbins*** has a branch near Astley Hall.

Getting There & Away

Bus The Delhi bus stand, beside the Hotel Drona, serves destinations on the plains. There are hourly deluxe buses to Delhi from 6.15 am to 1.15 pm (Rs 202, seven hours). Ordinary buses also leave hourly until 10.30 pm (Rs 120). There are half-hourly buses to Rishikesh (Rs 20, two hours), until 7.30 pm, hourly buses to Chandigarh (Rs 95, seven hours) and buses to Lucknow at 1.30 and 6.30 pm (Rs 235, 11 hours).

Dehra Dun is also well connected to Himachal Pradesh. A bus leaves for Dharamsala at 12.30 pm (Rs 220, 11 hours) and for Manali (Rs 250, 13 hours) via Kullu (Rs 215, 11½ hours). Buses to Shimla, via Nahan and Paonta Sahib, leave at 6, 8 and 10 am and 11 pm (Rs 130, 10 hours). Buses for Nainital in Kumaon leave every few hours (Rs 180 to 200, 10 hours). For Ramnagar (Corbett Tiger Reserve), there are buses at 4.30, 6.15 and 7.30 am (Rs 135).

Buses for destinations in Garhwal leave from the Mussoorie bus stand near the train station. There are half-hourly buses to the Library and Masonic Lodge bus stands in Mussoorie from 6 am to 8 pm (Rs 22, 1½ hours). Uttarkashi buses leave at 6, 8.30 and 10.30 am (Rs 125, eight hours). In season, there are at least four morning buses to Hanuman Chatti (for Yamunotri), charging Rs 100.

Train Services to Dehra Dun, the terminus of the Northern Railway, include the speedy *Shatabdi Express*, which leaves New Delhi at 7 am daily and reaches Haridwar at 11.20 am and Dehra Dun at 12.40 pm. The return trip leaves Dehra Dun at 5 pm (Haridwar at 6.10 pm) reaching Delhi at 10.40 pm. The fare is Rs 495 for a chair car seat.

The *Mussoorie Express* is an overnight train service from Delhi to Dehra Dun. It leaves Old Delhi station at 10.15 pm, arriving at Haridwar at 6 am and Dehra Dun at 8 am. On the return journey, it leaves Dehra Dun at 9.15 pm, Haridwar at 11 pm, arriving at Old Delhi at 7 am. The fare is Rs 146/451 sleeper/1st class. There are also useful services to Varanasi, Amritsar and Kolkata.

Taxi Share-taxis for Mussoorie leave until about 6 pm from a stand in front of the train station on Haridwar Rd (Rs 70, 1½ hours). For Rishikesh and Haridwar, you can pick up share-jeeps a block east of the Hotel Prince on Haridwar Rd (Rs 20/30).

Reserve taxis can be hired from opposite the Delhi bus stand and charge Rs 350 to Rishikesh or Mussoorie, Rs 450 to Haridwar, Rs 1325 to Delhi, Rs 1500 to Uttarkashi and Rs 2300 to Hanuman Chatti.

Getting Around

Six-seater vikrams run on fixed routes. Routes 1 and 2 run from the parade ground on Subhash Rd (east of the clock tower) to Astley Hall and on to the Forest Research Institute, returning along Rajpur Rd. The starting fare is Rs 4. Autorickshaws refuse to charge less than Rs 25 to anywhere.

MUSSOORIE

☎ 0135 • pop 35,000 • elevation 2000m

The hill station of Mussoorie was established by the British in 1823. Perched high above Dehra Dun, and with the nearest railhead just 34km away, it became hugely popular as a summer retreat for the Raj set in Delhi and picked up a reputation as the place to have an affair. The ghost of this time lives on in several splendid old hotels and summer palaces.

The crowds from Delhi still storm Mussoorie every summer, but these days most of the visitors are young Indian honeymooners. More than 100 hotels compete for the lucrative honeymoon trade and dozens of photographers stalk Gun Hill, Mussoorie's highest point, offering romantic portraits against a backdrop of Himalayan peaks.

Low-season room rates are very reasonable, but many visitors find Mussoorie prohibitively expensive in the high season (May to July).

Orientation

Mussoorie consists of two settlements, called Gandhi Chowk and Kulri Bazaar, which are joined by the road known as The Mall. It's a pleasant 2km walk between the two. Buses from Dehra Dun go to either Gandhi Chowk (Library bus stand) or Kulri Bazaar (Masonic Lodge bus stand), so make sure you get the right bus, as The Mall is closed to traffic during the high season.

Information

There's a UP Tourism office (☎ 632863) towards the Kulri Bazaar end of The Mall, near the ropeway station, and a GMVN booth (☎ 631281) at the Library bus stand in Gandhi Chowk, both open 10 am to 5 pm Monday to Saturday.

The State Bank of India at Kulri Bazaar will exchange American Express travellers cheques in US dollars only, and Thomas Cook and MasterCard cheques in US dollars and pounds sterling only. The Trek Himalaya office may change Visa travellers cheques.

The post office is on the Upper Mall in Kulri Bazaar. In the arcade beneath The Rice Bowl restaurant, the Mouse Trap Internet cafe charges Rs 100 per hour (open till 8 pm).

Gun Hill

A ropeway runs up to Mussoorie's highest point from 10 am to 6 pm daily (later in high

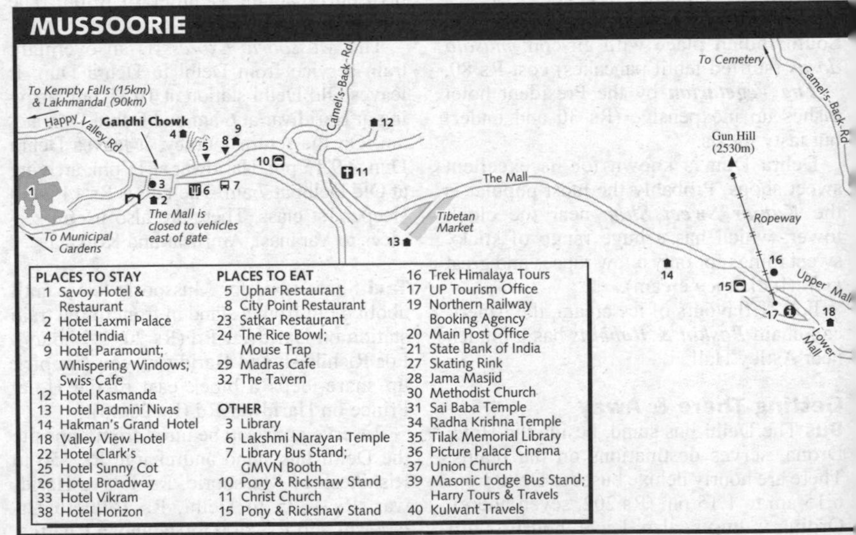

season) for Rs 30. From here there are views of several peaks including Bandarpunch. A steep path also runs up to Gun Hill.

At the top are a few dhabas and numerous photographers' stalls offering portraits in sequined Garhwali costumes for around Rs 50.

Walks

The walks around Mussoorie offer great views. **Camel's Back Rd** was built as a promenade and passes a rock formation that looks like a camel – hence the name. You can rent ponies or cycle-rickshaws (Rs 120/80). An enjoyable longer walk (5km) takes you through Landour Bazaar to **Childers Lodge** (Lal Tibba), another impressive lookout point, and Sisters' Bazaar.

Language Courses

The Landour Language School (☎ 631487, fax 631917) in the attractively forested Landour area has introductory courses in Hindi, with most classes held in an old Methodist church. The school is open between 9 February and 11 December. Private lessons cost Rs 70 an hour and group lessons Rs 45 an hour. Contact the principal, Mr Chitranjan Datt, Landour Language School, Landour, Mussoorie 248179. The nearby Hotel Dev Dar Woods (☎ 632644) offers discounts to students at the school (rates start at Rs 350 per night with breakfast).

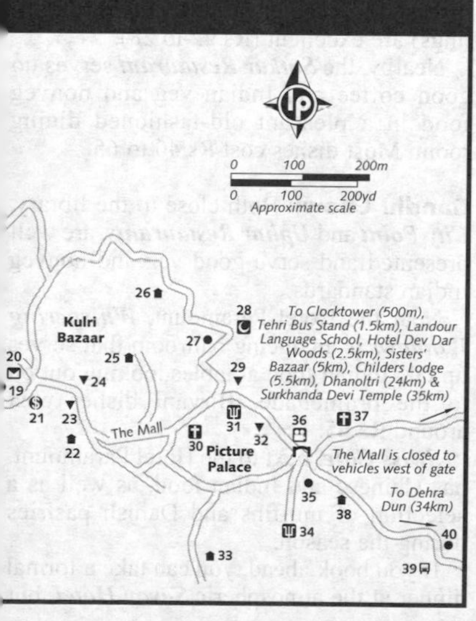

Organised Tours

The GMVN runs half-day tours to the most touristy Kempty Falls (Rs 50, three hours) at 10 am and 1 pm. Full-day tours to Kempty, Mussoorie Lake, the picnic site at Dhanoltri (with good Himalayan views) and the Surkunda Devi temple (also with good views) cost Rs 130 and leave at 10 am.

A respected trek operator is Trek Himalaya Tours (☎ 630491, fax 631302) on Upper Mall, which can arrange treks in the Garhwal area and farther afield. Harry Tours & Travels (☎ 631747) and Kulwant Travels (☎ 632717) near the Masonic Lodge bus stand can also organise treks, as well as booking air and train tickets.

Places to Stay

As with other hill stations, prices vary enormously according to the season. The rates quoted are for the high season (or rather honeymoon season!) from May to July. All hotels in Mussoorie drop their rates by up to 60% at all other times. You can also expect to pay high-season rates during the Christmas week celebrations and the Hindu festivals of Dussehra and Diwali.

Places to Stay – Budget

There are few budget places dotted around Mussoorie, but most hotels drop their rates to budget levels out of season. A double at any of the following hotels will cost around Rs 200 from August to April. They all have private bathroom, except where mentioned.

Kulri Bazaar The *Hotel Vikram (☎ 632 551)*, downhill from Kulri Bazaar in the alley beside the Tilak Memorial Library, has doubles from Rs 400 to 500. It's a quiet place with decent rooms and great views over the Doon Valley.

Hotel Sunny Cot (☎ 632789) is a friendly family run hotel on a hilltop with clean doubles for Rs 850. Take the alley leading uphill, just east of Hotel Clark's on the way to the Masonic Lodge bus stand.

Valley View Hotel (☎ 632324), on The Mall near the State Bank, is a well-managed place with friendly staff; clean rooms go for Rs 600 to 800 and there is a nonveg dining hall.

Hotel Broadway (☎ 632243), away from the centre on the road leading past the skating rink, is a friendly, well-kept place with some nice views, and is deservedly popular. Doubles cost from Rs 250 or there are a few singles with shared bathroom for Rs 150.

Gandhi Chowk Right on The Mall, ***Hotel Paramount*** *(☎ 632352)* has a variety of nice, small rooms from Rs 600 to 1500.

Hotel Laxmi Palace *(☎ 632774)* is a new place with clean, pleasant rooms and reliable hot water. The path down to the hotel is next to the arch on Gandhi Chowk. Doubles cost Rs 900 in season.

Hotel India *(☎ 632359)* is reached via the alley behind the City Point and Uphar Restaurants. It has simple doubles with private bathroom for Rs 600.

Places to Stay – Mid-Range & Top End

Most of Mussoorie's more expensive hotels are converted palaces from the Raj, and all offer TV, private bathroom and hot showers.

Kulri Bazaar The ***Hotel Clark's*** *(☎ 632 393)* has plenty of Raj-era character and boasts a billiard room with a full-size table. The well-maintained rooms are bright and spacious and cost Rs 850 to 1700.

Hakman's Grand Hotel *(☎ 632159)* is a great place for Raj-era nostalgia buffs. There's even a ballroom which once played host to stiffly formal British dances. Large dark rooms, which may not be to everyone's taste, start at Rs 750.

Hotel Horizon *(☎ 632899)* is a very good modern hotel with thick pile carpets, marble bathrooms, satellite TV and views across the valley. Doubles cost Rs 1400; there's a 40% discount in the low season.

Gandhi Chowk The splendid ***Hotel Kasmanda*** *(☎ 632424, fax 630007)*, uphill from Christ Church, was formerly a palace of the maharaja of Kasmanda. It has been beautifully maintained. There are acres of gardens and the rooms are decorated with pictures of tiger hunts and old lithographs. Rooms start at Rs 1400.

Hotel Padmini Nivas *(☎ 631093, fax 632793)*, 600m east of the library, once belonged to the maharaja of Rajpipla. The attractive rooms are warmed by the sun and ooze old-world charm. Doubles start from Rs 900, while well-appointed suites cost from Rs 1650.

Savoy Hotel *(☎ 632010, fax 632001)* is a vast British place covered with ivy and replete with faded touches of the Raj, including deer heads eaten down to the bone. Fittingly, it's said to have a resident ghost, one Lady Gore Ormsby, whose death allegedly provided inspiration for Agatha Christie's first novel *The Mysterious Affair at Styles*. Rooms (with three meals) start at Rs 1395/2295 single/double.

Places to Eat

Most of the better hotels have their own restaurants, and there are lots of good-value eating places in the Kulri Bazaar area. In the low season, restaurants generally close by 10 pm.

Kulri Bazaar The ***Madras Cafe*** is one of several veg places in Kulri Bazaar. It specialises in South Indian food, with the menu featuring 24 different types of dosa (Rs 10 to 30), plus plenty of *paneer* (cheese).

The Tavern, uphill from the Picture Palace cinema, specialises in Mughlai (nonveg) and Chinese cuisine and serves up some excellent dishes from the tandoor (clay oven). There's often live music in the season, but the restaurant closes down for the winter. Main dishes cost from Rs 70.

The Rice Bowl, downhill from Hotel Clark's, is a justly popular Tibetan restaurant that also rustles up Chinese and Thai dishes. The steamed mutton *momos* (dumplings) are excellent (Rs 22 to 28).

Nearby, the ***Satkar Restaurant*** serves up good coffee and Indian veg and nonveg food in a pleasant old-fashioned dining room. Most dishes cost Rs 40 to 65.

Gandhi Chowk Both close to the library, ***City Point*** and ***Uphar Restaurants***, are well presented and serve good veg and nonveg Indian standards.

Near the Hotel Paramount, ***Whispering Windows*** is an ageing ballroom that serves up OK Indian food at tables looking out on to the promenade. Biryani dishes cost around Rs 65.

Swiss Cafe, next to the Hotel Paramount, has Chinese and Indian food, as well as a selection of muffins and Danish pastries during the season.

If you book ahead, you can take a formal dinner at the atmospheric ***Savoy Hotel***, but only during the season. You may be rewarded with a glimpse of the ghost of Lady Gore Ormsby (who probably expired at the sight of the bill).

Getting There & Away

Bus Numerous buses leave from the Mussoorie bus stand (next to the train station) in Dehra Dun for Mussoorie between 6 am and 8 pm (Rs 22, 1½ hours). These go either to the Library bus stand (Gandhi Chowk) or Kulri Bazaar (Masonic Lodge bus stand).

Buses to Dehra Dun leave half-hourly to hourly from the Library and Masonic Lodge stands (Rs 22). For Delhi, there's a deluxe overnight service from the Library stand at 8.30 pm (Rs 172), and an ordinary express overnight service (Rs 139) from the Masonic Lodge stand at 8.30 pm.

Several daily buses to Hanuman Chatti (for Yamunotri) originate in Dehra Dun and collect passengers in Mussoorie about mid-morning at the Library bus stand (Rs 90, seven hours). For Uttarkashi and Gangotri, it's possible to take a bus to Tehri and change (the Tehri bus stand is a steep 45-minute walk towards Landour Bazaar), but you're probably better off going back down to Dehra Dun.

Train The Northern Railway booking agency (☎ 632846), at the Kulri Bazaar end of The Mall, has a small quota of tickets out of Dehra Dun, but needs 24 hours notice for bookings. It's open from 8 to 11 am and noon to 5 pm Monday to Saturday, from 8 am to 2 pm Sunday.

Taxi There are taxi stands at both bus stands offering identical rates to popular destinations in Garhwal and Kumaon. Destinations include Sisters' Bazaar (Rs 150 one way); Dehra Dun (Rs 350); Rishikesh (Rs 700); Haridwar (Rs 800); Uttarkashi, for Gangotri (Rs 1700); and Hanuman Chatti (Rs 3000).

Getting Around

The Mall is closed to traffic for most of the year, so to traverse the 2km between Kulri Bazaar and the Library area, you can either walk, rent a pony (officially Rs 20 per kilometre), or take a cycle-rickshaw (Rs 20).

AROUND MUSSOORIE

The most popular sight around Mussoorie is **Kempty Falls**, 15km north-west, which can be quite impressive but draws huge crowds. More peaceful is the trip up to **Dhanoltri**, a lovely picnic spot set among deodar forests 25.5km north-east of Mussoorie. There are great Himalayan views from the ridge. About 10km farther north is **Surkhanda Devi** temple, at a height of 3030m. The temple is a 2km hike from the road, and affords panoramic views of the Himalaya.

Altogether more interesting is **Lakhmandal**, 75km beyond Kempty Falls. This ancient temple complex features interesting statues and a stone sikhara-style temple dedicated, like most mountain shrines, to Lord Shiva. A return trip by taxi from Mussoorie costs Rs 1500.

Har-ki-Dun Valley Trek

Far above Mussoorie at an altitude of 3566m is the wonderfully remote Har-ki-Dun, a high-altitude meadow crisscrossed by glacial streams and surrounded by pristine forests and snowy peaks. The area is preserved as Govind Wildlife Sanctuary & National Park and foreigners are now charged Rs 350 to enter the region for up to three days (Rs 175 for subsequent days).

The trail begins at Sankri (Saur), accessible by a single early morning bus from Dehra Dun, where there's a ***GMVN Tourist Rest House*** with dorm beds for Rs 120 and doubles for Rs 360. From here it's a three- or four-day round trip to Har-ki-Dun; accommodation is available at Osla, but you'll have to camp in the valley itself.

HARIDWAR

☎ 0133 • pop 230,000

Propitiously located at the point where the Ganges emerges from the Himalaya, Haridwar is one of the most sacred cities in India for Hindus. Pilgrims flock here all year to ceremonially bathe in the Ganges, which at this point is crystal clear and very cold. The most interesting part of town is Har-ki-Pairi, the town's main bathing ghat, which is surrounded by a maze of shops selling religious paraphernalia. At dusk, the river comes alive with flickering flames as floating offerings are released onto the Ganges.

Within the spiritual architecture of India, Haridwar is much more significant than nearby Rishikesh, and there are numerous ashrams here where yoga study is possible, though most have extremely strict rules

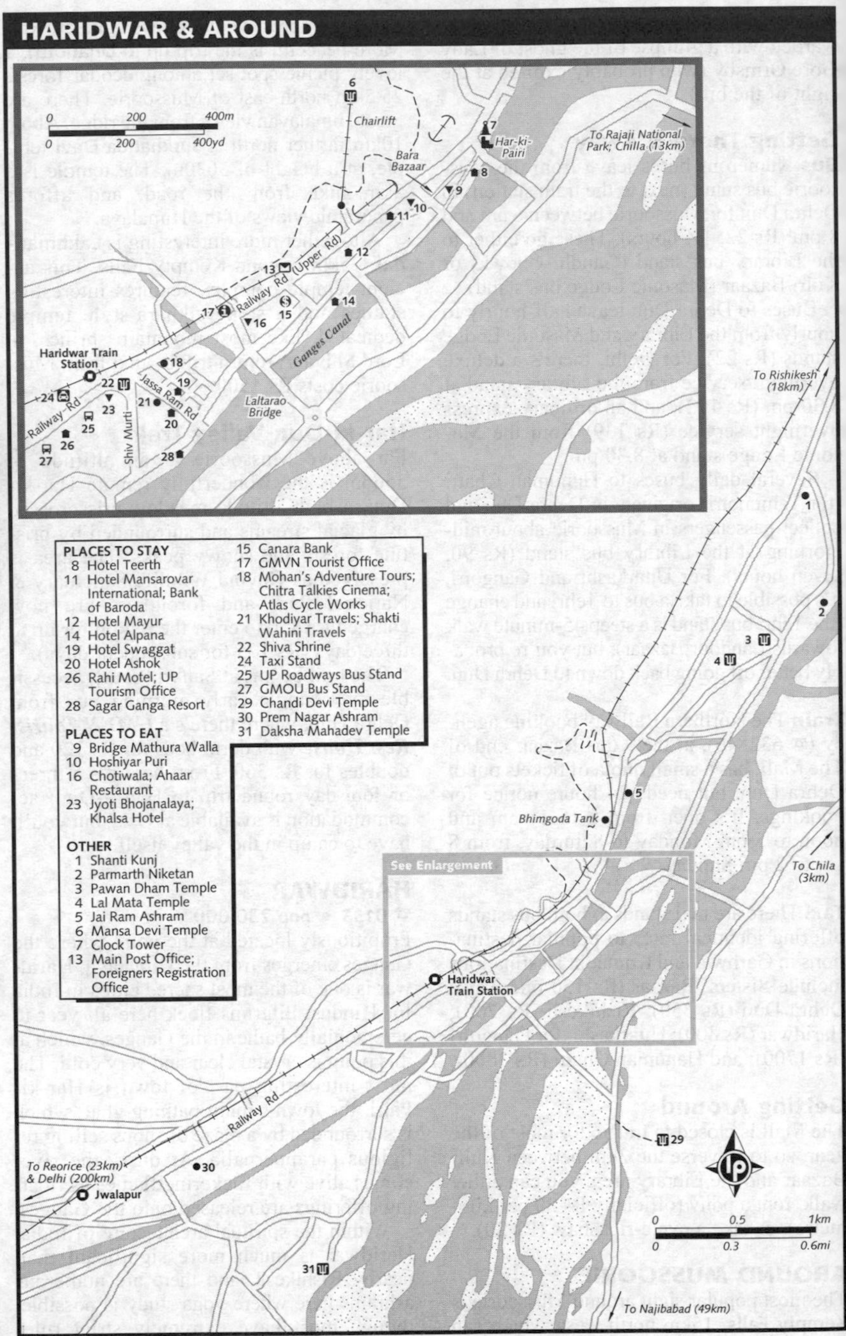

HARIDWAR & AROUND
0
200
400m
0
200
400yd
6
Chairlift
Bara
Bazaar
7
Har-ki-
Pairi
To Rajaji National
Park; Chilla (13km)
8
9
10
11
12
13
Railway Rd (Upper Rd)
15
14
17
16
Ganges Canal
Haridwar Train
Station
18
22
19
24
23
21
Jassa Ram Rd
Railway Rd
25
20
Laltarao
Bridge
26
Shiv Murti
28
27
To Rishikesh
(18km)
1
2
3
4
5
Bhimgoda Tank
See Enlargement
To Chila
(3km)
Haridwar
Train Station
Railway Rd
29
To Reorice (23km)
& Delhi (200km)
30
Jwalapur
31
0
0.5
1km
0
0.3
0.6mi
To Najibabad (49km)
PLACES TO STAY
8 Hotel Teerth
11 Hotel Mansarovar International; Bank of Baroda
12 Hotel Mayur
14 Hotel Alpana
19 Hotel Swaggat
20 Hotel Ashok
26 Rahi Motel; UP Tourism Office
28 Sagar Ganga Resort
PLACES TO EAT
9 Bridge Mathura Walla
10 Hoshiyar Puri
16 Chotiwala; Ahaar Restaurant
23 Jyoti Bhojanalaya; Khalsa Hotel
OTHER
1 Shanti Kunj
2 Parmarth Niketan
3 Pawan Dham Temple
4 Lal Mata Temple
5 Jai Ram Ashram
6 Mansa Devi Temple
7 Clock Tower
13 Main Post Office; Foreigners Registration Office
15 Canara Bank
17 GMVN Tourist Office
18 Mohan's Adventure Tours; Chitra Talkies Cinema; Atlas Cycle Works
21 Khodiyar Travels; Shakti Wahini Travels
22 Shiva Shrine
24 Taxi Stand
25 UP Roadways Bus Stand
27 GMOU Bus Stand
29 Chandi Devi Temple
30 Prem Nagar Ashram
31 Daksha Mahadev Temple

RICHARD I'ANSON

RICHARD I'ANSON

CHRISTINE OSBORNE

RICHARD I'ANSON

Top & middle left: In this fervently spiritual land, pontoon bridges support millions of pilgrims at the Allahabad Kumbh Mela and a holy man performs *puja* (prayers) at sunrise.
Middle right & bottom: Women at work and at prayer

SARA-JANE CLELAND

RICHARD I'ANSON

SARA-JANE CLELAND

At Varanasi, one of India's holiest places, the Ganges is the hub of life. On its *ghats* (steps) there are stalls selling offerings to the gods **(top right)**, pilgrims descending to bathe **(bottom)** and people drying off in the sun after an auspicious dip **(top left)**.

regarding silence and prayer. Every 12 years Haridwar is the site of the Kumbh Mela (festival), believed to be the world's largest religious gathering. The Kumbh takes place every three years, consecutively at Allahabad, Nasik, Ujjain and Haridwar (it last came to Haridwar in 1998), and attracts literally millions of pilgrims. The 2001 Kumbh took place in Allahabad. See the boxed text 'Kumbh Mela' under Nasik in the Maharashtra chapter for more information.

Orientation

Haridwar's main street is Railway Rd, which runs parallel to the Ganges Canal (the river proper is diverted around Haridwar). The road changes its name to Upper Rd north of the turn-off to the Laltarao Bridge, which leads towards Rishikesh. At the south-west end of Railway Rd are the tourist office, bus and train stations, while the Har-ki-Pairi ghat is about 2.5km to the north-east on Upper Rd. The very tight maze of religious shops known as Bara Bazaar is the most colourful part of town.

Information

Tourist Offices The well-informed GMVN tourist office (☎ 424240) is on Upper Rd, directly opposite the Laltarao Bridge. It's open 10 am to 5 pm Monday to Saturday. You can book Char Dham (the four great pilgrimage sites) packages here. For the time being, UP Tourism's regional office (☎ 427370; open 10 am to 5 pm Monday to Saturday) is at the Rahi Motel, west of the bus stand on Railway Rd. The Foreigners Registration Office (☎ 423980) is next to the post office on Railway Rd.

Money The Canara Bank on Railway Rd can exchange most major travellers cheques in US dollars and pounds sterling as well as dollars and pounds cash. The Bank of Baroda, next door to the Hotel Mansarovar International, gives cash advances on Visa, MasterCard and AmEx credit cards for a Rs 150 commission.

Post & Communications The main post office is on Upper Rd (Railway Rd) about 200m north-west of Laltarao Bridge. Slightly unreliable Internet access is possible at Mohan's Adventure Tours for Rs 2 per minute.

Yoga Centres Haridwar is a major yoga study centre with dozens of ashrams, but most offer formal tuition, with very strict rules regarding discipline, silence and attendance at prayer. Most travellers prefer to take the softer option of Rishikesh. Yoga centres and ashrams in Haridwar include:

Maha Prabhu Yoga & Natural Medicine Centre (☎ 425602) Kankhal
Parmarth Niketan (☎ 427099) Swami Shukdevanand Marg
Prem Naga Ashram (☎ 426345) Jwalapur Haridwar Rd
Shanti Kunj (☎ 426403) north of Har-ki-Pairi
Yogadham (☎ 424961) Arya Nagar

Har-ki-Pairi

Har-ki-Pairi (The Footstep of God) is supposed to be at the precise spot where the Ganges leaves the mountains and enters the plains. Consequently, the river's power to wash away sins at this spot is superlative and endorsed by a footprint Vishnu left in a stone here. Pilgrims hold on to chains set into the steps to ensure they don't get swept away. The ghat sits on the west bank of the Ganges Canal and every evening at sunset priests perform **ganga aarti** (the river worship ceremony) here, when floating lights are set on the water to drift downstream.

Non-Hindus were once forbidden to step on the ghat, but in a new spirit of friendliness, foreign visitors may now join the throngs of Hindu pilgrims. The price for this is a 'voluntary' donation which you will be approached for the moment you step onto the ghat. As well as official guards, Har-ki-Pairi has plenty of unofficial 'fundraisers' who will flash official looking documents and demand up to Rs 100 donation. In fact there is no obligation to give, though it's appropriate to make a small donation to the official guards.

Har-ki-Pairi is the centre of the Kumbh Mela celebrations (which will next come to Haridwar in 2010) and sees unbelievable numbers of visitors at this time. The Ardh Mela (next due in 2004) also attracts huge numbers of pilgrims. During interval years, pilgrims usually still gather from January to February for Magh Mela.

Between Har-ki-Pairi and Upper Rd is the very colourful **Bara Bazaar**. Along with the religious paraphernalia, or *prasad* (food offered to the gods, images of the deities, religious pamphlets etc), are scores of tiny stalls crammed along both sides of the bazaar selling an assortment of goods including *tiffins* (lunch-time snacks), shawls, Ayurvedic medicines (Indian herbal treatments), brassware, glass bangles, wooden whistles, bamboo canes and cane baskets.

Other Attractions

Pilgrims have been coming to Haridwar for centuries, but most of the temples here were constructed comparatively recently. It's worth taking the chairlift to the **Mansa Devi Temple**, devoted to Shiva's wife in her Shakti Devi form (appropriately 'The Inaccessible'), on the hill above the city. The path up to the chairlift is lined with vendors selling colourfully packaged prasad to take up to the goddess. Cable cars run up the hill from 8 am to 6 pm (Rs 25 return). You can also walk up 1.5km of steps (beware of prasad-stealing monkeys). Photography is forbidden in the temple.

Many visitors combine the Mansa Devi Temple with a trip up to **Chandi Devi**, erected on Neel Hill, 4km south-east of Haridwar, by Raja Suchet Singh of Kashmir in 1929. A similar chairlift operates here for Rs 50. Packages including both chairlifts and bus transfers between the two temples can be bought from the booking office at Mansa Devi (Rs 85).

About 4km to the south of Haridwar is the brand new **Pareshwar Mahadev Temple**. The temple houses a sacred lingam reputedly made of mercury. The **Daksha Mahadev Temple** (also known as Shri Dakheswar) is 2km from the centre on the riverbank at Khankhal. Daksha, father of Shiva's first wife Sati, refused to invite Shiva to a family sacrifice on this spot and the enraged Sati immolated herself in protest.

North of Haridwar on the road towards Rishikesh is the **Bhimgoda Tank**, said to have been formed by a blow from Bhima's knee (Bhima is the brother of Hanuman). About 150m farther north is the **Jai Ram Ashram**, which features pristine white sculptures of the gods and demons battling for the waters of humanity, and electronical displays from the Hindu epics. Other interesting temples in the area include the **Pawan Dham Temple**, famed for its fantastic glass and mirrorwork, and the **Lal Mata Temple**, a perfect replica of the Vaishno Devi Temple in Kashmir.

Organised Tours

The GMVN offers day tours which sprint around Mussoorie, Kempty Falls, Sahastradhara and Rishikesh for Rs 200. The GMVN is also the principal agent for Char Dham tours, which take in the four main pilgrimage sites of Yamunotri, Gangotri, Kedarnath and Badrinath. To cover all four temples takes up to 11 days, with accommodation provided in GMVN tourist bungalows, and costs Rs 5916. Tours run from May to November.

Every travel agent in town will also try to book you on a Char Dham trip. Most also offer day trips to Rishikesh (Rs 60) and Dehra Dun and Mussoorie (Rs 110) and expensive package tours to Rajaji National Park. Shakti Wahini Travels (☎ 427002) and Khodiyar Travels (☎ 423560) on Jassa Ram Rd are both long-established outfits. The undisputed Rajaji expert is Mohan's Adventure Tours (☎ 420910), by the Chitra Talkies cinema on Railway Rd, which offers day tours led by veteran guide Sanjeev Metha for Rs 1600 per day, including all fees.

Places to Stay

Seasonal rates apply in Haridwar, which means that most places are prohibitively expensive from May to July, and a veritable bargain from August to April. January and February also see large numbers of pilgrims. Rates given are for the high season and drop by 30% to 50% at other times. All have private bathroom.

Hotel Mayur *(☎ 427586, Upper Rd)*, near the chairlift, has basic singles/doubles for Rs 170/220 in the low season, and Rs 300/500 in the high season (May and June). Rooms have fans and geysers, and those at the front are larger.

The ***Hotel Mansarovar International*** *(☎ 426501, Upper Rd)*, towards Har-ki-Pairi, is relatively new. The rooms are a little plain for the money at Rs 500/600 (Rs 800/900 with air-con). There's a good restaurant (the Swagat) and major credit cards are accepted.

Hotel Teerth *(☎ 425311)*, in the heart of Bara Bazaar, is set right on the river, with great views over Har-ki-Pairi. Doubles are Rs 900/1200 with fan/air-con. All rooms have balconies facing the river, the staff are friendly and helpful and there's a restaurant.

Hotel Alpana *(☎ 424567)*, just south in the Bara Bazaar, is a swish air-con hotel.

Immaculate rooms with TV cost from Rs 1100 (Rs 500 in the low season).

Hotel Ashok *(☎ 426469, Jassa Ram Rd)* is in the area known as Shiv Mutri (near the roundabout with the Shiva shrine). It is a long-established place with budget singles with cold shower for Rs 150/110 in the high/low season. Doubles with hot shower cost from Rs 350/220.

Hotel Swaggat *(☎ 421581, fax 426553, Jassa Ram Rd)* is one of the better Shiv Mutri hotels. Clean modern doubles with TV cost from Rs 495 with fan and Rs 995 with air-con. In winter, the starting price for rooms drops to a very reasonable Rs 200.

Rahi Motel *(☎ 426430)* is handy for the bus stand and train station, but in a quiet location, and also houses the UP Tourism office. Air-cooled doubles are Rs 600 (Rs 900 with air-con) and you may be able to swing a Rs 100 discount for a single. The small dorm costs Rs 50 a bed. All rooms have colour TV and there's a restaurant.

Sagar Ganga Resort *(☎ 422115)* is a lovely Art Deco style lodge which once belonged to the King of Nepal, situated right on the river. Doubles cost Rs 750, and an enormous deluxe double costs Rs 1250. There's a lovely colonial-style dining room overlooking the Ganges.

Places to Eat

As a holy pilgrimage place, alcohol and meat are strictly prohibited and you won't find any of either in Haridwar. There is, however, a good selection of vegetarian restaurants.

Hoshiyar Puri, on Upper Rd near Har-ki-Pairi, has been serving thalis for over 50 years, and they're still good value. There are plenty of paneer options and a good choice of special thali, all with tasty dhal and *kheer* (rice pud).

Puri houses, right by the ghats, offer fast meals of *puri* (flat bread that puffs up when fried) with various veg curries for Rs 10.

Bridge Mathura Walla sweet shop in the heart of the Bara Bazaar has a range of sticky temptations for under Rs 10, including *ras malai* – a milk-and-sugar based sweet sprinkled with pistachio nuts.

Ahaar Restaurant, opposite the GMVN tourist office, has good Punjabi dishes and ***Chotiwala***, nearby, is a long-established South Indian place with good dosas.

Jyoti Bhojanalaya and ***Khalsa Hotel*** are superior *bhojanalyas* (veg snack bars) across from the train station. They offer veg standards such as *aloo gobi* (cauliflower and potato curry) and filling veg thalis for Rs 20 to 40.

Getting There & Away

Bus The UP Roadways bus stand (☎ 427037) is at the south-western end of Railway Rd. Buses leave every 30 minutes for Rishikesh (Rs 14, one hour) and Dehra Dun (Rs 26, 1½ to two hours). For Mussoorie, you'll need to change at Dehra Dun. There are ordinary bus services every 30 minutes up to 11 pm to Delhi (Rs 95, eight hours), and services to Agra every two hours or so from 5.40 am to 9 pm (Rs 149, 12 hours).

There are several early morning buses to Nainital, plus two night buses at 6.30 and 9.30 pm (Rs 135, seven hours). Almora buses leave at 5, 6.30 and 7.30 am and 4 pm (Rs 171, 10 hours) and Ranikhet buses leave at 6.30 am and 4.30 pm (Rs 150, nine hours).

Himachal Road Transport Company buses to Shimla leave at 6 and 8.30 am and 5, 7, 8.30 and 10 pm (Rs 179, 14 hours). For Dharamsala, a single bus leaves at 2.30 pm (Rs 227, 15 hours). There are also buses to Chandigarh (Rs 95, 10 hours) and Jaipur (Rs 207, 12 hours) – a superdeluxe Jaipur service leaves at 5 pm (Rs 368).

Heading towards the Char Dham pilgrimage sites, there are UP Roadways buses to Uttarkashi at 3.30, 6.20, 8.30 and 9.30 am (Rs 118, 10 hours). In yatra season, from April to October, the Garhwal Motor Owners' Union (GMOU; ☎ 426886) near the Rahi Motel has buses to Badrinath (via Joshimath) every few hours from 3.30 am to 2.30 pm (Rs 200, 15 hours). Buses to Kedarnath (Rs 150, 10 hours), Hanuman Chatti (Rs 190, 10 hours) and Gangotri (Rs 175, eight hours) leave between 3 and 5 am.

GMOU also has buses to Chilla (for Rajaji National Park) every few hours between 4 am and 1.30 pm (Rs 5). The last return trip leaves Chilla at 5.30 pm.

Train See Getting There & Away in Dehra Dun for details of trains between Haridwar and Delhi. Haridwar also has express trains to Kolkata (Rs 363/1592, sleeper/two-tier, 35 hours), Mumbai (Rs 380/1673, 40 hours), Varanasi (Rs 262/1149, 20 hours) and Lucknow (Rs 194/821, 11 hours). The most convenient train for Varanasi is the 6.15 pm *Varanasi Express*, which arrives at 6.15 pm the next day.

Taxi & Vikram The pricey Haridwar Taxi Union (☎ 427338), open 24 hours, is directly opposite the UP Roadways bus stand. Posted rates include Rishikesh (Rs 330), Dehra Dun (Rs 510), Chilla (for Rajaji National Park, Rs 410), Delhi (Rs 1510) and Uttarkashi (Rs 1510).

Shared Ambassador taxis to Delhi depart from near the train station and charge Rs 150 per seat.

Shared vikrams run between Haridwar and Rishikesh all day, charging Rs 15 for the hour-long bumpy ride. Drivers solicit for business near Laltarao Bridge.

Getting Around

You can get from the train station or UP Roadways bus stand to Har-ki-Pairi by cycle-rickshaw for Rs 15. Don't be tricked into taking an autorickshaw as motor vehicles are prohibited from Upper Rd.

Low-tech rattle-you-senseless bicycles can be hired from Atlas Cycle Works, Railway Rd, for an absurdly cheap Rs 3 per hour.

RAJAJI NATIONAL PARK

This beautiful park, covering 820 sq km in the forested foothills near Haridwar, is best known for its wild elephants, numbering around 445 in all. Unfortunately, their future is in question since human competition for land has severed their traditional migration route, which once stretched from here to Corbett Tiger Reserve. Plans for a migration corridor got as far as constructing an 'elephant tunnel' under the Chilla-Rishikesh road, but have since become bogged down in bureaucracy. Elephants are also threatened by the presence of Gujar tribespeople, who strip the trees for fodder to feed their buffalo herds.

As well as elephants, the park contains some very rarely seen tigers and leopards, chital (spotted deer), sambar (India's largest species of deer) and sloth bears, though most visitors report seeing very little wildlife of any kind.

The park is open from mid-November to mid-June and the entry fee is Rs 350 for up to three days (Rs 30 for Indians), and Rs 175 for each additional day. Entry into the park is not permitted between sunset and sunrise. Photography fees are Rs 50 for a still camera, and a staggering Rs 2500 for a video camera.

The village of **Chilla**, 13km north-east of Haridwar, is the only area which currently has an infrastructure in place for visitors. Elephant rides are offered in the morning and at dusk and cost Rs 100 (Rs 50 for Indians) and offer your best chance of seeing wildlife. These can be arranged at the Forest Ranger's office, close to the tourist bungalow at Chilla, where you also pay your entry fee.

About a kilometre beyond the entry gate is a *machaan* (hide), previously used by hunters, but now a vantage point from where visitors can unobtrusively view the park's inhabitants.

Places to Stay

***GMVN Tourist Bungalow** (☎ 01832-66 697)* at Chilla has fan-cooled doubles from Rs 590 to 720, while air-con rooms are Rs 1040. There are also dorm beds for Rs 130, and 'jungle huts' for Rs 650.

Forest resthouses, nine of them, are dotted around the park. Doubles at Beribara, Ranipur, Kansrao, Kunnao, Phandowala, Satyanarain and Asarodi cost Rs 225; at Motichur and Chilla, Rs 450. At these places (except Chilla) you'll need to bring your own food. For bookings contact the Director (☎ 0135-621669), Rajaji National Park Office, 5/1 Ansari Marg, Dehra Dun.

Getting There & Away

Buses to Chilla (Rs 5) leave the GMOU in Haridwar every few hours from 4 am to 1.30 pm. The last return trip leaves Chilla at 5.30 pm. Taxis charge Rs 410 return. It's also possible to walk from Haridwar; cross the Laltarao Bridge and walk to the roundabout, then turn left onto the Rishikesh road. The path breaks off to the right before the cable bridge and bears right over the dam, from where it's 5km to Chilla.

RISHIKESH

☎ 0135 • pop 82,000

In spite of its claim to being the 'Yoga Capital of the World', Rishikesh is a quieter and more easy-going place than Haridwar. The setting on the banks of the Ganges surrounded by hills on three sides is perfectly

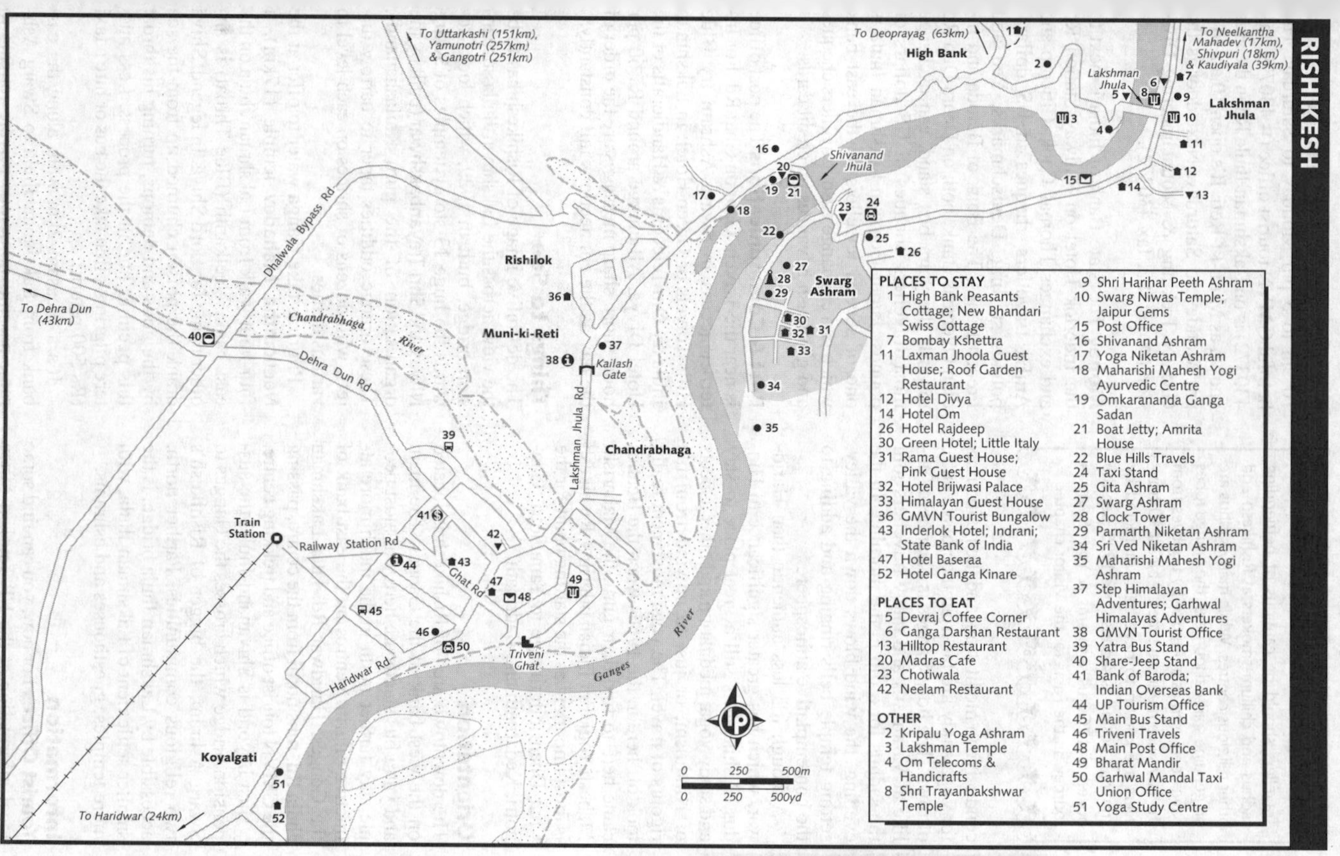
RISHIKESH
To Uttarkashi (151km), Yamunotri (257km) & Gangotri (251km)
To Deoprayag (63km)
High Bank
To Neelkantha Mahadev (17km), Shivpuri (18km) & Kaudiyala (39km)
Lakshman Jhula
Lakshman Jhula
Shivanand Jhula
Swarg Ashram
Rishilok
Muni-ki-Reti
Kailash Gate
Lakshman Jhula Rd
Chandrabhaga
Chandrabhaga River
Dhalwala Bypass Rd
Dehra Dun Rd
To Dehra Dun (43km)
Train Station
Railway Station Rd
Ghat Rd
Haridwar Rd
Triveni Ghat
Ganges River
Koyalgati
To Haridwar (24km)
0 250 500m
0 250 500yd
PLACES TO STAY
1 High Bank Peasants Cottage; New Bhandari Swiss Cottage
7 Bombay Kshettra
11 Laxman Jhoola Guest House; Roof Garden Restaurant
12 Hotel Divya
14 Hotel Om
26 Hotel Rajdeep
30 Green Hotel; Little Italy
31 Rama Guest House; Pink Guest House
32 Hotel Brijwasi Palace
33 Himalayan Guest House
36 GMVN Tourist Bungalow
43 Inderlok Hotel; Indrani; State Bank of India
47 Hotel Baseraa
52 Hotel Ganga Kinare
PLACES TO EAT
5 Devraj Coffee Corner
6 Ganga Darshan Restaurant
13 Hilltop Restaurant
20 Madras Cafe
23 Chotiwala
42 Neelam Restaurant
OTHER
2 Kripalu Yoga Ashram
3 Lakshman Temple
4 Om Telecoms & Handicrafts
8 Shri Trayanbakshwar Temple
9 Shri Harihar Peeth Ashram
10 Swarg Niwas Temple; Jaipur Gems
15 Post Office
16 Shivanand Ashram
17 Yoga Niketan Ashram
18 Maharishi Mahesh Yogi Ayurvedic Centre
19 Omkarananda Ganga Sadan
21 Boat Jetty; Amrita House
22 Blue Hills Travels
24 Taxi Stand
25 Gita Ashram
27 Swarg Ashram
28 Clock Tower
29 Parmarth Niketan Ashram
34 Sri Ved Niketan Ashram
35 Maharishi Mahesh Yogi Ashram
37 Step Himalayan Adventures; Garhwal Himalayas Adventures
38 GMVN Tourist Office
39 Yatra Bus Stand
40 Share-Jeep Stand
41 Bank of Baroda; Indian Overseas Bank
44 UP Tourism Office
45 Main Bus Stand
46 Triveni Travels
48 Main Post Office
49 Bharat Mandir
50 Garhwal Mandal Taxi Union Office
51 Yoga Study Centre

Wolves in Sadhu's Clothing

Travellers should be cautious of befriending sadhus and chillum-smokers at Rishikesh and other religious centres. While many sadhus are on genuine spiritual journeys, the orange robes have been used as a disguise by fugitives from the law since medieval times. At least 10 travellers are known to have been murdered by criminals posing as sadhus since 1995. See the boxed text 'Gurus, Ashrams & Your Spiritual Journey' in the Facts for the Visitor chapter.

conducive to meditation, and the main areas for yoga study are far from the noisy centre of town. The holy Ganges is clear here (unlike at Varanasi!) and many travellers join the sadhus for a dip in the morning. In the evening, the wind blows down the valley, setting temple bells ringing and adding to the contemplative atmosphere.

Although it's less authentic than Haridwar, which has greater significance to Hindus, Rishikesh is still a great place to stay and study yoga, meditation and other aspects of Hinduism, or just to unwind from the rigours of travel. The yoga movement really took off here in the 1960s when the Beatles came here to find their guru, the Maharishi Mahesh Yogi. For Indian pilgrims, Rishikesh is most important as the starting point for the Char Dham pilgrimage to Yamunotri, Gangotri, Kedarnath and Badrinath.

Orientation

The downtown area of Rishikesh is located on the west bank of the Ganges. The main and yatra bus stands are here, but most people stay farther north in the much more attractive pilgrim centres on the east bank of the Ganges. Haridwar Rd, later Lakshman Jhula Rd, runs north from the centre, passing the GMVN tourist office and trekking centre.

Just beyond is Shivanand Jhula, the suspension bridge which crosses the Ganges to Swarg Ashram, the bigger of Rishikesh's two religious communities. Farther north, accessible by Lakshman Jhula bridge, is the smaller settlement of Lakshman Jhula, with more temples, guesthouses and ashrams.

Information

Tourist Offices For now, you can find some local information at the UP Tourism office (☎ 430209) on Railway Station Rd. It's open 10 am to 5 pm Monday to Saturday. The helpful GMVN tourist office (☎ 430799, fax 430372) is on Lakshman Jhula Rd in the area known as Muni-ki-Reti. It's open 10 am to 5 pm Monday to Saturday. Next door is the GMVN Trekking & Mountaineering Division (☎ 431793, fax 430372).

Money The State Bank of India is next to the Inderlok Hotel on Railway Station Rd and exchanges Thomas Cook, Citicorp and AmEx travellers cheques in US dollars, pounds sterling, Deutschmarks, Yen and French francs. The Bank of Baroda and Indian Overseas Bank, both on Dehra Dun Rd towards the yatra bus stand, can exchange most travellers cheques in US dollars or pounds. Jaipur Gems in Lakshman Jhula is one of several jewellers on the east bank which can exchange cash, travellers cheques and give cash advances on credit cards.

Post & Communications The post office is near the Triveni Ghat on Ghat Rd. For Internet access in Swarg Ashram try Blue Hills Travels or Green Hotel; in Lakshman Jhula try Om Telecoms & Handicrafts or the Hotel Divya. All charge around Rs 60 per hour; short, sharp messages are the order of the day as the connections fail constantly.

Things to See

The definitive image of Rishikesh has to be the view across the Lakshman Jhula suspension bridge, built in 1929, which looks towards the huge 13-storey temples of **Swarg Niwas** and **Shri Trayanbakshwar** (built by the organisation of the guru Kailashanand). These orange oddities taper to narrow turrets, with dozens of shrines on each level to various deities.

Pilgrims take Ganga water to offer at the **Neelkantha Mahadev** temple (17km), a four-hour walk from Lakshman Jhula on the east bank. Neelkanth (Blue Throat) is another name for Lord Shiva. In legend, Shiva drank the poison churned up from the sea by the gods and demons, turning his throat this peculiar hue in the process. Less austere pilgrims often take the bus or hire a taxi (Rs 500 return).

It's a pleasant 2km walk along the east bank from Lakshman Jhula to Swarg Ashram, passing numerous private retreats in he woods. Swarg (which means heaven) Ashram is home to many vast yoga ashrams, with colourful murals and statues depicting scenes from the epics. The most flamboyant are **Parmarth Niketan Ashram**, which features a ghat topped by a sculpted arch, and **Swarg Ashram** itself, with many religious paintings and attractive gardens.

In downtown Rishikesh, the **Triveni Ghat** is an interesting place to be at dawn, when people make offerings of milk to the river and feed the huge fish. After sunset, priests set floating lamps on the water in the *ganga aarti* ceremony. Nearby is the **Bharat Mandir**, the oldest temple here.

Trekking

The GMVN Trekking & Mountaineering Division (☎ 431793, fax 430372) is next to the GMVN tourist office and offers various high- and low-altitude treks in the Garhwal Himalaya. You can hire tents, rucksacks, sleeping bags and cooking equipment at very reasonable rates. For all-inclusive trekking packages, rates start at Rs 2200 per day (minimum three persons). Otherwise, it's Rs 600 per day for a guide and Rs 250 to 550 for a porter. Possible summer destinations include Har-ki-Dun (nine days) and the Valley of Flowers (eight days).

In the vicinity of the GMVN are private operators who offer similar trekking trips and expeditions. Reliable operators include Step Himalayan Adventures (☎ 432581, fax 431558) and Garhwal Himalayas Adventures (☎ 433478, fax 431654).

Rafting & Other Activities

Blue Hills Travels (☎ 436179) in Swarg Ashram is the most popular rafting operator with travellers and charges Rs 300 for a day's rafting on the Ganges near Shivpuri, 18km from Rishikesh. The GMVN Rafting Resort (☎ 01378-62911) in Kaudiyala offers similar packages for Rs 350 per 'patch' (12km stretch) of the Ganges. Lodging is available for Rs 350 to 500 a double. You can book at the GMVN tourist office. Step Himalayan Adventures and Garhwal Himalayas Adventures can also organise rafting for Rs 350 to 450.

Meditation & Yoga Courses

There are many ashrams offering courses in meditation, yoga and Hindu philosophy. Some of the more reputable ashrams are included here, but ask around and you'll probably hear of others that are just as good.

Swarg Ashram & Koyalgati Close to the south-eastern end of Shivanand Jhula is the lavishly decorated **Parmarth Niketan Ashram** (☎ 434301), which offers daily classes in the hatha form of yoga at 7.30 am and 3.30 pm (classes are by donation). There's also a popular ganga aarti ritual on the riverside every evening at 5 pm.

East of Swarg Ashram is the extensive **Gita Ashram** (☎ 431998), which offers classes in hatha yoga at 7.30 and 9.15 am and 4 and 5.30 pm. Classes are by donation; inquire at the bookshop by the gatehouse for more information.

The huge **Sri Ved Niketan Ashram** (☎ 430 279) at the southern end of Swarg Ashram offers two-week or one-month courses in hatha yoga. Classes take place at 8 am and 6.30 and 9 pm daily except Sunday and cost Rs 100 per day. Accommodation is available in large but very spartan singles/doubles with hard beds for Rs 60/150 with private bathroom (bucket hot water) and Rs 50/120 with shared bathroom.

On Lakshman Jhula Rd, close to the western end of Shivanand Jhula, **Omkarananda Ganga Sadan** (☎ 431473) offers hatha yoga classes during the summer season at 7 am and 4 pm daily. Registration costs Rs 25, and a small fee is levied per class. Comfortable rooms with hot shower are available for Rs 175 to 250. Call ahead to check the current schedule.

Near Shivanand Jhula, **Shivanand Ashram** (☎ 430040) was founded by Swami Shivananda and is under the auspices of the Divine Life Society. There are yoga classes daily, with courses from three days to two months (all free). Two months' notice is required if you want to stay here: write to the Divine Life Society, PO Shivanandanagar 249192, District Tehri, Garhwal, Uttaranchal.

Close by, reached along a path leading up from Lakshman Jhula Rd and set in lovely gardens high above the Ganges, is the **Yoga Niketan Ashram** (☎ 430227). Classes on meditation and the pranayama form of hatha yoga are held throughout the year, although you must stay for a minimum of 15 days. The cost is Rs 225 per day, including basic accommodation.

South of Rishikesh on the Haridwar Rd, the well-regarded **Yoga Study Centre** (☎ 431 196) at Koyalgati runs three-week courses in the iyengar form of hatha yoga during February, April and September for beginners, intermediate and advanced students. Payment is by donation and accommodation can be arranged.

Lakshman Jhula Area Close to the eastern end of the Lakshman Jhula suspension bridge is the **Shri Harihar Peeth Ashram** (☎ 431182). This peaceful old complex offers hatha yoga classes at 7 am and 5 pm daily for Rs 50 per class. People studying here can stay in simple rooms with shared bathroom for Rs 50.

Popular with Italians, the **Kripalu Yoga Ashram** (☎ 430599) is a five-minute walk uphill from Lakshman Jhula on the road to Rishikesh. There are 10-day courses in hatha yoga with classes at 10 am and 4 pm daily for Rs 1000. Additional classes after this time cost Rs 50 per day. Accommodation at this relaxed centre costs from Rs 90/150 to 100/175 for a single/double.

Yoga

The most commonly practised form of yoga is the hatha system, which uses a series of body positions, breathing exercises and movements to increase physical and mental health. The main techniques of hatha yoga are asanas (fixed body positions), kriyas (movements designed to increase circulation) and mudras (exercises designed to promote secretions from the major endocrine glands). The goal of hatha is to cleanse and purge all the body organs.

Also important to hatha are the breathing exercises of pranayama yoga. Physical exercises are used to relax the lungs in order to achieve higher mental states required for meditation. The peak of yoga practise involves the arousal and control of the kundalini shakti, a vital force believed to lie dormant in the conus medullaris at the base of the spine.

The classes on offer in Rishikesh usually involve basic hatha techniques and pranayama exercises. Most centres offer a choice of day-by-day tuition or long-term residential study, but many foreigners report difficulties in finding one that satisfies them. Some have extremely rigid rules, some only accept people for long-term study, and some see foreigners as the source of a quick buck. It's worth going to a few lectures at different ashrams before you commit to a course.

Special Events

The **International Yoga Festival**, arranged by UP Tourism, is held annually in February. Yoga and meditation masters from around India converge on Rishikesh. Seven-day packages including meals, accommodation, transport from your hotel to venues, lectures and air-con deluxe coaches between Delhi and Rishikesh cost US$40/60 a single/double in ashram accommodation and US$60/100 in hotel accommodation. Bookings should be made at least two months in advance to the Director (☎ 0522-228349, fax 221776), UP Tourism, Chitrahar Bldg, 3 Naval Kishor Rd, Lucknow.

Organised Tours

As the principal leaping-off point for Char Dham pilgrimages, Rishikesh is very well equipped with travel agents offering package tours to the temples. The biggest and most reliable operator is the GMVN, which has a huge range of packages covering one, two, three or all four temples. The full Char Dham takes 10 days and costs Rs 5800 (Rs 8645 by taxi), while just Badrinath and Kedarnath costs Rs 3300 by bus (Rs 5222 by taxi) and takes six days. Prices include shared accommodation in GMVN tourist bungalows, but not meals. In winter, skiing packages to Auli near Joshimath can also be arranged.

Places to Stay

Swarg Ashram Area Centred around the huge Swarg Ashram on the east bank of the Ganges, this is the main centre for both pilgrims and travellers.

Green Hotel *(☎ 431242)*, a long-running establishment, is down a lane off the riverside path and has very clean downstairs doubles for Rs 125 (bucket hot water) and more spacious doubles upstairs with running hot water for Rs 250. The restaurant here serves great pizzas.

Hotel Brijwasi Palace *(☎ 435181)*, on the alley parallel to the riverside path, is a large modern place with a garden and perfectly OK singles/doubles for Rs 100/120 with bucket hot water. There are yoga classes at 10 am and 4 pm for Rs 50.

Himalayan Guest House *(☎ 435507)*, in the same maze of alleys, is popular but basic, with rooms for Rs 80 or Rs 120 upstairs with private bathroom. Yoga meditation sessions take place at 8 am and 4.30 pm.

Rama Guest House and ***Pink Guest House***, nearby, have tiny spartan rooms for Rs 40 upwards, which is about right for what you get.

Hotel Rajdeep *(☎ 432826, fax 433109)* is north of the bridge, on the lane that leads uphill from the taxi stand. Standard singles/doubles cost Rs 125/200 (bucket hot water), or there are better doubles with hot water for Rs 350, or Rs 925 with air-con. There's a travel desk and occasional yoga classes.

High Bank This small enclave on the west bank, high above the Ganges, has several peaceful retreats. Take the road to the left, 1km before Lakshman Jhula.

High Bank Peasants Cottage *(☎ 431167)* is family run and set in beautiful flower gardens and has a friendly communal atmosphere. Rooms start at Rs 300/350 with private bathroom (free bucket hot water), and the balcony has wicker chairs where you can sit and contemplate the Ganges.

New Bhandari Swiss Cottage *(☎ 431322)* is well run with large, pleasant rooms for Rs 100 with cold shower, or Rs 150 to 250 with hot water, plus a cafe and an Internet cafe. There's a quiet garden for relaxing and great views from the balcony.

Lakshman Jhula Many long-term residents now feel that Swarg Ashram is too commercial and have pulled back to this quieter settlement farther north. The best choices are all on the east bank.

Bombay Kshettra, just north of the bridge, is an atmospheric, colourful old building with rooms ranging from Rs 80 to 100, depending on the size, all with shared bathroom, and set around a pleasant courtyard.

Hotel Divya *(☎ 434938)* is a popular well-run modern place uphill from the road, with simple but clean rooms for Rs 150 with a view or Rs 100 at the back. All rooms have hot water bathroom and there's an Internet cafe and restaurant.

Laxman Jhoola Guest House *(☎ 435720)*, in the same area, has spartan but tidy rooms with private bathroom for Rs 100/150, as well as the friendly ***Roof Garden Restaurant***.

Hotel Om *(☎ 433272)*, at the southern end of the village, offers a range of clean rooms with private bathroom and hot water from Rs 150 to 250.

Downtown Rishikesh Most of Rishikesh's mid-range options are in the noisy market area.

Inderlok Hotel *(☎ 430555, Ghat Rd)* has standard singles/doubles for Rs 600/700 and air-con rooms for Rs 900/1000, all with TV, carpets, hot water and telephone.

Hotel Baseraa *(☎ 430720, fax 430888, Ghat Rd)*, on the far side of Haridwar Rd, is better than most, with neat, well-kept rooms for Rs 250/350 with fan and Rs 850/950 with air-con. All rooms have TV and hot water.

GMVN Tourist Bungalow *(☎ 430373)* is north of the centre on the far side of the train track. The hotel is set in lovely grounds and offers rooms for Rs 140/180 with cold shower, from Rs 340/420 with hot shower and Rs 620/840 with air-con. There's also a small dorm for Rs 70 per head, and a good restaurant.

Hotel Ganga Kinare *(☎ 431658, fax 435243, 16 Virbhadra Rd)*, the most upmarket option in Rishikesh, is about 2km south of the centre. It's a peaceful place with a restaurant, its own ghat and a quiet terrace with yoga and meditation classes. Well-appointed rooms cost from Rs 1650 a double, with all the luxuries you would expect.

Places to Eat

Rishikesh is a holy pilgrimage town, and is therefore strictly vegetarian.

Indrani at the Inderlok Hotel has a good range of Chinese cuisine, as well as specials such as *rajmah* – seasoned kidney beans (Rs 30).

Neelam Restaurant, run by the helpful Mr Singh, is a clean and friendly Italian-cum-Indian restaurant in a small lane just off Haridwar Rd. It's popular with Westerners tempted here by dishes such as macaroni (Rs 30), pizza and spaghetti, as well as the standard Indian fare.

Madras Cafe, on the west side of Shivanand Jhula, has a good range of dosas and other South Indian treats for Rs 20 to 30. It also has decent coffee.

Amrita House, down by the boat jetty, is another Italian-Indian place with excellent spaghetti and pizzas, made with home-made buffalo cheese. There are books to read and a great range of breakfasts.

Chotiwala, near the eastern end of Shivanand Jhula in Swarg Ashram, is worth a visit just for the gentlemen made up as the Chotiwala from the company's logo. Filling thalis range from Rs 35 to 70, with a free drink.

Little Italy at the Green Hotel serves excellent pizzas and other Western dishes as well as Indian standards. Most dishes are around Rs 50.

Devraj Coffee Corner, perched above the bridge in Lakshman Jhula, has great views over the 13-storied temples, good coffee and a wide range of tasty baked goods and snack meals, plus a well-stocked bookshop.

Ganga Darshan Restaurant, just north of the bridge on the east bank, has thalis for around Rs 30.

Hilltop Restaurant, up on the hill above Lakshman Jhula, is more upmarket with a fine range of Chinese, Indian, Tibetan and Italian dishes ranging from Rs 35 to 60.

Shopping

Rishikesh is a good place to pick up a *rudraksh mala*, the strings of beads used in *puja* (offerings) made from the nuts of the rudraksh tree. Prices start from around Rs 100, with beads of the smaller nuts commanding higher prices. Most ashrams boast their own Ayurvedic pharmacies which sell various cures and restoratives made from herbs collected from the Himalaya. The Maharishi Mahesh Yogi Ayurvedic Centre, on Lakshman Jhula Rd, is well regarded.

Getting There & Away

Bus From the main bus stand (☎ 430066) there are buses to Haridwar every 30 minutes from 4.30 am to 10.30 pm (Rs 14, one hour), continuing on to Delhi (Rs 112, seven hours). There are also half-hourly buses to Dehra Dun between 5.30 am and 7.30 pm (Rs 19, 1½ hours). There's one bus at 8.15 am to Ramnagar (Rs 99, seven hours) which continues to Nainital (Rs 135, 11 hours). Both Dehra Dun and Haridwar have connections to Shimla and Dharamsala.

Buses for the Char Dham leave from the yatra bus stand, behind Dehra Dun Rd. Schedules are fairly informal, but most buses leave early in the morning, between 3 and 7 am. There are several daily buses to Uttarkashi (Rs 92, seven hours), Kedarnath (Rs 127, 12 hours), Badrinath (Rs 152, 1[illegible] hours) and Joshimath (Rs 142, eight hours) and one or two buses to Gangotri (Rs 155, 10 hours) and to Hanuman Chatti (Rs 159, eight hours). Outside of the pilgrimage season, which runs from May to October, buses only run to Joshimath and Uttarkashi.

Train Bookings can be made at the train station (☎ 434167) from 8 am to 6 pm daily (until 2 pm Sunday). The station has a small allocation of seats for Haridwar. There are trains to Haridwar at 6.40 and 7.45 am and 2.20, 3.15 and 6.35 pm (Rs 5, one hour). The 6.40 am service continues to Delhi (Rs 146 sleeper class) arriving at 5.20 pm. The 6.35 pm train connects with the *Mussoorie Express* for Delhi.

Taxi & Jeep The main office for the Garhwal Mandal Taxi Union (☎ 430413) is on Haridwar Rd, just south of Ghat Rd. Official rates include: Haridwar (Rs 350), Dehra Dun (Rs 450), Uttarkashi (for Gangotri, Rs 1000), Delhi (Rs 1500) and Ramnagar (for Corbett Tiger Reserve, Rs 1800). To hire a taxi for the Char Dham costs Rs 9500, or for Badrinath and Kedarnath only, Rs 5500.

You can flag down share-jeeps for Dehra Dun anywhere along the Dehra Dun Rd. The cost to Dehra Dun is Rs 20. You may be able to get a share-taxi to Haridwar from the main bus stand (Rs 20). An alternative (and less comfortable) proposition is to pick up a shared vikram anywhere along the Haridwar Rd (Rs 15).

Share-jeeps leave from the corner of Dehra Dun Rd and Dhalwala Bypass Rd when full to Uttarkashi (Rs 120, five hours) and Joshimath (Rs 200, eight hours) between 8 am and 2 pm.

Getting Around

Vikrams run from Ghat Rd junction up to Shivanand Jhula (Rs 4) and Lakshman Jhula (Rs 6), but may try to give you a special trip for Rs 40. Taxis charge Rs 40/60 for the same trips. On the east bank of the river, a seat in a jeep between Lakshman Jhula and Shivanand Jhula costs Rs 4 (or Rs 40 for the whole jeep).

Between 8 am and 5.30 pm you can cross the river to Swarg Ashram by boat (particularly auspicious) for Rs 4.

TREKKING IN GARHWAL

The far north of Uttaranchal is best known as the home of the Char Dham which mark the sources of the four sacred rivers of Hinduism. All have spectacular locations and see thousands of pilgrims every year during yatra season. To escape, head for the beautiful Valley of Flowers, high above Joshimath, or the Har-ki-Dun valley (3566m), near the border with Himachal Pradesh. Other popular treks include the high-altitude lakes of Dodi Tal and Kedar Tal and Hem Kund.

There are some spectacular treks into the mountains surrounding Gangotri; the most popular is the overnight trip to Gaumukh (3890m) – the 'Cows Mouth' and the true source of the Ganges. There are a number of pilgrim rest stops and a ***GMVN Tourist Rest House*** (doubles Rs 520, dorm beds Rs 180, tents Rs 130) at Bhojbasa, just 4km short of Gaumukh. Other trekking destinations in the area include the meadow at Tapovan, 6km from Gaumukh, and Kedar Tal (4425m), 18km south of Gangotri.

The best time to trek is either in the pre-monsoon period (mid-May to the end of June), or the post-monsoon season (mid-September to mid-October), and guides are recommended. In July and August the region is subject to heavy rainfall, though this is the best time to appreciate the rich variety of wildflowers in the Valley of Flowers. Most temples and resthouses are closed over the winter, should you think of making a rash winter expedition. The GMVN Trekking & Mountaineering Division in Rishikesh can arrange organised treks in Garhwal for around Rs 2200 per day all-inclusive, and it also offers guides, porters and equipment hire. More information on trekking in Garhwal is given in Lonely Planet's *Trekking in the Indian Himalaya.*

UTTARKASHI

☎ 01374 • elevation 1158m

The pleasant town of Uttarkashi is 155km from Rishikesh on the bank of the Ganges, known locally as Bhagirathi. It is an important stop on the way north to the Char Dham. There are numerous temples here, the most significant being the **Vishwanatha Temple**, sacred to Shiva. Also here is the Nehru Institute of Mountaineering, where Bachhendri Pal, the first Indian woman to climb to the summit of Mt Everest, was trained.

There's a small tourist office (☎ 2290) on the main road and the town market is a good place to stock up on supplies for trekking farther north. Guides can be hired for between Rs 200 and Rs 500 per day. A popular local trek is the four-day hike to Dodi Tal, a high-altitude lake with great views, from where you can continue to Hanuman Chatti. On the day of **Makar Sakranti**, which usually falls in January, Uttarkashi hosts a colourful fair, when deities are borne aloft into the town on palanquins from outlying villages.

Accommodation in Uttarkashi includes a ***GMVN Tourist Rest House*** *(☎ 2271)* with dorms for Rs 70 and doubles from Rs 240 to 660, and the ***Hotel Hanslok*** *(☎ 22 290)* in the main bazaar, with basic doubles with bathroom for Rs 80. Nearby, the ***Hotel Bhadari*** *(☎ 22203)* is basic but clean with doubles from Rs 200. Buses depart in the morning for Gangotri (Rs 80), Rishikesh (Rs 92) and Dehra Dun (Rs 125).

THE CHAR DHAM

These four ancient temples mark the spiritual sources of the four sacred rivers of Hinduism, the Yamuna (Yamunotri), the Ganges (Gangotri), the Mandakini (Kedarnath) and the Alaknanda (Badrinath). All have spectacular locations and see thousands of pilgrims every year during yatra season. The yatra business is well developed, with luxury coaches, ponies and even palanquins on hand to make sure that anyone with the will (and the means) can make it around the four shrines. The plus side of this is that there is a very well-established network of resthouses and dhabas to provide shelter and food to hungry trekkers.

The pilgrimage season runs approximately from May to October, but the exact dates are declared by the priests each year. In season, the GMVN organises 12-day Char Dham packages from Delhi including transport and accommodation in GMVN resthouses, but not meals (Rs 7050 by deluxe bus; Rs 9850 by taxi). Similar pilgrimage tours are offered from Haridwar and Rishikesh.

Yamunotri

Yamunotri is the source of the Yamuna River, the second-most sacred river in India after the Ganges. This was once the source of the Saraswati River, one of the cradles of early Indian civilisation, before geological upheavals diverted its course. The river emerges from a frozen lake of ice and glaciers on the Kalinda Parvat mountain at an altitude of 4421m, 1km beyond the temple. In front of the rather plain temple are several hot springs where the priests cook potatoes to offer as prasad.

Buses go as far as Hanuman Chatti from Dehra Dun or Rishikesh, although you may have to change buses at Barkot. Hanuman Chatti has a ***GMVN Tourist Rest House*** with dorm beds for Rs 130, and expensive doubles for Rs 650, plus a simple restaurant. From Hanuman Chatti, it's a 13km trek to Yamunotri. Accommodation is provided at Yamunotri in the form of basic ***dharamsalas*** and a ***Tourist Rest House*** with dorm beds for Rs 130. Alternatively, you can stay in the ***Tourist Rest House*** in Janki Chatti (about halfway to Yamunotri from Hanuman Chatti), which also offers dorms for Rs 130 and doubles from Rs 330.

Gangotri

As the source of the Ganges (known as Bhagirathi until it reaches Deoprayag), Gangotri is one of the holiest places in India. In fact, the physical source of the river is 18km farther north at Gaumukh, but most pilgrims are content to make do with the spiritual source at the understated Gangotri temple, built by the Gorkha commander Amar Singh Thapa in the 18th century. The setting, at 3042m, is magnificent, and the attractive temple compound features a ghat where the devout dip in the freezing waters. Nearby is the rock on which Shiva is said to have received the Ganga in his matted locks.

Buses run right up to Gangotri village, where accommodation is available at the ***GMVN Tourist Rest House*** for the standard rates of Rs 130 for dorm beds, Rs 330 for doubles and Rs 720 for deluxe rooms. Gangotri also has a ***Forest Rest House*** and several ***dharamsalas***. In season there are frequent bus connections from Rishikesh and Haridwar.

Kedarnath

The highest of the Char Dham (at 3584m), Kedarnath is revered as the source of the Mandakini River but the temple is primarily dedicated to the hump that Shiva (who had taken the form of a bull) left behind when he dived into the ground to escape the Pandavas. Other portions of Shiva's body are worshipped at the other four Panch Kedar shrines: the arms at Tugnath; the mouth at Rudranth; the navel at Madmaeshwar; and the hair at Kalpeshwar. The actual source of the Mandakini is 12km past Kedarnath.

The attractive temple was built in the 8th century by guru Shankara, who is buried behind the shrine. Although the surrounding scenery is superb, the pilgrimage to Kedarnath is extremely popular, and the village simply groans with pilgrims during the yatra season. The site is so auspicious that pilgrims used to throw themselves from one of the cliffs behind the temple in the hope of instantly attaining *moksha* (salvation).

Accommodation is available at the ***GMVN Tourist Rest House*** *(☎ 01364-6210)* which has the usual dorm beds for Rs 130 and doubles from Rs 260. If it's full you can usually find a bed at one of the ***ashrams*** or ***dharamsalas*** between the temple and the bridge. There are plenty of inexpensive dhabas catering to the hordes.

Buses from Rishikesh to Kedarnath only run as far as Gaurikund, from where it's a steep 14km hike past an endless column of dhabas and chai stands to the temple. Ponies can be hired for the trip. Gaurikund also has a ***GMVN Tourist Rest House*** with cheap dorms and expensive doubles. A convoy of jeeps and buses leaves in the morning bound for Rishikesh and Rudraprayag, for connections to Joshimath and Kumaon.

Badrinath

Sacred to Lord Vishnu, Badrinath represents the source of the Alaknanda River and boasts a spectacular setting in the shadow of snow-topped Nilkantha (6558m). However, the uncontrolled construction of hotels and dharamsalas has eroded some of Badrinath's charm. The vividly colourful temple was founded by the guru Shankara in the 8th century, but the current structure is much more recent. Surrounding the temple is a colourful religious market.

The old village of Badrinath is just a short walk south, and here you can see some traditional mountain architecture. **Mana**, which is an ancient Buddhist village 4km beyond Badrinath, is an interesting detour, but may be off-limits to foreigners – ask about the current situation when you arrive. Devotees of Vishnu also visit the other four Panch Badri temples dotted around Joshimath.

The GMVN has the large ***Devlok Hotel*** *(☎ 01381-2212)* and a smaller ***Tourist Rest House*** with rooms from Rs 260 to 850 and dorms for Rs 50. You'll need to speak to the Badrinath Temple Committee on the east bank of the Alaknanda for permission to stay in one of their many ***dharamsalas***. In season, there are plenty of morning jeeps and buses to Rishikesh and Haridwar.

JOSHIMATH

☎ 01389 • elevation 1845m

This important administrative town is the gateway to the *dham* of Badrinath, and is where the yatra buses are organised into convoys for the final 44km stretch to Badrinath. Perched high above the confluence of the Saraswati and Dhauliganga Rivers, Joshimath was established by the guru Shankara in the 8th century and has some interesting temples including the brightly painted **Narsingh Temple**, dedicated to Vishnu in his lion form.

The small tourist office (☎ 22181) no longer hires out trekking gear; for this you'll have to go to the ski resort at Auli. Private trekking companies include Nanda Devi Mountain Travel (☎ 22170) and Garhwal Adventure Sports (☎ 22288), both in the Hotel Nanda Devi on the main bazaar in Joshimath.

As an alternative to staying in Auli, there are two ***GMVN Tourist Rest Houses*** in Joshimath. The *new* resthouse *(☎ 22226)* is the better of the two, with dorms for Rs 130 and doubles from Rs 460. The slightly neglected *old* resthouse *(☎ 22118)* has dorms for Rs 130 and doubles from Rs 260. Private hotels include ***Shailja*** *(☎ 22208)* and ***Kamet*** *(☎ 22155)*, with spartan but cheap rooms.

AULI

Just 13km from Joshimath by road, and easily reached by bus or jeep from Rishikesh, Auli is India's premier ski resort, managed by the GMVN. The resort boasts 5km-long slopes which drop from an altitude of 3049m to 2519m and there's a 500m chairlift running beside the main slope (Rs 50 per trip). The upper and lower slopes are linked by a 800m chairlift.

Open from January to March, Auli is usually assured of good snow, and a convenient 3.9km cable car links Joshimath to the resort (though it's prone to power cuts!) for Rs 250 return. The GMVN resort hires out skis and boots (Rs 175/225 for a half/full day; Rs 125/175 for children), gloves (Rs 100) and goggles (Rs 30). It's up to you to bring a hat and some suitably warm clothing. Daily lessons cost Rs 100/150.

Accommodation is provided in the comfortable ***GMVN Tourist Rest House*** at Auli *(☎ 01389-23208)* for Rs 900 a double, or Rs 70 in dorms. Seven- or 14-day ski packages, including all meals, lodging, equipment hire, ski lifts and lessons, are offered for Rs 4000/8000. To book, write in advance to the General Manager (☎ 0135-746817, fax 744 408), GMVN, 74/1 Rajpur Rd, Dehra Dun, Uttaranchal. Out of season, Auli is still worth a visit for the nearby impressive treks.

KUARI PASS TREK

Also known as the Curzon Trail (though Lord Curzon's party abandoned their attempt on the pass following an attack of wild bees), the trek over the Kuari Pass (4268m) offers magnificent views of the Garhwal Himalaya. The trailhead is at Auli, reached by bus or cable car from Joshimath, and various routes ascend to the pass and continue on the far side to Ghat (47km, four days), from where you can take a bus or jeep to Nandprayag on the Rishikesh-Joshimath road. An interesting alternative is to continue to Gwaldam on the border with Kumaon, via the sinister lake of Rup Kund (known as the 'mystery lake' on account of the numerous human skeletons found here).

VALLEY OF FLOWERS NATIONAL PARK & HEM KUND

Discovery of the legendary Valley of Flowers is attributed to a British mountaineer Frank Smythe in the 1930s, though the people of Garhwal have known about it for centuries. During the summer months (mid-June to mid-September) the valley is literally carpeted with an astonishing variety of wildflowers, framed by lofty peaks including Nilgiri Parbat (6474m).

Trekkers and livestock have taken their toll on the park in the past (by picking, walking on or eating the flowers) so access to the park has been restricted to daylight hours and camping is prohibited. Fortunately, there is accommodation available at the ***GMVN***

Tourist Rest House in Ghangaria, 4km below the valley, which has the usual dorms for Rs 130 and pricey doubles for Rs 590.

Access to the park is via Govind Ghat, served by local buses from Joshimath. The 13km trail to Ghangaria is well defined and follows the pretty gorge of the Laxman Ganga. An interesting detour is the trek to the lake at Hem Kund – identified as the spot where the Sikh guru Gobind Singh meditated in a former life. The trail to Hem Kund branches off the Valley of Flowers route 3km beyond Ghangaria, from where it's 6km to the lake.

TREKKING IN KUMAON

The summit of Nanda Devi (7816m), the highest peak wholly in India, is recognised as the northern border between Garhwal and Kumaon. The area to the east of Nanda Devi is one of the least visited parts of the Indian Himalaya and offers a multitude of treks, including the challenging hikes to the Pindari and Milam Glaciers, nestled up against the Tibetan border. Descending into the foothills, you'll find the peaceful hill stations of Ranikhet, Almora and Nainital. Corbett Tiger Reserve – the birthplace of Project Tiger and Kumaon's most famous attraction – sits right on the edge of the plains, while Banbassa in the far east of the state is an entry point for Nepal.

The best season for trekking, as in Garhwal, is either in the pre-monsoon period (mid-May to the end of June), or the post-monsoon season (mid-September to mid-October). Note that Kumaon is a sensitive border region, so many areas are off-limits to foreigners, including the area immediately surrounding Nanda Devi. The KMVN offices in Delhi and Nainital can organise all-inclusive trekking packages to the Pindari Glacier (Rs 2640, six days) and Milam Glacier (Rs 3660, eight days). Also on offer are week-long rafting expeditions on the Sarju and Kali Ganga Rivers, originating in Delhi.

CORBETT TIGER RESERVE

☎ 05947

Corbett Tiger Reserve was established in 1936 as India's first national park by the legendary tiger-hunter, Jim Corbett, who put Kumaon on the map with his book *The Man-Eaters of Kumaon*. The British hunter was greatly revered by local people for shooting tigers who had developed a taste for human flesh, but eventually shot more wildlife with his camera than with his gun. With the inclusion of the Sonanadi Wildlife Sanctuary to the west, Corbett has grown from 520 to 1318 sq km.

The reserve Jim Corbett established was the starting point for the India-wide Project Tiger program in 1973, inspiring the creation of 22 other reserves. However, tiger sightings are down to chance as the animals are neither baited nor tracked. If you really *must* see a tiger, your best chance is to come late in the season (April to mid-June) and stay in the park for several days.

Few visitors leave disappointed, as the park has a variety of wildlife and a beautiful location in the foothills of the Himalaya on the Ramganga River. More commonly seen wildlife include wild elephants, langur monkeys, rhesus macaques, peacocks, and several types of deer including chital (spotted deer), sambar, hog deer and barking deer. There are also leopards, mugger crocodiles, gharials (thin-snouted fish-eating crocodiles), monitor lizards, wild boars and jackals. Since the creation of the Ramganga Reservoir on the Ramganga River, large numbers of waterfowl have also been attracted. The best time of year for sightings is from mid-December to the end of March.

The differential price system means that Corbett is quite an expensive destination for foreigners (less so for Indians, who pay a tenth of the foreigner rates). Budget for around US$40 for a two-day visit (though you can do it cheaper by sharing a jeep ride or by hitching).

The park is open from mid-November to mid-June but much of the wildlife goes into hiding during the crowded weekends. It's a good idea to bring mosquito repellent, mineral water and binoculars.

The house formerly occupied by Jim Corbett at Veranda (26km from Ramnagar towards Nainital) has been opened as a museum (Rs 10 entry), and makes an interesting detour.

Orientation & Information

The Corbett Tiger Reserve encompasses both the original Corbett National Park, forming the eastern side of the reserve, and the Sonanadi Wildlife Sanctuary, forming the western side of the reserve.

The Corbett Tiger Reserve reception centre is at Ramnagar (☎ 51489, fax 51376), on the south-eastern perimeter of the park, and there is a second reception centre at Kotdwar (☎ 01382-24823), on the south-western edge of the park. Both centres are open 8.30 am to 1 pm and 3 to 5 pm daily, including holidays. Ramnagar is the nearest railhead and has several hotels and tour agents.

Dhikala, 51km north-west of Ramnagar inside the reserve, is the main accommodation centre and where most travellers stay, but it is only open to overnight guests, or as part of a tour booked through the reception centre at Ramnagar. Day-trippers are restricted to the Bijrani visitors centre closer to the edge of the reserve.

At Dhikala there's a library where interesting wildlife films are shown (free) in the evenings. The elephant rides at sunrise and sunset are not to be missed and cost Rs 100 each (minimum of four people) for about two hours. During the day you can sit in one of the *machaan* (observation towers) to unobtrusively watch for animals. Elephant rides are also available at Bijrani, where there's an interpretative centre and restaurant, and from the lodge at Khinnanauli.

Permits These are normally bought at Dhangarhi Gate (for Dhikala) or Amdanda Gate (for day trips to Bijrani). To stay at Dhikala you must first make an accommodation reservation at the park reception centre at Ramnagar. They will then give you a booking sheet, which you must show at Dhangarhi Gate.

Foreigners pay an entry fee of Rs 350 for a stay of up to three days, then Rs 175 per day (Indians pay Rs 30 then Rs 20 per day). There's no charge for a still camera, but a video camera costs a huge Rs 5000 (Rs 2500 for Indians). To take a car to Bijrani costs Rs 100, and you'll have to hire a (compulsory) guide for Rs 75 (for up to four hours; additional hours cost Rs 20). If you hire a jeep you will have to pay all these charges yourself. The guide fees at Dhikala are Rs 100 and Rs 20 per additional hour.

No walking or trekking is allowed in the park at any time (introduced after a British ornithologist was killed by a tigress in 1985). The gates are closed at sunset and no night driving is permitted. When leaving the park, you'll need to obtain a clearance certificate from your guide, which should be shown at the exit gate.

Organised Tours

UP Tourism in Delhi runs two/three-night fixed-departure tours to Dhikala from Delhi for Rs 3000/3500 per adult/child, including transport, accommodation, entrance fees, guide and one elephant ride.

The park reception centre in Ramnagar offers day trips by bus to Dhikala for Rs 1000, and Bijrani for Rs 600, including the entrance fee. This is the only way to visit Dhikala on a day trip. Buses leave the reception centre at 8.30 am.

Places to Stay & Eat

Most people choose to stay at Dhikala, Bijrani and Khinnanauli, where elephant rides are available. Rest houses are available at various locations; your chance of spotting wildlife will be reduced to sightings from the resthouses themselves, as venturing into the reserve on foot is prohibited.

Dhikala, Bijrani and Khinnanauli There are several choices at Dhikala, but all charge higher rates for foreign visitors (Indians pay one-third of the rate). All three following places can be booked at the reception centre at Ramnagar.

Log Huts have a very basic dormitory (like three-tier train sleepers!) for Rs 100.

Tourist Hutment has better-value triples (Rs 500). An extra charge (Rs 25) is made for mattresses and sheets in both these places.

Forest Rest House has more comfortable cabins and rooms, which cost Rs 900 and come with private bathroom.

Through a slightly perverse ruling, doubles at the ***Old Forest Rest House*** (Rs 1500) in Dhikala must be booked through the Chief Conservator of Forests in Dehra Dun (☎ 0135-745779) while the seven ***annexe rooms*** (Rs 900) must be booked through the KMVN in Delhi (☎ 011-3350481).

Dhikala has two ***restaurants***, one run by the KMVN.

The resthouse at ***Bijrani***, in the south-eastern corner of the reserve, has singles/doubles for Rs 500/900 and meals are available; access is via the Amdanda Gate. The resthouse at ***Khinnanauli*** is reached via the Dhangarhi Gate and costs Rs 1500 per room (Rs 100 extra to use the generator).

Ramnagar Next to the reception centre, ***KMVN Tourist Bungalow*** *(☎ 51225)* has good doubles from Rs 400 to 800. Dorm beds are Rs 60.

Along the main road in Ramnagar are several basic but clean guesthouses:

Corbett Guest House (no phone) has singles/doubles for Rs 150/200 with shared hot shower.

Govind Guest House *(☎ 51614)*, farther north, charges Rs 200 to 300 for really big clean doubles with fan and semi-private bathroom.

Hotel Everest *(☎ 51099)*, on the street opposite the bus stand, is friendly and has comfortable rooms for Rs 250 to 400 (Rs 200 at other times). More expensive rooms have TV and air-coolers. Meals can be arranged and there's a nice balcony.

Corbett Green Valley Restaurant, on the main road, has a wide menu of Indian favourites.

Other Areas With your own transport and food, there are numerous resthouses dotted throughout the park. Most convenient are the resthouses at ***Sarapduli*** and ***Gairal***, which cost Rs 500/900 a single/double, and the resthouse at ***Sultan***, which costs Rs 450. All have generator power (bring a flashlight just in case) and can be booked through Ramnagar reception.

Outside the Reserve There are several upmarket resorts strung along the Ramnagar-Ranikhet road, all outside the reserve precincts. All offer discounts of around 50% when the park is closed.

Infinity Corbett Lodge *(☎ 51279, fax 85278, Delhi 011-6444016)*, formerly known as Tiger Tops and 7km from Ramnagar, is a luxurious place with prices to match. Rooms start at US$95 per person in double rooms, including elephant rides, jeep trips, access to the pool and a wildlife slide show in the evenings.

Claridges Corbett Hideaway *(☎ 51959, Delhi 011-3010211)* has accommodation in attractive ochre cottages set in an orchard of mango trees. Air-con doubles cost from US$175, and rates include all meals.

Quality Inn Corbett Jungle Resort *(☎/fax 51230)*, in the Kumeria Forest Reserve on the north-east fringes of the park, has attractive cottages high above the river for Rs 3850, including all meals. This place features its own inhouse elephant so rides are assured.

Getting There & Away

UP Roadways and Delhi Transport Corporation buses for Delhi depart Ramnagar approximately every hour between 5 am and 7.30 pm (Rs 110, seven hours). For Dehra Dun (via Haridwar), buses leave hourly from 8 am to 1.30 pm (Rs 100). Nainital buses leave every few hours throughout the day (Rs 56, 3½ hours), passing through Veranda (Rs 19, one hour).

Various private buses leave from opposite the Corbett Tiger Reserve reception centre for destinations in Kumaon. To Ranikhet, buses leave every few hours until 2 pm (Rs 60, 4½ hours). The 9.30 am service continues to Almora (Rs 97). Regular local buses run up to Haldwani (Rs 17), from where there are jeep connections to Nainital, Almora and Ranikhet.

Ramnagar train station is 1.5km south of the main reception centre. The nightly *Ranikhet Express* leaves Ramnagar at 9.10 pm, arriving Delhi at 4.30 am (Rs 120 sleeper class). For other destinations, change at Moradabad. It's worth making a reservation before you visit the reserve.

Getting Around

Providing you have booked accommodation, you can take the local bus from Ramnagar to Dhikala at 3.30 pm (Rs 150, 2½ hours), returning to Ramnagar at 9.30 am the next day.

Jeeps can usually only be rented at Ramnagar, and will cost about Rs 600 for a one-way drop to Dhikala, or Rs 450 to 500 for a half-day safari to Bijrani, plus guide and car charges (see Permits earlier). Book through any hotel or deal directly with a driver.

Safaris on foot are strictly prohibited. The only other mode of transport is the ubiquitous elephant.

NAINITAL

☎ 05942 • pop 35,700

At 1938m, this attractive hill station was once the summer capital of Uttar Pradesh and is the largest town in Kumaon. Like most hill stations, Nainital was founded by homesick Brits, who were reminded of the Cumbrian Lake District. Things really took

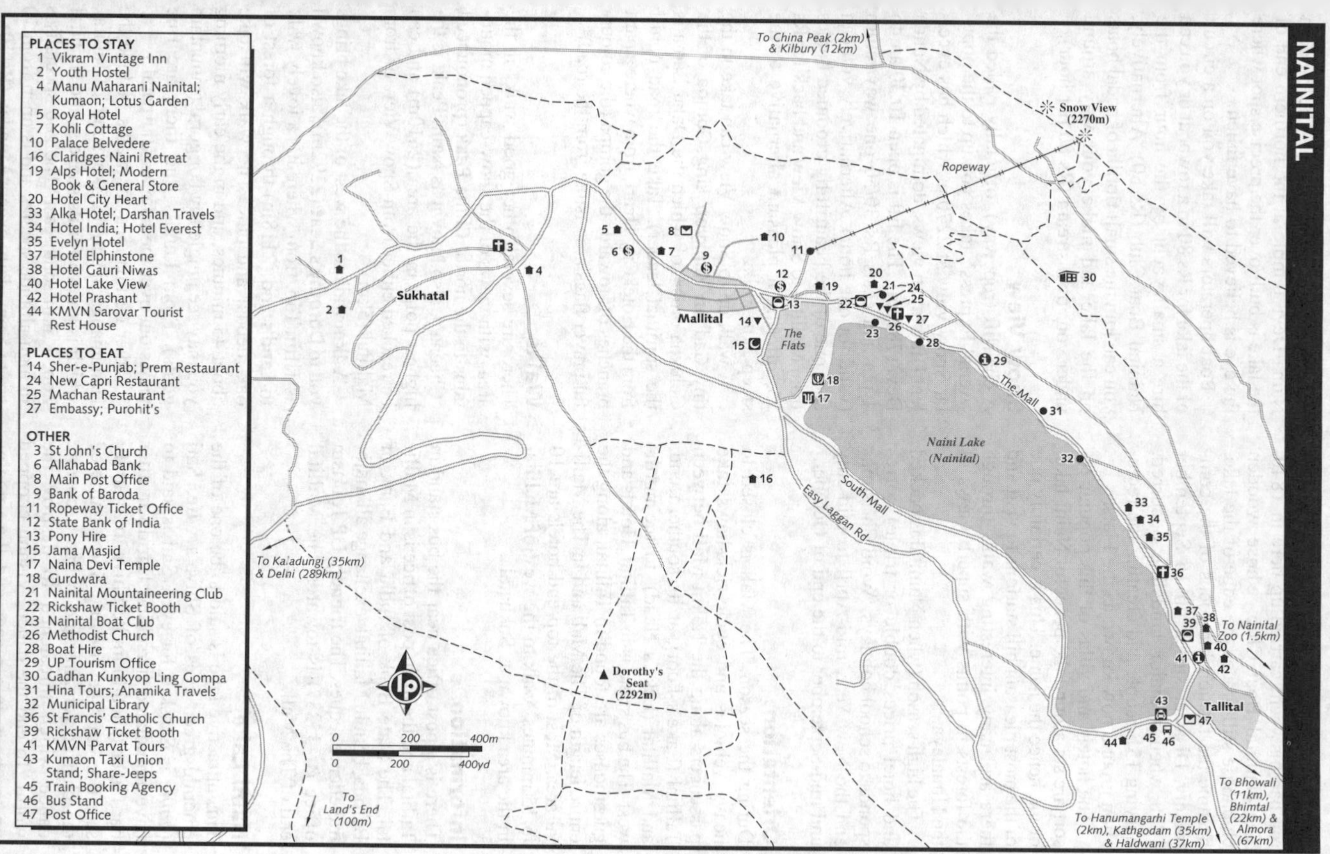
NAINITAL
PLACES TO STAY
1 Vikram Vintage Inn
2 Youth Hostel
4 Manu Maharani Nainital; Kumaon; Lotus Garden
5 Royal Hotel
7 Kohli Cottage
10 Palace Belvedere
16 Claridges Naini Retreat
19 Alps Hotel; Modern Book & General Store
20 Hotel City Heart
33 Alka Hotel; Darshan Travels
34 Hotel India; Hotel Everest
35 Evelyn Hotel
37 Hotel Elphinstone
38 Hotel Gauri Niwas
40 Hotel Lake View
42 Hotel Prashant
44 KMVN Sarovar Tourist Rest House
PLACES TO EAT
14 Sher-e-Punjab; Prem Restaurant
24 New Capri Restaurant
25 Machan Restaurant
27 Embassy; Purohit's
OTHER
3 St John's Church
6 Allahabad Bank
8 Main Post Office
9 Bank of Baroda
11 Ropeway Ticket Office
12 State Bank of India
13 Pony Hire
15 Jama Masjid
17 Naina Devi Temple
18 Gurdwara
21 Nainital Mountaineering Club
22 Rickshaw Ticket Booth
23 Nainital Boat Club
26 Methodist Church
28 Boat Hire
29 UP Tourism Office
30 Gadhan Kunkyop Ling Gompa
31 Hina Tours; Anamika Travels
32 Municipal Library
36 St Francis' Catholic Church
39 Rickshaw Ticket Booth
41 KMVN Parvat Tours
43 Kumaon Taxi Union Stand; Share-Jeeps
45 Train Booking Agency
46 Bus Stand
47 Post Office
To China Peak (2km) & Kilbury (12km)
Snow View (2270m)
Ropeway
Sukhatal
Mallital
The Flats
The Mall
Naini Lake (Nainital)
South Mall
Easy Laggan Rd
To Kaladungi (35km) & Delhi (289km)
Dorothy's Seat (2292m)
To Land's End (100m)
0 200 400m
0 200 400yd
To Nainital Zoo (1.5km)
Tallital
To Bhowali (11km), Bhimtal (22km) & Almora (67km)
To Hanumangarhi Temple (2km), Kathgodam (35km) & Haldwani (37km)

off here when a sugar-trader called Mr Barron had his yacht carried up here in 1840. The Nainital Boat Club, whose wooden clubhouse still graces the edge of the lake, became the fashionable focus of the community. Disaster struck on 16 September 1880 when a major landslide occurred, burying 151 people and creating the recreation ground now known as the Flats.

The hotels and villas of this popular resort are set around the peaceful Naini lake, or *tal*, hence the name. This is certainly one of the most pleasant hill stations to visit and there are many interesting walks through the forests to points with superb views of the Himalaya.

The high season (when Nainital is packed and hotel prices double or triple) corresponds to school holidays. Avoid Christmas and the New Year, mid-April to mid-July and mid-September to the end of October.

Orientation

During the season, The Mall is closed to heavy vehicles and cycle-rickshaws take passengers along the 1.5km Mall between Tallital (Lake's Foot), at its southern end, and Mallital (Lake's Head), to the north-west. The bus stand is in Tallital. Hotels and guesthouses are found in Tallital, along the entire length of The Mall and in The Mallital area. Most of the top-end hotels are 10 to 15 minutes' walk to the west of Mallital in the area known as Sukhatal.

Information

There is a post office near the bus stand in Tallital and the main post office is in Mallital. The State Bank of India and Bank of Baroda, both in Mallital, exchange all major travellers cheques. The friendly UP Tourism office (☎ 35337) is towards The Mallital end of The Mall.

Naini Lake

This attractive lake is said to be one of the emerald green eyes of Shiva's wife, Sati (*naina* is Sanskrit for eye). Sati is said to have immolated herself at Haridwar after her father failed to invite Shiva to a family sacrifice, and the grieving Shiva gathered the charred remains and began a cosmic dance which threatened to destroy the world. To end the dance, Vishnu chopped up the body into pieces and the remains were scattered across India. The modern Naina Devi Temple at the northern end of the lake is built over the precise spot where the eye is believed to have fallen.

Boat operators will take you on a circuit of the lake for Rs 80 in a rowboat or you can hire a small yacht by the hour from the Nainital Boat Club (Rs 60). Alternatively, you can join the small flotilla of pedal boats on the lake and make your way around under your own stream (Rs 80 per hour).

Snow View

A chairlift (ropeway), officially called the 'Aerial Express', takes you up to the popular Snow View at 2270m, which has excellent Himalayan views, dominated by Nanda Devi (7816m). The lift is open 10.30 am to 4 pm and costs Rs 30/50 one way/return (valid for one hour). Alternatively you can take one of the beautifully groomed horses from Mallital to Snow View and back for Rs 75, offering a pleasant alternative to the steep 2km walk.

A walk up to Snow View can take in the tiny **Gadhan Kunkyop Ling Gompa** of the Gelukpa order (of which the Dalai Lama is the spiritual leader). Take the road uphill from the Hotel City Heart, from where a path branches off towards the gompa (the colourful prayer flags are visible from the road).

Walks

There are several other good walks in the area, with views of the snow-capped mountains to the north. **China Peak** (pronounced 'Cheena'), also known as Naini Peak, is the highest point in the area (2610m) and can be reached either from Snow View or from Mallital (5km).

A 4km walk to the west of the lake brings you to **Dorothy's Seat** (2292m), also known as Tiffin Top, from where it's a lovely walk to **Land's End** (2118m) through a forest of oak, deodar and pine. The walk will take about 45 minutes, and in the early morning you may see jungle fowl or goral (mountain goats). From Land's End there are fine views out over the lake at Khurpatal.

Other destinations for walks include the Hanumangarhi temple, 3km south of Tallital, which is known for its sunsets, and **Nainital Zoo**, 1.5km south-east. The zoo specialises in high-altitude species and is open from 10 am to 5 pm, daily except Monday (Rs 10).

Other Activities

Opposite the Hotel City Heart, the Nainital Mountaineering Club (☎ 35051), offers **rock climbing** at nearby Bara Pattar for Rs 1100. It also adivises on local treks and helps you find guides and porters for trekking elsewhere in Kumaon. Tents and sleeping bags can be hired for around Rs 15 per day.

Organised Tours

Almost every travel agency run tours to sights around Nainital and farther afield in Kumaon. The standard offerings include day tours by bus to Ranikhet (Rs 200) and Mukteshwar Lake (Rs 150), two-day trips to Kausani (Rs 350 to 450 including accommodation) and one-day excursions to Bijrani in Corbett Tiger Reserve (Rs 1500). A half-day tour of the local lakes will cost Rs 100. The same tours are possible by taxi.

Among the travel agencies, Hina Tours (☎ 35860), Anamika Travels (☎ 35186) and Darshan Travels (☎ 35035), all on The Mall, are reliable operators. Parvat Tours (☎ 35656), at the Tallital end of The Mall, is run by the KMVN, and offers the usual tours, plus trips to Badrinath and Kedarnath (Rs 800, six days) during the yatra season, including dorm accommodation, transfers and evening meals. It can also book organised KMVN treks to the Pindari and Milam Glaciers and paragliding at Naukuchiatal, above Bhimtal Lake.

Places to Stay

There are over 100 places to stay, from gloomy budget guesthouses to five-star hotels. Prices listed here are for the high season and may appear expensive but, unless otherwise stated, all hotels offer *at least* a 50% discount in the low season. You may struggle to find a room during the Hindu festivals of Dussehra and Diwali and the peak summer periods.

Places to Stay – Budget

Tallital & The Mall There are several good budget choices at the Tallital end of the lake on the road which runs uphill from St Francis' Church.

Hotel Lake View *(☎ 35632, Ramji Rd)*, run by the charming Shah family, has doubles with private bathroom from Rs 300 to 550. The more expensive rooms have appealing views over the lake.

Hotel Gauri Niwas *(☎ 36617, Ramji Rd)* has double rooms with geysers from Rs 300 (no view) to Rs 1000 overlooking the lake.

Hotel Prashant *(☎ 35347)*, in the same area, has doubles ranging from Rs 700 to 800 with private bathroom and hot water. The more expensive rooms have good views but the cheaper rooms are a bit shabby. There's a good dining hall.

Hotel Elphinstone *(☎ 35534)*, up some steps above The Mall, is an atmospheric old building with a variety of comfortable rooms from Rs 300 to 800. Rooms are bright and airy (with hot water) and there's a pleasant dining hall.

Mallital & Sukhatal An excellent choice in the heart of Mallital, ***Kohli Cottage*** *(☎ 36368)* has doubles for Rs 300, Rs 400 and Rs 500, with private bathroom (24-hour hot water) and TV. Rooms are light, airy and clean and the manager is friendly and helpful. There are lovely views from the roof terrace.

Alps Hotel *(☎ 35317)* is a rather creaky centenarian, but has enormous doubles with basic private bathroom for Rs 200 to 300. There's a lovely old broad balcony for watching the promenaders on The Mall.

The ***Youth Hostel*** *(☎ 36353)* is set in a peaceful wooded location, but it's a long haul from anywhere else in town. The compensation is the prices: dorm beds (with lockers) cost Rs 22 for members, Rs 42 for nonmembers. Hot water is available in the mornings and filling vegetarian meals are available in the dining hall.

Places to Stay – Mid-Range & Top End

Tallital & The Mall The ***KMVN Sarovar Tourist Rest House*** *(☎ 35570)* is close to the bus stand. Doubles range from Rs 450 to 900 depending on the season, but the dorm is good value year round, from Rs 40 to 80.

Evelyn Hotel *(☎ 35457)* is a large hotel, one of several Victorian-looking places right on The Mall. All these hotels proudly announce that there is 'no climb' and charge high rates for the privilege, typically Rs 600 to 1200 for doubles with a view. Other choices include the ***Hotel India*** *(☎ 3517)* and the more expensive ***Hotel Everest*** *(☎ 36648)*.

***Alka Hotel** (☎ 35220)* is swish and stands out from the other places on The Mall with a fine restaurant. Rooms aren't bad for the money at Rs 1100 to 2000, though the low-season discount is only 30%.

Mallital & Sukhatal Sukhatal has the bulk of the top-end places.

***Hotel City Heart** (☎ 35228)* is a good mid-range choice, just uphill from the lake. The high-spirited owner is friendly and the spotless doubles are good value, with prices ranging from Rs 700 to 1400 in season (Rs 250 to 700 at other times). Cheaper rooms have no views, but you can always watch the sun sink behind the hills from the roof terrace.

***Royal Hotel** (☎/fax 35357)*, near the Allahabad Bank, is housed in a charismatic old building bedecked with hunting trophies and other Raj-era relics. Doubles with TV and fireplaces (wood is Rs 7 per bundle) cost from Rs 1000 to 1400.

***Palace Belvedere** (☎ 35082, fax 35493)* was formerly the palace of the raja of Awagarh and has a beautiful shady veranda. Take the road which leads up behind the Bank of Baroda. Doubles start from Rs 1500 and some of the rooms have very good lake views. There's a 30% low-season discount and credit cards are accepted.

***Claridges Naini Retreat** (☎ 35105, fax 35103)*, for comfort and peace and quiet, is on the hillside high above Mallital and has luxury doubles for Rs 3000 (Rs 3800 on half-board).

***Vikram Vintage Inn** (☎/fax 36177)*, farther along the same road, is a very stylish option with luxurious singles/doubles for Rs 1650/3000, including breakfast.

***Manu Maharani Nainital** (☎ 37341, fax 37350, Grasmere Estate)*, Nainital's top hotel, is also in Sukhatal. Rooms are splendidly appointed and most have lake views; rates start at Rs 3300 per night. There are two very good restaurants here.

Places to Eat

There's a wide range of eating establishments along the length of The Mall, and all of the top-end hotels have their own restaurants (visitors welcome).

Sher-e-Punjab and ***Prem Restaurant*** are cheap but good dhaba-style places in a small cul-de-sac in Mallital's main bazaar.

New Capri Restaurant, at the Mallital end of The Mall, has Indian, Chinese and continental cuisine. It's popular, and often full at lunch time. Nonveg dishes are around Rs 50.

Machan Restaurant, nearby, is popular and serves excellent soups (Rs 25 to 35) and a broad range of Indian, Chinese and European dishes for around Rs 55.

Embassy is considered one of the best restaurants by locals and serves up filling Indian staples and good value sizzlers from around Rs 65.

Purohit's, next door, serves vegetarian South Indian cuisine, including cheap thalis.

The ***restaurant*** at the Alka Hotel serves up good Gujarati food in a sophisticated setting. Expect to pay around Rs 150 for a meal.

There are two restaurants at the Manu Maharani Nainital hotel: the multicuisine ***Kumaon***, and the ***Lotus Garden***, serving Chinese cuisine. The Kumaon serves great European dishes and good Indian food for around Rs 140.

Getting There & Away

Bus From the bus stand at Tallital, there are several morning and afternoon buses to Delhi (Rs 142, nine hours). To Dehra Dun, ordinary buses leave at 5.30, 6 and 7 am and 4.30 pm (Rs 159, 10 hours), or there's a deluxe service at 8 pm (Rs 231). There are several early morning buses to Haridwar and one afternoon bus at 4.30 pm (Rs 133, eight hours). There's also a semideluxe service at 8 pm (Rs 170). There's a single daily bus to Rishikesh at 5 am (Rs 150, nine hours) and to Pithoragarh at 7 am (Rs 115, nine hours).

To Ramnagar, buses leave at 7 and 8.30 am (Rs 56, 3½ hours), but you're much better off taking one of the extremely regular buses to Haldwani (Rs 22, 1½ hours), the regional transport hub, and changing to a local bus there. Haldwani also has regular buses to Delhi and the Nepali border crossing at Banbassa. You can pick up the train to Delhi from either Haldwani or Kathgodam, on the northern outskirts of town.

Heading north, there are 7 am buses to Almora (Rs 42, three hours) and Kausani (Rs 70, five hours) and 12.30 and 2.30 pm buses to Ranikhet (Rs 39, three hours). A faster alternative is to take a bus to Bhowali at the junction of the Ranikhet and Almora

Share-Jeeps

A vast network of share-jeep routes criss-crosses Garhwal and Kumaon, linking towns and villages in the hills to important road junctions. If you can't go where you want directly, you should be able to leap-frog across to your destination from transport hub to transport hub in the relative comfort of a Tata Sumo or Maruti jeep. Jeeps usually solicit for customers on the highway in the direction of the next town or transport hub, and leave when full (or overfull), charging just a little more than the equivalent bus ride.

roads (Rs 8, 20 minutes), from where there are buses on to Almora, Ranikhet and Kausani about every 30 minutes. A single direct bus to Song leaves Bhowali at 6 am.

Many private agencies offer overnight deluxe coaches (two-by-two seating) to Delhi (Rs 250/350 deluxe/air-con) and Haridwar (Rs 250).

Train Kathgodam (35km south) is the nearest train station, but Haldwani, one stop earlier, is the major transport hub in the region. The train booking agency near the bus stand in Tallital has a quota for trains to Delhi, Moradabad and Kolkata. The *Ranikhet Express* departs Old Delhi station at 10.45 pm, arriving in Haldwani at 5.50 am and Kathgodam at 6.10 am. The return trip leaves Kathgodam at 8.45 pm and Haldwani at 9 pm, arriving at Old Delhi train station at 4.45 am (Rs 129/550 sleeper/two-tier). The office is open 9 am to noon and 2 to 5 pm Monday to Saturday; 9 am to 2 pm Sunday.

Taxi & Jeep A reserve taxi from the bus stand in Tallital will charge Rs 700 to Ramnagar, Rs 650 to Almora or Ranikhet and Rs 1200 to Kausani.

Share-jeeps leave when full from the bus stand and go to Bhowali (Rs 8), Kathgodam and Haldwani (Rs 40).

Getting Around

The official rate for a rickshaw from Tallital to Mallital is Rs 4; tickets can only be purchased at the booths at either end of The Mall and rickshaws cannot be flagged down anywhere else.

RANIKHET

☎ 05966 • elevation 1829m

North of Nainital, this peaceful hill station was established as a barracks and is still home to the Kumaon Regiment. There are good views of the Himalaya from the village, which has several places to stay, but all of the old Raj-era hotels are about 3km distant, on the far side of the cantonment. **Dwarahat**, 32km north, is an interesting detour for its 12th-century temples, which feature particularly fine carving.

There are several good walks, including the **Jhula Devi Temple** (1km south of West View Hotel) and the orchards at **Chaubatia** (3km farther on).

The tourist office (☎ 20227) is by the UP Roadways bus stand. The State Bank of India, on the road up to the cantonment, can change most travellers cheques in US dollars or pounds sterling, but there's a US$100 limit per day.

Places to Stay & Eat

There are several hotels in Sadar Bazaar between the bus stands, all offering basic rooms with squat toilet.

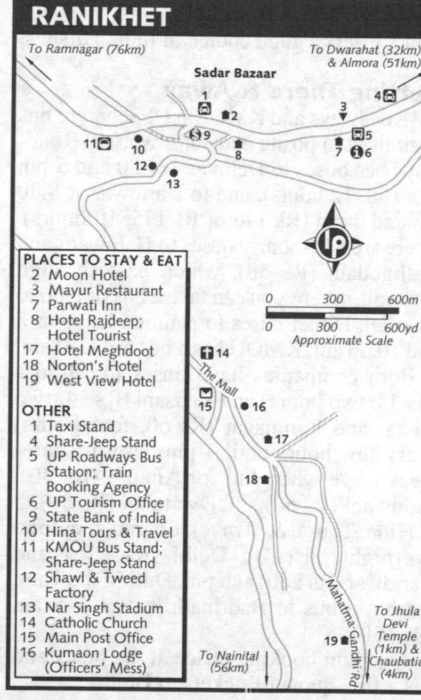

Hotel Rajdeep *(☎ 20017)* is the best of the cheap places, with a wide range of clean rooms from Rs 100 to 300, and a communal sitting area.

Hotel Tourist, next door, has simple rooms for Rs 80 to 100 and a nice balcony.

Moon Hotel *(☎ 20382)*, the large hotel across the road, has slightly overpriced rooms from Rs 650 to 1650, all with TV.

Parwati Inn *(☎ 20325)*, near the UP Roadways bus stand, is a modern complex with good rooms from Rs 500 (less 40% in the low season), and a restaurant and cinema.

There are three old Raj-era places in a tranquil location on the west side of the cantonment:

Hotel Meghdoot *(☎ 20475)* charges from Rs 450/650 for clean singles/doubles with hot water; it has a good restaurant.

Norton's Hotel *(☎ 20377)*, across the road, has a homely atmosphere and a cheery living room and charges Rs 300 to 400 for comfortable rooms with hot water.

West View Hotel *(☎ 20261)* is another former Raj establishment. Large rooms with fireplaces start at Rs 1500 (Rs 800 in the low season). There's afternoon tea, and croquet on the lawn.

Mayur Restaurant, opposite the bus stand, offers a good choice of Indian dishes.

Getting There & Away

UP Roadways and KMOU have separate bus stations at opposite ends of town. UP Roadways has buses to Delhi at 4, 4.30 and 5 pm (Rs 168, 12 hours), and to Haridwar at 8.30 am and 3 pm (Rs 146 or Rs 175, 10 hours). There are half-hourly buses to Haldwani and Kathgodam (Rs 58), which pass through Bhowali, where you can take a bus or jeep to Nainital. Direct buses to Nainital leave at 8 and 10.30 am; KMOU has a bus at 11.30 am.

Both companies have buses to Almora (Rs 34, two hours) and Kausani (Rs 34, two hours) and Ramnagar (Rs 60, four hours) every few hours until 3 pm. Useful share-jeeps leave when full for Almora (Rs 30), Haldwani (Rs 60) and Dwarahat (Rs 30).

Hina Tours & Travel operates deluxe overnight buses to Delhi (Rs 225) and Haridwar (Rs 260) at 6 pm. During the yatra season, a bus to Badrinath leaves at 5 am (Rs 550).

The train booking office at the bus stand has a tiny quota of tickets to Delhi.

ALMORA

☎ 05962 • pop 53,507 • elevation 1650m

This picturesque hill town was established as a summer capital by the Chand rajas of Kumaon in 1560 and is much more Indian in atmosphere than the other hill resorts in the area. The stone **Nanda Devi Temple**, reached through the colourful Lalal Bazaar area, is the only relic from the Chand days, but there are several stone houses and colonial-era buildings in town. In September, the temple is the setting for the Nanda Devi fair, which features a huge procession.

Like Ranikhet and Kausani, Almora offers good views of the mountains and great walks, including the 8km trek up to the **Kasar Devi Temple** where Swami Vivekananda came to meditate. There are impressive sunsets from **Bright End Corner**, 2.5km south-west of the town centre. The small **Pt GB Pant Museum** in town has displays on local temples and archaeology.

Information

There is a small and informal UP Tourism office (☎ 30180) near the Hotel Savoy. The State Bank of India will only exchange

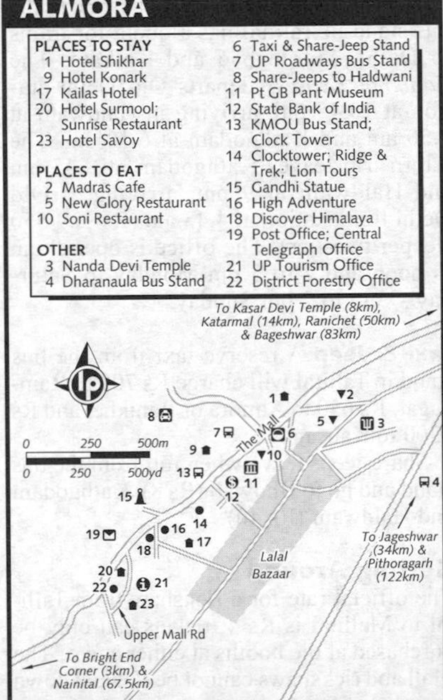

American Express travellers cheques in US dollars or pounds sterling. For treks in the local hills or farther afield to the Pindari or Milam Glaciers try High Adventure (☎ 32277), Discover Himalaya (☎ 31470) or Ridge & Trek (☎ 22492) on the main road. All charge around Rs 1000 per day with guides, porters, food and accommodation.

Places to Stay & Eat

Most of the places to stay are spread out along The Mall and all offer significant reductions in the low season.

Hotel Shikhar *(☎ 30253)*, right in the centre, has well-maintained rooms to suit all budgets, but the atmosphere is a little impersonal. Budget rooms start at Rs 150/200 with shared/private bathroom; better rooms with TV start at Rs 600.

Hotel Konark *(☎ 31217)*, opposite the State Bank of India, has spotless doubles from Rs 300 to 450 with private bathroom and hot water.

Kailas Hotel *(☎ 30624)*, nearby, is a colourful, slightly New Age hotel. Travellers seem to enjoy the eccentricities of the guesthouse itself and its elderly proprietors, Mr and Mrs Shah, and there are tasty home-cooked meals and excellent herbal teas. There are single/double rooms from Rs 75/125 in summer, and dorm beds for Rs 40.

Hotel Surmool *(☎ 22860)*, a five-minute walk east of the centre, has friendly staff and good-value rooms with private bathroom and geyser hot water from Rs 300/400 (Rs 450/500 with TV and geyser); dorm beds are Rs 150. The ***Sunrise Restaurant*** here is also good value.

Hotel Savoy *(☎ 30329, Upper Mall Rd)*, on the hill behind the Surmool, is a peaceful place with decent rooms and hot shower for Rs 400 or Rs 500 for upstairs rooms on the balcony. Prices drop by 30% in the low season.

Madras Cafe, in the Lalal Bazaar area, is gloomy but offers reasonably priced vegetarian food; main dishes are under Rs 25.

New Glory Restaurant, opposite, is a better vegetarian option, but look out for the low ceilings.

Soni Restaurant *(The Mall)* is a popular Sikh-run place offering veg and nonveg options in a slightly fast-food environment.

Almora's regional delicacy is *ball mithai* (fudge coated in sugar balls).

Getting There & Away

The KMOU and UP Roadways bus stands are both on The Mall (UP Roadways buses stop on the roadside opposite the museum). Private and public buses leave half-hourly for Ranikhet (Rs 32, two hours) and Kausani (Rs 32, two hours) from about 8 am to 3 pm. There are no direct services to Nainital, but buses run to Bhowali every 30 minutes (Rs 40).

Ordinary public buses to Delhi leave at 7 am and 3.30 and 4.30 pm (Rs 182, 12 hours) or there's a deluxe bus at 5 pm (Rs 225). Lion Tours (☎ 30860), on The Mall, offers daily deluxe buses to Delhi, Nainital and Kausani. For Pithoragarh (Rs 73, five hours) there are early morning and evening buses from The Mall and mid-morning buses from the Dharanaula bus stand on the east side of Lalal Bazaar. Trekkers may want to use the 5 am private bus to Munsyari (Rs 136, 12 hours) or the 5 am UP Roadways bus to Song (Rs 56, five hours).

One-way taxi fares include Ranikhet (Rs 500), Kausani (Rs 600), Nainital (Rs 600) and Bageshwar (Rs 700). For sightseeing, taxis offer return trips to Bright End Corner (Rs 150) and Katarmal (Rs 300).

Numerous share-jeeps operate from Almora to many destinations including Ranikhet (Rs 35), Kausani (Rs 40), Bageshwar (Rs 60), Haldwani (for trains to Delhi, Rs 70) and Gwaldam (for connections to Garwhal, Rs 70).

AROUND ALMORA

The hills around Almora are dotted with ancient temples; the 800-year-old Surya (Sun) Temple at **Katarmal** (12km to Kosi and then a 2km walk west) is worth a look. Buses to Ranikhet stop in Kosi.

About 38km north-east of Almora is the huge temple complex of **Jageshwar**, dating back to the 7th century AD, set in a forest of deodars. There are a staggering 124 temples here, from waist-high linga shrines to vast sikhara-style temples. The complex is a 4km walk through the forest from the village of old Jageshwar, where there's a ***KMVN Tourist Rest House*** with doubles from Rs 300 and dorms for Rs 60. There's a noon bus from Almora to Jageshwar, or you can take a Pithoragarh-bound bus to Artola and walk (or hitch) 3km north. Taxis charge Rs 600 for a return trip from Almora.

KAUSANI

☎ 05969 • elevation 1890m

There are even closer views of the Himalaya from the cluster of hotels along the ridge at Kausani, 51km north of Almora. The most easily identifiable peak is Trisul (7120m), shaped like a trident. It's a peaceful spot, and was home to the poet GB Pant, commemorated by a small museum. Gandhi stayed at the Anasakti Ashram in 1929 and wrote *Anasakti Yoga*.

Places to Stay & Eat

Uttarakhand Tourist Lodge (*☎ 45012*), at the top of the stairs leading up from the bus stand, has basic doubles with private bathroom from Rs 400 in high season and Rs 100 in low season. For hot water and TV, you'll pay Rs 1400/250. All rooms face the snows. Mountain biking tours depart from here in season.

Hotel Prashant (*☎ 45037*), up on the ridge, close to the Ashram, is a popular cheapie and the rates make up for the lack of a view. In season, rooms cost Rs 400 to 750; off-season they're Rs 175 to 300.

Krishna Mount View (*☎ 45008*), nearby, is an upmarket hotel with nice gardens, great views and the excellent ***Vaibhav restaurant***; plush doubles with TV cost from Rs 1025 in season (30% less at other times). There are other mid-range places farther along the ridge.

KMVN Tourist Rest House (*☎ 45006*) is a couple of kilometres beyond the village. It's very good value and has doubles from Rs 200 to 800 with great views, balconies and hot water. There are also dorm beds for Rs 60.

Anasakti Ashram has accommodation by donation, but you are required to attend prayers, and smoking, meat and alcohol are prohibited.

By the Sagar Hotel are several very similar restaurants, including the ***Hill Queen***, ***Ashoka*** and ***Sunrise***.

Getting There & Away

Buses to Almora pass through town approximately every hour between 7 am and 3 pm (Rs 32, 2½ hours), continuing to Nainital (Rs 70, six hours). Share-jeeps to Almora charge Rs 50. There are buses to Ranikhet at 6 and 9 am and 2 pm (Rs 42, four hours). There are also several buses to Bageshwar (Rs 23, 1½ hours), via Baijnath. A bus leaves between 7 and 8 am for Karnaprayag in Garhwal (Rs 56, three hours).

The nearest jeep hub is Garur, 10km downhill (Rs 10, 15 minutes), from where there are regular connections to Gwaldam (Rs 20), and Bageshwar (Rs 15). Taxis charge Rs 600 to Almora or Bageshwar and Rs 650 to Ranikhet.

BAIJNATH

☎ 05962

This peaceful village, 19km north of Kausani and 23km west of Bageshwar, is famous for its 12th-century sikhara-style temples. The main group (known collectively as Baijnath Temple) is devoted to Shiva and has a lovely location shaded by trees on the edge of the Gomti River. There are several other Shaivite shrines in the old village, a ten-minute walk north of Baijnath.

The only place to stay is the ***KMVN Tourist Rest House*** (*☎ 24101*), with doubles for Rs 200 and dorms for Rs 50. From Kausani, you can either take a Bageshwar bus or change to a Bageshwar jeep at Garur. Taxis charge Rs 250 return with an hour waiting.

BAGESHWAR

☎ 05963

This pleasant pilgrimage town is situated at the confluence of the Gomti and Sarju Rivers, 41km from Kausani and 78km from Almora. Indian pilgrims come here all year to pray at the ancient stone **Bagnath Temple**, which is devoted to Shiva and houses some impressive carvings. The town is an important transport hub and has some interesting ghats and bazaar backstreets.

There are several decent places to stay. Right by the bus stand, the ***Hotel Annpurna*** (*☎ 22109*) has a nice riverside terrace and simple rooms for Rs 175 (Rs 240 with TV and geyser). Farther along the main road is the ***Hotel Siddhartha*** (*☎ 22114*) with good value rooms with geyser and TV for Rs 250 a double.

There are several daily buses to Almora (Rs 55, three hours) and Ranikhet (Rs 65, three hours) via Kausani (Rs 23, 1½ hours), or you can take a share-jeep to Garur and change. Heading south, there are frequent buses to Bhowali (Rs 139, six hours) and Haldwani (Rs 155, 7½ hours). Jeeps and buses run up to Gwaldam (Rs 30, two hours) for connections on to Garhwal. For the Pindari Glacier, there's a 7 am bus to Song. For the Milam Glacier take the 9 am bus to Munsyari, or change at Thal.

Pindari Glacier Trek

Song, 36km north of Bageshwar, is the starting point for the trek to the Pindari Glacier on the southern rim of the Nanda Devi National Park. The trail passes through truly virgin country and offers wonderful views of Nanda Kot (6860m) and Nanda Khat (6611m). The return trip takes six days (a 100km round trip), but you can also include the Kafni Glacier (add two days) or continue west to Gwaldam (add two days). There are buses to Song from Bhowali and Bageshwar, or you can take a local bus to Bharari and change to a jeep there.

PITHORAGARH

☎ 05964 • pop 42,113 • elevation 1815m

Pithoragarh is the main town of a region that borders both Tibet and Nepal and has several Chand-era temples and an old fort. The town sits in a small valley that has been called 'Little Kashmir' and there are plenty of picturesque walks in the area, including the rewarding climb up to **Chandak** (7km) for views of the Panchchuli (Five Chimneys) massif.

There's a tourist office (☎ 25527) and a ***KMVN Rest House*** *(☎ 25434)*, with doubles for Rs 350 and dorm beds for Rs 50. The district magistrate's office in Pithoragarh (☎ 22202) is the place to inquire about Inner-Line Permits for the sensitive area around Nanda Devi. There are several other hotels, including ***Uttranchal Deep*** and ***Samrat***.

Several buses leave for Almora between 4.30 and 10 am (Rs 73, five hours). There are also regular buses to Haldwani, Delhi and Tanakpur (the railhead, 151km south), where you can take a local bus to the Nepali border crossing at Banbassa. Buses and jeeps run north to Munsyari, the trailhead for the Milam Glacier.

Milam Glacier Trek

This challenging trek passes through magnificent rugged country to the east of Nanda Devi (7816m), following the gorge of the Gori Ganga river. The trailhead is the spectacularly located village of Munsyari. Accommodation is limited to camping and the trek is best attempted with a guide (available in Munsyari). This is a politically sensitive area, and you'll need to show your passport and register with the Indo-Tibet Border Police (ITBP) at Milam village, who may not let you proceed any farther. Munsyari has a ***KMVN Rest House*** *(☎ 05961-22339)* with rooms from Rs 450 and dorms for Rs 60. There is a daily bus from Almora to Munsyari and several trips from Pithoragarh.

BANBASSA

Banbassa is the closest Indian village to the Nepali border post of Mahendrenagar. See Land in the Getting There & Away chapter for further information.

Bihar & Jharkhand

In November 2000 Bihar was split into two states to meet the demands of the Adivasi people. This movement gathered strength over the years and culminated in the creation of the new state, Jharkhand, which comprises 18 mineral-rich southern districts. This is not good news for poor Bihar, which will be even worse off without its more prosperous south.

There have been some teething problems with the creation of Jharkhand, including a petition in Patna's High Court from Members of the Legislative Council challenging its validity. Such issues will probably take a while to sort out, but travellers should notice few real changes when moving around the area of former Bihar.

Despite having areas of great beauty and historic religious links, Bihar is India's poorest state and is notorious for political uprisings. Both Bihar and Jharkhand are well known for Naxalite bandit activity and Ranchi, the capital of Jharkhand, has curfews to combat law and order problems.

Historically, Bihar has been closely linked with the life of Buddha as he spent most of his time here and attained enlightenment at Bodhgaya. Today Buddha's predictions continue to come true: the rivers periodically flood; per capita income is meagre; the literacy rate is one of the lowest in the country; and Bihar is considered to have the most widespread government corruption. Strikes and demonstrations are the order of the day and 'feud and fire' take the form of outbreaks of intercaste warfare and violence – dacoity (banditry) is still widespread.

Because of this lawlessness, political instability and the lack of tourism infrastructure, few travellers spend much time in Bihar or Jharkhand. This is a pity because there is much to see. There are areas of natural beauty such as lakes, waterfalls and hot springs; Bodhgaya is an excellent place to visit, particularly if you're interested in Buddhism; and Rajgir, Sasaram and especially Nalanda are some of the most fascinating places you'll find off the usual tourist trail.

History

The name Bihar is derived from the word *vihara*, meaning monastery. Bihar was a great religious centre for Jains, Hindus and, most importantly, Buddhists.

Buddha prophesied that, although a great city would arise in Bihar, it would always be in danger from 'feud, fire and flood'. From the 6th century BC to the 5th century AD, Bihar was coveted by a succession of rulers

Bihar & Jharkhand at a Glance

Population: 82.9 million (Bihar), 26.9 (Jharkhand)
Area: 173,877 sq km
Capital: Patna (Bihar), Ranchi (Jharkhand)
Main Language: Hindi
When to Go: Oct to Mar

Nepal
Patna p413
Gaya p421
Bodhgaya p417

- Soak up the Buddhist vibes under the sacred Bodhi Tree at Bodhgaya
- Explore Patna Museum, a little oasis of knowledge and artefacts
- Enjoy the peaceful tranquillity of the ruins at Nalanda University, an ancient seat of learning
- Relax just after the monsoon at one of the many beautiful waterfalls in the area around Ranchi
- Check out everything from chickens to elephants at Sonepur Fair, India's largest livestock fair

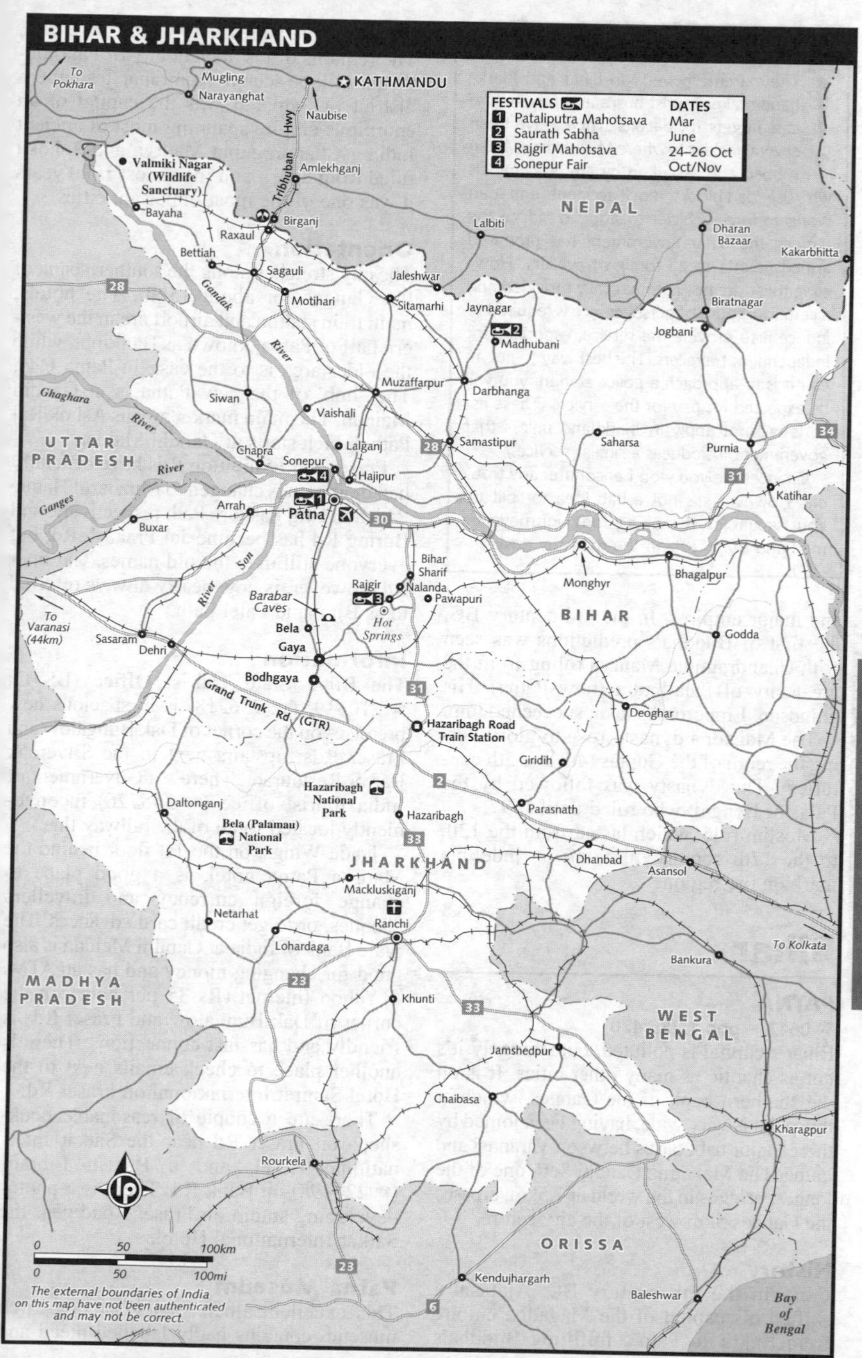

BIHAR & JHARKHAND
FESTIVALS
DATES
1 Pataliputra Mahotsava Mar
2 Saurath Sabha June
3 Rajgir Mahotsava 24–26 Oct
4 Sonepur Fair Oct/Nov
To Pokhara
Mugling
Narayanghat
KATHMANDU
Naubise
Tribhuban Hwy
Amlekhganj
Valmiki Nagar (Wildlife Sanctuary)
Bayaha
Birganj
Raxaul
Bettiah
Sagauli
Motihari
Gandak River
Jaleshwar
Sitamarhi
Jaynagar
Madhubani
Lalbiti
NEPAL
Dharan Bazaar
Kakarbhitta
Biratnagar
Jogbani
Muzaffarpur
Darbhanga
Siwan
Vaishali
Ghaghara River
UTTAR PRADESH
Chapra
Lalganj
Samastipur
Saharsa
Purnia
Katihar
Sonepur
Hajipur
Ganges River
Arrah
Patna
Buxar
Son River
Bihar Sharif
Nalanda
Rajgir
Pawapuri
Barabar Caves
Hot Springs
Monghyr
Bhagalpur
BIHAR
To Varanasi (44km)
Sasaram
Dehri
Bela
Gaya
Bodhgaya
Godda
Grand Trunk Rd (GTR)
Deoghar
Hazaribagh Road Train Station
Giridih
Hazaribagh National Park
Daltonganj
Parasnath
Hazaribagh
Bela (Palamau) National Park
Dhanbad
Asansol
JHARKHAND
Mackluskiganj
Netarhat
Ranchi
Lohardaga
To Kolkata
Bankura
MADHYA PRADESH
Khunti
WEST BENGAL
Jamshedpur
Chaibasa
Kharagpur
Rourkela
ORISSA
0 50 100km
0 50 100mi
Kendujhargarh
Baleshwar
Bay of Bengal
The external boundaries of India on this map have not been authenticated and may not be correct.
28
34
31
30
31
2
33
23
33
23
6

Warning

The extreme poverty in Bihar and Jharkhand makes tourist buses and private hire cars targets for dacoits. There have been several incidents where tourists have been robbed and assaulted by armed criminals who use road blocks, mock accidents and road works to force vehicles to stop. To reduce the danger, the Bihar government has promised armed escorts to all foreign travellers. However, these are not automatically provided and a certain amount of perseverance is required to induce it to provide the service, especially for independent travellers. The best way to get an escort is to approach a police station; you will be expected for pay for the service. (These escorts will not apply in Jharkhand unless that government introduces a similar service.)

Chances are you won't encounter any trouble. However, it's not a bad idea to split up your valuables if making long journeys by road and try to get off the roads by dusk.

and major empires. In the 3rd century BC, the first of Buddha's predictions was seen with Chandragupta Maurya ruling from the great city of Pataliputra (now Patna). His grandson, Emperor Ashoka, succeeded him.

The Magadha dynasty rose to glory during the reign of the Guptas (4th and 5th centuries). The dynasty was followed by the Palas of Bengal, who ruled until 1197.

Muslim rule, which lasted from the 12th to the 17th century, also left an indelible mark on the region.

Bihar

PATNA

☎ 0612 • pop 1,285,470

Bihar's capital is polluted, but strangely it's not as chaotic as many other cities. It is on the southern bank of the Ganges, which at this point is very wide, having been joined by three major tributaries between Varanasi and Patna. The Mahatma Gandhi Seti, one of the longest bridges in the world at 7.5km, crosses the Ganges 5km west of the city centre.

History

Early in the 5th century BC, Ajatasatru shifted his capital of the Magadha empire from Rajgir to Patna, fulfilling Buddha's prophecy that a great city would arise here. The remains of his ancient city of Pataliputra can still be seen in Kumrahar, a southern district of Patna. It was the capital of an enormous empire spanning most of ancient India – Chandragupta Maurya and Ashoka ruled from here – and for almost 1000 years it was one of the most important cities.

Orientation

The city stretches along the southern bank of the Ganges for about 15km. The hotels, main train station and airport are in the western half of Patna, known as Bankipur, while the older area is to the east, in Patna City. The 'hub' of the new Patna is at Gandhi Maidan. The main market area is Ashok Raj Path, which starts at Gandhi Maidan.

Fraser and Exhibition Rds have officially had their names changed to Muzharul Haque Path and Braj Kishore Path respectively, and Boring Rd has become Jal Prakash Rd, but everyone still uses the old names. Gardiner Rd, however, is now nearly always referred to as Birchand Patel Path.

Information

The Bihar State Tourist Office (BSTO; ☎ 210219, fax 236218) is in spacious new premises on the corner of Dak Bungalow and Fraser Rds; upstairs next to the Silveroak Bar & Restaurant. There's a Government of India tourist office (☎ 345776) inconveniently located south of the railway line.

Trade Wings, on the 1st floor behind the Maurya Patna hotel, is a good place to change foreign currency and travellers cheques, or to get credit card advances. The State Bank of India at Gandhi Maidan is also good for changing money and has an ATM.

Yahoo Internet (Rs 35 per hour) on the corner of Dak Bungalow and Fraser Rds is friendly and has fast connections. There is another place to check emails next to the Hotel Samrat International on Fraser Rd.

There are a couple of reasonable bookshops on Fraser Rd near the Satkar International Hotel, and a British Library (☎ 224198) on Bank Rd. There is a photo-developing studio on Fraser Road near the Satkar International Hotel.

Patna Museum

This excellent albeit somewhat dog-eared museum contains badly labelled metal and

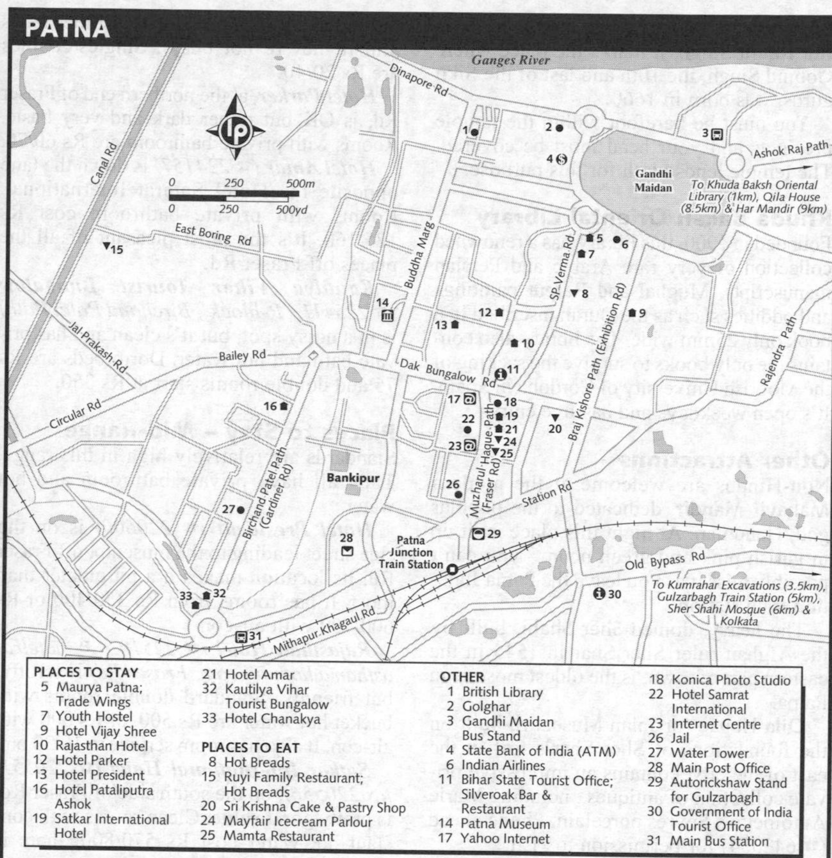

stone sculptures dating back to the Maurya and Gupta periods. It also houses the world's longest fossilised tree – 16m and 200 million years old. Stuffed wildlife includes the usual (tiger, deer) and the unusual (a young goat with three ears and eight legs). There is a fine collection of Chinese paintings and *thangkas* (Tibetan cloth paintings), but unfortunately this collection is frequently closed. The museum is open 10.30 am to 4.30 pm, Tuesday to Sunday. Entry costs Rs 2, and you need to ask permission before taking photos.

Kumrahar Excavations

The remains of Pataliputra, as well as the ancient capital of Ajatasatru (491–59 BC), Chandragupta (321–297 BC) and Ashoka (274–237 BC), have been uncovered in Kumrahar, south of Patna. A few large pillars from the assembly hall, dating back to the Mauryan period, and the foundations of the brick Buddhist monastery known as Anand Bihar are all that remain. There's a small display of clay figures and wooden beams that were discovered here.

The Kumrahar excavations are fairly esoteric and are likely to attract only those with a keen interest in archaeology and India's ancient history. They are set in a pleasant park and open 9 am to 5 pm Tuesday to Sunday; entry costs a hefty US$5 (Rs 230) for foreigners and a mere Rs 5 for Indians.

Har Mandir

At the eastern end of the city, in the Chowk area of old Patna, stands one of the holiest

Sikh shrines. Built of white marble by warrior Ranjit Singh, it marks the place where Gobind Singh, the 10th and last of the Sikh gurus, was born in 1660.

You must be barefoot within the temple precincts and your head must be covered. The temple lends cloth for this purpose.

Khuda Baksh Oriental Library

Founded in 1900, this library has a renowned collection of very rare Arabic and Persian manuscripts, Mughal and Rajput paintings and oddities such as the Quran inscribed in a book only 25mm wide. The library also contains the only books to survive the sacking of the Moorish University of Cordoba in Spain. It's open weekdays and has free entry.

Other Attractions

Non-Hindus are welcome at the modern **Mahavir Mandir**, dedicated to the popular god, Hanuman. At night this place is lit up in garish pink and green neon – you can't possibly miss it as you leave the Patna Junction train station.

The heavy, domed **Sher Shahi**, built by the Afghan ruler Sher Shar in 1545 in the eastern part of town, is the oldest mosque in Patna.

Qila House (or Jalan Museum), built on the foundations of Sher Shar's fort in the east of the city, contains an impressive private collection of antiques, including Marie Antoinette's Sévres porcelain. Phone ahead (☎ 642354) for permission to visit.

Organised Tours

BSTO sometimes operates a day trip that includes Patna, Rajgir, Nalanda and Pawapuri for Rs 125.

See also the boxed text 'The Buddhist Circuit' later in this chapter for information about tours of Bihar's Buddhist sites.

Special Events

Every March Patna comes alive with the **Pataliputra Mahotsava** featuring parades, sports, dancing and music.

Places to Stay – Budget

A lot of the cheaper hotels are tucked away in lanes off Fraser Rd.

The ***Youth Hostel*** *(SP Verma Rd)*, south of the Maurya Patna, has clean, spartan dorms and rooms. It only accepts members (although you can probably twist the staff's arm if they're not busy). Singles/doubles are Rs 20/40.

Hotel Parker, at the northern end of Fraser Rd, is OK but rather dark and very basic. Rooms with private bathroom are Rs 60/70.

Hotel Amar *(☎ 224157)* is down the lane opposite the Hotel Samrat International. Rooms with private bathroom cost Rs 125/160. It's the most pleasant of all the places off Fraser Rd.

Kautilya Vihar Tourist Bungalow *(☎ 225411, 'R-block', Birchand Patel Path)* is in a noisy spot, but it's clean and has private bath and hot water. Dorm beds are Rs 75 and double rooms start at Rs 350.

Places to Stay – Mid-Range

Standards are relatively high in this range. They all have private bathroom and hot water.

Hotel President *(☎ 220600)* is on the side street leading to the museum, off Fraser Rd. Its location makes it a bit quieter than most. It has rooms from Rs 350/400 or Rs 600/700 with air-con.

Rajasthan Hotel *(☎ 225102, ⓔ hotelrajasthan@hotmail.com, Fraser Rd)* is scruffy, but friendly. Standard double rooms with bucket hot water are Rs 500, or Rs 800 with air-con. It also has room service to 10.30 pm.

Satkar International Hotel *(☎ 220551, fax 220556)*, on the south side of Fraser Rd, is pretty good value. Clean rooms with constant hot water cost Rs 570/800; there is also a lift.

Hotel Vijay Shree *(☎ 685312, Exhibition Rd)* used to be Hotel Swayam Sidhi – it has had a tasteful makeover and is excellent value. Air-con rooms with TV and constant hot water are Rs 550/650.

Places to Stay – Top End

Maurya Patna *(☎ 222061, fax 222069)* overlooks Gandhi Maidan and is Patna's top hotel. You can count on the usual mod cons, including a pool. Rooms start at Rs 1900/2500, with breakfast. ***Hotel Pataliputra Ashok*** *(☎ 226270)*, south of Bailey Rd, is similar at Rs 1600/2000.

The ***Hotel Chanakya*** *(☎ 220590, fax 220598, ⓔ chanakya@gias101.vsnl.net.in)* is a central air-conditioned three-star place near the Tourist Bungalow and charges Rs 1700/2300.

Places to Eat

Bustling Fraser Rd is the best place to chow down.

Mayfair Icecream Parlour is a clean and very popular place with good *masala dosas* (curried vegetables inside a pancake) and other snacks, as well as 16-odd ice-cream flavours.

Mamta Restaurant is an intimate place for dinner. There's a fish tank with the biggest goldfish you'll ever see – fortunately fish isn't on the menu. Main courses start at around Rs 50 and beer costs Rs 65.

Rajasthan Hotel has a good vegetarian restaurant. It's not cheap, but the food is excellent and there's a good range of ice cream.

Sri Krishna Cake & Pastry Shop, around the corner on Dak Bungalow Rd, is a good place to pick up lunch. A couple of sandwiches and a drink will cost about Rs 40. It also does pizzas and lots of pastries.

Silveroak Bar & Restaurant, in the new building also housing BSTO on Fraser Rd, serves Indian and Chinese meals. It is clean, comfortable and affordable

Hot Breads sells excellent freshly baked breads, pastries and cakes and has two outlets, one on SP Verma Rd and one, which also sells ice cream, on East Boring Rd.

Ruyi Family Restaurant, next to Hot Breads on East Boring Rd, is the only restaurant in Bihar specialising in Chinese cuisine. While being quite expensive, it is well decorated, clean, friendly, nonsmoking and the service is first class.

Getting There & Away

Air Indian Airlines (☎ 226433) has two daily flights between Patna and Delhi (US$145); four weekly flights to Kolkata (Calcutta; US$100); and daily flights to Ranchi (US$70). A daily flight connects Patna with Lucknow (US$100); you can book tickets at the Indian Airlines office near Gandhi Maidan. Sahara Air has one flight a day to Varanasi (US$85) and Delhi. Necon Air flies four times a week between Kathmandu and Patna (US$75, plus Rs 50 airport tax).

Bus The main bus station is at Harding Park, just west of Patna Junction train station. It's a large place with departure gates spread out along the road. The fare varies according to the speed of the service. Buses from Gate 7 include:

destination	fare (Rs)	duration (hrs)
Gaya	50	4
Rajgir	50	3
Ranchi	142	9
Sasaram	70	6
Siliguri	175	12

The Gandhi Maidan bus stand is used by government buses going to many places in Bihar. There are night buses to Ranchi and a deluxe bus to Siliguri (Rs 165, daily).

Nepal Buses for Raxaul, on the Nepal border, depart from the main bus station (Rs 100, seven hours, Gate 6). There are hourly morning departures and less frequent afternoon services. A deluxe night bus also leaves the Gandhi Maidan bus stand (Rs 110, seven hours) at 10 pm. Buses from Birganj (on the Nepali side of the border) to Kathmandu cost about Rs 82 (Nep Rs 114).

Train The train booking office at Patna Junction is a joke – it's absolutely chaotic. If time is short, you might be better off paying a small commission to a tour company to buy tickets for you.

The fastest trains on the Kolkata to Delhi line take 12 hours to Delhi (Rs 324/926 in 2nd/1st class, 992km) and seven hours to Kolkata (Rs 202/640, 545km). There are a number of direct trains daily to Varanasi (Rs 115/346, five hours, 228km); Gaya (Rs 35/173, two hours, 92km); Ranchi (Rs 168/524, 10 hours, 591km); and Mumbai (Rs 397/1310).

If you're heading to Darjeeling or the north-eastern region, the fast *North East Express* from Delhi leaves Patna at 10.20 pm, arriving in New Jalpaiguri (Siliguri) at 9.40 am (Rs 132/951 in 2nd/2nd class air-con, 636km).

Getting Around

To/From the Airport The airport is 7km west of the city centre. There is a massive free-for-all for Immigration and Customs queues, and the security staff appear to double as porters. Indian Airlines runs a bus service from its office next to the Gandhi Maidan, cycle-rickshaws cost approximately Rs 60 and taxis should charge about Rs 130.

Autorickshaw Shared autorickshaws shuttle back and forth between the main

Patna Junction train station and Gulzarbagh train station (Rs 5). The other main route is from the train station to Gandhi Maidan bus stand (Rs 3).

SONEPUR

☎ 06654

Sonepur Fair, a two-week cattle fair, is held in October/November each year here. It takes place around the full moon of Kartika Purnima, the most auspicious time to bathe at the confluence of the Ganges and Gandak Rivers. Four times the size of Pushkar's Camel Fair, it's probably the largest animal fair in Asia. Not only cattle are traded at Haathi Bazaar – elephants change hands for anything from Rs 10,000 to 100,000, depending on their age and condition. If you're considering purchasing an alternative form of transport, Mark Shand's *Travels on my Elephant* is essential reading for the modern-day mahout.

The Bihar State Tourist Development Corporation (BSTDC) operates a tourist village during the fair. Double cottages cost Rs 500 (no single rates). There is also a 20-bed dorm for Rs 77 per person and several temporary huts, which are decorated with traditional Mithila paintings. The cost of the huts varies according to demand! For bookings contact BSTDC in Patna (☎ 0612-225411).

VAISHALI

☎ 06225

As long ago as the 6th century BC, Vaishali was the capital of a republic. Mahavira, a Jain *tirthankar* (teacher) was born here, and Buddha preached his last sermon here. There's little to see: an **Ashoka pillar** (with its lion capital intact), a few dilapidated **stupas** (one contains an eighth of Buddha's ashes) and a small **museum**. Admission to these ruins cost US$5 (Rs 230) for foreigners.

A ***BSTDC Tourist Youth Hostel & Tourist Bungalow*** has rooms for Rs 150/180 for singles/doubles with shared bathroom.

There are guided tours from Patna or buses from Lalganj and Muzaffarpur.

RAXAUL

☎ 06255

Raxaul is virtually a twin town with Birganj, just across the border in Nepal. Both are crowded and dirty. Cycle-rickshaws take 20 minutes (Rs 20) from the border (open 4 am to midnight) to the bus stand in

Mithila Paintings

Bihar's unique and most famous folk art is its *Mithila* or *Madhubani* paintings. Traditionally, wives from Madhubani and surrounding villages in the Mithila district started creating strong line drawings on the walls of their homes from the day of their marriage. Using pigments from natural products such as spices, minerals, charcoal and vegetable matter, the women painted local deities and scenes from mythology. Special events and aspects of everyday life were often incorporated with the images of gods and goddesses.

These paintings, both in black and white and strong primary colours, are now being professionally produced on paper, canvas and textiles for commercial purposes. Examples of the original wall paintings can still be seen in homes around Madhubani (approximately 160km north-east of Patna, five to six hours by bus) and in the Bihar government tourist village huts at the Sonepur Fair.

Each June, the Saurath Sabha is held in a mango grove in Saurath village. It is a unique gathering of Mithila Brahmins from all over India, who come for the biggest marriage market in the country. Parents of marriageable children come armed with horoscopes in the hope of negotiating suitable marriages for their offspring.

SIMON BORG

BIHAR & JHARKHAND

SARA-JANE CLELAND

SARA-JANE CLELAND

RICHARD I'ANSON

RICHARD I'ANSON

Top left: Bihar is closely linked with the life of Buddha and is home to many Buddhist devotees.
Top right: Bodhgaya's Mahabodhi Temple is a place of pilgrimage for all Buddhists.
Middle left & bottom: Monks light candles and perform *puja* (prayers) at the annual Ningma Monlam

MARK DAFFEY

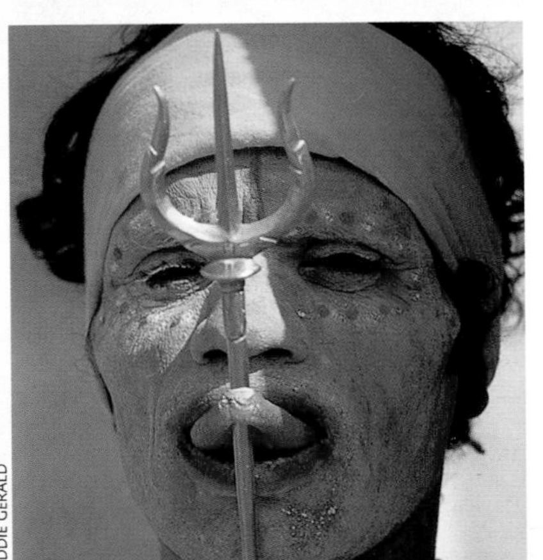

EDDIE GERALD

SARA-JANE CLELAND

PAUL BIGLAND

The sights of tropical Orissa: exploring the Udayagiri Caves in Bhubaneswar **(top)**; devotional sculpture in the holy seaside resort of Puri **(middle right)**; Konark's great Sun Temple **(bottom)**; and a devotee during Thaipusam, the time for penance **(middle left)**

Birganj. Visas for Nepal are available at the border for US$30. Be warned that US currency *only* is accepted as payment for visas.

Neither Raxaul or Birganj are places to hang around, but if you're stuck, ***Hotel Kaveri*** has rooms for Rs 100/120 for singles/doubles with shared bathroom.

Hotel Ajanta is better. It's down a side road near the bus stand and charges Rs 80/100 for a room with shared bathroom.

Getting There & Away

There are several buses a day from Raxaul to Patna (Rs 100, seven hours). Beware of touts selling combined bus and train tickets: it's more reliable to organise things yourself.

From Birganj, morning and evening buses to Kathmandu take around 12 hours (Rs 95); Pokhara buses take 10 hours (Rs 75). Most Kathmandu buses take the much longer road via Narayanghat and Mugling, rather than the scenic Tribhuvan Hwy via Naubise.

BODHGAYA

☎ 0631

For the traveller, Bodhgaya is probably the most interesting of all the holy sites associated with the life of Buddha, being much more of a working Buddhist centre than an archaeological site. It's also the most important Buddhist pilgrimage destination in the world.

The focal point is the Mahabodhi Temple, which marks the spot where Buddha attained enlightenment and set out on his life of preaching.

Buddhists from all over the world flock to Bodhgaya, along with non-Buddhists who come to learn about Buddhism and meditation. Bodhgaya is small and quiet, but growing rapidly and accumulating all the usual 'tourism' paraphernalia. However, it is still a pleasant place to stay a few days. The best time to visit is during winter, October to March, when Tibetan pilgrims come down from Dharamsala. The Dalai Lama often spends December here. The Tibetan refugee market, open at this time, is a great place to pick up some winter woollens, and you'll be helping the Tibetan community in exile.

Information

The tourist complex on the corner of Bodhgaya Rd and Temple St consists of two

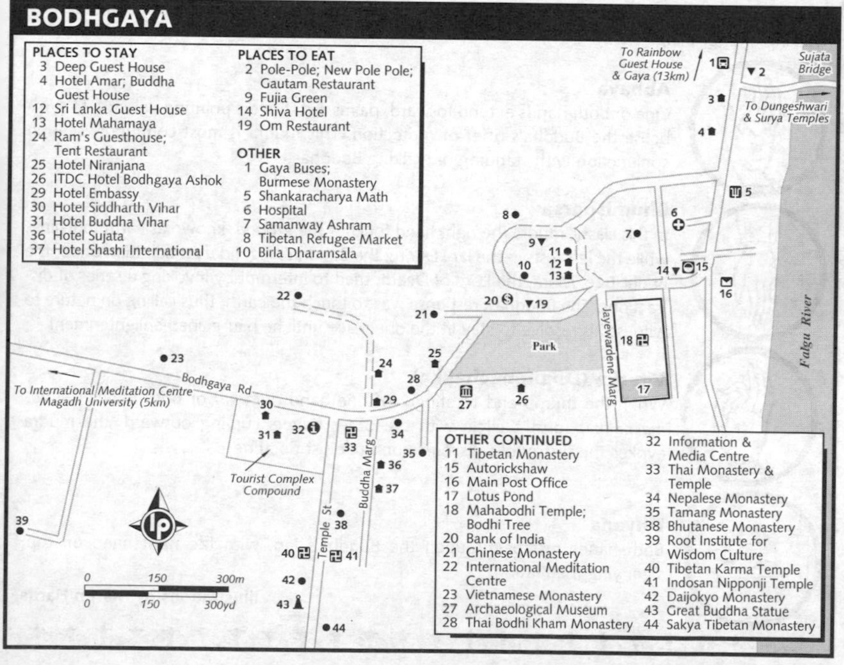

hotels, a restaurant, gardens and an 'Information & Media Centre' which is little more than a fancy building open from 10 am to 5 pm daily except Sunday.

There are a few banks, including a Bank of India, near Om Restaurant.

There were no email facilities at the time of research, but this will change – have a look around the Mahabodhi Temple area.

Mahabodhi Temple

Standing adjacent to a descendant of the original Bodhi Tree under which Buddha meditated on the excesses of life and formulated his philosophy of a balanced approach to it, this temple is a place of pilgrimage for all Buddhists.

A sapling from the original Bodhi Tree was carried to Anuradhapura in Sri Lanka by Sanghamitta (the Emperor Ashoka's daughter). That tree now flourishes there and, in turn, a cutting from it was carried back to Bodhgaya when the original tree died. A red sandstone slab under the tree is said to be the Vajrasan, or diamond throne, on which Buddha sat.

The Mahabodhi Temple stands on the site of a temple erected by Ashoka in the 3rd century BC. Topped by a 50m pyramidal spire, the ornate structure houses a large gilded image of Buddha. The current temple was restored in the 11th century and again in 1882. The stone railing around the temple, parts of which are still standing, is

Sculptural Symbolism

Buddha images throughout India are, for the most part, sculptured according to strict rules found in Buddhist art texts from the 3rd century AD. However, the tradition leaves room for innovation, allowing the various 'schools' of Buddhist art to distinguish themselves.

Most Buddha figures wear a simple long robe that appears to be transparent – the body is usually clearly visible underneath. In some earlier sculptures his hair is shown coiled.

Indian Buddha figures in all Indian religious sculpture, whatever the faith, can be distinguished from those of other countries by their body type – broad shoulders and chest, slim waist and a slight pot belly.

One aspect of the Buddhist tradition that almost never varies is the *asana* (posture) and *mudra* (hand position) of Buddha images. There are four basic postures and positions: standing, sitting, walking and reclining.

Abhaya

One or both hands extend forward, palms out, fingers pointing upward, to symbolise the Buddha's offer of protection. This mudra is most commonly seen in conjunction with standing or walking Buddhas.

Bhumisparsa

In this classic mudra the right hand touches the ground, known as earth touching, while the left rests in the lap. During the Buddha's legendary meditation under the Bodhi Tree, Mara, the Lord of Death, tried to interrupt by invoking a series of distractions. The Buddha's response was to touch the earth, thus calling on nature to witness his resolve to stay in the one place until he had gained enlightenment.

Vitarka (Dhammachakka)

When the thumb and forefinger of one hand *(vitarka)* or both hands *(dhammachakka)* form a circle with the other fingers curving outward, the mudra evokes the first public discourse on Buddhist doctrine.

Dhyana

Both hands rest palms upon the Buddha's lap, with the right hand on top, signifying meditation.

Illustrations by Martin Harris

BIHAR & JHARKHAND

considered to be from the Sunga period (around 184–72 BC). The carved and sculptured railing has been restored, although parts of it now stand in the museum in Kolkata and in the Victoria & Albert Museum in London. Stone stupas, erected by visiting pilgrims, dot the temple courtyard.

There is a great sense of peace and serenity within the temple compound. Pilgrims and visitors from all walks of life and religions come here to worship or just admire. Entry to the temple grounds, which are open 6 am to noon and 2 to 6.30 pm, is free, but there is a Rs 10/200 charge for cameras/video cameras. A relaxing way to finish the day is a stroll in the evening around the perimeter of the temple compound, threading your way through monks from all over the world, while soaking up the ambience of this sacred place.

For more information on Buddhism and Buddha's life, see Religion in the Facts about India chapter.

Monasteries

Most countries with a large Buddhist population have a temple or monastery here, usually built in a representative architectural style. Thus the Thai temple looks very much like the colourful wats you see in Thailand. The Tibetan Karma temple and monastery were built in 1934 and contain a large prayer wheel.

The Burmese, who led the campaign to restore the Mahabodhi Temple in the 19th century, built their present monastery in 1936. The Japanese temple (Indosan Nipponji) has a beautiful Buddha image from Japan – across the road is the Daijokyo Temple. There are also Chinese, Sri Lankan, Bhutanese, Vietnamese, Nepalese, Korean, Taiwanese and Bangladeshi monasteries. The Tai Bodhi Kham Monastery was built by tribes from Assam and Arunachal Pradesh.

Other Attractions

The archaeological museum (open 10 am to 5 pm Saturday to Thursday) has a small collection of Buddha figures and pillars found in the area. The Hindu Shankaracharya Math has a temple, and there's a sculpture gallery in the grounds. Across the river are the Dungeshwari and Suraya temples.

The 25m-high **Great Buddha Statue** in the Japanese Kamakura style was unveiled by the Dalai Lama in 1989. A Maitreya Buddha statue over 100m high is being built in Bodhgaya as a symbol of world peace.

Volunteer Work

If you're interested in working on social development projects in the area, contact Mr Dwarko Sundrani at the Samanway Ashram in Bodhgaya. This is a good place to do voluntary work (during which time you'll also be taught Indian beliefs and ways of life) or to make a donation.

The ashram works mainly with children from the lowest castes, performing thousands of eye operations every year; as a volunteer you can work with the children. There is also a dairy and agriculture farm that requires volunteer labour. At the time of research there were eight foreigners working here including Japanese, Australians and Danes. Ask for directions near the Mahabodhi Temple, as the ashram can be difficult to locate.

Sujata Charitable Society (☎ 400463) is run by Mr Sunil Kumar Sinha, the enthusiastic manager of Deep Guest House. He has opened a school that provides free education to illiterate children and adults. He also plans to make free medical services available for people in Bihar. Volunteers are welcome, as are donations.

Meditation & Buddhism Courses

Courses and retreats take place in the winter, mainly from October to early February.

Some of the most accessible courses (excellent for beginners) are run by the Root Institute for Wisdom Culture (☎ 400714, ⓔ rootinst@nda.vsnl.net.in). It runs basic eight-day meditation courses for Rs 2600 (this includes meals and accommodation). Courses include meditation teachings and discussion about adherence to the Buddhist lay vows; retreats are also held in the peaceful location on the edge of Bodhgaya.

Travellers who have spent some time here seem impressed, not only with the courses but by the way the institute is working to put something back into the local community with health, agricultural and educational projects.

Courses are also run by the International Meditation Centre (☎ 400707) near the Magadh University (5km from Bodhgaya), and another centre closer to town. These courses are far more informal and students can start and finish any time they choose.

The annual insight meditation *(vipassana)* and spiritual inquiry retreats, which have places for 130 people, take place from 7 to 15 January, 15 to 23 January, and 23 January to 4 February at the Thai Monastery. For information and bookings write to Gaia House (☎ 1626-333613), West Ogwell, Near Newton Abbot, Devon TQ12 6EN, UK or (from mid-October) you can contact the Thai Monastery, c/o Burmese Monastery (fax 400848) in Bodhgaya. There are often cancellations, so if you just turn up on the day there's a good chance you'll get a spot.

Other courses are sometimes advertised on the noticeboard in the Om Restaurant.

Places to Stay – Budget

Prices given here are for the low season; note that they increase substantially in the high season (December to March).

***Rainbow Guest House** (☎ 400308)* is the first hotel on the right-hand side of the road coming into town from Gaya. It's a new spot and is good value. Dorms are Rs 30, double rooms with bathroom are Rs 150/250 without/with fan. All rooms have squat toilets.

***Deep Guest House** (☎ 400463)*, on the road to Gaya and next to the Burmese Monastery, comes highly recommended. The shared bathrooms are tiled, clean and have hot water. Doubles cost Rs 200 with shared bathroom and Rs 300 with private bathroom. The staff are friendly and helpful.

***Hotel Amar** (☎ 400462)*, close by on the same road, is a basic little place with squat toilets. Doubles are around Rs 100.

***Buddha Guest House** (☎ 400934)*, next to Amar, is also basic but clean and has a good view from the rooftop. Double rooms with fan, hot water and squat toilet are Rs 150 and dorm beds are Rs 50.

***Sri Lanka Guest House** (☎ 400742)*, a Mahabodhi Society place near the Tibetan Monastery, is popular and well run. It accepts donations of around Rs 80 for rooms with private bathroom.

***Ram's Guesthouse** (☎ 400644)*, behind the Hotel Embassy, is a friendly family-run place. Double rooms with private bathroom and hot-water geyser are Rs 200. Doubles with clean, shared bathrooms are Rs 150.

Tourist Bungalows No 1 and No 2 in the tourist complex compound are next to each other and are also known by more imaginative names: ***Hotel Buddha Vihar** (☎ 400445)* has very comfortable dormitory accommodation. Beds with shared bathroom are Rs 50 and Rs 75 with private bathroom. ***Hotel Siddharth Vihar** (☎ 400445)* offers excellent, compact doubles with TV and private bathroom for Rs 200.

If you're planning a longer stay or don't mind roughing it a little, behaving in a dignified manner and abiding by some simple rules, it's possible to stay at some of the monasteries. The ***Burmese Monastery*** (particularly popular with Westerners for its study courses), the ***Bhutanese Monastery*** and the ***Tibetan Monastery*** all take guests and cost around Rs 50 a night.

Places to Stay – Mid-Range & Top End

The continuing spate of building in this range ensures competitive prices. All singles/doubles have private bathroom.

***Hotel Niranjana** (☎ 400475, Bodhgaya Rd)*, opposite the park, has good doubles with TV, although the bathrooms are a bit grotty for the price. Nonair-con singles/doubles are Rs 600/900.

***Hotel Embassy** (☎ 400711)*, with its rooftop seating, passes the white-glove test. Rooms with TV are Rs 500/800.

***ITDC Hotel Bodhgaya Ashok** (☎ 400700, 400790, fax 400788)*, near the Archaeological Museum, has rooms for Rs 1000/1500, or with air-con for Rs 1600/2400. Overpriced dorm beds are Rs 400.

***Hotel Sujata** (☎ 400761, 400481, ⓔ hotel_sujata@yahoo.com, Buddha Marg)* is an upmarket place with 24-hour room service, foreign exchange and restaurant. There is a Japanese-style bathroom and prayer hall. Singles/doubles cost Rs 1895/2295.

Next door, ***Hotel Shashi International** (☎ 400459, fax 400483, Buddha Marg)* has a restaurant serving Chinese and Thai cuisine. Small but spotless rooms are Rs 1000/1200.

***Mahamaya Hotel** (☎ 400221, ⓔ htl_mahamaya@hotmail.com)*, close to the Mahabodhi Temple, is a luxurious place in a very central spot. This large hotel with an impressive marble lobby has internal courtyards and comfortable, spacious rooms. Rooms start at Rs 1400/2000, but you may get a discount if it's not busy.

Places to Eat

The standard of food here is pretty low out of season and surprisingly high during winter, when the pilgrims arrive.

The cuisine at ***Shiva Hotel***, next to an autorickshaw stand, includes Japanese, Indian and Continental. A mushroom chow mein is Rs 40, chilli chicken is Rs 75 and burgers are Rs 35. The service is friendly.

Ram's Guesthouse has a cheap tent restaurant with a good selection of Sri Lankan, Japanese, Chinese, Tibetan and Western food.

Other tent restaurants that offer great value include ***Pole-Pole***, ***New Pole-Pole*** and the ***Gautam***, all opposite the Burmese monastery. All have varied menus, overworked jaffle machines, good music collections and are popular. The Gautam also has a bakery in winter.

There are also several Tibetan-run restaurants behind the Tibetan Monastery. Most operate in tents and only open during winter, but there are some perennial places that you can try. ***Om Restaurant*** is well established, and is a popular meeting place near the Bank of India. It has a particularly good breakfast menu and does good Tibetan and Japanese food. It's open only in winter. ***Fujia Green***, opposite the Tibetan refugee market, serves Tibetan and Chinese grub year-round.

Getting There & Away

Bodhgaya is 13km from Gaya, and shared autorickshaws shuttle between the two. They're phenomenally overloaded: a total of up to 15 people (plus animals, goods and so on) travel on a vehicle intended for three! The fare is Rs 8 (or from Rs 50 for the whole autorickshaw, but you'll probably pay closer to Rs 100).

There are frequent buses to Gaya (Rs 5) that are also very crowded. They leave regularly from outside the Burmese monastery.

GAYA

☎ 0631

Gaya is about 100km south of Patna. Just as nearby Bodhgaya is a major centre for Buddhist pilgrims, Gaya is a centre for Hindu pilgrims. Vishnu is said to have given Gaya the power to absolve sinners. Pilgrims offer *pindas* (funeral cakes) at the ghats along the river here, and perform a lengthy circuit of the holy places around Gaya to free their ancestors from bondage to the earth.

There's a BSTO at the train station. The nearest foreign exchange is in Bodhgaya.

Things to See & Do

In the crowded central part of the old town, the *sikhara* (spired) **Vishnupad Temple** was constructed in 1787 by Queen Ahalya Bai of Indore on the banks of the Falgu River.

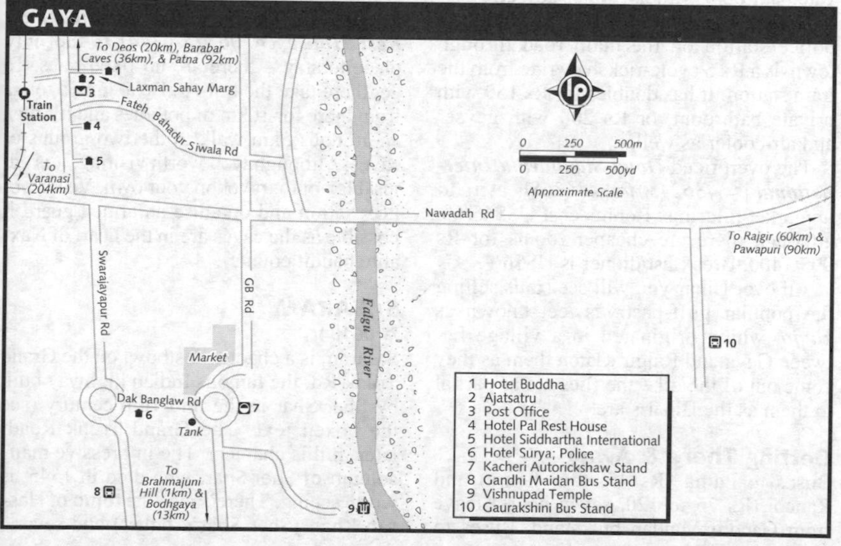

Inside the temple the 40cm 'footprint' of Vishnu is imprinted in solid rock and surrounded by a silver-plated basin. Note that non-Hindus are not permitted to enter.

During the monsoon, the river carries a great deal of water here but it dries up completely in winter. You can see cremations taking place on the riverbanks.

A flight of 1000 stone steps leads to the top of the **Brahmajuni Hill**, 1km south-west of the Vishnupad Temple. There's a good view over the town from the top. Gaya also has a small **archaeological museum** (open Tuesday to Sunday).

Places to Stay & Eat

There are many options around the station; most are spartan but OK for a short pause.

Hotel Buddha *(☎ 423428)* is down the lane opposite the train station. There is a roof garden and reasonable singles/doubles with private bathroom are Rs 150/200.

Hotel Pal Rest House *(☎ 436753)*, set back from the road, is quiet and cheap. Single/double rooms with private bathroom cost Rs 100/135. Singles with shared bathroom are only Rs 70.

At ***Ajatsatru*** *(☎ 434584)* rooms vary greatly; some are small, some dark, some have balconies and some are spacious and light. Doubles with fan and TV are Rs 300 or Rs 600 with air-con. All rooms have private bathroom with hot water geyser.

Hotel Surya *(☎ 424004)*, adjacent to the police station on the main road through town, is a Rs 5 cycle-rickshaw ride from the train station. It has doubles for Rs 150 with private bathroom, or Rs 200 with geyser and air-cooler as well.

The overpriced ***Hotel Siddhartha International*** *(☎ 436243, fax 436368)* caters to upmarket pilgrims. Rooms cost US$45/60, although there are cheaper rooms for Rs 995/1400. Breakfast/dinner is US$6/9.

All over Bihar you will see stalls selling the popular puff-pastry sweet known as *khaja*, which originated in a village between Gaya and Rajgir. Catch them as they come out of the oil – the flies are as partial to them as the Biharis are.

Getting There & Away

Buses to Patna (Rs 45, four hours) and Ranchi (Rs 75 to 120, seven hours) leave from Gandhi Maidan bus stand. Buses to Rajgir (Rs 35, three hours) leave from Gaurakshini bus stand, across the river.

Gaya is on the main Delhi-Kolkata railway line and there are direct trains to Delhi (Rs 174/310, 2nd class/2nd class sleeper); Kolkata (Rs 104/199/571, 2nd class/2nd class sleeper/1st class); Varanasi (Rs 61/115 /346, 2nd class/2nd class sleeper/1st class); Puri (Rs 156/282, 2nd class/2nd class sleeper); and Patna (Rs 31/198, 2nd class/ 1st class).

Autorickshaws from the train station to Bodhgaya (13km) should cost Rs 50 but they'll probably try for twice as much. From the Kacheri stand, a 25-minute walk from the station, shared autorickshaws cost Rs 8, plus Rs 4 for a rucksack. Local buses start at Rs 5.

Getting Around

From the train station it's Rs 10 by cycle-rickshaw to the Kacheri autorickshaw stand (for Bodhgaya) or Rs 15 to the Gaurakshini bus stand (for Rajgir). It's Rs 12 to Gandhi Maidan.

AROUND GAYA

At Deos, 20km to the north of Gaya, is a **temple of Surya** , the sun god.

The **Barabar Caves**, dating from 200 BC, are 36km north of Gaya. These are the 'Marabar' caves of EM Forster's *A Passage to India*. Two of the caves contain Ashokan inscriptions. The basic ***Barabar Siddhnath Rest House*** *(☎ 06322-6364)* is the only place to stay – there are no fixed rates. To get there take the train to Bela, grab a tonga from there for 10km of potholes and it's then an arduous 5km walk to the two groups of caves. Although well worth visiting, it is advisable not to travel on your own. Visit a police station and organise an armed guard if possible as the caves are in the heart of Naxalite bandit country.

SASARAM

☎ 06184

Sasaram is a chaotic dustbowl on the Grand Trunk Rd, the famous Indian highway built by Sher Shar in the mid-16th century (see the boxed text 'The Grand Trunk Road' later in this chapter). The impressive **mausoleum of Sher Shar**, who died in 1545, is worth seeing. There's also the **tomb of Hassan Khan** (Sher Shar's father) and several

BIHAR & JHARKHAND

other Muslim monuments. Entry is US$5 (Rs 230) for all.

Shershah Tourist Lodge is the best place to stay. Turn left onto the Grand Trunk Rd outside the train station and it's next to the second petrol station, 15 minutes' walk away. Doubles are Rs 110, or Rs 160 with private bathroom and Rs 370 with air-con. Dorm beds cost Rs 50.

There are buses to Patna (Rs 75, five hours). For Varanasi and Gaya, it's better to take a train. There are two direct trains from Varanasi – but it's possible to take a local bus from Varanasi train station to Mughal Serai (Rs 8, 17km), from where there are trains to Sasaram (Rs 23, three hours).

NALANDA

☎ 061194

Founded in the 5th century BC, Nalanda was one of the world's great universities and an important Buddhist centre until its sacking by the Afghans in the 12th century. When Chinese scholar and traveller Xuan Zang visited between AD 685 and 762, 10,000 monks and students resided here.

A credit to the curators, the site is peaceful, clean, well maintained and perfumed with the scent of roses and shrubs. Allow at least half a day for wandering as the ruins are extensive. The site is open from 7.30 am to 5 pm in winter and admission is US$5 (Rs 230) for foreigners.

The extensive brick-built remains include the **Great Stupa**, with steps, terraces and a few intact votive stupas around it, and the monks' cells. An **archaeological museum** (Rs 2, open 10 am to 4 pm Saturday to Thursday) houses the Nalanda University seal, sculptures and other remains. Pilgrims venerate Buddha figures in spite of signs saying 'Do not offer anything to the objects in the museum'! Guidebooks cost Rs 4.

The **Xuan Zang Memorial Hall** was recently built by the Chinese as a peace pagoda. Xuan Zang spent five years here as both a student and teacher.

There's also an international centre for the study of Buddhism, established in 1951.

Most people stay in Rajgir and visit on day trips, but you can stay at the Burmese, Japanese or Jain ***dharamsalas*** (pilgrims' resthouses) at Nalanda as well as the ***Public Works Department Rest House***. A bed at these places costs about Rs 50.

Getting There & Away

Ridiculously crowded shared Trekkers (jeeps) cost Rs 8 from Rajgir to Nalanda village from there it's Rs 8 for the 10-minute ride on a shared tonga to the university site. Take another jeep (Rs 5) from Nalanda village to Bihar Sharif, north of Nalanda, for buses to Patna (Rs 28, 3½ hours).

RAJGIR

☎ 06119

This was the capital of the Magadha empire until Ajatasatru moved to Pataliputra (Patna) in the 5th century BC. Today, Rajgir, 12km south of Nalanda, is a minor Indian holiday centre. In winter, visitors are drawn by the hot springs and healthy climate.

Rajgir is an important Buddhist pilgrimage site as Buddha spent 12 years here and the first Buddhist council after Buddha attained nirvana was held here. It's also an important place for Jains, as Mahavira spent some time in Rajgir and the hills are topped with Digambara (the 'sky-clad' Jain sect) shrines. A mention in the Mahabharata also ensures that there is a good supply of Hindu pilgrims.

Orientation & Information

The main road where you'll find the train station, bus stand and a number of hotels is about 500m west of town. There's a tourist complex by the hot springs, about 1km south of town along the main road.

The **Rajgir Mahotsava** (Indian Classical Performing Arts Festival) is held from 24 to 26 October every year. The festival includes performances of folk dance, ballet, opera, devotional song and instrumental music.

Things to See

Most people rent a tonga for half a day to see the sites, as they're spread out over several kilometres. This costs about Rs 60 but, with the brutal way these horses are treated, you might prefer to take a taxi.

Main sites include parts of the ruined city, caves and places associated with Ajatasatru and his father Bhimbisara, who he imprisoned and murdered. The pink building by the crowded hot springs is the **Lakshmi Narayan Temple**.

There's also a Burmese temple, an interesting **Jain exhibition** (Rs 10) and a modern Japanese temple. On the top of Ratnagiri

The Buddhist Circuit

Historically, Bihar has been closely linked with the life of Buddha. The Buddhist (or Lotus) Circuit is a pilgrims' trail following in the footsteps of Buddha, primarily in Bihar where he spent most of his time. The trail draws devotees from around the world. The following places are included in most itineraries.

Crawling with monks from all corners of the planet, **Bodhgaya** is the most holy of all Buddhist sites as it was here that Prince Siddhartha Gautama attained enlightenment more than 2500 years ago.

At the scruffy but excellent **Patna** Museum there's a collection of sculptures from Buddhist sites around Bihar. **Nalanda** was a place of great learning, and an important Buddhist centre, until it was levelled by the Afghans. Close by is **Rajgir** where Buddhist councils came into being.

The emperor Ashoka erected glorious monuments at **Sarnath**, where Buddha first preached his 'middle path' message. At **Vaishali** he announced his approaching nirvana.

Kushinagar in Uttar Pradesh is where Buddha is believed to have died and **Lumbini**, just over the border in Nepal, is recognised as his birthplace.

If you're interested in a tour, Potala Tours & Travels (☎ 3723284, 3722552, ⓔ potala@vsnl.com) 1011 Antriksh Bhavan, 22, KG Marg, New Delhi organises a 'Buddhist circuit' trip over 10 to 15 days with prices for most budgets. Check out its Web site at www.potalatours.com.

In Bihar, try the Buddha Travel Corporation (☎ 662443, fax 674589), Bhattacharya Rd, Patna.

Hill, 3km south of the hot springs, is the **Japanese Shanti Stupa**, reached by a chair-lift (Rs 20 return; 8.15 am to 5 pm daily).

Places to Stay & Eat

High season (October to March) rates are given below, but up to 50% discount applies out of season or if occupancy is low.

Hotel Anand (☎ 55030), near the bus stand, is one of the cheaper places. Gloomy singles/doubles with squat toilet and no hot water cost Rs 75/150. The Jain restaurant is strictly vegan and serves no eggs, onions or garlic.

Hotel Siddharth (☎ 55216), south of town near the hot springs, has a pleasant walled courtyard, and is known for its excellent food and friendly staff. Rooms are Rs 250/450 with private bathroom. They may give a 20% discount if you show this guidebook.

Hotel Rajgir (☎ 55266) is an old-fashioned Indian-style hotel with a garden. The basic rooms with private bathroom are a staggering Rs 210/310 plus Rs 5 for bucket hot water.

The BSTDC has three properties in Rajgir. The all-dorm *Ajatshatru (☎ 55027)* is clean and has squat toilets; a bed costs Rs 50. *Gautam (☎ 55273)* has dorm beds for Rs 50 and double rooms with TV and balcony for Rs 321, or Rs 535 with air-con. *Tathagat Vihar (☎ 55176)* has double rooms with flushing squat toilet for Rs 300 or Rs 600 with air-con.

Hotel Centaur Hokke (☎ 55245), 3km west of the hot springs, is Rajgir's top hotel. Although it looks a bit like a prison from the outside, it is a pleasant, Japanese-designed place with in-house communal bathhouse and temple. Rooms, in either Japanese or Western style, are US$86/124 (meals are an extra US$43 per person per day).

Getting There & Away

The nearest useful train station is at Gaya. There are regular buses to Gaya (Rs 35, three hours) and Pawapuri. For Nalanda take a share-jeep for Rs 8.

PAWAPURI

Mahavira, the final tirthankar and founder of Jainism, died and was cremated here in about 500 BC. It is said the demand for his sacred ashes was so great that a large amount of soil was removed around the funeral pyre, creating the lotus-filled tank. A marble temple, the **Jalmandir**, was later built in the middle of the tank and is now a major pilgrimage spot for Jains. You can get here by bus from Rajgir or Bihar Sharif.

Jharkhand

RANCHI

☎ 0651 • elevation 652m

At 652m, Ranchi doesn't really deserve its title of hill station, especially since it has now lost most of its tree cover. In British

BIHAR & JHARKHAND

times it was Bihar's summer capital; it is now capital of the new state of Jharkhand.

See the **Jagannath Temple**, a small version of the great Jagannath Temple at Puri. It's 6km south-west of Ranchi and visitors are welcome.

There are many beautiful waterfalls in the area, the most spectacular, especially at the end of the monsoon, are the **Hundru Falls**, 45km north-east of Ranchi.

About the same distance away to the north-west is **Macluskiganj**, a basically deserted hill station, once a holiday haven for Anglo-Indians. There's not a lot to see, but it does offer some pleasant walks through woods, gardens and orchards and the opportunity to view some of the old, albeit dilapidated, Victorian buildings.

There are a number of hills on the edges of Ranchi offering sunset views over the rocky landscape. There's also a Tribal Research Institute with a **museum of anthropology**.

Places to Stay & Eat

There are many hotels around the bus stand. All the ones listed have private bathroom unless indicated.

Hotel Konark *(☎ 307840)*, the best small place, is friendly with clean singles/doubles from Rs 150/175 and a good restaurant.

Hotel Paradise, with rooms at Rs 120/200, is another good place.

The ***Tourist Bungalow Birsa Vihar*** *(☎ 314826)* has dorms with shared bathroom for Rs 60 and double economy air-con rooms with private bathroom for Rs 200, or Rs 500 for the deluxe version.

Hotel Yuvraj *(☎ 300403)*, 'a house of respectable living', is 15 minutes from the train station with rooms from Rs 350/450.

Hotel Yuvraj Palace *(☎ 500326)*, nearby, is centrally air-conditioned with rooms from Rs 1200/1800. This is Ranchi's best hotel.

Getting There & Away

Ranchi has good air, bus and train connections. There are buses to Gaya (Rs 75 to 120, seven hours), Hazaribagh (Rs 35, three hours) and Netarhat (Rs 52, four hours). A direct bus to Puri in Orissa takes 15 hours.

The train station is 500m from the bus stand and there are daily trains to Patna (Rs 95/499, 2nd/1st class); Gaya (123/415, 2nd/1st class); and Delhi (326/1512, sleeper/2-tier air-con).

The Grand Trunk Road

India's Grand Trunk Rd (GTR) runs the breadth of the country, from the Pakistan border near Amritsar to Kolkata. It is by far the busiest road in the country and Rudyard Kipling described it as a 'river of life'; many of the events in his novel *Kim* take place along it.

Unfortunately the road has long been in decline, with little maintenance since the 17th century when it was lined with *khayabans* (trees) and became known among European travellers as the 'Long Walk'. The only significant realignment of the road was under the British, when the East India Company sought a more direct route between Kolkata and Varanasi. This route – the one that exists today – was completed in 1838 and is still a vital part of the Indian road network.

Nowadays, the GTR, especially the stretch crossing Bihar and Jharkhand, often descends into bone-shattering potholes and narrow sections that are more loose gravel and ditches than road. This causes considerable transport problems; you'll probably see more than one abandoned truck overturned, with its cargo sprawled along the roadside.

However, the GTR still does provide a vivid picture of Indians on the move: oil tankers from Assam, Tata trucks from Punjab; garish and battered buses, all with horns blaring; barefoot sadhus on a Ganga pilgrimage; farmers steering overloaded ox-carts; wayward cows; schoolkids on bicycles; and women on foot. Sit at a roadside *dhaba* (snack bar) and observe the passing parade, but be warned that you'll probably suffer industrial deafness from the racket.

HAZARIBAGH

☎ 06546 • elevation 615m

This pleasant leafy town lies 107km north of Ranchi. About the only reason for coming here would be to visit **Hazaribagh National Park**, 19km to the north.

Hotel Upkar *(☎ 2246)* is the best hotel in Hazaribagh, and good value with singles/doubles with private bathroom for Rs 175/300.

The train station, Hazaribagh Rd, is all of 67km away! Luckily, private minibuses to Gaya (Rs 50, four hours) leave from the bus station.

BELA (PALAMAU) NATIONAL PARK

Known as both Palamau and Bela, this park, 140km west of Ranchi, is part of Project Tiger and is one of the best places to see wild elephants. Permission to enter the park must be procured from the District Forest Officer in Bela, and although there are *machaans* (observation towers) for viewing the animals, wildlife is sparse since the government drove a major road through the area. Worse still, the World Bank is pumping funds into the construction of Kotku Dam, which will ensure the best forests in the park will need gills to survive.

Jeep safaris can be organised in Bela, the park's access point. Expect to pay around Rs 8 to 10 per kilometre for spins around the park's 250 sq km. There are also treetop and ground-level hideaways where you can watch the animals without being seen.

Accommodation is mostly in Bela, but you can also stay farther afield in Daltonganj (24km away). In Bela, the ***Forest Rest House*** or ***Tourist Lodge*** (built as a three-star ITDC hotel), are reasonable places to stay.

Bela is accessible by road from Ranchi and Gaya (both Rs 50, four to five hours).

Before going into the area it is imperative you seek security advice.

PARASNATH

☎ 0653232

Just inside the Jharkhand state boundary with West Bengal, and a bit north of the Grand Trunk Rd, Parasnath is the railhead for Sikayi, the major Jain pilgrimage centre in the east of India (Madhuban is the main town). Sikayi, at 1450m, is the highest point in Jharkhand and, like so many other pilgrimage centres, it is reached by a stiff climb on foot. You will see rich pilgrims from Kolkata being carried up in palanquins by porters.

The 24 temples, representing the Jain tirthankars, stand at an altitude of 1366m. Parasnath, the 23rd tirthankar, achieved nirvana here 100 years after his birth.

An internationally famous yoga school at Munger (☎ *06344-22430)*, known as the Bihar Yoga School, has courses.

There are a number of ***dharamsalas*** in Sikayi, but they are strictly vegan and, like those in Bodhgaya, there are strict rules of conduct. There is also a ***Tourist Bungalow***, built by the BSTDC and given to the Jain community at Madhuban, but it has no fixed rate.

Trains run to Patna and Kolkata, and Maruti vans and minibuses run between the train station and Madhuban.

Kolkata (Calcutta)

For many, contemporary Kolkata (formerly Calcutta) *still* conjures hideous images of interminable squalor – a skewed reputation largely built on antiquated stereotypes regurgitated by the (mainly Western) media. For first-time travellers to India, Kolkata – with its mass of humanity, crumbling buildings and frenetic streets – may well come across as a desperate, and even ugly, place. But after spending time in India's other major cities, it's plain to see that modern-day Kolkata has been unfairly stigmatised.

Get to know Kolkata and you'll see why it has long been acknowledged as the cultural capital of India. Although it may have some of the country's finest remnants of British colonial architecture, it possesses a distinct Bengali soul. Referred to as India's friendliest metropolis, Bengali humour is renowned and the Bengalis, so ready to raise arms against political wrongdoings, are also the poets and artists of India. Kolkata was the birthplace and/or home of many famous people including the inimitable Bengali poet Rabindranath Tagore, the novelist William Thackeray and the actress Merle Oberon, who appeared in films including *The Scarlet Pimpernel*. The house she lived in is on Lindsay St near New Market.

Kolkata has certainly had its share of problems. It has been plagued by chronic labour unrest resulting in a decline in productivity. Massive trade union rallies frequently block traffic in the city centre for hours at a time and the port has been silting up, limiting the size of ships that can use it. The Marxist government of West Bengal has had a lot of criticism over Kolkata's chaos, but as it has also pointed out, its apparent neglect and mismanagement of the city is combined with considerable improvement in the rural environment. Threats of flood or famine in the countryside no longer send hordes of refugees converging on the city as in the past.

As personal wealth has risen in Kolkata, so too have the number of fume-belching cars jostling for space on the already clogged streets. For the visitor, road travel can be a hair-greying experience, as drivers weave through the crazy traffic constantly swerving local buses travelling at breakneck

Kolkata at a Glance

Population: 14 million
Area: 18,733 sq km
Main Language: Bengali
Capital of: West Bengal
Telephone Area Code: 033
When to Go: Nov to Mar

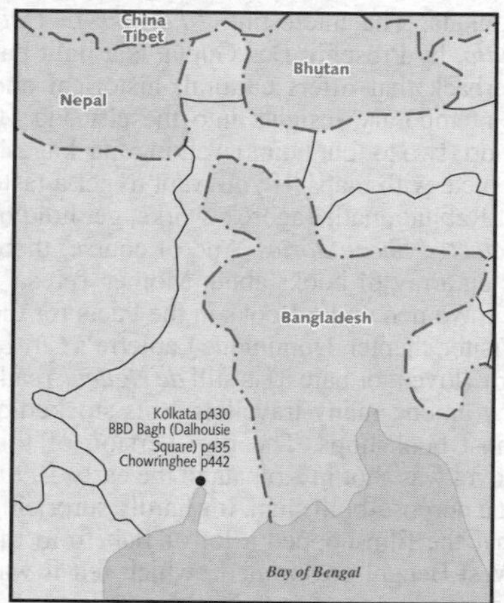

- Soak up the city's vibrant culture at a museum, gallery, drama performance, or by simply chatting to the friendly folk of Kolkata
- Visit the colossal colonial building, Victoria Memorial, one of India's most portentous remnants of the British Raj
- Stroll through the 'lungs', the Maidan of modern Kolkata, in the early morning or late afternoon as people exercise their dogs, power walk, do yoga or catch up with friends
- Witness the fascinating spectacle of the mighty Howrah Bridge set against the ethereal expanse of the Hooghly River, and the flurry of flower sellers below
- Kick back at the Botanical Gardens, a rare slice of serenity in bustling Kolkata, which features a spectacular 200-year-old banyan tree

KOLKATA (CALCUTTA)

speed. Indeed a drawback of sightseeing in Kolkata is the amount of time spent stuck in traffic jams – be mentally prepared. Sundays are best, as the roads are generally less congested (by Kolkata standards anyway).

The incredible contrasts and tenacity of this effervescent metropolis have enticed many to wax lyrical about Kolkata. Some good books include Geoffrey Moorhouse's classic 1971 study *Calcutta* and VS Naipaul's *India – A Million Mutinies Now*, which has some engaging chapters on Kolkata. The interesting *10 Walks in Calcutta*, by Prosenjit Das Gupta, is a light paperback that offers cultural, historical and contemporary insights into the city via 10 short (two to four hours) walking 'packages', replete with maps. If you want to get a taste of Rabindranath Tagore's works, get hold of *Selected Short Stories*. And of course, there is an array of books about Mother Teresa – see Women under Books in the Facts for the Visitor chapter. Dominique Lapierre's *City of Joy* (love it or hate it) is still *de rigueur* reading among many travellers so is stocked at most bookshops. The film version of this novel was shot in Kolkata in the early 1990s at a purpose-built slum. It's hardly surprising that the film copped a lot of flak from the West Bengal government, which felt it was yet another condescending and exaggerated Western depiction of Kolkata's poverty.

In late December 2000 the Indian government officially agreed to the West Bengal government's proposal to rename Calcutta with its traditional name, Kolkata. The two other major Indian hubs that have changed names in a nationalist move to reclaim their pre-colonial heritage are Mumbai (Bombay) and Chennai (Madras).

HISTORY

Kolkata isn't an ancient city like Delhi, with its impressive relics of the past. In fact, it's largely a British creation that dates back only some 300 years. It was the capital of British India until the beginning of last century.

In 1686 the British abandoned Hooghly, their trading post 38km up the Hooghly River from present-day Kolkata, and moved downriver to three small villages – Sutanati, Govindpur and Kalikata. Job Charnock, an English merchant who later married an Indian widow whom he dissuaded from committing *sati* (widow's act of suicide on her husband's funeral pyre), was the leader of the British merchants who made this move. At first the post was not a great success and was abandoned on a number of occasions, but in 1696 a fort was laid out near present-day BBD Bagh (Dalhousie Square) and in 1698, the Mughal ruler Aurangzeb's grandson gave the British official permission to occupy the villages.

Kolkata then grew steadily until 1756, when Siraj-ud-daula, the nawab of Murshidabad, attacked the town. Most of the British inhabitants escaped, but those captured were packed into an underground cellar where, during the night, most of them suffocated in what became known as 'the black hole of Calcutta'.

Early in 1757 the British, under Clive of India, retook Kolkata and made peace with the nawab. Later the same year, however, Siraj-ud-daula sided with the French and was defeated at the Battle of Plassey (now Palashi), a turning point in British-Indian history. A stronger fort was built in Kolkata and the town became British India's capital.

Much of Kolkata's most enduring development took place between 1780 and 1820. Later in the 19th century, Bengal became an important centre in the struggle for Indian independence, and this was a major reason for the British decision to transfer the capital to Delhi in 1911. Loss of political power did not alter Kolkata's economic control and the city prospered until after WWII.

Partition affected Kolkata more than any other major Indian city. Bengal and Punjab were the two areas of India with mixed Hindu and Muslim populations and the dividing line was drawn through them. The result in Bengal was that Kolkata, the jute-producing and export centre of India, became a city without a hinterland, while across the border in East Pakistan (now Bangladesh), jute (a plant fibre used in making sacking and mats) was grown without anywhere to process or export it. Furthermore, West Bengal and Kolkata were disrupted by tens of thousands of refugees fleeing from East Bengal, although fortunately without the communal violence and bloodshed that Partition brought to Punjab.

The massive influx of refugees, combined with India's own postwar population explosion, led to Kolkata becoming an international urban horror story. The work of

Mother Teresa's Kolkata mission focused worldwide attention on the city's festering problems. In 1971 the India-Pakistan conflict and the creation of Bangladesh led to another flood of refugees, and Kolkata's already chaotic condition further deteriorated.

ORIENTATION

Kolkata sprawls north–south along the eastern bank of the Hooghly River, which divides it from Howrah on the western bank. For travellers, the more relevant parts of Kolkata are south of the bridge in the areas around BBD Bagh and Chowringhee. BBD Bagh, formerly Dalhousie Square, is the hub of the central business district (CBD).

South of BBD Bagh is the open expanse of the Maidan, and east from here is the area known as Chowringhee. Here you'll find most of the lower priced hotels, as well as many of the restaurants, banks and airline offices. Sudder St runs off Chowringhee Rd and is the core of the city's travellers (especially budget) scene. Farther south down Chowringhee Rd, which runs alongside the eastern edge of the Maidan, is Park St, with upmarket restaurants and shops.

Street Names

The renaming of city streets, particularly those with Raj-era connotations, can make getting around slightly confusing. While many street signs still display the old names, some maps show new ones. Taxi and rickshaw-wallahs largely still go by the old (familiar) names; on this book's maps, we have provided the new name with the old name in brackets, however, in the text, the most commonly used name has been used. For instance, most people still know Jawaharlal Nehru Rd as Chowringhee Rd, so that's what we've gone with.

Adding to the confusion, in a bid to alleviate traffic problems, Kolkata has adopted 'timed' one-way streets, which flow in different directions depending on the time: In morning rush-hour a street might flow east to west, in the afternoon rush hour it will flow west to east, and in the middle of the day it might take two-way traffic.

Street Name Changes

old name	new name
Ballygunge Rd	Gurusday Rd
Central Ave	Chittranjan Ave
Chowringhee Rd	Jawaharlal Nehru Rd
Free School St	Mirza Ghalib St
Harrington St	Ho Chi Minh Sarani
Harrison Rd	Mahatma Gandhi Rd (MG Rd)
Kyd St	Dr M Ishaque Rd
Lansdowne Rd	Sarat Bose Rd
Lower Chitpur Rd	Rabindra Sarani
Lower Circular Rd	Acharya Jagadish Chandra (AJC) Bose Rd
Mirzapore St	Surya Sen St
Theatre Rd	Shakespeare Sarani
Wellesley St	Rafi Ahmed Kidwai Rd

INFORMATION
Tourist Offices

The helpful Government of India tourist office (☎ 2825813), 4 Shakespeare Sarani in Chowringhee, disseminates information about Kolkata as well as other destinations in India. The office has a couple of touch-screen computers enabling you to navigate your way through general tourist information, including local taxi rates. The office is open 9 am to 6 pm Monday to Friday and to 1 pm weekends.

West Bengal Tourism Centre (☎ 2488271), 3/2 BBD Bagh (on the opposite side to the main post office), specialises purely in West Bengal tourism matters and is open 10.30 am to 4 pm Monday to Friday, 10.30 am to 1 pm Saturday and 7 am to noon Sunday.

Both the state and national tourist offices have counters at the airport (☎ 5118299), and the West Bengal Tourism Centre has an office at Howrah train station (☎ 6602518) that's open 7 am to 1 pm daily. Both tourist offices can arrange sightseeing guides: the official rates for a half/full day are Rs 255/380 (one to four people), Rs 380/505 (five to 15 people) and Rs 505/825 (16 to 35 people).

Other states with tourist offices in Kolkata are as follows:

Andaman & Nicobar Islands (☎ 2472604) 3A Auckland Place
Arunachal Pradesh (☎ 3341243) Block-CE, 109–110 Salt Lake City
Assam (☎ 2295094) Assam Bhawan, 8 Russel St
Bihar (☎ 2803304) Neelkantha Bhawan, 1st floor, 26B Camac St
Gujarat (☎ 2101879) Room 28, ground floor, Martin Burn Bldg, 1 RN Mukharjee Rd

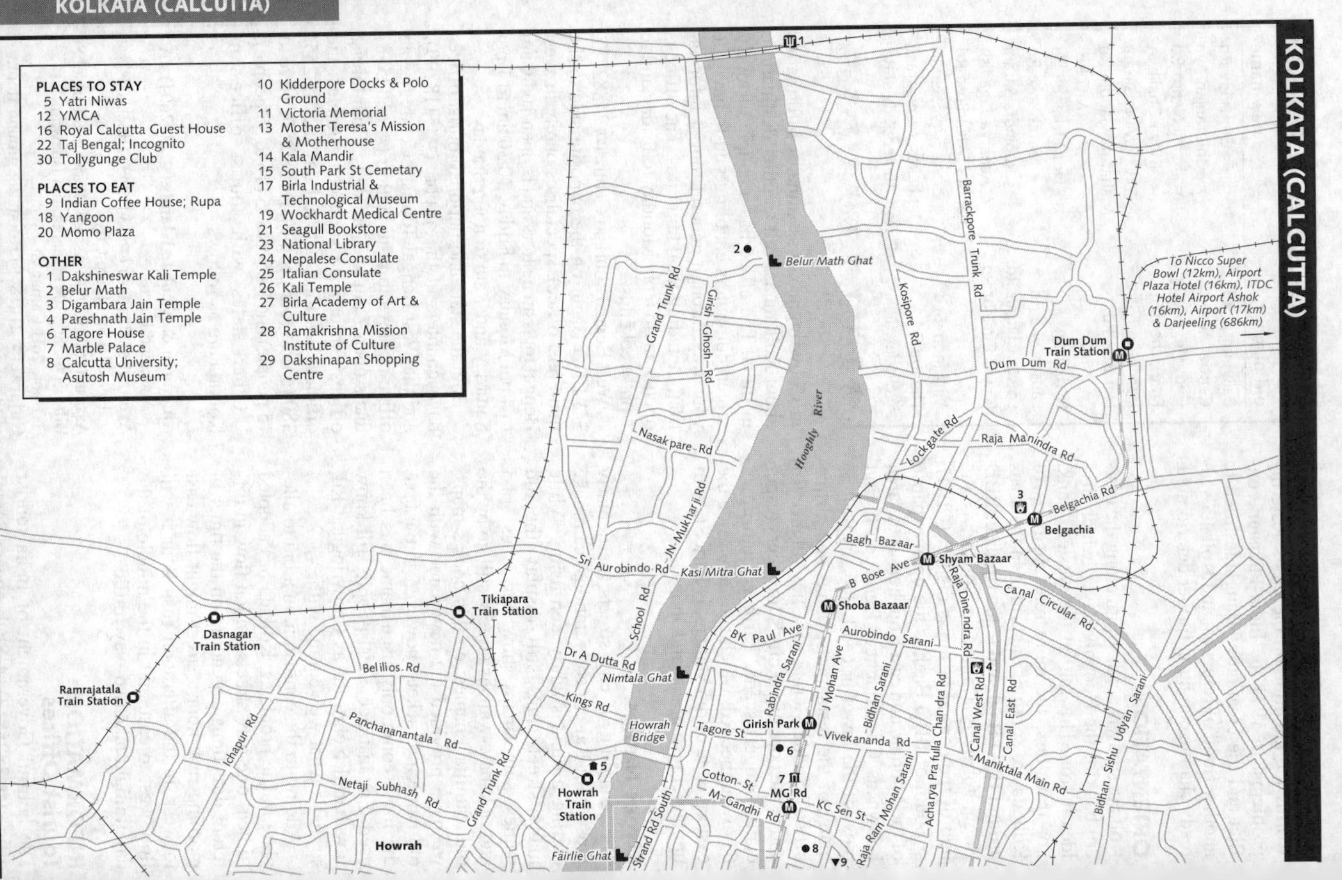
KOLKATA (CALCUTTA)
PLACES TO STAY
5 Yatri Niwas
12 YMCA
16 Royal Calcutta Guest House
22 Taj Bengal; Incognito
30 Tollygunge Club
PLACES TO EAT
9 Indian Coffee House; Rupa
18 Yangoon
20 Momo Plaza
OTHER
1 Dakshineswar Kali Temple
2 Belur Math
3 Digambara Jain Temple
4 Pareshnath Jain Temple
6 Tagore House
7 Marble Palace
8 Calcutta University; Asutosh Museum
10 Kidderpore Docks & Polo Ground
11 Victoria Memorial
13 Mother Teresa's Mission & Motherhouse
14 Kala Mandir
15 South Park St Cemetary
17 Birla Industrial & Technological Museum
19 Wockhardt Medical Centre
21 Seagull Bookstore
23 National Library
24 Nepalese Consulate
25 Italian Consulate
26 Kali Temple
27 Birla Academy of Art & Culture
28 Ramakrishna Mission Institute of Culture
29 Dakshinapan Shopping Centre
To Nicco Super Bowl (12km), Airport Plaza Hotel (16km), ITDC Hotel Airport Ashok (16km), Airport (17km) & Darjeeling (686km)
Dum Dum Train Station
Dum Dum Rd
Barrackpore Trunk Rd
Kosipore Rd
Belur Math Ghat
Grand Trunk Rd
Girish Ghosh Rd
Hooghly River
Nasak pare Rd
Lockgate Rd
Raja Manindra Rd
Belgachia Rd
Belgachia
JN Mukharji Rd
Bagh Bazaar
Shyam Bazaar
Sri Aurobindo Rd
Kasi Mitra Ghat
B Bose Ave
Raja Dinendra Rd
Canal Circular Rd
Tikiapara Train Station
Dasnagar Train Station
Shoba Bazaar
School Rd
BK Paul Ave
Aurobindo Sarani
Dr A Dutta Rd
Belilios Rd
Nimtala Ghat
Rabindra Sarani
J Mohan Ave
Bidhan Sarani
Ramrajatala Train Station
Kings Rd
Acharya Prafulla Chandra Rd
Canal West Rd
Canal East Rd
Bidhan Sishu Udyan Sarani
Ichapur Rd
Panchanantala Rd
Howrah Bridge
Tagore St
Girish Park
Vivekananda Rd
Maniktala Main Rd
Netaji Subhash Rd
Grand Trunk Rd
Howrah Train Station
Cotton St
MG Rd
M Gandhi Rd
KC Sen St
Raja Ram Mohan Sarani
Strand Rd South
Howrah
Fairlie Ghat

KOLKATA (CALCUTTA)

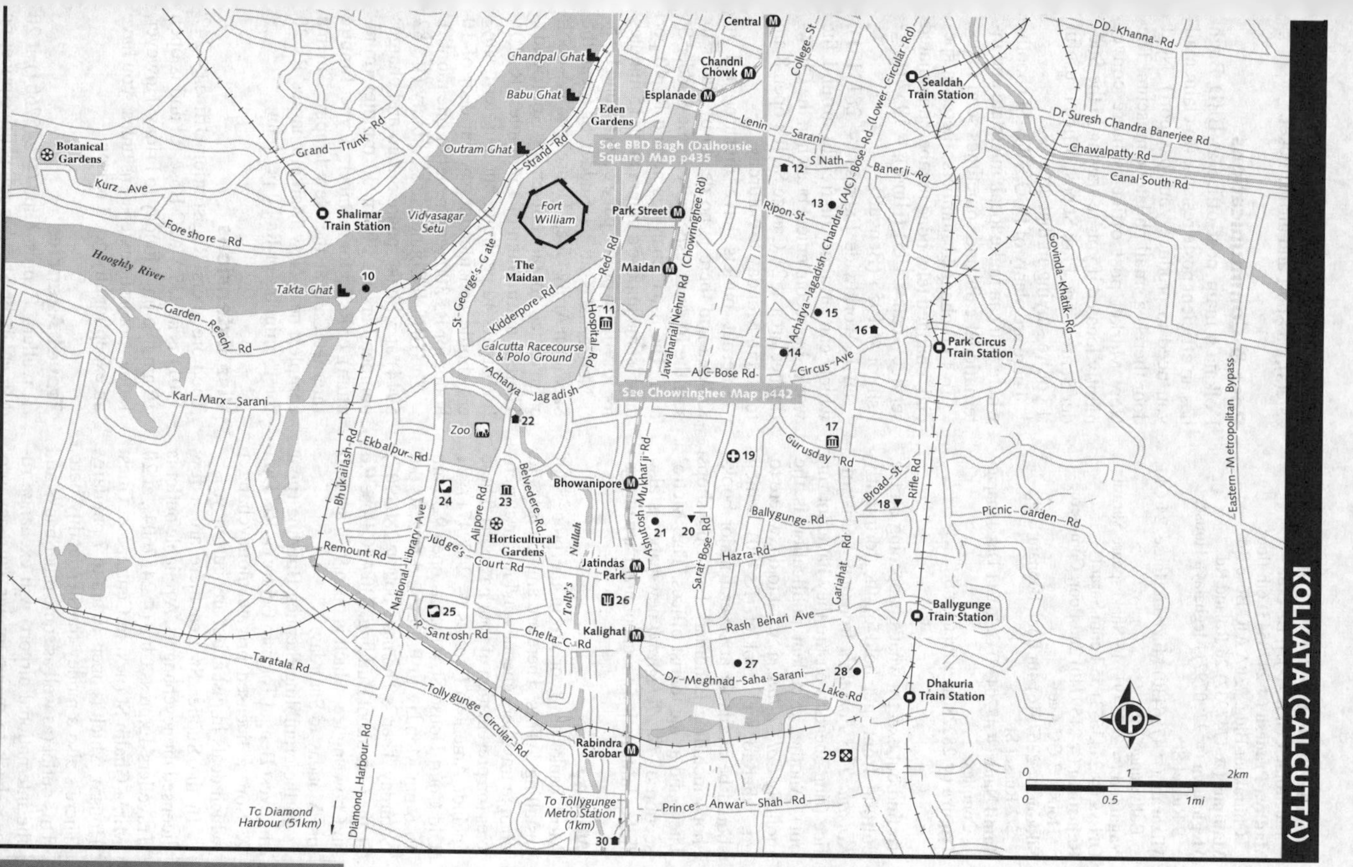

Himachal Pradesh (☎ 2219072) 1st floor, Electronic Centre, 1-1A, BAC St
Madhya Pradesh (☎ 2478543) 6th floor, Chitrakoot Bldg, 230A AJC Bose Rd
Manipur (☎ 4747937) 26 Roland Rd
Meghalaya (☎ 2290797) Meghalaya House, 9 Russel St
Mizoram (☎ 4756430) Mizoram House, 24 Old Ballygunge Rd
Nagaland (☎ 2823491) 13 Shakespeare Sarani
Orissa (☎ 2443653) 55 Lenin Sarani
Rajasthan (☎ 2159740) 2nd floor, Commerce House, 2 GC Ave
Sikkim (☎ 2267516) 4th floor, Poonam Bldg, 5/2 Russel St
Tamil Nadu (☎ 4720432) G-26 CIT Dakshinapan Complex
Tripura (☎ 2822801) 1 Pretoria St

To find out exactly what's happening on the cultural front, get hold of the fortnightly *Kolkata This Fortnight* from any tourist office (ring ahead to ensure they have not run out). Another excellent publication is the monthly *Cal Calling*, a 'what to do, where to go, what to see' booklet (Rs 20), which should be available at several major bookshops including Landmark (see Bookshops later) and at the tourist offices. The 'Metro' section of *The Telegraph* newspaper is also full of information about cultural happenings.

Money

Most banks have, or are in the process of installing, ATMs. There are ample places to change travellers cheques and major currencies (on presentation of your passport). These include American Express (☎ 2489471), 21 Old Court House St, which is open 9.30 am to 6 pm Monday to Friday and to 2.30 pm Saturday. There's Thomas Cook (☎ 2803907) in the Chitrakoot Building, 230 AJC Bose Rd in Chowringhee, which is open 9.30 am to 6 pm Monday to Saturday.

In the crumbling Stephen Building (near the West Bengal Tourism Centre) is RN Dutt & Son, a licensed private moneychanger which deals in just about any currency.

In the Sudder St area there are a few licensed moneychangers. A reliable outlet is Travellers' Express Club (☎ 2457604), at 20 Mirza Ghalib St (next to Centrepoint Guest House), which is open 10 am to 7 pm daily. There's also a money-transfer facility here. This outlet (as well as some other banks and the international airport) will exchange rupees back to major foreign currency provided you present your encashment certificate(s), passport and airline ticket.

Post & Communications

Kolkata's main post office at BBD Bagh has an efficient poste restante (to claim mail you need to produce your passport). Next door there's a small philatelic museum. The New Market post office is more conveniently located if you're staying in the Sudder St area. The Park St post office is useful if you're staying in that area.

There are plenty of PCO/STD/ISD booths where you can make local, interstate and international calls and sometimes send faxes.

To find changed numbers, there's a special 'changed telephone number' automated service – call ☎ 1951 (Hindi), ☎ 1952 (English) or ☎ 1953 (Bengali).

DHL Worldwide Express (☎ 2813131), which can arrange air-freight around the world, has a convenient branch in the Chowringhee area at 21 Camac St. It's open 8 am to 10 pm Monday to Saturday.

Internet outlets have mushroomed in Kolkata and there is no dearth of places to surf the Internet, especially in the Sudder St area. The usual charge is around Rs 40 per hour (some impose a minimum of 15 minutes for Rs 10). To print a page costs around Rs 5.

Netfreaks is at 2/1 Sudder St (near the Salvation Army Guest House) and is a cool, calm place to tap out emails to friends. There is a minimum of 15 minutes (Rs 10). It costs Rs 40 per hour, but long-term stayers should consider the special deal of 10 hours for Rs 300 (expires after one month).

The British Council has a library (☎ 282 5944) at 5 Shakespeare Sarani and charges nonmembers Rs 30 for 30 minutes (minimum), or Rs 15 for members. Cyber Empire Internet Cafe at the New Empire Cinema complex near New Market charges Rs 20 for 15 minutes or Rs 50 per hour.

Visa Extensions

The Foreigners' Registration Office (☎ 247 3301) is at 237A AJC Bose Rd and is open 10 am to 5 pm Monday to Friday. However, it does not issue extensions unless you have an exceptionally good reason.

Travel Agencies

Travellers' Express Club (☎ 2457604) at 20 Mirza Ghalib St offers competitive prices on domestic and international airline tickets. The helpful manager can also arrange specialist tours of India's Buddhist sites (see also its Web site: www.nirvana-tours.com). Kuka Travels (☎ 2260496), on the 1st floor of the Tourist Inn building on Sudder St, deals in domestic flight bookings.

Rail tickets can be purchased (for a commission) from several outlets in the Sudder St area, however some travellers have reported over-charging and bad service, so shop around. To avoid being hoodwinked, go to the tourist railway booking office at Fairlie Place near BBD Bagh (see Trains later in this chapter) – but be prepared to wait.

Photography

If you're heading off to Bangladesh, Nepal or elsewhere and need passport photos, a convenient option is North East Color Photos (☎ 2492098), near the corner of Sudder St and the small road directly opposite the entrance of the Salvation Army Guest House. The fee is Rs 50 for the standard four mug shots (including negatives), however you have to come back later in the day to collect them. To develop 36 colour prints costs Rs 18 plus Rs 3.50 per print. Although it also develops slide film, the most reputable place to get these processed is at Bourne & Shepherd (☎ 2281658), 141 SN Banerjee Rd (not far from the Sudder St area), which prides itself as being 'the oldest photographic studio in the world'. The charge is Rs 120 (cardboard mounts) or Rs 160 (plastic mounts) to develop 36 slides.

Bookshops

Kolkata has some brilliant bookshops and many around the Sudder St area sell second-hand books. The main bookshop area is along College St, opposite the Calcutta University east of BBD Bagh. In the same building as the Indian Coffee House here, Rupa has a decent range including its own publications. Newman's runs one of Kolkata's oldest bookshops – it's in the same block as the Great Eastern Hotel near BBD Bagh.

In the Chowringhee area, Cambridge Book & Stationery Company at 20D Park St is a good, small bookshop. A bit farther down Park St towards Chowringhee Rd, the swanky Oxford Book Shop is much larger and has plenty of well-stocked bookshelves. The small and unpretentious Classic Books, at 10 Middleton St, has a reasonably good collection, and the owner, Bharat, is a mine of information. Bookland is a modest street-front bookstall at the eastern end of Sudder St, opposite Khwaja restaurant. It sells new and second-hand books in various languages, and will buy them back for 50% of what you pay. There are other similar small swap-and-sell places on Mirza Ghalib St.

Landmark is on the 3rd floor of the modern Emami Shoppers City complex at 3 Lord Sinha Rd. It has a wide range of books, cards, stationary and music. While you're here, go down to the 2nd floor's ***Starlit Cafe*** for some refreshing organic ice cream (Rs 15 per scoop). The well-kept Seagull Bookstore, at 31A Shyama Prasad Mukherjee Rd (near Indira Cinema and opposite the Bhowanipore police station), is a real treasure trove. This place even publishes its own titles and sometimes has author talks.

Libraries & Cultural Centres

The British Council (☎ 2825944) on Shakespeare Sarani offers a full lending and reference library, plus an electronic media centre with Internet access (see Post & Communications). Membership costs Rs 600 per year or Rs 100 per month. Photocopying costs Rs 1 per sheet. There is a garden cafe that serves light meals and nonalcoholic drinks. The library is open 11 am to 7 pm Tuesday to Saturday.

Medical Services & Emergency

It's best to contact your country's embassy if you're in serious trouble (see Embassies & Consulates in the Facts for the Visitor chapter). For an ambulance call ☎ 102, for fire call ☎ 101 and for the police call ☎ 100. Medical concerns could be directed to any of the large hospitals. Some medical services follow:

Vital Medical Services (☎ 2825664) 6 Ho Chi Minh Sarani, Chowringhee. Open 9.30 am to 5.30 pm.

Wockhardt Medical Centre (☎ 4754320, 4754096) 2/7 Sarat Bose (Lansdowne) Rd, south of Chowringhee. Open 8 am to 8 pm.

CHOWRINGHEE AREA

Indian Museum

This museum, built in the mid 1870s, is a fine colonial building housing an impressive collection. The entrance hall is dominated by an original Mauryan lion capitol, India's national symbol, and the archaeological gallery houses the Barhut Gateway (2nd century BC), a massive structure decorated with a bas-relief depicting the life of Buddha. It has the best collection of Pala statues in the country and the art collection has many fine pieces from Orissan and other temples. It also has superb examples of Buddhist Gandharan art – an interesting meeting point between Greek artistry and Buddhist ideals that produced Buddha images and other sculptures of great beauty. The art and textile galleries are worth a look. Unfortunately, the natural history collection, while being vast, is disintegrating and exhibits are coated in dust. The museum is on the corner of Sudder St and Chowringhee Rd and is open from 10 am to 5 pm Tuesday to Sunday. Between December and February it closes 30 minutes earlier. Entry is Rs 10 for Indians and a whopping Rs 150 for foreigners. There's also a camera fee (Rs 25).

Asiatic Society

Founded on 15 February 1784 at the instigation of scholar and visionary Sir William Jones, the Asiatic Society was formed to preserve the science, civilisation and culture of India. The society established the first modern museum in Asia in 1814 in Kolkata, but due to a chronic lack of space and facilities, most of the priceless exhibits were eventually transferred to the Indian Museum on its completion in 1875. However, a small collection of valuable art and antiquities was retained and is now on display at the society's museum on Park St. Among the fabulous collection of paintings, *thangkas* (Tibetan cloth paintings), object d'art and botanical specimens, the Barhut Ashokan Rock Edict (circa 250 BC from Orissa) is unquestionably the most important piece, representing India's most famous and revered emperor and his conversion to Buddhism. Of great interest to scholars is the library, which contains more than 200,000 books, journals and manuscripts of rare antiquity.

Library hours are 8 am to 7 pm Monday to Friday and 8 am to 6 pm Saturday. Entry is free. The museum is open 8 am to 7 pm Monday to Friday. A small but informative quarterly publication, *The Asiatic Society*, is sold (Rs 100) at the society's offices.

MP Birla Planetarium

This planetarium (☎ 2231516), near the Government of India tourist office, is one of the largest in the world. For Rs 10 you'll get a much better view of the stars in here than in the polluted atmosphere outside. There are shows in English at 1.30 and 6.30 pm daily, but as these times may change, check in advance.

St Paul's Cathedral

Built between 1839 and 1847, St Paul's Cathedral stands at the southern end of the Maidan, just east of the Victoria Memorial, on Cathedral Rd. The steeple fell during an earthquake in 1897 and, following further damage in a 1934 quake, was redesigned and rebuilt. Inside, there's some impressive stained glass, including the great west window by Sir Edward Burne-Jones. It's open to visitors from 9 am to noon and 3 to 6 pm daily. There are Sunday services given in English at 7.30 and 8.30 am and 6 pm. A Bengali service is given at 10.30 am.

Academy of Fine Arts

The Academy of Fine Arts, on Cathedral Rd, has a permanent exhibition and runs an artists' studio. The academy is open from 3 to 8 pm daily, except Monday. Entry is free.

Nehru Children's Museum

The small Nehru Children's Museum, 94/1 Chowringhee Rd, has models depicting the Hindu epics, the Ramayana and the Mahabharata. It's open from 11 am to 6.30 pm Wednesday to Sunday and from 3 to 6.30 pm Tuesday; admission is Rs 5.

BBD BAGH AREA

BBD Bagh (Dalhousie Square)

When Kolkata was the administrative centre for British India, BBD (Binoy Badal Dinesh) Bagh was the centre of power. On the north side stands the huge **Writers' Building**, dating from 1880 (when clerical workers were known as writers). The East India Company's writers have now been replaced by modern-day West Bengal government employees, and this is where the quintuplicate forms, carbon copies and red ink come from.

Until it was abandoned in 1757, the original Fort William stood on the site of the present-day post office. It stretched from there down to the river, which has since

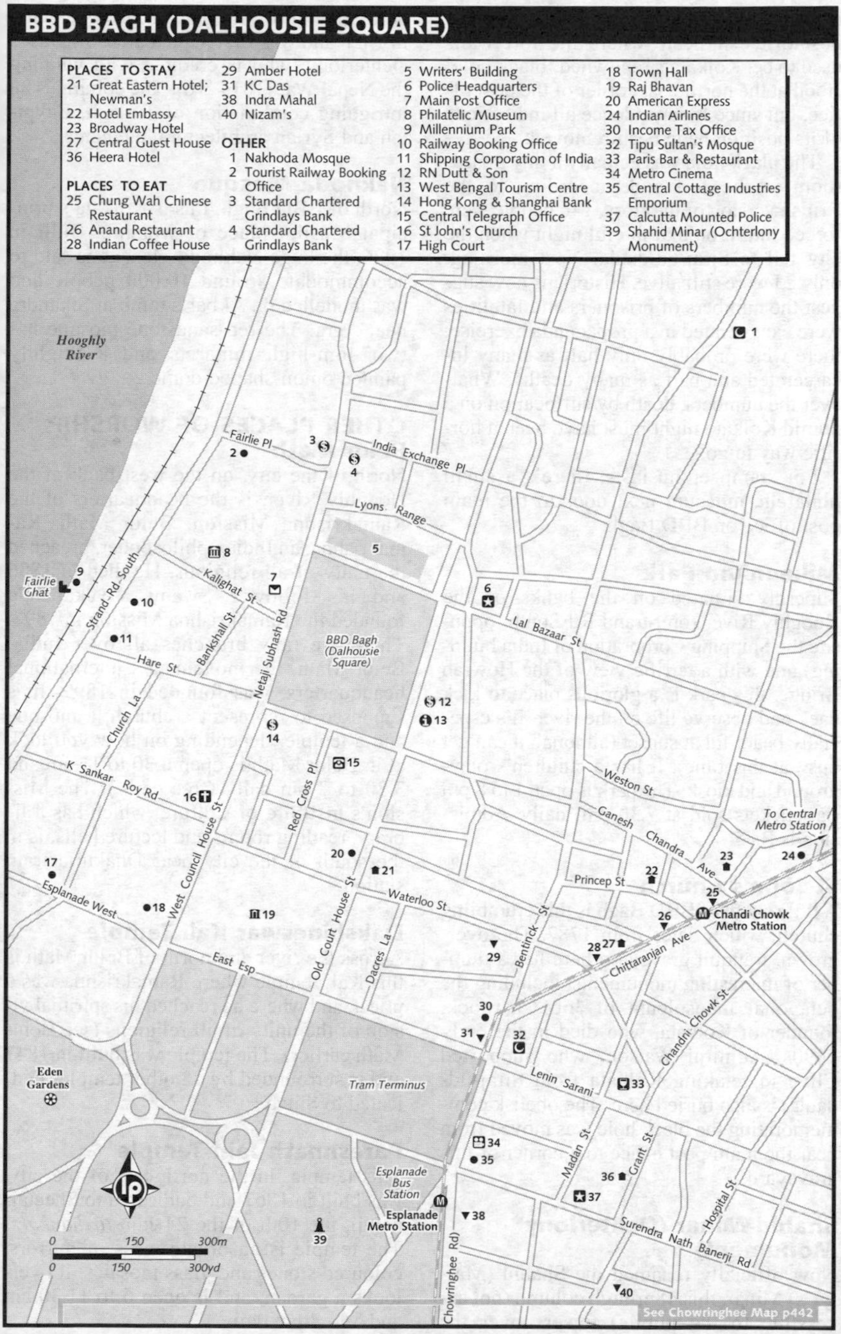

BBD BAGH (DALHOUSIE SQUARE)

PLACES TO STAY
21 Great Eastern Hotel; Newman's
22 Hotel Embassy
23 Broadway Hotel
27 Central Guest House
36 Heera Hotel
29 Amber Hotel
31 KC Das
38 Indra Mahal
40 Nizam's

PLACES TO EAT
25 Chung Wah Chinese Restaurant
26 Anand Restaurant
28 Indian Coffee House

OTHER
1 Nakhoda Mosque
2 Tourist Railway Booking Office
3 Standard Chartered Grindlays Bank
4 Standard Chartered Grindlays Bank
5 Writers' Building
6 Police Headquarters
7 Main Post Office
8 Philatelic Museum
9 Millennium Park
10 Railway Booking Office
11 Shipping Corporation of India
12 RN Dutt & Son
13 West Bengal Tourism Centre
14 Hong Kong & Shanghai Bank
15 Central Telegraph Office
16 St John's Church
17 High Court
18 Town Hall
19 Raj Bhavan
20 American Express
24 Indian Airlines
30 Income Tax Office
32 Tipu Sultan's Mosque
33 Paris Bar & Restaurant
34 Metro Cinema
35 Central Cottage Industries Emporium
37 Calcutta Mounted Police
39 Shahid Minar (Ochterlony Monument)

Hooghly River
Fairlie Pl
India Exchange Pl
Lyons Range
Fairlie Ghat
Strand Rd South
Kaliaghat St
Bankshall St
Netaji Subhash Rd
BBD Bagh (Dalhousie Square)
Lal Bazaar St
Hare St
Church La
K Sankar Roy Rd
Red Cross Pl
West Council House St
Old Court House St
Weston St
Ganesh Chandra Ave
To Central Metro Station
Princep St
Waterloo St
Esplanade West
East Esp
Dacres La
Bentinck St
Chandi Chowk Metro Station
Chittaranjan Ave
Chandni Chowk St
Lenin Sarani
Eden Gardens
Tram Terminus
Madan St
Grant St
Hospital St
Esplanade Bus Station
Esplanade Metro Station
Chowringhee Rd
Surendra Nath Banerji Rd
0 150 300m
0 150 300yd

See Chowringhee Map p442

changed its course. Brass markers by the post office indicate where the fort walls used to be. Kolkata's renowned 'black hole' stood at the north-east corner of the post office, but since Independence all indications of its position have been removed.

The **black hole** was actually a tiny guardroom in the fort and, according to the British version of the story, 146 people were forced into it on that fateful night when the city fell to Siraj-ud-daula. Next morning, only 23 were still alive. Historians now suggest the numbers of prisoners and fatalities were exaggerated in a propaganda exercise; there were probably only half as many incarcerated and half as many deaths. Whatever the numbers, death by suffocation on a humid Kolkata night must have been a horrific way to go.

For stamp enthusiasts, there's a small **philatelic museum** next door to the main post office on BBD Bagh.

Millennium Park

Superbly situated on the banks of the Hooghly River (on Strand Rd South, opposite the Shipping Corporation of India building) and with a terrific view of the Howrah Bridge, this park is a glorious place to kick back and observe life on the river. It's especially beautiful at sunset (although it can get busy at this time). It has a children's playground and kiosk. The park is open 1 to 8 pm (last tickets sold at 7.30 pm) daily. Admission is Rs 5.

St John's Church

A little south of BBD Bagh is this crumbling church, which dates from 1787. The overgrown, tranquil graveyard here has a number of interesting monuments, including the octagonal mausoleum of Job Charnock, founder of Kolkata, who died in the early 1690s. Admiral Watson, who supported Clive in retaking Kolkata from Siraj-ud-daula, is also buried here. The obelisk commemorating the black hole was moved from near the main post office to a corner of this graveyard.

Shahid Minar (Ochterlony Monument)

Now officially renamed the Shahid (Martyr's) Minar, this 48m-high column (not accessible to the public) towers over the northern end of the Maidan. It was erected in 1828 and was first named after Sir David Ochterlony, who is credited with winning the Nepal War (1814–16). The column is an intriguing combination of Turkish, Egyptian and Syrian architectural elements.

Nakhoda Mosque

North of BBD Bagh, this is Kolkata's principal Muslim place of worship. Built in 1926, the huge Nakhoda Mosque is said to accommodate around 10,000 people and was modelled on Akbar's tomb at Sikandra near Agra. The red-sandstone mosque has two 46m-high minarets and a brightly painted onion-shaped dome.

OTHER PLACES OF WORSHIP

Belur Math

North of the city, on the west bank of the Hooghly River, is the headquarters of the Ramakrishna Mission, Belur Math. Ramakrishna, an Indian philosopher, preached the unity of all religions. He died in 1886 and his follower Swami Vivekananda founded the Ramakrishna Mission in 1897. There are now branches all over India. Belur Math, the movement's international headquarters, was founded in 1899. It is supposed to represent a church, a mosque and a temple, depending on how you look at it. Belur Math is open 6.30 to 11 am and 3.30 to 7 pm daily (free entry). The Mission's **Institute of Culture**, which has a library, reading rooms and lecture halls, is in the south of the city near Dhakuria train station.

Dakshineswar Kali Temple

Across the river and north of Belur Math is this Kali temple where Ramakrishna was a priest, and where he reached his spiritual vision of the unity of all religions (see Belur Math earlier). The temple was built in 1847 and is surrounded by 12 other temples dedicated to Shiva.

Pareshnath Jain Temple

This temple, in the north-east of the city, was built in 1867 and dedicated to Sheetalnathji, the 10th of the 24 Jain *tirthankars*. The temple is an ornate mass of mirrors, coloured stones and glass mosaics. It overlooks a garden, and is open 6 to 11.30 am and 3 to 7 pm daily.

Kali Temple

Rebuilt in 1809 on the site of a much older temple, Kalighat (as it is also known) is believed to be the actual temple from which Kalikata (anglicised to Calcutta) took its name. According to legend, when Shiva's wife's corpse was cut up, one of her fingers fell here. Since then it has been an important pilgrimage site and is always extremely busy. Kali represents the destructive side of Shiva's consort and demands daily sacrifices. In the morning, goats are slaughtered to satisfy the goddess' bloodlust.

You'll probably be latched on to by temple 'priests' who will offer to whisk you around – for a donation of anything up to Rs 1000 (although some demand much more); don't be bullied. It's possible to view the temple's deity of Kali from around 6 am to 2 pm and 5 to 9 pm daily. Mother Teresa's **Hospital for the Dying Destitute** is next door to the temple.

The Kali Temple is about 2km south-east of the zoo and is easily accessible by the metro (Kalighat station).

CULTURAL CENTRES

Tagore House

The rambling old Tagore House is a centre for Indian dance, drama, music and other arts. This is the birthplace of Rabindranath Tagore, India's greatest modern poet, and his final resting place. It's just off Rabindra Sarani, north of BBD Bagh, and is open 10.30 am to 4.30 pm daily, except Monday. Entry to the museum is Rs 5 (shoes must be removed). There is a sound-and-light show in Bengali at 7 and 8 pm daily, except Monday and Thursday, from 1 February to 30 June; it's at 6 and 7 pm from 1 November to 31 January. Admission costs Rs 10. There are plans to commence a show in English.

PARKS & GARDENS

Botanical Gardens

The extensive Botanical Gardens, on the west bank of the Hooghly River, stretch for over 1km along the river and occupy 109 hectares. The gardens were founded in 1786 and administered by Colonel Kyd. It was from these gardens that the tea now grown in Assam and Darjeeling was first developed. The prime attraction is the 200-year-old **banyan tree**, claimed to have the second-largest canopy in the world (the largest is in Andhra Pradesh). It covers an area of nearly 400m in circumference and continues to flourish despite having its central trunk removed in 1925 due to fungus damage. The **palm house** in the centre of the gardens is also worth a look.

The gardens (open from sunrise to sunset) are a wonderful haven from the clamour of the city, although they can get very crowded on Sunday. You can get here by ferry from Babu Ghat, but this runs on a casual basis at sporadic times.

The Maidan & Fort William

After the events of 1756, when Siraj-ud-daula sacked the town, the British set out to replace the original Fort William, in the Maidan, with a massive and impregnable new fort. First they 'cleared out' the inhabitants of the village of Govindpur and in 1758 laid the foundations of a fort. By the time it was completed in 1781, the fort had cost the awesome total, for those days, of UK£2 million. Around the fort a huge expanse of jungle was destroyed to give the cannons a clear line of fire. However, the fort has never fired a single shot in aggression.

The fort is still in use today and visitors are only allowed inside with special permission (rarely granted). Even the trenches and deep fortifications surrounding the fort's massive walls seem to be out of bounds.

The area cleared around Fort William became the Maidan, the 'lungs' of modern Kolkata. This huge green expanse stretches 3km north to south and is more than 1km wide. The stream known as Tolly's Nullah is to the south and here you'll find a racecourse and the Victoria Memorial. In the north corner of the Maidan is Eden Gardens, while Raj Bhavan overlooks it from the north.

Within the gardens are cricket and football fields, ponds, trees and even musical fountains. Cows graze, political discussions are held, people stroll across the grounds or come for early morning yoga sessions.

Eden Gardens

At the northern corner of the Maidan are the small and pleasantly laid out Eden Gardens. A tiny **Burmese pagoda** was brought here from Prome, Myanmar (Burma) in 1856; it's set in a small lake and is extraordinarily picturesque. The gardens were named after the sister of Lord Auckland, the former governor general. The Calcutta Cricket Ground (Ranji Stadium), where international matches are held, is also within the gardens. Call the Cricket Association of Bengal on ☎ 2481528 for information.

Near the gardens you can take a pleasant **walk** along the banks of the Hooghly River. Ferries run across the river from several ghats and there are plenty of boat operators around offering to take you out on the water for a short **cruise**. There are no fixed prices for these cruises but expect to pay around Rs 80 per hour per boat.

In the corner of the gardens near the Raj Bhavan (old Government House; where a diagonal pathway joins the road), opposite the statue of Rash Behari Bose, there is a colony of small, virtually tame, **rats** that live in burrows. They may not be obvious at first – just scatter some food to entice them out of their cosy underground abode.

Zoo & Horticultural Gardens

South of the Maidan, Kolkata's 16-hectare zoo was opened in 1875. Some animals are displayed in near-natural environments, while others are not so blessed. It's open 9 am to 5 pm daily, except Thursday (Rs 5).

Just south of the zoo on Alipore Rd are the pleasant and quiet Horticultural Gardens. They're open 6 to 10 am and 1 to 5 pm daily (free entry).

OTHER MUSEUMS & GALLERIES

The **Asutosh Museum** at Calcutta University has a collection of art objects with an emphasis on Bengali folk art. It's open 11 am to 5 pm Monday to Friday and entry is free.

At 19A Gurusday Rd is the **Birla Industrial & Technological Museum**, open 10 am to 5.30 pm daily (Rs 7). The philanthropic (and very wealthy) Birlas have also provided the **Birla Academy of Art & Culture** at 109 Southern Ave, which is open 4 to 8 pm daily, except Monday (Rs 2). It has a good collection of sculpture and modern art. Also in the same area, Ballygunge, is the **Cima Gallery** at Sunny Towers, 43 Ashutesh Chowdhauri Ave. The gallery displays contemporary art and is open 11 am to 7 pm daily, except Sunday (free entry).

Victoria Memorial

At the southern end of the Maidan stands the Victoria Memorial, possibly the most awesome reminder of the Raj to be found in India. This huge white-marble museum houses a vast collection of memorabilia from the days of the British empire. There are portraits, statues and busts of almost all the main participants in British-Indian history. Scenes from military conflicts and the events of the Indian Uprising are illustrated. There are some superb watercolours of Indian landscapes and buildings that were executed by travelling Victorian artists. There's also a piano that Queen Victoria played as a girl and a huge painting depicting King Edward VII entering Jaipur in a regal procession in 1876. French guns captured at the Battle of Plassey are on show along with the black stone throne of the nawab defeated by Clive.

The **Calcutta Gallery**, opened in 1992, exhibits many early pictures of Kolkata as well as relics from the Raj, such as pistols. Upstairs is the **National Leaders Gallery**, which displays portraits of various political and social leaders of India, including Tagore. There is also a model of Fort William as well as historical documents including some pertaining to the struggle for Independence.

The memorial is open 10 am to 3.30 pm (to 4.30 pm in summer) daily, except Monday. Entry costs Rs 2; photography is not permitted inside.

There's an informative sound-and-light show: from October to February these are held 6.15 to 7 pm (Bengali) and 7.15 to 8 pm (English). Tickets can be bought from noon to 7.30 pm. From March to June the show takes place from 6.45 to 7.30 pm (Bengali) and 7.45 to 8.30 pm (English). The ticket counter is open 12.30 to 8 pm. Tickets cost Rs 10, but at the time of research there were unconfirmed reports that this would increase. See also the boxed text 'Cashing in on Foreign Tourists' under Money in the Facts for the Visitor chapter.

OTHER ATTRACTIONS

Howrah Bridge

Until 1943 the Hooghly River was crossed by a pontoon bridge that opened to let river traffic through. To alleviate fears that the building of a new bridge would affect river currents and cause silting, the Howrah Bridge (Rabindra Setu) was constructed to cross the river in a single 450m span – there are no pylons at all on the riverbed.

This amazing feat of engineering is similar in size to Australia's Sydney Harbour Bridge, but with a daily stream of some 100,000 vehicles and pedestrians too numerous to count, it is easily the busiest bridge in the world. It's intriguing to stand at one end of the bridge at morning rush-hour and watch the procession of buses, lumbering bullock carts, push carts, bicycles and cars. During rush-hour it can take 45 minutes to cross. The ferries running from below Howrah train station are a more convenient way to cross the river and also give you a good view of the bridge. However, if you are not too encumbered, walking is often the easiest way of crossing.

A second bridge, the Vidyasagar Setu, a Golden Gate Bridge lookalike, 2km downriver, was completed in 1994. Although it was supposed to relieve the crush on the old Howrah Bridge, the new bridge is now almost as chaotic itself.

Marble Palace

On Muktaram Babu St, a narrow lane off Chittaranjan Ave, this private mansion was built in 1835 by a Bengali zamindar (feudal landowner). The palace houses an incongruous collection of curios standing alongside significant statues and paintings (including works of Rubens and Sir Joshua Reynolds). There's a private zoo here too, but the inhabitants are only slightly more animated than the marble lions gracing the palace lawns. It's open 10 am to 4 pm daily, except Monday and Thursday. Entry is free with a permit from the Government of India tourist office.

South Park Street Cemetery

This peaceful cemetery is an evocative reminder of Kolkata's colonial past and is definitely worth a visit. Well-maintained and set under shady trees, there are some incredible tombs with poignant epitaphs (especially the children's). The more famous occupants include Colonel Kyd, founder of the Botanical Gardens, and Rose Aylmer, remembered only because her unfortunate death was supposed to have been caused by an addiction to pineapples.

Opening hours are 7.30 to 10.30 am and 3 to 4.30 pm Monday to Friday and 7.30 to 10.30 am Saturday. Entry is free. A booklet (Rs 40) about the cemetery is available.

Other British Buildings

Raj Bhavan, the old British Government House, built between 1799 and 1805 at the north end of the Maidan, is now occupied by the governor of West Bengal and entry is restricted. Near the Raj Bhavan is the Doric-style **Town Hall**, and next to that the **High Court**, which was copied from the Staadhaus at Ypres, Belgium, and completed in 1872. It has a 55m-high tower. Just south of the zoo on Alipore Rd is the **National Library**, the biggest in India, which is housed in Belvedere House, the former residence of the lieutenant-governor of Bengal.

ACTIVITIES

Meditation

Vyakti Vikas Kendra (☎ 4631018, ⓔ aritra@vsnl.com) offers meditation courses. A basic course is a minimum of six days and costs about Rs 800. At the time of writing, the manager of the Travellers' Express Club (see Travel Agencies earlier in this chapter) was planning to offer Buddhist meditation sessions with a Burmese monk.

Swimming

Unless you stay at an upmarket hotel, there are few options. The only hotels that allow nonguests to use their pool are the Hotel Hindustan International and ITDC Hotel Airport Ashok. Both charge Rs 350 per person (free for hotel guests), which includes a towel; the Hindustan's pool is better. You can use the Tollygunge Club's pools if you are a guest, a member or guest of a member.

Horse Riding

The Tollygunge Club (see Places to Stay) has horses and ponies that can be hired by guests or members for Rs 75 per hour. They can be ridden on the bridleway around the perimeter of the club.

Golf

The magnificent Royal Calcutta Golf Club at the Tollygunge Club is the oldest golf club in the world outside Britain. Established in 1829, the club was originally near the airport, but moved to Tollygunge in 1910. The title 'Royal' was conferred upon it by King George V and Queen Mary in 1911.

The fee is Rs 150 per round – but you can only play if you are staying at the club, are a club member or guest of a club member.

Mother Teresa

The late Mother Teresa, the 'Saint of the Gutters', came to epitomise selflessness because of her dedication to the destitute, the suffering and the dying. Born Agnes Gonxha Bojaxhiu in Serbia in 1910 to Albanian parents, she joined the Irish Order of Loreto nuns in 1929 and was sent to Darjeeling as a teacher. Moving to a school in Kolkata in 1937, she was horrified at the number of poor people who perished on the streets of the city because there was nowhere else for them to go. She began to feel that behind the secure walls of the nunnery she was too far removed from the people she wanted to help.

Mother Teresa formed a new order, the Missionaries of Charity, in 1950. Among the vows is the promise 'to give wholehearted and free service to the poorest of the poor'. This vow was put into action with the setting up of several homes including Nirmal Hriday (for the dying), Shanti Nagar (for lepers) and Nirmala Shishu Bhavan (the children's home). There are now homes in many other places around the world. In 1979 her work achieved world recognition when she was awarded the Nobel Peace Prize. For information about volunteer work, see the boxed text 'Helping Out' later in this chapter.

For all her saintliness, Mother Teresa was not without her critics. Feminist Germaine Greer, for example, accused her of being a religious imperialist, although anyone who has spent some time with the nuns and seen them at work could hardly call them Bible-bashing evangelists. Mother Teresa herself said that her's was contemplative work. Her inspiration was spiritual and Christian and was put into practice mainly by ministering to physical needs; she never sought to convert anyone. There have also been an increasing number of recent allegations that the mission adheres to antiquated health-care systems that compromise the quality of health care and that it lacks financial accountability.

ORGANISED TOURS

The Government of India tourist office operates a full-day sightseeing tour for Rs 100, departing 8 am daily (except Monday) from its office and returning at around 5 pm. It includes Belur Math, the Dakshineswar Kali Temple, Victoria Memorial, Indian Museum and more.

The West Bengal Tourism Centre offers a similar tour, also for Rs 100. This office can also arrange tours during the city's largest festival, Durga Puja (October), which includes a boat cruise down the Hooghly River to see the immersion of idols of the goddess Durga (for whom the festival is held) – prices are only available on application. This office also operates trips several times per week from October to March to the Sunderbans Wildlife Sanctuary (see Sunderbans Wildlife Sanctuary in the West Bengal chapter). In addition it has various packages around India, including tours of Darjeeling, Himachal Pradesh, Rajasthan, Sikkim and South India.

Walking Tours

Interesting and informative walking tours of BBD Bagh and north Kolkata (including areas off the tourist circuit) are conducted by the architect and conservationist, Manish Chakraborti. Tours leave from Great Eastern Hotel and cover historic buildings, heritage sites and history. The cost is Rs 350 per person and the tour takes two hours. For more information contact Footsteps (☎ 3375757, fax 3553188, ⓔ ashmon@cal2.vsnl.net.in), AA171A Salt Lake, Kolkata 700064.

Other Tours

Kali Travel Home (☎/fax 5587980, ⓔ refresh@cal2.vsnl.net.in) operates a two-week Kolkata 'Food & Culture Tour', which includes various cultural excursions, all meals, and Bengali cooking lessons by local women in their homes. These cost US$65 per person per day for groups of five and 15% extra per person for smaller groups. Three-hour cooking courses are also possible (US$13 per person). Advance bookings are essential. The same people also offer an 'Impressions of Kolkata Tour', which may appeal to those who sketch, photograph or write. Tailor-made tours of West Bengal and eastern India can also be arranged. For more details contact David Rowe or Martyn Brown at Kali Travel Home.

SPECIAL EVENTS

For 10 days in late January/early February the largest **book fair** in Asia is held on the

Mother Teresa

Early in 1997 Mother Teresa resigned her position at the Missionaries due to bad health, and named Sister Nirmala as her replacement. On 5 September 1997, a few days after her 87th birthday, and the day of Diana, Princess of Wales' funeral, Mother Teresa went to join her God. Not one to tolerate the restrictions of a hospital, she died surrounded by the sisters in her beloved Motherhouse in Kolkata. For one week her body lay in a glass case, draped with the Indian flag, in St Thomas' Church. Thousands of people, from the poor of Kolkata to dignitaries from around the world, came to pay their last respects. The government honoured Mother Teresa with a state funeral and her coffin was carried on a gun carriage that once bore the bodies of India's greatest statesmen, Mahatma Gandhi and Jawaharlal Nehru. The funeral service was attended by around 12,000 people.

Mother Teresa's coffin now rests in the Motherhouse; its only embellishment is a small marble tombstone inscribed with her name and the legend, 'Love one another as I have loved you'.

Maidan. The entry fee is nominal and there's a 10% discount on all books. Various other touring exhibitions occasionally take place on the Maidan (mainly during the cooler winter months) – inquire at the West Bengal Tourism Centre (see Information earlier).

The **Dover Lane Music Conference** held in January features Indian classical music. During **Durga Puja** in October it's auspicious to immerse idols of the goddess Durga in the Hooghly River. Theatre performances from India and neighbouring countries are held during the **National Theatre Festival** from 16 to 25 December.

PLACES TO STAY

Budget and mid-range accommodation in Kolkata is decidedly lacklustre, with most places hungry for a lick of paint and general sprucing up. Many have spartan rooms with rock-hard mattresses and pillows and a cell-like atmosphere due to the small or nonexistent windows. If you're planning a long stay here (as a volunteer for instance), you may like to bring along photos of your pet pooch and other loved ones to cheer up your home away from home. Colourful Indian bedspreads and fabrics also do wonders in brightening dreary rooms and are available in Kolkata at modest prices.

The din of traffic and dogs barking at night can be diabolical at some places, so request a quiet room (earplugs are recommended). Note that most budget and mid-range places lock their gates after about 11 pm, so if you're going to get back late, let them know in advance.

To stay with an Indian family, contact the Government of India tourist office (see Information earlier in this chapter), which can arrange paying guesthouse accommodation (ranging from around Rs 200 to Rs 2000 per night).

Most hotels whack an extra 10% service tax on their advertised room rates; air-con

Helping Out

Kolkata has long attracted volunteers from India and beyond. There are various charity organisations in Kolkata, ranging from the well-known Missionaries of Charity (see the boxed text 'Mother Teresa' to the lesser-known Calcutta Society for the Prevention of Cruelty to Animals (CSPCA). If you're interested in helping out in Kolkata (or other parts of West Bengal) see the Volunteer Work section in the Facts for the Visitor chapter.

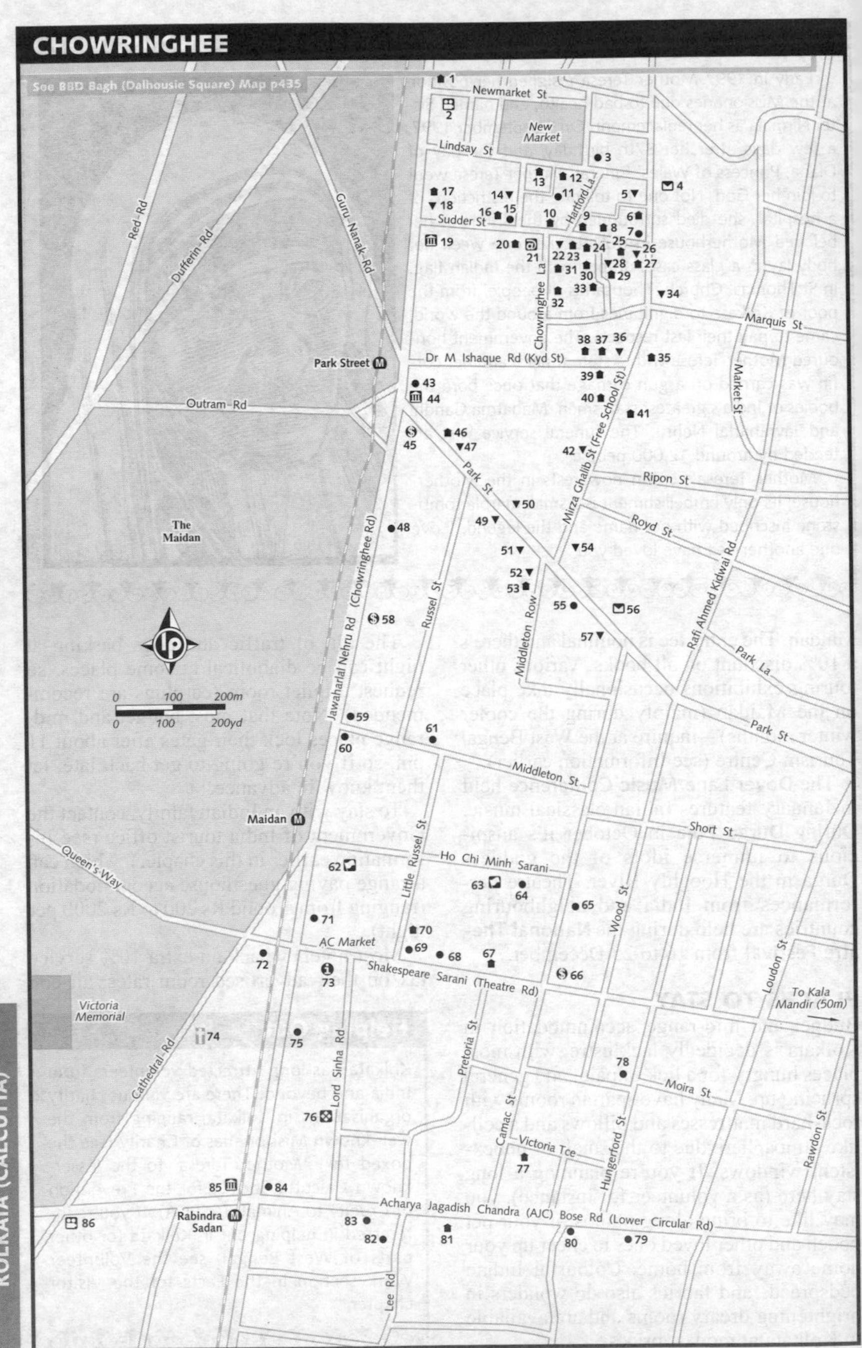
CHOWRINGHEE
See BBD Bagh (Dalhousie Square) Map p435
Newmarket St
New Market
Lindsay St
Sudder St
Hartford La
Chowringhee La
Marquis St
Dr M Ishaque Rd (Kyd St)
Park Street
Outram Rd
Red Rd
Dufferin Rd
Guru Nanak Rd
Market St
Mirza Ghalib St (Free School St)
Park St
Ripon St
Royd St
The Maidan
Jawaharlal Nehru Rd (Chowringhee Rd)
Russel St
Middleton Row
Rafi Ahmed Kidwai Rd
Park La
Middleton St
Short St
Maidan
Queen's Way
Ho Chi Minh Sarani
Little Russel St
Wood St
AC Market
Shakespeare Sarani (Theatre Rd)
Victoria Memorial
Cathedral Rd
Lord Sinha Rd
Pretoria St
Camac St
Hungerford St
Moira St
Loudon St
Rawdon St
Victoria Tce
To Kala Mandir (50m)
Acharya Jagadish Chandra (AJC) Bose Rd (Lower Circular Rd)
Rabindra Sadan
Lee Rd
0 100 200m
0 100 200yd

CHOWRINGHEE

PLACES TO STAY
1 The Oberoi Grand; Peerless Inn; Aaheli
6 Centrepoint Guest House; Travellers' Express Club
8 Hotel Astoria
9 Hotels Plaza & Diplomat; Titrupati's
10 Fairlawn Hotel
12 Hotel Lindsay; Gujral Guest House; Jharokha
13 CKT Inn
16 Lytton Hotel
17 YMCA
20 Salvation Army Guest House
23 Times Guest House; Hotel Hilson; Zurich's
24 Shilton Hotel; Tourist Inn; Kuka Travels
25 Hotel Maria
27 Gulistan Guest House; Hotel Royal Palace
29 Modern Lodge
30 Paragon Hotel; Hotel Galaxy
31 Hotel Palace
32 Capital Guest House
33 Timestar Hotel
35 Sonali Guest House
37 Hotel Neelam
38 Hotel Crystal
39 Hotel East End
40 Classic Hotel
41 Hotel VIP International; Shyamoli Paribahan (Bus Tickets To Dhaka); Gupta Restaurant
46 Park Hotel; Trinca's Restaurant; Jet Airways
53 YWCA
67 Astor Hotel
70 Kenilworth Hotel
77 Hotel Vic Terrace
81 Hotel Hindustan International

PLACES TO EAT
5 Kathleen Confectioners; Princess Restaurant & Bar
14 Khalsa Restaurant
18 Zaranj Restaurant
22 Blue Sky Cafe; Curd Corner
26 Khwaja
28 JoJo's Restaurant
34 Prince Restaurant
36 How Hua; Off Cum On Rambo Bar
42 Mocambo; Armenian College (Thackery's Birthplace)
47 Kwality; Oxford Book Shop
49 Junior Brothers
50 Bar-B-Q; Blue Fox
51 Flury's; Music World
52 Peter Cat
54 Golden Dragon
57 Waldorf Restaurant

OTHER
2 New Empire Cinema; Lighthouse Bar & Restaurant; On Cue; Cyber Empire Internet Cafe
3 Merle Oberon's House
4 New Market Post Office
7 Bookland
11 Treasure Island Market
15 North East Color Photos
19 Indian Museum
21 Netfreaks
43 Bangladesh Biman Airlines; Lufthansa
44 Asiatic Society
45 Standard Chartered Grindlays Bank
48 Japan Airlines
55 Cambridge Book & Stationary Company
56 Park St Post Office
58 State Bank of India
59 British Airways; RNAC
60 Cathay Pacific; KLM
61 Classic Books
62 British High Commission
63 US Consulate
64 Vital Medical Services
65 DHL Worldwide Express
66 ANZ Grindlays Bank
68 British Council & Library
69 AC Market
71 Swissair
72 MP Birla Planetarium
73 Government of India Tourist Office
74 St Paul's Cathedral; Academy of Fine Arts
75 Air India
76 Emami Shoppers City; Landmark; Starlit Cafe
78 Iskcon
79 Thai Airways International
80 Thomas Cook; Air France; Gulf Air
82 Singapore Airlines
83 Foreigners' Registration Office
84 Aeroflot
85 Nehru Children's Museum
86 Rabindra Sadan; Nandan Cinema

rooms attract an extra 10% luxury tax on top of that (taxes have not been included in this chapter). Checkout at most hotels is noon and discounts are usually offered in low season (around April to late September).

For quick reference, the following places to stay have been listed under the same name of the map on which they appear in this chapter.

PLACES TO STAY – BUDGET

Chowringhee Area

Sudder St is the budget travellers hang-out and rooms here can fill up fast. Being the tourist hotbed, there's a fair bit of the 'yes have a look! change money! buy something!' from the touts and others, but it's not as bad as Agra or parts of Rajasthan...yet. Having said that, numbers of beggars in the Sudder St area have risen in line with tourist numbers. Your money will probably go a longer way at one of Kolkata's charitable institutions (see the boxed text 'Helping Out'), but if you still want to give something, food offerings are best (packets should be opened to prevent them being resold on the black market). A recent 'scam' in Sudder St is for female beggars to ask you to buy milk for their baby. Sadly, this seemingly laudable request is a ploy – once you have handed over the milk, most of these women simply dash around the corner to resell it for cash.

Salvation Army Guest House (☎ *2450599, 2 Sudder St*) has long been popular, especially with volunteers working for Mother Teresa's mission. It's a mellow, well-kept place, with dorm beds for Rs 65 and doubles with private bathroom from Rs 200 to 700.

Hotel Maria *(☎ 2450860, 5/1 Sudder St)* is another favourite, with an equally laid-back atmosphere and strictly 'no drugs, no alcohol'. Basic singles/doubles with shared bathroom go for Rs 150/200, or Rs 200/250 with private bathroom. If you're strapped for cash, there are dorm beds for Rs 70.

Hotel Hilson *(☎ 2173896, fax 2463999, 4 Sudder St)*, near Zurich's restaurant, has singles with shared bathroom for Rs 150, doubles with private bathroom from Rs 350 and four-bed rooms for Rs 500. Some rooms are musty – choose carefully.

Times Guest House *(☎ 2451796, 3 Sudder St)*, near Zurich's, is a flophouse and is only worth considering if other places on Sudder St are full. Disheveled doubles with private bathroom are Rs 250. However, there are plans for renovation.

Shilton Hotel *(☎ 2451512, 5A Sudder St)* has single/double rooms with private bathroom for Rs 220/300. Some are rather gloomy, but otherwise OK.

Tourist Inn *(☎ 2450134, 2nd floor, 4/1 Sudder St)* is a small, decent place that has rooms with shared bathroom for Rs 100/200, or Rs 400 for a room for four with private bathroom. This place operates Kuka Travels on the 1st floor (see Travel Agencies earlier in this chapter).

Paragon Hotel *(☎ 2442445, 2 Stuart Lane)*, just off Sudder St, gets mixed reports from travellers. A dorm bed is Rs 60, small rooms with shared bathroom are Rs 130/140, and doubles with private bathroom start at Rs 250.

Hotel Galaxy *(☎ 2464565, ⓔ juvena@vsnl.com)*, next to the Paragon, is unpretentious, with just four rooms starting at Rs 400, all with private bathroom.

The nearby ***Timestar Hotel*** *(☎ 2450028)* is particularly popular with Japanese travellers and a bit quieter than other hotels in this area. Small rooms with private bathroom are Rs 175/250.

Modern Lodge *(☎ 2444960, 1 Stuart Lane)* is also popular, especially with long-term visitors. Rooms with shared bathroom are Rs 70/90 and doubles with private bathroom range from Rs 120 to 240.

Hotel Palace *(☎ 2446214, 13 Chowringhee Lane)* just off Sudder St, is a warren of a place but not a bad choice. There are rooms for Rs 200/300 with private bathroom. Request a room with a window.

Capital Guest House *(☎ 2450598, 11B Chowringhee Lane)*, near Hotel Palace, is in a quiet courtyard away from the noise of Sudder St. Doubles with private bathroom range from Rs 300 to 350. Rooms with shared bathroom go for Rs 150/200. Although some of the bathrooms here could be better, the rooms are acceptable.

Gujral Guest House *(☎ 2440620, fax 2455109, 8B Lindsay St)* is just north of Sudder St in the same building as Hotel Lindsay, but off to the side on the 2nd floor. It has reasonable (if somewhat musty and dark) rooms for Rs 250/450 with private bathroom and Rs 200/270 with shared bathroom. Air-con rooms cost Rs 850/950.

Centrepoint Guest House *(☎ 2448184, fax 2442867, 20 Mirza Ghalib St)* is a bustling place with dorm beds for Rs 75 and tiny rooms for Rs 250/300 with private bathroom.

Gulistan Guest House *(☎ 2260963, 30F Mirza Ghalib St)*, opposite the fire station, up a flight of stairs, is a popular choice with volunteers. The rooms (Rs 200/400 with private bathroom) are cleaner than many other cheapies in this area. In the same building is ***Hotel Royal Palace*** *(☎ 2455168)*, which is similar in price and standard.

Sonali Guest House *(☎ 2451844)*, farther south on Mirza Ghalib St, has rooms with private bathroom for Rs 150/350. Sonali gets variable reports from travellers, but the rooms are no worse than any other budget place.

Classic Hotel *(☎ 2297390)*, down an alley just off Mirza Ghalib St, has singles with shared bathroom for Rs 150. Doubles with private bathroom are Rs 260. Hot water is by the bucket (free) and the rooms are pretty good value.

Hotel East End *(☎ 2298921, 9/1 Dr M Ishaque Rd)* is nearby, and although the rooms are rather dull, it's run by friendly folk. Rooms with private bathroom start at Rs 250/350.

Hotel Neelam *(☎ 2269198, 11 Dr M Ishaque Rd)*, nearby, has ordinary but good-sized singles/doubles with private bathroom from Rs 175/300. Larger rooms cost Rs 400 a double.

The gloomy ***YMCA*** *(☎ 2492192, 25 Chowringhee Rd)* is a rambling building and not great value. Drab rooms with private bathroom are upwards of Rs 370/540.

All accommodation includes early morning tea, breakfast and dinner. There's a second ***YMCA*** *(☎ 2443814, 42 Surendra Nath Banerji Rd)* with simple rooms from Rs 250 per double with private bathroom.

YWCA *(☎ 2297033, 1 Middleton Row)* is an exceedingly better choice and you'll have no hassles here whatsoever. Despite the name, it accepts women and men. Rates include all meals: tidy rooms are Rs 300/500 with shared bathroom, or Rs 550/750 with private bathroom.

BBD Bagh Area

There is a paucity of respectable budget hotels in this part of town. ***Central Guest House*** *(☎ 2374876)* is a good choice in a city starved of quality budget accommodation. Singles/doubles with private bathroom go for Rs 200/275. The hotel (which is on the 2nd floor) fronts onto Chittaranjan (CR) Ave, but the entrance is around the corner at 18 Prafulla Sarkar St.

Elsewhere

Yatri Niwas *(☎ 6601742)*, in the new building next to Howrah train station, only accepts transit train or air passengers. It has dorm beds (Rs 75) and doubles with private bathroom for Rs 250, or Rs 450 with air-con. You can only stay here if you have a train/air ticket, and then only for two nights (one extra night on application). There are also ***retiring rooms*** at Howrah and Sealdah train stations (Rs 50 per bed), but these are nothing fancy.

For transit air passengers, moderately priced rooms are available at the airport. If you want to stay near the airport, try the small ***Airport Plaza Hotel*** *(Tarun Sengupta Sarani, No 1 Airport Gate)*. The rooms are basic but cheap at Rs 150/250 for singles/doubles with private bathroom (all with squat toilet). Try to have a look at a few rooms before deciding.

PLACES TO STAY – MID-RANGE

Kolkata's mid-range hotels are certainly nothing flash, but most come with private phone, cable TV and room service. All places included here have private bathroom and air-con unless otherwise indicated.

Chowringhee Area

Hotel Diplomat *(☎ 2468434, 10 Sudder St)* is a mid-range hotel that also has some budget rooms for Rs 150/200 a single/double with shared bathroom, or Rs 200/225 with private bathroom. The air-con rooms (Rs 495) are much more salubrious. Next door is the less impressive ***Hotel Plaza*** *(☎ 2446411, fax 2468434)*, with windowless doubles for Rs 400, or Rs 475 with air-con.

Hotel Astoria *(☎ 2451514, fax 2448589, e astoria@hotmail.com, 6/2 & 6/3 Sudder St)* looks seductively snazzy from the outside, but once you pass reception things take a turn for the worse. Many rooms are remarkably spacious, but rather scruffy and the corridors could be cleaner. Rooms cost Rs 600/850.

Hotel Lindsay *(☎ 2452237, fax 2450310, 8A Lindsay St)* offers small rooms for a hefty Rs 800/950, or Rs 1200/1400 with air-con.

The centrally air-conditioned ***CKT Inn*** *(☎ 2448246, fax 2440047, 12A Lindsay St)* is a small, cordial place with respectable rooms for Rs 825/1100 although it is often full.

Hotel VIP International (☎ 2290345, fax 2293715, *e hvipcal@mantraonline.com, 51 Mirza Ghalib St)* lacks panache, but the rooms are comfortable enough for Rs 1295 to 1695 a double.

Hotel Crystal *(☎ 2266400)* is close to the action off Dr M Ishaque Rd but the standards have dropped over recent years. Doubles cost Rs 500, or Rs 800 with air-con.

Astor Hotel *(☎ 2829917, fax 2827430, e astor@cal3.vsnl.net.in, 15 Shakespeare Sarani)* is a bit disappointing considering the price tag: Rs 1100/1300 for sloppy rooms. It's an option if all other places are booked out.

Hotel Vic Terrace *(☎ 2408788, fax 2404063, 1B Victoria Terrace)*, opposite Industry House, has rooms upwards of Rs 870/970. Although some of the cheaper ones are cramped, they are modern and tidy and the staff are obliging.

BBD Bagh Area

Hotel Embassy *(☎ 2379040, fax 2373288, 27 Princep St)* is an old, no-frills place with singles/doubles for Rs 400/500; with air-con they go for Rs 500/600.

Broadway Hotel *(☎ 2363930, fax 236 4151, e broadway@vsnl.com, 27A Ganesh Chandra Ave)* is more popular, with a range of reasonably well-kept rooms from Rs 340/440. It also has some cheaper rooms for Rs 285/400 with shared bathroom.

Heera Hotel *(☎ 2280663, fax 2280171, 28 Grant St)*, north of New Market, would have to have the world's smallest lift. Although the reception area is more glamorous than the rooms, it's not a bad choice. The rate is Rs 475/550, or Rs 700/825 with air-con.

Elsewhere

Royal Calcutta Guest House *(☎ 2800377, fax 2404823, 124 Karaya Rd)* is away from the central district (look for the preschool sign), but is delightfully homey and particularly good for long-term stays. There are just six spacious doubles, which are arranged in pairs with a common lounge and kitchen in between. Singles/doubles cost Rs 500/600, or Rs 750/850 with air-con. Car hire can be arranged.

PLACES TO STAY – TOP END

If you are cashed up and seeking some serious pampering, there are two hotels that stand out from the rest: The Oberoi Grand and Taj Bengal. Park Hotel is also quite ritzy, but other hotels in the top-end category lack the same 'wow' factor.

Chowringhee Area

The renowned ***Fairlawn Hotel*** *(☎ 2451510, fax 2441835, ⓔ fairlawn@cal.vsnl.net.in, 13A Sudder St)* is a slice of Kolkata where the Raj still prospers, albeit in a decidedly eccentric fashion that you may find quaintly amusing or downright irritating. Although atmospheric, the service here can be abrupt to the point of rudeness. Edmund Smith and his Armenian wife, Violet, still run the hotel more than 50 years after Independence. There's a lush courtyard garden and the interior is crammed with memorabilia, chintz and prewar furnishings. Some bathrooms have deep baths standing on ball and claw feet. A single/double room costs US$50/60, including three meals (set menu).

Lytton Hotel *(☎ 2491872, fax 2491747, ⓔ lytton@giascl01.vsnl.net.in, 14 Sudder St)* has a sterile ambience, but is adequately luxurious and friendly. The cheapest rooms cost Rs 1600/2200, but if you can afford it opt for the super deluxe rooms (Rs 2200/2700). There are two restaurants and a bar (see Entertainment, later).

The Oberoi Grand *(☎ 2492323, fax 2491217, ⓔ fo@oberoi-cal.com, 15 Chowringhee Rd)* has long been acknowledged as Kolkata's finest hotel and indeed one of the jewels in the Oberoi crown. Tasteful and immaculate rooms start at US$225/250 and there's an outdoor pool (guests only), three restaurants, and all the mod-cons you would expect of a world-class hotel.

Peerless Inn *(☎ 2280301, fax 2286650, ⓔ peerinn@giascl01.vsnl.net.in, 12 Chowringhee Rd)*, near The Oberoi Grand, is rather low on atmosphere, but some rooms boast magnificent city views. Good rooms start at Rs 2625/3250. The Aaheli restaurant gets positive reports (see Places to Eat).

Park Hotel *(☎ 2493121, fax 2497343, ⓔ resv.cal@theparkhotels.com, 17 Park St)* is a relatively large property, but has the ambience of a boutique hotel. Swish rooms start at US$225/250 and there are several good restaurants, an indoor pool (guests only) and more.

Kenilworth Hotel *(☎ 2828394, fax 2825136, 1–2 Little Russel St)* has old and new wings, but gets mixed reviews from travellers. Basic rates in the new wing are US$100/110; it costs US$140 (doubles only) in the old wing.

Quite popular, the ***Hotel Hindustan International*** *(☎ 2472394, fax 2472824, 235 AJC Bose Rd)* has a health club, shopping arcade, restaurants, bars and a swimming pool (open to nonguests – see Swimming earlier in this chapter). Attractive rooms start at US$150/165.

BBD Bagh Area

Great Eastern Hotel *(☎ 2482311, fax 2480289, ⓔ geh@vsnl.com, 1–3 Old Court House St)* is a rambling old Raj-style hotel, originally named The Auckland when it was built in 1840. It's not nearly as grandiose as other top-end hotels, but is mellow and atmospheric. There are some budget rooms for Rs 660/825 a single/double; more luxurious and spacious air-con rooms are upwards of Rs 1375/1980 (some are bigger and better than others so try to look at a few first).

Elsewhere

The well-known ***Tollygunge Club*** *(☎ 473 2316, fax 4731903)* is set on 44 hectares on the southern edge of Kolkata. It's got a fabulous golf course (see Golf earlier in this chapter) and although it's looking a little faded around the edges these days, it's still a good place to get an idea of how the other half frolicked in the days of the Raj. For decades it was run by Englishman Bob Wright who now lives in retirement on the property. Today, 'Tolly' is the playground of the city's elite. As well as the championship golf course, there are indoor and outdoor pools, grass and clay tennis courts, squash courts, a croquet lawn, a billiard room, badminton facilities and table-tennis rooms, and a stable of horses. As a foreign visitor, so long as you telephone, fax or write in advance (120 DP Sasmal Rd, Kolkata 700033), you may stay here and have temporary membership allowing you to use the facilities.

Although this club oozes charm, travellers have complained about the lackadaisical service and rather disheveled rooms. The cheapest rooms are in 'Hastings' (Rs 1150/1250 a single/double). The 'Grandstand' cottages go for Rs 2200/2400 and have small sitting areas overlooking the lush golf course. Most rooms in 'Tolly Towers' or 'Tolly Terrace' are similarly priced.

Taj Bengal *(☎ 2233939, fax 2231766, ⓔ tbhfo.cal@tajhotels.com)*, at the southern end of the Maidan, scores top marks for its slick service and impeccable interior. It has all the luxuries of a deluxe hotel, including a pool (guests only), several restaurants, a coffee shop (see Places to Eat) and a business centre. Suitably sumptuous rooms start at US$215/245 and shoot up to US$625 for the presidential suite.

The government-operated ***ITDC Hotel Airport Ashok*** *(☎ 5119111, fax 5119137, ⓔ airpotel@cal.vsnl.net.in)* is poor value for money and presumably manages to stay in business because of its proximity to the airport (1km away), making it a convenient stopover for transit passengers. Overpriced rooms start at Rs 4500/5500 and facilities include a nondescript swimming pool (open to nonguests – see Swimming earlier in this chapter). On the plus side, the 24-hour coffee shop is a relaxing place to kill time over a cup of chai (Rs 40) or toasted sandwich (Rs 80) while waiting for your flight (nonguests are welcome). If you're low on dough, there's a far cheaper (but much more basic) budget place nearby (see Places to Stay – Budget).

PLACES TO EAT

Fish (fried or curried) and rice are the focus of Bengali cuisine, but surprisingly, there are few restaurants that whip up the real stuff. If you're lucky enough to be invited to a Bengali home, that's where you'll indulge in authentic, lip-smacking Bengali fare.

Bengali sweet specialties include *misthi dhoi* (curd sweetened with *jaggery*, a sweetener made from palm sap) and *rasgulla* (sweet cream-cheese balls flavoured with rose-water), which can be found at virtually all sweet shops.

'Indianised' Chinese food is particularly popular with Kolkatans and you'll find at least several Chinese dishes tacked onto most menus. If money is no object, fine dining is available at the top-end hotels (see Places to Stay).

Many nonair-con restaurants levy an 8% to 12% tax on menu prices, while those with air-con generally charge between 15% and 17% (taxes have not been included in prices in this chapter).

Chowringhee Area

Most budget eateries, especially on tourist-laden Sudder St, offer the usual have-a-go-at-anything menu and most stay open throughout the day. Although the food and service can be a bit hit and miss, they're reasonably cheap and are ideal places to strike up a conversation with other travellers (sometimes unavoidable considering how tightly packed the tables are).

Sudder Street Area The small ***Blue Sky Cafe***, on the corner of Sudder St and Chowringhee Lane, has long been a travellers hang-out, but nowadays it has just as many detractors as fans. The menu is as jam-packed as the tables, offering everything from spaghetti fantasia (Rs 65), to various porridge concoctions (around Rs 20). ***Curd Corner***, next door on Sudder St, whips up some of the best curd and lassis in town at nominal prices.

Zurich's, close by, is not as buzzing as Blue Sky Cafe, but does get exceedingly rosier reports from travellers. Small and friendly, it serves Indian, Western and Chinese cuisine, including pizzas (around Rs 35) and apple pancakes (Rs 18).

Titrupati's, almost opposite Zurich's, is a tiny but busy street stall much patronised by volunteers for its cheap, wholesome preparations (Rs 10 to 25 per hearty feed). You may have to queue during lunch.

Khwaja is a tad more expensive than other cheapies in this area, but it's a rejuvenating retreat from the furore of the streets – an ideal place to kick back with a book (plenty available at Bookland, directly opposite), or to scribble letters. The soothing hot lemon (Rs 8) is a godsend for sore throats, and the cooks also do a good job at omelettes.

Khalsa Restaurant, just off Sudder St, looks pretty ordinary, but the food is satiating and the service is speedy. On top of that, it's darn cheap; veg curry is a mere Rs 10.

JoJo's Restaurant, a popular little spot with travellers and locals, is down the lane opposite Hotel Astoria. Although a tad gloomy inside, it's tidy and friendly and has a varied menu including egg curry (Rs 20) and the intriguing jelly belly (Rs 21).

The large ***Zaranj Restaurant***, on Sudder St, has wider menu choices but the bill hits harder. It's good for a splurge with some interesting North-Western Frontier dishes such as *gobi Peshawari* (cauliflower sauteed with spices and topped with roasted cumin seeds and mint leaves; Rs 150).

Jharokha, just north of Sudder St, is a rooftop indoor and outdoor restaurant 10 floors above Hotel Lindsay. It's worth visiting purely for its tremendous panoramic views over Kolkata. The food and interior are more upmarket than other places in this area – try the fish masala (Rs 65) or *palak paneer* (unfermented cheese in spinach gravy; Rs 50). If that breaks the bank, lick ice cream (Rs 30) while admiring the view.

Aaheli is at Peerless Inn (see Places to Stay), a couple of blocks north of Sudder St. According to Kolkatans, it's the best place to feast on authentic Bengali food. To sample various Bengali dishes, order the veg Aahelir Bhoj (Rs 225) or, for carnivores, the Aahelir Mahaabhoj (Rs 275). For cheaper Bengali food, there's ***Suruchi***, on Elliot Rd (by the Mallik Bazaar bus stop), which is only open for lunch. Although the food is not as exceptional as it once was, it's still OK; a veg thali is Rs 29.

Mirza Ghalib Street The ***Gupta Restaurant***, near Hotel VIP International, is a welcome escape from the hubbub and offers a tempting mix of Indian and Chinese food. For the adventurous there's brain masala (Rs 44); or there's vegetable korma (Rs 50), ginger fish (Rs 74) and plenty more.

Mocambo has an old-world ambience and boasts some curious Indian and continental creations, such as Greek drunken prawns (Rs 140). Other goodies include risotto with chicken liver (Rs 80), rogan josh (fiery lamb curry; Rs 70) and creme caramel (Rs 45).

Princess Restaurant & Bar is a relaxing place to dine. It does some particularly good Indian dishes, including chicken tikka (Rs 75) and dum aloo (Rs 50).

How Hua, a popular Chinese eatery, is another great escape from the tumultuous streets. The sweet and sour won tons (Rs 52 for 10 pieces) are delicious. Decent Chinese food can also be had at ***Golden Dragon***.

Prince Restaurant, a noisy streetfront place on the corner of Mirza Ghalib and Marquis Sts, is nothing fancy as far as decor goes, but is not bad for a cheap chow down. It specialises in Bengali fish preparations (ranging from Rs 20 to 40). A roti is just Rs 2.50.

Kathleen Confectioners proudly showcases its sugar-laden Western cakes, and although they may claim to be the best in town, their cakes are no match to those that grandma used to bake. The black forest (Rs 13 per slice) is probably the pick of the bunch. There's also a small outlet on AJC Bose Rd.

Park Street Area Ritzy Park St has a string of appealing eateries that are quite upmarket but won't totally decimate your cash stash.

Bar-B-Q is one of the most popular Chinese and Indian restaurants in this area and there is usually a queue after 7.30 pm. The service is good and the atmosphere buzzes. Fried chicken wings are Rs 60.

Next door is ***Blue Fox***, a pleasant multicuisine restaurant that features several Thai specialities such as *mee krob* (Thai crispy noodles; Rs 135). Other options include asparagus soup (Rs 65) and fish tikka (Rs 100).

Waldorf Restaurant has a Chinese emphasis but also turns a hand to Thai food. If you need a tofu fix, there are various dishes to choose from (Rs 60 to 70).

Junior Brothers churns out standard Indian fare, but is less pricey than other Park St places.

Kwality is a roomy restaurant with a seductive selection, including prawn curry (Rs 95) and a wicked chocolate sundae (Rs 57).

KRAIG LIEB

GREG ELMS

GREG ELMS

Top: Kolkata is sprawled along the Hooghly River, which is spanned by the mighty Howrah Bridge.
Middle: Effigies of Durga are immersed in the Hooghly River at the end of the Durga Puja.
Bottom: Fruit sellers display their produce just south of Howrah Bridge in New Market.

GREG ELMS

RICHARD I'ANSON

GREG ELMS

Top left & bottom: Pacing it out in Kolkata: Whether you're taking a leisurely stroll or a quick whirl in a rickshaw, there's never a dull moment in Kolkata.
Top right: The garland sellers beneath the Howrah Bridge provide a golden photo opportunity.

Trinca's Restaurant, near Park Hotel, has a band each night from 8 pm. The green peas masala (Rs 65) and tandoori chicken (Rs 72 for half a bird) are good. Light snacks, such as chutney sandwiches (Rs 35), are also available.

Peter Cat, just off Park St on Middleton Row, is a dimly lit, mellow bar and restaurant that is good for a frosty beverage with warm conversation. A bottle of Kingfisher is Rs 68. If you're feeling frazzled, a tequila (Rs 52 a shot) may hit the spot, or maybe the 'Gentle Murderer' (Rs 48) is more your poison.

Flury's, nearby on Park St, is a lively cafe-style spot that makes an invigorating tea 'n' treat break in-between shopping. It has savoury and sweet offerings, ranging from cheese croissants (Rs 39) to nut sundaes (Rs 48). The service can be sluggish.

Hare Krishna Bakery is a teeny-weeny corner place next to the Anokhi shop, just south of Park St. This snug little veg bakehouse sells satiating takeaway snacks as well as brown bread and small bags of home-made cookies. The pizza slab (Rs 25) is particularly pleasing.

BBD Bagh Area

The ***Chung Wah Chinese Restaurant*** *(Chittaranjan Ave)*, with private wooden booths, looks like something out of Shanghai in the 1930s. The fried chilli chicken (Rs 55) is a red-hot seller. There's another branch around the corner.

Anand Restaurant *(Chittaranjan Ave)*, nearby, is a very popular (and reasonably priced) vegetarian restaurant with some especially good South Indian specialities such as *dosas* (paper-thin lentil-flour pancakes).

Amber Hotel *(11 Waterloo St)* is in the centre of town on the narrow street that runs by Great Eastern Hotel. Although the food is tasty enough, it does not get the standing ovation it once did. The chicken *saag* (with leafy greens; Rs 69) is sublime.

Nizam's, just north of New Market, serves good-value mutton or chicken rolls, kebabs and other fast food that has Muslim influences.

You can buy Indian sweets (including Bengali) at various 'sweeteries' in Kolkata, including ***Indra Mahal*** on Chowringhee Rd and at ***KC Das*** on Lenin Sarani (near the corner of Bentinck St); the latter gets the most glowing reviews from locals and travellers.

Elsewhere

Indian Coffee House, near Calcutta University, was once the meeting place of the city's intellectuals. Nowadays it's popular with young undergraduates for its coffee and moderately priced snacks. There's a second (more central) branch in the BBD Bagh area.

Yangoon *(☎ 4401442 for reservations, 7D Swinhoe St)*, near Southpoint School, is an unpretentious little place that cooks up authentic Burmese food. The *ohn no khawshwe* (Rs 55) is positively divine and shouldn't be missed. Yangoon is only open for dinner (closed Thursday).

For real *momos* (Tibetan dumplings) make a beeline for ***Momo Plaza*** *(2A Suburban Hospital Rd)*, a modest eatery south of Chowringhee that has perfected the art of momo-making. A plate of five steamed chicken momos is a reasonable Rs 30.

To hobnob with Kolkata's yuppies, cruise over to the swish cafe-style ***Aqua Java*** *(79 Shambhu Nath Pandit St)* near the PG Hospital. The coffee concoctions are particularly innovative; a Black Forest cappuccino is Rs 65. There's a billiard table upstairs (Rs 50 per game) if you're pressed for conversation.

If you're sick of scrimping and want a budget-breaking luxury fix, brush your hair and seek out a suitable top-end hotel coffee shop (most are open 24 hours and welcome nonguests). One possibility is the coffee shop at ***Taj Bengal***: for a full-on splurge, there's lobster (Rs 1000), or Norwegian pink salmon with mango and lime sauce (Rs 650); for a minor splurge there are pizzas (Rs 225) and dosas (Rs 125) – if that still breaks the bank, share a banana split (Rs 125) or ask for several straws with your chocolate milkshake (Rs 90).

ENTERTAINMENT

Pubs & Bars

Most hotel watering holes are open to nonguests, but be warned that although the drinks may quench your thirst, too many will suck your wallet dry.

On Sudder St, Lytton Hotel's intimate, dimly-lit ***Sunset Bar*** charges Rs 80 for a bottle of beer and Rs 90 for a shot of cognac. The open-air forecourt at ***Fairlawn Hotel***, also on Sudder St, usually attracts an interesting crowd.

The more upmarket ***Someplace Else*** pub at Park Hotel on Park St, has a live band every night from 8 pm. Kenilworth Hotel's ***Big Ben*** *(Little Russel St)* is also a hip place to meet for a drink.

South of BBD Bagh, the somewhat seedy ***Paris Bar & Restaurant***, near Lenin Sarani, is a curious combination of Indian pub and nightclub. This large, dark cavern of a place has a casual atmosphere, but single women should be prepared to be ogled. Open 11 am to 11 pm daily, it has live bands and sells some knockout beers such as Thunderbolt and Haward's Turbo 5000 (each is Rs 65 per bottle), as well as the usual spirits including velvety Old Monk rum (Rs 40 per peg). If the Paris is too much of a scene, head back to Chowringhee and try the more conservative (but duller) ***Lighthouse Bar & Restaurant*** at New Empire Cinema complex near New Market. ***Off Cum On Rambo Bar*** (!) on Mirza Ghalib St is an absolute dive – probably best avoided by women on their own – but it does sell beer till late.

Discos

Some of the top-end hotels have pumping discos, but if you're not a hotel guest or member there's a hefty door charge (ranging from Rs 200 to 400 per couple). Solo shakers will need to find a friend of the opposite sex, as most discos have a 'couples only' policy. At the time of writing, the 'in' place was ***Tantra*** at the Park Hotel. Other recommended options include ***Incognito*** at Taj Bengal and ***Anticlock*** at Hotel Hindustan International, however the latter is only open to hotel guests.

Dance & Theatre

Kolkata is renowned for its film, poetry, music, art and dance. Current programs are listed in various publications, including the *Metro* section of *The Telegraph* newspaper and *Kolkata This Fortnight* (see Information earlier in this chapter).

A dance-drama performance, Bengali poetry reading or a similar event takes place on most nights at ***Rabindra Sadan*** *(☎ 2239936, Cathedral Rd)* in Chowringhee.

There are sometimes drama, music or dance performances in English at ***Kala Mandir*** *(☎ 2479086, 48 Shakespeare Sarani)*, and musical programs (mainly Bengali) at ***Sisir Mancha*** *(☎ 2239917, 1/1 AJC Bose Rd)*. The Government of India tourist office holds Indian regional dance performances by the Academy of Oriental Dance at its Shakespeare Sarani premises. These take place at 5.30 pm Monday to Friday and tickets cost Rs 100 for a 45-minute show.

Cinema

Foreign films and retrospectives are screened at the cinema in the ***Nandan*** complex near Cathedral Rd; some Chowringhee cinemas show recent-release US blockbusters (check local newspapers).

Billiards

On Cue, near the New Empire Cinema complex near New Market, has 10 billiard tables and is open 11 am to around 9 pm daily. Games cost Rs 30 (Rs 40 for the two full-sized tables) and you can synchronise shots to the beat of Western pop.

Ten-Pin Bowling

Although rather inconveniently located out at Nicco Park (about 12km from the city centre), the modern ***Nicco Super Bowl*** *(☎ 3578101)* boasts six good bowling alleys. You can also play billiards, but it's daylight robbery at Rs 40 for a mere 15 minutes (two people). There's a fast-food joint serving the usual array of deliciously sinful junk food.

This complex is open noon to 10 pm daily and there's an entry fee of Rs 25 per person. To bowl costs Rs 75 per person per game (20 bowls) from noon to 3 pm, or Rs 100 after 3 pm weekdays. On weekends the charge is Rs 125. To get here by taxi from Sudder St will set you back about Rs 100 (one way).

SHOPPING

Kolkata's local specialties are terracotta ware and handwoven cotton or silk saris. There are lots of interesting shops, including the Central Cottage Industries Emporium, lining Chowringhee Rd that sell everything from handicrafts to carpets. The shops along the entrance arcade to The Oberoi Grand hotel are worth a browse but are not as entertaining as Chowringhee's amazing variety of pavement vendors. Kolkata's administration has been trying to whisk away street hawkers to (as yet unbuilt) underground markets in an attempt to clear the footpaths, but the unionised street merchants have so far resisted attempts to uproot them.

New Market (formerly Hogg Market) is probably Kolkata's premier place for bargain shopping. Here you can find a little of almost everything, and it is worth an hour or so just wandering around. Other markets include the Treasure Island Market (between Sudder St and New Market), and the AC Market on Shakespeare Sarani, which specialises in imported foodstuffs. There's a good, reasonably cheap street market (mainly clothes) along Lenin Sarani in the evening. For designer products, there are upmarket boutiques around Park, Camac and Russel Sts.

The top-end hotels usually have an enticing arcade or two stocked with high-quality goods with high prices to match. The city's smattering of modern shopping complexes (such as Emami) are cheaper.

The Dakshinapan Shopping Centre is rather inconveniently located out on Gariahat Rd (near the Dhakuria flyover in southern Kolkata), but it has various Indian state government emporiums that sell some terrific regional fare at fixed prices.

For a wide range of Indian and Western music, go to Music World at 18G Park St (next to Flury's), which has some particularly good Indian regional CDs.

The Rabindra Sadan (Sarani) area sells an array of traditional Indian musical instruments at competitive prices.

GETTING THERE & AWAY

For details (including visa requirements) about air and land crossings to neighbouring countries such as Bangladesh (which now has a direct bus service between Kolkata and Dhaka), see the Getting There & Away chapter.

Air

Most airline offices are around Chowringhee:

Aeroflot (☎ 2829831) 58 Chowringhee Rd
Air France (☎ 2408646) Chitrakoot Bldg, 230A AJC Bose Rd
Air India (☎ 2822356) 50 Chowringhee Rd
Biman Bangladesh Airlines (☎ 2292844) 30C Chowringhee Rd

Flights from Kolkata

This table only lists domestic Indian Airline flights. Jet Airways offers the same fares, but currently only flies to Bagdogra, Bangalore, Chennai, Guwahati, Hyderabad, Imphal, Jorhat and Mumbai.

destination	duration (hrs)	frequency (per week)	fare (US$)
Agartala	¾	12	50
Ahmedabad	2½	6	230
Aizawl	1	3	90
Bagdogra	1	6	80
Bangalore	2½	14	265
Bhubaneswar	1	7	85
Chennai	2	14	220
Delhi	2	21	200
Dibrugarh	1½	4	95
Dimapur	2¼	4	90
Guwahati	1¼	19	70
Hyderabad	2	13	210
Imphal	1	9	80
Jaipur	2¼	6	220
Jorhat	1¼	4	90
Lucknow	2¼	7	155
Mumbai	2¼	35	230
Nagpur	1½	3	165
Patna	1	7	100
Port Blair	2	4	195
Silchar	1	6	75
Tezpur	1¼	2	80
Visakhapatnam	2¼	4	145

British Airways (☎ 2883451) 41 Chowringhee Rd; enter from Middleton St
Cathay Pacific (☎ 2403312, 2403211) 1 Middleton St
Gulf Air (☎ 2477783/5576) Chitrakoot Bldg, 230A AJC Bose Rd
Indian Airlines (☎ 2364433) 39 Chittaranjan Ave
Japan Airlines (☎ 2468370/1) 35A Chowringhee Rd
Jet Airways (☎ 2292227, 2292660) 18D Park St
KLM-Royal Dutch Airlines (☎ 2403151) 1 Middleton St
Lufthansa Airlines (☎ 2299365) 30A/B Chowringhee Rd
Royal Nepal Airlines Corporation (RNAC; ☎ 2888549) 41 Chowringhee Rd; enter from Middleton St
Singapore Airlines (☎ 2809898, 2808586) 1 Lee Rd
Swissair (☎ 2884643) 46C Chowringhee Rd
Thai Airways International (☎ 2801630/5) 229 AJC Bose Rd

Kolkata is good for competitive airfares to other parts of Asia, Europe and the USA's east coast. To hunt down the hottest deals, speak to fellow travellers and frequently check with agencies and airlines (see Air in the Getting There & Away chapter).

Open 24 hours, Kolkata's Indian Airlines office (☎ 2364433) is at 39 Chittaranjan Ave; its tourist counter is open 9 am to 7 pm daily. As well as its domestic routes (see the table 'Flights from Kolkata'), Indian Airlines also flies to Dhaka (Rs 2410, four times weekly), Bangkok (Rs 5825, six times weekly) and Kathmandu (US$96, five times weekly). Departure tax is Rs 150.

Bus

It's generally quicker and more comfortable to travel from Kolkata by train, though there are several useful bus routes to other towns in West Bengal. Apart from Bihar, Jharkhand and Orissa, there are very limited bus services to other states.

The only buses that travellers use with any regularity are those from Kolkata to Siliguri & New Jalpaiguri (for Darjeeling). The 'Rocket Service'(!) costs Rs 152 and leaves Kolkata at 6, 7 and 8 pm daily, arriving the next morning (travelling by train or air is still preferable). There's an air-con bus (Rs 440) that leaves Kolkata at 7 pm and arrives at Siliguri at around 7 am the next day.

Buses generally depart from the Esplanade bus station area at the northern end of the Maidan, near Chowringhee Rd, but there are a number of private companies that have their own stands. Buses to and from the south generally use the bus stand near Fort William at Babu Ghat.

Train

Kolkata has two major train stations, both of them frenetic. Howrah, on the west bank of the Hooghly River, handles most trains into the city, but trains going north to Darjeeling or the north-eastern region leave from Sealdah station on the east side of the Hooghly. Beware of pickpockets at both stations. At Howrah station, platforms 1 to 16 are in the old main building, platforms 17 to 22 are in the new annexe next door. A fair price to pay porters is about Rs 25 per bag.

The tourist railway booking office is on the 1st floor at 6 Fairlie Place near BBD Bagh. It's fully computerised and has a tourist quota, but be prepared to queue. It's open 8 am to 1 pm and 1.30 to 8 pm Monday to Saturday and 8 am to 2 pm Sunday. There's another booking office nearby at 14 Strand Rd South where you can buy advance tickets on routes into and out of Delhi, Chennai and Mumbai. Get a form and join the correct queue; the tourist quota isn't accessible from this office. Bookings can be made up to 60 days before departure for all trains apart from the *Shatabdi Express*, for which bookings are only open within 15 days of departure.

Both these places can attract long queues and the staff at Fairlie Place office demand to see encashment certificates (obtained whenever you change foreign currency) if you pay in rupees. There are other computerised booking offices that may be better for buying advance tickets out of Kolkata. The office at Tollygunge metro station is easy to get to and is rarely very busy. Alternatively, for a fee (about Rs 40), agents in and around Sudder St can buy tickets for you, often at short notice. But beware of some small-fry travel agencies who promise the best train/class, but actually give you a ticket on an inferior train/class. Only leave a small deposit, if any, and check the tickets before paying.

Boat

See the Andaman & Nicobar Islands chapter for details about boats from Kolkata.

Major Trains from Kolkata

destination	train No & name	departures	distance (km)	duration (hrs)	fare (Rs) 3rd/2nd air-con
Agra	2307 *Jodhpur Exp*	11.30 am H	1420	20¾	277/874
Ahmedabad	8034 *Ahmedabad Exp*	8.20 pm H	2090	41¼	428/1424
Ajmer	2315 *Ananaya Exp*	12.40 pm S	1760	32	420/1250
Amritsar	3005 *Amritsar Exp*	7.20 pm H	1829	38½	365/1235
Chennai	2841 *Coromandel Exp*	1.15 pm H	1636	28	406/1117
Delhi	2301 *Rajdhani Exp*	5 pm H	1441	17	1500/2470
	2303 *Poorva Exp*	9.15 am H	1441	24	383/1080
	2313 *Rajdhani Exp*	4.45 pm S	1441	17	1500/2470
Guwahati	5959 *Kamrup Exp*	3.35 pm H	991	25	290/806
Jodhpur	2307 *Jodhpur Exp*	11.30 pm H	1975	35	474/1240
Mumbai VT	2860 *Geetanjali Exp*	12.40 pm H	1960	33	433/1194
New Jalpaiguri	3143 *Darjeeling Mail*	7.15 pm S	573	12½	210/565
Patna	3231 *Danapur Exp*	9.05 pm H	545	11	202/555
Puri	8007 *Puri Exp*	9.45 pm H	500	10¾	206/565
Tirupati	7479 *Tirupati Exp*	11.30 pm H	1650	16½	377/889
Varanasi	3009 *Doon Exp*	10.15 pm H	670	12	230/787

Abbreviations for train stations: H – Howrah, S – Sealdah

GETTING AROUND

To/From the Airport

The airport (domestic and international terminals) is 17km north-east of the city centre. A public minibus runs from BBD Bagh to the airport for Rs 10. The metro line to Dum Dum stops 5km short of the airport; a bus from there will cost about Rs 5 (although there are plans to extend this all the way to the airport which will be far more convenient – check the current situation).

If you want to take a taxi from the airport, it's cheaper and more reliable to go to the prepaid taxi booth (after you clear customs) where you'll be assigned one. It costs about Rs 160 to Sudder St.

Although the airport is now officially called the Netaji Subhas Chandra Basu International Airport (the domestic terminal is here too), taxi drivers still commonly refer to it as Dum Dum; this was the site of the Dum Dum Barracks, where the explosive dumdum bullet, banned after the Boer War, was once made.

Bus

Local buses are passenger-crammed mechanical monsters that travel at frightening speed. Fares start at just Rs 2. There is also a private minibus service, which is even faster (fares start at Rs 2.25).

Tram

Kolkata's public tram service injects character to the city, even though they are like sardine tins in rush hour. Although they're pollution-free, there's been pressure to abolish them because they are a major cause of traffic jams. Tram enthusiasts, including a sister society in Melbourne, Australia, have campaigned to save the trams and they've succeeded – for now. Fares start at Rs 1.75.

Metro

Kolkata boasts India's first underground railway system. The southern sector, from Chandni Chowk to Tollygunge station, and the north sector to the west of BBD Bagh are most useful. There are two stations near Sudder St; to the north (almost opposite The Oberoi Grand hotel) and to the south (opposite Dr M Ishaque Rd).

The metro is clean and efficient, although still terribly crowded during peak hours (around 9 to 11 am and 5 to 7 pm Monday to Saturday). Trains run 8.15 am to 10 pm Monday to Saturday and 3 to 9.15 pm Sunday. Tickets range from Rs 3 (one sector) to Rs 7 (to the end of the line).

Taxi

You'll see two types of taxis in Kolkata: the yellow ones have permits to travel all over

Kolkata and West Bengal, while the black-and-yellow taxis are restricted to Kolkata.

For all taxi trips (other than those negotiated) add 20% to the reading on the meter. Meters are inevitably outdated, so it's best to see the fare conversion chart, which every driver should carry. Officially, taxi fares start at Rs 12 and go up by Rs 0.50 increments, but that can be more theory than practice. Not all drivers are willing to use the meter so you may have to firmly insist or choose another driver. Frustrating as it is, there are plenty of taxis, so shop around for a metered ride or a reasonable negotiated price. For a half/full day of sightseeing expect to pay around Rs 500/800.

At Howrah station there's a prepaid taxi rank outside, and from here it will cost you Rs 40 to Sudder St, although there may be a queue so be prepared to wait. There's also a prepaid booth at the airport (see To/From the Airport earlier).

Rickshaw

Kolkata is the last real bastion of the human-powered rickshaw. The city's rickshaw-wallahs rejected the new-fangled cycle-rickshaws when they were introduced elsewhere in India. After all, who could afford a bicycle? Many can't even afford to buy their own rickshaw and have to rent from someone who takes the lion's share of the fares.

You may find it morally unacceptable to have a man pulling you around in a carriage. The only compensation is that they wouldn't have a job at all if people didn't use them and you, as a tourist, naturally pay more than the locals. However, Kolkata's administration has long wanted to completely ban the rickshaws as part of a short-sighted traffic-management plan that equates slow-moving transport with slow-moving traffic. As it is, Kolkata's narrow lanes and poor drainage mean that, aside from walking, jumping in a rickshaw is often the only way to get somewhere. Anyway, these sort of rickshaws (as well as autorickshaws) are already restricted to small parts of central Kolkata. Across the river in Howrah or in the suburbs, there are auto and cycle-rickshaws.

A short ride in a cycle-rickshaw costs around Rs 10; a trip from Sudder St to the Motherhouse costs about Rs 25. A tip is heartily appreciated.

Rickshaws in Kolkata

Hand-pulled rickshaws still exist as tourist curiosities or historical oddities in very small numbers in several cities around the world. Only in Kolkata are hand-pulled rickshaws still in everyday use as real transport.

Although Kolkata has the last remaining hand-pulled rickshaws it did not have the first, even in India. The first Indian rickshaws made their appearance in 1880 in the Himalayan hill station of Shimla, a hot season retreat for officials of the British Raj. This was the same year rickshaws were first seen in Singapore. It was a further 20 years before the first rickshaws appeared in Kolkata and then only for conveying goods. The first Kolkata rickshaws were not only owned by Chinese residents, they were pulled by Chinese immigrants. The Chinese workers have long disappeared but even today Kolkata's rickshaw pullers are mainly outsiders from the neighbouring and even more poverty-stricken state of Bihar.

It was in 1914 before rickshaws were finally allowed to carry passengers but through the 1920s and 1930s the city's rickshaw fleet expanded rapidly, even though by that time rickshaw numbers were declining in other cities. In 1939 the city authorities decreed an absolute maximum of 6000 licences but after WWII the rickshaw population continued to grow. The combination of poverty, congestion and a ban on cycle-rickshaws in the city centre encouraged the hand-pulled rickshaw numbers to reach 30,000 to 50,000 in the late 1980s. In his bestselling novel, *City of Joy*, Dominique Lapierre estimated that Kolkata's 100,000 rickshaw pullers handled one million passengers a day and covered a greater distance than the entire Indian Airlines fleet of Boeing and Airbus aircraft.

Tony Wheeler, *Chasing Rickshaws*

Ferry

The ferries can be a quicker and more pleasant way to get across the river than the congested Howrah Bridge. From Howrah to Chandpal Ghat or Fairlie Ghat there are several crossings an hour between 8 am and 8 pm. Ferries to the Botanical Gardens go from Chandpal Ghat or Babu Ghat, but they are a 'casual' service on negotiation and not at any designated times. The fares are minimal (Rs 3 to 5).

West Bengal

The cradle of Indian renaissance and the national freedom movement, Bengal has long been considered by many as the cultural centre of India. After Partition, the state was split into East and West Bengal. East Bengal eventually became Bangladesh and West Bengal, a state of India with Kolkata (Calcutta) as its capital. The state is long and narrow, running from the delta of the Ganges river system in the Bay of Bengal to the south, up through the Ganges plain, to the heights of the Himalaya and Darjeeling in the north.

A land of aesthetes and political activists, West Bengal is famous for its eminent writers, poets, artists, spiritualists, social reformers, freedom fighters and revolutionaries.

South of Kolkata on the Bay of Bengal is the area known as the Sunderbans, one of the largest deltas in the world, and home to the elusive Royal Bengal tiger. To the north are the flourishing mango plantations and jute fields of the fertile river plains. Farther north again in the Himalayan foothills are the world-famous Darjeeling tea plantations.

West Bengal has plenty of historic sites, yet, apart from Kolkata and Darjeeling, this state receives relatively few foreign tourists. Several railway sabotage cases in northern Bengal in early 2000, which resulted in some near misses by passenger trains, did little to help tourism. Officials were quick to point the finger at Pakistan, but these allegations have not been proven. If you're concerned, check out the situation locally.

To put a halt to illegal immigration and smuggling between India and Bangladesh, the West Bengal government plans to construct a fence-like barrier (around 900km long) between the two countries.

History

Referred to as Vanga in the Mahabharata, this area has a long history that predates the Aryan invasions of India. It was part of the Mauryan empire in the 3rd century before being overrun by the Guptas. For three centuries from around the 9th century AD, the Pala dynasty controlled a large area based in Bengal and including parts of Orissa, Bihar and modern Bangladesh.

Bengal was brought under Muslim control by Qutb-ud-din, first of the sultans of Delhi,

West Bengal at a Glance

Population: 80.2 million
Area: 87,853 sq km
Capital: Kolkata (Calcutta)
Main Language: Bengali
When to Go: Oct to Mar

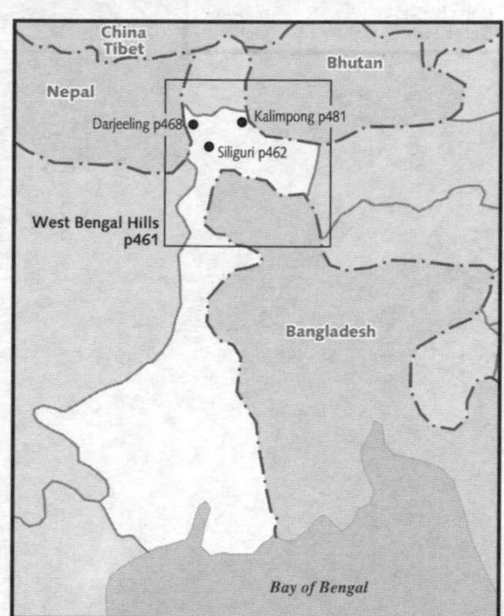

- Discover Sunderbans Wildlife Sanctuary and search for the prolific, but elusive, tigers at this picturesque World Heritage listed park
- Take an elephant ride through the lush Jaldhapara Wildlife Sanctuary, home to the Indian rhinoceros, tiger and other wildlife
- Relax in Mirik, a mellow 'minor' hill station with friendly folk and far less tourist hype than Darjeeling
- Experience the vibrant mix of statewide festivals, from the quaint folk fair of Paush Mela to the wildly exuberant Durga Puja celebrations
- Visit Darjeeling, a popular hill station replete with gompas and awesome views of the mighty Kanchenjunga
- Tour Darjeeling's Happy Valley Tea Estate and savour a cuppa back in town at Glenary's

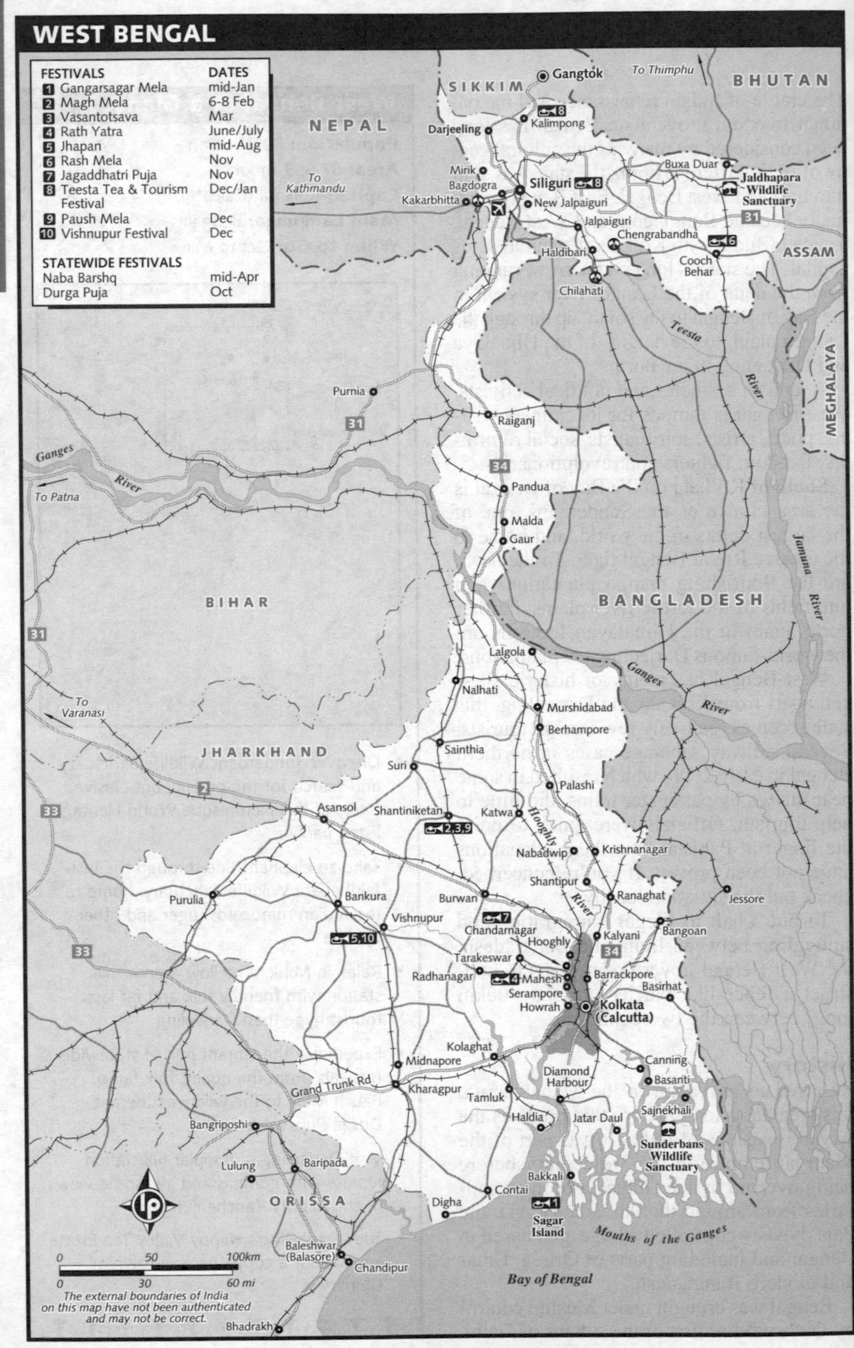
WEST BENGAL
FESTIVALS DATES
1 Gangarsagar Mela mid-Jan
2 Magh Mela 6-8 Feb
3 Vasantotsava Mar
4 Rath Yatra June/July
5 Jhapan mid-Aug
6 Rash Mela Nov
7 Jagaddhatri Puja Nov
8 Teesta Tea & Tourism Festival Dec/Jan
9 Paush Mela Dec
10 Vishnupur Festival Dec
STATEWIDE FESTIVALS
Naba Barshq mid-Apr
Durga Puja Oct
NEPAL
SIKKIM
Gangtok
To Thimphu
BHUTAN
Kalimpong
Darjeeling
Mirik
Bagdogra
Siliguri
Kakarbhitta
New Jalpaiguri
To Kathmandu
Buxa Duar
Jaldhapara Wildlife Sanctuary
Jalpaiguri
Chengrabandha
Haldibari
Cooch Behar
ASSAM
Chilahati
Teesta
River
MEGHALAYA
Purnia
Raiganj
Ganges
River
To Patna
Pandua
Malda
Gaur
Jamuna
River
BIHAR
BANGLADESH
Lalgola
Ganges
River
Nalhati
Murshidabad
Berhampore
To Varanasi
Sainthia
JHARKHAND
Suri
Palashi
Asansol
Shantiniketan
Katwa
Hooghly
Nabadwip
Krishnanagar
Shantipur
Purulia
Bankura
Burwan
River
Ranaghat
Jessore
Vishnupur
Chandarnagar
Bangoan
Hooghly
Kalyani
Tarakeswar
Radhanagar
Mahesh
Barrackpore
Serampore
Basirhat
Howrah
Kolkata (Calcutta)
Kolaghat
Midnapore
Canning
Grand Trunk Rd
Kharagpur
Diamond Harbour
Basanti
Tamluk
Sajnekhali
Haldia
Jatar Daul
Bangriposhi
Sunderbans Wildlife Sanctuary
Lulung
Baripada
Bakkali
Contai
ORISSA
Digha
Sagar Island
Mouths of the Ganges
Baleshwar (Balasore)
Chandipur
Bay of Bengal
0 50 100km
0 30 60 mi
The external boundaries of India on this map have not been authenticated and may not be correct.
Bhadrakh
31
34
33
2

at the end of the 12th century. Following the death of Aurangzeb in 1707, Bengal became an independent Muslim state.

Britain had established a trading post in Kolkata in 1698, which quickly prospered. Sensing rich pickings, Siraj-ud-daula, the nawab of Bengal, came down from his capital at Murshidabad and easily took Kolkata in 1756. Robert Clive defeated him the following year at the Battle of Plassey (now Palashi), helped by the treachery of Siraj-ud-daula's uncle, Mir Jafar, who commanded the greater part of the nawab's army. He was rewarded by succeeding his nephew as nawab but after the Battle of Buxar in 1764, the British took full control of Bengal. For entertaining background reading on this period as seen through the eyes of a modern-day traveller, Peter Holt's book *In Clive's Footsteps* is recommended. The author is the great-grandson, five times removed, of Clive.

Planning

Foreigners need a permit to visit the Sunderbans Wildlife Sanctuary (see later in this chapter). Permits are issued on presentation of your passport at the West Bengal Tourism Centre in Kolkata (see Information in the Kolkata chapter). There is no charge.

State government (West Bengal Tourism Development Corporation – WBTDC) hotels are scattered throughout the state and reservations for all of these can be made at the West Bengal Tourism Centre in Kolkata.

Special Events

Two important state-wide festivals are Naba Barshq, the Bengali new year, in mid-April. The other is Durga Puja in October – it is the largest Bengali festival and honours the goddess Durga.

Scores of festivals are held throughout the state; the major and most vibrant ones are included in this chapter. Although many have been attributed to one location, they may also take place in other areas. To find out about minor regional fairs, contact the West Bengal Tourism Centre.

South of Kolkata

DOWN THE HOOGHLY

The Hooghly River is very difficult to navigate due to constantly shifting shoals and sandbanks. River pilots have to stay in touch with it to keep track of its frequent course changes. **Falta**, 43km downriver, was the site of a Dutch factory. The British retreated here in 1756 when Kolkata was captured by Siraj-ud-daula. It's also from here that Clive recaptured Kolkata. Below Falta the Damodar River joins the Hooghly. The Rupnarain River also joins the Hooghly nearby and a little up this river is **Tamluk**, which was an important Buddhist centre over 1000 years ago. The James & Mary Shoal, the most dangerous on the Hooghly, is just above the point where the Rupnarain River enters. Its name comes from a ship wrecked here in 1694. Birdlife is abundant in areas south of Kolkata.

There is a catamaran service between Kolkata and Haldia (south of Kolkata) which operates on weekdays only. It leaves Kolkata at 7.45 am, returning at 5.30 pm. The one-way fare is US$9/23 for economy/1st class.

DIAMOND HARBOUR

A resort 51km south of Kolkata by road, Diamond Harbour is at the point where the Hooghly turns south and flows into the open sea. Launches run from here to Sagar Island. From Diamond Harbour you can visit the **crocodile breeding centre** at Bhagabatpur – catch a bus to Namkhana (Rs 15, 1½ hours) and from here, hire a boat to Bhagabatpur.

Sagarika Tourist Lodge (☎/fax 03174-55246) has air-con double rooms for Rs 650.

A bus from Kolkata takes 1½ hours (Rs 20).

SAGAR ISLAND

Accessible by bus and ferry from Diamond Harbour, this island, at the mouth of the Hooghly, is considered to be the point where the Ganges joins the sea, and a festival (Gangarsagar Mela) takes place. The festival attracts hundreds of thousands of Hindu pilgrims who come here to visit the Kapil Muni Temple and bathe at the confluence of the Ganges and the Bay of Bengal.

Cheap accommodation is possible at various ashrams and at the youth hostel (book through Youth Services India in Kolkata on ☎ 033-248 0626).

DIGHA & BAKKALI

Close to the border with Orissa, 185km south-west of Kolkata on the Bay of Bengal,

Digha is another self-styled 'Brighton of the East'. The 7km beach is very wide, but if a beach holiday is what you want, carry on south to Puri or Gopalpur-on-Sea. The Chandaneshwar Shiva Temple is just across the border in Orissa, 8km from Digha. Digha has a range of accommodation, including a ***WBTDC Tourist Lodge*** *(☎ 03220-66255, fax 66256)*, which has doubles from Rs 275 and dorm beds for Rs 80. There are several daily buses between Kolkata and Digha (Rs 60, six hours).

Sometimes referred to as Fraserganj, the beach resort of **Bakkali** is not as busy as Digha. It's 132km from Kolkata and has some wonderful birdlife. From here you can get boats to the small island of **Jambu Dwip** to the south-west. ***WBTDC Bakkali Tourist Lodge*** *(☎ 03210-25260)* has ordinary doubles for Rs 300, or dorm beds for Rs 80. Buses from Kolkata to Bakkali take about two hours (Rs 40).

SUNDERBANS WILDLIFE SANCTUARY

The innumerable mouths of the Ganges form the world's largest delta, and part of this vast mangrove swamp is a 2585 sq km wildlife reserve that extends into Bangladesh. The sanctuary is designated a World Heritage Site and, as part of Project Tiger, has one of the largest tiger populations of any of the parks on the planet. Tourist agencies capitalise on this fact, but in reality, few visitors get even a glimpse of one of the shy tigers (estimated to number just under 300 in 2000) that remain well-hidden in the sanctuary.

The tigers may be tourist shy, but they are partial to human flesh, killing a number of villagers each year. They generally stalk along the narrow channels that crisscross the estuarine forest. Since tigers are less likely to attack if they suspect they are being watched, fishermen and honey collectors have taken to wearing masks cleverly painted with human faces on the backs of their heads.

Winter and spring are the best time to visit the wildlife sanctuary, which is also home to spotted deer, wild pigs, monkeys and various bird species. The whole area is wonderfully peaceful after frenetic Kolkata.

At the **Sajnekhali visitors' centre** there's a shark pond, turtle hatchery and an interesting Mangrove Interpretation Centre. From here boats are available for excursions through the mangroves. Trips cost around Rs 800 per person for the whole day, or Rs 400 for four hours, and you need a guide and boat permits. There are watchtowers at several points around the park.

South of the Sunderbans are **Lothian** and **Halliday** islands, reached from Namkhana (three hours by bus from Kolkata).

Permission is required to visit Sunderbans; see Planning earlier. There's an entry fee to the reserve, payable at Sajnekhali.

Organised Tours

From October to March, the WBTC organises weekly boat tours, including food and accommodation. They cost Rs 1200 per person for one night or Rs 1500 for two nights. If you're expecting 'adventure at every corner', as one brochure suggests, forget it. One traveller described his trip as 'more like an uneventful three-day picnic on the water'.

Places to Stay & Eat

Sajnekhali Tourist Lodge *(☎ 03219-52560)*, at Sajnekhali, has doubles from Rs 525 and dorm beds for a whopping Rs 200 (but this includes one major meal and breakfast).

Getting There & Away

Travelling independently is more complicated than the WBTC boat tour (see Organised Tours) but is good for exploring the area at leisure – you could hire a guide from the West Bengal Tourism Centre in Kolkata (Rs 500 per day plus food and accommodation for any overnight stays). If you plan on visiting independently, ask the tourism centre about the current road routes etc. From Kolkata (Babu Ghat) it's quickest to get a bus to Basanti/Sonakhali (about three hours, Rs 30). Continuing from Basanti/Sonakhali the next step is a boat to Gosava (Rs 10, 1¼ hours). From here get a cycle-rickshaw for the 45-minute ride to Pakhirala (Rs 20), then a boat across the river to Sajnekhali.

There's also a direct boat (Rs 9) leaving Basanti for Sajnekhali at 3.30 pm. A private boat to Sajnekhali costs Rs 800, or Rs 400 from Basanti.

North of Kolkata

On the Hooghly River, 25km north of Kolkata, **Serampore** was a Danish centre until Denmark's holdings in India were transferred to the East India Company in 1845. The old Danish church and cemetery still stand. Across the river is **Barrackpore**. A few dilapidated buildings are all that are left of the East India Company's cantonment here. There is also a memorial to Gandhi by the river. **Mahesh**, 3km from Serampore, has a very old Jagannath temple. Each June/July the **Mahesh Rath Yatra** (Car Festival) takes place here. The festival is celebrated by the pulling of Lord Jagannath's chariot.

The historic town of **Hooghly** is 41km from Kolkata and was an important trading port long before Kolkata rose to prominence. In 1537 the Portuguese set up a factory here; before that time **Satgaon**, 10km farther north, had been the main port of Bengal but was abandoned because the river silted up. There are still a few traces of Satgaon's former grandeur, including a ruined mosque. After a lengthy siege, the Portuguese were expelled from Hooghly in 1632 by Shah Jahan, but were allowed to return a year later. The British East India Company also established a factory here in 1651. The *imambara* (a Shi'ite holy man's tomb), built in 1836, with its gateway flanked by lofty minarets, is the main sight. Only 1km or so south of Hooghly, **Chinsura** was exchanged by the Dutch for the British-held Indonesian island of Sumatra in 1825. There is a fort and the Dutch cemetery, with many old tombs, 1km to the west.

About 2km north of Hooghly, **Bandel** has a Portuguese church and monastery built in 1599. Destroyed by Shah Jahan in 1640, they were later rebuilt. Just 4km north of Bandel, **Bansberia** has the Vasudev Temple, with interesting terracotta wall carvings, and the Hanseswari Temple.

VISHNUPUR

This town of terracotta temples flourished as the capital of the Malla kings (great patrons of the arts) from the 16th to the early 19th centuries. The facades of the dozen or so **temples** are covered with ornate terracotta tiles depicting scenes from the Hindu epics. The main temples are the highly decorated Jor Bangla, the large Madan Mohan, the pyramidal Ras Mancha and the Shyam Rai.

Vishnupur is in Bankura district, famous for its **pottery** (particularly the stylised Bankura horse) and **silk**. In August, the **Jhapan Festival** draws snake charmers to honour the goddess Manasa who is the central figure of snake worship. In December, there is the Vishnupur festival of handicrafts and music.

Vishnupur Tourist Lodge *(☎ 03244-52013)*, not far from the train station, offers dorm beds (Rs 80) and doubles from Rs 300.

There are daily buses from Kolkata to Vishnupur (Rs 66, six hours).

SHANTINIKETAN

Shantiniketan takes its name from two Bengali words: *shanti*, meaning peaceful and *niketan*, meaning abode. The brilliant and prolific poet, writer, artist and nationalist Rabindranath Tagore (1861–1941) founded a school here in 1901. It later developed into the Visvabharati University with an emphasis on humanity's relationship with nature. Tagore went on to win the Nobel Prize for literature in 1913 and is credited with introducing India's historical and cultural greatness to the modern world. In 1915 Tagore was awarded a knighthood by the British, but he surrendered it in 1919 as a protest against the Amritsar massacre.

Points of interest to visitors include the **museum** and **art gallery** within the Uttarayan complex where Tagore lived. Of particular prominence are the **Shantiniketan Murals**; Seagull Books publishes the magnificently illustrated *The Shantiniketan Murals* by Jayanta Chakrabarti, R Siva Kumar & Arun K Nag (Rs 750).

There are several annual festivals held at Shantiniketan, including: **Magh Mela** on 6–8 February; **Vasantotsava**, held in March; and **Paush Mela** in December, a festival of folk music, dance, song and theatre.

If you're planning a long stay here, a cheap option may be ***university guesthouses*** – call ☎ 03463-52751 for details. WBTDC's ***Shantiniketan Tourist Lodge*** *(☎ 03463-52699, fax 52398)* has doubles from Rs 275 and dorm beds for Rs 80. For something more upmarket, there's ***Chhuti Holiday Resort*** *(☎ 03463-52692; 033-220 8307 in Kolkata)*, with singles/doubles from Rs 700/850.

There are rail connections between Shantiniketan and other parts of West Bengal.

NABADWIP & MAYAPUR

Nabadwip (also known as Nawadip), 114km from Kolkata, is an important Krishna pilgrimage centre, attracting throngs of devotees to its many temples. It is also an ancient centre of the Sanskrit culture. The last Hindu king of Bengal, Lakshman Sen, moved his capital here from Gaur.

Across the river from Nabadwip, Mayapur is a centre for the Iskcon (Hare Krishna) movement. There's a large temple and moderately priced accommodation is available at ***Iskcon Guest House*** *(☎ 033-4634959 in Kolkata)*. Iskcon runs a bus tour from Kolkata during winter (Rs 250) – for further details contact Iskcon (☎ 033-2476075), 3C Albert Rd, Kolkata.

MURSHIDABAD & BERHAMPORE

When Siraj-ud-daula was nawab of Bengal, **Murshidabad** was his capital, and it was here that he was assassinated after the defeat at Plassey (now Palashi). Murshidabad was also the major trading town between inland India and the port of Kolkata, 221km south. Today it's an insignificant, but peaceful town on the banks of the Bhagirathi River; a chance to see rural Bengali life.

Hazarduari, the classical-style Palace of a Thousand Doors, was built for the nawabs in 1837. In the renovated throne room a vast chandelier, a gift from Queen Victoria, is suspended above the nawab's silver throne. In the armoury downstairs is a cannon used at Plassey (Palashi). The palace is open from 10.30 am to 4.30 pm daily, except Friday. Entry is Rs 2. The library houses at least 10,000 books, 3000 manuscripts and a collection of magnificently illuminated Qurans. Though closed to the public, permission to view or use the collection is available from the Assistant Superintending Archaeologist, Archaeological Survey of India, Hazarduari Palace Museum, Murshidabad.

Across the grass from the palace is the deteriorating Great Imambara. Murshid Quli Khan, who moved the capital here in 1705, is buried beside the impressive ruins of the Katra Mosque. Siraj-ud-daula was assassinated at the Nimak Haram Deohri (Traitor's Gate). The Jain Parswanath Temple is at Kathgola, and south of the train station there's the Moti Jhil, or Pearl Lake, a fine place to view the sunset. It's worth taking a boat across the river to visit Siraj's tomb at Khusbagh, the Garden of Happiness.

Cycle-rickshaw-wallahs offer you guided tours of all the sites of Murshidabad for around Rs 80 for a half day. This is a good idea as everything's fairly spread out.

About 11km south of Murshidabad, **Berhampore** is a notable centre for silk production. In the old bazaar area of Khagra there are some dilapidated mansions, once belonging to European traders.

Places to Stay

In Berhampore, the best place to stay is ***Hotel Samrat*** *(☎ 03482-51147/51725, NH-34 Panchanantala)*, which has good-sized and tidy singles/doubles with private bathroom from Rs 100/125 (request a room with minimal traffic noise). There are also dorm beds (Rs 50).

In Murshidabad, the pick of the bunch is the tranquil ***Hotel Manjusha*** *(☎ 03482-70321)*, ideally located on the banks of the river, not far from the palace. The rooms downstairs cost Rs 125/200 a single/double with private bathroom (most with squat toilets), but it's worth paying a bit more for the better rooms upstairs. These cost Rs 250 (doubles only) and have sit-down flush toilets and balconies with splendid lake views.

The hotels in Berhampore are the best places to eat.

Getting There & Away

There are several trains a day between Kolkata and Berhampore/Murshidabad (about Rs 52 in 2nd class, six hours). A bus from Kolkata to Berhampore/Murshidabad costs around the same. There are also bus connections to other destinations in the state including Malda and Siliguri. Autorickshaws, taxis, and buses regularly whizz between Murshidabad and Berhampore (a share-rickshaw is Rs 5 per person).

West Bengal Hills

MALDA

Around 349km north of Kolkata, Malda (formerly known as English Bazaar or transliterated as Ingraj Bazar) is the base for visiting the ruined cities of Gaur and Pandua (see the following section), although it's now also renowned for its large Fajli mangoes.

The modest but pleasant ***Hotel Purbanchal*** *(☎ 03512-66183)* is the best value for money. Good singles/doubles with private bathroom range from Rs 200/250 to 550/800. There's a decent restaurant serving hearty mutton curry (Rs 40), chicken stew (Rs 45) and plenty more. If all the rooms here are full, there's the less impressive ***Malda Tourist Lodge*** *(☎ 03512-66123)* which is rather worn and weary, but acceptable for a night (check for frogs in the bathroom). Singles/doubles with private bathroom start at Rs 267/330 and meals are available. The ***retiring rooms*** at the train station cost Rs 50 for a dorm bed, Rs 250/400 for an air-con single/double with private bathroom.

Malda is on the main railway line to Kolkata (Rs 148 in 2nd-class sleeper, seven hours) and New Jalpaiguri (Rs 120 in 2nd-class sleeper, five hours). There are buses to Siliguri (Rs 90, six hours) for Darjeeling, Berhampore/Murshidabad (Rs 35, three hours) and Kolkata (Rs 117, eight hours).

GAUR & PANDUA

About 12km south of Malda and close to the border with Bangladesh, **Gaur** was first the capital of the Buddhist Pala dynasty, then it became the seat of the Hindu Sena dynasty, and finally the capital of the Muslim nawabs. The ruins of the extensive fortifications and several large mosques are all that remain. (There are also some ruins on the other side of the ill-defined border). Most impressive are the Bara Sona Mosque and the nearby brick Dakhil Darwajah built in 1425. Qadam Rasul Mosque enshrines a footprint of the Prophet Mohammed but it looks as if he was wearing flip-flops when

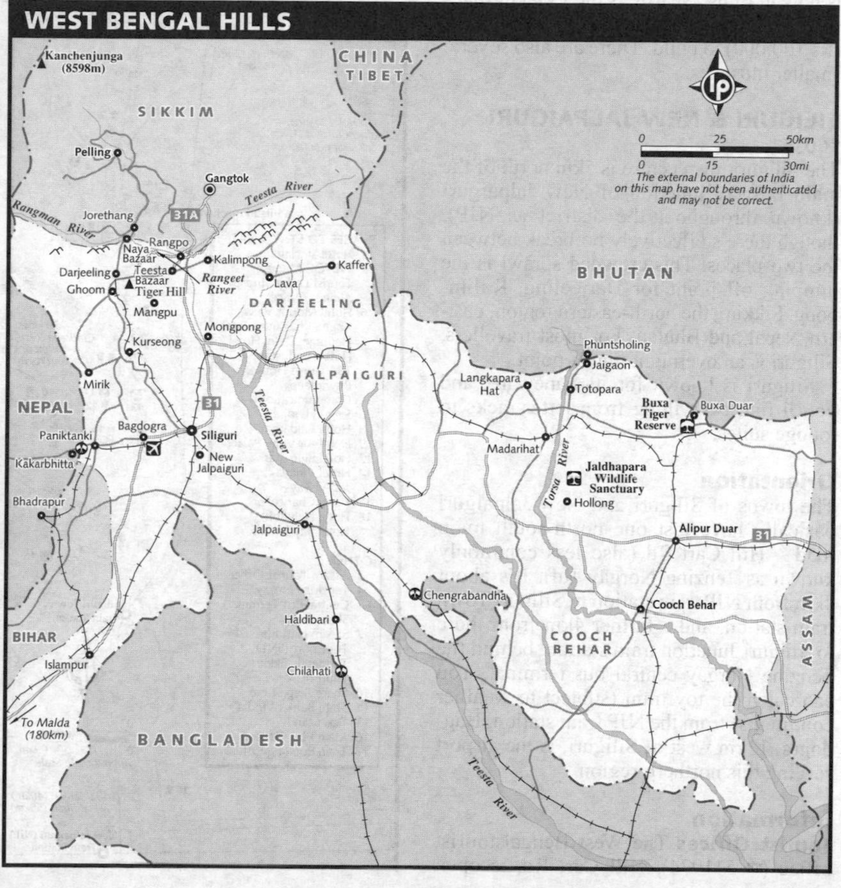

he made it! Fath Khan's tomb is nearby and a sign informs you that he 'vomited blood and died on this spot'. There are still some colourful enamelled tiles on the Gumti Gate and Lattan Mosque but few left on the Firoz Minar. The monuments are very spread out and not all easy to find. Some determined cycle-rickshaw-wallahs offer half-day trips from Malda for Rs 80 (return). Taxis cost about Rs 400 (return) and include Pandua.

Gaur once alternated with **Pandua** (18km north of Malda) as the seat of power. The main sites are at Adina, 2km north of the village of Pandua. The main place of interest is the vast Adina Mosque, built by Sikander Shah in the 14th century. Built over a Hindu temple, traces of which are still evident, it was one of the largest mosques in India but is now in ruins. Nearby is the Eklakhi mausoleum, so called because it cost Rs 1 lakh (Rs 100,000) to build. There are also several smaller mosques.

SILIGURI & NEW JALPAIGURI

☎ 0353

The Siliguri town centre is 5km north of the main railway junction of New Jalpaiguri (known throughout the district as NJP), though there's effectively no break between the two places. This crowded sprawl is the jumping off point for Darjeeling, Kalimpong, Sikkim, the north-eastern region, eastern Nepal and Bhutan. For most travellers, Siliguri is an overnight transit point.

Siliguri is known for its caneware, and you'll find everything from letter racks to lounge suites.

Orientation

The towns of Siliguri and New Jalpaiguri basically have just one north-south main road – Hill Cart Rd (also less commonly known as Tenzing Norgay Rd). It's about 4km from NJP train station to Siliguri Town train station, and a farther 4km from there to Siliguri Junction train station, behind the Tenzing Norgay central bus terminal. You can catch the toy train (subject to weather conditions) from the NJP train station. Bagdogra, 12km west of Siliguri, is the airport serving this northern region.

Information

Tourist Offices The West Bengal tourist office (☎ 511974), Hill Cart Rd, is open from 10.30 am to 5 pm weekdays. The staff are not particularly enthusiastic, so you may have to push for information. Here, it's possible to book accommodation in the Jaldhapara Wildlife Sanctuary (described later in this chapter), as well as arrange tours to Sikkim and Bhutan. There are also tourist counters at the airport and train stations.

Money There is a counter at Delhi Hotel (see Places to Stay), which changes travellers cheques and major currencies. It's conveniently open from 7 am to 9 pm daily. State Bank of India exchanges American Express (AmEx) travellers cheques in US dollars and pounds sterling only. It's open from 10 am to 2 pm weekdays and 10 am to noon Saturday.

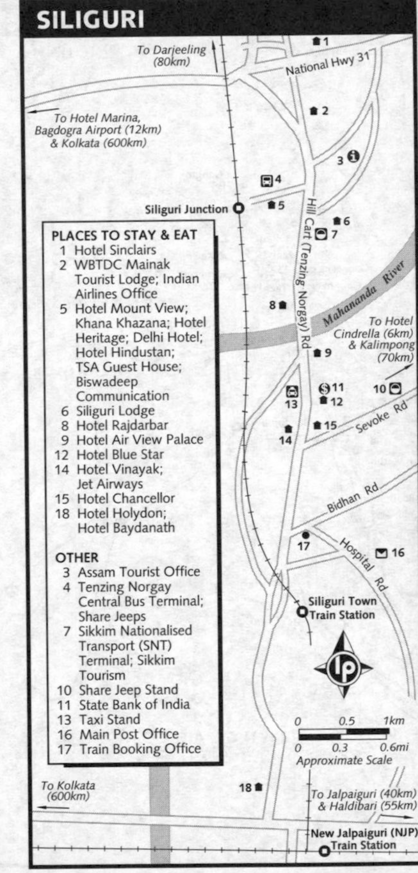

Internet Resources There were few places to surf the Net at the time of research. One fairly central place is Biswadeep Communication, near TSA Guest House, not far from the Tenzing Norgay central bus terminal just off Hill Cart Rd. It charges Rs 15 to send an email, Rs 15 to print a page and Rs 60 for 30 minutes of Internet use.

Permits Permits for Sikkim are available from Sikkim Tourism (☎ 432646) at the Sikkim Nationalised Transport (SNT) office, diagonally opposite the bus terminal. Sikkim Tourism is open from 10 am to 4 pm Monday to Saturday.

Places to Stay & Eat

There are dozens of hotels in town, many opposite the Tenzing Norgay central bus terminal, on Hill Cart Rd. The budget hotels are generally friendlier and better value for money than those in Kolkata and most have a noon checkout. The best places to eat are in the hotels.

Rooms attract a 10% service charge plus another 10% if they're air-con (taxes are not included here).

Siliguri Lodge *(☎ 533290, Hill Cart Rd)* has well-kept singles/doubles with shared bathroom for Rs 100/140; with private bathroom they start at Rs 200 a double. A four-bedded room with/without private bathroom is Rs 350/200.

About 1km to the north on Hill Cart Rd is ***WBTDC Mainak Tourist Lodge*** *(☎ 430 986)*. Rooms are a little dark, but otherwise OK. Doubles range from Rs 500 to 1000 and there is a good restaurant.

The no-frills but friendly Tibetan-run ***Hotel Chancellor*** *(☎ 432360)* on the corner of Sevoke and Hill Cart Rds, has tiny, basic rooms with private bathroom (some with squat toilets). Singles/doubles start at Rs 110/220. The front rooms can cop a fair bit of traffic noise. There's no restaurant, but meals can be arranged.

Hotel Vinayak *(☎ 431130, fax 531067, LM Moulik Complex, Hill Cart Rd)* is a good mid-range choice that also has some budget rooms. Rooms (doubles only) have private bathrooms and range from Rs 350 to 950. Good food is available at the restaurant.

The friendly ***Hotel Rajdarbar*** *(☎ 534316, Hill Cart Rd)* has acceptable singles/doubles with private bathroom from Rs 275/350 and a generous 1 pm checkout. There's a nice little restaurant; fish masala is Rs 40.

The calm ***Hotel Blue Star*** *(☎ 431550, 53 Hill Cart Rd)* is a splendid budget choice – cheerful and clean. Singles/doubles with private bathroom are from Rs 250/350. The restaurant serves Indian, continental and Chinese fare.

Opposite the Tenzing Norgay central bus terminal on Hill Cart Rd is ***Hotel Mount View*** *(☎ 425919)* with good-sized rooms, many with a fairyfloss pink paint job. Singles range from Rs 175 to 300, and doubles from Rs 250 to 400. It's quite a good choice, but you might have to get them to change the sheets. Tasty food is available at the plain-looking little restaurant; for more variety, pop next door to the pleasant ***Khana Khazana*** restaurant.

Hotel Heritage *(☎ 532510)*, nearby, has comfortable if somewhat drab doubles from Rs 400. If you are strapped for cash, cheap possibilities in this area include ***Delhi Hotel*** *(☎ 522918)*, with OK singles/doubles from Rs 100/150 with private bathroom (all with squat toilets); ***Hotel Hindustan*** *(☎ 526571)*, which has doubles with private bathroom (squat toilets) from Rs 250; and the similarly priced but slightly less impressive ***TSA Guest House*** *(☎/fax 432893)*.

Hotel Air View Palace *(☎ 431542/538337, Hill Cart Rd)* has clean doubles with private bathroom (some with squat toilets) from Rs 200/250, and a very good restaurant.

The three-star ***Hotel Sinclairs*** *(☎ 522674, fax 432743)*, 2km north of Tenzing Norgay central bus terminal, is a little faded around the edges but certainly comfortable enough. Doubles cost Rs 1210. There is a foreign-exchange facility, swimming pool, bar and restaurant.

A better choice is ***Hotel Cindrella*** *(☎ 547 136, fax 430615, ⓔ cindrella@dte.vsnl.net .in, 3rd Mile, Sevoke Rd)*, which although lacking in character, is away from the hustle and bustle (about 6km from the town centre). Facilities include a pool, health club, money-exchange facility and travel desk. Singles/doubles (all with air-con) start at Rs 2100/2300. For more information see the Web site: www.cindrellahotels.com

If you've got a flight to catch, an option near the airport is ***Hotel Marina*** *(☎ 551371)*, which has doubles with private bathroom (Rs 350). It's relatively quiet, has a restaurant, and provides a free cup of morning tea. Rooms here can fill up fast, so book ahead if possible. A taxi to/from the airport costs about Rs 100 (one way).

There are two good places near the NJP train station: ***Hotel Holydon*** *(☎ 564062)* has singles/doubles with shared bathroom for Rs 100/160; with private bathroom they're Rs 200/250. Next door is the similarly priced ***Hotel Baydanath***. Request a quiet room.

Getting There & Away

Air Bagdogra airport is 12km west of Siliguri. The Indian Airlines office (☎ 431509) is in the grounds of the WBTDC Mainak Tourist Lodge (see Places to Stay). It's open from 10 am to 1 pm and 2 to 5.30 pm daily. There are two flights a week between Siliguri (Bagdogra) and Kolkata (US$80, 55 minutes)/Delhi (US$185, four hours), and two a week to Guwahati (US$50, 50 minutes). Not all the flights to Delhi are direct; some backtrack to Guwahati first.

Jet Airways (☎ 435876) services the same destinations as Indian Airlines for the same fares, but the flight schedules are variable. The Jet Airways office (up a flight of stairs) is next to Hotel Vinayak and is open from 9 am to 6.30 pm daily.

Bus Most North Bengal State Transport Corporation (NBSTC) buses leave from the Tenzing Norgay central bus terminal. Private buses with services to hill regions (Darjeeling, Gangtok etc) also have counters at the terminal. Note that if you are travelling to West Sikkim, you will require a permit (see the Permits section in the Sikkim chapter for details).

NBSTC buses for Darjeeling (Rs 45, three hours), depart hourly between 6.30 am and 3 pm. There's a bus at 7 am for Kalimpong (Rs 45, three hours), and frequent services for Mirik (Rs 25, 2½ hours). There are private buses to Kolkata, which leave daily at 6, 7 and 8 pm and cost Rs 210. The 'Rocket' services to Kolkata leave at 6, 7 and 8 pm (Rs 177, 12 hours). Other destinations include Malda (Rs 90, six hours), Berhampore (Rs 130, eight hours) and Patna (Rs 170, 12 hours). The bus to Patna leaves from a stand near the Tenzing Norgay central bus terminal.

For Guwahati, there's a NBSTC Rocket service from Tenzing Norgay central bus terminal at 5 pm (Rs 175, 12 hours).

Sikkim Nationalised Transport (SNT) buses to Gangtok (Rs 60, five hours) leave the SNT terminal every hour between 7 am and 2 pm. There's also a deluxe bus, the *Sikkim Queen* (Rs 100) at 8 am and 1 pm.

Nepal For Nepal, local buses leave from in front of the Tenzing Norgay central bus terminal for Paniktanki (Rs 12, one hour) which is opposite the Nepal border town of Kakarbhitta. See Getting There & Away under Darjeeling earlier for more details.

Train The *Darjeeling Mail* leaves Sealdah (Kolkata) at 7.15 pm (12 hours, 570km). Tickets are Rs 210/600 in 2nd/1st class. The return trip leaves NJP train station at 7.20 pm, reaching Sealdah at around 8.30 am.

The *North East Express* is the fastest train to Delhi (33 hours, 1628km). It departs from NJP at 5.25 pm, travelling via Patna (16 hours, 636km). In the other direction this train continues to Guwahati (10 hours, 423km).

There's a train booking office on the corner of Hospital and Bidhan Rds. It's open from 8 am to 8 pm Monday to Saturday and to 2 pm Sunday.

Bangladesh For Bangladesh you can take a train from NJP to Haldibari, the Indian border checkpoint (Rs 20, two hours). From here it's a 7km walk along a disused railway line to the Bangladesh border point at Chiliharti, where there's a train station. See under Land in the introductory Getting There & Away chapter at the start of this book.

Toy Train Tickets for the toy train from Siliguri/New Jalpaiguri to Darjeeling can be purchased from NJP, Siliguri Town or Siliguri Junction train stations. As there are no advance reservations, it may be easier during the busy high season (May to mid-July) to pick up tickets at NJP, where the train originates. A daily service leaves at 8.30 am (also sometimes at 7.15 am during high season). The journey by steam engine takes an interminable nine hours to cover the 80km up to the hill station, or four hours to Kurseong, 30km short of Darjeeling. For more details see Getting There & Away under Darjeeling.

Taxi & Jeep The fastest and most comfortable way of getting around the hills is by share-jeep. There are a number of taxi stands, including one on Sevoke Rd and one outside the Tenzing Norgay central bus terminal, where you can get share-jeeps to destinations in the West Bengal Hills and Sikkim including: Darjeeling (Rs 50, 2 hours), Kalimpong (Rs 60, 2½ hours), Kurseong (Rs 30, two hours) and Gangtok (Rs 100, 4½ hours). Jeeps to Gangtok leave from the taxi stand opposite Sikkim Nationalised Transport.

Posted rates for a private taxi are: Darjeeling, Rs 750; Kalimpong, Rs 750; Mirik, Rs 500; Gangtok, Rs 1200; Malda, Rs 2000; Kolkata, Rs 6000 and Guwahati, Rs 4500. If you want to retain the car and driver, it will cost more (negotiable with driver).

Getting Around

From the Tenzing Norgay central bus terminal to NJP train station a taxi/autorickshaw will cost about Rs 150/75. Cycle-rickshaws cost about Rs 20 for the 45-minute trip from NJP to Siliguri Junction, or Rs 20 to Tenzing Norgay central bus terminal. There are infrequent bus services along this route (Rs 4).

A taxi between Bagdogra airport and Siliguri costs about Rs 250. Alternatively, take a taxi to Bagdogra bazaar (Rs 100, 3km) and get a frequent local bus from there into Siliguri (Rs 4, 9km).

JALDHAPARA WILDLIFE SANCTUARY

Although most visitors are keen to head for the hills after the commotion of Siliguri, it's worth making the 135km trip east to this rarely visited sanctuary. It protects 100 sq km of lush forests and grasslands, is cut by the wide Torsa River and is also a refuge for the Indian one-horned rhinoceros *(Rhinoceros unicornis)*, whose numbers have come under serious threat from poachers.

The best time to visit is from mid-October to May, particularly in March and April when wild animals are attracted by the growth of new grasses. The sanctuary is closed during the monsoon (around 15 July to 15 October). Apart from about 35 rhinos, other animals found in the park environs are tigers (rarely seen), wild elephants, and various deer. You can take elephant safaris from Hollong, inside the park. This costs Rs 65/70/140 for students/Indians/foreigners. The park entry fee is Rs 10/50 for Indians/foreigners, and Rs 25 per vehicle. A camera/video costs Rs 5/75.

The West Bengal tourist office in Siliguri (see Information under Siliguri) can organise tours to Jaldhapara – they leave the tourist office on Saturday at noon and return the next day at 5 pm (Rs 1100/1575 for Indians/foreigners, including an elephant ride, transport, accommodation and all meals).

Places to Stay & Eat

Within the park itself is ***Hollong Forest Lodge*** *(no phone)* with doubles for Indians/foreigners at Rs 425/850, plus Rs 110/ 160 per person (compulsory) for breakfast, dinner and a morning cup of tea. Outside the park precincts at Madarihat is ***Jaldhapara Tourist Lodge*** *(☎ 03563-62230)*. Doubles start at Rs 525. Both of these places must be booked in advance through the West Bengal tourist office in Siliguri, or at the West Bengal Tourism Centre in Kolkata.

Getting There & Away

From the Tenzing Norgay central bus terminal in Siliguri, buses ply the route to Madarihat, 9km from Jaldhapara (Rs 40, three hours). From here, a taxi to Hollong, inside the park, is Rs 250. To hire a taxi from Siliguri to Jaldhapara will cost about Rs 1200. The *Intercity Express* train leaves Siliguri at 6 am daily and arrives at Madarihat, near the Torsa River, at about 9.30 am (Rs 35). It also leaves Siliguri at 5 pm and arrives at 8.30 pm. There are also deluxe/air-con buses for Rs 200/400 from Kolkata to Siliguri which take about 14 hours.

MIRIK

☎ 0354

Being promoted as a 'new' or 'minor' hill station, Mirik (at an altitude of 1767m) is about 50km from both Siliguri and Darjeeling. It is still fairly pristine and far less commercial than Darjeeling, making it a much more serene place to stay. The artificial lake is the main attraction here (vendors on the bridge sell bread so you can feed the ravenous fish); there's a 3.5km path which meanders around it. The main tourist area is to the south of the lake, in the area known as Krishnanagar.

While this is certainly a pretty spot surrounded by tea estates, orange orchards and cardamom plantations (the views from the top of the hill are stunning), ambitious plans to overly 'develop' the area for tourism threaten the tranquil ambience.

At the time of research there was nowhere to change foreign currency in Mirik.

Things to See & Do

Perched high above the town is the **Bokar Gompa**, a small and brightly coloured gompa. On the west side of the lake, about a 10-minute walk from the taxi stand and set among banana trees, are three small **Hindu temples** dedicated to Hanuman, Kalamata (Durga as the Mother of Time) and Shiva.

Two-/four-seater **boats** can be hired on the east side of the lake for Rs 30/40 per 30 minutes. A good way to see the sights is by **pony ride**. Half-day (three hours) hire costs between Rs 300 and Rs 400; a half/full round of the lake costs Rs 20/40, or Rs 60 to the Mirik Swiss Cottages (see Places to Stay) at the top of the hill.

Places to Stay & Eat

Down a small lane opposite State Bank of India is the homey ***Lodge Ashirvad*** *(☎ 43272)*. Downstairs doubles with shared bathroom are Rs 130; upstairs doubles with private bathroom start at Rs 200. There are separate kitchen facilities for self-caterers.

Next door, ***Lodge Panchashil*** *(☎ 43284)* is also delightfully down-to-earth, with small but cheerful singles/doubles with private bathroom (some with squat toilets) for Rs 120/150, or larger doubles/triples for Rs 150/200. The manager is a friendly fellow, and there's a pleasant rooftop terrace.

Hotel Mhelung *(☎ 43300, Samendu Complex)* is also attractive and all rooms have polished timber floors. Rooms range from Rs 450 to 800.

Hotel Jagdeet *(☎ 43359)*, on the main road, is more upmarket than other places and has comfortable doubles with private bathroom from Rs 650 to 1600; a family room costs Rs 1200 (maximum eight people).

Slightly farther afield, but within easy walking distance of the lake, is ***Mirik Tourist Lodge*** *(☎ 42237)*, which was undergoing renovation at the time of research. Doubles with private bathroom are expected to cost Rs 550.

Also undergoing vigorous renovation was ***Mirik (Swiss) Cottages*** *(☎ 43612)*, which has 12 hilltop two-storey cottages affording glorious views of the township and surrounding countryside including Kanchenjunga. Rates are pegged at around Rs 1500 per cottage (each can accommodate four people).

Getting There & Away

Buses to Darjeeling leave frequently each day (Rs 30, three hours). There are buses to Siliguri (Rs 25, 2½ hours). Tickets can be purchased from the wooden shack next to Restaurant Liberty, near the lakeshore.

There are no share-taxis to Darjeeling. A private taxi to Darjeeling or Siliguri will cost about Rs 650.

KURSEONG

Kurseong (1458m) is 51km north of Siliguri and 30km south of Darjeeling. The name is said to be derived from the Lepcha word, *kurson-rip*, a reference to the small white orchid prolific in this area. It has a peaceful atmosphere and, like Mirik, is not nearly as commercial as tourist-laden Darjeeling. There are several good **walks**, including one to Eagle's Crag that affords splendid views down over the Teesta and the southern plains, and a four-hour walk along the ridge and through unspoilt forest to Ghoom.

Kurseong Tourist Lodge *(☎ 0354-44409)* has large rooms for Rs 600 a double. Meals are available.

There are buses to Darjeeling (Rs 30, 2½ hours) and Siliguri (Rs 30, 2½ hours). The toy train from Siliguri to Kurseong (weather permitting) takes about four hours.

DARJEELING

☎ 0354 • pop 83,000

Straddling a ridge at 2134m and surrounded by tea plantations, Darjeeling has been a popular hill station since the British established it as a rest and recreation centre for their troops in the early 19th century. Indians and foreigners still come here in droves to escape the heat, humidity and hassle of the north Indian plain; and to explore Buddhist monasteries, visit tea plantations, ride on a cable car, hunt for bargains in handicraft shops and arrange short hikes, longer treks or rafting trips.

The peak (tourist) season – mid-March to the end of May, and mid-September to mid-November – is when organised tours are more likely to be available and accommodation prices are higher. For mountain views, the best time to visit is mid-September to mid-December. During the monsoon (June to September), clouds obscure the mountains and the rain is often so heavy that whole sections of the road are washed away, but the town is rarely cut off for more than a few days at a time.

History

Until the beginning of the 18th century, the area between the present borders of Sikkim and the plains of Bengal, including Darjeeling and Kalimpong, belonged to the rajas (kings) of Sikkim. In 1706, they lost Kalimpong to the Bhutanese, and control of the remainder was wrested from them by the Gurkhas who invaded Sikkim from Nepal in 1780.

The annexations by the Gurkhas, however, brought them into conflict with the British East India Company. A series of battles were fought between the two parties, eventually leading to the defeat of the Gurkhas and the ceding of all the land they had taken from the Sikkimese to the British East India Company. Part of this territory was restored to the rajas of Sikkim, and the country's sovereignty guaranteed by the British, in return for British control over any disputes which arose with neighbouring states.

One dispute in 1828 led to the dispatch of two British officers to the area, and during their fact-finding tour they spent some time at Darjeeling. (It was then called Dorje Ling – Place of the Thunderbolt – after the lama who founded the monastery which once stood on Observatory Hill.) The officers were quick to appreciate Darjeeling's value as a site for a sanatorium and hill station, and as the key to a pass into Nepal and Tibet.

When the British arrived in Darjeeling, it was almost completely forested and virtually uninhabited. Development was rapid and, by 1840, a sanatorium and hotel, and roads and houses, had been built. By 1857, Darjeeling had a population of about 10,000.

The population increase was due mainly to the recruitment of Nepalese labourers to work the tea plantations established in the early 1840s. Even today, the vast majority of people speak Nepali as a first language.

The immigration of Nepali-speaking peoples (mainly Gurkhas) into the mountainous areas of West Bengal eventually led to political problems, including the call for the separate state of Gorkhaland in the mid-1980s. Resentment had been growing among the Gurkhas over what they felt was discrimination against them by the government of West Bengal: eg, their language was not recognised by the Indian constitution and government jobs were only open to those who could speak Bengali. In 1986 (and to a lesser extent in the late 1990s), riots orchestrated by the Gurkha National Liberation Front (GNLF) were held in Darjeeling.

A compromise was eventually hammered out in late 1988 whereby the GNLF, and the new Darjeeling Gorkha Hill Council (DGHC), were given a large measure of autonomy from the state government. However, the GNLF's reluctance to promote secession led to the formation of the breakaway Gorkhaland Liberation Organisation (GLO) in 1990. In late 2000, the local media reported the official formation of an armed group linked to the GLO in Darjeeling and Kalimpong. No other details are currently available, but it would be prudent to read local newspapers to determine if this, or any other similar, group is carrying out any violent activities in the region.

Orientation

Darjeeling sprawls over a west-facing ridge, spilling down the hillside in a complicated series of interconnecting roads and flights of steps. The town centre is Chowrasta, with the statue of Bhanu Bhakta Agharya, a Nepalese poet, at the upper (north-eastern) end. From Chowrasta, a series of paths head north and north-east, and Nehru Rd (still generally referred to as The Mall) heads south-west and joins Laden La and Gandhi Rds at a junction called Clubside.

Information

Tourist Offices The Tourist Bureau (☎ 54050), run by the West Bengal government, is below Bellevue Hotel at Chowrasta. Staff are helpful and can offer up-to-date pamphlets and a map of Darjeeling. It is open from 10 am to 4.30 pm weekdays. In the peak season, useful tourist booths are also opened up around town.

DGHC Tourism Office (☎ 54214, ⓔ dghctourism@hotmail.com) is virtually opposite Hotel Alice Villa, and accessible from either

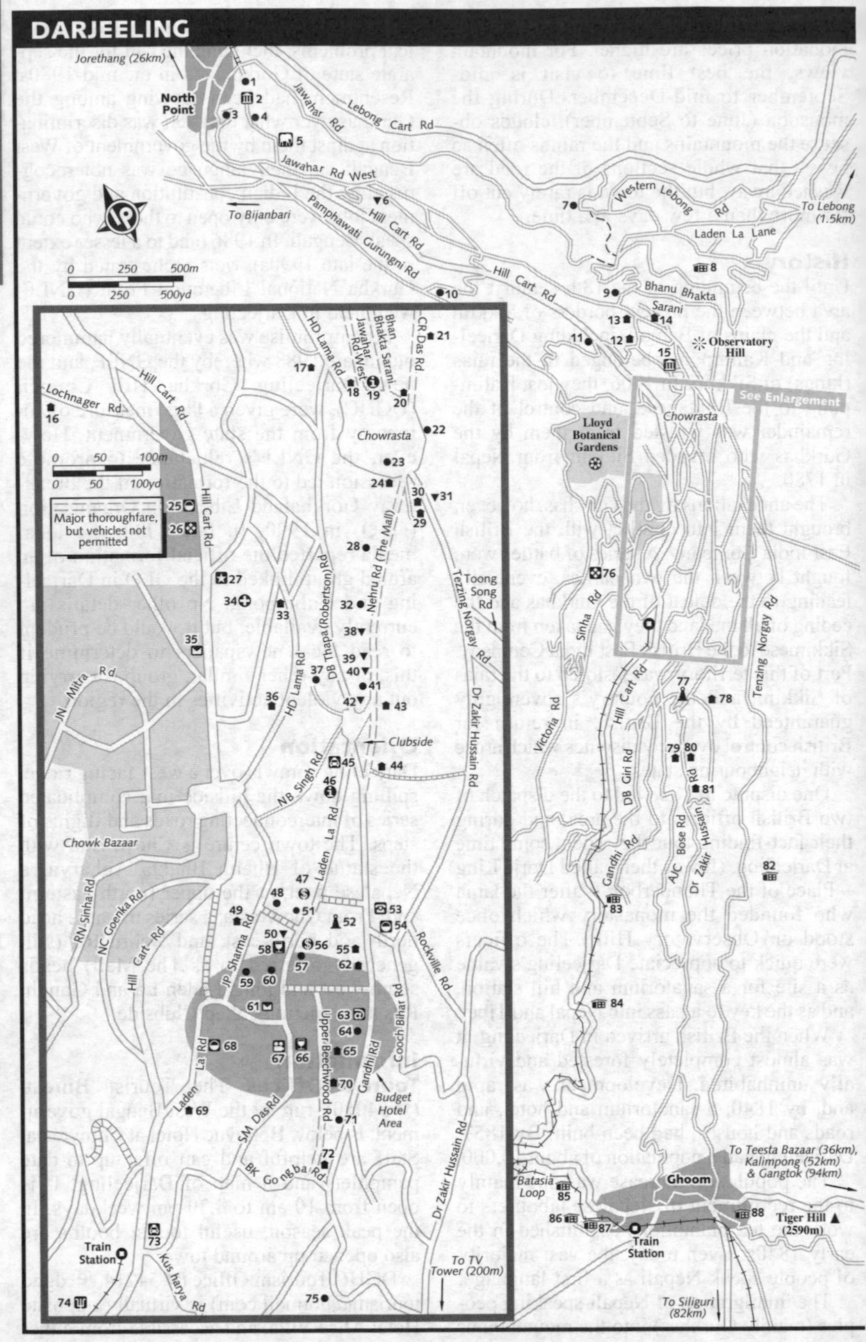
DARJEELING
Jorethang (26km)
North Point
Jawahar Rd
Lebong Cart Rd
Jawahar Rd West
To Bijanbari
Hill Cart Rd
Pamphawati Gurungni Rd
Western Lebong Rd
To Lebong (1.5km)
Laden La Lane
Bhanu Bhakta Sarani
Observatory Hill
See Enlargement
Chowrasta
Lloyd Botanical Gardens
Sinha Rd
Hill Cart Rd
Victoria Rd
DB Giri Rd
Gandhi Rd
A/C Bose Rd
Dr Zakir Hussain Rd
Tenzing Norgay Rd
To Teesta Bazaar (36km), Kalimpong (52km) & Gangtok (94km)
Batasia Loop
Ghoom
Train Station
Tiger Hill (2590m)
To Siliguri (82km)
0 250 500m
0 250 500yd
0 50 100m
0 50 100yd
Major thoroughfare, but vehicles not permitted
Lochnager Rd
HD Lama Rd
Jawahar Rd West
Bhanu Bhakta Sarani
CR Das Rd
Chowrasta
Toong Song Rd
Tezzing Norgay Rd
Dr Zakir Hussain Rd
DB Thapa (Robertson) Rd
Nehru Rd (The Mall)
JN Mitra Rd
NB Singh Rd
Clubside
Laden La Rd
Chowk Bazaar
RN Sinha Rd
NC Goenka Rd
JP Sharma Rd
Rockville Rd
Cooch Bihar Rd
Upper Beechwood Rd
Gandhi Rd
Budget Hotel Area
SM Das Rd
BK Gongba Rd
Train Station
Kushyarya Rd
To TV Tower (200m)

PLACES TO STAY
12 Maple Tourist Lodge
13 Mayfair Hill Resort
14 Darjeeling Tourist Lodge; Darjeeling Gymkhana Club
16 Hotel New Garden
17 New Elgin
18 Hotel Alice Villa
20 Windamere Hotel
21 Classic Guest House
24 Pineridge Hotel; Pineridge Travels
29 Main (Old) Bellevue Hotel
30 Bellevue Hotel; Tourist Bureau; Indian Airlines Office
33 Mohit Hotel; Moneychanger
36 Hotel Seven Seventeen; Moneychanger; Tibetan Medical & Astro Institute
43 The Darjeeling Club (The Planters); D&DMA Nursing Home
44 Hotel Dekeling; Kunga Restaurant
49 Hotel Tshering Denzongpa; Rhythm Internet Cafe
55 Hotel Springburn
62 Hotel Fairmont
65 Hotel Pagoda
69 Hotel Red Rose; Cyber Cafe
70 Hotel Shamrock
72 Hotel Hemadrie
78 Tower View Lodge & Restaurant
79 Triveni Guest House & Restaurant
80 Aliment Hotel & Restaurant
81 Tenzing Norgay Youth Hostel

PLACES TO EAT
6 Hot Stimulating Cafe
31 Stardust Restaurant; Police Assistance Booth
38 Glenary's Bakery, Bar & Restaurant
39 Frank Ross Cafe
40 Hasty Tasty
42 Keventer's Snack Bar
50 Park Restaurant; Hayden Hall; Third Eye

OTHER
1 Darjeeling Rangeet Valley Ropeway Station
2 Himalayan Mountaineering Institute
3 Snow Leopard Breeding Centre
4 Himalayan Nature Interpetation Centre
5 Padmaja Naidu Himalayan Zoological Park
7 Tibetan Refugee Self-Help Centre
8 Bhutia Busty Gompa
9 Raj Bhavan
10 Happy Valley Tea Estate
11 Office of the District Magistrate
15 Bengal Natural History Museum
19 DGHC Tourism Office
22 Pony Stand
23 Oxford Book & Stationery Company
25 Chowk Bazaar Bus/Jeep Station
26 Old Super Market Complex; Kasturi Tours & Travels Office; Diamond Treks, Tours & Travels Office
27 Police Station
28 Souvenir Shops
32 Das Studios
34 Sadar Hospital
35 Post Office
37 Manjushree Centre of Tibetan Culture
41 Trek-Mate Tours Office
45 Clubside Taxi Stand; Pool Cafe; Juniper Tours & Travels Office
46 Tourist Assistance Booth
47 Standard Chartered Grindlays Bank
48 Clubside Tours & Travels Office
51 Foreigners' Registration Office
52 Clock Tower
53 Telegraph Office
54 Jeep/Taxi Stand (to Siliguri)
56 State Bank of India
57 Samsara Tours, Travels & Treks Office
58 Golden Dragon Restaurant & Bar
59 Darjeeling Motor Service Co (Buses to Sikkim)
60 Nathmull's Tea Rooms
61 Head Post Office
63 Compuset Centre
64 Himalayan Travels Office
66 Joey's Pub
67 Rink Cinema; Video Parlours
68 Darjeeling Transport Corp (Jeeps to Gangtok)
71 Tibetan Refugee Self-Help Centre
73 Taxi Stand (for Ghoom)
74 Dhirdham Mandir
75 Nepali Girls' Social Service Centre
76 DGHC Lowis Jubilee Complex
77 TV Tower
82 Aloobari Gompa
83 Samdrub Dargye Choling Gompa
84 Thupten Sangag Choling Gompa
85 Samten Choling Gompa
86 Yiga Choling Gompa
87 Sakya Choling Gompa
88 Phin Choling Gompa

Senchal Rd

HD Lama Rd or Jawahar Rd West. Open from 8 am to 6 pm daily, it's the place to arrange an organised tour, a rafting trip or (maybe) a bus to the airport, but staff are not very helpful. The DGHC also has a tourist counter (☎ 0353-450714) at the Bagdogra airport near Siliguri, and at the train station in Darjeeling.

The DGHC's Web site is www.darjeelingtourism.com. Another useful private site about Darjeeling (and Kalimpong) is www.darjnet.com.

Money Standard Chartered Grindlays Bank, and State Bank of India (SBI), are both on Laden La Rd, and open from 10 am to 3 pm weekdays. Incredibly, Standard Chartered does not change cash, but *only* changes travellers cheques (of most major currencies and brands), and charges an outrageous Rs 200 fee per transaction. It also offers cash advances against a Visa card, with no commission.

The SBI only changes cash in US dollars and pounds sterling, and travellers cheques issued by AmEx (in US dollars) and Thomas Cook (in US dollars and pounds sterling). The commission rate is only Rs 20/25 for amounts of less/more than Rs 5000.

Moneychangers at Mohit Hotel and Hotel Seven Seventeen on HD Lama Rd, and at Pineridge Travels at Chowrasta, change major currencies in cash and travellers cheques.

Post & Communications The Head Post Office on Laden La Rd has a poste restante. A smaller post office is located in the Chowk Bazaar market.

Internet centres are springing up all over Darjeeling, but most of these will often only have two or three computers. The demand often exceeds the supply, and you will find that connections in this part of India are very slow.

The following Internet centres charge about Rs 1.25 per minute: Cyber Cafe, at Hotel Red Rose on Laden La Rd, is always crowded with waiting customers; Compuset Centre, on Gandhi Rd, has several computers and starts charging when a connection to Hotmail (or whatever) is made; and Rhythm Internet Cafe, near Hotel Tshering Denzongpa on JP Sharma Rd, has great Western music in the background.

Travel Agencies Most of the plethora of travel agencies in Darjeeling can arrange personalised local tours (see under Organised Tours later), and some can arrange treks, rafting trips and other interesting activities. A few of the more reliable agencies are listed here in alphabetical order:

Clubside Tours & Travels (☎ 54646, ⓔ clubside@dte.vsnl.net.in) JP Sharma Rd. Arranges treks and tours in northern Bengal, Sikkim and Assam, and specialises in wildlife tours in the north-eastern states.

Diamond Treks, Tours & Travels (☎ 53467) Old Super Market Complex, Hill Cart Rd. Has been operating for many years, and can arrange treks in Sikkim and luxury buses to Nepal.

Himalayan Travels (☎ 55405, ⓔ kkgurung@cal.vsnl.net.in) 18 Gandhi Rd. Also has many years' experience arranging treks and mountaineering expeditions in Darjeeling and Sikkim.

Juniper Tours & Travels (☎ 52095, fax 52625) Clubside. One of several nearby agencies offering a range of local and regional tours.

Kasturi Tours & Travels (☎ 53468, fax 54430) Old Super Market Complex, Hill Cart Rd. Organises tours to Kathmandu, Gangtok and Bhutan, and luxury buses to Nepal.

Samsara Tours, Travels & Treks (☎ 56370, ⓔ samsara@dte.vsnl.net.in) Laden La Rd. This very helpful and knowledgeable agency can also book rafting trips and hopes to offer treks in the future.

Trek-Mate Tours (☎ 74092, ⓔ odyssey@dte.vsnl.net.in) Singalila Arcade, Nehru Rd. Offers some budget-priced treks around Sikkim, Nepal and Darjeeling.

Anyone can hire trekking gear from Tenzing Norgay Youth Hostel, subject to a deposit to cover the value of the articles borrowed. (The deposit is returned, less hire charges, on return of the equipment.) The DGHC Lowis Jubilee Complex, on Dr SK Pal Rd, also rents trekking equipment to the public at minimal charges. Some travel agencies, such as Trek-Mate Tours, rent equipment to customers, and some of the budget hotels around the TV Tower area do the same for guests.

Bookshops The Oxford Book & Stationery Company at Chowrasta is unquestionably the best bookshop in Darjeeling. Open until late into the evening (so there's plenty of time for browsing), it sells a comprehensive selection of books about, and maps of, Tibet, Nepal, Sikkim, Bhutan and the Himalaya.

Photography Several photographic shops are located on Nehru Rd. They sell print and slide film, and can reliably and cheaply process print film (but not slide film) within 24 hours. Das Studios is probably the best.

Emergency There are pharmacies along Nehru Rd. Next to the Darjeeling Club, D&DMA Nursing Home (☎ 54327) is the best private hospital. The public Sadar Hospital (☎ 54218) is down some steps from HD Lama Rd. An alternative is the Tibetan Medical & Astro Institute, under Hotel Seven Seventeen on HD Lama Rd. It's open from 9 am to noon and 2 to 4 pm weekdays. The police station (☎ 52193) is along Hill Cart Rd, and there's a Police Assistance Booth near Stardust Restaurant at Chowrasta.

Permits for Sikkim If you're entering West Sikkim from Darjeeling, you'll need a permit (see the Sikkim chapter for details), which can be obtained in Darjeeling. Firstly, visit the Office of the District Magistrate (ODM) on Hill Cart Rd. If walking, take Bishop Eric Benjamin Rd from Chowrasta and keep left at the fork (the right-hand road goes to the museum). At Maple Tourist Lodge, keep zigzagging down and to the left along Kuchery Rd. When you first see Hill Cart Rd, walk straight ahead (don't turn left) and look for the large blue 'Office of the District Magistrate' sign. Alternatively, take a shared taxi from the Chowk Bazaar bus/jeep station.

At the ODM, find the entrance (at the back of the main building), go upstairs and look for the 'Sikkim Permit' sign. At the counter, which is open from 11 am to 1 pm and 2.30 to 4 pm weekdays, fill out a form and have it stamped. Then traipse back up to the Foreigners' Registration Office on Laden La Rd, which is open from 10 am to 5.30 pm daily, and get the form stamped again. Finally, return to the ODM, where your permit can be obtained while you wait. The paperwork takes about 15 minutes; the walking back and forth, about 45 minutes.

Tiger Hill

The highest spot in the area (2590m) is Tiger Hill, 11km from Darjeeling near Ghoom. The hill affords magnificent dawn views over Kanchenjunga and other eastern Himalayan peaks – but only if it's not

Anyone for Tea?

Tea is, of course, Darjeeling's most famous export. From its 80 gardens, employing over 40,000 people, the region produces the bulk of West Bengal's crop – almost 25% of India's total.

Although the region offers the right climatic conditions for producing fine tea bushes, the final result depends on a complex drying process. After picking, the fresh green leaves are placed 15 to 25cm deep in a 'withering trough' where the moisture content is reduced from 70 to 80% to 30 to 40% using high-velocity fans. Then the withered leaves are rolled and pressed to break the cell walls and express their juices onto the surface of the leaves. Normally, two rollings at different pressures are undertaken, and in between rolls the leaves are sifted to separate the coarse from the fine. The leaves, coated with their juices, are then allowed to ferment on racks in a high-humidity room, a process which develops their characteristic aroma and flavour. This fermentation must be controlled carefully since either over- or under-fermentation will ruin the tea.

This process is stopped by passing the leaves through a dry air chamber at 115 to 120°C on a conveyer belt to further reduce the moisture content to around 2 to 3%. The last process is the sorting of the tea into grades. In order of value they are: Golden Flowery Orange Pekoe (unbroken leaves), Golden Broken Orange Pekoe, Orange Fannings and Dust (the latter three consisting of broken leaves).

The tea from some estates in the Darjeeling region is of very high quality: the world record for the highest price paid for tea is US$220 per kg from the Castleton Estate.

The most convenient tea plantation to visit is the Happy Valley Tea Estate. Here, tea is still produced by the 'orthodox' method as opposed to the 'curling, tearing and crushing' method adopted on the plains. However, the estate is only worth visiting when plucking – and, therefore, processing – is in progress (April to November). The estate is open from 8 am to noon and 1 to 4.30 pm daily, except Sunday. An employee will latch on to you, whisk you around the factory and then demand an outrageous sum for his trouble; about Rs 20 per person is appropriate. The turn-off to the estate is about 500m down past the Office of the District Magistrate; look for the green sign.

cloudy. It can be very cold and crowded at the top, but coffee is available.

Every day in, umm, 'peak' season, a convoy of battered jeeps leaves Darjeeling at about 4.30 am for the 'sunrise trip' to Tiger Hill. Tickets for these trips (usually with a detour to Batasia Loop on the way back) can be purchased at the DGHC Tourism Office, or from one of the plethora of travel agencies around town. It's also easy enough to jump on a jeep going to Tiger Hill from along Gandhi or Laden La Rds between 4 and 4.30 am. This allows you to check possible cloud cover (by seeing if the stars are out) before deciding to go. A one-way/return trip costs about Rs 45/60.

The early start and discomfort are justified by the spectacular vision of a 250km stretch of the Himalayan massifs, with, from left to right, Lhotse (8501m) flanked by Everest (8848m) and Makalu (8475m), then an apparent gap before the craggy Kokang (5505m), flanked by Janu (7710m), Rathong (6630m), the apparently flat summit of Kabru (7338m), Kanchenjunga (8598m), Pandim (6691m), Simvo (6811m) and the cone-like Siniolchu (5780m).

Some people take the jeep one way to Tiger Hill and then walk back to Darjeeling. However, to avoid the awful traffic along the main road it's better to walk back as far as Batasia Loop, and visit a few gompas along the way, and then catch a bus or jeep to Darjeeling.

Mountain Views

At 8598m, Kanchenjunga is the world's third-highest mountain, and the biggest in India. The name 'Kanchenjunga' is derived from the Tibetan words for 'big five-peaked snow fortress' or 'big five-peaked treasury of the snow' (depending on whom you ask). Some of the best spots around Darjeeling for views of Kanchenjunga and other mountains (if it's not cloudy or foggy) are the several lookouts along Bhanu Bhakta Sarani, Observatory Hill (though some views are blocked by trees) and the roof of Keventer's Snack Bar at Clubside.

Observatory Hill

This place just north-west of Chowrasta is sacred to Hindus, who revere **Mahakala Mandir** temple located in a small cave down some stairs from the hill, and to Buddhists because the hill was once the site of the Dorje Ling monastery (from which Darjeeling got its name). The multicoloured prayer flags double as trapezes for monkeys which can be aggressive. The steps leading to the hill are not entirely obvious; they start about 300m on the left along Bhanu Bhakta Sarani from Chowrasta.

Gompas

The colourful monastery of **Bhutia Busty Gompa**, with Kanchenjunga providing a spectacular backdrop, was originally a branch of the Nyingmapa sect's Phodong Monastery in Sikkim, before it was transferred to Darjeeling in 1879. (The shrine here originally stood on Observatory Hill.) The gompa houses a library of Buddhist texts, including the original copy of the Tibetan Book of the Dead, and a fine mural (but permission is required to see it).

Follow CR Das Rd for about 800m from Chowrasta, and then head down to the right at the fork in the road; the monastery comes into view within a few hundred metres.

Yiga Choling Gompa is probably the most famous monastery in the region. Built in 1875, it enshrines an image of the Maitreya Buddha (Future Buddha), and the friendly monks belong to the Gelukpa order. Foreigners are allowed to enter the shrine and take photographs, but a small donation is customary. As Ghoom is frequently swathed in mists, and the monastery is old and dark, the gompa is sometimes affectionately called the 'Gloom Monastery'.

From Darjeeling, take a share-jeep or the Toy Train, or visit the gompa while walking back from Tiger Hill (see Tiger Hill earlier).

There are three other gompas in Ghoom: the very large, but relatively uninteresting, **Samten Choling Gompa** with its 8m-high stupa; the nearby and smaller **Sakya Choling Gompa**; and the **Phin Choling Gompa**.

About halfway between Ghoom and Darjeeling is **Thupten Sangag Choling Gompa**, inaugurated by the Dalai Lama in 1992. Westerners interested in Tibetan Buddhism often study there. Closer to Darjeeling, and along the same road, is the opulent **Samdrub Dargye Choling Gompa**.

Aloobari Gompa, along Tenzing Norgay Rd, also welcomes visitors. The monks often sell Tibetan and Sikkimese handicrafts and religious objects (usually hand bells). If the monastery is closed, ask someone at the cottage next door to let you in.

Padmaja Naidu Himalayan Zoological Park

This zoo was established in 1958 to study, conserve and preserve Himalayan fauna. It houses India's only collection of (massive) Siberian tigers, some rare species such as Himalayan black bears, and red pandas and Tibetan wolves – both of which the zoo has had great success in breeding. Compared to other zoos in India, the animals are reasonably well cared for by dedicated keepers.

Inside the park is the **Himalayan Nature Interpretation Centre**, a tacky indoor sound-and-light show, which can be avoided. Tickets to this cost an extra Rs 5.

The zoo is a pleasant 30-minute walk down from Chowrasta along Jawahar Rd West; alternatively, take a shared taxi from the Chowk Bazaar bus/jeep station. The zoo is open from 8 am to 4.30 pm daily, except Thursday. Entry is Rs 5 and an extra Rs 5/200 is charged for cameras/videos.

Himalayan Mountaineering Institute (HMI)

India's most prestigious mountaineering institute was founded in 1954. It boasts the **Mountaineering Museum**, with a collection of historic mountaineering equipment, specimens of Himalayan flora and fauna, and a relief model of the Himalaya showing the principal peaks. Next door, the fascinating **Everest Museum** traces the history of attempts on the highest peak, with photographs and biographies of all the summiteers.

The HMI is located within (and only accessible through) the zoo and has the same opening hours and admission fees. Next to

Tenzing Norgay

Tenzing Norgay, who conquered Everest with Edmund Hillary in 1953, lived in Darjeeling and was the director of the Himalayan Mountaineering Institute for many years. He died in 1986, but the climbing tradition of the Tenzings lives on: his eldest daughter, Pem Pen, was a climber of some note; his son, Jamling, climbed Everest in 1996; and his granddaughter, climbed it a year later.

the museums, there are a few ***chai stalls*** and a souvenir shop, and above it stands the **Tenzing Samadhi** statue.

Snow Leopard Breeding Centre

The snow leopards *(Panthera uncia)* were originally housed in the zoo, but due to the disturbance of visitors and the proximity of other animals breeding was largely unsuccessful. Pairs of these rare and beautiful animals are now housed in a large separate enclosure, and this has made all the difference. Most visitors may be disappointed, however: though you can get a lot closer to the leopards' cages, the centre is little more than an extension of the zoo.

The centre is a 10-minute walk farther along Jawahar Rd West from the entrance to the zoo. Otherwise, take a shared taxi from the Chowk Bazaar bus/jeep station and ask to be dropped off at the access road, which is not signposted along Hill Cart Rd. The centre is open from 8 am to 4 pm daily, except Thursday. Tickets cost Rs 10.

Darjeeling Rangeet Valley Ropeway

India's first 'ropeway' (cable car) connects North Point with Tukvar village, about 1.2km across the Rangeet Valley. It's an exhilarating ride, although a little scary if windy and pointless if the clouds or fog are thick. The return trip (including insurance) costs Rs 55, and takes about 50 minutes. The ropeway operates from about 10 am to 5 pm daily.

You can get off at Tukvar, but there's nothing more than a few simple ***cafes*** and ***bars***. The starting point is about a 15-minute walk along Hill Cart Rd from the zoo; or take a share-jeep to North Point from the Chowk Bazaar bus/jeep station.

Tibetan Refugee Self-Help Centre

Established in 1959, this centre now comprises a home for the aged, orphanage, school, clinic (☎ 53122), **gompa** and **craft workshops** which produce carpets, woodcarvings, leatherwork and wool items. The handicrafts, as well as Tibetan souvenirs and jewellery, are available for sale in the **showroom** (☎ 52552). Prices are similar to those in the souvenir shops at Chowrasta and along Nehru Rd, but the proceeds go straight back to the Tibetan community.

Visitors can wander around at leisure through the workshops: the shops with weaving/dyeing and woodcarving are particularly interesting, and the people are

Fight for Survival

The beautiful snow leopards can be found across the entire Indian Himalaya, from Kashmir in the west to Bhutan to the east; to the north, they're found in Tibet, Central Asia and the Altai mountains in Mongolia. Due to the inaccessibility of the terrain and the high altitudes (over 3600m) of their habitats, it's almost impossible to be accurate about the number of snow leopards in the wild, but it's estimated to be between 4000 and 5000. The snow leopard is a highly endangered and protected species, but tragically the smuggling of its pelt continues.

In captivity, snow leopards live approximately 14 years. Females have two breeding cycles per year, but are more likely to conceive in the winter cycle. The gestation period is from 92 to 100 days, and there are usually two cubs per litter, although this can be up to five in the wild.

While it is distressing to see these magnificent animals in cages, it's a sad fact that programs such as the Snow Leopard Breeding Centre in Darjeeling, which commenced in 1986 with two leopards brought from Switzerland, significantly enhance the snow leopard's prospects for survival as a species.

The International Snow Leopard Trust, which controls all breeding programs, was founded in the early 1970s. For further information contact: The Conservation Education Director (☎ 206-632 2421, fax 632 3967, ⓔ islt@serv.net), International Snow Leopard Trust, 4649 Sunnyside Ave Nth, Seattle, Washington 98103, USA.

friendly and welcoming. As the centre is self-funding, and a registered charity, donations are always welcome. (See also Volunteer Work in the introductory Facts for the Visitor chapter.) It's open daily, except Sunday, during daylight hours.

The centre is not easy to find, however. From Chowrasta, walk down CR Das Rd for about 800m until you come to a fork. The road to the left is signposted to the centre, but this steep vehicle road is about 4km long. If you take the road to the right at the fork, past the Bhutia Busty Gompa and keep heading downhill, it's shorter (about 1.2km) – but ask for directions along the way, and look out for the huge sign on the roof of the centre. Alternatively, take a shared or chartered taxi to the turn-off along Lebong Cart Rd.

Other Attractions

The most conspicuous Hindu temple in Darjeeling, **Dhirdham Mandir**, is modelled on the famous Pashupatinath Temple in Kathmandu. It's easy to find just below the Darjeeling train station.

If you're travelling on the Toy Train, or walking back from Tiger Hill (see Tiger Hill earlier), look out for the **war memorial** at the incredible **Batasia Loop** along the track. Entry is Rs 2, and it's open daily during daylight hours.

The unimpressive **Bengal Natural History Museum** offers a dilapidated collection of Himalayan and Bengali fauna, and an incongruous replica of a crocodile. It's open from 10 am to 4 pm daily, except Thursday. Entry is Rs 5. From Chowrasta, walk along Bishop Eric Benjamin Rd for two minutes, and take the lane to the right at the fork.

Lloyd Botanical Gardens contain an impressive representation of Himalayan plants and flowers, including orchids. The gardens are open from 6 am and 5 pm daily; the glasshouse, from 8 am and 5 pm. Follow the signs along Lochnager Rd from the Chowk Bazaar bus/jeep station. Admission is free.

White-Water Rafting

Teesta Bazaar is the centre for rafting along the Rangeet and Teesta Rivers. Although only about 16km from Kalimpong, most travellers will organise trips from Darjeeling. The rapids are graded from Grade II to Grade IV, and the best time for rafting is September to November and March to June.

Himalayan River Journey (☎ 53969, ⓔ jdriverjourney@rediffmail.com) charges from Rs 1200 (one hour) to Rs 2100 (4½ hours) for rafting trips, including transport from Darjeeling, food, equipment and guide. Longer trips are available on demand. Bookings can also be made at Samsara Tours, Travels & Treks (see under Travel Agencies earlier for contact details and also see under Around Kalimpong for more information on tours).

Other Activities

Membership of the Darjeeling Gymkhana Club (☎ 54341), along Jawahar Rd West, costs Rs 30/250/400/600 per day/week/fortnight/month. The activities here are not equestrian, however. (The word 'gymkhana' actually derives from the Hindi *gendkhana*, or 'ball house'.) Games on offer – at extra cost – include tennis, squash, badminton, roller-skating, table tennis and billiards. Ring the club to find out which games are available and when, or check the noticeboard in the foyer.

The grand Darjeeling Club (also called The Planters), at Clubside, offers temporary membership to visitors for Rs 50 per day. This allows free access to the billiard room, bar and library.

From Chowrasta, pony rides are available along any path without vehicles, eg, Jawahar Rd West as far as the zoo. The usual charge is a negotiable Rs 60 per hour. A pony can also be hired for longer treks from about Rs 250 per day (plus the cost of the pony-wallah).

Courses

Tibetan-language courses for beginners (three to six months) are conducted at the Manjushree Centre of Tibetan Culture (☎ 56714), 8 Burdwan Rd, just north of Clubside. The centre can also arrange Buddhist study courses for groups of six or more. Traditional Tibetan woodcarving is at the Tibetan Refugee Self-Help Centre; contact the head office (☎ 52346) at 65 Gandhi Rd.

Organised Tours

All travel agencies offer the same sort of organised local tours as the DGHC, but unless you can get enough other passengers to share the cost the agencies will often suggest you go on a DGHC tour – and the

DGHC needs a minimum number before any tour can start. If there's not enough demand for a half-day local tour, DGHC can arrange a taxi for Rs 350 per vehicle.

DGHC's half-day 'local sightseeing tour' (Rs 50 per person) includes the zoo, Himalayan Mountaineering Institute and Tibetan Refugee Self-Help Centre, but these places can be easily visited independently, and on foot. The DGHC's day trip (Rs 100) to Mirik is worthwhile, because going there on your own by public transport will cost about the same, and take longer. In the peak season, DGHC offers a 'Tiger Hill Tour', which also fits in a quick trip to the Samten Choling Gompa and Batasia Loop.

Special Events

Surprisingly, Darjeeling has no specific festivals worth mentioning. The New Years for the Sikkimese (December/January), Lepchas and Bhutias (January) and Tibetans (February/March) are celebrated enthusiastically, often at the major gompas. The five-day **Tihar Festival** is celebrated by the Nepalese in late October or early November.

Places to Stay

Only a limited selection of the massive number of hotels in Darjeeling is listed here. Prices vary widely according to the season: those listed are for the peak tourist season, but in the low season prices drop by about 50%. A lot of hotels don't offer single rates, and the 10% 'service charge' often added to the tariff is arbitrary and negotiable. Many places, particularly in the top-end range, offer an 'American Plan' including all meals, but this is never worthwhile (unless you're staying in a remote hotel), because there are plenty of good cheap restaurants around town.

Darjeeling suffers from chronic power and water shortages, and not all hotels have backup generators or permanent hot water. If there's a television in the room, make sure it has cable, which offers more variety (and English-speaking options) than local TV; and if heating is promised, find out the type and make sure it works.

Places to Stay – Budget

Near the TV Tower along Dr Zakir Hussain Rd there are four places which cater mostly to backpackers. The area is a little inconvenient, and sometimes hard to find at night, but it's clean and quiet. All (except the youth hostel) boast a book exchange, Internet centre and good, cheap restaurant. The best way to reach the TV Tower is to walk up Rockville Rd from opposite the clock tower, head left behind the Telegraph Office and then up to Dr Zakir Hussain Rd.

Tenzing Norgay Youth Hostel is perched on a ridge and undoubtedly has some of the best views in Darjeeling. (There's no need to go to Tiger Hill to watch the sunrise on Kanchenjunga – just wander out onto the balcony.) It's reasonably clean, if a little characterless, and good value with dorm beds for Rs 40 per person (membership of an international youth hostel organisation is not required). It has an informative travellers' comment book, and the staff can help with trekking information and equipment.

Triveni Guest House *(☎ 53878)* is basic, but very popular and friendly. Clean singles/doubles cost Rs 90/120 with shared bathroom; doubles (no singles) with private bathroom are Rs 130.

Aliment Hotel *(☎ 55068)* has clean rooms with shared bathroom (and squat toilet) for Rs 70/150, and doubles with spotless private bathrooms (and hot water) for Rs 200.

Tower View Lodge *(☎ 54452, ⓔ compuset@cal.vsnl.net.in)*, just down from the TV Tower, is simple but excellent value – so it's often full of long-term guests. Singles range from Rs 80 to 100, and doubles from Rs 100 to 150 – all have private toilets, but the showers (with hot water) are shared. Dorm beds cost Rs 40 per person. Visitors must stay at least two nights.

Along Upper Beechwood Rd, there are two charming, but very basic, choices. Neither have more than a handful of rooms, however, and they are not geared up for lots of travellers. ***Hotel Pagoda*** *(☎ 53498)* charges a bargain Rs 80/100 for tiny but clean rooms with shared bathroom and next door, ***Hotel Shamrock*** charges Rs 80/180 for similar facilities.

Hotel Hemadrie *(☎ 52967, ⓔ prashantpips@hotmail.com, 4 Gandhi Rd)* is a little inconvenient and noisy, but has been recommended by travellers. All rooms have cable TV and private bathroom (with squat toilet), and are very good value from Rs 165/275. Better doubles cost from Rs 385.

Other unexciting and noisy budget hotels costing about Rs 100/150 for basic rooms, often with private bathroom (cold water), can be found along the steps up from near Hotel Dekeling at Clubside, along the steps between Laden La and Gandhi Rds which lead to Upper Beechwood Rd, and around the train station.

The best of a bad lot around the Chowk Bazaar bus/jeep station is ***Hotel New Garden*** *(Lochnager Rd)*, down the quiet access road to the botanical gardens. A clean room with three beds, and a rudimentary private bathroom, costs Rs 200.

Places to Stay – Mid-Range

All rooms in the places listed here have private bathrooms (unless stated otherwise) with hot water (often mornings only).

Hotel Tshering Denzongpa *(☎ 56061, JP Sharma Rd)* is a friendly, Sherpa-run place with singles/doubles from Rs 350/600, and doubles with shared bathroom for Rs 250. The more-expensive rooms have better views. It's often full.

Hotel Springburn *(☎ 52054, Gandhi Rd)* has some character. The doubles for Rs 385 are large, clean and come with cable TV, but the bathrooms have squat toilets and the hot water is erratic. The rooms at the back have views of Kanchenjunga.

Bellevue Hotel *(☎ 54075)* is a charming old place at Chowrasta. Large, comfortable doubles range from Rs 440 to 660, but it's noisy because of the wooden floors and walls. For long-term guests, there are huge, but characterless, rooms (some with kitchens) at the back. Guests can enjoy the rooftop terrace, private Buddhist prayer room and cafe with views over Chowrasta.

Main (Old) Bellevue Hotel *(☎ 54178)* also has a great position at Chowrasta, and is constantly recommended by readers for its friendly staff. The Raj-era building at the back has large, musty doubles for Rs 400, and the newer wing has better rooms with great views for Rs 500.

Pineridge Hotel *(☎ 54074, ⓔ pineridge@dte.vsnl.net.in, Nehru Rd)* is a huge, rambling place with loads of character. All rooms are nicely furnished, with fireplaces and cable TV, and some have bay windows. Rooms range from Rs 400/550 to 600/700 for more space with views. The negotiable low-season discounts are particularly attractive.

Hotel Alice Villa *(☎ 54181, HD Lama Rd)* has charming doubles in the original building for Rs 825; or Rs 935 including breakfast and dinner. The rooms in the new annexe are disappointing, but cheaper: Rs 715/880 without/with two meals. All rooms have cable TV. The negotiable rates in low season make this excellent value.

The Darjeeling Club *(☎/fax 54348, Clubside)*, also known as The Planters, is a real ghost of the Raj era. Large musty doubles with a fireplace cost from Rs 660 to 1320; the superb 'suite' is Rs 2200.

Hotel Dekeling *(☎ 54159, ⓔ dekeling@dte.vsnl.net.in, Clubside)* is popular and friendly, but a little pricey. The double rooms, located mostly around convivial communal lounge areas, are small, but quaint, and range from Rs 660 with shared bathroom to 1210 with better views and private bathroom.

Hotel Fairmont *(☎ 53646, fax 53647, 10 Gandhi Rd)* offers very comfortable rooms with great views, cable TV and phone. It's particularly good value at Rs 1155/1650 for doubles/triples.

Hotel Seven Seventeen *(☎ 55099)* is probably the best of several similar hotels along HD Lama Rd. It's run by a welcoming Tibetan family, and offers four-star service and facilities at two-star prices. The comfortable singles/doubles/triples with cable TV are good value for Rs 880/1100/1430; slightly more for rooms with views.

Classic Guest House *(☎ 54106, CR Das Rd)*, just down from Chowrasta, is a delightful place, if expensive. It offers charming decor, great views and friendly service, and doubles with cable TV and a balcony for Rs 1000. It's popular, so book ahead.

Maple Tourist Lodge *(☎ 52813, Kuchery Rd)*, run by the West Bengal tourist department, is in a quiet location and surprisingly good value. Singles/doubles with shared (spotless) bathroom with hot water cost Rs 315/473. It's often full, so book ahead. See under Permits for Sikkim earlier in this chapter for details about getting to the lodge on foot from Chowrasta.

Darjeeling Tourist Lodge *(☎ 54411, ⓔ darjeeling@epages.webindia.com, Jawahar Rd West)* is above the Darjeeling Gymkhana Club. Most rooms are overpriced, but the doubles in the old annexe for Rs 400 are good value.

Places to Stay – Top End

Most top-end hotels only offer the 'American Plan', with breakfast, lunch and dinner included. The prices here are for the 'American Plan'.

New Elgin *(☎ 54114, ⓔ newelgin@cal.vsnl.net.in)*, off HD Lama Rd, retains its colonial ambience. Most of the elegantly furnished rooms have open fires, and all boast marble bathrooms, and the lovely gardens are a perfect place to relax and enjoy afternoon tea. Singles/doubles cost US$92/99.

Windamere Hotel *(☎ 54041, ⓔ windamere@vsnl.com)*, above Chowrasta, is a veritable institution among Raj relic aficionados, with Tibetan maids in starched frilly aprons and high tea served in the drawing room. The rooms are cosy and comfortable, and TVs are conspicuously (and deliberately) absent. Rates start from US$103/137.

Mayfair Hill Resort *(☎ 56376, ⓔ mayfair@cal2.vsnl.net.in)* is along Jawahar Rd West and opposite the Raj Bhavan (Government House). Originally a maharaja's summer palace, it's been extensively renovated so its origins are no longer apparent. It does, however, offer luxury in beautiful surroundings and fabulous views. Rooms and cottages are comparatively good value for Rs 3500/4500/5500 for singles/doubles/triples.

Places to Eat

Following is a small sample of the many fine places to eat in Darjeeling.

Keventer's Snack Bar *(Clubside)* has a deli on the ground floor selling uncooked sausages, cheese, ham and other goods. The range of meals at the small restaurant upstairs is limited, but it's ideal for a cooked breakfast. The service is slow, but this gives you time to enjoy the magnificent views.

Hasty Tasty *(Nehru Rd)* specialises in South Indian vegetarian snacks and meals, such as *dosas*. It's incredibly popular with Indian tourists, which is always a good sign.

Frank Ross Cafe *(Nehru Rd)* is also strictly vegetarian. It offers a decent range of pizzas (from Rs 40), burgers, South Indian snacks and even Mexican nachos (Rs 35).

Glenary's *(Nehru Rd)* has a classy restaurant and bar upstairs with a limited range of Indian, Chinese and continental dishes from Rs 50. The ***bakery*** underneath sells excellent pastries, cakes and chocolates, and is a wonderful place to enjoy a cup of Darjeeling's finest chai.

Stardust Restaurant is the best value at Chowrasta, and the views from the tables outside are staggering. Vegetarian (only) meals start from Rs 30, but inexplicably it does not serve tea.

Park Restaurant, near Hayden Hall on Laden La Rd, is probably the best place for a splurge. The service is excellent, the decor is charming and the meals (from Rs 50) are not as expensive as you'd imagine.

Kunga Restaurant, beneath Hotel Dekeling at Clubside, is small but very popular. It offers a huge range of authentic Tibetan and Chinese cuisine, including 36 varieties of soup (!), as well as decent pizzas. The servings are huge, eg, a plate of steamed *momos* (dumplings; Rs 30) is probably large enough for two people.

Opposite the Head Post Office along Laden La Rd, a number of tiny, cheap ***Tibetan restaurants*** serve simple, traditional cuisine; and, opposite Hotel Seven Seventeen on HD Lama Rd, several small ***Indian eateries*** serve excellent samosas and snacks.

Hot Stimulating Cafe *(Jawahar Rd West)*, perched over the mountainside on the road down to the zoo, offers beautiful views over the hills and valleys. The Nepalese owners make tasty and cheap food (such as momos), and serve excellent chai and coffee.

Entertainment

Golden Dragon Restaurant & Bar *(Laden La Rd)*, with its rainbow-painted walls and seedy 1920s ambience, is one of several similar dens where the beer, rather than the limited menu, is the main attraction. Decent restaurants which serve beer and other alcoholic drinks include the upstairs restaurant at ***Glenary's*** *(Nehru Rd)* and ***Park Restaurant*** *(Laden La Rd)*. The cosy bar at ***Hotel Seven Seventeen*** *(HD Lama Rd)* is inviting and pleasantly well lit.

The best place to meet other travellers is undoubtedly ***Joey's Pub*** *(SM Das Rd)*. It has friendly staff and Western music, and can even rustle some 'continental cuisine' (such as baked beans on toast!), but the drinks are expensive.

Rink Cinema, on SM Das Rd, shows mainly Indian films in Hindi. Nearby, several dingy video parlours show sleazy and violent films. ***Pool Cafe***, above the Juniper

Tours & Travels office at Clubside, is a great place to while away some time; pool tables cost Rs 100 per hour.

Shopping

Souvenirs Most souvenir shops are at Chowrasta and along Nehru Rd. They sell *thangkas* (rectangular Tibetan religious cloth paintings), brass statues, religious objects, jewellery, woodcarvings and carpets, but if you're looking for bargains, shop judiciously and be prepared to spend plenty of time looking. Thangkas in particular may look impressive at first sight, but you'll find little care has been taken over the finer detail in the cheaper ones.

Other great souvenirs are photographic prints of Kanchenjunga and nearby mountains, and of other places around Darjeeling, which cost from Rs 150 to 495. These are available from photographic shops along Nehru Rd, such as Das Studios.

Chowk Bazaar is huge and fascinating, although not the best place for souvenirs, except loose-leaf tea, spices and incense.

Tibetan Carpets One of the best places for Tibetan carpets is Hayden Hall on Laden La Rd. This women's co-operative sells *casemillon* (wool/synthetic mix) shawls, woollen hats, socks and mufflers. Virtually next door, Third Eye is an all-women enterprise which gives free training to female weavers and guarantees work at the end of their training. Shipping of carpets can be arranged.

Darjeeling Tea Tea is a popular souvenir. First Flush Super Fine Tippy Golden Flowery Orange Pekoe I has a forgettable name, but an unforgettable taste. To test the quality, take a small handful in your closed fist, breathe on it through your fingers, open your hand and smell the aromas released. At least it'll look as if you know what you're doing even if you don't have a clue. Avoid the tea in fancy boxes, because it's usually blended and packaged in Kolkata. A good supplier is Nathmull's Tea Rooms along Laden La Rd. Cheaper tea is available from stalls in Chowk Bazaar; it's sold loose, but can be packaged.

Getting There & Away

Air The nearest airport is 90km away at Bagdogra, about 12km from Siliguri. Refer to Getting There & Away under Siliguri & New Jalpaiguri earlier in this chapter for details about flights to/from Bagdogra.

The agents for Jet Airways in Darjeeling are Clubside Tours & Travels (☎ 54646, ⓔ clubside@dte.vsnl.net.in) on JP Sharma Rd; and Pineridge Travels (☎ 53912, ⓔ pineridge@dte.vsnl.net.in) at Chowrasta. The Indian Airlines office (☎ 54230) is beneath Bellevue Hotel at Chowrasta. These offices are closed on Sunday.

Clubside, Pineridge and some of the other companies listed under Travel Agencies earlier sell tickets for flights on Nepali airlines.

Bus From the Chowk Bazaar bus/jeep station, public buses go to Kalimpong (Rs 42, 3½ hours) at 8 am; to Mirik (Rs 30, three hours) every 30 minutes from 8 am to 3.15 pm; and to Siliguri (about Rs 45, three hours) every 30 minutes during the day. Tickets can be bought from counters along the ground floor of the Old Super Market Complex on Hill Cart Rd, but only buses to Gangtok and Kalimpong can be booked in advance.

No buses travel between Darjeeling and Jorethang, Pelling or anywhere else in Sikkim (except Gangtok) – so to get to West Sikkim, first take a share-jeep to Jorethang (described later). From the bus/jeep station, a public bus leaves at 7.30 am daily for Gangtok (Rs 80, six to seven hours). The agent for Sikkim Nationalised Transport (SNT) is the Darjeeling Motor Service Co (☎ 52101), 31 Laden La Rd; the SNT bus to Gangtok leaves from opposite the office at 12.30 pm daily.

Several travel agencies around the Old Super Market Complex on Hill Cart Rd, eg, Kasturi and Diamond, offer daily buses to Guwahati (Assam), via Siliguri, for Rs 285 to 320. Samsara Tours, Travels & Treks on Laden La Rd sells tickets for 'luxury' overnight buses to places all over northern India and Kolkata from Siliguri. Before buying a long-distance bus ticket from Darjeeling, determine the number and length of connections, because *all* long-distance bus services start and finish in Siliguri.

Nepal It's important to note that foreigners can only cross the border into Nepal at Kakarbhitta (not at Pasupati), so make sure your bus goes through the correct border crossing. The nearest Nepali consulate is in Kolkata, but visas are available at Kakarbhitta for US$30 (which must be paid in cash).

A number of travel agencies – such as Kasturi and Diamond at the Old Super Market Complex on Hill Cart Rd, and Samsara on Laden La Rd – sell tickets for daily buses between Darjeeling and Kathmandu (about Rs 450). These agencies sell you a ticket to Siliguri and a guaranteed, prepaid seat on a connecting bus (or jeep) from there.

Many people prefer to do the Darjeeling-Kathmandu trip independently, although this involves four changes – a bus/jeep from Darjeeling to Siliguri, bus/jeep (Rs 45) from Siliguri to Paniktanki on the Indian border, a rickshaw across the border to Kakarbhitta and a bus from Kakarbhitta to Kathmandu (Nepalese Rs 408, 13 hours). This is cheaper than the Darjeeling-Kathmandu package deal, and you get a choice of buses from the border and the option of travelling during the day and stopping at places along the way.

Taxis, Minivans & Jeeps Tickets for 'commander jeeps' to Gangtok (five hours) can be booked in advance from counters at the southern end of the Chowk Bazaar bus/jeep station. These jeeps travel via Teesta Bazaar and Rangpo, and cost Rs 100/1000 for a shared/chartered jeep. Darjeeling Transport Corp on Laden La Rd – and a few other agencies in the vicinity – also offer share-jeeps to Gangtok (about Rs 110 per person) at set times from outside their offices.

From the northern end of the bus/jeep station, shared/chartered taxis go to Jorethang (Rs 80/850, 2½ hours), from where it's easy to get a connection to anywhere in northern or West Sikkim. But remember: the section from Darjeeling to Naya Bazaar is tough, often steep, and subject to landslides during the monsoon; and you must have a basic permit for Sikkim if travelling on this route.

From inside the ground floor of the Old Super Market Complex, the agency for jeeps to Kalimpong (three hours) charges Rs 50 (for the back seat) or Rs 65 (front seat) in a share-jeep; Rs 750 if you charter it. Share-jeeps to Mirik (Rs 42, 2½ hours) leave from anywhere in the bus/jeep station, so ask around.

To Siliguri (Rs 60, three hours), jeeps and taxis leave every few minutes from around the bus/jeep station, from along Hill Cart Rd and outside the clock tower on Gandhi Rd. To New Jalpaiguri or Bagdogra, get a connection in Siliguri, or charter a jeep or taxi from Darjeeling for about Rs 650.

Train The nearest major train station is at New Jalpaiguri (NJP), near Siliguri (see Getting There & Away under Siliguri & New Jalpaiguri earlier in this chapter for details). Tickets – mostly 2nd-class sleepers only – can be bought for major services out of NJP at the Computerised Reservations Counter (☎ 52555) at Darjeeling train station between 8 am and 2 pm daily.

Toy Train The charming Toy Train has three different services, but note that wet weather causes landslides and services can be cancelled for months. Also, timetables change, so check the schedules at the stations for current details. No advance tickets are available on any service to NJP or Kurseong; tickets are available from one hour before departure. The fares for ordinary/1st class from Darjeeling are: to Ghoom (Rs 3/45), Kurseong (Rs 10/90), Siliguri (Rs 19/172) and NJP (Rs 22/202).

A train leaves Darjeeling for NJP at 9.10 am daily, and stops at Ghoom (at 9.56 am), Kurseong (noon), Siliguri (4.40 pm) and NJP (5.20 pm). It leaves NJP at 9 am, and stops at Siliguri (9.23 am), Kurseong (12.56 pm), Ghoom (2.57 pm) and Darjeeling (3.30 pm).

A 'local service' departs Darjeeling at 3 pm daily for Ghoom (arriving at 3.26 pm), and continues on to Kurseong (5.30 pm). It leaves Kurseong at 6.40 am and stops at Ghoom (8.31 am) on the way to Darjeeling (9.10 am).

A special tourist 'joy ride' departs at 10.30 am daily for a two-hour return trip to Ghoom, via Batasia Loop. Tickets (Rs 200) are limited to about 25, so book one day in advance if possible.

Getting Around

The DGHC tourist office runs a bus (Rs 65 per person) to the Bagdogra airport if there are 12 or more passengers (which is rare) – and at a time that suits the majority of passengers. If the bus doesn't leave Darjeeling, it won't be at Bagdogra airport for the return trip.

So, the alternatives from the airport to Darjeeling are: either a prepaid taxi to Siliguri bus station, and then a bus/jeep to Darjeeling; or charter (or ask around about sharing) a prepaid taxi, which costs from Rs 690 (2½ hours) to Rs 1150 (five hours, for the scenic route via Mirik). Chartered and shared taxi fares are a little cheaper outside the airport, and from Darjeeling to the airport.

Share-taxis to anywhere north of the city centre, eg, North Point, leave from the northern end of the Chowk Bazaar bus/jeep station.

KALIMPONG

☎ 03552 • pop 46,500

Although still relatively small, Kalimpong is a bustling and rapidly expanding bazaar town set among the rolling foothills and deep valleys of the Himalaya at an altitude of 1250m. It was part of the lands belonging to the rajas of Sikkim, until the beginning of the 18th century when it was taken from them by the Bhutanese. In the 19th century, Kalimpong passed into the hands of the British and thus became part of West Bengal. It became a centre for Scottish missionary activity, particularly by the Jesuits, in the late 19th century, and Dr Graham's orphanage and school is still running today.

Kalimpong is quieter (with far less Indian and foreign tourists), cheaper, warmer, smaller and flatter than Darjeeling, but is not as pretty and has fewer attractions.

Refer to History under Darjeeling earlier in this chapter about the possible activities of the Gorkhaland Liberation Organisation (GLO).

Information

The staff at the Darjeeling Gorkha Hill Council (DGHC) Tourist Reception Centre (☎ 57992), on DB Giri Rd, can't be too bothered with lots of questions from visitors, but it can arrange rafting trips and offer a left-luggage service. It's open from about 9 am to about 5 pm daily. Useful information is also available on the private Web site (www.kalimpong.org).

There is nowhere to change money: State Bank of India and Central Bank of India, both along Main (SDB Giri) Rd, will not. Mid-range and top-end hotels can usually change money for guests. The Odyssey Internet Cafe, upstairs in the shopping complex on the corner of Main (SDB Giri) and Rishi Rds, is the best place to send/receive email. It charges a reasonable Rs 1 per minute.

There is nowhere in Kalimpong to obtain permits for Sikkim, but free two-day extendable permits are available at the border at Rangpo (see the Sikkim chapter for details). Otherwise, get a permit in Darjeeling (see that section for details).

Gompas & Temples

Built in 1926, **Tharpa Choling Gompa** belongs to the Yellow Hat (Gelukpa) sect of Tibetan Buddhism, ie, the sect led by the Dalai Lama. It's a 45-minute walk (uphill) from town; head up Tripai Rd, turn right at KD Pradhan Rd and take the path to the right just before the Milk Collection and Extension Wing Building.

Lower down the hill, **Thongsa Gompa** (Bhutanese Monastery) is the oldest monastery in the area and was founded in 1692. The present building isn't so old, however: the original was destroyed by the Gurkhas during their rampage across Sikkim before the arrival of the British. Visitors are welcome.

Kalimpong's largest monastery, **Zong Dog Palri Fo-Brang Gompa**, is built on top of the spectacular Durpin Hill (1372m). In 1976, it was consecrated by the Dalai Lama, who donated a rare 108-volume edition of The Kangyur to the library. It also has impressive wall paintings in the prayer room, and a rare three dimensional mandala upstairs. The monastery is about 5km south of the town centre, and only accessible by chartered jeep. There are wonderful views from the unsigned **Jelepla Viewpoint**, about 300m below the gompa (look for the steps). Nearby, the DGHC's ***traditional tea house*** offers fine tea and meals, and exceptional vistas. This area is a military camp, but visitors are free to walk and drive around.

Mangal Dham, along Relli Rd, is a large and majestic temple. It is sacred to Krishna and notable for its contemporary architecture featuring white marble. It was closed at the time of research, but will re-open sometime in the future.

Dr Graham's Home

This orphanage and school was built in 1900 by a Scottish missionary, JA Graham, to educate the children of tea garden workers,

RICHARD I'ANSON

RICHARD I'ANSON

SARA-JANE CLELAND

RICHARD I'ANSON

Top & middle right: Darjeeling is home to mountain people from all over the eastern Himalaya.
Middle left: The Dussehra festival celebrates Durga's victory over the buffalo-headed demon.
Bottom: People have long come to Darjeeling to escape the heat of the North Indian plains.

LINDSAY BROWN

RICHARD I'ANSON

Top: Straddling a ridge and surrounded by tea plantations, Darjeeling commands a spectacular location, with magnificent views to the snowy peaks of Kanchenjunga.
Bottom: Elaborate paintwork adorns the walls of Ghoom Gompa, Darjeeling

and it now has more than 1300 students. The **chapel** above the school dates from 1925, and features fine stained-glass windows. (If the caretaker is around, he'll open the chapel.) Visitors are also welcome to visit the fine **school building**. Some visitors bring a picnic lunch to eat in the grounds.

The complex is about 3km up the *very* steep KD Pradhan Rd. It's really only accessible by chartered taxi or jeep, but it's a charming walk back to town.

Other Attractions

Kalimpong produces about 80% of India's gladioli, and is also an important orchid-growing area (flowers are exported from here to many cities in northern India). **Universal Nursery** is one of the more extensive nurseries in the region, but like most others it's more interested in serious customers than curious tourists. It's along Rishi Rd, about 3km from the town centre.

Deolo Hill (1704m) is surrounded by two reservoirs which provide water to the town. It offers fine views over Kalimpong and Sikkim on a clear day, and there's a ***chai stall*** at the end of the road. The small Hindu **Durga Mandir** is a short walk south-east from the hill. Deolo is about 8km from town along a steep, windy road. It's accessible by chartered taxi/jeep, and is a one-hour walk from Dr Graham's Home (but ask a lot of directions).

The **Nature Interpretation Centre** consists of a number of well-organised dioramas depicting the effects of human activity

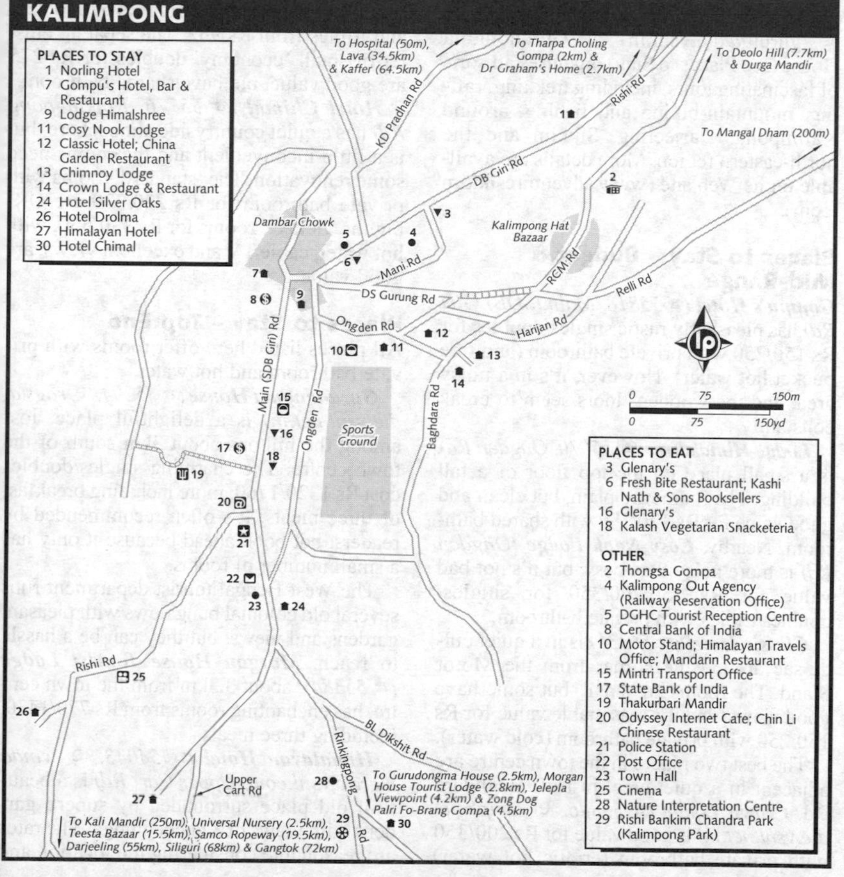

on the environment. It's an easy walk from the town centre along Rinkingpong Rd, and is open from 10 am to 1.30 pm and 2 to 4 pm daily, except Thursday. Admission is free. About 100m farther up the hill is the small but serene **Rishi Bankim Chandra Park** (also known as Kalimpong Park).

Organised Tours

Unlike Darjeeling, all of Kalimpong's attractions are accessible by road, and many are within walking distance of the town centre. The tourist office offers a half-day '11 point' sightseeing tour for Rs 400 per vehicle if there's enough demand (which is rare). This sort of tour can easily be arranged for about Rs 350 per vehicle through your hotel or a jeep agency at the Motor Stand, such as Himalayan Travels (☎ 55023).

Gurudongma Tours & Travels (☎ 55204, ⓔ gurutt@dte.vsnl.in) at Gurudongma House (see Places to Stay) organises all sorts of fascinating tours, including trekking, rafting, mountain-biking and fishing, around Kalimpong, Darjeeling, Sikkim and the north-eastern region. More details are available on its Web site (www.adventuresikkim.com).

Places to Stay – Budget & Mid-Range

Gompu's Hotel *(☎ 55818, Main (SDB) Giri Rd)* has pleasantly rustic singles/doubles for Rs 150/250 with private bathroom (and free bucket hot water). However, it's in a noisy area, and the wooden floors seem to creak constantly.

Lodge Himalshree *(☎ 55070, Ongden Rd)* is a small place on the top floor of a tall building. The rooms are plain, but clean and good value for Rs 120/180 with shared bathroom. Nearby, ***Cosy Nook Lodge*** *(Ongden Rd)* is more noisy than cosy, but it's not bad value for Rs 150/200/350 for singles/doubles/triples with private bathroom.

Classic Hotel *(☎ 56335)* is in a quiet cul-de-sac around the corner from the Motor Stand. The rooms are small, but some have good views, and it's reasonable value for Rs 150/250 with private bathroom (cold water).

The best two places in the town centre are adjacent in a quiet area, just off Baghdara Rd. ***Crown Lodge*** *(☎ 55846, ⓔ rampkg@dte.vsnl.net.in)* is good value for Rs 200/350 with private bathroom (erratic hot water) and cable TV. ***Chimnoy Lodge*** *(☎ 56264)* has tiny singles for Rs 150, and better doubles from Rs 250 to 300 (depending on the view) with cable TV – all rooms have private bathroom, with squat toilets and cold water. The helpful owner can organise tours and transport.

Norling Hotel *(☎ 57354, DB Giri Rd)* is run by a friendly Tibetan family. Clean rooms with private bathroom (hot water and squat toilet), cable TV and views cost Rs 250/350/450 for singles/doubles/triples, but the road is noisy at times.

Hotel Drolma *(☎ 55968, fax 55290, Rishi Rd)* is a renovated bungalow, which still exudes some old-fashioned charm, set in lovely gardens. The rooms around the communal TV lounge are unexciting, however, and a little pricey: doubles with private bathroom (hot water) range from Rs 620 to 825, and triples from Rs 962. The separate cluster of small 'economy' doubles for Rs 275 are good value, but have shared bathroom.

Hotel Chimal *(☎ 55776, Rinkingpong Rd)* has a quiet countryside atmosphere, but is a little inconvenient and the rooms need some renovation. The 'standard' rooms with private bathroom for Rs 220/330 are OK, but the 'deluxe' rooms for Rs 330/550, with hot water, cable TV and excellent views, are good value.

Places to Stay – Top End

All places listed here offer rooms with private bathroom and hot water.

Gurudongma House *(☎ 55204, ⓔ rags@dte.vsnl.net.in)* is a delightful place, lost among the hilltops about 3km south of the town centre. The charming singles/doubles cost Rs 1320/1760; more including breakfast or three meals. It's often recommended by readers, but book ahead because it only has a small number of rooms.

The West Bengal tourist department runs several old colonial bungalows with pleasant gardens and views, but they can be a hassle to reach. ***Morgan House Tourist Lodge*** *(☎ 55384)*, about 3.3km from the town centre, has enchanting rooms from Rs 770/1430, including three meals.

Himalayan Hotel *(☎ 54043, ⓔ windamere@vsnl.com, Upper Cart Rd)* is a beautiful old place surrounded by superb gardens with views of Kanchenjunga. The rates are reasonable considering the location and luxury: Rs 1430/2200 – but a lot more if you include all meals.

Hotel Silver Oaks *(☎ 55296, fax 55368, Rinkingpong Rd)*, once the home of a British family, is now a pretty hotel with delightful gardens. The rooms cost US$92/99, and are spacious, bright, well furnished and offer views of the valley or Kanchenjunga.

Places to Eat

Kalimpong cheese is a local speciality introduced by the Jesuits who established a dairy there. The dairy has since closed, but cheese is still produced in the area. Kalimpong lollipops are another speciality introduced by the sweet-toothed Jesuits. Both are available at shops around Dambar Chowk.

Glenary's (which is deservedly popular in Darjeeling) has two bakeries in Kalimpong: one on DB Giri Rd and another on Main (SDB Giri) Rd. Both serve pastries, cakes, burgers and small pizzas, and have informal eating areas inside.

Kalash Vegetarian Snacketeria *(Main (SDB Giri) Rd)* offers all sorts of meals and snacks, from pizzas to momos, but it's probably best to stick with what it does best: south Indian dosas, and hearty thalis (about Rs 35).

Gompu's Bar & Restaurant, in the hotel of the same name at Dambar Chowk, serves tasty meals, including breakfast, and is also a cheap and cheerful bar. ***Crown Restaurant***, next to the Crown Lodge off Baghdara Rd, has good service, pleasant decor and hearty meals from Rs 40.

For authentic Chinese food, try ***Mandarin Restaurant*** at the Motor Stand; ***Chin Li Chinese Restaurant***, on the ground floor of the shopping complex on the corner of Main (SDB Giri) and Rishi Rds; or the classy ***China Garden Restaurant***, in the hotel of the same name near the Motor Stand.

Fresh Bite Restaurant, above Kashi Nath & Sons Booksellers on DB Giri Rd, is a cosy place. The range of meals is impressive, the service is friendly and the prices are good.

Shopping

The Kalimpong Hat Bazaar market along Harijan Rd is held on Wednesday and Saturday, and is a great place to watch locals from nearby villages, often dressed in traditional gear. Several souvenir shops selling Tibetan jewellery and handicrafts are located around the streets in Dambar Chowk.

Getting There & Away

Air The nearest airport is at Bagdogra, near Siliguri (see Siliguri & New Jalpaiguri earlier in this chapter for details).

Bus, Taxi & Jeep All long-distance buses and jeeps leave from the Motor Stand. Taxis and jeeps can be chartered for local trips from along Main (SDB Giri) Rd.

To Siliguri (Rs 45, three hours), buses leave every 30 minutes or so from one of the agencies around the Motor Stand. A share-jeep to Siliguri costs Rs 40 (for the back seat) or Rs 50 (front seat); or about Rs 500 to charter it. The road to Siliguri follows the Teesta River after the bridge, so it's much cheaper and quicker than going via Darjeeling.

To Gangtok, via Rangpo, several agencies offer two or three buses each (Rs 55, three to four hours) every morning – these can (and should) be booked in advance. A shared/chartered jeep to Gangtok (three hours) costs Rs 70/700.

To Darjeeling (three hours), jeeps leave regularly, and cost Rs 50 (back seat) or Rs 65 (front); about Rs 700 if chartered. A bus (Rs 42, 3½ hours) also leaves for Darjeeling at about 8 am.

From the Himalayan Travels office at the Motor Stand, there's a daily (7.30 am) service to Kakarbhitta (Rs 65, five hours) on the border with Nepal, but jeeps (Rs 70/700 shared/chartered) are more frequent. Himalayan Travels, and Mintri Transport (☎ 55744) on Main (SDB Giri) Rd, provide buses to Bagdogra airport (Rs 120, three hours) at about 7 am. Mintri Transport can also book regional flights, including around Nepal.

Bhutan From Kalimpong, it's possible to visit Phuentsholing, just over the Bhutanese border. Although no permits are currently required for Phuentsholing, you *must* get a visa at least 15 days before your trip from a registered travel agency listed under the Tourism Authority of Bhutan (TAB). A bus leaves Kalimpong for Jaigaon (Rs 95, eight hours), on the Indian side of the border, at about 9 am daily. There are hotels and guesthouses in Phuentsholing, but not Jaigaon.

Train Bookings for trains from New Jalpaiguri station are possible at the Kalimpong Out Agency (☎ 55643) on Mani Rd. (Walk up the steps behind the building with the relevant sign along DS Gurung Rd.) The agency only has a small quota of tickets – mostly 2nd-class sleepers – and is open from 10 am to 1 pm and 4 to 5 pm daily.

AROUND KALIMPONG

Teesta Bazaar

About 16km from Kalimpong where the road divides for Darjeeling and Siliguri, Teesta Bazaar is becoming a centre for white-water rafting (see White-Water Rafting under Darjeeling earlier in this chapter).

The DGHC arranges trips from its office (☎ 09252-68261) in Chitrey Wayside Inn, about 1.5km up from Teesta Bazaar along the road to Gangtok and Kalimpong. It charges from Rs 350 (1½ hours) to Rs 650 (three hours), including equipment and guide, but not food or transport. Bookings can also be made at the DGHC tourist offices in Darjeeling and Kalimpong.

Chitrey Wayside Inn (☎ 09252-68261) offers dorm beds for Rs 80 per person, and pleasant doubles with private bathroom for Rs 365. It also has a ***restaurant***. Teesta Bazaar is about two hours from Darjeeling; take any bus or share-jeep (Rs 40) to Kalimpong.

Lava & Kaffer

About 35km east of Kalimpong, Lava (2353m) is a small village with a Kagyupa **gompa** and a bustling **market** on Tuesday. The summit of Kanchenjunga can be seen from Kaffer (1555m), also known as Lolegaon, about 30km farther east.

Dafay Munal Tourist Lodge at Kaffer is run by the DGHC. It charges Rs 450 for doubles with a private bathroom and cable TV. Dorms are usually available for Rs 50 per person.

Himalayan Travels at the Motor Stand in Kalimpong has two buses a day (8 am and 1 pm) to Kaffer (Rs 35, four hours), via Lava (Rs 21, 2½ hours)

Samco Ropeway

Thrill seekers should head for the Samthar Agriculture Marketing Co-operative (Samco) ropeway (chair lift), installed as part of an aid program to help villagers, and their produce, travel about 1.5km across, and some 40m above, the Teesta and Relli Rivers. At the other end, it's possible to walk around Samthar Plateau. However, if the idea of dangling from a piece of wire doesn't entice, give this a miss – it's definitely not for vertigo sufferers!

The ropeway operates from about 8 am to 4 pm daily, but usually not on Sunday. It's 20km from Kalimpong, along the main Siliguri-Gangtok road at a place known as 27th Mile. From Kalimpong, catch any bus/jeep towards Siliguri (about Rs 23, one hour).

Samthar Plateau

This gorgeous area offers awesome mountain views, traditional villages and forests – all ideal for short hikes.

Farm House has huts, rooms and camping in existing tents – ring Gurudongma House (see Places to Stay under Kalimpong earlier) for current rates and bookings. The occasional share-jeep (Rs 65, three hours) makes the journey from Kalimpong; alternatively, use the scary Samco Ropeway.

Orissa

The tropical state of Orissa lies along the eastern seaboard of India, on the Bay of Bengal. Its main attractions are what the tourist authorities call the 'Golden Triangle', ie, the temples of the capital Bhubaneswar, the long sandy beach at Puri and the majestic Sun Temple at Konark. Also increasingly popular these days are the Adivasi (tribal) areas of the south-west and the national parks to the north, but these places are difficult to reach for independent travellers.

Orissa is predominantly rural, with fertile green coastal plains rising to the hills of the Eastern Ghats. The state is also rich in minerals and a big exporter of iron ore. Orissa's economy is often destabilised by natural disasters, although flooding in the Mahanadi Delta, which used to occur regularly, has been much reduced by the building of Hirakud Dam, near Sambalpur.

The people of Orissa – of which about 25% are Adivasi – are very friendly and hospitable, and the atmosphere of the state is generally relaxed and safe. Orissa is also a great place to pick up souvenirs.

Cyclones & Droughts

A devastating cyclone lashed the state's coastal areas in October 1999. Officially, 9524 people died (the unofficial estimate is at least 50,000), about one million were left homeless and about 19 million were affected in some way.

The tidal waves (some of which reached 15km inland) destroyed thousands of hectares of rice, and other crops could not be harvested because of the death of draught animals. The subsequent high levels of saline in the soil, and the destruction of irrigation systems, paradoxically led to a severe drought in late 2000. This in turn caused mass migration from rural areas to the cities, an intolerable strain on natural water resources and widespread starvation.

In October 2000 another potentially destructive cyclone threatened the Orissan coast, but thankfully it stayed out to sea and soon dissipated.

These days, there is little evidence of the cyclone or drought in the main tourist areas, except for the eerie topless trees dotted along the road between Puri and Konark.

Orissa at a Glance

Population: 36.7 million
Area: 155,707 sq km
Capital: Bhubaneswar
Main Language: Oriya
When to Go: Nov to Mar

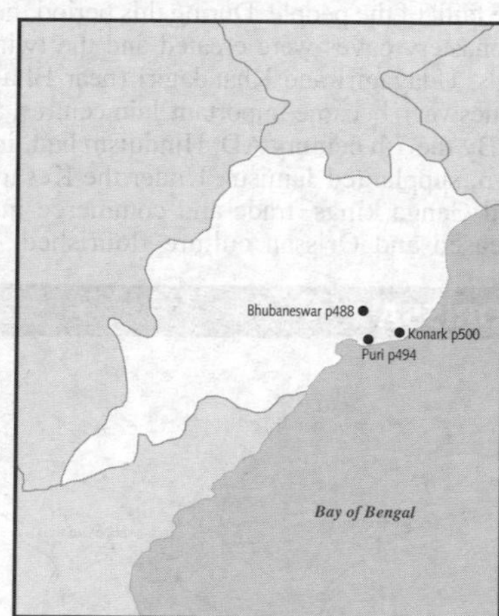

- Marvel at the erotic carvings of the mystery-shrouded Sun Temple at Konark
- Spot elephants and tigers among beautiful forests at Similipal National Park
- Witness the colourful spectacle of the Rath Yatra at Puri
- Wander around the myriad of Hindu temples in the capital Bhubaneswar
- Admire the abundant bird life in one of Asia's largest lakes at Chilka Lake
- Walk, swim and relax at the delightful seaside village of Gopalpur-on-Sea

History

Although known throughout the ancient world as a formidable maritime empire, with trading routes stretching to Bali, Sumatra and Java in Indonesia, the history of Orissa (once called 'Kalinga') is a little hazy until the demise of the Kalinga dynasty in 260 BC.

Near modern Bhubaneswar, Kalinga was conquered in a bloody battle by the great Indian emperor Ashoka. Appalled at the carnage, Ashoka forswore violence and converted to Buddhism, which he subsequently assisted in spreading to Sri Lanka and East Asia.

Around the 1st century BC, under the rule of Kharavela, the third Chedi king, Buddhism declined and Jainism was restored as the faith of the people. During this period the monastery caves were created and the twin hills, Udayagiri and Khandagiri (near Bhubaneswar), became important Jain centres.

By the 7th century AD, Hinduism had, in turn, supplanted Jainism. Under the Kesari and Ganga kings, trade and commerce increased and Orissan culture flourished – countless temples from that classical period stand today. The Orissans defied the Muslim rulers in Delhi until the region finally fell to the Mughals during the 16th century, when many of Bhubaneswar's temples were destroyed. Since then, Orissa has been successively ruled by Afghans, Marathas and the British (from 1803 to Independence).

In the last few years, a Hindu fundamentalist group, Bajrang Dal, has undertaken a violent campaign against Christians, mainly because of the missionaries success in converting the poor, especially in the tribal areas. In January 1999, an Australian missionary and his two sons were burnt alive while sleeping in their car. These activities resulted in the recent formation of a Christian youth group called Rashtriya Surakshya

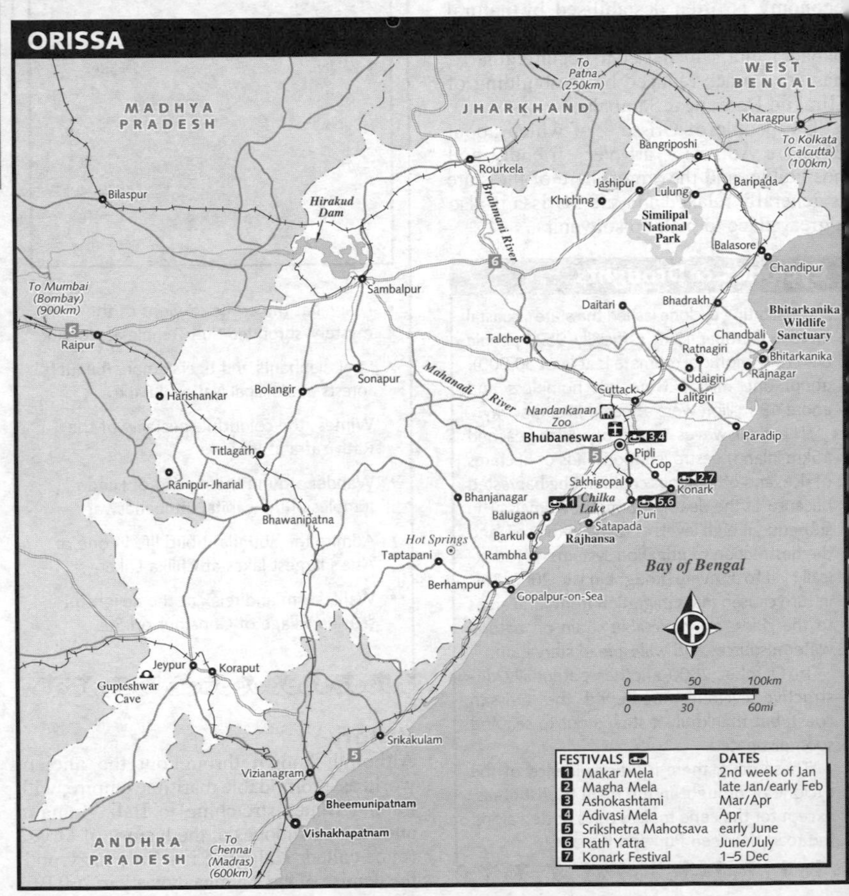

Vahni to 'protect' Christians, but this will possibly exacerbate the problem. Neither group specifically targets tourists, however.

The recent creation of Jharkhand state from neighbouring Bihar has increased the calls for the separate tribal-oriented state of Koshal, with Sambalpur the capital. Thankfully, no group has undertaken any violence to support this cause (so far).

Shopping

Orissa offers a very wide and distinctive selection of handicrafts. The gorgeous applique work of Pipli (near Bhubaneswar) features brightly coloured patches of fabric; Raghurajpur (near Puri) is famous for its *patachitra* (paintings on specially prepared cloth); and Cuttack is known for its exquisitely delicate silver filigree jewellery and ornaments.

More than 300,000 Orissans work as handloom weavers, producing numerous types of unique Orissan fabrics in silk and cotton. Sambalpur specialises in tie-dye and *ikat* fabrics, which involves tie-dying the thread before it's woven to produce material with an attractive pattern.

In Puri, brightly coloured carved wooden replicas of Jagannath and his two siblings are popular souvenirs; and at Balasore (in the north), lacquered children's toys and wooden masks are produced. Other favoured mementoes from around Orissa include horoscopes, religious texts and intricate images from the Kamasutra painstakingly inscribed or painted on palm leaves.

BHUBANESWAR

☎ 0674 • pop 528,390

With a juxtaposition of modern buildings and ancient temples, Bhubaneswar is a reasonably pleasant and manageable city, with enough to justify a stopover for a day or two. It's also a useful base for day trips to Dhauli, Nandankanan zoo and Cuttack.

Information

The Orissa Tourism Development Corporation (OTDC; ☎ 431299, ⓔ orotur@dte.vsnl.net.in) office is down a laneway by the Panthanivas Tourist Bungalow off Lewis Rd, but is not particularly helpful. It's open from 10 am to 5 pm daily, except Sunday. The OTDC counters at the airport (☎ 534006) and train station (☎ 404715, open 24 hours) can also handle bookings for OTDC hotels, bus trips and tours. OTDC also has a useful Web site (www.orissa-tourism.com).

The Government of India tourist office (☎ 432203) is not far from the museum, and signposted from Lewis Rd.

The State Bank of India on Raj Path provides quick and painless exchange for cash and travellers cheques. Some mid-range and top-end hotels also change money for guests.

The General Post Office, inconveniently located along National Hwy No 5, has the poste restante. A more convenient post office is in the Market Building, near Raj Path. The best Internet centre is Net4U, next to Hotel Sahara along Raj Path. It charge Rs 10 per 15 minutes.

Modern Book Depot, at Station Square, has a reasonable selection of maps and English-language books.

Temples

Some visitors may find that Lingaraj Mandir and the other smaller temples dotted around nearby Bindu Sagar are enough. If you wish to see a few more, then walk

Orissan Temple Architecture

All Orissan temples – whether it's the mighty Lingaraj Mandir (Bhubaneswar), Jagannath Mandir (Puri), Sun Temple (Konark) or one of the many smaller temples around the state – follow a similar architectural design. Basically, there are two structures: the *jagamohan* (assembly hall); and the *deul*, where the image of the temple deity is kept and above which the temple tower rises. The design is complicated in larger temples by the addition of other entrance halls in front of the jagamohan: the *bhoga-mandapa* (hall of offering) and *natamandir* (dancing hall).

The whole structure may be enclosed by an outer wall, and within the enclosure there may be smaller, subsidiary temples and shrines. The most notable aspects of the temple design are the soaring tower and the intricate carvings that cover every surface. These may be figures of gods, men and women, plants and trees, flowers, animals and every other aspect of everyday life. To some visitors, however, it's the erotic carvings which create the greatest interest, such as those at Konark, where the close-up detail is every bit as interesting as the temple's sheer size.

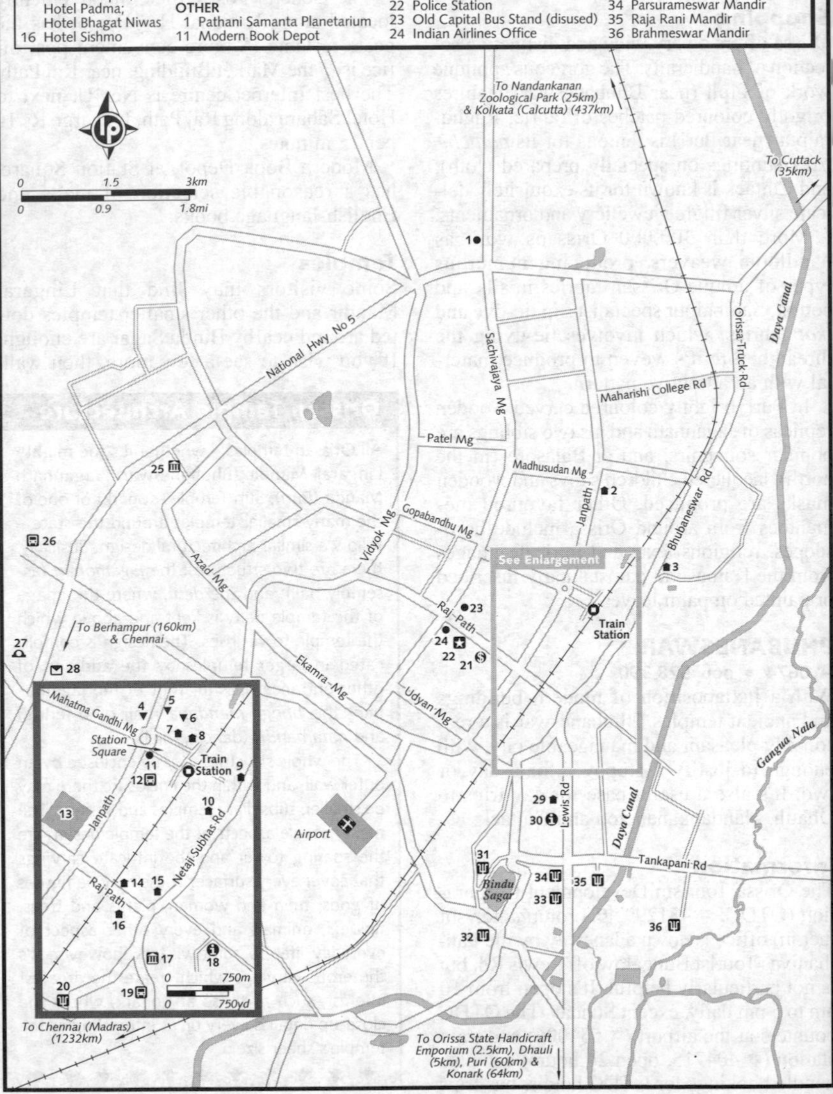
BHUBANESWAR
PLACES TO STAY
2 Hotel Prachi
3 Jatri Nivas
7 Hotel Keshari
8 Hotel Richi
9 Hotel Swagat
10 Bhubaneswar Hotel
14 Hotel Sahara; Park Inn Bar & Restaurant; Net4U
15 Hotel Pushpak; Hotel Padma; Hotel Bhagat Niwas
16 Hotel Sishmo
29 Panthanivas Tourist Bungalow & Maloki Restaurant; OTDC Bus Office
PLACES TO EAT
4 Bhuvanashree Vegetarian Restaurant
5 Brown & Cream; Hotel Swosti; Swosti Travels Office
6 Banjara Restaurant
OTHER
1 Pathani Samanta Planetarium
11 Modern Book Depot
12 City Bus Stand
13 Market Building; Suruchi Food Plaza; Post Office; Orissa State Handloom Cooperative (Utkalika)
17 State Museum
18 Government of India Tourist Office
19 Bus Stand (for Cuttack & Puri)
20 Maussi Maa Mandir
21 State Bank of India
22 Police Station
23 Old Capital Bus Stand (disused)
24 Indian Airlines Office
25 Scheduled Tribes Research & Training Centre
26 Baramunda Bus Station
27 Udayagiri & Khandagiri Caves
28 General Post Office
30 Orissa Tourism Development Corporation (OTDC)
31 Vaital Mandir
32 Lingaraj Mandir
33 Mukteswar & Siddheswar Mandir; Kedargauri Mandir; Raghunath Crafts
34 Parsurameswar Mandir
35 Raja Rani Mandir
36 Brahmeswar Mandir
To Nandankanan Zoological Park (25km) & Kolkata (Calcutta) (437km)
To Cuttack (35km)
0 1.5 3km
0 0.9 1.8mi
National Hwy No 5
Sachivalaya Mg
Orissa Truck Rd
Daya Canal
Maharishi College Rd
Patel Mg
Madhusudan Mg
Janpath
Bhubaneswar Rd
Vidyok Mg
Gopabandhu Mg
Azad Mg
See Enlargement
Train Station
Raj Path
To Berhampur (160km) & Chennai
Ekamra Mg
Udyan Mg
Gangua Nala
Mahatma Gandhi Mg
Station Square
Netaji Subhas Rd
Airport
Lewis Rd
Tankapani Rd
Bindu Sagar
0 750m
0 750yd
To Chennai (Madras) (1232km)
To Orissa State Handicraft Emporium (2.5km), Dhauli (5km), Puri (60km) & Konark (64km)

from Bindu Sagar to the cluster of temples west of Lewis Rd. To see all of the major temples, charter an autorickshaw from the city centre for two to three hours (about Rs 150), or take one to Bindu Sagar and then a cycle-rickshaw between each temple. The organised tour offered by the OTDC (see Organised Tours later in this chapter) includes reasonably long stops at Lingaraj and Mukteswar temples.

At the southern end of the entry road to Bindu Sagar is a large map showing the location of all local temples. The only temple that non-Hindus are not allowed to enter is Lingaraj; and the only one that charges an entrance fee is Raja Rani. There are plenty of places to eat and drink near each temple.

Bindu Sagar Also known as Ocean Drop Tank, it is said to contain water from every holy stream, pool and tank in India – so it's obviously a good place to wash away sin. A number of temples and shrines are scattered around the tank, several with towers imitating the ones at Lingaraj Mandir. In the tank's centre there is a water pavilion where once a year the Lingaraj Mandir's deity is brought for ritual bathing.

Lingaraj Mandir This 54m-high temple is dedicated to Tribhuvaneswar (Lord of the Three Worlds), also known as Bhubaneswar. Its present form dates from 1090 to 1104, although parts of it are over 1400 years old. The granite block, representing Tribhuvaneswar, is apparently bathed daily with water, milk and *bhang* (marijuana). The temple compound is about 150m square, and more than 50 smaller temples and shrines crowd the enclosure. In the north-east corner, the small temple to Parvati is interesting.

However, because the temple is surrounded by a wall and closed to non-Hindus, foreigners can only see it from a viewing platform – which is still worthwhile. Face the temple's main entrance, walk around to the right and ask directions to the laneway leading to the back of the temple and the viewing platform. You'll be asked for a 'donation' and shown a book to 'prove' that some people give over Rs 1000. How much you give is up to you, of course, but Rs 5 to 10 is enough.

Vaital Mandir This temple has a double-storey 'wagon roof' influenced by Buddhist cave architecture. It dates from the 8th century, and was a centre of Tantric worship. The presiding deity Chamunda (Kali) can be seen in the dingy interior, although her necklace of skulls and the corpse on which she sits are usually hidden beneath her temple robes.

Parsurameswar Mandir Just west of Lewis Rd is a cluster of about 20 smaller temples, including some of the most important in Bhubaneswar. The best preserved of these early temples is Parsurameswar Mandir, a small, single and ornate Shiva temple built in about AD 650. It has lively bas-reliefs of elephant and horse processions, lattice windows and Shiva images.

Mukteswar, Siddheswar & Kedargauri Mandirs Not far from Parsurameswar is the small 10th-century Mukteswar Mandir, one of the most ornate temples in the capital. The finely detailed carvings show a mixture of Buddhist, Jain and Hindu styles, but unfortunately some of the figures have been defaced. The ceiling carvings are particularly striking and the stone arch is revered for its architectural style. In front of the temple is a beautiful arched *torana* (architrave) clearly showing a Buddhist influence.

In the same compound, Siddheswar Mandir was built later than Mukteswar and is plainer, but has a fine standing Ganesh figure.

Across the path from Mukteswar, Kedargauri Mandir is one of the oldest temples in Bhubaneswar, although it has been substantially rebuilt.

Raja Rani Mandir This temple, built circa AD 1100 and surrounded by relaxing gardens, is famous for its ornate *deul* (place where the image of the temple deity is kept). Around the compass points there are pairs of statues representing the eight *dikpalas* (temple guardians), who protect the temple. Between them, nymphs, embracing couples, elephants and lions fill the niches and decorate the pillars. The complex is open from 6 am to 6 pm daily, and entry costs Rs 2.

Brahmeswar Mandir Standing in a courtyard flanked by four smaller structures, the 9th-century Brahmeswar Mandir is a smaller version of Lingaraj Mandir. It's notable for its finely detailed sculptures with erotic and sometimes amusing elements.

State Museum

This museum (and landmark) on Lewis Rd is worth a visit. It boasts a rich collection of rare palm-leaf manuscripts, traditional and folk musical instruments, Bronze-Age tools, an armoury and a fascinating display of Orissan tribal anthropology.

The natural history collection is also impressive, and most exhibits still retain their fur and feathers. The magnificent collection of Buddhist and Jain sculptures, which are displayed in chronological order, constitute the most important antiquities in the museum. It also boasts a gallery displaying the works of contemporary Orissan artists.

The museum is open from 10 am to 5 pm daily, except Monday. Tickets (Rs 1) are not sold between 1 and 2 pm, although the museum stays open at this time and visitors with tickets can still wander around.

Scheduled Tribes Research & Training Centre

Although this place (Museum of Man; ☎ 461635) is primarily an anthropological research centre, visitors are welcome. The outdoor display of indigenous Orissan housing was destroyed during the 1999 cyclone, but should be worth visiting when repaired. Buses between the city centre and Baramunda bus station pass by the centre; otherwise, charter an autorickshaw for about Rs 30.

Udayagiri & Khandagiri Caves

A few kilometres west of the city centre are two hills facing each other riddled with caves (most of which are numbered). Many caves are ornately carved, and most are thought to have been chiselled out for Jain ascetics in the 1st century BC. The hills are also wonderful spots to watch the sun rise or set.

Udayagiri (Sunrise Hill), to the north of the approach road, has the more interesting caves. At the base of the hill, and to the right is the two-storey **Rani ka Naur** (Queen's Palace Cave; cave 1). Both levels have eight entrances and the cave is extensively carved.

Return to the road via **Chota Hathi Gumpha** (3), with its carvings of elephants coming out from behind a tree. **Jaya Vijaya Cave** (5) is double-storeyed, and a bodhi tree is carved in the central compartment.

Back at the entrance, ascend the hill to **Swargapuri** (9) and **Hathi Gumpha** (Elephant Cave; 14). The latter is plain, but a 117-line inscription relates the exploits of its builder, King Kharaveli of Kalinga, who ruled from 168 to 153 BC.

Around the hill to the right, is the single-storeyed **Ganesh Gumpha** (10), which is almost directly above Rani ka Naur. The carvings tell the same tale as in the lower level cave, but are better made. Retrace your steps to Hathi Gumpha (14), then on to **Pavana Gumpha** (Cave of Purification), and the small **Sarpa Gumpha** (Serpent Cave), where the tiny door is surmounted by a three-headed cobra. About 15m from this is **Bagh Gumpha** (Tiger Cave; 12) – the entrance is through the mouth of the beast.

Across the road, **Khandagiri** offers a fine view back over Bhubaneswar from its summit. The steep path splits about one-third of the way up the hill. The right path goes to **Ananta Cave** (3), with its carved figures of athletes, women, elephants and geese carrying flowers. Further along is a series of **Jain temples** and, at the top, another Jain temple from the 18th century.

The whole complex (including all the caves) is open from 6 am to 6 pm daily. Entry is Rs 2. Guides are available for negotiable rates, but probably not worth hiring. An unimpressive government-run ***restaurant*** is nearby, and there are plenty of ***chai shops*** in the vicinity.

No public bus goes specifically to the caves, but plenty of buses (Rs 5) pass the nearby junction on National Hwy No 5. Alternatively, take an autorickshaw (about Rs 50 one way).

Pathani Samanta Planetarium

This surprisingly interesting planetarium on Sachivajaya Marg features 'out-of-this-world' shows every hour on the hour from 2 to 5 pm (4 pm in English); every day, except Monday. Tickets cost Rs 10.

Organised Tours

Bhubaneswar is not well set up for tourism, so if you want to organise a tour around Orissa, eg, to the tribal areas, consider doing it in Puri (a nicer place to stay anyway). Refer to boxed text 'The Adivasi' in the Puri section later in this chapter for information about tours to tribal areas.

One of the few travel agencies in the capital is Swosti Travels (☎ 508526, ⓔ swosti@cal.vsnl.net.in) in the Hotel Swosti complex on Janpath. It offers tours to tribal areas and Bhitarkanika Wildlife Sanctuary, but caters to upmarket tourists and charges accordingly. It has a Web site (www.swosti.com).

One agency recommended by readers is Travel Club (☎ 405830, fax 407819), which organises trips around tribal areas, Bhitarkanika and Similipal National Park.

The OTDC offers all-day city tours (except Monday), which include the Nandankanan zoo, Dhauli, the Lingaraj and Mukteswar temples, the State Museum and the Udayagiri and Khandagiri Caves (Rs 105 per person); and another day trip to Konark, Pipli and Puri (Rs 115). All tours require a minimum of five. Book at the OTDC offices/counters mentioned under Information earlier, or the OTDC bus office (☎ 431515) at the back of Panthanivas Tourist Bungalow on Lewis Rd.

Special Events

Bhubaneswar hosts a Hindu chariot race, Ashokashtami, at Lingaraj Mandir in March/April. In April, Bhubaneswar also hosts the Adivasi Mela, which features art, dance and handicrafts.

Places to Stay – Budget & Mid-Range

Like most of Orissa, hotel rates in Bhubaneswar drop 20% to 50% during the monsoons from June to September, so it always pays to ask for a discount. All places listed below include cable TV, a fan and private bathroom, unless stated otherwise.

Jatri Nivas *(☎ 575838, Bhubaneswar Rd)* is a friendly place, much like a youth hostel. Dormitory beds start from Rs 50 per person, but management claims that unused beds in the 18-bed dormitory must also be paid for! The normal rooms, which are grubby and have no TV, cost Rs 185 for triples with a shared bathroom and Rs 300 for nicer doubles with a private bathroom.

Three central, but noisy, places are located on Netaji Subhas Rd. ***Hotel Pushpak*** *(☎ 310185)* has double rooms for Rs 200, or Rs 300 with full board (ie, three meals), but the rooms are unexciting. Next door, ***Hotel Padma*** *(☎ 416626)* has two single rooms (without TV or private bathroom) for Rs 60, and many other good, clean doubles from Rs 160 to 200. Behind the Padma, ***Hotel Bhagwat Niwas*** has singles/doubles for Rs 160/250, but some are like cells.

Bhubaneswar Hotel *(☎ 416977, Netaji Subhas Rd)* is a flashy-looking place with a huge number of rooms, and surprisingly reasonable rates. A 'deluxe' room costs Rs 300/400 – some have balconies, and the management guarantees hot water. Cheaper rooms without TV start from Rs 125/175.

Hotel Swagat *(☎ 312686)* is just off Netaji Subhas Rd, so it's quiet. The rooms are large and clean, and range from Rs 175 for singles with a shared bathroom to Rs 275/300 for large 'deluxe' rooms with an 'air-cooler' (not an air-conditioner, but still refreshing) and private bathroom.

Hotel Sahara *(☎ 313631, Raj Path)* is central, clean, friendly and not too noisy. Small singles with a shared bathroom cost Rs 185, and huge, bright and airy doubles with a private bathroom are good value for Rs 395 (air-conditioned rooms cost about three times more).

Hotel Richi *(☎ 534619, Station Square)* is close to the train station and good value. Singles cost from Rs 220 to 250, and doubles, Rs 325 to 425 – and all rates include breakfast.

Although close to the temples, ***Panthanivas Tourist Bungalow*** *(☎ 432314, Lewis Rd)* is not great value, and has a nightmare checkout time (8 am). The large, musty doubles/triples cost Rs 375/450 (without TV), and doubles with air-con and TV cost from Rs 700.

Places to Stay – Top End

Hotel Keshari *(☎ 534994, e keshari@orissaindia.com, Station Square)* has all the inclusions expected of a three-star hotel, but the room rates are very reasonable and worth a splurge. A 'standard' room costs from Rs 675/775 for singles/doubles.

Hotel Sishmo *(☎ 433600, fax 433351, Raj Path)* is a luxurious place for Rs 2200/2900. One attraction is the swimming pool (which the public can use for Rs 100). Indian classical music recitals are sometimes held here in the evening.

Hotel Prachi *(☎ 522472, fax 503287, Janpath)* is a classy place with all mod-cons, but is overpriced from US$50/55. (Nonguests can use the swimming pool for Rs 100.)

Places to Eat

There are some cheap and acceptable ***south Indian eateries*** around the junction of Raj

ORISSA

Path and Janpath, and along the laneways behind Hotel Swosti. Most hotels listed have restaurants, some with attached bars (open to the public).

Suruchi Food Plaza, in the Market Building near Raj Path, is a little dark, but the food is tasty and cheap, and the service is good. The *thalis* (all-you-can-eat vegetarian plates) cost from Rs 25 and *dosas* (filled pancakes), from Rs 12, are popular among locals.

Brown & Cream, in the Hotel Swosti complex on Janpath, is the best place for pastries, cakes, sandwiches and burgers. Inside, there's a seating area. Prices start at Rs 3.

Park Inn Bar & Restaurant, next to Hotel Sahara on Raj Path, is one of the better hotel restaurants. The air-conditioning is freezing, but this keeps the beer cold! Meals range from Rs 15 to 65.

Maloki Restaurant, in Panthanivas Tourist Bungalow on Lewis Rd, is surprisingly good value (from Rs 30 per plate). You will inevitably end up there for lunch if you're on an OTDC 'city tour'.

Banjara Restaurant is along a laneway off Station Square. It's a no-frills place, popular with locals for the vast range of tasty food. A hearty meal costs about Rs 40.

Bhuvanashree Vegetarian Restaurant, on the corner of Janpath and Mahatma Gandhi Marg, offers a range of thalis from Rs 31 to 45 in a clean, comfortable setting.

Shopping

Orissan handicrafts, including applique and ikat work, can be bought at stalls and shops in and around the Market Building, near Raj Path, such as the Orissa State Handloom Cooperative (Utkalika). Other tourist-orientated souvenir shops – with prices to match – are the Orissa State Handicraft Emporium, on the road to Dhauli; and Raghunath Crafts, next to the entrance to Kedargauri Mandir.

Getting There & Away

Air Indian Airlines (☎ 530544), on Raj Path, has daily return flights between Bhubaneswar and Kolkata (Calcutta) for US$85 one way, and Bhubaneswar and Delhi (US $215); and flights four times a week to/from Vizianagram (US$120), in Andhra Pradesh, and Chennai (Madras) for US$200. Indian Airlines also offers services *to* – but not *from* – Mumbai (Bombay) for US$250, and Hyderabad (US$160) three times a week.

Bus The Baramunda Bus Station is just off National Hwy No 5, about 6km west of the city centre. From there, buses go every 15 to 30 minutes to Cuttack (Rs 15, one hour), Puri (Rs 15, 1¼ hours) and Konark (Rs 18, 1½ hours); and to Berhampur (Rs 50, five hours), via Balugaon (Rs 30, three hours), about every hour. Daily, there are also two late-afternoon departures to Kolkata (Rs 140, 12 hours), several each evening to Sambalpur (Rs 100, nine hours) and infrequent services to Baripada (Rs 85, seven hours).

From its office at the back of Panthanivas Tourist Bungalow on Lewis Rd, the OTDC offers overnight buses to Sambalpur (Rs 110, eight hours) and morning services to Berhampur (Rs 65, four hours).

To add to the confusion, buses to Cuttack also leave from the City Bus Stand, just off Station Square; to Cuttack and Puri they also depart from the top of Lewis Rd; and to Nandankanan, they go from near Lingaraj Mandir and outside the Old Capital Bus Stand on Raj Path.

Train Bhubaneswar is on the main line between Kolkata and Chennai, so plenty of trains go to these two cities, and many start/finish at Puri. For example, the *Puri Express* and *Dhauli Express* travel every night to Kolkata for Rs 52/99/490 (2nd class/1st class/air-con); and to Chennai, the *Howrah Mail* travels every night for Rs 80/210/1050.

There are also regular services (often daily) to Guwahati (Assam), Bangalore and Delhi, via Agra. Local trains regularly go to Puri, Cuttack and Berhampur, but buses are far quicker and more frequent.

Getting Around

Biju Patnaik airport is very close to town. Because there's no bus service, a prepaid taxi from the airport to central Bhubaneswar costs between Rs 70 and 100; taxis also go to Cuttack (Rs 300), Puri (Rs 500) and Konark (Rs 500). Alternatively, cycle-rickshaws (about Rs 35) and autorickshaws (about Rs 80) also link the city with the airport, but you have to walk the last 500m between the airport entrance and terminal.

AROUND BHUBANESWAR

Dhauli

In about 260 BC, King Ashoka had his famous edicts carved onto a large **rock** at

Dhauli, 8km south of Bhubaneswar. After murdering several members of his family to gain power, then hundreds of thousands on the battlefield as he enlarged his empire, Ashoka finally 'saw the light' and converted to Buddhism. This fascinating history is detailed on several notice boards at the rock, which is located along the main road at the bottom of **Dhauli Hill**.

At the top of the hill is a huge, white **Shanti Stupa** (Peace Pagoda) built by the Japanese in the 1970s. Older Buddha figures are set into the modern structure.

The turn-off to Dhauli is along the main Bhubaneswar-Puri Rd, and accessible on any bus (Rs 5) going to Puri or Konark. From the turn-off, it's a flat 3km walk to the rock, and then a short, steep walk to the stupa. By autorickshaw, a one-way trip to the stupa costs about Rs 90.

Nandankanan Zoological Park

This zoo is famous for its white tigers. There were 28 (the largest number in the world) until mid-2000, when eight died. See Endangered Species in the Facts about India chapter for more information.

The zoo also boasts lions and all sorts of reptiles, monkeys and deers, among other creatures. Just inside the gate, the small **Nature Interpretation Centre** has some minor displays about Chilka Lake and the major national parks and reserves in Orissa. Other attractions include **elephant rides** (Rs 4 per person, but only between 3 and 4.30 pm); a fun **toy train** (Rs 5); and **boat rides** (from Rs 15 to 40 per person for 30 minutes). Also, a fantastic 'ropeway' (**cable car**) crosses a lake (Rs 22 return), allowing passengers to get off half-way and walk down (300m) to the **State Botanical Garden** nearby. The highlight for many is the short **lion safari** (Rs 6) and **tiger safari** (Rs 6) in an 'armoured bus'.

The zoo is open from 10 am to 5 pm daily, except Monday. Tickets cost Rs 40; use of a still/video camera costs an extra Rs 5/200. Guides are available – but unnecessary – and charge Rs 50 per small group for about 90 minutes. There are plenty of places to eat and drink outside – but not inside – the zoo.

It's best to allow at least a half-day, so avoid the OTDC bus tour because it only stops there for an hour or so. From Bhubaneswar, frequent public buses (Rs 15, one hour) leave from near Lingaraj Mandir and outside the Old Capital Bus Stand for Nandankanan village, about 400m from the entrance to the zoo.

PURI

☎ 06752 • pop 142,665

Puri, is one of the four *dhams* (holiest Hindu pilgrimage places in India), and Buddhists believe Puri is the hiding place for Buddha's tooth before it was spirited away to Kandy in Sri Lanka. Religious life in Puri revolves around the great Jagannath Mandir and its famous Rath Yatra (Car Festival) held in June or July, which is similar to the annual *perahera* (procession) in Kandy.

Puri's other attraction is its long sandy beach. Unfortunately, much of it is now heavily polluted, but Puri still draws large numbers of visitors, mostly Indians from Kolkata. Whatever the drawbacks, Puri is a friendly place with a relaxed atmosphere. Many foreign visitors end up suffering from a local disorder known as 'Puri paralysis': Once there, they fall into a state of inertia and find it difficult to leave!

Being a holy place, Puri is one of those delightfully eccentric Indian towns where the use of bhang is legal. However, it's *only* available in the few official 'bhang shops', and buying, trading and smoking it outside these shops is illegal. See Drugs in the Facts for the Visitor chapter for more information.

Information

The OTDC tourist office (☎ 22664), on Station Rd, is inconvenient, but is still worth

ORISSA

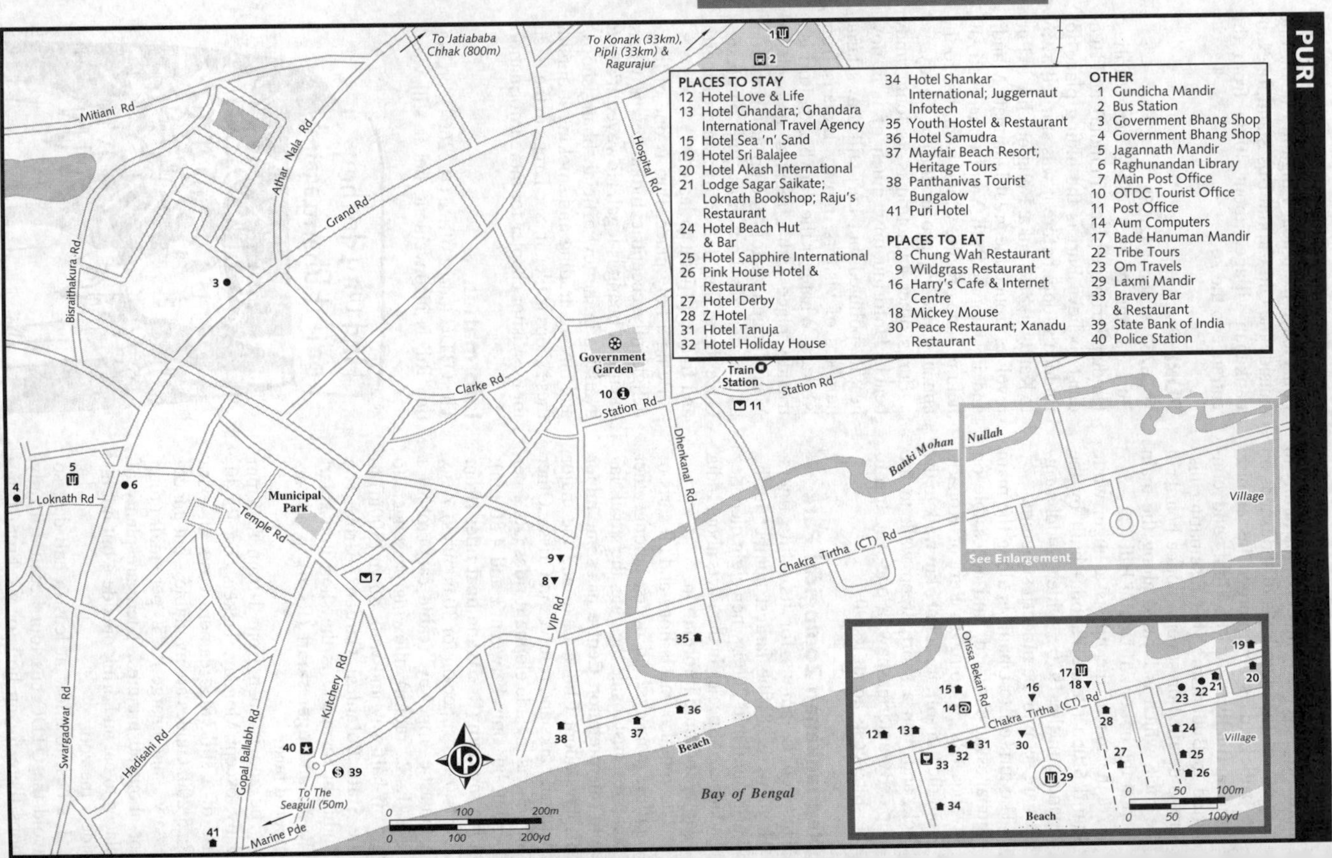
PURI
PLACES TO STAY
12 Hotel Love & Life
13 Hotel Ghandara; Ghandara International Travel Agency
15 Hotel Sea 'n' Sand
19 Hotel Sri Balajee
20 Hotel Akash International
21 Lodge Sagar Saikate; Loknath Bookshop; Raju's Restaurant
24 Hotel Beach Hut & Bar
25 Hotel Sapphire International
26 Pink House Hotel & Restaurant
27 Hotel Derby
28 Z Hotel
31 Hotel Tanuja
32 Hotel Holiday House
34 Hotel Shankar International; Juggernaut Infotech
35 Youth Hostel & Restaurant
36 Hotel Samudra
37 Mayfair Beach Resort; Heritage Tours
38 Panthanivas Tourist Bungalow
41 Puri Hotel
PLACES TO EAT
8 Chung Wah Restaurant
9 Wildgrass Restaurant
16 Harry's Cafe & Internet Centre
18 Mickey Mouse
30 Peace Restaurant; Xanadu Restaurant
OTHER
1 Gundicha Mandir
2 Bus Station
3 Government Bhang Shop
4 Government Bhang Shop
5 Jagannath Mandir
6 Raghunandan Library
7 Main Post Office
10 OTDC Tourist Office
11 Post Office
14 Aum Computers
17 Bade Hanuman Mandir
22 Tribe Tours
23 Om Travels
29 Laxmi Mandir
33 Bravery Bar & Restaurant
39 State Bank of India
40 Police Station
To Jatiababa Chhak (800m)
To Konark (33km), Pipli (33km) & Ragurajur
Mitiani Rd
Athar Nala Rd
Grand Rd
Hospital Rd
Bisraithakura Rd
Government Garden
Train Station
Station Rd
Clarke Rd
Banki Mohan
Nullah
Village
Loknath Rd
Municipal Park
Temple Rd
Dhenkanal Rd
Chakra Tirtha (CT) Rd
See Enlargement
VIP Rd
Kutchery Rd
Swargadwar Rd
Hadisahi Rd
Gopal Ballabh Rd
To The Seagull (50m)
Marine Pde
Beach
Bay of Bengal
0 100 200m
0 100 200yd
Orissa Bekari Rd
0 50 100m
0 50 100yd

visiting. The OTDC has a counter at the train station (☎ 23536), which can handle bookings for OTDC bus trips, tours and hotels.

The State Bank of India, on the corner of Chakra Tirtha (CT) and Kutchery Rds, changes cash and travellers cheques – eventually. Ghandara International travel agency, in the Hotel Ghandara complex on CT Rd, also changes cash and travellers cheques, but at about 5% lower than the normal bank rate. As a last resort, try an upmarket hotel.

A few Internet centres are located along, or just off CT Rd, eg, Harry's Cafe, Juggernaut Infotech and Aum Computers, but these are often small and access is expensive (about Rs 80 per hour).

Loknath Bookshop, near Lodge Sagar Saikate on CT Rd, is a good place to swap or buy second-hand books.

Jagannath Mandir

Because of this distinctive temple, Puri is one of the four dhams in India – the others are in Dwarka in Gujarat (in the west), Badrinath in Uttaranchal (north) and Rameswaram in Tamil Nadu (south). Jagannath Mandir's popularity among Hindus is partly due to the lack of caste distinctions – all Hindus are welcome inside (but non-Hindus are not).

The temple is dedicated to Jagannath, Lord of the Universe, who is an incarnation of Vishnu. It was built in its present form in 1198, and is protected by two surrounding walls. The conical tower of the temple is 58m high and topped by the flag and wheel of Vishnu, visible from far out to sea.

In front of the main entrance is a beautiful pillar, topped by an image of the Garuda, which originally stood in front of the Sun Temple at Konark. Guarded by two stone lions, the entrance is known as the Lion Gate and is used in the chariot procession. The southern, eastern and northern gates are guarded by statues of men on horseback, tigers and elephants respectively.

In the central jagamohan, pilgrims can see the images of Jagannath, his brother Balbhadra and sister Subhadra. The brothers have arms, but the smaller Subhadra does not. All three are garlanded and dressed for ceremonies and for the various seasons.

The temple employs about 6000 men to perform the temple functions and the complicated rituals involved in caring for the gods. An estimated 20,000 people – divided into 36 orders and 97 classes – are dependent on Jagannath for their livelihood and all are classed as the god's attendants.

Non-Hindus are not allowed inside the temple, but can partially observe it from the roof of the tallest building in the area, ie, the Raghunandan Library opposite (open from 9 am to 1 pm and 4 to 7 pm daily). The library provides great (free) views of the chaos on the street from the first floor. For views of the temple, ask permission from the librarian to climb to the top – if you do, a 'donation' is compulsory (about Rs 10). However, the views of the temple itself are limited and disappointing from anywhere inside the library.

Gundicha Mandir

Many other smaller temples around Puri (see the Puri map) can be visited by non-Hindus, but discretion is required and visitors should preferably be accompanied by a Hindu. Gundicha Mandir (Garden House) is where the images of the gods reside for seven days during Rath Yatra. The walls enclose a garden where the temple is built. It faces the bus station, and entrance costs Rs 1.

Beach & Village

Don't come to Puri expecting a tropical paradise – the beach is wide, exposed and there's not a scrap of shade anywhere. Also, to the east is a village where the beach doubles as a public lavatory. Between Pink House Hotel and Hotel Shankar International, the beach is comparatively uncrowded and unpolluted; further west, and parallel to Marine Parade, the beach is often crowded.

It's worth getting up before sunrise to watch the fishermen head out to sea from the village and, for a little financial incentive, they may take you with them. The crude construction of the boats is unusual: They're made of solid tree trunks and are enormously heavy – buoyancy is achieved purely from the bulk of the wood.

Warning

! Currents can be treacherous in Puri, so don't venture out of your depth; the occasional lifeguard will show you the safest places to swim. Also, muggings and attacks on women have been reported along isolated stretches, even during the day, so take care.

Organised Tours

Of the dozens of travel agencies in Puri, mostly dotted along CT Rd, only a handful are reputable and recognised by the OTDC, including:

Heritage Tours (☎ 23656, fax 24595, ⓔ heritage tours@hotmail.com) Mayfair Beach Resort. Caters more to the upmarket crowd, but offers a range of excellent tours to the tribal areas and handicraft villages, and trips around Konark, Puri, Chilka Lake and Bhubaneswar. Staff are competent and friendly.
Om Travels (☎ 24174, fax 27913) CT Rd. Offers all sorts of local and regional tours, and staff are knowledgeable and helpful.
Tribe Tours (☎/fax 24323, ⓔ tribe-tours@hotmail.com) CT Rd. Specialises in tribal tours.

The other travel agencies around Puri can often arrange train tickets, and can sell tickets for bus tours to Chilka Lake and Konark.

The OTDC runs tours daily, except Monday, to Chilka Lake, and very rushed and long day trips (from Rs 110 per person) to Konark, Dhauli, Bhubaneswar and Nandankanan zoo. Day trips to Gopalpur-on-Sea are also offered, if there's enough demand.

Tribal Tours Most organised tours start from Bhubaneswar or Puri and last at least five nights/six days – this is the recommended minimum because of the travel involved. Tours often concentrate on the more accessible areas in the south-west, and sometimes include side-trips to Gopalpur-on-Sea and Taptapani.

Prices range from US$35 to US$150 per person per day, including private transport, food, accommodation and guides, depending on the level of luxury and number of fellow passengers. Four recommended – and officially recognised – travel agencies offering tribal tours are:

Heritage Tours (Puri) Professional and extremely knowledgeable
Swosti Travels (Bhubaneswar) More upmarket option which charges accordingly
Travel Club (Bhubaneswar) Budget alternative (using tents or cheap hotels) which has been recommended by readers
Tribe Tours (Puri) Competent and reasonably priced

For more details about the travel agencies, see Organised Tours under Puri and Bhubaneswar; to get an updated list of recognised travel agencies offering tribal tours, contact the OTDC office in Puri; and to learn more about Adivasi culture, visit the Scheduled Tribes Research & Training Centre in Bhubaneswar.

The Adivasi

About 62 distinct tribal groups of indigenous people once inhabited the area now known as Orissa. Officially known as 'tribals' – but more accurately known as 'Adivasis' – they constitute more than one-quarter of the state's population. Many Adivasis have adapted to the mainstream Indian lifestyle, but some distinct groups remain.

The Kondh have a population of about one million and are based in the south-west, around Koraput, and near Sambalpur. The Santal, with a population over 500,000, live around Baripada and Khiching in the far north. The Saura, with a population over 300,000, live near Bolangir in the west. The Bonda, known as the 'Naked People', have a population of about 5000 and live in the hills near Koraput.

All the tribal groupings have their own fascinating customs, rituals and beliefs and have become something of a tourist attraction. Although there is always some controversy regarding the advisability and morality of visiting Adivasi areas, tourism does bring much-needed funds to these poor regions. It is important, however, to visit these areas on an organised tour because:

- Some areas require permits, which can only be obtained by a recognised travel agency.
- Some tribal areas are hard to find, and often not accessible by public transport.
- Adivasis often speak little Hindi or Oriya, and usually no English.
- Some tribes can get angry, even violent, if foreigners visit their villages uninvited and without official permission.

Special Events

One of India's greatest annual events, **Rath Yatra** (Car Festival), takes place in Puri each June or July, when a fantastic festival sets forth from Jagannath Mandir. It commemorates the journey of Krishna from Gokul to Mathura. The images of Jagannath, his brother and his sister are brought out from the temple and dragged in huge 'cars', known as *raths*, down Grand Rd to Gundicha Mandir.

The main car of Jagannath stands 14m high, over 10m square, and rides on 16 wheels, each over 2m in diameter – and in centuries past, devotees threw themselves beneath the wheels of the main car to die in the god's sight. To haul the cars takes over 4000 professional 'car pullers' – all employees of the temple. The huge and unwieldy cars take an enormous effort to pull, are virtually impossible to turn and, once moving, are nearly unstoppable. Hundreds of thousands of pilgrims (and tourists) flock from all over India to witness this stupendous scene.

Once the cars reach Gundicha Mandir, the gods take a week-long 'summer break' before being reloaded onto the cars and returned to Jagannath Mandir, in a virtual repeat of the previous week's procession. After the festival, the cars are broken up and used for firewood in the communal kitchens inside the temple, or for funeral-pyre fuel. New cars are constructed each year, mostly out of a special wood, thereby putting enormous pressure on the state's dwindling forests.

At intervals of eight, 11 or 19 years (or combinations of those numbers depending on various astrological occurrences), the gods themselves are also disposed of and new images made. In the past 150 years, new images were created in 1863, 1893, 1931, 1950, 1969, 1977 and 1996. The old ones are buried at a site near the northern gate of Jagannath Mandir.

Puri is the home of the **Srikshetra Mahotsava** held in early June which features art, dance and music.

Places to Stay

Prices listed below are at the high season (October to February), but healthy discounts can be negotiated outside this period, especially if you're staying more than three days. But watch out for checkout times – some are as early as 7 am!

All places listed below have a fan and private bathroom, unless stated otherwise, but most budget hotels have squat toilets. Blackouts are not uncommon, so anywhere with a generator is useful. Mosquito nets are sometimes offered in the cheaper places, mainly because they don't have generators and if the power shuts off the overhead fan doesn't work. Otherwise, mosquito nets are not necessary.

Places to Stay – Budget

Most budget hotels are in the eastern end of Puri, along or just off CT Rd. The places below are listed in order of location, from west to east.

The ***Youth Hostel*** *(☎ 22424)* is set in a pleasant garden, and very cheap. Dorm beds for members/nonmembers only cost Rs 20/40 per person. However, it's governed by the usual strict youth hostel rules, including a 10 pm curfew, and is away from the action along CT Rd.

Hotel Love & Life *(☎ 24433, fax 26093)* is friendly and cheap. The dorms (Rs 30), and singles/doubles for Rs 80/100 with a shared bathroom, are usually full, however, and the other rooms from Rs 100/200 are unexciting. At the back, the cottages cost from Rs 250 per double and are quiet, but not as nice as the outside suggests. Hot water is guaranteed in all shared and private bathrooms.

Hotel Ghandara *(☎ 24117, fax 25909)* has dorms from Rs 40/50 for men/women and singles with a shared bathroom for Rs 110 – but both types of accommodation are often full. The doubles from Rs 150 to 250 (depending on views) are reasonably comfortable and have mosquito nets.

Hotel Sea 'n' Sand *(☎ 27853)* is popular, because it's clean, comfortable and quiet (ie, off the main drag). It's also good value at Rs 150 per double.

Hotel Tanuja *(☎/fax 24823)* is a quiet, family-run place with small singles from Rs 80 with a shared bathroom, and unremarkable doubles from Rs 150 to 200 (with a huge bathroom).

Z Hotel *(☎ 22554, ⓔ zhotel@email.com)* is deservedly popular. Formerly the palace of a maharaja, it's an old, rambling building with large, airy rooms, many of them facing the sea. There are plenty of common areas, a lovely garden and roof terrace for sunbathing. Dorms cost Rs 60, and rooms with a shared bathroom and mosquito net are Rs 150/200. The huge, character-filled doubles, with a mosquito net and private bathroom in an enclosed balcony (!), are worth a splurge for Rs 300.

Hotel Derby *(☎ 23961)* offers fairly grubby singles for Rs 100, and more inviting rooms for Rs 150/200. Although nothing remarkable, it is popular because of its small, delightful garden and proximity to the beach.

Hotel Sapphire International *(☎ 22399)* is also on the beach. It offers small but clean doubles from Rs 150 to 250 – some have genuine sea views offering welcome breezes.

Pink House Hotel *(☎ 22253)* is another popular choice. The doubles facing the beach with a shared bathroom for Rs 150 are gloomy and airless (sort of like prison cells), but the other rooms for about Rs 250 are far nicer. Prices are very negotiable.

Hotel Beach Hut *(☎ 25704)* is almost on the beach, and boasts a garden, rooftop terrace and bar. Singles (Rs 100) are rarely available, but the doubles are large and clean, and range from Rs 150 to 300, depending on the views and size.

Lodge Sagar Saikate *(☎ 23253)*, also known as ***The Monali***, has tiny, grubby rooms with a shared bathroom for Rs 60/80, but the other doubles are slightly more appealing for Rs 100. The upstairs doubles are clean, still a little gloomy, but good value for Rs 150.

Hotel Sri Balajee *(☎ 23388)* is quiet, clean and family-run. It features a number of rooms around a courtyard, each with a veranda with table and chairs. Tiny singles with a shared bathroom cost Rs 50, and doubles range from Rs 150 to 350. It's popular, and often full.

Hotel Akash International *(☎ 24204)* has a large number of strangely shaped rooms – so there's always a vacancy. At Rs 75/100, it's also very good value.

Places to Stay – Mid-Range & Top End

Most hotels along Marine Parade are patronised almost exclusively by Indian tourists. ***The Seagull*** *(☎ 23618)* is often full, which is surprising because the rates (Rs 770/1150 for rooms with fan/air-con and cable TV) are high. ***Puri Hotel*** *(☎ 22114, ⓔ purihotel@satyam.net.in)* is better value. Rooms start from Rs 220/330 for doubles/triples, and from Rs 770 for doubles with air-con and cable TV.

Hotel Holiday House *(☎ 23782, CT Rd)* is large, clean and charmless, but pretty good value. Doubles with a balcony cost from Rs 250 to 475, depending on the sea views. Cable TV costs an extra Rs 75 per day.

Hotel Shankar International *(☎ 23637)*, just off CT Rd, has a range of unremarkable doubles from Rs 150 to 300, and better and larger cottages with cable TV, hot water and a sitting room for about Rs 500 per double. It's so close to the beach that guests can hear the waves, and the staff are friendly.

Hotel Samudra *(☎ 22705)* is right on the beach, and astoundingly good value for a classy mid-range place. Most rooms have a balcony facing the sea, and cost from Rs 550 for luxurious doubles; only Rs 825 with air-con. But beware of the 7 am checkout.

Mayfair Beach Resort *(☎ 27800, fax 24242)* is an upmarket place discreetly set in lush gardens. It has a swimming pool (only open to guests), and a semiprivate beach maintained by the hotel. Rooms cost from Rs 2800 with cable TV and breakfast.

The ***Panthanivas Tourist Bungalow*** *(☎ 22740)* has an enormous garden with access to the beach. All rooms come with cable TV, and cost from Rs 350 to 450; Rs 750 with air-con. The suites from Rs 1500 to 1800 are worth a splurge.

Places to Eat

Not surprisingly, the seafood is excellent in Puri. The cheapest places to eat are along the eastern end of CT Rd towards the village, eg, ***Raju's Restaurant*** near Lodge Sagar Saikate. The restaurant in the ***Youth Hostel*** is recommended for its excellent Orissan-style thalis. Four places close by, along CT Rd, cater almost exclusively to foreigners, and offer a large range of delicious Western food, as well as Indian and Chinese dishes. ***Harry's Cafe*** is an institution, but it has lost some character due to renovations. Nevertheless, the food is still tasty and the staff are friendly. The fish meals (about Rs 50) are good value, and it's open early for breakfast.

Mickey Mouse offers such delights as spaghetti, pizza and porridge, and 46 types of pancakes! It's an unassuming place, and the prices are very reasonable.

Peace Restaurant is a popular meeting place; the indoor section is unexciting, but the garden is delightful. The extensive menu features excellent food, including tasty tuna steaks. It's also open early for breakfast. ***Xanadu Restaurant*** is similar to the other three places.

Pink House, next to Pink House Hotel on the beach, is an open-air restaurant, which is probably more popular for its views and breezes than its food.

Chung Wah Restaurant, in the Lee Garden Hotel along VIP Rd, serves authentic Chinese cuisine and the prices are pleasingly reasonable (from about Rs 70 per dish).

Wildgrass Restaurant *(VIP Rd)* is unquestionably the nicest place in town. It offers a wide range of appealing meals, all at reasonable prices considering the impeccable service and lush gardens.

Bravery Bar & Restaurant *(CT Rd)* is one of the few bars around town, and is typically dingy and uninviting.

Shopping

Shops along Marine Parade sell crafts, fabric, beads, shells and bamboo work – mainly for Indian tourists. Stalls in the eastern end of town, nearer the village, sell Kashmiri and Tibetan souvenirs – mainly for foreigners.

Near Jagannath Mandir, numerous places sell palm-leaf paintings and engravings, handicrafts and Orissan hand-woven ikat fabric, which you can buy in lengths or as ready-made garments. Some visitors buy at least one Jagannath image – carved, sculpted or painted – and other popular souvenirs include exquisite, but remarkably cheap, silk-screen printed postcards.

Getting There & Away

Bus From the sprawling station (☎ 23786) near Gundicha Mandir, buses leave about every 10 minutes for Bhubaneswar (Rs 15, 1¼ hours) and Cuttack (Rs 23, two hours); once a day for Berhampur (Rs 110, six hours) and Taptapani (Rs 120, eight hours); two or three in the late afternoon for Sambalpur (Rs 110, 10 hours); and one or two for Kolkata (Rs 160, 13 hours).

Minibuses to Konark (Rs 10, one hour) leave every 20 to 30 minutes from a spot within the bus station area; and to Satapada (Rs 18, two hours), minibuses leave every 30 to 45 minutes from Jatiababa Chhak, about 2.5km north-west of Jagannath Mandir. To find either departure point, ask your auto/cycle-rickshaw driver to drop you off.

Train Between Puri and Kolkata, there are at least three direct trains a day (Rs 529/613/846 for 2nd class/1st class/air-con); and regular (often daily) trains as far as Delhi and Chennai. If there is no direct train from Puri to Chennai or Kolkata, get a connection at Khurda Road train station, 44km from Puri, rather than in Bhubaneswar.

The daily train to Sambalpur (Rs 421/663/1303) is more comfortable than the bus, but for local destinations, such as Cuttack and Bhubaneswar, buses are faster.

The railway booking office (☎ 131) is computerised, and open 8 am to noon and 12.30 to 3 pm Monday to Saturday; 8 am to noon Sunday. Book ahead during the pilgrim season, because trains to Chennai and Kolkata are often booked out 10 days ahead. Local travel agencies can usually book tickets for trains from Puri for a small fee.

Getting Around

Cycle-rickshaws outnumber autorickshaws in Puri, especially around CT Rd. Several places along CT Rd between Hotel Ghandara and Hotel Akash International rent pushbikes for about Rs 15 per day. They also rent 100cc Rajdoot or Yamaha motorcycles, and scooters and mopeds, from about Rs 150 per day – plus petrol and oil. None of these places offers insurance, however, so be extremely careful about noting any deficiencies, scratches etc before hiring anything. And remember: If you use a pushbike or motorbike on the beach, some places may charge an extra Rs 200/500 for cleaning!

AROUND PURI

Raghurajpur is famous for its patachitra paintings, which are done on cotton cloth coated with a mixture of gum and chalk and then polished before natural colours are applied. To get there, take a bus between Puri and Bhubaneswar, look for the 'Orissa Tourism Craft Village' signpost 11km north of Puri, and then walk (about 1km) or take an autorickshaw along the access road.

Pipli is notable for its brilliant applique craft, in which colourful materials are used to make bedspreads, temple umbrellas and wall hangings. These are for sale at stalls along the main road through the village. Pipli is easily accessible by any bus between Bhubaneswar and Puri or Konark.

KONARK

☎ 06758 • pop 12,681

Konark consists of the Sun Temple, some souvenir stalls and a few places to stay and eat. Although it's an easy day trip from Puri or Bhubaneswar, Konark is also a peaceful place to spend a few days – the temple certainly has more atmosphere once the day-trippers have left. Konark is protected as a Unesco World Heritage Site.

The tourist office (☎ 36821) inside Yatri Nivas hotel is the place to find out about local festivals including the famous **Konark Festival**. Staged between 1 and 5 December, it features enchanting music and dance from Orissa and elsewhere in India. It's held in the open-air auditorium, with the specially lit Sun Temple in the background. The **Magha Mela** (Sun Festival) is held on the seventh day of the bright half of the month of Magha (January/February). At this time, pilgrims bathe at the beach before sunrise and then proceed to the temple to worship.

ORISSA

Nine Planets' Shrine

This 6m chlorite slab, once the architrave above the main entrance of the jagamohan, is now the centrepiece of a small shrine just outside the temple walls. The carved seated figures represent Surya (the sun), Chandra (moon), Mars, Mercury, Jupiter, Venus, Saturn, Rahu and Ketu.

Archaeological Museum

This largish museum, along the main road outside the temple grounds, contains many sculptures and carvings found during the excavations of the Sun Temple. Some of the smaller pieces (eg, the statue of Agni, the Fire God) are particularly impressive. The museum is open from 10 am to 5 pm daily, except Friday; entry is free.

Konark Beach (Chandrabhaga)

The local beach is in an area known as Chandrabhaga. It's about 3km from the temple; either walk, hire a bicycle (Rs 20 per day from Yatri Nivas), charter an auto/cycle-rickshaw or use the Konark-Puri or the Konark-Bhubaneswar bus. This part of the beach is much quieter and cleaner than Puri, but beware of strong currents. If you don't like the tourist atmosphere, find a deserted stretch of sand from along the Konark-Puri road.

Places to Stay & Eat

Sunrise Lodging and ***Banita Lodge*** both offer basic doubles with a shared bathroom for about Rs 70. ***Konark Lodge*** has similar standards and prices, but is in a quieter location away from the crowds.

Yatri Nivas *(☎ 36820)* is a lovely building set in pretty gardens. Doubles with a fan and private bathroom cost Rs 150, and the ones with air-con, cable TV and hot water for Rs 325 are worth booking ahead.

Panthanivas Tourist Bungalow *(☎ 35831)* needs a lick of paint (like most other OTDC places). Unremarkable doubles with a fan,

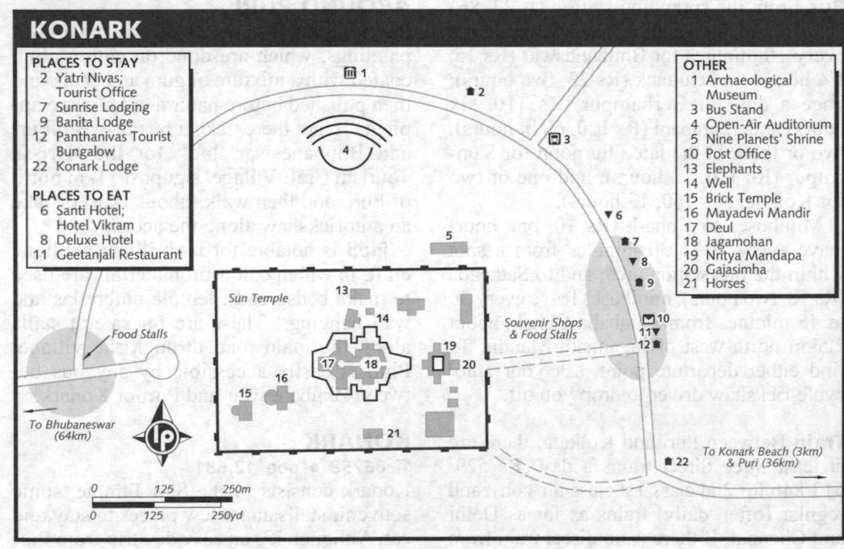

Sun Temple

The great Sun Temple of Konark was constructed in the mid-13th century, but remarkably little is known about its early history. It's thought to have been built by the Orissan king Narashimhadev I to celebrate his military victory over the Muslims. It probably fell into disuse in the early 17th century after being desecrated by one of Jehangir's envoys. (An information board at the entrance to the temple tries to make more sense of the early history.)

Originally nearer the coast (the sea has receded), Konark was visible from far out at sea and known as the 'Black Pagoda' by sailors, in contrast to the whitewashed temples of Puri. Konark was said to contain a great mass of magnetic iron which would draw unwary ships to the shore.

In 1904, debris and sand were cleared from around the temple base to reveal the sheer magnitude of the architect's imagination. The entire temple was conceived as a chariot for the sun god, Surya. Around the base of the temple are 24 gigantic carved stone wheels. Seven mighty stone horses haul at the temple and the immense structure is covered with carvings, sculptures, figures and bas-reliefs.

It's not known if the temple was ever completed. If the tower was finished, it would have soared to 70m, but archaeologists wonder if the sandy foundations could have supported such a structure. Part of the tower was still standing in 1837, but collapsed completely in 1869.

The ***gajasimha*** (main entrance) is guarded by two stone lions crushing elephants, and leads to the intricately carved ***nritya mandapa*** (dancing hall). Steps, flanked by straining horses, then rise to the ***jagamohan*** (assembly hall), which still stands, but the ***deul*** (temple sanctuary) behind it, in which the temple deity was kept, has collapsed. The three impressive chlorite images of the sun god Surya have been restored to their positions, aligned to catch the sun at dawn, noon and sunset. To the north is a group of **elephants**, and to the south a group of **horses** rearing and trampling men.

The image of the deity that resided here is thought to have been moved to Jagannath Mandir in Puri in the 17th century. Around the base of the Sun Temple, and up the walls and roof, is a continuous procession of carvings. Many are in the erotic style for which Konark, like Khajuraho in Madhya Pradesh, is famous and include entwined couples, as well as solitary exhibitionists; they are sometimes minute images on the spoke of a temple wheel, at other times they are life-size figures higher up the wall.

Of lesser importance around the grounds are a small shrine called **Mayadevi Mandir**; a deep, covered **well**; and the ruins of the **Brick Temple**.

As the temple's history is a complicated amalgam of fact and legend, it's worth hiring a guide (about Rs 60 an hour per small group); nothing much is signposted anyway. The stories they relate are fascinating and they can show you features which you might otherwise overlook – such as the dancer with high-heeled shoes, a giraffe (the first recorded sighting in India), and even a man treating himself for venereal disease! Be sure the guide is registered, because unlicensed (and unreliable) guides abound.

The temple grounds are open from sunrise to sunset daily. The best time to visit is late afternoon, when it's cooler and most day-trippers have left; it's also worth staying to see the temple illuminated (from dusk to about 9 pm). However, public transport back to Puri or Bhubaneswar is problematic after about 5 pm, so consider staying overnight in Konark.

mosquito net and private bathroom cost Rs 200; Rs 400 with cable TV and air-con.

Geetanjali Restaurant caters to upmarket day-trippers, but is one of the better places to sit and relax for a meal or drink.

There are numerous ***food stalls*** outside the temple entrance, and a dozen or more places along the main road serve cheap thalis (but little else), such as ***Santi Hotel***, ***Hotel Vikram*** and ***Deluxe Hotel***.

Getting There & Away

Overcrowded minibuses run along the pretty coastal road between Puri and Konark (Rs 10, one hour) very regularly until about 5 pm. There are also regular departures to Bhubaneswar (Rs 18, 1½ hours). Konark is often included in organised day trips by bus from Bhubaneswar and Puri. Because the Puri-Konark road is flat, some people even cycle from Puri (36km) and stay at Konark.

CHILKA LAKE

Chilka Lake is Asia's largest brackish lagoon, 1100 sq km in the monsoon season and 600 sq km by April/May. The shallow lake is separated from the Bay of Bengal by a 60km-long sand bar called Rajhansa.

The lake is noted for the one million or more migratory birds, including osprey, grey-legged geese, herons, cranes and flamingos that flock here in winter (November to January) from as far as Siberia and Iran. This is possibly the largest congregation of aquatic birds in the subcontinent, but because so many restrict themselves to a tiny area (3 sq km) within the **bird sanctuary** on Nalabana Island, they are sometimes poached. Other environmental problems, such as silting and commercial prawn fishing, are also threatening this important wetland area.

Besides the bird life on Nalabana, the other attractions are the **dolphins** near Satapada, the pristine **beach** along Rajhansa and **Kalijai temple** (on the island of the same name) where Hindu pilgrims flock for the **Makar Mela** festival in January.

There are OTDC tourist offices in two hotels: Barkul Panthanivas (☎ 06756-20855) and Satapada Yatri Nivas (no telephone at present).

ORISSA

Boat Trips

Dolphins are easier to see during a one-hour (return) boat trip from Satapada than from the jetty in Satapada village. To visit Nalabana and Kalijai Islands, charter a boat from Barkul or Rambha (two hours return). To Rajhansa, start from Satapada (three hours return). The standard price for boats at all three OTDC hotels is Rs 250/350/550 per hour per boat holding 6/7/22 people. Private boats are also available from Balugaon for about the same price. If you're on a tight budget, ask around for a seat on a boat, or talk the fishermen into taking you out (although fishing boats often don't have motors, which may limit you to a dolphin trip from Satapada).

Barkul Panthanivas hotel offers boat rides to Kalijai Island (Rs 40 per person one way) and Nalabana Island (Rs 120 per person) if there are enough passengers.

Organised Tours

The OTDC organises *long* (at least 10-hour) day trips (Rs 100 per person) by bus from Puri; book at the OTDC office/counter in Puri. Most travel agencies in Puri also sell tickets for day trips (about Rs 90) to Chilka.

Places to Stay & Eat

It makes sense to stay somewhere near the lake. All places listed below are managed by the OTDC, and have a ***restaurant*** serving fresh seafood.

Barkul Panthanivas *(☎ 06756-20488)*, near Barkul, is signposted 6km south of Balugaon and is 1km from the main road. It offers comfortable doubles on the lake for Rs 350/700 with fan/air-con, private bathroom and cable TV.

Rambha Panthanivas *(☎ 06810-78346)*, about 500m off the main road from Rambha, also boasts a pleasant location. Doubles with a private bathroom, cable TV and balcony overlooking the lake cost Rs 250/500 with fan/air-con. Rooms are available for the day (from 9 am to 5 pm) for half the normal rate.

Satapada Yatri Nivas *(☎ 06752-45564)*, in the middle of Satapada, has unremarkable doubles with a private bathroom, balcony (some with lake views) and clean beds for only Rs 150.

Heritage Tours (see Organised Tours in the Puri section earlier in this chapter) plans to open an 'ecocamp' with tents on the beach along Rajhansa.

Getting There & Away

All buses careering along the road between Bhubaneswar and Berhampur – including the more comfortable daily OTDC buses – stop anywhere along the main road hugging the lake. From Puri, minibuses regularly travel to Satapada (Rs 18, two hours) on the southern edge of the lake. From Satapada, a ferry (Rs 13, three hours) travels to Balugaon at midday, and returns from Balugaon at 7 am.

Trains travelling between Kolkata and Chennai, via Bhubaneswar, stop at several villages along the lake, including Balugaon and Rambha, and offer superb views.

GOPALPUR-ON-SEA

☎ 0680

Gopalpur is a delightfully peaceful seaside village. The **beach** is attractive, and the place is *far* less crowded and polluted than Puri. There's very little to do but laze around, go for walks and climb to the top of the **lighthouse** (open from 4 to 5 pm daily). Other than the hotels, there are very few facilities – you can't change money or send an email from here.

Places to Stay & Eat

Prices quoted below are for the high season (November to January), but hefty discounts are available at any other time. All hotels listed below are along, or just off, the beach road (called Beach Rd), or the main road through the village (called, umm, Main Rd). Most hotels have restaurants, but many only cater to guests. All rooms have a fan and private bathroom, unless stated otherwise.

As you face the beach at the end of Main Rd, there are several hotels to the right. ***Hotel Sea Pearl*** *(☎ 242556)* has spotless double rooms with a balcony (some looking straight into the walls of the neighbouring hotel) and cable TV for a pricey Rs 600. ***Hotel Kalinga*** *(☎ 242067)* is quaint and friendly, but surprisingly few rooms offer views or breezes. The doubles on the ground floor for Rs 200 are better than the windowless cubicles upstairs for Rs 300 with air-con and cable TV.

Facing the beach at the end of Main Rd, the first hotel on the left is ***Hotel Holiday Home*** *(☎ 242049)*. It offers doubles from Rs 250, and is popular with Indian families because some rooms hold four beds. The ***restaurant*** is open to the public.

Further along, ***Hotel Rosalin*** *(☎ 242071)* is friendly and in a pleasant location. Rooms with/without a private bathroom around a scrappy courtyard cost Rs 100/75, and are as basic as you'd expect for this price.

Hotel Sea Side Breeze *(☎ 242075)*, almost on the sand at the far end of Beach Rd, is a charming place with indifferent management. Spacious doubles facing the ocean cost about Rs 300.

Motel Mermaid *(☎ 242050)*, near the Sea Side Breeze, is popular with foreigners. Large, clean and comfortable singles/doubles with a balcony, but no sea views, cost from Rs 500/600 – and all rates include three meals.

Hotel Green Park *(☎ 242016)*, one street back from the Sea Side Breeze, is excellent. Doubles with cable TV cost from Rs 200 to 400 (with views); Rs 600 with air-con and views. Just a little farther along the same street, ***Gopalpur Panthanivas*** *(☎ 242088)* is decent enough for Rs 300/500 for doubles with fan/air-con. It sometimes offers dorm beds for Rs 70 per person. The ***restaurant*** is OK, and open early for breakfast.

Hotel Rohini *(☎ 242309)*, about 200m up Main Rd from the beach, has drab doubles with balcony (no views), but is good value for Rs 150. The unpretentious, but popular, ***Seaward Restaurant*** is attached.

The ***Youth Hostel***, down a street beside Rohini's, is run down. Dorm beds cost Rs 20/40 for members/nonmembers, and the shared bathroom is grimy.

Sea Shell Fast Food, opposite Hotel Rosalin, is the only restaurant with a genuine seaside location. The service is slow, but there's no reason to hurry while you're in Gopalpur. Meals start from Rs 15, and it's open for breakfast.

Getting There & Away

The only public transport to/from Gopalpur are the regular, crowded minibuses to the chaotic city of Berhampur (Rs 6, one hour). Between Berhampur and Bhubaneswar there are public buses (Rs 50, five hours) about every hour, and daily OTDC buses (Rs 65, four hours). Berhampur is also on the main Kolkata-Chennai train line.

TAPTAPANI

Apart from the small **hot springs** in this peaceful village in the hills west of Gopalpur-on-Sea, there's not much else to see.

For a great winter splurge, however, book one of the two rooms at ***Panthanivas Tourist Bungalow*** *(☎ 06814-47531)*, in which hot spring water is channelled directly to vast tubs in its Roman-style bathrooms. These doubles cost Rs 650 with cable TV and air-con; other rooms with a fan and private bathroom start from Rs 350. Both types of rooms can be rented for the day at half-price.

Buses regularly travel between Berhampur and Taptapani (Rs 18, two hours).

CUTTACK

☎ 0671 • pop 500,915

Cuttack is one of Orissa's oldest cities, and was the capital until 1950. Today, it's a chaotic and fairly uninteresting place, but the **shopping** is great: Silk and cotton textiles, horn and brass wares are manufactured here along with the exquisite, delicate silver filigree work for which Cuttack is famous.

The tourist office (☎ 612225) is along Link Rd, the main road from Bhubaneswar.

The 14th-century **Barabati Fort** is about 8km north of the city centre. It once boasted nine storeys, but only a gateway and the moat remain, so it's barely worth the effort. The stone **retaining wall** on the Kathajuri River, which protects the city from seasonal floods, dates from the 11th century. The 18th-century **Qadam-i-Rasool** shrine, in the city centre, is sacred to Hindus as well as Muslims (who believe it contains the footprints of the Prophet Mohammed).

Places to Stay & Eat

Most visitors come for the day from Bhubaneswar, but there are a number of comfortable hotels in Cuttack. Most hotels in the city have ***restaurants***.

Hotel Adarsh *(☎ 619898, Banwararilal Moda Market)* is a budget hotel with reasonable facilities. Singles with a shared bathroom cost Rs 80; doubles with a private bathroom cost from Rs 120 to 350.

The ***Panthanivas Tourist Bungalow*** *(☎ 621867, Buxi Bazaar)* has doubles with a private bathroom and cable TV for Rs 300/500 with fan/air-con. A decent ***restaurant*** is attached.

Hotel Neeladri *(☎ 614221, Mangala Bagh)* has singles/doubles with a private bathroom from Rs 180/250.

Hotel Ashoka *(☎ 613508, College Square)* has singles from Rs 220/550 with fan/air-con and doubles from Rs 280/660.

Getting There & Away

Cuttack is on the main line between Kolkata and Chennai, so there are plenty of interstate and local trains. Buses to Bhubaneswar (Rs 15, one hour), Puri (Rs 23, two hours) and Sambalpur (Rs 75, seven hours) leave from the bus station along the road from Bhubaneswar. To Rajnagar (Rs 35, four hours), on the outskirts of Bhitarkanika Wildlife Sanctuary, there's at least two buses a day.

LALITGIRI, UDAIGIRI & RATNAGIRI

Buddhist relics and ruins can be found at these three hilltop complexes about 60km north-east of Cuttack.

A gold casket, thought to contain relics of Buddha, was discovered at Lalitgiri and excavations are continuing. Udaigiri, 8km to the north, has its own **monastery complex** with a brick stupa. Ratnagiri, 5km north-east of Udaigiri, has the most interesting and extensive **ruins**. Two large monasteries flourished here from the 6th to the 12th centuries AD, and contained beautifully carved doorways, a large stupa and enormous Buddha figures.

There is nowhere to stay near any of the sites. The only public transport is between Cuttack and Lalitgiri (Rs 25, 1½ hours). Direct travel to Ratnagiri and/or Udaigiri means an expensive chartered taxi from Cuttack, or an autorickshaw from near the turn-off to Lalitgiri.

BHITARKANIKA WILDLIFE SANCTUARY

Bhitarkanika (672 sq km) is near the coast, between Paradip and Chandipur. It was proclaimed a sanctuary in 1975, and protects the nesting habitat of up to one million olive Ridley turtles which come to nest near the mouth of the Brahmani River in the **Gahirmatha (Marine) Wildlife Sanctuary** between January and March.

Within Bhitarkanika's protective environs and extensive waterways is a successful breeding and conservation program for saltwater crocodiles. The sanctuary is also home to more than 170 recorded species of resident and migratory birds. A large heronry on **Bagagaham Island** sees the colonial nesting of herons and other waterbirds. The birds start to arrive in early June and nesting finishes in November (but the most comfortable time for visitors is between mid-October and mid-April). For naturalists, another interesting feature of the sanctuary is the mangroves. Of the 72 species of mangroves worldwide, 63 are found in Bhitarkanika.

Most of the attractions and resthouses can only be reached by boat, so permission to enter the sanctuary – and bookings for all accommodation – must be made beforehand with the Divisional Forest Officer (☎ 06729-8460), Rajnagar, 754225. Entrance fees for foreigners are Rs 25 per day, plus Rs 10/250 for a still/video camera.

Facilities are very limited. There is accommodation at the ***Forest Rest House*** in Chandbali. Deep within the sanctuary there is

Rare olive Ridley turtles nest in their multitudes at Gahirmatha Wildlife Sanctuary.

also a ***Forest Inspection Bungalow*** at Dangmal (with dorm beds and rooms) and a ***Forest Rest House*** at Ekakula (with dorm beds and a cottage) on Gahirmatha beach – dorm beds cost about Rs 40 per person; rooms and cottages about Rs 200 per double. Camping is also permitted for Rs 25 per person.

Bring all food and water. The nearest train station is at Bhadrakh, along the line between Kolkata and Chennai. There are also daily buses from Cuttack to Chandbali and to the park entrance near Rajnagar.

Some of the travel agencies listed under Organised Tours in the Bhubaneswar and Puri sections earlier in this chapter can arrange trips to the sanctuary. Pugmarks Nature Resorts (☎ 033-287 1959, fax 240 7737) in Kolkata also offers tours; more details are available from its Web site (www.pugmarks.org).

BALASORE & CHANDIPUR

Balasore is the first major town in northern Orissa along the train line from Kolkata, and was once an important trading centre with Dutch, Danish, English and French factories. At **Remina**, 5km from Balasore, is the 19th-century Khirachora Gopinath Temple, an important pilgrimage centre; and **Panchalingeswar**, 30km from Balasore, has a cave and small waterfall. Panthanivas Tourist Bungalow offers half-day bus tours to these places, as well as to Balasore, for Rs 80 per person.

Along the coast 16km from Balasore, Chandipur has a **beach**, but the sea can be very shallow at low tide because it recedes up to 5km per day!

Many buses a day link Balasore with Chandipur. ***Panthanivas Tourist Bungalow*** *(☎ 06782-72251)*, in Chandipur, is probably the best option for accommodation. It offers dorm beds for Rs 70 per person, and doubles with a private bathroom and cable TV from Rs 300/625 with fan/air-con. A ***restaurant*** is attached.

SIMILIPAL NATIONAL PARK

☎ 06792

Hidden in the north-east of the state, Similipal (2750 sq km) is one of India's best secrets. As part of Project Tiger it boasts around 95 tigers, and there's also leopards, elephants, wolves, wild boars, deer and crocodiles, and over 300 species of birds. The scenery is exquisite and varied, with hills, waterfalls – including the spectacular 400m-high **Barheipani Waterfalls** – and undisturbed forest in which the wildlife remains well hidden.

The park is open from about 1 November to 15 June. Visitors must come on an organised tour or charter a vehicle to travel inside the park. Also, bring your own food, which a local *chowkidar* (caretaker) can cook.

Orientation & Information

The entrances to the park are at Jashipur on the north-western side, and (more conveniently) at Pithabata, near Lulung, about 25km west of Baripada. Entry permits can be obtained in advance from the Assistant Conservator of Forests (☎ 06797-2224), National Park, Jashipur, Mayurbhanj District, 757091; or the Field Director, Similipal Tiger Reserve Project (☎ 52593), LIC Colony, Baripada, Mayurbhanj District, 757002. Better still, get a permit in person at the Pithabata gate, open between 6 am and 2 pm daily. Entry fees for foreigners are Rs 100; an extra Rs 100/1000 per day for a still/video camera.

Organised Tours

If you want to avoid the hassles of arranging permits, food and accommodation, and finding transport, go on an organised tour. See Organised Tours under Bhubaneswar earlier in this chapter. Also, Pugmarks Nature Resorts (☎ 033-287 1959, fax 240 7737) in Kolkata runs tours and a camp site inside the park. More details are available from its Web site (www.pugmarks.org).

Places to Stay

The Forest Department has four sets of 'forest bungalows' dotted around the park. These cost from Rs 400 to 800 per double, and must be booked in advance with the Field Director, Similipal Tiger Reserve Project (see Orientation & Information). ***Barheipani*** offers impressive views; ***Chahala***, a former maharaja's hunting lodge near a salt lick, is brilliant in the evenings; and ***Newana*** and ***Joranda*** are great for wildlife viewing.

Aranya Nivas Tourist Lodge *(☎ 53297)*, about 10km inside the park and 35km south-west of Baripada, is run by the OTDC. It offers doubles with a private bathroom and fan for Rs 400, and dorm beds are often available for Rs 70 per person. Rooms must be booked in advance at the OTDC office (☎ 52710), Baghra Rd, Baripada, Mayurbhanj District, 757002.

Tourist Lodge, in Jashipur, charges Rs 80 for very basic doubles, and can arrange jeep hire and organised tours. There are also several budget hotels in Baripada, such as ***Hotel Durga*** *(☎ 53438)* and ***Hotel Mayura*** *(☎ 52343)*.

Getting There & Away

Baripada is on a branch train line from near Balasore. Buses leave daily from Bhubaneswar and Kolkata for Baripada and Jashipur, from where you must rent or charter a vehicle.

SAMBALPUR

☎ 0663 • pop 1,490,000

Located in the west near the border with Madhya Pradesh, Sambalpur is famous for its ikat **weaving**. Fabric, also known as *sambalpuri*, can be bought in the Gole Bazaar market and in government cooperative shops.

About 10km west of the city is the 24km-long **Hirakud Dam**. Built to control monsoon floods in the Mahanadi Delta around Bhubaneswar, it drains an area twice the size of Sri Lanka and is possibly the largest artificial lake in Asia. The OTDC runs afternoon tours (Rs 30 per person) from Sambalpur – book at the OTDC offices at the train station (☎ 21661) or Panthanivas Tourist Bungalow.

Places to Stay & Eat

Basic accommodation can be found near the bus station. ***Indhrapuri Guest House*** *(☎ 521712)* has small doubles with a shared bathroom from about Rs 100; and ***Rani Lodge***, nearby along the main street, is similar. A few decent places are clustered together on VSS Marg: ***Hotel Sujata*** *(☎ 521 403)* is a decent place with singles/doubles from Rs 170/395; and ***Hotel Uphar*** *(☎ 521 558)* has clean singles/doubles/triples for Rs 250/350/450; Rs 480 for doubles with air-con. The ***restaurant*** is only so-so.

The ***Panthanivas Tourist Bungalow*** *(☎ 521482)*, on top of a small hill at the end of the main street, offers fine views. Doubles with a private bathroom and cable TV are good value for Rs 225/400 with fan/air-con. The ***restaurant*** and bar are inviting.

Hong Kong Restaurant *(VSS Marg)* has Chinese food; also try ***Hotel Sujata*** and ***Central Hotel***, opposite Indhrapuri Guest House.

Getting There & Away

The bus station is in the city centre. Several buses go to Bhubaneswar (Rs 100, nine hours) and Puri (Rs 110, 10 hours) every afternoon, but these arrive late so it's better to catch a morning bus for Cuttack (Rs 75, seven hours), and then another to Puri.

More expensive 'deluxe video coaches' leave every night from the main street for Puri, Bhubaneswar and Raipur in Madhya Pradesh. The OTDC offers comfortable overnight buses between Bhubaneswar and Sambalpur (Rs 110, eight hours); book at OTDC offices/counters.

From the main train station (3km from the city centre), there are direct trains to Bilaspur (and sometimes on to Delhi) and Kolkata. Most of these trains also stop at Sambalpur Road station, a little closer to the city centre.

OTHER ATTRACTIONS

In northern Orissa, about 50km south-west of Jashipur, **Khiching** was once an ancient capital and has a number of ancient temples and a small museum. Bronze-casting is done in **Bolangir**, in the west and accessible by bus from Sambalpur and Bhubaneswar. **Harishankar**, west of Bolangir, has a number of temples and a waterfall. The twin villages of **Ranipur-Jharial**, in the far west, are noted for their collection of temples on a rock outcrop. These include a circular 64-*yogini* temple (female goddess attendants) which once had 64 cells for figures of yoginis who attended to the goddess Kali. **Gupteshwar Cave**, 85km west of Koraput in southern Orissa, is in an area inhabited by several Adivasi groups, mainly the Khond.

Sikkim

For many years, Sikkim was regarded as one of the last Himalayan 'Shangri-las' because of its remoteness, spectacular mountain terrain, varied flora and fauna, and ancient Buddhist *gompas* (monasteries). It was never easy to visit and, even now, you need a permit to enter Sikkim – although this is easy to obtain (see the Permits section later in this chapter). To ease potential resentment against the central government, India spends relatively large sums of money to subsidise Sikkim's road building, electrification, water supply and agricultural and industrial development. Much of this activity is also no doubt motivated by India's fear of Chinese military designs on Sikkim. Consequently, the state is more affluent than West Bengal, and being a tax-free zone helps further.

The best time for white-water rafting is March to late May, and mid-October to mid-December; wildflowers are at their most beautiful in March and April (orchids in late September). The ideal time for high-level trekking is October and November, while March and April are also fine at lower levels.

Sikkim at a Glance

Population: 540,493
Area: 7096 sq km
Capital: Gangtok
Main Language: Nepali
When to Go: Mar to late May; mid-Oct to mid-Dec

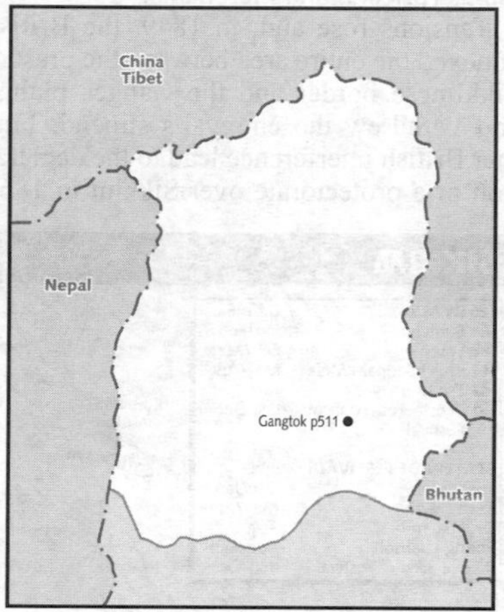

- Visit the friendly monks at Rumtek Dharma Chakra Centre near Gangtok, perhaps during a festival
- Walk the very accessible route from Pelling to Pemayangtse Gompa, one of the state's most important monasteries
- Take a wonderful journey through the Kanchenjunga National Park with a Yuksom-Dzongri-Goecha La trek
- Enjoy the wonderfully peaceful atmosphere at Sangachoeling Gompa, the second oldest gompa in Sikkim

History

The region was originally home to the Lepchas, a tribal people thought to have migrated from the hills of Assam, or possibly even from South-East Asia, around the 13th century. The Lepchas were peaceful forest foragers and small-crop cultivators who worshipped nature spirits.

Tibetans began migrating to Sikkim during the 15th century to escape religious strife between various Buddhist orders. In Tibet, the Gelukpa order (of which the Dalai Lama is the head) gradually gained the upper hand. The Nyingmapa order was introduced in Sikkim by three Tibetan lamas, Lhatsun Chempo, Kathok Rikzin Chempo and Ngadak Sempa Chempo. These lamas consecrated the first *chogyal* (king), Phuntsog Namgyal, at Yuksom, which became the capital of the kingdom (it was later moved to Rabdentse, near Pelling). In the face of waves of Tibetan migrants (known as Bhutias), the Lepchas retreated to remote regions.

When the kingdom of Sikkim was founded, the country included the area encompassed by the present state as well as part of eastern Nepal, the Chumbi Valley (Tibet), Ha Valley (Bhutan) and the Terai foothills down to the plains of India, including Darjeeling and Kalimpong. Much of this territory was later lost, however, during wars with Bhutan and the Gurkhas from Nepal.

In 1835, the British, seeking a hill station as a rest and recreation centre for their troops and officials, persuaded the chogyal to cede the Darjeeling area in return for an annual stipend. Tibet objected to this transfer of territory, regarding Sikkim as a vassal state – also Darjeeling's rapid growth as a trade centre began to make a considerable impact on the fortunes of Sikkim's leading *lamas* (priests) and merchants.

Tensions rose and, in 1849, the British annexed the entire area between the present Sikkimese border and the Ganges plains, and withdrew the chogyal's stipend. Further British interference lead to the declaration of a protectorate over Sikkim in 1861 and the delineation of its borders. Tibet, however, continued to regard these actions as illegal and, in 1886, invaded Sikkim to reassert its authority. The attack was soon repulsed by the British, who sent a punitive military expedition to Lhasa in 1888.

The British treaties with Sikkim passed to India at Independence. Demands within Sikkim for a democratic form of government as opposed to rule by the chogyal were growing. The Indian government supported these moves: It didn't want to be seen to be propping up an autocratic regime while doing its best to sweep away the last traces of princely rule in India itself.

The last chogyal, Palden Thondup Namgyal, came to the throne in 1963, but struggled to live up to the revered memory of his

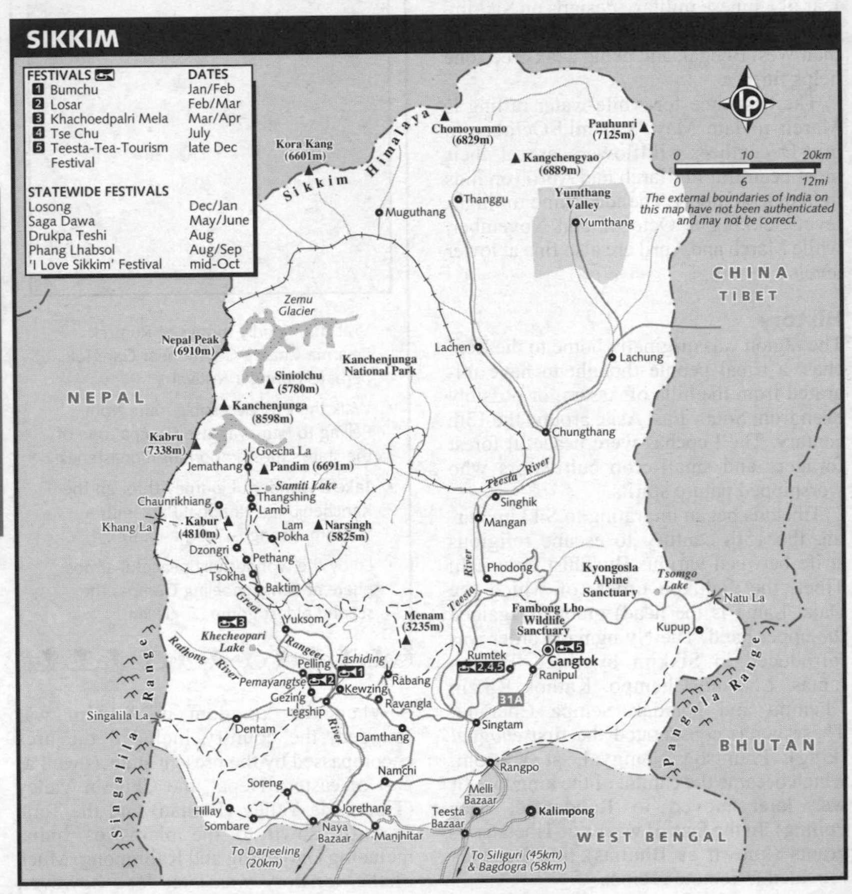

father, Tashi Namgyal. The Nepali population in Sikkim pushed for a greater say in government and impoverished Nepali farmers began attacking the larger landowning monasteries. The chogyal resisted demands for a change in the method of government until demonstrations threatened to get out of control. He was eventually forced to ask India to take over the country's administration.

In the 1975 referendum, 97% of the electorate voted for union with India. The current state government is led by the Sikkim Democratic Front (SDF), which helps to ensure elections by threatening to impose social boycotts on those who do not support the party. On the other hand, the SDF has earned a deserved reputation as the most environmentally conscious government in India.

Permits

A basic permit is required to enter Sikkim – but it's easy to obtain and extend, so don't let this put you off. This permit allows foreigners to visit 'Gangtok, Rumtek, Phodong and Pemayangtse' (which includes Pelling, Legship and Gezing). Although it doesn't say so on the permit, foreigners can also visit any town along the main roads between these four places, and the border towns of Rangpo and Jorethang.

A special endorsement on this permit (or your visa) allows foreigners to also visit Khecheopari Lake, Singhik, Yuksom and Tashiding, and anywhere on the way to, or near, these places. This endorsement can be obtained from the tourist office in Gangtok in a minute or two without a fee or photo.

Because of military sensitivities, foreigners need an additional special permit to visit Tsomgo Lake (valid for one day only), and anywhere between Singhik and Yumthang village (for a nonextendable five days/four nights only) – and foreigners can only travel to these areas on a tour organised by a travel agency in Gangtok. Officially, there must be at least four in the group, but the agency need only *apply* for four (or more) permits for a tour, and travelling in a group of four (or more) is rarely enforced at road blocks. Somehow, most agencies these days can even organise this permit for a group of two; and even if you're travelling alone, some agencies will look for another foreigner (or find one yourself) to complete a second permit application form (although the other/s need not accompany you on the trip). The agency will arrange the permit as part of their fee; you need to give them one passport-sized photo, and a photocopy of the pages in your passport with your personal particulars and Indian visa.

The Sikkim authorities are very slowly changing the permit requirements for the Yuksom–Dzongri–Goecha La trek, so check the tourist office in Gangtok for current information. By the time you read this, foreigners may be able to trek there independently, but if you go as part of an organised tour, the travel agency will arrange any permits as part of its fee. While the authorities are slowly opening up other areas of Sikkim – mainly for trekking – your chances of obtaining permission to travel anywhere not mentioned above is slim. To do so, apply to the Ministry of Home Affairs, Lok Nayak Bhawan, Khan Market, Delhi, 11003 – but each application will take at least three visits and a month or more of waiting and frustration. If all else fails, try for a permit at the Home Office in Gangtok.

There are two entry points to Sikkim: Jorethang (if travelling to/from Pelling) and Rangpo (if travelling to/from Gangtok). If coming through Jorethang, you must have a permit (or endorsed visa) beforehand. If travelling via Rangpo, you can get a (free) two-day permit at the border; the permit must then be extended within two days at Gangtok (see Extensions, later).

The basic permits (ie, for 'Gangtok, Rumtek, Phodong and Pemayangtse') are easy to obtain in India. You must fill out a form, which specifies your intended date of entry to Sikkim. (Note: You cannot enter Sikkim *before* this date.) You also have to provide one passport-sized photo, and possibly a photocopy of your passport pages with your personal details and Indian visa. There is no fee, and the permit is often available within one or two hours.

Permits are normally valid for 15 days from the specified date of entry. Note that re-entry into Sikkim within three months is not possible, even if you leave Sikkim before your 15-day permit expires. Basic permits can be obtained from any of the following places, although the Sikkim Tourist Information Centres are the best places to try:

Foreigners' Registration Offices Delhi, Mumbai (Bombay) & Kolkata (Calcutta)
New Sikkim House (☎ 011-611 6346) 14 Panchseel Marg, Chanakyapuri, Delhi
Office of the District Magistrate Hill Cart Rd, Darjeeling (see the West Bengal chapter for more information)
Sikkim Tourist Information Centres (☎ 0353-432646) SNT Colony, Hill Cart Rd, Siliguri (☎ 033-246 8983) 4C Poonam Building, 5/2 Russell St, Kolkata

When you apply for your Indian visa overseas, you can also ask for the visa to be endorsed with permission to travel to 'Gangtok, Rumtek, Phodong and Pemayangtse'. No entry date to Sikkim is normally specified on your visa (which is an advantage), but Indian embassies/consulates overseas charge an extra fee (up to US$30) for travel to Sikkim.

Basic permits (or endorsed visas) are checked, and your passport is stamped, when entering and leaving Sikkim, and usually on the Yuksom–Dzongri–Goecha La trek – but probably nowhere else in Sikkim.

Extensions Within two days of expiry, a basic permit can be extended twice by an extra 15 days (ie, 45 days is the maximum allowed in Sikkim). Firstly, fill out an application form at Tashi Ling (the Home Office), just off Bhanu Path in Gangtok. (Ignore the sign at the gate 'Tourists cannot enter from 10 am to 4 pm weekdays' – which are the official opening hours.) Then stroll down to the Foreigners' Registration Office on Kazi Rd (open 10 am to 4 pm weekdays, and 10 am to 2 pm on weekends). The whole process takes about 30 minutes.

National Parks Access to Kanchenjunga National Park – other than the Yuksom–Dzongri–Goecha La trek – is generally only permitted to mountaineering expeditions or experienced trekking parties using the services of a recognised travel agency. Most of the travel agencies listed in the Gangtok section can assist.

Special Events

Sikkim hosts many state-wide festivals.

Losong December/January. Celebrates Sikkimese New Year.
Saga Dawa May/June. Features processions to celebrate Buddha's birth.
Drukpa Teshi August. Celebrates Buddha's first teaching.
Phang Lhabsol August/September. Features Sikkimese dances devoted to Kanchenjunga.
'I Love Sikkim' Festival Mid-October. Features music, dance & food.

For information about other festivals held in Sikkim, see Gangtok, Enchey Gompa, Rumtek, Pemayangtse Gompa, Khecheopari Lake and Tashiding.

East Sikkim

GANGTOK

☎ 03592 • pop 90,000

The capital of Sikkim, Gangtok (which means 'hilltop'), sprawls down the west side of a long ridge flanking the Ranipul River. The scenery is truly spectacular, especially from the area known as 'the ridge', and many points in the city offer excellent views of the entire Kanchenjunga range.

Gangtok only became the capital of Sikkim in the mid-19th century. It has undergone a rapid and rather unattractive modernisation in recent years, but it's still a pleasant place with good facilities for visitors. In late December, Gangtok co-hosts (with Rumtek) the **Teesta-Tea-Tourism Festival**, which features music, food and flowers. In April or May **Buddha Jayanti** is celebrated when monks carry sacred scriptures through the streets.

Information

Tourist Office The Sikkim Tourist Information Centre (☎ 22064), at the northern end of MG Marg, should be the first point of call for all visitors. The notice board is a mine of information, and staff can advise on permits and festival dates. It's open from 8 am to 6 pm daily (March–May and October–December), and 10 am to 4 pm during the rest of the year.

Money Some mid-range and top-end hotels can change money for clients, but the best place is the State Bank of India, on MG Marg; open 10 am to 2 pm and 2.30 to 4 pm weekdays, and 10 am to 1 pm on Saturday. It changes US dollars and UK pounds in Thomas Cook and American Express travellers cheques, and cash in US

SIKKIM

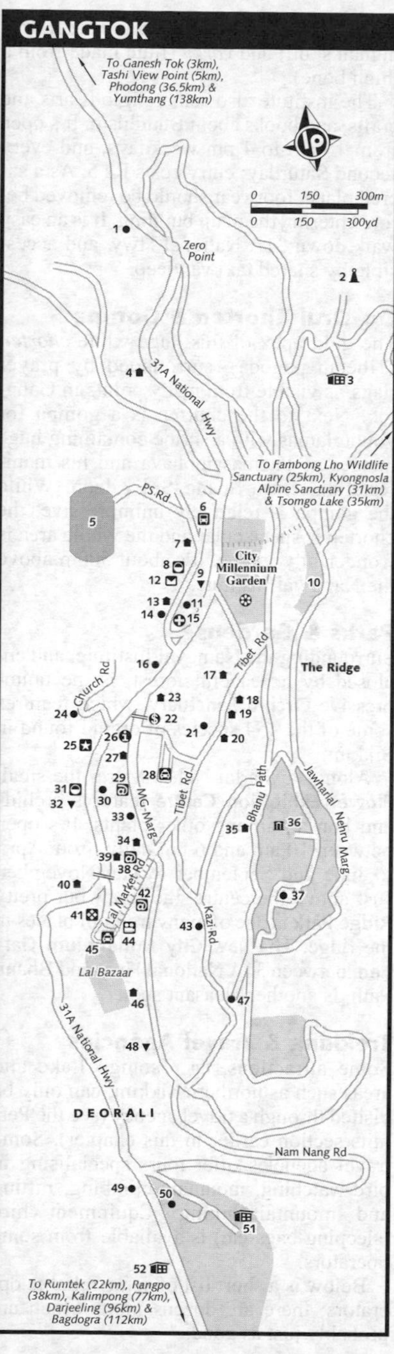

PLACES TO STAY

4 Hotel Superview Himalchuli; Yak & Yeti Travels
7 Hotel Lha Khar
13 Hotel Tibet
17 Hotel Sonam Delek; Oyster Bar & Restaurant
18 Hotel Heritage
19 Modern Central Lodge & Restaurant
20 Hotel Lhakpa
23 Gangtok Lodge
27 Green Hotel; Silk Route Tours & Travels
34 Hotel Golden Pagoda
35 Hotel Pomra
39 Hotel Orchid; Orchid Cafe
40 Hotel Central
46 Hotel Tashi Delek

PLACES TO EAT

9 Cafe Tibet
32 Hotel Hungry Jack; Tripti's
48 Oberoi's Barbique Restaurant

OTHER

1 Directorate of Handicrafts & Handlooms
2 Telecommunications Tower
3 Enchey Gompa
5 Palijor Stadium
6 SNT Bus Station; Railway Reservation Counter
8 Jeep Station
10 Flower Exhibition Centre; Ridge Park
11 Siniolchu Tours & Travels; Potala Tours & Travels
12 Main Post Office
14 Tibetan Souvenir & Handicrafts Stores
15 STNM Hospital
16 Jainco Booksellers
21 Blue Sky Treks & Travels
22 State Bank of India
24 Sikkim Tours & Travels
25 Police Station
26 Sikkim Tourist Information Centre; Blue Sheep Fast Food Centre & Restaurant; Wisdom Tours & Travels
28 Old Children's Park Taxi Station
29 Gokul (Internet Centre); RNC Enterprises; Parivar Restaurant; Khan Khazana (Restaurant)
30 Tashila Tours & Travels
31 Private Bus & Taxi Station
33 Good Books
36 Palace
37 Tsuk-La-Khang (Royal Chapel)
38 Sip 'n' Surf (Internet Centre)
41 Supermarket Complex
42 Logon.com (Internet Centre)
43 Foreigners' Registration Office
44 Denzong Cinema
45 Lal Bazaar Taxi Stand
47 Tashi Ling (Home Office)
49 Forest Department Office
50 Namgyal Institute of Tibetology; Orchid Sanctuary
51 Do-Drul Chorten & Gompa
52 Guru Lhakhang Gompa

dollars, UK pounds, French francs, Swiss francs and Japanese yen. It does not provide cash advances with any credit card.

Post & Communications The main post office along PS Rd has a poste restante. There is no shortage of public call offices (PCOs) for local and long-distance telephone calls around the streets.

Access at the many Internet centres is pleasingly reliable, and the standard rate is about Rs 1 per minute. The best three are probably Gokul, in an arcade off MG Marg; the trendy Sip 'n' Surf, at the top of the steps along Lal Market Rd; and Logon.com, farther along MG Marg.

Bookshops Good Books, at the end of an arcade off MG Marg, and Jainco Booksellers on 31A National Hwy, offer an impressive range of books and maps about Sikkim.

Emergency Useful emergency contact numbers are the police station (☎ 22033) and the STNM hospital (☎ 22944).

Enchey Gompa

This monastery is worth a visit, particularly when religious mask dances are performed during the Chaam festival in December/January. Built in 1909, it's now home to about 100 monks from the Nyingmapa order. The prayer hall is completely covered with exquisite paintings, and the roof is supported by four intricately carved pillars. The gompa sits on a spectacular ridge, with views across Gangtok and as far as Kanchenjunga. It's near the unmissable telecommunications tower, a steep 2km walk from the city centre.

Namgyal Institute of Tibetology

Established in 1958 and built in traditional Tibetan style, this unique institute promotes research into Mahayana Buddhism and the language and traditions of Tibet. It has one of the world's largest collections of books and rare manuscripts on Mahayana Buddhism, many religious works of art and a collection of finely embroidered silk *thangkas* (Tibetan cloth religious paintings). It also houses relics of monks from the time of Ashoka, examples of Lepcha script, masks, and ceremonial and sacred objects such as a *kapali* (bowl made from a human skull) and *varku* (flute made from a thigh bone).

The institute also sells religious arts and crafts, and books about Buddhism. It's open from 10 am to 4 pm weekdays, and every second Saturday; entry costs Rs 5. As a sacred place, footwear should be removed before entering the main building. It is an easy walk down 31A National Hwy, and accessible by shared taxi/van/jeep.

Do-Drul Chorten & Gompa

The gold apex of this huge white *chorten* (Tibetan pagoda), surrounded by prayer flags, is visible from many points in Gangtok. Next to the chorten is a gompa for young lamas with a shrine containing huge images of Padmasambhava and his manifestation, Guru Snang–Sid Zilzon. While the gompa is relatively unimpressive, the chorten is spectacular and the whole area is wonderfully serene. It's about 500m above the Namgyal Institute.

Parks & Gardens

Surrounding the Namgyal Institute, and enclosed by a peaceful forest, is the unimpressive **Orchid Sanctuary**, which features some of the 454 species of orchid found in Sikkim.

Along Jawharlal Nehru Marg, the small **Flower Exhibition Centre** features orchids and bonsai, among other plants. It's open between 10 am and 6 pm daily, from April to June and September to late November. Just above the centre, the small but pretty **Ridge Park** is one of many tranquil places in the ridge. The new **City Millennium Garden**, between 31A National Hwy and Bhanu Path, is another pleasant spot.

Trekking & Travel Agencies

Some attractions, eg, Tsomgo Lake and areas such as northern Sikkim, can only be visited through a travel agency (see the Permits section earlier in this chapter). Some travel agencies offer tours specialising in bird-watching, mountain-climbing, rafting and mountain-biking. Equipment hire (sleeping bags etc) is available from some operators.

Below is a short list of some reliable operators; there are dozens more which are probably just as good.

Blue Sky Treks & Travels (☎ 25113, ⓔ skar@cal2.vsnl.net.in) Tibet Rd. Offers several interesting budget-priced treks, and runs lodges in northern Sikkim.

Potala Tours & Travels (☎ 24434, ⓔ potala@dte.vsnl.net.in) PS Rd. One of several adjacent agencies, it offers the usual range of tours (including rafting) and treks at reasonable prices.

Sikkim Tours & Travels (☎ 22188, ⓔ sikkimtours@sikkim.org) Church Rd. An impressive and friendly outfit which can also organise photography and bird-watching tours.

Siniolchu Tours & Travels (☎ 25569, ⓔ siniolchu@dte.vsnl.net.in) PS Rd. Offers a wide range of treks, as well as cultural and mountain-biking tours.
Web site: www.sikkiminfo.com/siniolchu

Tashila Tours & Travels (☎ 22979, ⓔ tashilatt@hotmail.com) 31A National Hwy. Can also arrange special interest tours and rafting.
Web site: www.sikkiminfo.com/tashila

Wisdom Tours & Travels (☎ 20824, ⓔ baichungb@hotmail.com) Next to the tourist office on MG Marg. Friendly, convenient and competent.
Web site: www.wisdomtravels.com

Yak & Yeti Travels (☎/fax 24643, ⓔ yakyeti@dte.vsnl.net.in) Hotel Superview Himalchuli, 31A National Hwy. Informative, good value and specialises in mountain-climbing.

Activities

For something special (on a clear day), Sikkim Helicopter Service offers flights over West Sikkim (Rs 3250 per person, one hour); Yumthang (Rs 3750, 70 minutes); Kanchenjunga (Rs 5000, 90 minutes); and joyrides around Gangtok (Rs 1200, 20 minutes). See Getting There & Away later in this section for contact details.

Rafting trips down the Teesta River can be organised with several travel agencies, such as Tashila and Potala. These are good value: costing about Rs 350/600/900 per person for a one/two/3½ hour trip – including equipment and guide, but not transport. A minimum number (about six) is required.

Organised Tours

Any of the travel agencies listed earlier in this chapter can arrange customised local tours. These agencies, as well as local taxi drivers, also offer three types of 'official' tours: 'three point tours', including Ganesh Tok and Tashi view points (for Rs 300 per vehicle); 'five point tours', including Enchey Gompa, Flower Exhibition Centre and Namgyal Institute (Rs 420); and 'seven point tours' (basically the same as the 'five point tour', plus Rumtek) for Rs 600.

Unless you can get a group of four or five people together, these tours are way overpriced; and most attractions are within walking distance or easily accessible by chartered or shared taxi/van/jeep.

Places to Stay

In winter, it's important to inquire about the reliability and cost of hot water and heating. Few places have single rooms, and there's often no discount for single occupancy of a double room. A lot of mid-range and top-end hotels offer rates including meals, but these are not good value because there are plenty of good, cheap restaurants in Gangtok.

Low-season discounts (January–March and July–August) vary between 15% and 30%. The rates listed below are for the high season.

Places to Stay – Budget

Modern Central Lodge *(☎ 24670, Tibet Rd)* is popular and well set up for backpackers. Unexciting but clean singles/doubles with a shared bathroom cost Rs 100/180, and doubles with a private bathroom (and hot water) are Rs 250. A dormitory bed (eight in a room) costs only Rs 40 per person.

Plenty of hotels with decent rooms for about Rs 200/250 are dotted along the middle section of Tibet Rd. ***Hotel Lhakpa*** *(☎ 23002)* offers doubles (no singles) with a bathroom (cold water and squat toilets) for Rs 250. ***Hotel Heritage*** *(☎ 22701, ⓔ nirmal-mist@hotmail.com)* is one that boasts some imaginative decor. Pleasant rooms with a private bathroom (and hot water) cost a negotiable Rs 250/300; Rs 325/400 with cable TV. It also offers dorm beds for Rs 150 per person.

Green Hotel *(☎ 25057, ⓔ greenhot@dte.vsnl.net.in, MG Marg)* is comfortable and good value. It charges from Rs 150 for tiny singles to 250 for larger doubles; better doubles with cable TV cost Rs 350. All come with a private bathroom (with erratic hot water), and prices are negotiable.

Hotel Lha Khar *(☎ 25708, PS Rd)* is one of several budget places near the Main Post Office, and is convenient to the SNT Bus Station. This pleasant, quiet hotel has basic, but spotless, rooms for Rs 200/300 with a bathroom (hot water) and cable TV.

Hotel Orchid (☎ *23151, 31A National Hwy)* is another reasonable option, but the rooms with outside windows face the noisy road and the rooms without windows are gloomy. It is good value, however, and clean. Rooms with a shared bathroom cost Rs 100/200; and doubles (no singles) with a private bathroom are Rs 300.

Hotel Pomra *(☎ 26648, Bhanu Path)* has been recommended by readers, mainly because it's in a quiet area. Clean rooms (some with views) cost Rs 250/370, and the dorm beds for Rs 80 are good value.

Places to Stay – Mid-Range

All places listed below have private bathrooms (with continuous hot water) and cable TV.

Gangtok Lodge *(☎ 27319, ⓔ moderntreks@hotmail.com, MG Marg)* is friendly and central – but noisy. Standard doubles cost Rs 300, and very nice 'special' rooms (with lovely bathrooms) are Rs 800. Single rates are not available, but hefty discounts (of about 30%) are offered at most times.

Hotel Sonam Delek *(☎ 22566, ⓔ sonam.delek@gokulnet.com, Tibet Rd)* is pleasant and offers great views. The double rooms are bright and airy (most are quiet), and range from Rs 550 to 800 for the 'super deluxe' (ie, with the best views).

Hotel Superview Himalchuli *(☎/fax 24643, ⓔ himalchuli@usa.net, 31A National Hwy)* is in a more pleasant area, and boasts excellent views and helpful staff. Dorm beds cost Rs 75 per person; small 'standard' doubles are unremarkable, but adequate, for Rs 375; and spacious, well-furnished 'deluxe' rooms cost Rs 675/775 for doubles/triples.

Hotel Golden Pagoda *(☎ 26928, ⓔ goldenpagoda@hotmail.com, MG Marg)* is almost a top-end hotel with mid-range prices. It's central, but the rooms are smallish. Singles/doubles (some of which have great views) start from Rs 495/875.

Places to Stay – Top End

Top-end hotels add a 10% service charge (included in the rates below).

Hotel Tashi Delek *(☎ 22991, ⓔ tashidelek@sikkim.org, MG Marg)* has luxurious suites (Rs 4500) with awesome mountain views. The less-expensive singles/doubles (Rs 2500/2700) are comfortable, but only have views of other hotels.

Hotel Tibet *(☎ 22523, fax 26233, PS Rd)* is comfortable, popular and friendly. (You'll be welcomed by a doorman in full traditional Tibetan dress!) The cheaper rooms (from Rs 1012/1320) have no views, but the more expensive ones (from Rs 1265/1760) are well furnished, with traditional Tibetan decor, and have wonderful views.

Hotel Central *(☎ 22105, ⓔ hotel_central@hotmail.com, 31A National Hwy)* has been recommended by readers. It's friendly and convenient, but noisy, and offers very comfortable rooms for Rs 990/1430.

Places to Eat

Some of the best places to eat are in the hotels. ***Modern Central Lodge***, ***Hotel Lhakpa***, ***Hotel Lha Khar*** and ***Green Hotel*** have popular restaurants which offer cheap and tasty meals – usually Tibetan, Chinese and Indian – with some Western alternatives such as pancakes.

Oyster Bar & Restaurant, in Hotel Sonam Delek on Tibet Rd, is a bit more upmarket, and offers continental dishes, such as French toast, pizza and pancakes, as well as Chinese, Indian and Tibetan cuisine.

Hotel Golden Pagoda *(MG Marg)* has a rooftop vegetarian restaurant with lovely views and reasonable prices. It's open at 8 am for breakfast, but keep in mind that it doesn't serve omelettes.

Hotel Hungry Jack *(31A National Hwy)* has quick service, tasty meals and a reliable supply of cold beer. Underneath, ***Tripti's*** is the best bakery in town.

Cafe Tibet *(31A National Hwy)* is popular with local youth for sickly cakes, burgers, pizzas and milkshakes. ***Orchid Cafe***, underneath Hotel Orchid on 31A National Hwy, is similar.

Oberoi's Barbique Restaurant *(MG Marg)* is informal, clean and modern, and great for Western snacks, like club sandwiches, as well as Indian and Chinese meals.

Blue Sheep Fast Food Centre, next to the tourist office on MG Marg, does adequate burgers, while ***Blue Sheep Restaurant***, upstairs, is classy and good value.

Parivar Restaurant, downstairs along MG Marg, is a good choice for vegetarian food; and ***Khan Khazana***, at the back of the same arcade, has excellent service and delicious vegetarian food, including pizzas.

Entertainment

Numerous seedy little bars are dotted around town. All offer cheap prices (eg, a large bottle of tasty Dansberg beer costs about Rs 35), but finding a cold 'un is not always easy. More inviting places for a drink are Hotel Hungry Jack and Blue Sheep Restaurant. Full-moon and new-moon days are 'dry' days in Sikkim, but some bars still serve alcohol. For something different, try a mug of *chang*, known locally as *tongba* (fermented millet beer), from a shop in Lal Bazaar market.

Denzong Cinema, at Lal Bazaar, shows popular Indian films (in Hindi) for Rs 15/30 for front/upper circle seats.

Shopping

The Directorate of Handicrafts & Handlooms at Zero Point sells hand-woven carpets, blankets and shawls, patterned decorative paper, and beautifully carved Choktse tables. It's open from 9.30 am to 12.30 pm and 1 to 3 pm daily (except Sunday). It also hosts several craft fairs throughout the tourist season.

Many shops sell Tibetan handicrafts, especially along PS Rd. The Lal Bazaar is also worth a visit. It's open daily, but is especially lively on Sunday.

Getting There & Away

Air The nearest airport is at Bagdogra, near Siliguri – see Getting There & Away under Siliguri & New Jalpaiguri in the West Bengal chapter.

Sikkim Helicopter Service offers a daily flight between the Bagdogra airport and a helipad, 6km north of Gangtok (Rs 1500, 30 minutes). It leaves Gangtok at 11 am and returns from the airport at 2.45 pm. Book at RNC Enterprises (☎ 28652), upstairs along MG Marg, which is also the Jet Airways agent. The Indian Airlines agent is Silk Route Tours & Travels (☎ 23354), above Green Hotel on MG Marg.

Bus Sikkim Nationalised Transport (SNT), the main bus operator to/from Gangtok, offers plenty of decrepit buses from its well-organised bus station on PS Rd. The booking office is open 9 am to noon, and 1 to 2 pm.

SNT has several buses a day to Siliguri (Rs 55, five hours); and one a day to Darjeeling (Rs 83, six to seven hours) at 7 am, and to Kalimpong (Rs 55, three to four hours) at 1 pm. Within Sikkim, SNT buses go to Rumtek (Rs 17, 1½ hours) at 4 pm; Mangan (Rs 25, 2½ hours), via Phodong, at 8 am; Singhik (Rs 75, four hours) at 1.30 pm; and Jorethang at 7 am (Rs 55, four hours). SNT buses also leave for Pelling (Rs 70, 5½ hours) at 7 am, via Ravangla, Legship (for connections to Tashiding and Yuksom) and Gezing.

Private buses operate from the Private Bus & Taxi Station on 31A National Hwy to Siliguri (about every 30 minutes in the morning), and to Darjeeling and Kalimpong at least twice a day. These cost a little more than the SNT buses, but are faster and more comfortable. Tickets can be booked in advance at the station.

Train The Passenger Computerised Railway Service reservation counter (☎ 22014), at the SNT Bus Station, has a meagre allocation of tickets for services from New Jalpaiguri, near Siliguri. It's open from 8 am to 2 pm daily.

Shared Taxi & Jeep Shared taxis and jeeps are faster and more frequent than buses, but are potentially more dangerous and, if you're sitting in the back of a shared jeep, not necessarily as comfortable.

From the Private Bus & Taxi Station, on 31A National Hwy, shared jeeps regularly depart in the morning to Siliguri (Rs 90, four hours), Darjeeling (Rs 100, five hours), Kalimpong (Rs 65, three hours), Bagdogra (Rs 120, four hours) and Kakarbhitta (Rs 120, five hours) on the border with Nepal. These jeeps can often be booked in advance.

From the Old Children's Park Taxi Station, many shared jeeps go to Jorethang (Rs 70, three hours); two a day go to Gezing (Rs 95, 4½ hours), and on to Pelling (Rs 130, five hours), via Ravangla (Rs 60, three hours), at 7 am and 12.30 pm; and several a day go to Rangpo (Rs 35, two hours) and Mangan, via Phodong (Rs 40, two hours). Most can be booked in advance from a shed at the back of the station.

From Lal Bazaar, you can take shared jeeps to regional villages, such as Rumtek (Rs 20, one hour).

Getting Around

Taxis, jeeps and vans can be chartered from jeep/taxi stations for trips around Gangtok, eg, a trip across town costs about Rs 50. The rates for chartered taxis to tourist sites are officially fixed, and extortionate – but actually negotiable. Shared taxis, jeeps and vans stop at designated 'Taxi Stops' along 31A National Hwy; from the city centre to Namgyal Institute or Zero Point costs Rs 5.

AROUND GANGTOK

Rumtek

☎ 03592

In Rumtek village, on the other side of the valley from Gangtok, is the **Rumtek Dharma Chakra Centre**. It is the seat of the Gyalwa Karmapa, the head of the Kagyu order of Tibetan Buddhism, founded in the 11th century. Rumtek village co-hosts (with Gangtok) the Teesta-Tea-Tourism Festival in late December, which has music, food and flowers.

The main **monastery** is a recent structure, built by the 16th Gyalwa Karmapa in strict accordance with the traditional designs of his monastery in Tibet. The mural work here is not as refined as some of Sikkim's older gompas, however, and the **Golden Stupa** doesn't look too resplendent wrapped in plastic. Visitors are welcome to sit in on prayer and chanting sessions.

Behind the main monastery is the lavishly decorated **Karma Shri Nalanda Institute** of Buddhist studies. In the building opposite the entrance to the institute is a small hall featuring a beautiful jewel-studded **chorten**, which contains the ashes and bones of the 16th Gyalwa Karmapa.

The centre hosts many religious festivals, including **Tse Chu** in July which features Buddhist dancing, and it celebrates the Tibetan new year, **Losar**, in February/March with a big festival.

The centre is open every day from 8 am to 5 pm in summer, and 10 am to 5 pm in winter. A small booklet/map (Rs 20) about the Centre is available at the entrance. Visitors must register at the main gate to the village on arrival.

Places to Stay & Eat ***Sungay Guest House*** *(☎ 52221, ⓔ dechen@dte.vsnl.net.in)* is an obvious, friendly place surrounded by a pretty garden. It offers basic doubles, some with balconies and views, and an attached bathroom (with hot water), for a bargain Rs 150. Doubles with a bathroom (cold water), and no views, are Rs 100. The staff also serve basic Tibetan and Western meals for guests.

Sangay Hotel *(☎ 52238)* is down some steps at a corner near the centre. Tiny, basic but clean singles/doubles with a shared bathroom cost only Rs 50/100.

Hotel Kunga Delek, at the entrance to the centre, is run by the centre itself. The double rooms are ordinary, and comparatively overpriced for Rs 100/150 without/with a private bathroom.

A few ***stalls*** along the road to the Centre sells *chai* (tea), *momos* (dough parcels of vegetables or meat), and other snacks.

Getting There & Away Rumtek is only 26km from Gangtok. The official rate for a chartered jeep/taxi is a ridiculous Rs 240/400 one way/return, but bargaining down to a more reasonable Rs 300 return is not hard. Shared jeeps occasionally leave Lal Bazaar (Rs 20, one hour), and an SNT bus leaves every day from Gangtok at 4 pm (Rs 17, 1½ hours).

It's a pleasant 14km hike (downhill) from Rumtek to the turn-off along the highway, from where it's easy to get a ride for the 12km (uphill) to Gangtok. However, don't expect too much public transport after 3 pm.

Tsomgo (Changu) Lake

Sacred to the local Buddhists, Tsomgo Lake (also called Changu Lake) is perched about 3752m above sea level (about 1250m higher than Gangtok).

About 37km north-east of Gangtok, it's a great day trip, but don't bother if Gangtok's weather is cloudy or foggy because it will probably be a peasouper at the lake and the views will be very disappointing. Most of the lake is frozen from December until about mid-May, but it's still worth seeing if the weather is clear.

Around the lake, there are a few short **walking trails**, **yak rides**, plenty of ***stalls*** selling hot tea/coffee and momos, and the ***Alpine Lodge*** which serves the same sort of food and drink undercover. There are bizarre plans to build an artificial lake nearby for boating and fishing – activities which are not allowed at Tsomgo because it's sacred.

Currently, foreigners can only visit the lake on a day trip (see the Permits section

SIKKIM

earlier in this chapter) organised by a travel agency in Gangtok. The standard charge for foreigners is outrageous: US$10 (or the rupee equivalent) per person in a jeep with two to four people; US$8 per person for a jeep with six or more; and (if possible) US$15 to US$20 for a jeep with one person. If foreigners are eventually allowed to visit the lake independently, a chartered jeep (90 minutes one way) from Lal Bazaar will cost about Rs 700 return, or Rs 130 per person in a shared jeep, including waiting time. No-one is allowed to visit the lake in a private vehicle, and there is no bus service.

North Sikkim

More of this region is opening up to foreigners, but during the monsoons from June to August the roads are often cut off by landslides.

PHODONG

Phodong Gompa belongs to the same order as Rumtek, but is much smaller and less ornate. It's a fairly recent structure, although the original gompa was founded, like Rumtek, in 1740. It has a community of about 60 monks; many of them were born in India after the Chinese occupation of Tibet. They're friendly, and always happy to show visitors around.

Labrang Gompa, 1.2km farther up the road (and visible from Phodong Gompa), was established in 1844 and belongs to the Nyingmapa order.

There are a couple of basic places to stay in Phodong village. ***Hotel Northway*** has clean singles/doubles (some with good views), and a shared bathroom, for Rs 50/100. ***Hotel Yak & Yeti***, about 100m farther down the road, has bright, airy and clean doubles (no singles) for a negotiable Rs 120/150 without/with a private bathroom. Both places can rustle up some basic meals, and even some cold beer.

Phodong village straddles the main Gangtok-Mangan road, 38km north of the capital. The road (1.2km) to the gompa is unsigned but obvious, and starts about 1.5km south of the village. At the time of research, some of the Gangtok-Mangan road could only be crossed by jeep, so Phodong was not accessible by bus. Shared jeeps from Gangtok to Mangan travel via the gompa turn-off and village (Rs 40, two hours); to avoid the back seat, buy a fare for Mangan (Rs 60).

YUMTHANG VALLEY

Yumthang Valley, which lies 140km north of Gangtok at an elevation of 3564m, is now open to foreigners. You can go as far as Singhik with an endorsement of the basic permit, but to travel between Singhik and Yumthang village you technically need to join an organised tour (see the Permits section earlier in this chapter for details).

There is budget accommodation in Singhik, Chungthang and Lachung. An SNT bus usually leaves Gangtok for Singhik (Rs 75, four hours) at 1.30 pm. Otherwise, take a shared jeep to Mangan and another to Singhik or beyond.

South Sikkim

Most travellers rush through this region while going between Gangtok and Pelling, but the district headquarters of Ravangla is a pleasant base and stopover, and Jorethang is the border town with several places to stay if necessary.

RAVANGLA

☎ 03595

Ravangla has a spectacular setting along the highway between Gangtok and Pelling. About 15 minutes' walk (follow the road to Gangtok, and then to Namchi) from the jeep stand is the **Kunphenling Tibetan Settlement**, where you can buy authentic handmade carpets and other handicrafts. At the end of the village main street, flags indicate steps to the small but friendly **Mani Chokharling Gompa**.

Any hotel facing the mountains will initially ask an outrageous price, but negotiation is always possible. All places listed below have an attached bathroom (with hot water), unless otherwise stated; and all have a ***restaurant***.

Hotel 10zing (☎ *60705*), at the jeep stand, has spartan but clean singles/doubles for Rs 150/250, some with cable TV – but no views.

Hotel Kanchenjunga, up the hill from the jeep stand and behind the State Bank of

India, has large and quiet doubles (no singles) for Rs 200.

Hotel Meanamla (☎ *60666,* ⓔ *meanamla@hotmail.com)*, along the highway about 100m up from the jeep stand, has poor 'standard' doubles with a shared bathroom for Rs 495, but pleasant 'deluxe' doubles from Rs 660 with cable TV and views.

From the jeep stand, shared jeeps go to Siliguri (Rs 40, four hours) and Legship (Rs 32, two hours). For Gangtok or Pelling, wait near the jeep stand for a shared jeep or SNT bus to come past.

JORETHANG

☎ 03595

There is no need to stay at the border town of Jorethang – Darjeeling is only 26km to the south and Pelling 53km to the north – but there are several cheap places to stay and eat near the SNT Bus Station. ***Hotel Namgyal*** *(☎ 57263)* is the best: Decent singles/doubles, with a private bathroom (and a huge bath) and cable TV, cost Rs 150/300.

SNT buses go to Gangtok (Rs 55, four hours) at 7 am and 1.30 pm; to Siliguri (Rs 56, four hours) at 9 am; and to Pelling (Rs 35, three hours) at 9.30 am and 1 pm. Shared jeeps leave regularly (when full) from outside Hotel Namgyal to Darjeeling (Rs 80, 2½ hours); Gangtok (Rs 70, three hours); and Siliguri (Rs 80, 3½ hours). Jeeps leave less often to Yuksom (Rs 90, four hours), via Legship and Tashiding (Rs 75, 2½ hours); and to Pelling (Rs 60, three hours), via Gezing (Rs 35, 2½ hours).

SIKKIM

West Sikkim

The roads in this region are mostly sealed, but to Tashiding and Yuksom some of the roads are unsealed and subject to landslides.

GEZING (GAYSHING)

☎ 03595

Public transport between Gangtok and Pelling often bypasses the unexciting village of Gezing, but you may have to wait there for a connecting jeep or bus. Gezing is at its best on **market day** (Sunday).

Hotel Attri *(☎ 50602)*, 100m uphill from the town square, has large, clean and quiet singles/doubles, with an attached bathroom (and hot water), for Rs 385/495.

SNT buses to Gangtok (Rs 54, 4½ hours) leave at 9 am and 1 pm; and about every hour to Jorethang and Siliguri in the morning.

Shared jeeps to Pelling (Rs 15, 15 minutes) leave every 15 to 20 minutes. There are also regular jeeps to Gangtok (Rs 95, 4½ hours), via Jorethang or Ravangla every 30 minutes in the morning; several at about 7 am daily to Siliguri (Rs 95, four hours); and one per day to Tashiding (Rs 50, two hours) at 1 pm, and to Yuksom (Rs 70, three hours) at 12.30 pm.

PELLING

☎ 03593

The tiny village of Pelling, perched high on a ridge with great views of Kanchenjunga, is little more than a string of hotels, but it's a pleasant and popular place to relax and organise day trips and hikes.

Orientation & Information

Along the road from Gezing is 'Upper Pelling', with a handful of better hotels, the Sikkim Tourist Centre, post office, jeep/bus stand and several restaurants. The road continues up about 250m to an area known as the helipad (actually a soccer field), with a group of mid-range hotels. Another road at the jeep/bus stand winds down past 'Middle Pelling' and 'Lower Pelling', where there's a bunch of unexciting and inconvenient hotels, and eventually on to Yuksom.

Surprisingly for a place with about 50 hotels, there's nowhere to change money, send an email or even buy a newspaper.

Pemayangtse Gompa

Pemayangtse (Perfect Sublime Lotus) is one of the state's oldest and most important gompas. Reconstructed several times, it belongs to the Nyingmapa order, which was established by Padmasambhava in the 8th century. In February/March, the gompa celebrates Losar, Tibetan new year, with a big festival.

The monastery is a three-storey structure filled with wall paintings and sculptures. On the top floor is **Zandog Palri**, an amazing seven-tiered painted wooden model of the abode of Padmasambhava, complete with rainbows, angels and the whole panoply of Buddhas and Bodhisattvas on the third floor. The model was built single-handedly by the late Dungzin Rinpoche in five years. Pemayangtse is a 30-minute walk from Upper Pelling, and well signposted from the road down to Gezing.

Other Attractions

The ruins of **Rabdentse Palace**, in Sikkim's former capital, is an interesting place to explore, and the views are superb. Walk about 30 minutes farther down towards Gezing from the turn-off to Pemayangtse Gompa, turn left at the 'Archaeological Survey of India' sign, walk across the archery field and look for the start to the 2km track. It's fairly easy to then find your way downhill from the ruins to the Gezing-Pelling road.

A 45-minute walk south-west from the helipad brings you to **Sangachoeling Gompa**, the second oldest gompa in Sikkim. The monastery has a magical position high on a ridge, and it's a great spot at sunrise. Like Pemayangtse, the interior walls are highly decorated with paintings.

Places to Stay & Eat

All places listed below are in Upper Pelling and, unless stated otherwise, have an attached bathroom (with hot water). There is a massive oversupply of hotels throughout Pelling, so negotiation is possible.

Hotel Kabur *(☎ 50685)* is the first place you see as you come from Gezing. It offers plain singles/doubles for a reasonable Rs 150/300. The quaint ***restaurant*** has great views, but not everything on the menu is always available. Nearby, there are several other ***cheap hotels*** for about the same price.

Sikkim Tourist Centre *(☎ 50788)* is a few doors farther down. The rooms (all doubles) are smallish, and cost from Rs 550 to 660 (with better views), but they don't have TV. The ***restaurant*** on the top floor has good service, tasty meals and wonderful views.

Hotel Garuda *(☎ 50614)*, at the jeep/bus stand, is a popular travellers haunt. Dorm beds (four to a room) cost Rs 50 per person. Ordinary rooms with a shared bathroom cost from Rs 60/100, and better rooms with an attached bathroom and cable TV start from Rs 150/200. The ***restaurant*** offers a huge range of Western, Indian, Tibetan and Sikkimese meals.

Ladakh Guesthouse is a rustic Sikkimese house just down from the Garuda. It only has five rooms, all with a shared bathroom. At Rs 100 per double, and Rs 50 per dorm bed, not surprisingly it's often full.

Sister Guest House *(☎ 50569)* is a quaint, family-run place along the road to Lower Pelling just below the Garuda. Clean doubles with a shared bathroom cost Rs 190. Next door, ***Alpine Restaurant*** is a cosy place run by a friendly Tibetan family. The servings are large, and prices very reasonable.

Getting There & Away

Public transport is infrequent, so if nothing is available go to Gezing (9km downhill), and take a shared jeep or bus from there. Always check the current transport schedules from Pelling with hotel staff.

SNT buses leave Pelling for Jorethang (Rs 35, three hours) at 7 am and at 3.30 pm; the latter goes past the turn-off (Rs 25, 1½ hours) to Khecheopari Lake.

Simvo Tours & Travels, just down from the jeep/bus stand, has shared jeeps to Siliguri at 6 am (Rs 110, four hours) and 8.30 am (Rs 150), via Jorethang or Ravangla; to Kalimpong (Rs 110, three hours), via Jorethang, at 6 am; and to Gangtok (Rs 130, five hours) at 6 am and 12.30 pm. If there's enough demand, a jeep will leave for Darjeeling (Rs 170, five hours) – otherwise get a connection in Jorethang. Full fares are demanded for partial rides, and advance bookings are essential.

Shared jeeps to Gezing (Rs 15, 15 minutes) leave every 15 to 20 minutes. Shared jeeps between Gezing and Yuksom come through Pelling about every 30 minutes between about 6.30 and 9 am, but these are often full. To Yuksom and Tashiding, it's sometimes easier to start from Gezing, or hitch a ride from Legship.

KHECHEOPARI LAKE

This small and serene lake (pronounced 'catch a perry') lies in a depression surrounded by prayer flags and forested hills. It's a very holy place, so swimming and smoking is not allowed. The lake is about five minutes' walk from the end of the road to the lake, and about 1.5km above it is the small **Khecheopari Gompa**. In March/April, the lake hosts the Butter Lamp Floating Festival, **Khachoedpalri Mela**.

The ***Khecheopari Trekkers' Hut***, about 200m before the end of the road, offers clean, but very basic, dorm beds (Rs 30 per person) and rooms (Rs 60 per person). Simple Tibetan and Western meals are available for guests. It's also a good source of hiking information.

At the lake, the unsigned ***Pilgrims' Hut*** offers spotless dorm beds for Rs 40 per person – and some rooms only have two dorm beds. It also offers meals for guests. A ***chai stall*** nearby serves drinks and momos.

By road, the lake is about 27km from Pelling; the hiking trail is shorter, but much steeper (see the Trekking section later for details). The daily SNT bus from Pelling only goes as far as the turn-off (11km) up to the lake. Shared jeeps leave the lake from about 6 am and stop at Pelling and Gezing. To travel from Pelling directly to the lake, ask around about a shared jeep, join an organised (morning) tour from Pelling (Rs 75 per person) or charter a jeep (about Rs 500 one way).

TASHIDING

This friendly village is popular with trekkers, but is worth visiting anyway for the awesome setting.

Founded in approximately 1716, **Tashiding Gompa** is Sikkim's most sacred monastery and belongs to the Nyingmapa order. It's perched majestically atop a conical hill, a steep 45-minute walk from Tashiding village. A large Buddhist festival, **Bumchu**, is held here in January/February. During the festival, a pot of holy water is opened by the lamas, who tell the future of the coming year from the water.

Hotel Blue Bird, halfway up the village street, is a very basic but welcoming place with dorm beds from Rs 25 per person, and doubles with a shared bathroom from Rs 50. ***Mt Siniolchu Guest House***, at the end of the main street, has better doubles with a shared bathroom for Rs 100.

The SNT bus does not currently reach Yuksom, so the only way there is by shared jeep. Most leave Yuksom between 6 and 8 am; several travel daily to/from Gezing, via Pelling; to Jorethang; to Yuksom, when there's enough demand; and to Gangtok once a day.

YUKSOM

Yuksom is where the north-western road stops, and is the trailhead for anyone trekking to Dzongri or Goecha La. This peaceful village is where the three lamas of the Nyingmapa order arrived to establish Buddhism in Sikkim, and where the coronation of the first chogyal of Sikkim took place. The stone throne is next to a large **chorten** in a small hall not far from Hotel Tashi Gang.

Built in 1701, **Dubdi Gompa** was the first capital of Sikkim and is its oldest gompa. About 45 minutes' walk uphill from Yuksom, no monks are now based here, but a caretaker (check with your hotel for his whereabouts) will open it up. Police normally check permits along the Yuksom–Dzongri–Goecha La trek, so don't try setting off without one.

Khangchendzonga Conservation Committee, next to Hotel Wild Orchid, is an essential stop for anyone hiking/trekking in the area. It can provide excellent advice, organise guides and porters (if required) and rent equipment (gas stoves especially). It also plans to open a trekking agency later.

The following hotels are based around the village square. ***Hotel Wild Orchid*** has clean singles/doubles with a shared bathroom for Rs 75/100. ***Hotel Dzongrila*** has basic doubles for Rs 150, plus good food, beer and chang. ***Hotel Demazong*** is clean, well-run and has dorm beds from Rs 60 per person, and doubles from Rs 150/200 without/with a private bathroom. ***Gupta Restaurant*** offers tasty samosas and other Indian snacks.

Hotel Tashi Gang is unmissable on a hill above the village. The well-furnished rooms have fine views, cable TV and a private bathroom (with hot water), and are worth a splurge for Rs 710/990 for singles/doubles. The 'deluxe' rooms for Rs 990/1260, however, are not worth the extra. It also boasts a charming ***restaurant*** and bar.

Several shared jeeps go to Gezing, via Pelling, between about 5 and 7 am every morning; and about five jeeps go to Jorethang, via Tashiding, from about 6 am.

About 10km from Yuksom on the road to Pelling, the spectacular **Kanchenjunga Falls** is a popular stopoff.

Trekking

PELLING-LEGSHIP

This trek links some interesting villages and attractions in West Sikkim. You don't need a special additional permit, but you must get your basic permit endorsed in Gangtok to allow you to visit Khecheopari Lake and Tashiding.

The first stage takes you from Pelling to Khecheopari Lake along the main roads. For the second stage, the short cut to Yuksom heads downhill for about one hour, and then for the last two, ascends gradually into Yuksom. The short cut is confusing, so ask for advice at the lake before you start and whenever you meet anyone en route.

From Yuksom to Tashiding, follow the road, taking some of the obvious short cuts. Then it's an easy two or three hour walk along the road to Legship. Bring snacks because there's not much on offer along the way, and always check with locals for the best short cuts. To save the long uphill walk back (six hours) to Pelling from Legship, jump on a bus or shared jeep.

stage	route	duration (hrs)
1	Pelling to Khecheopari Lake	5–6
2	Khecheopari Lake to Yuksom	3
3	Yuksom to Tashiding	5–6
4	Tashiding to Legship	2–3

YUKSOM–DZONGRI–GOECHA LA–YUKSOM

This is the most popular trek in Sikkim, and offers superb views of Kanchenjunga. To start this trek, your basic permit must be endorsed for Yuksom, and to do the trek you must *currently* be in an organised group of at least four. However, this rule may be relaxed or even waived in the future (see the Permits section earlier in this chapter).

Even if independent trekking is allowed, inexperienced trekkers may wish to join an organised tour anyway. Most of the travel agencies mentioned in the Gangtok section earlier can arrange a tour from US$30 to US$60 per person per day, including food, yaks and porters.

There are ***trekkers' huts*** at Baktim, Tsokha, Dzongri, Thangshing and Samiti Lake, and these are the best bet if it's cold. At the height of the trekking season, there's sometimes not enough space in the huts so your travel/trekking agency will need to provide tents. And it's *imperative* not to trek too high too quickly. (See the Health section in the Facts for the Visitor chapter for advice about altitude sickness.)

From Yuksom (1630m), the trail follows the Rathong Valley through unspoilt forests to Baktim (2740m), from where there's a steep ascent to Tsokha (3050m). Above Tsokha, the trail enters magnificent rhododendron forests to an intermediary ***camp site*** at Pethang (3760m). It's a good idea to either bring tents and spend a night at Pethang, or spend two nights at Tsokha, to acclimatise.

The next stage brings you to Dzongri (4025m). From Dablakang, 200m above Dzongri, there are excellent mountain views. If spending more than one night at Dzongri to further acclimatise (recommended), walk up to Dzongri La (4550m) – four hours return – for more great mountain views.

From Dzongri, the trail drops steeply down to the river where there's a ***trekkers' hut***; then follow the river to Thangshing (3840m). The final stop is at Samiti Lake (4200m), from which an early morning assault is possible to the head-spinning Goecha La (4940m) for the best views of Kanchenjunga. After that it's down to Thangshing for the night, and then back to Yuksom two days later.

stage	route	duration (hrs)
1	Yuksom to Tsokha, via Baktim	6-7
2	Tsokha to Pethang	2–3
3	Acclimatisation Day	
4	Pethang to Dzongri	2–3
5	Dzongri to Samiti Lake, via Thansing	6–7
6	Samiti Lake to Goecha La & down to Thangsing	8–9
7	Thangshing to Tsokha	6–7
8	Tsokha to Yuksom	5–6

North-Eastern Region

The north-eastern region is the most varied yet the least visited part of India. Before Independence this beautiful area of rolling forested hills and lush green fields was known as Assam province, but it has since been gradually broken up into seven separate states. Nowadays, the state of Assam consists mostly of the plains around the Brahmaputra and Barak Rivers, while the other states (excluding Tripura) occupy the hills.

The north-east is the country's chief tribal area, with many different languages and dialects; in Arunachal Pradesh alone over 50 distinct languages are spoken. These Adivasis (tribal people) have many similarities to the hill tribes who live across an arc that stretches from the eastern end of the Himalaya through Myanmar (Burma) and Thailand into Laos.

India has always been touchy about the north-east, although the permit requirement for foreign tourists visiting Assam, Meghalaya and Tripura was lifted in 1995. Encompassing a sensitive border zone where India meets Bhutan, China, Myanmar and Bangladesh, the region is remote, and only the narrow Siliguri corridor connects it to the rest of India.

As well as the perceived threat from their neighbours, most of the states in the north-east have been, and continue to be, wracked by insurgencies and ethnic violence. The reasons for this unrest include a feeling of neglect by the central government – poor transport links and a lack of industrial development are two main issues. Very little of the oil wealth from Assam, for example, has found its way back to the state; and the whole region remains overwhelmingly agricultural.

Also of concern to the indigenous population is the inflow of 'foreigners' into the region. The poverty in crowded Bangladesh, and the oppression of that country's Hindu minority, has created a never-ending flow of Bangladeshis to the north-east. This has been so great that migrants now outnumber the indigenous population in Tripura. There has also been a significant migration of Nepalis to the hill states; despite the lack of shared borders, this is a

North-Eastern Region at a Glance

ARUNACHAL PRADESH
Pop: 1.1 million
Area: 83,743 sq km
Capital: Itanagar

ASSAM
Pop: 26.6 million
Area: 78,438 sq km
Capital: Dispur

MIZORAM
Pop: 891,058
Area: 21,081 sq km
Capital: Aizawl

MANIPUR
Pop: 2.4 million
Area: 22,327 sq km
Capital: Imphal

NAGALAND
Pop: 2 million
Area: 16,579 sq km
Capital: Kohima

MEGHALAYA
Pop: 2.3 million
Area: 22,429 sq km
Capital: Shillong

TRIPURA
Pop: 3.2 million
Area: 10,486 sq km
Capital: Agartala

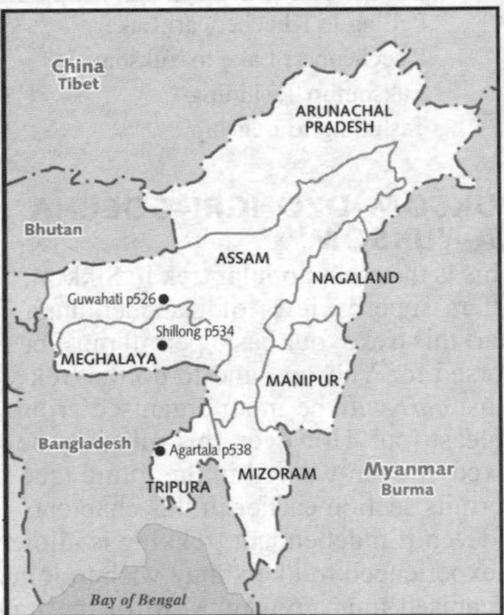

- See the endangered one-horned rhino in Assam's Kaziranga National Park
- Visit Assam's Hindu Vaishnavaite Monasteries, Majuli, the world's largest river island
- Splash around the pseudo-Scottish hill station of Shillong in Meghalaya
- Wander around Tripura's Neermahal, a majestic water palace attracting few tourists, but thousands of birds
- Contemplate Tawang Gompa in Arunachal Pradesh, one of the largest Buddhist monasteries in India

migratory flow seen in many parts of North India and in Bhutan.

Matters have been complicated by the demands of various ethnic minorities within the states. In Assam, for example, the Bodos are demanding a homeland separate from the rest of the state. In Manipur, there is bitter fighting between rival tribes, especially the Kukis and Nagas. In some states, like Tripura, insurgency has simply become a way of life, with good money to be made from kidnapping and extortion. Several hundred local people die each year in the north-east as a result of the troubles – and the situation continues to be bad.

Permits

Permits are no longer required for Assam, Meghalaya or Tripura – but still check to see if it's safe to go.

For Mizoram and Manipur, foreigners must travel in a group of four on a tour organised by an approved travel agency. If your patience knows no bounds and you want to try your luck at getting into these two states without joining an organised tour, you'll either need a very good excuse for visiting, or friends in *very* high places. It's worth contacting someone at the relevant state government office for advice before applying; a letter from them will improve your chances.

Foreigners may be issued a permit allowing independent travel in Arunachal Pradesh and Nagaland, but most visitors go on an organised tour anyway because it's easier and safer.

Restricted Area Permits (sometimes called Protected Area Permits) for these four states will be arranged by your travel agent if you're on an organised tour. If you are travelling independently, however, you should apply at:

- the state government offices (*bhavans*) listed in the relevant sections later in this chapter – certainly the best option
- Ministry of Home Affairs, Foreigners' Division, Lok Nayak Bhavan, Khan Market, New Delhi – where you can expect a bureaucratic nightmare
- a major Foreigners' Registration Office – eg, Chennai (Madras), Mumbai (Bombay) and Kolkata (Calcutta)
- the embassy/consulate where you applied for an Indian visa

Permits are usually valid for 10 days and normally extendable, and you need a separate permit for each state. Allow at least three weeks for each permit to be issued. Even in the states that openly accept tourism, red tape is alive and well; eg, if travelling by air, you'll be checked in (and out) by the police at the airport.

See the Warnings & Permits information in the individual sections later in this chapter for more details about obtaining permits for each state.

Warning

Because of constant rebel activity and ethnic violence, you are strongly advised to check the current situation before visiting the north-eastern region, especially Manipur and Nagaland. Don't underestimate the potential danger: At the time of research, large-scale massacres of locals were a weekly occurrence in all states (except Arunachal Pradesh), and over 100 police officers had been killed in this part of India in the previous 12 months.

The best – and, sometimes, only – way to know which areas are currently dangerous to visit is to read regional daily English-language newspapers such as *The Sentinel*, *The Assam Tribune* and *The Northeast Daily*.

A day or two after a massacre, a 12-hour daytime *bandh* (strike) is inevitably called by one or more regional political groups as a protest. All shops, offices and restaurants (except in hotels) are usually closed during a bandh, and all public transport around, and originating from, the area with the bandh ceases – but hotels, hotel restaurants and all interstate transport *to* the area continues to function.

To ensure that the bandh is effective, members (often fanatical) of the group(s) usually roam the streets, under the observation of many policemen and soldiers. If possible, avoid any area where a bandh is taking place (they are detailed in advance in local English-language newspapers), or at least stay in your hotel.

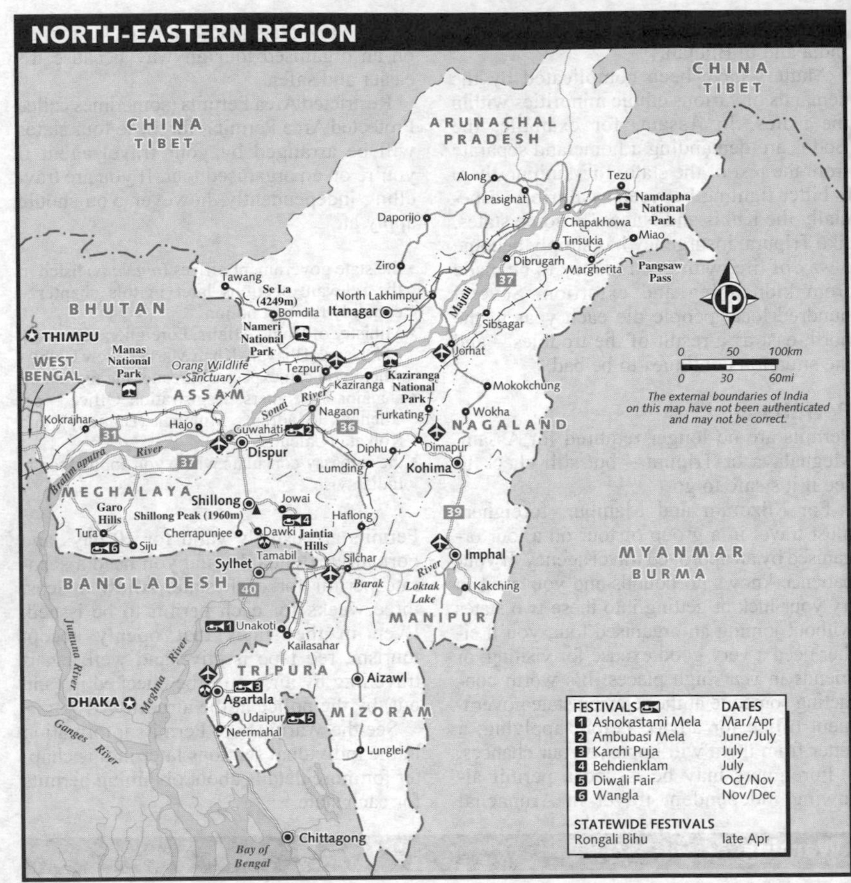

Organised Tours

Because of the difficulty of obtaining permits for, and possible problems about safety in, the north-eastern region, many travellers choose to join an organised tour. Many reliable operators offering tours around the north-east are based in Darjeeling and Kalimpong (West Bengal), Guwahati (Assam) and Gangtok (Sikkim) – see those sections or chapters for details.

Assam

The largest and most accessible of the north-eastern states, Assam grows about 60% of India's tea and produces a large proportion of the country's oil. The main attractions are Kaziranga National Park, home of India's rare one-horned rhinoceros, and the remarkable Majuli island.

History

Early Assamese history includes some semi-mythical Hindu rulers such as the great Narakasura, mentioned in the Mahabharata, who ruled from Pragjyotishpura (modern-day Guwahati). Branches of Hinduism based on *shakti* (power) worship and mystic-erotic Tantric cults are thought to have emerged in Assam, and these traditions continue at temples in Guwahati.

In the 13th century, the Ahoms, a Shan tribe from Myanmar (Burma), conquered Assam, adopted Hinduism and established a dynasty which lasted until 1826. The

Ahoms also repulsed some 17 invasions by the Mughals, thereby allowing Assam's Hindu culture to blossom in relative peace. The dynasty reached its peak under Rudra Singha (r. 1696–1714), who built trade links with Tibet and was renowned as a military strategist.

During the late 16th century, the philosopher-saint Sankardeva began a Vaishnavaite movement which rejected the Hindu caste system and the rituals of Tantric Hinduism. Instead a Hinduism based on community prayer was spread by *satras* (monasteries), eg, on Majuli island, which became centres for arts such as dance, manuscript painting and music.

The Ahom dynasty gradually declined until a Burmese invasion from 1817 to 1822 killed one in every three people. The British then drove out the Burmese and annexed the Ahom kingdom.

In the lead-up to Independence it took delicate manoeuvring, and the separation of the Muslim-majority Sylhet district, to stop the large Assam province joining East Pakistan (now Bangladesh) rather than staying in India. After Independence, old rivalries between peoples from the hills and plains, Hindus and Muslims and Adivasis and non-Adivasis, rose and Assam province gradually separated into seven north-east states.

Warnings & Permits

For the last 25 years, Assam has been subject to the militant actions of numerous groups. The United Liberation Front of Asom (ULFA), based primarily in Bangladesh and Bhutan, is pledged to the independence of Assam through armed struggle. In late 2000, the ULFA increased its rebel activities in upper Assam, especially near Dibrugarh, to include for the first time the wholesale massacre of innocent non-Assamese villagers. The ULFA's activities are currently widespread enough to affect the stability of all states in the north-eastern region.

The Bodo minority is campaigning for a separate state stretching along the border with Bhutan. Several militant groups, such as the Bodo Liberation Tiger Force (BLTF) and the National Democratic Front of Bodoland (NDFB), are operating in the north-western areas of Assam. Another active rebel group is the Muslim United Liberation Tigers of Assam (MULTA).

It's also imperative to note that travelling by train anywhere in upper (north-east) Assam is potentially dangerous because of the activities of armed dacoits (bandits).

No permits are required for travel within Assam. The major Assam government offices are at Bl Baba Kharak Singh Marg, New Delhi (☎ 011-334 3961), and 8 Russel St, Kolkata (☎ 033-298 331).

GUWAHATI

☎ 0361 • pop 580,000

Alongside the impressively wide Brahmaputra River is Guwahati, once known as Pragjyotishpura (The Light of the East). It has long been the region's most important city, and is now the service centre for the oil and tea industries.

Guwahati is sprawling and ugly, but as the gateway to Assam and the north-eastern region most travellers spend a few days there. The city is split into two on either side of the river. Most places of interest and use to visitors are in the southern section, simply known as Guwahati, while the northern section is called Uttar Guwahati. The state government is actually based in Dispur, a drab town about 8km to the south-east.

Information

Assam Tourism (☎ 544475, ⓔ astdcorp@gw1.dot.net.in) is based at the Tourist Lodge (hotel) on Station Rd. It isn't particularly helpful, but sells a useful map of the city (Rs 25). There's also a small tourism counter at the train station. Assam Tourism also has a Web site (www.assamtourism.com). The Government of India tourist office (☎ 547 407) is on the corner of B Barua and GS Rds.

Standard Chartered Grindlays Bank (SCB Grindlays) on GN Bordoloi Rd, and State Bank of India on MG Rd, change cash and travellers cheques. Stock up here on rupees before heading to anywhere else in the north-east.

There are a few Internet centres along MN Rd, such as NE Communication (which also has a pool table) and Nick Computers, just up from Ananda Lodge; and Cyberzone on B Barua Rd. The standard fee is about Rs 50 per hour.

Modern Book Depot, on HB Rd, has a wide range of books on the region.

For emergencies contact Guwahati Medical College (GMC) Hospital (☎ 562521), off GS Rd, about 5km south of the city centre; or the police station (☎ 555650) on HB Rd.

Temples (Mandirs)

Umananda Mandir The most interesting thing about this Shiva temple is its location, on Peacock Island in the middle of the river. Ferries and boats regularly leave Kachari and Umananda ghats near MG Rd between 7 am and 5 pm daily – but the exact departure points vary according to the tides. A return trip costs about Rs 10.

Navagrah Mandir On Chitrachal Hill to the north-east of the city centre, Navagrah Mandir (Temple of the Nine Planets) has long been known as a centre of astrology and astronomy. The nine planets are represented by nine linga (phallic symbols) inside the main temple.

Kamakhya Mandir Guwahati's best-known temple is Kamakhya Mandir on Nilachal Hill, about 8km west of the city. It is the centre for Shakti worship and Tantric Hinduism because worshippers believe that when Shiva sorrowfully carried away the corpse of his first wife, Shakti, her body disintegrated and her yoni (part of the female genitalia) fell there.

Although rebuilt in 1665, after being destroyed by Muslim invaders, the temple's origins are much older. It was probably an ancient sacrificial site used by the Khasi

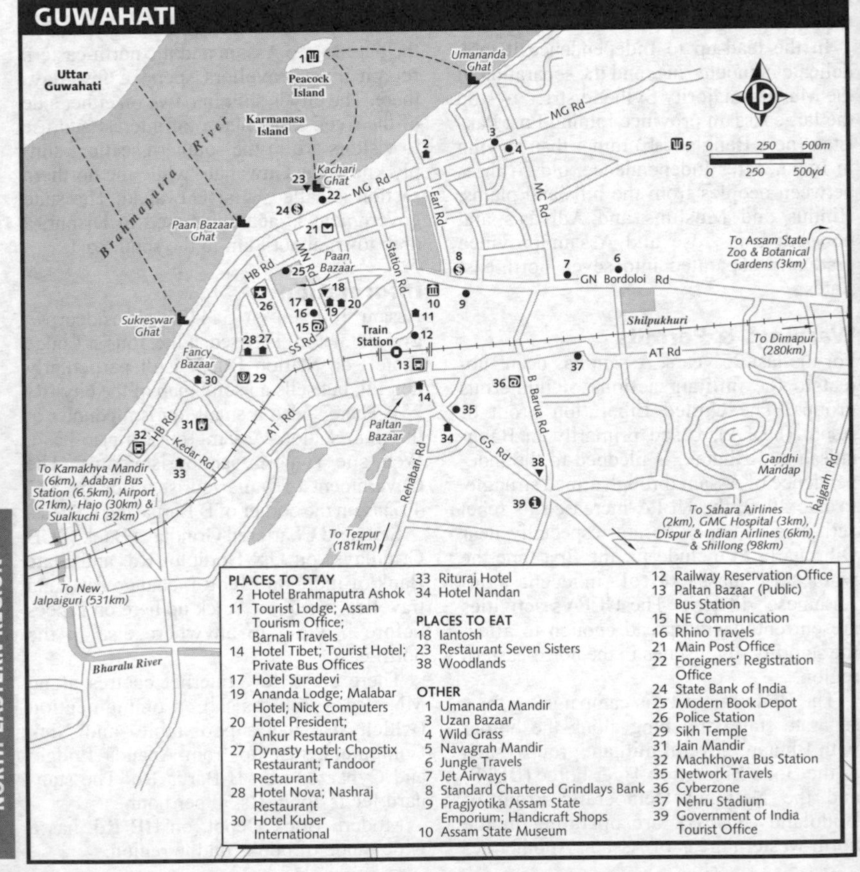

people from Meghalaya, and daily goat sacrifices are still part of worship. The temple attracts pilgrims from all over India, especially during **Ambubasi Mela** the statewide celebration of the end of the earth's menstrual cycle (June or July). **Rongali Bihu** is another festival held across Assam at the end of April to celebrate the start of the harvest.

Non-Hindus are usually allowed into the inner sanctum, but no photographs are permitted. Inside it's dark and quite eerie, and the floor is often sticky with the blood of sacrificial goats. Take bus No 15 from AT Rd (eg, at Paltan Bazaar), or charter an autorickshaw.

Assam State Museum

This large archaeological, ethnographic and natural history museum on GN Bordoloi Rd is well worth a visit. Particularly interesting is the 'walk-through' reconstructed village, the displays of weavings and musical instruments, and the explanations about the various tribal groups around Assam, such as the Karbi, Bodo, Rabha and Miri.

The museum is open from 10 am to 4.15 pm daily, except Monday (to 5 pm in summer). Tickets cost Rs 5; still/video cameras are an extra Rs 10/250.

Assam State Zoo & Botanical Gardens

The combined zoo and botanical gardens is spacious and well managed, and boasts tigers, leopards and, of course, Assam's famous one-horned rhinos – plus the African two-horned variety for comparison. It is about 5km south-east of the city centre, and is open from 8 am to 4 pm daily, except Friday. A combined ticket costs Rs 5; and still/video cameras are an extra Rs 5/250.

Organised Tours

As the gateway to the north-east, Guwahati is one of the best places to organise a tour around Assam and the other six states. Some of the more reliable travel agencies include:

Barnali Travels (☎ 544475) at Tourist Lodge, Station Rd. Associated with the Assam tourism office, this agency also offers day trips (Rs150 per person) to the local temples, zoo and museum; day trips to Hajo and Sualkuchi (Rs 250) and Shillong (Rs 250); and two-day trips to Kaziranga National Park (see that section for details). If, as often is the case, there aren't enough passengers for a bus trip, staff can arrange a taxi for the day for Rs 500.

Jungle Travels (☎ 520890, e jtxgau@gw1.vsnl.net.in) GN Bordoloi Rd. An impressive outfit offering rafting, trekking, fishing, 'jungle safaris' around all major regional national parks and all sorts of other interesting trips around the north-east.

Rhino Travels (☎ 540666) MN Rd. Offers a range of tours around Assam and the north-east, but office staff seem fairly disinterested.

Wild Grass (☎ 546827, fax 541186) Baruah Bhawan, 107 MC Rd. This helpful and knowledgeable agency runs an excellent resort at Kaziranga National Park, and tours to neighbouring states.

Places to Stay

There is a dire lack of decent budget hotels in Guwahati, and government taxes and service charges of up to 30% (which have been added to the prices) make accommodation fairly expensive anywhere in Assam. All places listed in this section have rooms with private bathroom and fan, unless stated otherwise.

Places to Stay – Budget

The hotels near the corner of GS and AT Rds in Paltan Bazaar are convenient to the private bus offices, public bus station and train station, but you won't get much sleep. ***Hotel Tibet*** *(☎ 539600, AT Rd)* is one of the better options, because it's friendly and clean. Singles/doubles cost Rs 150/250; more with cable TV. ***Tourist Hotel*** *(☎ 566882, AT Rd)* has a huge number of rooms for about the same price.

Ananda Lodge *(☎ 544832, MN Rd)* is nothing special, but it is friendly. Very small singles with a portable fan (if you're lucky) cost from Rs 60 to Rs 95 with shared bathroom, but it's often full and staff are sometimes reluctant to accept foreigners.

Tourist Lodge *(☎ 544475, Station Rd)*, run by Assam Tourism and close to the train station, used to be the only decent budget option. Clean and comfortable rooms used to cost Rs 170/210, but prices subsequently increased to a ridiculous Rs 324/383. Hopefully sense will prevail, and the rates will go down and/or the rooms will be improved considerably.

Hotel Suradevi *(☎ 545050, MN Rd)* is a large place with dorm beds for Rs 60 per person; basic, clean rooms for Rs 85/120 with shared bathroom; and Rs 95/150/195 for singles/doubles/triples with private bathroom. It's good value, which is why it's often full. Also, the managers may baulk at letting foreigners stay.

Hotel Kuber International *(☎ 520807, HB Rd)* is a little run-down but otherwise fine. Singles/doubles cost Rs 200/300; Rs 325/425 with air-con.

Rituraj Hotel *(☎ 522495, Kedar Rd)* has unexciting rooms for Rs 281/375 and is in an inconvenient location.

Places to Stay – Mid-Range & Top End

All hotels include cable TV and bathrooms with hot water.

Hotel Nova *(☎ 523464, SS Rd)* is convenient, clean and comfortable, and has helpful staff. Small singles/doubles cost Rs 845/858.

Hotel President *(☎ 544979, ⓔ presihot@gw1.dot.net.in, SS Rd)* is the same standard as the Nova, and has rooms from Rs 676/780.

Hotel Nandan *(☎ 540855, ⓔ nandan@gw1.dot.net.in, GS Rd)* is another comfortable and convenient three-star place. Rooms start from Rs 813/1235.

Hotel Brahmaputra Ashok *(☎ 541064, ⓔ brahmaputra@satyam.net.in, MG Rd)* is in an excellent location beside the river. Rooms are large and airy, and some have wonderful river views. Tariffs start from Rs 2000/3250.

Dynasty Hotel *(☎ 510499, fax 522112, SS Rd)* is a favourite with businesspeople. The comfortable rooms have air-con, and cost from Rs 1950/2600.

Places to Eat

Fish features on most menus, and is very tasty and often cheap (from Rs 15 to Rs 30). The most common varieties are known locally as *rahu*, *elish*, *puthi* and *chital*.

Malabar Hotel, near Ananda Lodge on MN Rd, specialises in South Indian vegetarian fare, and is cheap and convenient.

Woodlands *(GS Rd)* is a well-known South Indian vegetarian restaurant with filling thalis (all-you-can-eat plates) for about Rs 50. The food, and heavenly air-con, is worth the trip.

Hotel restaurants are generally the best places to eat: ***Nashraj Restaurant*** at Hotel Nova serves tasty, but expensive, Indian and Chinese cuisine; Dynasty Hotel offers the upmarket ***Chopstix*** (for Chinese) and ***Tandoor*** (Indian) restaurants; and ***Ankur Restaurant***, at Hotel President, is pricey (from Rs 60 per dish), but the food is excellent and worth a splurge.

Iantosh *(GN Bordoloi Rd)* is a clean, friendly and informal eatery offering the usual range of Chinese and Indian meals, as well as tasty burgers, fries and milkshakes at reasonable prices.

Restaurant Seven Sisters, at Kachari Ghat off MG Rd, is one of several 'floating' restaurants permanently moored along the Brahmaputra. It offers welcome breezes and views of the islands, and the prices are surprisingly reasonable – about Rs 50 for a hearty meal.

Shopping

Several places on GN Bordoloi Rd, such as Pragjyotika Assam State Emporium, sell Assam's *muga* silk, as well as other fabrics and handicrafts. The bazaars are fascinating and chaotic places to shop.

Getting There & Away

Air Indian Airlines (☎ 264425), on GS Rd in Dispur, has daily flights between Guwahati and Kolkata for US$70 one way, and several each week to/from Delhi (US$220), Agartala (US$45), Aizawl (US$55) and Imphal (US$50).

Jet Airways (☎ 520202), on GN Bordoloi Rd, has daily flights to/from Kolkata (US $70), and regular flights to/from Delhi (US$210), Imphal (US$50) and Bagdogra (US$50). Sahara Airlines (☎ 266667), 3.5km south of the city on GS Rd, has daily flights to/from Delhi (US$210) and Dibrugarh (US$55).

A quick and exhilarating alternative is offered by Meghalaya Helicopter Service, which has a daily service to Shillong (Rs 625, 30 minutes). Book at the airport office (☎ 840311).

Bus The well-organised Paltan Bazaar (public) bus station is at the southern exit of the train station. Most offices for the quicker and more comfortable private buses are near the corner of AT and GS Rds – the most reliable companies include Blue Inn, Green Valley and Blue Hill. Network Travels has an impressive…umm…'network' of bus routes; its office is further down GS Rd.

Private and public buses go to Shillong (about Rs 50, 3½ hours) every few minutes between 6 am and 5 pm. They also leave regularly for Dimapur (Rs 100, seven hours), Kohima (Rs 145, nine hours) and Imphal (Rs 232, 13 hours) and travel overnight to Itanagar (Rs 175, 12 hours), Siliguri (Rs 250, 13 hours), Bomdila (Rs 220, 18 hours) and Agartala (Rs 300, 25 hours).

Within Assam, private and public buses depart frequently for Tezpur (Rs 75, six hours), Kaziranga village (Rs 95, six hours), Jorhat (Rs 110, seven to eight hours), Haflong (Rs 180, nine to 10 hours), Sibsagar (Rs 145, eight to nine hours) and Silchar (Rs 215, 12 hours).

There are regular services to regional towns from the Machkhowa and Adabari bus stations.

Train Between Guwahati and Kolkata (993km, 24 hours), there are several trains daily; tickets cost about Rs 270/914/1253 for 2nd class/1st class/air-con. The Guwahati-Kolkata trains run daily and some of them start and finish in Chennai (Rs 472/1823/2213 from Guwahati). Most trains heading south and west stop at New Jalpaiguri (422km, eight hours), near Siliguri, for Rs 154/520/713.

The *Rajdhani Express* travels between Guwahati and New Delhi (Rs 402/143/1876) three times weekly. The *BP Mail* and *Kamrup Express* travel daily to Lower Haflong (Rs 111/373/535), sometimes detouring through Dimapur (Rs 100/336/508) in Nagaland. However, foreigners are not allowed to disembark there without a permit. The line heading from Lumding to Silchar (Rs 212/473/653 from Guwahati) is metre gauge.

The reservation office (☎ 520560) is on Station Rd.

Getting Around

Lok–Priya Gopinath Bordoloi airport is 23km south-west of Guwahati. Rhino Travels offers a daily bus (Rs 30) from outside its office on MN Rd to the airport at 10 am, and returns from the airport at 1 pm. Otherwise, shared taxis (Rs 70 per person) go from outside Hotel Nandan on GS Rd. Shared taxis are very easy to arrange from the airport.

Along the Brahmaputra, there are frequent ferries and boats (Rs 2 one way) from Paan Bazaar and Sukreswar ghats along MG Rd to Uttar Guwahati. One-hour boat cruises (Rs 50 per person) start from Sukreswar Ghat on the hour every hour between 4 and 8 pm daily.

AROUND GUWAHATI

On the northern bank of the Brahmaputra, **Hajo** is an important pilgrimage centre for Hindus, Buddhists and Muslims. The Hindus worship at the Hayagriba-Madhava Mandir; some Buddhists believe that Buddha attained nirvana here; and for Muslims, Pao-Mecca mosque is considered to have one-quarter of the holiness of the great mosque at Mecca. Buses link Machkhowa bus station in Guwahati with Hajo (Rs 15, 1¼ hours).

Sualkuchi is a famous silk weaving centre best known for its muga silk which is naturally golden-coloured, and not dyed. *Endi* and *pat* silks are also woven here, and prices are lower than in Guwahati (around Rs 350 per metre for muga, and Rs 170 for pat). Sualkuchi is accessible from the Machkhowa bus station in Guwahati, and is about 2km south of Hajo.

Manas National Park (360 sq km) is part of Project Tiger (an official agency of the Indian government, established in 1973 to save the Indian tiger from extinction), but is also home to langurs, elephants, rhinos and buffalos. However, Manas is currently too dangerous to visit because of the continuing activities of Bodo rebels in the area. Contact the local tourist office (☎ 03666-32749) for current information, and to book lodges at the park, if travel is possible.

TEZPUR

☎ 03712

Tezpur (named 'City of Blood' after a mythical war) is a centre for the regional tea industry. The town still retains a colonial atmosphere, and it's a pleasant place to stay.

Tezpur has several ancient temples, including **Mahabhairava Mandir**; and ancient Gupta sculptures at the ruins of the 6th-century **Da-Parbatia Mandir**, 5km west of Tezpur. In **Chitralekha Udyan** (also known as Cole Park), in the middle of Tezpur, there are the 9th-century sculptures and excavated sections of the palace belonging to the former king, Banasura. The lake in the park also offers **boat trips**, and there's a snack bar.

Places to Stay & Eat

Tourist Lodge *(☎ 21016)* is a pleasant place opposite the lake. Comfortable singles/doubles cost Rs 210/260 with private bathroom and mosquito net, but it's often full so book ahead. The tourist office is attached.

Hotel Meghdoot *(☎ 20714, Cemetery Rd)* has rooms with shared bathroom for Rs 90/110, and doubles with private bathroom from Rs 180. Some rooms have no outside windows, so it's a bit gloomy.

Hotel Luit *(☎ 22083)* has a large number and variety of rooms, all with cable TV and private bathroom. The rooms in the 'old wing' for Rs 192/275 are OK, and virtually the same as the overpriced 'new' doubles for Rs 330.

Gabharu Restaurant, at Hotel Luit, is overpriced and the food is nothing special. ***D'Oasis Restaurant & Bar*** *(Jonaki Rd)*, on the other side of the tank from Hotel Luit, is better.

Getting There & Away

Indian Airlines (☎ 22083) – based at Hotel Luit – has several flights a week between Saloni airport (16km from Tezpur) and Kolkata (US$80), often via Dimapur (US $35).

Since Tezpur is on a branch line, buses are more useful than trains. Buses frequently depart for Guwahati (Rs 75, six hours), Jorhat (Rs 60, four hours) and Kaziranga village (Rs 32, two hours), and there are several daily buses to Itanagar (Rs 100, six hours) and Tawang (Rs 185, 24 hours). Buses leave from the ASTC or CM Market bus stations; tickets can be booked at numerous agencies around town.

NAMERI NATIONAL PARK

This national park (212 sq km) protects forest and wetlands along the Bharali River, as well as endangered turtles, tigers, elephants and birdlife. The park is open between 1 November and 31 March.

At Potasali, 3km from the park entrance, ***Eco Camp*** *(☎ 03714-44246, ⓔ ripman@gw1.vsnl.net.in)* offers eco-friendly fishing (ie, tag the fish and throw them back), birdwatching, rafting, hiking (with an armed guard!), boat trips and elephant rides. It also offers accommodation in tents and dorm beds – contact them for current rates.

Tourist Lodge, at Bhalukpong on the border with Arunachal Pradesh, charges Rs 270/325 for singles/doubles with private bathroom.

The park entrance is 35km north of Tezpur, and best reached by chartered vehicle from Tezpur because public transport is unreliable.

KAZIRANGA NATIONAL PARK

Kaziranga National Park (430 sq km) has an official rhino population of over 1500, although in 1904 they were on the verge of extinction. It is famous as one of the last habitats of the one-horned rhino.

Kaziranga, which became a 'game sanctuary' in 1916 and a national park in 1974, also has gaurs (Indian bison), deer, elephants, tigers and bears, as well as prolific birdlife (best seen in December and January), including ibises, pelicans, eagles and storks. The most interesting way to see the wildlife is on an (albeit expensive) elephant ride.

The Great Indian Rhino

Assam is famous for the rare Great Indian One-Horned Rhinoceros *(Rhinoceros unicornis)*. Once widely distributed across the northern floodplains of the subcontinent, the rhino has been consistently killed to make way for tea plantations and villages, so it's now restricted to only a handful of national parks, such as Kaziranga in Assam (where the largest number is found) and Royal Chitwan in Nepal.

These rhinos are now on the Convention on International Trade in Endangered Species of Fauna and Flora (CITES) endangered list because less than 200 creatures remain. Large and formidable, the rhino has few natural predators, but a naturally slow population growth makes them especially vulnerable to illegal poaching. As in Africa, political turmoil has provided a cover for poachers, and there is an ever-present market for rhino products. In India and Nepal, there's little of a rhino's anatomy that is not prized for its aphrodisiac, medicinal or spiritual attributes.

Information

The park is open from 1 November to 30 April. Inside the park, the tourist information centre (☎ 036776-62423) at Bonani Lodge is where you must register, and where you can book accommodation, jeeps and elephant rides.

Entry to the park costs Rs 175. Other charges include: Rs 150 per day to bring in a vehicle; Rs 175/525 per day for a still/video camera; and Rs 525 for a one-hour elephant ride. A discount of 25% is usually given if you spend more than three days in the park (there are no discounts for the elephant ride). Jeeps are available from the main gate near Kaziranga village, or from the Bonani or Aranya lodges, for at least Rs 50 per person per hour (depending on the number of passengers).

Places to Stay & Eat

All accommodation listed here (except Wild Grass Resort) offers rooms with a fan and private bathroom; air-con costs about Rs 100 extra per room. All rooms, except at the Aranya and Wild Grass, should be booked in advance at the tourist information centre at Bonani.

Bonoshree Lodge costs Rs 150/210 (low/high season) for singles and Rs 200/260 for doubles; meals can be pre-ordered with staff. ***Bonani Lodge*** is Rs 250/350 for singles and Rs 310/410 for doubles, and has a ***restaurant***. ***Kunjaban Lodge*** has dorm beds without/with linen for Rs 25/50 per person, and basic meals can be ordered.

Other ***cottages*** around the park – with no cooking facilities or restaurant (so bring your own food) – cost Rs 650 per double (in any season).

Aranya Lodge *(☎ 03376-62429)* is the best of the lodges. The rooms with hot water (not always available) and a balcony cost Rs 250/410 for singles and Rs 350/510 for doubles in low/high season. The attached ***Rhino Restaurant*** is wonderful, but expensive – set meals are Rs 120.

Wild Grass Resort *(bookings: ☎ 0361-546827, fax 541186)* is an excellent eco-friendly private resort, signposted off the main road about 4km east of Kaziranga village. Accommodation is either in luxury tents or in a lodge. Doubles (no singles), with private bathrooms, cost Rs 1800, but discounts of 40% are readily available. The 'Jungle Plan' (Rs 2200 per person per day) includes accommodation, meals and trips into the park by elephant.

Getting There & Away

The nearest airport is at Jorhat (84km away), while the nearest train station is at Furkating (75km).

Buses between Guwahati (Rs 95, six hours) and Jorhat (Rs 45, 2½ hours) go through Kaziranga village (also known as Kohora), from where it's easy to walk or hitch a ride to the park entrance.

Allow at least three nights and four days in Kaziranga, so avoid organised tours from Guwahati, because they're too short (two days) and you'll spend most of that time on the bus and only have time for one wildlife drive. Tours are offered by Barnali Travels (see Organised Tours in the Guwahati section for details) for Rs 1440 per person including transport, meals, a guide, park fees, accommodation and an 'elephant safari'. Hotel Paradise in Jorhat can also arrange pricey tours.

UPPER ASSAM

Jorhat

☎ 0376

Jorhat is the gateway to Upper Assam, and a very pleasant stopover. Assam Tourism (☎ 321579) is at Tourist Lodge on MG Rd. State Bank of India on AT Rd changes cash and travellers cheques.

Along Biman Barua Rd, there's a laneway at the back of the ASTC bus station on AT Rd where there are several quiet, adjacent hotels. The three listed here have a restaurant, and rooms with a fan and private bathroom.

Hotel Dipti *(☎ 323502)* has simple but clean singles/doubles with a mosquito net for Rs 120/200. ***Hotel Dilip*** *(☎ 321610)* offers rooms for Rs 150/200; the rooms for Rs 300/500 with air-con are good value. ***Hotel Paradise*** *(☎ 321521)* is the best, and has large, comfortable rooms with cable TV for Rs 375/500.

Tourist Lodge *(☎ 321579, MG Rd)* is a comfortable alternative for Rs 210/260 with private bathroom, fan, mosquito net and balcony.

Indian Airlines (☎ 320011) and Jet Airways (☎ 325652) – both based in Hotel Paradise – have flights twice a week each to/from Kolkata (US$90). Jet Airways also flies to Imphal (US$80).

Long-distance buses to Sibsagar (Rs 18, 1½ hours), Kaziranga village (Rs 45, 2½ hours), Tezpur (Rs 60, four hours) and Guwahati (Rs 110, seven to eight hours) and leave from the ASTC bus station; local buses depart from the public bus station on the corner of AT and MG Rds. Trains are less convenient because Jorhat is on a branch line.

Majuli

In the midst of the mighty Brahmaputra, Majuli is famous as the world's biggest (albeit rapidly eroding) river island (886 sq km). However, it's more interesting for its 22 *satras*, important Hindu Vaishnavaite monasteries which also function as centres for Assamese arts.

The institution of the satra was founded in the 15th century by the Assamese poet, composer and philosopher Sankardeva. At the Majuli satras, Vishnu is worshipped through dance dramas re-enacting the stories of the *Mahabharata*, and with music and poetry. Sankardeva saw Vishnu as the pre-eminent deity without form – a concept that marks Assamese Hinduism apart from the other traditions. More information is available on an official Web site (www.auniati.bizland.com).

The main satras are at Kamalabari (the 'centre for learning'), Garamur (home of ancient weapons), Shamaguri (famed for mask-making), Auniati (with interesting jewellery and handicrafts), Dakhinpat (which hosts major festivals) and Bengenaati (with its centre of dance and arts). All are several kilometres apart, but accessible from Garamur, the main town, for about Rs 300/600 per day by autorickshaw/taxi.

It's possible to stay at some satras, but you should make a donation. ***Circuit House*** *(☎ 03775-74439)*, near Garamur, charges from Rs 100 per person for simple but clean rooms with private bathroom. Alternatively, ask about staying with a village family.

From Jorhat, ramshackle buses leave regularly from the public bus station to Nimati Ghat (Rs 12, 1¼ hours), from where ferries (Rs 5) leave at 10 am and 3 and 4 pm for Kamalabri on Majuli. The ferries depart Kamalabari for Nimati Ghat at 8 and 9 am and 2 pm. (Check current schedules with the tourist office in Jorhat.) Motorboats (Rs 15 per person) travel more regularly between Nimati Ghat and Kamalabari, from where there's public transport to Garamur.

Sibsagar

☎ 03772

Sibsagar was the ancient capital of the Ahom dynasty, which ruled Assam for over 600 years. It's now an important centre for the tea and oil industries.

The town is dominated by **Sibsagar Tank**, a huge artificial lake created in 1734. Beside the tank stand three temples, including **Shivadol Mandir**, possibly the tallest Shiva temple (33m) in India. About 6km west of the town centre are the ruins of the seven-storey 18th-century palace known as **Talatal Ghar**, and the nearby two-storey **Rang Ghar**.

About 13km to the east of Sibsagar is **Gargaon Palace**, the ruins of another 18th-century Ahom palace. Tombs of the Ahom kings are situated at the 13th-century capital of **Charaideo**, about 28km east of Sibsagar.

Tourist Lodge *(☎ 21814)*, by the tank in Sibsagar, has comfortable singles/doubles with private bathroom for Rs 210/260; Assam Tourism (☎ 22394) is also based there. ***Kareng Hotel*** *(☎ 22713, Temple Rd)* is pretty good value for Rs 90/150 with shared bathroom, and has a reasonable ***restaurant***. ***Hotel Brindavan*** *(☎ 22974, AT Rd)* has air-con doubles with private bathroom from Rs 600.

Simaluguri, the mainline train station, is 16km from Sibsagar. Buses are more convenient, and leave regularly for Guwahati (Rs 145, eight to nine hours) and Jorhat (Rs 18, 1½ hours).

SOUTH ASSAM

Haflong

Assam's only hill station is a friendly town based around the pretty **Haflong Lake**. The area is best known for **Jatinga** village (9km south of Haflong), where flocks of birds are said to 'commit suicide' between August and November. (What actually happens is that migrating birds passing by are attracted to lights set up by the villagers, and the birds land and end up in the villagers' cooking pots!)

Tourist Lodge *(☎ 03673-2468)* in Haflong has decent singles/doubles with private bathroom for Rs 210/260. ***Hotel Elite***, just above the market, is the best place to stay and eat. Doubles with private bathroom start from Rs 220.

At least two buses a day link Haflong with Silchar (Rs 60, four hours). From the station at Lower Haflong, two trains travel to/from Silchar and Guwahati daily.

Silchar

Silchar is a significant transport hub. If you need to spend the night, ***Tourist Lodge*** *(Park Rd)* has singles/doubles with private bathroom for Rs 210/260. Silchar is linked to Kolkata (US$75), via Imphal, most days by Indian Airlines. Several buses a day travel to Agartala, Aizawl, Shillong and Guwahati, and there are two trains a day to Haflong.

Meghalaya

Created in 1972, Meghalaya (The Abode of Clouds) is the home of the Khasi, Jaintia and Garo tribespeople, noted for their matrilineal society (ie, property and wealth are passed through the female rather than the male line). The gently rolling hills of Meghalaya are noted for growing fruit and betel nut, which locals enjoy immensely. The state – and, in particular its capital, Shillong – is one of the wettest places on earth, so come prepared.

History

Khasi and Jaintia tribes are closely related and are thought to have originally emigrated from South-East Asia, while the Garo came from Tibet. The Khasi and Jaintia trace their descent back to the Ri Hinniew Trep (Seven Families) – and the Khasi and Jaintia are collectively known as 'Hynniewtrep'. According to legend, there were 16 families – nine in heaven and seven on earth – connected by a golden vine ladder, but the link was severed when sin poisoned the earth.

Warring chiefs ruled the area before the arrival of the British, who established control by the 1820s by playing the tribes off against each other. Shillong's gentle rainy climate made it a favoured retreat from the plains for British tea planters and administrators of the region. Missionaries were permitted to work among the tribes, and nowadays more than half the population of Meghalaya is Christian.

Warnings & Permits

Meghalaya is comparatively safe from rebel activity. However, ethnic violence occasionally flares up in the south-west near the border with Bangladesh, so seek advice before travelling to Tura and the Garo Hills. One group based near Shillong is the A'chik National Volunteer Council, which strives for a 'Greater Garoland', but it is currently ineffectual.

Permits are not required for travel anywhere in the state. The major Meghalaya government offices are at 9–10 Russel St, Kolkata (☎ 033-229 0797); and 9 Aurangzeb Rd, New Delhi (☎ 011-301 4417).

Special Events

Behdienklam is a religious festival held in July during monsoon in the Jaintia Hills.

Wangla is a four-day festival of music held to celebrate the end of the harvest in the Garo Hills in November or December.

SHILLONG

☎ 0364 • pop 260,000

From 1874 until 1972, the hill station of Shillong was the capital of Assam, and known as the 'Scotland of the East'. The colonists here built a championship golf course (the world's wettest), and a polo ground, and soon the surrounding hills were dotted with neat Victorian bungalows and churches. These days, central Shillong is often heavily congested with road traffic, and a multitude of ugly concrete buildings have sprung up. However, it's still a very charming place.

Information

The Meghalaya Tourism office (☎ 226220), opposite the MTC bus station, is open from 7.30 am to 5 pm daily (to 11 am Sunday). It can't help much, but it is the place for booking organised tours (see later in this section). The Government of India tourist office (☎ 225632) is on GS Rd.

Cash and travellers cheques can be changed at State Bank of India on Kacheri Rd. Internet facilities are available at Aryans Dotcom on Police Bazaar Rd and Cyberzone on GS Rd. The standard rate is about Rs 40 per hour.

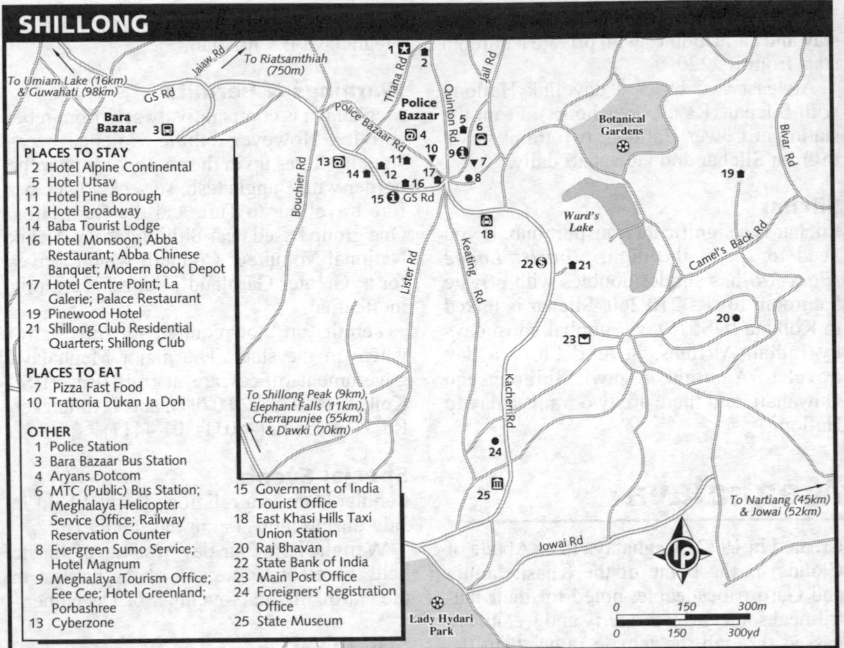

Parks & Waterfalls

As expected in a place with so much rain, there are numerous waterfalls and pretty spots in and around Shillong (see Around Shillong later).

The attractive **Ward's Lake**, named after the chief commissioner Sir William Ward, was the focus of European settlement. Entry to the surrounding park is Rs 15, and 20-minute **boat rides** cost Rs 60 per four-person boat. The **Botanical Gardens** are a few minutes' walk further north.

The spectacular **Elephant Falls** are 12km by autorickshaw or chartered taxi from central Shillong, and about 120 steps down from the car park when you get there.

The immaculate **Lady Hydari Park** is popular, particularly with young local couples, and features a mini-zoo. It's open during daylight hours, except Monday, and entry is Rs 2.

Museums

The unimpressive **State Museum** on Kacheri Rd provides dusty coverage to the flora, fauna, culture and anthropology of the state, but does have some interesting sculptures. It's open from 10.30 am to 4.30 pm daily, except Sunday. Entry is free.

More interesting is **Riatsamthiah**, also known as the Museum of Entomology, on Jaiaw Rd, 1.5km north of Police Bazaar. It breeds butterflies for conservation organisations around the world, and is open from 10 am to 4.30 pm weekdays and 10 am to noon Saturday.

Other Attractions

From the top of **Shillong Peak** (1965m) there are wonderful views of the town and surrounding hills. It's about 10km from the town centre, and accessible by chartered taxi or autorickshaw. Be careful where you wander off and point your camera – it's on restricted airforce land.

Umiam Lake (5 sq km), in the village of Barapani, is surprisingly undeveloped for tourism. A few motley boats are available for hire, but there's nothing else to do but admire the serenity. ***Orchid Lake Resort*** *(☎ 570258)* has large, clean and quiet singles/doubles with private bathroom near the lake from Rs 450/520. The main entrance to the lake is 400m off the road to Guwahati

(17km from Shillong), and accessible by any bus or jeep along that road.

Organised Tours

Despite all sorts of advertisements and promises, travel agencies only bother arranging local tours if you can find other passengers to share the cost. To see a few sights quickly, charter a taxi with the East Khasi Hills Taxi Union (see Getting Around later); or, better, jump on a tour organised by the tourist office. These tours leave at 8 am daily (Rs 100 per person, eight hours) for Cherrapunjee (see Around Shillong); and at 8.30 am (Rs 80, six hours) for places like Umiam Lake and Elephant Falls. Book tickets the day before, or from 7.30 am on the same day.

Places to Stay

All places listed offer rooms with private bathroom and cable TV, unless stated otherwise; very few have (or need) a fan, and none bother with air-con or heating. Shillong is a popular resort, so tariffs are seasonal and negotiable.

Hotel Utsav *(☎ 503268, Jail Rd)* is the best value around the MTC bus station area. Singles/doubles cost from Rs 165/265, but the rooms are fairly charmless and have no outside windows or TV.

Baba Tourist Lodge *(☎ 211285, GS Rd)* is the best value in the budget range. Tiny rooms with shared bathroom cost Rs 75/125, and the ones for Rs 182/265 with private bathroom are good value. Some rooms are better than others, so check out a few.

Hotel Broadway *(☎ 226996, GS Rd)* has small, clean rooms for Rs 165/265 with shared bathroom and Rs 275/495 with private bathroom. Some are gloomy, and avoid the ones near the busy kitchen area.

Clean and central, the ***Hotel Monsoon*** *(☎ 500064, ⓔ hotelmonsoon@123india.com, GS Rd)* has rooms facing the main road that are noisy and others that are gloomy. Singles/doubles/triples with fan cost Rs 265/495/605.

Hotel Pine Borough *(☎ 220698, Police Bazaar Rd)* is probably the best value, and surprisingly quiet despite its central location. Small, but clean and comfortable, rooms cost from Rs 198 to Rs 275 for singles, and about Rs 330 for doubles.

Hotel Centre Point *(☎ 225210, fax 225239, GS Rd)* is a central landmark in Police Bazaar. The rooms are comfortable and bright, and some boast pleasant views, but it's overpriced at Rs 605/715 for singles/doubles.

Shillong Club Residential Quarters *(☎ 226938, ⓔ shillongclublitd_resi@123india.com, Kacheri Rd)* boasts some real colonial charm. The rooms are large, comfortable and quiet, and cost Rs 478/565. The tariff includes temporary membership of the Shillong Club next door. It's worth a splurge and you should book ahead.

Hotel Alpine Continental *(☎ 223617 ⓔ alpineshillong@hotmail.com)*, on the corner of Thana and Quinton Rds, is a classy place and excellent value in the mid-range. Very comfortable rooms with hot water – but most with views of the building next door – cost Rs 708/828.

Pinewood Hotel *(☎ 223116, fax 224176)*, just off Camel's Back Rd, is a wonderful Raj-era place built in the early 20th century and set in attractive grounds. The rooms, which have high ceilings, large comfortable beds and open fireplaces, cost from Rs 660/990 to Rs 2400/3000 for the 'presidential room'.

Places to Eat

Some of the best restaurants are in the hotels. ***La Galerie***, in the Hotel Centre Point building, is a classy place with tasty Indian and Chinese cuisine, and marvellous views. In the same building, ***Palace Restaurant*** is an informal eatery serving Indian fast food, eg, samosas (pastry triangles stuffed with vegetables) and *dosas* (filled pancakes).

Trattoria Dukan Ja Doh *(Police Bazaar Rd)*, opposite the entrance to Hotel Pine Borough, is a simple cafe, and the best place to try authentic Khasi fare.

Abba Restaurant, beneath Hotel Monsoon on GS Rd, is a tiny place serving cheap Chinese and Tibetan meals. At the back of an adjacent arcade, the classy ***Abba Chinese Banquet*** is probably Shillong's finest restaurant. Meals cost around Rs 60, and the service is excellent.

Eee Cee, next to the tourist office on Jail Rd, is popular for cheap Chinese and Indian dishes, and pastries. Above this place, ***Hotel Greenland*** is one of the better places for a cheap and tasty curry; fish curry is a speciality (from Rs 25).

Pizza Fast Food *(Jail Rd)* does what the name suggests, and quite well, with pizzas from Rs 50.

Shopping

For handicrafts, try Porbashree, the emporium next to the tourist office on Jail Rd. Also, near the corner of Police Bazaar and Kacheri Rds several shops sell finely-woven baskets in all sizes.

The most interesting market takes place in Iewduh Bazaar (usually called Bara Bazaar) on Iewduh, the first day of the eight-day Khasi week. Khasi and Jaintia villagers come from all over eastern Meghalaya to buy and sell produce at the market, and Khasi food is sold at stalls. Ask the tourist office for current details.

Getting There & Away

The nearest airport and train station are at Guwahati (Assam). Meghalaya Helicopter Service offers daily flights to Guwahati (Rs 625, 30 minutes) and joy rides around Shillong from Rs 400 per person. The office (☎ 223200) is at the MTC bus station, where a computerised railway reservation counter is also located.

Between Shillong and Guwahati (3½ hours), public (MTC) buses run at least every hour (Rs 50); more comfortable private buses (Rs 60) leave as often. To Guwahati, shared taxis from Police Bazaar cost Rs 125 per person or Rs 625 per vehicle; and crowded shared jeeps (Rs 90) leave from the Evergreen Sumo Service office near Hotel Magnum in Police Bazaar.

MTC and the private companies also offer overnight buses to Silchar (Rs 105, eight hours), Dimapur (Rs 175, 15 hours) and Agartala (Rs 250, 21 hours).

Private bus companies, such as Green Valley Travels, Network Travels and Assam Valley Tours, have small offices near the corner of Police Bazaar and GS Rds. Private buses usually leave from the Bara Bazaar bus station, but those that leave before about 9 am often depart from the corner of Police Bazaar and GS Rds.

To/From Bangladesh See under Land in the Getting There & Away chapter at the start of this book for information about crossing the border to/from Bangladesh, via Dawki.

Getting Around

Shillong is too steep for cycle-rickshaws and too wet for autorickshaws, so the only private transport is the ubiquitous black-and-yellow taxis. These can be chartered for Rs 120 per hour, and a negotiable Rs 900 per day. Shared taxis to local areas leave from outside the East Khasi Hills Taxi Union station on Kacheri Rd (eg, to the airport near Guwahati, a shared/chartered taxi costs Rs 180/900). Jeeps can also be chartered for local tours from the Evergreen Sumo Service office at Police Bazaar.

Local buses depart from the Bara Bazaar bus station.

AROUND SHILLONG

Nohkalikai Falls at **Cherrapunjee** village are magnificent and are reputed to be the fourth-highest in the world. The village is the administrative and commercial centre for the Khasi people, where you'll find traditional houses built with curved walls and a sturdy arching roof to withstand the frequent storms. Cherrapunjee is about 56km south of Shillong. Buses leave from the Bara Bazaar bus station; otherwise, visit it on an organised tour.

In the Jaintia Hills, near the pleasant market town of Jowai, is **Krem Um Lawan**, India's longest cave (6.5km). At **Nartiang**, about 12km north of Jowai, are the atmospheric remnants of the ancient capital of the Jaintia kingdom. Jowai is accessible by bus from Bara Bazaar.

Tripura

The tiny state of Tripura is the second smallest in India, and almost surrounded by Bangladesh. Tribal customs, such as leaving parasols over ponds to commemorate the dead, can still be seen in rural areas, and official visitors to villages have bamboo arches built in their honour. The state is renowned for its vast array of cane-ware products.

Though 60% of Tripura is forested, the largest industry is handloom weaving. While there are 19 tribes in the state, the majority of the population is Bengali.

History

Tripura emerged as a distinct entity at the end of the 14th century under the Manikya dynasty, led by former Indo-Mongolian tribal chieftains who adopted Hinduism. The area was also once part of a large Hindu kingdom conquered by the Mughals in 1733. It was eventually taken over by the British in 1808, became a union territory of India in 1949 and a full state in 1972.

Under the British Raj, the Maharajas led a self-ruling princely state, although each ruler had to be firstly approved by the colonial overlords. At Independence, the Regent Maharani led the state into India, while the Sylhet district to the north joined East Pakistan (now Bangladesh).

Warnings & Permits

It is safe to travel to and around Agartala, but not in the north and, particularly, the far south where the National Liberation Front of Tripura (NLFT) continues to kill and kidnap indiscriminately. The victims are often Bengalis from Bangladesh, some of whom have sought equally violent retribution through the United Bengali Liberation Front (UBLF). Seek reliable advice before travelling outside of Agartala or Neermahal, or travelling overland to/from the capital.

No permits are required to travel anywhere within Tripura. The major Tripura government offices are at Chanakyapuri, Kautilya Marg, New Delhi (☎ 011-301 4607), and 1 Pretoria St, Kolkata (☎ 033-282 5703).

AGARTALA

☎ 0381 • pop 175,500

Tripura's sleepy capital, Agartala, was moved to its present site in 1850. It's pleasant enough, and the locals are very welcoming, but there's not a lot to see – it's really only a stopover for anyone travelling to or from Bangladesh.

Information

The very helpful Tripura Tourism office (☎ 225930), in the eastern wing of Ujjayanta Palace, is open from 10 am to 5 pm weekdays; and has an excellent Web site (www.tripura.nic.in). Staff can organise tours around Agartala and to Sepahijala Wildlife Sanctuary and Neermahal, but the chances of getting the minimum passengers required (about six) is remote. The tourist counter (☎ 422393) at the airport is useless.

Foreigners arriving and departing by air must register with the police at the airport.

State Bank of India on HGB Rd does not change money. If you're travelling to/from Bangladesh, use the moneychangers at the border. MediaNet, on Jagannath Bari Rd, offers Internet access for Rs 60 per hour.

The Bangladesh Visa Office (☎ 225260), on Palace Compound Rd, is open from 8.30 am to 4.30 pm weekdays. To obtain a visa, complete an application form, provide two photos and deposit the fee (in US dollars or Indian rupees) into its account at State Bank of India – the visa office will provide account details. One-month single-entry visas are available but costs vary by nationality and range from US$13 for Germans, US$45 for Americans, US$29 for Australians and US$40 for Brits. You may get your visa in less than two hours.

Things to See & Do

Built by Maharaja Radhakishore Manikya in 1901 in a mixed European-Mughal style, the **Ujjayanta Palace** is surrounded by 28 hectares of parkland and overlooks two large pools. Because the building now houses the Tripura State Legislative Assembly, it's not open to the public. The grounds, however, are open between 5 and 7 pm to see the 'Musical Fountain'; you can enter from the main gate.

Nearby, and open to all, are **Ummaneshwar Mandir** and **Jagannath Mandir** temples, both painted a striking ochre colour. At **Buddha Vihar**, on Airport Rd about 8km north of the city, there are Burmese statues of Buddha.

The small **Tripura Government Museum**, at the roundabout on HGB Rd, is reasonably interesting. The results of excavations within the state are on display, as well as old coins and sculptures. It's open from 10 am to 5 pm daily, except Sunday; entry is free.

The former capital, now known as **Old Agartala**, is 5km to the east. It is the site of **Chaturdasha Devata Mandir** – also known as the 'Temple of Fourteen Deities' – and draws thousands of devotees in July for the **Karchi Puja** festival which lasts seven days.

Places to Stay

All places listed offer rooms with private bathroom, unless stated otherwise.

Agartala Rest House *(Motor Stand Rd)* is about as basic as it comes – around Rs 50 for a rudimentary single room with shared

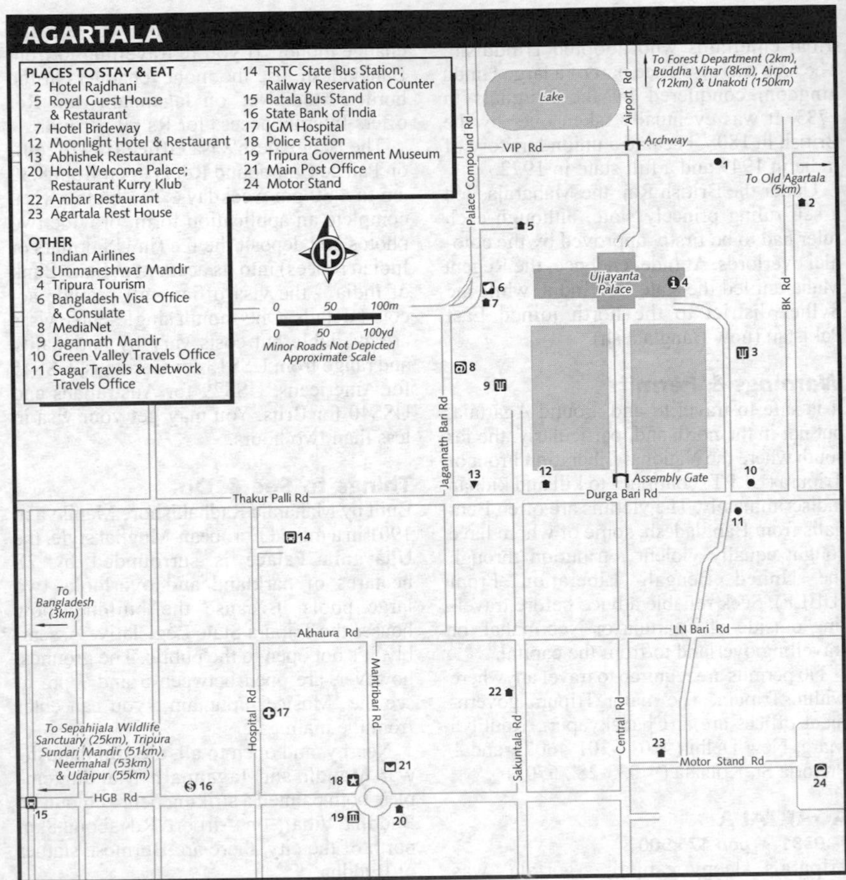

bathroom. Several other places of similar standard and price are located nearby.

Moonlight Hotel & Restaurant *(Durga Bari Rd)* is better known as a place to eat, but it also has some basic singles/doubles for Rs 80/100 with shared bathroom. The hotel is on a very noisy corner.

Hotel Brideway *(☎ 207298, Palace Compound Rd)* is also in a noisy location. It's not bad value if you crave air-con and cable TV (for Rs 440 per double), but the rooms with fan and mosquito net (Rs 275) are overpriced.

Royal Guest House *(☎ 225652)* is just off (but not signposted from) Palace Compound Rd. The rooms are unremarkable, but they're clean, quiet and good value. Singles cost from Rs 165 to Rs 275 and doubles are Rs 440; all rooms have cable TV and fan.

Hotel Rajdhani *(☎ 223387, BK Rd)* is also good value. Sing es with fan start from Rs 187 (but these are rarely available). Large, comfortable doubles with air-cooler, fan, hot water and cable TV cost just Rs 330.

Hotel Welcome Palace *(☎ 224940, ⓔ welcome_palace@usa.net, HGB Rd)* is worth a splurge and you should book ahead. It's new, spotless and central. Rooms start from Rs 220/330 with fan and Rs 440/550 with air-con – all have cable TV.

Places to Eat

Abhishek Restaurant *(Durga Bari Rd)* is the best in town, and turns into a pretty garden oasis at night. It's a little pricey (vegetarian dishes start from Rs 40), but the food is delicious and the service is efficient.

Ambar Restaurant *(Sakuntala Rd)* is a cheap, simple and friendly eatery. There are several others of similar standard and price nearby.

The best restaurants are in the hotels. ***Restaurant Kurry Klub***, at Hotel Welcome Palace, serves Chinese, Indian and passable Thai food. The uninviting dining room at ***Royal Guest House*** is also worth trying.

Getting There & Away

Travelling by air is the safest and most direct way to/from Agartala, so flights are often booked out. Indian Airlines (☎ 225470), on VIP Rd, has at least one flight daily to/from Kolkata (US$50), and three flights a week to/from Guwahati (US$45). Between the city centre and airport (12km), taxis/autorickshaws cost about Rs 150/80.

There are three bus stations in Agartala. From the TRTC station on Thakur Palli Rd, state-run buses go to Guwahati (Rs 300, 25 hours), via Shillong (Rs 250, 21 hours), and to Silchar (Rs 105, 12 hours). The TRTC station also has a computerised railway reservation counter (☎ 225533).

Private buses leave from Batala Bus Stand, on HGB Rd, and from Motor Stand, on the aptly named Motor Stand Rd. Companies with offices on Durga Bari Rd, such as Green Valley Travels, Sagar Travels and Network Travels, offer comfortable buses to Guwahati, Shillong and Silchar for a little more than the public buses.

Public buses and shared jeeps to local towns leave from Batala Bus Stand.

To/From Bangladesh For information about crossing the border to/from Bangladesh at Akhaura, near Agartala, see under Land in the Getting There & Away chapter at the start of this book.

AROUND TRIPURA

All of the places listed here are accessible by bus or shared jeep from Batala Bus Stand in Agartala.

Sepahijala Wildlife Sanctuary (18 sq km), 25km south of Agartala, has species of deer and monkey, and water birds, as well as a mini-zoo, toy train, elephant rides, orchard garden and boating lake. Entry costs Rs 5. ***Abasarika Forest Bungalow***, set in pleasant gardens near the lake, charges Rs 50 per person for dorm beds, and Rs 100 per person in a cottage. For bookings, contact the Forest Department (☎ 223779) on Airport Rd, Agartala.

On an island in the middle of Rudrasagar Lake (5 sq km) is Tripura's top attraction, the **Water Palace of Neermahal**, 53km from Agartala. The palace was built in 1930, but is now starting to fall into ruin. Still, it is a beautifully peaceful place that attracts migrating birds in winter. On the lakeshore, ***Sagarmahal Tourist Lodge*** has doubles with private bathroom for Rs 132/220 without/with air-con, and dorm beds for Rs 50; book at the tourist office in Agartala.

In the centre of the ancient Hindu capital, Udaipur (55km south of Agartala), is the **Jagannath Digthi tank**. On its banks is the ruined **Jagannath Mandir** which once held the famous Jagannath statue brought there from Puri (Orissa) in the 16th century. Nearby, are several **temples** to Vishnu, and the ruins of the **old royal palace**.

Tripura Sundari Mandir (also known as Matabari) is 4km from Udaipur. It's the most famous temple in southern Tripura and was built on a hilltop in the classic Bengali-hut style in 1501. A large **fair** is held there during Diwali (October/November). ***Matabari Pantha Niwas*** offers dorm beds for Rs 50.

The ancient pilgrimage centre of **Unakoti** is believed to date to the 8th century, and contains possibly the largest bas-relief in India. The annual cultural fair and pilgrim festival, **Ashokastami Mela**, is held here in March or April. There are also attractive waterfalls and pools nearby. It's 150km from Agartala, and 10km from Kailasahar where ***Uttarmegh Tourist Lodge*** has doubles for Rs 130; book at the tourist office in Agartala.

Other States in the North-East

Travelling around the other four states – Arunachal Pradesh, Manipur, Mizoram and Nagaland – is problematic, and in the case of Manipur and Nagaland, potentially dangerous. Seek reliable advice before venturing to these areas.

ARUNACHAL PRADESH

Because Arunachal Pradesh borders Bhutan, China and Myanmar (Burma), it is politically sensitive and has been off-limits to foreigners until recently. The state hosts about 65 tribes (although the 1971 census counted as many as 115), including the Adi (the largest group) in the Along area, the Mishmi in the ranges north-east of Pasighat and the Nishi around Itanagar.

History The Ahom dynasty in Assam had a policy of not interfering with the hill tribes, except for retaliatory raids. The British continued this policy and after declaring the region off-limits in 1873 ignored the place until the eve of WWII. After Independence, Nehru supported the policies of Verrier Elwin, a British-born anthropologist, to gradually prepare the tribes for the impact of the modern world.

Development was stepped up after China invaded Tawang in 1962 (this Buddhist mountain valley had until the late 1940s been claimed by Tibet). China advanced as far as Tezpur in Assam and then withdrew, so India moved quickly to build roads and military bases along the border. In 1972, Arunachal Pradesh became a Union Territory, and in 1987 a state. In 1999, the long-serving chief minister was deposed by his own party, but the feared ensuing political instability did not eventuate.

Warnings & Permits A stable and reasonably effective administration has helped Arunachal Pradesh avoid the ethnic violence of neighbouring states. However, it is a militarily and politically sensitive area, so foreigners (with permits) are only currently allowed to visit Bhalukpong, Bomdila, Seppa and Tawang in the west; Itanagar; the road from Itanagar to Pasighat along the Brahmaputra River or through Ziro, Daporijo and Along; and Namdapha National Park (including Miao).

All foreigners must obtain a Restricted (Prohibited) Area Permit. These can be obtained from Foreigners' Registration Offices in New Delhi and Kolkata, but it's probably quicker and easier at one of the Arunachal Pradesh government offices, eg, Block CE 109, Sector 1, Salt Lake City, Kolkata (☎ 033-358 9865), opposite the Salt Lake telephone exchange; or Kautilya Marg, Chanakyapuri, New Delhi (☎ 011-301 3915). You need to provide four passport-sized photos, and four photocopies of the passport pages with your personal details and Indian visa.

The Arunachal Pradesh government also charges foreigners US$50 (or the equivalent in Indian rupees) per day just to be in the state – this is payable at a state government office. (The state government, however, may relent in the future, and reduce the fee to an acceptable once-off US$50.)

In reality, individuals are still unlikely to get permits, so the best way to visit is on an organised tour. Travel agencies (eg, in Kolkata, Guwahati and Darjeeling) charge about US$150 per day (including the current daily fee), and will arrange the permit.

Getting Around Helicopters are an exhilarating way to travel to more remote places like Ziro, Along, Pasighat and Daporijo, and between Guwahati and Naharlagun. Schedules and prices are available from the Meghalaya Helicopter Service offices in Shillong and Guwahati (see those sections for contact details).

Itanagar

☎ 0360 • pop 17,700

The capital, Itanagar, is not particularly appealing. Attractions include **Buddha Vihar**, on the hill near Hotel Arun Subansiri; **Ganga Lake**, situated at the end of a rugged road and a short, steep track 6km from Itanagar; and **Jawaharlal Nehru Museum** in the city, open from 10 am to 5 pm Tuesday to Sunday.

In Ganga Market, ***Hotel Himalaya*** has basic doubles for Rs 150. ***Hotel Blue Pine*** *(☎ 212042)*, on the lane leading down to the ASTC bus station, is good value: Singles/doubles with private bathroom cost Rs 320/535. ***Hotel Arun Subansiri*** *(☎ 212677, Zero Point)* has comfortable singles/doubles/triples for Rs 600/800/900 with private bathroom and cable TV.

The nearest airport is 216km away at Tezpur (Assam). Green Valley and Blue Hills have several buses to Tezpur (Rs 100, six hours) and Guwahati (Rs 175, 12 hours).

West Arunachal Pradesh

Tawang Gompa is in a superb location near the border with Bhutan. Dating from the mid-17th century, it is the most important monastery in the north-east. The sixth Dalai Lama was born there, and it's now home to over 500 lamas (monks). It also boasts a fascinating collection of *thangkas* (Tibetan paintings on cloth) and a large gilded statue of Sakyamuni (the historical Buddha) in the prayer hall. Also, a **handicrafts centre** is located at the lower end of Tawang town, near the hospital.

In Tawang, ***Tourist Lodge*** has adequate doubles with private bathroom from Rs 400 to Rs 700; ***Inspection Bungalow***, uphill from the bus station, has basic accommodation for about Rs 100 per bed with shared facilities; and ***Hotel Paradise***, in the main market, has doubles from Rs 200 to Rs 500 with private bathroom.

Buses from Tezpur, via the 4249m Se La pass, take about 24 hours and cost Rs 185. Infrequent shared jeeps cost a little more, but are far quicker (12 to 15 hours).

About halfway between Tezpur and Tawang, the attractive town of **Bomdila** has a couple of Buddhist **gompas** (monasteries), and the unusual **Yak Research Centre**. The friendly ***Hotel Siphiyang Phong*** *(☎ 03782-22373)* has comfortable singles/doubles from Rs 435/685 with private bathroom.

At **Tipi**, a few kilometres from the state border with Assam, the **Orchid Research Centre** boasts over 7500 orchids (best visited in April/May).

Central Arunachal Pradesh

Ziro is the home of the Apatani people. ***Blue Pine Lodge*** has decent singles/doubles with private bathroom for Rs 200/300; and ***Circuit Bungalow*** has dorm beds for Rs 100 per person.

In the overgrown village of **Daporijo**, ***Circuit House*** has dorm beds for Rs 100 per person. **Along**, a quiet town mostly inhabited by the Adi people, also has a ***Circuit House*** (Rs 100 per person). **Pasighat** is a larger Adi town with shops selling locally made handicrafts, a few basic hotels and ***Circuit House*** (Rs 100 per person).

Namdapha National Park

This vast area (1850 sq km) is under the auspices of Project Tiger, and home to the four 'big cats' (tigers, leopards, clouded leopards and snow leopards). There aren't many treks or trails into the park, because it's mostly wilderness.

Forest Rest House and ***Tourist Bungalow*** at Deban inside the park are simple but pleasant. Doubles cost Rs 110 – book with the Namdapha National Park Field Director in Miao. Entry to the park is Rs 50.

MIZORAM

Mizoram (Hill People's Land) is a finger-like extension in the extreme south-east of the region poking between Myanmar and Bangladesh. Under the British, the area was known as 'Lushai Hills', a name that persisted until 1972 when it became a Union Territory.

History The Mizo people probably settled there some 300 years ago, perhaps from China. Under the British, they were among the few areas where missionaries were encouraged to operate, and today almost 95% of the Mizo population is Christian. Over 10,000 Mizos have even identified themselves as one of the lost tribes of Israel and converted to Judaism.

A natural crisis called *mautam* was one reason for a Mizo rebellion in 1959. Every 50 years the great bamboo forests burst into flower, attracting a plague of rats which devour the rice fields and vegetable gardens. The two-year famine which followed inspired the Mizo National Famine Front to fight for independence against what they regarded as an inept and uncaring Indian administration. In July 1986, after 20 years of bitter fighting, a peace deal which included statehood was made with the renamed Mizo National Front (MNF). The MNF government lasted one year, but regained power democratically in 1998.

Warnings & Permits Mizoram had been comparatively peaceful since achieving statehood in 1986, but the state and Indian governments have been fighting for the past five or so years against the Bru National Liberation Front and the Hmar People's Convention (Democrats). These groups are fairly ineffectual, however, and travelling around Mizoram is comparatively safe.

Foreigners can only obtain a permit if they travel on an organised tour of at least four arranged by a recognised travel agency. For more information, contact the Mizoram government offices at Circular Rd, Chanakyapuri, New Delhi (☎ 011-301 5951), and 24 AT Chowdury Ave, Kolkata (☎ 033-475 7034).

Aizawl

☎ 0389 • pop 160,000

Mizoram's capital clings to the sides of a central ridge at an altitude of 1130m. The staff at Mizoram Tourism (☎ 21227), Chandmary, are helpful.

Bara Bazaar, in the city centre, is interesting and one of several good places to buy handicrafts; others are the **Weaving Centre** and **Solomon's Cave**. The small **Mizoram State Museum**, at Babu Tlang, has a fascinating collection of traditional Mizo costumes and implements, and a mini-zoo.

Luangmual is a small ridge-top village, 7km from Aizawl with views, a handicraft centre and budget accommodation at ***Yatri Niwas***. In Aizawl itself, ***Hotel Embassy*** *(☎ 22570)*, near the tourist office, has singles/doubles with private bathroom for about Rs 250/ 320, and a decent ***restaurant***. Farther from the city centre, at Chatlang, is ***Tourist Lodge,*** similarly priced. ***Hotel Ritz***, in Bara Bazaar, is a little cheaper.

Several times a week, Indian Airlines flies between Guwahati and Aizawl (US$55). There are no railway lines anywhere near Aizawl, so all overland transport is by road through Silchar in Tripura (Rs 150, six hours).

MANIPUR

Manipur (Jewelled Land) borders Myanmar, and is inhabited by over two dozen tribes. Manipuri dancing is one of the great classical dance forms, and involves acrobatics on the part of the male dancers and slow graceful movements from the female participants. The favourite sport is polo and (along with several other places in Asia) Manipur claims to have invented the game. Agriculture and weaving form the basis of the economy.

History Manipur has a unique Hindu culture, fostered in the security of the hills. After a war against the Burmese, Manipur aligned itself with the British and signed the Treaty of Yandabo in 1826, thereby becoming a princely state within the Raj.

During WWII, most of the state was occupied by the Japanese. The Indian National Army, recruited from Indian prisoners of war, fought against British India and at Independence the Maharaja ceded his state to India. A movement to disown Vaishnavaite Hinduism and the Bengali script grew among the Meitei in the 1960s.

Warnings & Permits Violence, particularly between the Naga and Kuki tribes in the south, has continued for many years. These days, an estimated 50 separate guerrilla armies, such as the People's Liberation Army, Manipur People's Army and Kangleipak Communist Party, operate around Manipur. Travelling anywhere outside Imphal is not recommended. In any case, foreigners cannot currently travel overland into or out of Manipur: They can only fly to/from Imphal.

Foreigners can only obtain a permit if they travel on an organised tour of at least four arranged by a recognised travel agency. However, chances of getting a permit are slim. More information is available from the Manipur government offices at 2 Sardar Patel Marg, Chanakyapuri, New Delhi (☎ 011-301 3009), and 25 Ashutosh Shastri Rd, Kolkata (☎ 033-350 4412).

Imphal

☎ 0385 • pop 210,000

The capital is surrounded by wooded hills and lakes. The Vaishnavaite **Shri Govindajee Mandir** has two gold domes and often hosts ceremonial dances. Nearby, are the ruins of the **Old Palace**. **Khwairamband Bazaar** is a great place to buy Manipuri wickerwork, basketry and weavings – it's one of the biggest women's markets in India. In the middle of Tikendrajit Park is the huge war memorial, **Shaheed Minar**; and the **State Museum** is worth a look.

Imphal has a range of accommodation, including the government-run ***Hotel Imphal*** *(☎ 220459)* which charges Rs 250/375 for singles/doubles with private bathroom and air-con. Manipur Tourism is based there.

Indian Airlines (☎ 220999) and Jet Airways (☎ 230835) link Imphal with Kolkata daily for the same price (US$80), and both airlines fly regularly to Guwahati (US$50). Jet Airways also flies to Jorhat (US$80), and Indian Airlines goes to Delhi (US$240) and Silchar (US$45). Buses regularly depart for Kohima, Silchar and Guwahati.

Loktak Lake

Loktak Lake is the largest freshwater lake in the north-east, and much of it falls within the Keibul Lamjao National Park. Large areas of the lake are covered with 'islands' of thick matted weeds, and it's home to prolific birdlife and rare species of wildlife such as *sangai* (dancing deer). Accommodation is available at ***Tourist Home*** on Sendra Island; book at the tourist office in Imphal. The lake is accessible by bus (48km) from Imphal.

NAGALAND

South of Arunachal Pradesh and north of Manipur, the remote and hilly state of Nagaland shares a border with Myanmar.

History The 16 tribes of Nagaland were once head hunters dreaded by the neighbouring Assamese. Naga warriors collected heads during raids; the custom was linked to the beliefs that the soul can only be released when the head is severed and in the magic ability of the trophies to ensure the village harvest. After first encountering the Nagas in 1832, the British managed to crush them with difficulty only in 1879. Naga leaders campaigned for outright independence before the British left, but were unwillingly absorbed into India. Almost immediately a rebellion began, which continues with many factional splits and failed peace deals.

As with Mizoram, the main religion is Christianity, and churches are the centre of the communities. There are 16 Naga tribes, including the Angami, Rengma, Ao, Konyak, Wanchu, Sema and Lotha.

Warnings & Permits Various rebel groups including the National Socialist Council of Nagaland (Khaplang) – not to be confused with the National Socialist Council of Nagalim (Isak-Mulivah) – have been waging a war against the state and Indian governments (and among themselves) for many years. Clashes between Indian and Burmese forces along the border are also common.

At the time of research rumours abounded among tourist authorities about the relaxation of permits and restrictions for foreigners in 2001. However, foreigners still had to apply for a permit, and travel in a group of at least four or as a married (not de facto) couple. Individuals could not travel independently, but groups (of four or more) and couples could with a permit – ie, they didn't need to be part of an organised tour.

Travel around Nagaland is restricted to (and around) Kohima, Dimapur, Wokha and Mokokchung. You must register with the police when you visit each of these places, and at Dimapur airport if you arrive by air.

Permit forms are available from Indian embassies/consulates and Foreigners' Registration Offices in major cities (eg, New Delhi or Kolkata), but the best options are the Nagaland government offices at 29 Aurangzeb Rd, New Delhi (☎ 011-301 2296, fax 379 4240), or 11 Shakespeare Sarani, Kolkata (☎ 033-282 5247, fax 282 3491). A copy of the completed permit form must be sent by you – together with one passport photo, an itinerary and a photocopy of the personal details and Indian visa in your passport – to the Home Commissioner, Government of Nagaland, Kohima, 797001 (☎ 0370-270068, fax 270071). The authorities will mail, or even fax, the permit back to you. No fee is required, but allow about two weeks.

Kohima

☎ 0370

The capital of Nagaland, Kohima, is where the Japanese advance into India was halted in April 1944. To commemorate this, the **Kohima War Cemetery** has been established. Also worthwhile is the **State Museum**, with anthropological displays of the Naga tribes. The tourist office (☎ 22214) is helpful.

Yatri Niwas *(☎ 22708)* charges Rs 120/150 for basic but clean singles/doubles with shared bathroom. ***Hotel Japfu*** *(☎ 22721)* has comfortable rooms with private bathroom and cable TV from Rs 550/770.

The nearest airport and railhead are at Dimapur, four hours by road to the north. Buses regularly link Kohima with Imphal and Guwahati.

Dimapur

☎ 03862

Nagaland's gateway, near the border with Assam, is its commercial centre. In the 13th century, Dimapur was the capital of the Kachari tribal kingdom, and has decorative phallic symbols at **Kachari Ruins**.

Tourist Lodge *(☎ 26355)* offers comfortable singles/doubles with private bathroom for a reasonable Rs 150/220. ***Hotel Saramati*** *(☎ 20560)* has rooms with private bathroom from Rs 325/475; more with air-con.

Dimapur is an important transport hub served by air. Indian Airlines (☎ 20114) flies to Kolkata (US$90) several times a week, often via Tezpur (US$35).

Buses regularly travel to Kohima, Imphal and Guwahati.

Rajasthan

Rajasthan, the Land of the Kings, is India at its exotic and colourful best, with its battle-scarred forts, palaces of breathtaking grandeur and whimsical charm, riotous colours and even its romantic sense of pride and honour.

The state is diagonally divided into the hilly and rugged south-eastern region and the barren north-western Thar Desert, which extends across the border into Pakistan. There are plenty of historic cities, incredible fortresses awash with legends, and rare gems of impressionistic beauty, such as Udaipur. There are also a number of centres that attract travellers from far and wide, such as Pushkar with its holy lake, and the desert city of Jaisalmer, which resembles a fantasy from *The Thousand & One Nights*.

Rajasthan is one of India's prime tourist destinations. Nobody leaves here without priceless memories, a bundle of souvenirs, and an address book full of new friends.

Rajasthan at a Glance

Population: 51.5 million
Area: 342,239 sq km
Capital: Jaipur
Main Languages: Hindi, Rajasthani
When to Go: mid-Oct to mid-Mar

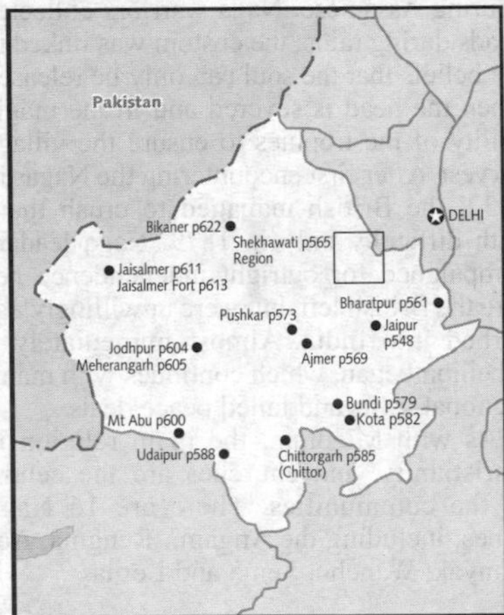

- Lose yourself in the medieval Jaisalmer Fort
- Join the pilgrims in the beautiful temple town of Pushkar, home to the Camel Fair
- Explore Udaipur, with its whitewashed temples, grand palaces by the lakeside, and the gorgeous Lake Palace
- Marvel at the blue city of Jodhpur, overlooked by the mighty Meherangarh
- Relax in Keoladeo Ghana National Park, a World Heritage–listed bird sanctuary
- Search for tigers and other wildlife at Ranthambhore and Sariska
- Enjoy Rajasthan's 'open-air gallery' of Shekhawati, with its scores of ornately painted *havelis*, or mansions
- Wander along the Dilwara temples in the exquisitely sculptured ancient Jain temple complex at Mt Abu

History

This diverse state is the home of the Rajputs, a group of warrior clans, who have controlled this part of India for 1000 years according to a code of chivalry and honour akin to that of the medieval European knights. While temporary alliances and marriages of convenience were the order of the day, pride and independence were always paramount. The Rajputs were therefore never able to present a united front against a common aggressor. Indeed, much of their energy was spent squabbling among themselves and the resultant weakness eventually led to their becoming vassal states of the Mughal empire. Nevertheless, the Rajputs' bravery and sense of honour were unparalleled.

Rajput warriors would fight against all odds and, when no hope was left, chivalry demanded that *jauhar* (mass suicide) take place. In this grim ritual, the women and children committed suicide by immolating themselves on a huge funeral pyre, while the men donned saffron robes and rode out to confront the enemy and certain death. In some of the larger battles, tens of thousands of Rajput warriors lost their lives in this way. Three times in Chittorgarh's long history, the women consigned themselves to the flames while the men rode out to their martyrdom. The same tragic fate befell many other forts around the state. It's hardly surprising that Akbar persuaded Rajputs to lead his army, nor that subsequent Mughal emperors had such difficulty controlling this part of their empire.

With the decline of the Mughal empire, the Rajputs gradually clawed back their independence through a series of spectacular victories, at least until the British arrived. As the Raj inexorably expanded, most Rajput states signed articles of alliance with the British, which allowed them to continue as independent states, each with its own maharaja (or similarly titled leader), subject to certain political and economic constraints.

These alliances proved to be the beginning of the end for the Rajput rulers. Indulgence and extravagance soon replaced chivalry and honour so that by the early 20th century, many of the maharajas spent much of their time travelling the world with scores of concubines and retainers, playing polo, racing horses, and occupying entire floors of the most expensive hotels in Europe and the USA. While it suited the British to indulge them in this respect, their profligacy was economically and socially detrimental. When India gained Independence, Rajasthan had one of the subcontinent's lowest rates of life expectancy and literacy.

At Independence, India's ruling Congress Party was forced to make a deal with the

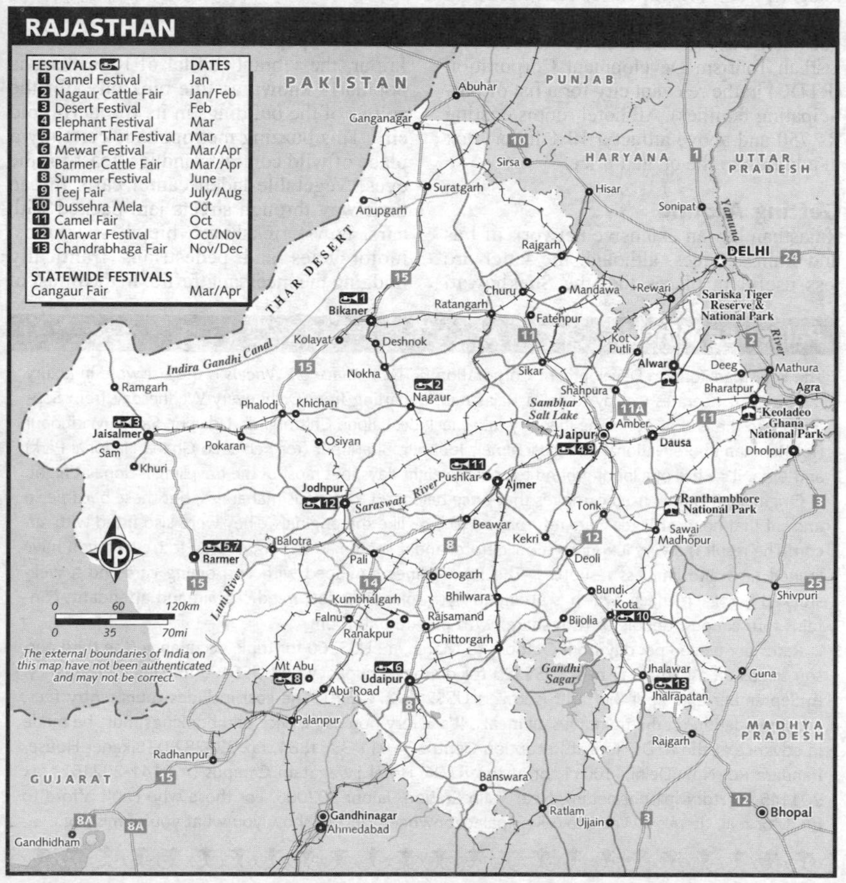

nominally independent Rajput states in order to secure their agreement to join the new India. The rulers were allowed to keep their titles, their property holdings were secured and they were paid an annual stipend commensurate with their status. It couldn't last forever, however, and in the early 1970s Indira Gandhi abolished both the titles and the stipends and severely sequestered the rulers' property rights.

While some of the rulers have survived this by converting their palaces into luxury hotels, many have fallen by the wayside, unable to cope with the financial and managerial demands of the late 20th century.

Accommodation

Rajasthan has accommodation to suit most budgets, from former palaces converted into exquisite hotels to cheap, family-run paying guesthouse accommodation (contact the Rajasthan Tourism Development Corporation (RTDC) in the relevant city for a list of participating families). All hotel rooms costing Rs 750 and above attract a 10% luxury tax in addition to the quoted price.

Getting Around

Rajasthan has an extensive network of bus and train services, although the latter are less useful in places like the Shekhawati region. Some rail services, particularly around Udaipur in the south, still operate on the slower metre-gauge system. The conversion to broad gauge is taking place but is a painfully slow process. Please note that all train prices quoted in this chapter do not include the Rs 20/25 reservation charge levied by Indian Railways on sleeper/three- and two-tier air-con (2A and 3A) berths.

An increasing number of travellers are engaging a private taxi and driver to get around. Costs start at Rs 4 per kilometre, although remember when calculating the costs that you also have to pay for the driver to return to his home base.

Eastern Rajasthan

JAIPUR

☎ 0141 • pop 1.86 million

Jaipur, the vibrant capital of Rajasthan, is popularly known as 'the pink city' for the colour of the buildings in its wonderful old city. This buzzing metropolis is certainly a place of wild contrasts and is a feast for the eyes. Vegetable-laden camel carts thread their way through streets jam-packed with cars, cows, rickshaws, bicycles, tempos, motorcycles and pedestrians frantically dodging the incessant traffic. In the midst of

Palace on Wheels

The Rajasthan Tourism Development Corporation (RTDC) *Palace on Wheels* is the last word in luxury rail travel. It operates weekly tours of Rajasthan, departing from Delhi every Wednesday from September to the end of April. The itinerary takes includes Jaipur, Chittorgarh, Udaipur, Sawai Madhopur (for Ranthambhore National Park), Jaisalmer, Jodhpur, Bharatpur (for Keoladeo Ghana National Park) and Agra. It's a hell of a lot of ground to cover in eight days, but most of the travelling is done at night.

Originally this train used carriages that once belonged to various maharajas, but these became so ancient that new carriages were refurbished to look like the originals. They were also fitted with air-con. The result is a very luxurious mobile hotel and it can be a memorable way to travel if you have limited time and limitless resources. The train comes equipped with two dining cars and a well-stocked bar. Each coach, which is attended by a splendidly costumed captain and attendant, contains four coupes (double or twin share) with private bathroom.

Rates per person per day from October to March are US$260 for triple occupancy (the third person sleeps on a fold-away bed), US$325 for double occupancy and US$460 for single occupancy. In September and April the tariff is lower: US$215/270/370. The cost includes tours, entry fees, accommodation on the train, plus all meals. It's a very popular service and bookings must be made in advance at the RTDC Tourist Reception Centre (☎ 011-3381884, fax 3382823), Bikaner House, Pandara Rd, New Delhi 110011, or at the RTDC Hotel Swagatam Campus (☎ 0141-202152, fax 201145, ⓔ rtdc@jp1.dot.net.in), Near Train Station, Jaipur 302006. For those who can't afford to do it for real, there's a Web site (www.palaceonwheels.net) to show you what you're missing.

it all, traditionally dressed Rajput men sporting bright turbans and swashbuckling moustaches discuss village politics outside restaurants serving spaghetti bolognaise and American ice-cream sodas. To cap it all, ramshackle roadside stalls selling *jootis* (traditional Rajasthani shoes) stand beside kitsch shops flogging a mishmash of modern trinkets.

Jaipur has long outstripped the confines of its city wall and is today among the most tumultuous and polluted places in Rajasthan. It can also feel at times as though many of the city's inhabitants are on the lookout for tourists. Despite this, it seldom disappoints the first-time visitor.

History

The city owes its name, its foundation and its careful planning to the great warrior-astronomer Maharaja Jai Singh II (1693–1743). His predecessors had enjoyed good relations with the Mughals and Jai Singh was careful to preserve this alliance.

In 1727, with Mughal power on the wane, Jai Singh decided the time was right to move down from his somewhat cramped hillside fort at nearby Amber to a new site on the plains. He laid out the city, with its surrounding walls and rectangular blocks, according to principles set down in the Shilpa-Shastra, an ancient Hindu treatise on architecture. In 1728, he built Jantar Mantar, the remarkable observatory that is still one of Jaipur's main attractions.

Orientation

The walled old city is in the north-east of Jaipur, the new parts spread to the south and west. The main tourist attractions are in the old city. The principal shopping centre in the old city is Johari Bazaar, the jewellers' market.

There are three main interconnecting roads in the new part of town: Mirza Ismail Rd (MI Rd), Station Rd and Sansar Chandra Marg. Along or just off these roads are most of the budget and mid-range hotels and restaurants, the main train and bus stations and many banks.

Information

Tourist Offices The RTDC Central Reservations Office (☎ 202152, fax 201145, ⓔ rtdc@jp1.dot.net.in) is behind the Hotel Swagatam; it's open from 10 am to 5 pm daily except Sunday. It has a range of literature and the staff are quite helpful. There are other tourist offices on platform No 1 at the train station (☎ 315714), open from 7 am to 6 pm daily, and outside the RTDC Tourist Hotel (☎ 375466). The Government of India tourist office (☎ 372200 or 1323) in the grounds of the Hotel Khasa Kothi can provide some good, if dated, brochures but is otherwise of limited use. It's open from 9 am to 6 pm weekdays and 9 am to 4.30 pm Saturday.

Money Thomas Cook (☎ 360940), on the ground floor of Jaipur Tower on MI Rd, will change most currencies and travellers cheques. It's open from 9.30 am to 6 pm daily. Nearby, also on MI Road, Tata Finance Amex (☎/fax 364223) is the local representative of American Express. The tiny Bank of Rajasthan (☎ 381416) in the Rambagh Palace changes money and is conveniently open from 7 am to 8 pm daily.

HDFC Bank on Ashoka Marg has a 24-hour ATM, which is the most convenient way to get cash from Visa, MasterCard and Cirrus cards. Andhra Bank (☎ 369906), on MI Rd, does cash advances on MasterCard, Visa and JCB (Japanese Credit Bureau) cards. Central Bank of India (☎ 317419), in the Anand Building on Sansar Chandra Marg, issues cash advances on MasterCard and Visa (minimum US$100).

Post & Communications The main post office (☎ 368740) on MI Rd is quite efficient and there's a man at the entrance who sews up parcels, sealing them with wax. It's open from 10 am to 5 pm Monday to Saturday.

DHL Worldwide Express (☎ 362826) is in a lane off MI Rd at C-Scheme, G7A Vinobha Marg. It operates air freight around the world, starting at Rs 3500 for a 10kg box and Rs 5500 for a 'jumbo' 25kg box to Australia and around Rs 500 more for Europe and the USA. Remember that unless you want the receiver to find a very nasty surprise in the mail, make sure you ask to pay any customs charges for the destination country upfront.

Jaipur is awash with hotels and Internet cafes advertising Internet access, although costs vary wildly (from Rs 45 to 180 per hour), as does the quality of the connection;

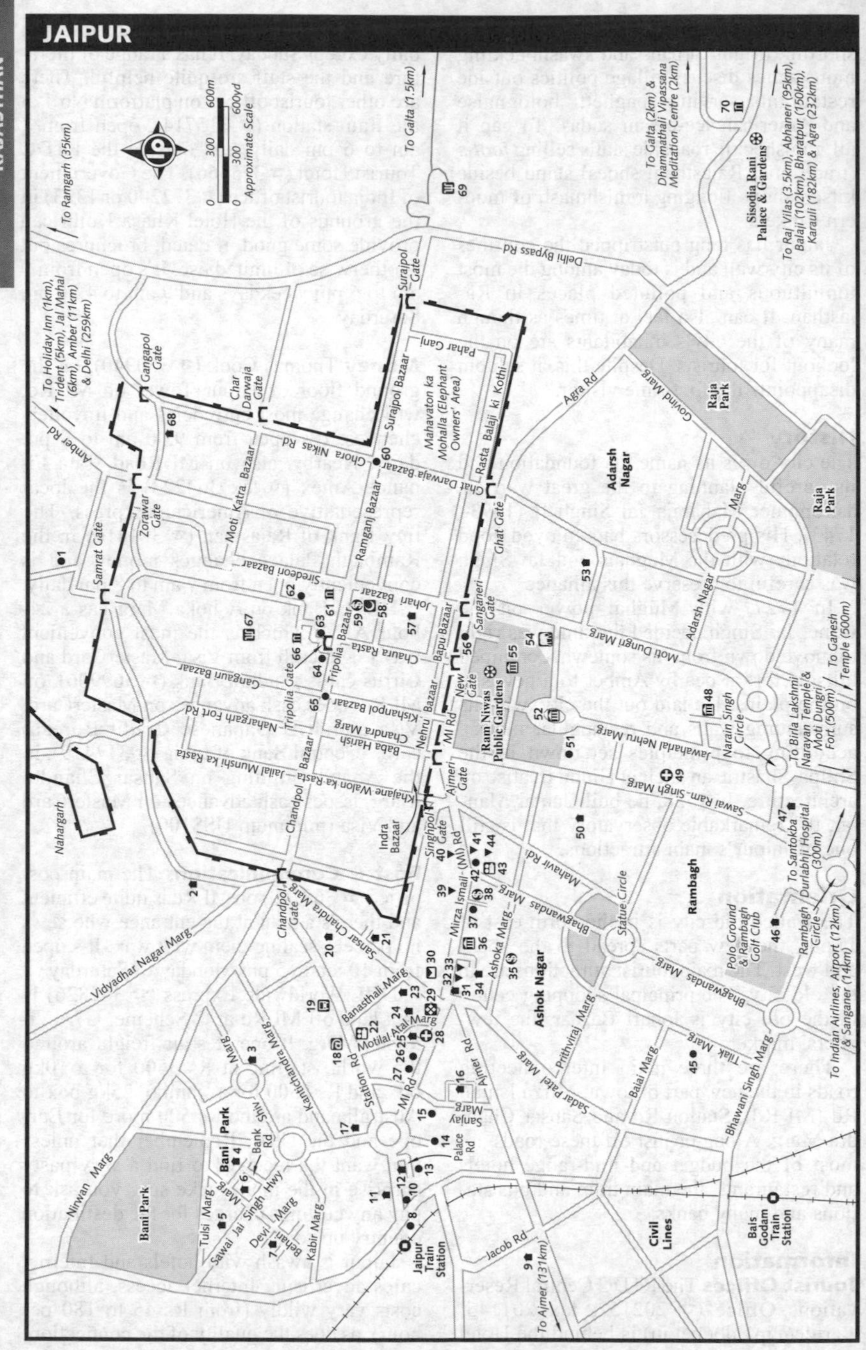
JAIPUR
To Ramgarh (35km)
Approximate Scale
0 300 600m
0 300 600yd
To Galta (1.5km)
To Galta (2km) & Dhammathali Vipassana Meditation Centre (2km)
Sisodia Rani Palace & Gardens
To Raj Vilas (3.5km), Abhaneri (95km), Balaji (102km), Bharatpur (150km), Karauli (182km) & Agra (232km)
Delhi Bypass Rd
Surajpol Gate
To Holiday Inn (1km), Trident (5km), Jal Mahal (6km), Amber (11km) & Delhi (259km)
Gangapol Gate
Char Darwaja Gate
Amber Rd
Pahar Ganj
Surajpol Bazaar
Mahavaton ka Mohalla (Elephant Owners' Area)
Rasta Balaji ki Kothi
Ghat Darwaja Bazaar
Chora Nikas Rd
Ramganj Bazaar
Moti Katra Bazaar
Zorawar Gate
Samrat Gate
Ghat Gate
Agra Rd
Govind Marg
Raja Park
Adarsh Nagar
Siredeori Bazaar
Johari Bazaar
Chaura Rasta
Tripolia Bazaar
Tripolia Gate
Gangauri Bazaar
Sanganeri Gate
Bapu Bazaar
Moti Dungri Marg
Adarsh Nagar Marg
Nahargarh Fort Rd
Kishanpol Bazaar
Chandra Marg
Baba Harish
Nehru Bazaar
New Gate
Ram Niwas Public Gardens
Jawaharlal Nehru Marg
Narain Singh Circle
To Ganesh Temple (500m)
To Birla Lakshmi Narayan Temple & Moti Dungri Fort (500m)
Jalal Munshi ka Rasta
Khajane Walon ka Rasta
Chandpol Bazaar
Indra Bazaar
MI Rd
Ajmeri Gate
Nahargarh
Sawai Ram Singh Marg
Singhpol Rd
Mirza Ismail (MI) Rd
Mahavir Rd
Chandpol Gate
Sansar Chandra Marg
Vidyadhar Nagar Marg
Bhagwandas Marg
Statue Circle
Rambagh
To Santokba Durlabhji Hospital (300m)
Rambagh Circle
Polo Ground & Rambagh Golf Club
Ashoka Marg
Ashok Nagar
Banasthali Marg
Motilal Atal Marg
Station Rd
Kanti Chandra Marg
Prithviraj Marg
To Indian Airlines, Airport (12km) & Sanganer (14km)
Shiv Marg
Bank Rd
Bani Park
Nirwan Marg
Tulsi Marg
Sawai Jai Singh Hwy
Devi Marg
Behari Marg
Kabir Marg
Jaipur Train Station
Palace Rd
Sanjay Marg
Ajmer Rd
Sadar Patel Marg
Bajaj Marg
Tilak Marg
Bhawani Singh Marg
Bais Godam Train Station
Civil Lines
Jacob Rd
To Ajmer (131km)

JAIPUR

PLACES TO STAY
- 2 Hotel Bissau Palace
- 3 Jaipur Inn
- 4 Umaid Bhawan Guest House
- 5 Hotel Meghniwas
- 6 Madhuban; Madhavanand Ashram
- 7 Shahpura House
- 9 Jai Mahal Palace Hotel
- 11 RTDC's Hotel Swagatam; RTDC's Central Reservations Office
- 12 Rajputana Palace Sheraton
- 16 Hotel Pearl Palace
- 17 RTDC's Hotel Teej
- 20 Alsisar Haveli
- 21 Hotel Arya Niwas
- 23 Mansingh Hotel; Central Bank of India
- 24 Hotel Neelam; Karni Niwas
- 25 Atithi Guest House; Aangan Guest House
- 31 RTDC's Tourist Hotel; Tourist Reception Centre; Rajasthali Emporium; Rajasthan Handloom House
- 34 Evergreen Guest House; Hotel Pink Sun; Ashiyana Guest House
- 46 Rambagh Palace; Bank of Rajasthan; & Polo Bar
- 47 Narain Niwas Palace Hotel
- 50 Hotel Diggi Palace
- 53 Nana ki Haveli
- 57 LMB Hotel & Restaurant
- 68 Samode Haveli

PLACES TO EAT
- 32 Copper Chimney
- 33 Handi Restaurant
- 39 Chanakya Restaurant
- 40 Lassiwala; Goyal Colour Lab; Charmica
- 41 Niro's; Surya Mahal; Natraj Restaurant
- 44 Bake Hut

OTHER
- 1 Royal Gaitor
- 8 Railway Reservation Office
- 10 Bicycle Hire
- 13 Crown Tours
- 14 Government of India Tourist Office; Hotel Khasa Kothi
- 15 RTDC's Hotel Gangaur
- 18 Mewar Cyber Cafe & Communication
- 19 Main Bus Station
- 22 Polo Victory Cinema
- 26 Jaipur Towers; Thomas Cook; Satyam Travels & Tours; Communicator; Web-Struk Cafe
- 27 British Airways
- 28 Galundia Clinic; Chic Chocolate; Tata Finance Amex
- 29 Ganpati Plaza; Swaad; Pizza Hut; Celebrations; Baskin 31 Robbins; Rajasthan Travel Service; Cybarea; Ganpati Books; Sentosa Colour Lab
- 30 Main Post Office
- 35 HDFC Bank (24-hour ATM)
- 36 Juneja Art Gallery (Lakshmi Complex)
- 37 DHL Worldwide Express
- 38 Andhra Bank
- 42 Books Corner
- 43 Raj Mandir Cinema
- 45 Anokhi Showroom
- 48 Museum of Indology
- 49 Sawai Mansingh Hospital
- 51 Maharaja College
- 52 Central Museum (Albert Hall)
- 54 Zoo
- 55 Ravindra Rangmanch Modern Art Gallery
- 56 Lufthansa; Singapore Airlines
- 58 Jama Masjid
- 59 Bank of Baroda
- 60 Ramganj Chaupar
- 61 Hawa Mahal
- 62 Jantar Mantar (Observatory)
- 63 Rajasthan Astrological Council & Research Institute
- 64 Iswari Minar Swarga Sal (Heaven Piercing Minaret)
- 65 Choti Chaupar
- 66 City Palace & Maharaja Sawai Mansingh II Museum
- 67 Govind Devji Temple
- 69 Temple of the Sun God (Monkey Temple)
- 70 Vidyadharji ka Bagh

many advertise rates of Rs 1 per minute, but the minimum charge is usually Rs 30. Communicator (☎ 360760, fax 374413, ⓔ pravin@jp1.dot.net.in), on the ground floor of the Jaipur Tower on MI Rd, is the cheapest, at Rs 45 per hour. Also good are Web-Struk Cafe (☎ 373333, ⓔ webstruk@usa.net) in the same building, Cybarea (☎ 379644, Ganpati Plaza, ⓔ cybarean@hotmail.com), and Mewar Cyber Cafe & Communication (☎ 204734, fax 206042, ⓔ mewar@jp1.dot.net.in, Station Rd), near the main bus terminal; all charge Rs 60 per hour. Mewar Cyber Cafe is open 24 hours to cater for insomniacs and party animals.

Photography Two of the best places for supplies and developing are Goyal Colour Lab, on MI Rd next to Lassiwala, and Sentosa Colour Lab (☎ 388748) in the Ganpati Plaza. The latter can also develop a roll of 36-exposure slide film, usually within 24 hours, for Rs 300 (including mounting).

Bookshops If you're on the hunt for reading material, there's a wide range of English-language books as well as magazines and maps at Books Corner (☎ 366323), on MI Rd (near Niro's restaurant), and Ganpati Books (☎ 388762) in the Ganpati Plaza; both sell a small range of Lonely Planet guidebooks. At Books Corner, you can pick up a copy of the informative *Jaipur Vision*, which contains useful information about the city.

Medical Services Highly recommended by a number of travellers is Galundia Clinic (☎ 361040), on MI Rd opposite All India Radio. Although the clinic doesn't look much from the outside, Dr Chandra Sen runs a highly professional service and is well versed in dealing with travellers' ailments. Importantly, he is also on call 24 hours (cell ☎ 9829061040) and will visit you in your hotel. He works with most travel insurance companies and a normal consultation costs Rs 300. The clinic should be your first port of call. It has a small number of beds, although should you need to be hospitalised, you may end up at Sawai Mansingh Hospital (☎ 560291), on Sawai Ram Singh Marg, or Santokba Durlabhji Hospital (☎ 566251), on Bhawani Singh Marg.

Emergency Emergency numbers are police ☎ 100; fire ☎ 101; and ambulance ☎ 102. For the police, you can also call ☎ 369796.

Old City (Pink City)

In 1876, Maharaja Ram Singh had the entire old city painted pink, traditionally a colour associated with hospitality, to welcome the Prince of Wales (later King Edward VII), a tradition which has been maintained. The old city is partially encircled by a crenellated wall with a number of gates – the major gates are Chandpol, Ajmer and Sanganeri. Broad avenues, more than 30m wide, divide the pink city into neat rectangles. In the early evening light, the pink and orange buildings have a magical glow which is complemented by the brightly clothed Rajasthanis.

A major landmark in this part of town is the **Iswari Minar Swarga Sal** (Heaven Piercing Minaret), near the Tripolia Gate. You can climb to the top between 9 am and 4.30 pm for Rs 5 (plus Rs 10/50 for a camera/video), for excellent views over the old city. The entrance is around the back – take the alley 50m west of the minaret along Chandpol Bazaar.

The main **bazaars** in the old city include Johari Bazaar, Tripolia Bazaar, Bapu Bazaar and Chandpol Bazaar.

Hawa Mahal Constructed in 1799, the Hawa Mahal, or Palace of the Winds, is one of Jaipur's major landmarks, although it is actually little more than a facade. This five-storey building, overlooking the main street of the bustling old city, is a stunning example of Rajput artistry, with pink, delicately honeycombed sandstone windows. It was originally built to enable ladies of the royal household to watch the everyday life and processions of the city. You can climb to the top of the Hawa Mahal for a fine view over the city. The palace was built by Maharaja Sawaj Pratap Singh and is part of the City Palace complex.

Entrance to the Hawa Mahal is from the rear of the building. To get there, go back to the intersection on your left as you face the Hawa Mahal, turn right and then take the first right again through an archway. It's open from 9 am to 4.30 pm daily and entry costs Rs 2. A still camera costs Rs 10/30 for Indians/foreigners, and a video camera is Rs 20/70.

City Palace Complex In the heart of the old city, the City Palace occupies a large area divided into a series of courtyards, gardens and buildings. The outer wall was built by Jai Singh, but other additions are much more recent, some dating from the start of the 20th century. Today, the palace is a blend of Rajasthani and Mughal architecture. The son of the last maharaja and his family still reside in part of the palace.

Before the palace proper you'll see the **Mubarak Mahal**, or Welcome Palace, which was built in the late 19th century by Maharaja Sawai Madho Singh II as a reception centre for visiting dignitaries. It now forms part of the **Maharaja Sawai Mansingh II Museum**, containing a collection of royal costumes and superb shawls, including Kashmiri *pashmina* (goats' wool) shawls. One remarkable exhibit is a set of the voluminous clothing of Sawai Madho Singh I, who was a stately 2m tall, 1.2m wide and weighed 250kg!

Other points of interest in the palace include the **Diwan-i-Am**, or the Hall of Public Audience, with its intricate decorations and manuscripts in Persian and Sanskrit, the **Diwan-i-Khas**, or Hall of Private Audience, with a marble-paved gallery, and the exquisite **Peacock Gate** in the Chandra Mahal courtyard.

Outside the buildings, you can see enormous silver vessels in which a former maharaja used to take holy Ganges water to England. Being a devout Hindu, he preferred not to risk the English water!

The palace and museum are open from 9.30 am to 4.30 pm daily. Entry is Rs 150 (including entry to Jaigarh – see the Around Jaipur section – and the ticket is valid for two days). Children between five and 12 years pay Rs 80. Photo opportunities are severely limited; photography is prohibited inside the museums. If you're still interested, a video camera costs Rs 100/150 for Indians/foreigners, but an inexplicable Rs 50 camera fee is only levied on Indians. There are guides for hire (Rs 150) inside the palace complex.

Jantar Mantar Next to the entrance to the City Palace is the Jantar Mantar, an observatory begun by Jai Singh in 1728. Jai Singh's passion for astronomy was even more notable than his prowess as a warrior and, before commencing construction, he sent scholars abroad to study foreign observatories. The Jaipur observatory is the largest and best preserved of the five he built, and was restored in 1901. Others are in Delhi (the oldest, dating from 1724), Varanasi and Ujjain. The fifth, the Muttra observatory, is gone.

At first glance, Jantar Mantar appears to be just a curious collection of sculptures, but in fact each construction has a specific purpose, such as measuring the positions of stars, altitudes and azimuths, and calculating eclipses. The most striking instrument is the sundial, with its 27m-high gnomon. The shadow this casts moves up to 4m per hour.

The observatory is open from 9 am to 4.30 pm daily and admission is Rs 4 (free on Monday). Photography is Rs 20/50 for Indians/foreigners; videos cost Rs 50/100.

Central Museum

This somewhat dusty collection is housed in the architecturally impressive Albert Hall in the Ram Niwas Public Gardens, south of the old city. Exhibits include models of yogis adopting various positions, tribal ware, dioramas depicting Rajasthani dances, and sections on decorative arts, costumes, drawings and musical instruments. The museum is open from 10 am to 4.30 pm daily except Friday. Entry is Rs 5/30 for Indians/foreigners (free on Monday). Photography is prohibited.

Nahargarh

Nahargarh, also known as the Tiger Fort, overlooks the city from a sheer ridge to the north, and is floodlit at night. The fort was built in 1734 and extended in 1868. An 8km road runs up through the hills from Jaipur,

TRUDI CANAVAN

An exquisitely carved ivory panel that is used as an inlay on a palace door.

or the fort can be reached along a zigzagging 2km footpath. The glorious views fully justify the effort and it's a great place to go for sunset. Entry is Rs 10, and a camera/video costs Rs 30/70.

There's a small restaurant on the top (with a toilet). You can even stay at the fort (see Places to Stay).

Royal Gaitor

The **cenotaphs** of the royal family are at Gaitor, just outside the city walls. The cenotaph of Maharaja Jai Singh II is particularly impressive. Entry is free, but there's a charge of Rs 10/20 for a camera/video (Rs 5/10 for Indians).

The cenotaphs of the maharanis of Jaipur are on Amber Rd, midway between Jaipur and Amber. Nearby is the **Jal Mahal** (Water Palace), in the middle of a lake and reached by a causeway.

Other Attractions

The Ram Niwas Public Gardens have a **zoo** with unhappy looking animals (open from 8 am to 5 pm daily except Tuesday; entry is Rs 5). Nearby, an old theatre houses Jaipur's **Modern Art Gallery**, on the 1st floor of the Ravindra Rangmanch Building (closed Sunday, free entry). The excellent **Juneja Art Gallery** (☎ 367448, fax 204237), in the Lakshmi Complex on MI Rd, has a full program of exhibitions of contemporary art by predominantly Rajasthani artists and is worth a visit.

The rather ramshackle **Museum of Indology** is an extraordinary private collection of folk art objects and other bits and pieces of interest – there's everything from a map of India painted on a rice grain, to manuscripts (one written by Aurangzeb), tribal ornaments, fossils, old currency notes, clocks and much more. The museum is signposted off J Nehru Marg, south of the Central Museum. It's open from 8 am to 6 pm daily. Entry is Rs 40 (including a guide). Cameras and videos are not allowed.

Farther south down Jawaharlal Nehru Marg, looming above the road to the left, is the small fort of **Moti Dungri** (closed to the public). At the foot of this fort is the large modern **Birla Lakshmi Narayan Temple**. There is a small **museum** next to the temple, which is open from 8 am to noon and 4 to 8 pm daily (free).

Meditation & Yoga

The Dhammathali Vipassana Meditation Centre (☎ 641520) at Galta (see the Around Jaipur section) runs meditation courses for a donation.

Yoga courses are available at the Madhavanand Ashram (☎ 200317), C19 Behari Marg, Bani Park.

Astrology

Dr Vinod Shastri (☎ 663338, 551117, ⓔ vshastri@jp1.dot.net.in) is the general secretary of the Rajasthan Astrological Council & Research Institute and works from his shop near the City Palace on Chandani Chowk, Tripolia Gate. It costs Rs 300 for a 20-minute consultation and you'll need to have your exact time and place of birth in order to get a computerised horoscope drawn up. A five-year prediction costs Rs 900 and a 30-year prediction costs a whopping Rs 3000. It's advisable to make an advance appointment; consultations take place from 2 to 8 pm daily.

Organised Tours

The RTDC offers half-/full-day tours of Jaipur and its environs for Rs 90/135. The full-day tours (9 am to 6 pm) do the major sites in Jaipur and around (including Amber Fort) and there's a lunch break at Nahargarh. Some travellers have reported that the lunch break can be as late as 3 pm, so have a big breakfast. Rushed, half-day tours are confined to the city limits and run from 8 am to 1 pm, 11.30 am to 4.30 pm and 1.30 to 6.30 pm. Entrance fees to monuments are extra. Tours depart daily from the train station (depending on demand), picking up people along the way at the RTDC Hotel Teej, Hotel Gangaur and Tourist Hotel. Contact any of the RTDC offices (see Tourist Offices under Information earlier in this section). The Central Office is not open Sundays. Just because the tours are a government operation, don't imagine that this means you are will be immune from prolonged shopping stops at emporiums along the way.

An expensive but more free-wheeling alternative is offered by Rajasthan Travel Service (☎ 365408, fax 376935, ⓔ dilip@datainfosys.net) in the Ganpati Plaza. For Rs 750/625 an air-con/nonair-con car with driver will take you to all the sights.

Special Events

Jaipur is home to a number of colourful festivals. **Teej** heralds the arrival of the monsoon and is celebrated in honour of the marriage of Lord Shiva and Parvati. During Teej (23–24 July 2001; 11–12 August 2002; 1–2 August 2003), flower-bedecked swings are hung from trees through out the city.

The **Elephant Festival** (9 March 2001; 28 March 2002; 17 March 2003) is the time to see elephants parading through the streets, elephant polo and a bizarre tug-of-war between elephants and men.

Gangaur is a statewide festival celebrated with particular excitement in Jaipur. Also celebrating the love between Lord Shiva and Parvati, colourful parades are the order of the day (28–29 March 2001; 15–16 April 2002; 4–5 April 2003).

Places to Stay

Getting to the hotel of your choice in Jaipur can be a headache. Autorickshaw drivers besiege most travellers who arrive by train (less so if you come by bus). A good rule of thumb is to pick the least pushy among them. If you don't want to go to a hotel of their choice, many will either refuse to take you or they'll demand at least double the normal fare. If you do go to their hotel, you'll pay through the nose for accommodation because the manager will be paying them a commission of at least 30% of what you are charged for a bed (and the charge won't go down for subsequent nights). Some enterprising rickshaw drivers openly declare their financial interest in getting you to a certain place which is, if nothing else in the absence of much competition, refreshingly honest. Ignore the 'ten rupees anywhere in Jaipur' crowd – 'anywhere' means the place of their choice or a sudden increase in price.

To get around this performance, go straight to the prepaid autorickshaw stands at both the bus and train stations, where rates are set by the government. Alternatively, some hotels will pick you up if you ring ahead.

Most hotels provide Internet access; those that don't probably will by the time you read this.

If you wish to stay with an Indian family, contact Mr SK Bhanot (☎ 200970), president of Jaipur's Paying Guest House Scheme, for a full list of participating families.

Places to Stay – Budget

Hotel Pearl Palace *(☎ 373700, fax 214415, ⓔ pearlpalaceindia@yahoo.com, Hari Kishan Semani Marg)*, off Sanjay Marg, has generated an enthusiastic following of satisfied customers since it opened in 1997. Good singles/doubles (all with private bathroom, some with balcony) cost Rs 250/350 and upwards. There are plans to turn the lovely rooftop area, from where there are superb views over the small Hathroi Fort next door, into a restaurant. The food is excellent and cheap (thalis cost Rs 40) and the hotel boasts one of the cleaner kitchens in India.

Jaipur Inn *(☎ 201121, fax 204796, ⓔ jaipurinn@hotmail.com, B17 Shiv Marg, Bani Park)* is an old-time favourite with travellers. Rooms range from cramped and spartan singles/doubles with shared bathroom for Rs 100/200 to Rs 350/400 for better rooms with private bathroom. Beds in the dorm cost Rs 80, and you can even camp on the lawn (Rs 50 per person) if you have your own tent. Mosquito nets can be hired for Rs 15 per day. Meals are available and the rooftop terrace commands sensational views.

Atithi Guest House *(☎ 378679, fax 379496, ⓔ tanmay@jp1.dot.net.in, 1 Park House Scheme Rd)*, between MI and Station Rds, is one of the better budget options. Squeaky-clean singles/doubles with private bathroom start at Rs 400/450. Despite its central location, the rooms are nice and quiet. Veg meals are available and there's a rooftop terrace as well as a small garden at the front. This is one place rickshaw drivers hate (always a good sign) because the owner refuses to pay commission.

Aangan Guest House *(☎ 373449, fax 204796, ⓔ aangan25@hotmail.com, Park House Scheme Rd)*, next door, isn't as good but is a little cheaper. Cells with private bathroom cost from Rs 175/250.

The friendly ***Karni Niwas*** *(☎ 365433, fax 375034, ⓔ karniniwas@hotmail.com, C5 Motilal Atal Marg)*, in a lane behind Hotel Neelam, is another good choice. The rooms are attractive, with nice terrace balconies, and range from Rs 275/300 up to Rs 650/700 for a room with TV and air-con. All rooms have private bathroom and the owners will gladly pick you up and drop you off at the train or bus station. Home-cooked meals are available.

Hotel Arya Niwas *(☎ 372456, fax 361871, ⓔ aryahotl@jp1.dot.net.in)*, just off Sansar Chandra Marg, is another very popular choice. This large hotel has clean singles/doubles with private bathroom from Rs 350/450, although some rooms are a little claustrophobic. There's a nice front lawn, a self-service veg restaurant and a laundry service. There are many reasons for staying at this well-run place, although the touts which are drawn to its perimeter are not among them.

Evergreen Guest House *(☎ 362415, fax 204234, ⓔ evergreen34@hotmail.com)* is just off MI Rd in the area known as Chameliwala Market. It's a good place to meet other backpackers and has a pleasant, sheltered garden area, a small swimming pool and a restaurant. Large, sometimes-clean singles/doubles with private bathroom start at Rs 150/175; stay here for the setting rather than the quality of the rooms.

Ashiyana Guest House *(☎ 375414)* is nearby if you find the Evergreen too much of a scene. Grubby rooms go for Rs 80/120 without/with private bathroom. No meals are available. Next door, ***Hotel Pink Sun*** has a decidedly relaxed approach to privacy and should be avoided by lone females (and possibly other travellers).

Hotel Diggi Palace *(☎ 373091, fax 370359, ⓔ diggihtl@datainfosys.net)*, just off Sawai Ram Singh Marg, about 1km south of Ajmer Gate, is another hang-out popular with budget travellers. Formerly the residence of the Thakur of Diggi, it has a lovely lawn area and a relaxing ambience. Reasonable singles/doubles with shared bathroom cost Rs 375/425. Although most leave satisfied, some travellers have found the welcome less than warm.

RTDC Hotel Swagatam *(☎ 200595)* is handy for the train station and has beds in a musty dorm for Rs 50; it also has luggage storage for Rs 5 per bag. ***RTDC Hotel Teej*** *(205482)* also has dorm beds for Rs 50, while ***RTDC Tourist Hotel*** *(☎ 360238)* must have been grand once but is now dingy and neglected; singles/doubles cost Rs 150/250.

Retiring rooms at the train station are handy if you're catching an early-morning train. Singles/doubles with shared bathroom are Rs 100/250, and Rs 150/300 with private bathroom. Air-con rooms start at Rs 500. Reservations can be made on the telephone inquiries number (☎ 131).

Places to Stay – Mid-Range

Madhuban *(☎ 200033, fax 202344, ⓔ madhuban@usa.net, D237 Behari Marg, Bani Park)* is heartily recommended if you crave a homey ambience with no hassles whatsoever. Run by the helpful 'Dicky' and his family, singles/doubles range from Rs 440/550 up to Rs 900/1000. The more expensive rooms are attractively furnished and even some of the cheaper rooms are elegantly decorated. Madhuban offers free pick-up from the bus and train stations (ring ahead). There's an indoor restaurant, or you can eat in the pleasant garden, where puppet shows are sometimes performed.

Umaid Bhawan Guest House *(☎ 206426, fax 201276, ⓔ umaidbhawan@yahoo.com, D1–2A Bani Park)*, behind the Collectorate via Bank Rd, is a family affair with a lovely personalised feel. Good singles/doubles start at Rs 450/550; some of the rooms are enormous. Renovations were under way when we visited, which should make this excellent place even better. There's a bar and a lovely swimming pool at the front.

Shahpura House *(☎ 202293, fax 201494, ⓔ shahpurahouse@usa.net, D257 Devi Marg, Bani Park)* is a beautifully restored house in a quiet street. Prices start at Rs 500 and rise to Rs 2200 for a luxury suite.

Alsisar Haveli *(☎ 368290, fax 364652, ⓔ alsisar@satyam.net.in, Sansar Chandra Marg)* is a gracious 19th-century mansion set in beautiful gardens. Although more pricey than other mid-range places, it's still a marvellous choice, with quaintly furnished rooms for Rs 1550/1850 plus tax; credit cards are not accepted. There's also a swimming pool.

Hotel Meghniwas *(☎ 202034, fax 201 420, ⓔ e@meghniwas.com, C9 Sawai Jai Singh Hwy, Bani Park)* is another excellent choice. Air-con singles/doubles start at Rs 1000/1100. Room Nos 201 and 209 guests (Rs 1650/1750) are like mini-apartments and are ideal for long-term accommodation. There's a swimming pool, lawn area with croquet, and a good restaurant. Major credit cards are accepted.

Hotel Bissau Palace *(☎ 304391, fax 304628, ⓔ sanjai@jp1.dot.net.in)*, north of Chandpol Gate, was built by the *rawal* (nobleman) of Bissau. The cheapest rooms cost Rs 990 and prices increase according to size, although some rooms have more character than others. There are two restaurants (one on the rooftop with fine views), a swimming pool and an interesting library. The attached travel agency has been recommended but it is expensive.

Narain Niwas Palace Hotel *(☎ 561291, fax 561045, Narain Singh Rd)* was once grand but is a little faded around the edges these days. Singles/doubles are Rs 1925/2395 plus 10% tax. There's a pool and a nice garden.

Nana-ki-Haveli *(☎ 615502, fax 605481, Fateh Tiba)*, off Moti Dungri Marg, is a nice place, although the transport yards nearby can make it noisy. Attractive rooms start at Rs 1095/1195 and the owners are friendly.

LMB Hotel *(☎ 565844, fax 562176)* is in the heart of the old city in Johari Bazaar. Noisy but OK singles/doubles cost from Rs 1075/1375.

Nahargarh, or ***Tiger Fort***, is a romantic choice, although there's only one double room (Rs 500) – it's located in one of the fort's parapets behind the restaurant and the views over Jaipur from the bed are unparalleled. Reservations should be made at the Tourist Reception Centre (☎ 0141-202152).

Places to Stay – Top End

Raj Vilas *(☎ 640101, fax 640202, e reservations@rajvilas.com, Goner Rd)*, about 8km from the city centre, is the most upmarket hotel in Jaipur, if not Rajasthan. Run by the Oberoi Group, this sophisticated boutique hotel has 71 rooms yet still manages to retain a personal touch. Set in more than 12 hectares complete with orchards and fountains, all rooms are immaculate and tastefully decorated. Deluxe singles/doubles are US$260/280, luxury tents are US$300 and villas (each with their own pool) range from US$600 to US$1000.

Rambagh Palace *(☎ 381919, fax 381098, e rambagh@jp1.dot.net.in, Bhawani Singh Marg)* was once the maharaja of Jaipur's residence, but is now a plush and palatial hotel operated by the Taj Group. Standard singles/doubles are US$185/205. The more-expensive rooms are more sumptuous, so if you've got a spare US$775, try the 'maharaja suite'. If you can't afford to stay, at least treat yourself to an evening drink at the Polo Bar (see Entertainment later in this section).

Jai Mahal Palace Hotel *(☎ 223636, fax 220707)* is on the corner of Jacob and Ajmer Rds. Most of the pleasant rooms (US$135/155 plus 20% tax) overlook the beautifully manicured Mughal gardens in which the hotel is located. The building itself is more than 250 years old.

Samode Haveli *(☎ 632407, fax 631397, Ganga Pol)* is one of the more romantic top-end places to stay. This 200-year-old building was once the town house of the rawal of Samode, who was also prime minister of Jaipur. Elegant singles/doubles cost Rs 1950/2750 (less from May to September). The only problem with staying in the breathtaking deluxe suite (Rs 3950), which is totally covered with original mirrorwork, is that you may no longer feel the need to visit any of the city's palaces.

Trident *(☎ 670101, fax 670303)*, about 5km north of the city, is modern but the rooms (Rs 4000/4500) have some nice touches and all have an electronic safe and individual balconies with great views; ask for one overlooking the Jal Mahal – the Water Palace. There is also a swimming pool.

Mansingh Hotel *(☎ 378771, fax 377582, e mansingh.jaipur@mailcity.com)*, off Sansar Chandra Marg in the centre of town, has rooms from Rs 1995/3000 plus tax. Amenities include a pool, health club and two restaurants, and its modern rooms have a little more character than some others in this price range.

Rajputana Palace Sheraton *(☎ 360011, fax 367848)* is between Station and Palace Rds. Run by Welcomgroup, it's not a palace as the name suggests, but rather a modern hotel built around a swimming pool. Standard singles/doubles cost US$130/140. There's a coffee shop, bar, two restaurants, a disco and a health club.

Places to Eat

Most of the best restaurants are along MI Rd.

Chanakya Restaurant *(☎ 376161)*, on the north side of MI Rd, is highly recommended. It's not as expensive as the decor and livery would suggest and the attentive staff are happy to explain the various pure veg menu items; continental dishes range from Rs 60 to 150 and most tandoori dishes are under Rs 70. It's worth booking ahead.

Niro's *(☎ 374493)* was established in 1949 and has long been a favourite with Indians and Westerners alike. There's an extensive menu offering veg and nonveg Indian, Chinese and continental food. Chicken pepper steak is Rs 130 and an American ice-cream soda will set you back a cool Rs 60. You will need to book ahead as it still fills up fast, especially on weekends, although many will tell you that it's trading on past glory. The nearby ***Surya Mahal*** *(☎ 369840)* is better value and specialises in excellent South Indian food with nothing over Rs 70.

Natraj Restaurant *(☎ 375804)*, near Niro's, is a very good veg place that's also popular for its Indian sweets and spicy nibbles. Its North Indian food is tasty; the vegetable bomb curry (Rs 70) is a blast. Veg dishes range from Rs 30 to 90. ***Lassiwala***, opposite Niro's, is the place to go for a thick, creamy lassi which will set you back Rs 10/20 for a small/jumbo cup.

Handi Restaurant *(☎ 364839)*, opposite the main post office, is tucked away at the back of the Maya Mansions building. The furnishings are nothing flash, but it offers scrumptious barbecue dishes and specialises in tandoori and Mughlai cuisine at reasonable prices.

Copper Chimney *(☎ 372275)*, nearby, offers veg and nonveg Indian, continental and

Chinese food in a pleasant setting. Main veg courses range from Rs 50 to 100, and between Rs 85 and 200 for nonveg. Try the Rajasthani dish *lal maas* (mutton in a thick spicy gravy) for Rs 85. In spite of the restaurant's name, smoking is not permitted.

Swaad *(Ganpati Plaza, MI Rd)* is recommended for a minor splurge. It has varied Indian, continental and Chinese cuisine; travellers' favourites include *subz malaai kofta-palak* (cottage cheese and herbs in spinach gravy) for Rs 60 and the sizzlers (Rs 95 to 170). Desserts start at Rs 45, up to Rs 105 for the baked Alaska. In the same complex is the swanky but less popular ***Celebrations***, which serves pure veg food.

Chic Chocolate *(☎ 204138)*, on MI Rd around the corner from Atithi Guest House, is a clean pastry shop serving up excellent cheese toast (Rs 15) and delicious fruit trifles (Rs 16). It also bakes its own bread. ***Bake Hut*** *(☎ 369840)*, close to Niro's, offers a selection of sweet treats including chocolate doughnuts (Rs 9) and little lemon tarts (Rs 11). It bakes birthday cakes to order.

LMB (Laxmi Mishthan Bhandar), in Johari Bazaar, has quaint 1970s-style decor, waiters in dinner suits and sandals and has been going strong since 1954, but the food and service is not as good as it once was. Main dishes range from Rs 35 to 80. Out the front, a counter serves snacks and colourful Indian sweets.

Jaipur Inn (see Places to Stay – Budget earlier in this section) boasts one of the city's only rooftop restaurants, with superlative views over Jaipur. The Indian veg buffet dinner costs Rs 100 (nonresidents should book in advance).

Entertainment

Entertainment in Jaipur is limited, although many hotels put on some sort of evening music, dance or puppet show.

The ***Polo Bar***, at the Rambagh Palace hotel, is Jaipur's most atmospheric watering hole; a large bottle of beer is Rs 165 and cocktails are around Rs 250.

Raj Mandir Cinema *(☎ 379372)*, just off MI Rd, is *the* place to go if you're planning to take in at least one Hindi film while you're in India. This opulent cinema is a Jaipur tourist attraction in its own right and is usually full, despite its immense size. Bookings can be made one day in advance (between 1 to 2 pm and 4 to 5 pm) at window Nos 7 and 8 – this is your best chance of securing a seat, although you can forget it in the early days of a new release. Alternatively, sharpen your elbows and join the queue when the ticket office opens 45 minutes before the curtain goes up. Tickets range from Rs 20 to 60; avoid the cheaper tickets, which are very close to the screen. Sessions are at noon, 3, 6.15 and 9.30 pm.

Rambagh Golf Club *(☎ 384482)*, near the Rambagh Palace hotel, charges US$25 for a round of golf, plus US$5 for equipment and Rs 100 for a caddie; left-handers are not catered for.

Shopping

Jaipur is *the* place to shop until you drop! It has a plethora of handicrafts ranging from

Warning – Gem Scams

Despite the warnings placed in previous editions, a disturbingly large number of travellers continue to succumb to promises of buying gems in Jaipur at 'low' prices for resale at a supposedly huge profit back home – don't fall for these rosy promises of easy money. For further details, see the boxed text 'Travellers Beware!' under Shopping in the Facts for the Visitor chapter.

Operators who practise such schemes are very good at luring trusting souls – they are invariably very friendly, often taking travellers to their homes and insisting on paying for meals and entry into sites. Mistaking smooth operators for genuine Indian hospitality, the unsuspecting traveller begins to trust his or her new-found friend. The asking price of US$500 or even up to US$10,000 a few days later for a bagful of gems seems too good to be true – it is. The gems are usually worth a tiny fraction of the price paid (or, if you agreed to have them sent, they never arrive even if you see them posted in front of you) and every year gem dealers in Western countries lend a sympathetic but wildly unprofitable ear to the stories of hardship. Hard-luck stories about an inability to obtain an export licence are not your problem. Don't let your desire for a quick buck cloud your judgment.

grimacing papier-mache puppets to exquisitely carved furniture. You'll have to bargain hard though – this city is accustomed to tourists with lots of money and little time to spend it. Shops around the tourist traps, such as the City Palace and Hawa Mahal, tend to be more expensive.

Jaipur is especially well known for precious stones, which seem cheaper here than elsewhere in India, and is even better known for semiprecious gems. There are many shops offering bargain prices, but you do need to know your gems. Marble statues, costume jewellery and textile prints are other Jaipur specialities.

The government-run Rajasthali emporium, in front of the RTDC Tourist Hotel (opposite the main post office), sells an interesting range of handicrafts from around the state and is a good place to get an idea of prices before launching into the bazaar. Rajasthan Handloom House is upstairs (although it was due to move to opposite the Ganpati Plaza when we visited), with a range of textiles. Another highly recommended place for textiles is the Anokhi showroom, at 2 Tilak Marg, near the Secretariat. It has high-quality products such as block-printed fabrics, tablecloths, bed covers and cosmetic bags.

Kripal Kumbh, B18A Shiv Marg in Bani Park, is a great place to see Jaipur's famous blue pottery. For good-quality jootis, go to Charmica (opposite Natraj restaurant) on MI Rd; a pair of jootis ranges from Rs 150 to 350.

Many rickshaw-wallahs are right into the commission business and it's almost guaranteed that they'll be getting a hefty cut from any shop they take you to.

Getting There & Away

Air Indian Airlines operates flights between Delhi and Jaipur (US$55, daily), Mumbai (US$155, daily), Udaipur (US$80, daily), Jaisalmer (US$125, three per week), Jodhpur (US$80, daily) and Kolkata (Calcutta; US$220, daily except Sunday; via Ahmedabad US$105, three per week). Jet Airways shadows many of these routes for a similar price.

You can book all domestic flights at a travel agency, such as Satyam Travels & Tours (☎ 378794, fax 375426), on the ground floor of the Jaipur Towers building, Rajasthan Travel Service (☎ 365408, fax 376935) in the Ganpati Plaza and Crown Tours (☎ 363310, fax 371751, ⓔ crown@jp1.dot.net.in), opposite the Rajputana Palace Sheraton; the latter is open Sundays. The Indian Airlines office (☎ 514500) is a little out of town on Tonk Rd, the southern extension of Sawai Ram Singh Marg.

Bus Rajasthan State Transport Corporation (RSTC) buses all leave from the main bus station on Station Rd, picking up passengers at Narain Singh Circle. There is a left-luggage office at the main station (Rs 5 per small bag for 24 hours, Rs 10 for larger items), as well as a prepaid autorickshaw stand. The deluxe (essentially nonstop) buses all leave from platform No 3, which is tucked away in the right-hand corner of the bus station. These buses should be booked in advance from the reservation office (☎ 205790) on platform No 3. For other bus inquiries call ☎ 206143.

There are deluxe buses to many destinations, including Delhi (Rs 206, 5½ hours), Jodhpur (Rs 161/98 for a day/night bus, seven hours), Kota (Rs 120, five hours), Ajmer (Rs 66, 2½ hours), Udaipur (Rs 201, 10 hours), Bikaner (Rs 168/99, eight hours), Bharatpur (Rs 88, 4½ hours), Bundi (Rs 102, five hours), Mt Abu (Rs 247, 13 hours), Jaisalmer (Rs 288/178, 15 hours), Chittorgarh (Rs 125, seven hours) and Jhunjhunu (Rs 88).

Train The reasonably efficient, reservation office (☎ 135) is in the building to your right as you exit the main train station. It's open (for advance reservations only) from 8 am to 2 pm and 2.15 to 8 pm Monday to Saturday; 8 am to 2 pm Sunday. Join the queue for 'Freedom Fighters and Foreign Tourists' (counter No 769). For same-day travel, you'll need to buy your ticket at the train station. For general train inquiries call ☎ 131. See the table 'Major Trains from Jaipur'.

Car The RTDC charges Rs 4.80 per kilometre with a minimum of 250km; the overnight charge starts at an extra Rs 100. Prices do not include tax but do include fuel. Private taxis charge a negotiable Rs 4 per kilometre. Remember that if your journey is one way, you'll have to pay for the driver to return to where you started.

Major Trains from Jaipur

destination	train No & name	departures	distance (km)	duration (hrs)	fare (Rs)
Abu Road	9106 *Ahmedabad Mail*	4.40 am	441	8½	99/154/713 *
Agra	2308 *Howrah Jodhpur Exp*	11.15 pm	310	7¼	77/120/564 *
Bikaner	4737 *Bikaner Exp*	9 pm	517	10	113/176/831 *
Delhi	2015 *Shatabdi Exp*	5.55 pm	308	4¼	495/985 ★
Delhi	2414 *Delhi-Jaipur Exp*	4.20 pm		5½	77/120/564 *
Jodhpur	2465 *Intercity Exp*	5.30 pm	320	5¼	79/237 ◆
Udaipur	9615 *Chetak Exp*	10.10 pm	431	12¼	96/149/692 *

* general/sleeper/2-tier air-con ◆ general/chair class ★ chair/executive chair class

Getting Around

To/From the Airport There is currently no scheduled bus service between the airport and the city. An autorickshaw/taxi will cost at least Rs 150/200 for the 15km journey into the city centre. Cut costs by sharing.

Autorickshaw There are prepaid autorickshaw stands at the bus and train stations. Rates are fixed by the government, so there's no need to haggle. If you want to hire an autorickshaw for local sightseeing it should cost about Rs 150/300 for a half/full day (including a visit to Amber but not Nahargarh). Prices are often inflated for tourists, so be prepared to bargain. Cycle-rickshaws are a cheaper option.

Bicycle Bicycles can be hired from some hotels and most bicycle shops, including the one to the right as you exit the main train station, opposite the reservation office (Rs 3/20 per hour/day).

AROUND JAIPUR

Amber

About 11km north of Jaipur, on the Delhi-Jaipur road, is Amber, the ancient capital of Jaipur state. Construction of the fort-palace was begun in 1592 by Maharaja Man Singh, the Rajput commander of Akbar's army. It was later extended by the Jai Singhs before the move to Jaipur. The fort is a superb example of Rajput architecture, stunningly situated on a hillside and overlooking a lake.

You can climb up to the fort from the road in about 10 minutes, and cold drinks are available within the palace if the climb is a hot one. A seat in a jeep up to the fort costs Rs 120 return. Riding up on elephants is popular at Rs 400 per elephant return (each can carry up to four people), although the elephant owners would prefer you to walk back down as the steep path is more challenging for the animals going down.

An imposing stairway leads to the **Diwan-i-Am**, or Hall of Public Audience, with a double row of columns and latticed galleries above. Steps to the right lead to the small **Kali Temple**.

The maharaja's apartments are on the higher terrace – you enter through a gateway decorated with mosaics and sculptures. The **Jai Mandir**, or Hall of Victory, is noted for its inlaid panels and glittering mirror ceiling. Regrettably, much of this was allowed to deteriorate during the 1970s and 1980s, but restoration proceeds. Opposite the Jai Mandir is the **Sukh Niwas**, or Hall of Pleasure, with an ivory-inlaid sandalwood door, and a channel that once carried cooling water running right through the room. From the Jai Mandir you can take in the fine views from the palace ramparts over the lake below.

Amber Palace is open from 9 am to 4.30 pm daily; entry costs Rs 50. A camera costs Rs 25 and a video camera Rs 100. Guides can be hired at the tourist office (at the fort entrance) for Rs 75/230/380 for 1½ hours/half day/full day (maximum four people).

There are frequent buses to Amber from near the Hawa Mahal in Jaipur (Rs 5, 25 minutes).

Jaigarh

The imposing Jaigarh, built in 1726 by Jai Singh, was opened to the public in mid-1983. The fort was never captured and so has survived virtually intact through the centuries. It's within walking distance of Amber and offers a great view over the plains from the Diwa Burj watchtower. The fort, with its water reservoirs, residential areas, puppet theatre and the cannon, Jaya Vana, is open from 9 am to 5 pm daily. Entry is Rs 15, plus Rs 50 per car, Rs 25 for a camera and Rs 100 for a video camera.

Galta

The temple of the sun god, also known as the Monkey Temple, at Galta is 2.5km above Jaipur to the east, a 100m climb from just beyond Surajpol. A deep, temple-studded gorge stands behind the temple and there are good sunset views over the surrounding plains.

Ramgarh

This green oasis, about 35km from Jaipur, has a picturesque lake (boating available), polo ground (☎ 0141-374791 in Jaipur for fixtures) and an ancient Durga temple.

Ramgarh Lodge *(☎ 01426-2217, fax 0141-381098)*, a former royal hunting lodge overlooking Ramgarh Lake, is the best place to stay (Rs 1600/2300 a single/double). Inside the lodge, there are a number of stuffed beasts, including a tacky elephant's trunk pot-plant holder.

Buses travel daily between Jaipur and Ramgarh (Rs 9, one hour).

Abhaneri

About 95km from Jaipur on the Agra road, this little village has one of Rajasthan's most awesome baoris. Flanking the baori is a small, crumbling palace, now inhabited by pigeons and bats.

From Jaipur, catch a bus to Sikandra, from where you can hire a jeep for the 10km trip to Abhaneri (Rs 200 return, including a 30-minute stop). Alternatively, from Jaipur get a bus to Gular, from where it's a 5km walk to Abhaneri.

Balaji

The extraordinary Hindu exorcism temple of Balaji is about 1.5km off the Jaipur-Agra road, 102km east of Jaipur. The exorcisms are sometimes very violent and many being exorcised don't hesitate to discuss their experiences. Most exorcisms take place on Tuesday and Saturday (go upstairs). Remove your shoes before entering the temple. Photography is prohibited.

From Jaipur there are numerous local buses to Balaji (Rs 26, 2½ hours).

BHARATPUR

☎ 05644 • pop 1.7 million

Bharatpur is renowned for its World Heritage–listed bird sanctuary, the Keoladeo Ghana National Park. This is one bird sanctuary that even nonornithologists should visit. In fact, many travellers rate it as a highlight of their visit to India.

In the 17th and 18th centuries, the town was an important Jat stronghold. Before the arrival of the Rajputs, the Jats retained their autonomy, both because of their prowess in battle and because of their chiefs' marriage alliances with Rajput nobility. They successfully opposed the Mughals on more than one occasion and their fort at Bharatpur, constructed in the 18th century, withstood an attack by the British in 1805 and a long siege in 1825. This siege eventually led to the signing of the first treaty of friendship between the Indian states of north-west India and the East India Company.

The town itself, surrounded by a decaying 11km wall, is of little interest. Bring mosquito repellent with you.

Orientation & Information

The Keoladeo Ghana National Park is 3km south of the city centre, and is easily accessed by cycle-rickshaw.

The helpful Tourist Reception Centre (☎ 22542) is opposite the RTDC Hotel Saras, about 700m from the park entrance. It's open from 10 am to 5 pm daily (except Sunday and every second Saturday of the month). A moderately useful map of Bharatpur (Rs 2) and the handy *Birds of Bharatpur – A Checklist* (Rs 50) are on sale here . A good map of the park is available at the park entrance (included in the ticket price). Books on birdlife are also available at a bookshop inside the park, about 1.5km from the main gate.

You can change money at the State Bank of Bikaner & Jaipur, near the Binarayan Gate.

Keoladeo Ghana National Park

The best time to visit the park is from October to late February, when many migratory birds can be seen, including the highly endangered Siberian crane. Only two of these birds have been arriving in the park each

October/November over the past decade, their numbers dwindling due to hunting over Pakistan and Afghanistan. Competition for scarce resources between local villagers and the tourist trade is also believed by some experts to have played a role. According to recent reports, around 354 species of birds have been identified at the beautiful Keoladeo sanctuary, a remarkable figure given that the park only covers 29 sq km. Apart from Siberian cranes, expect to see Saras cranes (the largest bird in the park), herons, egrets, geese, owls, cormorants, kingfishers and even pythons.

The sanctuary was formerly a vast semi-arid region, filling with water during the monsoon season only to rapidly dry up afterwards. To prevent this, the maharaja of Bharatpur diverted water from a nearby irrigation canal and, within a few years, birds began to settle in vast numbers. The maharaja was compelled not by conservationist motives, but by the desire to have a ready supply of waterfowl, affording fine shooting (and dining) possibilities. Indeed, Keoladeo continued to supply the maharajas' tables until as late as 1965. An inscription on a pillar near the small temple in the park bears testimony to the maharajas' penchant for hunting. It reveals that on one day alone, more than 5000 ducks were shot!

The park is open from 6 am to 6 pm daily. Entry is Rs 25/200 for Indians/foreigners, which entitles you to only one entrance per day; if you want to spend the day inside the park, get your hotel to provide a packed lunch. A still camera is free, but there's a typically steep Rs 200 video charge.

Only those cycle-rickshaws authorised by the government (recognisable by the yellow plate bolted onto the front) are allowed inside the park. Although you don't pay entry fees for the drivers of these cycle-rickshaws, you'll be up for Rs 30 per hour if you take one and they'll expect a tip on top of that. Some of the drivers actually know a lot about the birds and can be very helpful. A horse-drawn tonga costs Rs 60 per hour (maximum six people). If you wish to hire an experienced ornithologist guide, this will cost around Rs 35 per hour (maximum five people) or Rs 75 (more than five people). Guides can be hired at the park entrance and many hotels are run by qualified guides, who charge the same.

An excellent way to see the park is to hire a bicycle (around Rs 20 per day), either at the park entrance or from your hotel. This allows you to easily avoid the bottlenecks which occur at the nesting sites of the larger birds and increases your chances of seeing kingfishers, which are easily frightened away. A bicycle also enables you to avoid clocking up a large bill with a rickshaw driver. Try to visit the sanctuary at dawn (one of the best times to see the birds). The southern reaches of the park are virtually devoid of *humanus touristicus* but in dry years there is little water and even fewer birds.

A small display of photos, stuffed birds, nests and aquatic species found in the park's lakes is at the main entrance to the park (free entry). There's a small snack bar about halfway through the park, next to the Keoladeo Temple.

Lohagarh

Lohagarh, or Iron Fort, was built in the early 18th century and took its name from its supposedly impregnable defences. Maharaja Suraj Mahl, the fort's constructor and founder of Bharatpur, built two towers within the ramparts, the Jawahar Burj and Fateh Burj, to commemorate his victories over the Mughals and the British.

The fort occupies the entire small artificial island in the centre of the town, and the three palaces within its precincts are in an advanced state of decay. Entry costs Rs 50. One of the palaces houses a museum exhibiting sculptures, paintings, weapons and dusty animal trophies. The museum is open from 10 am to 4.30 pm daily except Friday. Entry is Rs 3 (free on Monday), and an additional Rs 10/20 for a camera/video.

Places to Stay & Eat

The commission system has reared its ugly head in Bharatpur – don't be pressured by touts at the train station or bus stand.

Park Precincts The following places are all within easy walking distance of the main entrance to the bird sanctuary, making them the most popular with travellers.

Spoonbill Hotel & Restaurant (☎ *23571, fax 29359,* ⓔ *hotelspoonbill@rediffmail.com)*, almost opposite the tourist office, has good singles/doubles with private bathroom for Rs 150/200 and dorm beds for Rs 50

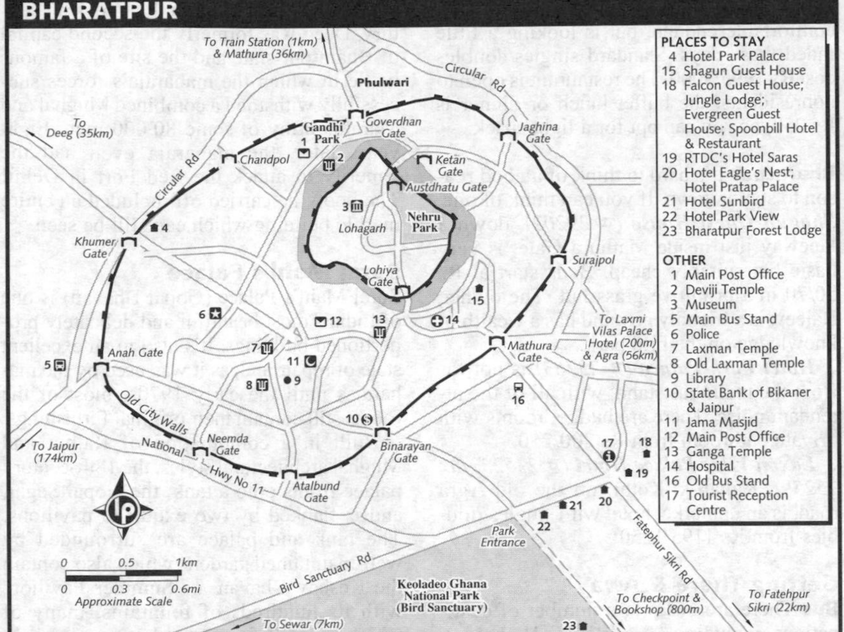

There's also one larger room which is good value for Rs 400/500. It has a restaurant and a campfire in winter.

Falcon Guest House *(☎ 23815)*, in the same area, is a well kept and homey place to stay. Good-sized singles/doubles go for Rs 150/200 with private bathroom; Rs 400/500 gets you a bigger room with a softer mattress and private balcony. There's a little garden restaurant.

Evergreen Guest House *(☎ 25917)* is a little more basic but is a good cheapie, with a garden restaurant serving delicious home-cooked meals. Rooms cost Rs 100 to 150. The staff are friendly once you get to know them and Viro, the owner, is an excellent guide for the park.

Jungle Lodge *(☎ 25622)*, nearby, has small but comfortable rooms with private bathroom from Rs 125/200 and better rooms for Rs 250/300. There's a lending library and a nice garden.

Hotel Park View *(☎ 20802, fax 2800…, e bharatpur007@yahoo.com)*, close to the park entrance, is quite good value, with rooms ranging from a dungeon with shared bathroom for Rs 40/60, up to doubles with private bathroom for between Rs 80 and Rs 150. The restaurant is pleasant; the Rajasthani *aloo deera* (potatoes lightly seasoned with cumin) costs Rs 25 and a chicken curry is Rs 45.

Hotel Pratap Palace *(☎/fax 25093, Bird Sanctuary Rd)* has faded but very spacious rooms for Rs 200/300 without/with private bathroom. Deluxe rooms with satellite TV cost Rs 600/700. The restaurant has an a la carte menu but the buffet lunches and dinners are good value at Rs 135.

Hotel Sunbird *(☎ 25701, fax 25265, e sunbird@jp1.dot.net.in)* is a well-run place further along Bird Sanctuary Rd, and the rooms in this popular place fill up fast. Decent singles/doubles with private bathroom start at Rs 300/500, including breakfast. Newer rooms out the back are quiet, if a little small, and cost Rs 550/750. The restaurant has a good range of dishes.

Hotel Eagle's Nest *(☎ 25144, fax 22310)* has comfortable rooms with satellite TV for Rs 500/650 and Rs 650/800 with air-con.

Bharatpur Forest Lodge *(☎ 22760, fax 22864)*, run by the Indian Tourism Development Corporation (ITDC), is inside the park,

1km beyond the park entrance gate. It's comfortable enough, but is looking a little faded these days. Standard singles/doubles cost Rs 1995/3000. The restaurant is open to nonresidents; the buffet lunch or dinner is Rs 250, or you can opt for a light snack.

Bharatpur It's hard to think of a good reason to stay in town. If you can think of one, ***Shagun Guest House*** *(☎ 29202)*, down a laneway just inside Mathura Gate, is very basic but suitably cheap. Beds start at Rs 50/70 in a primitive grass hut. The owner, Rajeev, is a friendly guy and has a wealth of knowledge on the bird park.

Hotel Park Palace *(☎ 23783)* is not far from the main bus stand, with all of the attendant noise. There are budget rooms with private bathroom from Rs 200/250.

Laxmi Vilas Palace Hotel *(☎ 23523, fax 25259)*, Kakaji-ki-Kothi, on the old Agra road, is an upmarket hotel with singles/doubles from Rs 1195/1250.

Getting There & Away

Bus There are buses to a number of destinations, including Agra (Rs 25, 1½ hours), Fatehpur Sikri (Rs 12, one hour), Jaipur (Rs 78, 4½ hours) and Deeg (Rs 15, one hour).

Train The *Janata Express* (9023/4) leaves New Delhi station at 2 pm and arrives in Bharatpur at 6.25 pm. It leaves Bharatpur at 8 am, arriving in the capital at 1.10 pm. The 175km trip costs Rs 52/81 in general/sleeper class. There are seven trains daily to Sawai Madhopur (Rs 52/81/234 general/sleeper/3A class).

Getting Around

Bharatpur has auto and cycle-rickshaws as well as tongas. An autorickshaw from the bus stand to the tourist office and most of the hotels should cost around Rs 15, and Rs 25 from the train station.

DEEG

☎ 05641 • pop 41,300

Few travellers make it to Deeg, about 36km north of Bharatpur. This is a pity because this small town with its massive fortifications, stunning palace and busy market is more interesting than Bharatpur itself (apart from the bird sanctuary, of course). It's an easy day trip from Bharatpur, Agra or Mathura.

Built by Suraj Mahl in the mid-18th century, Deeg was formerly the second capital of Bharatpur state and the site of a famous battle in which the maharaja's forces successfully withstood a combined Mughal and Maratha army of some 80,000 men. Eight years later, the maharaja even had the temerity to attack the Red Fort in Delhi! The booty he carried off included an entire marble building which can still be seen.

Suraj Mahl's Palace

Suraj Mahl's Palace (Gopal Bhavan) is one of India's most beautiful and delicately proportioned buildings. It's also in an excellent state of repair and, as it was used by the maharajas until the early 1970s, most of the rooms still contain their original furnishings.

Built in a combination of Rajput and Mughal architectural styles, the 18th-century palace fronts onto a tank, the Gopal Sagar, and is flanked by two exquisite pavilions. The tank and palace are surrounded by well-maintained gardens which also contain the Keshav Bhavan, or Summer Pavilion, with its hundreds of fountains, many of which are still functional but usually only turned on for local festivals.

The palace is open from 8 am to 5 pm daily and entry is Rs 200.

Deeg's massive **walls** (up to 28m high) and 12 bastions, some with their cannons still in place, are also worth exploring.

Places to Stay

RTDC Motel Deeg *(☎ 21000)*, not far from the bus stand, has just three air-cooled rooms with private bathroom for Rs 300/400 a single/double. If you have a tent, you can pitch it in the compound for Rs 40 per person (includes use of bathroom). Meals are available; a veg thali is Rs 55.

Getting There & Away

There are frequent buses between Deeg and Alwar; it costs Rs 23/30 by local/express bus (2½ hours express, three hours local). Buses for Bharatpur leave every 30 minutes and the one-hour journey costs Rs 12/15. There is one daily direct bus to Agra (Rs 45).

ALWAR

☎ 0144 • pop 258,600

Alwar was once an important Rajput state. It emerged in the 18th century under Pratap

Singh, who pushed back the rulers of Jaipur to the south and the Jats of Bharatpur to the east, and who successfully resisted the Marathas. It was one of the first Rajput states to ally itself with the fledgling British empire, although British interference in Alwar's internal affairs meant that this partnership was not always amicable.

The Tourist Reception Centre (☎ 21868) is not far from the train station and is open from 10 am to 1.30 pm and 2 to 5 pm Monday to Saturday. You can change foreign currency at the State Bank of Bikaner & Jaipur, near the bus stand.

Bala Quila

This imposing fort, with its 5km of ramparts, stands 300m above the city. Predating the time of Pratap Singh, it's one of the few forts in Rajasthan built before the rise of the Mughals. Unfortunately, the fort now houses a radio transmitter station and the inside can only be visited with special permission from the superintendent of police (☎ 337453).

Palace Complex

Below the fort sprawls the huge City Palace complex, its massive gates and tank lined by a beautifully symmetrical chain of ghats and pavilions. Today, most of the complex is occupied by government offices, but there's an interesting **government museum** housed in the former City Palace. It's open from 10 am to 4.30 pm daily except Friday and entry is Rs 3 (free on Monday). Photography is prohibited. Some of the museum's exhibits include stunning weapons, royal ivory slippers, and old musical instruments.

Places to Stay & Eat

Ankur *(☎ 333025)*, ***New Alankar*** *(☎ 20027)*, ***Atlantic*** *(☎ 21581)*, ***Akash Deep*** *(☎ 22912)* and ***Ashoka*** *(☎ 21780)* are a cluster of cheap hotels which all face each other around a central courtyard, about 500m east of the bus stand, set back from Manu Marg. The five hotels are each owned by one of five brothers. Without wishing to cause a family dispute, the Ashoka seems to be the best of the lot, with singles/doubles with private bathroom (Rs 3 for bucket hot water) for Rs 100/150 and Rs 200/250 with geyser. However, there's really not much difference between them, and prices are comparable at all the hotels.

Hotel Aravali *(☎ 332883, fax 332011)*, near the station, has dorm beds for Rs 100. Singles/doubles with private bathroom start at Rs 200/250 (request a quiet room). There's a restaurant, bar and pool (summer only).

RTDC Hotel Meenal *(☎ 22852)* is a respectable mid-range place, charging from Rs 300/400 for tidy singles/doubles. There's a little dining hall; a veg/nonveg thali costs Rs 55/70.

Alwar Hotel *(☎ 20012, fax 332250, 26 Manu Marg)*, set in a leafy garden, has decent rooms from Rs 300/450 with private bathroom. There's a good restaurant.

Narula's, near the Ganesh Talkies, whips up Indian, Chinese and continental cuisine. This pleasant restaurant, which is down a stairway, offers a good choice of dishes, including veg sizzlers (Rs 45) and strawberry milk shakes (Rs 25).

Getting There & Away

From Alwar, there are frequent local and express buses to Sariska (Rs 9/14 local/express, one/1½ hours), Bharatpur (Rs 45, 3½ hours express; Rs 29, 4½ hours local), Deeg (Rs 23/30, 2½/three hours) and Jaipur (Rs 45/61, 2½/two hours).

The very comfortable *Shatabdi Express* (2015/6) passes through Alwar daily except Sunday. It departs Alwar for Ajmer (Rs 480/950 chair/executive class, four hours) at 8.34 am and stops at Jaipur (Rs 145/315, two hours) along the way. For Delhi, it departs at 7.41 pm (Rs 350/670, 2½ hours). You have to be quick – the train only stops at Alwar for two minutes in either direction!

Getting Around

There are cycle-rickshaws, autorickshaws, tempos and some tongas. A cycle-rickshaw from the train station to the town centre should cost Rs 10. Bicycles can be hired near the train station (Rs 20 per day).

SARISKA TIGER RESERVE & NATIONAL PARK

☎ 0144

Located 107km from Jaipur and 200km from Delhi, this sanctuary is in a wooded valley surrounded by barren mountains. It covers 800 sq km (including a core area of 498 sq km) and has sambars, spotted deer, wild boars and, above all, tigers. Project Tiger has been in charge of the sanctuary since 1979.

As at Ranthambhore National Park (see later in this chapter) this park contains ruined temples, as well as a fort and pavilions built by the maharajas of Alwar. The sanctuary can be visited year-round, although during July and August your chance of spotting wildlife is minimal. The best time is between November and June. You'll see most wildlife in the evening, although tiger sightings are becoming more common during the day.

The park is open in winter (October to the end of February) from 7 am to 4 pm, and during the rest of the year from 6.30 am to 5 pm. The best way to visit the park is by jeep and these can be arranged at the Forest Reception Office (☎ 41333) on Jaipur Rd, directly opposite the Hotel Sariska Palace. Diesel/petrol jeeps cost Rs 500/600 per jeep (maximum five people). There's an entry fee of Rs 125 per jeep and an admission fee of Rs 25/200 for Indians/foreigners. Entry for Indians is free on Tuesday and Saturday (from 8 am to 3 pm), so try to avoid visiting on these days as the park can get busy. Using a still camera is free but a video camera will cost you Rs 200. Guides are available for Rs 50 per hour.

Places to Stay & Eat

***Hotel Sariska Palace** (☎ 41322, fax 41323)*, near the park entrance, is the imposing former hunting lodge of the maharajas of Alwar. It's a very pleasant place to stay, with rooms from Rs 2000/3000 a single/double. There's a small lending library, restaurant (lunch or dinner is Rs 350), and jeeps for hire.

***RTDC Hotel Tiger Den** (☎ 41342)* is cheaper and has a lovely garden, although the rooms are a bit run-down. Dorm beds are Rs 50, air-cooled singles/doubles with private bathroom are Rs 500/600, air-con rooms are Rs 700/800. Some travellers recommend bringing a mosquito net/repellent. A veg thali costs Rs 65.

Getting There & Away

Sariska is 35km from Alwar, a convenient town from which to approach the sanctuary. There are frequent buses that travel between Sariska and Alwar (Rs 14, one hour). It takes about three hours to Jaipur (Rs 48). Buses stop out the front of the Forest Reception Office.

SHEKHAWATI REGION

The semidesert Shekhawati region, in the triangular area between Delhi, Jaipur and Bikaner, is famous for its beautifully painted *havelis* (mansions), which were constructed by the merchants of the region. Most of the buildings date from the 18th century to the early 20th century, and the entire area has been dubbed by some as the 'open-air gallery of Rajasthan'. There are also forts, a couple of minor castles, baoris (stepwells) and *chhatris* (small, domed Mughal kiosks).

The major towns of interest in the region are Fatehpur, Nawalgarh, Mandawa, Ramgarh and Jhunjhunu, although virtually every town has at least a few surviving havelis. Many of these towns were important trading posts on the caravan routes emanating from the ports of Gujarat.

Ramgarh

The town of Ramgarh, not to be confused with the town of the same name 35km north-east of Jaipur, was founded by the extremely powerful Poddar merchant family in 1791, after they had left the village of Churu following a disagreement with the Thakur. It had its heyday in the mid-19th century and was one of the richest towns of the area.

The **Ram Gopal Poddar Chhatri** near the bus stand, and the **Poddar Havelis**, near the Churu Gate, are worth having a look at. This town is also known for its local handicrafts.

Fatehpur

Fatehpur was established in 1451 as a capital for Muslim *nawabs* (ruling princes or powerful landowners); however, it was taken over by the Shekhawati Rajputs in the 18th century.

Some of the main havelis of interest are the **Mahavir Prasad Goenka Haveli**, the **Geori Shankar Haveli**, the **Nand Lal Devra Haveli** and the **Harikrishnan Das Sarogi Haveli**.

***RTDC Hotel Haveli** (☎ 01571-20293)*, about 500m south of the bus stand, has dorm beds for Rs 50 and singles/doubles with private bathroom from Rs 150/250. There's a dining hall; you can buy a chicken curry for Rs 50 and a curd lassi will cost you Rs 15.

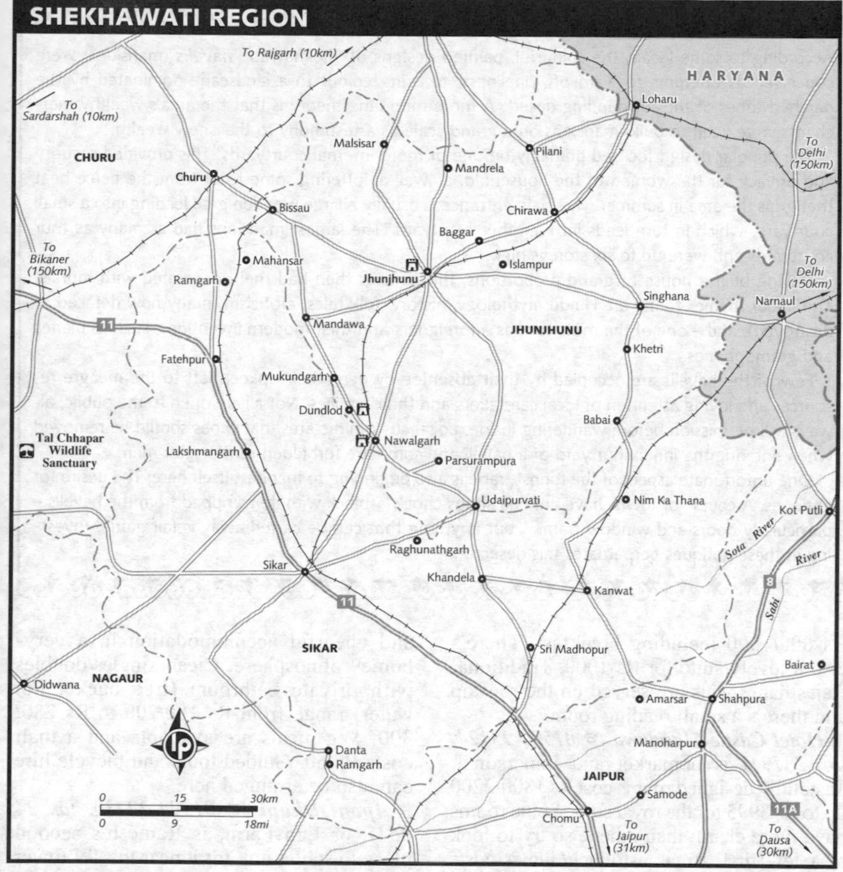

Mandawa

The compact and busy little market town of Mandawa was settled in the 18th century, and was fortified by the dominant merchant families. Increasingly, travellers are choosing this quiet town as a base for exploring the Shekhawati area.

The **Binsidhar Newatia Haveli** has curious paintings on its outer eastern wall – a boy using a telephone, and a European woman in a chauffeur driven car. The haveli is in the compound of the State Bank of Bikaner & Jaipur. The **Gulab Rai Ladia Haveli** has some defaced erotic images. There are also some fine **baoris** scattered around town.

Places to Stay Near the Subhash Chowk bus stand, ***Hotel Heritage Mandawa*** (☎ *01592-23742, fax 23243)* is an attractive old haveli with clean split-level singles/doubles with private bathroom from Rs 300/400; progressively larger and more elegant rooms range from Rs 700 to 1200. A tasty lunch/dinner is Rs 150/175 (open to nonresidents). There are plans to put a swimming pool in the rear courtyard.

Gayatri Niwas is another haveli (142 years old) run by the same owners and will be a good budget choice when renovations are complete. Rooms are expected to cost between Rs 150 and 300.

Hotel Mandawa Haveli (☎ *01592-23088,* ⓔ *hotelmandawahaveli@yahoo.com)*, close to Sonathia Gate, is also excellent. Located in a lovely 19th-century haveli, singles/doubles around the internal courtyard cost

Havelis

According to some locals, the colourful, painted designs of Shekhawati's *havelis* (mansions) were conceived as attempts to ward off loneliness, to bring colour to a landscape dominated by the parched tones of the surrounding desert. A more mundane theory is that the area's wealthy merchants were keen to build mansions on a grand scale as a testimony to their new wealth.

The popular design focused primarily on one or more internal courtyards. This provided security and privacy for the women of the household, as well as offering some relief from the fierce heat that grips the area in summer. The main entrance is usually a large wooden gate leading into a small courtyard, which in turn leads into another courtyard. The largest mansions had as many as four courtyards and were up to six storeys high.

Having built a house of grand proportions, the families then had them decorated with murals. The major themes found are Hindu mythology, history, folk tales, eroticism (many now defaced or destroyed), and – one of the most curious – foreigners and their modern inventions, such as planes and gramophones.

Few of the havelis are occupied by their absentee owners, their upkeep left to the meagre resources and loving attention of local caretakers and their families. Not all are open to the public; always ask permission before wandering inside. Local custom dictates that shoes should be removed when entering the inner courtyard of a haveli and some are forbidden territory for men.

One unfortunate aspect of the tourist trade is also beginning to manifest itself here: The desire for antiques. A couple of towns have antique shops chock-a-block with items ripped from the havelis – particularly doors and window frames, but anything that can be carted away is fair game. Investing in these antiques perpetuates this desecration.

Rs 600/1000 including breakfast. There's also a lovely suite for Rs 1000. Traditional Rajasthani meals are served on the rooftop and there's a small reading room.

Hotel Castle Mandawa *(☎ 01592-23124, fax 23171)* is upmarket and impersonal. Tastefully designed rooms cost Rs 1800/2200 up to Rs 3995 for the royal suite. Some rooms have more charm than others, so try to look at a few first. Breakfast/lunch/dinner costs Rs 250/400/450.

Nawalgarh

The main building in this town was the fort, founded in 1737 but today largely disfigured by modern accretions. Havelis of interest include the Aath Havelis, the Hem Raj Kulwal Haveli, the Bhagton-ki-Haveli and the Khedwal Bhavan. The Podar Haveli Museum, originally built in the 1920s on the eastern side of town, has been magnificently restored with wonderful, vibrant murals and a small collection of Rajasthani wedding costumes and miniature paintings. Entry is Rs 30.

Places to Stay & Eat Near the Maur Hospital, ***Ramesh Jangid's Tourist Pension*** *(☎ 01594-24060, fax 24061)* offers cheap and cheerful accommodation in a very-homey atmosphere. Clean singles/doubles with private bathroom (free bucket hot water) range from Rs 180/200 to Rs 280/300. Veg meals are available and a thali costs Rs 60. Guided tours and bicycle hire can also be arranged here.

Apani Dhani *(☎ 01594-22239, fax 24 061)*, or Eco Farm, is Ramesh's second place to stay. Look for it near the TV tower on the west side of the main Jaipur road. Rooms, decorated in traditional style with thatched roofs and mud plaster, are Rs 600/750. Alternative energy is used wherever possible.

Roop Niwas Palace *(☎ 01594-22008, fax 23388)*, 1km from the fort, is the most luxurious place to stay. Rooms cost Rs 1150/1300; try to look at a few rooms first, as some are much nicer than others. There's a restaurant and swimming pool.

Parsurampura

Located 20km south-east of Nawalgarh, this little village has among the best preserved and oldest paintings in Shekhawati. The paintings of the interior of the dome of the **Chhatri of Thakur Sardul Singh** date from the mid-18th century and are worth a look.

There is also the **Shamji Sharaf Haveli** and the small **Gopinathji Mandir**, an 18th-century temple constructed by Sardul Singh.

Jhunjhunu

Jhunjhunu is one of the largest towns of Shekhawati and is the district headquarters. The town was founded by the Kaimkhani nawabs in the mid-15th century, and stayed under their control until it was taken by the Rajput ruler Sardul Singh in 1730.

It was in Jhunjhunu that the British based their Shekhawati Brigade, a troop raised locally in the 1830s to try to halt the activities of the *dacoits* (bandits), who were largely local petty rulers who had decided it was easier to become wealthy by pinching other people's money than by earning their own.

The Tourist Reception Centre (☎ 01592-32909) is out of the town centre at the Churu bypass, Mandawa Circle. It's open from 10 am to 5 pm weekdays and every second Saturday.

Things to See The main item of interest here is the **Khetri Mahal**, a minor palace dating from around 1770. It's one of the most sophisticated buildings in the region, although it's not in the greatest condition. From the top, there are sensational views of the whole town. The **Bihariji Temple** is from a similar period and contains some fine murals, although these too have suffered over the years. The **Modi Havelis** and the **Kaniram Narsinghdas Tibrewala Haveli**, both in the main bazaar, are covered with murals.

Places to Stay & Eat East of the town centre, ***Hotel Shiv Shekhawati*** *(☎ 01592-32651, fax 38168)* is the most popular hotel with travellers, and deservedly so. Squeaky-clean rooms cost Rs 350/400 with private bathroom, and Rs 600/800 with air-con; prices are sometimes negotiable. Meals are available (veg breakfast/lunch/dinner costs Rs 75/150/150), although a la carte meals are also available.

Hotel Jamuna Resort *(☎ 01592-32871, fax 38168)* only has four rooms and there's a swimming pool (which nonguests can use for Rs 50). Singles/doubles cost Rs 700/800; some rooms are decorated with mirrorwork. There's a relaxing outdoor dining area, also open to nonresidents; a set veg/nonveg meal is Rs 150/200.

Hotel Sangam *(☎ 01592-32544, fax 33086)*, in the bus stand area, has reasonable singles/doubles with private bathroom (bucket hot water) from Rs 125/250. Checkout is 24 hours.

Hotel Shekhawati Heritage *(☎ 01592-35757, fax 33077, ⓔ Shekhawati_Heritage@yahoo.com)*, nearby, is arguably the pick of those in this area. Rooms with hot-water geyser start at Rs 400/500, although those for Rs 100 extra are better.

Mahansar

Although this sleepy little village does not have a great selection of painted havelis, it oozes old-world charm. Attractions include the mid-19th-century **Raghunath Temple**, the **Sona-ki-Dukan Haveli** and the **Sahaj Ram Poddar Chhatri**.

Narayan Niwas Castle *(☎ 01595-64322)*, in the old fort, is an authentic castle (without the commercial flavour of many of Rajasthan's royal hotels). Singles/doubles start at Rs 700/900 – see a few rooms first, as some have more atmosphere than others.

Getting There & Away

Access to the Shekhawati region is easiest from Jaipur or Bikaner. The towns of Sikar (gateway to the region, but with no notable havelis) and Fatehpur are on the main Jaipur-Bikaner road and are served by many buses.

Churu is on the main Delhi-Bikaner railway line, while Sikar, Nawalgarh and Jhunjhunu have several daily passenger train links with Jaipur and Delhi.

Getting Around

The Shekhawati region is crisscrossed by narrow bitumen roads, and all towns are quite well served by government or private buses. The local services to the smaller towns can get very crowded and riding 'upper class' (on the roof!) is quite acceptable – and often necessary.

If you have a group of four or five people, it's well worth hiring a taxi for the day to take you around the area. This is usually very easy to arrange in the towns that have accommodation, although finding a driver who speaks English can be a challenge. The official taxi rate is Rs 4 per kilometre, with a minimum of 300km per day. Alternatively, you could opt for a camel or horse safari; ask at your hotel.

AJMER

☎ 0145 • pop 493,000

Just over 130km south-west of Jaipur is Ajmer, a burgeoning town on the shore of the Ana Sagar, flanked by barren hills. Historically, Ajmer had considerable strategic importance and was sacked by Mohammed of Ghori on one of his periodic forays from Afghanistan. Later, it became a favourite residence of the mighty Mughals. One of the first contacts between the Mughals and the British occurred in Ajmer, when Sir Thomas Roe met with Jehangir here in 1616.

The city was subsequently taken by the Scindias and in 1818 it was handed over to the British, becoming one of the few places in Rajasthan controlled directly by the British rather than being part of a princely state. The British chose Ajmer as the site for Mayo College, a prestigious school opened in 1875 exclusively for the Indian princes, but today open to all those who can afford the fees. Ajmer is a major centre for Muslim pilgrims during the fast of Ramadan, and has some impressive Muslim architecture. However for most travellers, Ajmer is essentially just a stepping stone to nearby Pushkar.

Orientation & Information

The main bus stand is in the north-east of town. The train station and most of the hotels are on the east side of town.

The tourist office (☎ 627426) is in the RTDC Hotel Khadim compound and is open from 8 am to noon and 3 to 6 pm daily except Sunday. State Bank of India, opposite the Collectorate, changes travellers cheques and currency. Bank of Baroda on Prithviraj Marg, opposite the main post office, only changes travellers cheques, but also issues cash advances on MasterCard and Visa.

The convenient Cyber Planet (☎ 628721, ⓔ faakhirmoini@usa.net), 100m south of the train station on Station Rd, has Internet access for Rs 35 per hour. It's open from 11.30 am to 10.30 pm daily except Friday, when it opens at 2.30 pm.

Ana Sagar

This artificial lake was created in the 12th century by damming the River Luni. On its bank is a pleasant park, the **Dault Bagh**, containing a series of marble pavilions erected in 1637 by Shah Jahan. There are fine views from the hill beside the Dault Bagh, particularly just before sunset when the views back towards Ajmer are wonderful. Paddle boats can be hired for Rs 15 per person (minimum of two people). Life jackets are provided although if you fall in you're probably in greater danger from the polluted water than drowning.

The lake tends to dry up if the monsoon is poor, so the city's water supply is taken from **Foy Sagar**, 3km further up the valley.

Dargah

At the foot of a desolate hill in the old part of town, this is one of India's most important places for Muslim pilgrims. The Dargah is the tomb of a Sufi saint, Khwaja Muin-ud-din Chishti, who came to Ajmer from Persia in 1192. Construction of the shrine was completed by Humayun and the gate was added by the Nizam (hereditary title of the rulers of Hyderabad). Akbar used to make the pilgrimage to the Dargah from Agra once a year.

You have to cover your head in certain areas, so don't forget to take a scarf or cap – you can buy one in the bazaar leading to the shrine.

As you enter the courtyard, removing your shoes at the gateway, a mosque constructed by Akbar is on the right. The large iron cauldrons are for offerings, which are customarily shared by families involved in the shrine's upkeep. In an inner court, there is another mosque built by Shah Jahan. Constructed of white marble, it has 11 arches and a Persian inscription running the full length of the building.

The saint's tomb is in the centre of the second court. It has a marble dome and the actual tomb inside is surrounded by a silver platform. The horseshoes nailed to the shrine doors are offerings from successful horse dealers! Beware of 'guides' pestering for donations around the Dargah using the standard fake donation books or 'visitor registers' – you'll have to pay a generous donation if you sign up.

The tomb attracts hundreds of thousands of pilgrims every year on the anniversary of the saint's death, the Urs, in the seventh month of the lunar calendar (the dates are variable, so check with the tourist office). It's an interesting festival, but the crowds can be suffocating. As well as the pilgrims, sufis from all over India converge on Ajmer.

Adhai-din-ka-Jhonpra & Taragarh

Beyond the Dargah, on the very outskirts of town, are the ruins of the Adhai-din-ka-Jhonpra (Two-and-a-Half Days) Mosque. According to legend, its construction in 1153 took 2½ days, as its name indicates. Others say it was named after a festival lasting 2½ days. It was originally built as a Sanskrit college, but in 1198 Mohammed of Ghori seized Ajmer and converted the building into a mosque by adding a seven-arched wall in front of the pillared hall.

Although the mosque is now in need of restoration, it is a particularly fine piece of architecture – the pillars are all different and the arched 'screen', with its damaged minarets, is noteworthy.

About 3km and a steep 1½-hour climb beyond the mosque, the Taragarh, or Star Fort, commands a superb view over the city (accessible by car). This ancient fort was built by Ajaipal Chauhan, the town's founder. It was the site of much military activity during Mughal times and was later used as a sanatorium by the British.

Akbar's Palace

Back in the city, not far from the main post office, this imposing building was constructed by Akbar in 1570 and today houses the government museum, which has a limited collection. Items include a collection

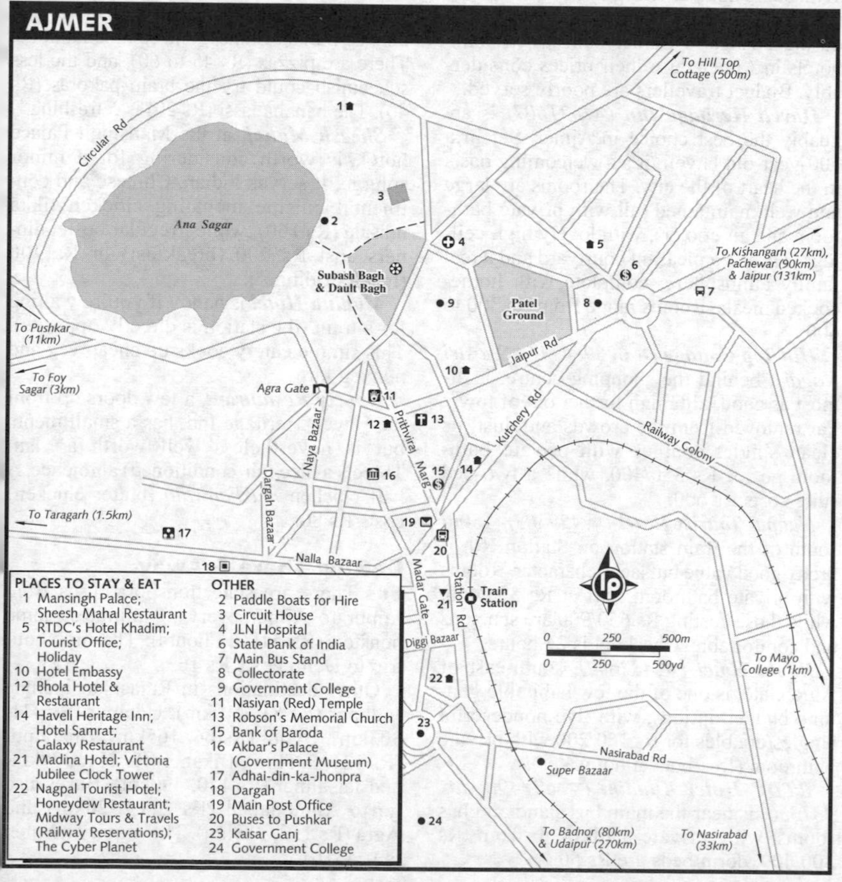

of stone sculptures, some dating back to the 8th century AD, old weapons and miniature paintings.

It's open from 10 am to 4.30 pm daily except Friday. Entry is Rs 3 (free on Monday). A camera costs Rs 10/20 for Indians/foreigners; a video is Rs 20/50.

Nasiyan (Red) Temple

The Red Temple on Prithviraj Marg, a Jain temple built last century, is definitely worth checking out. Its double-storey hall contains a fascinating series of large, gilt wooden figures from Jain mythology which depict the Jain concept of the ancient world. The temple is open 8.30 am to 6 pm daily (Rs 3).

Places to Stay

With some notable exceptions, Ajmer's hotels are generally poor value, especially during Pushkar's Camel Fair, when some hotels in Ajmer raise their prices considerably. Budget travellers are poorly served.

Haveli Heritage Inn *(☎ 621607)* is arguably the best choice in Ajmer. Set in a 100-year-old haveli, it's a welcoming oasis in the heart of the city. The rooms are large and well maintained (all with private bathroom and air cooler), with lovely high ceilings. There's a pleasant courtyard and a real family atmosphere, complete with home-cooked meals. Rooms range from Rs 300 to 600.

Hill Top Cottage *(☎ 623984, 164 Shastri Nagar)*, behind the shopping centre, is almost as good, although further out of town. Far removed from the crowds and dust, its clean singles/doubles with private bathroom go for Rs 350/400, while a two-bed suite costs Rs 600.

Nagpal Tourist Hotel *(☎ 429503)*, 150m south of the train station on Station Rd, is pretty good value but lacks character. Rooms with private bathroom start at Rs 350/450, while those costing Rs 650/900 are spacious and comfortable. Checkout is 24 hours.

Bhola Hotel *(☎ 432844)*, south-east of Agra Gate, is one of the few habitable genuine budget options, with five nondescript singles/doubles for Rs 150/200 with private bathroom (free bucket hot water).

RTDC Hotel Khadim *(☎ 627490, fax 431330)* is near the main bus stand and has rooms with private bathroom from Rs 300/400; dorm beds are Rs 50.

Hotel Embassy *(☎ 623859, ⓔ hotelembassy@satyam.net.in, Jaipur Rd)*, is a modern hotel with nice singles/doubles for Rs 450/550.

Mansingh Palace *(☎ 425702, fax 425 858, ⓔ mansingh.ajmer@mailcity.com, Circular Rd)*, overlooking Ana Sagar, is Ajmer's only top-end hotel. It's a long way from anywhere but the rooms (Rs 1995/3000) are attractive and there's a pleasant garden at the back. There's a bar and restaurant here (see Places to Eat).

Places to Eat

Bhola Hotel has a good veg restaurant at the top of a seedy staircase. Tasty thalis cost Rs 35, and there's also a variety of other dishes such as paneer kofta (Rs 40).

Honeydew Restaurant, next to Nagpal Tourist Hotel, has a good selection of veg and nonveg Indian, Chinese and continental food. There are pizzas (Rs 45 to 60), and the less squeamish could try the brain pakoras (Rs 40). The banana lassi (Rs 20) is refreshing.

Sheesh Mahal, at the Mansingh Palace hotel, is worth considering for a minor splurge. It serves Indian, Chinese and continental cuisine including chicken tikka masala (Rs 160), while irregular buffet dinners cost Rs 200 (breakfast) or Rs 400 (lunch or dinner).

Madina Hotel is handy if you're waiting for a train (the station is directly opposite). This simple eatery cooks up cheap veg and nonveg fare.

Galaxy Restaurant, a few doors up from the Haveli Heritage Inn, has a small menu, but is nevertheless well worth a visit. There's a nice (air-conditioned) ambience. A half chicken *makhanwala* (butter chicken) costs Rs 80.

Getting There & Away

Bus There are state transport buses from Jaipur to Ajmer every 30 minutes, some nonstop (Rs 51, 2½ hours). The nine-hour trip to Delhi costs Rs 163.

Other destinations in Rajasthan include Jodhpur (Rs 81, 210km), Udaipur (Rs 111, 303km), Bundi (Rs 66, 165km), Bharatpur (Rs 121, 305km), Bikaner (Rs 111, 277km) and Jaisalmer (Rs 140, 490km). Buses also go to Ahmedabad (Rs 211, 526km) and Agra (Rs 152, 388km). The inquiry number is ☎ 431615.

Many of these destinations are also served by private bus – most of the companies have offices on Kutchery Rd.

There are frequent buses from Ajmer to Pushkar (Rs 6, 30 minutes) which leave from the roadside 150m north of the train station, at the intersection of Station and Kutchery Rds. If arriving in Ajmer by private bus, some drivers will try to convince you that the Pushkar buses leave from the railway crossing – they don't and there are taxi drivers waiting.

Train There are no tourist quotas for many trains out of Ajmer, so it's worth booking as soon as you know your departure date. Midway Tours & Travels (☎ 628744) will prebook sleeper- and upper-class berths for Rs 15/25.

Ajmer is on the Delhi-Jaipur-Ahmedabad-Mumbai line and most of the trains on this line stop here. The comfortable *Shatabdi Express* (2016/5) travels daily, except Sunday, between Ajmer and Delhi (Rs 630/1250 chair/executive class) via Jaipur (Rs 320/615). This train leaves Delhi at 6.15 am and arrives in Ajmer at 12.45 pm. In the other direction, it leaves Ajmer at 3.30 pm, arriving in Jaipur at 5.25 pm and Delhi at 10.15 pm.

Another train that's useful is the *Delhi-Ahmedabad Mail* (9105/6), departing Ajmer at 8.33 pm and arriving in Delhi at 5.20 am (Rs 99/154/446 general/sleeper/3A class). Heading for Gujarat, the train leaves Ajmer at 7.35 am and arrives in Ahmedabad at 5.20 pm (Rs 107/166/482).

Getting Around

There are plenty of autorickshaws as well as some cycle-rickshaws and tongas. To travel anywhere in town by autorickshaw should cost you around Rs 15.

PUSHKAR

☎ 0145 • pop 13,500

Pushkar is a bewitching little town, despite its somewhat touristy feel these days. It is right on the edge of the desert and is only 11km from Ajmer but separated from it by Nag Pahar, the Snake Mountain.

Camel Fair

The Pushkar Camel Fair is one of India's grand epics. Each year, up to 200,000 people (of whom only around 6000 are tourists) flock to Pushkar for the Camel Fair, bringing with them some 50,000 camels and cattle for several days of pilgrimage, livestock trading, horse dealing and spirited festivities. The place becomes a flurry of activity, with musicians, mystics, comedians, tourists, traders, animals and devotees all converging on this small town. It's truly a feast for the eyes.

Check with the makeshift RTDC Tourist Information Tents (during fair time only), inside the gate of the RTDC Hotel Sarovar and outside the stadium for a list of events which include cultural performances and fiercely contested camel-judging competitions. They're also the people to see if you want to take a hot-air balloon ride over Pushkar for Rs 2000, although other travel agencies around town can also make the arrangements.

The exact date on which the Camel Fair is held depends on the lunar calendar but, in Hindu chronology, it falls on the full moon of Kartik Purnima, when devotees cleanse away their sins by bathing in the holy lake. It's strongly recommended that you get to the fair several days prior to the official commencement date in order to see the camel and cattle trading at its peak. The signing of deeds sometimes takes place a full two days before the official commencement date. Although the place assumes a carnival atmosphere, the Camel Fair is taken very seriously by livestock owners, who come from all over the country with the sole intent of trading. A good camel can fetch tens of thousands of rupees and is a vital source of income for many villagers.

We heard of one group of travellers in 2000 who got right into the spirit of the fair, purchasing a camel or two and a cart for luggage and set off from Pushkar, across the desert, heading for Jaisalmer.

This fair is the only one of its kind in the world and has featured in numerous magazines, travel shows and films. It can get noisy at night, so if you're a light sleeper, bring earplugs. Carry appropriate allergy medication if you are affected by dust and/or animal hair.

The fair takes place from 22 to 30 November 2001, 16 to 19 November 2002 and 5 to 8 November 2003, although check in advance as these dates are sometimes subject to change.

This traveller-friendly town clings to the side of the enchanting Pushkar Lake with its many bathing ghats and temples. For Hindus, Pushkar is a very important pilgrimage centre and you'll see plenty of *sadhus* (individuals on a spiritual search).

Pushkar is perhaps best known for its Camel Fair, which takes place on the full moon of Kartik Purnima. This massive congregation of camels, cattle, livestock traders, pilgrims, tourists and film-makers is a most incredible event. If you are anywhere within striking distance at the time, it's an event not to be missed (see the boxed text 'Camel Fair' on the previous page).

Being a holy place, alcohol, meat and even eggs are banned in Pushkar.

Information

Unfortunately, there is no tourist office in Pushkar (except at the time of the Camel Fair), but it's easy to find your way around. At the time of writing the State Bank of Bikaner & Jaipur (open from 10 am to 2 pm weekdays and 10 am to noon Saturday) only changes travellers cheques (not currency) – the wait can be long and the staff brusque. Every second shop along Sadar Bazaar Rd doubles as a moneychanger, doing both cash and travellers cheques at market rates, but check the commission before handing over your money. On the same road are plenty of places offering Internet services, although connections can be painfully slow.

For quality film processing (prints only), Rajasthan Colour Lab (which doubles as a bookshop) on Sadar Bazaar Rd charges Rs 5 per photo.

Temples

Pushkar boasts temples, although few are as ancient as you might expect at such an important pilgrimage site, since many were desecrated by Aurangzeb and were subsequently rebuilt. The most famous is the **Brahma Temple**, said to be one of the few temples in the world dedicated to this deity. It's marked by a red spire, and over the entrance gateway is the *hans*, or goose symbol, of Brahma, who is said to have personally chosen Pushkar as its site.

The one-hour trek up to the hilltop **Savitri Temple** overlooking the lake is best made early in the morning; the view is magical. The views from the closer **Pap Mochani Temple**, reached by a track behind the Marwar bus stand, are also worth the climb.

Ghats

Numerous ghats run down to the lake, and pilgrims are constantly bathing in the lake's sacred waters. If you wish to join them, do it with respect; remember, this is a holy place. Remove your shoes, don't smoke, refrain from kidding around and do not take photographs.

Priests, some genuine, some not, will approach you near the ghats and offer to do a *puja* (prayer) for which you'll receive a 'Pushkar passport' (a red ribbon around the wrist). Unfortunately, more and more travellers are reporting problems with pushy priests (although one traveller did write to tell us that one priest helped to cure his skin cancer). Don't be bullied into giving an exorbitant donation and agree on the price beforehand.

Another 'scam' involves 'priests' giving a traveller a flower. Once you take it, you are then asked to throw it into the holy lake – for a price! To avoid a scene, it's best to not take any flowers offered to you at all.

Massage & Yoga

For reiki, yoga and shiatsu, head to Honeymoon Hotel, not far from the Marwar bus stand, where Reiki Master Roshi Hiralal Verma (☎ 773298) is located. Costs depend on the duration and nature of your session. Women travellers have reported feeling comfortable here.

Tailors

Pushkar is an excellent place to get some clothes made. One reliable place recommended by a number of travellers is Navjyoti Tailors (☎ 772589, ⓔ yogeshnavjyoti@hotmail.com), opposite the Lake View (see Places to Stay – Budget). The relaxed yogi can make just about anything you want in one to two days and charges very reasonable prices.

Music Schools

The Saraswati Music School (☎ 773124) is an excellent place to learn classical *tabla* (drums) and singing. Birju, with over 12 years experience, charges Rs 100 for one hour and Rs 600 for three days of lessons.

He's open most days from 10 am to 10 pm and on many nights conducts performances from 8 to 9.30 pm.

Places to Stay

Most hotels in Pushkar are nothing fancy, but they're generally clean and freshly whitewashed. You should ask to see a few rooms before deciding, as many have a cell-like atmosphere owing to the tiny or non-existent windows. At the time of the Camel Fair, when demand for rooms is exceptionally high, most hotel tariffs blow sky high. To get the room of your choice at this time, you'll need to book ahead, although there are sometimes rooms to be found.

Places to Stay – Budget

Hotel VK *(☎ 772174)* is a popular cheapie. Acceptable singles with shared bathroom cost Rs 75 and doubles without/with private bathroom are Rs 125/175; Rs 200 gets you a room with a balcony. There are plans to extend upwards, which hopefully won't impinge upon the good rooftop restaurant.

Hotel Venus *(☎ 772323, ⓔ venushotel@yahoo.com)*, on the main thoroughfare nearby, offers doubles with private bathroom for Rs 150. Set in a shady garden, there's also a popular restaurant upstairs.

Krishna Guest House *(☎ 772461)* doesn't quite live up to the manager's claim that it's 'the best guest house in the world', but it's still a very pleasant place to stay. There are some very small rooms for Rs 40 and Rs 60, but most cost Rs 80/100 with shared bathroom and Rs 100/150 with private bathroom.

Hotel Om *(☎ 772672)* is similarly good, charging Rs 50/100 without bathroom and Rs 100/150 with private bathroom. The rooms are spacious, the owner relaxed and there are buffet dinners (Rs 40) in the garden.

Prince Hotel *(☎ 772674)*, closer to the lake, is quite basic, but cheap, friendly and quiet. It has rooms for Rs 50/80 with shared bathroom and Rs 100 for a double with private bathroom.

Hotel Kanhaia *(☎ 772146)*, also north-east of the lake, has clean doubles without/with private bathroom for Rs 80/100.

Hotel White House *(☎ 772147, fax 772950)*, north of the lake, is a very appealing place, with fine views from the rooftop restaurant. Spotless, airy and air-cooled

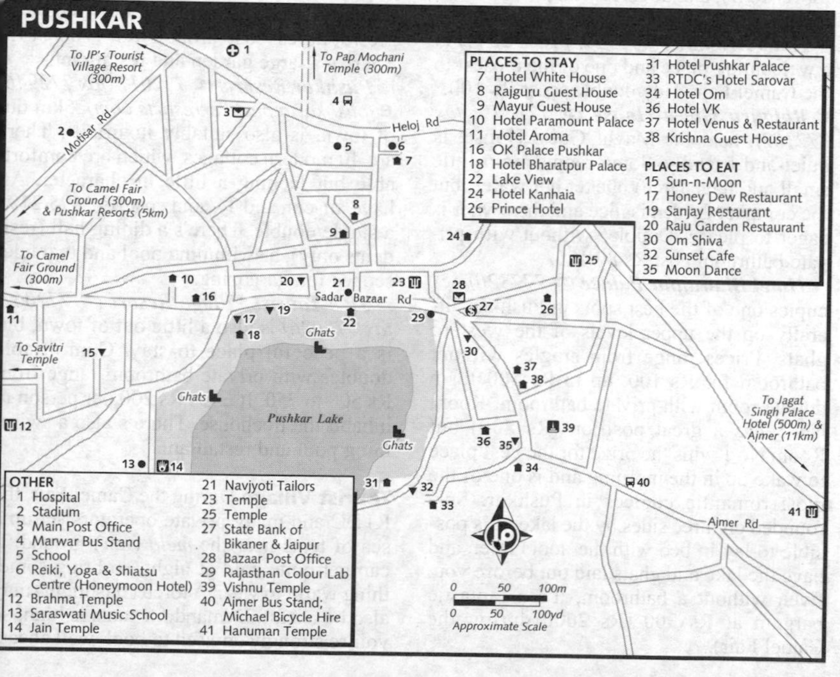

rooms cost from Rs 250, while Rs 350 and 450 gets you progressively larger rooms with balcony. The mango tea (complimentary on arrival) is refreshing and the meals are good.

Mayur Guest House *(☎ 772302)*, closer to the lake, is an unpretentious, relaxed place that gets a lot of repeat visitors. Rooms go for Rs 50/70 with shared bathroom and Rs 90/125 with private bathroom.

Lake View *(☎ 772106, fax 772106)* is wonderfully located above the ghats, with superb views over the lake from the roof. Doubles with private bathroom cost from Rs 200 to 300 but some of those without bathroom (Rs 150 to 200) have a balcony overlooking the lake. There are also other rooms for Rs 100.

Hotel Paramount Palace *(☎ 772428, fax 772244)* is another place with fine views over the town. Doubles with private bathroom range from Rs 100 to 450 depending on the size – the most expensive rooms (Nos 106, 108, 109 and 111) have balconies and are particularly good value.

Nearby, ***OK Palace Pushkar*** *(☎ 772868)* is good if you're suffering a cash crunch. Singles/doubles with shared bathroom go for Rs 40/80, and doubles with private bathroom cost Rs 100.

Hotel Aroma *(☎ 772729, fax 772244)* is a welcoming place and one of the closest to the Camel Fair. Tidy doubles cost Rs 100.

Rajguru Guest House *(☎ 772879, fax 772102)*, near the Mayur Guest House, is quiet and friendly. Some rooms are a little small and have (free) bucket hot water, but the compact garden is nice and the owner is eager to please. Doubles without/with private bathroom cost Rs 80/125.

Hotel Bharatpur Palace *(☎ 772320)* occupies one of the best spots in Pushkar, literally on the upper levels of the western ghats. Prices range from singles without bathroom for Rs 100, up to Rs 500 for a double room with private bathroom. Room No 5 has a great position (Rs 200) but Room No 1 wins the prize for the best place to wake up in the morning and is one of the most romantic choices in Pushkar. Surrounded on three sides by the lake, it is possible to lay in bed with the doors open and have the lake and ghats laid out before you. Even without a bathroom, it's a fantastic bargain at Rs 300 (Rs 2000 during the Camel Fair).

Places to Stay – Mid-Range & Top End

Hotel Pushkar Palace *(☎ 772001, fax 772226)*, near the lake, is a popular place, although it has had some mixed reviews in recent years. Once belonging to the maharaja of Kishangarh, the cheapest rooms cost Rs 600/745 without/with air-con. Better rooms start at Rs 1100/1195. The most expensive rooms (Rs 1900/1995) have superlative lake views for which you'll pay US$175 during the Camel Fair.

RTDC Hotel Sarovar *(☎ 772040)* is just along from Hotel Pushkar Palace but is approached from a different entrance. Set in its own spacious grounds at the far end of the lake and with a restaurant, it has more character than most other RTDC places, although some travellers have complained about the indifferent service. Singles/doubles with shared bathroom cost Rs 100/200 Rs 300/400 with private bathroom. Lake-view rooms cost Rs 500/600. There are also dorm beds for Rs 50.

Jagat Singh Palace Hotel *(☎ 772953, fax 772952)*, a little out of the main town area, is one of the most upmarket places in Pushkar. Designed like a fort and now a heritage hotel, attractively furnished singles/doubles cost around Rs 1100/1195. There's a large garden and restaurant.

Pushkar Resorts *(☎ 772017, fax 772946, ⓔ pushkar@pushkarresorts.com)*, 5km out of town, is also suitably luxurious. There are 40 modern cottages, which are comfortable but lacking a little in character. All have air-con and TV and cost Rs 1895/2195 a single/double. There's a dining hall (residents only), a swimming pool and two telescopes for stargazing.

JP's Tourist Village Resort *(☎ 772067, fax 772026)* is also a little out of town, but is a peaceful place to stay. Comfortable doubles with private bathroom range from Rs 500 to 750. It costs Rs 200 per person to inhabit the treehouse. There's also a swimming pool and restaurant.

Tourist Village During the Camel Fair, the RTDC and many private operators set up a sea of tents near the *mela* (fair) ground. It can get quite cold at night, so bring something warm to wear. A torch (flashlight) may also be useful. Demand for tents is high, so you're strongly advised to book well ahead

RTDC Tourist Village (☎ *772074*) has dorm tents for US$7 per person, and standard single/double tents with shared bathroom for Rs 4000/4500 including all meals. There are also more upmarket Swiss tents with private bathroom for Rs 5000/5500 and deluxe huts for Rs 5500/6000 including meals. These huts are open all year round, and are significantly cheaper outside fair time – Rs 150 to 400. For bookings, contact the General Manager, Central Reservations (☎ 0141-202152, fax 201145, ⓔ rtdc@jp1.dot.net.in), RTDC Hotel Swagatam Campus, Near Railway Station, Jaipur or the RTDC Hotel Sarovar in Pushkar. Full payment must be received 45 days in advance if you want to be sure of accommodation.

Royal Tents, owned by the maharaja of Jodhpur, seem to be the most luxurious tents, but you'll pay for this privilege. They cost US$175/225 a single/double with private bathroom (bucket hot water), including all meals. Reservations should be made in advance at the Umaid Bhawan Palace (☎ 0291-433316, fax 635373) in Jodhpur.

Royal Desert Camp (☎ *772957*), further away from the fairground, is another good option, with tents for US$85/100 with private bathroom and showers and others for US$115/125. There are also some cheaper tents with shared bathroom. The price includes all meals and a 'camel shuttle service' to and from the fair. Book well ahead at the camp or through Hotel Pushkar Palace (☎ 772001, fax 772226) in Pushkar.

Places to Eat

Pushkar has plenty of reasonably priced eating places, although hygiene standards sometimes leave a little to be desired. Strict vegetarianism that forbids even eggs limits the range of ingredients, but the cooks (sometimes) make up for this with imagination. You can even get an eggless omelette in some places, while others serve vegetarian spaghetti bolognaise. In general, steer clear of Western-style dishes, which tend to be a disappointment.

Buffet meals are popular, with many places offering all-you-can-eat meals for Rs 35 to 45.

There are a number of places where the view or location is better than the food. Surprisingly, one such place is the ***Hotel Pushkar Palace*** (see Places to Stay – Mid-Range & Top End) – a great place for a drink at sunset (a mango lassi is Rs 25), but eat elsewhere. Others include the ***Venus Restaurant***, which has a prime vantage point overlooking the main thoroughfare and its fascinating passing parade (the chocolate pancake with banana and honey Rs 25 isn't bad), and ***Sanjay Restaurant***, which has a great view over the lake.

Sunset Cafe, right on the eastern ghats, has long been a popular hang-out of travellers – a good place to swap stories about Goa, Kathmandu and beyond, which is just as well, as the service can be slow. This simple cafe offers the usual have-a-go-at-anything menu, including dosas (Rs 20) and sizzlers (from Rs 50 to 75). There's a German bakery too. The location by the lakeshore is perfect at sunset.

Om Shiva, near the State Bank of Bikaner & Jaipur, offers reasonably priced and tasty buffets (Rs 45). Feeding off the popularity of the original, there are at least three imitations with the same name around town.

Moon Dance is one place that gets consistently good reviews. It has tables in a laid-back garden and serves a wide range of food, including high-quality Indian, Mexican, Italian and Israeli dishes. A spectacular spinach and mushroom enchilada is Rs 55, a good spinach and mushroom burger is Rs 50 and great bruschetta costs from Rs 20. A cup of soothing cinnamon tea is Rs 5. There's also a pool table and you sit at tables or on cushions. The Indian food is surprisingly patchy and the service can be slow.

Raju Garden Restaurant serves a mish-mash of Western, Chinese and Indian fare. The prices are a little high, but the selection is good. If your tummy is screaming for something simple, try the baked potatoes (Rs 45). Birthday cakes can be ordered here (with advance notice); they range from a palatable Rs 65 to a mind-blowing Rs 1000!

Sun-n-Moon, not far from the Brahma Temple, has tables around a bodi tree, and is a peaceful place to eat. It offers a variety of Western and Indian food such as Kashmiri burgers (Rs 45), serves large breakfasts (Rs 55 to 75) and boasts the 'best apple pie in Pushkar' (Rs 45).

Honey Dew Restaurant, at the western end of Sadar Bazaar Rd, is a cosy place doing reasonable thalis for Rs 25.

Shopping

Pushkar's main bazaar is a tangle of narrow lanes lined with an assortment of interesting little shops – ideal for picking up gifts for friends back home. Here you'll come across everything from clothing shops catering to styles which were in vogue at the end of the 1960s to Rajasthani turbans, from musical instruments to incense sticks, from statues of Ganesh to the novels of Salman Rushdie. Particularly good buys include costume jewellery, embroidered fabrics such as wall hangings and groovy shoulder bags, Rajasthani puppets and traditional music. A lot of what is stocked here actually comes from the Barmer district south of Jaisalmer and other tribal areas of Rajasthan. You'll have to haggle over prices, as Pushkar has long been exposed to tourists with money to burn and not much time to burn it. There's the usual nonsense about 'last price' quotes which aren't negotiable – take your time and visit a few shops.

There are a number of bookshops in the main bazaar selling a tremendous range of second-hand novels in various languages, and they'll usually buy them back for around 50% of what you pay.

Getting There & Away

To Pushkar, buses depart Ajmer frequently for Rs 6 (although it's only Rs 4 when going from Pushkar to Ajmer – because of the road toll; for cars the toll is Rs 25). Like everything else in Pushkar, it all costs a bit more at fair time.

Travel agencies around town sell tickets for private buses to various destinations – shop around for the best price. These buses generally leave from Ajmer, but the agencies should provide you with free transport to Ajmer in time for the departures. Those that leave from Pushkar generally stop for an hour or more in Ajmer anyway. Be warned that some buses (particularly those via Jodhpur) don't go all the way in spite of promises and involve a change of bus *and* an extra fare. See Getting There & Away under Ajmer earlier in this section for destinations. Private buses go to Jaisalmer (Rs 180, 10½ hours), Jodhpur (Rs 100, 5½ hours), Udaipur (Rs 120, eight hours), Delhi (Rs 160, 10½ hours), Jaipur (Rs 80, four hours) and Agra (Rs 160, nine hours), among other destinations.

For around Rs 50, some agencies will book train tickets for services ex-Ajmer (including a free jeep transfer to Ajmer).

Getting Around

Fortunately, there are no autorickshaws in the town centre, but it's a breeze to get around by foot. Another good option is to hire a bicycle (Rs 5/25 per hour/day). A wallah can carry your luggage on a hand-drawn cart to or from the bus stand for around Rs 10.

RANTHAMBHORE NATIONAL PARK

☎ 07462

Near the town of Sawai Madhopur, midway between Bharatpur and Kota, Ranthambhore National Park is one of the prime examples of Project Tiger's conservation efforts in Rajasthan. Sadly, it also demonstrates the program's overall failure, for it was in this park that government officials were implicated in the poaching of tigers for the Chinese folk medicine trade. The visit of US president Bill Clinton in 2000 led to a rapid growth in the park's popularity, although, sadly, it also highlighted its problems: Bumbram, the tiger seen by President Clinton, could not be found when the park reopened in October 2000 after the monsoon, leading to fears that the now-famous tiger had been poached. Keen to play down the issue, park authorities denied the reports, although some doubts remained at the time of research.

According to a 1999 census, the park had a total of 42 tigers (32 adults and 10 cubs). There's a reasonable chance of seeing one, but you should plan on two or three safaris. Even if you don't see a tiger, it's worth the effort for the beautiful scenery alone: In India it's not often you get the chance to visit such a large area of virgin bush.

The park itself covers some 1334 sq km. A system of lakes and rivers is hemmed in by steep, high crags and on top of one of these is the Ranthambhore Fort, built in the 10th century. The lower ground alternates between open bushland and fairly dense forest and is peppered with ruined pavilions, *chhatris* (domed kiosks) and 'hides' – the area was formerly a hunting preserve of the maharajas.

Indian parliament has approved a law to rename the park the Rajiv Gandhi National

Park, although implementation of the decision has been put on hold indefinitely.

Orientation & Information

It's 10km from Sawai Madhopur to the first park gate, where you pay the entry fees, and another 3km to the main gate and the Ranthambhore Fort. Accommodation is stretched out along the road from the town to the park.

The helpful Tourist Reception Centre (☎ 20808) is in the grounds of the RTDC Vinayak Tourist Complex. It's open from 10 am to 1.30 pm and 2 to 5 pm daily except Sunday. You can change travellers cheques (not cash) at the State Bank of Bikaner & Jaipur, in Sawai Madhopur.

The Project Tiger office (☎ 20223, 21142) is 500m from the train station.

Wildlife Safaris

The best time to visit the park is between October and April; the park is closed during the monsoon from 1 July to 1 October. Early morning and late afternoon are generally the best times for spotting wildlife. If you are taking photos, it's worthwhile bringing some 400ASA or 800ASA film, as the undergrowth is dense and surprisingly dark in places.

There's an Rs 25/200 park entry fee for Indians/foreigners, plus Rs 100 for a video camera.

Jeeps are almost impossible to obtain during most of the season. To have any chance you need to book at least two months in advance and pay the hire charge (Rs 750) in advance. There are a limited number of jeeps but the main reason that demand outstrips supply is that the authorities wish to restrict the number of motorised vehicles within the park. Assuming you are able to plan your life that far in advance, contact either the Project Tiger office (☎ 20223, 21142) or the Tourist Reception Centre (☎ 20808) or find a travel agency (or local hotel) to make the booking and payment arrangements. Occupants of jeeps must pay an additional Rs 125 per jeep upon entry to the park.

A seat in a large, open-topped truck (called a *canter*), which can be arranged on arrival, costs Rs 80 per person. Try to ask for a minicanter, which feels a little less like a circus show. To increase your chances of seeing a tiger, it is a good idea to contact either the Project Tiger office or the Tourist Reception Centre the day before your safari to ask where the latest sighting took place and then arrange for a canter taking that route. It doesn't always work, but it's still worth trying, particularly if your time is short. Bookings can be made through most hotels, the Tourist Reception Centre or the Project Tiger office.

A guide is compulsory and is included in the ticket price for a canter, but will cost an extra Rs 150 if you go by jeep.

In winter (October to February), both canters and jeeps leave at 7 am and 2.30 pm; the safari takes three hours. In summer (March to June), they leave at 6.30 am and 3.30 pm. Bookings for morning trips can be made between 4 and 5 pm on the day before, and between 11 am and noon for the afternoon safari, although many hotels seem able to do it outside these hours.

Places to Stay & Eat

The best places to stay are on Ranthambhore Rd, but budget travellers will find the cheapest (and grimiest and noisiest) lodgings in uninspiring Sawai Madhopur.

Ranthambhore Road About 5km from the train station, ***Hotel Ranthambore Resort*** *(☎ 21645, fax 21430)* is the cheapest along Ranthambore Rd. Simple but clean and decent-sized doubles with private bathroom and constant hot water cost Rs 250. The hotel's ***City Heart Restaurant*** next door was due to open just after we were there and promised Punjabi, South Indian, Chinese and tandoori cuisine.

Hotel Tiger Safari Resort *(☎ 21137, fax 22391)*, 4 km from the station, has pleasant doubles with very clean bathrooms from Rs 300. There's a rooftop restaurant serving reasonably priced a la carte dishes.

Ankur Resort *(☎ 20792, fax 23303, ⓔ ankur@ranthambor.com)*, 3km from the station, is a popular choice, although a touch overpriced, with doubles from Rs 600. Deluxe rooms cost Rs 1200/1500 (the latter has satellite TV).

Hotel Ranthambore Regency *(☎ 21176, fax 22299, ⓔ ranthamboreregency@ranthambor.com)*, nearby, has attractive singles/doubles for Rs 600/800, while Rs 1300/1500 gets you an air-con cottage.

RTDC Castle Jhoomar Baori *(☎ 20495)* is a former royal hunting lodge stunningly located on a hillside, about 7km from the train station. The rooms are not really luxurious, but they do have character. Standard singles/doubles cost Rs 700/800. A 'panther' suite is Rs 900/1100, while a 'tiger' or 'leopard' suite is Rs 1200/1500.

RTDC Vinayak Tourist Complex *(☎ 21333)*, which is further along the road, has decent rooms for Rs 550/600. There's a nice lawn area and a campfire is lit in the winter.

Sawai Madhopur Lodge *(☎ 20541, fax 20718)*, 3km from the train station, once belonged to the maharaja of Jaipur. Run by the Taj Group, it's suitably luxurious, with a pool (open to nonresidents for Rs 300), bar, restaurant, library and 12 acres of lovely gardens. Rooms are Rs 2500/3500, and upmarket tented accommodation (with private bathroom) is Rs 2800 a double.

Sawai Madhopur ***The Hotel Chinkara*** *(☎ 20340, 13 Indira Colony, Civil Lines)* has large rooms for Rs 125/200 with private bathroom and semiconstant hot water.

Rajeev Resort *(☎ 21413, fax 33138)*, almost next door, is similar at Rs 125/200 for a decent room with private bathroom. It's not bad value.

The following places are really only for those for whom price is everything. At each, you'll probably need to ask them to change the sheets.

Vishal Hotel *(☎ 20504)*, in the main bazaar, offers just one dank single with shared bathroom for Rs 60 and dingy doubles with private bathroom (free bucket hot water) for Rs 80 to 175.

Hotel Pink Palace *(☎ 20722, plot A1, Bal Mandir Colony)* has pretty basic rooms with shared bathroom (free bucket hot water) for Rs 60/100 or Rs 125/150 with private bathroom. For Rs 200/250 you get a sit-down flush toilet, hot water geyser and a satellite TV, which sometimes works.

Shopping

The Dastkar Craft Centre, 3km beyond the park entrance on Ranthambore Rd, is worth a visit. The handicrafts, all of which are produced by low-caste women in local villages, include bedspreads, clothes and other textile pieces.

Getting There & Away

Bus There are buses to, among other places, Jaipur (Rs 45, 4½ hours) and Kota (Rs 45, four hours). Buses to these destinations via Tonk leave from the small bus stand near the petrol station not far from the overpass. To go via Dausa (on the Jaipur-Bharatpur road), buses leave from the roundabout near the main post office. Travelling to Bharatpur by bus invariably involves a change in Dausa – the train is infinitely preferable.

Train There's a computerised reservation office at the station, open from 8 am to 8 pm Monday to Saturday and until 2 pm Sunday.

For Delhi, the *Golden Temple Mail* (2903) leaves Sawai Madhopur at 1 pm, arriving in the capital at 7.35 pm (Rs 84/131/378 general/sleeper/3A class). It goes via Bharatpur, arriving at 3.35 pm (Rs 52/81/234). To Kota, there are seven trains daily, the most convenient of which is the *Avadh Express* (5063), leaving Sawai Madhopur at 9.55 am and arriving at 11.35 am (Rs 36/56/183).

Getting Around

Bicycle hire is available just outside the main entrance to the train station, and at the eastern end of the main bazaar (around Rs 20 per day).

Southern Rajasthan

BUNDI

☎ 0747 • pop 80,000

Visiting Bundi is like stepping back in time. It's a picturesque and captivating little town which has more or less retained a medieval atmosphere. Bundi is not a major tourist tramping ground, which is a big part of its charm. In the evening, people throng to the colourful and bustling markets that meander through the town's lanes. Unlike many other places in Rajasthan, in Bundi you're unlikely to be hounded by persistent shopkeepers and it's a friendly place.

The town's Rajput legacy is well preserved in the massive fort, which broods over the town in the narrow valley below, and the imposing palace which stands beneath it. In this palace are the famous Bundi murals.

Bundi was the capital of a major princely state during the heyday of the Rajputs. Although its importance dwindled with the rise of Kota during Mughal times, it kept its independence until its incorporation into the state of Rajasthan in 1947.

Information

There's a small tourist office (☎ 442697) in the grounds of the Circuit House. It's open from 10 am to 1.30 pm and 2 to 5 pm Monday to Saturday. Mukesh Mehta, at the Haveli Braj Bhushanjee (see Places to Stay & Eat) is also a terrific source of information. His Web site (www.kiplingsbundi.com) is worth a look. At the time of research, no banks were changing money. The small shopfront moneychanger just south of the palace will change US dollars for a few rupees less than the market rate but could be useful if you're stuck. Email can be accessed at the Haveli Braj Bhushanjee, and at Cyber Dream nearby.

Taragarh

The rather neglected Taragarh, or Star Fort, was built in 1354 and is a great place to ramble around at leisure. It is reached by a steep road leading up the hillside to its enormous gateway, topped by rampant elephants. Take the path up behind the Chittra Sala, east along the inside of the ramparts, then left up the steep stone ramp just before the small disused building 200m from the palace. Inside the ramparts are huge reservoirs carved out of solid rock, and the Bhim Burj, the largest of the battlements, on which is mounted a famous cannon. Views over the town (many of whose buildings are

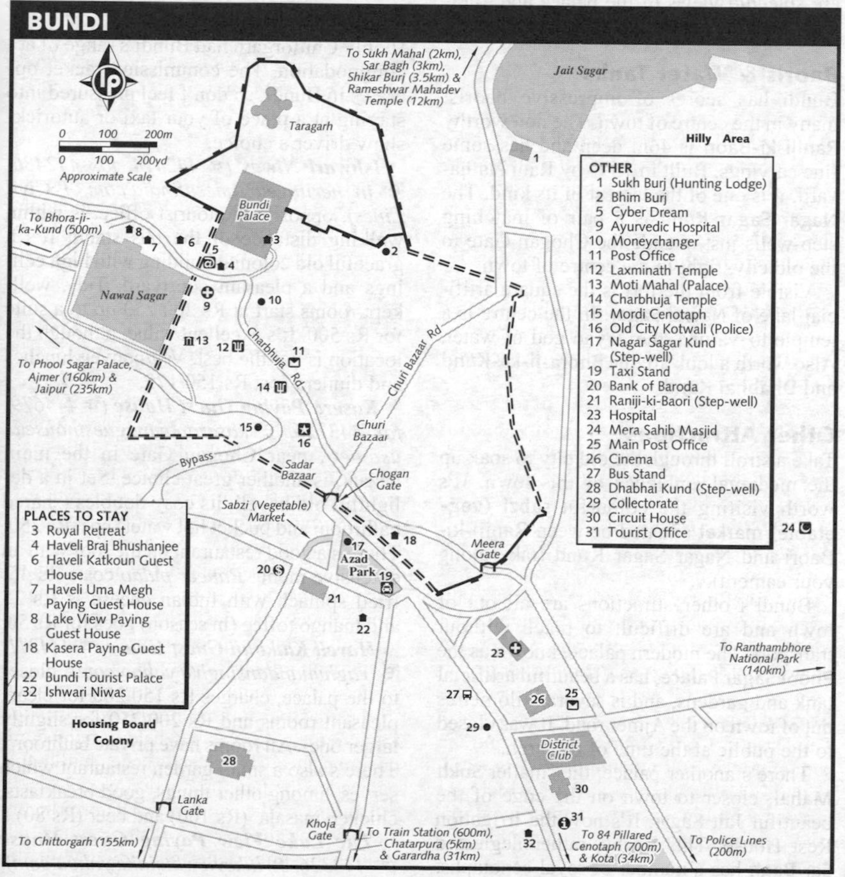

painted blue like in Jodhpur) and surrounding countryside are magical, especially at sunset. It's just a shame that the national broadcaster, Doordarshan, decided to build an ugly concrete transmission tower right next to the fort.

Bundi Palace

The palace is reached from the north-western end of the bazaar, through a huge wooden gateway and up a steep cobbled ramp. Only one portion of the outer perimeter of the palace, the Chittra Sala, is officially open to the public. If you want to see the renowned **Bundi murals** (found in the Chattra Mahal and Badal Mahal), you could try contacting the secretary of the maharaja of Bundi; most hotels are able to help out with this. There are splendid views of the palace and Taragarh from the south side of Nawal Sagar.

Baoris & Water Tanks

Bundi has scores of impressive baoris, many in the centre of town. The noteworthy **Raniji-ki-Baori** is 46m deep and has some fine carvings. Built in 1699 by Rani Nathavatji, it is one of the largest of its kind. The **Nagar Sagar Kund** is a pair of matching step-wells just outside the Chogan Gate to the old city, right in the centre of town.

Visible from the fort is the square artificial lake of **Nawal Sagar**. In the centre is a temple to Varuna, the Aryan god of water. Also worth a look are the **Bhora-ji-ka-Kund** and **Dhabhai Kund**.

Other Attractions

Take a stroll through the old city to soak up the medieval ambience of this town. It's worth visiting the colourful **sabzi (vegetable) market** situated between Raniji-ki-Baori and Nagar Sagar Kund (take along your camera).

Bundi's other attractions are all out of town and are difficult to reach without transport. The modern palace, known as the **Phool Sagar Palace**, has a beautiful artificial tank and gardens, and is several kilometres out of town on the Ajmer road. It was closed to the public at the time of research.

There's another palace, the smaller **Sukh Mahal**, closer to town on the edge of the beautiful Jait Sagar. It's now the Irrigation Rest House. The nearby, rather neglected **Sar Bagh** has a number of royal cenotaphs, some with terrific carvings. **Shikar Burj** is a small former royal hunting lodge on the road that runs along the north side of the Jait Sagar. South of town is the stunning **84 Pillared Cenotaph**, set in gardens and definitely worth a visit, especially at night when it is lit up.

About 32km from Bundi at the village of Garardha, you can see some ancient **rock paintings**. Found on some of the boulders flanking the river, these are believed to be about 15,000 years old. There's a curious depiction of a man riding a huge bird, as well as some hunting scenes. It's best to come here with a guide who is familiar with the area – contact Mukesh Mehta at the Haveli Braj Bhushanjee (see Places to Stay & Eat) for more information.

Places to Stay & Eat

If only Chittorgarh had Bundi's range of accommodation. The commission racket operates in Bundi, so don't feel pressured into staying at a place of your taxi or autorickshaw driver's choice.

Ishwari Niwas *(☎ 442414, fax 442486, ⓔ in_heritage@timesofindia.com, 1 Civil Lines)*, opposite the tourist office, is within walking distance of the bus stand. It's a graceful old colonial building with high ceilings and a pleasant courtyard. Tidy, well-kept rooms start at Rs 200/250 up to a suite for Rs 500. It's excellent value, although the location is not the best. Veg/nonveg lunches and dinners cost Rs 150/175.

Kasera Paying Guest House *(☎ 444679, fax 443126, ⓔ kaserapayingguesthouse@usa.net)*, near Chogan Gate in the main bazaar, is another great choice. Set in a delightful old haveli, its cosy doubles (shared bathroom and bucket hot water) cost Rs 250. There's a good restaurant on the roof with an extensive menu. *Paneer pulao* costs Rs 45, fried spinach with Indian cheese is Rs 25 and mango toffee (in season) goes for Rs 50.

Haveli Katkoun Guest House *(☎ 444311, ⓔ raghunandansingh@yahoo.com)*, closer to the palace, charges Rs 150/200 for clean, pleasant rooms and Rs 200/250 for slightly larger ones. All rooms have private bathroom. There's also a small garden restaurant which serves, among other things, good breakfasts, chicken masala (Rs 100) and beer (Rs 80).

The Lake View Paying Guest House *(☎ 442326, ⓔ lakeviewbundi@yahoo.com)*, not far away, has singles/doubles (mostly with shared bathroom) for Rs 100/150. Some rooms have lake views and room No 1 (Rs 150) is particularly good. Home-cooked meals are available.

Haveli Uma Megh Paying Guest House *(☎ 442191)*, almost next door, has a wide range of rooms, from small singles with shared bathroom (Rs 75) to a double with private bathroom, sit-down flush toilet and lake view (Rs 350). Some of the cheaper rooms also have a view. There's a nice garden restaurant by the water's edge.

Haveli Braj Bhushanjee *(☎ 442322, fax 442142, ⓔ res@kiplingsbundi.com)*, opposite the Ayurvedic Hospital just below the palace, has attractive rooms with private bathroom ranging from Rs 350 to 1400; all rooms have hot-water geyser and varying degrees of character. Credit cards are accepted, although they'd prefer you paid in rupees. Wholesome, but expensive, set veg meals are Rs 250 – the dining room is very atmospheric. They do free pick-ups from the bus stand and train station (advance notice appreciated).

Royal Retreat *(☎ 444426)*, ideally situated in the palace compound, is also a popular place, set around a quiet open-air courtyard. Rooms start at Rs 350/550.

Bundi Tourist Palace *(☎ 442650)*, opposite Azad Park, is pretty basic, but clean and friendly. Small singles/doubles cost Rs 70/120 with shared bucket hot-water bathroom. There are better places to stay but it's good for an early bus departure.

Getting There & Away

Roads to the east and west of Bundi are in an appalling condition, making the journey to Chittorgarh and Sawai Madhopur particularly tiring. There are semiregular express buses to Ajmer (Rs 67, five hours), Kota (Rs 15, one hour), Sawai Madhopur (Rs 44, 4½ hours), Udaipur (Rs 122, 8½ hours), Jodhpur (Rs 146, 10 hours), Bikaner (Rs 171, 10 hours), Jaipur (Rs 83, five hours) and Indore in Madhya Pradesh (Rs 147, 12 hours).

KOTA

☎ 0744 • pop 662,000

Kota is one of Rajasthan's less inspiring cities, although it is still worth a visit for its palace and gardens. Most travellers prefer to visit Kota on a day trip from Bundi.

Following the Rajput conquest of this area of Rajasthan in the 12th century, Bundi was chosen as the capital, with Kota as the land grant of the ruler's eldest son. This situation continued until 1624, when Kota became a separate state, remaining so until it was integrated into Rajasthan after Independence.

Building of the city began in 1264 following the defeat of the Bhil chieftains, but Kota didn't reach its present size until well into the 17th century, when Rao Madho Singh, a son of the ruler of Bundi, was made ruler of Kota by the Mughal emperor, Jehangir. Subsequent rulers have all added to the fort and palaces, which stand here now.

Today, Kota serves as an army headquarters. It's also Rajasthan's industrial centre (mainly chemicals), powered by the hydroelectric plants on the Chambal River – the only permanent river in the state – and the nearby nuclear plant.

Orientation & Information

Kota is strung out along the east bank of the Chambal River. The train station is well to the north; a number of hotels and the bus stand are in the centre.

The Tourist Reception Centre (☎ 327695) is in the grounds of the RTDC Hotel Chambal. It's open from 10 am to 5 pm Monday to Saturday. The State Bank of Bikaner & Jaipur, at Industrial Estate (opposite Rajasthan Patrika), changes travellers cheques and (sometimes) currency.

City Palace & Fort

Beside the Kota Barrage, overlooking the Chambal River, the City Palace and fort is one of the largest such complexes in Rajasthan. Some of its buildings are now occupied by schools, but most of the complex is open to the public. Entry is from the south side through the **Naya Darwaza**, or New Gate.

The **Rao Madho Singh Museum**, in the City Palace, is excellent. It's on the right-hand side of the complex's huge central courtyard and is entered through a gateway topped by elephants. Inside, you'll find well-displayed weapons, old costumes, stuffed beasts, and some of the best-preserved murals in the state. The museum is open from 10 am to 4.30 pm daily except Friday. Entry is Rs 7/50 for Indians/foreigners, plus Rs 50/75 for a camera/video.

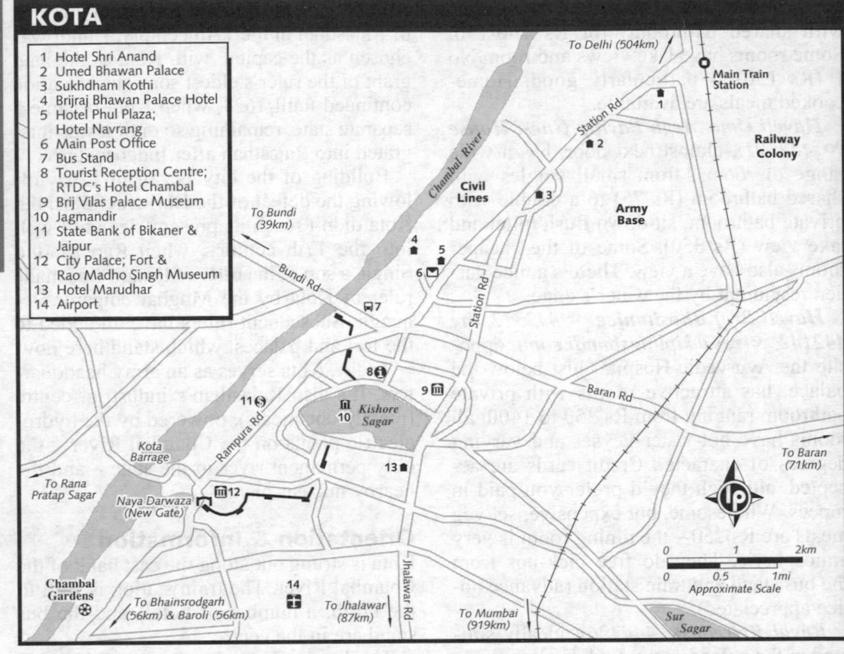

Jagmandir

Between the City Palace and the RTDC Hotel Chambal is the picturesque artificial lake of Kishore Sagar, constructed in 1346. In the middle of the lake, on a small island, is the enchanting little palace of Jagmandir. Built in 1740 by one of the maharanis of Kota, it's best seen early in the morning but is exquisite at any time of day. It's not currently open to the public, but you can take a close look at it by taking a boat (from 10 am to 5 pm daily except Monday). The cost is Rs 60 per boat for a 15-minute ride.

Brij Vilas Palace Museum

Near the Kishore Sagar, this small government museum is not as good as the City Palace museum. It has a collection of stone idols and other sculptural fragments, mainly from the archaeological sites at Baroli and Jhalawar. It's open from 10 am to 4.30 pm daily except Friday; entry is Rs 3 (free on Monday). Photography is prohibited.

Gardens

Kota has several well-maintained gardens – a sight for sore eyes in this industrial town. On the banks of the Chambal River, south of the fort, are the **Chambal Gardens**. The centrepiece is a murky pond stocked with crocodiles. Once common all along the river, by the middle of the 20th century crocodiles had been virtually exterminated through hunting. There are also some rare gharials (thin-snouted, fish-eating crocodiles).

Next to the RTDC Hotel Chambal are the **Chhattar Bilas Gardens**, a curious collection of neglected but impressive royal cenotaphs.

Special Events

The celebration of **Dussehra Mela** to commemorate the victory of Rama over Ravana has a special significance in Kota, where festivities take the form of a large mela, or fair. From 24 to 26 October 2001, 13 to 15 October 2002, 3 to 5 October 2003 the city will come alive with 22.5m-tall burning effigies in a fair to offer prayers to Lord Rama.

Places to Stay & Eat

Budget accommodation is limited and lacklustre. On the footpath outside the main post office, omelette and snack stalls set up in the early evening, and this can be a cheap way to eat. The mosquitoes can be a problem at some hotels in Kota, so come with a mosquito net or repellent.

Hotel Navrang *(☎ 323294, fax 450044)*, near the main post office, is much better than the exterior suggests. The rooms (some with more character than others) all have private bathroom and are arranged around an inner courtyard. Singles/doubles cost Rs 300/400 with air-cooling, or Rs 650/880 with air-con. All rooms do not include a 10% tax. There's a veg restaurant.

Hotel Phul Plaza *(☎ 329350, fax 322 614)*, next door, offers a range of rooms, all with private bathroom, from Rs 275/350. There's a good veg restaurant, with most dishes under Rs 40.

Hotel Shri Anand *(☎ 441157)*, a pink building 100m along the street opposite the train station, is useful if you're catching an early-morning train. The rooms are tiny and could be cleaner, but are cheap at Rs 150/200 with private bathroom and squat toilet. Veg meals are available.

Hotel Marudhar *(☎ 326186, fax 324415, Jhalawar Rd)*, between the fort and Kishore Sagar, also has a pink paint job. Small rooms with private bathroom cost Rs 225/250 and Rs 350/400 with air-con. This hotel fronts a busy road – ask for a quiet room.

The modest ***Brijraj Bhawan Palace Hotel*** *(☎ 450529, fax 450057)*, on an elevated site overlooking the Chambal River, is Kota's most interesting hotel. Named after the current maharaja of Kota, Brijraj Singh (who still lives here), this serene place has attractive rooms for Rs 1050/1450, and Rs 1800 for a magnificent suite. Unlike most palaces, this one is more homey than grand. There's a cosy dining room; the set lunch or dinner is Rs 240 (residents only).

Umed Bhawan Palace *(☎ 325262, fax 451110, Station Rd)* is more grandiose than the Brijraj Bhawan Palace; but while it looks OK, closer inspection reveals lack of attention to detail. Surrounded by sprawling gardens, this gracious palace has a restaurant, bar and billiard room. The cheapest singles/doubles cost Rs 1190/1790. There are also luxury rooms for Rs 1390/2190 and the royal chamber for Rs 1990/2990.

Sukhdham Kothi *(☎ 320081, fax 327781)* has comfortable rooms from Rs 735/875. Set in nice grounds in Civil Lines, this building is over 100 years old. There are 30% discounts when things are quiet. The set breakfast/lunch/dinner is Rs 110/200/225.

Getting There & Away

There are express buses to Ajmer (Rs 75, six hours), Chittorgarh (Rs 73, six hours), Jaipur (Rs 95, six hours), Udaipur (Rs 90, six hours), Jodhpur (Rs 175, 11 hours) and Bikaner (Rs 175, 12 hours). Buses leave for Bundi every 30 minutes (Rs 15, 50 minutes).

Kota is on the main broad-gauge Mumbai-Delhi line via Sawai Madhopur, so there are plenty of trains to choose from. For Sawai Madhopur, the 108km journey takes around two hours (Rs 36/56/183 general/sleeper/3A class). The 8½-hour trip to Delhi costs Rs 105/163/473 and the 16-hour journey to Mumbai costs 167/259/1203 in general/sleeper/2A class.

Getting Around

Minibuses link the train station and bus stand (Rs 2). An autorickshaw should cost Rs 15 for this journey. Cycle-rickshaws are a cheaper option.

AROUND KOTA

Baroli

One of Rajasthan's oldest temple complexes is at Baroli, 56km south-west of Kota. Many of the temples were vandalised by Muslim armies, but much remains. Some of the sculptures from these 9th-century temples are displayed in the Brij Vilas Palace Museum in Kota.

There are hourly buses to Baroli from Kota (Rs 15, 1½ hours).

Jhalrapatan

Known as the City of Temple Bells, and 94km south of Kota, Jhalrapatan contains the ruins of a huge 10th-century Surya temple which has impressive sculptures as well as one of the best-preserved idols of Surya (the sun god) in India. The 12th-century **Shantinath Jain Temple** is also worth visiting, as is the imposing **Gagron Fort**, 10km from nearby Jhalawar, which has a few accommodation options.

Every year (30 November to 2 December 2001, 19 to 21 November 2002, 8 to 12 November 2003), Jhalrapatan hosts the **Chandrabhaga Fair** – a cattle fair and a chance for thousands of pilgrims to bathe in the holy Chandrabhaga River. There are semi-regular buses between Jhalawar and Kota (Rs 38, 2½ hours).

CHITTORGARH (CHITTOR)

☎ 01472 • pop 87,400

The sprawling hilltop fort of Chittorgarh, or Chittor, epitomises the whole romantic, doomed ideal of Rajput chivalry. Three times in its long history, Chittor was sacked by a stronger enemy and, on each occasion, the end came in textbook Rajput fashion as *jauhar* (ritual mass suicide) was declared in the face of impossible odds. The men donned the saffron robes of martyrdom and rode out from the fort to certain death, while the women and children immolated themselves on a huge funeral pyre. Honour was always more important than death.

Despite the fort's impressive location and colourful history, Chittor is off the main tourist circuit and receives surprisingly few visitors (which accounts for the lacklustre accommodation options). It's well worth the detour – if you're pressed for time you could squeeze in a day trip to Chittor from Udaipur.

History

Chittor's first defeat occurred in 1303 when Ala-ud-din Khilji, the Pathan king of Delhi, besieged the fort in order to capture the beautiful Padmini, wife of the rana's uncle, Bhim Singh. When defeat was inevitable, the Rajput noblewomen, including Padmini, committed jauhar and Bhim Singh led the orange-clad noblemen out to their deaths.

In 1535 it was Bahadur Shah, the sultan of Gujarat, who besieged the fort and, once again, the medieval dictates of chivalry determined the outcome. This time, the carnage was immense. It is said that 13,000 Rajput women and 32,000 Rajput warriors died following the declaration of jauhar.

The final sacking of Chittor came just 33 years later, in 1568, when the Mughal emperor, Akbar, took the town. Once again, the fort was defended heroically but, once again, the odds were overwhelming and the women performed jauhar, the fort gates were flung open and 8000 orange-robed warriors rode out to their deaths. On this occasion, Maharaja Udai Singh II fled to Udaipur, where he re-established his capital. In 1616, Jehangir returned Chittor to the Rajputs, but there was no attempt at resettlement.

Orientation & Information

The fort stands on a 280-hectare site on top of a 180m-high hill, which rises abruptly from the surrounding plain. Until 1568 the town of Chittor was also on the hilltop within the fort walls, but today's modern town, known as Lower Town, sprawls to the west of the hill. A river separates it from the bus stand, railway line and the rest of the town.

The Tourist Reception Centre (☎ 41089) is near the train station and is open from 10 am to 5 pm (closed for lunch 1 to 2 pm) Monday to Saturday. You can change money at the State Bank of Bikaner & Jaipur.

Fort

According to legend, Bhim, one of the Pandava heroes of the Mahabharata, is credited with the fort's original construction. All of Chittor's attractions are within the fort. A zigzag ascent of more than 1km leads through seven gateways to the main gate on the western side, the Rampol.

On the climb, you pass two chhatris, memorials marking spots where Jaimal and Kalla, heroes of the 1568 siege, fell during the struggle against Akbar. The main gate on the eastern side of the fort is known as the Surajpol. Within the fort, a circular road runs around the ruins and there's a deer park at the southern end. From the western end of the fort, there are fine views over the town and across the surrounding countryside, as well as a less-than charming view of an enormous cement factory.

Today, the fort of Chittor is virtually a deserted ruin, but impressive reminders of its grandeur still stand. The main sites can all be seen in half a day (assuming you're not walking – see Getting Around later in this section) but, if you like the atmosphere of ancient sites, then it's worth spending longer as this is a very mellow place. Entry to the fort is free. Guides are available in the fort, usually at the Rana Kumbha Palace; they charge around Rs 200.

Rana Kumbha Palace After entering the fort and turning right, you come almost immediately to the ruins of this palace. It has elephant and horse stables and a Shiva temple. One of the jauhars is said to have taken place in a vaulted cellar. Across from the palace is the museum and archaeological office, and the treasury building, or Nau

Lakha Bhandar. The **Singa Chowri Temple** is nearby.

Fateh Prakash Palace Just beyond the Rana Kumbha Palace, this palace is much more modern (Maharaja Fateh Singh died in 1930). It houses a small, poorly labelled **museum**, and the rest of the building is closed. The museum is open daily except Friday 10.00 am to 4.30 pm. Entry is Rs 3 (free on Monday).

Tower of Victory Heading south around the fort, you come to the distinctive Jaya Stambh, or Tower of Victory, which was erected by Rana Kumbha between 1458 and 1468. It rises 37m in nine storeys and you can climb the narrow stairs to the 8th floor; it's open 8 am to 7 pm and costs a steep Rs 25/US$5 for Indians/foreigners. The view from the top is good but probably not worth it, especially as the exterior, with its exquisite Hindu sculptures, is most impressive; it's free to wander around the base. The dome was damaged by lightning and repaired during the 19th century. Watch your head on the lintels if you do decide to climb.

Close to the tower is the Mahasati, an area where the ranas were cremated during Chittorgarh's period as the Mewar capital. (Mewar is the area encompassing Chittorgarh and Udaipur.) There are many *sati* (the act of widowed self-immolation) stones here. The impressive **Sammidheshwar Temple** stands in the same area.

Gaumukh Reservoir Walk down beyond the temple and, at the very edge of the cliff, you'll see this deep tank. A spring feeds the tank from a carved cow's mouth in the cliffside – from which the reservoir got its name. The opening here leads to the cave in which Padmini and her compatriots are said to have committed jauhar.

Padmini's Palace Continuing south, you come to Padmini's Palace, built beside a large pool with a pavilion in its centre. Legend relates that, as Padmini sat in this pavilion, Ala-ud-din was permitted to see her reflection in a mirror in the palace. This glimpse was the spark that convinced him to destroy Chittor in order to possess her. The bronze gates in this pavilion were carried off by Akbar and can be seen in the fort at Agra.

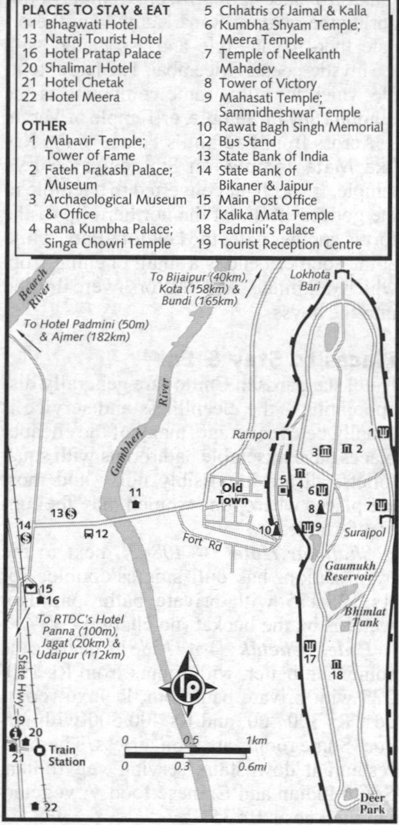

Continuing around the circular road, you pass the deer park, the Bhimlat Tank, the Surajpol and the Temple of Neelkanth Mahadev, before reaching the Tower of Fame.

Tower of Fame Chittor's other famous tower, the 22m-high Kirti Stambha, or Tower of Fame, is older (probably built around the 12th century) and smaller than the Tower of Victory. Built by a Jain merchant, it is dedicated to Adinath, the first Jain *tirthankar* (revered Jain teacher), and is decorated with naked figures of the various tirthankars, thus indicating that it is a *digambara*, or sky-clad, monument. A narrow stairway leads through the seven storeys to the top. The staircase is usually locked, although the gatekeeper will open the door for a small tip.

Other Buildings Close to the Fateh Prakash Palace is the **Meera Temple**, built during the reign of Rana Kumbha in the ornate Indo-Aryan style and associated with the mystic-poetess Meerabai. The larger temple which is in this same compound is the **Kumbha Shyam Temple**, or Temple of Varah.

Across from Padmini's Palace is the **Kalika Mata Temple**, an 8th-century Surya temple. It was later converted to a temple to the goddess Kali. At the northern tip of the fort is another gate, the **Lokhota Bari**, while at the southern end is a small opening from which criminals and traitors were hurled into the abyss.

Places to Stay & Eat

Hotel standards in Chittor are generally disappointing – the cleanliness and service is usually below average, many of the cheaper places have miserable bathrooms with squat toilets, all are impossibly noisy and most are places where lone women may feel uncomfortable.

Shalimar Hotel *(☎ 40842)*, next to the train station, has dull singles/doubles for Rs 125/175 with private bathroom. Hot water is by the bucket (no charge).

Hotel Chetak *(☎ 41588)*, nearby, is somewhat better, with rooms from Rs 150/275 with private bathroom. Deluxe rooms cost Rs 300/400, and Rs 400/500 with air-con. Some rooms are a bit airless. There's a restaurant downstairs serving veg Indian, South Indian and Chinese food. A vegetarian thali costs Rs 35.

Hotel Meera *(☎ 40266)*, in the same area, is a reasonable option. Singles/doubles with private bathroom range from Rs 250/325 to Rs 700/800. Quoted prices do not include an additional 'government tax', which none of the other hotels seemed to know about. The rooms are a tad sterile but most have geyser hot water. Meals are available.

Bhagwati Hotel *(☎ 46226)*, just over the river from the bus stand, is the best in this area, but still not that great. Simple rooms with private bathroom and bucket hot water cost Rs 100/150.

RTDC Hotel Panna *(☎ 41238)* is closer to town (ie, further away from the fort). Dorm beds are Rs 50, and singles/doubles with private bathroom start at Rs 150/250. Better, air-cooled rooms are Rs 300/400. The hotel has a seedy little bar and a restaurant (the veg/nonveg thali is Rs 45/55).

Hotel Pratap Palace *(☎/fax 40099)* is one of the most popular places to stay. Air-cooled rooms with private bathroom cost upwards of Rs 550/625 a single/double. The better rooms start at Rs 850 but they didn't exactly rock this author's world. There's a restaurant near the pleasant garden; a half tandoori chicken costs Rs 100 and *malai kofta* is Rs 35. Village safaris and visits to their castle in Bijaipur (see Around Chittorgarh, following) can be arranged.

Hotel Padmini *(☎ 41718, fax 47115)* is a little out of town near the Bearch River, but is the best and quietest place in Chittor. Pleasant, air-cooled rooms cost Rs 490/600 and Rs 1000/1200 for nicer but overpriced air-con rooms. Some rooms have a balcony and there are discounts of up to 15% if things are quiet. The veg restaurant serves Punjabi, South Indian and Chinese food; *palak paneer* is Rs 35.

Getting There & Away

Bus Express buses travel to various destinations, including Delhi (Rs 225, 14 hours, one bus daily at 8.45 pm), Ajmer (Rs 75, four hours), Jaipur (Rs 125, eight hours), Udaipur (Rs 45, three hours) and Bundi (Rs 68, 4½ hours).

Train The *Jaipur Express* (9770) leaves Chittor at 5.50 am, arriving in Jaipur at 2 pm (Rs 79/123/580 general/sleeper/2A class). The *Ajmer Express* (9672) leaves at an ungodly 3 am (Rs 53/83/426). For Udaipur, the *Chetak Express* (9615) leaves at 6.50 am, arriving at 10.25 am (Rs 36/56/350) and, going the other way, departs at 10 pm and arrives in Delhi at 1.10 pm (Rs 132/205/951). The *Ahmedabad Express* (9943) leaves at 1.45 pm, arriving in Ahmedabad at 6.35 am (Rs 95/148/684).

Getting Around

Autorickshaws charge around Rs 100 for a trip from the bus station area, around the fort compound, and back again (including waiting time at the various sites). A rickshaw between the bus and train stations should cost around Rs 15.

Bicycles can be rented near the train station (Rs 30 per day) to visit the fort but, as many Indian bikes lack gears, you may have to push the machine to the top. Still, they're great on the top and for the journey back down – but check the brakes first!

AROUND CHITTORGARH

Bijaipur

Castle Bijaipur, 40km from Chittor, is a converted 16th-century palace with pleasant rooms from Rs 800/850 to Rs 1350/1500 for a single/double room. The friendly owners can organise horse and jeep safaris to nearby villages. Reservations should be made through the Hotel Pratap Palace in Chittor (☎/fax 01472-40099). There are frequent daily buses from Chittor to Bijaipur (Rs 20, 1½ hours).

UDAIPUR

☎ 0294 • pop 378,000

Possibly no city in Rajasthan is quite as romantic as Udaipur. The French Impressionist painters, let alone the Brothers Grimm, would have loved this place. It's not without justification that Udaipur has been called the Venice of the East; the old city is a jumble of tangled streets.

Founded in 1568 by Maharaja Udai Singh II following the final sacking of Chittorgarh by the Mughal emperor, Akbar, Udaipur rivals any of the world-famous creations of the Mughals with its Rajput love of the whimsical and its superbly crafted elegance. The Lake Palace is certainly the best late example of this unique cultural explosion, but Udaipur is full of palaces, temples and havelis (ornate residences) ranging from the modest to the extravagant. It's also proud of its heritage as a centre for the performing arts, painting and crafts.

The Mewar Festival (28–29 March 2001, 15–16 April 2002, 4–5 April 2003) is a great time to be in town, with the women of Udaipur dressing up in their finest.

In common with most Indian cities, Udaipur's urban and industrial sprawl goes beyond the city's original boundaries, and pollution of various kinds can be discouraging. This will be your first impression of Udaipur if you arrive at the train or bus stations. Ignore it and head for the old city, where a different world awaits.

Orientation

The old city, bounded by the remains of a city wall, is on the east side of Lake Pichola. The train station and bus stand are both just outside the city wall to the south-east.

Information

Tourist Offices The Tourist Reception Centre (☎ 411535) is in the Fateh Memorial Building near Surajpol, less than 1km from the bus stand. The office is open from 10 am to 1.30 pm and 2 to 5 pm Monday to Saturday (closed on the second Saturday of every month). A much more accessible source of information is *Out & About in Udaipur*, an extremely informative bimonthly magazine available in most bookshops (Rs 10), or ask at your hotel.

Money You can change money at a number of places, including the Vijaya Bank and Thomas Cook, both in the City Palace complex. About 200m south-east of Delhi Gate, the Bank of Baroda changes US dollars and UK pounds and issues cash advances against Visa, MasterCard and Bobcard (open from 10 am to 2.30 pm weekdays and 10 am to 12.30 pm Saturday). You can also get cash advances on Visa and MasterCard at the Vijaya Bank (open from 10 am to 2 pm weekdays and to noon Saturday). LKP Forex (☎ 524746), next to the Rang Niwas Palace Hotel on Lake Palace Rd, changes all major (and many 'minor') currencies with a minimum of fuss.

Post & Communications The main post office is directly north of the old city, at Chetak Circle, but the poste restante is at the post office at Shastri Circle. There's also a small post office in the quadrant outside the City Palace Museum. The DHL Worldwide Express office (☎/fax 414388) is at 380 Ashok Nagar Rd, in the Shree Niketan Building (near Ayer Bridge). It has a free collection service within Udaipur.

There are loads of places where you can surf the Internet, particularly in the Lal Ghat area. Expect to pay around Rs 1 per minute. Mewar International (One Stop Shop; ☎ 419810) has the fastest connections, although be careful of overcharging on their bus and train bookings.

Lake Pichola

Placid Lake Pichola was enlarged by Maharaja Udai Singh II after he founded the city. He built a masonry dam, known as the

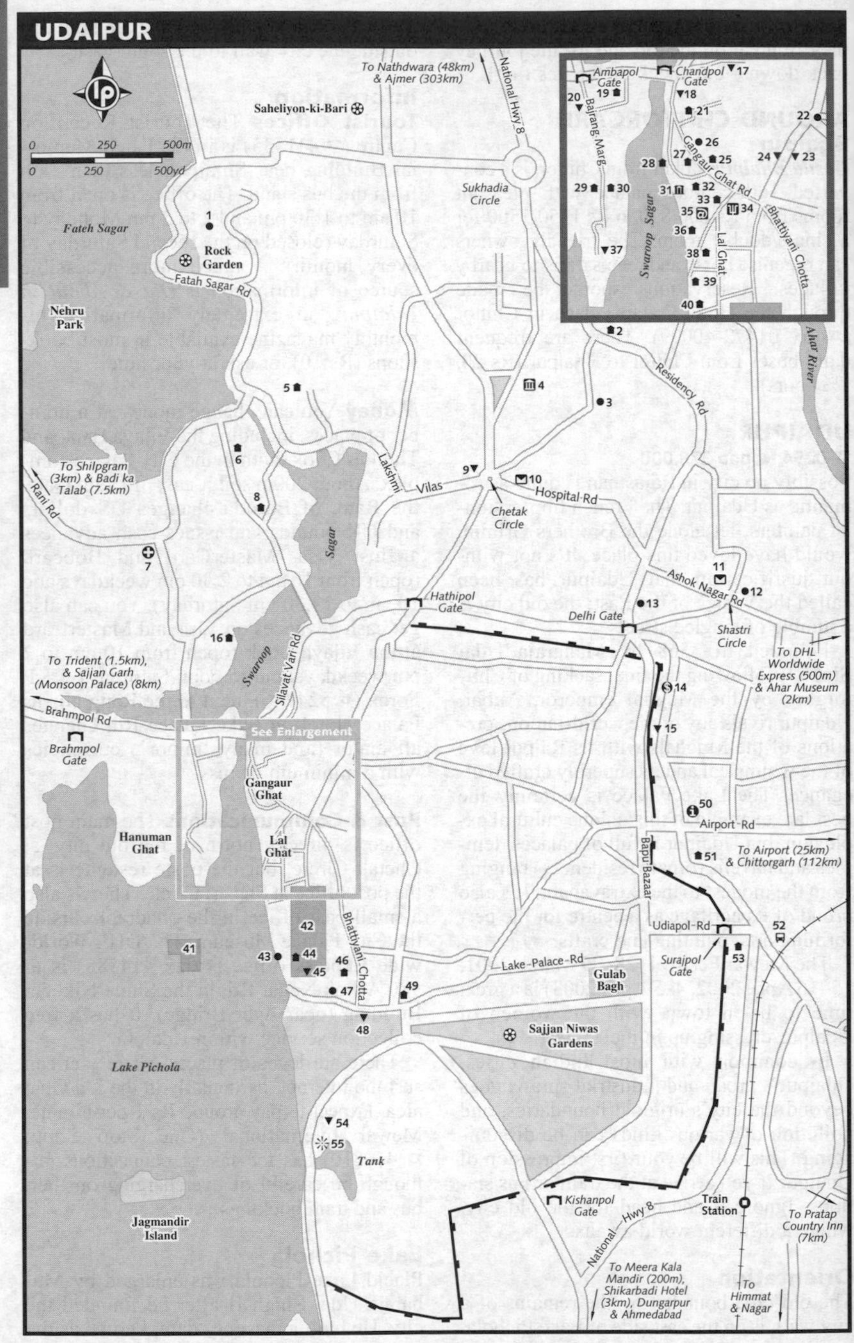
UDAIPUR
0 250 500m
0 250 500yd
To Nathdwara (48km) & Ajmer (303km)
National Hwy 8
Saheliyon-ki-Bari
Sukhadia Circle
Fateh Sagar
Rock Garden
Fatah Sagar Rd
Nehru Park
To Shilpgram (3km) & Badi ka Talab (7.5km)
Rani Rd
Lakshmi Vilas
Sagar
Hospital Rd
Chetak Circle
Hathipol Gate
Ashok Nagar Rd
Delhi Gate
Shastri Circle
To DHL Worldwide Express (500m) & Ahar Museum (2km)
Residency Rd
Ahar River
Swaroop
Silavat Vari Rd
To Trident (1.5km), & Sajjan Garh (Monsoon Palace) (8km)
Brahmpol Rd
Brahmpol Gate
See Enlargement
Gangaur Ghat
Lal Ghat
Hanuman Ghat
Airport Rd
To Airport (25km) & Chittorgarh (112km)
Bapu Bazaar
Udiapol Rd
Surajpol Gate
Lake Palace Rd
Gulab Bagh
Bhattiyani Chotta
Sajjan Niwas Gardens
Lake Pichola
Tank
Kishanpol Gate
National Hwy 8
Train Station
To Pratap Country Inn (7km)
Jagmandir Island
To Meera Kala Mandir (200m), Shikarbadi Hotel (3km), Dungarpur & Ahmedabad
To Himmat Nagar
Ambapol Gate
Chandpol Gate
Bajrang Marg
Gangaur Ghat Rd
Swaroop Sagar
Lal Ghat
Bhattiyani Chotta

UDAIPUR

PLACES TO STAY
- 2 Mewar Inn
- 5 Laxmi Vilas Palace Hotel
- 6 Hotel Hilltop Palace
- 8 Pahadi Palace
- 16 Hotel Natural
- 19 Dream Heaven Guest House
- 21 Nukkad Guest House
- 25 Hotel Badi Haveli; Lehar Paying Guest House; Heera Cycle Store
- 27 Hotel Gangaur Palace
- 28 Jheel Guest House
- 29 Udai Kothi
- 30 Lake Pichola Hotel; Lake Shore Hotel
- 32 Jag Niwas Guest House
- 33 Poonam Haveli; Coffee.com
- 36 Lalghat Guest House; Restaurant Natural View
- 38 Lake Ghat Guest House; Hotel Caravanserai
- 39 Kankarwa Haveli; Jagat Niwas Palace Hotel; Hotel Jagat Niwas & Restaurant
- 40 Lake Corner Soni Paying Guest House
- 44 Shiv Niwas Palace Hotel; Fateh Prakash Palace Hotel; Gallery Restaurant
- 46 Hotel Raj Palace
- 49 Rang Niwas Palace Hotel; LKP Forex
- 51 Apsara Hotel
- 53 Parn Kulti Hotel

PLACES TO EAT
- 9 Berry's Restaurant
- 15 Park View
- 17 Savage Garden Restaurant
- 18 Cafe Edelweiss
- 20 Queen Cafe & Guest House
- 23 Anna Restaurant
- 24 Maxim's Cafe
- 37 Ambrai Restaurant
- 45 Sunset View Terrace
- 48 Samor Bagh Restaurant
- 54 Cafe Hill Park

OTHER
- 1 Pratap Smarak (Moti Magri)
- 3 Jet Airways
- 4 Bhartiya Lok Kala Museum
- 7 Madan Mohan Malvai Ayurvedic College & Hospital
- 10 Main Post Office
- 11 Poste Restante
- 12 RTDC's Hotel Kajri
- 13 Indian Airlines
- 14 Bank of Baroda
- 22 Clock Tower
- 26 Prem Musical Instruments
- 31 Bagore ki Haveli
- 34 Jagdish Temple
- 35 Mewar International
- 41 Jagniwas Island (Lake Palace Hotel)
- 42 City Palace; Museums; WWF; Vijaya Bank; Thomas Cook; Heritage Hotels Reservation Office
- 43 Bansi Ghat (City Palace Jetty)
- 47 Ticket Office for Boat Rides
- 50 Tourist Reception Centre
- 52 Bus Stand
- 55 Sunset Point

Badipol, and the lake is now 4km long and 3km wide. Nevertheless, it remains fairly shallow and can actually dry up in severe droughts. Fortunately, this doesn't happen often. The City Palace extends a considerable distance along the east bank of the lake. North of the palace, you can wander along the lakeshore, where there are some interesting bathing and *dhobi* (laundry) ghats. Unfortunately, the lake can sometimes get choked with water hyacinth.

The lake has two islands: Jagniwas and Jagmandir. **Boat rides** leave regularly (10 am to 4 pm) from the City Palace jetty (known as Bansi Ghat). These cost Rs 100 for 30 minutes and Rs 200 for one hour (the latter includes a visit to Jagmandir Island). Tickets must be bought at the booth along the road running south of the City Palace, about 100m west of Samor Bagh restaurant.

Jagniwas Island Jagniwas, the Lake Palace Hotel island, is about 1.5 hectares in size. The palace was built by Maharaja Jagat Singh II in 1754 and covers the whole island. Formerly the royal summer palace, today it is the ultimate in luxury hotels, with shady courtyards, lotus ponds and even a small swimming pool shaded by a mango tree. Yes, this is the perfect place to fall in love, but casual visitors are not encouraged. Nonguests can only come over for lunch or dinner – and then only if the hotel is not full, which it often is. Bookings are essential and you will not be allowed on the boat unless you pay for your meal at the jetty, where your name will be on the list. Hotel launches cross to the island from the City Palace jetty. The Lake Palace, along with the Shiv Niwas Palace and Monsoon Palace in Udaipur, were used as sets in the James Bond movie, *Octopussy*.

Behind Jagniwas is a much smaller island called **Arsi Vilas**, which has been used in recent times as a helipad.

Jagmandir Island The other island palace, Jagmandir, was commenced by Maharaja Karan Singh, but takes its name from Maharaja Jagat Singh (1628–52), who made a number of additions to it. It is said that the Mughal emperor, Shah Jahan, derived some of his inspiration for the Taj Mahal from this palace after staying here in 1623–24 while leading a revolt against his father, Jehangir. Flanked by a row of enormous stone elephants, the island has an impressive chhatri carved from grey-blue stone. The view across the lake, to the city and its glorious golden palace, is a scene of rare beauty.

City Palace & Museums

The imposing City Palace, towering over the lake, is the largest palace complex in Rajasthan. Actually a conglomeration of buildings added by various maharajas, it still manages to retain a surprising uniformity of design. Construction was started by Maharaja Udai Singh II, the city's founder. The palace is surmounted by balconies, towers and cupolas and there are fine views over the lake and the city from the upper terraces.

The palace is entered from the northern end through the Baripol (1600) and the Tripolia Gate (1725), with its eight carved marble arches. It was once a custom for maharajas to be weighed under the gate and their weight in gold or silver distributed to the populace.

The main part of the palace is now preserved as a museum. It includes the **Mor Chowk** with its beautiful mosaics of peacocks, the favourite Rajasthani bird. The **Manak (or Ruby) Mahal** has glass- and mirrorwork, while **Krishna Vilas** has a remarkable collection of miniatures (no photography allowed). In the **Bari Mahal**, there is a pleasant central garden. The **Moti Mahal** has beautiful mirrorwork and the **Chini Mahal** is covered in ornamental tiles. There's an armoury section downstairs. More paintings can be seen in the **Zenana Mahal**. There's a large tiger-catching cage near the Zenana Mahal entrance, and a tiny World Wide Fund for Nature (WWF) shop nearby.

The museum is open from 9.30 am to 4.30 pm daily and admission is Rs 35. Enter from the north side (up the hill from the Jagdish Temple) unless you also want to pay the Rs 75 visitors fee. It costs Rs 75 for a camera, and a whopping Rs 300 for a video camera. A guide (Rs 70 for up to five people) is worthwhile; guides for non-Indian languages cost an extra Rs 25.

There's also a **government museum** (Rs 3; free Monday) within the palace complex. Exhibits include a stuffed kangaroo, a freaky monkey holding a small lamp and Siamese-twin deer. There's also more serious stuff, such as sculptures and paintings. In the large courtyard outside the City Palace Museum are a number of pricey handicraft shops, a currency-exchange facility, a kiosk and places to buy film.

The other part of the palace is against the lakeshore and has been partly converted into two luxury hotels: Shiv Niwas Palace and the Fateh Prakash Palace (see City Palace under Places to Stay – Top End later in this section).

There's a stunning **crystal gallery** at the Fateh Prakash Palace Hotel in the City Palace complex. This rare collection of Osler's crystal was ordered from England by Maharaja Sajjan Singh in 1877. Items include crystal chairs, tables and even beds. The gallery is open from 10 am to 1 pm and 3 to 8 pm daily; entry (Rs 250) includes a soft drink (soda), coffee or tea. No photography is allowed.

The Crystal Gallery overlooks the grandiose **durbar hall** with its massive chandeliers and striking portraits of former maharajas of Mewar. Many palaces in India have a durbar hall, or hall of audience. Historically, the durbar hall was used by India's rulers for official occasions such as state banquets. It was also used to hold formal or informal meetings. However, this is undoubtedly one of India's most impressive, with a lavish interior boasting some of the largest chandeliers in the country. The walls display royal weapons and striking portraits of former maharajas of Mewar (a most distinguished-looking lot). The illustrious Mewar rulers come from what is believed to be the oldest ruling dynasty in the world, spanning 76 generations.

The foundation stone of the durbar hall was laid in 1909 by Lord Minto, the viceroy of India, during the reign of Maharaja Fateh Singh. As a mark of honour to Lord Minto, the hall was originally named Minto Hall. The top floor of this high-ceilinged hall is surrounded by viewing galleries, where ladies of the palace could watch in veiled seclusion what was happening below.

Today, the durbar hall in Udaipur is open to visitors. It still has the capacity to hold hundreds of people and can even be hired for special functions, such as conferences or social gatherings. Entry to the durbar hall is Rs 50 (free if you're staying at either of the Fateh Prakash Palace or Shiv Niwas Palace Hotels).

Jagdish Temple

Only 150m north of the entrance to the City Palace, this fine Indo-Aryan temple was built by Maharaja Jagat Singh in 1651. It enshrines a black stone image of Vishnu as Jagannath, Lord of the Universe. A brass image of Garuda is in a shrine in front of the temple. The temple is open from 5 am to 2 pm and 4 to 10 pm daily.

Bagore-ki-Haveli

This gracious old haveli, on the water's edge in the Gangaur Ghat area, was built by a former prime minister in the late 18th century and has recently been opened to the public. There are more than 100 rooms as well as courtyards, terraces and elegant balconies. The mirror- and glasswork is quite lovely, as are the frescoes in the Chambers of the Royal Ladies. It's open from 10 am to 5 pm daily and entry is Rs 10. There are sometimes traditional Rajasthani dance performances in the evening.

Fateh Sagar

North of Lake Pichola, this lake is overlooked by a number of hills and is a hangout for young lovers. It was originally built in 1678 by Maharaja Jai Singh but, after heavy rains destroyed the dam, it was reconstructed by Maharaja Fateh Singh. In the middle of the lake is Nehru Park, a popular garden island with a boat-shaped cafe. You can get there by boat from near the bottom of Moti Magri for Rs 10. An autorickshaw from the old city should cost around Rs 20 (one way).

Bhartiya Lok Kala Museum

Exhibits at this small museum, which is also a foundation for the preservation of local folk arts, include dolls, masks, musical instruments, paintings and – the high point of the exhibits – puppets. It is open from 9 am to 5.30 pm daily and entry is Rs 10, plus Rs 20/50 for a camera/video. The puppet shows (Rs 30) are staged twice a day at 1 pm and 6 pm. Call ☎ 529296 for further details.

Saheliyon-ki-Bari

The Saheliyon-ki-Bari, or Garden of the Maids of Honour, is in the north of the city. This small and quaint ornamental garden, with its fountains, kiosks, marble elephants and delightful lotus pool, is open from 9 am to 6 pm daily. Entry is Rs 5 and there is also an extra payment of Rs 5 to turn the fountains on.

Shilpgram

Shilpgram, a crafts village 3km west of Fateh Sagar, has displays of traditional houses from Rajasthan, Gujarat, Goa and Maharashtra. There are also demonstrations by musicians, dancers and artisans from these states. Although it's much more animated during festival times (usually in early December, but check with the Tourist Reception Centre), there's usually something happening. It's open from 11 am to 7 pm daily; entry is Rs 5/10 for Indians/foreigners.

Next to the site, ***Shilpi Restaurant*** serves good Indian, continental and Chinese food. It also has a swimming pool (Rs 100), open from 11 am to 4 pm daily. Not far away is the less impressive ***Woodland Restaurant***.

A return autorickshaw trip (including a 30-minute stop) between the old city and Shilpgram is Rs 80.

Sajjan Garh (Monsoon Palace)

On a distant mountain range, this neglected palace was constructed by Maharaja Sajjan Singh in the late 19th century. It is now owned by the government, and is officially closed to the public, but the Rs 10 asked by the caretaker has been running so long it might as well be official. You also pay Rs 40 per person at the foot of the hill to enter the Sajjan Garh Wildlife Sanctuary, plus Rs 15 for the rickshaw. The main reason to come here is to take in the absolutely breathtaking views, particularly at sunset. The palace is illuminated at night and from a distance looks like something out of a fairytale. The return trip takes about one hour by car. The return trip by autorickshaw should cost Rs 180 (including waiting at the site).

Other Attractions

Not far from Cafe Hill Park is **Sunset Point**, which is also lovely at sunset (entry Rs 5). There's a musical fountain here, which plays each evening.

Madan Mohan Malvai Ayurvedic College & Hospital at Ambamata Scheme, near Fateh Sagar, prescribes natural medicines and conducts courses in Ayurveda.

Almost 5km beyond Shilpgram is **Badi ka Talab**, also referred to as Tiger Lake. This mammoth artificial lake, flanked by hills, is a pleasant picnic spot. Crocodiles apparently lurk in parts of the lake, so swimmers beware!

Music Lessons

Bablu at Prem Musical Instruments (☎ 430599) has been recommended by a number of travellers for sitar, tabla and flute lessons (around Rs 100 per hour). He also sells and repairs instruments and does performances on request.

Organised Tours

Five-hour city tours leave at 8 am daily from the RTDC Hotel Kajri. The cost is Rs 73.50 (excluding entry to sites). For information on boat tours, see Lake Pichola earlier in this section.

Places to Stay

The most romantic place to stay is close to the lakeshore, west of the Jagdish Temple, which has a good range of places to suit most budgets. Quieter, and often with even better views are the handful of excellent hotels and guesthouses just across the water in the Hanuman Ghat area.

Getting to the accommodation of your choice has been made easier by the police-supervised prepaid autorickshaw stands outside the train and government bus stations. Some unscrupulous operators will still try to take you to the hotel of their choice, but remember, they don't get reimbursed until you hand over the receipt at the end of your journey. If you do have any complaints (about rickshaw drivers – note the registration number – or hotels), contact the police on ☎ 413949 (☎ 100 in the case of an emergency) or report it to the Tourist Reception Centre (☎ 411535).

Udaipur pioneered the Homestay/Paying Guest House Scheme in Rajasthan, and there are now over 75 families involved. Expect to pay Rs 100 to 600 per night. The Tourist Reception Centre has a list of participating families.

Places to Stay – Budget

Lal Ghat Area If you're booking a hotel near Lake Pichola, ask for a lake-facing room (they usually cost a bit more). Most places have fabulous views over the lake and the central location is ideal.

There is a downside to this paradise. A look around the shores of Lake Pichola will reveal a growing collection of rubbish, fed primarily by the proliferation of hotels in the area. Actively encourage your hotel to dispose of all rubbish in a more environmentally friendly manner to prevent this magnificent place from being spoiled.

An autorickshaw from the bus stand to the Jagdish Temple should cost about Rs 25.

Lalghat Guest House *(☎ 525301, fax 418508, 33 Lal Ghat)*, by the lake, is a mellow place. The rooftop areas have excellent views over the lake and there's a back terrace which overlooks the ghats. A variety of rooms are available, ranging from dorm beds for Rs 50, small rooms with shared bathroom for Rs 75/100 for singles/doubles, larger doubles for Rs 150, and rooms with private bathroom for Rs 200/250. The best room costs Rs 350 a double. All the rooms have fans and mosquito nets. There is a small kitchen for self-caterers.

Hotel Gangaur Palace *(☎ 422303, fax 561121, 3 Gangaur Ghat Rd)* is a terrific choice in this area. It has large, clean doubles with private bathroom from Rs 250; Rs 350 gets you a lake-view room. There are also some rooms with shared bathroom for Rs 80/150. Those on the street can be a little noisy. There's a pastry shop near reception selling croissants (Rs 10), slices of apple pie (Rs 30) and coconut cookies (four for Rs 10).

Hotel Badi Haveli *(☎ 412588, Gangaur Ghat Rd)* is also good. Basic singles/doubles start at Rs 150/200 or Rs 200/350 for a nicer room with wall paintings. Most rooms have spotless shared bathrooms. There's a lovely sheltered and leafy courtyard surrounded by whitewashed walls and the rooftop has spectacular views. There's a vegetarian restaurant with thalis for Rs 55.

Lehar Paying Guest House *(☎ 417651, 86 Gangaur Ghat Rd)*, next door, has singles with shared bathroom for Rs 80, and Rs 100/150 for a better view over the town. There's a small rooftop restaurant.

Lake Ghat Guest House *(☎ 521636, fax 520023)*, across the road from the Lalghat Guest House, has OK singles/ doubles with private bathroom for Rs 100/150 (some have a balcony) and Rs 200/250 for those higher up. There are splendid views from the top, and a good restaurant.

Jag Niwas Guest House *(☎ 416022, 21 Gangaur Ghat Rd)* is a friendly little place with clean doubles with private bathroom from Rs 150, while Rs 300 gets you a lovely room with a sitting area. The rooftop has a veg restaurant.

Lake Corner Soni Paying Guest House, in the Lal Ghat area next to the wall of the City Palace, has rooms with shared bathroom and squat toilet for Rs 80/100, and Rs 100/125 with private bathroom.

Jheel Guest House *(☎ 421352, 56 Gangaur Ghat)* is at the bottom of the hill by the ghat, and is housed in an old haveli. Doubles start at Rs 100 for a basic room at the back, up to a nice room overlooking the lake in the newer building across the street (Rs 450). Prices are sometimes negotiable.

Nukkad Guest House *(56 Ganesh Ghati Rd)* has very cheap rooms which aren't bad value. Rooms cost Rs 40/60 with shared bathroom and Rs 80/100 for a room with private bathroom. Meals are available.

Bus Stand Area This is a very noisy and polluted area, and you'd have to be desperate, totally lacking in imagination or have an early departure to stay here.

Apsara Hotel *(☎ 420400)*, north of the bus stand, has dreary singles/doubles with bleak attached cold-water bathroom and squat toilet for Rs 100/150.

Parn Kulti Hotel *(☎ 586314, fax 521403)* has somewhat run-down but OK rooms with satellite TV for Rs 300/450.

Hanuman Ghat Directly across the water from the Lal Ghat area are some excellent options.

Dream Heaven Guest House *(☎ 431038, 22 Bhim Permashever Marg)* is a fantastic choice. Rs 80 gets you a clean, simple room, some of which have views, with private bathroom. Others cost Rs 150, with an unrivalled balcony overlooking the lake and Udaipur at its best.

Queen Cafe & Guest House *(☎ 430875)*, nearby, is another brilliant choice. The two simple rooms with shared bathroom cost Rs 100 to 150, or you can sleep on the roof.

Lakeshore Hotel is a laid-back place; a good escape from the hustle and bustle. It's fairly basic but OK, with just a few rooms, and a terrace with fine views over the water. Singles/doubles with shared bathroom are Rs 75/150; Rs 350 gets you a larger double with private bathroom and a view over the lake. The best room costs Rs 500.

Elsewhere Further away from Lake Pichola, ***Hotel Natural*** *(☎ 431979, ⓔ hotelnatural@hotmail.com, 55 Rang Sagar)* has basic but fine rooms with private bathroom (bucket hot water) for Rs 100/150; many rooms have a shared balcony.

Pahadi Palace *(☎ 481699, 18 Ambargarh, Swaroop Sagar)*, not far away, has spotlessly clean rooms and is great value for money. Well-kept doubles with private bathroom range from Rs 150 (some of which have great sunrise views) to rooms with alcove windows for Rs 450/600 without/with air-con.

Mewar Inn *(☎ 522090, fax 525002, ⓔ mewarinn@hotmail.com, 42 Residency Rd)* is not in a thrilling location, but it's cheap and gets consistently good reports from travellers. Basic singles/doubles with shared bathroom go for a mere Rs 39/49. The rooms with private bathroom range from Rs 79 to 99. A discount is given to YHA members. There's a rooftop veg restaurant and bicycles for hire (Rs 20 per day).

Pratap Country Inn *(☎ 583138, fax 583058)* is a serene and secluded country retreat at Titaradi village, about 7km outside Udaipur. It has doubles with private bathroom from Rs 300 to 1200.

Places to Stay – Mid-Range

Lal Ghat Area It's wise to book ahead, as these places (particularly their lakeside rooms) can fill up fast during the tourist season.

Kankarwa Haveli *(☎ 411457, fax 521403, 26 Lal Ghat)* has squeaky-clean doubles from Rs 400 to 1200; the more expensive rooms overlook Lake Pichola.

Jagat Niwas Palace Hotel *(☎ 420133, fax 520023, ⓔ jagat@jp1.dot.net.in, 25 Lal Ghat)*, on the lakeshore, is a charming converted haveli with overpriced rooms without view for Rs 1250, up to Rs 1895. The rooms for Rs 1400 overlook the lake and are the best value.

Hotel Jagat Niwas *(☎ 415547, fax 560414, ⓔ jagatniwas@yahoo.com)* has rooms away from the lake for Rs 450, up to Rs 1000/1200 for a lakeside room without/with air-con. It has a great restaurant (see Places to Eat) with tremendous lake views.

Poonam Haveli *(☎ 410303, ⓔ poonamhaveli@usa.net, 39 Lal Ghat)* has very nice rooms in need of a bit more furniture from Rs 300/350 to the 007 room with elegant arches for Rs 450/500.

Hotel Caravanserai *(☎/fax 521252, 14 Lal Ghat)* is a nice place with well-kept rooms for Rs 1195/1300.

Around Lake Palace Road An excellent choice is ***Rang Niwas Palace Hotel*** *(☎ 523 890, fax 527884, ⓔ rangniwas75@hotmail.com, Lake Palace Rd)*. Set in lovely gardens with a swimming pool, it's a very relaxed hotel with an attention to detail. Attractively furnished doubles with private bathroom range from Rs 550/770 to 2200/2500 for a suite. The only drawback is the tendency to push travellers towards the more expensive rooms.

Hotel Raj Palace *(☎ 410364, fax 410395, 103 Bhattiyani Chotta)* is another very good place to stay. It has comfortable doubles from Rs 400 to 1200, all with cushioned alcoves. Some of the rooms at the front can be a bit noisy. There's a lush courtyard restaurant which is a great place to chill out with a beer.

Hanuman Ghat One of Udaipur's best-value hotels is ***Udai Kothi*** *(☎ 432810, fax 430412, ⓔ udaikothi@yahoo.com)*. It has stylish, beautifully appointed rooms from Rs 750, with most costing Rs 995/1195. Deluxe doubles cost Rs 1295 and suites Rs 1495. It also possesses one of the city's most spectacular rooftop terraces with 360° views and where you can dine well or swim in Udaipur's *only* rooftop swimming pool.

Lake Pichola Hotel *(☎ 431197, fax 410575)*, directly opposite, also boasts excellent views, with singles/doubles for Rs 975/1000. It's worth paying Rs 1150/1195 to get a deluxe room, with a balcony and lake view. There's a good bar and restaurant.

Places to Stay – Top End

Trident *(☎ 432200, fax 432211, ⓔ reservations@tridentudp.com)* is out on a limb, beyond Chandpol, but is Udaipur's slickest hotel when it comes to service and attention to detail. Hidden in the hills, this modern property is part of the Oberoi Group and offers smart singles/doubles from US$140 up to US$225. The multicuisine restaurant (nonresidents welcome) is excellent and even has frothy cappuccinos. Other amenities include a swimming pool, bar, beauty parlour and health club. The Oberoi Group is planning to open Udai Vilas, an upmarket boutique hotel (similar to the Raj Vilas in Jaipur) complete with nine swimming pools – contact their Delhi corporate office (☎ 011-2914841, fax 2929800) for details.

Laxmi Vilas Palace Hotel *(☎ 529711, fax 526273, ⓔ gmlvp@jp1.dot.net.in)* is between Swaroop Sagar and Fateh Sagar, up on a hill. It's a pleasant four-star ITDC place where air-con rooms cost from Rs 3300/4000. There's a bar, restaurant and swimming pool.

Hotel Hilltop Palace *(☎ 432245, fax 432136, ⓔ hilltop@ad1.vsnl.net.in)* is a modern hotel atop another hill in the same area. Modern rooms start at Rs 1350/2100 and there's a pool, bar and restaurant. Although the ambience here is somewhat sterile, its rooftop terrace has good 360° views.

City Palace The ***Lake Palace Hotel*** *(☎ 528800, fax 528700, ⓔ lakepalace.udaipur@tajhotels.com)*, which appears to be floating in the middle of Lake Pichola, is one of the world's most spectacular hotels. It looks like something out of a romantic novel and few people would pass up an opportunity to stay here. This swanky white palace has a bar, restaurants (see Places to Eat), little shopping arcade, open-air courtyards, lotus ponds, and a small, tree-shaded swimming pool. The cheapest doubles are US$230 (no lake view, but they do overlook a lily pond); US$290 gets you a lake view. Sumptuous suites cost US$350 to US$600. You will need to book well in advance.

Shiv Niwas Palace Hotel *(☎ 528016, fax 528006, ⓔ sales@udaipur.hrhindia.com)* is another atmospheric place. The cheapest rooms (US$125 a double) aren't really good value – it's much better to get a room around the pool (from US$300 a double). For a real splurge there are some lavish suites; the lotus suite (room No 19, US $600) doesn't have much of a lake view but is very romantic. There's a good restaurant (see Places to Eat), bar, holistic health centre and marble pool (open to nonresidents for Rs 300 including a towel).

Fateh Prakash Palace Hotel *(☎ 528008, 528019, fax 528006, ⓔ sales@udaipur.hrhindia.com)* was built in the early 20th century during the reign of Maharaja Fateh Singh. The cheapest double rooms are US$125, but these are not in the main palace wing. Far more ornate suites (some with a lake view) cost US$250 to US$300 and are furnished with traditional palace pieces.

Places to Eat

Udaipur has scores of sun-kissed rooftop cafes catering to budget travellers, as well as fine dining at the top-end hotels. Many restaurants also boast terrific lake views. At places offering multicuisine menus, the chefs generally do a better job of the Indian food than Western dishes. Some restaurants in Udaipur serve bhang lassi – see the boxed text 'Beware of Those Bhang Lassis!' under Dangers & Annoyances in the Facts for the Visitor chapter.

Many of the budget restaurants try to lure customers by putting on a nightly screening of the James Bond movie *Octopussy*, which was partly filmed in Udaipur. These days, contemporary cult movies are also screened.

Sunset View Terrace, ideally situated on a terrace overlooking Lake Pichola, is *the* place to be at sunset. Located near the Fateh Prakash Palace Hotel in the City Palace complex, this place is worth visiting for the views alone (don't forget your camera). Live Indian classical music is played in the late afternoon and the menu offers a range of expensive light bites, such as pizzas (Rs 125), burgers (Rs 100) and milk shakes (Rs 60).

Ambrai Restaurant, in the Hanuman Ghat area, is also worth visiting for its superb location and good food. It is located just past the Lake Pichola Hotel, beyond Chandpol, and is a great place to kick back with a cold beer or hot masala tea. The beauty about this outdoor restaurant is that, unlike other places to eat, it sits right at water level. You can get Indian, Chinese and continental cuisine; chicken tikka masala is Rs 100.

Maxim's Cafe, near the Jagdish Temple, is probably the best value of the cluster of restaurants in this area. Menu items include paneer tikka (Rs 25) and Rajasthani pizza (Rs 30).

Anna Restaurant, not far away, is also good for cheap chow. The menu consists of Indian, continental and Chinese food, and includes a selection of cakes (around Rs 30) – perfect with a cup of mint tea (Rs 8).

Savage Garden, near Chandpol, is one of the few places that serves freshly ground coffee (Rs 25). Their food also gets good reports, including aubergine tomato for Rs 85.

Samor Bagh, at the Lake Palace Rd entrance to the City Palace, has slightly pricey Indian, Chinese and continental food. Its speciality is *paneer pasanda* (Rs 50). Other menu items include chicken *achari* (Rs 85) and fish tikka (Rs 80). You can sit in the large 'hut' or out in the garden, where a nightly puppet and dance show is performed at around 7.30 pm.

Restaurant Natural View, just along from the Lalghat Guest House, on the rooftop of the Evergreen Guest House, has fine lake views and the food is also good. It serves Indian, Chinese and continental fare; chicken palak is Rs 50, fish curry is Rs 60, aubergine tomato a bargain Rs 25 and the 'choco cake' (Rs 35) is to die for.

Queen Cafe, in Hanuman Ghat, has a wide range of dishes to choose from and the home-cooked Indian food is as good as you'll get anywhere (most dishes are under Rs 50).

Cafe Hill Park, south-west of the Sajjan Niwas Gardens on a hill overlooking Lake Pichola, attracts people for its views rather than its food. This rather ramshackle cafe offers Indian, continental and Chinese fare, including cheeseburgers (Rs 35) and chicken curry (Rs 45).

Park View, one of Udaipur's oldest restaurants, is opposite a small park in the main part of town, but there's absolutely no view. This dimly lit place is particularly good for its North Indian cuisine and is often packed with middle-class Indian families. A fish tandoori is Rs 80 and chicken curry is Rs 55. There's also cream of chicken soup and cheese naan.

Berry's Restaurant, at Chetak Circle, has a sterile feel to it but cooks up pretty good Indian food and is quite popular with the locals. The butter chicken is a hot seller (Rs 95 for half a bird) and there are also sizzlers (from Rs 85 to 135).

Of the German bakeries which have sprung up around town, ***Cafe Edelweiss***, near Chandpol, and ***Coffee.com***, next to the Poonam Haveli hotel, are probably the pick.

Udai Kothi hotel is hard to beat for views and value for money. The glorious terrace has fantastic views, the service is attentive and the food excellent – the paneer/chicken tikka (Rs 75/120) and fish a la Udai Kothi (Rs 125) are especially good.

Hotel Jagat Niwas (☎ *415547)* has an absolutely delightful restaurant with superlative lake views – great for a minor splurge. Its Western dishes are a little pricey, but the Indian food is very reasonably priced; palak paneer is Rs 50 and spaghetti bolognaise is Rs 95. The fish dishes are particularly good. It's wise to book ahead (especially for dinner), as this place can fill up in a flash.

The restaurant at ***Shiv Niwas Palace Hotel*** (*☎ 528016)* is highly recommended for a dose of pampering and is most captivating in the evening. There's seating indoors and in the pleasant open-air courtyard by the pool. The Indian food is best – try the *aloo chutneywale*, potatoes stuffed with Indian cottage cheese in a mango and mint chutney, for Rs 90. Indian classical music is performed each evening by the pool-side, creating a magical ambience. Nonresidents are welcome (although you probably won't get past the gate without forking out the Rs 75 visitors fee); it's wise to book ahead, especially for dinner.

Gallery Restaurant, at the Fateh Prakash Palace Hotel, serves a set continental lunch/dinner for Rs 550/650. For something more moneybelt-friendly, there's an afternoon tea served between 3 and 5 pm daily. A 'full cream tea' costs Rs 150, home-made biscuits and cakes cost Rs 100 and a pot of chocolate served with whipped cream is Rs 65.

Lake Palace Hotel is, of course, the ultimate dining experience, although there's no guarantee you'll get in. The sumptuous buffet dinner costs Rs 750 (including the boat crossing), and before your meal, you can take a drink at the sophisticated bar. A bottle of wine with your meal will cost around Rs 1000 (plus a whopping 60% tax). Make sure you go on an empty stomach. Reservations are essential, and reasonably tidy dress is expected. For something different, ask about their tiny ***floating pontoon*** on Lake Pichola, which arranges lunch/dinner for US$40 (maximum four people). If you don't want a waiter hanging around, you can request a cordless phone to be left in case you need anything. Wear something warm if you are dining at night in winter.

Entertainment

Before dinner, treat yourself to a drink at the plush pool-side ***Paanera Bar***, which has soft sofas to sink into. If it's been a tough day, there's tequila (Rs 180 a shot), or if you're in the mood, go wild on a bottle of bubbly – the Moet costs a cool Rs 5000!

Meera Kala Mandir *(☎ 583176, Sector 11, Hiran Magari)*, near the Paras Cinema, has one-hour Rajasthani folk dance and music performances at 7 pm daily except Sunday, from August to April. It costs Rs 60 per person. An autorickshaw from the City Palace area costs Rs 25. Closer to town, there are similar performances most nights at the Bagore-ki-Haveli on Gangaur Ghat.

Many hotels stage their own entertainment for guests – usually puppet shows or Rajasthani music/dance performances.

Shopping

Udaipur has oodles of little shops selling a jumble of things, from funky Western clothing to traditional antique jewellery. The town is popular for its local crafts, particularly miniature paintings in the Rajput-Mughal style. There's a good cluster of shops selling these on Lake Palace Rd, next to the Rang Niwas Palace Hotel, and others around the Jagdish Temple. Be prepared to bargain hard, as most places have ridiculously inflated prices for tourists. It's also a good place to buy leather-bound books and handmade paper. The bookshops stock a good range of titles, although the prices they offer for resale may not be quite what you're used to elsewhere.

Getting There & Away

Air The Indian Airlines office (☎ 410999, fax 410248) at Delhi Gate is open from 10 am to 1 pm and 2 to 5 pm Monday to Saturday and 10 am to 2 pm Sunday. Indian Airlines operates daily flights to Delhi (US$105) via Jodhpur (US$80) and Jaipur (US$85). There is also a daily flight to Mumbai (US$125). Jet Airways (☎ 561105, fax 561106) in the Blue Circle Business Centre near the main post office, has daily flights to Delhi via Jaipur and to Mumbai daily (except Saturday) for the same prices as Indian Airlines.

Bus Destinations served by RSTC buses include Jaipur (Rs 153/226 ordinary/deluxe, nine hours), Ajmer (Rs 111/163, six hours), Jodhpur (Rs 115/146, seven hours), Chittorgarh (Rs 43/61, three hours) and Delhi (Rs 275/404, 14 hours).

There are quite a few private bus companies which operate to Ahmedabad (Rs 100, six hours), Mumbai (Rs 300, 16 hours), Delhi (Rs 250, 14 hours), Indore (Rs 200, 10 hours) and Mt Abu (Rs 90, five hours). For Jaisalmer (Rs 200), you'll probably have to change buses in Jodhpur (Rs 90, six hours).

Train Lines into Udaipur are currently metre gauge only, but are scheduled to be converted to broad gauge – nobody is really sure when this will happen. It's quicker in most cases to catch a bus.

The *Chetak Express* (9616) departs at 6.10 pm, takes 19 hours to get to Delhi and costs Rs 145/225/1044 in general/sleeper/2A class. This train goes via Chittorgarh (Rs 35/55/348, arrives 9.40 pm), Ajmer (Rs 77/120/564, arrives 2.15 am) and Jaipur (Rs 99/154/713, arrives 5.45 am). The *Ahmedabad Express* (9943) departs at 9.15 pm, arrives in the Gujarati capital at 6.35 am and costs Rs 73/114/543.

Taxi Many drivers will show you a list of 'official' rates to places like Mt Abu, Chittorgarh and Jodhpur. Shop around (Rs 4 per kilometre is a good starting point), as you can often barter for better rates. For travel out of town, remember that taxis generally charge return fares even if you're only going one way.

Getting Around

To/From the Airport The airport is 25km from the city. There's no airport bus; an autorickshaw/taxi will cost at least Rs 180/220.

Autorickshaw These are unmetered, so you should agree on a fare before setting off. There are prepaid autorickshaw stands at both the main bus stand and train stations. Otherwise, the standard fare for tourists anywhere within the city appears to be around Rs 20. It costs Rs 180 to hire an autorickshaw for half a day of local sightseeing.

The commission system is in place with a vengeance, so if a rickshaw driver insists that the hotel of your choice has burnt down, suddenly closed, or the owner died in a freak accident, politely decline his kind offer. Unless your rickshaw is prepaid, ask for the Jagdish Temple when arriving, as it's a good place to start looking for accommodation.

Bicycle & Motorcycle You can hire bicycles all over town for around Rs 25 per day. Heera Cycle Store (☎ 523525), near the Hotel Badi Haveli, rents out bicycles/mopeds/motorcycles for Rs 25/150/300 per day.

AROUND UDAIPUR

Kumbhalgarh

About 84km north of Udaipur, this is the most important fort in the Mewar region after Chittorgarh. It's a secluded place, built by Maharaja Kumbha in the 15th century and, owing to its inaccessibility on top of the Aravalli Range at 1100m, it was taken only once in its history. Even then, it took the combined armies of the Mughal emperor, Akbar, and those of Amber and Marwar to breach its defences. It was here that the rulers of Mewar retreated in times of danger. The walls of the fort stretch some 36km and enclose many temples, palaces, gardens and water-storage facilities.

There's also a big **wildlife sanctuary** here, known for its wolves. The scarcity of waterholes between March and June makes this the best time to see animals. Other wildlife includes *chowsingha* (four-horned antelope), leopards and sloth bears. You need permission from the forest department in nearby Kelwara to enter the reserve, or from the Deputy Chief Wildlife Warden in Udaipur (☎ 0294-421361).

Aodhi Hotel *(☎ 02954-4222, 0294-528016 for reservations, fax 528006)* is by far the best place to stay. Rooms in this blissfully tranquil hotel cost Rs 1995/3300 for singles/doubles. There's a little bar, a restaurant (open to nonresidents) and an inviting pool. Horse/jeep safaris can be arranged. Nearby is ***Kumbhalgarh Fort Hotel*** *(☎ 02954-42372, fax 525106)* with rooms from Rs 1195/2395.

Hotel Ratnadeep *(☎ 02954-42217)* in nearby Kelwara is a bit further away from the fort, but has cheaper doubles with private bathroom (most with squat toilets) from Rs 400; dorm beds cost Rs 100.

There are several daily RSTC buses from Udaipur (Rs 30, 3½ hours) and one express bus each morning (Rs 38, 2½ hours).

Ranakpur

The exceptionally beautiful Ranakpur complex, 60km north of Udaipur, is one of the largest and most important Jain temples in India. It is in a remote valley of the Aravalli Range and is certainly worth seeing.

The main temple is the **Chaumukha Temple**, or Four-Faced Temple, dedicated to Adinath. Built in 1439, this huge, superbly crafted and well-kept marble temple has 29 halls supported by 1444 pillars – no two are alike. Within the complex are two other Jain temples to **Neminath** and **Parasnath** and, a little distance away, a **Sun Temple**. About 1km from the main complex is **Amba Mata Temple**.

The temple complex is open to Jains from 6 am to 8.30 pm daily and to non-Jains from 11 am to 5 pm. Shoes and all leather articles must be left at the entrance. Admission is free but there's a Rs 40/150 camera/video charge.

Places to Stay & Eat The ***Maharani Bagh Orchard Retreat*** *(☎ 02934-85151, 0291-433316 for reservations, fax 635373)*, 4km from Ranakpur, is the best place to stay. Set in a lush mango orchard, it offers accommodation in cottages from Rs 1600/1800 and Rs 2100/2390 with air-con. Hearty buffet meals are available (Rs 355) and nonresidents are welcome.

RTDC Hotel Shilpi *(☎ 02934-85074)* is conveniently located near the temple complex and has rooms with private bathroom from Rs 250/400. For the cash-conscious, there's a dorm for Rs 50. A veg thali in the dining room is Rs 55.

The Castle *(☎ 02934-85133)* is set in large grounds and offers singles/doubles for Rs 600/700.

Roopam Restaurant *(☎ 02934-3921)* has a few nice rooms for Rs 550/650 with private bathroom. The restaurant offers a buffet (Rs 150) and a la carte dining (Rs 35 to 60 for a main dish).

Getting There & Away From Udaipur there are four deluxe buses daily (Rs 35, three hours; at the time of research these were departing at 5.30 am and 3, 10 and 10.30 pm). Hiring a private taxi should cost around Rs 500 including waiting time – expensive, but it allows you to better appreciate the beautiful scenery en route and you can also combine it with a detour to Kumbhalgarh.

Deogarh

The attractive little town of Deogarh (pronounced Dev-gar), or Castle of the Gods, is 135km north of Udaipur. Surrounded by lakes, hills and rugged countryside, it's an ideal place to take a break from the rigours of travelling in India. Deogarh has lots of pleasant walks and is known for its school of miniature painting. The small cave temple of **Anjaneshwar Mahadev** is dedicated to Lord Shiva and is believed to be around 2000 years old. From the top of this hill there are good views of the countryside.

The delightful ***Deogarh Castle*** *(☎ 02904-52777, fax 52555, e deogarh@infosys.net)* is a family-run hotel with appealing doubles from Rs 2500 to 3995 for a suite. This well-managed castle has a good restaurant.

There's a deluxe bus from Udaipur (Rs 60, three hours) and railway connections to Udaipur.

Jaisamand Lake

Located 48km south-east of Udaipur, this stunningly located artificial lake, created by damming the Gomti River, was built by Maharaja Jai Singh in the 17th century. It's one of the largest artificial lakes in Asia, and there are beautiful marble chhatris around the embankment. The summer palaces of the Udaipur queens are also here and there's a wildlife sanctuary nearby.

Jaisamand Island Resort *(☎ 02906-2222, 0294-415100 for reservations, fax 523898, e resort@ad1.vsnl.net.in)* is a modern hotel in a secluded position 20 minutes by boat across the lake. Rooms start at Rs 1800/2700, although discounts are often available.

There are frequent RSTC buses from Udaipur (Rs 17, 1½ hours).

Dungarpur

Situated about 110km south of Udaipur, Dungarpur, the City of Hills, was founded in the 13th century. Between 9 am and 4 pm daily you can visit the deserted old palace, **Juna Mahal**, after obtaining a ticket (Rs 100) from the Udai Bilas Palace hotel. The former royal hunting lodge, on a nearby hilltop, has sensational views over the town and its many temples.

The beautiful **Deo Somnath Temple**, about 25km out of town, dates back to the 12th century.

Udai Bilas Palace *(☎ 02964-30808, fax 31008)* is an 18th-century palace which has partly been converted into a hotel. Singles/doubles cost Rs 1450/1900 and many rooms are decorated in Art-Deco style (some have a private balcony with lake views). Suites cost Rs 2600.

Hotel Pratibha Palace *(☎ 02964-30775, Shastri Colony)* has tiny singles/doubles with bath (squat toilet, bucket hot water) from Rs 50/100 to 150/250. No meals are available, but there are several cheap *dhabas* (snack bars) nearby.

Frequent RSTC buses travel to Dungarpur from Udaipur (Rs 35, three hours). There's also a slow train between Dungarpur and Udaipur (Rs 35/55 general/sleeper class).

MT ABU

☎ 02974 • pop 18,600 • elevation 1200m

Mt Abu, in the far south of the state, close to the Gujarat border, is Rajasthan's only hill station. It's a pleasant hot-season retreat from the plains of both Rajasthan and Gujarat. Mt Abu's pace is easy-going, although it can get impossibly crowded with people and traffic during summer and during certain festivals such as Diwali and Christmas.

Mt Abu has a number of important temples, particularly the breathtaking Dilwara group of Jain temples, 5km away. This is an important pilgrimage centre for Jains and boasts some of the finest marble carvings in all of Rajasthan, if not India. Also, like some other hill stations in India, Mt Abu has its own lake, which is the centre of activity.

If for some strange reason you are travelling through Rajasthan in the middle of the year, Mt Abu hosts the Summer Festival (1 to 3 June), which is dedicated to the classical and folk music of Rajasthan.

Orientation & Information

Mt Abu is on a hilly plateau about 22km long by 6km wide, 27km from the nearest train station (Abu Road). The main part of the town extends along the road in from Abu Road, down to Nakki Lake.

The Tourist Reception Centre (☎ 43151) is around the corner from the private bus stand and is open from 10 am to 1.30 pm and 2 to 5 pm Monday to Saturday. Money can be changed at the State Bank of Bikaner & Jaipur and Union Bank of India.

Nakki Lake

Nakki Lake is a big attraction with tourists. The lake takes its name from the legend that it was scooped out by a god, using only his nails, or *nakh*. It's a pleasant stroll around the lake – look for the strange **rock formations**. The best known, Toad Rock, looks just like a toad about to hop into the lake. Others, like Nun Rock, Nandi Rock and Camel Rock, require more imagination. The 14th-century **Raghunath Temple** stands beside the lake. You can hire your own boat (Rs 50 for 30 minutes in a two-seater paddle boat).

Viewpoints

Of the various viewpoints around town, **Sunset Point** is the most popular. Hordes stroll out here every evening to catch the setting sun. Other popular spots include **Honeymoon Point**, which also offers a view of the sunset, and **The Crags**. You can follow the white arrows along a path up to the summit of **Shanti Shikhar**, west of Adhar Devi Temple, where there are panoramic views.

For a good view over the lake, the best point is probably the terrace of the maharaja of Jaipur's former **summer palace**. No one seems to mind if you climb up here for the view and a photo.

Brahma Kumaris Spiritual University & Museum

The Brahma Kumaris teach that all religions lead to God and so are equally valid, and the principles of each should be studied. The university's stated aim is the establishment of universal peace through 'the impartation of spiritual knowledge and training of easy raja yoga meditation'. There are over 4500 branches in 70 countries around the world. You can attend an introductory course (seven lessons) while you're in Mt Abu; this would take a minimum of three days. There's no charge – the organisation is entirely supported by donations.

There's a museum (free) in the town outlining the university's teachings and offering meditation sessions. It's open from 8 am to 8 pm daily.

Dilwara Temples

These Jain temples are Mt Abu's main attraction and are among the finest examples of Jain architecture in India. The complex includes two temples in which the art of carving marble reached unsurpassed heights.

The older of the temples is the **Vimal Vasahi**, built in 1031 and dedicated to the

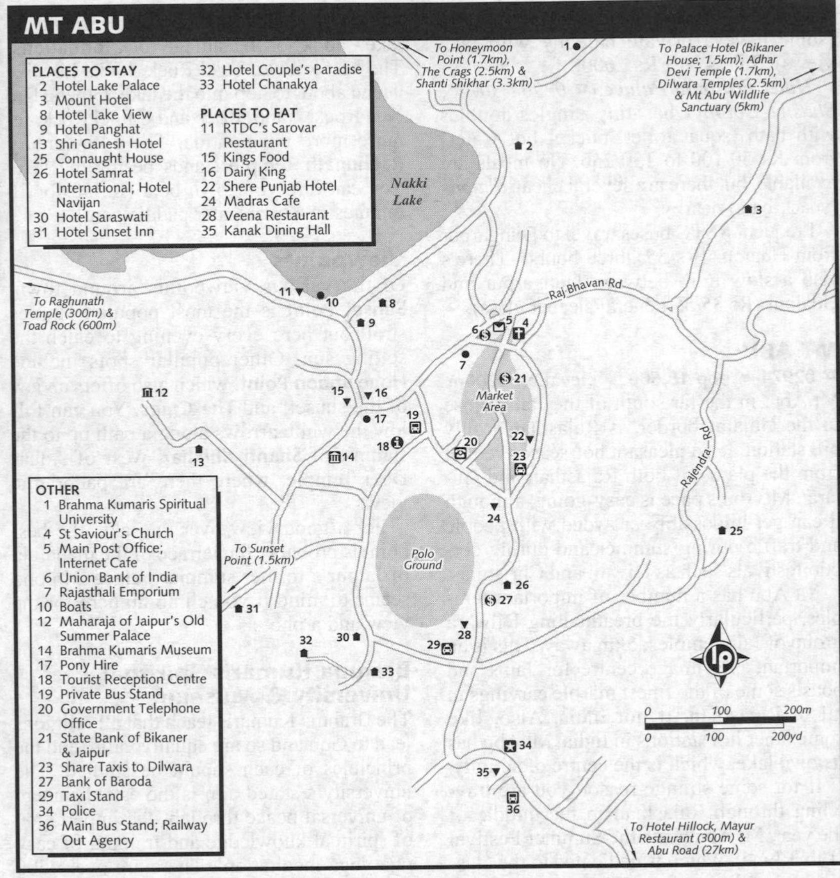

first tirthankar, Adinath. The central shrine has an image of Adinath, while around the courtyard are 52 identical cells, each with a Buddha-like cross-legged image. There are 48 elegantly carved pillars forming the entrance to the courtyard. In front of the temple stands the **House of Elephants**, with figures of elephants marching in procession to the temple entrance.

The later **Tejpal Temple** is dedicated to Neminath, the 22nd tirthankar, and was built in 1230 by the brothers Tejpal and Vastupal. Like Vimal, they were ministers in the government of the ruler of Gujarat. Although the Tejpal Temple is important as an extremely old and complete example of a Jain temple, its most notable feature is the brilliant intricacy and delicacy of the marble carving. The carving is so fine that, in places, the marble becomes almost transparent. In particular, the lotus flower which hangs from the centre of the dome is an astonishing piece of work. It's difficult to believe that this huge lace-like filigree actually started as a solid block of marble. The temple employs several full-time stone carvers to maintain and restore the work. There are three other temples in the enclosure, but they all pale beside the Tejpal Temple and Vimal Vasahi. There's a festival here in June (dates vary according to the lunar calendar).

The complex is open from noon to 6 pm (Jains can visit from sunrise to sunset). Photography is not allowed. As at other Jain temples, all articles of leather (belts as well as shoes) have to be left at the entrance (Rs 1). You can stroll out to Dilwara from the town in less than an hour, or take a share-taxi (see Getting Around later in this section).

Organised Tours

The RTDC has five-hour tours of all the main sites, leaving from the main bus stand at 8.30 am and 1.30 pm (later in summer). The tours cost Rs 36 plus all entry and camera fees. The afternoon tour finishes at Sunset Point. Reservations can be made at the inquiries counter of the main bus stand (☎ 43434).

Places to Stay

There is an explosion of hotels in Mt Abu. The high season is from mid-April to mid-November and prices rise considerably during this period. During Diwali (October/November), rooms are virtually unobtainable without advance booking and the tariffs are simply ridiculous. As Mt Abu's charm is its tranquillity, it's a good time to stay away.

In the low season (with the exception of Christmas and New Year), discounts of up to 50% are available and mid-range accommodation can be an absolute bargain. Negotiate a deal with hotel staff. The hotels usually have an ungenerous 9 am checkout time.

At all times of the year there are plenty of touts working the bus and taxi stands. In the low season you can safely ignore them; at peak times they can save you a lot of legwork as they'll know exactly where the last available room is.

Places to Stay – Budget

Shri Ganesh Hotel *(☎ 37292, ⓔ s_ganesh@datainfosys.net)*, up the hill towards the maharaja of Jaipur's old summer palace, is a popular place with travellers and deservedly so. The rooms are good value, starting at Rs 100 in the low season, and most rooms (with 24-hour hot water) cost Rs 150/175 year-round. There's a laundry service, Internet access (Rs 100 an hour), a kitchen for use by guests, and the restaurant serves good home cooking at reasonable prices (a veg thali costs Rs 40).

Hotel Lake View *(☎ 38659)* overlooks picturesque Nakki Lake. The rooms with private bathroom are decent value in low season, starting at Rs 100/200; we were quoted Rs 2000/2500 during Diwali, which is brazenly outrageous. Hot water is available between 7 and 11 am.

Hotel Panghat *(☎ 38886)*, nearby, charges from Rs 125 per room (and they are small and somewhat claustrophobic) up to Rs 200 for a larger one. Prices double in high season. All rooms have bathroom and bucket hot water (7 to 10 am).

Hotel Couple's Paradise *(☎ 43504)*, about 300m west of the taxi stand in Akshay Colony, is open only to couples and families and is terrific value. The tidy rooms with private bathroom (and constant hot water) cost Rs 150 and the ones at the front have private balconies. It's within walking distance of the centre of town but is nice and quiet. During Diwali, expect to pay Rs 650.

Hotel Saraswati *(☎ 38887, fax 38337)*, nearby, is also good. There are well-kept doubles with private bathroom and 24-hour hot water for Rs 100, and a range of other rooms from Rs 150 to 300. The vegetarian restaurant serves tasty Gujarati thalis (Rs 40).

Places to Stay – Mid-Range & Top End

Hotel Lake Palace *(☎ 37154, fax 38817, ⓔ savshanti@hotmail.com)* is a friendly place with singles/doubles/triples for Rs 800/900/1100 in the high season; bargain hard in the low season and you should be able to get the same rooms for Rs 450/550/660. Most rooms have semiprivate terrace areas overlooking the lake and are better than the exterior suggests.

Mount Hotel *(☎ 43150)* is a homey place in a tranquil location along the road to the Dilwara temples. Doubles range from Rs 400 to 600. Vegetarian meals (Rs 90) are available with advance notice.

Hotel Chanakya *(☎ 38154)* charges Rs 600/700 in the low season for a medium/large-sized double with private bathroom and hot water between 7 and 10 am.

Hotel Sunset Inn *(☎ 43194, fax 43515)*, on the western edge of Mt Abu, is a modern hotel with good doubles for Rs 990/1100 including all taxes. This is one of the few places in Mt Abu not to raise its rates from season to season, which makes it good value at peak periods; you can also book by calling the reservations number in Ahmedabad (☎ 079-6403906, fax 6469876).

Hotel Samrat International *(☎ 43153)* and ***Hotel Navijan*** *(☎ 43173)*, on the main road, are actually the same hotel. Attractive, spacious rooms (ask to see a few) are available in low season for Rs 650. Some have a sofa, a large sheltered balcony with rocking chair overlooking the polo ground, 24-hour hot water – great value in a central location.

Palace Hotel *(Bikaner House;* ☎ *43121, fax 38674)*, not far from the Dilwara temples, is the most atmospheric hotel in Mt Abu. It's a charming place to chill out, replete with shady gardens, a private lake, tennis courts and a restaurant (see Places to Eat). The cheapest singles/doubles are a reasonable Rs 1200/1550 plus 10% tax and it accepts Visa and MasterCard.

Hotel Hillock *(☎ 38463, fax 38467, ⓔ hillock.mtabu@POP3.gtsl.co.in)*, on the main road into town, is a stylish place in spite of the unattractive exterior. The staff here are more welcoming than at many top-end places and the rooms are beautifully appointed. Standard/deluxe rooms cost Rs 1590/2490 and the cheaper rooms are excellent value, particularly in the low season. There's a pool, a cosy bar, an elegant restaurant and a children's playground called Romp Pomp Pomp. Checkout is at noon and major credit cards are accepted.

Connaught House *(☎ 38560, 011-6561875 for reservations, ⓔ welcom@ndf.vsnl.net.in)*, just east of the town, has an English cottage feel and is a pleasant place to stay. Owned by the maharaja of Jodhpur, it's set in its own pleasant gardens – the perfect place to sit back with a good book. The rooms in the old building are Rs 1400/1750 and have more character than those in the new wing. Breakfast (Rs 150), lunch and dinner (both Rs 250) are available.

Places to Eat

Kanak Dining Hall, near the main bus stand, is popular. The all-you-can-eat Gujarati thalis are perhaps the best in Mt Abu (Rs 45); there's seating indoors and outdoors.

Veena Restaurant *(☎ 43448)* is further up the hill, next to the junction at the bottom end of the polo ground. Its Gujarati thalis (Rs 40) are also excellent.

Shere Punjab Hotel, in the market area, has reasonably priced Punjabi and Chinese food. It takes delight in its brain preparations (brain curry is Rs 35). There are also some more conventional dishes.

Madras Cafe *(☎ 43294)*, also in this area, is a pure veg place with an assortment of Indian and Western fare. There are even Jain pizzas (no garlic, onion or cheese) for Rs 35.

Kings Food, on the road leading down to the lake, has the usual have-a-go-at-anything menu and is good for cheap Chinese, Punjabi and South Indian food. ***Dairy King***, opposite, does a good range of ice creams for around Rs 30.

RTDC Sarovar Restaurant is on the water's edge. The food is nothing special (snacks and South Indian for Rs 40 and less) but it's a pleasant place from which to overlook the lake; the effect is diminished somewhat by the Hindi rock music blaring from its loudspeakers. There are pool tables inside which can be used for Rs 50 per hour.

Palace Hotel *(Bikaner House;* ☎ *43121)* is the best place to go for a special meal. The set lunch or dinner costs Rs 235 (veg) or Rs 295 (nonveg). It's a good idea to make an advance reservation. ***Mayur Restaurant*** at Hotel Hillock is also good for a splurge.

Getting There & Away

As you enter Mt Abu, there's a toll gate where bus and car passengers are charged Rs 5, plus Rs 5 for a car. If you're travelling by bus, this is an irksome hold-up, as you have to wait until the collector painstakingly gathers the toll from each and every passenger (keep small change handy).

Bus From 6 am onwards, regular buses make the 27km climb from Abu Road station up to Mt Abu (Rs 15/13 express/local buses, one hour. They leave from outside the main bus stand, next to the ticket booth. Some RSTC buses go all the way to Mt Abu, while others terminate at Abu Road.

In most cases you will find a direct bus faster and more convenient than going down to Abu Road station and waiting for a train. Deluxe RSTC buses (inquiries ☎ 43434) go to Jaipur (Rs 201, 11 hours), Ajmer (Rs 152, eight hours), Udaipur (Rs 75, five hours), Jodhpur (Rs 121, eight hours), Ahmedabad (Rs 85, six hours), Jaisalmer (Rs 176, 12 hours) and Delhi (Rs 305, 15 hours). Buses belonging to private bus companies leave, not surprisingly, from the private bus stand.

Train Abu Road, the railhead for Mt Abu, is on the broad-gauge line between Delhi and Mumbai via Ahmedabad. In Mt Abu there's a Railway Out agency (☎ 38697) near the main bus stand (opposite the police station), which has quotas on most of the express trains out of Abu Road. It's open from 10 am to 1 pm and 2 to 4 pm daily (10 am to noon Sunday).

From Abu Road, the *Ahmedabad Mail* (9106) leaves at 1.05 pm and reaches Ahmedabad at 5.20 pm (Rs 52/81/234 general/sleeper/3A class). Going the other way, it leaves Abu Road at 1.20 pm, arriving in Jaipur at 11.25 pm (Rs 99/154/446) and Delhi at 5.20 am (Rs 147/228/662). There are other connections to Jodhpur. For Bhuj and the rest of the Kathiawar peninsula in Gujarat, change trains at Palanpur, 53km south of Abu Road.

Retiring rooms at the train station are convenient if you're catching an early-morning train. They go for Rs 120 a double; a veg thali is Rs 40.

Taxi A taxi, which you can share with up to five people, into town from Abu Road costs about Rs 200. Some taxi drivers claim that this is only as far as the bus stand and ask an extra fee (as much as Rs 50) to take you to your hotel. To hire a jeep for local sightseeing costs around Rs 70/600 per hour/day (bargain hard and you may just bring it down).

Getting Around

Buses from the bus stand go to the various sites around Mt Abu, but it takes a little planning to get out and back without too much hanging around; it may be easier to take the five-hour tour (see Organised Tours earlier). For Dilwara it's easier to take a share-taxi (jeep). These leave when full from opposite the Madras Cafe in the centre of town; the fare is Rs 3 or Rs 4 per person (depending on the number of people), or Rs 30 all to yourself.

There are no autorickshaws in Mt Abu, but it's relatively easy to get around on foot.

AROUND MT ABU

Guru Shikhar

At the end of the plateau, 15km from Mt Abu, is Guru Shikhar, the highest point in Rajasthan, at 1721m. A road goes almost all the way to the summit. At the top is the **Atri Rishi Temple**, complete with a priest and good views all around.

Mt Abu Wildlife Sanctuary

This 290-sq-km sanctuary, 5.5km north-east of Mt Abu, is home to panthers, sambar, foxes, wild boar and bears. It's open from 8 am to 5 pm daily. Admission is Rs 5/40 for Indians/foreigners. Vehicle entry is Rs 125, and Rs 15 for a motorcycle.

Western Rajasthan

JODHPUR

☎ 0291 • pop 795,000

Jodhpur is at the edge of the Great Thar Desert and is the second-largest city in Rajasthan. The city is dominated by a massive fort, Meherangarh, topping a sheer rocky ridge in the middle of the town. From the fort, you can clearly see where the old city ends and the new begins; the view over the blue buildings of the old city is one of Rajasthan's most spectacular sights. Back at ground level, it's fascinating to wander around the jumble of winding streets in the old city, which is surrounded by a 10km-long wall (built about a century after the city was founded) and out of which eight gates lead. Part of the film *Rudyard Kipling's Jungle Book*, starring Sam Neill and John Cleese, was shot in Jodhpur and, yes, it was from here that those baggy-tight horse-riding trousers, jodhpurs, took their name.

Jodhpur's Got the Blues

One of the highlights of any visit to Rajasthan is the way in which the people of the state have converted their stark landscape into a mosaic of vivid colours. Apart from the Rajasthanis themselves, adorned in wildly colourful garments, a number of Rajasthan's major towns have adopted colourful identities – there's the pink city of Jaipur, the golden city of Jaisalmer and the blue city of Jodhpur.

Jodhpur is affectionately referred to as 'the blue city' because of the indigo-coloured houses in the old town. These can best be seen from the ramparts of the mighty Meherangarh, which looms high above the buzzing city.

Traditionally, blue signified the home of a Brahmin, but these days, non-Brahmins have also taken on the practice. Apart from looking fresh and lively, it is believed that the colour works as an effective mosquito repellent.

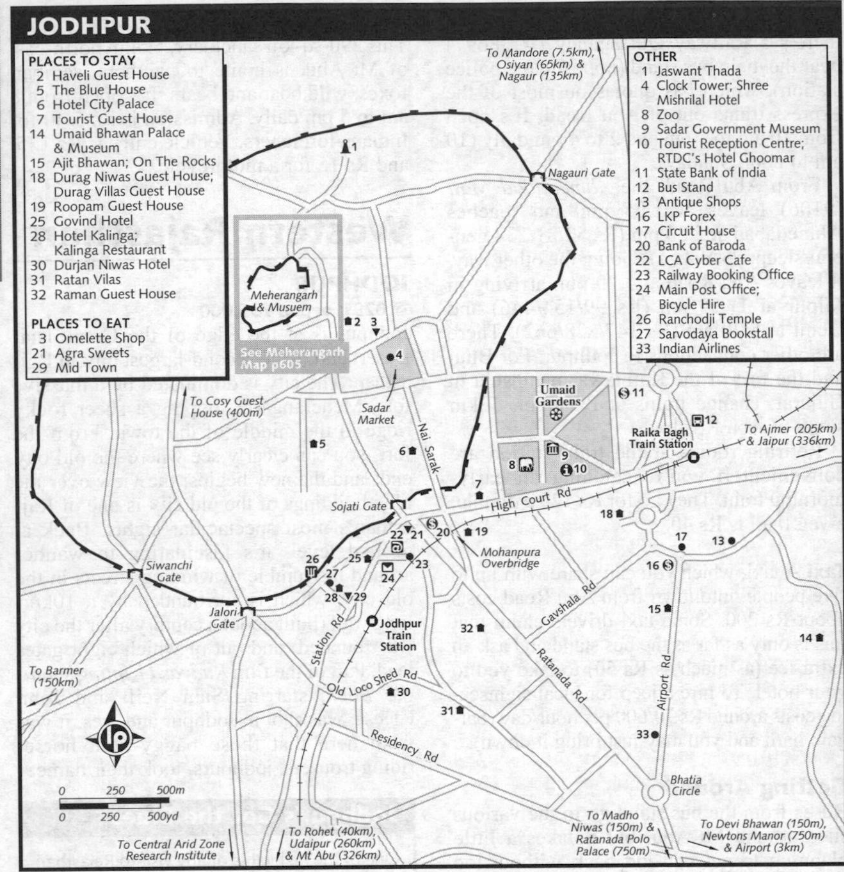

Jodhpur was founded in 1459 by Rao Jodha, a chief of the Rajput clan known as the Rathores. His descendants ruled not only Jodhpur, but also other Rajput princely states. The Rathore kingdom was once known as Marwar, the Land of Death.

Every year (31 October–1 November 2001, 19–20 October 2002, 8–9 October 2003), Jodhpur's Marwar Festival celebrates Rajasthan's heroes in music and dance.

Orientation

The Tourist Reception Centre, train stations and bus stand are all outside the old city. High Court Rd runs from the Raika Bagh train station, past the Umaid gardens, the RTDC Hotel Ghoomar, and round beside the city wall towards the main train station.

Information

Tourist Offices The Tourist Reception Centre (☎ 545083) is in the RTDC Hotel Ghoomar compound and is open from 7 am to 8 pm Monday to Saturday.

There's a helpful International Tourists Bureau (☎ 439052) at the main train station which provides information, has comfortable armchairs, a shower and a toilet. It stays open until the 11.15 pm train to Jaisalmer departs.

Money State Bank of India (High Court Rd branch) changes currency and travellers cheques. Bank of Baroda, around the corner from Agra Sweets, changes travellers cheques and, at the time of writing, issued cash advances against Visa and MasterCard. Reliable private operators that change a wider range of currencies include LKP Forex (☎ 512532), opposite Circuit House.

Email & Internet Access LCA Cybercafe (☎ 617825), in a lane opposite the Sojati Gate (same building as Lucky Bal Niketan school), is arguably the cheapest Internet place in the centre of town (Rs 30 per hour) and connections generally aren't bad. There are numerous other places scattered around town.

Meherangarh

Still run by the maharaja of Jodhpur, Meherangarh, the Majestic Fort, is just that. Sprawled across a 125m-high hill, this is the most formidable fort in fort-studded Rajasthan. A winding road leads up to the entrance from the city, 5km below. The second gate is still scarred by cannonball hits, indicating that this was a fort that earned its keep. The gates, of which there are seven, include the **Jayapol**, built by Maharaja Man Singh in 1806 following his victory over the armies of Jaipur and Bikaner, and the **Fatehpol**, or Victory Gate, erected by Maharaja Ajit Singh to commemorate his defeat of the Mughals.

The final gate is the **Lohapol**, or Iron Gate, beside which are 15 hand prints, the sati (self-immolation) marks of Maharaja Man Singh's widows who threw themselves upon his funeral pyre in 1843. They still attract devotional attention and are usually covered in red powder.

Inside the fort, there is a series of courtyards and palaces. The **palace apartments** have evocative names like the Sukh Mahal, or Pleasure Palace, and the Phool Mahal, or Flower Palace. They house a splendid collection of the trappings of Indian royalty, including an amazing collection of elephant howdahs (used when the maharajas rode their elephants in glittering procession through their capitals), miniature paintings from a variety of schools and the inevitable Rajput armoury, palanquins, furniture and costumes.

At the southern end of the fort, old cannons look out from the ramparts over the sheer drop to the old town beneath. You can clearly hear voices and city sounds swept up by the air currents from the houses far below. The views from these ramparts are

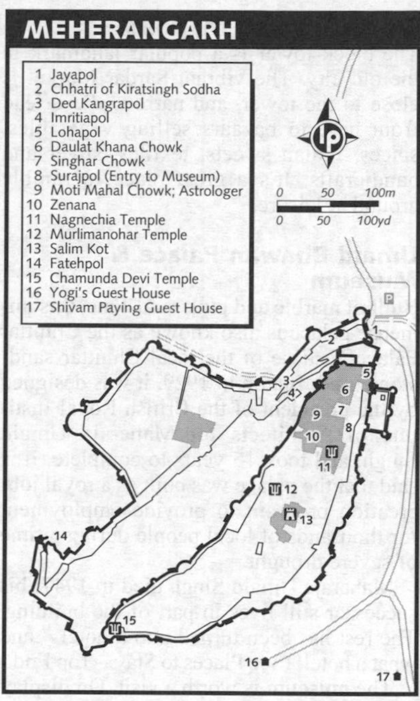

nothing less than magical. The **Chamunda Devi Temple**, dedicated to Durga, stands at this end of the fort.

The fort is open from 9 am to 1 pm and 2 to 5 pm daily. Entry costs Rs 10/50 for Indians/foreigners and there's a Rs 50/100 camera/video charge. Guides are available for around Rs 100. For weary travellers, an elevator will take you to the top of the fort for Rs 10. There is an **astrologer**, Mr Sharma, at the fort (☎ 548790 ext 39 or cell 9828032261); he charges Rs 150/300 for a 15-/30-minute consultation. Mr Sharma is available for consultations from 9 am to 1 pm and 2 to 5 pm daily.

Jaswant Thada

This white marble memorial to Maharaja Jaswant Singh II can be found a short distance from the fort, just off the fort road. The cenotaph, built in 1899, was followed by the royal crematorium and three other cenotaphs that stand nearby. There is some beautiful marble *jali* (lattice) work as well as some fine views from the terrace in front of the cenotaph. Admission is Rs 5/10 for Indians/foreigners.

Clock Tower & Markets

The clock tower is a popular landmark in the old city. The vibrant Sardar Market is close to the tower, and narrow alleys lead from here to bazaars selling vegetables, spices, Indian sweets, textiles, silver and handicrafts. It's a great place to ramble around at leisure.

Umaid Bhawan Palace & Museum

Built of marble and pink sandstone, this immense palace is also known as the Chhittar Palace because of the local Chhittar sandstone used. Begun in 1929, it was designed by the president of the British Royal Institute of Architects for Maharaja Umaid Singh, and took 15 years to complete. It is said that the palace was built as a royal job-creation program to provide employment for thousands of local people during a time of severe drought.

Maharaja Umaid Singh died in 1947; his successor still lives in part of the building. The rest has been turned into a hotel – and what a hotel! (See Places to Stay – Top End.)

The **museum** is worth a visit. On display is an opulent array of items belonging to the maharaja: weapons, fascinating antique clocks, dainty crockery, and hunting trophies. Attendants will ensure you don't stray into the hotel, where they let you know you clearly don't belong. Entry is Rs 10/40 for Indians/foreigners.

Umaid Gardens & Sadar Government Museum

The Umaid gardens contain the Sadar Government Museum, the library and the zoo. The museum's exhibits include moth-eaten stuffed animals, old weapons and sculptures; unfortunately the pieces aren't labelled. It's open from 10 am to 4.30 pm daily except Friday and entry costs Rs 1/3 for adults/students.

Organised Tours & Village Safaris

The Tourist Reception Centre has daily tours of Jodhpur from 9 am to 1 pm and 2 to 6 pm (Rs 85; entry fees extra). These take in the Umaid Bhawan Palace, Meherangarh, Jaswant Thada and Mandore gardens (see Around Jodhpur later in this section).

Jodhpur is known for its interesting 'village safaris'. You can visit villages of the Bishnoi, a Jain sect whose belief in the sanctity of the environment and the need to protect trees and animals dates from the 15th century. Just about every hotel can organise these excursions, although, typically, the quality varies. Recommended places include the Madho Niwas (☎ 434486), Durag Niwas (☎ 510692) and Durag Villas (☎ 512298) guesthouses. Most charge in the vicinity of Rs 400 for the day, including transport and lunch. Govind Hotel (☎ 622758) has a sliding scale from Rs 375 per person (including lunch and mineral water) for a minimum of two people, down to Rs 275 if there are five – good value if you can get a group together.

Places to Stay – Budget

Most places advertise wonderful fort views, but only a few deliver.

Haveli Guest House *(☎ 614615)* is inside the walled city at Makrana Mohalla. It is excellent value for money. Doubles with private bathroom are Rs 200 up to Rs 800. The rooftop vegetarian restaurant (meals around Rs 80) boasts some stunning views of the fort, Jaswant Thada and the blue city. The rooms at the front were being refurbished when we visited and will have great views and some period furnishings (around Rs 400 to 500).

Shivam Paying Guest House *(☎ 610688, ⓔ shivamgh@hotmail.com)*, not far from the clock tower, is one place to go if you want a traditional family atmosphere. Rooms without/with private bathroom cost Rs 150/200.

The Blue House *(☎/fax 621396, ⓔ bluehouse36@hotmail.com)*, in the heart of the old city, is also good. The atmospheric rooms range from Rs 200 for a small double to Rs 600 for a larger room with semiprivate terrace.

Yogi's Guest House *(☎ 643436, fax 619808)*, at the base of the fort walls and well signposted off the lanes leading to the fort, is another good choice with a homey atmosphere. Set in the 500-year-old Rajpurohitji-ki-Haveli, the rooms are simple but clean. Those without bathroom cost Rs 100 to 150, those with private bathroom and constant hot water go for Rs 250 to 350, depending on their size.

Cosy Guest House *(☎ 612066, Novechokiya Rd, Brahm Puri, Chuna-ki-Choki)*, formerly known as Joshi's Blue House, is an atmospheric little place in the old city. This blue-coloured house is pretty authentic (don't expect modern gadgets). Simple singles/doubles with shared bathroom start at Rs 90/150 (free bucket hot water).

Tourist Guest House *(☎ 541235, ⓔ udaibedi@hotmail.com)* is a great choice outside the old city on High Court Rd. Standard rooms cost Rs 150/250 with private bathroom, while there's an elegant, spacious room at the front which is great value for Rs 300, even after the private bathroom (under construction when we visited) is finished and the price rises.

Raman Guest House *(☎ 513980)*, opposite Kesar Bagh on Shiv Rd, is an increasingly popular place to stay. Rooms go for Rs 150/200 up to Rs 450.

The ***Govind Hotel*** *(☎ 622758, ⓔ govindhotel2000@yahoo.com)*, opposite the railway reservation office, is just a five-minute walk from the train station – great if you've got an early-morning train departure. The rooms are basic, but cheap and clean. Dorm beds go for Rs 60, singles/doubles with private bathroom for Rs 200/250 (bucket hot water) and Rs 300 for a double with constant hot water.

Madho Niwas *(Bhenswara House; ☎ 512486, fax 512086, New Airport Rd, Ratanada)* is inconveniently located well away from the centre, but it's a pleasant, homey place to stay, with a quiet lawn area. Doubles with private bathroom start at Rs 300 up to Rs 500.

Durag Niwas Guest House *(☎ 510692, 1 Old Public Park)* is a family-run place with doubles from Rs 200 to 250, and an enormous room for Rs 500 where you could conceivably sleep up to eight people.

Durag Villas Guest House *(☎ 512298)*, next door, is good value, with singles/doubles with private bathroom starting at Rs 150/200; nicer rooms go for Rs 250/300. It's a quiet, relaxed place.

Roopam Guest House *(☎ 627374, 7 Jagannath Bldg, Mohanpura Overbridge)* has one room with shared bathroom for Rs 200/250, and three rooms with private bathroom for Rs 400/500.

Places to Stay – Mid-Range

Ratan Vilas *(☎/fax 614418, Old Loco Shed Rd, Ratanada)* is a lovely, quiet family villa set in a nice garden. Comfortable, well-appointed doubles cost Rs 750 to 950 and there's a suite for Rs 1500. Delicious banquet-style meals are available (Rs 175).

Devi Bhawan *(☎ 511067, fax 512215, ⓔ devibhawan@satyamonline.com, 1 Ratanada Area)* is recommended and great value for money, even though it is a little inconveniently located. This green oasis has rooms for Rs 700/750 a single/double, and cottages for Rs 850. There's a good restaurant, and the garden would have to be one of the best in Jodhpur.

Durjan Niwas Hotel *(☎ 649546, fax 616991)*, off Old Loco Shed Rd, has elegant, quiet rooms for Rs 1195/1500, but they'll usually negotiate if things are quiet.

Newtons Manor *(☎ 430686, fax 610603, ⓔ info@newtonsmanor.com, 86 Jawahar Colony, Ratanada)* also has a nice atmosphere, although some readers have found the welcome less than warm and the location far from ideal. There are just five rooms, ranging from Rs 1095. Scrumptious home-cooked meals are also available here.

Hotel Kalinga *(☎ 627338, fax 627314, ⓔ kalingahotel@satyam.net.in)* is convenient if you want to be close to the main train station. Dull but comfortable and spacious rooms start at Rs 490/700 and Rs 540/800 including continental breakfast. Checkout is 24 hours.

Hotel City Palace *(☎ 649911, fax 639033, 32 Nai Sarak)* has comfortable singles/doubles from Rs 990/1190 and Rs 1040/1290 with breakfast. The upper rooms at the back have good views over the old city and are quieter.

Ajit Bhawan *(☎ 511410, fax 510674, ⓔ abhawan@del3.vsnl.net.in, Airport Rd)* has long been popular with travellers. Behind the gracious, main heritage building, there are a series of attractively furnished stone cottages arranged around a delightful garden for Rs 1895/2295. There's a restaurant, sensational swimming pool (nonguests Rs 250) and gift shop. Other services include babysitting (Rs 100 per hour), Internet access and a wonderful collection of vintage cars which can be rented for a small fortune – the 1939 Chevrolet convertible costs Rs 2400/4000 for a half/full day.

Places to Stay – Top End

Umaid Bhawan Palace *(☎ 433316, fax 635373)* is *the* place to stay if you have a passion for pure luxury. This very elegant palace has an indoor swimming pool, tennis court, billiard room, lush lawns and several restaurants (see Places to Eat). Standard rooms cost US$165/185, and suites range from US$325 to US$750 for the Maharani suite. If you can possibly afford it, opt for a suite, as the cheaper rooms are suitably comfortable, but hardly palatial.

Ratanada Polo Palace *(☎ 431910, fax 433118, Residency Rd)* is set in its own spacious grounds, but is a little lacking in character. It has a pool, restaurant and rooms for Rs 1800/2400.

Places to Eat

While you're in Jodhpur, try a glass of *makhania lassi*, a filling saffron-flavoured variety of that most refreshing of drinks.

Shree Mishrilal Hotel, at the clock tower, is nothing fancy to look at, but whips up the best lassis in town. A delicious glass of creamy special makhania lassi is Rs 10.

Agra Sweets, opposite Sojati Gate, also sells good lassis (Rs 10), as well as tasty Jodhpur dessert specialities such as *mawa ladoo* (Rs 5) and the baklava-like *mawa kachori* (Rs 9).

Omelette Shop, just through the gate behind the clock tower on the northern side of the square, claims to go through 1000 eggs a day. It's a small place and it's usually packed with locals. Two spicy boiled eggs cost Rs 5, while a two-egg omelette with chilli, coriander and four pieces of bread is a bargain Rs 12.

Kalinga Restaurant at the hotel of the same name, near the train station, is a pleasant place to eat. It has tasty veg and nonveg Indian, Chinese and continental food; chicken curry is Rs 65. It's open 7 am to 10.30 pm daily. ***Mid Town***, nearby, is a bit overpriced but not bad. Most mains cost between Rs 40 and Rs 65 and there are some Rajasthani specialities such as *chakki-ka-sagh* (wheat sponge cooked in rich gravy; Rs 55) and Rajasthani thalis (Rs 60).

On the Rocks, next to the Ajit Bhawan hotel is very popular, especially with locals. It serves tasty Indian cuisine outdoors; mushroom kebabs are Rs 55. The service can be sluggish, especially when it's busy. In the same compound, there's a bar and an excellent bakery (pastries cost Rs 15). It's open from 12.30 to 3 pm and 7 to 11 pm.

Umaid Bhawan Palace has four restaurants, including the very grand ***Marwar Hall*** (however, the buffet here is lacklustre). Overlooking the back lawn is ***The Pillars***, a breezy informal eatery recommended for a light bite; ***Risala***, which is more upmarket; and ***Kebab Konner***, an open-air restaurant which specialises in moderately priced barbecue Indian food (dinner only). Or, you may just like to have a drop of amber fluid at ***Trophy Bar***.

The ***refreshment room*** on the 1st floor of the main train station isn't bad. There's veg and nonveg food to munch on while waiting for your train; a veg/nonveg thali is just Rs 16/22.

Shopping

The usual Rajasthani handicrafts are available here, but Jodhpur particularly specialises in antiques. The greatest number of antique shops is along the road connecting the Ajit Bhawan hotel with the Umaid Bhawan Palace. These shops are well known to Western antique dealers, who come here with wallets stuffed with plastic cards. As a result, you'll be hard-pressed to find any bargains. The trade in antique architectural fixtures is contributing to the desecration of India's cultural heritage and is not condoned by Lonely Planet. Most places can make you a piece of furniture in the antique style and prices aren't bad. Shipping costs start at around US$150 per cubic metre; make sure you find out how much extra you'll end up paying for customs charges in your home country.

Getting There & Away

Air Indian Airlines (☎ 510757) is south of the centre on Airport Rd (open from 10 am to 1.15 pm and 2 to 4.30 pm daily). Daily flights depart to Delhi (US$105) via Jaipur (US$85) at 7.20 pm and to Mumbai (US$150) via Udaipur (US$65) at 8.30 am. Jet Airways (☎ 625094) also flies to Delhi (via Jaipur) and Mumbai (via Udaipur).

Bus RSTC buses depart regularly throughout the day from the bus stand to, among other places, Jaisalmer (Rs 92, five hours), Udaipur (Rs 105, eight hours), Jaipur (Rs 130, seven hours), Ajmer (Rs 82, four hours), Bikaner (Rs 101, five hours), Delhi (Rs 220, 12½ hours) and Ahmedabad (Rs

170, 10 hours). The Roadways inquiry number is ☎ 544686.

Private buses have offices opposite the train station and in the street leading to the Ranchodji Temple.

Train The computerised bookings office is on Station Rd, between the train station and Sojati Gate. There's a tourist quota (window No 788) and the office is open from 8 am to 8 pm Monday to Saturday (to 1.45 pm Sunday).

The *Jodhpur-Jaisalmer Express* (4810) leaves every night at 11.15, arriving in Jaisalmer around 5.30 am (Rs 82/130 general/sleeper class). The *Mandore Express* (2462) leaves Jodhpur at 7.30 pm, arriving in Delhi at 6.15 am (Rs 131/204/590 general/sleeper/3A class). To Jaipur, the *Intercity Express* (2466) leaves at 5.45 am, arriving at 10.35 am (Rs 104/162/749).

Getting Around

To/From the Airport The airport is only 5km from the city centre. It costs about Rs 50/110 in an autorickshaw/taxi.

Taxi & Autorickshaw There's a taxi stand near the main train station. Most autorickshaw journeys in town should cost no more than Rs 25.

AROUND JODHPUR

Mandore

Situated 9km north of Jodhpur, Mandore was the capital of Marwar prior to the foundation of Jodhpur. Today, its extensive **gardens** with high rock terraces make it a popular local attraction. The gardens also contain the cenotaphs of Jodhpur rulers, including the soaring memorial to Maharaja Dhiraj Ajit Singh.

The **Hall of Heroes** contains 15 figures carved out of a rock wall. The brightly painted figures represent Hindu deities, and local heroes on horseback. The Shrine of 33 Crore (330 million) Gods is painted with figures of deities and spirits.

Mandore Guest House *(☎ 0291-545620, fax 546959)* has delightful accommodation in a leafy garden. Singles/doubles with private bathroom cost Rs 350/500.

Rohet

Rohet Garh *(☎ 02936-68231)* is a heritage hotel in this small village, 40km south of Jodhpur, where Bruce Chatwin wrote *The Songlines* and William Dalrymple began *City of Djinns*. Good rooms start at Rs 1100/1700. Meals are available and there's a fantastic swimming pool. The hotel can also organise village safaris.

Osiyan

The ancient Great Thar Desert town of Osiyan, 65km north of Jodhpur, was a great trading centre between the 8th and 12th centuries when it was dominated by the Jains. The wealth of Osiyan's medieval inhabitants allowed them to build lavish and exquisitely sculptured temples, most of which have withstood the ravages of time. The sculptural detail on the Osiyan temples rivals that of the Hoysala temples of Karnataka and the Sun Temple of Konark in Orissa.

The Camel Camp *(☎/fax 0291-437023 in Jodhpur)* offers a range of tented accommodation in a magical location – atop a secluded sand dune overlooking Osiyan. Double-occupancy tents with shared bathroom are Rs 300. More-luxurious tents with private bathroom (and shower) are also available. There's a breezy bar with views of the temples, and camel safaris can be arranged. Advance bookings are essential. Contact The Safari Club, High Court Colony, Jodhpur.

For cheaper accommodation, contact Bhanu Prakash Sharma, a Brahmin priest with a ***guesthouse*** *(☎ 02922-74232)* for Rs 200 per room (maximum five people).

There are regular buses from Jodhpur to Osiyan (Rs 22, 1½ hours).

Nagaur

Nagaur, 135km north-east of Jodhpur, has the historic **Ahhichatragarh**, an ancient fort which is currently being restored (entry costs Rs 5/15 for Indians/foreigners, plus Rs 25/50 for a camera/video). Nagaur also sports a smaller version of Pushkar's Camel Fair; the **Nagaur Cattle Fair** (31 January–3 February 2001, 19–22 February 2002, 8–12 February 2003) in January/February attracts thousands of rural people from far and wide.

Royal Tents are available for US$175/225 a single/double at fair time. These most luxurious tents must be booked in advance through the Umaid Bhawan Palace *(☎ 0291-433316, fax 635373)* in Jodhpur .

RTDC Kurjan Nagaur *(no phone)* has two good rooms for Rs 300/400 with private bathroom (US$40/53 during the fair). For more details phone central reservations (☎ 0141-202152, fax 201145) at RTDC Hotel Swagatam Campus in Jaipur.

Hotel Mahaveer International *(☎ 01582-43158)* has rooms from Rs 250/350 with geyser hot water and colour TV and doubles with air-con for Rs 725.

JAISALMER

☎ 02992 • pop 48,000

Jaisalmer is a place that should exist only in the imagination. Nothing else in India is remotely similar to this enchanting city, which has been dubbed 'the Golden City' because of the honey colour imparted to its stone ramparts by the setting sun. The vision of Jaisalmer's massive fort thrusting heavenwards out of the barren desertscape is unforgettable, and the magic doesn't diminish as you approach its walls and bastions, and lose yourself in its labyrinthine streets and bazaars. The fort is home to several thousand people and this is what makes it so special. Although it is showing signs of decay, this desert fort is still like something out of *Tales of the Arabian Nights*.

However, there is a downside to Jaisalmer becoming one of Rajasthan's most popular tourist destinations. A major concern is that the poor plumbing and open drains have saturated the foundations, causing subsidence and collapse in buildings. For more information on the initiatives being taken to preserve Jaisalmer, contact Jaisalmer Conservation Initiative (☎ 011-463 1818, fax 461 1290), 71 Lodi Estate, New Delhi 110 003 or the British-registered charity Jaisalmer in Jeopardy (☎/fax 020-7460 8592, ⓔ jaisalmer@lineone.net), 20E Redcliffe Gardens, London SW10 9EX.

Jaisalmer hosts the Desert Festival in February each year (6 to 8 February 2001, 25 to 27 February 2002, 15 to 16 February 2003). It can be a little contrived, but is colourful enough, and it does give you the opportunity to try your hand at turban-tying competitions.

History

Centuries ago, Jaisalmer's strategic position on the camel train routes between India and Central Asia brought it great wealth. The merchants and townspeople built magnificent houses and mansions, all exquisitely carved from wood and golden sandstone.

The rise of shipping trade and the port of Mumbai (Bombay) resulted in the decline of Jaisalmer. Partition and the cutting of the trade routes through to Pakistan seemingly sealed the city's fate, and water shortages could have pronounced the death sentence. However, the 1965 and 1971 India-Pakistan Wars revealed Jaisalmer's great strategic importance.

Today, tourism rivals the military base as the pillar of the city's economy. The presence of the Border Security Force hardly impinges at all on the life of the old city and only the occasional sound of war planes ever disturbs the tranquillity of this desert gem.

While Jaisalmer largely escaped direct conquest by the Muslim rulers of Delhi, it did experience its share of sieges and sackings, with the inevitable Rajput jauhar being declared in the face of certain defeat. There is no other city in which you can more easily conjure up the spirit of those times.

Orientation

The massive fort which rises above the city is entered via the First Fort Gate. Within the fort walls is a warren of narrow, paved streets complete with Jain temples and the old palace of the former ruler – although you may think yourself lost at times, it's small enough not to matter.

The main market, Bhatia Market, and most of the city's attractions and important offices surround the fort to the north.

Information

Tourist Offices The Tourist Reception Centre (☎ 52406) is on Gadi Sagar Rd, about 2km south-east of the First Fort Gate. It's open from 7 am to 8 pm daily except Sunday.

Money The Bank of Baroda at Gandhi Chowk changes travellers cheques and issues cash advances on Visa, MasterCard and Bobcard for the usual 1% commission plus Rs 100. The State Bank of Bikaner & Jaipur, south of the fort, changes travellers cheques and major currencies. The more professional and reliable private moneychangers include SP Securities and LKP Forex (☎ 53679), which changes 32 currencies; both have offices on Gandhi Chowk.

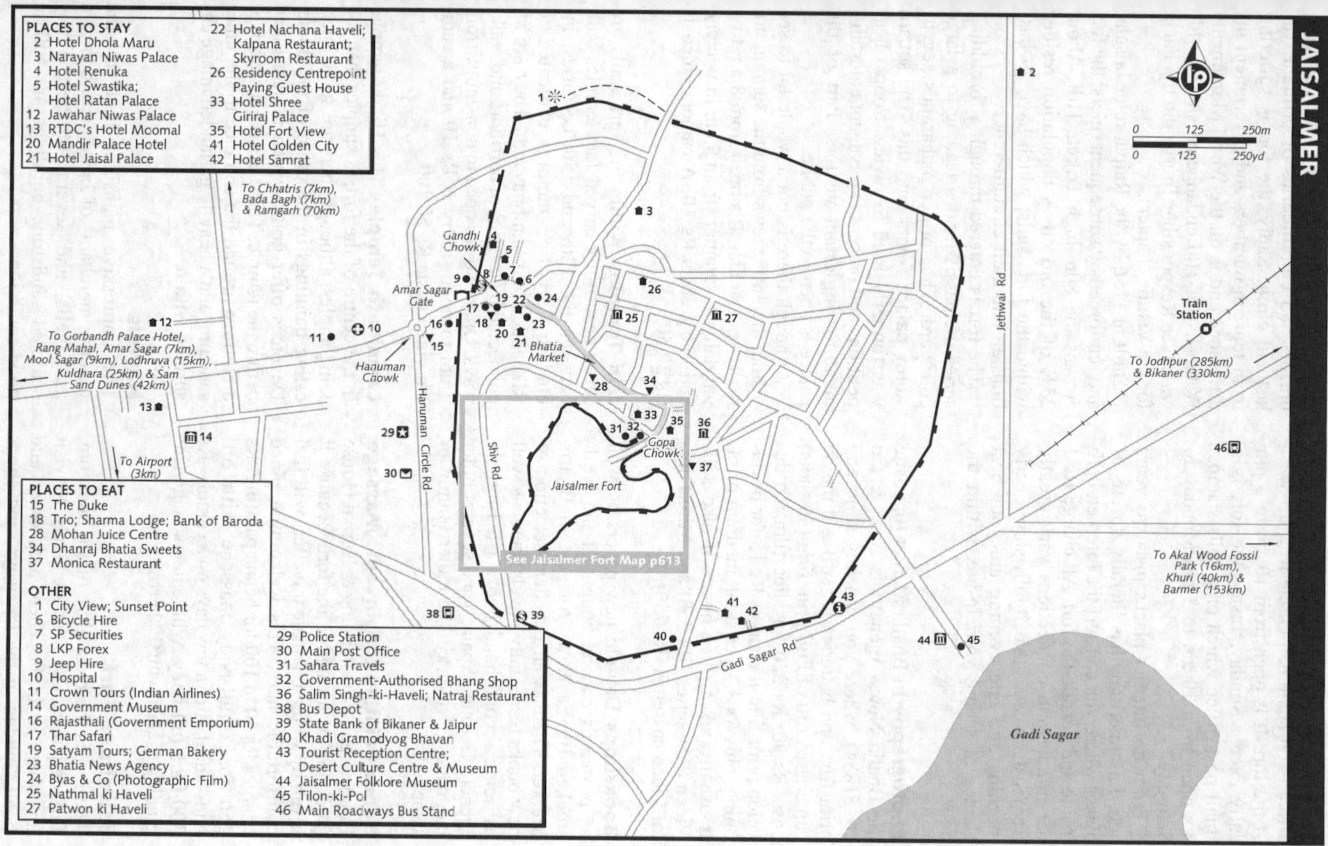
JAISALMER
PLACES TO STAY
2 Hotel Dhola Maru
3 Narayan Niwas Palace
4 Hotel Renuka
5 Hotel Swastika; Hotel Ratan Palace
12 Jawahar Niwas Palace
13 RTDC's Hotel Moomal
20 Mandir Palace Hotel
21 Hotel Jaisal Palace
22 Hotel Nachana Haveli; Kalpana Restaurant; Skyroom Restaurant
26 Residency Centrepoint Paying Guest House
33 Hotel Shree Giriraj Palace
35 Hotel Fort View
41 Hotel Golden City
42 Hotel Samrat
PLACES TO EAT
15 The Duke
18 Trio; Sharma Lodge; Bank of Baroda
28 Mohan Juice Centre
34 Dhanraj Bhatia Sweets
37 Monica Restaurant
OTHER
1 City View; Sunset Point
6 Bicycle Hire
7 SP Securities
8 LKP Forex
9 Jeep Hire
10 Hospital
11 Crown Tours (Indian Airlines)
14 Government Museum
16 Rajasthali (Government Emporium)
17 Thar Safari
19 Satyam Tours; German Bakery
23 Bhatia News Agency
24 Byas & Co (Photographic Film)
25 Nathmal ki Haveli
27 Patwon ki Haveli
29 Police Station
30 Main Post Office
31 Sahara Travels
32 Government-Authorised Bhang Shop
36 Salim Singh-ki-Haveli; Natraj Restaurant
38 Bus Depot
39 State Bank of Bikaner & Jaipur
40 Khadi Gramodyog Bhavan
43 Tourist Reception Centre; Desert Culture Centre & Museum
44 Jaisalmer Folklore Museum
45 Tilon-ki-Pol
46 Main Roadways Bus Stand
To Chhatris (7km), Bada Bagh (7km) & Ramgarh (70km)
To Gorbandh Palace Hotel, Rang Mahal, Amar Sagar (7km), Mool Sagar (9km), Lodhruva (15km), Kuldhara (25km) & Sam Sand Dunes (42km)
To Airport (3km)
Gandhi Chowk
Amar Sagar Gate
Hanuman Chowk
Hanuman Circle Rd
Shiv Rd
Bhatia Market
Gopa Chowk
Jaisalmer Fort
See Jaisalmer Fort Map p613
Jethwai Rd
Gadi Sagar Rd
Gadi Sagar
Train Station
To Jodhpur (285km) & Bikaner (330km)
To Akal Wood Fossil Park (16km), Khuri (40km) & Barmer (153km)
0 125 250m
0 125 250yd

Post & Communications The main post office is on Hanuman Circle Rd, just west of the fort. It is open from 10 am to 5 pm daily except Sunday. Inside the fort is a small post office which only sells stamps; it's open from 10 am to 3 pm Monday to Saturday.

From no Internet places just two years ago, Jaisalmer now has literally dozens of places where you can surf the Internet, both inside and outside the fort. All charge Rs 1 per minute and connections vary greatly from instantaneous to painfully slow – early morning and late evening are your best chance of seeing your in-box within the hour.

Photography In Bhatia Market (opposite the Bhatia News Agency) is Byas & Co (☎ 51884), where you can buy slide and print film and batteries for still and movie cameras. A roll of Fuji print film (36 shots) costs Rs 90; Rs 220 for slide film. To develop print film it charges Rs 15 for developing, plus Rs 3/4 per small/medium print. It usually takes three hours. It also sells Video 8 cassettes (Rs 250) and Mini Digital Video cassettes (Rs 750).

Bookshops Day-old newspapers as well as postcards can be bought at the well-stocked Bhatia News Agency, in Bhatia Market. There is an excellent selection of new books (especially novels) here, as well as some second-hand books (in English, French, German, Spanish and several other languages), which can be either bought or swapped.

Henna Painting & Ayurvedic Massage Bobby Henna Art Painting & Herbal House (☎ 54468) is located in the fort. Because it is run by women, female travellers will feel comfortable here. This welcoming place charges Rs 50 to 100 for henna painting, Rs 250 for a full-body massage with oil, and – ideal after a few days on a camel – Rs 300 for a full-body Ayurvedic massage (including facial) with 32 herbs.

Jaisalmer Fort

The fort is the most alive of any museum, fort or palace that you are likely to visit anywhere in India. There are homes and hotels hidden in the laneways, and shops and stalls swaddled in the kaleidoscopic mirrors and embroideries of brilliant Rajasthani cloth. Sadly, the fort is suffering from tourism numbers and government indifference and is on the World Monuments Watch list of 100 endangered sites worldwide (see Responsible Tourism in the Facts for the Visitor chapter).

Built in 1156 by the Rajput ruler Jaisala, and reinforced by subsequent rulers, the fort crowns the 80m-high Trikuta Hill. About 25% of the old city's population resides within the fort walls, which have 99 bastions around their circumference.

The fort is entered through a forbidding series of massive gates leading to a large courtyard. The former maharaja's seven-storey **palace** fronts onto this. The square was formerly used to review troops, hear petitions and present extravagant entertainment for important visitors. Part of the palace is open to the public.

Although there is not a whole lot to see inside, the 360° views from the summit are really spectacular. It's open from 8 am to 5 pm daily in summer (from 9 am in winter), and entry costs Rs 10. A camera/video is Rs 20/50.

Jain Temples Within the fort walls are seven beautifully carved Jain temples built between the 12th and 15th centuries, including very fine temples dedicated to Rikhabdev and Sambhavanth. They are all connected by a series of corridors and walkways. Only two are open to non-Jains, from 7 am to noon. Entry is Rs 10 and a camera/video costs Rs 50/100.

Laxminath Temple This Hindu temple, in the centre of the fort, is simpler than the Jain temples, although there are some interesting paintings in the drum of the dome. Devotees offer grain, which is distributed before the temple. There is a repousse silver architrave around the entrance to the inner sanctum, and a heavily garlanded image enshrined within.

Havelis

The impressive mansions built by the wealthy merchants of Jaisalmer are known as havelis, and several of these finely sculpted sandstone buildings are still in good condition.

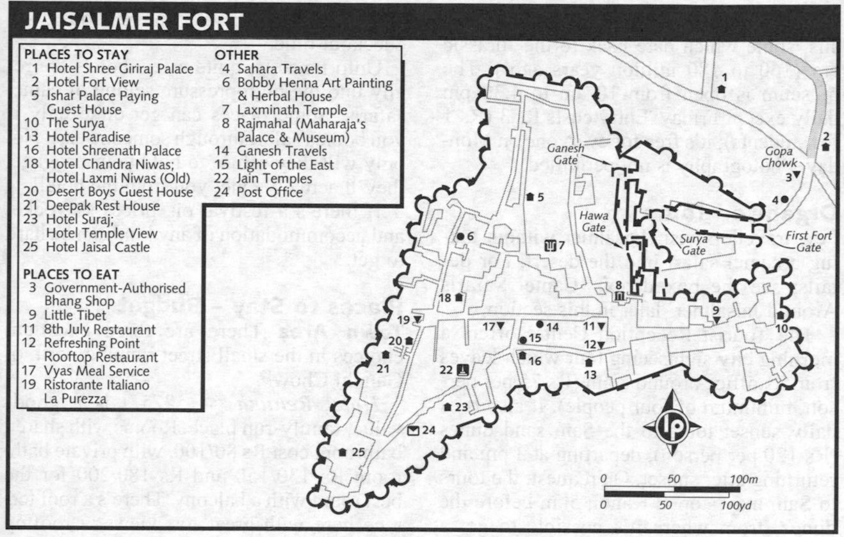

Patwon-ki-Haveli This most elaborate and magnificent of all the Jaisalmer havelis stands in a narrow lane. It was originally built between 1800 and 1860 by five Jain brothers who made their fortunes in trading jewellery and fine brocades. Although it's more impressive from the outside, the view back towards the fort from the roof is magnificent. There's a Rs 2 entry fee.

Salim Singh-ki-Haveli This private haveli was built about 300 years ago and part of it is still occupied. Salim Singh was the prime minister when Jaisalmer was the capital of a princely state, and his mansion has a beautifully arched roof with superb carved brackets in the form of peacocks. Entry costs Rs 15, and it's open daily between 8 am and 6 pm.

Nathmal-ki-Haveli This late-19th-century haveli was also a prime minister's house. The left and right wings of the building were carved by brothers and are very similar, but not identical. Yellow sandstone elephants guard the building, and even the front door is a work of art.

Gadi Sagar

This tank, south of the city walls, was once the water supply of the city and there are many small temples and shrines around it. A wide variety of waterfowl flock here in winter.

The attractive gateway which arches across the road down to the tank is said to have been built by a famous prostitute. When she offered to pay to have this gateway constructed, the maharaja refused permission on the grounds that he would have to pass under it to go down to the tank, and he felt that this would be beneath his dignity. While he was away, she built the gate anyway, adding a Krishna temple on top so the king could not tear it down.

Museums

Next to the Tourist Reception Centre is the **Desert Culture Centre & Museum**, which has textiles, old coins, fossils and traditional Rajasthani instruments among other things. Its aim is to preserve Rajasthan's cultural heritage and conduct research on local history. The museum is open from 10 am to 7.30 pm daily and there's a nightly puppet show from 6.30 to 7.30 pm (Rs 30). Admission is Rs 5/10 for Indians/foreigners, which includes entry to the **Jaisalmer Folklore Museum** – located on the road leading down to the lake (open between 9 am and 7 pm daily). The hill near this museum is a tremendous place to soak up the sunset.

Close to the RTDC Hotel Moomal is the small **government museum**, which has a limited but well-captioned collection of fossils, some which date back to the Jurassic era (160 to 180 million years ago!). The museum is open from 10 am to 4.30 pm daily except Friday. Entry costs Rs 3 (Rs 1 for students); it's free for everyone on Monday. Photography is not permitted.

Organised Tours

Few travellers visit Jaisalmer without taking a camel safari into the desert. For details, see the boxed text 'Camel Safaris Around Jaisalmer' later in this section.

The Tourist Reception Centre offers a morning city sightseeing tour which leaves from its office around 8 am (Rs 75 per person, minimum of four people). It also runs daily sunset tours to the Sam sand dunes (Rs 120 per person), departing at 3 pm and returning after sunset. On request, the tours to Sam may stop at Kanoi, 5km before the dunes, from where it's possible to get a camel to the dunes in time for sunset (for about Rs 50).

Places to Stay

Staying at one of the hotels within the fort itself is the most romantic choice, but there are equally good hotels outside the fort walls. Motorised traffic is not permitted in the narrow lanes beyond the main square at most times, which means you'll have to lug your backpack anywhere further into the maze – a 10-minute walk at most. Many hotels in Jaisalmer have an ungenerous 9 am checkout time.

Unfortunately, quite a few hotels are really into the high-pressure selling of camel safaris. Some places can get quite ugly if you book a safari through someone else. Not only will they refuse to hold your baggage, they'll actually evict you from the hotel!

If there's a festival on, prices skyrocket and accommodation of any kind can be hard to get.

Places to Stay – Budget

Town Area There are three excellent choices in the small street running north of Gandhi Chowk.

Hotel Renuka *(☎ 52757)* is a good-value, family-run place. Rooms with shared bathroom cost Rs 80/100, with private bathroom Rs 130/150 and Rs 180/200 for the best room with a balcony. There's a roof terrace here with great fort views, a rooftop restaurant, and the owner, Sunny, is a helpful chap. The same family also runs ***Hotel Ratan Palace*** *(☎ 53615)*, closer to Gandhi Chowk on the same street, with the same friendly approach. Larger, newer rooms cost between Rs 250 and 350.

Hotel Swastika *(☎ 52483)* also gets good reports from travellers, and deservedly so. It has simple, well-kept singles/doubles with shared bathroom for Rs 90/150 and a range of other rooms up to a larger room for Rs 220/250 with private bathroom.

Arrival in Jaisalmer

You realise that Jaisalmer is a tourist hotbed long before you arrive. Hotel and camel safari touts may even approach you in Bikaner or Jodhpur. Those travelling by bus will usually find the number of passengers suddenly increases about an hour before arrival, with touts knowing that they have a captive audience.

In the past few years, the local authorities have instituted various policies designed to keep the touts at bay. Most carriages on the overnight train have at least a couple of soldiers on board to try to ensure you get a good night's sleep, and they also patrol the relevant railway platform in Jodhpur, with varying degrees of vigilance. Perhaps the most surreal experience is stumbling out of the train in the pre-dawn light to find a small army of hotel owners kept behind a barricade about 20m from the station exit, holding up their signs and champing at the bit.

Once you cross that line, you're on your own.

Don't believe *anyone* who offers to take you 'anywhere you like' for just a few rupees, and take with a grain of salt claims that the hotel you want to stay in is 'full', 'closed', 'no good any more' or has suffered some other inglorious fate. If the hotel of your choice has a representative waiting for you, by all means accept the free ride. Alternatively, take a rickshaw and hope you get an honest one (they do exist) – pay no more than Rs 30.

Hotel Golden City *(☎/fax 51664, ⓔ khangazi@hotmail.com)* can be found in the southern section of the walled city, just off Gadi Sagar Rd. It's a laid-back place that has a real travellers' feel about it. Simple but clean rooms with private bathroom start at just Rs 40/50 and Rs 55/110 with private bathroom.

Hotel Samrat *(☎ 51498)*, in the same area, is another bargain, with a very clean single cell for Rs 30 and larger rooms with private bathroom for Rs 60/90. A dorm bed is a mere Rs 10.

Hotel Fort View *(☎ 52214)*, close to the entrance to the fort, has rooms from Rs 60/80 with private bathroom (some of the rooms are tiny). The best room costs Rs 300/350 and has a fort view. There's a popular restaurant on the top floor.

Hotel Shree Giriraj Palace *(☎ 52268)* is a little bit further west, just off Bhatia Market. This is a cheap and cheerful place, with singles/doubles for Rs 100/120 with shared bathroom, and Rs 150/200 with private bathroom and bucket hot water.

Residency Centrepoint Paying Guest House *(☎/fax 52883)*, near the Patwon-ki-Haveli, has five clean, spacious doubles with private bathroom for Rs 200. Room No 101 has a lovely antique balcony and nice fittings. This friendly, family-run place serves good home-cooked meals on the rooftop with superb views of the fort.

Fort In the western part of the fort, ***Deepak Rest House*** *(☎ 52665, fax 52070)* is a popular place. Most rooms are different, with singles from Rs 40 up to Rs 120, while doubles range between Rs 80 and 350. Rooms with a view and balcony (room Nos 8, 14, 17 and 21) cost Rs 200/250. The best room is No 9 (Rs 300/350), which is, not surprisingly, often occupied. A bed in the dorm is Rs 25.

Hotel Paradise *(☎ 52674)* is very popular. Its 23 rooms are arranged around a leafy courtyard, and there are palace views from the roof. Singles/doubles with shared bathroom are Rs 150/200, and doubles with private bathroom cost from Rs 350 to 650.

Hotel Chandra Niwas *(☎ 53277)* is a friendly place to stay, with just a handful of well-maintained double rooms, ranging from Rs 150 with shared bathroom to Rs 250 with private bathroom.

Ishar Palace Paying Guest House *(☎ 53062)* is near the Laxminath Temple. Rooms are spartan but quite clean, and cost from Rs 100 a double (a room with a bamboo roof on the top storey) with private bathroom. A bed in the dorm costs Rs 50. This was the home of a 19th-century prime minister, Ishar Singh, as evidenced by the statues of elephants before the building. You can even stay in his modest but atmospheric room with the balcony from which he used to address petitioners (Rs 150/200). There's also a nearby annexe, which can house five people for Rs 50 per person – ideal for families.

Hotel Temple View *(☎ 52832)* is a simple guesthouse with small but decent rooms for Rs 100/200 with shared bathroom, and Rs 250/300 with private bathroom.

The Surya *(☎ 50647)* is tucked away in the south-eastern corner of the fort and is a lovely, quiet family place. Doubles, all with shared bathroom, start at Rs 100, while the room for Rs 270 has great east-facing views.

Places to Stay – Mid-Range

Town Area The charming ***Hotel Nachana Haveli*** *(☎ 51910, Gandhi Chowk)* is a 280-year-old haveli that has been converted into a hotel. Comfortable air-cooled rooms are Rs 750/900, and deluxe air-cooled rooms are Rs 1100/1350. Meals are available with advance notice.

Hotel Jaisal Palace *(☎ 52717, fax 50257)*, nearby, is a clean and well-run place with smallish singles/doubles from Rs 700/850. Those on the south side have balconies facing the fort, or go up to the chair-swing on the roof terrace to soak up the view.

Mandir Palace Hotel *(☎ 52788, fax 51677, Gandhi Chowk)*, just inside the town walls, is a royal palace in part of which the erstwhile royal family still lives. The intricate stone latticework is exquisite and all rooms ooze an old-world charm, with antique furniture and fittings. Air-cooled rooms start at Rs 850/1350 and deluxe aircon suites are Rs 1250/2000.

Fort Close to the Jain temples, ***Hotel Shreenath Palace*** *(☎ 52907)* is a family-run establishment in a beautiful old haveli. The rooms reek with atmosphere, with little alcoves and balconies, and some have magnificent views over the temples. Omjee, the owner, claims descent from one of Jaisalmer's past prime ministers. Rooms (all doubles) cost Rs 350 with shared bathroom and free bucket hot water.

Hotel Suraj *(☎ 51623)*, nearby, is another atmospheric old haveli featuring a fine sculpture on the facade and good views from the roof. Each room is different, but they all have private bathroom with hot shower and start at Rs 300/350.

Hotel Jaisal Castle *(☎ 52362, fax 52101, ⓔ narayan@jp1.vsnl.net.in)* is another restored haveli, this one in the south-west corner of the fort. Its biggest attraction is its position, high on the ramparts overlooking the desert. The cheapest rooms are Rs 700/850, and both veg and nonveg meals are available.

Desert Boys Guest House *(☎ 53091, ⓔ desert_p@yahoo.com)*, not far away, has doubles from Rs 250 to 750. All have private sitting rooms and are comfortable and tastefully decorated.

Places to Stay – Top End

Rang Mahal *(☎ 50907, fax 51305)*, about 2.5km west of the fort, is a dramatic building with impressive rooms from Rs 1500/1850. The deluxe suites (Rs 3800) are divine and a pool is being planned.

Gorbandh Palace Hotel *(☎ 51511, fax 52749)*, nearby, is another upmarket modern hotel with traditional design elements. Constructed of local sandstone, the friezes around the hotel were sculpted by local artisans. Singles/doubles cost Rs 1999/3300 and a deluxe suite is Rs 5500. There's a coffee shop, bar, restaurant, travel desk, and superb pool (open to nonresidents for Rs 200).

Jawahar Niwas Palace *(☎ 52208, fax 52288, ⓔ jawaharniwaspalace@yahoo.com)*, about 1km west of the fort, is a stunning sandstone palace, standing rather forlornly in its own sandy grounds. Elegant, spacious rooms cost Rs 2000/2750. Those upstairs at the front have the best (if distant) fort views. Set lunch/dinner is Rs 400/450.

Narayan Niwas Palace *(☎ 52408, fax 52101, ⓔ narayan@jp1.vsnl.net.in)* is closer to the fort, and counts Britain's Princess Anne among its former guests. However, these days the rooms get mixed reports from travellers. Overpriced singles/doubles cost Rs 1500/2500. Suites are Rs 2650. There's a rather gloomy indoor swimming pool.

Hotel Dhola Maru *(☎ 52863, fax 53124, Jethwai Rd)*, to the north-east of the walled city, is a few kilometres from the fort entrance. It's a popular choice, and although the location is not great, this is compensated for by the comfortable rooms. Air-con rooms are Rs 1300/2000. There's an extraordinary little bar, which has incorporated tree roots into its decor, and a restaurant.

Places to Eat

Town Area Not far from the fort gate, ***Monica Restaurant*** gets lots of good reports from travellers. There's an extensive menu of Indian (including Rajasthani), continental and Chinese food. To taste authentic local specialities, try the Rajasthani thali (Rs 70). Ginger chicken (Rs 50) and potato peas curry (Rs 38) also aren't bad.

Natraj Restaurant is a few minutes walk down from the Monica and is also a good place to eat. Chicken masala is Rs 65, paneer kofta is Rs 55, and a beer will set you back Rs 80. For those with a sweet tooth, apple pie and fried ice cream (Rs 35 each) feature on the dessert list. The open-air top floor has a nice view of the upper part of the Salim Singh-ki-Haveli next door, and away to the south of town.

Trio, near the Amar Sagar Gate, is worth a try. This long-running Indian and continental restaurant is pricier than its neighbours, but the food is excellent, and musicians play in the evening. The *saagwala* mutton (with creamed spinach) for Rs 90 is delicious. There's even mashed potato (Rs 35) – ideal for tender tummies. The menu also includes a good nonveg tandoori thali (Rs 205).

Skyroom Restaurant, on Gandhi Chowk, has a somewhat limited menu, but has pretty good fort views. Half a tandoori chicken is Rs 80, a banana pancake is Rs 35 and a bottle of beer is Rs 80. It also does breakfasts for Rs 50 to 70.

Kalpana Restaurant, in the same area, has good banana lassis (Rs 15) or toasted chicken sandwiches (Rs 30).

Sharma Lodge (signed in Hindi) is a very simple eatery located beneath the Top Deck restaurant. It has a filling Indian thali for Rs 25.

German Bakery is a small, simple place near Satyam Tours at Gandhi Chowk. Items on offer include croissants (Rs 10), peanut cookies (Rs 10) and various cakes (Rs 25 per slice).

Mohan Juice Centre, at Bhatia Market, sells an assortment of interesting lassis, such as apple (Rs 12), honey (Rs 13) and even chocolate (Rs 10). A glass of fresh orange juice is Rs 15.

Bhang Shop, outside the First Fort Gate, not far from Sahara Travels, is a government-authorised bhang shop! Medium/strong lassis are Rs 30/35 per glass and bhang cookies, cakes and candy can be baked with advance notice. Bhang does not agree with everyone – see the boxed text 'Bhang Lassi Warning' under Drinks in the Facts for the Visitor chapter.

Dhanraj Bhatia Sweets, at Sadar Bazaar in Bhatia Market, has been churning out traditional sweet treats for the past 10 generations. It is renowned in Jaisalmer and beyond for its local speciality sweets, such as *ghotua* and *panchadhari ladoos* (Rs 4.50 each). This simple little shop is worth visiting just to watch the sweetmakers ply their trade.

The Duke, beside Hanuman Chowk, does a great mixed fruit lassi (Rs 25).

Fort Some of Jaisalmer's best restaurants are inside the fort. ***Little Tibet***, just east of the main square, has a cosy dining area, friendly service and large servings. The menu is extensive, with hearty soups (pumpkin and garlic costs Rs 25), a large plate of *momos* (dumplings) for Rs 40 and good enchiladas for around Rs 50. It's often full, so get there early or be prepared to wait.

Ristorante Italiano La Purezza, near the Desert Boys Guest House, serves excellent authentic pasta dishes for Rs 70 to 100 – if you've been travelling in Rajasthan for a while you'll appreciate what a treat this is. The bruschetta is also good (Rs 15 to 30), and this place does tiramisu (Rs 45), as well as espresso coffee and cappuccinos. The view from the tables is wonderful and it's a brilliant place to watch the sunset. The service is also good.

Vyas Meal Service, near the Jain temples, is a brilliant place to eat home-made food. This family-run veg restaurant offers traditional cuisine, with wholesome thalis and a good masala tea.

8th July Restaurant and ***Refreshing Point Rooftop Restaurant***, both above the main square in the fort, are good places to watch the passing human and bovine traffic, but the food is variable. At the latter is a small German bakery selling goodies such as choco banana croissants (Rs 20) and cheesecake (Rs 35 per slice).

Shopping

Jaisalmer is famous for embroidery, Rajasthani mirrorwork, rugs, blankets, old stonework and antiques. Watch out when purchasing silver items; the metal may be adulterated with bronze. Tie-dye and other fabrics are made at the Khadi Gramodyog Bhavan (Seemagram), at Dhibba Para, not far from the fort. Items for sale include tie-dye woollen shawls, cushion covers and cotton bed sheets.

On the laneway leading up to the Jain temples within the fort is Light of the East, which sells crystals and rare mineral specimens, including zeolite, which can fetch up to Rs 5000 depending on the quality.

Getting There & Away

Air Indian Airlines has, through its subsidiary Alliance Air, three flights a week from Jaisalmer to Delhi (US$155) via Udaipur (US$100) and Jaipur (US$125). The agents for Indian Airlines are Crown Tours (☎/fax 51912, ⓔ crown@jp1.dot.net.in), about 350m west of Amar Sagar Gate.

Bus The main Roadways bus stand (☎ 51541) is some distance from the centre of town, near the train station. Fortunately, all buses start at a bus depot more conveniently located just behind Hotel Neeraj.

To Jodhpur there are frequent deluxe buses (Rs 92, 5½ hours) and several daily direct deluxe buses which run to Bikaner (Rs 130, seven hours) and Ajmer (Rs 140, 9½ hours).

You can book luxury buses through most of the travel agencies. Quoted rates included Bikaner (Rs 130), Jaipur (Rs 175), Jodhpur (Rs 80) and Udaipur (Rs 150). Be aware that most private buses (except those going to Bikaner) require a change of bus at Jodhpur. Some travellers have found themselves in Jodhpur with an onward ticket that no-one will honour, so make sure you clarify exactly what you're getting for your money.

Train The reservation office at the train station is open from 8 am to 8 pm daily.

Camel Safaris Around Jaisalmer

Exploring the desert around Jaisalmer by camel safari is undoubtedly the most evocative way to sample desert life. If you follow a few simple precautions before setting out, you might just find it a highlight of your time in India. The best time to make a safari is from October to February.

Before Setting Out

Competition between safari organisers is cut-throat and standards vary considerably. None of the hotels have their own camels – these are all independently owned – so the hoteliers and the travel agencies are, with one notable exception (see Ganesh Travels under Safari Agencies later), just go-betweens.

Hotel owners typically pay the camel drivers around Rs 150 per camel per day to hire them, so if you're offered a safari at Rs 200 or even Rs 250 per day, this leaves only a small margin for food and the agent's profit. It's obvious that you can't possibly expect three reasonable meals a day on these margins, but this is frequently what is promised. As a result, a lot of travellers feel they've been ripped off when the food isn't what was offered. Beware of operators who claim (and charge for) three-day safaris when in actual fact you return after breakfast on the third day – hardly value for money.

Another precaution suggested by the tourist office is to ask the office through which you book for the camel or jeep driver's identity card and note down the registration number (written in red). If they can't produce one, you may want to look elsewhere.

The realistic minimum price for a basic safari is about Rs 350 per person per day. For this you can expect a breakfast of porridge, tea and toast, and a lunch and dinner of rice, dhal and chapatis – pretty unexciting stuff. Blankets are also supplied. You must bring your own mineral water. Of course, you can pay more for greater levels of comfort: tents, stretcher beds, better food, beer etc.

However much you decide to spend, make sure you know exactly what is being provided and make sure it's there before you leave Jaisalmer. Ensure you know where they're going to take you. Attempting to get a refund for services not provided is a waste of time. Take care of your possessions, particularly on the return journey. A recent scam involves the drivers suggesting that you walk to some nearby ruins while they stay with the camels and keep an eye on your bags. The police station in Jaisalmer receives numerous reports of items missing from luggage but seems unwilling to help. Nonetheless, any complaints you do have should be reported, either to the Superintendent of Police (☎ 52233) or the Tourist Reception Centre (☎ 52406).

If you're on your own it's worth getting a group of at least four people together before looking for a safari. Organisers will make up groups but four days is a long time to spend with people you might not get on with. Usually each person is assigned their own camel, but check this, as some agencies might try to save money by hiring fewer camels, meaning you'll find yourself sharing your camel with a camel driver or cook, which is not nearly as much fun.

What to Take

Bring something comfortable to sit on – many travellers fail to do this and come back with very sore legs and/or backsides! One traveller wrote to suggest that women wear nylon underwear. Women should also consider wearing a sports bra, as the trotting momentum of the camels can cause some discomfort after even just a few hours. A wide-brimmed hat (or Rajput-style turban), long trousers, toilet paper, sun cream and a personal water bottle (with a strap so you can secure it easily) are also recommended. It can get very cold at night, so if you have a sleeping bag bring it along even if you're told that lots of blankets will be supplied.

Safari Agencies

There are several independent camel safari agencies (not linked to any hotels) that have been recommended. Ganesh Travels (☎ 50138), inside the fort, is wholly owned by former and current camel drivers and gets consistently good reports from travellers. Sahara Travels (☎ 52609), by the First Fort Gate, is run by Mr Bissa, alias Mr Desert or India's Marlboro Man – the rugged model in the Jaisalmer

Camel Safaris Around Jaisalmer

cigarette ads. At both places, standard tours cost Rs 350 per day for two to four days. Remember that no place is perfect – recommendations here ought not be a substitute for doing your own research to see what suits your particular needs and budget. In previous editions, we have recommended Satyam Tours (☎ 50773) and Thar Safari (☎/fax 52722), both on Gandhi Chowk. These still get overwhelmingly positive reports, although not everyone has found that their safari lived up to expectations.

Whoever you book your safari through, insist that all rubbish is carried back to Jaisalmer, and not left at the Sam sand dunes or in remote villages where the wind will carry it across the desert.

Out on the Trail

The desert is surprisingly well populated and sprinkled with ruins. You often come across tiny fields of millet, girls picking berries or boys herding flocks of sheep or goats. The latter are usually fitted with tinkling neck bells and, in the desert silence, it's music to the ears. Unfortunately, the same cannot be said for the noises emitted by the notoriously flatulent camels!

Camping out at night, huddling around a tiny fire beneath the stars and listening to the camel drivers' yarns can be quite romantic. The camel drivers will expect a tip or gift at the end of the trip. Don't neglect to do this.

The reins are fastened to the camel's nose peg, so the animals are easily steered. At resting points, the camels are completely unsaddled and hobbled. They limp away to browse on nearby shrubs while the camel drivers brew sweet chai or prepare food. The whole crew rests in the shade of thorn trees by a tank or well.

Most safaris last three to four days and, if you want to get to the most interesting places, this is a bare minimum unless a significant jeep component is included. The usual circuit takes in such places as Amar Sagar (garden, step-wells and Jain Temple – Rs 25/50 for a camera/video), Lodhruva, Mool Sagar (garden, Shiva Temple – Rs 5), Bada Bagh (a fertile oasis with a huge old dam and the royal chhatris with beautifully carved ceilings – entry Rs 10) and Sam, as well as various abandoned villages along the way. It's not possible to ride by camel to the Sam sand dunes in one day; in 1½ days you could get a jeep to Sam, stay there overnight, and take a camel from there to either Kuldahra (then a jeep back to Jaisalmer) or to Kanoi (and catch a jeep from there to Jaisalmer). If you're really pressed for time, you could opt for a half-day camel safari (which involves jeep transfers).

In 2½ days you could travel by camel to Lodhruva, spend the second night at the Sam sand dunes, and return the following day to Jaisalmer by jeep. If you have more time, obviously you can travel at a more leisurely pace through these regions and forgo the jeep component.

MARTIN HARRIS

The *Jodhpur Express* leaves Jaisalmer daily at 10.25 pm, arriving in Jodhpur at 5.30 am (Rs 82/130 general/sleeper class). The *Jaisalmer Express* leaves Jodhpur at 11.15 pm and arrives in Jaisalmer around 5.30 am. There's also a daily passenger train in each direction.

Getting Around

Autorickshaw Rickshaw drivers can be rapacious in Jaisalmer, so bargain hard. An autorickshaw to Gadi Sagar costs about Rs 15 one way from the fort entrance. From the fort to the airport it costs around Rs 30.

Jeep It's possible to hire jeeps from the stand on Gandhi Chowk. To Khuri or the Sam sand dunes expect to pay Rs 300 return with a one-hour wait. For Lodhruva, you'll pay Rs 150 return with a one-hour stop. To cut the cost, find other people to share with (maximum of five people per jeep).

Bicycle A good way to get around is by bicycle. There are a number of hire places, including one at Gandhi Chowk directly opposite Skyroom Restaurant (Rs 3/20 per hour/day).

AROUND JAISALMER

Lodhruva

About 15km north-west of Jaisalmer are the deserted ruins of Lodhruva, which was the ancient capital before the move to Jaisalmer. The **Jain temples**, rebuilt in the late 1970s, are the only reminders of the city's former magnificence. The main temple enshrines an image of Parasnath, the 23rd tirthankar, and is finely wrought in silver and surrounded by fine sculptures. It's free to enter the temple (Rs 40/70 for a camera/video). There are three daily buses from Jaisalmer to Lodhruva (Rs 5).

Sam Sand Dunes

A desert national park has been established in the Great Thar Desert near Sam village. One of the most popular excursions is to the sand dunes on the edge of the park, 42km from Jaisalmer along a very good sealed road (which is maintained by the Indian army).

This is Jaisalmer's nearest real Sahara-like desert. It's best to be here at sunrise or sunset, and many camel safaris spend a night at the dunes. This place has become a massive tourist attraction, so don't set your heart on a solitary desert sunset experience. Nonetheless, it is still quite a magical place, and it's possible to frame pictures of solitary camels against lonely dunes.

One tragic consequence of the increasing number of visitors to the dunes is the debris and rubbish lying around. Please don't contribute to this problem. Visitors are charged Rs 2 to visit the dunes.

There are three daily buses to Sam (Rs 15, 1½ hours).

Khuri

Khuri is a small village 40km south-west of Jaisalmer, with its own desert sand dunes. It has far less tourist hype (at least for now) than the Sam sand dunes, and is becoming increasingly popular for camel/jeep safaris. It's a peaceful place, with houses of mud and straw decorated like the patterns on Persian carpets. There are, thankfully, no craftshop-lined streets or banana pancake restaurants. The attraction out here is the desert solitude and the brilliant star-studded sky at night.

Places to Stay & Eat Places to stay in Khuri are pretty basic, with charpoys and bucket hot water. All provide meals and most can arrange camel safaris. Accommodation is limited and you won't get any bargains; basically you're paying for the peace and quiet rather than the facilities, which are minimal.

Khuri Guest House is on the left of the main road as you enter the village. It has conventional rooms with shared bathroom for a reasonable Rs 75/100. Huts with shared bathroom are Rs 100/125 a single/double, and Rs 300 for a double with private bathroom.

Mama's Guest House is actually a cluster of thatched huts. The cheapest costs a hefty Rs 350 per night with shared bathroom, which includes meals and free bucket hot water. These cost Rs 200 in the low season, but would be hellishly hot. The huts are set in a semicircle around a campfire. There is a group of better thatched huts for Rs 450 each, while top-of-the-range huts are Rs 750, and include an electric fan. It's also possible to stay in a conventional room (but not nearly so romantic!) for Rs 300 with shared bathroom.

Sodha Guest House has doubles with shared bathroom for Rs 150. Lunch/dinner is Rs 100 per person.

Gangaur Guest House has huts ranging from Rs 150 to 300. Lunch/dinner is Rs 150.

Getting There & Away There are several buses daily to Khuri from Jaisalmer (Rs 14, two hours).

Barmer
Barmer is a centre for woodcarving, carpets, embroidery, block printing and other handicrafts, and its products are famous throughout Rajasthan. The small shops in the colourful Sadar Bazaar are a good place to start looking – you may also come across some of the artisans at work out the back. Otherwise, this desert town, 153km south of Jaisalmer, isn't very interesting. There are two annual fairs in Barmer: the Barmer Thar Festival in early March and the Barmer Cattle Fair (which is held at nearby Tilwara) in March/April. For details, contact the Tourist Reception Centre (☎ 52406) in Jaisalmer.

RTDC Khartal *(☎ 02982-22956)* has four neat singles/doubles with private bathroom for Rs 300/400. Other options include ***Hotel Krishna*** *(☎ 02982-20785)*, with rooms from Rs 100/200 (with shared bathroom), and the cheaper ***Kailash Sarover Hotel*** *(☎ 02982-20730)*.

From Barmer there are frequent daily express buses to Jaisalmer and Jodhpur.

Pokaran
At the junction of the Jaisalmer, Jodhpur and Bikaner roads, 110km from Jaisalmer, the **Pokaran Fort** rises from the desert and shelters a tangle of narrow streets lined by balconied houses. It's worth a quick look, especially as a stop at Pokaran breaks the long journey between Jodhpur and Jaisalmer. The fort is open from 7 am to 7 pm daily (entry is Rs 20; a camera or video is Rs 10).

It was in Pokaran in May 1998 that India detonated five nuclear devices.

Accommodation in town is lacklustre. ***RTDC Motel Godavan*** *(☎ 02994-22275)* conveniently rents out rooms with private bathroom for six hours (Rs 200), or per night (Rs 300).

There are frequent RSTC buses to Jaisalmer (2½ hours; Rs 30).

Khichan
This small village is a few kilometres from the large town of Phalodi, between Jodhpur and Jaisalmer. It has not yet been listed as a wildlife sanctuary, but is a must for bird lovers. From late August/early September to the end of March, it's possible to witness the spectacular sight of hundreds of demoiselle cranes descending on the fields around the village.

BIKANER
☎ 0151 • pop 510,000

This desert town, with its superb fort, is located in the north of Rajasthan and is becoming increasingly popular among travellers keen to extract themselves from the tourist hype of Jaisalmer. Bikaner has some wonderful Jain temples and an atmospheric old city. It's also a good base for camel safaris and for visiting the extraordinary Karni Mata Temple, 30km to the south, where thousands of holy rats are worshipped.

Bikaner was founded in 1488 by Rao Bika, a descendant of Jodha, the founder of Jodhpur. Like many others in Rajasthan, the old city is surrounded by a high crenellated wall and, like Jaisalmer, it was once an important staging post on the great caravan trade routes. The Ganga Canal, built between 1925 and 1927, irrigates a large area of previously arid land around Bikaner.

Bikaner hosts its own Camel Festival in January each year (8 to 9 January 2001, 27 to 29 January 2002, 17 to 18 January 2003). Though not as evocative as the fair at Pushkar, it's still worth a look.

Orientation & Information
The old city is encircled by a 7km-long city wall with five entrance gates, constructed in the 18th century. The fort and palace are outside the city walls to the north-east.

The well-organised Tourist Reception Centre (☎ 544125) is in the grounds of the RTDC Hotel Dhola Maru. It can provide lists of local doctors, as well as detailed bus and train timetables. It also has a small number of brochures and maps. It's open 10 am to 5 pm daily except Sunday.

You can change US dollars and UK pounds (cash and travellers cheques) at State Bank of Bikaner & Jaipur, at Ambedkar Circle, and at its public park branch (near Junagarh). The former branch is open from noon to 4 pm weekdays, the latter from 10 am to 2 pm. Bank of Baroda (1st floor), opposite the train station, changes travellers cheques only. At the time of writing, there were no banks in Bikaner issuing cash advances on credit cards.

Internet access is available at Net Yuppies (☎ 540560), behind Natraj off Kem Rd (Rs 65 per hour, open 9.30 am to 10.30 pm). Cyber City (☎ 529076), in the east of town, serves reasonable fast food and charges Rs 75 for one hour. Try also New Horizons, off Station Rd. You could also check out the hotels as an increasing number are gaining Internet access.

Junagarh

Constructed between 1588 and 1593 by Raja Rai Singh – a general in the army of the Mughal emperor, Akbar – this most impressive fort has a 986m-long wall with 37 bastions, a moat and two entrances. The Surajpol, or Sun Gate, is the main entrance to the fort. The palaces within the fort are on the southern side and make a picturesque ensemble of courtyards, balconies, kiosks, towers and windows. A major feature of this fort and its palaces is the magnificent stone carving and the interiors are among the most exquisite in India.

Highlights include: the Diwan-i-Khas; the Phool Mahal (Flower Palace), which is decorated with paintings and carved marble panels; and the Hawa Mahal, Badal Mahal and Anup Mahal.

The fort is open from 10 am to 5 pm daily, although the ticket office closes at 4.30 pm. Entry is Rs 10/50 for Indians/foreigners and there's a Rs 30/100 camera/video charge. A compulsory guide is included in the ticket price. It costs an extra Rs 25 to visit the museum and you will be charged Rs 20 to take in a camera.

Lalgarh Palace

About 3km north of the city centre, this mildly interesting red sandstone palace was built by Maharaja Ganga Singh (1881–1942) in memory of his father Maharaja Lal Singh. It's an imposing building with overhanging balconies and delicate latticework. The 1st floor contains the **Sri Sadul Museum**, which is open from 10 am to 5 pm daily except Wednesday; entry is Rs 5. Photography

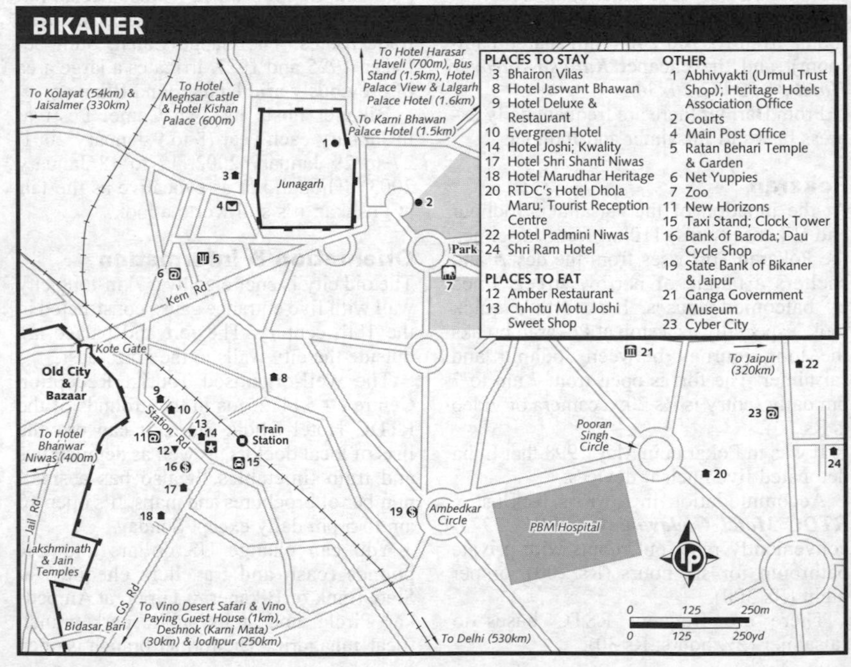

is not allowed. In front of the palace is a carriage from the maharaja's royal train.

Other Attractions

The narrow streets of the old city conceal a number of old havelis and a couple of notable **Jain temples**. The Bhandasar and Sandeshwar temples date from around the 15th century. The temples have colourful wall paintings and some intricate carving.

The **Ganga Government Museum** houses an interesting collection of sculptures, terracotta ware, paintings and musical instruments. It's open from 9.30 am to 4.30 pm daily except Friday and costs Rs 3 (video cameras are prohibited). Entrance is to the back left of the building.

Organised Tours

The Tourist Reception Centre can make arrangements for English-speaking guides (Rs 75 for two hours).

If you wanted to take a camel safari in Jaisalmer but didn't because it was too much of a scene, Bikaner is an excellent alternative. One good operator is Vino Desert Safari (☎ 204445, ⓔ vino_desertsafari@yahoo.com), opposite the Gopeshwar Temple. There are at least eight different camel treks available, ranging from two to seven days and costing from Rs 400 (minimum of six people and only for shorter treks) per person per day up to Rs 800. Check out the Web site at www.vinodesertsafari.com.

Places to Stay – Budget

The cheapest budget options are along the horrendously noisy Station Rd, near the train station. The better budget options are to the north of town.

Hotel Meghsar Castle *(☎ 527315, fax 522041, ⓔ MeghsarCastle@yahoo.com, 9 Gajner Rd)*, north of town, is popular with travellers and has clean rooms with private bathroom from Rs 250/300 a single/double. The front rooms can cop a bit of traffic noise. It's a well-run place, with Internet access, and meals available in the garden.

Next door is ***Hotel Kishan Palace*** *(☎ 527762, fax 522041)*, which is not quite as nice, but still comfortable at Rs 150/300. These same rooms can be bargained down to Rs 80/200 if things are quiet.

Hotel Marudhar Heritage *(☎ 522524, GS Rd)* is a great choice with rooms to suit most budgets. Rooms, all of which are comfortable and good value, range from Rs 250/350 up to Rs 900/999. It's a friendly place, with nice views from the roof, and Internet access (Rs 60 per hour). Hot water is available only from 7 am to 1 pm.

Shri Ram Hotel *(☎ 522651, fax 522548, ⓔ shriramhotel@yahoo.com)* is another excellent place. Located in a quiet area in the east of town, this place has doubles for Rs 150, Rs 250 and Rs 400, depending on their size. All rooms are spotless and have satellite TV.

Vino Paying Guest House *(☎ 270445, ⓔ vino_desertsafari@yahoo.com)*, south of town, is another homey choice. There are a small number of rooms available, from Rs 125 to 350.

Hotel Harasar Haveli *(☎ 209891, fax 525150, ⓔ harasar_haveli@yahoo.com)*, near the Karni Singh Stadium, is another great place to stay, with very clean singles/doubles from Rs 150/200, while better deluxe rooms cost Rs 300/400.

Evergreen Hotel *(☎ 542061)*, on Station Rd, is not a bad choice, although some of the rooms can be noisy. Singles/doubles/triples with private bathroom cost Rs 125/175/200. Hot water is by the bucket (Rs 5). There's a restaurant downstairs. Nearby, ***Hotel Deluxe*** *(☎ 528127)* has bare, basic and usually clean rooms from Rs 100/150.

Hotel Shri Shanti Niwas *(☎ 542320, fax 524231)* is on GS Rd, which leads out from opposite the train station. Basic but clean rooms are Rs 115/165.

RTDC Hotel Dhola Maru *(☎ 529621)*, 1km east of the city centre, has dorm beds for Rs 50.

Places to Stay – Mid-Range

Bhairon Vilas *(☎/fax 544751, ⓔ hbhairon@rediffmail.com)*, almost opposite the main post office, is the funkiest place to stay in Bikaner. Quaint doubles start at Rs 500/800.

Hotel Palace View *(☎ 543625, fax 522741)* is the closest hotel to Lalgarh Palace and is a good place to stay. Clean rooms are Rs 750/850, and smaller rooms are Rs 400/500.

Hotel Padmini Niwas *(☎ 522794, 148 Sadul Ganj)* has clean, pleasant singles/doubles from Rs 325/400, up to Rs 500/750 with air-con. The owner is relaxed, the restaurant is quite good and the small lawn area is very nice.

Hotel Joshi *(☎ 527700, fax 521213)*, near the train station, is a real step up in quality compared with other hotels on this street. Air-cooled singles/doubles start at Rs 300/375 and there's a veg restaurant here.

Hotel Jaswant Bhawan *(☎/fax 521834*, is a pleasant place to stay – handy for the train station without the noise of Station Rd. Attractive doubles cost Rs 400 and there's Internet access.

Places to Stay – Top End

Hotel Bhanwar Niwas *(☎ 529323, fax 200880)*, in the Rampuri Haveli, near the *kotwali* (police station) in the old city, is an excellent choice. This attractive pink sandstone building has enormous, opulent rooms around the internal courtyard for Rs 1999/3200. Prices drop by 30% from May to July.

Lalgarh Palace Hotel *(☎ 540201, fax 522253)*, 3km north of the city centre, is part of the maharaja's modern palace and has well-appointed singles/doubles for US$43/85 (US$40/70 from 15 April to 15 September). There's a bar, restaurant, billiard room, indoor pool and resident astrologer (Rs 600 per consultation) and masseur (Rs 150 for 30 minutes).

Karni Bhawan Palace Hotel *(☎ 524701, fax 522408)*, in Gandhi Colony, near Lalgarh Palace Hotel, is ugly, but peaceful and comfortable. Rooms cost Rs 1999/3300, and Rs 5500 for a huge suite. Good meals are available in the restaurant.

Places to Eat

Bikaner is noted for the spicy snacks known as *namkin*, sold in the shops along Station Rd, among other places.

Deluxe Restaurant, at the hotel of the same name on Station Rd, features a limited selection of cheap veg South Indian and Chinese dishes. All dishes are under Rs 40. There's an extensive ice-cream menu.

Amber Restaurant, diagonally opposite the Deluxe, is also popular for veg fare. Paneer korma costs Rs 42, a South Indian dosa is Rs 26 and cheese toast Rs 22.

Hotel Bhanwar Niwas welcomes non-guests to its vegetarian dining hall (with advance reservation). The set breakfast/lunch/dinner is Rs 150/300/325, or you can just come here for a drink in the courtyard.

Lalgarh Palace Hotel is good for a treat; the set breakfast/lunch/dinner costs US$8/10/12, or you can opt for a la carte dining.

Chhotu Motu Joshi Sweet Shop on Station Rd is Bikaner's most loved sweet stop, with an assortment of Indian treats. Prices vary, but Rs 100 per kilogram is a good benchmark.

Good ice cream is available at ***Kwality***, next door to Hotel Joshi.

Getting There & Away

Bus The bus stand is 3km north of the city centre, almost opposite the road leading to Lalgarh Palace Hotel. If your bus is coming from the south, ask the driver to let you out closer to the town centre. There are express buses to a variety of destinations, including Udaipur (Rs 180, 10 hours, 10.30 am), Ajmer (Rs 88, five hours), Jaipur (via Fatehpur and Sikar; Rs 115, seven hours), Jodhpur (Rs 85, 5½ hours), Jaisalmer (Rs 110, eight hours), Agra (Rs 199, 11 hours, 5 am) and Delhi (Rs 137, 11 hours) via Jhunjhunu (Rs 75).

Train To Jaipur, there's the *Jaipur-Bikaner Express* (4737/8), departing at 8.30 pm (Rs 113/176/831 general/sleeper/2A class, 11 hours), and the *Intercity Express* (2468/7), leaving Bikaner at 3 pm and arriving in Jaipur at 9.15 pm (Rs 113/348 general/chair class). The *Ranakpur Express* (4707) leaves for Jodhpur at 9.35 am (Rs 70/109/525 general/sleeper/2A class, 5½ hours). To Delhi (Sarai Rohilla station), the *Sarai Rohilla Express* (4790) leaves Bikaner at 8.30 am and arrives in the capital at 7 pm (Rs 104/162/749 general/sleeper/2A class).

Getting Around

An autorickshaw from the train station to the palace should cost Rs 15, but you'll probably be asked for more. Bicycles can be hired at the Dau Cycle Shop, opposite the police station on Station Rd (Rs 2/10 per hour/day for an old bicycle, Rs 3/15 for a new one).

AROUND BIKANER

Deshnok

A visit to the fascinating **Karni Mata Temple** at this village 30km south of Bikaner, is almost worth the trip to Bikaner on its own (see the boxed text 'Temple of Rats').

Temple of Rats

The Karni Mata Temple at Deshnok is one of India's more disconcerting and fascinating temples. According to legend, Karni Mata, an incarnation of Durga, who lived in the 14th century, asked the God of Death, Yama, to restore to life the son of a grieving storyteller. When Yama refused, Karni Mata reincarnated all dead storytellers as rats, in order to deprive Yama of human souls, which were later incarnated as human beings.

The thousands of holy rodents, known as *kabas*, are not for the squeamish. Once you've admired the silver doors and marble carvings donated by Maharaja Ganga Singh, you plunge into the rats' domain, hoping that some will scamper over your feet – most auspicious. Keep your eyes peeled for a rare white rat – it's considered good fortune if you spot one. Eating *prasad* (holy food offering) that has been salivated over by these holy rats is also claimed by believers to bring good luck, although most travellers are willing to take their word for it.

The temple is an important pilgrimage site and what may seem unusual to Western eyes is devoutly believed by pilgrims – this isn't a sideshow but a place of worship.

The temple is open from 4 am to 10 pm daily; there's a Rs 20 camera charge, and Rs 50 for a video. Don't conveniently forget to remove your shoes!

There are at least two buses every hour from Bikaner bus stand to Deshnok (Rs 10, 40 minutes). A slow rickshaw from the train station can be arranged for Rs 100 return, but Rs 150 is more common. A taxi (Rs 250) is better and safer.

Kolayat

This small temple town set around a lake, around 54km south of Bikaner, is occasionally referred to as a mini-Pushkar. It lacks the vibrant character of Pushkar, but is far less touristy. There's a fair here around the same time as the Pushkar Camel Fair (minus the camels and cattle, but with plenty of sadhus). There are many dharamsalas in Kolayat, but many won't accept tourists. One place worth trying is ***Bhaheti Dharamsala***, located on the main ghat by the lakeside. Simple rooms with shared bathroom cost Rs 100.

Every morning at 8.40 am, a special railbus heads for Kolayat. It takes two hours to arrive and costs Rs 11 one way. Buses (Rs 15, one hour) leave much more frequently throughout the day from Bikaner's bus stand or the old bus stand, next to the fort walls.

Gujarat

The west coast state of Gujarat is not one of India's busiest tourist destinations and although it is quite easy to slot Gujarat in between a visit to Mumbai (Bombay) and the cities of Rajasthan, few people pause to explore this interesting state.

Gujarat has always been a major centre for Jains, and some of its most interesting sights are Jain temple centres such as those at Palitana and at Girnar Hill, near Junagadh. The Jains are an influential and energetic group and, as a result, Gujarat is one of India's wealthier and most industrialised states. Gujarat is also the former home of a surprisingly large proportion of India's emigrants – around 40% of the Indians now living in the New York area are Gujaratis and the common Gujarati surname 'Patel' has come to be commonly identified as Indian.

Apart from its Jain temples, Gujarat's major attractions include the last remaining Asiatic lions (in the Gir Forest) and the fascinating Indo-Saracenic architecture of Ahmedabad. For more hedonistic pleasures, there are the pristine beaches at Diu, off Gujarat's southern coast.

Geographically, Gujarat can be divided into three areas. The eastern (mainland) region includes the major cities of Ahmedabad, Surat and Vadodara (Baroda). The Gulf of Cambay divides the mainland strip from the flat, often barren, plains of the Kathiawar peninsula, also known as Saurashtra. The Gulf of Kutch separates Saurashtra from Kutch (Kachchh), which is virtually an island, cut off from the rest of Gujarat to the east and Pakistan to the north by the low-lying *ranns* (deserts) of Kutch.

In January 2001, Gujarat shot to prominence for all the wrong reasons when a massive earthquake caused widespread destruction in the Kutch district and farther afield (see the boxed text 'The Day the Earth Shook' later in this chapter and 'Gujarat's Devastating Earthquake' in the Facts about India chapter).

Gujarat at a Glance

Population: 50.6 million
Area: 196,024 sq km
Capital: Gandhinagar
Main Language: Gujarati
When to Go: Oct to Mar

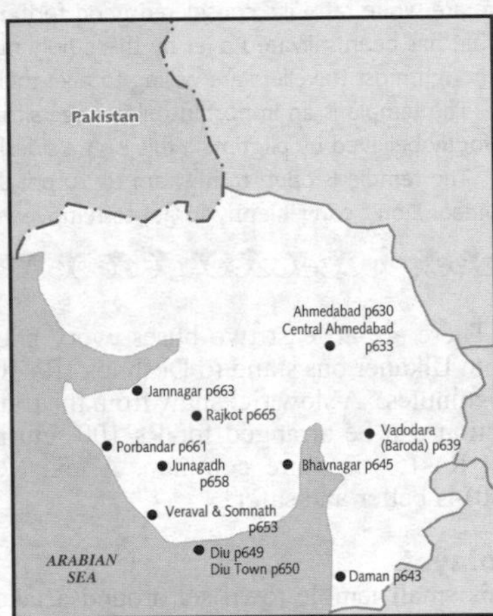

- Kick back in the easy-going little seaside town of Diu
- Visit Sasan Gir Wildlife Sanctuary, home of the last remaining population of the Asiatic lion
- Marvel at Ahmedabad's fascinating Indo-Saracenic architecture
- Climb to the magnificent hilltop temple enclosures of Palitana and Junagadh

History

If you want to go beyond history into the realm of legend, then Gujarat's Temple of Somnath was actually there to witness the creation of the universe. Along the south coast are the sites where many of the great events in Krishna's life took place.

On firmer historic footing, Lothal was the site of a Harappan or Indus Valley civilisation more than 4000 years ago. The main sites of this very ancient culture are now in Pakistan, but it is thought that Lothal may have survived the great cities of the Sindh by as much as 500 years. Gujarat featured in the exploits of the mighty Buddhist emperor, Ashoka, and one of his rock edicts can be seen near Junagadh.

Warning

As a result of the earthquake that hit Gujarat in January 2001, some of the information contained in this chapter may be subject to change. We visited Gujarat just prior to the quake and we have since contacted many hotels, restaurants and other sites in order to establish which ones were affected. Apart from the Kutch district, which was hardest hit, the impact upon tourist infrastructure has been minimal. Nonetheless, many towns throughout Gujarat were affected.

The damage in Ahmedabad was significant – some reports put the number of buildings that collapsed or were seriously damaged at over 300. Damage was, however, largely confined to the newly built residential high-rises in the outlying suburbs. The old city and central Ahmedabad area escaped largely unscathed. Eight out of Ahmedabad's 53 historical monuments sustained some damage, including the Bhadra Fort, Teen Darwaja, Jama Masjid and Raj Babri Mosque. Understandably, these are scheduled to be repaired only after many residential buildings have been reconstructed and the residents rehabilitated. In the meantime, some of these monuments have been cordoned off and access may be restricted until such time as the structures are determined to be safe for visitors.

Some damage was also reported in Rajkot, Jamnagar, Junagadh and Surat although many of the problems were on the outskirts of these towns which remain, thankfully, free of large-scale damage. The Little Rann of Kutch was, due to its low population density, spared great loss of life, although damage was reported in the town of Dhrangadhra. Transport links, primarily those which connect the Kutch districts with the rest of the state, were seriously affected and access to many of these routes is likely to remain restricted for some time. Most rail services elsewhere throughout the state were restored within weeks of the disaster.

Later, Gujarat suffered Muslim incursions from Mahmud of Ghazni and subsequent Mughal rulers, and was a battlefield between the Mughals and the Marathas. It was also an early point of contact with the West; the first British commercial outpost was established at Surat. Daman and Diu survived as Portuguese enclaves within the borders of Gujarat until 1961.

Saurashtra was never incorporated into British India, but survived in the form of more than 200 princely states right up to Independence. In 1956, the states were amalgamated into the state of Mumbai but, in 1960, Mumbai was in turn split, on linguistic grounds, into Maharashtra and Gujarat.

Eastern Gujarat

AHMEDABAD

☎ 079 • pop 5.68 million

Gujarat's principal city is Ahmedabad (also known as Amdavad), one of India's major industrial cities. It's been called the 'Manchester of the East' due to its textile industries and smokestacks. It's a noisy and polluted city and visitors in the hot season should bear in mind the derisive title given to Ahmedabad by the Mughal emperor, Jehangir: Gardabad, the City of Dust. Relief Rd gets our vote as one of the most polluted, congested and thoroughly chaotic strips of barely controlled mayhem in the country.

Nevertheless, this infrequently visited city has a number of attractions for travellers, with some excellent museums and the Sabarmati (Gandhi's) Ashram. It is also one of the best places to study the rich blend of Hindu and Islamic architectural styles known as Indo-Saracenic. If you're arriving from Rajasthan, you'll enjoy the fact that few of the smiles and greetings have an ulterior motive.

Makar Sakranti (13 to 15 January) is the time to see an extravaganza of kite flying in what has become an international festival.

History

Over the centuries Ahmedabad has had periods of grandeur and of decline. Founded in 1411 by Ahmed Shah, in the 17th century it was thought to be one of the finest cities in India. In 1615, the noted English ambassador, Sir Thomas Roe, judged it to be 'a goodly city, as large as London', but by the 18th century its influence had waned. Its industrial strength once again raised the city to prominence, and from 1915 it became famous as the site of Gandhi's ashram.

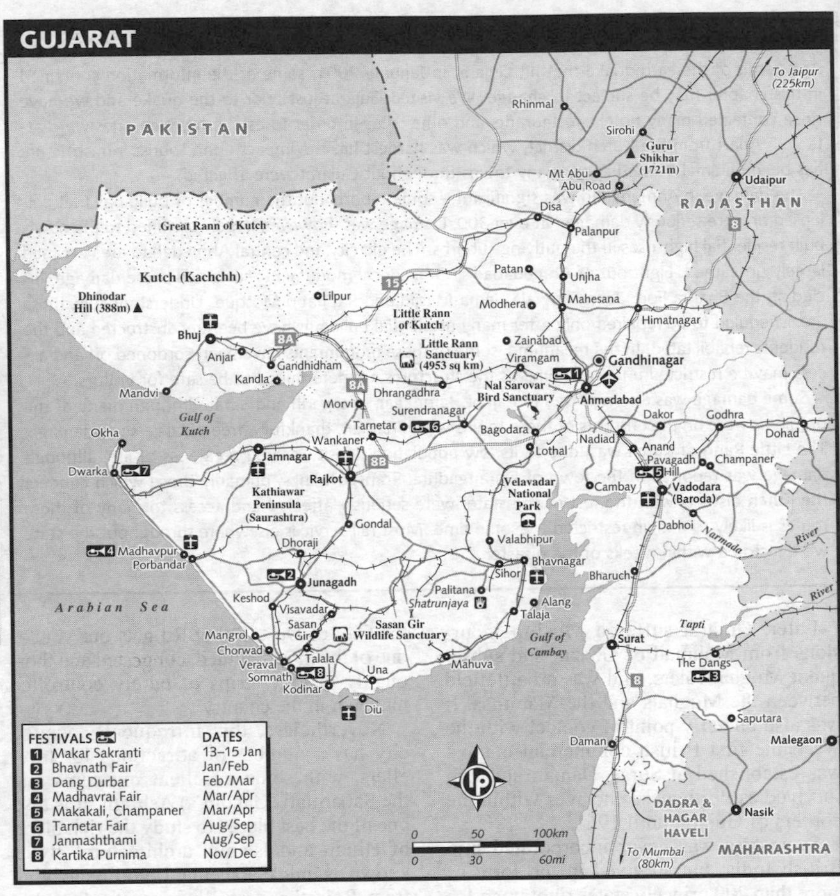

Orientation

The city straddles the Sabarmati River, which dries to a mere trickle in the hot season. On the eastern bank two main roads run east from the river to the train station, about 3km away. They are Mahatma Gandhi Rd and Relief Rd. The busy road flanking the western bank of the Sabarmati is universally known as Ashram Rd. This is the main road to the Sabarmati Ashram. The airport is off to the north-east of the city. Virtually all the old city walls are now demolished, but some of the gates remain.

Information

Tourist Offices The helpful state tourist office, Gujarat Tourism (☎ 6589172, fax 6582183, ⓔ ahmedabad@gujarattourism.com), is in a laneway just off Ashram Rd, across the river from the town centre. Ask rickshaw drivers for HK House or the BATA showroom (a more commonly known landmark). Opening hours are 10.30 am to 1.30 pm and 2 to 6 pm (closed Sunday and the second and fourth Saturday in the month). If you're there between 11 am and 1 pm Monday to Friday, ask for Professor H Pradhan, the Senior Tourist Officer, who is particularly friendly and a mine of information. The office has good brochures and maps of Ahmedabad and Gujarat state, and can also arrange car hire and tours. The latter might be worthwhile if your time in Gujarat is limited to fast-paced five-day tours to Saurashtra (Rs 2100) and northern Gujarat/southern

Rajasthan (Rs 2300). The quoted prices include all transportation, accommodation and guide fees.

Check out their excellent Web site at www.gujarattourism.com.

Money The State Bank of India branch (first floor) near Lal Darwaja (the local bus stand) and the Bank of Baroda, at the west end of Relief Rd, have money-changing facilities. For quicker money-changing, try either Green Channel Travel Services (☎ 6560489) – the local representatives for American Express – or Wall Street Finances (☎ 6426682), both on CG Rd, close to Mirch Masala Restaurant. The Bank of Baroda on Ashram Rd can give cash advances on Visa cards, while the HDFC ATM on Ashram Rd services Visa, MasterCard and Cirrus.

Post & Communications The main post office is central, just off Relief Rd. The central telegraph office is just south of Sidi Saiyad's Mosque.

Email & Internet Access The best connections are at Interscape Cyber Cafe (☎ 6404131, fax 6404134, ⓔ espey@interscapeworld.com) which is open 24 hours. It's on the first floor of the large white building, opposite the Standard Chartered Grindlays Bank on Panchwati Circle; it costs Rs 30 per hour. Another good option is itbaag.com Cyber Cafe (☎ 6585873, ⓔ itbaag@itbaag.com), close to the tourist office; Rs 25 per hour. On the east side of the river, try the private telephone office (☎ 5507498), 20m north of the Advance Cinema on the opposite side of the street; Rs 60 per hour.

Bookshops Crossword, in the Shree Krishna complex at Mithakali Six Rd, has a wide range of books, plus CDs, maps and a coffee shop. It's open from 10.30 am to 8.30 pm daily.

Medical Services & Emergency The Civil Hospital (☎ 2123721) is around 2.5km north of the Ahmedabad train station. For an ambulance call ☎ 102.

Bhadra Fort & Teen Darwaja

Bhadra Fort was built by the city's founder, Ahmed Shah, in 1411 and later named after the goddess Bhadra, an incarnation of Kali. It now houses government offices, where you can ask for access to the roof for views of the surrounding streets. There is a post office in the former Palace of Azam Khan, within the fort. Some of the bastions inside the fort fell during the recent earthquake, although the overall structure remains intact. To the east of the fort stands the Teen Darwaja (triple gateway), from which sultans watched processions from the palace to the Jama Masjid. It, too, was damaged by the tremors – at least one of the balconies collapsed.

Mosques & Mausoleums

The **Jama Masjid**, built in 1423 by Ahmed Shah, is beside Mahatma Gandhi Rd, to the east of the Teen Darwaja. Although 260 columns support the roof, the two 'shaking' minarets lost half their height in the great earthquake of 1819, and another tremor in 1957 completed their demolition. Sadly, the earthquake of 2001 also took its toll with significant cracks appearing in the domes and pillars. Much of the mosque was built using items salvaged from demolished Hindu and Jain temples.

The **Tomb of Ahmed Shah** stands just outside the east gate of the Jama Masjid. It was built shortly after his death in 1442. His son and grandson also have their cenotaphs in this tomb. Women are not allowed into the central chamber. Across the street on a raised platform is the tomb of his queens, which is now a market and is in very poor shape compared to his own tomb.

Dating from 1414, **Ahmed Shah's Mosque** was one of the earliest mosques in the city and was probably built on the site of a Hindu temple. It is to the south-west of the Bhadra Fort. The front of the mosque is now a garden.

Sidi Saiyad's Mosque is close to the river end of Relief Rd. It was constructed in 1573 by Sidi Saiyad, a slave of Ahmed Shah, and has beautiful carved stone windows depicting the intricate intertwining of the branches of a tree. These can be viewed from outside (women can't enter).

A little north of the city centre, **Rani Rupmati's Mosque** was built between 1430 and 1440 and was named after the sultan's Hindu wife. The minarets were partially brought down by the great earthquake of 1819. Note the way the dome is elevated to

GUJARAT

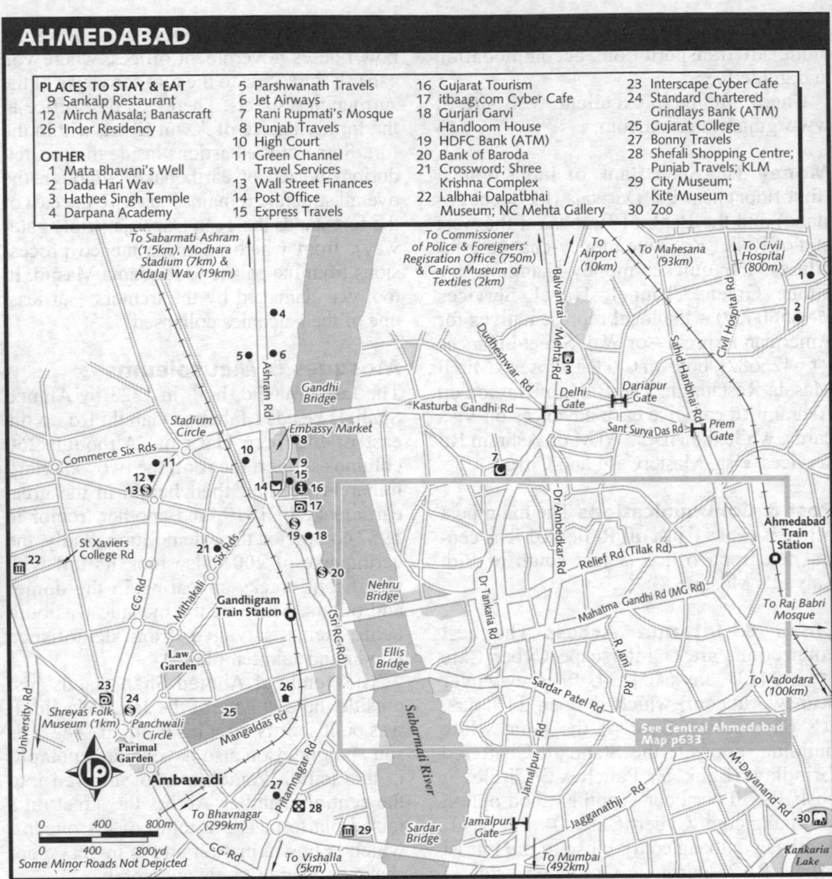

allow light in around its base. As with so many of Ahmedabad's early mosques, this one displays elements of both Hindu and Islamic design.

The small **Rani Sipri's Mosque**, southeast of the city, is also known as the Masjid-e-Nagira (Jewel of a Mosque) because of its extremely graceful and well-executed design. Its slender minarets again blend Hindu and Islamic styles. The mosque is said to have been commissioned in 1514 by a wife of Sultan Mahmud Begada after the latter executed their son for some minor misdemeanour – she is also buried here.

Just south of the train station, outside the Sarangpur Gate, the **Sidi Bashir Mosque** is famed for its *jhulta minars* or **shaking minarets**. It was believed that they were built to shake in order to protect against earthquake damage.

This technique didn't save the shaking minarets of the **Raj Babri Mosque**, southeast of the train station in the suburb of Gomtipur. One was partially dismantled by an inquisitive Englishman in an unsuccessful attempt to find out how it worked. They were rebuilt only to collapse again in January 2001 when the tremors proved too much. Undaunted, the city authorities are planning to rebuild the minarets.

Temples

Just outside the Delhi Gate, to the north of the old city, the **Hathee Singh Temple**, as with so many Jain temples, is made of white marble. Built in 1848, it is dedicated to

Dharamanath, the 15th Jain *tirthankar* (teacher).

For a complete change, you could plunge into the narrow streets of the old part of town and seek out the brightly painted, wood-carved **Swami Narayan Temple**. Enclosed in a large courtyard, it dates from 1850.

Baolis

Baolis (Step-wells) are strange constructions that are unique to northern India, and **Dada Hari Wav** is one of the best. Built in 1501 by a woman of Sultan Begara's harem, it has a series of steps leading down to lower platforms terminating at a small, octagonal well. The depths of the well are cool, even on the hottest day, and it must once have been quite beautiful. Today, it is completely neglected and often bone dry, but it's a fascinatingly eerie place with galleries above the well and a small portico at ground level.

The best time to visit and photograph the well is between 10 and 11 am; at other times the sun doesn't penetrate to the various levels. Entry is free. Bus No 111 (Rs 2.50) to Asarwa goes nearby.

Mata Bhavani's Well is about 200m north of Dada Hari's. Ask children to show you the way. Thought to be several hundred years older, it is much less ornate and is now used as a simple Hindu temple.

Museums

The **City Museum** (☎ 6578369), just west of the Sardar Bridge, is a well-organised exhibition of all aspects of Ahmedabad's history with sections on each of the city's religious communities, Gujarati literature and the independence struggle. There are some fine photos, examples of local contemporary art as well as beautiful textiles and carvings. This excellent museum is open 11 am to 8 pm Tuesday to Sunday and entrance is free. On the ground floor is the **Kite Museum** (which has the same opening hours and is also free).

The **Calico Museum of Textiles** (☎ 786 8172) exhibits antique and modern textiles including rare tapestries, wall hangings and costumes. Also on display are various old weaving machines. The museum is in Sarabhai House, a former *haveli* (mansion), in the Shahi Bagh Gardens, about 4.5km north of the city. You can only enter on one of the free guided tours which depart at 10.30 am and 2.45 pm. The museum is closed on Wednesday and photography is not allowed. To get there, take bus No 101, 102 or 105 (Rs 3) out through the Delhi Gate. An autorickshaw should cost Rs 30.

The **Lalbhai Dalpatbhai Museum** (☎ 6306883), on University Rd near Gujarat University, houses a fine collection of stone, marble and wood carvings from around India, bronzes, cloth paintings and coins. Among the sculptures is the oldest-known carved image of the God, Rama, a sandstone carving from Madhya Pradesh dating from the 6th century AD.

On the same campus is the **NC Mehta Gallery** (☎ 6302463, ext 31) which contains an important collection of illustrated manuscripts and miniatures from all over the country. It is particularly known for its *Chaurapanchasika* (the Fifty Love Lyrics of a Thief). These are attributed to Vilhana, an 11th-century Kashmiri poet who was sentenced to hang for loving the king's daughter. Just before his execution he composed the poems and so impressed the king that he gave his daughter to Vilhana in marriage. There are also some Rajasthani miniatures from the Mewar, Bundi, Kota and Bikaner schools. Both museums are free and open from 10.30 am to 5.30 pm (closed Monday). In summer, the hours are sometimes changed to 8 am to 1 pm, so ring before heading out there.

The **Shreyas Folk Museum**, about 2.5km west of the Sabarmati River in the suburb of Ambavadi, displays the folk arts and crafts of Gujarat, particularly textiles and clothing. It's open 9 am to noon and 3 to 5 pm Thursday to Tuesday. Take bus No 34 or 200 (Rs 3).

Sabarmati Ashram

About 5km from the centre of town, on the west bank of the Sabarmati River, this ashram (also known as Satyagraha Ashram) was Gandhi's headquarters during the long struggle for Indian independence. The ashram was founded in 1915 and moved to its current site a few years later. It was from here, on 12 March 1930, that Gandhi set out on his famous Salt March to the Gulf of Cambay in protest against government monopolies over the production and sale of salt, vowing not to return to the ashram until

India was free. Handicrafts, handmade paper and spinning wheels are still produced on the site. Gandhi's spartan living quarters are preserved as a small museum, and there's an excellent pictorial record of the major events in his life. There is also a bookshop selling books by and about the Mahatma and the library contains the letter sent by Gandhiji to Hitler on 23 July 1939 asking him to pull back from war.

The ashram is open from 8.30 am to 6 pm (to 7 pm between April and September). Admission is free. There is a sound-and-light show (65 min, Rs 5) at 7 pm (in Gujarati; daily) and 8.30 pm (in English on Sunday, Wednesday and Friday; in Hindi on other nights). The booking office (☎ 7556073) opens from 2 pm. Bus No 81, 83/1 or 84/1 (Rs 3) will take you there. An autorickshaw will cost about Rs 25.

Organised Tours

The Municipal Corporation (mobile ☎ 982 4032866) runs Heritage Walking Tours (Rs 25) through the old city every day. They start from the Swami Narayan Temple at 8 am and finish near the Jama Masjid around 10.30 am. There's no need to book; simply turn up a little before the appointed time. Some travellers have recommended the tours as an excellent way to get a feel for the city. Commentaries are given in English and there's sometimes a brief slide show before commencement. Brochures are available from Gujarat Tourism (see Information earlier in this chapter).

Places to Stay

Lots of cheap hotels are scattered along or close to Relief Rd. The real cheapies are opposite the train station, but most are assailed by Ahmedabad's horrendous noise and air pollution. The area around Sidi Saiyad's Mosque at the western end of Relief Rd is better, although it's still far from serene. Many hotels have 24-hour checkout although some top-end hotels have a stingy 9 am checkout. Except in the very cheapest hotels you can expect a 15% luxury tax to be added to your accommodation bill. In top-end places this can soar to 30%.

Places to Stay – Budget

A-One Hotel *(☎ 2149823)* is opposite the train station. The owner's claims to 'luxuriously furnished rooms' are decidedly ambitious. Basic singles/doubles go for Rs 90/140 without private bathroom or Rs 175/250 with cold water shower. The manager dismissed questions about hot water with the words, 'Ahmedabad is a very hot city'. He has a point.

Hotel Naigra *(☎ 384977)*, just off Relief Rd, has fairly quiet but cramped rooms which are airless and a little grubby. A single with shared bathroom goes for Rs 100 while a room with private bathroom costs Rs 160/180. Bucket hot water is available.

Hotel Roopalee Guest House *(☎ 5503135, Dr Tankaria Rd)*, near Sidi Saiyad's Mosque, is not a bad choice. Simple but pleasant and clean rooms with bucket hot water and TV cost Rs 150/200, or there's a dorm for Rs 55. The staff are friendly and a number of travellers have given this place the thumbs up.

Hotel Gulmarg *(☎ 5507202)*, across the alley, has a range of rooms from Rs 150/250, also with TV and hot water. It's a long climb up to the fifth floor if the lift isn't working, which is often.

Hotel Natraj *(☎ 5506048)*, near Lal Darwaja, is marginally better. Rooms cost Rs 130/ 220/300 for a basic single/double/triple with bathroom but no shower – bucket hot water is available in the morning. Some rooms have a balcony overlooking the pleasant gardens of Ahmed Shah's Mosque.

Hotel Sahil *(☎ 5507351)*, opposite the advance cinema near Lal Darwaja, is good value for a few more rupees. Rooms start at Rs 200/270, and for Rs 250/325 you get a deluxe double with fan, satellite TV, bathroom (geyser hot water) and squat toilet. Some rooms are better than others.

Hotel Mukam *(☎ 5509080, Khanpur Rd)*, near the Nehru Bridge, is also good value in the upper-budget range. Decent rooms with satellite TV start at Rs 275/370, though you'll pay more for air-con.

Places to Stay – Mid-Range

Hotel Serena *(☎ 5510136, Dr Tankaria Rd)*, not far from Sidi Saiyad's Mosque, is probably the best-value mid-range option. Pleasant, clean and modern rooms start at Rs 325/450 (children below 12 are free). There's an excellent restaurant.

The cluster of hotels close to the intersection of Relief and Dr Tankaria Rds all have

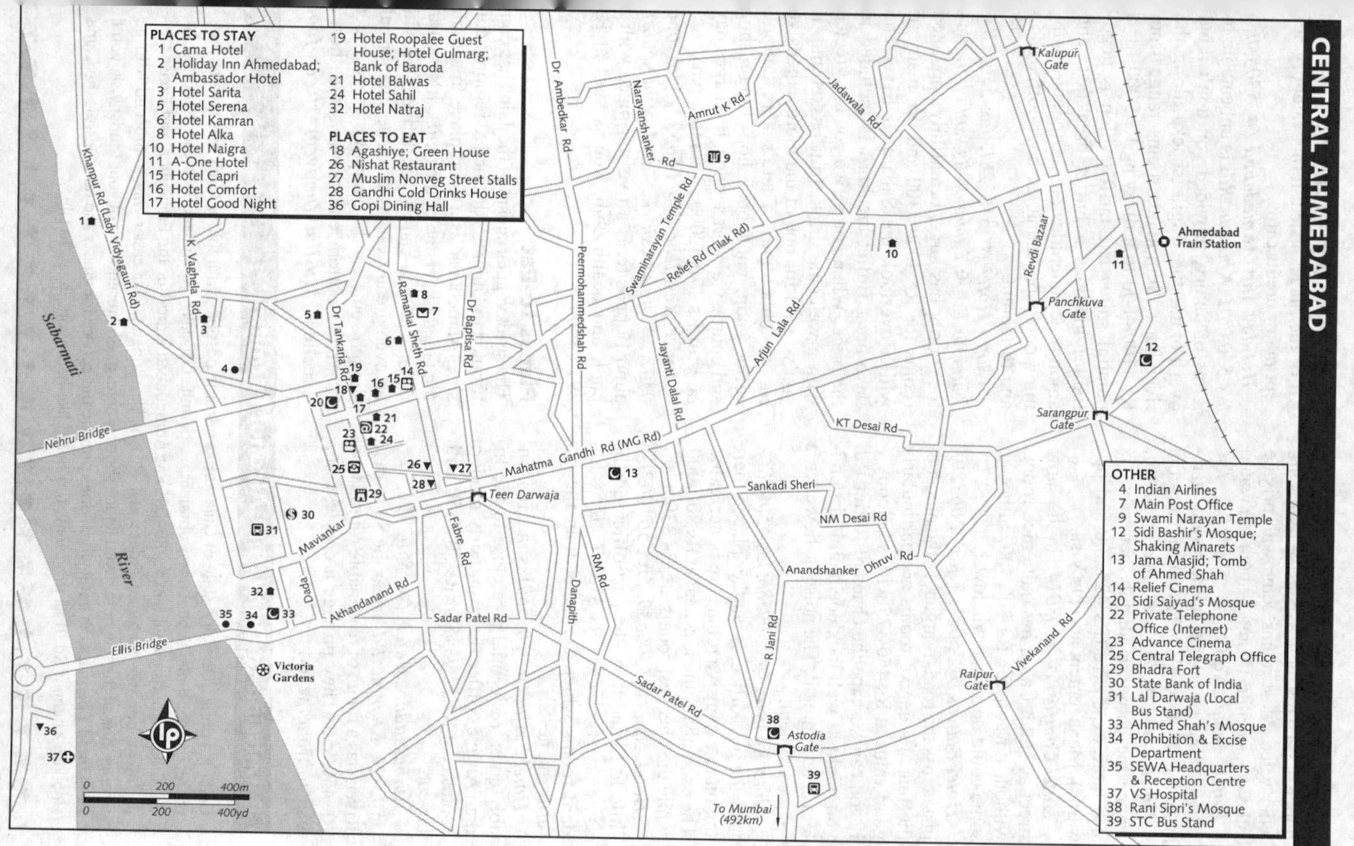
CENTRAL AHMEDABAD
PLACES TO STAY
1 Cama Hotel
2 Holiday Inn Ahmedabad; Ambassador Hotel
3 Hotel Sarita
5 Hotel Serena
6 Hotel Kamran
8 Hotel Alka
10 Hotel Naigra
11 A-One Hotel
15 Hotel Capri
16 Hotel Comfort
17 Hotel Good Night
19 Hotel Roopalee Guest House; Hotel Gulmarg; Bank of Baroda
21 Hotel Balwas
24 Hotel Sahil
32 Hotel Natraj
PLACES TO EAT
18 Agashiye; Green House
26 Nishat Restaurant
27 Muslim Nonveg Street Stalls
28 Gandhi Cold Drinks House
36 Gopi Dining Hall
OTHER
4 Indian Airlines
7 Main Post Office
9 Swami Narayan Temple
12 Sidi Bashir's Mosque; Shaking Minarets
13 Jama Masjid; Tomb of Ahmed Shah
14 Relief Cinema
20 Sidi Saiyad's Mosque
22 Private Telephone Office (Internet)
23 Advance Cinema
25 Central Telegraph Office
29 Bhadra Fort
30 State Bank of India
31 Lal Darwaja (Local Bus Stand)
33 Ahmed Shah's Mosque
34 Prohibition & Excise Department
35 SEWA Headquarters & Reception Centre
37 VS Hospital
38 Rani Sipri's Mosque
39 STC Bus Stand
Kalupur Gate
Ahmedabad Train Station
Panchkuva Gate
Revdi Bazaar
Sarangpur Gate
Raipur Gate
Astodia Gate
Teen Darwaja
Jadawala Rd
Amrut K Rd
Narayanshanker Rd
Swaminarayan Temple Rd
Relief Rd (Tilak Rd)
Arjun Lala Rd
KT Desai Rd
Jayanti Dalal Rd
Mahatma Gandhi Rd (MG Rd)
Sankadi Sheri
NM Desai Rd
Anandshanker Dhruv Rd
R Jani Rd
Vivekanand Rd
Sadar Patel Rd
RM Rd
Danapith
Peermohammedshah Rd
Dr Ambedkar Rd
Dr Baptisa Rd
Ramanlal Sheth Rd
Dr Tankaria Rd
Fabre Rd
Mavlankar
Dada
Akhandanand Rd
K Vaghela Rd
Khanpur Rd (Lady Vidyagauri Rd)
Nehru Bridge
Ellis Bridge
Victoria Gardens
Sabarmati River
To Mumbai (492km)
0 200 400m
0 200 400yd
GUJARAT

modern, clean and comfortable rooms, although at each the more expensive rooms are better value. Most rooms come with private bathroom, satellite TV and 24-hour hot water.

Hotel Good Night *(☎ 5507181, fax 5506998)* has somewhat sterile rooms starting at Rs 325/450 or Rs 475/600 with air-con.

Hotel Capri *(☎ 5507143, fax 5506646)*, around the corner, is slightly better but is also more expensive (Rs 425/500 and upwards). Management accepts Visa.

Hotel Comfort *(☎ 5503014)*, in the same street as Hotel Capri, has quite nice rooms without air-con for Rs 300/400, although some could do with a window.

Hotel Balwas *(☎ 5507135, fax 5506320)*, just across the road, is arguably the nicest of the four. Its deluxe rooms are particularly good value at Rs 450/575 with a balcony – if you can't escape the chaos of Relief Rd, you might as well look down on it for endless entertainment. The noise is, however, a major problem.

Hotel Kamran *(☎ 5509586, fax 5509586)*, near the post office, is another place where the more expensive rooms are better value. The executive suite is a steal at Rs 800/900, while the cheapest rooms are Rs 330/440.

Hotel Alka *(☎ 5500830, fax 5501002)*, a little to the north of the post office on the same street, charges Rs 375/475 for standard rooms which are better than the exterior suggests.

Hotel Sarita *(☎ 5501569)* is in a reasonably quiet, residential area close to the Indian Airlines office. Largish, fairly modern rooms cost Rs 325/375 or Rs 500/550 with air-con.

Ambassador Hotel *(☎ 5502490, fax 5502327, Khanpur Rd,)*, near the Sabarmati River, has a range of reasonable rooms from Rs 450/550. They provide a courtesy service to/from the airport.

Places to Stay – Top End

All of the places listed in this category accept major credit cards.

Holiday Inn Ahmedabad *(☎ 5505505, fax 5505501, Khanpur Rd)* is unbeatable in terms of luxury, provided you don't mind overlooking the fragile shacks along the river bank. Sumptuous rooms range from Rs 4100/4800 to a dizzying Rs 9000 for a palatial suite. The tariff (which is negotiable) includes a buffet breakfast, and among the amenities are an indoor swimming pool, spa, sauna, 24-hour coffee shop and restaurant.

Cama Hotel *(☎ 5505281, fax 5505285, Khanpur Rd,* e *camahotel@vsnl.com)*, farther north, has large, beautifully appointed rooms for Rs 3000/3300 and up, many of which overlook the Sabarmati River and lawn area. Buffet breakfast is included in the price. When you arrive you are greeted with a welcome drink, fruit basket and, if you've paid for one of the more expensive rooms, chocolates. There's a restaurant, coffee shop, pool, bookshop, liquor shop and courtesy airport service. It charges day rates of Rs 1700/2000 (9 am to 6 pm).

Inder Residency *(☎ 6565222, fax 656 0407,* e *inderresidency@ad1.vsnl.net.in)*, almost opposite, is a five-star place with a pool, and health club. Rooms start at Rs 2970/3600.

Places to Eat

The strict vegetarianism of the Jains has contributed to Gujarat's distinctive regional cuisine. Ahmedabad is a good place to sample the Gujarati version of the *thali* – it's the traditional all-you-can-eat vegetarian meal with an even greater variety of dishes than usual, though some can be overpoweringly sweet.

At the bottom end of the scale there's excellent ***Muslim (nonveg) street food***

Permission to Drink, Sir? Alcohol Permits

Getting a drink in the 'dry' state of Gujarat has become possible, with thirsty foreigners able to purchase and consume alcohol upon obtaining a permit. Officially, you'll need to present yourself to the Gujarat Tourism counter (☎ 2854095) at Ahmedabad airport or the Prohibition and Excise Department, opposite Victoria Gardens just east of Ellis Bridge. A far easier way to proceed is to go through one of the few hotels with liquor shops where, upon presentation of your tourist visa, you'll be granted a permit. One hotel which does provide this service for guests and nonguests is the Cama Hotel on Khanpur Rd. If all this seems too much like hard work, head to Diu.

available near Teen Darwaja on Bhathiyar Gali, a small street which runs parallel to Gandhi Rd. Stalls set up each evening and for around Rs 25 you can get a good feed. There are halal meat, fish and vegetarian dishes to choose from.

Nishat Restaurant *(☎ 5507335, Khas Bazaar)*, in the same area, is a friendly place which serves good tandoori dishes for under Rs 40 (save for a full chicken which costs Rs 72).

Gandhi Cold Drinks House, across the lane, is a popular spot with locals for a lassi or ice cream.

Gopi Dining Hall, just off the west end of Ellis Bridge, near VS Hospital, is one of the most popular thali places. Excellent all-you-can-eat Gujarati thalis are Rs 45 (lunch) or Rs 55 (dinner).

Sankalp Restaurant *(☎ 6583550)*, off Ashram Rd in the Embassy Market area, is worth a visit. This air-con restaurant boasts one of the longest dosas in India – 4 foot long! (Rs 400). The Rs 40 South Indian thalis also make a pleasant change from the sweet Gujarati cuisine.

Agashiye *(☎ 5506946, fax 5506535, e vcvl@vsnl.com, Dr Tankaria St)*, opposite Sidi Saiyad's Mosque, is one of Ahmedabad's best dining experiences right in the centre of town. Set atop one of the city's finest mansions (dating from the early 20th century), the lovely terrace area has faultless service and daily banquets for lunch (Rs 135, noon to 2.30 pm) and dinner (Rs 170, 7 to 11 pm). The dinner menu, which changes every day, includes introductory fruit juices, entrees, a multitude of veg main dishes, sweets and ice cream. It's a great place to sample quality Gujarati cuisine and pretend you're not really in one of India's most congested cities. Get there while you can – sadly the building is under threat of demolition by the municipal authorities, competing with the owner's plans to set up a Heritage Hotel and Internet cafe.

Green House, on the same property at street level in a covered garden, is of a similarly high standard, although it only serves snacks (11 am to 11 pm). The Coconut Coriander Tikka (Rs 35) is a sensation and the pineapple lassies are also good (Rs 35). You'll need to duck for cover whenever they turn the sprinklers on, although in summer it may just add to the attraction.

Vishalla, on the southern edge of town in Vasana, is a 'theme' dining experience that evokes the atmosphere of a Gujarati village. You eat in Indian fashion, seated on the floor in rustic wooden huts, and within the complex there are craft stalls, a puppet display and a utensils museum. Lunch (11 am to 2 pm) costs Rs 125; dinner (7.30 to 11 pm) is Rs 190 and is accompanied by music and dance performances. The veg-only food is a set all-you-can-eat meal, though dessert costs extra. Bus No 31 will get you within walking distance; an autorickshaw from the centre of town will cost Rs 30, but expect to pay about Rs 50 for the return trip.

Mirch Masala *(CG Rd)* also evokes a Gujarati village, this time with the aid of colourful murals. Although its a la carte menu is good for dinner (Rs 75 and up), the veg/nonveg lunch specials (Rs 85/125) are brilliant value. For your money, you get a salad, pappadams, five main dishes (if you're on your own it's quite a meal!), ice cream, sweets and as much buttermilk (definitely an acquired taste) as you can drink. It all happens from noon to 3.30 pm and the friendly staff accept Visa and MasterCard. It's something of an Ahmedabad institution, so you may have to queue.

Shopping

On Ashram Rd, just to the south of the tourist office, is the Gujarat state crafts

Things to Buy

With its busy, modern textile works, it's not surprising that Gujarat offers a number of interesting buys in this line. Extremely fine, and often extremely expensive, Patola silk saris are still made by a handful of master craftspeople in Patan. From Surat comes the *zari*, or gold-thread embroidery work. Surat is also a centre for silk saris. Less opulent, but still beautiful, are the block prints of Ahmedabad.

Jamnagar is famous for its tie-dye work, which you'll see throughout Saurashtra. Brightly coloured embroideries and beadwork are also found in Saurashtra, along with woollen shawls, blankets and rugs. Brass-covered wooden chests are manufactured in Bhavnagar, and Kutch is the centre for exquisite, fine embroidery, often with mirrorwork.

GUJARAT

emporium, Gurjari (☎ 6589505). The Garvi Handloom House is around the back. For hand-printed fabrics and other textiles, the Self-Employed Women's Association (SEWA; see the 'SEWA' boxed text) has a retail outlet called Banascraft (☎ 405784, ⓔ bdmsa@ad1.vsnl.net.in) at 8 Chandan Complex, above Mirch Masala Restaurant. Check out the Web site at www.banascraft.org.

Getting There & Away

The Ahmedabad edition of the *Times of India* has up-to-the-minute flight and rail information on page two.

Air Ahmedabad airport has international and domestic services. Many travel agents handle domestic and international bookings. Two recommended places are Parshwanath Travels (☎ 7544142, fax 7544144, ⓔ parshtrvl@ wilnetonline.net), almost opposite the Jet Airways office on Ashram Rd, and Express Travels (☎ 6588602, fax 6582533, ⓔ express@wilnetonline.net), around the corner from Gujarat Tourism. Both places accept all major credit cards.

International Air India (☎ 6585644), Premchand House, near the High Court building on Ashram Rd, has flights to New York (five per week) and on to Chicago (twice a week) via Mumbai and London. The one-way/return fare to the USA is Rs 27,000/40,000 while as far as London is Rs 22,000/31,000.

Indian Airlines (☎ 5503061; airport office ☎ 2869233) is on Relief Rd, near the Nehru Bridge. It has twice weekly flights to Sharjah (Rs 10,300/18,700 one way/return) and Kuwait (Rs 12,500/22,700), and flies three times a week to Muscat (Rs 10,300/18,700). Some of these Indian Airlines flights connect with KLM and British Airways for flights on to Europe.

Domestic Indian Airlines flies regularly to Chennai (Madras; US$235) via Mumbai (US$75; connections to Goa twice a week), Delhi (US$120), Kolkata (Calcutta; US$205) and Jaipur (US$95).

Jet Airways (☎ 7543304), Ashram Rd, has daily flights to Mumbai (US$75) and Delhi (US$120).

Bus STC (☎ 2144764) buses travel from the bus stand near Rani Sipri's Mosque to, among other places, Vadodara (Rs 45/52 for standard/semideluxe, 2½ hours), Palitana (Rs 68/77, five hours), Jamnagar (Rs 95/101, eight hours), Bhavnagar (Rs 65/74, four hours) and Rajkot (Rs 122 semideluxe only, 6½ hours).

If you're travelling long distances, private buses are a more expensive but much quicker alternative; many of their offices are just east

SEWA

The Self-Employed Women's Association (SEWA), is Gujarat's single largest union, comprising 215,000 members in India and 148,000 in Gujarat alone. Established in 1972, SEWA identifies three types of self-employed workers: hawkers and vendors; home-based workers such as weavers, potters and *bidi* (hand-made cigarette) rollers; and manual labourers and service providers such as agricultural labourers, contract labourers, construction workers, and laundry and domestic workers.

Adhering to a Gandhian philosophy of change through nonviolent means, SEWA aims to enable women to actively participate in the mainstream economy and to attain empowerment and self-reliance through financial autonomy. SEWA assists self-employed workers to organise into unions and cooperatives, so that they can ultimately control the fruits of their own labours. SEWA's focus is on areas such as health and childcare, literacy, appropriate housing and self-sufficiency, and the SEWA Academy conducts leadership training courses for its members. SEWA is also active in the campaign for a needs-based minimum wage of Rs 125 per day. Membership costs Rs 5 per annum.

SEWA has also set up a bank, giving many poor women their first access to a savings or lending body, since conventional banks are often unwilling to deal with people of such limited means.

The SEWA Reception Centre (☎ 079-5506444, fax 5506446, ⓔ sewamahila@wilnetonline.net) is at the eastern end of Ellis Bridge, opposite Victoria Gardens. They have a range of literature and visitors are welcome (open 10 am to 8 pm Monday to Saturday).

Major Trains from Ahmedabad

destination	train No & name	departures	distance (km)	approx duration (hrs)	fare (Rs)
Bhavnagar	9910 *Shetrunji Exp*	5.10 pm	299	5½	73/231 ◆
Delhi	9105 *Delhi Mail*	10.00 am	938	19¼	261/761 †
Dwarka	9005 *Saurashtra Mail*	6.15 am	453	10	162/468 †
Gandhidham	9031 *Kutch Exp*	2.00 am	300	6½	114/329 †
Mumbai	2902 *Gujarat Mail*	10.00 pm	492	8¾	166/482 †
Udaipur	9944 *Sarai Rohila Exp*	11.00 pm	297	9	114/329 †
Vadodara (Baroda)	2010 *Shatabdi Exp*	2.45 pm	100	1½	230/455 *

* Executive/Chair class ◆ General/Chair class † Sleeper/Air-con 3-tier sleeper

of the STC bus stand. Punjab Travels (☎ 6589200), Embassy Market, just off Ashram Rd near Gujarat Tourism, has a number of intercity services, including Ajmer (Rs 220, 13 hours), Aurangabad (Rs 300, 15 hours), Jaipur (Rs 250, 16 hours), Jodhpur (Rs 200, 15 hours), Mt Abu (Rs 140, seven hours) and Udaipur (Rs 100, eight hours). They have another office on Pritamnagar Rd in the Shefali Shopping Centre. Bonny Travels (☎ 6579265) in Pritamnagar Rd serves Jamnagar (Rs 120) and Rajkot (Rs 90) many times throughout the day.

Gujarat – by Rail & in Style

If you want to explore Gujarat quickly and in luxury, you should consider *The Royal Orient*, a special tourist train service which visits various Gujarati and Rajasthani destinations. Run by the Tourism Corporation of Gujarat and Indian Railways, it's a similar concept to the luxurious RTDC *Palace On Wheels* train that tours Rajasthan.

The eight-day trip leaves Delhi on Wednesday and travels to Chittorgarh, Udaipur, Junagadh, Veraval, Sasan Gir, Delwada, Palitana, Sarkhej, Ahmedabad and Jaipur.

Rates per person per day are US$175 in a three-berth cabin or US$200 in a two-berth cabin. Children between five and 12 years are half-price (free for kids under five), and all fares are reduced by 25% in April and September. Prices include tours, entry fees, accommodation on the train plus all meals. Bookings must be made in advance at Gujarat Tourism (see Information earlier this chapter), or via India-specialist travel agents worldwide.

Train There is a computerised booking office (☎ 135) to the left as you exit Ahmedabad train station. It's open 8 am to 8 pm Monday to Saturday, 8 am to 2 pm Sunday. Window No 6 handles the foreign-tourist quota, and you could try booking tickets with your credit card at Window No 7. Please note that all train prices do not include the Rs 20/25 reservation charge levied by Indian Railways on sleeper or three- or two-tiered air-con (2A or 3A) berths.

Getting Around

To/From the Airport The airport is 10km north of town; an autorickshaw costs about Rs 90. A cheaper option is a local bus from Lal Darwaja (Rs 5, bus No 102 or 105).

Autorickshaw Most autorickshaw drivers are willing to use the meter (it's the dial by their left knee); make sure they set it to zero at the outset. Travelling from Ahmedabad train station to Sidi Saiyad's Mosque costs about Rs 10, though drivers will sometimes quote much more, especially from the station.

Local buses depart from Lal Darwaja. Details of the routes, destinations and fares are all posted in Gujarati.

AROUND AHMEDABAD

Adalaj Wav

Nineteen kilometres north of Ahmedabad, Adalaj Wav is one of the finest of the Gujarati *baolis* (step wells), with carvings depicting intricate motifs of flowers and birds. The main corridor has four pavilions and the well is five storeys deep, each decorated with exquisite stone carvings. Built by Queen Rudabai in 1499 it provided a cool and secluded retreat during the hot summer

GUJARAT

months. The Ahmedabad-Gandhinagar bus will get you within walking distance (ask the conductor where to get off).

Nal Sarovar Bird Sanctuary

Between November and February, this 116 sq km lake, 60km south-west of Ahmedabad, is home to flocks of indigenous and migratory birds with as many as 250 species of bird passing through the park. Ducks, geese, pelicans and flamingos are best seen early in the morning and in the evening. One visitor has the following advice:

> You can hire a boat on Nal Sarovar with someone to punt you to the areas where the flamingos and pelicans are; but please avoid going too close and try to restrain the boatman from scaring the birds, as this causes them to fly away. One of the main reasons for the decline in population of some birds is excessive human disturbance. If possible, avoid weekends and holidays when it gets quite crowded.
>
> **Krys Kazmierczak, UK**

The sanctuary is most easily visited as a day excursion by taxi from Ahmedabad, as buses are infrequent and there is no convenient accommodation. Call the Conservator of Forests in Gandhinagar (☎ 02712-21951) to see if the Forest Rest House has reopened.

Lothal

About 85km south-west of Ahmedabad, and towards Bhavnagar, this important archaeological site was discovered in 1954. The city that stood here 4500 years ago is clearly related to the Indus Valley cities of Mohenjodaro and Harappa, both in Pakistan. It has the same neatly laid-out street pattern, the same carefully assembled brickwork and the same scientific drainage system.

The name Lothal actually means 'mound of the dead' in Gujarati, as does Mohenjodaro in Sindhi. Excavations have revealed a dockyard – at its peak, this was probably one of the most important ports on the subcontinent. Seals discovered at the site suggest that trade may have been conducted with the civilisations of Mesopotamia, Egypt and Persia.

The **archaeological museum** at the site displays jewellery, pots and other finds (open 10 am to 5 pm Monday to Saturday).

Accommodation is a problem in Lothal, though there is the expensive ***Utelia Palace***, 7km from the archaeological site, by the Bhugavo River.

Lothal is a long day trip from Ahmedabad (at least three hours travel each way). You can reach it by rail, disembarking at Bhurkhi on the Ahmedabad to Bhavnagar railway line, from where you can take a bus.

Modhera

The beautiful and partially ruined **Sun Temple of Modhera** was built by King Bhimdev I (1026–27) and bears some resemblance to the later, and far better known, Sun Temple of Konark in Orissa, which it predates by 200 years. Like that temple, it was designed so that the dawn sun shone on the image of Surya, the sun god, during the equinoxes. The main hall and shrine are reached through a pillared porch and the temple exterior is intricately and delicately carved. As with the Temple of Somnath, this fine temple was ruined by Mahmud of Ghazni.

Nonetheless, what remains is still impressive. This is hardly surprising given that the building work was first completed by Silavat stonemasons, renowned for their ability to turn the hardest stone into delicate carvings.

Within the main grounds, the **Surya Kund** is an extraordinary baoli containing over 100 shrines. Shrines to Ganesh, Vishnu and an incarnation of Shiva surround the tank on three sides while the main temple completes the rectangle and displays 52 intricately carved pillars which depict scenes from the Ramayana and the Mahabharata. The interior of the temple contains a hall whose walls have 12 niches representing the different manifestations of the Sun God in each month. Elsewhere in the complex, there are extensive panels of erotic sculpture.

The temple is open from 8 am to 6 pm daily.

Accommodation can pose a real problem here. There are a few cheap resthouses, but foreigners often find it difficult to get a bed at them.

Modhera is 102km north-west of Ahmedabad. There are direct buses (Rs 30, 3½ hours), or you can take the train to Mahesana and then catch a bus for the 26km trip to Modhera.

Patan

About 130km north-west of Ahmedabad, Patan was an ancient Hindu capital before it was sacked by Mahmud of Ghazni in 1024. Now a pale shadow of its former self, it still has more than 100 **Jain temples** and is famous for its beautifully designed Patola **silk saris**.

There's also the renovated **Rani-ki-Vav**, a baoli which boasts some of Gujarat's finest carvings. Built in 1050, the baoli is the oldest in Gujarat and is remarkably well preserved – a product of the restoration work completed in the 1980s to redress centuries of silting. The waters in the baoli once provided a natural air-cooling system in its chambers for members of the royal family who sought refuge here from the summer heat. It's very impressive and certainly warrants a visit.

Try looking for cheap accommodation near the bus stand and the train station, although what's on offer is generally unappealing.

Patan is 25km north-west of Mahesana. Buses from Ahmedabad take 3½ hours and cost Rs 40.

GANDHINAGAR

☎ 912 from Ahmedabad, ☎ 02712 from elsewhere • pop 393,000

Although Ahmedabad became the capital of Gujarat state when the old state of Mumbai was split, a new capital was planned 32km north-east on the west bank of the Sabarmati River. Named Gandhinagar after the Gujarat-born Mahatma Gandhi, it is India's second planned city after Chandigarh and, like that city, is laid out in rather dull, numbered sectors. The secretariat was moved here in 1970.

Gandhinagar's sole tourist sight is the splendid **Akshardham Temple** of the Hindu Swaminarayan sect, constructed out of 6000 tonnes of pink sandstone. It's on Ja Rd in Sector 20.

The ***Youth Hostel*** *(☎ 22364, Sector 16)* has beds for Rs 50 and offers cheap meals.

Hotel Haveli *(☎ 23905, fax 24057, Sector 11)* is a more upmarket option. Standard/deluxe rooms cost Rs 1600/2000 while a suite will set you back Rs 2500. Checkout is noon. There's a good restaurant here.

Getting There & Away

Buses to Gandhinagar (Rs 10) depart every 15 minutes from the back north-west corner of Lal Darwaja (the local bus stand) or one of the numerous stops along Ashram Rd.

VADODARA (BARODA)

☎ 0265 • pop 1.86 million

Baroda was the capital of the princely Gaekwad state prior to Independence. Today Vadodara (or Baroda, as it is still generally known), 100km south of Ahmedabad, is a pleasant, medium-sized city with

GUJARAT

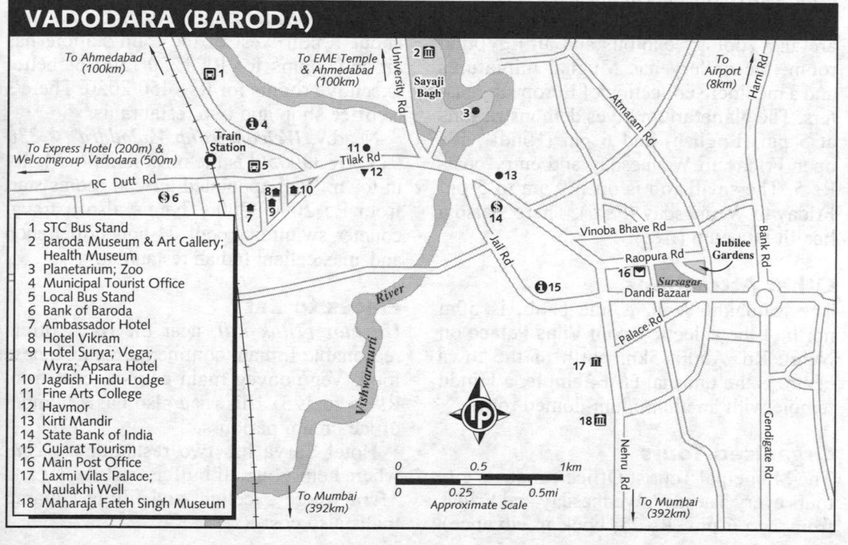

some interesting museums and art galleries and a fine park.

The city's Fine Arts College attracts students from around the country and abroad.

Orientation & Information

The train station, bus stand and a cluster of cheaper hotels are all on the west side of the Vishwarmurti River, which bisects the city. Tilak Rd connects the station with the main part of town. The state tourist office, Gujarat Tourism (☎ 427489), is on the ground floor of Narmada Bhavan, on Jail Rd. It's open from 10.30 am to 6 pm daily (closed Sunday and the 2nd and 4th Saturdays of every month).

There's also a Municipal Tourist Office (☎ 794456) opposite the train station, open 9.30 am to 6 pm daily. Not much English is spoken here but you can pick up the useful *Know Vadodara* booklet (Rs 25). The State Bank of India on Tilak Rd changes money, and the Bank of Baroda on RC Dutt Rd (west of the station) gives Visa cash advances.

Sayaji Bagh

This extensive park, encircled by a mini-railway, is a popular spot for an evening stroll. Within the park are several attractions. The most important is the **Baroda Museum & Art Gallery**, open from 10 am to 5 pm daily (Rs 1). The museum has some good Indian statues and carvings, but there are also zoology exhibits and an Egyptian room; the gallery has Mughal miniatures and a mediocre collection of European masters. The **planetarium** gives demonstrations at 5 pm (English) and 6 pm (Hindi); it's open Friday to Wednesday and entry costs Rs 5. The small **zoo** is open 9 am to 5 pm Friday to Wednesday (Rs 5). There's also a **health museum** (free).

Other Attractions

The **Naulakhi Well**, a fine baoli, is 50m north of the eclectic **Laxmi Vilas Palace** on Nehru Rd. About 5km north of the town centre is the unusual **EME Temple**, a Hindu temple with an aluminium-domed roof.

Organised Tours

The Municipal Tourist Office conducts city tours every Tuesday, Wednesday and Friday from 2 to 6 pm (Rs 25; book in advance). Ask at Gujarat Tourism about day trips that include the surrounding region.

Places to Stay – Budget

Jagdish Hindu Lodge *(☎ 361495)* is in the Sayaji Gunj district near the train station. It has fairly gloomy rooms arranged around a scruffy courtyard. Singles/doubles with private bathroom cost Rs 70/100.

Hotel Vikram *(☎ 361918)*, in the same street, is a small notch upmarket. It offers singles with cold water bathroom for Rs 125 or rooms with air-con for Rs 236/350.

Apsara Hotel *(no phone)*, in the next street west, is a well-maintained place with rooms for Rs 180/240 with private bathroom (bucket hot water).

Places to Stay – Mid-Range & Top End

All rooms in this class have colour TV, private bathroom and hot water (prices do not include tax).

Ambassador Hotel *(☎ 362726)* is opposite the Apsara Hotel. There are large, quiet rooms from Rs 225/336 or Rs 438/538 with air-con.

Hotel Surya *(☎ 361361)*, opposite, is one of the better-value places in town. This friendly place offers a courtesy coach to the airport and Internet access for guests. Rooms (including buffet breakfast) go for Rs 475/700 or Rs 700/900 with air-con.

Express Hotel *(☎ 337001, RC Dutt Rd)*, about 1.5km west of the train station, has air-con rooms for Rs 1250/1500 or better executive rooms for Rs 1450/2050. There's a coffee shop and two restaurants.

Nearby, ***Welcomgroup Vadodara*** *(☎ 330 033, fax 330050)* is the most luxurious hotel in town. Well-appointed air-con rooms start from Rs 2000/3300. There's also a travel counter, swimming pool, 24-hour coffee shop and an excellent Indian restaurant.

Places to Eat

Havmor *(Tilak Rd)*, near the river, offers reasonable Indian, continental and Chinese food. Veg/nonveg main courses cost from Rs 55 to 125. This road also has a number of ice-cream parlours.

Hotel Surya has two restaurants: ***Vega***, where help-yourself buffets cost Rs 75; and ***Myra*** where excellent and filling Gujarati thalis also cost Rs 75.

Ruchika, at the Welcomgroup Vadodara hotel, is recommended for a special treat. It serves scrumptious veg and nonveg Indian cuisine in pleasant surroundings. Be prepared to fork out a couple of hundred rupees. Otherwise try its coffee shop where the fare is cheaper.

Getting There & Away

Air The airport is 8km north-east of town. Indian Airlines (☎ 797447) has daily flights from Vadodara to Mumbai (US$55), Delhi (US$100) and Ahmedabad (US$40). Jet Airways (☎ 343441) has daily flights to Mumbai (US$55).

Bus The STC bus stand is 400m north of the train station, and there are buses to many destinations in Gujarat, western Madhya Pradesh and northern Maharashtra. Buses to Ahmedabad leave at least every 30 minutes (Rs 45/52 for normal/semideluxe, 2½ hours).

Many private bus companies have offices nearby.

Train The *Ahmedabad Express* (9129) leaves Vadodara at 6.10 pm, arriving in Ahmedabad at 8.40 pm (Rs 34/53 in general/sleeper class); the *Shatabdi Express* (2009) departs at 11.35 am and arrives at 1.20 pm (Rs 230/455 in executive/chair class). The *Mumbai Express* (2964) departs at 7.20 am and arrives at Bandra station in Mumbai at 1.50 pm (Rs 89/138/401 for general/sleeper/3A class).

AROUND VADODARA (BARODA)

Champaner (Pavagadh)

This city, 47km north-east of Vadodara, was taken by Sultan Mahmud Begara in 1484, and he renamed it Muhammadabad.

Among the site's exquisite mosques, the **Jama Masjid**, similar in style to the Jama Masjid of Ahmedabad, is the most impressive. Dating from 1513, it has a wonderful carved entrance, an imposing courtyard surrounded by galleries, lovely archways and slim minarets.

The **Hill of Pavagadh**, with its ruined fort, rises beside Champaner in three levels. In 1553 the Mughals, led by Humayun himself, scaled the fort walls using iron spikes driven into the rocks and captured both the fort and its city. Parts of the massive fort walls still stand. According to Hindu legend, the hill is actually a chunk of the Himalayan mountainside which the monkey god Hanuman carted off to Lanka in an episode of the Ramayana, hence the name Pavagadh, which means Quarter of a Hill.

Unfortunately, the site's neglect and increasing pressure from the tourist trade, have led to it being listed by the New York–based World Monuments Watch as one of the 100 most endangered monuments worldwide.

In the month of Chaitra (March/April), a major **festival** takes place at the foot of Pavagadh Hill, honouring the goddess Makakali.

Hotel Champaner *(☎ 02676-45641)* is run by Gujarat Tourism. Beds in a four-bed room which doubles as a dorm cost Rs 75 per person – this room only gets hot water around 7 am. Singles/doubles are Rs 269/400 or Rs 431/591 with air-con.

The trip from Vadodara takes 1½ hours: take a frequent bus to Halol then a minibus to Champaner.

BHARUCH

pop 213,000

This very old town was mentioned in historical records nearly 2000 years ago. It's on the main rail line between Vadodara and Surat, about one hour from each place.

The **fort** overlooks the wide Narmada River from a hilltop and at its base is the **Jama Masjid**. On the river bank, east of the city, is the **Temple of Bhrigu Rishi**, from which the city took its name, Bhrigukachba, later shortened to Bharuch.

The Narmada River has featured in the news both locally and internationally due to the construction of a large and extremely controversial dam, the Sardar Sarovar, upstream of Bharuch near the village of Manibeli (for more information, see the boxed text 'The Dam Debate' in the Facts about India chapter).

SURAT

☎ 0261 • pop 2.38 million

Surat stands on the banks of the Tapti River and was once one of western India's major ports and trading towns, although these days there's little reason for travellers to visit.

Parsis first settled in Surat in the 12th century and the town was the port of choice for the Mughals, British, Dutch and French down through the centuries.

Surat is no longer an important port though it is a major industrial centre, especially for the manufacture of textiles and chemicals, and the processing and finishing of diamonds. The city is probably best known these days as the site of an outbreak of pneumonic plague in 1994; at this time it was rated the filthiest city in India. Since then it has apparently transformed itself into India's second cleanest and healthiest city (after Chandigarh). However, a brief acquaintance with the noise and pollution of its traffic will make you question this statistic.

Things to See & Do

Built in 1546 by the Sultan of Gujarat, the **castle** is on the river bank, beside the Tapti Bridge. Since most of it has been given over to offices it is no longer of great interest, but there is a good view over the city and river from its bastions.

Surat has a number of mosques and Jain, Hindu and Parsi temples.

Places to Stay – Budget

Immediately to the left of the train station are various noisy, fairly grotty hotels.

Rupali Guest House *(☎ 423874)* is in the rock-bottom bracket and is very basic. It has dorm beds for Rs 40, singles with shared bathroom for Rs 80 and doubles with bathroom for Rs 150.

Simla Guest House *(☎ 442339)* is better, but it is still unremarkable. It has singles/doubles with bathroom for Rs 240/340 and singles with shared bathroom for Rs 120.

Sarvajanik Hotel *(☎ 426159)* is at the top end of this category, with rooms with bathroom for Rs 190/285.

Places to Stay – Mid-Range & Top End

Hotel Central Excellency *(☎ 425325, fax 441271)* is opposite the train station. It has rooms with private bathroom and TV from Rs 550/750 or from Rs 775/1250 with air-con. There's also a restaurant.

Hotel Yuvraj *(☎ 413001, Station Rd)*, nearby, has rooms with air-con from Rs 850/1050. The rooms costing Rs 1175/1400 include a chauffeur-driven car for sightseeing (up to 70km or seven hours). There's a Gujarati as well as a multicuisine restaurant.

Embassy Hotel *(☎ 443170, fax 443173, Station Rd)* next door is newer and slightly pricier at Rs 990/1200.

Rates at the above three places include breakfast.

Holiday Inn Hotel *(☎ 226565, fax 227294)*, near Bharti Park in Athwa Lines, 6km from the city centre, is Surat's finest hotel. Air-con rooms with plenty of buttons and switches are Rs 3375/4675. Facilities include a swimming pool, health club, coffee shop and restaurant.

Places to Eat

Sher-e-Punjab, next to the Hotel Central Excellency, offers good veg and nonveg Punjabi and Chinese dishes from around Rs 30.

Holiday Inn Hotel has a fine restaurant serving delicious (though pricey) Indian food. There's also a coffee shop in this hotel that serves a buffet dinner for Rs 250.

Getting There & Away

Surat is on the main Mumbai to Ahmedabad railway line. The 263km trip to Mumbai takes between 4½ and 6½ hours and costs Rs 67/104 in general/sleeper class. To Ahmedabad, the 229km trip takes around four hours and costs Rs 61/95.

AROUND SURAT

Twenty-nine kilometres south of Surat, **Navsari** has been a headquarters for the Parsi community since the earliest days of their settlement in India. **Udvada**, only 10km north of Vapi, the station for Daman, has the oldest Parsi sacred fire in India. It is said that the fire was brought from Persia to Diu, on the opposite coast of the Gulf of Cambay, in AD 700. **Sanjan**, in the extreme south of the state, is the small port where the Parsis first landed. A pillar marks the spot.

In the week preceding Holi (February/March), the Adivasi have a major festival in the forested region called The Dangs, east of Surat near the Maharashtra border – it's known as the **Dang Durbar**.

DAMAN

☎ 02602 • pop 90,000

In the far south of Gujarat is the 56 sq km enclave of Daman. Along with Diu and Goa, Daman was taken in 1961 from the Portuguese, who had seized Daman in 1531. The Portuguese had been officially ceded the region by Bahadur Shah, the last major Gujarati sultan, in 1559. For a time Daman and Diu were governed from Goa but both now constitute the Union Territory of Daman and Diu, which is governed from Delhi. Daman is a laid-back little town with a somewhat tropical flavour, although its beaches are rather drab and dirty. There's still a lingering Portuguese flavour to the town, with its fine old forts and churches, but it's definitely not a smaller version of Goa.

The streets of Daman are lined with bars selling beer, 'Finest Scotch Whisky – Made in India' and various other spirits such as *feni* (distilled from fermented cashew nuts or coconuts). You are forbidden to take alcohol out of Daman into Gujarat unless you obtain a permit (see the boxed text 'Permission to Drink, Sir?' earlier in this chapter); there are police checks as you leave Daman.

Information

The tourist office (☎ 55104) near the bus stand is open from 9.30 am to 1.30 pm and 2.30 to 6 pm weekdays.

No bank changes money, but Executive Travels & Tours, in the arcade below Hotel Maharaja, changes travellers cheques at only 50 paise below the bank rate. The main post office is south of the river in Moti Daman, but there's a more convenient branch in Nani Daman near the bridge.

Nani Daman

You can walk around the ramparts of the Nani Daman's **Fort of St Jerome**. They're a

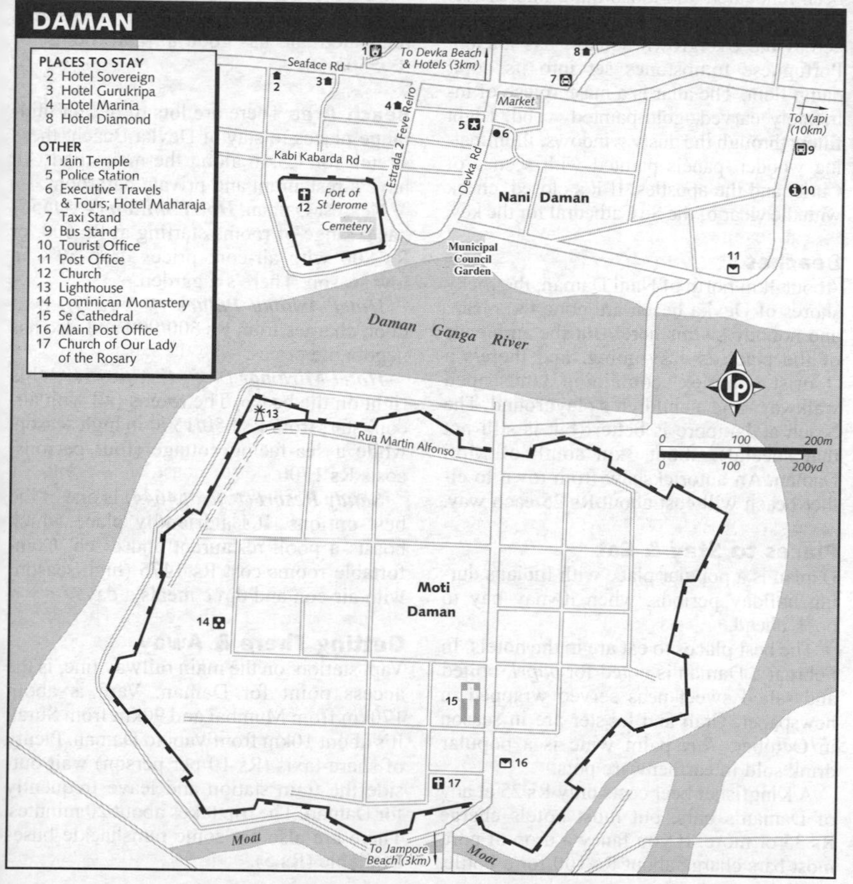

good place from which to watch the fish market and small fishing fleet which anchors alongside.

To the north is a **Jain temple**. If you inquire in the temple office, a caretaker should be able to show you around. The walls inside are completely covered with glassed-over 18th-century murals depicting the life of Mahavira, who lived around 500 BC.

Moti Daman

It's quite pleasant to wander around the wide streets within the fortified walls. The place has a sleepy atmosphere, and the views across the river to Nani Daman from the ramparts just near the lighthouse aren't bad.

The **Se Cathedral** dates from the 17th century and is totally Iberian. It has recently been renovated and looks quite impressive. The **Church of Our Lady of the Rosary**, across the overgrown square, has ancient Portuguese tombstones set into its cool, damp floor. The altar is a masterpiece of intricately carved, gold-painted wood. Light filters through the dusty windows, illuminating wooden panels painted with scenes of Christ and the apostles. If it's closed, check with the vicar of the Se Cathedral for the key.

Beaches

About 3km north of Nani Daman, the rocky shores of Devka beach are none too clean, and nobody swims here. But the ambience of the place is easy-going, and there's a 'tourist complex' containing landscaped walkways and a children's playground. The beach at Jampore is better (but is still not that special), about 3km south of Moti Daman. An autorickshaw from town to either beach will cost about Rs 25 each way.

Places to Stay & Eat

Daman is a popular place with Indians during holiday periods, when it may pay to book ahead.

The best places to eat are in the hotels. In February, Daman is noted for *papri*, boiled and salted sweet peas served wrapped in newspaper. Crab and lobster are in season in October. *Tari* palm wine is a popular drink sold in earthenware pots.

A Kingfisher beer costs only Rs 25 at any of Daman's bars, but most hotels charge Rs 35 or more. If you fancy a drop of port, most bars charge about Rs 100 for a bottle.

Town Area Most of the cheaper hotels in town are on Seaface Rd. They all have private bathrooms.

Hotel Marina *(☎ 54420)*, just off Seaface Rd, is one of the few surviving Portuguese-style houses and is good value. Singles/doubles cost Rs 150/175 or Rs 175/200 for deluxe rooms. There's a bar and restaurant downstairs.

Hotel Diamond *(☎ 55135)*, near the taxi stand, is a bit better. Decent rooms cost Rs 250/400. There's also a bar and restaurant.

Hotel Gurukripa *(☎ 55046, Seaface Rd)* has good, if slightly musty, air-conditioned rooms with TV for Rs 475/575. There's also a popular restaurant here that offers tasty vegetarian and nonvegetarian fare. Most dishes cost from Rs 50.

Nearby, ***Hotel Sovereign*** *(☎ 55023, fax 54433, Seaface Rd)* has been extensively renovated and has good air-con rooms for Rs 550/650.

Beach Area There are lots of decent mid-range places to stay at Devka Beach; these stretch for 1.5km along the main road. All have a restaurant and private bathroom.

Nearest Daman, ***Hotel Shilton*** *(☎ 54558)* has a range of rooms starting at Rs 600, or Rs 800 with air-con; prices drop 50% in low season. There's a garden.

Hotel Ashoka Palace *(☎ 54239)*, next door, charges from Rs 600/900 and also has negotiable prices.

Hotel Miramar *(☎ 54471, fax 54934)* is right on the beach. The rooms (all with air-con) start from Rs 850/1500 in high season, while a sea-facing cottage (four persons) costs Rs 1700.

Sandy Resort *(☎/fax 54644)* is one of the best options. It's a friendly place which boasts a pool, restaurant and disco. Comfortable rooms cost Rs 1475 (high season) with air-con and three meals a day.

Getting There & Away

Vapi station, on the main railway line, is the access point for Daman. Vapi is about 170km from Mumbai and 90km from Surat. It's about 10km from Vapi to Daman. Plenty of share-taxis (Rs 10 per person) wait outside the train station and leave frequently for Daman. The trip takes about 20 minutes. There are also are some ramshackle buses available (Rs 5).

Saurashtra

The often bleak plains of Saurashtra on the Kathiawar peninsula are generally inhabited by friendly but reserved people. Those in the country are distinctively dressed – the men wear white turbans, pleated jackets (short waisted and long sleeved) and jodhpurs (baggy seat and drainpipe legs) and often sport golden stud earrings. The women are nearly as colourful as the women of Rajasthan and wear embroidered backless *cholis* (sari blouses) which are known by various names but most commonly as *kanjeri*.

The peninsula, which is somewhat off the main tourist route, took its name from the Kathi tribespeople who used to roam the area at night stealing whatever was not locked into the many *kots* (village forts).

BHAVNAGAR

☎ 0278 • pop 775,000

Founded in 1743, Bhavnagar is still an important trading post for cotton goods manufactured in Gujarat. The Bhavnagar lock gate keeps ships afloat in the port at low tide. On the surface, it isn't the most exciting place to visit. It does, however, have an interesting bazaar area with overhanging wooden balconies, countless little shops, lots of local colour and rarely a tourist in sight.

Orientation & Information

Bhavnagar is a sprawling city with distinctly separate old and new sections. The bus stand is in the new part of town and the train station is at the far end of the old town, around 2.5km away. The State Bank of India in the old town changes cash.

Things to See & Do

Takhteshwar Temple sits on a small hillock, which is nevertheless high enough to provide good views over the city and out into the Gulf of Cambay. The temple itself is of minor interest.

North-east, by the clock tower, is the **Gandhi Smriti Museum**, with a moderate collection of Gandhi memorabilia and religious statues (free; closed Sunday and the second and fourth Saturday in the month).

For local colour, wander the atmospheric shopping streets in the old town, near the State Bank of India.

Places to Stay – Budget

The only cheap hotels in Bhavnagar are in the old bazaar area.

The ***Hotel Mini*** *(☎ 512915, Station Rd)*, located in the old city, close to the train station, is one of the better and friendlier budget hotels. It's clean and quiet with decent-sized singles/doubles for Rs 125/225 with private bathroom (check the shower nozzle

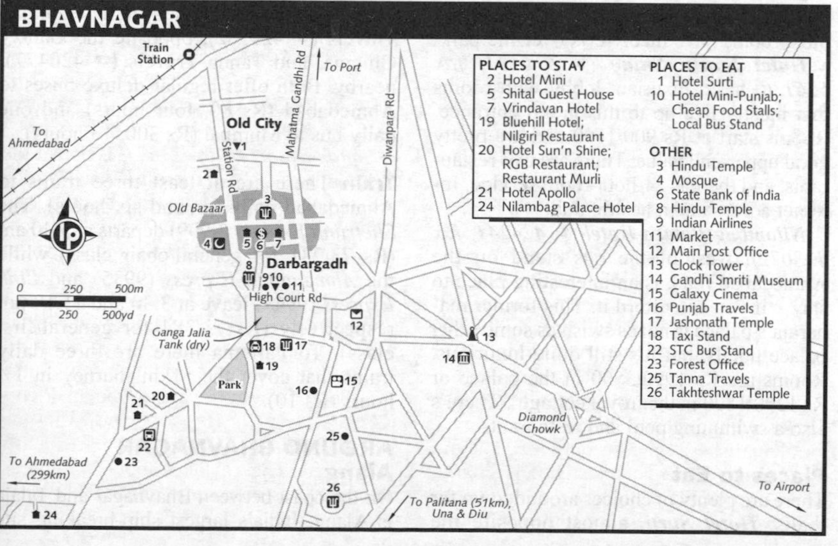

GUJARAT

works) or for Rs 25 less without a TV. Checkout is 24 hours and this place can rustle up breakfasts and thalis.

Shital Guest House *(☎ 428360, Amba Chowk)*, in the middle of the bazaar area, is not a bad choice. Enter through the rear of the building. Singles with shared bathroom cost Rs 75 while equally basic but clean doubles with private bathroom with bucket shower (hot water in the mornings) and squat toilet cost Rs 150.

Vrindavan Hotel *(☎ 519149, Darbargadh)*, not far from the Shital, is in a small lane just east of the grand State Bank of India. It's a huge, multistorey place set around a courtyard with rooms starting at Rs 100/200 or Rs 400/500 with air-con. The rooms are simple and the bathrooms clean. Reception is reached via the stairs on the right as you enter through the main archway.

Places to Stay – Mid-Range & Top End

Hotel Apollo *(☎ 425252, fax 412440)*, directly opposite the bus stand, is definitely the best mid-price deal. It has very comfortable and spacious rooms with TV for Rs 450/600 or Rs 650/800 with air-con. There are money-changing facilities (lowish rates) and there is a good restaurant.

Bluehill Hotel *(☎ 426951, fax 427313)*, down a quiet road from the taxi stand, is well appointed with air-con rooms from Rs 900/1350. There are two veg restaurants and most rooms have nice views over the park.

Hotel Sun'n Shine *(☎ 516131, fax 516130)* has a luxuriant lobby with rooms that mostly live up to this grand entrance. Rooms start at Rs 900/1100 and are pretty good upper-end value. There are two restaurants, and there is 24-hour room service, Internet access and a health club.

Nilambag Palace Hotel *(☎ 424241, fax 428072)*, west of the bus stand on the Ahmedabad road, is an interesting place to stay – if you can afford it. This former maharaja's palace is not as swish as some other palace hotels, but it's still quite luxurious. Rooms are Rs 1990/3500 in the palace or Rs 1200/1800 in the 'royal cottage'. There's also a swimming pool and restaurant.

Places to Eat

There are plenty of choices around town for thalis. ***Hotel Surti***, almost opposite the Hotel Mini, does reasonable thalis for Rs 30 and ***Hotel Mini*** is also good value (all you can eat for Rs 35). Those at the ***Vrindavan Hotel*** cost Rs 50 while ***Restaurant Murli*** is the place to go if you're happy to pay for the company of besuited waiters (Rs 60).

There are plenty of cheap ***food stalls*** on the northern side of Ganga Jalia Tank – the choice is greater when the amusement park is running. One relatively permanent and OK cheapie is ***Hotel Mini-Punjab***.

Of the mid- and upper-range hotels, the ***Nilgiri Restaurant*** in the Bluehill Hotel and the ***RGB Restaurant*** in the Hotel Sun'n Shine are probably the pick, with varied menus, good service and reasonable prices. The veg and nonveg restaurants at the ***Hotel Apollo*** also aren't bad.

Getting There & Away

Air The Indian Airlines office (☎ 426503) is just north of the Ganga Jalia Tank. There are four flights a week to Mumbai (US$75).

An autorickshaw to/from the airport costs around Rs 60.

Bus State transport buses connect Bhavnagar with Ahmedabad and other centres in the region. There are regular departures throughout the day for Una (for Diu; Rs 63, five hours), Palitana (Rs 18, 1½ hours) and half-hourly to Ahmedabad (Rs 65, four hours).

Private bus companies include Punjab Travels (☎ 424582), opposite the Galaxy Cinema, and Tanna Travels (☎ 420477), nearby. Both offer regular deluxe buses to Ahmedabad (Rs 80, four hours) and one daily bus to Mumbai (Rs 300, 13 hours).

Train There are at least three trains to Ahmedabad daily (around six hours). The *Shetrunji Express* (9909) departs at 5.40 am (Rs 73/231 for general/chair class) while the *Ahmedabad Express* (9935) and *Link Express* (9947) leave at 3.30 and 11.10 pm respectively (Rs 73/384 for general/first class). To Palitana there are three daily trains that cover the 51km journey in 1½ hours (Rs 10).

AROUND BHAVNAGAR

Alang

On the coast between Bhavnagar and Talaja is Alang, India's largest ship-breaking site where supertankers, container ships, warships and other vessels are dismantled – literally by hand – by 20,000 workers day and night. It's an epic, almost Dickensian scene, but almost impossible to see as a tourist.

According to a Gujarat Port Trust internal memo, 'It has come to our attention that foreign tourists are entering the port for sightseeing/photography on the pretext of an interest in buying ship's fittings'. You could try contacting the Gujarat Port Trust (☎/fax 0278-563132) for permission but chances are they'll send you on a paper trail that leads to Gandhinagar via Ahmedabad only to end up back where you started – unless, of course, you're serious about buying a ship. Some travellers have managed to sneak through the gate on a crowded local bus but more have been hauled off at the gatehouse. It's worth checking with the Port Trust to see whether regulations have changed, although this extraordinary sight is likely to be off limits for some time to come.

Velavadar National Park

This park, 65km north of Bhavnagar, is well known for its blackbucks, which sport impressive spiralling horns as long as 60cm in mature males. The best time to visit is from October to June; ask about current regulations at the Forest Office (☎ 0278-428644) or from the sanctuary superintendent (☎ 0278-426425) near Bhavnagar's bus stand – the latter is also the number for booking accommodation at the ***Tourist Lodge*** at the sanctuary; doubles cost around Rs 300.

Getting there by bus from Bhavagnar is possible (change at Valabhipur), but to visit on a day trip you would need to hire a taxi (no more than Rs 700).

PALITANA

☎ 02848 • pop 48,000

The town of Palitana, 51km south-west of Bhavnagar, is little more than a gateway to the pilgrimage site of Shatrunjaya.

Shatrunjaya

Strewn with 863 temples, the hilltop complex of Shatrunjaya (the Place of Victory) is one of Jainism's holiest pilgrimage sites. The temples were built over a period of 900 years on a hilltop dedicated entirely to the gods; at dusk, even the priests depart from the temples, leaving them deserted.

Almost all the temples are Jain, and this hill demonstrates their belief that merit is derived from constructing temples. The hilltops are bounded by sturdy walls and the temples are grouped into nine *tunks* (enclosures) – each with a central temple with many minor ones clustered around. Some of the earliest temples here were built in the 11th century, but were destroyed by Muslims in the 14th and 15th centuries; the current temples date from the 16th century onwards.

The hilltop affords a very fine view in all directions; on a clear day you can see the Gulf of Cambay beyond Bhavnagar. The most notable of the temples is dedicated to **Shri Adishwara**, one of the most important Jain *tirthankars*. Note the frieze of dragons around this temple. Adjacent is the Muslim shrine of **Angar Pir**. Women who want children make offerings of miniature cradles at this shrine.

Built in 1618 by a wealthy Jain merchant, the **Chaumukh**, or four-faced shrine, has images of Adinath facing out in the four cardinal directions. Other important temples are those dedicated to Kumar Pal, Sampriti Raj and Vimal Shah.

The temples are open from 6.30 am to 5.30 pm. A photography permit can be purchased for Rs 50 just inside the main entrance. (There are two entrances – the main one is reached by taking the left-hand fork as you near the top of the hill; the other is reached by the right-hand fork.) Shoes should be removed at the entrance to the compound, and leather items, including belts and bags, should not be brought onto the site.

A horse cart to the base of the hill costs Rs 20, or you can walk from the Palitana bus stand in about 30 minutes. The heat can be extreme by late morning, so it's a good idea to start early for the ascent. Water (not bottled) can be bought at intervals, and you can buy refreshing curd in pottery bowls outside the temple compound for Rs 10.

The 600m ascent from the base of the hill to the summit is 2km, up more than 3000 steps. At a moderate pace, the ascent will take about 1½ hours. You can be carried up the hill in a *doli* (rope chair) which costs from Rs 200 to 700 depending on comfort (the choice of quite a few affluent and obese pilgrims). The most conspicuous sight on first entering the temple compound is that of exhausted doli bearers resting in the shade.

Places to Stay & Eat

Palitana has scores of *dharamsalas* (pilgrim's guesthouses) but unless you're a Jain, you're unlikely to be allowed to stay at any of them.

Gujarat Tourism's ***Hotel Sumeru** (☎ 2327, Station Rd)*, 200m towards the train station from the bus stand, is really the best choice. Singles/doubles are Rs 377/538 or Rs 578/807 with air-con including taxes. Dorm beds are Rs 50. Prices almost halve from 15 June to 15 September. Its veg restaurant serves Gujarati thalis (Rs 45) as well as Punjabi and continental dishes.

***Hotel Shravak** (☎ 2428)*, opposite the bus stand, has basic singles with shared bathroom for Rs 100 or doubles/triples (with bathroom) for Rs 200/300. Dorm beds (men only) cost Rs 40. Checkout is 24 hours for rooms, 9.30 am for the dorm.

Across the alley, ***Jagruti Restaurant*** is a wildly busy 24-hour snack place offering *puris* (flat dough that puffs up when fried), *sabzi* (curried vegetables), curd, roasted peppers and *ganthia* (varieties of fried dough).

Havmor is a popular ice-cream parlour on the right as you approach the base of Shatrunjaya.

Getting There & Away

Bus STC buses make the 1½-hour trip to/from Bhavnagar every hour (Rs 18). There are also regular departures for Ahmedabad (Rs 68, five hours).

Infrequent buses go to Talaja, where you can switch to a bus to Una or Diu. The total journey to Talaja takes about six hours; it's a trip from hell, along bumpy village roads in dilapidated old rattletraps.

Train Sleepy Palitana station is only 800m from the bus stand heading away from Shatrunjaya. It only receives trains to/from Bhavagnar (though they stop at Sihor, which has connections to Ahmedabad). They depart Palitana at 9 am, 6.05 and 8.30 pm, and depart Bhavnagar at 6.30 am, 2.45 and 6.45 pm (Rs 10, 1½ hours).

DIU

☎ 02875 • pop 66,200

Diu is for many the highlight of Gujarat with its relaxed pace of life, decaying Portuguese architecture, huge fort and quiet beaches.

Like Daman and Goa, Diu was a Portuguese colony until it was taken over by India in 1961. Along with Daman, it is still governed from Delhi as a Union Territory rather than as part of Gujarat. The former colony includes the island of Diu, about 13km long by 3km wide, separated from the coast by a narrow channel. There are also two tiny mainland enclaves. One of these, where the village of Ghoghla stands, is the entry point to Diu from Una.

The northern side of the island, facing Gujarat, is tidal marsh and saltpans while the southern coast alternates between limestone cliffs, rocky coves and sandy beaches.

The island's main industry is fishing, followed by booze and salt. Kalpana Distillery at Malala produces rum from sugar cane. Diu town has many bars where visitors from the 'dry' mainland can enjoy a beer.

Diu is a popular hang-out with travellers and you'll probably see more foreigners here than anywhere else in Gujarat. Although the beaches are nothing compared to Goa's, it is still a great place to let your hair down and watch the world drift by.

History

Between the 14th and 16th centuries Diu was an important trading post and naval base from which the Ottomans controlled the shipping routes in the northern part of the Arabian Sea.

Portugal made an unsuccessful attempt to capture the island in 1531, during which Bahadur Shah, the Sultan of Gujarat, was assisted by the Turkish navy. The Portuguese finally secured control in 1535 by taking advantage of a quarrel between the sultan and the Mughal Emperor, Humayun.

Under pressure from both the Portuguese and the Mughals, Bahadur concluded a peace treaty with the Portuguese, effectively giving them control over the port at Diu. The treaty was soon cast to the wind and, although both Bahadur Shah and his successor, Sultan Mahmud III, attempted to contest the issue, the peace treaty that was eventually signed in 1539 ceded the island of Diu and the mainland enclave of Ghoghla to Portugal. Soon after the signing of this treaty, the Portuguese began constructing their fort.

The Indian government appears to have an official policy of playing down the

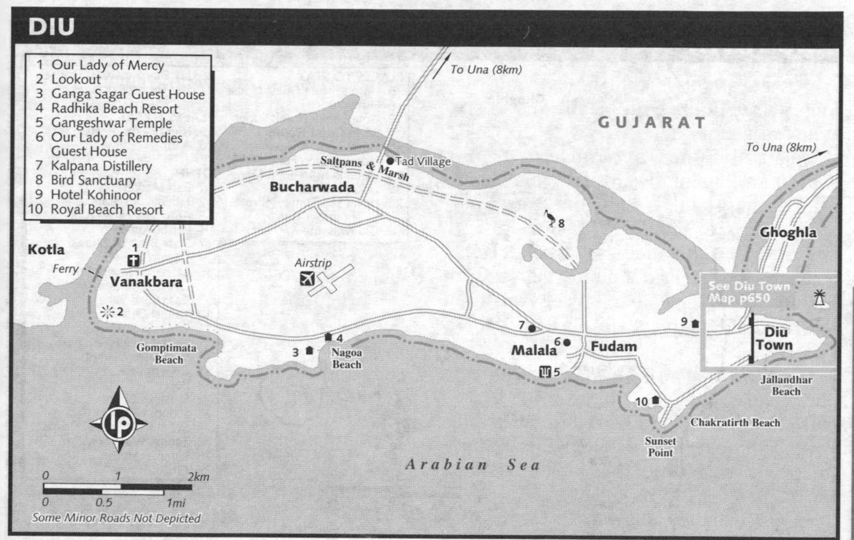

Portuguese era. Seven Rajput soldiers (six of them Singhs) and a few civilians were killed in Operation Vijay, which ended Portuguese rule in 1961. After the Indian Air Force unnecessarily bombed the airstrip and terminal near Nagoa, it remained derelict until the late 1980s. The old church in Diu Fort was also bombed and is now a roofless ruin.

Orientation & Information

The tourist office (☎ 52653) is on Bunder Rd, the main road that runs through Diu Town parallel to the waterfront. It has transport information and simple (free) maps. The office is open from 9.30 am to 1.30 pm and 2.30 to 6 pm Monday to Saturday.

You can change money at the State Bank of Saurashtra near the town square, but at lower rates than on the mainland. They are reluctant to change large amounts. Many shops around Diu Town also change money.

The main post office overlooks the town square and there's another branch at Ghoghla. Both Hotel Alishan (Rs 75 per hour) and Dee Pee Telecom (Rs 100; opposite the Tourist Office) have Internet access.

Diu Town

Laid-back Diu Town (population 38,500) was the first landing point for the Parsis when they fled from Persia, although they stayed only three years.

The town is sandwiched between the massive fort to the east and a huge city wall to the west. The main **Zampa Gateway** in the wall has carvings of lions, angels and a priest, while just inside the gate is a miniature chapel with an icon, dating from 1702. Just to the south, outside the wall, is the **Zampa Waterfall**, a strange artificial creation that is lit up at night.

St Paul's is the only church in town still fulfilling its original function and services the island's tiny Christian population. Nearby is St Thomas' Church, which houses the **Diu Museum** (entry by donation, open 8 am to 9 pm daily). There's an interesting collection of Catholic statues. If you thought the Hindu pantheon was confusing, take a look at the bewildering collection of Christian saints. There are also some stone remnants of a Jain temple which is thought to have once occupied the site. There is a guesthouse upstairs (see Places to Stay later in this section). Ask the caretaker to let you climb to the roof for spectacular views. **St Francis of Assisi** has been converted into a hospital.

Unlike Daman, many buildings in Diu show a significant Portuguese influence. The town is a maze of narrow, winding streets and many of the houses are brightly painted. Further away from this tightly packed residential quarter, the streets turn into

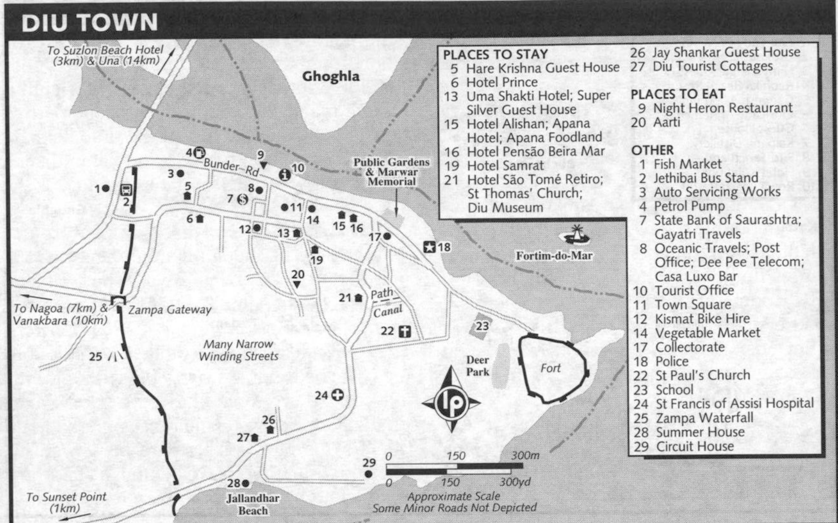

meandering and often leafy lanes and it's well worth a couple of hours exploring the area.

In a small park on the esplanade, between the square and the police station, the **Marwar Memorial**, topped by a griffin, commemorates the liberation of the island from the Portuguese.

Completed in 1541, the massive **Portuguese fort** with its double moat (one tidal) must once have been virtually impregnable, but sea erosion and neglect are leading to a slow but inevitable collapse. Piles of cannon balls litter the place and the ramparts have a superb array of cannons; many are still in good condition. A small chapel holds engraved tombstone fragments. The fort, part of which also serves as the island's jail, is open from 7 am to 6 pm daily. Entry is free. Photography is allowed.

Around the Island

Temple- and fort-satiated travellers used to head to **Nagoa** to catch up on some serious relaxation. Although it's still a pleasant palm-fringed beach and is safe for swimming, it's quite busy nowadays, and Western women tend to get unwanted attention from the numerous young Indian men hanging around. **Gomptimata**, to the west, is a sandy beach that is still relatively deserted, and gets big waves. Beaches within easy reach of Diu Town include, from east to west, **Jallandhar**, **Chakratirth** and the stunning **Sunset Point**.

Close to Diu Town, the village of **Fudam** has a huge church, Our Lady of Remedies, that's now used as a guesthouse. A large, old carved wooden altar with Madonna and child remains inside.

At the extreme west of the island, **Vanakbara** has a church (Our Lady of Mercy), fort, lighthouse, small bazaar, post office and fishing fleet. This little fishing village is worth a visit – wander through the town to the port area where you can see the locals mending nets and repairing their colourful fishing boats.

Places to Stay

Most hotels offer a discount in the low season, but it's worth bargaining at any time of the year, as places will slash prices by as much as 60% if they are not full. Your chances of success are greater if you're staying for more than a couple of days. Prices given here are for the peak season, which runs roughly from October to June and, unless stated otherwise, the rooms have a cold water bathroom (most of which in Diu are pretty ordinary) with squat toilet. Most places have a noon checkout time.

Diu Town *Hare Krishna Guest House* (☎ *52213)*, on the west side of town, is a small place with simple singles/doubles/triples for only Rs 75/100/150. Some rooms are better than others; Room 4 on the corner is good.

Hotel Prince *(☎ 52765)*, nearby, charges Rs 300 per double. Those on the second floor have good views from the balconies.

Hotel Samrat *(☎ 52354)*, a couple of blocks south of the town square, has very pleasant double rooms with nice bathrooms, balconies and satellite TV for Rs 350 and singles/doubles with air-con for Rs 500/650. Room service is available. There's a good restaurant and bar and, if the kitchen is not busy, the chef will cook fish bought by guests at the fish market for about Rs 50.

Super Silver Guest House *(☎ 52020)*, a block south of the vegetable market, is a new place with spotless and spacious rooms (good bathrooms) for a highly negotiable Rs 200/300. The owner is eager to please.

Uma Shakti Hotel *(☎ 52150)*, next door, is another good choice with decent doubles for Rs 200/600 without/with air-con. It's populated by the usual cast of thousands of brothers masquerading as staff. The terrace garden bar and restaurant on the roof is a lovely place for a meal, beer or breakfast (the cheese omelette for Rs 30 is particularly good).

Hotel Pensão Beira Mar *(☎ 53031, Bunder Rd)* is an old Portuguese villa, midway between the town square and fort, now converted into a semi-upmarket hotel. In previous incarnations it has been known as the Baron's Inn, Hotel Sanman and the totally misleading Fun Club. Staff seem to realise that the comfortable but unspectacular doubles are overpriced at Rs 1000 and will immediately drop to Rs 400, even in high season. Suites start at Rs 1200. There's a rooftop restaurant and bar.

Hotel Alishan *(☎ 52340, fax 52190, Bunder Rd)* next door, is better value with decent rooms with TV and balcony. Double rooms with views cost Rs 200/500 in low/high season or Rs 600/800 with air-con. There are cheaper rooms at the back and there is a restaurant, bar and Internet access. The restaurant does a good fish tandoor (Rs 100).

Hotel São Tomé Retiro is one of the better choices. Located on the southern fringes of Diu Town, upstairs in St Thomas' Church and museum, its five rooms are atmospheric, large and most have wonderful views. It's a homely, quiet place with the smaller rooms costing Rs 175/200 for short/long stays and larger rooms cost Rs 200/300. George D'Souza, the friendly, young manager, organises barbecue parties most evenings. The rest of the time his parents will cook Portuguese and Goan dishes (Rs 75) if you order in the morning.

Jallandhar Beach This is a lovely quiet area to stay in, though it's only an easy 10-minute walk to Diu Town. The Summer House lookout point is a stone's throw away.

Diu Tourist Cottages *(☎ 52654)* offers pleasant and spacious cottages with double or twin beds for Rs 650/800 without/with air-con. Many rooms have sea views, and its Pelican Bar & Restaurant is not bad, although it's more pleasant to be served on the individual terrace balconies. There are also some pool tables. It's a pretty mellow place. The same family runs the ***Royal Beach Resort*** *(☎ 52654)* at Sunset Point, charging from around Rs 400 a double.

Jay Shankar Guest House *(☎ 52420)*, near Diu Tourist Cottages, has doubles from Rs 100 to 250 (with balcony and sea view). It's good value. The attached Nilkanth Restaurant serves good fish dishes although the other offerings are a tad mediocre. Management can also help with bus bookings.

Fudam to Nagoa Beach ***Hotel Kohinoor*** *(☎ 52209, fax 52613)*, on the road to Fudam, has attractive, well-equipped villas grouped round a swimming pool and spa. Rooms (all with air-con) cost from Rs 1250 to 1650 with a bathtub and king-size bed. Suites cost Rs 2500. There's a good restaurant, pastry shop, disco and games room.

Ganga Sagar Guest House *(☎ 52249)* is right on Nagoa Beach. Small singles/doubles round a beachside garden cost Rs 100/ 300 with shared bathroom (bucket hot water) or Rs 500 with private bathroom. As well as the basic snack bar, the restaurant has the usual range of moderately priced Chinese and Indian food.

Resort Hoka *(☎ 53036)*, close by on the main road, has doubles for Rs 350 and the management seems eager to please.

Radhika Beach Resort *(☎ 52555)*, also in the vicinity, has come highly recommended by a number of travellers. Very comfortable rooms cost Rs 1000/1750, there's a nice swimming pool (guests only) and a good, reasonably priced restaurant.

Ghoghla *Suzlon Beach Hotel* (☎ *52212*) is in the village of Ghoghla on the mainland (where there's a good beach). This is the first building in Diu after you come through the barrier that marks the border with Gujarat. Renovated air-con doubles cost Rs 1400; a suite is Rs 1600. There's a pleasant restaurant and bar overlooking the sea.

Places to Eat

Beer and drinks are blissfully cheap in Diu – from Rs 30 for a large Kingfisher and even a Fosters. Food is rarely anything to write home about, although the fish is usually good. As well as the hotel restaurants featured in Places to Stay, there are a few others.

Apana Foodland, attached to the Hotel Apana, is probably the pick of the hotel restaurants with a pleasant outdoor setting overlooking the water. They do everything from breakfasts and South Indian (Rs 20 to 30) to Punjabi, Chinese and fish dishes.

Night Heron Restaurant, right on the water's edge near the tourist office, is an excellent place for a meal. The staff are friendly and it's very relaxed. Main dishes range from Rs 40 to 80. It's a great choice for breakfast.

Aarti is a relaxed traveller restaurant, with wall hangings and Western music. Pizzas (from Rs 50) are excellent and there are usually good fish specialities.

For a drink, ***Casa Luxo Bar***, next to Oceanic Travels, is highly recommended.

One traveller wrote to say that the milkshakes along Bunder Rd were the best in India. We found none living up to that lofty claim but hope you have better luck.

Gomptimata Beach has no cafes, so bring food with you.

Getting There & Away

Air Jet Airways flies to Mumbai (US$95) at 12.15 pm daily except Saturday. The Jet Airways agent is Oceanic Travels (☎ 52180), on the town square near the post office.

Bus STC departures from Jethibai bus stand are usually inconvenient. Buses to Rajkot via Veraval (Rs 30) leave at 4.15, 5 am and 2.15 pm. For Jamnagar and Ahmedabad it's 6 am, Porbandar 1 pm and Bhavnagar 7 am. There are more civilised and frequent departure times from Una. If you're travelling to Diu and arrive in Una, you'll have to get yourself the 10km or so to Ghoghla and Diu. Buses depart every 30 minutes from Una bus stand between 7.30 am and 8 pm (Rs 9, 40 minutes). Outside these hours, walk 1km to Tower Chowk in Una, from where crowded share-rickshaws go to Ghoghla or Diu for about the same as the bus fare. An autorickshaw from Una costs about Rs 100.

Buses go from Diu to Mumbai at 10 am (Rs 350, 22 hours) and to Ahmedabad at 7 pm (Rs 150, 10½ hours). Book in advance from Gayatri Travels (☎ 52346).

Train Delwada, between Una and Ghoghla and only about 8km from Diu, is the nearest railhead. A share-autorickshaw from there to Ghoghla costs about Rs 5. There's a direct train at 6 am from Delwada to Veraval (Rs 32/173 general/1st class, 96km). There is also a daily service to Junagadh (Rs 48/233, 164km) via Sasan Gir.

Getting Around

Autorickshaw drivers will demand Rs 100 from Diu Town to Una, and generally want higher prices. To travel anywhere within the town of Diu should cost no more than Rs 15. To Nagoa Beach pay about Rs 30, and to Sunset Point about Rs 20. Share-rickshaws to Ghoghla cost Rs 3 per person.

Mopeds are ideal for getting around the island – the roads are relatively deserted and are in good condition. The going rate per day is Rs 100 for a moped (plus fuel). Motorcycles with leg gears cost Rs 150. Most hotels can arrange mopeds although the quality is variable. Try Kismat (☎ 52971), which also rents bicycles, at the back of the town square, or the friendly Auto Servicing Works (☎ 52824) opposite the petrol pump on Bunder Rd. A deposit of Rs 500 is usually required.

Local buses from Diu Town to Nagoa Beach and Vanakbara leave from the Jethibai bus stand at 7 and 11 am and 4 pm. From Nagoa, they depart for Diu Town from near the police post at 1, 5.30 and 7 pm (Rs 4).

VERAVAL

☎ 02876 • pop 135,000

On the south coast of Saurashtra, Veraval was the major seaport for Mecca pilgrims before the rise of Surat. Apart from the port, and a quick look (from the outside) at the eerie **old Nawab's Palace** in the west of town, there's not a lot to see in Veraval. It still has some importance as one of India's major fishing ports (more than 1000 boats work from here) but the main reason to come here is as a base for a visit to Somnath Temple, 6km to the east.

For changing money, the State Bank of India will direct you to the State Bank of Saurashtra which will send you to JP Travels International (☎ 20110) nearby. It changes US dollars and British pounds (cash and travellers cheques) for a lowish exchange rate but charges no commission.

Places to Stay

There is wide selection of hotels along ST Rd between the bus stand and the clock tower. However, all hotels only have hot water in the morning.

Chetna Rest House (☎ *20688*), directly opposite the bus stand, with all of the accompanying noise, has clean and simple singles/doubles for Rs 65/130 with private bathroom with cold water and Rs 55/110 with bucket shower but shared squat toilet. Dorm beds for men are only Rs 35.

Hotel Satkar (☎ *20120, fax 43114*), around the corner, has a phone and TV (check that it works) in most rooms. Rates are from Rs 100/150 for a cramped room, with larger ones going for Rs 200/300 or Rs 400 with air-con. All rooms have private bathroom. Staff are obliging.

Toran Tourist Bungalow (☎ *46588*), not far from the lighthouse, is in a rather inconvenient location but is quiet and better maintained than most hotels run by Gujarat Tourism. Ordinary/deluxe/air-con singles cost Rs 225/275/425; the corresponding doubles are Rs 350/450/650. The deluxe rooms are very comfy with a balcony complete with swing chair and sunset and ocean views. Checkout is 9 am. The restaurant serves Gujarati and Punjabi food. One downside is the smell from the nearby chemical factory, although if the wind's blowing in the wrong direction, you'll be lucky to escape that anywhere in town.

Hotel Utsav (☎ *22306*), just up from the bus stand, has quite pleasant doubles with satellite TV for Rs 350/500 without/with air-con.

Places to Eat

Real Treats advertises continental and Chinese food, but delivers only good bottomless Gujarati thalis for Rs 40. The air-con dining area is pleasant.

Fast Food Restaurant, near the clock tower on the road to the station, has simple veg food for around Rs 25.

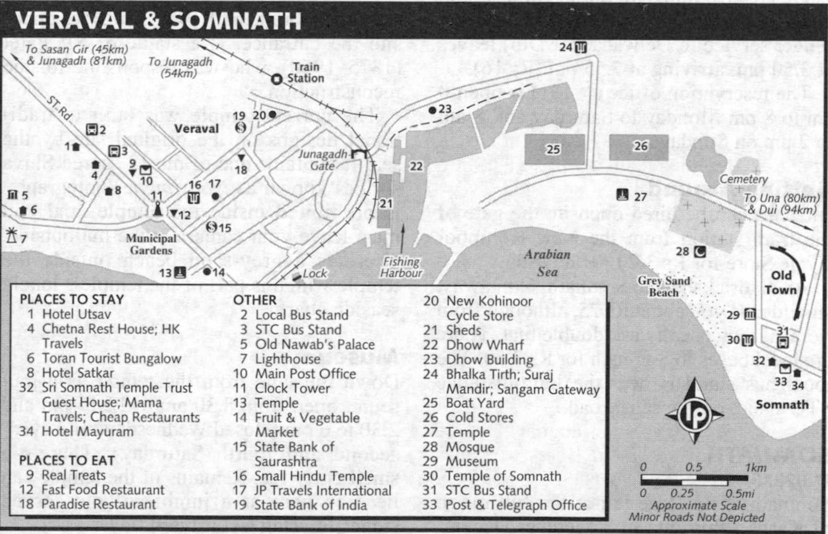

Paradise Restaurant *(☎ 41357)*, almost opposite the State Bank of India, does surprisingly good, reasonably priced, Chinese food. It's a friendly place and the won ton soup (Rs 50) is very tasty. There aren't many veg dishes to choose from.

Getting There & Away

Bus STC buses to Junagadh depart half-hourly from the bus stand from 5.45 am (Rs 30, two hours); to Porbandar from 6 am (Rs 43, three hours); and to Rajkot from 6 am (Rs 58, five hours). There are also regular departures for Sasan Gir (Rs 15, 1½ hours) and Ahmedabad (Rs 100, 10 hours). Buses direct to Diu leave at 7.30, 9.30 am and 4.40 pm (Rs 30, three hours). Departures are more frequent if you change at Una.

There are agents for the private bus companies opposite the bus stand, including HK Travels (☎ 21934) who have at least one nightly bus to Ahmedabad (Rs 130/170 for ordinary/sleeper berth).

Train It's 431km from Ahmedabad to Veraval. Fares for the 11½-hour trip are Rs 96/146/504 in general/sleeper/first class. The *Somnath Mail* (9923) leaves Veraval at 5 pm or the *Girnar Express* (9945) departs at 7.30 pm. The *Rajkot Mail* rolls out at 11.30 am, arriving in Rajkot at 4.50 pm (186km; Rs 52/273 in general/first class). There are also trains for Sasan Gir at 10 am and 9.20 pm (Rs 10, 1¼ hours). A daily passenger service to Delwada (for Diu) leaves at 3.50 pm, arriving at 7.55 pm (Rs 16).

The reservation office (☎ 131) is open 8 am to 8 pm Monday to Saturday and 8 am to 2 pm on Sundays.

Getting Around

Bicycles can be hired opposite the gate of the train station from the New Kohinoor Cycle Store for Rs 3/20 per hour/day.

An autorickshaw to Somnath, 6km away, should cost you about Rs 25, although from Veraval they usually ask double that. There are local buses to Somnath for Rs 3.50. The local bus stand is near the long-distance STC stand, on the same road.

SOMNATH

☎ 02876

Somnath has a large **fair** at the full moon of Kartika Purnima in November/December. Most travellers prefer to stay in Veraval, 6km away, where there is a wider range of accommodation, eating and transport options.

Temple of Somnath

This temple at Somnath, near Veraval and about 80km from Junagadh, has an extremely chequered past. Its earliest history fades into legend – it is said to have originally been built out of gold by Somraj, the moon god, only to be rebuilt by Rawana in silver, then by Krishna in wood and by Bhimdev in stone. A description of the temple by Al Biruni, an Arab traveller, was so glowing that it prompted a visit in 1024 by a most unwelcome tourist – Mahmud of Ghazni. At that time, the temple was so wealthy that it had 300 musicians, 500 dancing girls and even 300 barbers just to shave the heads of visiting pilgrims.

Mahmud of Ghazni, whose raids on the riches of India are legendary, descended on Somnath from his Afghan kingdom and, after a two-day battle, took the town and the temple. Having looted its fabulous wealth, he destroyed it for good measure. So began a pattern of Muslim destruction and Hindu rebuilding that continued for centuries. The temple was again razed in 1297, 1394 and finally in 1706 by Aurangzeb, the notorious Mughal fundamentalist.

After the 1706 demolition, the temple was not rebuilt until 1950. Outside, opposite the entrance, is a statue of SV Patel (1875–1950), who was responsible for the reconstruction.

The current temple was built to traditional designs on the original site by the sea. It contains one of the 12 sacred Shiva shrines known as *jyoti linga*. Photography is prohibited inside the temple, and you must leave your camera at the hut outside. There is a grey-sand beach outside the temple which is part of the temple's lonely seaside charm.

Museum

Down the lane from the temple is a museum, open from 8.30 am to 12.15 pm and 2.30 to 6 pm (closed Wednesdays and every second and fourth Saturday). There's a small entry fee. Remains of the temple can be seen here as a jumble of old carved stones littering a courtyard.

Other Attractions

Halfway between Veraval and Somnath is the **Bhalka Tirth** where Krishna was mistaken for a deer and wounded by an arrow while sleeping in a deerskin. The legendary spot is at the confluence of three rivers. You get to it through the small *sangam* (confluence gate), which is simply known as the Nana, or Small Gate. North of this sacred spot is the **Suraj Mandir**, or Temple of the Sun, which Mahmud of Ghazni also had a go at knocking down. This very old temple, with a frieze of lions with elephant trunks around its walls, probably dates from the same time as the original Somnath Temple.

Places to Stay & Eat

Don't expect too much hot water in Somnath.

Sri Somnath Temple Trust Guest House *(☎ 20212)* is rather dilapidated; its name is written only in Gujarati. Go to the booking office first, directly opposite the bus stand. The cheaper rooms are a bit dingy and cost Rs 60/100 for a double/triple. The best rooms cost Rs 350 or Rs 550 with air-con. This place is primarily for pilgrims.

Hotel Mayuram *(☎ 31286)*, just down the road heading away from the temple, has light doubles for Rs 400. Air-con rooms come with three beds and cost Rs 700.

There are dozens of ***cheap restaurants*** between the temple and Hotel Mayuram.

Getting There & Away

Bus Somnath has fewer departures than neighbouring Veraval, but the STC bus stand does service Jamnagar (Rs 72), Porbandar (Rs 48) and Dwarka (Rs 72). There are also daily departures to Diu (Rs 35, 10 am) and Rajkot (Rs 63, 5 pm). Unusually, the timetable is printed in English. Mama Travels (☎ 22286), directly opposite the bus stand, has a 9 pm departure to Ahmedabad (Rs 130, 10 hours).

SASAN GIR WILDLIFE SANCTUARY

☎ 0285

This last refuge of the Asiatic lion *(Panthera leo persica)* is 59km from Junagadh via Visavadar. The 1400 sq km sanctuary was set up to protect the lion and its habitat: Since 1980 numbers have increased from less than 200 to an estimated 325 in May 2000. However, while the lions have been the winners, the local *maaldharis* (herders) have lost valuable grazing land for their cattle. Moves by the Madhya Pradesh government to transfer 200 lions to the Pulpur Kuno sanctuary in Madhya Pradesh have been indefinitely halted by the Gujarat government, but there are no concrete plans to address the difficulties caused by the competition for scarce resources.

Although the lions seem remarkably tame, in recent years they have reportedly been wandering well outside the limits of the sanctuary in search of easy game – namely calves. One pride even ended up on the beaches of Diu in December 1995 while another responded to the mating calls at Junagadh zoo! The problem is compounded by the declining areas of forest outside the sanctuary, forcing villagers to forage for fuel within the sanctuary precincts, reducing the habitat of the lions.

Apart from lions, there are more than 30 other species, including leopards (268 in 1995), hyenas (137), foxes, wild boars and a number of deer and antelope. The deer include the largest Indian antelope (the nilgai), the graceful chinkara gazelle, the chowsingha and the barking deer. You may also see parrots, peacocks, crocodiles and monkeys.

The best time to visit the sanctuary is from December to April; it's closed from 16 June to 15 October, even later if there has been a heavy monsoon.

Information

The place to go for more information about the park is the Gir Orientation Centre which is next to the Forest Office inside the grounds of the Sinh Sadan Lodge. The centre is very well organised and informative and has displays and descriptions of the park's inhabitants, a replica Maaldhari hut and by pushing a button you can hear the calls of the lions and other animals. Outside, the Gir Welfare Association sells a range of postcards, books, T-shirts and caps. An aged film about the park is screened daily at 7 pm.

Safaris

The lions are elusive, but you'd be unlucky not to see at least one on a safari. If you're determined to spot one, allow for a couple of trips. Understandably, the lions retreat into the undergrowth during Indian holiday

The Last Lions in the Wild Outside Africa

In the 19th century, the territory of the Asiatic lion stretched from its current refuge in Gujarat's Gir Forest as far east as Bihar. Widespread hunting decimated the lion populations, with the last sightings recorded near Delhi in 1834, in Bihar in 1840 and in Rajasthan in 1870. The last lion to die in the Indian wild outside Gujarat's Kathiawar peninsula was recorded in 1884. Why did they survive in Gujarat? They almost didn't. Hunting pushed the Gir lion to the brink of extinction, with as few as 12 remaining in the 1870s. It was not until one of their erstwhile pursuers, the enlightened nawab of Junagadh, decided to set up a protection zone at the beginning of the 20th century, that the lion began to slowly recover. This zone now survives as the Sasan Gir Wildlife Sanctuary.

Separated from their African counterpart *(Panthera leo leo)* for centuries, the Asiatic lion has developed characteristics found only in the Gir Forest's small population. The mane of *Panthera leo persica* is less luxuriant and doesn't cover the top of the head or ears, while a prominent fold of skin runs the length of the abdomen. Its skin is also slightly lighter in colour. The Gir lions are also purely predatory, never feeding off carrion as do lions in Africa.

periods when convoys of jeeps roar through the park. Morning safaris are generally a better bet than those in the afternoon. Unfortunately, the standard of the local guides is variable and most speak little English.

The Gujarati government has drastically increased the cost of most of the park's services, meaning that a stay at Sasan Gir can be expensive. Before you can go on safari, you must get a permit. These are issued on the spot at the Sinh Sadan Forest Lodge office (see Places to Stay & Eat) and cost Rs 30/US$5 for Indians/foreigners. The permit is valid for the whole day. Vehicle entry costs Rs 50/US$10 for four hours, plus Rs 50/US$5 for a camera and a ridiculous Rs 2500/US$200 for a nonprofessional video. The guide's fee for a group is set at Rs 50/US$10, and if your guide's been keen and searched hard then a tip is certainly appreciated. Jeeps can be hired (US$10) from the lodge office from around 6 to 10 am and 3 to 5 pm every day during winter (October to February); there are shorter hours from March to June. Although prices are quoted in US dollars, payment is exclusively in rupees.

Private diesel vehicles cannot be used to tour the sanctuary. Whatever else you do, take a jeep and not a minibus. While the latter stick to the main tracks, the jeeps can take the small trails where you're much more likely to come across lions.

Gir Interpretation Zone

Twelve kilometres from Sasan village at Devalia, within the sanctuary precincts, is the **Gir Interpretation Zone**. The 4.12 sq km zone has a cross section of the wildlife in Gir, so you'd be certain to see a lion here if you've been unlucky in the main sanctuary. The cost to enter the zone, including your jeep, permit and guide, is around Rs 1050 per person, although cheaper minisafaris in a minibus cost around Rs 590. To get there from Sasan Gir, vehicles run from the main street for Rs 150. Although your chances of seeing lions here are good, it's all a bit stage-managed and not particularly good value for money as you're only likely to get 30 to 45 minutes looking for wildlife.

Places to Stay & Eat

There are only a few places to stay at Sasan Gir village. It's a good idea to make an advance booking, as rooms can suddenly fill up.

Sinh Sadan Forest Lodge *(☎ 85540)* is a five-minute walk from the train station and is the centre of most of the action. It is, however, outrageously priced at US$30/50 plus tax for a room without/with air-con; Indians pay Rs 500/1000. Even a dorm costs US$5 (Rs 50 for Indians). It's a pleasant place to stay but not *that* pleasant. Veg meals are available for Indians/foreigners at Rs 70/US$5, nonveg costs Rs 110/US$5, breakfast Rs 40/US$2 and tea or coffee is a silly Rs 7/US$1.

There are a couple of good cheaper options in town, although officials keen to cash in will try and push you towards the Sinh Sadan. ***Rajeshri Guest House*** *(☎ 85740)*, opposite the gate to Sinh Sadan, charges Rs 300 for a double with private bathroom outside holiday periods (Rs 500 during Diwali).

Hotel Umang *(☎ 85728)*, signposted off the main road 100m west, is quieter and pretty good value for Rs 500/800 a single/ double. There is a dining hall and the manager can arrange jeeps.

Gir Lodge *(☎ 85521, fax 85528)*, down by the river about 200m from the Sinh Sadan Forest Lodge, is a pleasant upmarket hotel operated by the Taj Group, although it's not quite up to the standard of other hotels in the chain. Well appointed, but nothing special, rooms including three meals (but not taxes) cost US$60/110 or US$71/ 120 with air-con. Checkout is noon. The hotel's restaurant is open to nonguests if things are quiet and you book ahead. Management can arrange jeeps for US$25, which may sound like a lot, but is possibly worth it if you want one to yourself in peak holiday periods.

The main street of Sasan village is lined with food stalls, grocery stores and a few restaurants doing not much more than thalis. ***Hotel Gulmohal***, at the western end, is probably the pick with reasonable South Indian and Punjabi food. ***Murlidhar Parotha House*** is more rough and ready, but is otherwise OK.

Getting There & Away

STC and express buses travel between Junagadh and Veraval via Sasan Gir regularly throughout the day. The 45km trip to Veraval takes 1½ hours (Rs 15). To Junagadh, the 59km trip takes around two hours (Rs 18). Trains run to Veraval (Rs 10, 1¼ hours, 11.54 am & 3.53 pm), to Delwada (for Diu, Rs 16, three hours, 9.04 am) and to Junagadh (Rs 15, 2½ hours, 5.25pm).

JUNAGADH

☎ 0285 • pop 233,000

Junagadh is at the base of the temple-studded Girnar Hill and is the departure point for visits to the Gir Forest. This interesting and unspoilt town has some exotic old buildings and is a fascinating place to explore. Some of the best buildings are in the streets and squares around the Durbar Hall museum.

The city takes its name from the fort that enclosed the old city (*jirna* means old). Dating from 250 BC, the Ashokan edicts near the town testify to the great antiquity of this site. At the time of Partition, the nawab of Junagadh opted to take his tiny state into Pakistan, but the inhabitants were predominantly Hindu and the nawab soon found himself in exile.

The **Bhavnath Fair** is held in the month of Magha (January/February). Folk music and dancing takes place and lots of *sadhus* (spiritual men) converge on the town. The first fair was allegedly organised by Lord Krishna to honour the Mahabharata hero, Arjuna, who had reached Saurashtra.

Information

The best source of information is Mr Sorathia, the owner of the Relief Hotel – the town's unofficial tourist centre. The State Bank of India, near Diwan Chowk, has money-changing facilities (11 am to 2 pm). Other banks are close by and travellers have reported efficient service from the Bank of Baroda next to the local bus stand. Credit cards can't be used in Junagadh.

Junagadh's main post office is inconveniently located south of the city centre at Gandhigram. There's a branch in a small street off MG Rd near the local bus stand. The telegraph office is on Jhalorapa Rd, near Ajanta Talkies. Internet access is available at Net@Cafe (☎ 628422, ⓔ netcafe@lovemail.com, Rs 30 per hour), downstairs from the Hotel Ashiyana, or Cyber Point (☎ 625655) near Geeta Lodge.

Uperkot Fort

This very old fort stands on the eastern side of Junagadh. It is believed to have been built in 319 BC by Chandragupta, though it has been rebuilt and extended many times over the centuries. In places, the walls are 20m high and an ornate triple gateway forms the entrance to the fort. It's said that the fort was once besieged for a full 12-year period. In all, it was besieged 16 times. It is also said that the fort was abandoned from the 7th to 10th centuries and, when rediscovered, was completely overgrown by jungle. The fort is open daily from 7 am to 6.30 pm, although you can stay inside until 7 pm; entry is Rs 1.

The **Jama Masjid**, the mosque inside the fort, was built from a demolished Hindu temple. Other points of interest include the **Tomb of Nuri Shah** and two fine baolis known as the **Adi Chadi** and the **Navaghan**

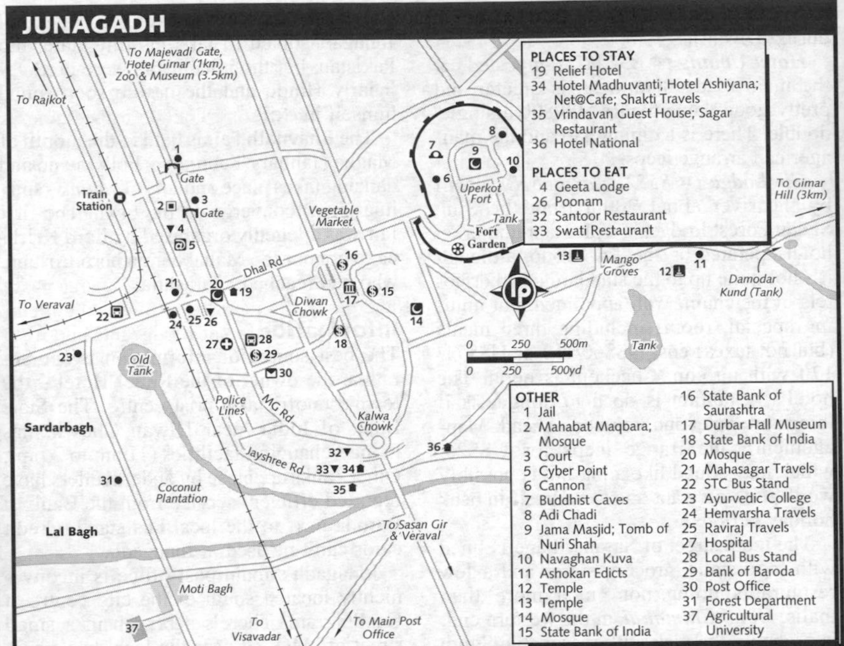

Kuva. The Adi Chadi is named after two of the slave girls who use to fetch water from it. The Navaghan Kuva is reached by a magnificent winding staircase cut into the rock.

Cut into the hillside close to the mosque are some ancient **Buddhist caves** which are thought to be at least 1500 years old. These eerie double-storey caves have six pillars with weathered carvings. Entry to the caves costs Rs 5/US$5 for Indians/foreigners.

The fort is a popular place with Indian tourists during holiday periods when you may feel like you're the main exhibit.

Mahabat Maqbara

This stunning mausoleum of a nawab of Junagadh is one of the finest examples of intricate Indo-Islamic architecture in Gujarat, resplendent with silver doors and minarets encircled by spiralling stairways. Completed in 1892, it is generally locked (the outside is more interesting anyway) – try to obtain the keys from the adjacent mosque.

Durbar Hall Museum

This museum has the usual display of weapons and armour from the days of the nawabs, with collections of silver chains and chandeliers, settees and thrones, howdahs and palanquins, and a few cushions and gowns, as well as a huge carpet that was woven in Junagadh's jail. There's a portrait gallery of the nawabs and local petty princes, including photos of the last nawab with his various beloved dogs.

It's open from 9 am to noon and 3 to 6 pm (closed Monday and the second and fourth Saturday of the month); entry is Rs 5.

Ashokan Edicts

On the way to the Girnar Hill temples, you pass a huge boulder on which Emperor Ashoka inscribed 14 edicts in Pali script around 250 BC. Later Sanskrit inscriptions were added around AD 150 by Emperor Rudradama and in about AD 450 by Skandagupta, the last emperor of the Mauryas. The 14 edicts are moral lectures, while the other inscriptions refer mainly to recurring floods destroying the embankments of a nearby lake, the Sudershan, which no longer exists. The boulder is actually housed in a small roadside building, on the right towards Girnar.

Girnar Hill

The climb up the 10,000 stone steps to the summit of Girnar is best begun early in the morning, preferably at dawn. The steps are well built and maintained; they were constructed between 1889 and 1908. The start of the climb is in scrubby teak forest, about 2km beyond the Damodar Kund, and the road actually takes you to around step No 3000 – which leaves you only 7000 to the top!

There are several refreshment stalls on the 2½-hour ascent, which sometimes sell chalk, so you can graffiti your name onto the rocks beside the path! If you really can't face the walk, *dolis* (rope chairs) carried by porters can be hired; for these you pay by weight so, before setting off, you suffer the indignity of being weighed on a huge beam scale, just like a sack of grain. From the summit, the views are superb.

Like Palitana, the temple-topped hill is of great significance to the Jains. The sacred tank of **Damodar Kund** marks the start of the climb. The path ascends through a wood to the temples near the summit. Five of them are Jain, including the largest and oldest – the 12th-century **Temple of Neminath**, the 22nd Jain tirthankar. There is a large black image of Neminath in the central shrine and smaller images around the temple.

The nearby triple **Temple of Mallinath**, the 9th tirthankar, was erected in 1177 by two brothers. During festivals, this temple is a favourite gathering place for sadhus and a great fair is held here during the Kartika Purnima festival. On top of the peak is the **Temple of Amba Mata**, where newlyweds are supposed to worship at the shrine of the goddess to ensure a happy marriage.

A No 3 or 4 bus from the local bus stand will take you to Girnar Taleti at the base of the hill. Buses run about once an hour from 6 am (Rs 2) and pass by the Ashokan edicts. An autorickshaw from town costs about Rs 30.

Other Attractions

If you are unable to visit the Sasan Gir Wildlife Sanctuary, Junagadh's **zoo** at Sakar Bagh, 3.5km from the town centre on the Rajkot road, has Gir lions. The zoo was set up by the nawab in 1863 specifically to save this lion from extinction and is surprisingly good, with lions, tigers and leopards being the main attractions. The zoo is open from 9 am to 6.30 pm (closed Wednesday) and entry costs Rs 10. There is also a fine **museum** at the zoo with paintings, manuscripts, archaeological finds and various other exhibits including a natural history section. Its opening hours are the same as for the zoo although the museum is also closed on the second and fourth Saturday of each month. Take a No 6 bus (Rs 2) or a rickshaw (Rs 15) – ask for Sakar Bagh.

The **Ayurvedic College** at Sardarbagh on the western edge of town is housed in one of the former nawab's palaces, and has a small museum devoted to Ayurvedic medicine. The staff are knowledgeable and it's a good place for information on this ancient traditional medicine. It is open from 9 am to 6 pm daily.

GUJARAT

Places to Stay

The following places all have bathrooms.

Relief Hotel *(☎ 620280, Dhal Rd)*, is a popular hang-out for travellers, and Mr Sorathia is an obliging and knowledgeable host. Singles/doubles cost Rs 125/200 or Rs 500 for air-con rooms. Good meals are available for guests including what one Indian newspaper described as 'the best biryani in Gujarat'. There's a secure parking area for those with their own vehicles.

Hotel Girnar *(☎ 621201, Majewadi Darwaja)* is a Gujarat Tourism hotel about 2km out of town. It offers rooms for Rs 225/400 or Rs 425/650 with air-con; prices include tea and breakfast. Most rooms are spacious and have a balcony (try to get one of these). Prices drop 40% from 15 June to 15 September. The restaurant serves Gujarati thalis for Rs 40.

Retiring Rooms at the train station cost Rs 50/100; dorm beds are Rs 30.

The ***Vrindavan Guest House*** *(☎ 622777, Jayshree Rd)* is basic but reasonably welcoming. Small rooms with hot water cost only Rs 70/125.

Opposite are two hotels in the same building. ***Hotel Madhuvanti*** *(☎ 620087, Jayshree Rd)* on the 1st floor has big, clean doubles for a negotiable Rs 300, which is a bit much. There's a pool hall on the same floor. ***Hotel Ashiyana*** *(☎ 620706, Jayshree Rd)* on the 2nd floor has decent rooms with TV from Rs 150/250.

Hotel National *(☎ 627891)*, off Kalwa Chowk, had rooms ranging from Rs 350 for a double up to Rs 700 with air-con. The more expensive rooms are particularly comfortable and spacious, although the other rooms (and the service) get decidedly mixed reviews from travellers.

Places to Eat

Junagadh is famous for its fruit, especially *kesar* (mangoes) and *chiku* (sapodilla) both of which are popular in milkshakes in November/December.

Geeta Lodge, close to the train station, has all-you-can-eat thalis for Rs 35.

Santoor Restaurant *(☎ 625090, MG Rd)* has quick service, good veg food (Rs 20 to 40) and tasty mango fruit shakes (Rs 15). The *paneer tikka masala* (Rs 35) is particularly tasty. It's a popular place with locals – always a good sign.

Sagar Restaurant *(☎ 623661)* and ***Swati Restaurant*** *(☎ 625296)*, both on Jayshree Rd, are of a similar standard and price to Santoor Restaurant. It is sometimes necessary to book at the Swati Restaurant during busy times.

Poonam, down a side road opposite Raj Guest House, is another veg place, with thalis for Rs 25. It's above an STD phone place (its sign is only in Gujarati).

Getting There & Away

Bus Just for something different, the timetable at the STC stand is entirely in Gujarati. Buses leave hourly for Rajkot (Rs 35, two hours) and for Sasan Gir (Rs 28, two hours), and there are other regular departures to Porbandar (Rs 42), Veraval (Rs 45), Una (for Diu, Rs 37), Jamnagar (Rs 45) and Ahmedabad (Rs 100).

Various private bus offices are nearby on Dhal Rd, near the rail tracks. Raviraj Travels (☎ 626988) has minibuses to Rajkot every 30 minutes (Rs 25, two hours). Hemvarsha Travels (☎ 620681), with a sign in Gujarati, has buses to Ahmedabad (Rs 110) and Mumbai (Rs 300). Shakti Travels (☎ 621913) and Maharsagar Travels (☎ 629919) are also good for long-haul travel.

Train The reservation office (☎ 131) is open 8 to 11 am and 3 to 5.30 pm.

The *Girnar Express* departs Junagadh at 9.13 pm, arriving in Ahmedabad at 6.05 am (377km, Rs 88/137/462 in general/sleeper/1st class). Few trains originate in Junagadh but plenty pass through en route to Rajkot (Rs 39/205 in general/1st class) and Veraval (Rs 23/173). They rarely stop at the station for longer than a couple of minutes so be prepared for a hasty entry or exit. At 6 am a train leaves for Sasan Gir (Rs 15, 2½ hours) and continues to Delwada (for Una and Diu) arriving at 12.50 pm (Rs 27 in general class only).

PORBANDAR

☎ 0286 • pop 189,300

On the south-east coast, midway between Veraval and Dwarka, modern-day Porbandar is chiefly noted as the birthplace of Mahatma Gandhi, beyond which there are few reasons to visit.

In ancient times, the city was called Sudamapuri after Sudama, a compatriot of Krishna, and there was once a flourishing trade from here to Africa and the Persian Gulf. The Africa connection is apparent in the number of Indianised blacks, known as Siddis, who form a separate caste of Dalits.

The State Bank of India, opposite the Hotel Flamingo, and the State Bank of Saurasthra, in Manek Chowk, are reluctant to change money for nonaccount holders, but may do so if pushed. Alternatively, try Divyaraj Foreign Exchange, south of the Jynbeeli Bridge, or Thankys Tours and Travels on MG Rd (see Getting There and Away later in this section).

Along the coast at Madhavpur near Porbandar, the **Madhavrai Fair** is held in the month of Chaitra (March/April) to celebrate Krishna's elopement with Rukmini.

Kirti Mandir

This memorial to Gandhi was built in 1950. There's a small bookshop and an exhibition of photographs, some with English captions (take the stairs by the entrance). Next door is Gandhi's actual birthplace – a three-storey, 300-year-old house. A swastika marks the spot where the great man was born on 2 October 1869. Entrance is free.

Places to Stay

New Rajkamal Guest House *(☎ 242674, MG Rd)* is not much different from the old guesthouse of similar name – dirt-cheap in every sense and only for real shoestringers. A single costs Rs 40 or Rs 50/80 will get you a single/double with grubby private bathroom and bucket cold water shower.

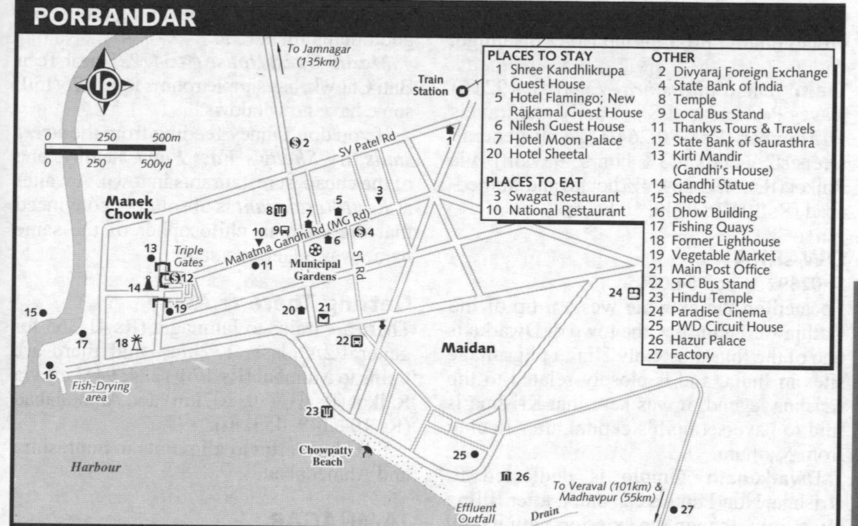

Nilesh Guest House *(☎ 252200, MG Rd)* has doubles with private bathroom, hot water and TV for Rs 150.

Hotel Flamingo *(☎ 247123, MG Rd)*, opposite, is a friendly place with a good restaurant. Rooms cost from Rs 100/150 or Rs 200/250 for better rooms with satellite TV; breakfast is (sometimes) included in the price. Some rooms have a balcony which looks straight into a wall. Checkout is 10 am.

Hotel Sheetal *(☎ 247596, fax 241821)*, opposite the main post office, is of a slightly better standard. Rooms have TV and hot water – prices start at Rs 150/250 up to 500 for an air-con double. Prices are likely to increase by Rs 50 to 100 when the renovations are completed. There is 24-hour room service and management can arrange secure parking for those with their own vehicles.

Shree Kandhlikrupa Guest House *(☎ 246655, SV Patel Rd)*, on the corner near the train station, offers good rooms with private bathroom with cold water for Rs 100/200 or Rs 400 with air-con and balcony. Look for the 'Welcome' sign – the only sign in English.

Hotel Moon Palace *(☎ 241172, fax 243248, ⓔ moonpalace@mail.com)* is the place to go if you're in search of a little more comfort. A few singles are available for Rs 125 though most rooms start at Rs 180/200. The management is decidedly reluctant to give the cheaper rooms to foreigners. Even so, the deluxe suite is good value at Rs 600/700 and as luxurious as you'll get in Porbandar.

Places to Eat

National Restaurant *(MG Rd)* serves only nonveg dishes. It's simple but not bad.

Swagat Restaurant on the eastern end of MG Rd is a popular place with Punjabi food from Rs 20.

Hotel Flamingo has a good air-con restaurant which offers a wide range of Punjabi, Chinese and South Indian food; a main dish costs from Rs 30 to 60. Nonguests are welcome.

Getting There & Away

Air Gujarat Airways has flights to Mumbai (US$110/Rs 5005, daily except Saturday), although how long they'll continue is anyone's guess. Bookings can be made with Thankys Tours & Travels (☎ 244344, fax 245128, ⓔ thankys@vsnl.com) on MG Rd.

An autorickshaw to/from the airport costs about Rs 30.

Bus The STC bus stand is a four-minute walk from MG Rd. There are regular services to Dwarka (Rs 52), Jamnagar (Rs 55), Veraval (Rs 50) and Junagadh (Rs 41/52 for local/

express bus). The private bus companies have offices on MG Rd, near the Hotel Flamingo.

Train The *Saurasthra Express* (9216) leaves Porbandar at 8 pm daily and travels to Mumbai (Rs 170/264/1224 in general/sleeper/2A class, 23½ hours, 959km), via Rajkot (Rs 59/92/464, 4½ hours) and Ahmedabad (Rs 104/162/749, 10 hours).

DWARKA

☎ 02892 • pop 54,000

Located on the extreme western tip of the Kathiawar Peninsula, the town of Dwarka is one of the four most holy Hindu pilgrimage sites in India, and is closely related to the Krishna legend. It was here that Krishna is said to have set up his capital after fleeing from Mathura.

Dwarkanath Temple is dedicated to Krishna. Non-Hindus can enter, after filling out a form, though the exterior, with its tall five-storey spire supported by 60 columns, is actually far more interesting than the interior.

Also worth a look are the carvings of **Rukmini Temple**, about 1km to the east, the many pillared **Sabha Mandapa**, reputed to be over 2500 years old, and the **Nageshwar Mandir** with its underground chamber.

Dwarka's **lighthouse** is open to the public between 4 and 6 pm, and affords a beautiful panoramic view and is a restful place (Rs 1).

Archaeological excavations have revealed five earlier cities at the site, all of which are submerged. Dwarka is the site of the important **Janmashthami Festival** which falls in August/September and celebrates Krishna's birthday.

A little north of Dwarka a ferry crosses from Okha to the **Island of Bet**, where Vishnu is said to have slain a demon. There are modern Krishna temples on the island, and a deserted beach on the northern coast; beware of unfriendly dogs.

Places to Stay & Eat

Most places are willing to negotiate significant discounts except when the town is awash with pilgrims.

Toran Tourist Bungalow *(☎ 34013)*, a state-run place, has dorm beds for Rs 50 and singles/doubles for Rs 200/300.

Meera Hotel *(☎ 34031)*, on the main approach road, has rooms with private bathroom for Rs 100/200. The dining room does good thalis for Rs 25.

Maruti Guest House *(☎ 34722)*, near Teen Bati Chowk, has simple rooms for Rs 75/150; some have no windows.

If you don't fancy feeding from the ***street stalls***, try ***Shetty's Fast Food***, nearby, one of the cheapest restaurants in town. A waiter at ***Kant Restaurant*** is absolutely convinced that the German philosopher of the same name was a German sadhu.

Getting There & Away

There are trains to Jamnagar (Rs 41/365 for general/2A class, 132km), and there are trains to Mumbai (Rs 170/1224, 945km) via Rajkot (Rs 61/470, 207km) and Ahmedabad (Rs 104/749, 453km).

STC buses run to all points in Saurashtra and Ahmedabad.

JAMNAGAR

☎ 0288 • pop 635,000

Prior to Independence, the princely state of Jamnagar was ruled by the Jadeja Rajputs. The city was built around the small Ranmal Lake, in the centre of which is a small palace, reached by a causeway.

Jamnagar has a long history of pearl fishing and *bandhani*, a very time-consuming process of tying thousands of tiny knots in a piece of fabric that has first been folded upon itself a number of times. This is then dyed in several stages using different colours. The knots are then pulled apart and the fabric unfolded to reveal a repeating pattern in a variety of hues. The process, believed to have been used in the area for up to 5000 years, is used for saris, shirts, shawls and other items.

Jamnagar is today equally well known for having the only Ayurvedic university in India and a temple listed in the *Guinness Book of Records*.

The old part of town, known as Chandni Chowk, has a number of delightful and decaying buildings and is a great place to wander around. The centre of the old town is known as Darbar Gadh, a semicircular gathering place where the former maharajas of Nawanagar once held public audiences.

Orientation & Information

The centre of the new part of town, where most places to stay are located, is Teen Batti

Chowk. The old town is to the south-east. The STC bus stand and the new train station are a long way to the west and north-west respectively.

The Lakshmi Vilas Bank, north of the town hall, is the best place to go for foreign exchange. Alternatively, you could also try Precious Money Exchange, which is further around the roundabout. The Hotel President will change US dollars, pounds sterling, euros and deutschmarks, but accept cash only.

Cyber City Club (☎ 676772), signposted simply as Cyber Cafe and opposite the town hall, charges Rs 30 an hour, while Sham Cyber World (☎ 672228), on the first floor next to the Hotel Swagat, charges Rs 35. Both are open 9 am to midnight.

Lakhota Palace

This diminutive palace once belonged to the maharaja of Nawanagar. Today it houses a small **museum** with displays from local archaeological sites. The museum is reached by a short causeway from the northern side of Ranmal Lake, and is open from 10.30 am to 1 pm and 3 to 5.30 pm daily (closed Wednesday and the second and fourth Saturday in the month). Entry costs Rs 2.

Bala Hanuman Temple

The Bala Hanuman Temple is on the south-eastern side of Ranmal Lake, and here, 24 hours a day since 1 August 1964, there's been continuous chanting of the prayer 'Shri Ram, Jai Ram, Jai Jai Ram' which honours and pays homage to the Gods. This

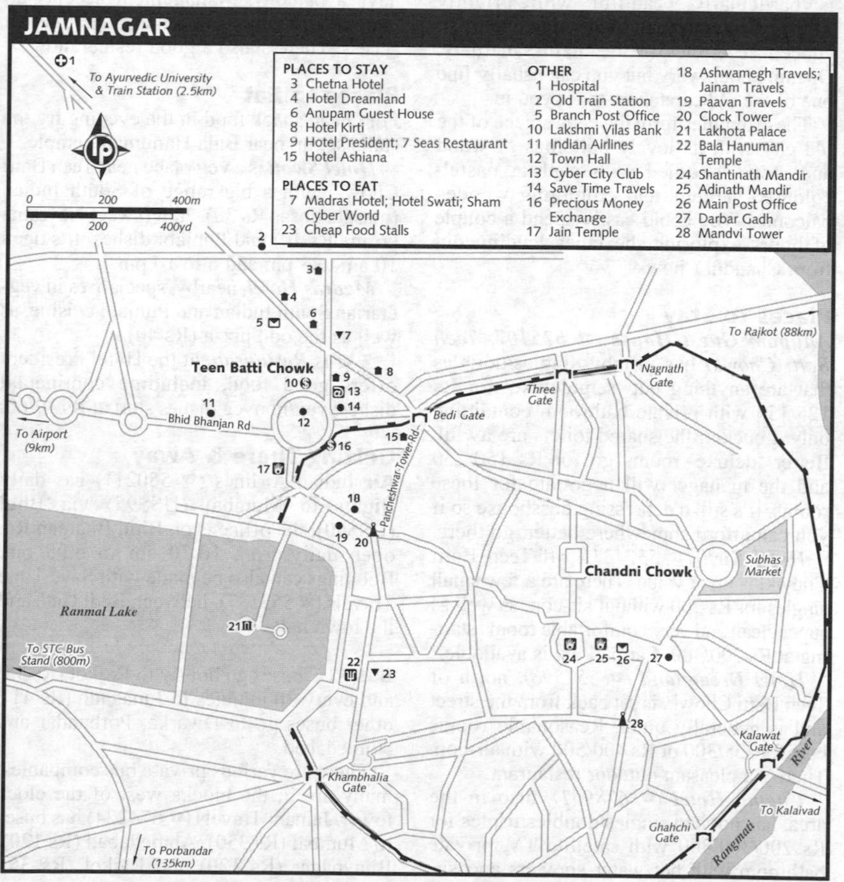

GUJARAT

devotion has earned the temple a place in the *Guinness Book of Records*. Early evening is a particularly good time to visit as it's fairly animated then. In fact this whole area on the south-eastern edge of the lake becomes very lively around sunset, when people come to promenade, and the usual chai and kulfi stalls set up and ply their trade.

Jain Temples

Two Jain temples, Shantinath Mandir and Adinath Mandir, in front of the main post office in Darbar Gadh, are very colourful with fine murals and domes. Dedicated to the sixteenth and first tirthankars respectively, these temples are strikingly located in the centre of the old city. The Shantinath Mandir is particularly beautiful with brightly coloured columns and a gilt-edged dome of concentric circles in the main sanctuary. Opening hours vary but you can usually find one of the old caretakers to let you in.

These temples form the centrepiece of the old city with its lovely buildings of wood and stone, adorned with peeling pastel-coloured shutters and crumbling wooden balconies. You could easily spend a couple of hours exploring the lanes leading out from Chandni Chowk.

Places to Stay

***Anupam Guest House** (☎ 675107, Teen Batti Chowk)* has grubby singles/doubles that are anything but 'semideluxe' for Rs 125/150 with private bathroom containing only a bucket; the shared toilets are awful. Better 'deluxe' rooms go for Rs 150/250 and the manager will negotiate for these rooms. It's still a depressing dosshouse so if you can afford somewhere better, go there.

***Hotel Kirti** (☎ 557121)*, off Teen Batti Chowk, is great value. There are a few small singles for Rs 200 without air-con, as well as super clean and very comfortable rooms starting at Rs 300/400. Car parking is available.

***Hotel Dreamland** (☎ 557598)*, north of Teen Batti Chowk, is set back from the street and is generally quiet. Reasonable rooms cost Rs 225/300 or Rs 400/500 with air-con. There's a pleasant outdoor restaurant.

***Chetna Hotel** (☎ 678951)*, also in the area, has not bad singles/doubles/triples for Rs 200/300/360 with satellite TV, private bathroom with hot water showers and sit-down flush toilet. There's also a dorm (Rs 60) and a restaurant which does good thalis.

***Hotel Ashiana** (☎ 559110, fax 551155)*, a vast, rambling place on the top floor of the New Super Market complex, is one place which takes price differences seriously. Decidedly ordinary semideluxe rooms cost Rs 200/300, the deluxe rooms are better at Rs 325/375 while the super deluxe rooms are huge, comfortable and excellent value. Some rooms have a balcony. There's a veg restaurant here.

***Hotel President** (☎ 557491, fax 558491, ⓔ president@wilnetonline.net, Teen Batti Chowk)* is arguably Jamnagar's best hotel. Rooms with private bathroom, hot water and TV are Rs 450/560 or Rs 650/790 with air-con; many of the very pleasant rooms have a balcony. Management accepts all major credit cards and can arrange Internet access. There's also a good restaurant.

Places to Eat

For cheap snack food in the evening try the stalls set up near Bala Hanuman Temple.

Hotel Swati is a veg place near Teen Batti Chowk with a big range of South Indian (masala dosas Rs 30), Jain (sweet Navratna korma Rs 40) and Punjabi dishes. It's open 10 am to 3 pm and 5 to 10 pm.

Madras Hotel, nearby, specialises in vegetarian South Indian and Punjabi cuisine, as well as the odd pizza (Rs 40).

7 Seas Restaurant at the Hotel President offers good food, including continental dishes; veg/nonveg dishes start at Rs 40/60.

Getting There & Away

Air Indian Airlines (☎ 550211) has daily flights to Mumbai (US$95) via Bhuj (US$40); the office is on Bhid Bhanjan Rd, open daily from 10.30 am to 6.05 pm. Bookings can also be made with Save Time Travels (☎ 553137), between Bedi Gate and the town hall.

Bus STC buses go hourly to Rajkot (Rs 35) and every 30 minutes to Junagadh (Rs 41); other buses go to Dwarka, Porbandar and Ahmedabad.

There are various private bus companies: many are in the blocks west of the clock tower. Jainam Travels (☎ 674224) has buses to Mumbai (Rs 350), Ahmedabad (Rs 120), Bhavnagar (Rs 120) and Rajkot (Rs 35).

Ashwamegh Travels costs the same and has seven daily departures to Ahmedabad and one to Mumbai at 2.35 pm. Paavan Travels (☎ 552002) is also nearby.

Train The *Saurasthra Mail* (9006) is one of many trains that runs between Jamnagar and Ahmedabad (Rs 79/123/356 in general/sleeper/3A class; 6½ hours) but it also continues on to Mumbai (Rs 157/244/707; 17½ hours). It departs Jamnagar at 2.40 pm daily. There are also trains to Dwarka and Rajkot.

Getting Around

There is no minibus service to the airport, which is a long way out. Autorickshaw drivers demand at least Rs 100. A rickshaw from the bus stand to the Bedi Gate area costs about Rs 10. From Teen Batti Chowk to the new train station, about 4km north of the city centre, expect to pay about Rs 25.

RAJKOT

☎ 0281 • pop 1.17 million

This bustling town was once the capital of the princely state of Saurashtra and is also a former British government headquarters. Mahatma Gandhi spent the early years of his life here, and his memory is marked with a statue.

The prestigious Rajkumar College dates back to the second half of the 19th century and is regarded as one of the best private schools in the country. It was set up by the British for the sons of nobility *(rajkumar* means prince).

Information

Rajkot's helpful tourist office (☎ 234507) is hidden away behind the old State Bank of Saurashtra building on Jawahar Rd, almost opposite the Galaxy Hotel. Opening hours are from 10.30 am to 1.30 pm and 2 to 6 pm weekdays and the first and third Saturday of the month.

The State Bank of India, to the north of the Jubilee Gardens, has moneychanging facilities. Entry is from the rear of the building. Some mid-range hotels will also change money, although usually only for guests.

For Internet access, head to the Interlink Cyber Cafe (☎ 227237, ⓔ interlinkindia@rajkotonline.com), in a lane opposite the Sarovar Restaurant. One hour costs Rs 30; this place is open 9 am to midnight.

Watson Museum & Library

The Watson Museum and Library, standing in the Jubilee Gardens, was built to commemorate the work of Colonel John Watson. Watson was Political Agent (Administrator) from 1886–89.

The entrance is flanked by two imperial lions. Among the exhibits are copies of artefacts from Mohenjodaro, 13th-century carvings, temple statues, natural history exhibits and dioramas of local Adivasi costumes and housing styles.

Perhaps the most startling exhibit is a huge marble statue of Queen Victoria seated on a throne, looking decidedly not amused. The museum is open from 9 am to 1 pm and 2 to 6 pm Thursday to Tuesday; admission costs Rs 2.

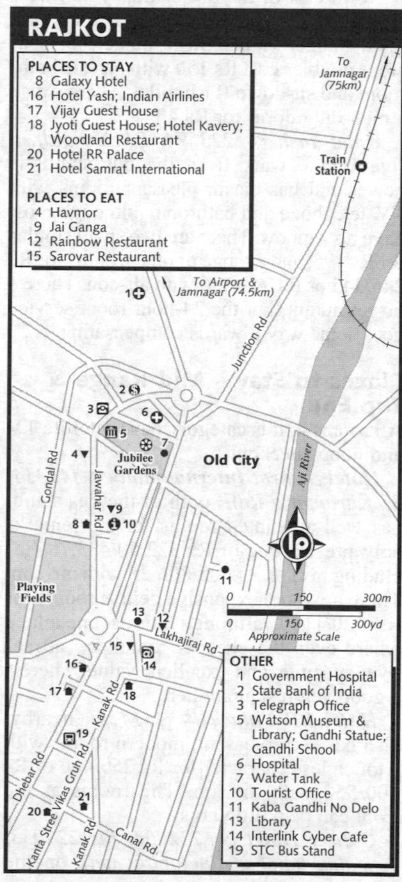

GUJARAT

GUJARAT

Kaba Gandhi No Delo

This is the house where Gandhi grew up, and it now holds a permanent exhibition of Gandhi items. The Mahatma's passion for the handloom is preserved in the form of a small weaving school. It's within the old city on Ghee Kanta Rd, and entry is free. Opening hours are flexible, from around 9 am to noon and 3 to 5.30 pm, Monday to Saturday. The surrounding streets of the old city are atmospheric places in which to wander around.

Places to Stay – Budget

Vijay Guest House *(☎ 236550)* north of the bus stand in a lane off Dhebar Rd, is basic but friendly with rooms for Rs 70/130/200 a single/double/triple. All rooms come with private bathroom and bucket hot water.

North-east of the bus stand, ***Jyoti Guest House*** *(☎ 225472, Kanak Rd)* is quiet and good budget value. Basic but clean, spacious doubles cost Rs 150 with private bathroom and sit-down flush toilet. There's also a men-only dorm for Rs 40.

Hotel Yash *(☎ 223574, Dhebar Rd)*, a five-minute walk from the bus stand, is newer and has clean, pleasant rooms with TV, telephone and bathroom, although most have no window. There are two small singles for Rs 195, and a range of other rooms for Rs 245/345 or Rs 345/586 with air-con. There's no restaurant, but the 24-hour room service goes some way towards compensating.

Places to Stay – Mid-Range & Top End

All rooms in this category have satellite TV and noon checkout.

Hotel Samrat International *(☎ 442234, 37 Karanpara Rd)*, south of the bus stand, has well-appointed rooms for the remarkably precise rate of Rs 322.50/483.75 (including tax) or Rs 605/806.25 with air-con. There are more expensive deluxe rooms for Rs 920/1100, although this is one place where even the cheaper rooms are attractive, spacious and excellent value. There's a good veg restaurant here.

Hotel RR Palace *(☎ 241473)*, nearby, also has very pleasant, modern rooms with a touch less character for Rs 250/400 or Rs 400/550 with air-con. The rooms at the front can be a little noisy.

Galaxy Hotel *(☎ 222904, fax 227053, e galaxyhotel@wilnetonline.net)*, on the 3rd floor of the Galaxy Commercial Centre on Jawahar Rd, is another excellent choice with a classy ambience. Spotless rooms cost Rs 440/660 or Rs 675/1010 with air-con. The rooms are spacious, the staff friendly and although there is no restaurant, management seems to be able to rustle up just about anything through the 24-hour room service. There's a pleasant open terrace area on the roof with swing chairs.

Places to Eat

Rainbow Restaurant *(Lakhajiraj Rd)* is very popular in the evenings and serves tasty and cheap South Indian cuisine. There's an air-con section upstairs. This place has an impressive selection of ice cream: See if you can resist the 'Nuts in Love'!

Havmor, near the Jubilee Gardens, serves Indian, Chinese and Western food from Rs 40 (veg and nonveg).

Jai Ganga, opposite the Galaxy Hotel, and ***Sarovar Restaurant***, north of the bus stand, are similarly good value.

The quality and ambience of the ***Woodland Restaurant*** *(Kanak Rd)* in the Hotel Kavery makes this place feel like an upmarket place, but the prices are very reasonable. Vegetarian dishes start at Rs 25; Gujarati thalis are Rs 65.

Getting There & Away

Air Indian Airlines has daily flights between Rajkot and Mumbai (US$75, 5.50 pm departure). The Indian Airlines office (☎ 227916, fax 233329) is on Dhebar Rd.

Bus STC buses (☎ 235025) connect Rajkot with Jamnagar (Rs 35), Junagadh (Rs 35), Porbandar (Rs 60), Veraval (Rs 58) and Ahmedabad (Rs 122).

There are a number of private buses that operate to Ahmedabad, Bhavnagar, Una (for Diu), Mt Abu, Udaipur and Mumbai. These companies' offices are on Kanak Rd, by the bus stand. The road between Rajkot and Bhuj was seriously damaged in the earthquake and transport links to the Kutch region are likely to be difficult for some time to come.

Train There are at least four trains daily between Rajkot and Ahmedabad (Rs 62/97/279 in general/sleeper/3A class, around six hours, 246km). Trains also go to/from

Jamnagar (Rs 28/44 for general/sleeper class, two hours, 75km), Porbandar (Rs 59/464 in general/2A, 4½ hours, 221km) and Mumbai (Rs 145/225/653 in general/sleeper/3A, 19 hours, 738km). There's a metre-gauge service to Veraval (Rs 52/273 in general/1st class, 5½ hours, 186km). For inquiries, call ☎ 443535 or ☎ 131.

Getting Around

A rickshaw to the airport from the city centre costs about Rs 50; to the train station expect to pay Rs 15.

AROUND RAJKOT

Tarnetar

Every year in the month of Bhadra (around September), the Trineteshwar Temple at Tarnetar, 65km north-east of Rajkot, hosts the three-day **Tarnetar Fair**. The fair is best known for the different *chhatris* (dome-shaped Mughal kiosk) made specifically for the occasion, and is an opportunity to find a spouse: One of the main functions of the fair is to enable villagers from the Bharwad community to form matrimonial alliances. Prospective candidates are bedecked in their finery, making this fair an extraordinarily colourful spectacle.

According to legend, Arjuna once danced at this site and the River Ganges flows into the tank here once a year.

Special state buses go to/from Rajkot during the fair.

Kutch

Kutch, the westernmost region of India, is virtually an island; during the monsoon period from May onwards, it really is an island. The Gulf of Kutch divides Kutch (known in the local dialect as Kachchh) from the Kathiawar peninsula. To the north, it is separated from the Sind region of Pakistan by the Great Rann of Kutch.

During the dry season, the Rann is a vast expanse of hard, dried mud. Then, with the start of the monsoon sometime in May, it is flooded first by sea water, then by the fresh river water. Kutch is also separated from the rest of Gujarat to the east by the Little Rann of Kutch.

The salt in the soil makes this low-lying marsh area almost completely barren. Only on scattered 'islands' above the salt level is there vegetation in the form of coarse grass, which provides fodder for the region's sparse wildlife. These grasslands are under threat from the *gando baval* plant which is spreading across the Rann at an alarming rate, threatening to destroy fragile ecosystems.

The Indus River once flowed through Kutch until a massive earthquake in 1819 altered its course, leaving behind a salt desert. The destructive earthquake in January 2001 similarly altered the fabric of Kachchhi life.

The villages of the Kutch region have long been renowned for their distinctive and high-quality handicrafts (especially exquisite, mirrored embroidery). These handicrafts, and the traditional Kachchhi culture which they represent, were also preserved by a number of cooperatives aimed at ensuring that the craftspeople got a fair cut of the profits. These included the Kutch Mahila Vikas Sangathan, an organisation comprising 4000 rural women that pays members a dividend of the profits and invests money at village level to meet social needs, Shrujan, the Kala Raksha Trust and Kutchcraft, the local representatives for SEWA (see the boxed text 'SEWA' earlier in this chapter). While the communities that ran these organisations have been devastated, you may come across outlets for these groups set up elsewhere in the state of Gujarat to assist the relief effort.

As they surrounded the epicentre of the earthquake, many of Kutch's villages were razed by the quake, with entire villages wiped off the map. For the foreseeable future, most will be off limits to travellers. As the region recovers, all requests for permission to visit should be directed to the Office of the District Superintendent of Police (Foreigners Registration Office) in Bhuj.

BHUJ

As the closest major town to the epicentre of the earthquake, Bhuj was reduced to rubble. Around 90% of the town's buildings were either destroyed or rendered uninhabitable and, although the final death toll may never be known, as much as 10% of the city's population of around 150,000 people were killed. A large proportion of the surviving inhabitants fled Bhuj and surrounding districts.

GUJARAT

The Day the Earth Shook

At around 8.46 am on 26 January 2001, as many of India's Republic Day celebrations were just getting under way, a massive earthquake hit Gujarat. Measuring 7.9 on the Richter scale (in the confused aftermath of the quake, reports of the tremor's magnitude ranged from 6.9 to 8.1) and with its epicentre about 20km north-east of Bhuj, the devastation it wrought was enormous. Apart from Bhuj, the towns of Bhachau (one of the closest towns to the epicentre), Anjar, Surendranagar and countless smaller villages across the Rann of Kutch were destroyed, with few buildings left standing and tens of thousands of lives lost. Further afield, at least 1000 people were killed in Ahmedabad, up to 100 in Morvi, over 300 in Rajkot, around 100 in Jamnagar and close to 50 in Surat.

It was a disaster which Gujarat could ill afford. Like much of western India, the state had been suffering the effects of a crippling drought for two years prior to the quake. As a result of crop failures and scarce water supplies many traditional farmers and other villagers had already left the land that had been worked by their ancestors for generations. Many had moved to the cities, spawning the precarious satellite suburbs ringing cities such as Ahmedabad, putting pressure on already strained resources and changing the demographic make-up of the Gujarati countryside. In the aftermath of the earthquake, as 147 aftershocks (including one which registered 5.9 on the Richter Scale two days after the quake) rocked the region between 26 January and 1 February, tens of thousands of Kachchhis were again reported to be leaving Kutch. The task of rebuilding for those who remain is staggering, and the state-wide ripples of trauma and social dislocation that will continue long after the tremors have ceased can hardly be imagined.

The Gujarati Government, and to a lesser extent the Indian Government, were slated for their slow response to the disaster, and for having contributed to its magnitude by tolerating the practices of unscrupulous builders. Many locals in Bhuj and Gandhidham blamed the large loss of life upon developers for ignoring local building laws limiting the height of new constructions to two storeys. The greatest problem in the quake's aftermath was not a shortage of relief materials, but rather incompetence in the coordination and distribution of supplies, highlighting official unpreparedness for such a large-scale disaster. This was in spite of the fact that both the Chief Minister of Gujarat and seismological experts had publicly predicted for over a year prior to the quake that Kutch would soon experience a high-intensity quake.

As political parties conducted an unseemly squabble for political points, it was the reaction of ordinary Indians that offered the most powerful reasons for hope. As survivors of the quake streamed out of Kutch, many Indians made the reverse journey in an effort to assist relief efforts, even if it meant removing the rubble with their bare hands. Expatriate Kachchhis from around the country (particularly the large community in Mumbai) and members of the sizeable Gujarati community around the world contributed generously to relief efforts. They were joined by expert rescue teams from as far away as Switzerland and Russia, and by thousands of volunteers from around the world. The international community, including Pakistan, also contributed millions of dollars in relief aid. In spite of everything, the bravery, resilience and solidarity of the Gujaratis left no-one in any doubt that Gujarat would be rebuilt.

Prior to the earthquake in January 2001, Bhuj was one of the highlights of any visit to Gujarat. This old, partially-walled city was an intricate maze of streets and alleys with attractive crenellated gateways, old palaces and brightly decorated Hindu temples. It was also the ideal base for exploring the tribal villages of the Kutch region.

It will be a long time before Bhuj and the entire Kutch region will be in a position to handle the arrival of tourists. Its tourist infrastructure was destroyed and the limited resources available in the quake's aftermath will necessarily be dedicated to rebuilding the lives and homes of those who remain.

It is not known which, if any, of Bhuj's tourist attractions remained intact. Most of Bhuj's architectural highlights were concentrated in the demolished old city. These once included the beautiful Aina Mahal (Old Palace) with its exquisite Hall of Mirrors and, just outside the city walls,

Kachchh Museum dating from 1877 – the oldest museum in Gujarat. Some royal tombs or chhatris south-west of Hamrisar Tank were also reduced to rubble. Remarkably, some eyewitness accounts suggest that the distinctive sandstone clock tower of the Prag Mahal (New Palace), right in the heart of the old city, is still standing.

AROUND BHUJ

Gandhidham

The new town of Gandhidham, near Kandla, was established to take refugees from the Sind following Partition. Gandhidham was similarly hard hit by the 2001 earthquake. The town has never contained much of interest to the traveller although in time it will once again become the railhead for neighbouring Bhuj.

MANDVI

Mandvi was, prior to the earthquake, being promoted as a beach resort, and the beach is generally good, long and clean, although, as in many towns along the coast, pollution is an increasing problem. The cleaner sections are away from the wind farm, down by the temple. The town also has a long history of shipbuilding. Mandvi is a pleasant seaside town with friendly people, and is a good place to unwind. Remarkably, Mandvi remained relatively unscathed by the earthquake which ravaged Bhuj, a mere 60km to the north-east. Previously, Kutch and the city of Bhuj were the only gateway for Mandvi and with such widespread damage to the region's roads, Mandvi will be difficult to reach for some time to come. That will change if the much-talked-about ferry between Mandvi and Jamnagar ever gets under way.

Places to Stay & Eat

Rukmavati Guest House *(☎ 20558)* is an eccentric but enjoyable hotel which is still operating. It's a converted hospital, still with hospital-style beds, and the owner uses the ambulance to conduct tours! Clean singles/doubles are Rs 150/300 (bucket hot water), dorms are a steep Rs 100; checkout is 24 hours.

You could also try ***Maitri Guest House*** *(☎ 20183, Bunder Rd)*, which has been recommended by travellers. Clean rooms with bathroom and hot water cost Rs 150/200.

Sahara Guest House *(☎ 20272)*, in the town centre, is also good. Rooms going for Rs 100/175 come with hot water and TV.

Zorba the Buddha, in the heart of the city, is a good place for cheap thalis (Rs 30).

LITTLE RANN OF KUTCH

The Little Rann of Kutch, the barren expanse of 'desert' (actually salt plains) which

Dharamanath: The Desolation of Kutch

The legends of Kutch speak of devastation. This is hardly surprising given the barren landscape and the tragic events of recent history.

One such legend speaks of a spiritual warrior named Dharamanath, who journeyed to Kutch in the 12th century to find a tranquil spot in which to practise penance. He settled himself under a tree near Raipur and, while focusing on matters spiritual, depended on the people of Raipur to attend to his material needs. However, the Raipurians were not exactly forthcoming so, in a fit of rage, Dharamanath invoked a curse upon them. The city became desolate and its inhabitants hastily removed themselves to Mandvi. Dharamanath, overcome by remorse, resolved to climb the highest hill he could find, in order to engage in a penance commensurate with his vengeful act. After being rejected by two hills, which refused to carry the burden of his guilt, he climbed *backwards* up a third hill – Dhinodar – and there proceeded to stand on his head...for 12 years. The gods, concerned at this excess, pleaded with Dharamanath to cease his penance. Dharamanath acceded, on condition that wherever his gaze fell, the region should become barren. Casting his gaze before him, the seas receded, leaving a barren, desolate wasteland – the Great Rann of Kutch.

On the highest peak of Dhinodar, a shrine dedicated to Dharamanath contains a red besmeared stone, which allegedly bore the head of the inverted ascetic during his extraordinary act of penance.

Dharamanath founded a community of sadhus at Than, known as the Kanphata (Split Eared), because they had to split open their ears upon joining. This is still done today with a heavy ring.

divides Gujarat's western region of Kutch from the rest of Gujarat, was described by one traveller as 'a striking desert of mud, salt and mirages'. It is home to the last remaining population of khur (Asiatic wild ass) in India. There's also a large bird population, particularly of lesser flamingos: The area is one of the few places in India where flamingos are known to breed naturally. Both are protected in the 4953 sq km Little Rann Sanctuary, which is approached from Dhrangadhra (see the boxed text 'Warning' earlier in this chapter for information on areas affected by the 2001 earthquake).

The Asiatic wild ass, of which there are around 2100 in the sanctuary, survives off the flat, grass-covered expanses or islands, known as *bets*, which spring up during the monsoon. This remarkable creature is capable of running at an average speed of 24km/h for up to two hours and can even reach speeds of 70km/h over shorter distances.

Before setting out, consider the following traveller's advice:

> The Rann can be treacherously difficult to explore as the desert consists of salt deposited at a time when the area formed part of the delta of the River Indus. This means that rain can quickly turn parts of the desert into a sea of mud, and what to the untrained eye looks like solid ground may in fact be a thin crust of dry silt with soft mud underneath. Hence it is essential to have someone along who is familiar with local conditions.
>
> **Krys Kazmierczak, UK**

The small town of **Zainabad**, 105km north-west of Ahmedabad, is very close to the Little Rann of Kutch. Desert Coursers (☎/fax 02757-41333; in Ahmedabad ☎ 079-6752883) is a family-run tour company that organises interesting safaris and cultural tours in the Little Rann. Prices are about Rs 1900 per day.

The same family runs ***Camp Zainabad***, offering *kooba* (traditional thatch-roofed huts) with private bathroom in a peaceful setting. It costs about Rs 1800 per person per night, including breakfast and dinner and unlimited safaris. Advance booking is advised. The self-contained huts are basic, but comfortable.

One guide, who has come highly recommended by a number of travellers, is Devji Bhai Dhamechs, a wildlife photographer who is based in Dhrangadhra (☎ 02754-50560, fax 50300). You can also stay at his home for Rs 1200 for two nights, including food (note that advance notice is essential). You could also try the ***Government Rest House***.

Permission is required to enter the sanctuary. Contact the Deputy Conservator of Forests in Dhrangadhra (☎ 02754-23016). Dhrangadhra is on the Gandhidham-to-Ahmedabad rail route 170km (3½ hours) from Gandhidham and 130km (3 hours) from Ahmedabad.

To get to Zainabad by road from Ahmedabad, you can take a bus to Dasada, 12km north-east of Zainabad (Rs 28, 2½ hours). From here Desert Coursers does free pick-ups, or there are local buses. There are also direct buses from Rajkot. Desert Coursers can arrange taxis for around Rs 2.50 per kilometre.

Madhya Pradesh & Chhatisgarh

/ladhya Pradesh is the geographical heart-and of the country, but is no longer as large n area. After years of lobbying by members f Madhya Pradesh's Assembly, the new tate of Chhatisgarh (also spelt Chhattis-;argh) came into existence in November :000, with the city of Raipur as its capital.

Consisting of the south-eastern corner of he old state, Chhatisgarh is industrially ackward and the infrastructure is poor; rought is a major problem and there is lit-e in the way of tourist attractions. The new overnment however has promised a new ocus on education, particularly literacy, to elp deal with the many issues facing the ew state.

Most of Madhya Pradesh is a high pla-eau and in summer it can be very dry and ot, but together with Chhatisgarh, it also as the highest percentage of forest in India, heltering a wide variety of wildlife, in-luding 22% of the world's tiger popula-ion. Virtually all phases of Indian history ave left their mark on Madhya Pradesh, istorically known as Malwa. There are still nany pre-Aryan Gond and Bhil Adivasis tribal people) in the state, but Madhya 'radesh is overwhelmingly Indo-Aryan.

Some of Madhya Pradesh's attractions are emote and isolated: Khajuraho, with its fab-lous temples, is in the north of the state – a ong way from anywhere; Jabalpur, with its narble rocks, is near the centre of the state; Kanha National Park, famous for its tigers, s 160km south-east of Jabalpur.

Most of the state's other attractions are on r near the main Delhi to Mumbai (Bombay) rain line. From Agra, just outside the state o the north, you can head south through Gwalior (with its magnificent fort) to Sanchi, Bhopal, Ujjain, Indore and Mandu.

History

Signs of habitation date back some 12,000 ears with the rock cave paintings at Bhim-etka near Bhopal – excavations have re-ealed a cultural succession from the late Stone Age. Madhya Pradesh's history how-ever can be traced back to the 3rd century BC, when the great Buddhist emperor Ashoka controlled the Mauryan empire in Malwa.

Madhya Pradesh & Chhatisgarh at a Glance

Population: 60.4 million (Madhya Pradesh), 20.8 million (Chhatisgarh)
Area: 443,446 sq km
Capital: Bhopal (Madhya Pradesh) & Raipur (Chhatisgarh)
Main Language: Hindi
When to Go: Sept to Feb

- Wander around Khajuraho's exquisite temples, India's visual *Kamasutra*, depicting love and life a millennium ago
- Explore Orchha – fortified palaces on a river island and magnificent temples
- Travel to Sanchi, with its ancient stupas revealing Buddhism's Indian origins
- See Bhimbetka's 12,000-year-old cave paintings depicting prehistoric India
- Escape the congestion of nearby cities at Mandu, a vast fortress complex
- Rumble around on an elephant or spot a tiger at Kanha and Bandhavgarh National Parks

At Sanchi you can see the Buddhist centre founded by Ashoka, the most important reminder of him in India. The Mauryas

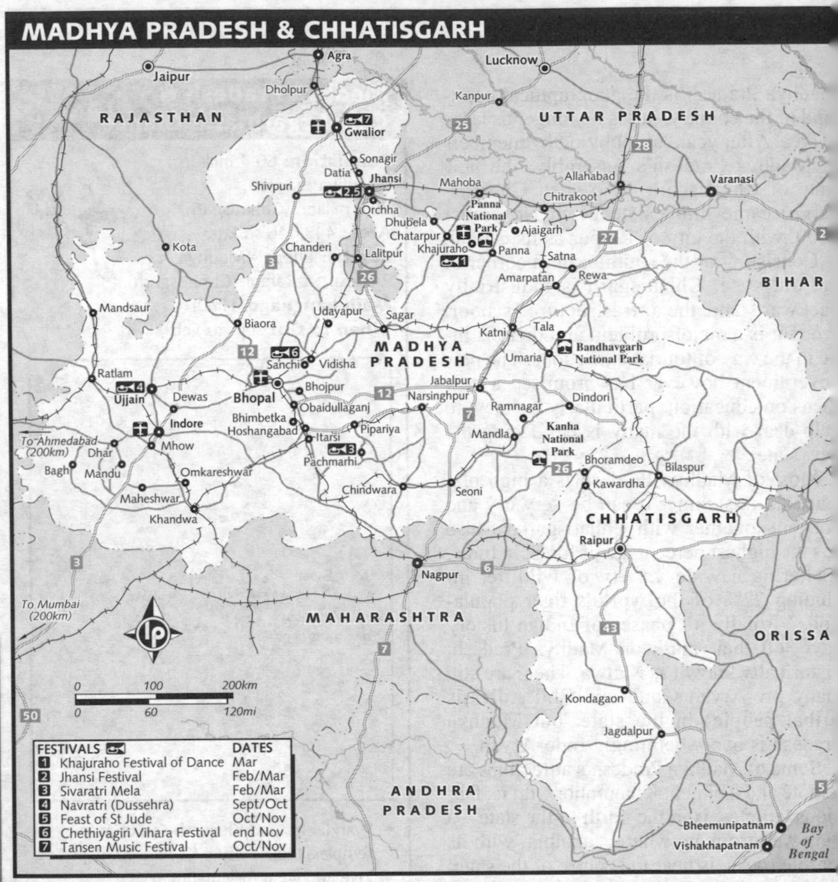

were followed by the Sungas and then by the Guptas, before the Huns swept across the state. Around 1000 years ago the Parmaras ruled in south-west Madhya Pradesh – they're chiefly remembered for Raja Bhoj, who gave his name to the city of Bhopal and also ruled over Indore and Mandu.

From AD 950 to 1050 the Chandelas constructed the fantastic series of temples at Khajuraho in the north of the state.

Between the 12th and 16th centuries, the region experienced continuing struggles between Hindu and Muslim rulers or invaders. The fortified city of Mandu in the south-west was frequently the scene for these battles, but finally the Mughals overcame Hindu resistance and controlled the region. The Mughals, however, met their fate at the hands of the Marathas who, in turn, fell t the British. With the States Reorganizatio Act of 1956, several former states were combined to form Madhya Pradesh.

Northern Madhya Pradesh

GWALIOR

☎ 0751 • pop 830,720

Just a few hours from Agra by train or road Gwalior is famous for its old and very large fort. Within the fort walls are several inter esting temples and ruined palaces. The dra matic and colourful history of the great for goes back over 1000 years.

History

Gwalior's legendary beginning stems from a meeting between Suraj Sen and the hermit Gwalipa, who lived on the hilltop where the fort stands. The hermit cured Suraj Sen of leprosy with a drink of water from the Suraj Kund, which still remains in the fort. He then gave him a new name, Suhan Pal, and said his descendants would remain in power so long as they kept the name Pal. His next 83 descendants did just that, but number 84 changed his name to Tej Karan and – you guessed it – goodbye kingdom.

What is more certain is that in 1398 the Tomar dynasty came to power in Gwalior and, over the next several centuries, Gwalior Fort was the scene of continual intrigue and clashes with neighbouring powers. In 1516 the fort was besieged and taken by Ibrahim Lodi after a long struggle. Later the Mughals, under Babur, took the fort and held it until 1754 when the Marathas captured it.

For the next 50 years the fort changed hands on several occasions, including twice to the British, and finally passed into the hands of the Scindias. At the time of the Indian Uprising in 1857, the maharaja remained loyal to the British but his troops didn't, and in mid-1858 the fort was the scene for some of the final, and most dramatic, events of the Uprising. It was near here that the British finally defeated Tantia Topi and it was in the final assault on the fort that the rani of Jhansi was killed (see Jhansi later in this chapter).

Orientation & Information

Gwalior is dominated by its fort, or *kila*, which tops the long hill to the north of Lashkar, the new town. The Old Town clings to the hill, north-east of the fort. The main market area, Jayaji Chowk, is Lashkar's hub, and nearby is Bada Chowk, where you'll find the post office and the State Bank of India.

MP Tourism (☎ 340370, fax 340371) is at Hotel Tansen, open weekdays, which you'll find about 500m south-east of the train station. There's another tourist office in the train station, but it's hopeless.

Email is available from the superior Cyber point 'n' Cafe Joint, Ashiana Complex, Moti Palace, Lashkar for Rs 25 per hour. It's just off the main road and is open from 8.30 am to 10.30 pm. Raja Cyber, near Hotel Safari, also has Internet connections, but is a bit more expensive.

Fort

Rising 100m above the town, the fort hill is about 3km long. Its width varies from nearly 1km to less than 200m. The walls, which encircle almost the entire hilltop, are 10m high and imposingly solid. Beneath them, the hill face is a sheer drop away to the plains. On a clear day the view from the fort walls is superb.

You can approach the fort from the south or the north-east. The north-eastern path starts from the archaeological museum and follows a wide, winding slope to the doors of the Man Singh Palace. The southern entrance, via Urbai Gate, is a long, gradual ascent by road, past cliff-face Jain sculptures.

An atmospheric sound-and-light show is held every evening at the open-air amphitheatre outside the Man Singh Palace. The English version is at 7.30 pm (the 6.30 pm showing is in Hindi); tickets are Rs 150.

There are several things to see in and around the fort, although most of the enclosed area is simply open space, fields and the grounds occupied by the prestigious private Scindia School. Admission to the fort, which includes all monuments, is US$5 (Rs 230), plus Rs 25 for a video camera and it's open from 8 am to 5 pm daily. Guides can be hired at the gate from around Rs 100 for two or three hours.

Jain Sculptures The long ascent on the southern side climbs up through a ravine to the fort gate. Along the rock faces flanking this road are many Jain sculptures, some impressively big. Originally cut into the cliff-faces in the mid-15th century, they were defaced by the forces of Babur in 1527 but were later repaired.

The images are in five main groups and are numbered. In the Arwahi group, image No 20 is a 17m-high standing sculpture of the first Jain *tirthankar* (revered teacher or saint), Adinath, while image No 22 is a 10m-high seated figure of Nemnath, the 22nd Jain tirthankar. The south-eastern group is the most important and covers nearly 1km of the cliff-face with more than 20 images.

Teli-ka-Mandir This temple probably dates from the 9th century but has been

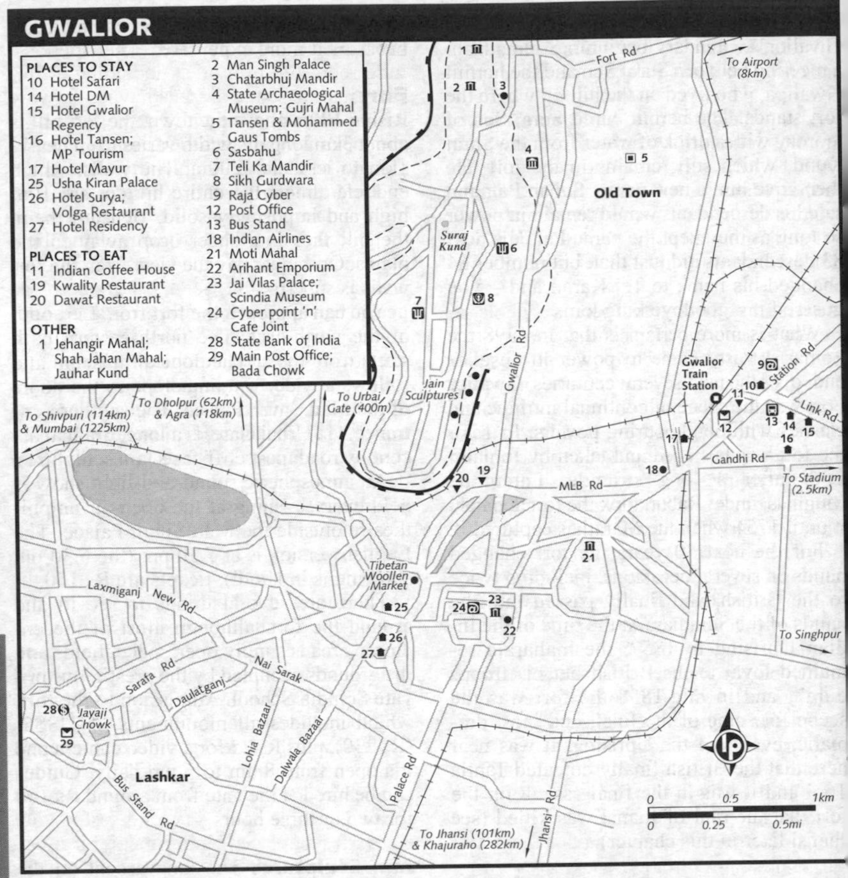

restored. Its peculiar design incorporates a Dravidian roof with Indo-Aryan decorations (the whole temple is covered with sculptures). A Garuda tops the 10m-high doorway.

Between the Teli Ka Mandir and the Sasbahu temples is an impressive gleaming white **Sikh gurdwara**, or temple.

Sasbahu Temples The Sasbahu, or Mother-in-Law and Daughter-in-Law temples, stand close to the eastern wall about midway along that side of the fort. The two temples are similar in style, and date from the 9th to 11th centuries. The larger temple has an ornately carved base and figures of Vishnu over the entrances, and four huge pillars support the heavy roof.

Man Singh Palace North of the Sasbahu the palace, a delightfully whimsical building, is also known as the Chit Mandir, or Painted Palace, because of the tiled and painted decorations of ducks, elephants and peacocks. Painted blue, with hints of green and gold, it still looks very impressive today.

The palace was built by Man Singh between 1486 and 1516, and was repaired in 1881. It has four levels, two of them underground and all of them now deserted. The subterranean ones were used as prison cells during the Mughal period.

There's a small **museum** next to the Man Singh Palace housing sculptures and carvings from around the fort. It's open from 1[illegible] am to 5 pm daily, except Friday (Rs 2).

Other Palaces There are other palaces clustered within the fort walls at the northern end. The **Karan Palace**, or Kirti Mandir, is a long, narrow two-storey building on the western side of the fort. At the northern end are the **Jehangir Mahal** and **Shah Jahan Mahal** with a very large and deep tank, the **Jauhar Kund**. It was here that the Rajput women of the harem committed mass *sati*, or self-immolation, after the raja was defeated in battle in 1232.

North-East Entrance There is a whole series of gates as you descend the worn steps of the path to the archaeological museum. The sixth gate, the **Hawa Gate**, originally stood within the palace but has been removed. The fifth gate, the **Hathiya Paur**, or Elephant Gate, is the entrance to the palace.

Descending, you pass a Vishnu shrine dating from AD 876 known as the **Chatarbhuj Mandir**, or Temple of the Four-Armed. From here a series of steps leads to rock-cut Jain and Hindu **sculptures**.

The interesting fourth gate was built in the 15th century and named after the elephant-headed god, Ganesh. There is a small pigeon house, or **Kabutar Khana**, here, as well as a small four-pillared **Hindu temple** to the hermit Gwalipa, after whom the fort and town were named.

The third gate is known as the **Badalgarh**, after Badal Singh, Man Singh's uncle. The second gate, the Bansur, or Archer's Gate, has disappeared. The first gate is the **Alamgiri Gate**, dating from 1660.

State Archaeological Museum The museum is within the **Gujri Mahal**. Built in the 15th century by Man Singh for his favourite queen, Mrignayni, the palace is now in a rather deteriorated condition. There's a large collection of Hindu and Jain sculptures and copies of the Bagh Caves frescoes. It's open from 10 am to 5 pm daily except Monday (entry is Rs 2 plus Rs 2 for a camera).

Jai Vilas Palace & Scindia Museum

Although the current maharaja still lives in the palace of the Scindia family, 35 rooms now form a museum. It's full of the bizarre items Hollywood maharajas are supposed to collect, such as Belgian cut-glass furniture (including a rocking chair), and what looks like half the tiger population of India, all shot, stuffed and moth-eaten. Then there's a little room full of erotica, including a life-sized marble statue of Leda having her way with a swan. But the *piéce de résistance* is a model railway that carried brandy and cigars around the dining table after dinner.

The main durbar hall is impressive. The gold paint used around the room is said to weigh 58kg, and the two giant chandeliers are incredible; they each hold 248 candles, are 12.5m high and weigh 3.5 tonnes – so heavy that before they were installed, elephants were suspended from the ceiling to check that it could take the weight.

If you go there by autorickshaw, ask for the museum, which is not at the palace entrance. The palace and museum are open from 9.30 am to 5.30 pm daily except Monday. Admission is a ridiculously royal Rs 175 plus Rs 25/75 for a camera/video.

Old Town

The Old Town of Gwalior is situated to the north of the fort hill. The 1661 **Jama Masjid** is a fine old building, constructed of sandstone quarried from the fort hill. On the eastern side of town is the **tomb of Mohammed Gaus**, a Muslim saint who played a key role in Babur's acquisition of the fort.

Nearby is the smaller **tomb of Tansen**, a singer much admired by Akbar. Chewing the leaves of the tamarind tree near his grave is supposed to do wonders for your voice. It is a place of pilgrimage for musicians during October/November, when the tree tends to look unseasonably autumnal, stripped by visiting enthusiasts.

Special Events

The **Tansen Music Festival** is held around October/November each year and attracts classical musicians and vocalists from all over India. Free performances are usually staged at Tansen's tomb in the Old Town.

Places to Stay – Budget

Most decent hotels in this range are within walking distance of the train station or bus stand.

Hotel Mayur *(☎ 325559, Padav)* is the best of the cheap places and is in a good location down a quiet alley, just a few minutes' walk across the bridge from the train station. A bed in the roomy, air-cooled dorm (no bunks) costs Rs 55. The dorm has two bathrooms, and there are lockers under each bed. Spotless air-cooled singles/doubles with private bathroom start from Rs 120/150, up to 300/350 with air-con. There is bucket hot water and squat toilets.

Hotel Safari *(☎ 340638, Station Rd)* is above shops on a busy road, but it's not bad value. Reasonably clean fan-cooled rooms with private bathroom (squat toilet) are Rs 135/170 and deluxe rooms with TV and hot water are Rs 200/235.

Hotel DM *(☎ 342083, Link Rd)* is a most peaceful place away from the hustle and bustle but close to the bus stand. Singles/doubles with private bathroom are good value at Rs 135/185, or bigger rooms with TV are Rs 185/225. There's a restaurant.

Hotel Residency *(☎ 320743, Inder Ganj, Lashkar)* is an excellent, centrally located hotel with clean rooms, constant hot water and is reasonably priced. Good-sized air-cooled rooms start at Rs 275/300.

Places to Stay – Mid-Range & Top End

Hotel Tansen *(☎ 340370, fax 340371, 6A Gandhi Rd)*, an MP Tourism place, is pleasantly situated in a shady area about 1km south-east of the train station. Rooms are spacious but not great value at Rs 390/450 (plus Rs 50 for an air-cooler), or Rs 650/750 with air-con. As with a lot of MP Tourism hotels, this place seems to be a breeding ground for mosquitoes. Checkout is noon and there's a restaurant and bar.

Hotel Surya *(☎ 331183, fax 310083, Jayendra Ganj, Lashkar)* has plain but comfortable air-cooled rooms for Rs 275/350 and air-con rooms for Rs 375/450.

Hotel Gwalior Regency *(☎ 340670, fax 343520, Link Rd)* has stylish, centrally air-conditioned rooms starting at Rs 750/975. There's a range of facilities including a health club and swimming pool.

Usha Kiran Palace *(☎ 323993, fax 321103, Jayendra Ganj, Lashkar)* is the town's top hotel. This serene former maharaja's palace is great for a splurge with opulent furnishings and huge rooms starting from US$65/120.

Places to Eat

Indian Coffee House below Hotel India is a good cheap place, with masala dosas for Rs 15 and other vegetarian snacks. It's staffed by the usual attentive waiters in fan-shaped headgear.

Kwality Restaurant is an air-con haven not far from the southern fort gate on MLB Rd. The food is fresh, the service is good and prices are reasonable with large veg mains from around Rs 38.

Dawat Restaurant, nearby on the same main road, is classier than Kwality with slightly higher prices to match.

Volga Restaurant is at Hotel Surya. There's nothing Russian about it, but very good Indian food is served.

Usha Kiran Palace restaurant is the place to eat out in style. The Mughlai food is excellent and it occasionally has a buffet as well as a la carte with mains from around Rs 110.

Shopping

The Arihant Emporium, a government approved shop, is a good place to find local handicrafts. It specialises in semiprecious silver jewellery. A simple ring may cost Rs 80 while an intricately styled necklace can cost up to Rs 10,000. It also specialises in silver carvings. For more atmosphere and better prices have a wander around Jayaji Chowk.

Getting There & Away

Air Indian Airlines (☎ 326872), MLB Rd, has a 'hopping' flight from Delhi (US$70) through Gwalior to Bhopal (US$80), Indore (US$105) and Mumbai (US$160). It flies from Delhi on Monday and Friday, and returns via the same route also on both of these days.

Bus From the government bus stand on Link Rd there are regular services to Agra (Rs 56, three hours), Jhansi (Rs 46, three hours) and Shivpuri (Rs 50, 2½ hours), and a few departures for Ujjain (Rs 187), Indore (Rs 224), Bhopal (Rs 175) and Jabalpur (Rs 200). There are two buses a day at 7 and 8.30 am to Khajuraho (Rs 129, nine hours), but it's better to take the train to Jhansi and a bus from there.

Train Gwalior is on the main Delhi to Mumbai train line. The superfast *Shatabdi Express* links Gwalior with Delhi (Rs 495/ 985 in chair/executive class, 3¼ hours), Agra (Rs 255/505, 1¼ hours), Jhansi (Rs 230/455, one hour) and Bhopal (Rs 545/ 1110, 4½ hours).

f you've got the money but not the time you ould use this reliable service for a day trip o Gwalior from Agra.

On other express trains it's five hours to)elhi (Rs 79/415 in 2nd/1st class, 317km), wo hours to Agra (Rs 36/189, 118km), 12 ours to Indore (Rs 205/693 sleeper/1st lass, 652km) and 24 hours to Mumbai Rs 310/1050, 1225km).

Slow passenger trains are useful if you vant to get off at Sonagir or Datia on the way o Jhansi, or Dholpur on the way to Agra.

;etting Around

'o/From the Airport Autorickshaws harge around Rs 90 for the 8km trip to the irport. A taxi costs around Rs 200.

.ocal Transport Gwalior is spread out ınd congested with traffic so finding your vay around on foot can prove futile. Autoickshaws are plentiful but the meters are ust fashion accessories; Rs 10 should cover hort trips. A ride from the train station to 3ada Chowk, the main square in Lashkar, vill cost Rs 20 – but you'll have to bargain. The frightening-looking *tempos* (large autoickshaws) are useful and cheap if you can vork out where they're going. They run ixed routes around the city; the fare is ₹s 6 from the train station to Bada Chowk.

AROUND GWALIOR

;hivpuri

☎ 07492

The old summer capital of the Scindias was ıt Shivpuri, 114km south-west of Gwalior ınd 94km west of Jhansi. Set in formal garlens, the **chhatris** (tombs) are the main atraction here. With Mughal pavilions and *ikhara* (Hindu temple-spires), these beauiful memorials to the Scindia rulers are inaid in *pietra dura* (marble inlay work) tyle, like the Taj Mahal.

Nearby is **Madhav National Park**, essenially a deer park (entry Rs 150). On the edge of the park is the Sakhya Sagar lake. Swimning from the old boat club pier here is unvise as there are crocodiles in the lake.

Accommodation includes ***Chinkara Motel*** *(☎ 21297),* MP Tourism's place in Shivpuri. ;ingles/doubles are Rs 350/450.

Tourist Village *(☎ 23760)* is near Bhadıiya Kund, only a few kilometres from Madhav National Park. It has comfortable rooms in attractive cottages for Rs 390/490, or Rs 590/690 with air-con.

There are frequent buses to/from Gwalior (Rs 50, 2½ hours) and Jhansi (Rs 40, four hours).

CHANDERI

At the time of Mandu's greatest power, Chanderi was an important place, as indicated by the many ruined palaces, *serais* (inns), mosques and tombs – all in a Pathan style similar to that of Mandu. The **Koshak Mahal** is a ruined Muslim palace and is worth a look.

Today the town is chiefly known for its gold brocades and saris. Accommodation in the town includes a ***Circuit House*** and the ***Rest House*** near the bus stand. Chanderi is 33km west of Lalitpur, which is 90km south of Jhansi on the main train line.

JHANSI

☎ 0517 • pop 456,895

Jhansi, 101km south of Gwalior, is actually just across the border in Uttar Pradesh, but for convenience we've included it here. Although Jhansi has played a colourful role in Indian history, for most visitors it's simply a convenient transit point for Khajuraho, and increasingly for Orchha, only 18km away.

The last of a string of rajas died in 1853 and the rani (Rani Lakshmibai) was forcibly retired by the British (who had conveniently passed a law letting them take over any princely state under their patronage if the ruler died without a male heir). When the Indian Uprising burst into flame four years later, she was in the forefront of the rebellion at Jhansi. The British contingent in Jhansi was all massacred, but the following year the rebel forces were still quarrelling among themselves, and the British retook Jhansi. The rani fled to Gwalior and, in a valiant last stand, she rode out against the British, disguised as a man, and was killed. She has since become a heroine of the Indian independence movement.

Orientation & Information

The old city is behind the fort, 3km from the train station. The town is spread out so you'll need to use autorickshaws to get around.

The Uttar Pradesh and Madhya Pradesh state governments have tourist booths at the train station, though neither of them is

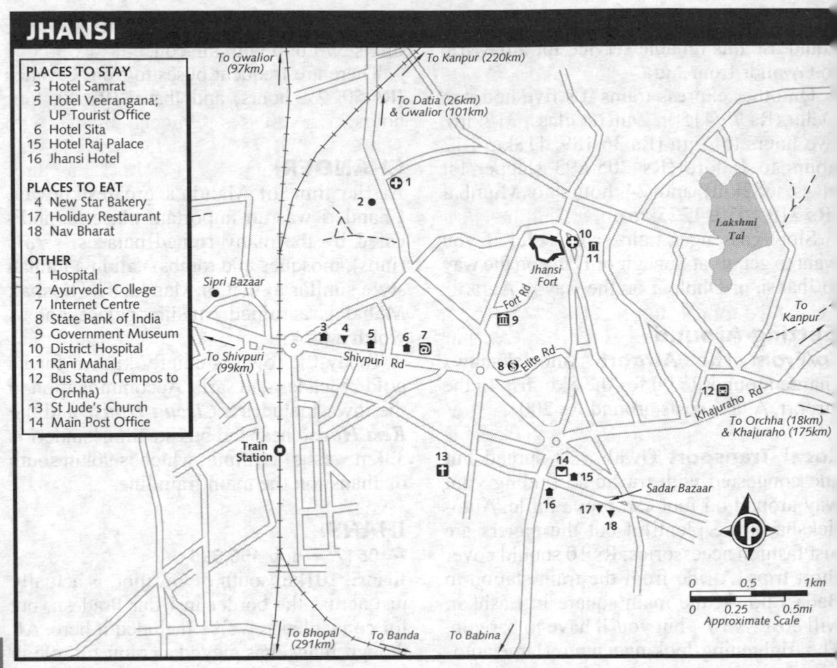

particularly good. There's a helpful UP tourist office (☎ 441267) open from 10 am to 5 pm weekdays, at Hotel Veerangana.

State Bank of India accepts only American Express travellers cheques (in US dollars). Try Hotel Sita or Jhansi Hotel for cash exchange.

There's an Internet cafe next to Hotel Sita. It's well signposted and costs Rs 60 per hour (open until 11 pm).

Things to See

Once used by the Indian army, **Jhansi Fort** was built in 1613 by Maharaja Bir Singh Deo of Orchha. There's nothing much to see, apart from the excellent views from the ramparts. Guides (around Rs 50) are on hand to show you around and tell some colourful tales. The fort is open from sunrise to sunset daily (US$5 or Rs 230).

Just below the walls as you approach the fort is a bizarre blood-and-guts diorama of the battle in which the rani of Jhansi died.

Rani Mahal, the former palace of Rani Lakshmibai, consists of arched chambers around an open courtyard and was built in the 18th century. The palace is now a museum containing hundreds of 9th- to 12th century sculptures. It's open from 9.30 am to 5.30 pm daily (entry is Rs 25; video cameras are an extra Rs 25).

Special Events

The **Jhansi Festival** is a lively arts and cultural event held in February/March. It is a locally organised program of music, art and dance. Jhansi is also known for the **Feast of St Jude** on 28 October when thousands of desperate Christian pilgrims converge on St Jude's Church to plead their case to the patron saint of lost causes. The big day is preceded by a 10-day novena.

Places to Stay

Jhansi has a range of accommodation, much of it strung along Shivpuri Rd.

Hotel Veerangana *(☎ 442402, Shivpuri Rd)* is a UP Tourism place with dorms at Rs 60 and singles/doubles from Rs 200/275 up to 525/600 with air-con (geyser hot water). Though it's a bit run-down, it's a large place with a garden and a good restaurant.

Hotel Samrat *(☎ 444943, Shivpuri Rd)* is pretty good value, with rooms costing from

Rs 200/250 with bathroom (bucket hot water) or Rs 250/275 with air-cooler and TV.

Jhansi Hotel *(☎ 470360, Shastri Marg)* is one of the best in town for old-fashioned charm. It was a hotel in British times and touches of the Raj are still evident. Big, slightly ragged doubles (bucket hot water) with colonial furniture are Rs 475/575. The restaurant here is very good, and the bar is open all day.

Hotel Raj Palace *(☎ 470554, Shastri Marg)* is a nondescript modern place with air-cooled rooms starting at Rs 245/325, or Rs 275/350 for better facilities. Air-con rooms are Rs 475/525. All rooms have a hot-water geyser.

Hotel Sita *(☎ 442956, fax 444691, Shivpuri Rd)* is the place to head if you like your creature comforts. Rooms in this clean and well-maintained three-star place have TV, phone and constant hot water and cost Rs 550/600, or Rs 875/925 with air-con.

Places to Eat

Most of the hotels have restaurants – those in ***Jhansi Hotel*** and ***Hotel Veerangana*** are recommended.

Holiday Restaurant, in the Sadar Bazaar near the Jhansi Hotel, is popular with a good range of North Indian and Chinese dishes, and tea served in fine china. Vegetarian dishes are between Rs 20 and Rs 35.

Nav Bharat runs a creditable second, and both places have good ice-cream parlours.

New Star Bakery *(Shivpuri Rd)* conjures up excellent sweets which you can enjoy with a coffee from the espresso machine set up on the road out the front.

Getting There & Away

Bus Deluxe buses to Khajuraho leave from the train station at 5.30 and 11 am (Rs 85, 4½ hours). Local buses (Rs 75, 5½ hours) leave more frequently from the bus stand east of town. Head to this bus stand for services to many other places including Gwalior (Rs 40, three hours), Shivpuri (Rs 40, four hours) and Datia (Rs 15, one hour). For Orchha, the tempos from here are better. They cost Rs 10 for the 40-minute journey and leave when (very) full. Buses to Orchha cost Rs 8.

Train Jhansi is on the main Delhi-Agra-Bhopal-Mumbai line. Tickets on the crack *Shatabdi Express* cost Rs 565/1030 in chair/executive class for Delhi; Rs 330/660 for Agra; Rs 230/460 for Gwalior; and Rs 480/960 for Bhopal.

Other expresses connect Jhansi with Delhi (Rs 95/478 in 2nd/1st class, 414km, eight hours), Agra (Rs 61/371, 215km, three hours), Gwalior (Rs 32/223, 97km, 1½ hours), Bhopal (Rs 176/476 for sleeper/1st class, 291km, 4½ hours), Indore (Rs 116/659, 555km, 10 hours) and Mumbai (Rs 332/1061, 1158km, 22 hours). There are also direct trains from Jhansi to Bangalore, Lucknow, Chennai (Madras), Pune and Varanasi.

Getting Around

The forecourt outside the train station is filled with predatory autorickshaw drivers. They charge around Rs 25 for the trip to the bus stand; crowded tempos will drop you there for Rs 6.

ORCHHA

☎ 07680

Once the capital city of the Bundelas, Orchha (hidden place) is now just a village, set among a wonderful complex of well-preserved palaces and temples. The main palaces were protected inside fortified walls on an island in the Betwa River. It's definitely worth a visit and a lot of travellers are beginning to discover Orchha's peaceful beauty. Tour groups do it in a couple of hours but it's a very relaxing place to stay, and you can even get a room in part of the palace here.

History

Orchha was founded in 1531 and remained the capital of a powerful Rajput kingdom until 1783, when nearby Tikamgarh became the new capital. Bir Singh Deo ruled from Orchha between 1605 and 1627 and built the Jhansi Fort. A favourite of the Mughal Prince Salim, he feuded with Akbar and in 1602 narrowly escaped the emperor's displeasure; his kingdom was all but ruined by Akbar's forces. Then in 1605 Prince Salim became Emperor Jehangir, and for the next 22 years Bir Singh was a powerful figure. In 1627, Shah Jahan became emperor and Bir Singh once again found himself out of favour; his attempt at revolt was put down by the 13-year-old Aurangzeb.

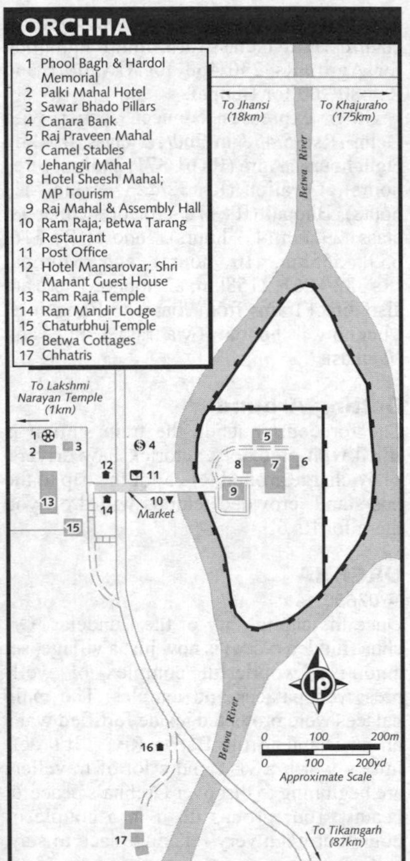

Orchha's golden age was during the first half of the 17th century. When Jehangir visited the city in 1606, a special palace, the Jehangir Mahal, was constructed for him. Later, both Shah Jahan and Aurangzeb raided the city.

Information

The helpful MP Tourism office is at Hotel Sheesh Mahal. Cash and travellers cheques can be changed at Canara Bank on the main road. You can only change US$100 or UK £50 here per day.

Entry to Orchha's sites is Rs 30, making it extremely good value in comparison to the escalating prices at similar attractions in the state – make sure you hold on to your ticket as it includes all the palaces, temples and the museum. It's an extra Rs 20/50 for a camera/video and the sites are all open from 9 am to 5 pm.

Palaces

Crossing the bridge over the Betwa River to the fortified island brings you to three 17th-century palaces. The **Jehangir Mahal** is an impressive, rambling complex with good views of the countryside from the upper levels. There's a small **archaeological museum** on the ground floor. The **Raj Mahal** nearby has superb murals. Below the Jehangir Mahal is the smaller **Raj Praveen Mahal**, a palace built near a garden. The *hammam* (bathhouse) and camel stables are nearby. Go-ahead MP Tourism has an excellent personal headset tour; you follow the arrows painted on the floor of the palaces in sync with the commentary. The English narration, sound effects and backing music really bring the empty rooms to life. It costs Rs 50 plus a Rs 500 deposit.

On the other side of the village, **Dinman Hardol's Palace** (also called **Palki Mahal**) next to the Ram Raja Temple, is also interesting, as is its story. The son of Bir Singh Deo, Dinman Hardol committed suicide to 'prove his innocence' over an affair with his brother's wife, achieving the status of a folklore hero through his martyrdom.

Temples

Orchha's impressive temples date back to the 16th century. They're still in use and are visited regularly by thousands of devotees. In the centre of the modern village is the **Ram Raja Temple** with its soaring spires. Originally a palace, it was turned into a temple when an image of Rama, temporarily installed, proved impossible to move. It now seems to have somehow made its way into the nearby **Chaturbhuj Temple**, where it is hidden behind silver doors. The **Lakshmi Narayan Temple** is linked to Ram Raja by a 1km-long path; it's worth the walk to see the well-preserved murals.

Other Attractions

The walled **Phool Bagh** gardens, a cool summer retreat beside the Palki Mahal, are a memorial to Dinman Hardol. Also worth seeing are the impressive **chhatris** (cenotaphs) to Orchha's rulers, down by the Betwa River, about 500m south of the village.

Places to Stay

Orchha has an increasingly good range of places to stay, including the wonderful Hotel Sheesh Mahal.

Hotel Mansarovar *(☎ 52628, Main Market)*, run by the Special Area Development Authority (SADA), looks shabby but has clean rooms for Rs 50/75 with shared bathroom (squat toilets).

Shri Mahant Guest House *(☎ 52715)* is a newly opened place right next to Mansarovar. It's possibly the best budget option in Orchha. Spotless rooms with tiled private bathroom (bucket hot water) are Rs 150, Rs 200 or Rs 250 depending on the space you want. Some rooms have squat toilets. It's very friendly and the balcony is an excellent meeting place.

Palki Mahal Hotel, another SADA place (check in at Hotel Mansarovar), is atmospherically set in part of the former palace of Dinman Hardol – though the rooms are anything but palatial. Simple doubles with shared bathroom are Rs 90 or a dorm bed is Rs 15. It's popular with backpackers.

Ram Mandir Lodge *(☎ 52669)*, opposite Mansarovar, has basic but clean double rooms with shared bathroom (bucket hot water and squat toilets) from Rs 100, and a balcony which overlooks the main street.

MP Tourism runs two fairly upmarket places in Orchha.

Betwa Cottages *(☎ 52618)*, in a peaceful location by the river about 500m from the village, is set in a spacious, well-tended garden with good views to the palace. Singles/doubles are Rs 490/590, or Rs 690/790 with air-con.

Hotel Sheesh Mahal *(☎ 52624)*, in a converted wing of the Jehangir Mahal, must be the most romantic place to stay in Madhya Pradesh. The ordinary rooms, with large private bathrooms, colonial furniture and views into the palace courtyard, are Rs 490/590 plus tax. The real luxury is found in the royal apartment (Rs 2990), with its own porch and dining area, huge marble bathroom and superb views over Orchha, or the equally luxurious room below it (Rs 1990). Book ahead, as it is often full.

Places to Eat

There are a few restaurants in the village on the road running between the Jehangir Mahal and the market. ***Ram Raja***, near the bridge is vegetarian and pretty good. ***Betwa Tarang***, next door, is a bit more upmarket with continental, Chinese and Indian (most curry dishes around Rs 30) cuisine. It's upstairs off the street and has an outdoor area.

The restaurant at ***Hotel Sheesh Mahal*** is the best place to eat in Orchha and is a good spot for breakfast before exploring the palaces. Excellent buffet dinners with traditional entertainment are occasionally held on the upstairs terrace.

Getting There & Away

There are regular buses (Rs 8) and tempos (Rs 10) from the Jhansi bus stand for the 18km journey to Orchha. An autorickshaw will cost around Rs 100.

KHAJURAHO

☎ 07686 • pop 7665

Close behind the Taj and up there with Varanasi, Jaipur and Delhi, the temples of Khajuraho are one of India's major attractions. Once a great Chandela capital, Khajuraho is now a quiet village. In spite of all the tourist attention it's still a mellow place to spend a few days, though the attention from hawkers immediately outside the western temple enclosure can be irritating.

Large numbers of visitors come to Khajuraho in March for the spectacular dance festival (see Special Events).

Orientation

The modern village of Khajuraho is a cluster of hotels, restaurants, shops and stalls near the western group of temples. About 1km east of the bus stand is the old village of Khajuraho. Around it are the temples of the eastern group and to the south are two further groups of temples.

Information

Tourist Offices The Government of India tourist office (☎ 72347, ⓔ goito@bom6.vsnl.net.in), open from 9.30 am to 6 pm weekdays, is the best place for information. There's also an office at the airport. The MP Tourism office is hardly worth visiting; it's hidden away at the Chandela Cultural Centre.

Money State Bank of India is the best place to change money – US$200 is the maximum you can change per day. Canara Bank down behind the bus stand is less

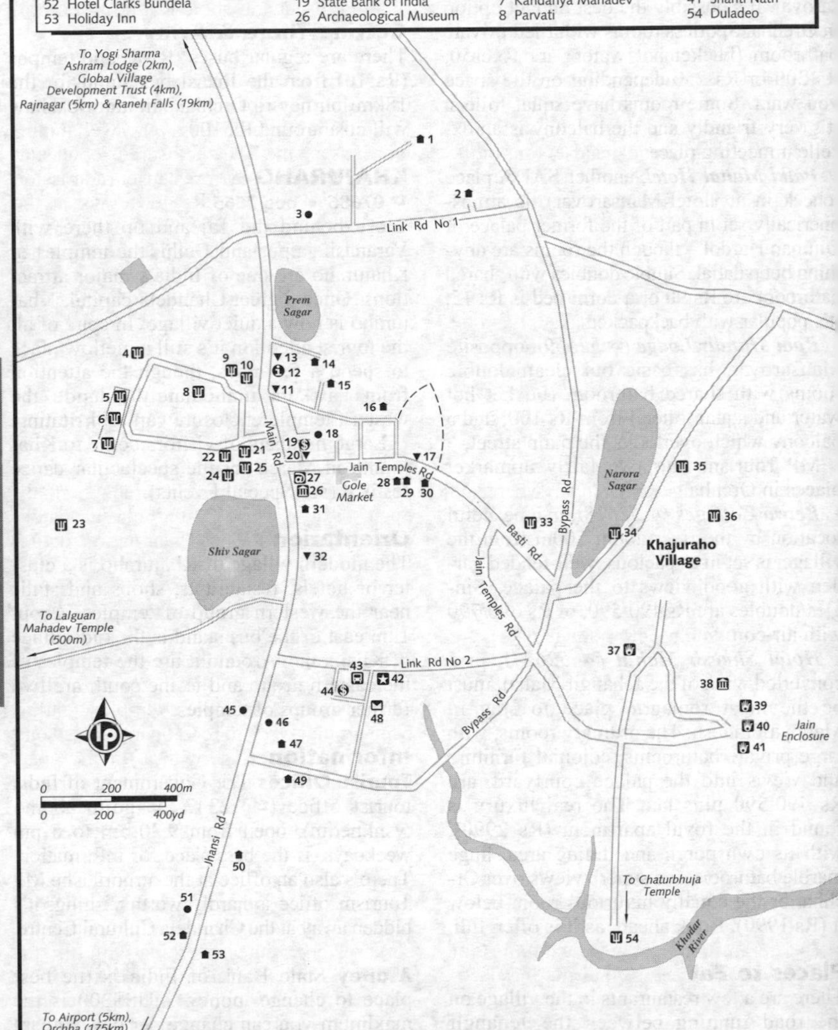
KHAJURAHO
PLACES TO STAY
1 Tourist Village
2 Hotel Payal
14 Hotel Casa Di William
15 Yogi Lodge & Guesthouse
16 Hotel Marble Palace
28 Hotels Jain, Surya & Gem Palace
29 Hotel Harmony; Shivam Restaurant
30 Hotel Zen
31 Hotel Lakeside
47 Hotel Jhankar
49 Hotel Jass Trident
50 Hotel Chandela
52 Hotel Clarks Bundela
53 Holiday Inn
PLACES TO EAT
11 Raja's Cafe
13 Blue Sky Restaurant
17 Mediterraneo Restaurant
20 Safari Restaurant
32 Shiva Janti; Paradise
OTHER
3 Chandela Cultural Centre; MP Tourism
12 Government of India Tourist Office
18 Chhatri
19 State Bank of India
26 Archaeological Museum
27 Internet Hut
38 Jain Museum
42 Police
43 Bus Stand
44 Canara Bank
45 Kandariya Art & Culture
46 Shilpgram
48 Main Post Office
51 Indian Airlines
TEMPLES
4 Chitragupta
5 Devi Jagadamba
6 Mahadeva
7 Kandariya Mahadev
8 Parvati
9 Vishvanath
10 Nandi
21 Lakshmi
22 Lakshmana
23 Chausath Yogini
24 Matangesvara
25 Varaha
33 Hanuman
34 Brahma
35 Vamana
36 Javari
37 Ghantai
39 Adinath
40 Parsvanath
41 Shanti Nath
54 Duladeo
To Yogi Sharma Ashram Lodge (2km), Global Village Development Trust (4km), Rajnagar (5km) & Raneh Falls (19km)
Link Rd No 1
Prem Sagar
Main Rd
Jain Temples Rd
Gole Market
Narora Sagar
Bypass Rd
Basti Rd
Khajuraho Village
Shiv Sagar
To Lalguan Mahadev Temple (500m)
Link Rd No 2
Jain Enclosure
0 200 400m
0 200 400yd
Jhansi Rd
To Chaturbhuja Temple
Khodar River
To Airport (5km), Orchha (175km) & Jhansi (188km)

busy than the State Bank of India and there are a few private moneychangers in the village offering lower rates than the banks.

Email & Internet Access Try Internet Hut near the Archaeological Museum for Internet access, costing Rs 80 per hour. Be warned – power failures in town can make connections haphazard. Private telephone booths sometimes provide connections but they charge about Rs 120 per hour.

Guides Government of India approved guides can be organised at tourist offices or at Raja's Cafe and cost Rs 255/380 per half/full day for up to four people. Multilingual guides are an extra Rs 125. MP Tourism also has a novel headset tour of the western group of temples for Rs 50 plus Rs 500 deposit. The narration is informative and easy to follow.

Temples

Khajuraho's temples were built during the Chandela period, a dynasty that survived for five centuries before falling to the Mughal onslaught. Most date from one century-long burst of creative genius from AD 950 to 1050. Almost as intriguing as the sheer beauty and size of the temples is the question of why and how they were built here. Khajuraho is a long way from anywhere and was probably just as far off the beaten track a thousand years ago as it is today. There is nothing of great interest or beauty to recommend it as a building site, there is no great population centre here and during the hot season Khajuraho is very hot and dry.

Having chosen such a strange site, how did the Chandelas manage to recruit the labour to turn their awesome dreams into stone? To build so many temples of such monumental size in just 100 years must have required a huge amount of human labour. Whatever their reasons, we can be thankful they built Khajuraho where they did, because its very remoteness helped preserve it from the desecration Muslim invaders were only too ready to inflict on 'idolatrous' temples elsewhere in India.

The temples are superb examples of Indo-Aryan architecture, but it's the decorations with which they are so liberally embellished that have made Khajuraho famous. Around the temples are bands of exceedingly artistic stonework showing many aspects of Indian life a millennium ago – gods and goddesses, warriors and musicians, real and mythological animals.

But two elements appear over and over again and in greater detail than anything else – women and sex. Stone figures of *apsaras* (celestial maidens) appear on every temple. They pout and pose for all the world like pin-up models posing for the camera. In between are the *mithuna* (erotic figures) running through a whole Kamasutra of positions and possibilities.

Western Group The main temples are in the western group, most contained within a fenced enclosure that is very well maintained as a park. The enclosure is open sunrise to 30 minutes before sunset (admission is a steep US$10 or Rs 460). Ask at the ticket office about the excellent Archaeological Survey of India guidebook to Khajuraho. It's often out of stock, but worth buying if available (Rs 20).

The temples are described here in a clockwise direction.

Lakshmi & Varaha Facing the large Lakshmana Temple are these two small shrines. The Varaha Temple, dedicated to Vishnu's boar incarnation or Varaha *avataar*, faces the Matangesvara Temple. Inside this small, open shrine is a huge, solid and intricately carved figure of the boar incarnation, dating from around AD 900.

Lakshmana The large Lakshmana Temple is dedicated to Vishnu, although in design it is similar to the Kandariya Mahadev and Vishvanath temples. It is one of the earliest of the western enclosure temples, dating from around AD 930 to 950, and is also one of the best preserved, with a full five-part floor plan and four subsidiary shrines. Around the temple are two bands of sculpture instead of the usual three; the lower one has fine figures of apsaras and some erotic scenes. Inside are excellent examples of apsaras acting as supporting brackets.

On the subsidiary shrine at the south-west corner is an architect working with his students – it is thought this may be the temple's designer including himself in the grand plan. Around the base of the temple is a continuous frieze with scenes of battles, hunting

Temple Terminology

The Khajuraho temples follow a fairly consistent and unique design pattern which has a five- or three-part layout.

You enter the temples through an entrance porch, known as the *ardhamandapa*. Behind this is the hall or *mandapa*. This leads into the main hall, or *mahamandapa*, supported with pillars and with a corridor around it. A vestibule or *antarala* then leads into the *garbhagriha*, the inner sanctum, where the image of the god to which the temple is dedicated is displayed. An enclosed corridor, the *pradakshina*, runs around this sanctum. The simpler three-part temples don't have a mandapa or pradakshina.

Externally the temples consist of successive waves of higher and higher towers culminating in the soaring *sikhara* (spire), which tops the sanctum. While the lower towers, over the mandapa or mahamandapa, may be pyramid-shaped, the sikhara is taller and curvilinear. The ornate, even baroque, design of all these vertical elements is balanced by an equally ornate horizontal element from the bands of sculptures that run around the temples.

The whole temple sits upon a high terrace, known as the *adisthana*. The finely carved entrance gate to the temple is a *torana*, and the lesser towers around the main sikhara are known as *urusringas*.

The temples are almost all aligned east to west, with the entrance facing east. Some of the earliest temples were made of granite, or granite and sandstone, but all those from the classic period of Khajuraho's history are made completely of sandstone.

The sculptures and statues play such an important part in the total design that many have their own terminology:

Apsara – heavenly nymph, beautiful dancing woman
Mithuna – Khajuraho's most famous image, the sensuously carved, erotic figures that have been shocking a variety of people, from Victorian archaeologists to busloads of blue-rinse tourists.
Nayika – the only difference between a surasundari and a nayika is that the surasundari is supposed to be a heavenly creature while a nayika is human.
Salabhanjika – female figure with tree, which together act as supporting brackets in the inner chambers of the temple. Apsaras also perform this bracket function.
Surasundari – when a surasundari is dancing she is an apsara. Otherwise she attends the gods and goddesses by carrying flowers, ornaments, mirrors or other offerings. She also engages in everyday activities like washing her hair, fondling herself, playing with pets and babies, playing musical instruments or posing seductively.
Sardula – a mythical beast, part lion, part some other animal or even human. Sardulas usually carry armed men on their backs, and can be seen on many of the temples.

and processions. The first metre or two consists of a highly energetic orgy, including one gentleman proving that a horse can be a person's best friend, while a stunned group of women look away in shock.

The temple platform gives you a good view of the Matangesvara Temple (see later in this section).

Kandariya Mahadev The first of the temples on the common platform at the back of the western enclosure is not only the largest, it is also artistically and architecturally the most perfect. Built 1025–50, it represents Chandela art at its finest. Although the four subsidiary shrines that once stood around the main temple are long gone, the central shrine is in superb condition and shows the typica five-part design of Khajuraho temples.

The main spire is 31m high, and the tem ple is lavishly carved. The English archae ologist Cunningham counted 226 statue inside the temple and a further 646 outsid – 872 in total with most of them nearly 1m high. The statues are carved around the temple in three bands and include gods, goddesses, beautiful women, musicians and, o course, some of the famed erotic groups The mithuna on the Kandariya Mahadev include some of the most energetic eroticism to be seen at Khajuraho.

Mahadeva This small and mainly ruinec temple stands on the same base as the

Kandariya Mahadev and the Devi Jagadamba. Although small and insignificant compared to its mighty neighbours, it houses one of Khajuraho's best sculptures – a fine sardula figure caressing a lion.

Devi Jagadamba The third temple on the common platform is slightly older than the Kandariya Mahadev and of a simpler, three-part design. It was probably originally dedicated to Vishnu, but later dedicated to Parvati and then Kali. Some students believe it may still be a Parvati temple and that the Kali image (or Jagadamba) is actually an image of Parvati, painted black. The sculptures around the temple are again in three bands. Many of the two lower band images are of Vishnu with sardulas in the inner recesses. But on the third and uppermost band the mithuna again come out to play.

Chitragupta The fourth temple at the back of the western enclosure does not share the common platform with the other three. Similar in design to the Devi Jagadamba, this temple is probably slightly newer and is unique at Khajuraho in being dedicated to Surya, the sun god.

Attempts have obviously been made at restoration, but it is not in as good condition as other temples. Nevertheless it has some very fine sculptures, which include processions, dancing girls, elephant fights and hunting scenes. In the inner sanctum, Surya can be seen driving his chariot and seven horses, while on the central niche in the south facade you can see an 11-headed statue of Vishnu. The central head is that of Vishnu himself; the 10 others are of his incarnations.

Parvati Continuing around the enclosure, you come to the Parvati Temple on your right. The name is probably incorrect since this small and not-so-interesting temple was originally dedicated to Vishnu and now has an image of Ganga riding on the back of a crocodile.

Vishvanath & Nandi Believed to have been built in 1002, this temple has the complete five-part design of the larger Kandariya Mahadev Temple, but two of its four subsidiary shrines still stand. The large image of Shiva's vehicle, the bull Nandi, faces the temple from the other end of the common platform. Steps lead up to this high terrace, flanked by lions on the northern side and elephants on the southern side.

The sculptures around the temple include the usual Khajuraho scenes, but the sculptures of women are particularly notable here. They write letters, fondle a baby, play music and, perhaps more so than at any other temple, languish in provocative poses.

Matangesvara Next to the Lakshmana Temple, this temple is not within the fenced enclosure because it is still in everyday use, unlike all the other old Khajuraho temples. It may be the plainest temple here (suggesting that it was one of the first built) but inside it sports a polished lingam, 2.5m high.

Early in the morning, flower-sellers do a brisk trade in garlands for the statue of Ganesh outside. People drape them around the elephant-headed statue, say a prayer and as they walk away the sellers whip the flowers off to resell!

Chausath Yogini & Lalguan Mahadev Standing beyond the tank, some distance from the other western group temples, this ruined temple is probably the oldest at Khajuraho, dating from AD 900 or earlier. It is also the only temple constructed entirely of granite and the only one not aligned east to west. Chausath means 64 – the temple once had 64 cells for figures of the 64 *yoginis* (female attendants) who attended the goddess Kali. A 65th cell sheltered Kali herself.

A further 500m west is the Lalguan Mahadev Temple, a small, ruined shrine dedicated to Shiva and constructed of granite and sandstone.

Eastern Group The eastern group of temples can be subdivided into two groups. The first is made up of interesting Jain temples in the walled enclosure. The other four temples are scattered through the old village of Khajuraho (as distinct from the modern village near the western temples).

Parsvanath The largest of the Jain temples in the walled enclosure is also one of the finest at Khajuraho. Although it does not approach the western enclosure temples in size, and does not attempt to compete in the sexual activity stakes, it is notable for the exceptional skill and precision of its construction, and for the beauty of its sculptures. Some of the best-known figures at Khajuraho can be seen here, including the classic figure of a woman removing a thorn from her foot and another of a woman applying eye make-up. Although it was originally dedicated to Adinath, an image of Parsvanath was substituted about a century ago; the temple takes its name from this newer image.

Adinath Adjacent to the Parsvanath Temple, the smaller Adinath has been partially restored over the centuries. It has fine carvings on its three bands of sculptures and, like the Parsvanath, is very similar to the Hindu temples of Khajuraho. Only the striking black image in the inner sanctum indicates that it is Jain rather than Hindu.

Shanti Nath This temple is a relatively modern one built about a century ago, but it contains many components from older temples around Khajuraho. The 4.5m-high statue of Adinath is said to have been sculpted in 1028. Groups of Digambara (Sky-clad, or naked) Jain pilgrims occasionally stay at the *dharamsala* (pilgrims' lodging) here.

Ghantai Walking from the eastern Jain temple group towards Khajuraho village, you come to this small, ruined Jain temple. Only its pillared shell remains, but it is interesting for the delicate columns with their bell-and-chain decoration and for the figure of a Jain goddess astride a Garuda that marks the entrance.

Javari Walk through the village, a typical small Indian settlement, to this temple. Dating from around 1075 to 1100, it is dedicated to Vishnu and is a particularly fine example of Khajuraho architecture on a small scale. The exterior has more of Khajuraho's maidens.

Vamana About 200m north of the Javari Temple, this temple is dedicated to Vamana, the dwarf incarnation of Vishnu. Slightly older than the Javari Temple, the Vamana Temple stands out in a field all by itself. It's notable for the relatively simple design of its sikhara. The bands of sculpture around the temple are, as usual, very fine with numerous celestial maidens adopting interesting poses.

Brahma & Hanuman Turning back (west) towards the modern village, you pass a granite and sandstone temple, one of the oldest at Khajuraho. It was actually dedicated to Vishnu and the definition of it as a Brahma temple is incorrect.

Taking the road directly from the modern village to the Jain enclosure, you pass a Hanuman Temple containing a large image of the monkey god. This 2.5m statue has on it the oldest inscription here – AD 922.

Khajuraho's Erotica

The most frequently asked question by visitors to Khajuraho is why all the sex? One theory has it that the erotic posturing was a kind of *Kamasutra* in stone, a how-to-do-it manual for adolescent Brahmin boys growing up segregated from the world in special temple schools. Another claims that the figures were thought to prevent the temples being struck by lightning, by appeasing the rain god Indra. This old lecher is supposedly a keen voyeur who wouldn't want the source of his pleasure damaged.

Rather more convincing is the explanation that these are Tantric images. According to this cult, gratification of the baser instincts is one way to blot out the evils of the world and achieve final deliverance. *Bhoga* (physical enjoyment) and *yoga* (spiritual exercise) are seen as equally valid in this quest for nirvana.

Probably the most accurate theory is that the Khajuraho sculptors were simply representing life as it was viewed by their society, with unhampered sexual expression. In spite of the fact that modern visitors are drawn as much for reasons of prurience as for cultural appreciation, this is not pornography. Although there are certainly large numbers of erotic images here, many other day-to-day scenes are also shown. The carvings should be seen as a joyous celebration of all aspects of life.

Jain Museum Outside the Jain enclosure is this modern circular gallery, with statues of the 24 tirthankars. It's open from 8 am to 5 pm daily (closed Sunday); entry is Rs 2.

Southern Group There are only two temples in the southern group.

Duladeo A dirt track runs to this isolated temple, about 1km south of the Jain enclosure. This is a later temple, and experts say that at this time the skill of Khajuraho's temple builders had passed its peak and the sculptures are more 'wooden' and 'stereotyped' than on earlier temples. Nevertheless, it's a fine and graceful temple with figures of women in a variety of pin-up poses and a number of mithuna couples.

Chaturbhuja South of the river, about 3km from the village and a healthy hike down a dirt road, this ruined temple has a fine 3m-high image of Vishnu.

Archaeological Museum

Close to the western enclosure, this small museum has a fine collection of statues and sculptures rescued from around Khajuraho. Unfortunately, admission is a laughable US$10, making it the most overpriced attraction in Madhya Pradesh. Give it a miss unless it's of special interest. It's open from 10 am to 5 pm daily except Friday.

Special Events

The **Khajuraho Festival of Dance** is a week-long event held every year in February/March. It attracts the cream of Indian classical dancers who perform amid the temples in the western enclosure. Performances are open-air, with the floodlit temples as a backdrop. MP Tourism's Web site (www.mptourism.com) is the best place to find a program.

There is also a relatively new Music Festival, in just it's third year – held on 28 and 29 November, it should become a regular on the calendar.

Places to Stay – Budget

On your arrival at the bus stand you'll be besieged by the usual rickshaw-wallahs offering Rs 5 rides – these are commission agents and you'll find bargaining for a room difficult if they take you to a hotel.

An Environmental Initiative

Global Village Development Trust (☎ 74237, 72250, e globalvillage@indiatimes.com), Rajnagan Rd, Khajuraho, is a new nongovernment organisation (NGO) committed to saving Khajuraho's fragile environment, which is coming under stress from increasing levels of tourism.

Global Village was born out of a collective frustration at the ineffectiveness of the government to make any real impact on the growing environmental problems in the area. It is embarking on a local education program in an attempt to help Khajuraho's community fight against plastic waste, diminishing water sources and vehicle pollution.

Importantly it is trying to come up with alternative materials to replace nonbiodegradable household items that are having such a negative effect on the environment.

Contact either Mr Ajay Awasthi or Mr Sharlesh Singh, if you're interested in donating to this very worthwhile cause or if you are interested in doing some voluntary environmental work. For people staying at one of the larger hotels, the Global Village recommends that you request biodegradable products from your hotel.

Yogi Lodge & Guesthouse *(☎ 74158)*, the most popular budget place, has singles/doubles with private bathroom from Rs 80/120. More-expensive rooms have a hot-water geyser and there is Internet access for Rs 80 per hour. For real tranquillity ask here about ***Yogi Sharma Ashram Lodge***, a large house with a garden about 2km north of the village. It has bright rooms for Rs 80/120 or dorm beds for Rs 40, all with shared bathroom, plus free meditation classes every morning with the Yogi Ramprakash Sharma.

There's a string of very good budget places side by side on Jain Temples Rd. ***Hotel Gem Palace*** *(☎ 74100)* has small singles/doubles for Rs 100/200, or bigger rooms for Rs 150/250, all with private bathroom and constant hot water. The ***Hotel Harmony*** *(☎ 74135)* is also good value. Comfortable rooms with private bathroom are Rs 200/250. The small walled garden is bright and immaculate.

Hotel Surya *(☎ 74145)*, next door, has a large garden with fruit trees and free yoga classes at dawn. Good rooms with private bathroom are Rs 150/200; rooms with balcony are Rs 250/350. ***Hotel Jain*** *(☎ 72352)* is a family-run place and an old favourite with travellers. There's a range of rooms from Rs 80/125 upwards, some with balconies.

Hotel Lakeside *(☎ 74120, Main Rd)* has clean rooms set around a central area. Rooms start at Rs 80 for a simple single, and singles/doubles with private bathroom and air-cooler start at Rs 150/250. You can get a good view of sunrise or sunset from the roof.

MP Tourism's ***Tourist Village*** *(☎ 74128)* is a somewhat shabby collection of cottages decorated with local carpets and furnishings for Rs 250. It's quiet and north of the village.

Places to Stay – Mid-Range

Hotel Marble Palace *(☎ 74353)* is a private hotel that lives up to its name with its marble floors and a winding staircase. Spacious, comfortable rooms with bathtubs are very nice but a little overpriced for Khajuraho at Rs 450/550, and Rs 750 with air-con.

Hotel Zen *(☎ 74228, fax 72408, Jain Temples Rd)* is a compact, immaculate place with a pleasant courtyard garden. Doubles start at Rs 150, or Rs 350 with bathtub and balcony facing the garden.

Hotel Casa Di William *(☎ 74244, fax 72252)*, on a side road just past the tourist office, has touches of the Mediterranean with its marble floors and whitewashed railings. Comfortable air-cooled/air-con double rooms are Rs 300/600 with constant hot water. There's a good restaurant serving Indian and Italian specialities.

Hotel Payal *(☎ 74064)*, near the Tourist Village, is a dilapidated place with a very sprawling garden and singles/doubles for Rs 340/390, or Rs 590/690 with air-con. It's clean and rooms have hot water and TV.

Hotel Jhankar *(☎ 74063, fax 74194)*, south of the village, is MP Tourism's flagship here. Slightly ageing rooms cost Rs 340/390, or Rs 590/690 for air-con, all with private bathrooms and constant hot water. There's a restaurant and cold beer.

Places to Stay – Top End

Most deluxe hotels attempt to outdo one another and are south of the modern village.

Hotel Jass Trident *(☎ 72344, ⓔ d_bhatial@indiatimes.com)* has singles/doubles for US$44/88 and a certain charm despite its box-like exterior. The hotel's pool is open to nonguests for Rs 150. From August to April there are folk dances (Rs 150). Year-round there is a nightly puppet show and a sitar and tabla recital (both free).

Hotel Chandela *(☎ 72355, fax 72366, Jhansi Rd)* has air-con rooms for US$42/70 with comfortable beds, and bathtubs. Diversions for 'templed-out' guests include tennis, yoga, archery, croquet and badminton. There's a good bookshop, two excellent restaurants and a coffee shop.

Hotel Clarks Bundela *(☎ 72386, fax 72385, Jhansi Rd)*, south of Hotel Chandela, charges US$45/85 and has a swimming pool (open to nonguests for Rs 100). Discounts of up to 50% are available in the low season.

Holiday Inn *(☎ 72301, ⓔ hi.khajuraho@vsnl.com, Jhansi Rd)*, further south again has a cavernous lobby, tastefully furnished rooms (for US$40/75) and helpful staff. It's probably the most luxurious of the five-star hotels in Khajuraho and has a pool, bar and two restaurants.

Places to Eat

Raja's Cafe has been here about 20 years and so has the Swiss woman who runs it. The large shady tree makes the restaurant's courtyard a popular gathering spot and there are good views to the temples from the terrace above. Tourist information and guides are also available here.

Blue Sky Restaurant, behind the tourist office, is a friendly place serving very good Indian, Japanese and Italian food. A veg kofta is Rs 30 and thali starts from Rs 20.

The hole-in-the-wall ***Shivam Restaurant*** *(Jain Temples Rd)* has plain thalis for Rs 20 and very good Gujarati thalis for Rs 30.

Safari Restaurant, opposite the Internet Hut, is good for reasonably priced breakfasts.

Mediterraneo Restaurant *(Jain Temples Rd)* is one of several popular places specialising in Italian food.

There's a string of decent restaurants on Main Rd with terraces overlooking the small Shiv Sagar – a good place to be in the early evening as the sun sets. ***Shiva Janti*** is a simple place with a good view of the lake. ***Paradise*** is a bit quieter than most and has a good menu – the management will also whip you up dishes not on the menu. Mango pancakes are Rs 40.

Recommended by readers is ***Gaylord Restaurant***, between the western temples and the airport.

The top-end hotels all have good restaurants – expect to pay around Rs 250 per person, excluding drinks.

Entertainment

The ***sound-and-light show*** at the western temples every night at 7 pm is excellent. The show (Rs 200) documents the history and culture of Khajuraho over the last 4000 years.

Kandariya Art & Culture *(☎ 74031)*, on the right-hand side of the Main Rd coming from the village, is a private set-up with cultural dance shows from India's different states every night, performed in a comfortable indoor theatre. One-hour shows start at 7 and 8.30 pm and cost Rs 250.

Shilpgram *(☎ 771606)*, on the opposite side of the road to Kandariya, is a government operation designed to promote Indian culture. It has classical and folk cultural events on the program and you can phone to see what's coming up. Entry is usually about Rs 100.

Hotel Jass Trident (see Places to Stay – Top End earlier) hosts various cultural and musical performances. There's also a pool open to nonguests.

Getting There & Away

Khajuraho is on the way from nowhere to nowhere, and while many travellers slot it in between Varanasi and Agra, it involves a lot of slow bus travel over small country roads. If affordable, flying is a good alternative.

Air Indian Airlines (☎ 74035) has a daily Delhi-Agra-Khajuraho-Varanasi flight that returns by the same route to Delhi. It's probably the most popular tourist flight in India and can often be booked solid for days by tour groups. It leaves Khajuraho (at 5.10 pm on Monday, Wednesday, Friday and Sunday and at 4.10 pm on Tuesday, Thursday and Saturday) for Delhi (US$100), Agra (US$80) and Varanasi (US$80). The fare to Mumbai, via Delhi, is US$275. Indian Airlines, next to Hotel Clarks Bundela, is open from 10 am to 5 pm daily.

Bus & Train Jhansi (Rs 75/90 ordinary/deluxe, 4½ to six hours) is the nearest approach to Khajuraho on the main Delhi to Mumbai train line, and there are about half-a-dozen buses a day on this popular route. There are also direct Agra-Gwalior buses (Rs 190).

There is no direct route to Varanasi from Khajuraho. Satna is the nearest reliable railhead for travellers from Varanasi and the east. It's on the Mumbai to Allahabad line so there are plenty of connections. There are five buses daily from Satna to Khajuraho (Rs 55, four hours). However, it may not be possible to get from Varanasi to Khajuraho in one day as the last bus from Satna leaves at 3.30 pm. A good option is to take the overnight *Muzaffarpur Lokmanya Tilak Express* at 11.30 pm, which gets you into Satna at 6.30 am.

You can also get to Khajuraho from Varanasi by taking a train to Mahoba (Rs 160, sleeper), 60km north of Khajuraho, then a bus (Rs 35, two hours) from there.

There's a 6 am daily bus to Jabalpur (Rs 135, 11 hours), but the train from Satna is more comfortable. Regular buses run to Panna (Rs 21, one hour) via Madla for Panna National Park.

You can get bus/train information at Madhur Cold Drinks Stand at the bus station.

Share-Taxi A taxi can be a good alternative if you find other travellers interested in sharing the cost. As a general guide it costs about Rs 5/10 per kilometre for nonair-con/air-con. Taxis will take you to Satna (Rs 1000), Varanasi (Rs 3500) and Agra (Rs 4000), all with air-con.

Getting Around

To/From the Airport Taxis to the airport charge Rs 80 for this short journey; cycle-rickshaws will pedal the 3km for Rs 40.

Local Transport The best way to get around Khajuraho is by bicycle, since it's flat and pleasantly traffic-free. Bicycles cost Rs 20 per day from several places in the new village. Cycle-rickshaws are generally a rip-off, but if you don't want to hire a bicycle, it's a long walk to the eastern group of temples.

A cycle-rickshaw should cost around Rs 100 for a half-day trip – make sure it includes stops at the southern temples and waiting time.

AROUND KHAJURAHO

Panna National Park

The road to Satna passes through this 543 sq km park along the Ken River, 32km from Khajuraho. It has large areas of unspoilt forest and a variety of wildlife including leopards, chittal (spotted deer), langur monkeys and sambar. There are about 22 tigers in the park but since they're not tracked (as at Kanha) you'd be very lucky to spot one.

Entry to the park is Rs 150 (Rs 10 for Indians) plus Rs 25/200 for a camera/video. Transport within the park is in petrol-driven 'Gypsys' only; they can be hired at the park's entrance in Madla, or Khajuraho – see Getting There & Away later in this entry.

The cooler months are the best time to visit; in summer it can be hotter than a furnace. The park is closed from June to October.

Day trips from Khajuraho (48km) often also take in a visit to the **diamond mines** at Majhgawan, the **Rajgarh Palace**, **Ranah Falls** and the **temples** of Panna town.

Places to Stay ***Giles Tree House***, on the Ken River 3km from the park entrance, is the best place to stay. It's literally a platform built in a tree with a few huts down by the river. Basic huts are Rs 300, rooms are Rs 500 and rooms by the river with private bathroom are Rs 800. Book at Raja's Cafe in Khajuraho.

Forest Rest House in Madla provides basic accommodation for Rs 275 per person. It can be booked at the office by the park entrance or through the director in Panna village *(☎ 07732-52135)*. You'll need to bring your own food here. There's another ***Forest Rest House*** (same booking details) on the opposite side of the park at Hinouta, about 50km from Khajuraho.

Getting There & Away Regular local buses run from Khajuraho to Panna (Rs 15, one hour) via Madla (45 minutes) – get off at Madla for the park.

Day trips (in six-seater Gypsys only) can be organised through travel agencies in Khajuraho or at Raja's Cafe. They cost around Rs 1500 excluding entry and guide fees.

SATNA

☎ 07672

You may find it convenient or necessary to stay here overnight on your way to or from Khajuraho. There's an MP Tourism office at the train station.

Places to Stay & Eat

The choice is basically between proximity to the bus stand or the train station. All hotels have free bucket hot water.

Hotel India *(☎ 51012, Rewa Rd)* is quite a decent place behind (east of) the bus stand. There are reasonably clean singles/doubles for Rs 95/126 with private bathroom; there's a good cheap restaurant downstairs, part of the ***Indian Coffee House*** chain.

Hotel Chanakya *(☎ 25026, Station Rd)*, about 500m from the train station, has large tidy rooms with TV for Rs 225/330, or with air-con for Rs 385/495.

Hotel Khajuraho *(☎ 23330)*, behind the road leading from the train station, has good air-cooled rooms with clean private bathrooms for Rs 250/350.

Saloni Restaurant *(Rewa Rd)* is an air-con vegetarian place opposite the bus stand. There are plenty of ***food stalls*** in the market around the bus stand.

Getting There & Away

Four buses to Khajuraho (Rs 45, four hours) leave from 6.30 am to 2.30 pm. For Bandhavgarh National Park you can take a bus to tiny Gorsari for tea and samosas with the locals while waiting for the bus from Rewa which continues to Tala. Otherwise you'll have to take a taxi for around Rs 1000.

There are direct trains from Satna to Varanasi (Rs 123/415 in sleeper/1st class, 316km, eight hours) and Jabalpur (Rs 53/279 in 2nd/1st class, 189km, three hours). Other direct expresses connect with Allahabad, Kolkata (Calcutta), Mumbai and Chennai.

Central Madhya Pradesh

BHOPAL

☎ 0755 • pop 1,278,030

The capital of Madhya Pradesh, was built on the site of the 11th century city of Bhojapal. It was founded by the legendary Raja Bhoj who is credited with having constructed the lakes around the city.

Today, Bhopal has a multifaceted profile. There is the old city with its crowded marketplaces, huge old mosques, and the palaces of the former begums who ruled over the city from 1819 to 1926. To the north sprawl the huge industrial suburbs and the slums that these developments in India inevitably give rise to. The new city with its broad avenues, high-rise offices and leafy residential areas is to the south. In the centre of Bhopal are two lakes that, while providing recreational facilities, are also the source of its plagues of mosquitoes.

Bhopal is hardly on every traveller's itinerary, but it has a relaxed feel for a state capital, a number of cultural attractions and is a good base for some excellent excursions.

Orientation

Both the train station and bus stand are within easy walking distance of the main hotel area along Hamidia Rd in Old Bhopal. When arriving by train, leave the station by platform No 4 or 5 to reach Hamidia Rd.

The new part of the city, which encompasses TT Nagar, site of most of the major banks and the tourist office, is a long way from either of the transport terminals. Old and New Bhopal are effectively separated by the Upper and Lower lakes.

Information

Tourist Offices There are helpful and efficient tourist information counters at both the train station and airport. The headquarters of MP Tourism (☎ 778383, fax 774289, ⓔ mail@mptourism.com) is in the Gangotri Complex, 4th floor, TT Nagar, in the new town, and there's a regional tourist office (☎ 553006) at Hotel Palash. MP Tourism can book its hotels throughout the state (it's best to book five days in advance). Its Web site is at www.mptourism.com.

MP Tourism can also organise a car and driver from Rs 4.50 per kilometre or Rs 500 per day.

Money You have to head over to TT Nagar to change travellers cheques or cash. State Bank of India (near the Rangmahal Talkies cinema), State Bank of Indore (beneath Hotel

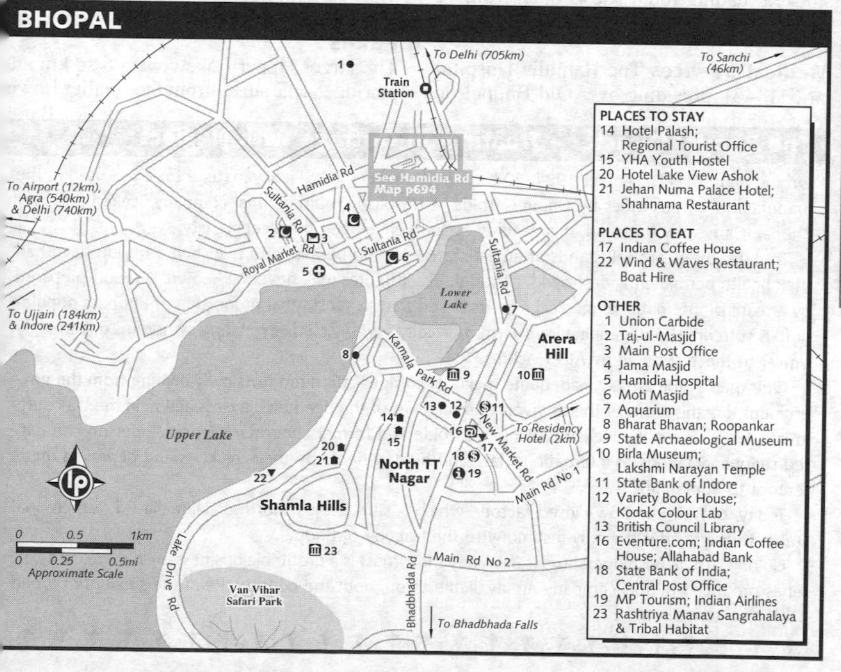

Panchanan) or Allahabad Bank, Bhadbhada Rd, will do the requisite transactions.

Post & Communications The main post office is on Sultania Rd, Old Bhopal, near the Taj-ul-Masjid.

Computera, on Hamida Rd not far from the bus stand, has quick Internet connections and charges Rs 40 an hour. If you're in New Bhopal, try Eventure.com between the Indian Coffee House and Allahabad Bank. It's a 24-hour place that charges Rs 35 per hour for email during the day and a mere Rs 25 per hour after 11 pm at night.

Bookshops Bhadbhada Rd, near MP Tourism in North TT Nagar, has a couple of bookshops with a small English-language range. Variety Book House has the best selection (as well as maps), and Books World stocks a lot of second-hand titles.

Cultural Centres The Alliance Française (☎ 466595, e afbpl@bom.vsnl.net.in) is in Arera Colony. The British Council Library (☎ 553767), GTB Complex, TT Nagar, just behind Variety Book House, has a well-stocked reading room and is open from 11 am to 7 pm Tuesday to Saturday.

Medical Services The Hamidia Hospital (☎ 511446), presiding over Old Bhopal on Royal Market Rd, is the city's best public hospital. There are also many pharmacies around here dispensing medical supplies.

Emergency The telephone number for the police is ☎ 100 and ☎ 102 for an ambulance.

Taj-ul-Masjid

Commenced by Shah Jahan Begum (1868-1901) but never really totally completed – construction recommenced in 1971 – the Taj-ul-Masjid is one of the largest mosques in India. It's a huge pink mosque with two massive white-domed minarets and three white domes over the main building. The entrance to the mosque is not on Sultania Rd despite the huge staircase here; go around the corner and enter from busy Royal Market Rd. It's closed to non-Muslims on Friday.

Other Mosques

The **Jama Masjid**, built in 1837 by Qudsia Begum, is surrounded by the bazaar and has squat minarets. The **Moti Masjid** was built by Qudsia Begum's daughter, Sikander Jahan Begum, in 1860. Similar in style to the Jama Masjid in Delhi, it is a smaller mosque with two dark-red minarets.

Lakes

The larger Upper Lake covers 6 sq km and a bridge separates it from the smaller Lower

The Bhopal Disaster – Treating an Outrage with Neglect

On the night of 3 December 1984, 40 tonnes of deadly methyl icocyanate, a toxic gas used in the manufacture of pesticides by Union Carbide, a US-based multinational company, leaked out over Bhopal. Carried by the wind, this deadly gas soon enveloped the sleeping city.

To date, the death toll stands at an estimated 16,000 people, and over half a million have had their health permanently destroyed, although exact figures may never be known. A report prepared by a team of international medical experts found that 'a substantial proportion of Bhopal's population' is suffering from 'genuine long-term morbidity', with victims exhibiting symptoms disturbingly similar to those suffered by AIDS victims.

Outraged at the grossly inadequate trickle of compensation money slowly coming from the government, organisations of the survivors and relatives of the dead filed a class action in the US courts in late 1999. The suit alleges that Union Carbide and former chairman Warren Anderson committed serious violations of international law and human rights by their 'reckless and depraved indifference to human life.'

Today, outside the now-closed factory, which is situated just north of Hamidia Rd, a memorial statue to the dead is the only testimony to the tragedy of Bhopal.

Union Carbide (also operating as Everyday Industries) is a profitable business once more, and batteries produced by this company are available throughout the country. Read the small print when buying batteries in India.

Lake. A veritable flotilla of boats is available for hire on the Upper Lake, including rowboats (Rs 50 for 30 minutes), pedal boats (Rs 60 per hour) and sailboats (Rs 100 per hour – only available in summer). There's a booking office at the bottom of the driveway leading to the Wind & Waves Restaurant.

There's a fairly dull **aquarium** near the Lower Lake, open from 3 to 8 pm daily except Monday (Rs 2).

Lakshmi Narayan Temple & Birla Museum

There are good views over the lakes to the Old Town from the Lakshmi Narayan Temple, also known as the Birla Mandir. Beside it on Arera Hill is an excellent museum, containing a small but very selective collection of local sculptures dating mainly from the Paramana period. The museum is open from 10 am to 5 pm daily except Monday (Rs 3).

State Archaeological Museum

Near the Lower Lake, this museum contains quite a small collection of 6th- to 10th-century Hindu sculptures, bronzes, prehistoric exhibits and copies of paintings from the Bagh caves. It's open from 10 am to 5 pm daily except Monday (free).

Bharat Bhavan

Bharat Bhavan (☎ 540353) is a complex for the verbal, visual and performing arts, designed by the well-known architect Charles Correa and opened in 1982. It's now regarded as one of the most important centres in the country for the preservation of traditional folk art. As well as the workshops and theatres that are here, there's the two-part **Roopankar Gallery**. To the right of the entrance is a superb exhibition of tribal folk art paintings, sculptures and carvings produced by previously unknown adivasi (tribal) artists. Among the most striking exhibits are the colourful murals depicting animals and village life. Across the central courtyard, the second gallery provides a contrast with some of India's finest contemporary urban photographs and sculptures. Bharat Bhavan is open from 2 to 8 pm daily, closed Monday in winter (Rs 5).

Rashtriya Manav Sangrahalaya

This 40 hectare complex in the hills overlooking the Upper Lake is an ambitious attempt to showcase the lives, culture, art and religion of a fraction of India's 450 plus adivasis. The complex started with **Tribal Habitat (Museum of Man)**, an open-air exhibition of some 25 tribal dwellings in authentic village-like settings. The three newer elements to the park, **Coastal Village** (which runs along the eastern edge of the lake), **Desert Village** and **Rock Heritage**, are designed along similar lines and there are prehistoric rock art sites scattered around the park. A huge indoor museum and gallery contains adivasi costumes, jewellery, ornaments, a multimedia display and an information database.

The complex is very much an educational project: There are two visitor information centres, as well as craft and pottery demonstrations, and film shows at 4 pm Saturday (one hour). Admission to the exhibits and the film are free. The display is open from 11 am to 6.30 pm daily, except Monday. You can walk between the exhibits (there's a sealed road) but it makes for a tiring visit. An autorickshaw costs around Rs 100 to take you up there, including waiting time.

Van Vihar Safari Park

This 445-hectare park is more of a zoo than a safari park, despite the promise of 'natural surroundings'. But if you're in the north during the monsoon, when all the national parks are closed, it's good to know you don't have to completely miss out on tigers, lions, leopards and crocodiles. The park is open from 7 to 11 am and 3 to 5.30 pm daily except Friday. Admission is Rs 100 (free for the disabled) and it costs Rs 10/20 for autorickshaw/car entry. A spin around Van Vihar in a rickshaw (from the city centre) should cost around Rs 120.

Places to Stay

Hamidia Rd in Old Bhopal is where most of the city's hotels are clustered. Although it can be difficult to find good cheap accommodation in Bhopal, there are some excellent reasonably priced mid-range hotels.

Places to Stay – Budget

Most of the following places have rooms with private bathrooms.

YHA Youth Hostel (☎ 550899, TT Nagar), near Hotel Palash, is dirt cheap but a bit of a disgrace by YHA standards. Members pay

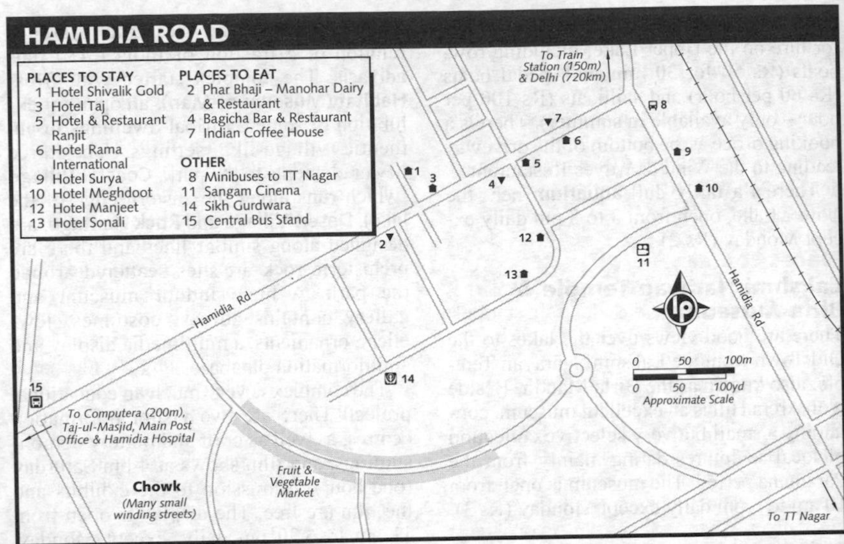

Rs 20 for a bed in a grimy dorm or Rs 60 for a double room. Nonmembers pay double.

Hotel Ranjit *(☎ 533511, ⓔ ranjit@bom6.vsnl.net.in, 3 Hamidia Rd)* is Bhopal's most popular moderately priced hotel. Very clean air-cooled singles/doubles are Rs 150/200, or Rs 325/375 with air-con.

Hotel Rama International *(☎ 535542, Hamidia Rd)*, nearby, is spacious, if a little shabby. Rooms are Rs 150/200, or Rs 250/300 with air-con.

Hotel Meghdoot *(☎ 713407)* has rather grimy rooms starting at Rs 126/172 or Rs 150/240 for better deluxe rooms. Hot water is by bucket and there are squat toilets.

Hotel Manjeet *(☎ 536168)*, just off Hamidia Rd near Hotel Ranjit, has smallish but very clean rooms starting at Rs 200/250, better rooms at Rs 250/275 and air-con rooms for Rs 425/465. The staff are friendly and the management efficient.

Places to Stay – Mid-Range

Hotel Sonali *(☎ 533880, fax 510337, Radha Talkies Rd)*, hidden just off busy Hamidia Rd, is possibly Bhopal's best-value hotel. The cheapest rooms are definitely mid-range standard and a bargain at Rs 210/285 with constant hot water, room service and balcony. There are also deluxe rooms for Rs 250/325 and air-con starting at Rs 450/525.

Hotel Taj *(☎ 533162, 52 Hamidia Rd)* is a big old hotel with a central courtyard. The cheap rooms are looking a bit ragged these days and they cost Rs 200/350; with air-con they are Rs 600/750 (plus 20% tax). There's a restaurant, but no bar.

Hotel Shivalik Gold *(☎ 536000, fax 710 224, 40 Hamidia Rd)*, behind the Taj, is a worn place with comfortable rooms starting at Rs 250/325, or Rs 450/550 with air-con.

Hotel Surya *(☎ 741701, Hamidia Rd)* is modern and well-run with standard rooms starting at Rs 250/300, air-con at Rs 500/600 and a good restaurant.

MP Tourism's ***Hotel Palash*** *(☎ 553006, TT Nagar)* is convenient if you want to stay in New Market and it's handy for the lake area. Rooms are not cheap, however, starting at Rs 550/650, or Rs 790/890 with air-con.

Places to Stay – Top End

Those who can afford it head for the hills.

Residency Hotel *(☎ 556001, 208 Zone 1, MP Nagar)* is a four-star hotel with a swimming pool and health club. Standard rooms are Rs 1140/1490 while deluxe rooms are Rs 1595/1945, plus a whopping 25% tax.

Hotel Lake View Ashok *(☎ 660090, fax 660096)* is a well-appointed, three-star hotel in the Shamla Hills with an excellent restaurant. All rooms have private balconies, and there are good views over the lake. Comfortable rooms are Rs 1600/2200, deluxe doubles are Rs 2800.

Jehan Numa Palace Hotel *(☎ 661100, fax 661720)*, only a stone's throw away, was formerly a palace built in the late 19th century and is Bhopal's stand-out hotel. Rooms start at Rs 2200/2750, or Rs 4300 for deluxe doubles, all with 10% tax; there's a restaurant and bar.

Places to Eat

The cheapest places to eat are the street stalls surrounding the bus and train stations. Many of the hotels around Hamidia Rd have good restaurants/bars.

Indian Coffee House is a good cheap place; there are outlets in both Old and New Bhopal. Some of its restaurants have separate areas for women and families.

Hotel Ranjit has an excellent (and well-deserved) reputation. Most dishes on the huge menu (there is even an 'everything' heading!) are around Rs 40, and ice-cold beer is Rs 60.

Bagicha Bar & Restaurant, a few doors down, also prepares a good range of food in a quieter, open-air setting. It's set a little way back from the cacophony of Hamidia Rd.

Phar Bhaji – Manohar Dairy & Restaurant has lots of gooey favourites such as *gulab jamun* (fried cake-like milk balls in a scented syrup), as well as an astonishing variety of ice cream. Dosas, *idlis* (South Indian rice dumplings) and veg burgers are also available. This place is very popular with locals.

Kwality Restaurant *(New Market Rd, TT Nagar)*, opposite the State Bank of Indore, does reasonable fast food, pizzas and Chinese and has an outdoor eating area.

Shahnama Restaurant at Jehan Numa Palace Hotel is the best place for a splurge. It's not cheap, with main dishes starting at Rs 110, but the food is excellent.

Wind & Waves Restaurant is a (fairly ordinary) snack shop, but you can enjoy a cold drink here (including beer) and there's a fantastic view of the Upper Lake. It's open until 11 pm.

Shopping

Bhopal's two main shopping areas are the new market area, in New Bhopal, and the old market area, or *chowk*, in Old Bhopal. While similar items can be found in both markets, prices are much more reasonable in the atmospheric chowk, just off Hamidia Rd near the bus stand. The labyrinthine streets and alleys here make this a fascinating area to wander around – dive in and count on getting totally lost! Here you'll find fine gold and silver jewellery, beautifully woven saris and hand-embroidered applique skirts at reasonable prices. Jari-made shoulder bags are a speciality of Bhopal. They are woven from cotton, and have colourful designs decorating the exterior. These can be purchased in the old market for about Rs 35.

Mrignayni is the registered trade name for MP state handicraft merchandise, which is mainly textiles and clay or brass sculptures – such items start at about Rs 50 and can cost anything up to Rs 2000 depending on your bargaining prowess. Many retail shops carry Mrignayni products.

Getting There & Away

Air Indian Airlines (☎ 770480) has daily flights to Mumbai (US$130), Indore (US$55) and Delhi (US$120), and two flights weekly to Gwalior (US$80). The office is in TT Nagar, adjacent to MP Tourism.

Bus From the bus stand on Hamidia Rd there are numerous daily buses to destinations that include Sanchi (Rs 15, 1½ hours; via Raisen, Rs 17); Vidisha (Rs 24, 2½ hours); Indore (Rs 78/144 in ordinary/deluxe, five to six hours); Ujjain (Rs 78, five hours); Pachmarhi (Rs 91, seven hours) and Jabalpur (Rs 154, 12 hours).

There's an overnight service to Khajuraho (about Rs 200), but it's better to go by train to Jhansi and connect by bus from there.

A computerised reservation system operates from 11 am to 8 pm for all deluxe and long-distance buses.

Train There's an efficient air-con reservation hall on the left as you exit the main terminal, and a separate counter for the *Shatabdi Express* within the terminal building itself. There's a 24-hour left-luggage facility at the train station.

Bhopal is on one of the two main Delhi to Mumbai railway lines. It's the terminus for the daily *Shatabdi Express*, from New Delhi. Cheapest fares from Bhopal (air-con chair class) are Rs 480 for Jhansi (three hours), Rs 545 for Gwalior (4¼ hours) and Rs 850 for Delhi (7¾ hours).

Other express trains connect Bhopal with Delhi (Rs 221/746 in sleeper/1st class, 705km, 12 hours), Mumbai (Rs 265/830, 837km, 14 hours), Agra (Rs 174/588, 506km, 8½ hours), Jhansi (Rs 112/378, 291km, 4½ hours) and Ujjain (Rs 53/279 in 2nd/1st class, 188km, three hours). Express trains leave for Sanchi (Rs 21 in 2nd class, 46km, one hour) at 8 am and 2.40 pm.

Getting Around

To/From the Airport The airport is 16km from Old Bhopal. Fixed rates operate for both taxis (Rs 180) and rickshaws (Rs 100).

Local Transport Autorickshaw drivers almost always use their meters (sheer luxury), except at night when you'll have to negotiate the fare. Hopelessly crowded minibuses for TT Nagar (No 2, 3 or 9) depart about every two minutes from Hamidia Rd near Hotel Red Sea Plaza (Rs 2). A rickshaw costs about Rs 30.

AROUND BHOPAL

Bhojpur

The legendary Raja Bhoj (1010–53) not only built the lakes at Bhopal but also built another one, estimated at 400 sq km, in Bhojpur, 28km south-east of the state capital.

Unfortunately, the lake no longer exists, having been destroyed by Hoshang Shah, the ruler of Mandu, in a fit of destructive passion in the early 15th century. What does survive here is the huge, partially completed **Bhojeshwar Temple**, which originally overlooked the lake.

A few local buses run to Bhojpur from Bhopal's bus stand, or you can take any Hoshangabad-bound bus (Rs 12) and get off at the turn-off to Bhojpur from where you should be able to pick up a tempo (Rs 2).

Bhimbetka

Like the Aboriginal rock paintings in the outback of Australia, the cave paintings of the Bushmen in the Kalahari Desert in Africa or the Palaeolithic Lascaux caves of France, the Bhimbetka caves are a must-see. Among forests of teak and sal in the craggy cliffs of an almost African setting 45km south of Bhopal, some thousand rock shelters have been discovered. Almost half contain ancient paintings depicting the life and times of the different people who lived here.

Because of the natural red and white pigments used by the painters, the colours have been remarkably well preserved and it's obvious in certain caves that the same surface has been used by different people at different times. There's everything from figures of wild buffalo (gaur), rhinoceros, bears and tigers, to hunting scenes, initiation ceremonies, childbirth, communal dancing and drinking scenes, religious rites and burials.

The extent and archaeological importance of the site was only recently realised and dating is still not complete. The oldest paintings are believed to be up to 12,000 years old, whereas some of the crude, geometric figures probably date from as recently as the medieval period.

The caves themselves are not difficult to find; 15 are accessible and signposted, and linked by a concrete path. A local guide (about Rs 20) can be useful for pointing out some of the more obscure paintings and explaining their significance. The **Zoo Rock Shelter** is one of the first you come to, famous for its variety of animal paintings. Rock shelter No 15 features a huge red bison attacking a helpless stick figure. There's nothing here other than the caves, so bring water.

Getting There & Away From Bhopal, 45km away, take any bus to Hoshangabad or Itarsi (Rs 15) via Obaidullaganj, 50 minutes south of Bhopal. Get off 6.5km after Obaidullaganj by the sign pointing right with '3.2' and some Hindi on it (ask the driver). Follow this sign, crossing the railway line for the 3km walk to the hills in front of you. (If you can't find the sign, try asking locals passing by for directions.)

To get back you can flag down a truck or bus on the main road. If you don't fancy the walk, pick up a rickshaw in Obaidullaganj. If you want to visit both Bhimbetka and Bhojpur it's worth springing for a taxi. You can hire a car and driver through MP Tourism in Bhopal for around Rs 500 per day (see Tourist Offices in the Bhopal section).

SANCHI

☎ 07482

Beside the main railway line, 46km north-east of Bhopal, a hill rises from the plain. It's topped by some of the oldest and most interesting Buddhist structures in India. It was the great Emperor Ashoka, Buddhism's most famous convert, who built the first stupas here in the 3rd century BC, and a great number of stupas and other religious structures were added over the succeeding centuries.

As Buddhism was gradually absorbed back into Hinduism in its land of origin, the site decayed and was eventually completely forgotten. In 1818 a British officer rediscovered the site, and in the following years amateur archaeologists and greedy treasure hunters did immense damage to Sanchi before a proper restoration was commenced in 1881. Finally, between 1912 and 1919, the structures were carefully repaired and restored to their present condition.

Sanchi is a very special place and is not to be missed if you're anywhere within striking distance. The site is also a good base for a number of interesting bicycle excursions.

Orientation & Information

Sanchi is little more than a small village at the foot of the hill on which the site is located. The site is open daily from dawn to dusk and tickets are available from the kiosk outside the museum. Entry costs US$10 (Rs 460) which covers both the site and the museum (if you plan on going up for the superb sunrise, you'll need to buy a ticket the day before). It's worth getting a copy of the *Sanchi* guidebook (Rs 12), published by the Archaeological Survey of India. There's also a museum guidebook on sale here.

The quickest way up to the site is via the stone steps off to the right of the tarmac road. There's a drink stall by the modern *vihara* (monastery) on Sanchi hill, and Buddhist publications are for sale in the vihara. Following is a brief description of the buildings at the site; the *Sanchi* guidebook describes all these buildings, and many others, in much greater detail.

Archaeological Museum

This museum has a small collection of sculptures from the site. The most interesting pieces are the lion capital from the Ashoka pillar, a *yakshi* (maiden) hanging from a mango tree and a beautiful Buddha figure in red sandstone. It's open from 10 am to 5 pm daily except Friday.

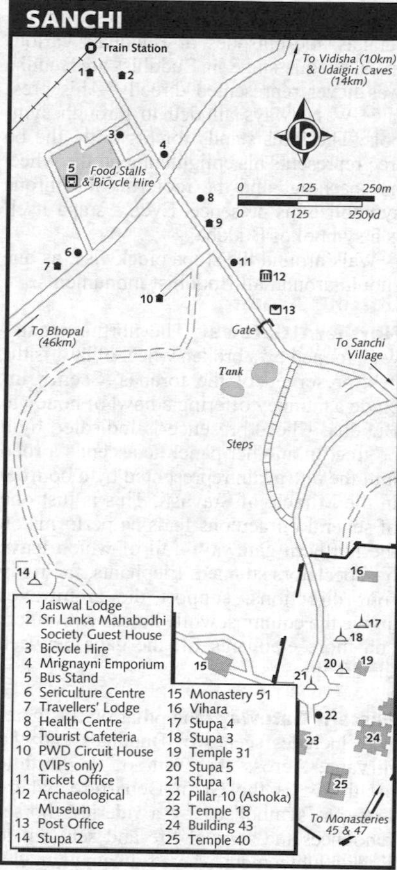

Great Stupa

Stupa 1, as it is listed on the site, is the main structure on the hill. Originally constructed by Ashoka in the 3rd century BC, it was later enlarged and the original brick stupa enclosed within a stone one. In its present form it stands 16m high and is 37m in diameter. A railing encircles the stupa and there are four entrances through magnificently carved gateways, or *toranas*. These toranas are the finest works of art at Sanchi and among the finest examples of Buddhist art in India.

Toranas The four gateways were erected around 35 BC and had all completely fallen down at the time of the stupa's restoration. The scenes carved onto the pillars and their triple architraves are mainly tales from the Jatakas, the episodes of Buddha's various lives. At this stage in Buddhist art Buddha was never represented directly – his presence was always alluded to through symbols. The lotus stands for his birth, the bo tree represents his enlightenment, the wheel his teachings and the footprint and throne symbolise his presence. Even a stupa itself is a symbol of Buddha.

Walk around the stupa clockwise, as one should around all Buddhist monuments.

Northern Gateway The northern gateway, topped by a broken wheel of law, is the best-preserved of the toranas. Scenes include a monkey offering a bowl of honey to Buddha, whose presence is indicated by a bo tree. In another panel he ascends a road into the air (again represented by a bo tree) in the Miracle of Sravasti. This is just one of several miraculous feats he performs on the northern gateway – all of which leave his spectators stunned. Elephants, facing in four directions, support the architraves above the columns, while horses with riders and more elephants fill the gaps between the architraves.

Eastern Gateway One pillar on this gateway includes scenes of Buddha's entry to nirvana. Across the front of the middle architrave is the Great Departure, where Buddha (symbolised by a riderless horse) renounces the sensual life and sets out to find enlightenment. Maya's dream of an elephant standing on the moon, which she had when she conceived Buddha, is also shown on one of the columns. The figure of a yakshi, hanging out from one of the architraves, is one of the best known images of Sanchi.

Southern Gateway The oldest of the gateways, this includes scenes of Buddha's birth and also events from Ashoka's life as a Buddhist. At the rear of the top architrave there is another representation of the Great Departure. As on the western gateway, the tale of the Chhaddanta Jataka features on this gateway.

Western Gateway The western gateway, with the architraves supported by dwarfs, has some of the most interesting scenes at the site. The rear face of one of the pillars shows Buddha undergoing the Temptation of Mara, while demons flee and angels cheer his resistance. The top front architrave shows Buddha in seven different incarnations, but since he could not, at the time, be represented directly, he appears three times as a stupa and four times as a tree.

The colourful events of the Chhaddanta Jataka are related on the front face of the bottom architrave. In this tale Buddha, in a lower incarnation, took the form of a six-tusked elephant, but one of his two wives became jealous; she managed to reincarnate as a queen and then arranged to have the six-tusked elephant hunted and killed. The sight of his tusks, sawn off by the hunter, was sufficient for the queen to die of remorse! Pot-bellied dwarfs support the architraves on this gateway.

Other Stupas

There are many other stupas on the hill, some of them tiny votive ones less than 1m high. Eight were built by Ashoka but only three remain, including the Great Stupa. **Stupa 2**, one of the most interesting of the lesser stupas, is halfway down the hill to the west. If you come up from the town by the main route you can walk back down via stupa 2. There are no gateways to this stupa, but the 'medallions' that decorate the surrounding wall are of great interest. Their design is almost childlike, but full of energy and imagination. Flowers, animals and people – some mythological – are found all around the stupa.

Stupa 3 stands north-east of the main stupa and is similar in design, though smaller. It has only one gateway and is thought to have been constructed soon after the completion of the Great Stupa. Stupa 3 once contained relics of two important disciples of Buddha. They were removed and taken to London in 185? but returned to Sanchi in 1953 and are now housed in the modern vihara.

Now almost totally destroyed, the 2nd century BC stupa 4 stands right behind stupa 3. Between stupa 1 (the Great Stupa) and stupa 3 is stupa 5, which is unusual in that it once had an image of Buddha, now displayed in the museum.

Pillars

Scattered around the site are pillars and the remains of pillars. The most important is **pillar 10**, which was erected by Ashoka and stands close to the southern entrance to the Great Stupa. Only the base of this beautifully proportioned and executed shaft now stands, but the fine capital can be seen in the museum. The four back-to-back lions that once topped the column are an excellent example of the Greco-Buddhist art of that era. They now form the state emblem of India and can be seen on every banknote.

Pillar 25, dating from the Sunga period (2nd century BC) and **pillar 35**, dating from the 5th century AD, are not as fine as the earlier pillar 10.

Temples

Immediately south of stupa 1 is **temple 18**, a *chaitya* (Buddhist temple, also prayer room or assembly hall) that is remarkably similar in style to classical Greek-columned buildings. It dates from round the 7th century AD, but traces of earlier wooden buildings have been discovered beneath it. Beside this temple is the small **temple 17**, also Greek-like in style. The large **temple 40**, slightly south-east of these two temples, in part dates back to the Ashokan period.

Temple 31, built during the 6th or 7th centuries but reconstructed during either the 10th or 11th centuries, is adjacent to stupa 5. This flat-roofed rectangular temple contains a well-executed image of Buddha. This appears to have been moved here from another temple during the reconstruction of temple 31, as it does not exactly fit its pedestal.

Monasteries

The earliest monasteries on the site were made of wood and are long gone. The usual plan is of a central courtyard surrounded by monastic cells. **Monasteries 45** and **47** stand on the higher, eastern edge of the hilltop. They date from the later period of building at Sanchi, a time of transition from Buddhism to Hinduism, and show strong Hindu elements in their design. There is a good view of the village of Sanchi below and Vidisha in the distance from this side of the hill.

Monastery 51 is partway down the hill on the western side towards stupa 2. Nearby is the **Great Bowl** in which food and offerings were placed for distribution to the monks. It was carved out of a huge boulder. The modern **vihara** on the hill was built to house the returned relics from stupa 3. The design is a poor shadow of the former artistry of Sanchi.

Special Events

In late November each year, the **Chethiyagiri Vihara Festival** attracts hundreds of Buddhist monks and pilgrims to see the relics of two of Buddha's early disciples, Sari Puttha and Maha Moggallana. The relics, originally discovered in stupa 3 in 1853, are now kept in the vihara and brought out for display during the festival.

Places to Stay & Eat

It's possible to take in all that Sanchi has to offer in just two or three hours. However, this is such a peaceful place that it's really worth spending the night here.

Sri Lanka Mahabodhi Society Guest House *(☎ 62739)* is where the visiting monks stay and is the best budget option in Sanchi. Spartan rooms are in a tranquil garden setting and cost Rs 50 with shared bathroom (cold water only). ***Jaiswal Lodge*** *(☎ 63908)*, over the road, has five rooms available for Rs 60.

MP Tourism runs two places in Sanchi, both with restaurants serving standard fare. ***Tourist Cafeteria*** *(☎ 62743)* has clean rooms with private bathroom for Rs 200/290. Rooms have ceiling fans, or there's a Rs 50 surcharge to use the air-cooler. ***Travellers' Lodge*** *(☎ 62723)*, on the main road to Bhopal about 250m from the crossroads, is a better hotel, but it's not as close to the stupas. Rooms cost Rs 250/350, or Rs 350/450 for the deluxe rooms.

The market area around the bus stand has a variety of fruit and ***food stalls***, as well as a couple of basic ***restaurants***.

Getting There & Away

Bus Local buses connect Bhopal with Sanchi (and other towns and villages in the area) about every hour from dawn to dusk, but there are two possible routes. The longer route (main road) goes via Raisen (see Around Sanchi following), costs Rs 17 and takes three hours for the 68km trip. The shorter route follows the railway line to Bhopal, costs Rs 15 and takes 1½ hours.

To Vidisha, buses depart from the Sanchi bus stand about every 30 minutes (Rs 5). A rickshaw to Vidisha can be bargained down to about Rs 25.

Train Sanchi is on the main Delhi to Mumbai railway line, 46km north of Bhopal. Slow passenger trains (Rs 10) can take over two hours to get to Bhopal, but there are two express trains each day (Rs 21, one hour). The expresses depart Bhopal at 8 am and 2.40 pm, and depart Sanchi at 10.18 am and 4 pm, so it's possible to visit on a day trip.

Getting Around

In Sanchi itself everything is within easy walking distance. For excursions to places nearby, like Vidisha (10km) and the Udaigiri caves (14km), you can rent bicycles in Sanchi's market for about Rs 20 per day.

AROUND SANCHI

Within cycling distance of Sanchi are more Buddhist sites, although none are of the scale or as well preserved as those at Sanchi. **Sonari**, 10km south-west of Sanchi, has eight stupas, two of them important. At **Satdhara**, west of Sanchi on the bank of the Beas River, are two stupas, one 30m in diameter. Another 8km to the south-east from Satdhara is **Andher**, where there are three small but well-preserved stupas. These stupas were all discovered in 1851, after the discovery of Sanchi.

Vidisha

pop 109,695

Vidisha was important in Ashoka's time. Then it was known as Besnagar and was the largest town in the area. The ruins of the 2nd century BC Brahmanical shrine here show traces of lime mortar – the earliest use of cement in India. Finds from the site are displayed in the **museum** near the train station.

From Sanchi you can reach Vidisha by bicycle (see under Udaigiri Caves for directions), bus (Rs 4, every 30 minutes), train (Rs 15), or rickshaw (Rs 35).

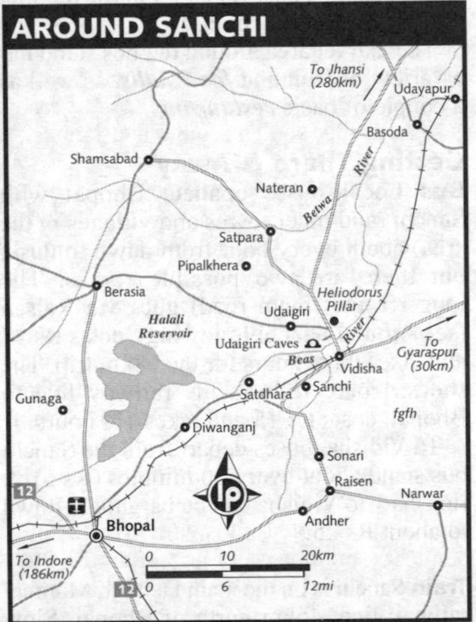

Udaigiri Caves

Cut into the sandstone hill, about 5km from Vidisha, are about 20 Gupta cave shrines dating from AD 320 to 606; two are Jain, the other 18 Hindu. In cave 5 there is a superb image of Vishnu in his boar incarnation. Cave 7 was cut out for the personal use of King Chandragupta II. Cave 20 is particularly interesting, with detailed Jain carvings. On the top of the hill are the ruins of a 6th-century Gupta temple.

From Bhopal or Sanchi take a bus or train to Vidisha, and from there take a tonga or autorickshaw to the caves. To reach the caves by bicycle from Sanchi, cycle towards Vidisha until you cross the river (6km). Turn left 1km further on (or carry straight on if you want to visit Vidisha first). After 3km you'll reach a junction in the colourful bazaar – turn left again. About 1km further is another left turn. Take this road for the caves (3.5km) or continue for 1km for the **Heliodorus Pillar**, erected in about 140 BC and dedicated to Vishnu.

Raisen

On the alternate road to Bhopal, 23km south of Sanchi, the huge and colourful hilltop **fort** of Raisen has temples, cannons, three palaces, 40 wells and a large tank. This Malwa fort was built around 1200, and although initially the centre of an independent kingdom, it later came under the control of Mandu. There are local buses to Raisen hourly from Sanchi (Rs 12), and regular departures from Bhopal's bus stand (Rs 14).

Gyaraspur

There are tanks, temples and a 9th or 10th century fort at this town, 51km north-east of Sanchi. The town's name is derived from the big fair that used to be held here in the 11th month, sometimes known as Gyaras. From Sanchi you'll have to change buses at Vidisha for the trip to Gyaraspur.

Udayapur

Udayapur is about 65km north of Sanchi. The large **Neelkantheswara Temple** here is thought to have been built in 1059. It's profusely and very finely carved with four prominent, decorated bands around the sikhara. The temple is aligned so that the first rays of the morning sun shine on the Shiva lingam in the sanctum.

From Sanchi or Vidisha, take a train to Basoda and then a local bus from there to Udayapur.

PACHMARHI

☎ 07578 • pop 14,700

Madhya Pradesh's peaceful hill station stands at an altitude of 1067m, nestled in the Satpura Ranges National Park 210km south-east of Bhopal.

Although nothing like a Himalayan hill station, Pachmarhi is a very attractive, relaxing place rarely visited by foreign tourists. The area draws quite a few artists, and gurus occasionally hold retreats up here.

There are fine views over the surrounding red sandstone hills, pools and waterfalls to bathe in, ancient cave paintings and some interesting walks through the sal forests.

Orientation & Information

The bus stand is at the north end of the small village. The main road continues south from here for about 3km to the seven-way junction called Jaistambha, which makes an excellent landmark for walks. Accommodation is spread over a wide area, so you'll need to use a taxi unless you're staying in the village itself.

There is a regional tourist information office (☎ 52100) next to Hotel Amaltas (open weekdays). It can provide brochures, fairly ordinary maps and arrange guides. There's no foreign exchange facilities in Pachmarhi.

There is an Internet centre charging Rs 65 per hour which has connections available after 11 am.

Things to See & Do

Built by Captain Forsyth in 1862, **Bison Lodge** was Pachmarhi's first forest lodge and is now a museum covering the history of the area and the flora and fauna of the Satpura region. A free wildlife film is shown in the open-air theatre here at 6 pm nightly, except Monday.

There are a number of interesting short **walks** around Pachmarhi, as well as longer treks for which you'll probably need a guide. **Jatashankar** is a revered cave temple in a gorge less than 2km from the bus stand. The small Shiva shrine is hidden under a huge overhanging rock formation.

Bee Falls are the most accessible of several waterfalls in the district – the drawback is the Rs 100 national park entry fee (Rs 10 for Indians) to get there. From the main road about 1km south of Jaistambha a trail leads down to the park entrance, then steps continue down to the falls.

About 2km east of Jaistambha, **Pandav Caves** are five 1000-year-old rock-cut caves overlooking an attractive garden. Legend has it the Pandavas lived here during their 12-year exile.

A recommended long day walk is to the hilltop shrine of **Chauragarh**, 4km from Mahadeo. You can see the cave paintings at **Mahadeo** on the way.

Special Events

Every February/March up to 100,000 Shaivite pilgrims, sadhus and adivasis attend the **Shivaratri Mela** celebrations at Mahadeo Temple, 10km south of Pachmarhi. The festival commemorates Lord Shiva and participants bring symbolic tridents and plant them on top of nearby Chauragarh hill.

Places to Stay

Most of the accommodation in Pachmarhi is run by MP Tourism or SADA, but there are a few private places in the village. High season is April to July and December and January.

Places to Stay – Budget

Hotel Pachmarhi *(☎ 52170, Patel Marg)*, in the village, has reasonable singles/doubles with squat toilets starting at Rs 250/350, with a 40% low-season discount.

Hotel Utkarsh *(☎ 52162)*, a short walk south of the bus stand just off the main road, has doubles with private bathroom and hot-water geyser for Rs 250, or Rs 125 in the low season.

Holiday Homes *(☎ 52099)* is the MP Tourism budget choice, and a pretty good one. Clean double rooms with private bathroom, TV and hot-water geyser are Rs 290. It's about 1km from the bus stand back towards Piparya.

New Hotel *(☎ 52017, Mahadeo Rd)* is a large place operated by SADA, about 4km from the village. There's a wide range of rooms from Rs 125 to 330 (with TV), and a 25% low-season discount.

Places to Stay – Mid-Range & Top End

The following are MP Tourism places, except Nilamber (SADA).

Satpura Retreat *(☎ 52097)* is another old Raj bungalow but much more atmospheric with a large veranda, comfortable rooms and vast private bathrooms. It's in a quiet location along the Mahadeo road. Standard doubles are Rs 690, but the good rooms are Rs 1390.

Nilamber Cottages *(☎ 52039)* are excellent. Perched up on a small hill about 3km south of the village, there's great east-west views from the verandas. Doubles with private bathroom, hot-water geyser and TV are worth the Rs 770.

Rock End Manor *(☎ 52079)*, just below Nilamber Cottages, is the swankiest address in Pachmarhi. It used to be the local maharaja's golf retreat, but has been converted into an elegant heritage hotel. Double rooms with panoramic views and all mod cons are Rs 1590, or Rs 1990 with air-con.

Places to Eat

The best places to eat are the hotel restaurants, especially ***China Bowl*** at Panchavati Huts & Cottages and ***The Club*** at Rock End Manor, but there are a few decent independent places and numerous cheap cafes in the bazaar area around the bus stand.

Mahfil Restaurant, near the bus stand, has cheap dosas and good veg burgers. ***Khalsa Restaurant*** has a pleasant outdoor setting by the lake and a range of good veg and nonveg food.

Getting There & Away

From the bus stand there are four services to Bhopal (Rs 91, seven hours) and the direct MP Tourism minibus at 2.30 pm (Rs 110, five hours). There are departures every few hours to Pipariya (Rs 25, 1½ hours).

Getting Around

Plenty of jeeps hang around the bus stand looking for passengers to take to Pachmarhi's viewpoints. A half-day trip costs at least Rs 300. They're also the local taxis (Rs 20 for a short trip). Bicycles can be hired from the shop just north of the bazaar for Rs 25 per day and are a good way to get to the various trailheads and viewpoints.

PIPARIYA

☎ 07576

Pipariya is the nearest road/rail junction to Pachmarhi, 47km away. If you get stuck here there's the MP Tourism ***Tourist Motel*** *(☎ 22299)* with doubles at Rs 150 (shared bathroom) and a restaurant. It's about 200m from the train station.

Local buses and jeeps leave from the bus stand behind the train station regularly for Pachmarhi. A local bus to/from Bhopal costs Rs 65 and takes six hours.

Western Madhya Pradesh

UJJAIN

☎ 0734 • pop 433,465

Only 56km from Indore, ancient Ujjain is one of India's holiest cities for Hindus. It gets its sanctity from a mythological tale about the churning of the oceans by the gods and demons in search of the nectar of immortality. When the coveted vessel of nectar was finally found, there followed a mad scramble across the skies with the demons pursuing the gods in an attempt to pinch the nectar from them. Four drops were spilt and they fell at Haridwar, Nasik, Ujjain and Prayag (Allahabad). As a result, Ujjain is one of the sites of the Kumbh Mela, which takes place here every 12 years and draws millions to bathe in the Shipra River.

Despite its relative obscurity today, Ujjain ranks equally as a great religious centre with such places as Varanasi, Gaya and Kanchipuram. The city really comes alive during Navratri (September/October). For non-Hindus, though, it can be a pretty dull place once you've explored the temples and ghats.

History

On an ancient trade route, Ujjain has a distinguished history with its origins lost in the mists of time. It was an important city under Ashoka's father, when it was known as Avantika. Later Chandragupta II (AD 380–414

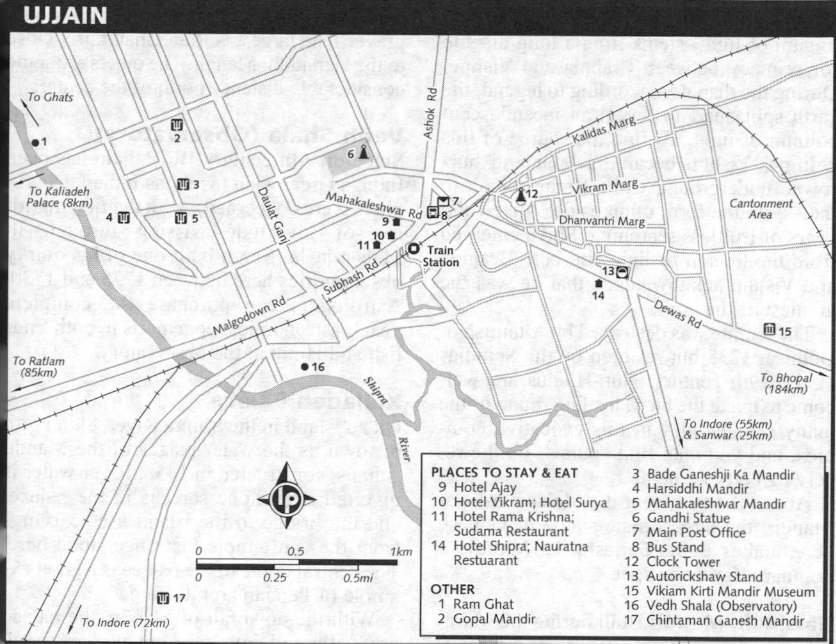

ruled from here rather than from his actual capital, Pataliputra. It was at his court that Kalidasa, one of Hinduism's most revered poets, wrote the *Meghdoot*, with its famous lyrical description of the city and its people.

With the passing of the Guptas and the rise of the Parmaras, Ujjain became the centre of a struggle for control of the Malwa region. The last of the Parmaras, Siladitya, was captured by the Muslim sultans of Mandu, and Ujjain thus passed into the hands of Mughal vassals.

An invasion by Altamish in 1234 resulted in the wholesale desecration of many of the temples, but that was halted during the reign of Baz Bahadur of Mandu. Bahadur himself was eventually overthrown by the Mughal emperor, Akbar. Later, under Aurangzeb, grants were provided to fund temple reconstruction.

Following the demise of the Mughals, Maharaja Jai Singh (of Jaipur fame) became the governor of Malwa, and during his rule the observatory and several new temples were constructed at Ujjain. With his passing, Ujjain experienced another period of turmoil at the hands of the Marathas until it was finally taken by the Scindias in 1750. When the Scindia capital was moved to Gwalior in 1810, Ujjain's commercial importance declined rapidly.

Orientation & Information

The train line divides the city: The old section, including the bazaar and most of the temples and ghats, is to the north-west of the city, and the new section is on the south-east side. The budget hotels are in front of the train station. Tourist information is available at the train station from MP Tourism and at Hotel Shipra. There's nowhere to change money in Ujjain – Indore and Bhopal are the closest places.

Temples

Mahakaleshwar Mandir The most important temple in Ujjain, the Mahakaleshwar Mandir is dedicated to Shiva. The temple enshrines one of India's 12 *jyoti linga* – naturally occurring lingam believed to derive currents of power *(shakti)* from within themselves as opposed to lingam ritually invested with *mantra-shakti* by the priests.

The myth of the *jyothirlingam* (the lingam of light) stems from a long dispute for primacy between Brahma and Vishnu. During the dispute, according to legend, the earth split apart to reveal an incandescent column of light. To find the source of this column, Vishnu became a boar and burrowed underground while Brahma took to the sky in the form of an eagle. After 1000 years of fruitless searching, Shiva emerged from the lingam of light and both Brahma and Vishnu acknowledged that he was the greatest of the gods.

The temple was destroyed by Altamish of Delhi in 1235 but restored by the Scindias in the 19th century. Non-Hindus are welcome to make the busy, jostling round of the many minitemples in this evocative complex, and you may find yourself on the receiving end of a puja.

Above the tank near the Mahakaleshwar Mandir, the large ornate statue of Ganesh here makes **Bade Ganeshji-ka-Mandir** a popular pilgrimage spot.

Harsiddhi Mandir Built during the Maratha period, this temple enshrines a famous image of the goddess Annapurna. The two large pillars adorned with lamps were a special feature of Maratha art and are spectacular when lit at Navratri (Dussehra) in September/October.

Gopal Mandir The marble-spired Gopal Mandir was built by the queen of Maharaja Daulat Rao Scindia in the 19th century and is a great example of Maratha architecture.

The silver-plated doors of the sanctum have quite a history. They were originally taken from the temple at Somnath in Gujarat to Ghazni in Afghanistan and then to Lahore by Mohammed Shah Abdati. From there they were rescued by Mahadji Scindia and shortly afterwards installed in the temple.

Chintaman Ganesh Mandir On the opposite bank of the Shipra River, this temple is believed to be of considerable antiquity. The artistically carved pillars of the assembly hall date back to the Parmara period.

Ghats

Since most of the temples are of relatively recent construction you may find more of interest on the ghats, especially at dawn and dusk when the locals frame their days with prayer. The largest is Ram Ghat, fairly close to the Harsiddhi Mandir. The others are some considerable distance north of the centre.

Vedh Shala (Observatory)

Since the 4th century BC, Ujjain has been India's Greenwich (as far as Indian geographers were concerned), with the first meridian of longitude passing through it. Maharaja Jai Singh built one of his quirky observatories here between 1725 and 1730. Astrologers can purchase the complete year's astronomical ephemeris in both English and Hindi at the observatory.

Kaliadeh Palace

On an island in the Shipra River, 8km north of town, is the water palace of the Mandu sultans, constructed in 1458. River water is diverted over stone screens in the palace, and the bridge to the island uses carvings from the sun temple that once stood here. The central dome of the palace is a good example of Persian architecture.

With the downfall of Mandu, the palace gradually fell into ruin but was restored, along with the nearby sun temple, by Madhav Rao Scindia in 1920.

Places to Stay

There's a few cheap hotels opposite the train station. They're basic but even the cheapest rooms have private bathrooms.

Hotel Ajay *(☎ 550856, 12 Dewas Gate, Mahakaleshwar Rd)* is one of the better budget choices. It's around the corner from the string of hotels in front of the train station, and has single/double rooms for Rs 100/150 with private bathroom or Rs 200/300 with TV and air-cooler. Bathrooms have squat toilets and bucket hot water.

Hotel Vikram *(☎ 562220, Subhash Rd)*, in front of the train station, has small rooms for Rs 60/80 and spacious rooms with TV for Rs 100/140. It's a pretty grubby place – avoid the grotty cells with shared bathrooms. All bathrooms have squat toilets and bucket hot water.

Hotel Surya *(☎ 560747)*, next door, has better rooms for Rs 95/110, or Rs 150/200 with TV. All rooms (theoretically) have constant hot water.

Hotel Rama Krishna *(☎ 557012, Subhash Rd)* charges Rs 125/150, or Rs 240/300

ANDREW LUBRAN

ANDREW LUBRAN

GREG ELMS

DAVID TIPLING

Visions of Rajasthan: camel-back safaris in the desert around Jaisalmer **(top)**; a villager outside a mud-brick house, near Udaipur **(middle right)**; marble *chhatris* (cenotaphs) punctuate the open desert landscape near Jaisalmer **(bottom)**; and elaborate *jali* (carved-marble lattice) windows at Amber Palace **(middle left)**

ANTHONY HAM

DAVID TIPLING

JOHN MOCK

Top: Chittorgarh's intricately patterned Sammidheshwar Temple, Rajasthan
Middle: Jodphur, evocatively named the 'blue city', viewed from Meherangarh
Bottom: A pilgrim poses on the trail to Savitri Temple, with Pushkar Lake in the background

with TV and air-con, and is a bit cleaner than its neighbours.

Retiring rooms at the train station have dorm beds for Rs 30, and rooms for Rs 100.

MP Tourism's ***Hotel Shipra*** *(☎ 551495)*, in a quiet, very pleasant setting just off Dewas Rd, has an impressive marble foyer, and extra-large rooms. Singles/doubles are from Rs 350/390, up to 690/790 with air-con, plus tax. The ***restaurant*** here is quite good, and there's a bar.

Places to Eat

There are a number of places to eat opposite the station.

Sudama Restaurant has good vegetarian dishes for under Rs 35 but the breakfasts are spooky.

Nauratna Restaurant at Hotel Shipra serves good food. The Nav Ratan curry (Rs 45) is good if you like a sweeter curry. Sandwiches are about Rs 25.

Getting There & Away

Bus There are buses roughly every 20 minutes to Indore (Rs 24, two hours), which are faster than the train. Buses to Bhopal (Rs 78/86 in ordinary/deluxe, four hours) go via Dewas. For Mandu you have to change at Indore. An early-morning bus connects Ujjain with Kota in Rajasthan (Rs 100, 256km).

Train The *Malwa Express*, departing at 2.35 pm, is the fastest link with Delhi. It takes 17½ hours (Rs 270/871 in sleeper/1st class, 885km), via Bhopal (Rs 104/298 2nd/1st class, 184km, four hours), Jhansi (Rs 183/577 in sleeper/1st class, 475km, nine hours), Gwalior (Rs 210/666 in sleeper/1st class, 572km, 10½ hours) and Agra (Rs 234/750 in sleeper/1st class, 690km, 13 hours).

The *Narmada Express* connects Ujjain with Indore (Rs 29/173 in 2nd/1st class, 2¼ hours) and, heading east: Bhopal (Rs 104/298 2nd/1st class, 184km, four hours), Jabalpur (Rs 117/615 2nd/1st class, 540km, 12½ hours) and Bilaspur (Rs 261/882 in sleeper/1st class, 929km, 25 hours).

The 5.20 pm *Avantika Express* is the only direct service to Mumbai (Rs 158/268 in 2nd/sleeper class, 11½ hours).

The *Bhopal-Rajkot Express* to Ahmedabad departs at 11 pm (Rs 102/179 in 2nd/sleeper class, 9½ hours).

Getting Around

Many of Ujjain's sights are a long way from the centre of town so you'll probably use quite a few autorickshaws or the more romantic horse-drawn tongas. There are registration booths at both the bus and train stations that autorickshaw drivers are obliged to use if you request it. The normal system of bargaining should work though – from the train station to the Mahakaleshwar Mandir costs around Rs 10 (Rs 20 for a tonga).

INDORE

☎ 0731 • pop 1,278,690

Indore is not of great interest, but it's a good base for visiting Mandu. The city is a major textile-producing centre and at Pithampur, 35km away, Hindustan Motors, Kinetic Honda, Bajaj Tempo and Eischer all have factories. Indians call Pithampur the Detroit of India, and Indore is its gateway.

Orientation & Information

The older part of town is on the western side of the railway line, the newer part on the east. If arriving by train, leave the station by platform No 1 for the east side of town and by platform No 4 for the west side.

The tourist office (☎ 528653) is by the Tourist Bungalow at the back of RN Tagore Natya Griha Hall, RN Tagore Rd. It's open from 10 am to 5 pm.

Cash and travellers cheques can be changed at the main branch of the State Bank of India, near the main post office.

Internet and email facilities are available at Indore Telecom's flash multimedia centre (Central Telegraph office) in Nehru Park. You have to remove your shoes to enter the spotless air-con room. Rates are very reasonable at Rs 30 per hour. It's open from 10 am to 6 pm daily except Sunday.

There's a good selection of reading material (including second-hand books) at Badshah Book Shop, in the City Centre shopping complex on MG Rd.

Things to See

On Jawahar Rd is the **Kanch Mandir** or Seth Hukanchand Temple. This Jain temple is very plain externally, but inside is completely mirrored with pictures of sinners being tortured in the afterlife.

The **museum** near the main post office, has one of the best collections of medieval and pre-medieval Hindu sculpture in Madhya Pradesh. It's open from 10 am to 5 pm daily, except Monday (free).

In the south-west of the city, surrounded by gardens, is the grand **Lal Bagh Palace**, built 1886–1921. It has all the usual over-the-top touches like entrance gates that are replicas of those at Buckingham Palace. It's open from 10 am to 6 pm daily, except Monday (entry is Rs 2 and it's Rs 10/50 if you want to use your camera/video).

The magnificent **Gandhi Hall** (town hall) is open to visitors from 10 am to 5 pm daily. Exhibitions are sometimes held here.

At the western end of MG Rd, the **Bada Ganapati Temple** contains an 8m-high bright-orange statue of Ganesh – reputed to be the world's largest.

In the old part of town, the multistorey gateway of the **Rajwada** looks out onto the palm-lined main square in the crowded streets of the Kajuri Bazaar.

Organised Tours

MP Tourism (☎ 528653) operates day tours to Mandu from July to September (and outside of these months if there are sufficient numbers) for Rs 225 as the monsoon is the high season for local tourists. It's a similar story for tours to Ujjain, Maheshwar and Omkareshwar (Rs 225). These tours include lunch and afternoon tea and a minimum of 10 people is required.

Places to Stay – Budget

The train station and the Sarwate bus stand are about a five-minute walk apart, and it's in this lively, polluted area that you'll find the budget hotels. The following places have rooms with private bathrooms and 24-hour checkout.

***Hotel Ashoka** (☎ 465991, 14 Nasia Rd)* is directly behind the bus stand. The cheapest rooms are way up on the 4th floor (no lift), but they're not bad at Rs 150/200 a single/double with hot-water geyser. For a shorter walk you pay Rs 185/235.

***Hotel Payal** (☎ 478460, Patel Bridge)* is a small place with reasonably priced singles/doubles/triples with TV and air-cooler for Rs 200/250/300. Free bucket hot water is available.

***Hotel Amrit** (☎ 465876, Patel Bridge)*, near Hotel Payal, is not a bad option with

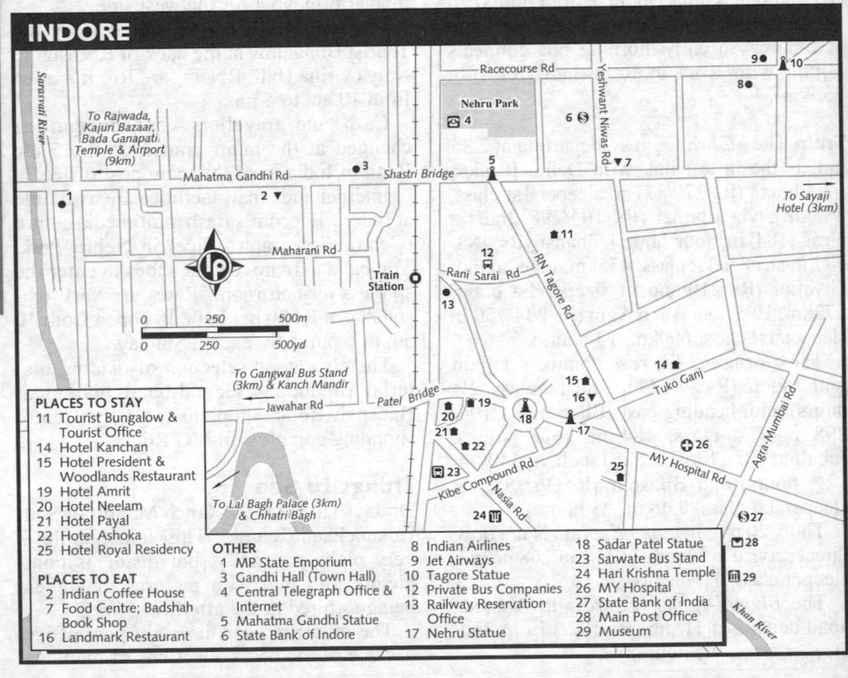

MADHYA PRADESH & CHHATISGARH

cheap rooms starting at Rs 100/150, or Rs 350/450 with TV and air-con.

Hotel Neelam *(☎ 466001, 33/2 Patel Bridge Corner)*, just around the corner from Hotel Payal, is a much smarter hotel and good value from Rs 180/230 with TV and hot water. The rooms are spotless but the white-tile decor is like sleeping in someone's bathroom.

Places to Stay – Mid-Range & Top End

Indore has a good selection of comfortable mid-range hotels, as befits a business city of this size.

Tourist Bungalow *(☎ 521818, RN Tagore Rd)* is at the back of the Tagore Natya Griha Hall. Very comfortable rooms are Rs 300/350, or Rs 390/490 with air-con.

Hotel Royal Residency *(☎ 764633, 225 RN Tagore Rd)* has well-appointed standard rooms that are good value at Rs 450/600; air-con starts at Rs 750/900.

Hotel Kanchan *(☎ 270871, ⓔ kanchan@bom4.vsnl.net.in)* is a small place in Kanchan Bagh, and maybe the best value in this range, with clean and comfortable rooms for Rs 400/550 and air-con for Rs 500/700. There's a bar and restaurant.

Hotel President *(☎ 528866, fax 512230, RN Tagore Rd)* describes its lobby as having an 'out of this world look'. The rooms, however, are definitely Indian and are looking a bit weary, although there is a health club and sauna. Rooms with air-con start at Rs 875/1075, including breakfast.

Sayaji Hotel *(☎ 552121, fax 553131, Vijay Nagar)*, 4km east of the town centre, is a huge place and Indore's top hotel. It's got a swimming pool, bowling alley, tennis and squash courts, health club and luxurious rooms starting at Rs 1450/1700.

Places to Eat

Indore is famous for its variety of *namkin* (prepackaged spicy nibbles) – Prakash brand is the best. If you're here during one of the festivals watch out for the *bhang gota* – samosas with added zing!

Indian Coffee House is always a good, cheap choice. There's a branch on MG Rd, near Gandhi Hall.

Food Centre is a busy cafeteria serving tasty South Indian food in the City Centre shopping complex on MG Rd.

Landmark Restaurant, next to Hotel President on RN Tagore Rd, is an astonishingly good continental-style place doing things rarely seen in India like delicious Waldorf salad and roast lamb. The service is attentive and prices are reasonable, considering the quality.

Most of the top hotels have restaurants and bars. ***Woodlands Restaurant*** at Hotel President is a good choice, and meals are very reasonably priced.

Getting There & Away

Air Indian Airlines (☎ 431595), on Racecourse Rd, has daily evening flights to Mumbai (US$90). There are also daily morning flights to Delhi (US$135), via Bhopal (US$55) and Gwalior (US$105, Monday and Friday only).

Bus There are departures from the Sarwate bus stand every 30 minutes to Ujjain (Rs 27, 1½ hours) and Bhopal (Rs 78/87 in ordinary/deluxe, five hours). For Mandu, take a bus to Dhar (Rs 28, two hours) and another to Mandu from there (Rs 15, 1½ hours). From Sarwate there are buses to Dhar at 5, 6, 7.45, 8.30 and 9 am.

There are also direct buses to Omkareshwar (Rs 34, three hours), most departing before 11 am. Two services go to Aurangabad (for the Ajanta and Ellora caves) at 5 am and 9.30 pm (Rs 182, 13 hours); the morning service stops at Ajanta but the overnight bus is direct to Aurangabad. There's a daily bus for Mumbai (Rs 244/368 in ordinary/deluxe, 16 hours) at 5 and 6.30 am.

From Gangwal bus stand, about 3km west along Jawahar Rd, there are departures to Dhar every 30 minutes.

Train Indore is connected to the main broad-gauge lines between Delhi and Mumbai by tracks from Nagda via Ujjain in the west and Bhopal in the east. The daily *Malwa Express* leaves Indore at 12.30 pm for New Delhi (Rs 287/903 in sleeper/1st class, 969km, 19 hours), via Ujjain (Rs 29/173, 80km, 1½ hours), Bhopal (Rs 67/352, 264km, 5½ hours), Gwalior (Rs 199/672, 652km, 12½ hours) and Agra (Rs 149/783, 770km, 14 hours). For Mumbai (Rs 284 in sleeper class, 829 km, 14½ hours), the *Avantika Express* leaves at 3.50 pm and arrives in Mumbai at 6.50 am the next morning.

There is also a metre-gauge line through Indore. Services on this line run from Jaipur in Rajasthan to Indore (Rs 160/225 in 2nd/sleeper class, 610km, 16 hours), and on to Khandwa and Purna.

Car An alternative to the slow public transport to Mandu, Omkareshwar and Maheshwar is a taxi or hired car and driver. MP Tourism (☎ 528653) can organise a car for Rs 4.50/km (minimum 250km per day). An overnight stay – essential if you want to visit all three places – costs an extra day. You may get a better price from a private taxi outside the bus or train station.

Getting Around

To/From the Airport The airport is 9km from the city. Autorickshaws charge Rs 80 and taxis Rs 250. You may find it cheaper than this to book your transport from your hotel.

Local Transport Indore's autorickshaws are cheap (most journeys are under Rs 10) and drivers will generally use their meters. Tempos operate along set routes and cost Rs 3 to 5 from point to point. The main stands are in front of the train station and at Gandhi Hall.

AROUND INDORE

Omkareshwar

This island at the confluence of the Narmada and Kaveri Rivers has drawn Hindu pilgrims for centuries on account of its jyothirlingam, one of the 12 throughout India, at the Shiva **temple of Shri Omkar Mandhata**. (For an explanation of the myth of the jyothirlingam see the Mahakaleshwar Mandir section under Ujjain earlier in this chapter.)

The temple is constructed from local soft stone that has enabled its artisans to achieve a rare degree of detailed work, particularly in the friezes on the upper parts of the structure.

The setting here is stunning. From the village on the banks of the Narmada, the island seems to loom out of the river, crowned by a former palace. A high footbridge connects the village with the island, or you can descend to the ghats and take a motorboat across the Narmada (Rs 5). The path up to the temple is lined with the usual colourful pilgrim paraphernalia – garlands of marigolds, coconuts, strings of beads and tacky souvenirs. Crowds gather for the puja that is performed in the temple three times a day.

There are other temples on this island including the **Siddhnath**, a good example of early medieval Brahminic architecture, and a cluster of other Hindu and Jain temples.

Places to Stay & Eat A concrete block place, ***Hotel Aishwarya*** *(☎ 07280-71325)*, the only hotel in the village, is easily the most comfortable place to stay. Clean rooms with private bathroom and bucket hot water are Rs 250/350. The restaurant serves simple, cheap vegetarian food. The hotel is on the other side of the village from the bus stand and is well-signposted from the main road.

Holkar Guesthouse is a bit difficult to find – it's the faded yellow building perched on a rocky outcrop with good views across to Omkareshwar Island. Ask for directions in the marketplace. Basic doubles with shared bathroom are Rs 100.

Yatrika Guest House, near the bus stand, has simple but clean rooms with private bathroom and bucket hot water for Rs 250.

There are ***stalls*** selling basic food around the bus stand.

Getting There & Away There are five direct buses daily to Indore (Rs 35, three hours). Coming from Indore, buses depart from Sarwate bus stand at regular intervals until about 11 am. There are four direct buses – on atrocious roads – to Maheshwar (Rs 35, 2½ hours), or you can take one of the regular buses to Barwaha and change there.

Maheshwar

Maheshwar was an important cultural and political centre at the dawn of Hindu civilisation and was mentioned in the Ramayana and Mahabharata under its former name of Mahishmati. It languished in obscurity for many centuries after that until revived by the Holkar queen, Rani Ahilyabai of Indore, in the late 18th century. It's from these times that most of the temples and the fort complex date.

The principal sights are the **fort**, which is now a museum displaying relics of the Holkar dynasty, the three **ghats** lining the banks of the Narmada River, and the tiered **temples**, distinguished by their overhanging balconies and intricately worked doorways.

Maheshwar saris are famous throughout the country for their unique weave and beautifully complex patterns. The Rewa Society, inside the fort, runs a **sari weaving factory** where you can see the weavers at work on handlooms. Saris are on sale here (around Rs 1000 for silk, Rs 500 for cotton), or you can shop around for them in the market.

Maheshwar is easily fitted in between Omkareshwar and Mandu, and the choice of accommodation is slim. ***Akashdeep Rest House***, on the road up to the fort, has very simple double rooms with shared bathroom for Rs 50, or try the ***Ahilya Trust Guesthouse***, also near the fort.

There is an afternoon bus from Indore (four hours). Otherwise, regular local buses run to Maheshwar from Barwaha and Dhar, both of which are easily reached by local bus from Indore.

MANDU

☎ 07292

The extensive and now mainly deserted hilltop fort of Mandu is one of the most evocative sights in central India. It's on an isolated outcrop separated from the tableland to the north by a deep and wide valley, over which a natural causeway runs to the main city gate. To the south of Mandu the land drops steeply away to the plains far below and the view is superb. Deep ravines cut into the sides of the 20 sq km plateau occupied by the fort.

Although it's possible to make a long day trip from Indore, Mandu is worth at least a night. In winter, Mandu is quite popular with foreign visitors but the local tourist season is during the monsoon, when the place turns verdant green and the buildings are mirrored in the lakes.

History

Mandu, known as the city of joy, has had a chequered history. Founded as a fortress and retreat in the 10th century by Raja Bhoj, it was conquered by the Muslim rulers of Delhi in 1304. When the Mughals invaded and took Delhi in 1401, the Afghan Dilawar Khan, Governor of Malwa, set up his own little kingdom and Mandu embarked on its golden age.

Although Dilawar Khan first established Mandu as an independent kingdom, it was his son, Hoshang Shah, who shifted the capital from Dhar to Mandu and raised it to its greatest splendour.

Hoshang's son ruled for only a year before being poisoned by Mohammed Shah, who became king himself and ruled for 33 years.

In 1469, Ghiyas-ud-din, Mohammed Shah's son, ascended the throne and spent the following 31 years devoting himself to women and song, before being poisoned at the age of 80 by his son, Nasir-ud-din. Finally, in 1526, Bahadur Shah of Gujarat conquered Mandu.

In 1534 the Mughal Humayun defeated Bahadur Shah, but as soon as Humayun turned his back an officer of the former dynasty took over. Several more changes of fortune eventually led to Baz Bahadur taking power in 1554. In 1561 he fled Mandu rather than face Akbar's advancing troops.

Even after Mandu was added to the Mughal empire by Akbar, it kept a considerable degree of independence, until taken by the Marathas. The capital of Malwa was then shifted back to Dhar, and Mandu became a ghost town. For a ghost town, however, it's very grandiose and impressive, and has one of the best collections of Afghan architecture in India.

Orientation & Information

The buildings of Mandu can be divided into three groups. The Royal Enclave, Mandu's most impressive group of temples, stands on the northern shoulder of the fort, but is only accessible by looping through Mandu village and entering from the south.

The village is about 2km from the gate and is where most of Mandu's inhabitants live. The buildings here are known as the village group. Continuing on, you'll eventually reach the Rewa Kund group at the extreme south of the fort.

You can get a copy of the Archaeological Survey of India's excellent guidebook *Mandu* for Rs 11 from the Taveli Mahal in the Royal Enclave.

The nearest bank for changing money is in Indore, although a traveller has reported being able to cash a travellers cheque at State Bank of India, next to the bus stand.

Royal Enclave Group

These are the only temples at Mandu for which you pay admission (US$5 or Rs 230, and Rs 25 if you want to use your video

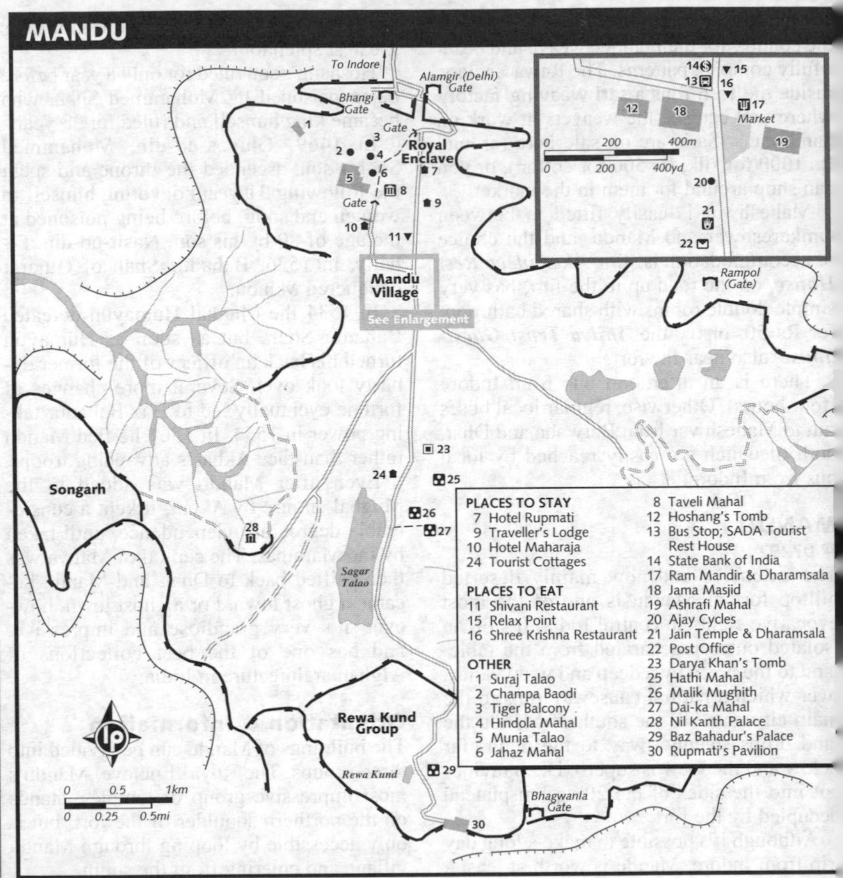

camera). The enclosure is open from sunrise to sunset.

Jahaz Mahal, or the Ship Palace, is probably the most famous building in Mandu. It really is shiplike, being far longer (120m) than it is wide (15m), and the illusion is completed by the two lakes that flank it to the east and west. It was constructed by Ghiyas-ud-din, son of Mohammed Shah, for his harem, reputed to number more than 15,000 maidens. The Jahaz Mahal with its lookouts, arches, cool rooms and beautiful pool was their playground.

Taveli Mahal is just south of the Jahaz Mahal and this palace is now the Archaeological Survey of India's Antiquity Gallery. This small museum is open from sunrise to sunset (entry to the Royal Enclave includes this museum). Exhibits include fragment of utensils and vessels found at the site, an some stone images.

Just north of Ghiyas' stately pleasur dome is a churchlike hall known as the **Hin dola Mahal**, or Swing Palace, because th inward slope of the walls is supposed t create the impression that the walls ar swaying. The wide, sloping ramp at th northern end of the building is said to hav been built to enable the ruler to be convey upstairs by elephant.

To the west of the first two Royal En clave structures is **Champa Baodi**, an inter esting step-well on the north edge of th tank. Its subterranean levels featured co wells and bathrooms and it was obviously popular hot-weather retreat.

Other buildings in the enclave include the 'house and shop' of Gada Shah and the 1405 **Mosque of Dilawar Khan**, one of the earliest Muslim buildings in Mandu.

Village Group

Jama Masjid This huge mosque built in 1454 dominates the village of Mandu. It is supposed to be the finest and largest example of Afghan architecture in India. Construction was commenced by Hoshang Shah, who patterned it on the great Omayyed Mosque in Damascus, Syria. The mosque features an 80 sq m courtyard. It's open from 8.30 am to 5.30 pm daily.

Hoshang's Tomb Immediately behind the mosque is the imposing tomb of Hoshang, who died in 1435. Reputed to be India's oldest marble building, the tomb is entered through a domed porch. Light enters the interior through stone jali (carved marble lattice screens), typical of the Hindu influence on the tomb's fine design. It has a double arch and a squat, central dome surrounded by four smaller domes. It is said that Shah Jahan sent his architects to Mandu to study this tomb before they embarked upon the design of the Taj Mahal.

To one side of the tomb enclosure is a long, low colonnade with its width divided into three by rows of pillars. Behind is a long, narrow hall with a typically Muslim barrel-vaulted ceiling, intended as a shelter for visiting pilgrims.

Ashrafi Mahal The ruin of this building stands directly across the road from the Jama Masjid. Originally built as a madrasa (Islamic college), it was later extended by its builder, Mohammed Shah, to become his tomb. The design was simply too ambitious for its builders' abilities and it later collapsed. The seven-storey circular tower of victory, which Mohammed Shah erected, has also fallen. A great stairway still leads up to the entrance to the empty shell of the building.

Jain Temple There are numerous buildings in this modern and ever-developing temple complex. The temples are richly decorated and feature tirthankars in marble, silver and gold, some with glinting jade eyes. Towards the back of the compound is a theme-park style Jain **museum**, which includes a walk-on replica of Shatrunjaya, the hilltop temple complex at Palitana, Gujarat, and a mural of colourful kitschy Jain homilies. One particularly explicit panel shows the terrible consequences of drinking and meat-eating: A drunk carnivore lies on the street with dogs pissing on him.

Rewa Kund Group

About 3km south of the village group, past the large Sagar Talao, is the Rewa Kund group.

Baz Bahadur's Palace Baz Bahadur was the last independent ruler of Mandu. His palace, constructed around 1509, is beside the Rewa Kund and there was a water lift at the northern end of the tank to supply water to the palace. A curious mix of Rajasthani and Mughal styles, it was actually built well before Baz Bahadur came to power.

Rupmati's Pavilion At the very edge of the fort, perched on the hillside overlooking the plains below, is the pavilion of Rupmati. The Malwa legends relate that she was a beautiful Hindu singer, and that Baz Bahadur persuaded her to leave her home on the plains by building her this pavilion. From its terrace and domed pavilions Rupmati could gaze down on the Narmada River, which is now dammed but which once wound across the plains far below.

The Perfect Escape

One of the wonderful things about Mandu is the sense of tranquility which seems to waft through its ancient palaces. After a few weeks in central India, escaping from the congestion and chaos of the cities is one of the most memorable things about spending a few days in the 'city of joy'. The palaces are still intact enough to get a sense of the Mandu of Dilawar Khan's time, and the echoes of this era resonate loudly through the impressive stone hallways. Fortunately, the flow of tourists has not yet reached the proportions that would rob the place of its magic. Wandering around a roofless, empty palace built for thousands and marvelling at the engineering ingenuity is absorbing and relaxing, particularly late in the day.

It's a romantic building, the perfect setting for a fairytale romance – but one with an unhappy ending. Akbar, it is said, was prompted to conquer Mandu partly due to Rupmati's beauty. And when Akbar marched on the fort Baz Bahadur fled, leaving Rupmati to poison herself.

For maximum romantic effect come here in the late afternoon to watch the sunset, or at night when the moon is full. Bring a torch (flashlight) as there's no lighting on the road back.

Darya Khan's Tomb & Hathi Mahal

To the east of the road, between the Rewa Kund group and the village, are these two buildings. The Hathi Mahal, or Elephant Palace, is so named because the pillars supporting the dome are of massive proportions – like elephant legs. Nearby is the tomb of Darya Khan, which was once decorated with intricate patterns of mosaic tiles.

Nil Kanth Palace

This palace, at the end of one of the ravines that cuts into the fort, is actually below the level of the hilltop and is reached by a flight of steps going down the hillside. At one time it was a Shiva shrine, as the name – God with the Blue Throat – suggests. Under the Mughals it became a pleasant water palace with a cascade running down the middle.

At the top of the steps, villagers sell the seeds of the baobab tree; Mandu is one of the few places in India where the baobab is found. It's difficult to miss – it's the tubby grey tree that looks as if it has been planted upside down with its roots in the air.

Organised Tours

Tours to Mandu are run from Indore from July to September, and outside these months if there are at least 10 people. See Organised Tours under Indore earlier in this chapter. Local guides loiter around the bus stand offering their services.

Places to Stay

Hotel Maharaja *(☎ 63288, Jahaz Mahal Rd)*, in a quiet location between the village and the Royal Enclave, is the best budget option. Basic doubles with private bathroom are Rs 125/200 and bucket hot water is Rs 5. There's a simple restaurant and friendly staff.

Tourist Rest House is a dull SADA place opposite the Jama Masjid. Rooms with private bathroom are dingy at Rs 125 – there are squat toilets and bucket hot water.

The following MP Tourism places should be booked at the ***tourist office*** in Indore *(☎ 0731-528653)* if you want to ensure a bed. ***Traveller's Lodge*** *(☎ 63221)* looks a little gloomy compared to the Rupmati a little further down the road, but it's comfortable enough with rooms at Rs 290/390 with private bathroom and hot water. ***Tourist Cottages*** *(☎ 63235)* is in a very pleasant location overlooking the Sagar Talao. Rooms cost Rs 350/450, or Rs 750/850 with air-con. Breakfast and dinner are served in the outdoor restaurant and nonguests are welcome.

Hotel Rupmati *(☎ 63270)* is the top hotel in Mandu. Its 10 spacious rooms have fine views over the gorge from back patios. The modern, comfortable rooms cost Rs 325/400. Air-con doubles are Rs 750. There's a pleasant terrace restaurant.

Places to Eat

The restaurants at Hotel Rupmati and the MP Tourism hotels are the best places to eat, but there are a few cheap independent places in the village. Look out for the green, hard-shelled seed of the baobab tree in the market. The locals love it, but it's a bit like eating sweet-and-sour chalk dust.

Relax Point has drinks and a shop but doesn't seem to cook food. You may be able to coax a menu out of ***Shree Krishna Restaurant*** next door. We've had reports that the food is good here.

Shivani Restaurant, further north, serves up good, reasonably priced veg food (between Rs 20 and 45) and breakfasts.

Getting There & Away

There are six daily buses direct from Mandu to Indore (Rs 40, 3½ hours), but coming the other way you must change at Dhar. There's one bus to Maheshwar at 7.30 am (Rs 25, 2½ hours).

For Bhopal, take the 6 am bus to Indore where you can connect with a bus or train to Bhopal. The buses stop near the Jama Masjid in the village.

The alternative is hiring a car; see Getting There & Away in the Indore section earlier in this chapter.

Getting Around

You can hire bicycles from Ajay Cycles, south of the Jama Masjid, or from the market for Rs 3 per hour or Rs 25 per day (24 hours). This is the best way to get around as the sights are quite far apart, and the terrain is relatively flat. This is also a fine area for walking.

There's just one autorickshaw in Mandu, which is available (of course) for a three- to four-hour tour of Mandu's sights (Rs 150). It costs Rs 20 return from the village to Rupmati's Pavilion.

Eastern Madhya Pradesh

JABALPUR

☎ 0761 • pop 1,065,025

Almost due south of Khajuraho and east of Bhopal, the large city of Jabalpur is principally famous today for the gorge on the Narmada River known as the Marble Rocks. It's also the departure point for a visit to the national parks of Kanha (160km) and Bandhavgarh (197km).

The tourist office (☎ 322111) is at the train station, and is open from 7 am to 9 pm daily. It can book MP Tourism accommodation for you at Kanha National Park (payment in full required) and Marble Rocks.

Money can be changed at the main branch of State Bank of India (opposite Hotel Rishi Regency) and at Jackson's Hotel.

Internet connections from Jabalpur are slow during the day but cheap. Cyber Estate, near Jackson's Hotel, is open until 9 pm and charges Rs 30 per hour.

Rani Durgavati Museum

South of the bazaar, next to the tempo stand, this museum's diverse collection is worth a look. The ground floor has 10th- and 11th-century sculptures from temples in the Jabalpur district. Upstairs are letters and photographs relating to Mahatma Gandhi, and models and photographs depicting the Gond people. It's open from 10 am to 5 pm daily, except Monday (entry is free).

Places to Stay – Budget

The cheapest places to stay are almost all down near the bus stand, about 3km from the train station. The commission racket for rickshaw-wallahs is alive and well in Jabalpur.

Hotel Mayur *(☎ 310035, Malviya Chowk)* is cheap, clean and only a short walk from the bus stand. Economy singles/doubles are Rs 120/220 and the better 'deluxe' rooms are Rs 150/250, all with private bathroom, squat toilets and bucket hot water.

Hotel Vijan Palace *(☎ 310972, 313 Vijan Market)* is a good choice in the heart of the bazaar. Basic rooms with private bathroom are Rs 250/300 and air-con rooms are Rs 500/600. You may get a better price if you try bargaining.

Swayam Hotel *(☎ 325377, Guru Nanak Market)* is grubby but cheap, with decent-sized rooms at Rs 65/130. Bathrooms have squat toilets and bucket hot water.

Hotel Rahul *(☎ 325525)*, next door, is only slightly better with rooms at Rs 100/130, or Rs 150/200 with TV and bucket hot water.

Places to Stay – Mid-Range

Hotel Roopali *(☎ 625566, Station Rd)* is popular and the best of a bunch of places on Station Rd. A range of clean rooms start from Rs 300/350, or Rs 600/700 with air-con.

Jackson's Hotel *(☎ 322320, fax 322066, Civil Lines)* must have been the best hotel in town at one time; these days it's a bit shabby, with a large population of mosquitoes, but still popular with travellers. Large, well-worn rooms with private bathroom and hot-water shower are Rs 450/500, or Rs 950/1200 with air-con. You can change travellers cheques, and baggage can be left here safely while you visit Kanha National Park. Jackson's is only about a 10-minute walk from the train station.

Hotel Kalchuri *(☎ 321491, Civil Lines)* is a well-maintained MP Tourism operation close to the train station. Rooms with hot-water geyser and balcony are Rs 450/550; Rs 750/850 with air-con.

Hotel Rishi Regency *(☎/fax 321804, Civil Lines)* is a three-star place near State Bank of India. It's Rs 550/750, or Rs 895/1095 with air-con. The cheaper rooms have squat toilets.

Places to Eat

Most of the hotels have restaurants.

Rooftop Restaurant at Jackson's Hotel has a wide range of decent food, comfy seating and cold beer. ***Haveli Restaurant*** in

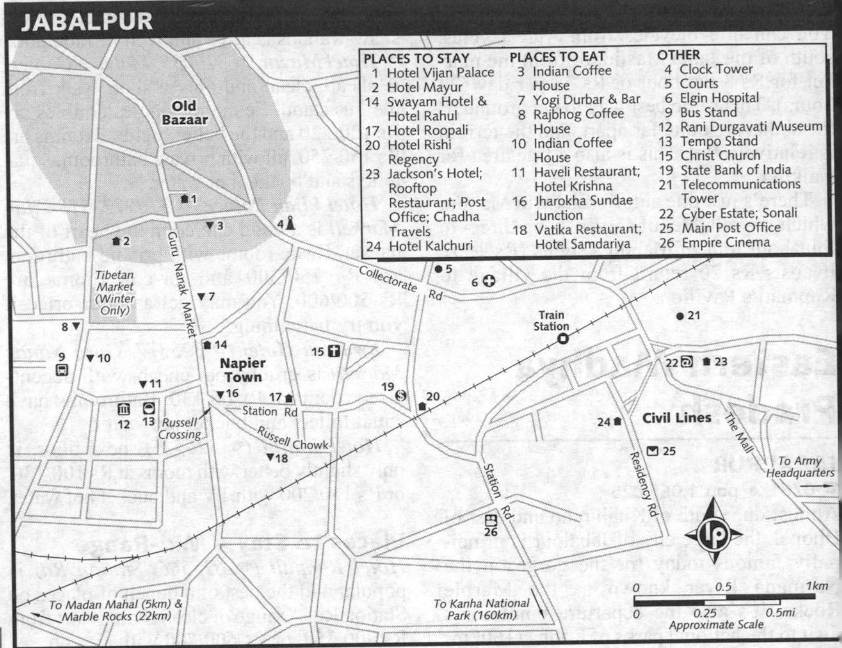

Hotel Krishna is another good place, though a little more expensive. ***Vatika Restaurant*** at the Samdariya has been recommended.

Rajbhog Coffee House, near the bus stand, is good for a snack. Masala dosa is Rs 14. The waiters have fan-shaped headgear and cummerbunds. The ***Indian Coffee House*** is similar and very good value.

Yogi Durbar & Bar is a popular place though it's a dimly lit cave inside. Good food is reasonably priced – where else can you get a full tandoori chicken for Rs 80? Most mains are Rs 25 to 35.

Jharokha Sundae Junction, next to Hotel Arihant Palace, is good for ice cream. Try ***Sonali***, next to Jackson's Hotel, for mouth-watering sweets.

Getting There & Away

Bus There are buses to Jabalpur from Allahabad, Khajuraho, Varanasi, Bhopal, Nagpur and other main centres. For overnight journeys the private buses are better – MP state transport buses are mostly in an advanced state of decay. The bus agencies are situated near the bus stand (across the road or nearby) and the private buses leave from outside these agencies. There's one bus a day to Khajuraho (Rs 125, 11 hours) leaving at 10 am but it's more comfortable to take the train to Satna from where there are regular bone-shattering buses to Khajuraho (Rs 55, four hours).

See Kanha National Park, later, for details on getting there from Jabalpur.

Train There are direct connections between Jabalpur and Satna (Rs 84/279 in sleeper/1st class, 189km, three hours), Varanasi (Rs 174/588, 505km, 13 hours) and Bhopal (Rs 126/426, 336km, 7½ hours).

For the Ajanta and Ellora caves, catch a train on the Mumbai line to Bhusaval (all the trains stop here) and another to Jalgaon. There are buses to the caves from there.

Getting Around

You'll be besieged by rickshaw-wallahs at the train station and bus stand offering cheap rides (to a hotel) – agree on a fare and a destination before getting in. If arriving by bus, most of the budget and mid-range hotels are within a 10-minute walk of the city bus stand.

Tempos trundle around town but the only time you're likely to use one is to get to Marble Rocks (Rs 8). The tempo stand is near the bus stand (opposite Hotel Krishna).

AROUND JABALPUR

Marble Rocks

Known locally as Bhedaghat (after the nearby village), this gorge on the Narmada River is 22km west of Jabalpur. The gleaming white (and sometimes pink, brown and black) cliffs rise sheer from the clear water and are a very impressive sight, especially by moonlight. On weekends and full moon nights the place is invariably packed with local tourists.

The trip up the 2km-long gorge is made in a shared rowboat – Rs 10 per person on a 20 seat boat, or it's possible to rent the whole boat for Rs 210. These go all day every day October to June from the jetty at the bottom of the gorge and leave when full. The first 500m is pretty dull, but as you glide upstream with the massive, naturally sculpted marble crags crowding in around you, it's difficult not to be impressed.

A worthwhile 1km walk from the jetty is the **Dhuandhar** or Smoke Cascade waterfall. Around the falls are hundreds of stalls selling marble carvings, mostly fairly standard, but you can find some decent pieces if you shop around. Along the way is the **Chausath Yogini** or Madanpur Temple. The circular temple has damaged ancient images of the 64 yoginis, or attendants of the goddess Kali.

Motel Marble Rocks (☎ *0761-83424*) is a very pleasant MP Tourism place overlooking the foot of the gorge. It has a well-kept garden and an excellent restaurant. The hotel is a comfortable ex-colonial bungalow with only four double rooms for Rs 450. Bookings can be made at the Jabalpur tourist office (☎ 322111). There are plenty of cheap ***cafes*** in the village.

Tempos run to Marble Rocks from the city tempo stand, which is near the museum in Jabalpur for Rs 8.

Narsinghpur

Narsinghpur, 84km west of Jabalpur, is just a sleepy town but worth a stop if you're interested in the Sleeman trail (see the boxed text 'Thugs'). There's a fascinating account of Sleeman's anti-thug detective work in Sir Francis Tuker's *The Yellow Scarf.*

Thugs

It was from Narsinghpur in the early 19th century that Colonel Sleeman waged his war against the bizarre Hindu Thuggee cult that claimed as many as one million lives over about 500 years. From as early as the 14th century, followers had roamed the main highways of India engaging in the ritual murder of travellers, strangling their victims with a yellow silk scarf in order to please the bloodthirsty goddess Kali.

Bizarre Thuggee rites included sugar sacrifices and axe-worshipping ceremonies and they resisted infiltration by using secret signs and developing their own jargon.

It was largely due to Sleeman's efforts that the Thuggee (from which the word 'thug' is derived) were wiped out. His campaign during the 1830s was sanctioned by the British governor-general Lord Bentinck and resulted in more than 400 thugs hanged and about 3000 imprisoned or banished, ensuring the virtual eradication of these scarf-wielding nasties.

Narsingh Mandir is an old temple with a honeycomb of tunnels beneath it. The caretaker may show you the room where Sleeman trapped some of the Thuggee leaders.

Lunawat Inn (☎ *07792-30034*) has singles/doubles with private bathroom and TV for Rs 250/450. It's about 100m from the train station (turn right at the exit).

Narsinghpur is on the main Jabalpur–Mumbai/Bhopal rail line and a handful of expresses stop here.

KANHA NATIONAL PARK

☎ 07649

Kanha, 160km south-east of Jabalpur, is one of India's largest national parks, covering 1945 sq km including a 'core zone' of 940 sq km. The setting for Kipling's *Jungle Book*, it's a beautiful area of sal forest and lightly wooded grassland with many rivers and streams. It is also part of Project Tiger.

Wildlife was first given limited protection here in 1933 but it wasn't until 1955 that the area was declared a national park. A policy of wildlife management over the past 30 years has seen a steady increase in the numbers of tigers and leopards, as well as sambar, chital (spotted deer), barasingha (swamp deer) and

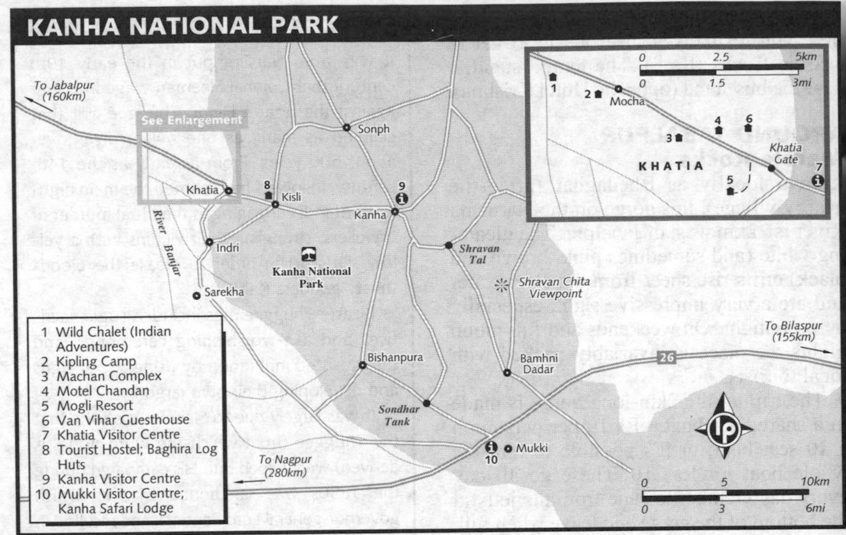

gaur (Indian bison). At the last census (1997) the tiger population was 114 and leopards numbered 86.

There's a good chance of sighting tigers, gaur and herbivores, and this is one of the best places in the state for bird-watching.

Orientation & Information

Kanha is completely closed from 1 July to 31 October, owing to the monsoons. Although it's possible to see wildlife throughout the season, sightings increase as the weather gets hotter in March and April and the animals move out of the tree cover in search of water. The hottest months are May and June, when the temperature can reach 42°C in the afternoon. December and January are the coolest months and, although it's warm during the day, as soon as the sun sets the temperature quickly plunges to zero and below.

Khatia village, at the western entrance to Kanha, is the best place to base yourself for visits to the park. Kisli, 3km further in, is the main gate where you pay the entry (Rs 200) and camera fees (Rs 25/200 for still/ video camera).

There are no facilities for changing money here, but there's a telephone, small shop and petrol pump at Kisli. You'll need fast film (400 ASA or higher) because of the low light during the early-morning and evening excursions.

The local market at **Sarekha** on Friday draws the colourful Baiga adivasis and is worth going to. A closer market is at **Mocha**, 5km back from Khatia, held on Wednesday

Visitor Centres There are three excellent visitor centres at Kanha (within the park), Khatia and Mukki with high-standard interpretive displays. The Kanha display is the most impressive, with five galleries and a research hall. There's a novel sound-and-light show 'Encounters in the Dark'.

A number of books and postcards are also sold. The centres are open from 8 am to noon and 3 to 7.30 pm daily (although these times change depending on the season), and a free outdoor film is shown each evening at the Khatia centre.

Wildlife Safaris

Excursions into the park are made in the early morning and evening; no night driving is allowed. Jeeps can be arranged by most of the accommodation places (which gives you a better chance of splitting the cost with others and the cost is calculated on a per kilometre basis. Expect to pay around Rs 500 (which can be shared by up to six people), plus Rs 90 for a compulsory guide. Park entry fees are extra but only need to be paid once a day. At the height of the season there may not be enough jeeps so book as soon as you arrive

Park gates open from sunrise to noon and 3 pm to sunset from 1 November to 15 February; sunrise to noon and 4 pm to sunset from 16 February to 15 April; and sunrise to 11 am and 5 pm to sunset from 16 April to 30 June.

You may need warm clothes for early-morning outings; choose your safari outfit carefully – a sign in the Khatia visitor centre warns: 'Avoid wearing colours that jar. Violators are liable to be prosecuted'!

Places to Stay & Eat

Accommodation is strung out over a distance of about 6.5km along the road from Jabalpur, so it's important that you get off the bus at the right place. Most accommodation is around Khatia, ranging from cheap guesthouses to the high-priced lodges operating on all-inclusive 'jungle plans'. Apart from the lodge restaurants, there are also a couple of basic *dhabas* (snack and chai shacks) serving veg food just outside Khatia Gate. Note that accommodation is considerably higher (40% to 50%) in the high season.

Khatia ***Van Vihar Guesthouse***, 400m from the road at Khatia Gate, is the best budget place. Basic doubles with private bathroom (squat toilets and bucket hot water) are Rs 100 per person. It's friendly and the resident family prepares good, cheap food.

Machan Complex is basic, charging Rs 30/150 for dorm beds/doubles with private bathroom. There are rather grotty squat toilets and bucket hot water. The menu at its restaurant has a handy Hindi language guide on the back.

Motel Chandan *(☎ 77220)* has better doubles with private bathroom for Rs 100 or Rs 250 and large deluxe rooms for Rs 300 that have hot-water geysers. There's a good restaurant here with Rs 30 thalis.

Mogli Resort *(☎ 77228)* is a modern place with little jungle character but clean and comfortable rooms. Excellent air cooled/air-con doubles with private bathroom are Rs 850/1400 and attractive cottages with fan and bathtub are Rs 850. There's also a smaller cottage for Rs 500. The jungle plan which includes all meals and safaris is the best deal of its type in town.

Wild Chalet *(☎ 77203)*, about 5km from Khatia, is by the river and very peaceful with friendly and knowledgeable staff. Double chalets with private bathroom are US$87 per person (single occupancy is 30% more) including meals and transport into the park (plus two wildlife drives per day). Staff also organise nature trails and bird-watching trips. Book with Indian Adventures (☎ 022-642 8244), 257 SV Rd, Bandra, Mumbai 400050, or direct with Wild Chalet and receive a 10% discount.

Kipling Camp *(☎/fax 77219)* has a certain toffy charm – it's staffed by enthusiastic Brits and run by Bob Wright, who can be contacted through the Tollygunge Club (☎ 033-473 4539, fax 473 1903), 120 DP Sasmal Rd, Calcutta 700033. Make advance bookings; it's not cheap at an all-inclusive Rs 4500 per day (less for three nights or more and there are discounts in the low season). It's also the home of Tara, the central character in Mark Shand's *Travels on My Elephant*.

Kisli There's nothing at Kisli apart from the forestry office and two MP Tourism hotels. ***Tourist Hostel*** has three eight-bed dorms at

On the Tiger Trail

Visitors to Kanha National Park might well be hoping for the triumph of a chance tiger spotting, but in reality it's all very well orchestrated.

The tigers are tracked each morning by rangers mounted on trained elephants. They listen for the distinctive warning calls of deer and monkeys that indicate a predator is in the vicinity, then try to pick up the trail of pug marks (footprints). Once a tiger is located, they radio back to the Kanha visitor centre where most of the jeeps and their passengers are waiting patiently. A flurry of activity then ensues as the jeep drivers race back to a base (eg, Kisli) to pick up a ticket that puts your vehicle in the 'queue' to view the tiger. The jeeps then park some distance from the tiger (which is hopefully still there) and you board an elephant (Rs 300 per person) for the final tramp through the undergrowth to view the tiger. On afternoon excursions sightings are left to chance, but the guides usually have a fair idea of where to look.

an overpriced Rs 250 per bed including all meals (vegetarian only) and hot showers.

Baghira Log Huts has reasonable air-cooled doubles for Rs 690, and a restaurant. Advance bookings can be made at the following MP Tourism offices, but full payment up front is required:

Bhopal (☎ 0755-778383) 4th floor, Gangotri, TT Nagar
Delhi (☎ 011-334 1187) 2nd floor, Kanishka Shopping Plaza, 19 Ashoka Rd
Kolkata (☎ 033-247 8543) 6th floor, Chitrakoot Bldg, 230A, AJC Bose Rd
Mumbai (☎ 022-218 7603) 74 World Trade Centre, Cuffe Parade, Colaba

Bookings less than five days in advance must be made through the tourist office (☎ 0761-322111) at the train station in Jabalpur.

Mukki ***Kanha Safari Lodge*** is another MP Tourism place in a pleasant but isolated location 36km from Khatia. It's worth trying if you're coming from Bilaspur or Kawardha but otherwise you're better off in Khatia. Doubles cost Rs 490, or Rs 690 with air-con and there's a restaurant. See the earlier Kisli section for booking information.

Getting There & Away

There are state transport buses from the city bus stand in Jabalpur to Khatia Gate three times daily at 8 am (six hours), 11 am (seven hours) and 2 pm (seven hours), which cost Rs 50. The same buses depart from Kisli at around 8 am and 12.30 pm. These buses are crowded and agonisingly slow. There are also some private buses from Jabalpur for around Rs 70.

BANDHAVGARH NATIONAL PARK

This national park is 197km north-east of Jabalpur in the Vindhyan mountain range. It's much smaller than Kanha but claims to have the highest density tiger population in India with between 46 and 52 tigers. There are also 27 leopards.

The park area is 448 sq km, of which 105 sq km is the 'core area'. Bandhavgarh's setting is impressive. It's named after the ancient fort built on 800m-high cliffs. There's a temple at the fort that can be visited by jeep and below it are numerous rock-cut cave shrines.

The core area of the park has a fragile ecology, but it supports a variety of wildlife such as nilgai, wild boar, jackals, gaur, sambar and porcupines as well as many species of birds. The ramparts of the fort provide a home for vultures, blue rock thrushes and crag martins. Bandhavgarh receives fewer visitors than Kanha and there's a good chance of spotting a tiger here.

Orientation & Information

The village of Tala is the access point for the park and the best place to stay. MP Tourism has an office at White Tiger Forest Lodge (see Places to Stay & Eat below) and there's a small visitor centre at the park gate. There's nowhere to change money in Tala.

Like Kanha, entry to the park is restricted to morning and evening visits in hired jeeps, or it's Rs 100 to bring in your own vehicle. The park is closed on Tuesday year-round. The park entry fee is Rs 200 (Rs 20 for Indians), Rs 25 for a camera or Rs 200 for a video camera. To hire a jeep (with up to six passengers) costs around Rs 550, including a guide. Bandhavgarh is closed from 1 July to 31 October. The telephone area code for Tala is ☎ 07653.

Bhaghela Museum

Attached to the Bandhavgarh Safari Camp in Tala, this museum is part of the private collection of the maharaja of Rewa. As well as the stuffed white tiger, Mohan, exhibits include the usual military and hunting paraphernalia, a carved ivory and silver chess set, and an extravagant swing bench made of Belgian cut glass and silver. It's open from 10 am to 3 pm and 5 to 8 pm daily (Rs 5).

Elephant Rides

Unlike at Kanha, elephants are still used for leisurely rides through the park. The cost is Rs 300 per person for one hour (maximum of four people) and can be arranged at the forestry office near the gate on Umaria Rd.

Places to Stay & Eat

Most of the accommodation is along Umaria Rd through Tala.

Tiger Lodge, situated where the bus stops, is the cheapest hotel around. Simple double rooms with grotty shared bathroom are Rs 150. The *dhaba* downstairs does good thalis for Rs 25 and basic breakfasts.

Kum Kum Home (☎ 65324) is a good budget option. There are four clean doubles with large private bathrooms (hot-water geyser) for Rs 200.

V Patel *(☎ 65323)* is a good choice if you want a bit more comfort at a reasonable price. Set well back from Umaria Rd, it offers pleasant singles/doubles for Rs 300/400 (room rate only), or US$65/120 including all meals, transport and park fees.

White Tiger Forest Lodge *(☎ 65308)* is a good MP Tourism place, with pleasant cottages overlooking the river where the elephants bathe. Singles/doubles with private bathroom cost Rs 590/690, or rooms set back from the river with air-con are Rs 790/890 (plus 10% tax). There's a good restaurant and a bar. Advance booking is advisable.

Bandhavgarh Jungle Lodge *(☎ 65317)* steps right up the price scale, operating a 'jungle plan' where all meals, park fees and safaris are included. It's hidden away near the park entrance where rustic thatched cottages of mud, dung and straw cost US$125 per night. Bookings are through Tiger Resorts (☎ 033-6853760, fax 6865212, ⓔ T-Resorts@indiantiger.com), suite 206, Rakeesh Deep, 11 Commercial Complex, Gulmohar Enclave, New Delhi.

Getting There & Away

Umaria, 32km away on the Katni to Bilaspur line, is the nearest railhead. Local buses run from there to Tala (Rs 14, one hour). Jeeps are also available from Tala to Umaria if demand is high enough.

From Satna there is an inconvenient bus service via Rewa: You're probably better off getting a taxi from there if there is a group of you; this should cost about Rs 1100.

Heading west, the only useful train service from Umaria is the *Bilaspur-Indore Express* through Katni, Jabalpur and Bhopal.

Chhatisgarh

BILASPUR

☎ 07752 • pop 282,230

Bilaspur is a bustling city in the north of the new state, Chhatisgarh. It has no 'attractions' to speak of, but you may find it convenient to stop here if heading from Kanha National Park to Puri in Orissa.

Natraj Hotel *(Link Rd)*, near the bus stand, is well located on the main street, and has singles/doubles from Rs 220/270.

Hotel Centrepoint *(☎ 24004, Anand Marg)* is a better-quality choice with rooms from Rs 300/400, to 600/650 for air-con.

The bus stand in the centre of town has regular departures for Kawardha, Nagpur, Raipur and Mukki (for Kanha National Park).

Bilaspur has rail connections with Jabalpur, Raipur, Bhopal, Sambalpur, Puri, Kolkata and Delhi. The train station is 3km from the town centre.

Mumbai (Bombay)

Mumbai is India's finance centre, the economic powerhouse of the nation, heart of the Hindi film industry and the industrial hub of everything from textiles to petrochemicals. But while it has aspirations to become another Singapore, it's also a magnet to the rural poor. It's these new migrants who continually re-shape the city in their own image, making sure Mumbai keeps one foot in its hinterland and the other in the global marketplace.

Mumbai is the glamour of Bollywood cinema, cricket on the *maidans* (open grassed areas), *bhelpuri* (a spicy sweet Mumbai snack) on the beach at Chowpatty, outstanding colonial architecture and red double-decker buses. It is also the infamous red-light district of Kamathipura, Asia's largest slums, communalist politics and powerful underworld dons. This tug-of-war for the city's soul is played out against a stately Victorian townscape more reminiscent of a prosperous 19th-century English industrial city than anything you'd expect to find on the edge of the Arabian Sea.

Most travellers miss out on the best of Mumbai, staying cocooned in the Colaba district and sticking around long enough only to organise transport to Goa. But this is an exciting, charismatic city that fully rewards exploration. It has vital streetlife, great nightlife, more bazaars than you could ever explore and the capacity to draw you in like no other Indian metropolis.

Mumbai at a Glance

Population: 16 million
Area: 440 sq km
Capital of: Maharashtra
Main Languages: Hindi, Marathi & Gujarati
Telephone Area Code: ☎ 022
When to Go: Oct to Feb

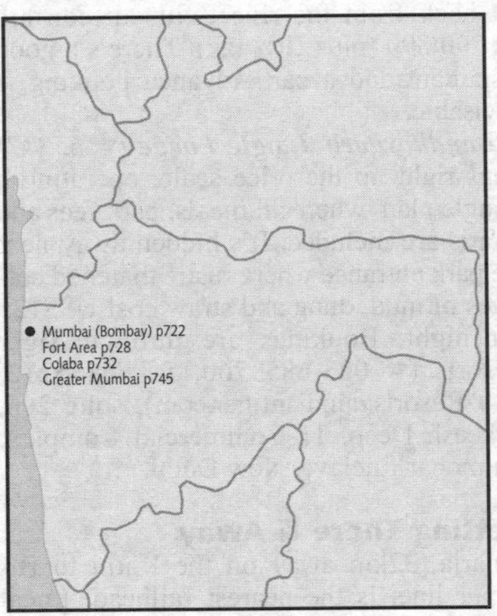

- Catch a ferry across the harbour to Elephanta Island and stand in awe before the triple-headed Shiva sculpture
- Lose yourself in the hectic bazaars of Bhuleshwar and Kalbadevi
- Experience India's nightlife at its best, from a beer with fellow travellers at Leopold's to mixing with Mumbai's glamorous young things at the Fashion Bar
- Stroll at sunset along Chowpatty Beach, before feasting on a sweet *bhelpuri* and getting a scalp massage in the sand

HISTORY

The islands that now form Mumbai were first home to the Koli fisherfolk as far back as the 2nd century BC; Koli shanties occupy parts of the city shoreline today. The islands were ruled by a succession of Hindu dynasties from the 6th century AD, invaded by Muslims in the 14th century and then ceded to Portugal by the sultan of Gujarat in 1534. The Portuguese did little to develop them before the major island of the group was included in Catherine of Braganza's dowry when she married England's Charles II in 1661. The British government took possession of the islands in 1665, but leased them three years later to the East India Company for the paltry annual rent of UK£10.

Then called Bombay, the area soon developed as a trading port and merchants were attracted from other parts of India by the British promise of religious freedom and land grants. Within 20 years the presidency of the East India Company was transferred to Bombay from Surat and it became the trading headquarters for the whole west coast of India.

Bombay's fort was built in the 1720s, and land reclamation projects began the process of joining the original seven islands into a single land mass. Although Bombay grew steadily during the 18th century, it remained isolated from its hinterland until the British defeated the Marathas and annexed substantial portions of western India in 1818. Growth was spurred by the arrival of steam ships and the construction of the first railway in Asia from Bombay to Thana in 1853. The first cotton mill was built in the city the following year, and the American Civil War – which temporarily dried up Britain's supply of cotton – sparked Bombay's cotton boom.

The fort walls were dismantled in 1864 and the city embarked on a major building spree as it sought to construct a townscape commensurate with its new-found wealth. Bombay played a formative role in the struggle for Independence, hosting the first Indian National Congress in 1885 and the launch of the 'Quit India' campaign in 1942. After Independence the city became capital of the Bombay Presidency, but this was divided on linguistic grounds into Maharashtra and Gujarat in 1960; Bombay then became the capital of Marathi-speaking Maharashtra.

The rise of a pro-Maratha regionalist movement, spearheaded by the Shiv Sena 'Shivaji's Army', broke the city's multicultural mould by actively discriminating against non-Maharashtrians and Muslims. The Shiv Sena won power in the city's municipal elections in 1985. Communalist tensions increased and the city's cosmopolitan self-image took a battering when nearly 800 people died in riots that followed the destruction of the Babri Masjid in Ayodhya in December 1992 and January 1993. They were followed by a dozen bombings on 12 March 1993, which killed more than 300 people and damaged the Bombay Stock Exchange and Air India Building.

In 2000, state elections saw the Congress Party win government from the BJP-Shiv Sena coalition, softening some – but not all – of the Sena's influence in Mumbai.

ORIENTATION

Mumbai is an island connected by bridges to the mainland. The principal part of the city is concentrated at the southern claw-shaped end of the island known as South Mumbai. The southernmost peninsula is known as Colaba and this is where most travellers gravitate since it has a decent range of hotels and restaurants and two of the city's best-known landmarks: the Gateway of India and the Taj Mahal Hotel.

Directly north of Colaba is the busy commercial area known as the Fort, where the old British fort once stood. On the northern

What's in a Name?

The city of Bombay officially became Mumbai in January 1996, a name change that had been part of the then democratically elected Shiv Sena's agenda for decades. They believe the new name reclaims the city's heritage and signifies its emergence from a colonial past. Others see the change as an assertion of Maratha identity (Mumbai is the Maratha name for the city) which is inappropriate in a city built and inhabited by people from all over India.

Supporters of 'Mumbai' believe the city's name is derived from the goddess Mumba, worshipped by the original Koli inhabitants at the Mumbadevi Temple, which stood on the present site of Victoria Terminus. When the Portuguese arrived they called the harbour Bombaim. This may have stemmed from 'buan bahia', meaning 'good bay' in Portuguese, or (much more likely) is a corruption of the original Koli name. When the islands were donated to the British, they anglicised Bombaim into Bombay.

The name changes are extending to street names and public buildings. Colonial street names such as Marine Drive and Colaba Causeway are still in popular usage, although they have officially been renamed with lengthy Marathi names (Netaji Subhashchandra Bose Rd and Shahid Bhagat Singh Rd respectively). In this chapter we stick to the names commonly used locally. Both the domestic (Santa Cruz) and international (Sahar) airports and Victoria Terminus (VT) have been renamed Chhatrapati Shivaji after the great Maratha leader, and there's a push to also name the Prince of Wales Museum after Shivaji.

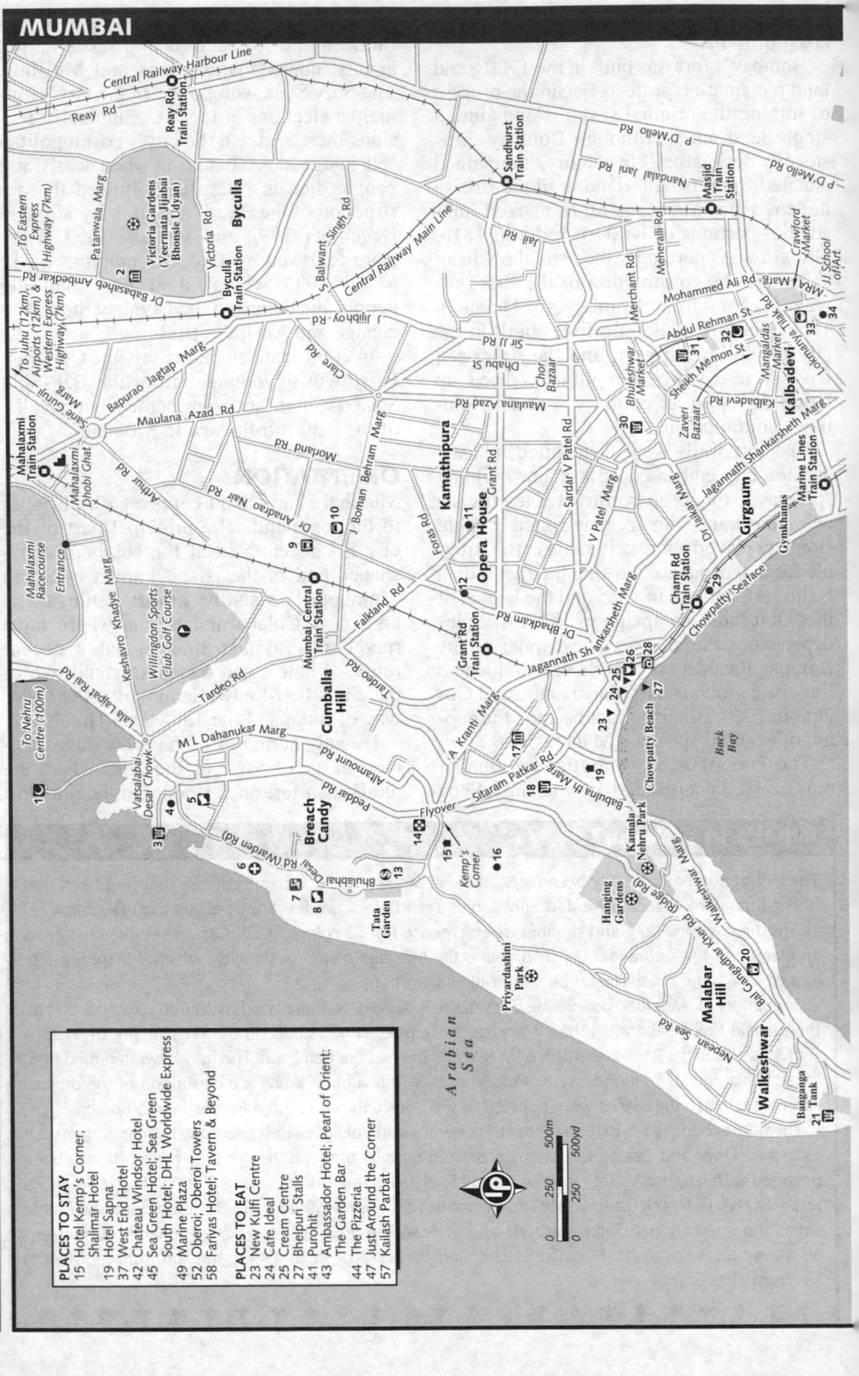

MUMBAI
PLACES TO STAY
15 Hotel Kemp's Corner; Shalimar Hotel
19 Hotel Sapna
37 West End Hotel
42 Chateau Windsor Hotel
45 Sea Green Hotel; Sea Green South Hotel; DHL Worldwide Express
49 Marine Plaza
52 Oberoi; Oberoi Towers
58 Fariyas Hotel; Tavern & Beyond
PLACES TO EAT
23 New Kulfi Centre
24 Cafe Ideal
25 Cream Centre
27 Bhelpuri Stalls
41 Purohit
43 Ambassador Hotel; Pearl of Orient: The Garden Bar
44 The Pizzeria
47 Just Around the Corner
57 Kailash Parbat
Arabian Sea
Back Bay
Chowpatty Beach
Malabar Hill
Walkeshwar
Breach Candy
Cumballa Hill
Kamathipura
Opera House
Girgaum
Kalbadevi
Byculla
Mahalaxmi Racecourse
Willingdon Sports Club Golf Course
Victoria Gardens (Veermata Jijabai Bhonsle Udyan)
Hanging Gardens
Kamala Nehru Park
Priyardashini Park
Tata Garden
Banganga Tank
Kemp's Corner
Mahalaxmi Train Station
Mahalaxmi Dhobi Ghat
Mumbai Central Train Station
Grant Rd Train Station
Charni Rd Train Station
Marine Lines Train Station
Byculla Train Station
Reay Rd Train Station
Sandhurst Train Station
Masjid Train Station
Central Railway Harbour Line
Central Railway Main Line
To Nehru Centre (100m)
To Juhu (12km), Airports (12km) & Western Express Highway (7km)
To Eastern Express Highway (7km)
Chor Bazaar
Bhuleshwar Market
Zaveri Bazaar
Mangaldas Market
Crawford Market
JJ School of Art
Gymkhanas
Chowpatty Seaface
Flyover
Vatsalabai Desai Chowk
Bhulabhai Desai Rd (Warden Rd)
Peddar Rd
Altamount Rd
M L Dahanukar Marg
Tardeo Rd
Lala Lajpat Rai Rd
Keshavro Khadye Marg
Falkland Rd
Dr Bhadkam Rd
Jagannath Shankarsheth Marg
Sardar V Patel Rd
V Patel Marg
Dr Jaikar Marg
Maulana Azad Rd
Mohammed Ali Rd
Abdul Rehman St
Sheikh Memon St
Kalbadevi Rd
Lokmanya Tilak Rd
Sitaram Patkar Rd
Babulnath Marg
Nepean Sea Rd
Bal Gangadhar Kher Rd (Ridge Rd)
Walkeshwar Marg
Arthur Rd
Sane Guruji Marg
Bapurao Jagtap Marg
Clare Rd
J Jijibhoy Rd
Dr Babasaheb Ambedkar Rd
Victoria Rd
Patanwala Marg
Reay Rd
P D'Mello Rd
Nandalal Jani Rd
Jail Rd
Meherali Rd
Merchant Rd
Sir JJ Rd
Dhabu St
Grant Rd
Foras Rd
Boman Behram Marg
Morland Rd
Dr Anadrao Nair Rd
S Balwant Singh Rd
A Kranti Marg
0 250 500m
0 250 500yd

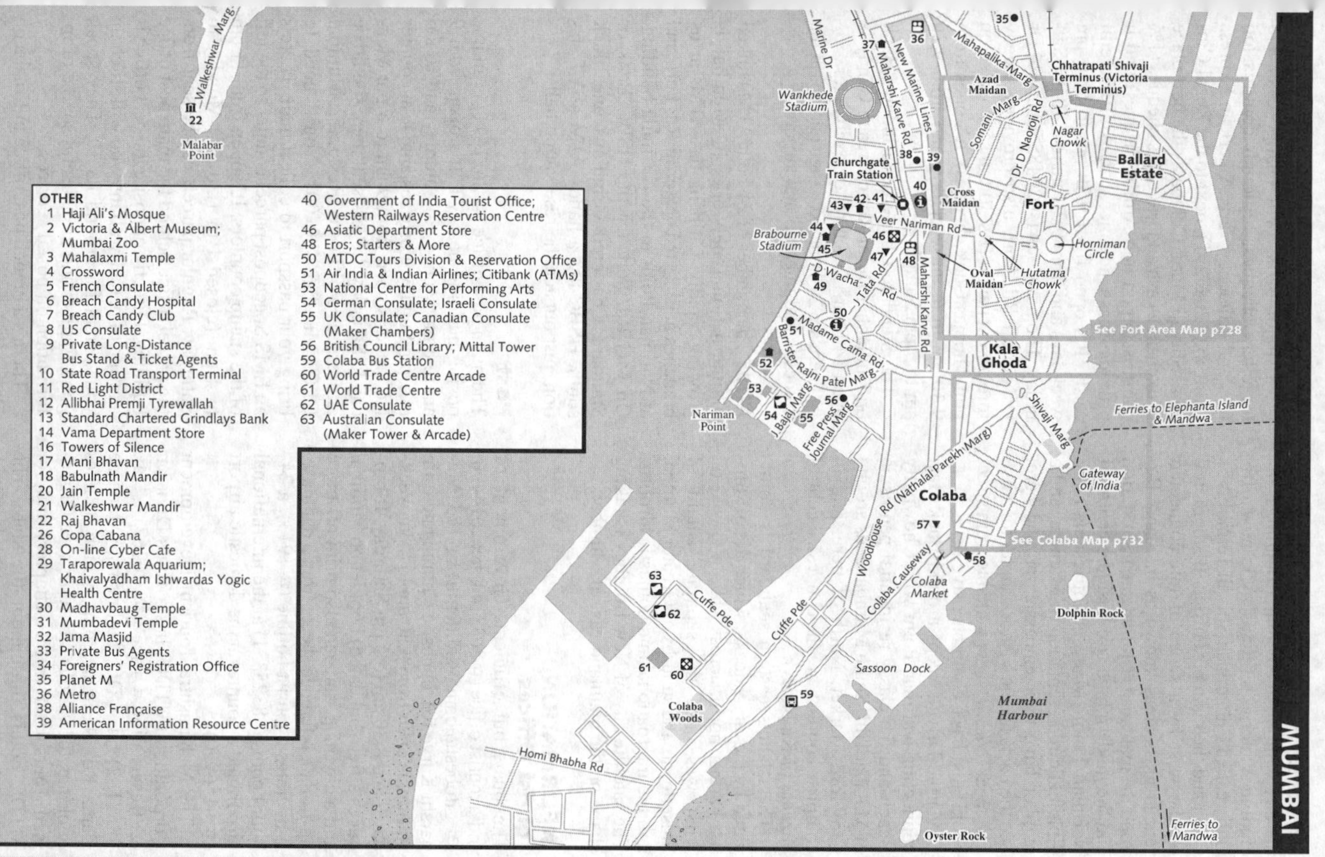
MUMBAI
OTHER
1 Haji Ali's Mosque
2 Victoria & Albert Museum; Mumbai Zoo
3 Mahalaxmi Temple
4 Crossword
5 French Consulate
6 Breach Candy Hospital
7 Breach Candy Club
8 US Consulate
9 Private Long-Distance Bus Stand & Ticket Agents
10 State Road Transport Terminal
11 Red Light District
12 Allibhai Premji Tyrewallah
13 Standard Chartered Grindlays Bank
14 Vama Department Store
16 Towers of Silence
17 Mani Bhavan
18 Babulnath Mandir
20 Jain Temple
21 Walkeshwar Mandir
22 Raj Bhavan
26 Copa Cabana
28 On-line Cyber Cafe
29 Taraporewala Aquarium; Khaivalyadham Ishwardas Yogic Health Centre
30 Madhavbaug Temple
31 Mumbadevi Temple
32 Jama Masjid
33 Private Bus Agents
34 Foreigners' Registration Office
35 Planet M
36 Metro
38 Alliance Française
39 American Information Resource Centre
40 Government of India Tourist Office; Western Railways Reservation Centre
46 Asiatic Department Store
48 Eros; Starters & More
50 MTDC Tours Division & Reservation Office
51 Air India & Indian Airlines; Citibank (ATMs)
53 National Centre for Performing Arts
54 German Consulate; Israeli Consulate
55 UK Consulate; Canadian Consulate (Maker Chambers)
56 British Council Library; Mittal Tower
59 Colaba Bus Station
60 World Trade Centre Arcade
61 World Trade Centre
62 UAE Consulate
63 Australian Consulate (Maker Tower & Arcade)
Walkeshwar Marg
Malabar Point
Marine Dr
Wankhede Stadium
Maharshi Karve Rd
New Marine Lines
Mahapalika Marg
Azad Maidan
Chhatrapati Shivaji Terminus (Victoria Terminus)
Somani Marg
Dr D Naoroji Rd
Nagar Chowk
Ballard Estate
Churchgate Train Station
Cross Maidan
Fort
Veer Nariman Rd
Brabourne Stadium
Horniman Circle
Oval Maidan
Hutatma Chowk
D Wacha Rd
J Tata Rd
Madame Cama Rd
Barrister Rajni Patel Marg
See Fort Area Map p728
Kala Ghoda
Nariman Point
J Bajaj Marg
Free Press Journal Marg
Shivaji Marg
Ferries to Elephanta Island & Mandwa
Woodhouse Rd (Nathalal Parekh Marg)
Gateway of India
Colaba
See Colaba Map p732
Colaba Causeway
Colaba Market
Cuffe Pde
Dolphin Rock
Sassoon Dock
Colaba Woods
Mumbai Harbour
Homi Bhabha Rd
Oyster Rock
Ferries to Mandwa

and western fringes of this area are most of the city's impressive colonial buildings, including Victoria Terminus (VT; now officially called Chhatrapati Shivaji Terminus or CST) and the main post office. It's bordered on the west by a series of interconnected fenced grass areas known as maidans. Beyond the maidans is Churchgate train station and the modern high-rise business centre of Nariman Point. Many countries maintain diplomatic representation in Mumbai, and a number have their embassies around here. See the Facts for the Visitor chapter for a list. The local *Yellow Pages* (available from street bookstalls) has a comprehensive list.

Marine Drive sweeps around Back Bay, connecting Nariman Point with Chowpatty Beach and the classy residential peninsula of Malabar Hill. South Mumbai ends around Crawford Market. North of here, and in complete contrast, are the congested central bazaars of Kalbadevi.

The island's eastern seaboard is dominated by the city's docks, which are off limits. Farther north, across Mahim Creek, on what was once the separate island of Salsette, are the suburbs of Greater Mumbai and the international and domestic airports. The satellite city of New Bombay is taking shape on the mainland east of Mumbai.

INFORMATION

Tourist Offices

The busy, but efficient, Government of India tourist office (☎ 2033144, fax 2014496, ⓔ gitobest@bom5vsnl.net.in) at 123 Maharshi Karve Rd, opposite Churchgate train station, is open from 8.30 am to 6 pm weekdays, and 8.30 am to 2 pm Saturday. It produces a free (but dated) booklet on Mumbai and a city map, and can also print off more up-to-date reference sheets from a database. It operates a tourist hotline (☎ 1913), a 24-hour booth (☎ 8325331) at the international airport and a counter at the domestic airport (☎ 6156920).

The Maharashtra Tourism Development Corporation (MTDC) has a Tours Division & Reservation Office (☎ 2026713, fax 2852182) at CDO Hutments, Madame Cama Rd, Nariman Point, which handles bookings for various city tours (see Organised Tours later in this chapter) and for MTDC hotels throughout the state. The cashier here accepts Visa and MasterCard.

Money

Most major banks will change cash and travellers cheques, although commission fees and efficiency vary. American Express (AmEx; ☎ 2048291), next to the Regal Cinema, Shivaji Marg, Colaba, is the best place to exchange cash and travellers cheques (1% commission on non-AmEx cheques) and it provides cash advances on AmEx credit cards. It's open from 9.30 am to 6.30 pm weekdays and from 9.30 am to 2.30 pm Saturday. Thomas Cook (☎ 2048556) at 324 Dr D Naoroji Rd, Fort, also provides speedy foreign exchange (Rs 30 transaction fee on non-Thomas Cook cheques). It's open from 9.30 am to 6 pm weekdays and from 9.30 am to 5 pm Saturday.

The Standard Chartered Grindlays Bank on Bhulabhai Desai Rd in Breach Candy is open 24 hours for currency exchange.

There are 24-hour exchange bureaus at the domestic and international airports.

ATMs The number of 24-hour ATMs linked to international networks in Mumbai is growing rapidly. Citibank has ATMs at its branches at 293 Dr D Naoroji Rd, Fort, and at Nariman Point in the Air India building. On MG Rd, Fort, try the HSBC Bank or Standard Chartered Grindlays one block south. HSBC has a handy ATM at VT station, just outside the reservation hall.

Post

The main post office (☎ 2621671) is an imposing building near VT. It's open from 9 am to 8 pm Monday to Saturday and 10 am to 5 pm Sunday. Poste restante is at counter No 4 and is open from 9 am to 6 pm Monday to Saturday. Letters sent there should be addressed c/o Poste Restante, Mumbai GPO, Mumbai 400 001. You'll need to bring your passport to collect mail. There's an EMS Speedpost parcel counter to the left of the stamp counters. It's open from 11 am to 4 pm (closed 1 to 1.30 pm) Monday to Saturday. Regular parcels can be sent from the parcel office behind the main post office building. Directly opposite the post office is a group of parcel-wallahs who will stitch up your parcel for around Rs 30. They speak good English and are a useful source of information on postal services.

There's a branch post office in Colaba on Henry Rd.

To send air freight parcels out of India, try DHL Worldwide Express (☎ 2837187) in the Sea Green South Hotel, 145A Marine Drive.

Telephone & Fax

Private phone/fax centres (labelled 'STD/ISD' or 'PCO') in Colaba and the Fort are convenient for STD and international calls. The international telecommunications centre run by Videsh Sanchar Nigam Limited (VSNL; ☎ 2624020, fax 2624027) is on Bhaurao Patil Marg in the fort area. It's most useful for home country direct, collect call and call-back services, but also has much cheaper ISD call rates than elsewhere (Rs 48 per minute to the USA; Rs 40 to the UK). Faxes can be sent for Rs 110 per page and there's a small Internet centre. It's open 8 am to 8 pm daily.

Email & Internet Access

There are many Internet cafes in South Mumbai, particularly around the Fort, Colaba and Marine Drive areas. They charge between Rs 40 and Rs 100 an hour, although rates will drop as competition hots up.

Just south of VT there are three convenient Internet cafes in the same building (Mahender Chambers). They're all a bit cramped, but they are air-conditioned and cheap for Mumbai. Netsurf is open from 8 am to 1 am daily and charges Rs 45 an hour. Kishco Cyber Plaza charges Rs 40 an hour and is open from 10 am to 10 pm. Cyber.com, on the 2nd floor, is probably the most pleasant place; it charges Rs 48 an hour and is open from 9 am to midnight.

In Colaba, the best place is the modern, spacious Satyam i-way, above Kamat Restaurant (the entrance is around the side on JA Allana Marg). The charge is Rs 48 an hour. There are several smaller places, including Access Infotech, down a laneway just off the causeway near Cafe Churchill's. On Marine Drive, On-line Cyber Cafe (Rs 50 an hour) is opposite Chowpatty Beach.

Visa Extensions

The Foreigners' Registration Office (☎ 2620446) is in Annexe Building No 2, CID, 3rd floor, Say-ed Badruddin Rd, near the Police Commissioner's Office. Walk north along Dr D Naoroji Rd and turn left into the laneway near the footbridge to VT. This office does not officially issue extensions on six-month tourist visas – even in emergencies they will direct you to Delhi. However, while we were there a traveller had managed to procure an emergency extension after a lot of waiting and considerable financial outlay (US$40).

Travel Agencies

Transway International (☎ 2626066, ⓔ transintl@ vsnl.com), in a tiny office on the 3rd floor of Pantaky House, 8 Maruti Cross Lane, off Maruti St, Fort, is a good place for travel information and advice. It can be a challenge to find because there are no obvious signs on the building, but the service is worth the hunt. Transway can provide advice on bus and rail travel, but does not issue tickets for either.

Thomas Cook and AmEx (see Money for details) are also reliable options. Magnum International Travel & Tours (☎ 2840016) at 10 Henry Rd is handy for those staying in Colaba.

Photography

Modern digital processing, print and slide film, video cartridges and camera accessories are available from Colour Vision (☎ 2612468), Image House, W Hirachand Marg, Fort, next to Hotel City Palace. You can get slide and black-and-white film processed on site here.

Bookshops

The best bookshop in the city is Crossword (☎ 4920253) on the 1st floor at 22 Bhulabhai Desai Rd, Breach Candy. The Strand Book Stall (☎ 2661994), just off Sir P Mehta Rd, Fort, also has a reasonable collection (closed Sunday).

Shankar Book Stall, outside Cafe Mondegar on Colaba Causeway, has an assortment of paperbacks, maps and guidebooks. A motley selection of bookstalls line the footpath on Veer Nariman Rd, between Flora Fountain and the maidans.

Newspapers & Magazines

The *Times of India* and the *Indian Express* both have Mumbai editions; the main local English-language paper is *Mid-Day*. India's only gay magazine is called *Bombay Dost*, which can be bought from street vendors on Veer Nariman Rd. *Mumbai: This Fortnight* is a free bimonthly listings magazine with a range of entertainment and shopping information. Many guesthouses have it, or you can get it from the tourist office.

Libraries & Cultural Centres

You have to be a member to take advantage of the facilities at the British Council Library (☎ 2823560) at Mittal Tower A Wing, 1st floor, Barrister Rajni Patel Marg, Nariman Point. A minimum monthly membership is Rs 250, annual membership is Rs 600. The library has an extensive collection of books, British newspapers and Internet access. It's open Tuesday to Saturday from 10 am to 6 pm.

The incredibly security-conscious American Information Resource Centre (AIRC; ☎ 2624590) on the 3rd floor, 4 New Marine Lines, Churchgate, has a good library, Internet access and 10-day old American newspapers. The library is open from 10 am to 6 pm (closed Wednesday and Sunday). It costs Rs 10 for a casual visit or Rs 200 for annual membership.

You can read French papers and browse the library for free at Alliance Française (☎ 2036187), at 40 New Marine Lines, from 9.30 am to 5.30 pm on weekdays and until 1 pm on Saturday. There's also Internet access and a regular cultural program here. Annual membership costs Rs 650. German speakers can use the library at Max Mueller Bhavan (☎ 2027542) on K Dubash Marg, Fort between 11 am and 6 pm Tuesday to Saturday.

Medical Services & Emergency

An Ambulance can be called on ☎ 102, and the Police can be contacted on ☎ 100. Medical service numbers in Mumbai include:

Apollo Pharmacy (☎ 2829707) 18 K Dubash Marg, Fort. A 24-hour chemist
Breach Candy Hospital (☎ 3685406) 60 Bhulabhai Desai Rd, Breach Candy

COLABA

This vibrant, fashionable suburb occupying the city's southernmost peninsula is Mumbai's travellers' centre. **Colaba Causeway** (Shahid Bhagat Singh Marg) is the busy commercial thoroughfare that runs the length of much of the promontory.

The causeway passes close to **Sassoon Dock**, a scene of intense and pungent activity at dawn when colourfully clad Koli fisherwomen sort the catch unloaded from fishing boats at the quay. The fish drying in the sun are *bombil*, which are deep fried to make Bombay Duck. Photography at the dock is forbidden without permission from the Mumbai Port Trust (☎ 2614321, fax 2611011). Most travellers tend to hang around at the northern end of Colaba, but the real local activity is farther south on the backstreets of **Colaba Market**.

Gateway of India

The Gateway of India is an exaggerated colonial marker conceived of after the visit of King George V in 1911. The yellow basalt arch of triumph, derived from the Muslim styles of 16th-century Gujarat, faces out to Mumbai Harbour at the tip of Apollo Bunder in Colaba. Officially opened in 1924, it was redundant just 24 years later when the last British regiment ceremoniously departed India through its archway.

The gateway has become a popular emblem of the city and is a favourite gathering spot for locals in the evening and on weekends. Boats depart from the gateway's wharfs for Elephanta Island, and touts, balloon sellers, photographers and snake charmers give the area the hubbub of a bazaar. Nearby are statues of the religious reformer Swami Vivekananda, and of the Maratha leader Shivaji astride his horse.

Taj Mahal Hotel

This majestic hotel, a Mumbai institution, overlooks Apollo Bunder and has good views of the gateway from its top-floor bar. It was built in 1903 by the Parsi industrialist JN Tata, supposedly after he was refused entry to one of the European hotels on account of being 'a native'. It's a beautiful hotel and it's worth seeing the grand central stairway in the hotel's old wing. Nearby is the august **Royal Bombay Yacht Club**, where the clock seems to have stopped in the late 19th century.

KALA GHODA

Kala Ghoda is the name given to the area wedged between Colaba and the Fort that contains Mumbai's main galleries and museums, along with a wealth of colonial buildings, some of them in a poor state of repair. The Institute of Science, Elphinstone College and David Sassoon Library are among the impressive buildings lining the southern end of MG Rd.

The **Kala Ghoda Fair**, an exhibition of regional arts and crafts, is held along K Dubash Marg every Sunday between November and January. The area is named after a statue of King Edward IV astride a black horse *(Kala Ghoda)* that once stood here, but is now in Victoria Gardens.

National Gallery of Modern Art

The National Gallery of Modern Art (☎ 2852457) in the Sir Cowasji Jehangir Public Hall on MG Rd is a bright, modern exhibition space showcasing a range of changing exhibitions. There's a small permanent collection of contemporary Indian art in the top floor Dome Gallery. The gallery is open from 11 am to 6 pm daily, except Monday (Rs 5). There are free guided tours at noon and 4 pm.

Prince of Wales Museum

The Prince of Wales Museum (☎ 2844519) was built to commemorate King George V's first visit to India in 1905 (while he was still Prince of Wales), though it did not open until 1923. Designed by George Wittet in grand Indo-Saracenic style, it is set in an ornamental garden and boasts a galleried central hall topped by a huge dome, said to have been inspired by the Golgumbaz in Bijapur (Karnataka).

Its collection includes impressive sculptures from Elephanta Island, Gujarat and Karnataka; terracotta figurines from the Indus Valley; Gandharan Buddhas; miniature paintings; porcelain and weaponry. There's an interesting natural history section and a collection of second-rate European paintings.

The museum is open from 10.15 am to 6 pm daily except Monday. Entry is Rs 150 for foreigners and Rs 10 for Indians. Foreign students can get in for Rs 6 with a valid International Student Identity Card (ISIC). A camera/video permit is Rs 30/200. Bags must be left at the entrance gate cloakroom. If the Shiv Sena gets its way, the museum will be renamed Chhatrapati Shivaji Museum.

Jehangir Art Gallery

The Jehangir Art Gallery (☎ 2048212) at 161B MG Rd used to be the city's principal exhibition space and still hosts interesting weekly shows by Indian artists. Most of the works on display are for sale. It's open from 11 am to 7 pm daily (entry is free). In the same building is the **Gallery Chermould**, the mediocre **Terrace Art Gallery** and a pleasant cafe (closed Sunday).

FORT AREA

Flora Fountain

This cherished, but undistinguished, fountain stands at the established business centre of Mumbai. Though named after the Roman goddess of abundance, it was erected in 1869 in honour of Sir Bartle Frere, the governor of Bombay who was responsible for dismantling the fort and shaping much of modern Mumbai.

The goddess now shares her diminished area with a monument honouring those who died fighting to carve the state of Maharashtra out of the Bombay Presidency – hence the area's new name, Hutatma Chowk or Martyr's Square.

Horniman Circle

This stately, arcaded circle of buildings, laid out in the 1860s around the sole surviving section of Bombay's original Cotton Green, was the result of a British attempt to stamp some discipline on the disorder of the fort.

The circle is overlooked from the east by the neoclassical **town hall**, which contains the august members-only Asiatic Society of Bombay Library and Mumbai's State Central Library. Behind the town hall, in the inaccessible dockland, are the **Mint** and the remains of the original **Bombay Castle**.

The pretty **St Thomas' Cathedral** nearby is the oldest English building standing in Mumbai. Construction began in 1672, but remained unfinished until 1718. Its airy, whitewashed interior is full of poignant colonial memorials, including one to Henry Robertson Bower, lieutenant of the Royal Indian Marine, 'who lost his life returning from the South Pole with Scott'.

Victoria Terminus

The city's most exuberant Gothic building looks more like a lavishly decorated palace or cathedral than anything as mundane as a transport depot – don't wait until you have to catch a train to see it. It was designed by Frederick Stevens as the headquarters of the Great Indian Peninsular Railway Company

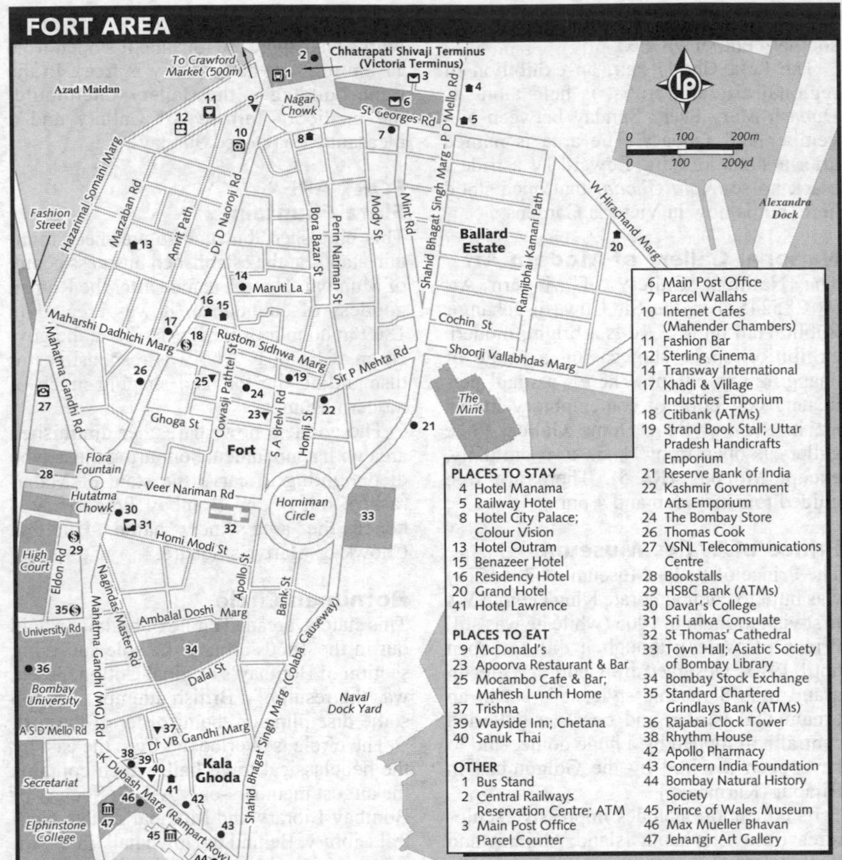

and was completed in 1887, 34 years after the first train in India left this site on its way to nearby Thana. Carvings of peacocks, gargoyles, monkeys and lions are mixed up among the buttresses, domes, turrets, spires and stained-glass windows. Topping it all is a 4m-high statue of 'Progress' – though the rest of the building looks more like a celebration of pandemonium. In 1998 the station was officially renamed Chhatrapati Shivaji Terminus (CST), but it's still better known locally as VT.

Bombay University & High Court

Many of Mumbai's impressive Victorian buildings were constructed on the edge of Oval Maidan during the building boom of the 1860s and '70s. The maidans were on the seafront in those days, and a series of grandiose structures, including the Secretariat, Bombay University, the High Court and the Western Railway Building, faced directly onto the Arabian Sea.

The most impressive of these buildings is Bombay University, designed by Gilbert Scott of St Pancras Station (London) fame. It looks like a 15th-century Italian masterpiece dropped into the middle of an Indian metropolis. It consists of the exquisite **University Library**, **Convocation Hall** and the 80m-high **Rajabai Tower**, whose clock used to play 'God Save the Queen' and 'Home Sweet Home' to mark the hour.

The neighbouring High Court was obviously designed to dispel any doubts about the weightiness and authority of the justice dispensed inside. Local stone carvers, who often worked independently, presumably saw things differently: They carved a one-eyed monkey holding the scales of justice on one of its pillars.

OTHER ATTRACTIONS

Marine Drive

Built on land reclaimed from Back Bay in 1920, Marine Drive (Netaji Subhashchandra Bose Rd) runs along the shore of the Arabian Sea from Nariman Point past Chowpatty Beach to the foot of Malabar Hill. It's a grand sweeping affair that's poorly landscaped and lined with flaking Art Deco apartments. This is one of Mumbai's most popular promenades and sunset-watching spots. During Diwali the machine-gun rattle of firecrackers and pungent gunpowder smoke fills the air along here.

Tourist brochures are fond of dubbing Marine Drive the Queen's Necklace, because of the dramatic curve of its streetlights at night – best seen from Kamala Nehru Park on Malabar Hill or around the other side of the bay on the upper floors of the Ambassador Hotel or the Oberoi Towers.

The uninspiring **Taraporewala Aquarium** is on Marine Drive, near Chowpatty Beach. It's open from 10 am to 7 pm daily, except Monday (to 8 pm on Sunday) and entry is Rs 4. There are plans for a major overhaul of the aquarium, which might lift it from complete mediocrity.

Chowpatty Beach

Although a lot of the 'unsavoury elements' that once gave this little stretch of sand its character have been moved on, Chowpatty is still a favourite evening spot for courting couples, families, political rallies and anyone out to enjoy the fresh air. Eating bhelpuri at the collection of stalls on the edge of the beach at night is an essential part of the Mumbai experience (see Places to Eat), as is getting a vigorous head rub from a *malish-wallah* (head masseur). Forget about visiting during the day for a sunbathe or a dip.

The highlight of the year at Chowpatty is during **Ganesh Chaturthi** (August/September) when huge crowds gather to watch images of the elephant-headed god of good fortune, Ganesh, paraded through the city streets and immersed in the sea.

A malish-wallah applies a soothing head massage. Well...it's soothing when he stops.

Malabar Hill

On the northern promontory of Back Bay is the expensive residential area of Malabar Hill, favoured for its cool breezes and fine views. The colonial bungalows that peppered the hillside in the 18th century have now been replaced by the apartment blocks of Mumbai's nouveau riche.

On the main road climbing Malabar Hill is a gaudy **Jain temple**, built in 1904, dedicated to the first Jain *tirthankar* (teacher), Adinath.

The formal **Hanging Gardens** (Pherozeshah Mehta Gardens) on top of the hill are a reasonable place for a stroll, while the smaller **Kamala Nehru Park** opposite has views of Chowpatty Beach, Marine Drive and the city. Signs in both parks warn that exercise and eating are not allowed (spoil sports).

Beyond the Hanging Gardens, but carefully shielded from view, are the Parsi Towers of Silence. Parsis hold fire, earth and water sacred so do not cremate or bury their dead. Instead the corpses are laid out within the towers to be picked clean by vultures. Elaborate precautions are taken to keep sightseers out, so don't come here expecting to see anything. In any case, a shortage of vultures around Mumbai has meant that the Parsis have sometimes had to resort to chemical methods to dissolve their dead.

Towards the southern end of the promontory is the sacred precinct of **Banganga Tank**. Bathing pilgrims, picturesque old *dharamsalas* (pilgrims' resthouses), a dozen temples

Mumbai's Magical Markets

Crawford Market

This colourful market (officially called Mahatma Phule Market) is the last outpost of British Bombay before the tumult of the central bazaars begins. Bas-reliefs by Rudyard Kipling's father, Lockwood Kipling, adorn the Norman-Gothic exterior, and a gaudy fountain he designed stands buried beneath old fruit boxes in the market's central courtyard. The animal market at the rear sells everything from sausage dogs to cockatoos, most kept in cruelly small cages. The meat market is for the brave only, being one of the few places you can expect to be accosted and asked to buy a bloody goat's head. The fish market is just across MRA Marg. South of the market, on the opposite side of Dr D Naoroji Rd, is the JJ School of Art, an important institution in the development of Indian art. Rudyard Kipling was born here in 1865; his birthplace is now the dean's residence.

Bazaars of Kalbadevi & Bhuleshwar

No visit to Mumbai is complete without a foray into the bazaars of Kalbadevi & Bhuleshwar to the north of Crawford Market. The narrow lanes of this area are in complete contrast to the relative orderliness of South Mumbai, and a seething mass of people bring Mumbai's traffic to a standstill. Highlights include Mangaldas Market, Zaveri Bazaar, Bhuleshwar Market and Chor Bazaar (see Shopping later in this chapter). You'll also find the Jama Masjid and the interesting Mumbadevi Temple, dedicated to the patron goddess of the island's original Koli inhabitants. It's best to venture into this area without a clear destination in mind and wander aimlessly; when you've had enough and need to get your bearings, head east until you hit the main thoroughfare of Mohammed Ali Rd. Catch bus No 1, 3 or 21 from Colaba or Flora Fountain.

and scores of curious kids make this neighbourhood an oasis from the intrusive apartment blocks towering above. The **Banganga Festival**, a music festival organised by the MTDC, is held here in January.

The most important temple in the area is the **Walkeshwar Mandir** (Sand Lord Temple), on the tank's western flank. Rama is said to have constructed a lingam of sand at the site while on his way to Lanka to rescue Sita in the Hindu epic Ramayana. The original temple was possibly built 1000 years ago; the current unimpressive structure dates only to the 1950s.

At the end of the promontory is the inaccessible **Raj Bhavan**, once the British governor's house and now home to the governor of Maharashtra.

Mani Bhavan

The building where Mahatma Gandhi stayed during his visits to Bombay from 1917 to 1934 is now a small, but engrossing, museum. Gandhi's simple room remains untouched and there's an excellent photographic record of his life, along with original documents such as letters he wrote to Hitler and President Roosevelt. Mani Bhavan (☎ 3805864) is at 19 Laburnum Rd, near August Kranti Maidan where the campaign to persuade the British to 'Quit India' was launched in 1942. It's open from 10 am to 5.30 pm daily (free).

Haji Ali's Mosque

At the end of a long causeway poking into the Arabian Sea is a whitewashed mosque containing the tomb of the Muslim saint Haji Ali. The saint is believed to have been a wealthy local businessman who renounced the material world and meditated on a nearby headland after a pilgrimage to Mecca. The mosque and tomb were built by devotees in the early 19th century. Alternative versions say Haji Ali died while on a pilgrimage to Mecca and his casket miraculously floated back to Mumbai and landed at this spot.

The mosque becomes an island at high tide, but is accessible at other times via the concrete causeway lined with beggars and change (coin) vendors.

Mahalaxmi Temple

This popular Hindu temple, dedicated to the goddess of wealth, is perched on a headland not far from Haji Ali's mosque. It's the focus for Mumbai's Navrati (Dussehra) celebrations in September/October.

Victoria Gardens

These gardens, officially renamed 'Veermata Jijabai Bhonsle Udyan' contain the **Victoria & Albert Museum** (Dr Bhau Daji Lad Museum) and the city zoo. The museum (☎ 3757943) is a fine old building housing a hotch-potch of fairly unexciting educational-style exhibits, many of them models depicting community life, temples and architecture. The best displays are old maps of Bombay, a model of a Parsi Tower of Silence and a brass statue of Ganesh. The museum is open from 10.30 am to 4.30 pm daily, except Wednesday (Rs 2). A camera permit costs Rs 30 and it's a ridiculous Rs 1500 to use a video camera.

The city **zoo** (☎ 3725799) is set in well-maintained gardens; the state of the animal enclosures varies, but most aren't too bad for an Indian zoo. There has been some local pressure, however, to close the zoo down and shift it to a more spacious location outside the city centre. The zoo is open from 9 am to 6 pm daily except Wednesday (Rs 4). It costs Rs 5/20 for a camera/video.

The gardens, which have officially been renamed Veermata Jijabai Bhonsle Udyan, are in Byculla, north of the city centre. Catch bus No 1, 4, 6, 7 or 8 from Colaba or Flora Fountain, or take a train to Byculla train station from VT.

Mahalaxmi Dhobi Ghat

At Mumbai's municipal laundry or *dhobi ghat* at Mahalaxmi, some 5000 men use rows of open-air troughs to beat the dirt out of the thousands of kilograms of soiled clothes brought from all over the city each day. The best view is from the bridge across the railway tracks near Mahalaxmi train station, which can be reached from Churchgate station. The ghats make a good photo opportunity, but the presence of persistent beggars makes it uncomfortable to hang around. See the boxed text 'India's Washing Wizards' in the Facts for the Visitor chapter.

Juhu Beach

A decade ago the luxury hotels fronting Juhu Beach were the height of glamour for Mumbai's wealthy film crowd. The allure has become a little jaded these days, but Juhu's reputation is still strong enough to make it a must-do for all Indian tourists visiting Mumbai.

It's a pleasant enough beach if you're not expecting a sunbathe or a swim, and on weekend afternoons it develops a carnival atmosphere as crowds of locals and tourists paddle in the sea, play cricket, ride horses and enjoy the fresh air. There are heaps of snack stands and fruit vendors, fairground rides, toy sellers, fortune tellers and every other type of Indian beach entertainment.

The Hare Krishna **Iskcon** complex is nearby, and is worth a peek when the temple is open (7.15 am to 1 pm and 4 to 9 pm).

Juhu is 25km north of the city centre, not far from Mumbai's airports. Catch bus No 231 from Santa Cruz train station or an autorickshaw from Vile Parle train station.

ACTIVITIES

Swimming

Mumbai is hot and sticky year-round, but don't be tempted by the lure of Back Bay, or even the open sea at Juhu. If you want to swim and you aren't staying at a luxury hotel, the Fariyas Hotel in Colaba has a tiny pool (Rs 330), or splash out at the Breach Candy Club (☎ 3674381) on Bhulabhai Desai Rd, which has a pool built in the shape of India. Day tickets to the club (which is open only to members and foreigners) cost Rs 200/300/500 on weekdays/Saturday/Sunday.

Yoga

Serious yoga classes are held at the Khaivalyadham Ishwardas Yogic Health Centre (☎ 2818417, ⓔ kaivalya@bom7.vsnl.net.in) on Marine Drive, Chowpatty. The centre is open daily except Sunday. Membership costs a minimum Rs 300 for a month and you are expected to attend a one-hour class six days a week for the whole month. You must undergo a routine physical examination before enrolling, for which you should make a personal appointment (ie, not by phone). The emphasis here is on yoga for better health and curative purposes.

Hindi Classes

Davar's College (☎ 2042007), 3rd floor, Jehangir Building, Flora Fountain, offers Hindi and Marathi language classes suitable for beginners. A one-month course in basic grammar and conversational Hindi costs Rs 4500, with one 45-minute class held every weekday.

ORGANISED TOURS

The MTDC operates uninspiring city tours at 2 pm daily (Rs 60) and suburban tours from 9.15 am to 6 pm (Rs 120). Admission fees are not included. It also has one-hour open-deck bus tours of the city's illuminated heritage buildings at 7 and 8.30 pm weekend evenings (Rs 50). All can be booked at the MTDC office on Madame Cama Rd.

The Government of India tourist office can arrange multilingual guides if you wish to explore Mumbai at your own pace. They cost Rs 255/380 for a half/full day, plus Rs 125 for a guide using a foreign language other than English.

Cruises on Mumbai Harbour are a good way to escape the city and offer the chance to see the Gateway of India as it was intended. Short ferry rides (1½ hours) cost Rs 25.

SPECIAL EVENTS

Mumbai features a lot of festivals. Some of the most popular are:

Banganga 8–9 January – music festival, Banganga Tank
Elephanta Festival February– Classical dance and music festival, Elephanta Island
Kala Ghoda Arts Festival February – 14 days featuring performing arts, Kala Ghoda
Nariyal Poornima August – celebrates the start of the fishing season, Colaba & Versova
Ganesh August/September – 10 day festival featuring street parades, Chaturthi Chowpatty Beach
Diwali October/November – features raucous festivities, Marine Drive
Kala Ghoda Fair Each Sunday, November to January – features performing arts, K Dubash Marg

PLACES TO STAY

Mumbai is India's most expensive city to stay in – hardly surprising since real estate here is among the most expensive in the world. Pressure for accommodation can be intense during the Christmas season so it pays to plan well ahead. A budget place here is one that costs anything under Rs 1000 for a double, but you can get a reasonable room for half that.

Most travellers head towards Colaba, which has plenty of budget and mid-range hotels, and is a lively, well-placed area. The Fort area is also convenient and everyone is far too busy going about their business

to take any notice of foreigners. To stay with a local family, contact the Government of India tourist office for a list of homes participating in Mumbai's paying guest scheme.

PLACES TO STAY – BUDGET

Colaba

The ***Salvation Army Red Shield Hostel*** *(☎ 2841824, 30 Mereweather Rd)* is the cheapest place to stay in Colaba and the best option if you're travelling alone on a tight budget. A bed in a separate-sex dorm costs Rs 130 including breakfast or Rs 190 with full board. It's a little institutional and some travellers report problems with bed bugs. Full board in a double with private bathroom costs Rs 460, including tax. Dorm beds are leased on a first-come first-served basis. The maximum stay is one week and checkout time is 9 am. Lockers are available (Rs 5 per day).

Apollo Guest House *(☎ 2045540, fax 2883991, 43/45 Mathuradas Estate Building, 1st floor, Colaba Causeway)* has clean but cramped singles/doubles with shared bathroom for Rs 338/440, and tidy air-con doubles with private bathroom for Rs 728, or Rs 832 with air-con, including tax.

Hotel Volga II *(☎ 2824755, Rustam Manzil, 1st floor, Nawroji F Rd)*, just near Leopold's, has doubles with shared/private bathroom for Rs 450/600. This place is surviving essentially on its location.

There's a group of three budget hotels in a building called Kamal Mansion on Arthur Bunder Rd. ***Sea Shore Hotel*** *(☎ 2874237, 1/49 Kamal Mansion, 4th floor, Arthur Bunder Rd)* has spartan, windowless rooms with TV and shared bathroom for Rs 320/420, or better doubles with small harbour views for Rs 500. The singles are tiny, but the place is clean enough.

India Guest House *(☎ 2833769, 1/39 Kamal Mansion, 3rd floor, Arthur Bunder Rd)* is basic with hardboard partitions that don't reach the ceiling, but it's usually busy. Rooms with shared bathroom are overpriced at Rs 370/ 420, and there's one minuscule single for Rs 250. Rooms with windows cost a little more.

Hotel Sea Lord *(☎ 2845392)*, which is on the 2nd floor of the same building, has windowless doubles for Rs 350 and singles/doubles with air-con, TV, window and shower (but no toilet) for a very reasonable Rs 500/600.

Hotel Prosser's *(☎ 2841715, 2 Henry Rd)* is decrepit and ramshackle in appearance, but the rooms are reasonably well kept and decent value. Doubles/triples with shared bathroom cost Rs 400/600. The bathrooms have hot water and sit-down flush toilets.

Bentley's Hotel *(☎ 2841474, fax 2871846, e bentleyshotel@hotmail.com, 17 Oliver Rd)* is a successful, friendly hotel with two annexes to complement the main building, and a cheaper ***guesthouse*** *(☎ 2881706)*, which is a block away in Henry Rd. Doubles range from Rs 650 to 970, including TV, breakfast and tax. The more expensive rooms are spacious and excellent value. The best are the huge rooms without private bathroom. Air-con costs Rs 150 to 200 extra. Reservations here are recommended. Each take email bookings and accept major credit cards.

Hotel Whalley's *(☎ 2821802, 41 Mereweather Rd)* has a range of old-fashioned but well-kept rooms starting from Rs 500/600 with shared bathroom and Rs 650/750 with private bathroom. A cavernous double goes for Rs 1000 and an air-con double is Rs 1200; tax and breakfast are included in the room rate.

Fort Area

Hotel Lawrence *(☎ 2843618, 3rd floor, 33 Sri Sai Baba Marg)* is a good-value budget hotel with clean, plain singles/doubles/triples with shared bathroom for Rs 300/400/600, including taxes. Book ahead. It's down a lane (formerly known as Rope Walk Lane) behind the Prince of Wales Museum.

Hotel City Palace *(☎ 2615515, fax 2676897, 121 City Terrace, W Hirachand Marg)* is cramped but clean and surprisingly quiet given the location. Singles/doubles/triples with bathroom and TV cost Rs 750/900/1100. Air-con costs an extra Rs 350. It's opposite CST and a good place to stay if you are only in Mumbai a short time.

Hotel Outram *(☎ 2094937, Marzaban Rd)* is in a quiet but central location between VT and the maidans. Rooms with private bathroom are reasonably clean (despite the mildewed walls) and there's 24-hour hot water. Single/double rooms cost Rs 600/700 and small rooms with shared bathroom cost Rs 310/415.

***Residency Hotel** (☎ 2625525, fax 26 9164, ⓔ residencyhotel@vsnl.com, 26 Rustom Sidhwa Marg)* is one of the few comfortable options in the heart of the Fort. It has a marble lobby and spotless air-con singles/doubles with private bathroom and TV starting at Rs 1200/1300. Bookings are recommended.

***Benazeer Hotel** (☎ 2611725, ⓔ benazeer@bom7.vsnl.net.in, 16 Rustam Sidhwa Marg)* has reasonable air-con rooms with private bathroom and TV for Rs 832.

***Hotel Manama** (☎ 2613412, fax 2613 860, 221/225 P D'Mello Rd)* has average doubles with TV for Rs 400/600 with shared/private bathroom, or Rs 750 with air-con, including tax. It makes a good budget option close to VT.

***Railway Hotel** (☎ 2616705, fax 2658049, 249 P D'Mello Rd)* is a clean place with old-style carpeted rooms. Singles/doubles cost from Rs 800/1100 with private bathroom, TV and fridge or Rs 1100/1500 with air-con.

Airport Area

There are a couple of budget hotels in Vile Parle (pronounced 'Veelay Parlay'), which is a middle-class suburb adjoining the Santa Cruz Domestic Airport.

***Shangri-La** (☎ 6128983, Nanda Patkar Rd, Vile Parle East)* is the cheapest budget hotel close to the domestic airport and it's easy to see why. Very ordinary doubles with bathroom start at Rs 390, including tax. Air-con doubles cost Rs 780. Head west on Nehru Rd at the crossroads outside the airport, and take the second left-hand turn. It's a 10-minute walk from the terminal or under Rs 10 in an autorickshaw.

***Hotel Aircraft International** (☎ 6121419, fax 6182942, 179 Dayaldas Rd, Vile Parle East)* is opposite the domestic airport entrance, just off the Western Express Hwy. It has clean air-con singles/doubles with private bathroom and TV for Rs 1000/1150, which is not bad for this overpriced area. Checkout time is 24 hours.

PLACES TO STAY – MID-RANGE

Unless otherwise indicated all mid-range hotels offer air-con rooms with private bathroom, TV and fridge.

Colaba

***Shelleys Hotel** (☎ 2840229, fax 2840385, ⓔ shelleyshotel@vsnl.com, 30 PJ Ramchandani Marg)* overlooks the waters of Mumbai Harbour. It's an excellent place with a slight hint of the Raj about it. Doubles start at Rs 1415 and rise to 1900 with water views, including tax.

***Harbour View Hotel** (☎ 2821089, 4th floor, 25 PJ Ramchandani Marg, ⓔ parkview@bom3.vsnl.net.in)* is a tastefully refurbished hotel with spotless doubles from Rs 2190, rising to Rs 2475 for rooms with those namesake harbour views, plus 20% tax. Its rooftop restaurant is a major plus.

***Regency Inn** (☎ 2020292, fax 2855226, 18 Lansdowne House, Mahakavi Bhushan Marg)* has compact rooms with shared bathroom for Rs 750, and spacious rooms with private bathroom for Rs 1200/1490, including tax. It's good value.

***Hotel Suba Palace** (☎ 2020636, fax 2020812, ⓔ subapalace@hotmail.com, Battery St)* has comfortable, modern air-con singles/doubles for Rs 1450/1950, plus 14% tax. It's well located and gets positive reviews from travellers. Book ahead.

***Regent Hotel** (☎ 2871854, fax 2020363, ⓔ hotelregent@vsnl.com, 8 Best Marg)* is a bit more upmarket with decent motel-style single/double rooms for Rs 2080/2388, including tax.

***Hotel Causeway** (☎ 2817777, fax 2810999, 43/45 Mathuradas Estate Building, 3rd floor, Colaba Causeway)* is central and has adequate air-con rooms that start at Rs 1000/1200.

Fort Area

***Grand Hotel** (☎ 2618211, ⓔ grandh@bom3.vsnl.net.in, 17 Shri Shiv Sagar Ramgulam Marg, Ballard Estate)* fails to live up to its name, but it has clean, spacious single/double rooms with dowdy furniture for Rs 1980/2392, including tax (no fridge).

***West End Hotel** (☎ 2039121, fax 205 7506, ⓔ westhotel@vsnl.com, 45 New Marine Lines)* is a very clean, old-fashioned place with some huge rooms. No frills singles/doubles start at Rs 2160/2622 (including tax) and there are suites for Rs 4800.

Marine Drive

***Chateau Windsor Hotel** (☎ 2044455, fax 2026459, ⓔ munshi@vsnl.com, 5th floor, 86 Veer Nariman Rd, Churchgate)* is well run and has spotless fan-cooled rooms with shared bathroom for Rs 940/1190 and singles/doubles with private bathroom for Rs 1190/1440. Air-con doubles cost Rs 1890.

Sea Green Hotel *(☎ 2822294, fax 283 6158, 145 Marine Drive)* and the ***Sea Green South Hotel*** *(☎ 2821613, fax 283 6303, ⓔ sgsh@vsnl.com, 145A Marine Drive)* are identical hotels offering spacious but spartan air-con rooms for Rs 1500/1775, plus 20% tax. Ask for a sea view as the rooms fronting Marine Drive cost the same.

Chowpatty & Kemp's Corner

Hotel Sapna *(☎ 3670041, fax 3619115, Pandita Ramabai Marg, Chowpatty)*, opposite Bharatiya Vidhya Bhavan, is cramped and overpriced, but it's in an interesting location, close to Chowpatty Beach and Mani Bhavan. Singles/doubles start at Rs 1395/1645, plus 20% tax. Its brochure states, 'Only for families and business tycoons', but it hardly seems suitable for either!

Hotel Kemp's Corner *(☎ 3634646, fax 3634732, 131 August Kranti Marg)* has very clean and very white rooms with air-con and TV for Rs 1050 for a small single, Rs 1300/1400 for larger singles/doubles and Rs 1500/1600 for deluxe rooms. Bookings are recommended.

Shalimar Hotel *(☎ 3631311, August Kranti Marg, ⓔ shalimar@giasbm01.vsnl.net.in)* is a decent air-con hotel with three restaurants. Rooms are pricey at US$100/120, plus 20% tax.

Juhu Beach

Juhu Hotel *(☎ 6184012, fax 6192578, ⓔ juhuhotel@vsnl.com, Juhu Tara Rd)* is a small, single-storey beachfront hotel with ageing apartment-style double rooms from Rs 1150 to 2800 plus tax. The more expensive rooms are spacious, but the ordinary rooms are quite small. It attracts a fashionable, young crowd and has a popular nightclub (the Raspberry Rhinocerous).

Iskcon *(☎ 6206860, fax 6205214, ⓔ guest.house.bombay@com.bbt.se, 111 Hare Krishna Land)* is a garish-looking, efficiently run high-rise place with fan-cooled singles/doubles with private bathroom for Rs 960/1150; air-con rooms cost Rs 1050/1440, plus 4% tax (no TV or fridge). Book ahead.

Airport Area

There are about half-a-dozen mid-range hotels clustered on Nehru Rd Extension close to the entrance to the domestic airport. They're twice the price of equivalent rooms in the city and there's no compelling reason to stay in the Vile Parle area unless you're just filling in time between flight connections. Bookings are recommended; most offer courtesy airport pick-up.

Hotel Bawa International *(☎ 6113636, fax 6107096, Nehru Rd Extension, Vile Parle East)* is a modern, well-appointed hotel with a restaurant, coffee shop and a nightclub (which starts up around 10 pm on weekend nights). Comfortable rooms with TV, fridge and air-con cost Rs 3300/3800, plus 20% tax.

Kumaria Presidency *(☎ 8352601, fax 8373850, ⓔ kumaria@bom2.vsnl.net.in Anderhi-Kurla Rd)*, facing Sahar international airport, has reasonable rooms for Rs 2145/2420.

PLACES TO STAY – TOP END

Hotels in this category generally charge 10% luxury tax, plus another 10% service tax, and accept major credit cards. Taxes have not been included in the following prices.

Colaba

Taj Mahal Hotel *(☎ 2023366, fax 2872711, ⓔ gateway@bom4.vsnl.net.in, Apollo Bunder)*, next to the Gateway of India, is one of the best hotels in the country. Singles/doubles in the superb heritage wing start at US$310/330, rising to US$330/345 with a harbour view, plus 20% tax. Rooms in the modern wing are 20% cheaper. The Taj is a second home to Mumbai's elite and has every conceivable facility, including three quality restaurants, several bars, a stylish 24-hour cafe, swimming pool, gymnasium and nightclub.

Fariyas Hotel *(☎ 2042911, fax 2834992, ⓔ info@fariyas.com, 25 Justice Devshanker V Vijas Marg)* is a comfortable, modern four-star establishment offering quality rooms starting at US$125. It has a tiny pool, a restaurant and popular bar.

Marine Drive

Oberoi *(☎ 2325757, fax 2043282, ⓔ reservations@oberoi-mumbai.com, Marine Drive, Nariman Point)* competes with the Taj Mahal in a bid to be South Mumbai's most opulent hostelry. It's a modern, service-oriented, luxury business hotel overlooking the Arabian

Sea. Rooms start at US$300/320, rising to US$325/345 with a sea view. It has a pool, a gymnasium, three restaurants and a bar.

Oberoi Towers *(☎ 2324343, Marine Drive, Nariman Point)* attracts upmarket travellers, businesspeople and airline crews, many of them drawn by the fantastic views of Back Bay and the city from the upper floors and the fact that it's marginally cheaper than its neighbour. Rooms start from US$275/290. There's an ordinary pool, a gymnasium, two restaurants and a bar. It's connected to the Oberoi, and guests can make use of both hotels' facilities. Email and fax bookings are the same as for the Oberoi.

Marine Plaza *(☎ 2851212, fax 2828585, 29 Marine Drive, Nariman Point)* is a modern boutique five-star hotel with Art Deco flourishes. It has stylish rooms starting at US$250 with sea views. Facilities include a gymnasium, restaurant, coffee shop and popular bar.

Juhu Beach

Holiday Inn *(☎ 6704444, fax 6701710, ⓔ hib@holidayinnbombay.com, Balraj Sahani Marg)* has a beachfront location, a decent pool, a good 24-hour coffee shop and a relaxing ambience. Fine rooms start at US$220, including a buffet breakfast. It also offers free airport pick-up.

Airport Area

Leela Kempinski *(☎ 6911234, fax 6911455, ⓔ leela.bom@leela.sprintrpg.ems.vsnl.net.in)* is opposite the international airport. It's the only five-star hotel in Mumbai that can compete with the Oberoi and the Taj. Singles/doubles start from US$315/345.

The Orchid *(☎ 6164040, ⓔ info@orchidhotel.com)*, off Nehru Rd Extension in Vile Parle East, is a stylish five-star hotel next to the domestic airport and the first certified 'ecofriendly' hotel in Asia. Excellent rooms start at US$250.

PLACES TO EAT

Mumbai has the best selection of restaurants in India. You could trace the cultural history of the metropolis by trawling through the variety of food available: from Parsi *dhan-saak* (meat with curried lentils and rice), Gujarati *thalis* (meals) and Muslim kebabs to a Goan vindaloo and Mangalorean seafood. The city's delicious seafood is safe to eat, even during the monsoon months of mid-June to early September. Very few restaurants serve it, but if you find it on a menu, Bombay Duck is a *bombil* (small fish) dried in the sun and deep fried.

Make sure to try Mumbai's famous bhelpuri – a tasty snack of crisp vermicelli, puffed rice, spiced vegetables, chutney and chillies. During the Muslim holy month of Ramadan, fantastic night food markets line Mohammed Ali and Merchant Rds.

Most budget restaurants and cafes open from breakfast to around 11 pm daily. Smarter restaurants tend to open only for lunch and dinner; they generally accept credit cards. A tip of 5% to 10% is appropriate for good service.

A 24-hour telephone information service (☎ 8888888) can provide additional information on Mumbai's restaurants.

If you're self-catering, the Colaba market on Lala Nigam St has plenty of fresh fruit and vegetables, and there's the ***Saharkari Bhandar Supermarket*** *(☎ 2022248)* at the north of Colaba Causeway. ***Suryodaya*** *(☎ 2040979)* is a well-stocked supermarket next to Churchgate train station on E Road. It's open from 7.30 am to 8.30 pm.

Colaba

Leopold Cafe & Bar *(☎ 2020131)* at the corner of Colaba Causeway and Nawroji F Rd, is a Mumbai institution dating back to 1871. It's also the most popular travellers' hang-out in the city and is invariably packed with visitors arriving from less salubrious parts of India. There's an extensive Chinese, continental and Indian menu, an excellent juice bar, and consistently good food. Soups and sandwiches cost around Rs 45, Indian and Chinese mains are around Rs 70 to 160, plus 12% tax.

Cafe Churchill *(☎ 2844689, 103B Colaba Causeway)* serves some of the best comfort food in the neighbourhood. It's a tiny place with booth seating so it can be hard to get a table in the evening. It does ace sandwiches (Rs 50), reasonable pasta meals and some interesting desserts such as honey walnut tart (Rs 40). There's a good all-day breakfast menu, but unfortunately it doesn't open till 11 am.

Bade Miya *(☎ 2841649)*, on Tulloch Rd, is an evening street stall with a city-wide

CHRISTINE OSBORNE

LINDY HICKMAN

KAREN TRIST

DAVID COLLINS

Colourful Mumbai: Crawford Market **(top)**; a Hindi film poster advertising a Bollywood blockbuster **(middle right)**; local crowds cool off at Juhu Beach **(bottom)**; and the washing wizards at the *dhobi ghat* or laundry **(middle left)**

DAVID COLLINS

GREG ELMS

GREG ELMS

DAVID COLLINS

EDDIE GERALD

Reminders of British imperialism in the form of some imposing buildings in Mumbai: the Gateway of India, next to the Taj Mahal Hotel **(top)**; the BMC building **(bottom left)**; and Victoria Terminus **(bottom right)**. However, the real spirit of India is captured by snack sellers on Chowpatty Beach **(middle)**.

reputation. It serves excellent kebabs, tikkas and rotis to customers milling on the street or seated at tables on the roadside.

Kailash Parbat, *(☎ 2874823, 5 Sheela Mahal, 1st Pasta Lane)* is a Mumbai legend thanks to its inexpensive Sindhi-influenced pure vegetarian snacks and its mouthwatering sweets.

Indigo *(☎ 2856316, 4 Mandlik Rd)* is the trendiest new place in Colaba and it can be difficult to get a seat in the evening without a booking. It's a stylish, modern restaurant with casual furniture and a rooftop dining area – though most diners prefer the ambience of the downstairs restaurant. The food is largely continental and not cheap, with dinner mains starting at around Rs 275 for the seared prime fillet mignon.

Fort Area

Wayside Inn *(☎ 2844324, 38 K Dubash Marg)* is a comfortable historic spot to hang out in central Mumbai. Dr Ambedkar must have felt that way, since he wrote parts of the draft of the Indian constitution here. The decor, with leadlight windows and red-and-white check tablecloths, is like a rural Italian cafe and the simple menu reads like an English greasy spoon. Mixed grill is Rs 140, sausage and onion Rs 85 and fish and chips Rs 85. The beer is cold, making this a great place to while away a few hours in the afternoon (a nice change from Leopold's). It's open from 9 am to 7 pm daily except Sunday.

Chetana *(☎ 2844968, 34 K Dubash Marg)* opened the year before Independence and played a key role in the development of Indian contemporary art. It's a popular lunch spot and a great place to deconstruct the mysteries of the North Indian vegetarian thali (Rs 150 to 185).

Mocambo Cafe & Bar *(☎ 2870458, 23A Sir P Mehta Rd)* has an open street frontage that lets you absorb the atmosphere of the Fort. It's a convenient spot for breakfast, sandwiches and cold beer, and most dishes are under Rs 40.

Mahesh Lunch Home *(☎ 2870938, 8B Cawasji Patel St)* is the place to try Mangalore seafood. Renowned for its ladyfish, pomfret and crabs, the *rawas tikka* (marinated white salmon) and pomfret tandoor are superb.

Another excellent Mangalorean seafood specialist is ***Apoorva Restaurant and Bar*** *(☎ 2870335, Noble Chambers, SA Brelvi Rd)*. Its mouthwatering crabs and prawn *gassis* (coconut-based curry) are known throughout South Mumbai. Seafood dishes, including Bombay Duck, start at Rs 50 and rise to Rs 375. The main lobster and crab dishes are priced by weight.

Trishna *(☎ 2672176, 7 Sai Baba Marg)* is a high-quality restaurant specialising in seafood, and good for a splurge. The service and ambience match the food. Dishes range from Rs 100 to 650. Bookings are advisable.

Sanuk Thai *(☎ 2044233, 30 K Dubash Marg)* is a stylish new split-level Thai restaurant behind the Prince of Wales museum. Green curry is Rs 250, pad Thai is Rs 220 and a bottle of beer is Rs 100. Unlike some places, the menu sticks to the chosen style of cuisine and the food is authentic.

McDonald's, opposite VT station is incredibly busy around lunch time and has a pleasant alfresco eating area. A Maharaja Mac burger is Rs 54.

Churchgate

The Pizzeria *(☎ 2843646, Soona Mahal, 143 Marine Drive)* has decent pizzas and fine views of Back Bay and the lights of Malabar Hill at night. Pizzas cost from Rs 110 to 350.

Purohit *(☎ 2049231, Veer Nariman Rd)* looks new, but has been serving vegetarian food for over 60 years. It knows a thing or two about Gujarati thalis (Rs 120) and has an extensive a la carte menu (with prices around Rs 80).

Pearl of the Orient *(☎ 2041131, Veer Nariman Rd)*, at the Ambassador Hotel, is a pricey revolving restaurant, but it's worth a splurge for the views. Thai, Japanese and Chinese food are the specialities.

Just Around the Corner *(☎ 2886737)*, opposite Eros Cinema, is a bright, clean salad bar with soups and sandwiches. It's self-service so pile it on – a salad costs Rs 125.

Starters & More *(☎ 2814124, 42 Maharshi Karve Rd)* is a new Art Deco restaurant overlooking Oval Maidan. The menu is Indian and international and a lunch buffet costs Rs 225. There's a small cocktail bar.

Chowpatty Beach & Malabar Hill

The ***stalls*** at Bhel Plaza on Chowpatty Beach open up in the evening and are the most atmospheric spots to snack on bhelpuri (Rs 10), *panipuri* (deep-fried rote filled with dahl) and ice cream.

Cafe Ideal *(☎ 3630943, Fulchand Niwas, Chowpatty Seaface)* is a bustling cafe, of the type made popular by Iranian parsis early in the 20th century, with a CD jukebox and a Chinese and continental menu. Most dishes cost around Rs 50; beer is more popular at Rs 75.

New Kulfi Centre, on the corner of Chowpatty Seaface and Sardar V Patel Rd, makes some of the most delicious kulfi (Rs 12 to 30) in Mumbai. It's weighed into 100g slabs, cut into cubes, and served on plates to customers gathered on the pavement.

Cream Centre *(☎ 3692025, Chowpatty Seaface)* is an iconic vegetarian snack bar and ice-cream parlour that's been gracing Chowpatty for over 40 years. It serves delicious *puris* (deep-fried flat dough), samosas and sandwiches, plus ready-made and create-your-own sundaes (around Rs 60).

ENTERTAINMENT

The daily English language tabloid *Mid-Day* incorporates 'The List', a guide to Mumbai entertainment. Newspapers have information on mainstream events and film screenings.

Bars & Nightclubs

Compared with most Indian cities Mumbai has a relaxed attitude to alcohol and good nightlife. In some clubs entry is restricted to couples or women; sober, appropriately dressed foreigners may find it possible to circumvent these rules. A bottle of beer in a bar or restaurant costs between Rs 70 and Rs 100 – more in a nightclub or fashionable drinking spot.

Cafe Mondegar *(☎ 2020591, Metro House, 5A Colaba Causeway)* is a cramped cafe-bar with a CD jukebox that's popular with travellers. It's open from 8 am daily.

Leo's Square, above Leopold's (there's a door at the rear of the cafe) is a good spot for a drink, with modern decor and Western music. It's open till midnight.

Gokul Bar *(☎ 2848428)* on Tulloch Rd in Colaba is a serious, 100% male, Indian drinking den. It can get pretty lively and the beer is cheap (starting at Rs 45). It's open from 11 am daily.

Voodoo Pub *(☎ 2841959, 2/5 Kamal Mansion, Arthur Bunder Rd, Colaba)* is a dark, clubby grunge bar. Saturday night is gay night. It's open nightly from 7.30 pm and there's a Rs 120 cover charge after 8.30 pm.

Tavern & Beyond *(☎ 2042911, 25 Justice Devshanker V Vijas Marg, Colaba)*, at the Fariyas Hotel, is an air-con bar popular with 30-something Indians. It's open from midday to midnight.

Three Flights Up *(☎ 2829934, Narang House, 1st floor, 34 Shivaji Marg, Colaba)* is a stylish club above the Central Cottage Industries Emporium. It's a converted warehouse space and boasts the longest bar in India. Gents pay Rs 200 weekdays and Rs 400 on Friday and Saturday, but this is redeemable at the bar.

The Garden Bar *(☎ 2041131, 14th floor, Ambassador Hotel, Veer Nariman Rd, Churchgate)* was closed for renovation at the time of writing, but when it re-opens its superb 360-degree panorama of the bay and city should make it worth a visit.

Fashion Bar *(☎ 2077270, 1st floor, Dhiraj Chambers Annex, 16 Marzaban Rd, Fort)* is still one of the hippest spots in town. There's a cover charge of Rs 200 per person (Rs 300 on Friday and Saturday), which is redeemable at the bar. It's open from 7 pm daily; couples only.

Copa Cabana *(☎ 3680274, Darya Vihar, 39 Chowpatty Seaface)* is a small, buzzing, Latin-flavoured club/bar with decent music, fine margaritas (Rs 200) and no elbow room. Draught beer costs Rs 60. It's open from 6.30 pm to 12.30 am daily (entry free).

Cinema

There are well over 100 cinemas in Mumbai. ***The Regal*** *(☎ 2021017, Colaba Causeway)* and ***Sterling*** *(☎ 2075187, Marzaban Rd)* in the Fort show first-run English-language movies (Rs 60 to 87). To check out a Bollywood blockbuster, try ***Eros*** *(☎ 282 2335)* opposite Churchgate train station or ***Metro*** *(☎ 2030303)* on MG Rd (Rs 35 to 80).

It's worth reserving tickets in advance, especially for weekend screenings. Advance tickets go on sale up to a week before films are screened; current tickets are usually available about one hour before the show. The cheapest seats are in the stalls, better seats are in the dress circle or the balcony.

Music, Dance & Theatre

The ***National Centre for the Performing Arts*** (NCPA; *☎ 2833737)*, located at the tip of

Bollywood Nights

Mumbai is the centre of India's huge Hindi film industry, though falling production means it now produces about 120 feature films a year so is as good a place as anywhere to catch a Bollywood blockbuster. Much of the glamour associated with the city stems from its pivotal position as the dream factory of the nation.

The local film industry is known as Bollywood and the films it produces tend to be spectacular melodramatic fantasies, known as 'masala movies' because they're made to an established formula that mixes a variety of ingredients – action, violence, music, dance, romance and moralising – into one outrageous blend. Bollywood movies remain exuberant, spectacle-driven entertainment and the success of a film is determined by its stars, film score, choreography and playback singers (all songs are dubbed), not by its message.

Unfortunately, there are no organised tours of Mumbai's film studios, and it's difficult to get beyond the front gates without a good reason. Permission to visit sets may be possible if you sweet talk the public relations officers of Film City (☎ 840 1533) in Goregaon East; RK Studio (☎ 5563252) in Chembur-Sion; or Kamal Amrohi Studio (☎ 8371160) 6, Jogeshwari Vikhroli Link Road, Andheri (East). Otherwise you'll have to do what locals do: flick through the pages of filmzines like *Cineblitz*, check out the latest offerings on TV channels like Zee Cinema or pay a visit to a downtown cinema.

See 'Behind the Scenes of Indian Cinema' in the Facts about India chapter for more information.

Nariman Point, is the hub of Mumbai's music, theatre and dance scene. In any given week, it might host Marathi theatre, dance troupes from Bihar, ensembles from Europe, and Indian classical music. It also contains the ***Tata Theatre*** (which occasionally has English-language plays) and the ***Experimental Theatre***. The box office (☎ 2824567), at the southern end of Nepa Marg, is open for bookings from 9 am to 1.30 pm and 4.30 to 6.30 pm. Tickets range from Rs 30 to 200.

Most of the cultural centres (see the Libraries & Cultural Centres section earlier in this chapter) host regular music, dance and theatre performances.

You can see regional artists perform on K Dubash Marg every Sunday evening during the Kala Ghoda Fair, which takes place on Sunday from November to January.

English-language plays are performed at the ***Nehru Centre*** *(☎ 4928086)*, Dr Annie Besant Rd, Worli. The ***Privthi Theatre*** *(☎ 614 9546)* at Juhu Beach is a good place to see both English-language and Hindi theatre.

Planet M *(☎ 2620271)*, in the Times of India building on Dr D Naoroji Rd, is primarily a music store, but it's a possibility for live entertainment. It often features live performers and record launches, including Hindi pop stars and Western bands. It has its own in-house radio station, a CD jukebox and a mezzanine cafe. It's open from 10.30 am to 9 pm daily. Check the *Times of India* to find out what's on.

SPECTATOR SPORTS

The *Times of India* lists the day's sporting events in a handy box-out on its back page.

Cricket

The cricket season runs from October to April. Test matches and One Day Internationals are played a handful of times a year at Wankhede Stadium (☎ 2811795), just off Marine Drive. See Spectator Sports in the Facts for the Visitor chapter for information on buying tickets.

You can see spirited local club cricket matches for free at the maidans in south Mumbai, particularly Oval Maidan with the university clock tower as a backdrop.

Horse Racing

Mumbai's horse-racing season runs from November to April. Races are held on Sunday and Thursday afternoons (Saturday and Sunday towards the end of the season) at Mahalaxmi Racecourse (☎ 3071401). The big races, such as the Indian Derby, are major social occasions. Entry costs Rs 12 in the public enclosure, or Rs 70 if you can get a member to sign you in as a guest in the Member's Enclosure. The dress code for men in the latter is a shirt with jacket or tie, Indian national dress or, of course, a safari suit.

Football

The Cooperage Football Ground (☎ 202 4020), Maharshi Karve Rd, Colaba hosts soccer matches between November and February. Tickets are available at the gate (Rs 25).

SHOPPING

Mumbai is India's great marketplace with some of the best shopping in the country.

Markets

You can buy just about anything in the dense bazaars north of the Fort. The main areas are Crawford Market (fruit and veg), Mangaldas Market (silk and cloth), Zaveri Bazaar (jewellery), Bhuleshwar Market (fruit and vegetables) and Chor Bazaar (Mumbai's 'thieves' market', for antiques).

Specialist streets worth checking out in Kalbadevi include Shamsheth Lane, two streets north of the Jama Masjid, for lace; and Dhabu St in Chor Bazaar, which is still worth a peek for leather goods. Mutton St in Chor Bazaar specialises in antiques, ingenious reproductions and miscellaneous junk.

Colaba Causeway is lined with hawkers' stalls. You'll probably get sick of the approaches from drum sellers, but there are some cheap clothes, bags and crafts to be found here. The shops lining the causeway stock better quality garments, including genuine sporting apparel.

Handicrafts & Gifts

You can pick up handicrafts from various state government emporiums in the World Trade Centre Arcade near Cuffe Parade; there's more on Sir P Mehta Rd, Fort. The Central Cottage Industries Emporium (☎ 2027537) on Shivaji Marg, Colaba, has the biggest selection of mass-produced trinkets, and is a convenient place to buy gifts.

If you're looking for something that won't look incredibly tacky the moment you take it home, try the Bombay Store (☎ 2885048) on Sir P Mehta Rd, Fort. It sells rugs, textiles, home furnishings and bric-a-brac.

Antiques & Curios

Small antique and curio shops line Mereweather Rd behind the Taj Mahal Hotel. Prices aren't cheap, but the quality is definitely a step up from government emporiums. If you prefer Raj-era bric-a-brac, head to Chor Bazaar (see Markets).

Clothing & Department Stores

You can save a small fortune by buying your backpacking wardrobe at 'Fashion Street', the stalls lining MG Rd between Cross and Azad maidans. Colaba Causeway shops sell cheap and decent Western-style clothing.

For something unique, check out the cluster of boutiques at Kemp's Corner, between the flyover and the junction with Nepean Sea Rd. Pieces by Indian designers sell here for half the price of off-the-shelf gear back home.

Ready-made traditional Indian clothing can be picked up at the Khadi & Village Industries Emporium (☎ 2073280) at 286 Dr D Naoroji Rd, Fort, where time seems to have stopped somewhere in the 1940s.

The Asiatic Department Store (☎ 287 2815) on Veer Nariman Rd, Churchgate, is a handy shop with a pharmacy and photo lab. Vama Department Store (☎ 3871450), 72 Peddar Rd, Kemp's Corner, has Western labels such as Benetton, Levi's and Nike.

Miscellaneous

With a bit of sifting, you can pick up decent belts and wallets from the stalls on Dr D Naoroji Rd. It is still worth trawling Dhabu St in Kalbadevi, but the cheapest leather goods are now found in Dharavi, north of the city centre towards Juhu.

Inshaallah Mashaallah (☎ 2049495) on Best Marg, Colaba, has a vast range of perfumes and helpful staff to guide you through the olfactory chaos.

Music stores, selling CDs, tapes and videos of Hindi and Western music, Bollywood film soundtracks and Indian classical music, are becoming all the rage. Planet M (☎ 2620271), in the Times of India building on Dr D Naoroji Rd, has its own in-house radio station and a cafe. Groove (☎ 2812206), on Tata Rd across from Churchgate station, has a large selection. Rhythm House (☎ 284 2835), near the Jehangir Art Gallery, is also a good place to browse.

Singh Musical Instruments (☎ 2841373) at Ram-Nimi, Mandlik Marg, Colaba, sells tablas, sitars and guitars.

GETTING THERE & AWAY

Air

Mumbai is the main international gateway to India. It also has the busiest network of domestic flights. The international terminal (officially called CST, but still better known as Sahar) is about 4km away from the domestic airport, Santa Cruz. There's a free shuttle bus between the airports if you have a connecting flight. They are 30km and 26km respectively north of Nariman Point in downtown Mumbai.

Facilities in Sahar's arrival hall include a duty-free shop, several foreign-exchange counters offering reasonable rates, a Government of India tourist office (☎ 8325331), a hotel reservation counter (☎ 6155239) and a prepaid taxi booth – all open 24 hours. There's a left-luggage shed in the car park, about 200m left of the arrivals hall exit.

If you're leaving India from Mumbai, reconfirm your ticket three days before departure.

Mumbai's Santa Cruz Domestic Airport has two terminals, a couple of minutes' walk apart. Terminal A handles Indian Airlines flights, while terminal B caters to Jet Airways and Sahara Airlines. Planes start departing and arriving around dawn and stop around midnight. You're advised to check in one hour before departure.

Both terminals have foreign-exchange bureaus, ticketing counters and a restaurant-bar. The 24-hour left-luggage facility is midway between the two terminals. Note that flights on domestic sectors of Air India routes depart from the international airport.

Mumbai: This Fortnight has a list of major international airline offices in Mumbai, or consult the *Yellow Pages* for a more comprehensive list. Travel agents are a better bet for booking international flights, and will reconfirm your flight for a small fee.

Domestic Airlines

Domestic carriers servicing Mumbai include:

Indian Airlines (☎ 2023031; 24-hour reservations ☎ 141) Air India Bldg, Nariman Point
Jet Airways (☎ 8386111) Amarchand Mansion, Madame Cama Rd
Sahara Airlines (☎ 2855788), 7 Tulsiani Chambers, Free Press Journal Marg, Nariman Point

Domestic Flights from Mumbai There are flights to more than 30 Indian cities, including daily flights to Bangalore (US$140 one way), Kolkata (Calcutta; US$230), Chennai (Madras; US$160), Delhi (US$175), Goa (US$85) and Varanasi (US$235). Travellers under 30 years old can take advantage of youth fares, which are 25% cheaper. Indian Airlines offers check-in at its city office for passengers with hand luggage. This also applies to passengers booked on its subsidiary, Alliance Air.

Arriving Late at Night

Most long-haul international flights to Mumbai arrive in the middle of the night. Many travellers, wary of tramping around an unfamiliar city in the early hours of the morning, either wait until dawn before heading into the city or book expensive rooms in hotels close to the airport. This is unnecessary and can be avoided by reserving a room in advance and informing the hotel of your arrival time or calling a hotel yourself from the airport. Alternatives are to ask the 24-hour Government of India tourist office or the hotel reservation counter in the airport arrivals hall to book a room for you.

Mumbai is not a dangerous city for foreign travellers and the taxi ride from the airport is much quicker at night than during the morning or afternoon rush hour (though also slightly more expensive). Virtually all hotels claim to have 24-hour reception, though in some budget places this still means you'll have to wake the security guard or bang on a few doors to gain entrance.

Bus

Numerous private operators and state governments run long-distance buses to and from Mumbai. Private operators provide faster service, better comfort and simpler booking procedures.

Private long-distance buses depart for all points from Dr Anadrao Nair Rd, near Mumbai Central train station. Fares for non aircon deluxe buses include Goa (Panaji) for Rs 200 (14 to 18 hours), Pune for Rs 180 (six hours), Aurangabad for Rs 200 (10 hours), Mahabaleshwar for Rs 200 (seven hours), Ahmedhabad for Rs 250 (13 hours), Udaipur for Rs 400 (16 hours) and Bangalore for Rs 500 (24 hours). There are also sleeper buses to Goa costing Rs 400. Note that fares to popular destinations such as Goa are 25% higher during holiday periods, eg, Diwali and Christmas. To check on departure times and current prices, try National Travels on Dr Anadrao Nair Rd (☎ 3070780).

Private buses to Goa also depart roughly every 30 minutes between 2 and 6 pm from MG Rd, just south of the Metro cinema. Some buses to South India depart from MRA Marg at the rear of Crawford Market. It's best to purchase tickets directly from agents clustered in either of these areas.

Long-distance state-run buses depart from the state road transport terminal close to Mumbai Central train station. Buses service major towns in Maharashtra and neighbouring states. They're slightly cheaper and more frequent than the private services, but they're also decrepit, crowded vehicles. There's a helpful information office (☎ 3074272) on the 1st floor, open from 8 am to 8 pm daily.

The MTDC reservation office on Madame Cama Rd has daily buses to Mahabaleshwar (Rs 230) and Ganpatipule (Rs 230).

Train

Two train systems operate out of Mumbai. Central Railways (☎ 134 for inquiries) handles services to the east and south, plus a few trains to the north. It operates from Chhatrapati Shivaji Terminus (CST), still better known locally as Victoria Terminus (VT). The reservation centre is at the back of the station where the taxis gather and is open from 8 am to 8 pm Monday to Saturday, to 2 pm on Sunday. Tourist-quota tickets (which can be fully booked weeks in advance during the high season) and Indrail passes can be bought at counter No 7 (closed Sunday).

A few Central Railways, trains depart from Dadar (D), half-a-dozen stations north of CST or Churchgate. They include the *Chennai Express*, the fastest train to Chennai. Another handful of express trains depart from Lokmanya Tilak (T), 16km north of

Major Trains from Mumbai

destination	train No & name	departures	distance (km)	duration (hrs)	fare (Rs)
Agra	2137 *Punjab Mail*	7.10 pm CST	1344	21½	326/945
Ahmedabad	2009 *Shatabdi Exp*	6.25 am MC	492	7	630/1270
	2901 *Gujarat Mail*	9.50 pm MC	492	9	165/477
Aurangabad	1003 *Devagiri Exp*	9.20 pm CST	374	7½	137/638
	7617 *Tapovan Exp*	6.10 am CST	374	7½	88/267
Bangalore	6529 *Udyan Exp*	7.55 am CST	1210	24½	310/1440
Bhopal	2137 *Punjab Mail*	7.10 pm CST	831	14	244/707
Kolkata	2859 *Gitanjali Exp*	6.00 am CST	1968	33½	393/1139
	8001 *Howrah Mail*	8.15 pm CST	1968	36	393/1139
Chennai	6011 *Chennai Exp*	2 pm CST	1279	26½	314/1455
Delhi	2951 *Rajdhani Exp*	4.55 pm MC	1384	17	1485/2405
	2925 *Paschim Exp*	11.35 am MC	1384	23	329/954
	2137 *Punjab Mail*	5.10 pm CST	1538	25¼	343/995
Goa	0111 *Konkan Kanya Exp*	10.40 pm CST	588	12	193/558
	0103 *Mandavi Exp*	5.15 am CST	588	13	125/375
Hyderabad	7001 *Hussainsagar Exp*	9.55 pm CST	790	15¼	235/680
Indore	2961 *Avantika Exp*	7.25 pm MC	829	14½	244/707
Jaipur	2955 *Jaipur Exp*	7.05 pm MC	1200	17½	304/882
Kochi	6345 *Netravati Exp*	11 pm T	1314	29½	321/932
	1081 *Kaniya Kumari Exp*	3.35 pm CST	1817	39	380/1103
Pune	2123 *Deccan Queen*	5.10 pm CST	191	3½	83/170
	1007 *Deccan Exp*	6.35 am CST	191	4½	53/170
Varanasi	1065 *Gorakhpur Exp*	6.35 am D	1490	30¼	340/986

Abbreviations: CST – Chhatrapati Shivaji Terminus, MC – Mumbai Central, T – Lokmanya Tilak, D – Dadar

Note: Fares are for sleeper/air-con 3-tier sleeper on overnight trips (2-tier if the train does not have 3-tier carriages), except for *Shatabdi* and *Rajdhani Express*, which are air-con chair with meals included.

CST on the suburban main line. You can book tickets for all these trains at VT.

The other train system is Western Railways (☎ 131), which has services to the north (including Rajasthan) from Mumbai Central (MC) train station (still usually called Bombay Central). The easiest place to make bookings for Western Railways trains is at the crowded reservation centre opposite Churchgate train station, open from 8 am to 8 pm Monday to Saturday, from 8 am to 8 pm Sunday. The foreign tourist-quota counter (open 9.30 am to 4.30 pm weekdays and until 2 pm on Saturday) is upstairs next to the Government of India tourist office, but tourist-quota tickets are only sold 24 hours before departure and you must pay in foreign currency. There's a reservation centre adjacent to Mumbai Central, but it doesn't sell tourist-quota tickets.

See the table 'Major Trains from Mumbai' for a selection of trains. The useful *Trains at a Glance* (Rs 25) is available from bookstalls at VT, Churchgate and Mumbai Central stations. The electronic touch-screen machines in the reservation halls at VT and Churchgate can be used to check seat availability and to check confirmation status if you have a waitlisted ticket.

GETTING AROUND

To/From the International Airport

There's a prepaid taxi booth at the international airport with set fares to various places. To Colaba, the Fort and Marine Drive the fare is Rs 260 during the day (Rs 325 for air-con). There's a 25% surcharge between midnight and 5 am and a charge of Rs 5 per bag. The journey takes about one hour at night and 1½ to two hours during the day. To Juhu the day fare is Rs 93, to Chowpatty Rs 225 and to Mumbai Central station Rs 191. These fares may have increased – taxi drivers regularly strike for higher fares. Don't try to catch an autorickshaw from the airport to the city: They're prohibited from entering downtown Mumbai and will drop you a few kilometres down the road at Mahim Creek. Taxis loitering there will take maximum advantage of your predicament.

The cheap alternative is to catch an autorickshaw (around Rs 25) to Andheri train station and catch a suburban train (Rs 5, 45 minutes) to Churchgate or VT. It's unlikely that you'll be up for this after a long-haul flight; don't attempt it during rush hours (particularly the morning rush into the city from around 7 to 10 am) or if weighed down with luggage. At the very least, buy a first-class ticket (Rs 56).

Minibuses outside the arrival hall offer free shuttle services to the domestic airport and Juhu hotels. There's also a free Air India shuttle service between the international and domestic airports.

A taxi from the city centre to the international airport costs around Rs 300, plus extra for baggage; taxi drivers in Colaba usually ask for Rs 350. You'll pay about 30% more between midnight and 5 am.

To/From the Domestic Airport

Taxis and autorickshaws queue up outside both domestic terminals. There's no prepaid taxi counter, but the taxi queue outside is controlled by the police – make sure your driver uses the meter and conversion card. A taxi takes between one and 1½ hours to reach the city centre and costs around Rs 250, plus extra for baggage.

If you don't have too much luggage, bus No 2 stops on nearby Nehru Rd, opposite the junction to Nanda Patkar Rd, and terminates at the Prince of Wales Museum, right near Colaba. It stops on the highway opposite the airport when heading out of the city.

A better alternative is to catch an autorickshaw between the airport and Vile Parle train station (Rs 15), and catch a suburban train between Vile Parle and Churchgate or VT (Rs 5, 45 minutes). Don't attempt this during rush hour. Note that Vile Parle is the closest station to Santa Cruz Domestic Airport – not Santa Cruz station.

Most airport and Juhu hotels offer free airport pick-up.

Bus

Mumbai's red single and double-decker buses are one of the best ways to travel short distances in the city, though they are best avoided during rush hours. Fares around South Mumbai cost less than Rs 5 so make sure you have some small change available; pay the conductor once you're aboard. The service is run by BEST, which has its main depot in Colaba (☎ 4143611).

Route numbers and destinations on the front of buses are written in Marathi and English signs are on the side. Get a spot at

Local Bus Services in Mumbai

destination	bus No
Breach Candy	132, 133
Chowpatty	103, 106, 107, 123
Churchgate	70, 106, 123, 132
Haji Ali	83, 124, 132, 133
Hanging Gardens	103, 106, 107
Mani Bhavan	123
Metro Cinema	103, 124, 125
Mohammed Ali Rd	1, 3, 21
Mumbai Central Train Station	124, 125
Mumbai Zoo	3, 6, 7
CST (VT) & Crawford Market	1, 3, 21, 103,124
Walkeshwar	103,106, 107

Note: The above buses all depart from Colaba Causeway and pass Flora Fountain.

the bus stop where you can read the English signs as the bus pulls to a stop. Some destinations and bus numbers are shown above.

Train

Mumbai has an efficient but overcrowded suburban train network – it's virtually the only place in India where it's worth taking trains for travel within a city.

There are three main lines, making it easy to navigate. The most useful service operates from Churchgate heading north to stations such as Charni Rd (for Chowpatty Beach), Mumbai Central, Mahalaxmi (Dhobi Ghats), Vile Parle (Santa Cruz Domestic Airport), Andheri (Sahar International Airport) and Borivali (Sanjay Gandhi National Park). A couple of other suburban lines operate from VT, servicing places such as Dadar, and as far as Neral (for Matheran). Trains begin operating just after 4 am and run until almost 1 am. From Churchgate, 2nd/1st-class fares cost Rs 3/15 to Mumbai Central, Rs 5/56 to Vile Parle and Rs 8/82 to Borivali.

Avoid rush hours when trains are jam-packed, even in 1st class. Women should take advantage of the ladies-only carriages. Trains stop at suburban train stations for about 10 seconds. Watch your valuables.

Taxi & Autorickshaw

Every second car on Mumbai's streets seems to be a black and yellow Premier taxi (India's version of a 1950s' Fiat), so you'll have no problems finding one. They're the most convenient way to get around the city and in South Mumbai drivers almost always use the meter without prompting and give the correct change; autorickshaws are confined to the suburbs north of Mahim Creek.

Taxi meters are out of date, so the fare is calculated using a conversion chart, which all drivers carry – ask to see it at the end of the journey. The rough conversion rate during the day is around 13 times the meter reading. The minimum fare is Rs 13 for the first 1.6km (flagfall) and Rs 7 per kilometre after this. It's about 25% more expensive between midnight and 6 am. A steep rise in fuel prices in late 2000 will almost certainly result in an increase in these fares.

Cool Cabs (☎ 8246216) operates correctly metered, blue air-con taxis. They're about 33% more expensive than regular cabs and can be booked by telephone.

If you're north of Mahim Creek and not heading into the city, it's best to catch autorickshaws. They're metered but also use a conversion chart. The fare is roughly 7.5 times the meter reading.

Car

Cars are generally hired for an eight-hour day and with a maximum of 80km; additional charges rack up if you exceed these limits.

Agents at the Apollo Bunder ticket booths near the Gateway of India, can arrange a non air-con Maruti with driver for a half-day of sightseeing for Rs 600. Regular taxi drivers in this area accept a similar price.

Autoriders International (☎ 4921838), 139 Autoworld, Tardeo Rd, Tardeo, is affiliated with Hertz and has self-drive air-con Marutis at Rs 1750 for 24 hours (minimum age 25 years) or Rs 1650 with driver (eight hours, 80km).

Motorcycle

Mumbai is no place to learn how to ride a motorcycle, but it's as good a place as any to start touring. Allibhai Premji Tyrewallah (☎ 3099313, e apt@premjis.com) at 205 Lamington Rd, Opera House, near Grant Rd station, is the place to rent or purchase a motorcycle. Hire costs around Rs 2500 per week for a 350cc or 500cc Enfield, or Rs 2000 a week for a 100cc scooter. It prefers to operate on a purchase and buy-back scheme which, over a period of two months or more, works out cheaper anyway. You can get a second-hand Enfield for less than Rs 53,000 and the buy-back price after three months is around Rs 18,000 less than the original price. Grant Rd is the closest suburban train station.

Boat

Ferries shuttle between the Gateway of India and Elephanta Island (see the Greater Mumbai section), and between the Gateway and Mandwa on the mainland. The latter is useful to access Murud-Janjira and other parts of the Konkan coast by bus (see the Maharashtra chapter).

Greater Mumbai

ELEPHANTA ISLAND

The rock-cut temples on Elephanta Island, 9km north-east of the Gateway of India, are Mumbai's premier tourist attraction. Little is known about their origins, but they are thought to have been created between AD 450 and 750, when the island was known as Gharapuri (Place of Caves). The Portuguese renamed it Elephanta because of a large stone elephant near the shore. This statue collapsed in 1814 and the British moved and reassembled the remaining pieces at Victoria Gardens, where it stands today. There is one main cave with a number of large sculptured panels, all relating to Shiva. The most famous of the panels is the Trimurti, or triple-headed Shiva, where the god is depicted as destroyer, preserver and creator. The central bust of Shiva, its eyes closed in eternal contemplation, may be the most serene sight you witness in India.

There are also figures of Shiva dancing the Tandava, the marriage of Shiva and Parvati, Ravana shaking Kailasa, a scary carving of Shiva killing the demon Andhaka, and one in which Shiva appears as Ardhanari, uniting both sexes in one body.

The caves are open from 9 am to 5.30 pm daily except Monday. Entry for foreigners is about Rs 460, which most will find is way over the top. Indians pay Rs 10, and a video camera permit costs Rs 25. It's worth making use of the free English-language guide service offered to travellers with deluxe launch tickets. Tours depart every hour on the half-hour from the ticket booth. If you prefer to explore independently, pick up Pramod Chandra's *A Guide to the Elephanta Caves* from the stalls lining the stairway.

There's also a small museum on site, which has some informative pictorial panels on the origin of the caves and the history of Maharashtrian rock-cut architecture.

The best time to visit Elephanta is during the week when there are fewer visitors. The MTDC holds the **Elephanta Festival**, an annual celebration of classical music and dance, in front of the cave temple here, usually in February.

The terrace of the MTDC's ***Chalukya Restaurant & Beer Bar*** (☎ *284 8323*) at the top of the stairway, is a good spot to relax after a visit to the caves. Despite the accommodation sign here, visitors are not permitted to stay overnight on the island.

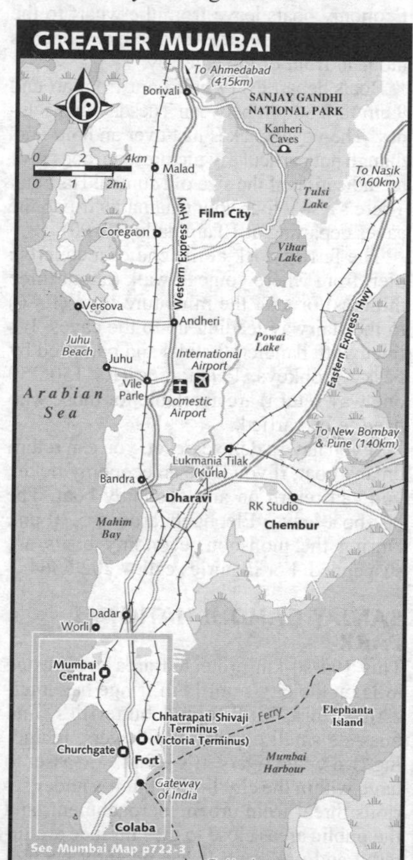

The state government has been criticised for its failure to maintain both the monument and the island's environment, but with the hike in the admission price there should be no excuse for not spending money on its upkeep. Travellers can help by carrying their rubbish with them back on the boat to Mumbai.

Getting There & Away

Launches head to Elephanta Island from the Gateway of India. Small economy boats cost Rs 65 return and more spacious 'deluxe' launches cost Rs 85 return, although there's not a great deal of difference between the boats. Tickets are sold by touts at the gateway and at booths lining the southern end of Shivaji Marg at Apollo Bunder, but they cost the same no matter where you buy them. Economy boats leave from the wharf to the left (north) of the gateway; deluxe launches moor in front of the gateway.

Boats depart every half-hour from around 9 am to 2.30 pm between Tuesday and Sunday. The voyage takes just over an hour and, though not particularly picturesque, does give an indication of the size of Mumbai Harbour. There's also a four-hour catamaran trip to the caves departing at 10 am daily (Rs 90).

The ferries dock at the end of a concrete pier, from where you can walk (about three minutes) or take the miniature train (Rs 6) to the stairway leading up to the caves. It's lined with handicraft stalls and patrolled by pesky monkeys. Palanquins (Rs 150/250 one way/return) are available for those who need to be carried.

If you have a deluxe ticket, you can return on any boat; if you have an economy ticket, you can return on any economy boat. The last boat leaves Elephanta around 5.30 pm. During the monsoon, economy boats are suspended. For inquiries call ☎ 202 6364.

SANJAY GANDHI NATIONAL PARK

This 104-sq-km protected area of forested hills on the city's northern fringe has interesting flora, birdlife and butterflies, and boasts a small population of tigers, including two white tigers. It's a fantastic asset to have within the city limits, but it's under serious threat from urban encroachment, and the public areas close to the entrance are littered and unkempt. It has recently been at the centre of controversy involving slum dwellers and environmentalists who have been setting up within the park boundaries.

The Bombay Natural History Society runs a **Conservation Education Centre** (☎ 842 1174) close to the park's southern entrance. There's also an information centre with a small exhibition on the park's wildlife, just inside the main northern entrance. The park is open from 7.30 am to 7.30 pm daily, except Monday (Rs 4). The best time to see birds is October to April; the best time to see butterflies is August to November.

For many visitors (mostly Indian families) the main attraction is the **lion & tiger safari**. These depart from the Tiger Orientation Centre (a free display explaining the demise of the tiger), about 1km in from the northern entrance. Tickets cost Rs 30 for a whirlwind 20-minute jaunt by bus through the two separate areas of the park housing the tigers and lions. There's a good chance of seeing one of the big cats. Safari buses leave roughly every 20 minutes from 9 am to 12.40 pm and 2 to 5.20 pm daily except Monday. Cameras can be used free, but there is a Rs 500 fee for video cameras.

Another major attraction in the park is the 109 **Kanheri Caves**, which line the side of a rocky ravine 5km from the northern park entrance. They were used by Buddhist monks between the 2nd and 9th centuries as *viharas* (monasteries) and *chaityas* (temples).

The most impressive is cave 3, the Great Chaitya cave, which is flanked by two huge Buddha statues and has a long colonnade of decorated pillars and a 5m high *dagoba* (hemispherical relic chamber topped by a spire) at the back. The caves are open from 9.30 am to 5.30 pm daily except Monday; admission is US$5 for foreign tourists and Rs 5 for Indians. From the northern gate you can walk to the caves in about two hours, or take a private car for about Rs 450 return, including an hour at the caves.

Getting There & Away

Take the train from Churchgate to Borivali train station (Rs 8, one hour). From the station, you can either walk (10 minutes), take an autorickshaw (Rs 10) or catch any bus to the park entrance. It's a farther 10-minute walk from the entrance to the safari parks.

The safaris and the caves can also be visited on the MTDC's suburban tour. See the Organised Tours section earlier.

Maharashtra

Maharashtra is a large, populous and economically important state. From the capital Mumbai (Bombay) most travellers head south to the beaches of Goa, south-east to Pune and its famous ashram, or north-east to the World Heritage-listed cave temples of Ajanta and Ellora. The state also has some interesting ruined forts, mostly associated with the Marathas.

The Western Ghats run parallel with the coast. South of Mumbai the thin strip between the ghats (hills) and the Arabian Sea is known as the Konkan Coast and there are some surprisingly good, virtually undiscovered, beaches along here. The rest of the state stands on the high Deccan plateau, stretching some 800km east, and includes two hill stations, Matheran and Mahabaleshwar.

History

Mughal power dominated much of central and southern India in the 16th century until the Deccan (literally 'south') became the epicentre of the Maratha empire in the 17th century. With a relatively small army, legendary Maratha leader Shivaji established a base at Pune and later Raigad from where he controlled the Deccan. From the early 18th century the Maratha empire came under the control of the Peshwas who retained power until they upset the British in 1817.

After Independence, western Maharashtra and Gujarat were joined to form Bombay state. Today's state, with Mumbai as capital, was formed in 1960 when the Marathi and Gujarati-speaking areas were once again separated.

In the 1999 elections Congress won power in Maharashtra, forcing out the Hindu fundamentalist BJP-Shiv Sena alliance.

Maharashtra at a Glance

Population: 96.8 million
Area: 307,690 sq km
Capital: Mumbai
Main Language: Marathi
When to Go: Oct to Mar (coast); Sep to mid-June (hills)

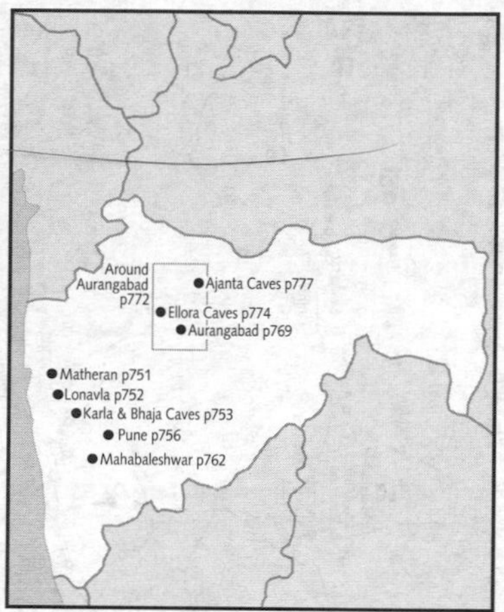

- Admire the hand-carved extravagance of Ellora's Kailasa Temple and a string of rock-cut caves
- Appreciate Ajanta's stunning setting and extraordinary Buddhist art in a series of man-made caves
- Take the toy train ride up to the traffic-free hill station of Matheran and enjoy the views
- Make a pilgrimage to Nasik, virtually devoid of Western tourists; the ghats on the Godavari River are a sublime place to watch Hindu life unfolding and learn a bit about the Ramayana
- Spend a couple of days spinning yarn and meditating at Gandhi's famous ashram at Sevagram
- Drop in for a quick tour of the ashram of Osho the Bhagwan, and enjoy some nightlife in Pune

Southern Maharashtra

THE KONKAN COAST

Maharashtra's Konkan Coast – the narrow strip between the Western Ghats and Arabian Sea – is a region of deserted beaches, stands of coconut and banana palms, abandoned forts and isolated fishing communities.

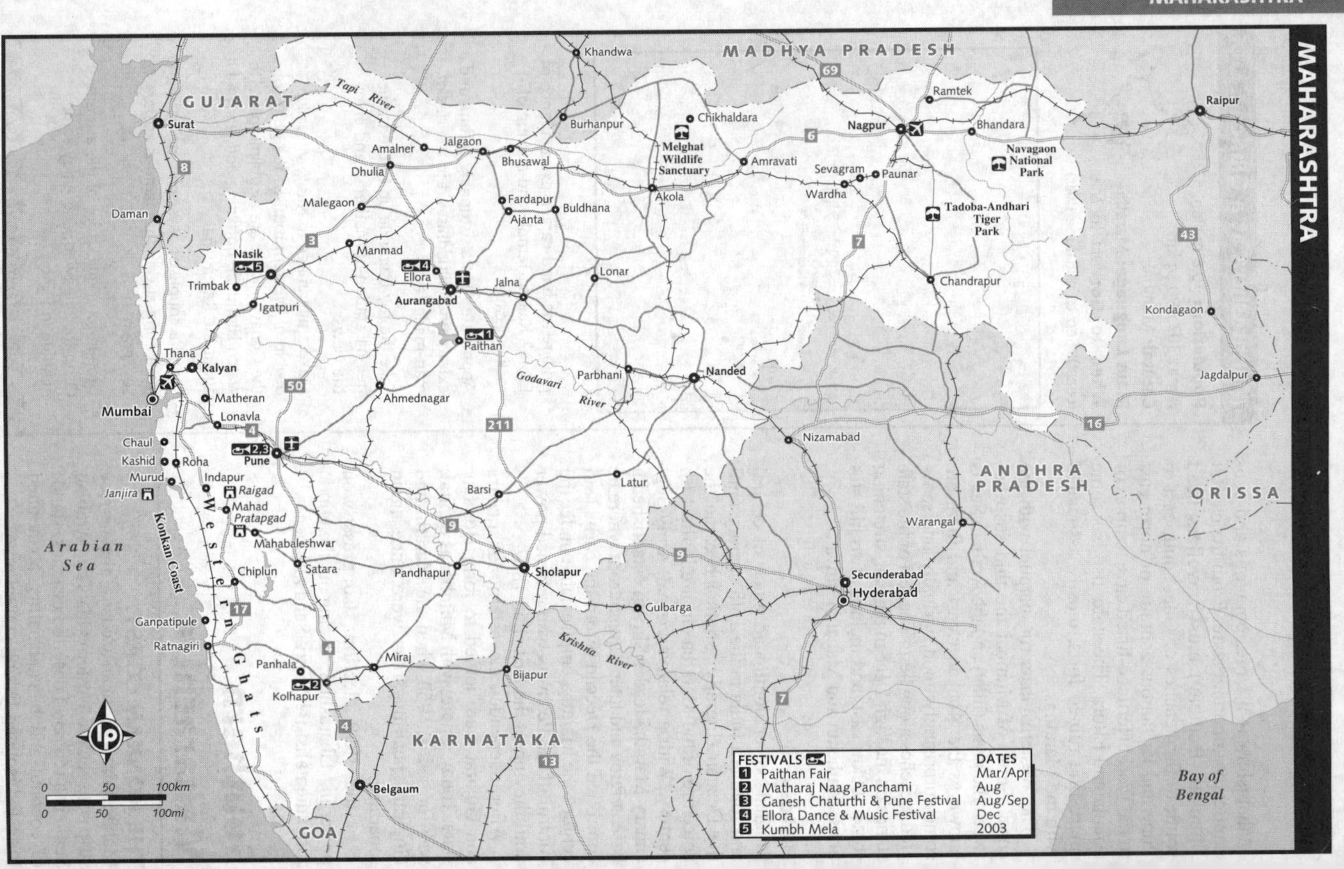
MAHARASHTRA
FESTIVALS
1 Paithan Fair
2 Matharaj Naag Panchami
3 Ganesh Chaturthi & Pune Festival
4 Ellora Dance & Music Festival
5 Kumbh Mela
DATES
Mar/Apr
Aug
Aug/Sep
Dec
2003
MADHYA PRADESH
GUJARAT
ORISSA
ANDHRA PRADESH
KARNATAKA
GOA
Bay of Bengal
Arabian Sea
Western Ghats
Konkan Coast
Tapi River
Godavari River
Krishna River
Khandwa
Raipur
Ramtek
Nagpur
Bhandara
Navagaon National Park
Tadoba-Andhari Tiger Park
Chandrapur
Kondagaon
Jagdalpur
Chikhaldara
Melghat Wildlife Sanctuary
Burhanpur
Amravati
Sevagram
Paunar
Wardha
Akola
Surat
Amalner
Jalgaon
Bhusawal
Dhulia
Malegaon
Fardapur
Ajanta
Buldhana
Daman
Manmad
Nasik
Trimbak
Igatpuri
Ellora
Aurangabad
Jalna
Lonar
Paithan
Parbhani
Nanded
Thana
Kalyan
Mumbai
Matheran
Lonavla
Ahmednagar
Pune
Chaul
Kashid
Roha
Murud
Janjira
Indapur
Raigad
Mahad
Pratapgad
Mahabaleshwar
Nizamabad
Latur
Barsi
Warangal
Chiplun
Satara
Pandhapur
Sholapur
Secunderabad
Hyderabad
Gulbarga
Ganpatipule
Ratnagiri
Panhala
Kolhapur
Miraj
Bijapur
Belgaum
0 50 100km
0 50 100mi

Although the completion of the Konkan Railway has made the area more accessible to visitors, it's still difficult to explore in any depth by public transport as the line runs some distance in from the coast. Dilapidated local buses fill the gaps, so if discovering beaches and fishing villages rarely seen by Western tourists is of interest to you, it's worth the effort.

Murud

☎ 021447

The main reason for visiting the sleepy fishing town of Murud, about 160km south of Mumbai, is to visit the commanding island fortress of **Janjira**, 5km south of the village.

The fortress was built in 1140 by Siddi Jahor and became the 16th-century capital of the Siddis of Janjira, descendants of sailor-traders from the Horn of Africa. Remarkably, its inhabitants were still living here until Independence in 1947, when they shifted up to the Murud Palace.

Although built on an island, its 12m-high walls appear to emerge straight from the sea. This made the fort impregnable to everyone, even the Marathas – Shivaji tried to conquer it by sea and his son, Sambhaji, even attempted to tunnel to it. The interior of the fort is overgrown and has fallen into disrepair, but you can walk along the outer walls, explore the 22 watch towers, battlements and rusting remains of cannons and get a feel for the romance of this island stronghold.

The only way to reach Janjira is by local boat (Rs 9.50, 10 minutes) from Rajpuri Port, about 5km south of Murud. Boats depart from 7 am to 6 pm daily, but require a minimum of 20 passengers. On weekends and holidays you won't have to wait long. To get to Rajpuri, either take an autorickshaw (Rs 30 each way) or hire a bicycle (Rs 3 an hour) from the small shop opposite the temple shrine in the middle of town.

Places to Stay & Eat There are quite a few places strung out along the beach road in Murud, but don't expect anything dirt cheap.

The Nest *(☎ 76144, Darbar Rd)*, on the beach road just north of the temple shrine, has basic bamboo huts set among the palm trees with easy access to the beach. They have private bathroom (bucket hot water) and cost Rs 350 for a double, though you should be able to get a reduction when it's quiet.

Golden Swan Beach Resort *(☎ 4078, ⓔ beachresort@goldenswan.com, Darbar Rd)* has a good location on the beachfront at Murud. Pleasant cottage-style double rooms with private bathroom cost Rs 750/950 on weekdays/weekends. There is also a decent restaurant here.

Getting There & Away The best way to get to Murud from Mumbai is to hop on one of the regular ferries from the Gateway of India (Colaba) to Mandwa on the mainland and take a bus from there. There are regular ferries (Rs 45, one hour) and faster catamarans (Rs 75 to 100, 45 minutes). The ticket includes a free shuttle bus to Alibag (30 minutes), from where you can pick up one of the regular local buses heading down the coast to Murud (Rs 26, two hours), via Chaul and Kashid.

Alternatively, buses from Mumbai Central take around five hours to Murud.

The nearest railhead on the Konkan Railway is Roha, which you can reach by bus (Rs 21, two hours).

Ganpatipule & Ratnagiri

Ganpatipule, on the coast 375km south of Mumbai, has several kilometres of almost pristine beach and good swimming. The attraction for thousands of Hindu pilgrims, however, is the **Swayambhu Ganpati** or 'naturally formed' monolithic Ganesh.

MTDC's ***Resort*** *(☎ 02357-35248, fax 35328)*, pleasantly ensconced among the palms on the beachfront, has the only decent accommodation at Ganpatipule. The cheapest option here is its ***Tent Resort*** *(☎ 02357-35348)* with two/four-bed tents at Rs 300/400, or a range of pricey double rooms from Rs 700 up to 2000 for the aircon 'sea view cottages'. Rates drop by 30% outside high season.

MTDC's ***Tarang Restaurant*** is the best place to eat, with a range of local fish specialities on the menu from Rs 50, including Bombay Duck and Malvani fish curry.

The Maharashtra Tourism Development Corporation (MTDC) has an overnight semideluxe bus direct from Mumbai to Ganpatipule departing at 8.30 pm from its office in Nariman Point (Rs 230). The bus returns from Ganpatipule at 7.30 pm.

Around 50km south of Ganpatipule, **Ratnagiri** is the largest town on the state's south coast and the main transport hub (it's on the Konkan rail line). It was the birthplace of freedom fighter Lokmanya Tilak (you can visit his home), and was where the British interned the last Burmese king, Thibaw, from 1886 until his death in 1916.

Hotel Kanchen *(☎ 02352-28250, P55 Mirjole Block)* is the closest hotel to the station (about 2km). Doubles with private bathroom are simple but clean for Rs 350 and there's a restaurant and swimming pool here.

The newly built Ratnagiri station is about 6km from the bus stand and all express trains stop here. From Ratnagiri's bus stand there are government buses to Kolhapur (Rs 58, four hours) and Goa (Rs 80, six hours). Buses to Ganpatipule depart hourly until about 6 pm (Rs 21, 1¾ hours).

MATHERAN

☎ 02148 • pop 6000 • elevation 803m

Matheran, which means jungle topped, is the nearest hill station to Mumbai and Maharashtra's most pleasant retreat. It's an undulating hilltop cloaked in shady trees and ringed by walking tracks leading to lookouts that drop sheer to the plains.

Hugh Malet, Collector for the Thane district, is credited with the 'discovery' of Matheran in 1850 while climbing the path known as Shivaji's Ladder, and it soon became a popular hill station during the days of the Raj.

Matheran owes its tranquillity to a complete ban on motor vehicles (and bicycles), but on weekends the town can be overrun by day-trippers and the pleasant trails are clogged with people.

Matheran's true high season is during the peak holiday periods of April-June, Diwali and Christmas when it's uncomfortably packed and accommodation prices are ludicrous. During the monsoon (mid-June to early-October) the village virtually closes up and the dirt walking trails and roads become very muddy.

Getting to Matheran is half the fun; from Neral Junction you take a narrow-gauge toy train up the 21km route to the heart of the hill station. It's a scenic two-hour ascent as the train winds its way around the steep slopes.

Information

Entry to Matheran costs Rs 20 (Rs 10 for children), which you pay on arrival at the train station or at the Dasturi car park. Beware of 'coolies' (porters) or touts trying to drag you into a particular hotel – they're mainly interested in the highest commission.

There's no tourist office, but some shops and hotels have a basic map of Matheran. The Union Bank of India on MG Rd, the main road through the bazaar, changes travellers cheques only.

Walks & Views

You can walk to most of Matheran's viewpoints in a matter of hours. The best views are seen in the early morning and about an hour before sunset. Louisa Point (Sunset View), Panorama Point, Porcupine Point and Little Chouk Point have the finest views. You can reach the valley below One Tree Hill down the path known as **Shivaji's Ladder**, so called because the Maratha leader is said to have used it.

Ponies can be hired for rides to lookout points for about Rs 100 an hour.

Places to Stay

There are a few budget places close to the train station, but most of the mid-range and expensive 'resort' accommodation is a 10- to 20-minute walk away. Early-morning check-out times are the norm in Matheran – they can be as early as 7 am. Unless otherwise stated, rates quoted here are outside high season (Christmas, Diwali etc). If you're mad enough to come then, expect to pay between 30% and 200% more.

Khan's Hotel *(☎ 30240, ⓔ khansparkview@india.com, MG Rd)*, a slightly rundown and officious place, has a tiny single with running water (but no bathroom as such) for Rs 120, and small doubles with private bathroom for Rs 200. There's a vegetarian and nonvegetarian restaurant here. Check-out is noon.

Hope Hall Hotel *(☎ 30253, MG Rd)* should be your first choice in this range. Run by a lovely Christian family, it's a rambling, welcoming lodge set in pleasant gardens. Large, clean singles/doubles with mosaic tiled floors cost Rs 190/250 and a room sleeping five is Rs 375. Rooms have private bathroom with bucket hot water.

Hanjar House *(☎ 30536, Usman Valge Rd)*, just north of the train station and on the same side, is a family-run place with spotless doubles with private bathroom and

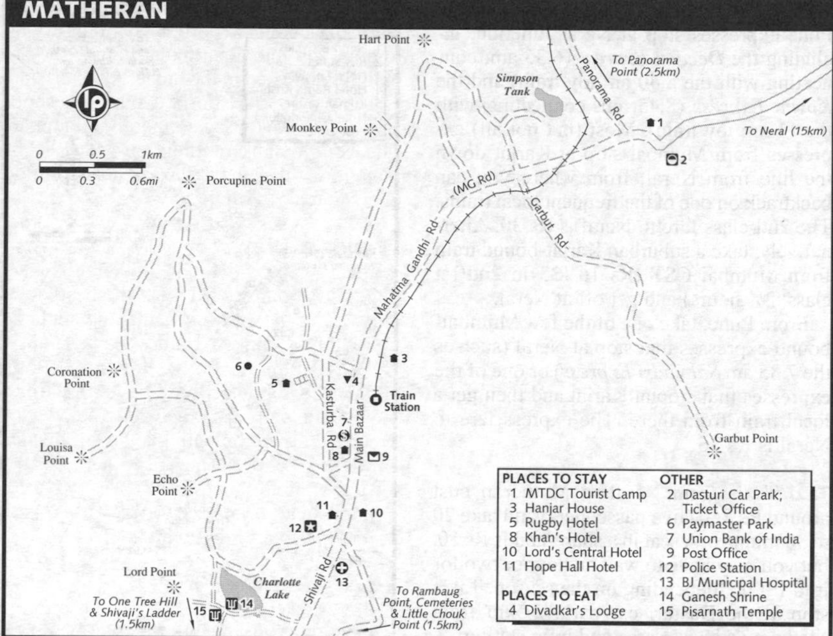

cable TV for Rs 300 (no singles) – rising to a crazy Rs 1200 in season.

MTDC Tourist Camp *(☎ 30277)*, next to the Dasturi car park 2.5km north-east of the train station is in a peaceful wooded location, but the cheapest rooms are not cheap enough at Rs 520 for a double with private bathroom and TV. It's convenient if you arrive in Matheran by car.

Lord's Central Hotel *(☎ 30228, fax 30595, e lord@wspl.net.in; ☎ 022-386 7776 in Mumbai)*, presided over by the genial Mr Lord, is easily the most charming place to stay in Matheran. Rates, including full board, are Rs 1700 in the regular rooms (Rs 1225 for single occupancy). Valley view rooms cost Rs 2200 (Rs 1650 for singles) and the suites are Rs 2800 (double only). There's a beautifully situated swimming pool, small library, bar and a dining room.

Places to Eat

Most of the resort hotels cater for their own guests, but there are numerous small eateries catering to day trippers in the bazaar. Lord's Central Hotel is well worth a visit. Nonguests can dine here any time for lunch or dinner, but on Saturday evening there's a sumptuous garden buffet (Rs 250) and midweek there's a poolside barbecue. ***Divadkar's Lodge*** has a reasonable restaurant and a bar.

Matheran is famed for its locally produced honey and for *chikki*, a rock-hard toffee-like confection made of *gur* (unrefined sugar made from cane juice) and nuts which is sold at many 'chikki marts' and shops on MG Rd.

Getting There & Away

Train The toy train departs from Neral Junction train station at 8.40 and 11 am and 5 pm; in the opposite direction it leaves Matheran at 5.45 am and 1.10 and 2.35 pm. In April and May there's one extra service from both points (departing Neral at 10.20 am and Matheran at 4.10 pm). During the monsoon there is only one train per day – it departs Neral at 8.40 am and Matheran at 1.10 pm. The fares are Rs 24/190 in 2nd/1st class. The toy train can be booked in advance from Mumbai or Pune, which is a good idea in the high season. Reservations are accepted up to three days in advance at Neral or Matheran, but tickets for same-day departure only go on sale 45 minutes beforehand.

From Mumbai CST, only a few of the Pune expresses stop at Neral Junction, including the *Deccan Express* (6.35 am, connecting with the 8.40 am toy train) and the *Koyna Express* (8.45 am, connecting with the 11 am toy train). Most (but not all) expresses from Mumbai stop at Karjat down the line from Neral, from where you can backtrack on one of the frequent local trains. The 2nd-class fare to Neral is Rs 30. Alternatively, take a suburban Karjat-bound train from Mumbai CST (Rs 16/133 in 2nd/1st class, 2½ hours) and get off at Neral.

From Pune, take one of the few Mumbai-bound expresses that stop at Neral (such as the 7.35 am *Sahyadri Express*) or one of the expresses that stop at Karjat and then get a local train from there. The express fare to Neral is Rs 36.

Taxi Taxis from Neral to Matheran cost around Rs 250 (five passengers) and take 20 to 30 minutes. A seat in a share-taxi is Rs 50, but you may have to wait an hour or two for it to fill up, depending on the season. Taxis stop at the Dasturi car park, 2.5km from Matheran's bazaar area and train station.

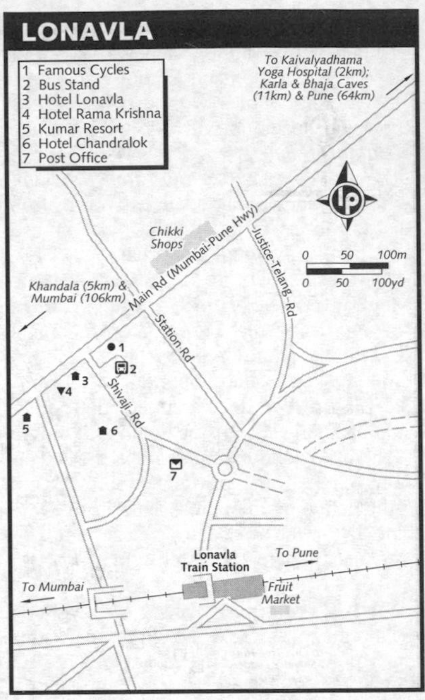

Getting Around

Matheran is one of the few places left in India where you'll find hand-pulled rickshaws; along with horses and your own feet, they're the only transport options here. From the Dasturi car park, it's a 30-minute walk to the centre (porters are available), or you can hire a horse (Rs 80). Walking is quicker and less embarrassing than being pulled along in a rickshaw (Rs 120).

LONAVLA

☎ 02114 • pop 60,000

Situated 106km south-east of Mumbai in the hills on the main railway line to Pune, Lonavla and nearby Khandala are twin hill resorts catering to weekenders and conference groups from Mumbai. Unless you're particularly fond of chikki, there is little of interest in the towns themselves, but Lonavla is the most convenient base from which to visit the Karla and Bhaja caves.

Hotels, restaurants and the main road to the caves are north of the train station (exit from platform one), but most of Lonavla town, including the busy market, is south of the station.

Change money at Mumbai or Pune as none of the banks here make a habit of foreign exchange. Internet access is available at the Kumar Resort (Rs 60 an hour).

Bicycles can be hired from Famous Cycles, on the main road, for Rs 5 an hour.

Kaivalyadhama Yoga Hospital

About 2km from Lonavla on the road to the Karla and Bhaja caves, this ashram is popular with Indians seeking yogic healing. It was founded in 1924 by Swami Kuvalayanandji and combines yoga courses with a research centre and a training college. The minimum course is eight days and the all-inclusive cost is US$10/15 per day in a single room with shared/private bathroom or US$16/20 in a double. Indians pay a little less. Bookings are advised (☎ 73039, fax 71983).

Places to Stay & Eat

Hotel Chandralok *(☎ 72921,* ⓔ *hotelchandralok@vsnl.com)* is a clean, friendly place in a handy location. Singles/doubles with private bathroom, constant hot water and TV cost 390/490; air-con doubles are Rs 600/790. Checkout is 10 am.

Hotel Lonavla *(☎ 72914)* faces the Mumbai-Pune highway, but it's a new place so it's in spritely condition and is good value at Rs 595/895 for doubles without/with air-con. Rooms are spacious, with TV and hot water.

Kumar Resort *(☎ 73091, ⓔ kumar_resort@vsnl.com; ☎ 022-604 5669 in Mumbai)* has a range of large, air-con rooms from Rs 1850 to 2750, plus an in-house amusement park, wave pool and a bar.

The best places to eat are at the hotel restaurants. The ***Hotel Rama Krishna*** *(☎ 73600)* and the ***Kumar Resort***, on the old Mumbai-Pune highway have excellent (though a little pricey) open-air restaurants. The ***Chandralok*** does a superb bottomless Gujarati thali (Rs 70) for lunch and dinner.

There's a good ***fruit market*** in the bazaar, south of the train station. At the other end of the dental appreciation scale, Lonavla is famous for the rock-hard sweet, chikki – every second shop is a chikki mart.

Getting There & Away

At the time of writing, the expressway linking Mumbai and Pune was open between Lonavla and Pune, and the remainder was expected to be completed in 2001. Until then, rugged MSRTC (Maharashtra State Road Transport Corporation) buses take up to four hours to get to Mumbai – the train, although crowded, is better. There are frequent local buses to Pune (Rs 28) and more comfortable Asiad buses (Rs 45). Buses using the expressway should take only one hour.

All express trains from Mumbai to Pune stop at Lonavla. The three-hour trip to Mumbai costs Rs 39/61 in 2nd/sleeper. To Pune (64km) there are express trains (Rs 26/41, one hour) and hourly shuttle trains (Rs 12, two hours).

KARLA & BHAJA CAVES

Dating from around the 2nd century BC, the rock-cut caves in the hills near Lonavla are among the oldest and finest examples of Early Buddhist rock temple art in India.

It's possible to visit the caves in a day trip from either Mumbai or Pune if you hire an autorickshaw from Lonavla for the day. Visiting both caves will cost US$10 in admission alone; if you only want to visit one site, Karla has the most impressive single cave, but Bhaja is a more enjoyable site to explore.

Karla Cave

A steep 20-minute climb via stone steps from the car park brings you to the impressive Karla cave, the largest Early Buddhist *chaitya* (shrine) in India. Completed in 80 BC, the chaitya is around 40m long and 15m high, carved by monks and artisans from the rock in imitation of more familiar wooden architecture.

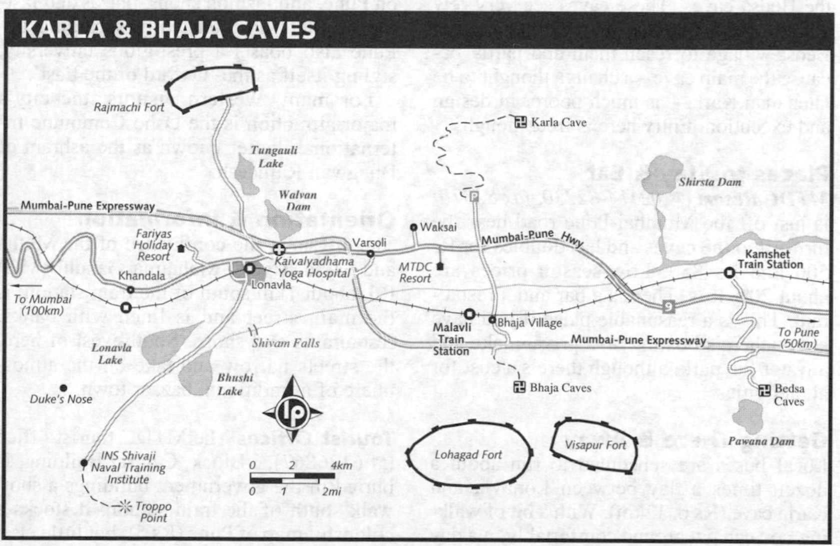

A semicircular 'sun window' filters light in towards the cave's representation of Buddha – a *dagoba*, or stupa, protected by a carved wooden umbrella. The 37 pillars which form the aisles are each topped by kneeling elephants. The roof of the cave is ribbed with teak beams said to be original. On the sides of the vestibule are carved elephant heads, which once had ivory tusks.

The cave is open from 9 am to 5 pm. Entry is as steep as the walk up at US$5 (Rs 230) for foreigners; Indians pay Rs 5, and there's a Rs 25 charge for video cameras.

Bhaja Caves

It's a 3km walk or ride from the main road to the Bhaja caves (crossing over the new expressway), where the setting is lusher, greener, and more peaceful than Karla cave. Thought to date from around 200 BC, 10 of the 18 caves here are *viharas* (monasteries), while Cave 12 is an open chaitya, earlier than Karla, containing a simple dagoba, but no sculpture. Beyond this is a strange huddle of 14 stupas, five inside and nine outside a cave.

Admission here is another US$5 (Rs 230) for foreigners (Rs 5 for Indians).

Bedsa Caves

About 15km past the Karla/Bhaja turn-offs, and 6km south-east of Kamshet station, are the Bedsa caves. These caves see very few visitors, partly because of the 3km walk from Bedsa village to reach them and partly because the main cave – a chaitya thought to be later than Karla – is much poorer in design and execution. Entry here is free, though.

Places to Stay & Eat

MTDC Resort *(☎ 02114-82230, fax 82370)* is just off the Mumbai-Pune road near the turn-off to the caves and has doubles for Rs 500 and Rs 850. Low-season prices are about 20% less. There's a bar and a restaurant. This is a reasonable place if you have kids – there's boating on a private lake and a water fun park, although there's a cost for all activities.

Getting There & Away

Local buses are scheduled to run about a dozen times a day between Lonavla and Karla cave (Rs 6, 12km). With a bit of walking you can get around comfortably in a day by public transport. First, catch the 8 or 9 am bus from Lonavla to Karla cave, walk to Bhaja (1½ hours, 5km), then walk back to Malavli station (one hour, 3km) and catch a local train back to Lonavla. You can cut out the long walk by taking an autorickshaw from Karla to Bhaja for around Rs 60.

Autorickshaws are plentiful and the price usually includes waiting time at the sites (about three hours all up). A return trip from Lonavla to the Karla and Bhaja caves will cost around Rs 250 to 300 depending on the season, a little more if you include Bedsa.

PUNE

☎ 020 • pop 2.8 million

Shivaji, the great Maratha leader, was raised in Pune, which was granted to his grandfather in 1599. Later it became the seat of power for the Brahmin Peshwa family until 1817 when it fell to the British and became their alternative capital during the monsoon.

Pune (pronounced and often spelt 'Poona') has a more pleasant climate than muggy Mumbai, and is a growing centre for industry and software production. Many people who can't afford the sky-high prices of accommodation in Mumbai commute daily between the two cities and that fashion will only increase with the opening of the new six-lane Mumbai-Pune expressway. As a result, the big-city influence has rubbed off on Pune, and fashion shops, plazas and fast-food outlets are constantly springing up. Pune also boasts a prestigious university, styling itself as the 'Oxford of the East'.

For many Western visitors, the city's major attraction is the Osho Commune International, better known as the ashram of Bhagwan Rajneesh.

Orientation & Information

The city is at the confluence of the Mutha and Mula Rivers. Mahatma Gandhi (MG) Rd, about 1km south of the train station, is the main street and is lined with banks, restaurants and shops. South-west of here, the streets narrow and take on the atmosphere of a traditional bazaar town.

Tourist Offices The MTDC tourist office (☎ 6126867), I Block, Central Building, is buried in the government buildings a short walk south of the train station. It stocks a colourful map of Pune (Rs 5), but little else.

Money American Express (☎ 6055337), next to Aurora Towers on MG Rd, and Thomas Cook (☎ 648188), 13 Thacker House, 2418 G Thimmaya Rd (between East St and MG Rd) open from 10 am to 5 pm Monday to Saturday for foreign exchange.

Citibank has 24-hour ATMs accepting foreign cards at two locations: The main branch is on East St just south of Thousand Oaks pub, and there's another ATM on Bund Garden Rd, handy for Koregaon Park. The Central Bank on MG Rd gives credit card cash advances (Rs 100 commission).

Post & Communications The main post office on Sadhu Vaswani (Connaught Rd) is open 10 am to 6 pm Monday to Saturday, but the parcel office closes at 4 pm. Post restante is at the inquiry counter (No 8).

Internet cafes are scattered around the city, including several on MG Rd and in Koregaon Park. They generally charge between Rs 20 and Rs 30 an hour. NetXs (☎ 4004013), in the west wing of the Aurora Towers building, is a modern place open 24 hours and charging only Rs 15 an hour. Cybersite, shop 43, on the ground floor of the Ashok Vijay Complex, 326 MG Rd, is also good.

Travel Agencies One of the best travel agents in town for flights and tours is Sunder Travel Shoppe (☎ 6131848, fax 613 1534), Sunder Plaza, 19 MG Rd.

Bookshops The best bookshop is Manneys Booksellers (☎ 6131683), Clover Centre, 7 Moledina Rd, open 9.30 am to 1.30 pm and 4 to 8 pm Monday to Saturday (credit cards accepted). Also good is the Modern Bookshop (☎ 633597), Radiant Plaza, just off MG Rd.

Osho Commune International

The Bhagwan Rajneesh's famous ashram (☎ 6136655, fax 6139955, ⓔ commune@osho.com, 17 Koregaon Park) is in a leafy northern suburb of Pune. Styling itself as a 'spiritual health club', it has continued to prosper since the Bhagwan's death in 1990 and attracts thousands of visitors each year,

Osho, the Bhagwan

Bhagwan Shree Rajneesh (1931–90), or Osho as he preferred to be called, was one of India's most popular and flamboyant 'export gurus' and without doubt the most controversial. He followed no particular religion, tradition or philosophy and his often acerbic criticism and dismissal of various religious and political leaders made him many enemies the world over. What particularly outraged his Indian critics was his advocacy of sex as a path to enlightenment, an approach which earned him the epithet 'sex guru' from the Indian press.

Rajneesh used a curious blend of Californian pop psychology and Indian mysticism to motivate his followers. His last technique, tagged the Mystic Rose, involved following a regime of laughing for three hours a day for one week, crying for three hours a day the next week, followed by becoming a 'watcher on the hill' (ie, sitting) for three hours a day for another week. The Bhagwan felt that it was 'the most important breakthrough in meditation since Buddha's *vipassana*, created 25 centuries ago'.

In 1981, Rajneesh went to the USA and set up the agricultural commune and ashram of Rajneeshpuram in Oregon. It was here that he drew the attention of the international media, and the ashram's notoriety (along with its highly publicised fleet of Rolls Royces) grew and grew. Eventually, with rumours and local paranoia about the ashram's activities running wild, the Bhagwan was charged with immigration fraud, fined US$400,000 and deported to India in November 1985.

In January 1987, Rajneesh took up residence again at the Pune ashram, and soon thousands of foreigners were flocking to attend his nightly discourses and meditation courses. From early 1989 until his death, Rajneesh reverted to silence as he had done so once in America.

Before his death, the orange clothes and the *mala* (the string of beads and photograph of the Bhagwan worn around the neck), which used to be the distinctive mark of Bhagwan followers, had been discarded. This was done so that his followers could (according to the ashram press office) 'avoid harassment and molestation by the authorities'. These days followers are required to wear maroon while inside the ashram, in order to keep the spiritual energy at an even level (apparently).

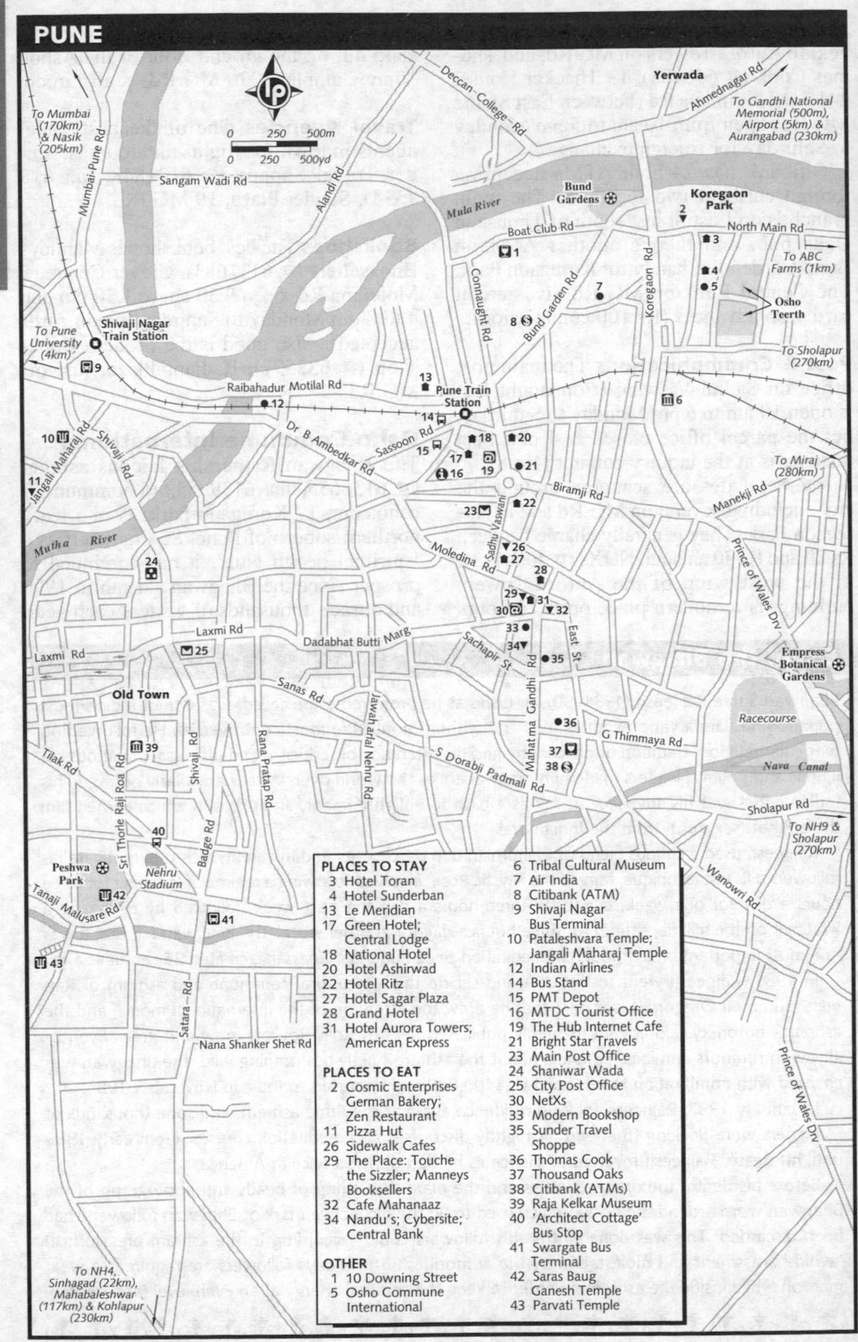

PLACES TO STAY
- 3 Hotel Toran
- 4 Hotel Sunderban
- 13 Le Meridian
- 17 Green Hotel; Central Lodge
- 18 National Hotel
- 20 Hotel Ashirwad
- 22 Hotel Ritz
- 27 Hotel Sagar Plaza
- 28 Grand Hotel
- 31 Hotel Aurora Towers; American Express

PLACES TO EAT
- 2 Cosmic Enterprises German Bakery; Zen Restaurant
- 11 Pizza Hut
- 26 Sidewalk Cafes
- 29 The Place: Touche the Sizzler; Manneys Booksellers
- 32 Cafe Mahanaaz
- 34 Nandu's; Cybersite; Central Bank

OTHER
- 1 10 Downing Street
- 5 Osho Commune International
- 6 Tribal Cultural Museum
- 7 Air India
- 8 Citibank (ATM)
- 9 Shivaji Nagar Bus Terminal
- 10 Pataleshvara Temple; Jangali Maharaj Temple
- 12 Indian Airlines
- 14 Bus Stand
- 15 PMT Depot
- 16 MTDC Tourist Office
- 19 The Hub Internet Cafe
- 21 Bright Star Travels
- 23 Main Post Office
- 24 Shaniwar Wada
- 25 City Post Office
- 30 NetXs
- 33 Modern Bookshop
- 35 Sunder Travel Shoppe
- 36 Thomas Cook
- 37 Thousand Oaks
- 38 Citibank (ATMs)
- 39 Raja Kelkar Museum
- 40 'Architect Cottage' Bus Stop
- 41 Swargate Bus Terminal
- 42 Saras Baug Ganesh Temple
- 43 Parvati Temple

many of them Westerners. Facilities include a swimming pool, sauna, tennis and basketball courts, massage and beauty parlour, bistro and bookshop. The main centres for meditation or spiritual dance are the Gautama Buddha Auditorium (where the 'White Robe Brotherhood' gathers every evening) and the Osho Samadhi, where the guru's ashes are kept. A tranquil five-hectare Zen garden, known as **Osho Teerth**, is behind the ashram and is open to the public from 6 to 9 am and 3 to 6 pm daily.

The commune is big business – its 'Multiversity' runs a plethora of (expensive) courses in traditional meditation as well as New Age techniques, all with computerised booking facilities. Those wishing to meditate at the commune must fill out an application form (complete with two passport photographs, and your passport), prove HIV-negative to an on-the-spot test given at the centre (Rs 125; make sure a sterile package needle is used) and purchase three tunics (two maroon and one white). Meditation is then Rs 130 per day (Rs 40 for Indians) and you can come and go as you please. You must arrange your own accommodation outside the ashram.

Casual visitors can watch a video presentation at the visitor centre and, if they wish, take a brief tour of the facilities (Rs 10) between 10 and 11 am and 2 and 3 pm daily. Even if you do not decide to enter the ashram, it is worth having a look inside and mingling briefly with the maroon-clad soul-searchers – though there are just as many wandering around Koregaon Park outside the ashram.

Raja Kelkar Museum

This fascinating museum is one of Pune's real delights. The exhibits are the personal collection of Sri Dinkar Gangadhar (AKA Kaka Kelkar) who died in 1990. Among the 17,000 or so artworks and curios he collected over 70 years are Peshwa and other miniatures, a bizarre collection of musical instruments, carved doors and windows, hookah pipes, oil lamps and a superb collection of betel-nut cutters, adorned brass foot scrubbers, carved wooden noodle makers and hair-drying combs.

The museum is open from 8.30 am to 6 pm daily (Rs 40/120 children/adults, Rs 10 for Indians).

Shaniwar Wada

The ruins of this fortress-like palace stand in the old part of the city. Built in 1736, the palace of the Peshwa rulers burnt down in 1828, but the massive walls remain. Today there's an unkempt two-hectare garden inside and not a lot to see, which makes the US$5 entry fee a little galling. The sturdy palace doors are studded with spikes designed to dissuade enemies from leaning too heavily against the entrance with their elephants, and in a nearby street the Peshwa rulers executed offenders by having elephants trample them. The palace is open from 8 am to 6 pm daily; entry for foreigners is US$5 (Rs 230), Rs 5 for Indians.

Pataleshvara Temple

Just across the river on Jangali Maharaj Rd is the wonderful rock-cut Pataleshvara Temple (aka Panchalesvara cave), a small 8th-century temple similar in style to the much grander rock temple at Elephanta, but never completed. It's an active temple with many people coming here for worship or simply to relax in the gardens. In front of the excavation is a circular Nandi *mandapam* (pavilion). Adjacent is the **Jangali Maharaj** (Lord of the Jungle) temple, dedicated to a Hindu ascetic who died here in 1818.

Tribal Cultural Museum

About 1.5km east of the Pune train station at 28 Queens Gardens, this excellent museum documents the cultures of Maharashtran Adivasi communities, particularly those from the Sahyadri and Gondwana regions. It's open from 10.30 am to 5.30 pm daily (free).

Gandhi National Memorial

Across the river in Yerwada is this fine memorial set in 6.5 hectares of gardens. Built by Imamsultan Muhammad Sha Aga Khan III in 1892, it was the Aga Khan's palace until 1956 after which it became a school. In 1969 it was donated to India by the Aga Khan IV.

After Mahatma Gandhi delivered his momentous Quit India resolution in Bombay in 1942, the British interned him and other leaders of India's independence movement here for nearly two years. Both Kasturba Gandhi, the Mahatma's wife, and Mahadoebhai Desai, his secretary for 35 years, died here during this period of imprisonment. Their ashes are kept in memorial *samadhis* (tombs) in the gardens.

A photographic exhibition details some of the highlights of Gandhi's long career, but it is the simple personal effects (including a pair of sandals and a thermos) and the personal tragedies of the Mahatma during this period that leave the deepest impression. The memorial is open from 9 am to 5.45 pm daily (Rs 5).

Gardens

The **Empress Botanical Gardens** have fine tropical trees and a there's a small zoo nearby. The moated Saras Baug Ganesh Temple is in **Peshwa Park** (open 9.30 am to 5.30 pm; Rs 2) and there are dozens of food stalls set up outside in the evening.

Organised Tours

All-day city bus tours of Pune leave the Pune Municipal Transport (PMT) depot near the train station at 9 am daily (Rs 100). They cover all the main sights and are reasonable value if you're in a hurry. Book at the PMT office or inquire at the tourist office.

Special Events

While **Ganesh Chaturthi** is celebrated all over India, the festival is most extravagant at Mumbai and Pune. Traditionally a household affair, it was made a public celebration a century ago when the freedom fighter Lokmanya Tilak used it to unite the masses for the freedom struggle. Ganesh is, after all, the remover of obstacles.

At the end of the 11-day festival in August or September, plaster and clay images of Ganesh, some of them 6m high, are taken from homes and street *mandals* (shrines) and carried in huge processions to be immersed in the river.

The procession of Ganesh is the climax of the very popular **Pune Festival**, which features classical dance and music concerts, folk dance and a village festival including bullock cart races and wrestling. The opening ceremony presents some of the country's best musicians and dancers. The festival will be held from 22 August to 1 September in 2001, and from 10–20 September in 2002.

In August the **Matharaj Naag Panchami**, a snake worshipping festival, is held here and in Kolhapur.

Places to Stay

There are plenty of hotels in Pune, but it's difficult to find a decent cheap place. If you're planning on staying a while to hang out at the Osho Commune, ask around at the cafes and 'robe stalls' near the ashram – rooms in homes or apartments are usually available for rent on a monthly basis from around Rs 5000.

Places to Stay – Budget

There's a cluster of cheap hotels opposite the train station in an area known as Wilson Garden. Some (if not most) are dives, but there are some acceptable choices.

The ***National Hotel*** *(☎ 6125054, 14 Sassoon Rd)*, opposite the train station, is a good choice. Bahai-run, it is a ramshackle old colonial mansion with verandas and high ceilings set in a pleasant garden. Most of the rooms were about to be renovated at the time of writing. Doubles with private bathroom cost around Rs 450, triples Rs 550, and small cottages (stables in a previous life) with private bathroom and a little porch cost Rs 400.

Green Hotel *(☎ 6125229, 16 Wilson Gardens)* is a Georgian building with a touch of character, but forlorn and grubby rooms. Singles with shared bathroom are Rs 200, and doubles/triples with private bathroom are Rs 250/350. There's hot water in the morning and checkout is 5 pm.

Central Lodge *(☎ 6121313, 13 Wilson Gardens)* is not very welcoming, but it is a cheap option; doubles/triples with shared bathroom cost Rs 140/180, dorm beds are Rs 60.

Grand Hotel *(☎ 6360728, MG Rd)* is a crumbling old place in private grounds on MG Rd. Single 'cabins' (beds separated by partition walls) cost Rs 100 with shared bathroom. Bare double rooms looking like they might have once been colonial servants' quarters cost Rs 320. They have private bathroom (bucket hot water). The hotel has its own beer bar, patio and restaurant and is a friendly, relaxing place suited to backpackers.

Hotel Toran *(☎ 613 7171, 23 North Main Road)* is a good budget choice near the Osho Commune. Even if you're not visiting the ashram, Koregaon Park is a pleasant area to stay. Singles/doubles with shared bathroom cost Rs 150/250 and there's a variety of rooms with private bathroom from Rs 300/400.

Places to Stay – Mid-Range

Add between 5% and 20% tax to prices quoted for the mid-range and top-end hotels.

Hotel Ritz *(☎ 6122955, fax 6136191, 6 Sadhu Vaswani Path)*, opposite the post office, is the best value in this range. It's a renovated heritage hotel with more character than most. Comfortable singles/doubles with TV and hot shower cost Rs 950/1100 or Rs 1199/1550 with air-con (plus 14% tax). Ask for a first floor room with balcony (at the front). There's a pleasant garden restaurant and a speciality restaurant serving excellent Gujarati thalis. Credit cards are accepted.

The ***Hotel Ashirwad*** *(☎ 6128585, fax 6126121, 16 Connaught Rd)* is close to the station. Clean rooms with balcony and TV cost Rs 850/1000 or Rs 1100/1400 with air-con. Attached is a decent vegetarian restaurant.

Hotel Sunderban *(☎ 6124949, fax 612 3535, 19 Koregaon Park)*, next to the ashram, is a reasonably well-kept heritage property with a large garden. There's a wide variety of old-fashioned rooms available from Rs 600 (shared bathroom) and Rs 975 (private bathroom), up to huge, but hugely overpriced, deluxe rooms from Rs 2100. There are 25% discounts between May and October.

Places to Stay – Top End

Hotel Sagar Plaza *(☎ 622622, fax 622633, ⓔ sparkplaza@wmi.co.in, 1 Bund Garden Rd)*, off Moledina Rd, has well-appointed air-con rooms from Rs 2700/3100 including a buffet breakfast. There's a bar, coffee shop, restaurant, small swimming pool and bookshop.

Hotel Aurora Towers *(☎ 631818, fax 631826, ⓔ hotelaurora@usa.net, 9 Moledina Rd)*, at the junction of MG Rd, has air-con economy singles/doubles for Rs 1850/2350; suites start at Rs 3500. Facilities include a shopping arcade, rooftop swimming pool with city views, a bar, two restaurants and a 24-hour coffee shop.

Le Meridien *(☎ 6050505, fax 6050506, ⓔ meridien@pn2.vsnl.net.in, RMB Rd)*, behind the train station, is a sumptuous new hotel designed in Mughal and Rajput styles with a cavernous interior. The rooms are compact, but comfortable. Standard rooms are US$150.

Places to Eat

Cafe Mahanaaz, opposite Aurora Towers on MG Rd, is a busy, no-nonsense cafe and bakery. It's a great place for breakfast (if you've forgotten what real toast tastes like, this is the place) and there's nothing over Rs 17 on the menu.

The ***sidewalk cafes*** lined up along Lothion Rd just south of the post office are the best place to head in the evening for a cheap meal. They offer a variety of food including Indian and Chinese, and fresh fruit juices. Touts wave menus and beckon you to sit as you walk past. ***Nandu's***, down an alley just off MG Rd, is well known locally for making the best *parathas* (bread) and Punjabi vegetarian dishes around.

For Western fast food you'll find ***McDonald's*** and ***Pizza Hut*** on Jangali Maharaj Rd.

The Place: Touche the Sizzler *(☎ 613 4632, 7 Moledina Rd)* is a popular two-tier air-con restaurant specialising in sizzlers from Rs 125, but it also offers cheaper Indian, tandoori, seafood and continental dishes. The home-made ice creams (Rs 40 to 65) are something special. It's open for lunch and dinner.

Cosmic Enterprises German Bakery in Koregaon Park churns out great muesli, coffee, cakes and lassis. It's so busy that there's a sign up asking 'please do not sit for a long time'.

Zen Restaurant is right behind and is a good place for dinner. There's always an interesting international crowd of Osho *sanyasins* (seekers) at these places.

About 2km east along North Main Rd is ***ABC Farms*** *(☎ 676555)*, a cheese-producing dairy farm which houses five very different restaurants: Thai, Swiss, Japanese, Hyderabadi and Italian/Mexican. It's upmarket dining, but an interesting place to go for dinner.

Entertainment

Pune has a handful of lively pubs and clubs. ***Thousand Oaks*** *(☎ 6343194, 2417 East St)* is a cosy pub-style bar with Western DJ music and a pleasant outdoor terrace area. It's open from noon to 3 pm and 7 pm to midnight daily, but on Saturday night only couples are admitted into the bar (others are relegated to the terrace).

10 Downing Street *(☎ 6128343, 2nd floor, Gera Plaza, Boat Club Rd)*, not far from Koregaon Park, is another pub with a lively upstairs nightclub (Rs 200 entry per couple) on Friday and Saturday nights.

Jazz Garden (☎ *6817412, North Main Rd*), at ABC Farms, has jazz nights and other live music, along with an open-air restaurant and bar. It's open from 7 to 11.30 pm.

Getting There & Away

Air Airline offices in Pune include:

Air India (☎ 6216990) 4 Hermeskunj Mangaldas Rd
Indian Airlines (☎ 140 or 141) 39 Dr B Ambedkar Rd
Jet Airways (☎ 6127524) 243 Century Arcade, Naurangi Baug Rd

Indian Airlines flies daily to Delhi (US$205) and four times a week to Bangalore (US$145). Jet Airways has two to three flights daily to Mumbai (US$85), and daily flights to Bangalore (US$145) and Delhi (US$205).

Bus Pune has three bus terminals: Pune train station terminal for Mumbai and points south – including Goa, Belgaum, Kolhapur and Mahabaleshwar; Shivaji Nagar terminal for points north and north-east – Ahmednagar, Aurangabad, Lonavla and Nasik; and Swargate terminal – for Sinhagad, Bangalore and Mangalore. Deluxe buses shuttle from the train station bus stand to Dadar (Mumbai) every 15 minutes (Rs 110).

The MSRTC buses are pretty rough and in some cases are only marginally cheaper than the private buses; for Mumbai (and points along the way) and Kolhapur the train is a better option. There are plenty of private deluxe buses to most centres including Goa (Rs 250, sleeper Rs 300, 12 hours), Nasik (Rs 120, five hours) and Aurangabad (Rs 120, six hours). Most agencies are sound, but beware of being dumped on a regular MSRTC bus, and make sure you know where the bus will drop you off (going to Mumbai, for instance, some private buses get no farther than Borivali). Try Bright Star Travels (☎ 6139666) on Connaught Rd; their buses depart from the service station near the roundabout.

Train Pune is an important rail hub with connections to many parts of the state. The computerised booking hall is in the building to the left of the station as you face the entrance.

The *Deccan Queen*, *Sinhagad* and *Pragati Express* are fast commuter trains to Mumbai, taking three to four hours.

For Matheran, the only express train stopping at Neral is the *Sahyadri Express*, which leaves at 7.35 am. See the Matheran section, earlier in this chapter, for further details.

Taxi Long-distance share-taxis (four passengers) connect Pune with Dadar in Mumbai around the clock. They leave from the taxi stand in front of Pune train station (Rs 220 per seat, four hours). A similar service operates from Shivaji Nagar train station to Nasik (Rs 220) and Aurangabad (Rs 240).

Getting Around

The airport is 8km north-east of the city (autorickshaws there cost Rs 60, taxis Rs 150).

City buses gather at the Pune Municipal Transport (PMT) depot across from Pune train station, but they are slow going. Useful buses include No 4 to Swargate, No 5 to Shivaji Nagar bus terminal, and No 159 to Koregaon Park and the Aga Khan Palace.

Trains from Pune

destination	train No & name	departures	distance (km)	approx duration (hrs)	fare (Rs)
Bangalore	6529 *Udyan Exp*	noon	1019	20½	284/1318
Chennai	6011 *Chennai Exp*	6.15 pm	1088	22½	290/1347
Delhi	1077 *Jhelum Exp*	5.35 pm	1595	27¾	346/1615
Hyderabad	7031 *Hyderabad Exp*	4.50 pm	600	13½	194/900
Mumbai CST	2124 *Deccan Queen*	7.15 am	191	3½	83/170
	2028 *Shatabdi Exp*	5.35 pm	191	3¼	365/720

Fares are for sleeper/2-tier air-con, except for *Deccan Queen* (2nd/chair car) and *Shatabdi Express* (air-con chair/executive)

Autorickshaws are everywhere and the best option for most trips around town – generally drivers are pretty good about using their meters and conversion cards. Official rates are Rs 6 for the first kilometre and Rs 4 per kilometre after that (or around five times the rate shown on the out-of-date meters). If you're going to be around for a few days, you can pick up a conversion card from some shops and newsstands (Rs 5). After dark you'll almost certainly have to negotiate a fare.

A ride from the train station to Koregaon Park costs around Rs 15.

AROUND PUNE

Sinhagad

Sinhagad, the Lion Fort, is 24km south-west of Pune and makes an excellent day trip. The nearly ruined fort stands on top of a steep hill, where there are also a number of old bungalows; including one where Gandhi met with the freedom fighter Tilak in 1915.

In 1670 Shivaji's general, Tanaji Malusre, led a force who scaled the steep hillside in the dark and defeated the unprepared forces of Bijapur. Legends about this dramatic attack relate that the Maratha forces used trained lizards to carry ropes up the hillside!

A road winds up to the fort, but if you come by local bus it's a sweaty 1½- to two-hour walk to the top. Bring water and food with you. The Pune city bus No 50 runs frequently to Sinhagad Village (from where you must walk) from 5.25 am until evening. It leaves either from Swargate or from the 'Architect College' bus stop opposite Nehru Stadium (Rs 12.50, 45 minutes).

MAHABALESHWAR

☎ 02168 • pop 12,000 • elevation 1372m

The terraced hills of Maharashtra's most popular hill station are a welcome escape from the noise and fumes of Mumbai and Pune. Mahabaleshwar has pleasant walks and panoramic lookouts, and the area has strong historical connections with Shivaji. Founded in 1828 by Sir John 'Boy' Malcolm, it was the summer capital of the Bombay presidency during the days of the Raj.

Like most hill stations, Mahabaleshwar virtually closes up for the monsoon (late June to mid-September) when an unbelievable 6m of rain falls. Local buildings are clad with *kulum* grass to prevent damage from the torrential downpour. Mahabaleshwar is hopelessly crowded during the peak periods of summer school holidays (April to June), Christmas and Diwali, and is best avoided then.

Orientation & Information

Most of the action is in the main bazaar (Main Rd, also called Dr Sabane Rd) – a 200m strip of ice cream and chikki parlours, video games, flashing lights and tacky stalls, with the bus stand at the western end. A Rs 5 entry fee is payable on arrival.

The small tourist kiosk (☎ 60271) near the bus stand hands out a poor map and is generally not very helpful.

The Bank of Maharashtra, in the main bazaar, changes cash and travellers cheques. There's Internet access (Rs 60 an hour) at Vedant (☎ 60237) in the bazaar.

Things to See & Do

Some faded traces of the Raj persist in Mahabaleshwar in the many preserved and dilapidated buildings and the various 19th-century lodges and colonial homes dotted around the town. **Mount Malcolm**, built as government house and residence of 'Boy' Malcolm in 1829, was once a magnificent country residence, but it's now derelict, overgrown and a little spooky. You can visit it on the way up to **Wilson's Point**, a reasonable lookout within easy walking distance of the town. Also worth a detour is **Morarji Castle**, where Mahatma Gandhi lived during 1945.

Elphinstone, Babington, Bombay and Kate's points offer fine **views** from the wooded plateau to the plains below. The best viewpoint is **Arthur's Seat**, 12km from Mahabaleshwar, which looks out over a sheer drop of 600m to the Konkan coastal strip. There are pleasant **waterfalls** around Mahabaleshwar, such as Chinaman's, Dhobi's and Lingmala falls, and boating on **Venna Lake**.

In the village of **Old Mahabaleshwar** there are two ancient temples worth visiting. The Krishnabai, or Panchganga Mandir, is said to contain the springs of five rivers, including the sacred Krishna River which issues from the mouth of a sculpted cow suckling a calf. The Mahabaleshwar Mandir is of interest for its naturally occurring lingam.

Organised Tours

In the peak season, the MTDC organises separate tours of Mahabaleshwar, Pratapgad Fort and Panchgani, the smaller hill station above Mahabaleshwar, each costing Rs 70 per person. These can be booked at the tourist kiosk. At other times taxi drivers will fall over themselves to get you on their 14-point tour of Mahabaleshwar's sights for a fixed Rs 280. This amounts to a ride out to Arthur's Seat and back with a stop at Old Mahabaleshwar along the way. There's also a tour of the lookout points south of town (Rs 280) and one to Panchgani (Rs 300).

Places to Stay

Accommodation prices are all about supply and demand in Mahabaleshwar – prices rocket phenomenally during the well-defined high season of Christmas, Diwali and April to June (school holidays). Outside these times some of the budget and mid-range lodges are good value. Most of the budget places are around the main bazaar near the bus stand, and in the two roads running parallel to it, but there are dozens of resort-style lodges (most offering full board) scattered around the village.

Hotel Blue Star (*☎ 60678, 114 Main Rd*) has decent doubles with TV, private bathroom and hot water in the morning for Rs 200, rising to 1200 in peak season.

Hotel Sai Regency (*☎ 60157, Main Rd*) has spacious rooms with cable TV – better than most in this price range. Doubles/triples cost Rs 250/350 (Rs 750/950 in high season).

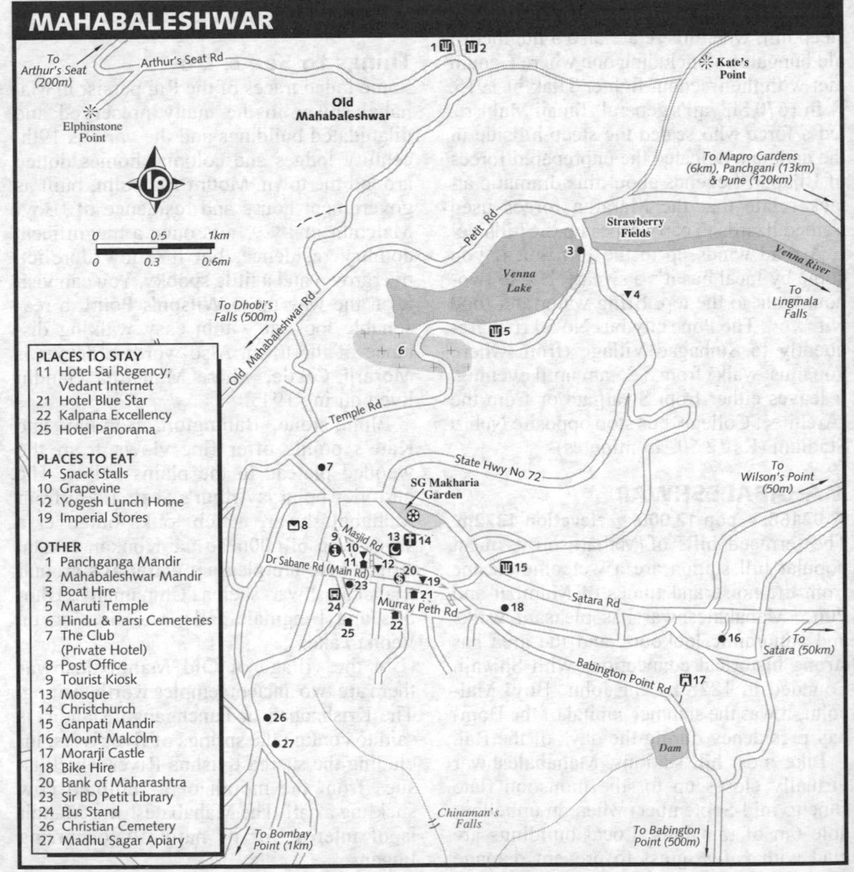

Kalpana Excellency *(☎ 60419, Murray Peth Rd)* is one of the best of a string of hotels along the road south of the bazaar. Rooms around a Mediterranean-style courtyard cost from Rs 400, but the better rooms are Rs 520 (Rs 1200 in the high season).

Hotel Panorama *(☎ 60404, fax 61234)* has all the mod cons and a pool that features its own waterfall and paddle boats. Well-appointed double rooms, all with air-con, start from Rs 850/1400 in low/high season.

Places to Eat

There are plenty of cafes and cheap fast-food places lining the bazaar, and most hotels have attached restaurants. The restaurant at Hotel Panorama is the best in town for pure vegetarian food.

The ***Imperial Stores*** at the far end of Main Rd was once victualler to the Raj and now turns out pizzas, toasted sandwiches, burgers and other snacks, though there are only a couple of tables at the front. Inside is a cluttered ***supermarket***.

Yogesh Lunch Home in the bazaar is great for a cheap plate of vegetables and rice (Rs 25).

The ***Grapevine*** *(☎ 61100, Masjid Rd)* is a stylish little place with a small bar. It has a reasonable go at Thai and a handful of Indian dishes (from around Rs 100) and seafood (from Rs 90 to 150). A bottle of icy cold beer is Rs 80.

Mahabaleshwar is famous for its berries, which you can buy fresh (in season) or as juice, ice cream and jams. Chikki, that rock-hard conglomeration of nuts and gur sugar, is also popular here.

Getting There & Away

Frequent buses run to Satara (Rs 24, two hours), Panchgani (Rs 10, 30 minutes) and Mahad (for Raigad Fort; Rs 33, one hour) and there are several daily services to Kolhapur (Rs 82, five hours) and Pune (Rs 65, four hours). There are four daily buses to Mumbai Central Station (Rs 120, 10 hours), and two expensive MTDC luxury buses at 9.30 am and 12.30 pm (Rs 230, seven hours). Going to Mahabaleshwar, the MTDC buses leave from Nariman Point in Mumbai at 6.30 am and 11 pm.

There are plenty of private bus booking agents in the bazaar for luxury buses to destinations within Maharashtra or to Goa

Strawberry Fields Forever

Mahabaleshwar and its smaller twin Panchgani, 19km east, are famous for producing some of India's finest strawberries, as well as raspberries, mulberries and gooseberries.

Along the road between the two hill stations stretches some 5km of strawberry fields producing varieties such as Californian, Australian and Sweet Chandler. Planting begins soon after the monsoon and fruits are harvested from late November to June with the best crops coming around February. You can visit the farms and buy direct, or get them from the berry vendors who sit cross-legged in Mahabaleshwar's bazaar presiding over neat pyramids of strawberries, raspberries and mulberries. There's also a big industry in fruit drinks, sweets, fudges and jams. The main processor, Mapro (☎ 40112), has its plant near Panchgani, which you can visit for a free tour of the factory and to sample the many products.

(Rs 330, 12 hours via Surul). They all quote similar prices and timings, but it pays to find out exactly where they intend to drop you at your destination. None of the luxury buses to Mumbai (Rs 200) go into the city – the furthest you'll get is Borivali. Private buses to Pune (Rs 140) drop off at Swargate.

Getting Around

Mahabaleshwar has no autorickshaws, but there are plenty of taxis and Maruti vans hanging around near the bus station to take you around the main viewpoints or to Panchgani (see Organised Tours earlier in this section).

Cycling is a good option; there's little traffic, though the narrow lanes have many blind corners and require extra care if you're planning to ride to the viewpoints. Reasonable bikes can be hired from a shop at the eastern end of Main Rd for Rs 5 an hour.

AROUND MAHABALESHWAR

Pratapgad & Raigad Forts

From Mahabaleshwar you can visit two impressive hill forts associated with Shivaji.

Built in 1656, Pratapgad Fort dominates a high ridge 24km west of Mahabaleshwar, and was the setting for one of the most enduring legends involving the Maratha leader. In 1659, Shivaji agreed to meet the Bijapuri general Afzal Khan below the fort walls in an attempt to end a stalemate. Despite a truce the two men arrived armed and Shivaji disembowelled his enemy with a set of iron *waghnakh* (tiger's claws). A tomb marks where the encounter took place, and a tower was erected over the Khan's head.

The fort is reached by a 500-step climb, which affords spectacular views. The cheapest way to get here from Mahabeleshwar is to take the 9.30 am government bus (Rs 44 return, one hour). It waits at the site for an hour before returning. A taxi to Pratapgad and back costs around Rs 450.

Raigad Fort, 80km north-west of Mahabaleshwar, also has fine views from its isolated hilltop location, reached by a long, steep ascent. It was here that Shivaji was crowned in 1648 and where he died in 1680. Raigad is most easily reached from Mahad, 27km away on the Mumbai-Goa highway. Admission is US$5 for foreigners. Although isolated, the MTDC has a basic ***guesthouse*** *(☎ 02145-22898)* within the fort walls, with dorm space (no beds) for Rs 35 and doubles for Rs 150.

KOLHAPUR

☎ 0231 • pop 480,200

Kolhapur was once the capital of an important Maratha state. These days it's famous for turning out some of India's best wrestlers and trendiest leather *chappals* (sandals). In August the **Matharaj Naag Panchami**, a snake worshipping festival, is held here and in Pune. Kolhapur is worth exploring for a day or two if you're passing through.

Information

You can pick up a city map (Rs 5) from the MTDC tourist office (☎ 652935), next to the Hotel Tourist on Station Rd. It's open from 10 am to 6 pm Monday to Saturday.

For foreign exchange, the State Bank of India is a Rs 10 autorickshaw ride southwest of the train station near Hutatma Park.

Kolhapur has plenty of Internet cafes charging around Rs 20 an hour. Internet Zone (☎ 680246), near the MTDC office, is open 24 hours.

Nakoda Travels (☎ 651031), across from the bus stand, has a daily tour of Kolhapur and Panhala starting at 9 am (Rs 100), which is not bad value if you are in a hurry.

Maharaja's Palace

The maharaja's 'new' palace, completed in 1881, houses the **Shahaji Chhatrapati Museum** (☎ 656020), one of the most bizarre collections of memorabilia in the country. The building was designed by 'Mad' Charles Mant, the British architect who fashioned the Indo-Saracenic style of colonial architecture and is a cross between a Victorian train station (clock tower included) and the Addams Family mansion.

The palace contains a weird array of the old maharaja's possessions including his clothes, old hunting photos, silver peacock-shaped elephant saddles and the memorial silver spade he used to 'turn the first sod of the Kolhapur State Railway' in 1888.

Dominating every room in the palace are reminders of the maharaja's macabre passion: killing wild animals to decorate his palace. Skins cover floors and furniture, while trophy heads stare blankly from the walls, ashtrays and coffee tables are made from tiger and elephant feet, lamp stands from ostrich legs and zebra hoofs. The variety of stuffed animals includes black bear, rhino, pangolin, panther and an entire family of tigers in a forest diorama.

The palace is a few kilometres north of the centre, Rs 15 in an autorickshaw. The museum is open from 9.30 am to 12.30 pm and 2.30 to 5.30 pm daily. Entry is Rs 22 and you must buy your ticket at the gates to the palace grounds, not at the palace itself.

Other Attractions

The **Mahalaxmi Temple**, dedicated to the goddess Amba Bai, dominates the old town. Of particular interest is the carved ceiling of the columned mandapam. Nearby, the **Old Palace** (Rajwada) still accommodates members of the maharaja's family, but the ground floor, with its cool atrium (open 10 am to 6 pm daily) now acts as a temple to the goddess Bhawani.

An alley leads from the front of the palace to Kolhapur's famous **wrestling ground**, a red earth arena in a natural sunken stadium. Kolhapur has produced several Indian national wrestling champions, and you can see the athletes training most days in the early morning or evening at one of the local wrestling clubs. Ask around for the *kusti akhada* (wrestling ground) or the Kasbagh Maidan.

The town hall, built by Mant in 1872–76, houses a small but satisfying **museum** (☎ 520481) exhibiting pottery and bronze artefacts found during archaeological excavations on nearby Brahmapuri Hill, as well as paintings, sculpture and weaponry; it's open from 10.30 am to 1 pm and 1.30 to 5.30 pm daily, except Monday (Rs 3).

Places to Stay

The main hotel and restaurant area is around the square opposite the bus stand, 10 to 15 minutes' walk east of the centre of town and the train station.

City Lodge *(☎ 651748)*, above the shops on the western side of the square, is a reasonably clean budget place. Rooms with private bathroom are Rs 170/210. There's hot water and a 24-hour check-out.

Hotel Maharaja *(☎ 652140, Station Rd)* is very cheap for the standard of rooms, which is why it's often full. There are no advance bookings. Singles/doubles with shared bathroom cost Rs 75/150 or Rs 150/250 with private bathroom and hot water (mornings only). The front rooms have a little balcony with a stunning view of the bus stand.

Hotel Tourist *(☎ 650421, ⓔ tourist@pn3.vsnl.net.in, Station Rd)*, a few minutes' walk east of the bus station, is a step up in comfort and service. Comfortable, spacious singles/doubles with bath, TV and phone are good value at Rs 275/325. Air-con rooms start from Rs 400/450. Major credit cards are accepted and check-out is noon. There's a reasonable restaurant and a bar.

Farther east are a couple of mid-range places. ***Hotel International*** *(☎ 652441, fax 652446, 517 A1 Shivaji Park)* has rooms from Rs 350/400 or Rs 600/675 with air-con, all with TV and phone.

Hotel Shalini Palace *(☎ 620401, fax 620407, Lake Rankala)* is the top place to stay in Kolhapur. Situated on the lake 5km south-west of the bus stand or train station, this is the maharaja's old summer palace. It dates back only to the 1930s, but has plenty of regal grandeur with huge rooms, marble balconies and four-poster beds. The standard rooms are spacious, open out onto the marble balcony, and cost Rs 800/1150. To really savour the atmosphere of this place you need to lash out on the Maharaja or Maharani suites at Rs 2100.

Places to Eat

Cheap restaurants are clustered around the bus station square. ***Subraya Restaurant*** has North Indian vegetarian and nonvegetarian dishes and regulation thalis. ***Surabhi***, opposite and beneath the Hotel Sayhadri, is a busy vegetarian restaurant with some Kolhapuri specialities such as *misal* (a spicy snack not unlike bhelpuri), dosas, fresh fruit juices and lassis.

Harvest Garden Bar & Restaurant, at the Hotel International, has an unusual pure vegetarian menu, with local specialities between Rs 55 and Rs 80, and a pleasant garden setting.

In the evening, ***snack stalls*** set up opposite the bus stand and there are plenty of fruit stalls here during the day. Opposite the Old Palace, ***Shetkari Bazaar*** is a well-stocked supermarket open daily except Saturday.

Getting There & Away

There are regular government buses to Pune (Rs 108, five hours) via Satara (Rs 63), Mahabaleshwar (Rs 75, four hours) and Ratnagiri (Rs 58, four hours), as well as direct services to Belgaum and Bijapur. For Mumbai, Goa, Aurangabad, Bangalore and other popular long hauls, you're better off with the deluxe private buses. Most of the private bus companies are on the western side of the square at Mahalaxmi Chambers, just across from the bus stand. There are air-con overnight buses to Mumbai (Rs 300, 10 hours; Rs 450 for the sleeper bus) and Aurangabad (Rs 250, 10 hours); and non air-con overnight buses to Panaji in Goa (Rs 150, 5½ hours) and Bangalore (Rs 300, 11 hours).

The train station is 10 minutes' walk west of the bus station, towards the centre of town. There are three daily expresses to Mumbai (Rs 113/509 in sleeper/three-tier air-con, 13 hours) via Pune (Rs 123/356, eight hours).

Northern Maharashtra

NASIK

☎ 0253 • pop 834,000

This absorbing town, peppered with hundreds of temples and colourful bathing ghats, stands on the Godavari River, one of the holiest rivers of the Deccan.

Nasik has many associations with the Hindu epic Ramayana. It was here that Lord Rama and his wife Sita were sent to exile. Lakshmana was said to have cut off the nose *(nasika)* of Ravana's sister here, thus giving the city its name.

Nasik is a popular base for pilgrims visiting Trimbak (see Around Nasik) or Shirdi (birthplace of Sai Baba), but it's not a tourist town, and that alone makes it worth a visit. Nasik's biggest event is the phenomenal Kumbh Mela, which occurs here every 12 years – next in 2003.

Orientation & Information

MG Rd, a couple of blocks north of the central bus stand, is Nasik's hub. The Godavari River, lined with temples and bathing ghats, flows through town just east of here.

The MTDC tourist office (☎ 570059) about 1.5km south of the bus stand, has a map of Nasik and staff are helpful. The State Bank of India, less than 100m from the bus stand on Old Agra Rd, changes cash and travellers cheques (eventually).

Ramkund

This holy bathing tank, 1.5km north-east of the town centre on the Godavari, is the focus for pilgrims filing into Nasik. Surrounded by ghats and the riverside market, it's a lively and interesting area to explore.

The Ramkund is said to have been used by Rama and Sita during their exile. Like the Ganges at Varanasi, its holy water is believed to provide *moksha*, or liberation of the soul, to those whose ashes are immersed here – Indira Gandhi and Jawaharlal Nehru are among those to have had this treatment. Nearby is a lively riverside **market** best visited in the early morning.

Kala Rama Mandir

A short walk east of the Ramkund, the Kala Rama, or Black Rama, is the city's holiest temple. The black stone temple is in a 96-arched enclosure and contains icons of Rama, Sita and Lakshmana as well as a huge bell.

Other Attractions

Near Kala Rama is the **Sita Gumpa cave**. According to the Ramayana it was from here that Sita, the deity of agriculture and wife of Rama, was carried off to the island of Lanka by the evil king Ravana. For a small donation you can join the queue crawling through the narrow opening, but there's not much to see.

Among the many temples in Nasik, the **Sundar Narayan Temple** at the western end of Victoria Bridge is worth a visit. The **Muktidham Temple**, near the train station about 7km south-east of the city, is a modern and

Kumbh Mela

Welcome to the greatest congregation of humanity on Earth!

The Kumbh Mela – the world's biggest religious gathering – attracted a mind blowing 30 million Hindu pilgrims to Allahabad in 2001 (although it was probably fewer than this estimate) and it will next be held at Nasik and Trimbak in 2003. According to Hindu creation myths, the gods and demons once fought a great battle for a *kumbh* (pitcher) containing the nectar of immortality. Vishnu got his hands on the container and spirited it away, but during his flight four drops of nectar spilt on the earth – at Allahabad, Haridwar, Nasik and Ujjain. The fight lasted 12 days, but the gods finally triumphed and got to quaff the nectar – a scene often portrayed in illustrations of Hindu mythology.

The event is noted for the huge number of Hindu holy men it attracts, especially the naked sadhus or *nagas* of militant Hindu monastic orders.

The Kumbh Mela doesn't belong to any caste or creed in India. The festival, perhaps more than any single event in India, captures the huge mix of religious and cultural backgrounds that swarm together to form the fabric of Indian society.

Mark Tully's *No Full Stops in India* has a fascinating chapter on the politics, logistics and significance of Allahabad's 1989 Kumbh Mela.

In Nasik the centre of attention is the holy tank of Ramkund, through which the Godavari River flows, but much of the month-long celebration takes place out at Trimbak, 33km away, where the Trimbakeshwar Temple houses one of India's 12 *jyoti linga* (naturally occurring linga).

strikingly white marble structure. The walls of its vast interior are lined with the 18 chapters of the Bhagavad-Gita.

Organised Tours

An all-day tour of Nasik, including Trimbak and Pandu Lena, departs daily at 7.30 am from the central bus stand (Rs 63). It's a long day and the guide speaks Marathi only, but if you want to see a few of Nasik's estimated 2000 temples, it's as good a way as any.

Places to Stay & Eat

Hotel Panchavati *(☎ 575771, 430 Vakilwadi)*, just off MG Rd, is a large hotel and restaurant complex right in the centre of Nasik. There are three accommodation sections: Cheapest is ***Panchavati Guest House*** *(☎ 581071)* at the rear of the complex with share beds (four in a room) for Rs 150 per person and decent singles/doubles with private bathroom and TV for Rs 300/395. ***Panchavati Yatri*** *(☎ 572290)* has rooms for Rs 440/590, or Rs 630/720 with air-con; and the main hotel charges Rs 540/740. The complex includes a couple of very good restaurants, an ice-cream parlour and a bar.

Rajmahal Lodge *(☎ 580501, ⓔ rajmahallodge@vsnl.com, Sharanpur Rd)* opposite the central bus stand, has a range of clean rooms with private bathroom from Rs 300/350, all with TV and hot shower, and a single with shared bathroom for Rs 190.

There's a bunch of hotels around the Dwarka Circle, the junction of the main roads to Mumbai and Pune, a couple of kilometres south of the town centre. All have private bathroom.

Sun Moon Guest House *(☎ 596748)* has a grubby dorm with beds at Rs 40 and Rs 50, small doubles for Rs 200 or cleaner rooms with private bathroom with hot water and TV for Rs 200/300.

Hotel Blue Moon *(☎ 590548)*, directly across the laneway, is a new place with immaculate rooms not lost in the usual 1970s time warp. They start at Rs 300/350 with TV, or Rs 500/600 with air-con.

The ***Tandoor***, off Shivaji Rd, is a simple North Indian place offering reasonably cheap tandoori dishes – chicken in a basket is a bargain at Rs 33.

Hotel Samrat *(☎ 577211, Old Agra Rd)* has a restaurant serving good Gujarati thalis and there's a bar.

Getting There & Away

Bus Nasik is a major road transport hub and frequent state government buses operate virtually round the clock to Mumbai (Rs 90, six hours), Pune (Rs 110, five hours) and Aurangabad (Rs 102, five hours). There are also regular services to Shirdi (Rs 45, three hours). Half-hourly buses to Trimbak (Rs 13, one hour) depart from a separate bus stand across the road.

There are plenty of private bus agents near the bus stand and most buses depart from Old Agra Rd. They include Pune (Rs 120), Mumbai (Rs 120 or Rs 200 for air-con), Aurangabad (4.30 and 11.30 pm only; Rs 120). For the 11-hour overnight trip to Ahmedabad you can go by sleeper (Rs 350) or regular bus (Rs 300). If you're heading to Mumbai ask where the bus terminates, as most only go as far as Dadar.

Train The Nasik Rd train station is 8km from the town centre, but there's a very useful railway reservation office in a small lane off Deshpande Peth, just north of MG Rd (open 8 am to 2 pm and 4.15 to 8 pm Monday to Saturday, 8 am to 2 pm Sunday). The fastest train to Mumbai is the 7.02 am *Panchvati Express*, which takes four hours (Rs 53/170 in 2nd/chair class). The *Tapovan Express* is the only convenient direct train to Aurangabad, departing at 10.08 am and taking 3½ hours (Rs 52/161). Local buses ply between the Nasik Rd train station and the bus stand (Rs 5). An autorickshaw costs about Rs 50.

AROUND NASIK

Pandu Lena

Set in a hillside about 8km south of Nasik, close to the Mumbai road, is a group of 24 Early Buddhist caves dating from around the 1st century BC to the 2nd century AD. The caves are reached by a 10-minute walk up a stone stairway. Admission is stiff at US$5 (Rs 230) for foreigners, Rs 5 for Indians. Local buses (Rs 5) run past the caves from the second stop north of the central bus stand on Old Agra Rd. A return autorickshaw ride (including waiting time) costs around Rs 80.

Trimbak

From a spring high on a steep hill above Trimbak, 33km west of Nasik, the source of the Godavari River dribbles into the **Gangasagar bathing tank** whose waters are reputed to wash away sins. From this tiny start the Godavari eventually flows down to the Bay of Bengal, clear across India.

The **Trimbakeshwar Temple** is one of India's most sacred, containing one of the 12 *jyoti linga* (naturally occurring linga) of Shiva. The temple is open to Hindus only, but it's possible to see into the courtyard to the shrine, and it's interesting to watch pilgrims going about their ritual business around the main tank.

The walk up **Brahmagiri Hill** makes a good day hike. Continue on the road past the MTDC Resort and it's a four-hour return walk to the temples high above the town.

MTDC Resort has overpriced singles/doubles for Rs 250/300. Regular buses run from the bus stand alongside Hotel Padma in Nasik to Trimbak (Rs 13, one hour).

Igatpuri

About 44km south of Nasik on the rail line to Mumbai, the village of Igatpuri would be of little interest to travellers if it wasn't the home of the world's largest Vipassana centre, the **Vipassana International Academy**.

Also known as Dhamma Giri, the centre (☎ 02553-84076) can accommodate up to 600 students and conducts regular 10-day residential courses in this strict form of Buddhist meditation. Courses are free (or by donation), but students must stay on site and observe a regime of 'noble silence' in order to achieve 'mental purification'. Vipassana was first taught by Gautama Buddha in the 6th century BC, but was reintroduced to India by teacher SN Goenkar in the 1960s.

Igatpuri is easy to reach by rail with eight trains a day from Mumbai (Rs 64 sleeper class, three hours). Trains and buses from Nasik take only one hour. The centre is a 15-minute walk from the station, but there are plenty of autorickshaws around.

AURANGABAD

☎ 0240 • pop 682,000

Aurangabad is central Maharashtra's most visited city since it's the logical base for visiting the famous Ellora and Ajanta caves.

The city was originally founded in 1610 on the site of a village called Khirki, by Malik Ambar, prime minister of the Murtaza Nizam Shah II. Ambar's son, Fateh Khan, succeeded the throne in 1626, renaming the city Fatehpur, before Aurangzeb moved in and made it his capital in 1653. The city is named after him.

Aurangabad is becoming something of an industrial centre: About 10km from the city, the Bajaj-Kawasaki factory is the biggest producer of two-wheelers (motorcycles) in India. There are also at least half-a-dozen breweries here supplying most of Maharashtra's beer.

Orientation & Information

The train station, tourist office and cheap hotels and restaurants are clustered in the south of the town. The bus stand is 1.5km to the north along Station Rd West. North-east of here is the crowded old town with its narrow streets and distinct Muslim quarter.

Tourist Offices The Government of India tourist office (☎ 331217) on Station Rd West has a decent range of brochures and will try to answer almost any query. The manager Mr Yadav is very knowledgeable and one of the most passionate tourism officials you'll meet anywhere. The office is open from 8.30 am to 6 pm weekdays and until 1.30 pm on Saturday. The MTDC office (☎ 331513), on Station Rd East, is only good for booking MTDC tours and accommodation. It's open from 7 am to 10 pm. There are also information counters at the airport and train station.

Money The quickest place to change cash and travellers cheques is Trade Wings Foreign Exchange (☎ 357480), opposite Hotel Printravel on Station Rd West, although there's a hefty Rs 50 transaction fee. It's open from 8 am to 7 pm daily. The Bank of Baroda, near the Paithan Gate on Pattan Darwaza Rd, gives cash advances on Visa and MasterCard between 1 and 2.30 pm Weekdays, and 10.30 am and 12.30 pm Saturday.

Post & Communications Poste restante can be collected from the busy main post office at Juna Bazaar 10 am to 5 pm Monday to Saturday.

There are plenty of Internet cafes in Aurangabad, particularly along the east and west extensions of Station Rd. Most charge around Rs 20 per hour.

Travel Agencies Classic Travels (☎ 335 598, ⓔ classictours@vsnl.com) is based at the MTDC hotel and is a good place for booking transport, tours and even accommodation. Trade Wings (☎ 357480) also has travel services.

Bibi-ka-Maqbara

The so-called 'poor-man's Taj Mahal' was built in 1679 as a mausoleum for Aurangzeb's wife, Rabia-ud-Daurani. It's a modest imitation of the Taj in both design and execution, but the inevitable comparisons are a bit unfortunate because it's still an impressive piece of work. It's particularly atmospheric at night when floodlit. If you don't want to pay the entrance fee, you can still go along and view the exterior and gardens from the entrance archway, or climb the small hill behind the Bibi-ka-Maqbara and look down on it.

The building is open from sunrise to 10 pm; admission is US$5 (Rs 235), or Rs 5 for Indians.

Panchakki

Panchakki (Water Wheel) takes its name from the mill that, in its day, was considered a marvel of engineering. Driven by water brought through earthen pipes from the river 6km away, the mill once ground grain for pilgrims. The mill (still working) is to the right of the first tank as you enter.

Baba Shah Muzaffar, a Sufi saint and spiritual guide to Aurangzeb, is buried here, and the garden, with its series of fish-filled

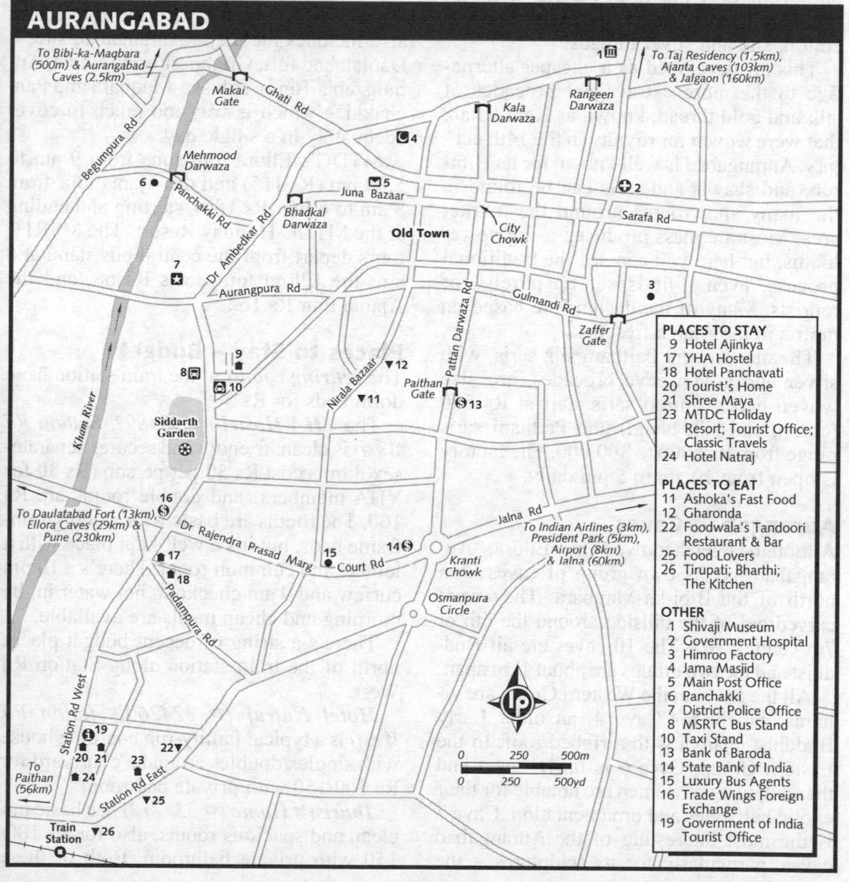

tanks, serves as his memorial. It is open from 8 am to 8 pm daily (Rs 5).

Shivaji Museum

This spacious new museum is dedicated to the life of the Maratha hero, Shivaji – focusing mostly, of course, on his military prowess. Most of the exhibits here are from the collection of the former Purwar Museum and include a 500-year-old chain-mail suit, a copy of the Quran handwritten by Aurangzeb and an 800-year-old Paithani sari.

It's open from 10.30 am to 1.30 pm and 3 to 6 pm daily, except Monday (Rs 5).

Himroo Factory

Tucked away in the old town near Zaffar Gate, this small workshop (☎ 351745) is one of the only places in the city that still produces hand-woven Himroo shawls from cotton, silk and silver threads.

This art developed as a cheaper alternative to the more extravagant brocades of silk and gold thread, known as Kam Khab, that were woven for royalty in the 14th century. Aurangabad is well known for its Himroo, and shawls and saris can be found in the many showrooms around the market area. Most are mass produced using power looms, but here you can see the traditional process, even if it is set up purely for tourists. Many of the designs are based on motifs in the Ajanta frescoes.

The magnificent Paithani silk saris, with silver and gold weave brocades, are also woven here. Himroo saris start at Rs 500 (cotton and silk blend) and Paithani saris range from Rs 6000 to 300,000. The factory is open from 10 am to 5 pm daily.

Aurangabad Caves

Although overshadowed by Ellora, Aurangabad has its own group of caves 2km north of the Bibi-ka-Maqbara. They were carved out of the hillside around the 6th or 7th century AD. The 10 caves are all Buddhist and the two groups are about 1km apart.

All the caves in the Western Group are viharas, except for Cave 4, an older Early Buddhist chaitya with a ribbed roof. In the Eastern Group, Cave 6 is fairly intact and the sculptures of women are notable for their exotic hairstyles and ornamentation. Cave 7 is the most interesting of the Aurangabad caves, particularly for its sculptures – the figures of women, scantily clad and ornately bejewelled, are indicative of the rise of Tantric Buddhism during this period.

You can walk up to the caves from the Bibi-ka-Maqbara or take an autorickshaw up to the eastern group, walk back down the road to the western group and then cut straight back across country to the Bibi-ka-Maqbara.

Unfortunately, the US$5 (Rs 235) entry charge probably means few foreigners will bother with these caves. The attendants arrive at around 8 am, but there's nothing to stop visitors arriving earlier (yet).

Organised Tours

The MTDC (☎ 331513) and the MSRTC (☎ 331647) run almost identical daily tours to the Ajanta and Ellora caves. These include an accompanying guide, but not admission fees. In each case the Ellora tour also includes the major Aurangabad sites – Daulatabad fort, Grishneshwar Temple, Aurangzeb's Tomb, Bibi-ka-Maqbara and Panchakki – which is way too much to cover adequately in a single day.

MTDC's Ellora tour runs from 9 am to 5.30 pm (Rs 115) and the Ajanta tour from 8 am to 6 pm (Rs 150), starting and ending at the MTDC Holiday Resort. The MSRTC tours depart from the central bus stand at 8 am; the Ellora tour costs Rs 68, and the Ajanta tour Rs 162.

Places to Stay – Budget

The ***retiring rooms*** at the train station have dorm beds for Rs 50.

The ***YHA Hostel*** *(☎ 334892, Station Rd West)* is clean, friendly and secure. Separate-sex dorms cost Rs 50 per person (Rs 30 for YHA members) and double rooms are Rs 100. The rooms are basic with wobbly iron-frame beds, but it's a well-kept place with a lounge and common room. There's a 10 pm curfew and 9 am checkout, hot water in the morning and cheap meals are available.

There's a string of decent budget places north of the train station along Station Rd West.

Hotel Natraj *(☎ 324260, Station Rd West)* is a typical family-run boarding house with singles/doubles around a courtyard for Rs 100/150 with private bathroom.

Tourist's Home *(☎ 337212)* has basic but clean and spacious rooms, also for Rs 100/150 with private bathroom. Both of these places have squat toilets and bucket hot water available in the morning.

Hotel Panchavati *(☎ 328755, Padampura St)*, near the youth hostel, has good-value rooms with bath for Rs 100/150 (hot water in the mornings). It's basic, but the staff are amiable and there's a good restaurant and bar.

Shree Maya *(☎ 333093, Bharuka Complex)*, only a few minutes' walk from the train station, is easily the best of the budget places. It's immaculately kept, well run and traveller-friendly. Spacious doubles with private bathroom (hot shower in the mornings) and TV cost Rs 275, or Rs 350 with air-con. There are no singles, but there is a three-bed share room at Rs 145 per bed. The buffet breakfast on the terrace (Rs 45) is unbeatable.

For some reasonable places close to the bus stand, walk down the small road directly opposite and turn left into Nehru Place. ***Hotel Ajinkya*** *(☎ 335601, Nehru Place)* is the best of the cheap places with a variety of rooms starting at Rs 160/210 or Rs 500/550 with air-con.

Places to Stay – Mid-Range & Top End

MTDC Holiday Resort *(☎ 331513, Station Rd East)* is set in its own shady grounds. Comfortable, spacious doubles with bath are Rs 500 in the 'Ajanta' section or Rs 550 in the 'Ellora' suite. Curiously, the cheaper Ajanta rooms are better. Air-con rooms are Rs 600/700. There's no discount for single occupancy and checkout is an uncharitable 8 am. There's a restaurant, bar and travel agent on site.

President Park *(☎ 486201, fax 484823, ⓔ hpp@bom4.vsnl.net.in, Jalna Rd)* is a very classy three-star a little farther out towards the airport; it's excellent value at Rs 1500/2000. The best feature of this hotel is its semicircular swimming pool set in gardens with a poolside bar. It also has a travel desk, gym, multicuisine restaurant and coffee shop.

Taj Residency *(☎ 381106, fax 381053, Ajanta Rd)* is a gleaming oasis in the northern fringes of Aurangabad. The hotel sweeps around an immaculate garden and swimming pool. Well-appointed rooms start at Rs 1995/2495.

Places to Eat

There's a clutch of rock-bottom restaurants along Station Rd East, including the ***Tirupati***, ***Bharthi*** and ***The Kitchen***, which specialise in cheap South Indian meals. The ***food stalls*** around the bus stand do great omelettes.

Aurangabad's modern fast-food hub is Nirala Bazaar, just west of Paithan Gate. Here you'll find plenty of neon signs and a youthful crowd dining on an Indian-American fusion of pizzas, burgers, shakes and ice cream (the food is usually vegetarian and a little spicy).

Ashoka's Fast Food is one of the more popular places and has an outdoor terrace as well as an indoor dining area. Most dishes are Rs 20 to 40, although you can get a kilo of black forest cake for Rs 160!

Also in this area, ***Gharonda*** is a locally recommended air-con place serving good Indian and Chinese fare – expect around Rs 200 a head.

Food Lovers is a garden restaurant near the train station and has the best ambience in town – earthen floor, thatched walls and an ingenious cooling system on hot days. The Punjabi and Chinese food is delicious. It's open until midnight.

Foodwalas Tandoori Restaurant & Bar is farther up Station Rd East and offers reasonable tandoori dishes.

Getting There & Away

Air The airport is 10km east of town on the Jalna road. En route you'll find the Indian Airlines office (☎ 485421) and Jet Airways (☎ 441770), almost opposite. Indian Airlines has daily flights to Mumbai (US$65) and Delhi (US$175). Jet Airways flies daily to Mumbai (US$69).

Bus There are regular MSRTC buses from Aurangabad to Pune (Rs 101, six hours), Nasik (Rs 105, five hours) and Mumbai (Rs 201, 10 hours). The luxury bus agents congregate around the corner where Dr Rajendra Prasad Marg becomes Court Rd and there are a few closer to the bus stand on Station Rd. A deluxe overnight bus to Mumbai, Ahmedabad or Nagpur is Rs 250.

To Ellora & Ajanta Caves There are local buses to Ellora every half hour (Rs 12, 45 minutes), four morning buses direct to Ajanta (Rs 50, three hours) and hourly services to Jalgaon (Rs 66, 4½ hours), which can drop you at Fardapur, the nearest village to the Ajanta caves.

Train Aurangabad is not on a main line, but there are two direct trains daily to/from Mumbai (375km), which are often heavily booked. The *Tapovan Express* departs at 2.40 pm and costs Rs 88/267 in 2nd/chair car (the only classes available), arriving at Mumbai CST at 10.50 pm. Coming from Mumbai, the same train leaves at 6.10 am. The overnight *Devgiri Express* departs from Aurangabad at 9.05 pm and arrives at Mumbai CST at 5.35 am (Rs 135/627 sleeper/two-tier air-con).

Alternatively, you can get a bus or a local train to the nearest main line train station, Manmad, 113km north-west of Aurangabad, from where there are more frequent express trains to Mumbai.

To Hyderabad (Secunderabad), the daily *Manmad Express* departs from Aurangabad at 6.22 am for the 12-hour journey (Rs 132/951 in sleeper/two-tier air-con). To reach northern or eastern India by train (eg, Delhi or Kolkata), take a bus up to Jalgaon and one of the major trains from there.

Getting Around

The taxi stand is next to the bus stand; share jeeps also depart from here for destinations around Aurangabad, including Ellora and Daulatabad.

A bicycle is a good way to get around to some of the city sights and they can be hired from stalls near the bus stand.

AROUND AURANGABAD

Daulatabad

Halfway (13km) between Aurangabad and the Ellora caves is the magnificent **hilltop fortress** of Daulatabad. The fort is surrounded by 5km of sturdy walls, while the central bastion tops a 200m high hill, which was originally known as Devagiri, the Hill of the Gods.

In the 14th century it was renamed Daulatabad, the City of Fortune, by Mohammed Tughlaq. This unbalanced sultan of Delhi conceived the crazy plan of not only building himself a new capital here, but marching the entire population of Delhi 1100km south to populate it. His unhappy subjects proceeded to drop dead like flies on this forced march, and 17 years later he turned around and marched them all back to Delhi.

Climb to the top for the superb views over the surrounding countryside. Along the way you'll pass through a complicated and ingenious series of defences, including multiple doorways with spike-studded doors to prevent elephant charges. A magnificent tower of victory, known as the **Chand Minar** (Tower of the Moon), built in 1435, soars 60m.

Higher up is the blue-tiled **Chini Mahal** where the last king of Golconda was imprisoned for 13 years until his death. Finally, you climb to a 6m **cannon**, cast from five different metals and engraved with Aurangzeb's name.

The final ascent to the top goes through a pitch black spiralling tunnel, down which the fort's defenders could hurl burning coals at invaders, and a bat infested cave. Of course, your guide may tell you that the fort

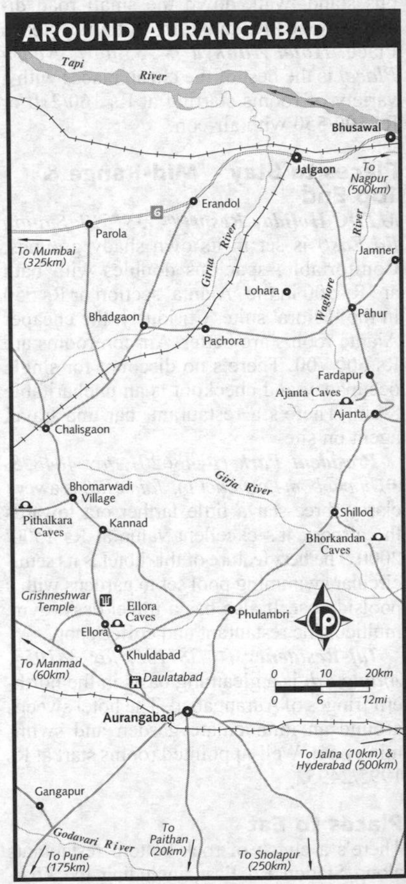

was once successfully conquered despite all these elaborate precautions – by simply bribing the guard at the gate.

If you take one of the MTDC bus tours to Daulatabad and Ellora, you won't have time to climb to the summit. The fort is open until 6 pm and entry for foreigners is US$5 (Rs 5 for Indians).

Khuldabad

Khuldabad, the Heavenly Abode, is a walled town just 3km from Ellora. It is the Karbala (holy shrine) of Deccan Muslims. A number of historical figures are buried here, including Aurangzeb, the last great Mughal emperor. His final resting place is a simple affair of bare earth in a courtyard of the **Alamgir Dargah** at the centre of the town.

Within the building there is supposed to be a robe worn by the prophet Mohammed; it is only shown to the faithful once each year. Another shrine across the road from the Alamgir Dargah is said to contain hairs of the prophet's beard and lumps of silver from a tree of solid silver, which miraculously grew at this site after a saint's death.

PAITHAN

Paithan, 56km south of Aurangabad, is famous for its Paithani silk saris. These highly sought after saris are brocaded with pure gold thread and can take up to a year and a half to weave. Apart from the Paithani weaving centre, the main attraction here is the Gyaneshwar Gardens, the largest in Maharashtra. The Paithan Fair, a 10-day celebration for St Eknath, is held here in March or April. Local MSRTC buses go to Paithan from Aurangabad, or you can join the MTDC half-day tour on Monday (Rs 115).

ELLORA

The World Heritage-listed cave temples of Ellora, about 30km from Aurangabad, are the pinnacle of Deccan rock-cut architecture.

Over five centuries, many generations of Buddhist, Hindu and Jain monks carved monasteries, chapels and temples from a 2km-long escarpment and decorated them with a profusion of sculptures of remarkable imagination and detail. Because of the escarpment's gentle slope, in contrast to the sheer drop at Ajanta, many of the caves have elaborate courtyards in front of the main shrines.

In all there are 34 caves at Ellora: 12 Buddhist (AD 600–800), 17 Hindu (AD 600–900) and five Jain (AD 800–1000). Ellora represents the renaissance of Hinduism under the Chalukya and Rashtrakuta dynasties, the subsequent decline of Indian Buddhism, and a brief resurgence of Jainism under official patronage. The sculptural work at Ellora shows the increasing influence of Tantric elements in India's three great religions, and their coexistence at one site indicates a prolonged period of religious tolerance.

The masterpiece of Ellora is the astonishing Kailasa Temple (Cave 16). Dedicated to Shiva, it is the world's largest monolithic sculpture, hewn from the rock by 7000 labourers over a 150-year period. For three days in December the Kailasa Temple is the backdrop for the annual **Ellora Dance & Music Festival**.

Entry to Ellora is free, except to the Kailasa Temple which costs US$10 for foreigners, Rs 10 for Indians. The caves are closed on Monday.

Official guides can be hired at the ticket office in front of the Kailasa Temple for Rs 245 for up to four hours. They speak English reasonably well and have a sound knowledge of the cave architecture. There's a selection of pictorial guidebooks available at the site.

Buddhist Caves

The southernmost 12 caves are all Buddhist viharas, except Cave 10, which is a chaitya. While the earliest caves are quite simple, Caves 11 and 12 are much more ambitious, probably in an attempt to compete with the more impressive Hindu temples.

Cave 1 is the simplest vihara and may have been a granary. **Cave 2** is notable for its ornate pillars and its imposing seated Buddha facing the setting sun, his huge feet planted solidly on the earth. **Caves 3 and 4** are earlier, simpler and less well preserved.

Cave 5 is the largest vihara in this group, 18m wide and 36m long; the rows of stone benches indicate that it may have been an assembly or dining hall.

As well as the large seated Buddha in the shrine room, **Cave 6** is an ornate vihara with wonderful images of Tara (on the left), consort of the Bodhisattva Avalokiteshvara, and of the Buddhist goddess of learning,

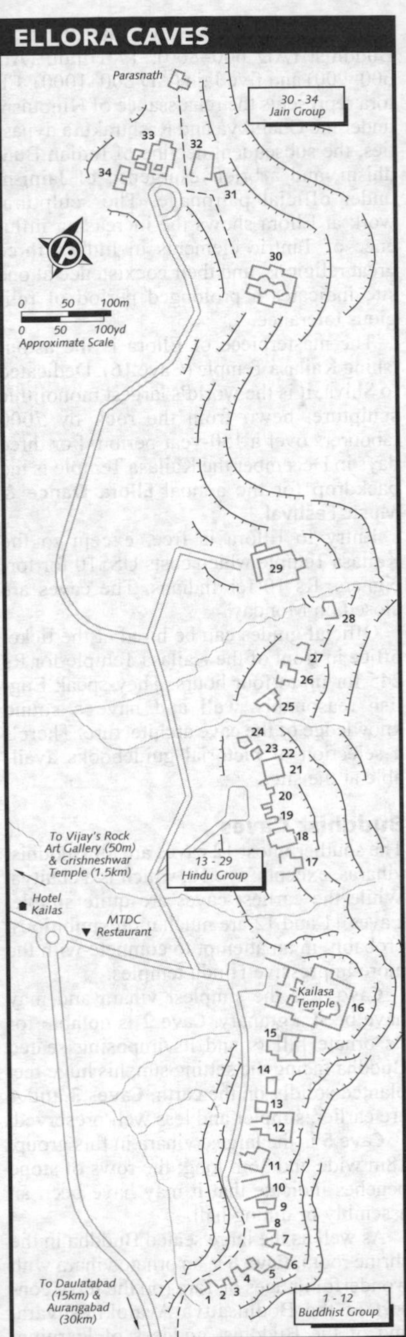

Mahamayuri, looking remarkably similar to her Hindu equivalent, Saraswati. **Cave 9** is notable for its wonderfully carved facade.

Cave 10, the Viswakarma or Carpenter's Cave, is the only chaitya in the Buddhist group, and one of the finest in India. It takes its name from the ribs carved into the roof, in imitation of wooden beams; steps from the left of the courtyard lead to the balcony and upper gallery for a closer view of the ceiling and a frieze depicting amorous couples. A small, decorative window gently illuminates an enormous teaching Buddha.

Cave 11, the Do Thal (Two Storey) Cave, is entered through its third, basement level, not discovered until 1876. Like Cave 12 it probably owes its size to competition with the more impressive Hindu caves of the same period.

Cave 12, the enormous Tin Thal (Three Storey) Cave, is entered through a courtyard. The (locked) shrine on the top floor contains a large seated Buddha flanked by his seven previous incarnations. The walls are carved with relief pictures, as in the Hindu caves.

Hindu Caves

Where calm and contemplation infuses the Buddhist caves, drama and dynamic energy characterise those of the Hindu group (Caves 13 to 29) in the middle of the escarpment. In terms of scale, creative vision and skill of execution, these are in a totally different league to the neighbouring Buddhist and Jain caves.

All these temples were cut from the top down, so that it was never necessary to use scaffolding – the builders began with the roof and moved down to the floor. The planning and coordination required over several generations must have been unbelievably precise – there was no way of adding a panel or a pillar if things didn't work out as expected.

Cave 14, the Ravana-ki-Khai, is a Buddhist vihara converted to a temple dedicated to Shiva some time in the 7th century. Familiar scenes include Shiva dancing the *tandava*, a victory dance over the demon Mahisa; Shiva playing chess with his wife Parvati; and Durga defeating the buffalo demon. Vishnu makes several appearances, including as Varaha the boar.

The Das Avatara (Ten Incarnations of Vishnu) Cave, **Cave 15**, is one of the finest at Ellora. The two-storey temple is reached

Kailasa – Temple of the Gods

Ellora's Kailasa Temple (Cave 16) is one of the most audacious feats of architecture ever conceived. Built by King Krishna I of the Rashtrakut dynasty in AD 760, the idea was not only to build an enormous and fantastically carved representation of Mt Kailasa (Kailash), Shiva's home in the Himalaya, but to create it from a single piece of stone by first cutting three huge trenches into the rock of the Ellora cliff face and then 'releasing' the shape of the temple using hammers and chisels. The sheer scale of the undertaking is overwhelming. It covers twice the area of the Parthenon in Athens, is 1½ times as high, and it entailed removing 200,000 tonnes of rock!

The temple consists of a huge courtyard, 81m long, 47m wide and 33m high at the back. In the centre, the main temple rises up and is connected to the outer enclosure by a bridge. Around the enclosure are galleries, while towards the front are two large stone elephants with two massive stone 'flagstaffs' flanking the Nandi Pavilion, which faces the main shrine. Originally the entire structure was covered in white plaster to more closely resemble the snowy peak of Mt Kailasa.

Apart from the technical genius evident in its creation, Kailasa Temple is remarkable for its prodigious sculptural decoration. Around the temple are dramatic and finely carved panels, depicting scenes from the Ramayana, the Mahabharata and the adventures of Krishna. The most superb panel depicts the demon king Ravana flaunting his strength by shaking Mt Kailasa. Unimpressed, Shiva crushes Ravana's pride by simply flexing a toe.

Admission to the Kailasa Temple now costs US$10 for foreigners (Rs 10 for Indians) and it's open from 6 am to 6 pm daily except Monday. You can climb the path to the south and walk right around the top perimeter of the 'cave' for free. From here you can really appreciate the massive scale of the temple and get a good view of the roof, topped by four lions and a pyramidal tower. It doesn't allow you to appreciate the exquisite rock carving up close, though.

through its courtyard by a long flight of steps. Many of the familiar scenes involving Shiva are here, including a mesmerising Shiva Nataraja, and Shiva emerging from a lingam while Vishnu and Brahma pay homage.

The other Hindu caves pall beside the majesty of the Kailasa, but several are worth a look. **Cave 21**, known as the Ramesvara, features interesting interpretations of the familiar Shaivite scenes depicted in the earlier temples. The goddesses Ganga and Yamuna are also depicted; the figure of Ganga, standing on her crocodile or *makara*, is particularly notable.

The very large **Cave 29**, the Dumar Lena, is thought to be a transitional model between the simpler hollowed-out caves and the fully developed temples exemplified by the Kailasa. It has a wonderfully peaceful outlook over the nearby waterfall and it's possible to walk under the waterfall (though it's sometimes dry) to Cave 28, or vice versa.

Jain Caves

The Jain caves mark the final phase of Ellora. They do not have the drama and high-voltage energy of the best Hindu temples nor are they as ambitious in size, but they balance this with their exceptionally detailed work. There are only five Jain temples, and they're 1km north of the last Hindu temple (Cave 29) at the end of the bitumen road.

Cave 30, the Chota Kailasa or Little Kailasa, is a poor imitation of the great Kailasa Temple. It stands by itself some distance from the other Jain temples.

Cave 32, the Indra Sabha (Assembly Hall of Indra), is the finest of the Jain temples. Its ground-floor plan is similar to that of the Kailasa, but the upstairs area, reached by a stairway, is as ornate and richly decorated as downstairs is plain. There are images of the Jain *tirthankars* Parasnath and Gomateshvara, the latter surrounded by vegetation and wildlife. Inside the shrine is a seated figure of Mahavira, the 24th and last tirthankar, and founder of the Jain religion.

Cave 31 is really an extension of 32. **Cave 33**, the Jagannath Sabha, is similar in plan to 32 and has some particularly well-preserved sculptures. The final temple, the small **Cave 34**, also has interesting sculptures. On the hilltop over the Jain temples, a 5m-high image of Parasnath looks down on Ellora.

Places to Stay & Eat

Hotel Kailas *(☎ 02437-44543, fax 44467, e kailas@bom4.vsnl.net.in)*, close to the caves, is Ellora's only real hotel. Attractive double-bed cottages cost Rs 700, or Rs 1000 for rooms with a view of the caves. There's a 20% discount for singles, and a budget annexe where two basic doubles with private bathroom cost Rs 250 each. The restaurant has Indian and Chinese fare, and is cheaper than the nearby ***MTDC restaurant***.

Vijay's Rock Art Gallery *(☎ 02437-44552)*, a short walk farther along the road past the Kailas, has a few very basic and not too clean rooms set up behind artist Vijay Kulkarni's gallery and studio from Rs 250 to 350. Vijay's passion and life's work is reproducing the cave paintings of Ajanta.

Getting There & Away

There are regular buses from Aurangabad to Ellora (Rs 12); the last returns from Ellora at around 7 pm. There are also share-jeeps that leave when jam-packed and stop outside the bus stand in Aurangabad (Rs 11). An autorickshaw/taxi tour to Ellora with stops en route costs around Rs 300/500.

AJANTA

The Buddhist caves of Ajanta – 166km north-east of Aurangabad, and about 60km south of Jalgaon – date from around 200 BC to AD 650, predating those at Ellora. As Ellora developed and Buddhism gradually declined, the Ajanta caves were abandoned and eventually forgotten. But in 1819 a British hunting party stumbled upon them, and their remote beauty was soon unveiled. Their isolation contributed to the fine state of preservation in which some of their remarkable paintings remain to this day. Ajanta is listed as a World Heritage Site by Unesco.

Information

The caves are open from 9 am to 5.30 pm daily except Monday. Entry is US$10 for foreigners (Rs 10 for Indians) plus a Rs 5 lighting fee (required for Caves 1, 2, 16 and 17, where flash photography is strictly prohibited) and Rs 25 for a video camera.

Many of the caves are dark and a torch comes in useful. If possible, avoid coming here on weekends or public holidays when Ajanta can get very crowded with local tourists. The hawkers at Ajanta are persistent, too; most of them flogging pictorial guidebooks and crystalline rocks – if you don't want to buy, don't accept 'gifts' or make promises to 'just look'.

There's a free guarded cloakroom near the entrance where you can safely leave gear, so it is possible to arrive on a morning bus from Jalgaon, look around the caves, and continue to Aurangabad in the evening, or vice versa.

Government of India tourist office guides can be hired from the ticket office for Rs 245. It's worth at least having a guide for the main caves as they really bring the frescoes to life and can explain the complex stories behind them. Guides are included with tours, but the groups are often quite large.

The Caves

The 29 caves are cut into the steep face of a horseshoe-shaped rock gorge on the Waghore River. They are sequentially numbered from one end of the gorge to the other, but do not follow a chronological order; the oldest are mainly in the middle and the newer ones are close to each end.

Five of the caves are chaityas while the other 25 are viharas. Caves 8, 9, 10, 12 and 13 are older Early Buddhist caves, while the others are Mahayana (dated from around the 5th century AD). In the simpler, more austere Early Buddhist school, Buddha was never represented directly – his presence was always alluded to by a symbol such as the footprint or wheel of law.

Cave 1 This Mahayana vihara is one of the latest excavated and is the most beautifully decorated of the Ajanta caves.

A veranda at the front leads to a large congregation hall, with elaborate sculptures and narrative murals. Of particular interest is the use of perspective in the paintings and the details of dress and daily life. Many of the facial expressions are also wonderfully executed. The colours in the paintings were created from local minerals, with the exception of the vibrant blue made from Central Asian lapis lazuli.

Paintings include scenes from the *jatakas* (tales from Buddha's various lives), and portraits of the Bodhisattvas Padmapani (holding a lotus flower) and Vajrapani.

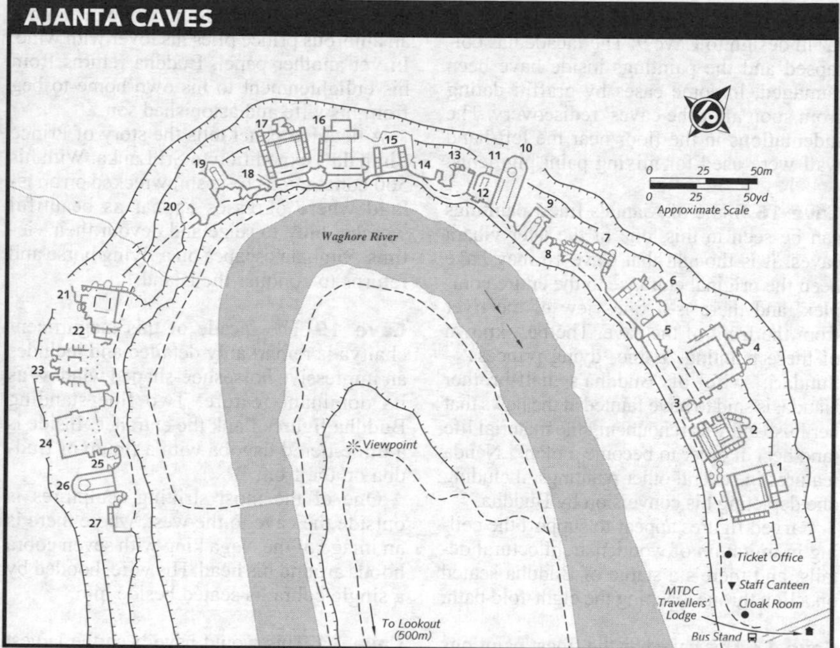

Among the interesting sculptures is one of four deer sharing a common head.

Don't leave Cave 1 without seeing the three aspects of Buddha (you'll need to ask an attendant to move the spotlight): A large statue of Buddha preaching in the deer park is illuminated from each side and then from below to reveal distinct facial expressions of solemnity, joy and serenity.

Cave 2 This is also a late Mahayana vihara with deliriously ornamented columns and capitals and some fine paintings. As well as murals, the ceiling is decorated with geometric and floral patterns. The mural scenes include a number of jatakas and events surrounding Buddha's birth, including his mother's dream of a six-tusked elephant, which heralded Buddha's conception.

Cave 4 This is the largest vihara at Ajanta and is supported by 28 pillars. Although never completed, the cave has some fine sculptures, including scenes of people fleeing from the 'eight great dangers' to the protection of Buddha's disciple Avalokiteshvara. Caves 3 and 5 were never completed.

Cave 6 This is the only two-storey vihara at Ajanta, but parts of the lower storey have collapsed. Inside is a seated Buddha figure and an intricately carved door to the shrine. Upstairs the hall is surrounded by cells with fine paintings on the doorways.

Cave 7 This cave is of unusual design in that the veranda does not lead into a hall with cells down the sides and a shrine room at the rear. Here there are porches before the veranda, which leads directly to the four cells and the elaborately sculptured shrine.

Cave 9 This is one of the earliest chaityas at Ajanta. Although it dates from the Early Buddhist period, the two figures flanking the entrance door were probably later Mahayana additions. Columns run down both sides of the cave and around the 3m-high dagoba at the far end. At the front there's a horseshoe-shaped window above the entrance, and the vaulted roof has traces of wooden ribs.

Cave 10 This is thought to be the oldest cave (200 BC) and was the one first spotted by the British soldiers who rediscovered

Ajanta. It is the largest chaitya and is similar in design to Cave 9. The facade has collapsed and the paintings inside have been damaged, in some cases by graffiti dating from soon after the caves' rediscovery. The indentations in the floor near the left-hand wall were used for mixing paint pigments.

Cave 16 Some of Ajanta's finest paintings can be seen in this, one of the later vihara caves. It is thought that Cave 16 may have been the original entrance to the entire complex, and there is a fine view of the river from the front of the cave. The best known of these paintings is the 'dying princess' – Sundari, wife of Buddha's half-brother Nanda, is said to have fainted at the news that her husband was renouncing the material life (and her) in order to become a monk. Nanda features in several other paintings, including one depicting his conversion by Buddha.

Carved figures appear to support the ceiling in imitation of wooden architectural details, and there's a statue of Buddha seated on a lion throne teaching the eight-fold path.

Cave 17 This cave has the finest paintings at Ajanta. Not only are they in the best condition, they are also the most numerous and varied. They include beautiful women flying overhead on the roof while carved dwarfs support the pillars. One of Ajanta's best-known images shows a princess, surrounded by attendants, applying make-up. In one there is a royal procession, while in another an amorous prince plies his lover with wine. In yet another panel, Buddha returns from his enlightenment to his own home to beg from his wife and astonished son.

A detailed panel tells the story of Prince Simhala's expedition to Sri Lanka. With his 500 companions he is shipwrecked on an island where ogresses appear as beautiful women, only to seize and devour their victims. Simhala escapes on a flying horse and returns to conquer the island.

Cave 19 The facade of this magnificent chaitya is remarkably detailed and includes an impressive horseshoe-shaped window as its dominant feature. Two fine standing Buddha figures flank the entrance. Inside is a three-tiered dagoba with a figure of Buddha on the front.

One of the most striking sculptures is outside the cave to the west, where there is an image of the Naga king with seven cobra hoods around his head. His wife, hooded by a single cobra, is seated beside him.

Cave 24 This would have been the largest vihara at Ajanta if it had been finished, and shows how the caves were constructed – long galleries were cut into the rock, and then the rock between them was broken through.

Caves 26 & 27 The fourth chaitya's facade has fallen and almost every trace of its

The 'Frescoes' of Ajanta

The famous Ajanta 'frescoes' are technically not frescoes at all. A fresco is a painting done on a wet surface that absorbs the colour. The Ajanta paintings are more correctly *tempera*, since they used animal glue and vegetable gum mixed with the paint pigments to bind them to the dry surface. The rough-hewn rock walls were coated with a 1cm-thick layer of clay and cow dung mixed with rice husks. A final coat of lime was applied to produce the finished surface on which the artist painted. This was then polished to produce a high gloss. The colours were obtained from a variety of minerals and ochres – the striking blue comes from the semiprecious lapis lazuli.

The paintings initially suffered some deterioration after their rediscovery, and some heavy-handed restoration also caused damage, but between 1920 and 1922, two Italian art experts conducted a meticulous restoration process, and the paintings have been carefully preserved ever since.

Early attempts to record the paintings also ended in disaster. A Major Robert Gill spent 27 years at the site from 1844, meticulously recording the paintings. They were displayed at the Crystal Palace in London, but were lost in December 1866 when the building burnt to the ground. Gill returned to Ajanta to recommence his labours, but died only a year later. In 1872, John Griffiths of the Bombay School of Art arrived at the site and spent 13 years recording the paintings. Tragically his work was also lost in a fire at the Victoria and Albert Museum in London.

paintings has disappeared. Nevertheless, there are some fine sculptures remaining. On the left wall is a huge figure of the 'reclining Buddha', lying back as he prepares to enter nirvana. Other scenes include a lengthy depiction of Buddha's temptation by Mara. Cave 27 is virtually a vihara connected to the Cave 26 chaitya.

Viewpoints

There are two lookouts from where you can get a good view of the whole horseshoe-shaped gorge from which the Ajanta caves were carved. The first is an easy 10-minute walk beyond the river crossing below Cave 27 (a path leads down from Cave 16 through a small park to the concrete bridge). A farther 20-minute uphill walk from here leads to the lookout from where the British party first spotted the caves. It's also possible to take a taxi up to the latter viewpoint from the car park outside the caves.

Places to Stay & Eat

It's a long day trip to Ajanta from Aurangabad and many visitors prefer to stay close by, although the MTDC hotels are not the bargain they once were.

MTDC Travellers' Lodge *(☎ 02438-4226)* is right by the entrance to the caves. Rooms with shared bathroom cost Rs 200/250. Checkout is 9 am. The food in the restaurant is reasonably good.

MTDC Holiday Resort *(☎ 02438-4230)* at Fardapur, 5km from the caves, is quieter and has nicer rooms (TV, hot shower), but the price is steep at Rs 520 for a double, or Rs 624 with air-con. There's a basic restaurant.

Near the ticket window at the caves themselves, the ***staff canteen*** is open to all (in fact, the staff make every attempt to drag you in) and serves good cheap thalis and other vegetarian snacks as well as cold drinks.

Getting There & Away

For information on buses from Aurangabad or Jalgaon, see those sections. Buses pull up in front of the caves and there's a timetable posted in the MTDC Travellers' Lodge. The last bus back to Aurangabad is at 5.45 pm and the last one to Jalgaon at 5.35 pm.

The caves are 4km off the main road from Aurangabad to Jalgaon and Fardapur is 1km farther down the main road towards Jalgaon. If you don't get a direct bus to Ajanta you may have to hang around at Fardapur waiting for a local bus, or an autorickshaw should take you for Rs 30.

Share-taxis or jeeps operate between the caves, Fardapur and Jalgaon. Prices are negotiable, but expect to pay around Rs 10 from Ajanta to Fardapur and Rs 500 for the whole taxi to Jalgaon.

JALGAON

☎ 0257

Jalgaon is on the main railway line from Mumbai to the country's north-east, and is a hub for trains in all directions. For many it's a practical or essential overnight stop en route to the Ajanta caves, 60km to the south.

Places to Stay & Eat

The ***retiring rooms*** at the station aren't bad value with dorm beds for Rs 40 and doubles at Rs 60 per person, but Jalgaon is blessed with some very decent hotels right in front of the train station.

Hotel Plaza *(☎ 227354, Station Rd)*, about 150m up from the station on the left-hand side, is one of the cleanest and most welcoming budget hotels in Maharashtra. Spotless rooms with white tiled floors, private bathroom and cable TV cost Rs 150 or Rs 180 for singles, Rs 220 or Rs 280 for doubles. The effusive manager/owner is a mine of useful information.

The ***Anjali Guest House*** *(☎ 225079, Station Rd)*, on the right past the autorickshaw stand, is also a very clean place with rooms from Rs 200/225. There's a good vegetarian restaurant downstairs.

Hotel Galaxy *(☎ 223578, Jilha Rd)* is right next to the bus stand, about 2km from the train station. Reasonable rooms with TV cost Rs 250/300, there's a smaller single for Rs 190, and air-con doubles are Rs 550.

Getting There & Away

Several express trains between Mumbai and Delhi or Kolkata (Calcutta) stop briefly in Jalgaon. The trip to Mumbai (eight hours, 420km) costs Rs 148/428 in sleeper/three-tier air-con. There are no decent arrival times from Mumbai unless you leave from Dadar or Lokmanya Tilak stations. For Agra and Delhi, take the 6.35 am *Amritsar Express*.

From Jalgaon there are hourly buses to Fardapur (Rs 26, two hours), continuing on to

Aurangabad (Rs 66, four hours). If you want to get straight to the caves there are three direct buses to Ajanta in the morning at 6.20, 8.45 and 10.30 am. Jalgaon's train and bus stations are about 2km apart (Rs 15 by autorickshaw). There are plenty of luxury bus offices on Station Rd with departures to Mumbai (Rs 200, 11 hours), Nagpur (Rs 220, 10 hours), Aurangabad (Rs 120, 3½ hours).

LONAR METEORITE CRATER

Near the village of Lonar, on a flat plain about 140km east of Aurangabad, is a huge meteorite crater. Believed to be about 50,000 years old, the crater is 2km in diameter and 170m deep, with a shallow lake at the bottom. A plaque at the rim states that it is 'the only natural hypervelocity impact crater in basaltic rock in the world'. Scientists suspect that the meteor is still embedded about 600m below the south-eastern rim of the crater.

There are several **Hindu temples** on the crater floor, and langur monkeys, peacocks, gazelles and an array of birds inhabit the bushes by the lake. You can spend an enjoyable afternoon wandering around here. The crater is about 15 minutes' walk from the bus stand – ask for directions to Lonar Tank.

At the time of writing, the MTDC was constructing a ***guesthouse*** at Lonar crater, which will certainly be the most comfortable place to stay. Contact the MTDC in Aurangabad or Fardapur for rates and booking.

Getting There & Away

There are some direct buses to Lonar from Aurangabad (Rs 70, five hours), or take a bus or a train to Jalna and change there. Lonar can also be reached by bus from Fardapur with a change at Buldhana.

It's possible to visit Lonar on a day trip from Aurangabad if you hire a car and driver. Classic Travels (☎ 337788) in Aurangabad has cars for around Rs 1400 (Rs 2000 with overnight stop), or shop around for taxis outside the bus stand.

NAGPUR

☎ 0712 • pop 1.8 million

Situated on the River Nag in the north-eastern corner of the state, Nagpur is India's orange-growing capital. It was once the capital of the central province, but was later incorporated into Maharashtra. Long ago it was a centre for the aboriginal Gond tribes who remained in power until the early 18th century; many Gonds still live in the region. Its final place in Maharashtra is still not assured – Nagpur is the centre of the Vidarbha region, in which there is a growing movement for a separate state.

On 18 October each year the city hosts thousands of Buddhists celebrating the anniversary of Dr Ambedkar's conversion to Buddhism in 1956. The main centre of the Buddhist movement is **Digsha Bumi**, where a huge white stupa has been constructed.

Dr Ambedkar's Conversion

One of Maharashtra's most important figures in recent history was Dr Bhimrao Ramji Ambedkar, a low-caste Hindu, Law Minister and Scheduled Castes leader.

Dr Ambedkar was born into a Dalit household in the district of Ratnagiri in 1891. After graduating from Bombay's Elphinstone College he was offered the chance to study abroad where he earned impressive qualifications in Britain and the USA. On returning to India in 1923, his work life became intolerable when his associates refused to directly hand him anything for fear of ritual pollution. The following year he launched his legal and political fight for Dalit rights and spent the next two decades skilfully using the courts to seek equality for depressed classes. Among his publicised struggles was a march in Mahad in 1927 to establish rights for Untouchables to drink from the public water supply, and a movement at the Kalaram Temple in Nasik to allow Dalits temple access.

Dr Ambedkar fought to secure an allotment of places for Dalits in parliament and is regarded as one of the key architects of the Indian constitution – a document that officially wiped out untouchability in India.

Despite these successes, Dr Ambedkar eventually lost faith that Hindu discrimination against Dalits would ever be overcome and, on 14 October 1956, he converted to Buddhism at Digsha Bumi in Nagpur – an act that was repeated by an estimated three million low-caste Hindus. He died only weeks later on 6 December, 1956.

There is little of interest for travellers here, except those heading for Gandhi's ashram at Sevagram, the remote Navagaon or Tadoba national parks, or taking a break on the long journey across the subcontinent.

Information

Nagpur has an MTDC office (☎ 533325), though staff here blithely tell you there is nothing to see or do in Nagpur. It's at Sanskritik Bachat Bhavan, Sitabuldi (opposite Hotel Hardeo).

The most reliable place to change money is the State Bank of India on Kingsway, a two-minute walk west of the train station.

If you're heading up to Madhya Pradesh, there's a useful MP Tourism office (☎ 523 374) on the 4th floor, Lokmat Bhavan. On the same floor is Cyber Den Internet cafe.

There are a couple of Internet centres on Central Ave charging Rs 20 an hour. Computrek (☎ 727435), 18 Central Ave, is open from 7 am to 9 pm daily.

Places to Stay

The best area for budget and mid-range hotels is Central Ave, a 15-minute walk east of the train station. Turn right as you leave the station concourse, then right again across the bridge over the railway tracks into Central Ave. If you arrive by bus, an autorickshaw to Central Ave will cost around Rs 20.

Hotel Blue Diamond *(☎ 727461, ⓔ bluediamond@nagpurkhoj.com, 113 Central Ave)* is probably the best of the budget places. Small singles/doubles are Rs 100/150 with shared bathroom, Rs 130/200 with private bathroom and Rs 350/450 with air-con. Air coolers and TVs are available for an extra charge and the hotel has a restaurant and bar.

Hotel Blue Moon *(☎ 726061, ⓔ micron@bom3.vsnl.net.in)* is one of the first places you come to if walking from the train station. It's an ageing but friendly hotel with singles/doubles with private bathroom and TV from Rs 225/400 and air-con rooms for Rs 550/650.

Hotel Skylark *(☎ 724654, fax 726193, 119 Central Ave)*, farther east, is a better option. Singles/doubles with private bathroom and TV cost Rs 350/450, or Rs 600/700 with air-con.

Hotel Pal Palace *(☎ 724725, fax 722337, 25 Central Ave)* is comfortable enough with singles/doubles from Rs 250/350 to Rs 550/650 (air-con); suites are Rs 1200 (all plus 14% tax).

Places to Eat

There are dozens of cheap *dhabas* (snack bars), food stalls and fruit stands directly opposite the train station, most of which liven up in the evening.

Krishnum, on Central Ave, has cheap dosas, samosas, vegetarian pizzas and thalis (Rs 25 to 45), as well as ice creams, fresh fruit juices and shakes. The ***bakery*** and sweet shop downstairs also has a good selection.

The ***Host Restaurant*** at Hotel Pal Palace has a good range of Indian, Chinese and continental dishes, including such rarities as chicken kiev (Rs 90).

The Grill at Hotel Skylark is also good.

Getting There & Away

Air Indian Airlines (☎ 533962), on RN Tagore, Civil Lines, has two daily flights to Mumbai (US$130), one to Delhi (US$150), and flights on Wednesday, Friday and Sunday to Hyderabad (US$115) and Kolkata (US$165).

Bus The main MSRTC bus stand is 2km south of the train station and hotel area. There are regular departures for Wardha (Rs 33, two hours) and Ramtek (Rs 21, 1½ hours), two daily buses to Jalgaon (Rs 179, 10 hours) and deluxe buses to Hyderabad (Rs 300, 12 hours). Buses to Madhya Pradesh operate from a separate stand about 500m west of the station, and include regular services to Jabalpur (Rs 115/137 ordinary/deluxe, seven hours), and two daily buses to Bhopal (Rs 187, 12 hours) and Indore (Rs 278, 16 hours).

Train Nagpur Junction train station is an impressive edifice in the centre of town. Nagpur is on the main Mumbai-Howrah line so there are several daily expresses in each direction. The overnight *Vidharba Express* originates in Nagpur, departing for Mumbai CST at 3 pm (Rs 244/707 sleeper/three-tier air-con) and takes 15 hours. The same train departs Mumbai nightly at 7.35 pm for Nagpur. Heading north to Kolkata the *Mumbai Howrah Mail* departs from Nagpur at 11.30 am and arrives at Howrah at 7.40 am (Rs 297/860). Five Mumbai-bound expresses stop at Jalgaon (for Ajanta caves). Nagpur also has good connections to Bangalore, Delhi and Hyderabad.

AROUND NAGPUR

Ramtek

About 40km north-east of Nagpur, Ramtek has a number of picturesque 600-year-old **temples**, spectacularly situated on the Hill of Rama above the town. Rama is said to have spent time here with Sita and Lakshmi in the epic Ramayana.

Along the road to the temples is a **memorial** to the Sanskrit dramatist Kalidasa, and east of the Hill of Rama is the Ramsagar Tank, lined with bathing ghats and smaller temples. Autorickshaws will take you the 5km from the bus stand up to the temples for Rs 30, but it's worth walking back down via the steps from the back of the temple and through the village.

The hilltop ***Rajkamal Resort*** *(☎ 07114-55620)* has rooms for Rs 400 a double, but they are clean, with hot water shower and TV, and there's a basic restaurant.

Buses run roughly every half an hour between Ramtek and the MSRTC bus stand in Nagpur (Rs 21, 1½ hours). The last bus back to Nagpur is at 8.30 pm.

SEVAGRAM

If you are at all interested in the life and philosophy of Mahatma Gandhi, it's well worth making the long trek to the heart of India to visit Sevagram, the Village of Service, where Gandhi established his ashram in 1933. For the 15 years from then until India achieved Independence, Gandhi's headquarters was in some ways the alternative capital of India – the British considered it important enough to install a telephone box here with a hotline to Delhi.

The ashram encompasses 40 hectares of farmland, as well as residences and research centres, though the central complex itself is quite small. The original adobe huts of the ashram are still preserved, as are the Mahatma's personal effects, including his famous spinning wheel and spectacles.

Across the road from the ashram, there's an interesting photo exhibition following the events in Gandhi's life.

Nondenominational prayer services are held daily at 4.45 am and 6 pm under the pipal tree planted by Gandhi in 1936. Ashramites follow a strict daily routine and while visitors aren't required to work, they are encouraged to participate in half an hour of community spinning each day, and to be on time for meals. At other times, life at Sevagram is extremely leisurely.

Hand-spun cloth *(khadi)* is for sale at the ashram, as are volumes of Gandhi's writings.

Places to Stay & Eat

Accommodation at the ashram is basic, but clean and naturally very cheap.

Rustam Bhavan has four double rooms with private bathroom for Rs 25 per person. The ashram can be contacted on ☎ 07152-43526 to check availability of rooms. Vegetarian meals are served communally in the dining hall for a nominal sum.

MTDC Holiday Resort *(☎ 07152-43872)* in Wardha offers less interesting but more comfortable singles/doubles for Rs 150/220. Turn right as you exit the train station and it's a five minute walk, across the road from the bus stand.

Getting There & Away

The ashram can be reached from Wardha or Sevagram train stations, both on the Central Railway. Express trains from Nagpur to Sevagram (76km, Rs 28 in 2nd class) take a little over an hour. Express MSRTC buses run frequently between Nagpur and Wardha (Rs 33, two hours).

There are regular local buses to the ashram from Wardha (Rs 3, 20 minutes), or an autorickshaw will cost Rs 40 for the 8km trip.

AROUND SEVAGRAM

Paunar

At Paunar, just 3km from Sevagram on the road to Nagpur, is the ashram of Vinoba Bhave, Gandhi's disciple. This persistent soul walked through India encouraging rich landlords to hand over tracts of land for redistribution to the landless and poor – he managed to persuade them to hand over a total of 1.6 million hectares.

The ashram, run almost entirely by women, is dedicated to *swarajya*, or rural self-sufficiency. It is an interesting working ashram, operated on a social system of consensus with no central management. Basic accommodation at a nominal cost is available at the ashram and, while women are preferred, it is open to all.

Goa

The former Portuguese enclave of Goa has beckoned travellers for many years with its palm-fringed beaches, liberal attitudes and renowned 'travellers' scene'. Times are changing for India's laid-back holiday state, though. Central government laws banning loud music in open spaces after 10 pm has virtually ended the famous all-night rave parties; while the increase in charter and package tourism has resulted in runaway development at many of the beach resorts.

But away from tourism, Goa has a character quite distinct from the rest of India and offers much more than just the hedonism of sun, sand and sea. Despite four decades of 'liberation' from Portuguese colonial rule, Roman Catholicism remains a major religion in Goa, skirts far outnumber saris, and the people display an easy-going tropical indulgence, humour and civility.

Gleaming, Portuguese-style whitewashed churches, paddy fields, dense coconut palm groves, and crumbling forts guarding rocky capes make up the Goan landscape. Markets are lively, colourful affairs, and siesta is widely observed during the hot afternoons. Goans love to celebrate and this is reflected in the huge number of feasts and festivities.

Farming, fishing, tourism and iron-ore mining form the basis of the economy, although the last two sources of income are sometimes incompatible with the former. Mining has caused damage to paddy fields, and the five-star tourist resorts, with their swimming pools, have placed a heavy strain on water supplies.

History

Goa's history stretches back to the 3rd century BC when it formed part of the Mauryan empire. Later it was ruled by the Satavahanas of Kolhapur and eventually passed to the Chalukyans of Badami control from AD 580 to 750.

Goa fell to the Muslims for the first time in 1312, but the invaders were forced out in 1370 by Harihara I of the Vijayanagar empire, whose capital was at Hampi. During the next 100 years Goa's harbours were important landing places for ships carrying Arabian horses to Hampi to strengthen the Vijayanagar cavalry.

Goa at a Glance

Population: 1.3 million
Area: 3701 sq km
Capital: Panaji
Main Languages: Konkani, Marathi, English & Hindi
Telephone Area Code: 0832
When to Go: Oct to Mar

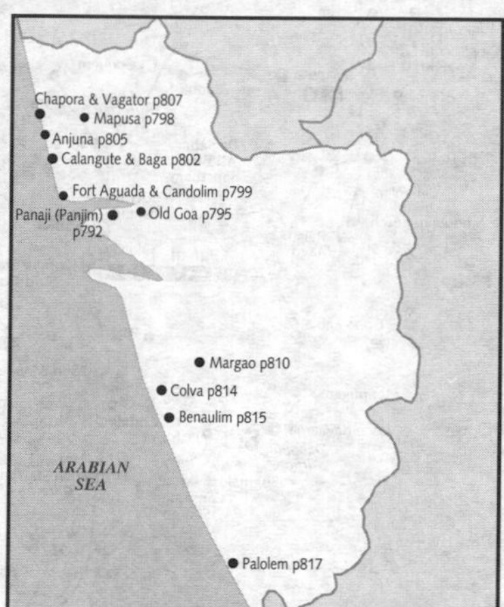

- Wander the lanes of the old Portuguese quarter of Panaji and enjoy a beer or *feni* on the balcony of Hotel Venite
- Explore the magnificent cathedrals in Old Goa, the fallen city that once rivalled Lisbon
- Check out Anjuna's famous Wednesday flea market and then party on at the Shore Bar
- Relax under coconut palms at Palolem, one of Goa's most idyllic beaches
- Hire a scooter or motorcycle and explore Goa at your own pace
- Time your visit for one of Goa's riotous festivals such as Carnival, prior to Lent

Blessed as it is by natural harbours and wide rivers, Goa was the ideal base for the seafaring Portuguese, who arrived in 1510 aiming to control the spice route from the

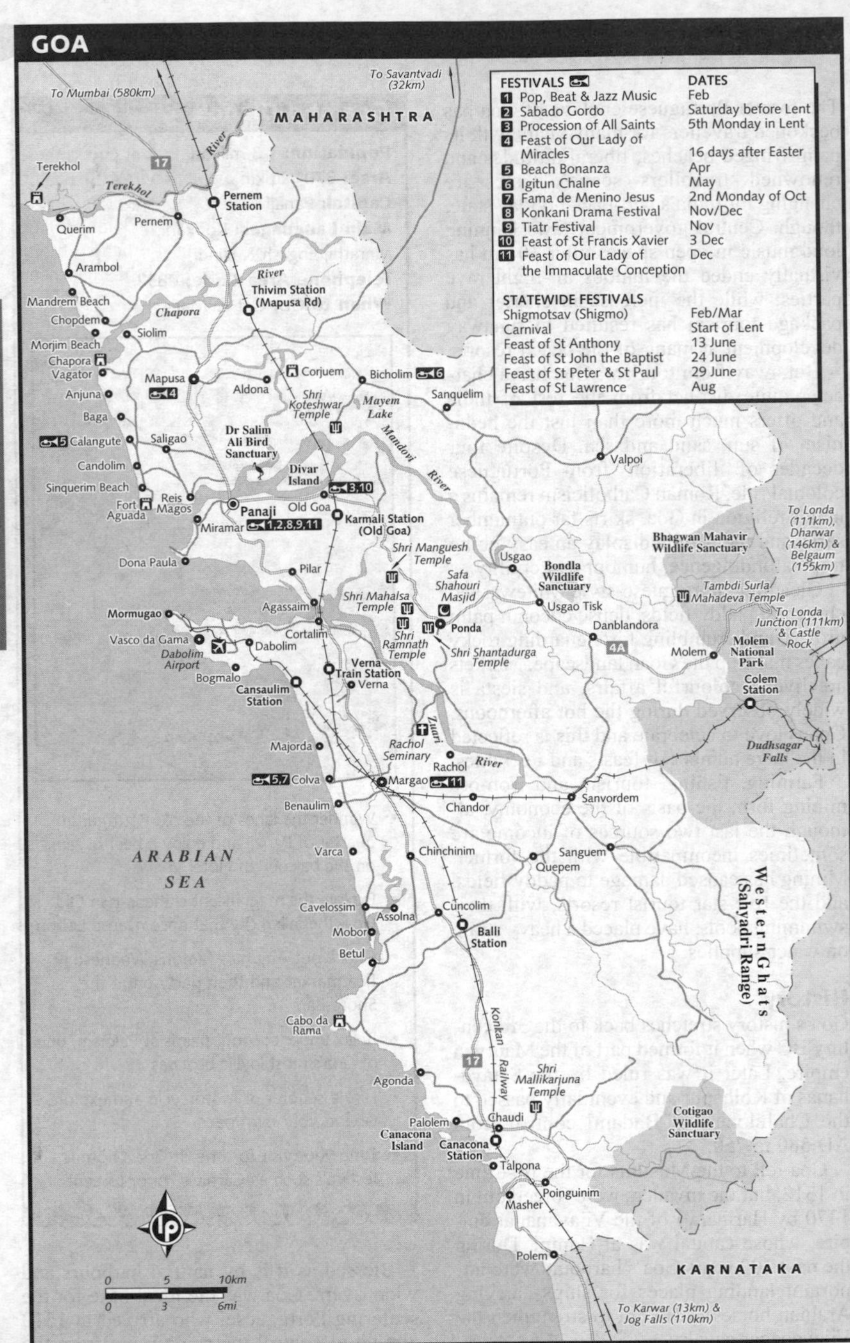
GOA
FESTIVALS
1 Pop, Beat & Jazz Music — Feb
2 Sabado Gordo — Saturday before Lent
3 Procession of All Saints — 5th Monday in Lent
4 Feast of Our Lady of Miracles — 16 days after Easter
5 Beach Bonanza — Apr
6 Igitun Chalne — May
7 Fama de Menino Jesus — 2nd Monday of Oct
8 Konkani Drama Festival — Nov/Dec
9 Tiatr Festival — Nov
10 Feast of St Francis Xavier — 3 Dec
11 Feast of Our Lady of the Immaculate Conception — Dec
STATEWIDE FESTIVALS
Shigmotsav (Shigmo) — Feb/Mar
Carnival — Start of Lent
Feast of St Anthony — 13 June
Feast of St John the Baptist — 24 June
Feast of St Peter & St Paul — 29 June
Feast of St Lawrence — Aug
To Mumbai (580km)
To Savantvadi (32km)
MAHARASHTRA
KARNATAKA
ARABIAN SEA
Western Ghats (Sahyadri Range)
To Londa (111km), Dharwar (146km) & Belgaum (155km)
To Londa Junction (111km) & Castle Rock
To Karwar (13km) & Jog Falls (110km)
Terekhol
Querim
Pernem
Pernem Station
Arambol
Mandrem Beach
Chopdem
Morjim Beach
Chapora
Vagator
Siolim
Thivim Station (Mapusa Rd)
Anjuna
Mapusa
Aldona
Corjuem
Bicholim
Sanquelim
Baga
Calangute
Saligao
Candolim
Sinquerim Beach
Fort Aguada
Reis Magos
Dr Salim Ali Bird Sanctuary
Divar Island
Shri Koteshwar Temple
Mayem Lake
Mandovi River
Chapora River
Terekhol River
Panaji
Miramar
Old Goa
Karmali Station (Old Goa)
Valpoi
Dona Paula
Pilar
Shri Manguesh Temple
Safa Shahouri Masjid
Shri Mahalsa Temple
Shri Ramnath Temple
Shri Shantadurga Temple
Ponda
Usgao
Bondla Wildlife Sanctuary
Usgao Tisk
Bhagwan Mahavir Wildlife Sanctuary
Tambdi Surla Mahadeva Temple
Danblandora
Molem
Molem National Park
Colem Station
Dudhsagar Falls
Mormugao
Vasco da Gama
Dabolim Airport
Dabolim
Agassaim
Cortalim
Bogmalo
Cansaulim Station
Verna Train Station
Verna
Rachol Seminary
Rachol
Zuari River
Majorda
Colva
Margao
Benaulim
Chandor
Sanvordem
Varca
Chinchinim
Sanguem
Quepem
Cavelossim
Assolna
Cuncolim
Mobor
Balli Station
Betul
Cabo da Rama
Konkan Railway
Agonda
Shri Mallikarjuna Temple
Palolem
Chaudi
Canacona Island
Canacona Station
Cotigao Wildlife Sanctuary
Talpona
Poinguinim
Masher
Polem
17
4A
0 5 10km
0 3 6mi

east. They also had a strong desire to spread Christianity. Jesuit missionaries led by St Francis Xavier arrived in 1542. For a while, Portuguese control was limited to a small area around Old Goa, but by the middle of the 16th century it had expanded to include the provinces of Bardez and Salcete.

Fortunes made from the spice trade led to Goa's golden age. The colony became a viceregal seat of the Portuguese empire. But competition from the British, French and Dutch in the 17th century led to decline.

The Marathas almost vanquished the Portuguese in the late 18th century and there was a brief occupation by the British during the Napoleonic Wars in Europe. But it was not until 1961, when they were ejected by India, that the Portuguese finally disappeared from the subcontinent.

Dangers & Annoyances

As with any tourist enclave, security can be a problem in Goa. Theft from rooms is something to watch out for, particularly on party nights at places like Anjuna and Vagator, or if you're renting a flimsy beach shack. Never leave money, passport or other valuables in your room. Many guesthouses and hotels provide safe deposit boxes.

Muggings have been reported in Goa, particularly in quiet, unlit lanes away from the beach. Avoid being alone at night unless there are plenty of people around. More disturbing are reports of attacks on young women – solo women travellers shouldn't walk alone on the beach at night, or go unaccompanied along unlit village lanes. Street lighting has been added to many lanes in places such as Colva and Benaulim in recent years, but it is little help if nobody else is around.

The Arabian Sea can be a little deceptive and every year people drown here. Most of the main beaches are safe enough, but there are no beach patrols so ask local advice about undercurrents and rips. It's not a good idea to go for a midnight dip on your own, especially if you've been drinking, and the sea is definitely not safe for swimming during the monsoon. Look out for jellyfish, which can occasionally drift in from deeper waters.

Hotel and taxi touts are becoming a major annoyance at Goa's beach resorts. If

GOA

The Beach Files

Goa's biggest attraction for Western visitors is its beaches. The beaches, associated villages and resorts that have grown up around them have changed over the years, but all still have a very different character. The following is a brief rundown of Goa's beaches from north to south.

Arambol This is a quiet village with a rocky headland and chilled-out scene, although it's developing fast. Many travellers rent rooms long-term here.

Mandrem & Morjim The beaches here are clean, but uninspiring; it's a peaceful, area where you can get away from it all. There's some great places to stay; it's destined to be the next Arambol.

Chapora & Vagator There's a picturesque beach and rocky headland here with a laid-back village attracting backpackers, long-term hippies and ravers.

Anjuna There's a good stretch of beach near the flea market. Anjuna is still popular with the party crowd, though the parties themselves have waned.

Baga & Calangute The long stretch of very crowded beach here has loads of beach shacks and sun beds. This is package-tourism central, though many backpackers still prefer the upbeat atmosphere here to further north.

Candolim This place has upscale tourism and a quieter beach than Calangute.

Bogmalo The small, exclusive beach here has water sports (it's the main diving centre for Goa).

Colva & Benaulim There's a similar beach to Calangute, but it's much quieter and still has a noticeable fishing industry. There's a mix of package tourists, Indian tourists and backpackers.

Varca & Cavelossim Five-star luxury resorts here are surrounded by relatively empty beaches.

Agonda There's an average beach, but it's a good place to chill out – mostly attracting laid-back travellers doing as little as possible.

Palolem This is Goa's 'paradise lost' according to some. It's still the most idyllic beach in the state, but fast filling up with travellers and the businesses set up to service them. Accommodation is still mostly in beach shacks and village homes.

a driver tells you the hotel you want is full, closed, burnt down or whatever, it's because he wants to take you to one that will pay him commission. Treat touts with suspicion and always ask to be taken to the place of your choice first.

Legal Matters

Drugs Acid, ecstasy and marijuana – the drugs of choice for many party goers – are illegal (though still very much available) and any attempt to purchase them is fraught with danger. Fort Aguada prison houses some foreigners serving lengthy sentences for drug offences, because for some time now authorities have been taking a hard line on the parties and the drugs.

Possession of even a small amount of *charas* (hashish) can mean 10 years in prison. There have been cases of policemen approaching hapless tourists and threatening to 'plant' drugs on them unless they pay a relatively large amount of money on the spot. Most travellers comply – the prospect of several months awaiting trial, and then possibly a jail sentence, makes it only wise to do so.

Probably the best way to deal with the problem should it happen to you is to try persuasion, but if that fails, pay the baksheesh. While doing this, make a mental note of every distinguishing feature of the policeman you are paying. Immediately after the incident, write a letter describing exactly what happened, with as much detail as possible.

Copies of the letter should go to the Government of India tourist office in Panaji (not the Goan Tourist Department), any one (or all) of the three daily English-language newspapers in Goa, and the Government of India tourist office in your own country.

Sun-bathers should be aware that nudism (including topless bathing for women) is illegal in Goa.

Special Events

There is a strong Christian influence in Goa and this is reflected in the number of feast days and festivals that follow the religious calendar. As well as the more popular Christian holidays (Christmas, Easter etc) Goans use feast days to celebrate events such as the arrival of the monsoon.

Igitun Chalne (fire-walking), held at Sirigao Temple in Bicholim province in May, is one of Goa's most distinctive festivals. The high point of the festival comes when devotees of the goddess Lairaya walk across burning coals to prove their devotion.

The **Feast of St Anthony** in June, has also taken on local significance. It is said that if the monsoon has not arrived by the time of this feast day, a statue of the saint should be lowered into the family well to hasten the arrival of the rain. The Feast of St John in June is a thanksgiving for the arrival of the monsoon. Wells start to fill up again, and to mark the event young men jump into the water. Since each well owner by tradition has to supply *feni* (liquor distilled from coconut milk or cashews – the fruit, not the nut) to the swimmers, the feast day is marked by increasingly high spirits.

Shigmotsav (Shigmo) of Holi is Goa's version of the Hindu Holi festival, and it marks the beginning of spring. Coloured water and red powder are thrown around at everyone and anyone and parades are sometimes held in the main towns.

Fat Saturday is part of the state-wide **Carnival** and is held on the Saturday before Lent. It's celebrated in Panaji by a procession of floats and raucous street partying.

Accommodation

Accommodation prices in Goa are based on high, middle and low seasons. High season is mid-December to late January, the middle (shoulder) period is from October to mid-December and February to June, and the low season is from July to September. Unless otherwise stated, prices quoted here are high-season rates. If you're in Goa during the rest of the year, then expect discounts of about 25/60% in middle/low season. There's a fourth season when prices rise again, sometimes ridiculously, over the peak Christmas period from around 22 December to 3 January. This usually applies to short-term stays and is prevalent in package-tourist hotels.

Year round, there's a state-imposed 'luxury tax' of 8% on rooms over Rs 100 and 12% on rooms over Rs 800. Many budget places include this in the quoted price, but in mid-range and top-end hotels it will be added to the bill.

Food & Drink

Goans are passionate about their food and there are several local specialities, including the popular pork vindaloo. Other pork specialities include the *chourisso* (Goan sausage), and the pig's liver dish known as *sorpotel*. *Xacutí* is a spicy chicken or meat dish; *bangra* is Goan mackerel; *sanna* are rice 'cupcakes' soaked in palm toddy before cooking; *dodol* and *bebinca* are special Christmas sweets, the latter made from layers of sweet pancake.

Commercially produced alcohol is readily available and inexpensive in Goa, but that hasn't stopped the Goans from enjoying their own brand of firewater. Most common of these is feni. A bottle bought from a liquor shop costs only slightly more than a bottle of beer bought at a restaurant. It's very strong, both in taste and in effect, and is best mixed with a soft drink (soda) such as Limca. Reasonably palatable wines are also turned out in Goa. The dry white is not bad; the red is basically a port.

Getting There & Away

Air Goa's airport, Dabolim, is 29km from Panaji, on the coast near Vasco da Gama. Most of India's domestic airlines operate services here, as well as several direct charter companies that fly into Goa from the UK and Germany. Dabolim was declared an international airport in 2000, but charter flights into and out of Goa are controlled – it's illegal to fly into India on a scheduled flight and out on a charter flight. If you book an international flight from Goa, it will involve a domestic flight to Mumbai (Bombay; or another international airport) and a connection there.

There are numerous flights between Goa and Mumbai. Indian Airlines flies daily for US$85, and Jet Airways has three flights daily (two on Tuesday and Sunday) for US$93. Sahara Airlines also flies direct to Mumbai (US$85) and Delhi (US$235).

Indian Airlines has daily direct flights to Delhi (US$235), Bangalore (US$105) and Pune (US$120), two flights a week to Chennai (Madras; US$140), Cochin (US$125) and Calicut (US$105), and two flights also to Agra (US$230, Tuesday and Saturday). In the case of the Pune and Agra services, the flights only operate one way (ie, there is no direct Agra-Goa service).

Bus Long-distance interstate buses operate to/from Panaji, Margao, Mapusa and Vasco. See those sections for more information.

Train The 760km Konkan Railway linking Mumbai with Mangalore opened in 1998, finally making Goa accessible by train. The main Konkan Railway station in Goa is Margao, but expresses and passenger trains stop at most other stations along the line.

There are two daily expresses between Margao and Mumbai CST (plus two more from Lokmanya Tilak, 16km north of Mumbai CST). From Mumbai CST the overnight *Konkan Kanya Express* is the best option (Rs 193/558 in sleeper/three-tier air-con, 12 hours). There are seven expresses between Margao and Mangalore, with most stopping at Mangalore's Kankanadi station (4½ hours, 317km).

The South Central Railway operates from Vasco da Gama via Margao and Londa, and runs to Pune, Delhi and Bangalore. Getting to Delhi on the *Nizamuddin-Goa Express* (2200km) takes about 41 hours and the fare is Rs 410/1939 in sleeper/two-tier air-con.

Seats and sleepers can be booked at Margao and Vasco da Gama station, or at the train reservation office in Panaji's Kadamba bus stand. Other useful stations on the Konkan route are Pernem for Arambol; Thivim (Mapusa Road) for Mapusa and the northern beaches; Karmali (Old Goa) for Panaji and Canacona for Palolem.

Getting Around

Bus The state-run Kadamba bus company is the main operator, although there are also private companies. Local buses are cheap, services are frequent and they run to just about everywhere, eventually. The going can be slow on some routes because of the frequent stops. Destination signs at the bus stands are in English and there are information counters at the main depots.

Car Self-drive car rental is available in Goa, but it's expensive. Sai Service has a counter at the airport (☎ 514817) and an office at Alto Porvorim (☎ 417063, fax 417064). A non air-con Maruti car costs Rs 900 for 24 hours with 150km per day. It's generally cheaper to rent a taxi or car and driver for a specific trip or for a day's sightseeing.

Perhaps the biggest threat to your sanity at Goa's beach resorts is the taxi men. You can't walk a few metres without being asked if you want one (a taxi, that is). It's a form of local mental torture.

Motorcycle Goa is one of the few places in India where hiring a motorcycle or scooter is cheap and easy, and the relatively short distances make travel a breeze. Many travellers find that having their own transport is the only way to enjoy Goa. Bikes available include old Enfields, more modern Yamaha 100s and the gearless Kinetic Honda scooters. What you pay for, with some exceptions, is what you get, and prices also vary according to season and the length of rental. In peak Christmas season, on a daily basis, you're looking at up to Rs 300 for a scooter, Rs 400 for the small bikes and Rs 500 for an Enfield. Outside this time, when there's a glut of idle bikes, especially at the northern beach resorts, you should only pay Rs 100/250/350 per day for scooters/small bikes/Enfields if you hire for a week or more. In most cases you don't need to provide a deposit, but you'll probably be asked for your passport details (don't hand over the passport itself) and the name of your hotel. Guesthouses and hotels are good places to rent a bike, but you'll get plenty of offers on the street.

While most bikes will have some sort of insurance, if you're involved in an accident you'll probably be required to pay for the damage to the rental bike, at the very least.

Although Goan lanes – and the main highway for that matter – are probably safer than most Indian roads, inexperienced, helmetless foreigners on motorcycles are extremely vulnerable. Each season, more than a few tourists travel home in a box via the state mortuary in Panaji. Never forget that the Highway Code in India can be reduced to one essential truth – 'might is right' – and on a motorcycle, you're pretty low on the hierarchy. India is certainly no place to learn how to ride a motorcycle, or even a scooter. Also make sure that the machine you rent is in a reasonable state of repair (with working horn, indicators and brakes). In fact, helmets are now compulsory for all motorcycle riders and their pillion passengers in Goa. This affects travellers renting motorcycles and motorcycle taxis, which must provide a spare helmet for their passengers. At the time of research, this new law was being strongly opposed by Goa's motorcycle taxi pilots.

Make sure that you carry the necessary paperwork (licence, registration and insurance) at all times because licence checks on foreigners have traditionally been a lucrative source of baksheesh for the police. British licences are valid in Goa, otherwise you should carry an International Driving Permit. Breath-testing for alcohol was introduced in Goa in 2000, which is another reason to leave the bike at home if you're going out partying.

Motorcycle Taxi Motorcycles are a licensed form of taxi in Goa. They are cheap, common, backpacks are no problem and they can be identified by a yellow front mudguard. At the northern beaches, young Goan motorcycle owners make a bit of extra money ferrying party goers around in the evening. Prices are negotiable.

Bicycle There are plenty of places to hire bicycles in all the major towns and beach resorts – around Rs 40 for a full day.

Boat One of the joys of travelling around Goa is the passenger/vehicle ferries that cross the state's many rivers. Most operate a half-hourly service from early morning until late evening. Foot passengers ride for free, motorcycles cost Rs 4. There are more than 20 in daily operation, but bridges being built over several rivers may eventually put the ferries out of business. The main ferries of interest to travellers are: Siolim-Chopdem, for Arambol, Mandrem and places north; Querim-Terekhol for Terekhol Fort; Old Goa-Divar Island; Ribandar-Chorao, for Dr Salim Ali Bird Sanctuary; and Cavelossim-Assolna, for the coastal ride from Benaulim to Palolem.

North Goa

Goa neatly splits into two districts: North and South Goa. North Goa has the state capital, Panaji; the former capital of Old Goa, with its fascinating churches and cathedrals; and a string of beaches running right up the coast to Maharashtra.

PANAJI (PANJIM)

pop 93,000

Panaji is one of India's smallest and most pleasant state capitals. Built on the south bank of the wide Mandovi River, it officially became the capital of Goa in 1843 when Old Goa was finally abandoned.

Most travellers pass through Panaji on their way to the beaches or to Old Goa, but the town is well worth exploring.

Information

Tourist Offices The Goan Tourist Development Corporation (GTDC, also known as Goa Tourism) office (☎ 225583, ⓔ gtdc@goa.goa.nic.in) is in the government-run Patto Tourist Home between the Kadamba bus stand and the Ourem Creek. Reasonable maps of Goa and Panaji are available (Rs 12). A more useful place for information, however, is the GTDC counter (☎ 225620) at the Kadamba bus stand.

The Government of India tourist office (☎ 223412, ⓔ goitour@goa.goa.nic.in) in the Communidade Building, Church Square, is helpful for onward travel plans and information outside Goa.

Money There are plenty of efficient private foreign exchange places in Panaji. Thomas Cook (☎ 221312) on Dayanand Bandodkar Marg is open from 9.30 am to 6 pm Monday to Saturday and 10 am to 5 pm Sunday (October to March only). The Bank of Baroda, on the Azad Maidan, provides Visa and MasterCard cash advances (Rs 100 fee plus 1% commission) from 10 am to 1 pm weekdays and 10 to 11 am Saturday.

HDFC bank has 24-hour ATMs accepting international cards (MasterCard, Cirrus, Maestro, Visa) at its branch on 18th June Rd (diagonally opposite the branch is the ATM). Centurion Bank, on MG Rd, also has an ATM accepting MasterCard and Cirrus.

Post & Communications The main post office is on MG Rd and has a Speedpost parcel service. Poste restante is open from 9 am to 5 pm Monday to Saturday. You can make international telephone calls from the 24-hour central telegraph office on Dr A Borkar Rd, but there are plenty of private STD/ISD offices charging similar rates.

There are a growing number of Internet cafes in Panaji, and many STD/ISD offices have a few terminals. Clasik Cybercafe (☎ 222237), opposite the Municipal Gardens (upstairs at the back of Kamat Hotel) charges Rs 55 an hour. Little.dot.com Cyber Cafe (☎ 420550), in the Padmavati Towers shopping complex on 18th June Rd, charges Rs 40 an hour and is open from 9.30 am to midnight. There are a couple of terminals at Shrut Communications, below Hotel Venite.

Bookshops & Libraries The Mandovi and Fidalgo hotels have good bookshops that stock international magazines. The Goa Book Centre, down a laneway off 18th June Rd, also has a good range. Panaji Central Library is on the west side of the Azad Maidan, next to the police headquarters.

Church of Our Lady of the Immaculate Conception

This striking whitewashed edifice is Panaji's main church. It stands above the square in the main part of town. The original construction was consecrated in 1541. Panaji was the first port of call for voyages from Lisbon, so Portuguese sailors would visit this church to give thanks for a safe crossing before continuing to Old Goa. Mass is held here daily in English, Konkani and Portuguese.

Goa State Museum

This modern, roomy museum (☎ 226006) has several galleries featuring Christian art, Hindu and Jain sculpture and bronzes, and paintings from all over India. An interesting exhibit is the pair of huge rotary lottery machines containing thousands of wooden balls. The first draw was in 1947. The museum is in a forlorn area near the bus stand, open from 9.30 am to 5.30 pm weekdays (free).

Fontainhas & Sao Tomé

Just west of the Ourem Creek, these old Portuguese districts are Panaji's most interesting areas. The narrow cobbled streets, tiled buildings, shuttered windows and tiny overhanging balconies. Local men sip feni in tiny darkened bars and some of Panaji's best guesthouses are in this quarter.

The **Chapel of St Sebastian** stands at the end of a picturesque street in Fontainhas. Although it dates only from the 1880s, it contains a number of interesting features, in particular a striking crucifix that originally stood in the Palace of the Inquisition in Old Goa.

Other Attractions

The **Secretariat building** dates from the 16th century, and was originally the palace of Adil Shah, ruler of the Adil Shahi dynasty of Bijapur, before becoming the viceroy's

Hypnotist Abbé Faria is enshrined in stone as a statue in Panaji.

official residence in 1759. The bizarre **statue** of a man apparently about to strangle a woman is of Abbé Faria, a famous hypnotist, and his assistant. Born in Candolim in 1756, he emigrated to France, where he became a celebrated hypnotic medium.

The modern **Mahalaxmi Temple** is a reminder that there's a thriving Hindu community in Panaji. For good views over the town, walk up to the **Altinho** district. You can get there by walking south from Fontainhas or following the road up past Our Lady of the Immaculate Conception church.

Organised Tours

A variety of tours are offered by Goa Tourism and private agencies. Some of the day tours pack too much in, so you end up seeing very little.

The North Goa tour visits Panaji, Mapusa, Mayem Lake, Vagator, Anjuna, Calangute and Fort Aguada. The South Goa tours take in Miramar, Dona Paula, Colva, Margao, Shantadurga Temple, Mangesh Temple, Ancestral Goa and Old Goa. These cost Rs 90 (or Rs 110 for air-con buses) in the high season and depart at 9.30 am daily, returning to Panaji at 6 pm (8 pm for the South Goa tours). Other tours include a two-day trip to Dudhsagar Falls and the Bondla Wildlife Sanctuary, staying at Molem (Rs 400).

Goa Tourism also has enjoyable hour-long cruises along the Mandovi River aboard the *Santa Monica*. There's a sunset cruise (6 pm) and sundown cruise (7.15 pm), which cost Rs 90. They include a live band performing Goan folk songs and dances. Drinks and snacks are available. On full-moon nights, there is a two-hour cruise at 8.30 pm (Rs 130). Cruises depart from the Santa Monica jetty next to the huge Mandovi bridge and tickets can be purchased here. A couple of private operators also have cruises from Santa Monica jetty each evening (Rs 100), as well as open-sea 'dolphin cruises' (Rs 500) from 10 am to 1 pm. Their boats are bigger and rowdier than the *Santa Monica*.

There's also a 'Goa By Night' bus tour at 6.30 pm, which includes a river cruise and illuminated sights (Rs 120).

Special Events

The **Konkani Drama Festival** is held over November and December with a program of Konkani music, dance and theatre held at Panaji's Kala Academy – it is a competition, with prizes awarded to the best performing group at the end.

The **Tiatr Festival**, held in November, is another drama/arts program held as a competition at the Kala Academy.

Around 8 December, a large fair and a church service during the **Feast of Our Lady of the Immaculate Conception** is held at Panaji's Church of Our Lady of the Immaculate Conception.

The **Pop, Beat & Jazz Music Festival** is held in February.

Sabado Gordo, with its Christian float processions, is held on the Saturday before Lent.

Places to Stay – Budget

The ***Youth Hostel*** *(☎ 225433)* is at Miramar, 3km west of Panaji, in a shady she-oak garden by the water. It has an institutional air, is inconveniently located and there's an 8 am checkout and 10 pm curfew. Dorm beds cost Rs 20 (Rs 40 for nonmembers).

Udipi Boarding & Lodging *(☎ 228047)* is one of several good, cheap places to stay in the old part of town. It has basic double rooms with shared bathroom for Rs 100. ***Hotel Venite*** *(☎ 225537, 31st January Rd)*, better known for its restaurant, has two double rooms (with shared bathroom) for Rs 150.

Mandovi White House *(☎ 223928)*, behind the Tourist Hotel, has four rooms. Doubles with bathroom cost Rs 250 (Rs 495 over Christmas). Checkout is 8.30 am.

Republica Hotel *(☎ 224630, Jose Falcao Rd)* is an interesting old place with good views from the balcony over to the river and the Secretariat and Panaji's tiled rooftops. Bright rooms with stained-glass windows and private bathroom cost Rs 150/259 for singles/doubles.

Afonso Guest House *(☎ 222359)*, on the same street as the Chapel of St Sebastian, is a friendly place. Spotless doubles with hot-water are a bit above budget range, but worth the Rs 380 (Rs 760 over Christmas).

Park Lane Lodge *(☎ 220238, ⓔ pklaldg@goatelecom.com)* is an old Portuguese house with a bit of character and a variety of rooms, though travellers give it mixed reports. A double with private bathroom is Rs 300 (Rs 450 over Christmas). It also has two cheaper rooms with shared bathroom, which they may let as singles.

Orav's Guest House *(☎ 426128, 31st January Rd)* lacks character, but is clean, family run and quite good. Singles/doubles with bathroom are Rs 200/300 (Rs 300/550 over Christmas) and the front rooms have little balconies.

Places to Stay – Mid-Range

Panjim Inn *(☎ 226523, ⓔ panjimin@goa1.dot.net.in, 31st January Rd)* is by far the most charming place to stay in this range. It's a beautiful 300-year-old mansion with a large 1st-floor veranda and leafy garden. All rooms have four-poster beds and colonial furniture. High season rates are Rs 720/990 (Rs 900/1130 from 28 December to 3 January). Ask to see a few rooms as they are all different. Across the road, ***Panjim Pousada*** is under the same management and is also a comfortable, well-furnished place. The rooms here, from Rs 675/900, are perhaps even more pleasant than at the Panjim Inn.

Mayfair Hotel *(☎ 223317, ⓔ mayfair@goatelecom.com, Dr Dada Vaidya Rd)* is a friendly, established hotel with mosaic tile murals in the lobby. Standard rooms at Rs 350/480 are small but clean, and have touches of character such as Goan oyster-shell windows. Air-con is Rs 600. Doubles are Rs 700 over the Christmas period.

Garden View Hotel *(☎ 227844, Diogo de Couto Rd)* is in a pleasant spot overlooking the Municipal Gardens. Plain but decent-sized doubles cost Rs 300 and air-con is Rs 500.

Hotel Bareton *(☎ 226405, Luis Menezes Rd)* is just a small place in Sao Tomé with decent doubles from Rs 425 (Rs 850 over Christmas).

GTDC Tourist Hotel *(☎ 227103, MG Rd)* is an unremarkable place on a busy road, but it's popular with travellers. Doubles cost Rs 500, or Rs 650 for air-con (Rs 750 for front rooms). There's a terrace restaurant, bar and bookshop.

Hotel Aroma *(☎ 43519, Cunha-Rivara Rd)* is a modern place that fronts onto the Municipal Gardens. The clean, airy double rooms with private bathroom are relatively good value at Rs 450.

Places to Eat – Top End

Hotel Mandovi *(☎ 426270, fax 225451, ⓔ mandovi@goatelecom.com, Dayanand Bandodkar Marg)* is the best of the central top-end places. Rooms in this air-con colonial hotel start at Rs 1000/1300 (Rs 1400/1750 over the peak Christmas period). River-facing rooms are more expensive. There's a good restaurant on the 1st floor and a pleasant bar on the balcony.

Hotel Nova Goa *(☎ 226231, fax 224958, ⓔ novagoa@goa1.dot.net.in, Dr Atmaram Borkar Rd)* is a more modern and anonymous hotel. Singles/doubles start from Rs 990/1400 (Rs 2500 a double over Christmas), including a buffet breakfast. There are also more-expensive suites, and a shaded pool.

Goa Marriott Resort *(☎ 437001, fax 437020)*, out at Miramar, is a sumptuous new five-star hotel. It has a riverside swimming pool with bar, two restaurants, health club, squash and tennis courts. Luxury costs from US$114 for a double room, up to US$262 between 28 December and 2 January.

Places to Eat

Hotel Venite *(31st January Rd, Sao Tomé)* is one of the most character-laden restaurants in Goa. With four tiny balconies hanging over the street and rustic Portuguese decor it's a fine place to enjoy a meal or just a cold beer during siesta. The Goan dishes and seafood are excellent, though not cheap by local standards with mains around Rs 80. Goan sausages, chicken *cafrial* and tiger prawns are among the specialities. The Venite is open for breakfast, lunch and dinner Monday to Saturday.

Udipi Boarding & Lodging, one street east of the Venite, also has a 1st-floor

GOA

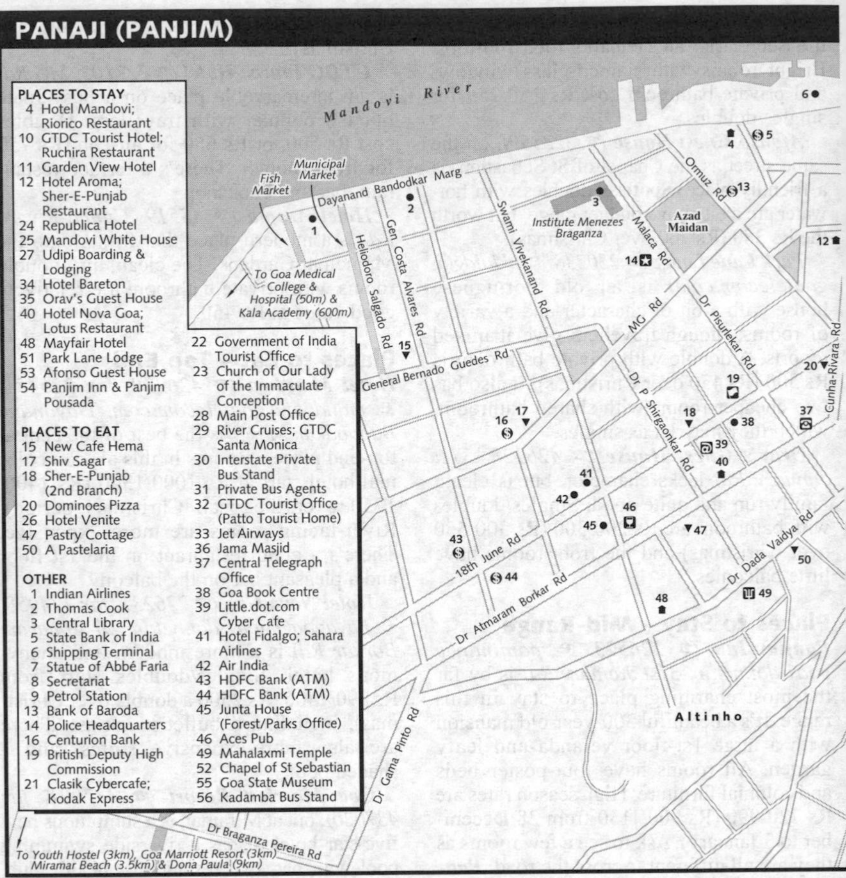

restaurant with a balcony overlooking the street below. Although it doesn't attract many foreigner travellers, it's always crowded with Goans, and serves simple but tasty food.

New Cafe Hema *(General Bernado Guedes Rd)* is a cheap, clean place near the municipal market serving a good fish curry and rice for Rs 20 and cheap veg snacks for Rs 10.

Shiv Sagar *(☎ 436308, MG Rd)* is a recommended pure veg restaurant with South Indian snacks for Rs 15 to 30 and North Indian veg dishes around Rs 45.

Ruchira Restaurant, upstairs at the Tourist Hotel, has a pleasant veranda overlooking the Mandovi River, as well as an enclosed air-con dining room. The balcony is a popular place for breakfast. Service is a little slow, but the food is OK.

Sher-E-Punjab, at the Hotel Aroma, is a flash place serving arguably the best tandoori in town. There's a second branch on 18th June Rd.

Riorico, at the Hotel Mandovi, is reputedly the city's best restaurant for Goan cuisine; while it certainly is high quality, the service is second-rate. Prawn *balchao* is Rs 125, *peixe caldeirada* (fish and potato stew with wine) is Rs 140 and the Goa seafood fiesta is a treat at Rs 650. There's a pleasant balcony overlooking the Mandovi River, but you can only take drinks out here.

Palmeira Restaurant *(☎ 437014)* at the Marriott in Miramar has a full buffet daily (Rs 300 for lunch, Rs 450 for dinner). There's

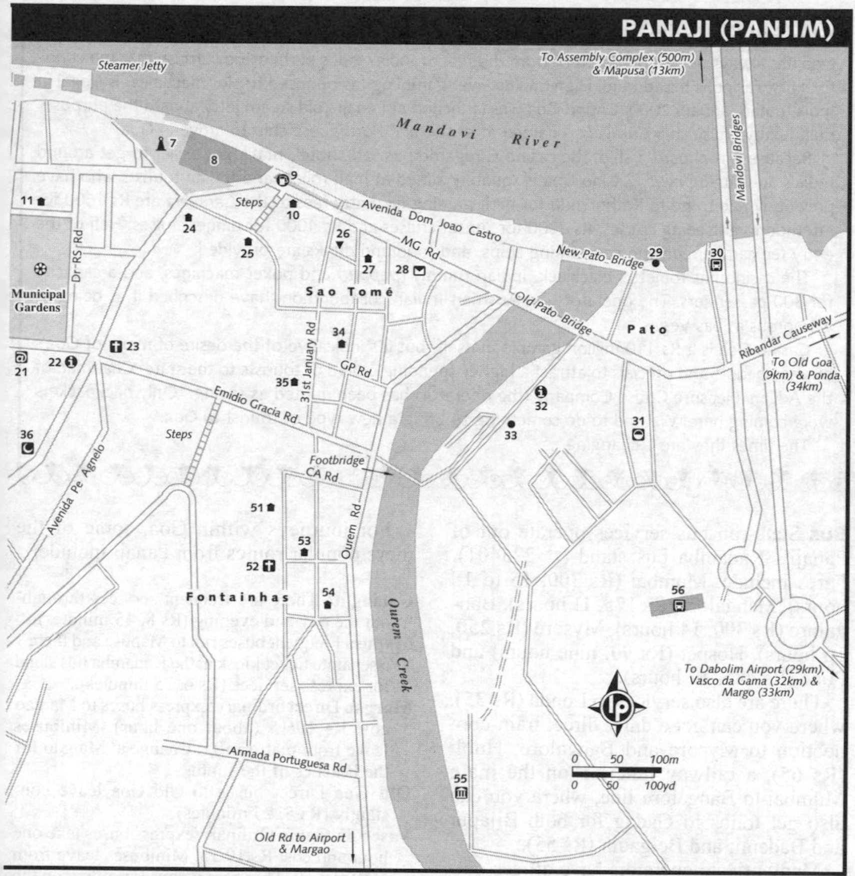

also a Sunday brunch special with free champagne, buffet lunch and free use of the swimming pool for Rs 430 plus tax.

There are several pastry shops in Panaji: Try ***Pastry Cottage***, near the Hotel Nova Goa, or ***A Pastelaria*** on Dr Dada Vaidya Rd. ***Dominoes Pizza*** *(☎ 1600-111123 for delivery)* has a branch in the centre of town opposite the Municipal Gardens.

Entertainment

Kala Academy *(☎ 223280, Dayanand Bandodkar Marg)*, on the west side of the city, has a cultural program of dance, music and art exhibitions throughout the year, and there are occasional English language productions. Panaji has a few pubs, mostly frequented by young Goans rather than foreign tourists, but they make an interesting change from the beach resort bars. ***Aces Pub***, opposite Junta House, is a tiny two-tier place like a little cocktail bar. Draught beer is Rs 20, cocktails Rs 60 to 150 and it's open to 11 pm.

Getting There & Away

Air Indian Airlines (☎ 223826) is at Dempo Building, Dayanand Bandodkar Marg. Air India (☎ 224081) is next to Hotel Fidalgo, on 18th June Rd. Other airlines with offices in Panaji include Jet Airways (☎ 431472), Shop 7–9, Sesa Ghor, Patto Plaza, and Sahara Airlines (☎ 230237) at Hotel Fidalgo.

See Getting There & Away at the start of this chapter for information on flights from Goa.

Goa's Floating Casino

Goa has always been a bit different from the rest of India, so it's perhaps no surprise that the country's first casino is based here. High-stakes 'live' gambling (as opposed to slot machines) is illegal in India, but in January 2000, Casino Goa was launched at Panaji's old steam jetty aboard the purpose-built luxury cruise ship *Caravela* – named after the first Portuguese ship to arrive in Goa.

Because it is aboard a ship, the casino is regarded as 'off-shore', making it easier to get around India's antigaming laws. Casino Goa is squarely aimed at high rollers and Indian tourists who have previously had to go to Kathmandu for their gaming fix. Entry fees to the *Caravela* are Rs 1600 for afternoon sightseeing cruises, Rs 3000 for sunset cruises and Rs 4000 for dinner cruises. Half of the entry fee can be redeemed as gaming chips, and food and drinks are provided.

The casino has roulette, blackjack, Indian rummy *(papplu)* and poker machines, and a capacity for 300 passengers. The operators, an Austrian-Indian collaboration, have described it as being as glamorous as Las Vegas.

Casino Goa is a Rs 110 million gamble in itself, but it's indicative of the desire of many of Goa's businesspeople and officials to attract a higher-spending crowd of tourists to the state. Chairman of the Advani Pleasure Cruise Company (the operator) has been quoted as saying: 'Only backpackers were coming here. We had to do something to bring a new type of tourist to Goa.'

The times they are a changing.

GOA

Bus State-run bus services operate out of Panaji's Kadamba bus stand (☎ 225401). Fares include: Mumbai (Rs 300, 15 to 18 hours), Mangalore (Rs 175, 11 hours), Bangalore (Rs 300, 14 hours), Mysore (Rs 250, 16 hours), Hospet (Rs 90, nine hours) and Pune (Rs 285, 12 hours).

There are also services to Londa (Rs 35), where you can get a daily direct train connection to Mysore and Bangalore; Hubli (Rs 65), a railway junction on the main Mumbai to Bangalore line, where you can also get trains to Gadag for both Bijapur and Badami; and Belgaum (Rs 55).

Many private operators have offices outside the entrance to the bus stand, with luxury and air-con buses to Mumbai, Bangalore, Hampi and other destinations. These are better for long-distance travel. Most private interstate buses arrive and depart from a separate bus stand next to the Mandovi Bridge. Paulo Tours & Travel (☎ 223736), just north of the bus stand, has nightly sleeper coaches to Hampi (Rs 400), Mumbai (Rs 300) and Bangalore (Rs 350), though these prices fluctuate. The sleeper buses aren't the pinnacle of comfort – they can be cramped, and typically erratic Indian driving and rough roads make sleep a lottery. Ordinary non air-con buses cost Rs 200 to Mumbai and Rs 350 to Hampi. Luxury buses can also be booked through agents in Margao, Mapusa and the beach resorts, but they still depart from Panaji.

For journeys within Goa, some of the more popular routes from Panaji include:

Calangute There are frequent services throughout the day and evening (Rs 8, 45 minutes).

Mapusa Frequent buses run to Mapusa and there's a separate ticket kiosk at the Kadamba bus stand for express services (Rs 6, 25 minutes).

Margao Direct ordinary/express buses to Margao cost Rs 10/15 (about one hour). Minibuses leave from platform 11. Change at Margao for the beaches of the south.

Old Goa Direct buses to Old Goa leave constantly (Rs 5, 25 minutes).

Vasco da Gama Ordinary/express buses take one hour and cost Rs 10/15. Minibuses leave from platform 10. There are no buses running on the route via Cona Paula as the ferry to Mormugao is no longer operating.

Train The train is a better than the bus for Mumbai and Mangalore – see Getting There & Away at the start of this chapter. The nearest train station to Panaji is Karmali, 11km to the east near Old Goa. There's a reservation office at Panaji's Kadamba bus stand, open 9 am to 1 pm and 3 to 5 pm; it's very busy.

Getting Around

Getting taxi and autorickshaw drivers to use their meters is difficult. Agree on the fare before heading off.

It's easy enough to rent a motorcycle or scooter in Panaji, though if you intend to spend most of your time at the beach resorts it's more convenient to hire one there. There are no hire shops as such – ask at your guesthouse or head to the cluster of bikes opposite the main post office on MG Rd.

OLD GOA

Just 9km east of Panaji, half a dozen imposing churches and cathedrals (among the largest in Asia) are all that remain of the Portuguese capital that was once said to rival Lisbon in magnificence. Some of the old buildings have become museums maintained by the Archaeological Survey of India.

The Archaeological Survey of India publishes *Old Goa* (Rs 10). It's available from the archaeological museum.

History

Even before the arrival of the Portuguese, Old Goa was a thriving and prosperous city, and the second capital of the Adil Shahi dynasty of Bijapur. At that time, it was a fortress surrounded by walls, towers and a moat, and contained temples, mosques and the large palace of Adil Shah. Today, none of these structures remain except for a fragment of the palace gateway.

Under the Portuguese, the city grew rapidly in size and splendour, despite an epidemic in 1543 that wiped out a large part of the population. The city's decline was accelerated by the Inquisition and another devastating epidemic that struck in 1635. Indeed, if it hadn't been for the treaty between the British and the Portuguese, Goa would probably have either passed to the Dutch or been absorbed into British India. In 1843 the capital shifted to Panaji.

Se Cathedral

The largest of the churches in Old Goa, Se Cathedral was begun in 1562 during the reign of King Dom Sebastião (1557–58). It was completed by 1619, though the altars were not finished until 1652. The cathedral was built for the Dominicans and paid for by the sale of crown property.

The building's style is Portuguese-Gothic with a Tuscan exterior and Corinthian interior. The remaining tower houses a famous bell, one of the largest in Goa, often called the Golden Bell because of its rich sound. The main altar is dedicated to St Catherine of Alexandria, and paintings on either side of it depict scenes from her life and martyrdom.

Convent & Church of St Francis of Assisi

This is one of the most interesting buildings in Old Goa. The interior contains gilded and carved woodwork, a stunning *reredos* (ornamented screen behind the altar), old murals depicting scenes from the life of St Francis, and a floor made of carved gravestones – complete with family coats of arms dating

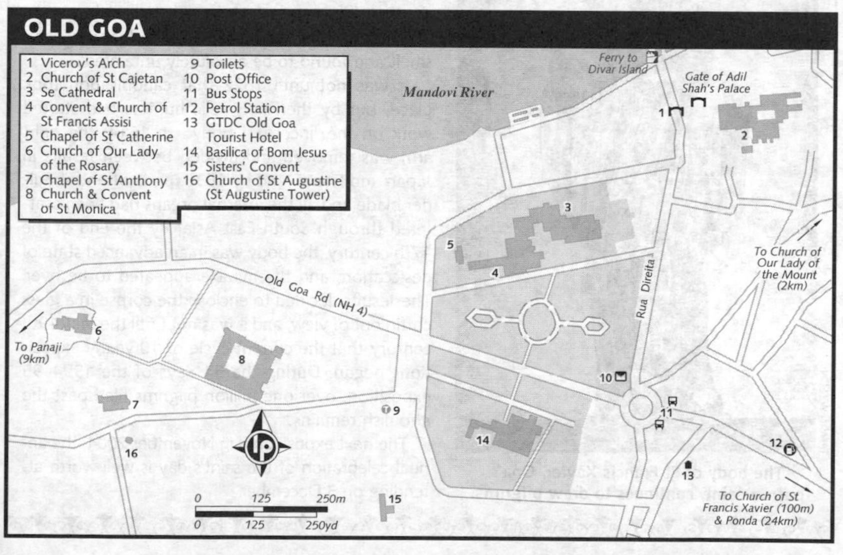

back to the early 16th century. The church was built by eight Franciscan friars who arrived here in 1517 and constructed a small chapel consisting of three altars and a choir. This was later pulled down and the present building was built on the same spot in 1661.

A convent behind this church is now the **archaeological museum** (open from 10 am to 5 pm Saturday to Thursday, Rs 5). It houses portraits of the Portuguese viceroys, most of them inexpertly restored; sculpture fragments from Hindu temple sites; and stone Vetal images from the animist cult that flourished in this part of India centuries ago.

Basilica of Bom Jesus

The Basilica of Bom Jesus is famous throughout the Roman Catholic world. It contains the tomb and mortal remains of St Francis Xavier who, in 1541, was given the task of spreading Christianity among the subjects of the Portuguese colonies in the east.

A former pupil of St Ignatius Loyola, the founder of the Jesuit Order, St Francis Xavier's missionary voyages became legendary and, considering the state of transport at the time, were nothing short of miraculous.

Apart from the richly gilded altars, the interior of the church is remarkable for its simplicity. This is the only church that is not plastered on the outside (although it was originally). Construction began in 1594 and it was completed in 1605. The focus of the church is the three-tiered marble tomb of St Francis, which took 10 years to build and was completed in 1698. The remains of the

The Incorrupt Body of St Francis Xavier

Goa's patron saint, Francis Xavier, spent 10 years as a tireless missionary in South-East Asia. His death on 2 December 1552 gave rise to his greatest influence on the region.

He died on the island of Sancian, off the coast of China. A servant is said to have emptied four sacks of quicklime into his coffin to consume his flesh in case the order came to return the remains to Goa. Two months later, the body was transferred to Malacca, where it was observed to be still in perfect condition – refusing to rot despite the quicklime. The following year it was returned to Goa, where the people were declaring the preservation a miracle.

The church was slower to acknowledge it, requiring a medical examination to establish that the body had not been embalmed. This was performed, in 1556, by the viceroy's physician, who declared that all internal organs were still intact and that no preservative agents had been used. He noticed a small wound in the chest and asked two Jesuits to put their fingers into it. He noted, 'When they withdrew them, they were covered with blood which I smelt and found to be absolutely untainted'.

TAMSIN WILSON

The body of St Francis Xavier, Goa's patron saint, continues to draw pilgrims.

It was not until 1622 that canonisation took place, but by then holy relic hunters had started work on the 'incorrupt body'. In 1614, the right arm was removed and divided between Jesuits in Japan and Rome, and by 1636, parts of one shoulder blade and all the internal organs had been scattered through South-East Asia. By the end of the 17th century, the body was in an advanced state of desiccation, and the miracle appeared to be over. The Jesuits decided to enclose the corpse in a glass coffin out of view, and it was not until the mid-19th century that the current cycle of 10 yearly expositions began. During the 54 days of the 1994–95 exposition, over one million pilgrims filed past the ghoulish remains.

The next exposition is in November 2004; the annual celebration of the saint's day is well worth attending on 3 December.

body are housed in a silver casket, which at one time was covered in jewels. On the walls surrounding it are murals depicting scenes from the saint's journeys, and one of his death on Sancian Island.

The **Professed House**, next door to the basilica, is a two-storey laterite building covered with lime plaster. It was completed in 1585, despite much opposition to the Jesuits. Part of the building burned down in 1633 and was partially rebuilt in 1783. There is a modern **art gallery** attached to the basilica.

Church of St Cajetan

Modelled on the original design of St Peter's in Rome, this church was built by Italian friars of the Order of Theatines, who were sent by Pope Urban III to preach Christianity in the kingdom of Golconda (near Hyderabad). The friars were not permitted to work in Golconda, so settled at Old Goa in 1640. The construction of the church began in 1655. Historically, it's of much less interest than the other churches.

Church of St Augustine Ruins

All that is really left of this church is the enormous 46m tower that served as a belfry and formed part of the facade of the church. It was constructed in 1602 by Augustinian friars who arrived in 1587. It was abandoned in 1835 due to the repressive policies of the Portuguese government, resulting in the eviction of many religious orders from Goa. The church fell into neglect and the vault collapsed in 1842. In 1931, the facade and half the tower fell down.

Church & Convent of St Monica

This huge three-storey laterite building was completed in 1627, only to burn down nine years later. Reconstruction started the following year, and it's from this time that the buildings date. Once known as the Royal Monastery, due to the royal patronage that it enjoyed, the building is now used by the Mater Dei Institute as a nunnery and it was inaugurated in 1964.

Other Buildings

Other monuments of minor interest in Old Goa are the Viceroy's Arch, Gate of Adil Shah's Palace, Chapel of St Anthony, Chapel of St Catherine and the Church of Our Lady of the Rosary.

Special Events

The **Procession of All Saints**, on the fifth Monday in Lent, is the only procession of its sort outside Rome. Thirty statues of saints are brought out from storage and paraded around Old Goa's neighbouring villages.

Another major festival here is the **Feast of St Francis Xavier** on 3 December, preceded by a 10-day Novena.

Places to Stay

Most people visit Old Goa as a day trip, but there is one hotel. The GTDC ***Old Goa Tourist Hotel*** *(☎ 286127)* has basic singles/doubles for Rs 170/250.

Getting There & Away

Frequent buses to Old Goa leave the bus stand at Panaji (Rs 5, 25 minutes) and stop on the east side of the main roundabout.

MAPUSA

pop 34,800

Mapusa (pronounced 'Mapsa') is the main population centre in the northern *talukas* (provinces) of Goa and the main town for supplies if you are staying at Anjuna or Vagator. There's not much to see in Mapusa, though the Friday market (8 am to 2 pm) is worth a visit. A Hindu and Christian feast day, Feast of Our Lady of Miracles, is held here 16 days after Easter.

Places to Stay & Eat

Accommodation at the nearby beaches of Anjuna, Vagator and Calangute is far preferable to that on offer in Mapusa.

Hotel Vilena *(☎ 263115, Feira Baixa Rd)* is a good, clean place with doubles with shared bathroom for Rs 200, or Rs 300 with private bathroom. There's a decent restaurant and bar here.

Hotel Suhas *(☎ 262700)* is a cheap option; dorm beds are Rs 60 and doubles with private bathroom are Rs 150, but in high season the dorms become four-bed rooms at Rs 360.

GTDC Tourist Hotel *(☎ 262794)*, on the southern roundabout, is popular and has singles/doubles for Rs 220/300, four-bed rooms for Rs 400.

Hotel Satyaheera *(☎ 262849, ⓔ satya@goa.dot.net.in)*, near the Maruti Temple on the northern roundabout, is the best Mapusa has to offer. Doubles are Rs 400 (Rs 750 with air-con), all with TV and private bathroom.

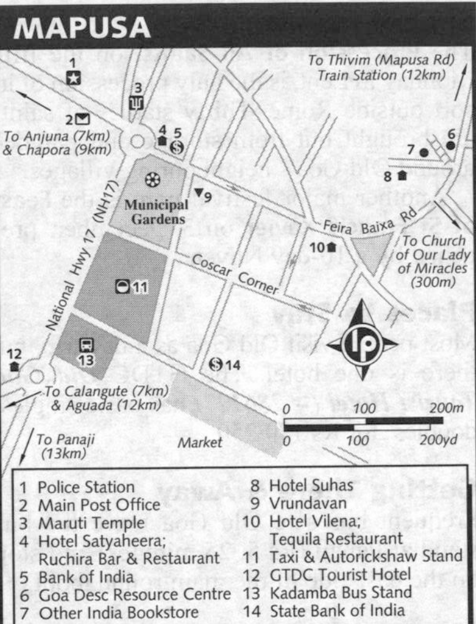

***Ruchira Bar & Restaurant** (☎ 263869)* on the top floor, is one of Mapusa's best.

Vrundavan, near the Municipal Gardens, is a good, cheap thali place (closed Tuesday).

Getting There & Away

If you're coming from Mumbai, Mapusa is the jumping off point for the northern beaches. From the Kadamba bus stand, there are afternoon and evening buses to Mumbai (Rs 255 for a 'luxury' bus, 17 hours) as well as Pune, Hubli and Belgaum. Private operators have kiosks by the taxi and autorickshaw stand, with services to Mumbai and Pune only (both Rs 200).

There are frequent local buses to Panaji (Rs 5, 25 minutes), and buses every 30 minutes to Calangute and Anjuna (both Rs 5). Other buses go to Chapora, Candolim and Arambol (Rs 12). A motorcycle taxi to Anjuna or Calangute costs Rs 50.

Thivim, about 12km north-east of town, is the nearest train station on the Konkan Railway. Local buses meet trains (Rs 5); an autorickshaw will cost Rs 80.

FORT AGUADA & CANDOLIM

The beaches of North Goa extend from Fort Aguada in an almost uninterrupted 30km sandy stretch to the border with Maharashtra. Sinquerim, the beach below the fort, and Candolim are popular with package tourists – there's not much here for those on a very tight budget.

Guarding the mouth of the Mandovi River, **Fort Aguada** was built by the Portuguese in 1612. It's worth visiting the moated ruins on the hilltop for the views, which are particularly good from the old lighthouse. Nearby, the new **lighthouse** can be visited from 4 to 5.30 pm; photography from it is forbidden.

To the east is **Aguada Jail**; most inmates (including Westerners) are in on drug charges. They're only allowed one visit a month, so although they usually appreciate visits from other foreigners, you need to make sure you won't be denying them the visit of someone they're expecting. You'll also need to contact your embassy for a list of names.

Thunderwave, on the beach outside the Taj Holiday Village, offers a range of pricey **water sports**, including parasailing (Rs 1300) and jet skiing (Rs 750) at the southern end of Sinquerim Beach, so this is not a great spot for swimming. It's much quieter further up along Candolim Beach.

There are various **boat cruises** on offer. Thunderwave has a dolphin cruise for Rs 350. John's Boat Trips (☎ 277780), further up behind Candolim Beach, has half-day dolphin trips with lunch and beers on the boat for Rs 550 and a variety of other trips such as the full-day 'Crocodile Dundee' river trip including lunch with a Goan family and free drinks for Rs 950.

Places to Stay

Accommodation along here is mostly overpriced mid-range hotels catering to package tourists, with a couple of five-star places and the odd gem of a family guesthouse. Prices listed here are for doubles with private bathroom in the high season, but not the peak Christmas period when many hotels are taken over entirely by package groups.

At the Calangute end is a clutch of places from Rs 500 to 700 in an excellent position very close to the beach. These include ***Dona Florina Beach Resort** (☎ 275051, fax 276878)* with rooms for Rs 550/650.

A good area to look for family-run guesthouses is further south in a warren of back lanes reached from the road opposite the post office. Inexpensive options with doubles around Rs 250 to 350 include ***Manuel***

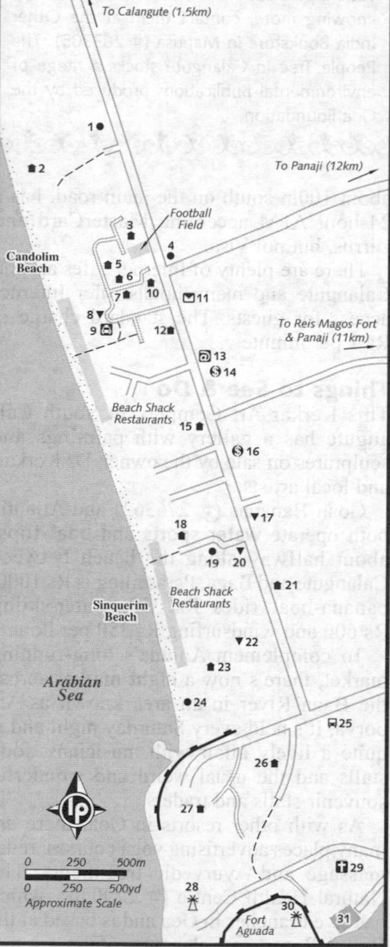

Guest House (☎ *277729*), ***Moonlight Bar & Restaurant*** (☎ *279249*) and ***Ave Maria*** (☎ *277336*). ***Pretty Petal Guest House*** (☎ *276184*) is a lovely place with a large garden and spacious singles/doubles from Rs 350/500. Larger rooms with balcony and fridge cost Rs 600.

Tropicano Beach Resort (☎ *277732, 835B Camotim Vaddo*) is an excellent choice with pleasant doubles for Rs 250 (Rs 450 with breakfast). There's a shady garden and the doors of this traditional house feature Goan glazing made from sea shells.

Moving south, there's a group of hotels with swimming pools in the Rs 500 to 850 price range. ***Sea Shell Inn*** (☎ *276131,* e *seashellgoa@hotmail.com*), on the main road, has comfortable rooms in an old colonial house for Rs 650 (Rs 900 over Christmas); the homey ***Per Avel*** (☎ *277074, fax 277074*) charges Rs 850.

Villa Ludovici Tourist Home (☎ *275684*) is a traditional Goan house with four old-fashioned and homey rooms at Rs 350.

Marbella Guest House (☎ *275551, fax 276509*) is one of the nicest places in the area. It's a beautifully restored Portuguese villa hidden down a quiet lane behind the Fort Aguada Beach Resort. The six airy rooms, each charmingly decorated in a different style (such as Rajasthani and Mughal), cost Rs 1000 to 1950 (Rs 850 to 1700 mid-season), including tax.

The Taj Group (☎ *276201, fax 276044,* e *village.goa@tajhotels.com*) operates a complex of three five-star deluxe hotels beside Sinquerim Beach. The beachside ***Taj Holiday Village*** charges US$125/140 for a standard room. Within the outer walls of the old fort, ***Fort Aguada Beach Resort*** has singles/doubles for US$135/150. Above it is the luxurious ***Aguada Hermitage***, with northern views and rooms for US$225 (US$475 over Christmas and New Year!).

Places to Eat

Most hotels have restaurants, and down on the beach are dozens of beach shacks serving the obligatory Western breakfasts, seafood dishes and cold drinks. There's a good selection of beach shacks on Candolim Beach at the end of the road opposite the post office.

Tibet Kitchen, down this same road near the taxi stand, offers a good selection of seafood and *momos* (Tibetan dumplings). It has a water filter from which you can fill your bottle.

Back on the main Calangute road, ***Stone House*** is a mellow place, with tables laid out in a garden. It's open for dinner only.

Santa Lucia is an Italian place (with a Swiss chef) and one of the best restaurants in Candolim for food and ambience. Pasta dishes are Rs 85 to 130 and there's a pasta buffet for Rs 150.

Banyan Tree, in the grounds of the Taj Holiday Village, is a semi open-air restaurant serving fine Thai and Chinese cuisine from Rs 150.

Getting There & Away

Buses run from Panaji to Sinquerim (14km) and continue north to Calangute. A prepaid taxi from the airport costs Rs 450.

CALANGUTE & BAGA

Calangute's heyday as the Mecca of all expat hippies has passed – it's now the Mecca of package tourists winging in from the UK. These days – in high season at least – central Calangute is the most overhyped, overpriced, overcrowded strip of mayhem in Goa.

The beach is long and sandy, but it isn't one of the best in Goa and many people will find it far too crowded – dotted, as it is, with sun beds, deck chairs and slowly burning bodies. There is, however, plenty going on, and lots of good places to stay and eat. Up near the mouth of the river, Baga is a more interesting area, and it's handy for those wanting to commute to the nightlife at Anjuna and Vagator.

Orientation & Information

Most services cluster around a single street, where you'll find the market and bus stand.

Limited tourist information is available from the GTDC Calangute Tourist Resort (☎ 276024). Rama Bookshop offers a great range of books in many languages and offers book exchange. MGM International Travels (☎ 276249) is a reputable travel agency nearby.

Bank of Baroda, on the main Anjuna road near the market, gives cash advances on MasterCard or Visa, and there are many exchange offices scattered around that will change cash or travellers cheques, including a branch of Thomas Cook. Centurion Bank, about 100m south on the main road, has a 24-hour ATM accepting MasterCard and Cirrus, but not Visa.

There are plenty of Internet cafes around Calangute and many hotels offer Internet access for guests. The standard charge is Rs 1 per minute.

Green Goa

Increased tourism, overuse of water and mining are all posing a threat to the environment in Goa. As a traveller, you can help by responsibly disposing of litter, conserving water when showering and patronising the few restaurants that have installed water filters. Discarded plastic bottles are a major problem, which prompted a Clean Up Calangute project in 2000. The Goa Foundation is the state's main environmental pressure group and has been responsible for a number of conservation projects since its inauguration in 1986, as well as producing numerous conservation publications. If you're interested in knowing more, contact them at the Other India Bookstore in Mapusa (☎ 263305). The People Tree in Calangute stocks a range of environmental publications produced by the Goa Foundation.

Things to See & Do

This Kerkar Art Complex in South Calangute has a gallery with paintings and sculptures on sale by the owner, Dr Kerkar, and local artists.

Goan Bananas (☎ 276362) and Atlantis both operate **water sports** and **boat trips**, about halfway along the beach between Calangute and Baga. Parasailing is Rs 1000, banana-boat rides Rs 350, water-skiing Rs 600 and windsurfing Rs 350 per hour.

To complement Anjuna's long-running market, there's now a **night market** across the Baga River in an area known as Arporva. It's held every Saturday night and is quite a lively affair with musicians, food stalls and the usual weird and wonderful souvenir stalls and traders.

As with other resorts in Goa, there are many places advertising yoga courses, reiki, massage and Ayurvedic treatments. The Natural Health Centre (☎ 279036), which has five branches in Goa and is based at the Breiza Resort in Calangute, offers a range of Ayurvedic treatments including massage (Rs 500 for one hour), reflexology, aromatherapy, acupressure and yoga. There's also a range of herbal medicines on offer and a free consultation by a Keralan doctor.

Special Events

Calangute hosts the Youth Fete, a music and dance festival, part of **Beach Bonanza**, held from mid-April.

Places to Stay

It's a solid line of hotels for about 3km along the main Calangute-Baga road and between the road and the beach. Prices quoted here are for doubles with private bathroom during high season, but not the peak Christmas period (roughly 20 December to 3 January) unless otherwise noted. At this time many hotels are booked solid and, even if they weren't, walk-in rates are ludicrous.

Central Calangute The centre of Calangute is the area either side of the main road down to the beach. There are a few good budget options, but generally this is a crowded, noisy area.

***Angela Guest House** (☎ 277269)*, south of the main drag in a pleasant area of coconut groves, offers basic doubles for Rs 150 so it's popular with backpackers. If it's full, there are several other places nearby, including ***Alfa Guest House** (☎ 275986)* further along the main road with doubles for Rs 300. ***Coco Banana** (☎ 279068)*, nearby, is a big step up in quality. It's run by a friendly and very helpful Goan-Swiss couple. Spotless, secure rooms with comfortable beds are set around a quiet courtyard and cost Rs 500 a double (Rs 850 from mid-December to mid-January).

Ugly ***GTDC Calangute Tourist Resort** (☎ 276024)* at the end of the beach road is not great value at Rs 450 a double, but its annexe (☎ 276009) has dorm beds for Rs 60.

***Garden Court Resort** (☎ 276054)*, in the thick of things at the roundabout at the start of the Calangute-Baga road, is a lovely old place run by a traveller-friendly family. There are a couple of budget rooms at Rs 250 and Rs 300, but the best rooms cost Rs 800 (Rs 1000 with air-con). There's a room with kitchenette for Rs 600.

***Albenjoh** (☎ 276422)* is a good choice, with clean rooms from Rs 300 to 600, all with hot water. More-expensive rooms have balconies and some have a fridge.

South Calangute It's generally quieter and more rustic here than further north. There are a few cheap places left, but they're in the minority. ***NV Guest House** (☎ 279749)* enjoys an excellent location close to the beach. It's run by a friendly family, and there's a variety of rooms. Newer ones are Rs 350 (Rs 500 at Christmas) with private bathroom and hot water, while the budget rooms are Rs 100. The restaurant, only a few metres from the beach, serves fresh seafood.

In the Rs 500 to 1000 range, there's a group of small hotels notable only for their position near the beach. ***Hotel Golden Eye** (☎ 277308)*, on the beach, charges Rs 325/650 for singles/doubles (Rs 500/1000 over Christmas). It has a beachfront restaurant. ***Dona Cristalina** (☎ 279012)*, and the Mediterranean-style ***White House** (☎ 277938)* are great value with clean, comfortable double rooms for Rs 450 and Rs 500 respectively.

***Gabriel's Guest House** (☎ 279486)*, further back from the beach, is a pleasant family home with rooms for Rs 500. The Goan and Italian food here is highly regarded.

The stylish ***Kerkar Retreat** (☎ 276 017, e subodhkerkar@satyam.net.in)* has just six individually designed rooms. These cost Rs 1000 a double, rising to 2500 during the Christmas period.

Calangute to Baga Many hotels in this area have been tarted up to pull in the package tourists, so it's no surprise that prices are relatively high.

***Johnny's Hotel** (☎ 277458, e johnnys@rediffmail.com)* is close to the beach down one of the first lanes you come to as you head north. There's a variety of clean rooms in this two-storey house from Rs 250/300 (Rs 600 a double over Christmas).

***Stay Longer Guest House** (☎ 277460)* is one of the smaller places on the main road heading north. It's run by a friendly family and has simple doubles at Rs 200 (Rs 350 in high season).

***Venar Holiday Home** (☎ 276827)* is an old Portuguese house with three large doubles at Rs 200 (all year). It makes a refreshing change from the modern hotels around it.

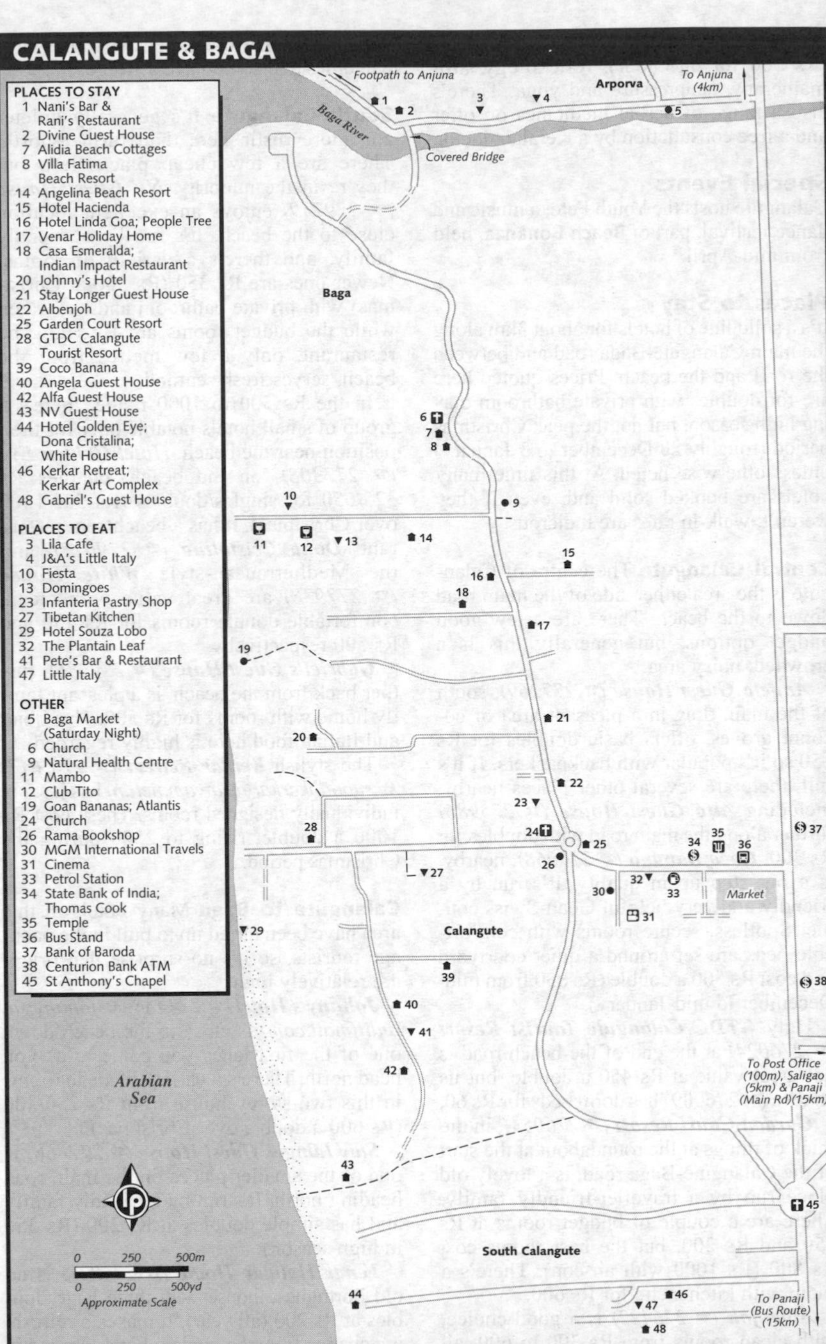
CALANGUTE & BAGA
PLACES TO STAY
1 Nani's Bar & Rani's Restaurant
2 Divine Guest House
7 Alidia Beach Cottages
8 Villa Fatima Beach Resort
14 Angelina Beach Resort
15 Hotel Hacienda
16 Hotel Linda Goa; People Tree
17 Venar Holiday Home
18 Casa Esmeralda; Indian Impact Restaurant
20 Johnny's Hotel
21 Stay Longer Guest House
22 Albenjoh
25 Garden Court Resort
28 GTDC Calangute Tourist Resort
39 Coco Banana
40 Angela Guest House
42 Alfa Guest House
43 NV Guest House
44 Hotel Golden Eye; Dona Cristalina; White House
46 Kerkar Retreat; Kerkar Art Complex
48 Gabriel's Guest House
PLACES TO EAT
3 Lila Cafe
4 J&A's Little Italy
10 Fiesta
13 Domingoes
23 Infanteria Pastry Shop
27 Tibetan Kitchen
29 Hotel Souza Lobo
32 The Plantain Leaf
41 Pete's Bar & Restaurant
47 Little Italy
OTHER
5 Baga Market (Saturday Night)
6 Church
9 Natural Health Centre
11 Mambo
12 Club Tito
19 Goan Bananas; Atlantis
24 Church
26 Rama Bookshop
30 MGM International Travels
31 Cinema
33 Petrol Station
34 State Bank of India; Thomas Cook
35 Temple
36 Bus Stand
37 Bank of Baroda
38 Centurion Bank ATM
45 St Anthony's Chapel
Footpath to Anjuna
To Anjuna (4km)
Arporva
Baga River
Covered Bridge
Baga
Calangute
South Calangute
Market
Arabian Sea
To Post Office (100m), Saligao (5km) & Panaji (Main Rd)(15km)
To Panaji (Bus Route) (15km)
0 250 500m
0 250 500yd
Approximate Scale
GOA

Casa Esmeralda *(☎ 277194)*, a little way along the next lane to the north, is good value outside the Christmas period when rooms are Rs 350 (Rs 1500 in peak season). There's also a good restaurant here.

Hotel Linda Goa *(☎ 276066, ⓔ lindagoa@hotmail.com)* is one of a number of package tour hotels on the main road that are reasonably priced outside the mid-December to early January high season when rooms are Rs 450/550 or Rs 650/750 with air-con. It has a pool, games room, bar and restaurant. ***Hotel Hacienda*** *(☎ 277348)*, down a lane away from the beach, is a bright and friendly place with a leafy garden and doubles with veranda for Rs 350 and Rs 400.

Angelina Beach Resort *(☎ 279268)* is one of several good family-run places along the next lane leading to the beach (before you get to Tito's). It's set a little back from the lane so it's reasonably peaceful. Spotless doubles cost Rs 300 (Rs 500 in peak season).

Baga These days it's hard to tell where Calangute ends and Baga begins.

Villa Fatima Beach Resort *(☎ 277418)*, set back from the road, is well-run and popular among backpackers. Double rooms with private bathroom range from Rs 200 to 600. There's a restaurant and TV area, and you can rent a safety deposit box for Rs 100.

Alidia Beach Cottages *(☎ 276835)* is another excellent place to stay; the rooms are well back from the road, fronting on to the beach. Cottages with veranda cost Rs 600 (Rs 800 over Christmas).

Across the Baga River (cross through the extraordinarily ugly covered bridge and turn left) are several lovely family-run places. ***Divine Guest House*** *(☎ 279546)* has spotless rooms for Rs 250 and Rs 350 (upstairs) and a pleasant garden restaurant.

Nani's Bar & Rani's Restaurant *(☎ 276 313)*, further around this road, is a big old Portuguese house with a variety of simple and very rustic rooms from Rs 200. The eight rooms are all different and they're offered on a first-come-first-served basis. There's a lovely garden and meals are served on the veranda.

Places to Eat

Calangute's restaurant scene has improved over the years and it now boasts some of the best dining in Goa. There are literally hundreds of small restaurants crammed into every available bit of space, and the endless bamboo beach shacks are a great place to watch the sun go down with a cold beer and a plate of seafood.

Lila Cafe *(☎ 279843)*, north of the river in Baga, is the best spot in Goa for breakfast. There's a German bakery, superb croissants, muesli, fresh fruit juices and home-made marmalade, all served in a relaxing garden. It's not the cheapest place around, but this is a restaurant where hippies rub shoulders with package tourists. It's open from 8.30 am to 6.30 pm.

Infanteria Pastry Shop, near the main roundabout in central Calangute, is also great for breakfast with an all-you-can-eat buffet for Rs 80.

Hotel Souza Lobo *(☎ 276463)*, facing the main beach, is an established favourite and the quality of the seafood is hard to beat, though it's not cheap. Fish curry is Rs 60, promfret with prawns is Rs 190 and lobster dishes top Rs 700.

Pete's Bar & Restaurant, beside the Angela Guest House, is a good cheap travellers' place where you can sit around with a few cold beers.

Tibetan Kitchen offers momos and other Tibetan food in a relaxed setting. ***The Plaintain Leaf***, near the market, is the best vegetarian restaurant around. It's pure veg with thalis from Rs 35.

Little Italy is a pricey Sicilian-run restaurant in South Calangute. ***J&A's Little Italy*** (no relation), across Baga River, also serves authentic Italian food at a price and has a pleasant outdoor dining area. Gourmet wood-fired pizzas (from Rs 150) are recommended. Wine is available by the glass and filtered mineral water is provided free to patrons.

Domingoes is a simple palm-thatch place just off the lane leading to Tito's. It specialises in excellent home-made pasta (around Rs 70) and some of the best beef steaks in Calangute (Rs 110). It's open from 6.30 pm.

Nearby on the same lane, ***Fiesta*** is one of Calangute's best restaurants for food and ambience, with an alfresco dining area overlooking the beach. It specialises in Mediterranean cuisine with paella (Rs 185) and tiramisu (Rs 95) featuring on the menu. Most mains are between Rs 125 and Rs 185.

Entertainment

Kerkar Art Complex *(☎ 276017)* hosts performances of Indian classical music and dance at 8.30 pm on Tuesday (Rs 250).

Calangute doesn't have a great deal of nightlife beyond the beach bars and small pubs, most of which close around midnight. ***Club Tito*** has long been the centre of nocturnal activity. There's a garden bar, a big screen showing latest release movies, and the small (slightly seedy) disco is open to 3 am (Rs 200). There's often reports of trouble in this area late at night – solo travellers, particularly women, should take care. ***Mambo***, closer to the beach, is a lively bar.

Club West End *(☎ 98230809)* is a new place out at Saligao, about 7km inland from Calangute. Parties here, usually on a Friday, go into the early hours and feature top Goan DJs. Taxi drivers know where to find it.

Getting There & Away

There are frequent buses to Panaji (Rs 8, 35 minutes) and Mapusa (Rs 6) from the bus stand opposite the main market. A taxi from Calangute or Baga to Panaji costs Rs 150 to 200 and takes about 30 minutes.

On Wednesday, boats leave regularly from Baga beach for the Anjuna flea market (Rs 50 per person).

ANJUNA

Famous throughout Goa for its Wednesday flea market, Anjuna is still a popular meeting point for backpackers, European ravers and long-term hippies, but times are changing and comfy hotels and package tourism are beginning to make their mark. The full-moon parties and the rave scene are almost throttled, though attempts to get around the new laws are still being attempted. Anjuna is still a more relaxing place to stay than Calangute, Baga or Colva, though many travellers that once made this their first stop are now heading to more remote beaches like Arambol to the north and Gokarna, south of the border in Karnataka.

Orientation & Information

Anjuna is quite spread out and much of the land behind the beach is still farm land. There are three distinct areas: the main crossroads and bus stand where paths lead down to the beach; the back part of the village where you'll find the post office and convenience stores; and the flea market area to the south, which also marks the southern end of the beach.

There are numerous travel agencies where you can make onward travel bookings, get flights confirmed and change foreign currency. MGM Travels (☎ 274317), on the main road, and Kwick Travels (☎ 273477) at the Manali Guest House are both good.

Internet access is available at a number of places, including the Manali Guest House and Colours Internet. The cost is around Rs 1 per minute.

The Bank of Baroda gives cash advances on Visa and MasterCard.

Anjuna Flea Market

The Wednesday flea market at Anjuna is a major attraction for people from all the Goan beaches. It's a wonderful blend of Tibetan and Kashmiri traders, colourful Gujarati tribal women and blissed-out 1960s-style hippies. It's quite a scene. Whatever you need, from a used paperback to a haircut, you'll find it here – along with hundreds of stalls selling jewellery, carvings, T-shirts, sarongs, chillums, spices and everything else you can think of. You have to bargain hard to get a reasonable deal as plenty of well-heeled tourists also make their way here and the traders start high with their prices. This is also the place to get body piercing, a massage or palm reading.

There's lots of good Indian and Western food available, as well as a couple of bars, and when it all gets too much you can wander down to a makeshift chill-out tent on the beach. Traditional-style fishing boats are available for transport to the market from Baga and Arambol.

The market starts in the morning, but does not warm up until mid-afternoon and continues until the crowds drift away after sunset.

Bungee Jumping

Gravity Zone, towards the beach near the bus stand, offers bungee jumps from a 25m crane (Rs 500). There's a cafe, bar and occasional party nights here. It's open from 10 am to 1.30 pm and 3 to 9.45 pm.

Places to Stay

There are plenty of guesthouses around the village, but finding a place to stay during peak season can still be a problem. If you're planning to stay long term look out for 'To Let' signs on houses – there are plenty along the back lanes leading to the flea market. If you arrive before about 15 December you should be able to find a place.

Poonam Guest House *(☎ 273247)* is an attractive place built around a garden and it has some of the nicest rooms in Anjuna. They're not cheap though; doubles with private bathroom and no view start at Rs 600 while newer rooms and upper-floor rooms with a view start at Rs 800.

Several of the beach bars and restaurants along the path leading south from the bus stand have a few rooms from Rs 150 to 350. They include ***Guru Bar*** *(☎ 273319)* and ***Crab Key*** *(☎ 274554)*. Further down towards the Shore Bar you'll find ***Sunset Bar & Guesthouse*** *(☎ 273917)* with big old rooms with shared bathroom for Rs 100 and Rs 150.

Palmasol Beach Resort *(☎ 273258)* is a bargain with comfortable rooms with private bathroom and hot water for Rs 314 (Rs 410 over Christmas).

Red Cab Inn *(☎ 274427)* has some unusual though slightly run-down rooms and cottages from Rs 300 for a double with private bathroom, up to Rs 600 for a large split-level room. There's a good bar and restaurant here and the management is helpful.

Starco Bar & Restaurant has a collection of comfortable bungalows for Rs 400/500 a single/double, and some small doubles for Rs 300 over December/January.

Manali Guest House *(☎ 273477)* is a central place with good-value rooms for Rs 150 with shared bathroom.

Coutino's Nest *(☎ 274386)* is a clean home on the road into Anjuna. Rooms with shared bathroom cost Rs 150 (Rs 300 in season) and Rs 250 to 600 with private bathroom. It's run by a friendly family and there's a pleasant terrace.

Palacete Rodrigues *(☎ 273358)*, on the outskirts of Anjuna, is a lovely old colonial house built around a courtyard. Spacious, nicely furnished doubles are great value at a fixed Rs 650, or Rs 750 for the suite.

The Bougainvillea *(☎ 273273, fax 274370, ⓔ granpas@hotmail.com)*, also known as Granpa's Inn, is well back from the beach on the road to Mapusa. It's an upmarket place, but with an old-fashioned

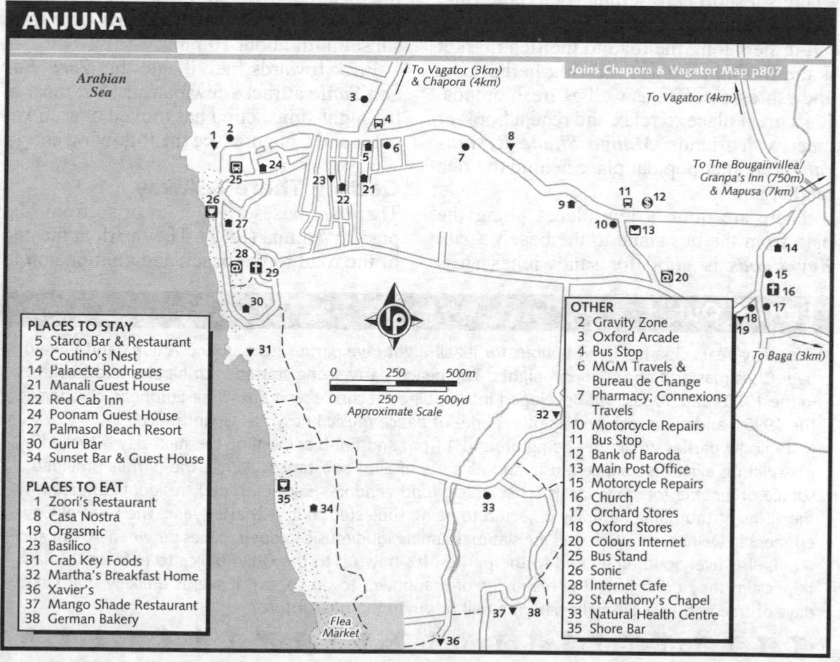

resort-style feel. Comfortable rooms cost from Rs 1250 to 1900 (Rs 1950 to 2950 over Christmas). There's a pool and a relaxing garden.

Places to Eat

Anjuna doesn't have beach shacks like Calangute, but there are a handful of beachside restaurants and some refreshingly different places to eat.

The retail needs of the expat community are served by the ***Oxford Stores*** and the ***Orchard Stores***, which stand opposite each other, and there's the newer ***Oxford Arcade***, closer to the beach. Here you can get everything from a loaf of bread to a Christmas turkey, and such 'exotic' goodies as Vegemite, Heinz baked beans etc.

There are quite a few interesting places on the road leading to the flea market. ***Martha's Breakfast Home*** (☎ *273365*) is a good place to start the day. The breakfasts aren't particularly cheap, but they're excellent and served in a pleasant, shady garden. They also have a few rooms to rent. Stylish ***Orgasmic*** (☎ *273990*) is a Tibetan and veg restaurant specialising in organic food. There's a shop here selling Ayurvedic oils, herbs and books.

Further along the road to the flea market is the ***German Bakery***, serving herbal teas and espresso coffee as well as fresh breads. It's a great place to relax and read a book or meet with friends. ***Mango Shade Restaurant*** is another popular place behind the flea market site.

There are quite a few places along the path from the bus stand to the beach. ***Crab Key Foods*** is good for sandwiches (less than Rs 30) and fresh seafood. You can choose a live crustacean from the pond in the middle of the dining area – stuffed crab is Rs 130.

Down on the cliffs near the bus stand, ***Zoori's Restaurant*** is a relaxing place with cushions on the floor and a great location. Breakfast is the speciality, as well as sushi from Rs 130 to 160.

There is a string of good but unremarkable cafes and restaurants around the crossroads in the main part of the village and along the road leading to Mapusa. ***Casa Nostra*** turns out pretty good Italian fare. Pasta dishes are around Rs 100 and you can wash it down with a red wine. Another good Italian place is ***Basilico***, tucked in behind the Red Cab Inn. Both places are open for dinner only.

Xavier's, hidden away behind the flea market area, is recommended as the best place for seafood in Anjuna. Most dishes are between Rs 150 and Rs 350, and it's open from around 7 pm.

Entertainment

Shore Bar is still a popular spot to sink a few beers and watch the sun go down. On market day there's usually a party here from sunset until about 10 pm.

Back towards the village, the ***Guru Bar*** and ***Sonic*** attract a few patrons, but most of the night-time action has moved over to Vagator and Chapora (see the following entry).

Getting There & Away

There are buses every hour or so from Mapusa to Anjuna (Rs 7). They park at the end of the road to the beach and continue on to

Partied Out

For many years Goa has been famous for its all-night rave parties held around Anjuna and Vagator over Christmas and on full-moon nights. The beach-party scene started with hippies and travellers in the 1970s and 1980s, but developed into a full-on techno scene attracting European clubbers in the 1990s, and even spawned its own genre of dance music known as Goan trance.

Typically parties would get going around 11 pm and finish some time the next day – fuelled by ear-splitting electronic dance music and all sorts of illicit substances. While the parties provided a source of income for some locals (chai ladies, food vendors, baksheesh etc), residents affected by the all-night thumping naturally objected to being subjected to it year after year. The Central Government in Delhi has now passed legislation banning loud music in open spaces between 10 pm and 6 am, effectively putting an end to the parties. It's now up to the Goan police to enforce this law; they claim they don't have the resources or manpower to do so, but it seems unlikely that Goa's days of free and easy all-night partying will return in the near future.

Vagator, Chapora and up to Arambol. Plenty of motorcycle taxis gather at the central crossroads and you can also hire scooters and motorcycles easily from here.

CHAPORA & VAGATOR

This is one of the most beautiful and interesting parts of Goa's coastline. Much of the inhabited area nestles under a canopy of dense coconut palms, and Chapora village is dominated by a rocky hill on top of which sits an old Portuguese **fort**. The views from its ramparts are excellent.

Secluded, sandy coves are found all the way around the northern side of this rocky outcrop, though Vagator's main beaches face west towards the Arabian Sea. Little Vagator, the beach to the south, is very popular and, thanks largely to the cliffs, there is very little beachside development here.

Information

There are STD/ISD phone places in the main street of Chapora as well as a small bookstall. Soniya Travels (☎ 273344) in Chapora is a good agency for transport bookings, foreign exchange and Internet access (Rs 60 per hour). It's also an agent for Western Union. In Vagator, you'll find Internet access at several places near the beach (try Eddie's Cyberzone or Mira Cybercafe), and further back in the village.

Places to Stay

Most people who come here tend to stay a long time in cheap rooms. With a group you can rent a whole house for next to nothing. It may not be luxury – it might not even have beds – but it's a great way to spend the winter. If you arrive before peak season, look around for 'To Let' signs for rooms in private houses and expect to pay around Rs 50 per night for basic accommodation (shared bathroom).

Chapora The ***Shertor Villa*** *(☎ 274335)* has about 20 basic rooms at Rs 160 for a double with shared bathroom or Rs 250 with attached bathroom (reductions for long stays). If there's nobody here, check over the road at Noble Nest restaurant.

Baba Restaurant *(☎ 273213)* has six rooms with shared bathroom for Rs 150 (Rs 120 in low season). They're building four more rooms with private bathrooms.

Helinda Restaurant *(☎ 274345)* has some of the best rooms in Chapora. It's clean, and relaxed, but is often full. Doubles without/with private bathroom are Rs 200/300.

Vagator Vagator has many more options than Chapora, including several upmarket places. As well as trying the following guesthouses, you can ask around for rooms at any of the local restaurants.

Dolrina Guest House *(☎ 273382)* is near the beach and has a good range of rooms. Doubles with shared/private bathroom are Rs 275/350 in the original sections, and the spotless new rooms cost Rs 450. It's run by a very friendly family.

Reshma Guest House *(☎ 273568)*, across the road and down a lane, has doubles with

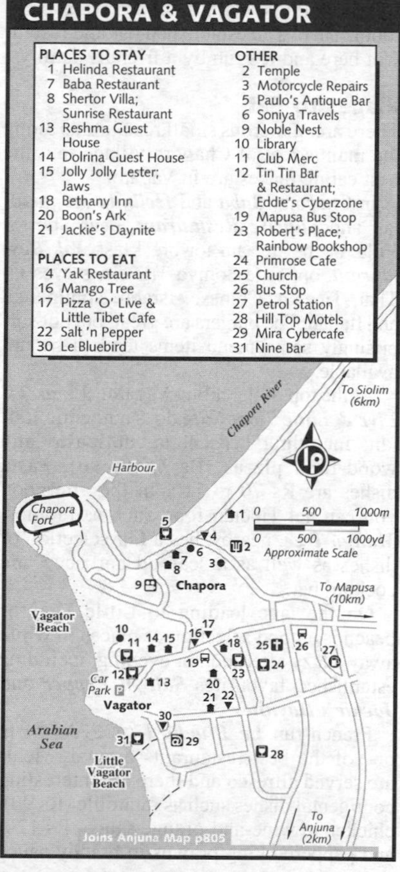

shared bathroom from Rs 150 to 300, or Rs 400 with private bathroom.

Jolly Jolly Lester *(☎ 273620)* has better doubles with private bathroom behind its restaurant at Rs 500 (Rs 800 over Christmas).

Bethany Inn *(☎ 273731)*, further back from the beach, has a range of spacious, clean doubles and a fluid pricing policy depending on how busy the season is. As far as we can tell, doubles cost from Rs 250 to 500. There are a couple of four-bed rooms with fridge and balcony that are great value at Rs 600. ***Boon's Ark*** *(☎ 274045)*, nearby on the same road, is a new place with pleasant cottage-style rooms from Rs 400 to 500 (Rs 800 to 1000 over Christmas).

There are several places on the road leading to Little Vagator Beach. ***Jackie's Daynite*** *(☎ 274320)* has some immaculate new rooms for Rs 400/600 with shared/private bathroom. There's an established bar and restaurant here and it's run by a friendly family.

GOA

Places to Eat

There are numerous small restaurants along the main street of Chapora village, but the best eating places are in Vagator.

In Chapora, ***Baba*** and ***Helinda*** are popular, and ***Sunrise Restaurant***, near Shertor Villa, opens at 7 am for breakfast. ***Yak Restaurant***, opposite Soniya Travels, serves up Thai, Tibetan, Chinese, Israeli, continental and Italian. The burgers are great, but not surprisingly some menu items tend to be unavailable.

At the top of the hill in Vagator, ***Pizza 'O' Live & Little Tibet Cafe*** does authentic Italian, including bruschetta, antipasto and wood-fired pizzas (Rs 45 to 90). Pasta dishes are Rs 70 to 110. In the afternoon you can get Tibetan food such as momos. ***Mango Tree***, nearby, has a fair selection of dishes as well as a seafood barbecue and cocktail bar.

On the lane leading to Little Vagator beach is a good selection of places to while away a lazy afternoon or evening, including established favourites ***Salt 'n Pepper*** and ***Jackie's Daynite***.

French-run ***Le Bluebird*** *(☎ 273695)* is one of the best restaurants around. Meals are served alfresco and there are interesting continental dishes such as ratatoille (Rs 90), chicken in wine-and-orange sauce (Rs 120) and peppered king prawns in brandy sauce (Rs 250). There's a good breakfast menu and a range of vegetarian dishes, plus wine by the bottle or glass.

Entertainment

Vagator is the centre of Goa's party scene, especially now that the future of late-night raves at places like the Bamboo Forest is in doubt, and Chapora has some great little bars on its main street. The evening usually starts at the ***Nine Bar*** overlooking Little Vagator beach. By 10 pm the party is up at ***Primrose Cafe***, or the smaller ***Robert's Place***, virtually across the road.

Hill Top Motels often has outdoor parties. The latest place on the party scene is ***Club Merc***, down near Vagator beach, which was managing to evade some of the late night music restrictions.

New-release movies are shown nightly at ***Jaws*** in Vagator and ***Noble Nest*** in Chapora, and you can occasionally see live music or just play pool at ***Tin Tin Bar & Restaurant*** in Vagator. ***Paulo's Antique Bar*** in Chapora is tiny, but has a friendly atmosphere and cheap beer (Rs 15 for a small King's).

Getting There & Away

Fairly frequent buses run to both Chapora and Vagator from Mapusa throughout the day. Many go via Anjuna. The bus stop is near the road junction in Chapora village. Most people hire a motorcycle to get around; ask at hotels and restaurants.

CHAPORA TO ARAMBOL

The ride up the coast between Chapora and Arambol offers the opportunity to detour to some relatively deserted beaches. The trip also involves crossing the Chapora River by vehicle ferry at Siolim. A monstrous bridge from Siolim to Chopdem is nearing completion (has been for years), which will unfortunately put an end to this ferry ride.

From Chopdem you can head east to **Morjim Beach**, which has a handful of beach shacks and several places to stay at its northern end. Rare olive Ridley turtles nest at the southern end of Morjim Beach from September to February, so this is a protected area.

Continuing north, you pass though **Asvem Beach** on the way up to **Mandrem Beach**, a peaceful area with some great places to stay. As with Morjim the beach is not idyllic to look at, but it's a good place to get away from it all – while you still can.

River Cat Villa *(☎ 297346)* is a stylish Portuguese house with large rooms for Rs 600, or Rs 700 with private bathroom. ***Dunes*** *(☎ 297219, ⓔ dunes13@rediffmail.com)*, is a laid-back new place among the palms with a choice of tepees (Rs 150), thatched huts (Rs 250) or rooms in a stone cottage (Rs 250). The owner plans to hold yoga and naturopathy courses here. Further north, ***Sea Paradise*** consists of six thatch huts just back from the beach. They have lights, fans and mosquito nets and cost Rs 250 per double in season.

ARAMBOL (HARMAL)

Although Arambol is one of Goa's more far flung beaches, travellers have been drifting up here for years and a mushrooming industry of facilities is appearing to service them. Arambol is still a good place to get away from the crowds, but not if you want complete solitude.

The beach is an open and fairly deserted stretch of clean sand with a rocky headland at the northern end. The main beach is good for swimming, but over the headland are several more attractive bays.

Arambol village is quiet and friendly, with just a few hundred locals, mostly fishing people. Accommodation here is still pretty basic, but there's enough of it, along with restaurants, travel agencies (handling foreign exchange), Internet and other services. Most of this is concentrated on the road leading to the northern end of the beach. There are also a few stores back in the village.

The headland at Arambol is a popular place for **paragliding**. There's an outfit based at the Relax Inn (on the beach) which charges Rs 900 for a tandem flight and also offers certified courses.

Buses from Mapusa stop on the main road at Arambol, where there's a church and a few shops. From here, a side road leads 1km down to the village, and the beach is about 500m further on.

Places to Stay & Eat

The most pleasant accommodation is in the little ***chalets*** on the next bay to the north of the main beach. Some are basic, but many now have private bathrooms and running water, and the sea views are superb. Rooms range from Rs 300 to 400 for a double in high season, but discounts are available at other times. ***Om Ganesh*** *(☎ 297657)* is the main place, or just ask at the cafes on the north side of the headland.

Welcome Inn *(☎ 297733)*, among the group of restaurants on the lane leading to the beach, has nine clean doubles with private bathroom, constant hot water and fan from Rs 100 to 350 depending on the season.

About 1km south, closer to the village, the ***Ave Maria Guest House*** *(☎ 297674, ⓔ avemaria_goa@hotmail.com)* is a solid old home run by a friendly family. A single/double with shared bathroom is Rs 120/150, a double with private bathroom is Rs 200, and there are dorm beds for Rs 30. There's a good rooftop restaurant.

There are several bars and shacks lining the main beach and an increasing number of decent restaurants on the road leading back to the village. ***Garden of Meals*** has a different set special each night. ***Fellini*** is a good place for Italian food.

TEREKHOL FORT

At Terekhol (Tiracol), on the north bank of the river of the same name, is a small Portuguese fort with a little church within its walls. It's now a hotel, the ***Hotel Tiracol Fort Heritage*** *(☎ 02366-68248 or 0832-782240, ⓔ tiracol@usa.net)*, which is a peaceful and atmospheric place to stay. There's little else here, but the setting is spectacular, and the rooms in the old fort are unique. Singles/doubles are Rs 800/850, and the deluxe suites (complete with a huge circular bath) cost Rs 1750. The owners organise backwater boat trips up the Terekhol River.

The trip to the fort makes a good outing on a motorcycle, and you could stop for a swim on deserted **Querim Beach**.

There are occasional buses from Mapusa or Pernem to Querim, on the south bank of the river, opposite Terekhol, and also between Arambol and Querim. The ferry between Querim and Terekhol runs every 30 minutes from 6 am to 9.30 pm.

South Goa

South Goa's beaches include travellers' centres like Colva and Benaulim, and a sprinkling of upmarket resorts, but there's generally less tourist development here and a more laid-back feel than in the north. Margao is both the capital of the region and the transport hub. Goa's Dabolim airport is near Vasco da Gama.

MARGAO (MADGAON)

pop 79,800

The capital of Salcete province, Margao is the main population centre of South Goa and is probably the busiest town in the state – the traffic in the town centre makes Panaji look positively comatose.

Though Margao is not really of great interest to travellers, the richly decorated **Church of the Holy Spirit** is worth a visit, and the **covered market** is the best of its kind in Goa.

Around 8 December, Margao celebrates the **Feast of Our Lady of the Immaculate Conception** with a large fair.

Information

The tourist office (☎ 715204) is in the GTDC Tourist Hostel, in the centre of town. The State Bank of India is opposite the Municipal Gardens, and you can get Visa or MasterCard cash advances at the Bank of Baroda near the covered market. HDFC Bank has a 24-hour ATM on the ground floor of the Caro Centre opposite the Municipal Gardens, while Centurion Bank has an ATM (MasterCard and Cirrus only) just off Luis Miranda Rd.

The main post office is on the north side of the Municipal Gardens, but the poste restante (open 8.30 to 10.30 am and 3 to 4.30 pm)

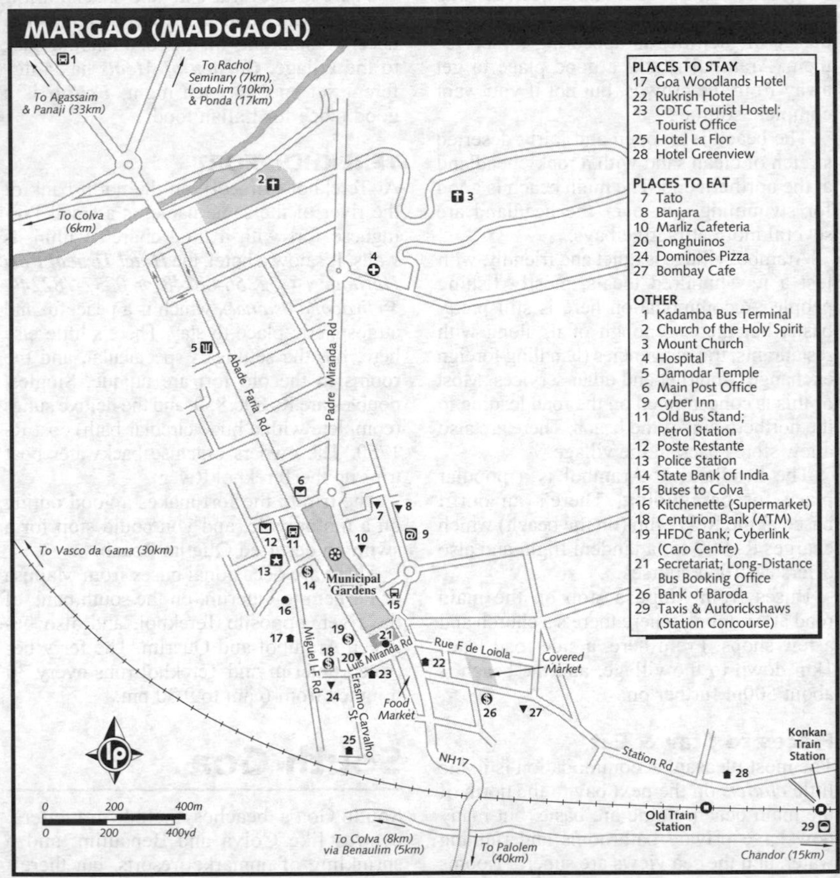

has its own office, about 100m away. Cyber Inn, in the Kalika Chambers, has Internet access for Rs 45 per hour and is open from 9 am to 8 pm weekdays. Cyberlink, in the Caro Centre, charges Rs 30 per hour.

Places to Stay

Rukrish Hotel *(☎ 721709)* is probably the best of an unappealing range of cheapies cented around the bazaar area. Reasonably clean single/double rooms with shared bathroom cost Rs 90/130; doubles with tiny private bathrooms cost Rs 238. Checkout time is 24 hours.

Hotel Greenview *(☎ 715489)*, across the road from the old train station, is better, but still basic with singles/doubles/triples with private bathroom for Rs 130/190/250.

Hotel La Flor *(☎ 731402, fax 731382, Erasmo Carvalho St)* is friendly and in a quiet but central location. Rooms with TV and private bathroom cost from Rs 350/420, or Rs 460/520 with air-con, plus 18% tax.

Goa Woodlands Hotel *(☎ 705121, fax 738 732, ⓔ woodland@goa1.dot.net.in, Miguel Loyola Furtado Rd)* is one of Margao's better hotels, which unfortunately doesn't say a lot for Margao. There's a wide range of rooms from basic singles/doubles with bathroom, TV and balcony for 240/300 to air-con suites for Rs 610/670. There's a bar and restaurant.

Places to Eat

Bombay Cafe is a busy vegetarian place with cheap snacks such as samosas and dosas – nothing over Rs 8. ***Tato***, to the east of the Municipal Gardens, is an excellent vegetarian restaurant. A thali costs Rs 22, and the place is kept very clean.

Longhuinos *(☎ 739908, Luis Miranda Rd)*, opposite the GDTC Tourist Hotel, is the place to sit and while away the siesta hours over a cold beer. It has an old fashioned ambience and is recommended for Goan cuisine such as chourisso (Rs 35) or prawns vindaloo (Rs 60). It also does pastries and sweets.

Marliz Cafeteria is a modern open-fronted cafe looking out at the busy town centre. It's a great spot for coffee and cake.

Banjara *(☎ 714837)* is Margao's best Indian restaurant, specialising in North Indian dishes (around Rs 95) and seafood. The subterranean dining room is cosy and the service is good.

There's a branch of ***Dominoes Pizza*** (takeaway only) on Luis Miranda Rd.

Getting There & Away

Bus All local buses operate from the busy Kadamba bus terminal north of town, but many also stop at the old bus stand in the centre of town. Catch buses to Colva and Benaulim from Kadamba or from the bus stop on the east side of the Municipal Gardens.

There are hourly buses to Colva from around 7 am to 7 pm (Rs 5, 20 minutes). Some go via Benaulim. Buses to Panaji run every 15 minutes and take about one hour (Rs 10/15 ordinary/express). There are around eight buses a day direct to Palolem (Rs 10, one hour) and others heading to Karwar that stop in nearby Chaudi. There are also local buses to Vasco (for the airport), Ponda, Chandor and Rachol.

There is one deluxe daily bus to Mumbai at 2.30 pm (Rs 265, 16 hours), Bangalore at 6.30 pm (Rs 302, 14 hours) and Hospet at 7 pm (Rs 120, nine hours). There are also buses to Pune (Rs 240, 15 hours), Hubli (Rs 67, six hours) and Belgaum (Rs 57, five hours). There's a booking office for long-distance buses in the Secretariat building.

There are private bus agents in the town centre near the GDTC Tourist Hostel.

Train Margao's new station is about 1.5km east of the town centre; vehicle access is via the road south of the train line, not Station Rd (which leads to the now closed old station). If you're walking there, however, you can cross the tracks at the footbridge past the old station. There's a reservation hall within the main building. For inquires phone ☎ 712790. See Getting There & Away at the start of this chapter for train information.

Taxi To get to Colva or Benaulim, you can take a motorcycle taxi for about Rs 30 (no objection to taking backpacks), autorickshaw (around Rs 50) or taxi (Rs 70).

AROUND MARGAO (MADGAON)

About 6km from Margao, near the village of Raia, is the **Rachol Seminary and Church**. The Museum of Christian Art here has some interesting displays including textiles, some of the silver once used in the churches of Old Goa, a magnificent 17th-century silver monstrance in the shape of a swan, and a mobile mass kit (complete with candlesticks) – standard issue for missionaries out in the jungle. The museum is open from 9 am to 1 pm and 2 to 5 pm Tuesday to Sunday (Rs 5).

The church dates from 1610 and the seminary has interesting architecture, a decaying library and paintings of Christian characters done in Indian styles. This is not a tourist site, so you should ask before wandering around.

In the village of Chandor, 20km east of Margao, are several interesting colonial mansions. One of the grandest, **Braganza House**, is open to the public (see the boxed text 'Braganza House').

VASCO DA GAMA

Close to Mormugao Harbour and 3km from Dabolim airport, Vasco da Gama is a busy

Braganza House

Taking up one complete side of the village square in front of the church, the Braganza House is not one house, but two. Built by two brothers, the east and west wings of the house stretch outwards from a common front entrance – giving the place its incredibly long facade.

During the 400 years since the work was started the original houses have been extended so that you come to newer sections of each house working outwards from the central staircase. Over this time too, the families have acquired different names. In the east wing of the house is the Braganza Pereira family, while in the west wing is the Menezes Braganza family. The latter is one of the most famous names in Goa – Luís de Menezes Braganza was a journalist and leading light in the Goan Independence movement.

Although there is no entry fee to either house, the owners must bear maintenance expenses and a contribution of some sort is expected – a minimum of Rs 50 is reasonable. Both houses are open during normal hours (ie, don't turn up during siesta) but it's well worth getting the nearest branch of the tourist office to ring for you in advance to ensure the owners will be there. There are frequent buses to Chandor from Margao's Kadamba bus terminal.

The east wing, or the **Braganza Pereira House**, is less well preserved than the west wing, although the slight air of decay, and the clutter of bric-a-brac collected by the family over the years, gives it an air of faded magnificence.

The first room you are shown into contains a mass of Goan-made furniture beautifully carved from rosewood, with the family initials worked into the designs of the chair backs. Among the other items is a marble-topped table imported from Italy. The ballroom, despite its rather battered looking ceiling and dusty furniture, must have been magnificent in its time. The gallery beyond contains a jumble of collected items, from crocodile and snake skins to an old 78 rpm record, a faded photo of Elizabeth Taylor, and a couple of old palanquins in which members of the family were accustomed to being carried around.

At the back of the house is a small family chapel, again looking rather bare, but fascinating nonetheless. A chest in the adjoining room contains 200-year-old vestments, chalices and other paraphernalia used in the services occasionally held in the chapel. The family proudly possesses its very own relic of St Francis Xavier – a fingernail – which is kept carefully hidden in the house.

The west wing, or the **Menezes Braganza House**, is in much better condition as large parts of it have been renovated. Carved rosewood furniture again fills almost every room, along with large amounts of Chinese porcelain – some of it has plain blue-and-white patterns and is from Macau and other items are multicoloured. Some of the ceramics such as the large vase in the ballroom were even ordered especially for the house.

The two large rooms behind the entrance halls contain Dr Menezes Braganza's extensive library. Passing beyond them you go through the journalist's study to the beautifully renovated ballroom. Nowhere in Goa today will you get a better idea of the lifestyle of the Goan landowners during the peak of their fortunes. The ballroom is paved with Italian marble and hung with enormous gilt-edged mirrors and chandeliers from Belgium. The arches of the doors are gilded with gold leaf. The last big party held here, according to Mrs Aida de Menezes Braganza, was some 50 years ago. The orchestra sat in the study with the double doors open to the ballroom, and played waltzes and mandos. At the back of the house, with windows opening to the orchard, is the huge official dining room.

industrial town with a rather seedy feel about it – not helped by the presence of a well-known red light district. With the new station at Margao taking over as the main rail hub, few travellers will bother to venture up to this unexciting town. If you fly into Goa, it's possible you may want to stay overnight in Vasco rather than take a taxi further afield.

There's tourist information (☎ 512673) at the GTDC Vasco Tourist Hotel. HDFC Bank has a 24-hour ATM on Swatantra Path.

Places to Stay & Eat

***Twiga Lodge** (☎ 512682)*, near the main bus stand, is a good budget option. The dilapidated old Portuguese house is run by a friendly family and has just five basic rooms at Rs 100 for a double with private bathroom.

The GTDC's ***Vasco Tourist Hotel** (☎ 513 119)* is large and central, but a bit run-down. Rooms with private bathroom are Rs 200/260 a single/double.

The more upmarket ***Hotel Karma Plaza** (☎ 518928, ⓔ karmahotel@123india.com, Rajendra Prasad Ave)* is a good choice at Rs 800 for a standard double, or Rs 1000 for a deluxe, all with air-con. The hotel is part of a shopping complex that includes fast-food outlets and an Internet cafe.

***Hotel Annapurna** (☎ 513375, D Deshpande Rd)* is a good cheap option with veg thalis under Rs 20.

The Karma Plaza shopping centre on Rajendra Prasad Ave has clean, modern restaurants, including ***Ginza*** for Chinese and Japanese and ***Temptations*** for burgers.

Getting There & Away

Express minibuses run nonstop from the city bus stand north of the train station to Margao (Rs 10) and Panaji (Rs 15). Both trips take about 45 minutes. There are also buses from here to the airport (Rs 3) and Bogmalo (Rs 5). Normal buses operate from the main bus stand to Margao and Panaji and interstate to Mumbai (Rs 265, 15 hours) and Bangalore (Rs 312, 16 hours). Long-distance private buses can be booked outside the train station.

A taxi from the airport costs Rs 60 and an autorickshaw is Rs 50.

BOGMALO

Bogmalo, 8km from Vasco da Gama and 4km from the airport, is a small, sandy cove dominated by the five-star high rise Bogmalo Beach Resort, which evaded the restriction requiring all hotels to be built at least 500m from the beach.

There's little here apart from a pleasant and reasonably exclusive beach with several pricey beach shack cafes (in some places menu prices are quoted in pounds sterling!), water sports facilities and the small village of Bogmalo.

Goa Diving (☎ 555117, ⓔ goadivin@goatelecom.com) is based at Joets Guest House. A single tank dive costs Rs 1300 and a PADI open water course is Rs 14,000.

Places to Stay & Eat

***Saritas Guest House** (☎ 555965, ⓔ saritas@expl.com)* on the beach, has clean but small and unremarkable rooms for Rs 550 (Rs 1100 over Christmas).

***Joets Guest House** (☎ 555036)*, further down the beach, is a nice place with doubles for Rs 700, but it's usually booked up by package companies.

***Coconut Creek** (☎ 556100, fax 556300 ⓔ joets@goal.dot.net.in)* is a very stylish new resort set back from the beach in the coconut groves. There's a shady pool surrounded by ten double-storey cottages. The ground-floor air-con rooms are Rs 2500 (Rs 3500 over Christmas) and the 1st-floor rooms with fan are Rs 2000 (Rs 3000 over Christmas). There's a good restaurant serving Italian and Goan cuisine here.

Getting There & Away

Frequent buses run between Bogmalo and Vasco da Gama (Rs 5), from where you can pick up buses to Margao and Panaji.

COLVA & BENAULIM

About 20 years ago, precious little disturbed Colva, except the local fishing people who pulled their catch in by hand cach morning, and a few of the more intrepid hippies who had forsaken the obligatory sex, drugs and rock and roll of Calangute for the soothing tranquillity of this paradise. Since there were only a couple of cottages for rent, most people stayed either on the beach itself or in palm-leaf shelters, which they constructed themselves.

Those days are gone, but development is still more low key here than in the north. You'll still see fishing boats on the main beach and the odd fisherman mending a net,

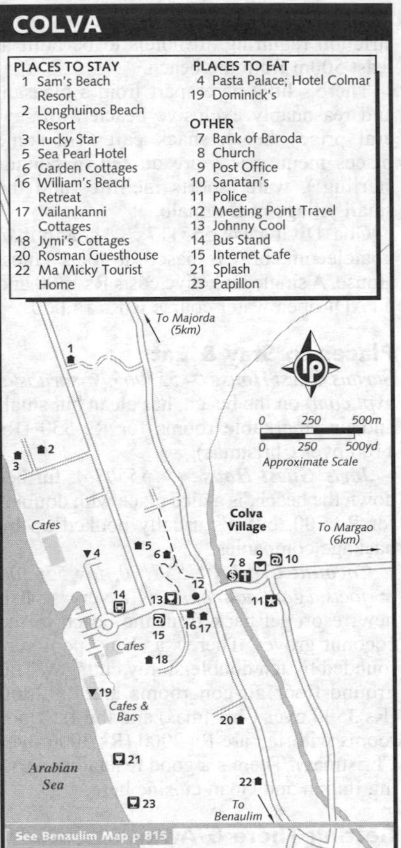

although most now have motorised trawlers standing anchored in a line offshore.

Colva village itself has suffered, with ugly shops, hotels and souvenir stalls clustered at the end of the road from Margao. In peak season this area is crammed with holiday-makers. Walk 2km in either direction, and you'll get close to what it used to be like before the cement mixers began chugging away. Benaulim, 2km south of Colva, is still a very peaceful village, consisting more of family guesthouses than resort hotels.

In April, Colva hosts a music and dance festival, **Beach Bonanza**, from mid-April. **Fama de Menino Jesus** is a feast day held on the second Monday in October when the Menino Jesus (a statue of the infant Jesus said to perform miracles) is paraded.

With fewer people than the northern beaches and quiet back lanes, occasional robberies occur in Benaulim, although additional street lighting has improved things. Avoid walking from the beach alone at night.

Information

The nearest post office is in Colva village, where letters can be sent poste restante. There's a small Bank of Baroda next to the church, and several travel agencies in both Colva and Benaulim that will change cash and travellers cheques – try Meeting Point Travel (☎ 710413) in Colva.

There are several small shops on Colva's main beach offering Internet access.

Organised Tours

If you're not planning to stay at any of the northern beaches, it's worth making the day trip to the Wednesday flea market at Anjuna. Trips are advertised at the beach bars and cost about Rs 75. Tackling this trip by public bus involves three or four changes.

Dominick's (see Places to Eat) also organises boat trips to Palolem beach every Sunday (and sometimes Friday). They cost Rs 375 including a buffet lunch and a drink. The boat trip there takes 2½ hours and there's a good chance of seeing dolphins; the return trip is by bus.

Places to Stay

It's easy to rent houses long term in Colva and Benaulim, particularly if you arrive early in the season – just ask around in the restaurants and shops. Most houses are a 20-minute walk back from the beach.

Colva About 1km north of the main road, ***Sam's Beach Resort*** *(☎ 735304)* has pleasant rooms around a courtyard garden. It's quiet and good value at Rs 200 per double with private bathroom.

Lucky Star *(☎ 788071,* ⓔ *pradorbarad@hotmail.com)* is close to the beach and has a range of comfortable doubles with bathroom from Rs 350. Each room has a safe and there's a good restaurant and bar here.

Sea Pearl Hotel *(☎ 730070)* offers clean, spacious doubles with balcony for Rs 265. Its popular restaurant has excellent seafood.

Garden Cottages, in the quiet, palm-fringed 4th Ward, is a friendly place with only six rooms at Rs 200 per double.

Vailankanni Cottages *(☎ 788584)*, back on the main road to the beach, is popular with travellers for its friendly atmosphere and clean rooms from Rs 150 to 250 with private bathroom.

Jymi's Cottages *(☎ 788016)* is run by a friendly family and is close to the beach tucked just south of the main drag. Doubles with private bathroom are pretty basic at Rs 250 to 350.

There's a string of small family-run guesthouses along the road leading to Benaulim. ***Rosman Guesthouse*** *(☎ 788735)* is a friendly place with rooms for Rs 100/150 with shared/private bathroom. ***Ma Mickey Tourist Home*** *(☎ 788190)* is another lovely place with singles/doubles at Rs 100/150, all with shared bathroom.

William's Beach Retreat *(☎ 788153, ⓔ wbretreat@satyam.net.in)* is a superior place, but still family run. Comfortable ground-level rooms around a pool cost Rs 650, or Rs 850 with air-con, including breakfast and tax. Prices increase over Christmas. Nonguests can use the pool – which has a nifty pool bar – for Rs 50 per half day.

Longhuinos Beach Resort *(☎ 788068, fax 788070, ⓔ lbresort@goatelecom.com)* is in an excellent location near the beach. The rooms are simply furnished, but most have balconies and sea views. Rates are from Rs 800/900 (Rs 1200/1400 over Christmas) with hot water and satellite TV. Breakfast is included and there's a small garden with beach access.

Benaulim Less than 2km from Colva, Benaulim is much more peaceful and rustic, with numerous guesthouses and small hotels spread over a wide area. There are several places on the beach 1km or so from Benaulim village. Note that some telephone numbers in Benaulim were due to change early in 2000. You can make inquiries on ☎ 197.

Furtado's Beach House *(☎ 705265)* has a prime beachfront location, a restaurant and 10 simple double rooms for Rs 300 with private bathroom. ***Camilson's Beach Resort*** *(☎ 788722)*, 50m north, has a variety of rooms set in a large garden just back from the beach. Doubles with private bathroom cost from Rs 300 to 600 (Rs 350 to 800 over Christmas).

GOA

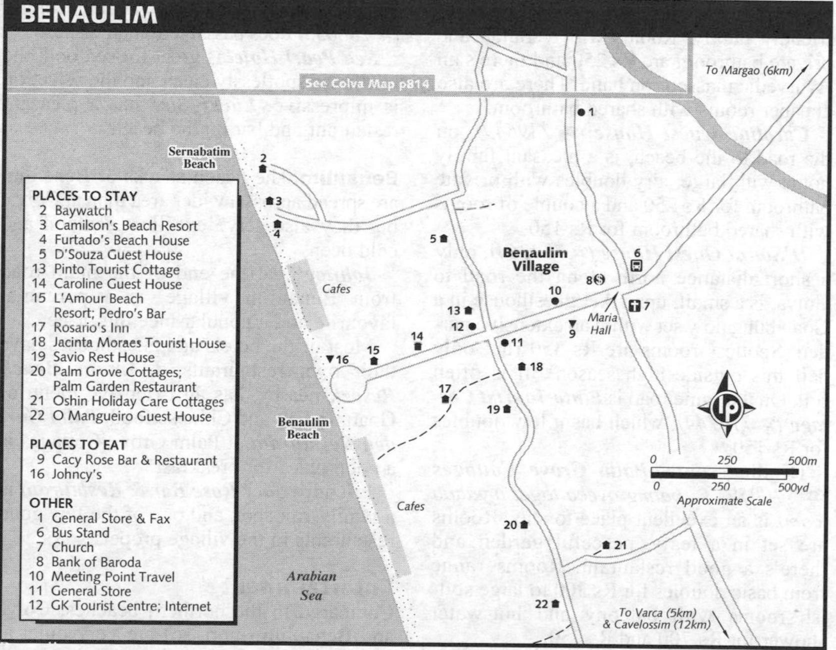

More expensive is ***Baywatch*** *(☎ 730075, Sernbabatim Beach)* but it has an excellent set-up with safari tents, complete with private bathroom (toilet and shower) and electricity for Rs 800 (Rs 1200 over Christmas). There are also spacious, clean rooms for Rs 600. There's a bar, restaurant and occasional disco here.

L'Amour Beach Resort *(☎ 737960)* is a semi-upmarket place in a well-kept garden. Worn rooms with private bathroom cost from Rs 400.

Most other places are scattered around the village of Benaulim, about 1km from the beach, where accommodation is generally cheaper.

Savio Rest House *(☎ 736249)* is hidden behind a decrepit-looking building, but it's not a bad option and you can't beat the price. Reasonable doubles are Rs 80/95 without/with private bathroom, and some upstairs rooms have a balcony.

Nearby on the same road, ***Jacinta Moraes Tourist House*** *(☎ 770187)* has nice doubles for just Rs 100 with private bathroom, Rs 90 with shared bathroom, and it's run by a friendly family.

Rosario's Inn *(☎ 734167)*, next to the football pitch, is a big place run by a friendly family. Rooms with veranda and private bathroom are Rs 250 and there's an Ayurvedic masseur on hand. There are also cheaper rooms with shared bathroom.

Caroline Guest House *(☎ 739649)*, on the road to the beach, is a pleasant family home with large, airy doubles with private bathroom for Rs 250 and a couple of rooms with shared bathroom for Rs 150.

D'Souza Guest House *(☎ 734364)*, only a short distance north along the road to Colva, is a small, upmarket guesthouse in a Goan bungalow set within an extensive garden. Spotless rooms are Rs 350 (but only half this outside high season). It is often full. On the same road is ***Pinto Tourist Cottage*** *(☎ 710744)*, which has a few doubles for Rs 150.

Heading south, ***Palm Grove Cottages*** *(☎ 770059, ⓔ palmgrovecottages@yahoo.com)* is an excellent place to stay. Rooms are set in a leafy, peaceful garden and there's a good restaurant. Rooms range from basic doubles for Rs 300 to large stylish rooms with balcony and hot-water shower for Rs 700 and Rs 750.

O Mangueiro Guest House *(☎ 734164)* has rooms in the family house (with shared bathroom) for Rs 150 and spotless double rooms with private bathroom in the newer section for Rs 400. A garden is rapidly taking shape here.

Oshin Holiday Care Cottages *(☎ 770 069)* is hidden away in a peaceful area, back about 100m from the main road. Singles/doubles with private bathroom in this well-kept house are Rs 250/400.

Places to Eat

Colva The most popular places to eat (and drink) are the open-air, wooden restaurants lining the beach either side of where the road ends. They're all individually owned and the standard of food is generally very high. Seafood is, of course, the staple of the menu and the best stuff is brought in fresh daily from the Margao market. These restaurants are also well tuned in to what travellers like for breakfast; cold beer is also available. Among the beach shacks, ***Dominick's*** is consistently good. Dominick comes around at dinner with a selection of fresh seafood so you can see what's on offer.

Back from the beach are plenty more places. ***Pasta Palace*** at Hotel Colmar *(☎ 788053)* does passable Italian dishes.

Sea Pearl Hotel is great for seafood; the kitchen is spotlessly clean and the selection is impressive. ***Lucky Star*** has a pleasant restaurant and bar on the beach.

Benaulim The beach shacks at Benaulim are spread across a wider area than at Colva, but they also serve excellent seafood and cold beer.

Johncy's, at the end of the main road from Benaulim village, is a perennial favourite and a popular meeting place.

Most of the hotels and guesthouses have their own restaurants. ***L'Amour Beach Resort***, nearby, has an extensive menu of Goan, Indian and Chinese food. ***Palm Garden Restaurant*** at Palm Grove Cottages is a good place for breakfast.

Friendly ***Cacy Rose Bar & Restaurant*** is a family-run spot, and one of the few good restaurants in the village proper.

Entertainment

Compared to the northern beaches, Colva and Benaulim (more so) are very quiet at

GREG ELMS

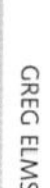

CHRISTINE NIVEN

NEIL SETCHFIELD

LINDY HICKMAN

GREG ELMS

The land of plenty: Goa's Anjuna Flea Market is a meeting place for traders and for travellers alike. Whether you're after intricately worked handicrafts **(top right)** or tantalisingly fresh produce **(others)**, you'll find something here.

GREG ELMS

SARA-JANE CLELAND

GREG ELMS

BRYN THOMAS

With over 100km of almost uninterrupted coastline and hours of sunshine, Goa remains one of India's most popular destinations. Fishing is central to life at Benaulim **(top & middle right)** and other coastal villages **(middle left)**, and for many the Anjuna Flea Market is the highlight of each week **(bottom)**.

night, with most people content to eat out and enjoy a few drinks. Some of the resort hotels put on live bands and floor shows during the high season.

The area of beachside to the south of the roundabout at Colva stays fairly active, however. ***Splash*** has a dance floor by the beach, pool tables and a rustic bar. Solo women should take care around here late at night. Further south along the beach, ***Papillon*** is a much more laid-back beach bar where you're more likely to hear Bob Marley playing than Ibiza techno.

Johnny Cool, rapidly disappearing behind two new hotels on the main road in Colva, is a small bar with a good selection of beers.

Over at Benaulim, ***Baywatch*** *(☎ 730075)* on Sernabatim Beach, is a little isolated, but it has a good bar with an enclosed disco with occasional party nights.

Getting There & Away

Buses run from Colva to Margao roughly every 30 minutes (Rs 5, 20 minutes) from 7.30 am to about 7 pm. Buses from Margao to Benaulim are also frequent; some of them continue south to Varca and Cavelossim. Buses arrive and depart at the roundabout at the end of the beach road. In Benaulim buses stop at the crossroads known as Maria Hall.

BENAULIM TO PALOLEM

The 10km strip of pristine beach south of Benaulim has become Goa's upmarket resort beach, with at least six hotels of varying degrees of luxury. As far as resorts go, some of them are quite good – being self-contained luxury bubbles – and they are certainly isolated from anything that might disturb the peace. **Varca** is 5km south of Benaulim, and **Cavelossim**, with an impressive church, is 7km further on.

If you're planning on riding down to Palolem, this road is more enjoyable than taking the national highway from Margao and there are a couple of things to see en route. To get across the estuary you'll need to take the ferry from Cavelossim to Assolna – turn left at the sign saying 'village panchayat Cavelossim' before you get to Mobor, and continue for 2km to the river. From there you can continue to the fishing village of **Betul**.

The road from Betul to Agonda winds over hills and is pretty rough in places. You can detour to the old Portuguese fort of **Cabo da Rama**. There's not a lot to see, but the views from the ruined ramparts are good.

Agonda, the next village, has an empty 2km stretch of sand and several places to stay. This place is popular with travellers wanting to escape the resort scenes, but with Palolem already getting overcrowded, the peace probably won't last. About 1km past the village, along the beach road, you'll find a string of small guesthouses.

Dersy Bar *(☎ 647503)* has very clean doubles for Rs 300 with three adjoining rooms sharing one bathroom. Across the road on the beach side they have set up some beach huts for Rs 150 to 200. ***Dunhill Bar and Restaurant*** *(☎ 647328)* is an established place with 12 cottage-style rooms with private bathroom for Rs 250 (Rs 350 over Christmas) and two with shared bathroom for Rs 150. There's a shady bar and restaurant.

Fatima Restaurant *(☎ 647377)* has a few rooms with private bathroom for Rs 200 and Rs 250.

GOA

PALOLEM

Palolem is arguably Goa's most beautiful and idyllic beach – the argument being whether or not the addition of wall-to-wall beach shacks beneath those leaning palms has spoilt it. In any case, the sweeping crescent of white sand fringed by a shady rim of

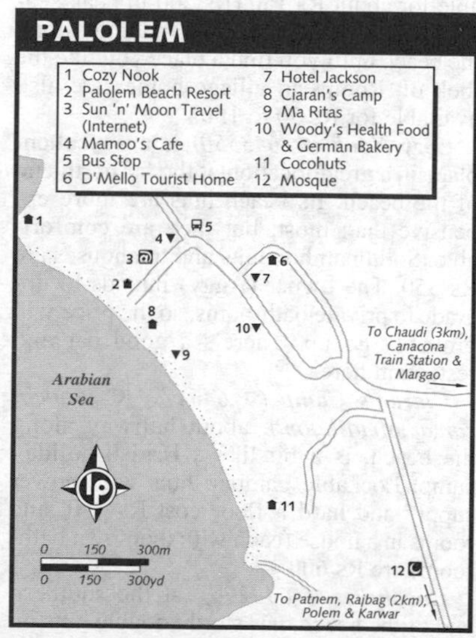

coconut palms is a postcard picture. The beach is hemmed in at either end by rocky crags and there's a small island (Green Island) off the northern tip that you can walk across to at low tide.

Palolem is remote in the sense that it's the most southerly of Goa's developed beaches, but in the last few years it has really been discovered. During the high season the beach is crowded with a mix of day-trippers coming down from Colva and Cavelossim, travellers drifting down from the northern beaches to chill out, and baleful long-termers wondering what the hell happened to their paradise.

Still, the development is very earthy and Palolem remains to this day one of Goa's most laid-back beaches. Most accommodation is in simple (though increasingly sophisticated) beach huts or in villagers' homes, with a handful of more solid guesthouses scattered around.

Palolem village is nestled in the palms back from the beach. All the facilities you need are here, including Internet access, some pretty good restaurants, motorcycle hire and foreign exchange (through several travel agencies).

GOA

Places to Stay & Eat

Along the edge of the beach are numerous groups of palm thatch or bamboo huts available for about Rs 150 (Rs 200 in peak season). It's just a matter of wandering along the beach until you find a place you like the look of. Rooms in village homes are also available for Rs 50 to 150.

Cozy Nook *(☎ 643550)* is an excellent place in a great location at the far north end of the beach. Its beach huts are more expensive than most, but they are comfortable. Solid bamboo huts and treehouses are Rs 350. The owner (Aggy) intends to upgrade to private bathrooms, so the price will probably go up. There's a good bar and restaurant here.

Ciaran's Camp *(☎ 643477, e johnciaran@hotmail.com)*, about halfway along the beach, is a bit like a British holiday camp. Lockable bamboo huts with power supply and hard a floor cost Rs 350, and rooms in a house (each with their own bathroom) are Rs 600.

Cocohuts *(☎ 643296)*, at the southern end of the beach, has sturdy double huts on stilts, but they're a bit overpriced at Rs 400 (Rs 450 over Christmas).

Palolem Beach Resort *(☎ 643054)* is more upmarket but still low-key. Cottages with shared bathroom are Rs 350, tents with solid floor and electricity are Rs 300 and rooms with private bathroom (at the back of the complex) are Rs 400.

There are several guesthouses in the village. ***D'Mello Tourist Home*** *(☎ 643057)* has doubles from Rs 200 to 350.

The diverse range of travellers coming to Palolem has spawned a diverse range of restaurants. You can now get reasonable Italian, Mexican, Chinese, continental as well as Goan and, of course, seafood.

Ma Rita's *(☎ 643674)* is a great little beachside restaurant serving delicious seafood. It's a good spot to watch Palolem's legendary sunset. ***Hotel Jackson***, on the road behind the beach, has a good reputation for seafood and is usually full as a result.

Woody's Health Food & German Bakery is good for breakfast. There's a wide range of fresh breads, cakes and cheeses here and there's a water filter from which you can fill your bottle for free if you eat here. ***Mamoo's Cafe***, near the bus stand, does reasonable Italian including highly-rated lasagne.

Getting There & Away

There are hourly buses to Margao (Rs 15, one hour) from the bus stand on the main road down to the beach. There are also regular buses to Chaudi, the nearest town, and you can get off on the way to Chaudi to reach Canacona station on the Konkan Railway. Two expresses between Marago and Mangalore stop at Canacona.

Autorickshaws and motorcycle taxis hang around at the entrance to the beach, and motorcycles can be hired from here.

PONDA & AROUND

The inland town of Ponda is of little interest to travellers, but there are a number of unique Hindu temples in the surrounding area.

The five main temples were rebuilt from originals destroyed by the Portuguese and their lamp towers are a distinctive Goan feature. The Shiva temple of **Shri Manguesh** is at Priol-Ponda Taluka, 22km from Panaji (5km from Ponda). This tiny 18th-century hilltop temple, with its white tower, is a local landmark. Less than 2km further down the road is **Shri Mahalsa**, a Vishnu temple.

Near Shri Manguesh are two temples; **Shri Ramnath** and the **Shri Shantadurga Temple**. Dedicated to Shantadurga, the goddess of peace, this temple sports an unusual, almost pagoda-like, structure with a roof made from long slabs of stone.

The oldest mosque remaining in Goa is the **Safa Shahouri Masjid**, located on the outskirts of Ponda. It was built by Ali Adilshah in 1560.

There are regular buses from Panaji and Margao to Ponda, but to get to the temples it's best to have your own transport. They are included in the GTDC's North Goa tour (see Organised Tours under Panaji in the North Goa section).

BONDLA WILDLIFE SANCTUARY

Up in the lush foothills of the Western Ghats, Bondla is the smallest of the Goan wildlife sanctuaries (8 sq km), but the easiest to reach. It's 52km from Panaji and 38km from Margao.

There's a botanical garden, fenced deer park and a zoo. Fauna in the wild here includes gaur and sambar, but unless you're prepared to spend a few days and put in the time on an observation platform, you're unlikely to see much in the wild. Entry to the park is Rs 5, plus Rs 25 for a camera.

There's chalet ***accommodation*** (☎ *611 144)* at Rs 150 per double or Rs 30 for a dorm bed. Bookings can also be made in advance at the office of the Department of Forestry in Panaji (☎ 229701).

To get to Bondla, take any bus heading east out of Goa along the NH4A, and ask to be let out at Usgao Tisk. From there catch a taxi or motorcycle taxi to the park, or you can take the Forest Department bus (Rs 5), which leaves daily at 11 am and 7.30 pm.

DUDHSAGAR FALLS

On the eastern border with Karnataka are Goa's most impressive waterfalls; however, reaching them is no longer cheap and easy as the train from Margao doesn't stop at Dudhsagar. You have to get off at Colem station and pay an extortionate Rs 1800 for a jeep (up to five people) to take you up to the falls. Getting to the falls would be difficult by motorcycle as there are several rivers to ford.

BHAGWAN MAHAVIR & COTIGAO WILDLIFE SANCTUARIES

These wildlife sanctuaries are larger than Bondla, but you will need your own transport to get to them. Bhagwan Mahavir incorporates the Molem National Park and the village of Molem is the best base. There's a tree-top watchtower in Cotigao, but the animals (including gaur, sambar, leopards, spotted deer and snakes) manage to remain well hidden, so you won't see much. Cotigao is only about 9km from Palolem so it makes a good day trip from there.

Accommodation is available at Molem in the GTDC ***Forest Resort*** *(☎ 612238)*. Rooms cost Rs 180/220 a single/double, and meals are available if booked in advance. At Cotigao sanctuary there are three ***tents*** (Rs 50 per person) at the park entrance. Contact the Department of Forestry in Panaji (☎ 229701) for information on both these parks.

Karnataka

Karnataka offers a terrific balance of natural attractions and magnificent historic architecture. It appeals equally to temple lovers, wildlife enthusiasts, trekkers and beach bums, yet Karnataka receives few travellers compared to Goa, Kerala and Tamil Nadu.

The state consists of a narrow coastal strip backed by the monsoon-drenched Western Ghats and a drier, cooler interior plateau that turns semi-arid in the far north. It's a major producer of coffee, spices and betel nut, and supplies 60% of the country's silk. The capital, boomtown Bangalore, is a centre of India's software and technology industries and is one of Asia's fastest growing cities.

Karnataka at a Glance

Population: 52.8 million

Area: 191,791 sq km

Capital: Bangalore

Main Languages: Kannada, Urdu, Telugu

When to Go: Sep to Feb

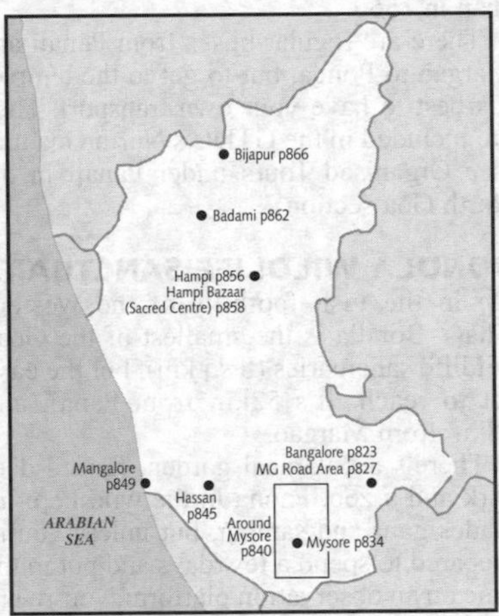

- Wander through the palaces and bazaars of Mysore
- Walk through plantations and hills in the Kodagu region
- Marvel at the exquisitely sculpted temples at Belur and Halebid
- Visit a 17m-high statue of a Jain saint in the pilgrimage village of Sravanabelgola
- Watch the waves roll in on a beach at Gokarna
- Cycle around the awesome ruins of the Vijayanagar capital at Hampi
- Discover the ancient caves and temples of Badami, set in a stunning red cliff

History

A multitude of religions, cultures and kingdoms have unrolled across Karnataka, including Vijayanagar, the last great Hindu empire. In the 3rd century BC Chandragupta Maurya, India's first great emperor, retreated to Sravanabelagola after embracing Jainism. In the 6th century, the Chalukyas built some of the earliest Hindu temples near Badami.

Other Indian dynasties, such as the Cholas and Gangas, played their part in Karnataka's history, but it was the Hoysalas (11th–14th century), who left the most vivid mark. The beautiful Hoysala temples at Somnathpur, Halebid and Belur are architectural gems, with intricately detailed sculptures rivalling anything found in India.

In 1327 the Muslim army of Mohammed Tughlaq sacked the Hoysala capital at Halebid, but his impact was brief and in 1346 the Hindu empire of Vijayanagar annexed it. This dynasty, with its capital at Hampi, peaked in the early 1550s, but in 1565 it fell to the united forces of the Deccan sultanates and Bijapur became the most important city of the region.

With the demise of Vijayanagar, the Hindu Wodeyars (the former rulers of Mysore state) grew in importance. They quickly established their rule over a large part of southern India, with their capital at Srirangapatnam. Their power remained largely unchallenged until 1761 when Hyder Ali (one of their generals) deposed them.

The French helped Hyder Ali and his famous son, Tipu Sultan, to consolidate their rule in return for support in fighting the British. However, in 1799 the British defeated Tipu Sultan, annexed part of his kingdom, and put the Wodeyars back on Mysore's throne.

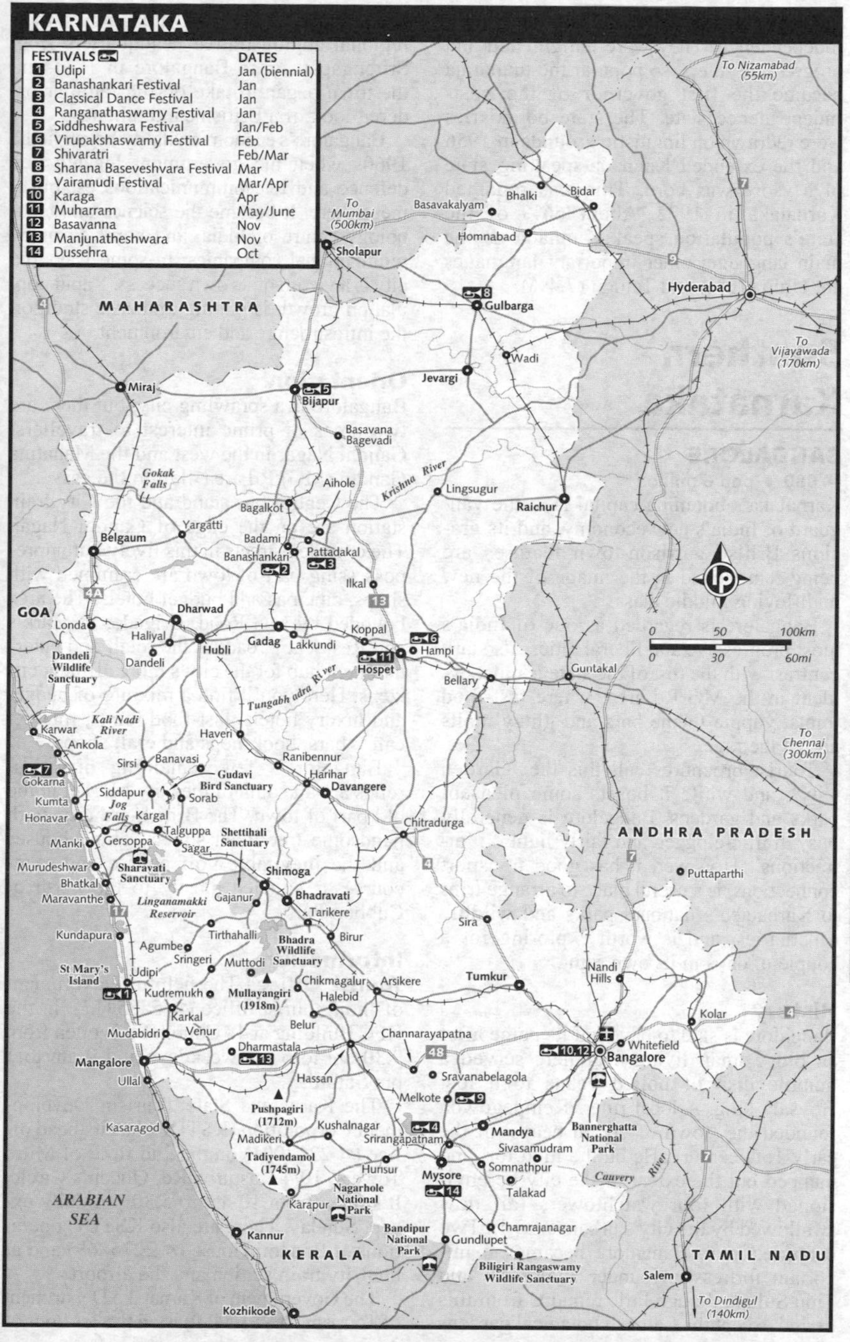
KARNATAKA
FESTIVALS
DATES
1 Udipi Jan (biennial)
2 Banashankari Festival Jan
3 Classical Dance Festival Jan
4 Ranganathaswamy Festival Jan
5 Siddheshwara Festival Jan/Feb
6 Virupakshaswamy Festival Feb
7 Shivaratri Feb/Mar
8 Sharana Baseveshvara Festival Mar
9 Vairamudi Festival Mar/Apr
10 Karaga Apr
11 Muharram May/June
12 Basavanna Nov
13 Manjunatheshwara Nov
14 Dussehra Oct
MAHARASHTRA
ANDHRA PRADESH
KERALA
TAMIL NADU
GOA
ARABIAN SEA
To Nizamabad (55km)
To Mumbai (500km)
To Vijayawada (170km)
To Chennai (300km)
To Dindigul (140km)
Hyderabad
Bidar
Bhalki
Basavakalyam
Homnabad
Sholapur
Gulbarga
Wadi
Jevargi
Miraj
Bijapur
Basavana Bagevadi
Krishna River
Aihole
Lingsugur
Raichur
Gokak Falls
Bagalkot
Yargatti
Belgaum
Badami
Pattadakal
Banashankari
Ilkal
Dharwad
Londa
Haliyal
Hubli
Gadag
Lakkundi
Koppal
Hampi
Hospet
Dandeli
Dandeli Wildlife Sanctuary
Bellary
Guntakal
Tungabhadra River
Kali Nadi River
Karwar
Ankola
Haveri
Ranibennur
Sirsi
Banavasi
Gudavi Bird Sanctuary
Harihar
Davangere
Gokarna
Siddapur
Sorab
Kumta
Jog Falls
Kargal
Honavar
Chitradurga
Manki
Gersoppa
Talguppa
Sagar
Shettihali Sanctuary
Murudeshwar
Sharavati Sanctuary
Bhatkal
Shimoga
Puttaparthi
Maravanthe
Gajanur
Bhadravati
Linganamakki Reservoir
Tarikere
Sira
Kundapura
Tirthahalli
Birur
Bhadra Wildlife Sanctuary
Agumbe
Sringeri
Muttodi
St Mary's Island
Udipi
Nandi Hills
Mullayangiri (1918m)
Chikmagalur
Arsikere
Tumkur
Kudremukh
Halebid
Karkal
Belur
Kolar
Mudabidri
Venur
Channarayapatna
Dharmastala
Whitefield
Bangalore
Mangalore
Hassan
Sravanabelagola
Ullal
Melkote
Pushpagiri (1712m)
Kasaragod
Kushalnagar
Mandya
Bannerghatta National Park
Madikeri
Srirangapatnam
Sivasamudram
Tadiyendamol (1745m)
Hunsur
Mysore
Somnathpur
Cauvery River
Talakad
Nagarhole National Park
Karapur
Chamrajanagar
Kannur
Bandipur National Park
Gundlupet
Biligiri Rangaswamy Wildlife Sanctuary
Salem
Kozhikode
0 50 100km
0 30 60mi

KARNATAKA

The Wodeyars ruled Mysore state until Independence. They were enlightened and progressive rulers, so popular the maharaja became the first governor of the post-Independence state. The state boundaries were redrawn on linguistic grounds in 1956 and the extended Kannada-speaking state of Mysore was born. This was renamed Karnataka in 1972. About 66% of the state's population speak Kannada as the main language; other important languages are Urdu (10%) and Telugu (7.4%).

Southern Karnataka

BANGALORE

☎ 080 • pop 6 million

Karnataka's booming capital is in the vanguard of India's new economy, and its gracious British garrison-town features are being remodelled in the image of the new mall-loving middle class.

Bangalore is regarded as one of India's most progressive and liberal cities. Its stark contrast with the rest of the state is most evident in the MG Rd area, where fast-food joints, yuppie theme bars and glitzy malls are all the rage.

Tourist brochures call this the 'Garden City', and while it boasts some pleasant parks and gardens, Bangalore is generally busy, traffic-clogged and fairly light on 'attractions'. However, it has good transport connections, is a useful place to arrange trips to Karnataka's national parks and wildlife sanctuaries, and is worth exploring for a couple of days in its own right.

History

Bangalore is said to have got its name after an old woman living near here served a humble dish of boiled beans to a lost Hoysala king. A local ruler, Kempegowda founded the 'town of boiled beans' in the early 16th century. He built a mud fort and mapped out the extent of the city he envisioned with four watchtowers (all now swallowed by the city's urban sprawl). Two centuries later, Bangalore became an important fortress city under Hyder Ali and Tipu Sultan, though little remains from this period except the Lalbagh botanical gardens and a small palace. The British moved their regional administrative headquarters from Srirangapatnam to Bangalore in 1831 and the town began to take on the familiar ordered look of a British cantonment.

Bangalore's economic vitality began in the 1960s when the government located key defence and telecommunications establishments here. It became the science and technology centre of India, and home to many multinational companies. In some ways the city is a victim of its own success. Rapid population growth is putting immense strain on the infrastructure and environment.

Orientation

Bangalore is a sprawling city, but there are two areas of prime interest to travellers: Gandhi Nagar in the west and the Mahatma Gandhi (MG) Rd area 4km to the east.

The Central bus stand and the City train station are on the edge of Gandhi Nagar. The crowded streets in this lively but unprepossessing part of town are crammed with shops, cinemas and budget hotels. The area bounded by MG Road, Brigade, St Mark's and Residency roads is the retail and entertainment hub for the city's more affluent citizens. Here you'll find a mixture of budget and luxury hotels, fast-food joints, Internet cafes, bars, bookshops and craft shops.

Bangalore's few remaining historical relics are all south of the City Market in the old part of town. The British-era city, with handsome tree-lined streets, grand houses and the inevitable golf course and racecourse, is situated mostly to the north of Cubbon Park.

Information

Tourist Offices The helpful Government of India tourist office (☎ 5585417), in the KFC Building at 48 Church St, is open from 9.30 am to 6 pm weekdays and 9 am to 1 pm Saturday.

The Karnataka State Tourism Development Corporation (KSTDC) has its head office (☎ 2212901) on the 2nd floor of Mitra Towers, 10/4 Kasturba Rd, Queen's Circle. It's open from 10 am to 5.30 pm daily except Sunday. There are also KSTDC operations at Badami House (☎ 2275869) and at the City train station and the airport.

The Government of Karnataka Department of Tourism (☎ 221 5489) is on the 1st floor of

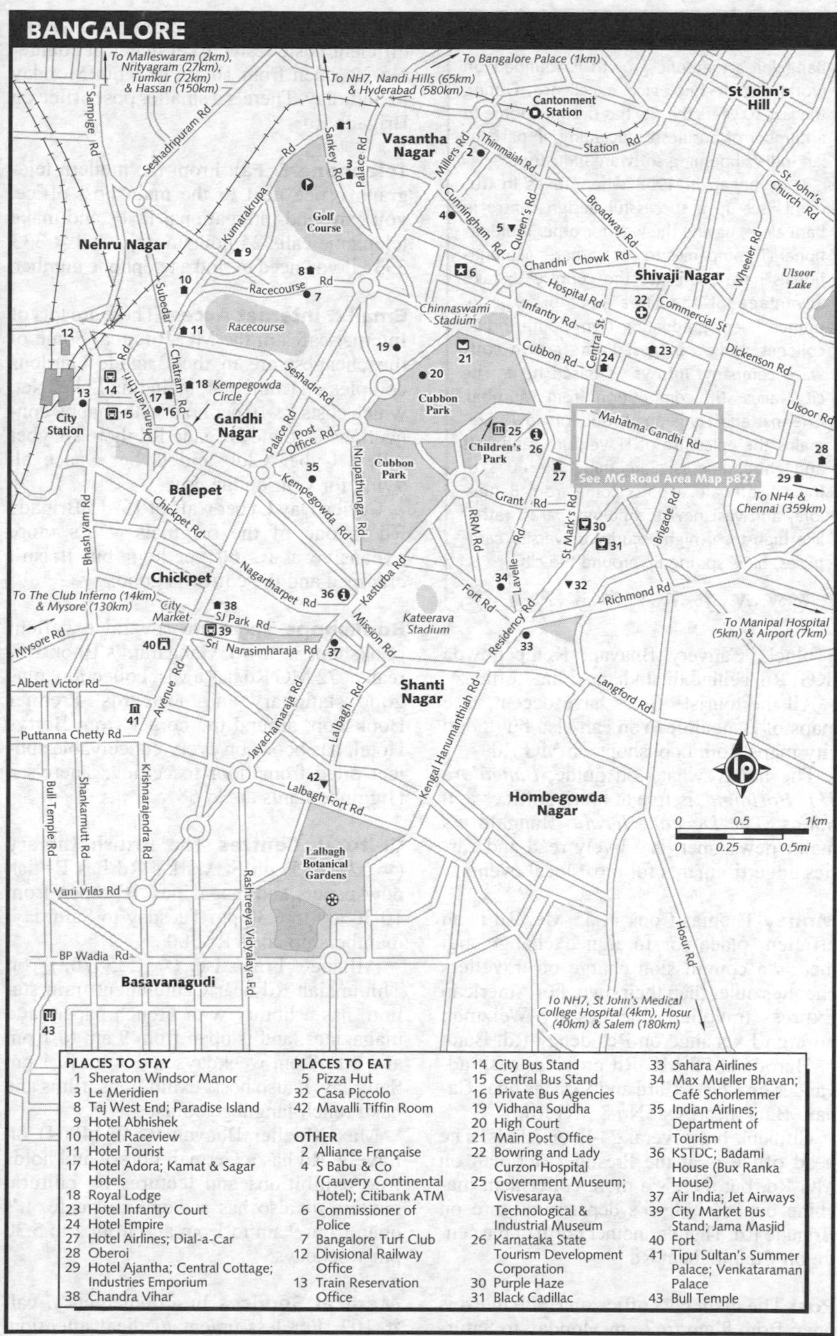

BANGALORE
To Malleswaram (2km), Nrityagram (27km), Tumkur (72km) & Hassan (150km)
To Bangalore Palace (1km)
To NH7, Nandi Hills (65km) & Hyderabad (580km)
Cantonment Station
St John's Hill
Vasantha Nagar
Sampige Rd
Seshadripuram Rd
Sankey Rd
Palace Rd
Millers Rd
Thimmaiah Rd
Station Rd
St John's Church Rd
Golf Course
Cunningham Rd
Queen's Rd
Broadway Rd
Wheeler Rd
Nehru Nagar
Kumarakrupa Rd
Chandni Chowk Rd
Shivaji Nagar
Ulsoor Lake
Subedar
Racecourse Rd
Hospital Rd
Infantry Rd
Chinnaswami Stadium
Commercial St
Racecourse
Chatram Rd
Dhanvanthri Rd
Seshadri Rd
Cubbon Rd
Central St
Dickenson Rd
Kempegowda Circle
Cubbon Park
Ulsoor Rd
City Station
Gandhi Nagar
Post Office Rd
Palace Rd
Children's Park
Mahatma Gandhi Rd
Nrupathunga Rd
Kempegowda Rd
See MG Road Area Map p827
Balepet
Bhashyam Rd
Chickpet Rd
Grant Rd
To NH4 & Chennai (359km)
RRM Rd
Lavelle Rd
St Mark's Rd
Brigade Rd
Nagarthpet Rd
Kasturba Rd
Chickpet
To The Club Inferno (14km) & Mysore (130km)
City Market
SJ Park Rd
Fort Rd
Richmond Rd
Kateerava Stadium
Mission Rd
Residency Rd
To Manipal Hospital (5km) & Airport (7km)
Mysore Rd
Sri Narasimharaja Rd
Albert Victor Rd
Avenue Rd
Shanti Nagar
Lalbagh Rd
Jayachamaraja Rd
Kengal Hanumanthiah Rd
Langford Rd
Puttanna Chetty Rd
Lalbagh Fort Rd
Hombegowda Nagar
Shankarmutt Rd
Bull Temple Rd
Krishnarajendra Rd
0 0.5 1km
0 0.25 0.5mi
Lalbagh Botanical Gardens
Rashtreeya Vidyalaya Rd
Vani Vilas Rd
BP Wadia Rd
Hosur Rd
Basavanagudi
To NH7, St John's Medical College Hospital (4km), Hosur (40km) & Salem (180km)
PLACES TO STAY
1 Sheraton Windsor Manor
3 Le Meridien
8 Taj West End; Paradise Island
9 Hotel Abhishek
10 Hotel Raceview
11 Hotel Tourist
17 Hotel Adora; Kamat & Sagar Hotels
18 Royal Lodge
23 Hotel Infantry Court
24 Hotel Empire
27 Hotel Airlines; Dial-a-Car
28 Oberoi
29 Hotel Ajantha; Central Cottage; Industries Emporium
38 Chandra Vihar
PLACES TO EAT
5 Pizza Hut
32 Casa Piccolo
42 Mavalli Tiffin Room
OTHER
2 Alliance Française
4 S Babu & Co (Cauvery Continental Hotel); Citibank ATM
6 Commissioner of Police
7 Bangalore Turf Club
12 Divisional Railway Office
13 Train Reservation Office
14 City Bus Stand
15 Central Bus Stand
16 Private Bus Agencies
19 Vidhana Soudha
20 High Court
21 Main Post Office
22 Bowring and Lady Curzon Hospital
25 Government Museum; Visvesaraya Technological & Industrial Museum
26 Karnataka State Tourism Development Corporation
30 Purple Haze
31 Black Cadillac
33 Sahara Airlines
34 Max Mueller Bhavan; Café Schorlemmer
35 Indian Airlines; Department of Tourism
36 KSTDC; Badami House (Bux Ranka House)
37 Air India; Jet Airways
39 City Market Bus Stand; Jama Masjid
40 Fort
41 Tipu Sultan's Summer Palace; Venkataraman Palace
43 Bull Temple

India's Silicon Valley

Bangalore's meteoric growth is founded on world-class technological excellence. During the last 30 years the city has become home to a number of businesses including, in particular, India's booming software industry.

It all began in 1958 when Texas Instruments set up a successful design centre in Bangalore, paving the way for other multinational IT companies to set up here. Multinationals have piled into the country to take advantage of the large pool of expertly trained talent graduating from South India's colleges. India's biggest home-grown software company, Infosys, is based here. The city faces stiff competition from Mumbai, Chennai and Hyderabad, but for now it remains the epicentre of IT venture capitalists and entrepreneurs. Something like 60% of India's software exports come from Bangalore, and vast new technology parks, rather like high-tech, high-security university campuses, have sprung up around the city.

F block, Cauvery Bhavan, Kempegowda (KG) Rd, behind the Indian Airlines office.

All the tourist offices have decent, free maps of Bangalore. You can also buy good city maps from bookshops on MG Rd.

The handy what's-on guide, *Bangalore This Fortnight*, is free at tourist offices and hotels. The *Deccan Herald*, Bangalore's major newspaper, is a lively read and carries advertisements for most local events.

Money Thomas Cook at 55 MG Rd is an efficient place for foreign exchange, but there's a commission charge on travellers cheques other than their own. For American Express travellers cheques try Weizman Foreign Exchange on Residency Rd. Bank of Baroda at 72 MG Rd provides cash advances on MasterCard and Visa, as does Canara Bank nearby at No 8 MG Rd.

Citibank has several 24-hour ATMs. The head office is at the Prestige Meridian on MG Rd, but there's a more convenient machine outside Nilgiri's deparment store on Brigade Rd. There's another north of the centre on Cunningham Rd.

Post The main post office on Cubbon Rd is open from 8 am to 7 pm Monday to Saturday and 10.30 am to 1.30 pm Sunday. The efficient poste restante service is at counter No 22, open from 10 am to 6 pm Monday to Saturday. There's a smaller post office on Brigade Rd.

Telephone & Fax From the modern telegraph office next to the main post office, you can send international faxes and make telephone calls 24 hours a day. Call ☎ 333 3333 if you need to find a telephone number.

Email & Internet Access There are lots of Internet cafes in the MG Rd area. Some of the cheapest are in the Brigade Gardens complex on Church St, including Lake2Net, which costs Rs 10 per hour with snappy connections. Around Brigade Rd there's Cyber Alley, Cyber Club and Cyber Space all vying for your online time.

Coffee Day Cyber Cafe at 13–15 Brigade Rd is one of the originals – it's more expensive at Rs 60 per hour but it isn't cramped and the coffee is good.

Bookshops There are several excellent bookshops in town. Gangaram's Book Bureau at 72 MG Rd has a vast collection, plus good stationary and postcards. Premier Bookshop, around the corner from Berrys Hotel, has books on every conceivable subject piled from floor to ceiling. There's a Higginbothams at No 68.

Cultural Centres The British Library (☎ 2213485) on St Mark's Rd has British newspapers and magazines. It's open from 10.30 am to 6.30 pm Tuesday to Saturday; membership costs Rs 300.

Alliance Française (☎ 2258762), on Thimmaiah Rd near Cantonment train station, has a library with French papers and magazines, and is open from 9 am to 1 pm and 3 to 7 pm weekdays and 9 am to 1 pm Saturday. It also hosts exhibitions, films and has French-language courses.

Max Mueller Bhavan (☎ 2214964) on Lavelle Rd has a German library and holds free exhibitions and lectures on cultural matters. It also has a wonderful cafe. It's open from 9 am to 1 pm and from 2 to 5.30 pm weekdays.

Medical Services In an emergency, call ☎ 102. For less-urgent medical attention, there's the government-run Bowring and Lady Curzon Hospital (☎ 5591325), on Hospital Rd; St John's Medical College Hospital (☎ 5530725), Sarjapur Rd, Koramangala (off Hosur Rd); and the private Manipal Hospital (☎ 5287751), Airport Rd.

National Parks To arrange Forest Department accommodation in Bandipur National Park, contact the Chief Wildlife Warden (☎ 3341993), Aranya Bhavan, 18th Cross, Malleswaram, Bangalore. This can also be done in Mysore (see that section). It's also possible to make bookings in Bangalore for Nagarhole National Park, but it's better to do this at Hunsur. See the Nagarhole National Park section later in this chapter for details on accommodation in the park.

Jungle Lodges & Resorts Ltd (☎ 5597025, fax 5586163, ⓔ infodesk@karnatakatourism.com), in the Shrungar Shopping Centre between MG Rd and Church St, arranges excellent (but expensive) private at Nagarhole National Park and several other reserves around the state.

Vidhana Soudha

At the north-western end of Cubbon Park, this massive, granite, neo-Dravidian style building is one of Bangalore's most imposing. Built in 1954 by convicts, it houses the secretariat and the state legislature. It's floodlit on weekend evenings but isn't open to the public.

Lalbagh Botanical Gardens

This beautiful 96-hectare park south of city centre was laid out in the 18th century by Hyder Ali and his son Tipu Sultan. It was named for its profusion of red roses; *lalbagh* means 'red garden'. It contains many labelled, centuries-old trees, one of India's largest collections of rare tropical and subtropical plants, a glasshouse modelled on London's Crystal Palace, one of Kempegowda's watchtowers and a surreal lawn clock surrounded by Snow White and the seven dwarfs. It's great for people watching, especially the young and bashful courting couples.

There are major flower displays here in the week preceding Republic Day (26 January) and the week before Independence Day (15 August). The gardens are open from sunrise to sunset daily (Rs 2).

Cubbon Park & Museums

This scruffy 120-hectare park is one of the main 'lungs' of the city. On its fringes are the superbly restored neoclassical High Court, the grand Public Library, two municipal museums and a dull aquarium.

The **Government Museum**, one of the oldest in India, was established in 1886 and houses a poorly presented collection of stone carvings, pottery, weapons, paintings, and some good pieces from Halebid. It's open from 10 am to 5 pm daily except Monday (Rs 4).

The **Visvesvaraya Technological & Industrial Museum** is usually full of school children pressing buttons on exhibits that reflect India's technological progress. It's open from 10 am to 6 pm daily (Rs 10).

City Market

This bustling market south-west of Cubbon Park is all you need to remind you that you're still in India if you've spent most of your time on MG Rd. It contains a tarpaulin-covered fruit and vegetable bazaar, a spice market, plenty of garland sellers, cloth shops and an entire colourful street lined with hole-in-the-wall tailor shops. Also in this bustling area is the imposing, white **Jama Masjid**.

Fort & Tipu Sultan's Palace

Kempegowda built a mud-brick defence structure on this site in 1537, and in the 18th century Hyder Ali and Tipu Sultan solidly rebuilt it in stone. It's a sturdy little fort, though much of it was destroyed during the wars with the British. It's worth a quick visit if you're exploring the City Market.

Tipu Sultan's modest palace is notable for its elegant teak pillars. It was begun by Hyder Ali, and completed by Tipu in 1791. The palace is a five-minute walk south-west of the City Market. Entry is Rs 5 and Rs 25 for a video camera. Next to the palace is the small but ornate 250-year-old Venkataraman Temple.

Bull Temple

Situated on Bugle Hill at the southern end of Bull Temple Rd, this is one of Bangalore's oldest temples. Built by Kempegowda in the Dravidian style in the 16th century, it contains a huge granite monolith of Nandi. Non-Hindus are allowed to enter the temple and the priests are friendly, though prone to hit you for a donation. The basic *puja* (literally 'respect'; offering or prayers) costs Rs 10. It's especially interesting on weekends, when there are often musicians, wedding processions and even pujas to bless new motor cars. Bus No 31, 31E, 35 or 49 from the City bus stand will get you to Bull Temple.

Bangalore Palace

You wouldn't expect to find a replica of Windsor Castle in the middle of India, but here it is, complete with granite turrets, towers and battlements. The palace was built in 1880 and later bought and extended by the Wodeyar rajas of Mysore. The grounds are massive, and include a formal garden. The Wodeyar family and the Karnataka government have been engaged in a long struggle over who owns this valuable piece of real estate, so the palace is not officially open. However the gatekeeper lets people have a look around the gardens, as long as the Wodeyars aren't in residence. The palace is on Palace Rd (of course) just north of the railway line.

Swimming

There's a public swimming pool (membership Rs 100), with regulated separate-sex swimming hours, at Ulsoor Lake. For something more fancy, nonguests can use the pools at Le Meridien (Rs 350) or Taj West End (Rs 500).

Organised Tours

The KSTDC offers a huge range of tours, which can be booked at any of its offices. They all start at Badami House (aka Bux Ranka House). The city sightseeing tour runs twice daily at 7.30 am and 2 pm (Rs 80). It quickly covers Bangalore's main attractions with an obligatory stop at a government-owned silk and handicraft emporium – not bad value if you really want to see everything, but it's a bit dull. There's also a tour to Srirangapatnam, Mysore and Brindavan gardens departing daily at 7.15 am and returning at 11 pm (Rs 230 for non air-con bus, Rs 300 for air-con bus, including entrance fees). There is also a tour of Belur, Halebid and Sravanabelagola and a weekend tour to Hampi, which involve a lot of travelling and little time for anything but a quick photo opportunity.

Special Events

Basavanna, a groundnut fair, is held in November; **Karaga**, a festival honouring the goddess Draupadi, is held in April.

Places to Stay – Budget

In Karnataka, rooms costing less than Rs 200 are hit with a 5% tax, between Rs 200 to 399 it's 10%, Rs 400 to 599, 12.5%, and more than Rs 600, 15%.

Bus Stand Area A dozen or more budget hotels line Subedar Chatram Rd (SC Rd) in the heart of Gandhi Nagar, just east of the bus stands.

Royal Lodge *(☎ 2266575, 251 SC Rd)* is one of the cheapest, largest and oldest places. It has clean singles/doubles with shared bathroom for Rs 110/150 and doubles with private bathroom and hot water in the morning for Rs 275.

Hotel Adora *(☎ 2872280, 47 SC Rd)*, almost opposite, has decent rooms with private bathroom for Rs 168/275.

Hotel Tourist *(☎ 226 2381, 5 Racecourse Rd)* is a little further afield. It's reasonable value at Rs 80/140 for rooms with private bathroom and hot water in the morning.

MG Rd Area Set in a quiet compound, ***Hotel Ajantha*** *(☎ 5584321, MG Rd)* is a good value budget hotel with friendly staff, a restaurant and a small shop. The rooms are functional but large and clean, and have TV. They cost Rs 190/325, while air-con doubles cost Rs 600.

Airlines Hotel *(☎ 2273783, 4 Madras Bank Rd)* is set back from the road in its own leafy grounds and has a wide range of facilities including a garden restaurant, bakery and an Internet cafe (Rs 40 per hour). Singles/doubles with private bathroom and hot water in the morning cost from Rs 125/250, or Rs 330/450 for deluxe (with TV). Unfortunately it's so popular that you will need to make a reservation 10 to 15 days in advance.

Brindavan Hotel *(☎ 5584000, 108 MG Rd)* has decent rooms with private bathroom from Rs 200/300 and air-con doubles for Rs 400. The hotel is fairly quiet since it's set back from the road, but it's also often full – book 10 days ahead.

Hotel Empire *(☎ 5592821, ⓔ hotelempire@usanet, 78 Central St)* is a new hotel on a busy street, with good-value rooms for Rs 400/550, and air-con doubles for Rs 750. There's a flashy restaurant on the ground floor, and checkout is 24 hours.

Hotel Imperial *(☎ 5585473, 93–94 Residency Rd)* is an emergency option. Singles/doubles with private bathroom cost Rs 180/320. It's in a noisy area and the staff are more concerned with running the restaurant.

City Market Area This is where to stay if you enjoy being in the thick of the bustling bazaar. It's a 25-minute walk south from the City train station.

Chandra Vihar *(☎ 2224146, Avenue Rd)* charges Rs 168/303 for clean, decent-sized rooms with private bathroom and hot water in the morning, or Rs 145 for a smaller single. There are great views of the market from some rooms.

Places to Stay – Mid-Range

Most of the hotels in this price range are in the MG Rd area, but there are a few near the racecourse, a relatively dull area that's a short autorickshaw ride from the City train station and Central bus stand.

MG Rd Area The large, comfortable ***Ballal Residency*** *(☎ 559 7277, fax 559 7276, ⓔ ballalry@bgl.vsnl.net.in)* is set back from Residency Rd, down an alley next to the Baskin & Robbins ice-cream parlour. Rooms are large and clean with all mod cons, including air-con, for Rs 1400/1750. There's a garden cafe, which serves pure vegetarian food.

Highgates Hotel *(☎ 5597172, fax 559 7799, 33 Church St)* is a tasteful, modern, three-star hotel at the top of this price range. Comfortable air-con rooms with TV, fridge and private bathroom cost Rs 1595/1995. It has a restaurant, a lobby coffee shop and a patio. Reservations are recommended.

Hotel Infantry Court *(☎ 5591800, fax 5592276, ⓔ hotelic@vsnl.com, 66 Infantry Rd)* is part of the Comfort Inn chain and is a very comfortable, well-run hotel. Modern air-con rooms are Rs 1950/2250 including breakfast.

Nilgiri's Nest *(☎ 5588401, fax 5585348, ⓔ nilgirisnest@vsnl.net, 171 Brigade Rd)* is in the thick of things on the 3rd floor above the supermarket of the same name. It has clean, spacious, airy rooms with TV and

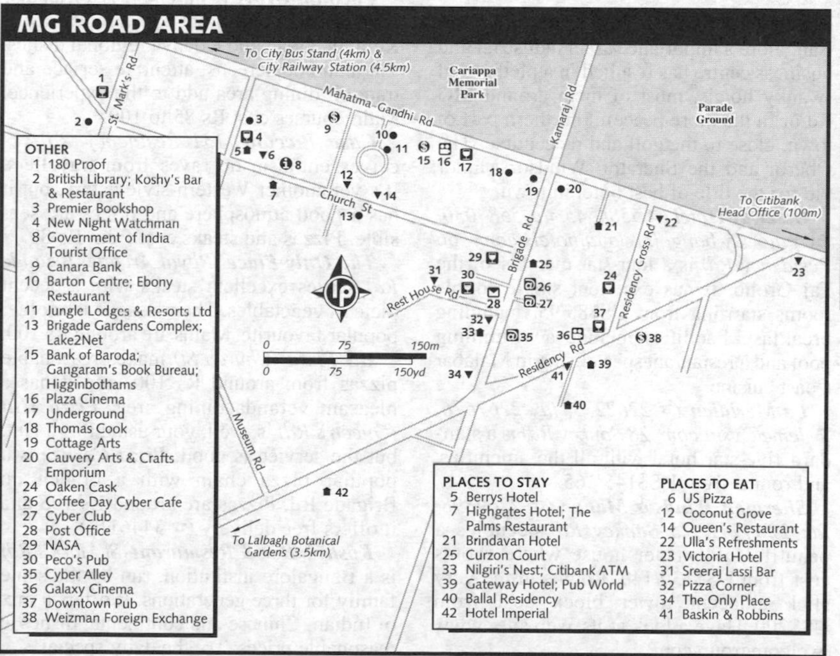

private bathroom for Rs 900/1200, or Rs 1100/1450 with air-con, but it's nothing special for these prices. Checkout is 24 hours.

Berrys Hotel *(☎ 5587211, 46/1 Church St)* is a large, standard, place with better rooms than the shabby reception suggests. It's rarely full, but well located. Decent rooms with TV and hot water cost Rs 500/600, or Rs 600/675 for the suite.

Curzon Court *(☎ 5582997, fax 558 2278, 10 Brigade Rd)* has a central location but it's a bit dark and dingy inside. The rooms are comfortable though; air-con rooms with TV and hot shower cost from Rs 800/1000, to 850/1200 for the suite.

Racecourse Area At ***Hotel Raceview*** *(☎ 2203401, 25 Racecourse Rd)* doubles (no singles) cost Rs 500. Keen punters may be interested to know that some of the more expensive rooms here have a good view of the racetrack.

Hotel Abhishek *(☎ 2262713, fax 226 8953, ⓔ hotelabhishek@vsnl.net, 19/2 Kumarakrupa Rd)* has singles/doubles with TV and private bathroom for Rs 810/900, or Rs 900/990 with air-con.

KARNATAKA

Places to Stay – Top End

Bangalore's importance as an industrial and business centre has resulted in a plethora of swanky hotels, most of them around MG Rd or in the more peaceful northern part of town, close to the golf and racecourse. The Oberoi and the Sheraton Windsor Manor vie for the title of best hotel in town.

Gateway Hotel *(☎ 5584545, fax 5584030, ⓔ gateway.bangalore@tajhotels.com, 66 Residency Rd)* is a four-star member of the Taj Group. It has excellent single/double rooms starrting from US$85/95, including breakfast. Facilities include a swimming pool and a restaurant specialising in Malabar Coast cuisine.

Le Meridien *(☎ 2262233, fax 2267676, ⓔ leme@vsnl.com, 28 Sankey Rd)* is a standard five-star hotel with all the amenities, and rooms from US$145/165.

Sheraton Windsor Manor *(☎ 2269898, fax 2264941, 25 Sankey Rd)* occupies a beautiful old manor house where rooms cost from US$130/140. Rooms in the very slick adjacent tower block cost from US$200. Have a look at its Web site: www.welcomgroup.com.

Oberoi *(☎ 5585858, fax 5585930, ⓔ unitresvn@oberoiblr.com, 37–39 MG Rd)* has luxurious rooms that open onto an immense tranquil garden at US$230/255 for standard rooms to US$285/315 for deluxe rooms. It does get some pollution from MG Rd though. There's a swimming pool and all the usual five-star amenities.

Taj West End *(☎ 2255055, fax 2200010, ⓔ westend.bangalore@tajhotels.com, Racecourse Rd)* is a five-star hotel occupying a 19th-century mansion and several villas set in a beautiful eight – hectare garden. Some of the villas haven't been well maintained though. Rooms start from US$195/215.

Places to Eat

MG Rd Area There are many places here, though most are expensive and mediocre imitations of Western fast-food or pizza joints. Their attractiveness will probably be determined by how long you've been in India.

Ulla's Refreshments, on the 1st floor of General Hall, MG Rd, is a local favourite and a great spot for snacks and South Indian vegetarian dishes. It has an indoor area and a big, convivial terrace.

Coconut Grove *(Church St)* is a friendly, semi open-air restaurant with a fine array of Keralan, Goan and Kodava regional dishes. The bamboo screens, attentive service and tranquil dining area add to the experience. Main courses cost Rs 85 to 100.

Casa Piccolo *(131 Residency Rd)* receives enthusiastic raves from travellers. It's yet another Western-style eatery, but it has a good atmosphere and prices are sensible. Pizzas and steaks cost from Rs 80.

The Only Place *(Royal Arcade, Brigade Rd)* serves excellent steaks with a decent plate of vegetables. Their lasagne is another popular favourite. Mains are around Rs 100.

US Pizza *(Church St)* makes reasonable pizzas from around Rs 100, and it has a pleasant veranda dining area. ***Pizza Hut*** *(Queen's Rd)* is, well, your usual Pizza Hut, but the service is good. ***Pizza Corner*** is a popular pizza chain with a branch on Brigade Rd. Pizzas are around Rs 105 and it offers free delivery (☎ 3446111).

Koshy's Bar & Restaurant *(St Mark's Rd)* is a Bangalore institution, run by the same family for three generations. It offers a mix of Indian, Chinese and continental dishes at reasonable prices. Try the daily special.

Victoria Hotel *(47–48 Residency Rd)* has a garden restaurant and an old-fashioned dining hall that are both interesting eating places, and a good place for a drink too.

Queen's Restaurant *(Church St)* has an earthy atmosphere with mud walls, tribal decorations and cane furniture. It's popular and serves reasonably priced Indian and Chinese food.

Ebony *(MG Rd)* is up on the 13th floor of the massive Barton Centre, with tables on a terrace overlooking the city. It offers Thai, French and Parsee cuisine, with mains around Rs 120 and salads for Rs 70.

The reliable ***Baskin & Robbins*** *(Residency Rd)* is a good place to go for ice cream. ***Sreeraj Lassi Bar*** *(Rest House Rd)* offers terrific lassis in a wide range of flavours.

Elsewhere Two good options in Subedar Chatram Rd in Gandhi Nagar are ***Kamat Hotel*** and ***Sagar Hotel***. The former has vegetarian fare, and the latter Andhra-style cuisine.

Mavalli Tiffin Room, near Lalbagh botanical gardens is a legendary *dosa* (lentil-flour pancakes), thali and snack joint. The lunches are particularly good.

Paradise Island at the Taj West End is the most interesting of the five-star hotel restaurants. Set in a beautiful garden pavilion, it serves excellent Thai and Chinese cuisine.

Café Schorlemmer on the roof of Max Mueller Bhavan on Lavelle Rd is a terrific German cafe, with fresh pastries, coffee and lunches (Rs 80 to 120). It's open until 8 pm Monday to Saturday.

Entertainment

Bars Bangalore's pub culture is renowned among middle-class Indians. Flashy bars, draught beer and well-lit discos are all the rage with well-heeled young people and office workers. Bars are open during lunch time and from 5 pm to a dismally early 11 pm. Draught beer costs around Rs 35 for a small mug, Rs 80 for a large mug and Rs 150 to 175 for a pitcher. Nearly all bars serve snacks.

Peco's Pub, on Rest House Rd, must be a true original – a 1960s acid-rock theme bar. It's a slightly battered but cheerful little place on several floors, including a roof garden.

Pub World, next to Gateway Hotel, squeezes a British pub, German beer hall, wild west saloon and Manhattan cocktail bar into one room, though you may have trouble realising which one you're meant to be in.

NASA *(Church St)* is decked out like a spaceship and has laser shows, but seems to be on the decline. If you like this place, you'll also like the ***Underground*** *(MG Rd)*, which is loosely modelled on a London tube station.

New Night Watchman, near Berrys Hotel, has a nifty cubist park bench arrangement but thankfully no theme decor, and is a good place for a beer.

Oaken Cask, just around the corner from Residency Rd, is another British-style pub that's quieter than most.

Black Cadillac *(50 Residency Rd)* has quieter music, more-expensive drinks and a cover charge on Friday and Saturday night. Opposite is ***Purple Haze***, which attracts a cheerful mixed crowd, which seems inordinately fond of Queen and Bon Jovi.

Downtown Pub, opposite Gateway Hotel, has good music, a relaxed atmosphere and a couple of pool tables.

The two nicest places for a beer have nothing to do with Bangalore's pub culture: Try the veranda of the ***Victoria Hotel*** and the old fashioned tea-room ambience of ***Koshy's Bar & Restaurant*** *(St Mark's Rd)*.

Nightclubs Bangalore's trend-conscious nightclub scene is constantly changing. ***180 Proof*** on St Mark's Rd is the flashiest and the most expensive; on weekends you have to dress sharp and queue for up to an hour. Drinks aren't cheap but the elegant decor and sharp sound system is as good as you'll find outside of Mumbai. ***The Club Inferno***, on the Mysore road, about 14km from the city centre, is also popular. Police periodically shut nightclubs outside the city, allegedly because of moral outrages like couples dancing and drinking together. Cynics suggest there are financial motives as well.

Cinema For first-run English-language films, try ***Plaza*** *(MG Rd)* and ***Galaxy*** *(Residency Rd)*. Late shows are the preserve of large, rowdy groups of young men. Regional films are best watched at one of the many cinemas along KG Rd in Gandhi Nagar.

Spectator Sports

Horse Racing Bangalore's winter race season runs from November to February and its summer season from May to July. Races are generally held on either Friday or weekends and can be a lot of fun. Contact the Bangalore Turf Club (☎ 2262391) for details.

Cricket If you want to see India's sporting passion up close, Bangalore's Chinnaswami Stadium hosts regular matches. Contact the Karnataka Cricket Association (☎ 2864487) for information. A range of tickets are sold on the day, though there are the inevitable queues. Rs 100 buys a good seat in a not-too-crowded area.

Shopping

Bangalore is a good place to purchase silk, sandalwood and rosewood items, and Lambani tribal jewellery.

There are plenty of handicraft shops on MG Rd and Commercial St, north of MG Rd. Cauvery Arts & Crafts Emporium at 23 MD Rd stocks the same range of statues, jewellery, ceramics, carpets and *agarbathi* (incense) that you've seen in a thousand other tourist towns across the country. Cottage Arts at 52 MG Rd and Central Cottage Industries Emporium at 144 MG Rd also stock the usual range of artefacts.

There are a number of shops around MG Rd selling cheap new release CDs and cassettes of Western and Hindi music. The cassettes are a bargain at around Rs 100.

Getting There & Away

Air The Indian Airlines office (☎ 2211914) is in the Housing Board Buildings, Kempegowda (KG) Rd. The Jet Airways office (☎ 2226617) is in the Unity Buildings, Jayachamaraja Rd, and Sahara Airlines is in the Sahara Nirvana Building, Richmond Circle, Richmond Rd (☎ 2246435).

There are daily flights to Mumbai (Bombay; US$140), Kolkata (US$265), Delhi (US$255), Hyderabad (US$105), Chennai (Madras; US$95), plus flights to Ahmedabad (US$200), Goa (US$105), Kochi (US$80), Mangalore (US$80), Pune (US$145) and Thiruvananthapuram (US$120).

International airlines that have offices in Bangalore include:

Air France (☎ 5589397) Sunrise Chambers, 22 Ulsoor Rd
Air India (☎ 2277747) Unity Bldgs, Jayachamaraja Rd
British Airways (☎ 2271205) 7 St Mark's Rd
KLM (☎ 2268703) West End Hotel, Racecourse Rd
Lufthansa (☎ 5588791) 44/2 Dickenson Rd
Malaysia Airlines (☎ 2215326) Parvathi Plaza, Richmond Rd
Singapore Airlines (☎ 2213833) 51 Richmond Rd

Bus Bangalore's huge and well-organised Central bus stand is directly in front of the City train station. All the regular buses within the state are operated by the Karnataka State Road Transport Corporation (KSRTC; ☎ 2873377). Interstate buses are operated by KSRTC as well as the state transport corporation of Andhra Pradesh (APSRTC; ☎ 2873915, platform No 15), Tamil Nadu's JJTC (☎ 287 6974, platform No 14) and Goa's Kadamba Transport Corporation. Computerised advance booking is available for all KSRTC super-deluxe and express buses as well as for the bus companies of neighbouring states. All have booths in the main reservations office. It's advisable to book in advance for long-distance journeys.

KSRTC operates horrifyingly fast buses to Mysore every 15 minutes from 5 am to midnight (Rs 46/73 ordinary/deluxe, three hours, platform Nos 17 and 18). It also has six daily departures to Ernakulam (16 hours), 12 to Hospet (nine hours), four to Jog Falls (eight hours), 10 to Chennai (eight hours), three to Mumbai (24 hours), three to Ooty (eight hours) and two to Panaji (15 hours). The KSTDC has a deluxe bus to Hospet (for Hampi), departing every morning from Badami House.

Kadamba buses depart for Panaji at 6 pm (Rs 243, 11 hours). The APSRTC has plenty of buses to Hyderabad (Rs 244, 12 hours); one departs at 7.45 am and the rest leave in the evening. JJTC has frequent departures to Madurai (10 hours) and Coimbatore (11 hours), plus nine daily buses to Chennai (Rs 149, eight hours).

In addition to the various state buses, there are numerous private companies offering more comfortable and only slightly more expensive buses between Bangalore and the other major cities in central and southern India. You'll find private operators lining the street facing the Central bus stand. Most private buses depart Bangalore in the evening.

Train There are two train stations in Bangalore. The main one, the City train station,

Major Trains from Bangalore

destination	train No & name	departures	distance (km)	duration (hrs)	fare (Rs)
Chennai	2608 *Lalbagh Exp*	6.30 am	361	5½	266 *
	2640 *Brindavan Exp*	2.30 pm		5¾	
	2008 *Shatabdi Exp*	4.25 pm		5	530/1075 ◆
Delhi	2627 *Karnataka Exp*	6.25 pm	2444	41¾	436/1265 †
	2429 *Rajdhani Exp*	6.35 am Mon, Wed, Thu & Sun		34½	2205/6385 ✤
Ernakulam	6526 *Kanniyakumari Exp*	9 pm	638	13	193/893 ✱
Hospet	6592 *Hampi Exp*	10 pm	491	10	163/756 ✱
Hyderabad	7086 *Secunderabad Exp*	5.05 pm	790	13½	242/702 ✱
Kolkata	5625 *Guwahati Exp*	11.30 pm Wed & Fri	2025	38	397/1152 ✱
Mumbai	6530 *Udyan Exp*	8.30 pm	1279	24	310/1440 ✱
Mysore	6222 *Mysore Exp*	7.10 am	139	2½	41/365 ✧
	6206 *Tipu Exp*	2.15 pm			41/138 *
	6216 *Chamundi Exp*	6.15 pm			41/138 *
	2007 *Shatabdi Exp*	11 am		2	280/550 ◆
Thiruvananthapuram	6526 *Kanniyakumari Exp*	9 pm	851	18¼	242/1124 ✱

* 2nd/chair class ◆ air-con chair/air-con exec † sleeper/3-tier air-con
✤ 3-tier air-con/1st air-con ✱ sleeper/2-tier air-con ✧ 2nd/2-tier air-con

is the place to make reservations. Cantonment train station is a useful spot to disembark if you're arriving in Bangalore and heading for the MG Rd area.

Rail reservations in Bangalore are computerised but there are no tourist quotas and bookings are heavy on most routes. It's usually possible for travellers to get into the emergency quota. First you have to buy a ticket (waitlisted), then fill out a form at the Divisional Office building immediately to the left of the City train station. You find out about six hours before departure whether you're on (a good chance); if not, the ticket is refunded. The reservation office, where there is a foreign tourist counter is on the left as you're facing the station and is open from 8 am to 8 pm Monday to Saturday and 8 am to 2 pm Sunday. Luggage can be left at the City train station.

Direct daily express trains connect Bangalore with all the main cities in southern and central India. For Goa, catch the daily *Rani Chennamma Express* (No 6589) at 8 pm and change trains at Londa. The journey takes 10½ hours and costs Rs 185/857 in sleeper/2-tier air-con. The only line disrupted by conversion from metre to broad gauge is the stretch between Hassan and Mangalore.

See the 'Major Trains from Bangalore' table for more information.

Getting Around

To/From the Airport The airport is 13km east of the City train station and about 9km east of the MG Rd area. There are prepaid taxis from the airport to the city (Rs 150); in the other direction you'll probably have to haggle for a price – count on around Rs 130 for a taxi or Rs 50 for an autorickshaw. Bus Nos 13 and 333 go from the City bus stand to the airport for around Rs 8.

Bus Bangalore has a comprehensive but often crowded local bus network. Peak-hour services are packed, and locals warn that women on their own should think twice about taking buses after dark. Most local buses (light blue) run from the City bus stand next to the Central bus stand; a few operate from the City Market bus stand to the south.

KARNATAKA

To get from the City train station to the MG Rd area, catch any bus from platform No 17 at the City bus stand. For the City market, take bus No 31, 31E, 35 or 49 from platform No 8.

Car There are plenty of places around Bangalore to hire a car with driver or (if you're brave enough) self-drive. Standard rates for a Hindustan Ambassador car are Rs 4.5 per kilometre for a minimum of 250km, plus an allowance of Rs 100 for the driver (Rs 1225 per day. Agencies include Europcar (☎ 221 9502), 85 Richmond Rd, and Dial-a-Car (☎ 5261737) is also good value and has an office at the Airlines Hotel.

Autorickshaw The city's autorickshaw drivers are required by law to use their meters (which are properly calibrated), and locals insist on them being used. Do likewise! After dark you may have to bargain, or pay 50% above the metered rate. Flagfall is Rs 8.80 and then Rs 4 for each extra kilometre. There is a prepaid autorickshaw stand at City train station, on the left side of the courtyard outside the exit. From City train station to MG Rd costs about Rs 25.

KARNATAKA

AROUND BANGALORE

Nrityagram

This dance village, 30km north-west of Bangalore, was established in the early 1990s to revive Indian classical dance. Founded by the late Odissi dancer, Protima Gauri, it offers the long-term study of classical dance and its allied subjects, such as choreography, philosophy, music, mythology and painting. The village, designed by award-winning Goan architect, Gerard Da Cunha, welcomes visitors and accommodates guests. Guided tours cost Rs 250, including lunch, dance demonstrations and a short lecture. Contact Nrityagram's Bangalore office (☎ 8466314).

Nandi Hills

☎ 08156 • elevation 1615m

Nandi Hills, 68km north of Bangalore, is one of the most majestic places in the region and is well worth a visit. It was a popular summer retreat even in Tipu Sultan's days. **Tipu's Drop**, a 600m-high cliff face, not only provided a good view over the surrounding country, it was also a convenient place to dispose of enemies. There are two notable **Chola temples** here.

Entry is Rs 25 and it's open daily during daylight hours. Avoid Sunday when the day-tripping crowds are out in force.

Places to Stay & Eat The *Nehru Nilaya Guest House (☎ 78621)* has clean doubles for Rs 150 or a quaint cottage for Rs 200.

KSTDC's Hotel Mayura Pine Top (☎ 78624) has only two rooms and they're in bad shape; a pity because the setting is great. Booking is essential – either directly with the hotel or at the KSTDC office (☎ 2212901) in Bangalore. Singles/doubles cost Rs 190/220. Both places have restaurants.

Getting There & Away There are around six KSRTC buses a day to Nandi Hills (Rs 19, two hours) from Bangalore's Central bus stand.

MYSORE

☎ 0821 • pop 735,000

It's easy to see why this charming city has long been a favourite with travellers – it's a manageable size, enjoys a good climate and has chosen to retain and promote its heritage rather than replace it. The city is famous for its silk and is also a thriving sandalwood and incense centre, though don't expect the air to be any more fragrant than that of the next town.

Until Independence, Mysore was the seat of the maharajas of Mysore, a princely state covering about one-third of present-day Karnataka. The maharajas' palace is a major tourist attraction.

History

Mysore was named after the mythical Mahisuru, where the goddess Chamundi slew the demon Mahishasura. The Mysore dynasty was founded in 1399, but up until the middle of the 16th century its rulers, the Wodeyars, were in the service of the Vijayanagar emperor. With the fall of the empire in 1565 the Mysore rulers were among the first to declare their independence.

Apart from a brief period in the late 18th century when Hyder Ali and Tipu Sultan usurped the throne, the Wodeyars continued to rule until Independence in 1947. In 1956, when the new state was formed, the former maharaja was elected governor.

Orientation

The train station is on the north-western fringe of the city centre, about 1km from the main shopping street, Sayyaji Rao Rd. The Central bus stand is on the Bangalore-Mysore road, on the north-eastern fringe of the city centre. Mysore Palace occupies the entire south-eastern sector of the city centre. Chamundi Hill is an ever visible landmark to the south.

Information

Tourist Offices The KSTDC tourist office (☎ 442096, fax 441833) is in the Old Exhibition Building on Irwin Rd and is open from 10 am to 5.30 pm Monday to Saturday. There are also counters at the train station, the Central bus stand, and a transport office next to Hotel Mayura Hoysala.

Money The State Bank of Mysore, on the corner of Irwin and Ashoka Rds, has efficient foreign exchange facilities, as does its branch office on Sayyaji Rao Rd. Bank of Baroda on Gandhi Square gives cash advances on MasterCard and Visa.

Post & Communications The main post office is on the corner of Irwin and Ashoka Rds. It's open from 10 am to 6 pm Monday to Sunday, 10.30 am to 1.30 pm Sunday. The poste restante facility is only open until 4 pm. There's a handy local post office on the 1st floor of a building fronting KR Circle.

The central telegraph office is on the western side of the palace and is open 24 hours.

There are several Internet cafes: Coca-Cola Cyber Space on Nazarbad Main Rd is central and open from 9 am to 10 pm daily. Rates for Internet access are Rs 60 per hour (minimum 30 minutes). Cyber Net Corner, at the Hotel Indra Bhavan building on Dhanvanthri Rd, also costs Rs 60 per hour.

Bookshops Geetha Book House, on KR Circle, and Ashok Book Centre on Dhanvanthri Rd are the best bookshops in town.

Medical Services Basappa Memorial Hospital (☎ 512401) is on Hunsur Rd about 2km west of the city.

National Parks Accommodation and transport for Bandipur National Park (80km south of Mysore) should be booked with the Field Director (☎ 480901), Aranya Bhavan, Ashokapuram, Mysore. Take an autorickshaw or a No 61 bus from the City bus stand.

Mysore Palace

The beautiful profile of this walled Indo-Saracenic palace, the seat of the maharajas of Mysore, graces the city's skyline. An earlier palace burnt down in 1897 and the present one, designed by English architect Henry Irwin, was completed in 1912 at a cost of Rs 4.2 million. The former maharaja is still in residence at the back of the palace.

Inside it's a kaleidoscope of stained glass, mirrors, gilt and gaudy colours. Some of it is undoubtedly over the top but there are also beautiful carved wooden doors and mosaic floors, as well as a whole series of mediocre, though historically interesting, paintings depicting life in Mysore during the Edwardian Raj. The palace has a selection of Hindu temples within its grounds, including the Shweta Varahaswamy Temple with its *gopuram* (Dravidian gateway tower) that influenced the style of the later Sri Chamundeswari Temple on Chamundi Hill.

The main rooms of the palace are open to the public from 10.30 am to 5.30 pm daily, and the crowds can sometimes rival those in the departure lounge of a major international airport. The Rs 10 entry fee is paid at the southern gate of the palace grounds, though you need to retain the ticket to enter the palace building itself. Cameras must be deposited at the entrance gate (free); visitors can only take pictures of the outside of the buildings. Shoes are left at the shoe deposit counter near the palace entrance. There's an Archaeological Survey of India storeroom in the palace grounds, full of books (available for sale) on various historical sites.

The **Residential Museum**, incorporating some of the palace's living quarters and personal effects belonging to the maharaja's family, costs an extra Rs 15 and is rather dull after the magnificence of the palace itself.

On Sunday night and during the entire Dussehra Festival, there's a carnival atmosphere around the palace as 97,000 light bulbs illuminate the building from 7 to 8 pm.

Chamundi Hill

Overlooking Mysore from the 1062m summit of Chamundi Hill, the **Sri Chamundeswari Temple** makes a pleasant half-day

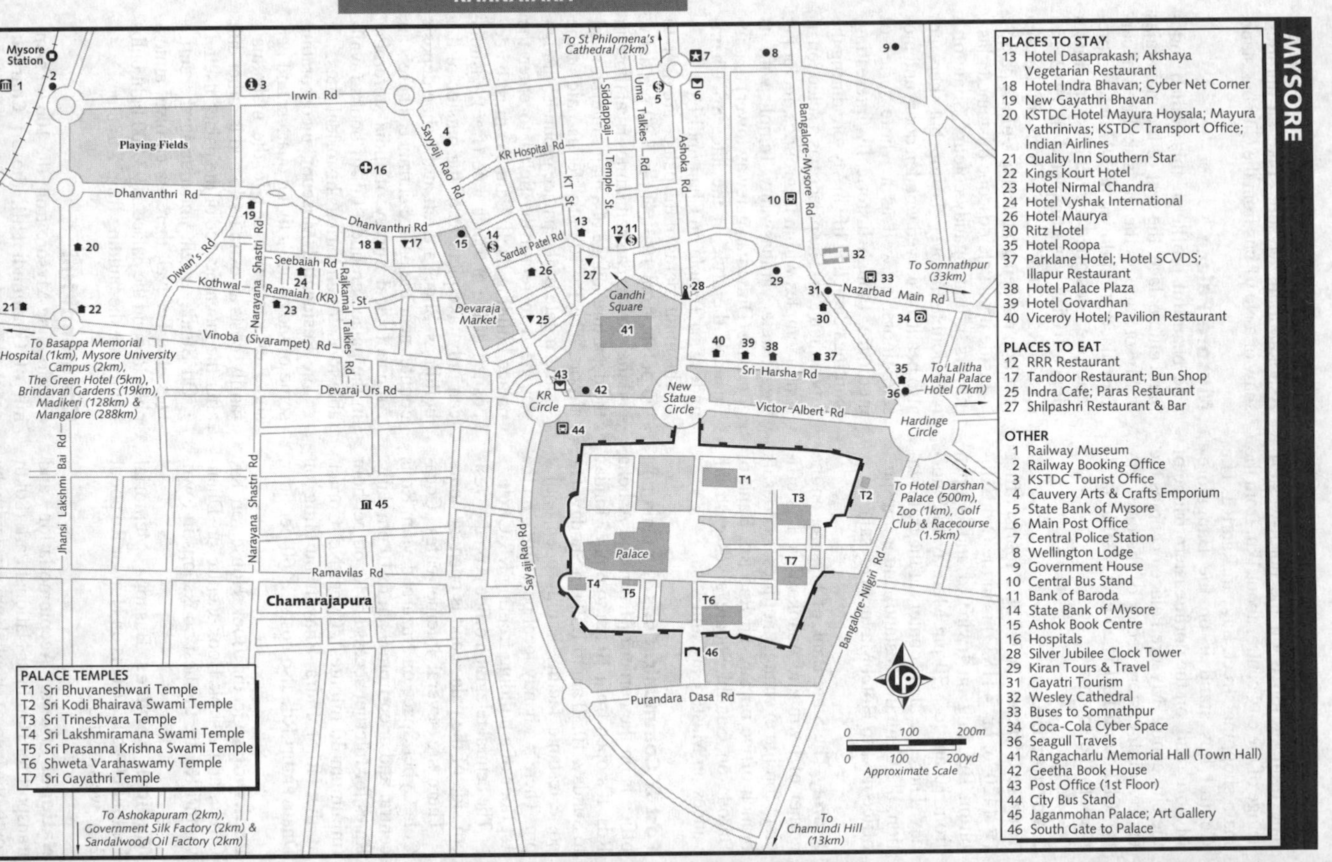
MYSORE
PLACES TO STAY
13 Hotel Dasaprakash; Akshaya Vegetarian Restaurant
18 Hotel Indra Bhavan; Cyber Net Corner
19 New Gayathri Bhavan
20 KSTDC Hotel Mayura Hoysala; Mayura Yathrinivas; KSTDC Transport Office; Indian Airlines
21 Quality Inn Southern Star
22 Kings Kourt Hotel
23 Hotel Nirmal Chandra
24 Hotel Vyshak International
26 Hotel Maurya
30 Ritz Hotel
35 Hotel Roopa
37 Parklane Hotel; Hotel SCVDS; Illapur Restaurant
38 Hotel Palace Plaza
39 Hotel Govardhan
40 Viceroy Hotel; Pavilion Restaurant
PLACES TO EAT
12 RRR Restaurant
17 Tandoor Restaurant; Bun Shop
25 Indra Cafe; Paras Restaurant
27 Shilpashri Restaurant & Bar
OTHER
1 Railway Museum
2 Railway Booking Office
3 KSTDC Tourist Office
4 Cauvery Arts & Crafts Emporium
5 State Bank of Mysore
6 Main Post Office
7 Central Police Station
8 Wellington Lodge
9 Government House
10 Central Bus Stand
11 Bank of Baroda
14 State Bank of Mysore
15 Ashok Book Centre
16 Hospitals
28 Silver Jubilee Clock Tower
29 Kiran Tours & Travel
31 Gayatri Tourism
32 Wesley Cathedral
33 Buses to Somnathpur
34 Coca-Cola Cyber Space
36 Seagull Travels
41 Rangacharlu Memorial Hall (Town Hall)
42 Geetha Book House
43 Post Office (1st Floor)
44 City Bus Stand
45 Jaganmohan Palace; Art Gallery
46 South Gate to Palace
PALACE TEMPLES
T1 Sri Bhuvaneshwari Temple
T2 Sri Kodi Bhairava Swami Temple
T3 Sri Trineshvara Temple
T4 Sri Lakshmiramana Swami Temple
T5 Sri Prasanna Krishna Swami Temple
T6 Shweta Varahaswamy Temple
T7 Sri Gayathri Temple
Mysore Station
To St Philomena's Cathedral (2km)
To Somnathpur (33km)
To Lalitha Mahal Palace Hotel (7km)
To Hotel Darshan Palace (500m), Zoo (1km), Golf Club & Racecourse (1.5km)
To Chamundi Hill (13km)
To Ashokapuram (2km), Government Silk Factory (2km) & Sandalwood Oil Factory (2km)
To Basappa Memorial Hospital (1km), Mysore University Campus (2km), The Green Hotel (5km), Brindavan Gardens (19km), Madikeri (128km) & Mangalore (288km)
Playing Fields
Gandhi Square
Devaraja Market
Palace
Chamarajapura
KR Circle
New Statue Circle
Hardinge Circle
Irwin Rd
Dhanvanthri Rd
KR Hospital Rd
Sayyaji Rao Rd
Sayaji Rao Rd
Siddappaji Temple St
Uma Talkies Rd
Ashoka Rd
KT St
Sardar Patel Rd
Bangalore-Mysore Rd
Nazarbad Main Rd
Seebaiah Rd
Kothwal Ramaiah (KR) St
Narayana Shastri Rd
Rajkamal Talkies Rd
Diwan's Rd
Vinoba (Sivarampet) Rd
Devaraj Urs Rd
Sri Harsha Rd
Victor Albert Rd
Jhansi Lakshmi Bai Rd
Ramavilas Rd
Bangalore-Nilgiri Rd
Purandara Dasa Rd
0 100 200m
0 100 200yd
Approximate Scale

excursion. Pilgrims are supposed to climb the 1000-plus steps to the top; those not needing to improve their karma will find descending easier on the leg muscles. There's a road to the top; bus No 201 departs from the City bus stand in Mysore for the summit every 40 minutes (Rs 3). A taxi to the top from Mysore will cost around Rs 200.

Before exploring the temple, visit the free **Godly Museum** near the car park where you can ponder the price of various sins.

The Chamundeswari Temple is dominated by a towering seven storey, 40m-high gopuram. The statue in the car park is of the demon Mahishasura, who was one of the goddess Chamundi's victims. The goddess was the family deity of the maharajas and Mysore derived its name from Mahishasura. The temple is open from 6 am to 2 pm and 4 to 8 pm.

After visiting the temple start back to the car park and look for the top of the stairway, behind the Mahishasura statue, marked by a sign proclaiming 'Way to Big Bull'. It's a pleasant descent and the views over the city and surrounding countryside are superb.

One-third of the way down you come to the famous 5m-high **Nandi** (Shiva's bull vehicle), carved out of solid rock in 1659. It's one of the largest in India and is visited by hordes of pilgrims offering *prasad* (food offering used in religious ceremonies) to the priest in attendance there. The garlanded statue has a flaky black coating of coconut husk charcoal, mixed with ghee.

You'll probably have rubbery legs by the time you reach the bottom of the hill and it's still about 2km back into the centre of Mysore. Fortunately there are usually autorickshaws waiting to ferry pedestrians back to town for around Rs 35.

Devaraja Fruit & Vegetable Market

The Devaraja Market, stretching along the western side of Sayyaji Rao Rd, south of Dhanvanthri Rd, is one of the most colourful in India and provides excellent subject material for photographers.

Jaganmohan Palace & Art Gallery

The Jayachamarajendra Art Gallery in the Jaganmohan Palace, just west of Mysore Palace, has a collection of kitsch objects and memorabilia from the Wodeyars, including weird and wonderful musical machines, rare instruments and paintings by Raja Ravi Varma. The palace was built in 1861 and served as a royal auditorium. It's open from 8 am to 12 noon and 2.30 to 5 pm daily (Rs 10).

Mysore Zoo

Mysore has one of India's better kept zoos. It's set in parched but pretty gardens on the eastern edge of the city centre. Among the attractions are a couple of white tigers and several Bengal tigers, as well as the usual range of primates, elephants, bears, birds and rhinos. Come in the morning or evening if you want to see the tigers roaming in their enclosures rather than in the depressing cages. The zoo is open 8 to 11.30 am and 2 to 6 pm daily except Tuesday (Rs 10).

Rail Museum

Mysore's paltry rail museum boasts a maharani's saloon carriage, complete with royal toilet, dating from around 1899. It's west of the train station, just across the railway track, and is open from 8 am to 1 pm and 2 to 6 pm daily; entry is Rs 2.

Folklore Museum

This small museum is in the Mysore University Campus, north-east of the city centre. Among the exhibits is a superb collection of carved wooden figures from Karnatakan villages, decorative masks and ceremonial headdress, and a display of *thogalu bomba* (leather shadow puppets) used to perform stories from the Ramayana and Mahabharata – similar to the *wayang kulit* of Java in Indonesia. There are also wooden puppets, including one of a 10-headed demon Ravana. The museum is open from 10 am to 1.30 pm and 2.30 to 5.30 pm daily except Sunday (and every second Saturday; admission is free). It's in the building behind the university canteen.

Other Attractions

Mysore has several fine buildings and monuments in a variety of architectural styles. Dating from 1805, **Government House**, formerly the British Residency, is a 'Tuscan Doric' building set in 20 hectares of gardens. West of Government House is **Wellington Lodge**, where Arthur Wellesley (later the Duke of Wellington) lived after the defeat of Tipu Sultan.

In front of the north gate of Mysore Palace, a 1920 **statue** of Maharaja Chamarajendar Wodeyar stands in the New Statue Circle, facing the 1927 **Silver Jubilee Clock Tower**. If he glanced sideways he'd see the imposing town hall, the **Rangacharlu Memorial Hall** of 1884. The next traffic circle west is the 1950s **Krishnaraja Circle** (KR Circle), graced by a statue of Maharaja Krishnaraja Wodeyar.

Towering **St Philomena's Cathedral**, built between 1933 and 1941 in neo-Gothic style, is one of the largest in India. Beneath the altar a subterranean chapel contains a relic of St Philomena, a 3rd-century martyr said to have performed miracles after her death.

The Royal City by TP Issar, available from Mysore bookshops, is a comprehensive survey of the city's architecture.

Organised Tours

The KSTDC's Mysore city tour covers the city sights plus Chamundi Hill, the Keshava Temple at Somnathpur, Srirangapatnam and Brindavan gardens. The tour starts daily at 7.30 am, ends at 8.30 pm and costs Rs 115. It's a bit rushed, and may include a lengthy unscheduled stop at a handicraft emporium.

The KSTDC also runs a Belur, Halebid and Sravanabelagola tour every Tuesday, Wednesday, Friday and Sunday (daily in the high season) at 7.30 am, ending at 9 pm (Rs 210). Buses leave from KSTDC Hotel Mayura Hoysala. It's worthwhile if your time is limited, but again you spend far more time on the bus (nine hours!) than at the sites.

Special Events

The 10-day **Dussehra Festival** in the first two weeks of October is a wonderful time to visit Mysore. The palace is illuminated every night and on the last day the former maharaja leads one of India's most colourful processions. Richly caparisoned elephants, liveried retainers, cavalry, and flower-bedecked images of deities make their way through the streets to the sound of jazz and brass bands and inevitable clouds of incense.

Places to Stay

Accommodation can be hard to find during the Dussehra Festival, so if you're arriving in October book ahead.

Places to Stay – Budget

Mysore has plenty of budget hotels. The main areas to look are around Gandhi Square and in the area between Dhanvanthri and Vinoba Rds.

Parklane Hotel *(☎ 434340, fax 428424, 2720 Sri Harsha Rd)* is more of a restaurant than a hotel, with only eight rooms. Nevertheless it's good value, with singles/doubles for Rs 125/149. At peak times it would be helpful to make a reservation.

Hotel Govardhan *(☎ 434118, Sri Harsha Rd)* is a large hotel with rooms for Rs 149/190; it's characterless, but a reasonable standby option.

Hotel Maurya *(☎ 26677, Hanumantha Rao St II)* is reasonably good. Clean singles/doubles/triples with private bathroom and bucket shower cost Rs 105/195/280 and open onto a courtyard.

Hotel Dasaprakash *(☎ 442444, Gandhi Square)* is part of a South Indian hotel chain. It's a huge, airy place built around a central courtyard with basic but acceptable rooms with private bathroom from Rs 145/300. Checkout is 24 hours. There's a vegetarian restaurant, an ice-cream parlour, a travel agency and, for emergencies, an astro-palmist on call.

There's a string of hotels in the Dhanvanthri Rd area with not much to distinguish between them.

New Gayathri Bhavan *(☎ 421224, Dhanvanthri Rd)* is handy for the train station. It's a cheap, friendly, large place with double rooms from Rs 185 with private bathroom.

Hotel Nirmal Chandra *(☎ 432238, 58 Kothwal Ramaiah St)*, nearby, is a pleasant lodge with singles/doubles/triples for Rs 125/175/225.

Hotel Indra Bhavan *(☎ 423933, Dhanvanthri Rd)* has simple, clean rooms and a balcony with wicker furniture. Singles/doubles with private bathroom cost Rs 170/180. There's a 'meals' hall downstairs.

Places to Stay – Mid-Range

Ritz Hotel *(☎ 422668, Bangalore-Mysore Rd)*, a few hundred metres from the Central bus stand, is an old hotel with loads of colonial charm and huge rooms with four-poster beds. There are only four rooms: Spacious doubles with mosquito nets and 24-hour hot water are Rs 300, and a four-bed room costs Rs 450. Book in advance. There's a good restaurant and bar downstairs and a comfortable guests' dining area upstairs.

KSTDC Hotel Mayura Hoysala *(☎ 425 349, 2 Jhansi Lakshmi Bai Rd)* is a good place on the opposite side of the city centre. It has a relaxing ambience with its own quiet gardens, and offers decent rooms (with enormous private bathroom) for Rs 350/400. There's a bar and restaurant here.

Hotel Palace Plaza *(☎ 430034, fax 421070, Sri Harsha Rd)* is a modern hotel offering a variety of rooms ranging from Rs 400/500 with TV and private bathroom to 650 with air-con.

Viceroy Hotel *(☎ 428001, fax 433391, Sri Harsha Rd)*, nearby, caters to a business clientele; you can be pampered here without spending a fortune. Rooms are Rs 625/775, or Rs 1075/1175 with air-con.

Hotel Vyshak International *(☎ 421777, Seebaiah Rd)* is a new hotel with regular rooms for Rs 400/500, and deluxe rooms for Rs 600/700.

Hotel SCVDS *(☎ 421379, fax 426297, Sri Harsha Rd)*, next to Parklane Hotel, is a last resort. It has doubles with mosquito nets, TV and private bathroom from Rs 250, or Rs 550 with air-con. Some rooms are a bit frayed, so check first.

Places to Stay – Top End

The Green Hotel *(☎ 512536, fax 516139, ⓔ grenhotl@glasbg01.vsnl.net.in, Vinoba Rd, Jayalakshmipuram, Mysore)* is a 100-year-old palace built as a country retreat for the Wodeyar princesses. The hotel has won awards for ecological awareness, and profits go to charity. The management has kept the palace's elegant atmosphere intact, with a library, chess sets, croquet lawn and bar. Double rooms in the palace cost Rs 3000 to 3500, while there's a modern wing facing the garden where deluxe rooms cost Rs 1400/1700, and ordinary rooms are Rs 1100/1300. The hotel is 5km west of the city centre; they'll send a vehicle to collect you if you book, or an autorickshaw costs Rs 40.

Kings Kourt Hotel *(☎ 421142, fax 438384, ⓔ kingskourt@vsnl.com, Jhansi Lakshmi Bai Rd)* is a large, modern establishment. It charges Rs 650/750, or Rs 1390/1690 for air-con rooms. Some rooms are in better shape than others.

Quality Inn Southern Star *(☎ 426426, fax 421689, ⓔ southernstar@vsnl.com, 13–14 Vinoba Rd)* is a plush, modern hotel. It boasts a swimming pool, health club, poolside barbecue, restaurant and coffee shop. Centrally air-conditioned rooms cost Rs 2100/3200.

Lalitha Mahal Palace Hotel *(☎ 571265, fax 571770)*, 7km from the city centre, was once one of the maharaja's palaces. It's government-run, so service and maintenance isn't what it could be. Standard rooms cost US$154/176, though there are some cramped 'turret' rooms for US$66/77, all plus 25% tax. The rooms in the older part of the building have the most character, but they can be gloomy and lack balconies. Facilities include an ordinary swimming pool, a tennis court, and a large bar with reputedly the best billiard table in India.

Places to Eat

Shilpashri Restaurant & Bar *(Gandhi Square)* is very good, the prices are reasonable and the rooftop is a lovely place to dine in the evening. The service is good, even if there's a cricket match on TV. It serves Western breakfasts and Indian, Chinese and continental mains for around Rs 50.

Ritz Hotel is also worth checking out, with good value Indian and continental meals, and it serves alcohol. There's a courtyard at the rear of the building. Vegetarian dishes cost around Rs 40 and non-vegetarian meals cost from Rs 65.

RRR Restaurant *(Gandhi Square)* is a typical vegetarian place and travellers rave about the all-you-can-eat thalis.

Parklane Hotel *(Sri Harsha Rd)* has a convivial courtyard restaurant that's long been a travellers' favourite, and it's often full. It serves everything from tandoori chicken and chop suey to sandwiches and beer.

Paras Restaurant *(Sayyaji Rao Rd)* is a popular local eatery serving south (Rs 22) and North Indian (Rs 45) thalis at lunch time.

Tandoor Restaurant *(Dhanvanthri Rd)* is a hole-in-the-wall eatery serving Punjabi fare and cheap Western breakfasts. The nearby ***Bun Shop*** sells tasty potato buns that make a fine light lunch.

Pavilion Restaurant at the Viceroy Hotel is a smart place with mains from Rs 60.

Akshaya Vegetarian Restaurant in the Hotel Dasaprakash has meals from Rs 25. There's also a good ice-cream parlour in the courtyard.

Quality Inn Southern Star has buffet lunches for Rs 175.

Lalitha Mahal Palace Hotel offers the city's grandest dining experience, complete with baby-blue Wedgwood-style decor in the dining hall. Dinner for two here costs around Rs 600, excluding drinks. The a la carte menu is replaced by a buffet outside the busy tourist season.

Shopping

Mysore is famous for carved sandalwood, inlay work, silk saris and wooden toys. You can see the whole range at the Cauvery Arts & Crafts Emporium on Sayyaji Rao Rd, although it's not cheap. It accepts credit cards, foreign currency or travellers cheques and will arrange packing and export. There are a number of other souvenir and handicraft shops in the precincts of the Jaganmohan Palace and along Dhanvanthri Rd. Silk shops can be found along Devaraj Urs Rd.

You can buy silk and see weavers at work at the Government Silk Factory on Jhansi Lakshmi Bai Rd. The factory is open to visitors from 10.30 am to noon and 2.30 to 4 pm and you need to get a permit from just inside the front gate. Mysore is one of India's major incense manufacturing centres, and scores of small, family-owned agarbathi factories around town export their products worldwide.

Usually handmade by women and children – a good worker can turn out at least 10,000 a day – they are made with thin slivers of bamboo, dyed red or green at one end, onto which is rolled a sandalwood putty base. The sticks are then dipped into small piles of powdered perfume and laid out to harden in the shade. You can also visit a sandalwood oil extracting plant in the suburb of Ashokapuram, about 2km southeast of Mysore Palace, and purchase oil and scented incense sticks here.

KARNATAKA

Getting There & Away

Air There are no flights to Mysore but Indian Airlines (☎ 421846) has an office next to KSTDC Hotel Mayura Hoysala, open from 10 am to 1.30 pm and 2.15 to 5 pm Monday to Saturday.

Bus The Central bus stand handles all of the KSRTC long-distance buses. The City bus stand, on KR Circle, is for city, Srirangapatnam and Chamundi Hill buses. Private long-distance bus agencies are clustered around the road junction near the Wesley Cathedral.

Nonstop KSRTC buses hurtle off to Bangalore (Rs 47/67 ordinary/semi-deluxe, three hours) every 15 minutes. For Belur, Halebid or Sravanabelagola, the usual gateway is Hassan (Rs 40, three hours). Buses depart every 30 minutes. There are only four buses to Sravanabelagola (Rs 24, 2½ hours), but services every 30 minutes to Channarayapatna (Rs 20) from where you can catch a connection. There are three buses to Hospet (Rs 145, 12 hours), where you change for Hampi. There are 13 daily buses to Ooty (Rs 54, five hours) via Bandipur National Park. Plenty of buses travel to Mangalore (Rs 80, seven hours) and there are four buses to Ernakulam (Rs 195, 12 hours). One bus heads to Gokarna (Rs 220, 14 hours) at 6 am and two go to Chennai ('superdeluxe' Rs 178, 10 hours) at 5 pm.

In addition to the KSRTC buses, there are private bus companies that run to such places as Bangalore, Mumbai, Goa, Hyderabad, Chennai, Mangalore, Ooty and Pune. Fares are higher than the KSRTC buses, but the private ones are more comfortable. To book, try Gayatri Tourism, opposite the Ritz Hotel, and nearby Kiran Tours & Travel.

From the City bus stand, bus Nos 301, 304, 305 and 306 go to Brindavan gardens (Rs 4.50), departing every 30 minutes. Bus Nos 313 and 316 leave every 40 minutes for Srirangapatnam (Rs 5). A direct private bus to Somnathpur (1½ hours) runs along Nazarabad Main Rd at around 11.45 am (Rs 14), but buses run every hour to Tirumakudal Narsipur and Bannur, where you can change to another bus for Somnathpur.

Train The booking office is open from 8 am to 2 pm and 2.15 to 8 pm Monday to Saturday and 8 am to 2 pm Sunday. There are four daily express trains to Bangalore (Rs 41/138 in 2nd/chair class, three hours), plus the air-con high-speed *Shatabdi Express* (Rs 250/550 in air-con chair/air-con executive, two hours), which departs at 2.10 pm daily except Tuesday. The *Shatabdi* continues to Chennai (Rs 630/1270 in air-con chair/air-con executive, seven hours). There are also six daily passenger trains to Bangalore (Rs 25, 2nd class only 3½ hours,), and stop at Srirangapatnam (Rs 3).

There are two passenger trains daily to Arsikere and Hassan, and one express to Mumbai on Saturday at 6 am.

Getting Around

Bus From the City bus stand, bus No 201 travels to Chamundi Hill (Rs 3.50) aproximately every 40 minutes.

Car If you intend to explore the many sights around Mysore in a car, numerous agencies at hotels and around town rent out cars from Rs 3.80 per kilometre, for a minimum of 250km per day, plus Rs 100 for the driver.

Taxi & Autorickshaw There are plenty of autorickshaws, and drivers are usually willing to use the meter. Flagfall is Rs 7 and then around Rs 3 per kilometre. Taxis are considerably more expensive and do not have meters so fares must be negotiated.

AROUND MYSORE

Somnathpur

☎ 08227

The **Keshava Temple** stands at the edge of the tranquil village of Somnathpur, 33km east of Mysore. Built in 1268 during the heyday of the Hoysala kings, it's an astonishingly beautiful building. It's also complete, unlike the larger Hoysala temples at Belur and Halebid. For more details on Hoysala architecture, see the boxed text 'Hoysala Architecture' under Belur & Halebid later in this chapter.

The walls of this star-shaped temple are covered with superb stone sculptures depicting various scenes from the Ramayana, Mahabharata and Bhagavad Gita and the life and times of the Hoysala kings. No two friezes are alike. The carved frieze, which goes around the temple, has six strips, starting with elephants at the bottom, followed by horses, a floral strip, crocodiles or lions and, finally, geese.

The temple is open from 9 am to 5.30 pm daily (US$5 in rupees). Somnathpur is just a few kilometres south of Bannur and 10km north of Tirumakudal Narsipur. It's an easy day trip from Mysore – see the earlier Mysore Getting There & Away section for public transport details.

Talakad & Sivasamudram

The remains of the capital of the 4th to 5th century Ganga dynasty, built on a bank of the Cauvery River at Talakad, are now largely buried by sand. A few buildings, including a 12th-century Hoysala temple, still poke through the surface. Once every 12 years this surreal temple is dug out for the performance of Panchalinga Darshan, and soon smothered by sand again. Talakad is 50km south-east of Mysore.

A further 25km downstream, the Cauvery suddenly drops more than 50m at the twin waterfalls at Sivasamudram; it's best seen immediately after the monsoon.

Srirangapatnam

On the Bangalore road 16km from Mysore stand the ruins of Hyder Ali's and Tipu Sultan's capital, from where they ruled much of southern India during the 18th century. In 1799, the British conquered them with the help of disgruntled local leaders. Tipu's defeat marked the real beginning of British territorial expansion in southern India.

Srirangapatnam was built on a long island in the Cauvery River. There isn't much left of it since the British did a good job of demolishing the place, but **ramparts**, battlements and some of the gates still stand.

The dungeon where Tipu held a number of British officers has been preserved. Inside the fortress walls there's a mosque and the handsome **Sri Ranganathaswamy Temple**.

About 1km east of the fort, set in ornamental gardens, is Tipu's summer palace, known as the **Daria Daulat Bagh**. After Tipu's defeat, it was temporarily the home of Colonel Arthur Wellesley (later the Duke of Wellington). Its highly decorated interior now houses a **museum** with a motley collection of family memorabilia and paintings depicting Tipu's campaigns against the British. The museum is open from 10 am to 5 pm daily except Friday (US$5 in rupees).

About 2km further east is the impressive onion-domed **Gumbaz**, or mausoleum, of Tipu and his father, Hyder Ali.

Places to Stay The best place to stay is the ***KSTDC Hotel Mayura River View*** *(☎ 08236-52114)*, beside the Cauvery River, a few kilometres from the bus stand and train station. It has eight double cottages from Rs 500 (no singles) plus an indoor/outdoor restaurant-bar. You can arrange a coracle (a saucer-shaped raft) ride with a local, but don't swim unless you want to be crocodile bait.

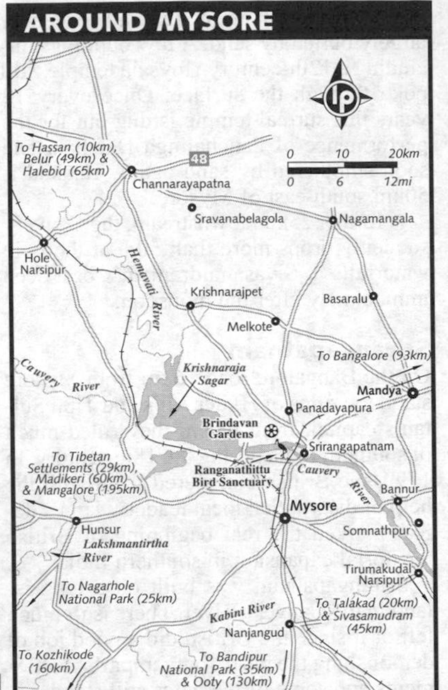

Getting There & Away Many buses ply the Mysore to Bangalore road. It's also possible to get to Srirangapatnam by passenger train. See the earlier Mysore Getting There & Away section for details.

Getting Around The points of interest are very spread out so the best plan is to hire a bicycle on the main street in the fort, about 500m from the bus stand. All the sites are signposted so it's not difficult to find your way around. There are also tongas and autorickshaws for hire. Hiring a tonga for three hours costs about Rs 75.

Ranganathittu Bird Sanctuary

This sanctuary is on one of three islands in the Cauvery River, 3km upstream from Srirangapatnam. It's a good place to see storks, ibis, egrets, spoonbills and cormorants.

The sanctuary is open from 9 am to 6 pm daily, but you should try to get there in the early morning or late afternoon to see the most birdlife. There's a foreigners' entry fee of Rs 100. It's open all year, but the best time to visit is June to November. Boats are available for hire here.

Brindavan Gardens

These tranquil ornamental gardens, laid out below the immense Krishnaraja Sagar dam, are a popular picnic spot and crowds come each night to see the illuminated fountains.

The gardens are illuminated from 6.30 to 7.25 pm (7 pm to 7.55 pm in summer) weekdays to the accompaniment of movie tunes, and to 8.25 pm (to 8.55 pm in summer) on weekends. Entry is Rs 5, plus Rs 25 for a camera permit. If you arrive by car after 4.30 pm or without a hotel booking, you'll have to walk the pleasant 1.5km stretch from the main gate, across the top of the dam, to the gardens as the road is closed to cars then.

Places to Stay *Hotel Mayura Cauvery* (☎ *08236-57252)* is the only place to stay here. Clean, basic rooms with private bathroom and partial views of the garden cost Rs 135/200. It has a restaurant with a limited menu.

Getting There & Away The gardens are 19km north-west of Mysore, and one of the KSTDC tours stops here briefly. See the earlier Mysore Getting There & Away section for details.

Tibetan Settlements

There are many Tibetan refugee settlements in the rolling hills west of Mysore, between Hunsur and Madikeri. The **Bylakuppe** area has 20 or so villages. The villages are spread out, so it's a good idea to have your own transport or to spend a couple of days and wander at your leisure. **Sera** village is the site of the Sera Je and Sera Mey monasteries, with 2500 monks. About 8km from the main road, the settlement has a guesthouse and an enormous prayer hall. There are several handicrafts operations in the area, including carpet factories (where you can get Tibetan carpets made to your own design), an incense factory and various social organisations. There are other monasteries at neighbouring settlements, including the 25-year-old Tashi Lhunpo monastery which has some 500 monks.

Sera-Jhe Health Care Committee Guest House *(☎/fax 08223-54672)* has 10 clean doubles with private bathroom for Rs 125, and there's a good restaurant downstairs. The atmosphere is very welcoming.

Mandya District

There are several beautiful Hoysala temples in the Mandya district, which stretches north and east of Mysore. The Cheluvarayaswami Temple at **Melkote**, approximately 50km north of Mysore via the town of Pandayapura, was built in the 12th century and later came under the patronage of the Mysore maharajas and even Tipu Sultan. It's an important religious centre and the **Vairamudi Festival** is held here each year during March/April, when the temple image is adorned with jewels belonging to the former maharajas of Mysore.

North of Melkote is **Nagamangala**, which was an important town even in the days of the Hoysalas. Its principal attraction is the Saumyakeshava Temple, which was built in the 12th century and later added to by the Vijayanagar kings.

Approximately 20km west of Melkote, near Krishnarajpet, is the village of **Hosaholalu**. Here you'll find the Lakshminarayana Temple, a superb example of 13th-century Hoysala temple architecture that rivals the temples at Belur and Halebid in artistry.

The village of **Basaralu**, some 25km north of Mandya, is home to the exquisite 12th-century Mallikarjuna Temple, executed in early Hoysala style. It's adorned with beautiful sculptures, including a 16-armed Shiva dancing on Andhakasura's head, and Ravana lifting Mt Kailash.

Getting to any of these towns involves the use of numerous local buses; you'll have to ask around to find the right ones as the timetables are all in Kannada. Mysore is your best base for all of them except Basaralu, for which Mandya might be better. There's a range of modest accommodation in Mandya.

BANDIPUR NATIONAL PARK

About 80km south of Mysore on the Mysore to Ooty road, this wildlife sanctuary covers 865 sq km and is part of a larger national park that also includes the neighbouring wildlife sanctuaries of Mudumalai in Tamil Nadu and Wayanad in Kerala. This was once the Mysore maharajas' private wildlife reserve.

The sanctuary is noted for herds of gaur (Indian bison), chital (spotted deer), elephants, sambar, sloth bears and langur. There are supposed to be 75 tigers, but they are rarely seen. The vegetation is a mix of deciduous and evergreen forest and scrubland.

Information

The best time to see wildlife is March to April, but the most comfortable time to visit is winter (November to February). The park is sometimes closed because of the activities of the bandit Veerappan (see the boxed text 'They Seek Him Here' in the Tamil Nadu chapter).

The park entry fee is Rs 150 per day (for foreigners) plus Rs 30 for a camera and Rs 100 for a video camera. The only way to tour the park is in the Forest Department's bus, which leaves from 6 to 9 am and 4 to 6 pm hourly and daily (Rs 15, one hour), or on elephant rides (Rs 30 per person, minimum four). Private vehicles are not allowed to tour the park. Try to avoid coming on weekends (especially Sunday), when hordes of tourists from Mysore and Ooty shatter the serenity.

Bus tours and Forest Department accommodation should be booked in advance. For reservations, contact either the Chief Wildlife Warden (☎ 080-3341993), Aranya Bhavan, 18th Cross, Malleswaram in Bangalore or the Field Director (☎ 0821-480901), Aranya Bhavan, Ashokapuram, Mysore.

Places to Stay & Eat

The Forest Department's huge deluxe ***bungalows*** have private bathroom and hot water (if there's no water shortage) and cost Rs 400. The caretaker can prepare meals if notified in advance. The bungalows must be booked at the department's wildlife offices in Mysore or Bangalore.

KSTDC's Hotel Mayura Prakruti *(☎ 08229-7301)* is on the Mysore road, 3km outside the park. Singles/doubles in the pleasant cottages cost Rs 300/400, and there are also double rooms in the main building. You can book direct or at the tourist offices in Mysore or Bangalore.

Bush Betta is a private resort about 4km from the Bandipur reception centre, off the road to Mudumalai. It has singles/doubles for US$100/180, including all meals, an elephant ride and a jeep safari. Book through the resort's Bangalore office (☎ 080-5512631, fax 5593451, ⓔ bushbetta@vsnl.com) at Gainnet, Raheja Plaza, Ground Floor, Richmond Rd. Resort guests are picked up at the Bandipur reception centre.

Tusker Trails resort is on the eastern edge of the park near Mangala village. Run by a maharaja's daughter, it has 12 twin-bed cottages, a swimming pool and a private atmosphere. Doubles are US$88 including three meals and two tours of the park. Bookings should be made in advance at Hospital Cottage (☎ 080-3342862, fax 3342862), Bangalore Palace, Bangalore.

Getting There & Away

All buses between Mysore (2½ hours) and Ooty (three hours) will drop you at Bandipur, Gundlupet or Hotel Mayura Prakruti. For other resorts you'll have to arrange private transport.

NAGARHOLE NATIONAL PARK

This 643 sq km wildlife sanctuary (also known as Rajiv Gandhi National Park) is in an isolated pocket of the Kodagu region, 93km south-west of Mysore. There are about 55 to 60 tigers as well as leopards and elephants, but you're more likely to see gaur, muntjac (barking deer), wild dogs, bonnet macaques and common langur. Facilities are minimal, but the lush forest is more attractive than Bandipur's scrubby vegetation.

As with Bandipur, foreigners pay a Rs 150 per day fee to enter the park and the only way to get around is on the bus tour (included in the fee). The best time to view wildlife is the hot months (April to May), but winter is a much more pleasant time (November to February).

KARNATAKA

Places to Stay & Eat

In Nagarhole, there are two Forest Department ***dorms*** (Rs 20 per bed), and rustic but charming ***bungalows*** (Rs 100 to 150 per double). Bookings must be made 15 days in advance with the Deputy Conservator of the Forest & Wildlife Division (☎ 08222-52041).

Kabini River Lodge, near Karapur on the Mysore to Mananthavadi road, is a former maharaja's hunting lodge. It costs US$110 per person per double, including full board and wildlife safaris. The lodge is on the southern fringe of the park, about 65km from the sanctuary's reception centre, and has access to far more of the park than the Forest Department accommodation. Book through Jungle Lodges & Resorts (☎ 080-5597025, fax 5586163, ⓔ infodesk@karnatakatourism.com) in the Shrungar Shopping Centre, MG Rd, Bangalore.

Getting There & Away

Direct buses to Nagarhole leave from Mysore's Central bus stand at 7 am and 1.30 pm and take four hours to reach the park. Jungle Lodges & Resorts can arrange private transportation to Kabini River Lodge.

MADIKERI (MERCARA)

☎ 08272 • pop 31,200

The market town of Madikeri is the capital of the Kodagu (Coorg) region, a cool green mountainous area in the south-west of Karnataka. The town centre is not particularly pretty, but it has a pleasant climate, it's a good place to organise treks and is surrounded by picturesque hills where the roads are lined with hedgerows, flowering trees, spice plantations and coffee estates.

If it seems a world apart from the rest of Karnataka, that's because Kodagu was a state in its own right until 1956. Local politicians are pushing for statehood to be restored, or at least for more local autonomy.

Orientation & Information

Madikeri is spread out along a series of ridges. The bus stand as well as most of the hotels and restaurants are in a compact area in the centre.

There's a useless tourist office in the poorly signed PWD Bungalow beside the first roundabout on the Mysore road. See Trekking following for local trekking information. Canara Bank on Gandhi Chowk changes cash and travellers cheques. Otto Cyber Centre is just downhill from the fort on the road to the bus station and costs Rs 60 per hour.

Things to See

Madikeri's **fort** was built in 1812 by Raja Lingarajendra II, and is now the municipal headquarters. The austere **Omkareshwara Temple**, just below the fort and accessible via steps going down past the police station, is an interesting blend of Keralan and Islamic architectural styles. The view from **Raja's Seat**, the garden and lookout close to Madikeri's KSTDC hotel, is superb. There is an interesting little Kodava-style **temple** next to the Raja's Seat gardens. The scenic

Abbi Falls are about 8km from the town centre. You can hike there and visit the **Raja's Tombs** on the way, or an autorickshaw will cost about Rs 120 for the return trip.

Trekking

The Kodagu region has superb trekking opportunities. Facilities are limited but there are several people in Madikeri and in guesthouses in the area who arrange guides, food, transport and accommodation. Most treks last two to three days, but longer treks of up to 10 days are possible. Overnight accommodation is usually in local houses or schools, though on one trek you can bunk down in an old palace.

The trekking season lasts from November to March. A guide is essential since you will easily get lost in the labyrinth of forest tracks without one. Trekking some obscure routes requires prior permission from the Forestry Department, which generally takes locals two days to procure. The most popular treks – to the 1700m-high peaks of Tadiyendamol and Pushpagiri, and to smaller Kotebetta – don't require permission.

Ganesh Aiyanna at Hotel Cauvery arranges all-inclusive treks for around Rs 500 per day, with a few day's advance notice. Mr Muktar at Hotel Chitra is an English-speaking guide who gets good reports. Raja Shekhar, Project Coordinator of the YHA, is another recommended trek organiser. He can be found at Friends Tours & Travels (☎ 29974) on College Rd, or (if he's away trekking) contact Rao Ganesh at Sri Ganesh Automobile on Hill Road, just up from the private bus stand. He arranges one- to three-day treks with guides costing around Rs 200 per day per person (minimum of two), plus accommodation and food (around Rs 12). Short treks will take only a day or two to prepare.

Another place to arrange treks is Coorg Tourist Travel Agency (☎ 25817) at Vinayaka Lodge.

Places to Stay

Hotel Cauvery *(☎ 25492, School Rd)* is clean, friendly and good value. Singles/doubles with private bathroom cost Rs 150/300, and there's hot water in the morning. It's central, near the main bus stand, and the owner can arrange treks as well as visits to local homes.

Vinayaka Lodge *(☎ 29830)* is virtually next to the main bus stand and is a reasonable budget option. Basic rooms with private bathroom cost Rs 130/275.

Hotel Chitra *(☎ 25191, School Rd)*, near the Cauvery, is a more upmarket place with large, clean rooms for Rs 275/330.

KSTDC'S Hotel Mayura Valley View *(☎ 28387, MG Rd)* is a 20-minute walk from the town centre near Raja's Seat. Rooms with private bathroom cost too much at Rs 300/400, dropping to 275/330 in the low season (mid-June to mid-September). It looks run-down from outside but the rooms are in reasonable shape. It also has a restaurant and great views.

Capitol Village Resort *(☎ 25929, Chettali-Siddapur Rd)*, 8km from Madikeri, is a charming lodge, beautifully located among coffee, cardamom, pepper and citrus plantations. Beds in the comfortable dorm cost Rs 250, modern cottages with private bathroom cost Rs 750 for a double, and full board is available. You can get there by hourly bus from Madikeri, or by autorickshaw (Rs 40), but call ahead as it may be full (or you can book at the Hotel Cauvery).

Hotel Rajdarshan *(☎ 29142, fax 29142, e hrdvij@vsnl.net, 116/2 MG Rd)*, on the way up to Raja's Seat, is a modern hotel and the best in town. Facilities include the Peg House, 'a well-stocked bar which would make you crazy'! Comfortable rooms cost Rs 600/700, suites are Rs 1150.

Places to Eat

The slightly gloomy restaurant at ***Hotel Cauvery*** serves the local speciality, *pandhi* (pork) curry. It's absolutely delicious, and the porkers are raised on the owner's estate. The restaurant at ***Hotel Rajdarshan*** is more expensive but the ambience is brighter. It serves the usual Indian/Chinese standards.

Hotel Veglands near the fort and ***Guruprasad***, near the bus station, is a popular cheap pure vegetarian restaurant.

Chitra Lodge and ***Hotel Mayura Valley View*** have standard hotel restaurants (and bars) – the terrace of the Mayura, overlooking the valley, is a great place for breakfast.

Getting There & Away

The KSRTC bus stand is close to the centre of town and handles public buses to destinations outside Kodagu. There are frequent buses (roughly every 30 minutes) to Bangalore (Rs 86/114 semi/superdeluxe, six hours) and Mysore (Rs 40/46, three hours) from 6.30 am to 11 pm. Regular buses also go to Mangalore (Rs 46/61, four hours), Hassan (Rs 40, 3½ hours) and Shimoga (Rs 86, seven hours).

The private bus stand is predominantly for local buses within the Kodagu region. Early morning buses are less crowded than later ones. The scenery on local roads is beautiful.

AROUND MADIKERI

Several guesthouses and resorts, highly recommended by travellers, have opened in the **Kodavu Hills**. The owners can arrange plantation tours and recommend local hiking routes. It's a good area for bird-watching and its tropical variant – bug-watching.

Kakkabe

The village of Kakkabe, 35km from Madikeri, is close to plantation guesthouses. One, ***Honey Valley Estate*** *(☎ 08272-38339)*, is in the middle of a forest, so it doesn't get much more peaceful. Rooms cost Rs 200/350. The guesthouse also has small library. It's only accessible by jeep or by walking; call in advance to arrange transport.

Yavakapudi

Palace Estate *(☎ 08272-38446)*, at Yavakapudi, a Rs 50 jeep ride from Kakkabe, gets high praise for hospitality and home cooking. Rooms cost Rs 200/300.

Bittangala

Near Virajpet, 35km south of Madikeri at Bittangala village is ***Cicada Trails Guesthouse*** *(☎ 08272-54826, 57399)*. Double rooms are Rs 600, dorm beds Rs 175, with a large lower veranda for relaxing on. The guesthouse arranges treks.

Ammathi

Alath-Cad Estate Bungalow *(☎ 08274-52190, fax 52589, ⓔ alathcd@vsnl.com)* is on a 26-hectare coffee plantation about 28km from Madikeri, 1.5km from the town of Ammathi. Double rooms in the 100-year-old house cost Rs 750 and Rs 900.

Gallibedu

Mojo Plantation Guesthouse *(☎ 08272-24136, fax 28638, ⓔ wapred.india@vsnl.com)* is situated on an organically farmed plantation about 12km from Madikeri near Gallibedu. There are two comfortable double rooms for Rs 1500, an extensive collection of blues music and the opportunity for bird-watching, local walks and learning about their environmental activities. A number of French travellers have raved about the food here.

Siddapur

The village of Siddapur, 32km south of Madikeri, is home to the highly rated ***Orange County Resort***. Situated on a 120-hectare plantation, accommodation is in mock Tudor cottages with all mod cons. The adjoining Dubare Reserve Forest extends to Nagarhole National Park, which some people visit from here. Including taxes, twin cottages cost from Rs 4290 to 5270, while four-person cottages are Rs 9950. Book through Ramapuram Holiday Resorts *(☎ 558 2380, fax 558 2435, ⓔ rhrl@vsnl .com)* in Bangalore.

HASSAN

☎ 08172 • pop 121,000

Hassan is a convenient base from which to explore Belur (38km), Halebid (33km) and Sravanabelagola (48km), since it's the nearest big town with a range of hotels and the closest railhead to all three sights. However, rail services to Mangalore have been disrupted for several years due to line conversion work; see Getting There & Away at the end of this section.

There are ample bus connections to compensate for the rail disruption, so you'll still almost certainly pass through here, but apart from a few reasonable hotels, Hassan has nothing to offer.

Information

The tourist office (☎ 68862), which is in the Vartha Bhavan building on the Bangalore-Mangalore Rd, is open from 10 am to 5.30 pm daily except Sunday. For foreign exchange, go to the State Bank of Mysore on Bus Stand Rd. Cyber Park, next to Vaishnavi Lodging on Harsha Mahal Rd, costs Rs 35 per hour for Internet access.

Places to Stay

Vaishnavi Lodging *(☎ 67413, Harsha Mahal Rd)*, a one-minute walk from the bus stand, is good value at Rs 110/170 for clean singles/doubles with private bathroom.

Hotel Lakshmi Prasanna *(☎ 68391, Subhas Square)*, in the centre of town, has decent cheap rooms with private bathroom and bucket hot water for Rs 95/140.

Hotel DR Karigowda Residency *(☎ 65406)*, on Bangalore-Mangalore Rd, is great value – clean and quiet with large rooms for only Rs 200/250.

Hotel Suvarna Regency *(☎ 64006, fax 63822, Bangalore-Mangalore Rd)* is slightly more upmarket, but still good value, with rooms for Rs 275/400, and air-con doubles for Rs 550.

Hotel Hassan Ashok *(☎ 68731, fax 68324, Bangalore-Mangalore Rd)* is government-run and overpriced. Rooms cost Rs 1200/1600, or Rs 1600/2300 with air-con and there's a restaurant.

The best hotel in town is ***Southern Star*** *(☎ 51816, fax 68916, e sshassan@vsnl.com, Bangalore-Mangalore Rd)*. Its well-appointed, comfortable rooms cost Rs 850/1050, or Rs 1050/1250 with air-con. Any complaints? It gets some noise from the nearby highway.

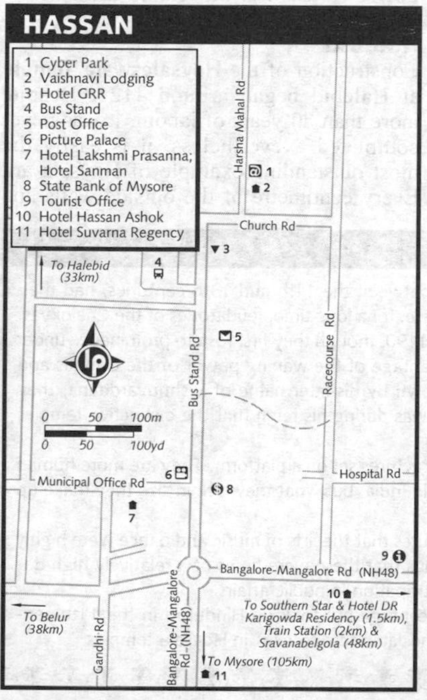

Places to Eat

Hotel Sanman and ***Hotel Lakshmi Prasanna*** have very popular vegetarian restaurants serving thalis for Rs 15.

Hotel GRR across from the bus stand offers cheap, filling Andhra-style thalis on plantain leaves for Rs 15.

Karwar Restaurant, in the Southern Star hotel, is the fanciest in town and offers vegetarian, nonvegetarian and Chinese dishes. Chicken curries cost around Rs 80.

Getting There & Away

Bus If you intend visiting Belur and Halebid on the same day from Hassan, go to Halebid first as there are more buses from Belur to Hassan and they run until much later.

There are hourly buses from Hassan to Halebid (Rs 11, one hour). The first bus departs at 7.15 am, and the last bus back to Hassan leaves Halebid at 6.30 pm. There are also lots of buses from Hassan to Belur (Rs 13, 1½ hours). The first leaves Hassan at 6 am and there are buses from Belur to Hassan until late in the evening.

There are four direct buses to Sravanabelagola (Rs 15, 1½ hours), but the first one doesn't leave until 12.45 pm. It's easier to catch one of the frequent buses to Channarayapatna (Rs 13, one hour) and then another bus or minivan to Sravanabelagola from there.

There are frequent buses to Mysore (Rs 31, three hours) and Bangalore (Rs 48, four hours). The first bus to both cities leaves at 5.15 am and the last departs at 7.45 pm.

Train The train station is about 2km east of town; Rs 10 by autorickshaw. There are passenger trains to Mysore at 6 am and 6.30 pm (Rs 22, three hours). There are no services to Mangalore until the line has been converted to broad gauge.

Taxi Hordes of taxi drivers hang out on the road just north of the bus stand so it's easy to negotiate a good fare for a tour of Belur and Halebid. Expect to pay around Rs 500 for the day. A taxi to Sravanabelagola costs about Rs 300.

BELUR & HALEBID

☎ 08177

The Hoysala temples at Halebid (Halebeed, Halebidu) and Belur, along with the one at

Somnathpur, east of Mysore, are the cream of one of the most artistically exuberant periods of Hindu cultural development. Their sculptural decoration rivals that of Khajuraho (Madhya Pradesh) and Konark (Orissa).

Belur

The **Channekeshava Temple** at Belur is the only one at the three major Hoysala sites still in daily use – try to be there for the daily ceremonies at around 10 am and 7 pm. Begun in 1116 to commemorate the Hoysala's victory over the Cholas at Talakad, it was worked on for over a century. Its exterior is not, in the lower friezes, as extensively sculptured as the other Hoysala temples, but the work higher up on the walls is unsurpassed in detail and artistry. Particularly interesting are angled bracket figures depicting female figures dancing or in ritual poses. Much decorative work can also be found on the internal supporting pillars and lintels. It is said that every major Hindu deity is represented here.

The temple, which is enclosed in a paved compound, includes a well and also a bathing tank. The temple's 14th-century seven-storey gopuram has some sensual sculptures explicitly portraying the apres-temple activities of dancing girls.

Open daily from sunrise to sunset (free). Guides can be hired for Rs 50 and are very helpful in explaining the significance of the detailed sculptural work.

The other, lesser, Hoysala temples at Belur are the **Chennigaraya** and the **Viranarayana**.

Places to Stay & Eat The new ***Hotel Vishnu Regency*** *(☎ 23011, Kempegowda Rd)* has marble floors and comfortable beds. The cheapest rooms are good value at Rs 125/250, while larger doubles cost Rs 300 or Rs 400 with air-con. From the bus stand, walk up Temple Rd and turn left at the statue; it's about 150m further on. There's a North Indian restaurant here.

KSTDC Hotel Mayura Velapuri *(☎ 22 209, Temple Rd)* is basic but serviceable – some rooms are in better condition than others. Singles/doubles cost Rs 160/190. There's a fairly bland restaurant/bar serving vegetarian/nonvegetarian food and Western breakfasts. The hotel is between the bus stand and the temple.

Sri Vishnu Krupa *(☎ 22263)* is on the town's main road, a short walk from the bus stand. It has reasonable but uninspiring doubles with private bathroom for Rs 125 and Rs 250 (with TV) and small, cheaper rooms with hard beds for Rs 50/75. It also has a vegetarian restaurant.

Hotel Shankar, 200m before the temple, is the most popular of the town's handful of basic restaurants. There's also an ***Indian Coffee House*** near the temple entrance.

Halebid

Construction of the **Hoysaleswara Temple** at Halebid began around 1121. Despite more than 80 years of labour, it was never completed. Nevertheless, it is easily the most outstanding example of Hoysala art. Every centimetre of the outside walls and

Hoysala Architecture

The Hoysalas, who ruled this part of the Deccan between the 11th and 13th centuries, had their origins in the hill tribes of the Western Ghats and were, for a long time, feudatories of the Chalukyas. They did not become fully independent until about 1190, though they first rose to prominence under their leader Tinayaditya (1047–78), who took advantage of the waning power of the Gangas and Rashtrakutas. Under Bittiga (1110–52), better known by his later name of Vishnuvardhana, they began to take off on a course of their own and it was during his reign that the distinctive temples at Belur and Halebid were built.

Typically, these temples are squat, star-shaped structures set on a platform. They are more human in scale than the soaring temples found elsewhere in India, but what they lack in size they make up for in sheer intricacy.

It's quickly apparent from a study of these sculptures that the arts of music and dance were highly regarded during the Hoysala period. It's also obvious that these were times of a relatively high degree of sexual freedom and prominent female participation in public affairs.

The Hoysalas converted to Jainism in the 10th century, but took up Hinduism in the 11th century. This is why images of Shaivite, Vaishnavite and Jain sects co-exist in Hoysala temples.

much of the interior is covered with an endless variety of Hindu deities, sages, stylised animals and birds, and friezes depicting the life of the Hoysala rulers.

The temple is set in a well-tended garden, and there's a small **museum** adjacent to it housing a collection of sculptures. The temple is open from sunrise to sunset daily; admission is free. The museum is open from 10 am to 5 pm daily except Friday.

Halebid also has a smaller temple known as **Kedareswara** and a little-visited enclosure containing three **Jain *bastis*** (temples), which also have fine carvings.

Places to Stay & Eat The only place to stay here is the peaceful ***KSTDC Mayura Shantala*** (☎ *73224)*, set in a pleasant garden across the road from the Hoysaleswara Temple. There are four clean rooms with private bathroom for Rs 150/200, or one cheaper room for Rs 100/150. There's a restaurant that serves basic meals, and also a couple of rustic local eateries along the main road.

Getting There & Away

Belur and Halebid are only 16km apart. Crammed small trucks shuttle between the two towns every 30 minutes from around 6 am to 9 pm (Rs 5). See the previous Hassan section for details of buses to/from there. There are a few buses a day from Halebid to Mysore and many buses from Belur to Mysore. Belur is something of a transport hub, with direct buses to Bangalore, Mangalore, Dharmastala, Sravanabelagola (11.30 am) and Arsikere (for trains to Bangalore). If you're heading to Hampi, you'll need to catch a bus from Halebid to Shimoga (three hours) and pick up a bus to Hospet (five hours), Hampi's access point, from there.

SRAVANABELAGOLA

☎ 08176 • pop 4000

This is one of the oldest and most important Jain pilgrimage centres in India, and the site of the huge 17m-high naked statue of Gomateshvara (Bahubali). Said to be the world's tallest monolithic statue, it overlooks the sedate country town of Sravanabelagola from the top of the bald rock of Vindhyagiri Hill. Its simplicity and serenity is in complete contrast to the complexity and energy of the sculptural work at the temples of Belur and Halebid. The word Sravanabelagola means the Monk of the White Pond.

History

Sravanabelagola has a long pedigree, going back to the 3rd century BC when Chandragupta Maurya came here with his guru, Bhagwan Bhadrabahu Swami, after renouncing his kingdom. Bhadrabahu's disciples spread his teachings all over the region, firmly establishing Jainism in the south. The religion found powerful patrons in the Gangas who ruled southern Karnataka between the 4th and 10th centuries, the zenith of Jainism's influence.

Information

The helpful tourist office is at the foot of the stairway up Vindhyagiri Hill and is open from 10 am to 5.30 pm daily except Sunday. There's no entry fee to the site, but a donation is encouraged.

Gomateshvara Statue

The statue of Gomateshvara (Bahubali) was created during the reign of the Ganga king, Rachamalla. It was commissioned by a military commander in the service of Rachamalla and carved out of granite by the sculptor Aristenemi in AD 981. Bahubali's father was the great Emperor Vrishabhadeva, who became the first Jain *tirthankar* (revered Jain teacher, literally 'ford crosser'), Adinath. Bahubali and his brother Bharatha competed fiercely for the right to succeed their father but, on the point of victory, Bahubali realised the futility of the struggle and renounced his kingdom. He withdrew from the material world and entered the forest, where he began to meditate in complete stillness until he attained enlightenment. The statue has vines curling around his legs and an anthill at his feet, signs of his utter detachment. The gallery around his statue has many smaller images of Jain tirthankars.

The statue stands atop Vindhyagiri Hill and is reached by 614 rock-cut steps. You must leave your shoes at the foot of the hill, which is a problem in summer since the steps become scalding. You're not supposed to wear socks, but it might well be necessary.

Every 12 years, the statue of Bahubali is anointed with thousands of pots of coconut milk, yogurt, ghee, bananas, jaggery, dates, almonds, poppy seeds, sandalwood, milk

KARNATAKA

and saffron during the Mahamastakabhisheka ceremony. The next ceremony is to be held in 2005.

Temples

In addition to the statue of Bahubali there are several interesting Jain *bastis* (temples) and *mathas* (monasteries) in the town and on Chandragiri Hill, the smaller of the two hills between which Sravanabelagola nestles.

Two of these, the **Bhandari Basti** and the **Akkana Basti**, are in the Hoysala style, and a third, the **Chandragupta Basti**, is believed to have been built by Emperor Ashoka. The well-preserved paintings in one of the temples are like a 600-year-old comic strip of Jain stories.

Places to Stay & Eat

Nearly all of Sravanabelagola's accommodation is run by the local Jain organisation SDJMI, whose central accommodation office (☎ 57258) handles bookings for 21 guesthouses in town. Most are efficiently run and indistinguishable. They generally cost Rs 135, for a double, though the pick of the bunch, ***Yatri Nivas***, costs Rs 160/210 for a double/triple. The accommodation office is behind the Vidyananda Nilaya Dharamsala, just before the bus stand on the way into town.

Hotel Raghu *(☎ 57238)*, about 50m from the bottom of the stairway climbing Vindhyagiri Hill, is the only privately owned establishment. Basic but decent singles/doubles/triples with private bathroom and hot water in the mornings cost Rs 50/100/150. It also has a popular vegetarian restaurant downstairs.

There are chai shops and basic vegetarian restaurants in the street leading to the foot of Vindhyagiri Hill.

Getting There & Away

There are four buses a day to Hassan (Rs 14, one hour); three to Belur (Rs 28, 2½ hours); four to Bangalore (Rs 41, three hours); and one to Mysore at 7.30 am (Rs 24, 2½ hours). Nearly all long-distance buses leave in the morning or at lunch time; there's very little transport after 2 pm. If you miss one of the early buses, catch a local bus 10km northwest to Channarayapatna, which is on the main Bangalore-Mangalore road and has plenty of connections.

Coast & Western Ghats

MANGALORE

☎ 0824 • pop 480,000

At one time Mangalore was the major port of Hyder Ali's kingdom; today it's a centre for the export of coffee and cashew nuts and the production of rust-red Mangalore roof tiles. It has a languid tropical atmosphere and a significant Catholic community dating back to the arrival of the Portuguese in 1526. The language of the surrounding district is Tulu, a Dravidian tongue related to Malayali and Kannada. If you're passing this way, it can make a convenient overnight stop, and there are some interesting local sights.

Orientation

Mangalore is hilly and has winding, disorienting streets. Fortunately, all the hotels and restaurants, the City bus stand and the train station are in or around the hectic city centre. The KSRTC long-distance bus stand is 3km to the north; you'll need to take an autorickshaw (about Rs 15).

Information

The tourist office (☎ 442946) is in the former Hotel Indraprastha. It's open 10.30 am to 5.30 pm daily except Sunday.

Several banks have foreign exchange facilities; more efficient (for travellers cheques) is Trade Wings travel agency on Lighthouse Hill Rd. Bank of Baroda, nearby on Balmatta Rd, gives cash advances on Visa and MasterCard for the usual Rs 100 plus 1% commission.

For Internet access I-Net 107 Cyber Cafe on KS Rao Rd is a stylish setup charging Rs 60 per hour. It's open from 9 am to 11.30 pm daily. Kohinoor Computer Zone on Lighthouse Hill Rd is cheaper at Rs 50 per hour, but it's hot and stuffy inside.

Athree Book Centre on Balmatta Rd is full of books on a range of subjects.

Things to See

The main remnant of the past is the **Sultan's Battery**, a stone watchtower 4km from the centre on the headland of the old port. A No 16 bus from the city centre will get you there.

EDDIE GERALD
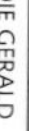

GREG ELMS

GREG ELMS

The sensuous and the spiritual combine in Karnataka: exquisite silks and floral garlands are worn by a bridal couple at a Hampi wedding **(top)**; colourful *tikka* powder is sold to devout Hindus to mark their foreheads **(bottom right)**; and fragrant garlands are sold in a Mysore stall **(bottom left)**

SARA-JANE CLELAND

EDDIE GERALD

Top: Once the capital of one of the largest Hindu empires, Vijayanagar features some of India's most fascinating ruins and is today one of Karnataka's most visited sights.
Bottom: Nandi (Shiva's bull vehicle) is found on Karnataka's Chamundi Hill overlooking Mysore.

Shreemanthi Bai Memorial Government Museum is about 1km east of the KSRTC bus stand (take bus No 19). It's open from 9 am to 5 pm daily except Monday. The town boasts some attractive temples. The Keralan-style **Kadri Manjunatha Temple**, whose Lokeshwara statue is one of the best bronzes in India (take bus No 3, 4 or 6), and the painted ceiling of **St Aloysius College Chapel** (open from 8.30 to 10 am, 12.30 to 1 pm and 3.30 to 6 pm) are also worth a look. If you've still got time, try **Rosario Cathedral**, **Sri Gokarnanatha Temple** or **Mangladevi Temple** (the latter gave the town its name).

Places to Stay – Budget

Hotel Manorama *(☎ 440306, KS Rao Rd)* has large and clean single/double rooms with private bathroom costing from Rs 145/231. Air-con doubles go for Rs 450.

Hotel Roopa *(☎ 421271, Balmatta Rd)* has OK rooms with private bathroom for Rs 125/184 and air-con doubles for Rs 450. There are a couple of good restaurants here.

Places to Stay – Mid-Range & Top End

Hotel Srinivas *(☎ 440061, GHS Rd)* is a massive hotel one block west of KS Rao Rd, with a range of rooms. Singles/doubles start from Rs 250/300, while air-con doubles are Rs 600.

Hotel Mangalore International *(☎ 444 860, KS Rao Rd)* is a business class hotel with well-appointed rooms from Rs 530/630, or Rs 750/850 with air-con, including

MANGALORE

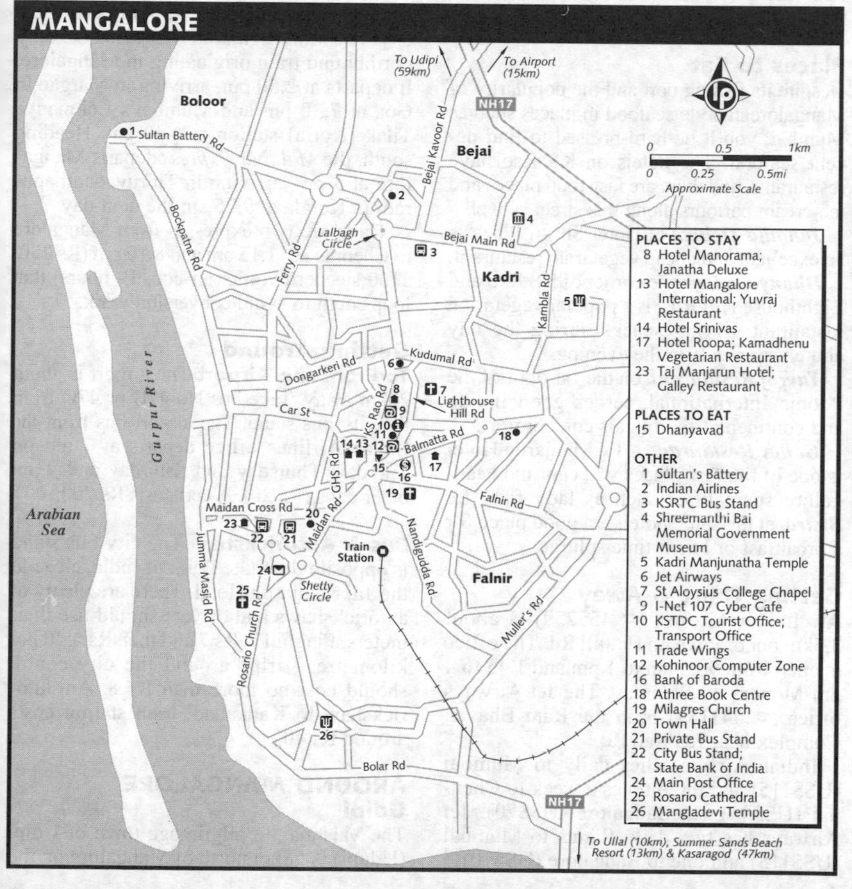

KARNATAKA

breakfast. There are a couple of restaurants and fast-food places in this complex, but alcohol is not permitted. You must check out within 24 hours.

Taj Manjarun Hotel *(☎ 420420, fax 420585,* **e** *manjarun.mangalore@tajhotels.com, Old Port Rd)* is the top hotel in town. Air-con rooms cost from US$30/45, up to US$95 for the suite. It has a good restaurant and a swimming pool.

Summer Sands Beach Resort *(☎ 467 690, fax 467693,* **e** *summer@satyam.net.in)* is 13km south of Mangalore on pristine Ullal Beach. Pleasant rooms in bungalows cost Rs 580/780, while suites cost Rs 695/865. You can spend a day at the beach here for Rs 25 (the fee is redeemable at the restaurant). An autorickshaw from Mangalore costs Rs 65, or catch bus No 44D from the City bus stand.

Places to Eat

Despite its fishing port and the popularity of Mangalorean-style seafood in places such as Mumbai, you'll be hard-pressed to find decent seafood. The hotels on KS Rao have restaurants, and there are fast-food places and ice-cream parlours along this street as well.

Janatha Deluxe at Hotel Shaan Plaza is an excellent and cheap vegetarian restaurant.

Dhanyavad, on the corner of KS Rao and Lighthouse Hill Rds, is a popular vegetarian restaurant serving snacks during the day and cheap meals in the evening.

Yuvraj Restaurant, on the 1st floor of the Poonja International, serves good Indian and continental food in air-con comfort.

Galley Restaurant at Taj Manjarun Hotel is one of the few places you can find Mangalore specialities such as lady fish. ***Le Bistro***, at the same hotel, is a good place for a breakfast or lunch-time splurge.

Getting There & Away

Air Indian Airlines (☎ 455259) is about 3.5km out of town on Hathill Rd. The office is open from 9.25 am to 1 pm and 1.45 to 4 pm Monday to Saturday. The Jet Airways office (☎ 441181) is in the Ram Bhavan Complex near KS Rao Rd.

Indian Airlines flies daily to Mumbai (US$115) and three times a week to Chennai (US$95) via Bangalore (US$70). Jet Airways has two daily flights to Mumbai (US$115) and one to Bangalore (US$70).

Bus The KSRTC long-distance bus stand is about 3km north of the city centre. It's fairly orderly with daily deluxe departures to Bangalore (Rs 117/186, ordinary/deluxe, nine hours), Panaji (Rs 193 deluxe, 10 hours), Hassan (Rs 67/90, six hours), Madikeri (Rs 46/73, four hours), Mysore (Rs 86/134, seven hours) and Kochi (Rs 250 deluxe, 10 hours). There are also long-distance departures to Mumbai, Chennai and Hospet.

Private buses running to other destinations (including Udipi, Sringeri and Mudabidri) operate from the bus stand opposite the city bus stand.

Several private bus companies have their offices on Falnir Rd.

Train The train station is south of the city centre. However, Konkan Railway trains stop at Kankanadi station, 5km east of the city. The *Matsyagandha Express* is the only northbound train originating in Mangalore. It departs at 2.50 pm, arriving in Margao in Goa at 7.30 pm and Mumbai's Lokmanya Tilak (Kurla) station at 6.40 am. Heading south, the *Malabar Express* departs Mangalore at 5 pm, arriving in Thiruvananthapuram in Kerala at 9.25 am the next day.

There are two expresses from Mangalore to Chennai at 11.15 am and 8.10 pm (Rs 250/1160 sleeper/two-tier air-con, 19 hours) that loop south to avoid conversion work.

Getting Around

To/From the Airport The airport is about 20km away. Take bus No 47B or 47C from the city bus stand. The airport bus from the Indian Airlines office departs at 7 am on Tuesday, Thursday and Saturday and 9 am other days (Rs 20). A taxi costs Rs 200.

Bus & Autorickshaw The city bus stand is opposite the State Bank of India, close to the Taj Manjarun Hotel. There are plenty of autorickshaws and drivers should use their meters. Flagfall is Rs 7 and then Rs 4.20 per kilometre – trips around the city centre should cost no more than Rs 8. An autorickshaw to Kankanadi train station costs around Rs 40.

AROUND MANGALORE

Udipi

The Vaishnavite pilgrimage town of Udipi (Udupi) is 58km north of Mangalore on the

Buffalo Surfing

Kambla, the Canarese sport of buffalo racing, first became popular in the early part of the 20th century, when farmers would race their buffalo home after a day in the fields. The event took off in the 1950s and 1960s, and today the best of the races are big business. Up to 50,000 spectators may attend top events. The racing buffaloes are extremely valuable, and are pampered and prepared like thoroughbreds. A good animal can cost over Rs 300,000.

The events are held in the Dakshina Kannada region, between about October and March every year, when the paddy fields have enough water in them for racing. Although the racing 'season' is still observed, the exact timings are becoming less important as nowadays specially prepared tracks are often laid out. The 120m-long tracks are laid parallel to each other and the fastest pairs of buffalo can cover the distance through water and mud in around 14 seconds. There are two versions: In one, the man runs alongside the buffalo; in the other, he rides on a board fixed to a ploughshare, literally surfing his way down the track behind the beasts. It's an amazing sight. For those who don't believe that these lumbering beasts can really move, look out!

coastal road. The 13th-century religious leader, Madhvacharya, lived and preached here, and the town's Krishna Temple draws many pilgrims. The modern town is an unprepossessing mix of hotels, shopping centres and traffic.

The Krishna Temple, in the centre of town, is not too impressive to look at, but it's worth being around for the commotion when one of the daily ceremonies begins. There are 14 daily acts of worship by the swami in charge of the temple – pilgrims are herded out of the way, the temple elephants trumpet and a row of chanting monks pass in procession.

Frequent buses run to Mangalore and points further north.

Sringeri

The southern seat of the orthodox Hindu hierarchy is in Sringeri, a small, unspoilt town nestled among the lush coffee-growing hills of Chikmagalur, about 100km north-east of Mangalore. The interesting Vidyashankar Temple has zodiac pillars and a huge paved courtyard. A second temple is dedicated to Sharada, the goddess of learning. The Tunga River flows past the temple complex and hundreds of fish gather at the ghats to be hand-fed by pilgrims. There's a range of cheap pilgrim accommodation; report to the reception centre (☎ 50123) next to the temple entrance to be allocated a room.

Dharmastala

There are a number of Jain bastis in Dharmastala, 75km east of Mangalore, including the famous Manjunatha Temple. There's also a 14m-high statue of Bahubali, which was erected in 1973, and a museum (Rs 1). The height of the festival season begins here with Diwali, and includes the three-day **Manjunatheshwara Festival** in November. There are regular buses to Dharmastala from in Mangalore.

Venur

Venur, approximately 50km north-east of Mangalore, has eight bastis and the ruins of a Mahadeva temple. An 11m-high **Bahubali statue**, dating back to 1604, stands on the southern bank of the Gurupur River.

Mudabidri

There are 18 bastis in Mudabidri, 35km north-east of Mangalore. The oldest of them is the 15th-century Chandranatha Temple, known colloquially as the 1000-pillar hall.

Karkal

A further 20km north of Mudabidri, at Karkal, are several important temples and a 13m-high Gomateshvara (Bahubali), finished in 1432. The statue is on a small, serene hillock on the outskirts of the town. There are good views of the Western Ghats.

JOG FALLS

☎ 08186

Jog Falls may be the highest in India, but they're not the most spectacular: The Linganamakki Dam further up the Sharavati River limits the water flow. The falls are more voluminous during the monsoons. There are actually four falls; the longest drop of 253m is known as The Raja.

The setting is superb and the countryside is perfect for gentle hiking. You can hike to the bottom of the falls by following the steps that start close to the bus stand; watch out for leeches during the wet season.

Places to Stay & Eat

There are two ***forest resthouses*** with rooms costing Rs 75 per person. One is on the left, about 1km down the road to the coast from the falls; the other is 300m farther down on the right and unsigned behind a blue and green fence.

KSTDC'S Hotel Mayura Gerusoppa *(☎ 44732)* is wonderfully situated overlooking the falls, about 150m from the car park. It offers quiet rooms for Rs 150/200 and a restaurant. But like many KSTDC hotels, it isn't as well maintained as you'd like.

Woodlands Hotel *(☎ 47325)* has basic rooms from Rs 65/150 to 150/250.

One side of the car park at the falls is lined with about a dozen ***chai stalls***. Most serve cheap and tasty omelettes, thalis, fried noodles and fried rice, as well as hot and cold drinks.

Getting There & Away

Bus Jog Falls has good bus connections. The roads to/from the coast are fairly tortuous – the road from Manki is more spectacular, but also more likely to make you sick than the road from Bhatkal.

There are buses about every 45 minutes to Shimoga (2½ hours), three a day to Siddapur, two to Karwar and one to Gokarna (via Kumta) and to Bhatkal.

Train The nearest train station is at Talguppa, between Sagar and Jog Falls. There are two trains a day to Shimoga, on a wonderfully slow and scenic narrow-gauge line.

GOKARNA

☎ 08386

The town of Gokarna (Cow's Ear), 50km south of Karwar, attracts an unlikely mixture of Hindu pilgrims, Sanskrit scholars, beach-loving travellers and a hardcore hippy element, which shifted here when things got way uncool in Goa. For Hindus, Gokarna is one of the most sacred sites in South India. It's a sleepy, charming town with wooden houses on the main street and some attractive traditional houses in nearby alleys. Some of locals feel the foreign influx has debased the holy atmosphere, but others are quite happy with the extra income generated.

Information

You can change cash and travellers cheques at poor rates at the Om Lodge. The Pai STD shop on Main St gives slightly better rates but for a bank you'll need to go to Karwar. There's a small sub post office at the junction of Car and Main Sts, and you can make international calls from several STD/ISD places. Internet at Hotel Om costs Rs 60 per hour, but connections are pretty bad.

Temples

At the western end of Car St is the **Mahabaleshwara Temple**, home to a revered Shiva lingam. Nearby is the **Ganapati Temple**, which honours the role that Ganesh played in rescuing the lingam. Near the temple are two enormous **chariots**, which are dragged along the main street on Shivaratri in Febrary/March, the night when Shiva danced the cosmic *tandava* dance.

At the eastern end of the streets is the **Venkataraman Temple** and 100m south of this is **Koorti Teertha**, the large temple tank, where locals, pilgrims, and immaculately dressed Brahmins perform their ablutions next to dhobi-wallahs (people who wash clothes) on the ghats.

Beaches

Travellers have been drifting into Gokarna for some time now, lured by stories of beaches that rival anything Goa has to offer. Although Gokarna village has its own beach, the closest decent stretch of sand is **Kudle Beach** (pronounced 'kood-lee'), a 20-minute walk to the south. To reach it, follow the footpath that begins on the southern side of the Ganapati Temple and heads southwards (if you reach the bathing tank, you've taken the wrong path).

The track soon climbs to the top of a barren headland with expansive sea views. On the southern side of the headland is the first in a series of four perfect half-moon beaches, hemmed in by headlands and backed by the foothills of the Western Ghats. There are five or six chai shops on Kudle Beach, all offering basic snacks, drinks and accommodation.

At the southern end of Kudle a track climbs over the next headland and a further 20-minute walk brings you to **Om Beach**. A dusty road provides vehicle access to this beach but it's almost deserted on weekdays. On weekends there can be carloads of Indian men parading on the beach in their Y-fronts, ogling the allegedly hot-for-it foreign women. There's a handful of chai shops and beach shacks here. The other beaches – **Half-Moon** and **Paradise** – are a series of 30-minute walks to the south, each one more isolated. There's a couple of palm-thatch shelters for rent on Paradise Beach, but nothing permanent on Half Moon. It's risky to walk between the beaches and Gokarna after dark – it's easy to get lost and muggings have occurred. It's safe to leave valuables and bulk belongings at the Vaibhav Niwas and Nimmu lodges in Gokarna, which charge small fees for storage.

Places to Stay

The choice in Gokarna is between the rudimentary huts right on the beach or the basic but more comfortable options in town. The advantages of being on the beach are obvious and, since it's a decent hike from town, you're pretty much left to your own devices – highly appreciated by those travellers who like the odd chillum for breakfast.

Beaches The ***huts*** on the beach, mainly at Kudle and Om, cost from Rs 30 for basic palm-thatch shacks to Rs 75 for lockable mud or brick huts in high season (December and January). They're mostly just a space to stash your gear and sleep on the floor at night, so bring a sleeping bag or a bedroll. Padlocks are provided and the huts are secure. Communal washing and toilet facilities are basic but there is fresh water.

Exceptions include ***Shiva Prasad***, at the south end of Kudle Beach, and ***Namaste*** on Om Beach. Both have basic rooms with fan and shared bathrooms for Rs 100.

Gokarna There are a handful of good guesthouses in town.

Nimmu House *(☎ 56730, ⓔ amithgn@blr.vnsl.net.in)* is a relaxed family-run place just back from the town beach, on a side street near the Mahabaleshwara Temple. Simple doubles with shared bathroom cost Rs 70 to 100, and the upstairs doubles with private bathroom are Rs 125; there are discounts in the low season. Internet use is Rs 100 per hour.

Vaibhav Niwas *(☎ 46714)* is a cosy, relaxed guesthouse set back from the main road on the way into town. Small but acceptable rooms with shared bathroom cost Rs 40/75 and doubles with private bathroom cost Rs 100 to 125.

New Prasad Nilaya *(☎ 57135)* is a friendly, modern hotel. It has plain rooms with private bathroom for Rs 150 and larger rooms with balcony for Rs 200. The hotel is on a small side road off the main street near the bus stand.

Om Lodge *(☎ 56445)*, nearby on the same lane, has shabby doubles with private bathroom for Rs 100 and four-bed rooms for Rs 200.

Shastri Guest House *(☎ 56220, Main St)* is a reasonable budget option near the bus stand. Quite large rooms with balconies cost Rs 50/100/160.

Hotel Gokarn International *(☎ 56622)* about 500m up the main road from the bus stand is a decent new place with a mostly Indian clientele. Rooms are Rs 150/200, deluxe doubles are Rs 300 and air-con doubles cost Rs 600. There's a bar, two small restaurants (vegetarian and nonvegetarian) and an ice-cream parlour.

Places to Eat

The ***chai shops*** on all of the beaches can rustle up basic snacks and meals.

Ganga Cafe, at the northern end of Kudle Beach, is a pleasant place for a meal or cold drink. ***Namaste Cafe*** at the start of Om Beach is also very good, and sometimes offers fresh seafood as well as cold beers.

Prema Restaurant, upstairs in the alley next to the Mahabaleshwara Temple, serves good masala dosas (Rs 13) and coffee milkshakes, as well travellers' fare such as pasta (Rs 40) and papaya porridge. ***Vaibhav Niwas*** also serves travellers' fare. ***Pai Restaurant***, halfway along Main St, has cheap, light vegetarian meals and masala dosas.

Getting There & Away

Bus Gokarna has an oversized bus stand just off Main St as you enter town.

Buses head to Karwar every hour (Rs 20, 1½ hours), but there are frequent private buses to Ankola where you can change to a local Karwar-bound bus. Karwar is also the place to pick up a bus for Goa. There are four buses to Hubli in the morning and one just after lunch. There's a direct 6.45 am bus to Mangalore. If you miss this, catch a local bus to Kumta (25km south), then one of the more-frequent Mangalore buses from there.

There's one deluxe bus to Bangalore (Rs 242, 12 hours), one to Hospet (for Hampi; Rs 105, 10 hours) at 7 am and one deluxe bus to Mysore (Rs 225, 12 hours).

Train The Konkan Railway is the best way to reach Goa, Mangalore and everywhere else along this line, even though only a couple of slow passenger trains currently stop at Gokarna Road station, 9km from town. Buses run out to the station at 11 am in time for the 11.30 am train to Margao. The south-bound train departs Gokarna Road at 4.25 pm. Autorickshaws want about Rs 75 to take you out to the station. Many of the hotels as well as small travel agencies on Main St can book tickets.

Express trains stop at Ankola and Kumta stations, both about 25km from Gokarna and accessible by local bus.

KARNATAKA

KARWAR

☎ 08382

Karwar is a dull, sleepy port town near the mouth of the Kali Nadi River, only a short distance south of Goa. While the town isn't very interesting, the area immediately south is picturesque since the foothills of the Western Ghats come right to the coast, forming headlands that are separated by sweeping sandy bays. Their peacefulness and beauty could change radically when work finally begins on a new naval base.

Karwar's Indian Bank changes travellers cheques (but not cash).

Places to Stay & Eat

Anand Lodge *(☎ 26156)*, a two-minute walk from the bus stand, has acceptable doubles (only) with private bathroom and balconies for Rs 120.

Hotel Bhadra *(☎ 25212)*, just south of the Kali Nadi bridge, has doubles with private bathroom for Rs 250, and air-con doubles for Rs 600. It has a vegetarian/nonvegetarian restaurant and a bar.

Devbag Forest Beach Resort *(☎ 26596, ⓔ infodesk@karnatakatourism.com)* is administered by Jungle Lodges & Resorts from its office opposite Hotel Bhadra. It's a peaceful resort (reached by a 10-minute boat ride) with accommodation in comfortable huts on stilts, but it's not cheap. A package including meals and use of recreational facilities is US$60 per night (Rs 1000 for Indians). It also offers scuba diving.

Udipi Hotel and its sister restaurant ***Hotel Savita***, both on Main Rd, are clean, vegetarian snack and 'meals' (or thali) specialists.

Hotel Sitara, nearby, has a comfortable air-con restaurant upstairs serving a wide range of Indian, Chinese and continental dishes, and there's also a balcony dining area.

Getting There & Away

Karwar is a main station on the Konkan Railway so most expresses stop here. Heading south to Mangalore (Kankanadi) there's an express at 9.05 am, and north to Margao at 9.11 am and 7.30 pm.

The Karwar bus stand is on the southern edge of the town centre. There are numerous buses to Panaji (four hours) and Mangalore (Rs 84). There are two buses to Jog Falls (Rs 52, five hours), one to Hassan and one direct to Hospet at 9.30 am (Rs 95, eight hours).

There are five direct KSRTC buses to Gokarna daily (Rs 20), but more-frequent private buses shuttle between Karwar and Ankola, where you can change for Gokarna. They depart from just in front of the bus stand entrance.

Getting Around

The train station is 8km from town. A local bus meets incoming trains (Rs 3), but many more Karwar-bound buses pass along the main road about 50m from the station.

There are plenty of autorickshaws, but a good way to get to Kali Nadi bridge or the beaches around Karwar is by bicycle. They can be hired at several shops on Main St for Rs 2 per hour.

AROUND KARWAR

The nearest beaches to Karwar are **Binaga** and **Arga**, 3km and 5km south of the town respectively. They're both scimitar-shaped swathes of sand and are generally deserted.

Krishna Rest House *(☎ 21613)*, set back from the beach at Binaga, is a great place to stay if you want some peace and quiet. It's a basic family-run guesthouse with a few rooms with shared bathroom and a small cottage, all for Rs 150. You can either self-cater or arrange food in advance with the owner. It's Rs 40 by autorickshaw or Rs 4 by bus from Karwar.

At the small town of **Ankola**, 37km south of Karwar, are the 15th-century ruined walls of King Sarpamalika's fort and the equally old Sri Venkataraman Temple.

The Western Ghats inland of Karwar have some interesting tribal communities. The Suddha people are of African descent, whose ancestors were brought to Goa by Portuguese slave traders to be sold to local rulers.

Central Karnataka

HAMPI

☎ 08394 • pop 1000

The ruins of Vijayanagar, near the village of Hampi, are some of the most fascinating in India. They're set in a strange and beautiful boulder-strewn landscape that has an almost magical quality.

Hampi is a thriving travellers' centre, the kind of place you can't seem to leave. If you're in a hurry, it is possible to see the main sites in one day – either by bicycle or, if you start early, on foot – but this defeats the laid-back nature of Hampi. Signposting in some parts of the site is inadequate, but you can't really get lost. Unfortunately it's not safe to wander around the ruins alone at dawn or dusk, particularly on the climb up Matanga Hill.

Orientation

There are two main points of entry to the ruins: Hampi Bazaar and the small village of Kamalapuram to the south. Kamalapuram is a sleepy village with the KSTDC hotel and the museum. The main travellers' scene is Hampi Bazaar, a bustling village with a burgeoning array of cheap lodges and restaurants, all dominated by the Virupaksha Temple. The ruins themselves can be divided into two main areas: the Sacred Centre, around Hampi Bazaar, and the Royal Centre, to the south around Kamalapuram.

Information

The tourist office (☎ 51339) is on the main street of Hampi Bazaar and is open from 10 am to 5.30 pm daily except Sunday. It can arrange guides for Rs 450 per day or Rs 250 for half a day. There are good books and maps of Hampi available from Aspiration Stores, near the entrance to the Virupaksha Temple in Hampi Bazaar.

You can change travellers cheques and get cash advances on Visa and MasterCard at Canara Bank in Hampi Bazaar from 11 am to 2 pm on weekdays (except Wednesday) and 11 am to 12.30 pm Saturday. There are numerous authorised moneychangers, offering slightly worse rates, on the main street. There are numerous Internet cafes around town, but connections are unreliable.

Foreigners are asked to register at the police station inside the Virupaksha Temple on arrival. The station, which is just inside the temple entrance on the right, has a photo gallery of crooks.

The Ruins of Vijayanagar

Vijayanagar (Hampi) was once the capital of one of the largest Hindu empires in Indian history. Founded by the Telugu princes Harihara and Bukka in 1336, it reached the height of its power under Krishnadevaraya (1509–29), when it controlled the entire peninsula south of the Krishna and Tungabhadra Rivers, except for a string of commercial principalities along the Malabar Coast.

Comparable to Delhi in the 14th century, the city, which covered an area of 33 sq km, was surrounded by seven concentric lines of fortification and was reputed to have had a population of about 500,000. It maintained a mercenary army of more than one million, according to the Persian ambassador Abdul Razak, and ironically included Muslim mounted archers to defend it from the Muslim states to the north.

Vijayanagar's wealth was based on control of the spice trade to the south and the cotton industry of the south-east. Its busy bazaars, described by European travellers such as the Portuguese Nunez and Paes, were centres of international commerce.

The empire came to a sudden end in 1565 after the disastrous battle of Talikota when the city was ransacked by a confederacy of Deccan sultanates (Bidar, Bijapur, Golconda, Ahmednagar and Berar).

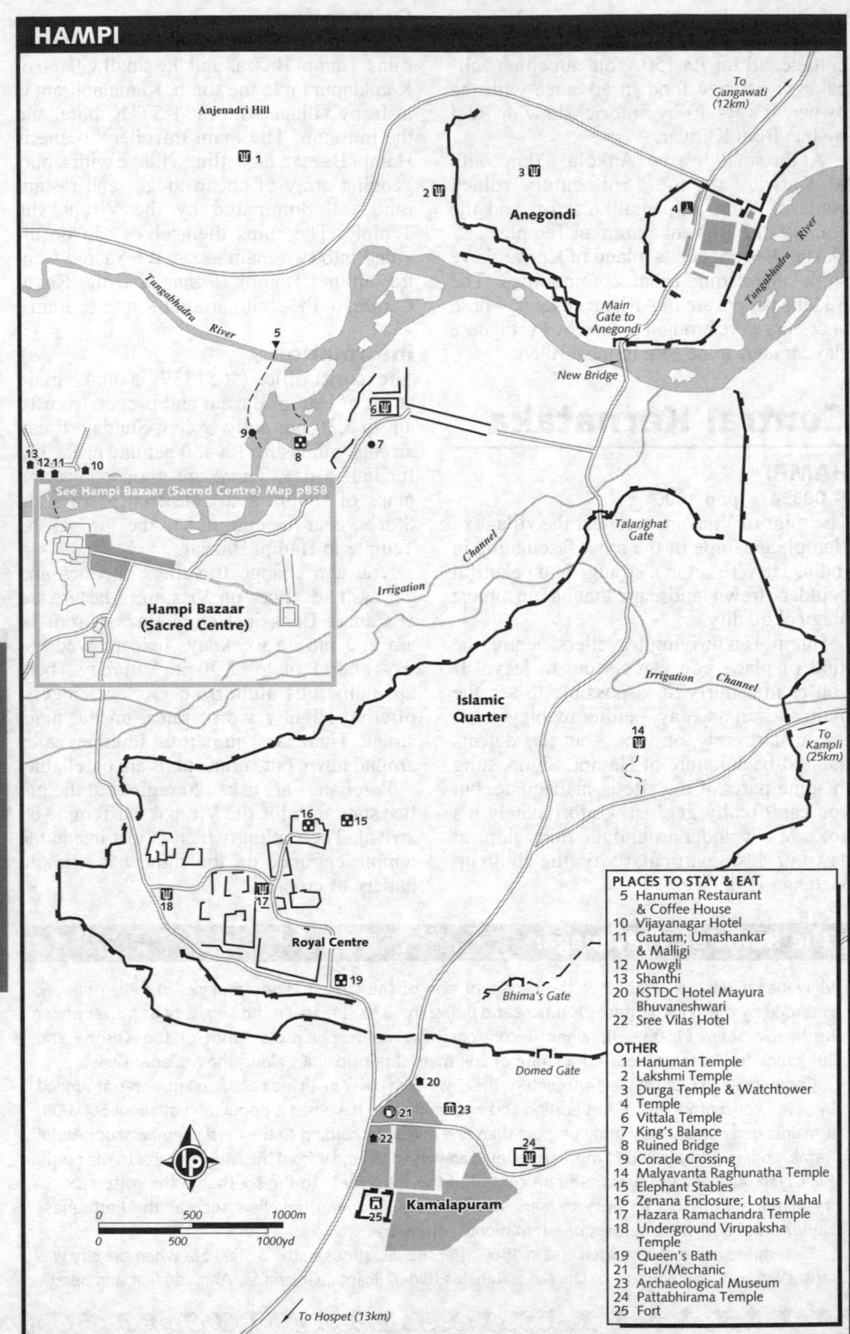
HAMPI
To Gangawati (12km)
Anjenadri Hill
Anegondi
Tungabhadra River
Main Gate to Anegondi
New Bridge
See Hampi Bazaar (Sacred Centre) Map p858
Hampi Bazaar (Sacred Centre)
Irrigation Channel
Talarighat Gate
Islamic Quarter
To Kampli (25km)
Royal Centre
Bhima's Gate
Domed Gate
Kamalapuram
To Hospet (13km)
0 500 1000m
0 500 1000yd
PLACES TO STAY & EAT
5 Hanuman Restaurant & Coffee House
10 Vijayanagar Hotel
11 Gautam; Umashankar & Malligi
12 Mowgli
13 Shanthi
20 KSTDC Hotel Mayura Bhuvaneshwari
22 Sree Vilas Hotel
OTHER
1 Hanuman Temple
2 Lakshmi Temple
3 Durga Temple & Watchtower
4 Temple
6 Vittala Temple
7 King's Balance
8 Ruined Bridge
9 Coracle Crossing
14 Malyavanta Raghunatha Temple
15 Elephant Stables
16 Zenana Enclosure; Lotus Mahal
17 Hazara Ramachandra Temple
18 Underground Virupaksha Temple
19 Queen's Bath
21 Fuel/Mechanic
23 Archaeological Museum
24 Pattabhirama Temple
25 Fort
KARNATAKA

Hampi Bazaar & Virupaksha Temple

Now that locals are occupying the ancient buildings lining the main street, Hampi Bazaar is once more a bustling village. The Virupaksha Temple at the western end is one of the earliest structures in the city. The main gopuram, almost 50m high, was built in 1442, with a smaller one added in 1510. The main shrine is dedicated to Virupaksha, a form of Shiva.

Overlooking Virupaksha Temple to the south, **Hemakuta Hill** has a scattering of early ruins including Jain temples and a monolithic sculpture of Narasimha (Vishnu in his man-lion incarnation). It's worth the short walk up for the view over Hampi Bazaar.

Vittala Temple

From the eastern end of Hampi Bazaar an obvious track, navigable only on foot, leads left to the Vittala Temple, about 2km away. The undisputed highlight of the ruins, the 16th-century Vittala Temple, is a World Heritage monument. It's in a good state of preservation, though purists may have reservations about the cement-block columns erected to keep the main structure from falling down.

Work is thought to have started on the temple duing the reign of Krishnadevaraya (1509–29) and, despite the fact it was never finished or consecrated, the temple's incredible sculptural work is the pinnacle of Vijayanagar art. The outer pillars are known as the musical pillars as they reverberate when tapped, although this is discouraged to avoid further damage. There's an ornate stone chariot in the temple courtyard containing an image of Garuda. The chariot's stone wheels used to be capable of turning. It costs foreigners US$10 in rupees to enter the temple complex.

Sule Bazaar & Achyutaraya Temple

Halfway along the path from Hampi Bazaar to the Vittala Temple, a track to the right leads to deserted Sule Bazaar, which gives you some idea of what Hampi Bazaar might have looked like if it hadn't been repopulated. At the southern end of this area is the Achyutaraya Temple. Its isolated location at the foot of Matanga Hill makes it even more atmospheric than the Vittala Temple.

Royal Centre

This area of Hampi is quite different from the northern section, since most of the rounded boulders that once littered the site have been used to create a mind-boggling proliferation of beautiful stone walls. It's a 2km walk from the Achyutaraya Temple on a poorly signposted track, so most people get to it from the Hampi Bazaar-Kamalapuram road. This area is easily navigable by bicycle since a decent dirt road runs through the heart of it.

Within various stone-walled enclosures here are the rest of Hampi's major attractions, including the **Lotus Mahal** and the **Elephant Stables**. The former is a delicately designed pavilion in a walled compound known as the Zenana Enclosure. It's an amazing synthesis of Hindu and Islamic style and it gets its name from the lotus bud carved in the centre of the domed and vaulted ceiling. It costs US$10 in rupees to enter the Zenana Enclosure.

The Elephant Stables is a grand building with domed chambers, which once housed the state elephants.

Further south is the Royal Centre area, with its various temples and elaborate waterworks, plus the **Underground Virupaksha Temple** and the impressive **Queen's Bath**.

Museum

The archaeological museum at Kamalapuram now costs foreigners US$10 in rupees, something of a hike on the old entrance fee of Rs 2 (US$0.04). Apparently it has a modest collection of sculptures and a large floor model of the Vijayanagar ruins.

Anegondi

North of the river is the ruined fortified stronghold of Anegondi. There's not a lot to see here today, although much of the old defensive wall is intact and there are numerous small temples, including the tiny whitewashed **Hanuman Temple**, perched on top of a prominent rocky hill.

To get to Anegondi you need to take a coracle across the river then follow the dusty road north.

Places to Stay

Hampi Bazaar There are dozens of basic but adequate lodges in the alleys leading off the main road. These rates are for the high season, but prices shoot up by 50% or more

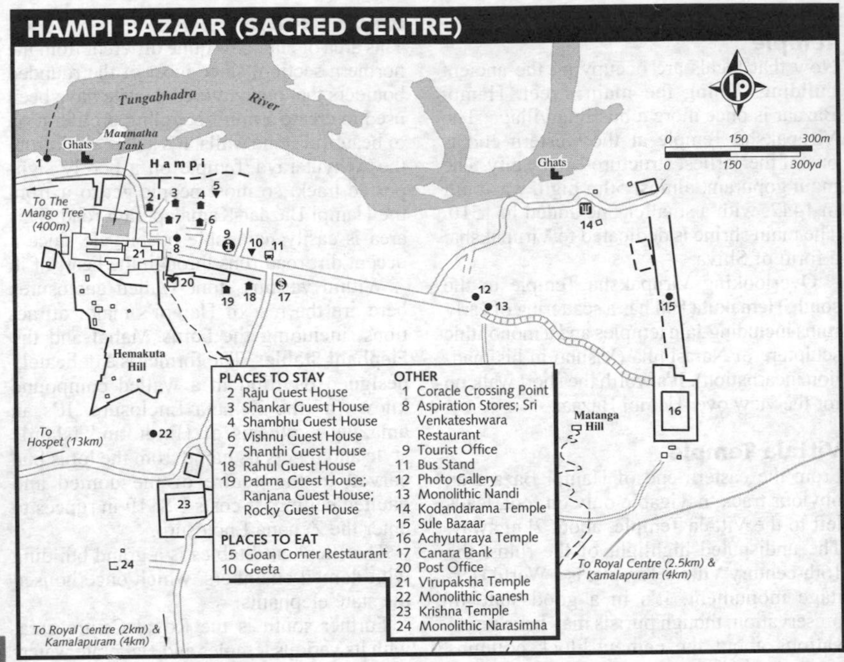

during the busiest fortnight around New Year's Day.

Shanthi Guest House *(☎ 51368)* is a popular travellers' haunt. Bare rooms with shared bathroom are a bit overpriced at Rs 100/120, but there's a pleasant garden courtyard and it's clean.

Vishnu Guest House *(☎ 41611)* is a friendly family home. Doubles with private bathroom and bucket hot water are Rs 150.

Raju Guest House, across the street from Shanti Guest House, has clean simple rooms with shared bathroom for Rs 60/80. It has a rooftop eating area where you can relax when your room gets claustrophobic.

Rahul Guest House *(☎ 41648)*, south of the bus stand in the street running parallel to the bazaar, is a popular place with congenial common areas. Clean, spartan rooms with mattresses on the floor and shared bathroom cost Rs 50, rooms with beds Rs 75 and air-con doubles Rs 300.

There are a couple of other good places in this area. ***Ranjana Guest House*** *(☎ 41696)* is run by women and has three very clean doubles with private bathroom (and shower) for Rs 200. ***Padma Guest House*** *(☎ 41331)* is a small friendly place with five doubles with private bathroom for Rs 250.

There are many more places: ***Shankar Guest House*** and ***Shambhu Guest House*** both have rooms for Rs 100/150 and the latter has a rooftop restaurant. ***Rocky Guest House*** has five simple rooms for Rs 80/100 and a good little restaurant.

North of the River The most laid-back 'scene' in Hampi is across the river where a string of guesthouses cater for those who find even Hampi Bazaar too busy. To get across take a coracle (Rs 5) from the ghats north of the Virupaksha Temple. In the monsoon season, when the river is running high, boats may not make the crossing.

Vijayanagar Hotel is the first place you come to. Basic rooms in a concrete building cost Rs 30/60, little thatched huts cost Rs 30, and there's a restaurant. The compound is spacious and the manager is friendly.

Gautam, further west, is run by a local farming family. It has rustic palm-thatched mud huts for Rs 40/50, and there's a small cafe. ***Umashankar*** and ***Malligi*** guesthouses are similar.

Mowgli is a more elaborate set-up, with basic huts with shared bathrooms for Rs 80/100 up to 250 for bigger huts with private bathroom. The compound has pleasantly shady trees.

Shanthi, the next place along, is friendly and relaxed, and has a range of rooms and huts. The cheapest cost Rs 70/100, while new huts with private bathrooms cost Rs 250. The kitchen here does excellent thalis and pizzas.

Kamalapuram On the northern outskirts of Kamalapuram, ***KSTDC Hotel Mayura Bhuvaneshwari*** *(☎ 41574)* is modern and fairly well-maintained, with spacious grounds. Decent singles/doubles with private bathroom and mosquito nets cost Rs 250/300, or Rs 400/450 with air-con (including tax). The hotel has a vegetarian/ nonvegetarian restaurant and a basic bar.

Places to Eat

There are a few simple restaurants on the main street of Hampi Bazaar and newer places among the guesthouses in the dusty streets behind the tourist office. There's very little to distinguish between them, since they all serve standard Indian fare and western standbys and all cater exclusively to the travelling community. Despite their extensive menus, most can only produce limited offerings.

Sri Venkateshwara, on the right as you near the Virupaksha Temple, is the most established restaurant. It serves tiffin and Western snacks at lunch and thalis in the evening. ***Geeta*** is a popular alternative. North of the bazaar, ***Goan Corner Restaurant*** is popular. Many of the guesthouses have good rooftop restaurants.

The Mango Tree is away from the crowds, about 400m west of the ghats down a path through a banana plantation. Excellent thalis are served on mats on the earthen terrace.

There are a few humble eateries in Kamalapuram, the most notable being ***Sree Vilas Hotel***, opposite the bus stop. It closes at 7.30 pm.

Due to Hampi's religious significance, alcohol is not permitted – but that doesn't mean you can't get a discreet beer or two. If you want a legal drink, there's a bar at ***Hotel Mayura Bhuvaneshwari*** in Kamalapuram.

Getting There & Away

While private buses from Goa and Bangalore will drop you in Hampi, you have to go to Hospet to catch a bus out (because local autorickshaw drivers complained about lost business). Local buses run roughly every hour from Hampi Bazaar to Hospet (Rs 10, 30 minutes). The first bus from Hospet is at 6.30 am, the last one back leaves Hampi at 8.30 pm. A rickshaw costs Rs 80.

If you're going to or coming from Goa, the overnight sleeper bus (Rs 400) is a popular option. A couple of noisy stops along the way and some terrifying cornering that can fling you out of your 'bed' make sleep a bit erratic. Solo travellers have to share a bunk. There are several travel agents in Hampi Bazaar that can book onward bus, train and plane tickets or arrange a car and driver.

Getting Around

It makes a lot of sense to hire a bicycle to explore the ruins once you've seen the Vittala and Achyutaraya Temples and Sule Bazaar. The road between Hampi Bazaar and Kamalapuram can be used to get to the ruins; key monuments are haphazardly signposted along its length. Bicycles cost around Rs 30 per day in Hampi Bazaar.

Walking is the only way to explore all the nooks and crannies, but expect to cover at least 7km just to see the major ruins. Autorickshaws and taxis are available for sightseeing, and will drop you as close to each of the major ruins as they can. A five-hour autorickshaw tour costs Rs 300.

Organised tours depart from Hospet; see that section for details.

HOSPET

☎ 08394 • pop 151,900

Hospet is a bustling regional centre with none of Hampi's atmosphere. You'll need to come here to make transport connections though. It has some upmarket accommodation, but otherwise there's no reason to stay.

Information

The tourist office (☎ 28537) is on Old Bus Stand Rd (7.30 am to 10 pm daily). It has maps and information on Hampi and sights in northern Karnataka. Hotel Malligi changes travellers cheques and Andhra Bank on Station Rd near the small canal gives cash advances on Visa and MasterCard.

Firewalking in Hospet

Hospet comes alive during the Shiah Muslim festival of Muharram, which commemorates the martyrdom of Mohammed's grandson, Imam Hussain, in May or June. If you're here at this time, don't miss the firewalkers, who walk barefoot across the red-hot embers of a fire that's been going all day and night. Virtually the whole town turns out to watch or take part and the excitement reaches fever pitch around midnight. The preliminaries, which go on all day, appear to be a bewildering hybrid of Muslim and Hindu ritual. Those who are scheduled to do the firewalking must be physically restrained from going completely berserk just before the event.

Organised Tours

The daily KSTDC tour to the three main sites at Hampi (Hampi Bazaar, Vittala Temple and the Royal Centre) and to Tungabhadra Dam departs at 9.30 am and returns at 5 pm (Rs 80). Whether you get an informative guide or one who wants to rush through the ruins is a matter of chance. Bookings can be made at the Hospet tourist office or Hotel Malligi.

Places to Stay & Eat

Hotel Malligi *(☎ 28101, fax 27038, ⓔ malligi@blr.vsnl.net.in, 6/143 Jabunatha Rd)* is near the southern canal, which runs through Hospet. The modernistic new wing has pleasant air-con rooms from Rs 550 to 2250. The older wing is much cheaper but nothing special – you're better off staying in Hampi. The swimming pool costs Rs 25 for nonguests.

Hotel Karthik *(☎ 24938, Sardar Patel Rd)* is a new place with well-appointed double rooms for Rs 250. Deluxe rooms are Rs 300 and air-con rooms are Rs 500.

Madhu Paradise, at Hotel Malligi, serves reasonably priced South and North Indian vegetarian fare and Western breakfasts. ***Waves*** multicuisine restaurant is opposite the Malligi. ***Shanbagh Hotel***, near the tourist office, is a decent vegetarian restaurant.

Getting There & Away

Bus The busy bus stand in Hospet is fairly well organised, though buses in this part of the state are generally crowded and you'll need to fight to get on. A large backpack can make this an uncomfortable experience.

Buses to Hampi depart from bay No 10 every 30 minutes (Rs 5).

More than 10 express buses run daily to Bangalore (Rs 117/166 ordinary/deluxe, nine hours). They are nearly all morning or night departures: No Bangalore buses depart between 1 and 9.30 pm. The KSTDC runs its own overnight deluxe bus to Bangalore at 10 pm daily (Rs 160). There are regular public buses to Hubli (Rs 42, four hours).

There are three buses a day to Badami, or catch one of the many buses to Gadag or Ilkal and transfer to another bus there. The journey takes five hours via Gadag and close to six hours via Ilkal. It's more comfortable to take the train.

There are four buses to Bijapur (Rs 77, six hours); five buses to Hyderabad (Rs 143, nine hours); and also daily departures to Hassan, Mangalore and Shimoga. Two buses head to Gokarna (Rs 107, eight hours) daily at 9 am and 1 am.

Train Hospet train station is a 20-minute walk or Rs 10 autorickshaw ride from the centre of town. There is one direct train daily to Bangalore at 8.20 pm (Rs 151/531 in sleeper/1st class, 10½ hours) or go to Guntakal (three hours), and get an express to Bangalore from here; and two expresses to Hubli (four hours). To get to Badami and Bijapur, catch a Hubli train to Gadag and pick up a connection from there.

HUBLI

☎ 0836 • pop 728,000

Hubli is important to travellers mainly as a railway junction on the routes from Mumbai to Bangalore, Goa and northern Karnataka.

All the main services (hotels, restaurants etc) are conveniently close to the train station. The bus stand is on Lamington Rd, a 15-minute walk from the train station.

Places to Stay

Ashoka Towers Hotel *(☎ 362271, Lamington Rd)*, about 500m from the train station, has single/double rooms with private bathroom for Rs 130/175. Air-con doubles cost Rs 350.

Hotel Kailash *(☎ 352235, Lamington Rd)*, opposite the Ashoka, is more upmarket. Comfortable rooms with hot water and TV cost Rs 300/450. Air-con doubles are Rs 630.

KARNATAKA

Hotel Ajanta *(☎ 362216)* is a short distance off the main street and visible from the train station. It's a huge place so you'll always be able to find accommodation here. Average rooms cost Rs 60/100 with shared bathroom or Rs 110/160 with private bathroom. Checkout is 24 hours.

Hotel Ayodhya *(☎ 351951, Station Rd)* is the best of the hotels near the bus stand. Singles/doubles cost Rs 150/220.

Hotel Naveen *(☎ 372283, fax 372730, Poona-Bangalore Rd, Unkal)* is Hubli's best, situated beside a lake about 5km from the town centre. Rooms cost from Rs 1230/1500 to 6000 for a large suite. There's a multicuisine restaurant and a swimming pool.

Places to Eat

Parag Bar & Restaurant, on the street facing the train station, has a British pub-style restaurant and an open-air rooftop section serving passable vegetarian and nonvegetarian Indian and Chinese dishes.

Royal Palace, on a side street near Ashoka Towers Hotel, is the best restaurant in this part of the city. North Indian mains cost around Rs 60.

There are plenty of late-night food stalls around the bus stand and train station.

Getting There & Away

Bus Hubli has a large and busy bus stand with a well-organised reservation and ticket hall in a separate building. The KSRTC has lots of deluxe buses to Bangalore (Rs 169, nine hours) and Hospet (Rs 42, four hours). There are also four buses daily to Mumbai (Rs 194, 15 hours); three to Mysore (Rs 161, 10 hours); two to Mangalore (Rs 128, 10 hours); and at least one daily departure to Bijapur, Gokarna and Jog Falls.

There are four KSRTC buses to Panaji (Rs 55, five hours), and Goa's Kadamba Transport Corporation also runs a number of services.

Opposite the bus stand are plenty of private companies operating deluxe buses to Bangalore, Bijapur, Goa, Mangalore, Mumbai and Pune.

Train The railway reservation office is open from 8 am to 8 pm daily. If you're heading for Hospet (four hours), there are expresses at 1 and 8 pm. To reach Bijapur, you'll have to catch one of these trains and change at Gadag (one hour). There are two to three expresses a day to Bangalore (Rs 162/749 in sleeper/two-tier air-con, nine hours) and usually two expresses to Mumbai (Rs 205/951 in sleeper/two-tier air-con, 17 hours) via Londa (Rs 30 in 2nd class, two hours). Londa is the closest junction with rail connections to Goa.

Northern Karnataka

BADAMI

☎ 08357 • pop 18,200

Set in beautiful countryside at the foot of a stunning red sandstone ridge, the village of Badami was once the capital of the Chalukyan empire, which covered much of the central Deccan between the 4th and 8th centuries AD. Here, and at nearby Aihole and Pattadakal, you can see some of the earliest and finest examples of Dravidian temples and rock-cut caves. The forms and sculptural work at these sites provided a great deal of inspiration for later South Indian Hindu empires.

History

Badami was the Chalukyan capital from about AD 540 until AD 757. The surrounding hills are dotted with temples, fortifications, carvings and inscriptions dating not just from the Chalukyan period, but also from other times when the site was occupied as a fortress. After it fell to the Rashtrakutas, Badami was occupied successively by the Chalukyas of Kalyan (a separate branch of the Western Chalukyas), the Kalachuryas, the Yadavas of Devagiri, the Vijayanagar empire, the Adil Shahi kings of Bijapur and the Marathas.

All these various rulers left their mark at Badami, and there's even a Pallava inscription dating back to AD 642 when their king, Narasimha Varman I, briefly overwhelmed the Chalukyas and occupied Badami for 13 years before being driven out.

Orientation & Information

The main street of Badami (Station Rd) has a few hotels and restaurants, and Badami village itself is squeezed between this road and the hilltop caves. The tourist office (☎ 65414), open from 10 am to 5.30 pm Monday to Saturday, is in the new wing of

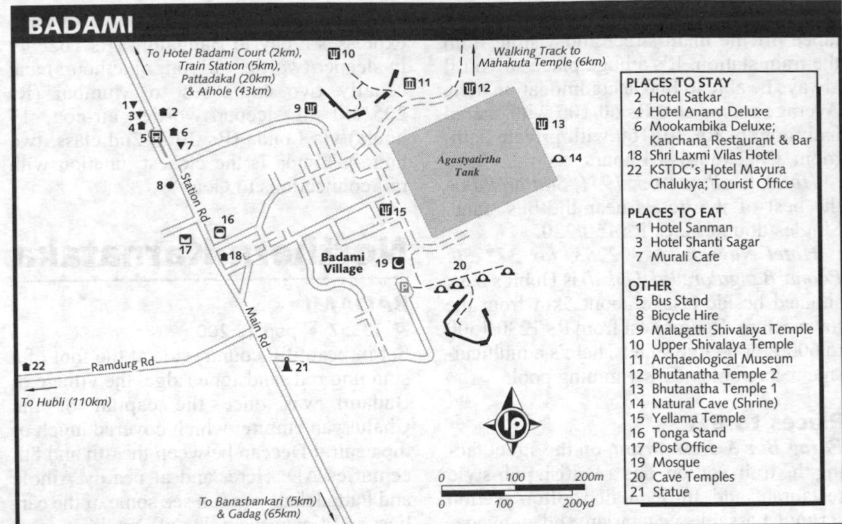

the KSTDC'S Hotel Mayura Chalukya on Ramdurg Rd.

The Badami Court and Mookambika Deluxe hotels will change travellers cheques, but with a high commission charge.

Caves

Badami is best known for its beautiful cave temples, which are open 6 am to 6 pm (US$5 in rupees). Guides charge Rs 150 for a tour of the caves, or Rs 350 for the whole site.

Cave One This cave, just above the entrance to the complex, is dedicated to Shiva. It is the oldest of the four caves, thought to have been carved during the 6th century. On the cliff wall to the right of the porch is a beautiful image of Nataraja striking 81 dance poses and whose 18 arms hold, among other things, a snake, a musical instrument and a *trishula* (trident).

On the right of the porch area is a huge figure of Ardhanarishvara. The right half of the figure shows features of Shiva, such as matted hair and a third eye, while the left half of the image has aspects of Parvati, including braided hair and ornaments. On the opposite wall is a large image of Harihara, the right half of which represents Shiva, and the left half Vishnu. A headless Nandi sits in the middle of the cave, facing a tiny sanctuary, which is carved into the back wall.

Cave Two This cave is simpler in design, and is dedicated to Vishnu. As with caves one and three, the front edge of the platform is decorated with images of pot-bellied dwarfs in various poses. Four pillars support the veranda, the top of each of which is carved with a bracket in the shape of a *yali*, or mythical beast. On the left wall of the porch is the pig-headed figure of Varaha, an incarnation of Vishnu and the emblem of the Chalukya empire. To his left is an image of Naga, the snake. On the right wall is a large sculpture of Trivikrama, another incarnation of Vishnu, booting out a demon while in his eight hands he holds a variety of weapons including a discus, a bow and a sword. The ceiling panels contain images of Vishnu riding Garuda, *gandharva* couples, swastikas and fish arranged in a wheel.

Between the second and third caves are two sets of steps to the right. The first leads to a **natural cave**, the eastern wall of which contains a small Buddhist image of Padmapani (an incarnation of Buddha). The second set of steps leads to the hilltop **South Fort**; sadly these steps are barred by a metal gate.

Cave Three This cave was carved under the orders of Mangalesha, the brother of King Kirtivarma, in AD 578. It is dedicated to Vishnu and contains some of the best sculptures in the complex.

On the left-hand wall of the cave is a large carving of Vishnu, sitting on the coils of the snake; nearby is an image of Varaha with four hands. The pillars here have carved brackets in the shape of *yalis* (mythical lion creatures) and the sides of the pillars are also carved. The ceiling panels contain images including Vishnu, Indra riding an elephant, Shiva on a bull, and Brahma on a swan.

Cave Four Dedicated to Jainism, Cave Four is the smallest of the set and was carved from the 7th to 8th century. The pillars, with their roaring yalis, are of a similar design to the other caves. The right wall of the cave has an image of Suparshvanatha (the 7th Jain tirthankar or teacher), surrounded by more than 20 Jain tirthankars. The sanctum contains an image of Adinath, the first Jain tirthankar.

Other Attractions

The caves overlook the livid green 5th century **Agastyatirtha Tank** and the peaceful waterside **Bhutanatha temples**. On the other side of the tank is the **archaeological museum**, which houses superb examples of local sculpture, including remarkable Lajja-Gauri images of a fertility cult that flourished in the area. It's open from 10 am to 5 pm daily except Friday (Rs 2). The stairway behind the museum climbs through a sandstone chasm and fortified gateways to reach the various temples and ruins of the **north fort**. The fort has expansive views and overlooks the rooftops of Badami.

It's worth exploring Badami's laneways, where you'll find old houses, tiny squares, a wide range of domestic and farm animals and the occasional Chalukyan ruin.

Places to Stay

Hotel Anand Deluxe *(☎ 20074, Station Rd)* has a range of rooms from cramped singles at the back for Rs 70 to doubles ranging from Rs 120 to 250 and air-cooled doubles with TV for Rs 300. Check out a few rooms before deciding.

Shri Laxmi Vilas Hotel *(☎ 20077, Station Rd)*, near the tonga stand, is a basic cheapie with doubles for Rs 125, with a restaurant downstairs.

KSTDC's Hotel Mayura Chalukya *(☎ 20046, Ramdurg Rd)* is about 500m from Station Rd. It's in reasonable shape, and has tranquil gardens and singles/doubles/triples for Rs 160/190/250.

Hotel Satkar *(☎ 20417, Station Rd)* is a final option – hard beds, grubby rooms and squat toilets for Rs 70/100. There's a bar next door.

Mookambika Deluxe *(☎ 65067, Station Rd)*, opposite the bus stand, has gone upmarket with all its rooms now in the 'deluxe' category. In high season it charges Rs 300 for clean standard rooms, or Rs 500 with TV and bathtub. The bathrooms are modern, with hot water all day.

Hotel Badami Court *(☎ 20230, fax 20207, Station Rd)*, 2km from the town centre towards the train station out in the countryside, is Badami's top hotel. Air-con singles/doubles with bathtub and TV cost US$42/54, taxes included. Non-guests can use the swimming pool for Rs 100. For more information, check out the hotel's Web site: www.hotelbadamicourt.com.

Places to Eat

Kanchana Restaurant & Bar, attached to Mookambika Deluxe, is not the cheapest place around, but it serves a good range of vegetarian and nonvegetarian food, Western breakfasts and has a pleasant upstairs terrace. Vegetable biryani costs Rs 50.

Hotel Sanman, nearby, is popular with travellers and locals. It has cheap veg/non-veg food and cold beers.

Murali Cafe is a basic vegetarian restaurant serving thalis at lunch time.

Hotel Shanti Sagar next to Hotel Anand Deluxe does good Udupi vegetarian food.

Pulikeshi Dining Room in Hotel Badami Court is an upmarket, multicuisine, silver-service restaurant where dinner costs around Rs 200 per person.

Getting There & Away

Bus There are six buses daily to Bijapur (four hours) and Hubli (three hours), and four buses to Bangalore (Rs 150 deluxe, 12 hours). There are five buses direct to Hospet (five hours), or you can catch any of the buses to Gadag (two hours) or Ilkal (two hours) to pick up a connection.

Train Trains only run to Gadag and Bijapur and nearly all are 2nd-class passenger trains. Still, it's more comfortable than the buses.

Tickets for passenger trains go on sale about 30 minutes before the train arrives. Five trains head to Bijapur (Rs 24, four hours), and there are five to Gadag, where it's easy get a connecting train to Hospet or Hubli.

Getting Around

Badami train station is 5km from town. A tonga from the station into town costs about Rs 25. You have the choice of a tonga, autorickshaw (Rs 35) or taxi (Rs 55) when heading from town out to the train station. You can hire bicycles in Badami for Rs 3 per hour.

The best way to explore the surrounding area is by local bus, since they're fairly frequent and run pretty much to schedule. You can easily visit both Aihole and Pattadakal in one day from Badami if you start early. Start with Aihole since the last bus back from Aihole to Badami is around 4.30 pm; the last bus from Pattadakal to Badami is at 6 pm. There are plenty of buses from Badami to Aihole (Rs 15, two hours). From Aihole, there should be buses at 11.30 am and 1 pm (the schedule is very flexible) to Pattadakal (30 minutes), from where there are hourly buses and minibuses back to Badami. It's a good idea to take food and water with you.

Taxis cost Rs 500 to 600 for a day trip taking in Pattadakal, Aihole and Mahakuta – good value when shared between three or four people. Badami's hotels arrange taxis.

KARNATAKA

AROUND BADAMI

Pattadakal

This village, 20km from Badami, was the second capital of the Badami Chalukyas and was used in particular for the royal coronations. While most of the temples here were built during the 7th and 8th centuries, the earliest remains date from the 3rd and 4th centuries, and the latest structure is a Jain temple of the Rashtrakuta period (9th century). It costs foreigners a ridiculous US$10 in rupees to enter, but you can get a decent view.

Pattadakal, like Aihole, was a developing ground for South Indian temple architecture. In particular, two main types of temple towers were tried out here. On the one hand there are the curvilinear towers of the Kasivisvesvara, Jambulinga and Galaganatha temples, while on the other, the Mallikarjuna, Sangamesvara and Virupaksha temples have a square roof and receding tiers.

The main **Virupaksha Temple** is a huge structure. The massive columns are covered with intricate carvings depicting episodes from the Ramayana and Mahabharata, and showing battle scenes, lovers and decorative motifs. Around the roof of the inner hall are sculptures of elephants' and lions' heads. To the east, and facing the temple, is a pavilion containing a massive Nandi. The exterior of the temple is covered with sculpture and ornamentation, some of it fairly eroded, but much of it still in good shape. The **Mallikarjuna Temple**, next to the Virupaksha Temple, is slightly more worn but almost identical in design. About 500m south of the main enclosure is **Papanatha Temple**.

A **classical dance festival** is held at Pattadakal, normally at the end of January.

Aihole

Aihole was the Chalukyan regional capital between the 4th and 6th centuries. Here you can see Hindu temple architecture in its embryonic stage, from the earliest simple shrines, such as those in the Kontigudi Group and the Lad Khan Temple, to the later and more complex buildings such as the Meguti Temple.

In the centre of the village is a fenced enclosure with the most impressive building in Aihole – the **Durga Temple**, which dates from the 7th century. The temple is notable for its semicircular apse, which was copied from Buddhist architecture, and for the remains of the curvilinear *sikhara* (Hindu temple spire). Even more striking than the formal layout are the outstanding carvings crowding the colonnaded passageway around the sanctuary. The small **museum** behind the Durga temple contains further examples of the Chalukyan sculptors' work, and is open from 10 am to 5 pm daily (closed Friday). Foreigners pay US$5 in rupees to enter the fenced enclosure.

To the south of the Durga temple are several other collections of buildings including some of the earliest structures in Aihole – the Gandar, Ladkhan, Kontigudi and Hucchapaya groups, which are of the pavilion type with slightly sloping roofs. About 600m to the south-east, on a low hilltop, is the Jain **Meguti Temple**.

Tourist Home *(☎ 08351-34541)* is excellent value, with dorm beds for Rs 40 and rooms for Rs 100/200. There are cheaper rooms in the old wing. It's well run and the helpful manager arranges guides to some of the dozens of temples scattered around for Rs 200 per day. The hotel is 1km from the village centre on the Amingad road. Food is available by arrangement.

Mahakuta Temple

About 10km east of Badami, this temple is easily visited en route to Aihole. Mahakuta was made sacred by the presence of the sage Agastya, who lived here, and the temple is still active as a pilgrimage site. Within the walled courtyard are two main temples on either side of an old tank. The first of these, nearest the entrance, is still in use but the other one is now deserted. A number of small Shiva shrines are arranged around the outside of the courtyard.

Banashankari

This small village, about 5km south-east of Badami, is home to an attractive temple, with a huge tank surrounded by a pillared cloister. Banashankari is particularly worth visiting during the annual **temple festival**, which usually falls in January. For days on end the streets around the temple are taken over by a huge fair, which is best visited in the evening.

BIJAPUR

☎ 08352 • pop 217,500

As a city Bijapur hit its peak about 400 years ago and seems to have been declining ever since. Nevertheless, it is blessed by a wealth of 15th- to 17th-century Muslim architecture. It is dotted with mosques, mausoleums, palaces and fortifications, including the famous Golgumbaz, with its vast dome said to be the world's third largest. The austere grace of Bijapur's monuments is in complete contrast to the sculptural extravagance of the Chalukyan and Hoysala temples further south. The Ibrahim Roza Mausoleum, in particular, is considered to be one of the most finely proportioned Islamic monuments in India.

Bijapur was the capital of the Adil Shahi kings (1489–1686), and one of the five splinter states formed when the Bahmani Muslim kingdom broke up in 1482. The others, formed at roughly the same time, were Bidar, Golconda, Ahmednagar and Gulbarga. The town still has a strong Muslim character, but is also a centre for the Lingayat brand of Shaivism. Inspired by the 12th-century religious revolutionary Basavanna (Basaveshwara), the Lingayat faith emphases a single personalised god, the 'chosen linga'. Basavanna's poems and hymns mock the rituals and legends of Vedic Hinduism.

Orientation

The two main attractions, the Golgumbaz and the Ibrahim Roza, are at opposite ends of the town. Between them runs Station Rd (MG Rd) along which you'll find most of the major hotels and restaurants. The bus stand is a five-minute walk from Station Rd; the train station is 2km east of the centre.

Information

The tourist office is behind KSTDC's Hotel Mayura Adil Shahi Annexe on Station Rd, but there's not much information and it doesn't operate city tours. The post office, also on Station Rd, is open from 8.30 am to 6 pm Monday to Saturday.

To change travellers cheques head to Canara Bank, north of the market. You'll need to provide the bank with photocopies of the ID pages of your passport.

Golgumbaz

Bijapur's largest and most famous monument is the Golgumbaz. Built in 1659, it's an enormous, bulky, ill-proportioned building, containing an immense hall, buttressed by octagonal seven-storey towers at each of its corners. The structure is capped by an enormous dome, 38m in diameter, said to be the world's third largest.

Around the base of the dome, high above the hall, is a gallery known as the 'whispering gallery'; if you speak into the wall a person listening on the opposite side of the gallery should hear you clearly. The acoustics here are such that any sound made is said to be repeated 10 times over. Unfortunately groups of children like to test the acoustics by shouting a lot. Access to the gallery is via a narrow staircase in the south-eastern tower and there are views of Bijapur from the outside of the dome. It's best to come in the early morning, before any school groups arrive.

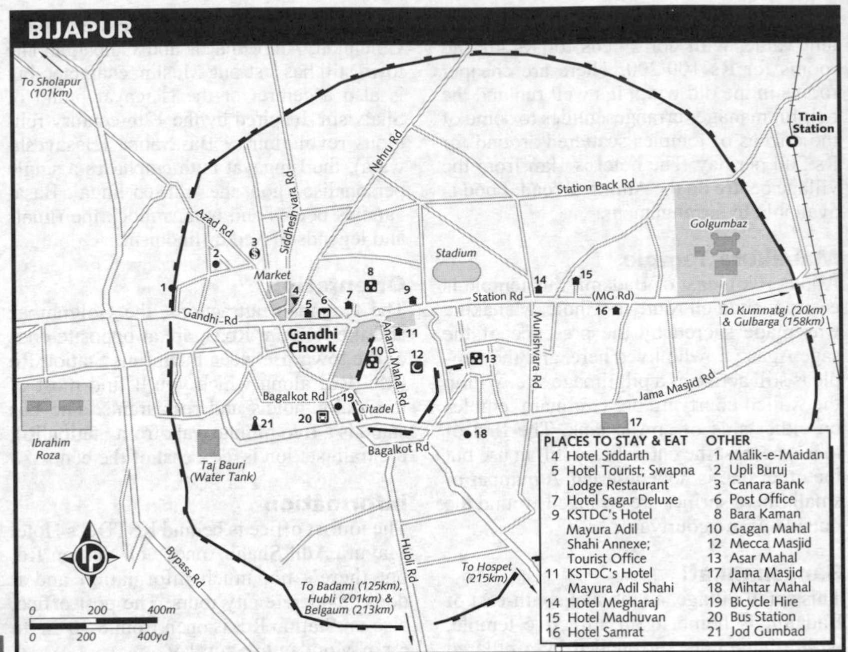

KARNATAKA

The Golgumbaz is the mausoleum of Mohammed Adil Shah (1626–56), his two wives, his mistress (Rambha), one of his daughters and a grandson. Their caskets stand on a raised platform in the centre of the hall, though their actual graves are in the crypt, accessible by a flight of steps under the western doorway.

The mausoleum is open from 6 am to 6 pm, and for foreigners costs US$5 in rupees. Shoes should be left outside near the entrance to the hall.

An **archaeological museum** in the ornamental gardens is open from 10 am to 5 pm daily except Friday.

Ibrahim Roza

The beautiful Ibrahim Roza was built at the height of Bijapur's prosperity by Ibrahim Adil Shah II (1580–1626) for his queen. Unlike the Golgumbaz, which is impressive for its immensity, the emphasis here is on elegance and delicacy. Its 24m-high minarets are said to have inspired those of the Taj Mahal. It's also one of the few monuments in Bijapur with substantial stone filigree and other decorative sculptural work.

Interred here are Ibrahim Adil Shah, his queen, Taj Sultana, his daughter, two sons, and his mother, Haji Badi Sahiba. Entry costs US$5 in rupees; shoes should be left on the steps up to the platform.

Citadel

Surrounded by fortified walls and a wide moat, the citadel once contained the palaces, pleasure gardens and durbar hall of the Adil Shahi kings. Most are in ruins, though some impressive fragments remain. The best is the **Gagan Mahal**, built by Ali Adil Shah I around 1561 to serve the dual purpose of a royal residence and a durbar hall.

Mohammed Adil Shah's seven-storey palace, the **Sat Manzil**, is nearby, but substantially in ruins. Just across the road stands the delicate **Jala Manzil**, once a water pavilion surrounded by secluded courts and gardens. On the other side of Station Rd are the graceful arches of **Bara Kaman**, the ruined mausoleum of Ali Roza.

Jama Masjid

The finely proportioned Jama Masjid has graceful arches, a fine dome and a large inner courtyard with room for 2250 worshippers. Spaces for them are marked out in black on the polished floor of the mosque. The flat roof is accessible by several flights of stairs. It was constructed by Ali Adil Shah I (reigned 1557–80), who was also responsible for erecting the fortified city walls and the Gagan Mahal, and for installing a public water system.

Other Monuments

The **Asar Mahal**, to the east of the citadel, was built by Mohammed Adil Shah in about 1646 to serve as a Hall of Justice. The building once housed two hairs from the Prophet's beard. The rooms on the upper storey are decorated with frescoes and the front is graced with a square tank. Women are not allowed inside. The stained but richly decorated **Mihtar Mahal** to the south serves as an ornamental gateway to a small mosque.

Upli Buruj is a 16th-century, 24m-high watchtower built on high ground near the western walls of the city. An external flight of stairs leads to the top, where there are a couple of hefty cannons and good views of the city and plains.

The **Malik-e-Maidan** (Monarch of the Plains) is a huge cannon measuring over 4m long, almost 1.5m in diameter, and estimated to weigh 55 tonnes. It was cast in 1549 and brought to Bijapur as a war trophy thanks to the effort of 10 elephants, 400 oxen and hundreds of men. Legend has it that the gunners would jump into the moat after lighting the fuse, rather than be deafened. In a whimsical touch, the head of the cannon is shaped like a tiger (Islam), whose razor-sharp jaws are closing on a cartoonish bug-eyed elephant (Hinduism) trying to flee.

In the south-west of the city stands the twin **Jod Gumbad** tombs with handsome bulbous domes, where an Adil Shahi general and his spiritual adviser, Abdul Razzaq Qadiri, are buried. The surrounding gardens are a popular picnic spot. Nearby is the **Taj Bauri**, a large, polluted water tank with fine gateway.

Special Events

Bijapur's **Lingayat Siddeshwara Festival** runs for eight days in January/February.

Places to Stay

Hotel Sagar Deluxe *(☎ 59234, Barakaman Rd)*, in the centre of town, is the best budget option. The rooms are on the small side but are clean and comfortable. Singles/doubles cost Rs 125/150 (a TV is Rs 50 extra), and there's an air-con suite for Rs 750.

Hotel Tourist *(☎ 20655, Gandhi Rd)*, further west, is very basic but in reasonable shape, besides a few stains on the walls. Ordinary doubles are Rs 120.

Hotel Megharaj *(☎ 51458, Station Rd)* is of a similar standard; the ordinary doubles for Rs 130 are better value than the deluxe doubles for Rs 210.

Hotel Samrat *(☎ 21620, Station Rd)* has bearable rooms with private bathroom for Rs 120/150, or deluxe doubles with TV and air-cooler for Rs 220.

KSTDC's Hotel Mayura Adil Shahi Annexe *(☎ 50401, Station Rd)* is a bit shabby but the rooms are big; air-con doubles cost Rs 445. Rooms at ***KSTDC's Hotel Mayura Adil Shahi*** on Anand Mahal Rd are horrid and swarming with mosquitoes.

Hotel Madhuvan *(☎ 55571, fax 53254, e madhuvan_hotel@yahoo.com, Station Rd)* a modern and very comfortable hotel set back from the main road. Singles/doubles with TV and private bathroom are US$25/29, or US$31/41 with air-con. They will change money for guests.

Places to Eat

Swapna Lodge Restaurant, on the 2nd floor of the building next to Hotel Tourist, has good vegetarian and nonvegetarian food, good service as well as cold beer. Its open-air terrace is perfect for evening dining.

Hotel Siddharth, in the busy market just north of Station Rd, is one of Bijapur's best vegetarian places, and it also has a range of ice creams.

KSTDC's Hotel Mayura Adil Shahi is not a bad place for a beer in its garden courtyard, but the food is below average and service is very slow.

Hotel Madhuvan is probably the most cheerful restaurant in town, with all the usual Indian/Chinese/continental standards and air-con.

Getting There & Away

Bus There are daily services to Badami (Rs 46, four hours), Belgaum (Rs 56, five hours), Gulbarga (Rs 55, four hours), Bidar (Rs 70, seven hours), Hubli (Rs 55, 4½ hours) and Sholapur (Rs 44, two hours).

There are six evening services to Bangalore (Rs 203 in 'ultra-deluxe', 12 hours) via Hospet; four buses to Hyderabad and to Pune; and a couple to Bidar.

Private bus agencies near the bus stand have services to Bangalore and Mumbai.

Train Conversion to broad gauge line is complete between Bijapur and Sholapur, but is still continuing to Gadag. Once normal services resume it should be easy to get express connections to Sholapur and Gadag (via Badami). Sholapur has connections to Mumbai, Hyderabad and Bangalore; Gadag has connections to Hospet, Hubli and Bangalore. Bijapur station has a healthy quota of sleeping berths allotted to it on all major expresses. Note that the 12.10 pm departure to Gadag connects with the *Hampi Express* to Bangalore.

Getting Around

The uncrowded local bus system has only one useful route – from the train station, along Station Rd to the gate at the western end of town. Buses run every 15 minutes.

Autorickshaw drivers charge what they think you will pay – intense haggling and Rs 20 should get you between the train station and the town centre. Between the Golgumbaz and Ibrahim Roza costs about Rs 25. Tonga drivers are eager for business but charge around the same.

You can rent bicycles from the stall opposite the bus stand, or from outside Hotel Sanman for Rs 2 per hour.

THE NORTH-EAST

Gulbarga

☎ 08472 • pop 349,500

This scruffy town was the Bahmani capital from 1347 until its transfer to Bidar in 1428. Gulbarga's **fort** is in a deteriorated state. It includes the **Jama Masjid**, reputed to have been built by a Moorish architect who imitated the great mosque in Cordoba in Spain. Gulbarga also has a number of imposing **tombs** of Bahmani kings, a shrine to an important Muslim saint and the **Sharana Basaveshwara Temple**, where a 15-day **festival to Shiva** in March attracts an estimated 100,000 people.

Places to Stay & Eat At ***Hotel Pariwar*** *(☎ 21421, Station Rd)* you'll find clean rooms, hot water all day and a basic vegetarian restaurant. Ordinary rooms cost Rs 250/350 with TV.

Hotel Southern Star *(☎ 24093, SB Temple Rd)* is tucked between the tank and the fort. Simple, decent doubles cost Rs 220, or Rs 500 with air-con.

Kamat Cafe on Station Bazaar, the traffic circle at the south end of Station Rd, is clean and serves good vegetarian food. There's an air-con dining room.

Getting There & Away There are plenty of buses to Bijapur (Rs 55, five hours) and Bidar (Rs 33, three hours), plus overnight buses to Bangalore. Four buses depart for Hyderabad, all of them in the evening.

Many express trains pass through Gulbarga, giving it good connections to Mumbai, Bangalore and Hyderabad.

Bidar

☎ 08482

This walled town in the extreme north-eastern corner of the state was the capital of the Bahmani kingdom from 1428, and later the capital of the Barid Shahi dynasty. It features a magnificent 15th-century **fort** containing the evocative ruins of the Rangin Mahal, Takht Mahal and Tarkash Mahal **palaces**. The fort has a triple moat carved from red rock, intricate battlements and an imposing gateway, all well preserved.

The *Bidriware* of Bidar

During its heyday, the Persian craftsmen of Bidar came up with a form of damascening now known as *bidriware*. It involves moulding imaginative blends of blackened zinc, copper, lead and tin, which are then embossed, and overlaid or inlaid with pure silver. In both design and decoration, the artefacts are heavily influenced by the typically Islamic decorative motifs and features of the time. Finely crafted pieces such as hookahs, goblets, *paan* boxes and bangles are exquisitely embellished with interwoven creepers and flowing floral patterns, and occasionally framed by strict geometric lines. The effect of the delicate silver filigree against the ebony-toned background is striking. These days artists still tap away at their craft in the backstreets of Bidar, as well as in Hyderabad.

The **Khwaja Mahmud Gawan Madrasa** in the middle of town has a few colourful remains of typical Islamic mosaics. The huge domed **tombs** of the Bahmani and Barid kings are also worth seeing. These abandoned structures, that dot the countryside to the west and east of town, have an enticingly desolate aura, broken only by the noise of jets from the nearby air-force base.

Bidar lent its name to the handicraft *bidriware* (for details see the boxed text 'The Bidriware of Bidar').

Places to Stay & Eat You'll find ***Hotel Kailash*** *(☎ 27727)*, right near the old bus stand, clean, safe and comfortable with a helpful manager. Ordinary doubles cost Rs 130, deluxe doubles are Rs 230 and air-con doubles are Rs 410.

Hotel Ashoka *(☎ 26249)*, near Deepak Theatre, isn't quite so clean but is still good value. Rooms cost Rs 130/170 and air-con doubles are Rs 400. The Ashoka has a popular bar/restaurant with private booths and generous servings of North Indian and 'Chindian' (eg, fried noodles) dishes.

Among the cheap hotels, ***Hotel Prince*** *(☎ 25747)* is probably the 'least worst'. Singles/doubles with private bathroom cost from Rs 60/90. It's just one block from Hotel Kailash, past a couple of small Internet cafes.

Hotel Mayura Restaurant, opposite the bus stand, is a clean establishment where you can get reasonable vegetarian and non-vegetarian food and a cold beer.

Udipi Krishna Restaurant at the main intersection offers cheap pure vegetarian meals and has a separate room for women.

Getting There & Away Bidar has a number of bus connections to Gulbarga and Hyderabad, plus a few buses to Bijapur and Bangalore.

Andhra Pradesh

Andhra Pradesh is situated on the Deccan (south) plateau – one of the oldest geological formations in India. The Godavari and Krishna Rivers cut their way through the plateau, forming large deltas before entering the Bay of Bengal.

With its recent foray into information technology, Andhra Pradesh is promoting itself as the 'No 1 State'. Yet much of the state remains poor and undeveloped. Less than half the population is literate. Few travellers explore Andhra Pradesh, daunted by the long distances and lack of facilities. But Andhra Pradesh still attracts huge numbers with Tirumala and Puttaparthi in the south being two of the most visited pilgrim sites in the world.

Hyderabad-Secunderabad, the twin-city capital, is also a magnet due to its Muslim heritage while elsewhere in the state, Warangal, Vijayawada and Nagarjunakonda provide opportunities for observing the evidence of early Hindu-Buddhist societies and ancient architecture.

Andhra Pradesh at a Glance

Population: 76 million
Area: 276,754 sq km
Capital: Hyderabad
Main Language: Telugu
When to Go: Oct to Feb

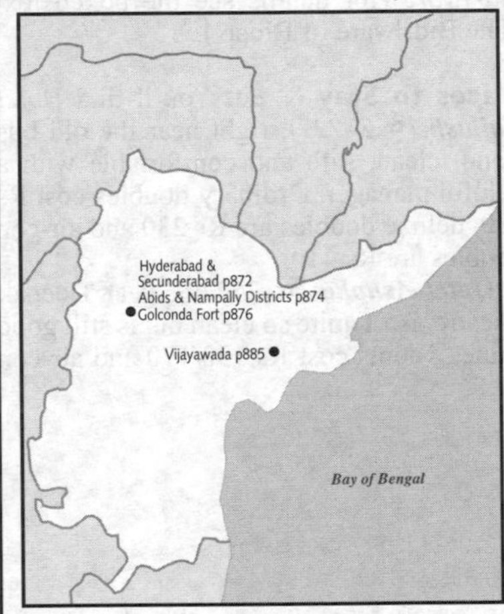

- Ascending the ancient spiral steps of the 400-year-old Charminar for a breathtaking view of Hyderabad
- Wandering through the colourful bazaars, especially Laad Bazaar of Hyderabad
- Tasting the aromatic flavours pounded and blended during the Ramadan fast
- Enjoying a picnic atop the ruins of the 16th-century Golconda Fort
- Mingling with the pilgrims at Tirupathi as they shed their hair in honour of their deity
- Experiencing the splendour of the ancient sculptures in the temple at Lepakshi

History

By the 1st century AD the flourishing Satavahana dynasty reigned throughout the Deccan plateau. It evolved from the Andhra people whose presence in southern India may date back as far as 1000 BC. In the 3rd century BC, the Andhras embraced Buddhism and built huge edifices in its honour.

From the 7th to the 10th century the Chalukyas established their Dravidian style of architecture, especially along the coast. The Chalukya and Chola dynasties merged in the 11th century to be overthrown by the Kakatiyas who introduced pillared temples into South Indian religious architecture. Following the Kakatiya rule, the Vijayanagars rose to become one of the most powerful empires, not only in the region, but of India.

By the 16th century the Islamic Qutb Shahi dynasty was established in Hyderabad. The Hyderabad rulers, known as nizams, managed to retain control throughout the 17th and 18th centuries as the British and French vied for trade. The region became part of the new independent India in 1947 and, in 1956, the state of Andhra Pradesh was created – an amalgamation of the Telugu-speaking areas.

Special Events

Like elsewhere in India, Andhra Pradesh hosts many vibrant festivals.

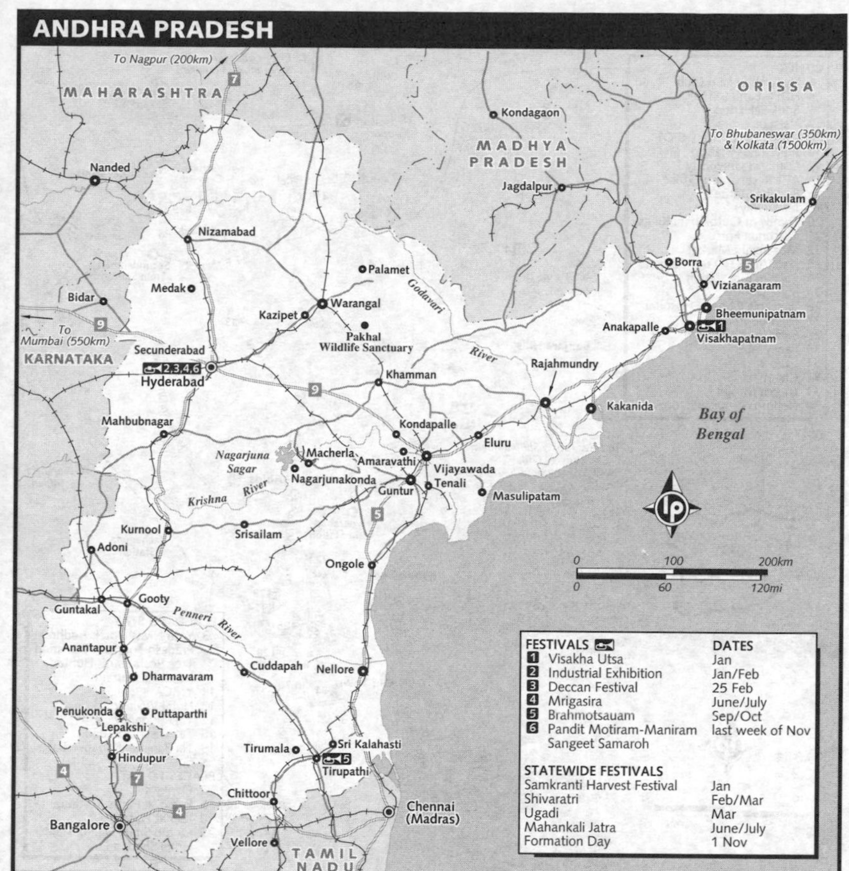

Samkranti Harvest Festival, in January, celebrates the end of the harvest season. Women create colourful *kolams* (rice flour designs, also known as *rangolis*) at the entrance to their homes and in public places people fly kites.

In February/March, during the time of the absent moon, **Shivaratri** celebrates the night of Shiva. The deity is honoured with prayers and special foods. This is a time of reflection, with the darkness of night becoming a metaphor for opposites – as night follows day, so too death follows birth. It's a time to enjoy success and prosperity, but to refrain from arrogance and egoism.

March marks the time of **Ugadi**, the Telugu new year. People make *puja* (worship) and celebrate with sweets and special foods.

In June/July, it is Kali, the goddess in her powerful and wrathful form, who is honoured in the **Festival of Mahankali Jatra**. Walking in colourful processions, people convey pots of food offerings to the deity.

On 1 November the state celebrates **Formation Day**, which commemorates its constitution as a state.

HYDERABAD & SECUNDERABAD

☎ 040 • pop 4.3 million

Hyderabad-Secunderabad, the capital of Andhra Pradesh, combines influences from both the Hindu and Islamic traditions. It's a busy place, where ancient lanes meet vehicle-choked highways. Centuries-old Islamic monuments stand alongside modern buildings. As the capital to a 95% Hindu

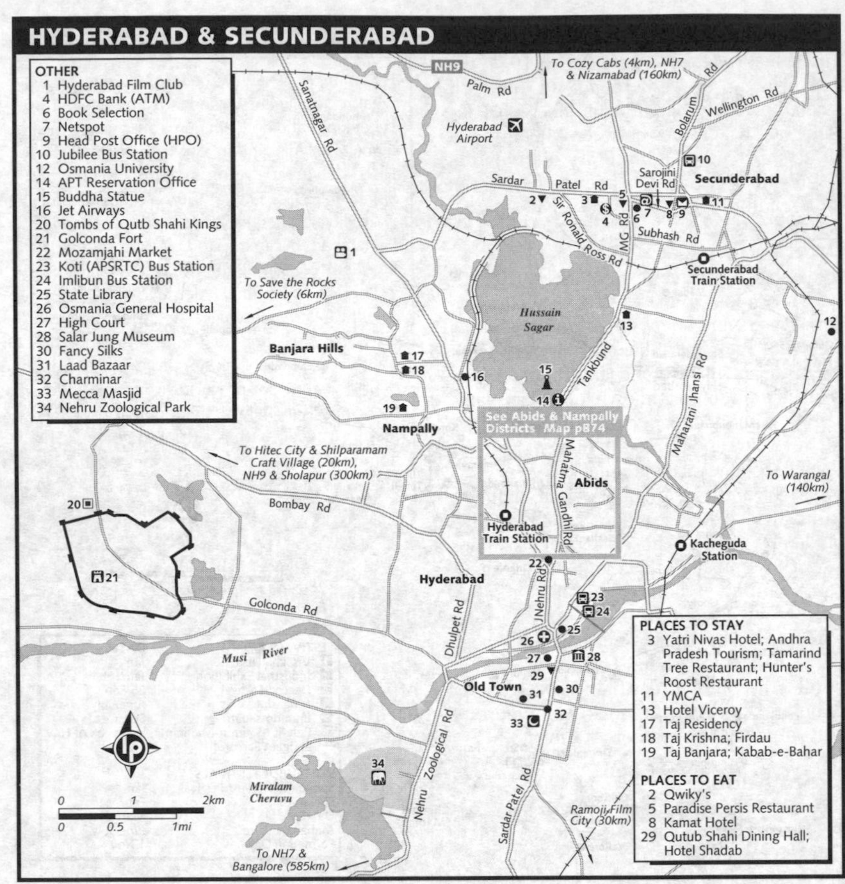

state, Hyderabad's population is almost 50% Muslim.

An important centre of Islamic culture, Hyderabad is central India's counterpart to the Mughal splendour of the northern cities of Delhi, Agra and Fatehpur Sikri.

As Hyderabad embraces technology, a third city is emerging – Hitec City, and in some circles Hyderabad is now referred to as Cyberabad (see the boxed text 'Cyberabadic Contradictions').

History

Hyderabad owes its existence to a water shortage. Towards the end of the 16th century, the banks of the Musi River proved to be a preferable location for Mohammed Quli, of the Qutb Shahi dynasty. So the royal family moved from Golconda Fort to establish the new city of Hyderabad. In 1687, it was overrun by the Mughal emperor Aurangzeb. Subsequently the rulers of Hyderabad were viceroys, installed by the Mughal administration in Delhi.

In 1724 the Hyderabad viceroy, Asaf Jah, took advantage of waning Mughal power and declared Hyderabad an independent state with himself as its head. So began the dynasty of the nizams of Hyderabad, under which the traditions of Islam flourished. Hyderabad became a focus for arts, culture and learning and the centre of Muslim India. Its abundance of rare gems and minerals furnished the nizams with enormous wealth.

In the early 19th century the British established a military barracks at Secunderabad, named after the nizam at the time, Sikander Jah. When Independence came in 1947, the then Nizam of Hyderabad, Osman Ali Khan, considered amalgamation with Pakistan, but the tensions between Muslims and Hindus increased and military intervention resulted in Hyderabad becoming part of the Indian union.

Orientation

Hyderabad has three distinct areas. The ancient city, close to the Musi River has bustling bazaars and many important landmarks including the Charminar. Just north of the river is the main bus stand (Imlibun), the Hyderabad train station (known locally as Nampally station) and main post office. Here too are the Abids and Nampally districts, a good place for budget accommodation.

Farther north again and beyond the huge artificial lake, the Hussain Sagar, lies Secunderabad. The head post office is here and many trains terminate at Secunderabad train station. Hyderabad airport is 8km north of the city.

The area west of Hussain Sagar is where the well heeled reside. The jewel in this middle-class crown is Hitec City with its landmark Cybertower housing numerous software development corporations.

Information

Tourist Offices Andhra Pradesh Tourism (APT) has several offices, all of which focus on organised tours. There's an office on the Tankbund road (☎ 3453036) and another at Yatri Nivas Hotel (☎ 7816375), Sardar Patel (SP) Rd, Secunderabad. Both offices open from 7 am to 7 pm daily.

The Government of India tourist office (GITO; ☎ 7630037) in the Sandozi Building, Street No 1, Himayatnagar, is open from 7 am to 7 pm weekdays.

If you wish to visit any national parks or sanctuaries, you'll need a permit from the Forest Office (☎ 3544355), Secretariat Rd.

For useful 'what's on' information pick up a copy of *Channel 6* (Rs 12) or *Prism* (Rs 10) from any newsstand.

Money You can change money at State Bank of India on Bank St or State Bank of Hyderabad on MG Rd. Thomas Cook (☎ 3231988) is in the Nasir Arcade on the 1st floor, AG's Office Rd. And there's a very convenient 24-hour ATM, which accepts most cards, at HDFC Bank just near the corner of MG and SP Rds.

Cyberabadic Contradictions

Hyderabad has always been renowned for its wealth, intelligentsia and artisans. Now the cyber kings and dot.com gurus are making their mark. So significant are the new changes that Hitec (Hyderabad Information Technology Engineering Consulting) City, a centre of software development situated on the outskirts of Hyderabad, became a stop over for former US President Clinton during his 2000 Indian tour.

There's no doubt Hyderabad deserves to celebrate its technological achievements. But contradictions abound. Of the state's population, 55% remain illiterate; millions lose crops due to insufficient power or irrigation. While the computer literate shelter in their cyber tower travelling the virtual highway, the homeless know the harsh realities of the *real* highways of Hyderabad.

Post & Communications The main post office is on Abids Circle, Hyderabad, and is open for general business from 9.30 am to 8 pm daily and for poste-restante collection from 10 am to 3 pm weekdays (to 1 pm Saturday). In Secunderabad the head post office, on Rashtrapati Rd, has the same hours.

There are plenty of telephone and fax kiosks around town. Internet connection can be very slow. Efficient places are usually in the plush areas. In Secunderabad, try Netspot, Shop 35, Chandralok Complex, Sarojini Dev (SD) Rd. In Abids, Aura Studio, next to the Government of India Tourist Office, provides good service. Both charge Rs 30 per hour.

Bookshops & Cultural Centres Hyderabad has many bookshops: AA Hussain & Co is on MG Rd (also known as Abids Rd) and Book Selection is in SD Rd in Secunderabad.

Alliance Française (☎ 3236646, fax 323 1684) is next to Birla Planetarium. It screens weekly movies in French and organises cultural events.

British Library (☎ 3230774), on Secretariat Rd, is a good place to catch up with current British newspapers and magazines. It's open from 11 am to 7 pm (closed Sunday and Monday).

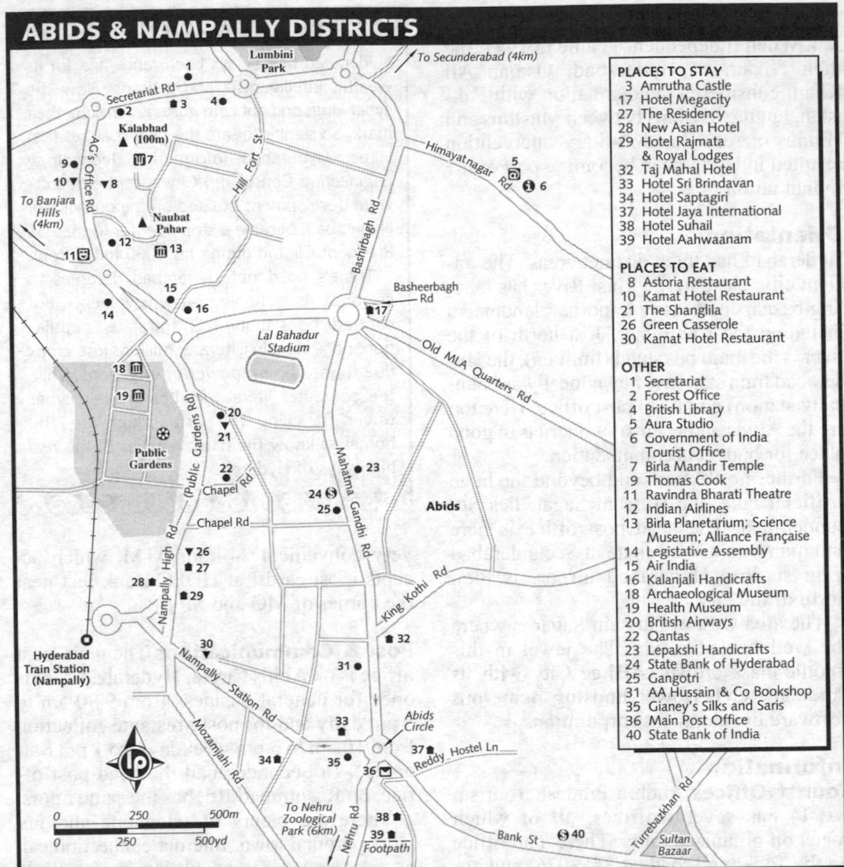

The State Library (☎ 4600107) with more than three million books is open 8 am to 8 pm daily, except Friday and public holidays.

Charminar & Bazaars

Hyderabad's principal landmark, the Charminar (four towers) was built by Mohammed Quli Qutb Shah in 1591, reputedly to commemorate the end of a devastating epidemic. This four-columned structure stands 56m high and 30m wide, creating four arches facing each of the cardinal points. Each column has a minaret on top.

The small mosque with 45 prayer spaces on the 2nd floor is the oldest in Hyderabad. Spiral staircases lead up the columns to views of the city. With luck, the man with the key will let you in for Rs 50.

The lower area of the Charminar is open from 9 am to 4.30 pm daily. The structure is illuminated from 7 to 9 pm daily.

West from the Charminar is the famous **Laad Bazaar** where you'll find just about everything from the tackiest of merchandise to the most exquisite perfumes, jewels and fabrics. You can also see artisans creating their works of fine *bidri* (inlaid silverware), large pots and musical instruments. The lanes around the Charminar form the centre of India's pearl trade. Browsing these lanes is a highlight of a visit to Hyderabad.

Mecca Masjid

Adjacent to the Charminar is the Mecca Masjid, one of the largest mosques in the world – accommodating up to 10,000 worshippers. Construction began in 1614 during the reign of Mohammed Quli Qutb Shah, but wasn't finished until 1687, by which time the Mughal emperor Aurangzeb had annexed the Golconda kingdom. The minarets were originally intended to be much higher but, as he did with the Bibi-qa-Maqbara in Aurangabad, Aurangzeb sacrificed aesthetics to economics.

Several bricks embedded above the gate are said to be made with soil from Mecca – hence the name. The colonnades and door arches, with their inscriptions from the Quran are made from single slabs of granite. These massive stone blocks were quarried 11km away and dragged to the site by a team of 1400 bullocks.

The mosque has been disfigured by huge wire mesh awnings, erected in a vain attempt to stop birds nesting.

To the left of the mosque is an enclosure containing the tombs of Nizam Ali Khan and his successors.

Non-Muslims cannot enter the Mecca Masjid, but they can appreciate the structural and architectural features from the outside.

Salar Jung Museum

This museum's huge collection, dating back to the 1st century, was put together by Mir Yusaf Ali Khan (Salar Jung III), the prime minister, or grand vizier, of the seventh nizam, Osman Ali Khan. The 35,000 exhibits from every corner of the world include sculptures, woodcarvings, religious and devotional objects, Persian miniature paintings, illuminated manuscripts, weaponry, and over 50,000 books.

The museum is open from 10 am to 5 pm daily except Friday, but avoid Sunday when it's bedlam. Entry is Rs 5. From any of the bus stands in the Abids area, take bus No 7, which will drop you at the Musi River Bridge; just cross the river and take the first turn left.

Not far west of the Musi River Bridge, facing each other across the river, are the spectacular **High Court** and **Osmania General Hospital** buildings, built in the Indo-Saracenic style.

Birla Mandir Temple & Planetarium

The Birla Mandir Temple, which was constructed of white Rajasthani marble in 1976, graces one of the twin rocky hills, Kalabahad (black mountain) overlooking the southern end of Hussain Sagar. Dedicated to Lord Venkateshwara, the temple is a popular Hindu pilgrimage centre. There are excellent views over the city from the temple, especially at sunset. It's open to Hindus and non-Hindus from 7 am to noon and 2 to 9 pm daily.

On Naubat Pahar (Drum Rock), the hill adjacent to the Birla Mandir Temple, are the Birla Planetarium & the Science Museum (☎ 3235081). The planetarium has daily sessions in Telugu, Hindi and English. Admission is Rs 10. The museum is open from 10.30 am to 8.15 pm daily (closed on the last Tuesday of each month) and admission is Rs 6.

Buddha Statue & Hussain Sagar

Hyderabad boasts one of the largest stone Buddhas in the world. Work on the project began in 1985 at Raigir, 50km from Hyderabad, and was completed in early 1990. The 17.5m-high, 350-tonne monolith was transported to Hyderabad and loaded onto a barge for ferrying across Hussain Sagar to be erected on the dam wall.

Unfortunately, disaster struck and the statue sank into the lake taking with it eight people. There it languished for two years. Finally, in 1992, a Goan salvage company raised it (undamaged!) and it is now on a plinth in the middle of the lake.

Frequent boats make a 30-minute return trip to the statue from **Lumbini Park** from 10 am to 8 pm for Rs 20 per person. The park is open from 9 am to 9 pm Tuesday to Sunday, and entry is Rs 2. Lumbini Park is a pleasant spot to enjoy Hyderabad's blood-red sunsets and the popular (though somewhat absurd) musical fountain. There's a fairground for children.

The Tankbund skirts the eastern shore of Hussain Sagar. It has great views of the Buddha statue and is a popular promenade and jogging track.

Archaeological Museum

The Archaeological Museum contains a small collection of archaeological finds from the area, together with copies of paintings from the Ajanta Caves in Maharashtra. Opening hours are from 10.30 am to 5 pm daily, except Friday, and entry is Rs 1.

Also worth a quick visit is the nearby **Health Museum**, where you'll see a bizarre and eclectic collection of medical and public health paraphernalia. It's open from 10.30 am to 1.30 pm and 2 to 5 pm daily; admission is free.

There's an **aquarium** nearby in Jawahar Bal Bhavan. It's open from 10.30 am to 5 pm daily, except Sunday.

Nehru Zoological Park

One of the largest zoos in India, the Nehru Zoological Park is spread over 1.2 sq km of landscaped gardens. The 3000 animals and birds here live in large, open enclosures and don't look any less bored than animals in zoos elsewhere in the world. There's a prehistoric animal section, a toy train (Rs 2, every 15 minutes) a lion safari trip (Rs 10, every 15 minutes) and a nocturnal section.

The park is open from 9 am to 5 pm daily, except Monday; entry costs Rs 2. Take bus Nos 74, 94A, 95k, 95P or 95S from Koti bus station.

Golconda Fort

This 16th-century fortress is a must-see. Like many of the great forts in India, Golconda exudes a palpable sense of history.

It has experienced many waves of occupation and abandonment. Although the bulk of the fort dates from the time of the Qutb Shah kings (16th to 17th century) its origins have been traced to the earlier Hindu periods when the Yadavas and, later, the Kakatiyas ruled this part of India.

For nearly 80 years Golconda was the capital of the independent state Telangana, but in 1590, Sultan Quli Qutb Shah abandoned the fort and moved to the new city of Hyderabad.

In the 17th century, Mughal armies from Delhi were sent against the Golconda kingdom to enforce payment of tribute. Abul Hasan, the last of the Qutb Shahi kings, held out at Golconda for eight months against the massive army of emperor Aurangzeb. The emperor finally succeeded via the treacherous actions of an insider, Abdullah Khan Pani.

Following Aurangzeb's death early in the next century, his viceroys (later the nizams) made Hyderabad their capital once again, and Golconda was abandoned.

When standing at the top of the fort, it's easy to see how the Mughal army came close to total defeat. The citadel is built on a granite hill 120m high and is surrounded by crenellated ramparts constructed of large masonry blocks. The massive gates are studded with large pointed iron spikes, intended to obstruct war elephants. Outside the citadel stands another crenellated rampart, surrounding the base of the hill, with a perimeter of 11km. Outside this wall is a third wall.

Survival within the fort was attributable not only to the walls, but also to water and sound. A complex series of concealed glazed earthen pipes ensured a reliable water supply and the acoustics guaranteed that even the smallest sound from the Grand Portico would echo across the fort complex, making anonymity impossible. Even today, silence only comes with stillness, and it is worth being still to consider the great tides that have moved through the fort.

Knowledgeable guides congregate at the entrance. They'll start asking Rs 250 for a 1½-hour tour and rapidly lose interest in any offer below Rs 150. Alternatively, the *Guide to Golconda Fort & Qutb Shahi Tombs* (Rs 10) may be on sale.

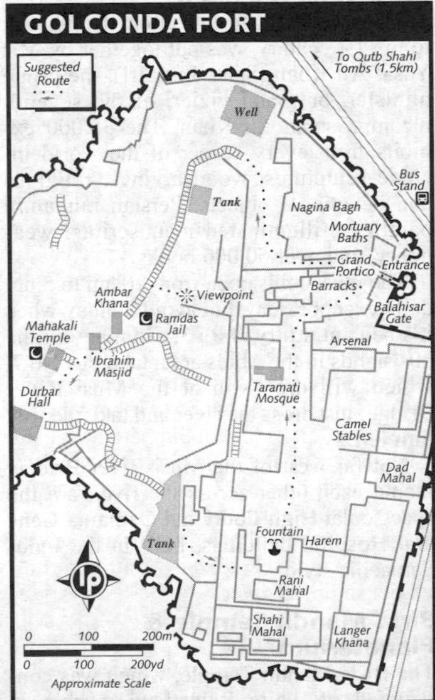

The fort is open from 8 am to 6.30 pm daily, and entry is Rs 2 (free on Friday). Many city buses will get you to the fort's main entrance, Balahisar Gate. See the list under Bus in Getting Around later. An autorickshaw from Abids costs around Rs 150 return, including waiting time. Early morning is best for relative peace and quiet – tour groups arrive from 11 am.

There's also a sound-and-light show here; for more information see Organised Tours later in this section.

Tombs of Qutb Shahi Kings

These graceful domed tombs are about 1.5km north-west of Golconda Fort's Balahisar Gate. Surrounded by landscaped gardens, they are open from 9.30 am to 4.30 pm daily, except Friday and entry is Rs 2. Most people walk from Golconda to the tombs, but there are usually a few autorickshaws willing to take you for a handsome price.

Ramoji Film City

Situated 35km south-east of Hyderabad, this 800-hectare complex is claiming to lure film production away from Mumbai (Bombay). If you enjoy being herded like cattle for four hours to see clapped out film sets, it's worth a visit. To get there take bus No 205 from Koti (Rs 8, one hour). You'll need to wait at the bus station opposite the Osmania University Women's College, 100m from the main Koti bus station. Ramoji Film City is open from 9 am to 6 pm (it's best to arrive before 2 pm). Entry is Rs 150 (Rs 200 on weekends). A 'royal package' (Rs 650) includes transport within film city in a small bus and lunch at a five-star hotel.

Hitec City & Shilparamam Craft Village

If glass towers housing software companies excite you, then take a bus (30km west) to Hitec City. The adjacent Shilparamam Craft Village (entry Rs 2) is a pleasant garden setting with boating, craft displays and occasional performances. Bus No 10H from Secunderabad will bring you here (see the boxed text 'Cyberabadic Contradictions' earlier in this chapter).

Organised Tours

The APT conducts numerous tours including half-day city (Rs 100), full-day city (Rs 130), Ramoji Film City (Rs 350) and longer tours to Nagarjuna Sagar (Rs 225) and Tirupathi (Rs 950, three days). The evening city tour (Rs 100) takes in Hitec City, Shilparamam Craft Village and a sound-and-light show at Golconda Fort. If you make your own way to the fort you can see the sound-and-light show for Rs 20. It starts at 6.30 pm (November to February) and 7 pm (March to October), daily except Monday. Sessions are in Telugu, Hindi and English.

Beating the Bhattis

If you happen to be travelling around Andhra Pradesh during the month of Ramadan (known locally as Ramazan), look out for the clay ovens known as Bhattis. You'll probably hear them before you see them. Men gather around and take turns in vigorously pounding the *haleem* (a mixture of meat and wheat) inside the purpose built structures. Come nightfall, the serious business of eating begins. The taste is worth the wait.

Special Events

Hyderabad is a popular venue for cultural festivals, exhibitions, book fairs and car rallies. The city guide *Channel 6* or the daily papers will have details. In January/February, the huge **Industrial Exhibition**, displays products including machinery, appliances and fabrics from throughout the country. The **Deccan Festival**, on 25 February, features cultural performance, while in the last week of November the **Pandit Motiram-Maniram Sangeet Samaroh** celebrates Hindustani music, with a four-day festival of music and dance. **Mrigasira Hyderabad**, in June/July, marks the beginning of the monsoon. It is celebrated with a feast of local fish. A fascinating aspect of this time is the medical treatment administered to thousands of asthma sufferers. The treatment, a tradition more than 150 years old, involves swallowing live fish, which have in turn consumed a unique herbal remedy. It's believed the remedy was revealed by a sage to the ancestors of the physicians who now dispense it.

Places to Stay – Budget

The best of the cheap hotels are all in the Nampally/Abids area between Abids Circle and Hyderabad (Nampally) train station.

Royal Home, ***Royal Hotel*** (☎ *3201194)* and ***Neo Royal Hotel*** (☎ *3201029)* are built around a courtyard opposite the station on Nampally High Rd (Public Gardens Rd). They're all similar – at Rs 130/230 for singles/doubles with not-very-clean private bathrooms, squat toilets and hot water in the morning only.

Hotel Rajmata (☎ *3204111, fax 320 4133)* has 'deluxe' rooms with TV and phone for Rs 390/490. This is a good-value place. There's a restaurant here with vegetarian and nonvegetarian food.

New Asian Hotel (☎ *3202655)*, also called Asian Lodge, is a typical, no-frills boarding house. Cage-like rooms with squat toilets and cold water only are Rs 100/150.

Hotel Sri Brindavan (☎ *320970)* near Abids Circle is good value. It offers singles/doubles with squat toilets for Rs 250/ 300, with hot water from 4 to 7.30 am. Rooms are set around a quiet courtyard.

Hotel Suhail (☎ *4610299, 4-1-527 Troop Bazaar)* is quiet with standard rooms for Rs 120/175, deluxe rooms for Rs 180/250 and air-con doubles for Rs 450. All rooms have a TV and most have a balcony.

YMCA (☎ *7564670)* accepts male and female guests and has six branches. The Secunderabad branch at the northern end of Station Rd has rooms for Rs 70/100 with a shared bathroom and squat toilets.

Only Secunderabad train station has ***retiring rooms***. Air-con rooms are Rs 175/250 and non air-con rooms cost Rs 75/100. Dorm rates are Rs 40 for 24 hours.

Places to Stay – Mid-Range

Yatri Nivas Hotel (☎ *7816881, fax 772 9129, Sardar Patel Rd)* in Secunderabad has large, clean rooms for Rs 425/550 or Rs 650/750 with air-con. It has two good restaurants, a trendy pub and a tourist office.

Hotel Megacity (☎ *3229267, fax 322 9969, Basheerbagh Rd)* has clean, reasonable rooms for Rs 375/450. The attached bar/restaurant is pleasant, well priced and has a good selection.

Hotel Saptagiri (☎ *4603601, Nampally Station Rd)* has small but good-value rooms with balconies for Rs 150/200, and Rs 400 for a double with air-con.

Hotel Aahwaanam (☎ *4740301)*, opposite the noisy Ramakrishna Cinema, is huge with decent rooms with TV for Rs 260/295 or Rs 600/650 with air-con.

Hotel Jaya International (☎ *4752929, fax 4753919, Reddy Hostel Lane)*, off Bank St, has comfortable rooms for Rs 300/400 (plus Rs 50 for TV) or Rs 600/750 with air-con.

Taj Mahal Hotel (☎ *4758221)*, on the corner of MG and King Kothi Rds, is rambling and deservedly popular. Spacious rooms with hot water from 5 am to noon and TV cost Rs 350/500, or Rs 500/700 with air-con. Facilities include two vegetarian restaurants and a coffee shop.

The Residency (☎ *3204060, fax 320 4040, Nampally High Rd)* has thoughtful, attentive service, but its rooms, ranging from Rs 1395/1750 to 3000, are tacky. There's a pleasant lobby, a pub and a 24-hour coffee shop.

Amrutha Castle (☎ *3299899, fax 324 1850, Secretariat Rd)* is eccentric on the outside, but ordinary inside. Rooms start at Rs 1200/1600, and suites go for Rs 3000 to 5000. Facilities include a fax in every room, a restaurant, gym and a rooftop pool.

Places to Stay – Top End

Hotel Viceroy (☎ *7538383, fax 7538797)*, on the Tankbund, has overpriced but comfortable, well-appointed singles/doubles for Rs 2200/2600 or Rs 2500/2900 with a lake view. All rates include a buffet breakfast. This centrally air-conditioned hotel has the usual facilities, including Internet access (for nonguests, too). The travel desk can organise car hire, but has little other information.

The five-star hotels are on Road No 1 at Banjara Hills. They are all centrally air-conditioned with excellent restaurants, shopping arcades and facilities; all charge a 20% tax.

Taj Residency (☎ *3993939, fax 339 2684)* has rooms from Rs 2600 to 7500, including breakfast.

Taj Krishna (☎ *3392323, fax 3393079)* ranges from US$120/140 to US$500 for the presidential suite.

Taj Banjara (☎ *3399999, fax 3392218)* is a palatial hotel with rooms costing from Rs 2600/2900 (Indian residents) and US$90/105 (foreigners). The presidential suite is Rs 10,000 or US$300. One of its four restaurants is set outside next to a small lake.

Places to Eat

The cuisine of Andhra Pradesh has two major influences. The northern Mughals and the former local nizam palaces brought the tasty biryanis of spiced meats, vegetables and rice, *haleen* (pounded spiced wheat with mutton – see boxed text 'Beating the Bhattis') and kebabs. The Andhra styles combine vegetables with spices, particularly chilli and mustard. Andhra pickle (chilli, lime peel and mango) is a hot favourite. Mozamjahi Market on the corner of Mukkarramjahi and Jawaharlal Nehru Rds is a great place to buy fruits and vegetables, and you can enjoy its alluring architecture at the same time.

Woodland, at Hotel Saiprakash, Nampally Station Rd, does great South Indian vegetarian breakfasts, snacks and meals.

The ***Kamat Hotel*** chain continues to dish up good cheap meals. The main dishes are Rs 15 to 30. There's one in Secunderabad on Sarojini Devi Rd, another in Abids on AG's Office Rd, and a third on Nampally Station Rd.

Astoria Restaurant, opposite Kamat Hotel on AG's Office Rd, is a popular open-air dinner spot.

Green Casserole serves everything on green crockery. There's an extensive vegetarian menu and the food's good. Average main courses cost Rs 45.

The Shanglila has good multicuisine fare.

Qutub Shahi Dining Hall (downstairs) and ***Hotel Shadab*** (upstairs), at High Court Rd, Madina Circle, have sumptuous Andhran and North Indian meals from Rs 45.

Paradise Persis Restaurant, on the corner of SD and MG Rds, Secunderabad, is famous for its authentic Hyderabadi cuisine. This is *the* place to eat. It's a multi-layered maze of eating venues with flashing fairy lights. On the footpath take-away try the juicy kebabs for Rs 100.

Hunter's Roost and ***Tamarind Tree*** are relaxing and attractive outdoor venues attached to Yatri Nivas. Hunter's Roost has multicuisine and a bar.

Qwiky's, part of the American chain, on SP Rd, offers cocktails or coffee (Rs 40). The coffee's good but it's no match for the excellent South Indian coffee elsewhere.

Top-end hotels all have excellent restaurants and coffee shops, including ***Firdau*** at the Taj Krishna. Expect to pay at least Rs 250 to 500 per person. The Taj Banjara's ***Kabab-e-Bahar*** is a less formal barbecue/kebab restaurant set outdoors on a small lake, with excellent vegetarian and nonvegetarian dishes for around Rs 500.

Entertainment

The ***Ravindra Bharati Theatre*** has regular performances of music, drama and dance. Details are available from local papers.

With the relaxation of liquor laws, many hotels are now providing music and dance venues. There are several pubs, including those at ***Hotel Residency*** and ***Yatri Nivas***, but they tend to be smoky clubs for the blokes.

There is a plethora of cinemas in Hyderabad showing Tamil and Telugu films. ***Hyderabad Film Club*** *(☎ 3730265, 7-1-209/3 Ameerpet)* shows foreign films, sometimes in conjunction with the Alliance Française.

If you're into rocks, ***Save the Rocks Society*** *(☎ 3552923, 1236 Rd, No 60 Jubilee Hills)* organises walks through the surreal Andhran landscape to raise awareness of the damage of intensive quarrying.

Shopping

The bazaars near the Charminar are the most exciting places to shop. Here you'll find exquisite pearls, silks and fabrics. Silk and sari shops dominate the lower section of Nampally Station Rd nearby. One of the biggest is Gianey's Silks and Saris and there's also Fancy Silks, 21-2-28, Pathergatti.

One of the best places for Indian arts and crafts is Kalanjali on Nampally High Rd. Along MG Rd you'll find the state outlets for Uttar & Andhra Pradesh – Gangotri (which has fine furniture and other crafts) and Lepakshi with its wide range of Andhra crafts.

Getting There & Away

Hyderabad has air, road and rail links to most major Indian cities. There are also some international flights.

Air The airport is 8km north of the city. The Air India office (☎ 7811395) is opposite the Legislative Assembly. International flights leave for Kuwait (twice weekly), Muscat (three weekly) and Sharjah (twice weekly). Air India also has flights to Mumbai (Bombay; six weekly).

Indian Airlines (☎ 3299333) nearby is open from 10 am to 1 pm and 2 to 5.25 pm daily. It has flights between Hyderabad and Bangalore (Rs 3055/US$105 for Indians/foreigners, once daily), Mumbai (Rs 3490/US$120, three daily), Kolkata (Calcutta; Rs 6405/US$210, once daily), Delhi (Rs 6075/US$205, twice daily), Chennai (Madras; Rs 3005/US$105, once daily), Vizag (Rs 3175/US$110, once daily) and Tirupathi (Rs 2410/US$85, twice weekly).

Jet Airways (☎ 3301222), with similar prices, flies daily to Bangalore, Chennai, Delhi, Kolkata, Mumbai, Tirupathi and Vizag. Other airlines with offices in Hyderabad are:

British Airways (☎ 3241802) 5-9-88/4 Chapel Rd
Qantas (☎ 3298495) 3-A4-9-93 Chapel Rd

Bus There are numerous bus stands in Hyderabad, and three main bus stations – Imlibun, Jubilee and Koti (also known as the Andhra Pradesh State Road Transport Corporation – APSRTC bus station). Buses leave Imlibun bus station (☎ 4613955) for all parts of the state and interstate. They are well organised with timetables in Telugu and English. A computerised advance booking office is open from 8 am to 9 pm daily. Jubilee bus station (☎ 7802203), Secunderabad, operates a similar service with buses to destinations in the north and west. From Koti you'll catch local buses. See the table 'Buses from Hyderabad'.

Private bus companies have superdeluxe video services to Bangalore, Mumbai, Chennai, Nagpur and Tirupathi. Most of their offices are on Nampally High Rd near the entrance road to Hyderabad station. Daily departures are usually in the late afternoon. To Bangalore or Nagpur it's Rs 220 (12 hours); to Mumbai or Chennai it's Rs 250 (14 hours).

Buses from Hyderabad

destination	distance (km)	frequency (per day)	fare (Rs)
Bangalore	574	12 ★	210
Chennai	700	1 ◆	240
Guntur	311	6	105
Medak	96	19	35
Tirupathi	550	7	200
Vijayawada	276	44	120

★ mainly evening ◆ 4.30 pm

Train There are three main train stations in Hyderabad – Secunderabad, Hyderabad (also known as Nampally) and Kacheguda. Secunderabad is the station where you catch most through trains (trains not originating in Hyderabad). Most stop at Kacheguda, a convenient set-down for Abids and the old city. See the table for major trains departing Hyderabad. Bookings for any train can be made at Hyderabad and Secunderabad stations from 8 am to 8 pm Monday to Saturday (4 pm Sunday). Both stations have a tourist counter. For general inquiries phone ☎ 1332 (Telegu); ☎ 1333 (Hindi); ☎ 1311 (English). For reservations (all languages) phone ☎ 1345.

Getting Around

The system of multinumbered addresses makes Hyderabad a confusing city to negotiate. Languages other than Telugu, Hindi and Urdu are rarely spoken or understood. However, new signs with street names and numbers are making the system a little easier and local cooperation and assistance is always there.

To/From the Airport The airport is at Begampet, 8km north of Abids. There is no airport bus. An autorickshaw from Abids costs about Rs 40 (about Rs 25 if you're local or a good negotiator). Taxis ask about Rs 120.

Bus Buses you might find useful include:

Nos 2C, 2R, 2U, 2V, 8A, 8B, 8C, 8D & 8U Jubilee station to Charminar
Nos 1, 2J, 7C, 7U, 8A, 8B & 8D Jubilee station to Afzalgang – catch these if you're heading for Abids, as they go down Tankbund and Nehru Rd via the main post office
Nos 8C, 8D, 8N, 8S, 8U, 8V, 20P, 20N & 20V Jubilee station to Hyderabad station
Nos 65G, 66P & 66G Charminar to Golconda Fort
65G & 142K Koti to Golconda Fort
2G & 5G Jubilee station to Golconda Fort

The 'Travel As You Like' ticket, available at any of the major bus stands or Secunderabad train station, permits unlimited bus travel anywhere within the city area for the day of purchase.

Car You can rent a car and driver from Cozy Cabs (☎ 7762023), Karan Apartments,

Major Trains from Hyderabad

destination	train No & name	departures	distance (km)	duration (hrs)	fare (Rs) 2nd/1st
Bangalore	5092 *G/S-Bangalore Exp**	6.20 pm S	790	15¾	235/793
Chennai	7054 *Hyderabad-Chennai Exp*	3.30 pm H	794	14½	236/798
	2760 *Charminer Exp*	7 pm H	794	14¼	236/798
Delhi	2723 *Andhra Pradesh Exp*	6.40 am H	1397	26¼	329/1113
	7021 *Dakshin Exp*	9.30 pm H	1397	31	329/1113
Kolkata	7046 *East Coast Exp*	7 am H	1591	30	346/1209
Mumbai	7032 *Hyderabad-Mumbai Exp*	8.40 pm H	800	15½	236/798
Tirupathi	7497 *Venkatadri Exp*	6.55 pm K	741	13	228/772

S – Secunderabad, H – Hyderabad, K – Kacheguda
* Gorakhpur/Secunderabad-Bangalore Express

Begumpet. It has reliable drivers with good local knowledge. Within the city it's about Rs 500 (half day). Outside the city, rates vary from Rs 4 per kilometre to Rs 6 with air-con.

Autorickshaw By the meter, autorickshaws cost Rs 7 for the first 2km plus Rs 3 for each additional kilometre. There's a minimum fee of Rs 7. Most drivers prefer a negotiated price rather than the metered one. Between 10 pm and 5 am you may have to pay a 50% surcharge.

NAGARJUNAKONDA

☎ 08680

Nagarjunakonda is 150km south-east of Hyderabad. Prehistoric remnants suggest that human activity began here some 200,000 years ago. From the 2nd century BC until the early 3rd century AD, Nagarjunakonda and nearby Amaravathi became the sites of powerful Hindu and Buddhist empires.

Nagarjunakonda may be named after Nagarjuna, the revered Buddhist monk, who governed the *sangha* (Buddhist monastery) for nearly 60 years around the turn of the 2nd century AD. He founded the Madhyamika school, which studied and developed the teachings of Mahayana Buddhism.

The ancient remains at the site were discovered in 1926 by archaeologist AR Saraswathi. In 1950 the area was chosen as the site for a huge reservoir, the **Nagarjuna Sagar**, for irrigation and the generation of electricity. Before the flooding in 1960, excavations unearthed Buddhist ruins: stupas, *viharas* (monasteries), *chaityas* (temples) and *mandapams* (pillared pavilions), as well as some outstanding examples of white marble depictions of the life of the Buddha. Many of these ancient monuments and structures were removed and rebuilt on an island in the middle of the dam.

Nagarjunakonda Museum is also on the island. It's well laid out with information in Telugu, Hindi and English. Stone Age picks, hoes and spears are on show. Impressive sculptures of large, voluptuous women stand next to exquisite Buddha statues.

The museum is open from 9 am to 4 pm daily (except Friday). Launches depart for the island from the village of Vijayapuri, on the banks of Nagarjuna Sagar at 9.30 am and 1.30 pm daily (except Friday). The one-hour trip costs Rs 10/20 per child/adult.

The launch stays at the island for 30 minutes. To do the place justice take the morning launch out to the island and the afternoon one back. You may be told that you require a permit to do this – you don't. Weekends and holidays are crowded, so extra express launches may run for Rs 20/30. Light refreshments only are available on the island.

Places to Stay

Nagarjunakonda is popular and accommodation can be tight during May school holidays. It's also rather basic; sleeping sheet territory!

Vijay Vihar Complex *(☎ 77362)* is operated by the APT. The beds in this spacious, crumbling hotel are in urgent need of replacement. Singles/doubles are Rs 500/600. The downstairs restaurant has a good range of vegetarian and nonvegetarian meals.

Project House (☎ *76540)* is also APT operated. About 3km from the jetty in a landscaped garden at Hill Colony, it offers basic rooms for Rs 300/500. The vegetarian restaurant is OK.

There is also an OK ***youth hostel*** at Hill Colony; a bed costs Rs 15 to 25, depending on the size of the room.

A number of basic, clean, and private ***rooms*** are available near Project House for around Rs 100 per room per day. For details check at Suranthi Wine Shop.

Getting There & Away

The easiest way to visit Nagarjunakonda from Hyderabad is to take the APT (☎ 040-3453036) tour. It departs Hyderabad daily (if demand warrants it) at 6.45 am from Yatri Nivas Hotel, returns at 9.45 pm and costs Rs 150/225 per child/adult. The tour includes visits (but not entrance fee) to the Nagarjunakonda Museum (closed Friday), Nagarjuna Sagar and Ethipothala Waterfalls.

If you'd prefer to make your own way there, regular buses link Hyderabad, Vijayawada and Guntur with Nagarjuna Sagar. The nearest train station is 22km away at Macherla (a branch line running west from Guntur) from where buses leave regularly for Nagarjuna Sagar.

WARANGAL

☎ 08712 • pop 537,000

About 157km north-east of Hyderabad, Warangal was the capital of the Kakatiya kingdom, which covered the greater part of present-day Andhra Pradesh from the late 12th to early 14th century until it was conquered by the Tughlaqs of Delhi. The Hindu Kakatiyas were great patrons of the arts, and during their reign the Chalukyan style of temple architecture reached its pinnacle.

If you have an interest in Hindu temple development then an outing to Warangal is worthwhile. Facilities are adequate for an overnight stop, or it can be visited in a long day trip from Hyderabad.

Warangal is a cotton market town. There's also a colourful **wool market** around the bus stand area in the cooler months.

Orientation & Information

The main locations of interest and information are Warangal, Hanamkonda (3km north-west of Warangal) and Kazipet (10km south-west of Warangal).

The Warangal train station and bus stand are opposite each other. Station Rd, running left as you leave the train station, is the main area for facilities including the post office and police station. Main Rd connects Warangal and Hanamkonda.

Kazipet, the train junction for north-bound trains, has a tourist kiosk. The Regional Tourist Information Bureau is 3km north of here at the Tourist Resthouse and the Forest Department is nearby, but all have very limited resources.

Bank hours are from 10.30 am to 2.30 pm weekdays (to 12.30 pm Saturday). For foreign exchange, go to State Bank of Hyderabad (closed weekends), opposite the Regional Tourist Information Bureau. Few places accept credit cards.

There's no shortage of local/STD/ISD booths; many are open 24 hours.

Fort

Warangal's fort was a huge construction with three distinct circular strongholds surrounded by a moat. Four paths with decorative gateways, set according to the cardinal points, led to the centre where a huge Shiva temple once existed. The gateways are still obvious, but much of the fort is in ruins.

The fort is around from Warangal at Mantukonda and can be easily reached by bus or autorickshaw.

Hanamkonda

Built in 1163, the **1000-Pillared Temple** on the slopes of Hanamkonda Hill, 400m from the Hanamkonda crossroads, is a fine example of Chalukyan architecture. Dedicated to three deities – Shiva, Vishnu and Surya, it has been carefully restored with intricately carved pillars and a central, very impressive Nandi. It's open from 6 am to 6 pm.

Down the hill and 3km to the right is the small **Siddheshwara Temple**. The **Bhadrakali Temple** featuring a stone statue of the goddess Kali, seated with a weapon in each of her eight hands, is high on a hill halfway between Hanamkonda and Warangal.

Palampet

About 60km north-east of Warangal, the **Ramappa Temple**, built in 1234, provides another attractive example of Kakatiya architecture. Its pillars are ornately carved and its eaves shelter fine statues of female forms. The temple is open from 6 am to 6.30 pm daily.

Just 1km south, the **Ramappa Cheruvu**, an artificial lake, now assumes a natural presence within the landscape. ***Vanavihar Guesthouse***, on the lakeshore, has double rooms for Rs 15 per person. You must book with the tourist information bureau in Kazipet and you'll need to bring all your own provisions.

Places to Stay

Accommodation facilities are modest. In addition to room charges, several hotels have a once-only guest charge of up to Rs 30.

Vijaya Lodge *(☎ 61781)* on Station Rd, three minutes from the train station, is OK value at Rs 75/120, or Rs 110 for a double room with phone. There are both squat/sit-down flush toilets and morning hot water.

Ashok *(☎ 85491, Main Rd)* at Hanamkonda, is 7km from Warangal train station and has singles/doubles for Rs 200/275; with air-con it's Rs 380/450. It's spacious and noisy with occasional hot water. It has two good restaurants and one of them serves alcohol.

Hotel Ratna *(☎ 60645, fax 60096)*, newer than Ashok, has singles/doubles for Rs 250/320 and air-con doubles for Rs 550 and Rs 750. It accepts MasterCard and Visa.

AP Tourist Resthouse *(☎ 32312)* is on the main road (3km before Kazipet bus stand) opposite the Regional Engineering College. The basic but spacious double rooms (no singles) are Rs 150. A dorm of six beds costs Rs 350 (total). There's a good vegetarian restaurant and the Regional Tourist Information Bureau is also here.

Retiring rooms at Warangal train station are Rs 50/75 (non air-con) and Rs 85/130 (air-con). There are also ***retiring rooms*** at Kazipet train station.

Places to Eat

There are several small snack houses, but few eating places in Warangal. ***Ashok*** and ***Hotel Ratna*** have restaurants with good food. ***Ruchi Restaurant*** on Station Rd serves nonvegetarian dishes. ***Kapila Restaurant*** at the Hanamkonda crossroads has vegetarian meals from Rs 25 and nonvegetarian food from Rs 100.

Getting There & Away

Regular buses run between Warangal and Hyderabad, Nizamabad and other major centres. Local buses connect Warangal with Kazipet and Hanamkonda.

Warangal is a major rail junction and there are regular trains to main cities such as Delhi and Chennai, as well as Hyderabad or Secunderabad (Rs 46/242 in 2nd/1st class, 152km, three hours) and Vijayawada (Rs 90/306, 209km, four hours). The three-hour journey from Hyderabad makes a day trip to Warangal and surrounds possible.

Getting Around

The bus stand is opposite the train station. Bus No 28 goes to the Warangal Fort at Mantukonda. Regular buses go to all the other sites. You can rent bicycles in Station St (Rs 5/20 per hour/day). Autorickshaws and cycle-rickshaws are other transport alternatives.

VISAKHAPATNAM

☎ 0891 • pop 1.15 million

This coastal city is the commercial and industrial heart of Andhra Pradesh's isolated north-east corner, and is home to India's largest shipbuilding yard.

Orientation & Information

The train station and bus stand are about 1.5km apart. Both are about 2km from the city centre, which is based loosely around the Poorna Market area. The beach hotels are all in Waltair, which is the most pleasant place to stay. The tourist office in the train station has little information.

Things to See & Do

These days the town has little to offer tourists. The best known sight is the rocky promontory known as the **Dolphin's Nose** (accessed only from 3 to 5 pm daily) jutting into the harbour. Waltair, the hilly seaside area, is edged by long beaches affording views across the Bay of Bengal and the busy Kolkata-Chennai shipping lane.

At Simhachalam Hill, 16km north-east, is a fine 11th-century **Vishnu Temple** in Orissan style. It's open from 6 to 10 am and 4 to 6 pm daily for puja and costs Rs 2, Rs 10 or Rs 30 – depending on the level of *darshan* (viewing of the god). The best beach is **Rushikonda**, 10km north-east.

The APT (☎ 596761) operates full-day **city tours** (including Vishnu Temple) for Rs 125 per person and day tours to the Araku Valley and Borra Caves for Rs 300.

About 25km north-east of Vizag, **Bheemunipatnam**, is one of the east coast's oldest Dutch settlements. Apart from a few tombs, little remains. A little way inland from here is **Hollanders Green**, the Dutch cemetery.

Some 90km north of Vizag are the million-year-old limestone **Borra Caves** which are filled with stalagmites and stalactites. A farther 30km north is the **Araku Valley**, home to isolated tribal communities.

Places to Stay & Eat

There's no shortage of places to stay for any budget. The ***retiring rooms*** include men-only dorm beds for Rs 20 and comfortable doubles at Rs 180.

A good area for cheap hotels is Main Rd near the Poorna Market.

Central The ***Hotel Poorna*** *(☎ 502344)* off Main Rd, has clean rooms from Rs 100/180, plus a once-only guest charge of Rs 30.

Hotel Daspalla *(☎ 564825, fax 563141)* has rooms (air-con only) for Rs 650/775 or Rs 750/875 for executive style. The three-star hotel has several restaurants serving Chinese, continental, tandoori and spicy local cuisine.

Dolphin Hotels Limited *(☎ 567000, fax 567555)* is a central four-star place with a swimming pool and three restaurants – South Indian, multicuisine and a 24-hour coffee shop. Rooms range from Rs 695/895 to 1195/1325, and breakfast is included in rooms priced above Rs 895.

Beach Area The ***Palm Beach Hotel*** *(☎ 754 026)* is old and run-down, but it's OK if you just want to be close to the beach. Rooms are Rs 450/500 or Rs 600/800 with air-con.

Park Hotel *(☎ 754488, fax 754181)*, next door, looks ugly from the outside but it is modern, friendly and comfortable. Air-con rooms, all with sea views, cost Rs 1850/2100. There's a pool and three restaurants.

Taj Residency *(☎ 567756, fax 564370)*, Vizag's best, is a luxurious, tiered hotel that climbs the hill from Beach Rd. It has a pool and restaurant, and room prices range from Rs 2000 to 5500.

Getting There & Away

Air Vizag's airport is 13km west of town and it costs Rs 150 by autorickshaw to get there. Indian Airlines (☎ 546501) flies to Chennai (Rs 3360/US$220 for Indians/foreigners) and Kolkata (Rs 4195/US$145) on Monday, Wednesday, Friday and Sunday; and to Hyderabad (Rs 3175/US$110) daily.

Train Visakhapatnam Junction station is on the Kolkata-Chennai line. To Kolkata, the overnight *Coromandel Express* is fast (Rs 250/846 in 2nd/1st class, 879km, 15 hours). Heading south, it goes to Vijayawada (Rs 128/431, 352km, 5½ hours) and Chennai Central (Rs 235/793, 784km, 15 hours).

Bus From the well-organised bus stand, the APSRTC (☎ 546400) has services to destinations within Andhra Pradesh, as well as Puri in Orissa.

Boat Boats for Port Blair in the Andaman Islands leave once every two months. Bookings for the 56-hour journey can be made at the Shipping Office (☎ 565597, fax 566507), AV Bhanoji Row, within the port complex. See Port Blair in the Andaman & Nicobar Islands chapter for more details.

VIJAYAWADA

☎ 0866 • pop 853,300

Vijayawada, at the head of the delta of the mighty Krishna River, has established itself as a major port and an important junction on the east coast train line from Kolkata to Chennai. About 265km east of Hyderabad and 70km inland from the sea, it's an important industrial centre and a hectic town.

For many, Vijayawada is the heart of Andhra culture and language. The main attractions here are the temples, including the ancient rock-cave temples.

There's a tourist information kiosk at the train station (try your luck) and Krishnaveni Motel (see Places to Stay & Eat). There are many Internet places, but the District Telecom Office has fast access at Rs 40 per hour. Money can be changed at State Bank of Hyderabad and Millennium Foreign Exchange (open from 10 am to 8.30 pm, except Sunday). A 2% commission is charged on travellers cheques. Lepakshi Handicrafts Emporium (☎ 573129) is in Ghandinagar near Hotel Ilapuram.

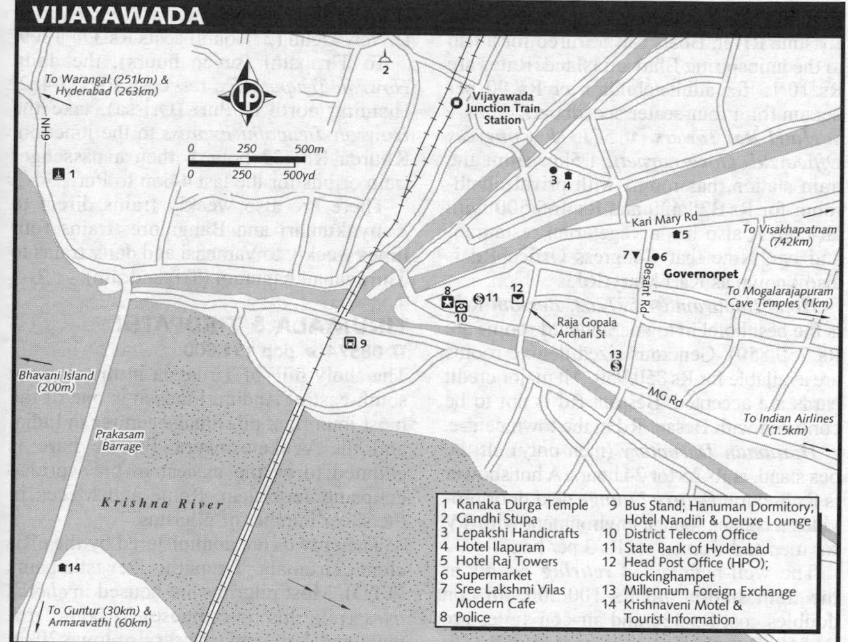

Kanaka Durga Temple

This temple on Indrakila Hill is dedicated to the goddess and protector of the city. Legend has it that she eradicated the area of powerful demons. She now receives continual gratitude from her followers, who credit her with the prosperous development of Vijayawada.

Cave Temples

About 8km west from Vijayawada, the 7th-century Hindu cave temples of **Undavalli** house a huge statue of the reclining Vishnu. Find the man with the key to let you in and he'll light a candle to display the sculpture. Other shrines are dedicated to the Trimurti (the triad – Brahma, Vishnu and Shiva). The caves are well worth a visit. You can get there by bus from Vijayawada.

Amaravathi

Amaravathi, 30km west of Vijayawada, is a significant ancient Buddhist centre and former capital of the Andhras. Here you'll see the remnants of a 2000-year-old **stupa** – a grass hump and a few stones. In the nearby **museum**, you'll see a small replica. It's open from 10 am to 5 pm daily, except Friday and public holidays (entry is free).

If you're into Buddhist history, you will no doubt wish to visit Amaravathi. But the best of the remaining sculptures are now in the Chennai Museum. There's no direct route from Vijayawada so it's necessary to travel 30km to Guntur and then a farther 30km to Amaravathi. Buses run from Vijayawada to Amaravathi (via Guntur) every hour from 6 am to 9 pm. The APT organises bus tours for Rs 65, and also boat trips for Rs 80 return. Ask at the tourist offices in Vijayawada. There's no accommodation at Amaravathi and few places to get drinks and snacks.

Places to Stay & Eat

Sree Lakshmi Vilas Modern Cafe *(☎ 572 525, Besant Rd)* at Governorpet, has single/double rooms with shared bathroom for Rs 90/100, or Rs 135/175 with private bathroom and bucket shower. The hotel has a good vegetarian restaurant and a 'conveyance service' to the bus or train station.

Krishnaveni Motel *(☎ 426382)* has singles/doubles for Rs 300/400. It's away

ANDHRA PRADESH

from the chaos of the city with views of the Krishna River. Boats can be hired for a trip to the uninspiring Bhavani Island. Rates are Rs 10/15 for adults/children or Rs 90 per person for a four-seater speedboat.

Hotel Raj Towers *(☎ 571311, Congress Office Rd, Governorpet)*, 1.5km from the train station, has rooms with private bathroom for Rs 325/420 and Rs 465/500 with air-con. It also has a vegetarian restaurant and bar. Note that Congress Office Rd is also known as Kari Mary Rd

Hotel Ilapuram *(☎ 571262, Bessant Rd)*, is the best hotel in town. Standard rooms are Rs 750/850). Generous sized deluxe rooms are available for Rs 850/950. All major credit cards are accepted. Bessant Rd is not to be confused with Besant Rd in the town centre.

Hanuman Dormitory (men only), at the bus stand, is Rs 25 for 24 hours. A hot shower is Rs 3 extra. ***Deluxe Lounge*** next door provides a banana lounge environment with TV for men and women for Rs 3 per hour.

The well-maintained ***retiring rooms*** at the train station are Rs 100/200, air-con doubles cost Rs 320 and air-con suites are Rs 350. Dorms (men only) cost from Rs 40; Rs 125 for air-con.

Hotel Nandini, at the bus stand (upstairs), serves South Indian vegetarian meals from 10 am to 3 pm and 7 to 10 pm. The downstairs restaurant is open 24 hours.

Getting There & Away

The enormous bus stand is 1.5km from the train station. It's well organised with dorms, waiting rooms, a cloakroom and restaurant. Signs here are in Telugu, but for non-Telugu speakers there is a helpful inquiry desk. From here, buses travel to all parts of Andhra Pradesh: every 30 minutes to Hyderabad (Rs 130, six hours), every 45 minutes to Amaravati (Rs 17), eight times daily to Warangal (Rs 115, six hours) and twice daily to Chennai (Rs 150, 10 hours).

Vijayawada is on the main Chennai to Kolkata and Chennai to Delhi lines and all express trains stop here. The quickest train from Vijayawada to Chennai is the *Coromandel Express* (Rs 140/473 in 2nd/1st class, seven hours). The same train to Kolkata (20 hours) costs Rs 312/1056.

There are plenty of trains via Warangal to Hyderabad (Rs 104/352, 6½ hours); one of the quickest is the 2703 *Falaknuma Express* (Rs 131/441). The 2621 *Tamil Nadu Express* to New Delhi (27 hours) costs Rs 374/1309.

To Tirupathi (seven hours), the daily *Howrah-Tirupathi Express* costs Rs 137/462. Heading north to Puri (Orissa), take the *Howrah-Tirupathi Express* to the junction, Khurda Rd (32 hours), then a passenger train or bus for the last 44km to Puri.

There are also weekly trains direct to Kanyakumari and Bangalore, trains four times weekly to Varanasi and daily trains to Thiruvananthapuram (Trivandrum).

TIRUMALA & TIRUPATHI

☎ 08574 • pop 191,000

The 'holy hill' of Tirumala in the extreme south-east of Andhra Pradesh is one of the most important pilgrimage centres in India, and the Venkateshwara Temple here is claimed to be the busiest in the world – eclipsing Jerusalem, Rome and Mecca in the sheer number of pilgrims.

The crowds are administered by the efficient Tirumala Tirupathi Devasthanams (TTD). Most pilgrims are housed in *choultries* (pilgrims' guesthouse) in both Tirumala and Tirupathi (the service town 20km away at the bottom of the hill). Buses constantly ferry pilgrims up and down the hill between Tirupathi and Tirumala from before dawn until well after dusk.

Tirumala is an engrossing place. It's one of the few places in India that allows non-Hindus into the sanctum. Despite this, the place receives few non-Hindu visitors. It's worth a visit, even if you're not a pilgrim; see the boxed text 'Venkateshwara Temple'. Down the hill from the main temple is **Sri Padmavathi Amma Vari Temple** dedicated to Lakshmi – the goddess of abundance.

The **Brahmotsavam**, the annual nine-day festival, is held in September/October. Initiated by Brahma himself, the festival sees the temple donned in decorations. Special pujas and colourful chariot processions are an important part of the festivities.

Organised Tours

The APT runs weekend tours to Tirupathi from Hyderabad. The tours leave at 3.30 pm Friday and return at 7 am Monday and include accommodation and 'special *darshan*' (viewing of a god). The cost is Rs 600/700 per child/adult. It's also possible (but not advisable) to take the bus; this costs Rs 175

Venkateshwara Temple

Pilgrims flock to Tirumala to visit the ancient temple of Venkateshwara, an avatar of Vishnu. Among the powers attributed to Venkateshwara is the granting of any wish that is made in front of the idol at Tirumala. It's considered auspicious to have your head shaved when visiting the temple and hundreds of barbers attend the devotees.

There are never less than 5000 pilgrims here at any one time and, in a single day, the total is often as high as 100,000. The temple staff alone number 18,000. Such popularity makes the temple one of the richest in India, with an annual income of a staggering one billion rupees. This is administered by a temple trust which ploughs the bulk of the money back into hundreds of *choultries* (pilgrims' guesthouses) and charities such as orphanages, schools, colleges and art academies.

Special *Darshan* at Tirumala

For Rs 30 you can have 'special *darshan*' (viewing of a god) at Tirumala. This not only allows you to enter the Venkateshwara Temple, but it gives you priority – you get to go ahead of all those who have paid nothing for their ordinary darshan and who have to queue – often for 12 hours or more – in the claustrophobic wire cages that ring the outer wall of the temple.

Although special darshan is supposed to get you to the front of this immense queue in two hours, on weekends when the place is much busier it can take as long as five hours, and you still have to go through the cages. A signboard at the entrance keeps you briefed on the waiting time.

No matter which darshan you experience, once inside the temple, you'll have to keep shuffling along with everyone else and, before you know it, you'll have viewed Venkateshwara and will be back outside again.

You can, however, pay considerably more than Rs 30 and secure a position for other special darshans, some of which involve minimal waiting.

one way. It's probably best to approach Tirupathi from Chennai; for more information see Organised Tours in the Chennai chapter.

Places to Stay & Eat

Hotel prices can vary, especially at festival times when there may be dramatic increases.

Tirumala There's a variety of accommodation options on the Tirumala Hill close to the temple. It's well organised and pleasant, and has a post office, several shopping complexes and a hospital.

Most pilgrims stay in the vast ***dormitories*** that ring the temple – beds here are free to pilgrims. If you want to stay, check in at the Central Reception Office, right near the Tirumala bus stand, and you'll be allocated a bed or a room. It's best to avoid weekends when the place becomes outrageously crowded.

Guesthouses and cottages range from Rs 250 for a suite to 8000 for an entire guesthouse. Accommodation in these is organised through the Central Reception Office.

You can also book accommodation. Write (not phone) giving all details of your requirements, and include a bank draft for Rs 100, to the Assistant Executive Officer (Reception-I), TTD, Tirumala 517504. During festivals there are no reservations.

Huge ***dining halls*** in Tirumala serve thousands of free meals daily to pilgrims. There are also numerous very good restaurants serving vegetarian meals.

Tirupathi The town and transport hub at the bottom of the hill is Tirupathi. It has plenty of hotels and lodges, so there's no problem finding somewhere to stay. A number of hotels are clustered around the main bus stand, 500m from the centre of town, and there are retiring rooms at the train station.

Vasantha Vihar Lodge *(☎ 20460, 141 G Car St)* is a friendly place about a one-minute walk from the train station. It has small, basic singles/doubles for Rs 65/90 with fan and shower.

Hotel Bhimas Paradise *(☎ 25747, fax 25568, Renigunta Rd)* has doubles only from Rs 450; Rs 750 to 950 for air-con. As well as the 10% tax, there's a guest charge of Rs 100.

Hotel Bhimas *(☎ 25744, 42 G Car St)*, a block away, has rooms for Rs 185/275 and doubles with air-con for Rs 600.

Bhimas Deluxe Hotel *(☎ 25521, 34–38 G Car St)*, opposite, and apparently not associated with its namesakes, is a two-star hotel with air-con rooms for Rs 540/650. All rooms have private bathroom and TV, and good views to the hills.

Hotel Mayura *(☎ 25925, fax 25911, 209 TP Area)* is a three-star hotel close to the bus stand. Rooms with private bathroom cost Rs 475, or Rs 700/750 with air-con. There's a restaurant and it has some good views.

The newer ***India Quality Inn Bliss*** *(☎ 21650, fax 29514)* has singles/doubles for Rs 750/950 with air-con and Rs 395/475 without. All rooms have TV. There are two restaurants, a cake shop and a bar. It's a friendly place with great views.

Lakshmi Narayana Bhavan is a good vegetarian place opposite the main bus stand in Tirupathi. ***Bhimas Deluxe Hotel's*** popular basement restaurant serves both North and South Indian cuisine until late at night.

Getting There & Away

It's possible to visit Tirupathi on a long day trip from Chennai, but staying overnight makes it far less rushed. If travelling by bus or train, it's possible to buy 'link tickets' (at place of ticket purchase) that cover the transport to Tirupathi and then up the mountain to Tirumala. These can save considerable time and confusion once you arrive.

Air The Indian Airlines office (☎ 22349) is in the Hotel Vishnupriya complex, opposite the main bus stand in Tirupathi. Flights come from Hyderabad (Monday and Friday) for Rs 2410/US$85 for Indians/foreigners. Jet Airways also has a service for the same fare.

Bus APSRTC runs 30 buses per day from Chennai, starting from 5 am. Ordinary buses are more frequent but much slower. The express buses take about five hours to do the 150km trip, cost Rs 55 and can be booked in advance in Chennai.

To Chennai, there are express buses from Tirupathi's main bus stand every 20 minutes from 2.30 am.

Several express and luxury buses travel to Hyderabad (Rs 450, 12 hours); there are also cheaper, less comfortable options. There are hourly buses to Vijayawada (Rs 140) as well as plenty of services to Vellore (Rs 185, 2½ hours) in Tamil Nadu and most other major towns in Andhra Pradesh and Tamil Nadu.

Train Tirupathi is well served by express trains. There are three trains daily to Chennai (147km, three hours), which cost Rs 67/226 in 2nd/1st class. The daily *Venkatadri Express* runs to Secunderabad (Rs 228/772, 741km, 17½ hours) and there are three daily express trains to Vijayawada (Rs 138/468, 389km, nine hours). There's also an express train to Madurai (Rs 208/704, 663km, 18 hours) via Vellore, Chidambaram and Tiruchirappalli, as well as a service to Mumbai (Rs 297/1003, 1132km, 31 hours) twice weekly.

Getting Around

Bus Tirumala Link buses operate from two bus stands in Tirupathi: the main bus stand, which is about 500m from the centre of town, and the Tirumala bus stand, which is near the train station. The 20km trip takes 45 minutes and costs Rs 15/25 one way/return on an ordinary bus and Rs 25/45 on an express bus.

To get on a bus in either Tirupathi or Tirumala, you usually have to go through a system of crowd-control wire cages, which are definitely not for the claustrophobic. At busy times (weekends and festivals), it can take up to two hours to file through and get on a bus. If you're staying in Tirupathi, buy a return ticket, which saves some queuing time. You can avoid the cages at Tirupathi by catching a bus from the main bus stand.

To find the bus queue at the Tirumala bus stand, walk through a choultry to reach the cages and ticket office – the choultry is about 200m from the entry to Tirupathi train station (turn to the right as you exit the station) opposite the bottom of the footbridge over the train line. If you're in a hurry, or don't like the cages, there are share taxis available. Seats cost around Rs 55, depending on demand. A taxi of your own costs about Rs 350 one way.

You can walk with pilgrims up a pleasant 15km path in four to six hours. Leave your luggage at the toll gate at Alipiri near the Hanuman statue. It will be transported for free to the reception centre. It's best to walk in the cool of the evening, but there are rest points protected from the sun on the way, and there's even a canteen.

PUTTAPARTHI

☎ 08555

Prasanthi Nilayam, Abode of Highest Peace, the main ashram of Sri Sathya Sai Baba, is in the south-western corner of Andhra

The God of Big Things

Around 20,000 people live in the small town of Puttaparthi. Many times a year however, the population swells to more than 50,000. The drawcard of course is Sai Baba and Puttaparthi is his birth place and the place where he established his main ashram, Prasanthi Nilayam.

It's difficult to overestimate the pulling power of this man who, at the age of 14, declared himself to be the reincarnation of a saintly figure named Sai Baba who died in 1918.

In November 2000, an estimated one million people gathered in and around the ashram to celebrate Sai Baba's 75th year. The massive gig rivalled the Sydney Olympics opening ceremony. Sai Baba's elaborately adorned elephant, Sai Gita, led a procession of bands, dancing troupes and flag bearers from 165 countries. Many devotees regard Sai Baba as a true avatar.

Everything about Sai Baba is big. There's his afro hair-do. There are the big name devotees including film stars, politicians and other 'gods' such as current Indian cricket superstar Sachin Tendulkar. There's the big money (millions of dollars) pumped into the nearby hospital, schools and university. And there's the big controversy. Serious allegations of sexual misconduct have led some devotees to lose faith. Others, however, regard such controversy as simply another terrestrial test for their avatar.

Pradesh at Puttaparthi. Sai Baba has a huge following in India and around the globe. He set up this ashram 40 years ago. He spends most of the year here but sometimes moves to Whitefields Ashram near Bangalore, or Kodaikanal in Tamil Nadu in the hot season.

Places to Stay & Eat

Most people stay at the ***ashram*** *(☎ 87583)*, a small village with all amenities. Ashram accommodation, although basic, is well kept, comfortable and cheap. Advance bookings are not taken. Meal costs are low, starting at Rs 2 for a breakfast of tiffin.

Accommodation outside the ashram is mostly run by Sai Baba devotees and rules (no alcohol, early to bed) apply. ***Hotel Sai Sree Nivas*** *(Main Rd)* is typical of outside accommodation. It's basic, with singles/doubles with private bathroom for Rs 175/350. Prices fluctuate with demand. ***Sri Sathya Sai Village***, about 2km from the ashram towards the airport, is a new village with all facilities and a multicuisine restaurant. Prices range from Rs 750 (double rooms only) to 1250 (double room with full board). All rooms have aircon. Advance bookings can be made in Chennai (☎ 044-4896060, fax 4896069).

Big Pizza – Long Noodles Restaurant, in the Sai Jyothi Complex just off Chitravanthi Rd, has omelettes for Rs 24 and noodles for Rs 26. ***Sai Bestways*** has good paneers for about Rs 35 and dhal for Rs 15.

Getting There & Away

Puttaparthi is most easily reached by bus from Bangalore and there are regular departures to Bangalore from Puttaparthi. From Bangalore or Hyderabad you can catch the train to Dharmavaram where regular buses connect to Puttaparthi. From Bangalore the train takes four hours (Rs 97/326 in 2nd/1st class, 235km). Many people take a taxi from Bangalore (Rs 850 to 1200).

If you're coming from Chennai the overnight 'high-tech' bus (softer seats, generally more comfortable and usually with a video) handles the bumpy ride. It leaves Parry's Corner at 7 pm daily (Rs 195, 11 hours). Indian Airlines flies to Puttaparthi from Mumbai (Rs 4095/US$140 for Indians/foreigners on Wednesday and Sunday).

Getting Around

Puttaparthi is well-organised and you should have no trouble finding your way. For travel farther afield, the large bus station has regular buses to surrounding areas such as Dharmavaram and Hindupur. The timetable is listed in Telugu, Hindi and English. Autorickshaws and cars can be hired from travel agencies. Try Sri Sai Ravitheja (☎ 87429) opposite the ashram on Main Rd.

LEPAKSHI

If you're travelling between Puttaparthi and Bangalore, it's well worth detouring to the **Veerbhadra Temple** at Lepakshi.

At the town entrance is a huge, monolithic Nandi (Shiva's bull vehicle). Just 500m on is the temple. Leave plenty of time to enjoy the splendour of this temple. Information booklets in Hindi and Telugu are available and there's a good English-speaking guide.

Kerala

Kerala, the narrow, fertile strip on the southwest coast of India, is sandwiched between the Lakshadweep Sea and the Western Ghats. The Western Ghats, with their dense forests and extensive ridges, have sheltered Kerala from many mainland invaders, and the long coastline has encouraged maritime contact with the outside world, resulting in an intriguing blend of cultures.

The state's sheltered location has allowed many distinctive customs, art forms and festivals to thrive. Kerala's biggest cultural celebration is the harvest festival Onam, when the state celebrates the golden age of mythical King Mahabali Kerala for four days in late August or early September. It includes elephant processions, cultural performances boat races for the public, and feasts and floral decorations in the home.

Kerala offers beautiful beaches, trips through peaceful lagoons and canals, hill stations, wildlife sanctuaries and complex cultural customs. With a high literacy rate and little of the poverty of say, Bihar, Kerala shows a much gentler and more relaxed side of India.

Kerala at a Glance

Population: 32 million
Area: 38,864 sq km
Capital: Thiruvananthapuram
Main Language: Malayalam
When to Go: Oct to Mar

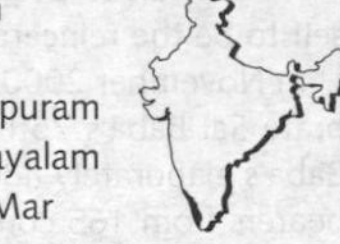

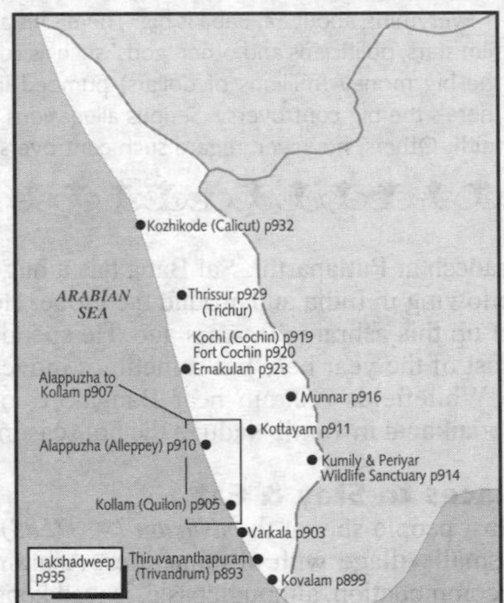

- Explore the backwaters at Kollam aboard a *kettuvallam* (rice-barge houseboat)
- Watch the spectacle of the Nehru Cup Snake Boat Race Alappuzha
- Soak up the sun, surf and seafood on busy beach resorts at Kovalam & Varkala
- Take a look at the wildlife or go on a jungle walk, boat trip or trek at Periyar Wildlife Sanctuary
- Walk around and take in the mountain vistas and tea gardens at Munnar
- Admire the Portuguese, Dutch and South Indian architecture at Kochi
- Laze on the beautiful palm-fringed atolls of Lakshadweep

History

Traders have been sailing to Kerala seeking spices and ivory for at least 3000 years. The coast was known to the Phoenicians, Romans, Arabs and Chinese. Kerala was also a trans-shipment point for spices from the Moluccas (eastern Indonesia), and it was through Kerala that Chinese products and ideas found their way to the West.

The kingdom of the Cheras ruled much of Kerala until the early Middle Ages. Its fortunes waxed and waned as it competed with kingdoms and small fiefdoms for territory and trade.

Vasco da Gama's arrival in 1498 heralded an era of European contact as Portuguese, Dutch and English interests fought the Arab traders and then each other for control of the spice trade.

The present-day state of Kerala was created in 1956 from the former states of Travancore, Cochin and Malabar. Traditional concern for the arts and education resulted in a post-Independence state that is one of the most progressive in India.

Kerala had the first freely elected communist government in the world, elected in 1957. The participatory political system has resulted in a more equitable distribution of land and income, low infant mortality and a 91% literacy rate.

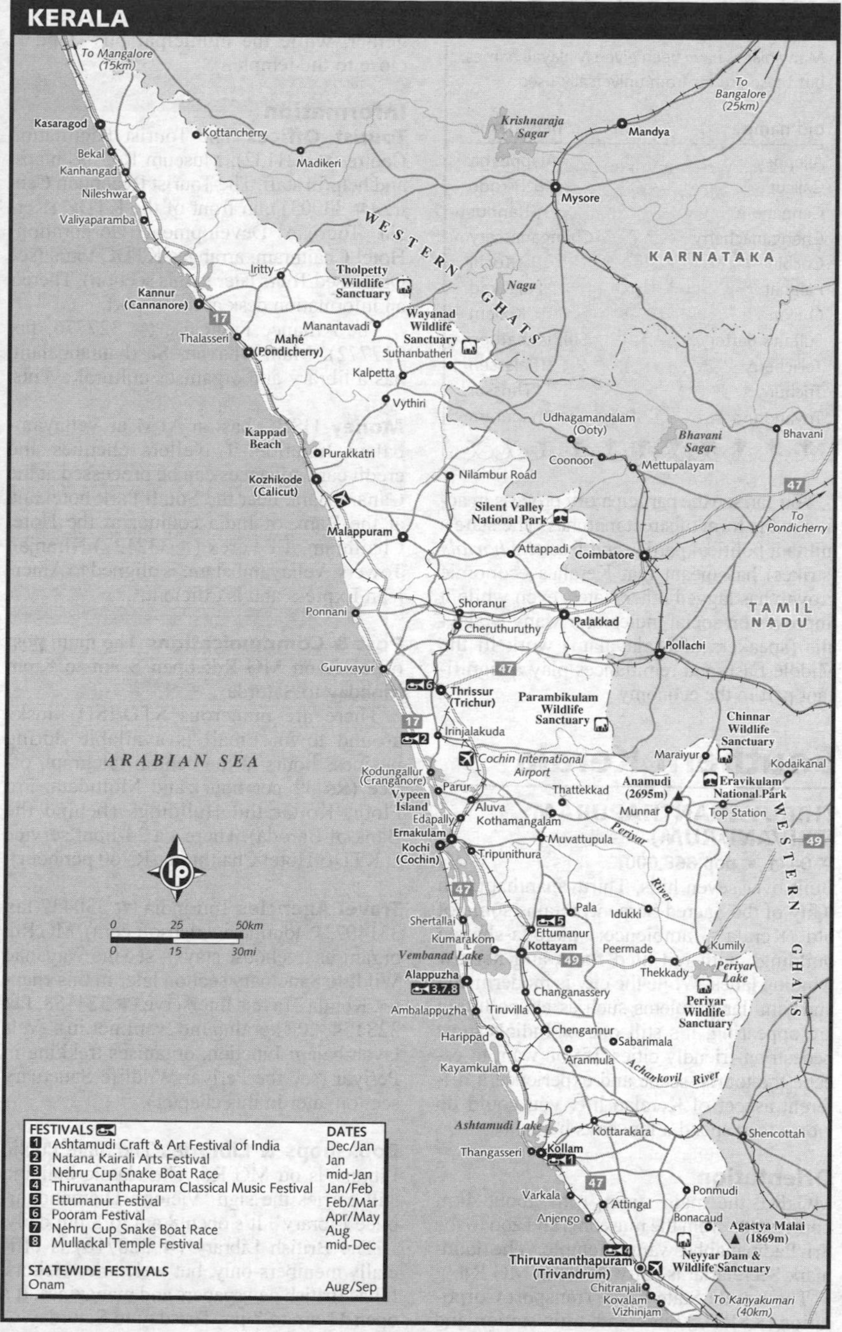
KERALA
To Mangalore (15km)
Kasaragod
Bekal
Kanhangad
Nileshwar
Valiyaparamba
Kottancherry
Madikeri
Iritty
Kannur (Cannanore)
17
Thalasseri
Mahé (Pondicherry)
Tholpetty Wildlife Sanctuary
Wayanad Wildlife Sanctuary
Manantavadi
Suthanbatheri
Kalpetta
Vythiri
WESTERN GHATS
Krishnaraja Sagar
Mandya
To Bangalore (25km)
Mysore
KARNATAKA
Nagu
Udhagamandalam (Ooty)
Coonoor
Mettupalayam
Bhavani Sagar
Bhavani
47
To Pondicherry
Kappad Beach
Purakkatri
Kozhikode (Calicut)
Nilambur Road
Silent Valley National Park
Malappuram
Attappadi
Coimbatore
TAMIL NADU
Shoranur
Cheruthuruthy
Palakkad
Ponnani
Pollachi
Guruvayur
47
6
Thrissur (Trichur)
Parambikulam Wildlife Sanctuary
17
2
Irinjalakuda
Chinnar Wildlife Sanctuary
ARABIAN SEA
Cochin International Airport
Maraiyur
Kodaikanal
Kodungallur (Cranganore)
Parur
Vypeen Island
Aluva
Thattekkad
Anamudi (2695m)
Eravikulam National Park
Munnar
Top Station
Edapally
Kothamangalam
Ernakulam
Kochi (Cochin)
Muvattupula
Periyar River
49
Tripunithura
WESTERN GHATS
47
Pala
Idukki
Shertallai
5
Ettumanur
Kumarakom
Kottayam
Peermade
Kumily
Vembanad Lake
49
Thekkady
Periyar Lake
Alappuzha
3,7,8
Periyar Wildlife Sanctuary
Changanassery
Ambalappuzha
Tiruvilla
Chengannur
Harippad
Sabarimala
Aranmula
Achankovil River
Kayamkulam
0 25 50km
0 15 30mi
Ashtamudi Lake
Kottarakara
Shencottah
Thangasseri
Kollam
1
47
Ponmudi
Varkala
Attingal
Anjengo
Bonacaud
Agastya Malai (1869m)
4
Neyyar Dam & Wildlife Sanctuary
Thiruvananthapuram (Trivandrum)
Chitranjali
Kovalam
Vizhinjam
To Kanyakumari (40km)
FESTIVALS
DATES
1 Ashtamudi Craft & Art Festival of India Dec/Jan
2 Natana Kairali Arts Festival Jan
3 Nehru Cup Snake Boat Race mid-Jan
4 Thiruvananthapuram Classical Music Festival Jan/Feb
5 Ettumanur Festival Feb/Mar
6 Pooram Festival Apr/May
7 Nehru Cup Snake Boat Race Aug
8 Mullackal Temple Festival mid-Dec
STATEWIDE FESTIVALS
Onam Aug/Sep

Name Changes

Many places have been given Malayali names, but these are far from universally used.

old name	new name
Alleppey	Alappuzha
Calicut	Kozhikode
Cannanore	Kannur
Changanacherry	Changanassery
Cochin	Kochi
Palghat	Palakkad
Quilon	Kollam
Sultan's Battery	Sulthanbatheri
Tellicherry	Thalasseri
Trichur	Thrissur
Trivandrum	Thiruvananthapuram

You can see the participatory process in action in the form of street marches. The state's militant political parties and frequent *hartals* (strikes) has meant that Kerala's economic growth has lagged other states, even while it improves on social indicators. Many Malayalis (speakers of Malayalam) work in the Middle East, and remittances play a significant part in the economy.

Southern Kerala

THIRUVANANTHAPURAM (TRIVANDRUM)

☎ 0471 • pop 868,000

Built over seven hills, Thiruvananthapuram (City of the Sacred Serpent) retains some of old Kerala's ambience: pagoda-shaped buildings with red-tiled roofs and narrow winding lanes. While the city is modernising and familiar problems such as air pollution are appearing, it's still one of India's most pedestrian-friendly cities. If you want to escape the tourist scene and experience a different aspect of Keralan life, you could do worse than spend a few days here.

Orientation

MG Rd, the main street, runs about 4km north–south from the museums and zoo to the Sri Padmanabhaswamy Temple. The landmark Secretariat is halfway along MG Rd.

The Kerala State Road Transport Corporation (KSRTC) bus stand, train station and many of the budget hotels are close together, while the municipal bus stand is close to the temple.

Information

Tourist Offices The Tourist Facilitation Centre (☎ 321132), Museum Rd, has maps, and helpful staff. The Tourist Reception Centre (☎ 330031), in front of the KTDC (Kerala Tourism Development Corporation) Hotel Chaithram, arranges KTDC tours (see Organised Tours later in this section). There's an information desk at the airport.

The Alliance Française (☎ 327776, fax 327772), Mani Bhavan, Sasthamangalam, has a library and organises cultural events.

Money HSBC has an ATM at Vellayambalam Junction. Travellers cheques and credit card advances can be processed at the Canara Bank near the South Park hotel and at the Bank of India counter at the Hotel Chaithram. TT Forex (☎ 332127) Niranjan Towers, Vellayambalam, is aligned to American Express and is efficient.

Post & Communications The main post office is on MG Rd; open 8 am to 8 pm Monday to Saturday.

There are numerous STD/ISD kiosks around town. Email is available during business hours at the central telegraph office (Rs 32 per hour) and Multidata, 3rd Floor, Kottarathil Buildings (behind the Bank of Baroda). There's a 24-hour service at KTDC Hotel Chaithram (Rs 60 per hour).

Travel Agencies Tourindia (☎ 330437 fax 331407, ⓔ tourindia@richsoft.com), MG Rd, organises treehouse stays – see the Wayanad Wildlife Sanctuary section later in this chapter. Kerala Travels Interserve (☎ 324158, fax 323154, ⓔ keralt@md2vsnl.net.in), Vellayambalam Junction, organises trekking in Periyar (see the Periyar Wildlife Sanctuary section later in this chapter).

Bookshops & Libraries The State Public Library is on MG Rd. The classic building still carries the sign 'Victoria Diamond Jubilee Library'. It's open 8 am to 8 pm daily.

The British Library (☎ 328716) is officially members-only, but welcomes visitors. It has British newspapers and magazines. It's open 11 am to 7 pm Tuesday to Saturday.

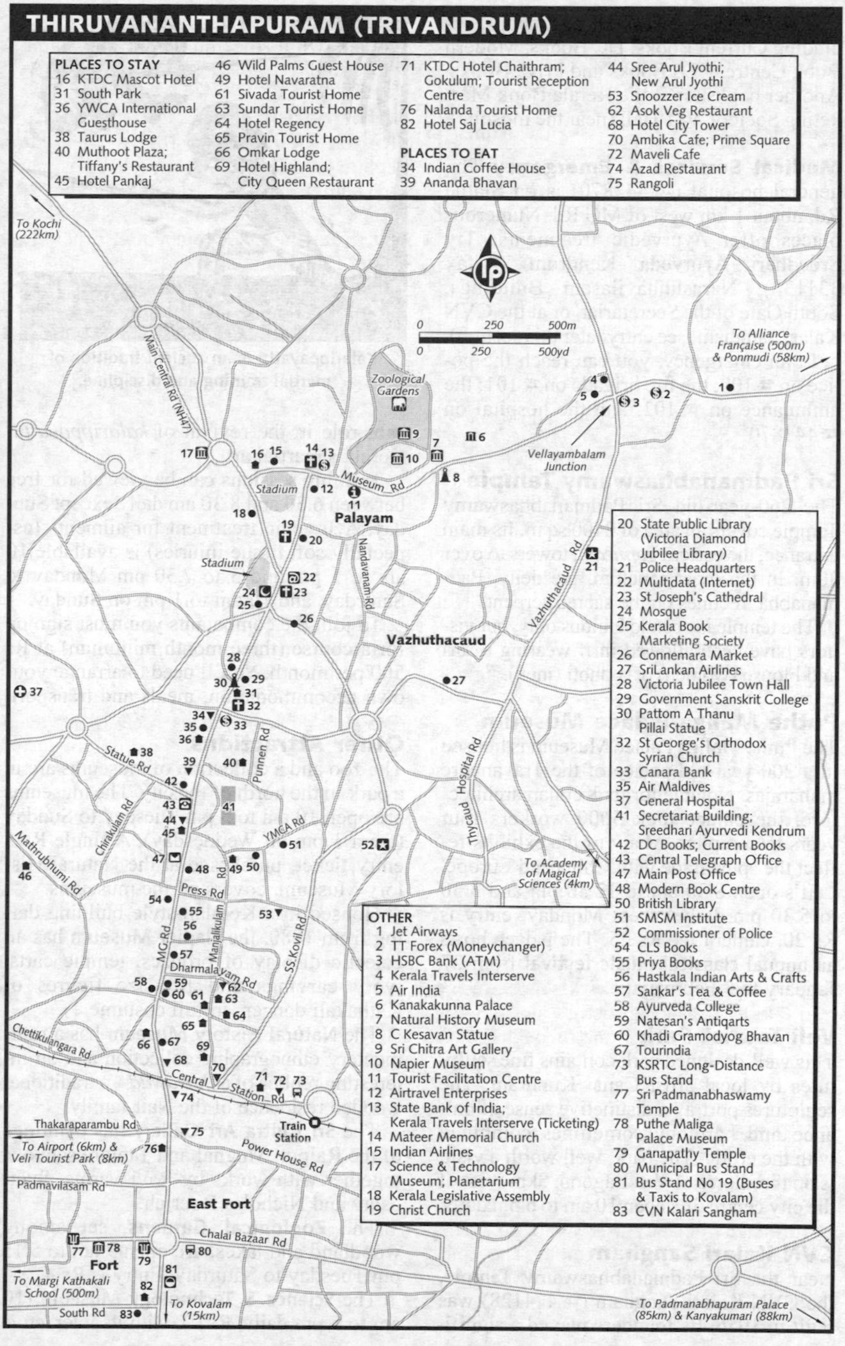

THIRUVANANTHAPURAM (TRIVANDRUM)

PLACES TO STAY
16 KTDC Mascot Hotel
31 South Park
36 YWCA International Guesthouse
38 Taurus Lodge
40 Muthoot Plaza; Tiffany's Restaurant
45 Hotel Pankaj
46 Wild Palms Guest House
49 Hotel Navaratna
61 Sivada Tourist Home
63 Sundar Tourist Home
64 Hotel Regency
65 Pravin Tourist Home
66 Omkar Lodge
69 Hotel Highland; City Queen Restaurant
71 KTDC Hotel Chaithram; Gokulum; Tourist Reception Centre
76 Nalanda Tourist Home
82 Hotel Saj Lucia

PLACES TO EAT
34 Indian Coffee House
39 Ananda Bhavan
44 Sree Arul Jyothi; New Arul Jyothi
53 Snoozzer Ice Cream
62 Asok Veg Restaurant
68 Hotel City Tower
70 Ambika Cafe; Prime Square
72 Maveli Cafe
74 Azad Restaurant
75 Rangoli

20 State Public Library (Victoria Diamond Jubilee Library)
21 Police Headquarters
22 Multidata (Internet)
23 St Joseph's Cathedral
24 Mosque
25 Kerala Book Marketing Society
26 Connemara Market
27 SriLankan Airlines
28 Victoria Jubilee Town Hall
29 Government Sanskrit College
30 Pattom A Thanu Pillai Statue
32 St George's Orthodox Syrian Church
33 Canara Bank
35 Air Maldives
37 General Hospital
41 Secretariat Building; Sreedhari Ayurvedi Kendrum
42 DC Books; Current Books
43 Central Telegraph Office
47 Main Post Office
48 Modern Book Centre
50 British Library
51 SMSM Institute
52 Commissioner of Police
54 CLS Books
55 Priya Books
56 Hastkala Indian Arts & Crafts
57 Sankar's Tea & Coffee
58 Ayurveda College
59 Natesan's Antiqarts
60 Khadi Gramodyog Bhavan
67 Tourindia
73 KSRTC Long-Distance Bus Stand
77 Sri Padmanabhaswamy Temple
78 Puthe Maliga Palace Museum
79 Ganapathy Temple
80 Municipal Bus Stand
81 Bus Stand No 19 (Buses & Taxis to Kovalam)
83 CVN Kalari Sangham

OTHER
1 Jet Airways
2 TT Forex (Moneychanger)
3 HSBC Bank (ATM)
4 Kerala Travels Interserve
5 Air India
6 Kanakakunna Palace
7 Natural History Museum
8 C Kesavan Statue
9 Sri Chitra Art Gallery
10 Napier Museum
11 Tourist Facilitation Centre
12 Airtravel Enterprises
13 State Bank of India; Kerala Travels Interserve (Ticketing)
14 Mateer Memorial Church
15 Indian Airlines
17 Science & Technology Museum; Planetarium
18 Kerala Legislative Assembly
19 Christ Church

0 250 500m
0 250 500yd

To Kochi (222km)
To Alliance Française (500m) & Ponmudi (58km)
Zoological Gardens
Vellayambalam Junction
Main Central Rd (NH47)
Museum Rd
Stadium
Palayam
Nandavanam Rd
Vazhuthacaud Rd
Vazhuthacaud
Statue Rd
Punnen Rd
Thycaud Hospital Rd
Chirakulam Rd
Mathrubhumi Rd
YMCA Rd
Press Rd
To Academy of Magical Sciences (4km)
MG Rd
Manjalikulam Rd
SS Kovil Rd
Dharmalayam Rd
Chettikulangara Rd
Central Station Rd
Thakaraparambu Rd
Train Station
To Airport (6km) & Veli Tourist Park (8km)
Power House Rd
Padmavilasam Rd
East Fort
Chalai Bazaar Rd
Fort
To Margi Kathakali School (500m)
To Kovalam (15km)
South Rd
To Padmanabhapuram Palace (85km) & Kanyakumari (88km)

MG Rd has many small bookshops, including Current Books, DC Books, Modern Book Centre, CLS Books and Priya Books. Another bookshop is the Kerala Book Marketing Society, VJT Hall (near the mosque).

Medical Services & Emergency The general hospital (☎ 443870) is on Statue Rd, about 1 km west of MG Rd. Numerous places offer Ayurvedic treatments. Try Sreedhari Ayurveda Kendrum (☎/fax 331138), Narasimhavilasam Buildings, South Gate of the Secretariat, or at the CVN Kalari Sangham (see entry later this section).

In an emergency, you can reach the police on ☎ 100; the fire brigade on ☎ 101; the ambulance on ☎ 102; and the hospital on ☎ 443870.

Sri Padmanabhaswamy Temple

The 260-year-old Sri Padmanabhaswamy Temple covers an area of 2400 sq m. Its main entrance, the eastern *gopuram*, towers to over 30m. In the inner sanctum, the deity, Padmanabha reclines on the sacred serpent.

The temple is open to Hindus only, but visitors have been allowed in if wearing a sari and blouse (women) or a dhoti (men).

Puthe Maliga Palace Museum

The Puthe Maliga Palace Museum is housed in a 200-year-old palace of the Travancore maharajas. Notable for its Keralan architecture, the palace took 5000 workers four years to complete. Many of the exhibits reflect the spice trade with China and Europe.

It's open 8.30 am to 12.30 pm and 3.30 to 5.30 pm daily except Monday; entry is Rs 20, camera fee Rs 25. The palace hosts an annual **classical music festival** from 27 January to 3 February.

Veli Tourist Park

This well-designed park contains fine sculptures by local artist Canai Kunuram. The sculptures portray a distinctive sense of balance and harmony sometimes combined with the erotic. The park, well worth a visit, is on the shores of Veli Lagoon, 8km west of the city centre. It's open 10 am to 6 pm daily.

CVN Kalari Sangham

Near the Sri Padmanabhaswamy Temple, the CVN Kalari Sangham (☎ 474128) was built in 1956. Its founders played a significant role in the revival of *kalarippayattu*, Kerala's martial art.

JENNY BOWMAN

Kalarippayattu is an ancient tradition of martial training and discipline.

Training sessions can be viewed for free between 6.30 and 8.30 am daily except Sunday. Ayurvedic treatment for ailments (especially soft tissue injuries) is available 10 am to 1 pm and 5 to 7.30 pm Monday to Saturday, and 10 am to 1 pm on Sunday.

To join the combatants you must sign up for a course (three month minimum) at Rs 500 per month. You'll need to arrange your own accommodation, meals and transport.

Other Attractions

The zoo and a collection of museums are in a park in the north of the city. The museums are open 10 am to 5 pm Tuesday to Sunday (from 1 pm on Wednesday). A single Rs 5 entry ticket, purchased at the Natural History Museum, covers all the museums.

Housed in a Keralan-style building dating from 1880, the **Napier Museum** has an eclectic display of bronzes, temple carts, ivory carvings and life-size figures of Kathakali dancers in full costume.

The **Natural History Museum** has a rudimentary ethnographic collection and an interesting replica of a *tharawad* – a traditional wooden residence of the Nair family.

The **Sri Chitra Art Gallery** has paintings of the Rajput, Mughal and Tanjore schools, together with works by Ravi Varma, Svetoslav and Nicholas Roerich.

The **Zoological Gardens**, set among woodland and lakes, are open 9 am to 5.15 pm Tuesday to Saturday. Entry is Rs 4.

The **Science & Technology Museum** (10 am to 5 pm daily, Rs 2), with its interactive displays, is about 100m west of the KTDC Mascot Hotel. The nearby **Planetarium** (☎ 446976) has daily 40-minute shows for Rs 10 (in Malayalam at 10.30 am, 3 and 5 pm and English at noon). It's closed Monday.

Courses

Courses in Kathakali (see the boxed text 'Kathakali' under Kovalam) and Kootiattam (traditional Sanskrit drama) are conducted for genuine students at the Margi Kathakali School, West Fort (☎ 434066). Tuition is for beginners (no experience necessary) as well as advanced students. Fees must be organised with teachers. If you are interested write to or phone the treasurer, Mr Ramaiyer.

Organised Tours

KTDC offers a range of tours around the city and beyond. They give a quick overview of major attractions. All tours leave from in front of the KTDC Hotel Chaithram:

Kanyakumari Day Tour This tour goes to the Padmanabhapuram Palace, Suchindram Temple and Kanyakumari (Rs 230).

Other Long-Listance Tours Tours also go to Munnar (Rs 475, three days) and Thekkady (Rs 370, two days).

Ponmudi Day Tour (Rs 195).

Thiruvananthapuram City Day Tour The tour goes to Sri Padmanabhaswamy Temple (non-Hindus usually not admitted), art gallery, zoo, Veli Lagoon and Kovalam Beach (Rs 95).

Thiruvananthapuram Half-Day Tour This half-day tour goes to Kovalam Beach, aquarium and Veli Lagoon (Rs 65).

Places to Stay – Budget

The best hunting ground is Manjalikulam Rd, which runs parallel to MG Rd. Despite its central location, it's quiet and has a collection of cheap to mid-range hotels.

Pravin Tourist Home *(☎ 330753)* is a cheerful place with large singles/doubles/triples for Rs 140/220/285.

Sundar Tourist Home *(☎ 330532)* has simple singles/doubles for Rs 40/75; Rs 80/115 with private bathroom.

Sivada Tourist Home *(☎ 330320)* has rooms with private bathroom for Rs 100/180.

Nalanda Tourist Home *(☎ 471864)* is on busy MG Rd, but the rooms at the back are not too noisy and it's cheap at Rs 70/100.

Omkar Lodge *(☎ 451803, MG Rd)* also suffers from street noise but the staff are friendly and it's not bad value at Rs 85/140.

YWCA International Guesthouse *(☎ 477 308, MG Rd)* has eight clean single/double/family rooms with bathroom for Rs 200/305/400. An air-con double costs Rs 500.

Taurus Lodge *(☎ 477071, fax 331704)* is popular with long-term visitors. It's in a quiet laneway off Statue Rd. Look for the Mayfair Hotel on Statue Rd (it has a red neon sign reading 'Bar'), and the lodge is up the laneway across the road. It has 18 simple rooms, with doubles costing Rs 150.

Places to Stay – Mid-Range

Wild Palms Guest House *(☎ 471175, fax 461971,* ⓔ *wildpalm@md3.vsnl.net.in, Mathrubhumi Rd)* offers a welcome break from the hotel environment. This often-recommended guesthouse has spacious rooms starting at Rs 595; Rs 1145 with air-con. It's hard to find on your own, so call and give a pick-up point and they'll send a car.

The ***KTDC Hotel Chaithram*** *(☎ 330977, fax 331446, Central Station Rd)*, next to the KSRTC long-distance bus stand, is noisy. Rooms cost Rs 475/575; Rs 750/900 with air-con. Facilities include a Bank of India branch, a bar, a good air-con veg restaurant and an average nonveg restaurant.

Hotel Highland *(☎ 333200, fax 332645, Manjalikulam Rd)* has a good choice of rooms starting at Rs 225/280; Rs 480/580 with air-con and extra for a TV. There's also an air-con multicuisine restaurant.

Hotel Regency *(☎ 331541, fax 331696,* ⓔ *hotelregency@satyam.net.in, Manjalikulam Cross Rd)* has comfortable rooms for Rs 250/400; Rs 750/950 with air-con. There's also a restaurant.

Hotel Residency Tower *(☎ 331661, fax 331311, Press Rd)* is clean and comfortable with friendly staff. Rooms cost Rs 390/590, Rs 790/990 with air-con. It has a bar and nonveg restaurant.

Hotel Navaratna *(☎ 333494, YMCA Rd)* is a favourite of business travellers, with rooms for Rs 250/280; Rs 700 for an air-con suite. There's a restaurant and coffee shop.

Places to Stay – Top End

Muthoot Plaza *(☎ 337733, fax 337734,* ⓔ *muthoot@eth.net, Punnen Rd)* is an ultra-modern business hotel, with the best facilities in town. Rooms cost US$40/50; US$70 for a suite. It has a plush restaurant and a 24-hour coffee shop.

South Park *(☎ 333333, fax 331861, ⓔ mail@thesouthpark.com)*, a swanky, centrally air-conditioned hotel on MG Rd, has rooms from US$60/70 to US$110/120. It has one of the city's best restaurants, a coffee shop, a terrific cake shop and a bar.

Hotel Pankaj *(☎ 464645, fax 465020, ⓔ hlpankaj@md5.vsnl.net.in, MG Rd)* has central air-con and rooms from US$35/45 up to US$75 a suite. The cheaper rooms are small and musty, the deluxe rooms are fair value. There's a bar and restaurants.

Hotel Saj Lucia *(☎ 463443, fax 463347, ⓔ sajlucia@md2.vsnl.net.in)*, in East Fort, has unexciting air-con rooms in a conspicuously ugly building starting at US$40/50. There's a bar, restaurant, coffee shop, bookshop, business centre and pool.

The ***KTDC Mascot Hotel*** *(☎ 318990, fax 317745, Museum Rd)* is a large, slightly faded government-run hotel. Rooms all have air-con and start at Rs 995/1195. There's a restaurant, coffee shop and pool-side bar.

Places to Eat

Maveli Cafe is an Indian Coffee House with good, cheap food in a brilliant, spiralling tower. Watch your knees on the tables.

Ambika Cafe, at the junction of Central Station and Manjalikulam Rds, is a good spot for a cheap breakfast.

Prime Square, adjacent to the Ambika Cafe, has good-value veg and nonveg restaurants and is deservedly popular.

Asok Veg Restaurant, further north along Manjalikulam Rd, is a typical good-value 'meals' restaurant.

Indian Coffee House is just off MG Rd, behind Spencer's Store.

Hotel City Tower *(MG Rd)*, near the railway bridge, is another popular lunch spot; *thalis* are Rs 15.

There are several good, cheap vegetarian places opposite the Secretariat on MG Rd, including ***Sree Arul Jyothi***, ***New Arul Jyothi*** and ***Ananda Bhavan***.

Rangoli, south of the railway line, on MG Rd, is reputedly the best place for Keralan breakfasts.

Azad Restaurant, a few doors north, is also clean, air-conditioned and good value.

There are restaurants in many of the hotels. ***City Queen Restaurant***, in the Hotel Highland on Manjalikulam Rd, does good Indian, Chinese and Western food, as does ***Tiffany's*** at the Muthoot Plaza. ***Gokulum***, in the KTDC Hotel Chaithram, is a good air-con veg restaurant. ***Mascot Hotel***, ***Hotel Pankaj*** and in particular the ***South Park*** all have popular lunchtime buffets. The ***Hotel Regency*** has a restaurant.

To escape the midday heat try the engagingly named ***Snoozzer*** ice-cream parlour on Press Rd.

Entertainment

The ***Academy of Magical Sciences*** *(☎ 345 910, fax 345920, Poojapurra)* was established in 1996 to revive some of the traditional magic of India. Under the directorship of Gopinath Muthukad, the academy holds regular shows and visitors are welcome. Telephone first for times.

Shopping

The SMSM Institute, YMCA Rd, is a government-sponsored handicrafts outlet with the usual sandalwood carvings, textiles and bronzes. Natesan's Antiqarts and Khadi Gramodyog Bhavan, opposite the Ayurvedic college on MG Rd, have collections of bronzes and Keralan furniture. Hastkala Indian Arts & Crafts, off MG Rd, is a Kashmiri shop with all the usual artefacts. For nuts, tea and coffee try Sankar's Tea & Coffee, MG Rd.

Getting There & Away

Air Indian Airlines (☎ 438288) is on Museum Rd, next to the KTDC Mascot Hotel. Jet Airways (☎ 325267) is at Akshaya Towers, Sasthamangalam Junction. Other airlines flying from Thiruvananthapuram include:

Air India (☎ 328767)
Air Maldives (☎ 461315)
Gulf Air (☎ 328003)
Kuwait Airways (☎ 328651)
SriLankan Airlines (☎ 328767)

Jet Airways has daily flights to Mumbai (Bombay; US$195) and Chennai (Madras; US$105), while Indian Airlines flies to Bangalore (US$120, daily) and Delhi (US$360, twice daily). Gulf Air, Kuwait Airways, Air India and Indian Airlines fly to the Arabian Gulf. For Colombo, Air Lanka flies daily and Indian Airlines twice weekly (Rs 2535). Air Maldives and Indian Airlines have four flights a week to Malé in the Maldives for Rs 3150.

All airline bookings can be made at the efficient Airtravel Enterprises (☎ 327627, fax 331704, ⓔ ate@vsnl.com), New Corporation Building, Palayam.

Bus From the chaotic KSRTC bus stand (☎ 323886), opposite the train station, buses operate to Varkala (Rs 21, 1¼ hours), Kollam (Rs 25, 1½ hours), Alappuzha (Rs 55, 3½ hours), Ernakulam (Rs 65, five hours) and Thrissur (Rs 105, 7½ hours). Buses depart hourly for the two-hour trip to Kanyakumari. Two morning buses go to Thekkady (Rs 85, eight hours) for Periyar Wildlife Sanctuary.

Most Tamil Nadu bus services are operated by State Express Transport Corporation (SETC); its office is at the eastern end of the long-distance bus stand. It has services to Chennai (17 hours, eight daily), Madurai (seven hours, 10 daily) and Pondicherry (16 hours, one daily), as well as to Nagercoil and Erode.

Bus No 111 goes to Kovalam Beach (Rs 5, every 30 minutes) between 5.30 am and 9.30 pm from East Fort, stand 19, on MG Rd.

Train The reservation office (open 8 am to 8 pm Monday to Saturday, 8 am to 2 pm Sunday) is on the 1st floor of the station building. Make reservations as far in advance as possible because trains are often heavily booked. If you're just making your way up the coast in short hops or to Kochi, there's no need to reserve a seat.

Numerous trains run up the coast via Kollam and Ernakulam to Thrissur. Some trains branch off at Kollam and head for Shencottah. Beyond Thrissur, many others branch off east via Palakkad (Palghat) to Tamil Nadu. It's 436km to Coimbatore (Rs 96/149/692 for 2nd class/sleeper/two-tier air-con, nine hours). Coimbatore has connections to Udhagamandalam (Ooty).

Trains that go all the way up the coast as far as Mangalore in Karnataka include the daily *Parasuram Express* (departs 6 am; 16 hours) and *Malabar Express* (departs 5.45 pm). These trains travel via Ernakulam, along with daily expresses to Ernakulam (for Kochi) such as *Shoranur Venad Express* (departs 5 am) and the *Cannanore Express* (departs 9 pm).

It's about 42km (by train) from Thiruvananthapuram to Varkala (Rs 21/114 in 2nd/chair class, 45 minutes), 65km to Kollam (Rs 26/114, 1¼ hours); 224km to Ernakulam (Rs 61/275 in 2nd class/three-tier air-con, five hours); and 414km to Kozhikode (Rs 95/148/428 for 2nd class/sleeper/three-tier air-con, 10 hours).

South of Thiruvananthapuram, it's 87km to Kanyakumari (Rs 30/159 in 2nd class/three-tier air-con, two hours). For long-haulers, there's the Monday-only *Himsagar Express* to Jammu Tawi, via Delhi.

Getting Around

The airport is 6km from the city and 15km from Kovalam Beach. A No 14 local bus from the municipal bus stand will take you there for Rs 3. Prepaid taxi vouchers from the airport cost Rs 100 to the city; Rs 200 to 240 to Kovalam.

Autorickshaws are your best transport around the city. Standard rates are Rs 8.50 flag fall, then Rs 4.5 per kilometre.

Cars, with driver, may be hired from any number of travel agencies including Kerala Travels Interserve (☎ 324158, fax 323154), near Vellayambalam Junction. Prices average Rs 4.5 per kilometre, or Rs 7 with air-con, for a minimum of 200km per day, plus Rs 100 for the driver per day.

AROUND THIRUVANANTHAPURAM

Ponmudi & The Cardamom Hills

Ponmudi, a small hill resort just 61km north-east of Thiruvananthapuram, makes for a pleasant excursion. Arrange accommodation in the ***Government Guest House*** by ringing the manager (☎ 0471-890230). Rooms and cottages cost from Rs 250 to 600. The KTDC runs a restaurant/beer parlour, popular with carloads of young men.

On the road to Ponmudi you will pass the turn-off to **Neyyar Dam** and the surrounding **Neyyar Wildlife Sanctuary**. The sanctuary has a lion park and a crocodile breeding park. These are popular for picnics and day-trips. Boats to view deer and other wildlife on an island in the dam are Rs 10 and Rs 40 (depending on the size of the boat).

Just near the Neyyar Dam the **Sivananda Yoga Vedanta Dhanwantari Ashram** (☎/fax 0472-273093, ⓔ yogaindia@sivananda.org), established in 1978, conducts hatha yoga courses. Costs (donations) for a two-week course range from Rs 300 to 400 depending on the type of accommodation. Prices include tuition and all meals. Prior bookings (up to 15 days) are required.

Getting There & Away Six KSRTC buses daily go to Ponmudi from the long-distance bus stand. Change at Nedumangad for a smaller bus capable of negotiating the hairpin corners. A taxi will cost about Rs 900 for a day trip. The KTDC organises tours (Rs 195) that include Ponmudi and Neyyar Dam.

Padmanabhapuram Palace

The Padmanabhapuram Palace was once the seat of the rulers of Travancore, a princely state for more than 400 years that included a large part of present-day Kerala and the western coast of Tamil Nadu.

The palace is superbly constructed of local teak and granite, the oldest parts dating from 1550. The architecture is exquisite, with rosewood ceilings carved in floral patterns, windows laid with jewel-coloured mica, and floors finished to a high polish with a special compound of crushed shells, coconuts, egg white and the juices of local plants.

The 18th-century murals in the *puja* (prayer) room on the upper floors have been beautifully preserved, and surpass even those at Mattancherry in Kochi.

Chinese traders sold tea and bought spices here for centuries and their legacy is evident. There are intricately carved rosewood chairs, screens and ceilings as well as large Chinese pickle jars. With its banqueting halls, audience chamber, women's quarters, and galleries, the palace shouldn't be missed.

The palace is open 9 am to 4.30 pm Tuesday to Saturday. Entry costs Rs 6.

Getting There & Away Padmanabhapuram is just inside Tamil Nadu, 65km southeast of Thiruvananthapuram. To get there, catch a local bus from Thiruvananthapuram (or Kovalam Beach) to Kanyakumari and get off at Thuckalay, from where it is a short rickshaw ride or 15-minute walk. Alternatively, take one of the tours organised by the KTDC (see Organised Tours in the Thiruvananthapuram section earlier for details) or organise your own taxi (about Rs 900 return).

KOVALAM

☎ 0471 • pop 18,000

Thirty years ago Kovalam was a hippie cliche: a tropical beach with a fishing village offering seafood, fruit and toddy (coconut beer). Today this tiny beach is the focus of a multimillion dollar business, drawing thousands of tourists for a two-week dose of UV and a sanitised Indian 'experience'. The results are predictable. Exorbitant prices, an influx of get-rich-quick merchants, chaotic beachfront development, an avalanche of garbage, and desperate souvenir sellers coping with a declining market go a long way to ruining the postcard image. It's not bad if you crave fish and chips, beer (served discreetly) and the company of foreigners, but essentially it's about as Indian as bikinis and Bob Marley.

Orientation

Kovalam consists of two coves (Lighthouse Beach and Hawah Beach) separated from less-populated beaches north and south by rocky headlands. The southern headland is marked by a lighthouse; the northern headland by the Kovalam Ashok Beach Resort. It's a 15-minute walk from one headland to the other.

Information

There's a helpful tourist office inside the entrance to the Ashok Beach Resort and another at Hawah Beach Restaurant.

There are numerous moneychangers along the beach. Wilson Tourist Home has official money-changing facilities as does Pournami Handicrafts.

The GPO is open 9 am to 5 pm daily and there are STD/ISD, fax and email facilities.

There is a huge number of travel agencies which arrange ticketing, tours and car hire. It definitely pays to check around a few before deciding.

Dangers & Annoyances

A local newspaper reported that beach-goers get hassled by hawkers every three minutes on average, even if they're sleeping.

Theft does occur, from hotels and the beach. Lock the doors and windows and watch your possessions at the beach.

Strong rips at both ends of Lighthouse Beach carry away several swimmers every year. Swim only between the flags, in the area patrolled by lifeguards.

Kovalam has frequent blackouts and the footpaths behind Lighthouse Beach are unlit, so carry a torch (flashlight) after dark.

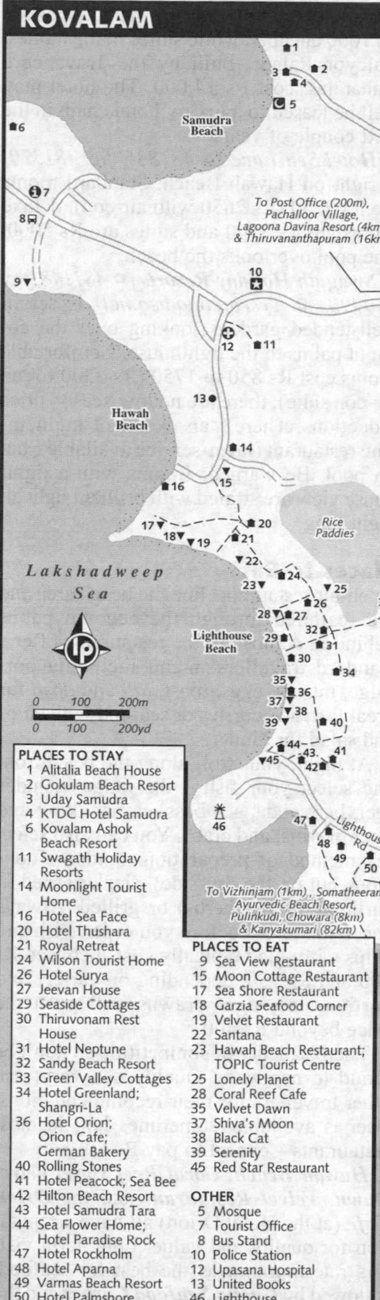

Places to Stay

Kovalam is packed with hotels. From about 15 December to 7 January is the high season, otherwise it can be a buyer's market if you shop around – prices can drop by 50% to 75%. The prices quoted here are high-season rates (not including tax of 10% to 20%).

Places to Stay – Budget

Green Valley Cottages *(☎ 480636)*, in a wonderfully peaceful location next to the paddy fields, has clean, neat and colourful rooms with bathroom for Rs 500.

Hotel Greenland, also well back from the beach, is attached to the well-known Shangri-La restaurant. Simple but clean rooms cost Rs 300 (single or double occupancy).

Jeevan House *(☎/fax 480662)*, right behind the Coral Reef Cafe, has a range of accommodation from Rs 350 to 1200.

Sandy Beach Resort *(☎ 480012)* has doubles from Rs 300 to 500 and a restaurant.

Other places to consider include the ***Hotel Surya*** *(☎ 481012)* just back from the beach with rooms starting at Rs 240, and the beachfront ***Sea Flower Home*** *(☎ 480554, fax 481069)*, a touch close to the drain but friendly and clean with rooms for Rs 250 downstairs and Rs 450 with a balcony. ***Hotel Paradise Rock*** *(☎ 480658)*, nearby, offers clean, small rooms for Rs 120/160.

Seaside Cottages *(☎ 481937)* has rooms for Rs 260 (single and double). ***Thiruvonam Rest House*** *(☎ 480661)* is not bad value with rooms from Rs 350 to 550 (with a balcony) – an air-cooler is Rs 130. ***Rolling Stones*** has basic rooms for Rs 250 (single and double).

Hotel Samudra Tara *(☎ 481608)*, farther down Lighthouse Rd towards the beach, has clean and comfortable nonair-con rooms for Rs 400 (Rs 500 with a balcony) and air-con rooms for Rs 1000.

The friendly ***Hotel Orion*** *(☎ 480999)* overlooks Lighthouse Beach just 20m from the high-tide mark. Doubles are Rs 400, and the female owner offers home cooking.

Places to Stay – Mid-Range

Lighthouse Rd is the best place for mid-range hotels.

Hotel Rockholm *(☎ 480306, fax 480607, e rockholm@techpark.net)*, farther up Lighthouse Rd (ie, away from the beach), is an excellent choice. It has great views over the small cove beyond the lighthouse. Rooms cost Rs 1100/1250 with 25% discount in the low season.

Hotel Aparna *(☎ 480950)* is a nice, small hotel with only eight rooms for Rs 800/1000.

Varmas Beach Resort *(☎ 480478, fax 276022, ⓔ varmabeach@hotmail.com)* has balconies overlooking a small cove. Doubles with air-con are Rs 1200; without air-con Rs 800.

Hotel Palmshore *(☎ 481481, fax 480495)* fronts onto the private sandy cove south of the lighthouse headland, but the rooms are a bit musty. Doubles cost Rs 2000; Rs 2400 with air-con.

Hilton Beach Resort *(☎ 481476, fax 481476)*, off Lighthouse Rd, has shabby air-con rooms for Rs 850/1300.

Hotel Peacock *(☎ 481395)* has nonair-con rooms for Rs 350 and air-con rooms with fridge for Rs 950. There's a restaurant, the Sea Bee.

Hotel Neptune *(☎ 480222, fax 460187, ⓔ replica@vsnl.com)* is set back from Lighthouse Beach and has standard rooms for Rs 550, balcony rooms for Rs 600 and air-con suites for Rs 1100.

Wilson Tourist Home *(☎/fax 480051, ⓔ wilson6@vsnl.net.in)* is large and friendly, with a range of nonair-con rooms starting at Rs 500 during the high season and air-con courtyard rooms for Rs 1000.

Hotel Thushara *(☎ 480692, fax 481693, ⓔ thushara@shyamnet.com)*, back in the coconut palms, has superbly built and beautifully furnished cottages for Rs 800.

Royal Retreat *(☎ 481080)*, next door, is a cluster of brand new air-con cottages from Rs 850 to 1000 a double. There are also nonair-con singles from Rs 350 to 800.

Moonlight Tourist Home *(☎ 480375, fax 481078)*, 300m south of the Upasana Hospital, is popular and squeaky clean. The spacious rooms have poster beds; doubles, some with small balconies, cost Rs 900; Rs 1000/1400 with air-con. You can rent motorcycles here.

Places to Stay – Top End

The ***Kovalam Ashok Beach Resort*** *(☎ 480101, fax 481522)* is superbly located on the headland of the second cove. The hotel has central air-con, a bar, restaurants, three swimming pools, sports and massage facilities, bank and bookshop. Room prices are Rs 5000/6000; uninspiring cottages are Rs 1000 cheaper, while suites in the modest Halcyon Palace, built by the Travancore maharajas, cost Rs 14,000. The hotel may well be leased to a luxury hotel chain in the next couple of years.

Hotel Sea Face *(☎ 481835, fax 481320)* is right on Hawah Beach. Standard rooms are Rs 2250 (Rs 2650 with air-con), deluxe rooms are Rs 3500 and suites are Rs 5000. The pool overlooks the beach.

Swagath Holiday Resorts *(☎ 481148, fax 330990, ⓔ prsrajcot@usa.net)* is set in well-tended gardens looking over the coconut palms to the lighthouse. Comfortable rooms cost Rs 850 to 1750 (Rs 3500 for an air-con suite); there are no low-season price reductions. There's an excellent multicuisine restaurant (lawn-service available), but no pool. Be warned: Rooms with a lighthouse view are strafed with brilliant light all night long.

Places to Eat

Open-air restaurants line the beach area and are scattered through the coconut palms behind it. Almost all the restaurants offer a standard travellers' menu including porridge, muesli, eggs, toast, *idli* and *dosa* for breakfast, and curries or seafood with chips and salad for dinner.

At night, you stroll along the beachfront and select your fish – the range includes seer, barracuda, sea bass, catfish, king and tiger prawns, and crabs. You can also select the method of preparation: tandoor (delicious but on the dry side), sizzler (fried in garlic and other herbs) or grilled. Always check the prices before you order. Fish and chips with salad typically costs between Rs 100 and Rs 150, depending on variety and portion size; tiger prawns will push the price beyond Rs 400.

There's plenty of competition so don't be afraid to negotiate. Quality can vary; ask other travellers for their recommendations. Beer is available, sometimes hot, in most restaurants – expect to pay Rs 80.

Hawah Beach, ***Coral Reef Cafe***, ***Velvet Dawn***, ***Velvet Restaurant*** and the ***Orion Cafe*** (at the Hotel Orion) all have a reputation for quality and value. Long-term visitors rate ***Santana*** as the best for seafood, followed by ***Garzia Seafood Corner*** and the ***Sea Shore Restaurant***. But almost without exception you'll have a long wait – 30 minutes – while the fish marinates.

Serenity, at the southern end of the beach, turns out recognisable travellers' fare; nearby ***Black Cat***, ***Shiva's Moon*** and ***Sea View Restaurant*** are similar. For cappuccino, apple strudel and croissants visit the rooftop ***German Bakery*** at the Hotel Orion.

Red Star Restaurant is just about the last relic of the old Kovalam – a simple hut with cheap thalis (Rs 15) and one table outside.

There are quite a few places back from the beach, although seafood is not the number one concern.

Lonely Planet vegetarian restaurant is nicely situated by a water lily pond. Excellent meals include South and North Indian as well as continental cuisine, and there's a good range of magazines to browse through. Incidentally, Lonely Planet has nothing to do with it and we are not planning to open a franchised chain!

The ***Shangri-La*** and ***Moon Cottage Restaurant*** are also worth a look.

If you get tired of waiting for meals at the beachside places, try the mid-range hotels, which have better equipped kitchens and can turn out more consistent food with greater speed.

For a splurge, head to the ***Ashok Beach Resort*** or the ***Swagath Holiday Resorts***, but don't expect a warm welcome if you haven't scrubbed up first, and drinks like gin and tonic push the bill out to astronomical levels.

On the beach, women sell fruit to sunbathers. The ring of 'Hello. Mango? Papaya? Coconut?' will become a familiar part of your day. Once you establish the going rate, they'll remember you so you don't have to repeat the performance. If you deal with the same people every day, the others will leave you alone – eventually. They rarely have change, but they're reliable about bringing it later. Toddy (coconut beer) is also available.

Entertainment

During the holiday season, a shortened version of Kathakali is performed every night except Sunday: On Monday, Wednesday and Saturday you can see it at ***Hotel Neptune***, and on Tuesday and Friday at ***Ashok Beach Resort***. You can watch make-up and dressing from 5 to 6.45 pm. The performance is from 6.45 to 8.15 pm and entry costs Rs 100.

On weekends, cultural programs involving music and dance are sometimes performed on the beach. You'll see the flags notifying all the details.

For less cultural pursuits, Western videos are shown twice a night in a few restaurants. There are no nightclubs or discos, just bars where people drink and listen to an endless soundtrack of reggae, trance music and classic rock.

Shopping

Kovalam Beach has numerous craft and carpet shops (usually of Tibetan, Kashmiri and Rajasthani origin), clothing stores (ready to wear and made to order), book exchanges, general stores selling everything from cornflakes to sunscreen, travel agencies and even yoga schools. Beach vendors sell batik *lungis* (sarongs), beach mats, sunglasses and leaf paintings, while others offer illegal Kerala grass, hashish and harder drugs, often to support their own addictions.

Kathakali

Kathakali, the renowned stage drama of Kerala, possibly had its beginnings in ancient drama methods of the 2nd century AD. However, the contemporary form dates from the 17th century.

Kathakali literally means story play, and the Kathakali performance is the dramatised presentation of a play. Originally there were over 100 plays but now only about 30 are performed. Based on the Indian epics the Ramayana and the Mahabharata, as well as the Puranas, the themes explored are all those canvassed in the great stories – righteousness and evil, frailty and courage, poverty and prosperity, war and peace, the terrestrial and the cosmic. And with each great story there are complex characters. Kathakali performers, through skilful movement, gesture and expressions, dramatise the traits of the various characters of the play, while singers and musicians narrate the story.

Traditional performances take many hours, but for the visitor there are shortened versions. You can see Kathakali at several venues throughout Kerala and particularly at Kovalam, Varkala and Kochi. Traditional performances are held in Kochi and also in the Sree Vallabha Temple, Tiruvilla.

Getting There & Away

Bus The local No 111 bus between Thiruvananthapuram and Kovalam Beach runs every 30 minutes between 5.30 am and 9.30 pm and costs Rs 5. The bus leaves Thiruvananthapuram, East Fort, Stand 19, on MG Rd, 100m south of the municipal bus stand. At Kovalam, the buses start and finish at the entrance to the Ashok Beach Resort.

There are also direct services to Ernakulam (Rs 68, 5½ hours) and Kanyakumari (Rs 24, 1½ hours, four daily) – good ways of avoiding the Thiruvananthapuram crush. Every morning a bus leaves for Thekkady in the Periyar Wildlife Sanctuary (Rs 100, 8½ hours). Direct buses go to Kollam (Rs 22, two hours).

Taxi & Autorickshaw A taxi between Thiruvananthapuram and Kovalam Beach costs approximately Rs 250; autorickshaws are about Rs 100. It's best to arrive at the lighthouse (Vizhinjam) end of the beach because it's closer to the hotels and there are fewer touts. Prepaid taxis from Thiruvananthapuram airport to the beach cost around Rs 190 to 225. Don't assume a rickshaw will be cheaper than a taxi – shop around.

AROUND KOVALAM

Pulinkudi & Chowara

Eight kilometres south of Kovalam are several interesting alternatives to Kovalam's crowded beaches. Prices quoted here are high season (and exclude 20% tax). Low-season rates may drop by 50%.

The Surya Samudra Beach Garden *(☎ 480413, fax 481124, ⓔ suryasamudra@vsnl.com)* is a small resort with individual cottages, many of them constructed from transplanted traditional Keralan houses. There are private beaches, a rock swimming pool, and cultural performances at night. Room rates range in price from US$80 to US$280.

Somatheeram Ayurvedic Beach Resort *(☎ 481600, fax 480600, ⓔ soma@md2.vsnl.net.in)*, which is a little farther south at Chowara, combines relaxing beach life with Ayurvedic medical treatment. Room prices range from US$40 to US$200. Various treatment packages are available. There is also a sister resort, ***Manaltheeram***, nearby.

Samudra Beach & Pozhikkara Beach

Samudra Beach, about 4km north of Kovalam, has a number of resorts competing for space with the local fishing villages. The steep and rough beach is not as amenable for swimming as the beaches further south.

The ***KTDC Hotel Samudra*** *(☎ 480089, fax 480242, ⓔ samudra@md3.vsnl.net.in)*, a pleasant retreat from Kovalam, has spacious grounds and its own bar and restaurant. Air-con singles/doubles cost Rs 2290/5200.

Uday Samudra *(☎ 481654, fax 481578, ⓔ udaykov@md4.vsnl.net.in)* is a new resort right on the beach, with air-con doubles for Rs 2900 and suites for Rs 3900.

Alitalia Beach House *(☎ 480042)*, run by the amiable Shah Jahan, has singles for Rs 500 and doubles for Rs 1000.

Gokulam Beach Resort *(☎ 481624, ⓔ gokulam_kovalam@usa.net)* is basically four rooms in a simple but comfortable family home. Doubles cost Rs 800; Rs 1500 with air-con.

Lagoona Davina *(☎ 380049, fax 462935, ⓔ davina@india.com)*, at Pachalloor village, behind Pozhikkara Beach, 5km north of Kovalam, is a small, exclusive boutique resort with six double rooms for Rs 5500, Maharajas tents for Rs 3500 and a couple of rooms in cottages for Rs 2900. You can also come here for dinner; a three-course a la carte meal with French wines costs Rs 700 per person.

VARKALA

☎ 0472 • pop 41,400

Varkala's beach scene is what Kovalam used to be like, though one look and it's apparent the same mistakes are being repeated. Inappropriate developments already mar the area, and many new hotels are springing up. Still, an Arabian Sea sunset viewed from the cliff-top is unlikely to be forgotten, and Papanasham Beach is relatively free of hawkers and gawkers.

Idyllic as the sea appears, there are very strong currents and no lifeguards. Even experienced surf swimmers have been swept away, so be careful.

Orientation & Information

The town and the train station are 2km from the beach. The police aid post and District Tourism Promotion Council (DTPC) tourist

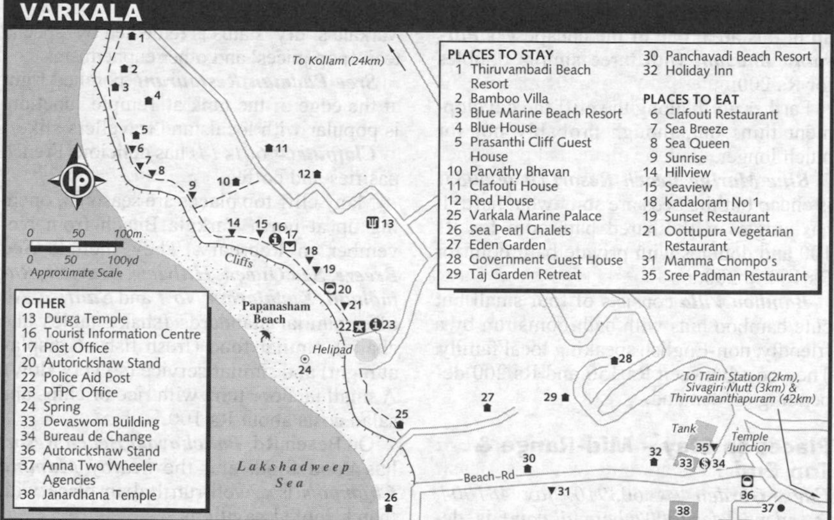

information office (open 8.30 am to 6.30 pm daily) are at the helipad.

The Bureau de Change (☎ 602749) at Temple Junction cashes travellers cheques, has STD/ISD, Internet access (Rs 60 per hour) and bus and train timetables. It's open 9 am to 10 pm daily.

There is also a privately run tourist information centre near the post office. The centre is primarily for ticketing and tour bookings.

Stores on the cliff-top have food items plus a essentials such as soap and batteries.

Things to See & Do

Varkala is first and foremost a temple town and the **Janardhana Temple** is on Beach Rd. Non-Hindus may not enter but may be invited into the temple grounds where there is a huge banyan tree and shrines to Ayyappan, Hanuman and other Hindu deities.

Sivagiri Mutt is the headquarters of the Sree Narayana Dharma Sanghom Trust (☎ 602221, fax 550651), the ashram devoted to Sree Narayana Guru (1855–1928) who preached 'one caste, one religion, one god for people'. Inquiries are welcome.

There are numerous centres for **yoga** and **massage** and the quality of offering varies.

Places to Stay

Most places to stay are at the beach, and they disappear almost entirely during the monsoon to be reborn in time for the tourist onslaught. Budget and mid-range accommodation is generally very good value, as are the top-end places in the low season. The quietest places are either situated inland, at the northern end of the cliff, or on Beach Rd. Prices quoted here are high season (December to February); considerable discounts apply in low season.

Places to Stay – Budget

Holiday Inn *(Beach Rd)* has small, clean singles/doubles for Rs 100/150.

Varkala Marine Palace *(☎ 603204)* has rooms from Rs 200 to 500 with an open-air tandoor restaurant overlooking the beach.

Government Guest House *(☎ 602227)*, inland near the Taj Garden Retreat, has cavernous rooms in a former palace of the Travancore rajas. It's spacious and quiet, though the housekeeping isn't fabulous. Still, it only costs Rs 150 for a room in the main building, or Rs 100 for very basic huts.

On the cliffs, 10 minutes' walk north, accommodation is provided by small hotels and families. Some of these places haven't yet acquired names, so just look for the ***Blue House*** or ***Red House***, with rooms at around Rs 100 to 300.

Prasanthi Cliff Guest House *(☎ 604716)* has three small, charmingly decorated rooms with shared bathroom for Rs 250.

There are many new guesthouses coming up in this area; one of the cheapest is ***Parvathy Bhavan***, with three simple doubles for Rs 200.

Farther north along the cliff the development thins out, though probably not for much longer.

Blue Marine Beach Resort *(☎ 606085)* is cheap but the beds are somewhat hard. It has singles with shared bathroom for Rs 100 and doubles with private bathroom for Rs 150 to 200.

Bamboo Villa consists of four small but cute bamboo huts with bathrooms run by a friendly, non-English speaking local family. They cost between Rs 150 and Rs 200 depending on demand.

Places to Stay – Mid-Range & Top End

Eden Garden *(☎ 603910, fax 481004, ⓔ edengarden2000@hotmail.com)* is delightfully situated, overlooking paddy fields. The 10 rather small, low-ceilinged double rooms are Rs 350 to 450. There's an in-house masseur and a female Ayurvedic practitioner who gets good reports.

Panchavadi Beach Resort *(☎ 600200)* is a secure place run by a personable French woman. There are five small but comfortable rooms for Rs 300 and two family rooms (each with two double beds) for Rs 500.

Clafouti House *(☎ 601414)* offers an intimate, homey atmosphere with the wafting smell of French pastries and clean double rooms for Rs 500.

Sea Pearl Chalets *(☎ 605875)* consists of concrete wigwams on the headland south of Beach Rd. Rooms overlooking the sea cost Rs 1000 a double, the others are around Rs 800 or Rs 600.

Thiruvambadi Beach Resort *(☎ 601028, fax 604345)* is a villa built in the grandiose style favoured by Malayalis who have made their money in the Gulf States, situated at the very northern end of the cliff. Comfortable doubles in a separate wing cost around Rs 600, and they have hot water, hammocks and gardens.

Taj Garden Retreat *(☎ 603000, fax 602296, ⓔ retreat.varkala@tajhotels.com)*, a resort overlooking the beach, has standard air-con rooms for US$95/105 to US$115/125. There's a restaurant, bar, pool, tennis courts and health club.

Places to Eat

Varkala's 'dry' status is remedied by 'special tea', 'pop juices' and other euphemisms.

Sree Padman Restaurant, perched right at the edge of the tank at Temple Junction, is popular with locals and travellers alike.

Clafouti *(☎ 601414)* has delicious French pastries and coffee.

Many cliff-top places are seasonal, opening up at north Varkala Beach from November to February. They include ***Sea Breeze***, ***Sea Queen***, ***Hillview***, ***Seaview***, ***Rajadhani***, ***Kadaloram No 1*** and ***Sunrise***. All offer similar standards (shaky tables and chairs), similar food (fresh fish on display at night) and similar service (so very slow). A small tandoor tuna with rice or chips and salad costs about Rs 100.

On Beach Rd, ***Panchavadi Beach Resort*** has good food, and the nearby ***Mamma Chompo's*** is a well-run Italian place with thatch-roofed pavilions.

For vegetarians, ***Oottupura*** serves a decent range of dishes.

Entertainment

Kathakali performances in the atmospheric surroundings of the old Devaswom building are held every Sunday, Wednesday and Friday during December and January for Rs 100. Make-up and dressing is from 5 to 6.45 pm and the performance with English commentary is from 6.45 to 8.15 pm.

Getting There & Away

Varkala is 41km north of Thiruvananthapuram by train (Rs 21/114 in 2nd/chair class, 45 minutes) and just 24km south of Kollam (Rs 18/114, 35 minutes). There are regular buses to/from Thiruvananthapuram (Rs 21, 90 minutes) and Kollam that stop at Temple Junction. It's easy to get to Kollam in time for the morning backwater boat to Alappuzha (see the boxed text 'The Backwaters' later in this chapter). A taxi from Thiruvananthapuram to Varkala costs about Rs 550 (Rs 650 from Kovalam).

Getting Around

Autorickshaws between the train station and Varkala's Temple Junction are Rs 20. A taxi to the beach costs about Rs 60. You can hire a 350cc Enfield Bullet (Rs 350 per day), and other bikes from Anna Two Wheeler Agencies.

KOLLAM (QUILON)

☎ 0474 • pop 362,572

Surrounded by coconut palms and cashew plantations on the edge of Ashtamudi Lake, Kollam, still referred to as Quilon (pronounced 'koy-lon'), is a busy Keralan market town. Away from the teeming main streets there are old wooden houses whose red-tiled roofs overhang winding alleys.

The Malayalam era is calculated from the founding of Kollam in the 9th century.

Kollam is the southern gateway to the backwaters of Kerala, and is well known for the Kollam-Alappuzha backwater cruise.

Information

There's a helpful DTPC tourist information centre near the KSRTC bus stand (open 8 am to 7 pm daily), and another at the train station.

You can cash travellers cheques at the Bank of Baroda, or more quickly at the DTPC tourist information centre, between 10 am and 2 pm. It's quicker to change cash or get a credit card advance at UAE Money Exchange in the Bishop Jerome Nagar Complex. There are also several efficient Internet cafes at the Bishop Jerome Nagar Complex, including RJS (Rs 40 per hour).

Things to See & Do

To promote Kollam as more than a jetty for backwater tours, DTPC has a wide range of activities for all budgets. An example of its entrepreneurial acumen is the new monsoon package for Middle Eastern visitors, keen to experience a real tropical downpour. Other activities include the annual **Ashtamudi Craft & Art Festival of India**, from 26 December to 10 January, which involves artists from all over India. Workshops, demonstrations and exhibitions showcase the art at Asraman Maidan and entry is free.

There are several churches of interest. In town is the extraordinary **Shrine of Our Lady of Velamkanni** and at **Thangasseri**, 5km from Kollam's centre, there are 18th-century sites.

Organised Tours

Guided tours (from Rs 300 per person with a minimum of two) through the myriad paths and canals of **Monroe Island** in Ashtamudi Lake are organised by the DTPC. Tours include observation of prawn and fish farming, coir making, and even matchstick making, as well as opportunities for bird-watching.

Places to Stay – Budget

The ***Government Guest House*** *(☎ 743620)*, 3km north of the centre on Ashtamudi Lake, is a classic relic of the Raj. Immense, newly renovated rooms are a bargain at Rs 165 per person but getting into town can be difficult because of the scarcity of autorickshaws.

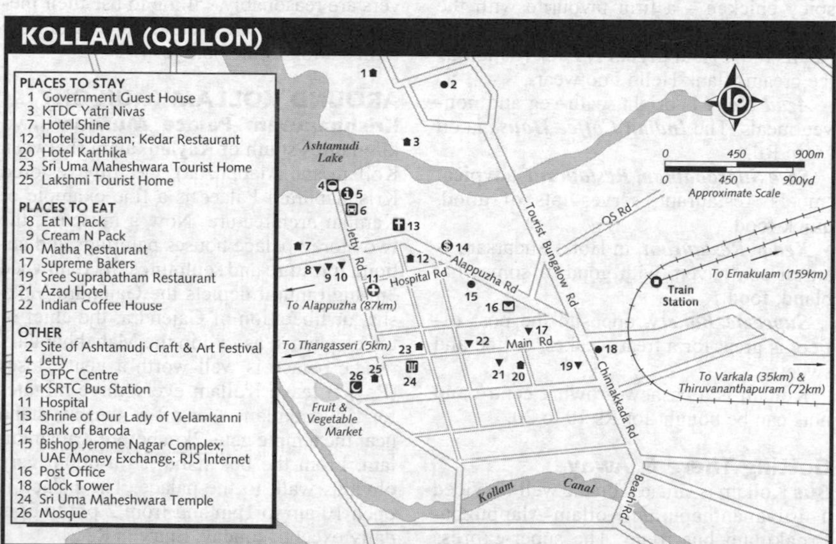

Hotel Karthika *(☎ 745538)* is a large, popular place built around a central courtyard. Decent rooms are Rs 140/225 with private bathroom; Rs 350 with air-con.

Lakshmi Tourist Home *(☎ 741067)* is a no-frills lodge with clean rooms for Rs 70/130 with private bathroom.

Sri Uma Maheswara Tourist Home *(☎ 743712)* is very basic and has doubles with private bathroom for Rs 145. Staff are friendly and the premises clean.

Hotel Shine *(☎ 752452)* offers rooms for Rs 130/180 with bathroom.

There are ***retiring rooms*** at the station.

Places to Stay – Mid-Range & Top End

Hotel Sudarsan *(☎ 744322, fax 740480)* is welcoming and good value at US$9/10; from US$15/18 with air-con. Back rooms are quieter. All rooms have TV and there are restaurants and a bar.

The ***KTDC Yatri Nivas*** *(☎ 745538, fax 314406)* has a pleasant riverside location, diffident staff and slightly musty rooms. Rooms cost from Rs 165/200 to 220/275, or Rs 440 for an air-con double. You can get across to the boat jetty in the hotel's speedboat or by autorickshaw for Rs 20.

Places to Eat

Matha Restaurant serves up a wickedly spicy chicken – a firm favourite with the rickshaw drivers. Next door, ***Eat N Pack*** (thalis Rs 12) and ***Cream N Pack*** (delicious ice cream) flank Hello Footwear.

Azad Hotel is bright, with veg and non-veg meals. The ***Indian Coffee House*** is on Main Rd.

Sree Suprabatham Restaurant, a typical 'meals' restaurant, serves lots of good, quick food.

Kedar Restaurant, in Hotel Sudarsan, is an air-con haven, with good, if somewhat bland, food.

Supreme Bakers, opposite the post office, is great for a treat – cakes, coffee and sweets.

Kollam is a cashew-growing centre and nuts can be bought for Rs 10 to 20.

Getting There & Away

Bus Kollam is situated on the well-serviced Thiruvananthapuram-Kollam-Alappuzha-Ernakulam bus route. The super-express services (reservations possible) take 1½ hours to Thiruvananthapuram (Rs 30); 1¾ hours to Alappuzha (Rs 33); and 3½ hours to Ernakulam (Rs 65).

Train Kollam is 159km south of Ernakulam and the three- to four-hour trip costs Rs 47/212 in 2nd class/three-tier air-con. The *Trivandrum Mail* from Chennai goes through Kollam, as does the *Mumbai-Kanyakumari Express* and Mangalore-Thiruvananthapuram services.

Boat See the boxed text 'The Backwaters' for information on backwater cruises to Alappuzha. There are public ferry services across Ashtamudi Lake to Guhanandapuram (one hour), Muthiraparam (2½ hours) or Perumon (2½ hours); fares are around Rs 6 return. The daily Alleppey Tourism Development Cooperative (ATDC) and DTPC tourist boats to Alappuzha can be booked at various hotels around town; substantial discounts are given for direct bookings, with further discounts for students and pensioners. The tours start by bus from the KSRTC bus stand or from one of the town jetties.

Getting Around

The KSRTC bus stand and the boat jetty are side by side, but the train station is on the opposite side of town. Autorickshaw drivers are reasonably willing to use their meters; expect to pay around Rs 15 from the train station to the boat jetty.

AROUND KOLLAM (QUILON)

Krishnapuram Palace Museum Two kilometres south of Kayamkulam (between Kollam and Alappuzha), the fully restored Krishnapuram Palace is a fine example of Keralan architecture. Now a museum, the two-storey palace houses paintings and antique furniture and sculptures. Its renowned 3m-high mural depicts the Gajendra Moksha, or liberation of Gajendra, the chief of the elephants, as told in the Mahabharata.

The palace is well worth a visit. Buses (Rs 12) leave Kollam every three minutes for Kayamkulam. Get off at the bus stand near the temple gate, 2km before Kayamkulam. From the bus stand it's a 600m very obvious walk to the palace. The palace is open 10 am to 1pm and from 2 pm to 5pm daily except Monday. Entry is Rs 2.

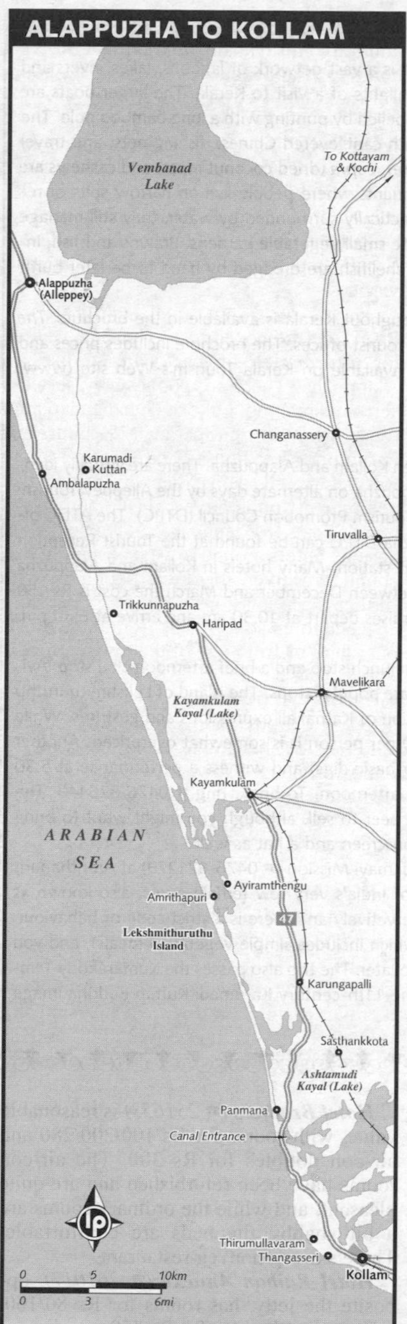

ALAPPUZHA (ALLEPPEY)

☎ 0477 • pop 264,969

This fairly pleasant market town is built on canals and surrounded by coconut trees. A walk through the streets present many examples of Keralan architecture. If you arrive in mid-December you can enjoy the festivities at the **Mullackal Temple** when some of India's finest temple musicians perform in the main hall. In August, the annual **Nehru Cup Snake Boat Race** is not to be missed. And of course there are many opportunities for backwater tours (see the boxed text 'The Backwaters').

Orientation & Information

The bus stand and boat jetty are close to each other, and to most of the cheap hotels. The train station is 4km south-west of the town centre. The DTPC Tourist Reception Centre and the Alleppey Tourism Development Cooperative (ATDC) are both very helpful. The Bank of India on Mullackal Rd cashes travellers cheques.

Nehru Cup Snake Boat Race

This famous regatta on Vembanad Lake takes place on the second Saturday of August each year. Scores of long, low-slung *chundan vallams* (snake boats) compete for the Nehru Cup. Each boat is crewed by up to 100 rowers shaded by gleaming silk umbrellas. Watched avidly by thousands of spectators, the annual event celebrates the seafaring and martial traditions of ancient Kerala.

Tickets, available from numerous ticket stands, entitle you to seats on bamboo terraces, which are erected for the races. Ticket prices range from Rs 10 for standing room to Rs 500 for the best seats in the Tourist Pavilion, which offers views of the finishing point. The race is now repeated for tourists in mid-January.

Take food, drink and an umbrella to protect you from the monsoon rains or blistering sunshine.

Places to Stay – Budget

YMCA *(☎ 245313)* rents most of its rooms to students but visitors may get a place. The reception isn't staffed on public holidays. There's a restaurant and clean, basic double rooms are Rs 200; Rs 300 with air-con.

Komala Hotel *(☎ 243631)*, just north of the North Canal, has singles/doubles/triples

The Backwaters

Fringing the coast of Kerala and winding far inland is a vast network of lagoons, lakes, rivers and canals. Travelling the backwaters is one of the highlights of a visit to Kerala. The larger boats are motorised but there are numerous smaller boats propelled by punting with a long bamboo pole. The boats cross shallow, palm-fringed lakes studded with cantilevered Chinese fishing nets, and travel along narrow, shady canals where *coir* (coconut fibre), *copra* (dried coconut meat) and cashews are loaded onto boats. Along the way are small settlements where people live on narrow spits of reclaimed land only a few metres wide. Although practically surrounded by water, they still manage to keep cows, pigs, chickens and ducks and cultivate small vegetable gardens. Prawns and fish, including the prized *karimeen*, are also farmed, and shellfish are dredged by hand to be later burnt with coal dust to produce lime.

A comprehensive listing of backwater tours throughout Kerala is available in the brochure *The Backwaters of Kerala Tourist Guide*, available from tourist offices. The brochure includes prices and telephone booking contacts. More information is available on Kerala Tourism's Web site (www.keralatourism.org).

Tourist Cruises

The most popular cruise is the eight-hour trip between Kollam and Alappuzha. There are virtually identical daily cruises operated between Kollam and Alappuzha on alternate days by the Alleppey Tourism Development Cooperative (ATDC) and the District Tourism Promotion Council (DTPC). The ATDC office is in Komala Rd, Alappuzha, while the Alappuzha DTPC can be found at the Tourist Reception Centre. In Kollam, the DTPC is near the KSRTC bus station. Many hotels in Kollam and Alappuzha take bookings for one or other of these services. Between December and March the cost is Rs 150 one way, or Rs 100 for students with ISIC cards. Cruises depart at 10.30 am and arrive at 6.30 pm. Between April and November it costs Rs 250.

Generally, there are only two major stops: a noon lunch stop and a brief afternoon chai stop. Ayiramthengu or the coir village of Thrikkunnappuha are popular stops. The island of Lekshmithuruthu is the lunch stop, where you can see a demonstration of Kathakali expressions and gestures. While this helps to understand a performance, at Rs 250 per person it is somewhat overpriced. Another option is to stay overnight (Rs 200 per double for basic digs) and witness a performance at 5.30 pm. You can then pick up the boat the following afternoon. To book, ring ☎ 0476-826449. The crew have an ice box full of fruit, soft drinks and beer to sell, although you might want to bring along additional refreshments and snacks. Bring sunscreen and a hat as well.

Boats drop visitors off at the Matha Amrithanandamayi Mission (☎ 0476-621279) at Amrithapuri, the residence of Matha Amrithanandamayi, one of India's very few female gurus, also known as 'The Hugging Mother'. Visitors should dress conservatively and there is a strict code of behaviour. You can stay at the ashram for Rs 150 per day (which includes simple vegetarian meals), and you can pick up an onward or return cruise a day or two later. The trip also passes the Kumarakody Temple, and close to Alappuzha there's a glimpse of the 11th-century Karumadi Kuttan Buddha image near the canal bank.

for Rs 120/172/195 and air-con singles/doubles for Rs 495/605.

***Sheeba Lodge** (☎ 244871)*, behind the Komala, is cheap and fairly habitable at Rs 100/150. However, it's uncomfortably close to a loud mosque.

***St George's Lodging** (☎ 251620, CCNB Rd)*, opposite South Canal, is the best of the cheapies. Rooms cost Rs 45/80, or Rs 67/115 with private bathroom.

***Hotel Brothers** (☎ 251653)* is reasonable value, with rooms for Rs 100/200/280 and air-con doubles for Rs 300. The air-con rooms have been refurbished and are quite pleasant, and while the ordinary rooms are a bit shabby the beds are comfortable. There's a veg/nonveg restaurant.

***Hotel Raiban Annexe** (☎ 261017)*, opposite the jetty, has rooms for Rs 80/160, and air-con doubles for Rs 350.

The Backwaters

The cruise between Alappuzha and Kottayam is about 4½ hours (it follows a longer route than the public ferry, see below). The operator is the Bharath Tourist Service Society (BTSS; ☎ 0477-262262), based in Alappuzha at the Raiban Shopping Complex on Boat Jetty Rd, and the cost is Rs 100 one way. Boats depart Alappuzha at 9.30 am, and Kottayam at 2.30 pm. The DTPC also runs a four-hour cruise which departs Alappuzha at 10 am and returns at 2 pm. This cruise leaves daily during December and January, and on weekends during the rest of the year. The cost is Rs 100; Rs 60 concession (students and children).

Houseboats & Charters

A popular, but at times overpriced, option is to hire a houseboat designed like a *kettuvallam* (rice barge). Boats can be chartered through the DTPC in Kollam and Alappuzha. Houseboats cater for groups (up to eight bunks) or couples (one or two double bedrooms). They can be hired either on a day basis (Rs 3500 per boat) or overnight (Rs 5000), allowing you to make the Kollam-Alappuzha trip over two days. Food can be provided (including a cook) for an extra Rs 400 per person. The DTPC also hires four-seat speedboats for Rs 300 per hour, and six-seaters for Rs 200 per hour. In Alappuzha, the tourist boats are moored across the North Canal from the boat jetty. A one-way trip to Kottayam costs about Rs 500. Alternatively, there are boat operators like Penguin Tourist Boat Service (☎ 0477-261522) on Boat Jetty Rd, who have a long list of suggested trips from Alappuzha. Vembanad Tourist Services (☎ 0477-251395) and Blue Lagoon (☎ 0477-260103), both in Alappuzha, also have boats for hire.

Backwater Village Tours

These usually involve small groups of less than 10 people, a knowledgeable guide and an open work boat or covered kettuvallam. The tours last from 2½ to six hours. You visit villages to watch coir making, boat building, toddy tapping and fish farming, and on the longer trips a traditional Keralan lunch is provided.

Public Ferries

Most passengers on the eight-hour Kollam-Alappuzha cruise will be Western travellers. If you want the local experience or a shorter trip, there are State Water Transport boats between Alappuzha and Kottayam (Rs 6, 2½ hours, six boats daily) and Changanassery (Rs 9, three hours, two boats daily). The trip to Kottayam crosses Vembanad Lake and has a more varied landscape than the Alappuzha cruise. Changanassery, 18km south of Kottayam and 78km north of Kollam, has good road and rail links.

JENNY BOWMAN

Devotees from around the world flock to be hugged by Matha Amrithanandamayi.

Places to Stay – Mid-Range & Top End

Hotel Raiban *(☎ 251930)*, south of South Canal, has rooms for Rs 160/225; Rs 650 for an air-con double.

Yatri Nivas *(☎ 244460)*, 2km north of town, offers clean, basic doubles with private bathroom for Rs 250; Rs 400 with air-con.

The recently renovated ***Hotel Arcadia*** *(☎ 251735)* is opposite the boat jetty. Rooms cost Rs 200/300; air-con doubles are Rs 600. It has a restaurant and a bar.

Alleppey Prince Hotel *(☎ 243752, fax 243758, ⓔ alleppeyprincehotel@indiaatbest.com, AS Rd)*, 3km north of the centre, has central air-con but is somewhat overpriced. It has a bar, restaurant with musicians playing *filmi* (movie music) hits and classics (opens 7 pm) and an inviting pool. Rooms are Rs 1000/1275; Rs 1700 for a suite.

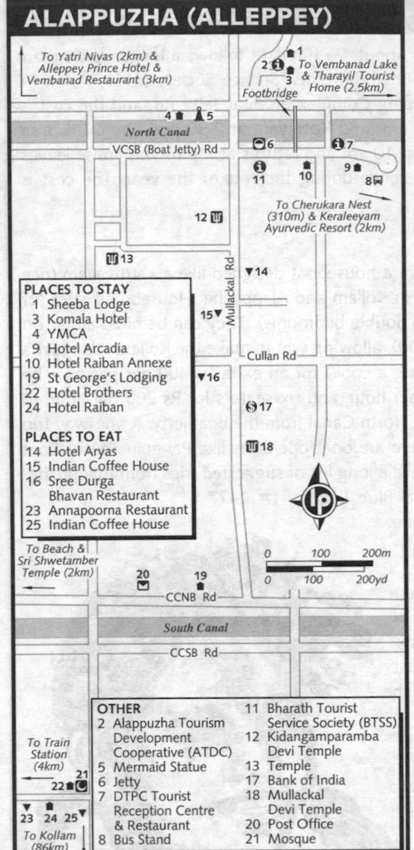

Guesthouses, in the form of converted private homes, are becoming a popular alternative to hotels for travellers. This style of accommodation is particularly suitable for families.

Cherukara Nest *(☎ 251509, fax 243164, e zachs@md4.vsnl.net.in)* is a handsome century-old family home, with several spacious doubles from Rs 550; deluxe rooms are Rs 950.

Tharayil Tourist Home *(☎ 236745, 233543, Lake Punnamada Rd, Thathampally)* is 2.5km north-east of town, near the finishing point of the snake boat race. It's deservedly popular, with clean, bright rooms for Rs 350 and Rs 400, Rs 750 with air-con. An autorickshaw from town should cost Rs 15.

Places to Eat

The restaurant at the DTPC ***Tourist Reception Centre*** on the North Canal is cheap, clean and offers a varied menu.

There's an ***Indian Coffee House*** branch on Mullackal Rd and another south of the South Canal.

Hotel Aryas *(Mullackal Rd)* serves good, cheap vegetarian meals. ***Hotel Rajas*** is a basic veg/nonveg restaurant.

Sree Durga Bhavan is a cheerful place where a good *masala dosa* is only Rs 10.

Komala Hotel and ***Hotel Raiban*** have OK restaurants, and there are two ***Annapoorna*** veg restaurants: one next door to the Hotel Raiban and the other on Boat Jetty Rd.

Vembanad Restaurant at the Alleppey Prince Hotel is air-conditioned and comfortable (or you can elect to eat by the pool). It serves decent veg/nonveg food.

Getting There & Away

Bus Buses on the Thiruvananthapuram-Kollam-Alappuzha-Ernakulam route operate frequently. From Thiruvananthapuram, it's about 3¼ hours (and Rs 47/65) to Alappuzha by super-fast/express bus. It takes 1¾ hours and costs Rs 20/27 to reach Ernakulam from Alappuzha. To Kottayam a super-fast is Rs 18.

Train The train station is about 4km south-west of the town centre. An autorickshaw from town costs about Rs 30. The 57km journey to Ernakulam takes one hour and costs Rs 24/158 in 2nd/three-tier air-con. There are also plenty of trains to Kayamkulam (Rs 21/158).

Boat Like Kollam, Alappuzha is a point from which to explore the backwaters. See 'The Backwaters' boxed text in the Around Kollam section.

KOTTAYAM

☎ 0481 • pop 166,552

When the Portuguese began forcing Keralan Christians to switch allegiance to Catholicism in the 14th century, the hierarchy of the Orthodox churches moved inland to Kottayam. The city is now a place of churches and seminaries and an important centre for rubber production, perched between the foothills of the Western Ghats on one side and the backwater rivers and canals on the

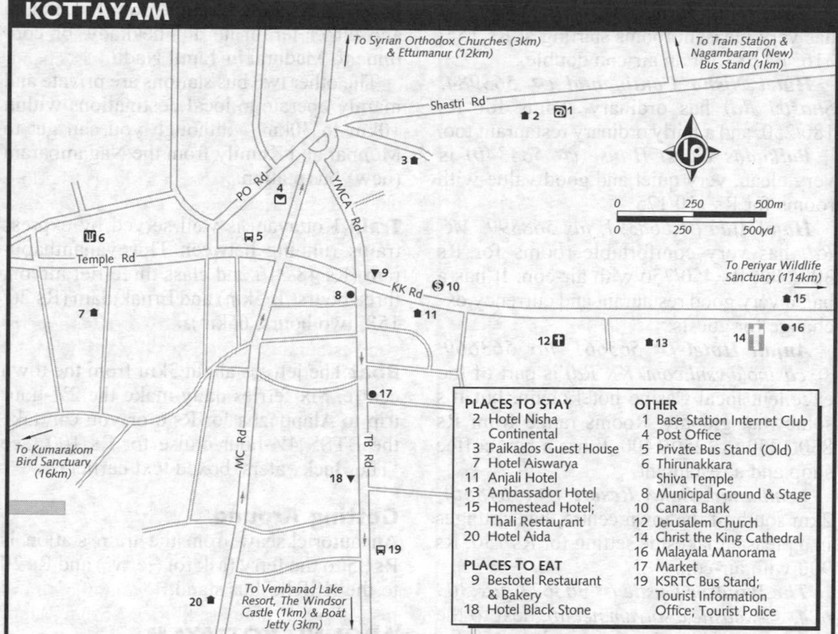

other. The town centre is a rather ugly mess of concrete buildings and traffic, but the residential areas are green and pleasant.

Kottayam district was the first in India to achieve total literacy, and today it is the headquarters of the daily newspaper *Malayala Manorama*. Published in Malayalam, with a circulation of 1.2 million (and a readership of around 8 million), it's second only to the English-language daily the *Times of India*. Arundhati Roy, author of *The God of Small Things*, was raised near Kottayam.

Orientation & Information

The train station, boat jetty and KSRTC bus stand are all a few kilometres from the centre. There is a helpful tourist information office at the KSRTC. The tourist police are also here. Email is available from the efficient Base Station Internet Club (Rs 60 per hour). You can cash travellers cheques and get Visa cash advances at the Canara Bank on KK Rd.

Things to See

The **Thirunakkara Shiva Temple**, in typical Keralan style, is noted for its Kootiattam, traditional Sanskrit drama. Sometimes visitors are admitted; chances improve if you don the correct garb (dhotis for men, saris for women). At the **Municipal Stage**, in the town centre, regular dramas are performed for free. About 3km north-west of the centre are two Syrian Christian churches. **Cheriapally**, St Mary's Orthodox Church, has an elegant facade with an interior noted for its 400-year-old paintings. **Valiyapally**, another St Mary's church, is 100m away. Built in 1550, its guestbook dates from 1899, and was signed by (among others) the late Emperor of Ethiopia Haile Selassie in 1956. **Backwater** trips can be made to Kollam (see boxed text 'The Backwaters' earlier).

Places to Stay

The multistorey ***Hotel Aiswarya*** *(☎ 581440, fax 581254)*, just off Temple Rd, has singles/doubles for Rs 150/250, to 300/400 (deluxe) and Rs 600/750 with air-con. It has a multicuisine restaurant.

The ***Ambassador Hotel*** *(☎ 563293, KK Rd)* is off the road – look for the driveway. Spartan singles/doubles are Rs 150/300. There's a bakery and a good restaurant.

Homestead Hotel *(☎ 560467, KK Rd)* has very pleasant rooms starting at Rs 154/316; Rs 687 for an air-con double.

Hotel Nisha Continental *(☎ 563984, Shastri Rd)* has ordinary rooms for Rs 180/250, and a fairly ordinary restaurant too.

Paikados Guest House *(☎ 584340)* is very clean, very quiet and good value with rooms for Rs 110/175.

Hotel Aida *(☎ 568391, fax 568399, MC Rd)* has very comfortable rooms for Rs 300/600; Rs 450/750 with air-con. It has a bar, a very good restaurant and currency exchange for guests.

Anjali Hotel *(☎ 563661, fax 563669, ⓔ casino@vsnl.com, KK Rd)* is part of the excellent local Casino hotel chain, but it's somewhat gloomy. Rooms range from Rs 850/1250 to 1250/1400. It has a bar, coffee shop and a restaurant.

Vembanad Lake Resort *(☎ 564866)*, 2km south of the town centre, has cottages in a pleasant lakeside setting for Rs 750; Rs 900 with air-con.

The Windsor Castle *(☎ 303623, fax 303 624, ⓔ wcastle@satyam.net.in)*, next to the Vembanad, is a grandiose carbuncle of a building with rooms for Rs 1950/2300. It also has attractive cottages in an approximation of traditional Keralan design for Rs 3700, set in spacious grounds. The hotel also has a swimming pool and several restaurants.

Places to Eat

Hotel Black Stone *(TB RD)* has basic veg food. ***Bestotel Restaurant & Bakery*** *(KK RD)* is a typical South Indian restaurant fronted by a bakery.

The excellent, partly air-con ***Thali Restaurant*** *(KK Rd)*, at the Homestead Hotel, does good thalis for Rs 20.

The restaurant at ***Hotel Aida*** has very good food, and the ***Ambassador Hotel*** has a buffet lunch of Keralan delights for Rs 100.

Vembanad Lake Resort offers outdoor eating, while ***The Windsor Castle*** has a restaurant set in an open-walled pavilion where non-veg mains start at Rs 90.

Getting There & Away

Bus Kottayam has three bus stations. The KSRTC bus stand, on TB Rd, has numerous buses to Thiruvananthapuram. Buses take about four hours and cost Rs 38 to Thekkady (Periyar Wildlife Sanctuary). Seven express buses daily come through from Ernakulam and either terminate at Thekkady, or continue to Madurai in Tamil Nadu.

The other two bus stations are private and mainly operate to local destinations within 10km to 30km – although you can get to Munnar and Kumily from the Nagambaram (new) bus station.

Train Kottayam is well served by express trains running between Thiruvananthapuram (Rs 48/216 2nd class/three-tier aircon, three hours, 165km) and Ernakulam (Rs 26/158, two hours, 65km).

Boat The jetty is about 3km from the town centre. Six ferries daily make the 2½-hour trip to Alappuzha for Rs 6 or you can take the BTSS 4½-hour cruise for Rs 100 (see 'The Backwaters' boxed text earlier).

Getting Around

An autorickshaw from the train station is Rs 35 to the ferry (ask for 'jetty') and Rs 20 to the KSRTC bus stand.

AROUND KOTTAYAM

The **Kumarakom Bird Sanctuary** on Vembanad Lake is 16km west of Kottayam. Between October and February is the time for cormorants and ducks. From February to July the night herons and Siberian storks take their turn. The best time to see the most birds is around 6.30 am.

There are several luxury resorts here. The ***KTDC Kumarakom Tourist Village*** *(☎ 524258)* has houseboats for Rs 1500 (one double bedroom) and Rs 2500 (two double bedrooms).

Coconut Lagoon Resort *(☎ 524491, fax 524495, ⓔ casino@vsnl.com)*, part of the luxury Casino Group, has bungalow rooms for US$110/120 and mansion rooms for US$120/130 in a beautiful setting.

Taj Garden Retreat *(☎ 524371; in Kochi ☎ 0484-668377)* is small but luxurious and similarly priced.

Regular buses operate from Kottayam to Kumarakom.

Ettumanur

The **Shiva temple** at Ettumanur, 12km north of Kottayam, has inscriptions dating from 1542, but parts may be older than this. It is noted for its superb woodcarvings and murals similar to those at Kochi's Mattancherry Palace. The annual **festival**, involving exposition of the idol (Shiva in his fierce form) and elephant processions, is held in February/March.

Vijnana Kala Vedi Centre

The Vijnana Kala Vedi Cultural Centre at Aranmula, 10km from Chengannur, offers courses in Indian arts under expert supervision. Subjects include Kathakali, Mohiniattam (classical dance) Carnatic music (South Indian classical dance) woodcarving, painting, Keralan cooking, languages, *kolams* (auspicious decorations) and kalarippayattu (Keralan martial art). It also arranges for visitors to meet experts in Ayurvedic medicine, astrology, religion and mythology.

You can customise your course and stay as long as you like, though a minimum commitment of one month is preferred. Fees, which include full board and two subjects of study, start at around US$200 a week – less for longer stays. For further details, contact The Director, Vijnana Kala Vedi Cultural Centre (☎ 0473-314483, fax 0479-452668), Tarayil Mukku Junction, Aranmula 689533, Kerala, or see the Web site (www.vijnanakalavedi.org).

Sree Vallabha Temple

Traditional, all-night **Kathakali** performances are staged almost every night at this temple, 2km from Tiruvilla. Non-Hindus may watch. Tiruvilla, 35km south of Kottayam, is on the rail route between Ernakulam and Thiruvananthapuram. The ***DTPC Complex***, 100m before the temple, has very basic double rooms for Rs 60.

The Western Ghats

PERIYAR WILDLIFE SANCTUARY

☎ 0486

Periyar is South India's most popular wildlife sanctuary. It encompasses 777 sq km, with a 26-sq-km artificial lake, created by the British in 1895. It's home to bison, antelopes, sambar, wild boar, langur, some 750 elephants and an estimated 35 tigers. The mountain scenery on the road up, the lake cruise and a jungle walk make for an enjoyable visit, though it does get busy on weekends. Bring clothing that's warm and waterproof.

Orientation & Information

Kumily, 4km from the sanctuary and the closest town, is a small, touristy strip of hotels, spice shops and Kashmiri emporiums. Thekkady is the centre inside the park with the KTDC hotels and boat jetty. When people refer to the sanctuary, they tend to use Kumily, Thekkady and Periyar interchangeably, which can be confusing. 'Periyar' is used to refer to the whole park.

There's a Wildlife Information Centre in Thekkady, and if you think you've come to terms with the DTPC, KTDC, ATDC etc, now try the IDTIO (Idukki District Tourist Information Office) and the TTDC (Thekkady Tourist Development Council). DC Books has an excellent selection and the Nature Shop (☎ 322763) markets World Wide Fund for Nature (WWF) merchandise. You can change money at the State Bank of Travancore behind the bus stand, have an oily massage at the Ayurvedic Hospital or visit a spice garden.

The post office is near the park entrance and there are numerous STD/ISD kiosks. Rissas Communications has email in a back room with a leaky roof (Rs 60 per hour).

Visiting the Park

Admission to the park costs Rs 60 for foreigners, and Rs 10 for each subsequent visit (keep your ticket).

Two-hour **boat trips** on the lake are the usual way of touring the sanctuary. Entry to the park doesn't guarantee a place on the boat. If you miss out, hang around and pursue other possibilities – a place may miraculously appear. Boat tickets cost Rs 40/80 on the lower/upper deck in the larger KTDC craft, or Rs 15 in the more decrepit Forest Department craft. There are five KTDC cruises a day (7, 9.30 and 11.30 am and 2 and 4 pm) and four Forest Department cruises (same times minus the 7 am departure). The first and last departures offer the best wildlife-spotting prospects. It's better to get a small group together (the smaller the better) and charter your own boat. They're available in a variety of sizes from Rs 600 per cruise for a 12-person boat. Tickets for video cameras cost Rs 25 from the Wildlife Information Centre. Don't forget to get one; they're strictly policed.

Guided **jungle walks** depart at 7.30 am, 10 am and 2 pm for about three hours and

KUMILY & PERIYAR WILDLIFE SANCTUARY

PLACES TO STAY & EAT	OTHER
5 Hotel Regent Tower; Maharani	1 Tamil Nadu Bus Station
6 Muckumkal Tourist Home; Little Chef Restaurant	2 State Bank of Travancore
9 Lake Queen Tourist Home; Lakeland Restaurant	3 Bus Stand & Tourist Taxis
11 Rolex Tourist Home; Thekkady Tourism Development Council	4 Post Office
17 Michael's Inn	7 Mosque
19 Spice Village	8 Rissas Communications
20 Taj Garden Retreat	10 Lourdes Church
21 Claus Garden	12 Idukki District Tourist Information Office
23 Hotel Ambadi	13 St George Orthodox Church
25 Coffee Inn	14 Ayurvedic Hospital
28 Periyar House	15 DC Books
29 Aranya Nivas	16 Kumily Central Hospital
	18 Ninja Tailoring & Spices
	22 Wildlife Preservation Office
	24 Nature Shop
	26 Post Office
	27 Park Entry Post
	30 Wildlife Information Centre
	31 Jetty

cost Rs 60 per person. Many visitors find these disappointing due to the lack of information and the often large and noisy groups. For walks further into the park guides can be arranged from the Wildlife Information Centre. Leeches are very common after rain.

More serious **trekking** can be organised at the Nature Shop but it's best arranged in Thiruvananthapuram before leaving for Thekkady. Contact Kerala Travels Interserve (☎ 0471-324158, fax 323154) Mangala Saudham, Vellayambalam. Prices start at US$250 per person for two days.

Another way to see wildlife is to spend a night in an observation tower or resthouse (see Places to Stay). Elephant rides (Rs 30 for two people for 30 minutes) are for fun, not for serious wildlife viewing.

The best time to visit the sanctuary is from September to May. Although the hot season (February to May) may be less comfortable, with other water resources drying up more animals go to drink at the lakeside.

Spice Gardens

Spice Tours are organised by almost every spice shop and cost Rs 400 for about 3½ hours. They're good value if you get a knowledgeable guide. The Thekkady Tourism Development Council (TTDC) at Rolex Tourist Home and Ninja Tailoring & Spices are two possibilities.

Places to Stay & Eat

Prices quoted here are for the high season (21 December to 20 January). Discounts are available out of season.

Inside the Sanctuary The KTDC has three hotels in the park, all rather expensive for what you get. It's a good idea to make reservations (at any KTDC office or hotel), particularly for weekends.

Periyar House *(☎ 322026, fax 322526)* is the cheapest of the three, with rooms starting at Rs 550/750, including breakfast and either lunch or dinner. Bike hire, massage and money changing are available.

Aranya Nivas *(☎ 322023, fax 322282, e aranyanivas@vsnl.com)* has seriously overpriced rooms for Rs 2425/3500 and aircon suites for Rs 2800/4000. There's a bar, a restaurant (poor service, readers report) and a garden area.

Lake Palace *(reservations Aranya Nivas ☎ 322024, fax 322282, ⓔ ktdc@vsnl.com)* is well away from the noise of day-trippers. Guests should arrive at the Thekkady boat jetty by 4 pm (the final trip of the day) for transport to the hotel. The six suites in the palace – once the maharaja's game lodge – cost Rs 4000/6000, including meals.

There are ***resthouses*** in the sanctuary at Manakavala (8km from Kumily), Mullakudy (39km) and Edappalayam (5km), but in reality they're rarely available. Book at the Wildlife Preservation Office (☎ 322028) in Kumily. The resthouses cost Rs 200/300 and three meals a day cost Rs 60.

There are also ***observation towers*** for Rs 175, which can theoretically be booked at the Wildlife Information Centre (☎ 322028). Although primitive (some are poorly maintained), and you must provide all your own food and bedding, they give you the best chance of seeing animals.

Outside the Sanctuary Quite a few new resorts are opening on the road to the park, mostly upmarket places with grandiose buildings quite out of character with their surroundings. The following is only a selection.

Coffee Inn *(☎ 322763, ⓔ coffeeinn@satyam.net.in)* has a range of basic accommodation, from bamboo huts on stilts for Rs 75 per person to rooms in cottages with bathroom and hot water for Rs 250. It also has a laid back cafe offering spaghetti, home-made bread and muzak.

Lake Queen Tourist Home *(☎ 322084)* has 54 rooms starting at Rs 120/200. Run by the Catholic church, its profits go to charity. The ***Lakeland Restaurant*** is downstairs.

Muckumkal Tourist Home *(☎ 322070)* has quieter rooms, away from the generator. Rooms with bathroom are Rs 100/200. The ***Little Chef Restaurant*** here is OK.

Hotel Regent Tower *(☎ 322570)*, nearby, has rooms for Rs 150/250, and there's a restaurant, the ***Maharani***.

Rolex Tourist Home *(☎ 322081)* has clean, spartan singles/doubles with bathroom for Rs 100/250. The owners rent out a cottage in a plantation for Rs 600.

Claus Garden, a couple of kilometres out of Kumily, is a private house with a few basic rooms for rent for Rs 100/180. You can prepare your own food in the kitchen. To get there turn off the Kumily-Thekkady Rd to the tank. From the tank it's a 100m walk uphill; turn right at the top of the hill and walk for another 100m.

Michael's Inn *(☎ 322355, fax 322356)* has 15 clean, almost clinical rooms for Rs 600/800; it's Rs 1300 for an air-con double. There's also a restaurant here.

Hotel Ambadi *(☎ 322193, fax 322192, ⓔ info@hotelambadi.com)* has dank cottages (that some travellers find OK) for Rs 425 to 690, and rooms in a new building for Rs 990. There's also a reasonably good multicuisine restaurant.

Taj Garden Retreat *(☎ 322041, fax 22106)* has rooms for US$105/120 for foreigners, with the usual high standards associated with the luxury Taj chain of hotels.

Spice Village *(☎ 322314, fax 322317, ⓔ casino@vsnl.com)* has thoughtful service. Very attractive cottages in a pleasant garden are US$115/125, or US$150 for deluxe bungalows. Lunch and dinner buffets in the salubrious restaurant are Rs 400.

There are cheap meals places along Kumily's main drag.

Around Periyar The ***Shalimar Spice Garden*** *(☎ 322132, ⓔ shalimar_resort@vsnl.com)*, about 7km from Kumily, just 3km off the Kottayam road, offers individually designed luxury cottages for US$70/80 to US$90/105. The restaurant serves Indian and Italian food. Ayurvedic packages are available.

Carmelia Haven *(☎ 370252, fax 370268, ⓔ carmelia@eth.net)*, on the Munnar road, 20km from Kumily, has rooms starting at Rs 1750/2000; Rs 4000 for a treehouse. The resort has 20 hectares of grounds with a swimming pool and tennis court.

Getting There & Away

All buses originating or terminating at Periyar start and finish at Aranya Nivas, but they also stop at the Kumily bus stand, at the eastern edge of town.

At least 10 buses daily operate between Ernakulam and Kumily (Rs 57, six hours) and buses leave every half hour for the 114km trip to Kottayam (Rs 38, four hours).

At least two direct buses daily make the eight-hour trip to Thiruvananthapuram (Rs 86). Another goes to Kovalam (nine hours), and another to Kodaikanal, in Tamil Nadu

(6½ hours). Only private buses go to Munnar (Rs 41, 4½ hours). They all leave Kumily in the morning (from 6 to 9.45 am).

Getting Around

Although Kumily is 4km from Periyar Lake, you can catch the semi-regular bus (almost as rare as the tigers), take an autorickshaw (Rs 35 plus Rs 5 entrance for the auto), hire a bicycle (from Periyar House or Aranya Nivas for Rs 25 a day) or set off on foot; it's a pleasant, shady walk into the park.

MUNNAR

☎ 0486

Set amid dramatic mountain scenery in what was once known as the High Range of Travancore, the hill town of Munnar (1524m) is the commercial centre of some of the world's highest tea-growing estates.

The combination of the craggy peaks, manicured tea estates and crisp mountain air makes Munnar an ideal retreat. The centre of the town is noisy and grubby, but there are good places to stay on the periphery.

Information

There are several tourist offices, but the only one you need is the private Tourist Information Service (☎ 530349), opposite the Gandhi statue. Mr Joseph Iype supplies maps, copies of various guidebooks for Rs 50, and can be helpful for advice on local walks depending on how much business you do with him. The small Munnar Tourist Information centre (☎ 531136) arranges tours, while the DTPC Tourist Information Office is barely operational.

STD/ISD booths are everywhere, but fax machines are rare and transmissions can only be made within India. Alpha Internet, next to Misha Tourist Home, charges Rs 60 per hour.

For changing money, the Federal Bank changes travellers cheques only. The Wildlife Warden's Office is just beyond the PWD Guest House.

Things to See & Do

The stone **Christ Church** (1910), now administered by the Church of South India, has fine stained glass. Inside, brass plaques honour the memory of the tea planters.

Walks around Munnar offer spectacular views. It is worth taking an autorickshaw

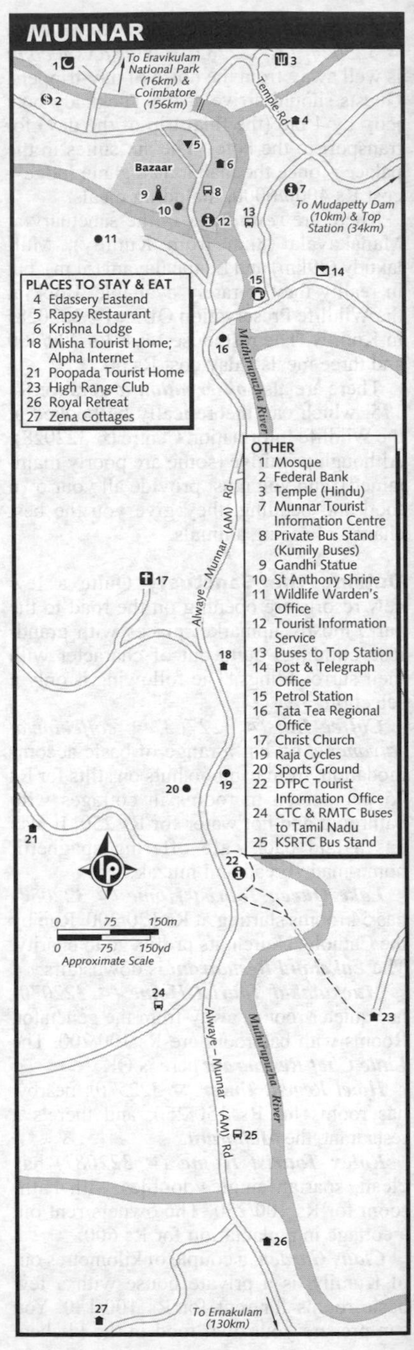

(Rs 125 return) for the 16km to **Eravikulam National Park** (entry costs Rs 10/50 for Indians/foreigners) where you can see the rare, but almost tame, Nilgiri tahr (a type of mountain goat), and walk around the Rajamala hills. Ten kilometres from Munnar on the way to Top Station, **Mudapetty Dam** is open daily for boating and short horse rides.

From many places in Munnar you'll see **Anamudi** (2695m), South India's highest peak. Classified as a core forest area, it may not be climbed except for study purposes. See the Around Munnar section for more information on sights within the vicinity of the town.

Places to Stay

Most accommodation is in the middle to top-end range with most of the few budget options near the noisy bazaar. Generally, in all categories, the accommodation here is nothing to get excited about.

Misha Tourist Home *(☎ 530376, AM Rd)*, is a standard Indian hotel with basic rooms for Rs 150/280 and some newer doubles for Rs 450.

Krishna Lodge *(☎ 530669)*, in the noisy bazaar, has basic rooms for Rs 100/200 with bathroom.

Zena Cottages *(☎ 530349)*, run by Mr Iype at the Tourist Information Service, is one cottage surrounded by tea gardens. There are three double rooms costing Rs 500. There is hot water and plenty of peace and quiet.

Poopada Tourist Home *(☎ 530223)*, about 400m west of the DTPC, has doubles starting at Rs 460, and better doubles for Rs 550. It has a good, cheap restaurant.

Royal Retreat *(☎ 530240, fax 530440)* is a comfortable, well-run place with rooms starting at Rs 850/950. The restaurant here is cosy and the food well prepared.

Edassery Eastend *(☎ 530451, fax 530 227)* has double rooms in a modern wing for Rs 850 and rooms in plantation house buildings starting at Rs 1250.

High Range Club *(☎ 530253, fax 530-333)* is somehow more British than Britain, a place where dress standards are still taken seriously (shirts with collar, thank you gentlemen) and the bar is decorated with hunting trophies. Membership is restricted to managers of local tea estates, but commoners can rent one of 10 comfortable cottages for Rs 1950 to 2250. Book at least one month in advance.

Places to Eat

Early morning ***food stalls*** in the bazaar serve breakfast snacks. In the evening, outdoor eating places set up near the Gandhi statue.

Rapsy Restaurant, in the arcade running off the bazaar, has excellent chicken biryani.

Edassery Eastend has two good restaurants: upstairs it's upmarket; downstairs it's simple, cheaper and slow.

The other middle and top-end hotels have good multicuisine restaurants.

Getting There & Away

The roads around Munnar are in poor condition and may be seriously affected by monsoons. Bus timings therefore may vary. Munnar, 130km east of Kochi, is best reached by direct bus from Kochi (4½ hours, eight daily); Kottayam (five hours, seven daily); Kumily (4½ hours, four daily); Thiruvananthapuram (nine hours, five daily); Coimbatore (six hours, two daily); or Madurai (six hours, one daily).

Getting Around

The DTPC hires out bikes (Rs 10 for four hours), but they're quick to point out cheaper options. At Raja Cycles, rates are only Rs 5 for the same time.

AROUND MUNNAR

At Maraiyur, north-east of the Eravikulam National Park and 42km from Munnar, you can experience the peace and beauty of a **sandalwood forest**. Some 10km past here is the **Chinnar Wildlife Sanctuary**, home to elephants, leopards and bears. There's a watchtower, but many visitors find the allocated viewing time – 10 minutes – insufficient. This may be extended for a 'small consideration'. Returning to Munnar at night is not advisable, and, contrary to official advice, you can't stay in the Forest Rest House. Instead try the ***Marayoor Tourist Home*** *(☎ 04865-52231)*, with double rooms for Rs 150. The more upmarket ***Chandana Residency*** *(☎ 04865-52222)* is 5km east of town, and has rooms starting at Rs 600.

Top Station, on Kerala's border with Tamil Nadu, has spectacular views over the Western Ghats. From Munnar eight daily buses (Rs 11, from 7.30 am) make the steep

32km climb in around an hour. Jeeps (Rs 600 per day) and rickshaws (Rs 300) can also be hired from along the main street in Munnar for the return trip.

The **Thattekkad Bird Sanctuary** is home to Malabar grey hornbills, woodpeckers, parakeets, and rarer species such as the Sri Lankan frogmouth and rose-billed roller. The 25-sq-km sanctuary was established in 1983 by the renowned ornithologist, Salim Ali, and is an important research area. Entry is Rs 25/5 for foreigners/Indians. The best viewing time is from 5 to 6 am and the best visiting time is from October to March.

Thattekkad is 15km north-east of Kothamangalam, which is on the Ernakulam-Munnar road, halfway between the two towns. There is an inspection bungalow and a dormitory at Thattekkad. The ***Hornbill Bungalow*** has double rooms for Rs 300 and dorm beds for Rs 50; meals can be arranged.

To get to Thattekkad, take a direct bus from Ernakulam to Kothamangalam or a more frequent bus to Muvattupula, and change there for Kothamangalam – a farther 8km. From Kothamangalam, you take the Thattekkad bus for the next 15km which takes about 30 minutes. Then you and the bus will be ferried along the Periyar River to Thattekkad.

PARAPARAMBIKULAM WILDLIFE SANCTUARY

The Parambikulam Wildlife Sanctuary, 135km from Palakkad (via Pollachi), stretches around the Parambikulam, Thunakadavu and Peruvaripallam dams, and covers an area of 285 sq km. It's home to elephants, bison, gaur, sloth bears, wild boars, sambar, chital, crocodiles and a few tigers and panthers. The sanctuary is open all year, but is best avoided from June to August due to the monsoon.

The sanctuary headquarters are at Thunakadavu, where the Forest Department has a ***Forest Rest House*** and a treetop hut; book through the Forest Inspection Bungalow (☎ 0425-367233) at Thunakadavu. At Parambikulam, there's a ***PWD Rest House*** and ***Tamil Nadu Government Inspection Bungalow*** (book through the Junior Engineer, Tamil Nadu PWD, Parambikulam). There are also two **watchtowers**: one at Anappadi (8km from Thunakadavu) and another at Zungam (5km from Thunakadavu).

The best access to the sanctuary is by bus from Pollachi (40km from Coimbatore and 49km from Palakkad). There are four buses in either direction between Pollachi and Parambikulam via Anamalai daily. The trip takes two hours.

Central Kerala

KOCHI (COCHIN)

☎ 0484 • pop 1.7 million

With its wealth of historical associations and its setting on a cluster of islands and narrow peninsulas, the city of Kochi perfectly reflects the eclecticism of Kerala. Here you can see the oldest church in India, winding streets with mosques and 500-year-old Portuguese houses, cantilevered Chinese fishing nets, a Jewish community with ancient roots, a 16th-century synagogue, and a palace built by the Portuguese and given to the raja of Cochin. The palace, which was later renovated by the Dutch, contains some of India's most beautiful murals. Another must-see is a (world-famous) performance of Kathakali drama.

The older parts of Fort Cochin and Mattancherry are an unlikely blend of medieval Portugal, Holland and an English country village grafted onto the tropical Malabar Coast – a radical contrast to the bright lights of mainland Ernakulam.

Kochi is one of India's largest ports and a major naval base. Huge merchant ships can be seen anchored off Fort Cochin, waiting for a berth in the docks of Willingdon Island, an artificial island created with material dredged up when the harbour was deepened. All day, ferries scuttle back and forth between the various parts of Kochi. Dolphins can often be seen in the harbour.

Orientation

Kochi consists of mainland Ernakulam; the islands of Willingdon, Bolgatty and Gundu in the harbour; Fort Cochin and Mattancherry on the southern peninsula; and Vypeen Island, north of Fort Cochin. All these areas are linked by ferry; bridges also link Ernakulam to Willingdon Island and the Fort Cochin/Mattancherry peninsula. Ernakulam is where you'll find banks, the main train station, the bus stand and the Tourist Reception Centre.

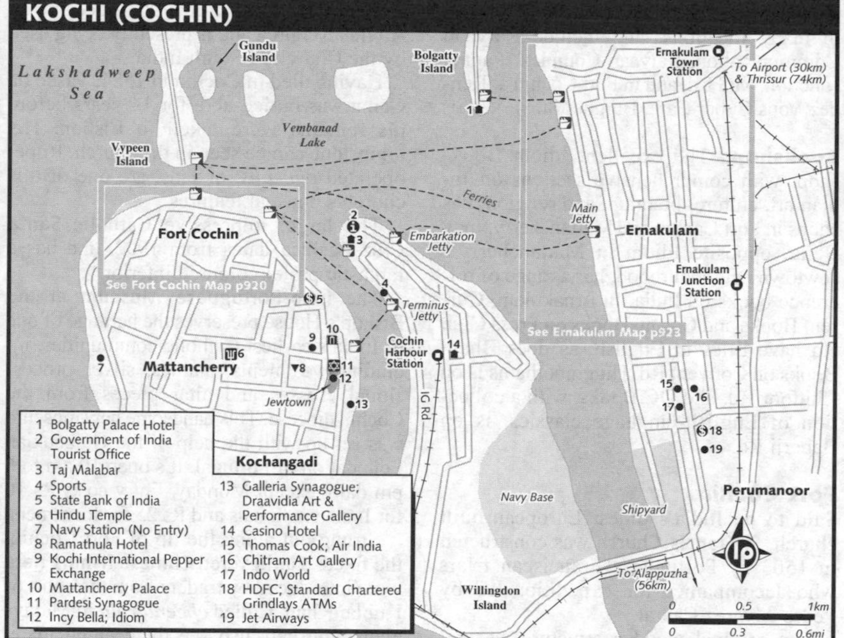

Almost all the historical sites are in Fort Cochin or Mattancherry, a more tranquil setting than Ernakulam. Two of the top hotels are on Willingdon Island. The airport (domestic and international) is 30km northeast of Kochi at Nedumbassery.

Information

Tourist Offices The KTDC Tourist Reception Centre (☎ 353234) on Ernakulam's Shanmugham Rd organises harbour cruises. The office is open 8 am to 7 pm daily. The very helpful Mr PJ Varghese at the tourist desk (☎ 371761) at Ernakulam's main ferry jetty is a mine of information. It's open from 9 am to 7 pm daily; you can also book accommodation and tours here. There's also a DTPC tourist information centre on Park Ave, Ernakulam (☎ 381743).

The Government of India tourist office (☎ 668352) near the Taj Malabar Hotel on Willingdon Island offers a range of leaflets and maps. The airport tourist information counter is staffed for flight arrivals.

Ernakulam's tourist police are specially trained to deal with visitor queries. You'll find them near the KTDC Tourist Reception Centre (☎ 353234). They also maintain a presence at Fort Cochin at the airport and Ernakulam Junction station.

Visa Extensions Apply at the office of the Commissioner of Police (☎ 360700), at Shanmugham Rd, Ernakulam. Visa extensions can take up to 10 days, you have to leave your passport for processing, and there's no guarantee that an extension will be granted.

Money In Ernakulam there's a State Bank of India on Shanmugham Rd and a very efficient Thomas Cook office on MG Rd. HDFC and ANZ Grindlays have ATMs at the southern end of MG Road, while HDFC has another at Palarivattom Junction, just off the NH47 about 1.2km east of Ernakulam Town Station. In Fort Cochin the State Bank of India is near Mattancherry Palace.

Post & Communications The main post office (including poste restante) is at Fort Cochin. Mail can be sent to the post office on Hospital Rd, Ernakulam, if it's specifically addressed to that office. STD/ISD booths are all over town. Internet cafes are springing up in many locations, and include Raiyaan Communication, Raiyaan Complex, Padma Junction, MG Rd, and in Fort Cochin at Rendez Vous Cyber Cafe, Burgher St.

Bookshops The excellent Idiom Bookshop, with comprehensive sections on Indian art, culture, literature and religion, has shops in Fort Cochin and Mattancherry. Incy Bella, opposite Idiom in Mattancherry's Jewtown neighbourhood, has a range of reference books on India. In Ernakulam, Current Books and Cosmo Books on Press Club Rd have titles in English, as does Bhavi Books on Convent Rd. Higginbothams is on Chittoor Rd, and DC Books, with a collection of English-language classics, is on Banerji Rd.

Fort Cochin

Said to be India's oldest European-built church, **St Francis Church** was constructed in 1503 by Portuguese Franciscan friars who accompanied the expedition led by Pedro Alvarez Cabral.

The original wooden structure was rebuilt in stone around the mid-16th century; the earliest Portuguese inscription in the church is dated 1562. The Protestant Dutch captured Kochi in 1663 and restored the church in 1779. After the occupation of Kochi by the British in 1795, it became an Anglican church and is presently being used by the Church of South India.

Having died in Cochin in 1524, Vasco da Gama was buried here for 14 years before his remains were taken to Lisbon. His tombstone can be seen in the church. Rope-operated *punkahs*, or fans, are one of this church's unusual features.

The large, impressive Catholic **Santa Cruz Basilica** dates from 1902, and has a fantastic pastel-coloured interior.

The **Indo-Portuguese Museum** at the Bishop's House preserves the heritage of one of India's earliest Catholic communities, including vestments, statues, silver processional crosses and altar pieces from the Cochin diocese. This handsome new museum was set up with the help of the Gulbenkian Foundation of Portugal. It's open 10 am to 6 pm daily except Monday. Entry costs Rs 10 for Indian nationals and Rs 25 for foreigners.

Strung out along the tip of Fort Cochin, the fixed, cantilevered **Chinese fishing nets** were introduced by traders from the court of Kublai Khan. Called *cheena vala* in Malayalam, you can also see them along many backwaters. They're mainly used at high tide, requiring at least four men to operate their system of counterweights.

The **Dutch Cemetery** was consecrated in 1724 and contains many European graves.

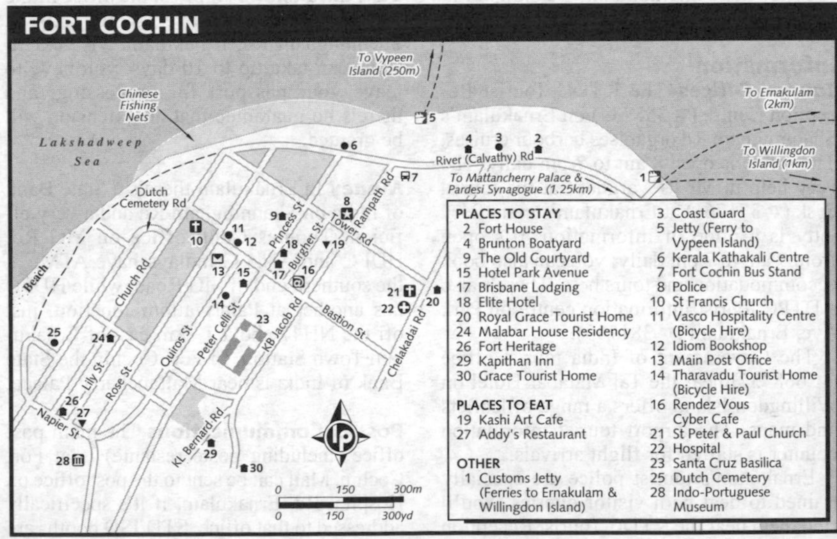

The Jews of Kochi

The Jewish diaspora extends all the way to Kochi (Cochin), home to a tiny Jewish community descended from those who fled Palestine 2000 years ago. The first Jewish settlement was at Kodungallur (Cranganore), north of Kochi. Like the Syrian Orthodox Christians, the Jews became involved in the trade and commerce of the Malabar Coast. Preserved in the Mattancherry synagogue are a number of copper plates bearing an ancient inscription granting the village of Anjuvannam (near Kodungallur) and its revenue to a Jewish merchant, Joseph Rabban, by King Bhaskara Ravi Varman I (962–1020). You can see these plates with the permission of the synagogue guardian.

Concessions given to Joseph Rabban by Ravi Varman I included permission to use a *palanquin* (carrying chair) and parasol. Given that palanquins and parasols were the prerogative of rulers, Ravi Varman I had in effect legitimised a tiny Jewish kingdom. On Rabban's death, his sons fought each other for control of the 'kingdom' and this rivalry led to its break-up and the move to Mattancherry.

The community has been the subject of much research. One study by an American professor of ethnomusicology found that the music of the Cochin Jews contained strong Babylonian influences, and that their version of the Ten Commandments was almost identical to a Kurdish version housed in the Berlin Museum Archives. Of course, there has also been much local influence, and many of the hymns are similar to ragas. The community was divided into three groups, the black (Myuchasim), brown (Meshuchrarim) and white (Pardesi).

Migration to Israel has reduced the community to less than 20. In spite of such low numbers, however, the community remains active with the synagogue as its focus. There has been no rabbi within living memory but all the elders are qualified to perform religious ceremonies and marriages.

Mattancherry Palace

Built by the Portuguese in 1555, Mattancherry Palace was presented to the raja of Cochin, Veera Kerala Varma (1537–61), as a gesture of goodwill (and probably as a means of securing trading privileges).

The Dutch renovated the palace in 1663, hence its alternative name, the Dutch Palace. The two-storey building surrounds a courtyard containing a Hindu temple.

The central hall on the 1st floor was the coronation hall of the rajas. The astonishing **murals**, depicting scenes from the Ramayana, Mahabharata and Puranic legends, are one of the wonders of India. The ladies' bedchamber downstairs features a cheerful Krishna using his six hands and two feet to engage in foreplay with eight happy milkmaids.

The palace is open 10 am to 5 pm Saturday to Thursday; entry is Rs 2. Photography is prohibited.

Pardesi Synagogue

Originally constructed in 1568, the synagogue was destroyed by the Portuguese in 1662 and rebuilt two years later when the Dutch took over Kochi. It features hand-painted willow pattern floor tiles brought from Canton in China in the mid-18th century by Ezekial Rahabi, who was also responsible for the building's clock tower.

A synagogue built in the Kochangadi neighbourhood (about 1km south of the present synagogue) in 1344 has since disappeared, although a stone slab from this building, inscribed in Hebrew, can be found on the inner surface of the wall that surrounds the Mattancherry synagogue.

The area around the synagogue is known as **Jewtown** and is one of the centres of the Kochi spice trade. Scores of small firms huddle together in old, dilapidated buildings and the air is filled with the pungent aromas of ginger, cardamom, cumin, turmeric and cloves. Many Jewish names are visible on premises, and there are several curio shops on the street leading to the synagogue.

The synagogue is usually open from 10 am to noon and from 3 to 5 pm Sunday to Friday (not including Jewish holidays). Entry is Rs 2.

Ernakulam

The **Parishath Thampuram Museum** contains 19th-century oil paintings, old coins, sculptures and paintings, but apart from some interesting temple models, it's nothing special. Housed in a traditional Keralan building on Durbar Hall Rd, it's open 10 am to 12.30 pm and 2 to 4.30 pm Tuesday to Sunday; entry is free.

Vypeen Island

Ferries shuttle across the narrow strait from Fort Cochin to Vypeen Island. There are miles of surf beaches, but bathers would feel most comfortable at **Cherai Beach**, 5km from the ferry, where there are a couple of basic cafes and guesthouses. A rickshaw will cost about Rs 25. Vypeen Island also boasts a **lighthouse** at Ochanthuruth (open 3 to 5 pm daily), good **beaches** and the early-16th-century **Pallipuram Fort** (open Thursday).

Places to Stay

Ernakulam's range of accommodation is greater than Fort Cochin's and while it may appear frenetic it has many quiet possibilities. Fort Cochin is slowly succumbing to commercialisation which is affecting the very fabric of the community, so it's probably better to stay in Ernakulam. Willingdon Island has mid-range and two top-end places. During December/January hotel space is severely limited.

Places to Stay – Budget

Fort Cochin On the corner of Bastion and Peter Celli Sts, the ***Hotel Park Avenue*** *(☎ 222671, fax 224670)* is a marble-clad travesty of a redevelopment, but it's a well-run and friendly hotel. Singles/doubles cost from Rs 200/300 to 500/800 with air-con.

Royal Grace Tourist Home *(☎ 223584)* is a modern, concrete budget hotel with large double rooms with private bathroom starting at Rs 150 (downstairs) and Rs 250 (upstairs, breezy and brighter), or Rs 560 with air-con. Under the same management is the smaller, but similarly priced, ***Grace Tourist Home*** *(KB Jacob Rd)*, south of the basilica. Checkout is 10 am.

Elite Hotel *(☎ 225733, fax 225733, Princess St)* is a long-term favourite and has doubles with bathroom from Rs 150 to 300.

Brisbane Lodging *(☎ 225962)*, a couple of doors away, has seven presentable rooms from Rs 150 to 175.

Kapithan Inn *(☎ 226560, fax 228037, KL Bernard Rd)* is a scrupulously clean family home with seven rooms and two cottages, starting at Rs 250 for a single, Rs 400 to 600 for a double room.

Ernakulam Ernakulam's budget options include the following:

YMCA International House *(☎ 353479, fax 364641, Chittoor Rd)* is bright, clean and friendly. Rooms with bathroom are Rs 150/200 (economy), Rs 250/300 (executive) and Rs 500/650 (with air-con). There's also a multicuisine restaurant.

Basoto Lodge *(☎ 352140, Press Club Rd)* is small, simple, friendly and popular, so get there early. Singles with shared bathroom cost Rs 70, and doubles with private bathroom are Rs 140.

Hotel Seaking *(☎ 355341, fax 370073, MG Rd)* has good rooms for Rs 200/330; Rs 500 with air-con. There's a restaurant.

Maple Tourist Home *(☎ 355156, fax 371712, Cannon Shed Rd)* has good-value doubles from Rs 250 to 350; Rs 450 with air-con. The rooftop garden overlooks the jetty.

Bijus Tourist Home *(☎ 381881, corner of Cannon Shed and Market Rds)* is a friendly place with rooms for Rs 165/300, and air-con doubles for Rs 550.

Queen's Residency *(☎ 365775, fax 352845, Narakathara Rd, Shenoys Junction)* is a quaint hotel, airy and aesthetically pleasing, with rooms starting at Rs 165/220; Rs 550 with air-con.

Hotel KK International *(☎ 366010, Caravara Rd)* is good value with rooms at Rs 162/270.

Geetha Lodge *(☎ 352136, MG Rd)* has simple rooms for Rs 180/280.

Hotel Luciya *(☎ 381177)*, with efficient and friendly staff, has good-value rooms for Rs 130/250; Rs 250/375 with air-con. It has a restaurant and TV lounge.

Places to Stay – Mid-Range

Fort Cochin As well as the listings below, see the previous budget-hotel listings, some of which offer mid-priced rooms.

Fort House *(☎ 226103, fax 222066, Calvathy Rd)* has a lovely courtyard sculpture garden and clean, comfortable doubles for Rs 850 (including breakfast and taxes).

The Old Courtyard *(☎ 226302, ⓔ kuruvi@md3.vsnl.net.in, Princess St)* is a 200-year-old house. The eight large double rooms feature wooden floors and four-poster beds. Rooms cost from Rs 1000 to 1500.

Fort Heritage *(☎ 225333, fax 221455, ⓔ hapynest@satyam.net.in, Napier St)* has been run by the same family for years. It's an old Dutch building, with spacious rooms furnished with antique rosewood furniture.

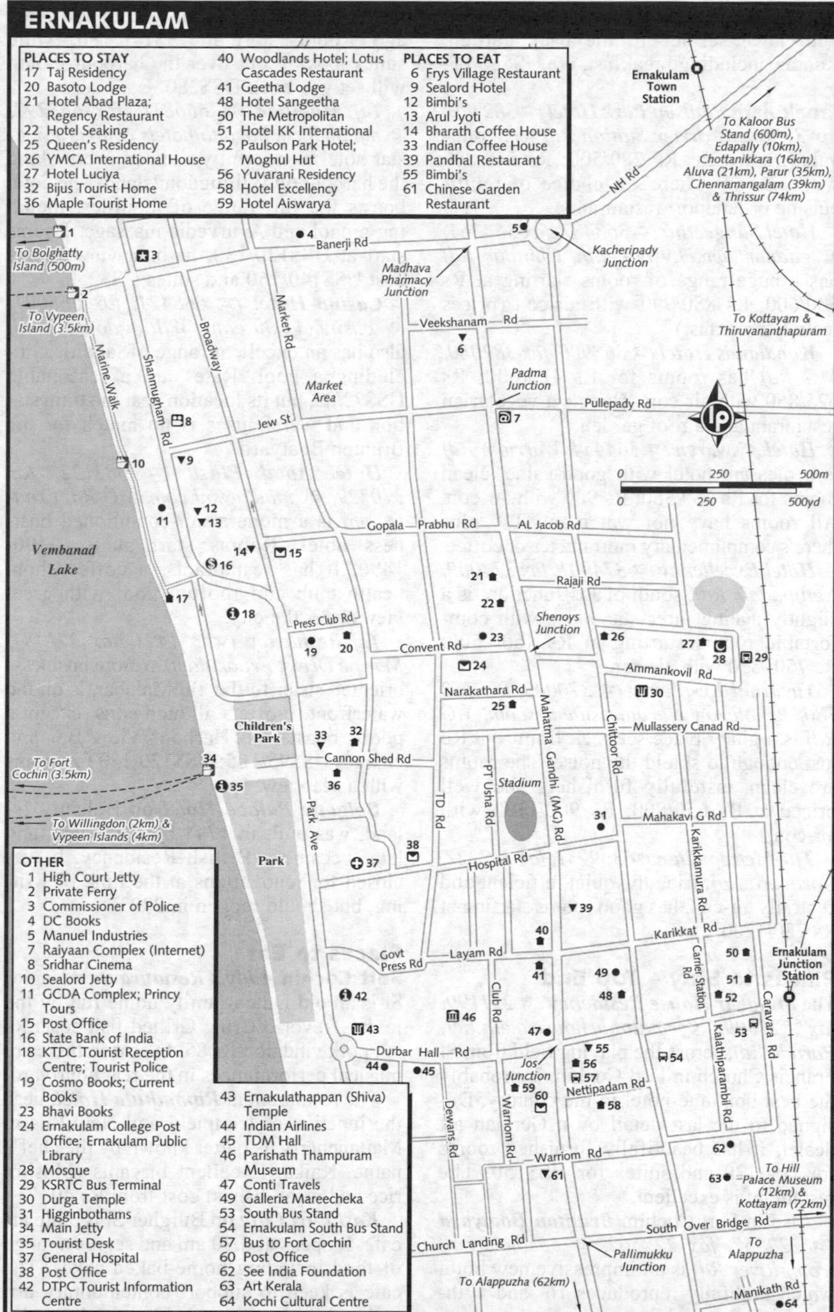
ERNAKULAM
PLACES TO STAY
17 Taj Residency
20 Basoto Lodge
21 Hotel Abad Plaza; Regency Restaurant
22 Hotel Seaking
25 Queen's Residency
26 YMCA International House
27 Hotel Luciya
32 Bijus Tourist Home
36 Maple Tourist Home
40 Woodlands Hotel; Lotus Cascades Restaurant
41 Geetha Lodge
48 Hotel Sangeetha
50 The Metropolitan
51 Hotel KK International
52 Paulson Park Hotel; Moghul Hut
56 Yuvarani Residency
58 Hotel Excellency
59 Hotel Aiswarya
PLACES TO EAT
6 Frys Village Restaurant
9 Sealord Hotel
12 Bimbi's
13 Arul Jyoti
14 Bharath Coffee House
33 Indian Coffee House
39 Pandhal Restaurant
55 Bimbi's
61 Chinese Garden Restaurant
OTHER
1 High Court Jetty
2 Private Ferry
3 Commissioner of Police
4 DC Books
5 Manuel Industries
7 Raiyaan Complex (Internet)
8 Sridhar Cinema
10 Sealord Jetty
11 GCDA Complex; Princy Tours
15 Post Office
16 State Bank of India
18 KTDC Tourist Reception Centre; Tourist Police
19 Cosmo Books; Current Books
23 Bhavi Books
24 Ernakulam College Post Office; Ernakulam Public Library
28 Mosque
29 KSRTC Bus Terminal
30 Durga Temple
31 Higginbothams
34 Main Jetty
35 Tourist Desk
37 General Hospital
38 Post Office
42 DTPC Tourist Information Centre
43 Ernakulathappan (Shiva) Temple
44 Indian Airlines
45 TDM Hall
46 Parishath Thampuram Museum
47 Conti Travels
49 Galleria Mareecheka
53 South Bus Stand
54 Ernakulam South Bus Stand
57 Bus to Fort Cochin
60 Post Office
62 See India Foundation
63 Art Kerala
64 Kochi Cultural Centre
Ernakulam Town Station
To Kaloor Bus Stand (600m), Edapally (10km), Chottanikkara (16km), Aluva (21km), Parur (35km), Chennamangalam (39km) & Thrissur (74km)
NH Rd
Kacheripady Junction
Madhava Pharmacy Junction
Banerji Rd
To Bolghatty Island (500m)
To Vypeen Island (3.5km)
To Kottayam & Thiruvananthapuram
Veekshanam Rd
Market Rd
Broadway
Shanmugham Rd
Marine Walk
Market Area
Padma Junction
Pullepady Rd
Jew St
0 250 500m
0 250 500yd
Gopala Prabhu Rd
AL Jacob Rd
Vembanad Lake
Rajaji Rd
Press Club Rd
Shenoys Junction
Convent Rd
Ammankovil Rd
Narakathara Rd
Mullassery Canad Rd
Children's Park
Cannon Shed Rd
To Fort Cochin (3.5km)
To Willingdon (2km) & Vypeen Islands (4km)
Mahatma Gandhi (MG) Rd
Chittoor Rd
Stadium
PT Usha Rd
TD Rd
Park Ave
Mahakavi G Rd
Karikkamura Rd
Park
Hospital Rd
Karikkat Rd
Govt Press Rd
Layam Rd
Club Rd
Carrier Station Rd
Ernakulam Junction Station
Durbar Hall Rd
Jos Junction
Nettipadam Rd
Kalathiparambil Rd
Caravara Rd
Dewans Rd
Warriom Rd
To Hill Palace Museum (12km) & Kottayam (72km)
South Over Bridge Rd
Church Landing Rd
Pallimukku Junction
To Alappuzha
To Alappuzha (62km)
Manikath Rd

It has a good restaurant including tandoori with lawn service in the back garden. Rooms, including breakfast, are US$55/65.

Ernakulam ***Paulson Park Hotel*** *(☎ 382170, fax 370072, Carrier Station Rd)* has good-value rooms for Rs 280/500; Rs 540/800 with air-con. There's a choice of multi-cuisine or tandoori restaurants.

Hotel Sangeetha *(☎ 368487, fax 354261, ⓔ gaanam@md3.vsnl.net.in, Chittoor Rd)* has a huge range of rooms starting at Rs 500/600; Rs 880/990 with air-con (prices include breakfast).

Woodlands Hotel *(☎ 368900, fax 382080, MG Rd)* has rooms for Rs 425/600; Rs 625/850 with air-con. There's a vegetarian restaurant and a roof garden.

Hotel Aiswarya *(☎ 364454, Warriom Rd)* is a pleasant hotel with good-value, clean rooms for Rs 260/360; Rs 900 with air-con. All rooms have hot water and TV, plus there's complimentary morning tea or coffee.

Hotel Excellency *(☎ 374001, fax 374009, Nettipadam Rd)*, south of Jos Junction, is a slightly ageing three-star place with comfortable rooms starting at Rs 450/ 500; Rs 750/ 850 with air-con.

Yuvarani Residency *(☎ 370040, fax 352 780, ⓔ hotel@yuvaraniresidency.com, MG Rd)* is a glitzy place set back from MG Rd just enough to shield the noise. The rooms are clean, tastefully furnished, and well priced at Rs 650/800; Rs 900/1100 with air-con.

The Metropolitan *(☎ 369931, fax 382227, Caravara Rd)*, friendly, quiet, efficient and centrally air-con, has good rooms starting at Rs 750/1200.

Places to Stay – Top End

The ***Malabar House Residency*** *(☎ 221199, fax 221599, ⓔ malabarhouse@eth.net, Parade Rd)*, across the playing field from St Francis Church in Fort Cochin, is probably the best boutique hotel in the country. Designed to the last detail by a German art dealer, it has beautifully furnished rooms for US$120 and suites for US$150. The restaurant is excellent.

Also in Fort Cochin, ***Brunton Boatyard*** *(☎ 222557, fax 222562, ⓔ casino@vsnl.com, River Rd)* is an impressive new hotel which faithfully reproduces 16- and 17th-century Dutch and Portuguese architecture, rather like a movie set of Cochin 300 years ago. Rooms start at US$170/180, while suites looking out over the harbour mouth will set you back US$280.

Taj Malabar *(☎ 666811, fax 668297, ⓔ malabar.cochin@tajhotels.com)* is a five-star hotel wonderfully situated overlooking the harbour on Willingdon Island. The hotel boasts the full range of facilities, includ ing a pool and Ayurvedic massage. Rooms start at US$120/130, harbour-view rooms cost US$140/160 and suites US$250.

Casino Hotel *(☎ 668421, fax 668001, ⓔ casino@vsnl.com, Willingdon Island)* also has an excellent range of facilities, including a pool. Rates are a reasonable US$72/82, but its location near the train station and warehouses is no match for the Brunton Boatyard.

Hotel Abad Plaza *(☎ 381122, fax 370729, ⓔ abad@vsnl.com, MG Rd, Ernakulam)* is a modern, air-conditioned business hotel. Rooms start at Rs 1190/ 1490. It has restaurants, a coffee shop, health club and rooftop pool with great views over the city.

Taj Residency *(☎ 371471, fax 371481, Marine Drive, Ernakulam)*, a more business-oriented sister to the Taj Malabar, is on the waterfront. It offers all mod cons (except a pool), boasts the Harbour View Bar and charges US$95/105; US$120/140 for rooms with a sea view.

Bolgatty Palace Hotel on Bolgatty Island, was built in 1744 by the Dutch, and later became a British Residency. It was closed for renovations at the time of writing, but should reopen in 2002.

Places to Eat

Fort Cochin ***Addy's Restaurant*** on Napier St is an old Dutch family home run by the jovial Trevor d'Cruz. Grilled fish costs Rs 90, pork vindaloo Rs 85. In season there are musical performances in the rear courtyard.

The restaurant at ***Ramathula Hotel***, near the junction of Irimpichi and New Rds in Mattancherry, is better known by the chef's name, Kaika. Excellent biryanis (Muslim rice and meat dishes) cost from Rs 40.

Kashi Art Cafe on Burgher St is a hip art cafe. It opens at 8.30 am and serves a range of food including home-baked cakes. The cafe is keen to support contemporary art, and exhibitions, workshops and theatre performances are organised and held here. Interested artists can contact the cafe for possible residencies and networking.

The top-end hotels have good quality restaurants. ***Malabar House Residency*** serves top-quality Indian and Italian dishes; main courses cost around Rs 150. ***The Old Courtyard*** has a Filipino chef and an international menu; slightly expensive at around Rs 300 to 400 per head for dinner but worth a splurge. ***Fort House*** has a good reputation for seafood but two hours' notice is required.

Behind the Chinese fishing nets are a couple of ***fishmongers***. The idea is you buy a fish (or prawns, scampi, lobster; Rs 50 to 300 per kilogram), then take your selection to a kitchen where they will cook it and serve it to you (about Rs 30 for a large fish). Of course it's important to determine the freshness of the catch.

The restaurant at the ***Elite Hotel*** does all the usual travellers fare, sometimes quite well and sometimes indifferently. It's a good place to hang out and tap into the backpacker information network though.

Ernakulam The ***Indian Coffee House*** on the corner of Cannon Shed Rd and Park Ave has quaintly uniformed waiters in cummerbunds offering good snacks and breakfasts. It's popular and always busy.

Bimbi's *(Shanmugham Rd)* is a modern, self-serve restaurant with fast food (North and South Indian plus some Western snacks) as well as sweets. An excellent masala dosa costs Rs 12. There's another branch near Jos Junction.

Lotus Cascades *(MG Rd),* in the Woodlands Hotel, turns out excellent vegetarian thalis for Rs 30.

Frys Village Restaurant on Veekshanam Rd near Padma Junction is the place to go for authentic Keralan food.

Pandhal Restaurant *(MG Rd)* could easily be a Western chain restaurant. It has excellent North Indian food and fish dishes.

Chinese Garden Restaurant *(Warriom Rd)* has good food and attentive service.

Arul Jyoti *(Shanmugham Rd)* is a straightforward 'meals' place with basic veg meals for Rs 15. The ***Bharath Coffee House*** *(Broadway)* offers similar fare.

Sealord Hotel *(Shanmugham Rd)* has two restaurants: Chinese and Indian/continental. The reasonably priced food is consistently good. The choice is between air-con and live 'easy-listening' rock, or the roof where conversation is accompanied by traffic noise wafting up on photochemical thermals.

The classy but reasonably priced ***Regency Restaurant*** *(MG Rd),* in the Hotel Abad Plaza, offers good Indian, Chinese and Western food.

The Paulson Park Hotel, near the Ernakulam Junction train station, has the ***Moghul Hut*** tandoori restaurant in its central atrium area.

Entertainment

The ***Sridhar Cinema*** *(Shanmugham Rd, Ernakulam)* screens films in Malayalam, Hindi, Tamil and English.

There are several places in Kochi where you can see Kathakali (see the 'Kathakali' boxed text in the Kovalam section).

Art Kerala *(☎ 366238)*, near the See India Foundation, Ernakulam, stages rooftop performances for Rs 100. Make-up begins at 6 pm and the show runs from 7 to 8.30 pm.

Kochi Cultural Centre *(☎ 368153)*, Souhardham, Manikath Rd, is south of Ernakulam Junction train station. The performance is held in a specially constructed, air-conditioned theatre designed to resemble a temple courtyard. Make-up begins at 5 pm and the performance runs from 6.30 to 8 pm. The cost is Rs 125.

Kerala Kathakali Centre stages performances at the Cochin Aquatic Club on River (Calvathy) Rd, Fort Cochin, near the bus stand. Enthusiastic performances from young Kathakali artists nicely balance the more formal introduction to the art at the See India Foundation. Make-up begins at 5 pm, and the performance runs from 6.30 to 7.30 pm. The last ferry from Fort Cochin to Ernakulam departs after the performance at 9.30 pm. Admission is Rs 100.

See India Foundation *(☎ 371571)*, Devan Gurukalum, Kalathiparambil Rd, is near the Ernakulam Junction train station. The show features an extraordinary presentation by PK Devan, who explains the dance's history and makes a plucky attempt to simplify the main elements of Hinduism for visitors. Make-up begins at 6 pm, and the performance runs from 6.45 to 8 pm, with time for questions afterwards. It costs Rs 125, though you may be offered a discounted ticket from hotel staff in Ernakulam.

If, after viewing one of these performances, you wish to experience more of this fascinating art, you can attend a traditional all-night performance. Once a month the Ernakulam Kathakali Club hosts all-night performances by major artists at the TDM Hall on Durbar Hall Rd, Ernakulam. Programs covering the story in English are distributed from tourist offices a week in advance. The cost is Rs 100 (as donation).

Shopping

There are a number of handicraft and antique emporiums along MG Rd, Ernakulam, just south of Durbar Hall Rd. In Jew St, Mattancherry, there's a plethora of shops selling antiques and reproductions.

One of the more exciting developments in Kochi has been the encouragement of contemporary artists, including home-town talent. You can view and buy their work at Kashi Art Cafe, Burgher St, Fort Cochin, and Draavidia Art & Performance Gallery, Jew St, Mattancherry and Galleria Synagogue, also in Mattancherry.

In Ernakulam Galleria Mareecheka, Chittoor Rd, and Chitram Art Gallery, opposite Air India at the southern end of MG Rd, both exhibit works by well-known and emerging artists. If you fancy picking up a sitar or set of tabla, head to Manuel Industries, Banerji Rd, Ernakulam. A sitar costs approximately Rs 3500, while a set of tabla is Rs 1500.

Getting There & Away

Air The Indian Airlines office (☎ 352065) is in Ernakulam on Durbar Hall Rd, next to the Bharat Hotel. Air India (☎ 351295) is on MG Rd opposite Thomas Cook. Jet Airways (☎ 369212), MG Rd, has daily services to Mumbai (US$150), Chennai (US$120) and Bangalore (US$80). Indian Airlines flies daily to these cities for the same prices, and also has two flights a week to Goa (US$125).

Bus The KSRTC bus stand, also known as the central bus stand (☎ 372033), is by the railway line in Ernakulam, between the train stations. Because Kochi is in the middle of Kerala, many of the buses passing through Ernakulam originated in other cities. Although it's still possible to get a seat, you cannot make advance reservations; you simply have to join the scrum when the bus turns up. You can make reservations up to five days in advance for many of the buses that originate in Ernakulam. The timetable is in Malayalam and English, and the staff are very helpful.

There are also private bus stands: the Kaloor stand is north-east of Ernakulam Town train station, and the Ernakulam South stand is right outside the entrance of Ernakulam Junction train station.

The fares and times that follow are for superexpress buses from the KSRTC bus stand, unless otherwise noted. Superfast services are usually a few rupees cheaper and stop more often.

Southbound There are two routes to Thiruvananthapuram (221km): one via Alappuzha and Kollam, and the other via Kottayam. Over 60 KSRTC buses a day take the Alappuzha-Kollam route. Superexpress buses take 4½ hours to Thiruvananthapuram and cost Rs 85. The fares, times and intermediate distances for superexpress buses are: Alappuzha (Rs 27, 1½ hours, 62km), Kollam (Rs 65, three hours, 150km) and Kottayam (Rs 35, 1½ hours, 76km). There are also at least two direct buses a day to Kanyakumari, in Tamil Nadu (Rs 118, 9 hours, 302km).

Eastbound At least four direct buses a day run to Madurai (Rs 122, 9¼ hours, 324km). For those with phenomenal endurance, there are direct buses to Chennai (Rs 250, 16 hours, 690km).

The Madurai buses pass through Kumily, near the Periyar Wildlife Sanctuary on the Kerala–Tamil Nadu border. They cost Rs 57 by fast passenger bus (six hours, 192km). Departure times are 7.30 and 8.15 am, and 8.15 and 9.30 pm, and you can book a seat on the morning departures. You will need to book your journey through to Kumbam (the end of a section) but disembark at Kumily.

There are several KSRTC buses a day to Munnar (Rs 46).

Northbound Buses run every half hour to Thrissur (Rs 30, two hours, 74km) and Kozhikode (Rs 83, five hours, 219km). Three daily buses run up the coast beyond Kozhikode to Kannur (Cannanore), Kasaragod and Mangalore.

Major Trains from Ernakulam Town

destination	train No & name	departures	distance (km)	duration (hrs)	fare (Rs)
Bangalore	6525 *Kanniya Kumari-Bangalore Exp*	2.40 pm	637	14	193/893 *
Chennai	6320 *Chennai-Trivandrum Mail*	7.10 pm	697	13	211/980 *
Delhi	2625 *Kerala Exp*	3.50 pm	2833	48	489/1418 ◆
Mangalore	6329 *Malabar Exp*	11.05 pm	414	9½	148/684 *
	6349 *Parasuram Exp*	10.50 am		10	94/298 †
Mumbai	6332 *Kanniyakumari-Mumbai Exp*	12.30 pm	1815	41	380/1103 ◆
Thiruvananthapuram	6350 *Parasuram Exp*	1.55 pm	224	5	61/199 †

* sleeper/2-tier air-con ◆ sleeper/3-tier air con † second/chair class

Half a dozen interstate express buses go to Bangalore (Rs 220, 15 hours, 565km) daily via Kozhikode, Sultanbatheri and Mysore.

In addition to the KSRTC state buses, there are a number of private bus companies that have super-deluxe video buses daily to Bangalore, Mumbai and Coimbatore. Check out Princy Tours (☎ 354712), in the GCDA Complex on Shanmugham Rd, and Conti Travels (☎ 353080), at the Jos Junction of MG Rd.

Train Ernakulam has two stations, Ernakulam Junction and Ernakulam Town (the one you're most likely to use). Reservations for both have to be made at Ernakulam Junction. None of the through trains on the main trunk routes go to the Cochin Harbour station on Willingdon Island.

Trains regularly run from Thiruvananthapuram via Kollam and Kottayam to Ernakulam; less frequently they continue on to Thrissur, Kozhikode, Thalasseri and Kasaragod. See the table Major Trains from Ernakulam Town.

Getting Around

To/From the Airport Kochi International Airport is at Nedumbassery, 30km northeast of Ernakulam. Taxis cost Rs 200.

Local Transport There are no convenient bus services between Fort Cochin and the Mattancherry Palace or the synagogue, but it's a pleasant 30-minute walk through the busy warehouse area along Bazaar Rd. Autorickshaws are available and you'll need to haggle hard – this is tourist territory.

In Ernakulam, autorickshaws are the most convenient mode of transport. The trip from the bus or train stations to the Tourist Reception Centre on Shanmugham Rd should cost about Rs 25.

Local buses are very good and economical. If you have to get to Fort Cochin after the ferries stop running, catch a bus in Ernakulam on MG Rd, south of Durbar Hall Rd. The fare is Rs 3. Autorickshaws will demand at least Rs 80 once the ferries stop running after about 10 pm.

Taxis charge round-trip fares between the islands, even if you only want to go one way. Ernakulam to Willingdon Island could cost up to Rs 150 late at night.

Bicycles can be hired in Fort Cochin at Vasco Hospitality Centre (Rs 5 per hour or Rs 35 per day) and Tharavadu Tourist Home (Rs 35 per day).

Boat Ferries are the main form of transport between the various parts of Kochi. Nearly all the ferry stops are named, making identification easy. The stop on the eastern side of Willingdon Island is Embarkation; the west one, opposite Mattancherry, is Terminus, and the main stop at Fort Cochin is Customs.

Getting a ferry at Ernakulam can sometimes involve scrambling across several ferries to get to the boat you want. Make sure you get the right ferry or you may find yourself heading for the wrong island – ask the skipper or deck hand. Ferry fares are all Rs 2 or less.

From Ernakulam There are services to Fort Cochin every 45 minutes (around 6 am to 9.30 pm) from Main jetty. It's a pleasant 20-minute walk from the Fort Cochin pier to

Mattancherry. There are also six ferries a day direct to/from Mattancherry. The ticket office in Ernakulam opens 10 minutes before each sailing.

To Willingdon and Vypeen islands, ferries run every 20 minutes (6 am to 10 pm) from Main jetty. There are also ferries to Vypeen Island (sometimes via Bolgatty Island) from the High Court jetty on Shanmugham Rd.

Ferries for Bolgatty Island depart from the High Court jetty every 30 minutes between 6.15 am and 10.30 pm. It's a five-minute walk from the public jetty to Bolgatty Palace Hotel.

From Fort Cochin Ferries operate between Customs jetty and the Taj Malabar/tourist office jetty on Willingdon Island about 18 times from 6.30 am to 9 pm daily except Sunday.

Ferries cross to Vypeen Island virtually nonstop from 6 am until 10 pm. There is also a vehicular ferry every half hour or so.

Hire Boats Motorised boats of various sizes can be hired from the Sealord jetty or from the small dock adjacent to the Main jetty in Ernakulam. They're an excellent way of exploring Kochi Harbour at your leisure and without the crowds; rates start at around Rs 300 an hour. Rowboats shuttle between Willingdon Island and Fort Cochin or Mattancherry on request for about Rs 40.

AROUND KOCHI (COCHIN)

Tripunithura

The **Hill Palace Museum** at Tripunithura, 12km south-east of Ernakulam en route to Kottayam, houses the collections of the Cochin and Travancore royal families. It's open 9 am to 12.30 pm and 2 to 4.30 pm Tuesday to Sunday; entry is Rs 1. Bus No 51 or 58 from MG Rd will take you there.

Edapally

The **Museum of Kerala History**, at Edapally, 10km north-east of Ernakulam en route to Aluva (Alwaye) and Thrissur, is open 10 am to 12.30 pm and 2 to 4 pm Tuesday to Sunday; entry is Rs 5. Bus No 22 from MG Rd runs to Edapally.

Parur & Chennamangalam

About 35km north of Kochi, Parur encapsulates the cultural and religious medley of this region. There's a dusty synagogue, built around the same time as its famous counterpart in Mattancherry. Nearby is an *agraharam* (place of Brahmins), a small street of closely packed houses that was settled by Tamil Brahmins. Parur also boasts a Syrian Orthodox church, a Krishna temple and a temple to the goddess Mookambika.

Four kilometres from Parur is Chennamangalam, with the oldest **synagogue** in Kerala – slowly disintegrating.

There's a **Jesuit church** and the ruins of a Jesuit college. The Jesuits first arrived in Chennamangalam in 1577 and, soon after their arrival, the first book in Tamil (the written language then used in this part of Kerala) was printed here by John Gonsalves.

You can walk to the **Hindu temple** on the hill overlooking the Periyar River. On the way you'll pass a 16th-century **mosque** as well as Muslim and Jewish **burial grounds**.

Whereas Parur is compact and locals can point you in the right direction, Chennamangalam is best visited with a guide. Indo World (☎ 0484-370127, fax 380968), 39/4155 Heera House, MG Rd, Ernakulam, can organise transport and a local retired history teacher to guide you.

For Parur, catch a bus from the KSRTC bus stand in Kochi. From Parur you can catch a bus or autorickshaw to Chennamangalam.

THRISSUR (TRICHUR)

☎ 0487 • pop 275,053

Thrissur has long been regarded as Kerala's cultural capital. Today it continues to assume the role with its numerous festivals, art schools and institutions. Thrissur is also home to a community of Nestorian Christians, whose denomination dates back to the 3rd century AD.

Orientation & Information

Thrissur radiates from the Vadakkunathan Kshetram temple with the encircling roads named after the four directions. The DTPC tourist information centre on Palace Rd has little to offer.

The State Bank of India on Town Hall Rd cashes American Express and Thomas Cook travellers cheques but doesn't handle cards. HDFC Bank on Palace Road has an ATM which accepts foreign cards. Canara Bank on Round South can handle cash advances on Visa cards.

PAUL BEINSSEN

MARTIN HUGHES

MARTIN HUGHES

EDDIE GERALD

The gentle rhythms of Kerala: a woman carries water near Kottayam **(top right)**; a traditional river craft sails the backwaters between Alappuzha and Kollam **(bottom)**; women sift ginger in Mattancherry, near Kochi **(middle left)**; and an elephant takes part in the Pooram Festival in Thrissur **(top left)**

PAUL BEINSSEN

EDDIE GERALD

PAUL BEINSSEN

PAUL BEINSSEN

Festivals play a big part of life in Kerala: Thrissur's Pooram Festival is one of the largest in the state and features a procession of decorated elephants **(top)**; frenetic drummers **(middle right)**; Kathakali dancers **(bottom)**; and stage performers **(middle left)**

Email is available at IRS Computers & Communications for Rs 45 per hour.

Things to See & Do

In the centre of Thrissur, the Hindu-only **Vadakkunathan Kshetram** temple is famed for its artwork. To the west and east are the lesser known **Thiruampady** and **Paramekkavu temples**. Several festivals are celebrated at the temples. The annual April/May **Pooram Festival**, which includes colourful processions of decorated elephants, is one of the biggest.

There are several interesting churches, including the large **Our Lady of Lourdes Cathedral**, **Puttanpalli Church** and the **Chaldean (Nestorian) Church**. Skip the sad zoo, and the amazingly decrepit state museum in the zoo grounds. However, the **Archaeological Museum**, farther along Museum Rd, is worth a visit. It has temple models, stone reliefs, Gandharan pieces and reproductions of some of the Mattancherry murals. It's open 10 am to 5 pm. The zoo and museums are closed Monday.

Places to Stay

The ***Ramanilayam Government Guest House*** (☎ *332016*), on the corner of Palace Rd and Museum Rd, is excellent value at Rs 45/50 for singles/doubles, Rs 175/275 with air-con, but ring first as it's often full.

KTDC Yatri Nivas (☎ *332333, Stadium Rd*), nearby, has rooms for Rs 100/150, or Rs 350/400 with air-con. There's a restaurant and bar.

THRISSUR (TRICHUR)

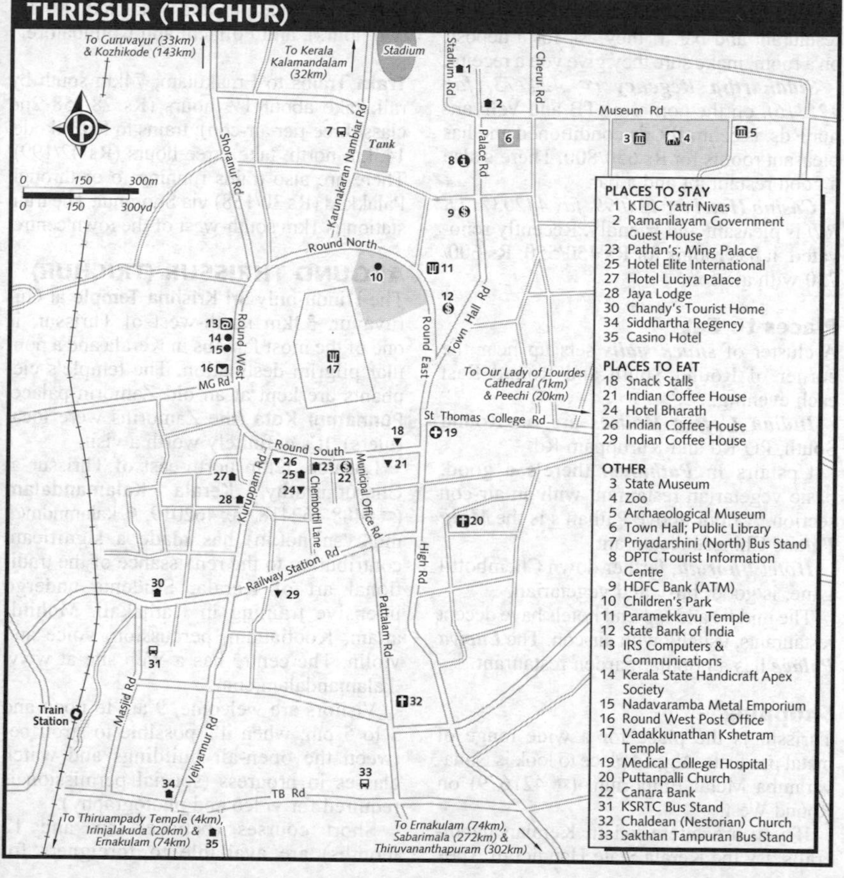

Chandy's Tourist Home *(☎ 421167, Railway Station Rd)* has rooms for Rs 80/150 with shared bathroom, Rs 150/300 with private bathroom. There are several lodges nearby with similar standards and prices.

Jaya Lodge *(☎ 423258, Kuruppam Rd)*, around the corner, is unexciting but cheap. Rooms are Rs 70/100; doubles with bathroom are Rs 120.

Pathan's *(☎ 425620, Chembottil Lane)* has rooms for Rs 175/250. The larger doubles for Rs 300 are good value.

Hotel Elite International *(☎ 421033, fax 442057)*, across the road, has rooms for Rs 210/260; Rs 420/500 with air-con. It has a bar and restaurant.

Hotel Luciya Palace *(☎ 424731, fax 427290, Marar Rd)* has comfortable rooms for Rs 350/475; Rs 575/675 with air-con. There's an air-con restaurant, a garden restaurant and bar. If they ask for a deposit on a room, make sure they give you a receipt.

Siddhartha Regency *(☎ 424773, fax 425116)*, on the corner of TB and Veliyannur Rds, is centrally air-conditioned and has pleasant rooms for Rs 650/800. There's also a good restaurant and a bar.

Casino Hotel *(☎ 424699, fax 442037, TB Rd)* is pleasant and friendly. Recently renovated, it has rooms for Rs 450/550; Rs 600/750 with air-con.

Places to Eat

A cluster of ***snack stalls*** sets up near the corner of Round South and Round East each evening.

Indian Coffee Houses are on Round South, PO Rd and Kuruppam Rd.

Upstairs in ***Pathan's***, there's a good, basic vegetarian restaurant with an air-con section. A floor above Pathan's is the ***Ming Palace*** Chinese restaurant.

Hotel Bharath, farther down Chembottil Lane, is good, busy and vegetarian.

The middle and top-end hotels have decent restaurants, usually with air-con. The ***Luciya Palace*** has a popular garden restaurant.

Shopping

Thrissur is the place for a wide range of metal products. A good place to look is Nadavaramba Metal Emporium (☎ 421679) on Round West.

If you are interested in Keralan handicrafts, try the Kerala State Handicraft Apex Society (☎ 420865) on Round West. It's open 10 am to 7.30 pm Monday to Saturday.

Getting There & Away

Bus There are three bus stands in Thrissur: The KSRTC and Sakthan Tampuran stands in the south and the Priyadarshini (also referred to as North) stand in the north.

KSRTC buses go to Thiruvananthapuram (Rs 105, 7½ hours), Ernakulam (Rs 30, two hours), Kozhikode (Rs 43, 3½ hours) and Palakkad (Rs 24, 1½ hours). There are also buses to Ponnani, Kottayam and Prumpavoor (for connections to Munnar).

The large, private Sakthan Tampuran stand has buses bound for closer towns such as Kodungallor, Irinjalakuda and Guruvayur (Rs 8, one hour). The smaller, private Priyadarshini bus stand has many buses bound for Shoranur and Palakkad (Rs 15, two hours), and Pollachi and Coimbatore.

Train Trains to Ernakulam, 74km south by rail, take about 1½ hours (Rs 28/158 2nd class/three-tier air-con); trains to Kozhikode, 143km north, take three hours (Rs 42/199). There are also trains running to or through Palakkad (Rs 30/158) via Shoranur. The train station is 1km south-west of the town centre.

AROUND THRISSUR (TRICHUR)

The Hindu-only **Sri Krishna Temple** at Guruvayur, 33km north-west of Thrissur, is one of the most famous in Kerala and a popular pilgrim destination. The temple's elephants are kept at an old Zamorin palace, **Punnathur Kota** (the Zamorins were local rulers). It's definitely worth a visit.

Located 32km north-east of Thrissur at Cheruthuruthy, **Kerala Kalamandalam** (☎ 0488-462418, fax 462019, ⓔ kalamndm@md4.vsnl.net.in) has made a significant contribution to the renaissance of the traditional art of Kerala. Students undergo intensive training in Kathakali, Mohiniattam, Kootiattam, percussion, voice and violin. The centre has a Web site at www.kalamandalam.com.

Visitors are welcome, 9 am to noon and 3 to 5 pm, when it's possible to stroll between the open-air buildings and watch classes in progress (special permission is required for video and photography).

Short courses (between six and 12 months) are available to foreigners for around Rs 1000 per month (plus Rs 1000 for accommodation).

The **Natana Kairali Research & Performing Centre for Traditional Arts** (☎ 0488-825559), 20km south of Thrissur near Irinjalakuda, offers training in traditional arts including rare forms of puppetry and dance. The centre hosts a 12-day **festival** in January. Short appreciation courses (usually about one month) are available to foreigners. For details of performances or enrolments, telephone or write to the Director, Natana Kairali Research & Performing Centre for Traditional Arts, Ammannu Thakyar, Mathom, Irinjalakuda, Thrissur District.

Northern Kerala

KOZHIKODE (CALICUT)

☎ 0495 • pop 801,190

The landing of Vasco da Gama near Kozhikode in 1498 heralded the period of Portuguese colonisation in India. The Portuguese attempted to conquer Kozhikode and the local rulers, the Zamorins, but their attacks in 1509 and 1510 were repulsed. Tipu Sultan took control of the whole region in 1789, with British rule established in 1792. The modern city is a typically busy Indian metropolis with few imprints of its long history, but the network of rivers and lagoons nearby offers a much less touristy backwater experience than the Kollam-Alappuzha backwaters.

Information

Money can be changed at the State Bank of India in Bank Rd or the faster PL Worldways, Lakhotia Computer Centre.

There are numerous STD/ISD booths, and a growing number of Internet cafes. Try SR Enterprises on the corner of Mavoor (Indira Gandhi) and Bank Rds, which charges Rs 60 per hour.

Things to See

There are few indicators of Kozhikode's colourful past. **Mananchira Square** was the former courtyard of the Zamorins. Temples, mosques and churches illustrate the region's acquaintance with the major belief systems. Of note are the **Tali Temple** (Hindus only), the **Kuttichira Mosque** and the **Church of South India**. The impressive **Mananchira Library** reflects the significance Kozhikode places on literature.

Five kilometres north of town, at East Hill, archaeological displays at the **Pazhassirajah Museum** include copies of ancient murals, bronzes, coins and models of megalithic monuments – the earliest monuments of Kerala. Next door, the **Krishna Menon Museum** has memorabilia of this former foreign minister, while the **art gallery** has paintings by Raja Ravi Varma (1848–1906), an internationally recognised artist. He specialised in portraits influenced by European styles.

The three places are open 10 am to 5 pm Tuesday to Sunday, except on Wednesday when the Krishna Menon Museum and the art gallery open at noon.

Sixteen kilometres north, on the way to Kannur, there's a nondescript memorial for da Gama's landing at **Kappad Beach**.

Malabar Houseboats (☎ 452045, fax 765 066, e malabarhouseboat@hotmail.com) offers backwater cruises. A 24-hour cruise for two people costs Rs 6250, while a 7½-hour day cruise costs Rs 3000. Popular destinations include the Kallai River and the Canoli Canal. Malabar Houseboats provides transport from your hotel to and from the jetty at Purakkatri, 12km north of Kozhikode.

Places to Stay – Budget

All of the following have private bathrooms.

Metro Tourist Home *(☎ 766029),* on the corner of Mavoor and Bank Rds, has singles/doubles for Rs 130/200 and air-con rooms with TV for Rs 500.

Hotel Sajina *(☎ 722975, Mavoor Rd)* has basic rooms for Rs 145/250.

NCK Tourist Home has double rooms (no hot water) for Rs 145. Across the way the ***Delma Tourist Home*** charges Rs 200. Women travellers will find better options elsewhere.

Hotel Maharani *(☎ 722541, Taluk Rd)* is slightly off the beaten track, and quiet. Rooms are Rs 150/185; Rs 470 for an air-con double. There's a bar and a garden.

The ***KTDC Hotel Malabar Mansion*** *(☎ 722391, Mananchira Square)* has rooms for Rs 185/235; Rs 370/420 with air-con. There's a restaurant and beer parlour.

Kalpaka Tourist Home *(☎/fax 720222, Town Hall Rd)*, run by women, has rooms for Rs 180/225; Rs 550 for air-con. There is an OK restaurant.

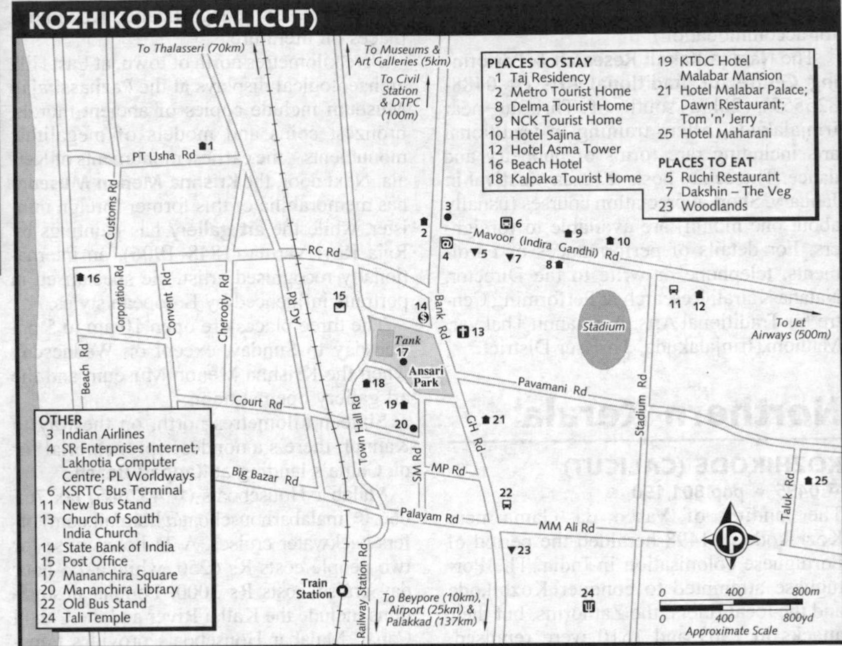

Places to Stay – Mid-Range & Top End

The ***Beach Hotel*** *(☎ 365363, ⓔ beachhotel@rediffmail.com)* was once the Malabar British Club and is now a comfortable small hotel with 10 rooms. Standard air-con rooms cost Rs 500, while beach-facing suites are Rs 1200.

Hotel Asma Tower *(☎ 723560, Marvoor Rd)* is friendly and good value. Rooms are Rs 250/300; Rs 375/475 with air-con.

Hotel Malabar Palace *(☎ 721511, fax 721794, GH Rd)* has central air-con and rooms for Rs 1150/1475.

Taj Residency *(☎ 765354, fax 766448, ⓔ tajclt@md3.vsnl.net.in, PT Usha Rd)* has rooms starting at US$45/75.

Places to Eat

The glossy ***Woodlands*** vegetarian restaurant is in the easily spotted White Lines building on GH Rd.

Dakshin – The Veg and nearby ***Ruchi Restaurant*** *(Mavoor Rd)* both serve very good vegetarian food.

The restaurants in the ***Metro*** and ***Kalpaka Tourist Homes*** and in the ***Malabar Mansion*** hotel are reasonably priced.The air-con ***Dawn Restaurant*** at the Malabar Palace is good and there's an ice cream parlour, ***Tom 'n' Jerry***, outside.

The garden restaurant at the ***Beach Hotel*** has good food and cold beer.

Getting There & Away

Air Jet Airways (☎ 356518), 29 Mavoor Rd, flies daily to Mumbai (US$140). Indian Airlines (☎ 766243), Eroth Centre, Bank Rd, flies daily to Mumbai, Coimbatore (US$40) and Chennai (US$90).

Bus The KSRTC bus stand is on Mavoor Rd, close to the junction with Bank Rd. There's also the new bus stand, farther east along Mavoor Rd, for long-distance private buses, and the old bus stand, at the intersection of GH and MM Ali Rds, for local buses. There are regular buses to Bangalore, Mangalore, Mysore, Ooty, Madurai, Coimbatore, Pondicherry, Thiruvananthapuram, Alappuzha, Kochi and Kottayam.

Train The train station is south of Mananchira Square, about 2km from the New bus stand. It's 242km north to Mangalore (Rs 62/279 in 2nd class/three-tier air-con, 4½ to 5½ hours), 190km south to Ernakulam (Rs 53/239, five hours) and 414km to Thiruvananthapuram (Rs 95/424, 9½ to 11 hours).

Heading south-east, there are trains to Coimbatore (Rs 52/234) via Palakkad (Rs 41/188). These trains then head north to the centres of Bangalore, Chennai and Delhi.

Getting Around

There's no shortage of autorickshaws in Kozhikode, and the drivers will use their meters. It's about Rs 10 from the station to the KSRTC bus stand or most hotels.

WAYANAD WILDLIFE SANCTUARY

Also known as Muthanga Wildlife Sanctuary, Wayanad is a remote rainforest reserve connected to Bandipur National Park in Karnataka and Mudumalai Sanctuary in Tamil Nadu. Wayanad is not really geared up for visitors. The Forest Department staff are very helpful but you'll probably just get a short jeep trip on the outskirts of the sanctuary through plantations.

If chasing forest officers for permits gets too much you may like to try a treehouse experience at ***Green Magic Nature Resort***, Vythiri, 65km north-east of Kozhikode. All essentials must be carried in. Accommodation and meals for two people is US$150, in a cabin 40m up in the treetops. Guided walks through the Wayanad forest are also available. All bookings must be made through Tourindia (☎ 0471-330437, fax 331 407, ⓔ tourindia@richsoft.com), on MG Rd in Thiruvananthapuram.

KANNUR (CANNANORE)

☎ 0497 • pop 463,962

Kannur's days of glory were under the Kolathiri rajas, and its importance as a spice-trading port was even mentioned by the Venetian traveller Marco Polo. From the 15th century various colonial powers exerted their influence, including the Portuguese, Dutch and British. Many circus performers are based in Kannur.

Information

Give the DTPC (☎ 706336) a miss. Opposite, the State Bank of Travancore will cash American Express travellers cheques. For other brands and for cash advances on credit cards try the State Bank of India on Fort Rd.

Things to See

The Portuguese built **St Angelo Fort** in 1505 on the promontory north-west of town. Under the British it became a major military base, and the Indian army occupies the cantonment area beside the fort. The fort is a Rs 10 rickshaw ride from town (entry is free). The solid laterite fortifications were modified by the British who also remodelled many of the buildings within the walls.

At the **Kanhirode Weavers Co-operative** (☎ 851259, fax 851865), 13km north-east of Kannur, you can see the 385 members turn out high-quality furnishing fabrics, saris, dhotis and fine silks. Visitors (by appointment only – phone the secretary) can buy direct for 20% below showroom prices.

The co-op, on the Kannur-Mysore road, is easily reached by bus (or rickshaw, Rs 200) from Kannur. Ask to get off at Kudukkimotta.

Four kilometres from the weaving co-op, farther along the road towards Mysore, you'll see the **Dinesh Beedi Co-op** – the makers of the popular *beedi* cigarettes and a significant player in the Keralan economy. Visitors are welcome.

At the **Parasinikadavu Temple**, 18km north-east of Kannur, there are regular Teyyam (ritual temple dance) performances (October to February) usually 4 am to 9 am. Times and days vary so ask the locals (but not tourist officials – they're likely to give incorrect information).

Places to Stay & Eat

Government Guest House *(☎ 706426)* is for government ministers, but it's let to visitors if there's room. It's the best place to stay and at Rs 150 for a double room is very good value. Phone the manager first to make sure there's room.

Centaur Tourist Home *(☎ 768270)*, directly across from the train station entrance, on MA Rd, has basic singles/doubles for Rs 120/193. There are plenty of similar lodges in the vicinity.

Malabar Residency *(☎ 765456, fax 778817, Thavakkara Rd)* has air-conditioned rooms for Rs 800/950, all with balconies overlooking a busy road. It has a 24-hour coffee shop and multicuisine restaurant.

Parkin's Chinese restaurant, New Subway, Thavakkara, serves huge, OK meals for reasonable prices.

Getting There & Away

There are direct buses to/from Mysore as well as regular buses to Mangalore and Kozhikode. Kannur is on the main train link between Mangalore and Kozhikode.

BEKAL

☎ 0499

Bekal, in the far north of the state, has palm-fringed beaches and a rocky headland topped by the huge Bekal Fort, built between 1645 and 1660. This fort, with views from the battlements north and south, has an obscure early history but it has been under the control of the Kolathiri rajas and the Vijayanagar empire. The British occupied it for a period after Tipu Sultan's defeat. There are slow-moving plans to establish resorts here. The beach has fine sand and calm waters, but swimmers should beware of shifting sand bars.

Places to Stay & Eat

You can stay inside the Bekal Fort walls at the ***Tourist Bungalow***. There are just two double rooms for Rs 60 with bathroom (singles are charged Rs 40). To book, ring the District Collector, Kasaragod (☎ 430400). Cold mineral water and soft drinks are available but for food you'll have to head to the villages north of the fort – take a torch (flashlight).

Hotel Sri Sistha, nearby, is a fairly basic restaurant but one of the few open during Ramadan. Meals can be had for under Rs 10.

Eeyem Lodge *(☎ 736343)*, 2km north of Bekal close to Kappil Beach, is good value at Rs 100/150 to 300 for a large double room. There's an air-con restaurant here.

Fortland Tourist Home *(☎ 736600, Main Rd)* is a few kilometres farther north at the village of Udma. Comfortable rooms cost Rs 75/125; Rs 400 with air-con. The attached ***Sealord*** restaurant is good value.

Nalanda Resort *(☎ 782662, fax 780199, ⓔ nalanda@md5.vsnl.net.in)*, 14km south of Bekal on the edge of the highway, is a very attractive riverside resort with rooms from Rs 500/800 to 800/1100, with air-con. It can arrange fishing trips, treks in the Western Ghats and visits to temple dance performances.

Getting There & Around

The train station for Bekal Fort is Kotikulum in the village of Palakunnu, and trains stop regularly. There are many buses to/from Kasaragod (Rs 3 to 5.50), the nearest town of any size, and it's not too hard to find an autorickshaw or a bus at Bekal Junction to take you to/from Palakunnu and Udma.

KASARAGOD

☎ 0499 • pop 60,000

Kasaragod is about 20km north of Bekal and 47km south of Mangalore. There is a small 17th-century fort nearby at Chandragiri. Like many north Keralan towns, it has a large Muslim population who rely on fishing and remittances from the Middle East.

Places to Stay & Eat

There are a number of hotels along MG Rd, near the junction with National Highway 17.

Enay Tourist Home *(☎ 421164)* has single or double rooms for Rs 100 with shower. Of a similar standard are the ***Ceeyel Tourist Home*** *(☎ 430177)* and the ***Aliya Lodge*** *(☎ 430666)*, behind the post office.

Hotel City Tower *(☎ 430562, fax 430 235)*, the green-and-cream landmark at the bus stand end of MG Rd, has rooms for Rs 200/280, or Rs 495 with air-con. It has a restaurant serving veg and nonveg food.

Hotel Apsara Regency *(☎ 430124)*, opposite the KSRTC bus stand, has good rooms (quieter at the back) for Rs 160/260, and Rs 360/495 with air-con. The attached ***Sri Nivas*** veg is very good food.

Getting There & Away

Private buses leave for Bekal and Mangalore from the Municipal bus stand near the Hotel City Tower. More regular buses leave from the KSRTC bus stand 1.5km south of the Municipal stand. Buses to Kahangad will drop you off at Udma, Palakunnu or Bekal.

The train station is a few kilometres south of town. It's 1½ hours between Kasaragod and Mangalore by express train (Rs 22).

Lakshadweep

☎ 0484 • pop 58,000

The palm-covered islands of Lakshadweep add up to only 32 sq km, scattered around 4200 sq km of lagoon waters. The archipel-

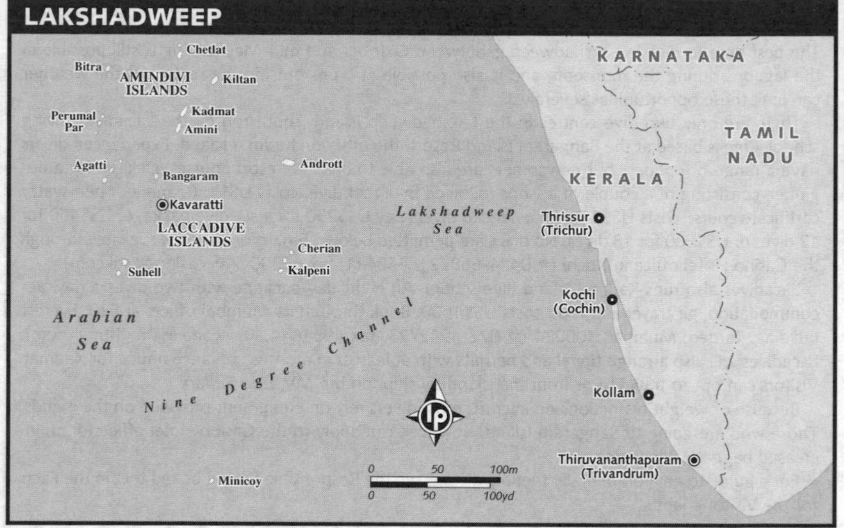

ago lies 300km west of Kerala, and is divided into the northern Amindivi group, the Laccadive group and isolated Minicoy in the south. Only 10 of the 35 islands are inhabited, not including the resort island of Bangaram. The population is 93% Sunni Muslim. Malayalam is the main language, but the southernmost island of Minicoy speaks Mahl, which is also spoken in the neighbouring Maldives. Fishing and coir production are the main economic activities. A caste system divides the islanders between Koya (land owners), Malmi (sailors) and Melachery (farmers).

While several islands have opened to visitors in recent years, foreigners are limited to day trips to islands on a boat cruise, or staying in pricey resorts. A special permit is required to visit Lakshadweep, which is organised by tour operators. Foreigners can stay on Bangaram, Agatti and Kadmat, and make day visits to Kalpeni and Minicoy. Indian nationals can also make day trips to Andrott and Kavaratti.

The archipelago's pristine lagoons, unspoiled coral reefs and average November to March temperatures of 24° to 34°C make it a diver's dream.

History

A popular story is that the islands were discovered when the legendary ruler of Kerala, Cheraman Perumal, converted to Islam and set off for Mecca. Relatives sent a search party to bring him back, but the ships were wrecked on Bangaram Island. Having made their repairs, the mariners sailed home to report what they had found, and were rewarded with the right to settle the islands. There is no concrete evidence to suggest who the first settlers really were.

Around the 12th century the islands came under the control of the mainland rulers, the Ali rajas of Cannanore. In 1525 the Portuguese began their brutal occupation. When their power waned the Ali rajas returned (with an equally brutal regime). In 1783 Hyder Ali assumed control. When the British defeated his son (Tipu Sultan) they took over the islands and in 1908 the entire region was ceded to the British government.

In 1956, nearly 10 years after Indian Independence, the islands became centrally administered by the government in Delhi as a Union Territory. In 1973 they became officially known as Lakshadweep.

Information

The Society for the Promotion of Recreational Tourism & Sports in Lakshadweep (Sports) is the main tourism organisation. Its office (☎ 0484-668387, fax 668155) is on IG Rd, Willingdon Island, Kochi, 682003.

Diving

The best time to dive in Lakshadweep is between October and mid-May. Diving is still possible in the lagoons during the monsoon, and is also possible at times outside the reefs, but the weather can limit these opportunities severely.

There are only two dive centres in the Lakshadweep Islands, both run by the Lacadives diving school. One is based at the Bangaram Island Resort, the other on Kadmat Island. Experienced divers have a range of options, but newcomers are also able to dive. A 'resort course' package for a beginner, consisting of a couple of lessons followed by a reef dive, costs US$150, and an open-water certificate course costs US$300. Experienced divers pay US$250 for a six-dive package, US$450 for 12 dives or US$600 for 18 dives. No dives are permitted below 35m. Information is available through the Casino Hotel office in Kochi (☎ 0484-668221, 668421, fax 668001, ⓔ casino@vsnl.com).

Lacadives also runs Kadmat Island dive school. An eight-day package with two dives a day, accommodation, air travel and food costs US$1500. Book through its Mumbai office, at E20, Everest Building, Tardeo, Mumbai, 400034 (☎ 022-4942723, fax 4951644, ⓔ lacadives@rediffmail.com). Lacadives will also arrange travel and permits with at least two months' advance notice for Kadmat. Visitors can opt to travel to or from the island by ship, on the MV *Tipu Sultan*.

Because of weight restrictions on aircraft, most divers rely on equipment provided on the islands. Those who are going to Bangaram Island, however, can apply to the Casino Hotel office for an increased baggage allowance.

For a guide to environmentally friendly diving, see the Responsible Diving boxed text in the Facts for the Visitor chapter.

Places to Stay & Eat

The ***Bangaram Island Resort*** is run by Casino Hotels, and is administered from its hotel in Kochi *(☎ 0484-668221, fax 668 001, ⓔ casino@vsnl.com)*.

There are 30 rooms and a maximum of 60 guests. Double rooms with full board are US$240 (plus 10% tax) between mid-December and May; single occupancy is US$230, while a four-person deluxe cottage costs US$500. Prices drop in the low season. It's worth shopping around before you leave home – some operators book through Casino Hotels and can secure a better deal.

The resort has a restaurant and bar, but no TV, newspapers or telephones. The 128-acre island is fringed with pure sand, and the sight of the moon slipping beneath the lagoon horizon is very nearly worth the expense. Activities include diving, snorkelling, deep-sea fishing and sailing. Casino Hotels organises permits with one month's notice.

Agatti Island Beach Resort *(☎ 0484-362232, fax 362234, ⓔ aiber@md4.vsnl.net.in)* offers a range of packages. It costs US$150 per person for three nights, US$225 for five nights and US$300 for seven nights. The resort has 10 simple, low-rise cottages on the beach cleverly designed to be comfortable without air-conditioning, and a restaurant for 20. The village on this 2.7-sq-km island has several mosques, which you can visit if dressed modestly. There's no alcohol on the island – one otherwise satisfied guest suggested stashing your favourite bottle. Snorkelling and boat trips to nearby islands can be arranged.

On the other islands, Sports runs modest tourist bungalows, and there are a few government guesthouses. The Lacadives diving school uses the Tourist Cottage on Kadmat island (see the Diving boxed text earlier).

Getting There & Away

Indian Airlines has daily flights (except Sunday) from Kochi to Agatti Island (US$300 return). Between 16 September and 15 May there are flights from Goa every Monday, Wednesday and Friday for US$310 return. The plane is a tiny Dornier 228 propeller aircraft and passengers are restricted to 10kg of luggage. If staying on Bangaram, extra luggage can be left in the Casino Hotel in Kochi. The 1½-hour transfer by boat from Agatti to Bangaram costs an extra US$30 or, if seas are rough, US$80 by helicopter.

The MV *Tipu Sultan* operates five-day cruises for between Rs 6500 and Rs 11,000. Timetables are available from the Sports office on Willingdon Island.

Chennai (Madras)

The fourth-largest city in India and the capital of Tamil Nadu, Chennai has grown from the merging of a number of small villages, including its former namesake Madraspatnam. Many still call it Madras, but officially it's now Chennai. The city sprawls over more than 70 sq km and rather than claiming a centre, retains its former regional hubs.

Billboards are the most striking outward expressions of the city. These gargantuan icons of popular culture dwarf city buildings in their eagerness to promote everything from soap to blockbuster movies. In fact, Chennai is the centre for Tamil film making.

Many of the Indian languages are spoken in Chennai, though the main language is Tamil. The Tamil people are zealous guardians of their language and have been among the most vociferous opponents to Hindi becoming the national language.

With many esteemed educational institutes and a strong and sometimes volatile tradition of journalism and publishing, Chennai remains a focus for serious and diverse public discourse.

The pollution in Chennai is horrendous and at times breathing feels positively dangerous. Yet Chennai still conveys a sense of spaciousness and ease.

For travellers with an interest in the colonial history of India, Chennai has much to explore and abundant transport options make other parts of the country readily accessible.

Chennai at a Glance

Population: 5.9 million
Area: 174 sq km
Capital of: Tamil Nadu
Main Language: Tamil
Area Code: 044
When to Go: Nov to Feb

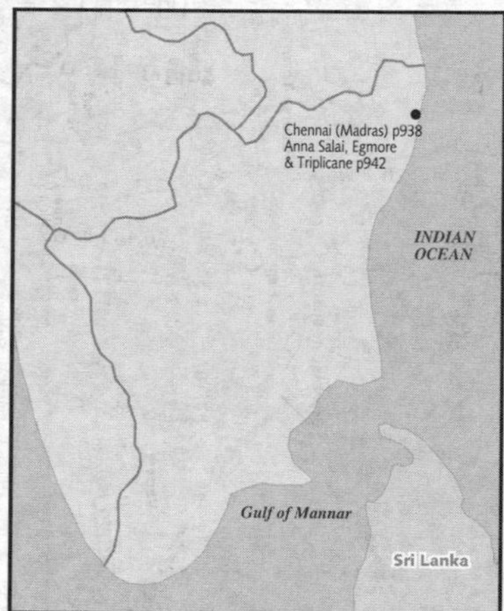

- Attend a performance of traditional dance at the Kalakshetra Arts Village
- Comb the labyrinthine markets and bargain hard for some fine silks
- Hang around the film studios and try your luck at 'being discovered'
- Haggle with autorickshaw drivers and test your negotiating skills

HISTORY

For more than 2000 years the Chennai area has been popular with seafarers, spice traders and cloth merchants. The 16th century resulted in the arrival of the Portuguese, followed by the Dutch. In 1639, the British East India Company established a settlement in the fishing village of Madraspatnam.

Fort St George was constructed over a period of 15 years and finally completed in 1653. George Town grew in the area of the fort and was granted municipal charter in 1688 by James II, making it the oldest municipality in India.

During the 18th and 19th centuries, French and British traders competed for supremacy in India. A key player in the British campaign against the French was Robert Clive (known as Clive of India). Recruiting an army of around 2000 sepoys (locally engaged troops), he launched a series of military expeditions in what became known as the Carnatic Wars. In 1756, the French were forced to withdraw to Pondicherry, leaving the British to develop Fort St George.

In the 19th century, the city became the seat of the Madras presidency, one of the four divisions of British imperial India. After Independence, it continued to grow into what is now a significant southern gateway.

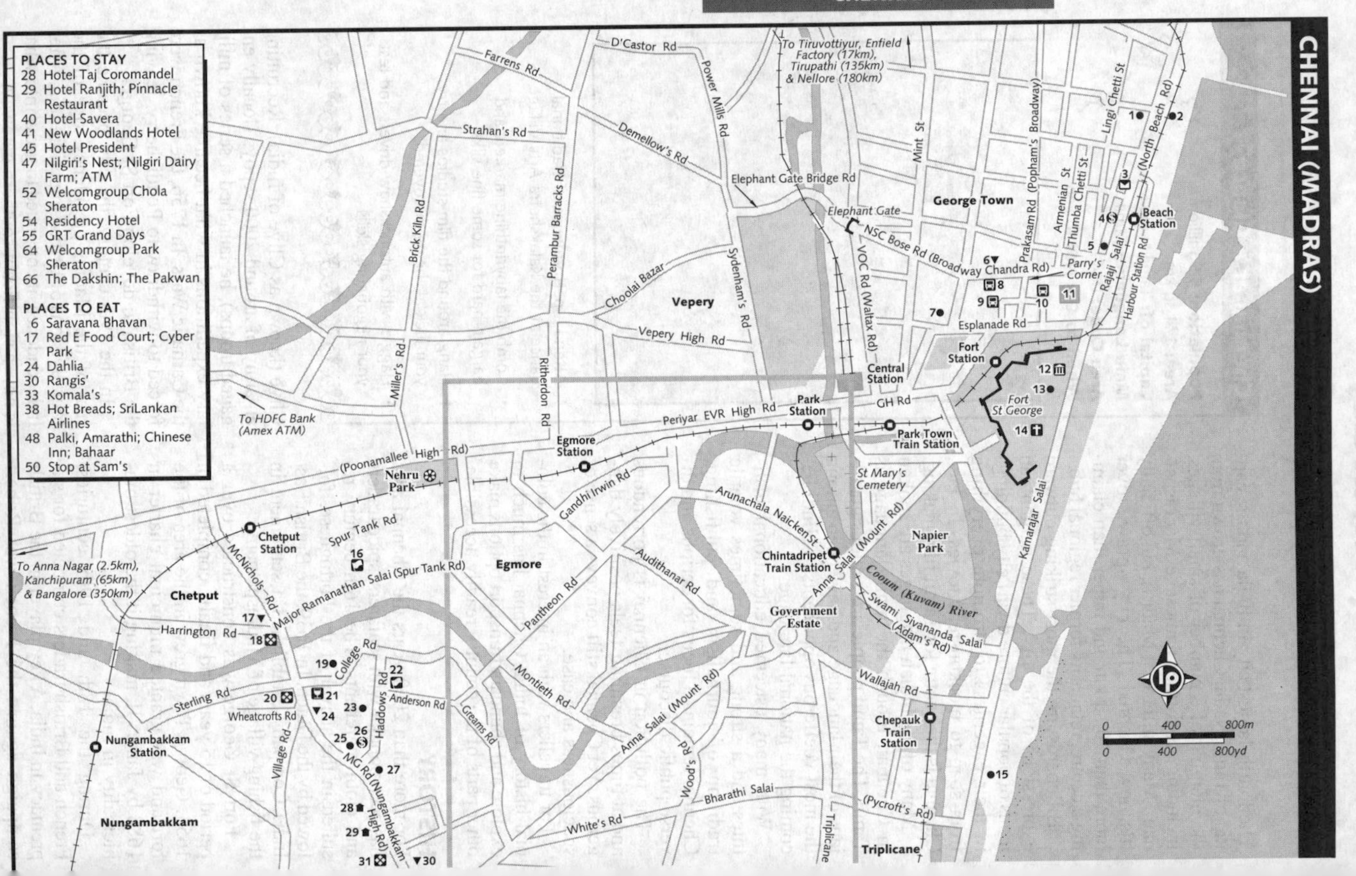
CHENNAI (MADRAS)
CHENNAI
PLACES TO STAY
28 Hotel Taj Coromandel
29 Hotel Ranjith; Pinnacle Restaurant
40 Hotel Savera
41 New Woodlands Hotel
45 Hotel President
47 Nilgiri's Nest; Nilgiri Dairy Farm; ATM
52 Welcomgroup Chola Sheraton
54 Residency Hotel
55 GRT Grand Days
64 Welcomgroup Park Sheraton
66 The Dakshin; The Pakwan
PLACES TO EAT
6 Saravana Bhavan
17 Red E Food Court; Cyber Park
24 Dahlia
30 Rangis'
33 Komala's
38 Hot Breads; SriLankan Airlines
48 Palki, Amarathi; Chinese Inn; Bahaar
50 Stop at Sam's
To Tiruvottiyur, Enfield Factory (17km), Tirupathi (135km) & Nellore (180km)
To HDFC Bank (Amex ATM)
To Anna Nagar (2.5km), Kanchipuram (65km) & Bangalore (350km)
George Town
Vepery
Egmore
Chetput
Nungambakkam
Triplicane
Fort St George
Napier Park
Government Estate
St Mary's Cemetery
Cooum (Kuvam) River
Beach Station
Fort Station
Central Station
Park Station
Park Town Train Station
Egmore Station
Chintadripet Train Station
Chepauk Train Station
Chetput Station
Nungambakkam Station
Nehru Park
Parry's Corner
Elephant Gate
D'Castor Rd
Farrens Rd
Power Mills Rd
Strahan's Rd
Demellow's Rd
Elephant Gate Bridge Rd
Mint St
Lingi Chetti St
(North Beach Rd)
Prakasam Rd (Popham's Broadway)
Armenian St
Thumba Chetti St
Rajaji Salai
Harbour Station Rd
NSC Bose Rd (Broadway Chandra Rd)
VOC Rd (Waltax Rd)
Esplanade Rd
Brick Kiln Rd
Perambur Barracks Rd
Sydenham's Rd
Choolai Bazar
Vepery High Rd
Miller's Rd
Ritherdon Rd
Periyar EVR High Rd
GH Rd
(Poonamallee High Rd)
Gandhi Irwin Rd
Arunachala Naicken St
Anna Salai (Mount Rd)
Kamarajar Salai
Spur Tank Rd
Major Ramanathan Salai (Spur Tank Rd)
McNichols Rd
Audithanar Rd
Pantheon Rd
Swami Sivananda Salai (Adam's Rd)
Harrington Rd
College Rd
Montieth Rd
Wallajah Rd
Sterling Rd
Wheatcrofts Rd
Haddows Rd
Anderson Rd
Greams Rd
Village Rd
MG Rd (Nungambakkam High Rd)
Wood's Rd
Bharathi Salai
(Pycroft's Rd)
White's Rd
Triplicane
0 400 800m
0 400 800yd

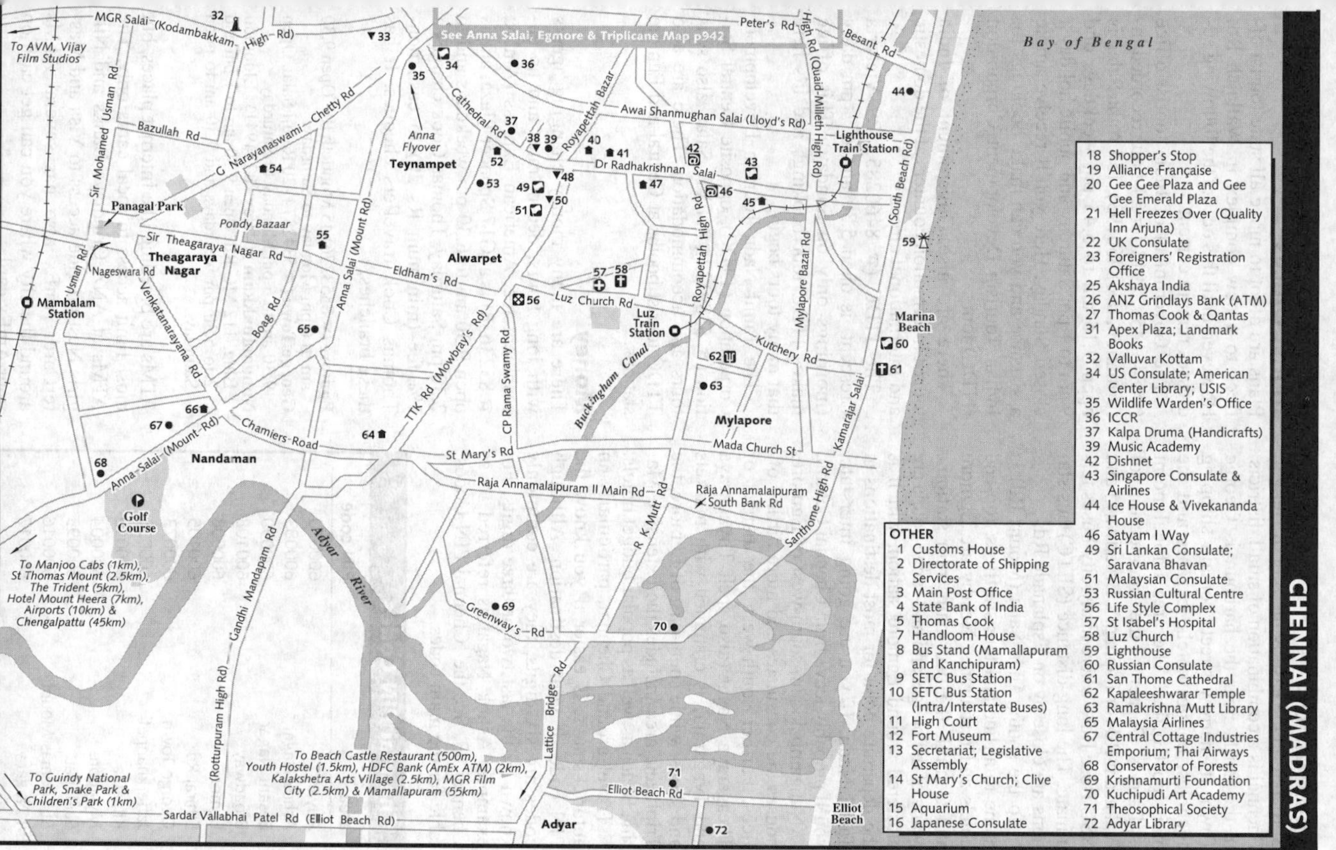
CHENNAI (MADRAS)
Bay of Bengal
See Anna Salai, Egmore & Triplicane Map p942
OTHER
1 Customs House
2 Directorate of Shipping Services
3 Main Post Office
4 State Bank of India
5 Thomas Cook
7 Handloom House
8 Bus Stand (Mamallapuram and Kanchipuram)
9 SETC Bus Station
10 SETC Bus Station (Intra/Interstate Buses)
11 High Court
12 Fort Museum
13 Secretariat; Legislative Assembly
14 St Mary's Church; Clive House
15 Aquarium
16 Japanese Consulate
18 Shopper's Stop
19 Alliance Française
20 Gee Gee Plaza and Gee Gee Emerald Plaza
21 Hell Freezes Over (Quality Inn Arjuna)
22 UK Consulate
23 Foreigners' Registration Office
25 Akshaya India
26 ANZ Grindlays Bank (ATM)
27 Thomas Cook & Qantas
31 Apex Plaza; Landmark Books
32 Valluvar Kottam
34 US Consulate; American Center Library; USIS
35 Wildlife Warden's Office
36 ICCR
37 Kalpa Druma (Handicrafts)
39 Music Academy
42 Dishnet
43 Singapore Consulate & Airlines
44 Ice House & Vivekananda House
46 Satyam I Way
49 Sri Lankan Consulate; Saravana Bhavan
51 Malaysian Consulate
53 Russian Cultural Centre
56 Life Style Complex
57 St Isabel's Hospital
58 Luz Church
59 Lighthouse
60 Russian Consulate
61 San Thome Cathedral
62 Kapaleeshwarar Temple
63 Ramakrishna Mutt Library
65 Malaysia Airlines
67 Central Cottage Industries Emporium; Thai Airways
68 Conservator of Forests
69 Krishnamurti Foundation
70 Kuchipudi Art Academy
71 Theosophical Society
72 Adyar Library
To AVM, Vijay Film Studios
Mambalam Station
Panagal Park
Pondy Bazaar
Theagaraya Nagar
Anna Flyover
Teynampet
Alwarpet
Nandaman
Mylapore
Luz Train Station
Lighthouse Train Station
Marina Beach
Elliot Beach
Adyar
Golf Course
Adyar River
Buckingham Canal
To Manjoo Cabs (1km), St Thomas Mount (2.5km), The Trident (5km), Hotel Mount Heera (7km), Airports (10km) & Chengalpattu (45km)
To Guindy National Park, Snake Park & Children's Park (1km)
To Beach Castle Restaurant (500m), Youth Hostel (1.5km), HDFC Bank (AmEx ATM) (2km), Kalakshetra Arts Village (2.5km), MGR Film City (2.5km) & Mamallapuram (55km)
MGR Salai (Kodambakkam High Rd)
Sir Mohamed Usman Rd
Bazullah Rd
G Narayanaswami Chetty Rd
Sir Theagaraya Nagar Rd
Nageswara Rd
Usman Rd
Venkatanarayana Rd
Boag Rd
Anna Salai (Mount Rd)
Eldham's Rd
TTK Rd (Mowbray's Rd)
CP Rama Swamy Rd
Cathedral Rd
Royapettah Bazar
Awai Shanmughan Salai (Lloyd's Rd)
Dr Radhakrishnan Salai
Royapettah High Rd
Luz Church Rd
Kutchery Rd
Mylapore Bazar Rd
Peter's Rd
High Rd (Quaid-Milleth High Rd)
Besant Rd
(South Beach Rd)
Kamarajar Salai
Santhome High Rd
Mada Church St
St Mary's Rd
Chamiers Road
Raja Annamalaipuram II Main Rd
Raja Annamalaipuram South Bank Rd
R K Mutt Rd
Greenway's Rd
Gandhi Mandapam Rd
(Rotturpuram High Rd)
Lattice Bridge Rd
Elliot Beach Rd
Sardar Vallabhai Patel Rd (Elliot Beach Rd)
CHENNAI

ORIENTATION

Bordered on the east by the Bay of Bengal, Chennai is a combination of small districts. In the north, near the harbour, is George Town. Its narrow streets contain shipping agencies, budget hotels, bazaars and the main post office. The area's focal point is Parry's Corner – the intersection of Prakasam Rd (or Popham's Broadway) and NSC Bose Rd – where many city buses terminate. The long-distance (SETC) bus stations are close by on Esplanade Rd.

To the south, Anna Salai (Mount Rd) is home to airline and tourist offices, top-end hotels and restaurants. Nearby are Egmore and Central, the two main train stations. Many of the budget and mid-range hotels are clustered around Egmore station, which is the departure point for most destinations in Tamil Nadu. If you are going interstate, you'll probably leave from Chennai Central.

Nungambakkam, south-west of Egmore, houses the consulates and more airline offices. Farther south-west, the district of Theagaraya Nagar (also spelt Thyagaraya and Tyagaraja) is crammed with markets and shops, while south-east of Egmore, the Triplicane area includes the extensive Marina Beach as well as popular budget hotels.

Travel around Chennai, particularly in autorickshaws, is easier if you know the PIN code of your destination. Although codes are six digits, they are commonly known by the last two or three digits. For example, Ashok Nagar is referred to as Chennai 83. See the 'Chennai PIN Codes' table for the main codes.

Chennai PIN Codes

area	PIN code
Adyar	600020
Ashok Nagar	600083
Besant Nagar	600090
Broadway	600108
Egmore	600008
Ethiraj Rd	600105
George Town	600073
Jafferkhanpet	600095
Kilpauk	600010
Mylapore	600004
Saidapet	600093
St Thomas Mount	600016
T Nagar	600017

INFORMATION

Tourist Offices

Plans are afoot to move all state tourist offices to a new complex in Wallajah Rd. However, until this occurs the following addresses remain current.

The Government of India tourist office (☎ 8461459, 1913 for 24-hour recorded information, fax 8460193), 154 Anna Salai, is open 9.15 am to 5.45 pm weekdays and 9 am to 1 pm Saturday and public holidays; closed Sunday. Here you'll receive ample assistance and you can make bookings for Indian Tourism Development Corporation (ITDC) tours.

There are also Government of India tourist information counters at the domestic and international airports.

The ITDC (☎ 8460285), 29 Victoria Crescent, is open 5.30 am to 7 pm daily (mornings only on Sunday). This office makes ITDC tour bookings and it's here that many tours begin.

The Tamil Nadu Tourism Development Corporation (TTDC), opposite Central Station (☎ 5389132), 4 EVR Salai, also sells tours and accommodation. There are also TTDC tourist booths at Central and Egmore stations.

Money

There are many money changing agents with long hours, decent rates and no encashment fee. American Express (AmEx; ☎ 8523638) is at G17 Spencer Plaza, and is open 9.30 am to 6.30 pm weekdays and to 2.30 pm Saturday. Thomas Cook charges a 1% fee (minimum Rs 20) to cash non-Thomas Cook travellers cheques. It has these branches:

Egmore (☎ 8553276) 45 Montieth Rd. Open 9.30 am to 6 pm Monday to Saturday.
George Town (☎ 5342374) 20 Rajaji Salai. Open 9.30 am to 6 pm Monday to Saturday.
Nungambakkam (☎/fax 8274941) Eldorado Bldg, 112 MG Rd. Open 9.30 am to 1 pm and 2 to 6.30 pm weekdays and 9.30 am to noon Saturday.

ATMs are breeding like Internet places, but most limit access to local cards only. The ATMs at ANZ Grindlays Banks and Nilgiris Nest provide access to Visa and MasterCard. AmEx also has several ATMs around the city where you can get cash on your AmEx card:

Street Name Changes

It's not only the city that's been renamed; many streets have had official name changes (several times), so there's a confusing mixture of names used in the vernacular.

old name	new name
Adam's Rd	Swami Sivananda Salai
Broadway	NSC Chandra Bose Rd
Chamiers Rd	Pasumpon Murthuramalingam Salai
C-in-C Rd	Ethiraj Rd
Harris Rd	Audithanar Rd
Lloyd's Rd	Awai Shanmughan Salai
Marshalls Rd	Rukmani Lakshmi Pathy Rd
Mount Rd	Anna Salai
Mowbray's Rd	TTK Rd
North Beach Rd	Rajaji Salai
Nungambakkam High Rd	MG Rd
Poonamallee	Periyar High Rd
Popham's Broadway	Prakasam Rd
Pycroft's Rd	Bharathi Salai
Triplicane High Rd	Quaid-Milleth High Rd
South Beach Rd	Kamarajar Salai
Spur Tank Rd	Major Ramanathan Salai
Waltax Rd	VOC Rd

Adyar HDFC Bank, Arunachala Apartments, Plot 12, MG Rd
Anna Nagar HDFC Bank, Block Y, No 206, Plot 4522, 5th Ave

State Bank of India's main branch is on Rajaji Salai in George Town. There are also branches on Anna Salai and at the international (open 24 hours) and domestic (open 5 am to 8 pm) airport terminals.

Several of the banks in Spencer Plaza give cash advances on MasterCard and Visa.

Post & Communications

The main post office is on Rajaji Salai. There's also a post office in Kennet Lane, near Egmore station, and on Anna Salai. For poste restante it's more convenient to use the Anna Salai post office. The full address is Poste Restante, Anna Salai (Mount Rd) Post Office, Anna Salai, Chennai 600002. Poste restante is open 10 am to 6 pm Monday to Saturday; the post office itself is open 8 am to 8.30 pm Monday to Saturday and 10 am to 5 pm Sunday. The Anna Salai post office is also the best place to post parcels. It's much less congested than the main post office and there's a super-efficient 'professional parcel packer' just inside (from 10 am). There are numerous STD/ISD/fax kiosks around here.

Internet Resources

Email centres are now on almost every corner. Services are invariably good and range in price from Rs 30 per hour. Dishnet, at 45 Royapettah Rd, has 40 terminals and is open from 6 am to midnight daily, except public holidays. It's quick and efficient; rates are Rs 20 for 30 minutes; Rs 30 for one hour. Almost opposite, Satyam I Way has similar services and prices. Both have numerous offices and packages (the more you browse the less you pay) throughout the city.

Cyber Park (☎ 8251790) at 107 Harrington Rd (adjacent to the Red E Food Court) is open 9 am to 11 pm daily.

Foreign Consulates

Foreign missions in Chennai are open weekdays and are listed in the Facts for the Visitor chapter.

Visa Extensions & Permits

The Foreigners' Registration Office (FRO; ☎ 8278210) is in the Shashtri Bhavan annexe (rear building, on the ground floor) at 26 Haddows Rd, Nungambakkam. Visa extensions (Rs 960 for three months; Rs 1800 for six months) are possible, but can be very difficult to obtain. The office is open 10 am to 1 pm and 2 to 5 pm weekdays.

If you're planning to visit the Andaman & Nicobar Islands by air or boat, you can apply for a permit on arrival at Port Blair, the capital. Charges for permits have been waived. If you're travelling by ship, you can also apply beforehand to the Directorate of Shipping Services (☎ 5226873) at 6 Rajaji Salai in George Town. If you apply in the morning, you should be able to collect the permit the same day between 4 and 5 pm. Application on arrival in Port Blair is much easier.

For accommodation and access permits for national parks you'll need to approach the following offices:

Conservator of Forests (☎ 4321139, 4320994) 8th floor, Panangal Bldg, Saidapet. Conservator issues permits for all areas other than Vedantagal Bird Sanctuary, but only to researchers.

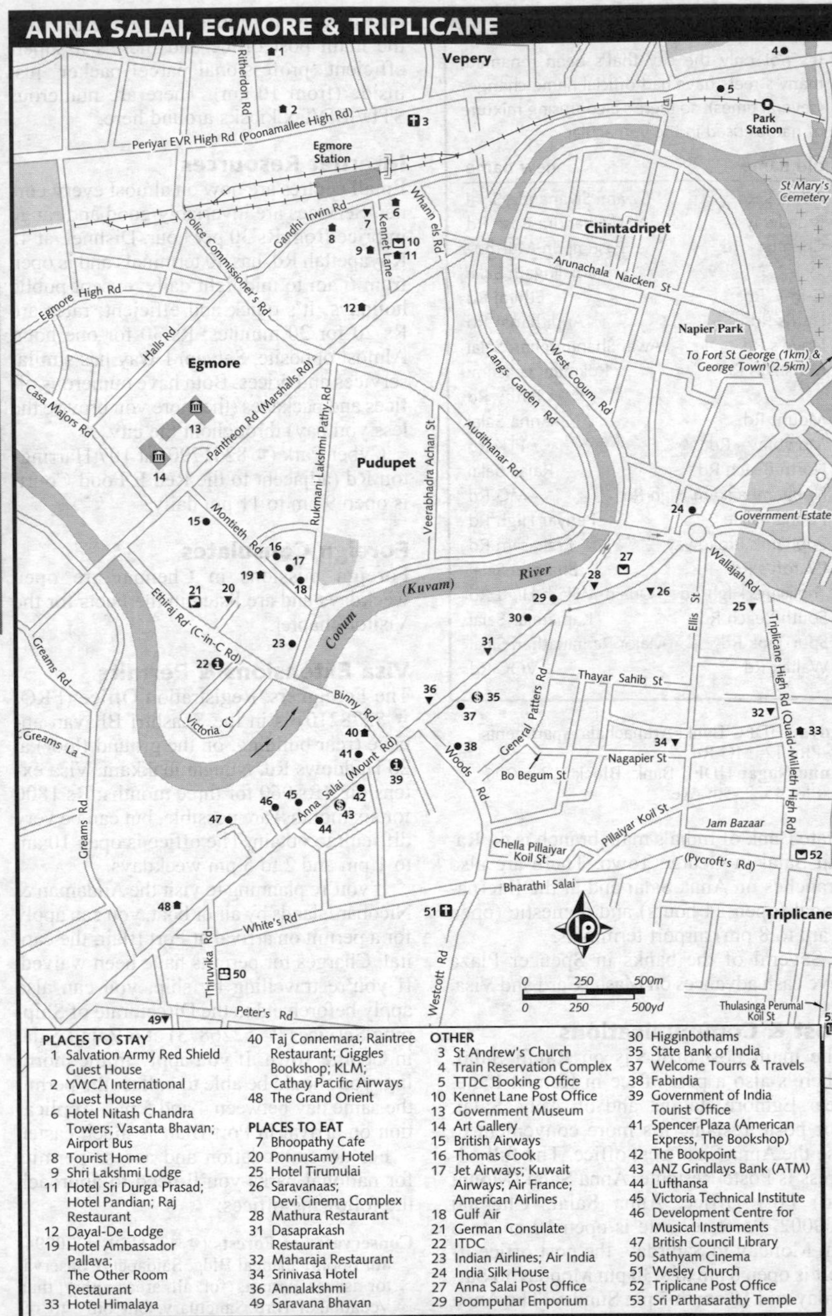
ANNA SALAI, EGMORE & TRIPLICANE
Vepery
Ritherdon Rd
Periyar EVR High Rd (Poonamallee High Rd)
Egmore Station
Park Station
St Mary's Cemetery
Chintadripet
Gandhi Irwin Rd
Kennet Lane
Whannels Rd
Police Commissioner's Rd
Egmore High Rd
Arunachala Naicken St
Napier Park
To Fort St George (1km) & George Town (2.5km)
Halls Rd
Egmore
Casa Majors Rd
Pantheon Rd (Marshalls Rd)
Rukmani Lakshmi Pathy Rd
Veerabhadra Achan St
Langs Garden Rd
West Cooum Rd
Audithanar Rd
Pudupet
Montieth Rd
Government Estate
Wallajah Rd
River
(Kuvam)
Cooum
Ethiraj Rd (C-in-C Rd)
Greams Rd
Greams La
Binny Rd
Victoria Ct
Anna Salai (Mount Rd)
Woods Rd
General Patters Rd
Thayar Sahib St
Ellis St
Triplicane High Rd (Quaid-Milleth High Rd)
Nagapier St
Bo Begum St
Pillaiyar Koil St
Chella Pillaiyar Koil St
Jam Bazaar
(Pycroft's Rd)
Bharathi Salai
Triplicane
White's Rd
Thiruvika Rd
Westcott Rd
Peter's Rd
Thulasinga Perumal Koil St
0 250 500m
0 250 500yd
PLACES TO STAY
1 Salvation Army Red Shield Guest House
2 YWCA International Guest House
6 Hotel Nitash Chandra Towers; Vasanta Bhavan; Airport Bus
8 Tourist Home
9 Shri Lakshmi Lodge
11 Hotel Sri Durga Prasad; Hotel Pandian; Raj Restaurant
12 Dayal-De Lodge
19 Hotel Ambassador Pallava; The Other Room Restaurant
33 Hotel Himalaya
40 Taj Connemara; Raintree Restaurant; Giggles Bookshop; KLM; Cathay Pacific Airways
48 The Grand Orient
PLACES TO EAT
7 Bhoopathy Cafe
20 Ponnusamy Hotel
25 Hotel Tirumulai
26 Saravanaas; Devi Cinema Complex
28 Mathura Restaurant
31 Dasaprakash Restaurant
32 Maharaja Restaurant
34 Srinivasa Hotel
36 Annalakshmi
49 Saravana Bhavan
OTHER
3 St Andrew's Church
4 Train Reservation Complex
5 TTDC Booking Office
10 Kennet Lane Post Office
13 Government Museum
14 Art Gallery
15 British Airways
16 Thomas Cook
17 Jet Airways; Kuwait Airways; Air France; American Airlines
18 Gulf Air
21 German Consulate
22 ITDC
23 Indian Airlines; Air India
24 India Silk House
27 Anna Salai Post Office
29 Poompuhar Emporium
30 Higginbothams
35 State Bank of India
37 Welcome Tourrs & Travels
38 Fabindia
39 Government of India Tourist Office
41 Spencer Plaza (American Express, The Bookshop)
42 The Bookpoint
43 ANZ Grindlays Bank (ATM)
44 Lufthansa
45 Victoria Technical Institute
46 Development Centre for Musical Instruments
47 British Council Library
50 Sathyam Cinema
51 Wesley Church
52 Triplicane Post Office
53 Sri Parthasarathy Temple

Wildlife Warden's Office (☎ 4321471, 4321738) 4th floor, DMS office, 259 Anna Salai, Teynampet. Wildlife issues permits for accommodation at Vedantagal Bird Sanctuary.

Travel Agencies

Thomas Cook (☎ 8554600), 45 Montieth Rd, Egmore, and the AmEx Travel Service (☎ 852 3592), in Spencer Plaza, are good.

Welcome Tourrs (sic) and Travels (☎ 846 0908, fax 8461645), 150 Anna Salai, is approved by the Government of India Tourist Board and can organise everything from visas, accommodation, car hire, air or train tickets to customised individual or group tours. The drivers are well trained, good humoured and safety conscious. Further information is available at www.welcometourrsandtravel.com

Akshaya India (☎ 8224617, fax 8251783), A1/2, Kushkumar Rd, Nungambakkam, www.akshayaindia.com, is also recognised by the Government of India and promotes itself as a company geared for 'families' with tours tailored for 'baby to grandma'.

Film Processing

For print and slide processing you can try The Image Park (☎ 8276383) Shop No 2, Gee Gee Plaza, Wheatcrofts Rd.

Bookshops

Landmark Books in Apex Plaza (3 MG Rd) has an excellent selection. It's open 9 am to 9 pm weekdays and noon to 9 pm weekends.

The popular Higginbothams is at 814 Anna Salai with kiosks at Central Station and the domestic airport. The Bookpoint at 160 Anna Salai and The Bookshop in Spencer Plaza are both well stocked.

The tiny Giggles bookshop at the Taj Connemara redefines 'bookworm'. Here you need to wriggle your way through the mountains of books. But don't be deterred – you'll easily locate your desired tome; the collection is excellent and so is the proprietor's knowledge.

Libraries & Cultural Centres

The Indian Council for Cultural Relations (ICCR; ☎ 8274519), 201 Awai Shanmughan Salai (formerly Lloyd's Rd), facilitates cultural programs and visits from international artists. The daily paper will give you all the details.

In Mylapore district, Ramakrishna Mutt Library at 16 Ramakrishna Mutt Rd, specialises in philosophy, mythology and Indian classics. Adyar Library (☎ 4913528), in the grounds of the Theosophical Society, has a huge collection on religion and philosophy.

British Council Library (☎ 8525002), 737 Anna Salai, offers temporary membership for Rs 100 a month. It's open 11 am to 7 pm Tuesday to Saturday.

American Center Library (☎ 8273040), attached to the US consulate, is open 9.30 am to 6 pm daily, except Sunday. Alliance Française de Madras (☎ 8279803), at 40 College Rd, Nungambakkam, is open 9 am to 1 pm and 3.30 to 6.30 pm weekdays and on Saturday morning. The library hours are similar to office hours but it's closed Wednesdays as well as Sundays. Check out the Web site for more information: www.afmadras.org

Medical Services & Emergency

For 24-hour medical services, head to St Isabel's Hospital (☎ 4991081), 18 Oliver Rd, Mylapore. There's no shortage of optical services in the city where you can obtain new glasses or lenses within a couple of days from Rs 1250 (less if you already have a prescription).

In an emergency you can call the police on ☎ 100; the fire brigade on ☎ 101; and an ambulance on ☎ 102.

PLACES OF WORSHIP

St Mary's Church

Built between 1678 and 1680, this was the first English church in Madras, and is the oldest surviving British church in India. There are reminders in the church of Clive, who was married here in 1753, as well as Elihu Yale, the early governor of Madras, who later founded the famous American university bearing his name. About 1km west of St Mary's church is the cemetery in Pallavan Salai.

St Andrew's Church

Near Egmore station, St Andrew's Church was completed in 1821 in the classical style. Inside, the impressive blue dome is decorated with gold stars. There are excellent views from the 55m steeple. Services are at 9 am and 6 pm Sunday.

Workers in the Shadows

They leave their slum dwellings at around 5 am to begin work in the city by 6 am. They scurry swiftly and silently across the city streets, keeping to the shadows and working mostly in pairs. They are the waste-pickers – mostly women and sometimes children. They spend up to 10 hours a day rummaging through piles of domestic and industrial waste and separating it into bags of metal, plastic, paper, cloth and other items that can be recycled. Usually they sell their bundles to the middlemen who then sell to the recycling companies. For this dangerous and dirty work they earn around Rs 45 a day. With assistance from NGOs, some waste-pickers have formed cooperatives and successfully bypassed the middlemen, thereby boosting their earning potential.

Waste-pickers ply their trade in all major Indian cities. No-one really knows how many operate in Chennai. The estimate is between 2000 and 3000. But the authorities agree that their labour contributes significantly to a cleaner and more sustainable environment.

Sri Parthasarathy Temple

This temple is dedicated to Krishna. Built in the 8th century by the Pallavas, and renovated in the 16th century by the Vijayanagars, it's one of the oldest surviving temples in Chennai. It's open 6 am to noon and 4 to 8 pm daily.

To get there take bus No 27 or 27B from Egmore, bus No 1 or 4E from Central Station or bus No 6D or PP42 from Fort St George.

San Thome Cathedral

Built in 1504, then rebuilt in neo-Gothic style in 1893, this Roman Catholic church near Kapaleeshwarar Temple is said to house the remains of St Thomas the Apostle (Doubting Thomas). A crypt can be entered by a stairway, which is just before the altar.

Kapaleeshwarar Temple

This ancient Shiva temple, off Kutchery Rd in Mylapore, is constructed in Dravidian style and displays the architectural elements – *gopurams*, *mandapams* and a tank – that are found in the famous temple cities of Tamil Nadu.

The temple is open for *puja* (worship) 4 am to noon and 4 to 8 pm daily.

Luz Church

Dedicated to Our Lady of Light, this 16th-century church is the oldest church in Chennai. It was built by Portuguese sailors who believed they owed their survival to Our Lady.

Numerous buses go to the Luz Church. From Broadway, take bus No PP51 or 60E, or from Parry's Corner, take No 21B, 21D, 21E or PP25.

Little Mount Church

This tiny cave is where St Thomas is believed to have lived when he came to India around AD 58. Known locally as Chinnamalai, the cave is entered via the Portuguese church that was built in 1551.

Daily services are held at 6.30 am, except Sunday when it's 7 am. To get here take bus No 18E from Parry's Corner or any of the 88 series from Broadway or other city bus stands. You can also catch the train from Central Station to St Thomas Mount station then walk, bus or rickshaw the remaining 1km.

MUSEUMS & GALLERIES

Government Museum

Well worth visiting, the Government Museum is on Pantheon Rd, between Egmore station and Anna Salai. The buildings forming the complex originally belonged to a group of eminent British citizens, known as the Pantheon Committee, who were charged with improving the social life of the British in Madras.

The main building has a fine **archaeological section** representing all the major South Indian periods including Chola, Vijayanagar, Hoysala and Chalukya. It also houses a good ethnology collection.

The **bronze gallery** has a superb collection of Chola art. One of the most impressive is the bronze of Ardhanariswara, the androgynous incarnation of Shiva.

The museum complex is open 9.30 am to 5 pm daily, except Friday and public holidays. Entry costs Rs 3.

Valluvar Kottam

The Valluvar Kottam, on the corner of MGR Salai and Village Rd, honours the acclaimed

Tamil poet, Thiruvalluvar, whose classic work, the *Kural*, is reputed to be about 2000 years old. Established in 1976, Valluvar Kottam replicates ancient Tamil architecture with the 1330 verse *Kural* inscribed on panels and depicted in contemporary art. It's open 8 am to 6 pm daily. Entry is Rs 1.

Development Centre for Musical Instruments

Ancient and modern Indian musical instruments are made and exhibited here. The centre is in the Tamil Nadu Handicrafts building at 759 Anna Salai and is open 9.30 am to 6 pm weekdays and 9.30 am to 1 pm Saturday.

OTHER ATTRACTIONS

High Court Building

This red Indo-Saracenic structure at Parry's Corner is the main landmark in George Town. Built in 1892, it is said to be the largest judicial building in the world after the Courts of London.

Fort St George

Built around 1653 by the British East India Company, the fort has undergone many alterations. It presently houses the Secretariat and the Legislative Assembly. The 46m-high flagstaff at the front is actually a mast salvaged from a 17th-century shipwreck.

The **Fort Museum** has a fascinating collection of memorabilia from both the British and French East India Companies, as well as the Raj and Muslim administrations. Entry is Rs 2 and it's open 9 am to 5 pm Saturday to Thursday.

Marina & Aquarium

The stretch of beach known as the Marina extends for 13km. South of the pitiful aquarium is the **Ice House**, once used to store massive ice blocks transported by ship from North America. It later became the venue from which Vivekananda preached his ascetic philosophy. If you're tempted to take a dip in the waters at Marina Beach, don't. The rips are hazardous and unforgiving. Many people have drowned here.

Guindy National Park, Snake Park & Children's Park

These parks are adjacent to each other, just 1km from Guindy station. Guindy National Park supposedly has much wildlife, but it's a scraggy place and you're unlikely to see much.

The children's park is small and pleasant with enclosures containing over 30 animal species including peacocks, hyenas, otters and porcupines. At the end, about 100m in, there are two good-looking elephants under the watchful eyes of their mahout. Two playgrounds provide swings, slides and climbing equipment.

The parks are open 8.30 am to 5 pm daily, except Tuesday. Entry is Rs 2 (Rs 10 for a camera).

Snake Park with its lizards, crocodiles and turtles is more interesting. Generous and well-maintained enclosures display information boards which debunk many myths about reptiles. The hourly demonstration is truly pythonesque! The park is open at the same times as the others and entry is Rs 3 (Rs 5 for a camera).

The train from Egmore station will take you to Guindy station. From there you can either walk 1km east, or you could catch an autorickshaw.

Film Studios

The film industry in Chennai now rivals Bollywood (Mumbai) for output. One of the biggest studios is MGR Film City (☎ 2352212). This is the only one routinely open to the public. If you have always fancied your chances as a film star, extras are occasionally needed. You can telephone the studios or simply try your luck and hang about waiting to be spotted.

MGR Film City is near Indira Nagar, about 10km south of Egmore. The studios open 8 am to 8 pm daily and entry is Rs 15.

Enfield Factory

Tiruvottiyur, 17km north of Chennai, is the site of the Enfield motorcycle factory. Factory tours can be arranged by contacting the product manager (☎ 544442, fax 545720). For more information, take a look at the Web site at www.royalenfield.com.

ORGANISED TOURS

TTDC and ITDC both conduct tours of Chennai and surrounds. For information on where to book, see Tourist Offices at the start of this chapter. TTDC tours can also be booked at Central Station (☎ 5353351).

CHENNAI

Available tours include:

City Sightseeing Tour This tour includes Fort St George, Government Museum, Valluvar Kottam, Snake Park, Kapaleeshwarar Temple and Marina Beach. The daily tours are good value, although rushed. The morning tour is from 8 am to 1.30 pm and the afternoon tour 1.30 to 6.30 pm; Rs 85 or Rs 130 for air-con.

Cultural & Spiritual Tours Faith Pandian's Window to the World (☎ 431-436052, fax 431-430832), 44A Royar Thoppu, Srirangam, Trichy, specialises in cultural tours. There's an Australian office (☎/fax 612-6493 8595), 36 Fieldbuckets Rd, Quaama, NSW 2550. Check out the Web site at www.window.totheworld.com.au

Kanchipuram & Mamallapuram (Mahabalipuram) This full-day tour costs Rs 200 or Rs 325 for air-con bus, and includes breakfast and lunch and a visit to a crocodile farm.

Tirupathi You can choose a day (6 am to 9.30 pm) or night (10.30 pm to 4 pm the next day) trip taking in the famous Venkateshwara Temple at Tirumala in southern Andhra Pradesh and the 'special darshan' (viewing the idol of the god). Darshan usually takes two hours, but can take five hours, which means you'll get back to Chennai much later than planned. The fare is Rs 350, or Rs 500 (air-con), and includes breakfast and lunch. The night trip is Rs 50 more. Night or day, this tour involves 12 hours on a bus.

SPECIAL EVENTS

Chennai hosts a wide range of events from classical and contemporary concerts and theatre to art exhibitions and trade shows. See the daily papers for listings. The **Festival of Carnatic Music & Dance**, which takes place mid-December to mid-January, is one of the largest of its type in the world. See the boxed text 'South Indian Music & Dance'.

At the Kalakshetra Arts Village (or Temple of Art) in Tiruvanmiyur, a special 10-day **arts festival** takes place over December and January. Tickets are available during the day at the Bharata Kalakshetra Auditorium and cost Rs 20 to 100. Entry is through the main gate on the northern side opposite the auditorium. During the festival, some hotels run free shuttle buses between Kalakshetra and the city. Check with any tourist office.

South Indian Music & Dance

The Festival of Carnatic Music & Dance is a celebration of the classical music of South India, with songs in all the main languages – Tamil, Telugu, Malayalam and Kannada. Most performances are preceded by a lecture and demonstration. Concerts usually start with a *varnam*, an up-tempo introduction, followed by several songs, *kirtis*, or *kirtanas*, before the main number. The *raga* is the basis of Carnatic music: five, six or seven notes arranged in ascending or descending scales.

The main instruments used are the violin, wooden flute, *veena* (a large stringed instrument), *gottuvadyam* (similar to the veena but without frets), *nagaswaram* (pipe), *thavil* (percussion instrument), *mridangam* (drum), and even a *ghatam* (mud pot). Check the daily papers for details.

PLACES TO STAY

Chennai is always tight for accommodation, so it's best to book. Egmore, on and around Kennet Lane, is the main budget accommodation hub but you may find George Town and Triplicane to be less chaotic. The top hotels are mainly along Anna Salai and the roads leading off it. If you'd like to stay in a private home, contact the Government of India tourist office for a list of home-stays. Prices range from Rs 100 to 600 per person per week.

Unless otherwise stated all rooms covered here have private bathroom with constant hot water, sit-down flush toilets and accept cash only.

PLACES TO STAY – BUDGET

Egmore

Salvation Army Red Shield Guest House *(☎ 5321821, 15 Ritherdon Rd)* welcomes both men and women. It's a quiet, friendly place, popular with budget travellers. Dorm beds (10 beds) cost Rs 70 with cold water only. Double/triple rooms with constant hot water and squat and sit-down flush toilets are Rs 250/280. There's an air-con room for Rs 500. Checkout time is 9 am.

Tourist Home *(☎ 8250079, 21 Gandhi Irwin Rd)* has singles/doubles for Rs 130/160; a double with air-con is Rs 250.

Shri Lakshmi Lodge *(☎ 8254576, 16 Kennet Lane)* is clean and costs Rs 175/350, or Rs 140/199 without air-con. The rooms face a quiet central courtyard. The nearby ***Hotel Sri Durga Prasad*** *(☎ 8253881, 10 Kennet Lane)* is similarly priced. Both have squat toilets and bucket hot water.

Hotel Tax

Hotel tax in Tamil Nadu is currently among the highest in the country – 15% on rooms costing Rs 100 to 199, and 20% for anything above. The top hotels add a further 5% to 10% service charge. Prices given in this section *do not* include taxes.

***Dayal-De Lodge** (☎ 8227328, 486 Pantheon Rd),* at the southern end of Kennet Lane, has reasonable rooms from Rs 185/299 with squat/sit-down flush toilets.

***Hotel Masa** (☎ 8252966, 15 Kennet Lane)* has singles/doubles/triples with private bathroom from Rs 258/330/375. There are also air-con doubles/triples for Rs 450/500. Singles have squat toilets; doubles have sit-down flush toilets. This is a great place for those who can't tolerate silence.

The ***retiring rooms*** at the Central and Egmore Stations have doubles from Rs 175 or Rs 350 with air-con. Dorm beds (men only) are Rs 90 for 12 hours and are quiet, clean and have air-con.

Triplicane

On what was formerly known as Triplicane High Rd, ***Hotel Himalaya** (☎ 8547522, 54 Quaid-Milleth High Rd)* is not a bad option, with singles/doubles/triples with squat and sit-down flush toilets from Rs 345/425/510 and also some air-con rooms. There's direct dial phones, TV and a veg restaurant.

Indira Nagar

***Youth Hostel** (☎ 4420233, 2nd Ave, Indira Nagar)* is about 10km south of Egmore in a peaceful residential area. Dorm beds cost Rs 40 for nonmembers, Rs 20 for members, and you can camp in the garden. Phone in advance for a reservation and directions, and bring a padlock for your locker. Meals are available on request (Rs 10 for a thali). This is a good place for genuine shoestringers.

PLACES TO STAY – MID-RANGE

Egmore

On what was formerly known as Poonamallee High Rd, ***YWCA International Guest House** (☎ 5324234, fax 5324263, 1086 Periyar EVR High Rd)* has bright, clean, spacious rooms. Singles/doubles are Rs 450/580, triples are Rs 800 and singles/doubles with air-con are Rs 630/750. Rates include breakfast. The guesthouse accepts both men and women, but there's a transient membership fee of Rs 20 – valid for one month. The restaurant serves Indian, Chinese and Western food. There are several small sitting areas and one large comfortable one with TV. Because this is a service organisation, taxes do not apply, except for a 5% service charge. However, certain rules do apply: visitors are forbidden in the rooms, lunch and dinner in the restaurant must be ordered in advance, alcohol is not served and meals usually finish by 9 pm.

***Hotel Pandian** (☎ 8252901, fax 825 8459, 9 Kennet Lane)* is as jovial as ever and deservedly popular. Small but comfortable singles/doubles are Rs 450/550; air-con rooms start at Rs 800/950. Larger deluxe rooms (Rs 1200) have stocked bar fridges. There are squat/sit-down flush toilets and hot water for three hours each morning and evening. The hotel has an excellent veg/nonveg restaurant, and a bar.

The ***Hotel Nitash Chandra Towers** (☎ 8233344, fax 8251703, 9 Gandhi Irwin Rd)* has a lush lobby that belies the somewhat cramped, centrally air-con singles/doubles for Rs 1095/1295. There's a good restaurant, a 24-hour coffee shop, a bar and several other promoted (but nonexistent) services.

Mylapore

***New Woodlands Hotel** (☎ 8113111, fax 8110460, 72–75 Dr Radhakrishnan Salai)* is a sprawling complex with 170 rooms and a certain eccentric style and hospitality. It's a great place to start your Indian journey. Singles start from Rs 300, and doubles with air-con are Rs 675. Spacious deluxe rooms are Rs 975. The hotel has a billiard room and is renowned for its excellent veg food. There's a decent pool (Rs 75 for two swims a day), Ayurvedic massage and the opportunity to watch colourful weddings. MasterCard is accepted.

***Nilgiri's Nest** (☎ 8115222, fax 8110214, 58 Dr Radhakrishnan Salai)* has singles/doubles from Rs 950/1300 to 1500/2250, including breakfast. Nilgiri's Nest has a good restaurant, there's a supermarket next door and crowds of rickshaw drivers at the entrance to drive you anywhere, especially crazy. Major cards are accepted.

Nungambakkam

On what is also known as Nungambakkam High Rd, ***Hotel Ranjith*** *(☎ 8270521, fax 8277688, 9 MG Rd)* is convenient for the consulates and airline offices. Rooms, with direct dial phones and TV are Rs 750/950, or Rs 1250/1380 with air-con. There are numerous restaurants (the rooftop is excellent), a bar and major cards are accepted.

Airport

Hotel Mount Heera *(☎ 2349563, fax 2331236, 287 MKN Rd, Alandur)* has pleasant staff and single/double rooms for Rs 677/800 (including tax). It's about 20 minutes by taxi from the airport.

PLACES TO STAY – TOP END

Unless otherwise stated, all the following hotels have central air-con, a swimming pool, multicuisine restaurants, bar and accept major cards.

Grand Orient *(☎ 8524111, fax 8523412, 693 Anna Salai)* has pleasant rooms starting at Rs 1195/1800.

Residency Hotel *(☎ 8253434, fax 825 0085, ⓔ resmds@vsnl.com, 49 GN Chetty Rd, Theagaraya Nagar)* is popular, comfortable and friendly. Singles/doubles start at Rs 1900/2300. A suite is Rs 3600 and some rooms have city views.

Hotel Savera *(☎ 8114700, fax 8113475, 69 Dr Radhakrishnan Salai)* has well-appointed rooms, but a bit shabby for the price (Rs 2000/2400 to 7000). There's a health club and some fine restaurants.

Hotel President *(☎ 8532211, fax 853 2299, 16 Dr Radhakrishnan Salai)* is a big place with spacious rooms starting at Rs 1250/1575. It has a 24-hour coffee shop.

The Dakshin *(☎ 4330866, fax 4322639, 35 Venkatanarayana Rd)* is a pleasant place with friendly staff. Standard singles/doubles, with shabby carpet, start at Rs 1295/1800 and suites are Rs 2700. There's no pool but there's an excellent restaurant and a 24-hour coffee shop.

GRT Grand Days *(☎ 8220500, fax 8230778, ⓔ grtgranddays@vsnl.com, 120 Sir Theagaraya Rd, Pondy Bazaar)* is plush and serene amid the bustling Theagaraya markets. Quality rooms start at Rs 2950/23450, with suites at Rs 5500. There's Internet access (Rs 250 per hour), which may be extended to every room.

Hotel Ambassador Pallava *(☎ 8554476, fax 8554492, 53 Montieth Rd)* offers a range of services including 1kg cakes for birthdays and anniversaries. But this does not compensate for its lacklustre standards. Rooms range from US$80 to US$100.

Chennai has no shortage of five-star hotels where rooms start at US$150/200. ***Taj Connemara*** *(☎ 8520123, fax 8523361, Binny Rd)* is off Anna Salai and offers charm and comfort. Singles/doubles cost Rs 3950/4550 to 8000/ 9500. There's a shopping arcade and business centre.

Hotel Taj Coromandel *(☎ 8272827, fax 8257104, 37 MG Rd)* is luxurious at US$195 to US$750 for the presidential suite.

The Trident *(☎ 2344747, fax 2346699, 1/24 GST Rd)* is the closest luxury hotel to the airport (5km), but it is a long haul from the city centre. Rooms cost Rs 5000 to 7500 (plus 35% tax).

The ***Welcomgroup Chola Sheraton*** *(☎ 8280101, fax 8278779, 10 Cathedral Rd)* is closer to the centre than the Park Sheraton. Rooms cost Rs 3500/3800 to 6500/6800. The ***Welcomgroup Park Sheraton*** *(☎* 4994101, 132 TTK Rd, Alwarpet) epitomises executive-class opulence. Rooms cost Rs 3500/3800 to 6500/6800; suites are Rs 8500 to 22,000.

PLACES TO EAT

There are numerous vegetarian restaurants in Chennai, ranging from the simple 'meals' restaurants where a thali lunch is served on a banana leaf for under Rs 20 to sumptuous spreads for 20 times that amount in the major hotels. Breakfast at the simpler restaurants, which open shortly after dawn, consists of *dosa*, *idli*, curd and coffee.

For excellent veg meals try the ***Saravanaas/Saravana Bhavan*** chain. These range from clean, inexpensive self-service restaurants to upmarket ones usually open 7 am to 11.30 pm. South and North Indian dishes are served, as well as Chinese food and pizzas.

With the growing demand for meat, you will find that nonvegetarian restaurants are on the increase.

George Town

There are few eating places here. You'll find ***Saravana Bhavan*** opposite the High Court on NSC Bose Rd and that's about it.

Egmore

Most of the restaurants are along Gandhi Irwin Rd, in front of Egmore station.

Bhoopathy Cafe directly opposite the station, is popular.

Vasanta Bhavan on the corner Gandhi Irwin Rd and Kennet Lane is bustling with waiters and features an upstairs dining hall.

Raj Restaurant at Hotel Pandian serves good veg and nonveg dishes (Rs 55 to 90).

Ponnusamy Hotel *(Wellington Estate, 24 Ethiraj Rd)* serves meat and fish curry and biryani dishes starting from Rs 35. A few veg dishes are also on the menu.

Triplicane

Maharaja Restaurant on Triplicane High Rd is popular with backpackers and has a varied veg menu available to midnight.

Hotel Tirumulai on Triplicane High Rd serves luscious banana-leaf thalis (Rs 30) and gigantic dosas. ***Srinivasa Hotel*** *(Ellis St)* is also a favourite.

Anna Salai Area

Saravanaas has a branch in the forecourt of the Devi Theatre on Anna Salai. It's a great place for a quick meal. Its upmarket branch is at 293 Peter's Rd. Here, on the ground floor, you'll find the usual Saravana offerings, but on the 2nd and 3rd floors you can dine in style with fine dinner sets and silver cutlery. At ***Swathi*** *(2nd floor, Devi Theatre)* prices start at Rs 60 for the business thali, a limited (although very substantial) version of the special thali for Rs 110. On the 3rd floor, ***Swayam*** has a buffet – 500g of your choice of food for Rs 100. Whichever floor you choose, the food is excellent. ***Mathura Restaurant*** *(2nd floor, Tarapore Tower, Anna Salai)* is an excellent upmarket veg restaurant. Its Madras thali (Rs 60) comes with all the usual delicacies.

Dasaprakash Restaurant *(806 Anna Salai)*, also known as AVM Dasa, is an excellent upmarket cafe-style restaurant. It serves veg fare, with some interesting choices such as broccoli crepes.

The Other Room at Hotel Ambassador Pallava has great service, disappointing dishes and high prices (Rs 1500 for two). It sometimes has pool-side buffets for a set price of Rs 500.

Annalakshmi *(804 Anna Salai)* has veg fare with meals starting at Rs 150. This place is run by the devotees of Swami Shantanand Saraswati who established Shivanjali, an education trust. Annalakshmi is open noon to 3 pm and 7.30 to 10 pm daily, except Monday. Should you have the need (and the money) you can even buy the furniture.

Just of Anna Salai, ***Komala's*** *(3A MGR Salia)* brings a Singaporean flavour to Chennai, with a vegetarian range of snacks (idli and vadai from Rs 12 to 15) and meals (thali and biryani from Rs 25 to 45). Choose self service or table service.

Qwiky's, the USA coffee chain, has several outlets in Chennai including the Life Style Complex and the Gee Gee Emerald Plaza.

Taj Connemara has a lunch-time buffet in its coffee shop for Rs 350. Its ***Raintree*** restaurant is open in the evening for meals (about Rs 650). The outdoor setting is superb, with live classical dancing and music some nights.

Mylapore

Welcomgroup Chola Sheraton has a great dinner buffet for Rs 450, including taxes.

The restaurant at ***New Woodlands Hotel*** is popular with locals. The dosas, tandoori and milk *burfis* (a delicious sweet made with coconut, nuts and sometimes eggs and fruit) all get rave reviews.

Across the road from the Music Academy there's a plethora of fine restaurants. ***Palki*** is a North Indian specialist, while ***Amarathi*** serves exciting Andhra dishes. ***Chinese Inn*** has excellent Sechwan fare (mains Rs 60) and ***Bahaar*** provides an outdoor barbecue with Hyderabadi dishes.

Stop at Sam's, TTK Rd, is a groovy place modelled on a Western-style coffee shop with live music and contemporary art (for sale). Western and Indian dishes are available from around Rs 60.

Nungambakkam & Chetput

The Pinnacle rooftop restaurant at Hotel Ranjith is deservedly popular, where one delicious tandoori platter is sufficient for two.

Rangis' *(142 Uttamar Gandhi Salai)*, across the road from Landmark Books, is an intimate Chinese restaurant with Indianised dishes for Rs 30 to 60.

Dahlia *(Kaveri Complex, 96 & 104 MG Rd)* is one of the few Japanese restaurants in town. The food is good and you'll pay Western prices – around Rs 500 per person.

The Red E Food Court *(107 Harrington Rd)* offers fast Indian, Chinese, Mexican and Western dishes.

Hot Breads produces fresh breads (foot-long rolls), seductive pastries and (in some outlets) good coffee. There's a branch at Nilgiri's, and another just near SriLankan Airlines.

Elsewhere

Beach Castle Restaurant *(34 Elliot Beach Rd)*, right on the beach, has been renovated in a 'foreign style'. A coke bar and pizza are its new offerings with promises to retain its fine seafood.

The Pakwan at Dakshin Hotel, is just around the corner from the Central Cottage Industries Emporium. The multicuisine fare is very good. A two-course meal is around Rs 250. The 24-hour coffee shop has less exciting offerings.

Nilgiri Dairy Farm supermarket, next to Nilgiri's Nest Hotel, is a good place to buy dairy products, boxed tea, coffee and other edibles (closed Tuesday).

If you're after fruit and vegetables or spices, head south along Ellis St to the junction of Bharathi Salai where you'll find the colourful ***Jam Bazaar***.

ENTERTAINMENT

Bars & Nightclubs

In Chennai, discos and nightclubs come and go quicker than strobe lights. Some of the plush hotels have bars, but some are dark dingy places. ***Taj Connemara*** has a plush bar with plush prices and overamplified music.

The latest funky place to hit town is the very cool ***Hell Freezeth Over*** *(☎ 8259090, 144 Sterling Rd)* at Quality Inn Arjuna. Entrance is Rs 300 per couple (woman and man or two women) and things start to really heat up from 11 pm to 2 am.

Classical Music & Dance

Music Academy *(☎ 8115619)*, on the corner of TTK Rd and Dr Radhakrishnan Salai, is Chennai's most popular public venue for Carnatic classical music and Bharata Natyam dance. Check newspapers. Expect to pay about Rs 200 for a good seat, but there are also many free performances.

Another venue is ***Kalakshetra Arts Village*** *(☎ 4911169, fax 4914359)*, which was founded in 1936 and is committed to the revival of classical dance and music and of traditional textile design and weaving. The college puts on regular performances and visitors can also watch classes from 9 to 11.15 am weekdays. For small groups, a lecture explaining the techniques and history is possible with prior arrangement.

Kuchipudi Art Academy *(☎ 4937260, 105 Greenway's Rd)* was founded in 1963 by the eminent teacher Dr Vempati Chinna Satyam. The vigorous and graceful Kuchipudi dance originated in northern Andhra Pradesh. The academy offers free teaching and accommodation to serious students, many of whom come from overseas.

Cinema

There are over 100 cinemas in Chennai – a reflection of the vibrant film industry here. Most cinemas screen Tamil films; some screen foreign-language movies. ***Devi Complex*** *(☎ 8555660, Anna Salai)* and ***Sathyam Cinema*** *(☎ 8523813, 8 Thiruvika Rd)* often show English-language films. Check local papers for details.

The ***British Council*** *(737 Anna Salai)* and ***Alliance Française*** have weekly film screenings. Film festivals are held at the ***United States Information Service*** *(USIS; ☎ 8273040, 220 Anna Salai)*, and at the ***Russian Cultural Centre*** *(☎ 4982320, 27 Kasturi Ranga Rd)*. ***Madras Film Club*** *(☎ 8540984)* has regular screenings of Indian and foreign films.

SHOPPING

Chennai shopping is changing fast. New plazas are springing up while traditional stores are extending services.

Ready-made or tailored clothing, crafts from all corners of India, contemporary artworks, genuine antiques, jewellery, musical instruments and quality fabrics are readily available.

For conventional souvenirs at fixed prices, including carvings and bronzes, head to the government emporiums along Anna Salai. These are usually open 10 am to 6 pm weekdays and 10 am to 1 pm Saturday; closed Sunday. Worth visiting are Poompuhar Emporium, 818 Anna Salai; Victoria Technical Institute, 765 Anna Salai (revenue from certain items supports various development groups); and the more upmarket Central Cottage Industries Emporium in Temple Towers, 672 Anna Salai, Nandanam. With minimum fuss and maximum efficiency, this emporium will assist you with purchasing and shipping.

Private emporiums with their somewhat negotiable prices close at 9 pm. Every rickshaw driver will want to take you to them often for no fee, so you can imagine the payoff to them from the emporium owners – a pay-off that will be added to your bill. Some private places have even adopted pseudo titles ('cottage industries' etc) giving the unsuspecting buyer the impression that they are actually community or government establishments.

An exception to the pressurised buying operations is Kalpa Druma (☎ 8267652), 61 Cathedral Rd, opposite Chola Sheraton, which has an exquisite range of textiles, handicrafts and furniture at fixed prices.

For top-grade silks and cottons head to either the government-sponsored Handloom House, 7 Rattan Bazaar, George Town, (open 10 am to 1 pm and 3 to 8 pm daily, except Sunday) or the more expensive India Silk House on Anna Salai.

If you like large air-conditioned complexes go to Spencer Plaza, Shopper's Stop (Harrington Rd), Life Style (sandwiched between CP Rama Swamy, TTK and Luz Church Rds) or Gee Gee Emerald Plaza (MG Rd). All have a wide range of shops selling clothing, books, music, fabrics and children's gear. Also for fabrics call in at Fabindia, 3 Woods Rd, with its small but discriminating range of textiles, house linen and furnishings.

The Theagaraya Nagar district (known locally as T Nagar) is a great place to shop, especially at Pondy Bazaar and the bustling markets around Panagal Park. For an exciting array of silks and cottons, saris, satins and crepes, visit Pothys in Usman Rd and nearby Nalli in Nageswara Rd, both at Panagal Park.

GETTING THERE & AWAY

Air

Anna international airport is efficient and not too busy, making Chennai a good entry or exit point. Next door is the relatively new domestic airport.

A departure tax of Rs 150 is payable for flights from Chennai to Sri Lanka and the Maldives, Rs 500 for other international destinations.

Domestic Airlines

Domestic carriers that fly into Chennai include the following:

Indian Airlines (☎ 8553039, fax 8555208) 19 Rukmani Lakshmi Pathy Rd (formerly Marshalls Rd), Egmore. Open 8 am to 8 pm Monday to Saturday.
Jet Airways (☎ 8414141) 43 Montieth Rd, Egmore

It is worth inquiring about Jet Airways' youth fares, which apply to some routes and are about 15% less than the usual fare.

International Airlines

International airlines with offices in Chennai include:

Air France (☎ 8554899) Thapar House, 43–44 Montieth Rd, Egmore
Air India (☎ 8554477) 19 Rukmani Lakshmi Pathy Rd, Egmore
American Airlines (☎ 8592915) Thapar House, 43–44 Montieth Rd, Egmore
British Airways (☎ 8554680) Alsamall, Khaleeli Centre, Montieth Rd, Egmore
Cathay Pacific Airways (☎ 8522418) Taj Connemara, Binny Rd
Gulf Air (☎ 8553091) Indian Red Cross Bldg, 52 Montieth Rd, Egmore
KLM-Royal Dutch Airlines (☎ 8524427) Taj Connemara, Binny Rd
Kuwait Airways (☎ 8554111) Thapar House, 43–44 Montieth Rd, Egmore
Lufthansa Airlines (☎ 8525095) 167 Anna Salai
Malaysia Airlines (☎ 4349651, fax 4349958) Karumuttu Centre, 498 Anna Salai
Qantas Airways (☎ 8278680, fax 8240608) G3, Eldorado Bldg, 112 MG Rd (formerly Nungambakkam High Rd)
Singapore Airlines (☎ 8522871) West Minster, 108 Dr Radhakrishnan Salai
SriLankan Airlines (☎ 8261535) Cathedral Rd
Thai Airways International (☎ 4330098) Stic Travels, Temple Towers, 476 Anna Salai

Bus

All bus stations are in the vicinity of the High Court in George Town. Long-distance buses depart from the State Express Transport Corporation (SETC) bus station on either side of Prakasam Rd.

The eastern terminal is for most long-distance services. The intrastate (☎ 5341835) and interstate (☎ 5341836) bus reservation offices are upstairs. They are computerised and open 7 am to 9 pm daily. There's a Rs 5

CHENNAI

Domestic Flights from Chennai

destination	frequency	airline	duration (hrs)	fare Rs/US$
Bangalore	3d	IC/CD	45 min	2010/65
	5d	9W	45 min	2315/65
Bhubaneswar	4w	IC	2½	5905/200
Coimbatore *	2w	IC	1	2745/90
Coimbatore	7w	CD	2	
	1d	9W		3005/90
Delhi	2d	IC	2½	7720/260
	4w	CD	5½	7720/260
	3d	9W	3 to 4	8480/260
Goa	2w	IC	2¾	4075/140
Hyderabad	2d	IC	1	3005/105
	1d	9W		3290/105
Kochi (Cochin) *	9w	IC	1 to 2	3430/120
	1d	9W		3760/120
Kolkata	1d	IC	2	6725/200
	1d	9W		7385/220
Kozhikode (Calicut)	4w	IC	2¼	2745/90
Madurai	1d	IC	1	2625/90
Mumbai (Bombay)	3d	IC	1¾	4825/160
	4d	9W		5295/160
Port Blair	4w	IC	2	5920/195
	1d	9W		5920/367
Thiruvananthapuram	1d	IC	1¼	3500/155
	1d	9W		3840/105
Tiruchirappalli (Trichy) *	5w	IC	50 min	2185/80
Visakhapatnam	4w	CD	1	3360/120

Note: Fares given are one way only. Rs fares apply to Indian travellers only.
Frequency abbreviation: d daily; w weekly
Airline codes: IC–Indian Airlines, CD–Alliance Air, 9W–Jet Airways
* Departure from International Airport

reservation fee plus Rs 0.25 for the form! In addition to the SETC services the Karnataka and Andhra Pradesh State Road Transport Corporations operate services to their respective states from the SETC bus station. See the 'Bus Services from Chennai' table.

The station west of Prakasam Rd is used mainly for depot purposes; few buses depart from here. The stations are well organised; you'll get plenty of help at the office and if you're still stuck, there are many people who'll find your bus for a few rupees.

Buses to Mamallapuram and Kanchipuram leave from a station opposite the Saravana Bhavan while city buses set down and pick up nearby at Parry's Corner.

There are also private bus companies with offices opposite Egmore station that run superdeluxe video buses daily to cities such as Bangalore, Coimbatore, Madurai and Trichy. Prices are similar to the state buses.

Train

The reservation office at Central Station is on the 1st floor of the Train Reservation Complex next to the station. For reservations and general inquiries call ☎ 131/2 (operator assistance), ☎ 1361 (English), ☎ 1362 (Hindi), ☎ 1362 (Tamil) or ☎ 1363 (Kannada and Malayalam). You can make reservations here for trains originating in most larger cities. The very helpful Foreign Assistance Tourist Cell, in the reservation

Bus Services from Chennai

destination & bus No	frequency (daily)	distance (km)	duration (hrs)	fare (Rs)
Bangalore 628, 831, 863	30	351	8	140
Chidambaram 300	8	240	7	56
Kanyakumari 282S, 282T	7	705	16	189
Kodaikanal 461	1	511	12	120
Madurai 135, 137 (S&F)	37	447	10	125
Mysore 863	2	497	11	167
Ooty 468S, 860	2	565	15	157
Pondicherry 803, 803F	37	162	5	43
Rameswaram 166	1	570	13	153
Thanjavur 323 (F&S)	18	321	18	87
Thiruvananthapuram 794	6	752	17	237
Tiruchirappalli 123 (A&F), 124	46	319	8	93
Tirupathi 902/911, 811, 848, 863	83	150	4	52
Vellore 831, 863	26	145	4	47

office at Central Station, deals with Indrail Pass and tourist-quota bookings.

The office is open 8 am to 2 pm and 2.15 to 8 pm Monday to Saturday and 8 am to 2 pm Sunday. At Egmore the booking office (☎ 5353545) is in the station itself, and keeps the same hours as the office at Central Station. See the 'Major Trains from Chennai' table for a selection of trains from Chennai.

Boat

There are various services to the Andaman Islands, but they're prone to change, so check the latest schedules. For foreigners, there is no service between May and August. The boat, *MV Nancowry*, sails from Chennai every 14 days to Port Blair (50 to 60 hours). Once a month, it sails via Car Nicobar, but only residents may disembark here. This voyage takes an extra two days.

The categories of accommodation include deluxe cabin (two berth, Rs 4140), 1st-class cabin (usually two berth, Rs 3420), 2nd-class A cabin (four to six berth, Rs 2700) and 2nd-class B cabin (similar to A but smaller, Rs 2070). Some ships have an air-con dorm for Rs 1449. If you can get a ticket for bunk class, it will cost Rs 1150. For residents of the Andaman or Nicobar Islands, fares are 40% cheaper. All prices are per person. Food (thalis for breakfast, lunch and dinner) costs around Rs 120 per day. Almost everyone complains so you may wish to bring something to supplement this. Some bedding is supplied, but if you're travelling dorm or bunk class, bring a sleeping sheet.

Tickets are issued at the Andaman Shipping Service Office, Directorate of Shipping Services (☎ 5226873), 6 Rajaji Salai (opposite the Customs House, in the little office by Gate No 5) in George Town.

Foreigners can get a permit in Chennai or when they arrive on the islands (see Visa Extensions & Permits under Information at the start of this chapter).

GETTING AROUND

To/From the Airport

The domestic and international terminals are 16km south of the city centre. The cheapest way to reach them is by suburban train from Egmore to Tirusulam, which is only about 500m across the road from the terminals. The trains run from 4.15 am until 11.45 pm, the journey into the city takes about 40 minutes, and the fare is Rs 7/85 in 2nd/1st class. These trains are not overly crowded, except during peak hours.

Public buses are not such a good bet, particularly if you've got a lot of luggage. Nos 18J, 52, 52A/B/C/D and 55A all start and finish at Parry's Corner and go along Anna Salai.

There's also a minibus service for Rs 100 (Rs 60 during the day) between the airport and the major hotels and sites. It is slow, but efficient and friendly. The booking counter is next to the taxi counters at the

Major Trains from Chennai

destination	train No & name	departures	distance (km)	duration (hrs)	fare (Rs) (2nd/1st)
Bangalore	2007 *Shatabdi Exp* *	6 am CC	356	5	530/–
	6007 *Bangalore Mail*	10.15 pm CC		7¼	87/457
Kolkata	2842 *Coromandel Exp*	9.05 am CC	1669	28	366/1255
	6004 *Howrah Mail*	10.30 pm CC		32¼	366/1062
Coimbatore	2675 *Kovai Exp*	6.15m CC	494	6½	107/562
Delhi	2621 *Tamil Nadu Exp*	10 pm CC	2194	34	410/1545
Hyderabad	2759 *Charminar Exp*	6.10 pm CC	794	14¼	222/751
Kanyakumari	6119 *Nellai Exp*	7.15 pm CE	744	16½	225/762
Kochi (Cochin)	6041 *Alleppey Exp*	7.45 pm CC	700	13½	214/725
Madurai	6717 *Pandian Exp*	8 pm CE	556	10¼	166/562
Mettuppalayam	6605 *Nilgiri Exp*	8.15 pm CC	630	9¼	205/693
Mumbai	1064 *Chennai Exp*	6.40 am CC	1279	30	315/1066
	6010 *CST Mail*	9.30 pm CC		30	315/1462
Mysore	2007 *Shatabdi Exp* *	6 am CC	500	7	630/–
Rameswaram	6713 *Sethu Exp* †	1 pm CE	656	17½	210/709
Thanjavur	6853 *Cholan Exp* †	8.45 am CE	351	9	131/441
Thiruvananthapuram	6319 *Trivandrum Mail*	7 pm CC	921	19	259/887
Tiruchirappalli	2635 *Vaigai Exp* ◆	12.25 pm CE	337	5¼	145/489
Tirupathi	6057 *Saptagiri Exp*	6.25 am CC	147	3	46/242
Varanasi	6039 *Varanasi Exp* ††	5.30 pm CC	2144	37	407/1518

CC – Chennai Central, CE – Chennai Egmore

* Daily except Tuesday; air-con chair only; fare includes meals and drinks

◆ Daily except Wednesday; air-con only; fare includes meals and drinks

† Board CE, change at Tambaram (after gauge work completed, no change required)

†† Monday and Saturday only

international terminal. When the booking counter is closed, taxi drivers may tell you the service is no longer running; the bus should nevertheless be waiting outside and you can pay on board.

An autorickshaw to the airport costs about Rs 150/250 for a day/night trip.

A yellow-and-black taxi costs Rs 250. At the prepaid taxi kiosk inside the international airport, you can buy a ticket into Chennai for Rs 200 to 250 (depending on the distance). There's another prepaid kiosk in the baggage collection area inside the domestic terminal.

Bus

The bus system in Chennai is run by the Metropolitan Transport Corporation (MTC). It's less overburdened than those in the other large Indian cities, although peak hour is still best avoided.

See the 'Chennai Buses' table, following, for some bus routes within Chennai.

Train

The suburban train is an excellent way to get between Egmore and Central Stations (Rs 2.5), Egmore and George Town (Rs 2.5), to Guindy (Rs 5) or the airport (Rs 5). There are relatively uncrowded ladies' compartments.

To move quickly across the city, catch the more recently introduced north–south MRTS (Mass Rapid Transport System). All tickets are Rs 2.50 no matter how far or long you travel. Stations include Beach, Fort, Park Town, Chintadripet, Chepauk, Lighthouse and Luz (with extensions planned.

Car

Almost without exception, car hire means you hire the car and a driver. It's wise to use

Chennai Buses

from	to	bus
Central Station	Egmore Station	M4
Egmore Station	Anna Salai	16, 23C, 27, 27B, 27D, 29, 29A
High Court	Guindy	21G
Parry's Corner	Little Mount	18C
Parry's Corner	St Thomas Mount	18E
Mylapore	T Nagar	5B
Parry's Corner	Adyar	5LSS, 21B
Parry's Corner	Anna Salai	11, 11A, 11B, 11D, 17A, 8, 8J
Parry's Corner	Central & Egmore Stations	9, 9A, 9B, 10, 17D, 17E, 17K
Parry's Corner	T Nagar	9, 10, 11

a travel agency approved by the Government of India or one of the many hotels that have travel desks. Rates can vary but a general guide for travelling within the city is Rs 800 per day (eight hours). For travelling beyond city limits costs are Rs 5 per kilometre (Rs 7 with air-con) with a minimum of 250km per day. Driver fees (for food and accommodation) are often additional, up to Rs 125 per day. See the Travel Agency section above for company details. Or, if you want to support a group of very enterprising drivers, many of whom have worked to save and purchase their own cars and now form a cooperative, contact the government approved Manjoo Cabs (☎ 4851083, fax 4852533, ⓔ manjoocabs@yahoo.com), 1 Subramaniyaswamy Koil West St, Saidapet.

Motorcycle

Mopeds are available from U-Rent (☎ 491 0838), No 1 1st St, Main Rd, Gandhinagar. Charges are Rs 175 per day but a year's membership of their rental scheme is also required (Rs 250). Helmets and insurance are mandatory and cost Rs 35 each per day. An international driving licence is generally needed but your home-country licence may be accepted. You'll also need your passport, two passport photos and two references from local residents.

Taxi

Rates are Rs 25 for the first 1.5km and Rs 5 for each subsequent kilometre. Most drivers will quote you a fixed price rather than use the meter, so negotiate hard. Expect to pay more for travel at night and on Sunday and public holidays.

Autorickshaw

On the meter it's Rs 7 for the first kilometre, then Rs 3.5 per kilometre, but drivers will rarely use a meter, so it's down to hard bargaining. There's a prepaid booth outside Central Station. Prices are at least 25% higher after 10 pm. Drivers have redefined the 'shop-till-you-drop' mantra. They receive handsome commissions from large emporiums, whether or not you buy. So for them a drop (even if you don't shop) is worthwhile and many will hassle (even waive the fare) in their attempt to get their commission. Rather than haggling with one at your hotel, it's often easier to simply walk a short distance and hail one in the street. The hassle and the price are often lower.

Tamil Nadu

In the southernmost part of India, Tamil Nadu is referred to as the cradle of Dravidian culture, an ancient culture distinguished by unique customs. The cultural icons are everywhere – huge temples with their towering *gopurams* (gateways), intricate rock carvings, evocative music and, of course, the complex classical dance. Throughout Tamil Nadu pilgrims pour into the ancient sites of Kanchipuram, Chidambaram, Kumbakonam, Tiruchirappalli, Thanjavur, Madurai, Kanyakumari and Rameswaram. These names are on the tourist map, but it is their significance as potent contours on the cultural map that guides pilgrims in their celebration of the land and its legends.

The coastline has resorts and delightful fishing villages while mountain towns, such as Udhagamandalam (Ooty) and Kodaikanal, provide a cool haven from the hot summer.

Tamil cuisine, traditionally vegetarian, consists of *dosas* (crispy pancakes) and *idlis* (steamed rice dumplings), delicately spiced vegetables and mounds of rice. Sweets are a favourite, and coffee is more popular than tea. Alcohol is more likely to be available in nonvegetarian restaurants.

The Tamil Nadu Tourist Commission has a Web site (www.tamilnadutourism.com) for inquiries and reservations.

Many of Tamil Nadu's towns have been renamed. However, since the new names are not widely used, both versions are included throughout this chapter.

Tamil Nadu at a Glance

Population: 62.1 million
Area: 130,058 sq km
Capital: Chennai (Madras)
Main Language: Tamil
When to Go: Dec to Feb

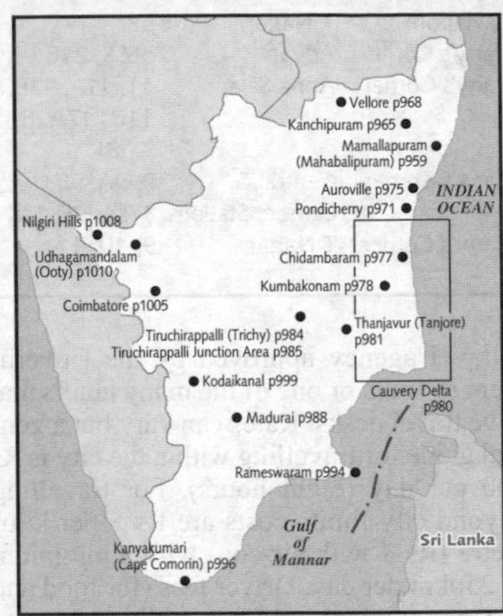

- Visit Mamallapuram, a place of unique rock sculptures and skilful artisans
- Meander through Madurai and absorb the magnificence of the Sri Meenakshi Temple
- Meditate at the convergence of three great oceans at Kanyakumari, the most southerly tip of the Indian mainland
- Hike through the cool shola forests of the Nilgiris, near Ooty
- Ride the miniature train as it climbs from the plains to the cool hill station of Ooty

History

Tamil Nadu is the home of the Tamils and their Dravidian culture. It is not known exactly when the original Dravidians came or where they came from. There is speculation that the first Dravidians were part of early Indus civilisations and came south around 1500 BC. But human activity in the area may have begun as early as 300,000 years ago. By 1200 BC, a civilisation distinguished by huge stone sculptures existed in South India. By 300 BC the region was controlled by three major dynasties – the Cholas in the east, Pandyas in the central area and Cheras in the west. This was the classical period of Tamil literature – the Sangam Age – that continued until around AD 300.

The domains of these three dynasties changed many times over the centuries. At times other sovereignties became powerful. The Pallava dynasty was influential, particularly in the 7th and 8th centuries, when it constructed many of the monuments at Mamallapuram. Although all these dynasties engaged in continual skirmishes, their steady patronage of the arts served to consolidate and expand Dravidian civilisation.

TAMIL NADU

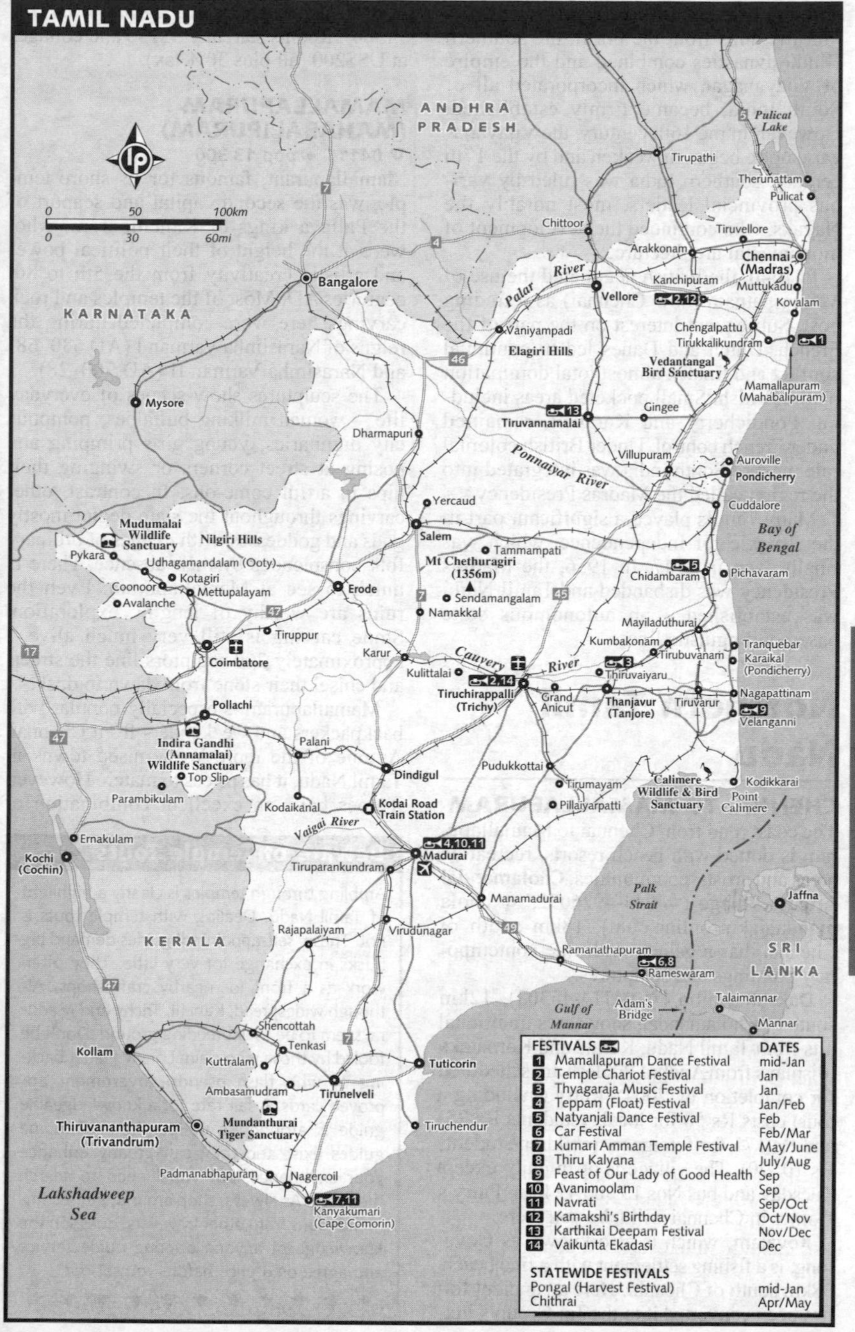

FESTIVALS	DATES
1 Mamallapuram Dance Festival	mid-Jan
2 Temple Chariot Festival	Jan
3 Thyagaraja Music Festival	Jan
4 Teppam (Float) Festival	Jan/Feb
5 Natyanjali Dance Festival	Feb
6 Car Festival	Feb/Mar
7 Kumari Amman Temple Festival	May/June
8 Thiru Kalyana	July/Aug
9 Feast of Our Lady of Good Health	Sep
10 Avanimoolam	Sep
11 Navrati	Sep/Oct
12 Kamakshi's Birthday	Oct/Nov
13 Karthikai Deepam Festival	Nov/Dec
14 Vaikunta Ekadasi	Dec

STATEWIDE FESTIVALS	
Pongal (Harvest Festival)	mid-Jan
Chithrai	Apr/May

In the 13th century, with threats of Muslim invasions from the north, the southern Hindu dynasties combined and the empire of Vijayanagar, which incorporated all of South India, became firmly established. However, in the 16th century, the Vijayanagar empire began to weaken and by the 17th century, southern India was ruled by various provincial leaders, most notably the Nayaks, who continued the development of monumental architecture.

In 1640, the British negotiated the use of Madraspatnam (now Chennai) as a trading post. Subsequent interest on the part of the French, Dutch and Danes led to continual conflict and finally, almost total domination by the British. Small pocketed areas including Pondicherry and Karaikal, remained under French control. Under British colonial rule most of South India was integrated into the region called the Madras Presidency.

Many Tamils played a significant part in the struggle for Independence, which was finally won in 1947. In 1956, the Madras Presidency was disbanded and Tamil Nadu was established – an autonomous state based on linguistic lines.

Northern Tamil Nadu

CHENNAI TO MAMALLAPURAM

The coast road from Chennai to Mamallapuram is dotted with beach resorts, recreation areas and artists' communities. **Cholamandal Artists' Village** (☎ 044-4926092, ⓔ cholamandal@kmronline.com), 18km south of Chennai, has a gallery with fine contemporary paintings and sculptures.

Dakshinachitra (☎ 04114-45303), 12km south of Cholamandal, showcases traditional arts from Tamil Nadu, Kerala and Karnataka (displays from Andhra Pradesh are scheduled for completion by 2004). Entry (including a tour) costs Rs 50 for locals (students Rs 25) and Rs 175 for foreigners (children/students Rs 10/ 70). The village is open daily except Tuesday and bus Nos 19 and 49 from Parry's Corner in Chennai will take you there.

Kovalam, which is also known as Covelong, is a fishing settlement with a fine beach, 38km south of Chennai. Here an ancient fort has been converted into the Taj Group's luxurious ***Fisherman's Cove Resort*** *(☎ 04114-74304)*. Rooms start at US$150 and cottages at US$200 (all plus 30% tax).

MAMALLAPURAM (MAHABALIPURAM)

☎ 04114 • pop 13,300

Mamallapuram, famous for its shore temple, was the second capital and seaport of the Pallava kings of Kanchipuram, who, were at the height of their political power and artistic creativity from the 5th to 8th centuries AD. Most of the temples and rock carvings here were completed during the reigns of Narasimha Varman I (AD 630–68) and Narasimha Varman II (AD 700–28).

The sculptures show scenes of everyday life – women milking buffaloes, pompous city dignitaries, young girls primping and posing at street corners or swinging their hips in artful come-ons. In contrast, other carvings throughout the state depict mostly gods and goddesses, with images of ordinary folk conspicuous by their absence. There is much to see at Mamallapuram. Even the ruins are worthy of lengthy exploration. Stone carving is still very much alive – approximately 200 sculptors line the streets and chisel their stone from dawn to dusk.

Mamallapuram is especially popular with backpackers and weekenders from Chennai. As one of the more Westernised towns in Tamil Nadu, it has prices to match. However, it does have an excellent combination of

Beware of Temple Touts

Ambling through temples is clearly a highlight of Tamil Nadu. Dealing with temple touts is not. These 'self-appointed' guides demand big bucks in exchange for very little. They often work as a front for nearby craft shops. Although widespread, Kanchi, Trichy and Madurai seem to be their breeding ground. Don't be fooled by those who claim Lonely Planet backing or who flash pseudo-government approved cards. A fair rate for a knowledgeable guide is around Rs 60 per hour. Genuine guides exist and they can greatly enhance your experience. But you'll need to search them out. As always, shop around, get recommendations from other travellers, question the knowledge of anyone offering guide service and agree on a price before you set out.

KOLKATA (CALCUTTA) 427

WEST BENGAL 455

ORISSA 485

SIKKIM 507

NORTH-EASTERN REGION 522

RAJASTHAN 544

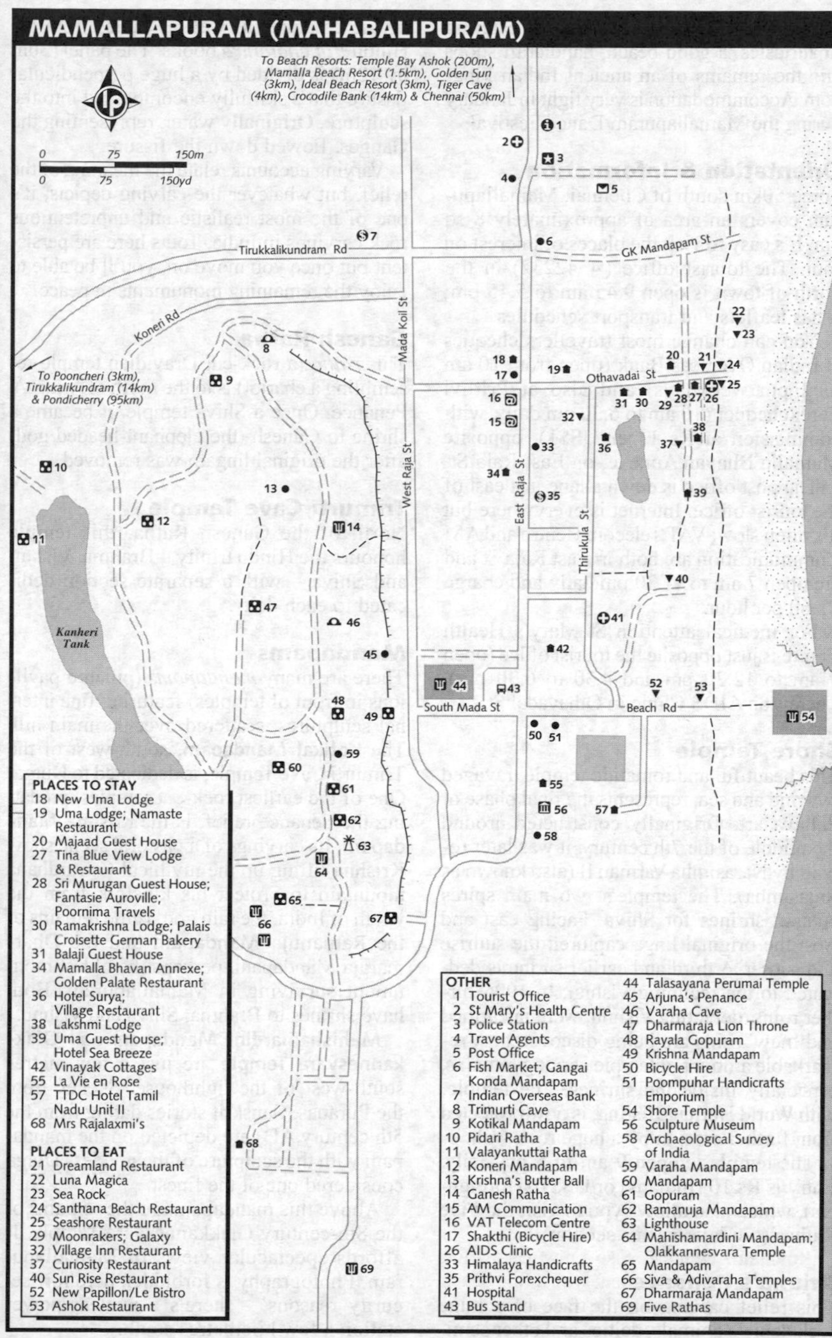
MAMALLAPURAM (MAHABALIPURAM)
To Beach Resorts: Temple Bay Ashok (200m), Mamalla Beach Resort (1.5km), Golden Sun (3km), Ideal Beach Resort (3km), Tiger Cave (4km), Crocodile Bank (14km) & Chennai (50km)
0 75 150m
0 75 150yd
Tirukkalikundram Rd
GK Mandapam St
Koneri Rd
Mada Koil St
To Pooncheri (3km), Tirukkalikundram (14km) & Pondicherry (95km)
Othavadai St
West Raja St
East Raja St
Thirukula St
Kanheri Tank
South Mada St
Beach Rd
TAMIL NADU
PLACES TO STAY
18 New Uma Lodge
19 Uma Lodge; Namaste Restaurant
20 Majaad Guest House
27 Tina Blue View Lodge & Restaurant
28 Sri Murugan Guest House; Fantasie Auroville; Poornima Travels
30 Ramakrishna Lodge; Palais Croisette German Bakery
31 Balaji Guest House
34 Mamalla Bhavan Annexe; Golden Palate Restaurant
36 Hotel Surya; Village Restaurant
38 Lakshmi Lodge
39 Uma Guest House; Hotel Sea Breeze
42 Vinayak Cottages
55 La Vie en Rose
57 TTDC Hotel Tamil Nadu Unit II
68 Mrs Rajalaxmi's
PLACES TO EAT
21 Dreamland Restaurant
22 Luna Magica
23 Sea Rock
24 Santhana Beach Restaurant
25 Seashore Restaurant
29 Moonrakers; Galaxy
32 Village Inn Restaurant
37 Curiosity Restaurant
40 Sun Rise Restaurant
52 New Papillon/Le Bistro
53 Ashok Restaurant
OTHER
1 Tourist Office
2 St Mary's Health Centre
3 Police Station
4 Travel Agents
5 Post Office
6 Fish Market; Gangai Konda Mandapam
7 Indian Overseas Bank
8 Trimurti Cave
9 Kotikal Mandapam
10 Pidari Ratha
11 Valayankuttai Ratha
12 Koneri Mandapam
13 Krishna's Butter Ball
14 Ganesh Ratha
15 AM Communication
16 VAT Telecom Centre
17 Shakthi (Bicycle Hire)
26 AIDS Clinic
33 Himalaya Handicrafts
35 Prithvi Forexchequer
41 Hospital
43 Bus Stand
44 Talasayana Perumal Temple
45 Arjuna's Penance
46 Varaha Cave
47 Dharmaraja Lion Throne
48 Rayala Gopuram
49 Krishna Mandapam
50 Bicycle Hire
51 Poompuhar Handicrafts Emporium
54 Shore Temple
56 Sculpture Museum
58 Archaeological Survey of India
59 Varaha Mandapam
60 Mandapam
61 Gopuram
62 Ramanuja Mandapam
63 Lighthouse
64 Mahishamardini Mandapam; Olakkannesvara Temple
65 Mandapam
66 Siva & Adivaraha Temples
67 Dharmaraja Mandapam
69 Five Rathas

cheap accommodation, restaurants catering to all tastes, a good beach, handicraft shops *and* the remains of an ancient Indian kingdom. Accommodation is very tight in January during the Mamallapuram Dance Festival.

Orientation & Information

Some 50km south of Chennai, Mamallapuram covers an area of approximately 8 sq km. It's easy to visit the places of interest on foot. The tourist office (☎ 42232) in the north of town is open 9.45 am to 5.45 pm; it has leaflets and transport schedules.

You can change most travellers cheques at Indian Overseas Bank (open from 10 am to 2 pm weekdays) and also at Prithvi Forexchequer (10 am to 6.30 pm daily, with commission at Rs 1 per US$1), opposite Mamalla Bhavan Annexe, on East Raja St.

The post office is down a lane just east of the tourist office. Internet is everywhere but it's often slow; VAT Telecom Centre and AM Communication are both in East Raja St and are open 7 am to 11.30 pm daily and charge Rs 60 per hour.

For medical attention St Mary's Health Centre is just opposite the tourist office (open 9 am to 12.30 pm and 4.30 to 6.30 pm). There's an AIDS Clinic in Othavadai St.

Shore Temple

This beautiful and romantic temple, ravaged by wind and sea, represents the final phase of Pallava art. Originally constructed around the middle of the 7th century, it was later rebuilt by Narasimha Varman II (also known as Rajasimha). The temple's two main spires contain shrines for Shiva. Facing east and west the original linga captured the sunrise and sunset. A third and earlier shrine is dedicated to the reclining Vishnu. In 1996 further ruins, depicting Vishnu, were unearthed and 'new' ruins are being discovered. A remarkable amount of temple carving remains, especially inside the shrines. The temple, with World Heritage listing, is now protected from further erosion by a huge rock wall.

The temple is open 9 am to 5 pm daily. Entry is Rs 10 (Indians) or US$10 (foreigners), which also allows you to visit the Five Rathas (see later in this section).

Arjuna's Penance

This relief carving on the face of a huge rock depicts animals, deities and other semi-divine creatures as well as fables from the Hindu *Panchatantra* books. The panel (30m by 12m) is divided by a huge perpendicular fissure that's skilfully encompassed into the sculpture. Originally water, representing the Ganges, flowed down the fissure.

Varying accounts relate the meaning of the relief, but whatever the carving depicts, it's one of the most realistic and unpretentious rock carvings in India. Touts here are persistent but once you move on, you'll be able to enjoy the remaining monuments in peace.

Ganesh Ratha

This *ratha* (a rock-cut Dravidian temple resembling a chariot) is to the north of Arjuna's Penance. Once a Shiva temple, it became a shrine to Ganesh (the elephant-headed god) after the original lingam was removed.

Trimurti Cave Temple

North of the Ganesh Ratha, this temple honours the Hindu trinity – Brahma, Vishnu and Shiva – with a separate section dedicated to each deity.

Mandapams

There are many *mandapams* (pillared pavilions in front of temples) featuring fine internal sculptures, scattered over the main hill. The **Kotikal Mandapam**, south-west of the Trimurti Cave Temple, is dedicated to Durga. One of the earliest rock-cut temples, predating the penance relief, is the **Krishna Mandapam**. Its carvings of a pastoral scene show Krishna lifting up the mythical Govardhana mountain to protect his kinsfolk from the wrath of Indra, the rain god. Little remains of the **Ramanuja Mandapam** and the Dharmaraja Mandapam, perhaps the oldest monument surviving in Mamallapuram. Both have shrines to Brahma, Shiva and Vishnu.

Mahishamardini Mandapam and **Olakkannesvara Temple** are just a few metres south-west of the lighthouse. Scenes from the Puranas (Sanskrit stories dating from the 5th century AD) are depicted on the mandapam with the sculpture of the goddess Durga considered one of the finest.

Above this mandapam are the remains of the 8th-century Olakkannesvara Temple. It affords spectacular views of Mamallapuram. Photography is forbidden here for 'security reasons' – there's a nuclear power station a few kilometres south.

EDDIE GERALD

GREG ELMS

PAUL BEINSSEN

PETER DAVIS

Aspects of Tamil Nadu culture are expressed in the graceful steps of the Bharata Natyam dancers **(top)**; in the artistry of an outdoor tailor **(right)**; in morning prayer at the Mamallapuram rock temples **(bottom left)**; and in the gentle solicitations of a betel-leaf seller **(middle left)**.

MARK DAFFEY

TERESA CANNON

EDDIE GERALD

Top & middle: One of the nine *gopurams* (pyramidal gateways) of the Sri Meenaskshi Temple, Madurai, Tamil Nadu, adorned with a profusion of multicoloured sculptures
Bottom: Tamil Nadu's Brihadishwara Temple, Thanjavur, the crowning glory of Chola temple architecture

Five Rathas
The Five Rathas are sculptured temples in the style of chariots. Just 300m from the sea, and carved from solid rock, they provide another fine example of Pallava architecture. These structures were hidden in the sand until excavated by the British 200 years ago. You can see photos in the museum documenting the excavation process.

The Five Rathas derive their names from the champions of the Mahabharata; the Pandavas, and their collective wife, Draupadi.

The first ratha, **Draupadi Ratha**, on the left after you enter the gate, is dedicated to the goddess Durga. Within, the goddess stands on a lotus, her devotees on their knees in worship. Outside, the huge sculptured lion stands proud in front of her temple.

Behind the goddess shrine, a huge Nandi (Shiva's bull vehicle) heralds the next chariot, the **Arjuna Ratha**, dedicated to Shiva. Numerous deities, including Indra, the rain god, are depicted on the outer walls.

The next temple chariot, **Bhima Ratha,** honours Vishnu. Within its walls a large sculpture of this deity lies in repose.

The **Dharmaraja Ratha** is the tallest of the chariots and the farthest south. The outside walls portray many deities, including both the sun god, Surya, and the rain god, Indra. The final ratha, the **Nakula-Sahadeva Ratha,** is dedicated to Indra. His mount is represented in the fine sculptured elephant standing next to the temple. Approaching from the north, as you enter the gate, you'll see its back first, hence its name; **gajaprishthakara** (elephant's backside). The life-sized image is regarded as one of the most perfectly sculptured elephants in India.

Sculpture Museum
On East Raja St, the museum contains more than 3000 sculptures by local artisans who work with wood, metal, brass and even cement. Some fine paintings are also on display. It's open 9 am to 6 pm daily. Entry is Rs 0.50.

Beach
The village is only about 200m from the wide beach, north of the Shore Temple, where local fishers pull in their boats. Be warned – the local toilet is also here. Either further north, or to the south of the Shore Temple, the beach becomes cleaner and you can take long unimpeded walks. Take care, however, if you decide to swim. There are dangerous rips and all too often lives are lost.

Massage, Yoga & Ayurveda
There are numerous places offering massage, reiki, yoga and other ayurvedic practices. Sessions cost around Rs 350 for 30 to 45 minutes. Krishna at Sri Murugan Guest House, is recommended by both male and female travellers. There are many operators in town and rates and timings vary. As always, and especially for such an intimate service, ask fellow travellers, question the masseur carefully and if you have any misgivings, don't proceed.

Courses
You can learn a traditional Indian musical instrument from K Saikumar on School St at Pooncheri Village, 3km from Mamallapuram, on the road to Chengalpattu. The New Papillon Le Bistro will give you all the details and arrange a translator.

Special Events
For four weeks each January, the **Mamallapuram Dance Festival** showcases dances from all over India, including the Bharata Natyam (Tamil Nadu), Kuchipudi (Andhra Pradesh) tribal dance, and performances including Kathakali (Kerala drama), puppet shows and classical music. Many events take place against the imposing backdrop of Arjuna's Penance. Pick up a leaflet at the tourist office or in Chennai. Local hotels can also assist with programs and tickets.

Places to Stay
If you don't mind roughing it, you can stay in ***home accommodation*** with families near the Five Rathas. Rooms are basic but travellers' reports are positive. Touts will find you accommodation in the village but, of course, you'll pay more. The usual cost is around Rs 50 per day, or Rs 300 per week (more if a tout takes you).

Hotel accommodation is abundant but can be tight at holiday times. Be careful of the scams operating at the bus station where autorickshaw drivers convince you that your desired hotel is full and whisk you to one where they receive a substantial commission that eventually comes out of your pocket. The best strategy is to check out places yourself.

Places to Stay – Budget

Mrs Rajalaxmi's place still rates well and deservedly so. It's friendly, homey and well maintained. The rooms (Rs 50) have fans and electricity, and there's a communal squat toilet. Take water from the well for a bucket shower. Meals are available on request.

Majaad Guest House *(☎ 42908, 44 Othavadai St)* is also friendly and homey. The rooms are small and basic with cold water only, but quite OK at Rs 100/150 for a single/double.

Lakshmi Lodge *(☎ 42059, fax 42511)*, near the beach, is very popular with backpackers. Light, airy rooms are Rs 150 to 250 with cottages for Rs 450 and air-con for Rs 750. There are both squat and sit-down flush toilets and bucket hot water is provided on request from 6 am to 10 pm. Indian and Western food is served on private terraces or on the roof under the stars.

Tina Blue View Lodge & Restaurant *(☎ 42319, 34 Othavadai St)*, set in a leafy garden, has basic rooms for Rs 100/198. It's Rs 50 for each extra person. Bucket hot water is available anytime. There's a pleasant music cum games room, ideal for families or getting together with other travellers. The upstairs restaurant, is a great place to eat or to linger over a beer.

Uma Lodge *(☎ 42322)*, in the same area, has doubles without bathroom/with bathroom (with bucket hot water) for Rs 100/150. The Namaste Restaurant (formerly Pumpernickel Bakery) is here.

New Uma Lodge *(☎ 43369, 10 East Raja St)* is a slightly upmarket version of its predecessor. It's fairly clean with rooms for Rs 125/150/190 for singles/doubles/large doubles. There's cold water only.

Uma Guest House *(☎ 42697, 11 Othavadai Cross St)* is evidence that Uma has been busy. Doubles (no singles) are Rs 150 to 190 (with bucket hot water) and Rs 480 with air-con and constant hot water.

Vinayak Cottages *(☎ 42445)* may be a victim of tout scams, with many people supposedly being told it doesn't exist – a shame because it's good value. There are older-style cottages with thatched roofs for Rs 250, and newer, larger cottages (with cleaner bathrooms) from Rs 250 to 450, with air-con at Rs 600.

Balaji Guesthouse *(☎ 42546, fax 42511, 9 Othavadai St)* is a pleasant lodge with small doubles (no singles) for Rs 200 and larger family rooms for Rs 400.

Sri Murugan Guest House *(☎ 42662, 42 Othavadai St)* is close to the beach with clean, well-priced rooms at Rs 150 downstairs and Rs 250 upstairs (only doubles). An Ayurvedic masseur operates from this guesthouse.

Ramakrishna Lodge *(☎ 42431, 8 Othavadai St)* is clean, friendly and justifiably popular. Rooms begin at Rs 100/150 but prices can be higher in the high season. Bucket hot water is available and the roof terrace has a great bakery and restaurant – Palais Croisette German Bakery.

Places to Stay – Mid-Range & Top End

Mamalla Bhavan Annexe *(☎ 42260, fax 42160, ⓔ mamalla@vsnl.com, 104 East Raja St)* continues to be very popular. What it lacks in the plumbing and electrical departments it makes up for with its thoughtful staff. All rooms are doubles and have phone and TV. Prices range from Rs 350 (nonair-con) to 550 (air-con). You can eat in the veg restaurant, on the balconies or in the courtyard. Credit cards (MasterCard, Visa and AmEx are accepted.

Hotel Sea Breeze *(☎ 43035, fax 43065, ⓔ seabreezehotel@hotmail.com)*, set among coconut trees, with a swimming pool, is good value for Rs 250/450 for singles/doubles, and Rs 700 for doubles with air-con.

La Vie en Rose *(☎ 42522)*, better known as a restaurant, has a few pleasant, clean rooms for Rs 250/300 with many facing a central courtyard.

Hotel Surya *(☎ 42292, Thirukula St)* with its archaeologist proprietor makes for an interesting stay. Surya's a friendly place with very clean rooms starting at Rs 200/350. Double rooms with a balcony overlooking either the sculpture garden or the lake are Rs 400/450, air-con rooms are Rs 750, deluxe are Rs 850.

TTDC Hotel Tamil Nadu Unit II *(☎ 42287)*, near Beach Rd in pleasant shady grounds, has double cottages at Rs 300 to 350. The hotel's facilities include a bar, restaurant and a children's play area. There are dorms (with 12 to 15 well-spaced beds per room) for Rs 50. And you can camp – Rs 100 per tent. For the price and facilities, it's not a bad choice.

The other mid-range and top-end hotels are scattered for several kilometres along the road north to Chennai. Each is positioned on its own narrow strip of land, about 300m from the road and as close as possible to the beach. All of these so-called beach resorts offer a range of facilities that usually include a swimming pool, bar, restaurant(s) and credit card facilities.

Temple Bay Ashok Beach Resort *(☎ 42251, fax 42257, ⓔ tbabr@md3.vsnl.net.in)* is 200m from the edge of town set in pleasant gardens with a children's playground. Singles/doubles with air-con cost Rs 1995/3900 in either the main block or the detached cottages, some with slate floors and thatched roofs. Nonguests can use the small pool for Rs 100 per day.

Mamalla Beach Resort *(☎ 42375, fax 42160)* is farther north, but not as close to the sea. It's a good place with clean doubles from Rs 500 to 600, and Rs 780 for air-con. There's a veg/nonveg restaurant with particularly friendly staff.

Golden Sun Beach Resort *(☎ 42245, fax 044-4982669 in Chennai)* is 3km from Mamallapuram. Rooms here start at Rs 800/850, or Rs 1100/1200 with air-con. There are sea-facing rooms starting at Rs 1400/1500. There's also a health club and pool. This place is popular and is often full.

Ideal Beach Resort *(☎ 42240, fax 42243)*, also 3km from town, is one of the best. This place is small enough to retain the owner's intended warm and intimate atmosphere. Rooms/cottages cost Rs 1350/1500. There's great food and a pool that nonguests can use for Rs 100.

Places to Eat

Mamallapuram is a gastronome's delight. Beachside restaurants serve attractively presented seafood in relaxed settings. Most will show you the fresh fish, prawns, crabs and squid before cooking them so you can make your choice. Be sure, however, to ask the price before giving the go-ahead, as some items – king prawns for example – can be very expensive. At many of the restaurants it is possible to 'customise' your meal according to budget and/or appetite. Beer usually costs Rs 50 at the beach bars and Rs 35 in the numerous wine shops.

Seashore Restaurant, ***Santhana Beach Restaurant***, ***Luna Magica*** and ***Sea Rock*** are all on the beach, offering excellent fresh seafood, including tiger prawns (Rs 50 each), lobster, crab (small Rs 200) and whole fish (Rs 200). Other meals are about Rs 40 to 50.

Moonrakers *(Othavadai St)* is a late night 'hang-out'; a great place to meet people. Run by three friendly brothers, it has good food and ambience. ***Galaxy***, next door, has similar fare with good coffee and pancakes.

Village Inn Restaurant has an indoor section plus an intimate garden terrace where you can dine under coconut palms. Multicuisine food including fresh seafood starts from a few rupees to Rs 500 for seafood.

Village Restaurant, just down from Village Inn and near Hotel Surya in Thirukula St, serves multicuisine fare.

Tina Blue View Lodge & Restaurant is a good place to eat, especially in the heat of the day, as the shady upstairs area catches any breeze that might be around. The service is slow but the mellow atmosphere makes up for that. Beer is available.

Dreamland Restaurant, opposite Tina Blue, also has an upstairs section and multicuisine menu.

Namaste Restaurant, on the terrace at Uma Lodge, is a great place to go for any meal. Nepali run, it's truly international with German and French pastries, Italian pastas and Indian dishes.

New Papillon/Le Bistro, on the road to the Shore Temple, is a tiny place run by an enthusiastic crew. Cold beers are available, as well as early morning breakfasts.

Sun Rise Restaurant, behind New Papillon and across the playing field, has a wide range of fish dishes that are good value.

Curiosity Restaurant is opposite Lakshmi Lodge. The food, especially breakfast, is good and the prices are still on the high side.

La Vie en Rose, on the 1st floor of a building at the southern end of East Raja St, is partly French run. This lovely little place offers a different nonvegetarian menu each day and has main courses for about Rs 70, and good coffee.

Golden Palate Restaurant in the Mamalla Bhavan Annexe is a top veg restaurant. The eggplant masala fry with special cashew gravy (Rs 25) is excellent.

Ashok Restaurant is set in pleasant gardens near the Shore Temple. It's not bad for breakfast with dosas from Rs 15.

Shopping

Mamallapuram has revived the ancient crafts of the Pallava sculptors, and the town wakes each day to the sound of chisels on granite. Sculptures are exported throughout the world. You can buy the work from the government-run Poompuhar Handicrafts Emporium (fixed prices – in theory) or from the craft shops that line the main roads (prices negotiable). Sculptures range from Rs 300 (for a small piece to fit in your baggage) to 400,000 for a massive Ganesh that needs to be lifted with a mobile crane. Shipping to Europe or the USA takes three months with costs dependent on weight. Soapstone images of Hindu gods, woodcarvings, jewellery and hammocks are all available as well as the usual handicrafts from Kashmiri shops – you can't miss them, they're at every turn, a voice inviting (sometimes haranguing) you into yet another sale. Fantasie Auroville, with its excellent crafts, is in the Sri Murugan Guest House building. Near the Shore Temple you can buy a stuffed mongoose! For book exchange, try Himalaya Handicrafts, East Raja St.

Getting There & Away

The most direct route to/from Chennai (Rs 25, two hours, 50km, 20 daily) is on bus Nos 188 and 188A/B/D/K. Buses from Chennai leave opposite the Saravana Bhavan near Parry's Corner. Bus Nos 19C and 119A, from the bus station on the corner of East Raja and South Manda Sts, go to Chennai via Kovalam (26 daily). To Chennai via the airport you take No 108B (12 daily).

To Pondicherry (Rs 30, 3½ hours, 95km, nine daily) take bus No 188 or 188A. There are five daily buses (No 212A/H) to Kanchipuram (Rs 12, two hours, 65km) via Tirukkalikundram and Chengalpattu (Chingleput). Alternatively, take a bus to Chengalpattu and then another bus from there to Kanchipuram.

To Madurai catch a bus to Chengalpattu (one hour) then a train from there (Rs 576/167 in 1st/2nd class, 15 hours).

Taxis are available from the bus station. Long-distance trips may require haggling before the price becomes reasonable. It's about Rs 450 to Chennai airport.

Getting Around

The easiest way to get around is on foot. You can hire bicycles from several places, including the bicycle shop near the bus station, for around Rs 25 per day. You can hire mopeds from either Lakshmi Lodge, Shakthi, 137 East Raja St, or Poornima Travels (☎ 42463) at 33 Othavadai St. Costs are around Rs 175 per day. Helmets are not available, you don't need a licence and you don't need to surrender your passport.

Autorickshaws are available but, since this is a tourist town, negotiation is more cryptic than usual. Many travellers find that sharing a taxi is a good option to see places nearby.

AROUND MAMALLAPURAM

Almost 5km north of Mamallapuram, in the village of Salavankuppam the **Tiger Cave** is a rock-cut shrine, possibly dating from the 7th century. It's dedicated to Durga and has a small mandapam featuring a crown of carved *yali* (mythical lion creature) heads.

About 14km from Mamallapuram, Tirukkalikundram is a pilgrimage centre with a hilltop temple dedicated to Shiva. According to legend two eagles come here each day at noon from Varanasi (Benares). But they often don't turn up!

Steps (550) lead to the hilltop and you must ascend bare-footed. The temple contains two beautiful shrines. Unless you're Hindu, it's best to go when it's closed – the custodian will let you in, for a small consideration. When it's open, the pressuring of priests for large donations, under the guise of prayer, can become unpleasant. Views from the top encompass the larger Bhaktavatsaleshavra Temple, rocky hills and rice paddies. You can get here from Mamallapuram by bus or bicycle. The temple is open 8.30 am to 1 pm and 5 to 7 pm. Entry is Rs 2.

VEDANTANGAL BIRD SANCTUARY

Located about 52km from Mamallapuram, this is an important breeding ground for waterbirds. Cormorants, egrets, herons, ibis, storks, spoonbills, grebes and pelicans migrate here from October to March. At the height of the breeding season (December and January) there can be up to 30,000 birds here. The best viewing times are early morning and late afternoon. The sanctuary is open 6 am to 6 pm daily and entry is Rs 1.

Basic accommodation is available at ***Forest Department Resthouse***, just 500m before the sanctuary. Charges are Rs 30 per person. Book with the Wildlife Warden (☎ 044-413947), 4th floor, DMS Office, Teynampet, Chennai. But if you arrive and there's a vacancy, you're in.

To get to Vedantangal take a bus from Chengalpattu to the Vedantangal bus station, then walk the remaining 1km south. Often the buses will take you there. An alternative is to get a bus from any of the major centres to Madurantakam, the closest town of any size, and then hire transport for the last 8km.

KANCHIPURAM

☎ 04112 • pop 184,000

The temple town of Kanchipuram is famous for its temples and its silks. Other than that, Kanchipuram is a dusty and fairly nondescript town. Its attraction for pilgrims and tourists has led to a culture of harassment and at some temples and silk shops this is particularly prevalent. Large tour companies are in cohorts with the silk manufacturers – the more customers they bring, the more commission they get. Remember, if someone (bus/car driver, tout) takes you to the silk shop, the commission they receive comes out of your pocket. For the temples, have plenty of small change handy to meet demands for 'small considerations' from caretakers, shoe minders, guides and assorted priests. All the temples close from noon to 4 pm.

History

By the 3rd century AD Kanchipuram was reputedly a sophisticated city with diverse cultures and languages. It was significant for Buddhist scholarship, although Hinduism and Jainism were also prevalent. When Kanchipuram became the Pallava capital (from the 6th to 8th centuries), the arts, especially literature, music and dance, prospered and the first South Indian stone temples were constructed. Subsequent dynasties, among them the Cholas and Pandyas, continued to support a prosperous Kanchipuram. New temples were built, old ones were renovated.

Today it's silk trade and tourism that dominate Kanchipuram; even within the sacred precincts of the temples.

Orientation & Information

Kanchipuram, also known as Kanchi, is on the main Chennai to Bangalore road, 76km south-west of Chennai.

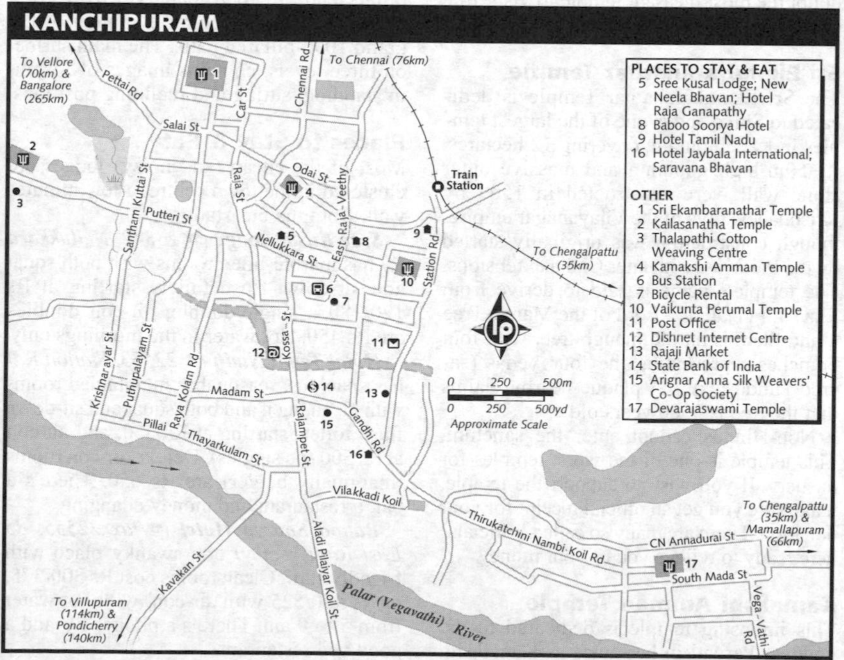

The tourist information counter at Hotel Tamil Nadu (☎ 22461) is interested in promoting friends in the silk trade. The post office is on Station Rd and there's Internet access at Dishnet, 81C Kamaraja St (also known as Kossa St). There are banks but they do not accept travellers cheques. Some hotels (and silk shops) accept credit cards.

Kailasanatha Temple

Dedicated to Shiva, Kailasanatha is the oldest temple in Kanchi. Reflecting the freshness of early Dravidian architecture, it was built by the Pallava king, Rayasimha, in the late 7th century, though its front was added later by his son, King Varman III.

Fragments of the 8th-century murals are a visible reminder of how magnificent the original temple must have looked. There are 58 small shrines honouring Shiva and Parvati and their sons, Ganesh and Murugan.

The temple is run by the Archaeology Department. Non-Hindus are allowed into the inner sanctum, where there is a prismatic lingam – the largest in Kanchi and third-largest in Asia. The guide and priest here are generous with information and this is no doubt the most pleasant temple to visit, free of the harassment metered out at the others.

Sri Ekambaranathar Temple

The Sri Ekambaranathar Temple is dedicated to Shiva and is one of the largest temples in Kanchipuram, covering 12 hectares. Its 59m-high gopuram and massive outer stone wall were constructed in 1509 by Krishnadevaraya of the Vijayanagar empire, though construction was originally started by the Pallavas, with later Chola extensions. The temple's name is said to derive from Eka Amra Nathar – Lord of the Mango Tree – and there is an old mango tree, with four branches representing the four Vedas (sacred Hindu texts). A plaque nearby claims that the tree is 3500 years old.

Non-Hindus cannot enter the sanctum. This temple is one of the worst temples for hustlers. If you wish to support the temple, make sure you get an official receipt for your donation. There are many so called 'officials' here ready to relieve you of your money.

Kamakshi Amman Temple

This imposing temple is dedicated to the goddess Parvati in her guise as Kamakshi, the goddess who accedes to all requests. To the right of the temple's entrance is the marriage hall, which has wonderful ornate pillars, and directly ahead is the main shrine topped with gold. Each February/March wooden carriages housing statues of deities are hauled through the streets in a most colourful procession. The goddess' birthday is in October/November.

Devarajaswami Temple

Dedicated to Vishnu, this enormous monument was built by the Vijayanagars. It has a beautifully sculptured pillared hall as well as a marriage hall commemorating the wedding of Vishnu and Lakshmi. One of the temple's most notable features is a huge chain carved from a single piece of stone.

Every 40 years the waters of the temple tank are drained revealing a huge statue of Vishnu. You may like to hang around for the next viewing – in 2019.

Vaikunta Perumal Temple

Dedicated to Vishnu, this temple was built shortly after the Kailasanatha Temple. The cloisters inside the outer wall consist of lion pillars and are representative of the first phase in the architectural evolution of the grand 1000-pillared halls. The main shrine, on three levels, contains images of Vishnu in standing, sitting and reclining positions.

Places to Stay & Eat

Most of the cheap (and noisy) lodges are clustered in the town centre, a few minutes walk from the bus station.

Sree Kusal Lodge *(☎ 23342, Nellukkara St)* has marble-lined rooms with both squat and sit-down flush toilets starting at Rs 120/180 a single/double; air-con doubles are Rs 450. Hot water in the mornings only.

Hotel Tamil Nadu *(☎ 22553, Station Rd)* has spacious, reasonably maintained rooms with clean linen and both squat and sit-down flush toilets starting at Rs 350, and air-con at Rs 500 (no singles). Deluxe air-con rooms (marginally bigger) are Rs 650. There's a bar, a restaurant and money changing.

Baboo Soorya Hotel *(☎/fax 22555, 85 East Raja Veethy)* is a swanky place with friendly staff. Clean rooms cost Rs 300/375, or Rs 450/525 with air-con, with hot water from 5 to 9 am. There's a phone, TV and a good veg restaurant.

Hotel Jaybala International *(☎ 24348, 504 Gandhi Rd)* has rooms with clean linen, but bathrooms are a tad grotty. Prices range from Rs 125/350 to 450/500 with air-con. There's hot water from 6 to 10 am, both squat and sit-down flush toilets, showers in the air-con rooms, TV and email facilities. All major credit cards are accepted.

The best meals are available from ***Saravana Bhavan*** at Hotel Jaybala International.

New Neela Bhavan and the popular ***Hotel Raja Ganapathy*** are next to Sree Kusal Lodge. Both offer cheap and good South Indian veg dishes.

Getting There & Away

Bus The bus station is well set up. Look for direct, or 'Point-to-Point' buses; they're the fastest – No 76B runs to Chennai (Rs 14, 1½ hours). There are five No 212A buses daily to Mamallapuram (Rs 12, about two hours). Alternatively, take one of the more frequent buses to Chengalpattu and then catch another one from there to Mamallapuram.

There are direct State Express Transport Corporation (SETC) buses to Tiruchirappalli (No 122), Chennai (No 828) and Bangalore (No 828).

There are numerous regional buses to Chennai, Vellore and Tiruvannamalai, as well as private ones to Pondicherry.

Train From Chennai Egmore station change at Chengalpattu (Chingleput) for Kanchipuram. Trains are infrequent so it's probably best to get a bus.

Getting Around

Bicycles can be rented for Rs 5 per hour (Rs 50 for a day) from shops near the bus station. There are cycle and autorickshaws – all the way to Mamallapuram for Rs 500.

VELLORE

☎ 0416 • pop 330,200

Vellore, 145km west of Chennai, is a dusty, bazaar town, noteworthy for the Vijayanagar Fort and temple, which are in an excellent state of preservation. Vellore is also famed for its CMC Hospital – a leader in research and health care. The people who come here from all over India for medical care give this unassuming town a cosmopolitan feel.

The post office is off Minny St; money can be exchanged at State Bank of India.

Vellore Fort

Vellore Fort was built in the 16th century and passed briefly into the hands of the Marathas in 1676. The British occupied the fort in 1760 following the fall of Srirangapatnam and the death of Tipu Sultan. Open 7 am to 7 pm daily, it now houses various public and private offices.

The small **museum** (closed Friday), inside the fort complex, contains sculptures dating back to Pallava and Chola times.

Jalakanteshwara Temple

This temple, a gem of late Vijayanagar architecture, was built about 1550. During the invasions by the Adil Shahis of Bijapur, the Marathas and the Carnatic nawabs, the temple was occupied by a garrison and temple rituals ceased. However, it has reopened and is now a popular place of worship.

Within the temple, its pillared mandapam, famed for its sculptures of yali and other mythical creatures, is considered a masterpiece of its time. Large statues of Ganesh grace the entrance and mandapam. The temple is open 6 am to 1 pm and 3 to 8 pm daily.

Places to Stay

Vellore's cheap hotels are concentrated along the roads south of and parallel to the hospital.

Srinivasa Lodge *(☎ 26389, 14 Beri Bakkali St)* is a clean place run by friendly people. Rooms with hot water in the morning start at Rs 120/150 for a single/double.

VDM Lodge *(☎ 24008, 13 Beri Bakkali St)* is a large place with ordinary rooms at Rs 100/150 and deluxe rooms with TV at Rs 250/300. There's morning hot water.

Nagha International Lodge *(☎ 26731, 13 KVS Chetty St)* is a large, modern hotel with rooms from Rs 150/200 to 550 for an air-con double.

Hotel River View *(☎ 25251, Katpadi Rd)* is 1km north of the town centre. It's modern and clean, but where's the view? Rooms cost Rs 370/420, or Rs 550/650 with air-con; there are three restaurants, a bar and a garden.

Hotel Prince Manor *(☎ 27726, Katpadi Rd)* is an upmarket hotel with double rooms starting at Rs 650, or Rs 950 with air-con. There are three restaurants – veg, nonveg and a roof garden.

More hotels to suit a range of budgets are on Filterbed Rd in the south of town.

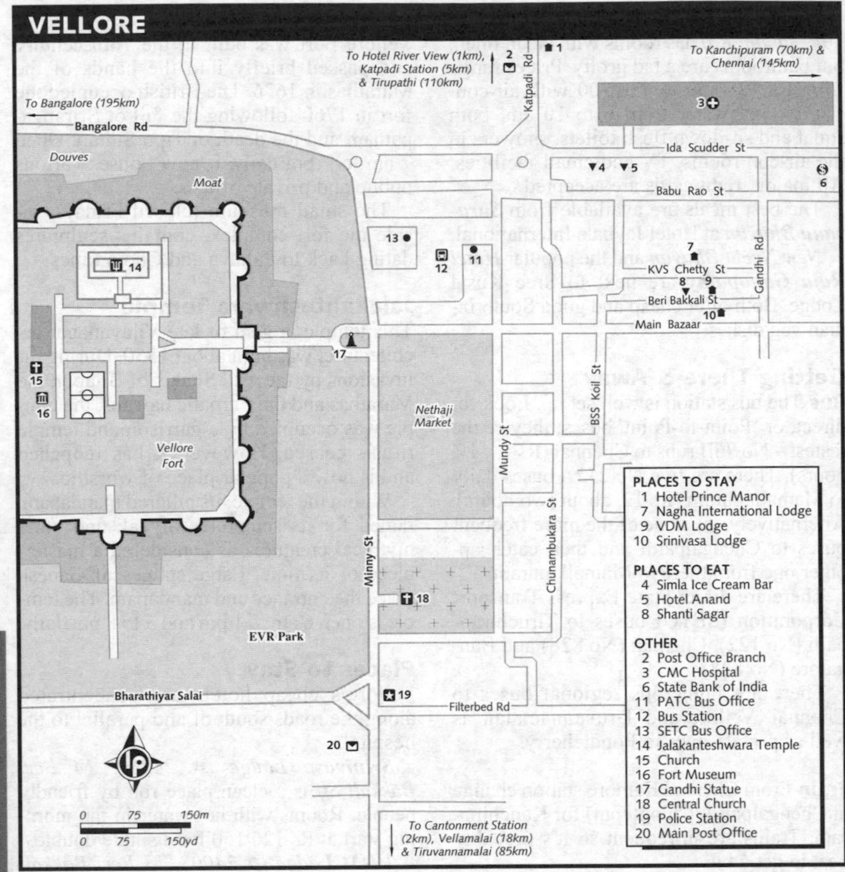

TAMIL NADU

Places to Eat

Simla Ice Cream Bar *(Ida Scudder St)* is not an ice-cream bar but an excellent North Indian vegetarian cafe.

Shanti Sagar *(Beri Bakkali St)*, next door to VDM Lodge, is a buzzing veg restaurant with an attractive open-air courtyard. ***Hotel Anand*** *(Ida Scudder St)* is an upmarket veg restaurant with an air-con room.

River Room, one of three restaurants at Hotel River View, has fish and chips for Rs 70 and pepper steak for Rs 80.

Getting There & Away

Bus SETC bus Nos 139 and 280 run to Chennai (Rs 33), No 104 to Tiruchirappalli (Rs 58) and Nos 168, 866 and 983 to Madurai (Rs 72). All these buses originate in Vellore and can be booked in advance at the offices by the bus stations. Others, which pass through en route from Chennai and Bangalore (and may be full), go to Bangalore, Tirupathi (2½ hours), Thanjavur and Ooty. There are 30 buses a day to Kanchipuram (Rs 12, 2½ hours) from 5 am.

Buses wait outside Katpadi train station and the journey into Vellore (Rs 2) takes anything from 15 to 30 minutes. Autorickshaws charge Rs 60.

Train Vellore's main train station is 5km north at Katpadi. The 228km trip from Katpadi to Bangalore (4½ hours) costs Rs 321/95 in 1st/2nd class. To Chennai (two hours, 130km) it's Rs 205/39. For Tirupathi (three hours) it's either a 2.20 am departure, or you could take the 10.30 pm train that gets you there at 2 am.

TIRUVANNAMALAI

☎ 04175 • pop 100,000

The small town of Tiruvannamalai, 85km south of Vellore, sits at the base of Arunachala Hill. This is an important Shaivite town, where Shiva is revered as Arunachaleswar, an aspect of fire. The site is becoming very popular and each full moon it swells with thousands of pilgrims who circumnavigate the base of the mountain.

The **Arunachaleswar Temple** itself covers some 10 hectares and is one of the largest in India. It dates from the 11th century, but much of the structure is actually from the 17th to 19th centuries. It has four large gopurams, one at each cardinal point, with the eastern one rising to 66m. It's open 6 am to 1 pm and 5.30 to 10 pm. The small **Sri Ramanasramam Ashram**, 2km south-west of Tiruvannamalai, draws devotees of Sri Ramana Maharishi, a guru who died in 1950 after nearly 50 years in contemplation. Day visits are permitted and *devotees only* may stay by applying in writing at least three months in advance to the President, Sri Ramanasramam, PO Tiruvannamalai. Office hours (☎/fax 22491) are 8 to 11 am and 2 to 5 pm .

The main post office is just off the road to Gingee and Internet is available almost next to State Bank of India at Shree Super Shop, 81B Krishnan St.

The Lingam of Fire

Legend has it that Shiva appeared as a column of fire on Arunachala Hill in Tiruvannamalai, creating the original symbol of the lingam. Each November/December full moon, the Karthikai Deepam Festival, one of India's oldest festivals, celebrates this legend throughout India but the festival is particularly significant at Tiruvannamalai. Here, a huge fire, lit from a 30m wick immersed in 2000L of ghee, blazes from the top of Arunachala Hill for days. In homes it is lamps that honour Shiva and his fiery lingam. The fire symbolises Shiva's light, which eradicates darkness and evil.

At festival time up to half a million people come to Tiruvannamalai. In honour of Shiva, they scale the mountain or circumnavigate its base (14km). On the upward path steps quickly give way to jagged and unstable rocks. There's no shade and the sun is relentless. And the journey must be undertaken in bare feet – a mark of respect to the deity. None of this deters the thousands of pilgrims who quietly and joyfully make their way to the top and the abode of their deity.

Places to Stay & Eat

There are several lodges near the temple. At festival time (November/December) prices can rise by an astronomical 1000% and you'll need to haggle hard to get a reduction.

Swathi Lodge *(☎ 26426, 27 Othavadai St)* has singles/doubles for Rs 100/150; Rs 350 for air-con. There are both squat and sit-down flush toilets and bucket hot water anytime. More-expensive rooms have a phone and TV.

Trishul Hotel *(☎ 22219, 6 Kanakaraya Mudali St)*, 500m east of the temple, has comfortable rooms for Rs 450/495, or Rs 650/700 with air-con. The staff are particularly accommodating and there's an OK veg restaurant.

Hotel Ramakrishna *(☎ 25004, fax 25008, 34F Polur Rd)* is a few kilometres out of town and the best place for accommodation and food. Double rooms are Rs 195 to 475 (air-con, TV and phone). Hot water is available from 4 to 11 am, there's an email facility and free pick-up from the train and bus stations.

Getting There & Away

The daily *Tirupati-Trichy Express* (No 6801) passes through Tiruvannamalai, southbound at 9.13 pm and northbound at 11 pm. Buses leave for Chennai every 15 minutes (Rs 49, express buses every hour). Regular buses also go to Pondicherry and all major centres.

GINGEE (SENJI)

The fort at Gingee (pronounced shingee) is 37km east of Tiruvannamalai. Constructed mainly in the 16th century by the Vijayanagars (though some structures date from the 13th century), the fort has been occupied by various armies, including the forces of Adil Shah from Bijapur and the Marathas, who assumed control from 1677. In 1698 the Mughals took over. Then came the French, who remained until the British defeated them at Pondicherry.

Nowadays the fort is delightfully free of human activity except for picnickers or workers undertaking renovations. A walk around can take an entire day. Buildings within the fort include a granary, a Shiva temple, a mosque and the most prominent – the recently restored audience hall. Open 9 am to 5 pm, the fort siren at 4.45 pm warns stragglers the gates are about to be locked. Entry is Rs 2/250 for Indians/foreigners.

Devi Lodge *(☎ 04145-22210)* is on the main road, 1.5km east of town. It's a cheerful place with basic rooms (some with a fort view) for Rs 60/80. ***ANA Hotel*** *(☎ 04145-22699, 191 Tiruvannamalai NH Rd)* is a more upmarket place where standard rooms are Rs 215/410 and those with air-con, TV and phone are Rs 260/495. There's a great restaurant here.

Buses leave almost every hour from Tiruvannamalai. Ask to be let off at 'the fort'; it's 2km before Gingee. Day trips from Pondicherry are also possible.

PONDICHERRY

☎ 0413 • pop 789,416

Pondicherry, the former French colony settled in the early 18th century, is a charming coastal town with a few enduring pockets of French culture, and an ashram. Together with the other former French enclaves of Karaikal (also in Tamil Nadu), Mahé (Kerala) and Yanam (Andhra Pradesh), it now forms the Union Territory of Pondicherry.

The French relinquished control of 'Pondy' some 50 years ago, but reminders of the colonial days remain; the Tricolour flutters over the grand French consulate, there's a *hôtel de ville* (town hall), and red *kepis* (caps) and belts are worn by the local police.

Hotels are excellent value since Tamil Nadu's punitive taxes do not apply here. Beer is only Rs 40.

You may come here to see the Sri Aurobindo Ashram, to experience Indian/French culture or to check up on ancestry; whatever, you'll probably stay longer than you'd intended.

Orientation & Information

Navigating the town is easy, but there are some eccentricities with street names. Many have one name at one end and another at the other end. See the Renamed Streets table.

Renamed Streets

street name	alternative name
Mission St	Cathedral St
Ambour Salai	HM Kasim St
AH Madam St	Kosakadai St
Beach Rd	Goubert Ave
La Bahabhur St	Bussy St
Gingee Salai	NC Bose St

The booklet *Experience! Pondicherry* (Rs 20 from any bookshop) will give you the current lowdown on events and attractions, and the net proceeds go to charity.

Tourist Offices The Pondy tourist office (☎ 339497), on Goubert Ave (Beach Rd), is open 8.45 am to 5 pm daily. The office runs half-day sightseeing tours (Rs 52.50) that take you to the museum, boat house, Auroville and the ashram. Day tours (Rs 63) run if there are sufficient numbers (more than six). Tours leave from the tourist office at 9.30 am (full day) and 2 pm (half day).

Money Many visitors find Andhra Bank in Mission St to be most convenient for changing money. There's also Sterling Holiday Financial Services Ltd (☎ 346390) at 29 St Louis St, open 9.30 am to 5 pm weekdays and 9.30 am to 1.30 pm Saturday.

Post & Communications The main post office, on Rangapillai St, is open 10 am to 7.30 pm Monday to Saturday. There are numerous STD/ISD/fax booths and email is available at Raji Internet Corner, 143A MG Rd. On Nehru St there's Net Info Kiosk and also Info-Graphics.

Bookshops Higginbothams and Focus Books are both in town.

Libraries The library in Rangapillai St is open between 8.30 am to 8.30 pm (closed Monday).

Cultural Centres Alliance Française (☎ 338146), 38 Suffren St, runs French, English and Tamil classes and has a library and computer centre. Its small monthly newsletter, *Le Petit Journal*, details forthcoming events. The library (☎ 334351) is

TAMIL NADU

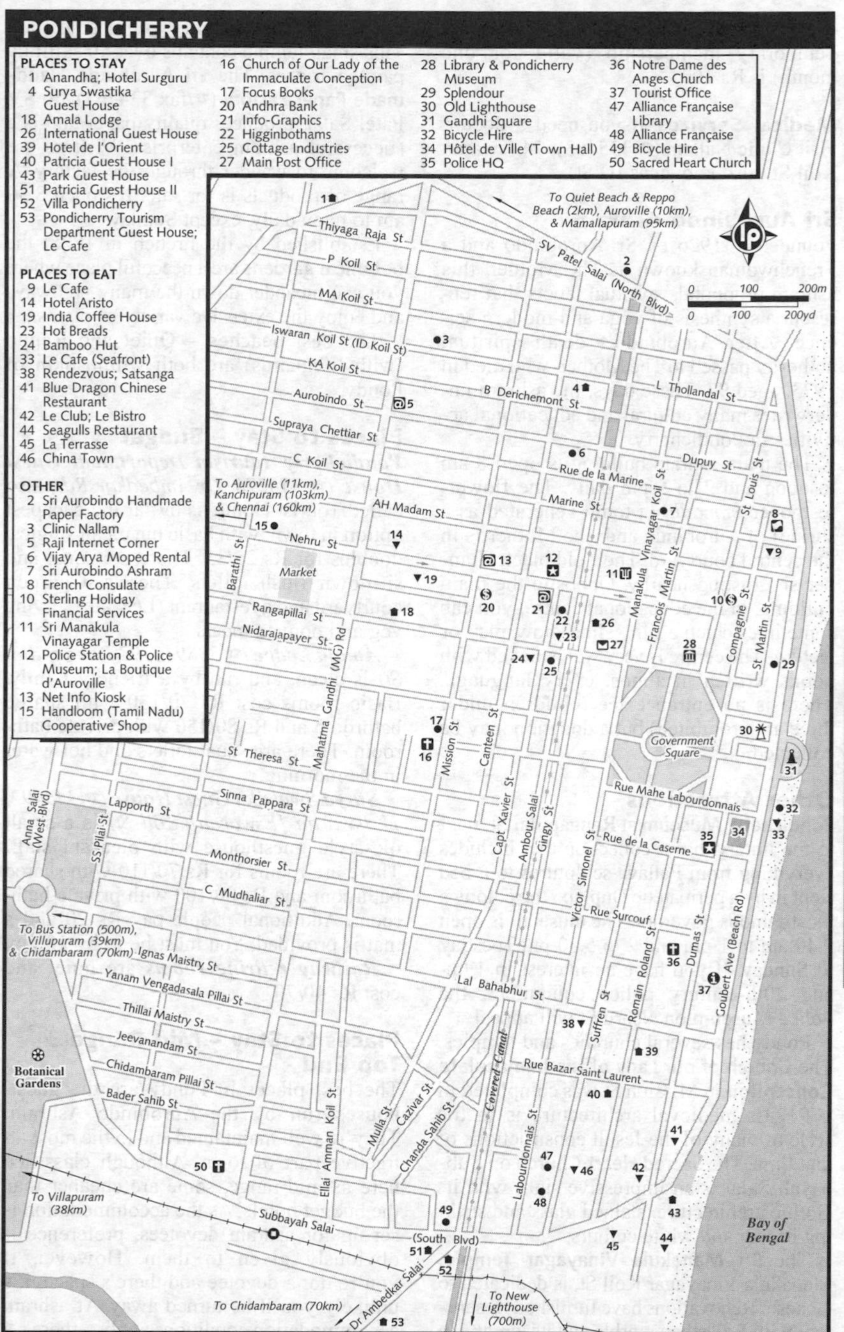
PONDICHERRY
PLACES TO STAY
1 Anandha; Hotel Surguru
4 Surya Swastika Guest House
18 Amala Lodge
26 International Guest House
39 Hotel de l'Orient
40 Patricia Guest House I
43 Park Guest House
51 Patricia Guest House II
52 Villa Pondicherry
53 Pondicherry Tourism Department Guest House; Le Cafe
PLACES TO EAT
9 Le Cafe
14 Hotel Aristo
19 India Coffee House
23 Hot Breads
24 Bamboo Hut
33 Le Cafe (Seafront)
38 Rendezvous; Satsanga
41 Blue Dragon Chinese Restaurant
42 Le Club; Le Bistro
44 Seagulls Restaurant
45 La Terrasse
46 China Town
OTHER
2 Sri Aurobindo Handmade Paper Factory
3 Clinic Nallam
5 Raji Internet Corner
6 Vijay Arya Moped Rental
7 Sri Aurobindo Ashram
8 French Consulate
10 Sterling Holiday Financial Services
11 Sri Manakula Vinayagar Temple
12 Police Station & Police Museum; La Boutique d'Auroville
13 Net Info Kiosk
15 Handloom (Tamil Nadu) Cooperative Shop
16 Church of Our Lady of the Immaculate Conception
17 Focus Books
20 Andhra Bank
21 Info-Graphics
22 Higginbothams
25 Cottage Industries
27 Main Post Office
28 Library & Pondicherry Museum
29 Splendour
30 Old Lighthouse
31 Gandhi Square
32 Bicycle Hire
34 Hôtel de Ville (Town Hall)
35 Police HQ
36 Notre Dame des Anges Church
37 Tourist Office
47 Alliance Française Library
48 Alliance Française
49 Bicycle Hire
50 Sacred Heart Church
To Quiet Beach & Reppo Beach (2km), Auroville (10km), & Mamallapuram (95km)
0 100 200m
0 100 200yd
Thiyaga Raja St
P Koil St
MA Koil St
SV Patel Salai (North Blvd)
Iswaran Koil St (ID Koil St)
KA Koil St
Aurobindo St
B Derichemont St
L Thollandal St
Supraya Chettiar St
C Koil St
Dupuy St
Rue de la Marine
Marine St
St Louis St
To Auroville (11km), Kanchipuram (103km) & Chennai (160km)
AH Madam St
Nehru St
Market
Barathi St
Manakula Vinayagar Koil St
Francois Martin St
Rangapillai St
Nidarajapayer St
Compagnie St
St Martin St
Mahatma Gandhi (MG) Rd
Mission St
Canteen St
Government Square
St Theresa St
Sinna Pappara St
Lapporth St
Anna Salai (West Blvd)
SS Pilai St
Capt Xavier St
Ambour Salai
Gingy St
Rue Mahe Labourdonnais
Rue de la Caserne
Monthorsier St
C Mudhaliar St
Victor Simonel St
Rue Surcouf
Dumas St
To Bus Station (500m), Villupuram (39km) & Chidambaram (70km)
Ignas Maistry St
Yanam Vengadasala Pillai St
Romain Roland St
Lal Bahabhur St
Thillai Maistry St
Suffren St
Goubert Ave (Beach Rd)
Jeevanandam St
Botanical Gardens
Chidambaram Pillai St
Rue Bazar Saint Laurent
Bader Sahib St
Cazivar St
Mulla St
Chanda Sahib St
Covered Canal
Labourdonnais St
Ellai Amman Koil St
To Villapuram (38km)
Subbayah Salai
(South Blvd)
Bay of Bengal
Dr Ambedkar Salai
To Chidambaram (70km)
To New Lighthouse (700m)

TAMIL NADU

open 9 am to noon and 4 to 7 pm daily. Temporary membership (valid for one month) is Rs 100.

Medical Services If you need a doctor, visit Clinic Nallam (☎ 335463), 74 Iswaran Koil St (also known as ID St).

Sri Aurobindo Ashram

Founded in 1926 by Sri Aurobindo and a Frenchwoman known as The Mother, this ashram propounds spiritual tenets that represent a synthesis of yoga and modern science. After Aurobindo's death spiritual authority passed to The Mother, who died in 1973, aged 97. These days, the ashram underwrites many cultural and educational activities in Pondicherry.

The main ashram building is open 8 am to noon and 2 to 6 pm daily. The flower-festooned *samadhi* (a tomb venerated as a shrine) of Aurobindo and The Mother is in the central courtyard. Their old black Humber sits rusting nearby. Opposite the main building, in the educational centre, you can sometimes catch a film, slide show, play or lecture. The centre is very well stocked with books written in almost every language. There is no entrance fee (children under three are prohibited) but a donation may be collected.

Other Attractions

Pondicherry Museum at Rangapillai St, next to the library, has a collection that includes everything from Pallava sculptures to a bed slept in by a peripatetic Dupleix, the colony's most famous governor. The museum is open 9.40 am to 1 pm and 2 to 5.30 pm Tuesday to Sunday. If you have an interest in 19th- and 20th-century police equipment, the **Police Museum** on Nehru St will appeal.

Pondy has several churches and temples. The **Church of our Lady of the Immaculate Conception** in Mission St was completed in 1791. Its medieval architecture is in the style of many of the Jesuit constructions of that time. The **Sacred Heart Church** on Subbayah Salai is an impressive sight with its Gothic architecture, stained glass and striking brown and white colours.

The **Sri Manakula Vinayagar Temple**, Manakula Vinayagar Koil St, is dedicated to Ganesh. Renovations have furnished its sanctum with Rajasthan marble and its *vimana* (a tower over the sanctum) with a gold roof. This small temple contains over 40 skilfully painted friezes. The **Sri Aurobindo Handmade Paper Factory** (☎/fax 334763), 50 SV Patel Salai, produces quality paper and is a successful ashram enterprise. Visitors are welcome to wander through the factory. A range of products is for sale. It's open 8.30 am to noon daily, except Sunday.

Established by the French in 1826, the **botanical gardens** are a peaceful place where you can meander down the many pathways and enjoy the extensive variety of plants.

The best **beaches** – Quiet and Reppo (with lifeguards) are both within 6km of Pondy.

Places to Stay – Budget

Pondicherry Tourism Department Guest House *(☎ 358276, Dr Ambedkar Rd)*, also called Tourist Home, is by far the cheapest option in town, with basic but clean singles/doubles for Rs 25/35. There are squat and sit-down flush toilets. There's a garden courtyard and a restaurant (Le Cafe) serving veg and nonveg meals.

Amala Lodge *(☎ 338910, 92 Rangapillai St)* is clean, and run by a friendly family. Basic rooms cost Rs 70/130 with shared bathroom and Rs 80/150 with private bathroom. There are squat toilets and hot water in the morning.

Surya Swastika Guest House *(☎ 343092, 11 Iswaran [Eswaran] Koil St)* is a small old-style guesthouse with pleasant staff. There are rooms for Rs 70/110 with shared bathroom and Rs 80/100 with private bathroom. Additional people pay Rs 20 and a mat is provided. You must be in by 10 pm.

Railway retiring rooms are quiet and cost Rs 40/70.

Places to Stay – Mid-Range & Top End

The best places in Pondy are the guesthouses run by the Aurobindo Ashram. They're well maintained and in the most attractive part of town. Although classified here as mid-range, some are cheaper than the budget hotels. As the accommodation is set up for ashram devotees, preference is obviously given to them. However, if you're not a devotee and there's space, it's unlikely you'll be turned away. At ashram accommodation conditions apply – there's a

10.30 pm curfew, and smoking and alcohol are banned. ***Park Guest House*** *(☎ 334412, Goubert Ave)* has the best facilities and position; all front rooms face the sea and have a balcony. Doubles (concessions for singles) range from Rs 300 to 400. There's a veg restaurant. ***International Guest House*** *(☎ 336699, Gingy St)*, also run by the ashram, has single/double rooms from Rs 80/110 in the old wing. Doubles in the new wing cost Rs 200, or Rs 400 with air-con, and hot water on request.

The following places are not operated by the ashram. ***Hotel Surguru*** *(☎ 339022, fax 334377, 104 SV Patel Salai)* is deservedly popular. Bright, clean rooms, with both squat/sit-down flush toilets, range from Rs 410/540 and Rs 620/780 for nonair-con/air-con, Star TV and phone. The rear rooms are less noisy. The hotel has a good veg restaurant and MasterCard and Visa are accepted.

Patricia Guest House I at Romain Rolland St and ***Patricia Guest House II*** on Dr Ambedkar Salai are two delightful colonial places with a range of rooms (with shared and private bathrooms), facilities and prices ranging from Rs 400 to 1600. Private verandas and garden courtyards add to the character. Bookings for both places may be made at ☎ 335130, fax 332776.

Villa Pondicherry *(☎ 334677, fax 334230, 23 Dr Ambedkar Salai)* is another charming colonial residence. Rooms with shared bathroom start at Rs 525; those with air-con are Rs 850.

Anandha *(☎ 330711, fax 331241, SV Patel Salai)*, the top hotel in town, is a flashy neoclassical place with all luxuries. Air-con rooms are Rs 1300/1650, there's a bar, good nonveg and veg restaurants and an efficient travel desk. Major cards are accepted.

Hotel de l'Orient *(☎ 343067, fax 227829, e orient1804@satyam.net.in)* is a grand French colonial building, tastefully renovated and furnished. There are 10 rooms, individually designed. Four-poster beds, comfortable old-style furniture, Jaipur *dhurries* (rugs) and fine etchings decorate each room. There's a garden courtyard and prices range from Rs 1000/1500 to 2000/2500 (singles/doubles).

Places to Eat

Pondicherry has good places to eat, some open air, and most serve cheap beer. One of the cheapest places is the ***ashram***. For an advance-purchase meal ticket (Rs 15) you can have lunch or dinner in peaceful, mandatory silence.

The Hotel Aristo *(Nehru St)* has a popular rooftop restaurant with most main dishes ranging from Rs 40 to 55. ***India Coffee House*** *(Nehru St)* is good value for breakfast and snacks.

Bamboo Hut *(3 Rangapillai St)* serves well-priced Chinese dishes from its rooftop garden.

Le Cafe *(Marine St)*, a snack bar opposite the French consulate (not to be confused with the seafront Le Cafe or Le Cafe at Pondicherry Tourism Development Guest House) offers good tea and samosas.

Le Cafe *(Goubert Ave)*, is a crumbly old place, popular for popcorn and ice creams.

Seagulls Restaurant *(19 Dumas St)* is beside the sea and serves good multicuisine food, but most things on the menu are unavailable. Alcohol is available (Rs 30 for beer; Rs 150 for cocktails).

Blue Dragon Chinese Restaurant *(33 Dumas St)* serves good food as does ***China Town*** *(Suffren St)*. ***La Terrasse*** *(5 Subbayah Salai)*, open air and multicuisine, is most popular for its pizzas. It's open 8.30 am to 10 pm daily, except Wednesday.

Rendezvous *(30 Suffren St)* with decor which is straight out of rural France, including wicker chairs and gingham tablecloths, has *bouillabaisse* (seafood soup; Rs 70), grilled prawns (Rs 170) and tandoori food. Open from 8 to 11 am, noon to 3 pm and 6 to 10.30 pm, you can have your meals on the attractive roof terrace.

Hot Breads *(Ambour Salai)*, near Higginbothams, has coffee, cakes and baguettes.

Satsanga *(Suffren St)* is French run and the food is as good as it sounds – *soupe de poisson* (fish soup; Rs 55) and *terrine de lapin* (rabbit casserole; Rs 60). The coffee is superb, as is the crème caramel, and you can sit in the garden.

Le Club *(33 Dumas St)*, in a rambling old mansion, just isn't what it used to be. It has great atmosphere, wonderful service and very disappointing food. Expect to pay Rs 160 for the mains which are supposedly French, and Rs 60 for dessert. It's not worth it. ***Le Bistro***, which is situated in the garden, serves Vietnamese food and is much better value for money.

Shopping

Fine handmade paper is sold from the Sri Aurobindo factory and jewellery, batiks, *kalamkari* (similar to batik) drawings, carpets and woodcarvings may be purchased from La Boutique d'Auroville on Nehru St. Also on Nehru St is the Handloom (Tamil Nadu) Cooperative shop. Cottage Industries on Rangapillai St has a range of crafts while Splendour, at 16 Goubert Ave (closed Wednesday), has distinctive postcards.

Getting There & Away

Bus The bus station is 500m west of town.

destination	daily departures
Bangalore	6
Chennai	80
Chidambaram	50
Coimbatore	4
Kanchipuram	5
Karaikal	10
Kumbakonam	5
Mamallapuram	5
Nagapattinam	3
Tiruchirappalli	4
Tirupathi	2
Tiruvannamalai	9
Vellore	7

Train There are four passenger trains to Villupuram daily (Rs 9, one hour), from where you can connect to other services. They depart Pondicherry at 5 and 7.45 am and 4.05 and 5.20 pm. From Villupuram it's 6.10 and 11.45 am and 3.45 (not Sunday) and 10.20 pm (not Sunday) but these times tend to fluctuate so it's best to check. The computerised booking service at the station covers all of the trains on the southern railway.

Taxi Taxis between Pondicherry and Chennai cost Rs 1100 and to Chennai airport it's Rs 1000.

Getting Around

One of the best ways to get around is by walking. Large three-wheelers shuttle between the bus station and Gingy St for Rs 5, but they're so overcrowded you might not want to use them. Cycle and autorickshaws are plentiful. Although official fares for autorickshaws (Rs 7 flagfall and Rs 3.5 per km) are posted near the main stands, you'll have to haggle hard to get something resembling these prices.

The most popular transport is bicycle – a good idea if you're going to Auroville. Bicycle hire shops line many of the streets, especially MG Rd and Mission St. You'll also find hire shops in Subbayah Salai and Goubert Ave and usual rental is Rs 5 per hour, or Rs 20 per day, but some places ask Rs 70.

Mopeds can be rented from Vijay Arya (☎ 336179), 9 Aurobindo St, near the corner with Ambour Salai, for Rs 120 per day. You need to leave some ID (passport or driving licence) and a Rs 500 deposit.

AUROVILLE

☎ 0413

Just over the border from Pondicherry in Tamil Nadu is the community of Auroville, whose international residents aim to develop a harmonious environment through the implementation of socially useful projects.

Auroville is the brainchild of The Mother, 'an experiment in international living where people could live in peace and progressive harmony above all creeds, politics and nationalities'. Designed by French architect Roger Anger, its opening ceremony on 28 February 1968 was attended by the president of India and representatives of 121 countries, who poured the soil of their lands into an urn to symbolise universal oneness.

The project has 80 settlements spread over 20km, and about 1500 residents (two-thirds of whom are foreigners). The settlements include: Forecomers, involved in alternative technology and agriculture; Aurelec, devoted to computer research; Fertile, Nine Palms and Meadow, all engaged in tree planting and agriculture; Fraternity, a handicrafts community working in cooperation with Tamil villagers; and Aspiration, an educational, health care and village industry project.

The project is not a tourist attraction, but as long as certain customs are observed, day-trippers are welcome to call in to the visitor's centre and visit the meditation centre. Prior arrangements must be made if you wish to venture further.

Information

In Pondicherry, La Boutique d'Auroville (☎ 337264) on Nehru St has information on the community and if you want to stay it's very important to drop by here to organise

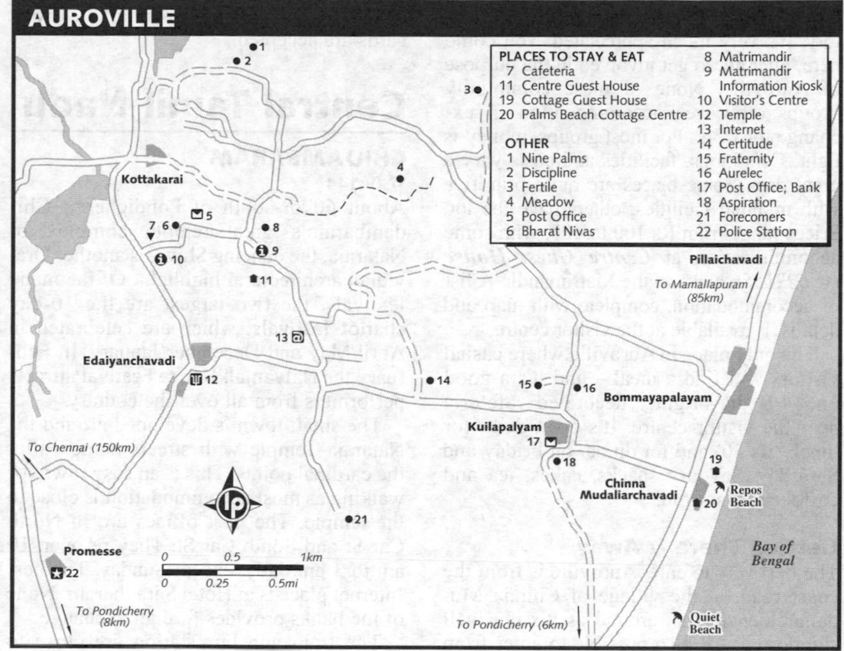

accommodation before you head out. At Auroville itself, there is a visitor centre (☎ 622373) near Bharat Nivas. This centre has a permanent exhibition of the community's activities and the helpful staff will address any queries. It's open 9.30 am to 5.30 pm daily. Next door is an Auroville handicrafts shop (closed Sundays) and a cafeteria.

The Auroville Handbook, available at the visitor centre, has a complete rundown on the community, its history and projects. You can also check out the excellent Auroville Web site at www.auroville.org.

Matrimandir

The Matrimandir was designed to be the spiritual and physical centre of Auroville. The meditation chamber and the main structure are now finished with total completion expected soon.

The meditation chamber is lined with white marble and houses a solid crystal (reputedly the largest in the world) 70cm in diameter. Rays from the sun are beamed into this crystal from a tracking mirror located in the roof. On cloudy days, solar lamps do the job. You can wander around the gardens between 9.30 am and 3.30 pm. Only between 4 and 4.45 pm are visitors allowed inside the Matrimandir, but you need to get a pass (free) from the information kiosk between 3.30 and 4.30 pm and once on your way you must observe total silence. The Matrimandir is closed on rainy days and photography is prohibited.

Places to Stay & Eat

Palms Beach Cottage Centre is at Chinna Mudaliarchavadi, on the way to Auroville from Pondy. Clean toilets and showers are shared, and there's an open-air gazebo for eating and relaxing in. Meals are around Rs 50. Singles/doubles cost Rs 90/160.

Cottage Guest House, a little further on, down the lane on the right opposite the turn-off to Auroville, offers basic rooms in a thatched-roof, semiconcrete block for Rs 70/140 with shared bathroom. Doubles with private bathroom in the new block are Rs 200. There's a communal dining area.

People with a serious interest in the aims of Auroville can stay with any one of the 40 community groups here. A stay – no shorter than a week and, if possible, no longer –

is preferred and although work isn't obligatory, it's very much appreciated. You come here, after all, to get involved in the purpose of Auroville. None of these community groups offer free accommodation in exchange for work. For most groups, money is tight. Conditions, facilities and costs vary a great deal. Some places are quite primitive with minimal facilities; others have the lot. Prices range from Rs 100 to 400, with some accommodation at ***Centre Guest House*** *(☎ 622155)*, close to the Matrimandir. A list of accommodation, complete with map and details, is available at the visitor centre.

The only place in Auroville where casual visitors will find a meal – and it's a good one – is the brightly decorated cafeteria near the visitor centre. It's open daily for lunch (Rs 30) and for dinner on Friday and Saturday. Savoury snacks, cakes, tea and coffee are also sold.

Getting There & Away

The best way to enter Auroville is from the coast road, at the village of Chinna Mudaliarchavadi. Ask around as it's not well signposted. It's also possible to enter from the main Pondicherry to Chennai road near Promesse. The turn-off, 1km after the police station, is signposted.

YERCAUD

☎ 04281

This hill station (altitude 1500m) is 33km uphill from Salem. Surrounded by coffee plantations in the Servaroyan hills, it's a good place for relaxing, walking, or boating on the town's artificial lake.

Places to Stay

If you prefer solitude, stay away from the lake, which is continually blasted by raucous music. ***Hotel Tamil Nadu*** *(☎ 22273, Yercaud Ghat Rd)*, near the lake, is a friendly place with OK double rooms from Rs 350 to 500 (Rs 450 and Rs 650 in high season). Dorm beds cost Rs 75. There's a restaurant and bar, but in spite of nearby coffee plantations, it's instant coffee here. There's a playground as well as boating facilities.

Hotel Shevaroys *(☎ 22288, fax 22387, Hospital Rd)* has standard doubles/suites from Rs 475/1225 in low season and Rs 575/1475 in high season. It has two restaurants, offering Indian and Chinese food, a bar, fitness centre and supermarket. Credit cards are accepted.

Central Tamil Nadu

CHIDAMBARAM

☎ 04144

About 60km south of Pondicherry, Chidambaram's great temple complex of Nataraja, the dancing Shiva, is another Dravidian architectural highlight. Of the many festivals, the two largest are the 10-day **chariot festivals**, which are celebrated in April/May and December/January. In February the **Natyanjali Dance Festival** attracts performers from all over the country.

The small town is developed around the Nataraja Temple with streets named after the cardinal points. This is an easy town for walking as most accommodation is close to the temple. The post offices are in North Car St and South Car St. They're open 10 am to 3 pm daily, except Sunday. The best Internet place is at Hotel Saradharam. None of the banks provides foreign exchange.

The train and bus station are close to town. The tourist office (☎ 22739) is at the TTDC Hotel Tamil Nadu, and is open 9 am to 5 pm weekdays, but often there's no-one home. If you want to shop, the small Khadi Gramodyog Bhavan will enable you to make a few gift purchases.

There's a bicycle hire shop on South Car St (Rs 5 per hour). No deposit is required. Only bikes with bars are available.

Nataraja Temple

Chidambaram was a Chola capital from 907 to 1310 and the Nataraja Temple was erected during the later time of the administration. The 22-hectare complex has four gopurams with finely sculptured icons depicting Hindu myths. The temple is renowned for its prime examples of Chola artistry and has since been patronised by numerous dynasties.

The temple courtyard with its many shrines is open 4 am to noon and 4.30 to 9 pm daily. The daily *puja* (worship) is held about 5 pm. Although non-Hindus are not allowed into the inner sanctum, there are usually priests who will take you in for a fee. You may wish to support this magnificent building by way of donation, but don't be intimidated by priests who try to pressure you.

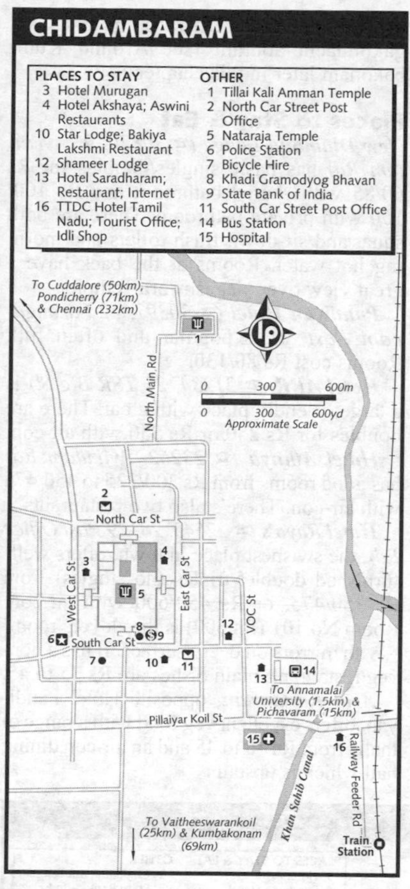

Pichavaram

About 15km east of Chidambaram, the seaside resort of Pichavaram, with its backwaters and mangroves, is the perfect place for leisurely boating. Here you can navigate the 4000 canals and 1700 islands – with a guide so you don't get lost. Until the Tourist Complex is restored there's nowhere to stay, so you'll need to make it a day trip only.

Places to Stay

Most of the current accommodation in Chidambaram is in lodges, which are well positioned away from the noise, with balconies and fine village views.

Railway retiring rooms are under repair with no completion date determined. ***Star Lodge*** *(☎ 22743, 101–102 South Car St)* has OK singles/doubles for Rs 60/80 (four-bed rooms Rs 150) all with squat toilets. It's friendly and there's a good restaurant.

Shameer Lodge *(☎ 22983, Venugopal Pillai St)* is good value at Rs 70/100/150 for rooms with clean sheets. ***Hotel Murugan*** *(☎ 20419, West Car St)* is similar. You receive a hearty welcome and train and bus schedules are listed. Basic rooms are Rs 70/150, and an air-con double is Rs 250. The dorm (good value for a family) with five beds costs Rs 250.

TTDC Hotel Tamil Nadu *(☎ 38056, fax 38061, Railway Feeder Rd)* has basic rooms at Rs 150/200, or Rs 460/900 for air-con. Some rooms have phone and TV or you can hire one for Rs 60. Dorm rooms are Rs 50 and there's a multicuisine restaurant and bar.

Hotel Akshaya *(☎ 20192, fax 22265, ⓔ akshayahotel@satyam.net.in, 17–18 East Car St)* has helpful staff, with rooms for Rs 175/199 and air-con rooms are Rs 480. There are both squat and sit-down flush toilets, a multicuisine restaurant, bar and gift shop.

Hotel Saradharam *(☎ 21336, fax 22656, ⓔ hsrcdm@vsnl.com, 19 VGP St)* is the best place in town. For Indians ordinary rooms with TV are Rs 300/450 and air-con rooms are Rs 500/575. For non-Indians it is 30% dearer. There are both squat and sit-down flush toilets, major credit cards are accepted and there's a functioning Internet cafe.

Places to Eat

Bakiya Lakshmi Restaurant (formerly Babu Restaurant), on the ground floor of Star Lodge, offers good veg meals.

TTDC Hotel Tamil Nadu has veg and nonveg restaurants plus a very pleasant rooftop bar (beer is Rs 75).

Hotel Saradharam is an excellent place to eat; the veg and nonveg restaurants are inexpensive, service is good, there's a bar and the beer's really cold! You need to get there early for lunch or dinner as it's very popular.

The Idli Shop, next to Hotel Tamil Nadu, serves idli-addicts from morning to evening.

The ***Aswini*** veg and nonveg restaurants at Hotel Akshaya offer good food (Rs 30 to 70 for mains, beer Rs 65) and there's a multicuisine rooftop restaurant.

Getting There & Away

The train station is a 20-minute walk southeast of the temple, or it costs Rs 25 to get there by cycle-rickshaw. Express and passenger trains leave for Chennai (six times daily), Kumbakonam, Thanjavur (twice daily), Tiruchirappalli and Madurai.

The bus station, used by both SETC and local buses, is more central. Bus No 157 (seven per day) is the quickest to Chennai. Services for Pondicherry every 30 minutes continue to Chennai (Nos 300, 324 and 326, Rs 42, seven hours). To Madurai take No 521 (Rs 64, eight hours).

KUMBAKONAM

☎ 0435

This busy, dusty commercial centre, nestled along the Cauvery River some 37km north-east of Thanjavur, is noted for its many temples with their colourful semi-erotic sculpture. **Sarangapani Temple** is the largest Vishnu temple in Kumbakonam, while **Kumbeshwara Temple** is the largest Shiva temple. **Nageshwara Temple**, also a Shiva temple, is dedicated to him in the guise of Nagaraja, the serpent king. Just 600m south-east of here is the palindromic **Mahamakham Tank**. Current belief is that every 12 years, the waters of the Ganges flow into the tank and at this time a festival is held. The next festival will be in early 2004. All the temples are closed between noon and 4.30 pm.

Kumbakonam also makes a good base from which to visit the very interesting nearby temples at Dharasuram and Gangakondacholapuram (see Around Kumbakonam later in this chapter).

Places to Stay & Eat

New Diamond Lodge *(☎ 30870, 93 Ayikulam Rd)* has basic singles/doubles for Rs 60/85 with shared bathroom and Rs 100/150 with private bathroom. There are both squat and sit-down flush toilets and morning hot water. Rooms at the back have a great view over Nageshwara Temple.

Pandiyan Hotel *(☎ 30397, 52 Sarangapani East St)* is popular and often full. Rooms cost Rs 80/130.

Hotel ARR *(☎ 21234, 21 TSR Big St)* is a large, friendly place with a bar. There are doubles for Rs 250 or Rs 550 with air-con.

Hotel Athitya *(☎ 23262, Ayikulam Rd)* has good rooms from Rs 300/325 to 450/475 with air-con. There's also two restaurants.

Hotel Raya's *(☎ 22545, 28–29 Post Office Rd)*, the swishest place in town, offers well-furnished doubles/triples (no singles) from Rs 350/475, or Rs 450/600 with air-con. Room No 101 (Rs 600) is the 'lovers room' – with mirrors on every surface. It has a non-veg restaurant; main dishes are Rs 35 to 45.

Arul Restaurant, opposite Hotel Pandiyan, offers excellent veg food with a range of thalis from Rs 10 to 45 and an air-con dining hall which is upstairs.

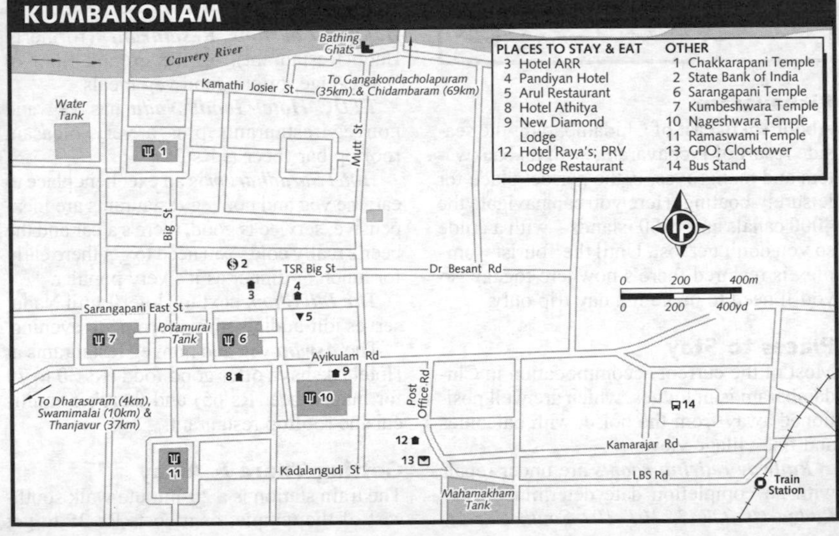

TAMIL NADU

PRV Lodge Restaurant, next to Hotel Raya's, has good veg food with meals from Rs 15 and Rs 20 for specials. Breads are very good.

Getting There & Away

The bus stand and train station are about 2km east of the town centre.

SETC has four buses a day to Chennai (No 303, Rs 60, seven hours) and there are frequent departures to Thanjavur via Dharasuram and to Gangakondacholapuram. Other buses pass through to Madurai, Coimbatore, Bangalore, Tiruvannamalai, Pondicherry and Chidambaram. Bus No 459 connects Kumbakonam with Karaikal. Four daily express trains go to Chennai via Chidambaram, four go to Madurai and three to Thanjavur and Tiruchirappalli.

AROUND KUMBAKONAM

Not far from Kumbakonam are two Chola temples, Dharasuram and Gangakondacholapuram. Both have been restored by the Archaeological Survey of India. They have knowledgeable guides to show you around. Few visitors go to these temples, so you can appreciate their beauty in peace.

Dharasuram

The small town of Dharasuram is 4km west of Kumbakonam. Its **Airatesvara Temple**, constructed by Raja Raja II (1146–63), is an absolutely superb example of 12th-century Chola architecture.

The temple is fronted by columns with unique miniature sculptures. In the 14th century, the row of large statues around the temple was replaced with brick and concrete statues similar to those found at the Thanjavur Temple. Many were removed to the art gallery in the raja's palace at Thanjavur, but have since been returned to Dharasuram. The remaining empty niches are awaiting their replacements. The remarkable sculptures depict, among other things, Shiva as Kankala-murti – the mendicant. Stories from the epics are also depicted.

At the main shrine, a huge decorated lingam stands, the natural light illuminating it from sunrise to sunset.

There's a English-speaking priest available (for a small fee) from 8 am to 8 pm daily. You can get to Dharasuram by bus (Rs 5) or train (Rs 5) on the Chennai to Thanjavur line.

Gangakondacholapuram

This temple, 35km north of Kumbakonam, was built by the Chola emperor Rajendra I (1012–44) in the style of (and with the same name as) the Brihadishwara Temple at Thanjavur, built by his father. Later additions were made in the 15th century by the Nayaks. The ornate tower is almost 55m high and is said to weigh 80 tonnes. Within the recesses of the temple walls stand many beautiful statues, including those of Ganesh, Nataraja and Harihara.

The temple has a knowledgeable guide and is open 6 am to noon and 4 to 8 pm daily.

Next to the temple there's a small **museum** (closed Friday), which exhibits the excavated remains of the palace that once existed nearby.

There are buses from Kumbakonam bus stand to the temple (Rs 10).

CAUVERY DELTA

Tranquebar (Tharangambadi)

About 80km south of Chidambaram, Tranquebar was a Danish post, established in 1620. The **Danesborg Fort** was occupied by the British in 1801. Now it houses a small but fascinating museum (closed Friday) reflecting aspects of Danish history here.

Velanganni (Vailankanni)

☎ 04365

Velanganni is the site of the Roman Catholic **Basilica of Our Lady of Good Health**. This impressive white neo-Gothic structure was elevated to the status of basilica in 1962 during the Pope's visit. The annual nine-day festival culminates on 8 September, the celebration of Mary's birth.

Hotel Picnic *(☎ 63510)*, located on the main road near the basilica, offers basic but clean double rooms for Rs 180, or Rs 260 with air-con.

The Retreat *(☎/fax 63534, 64 Nagapattinam Main Rd)* is the best hotel with clean rooms and friendly service. High-season doubles are Rs 550, or Rs 650 with air-con. Cottages are Rs 750, or Rs 900 with air-con.

Calimere Wildlife & Bird Sanctuary

Also known as Kodikkarai, this 333 sq km sanctuary is 90km south-east of Thanjavur. Noted for its vast flocks of migratory waterfowl, Calimere's tidal mud flats are home to

teals, shovellers, curlews, gulls, terns, plovers, sandpipers, shanks and herons from November to January. In February/March, koels, mynas and barbets come here for the wild berries.

The easiest way to get to Calimere is by bus (Rs 5, every hour) or taxi from Vedaranyam, 12km away and the nearest town linked by frequent buses to Nagapattinam or Thanjavur.

The sanctuary is open 6 am to 6 pm daily and entry is Rs 5. There's a ***Forest Department Resthouse*** *(☎ 72424)* offering basic accommodation at only Rs 20 per person per night. Officially, reservations must be made with the wildlife warden in Nagapattinam (☎ 22349), but many travellers just turn up and get a room.

THANJAVUR (TANJORE)

☎ 04362 • pop 217,000

Thanjavur was the ancient capital of the Chola kings whose origins (like those of the Pallavas, Pandyas and Cheras with whom they shared the tip of the Indian peninsula) go back to the beginning of the Christian era. Power struggles between these groups were continual, with one or other gaining the ascendancy at various times. The Cholas' turn for empire building came between AD 850 and 1270 and, at the height of their power, they controlled most of the Indian peninsula, including parts of Sri Lanka and, for a while, the Srivijaya kingdom of the Malay Peninsula and Sumatra.

Probably the greatest Chola emperors were Raja Raja (985–1014), who was responsible for building the Brihadishwara Temple (Thanjavur's main attraction), and his son Rajendra I (1014–44), whose navy competed with the Arabs for the Indian Ocean trade routes. The Cholas also constructed the temples at Thiruvaiyaru, Gangakondacholapuram and Dharasuram and contributed to the enormous temple complex at Srirangam near Tiruchirappalli – probably India's largest.

Thanjavur is famous also for its distinctive art style, which is usually a combination of raised and painted surfaces. Krishna is the most popular deity depicted, and in the Thanjavur school his skin is white, rather than the traditional blue-black. Set on a fertile delta, agriculture is important and makes Thanjavur a great place to be during Pongal (harvest) celebrations in January.

Orientation & Information

The main road, Gandhiji Rd (also known as Railway Station Rd), runs north-south and has most of the hotels and restaurants. The train and new bus station are in the south, the Brihadishwara Temple mid-west and the Royal Palace Museum in the north.

The Tamil Nadu Tourism Development Corporation tourist office (TNDC; ☎ 23017) in Jawans Bhavan is open 9 am to 4.45 pm weekdays. There's also a branch counter at the TTDC Hotel Tamil Nadu open daily. Here you'll get brochures and helpful information.

State Bank of India is the only bank that changes travellers cheques. The more expensive hotels do too, but rates are usually better at the bank. Canara Bank will pay you cash from a credit card, but by the time you get your money, inflation may have rendered it worthless.

The main post office, near the train station, is open 10 am to 4 pm daily (Sunday from noon). Internet and email is available at Netcafe Internet Zone (☎ 38148), Shop 30, Gandhiji Shopping Complex, Gandhi Rd, for Rs 40 per hour. Access is quick; so is time out.

The police (☎ 30451) are near the Royal Palace Museum.

Brihadishwara Temple & Fort

Built by Raja Raja in 1010, the Brihadishwara Temple is the crowning glory of Chola temple architecture. This superb and fascinating monument is one of only a handful in India with World Heritage listing and is worth a couple of visits.

The temple, set in spacious grounds, has several pillared halls and shrines and 250 linga enshrined along the outer walls. Inscriptions record the names of dancers, musicians and poets – a reminder of the significance of this area to the development of the arts. A huge Nandi, 6m long by 3m high, faces the inner sanctum. Created from a single piece of rock, it weighs 25 tonnes and is one of India's largest Nandi statues.

Constructed from a single piece of granite weighing an estimated 80 tonnes, the dome was hauled into place along a 4km earthwork ramp in a manner similar to that used for the Egyptian pyramids.

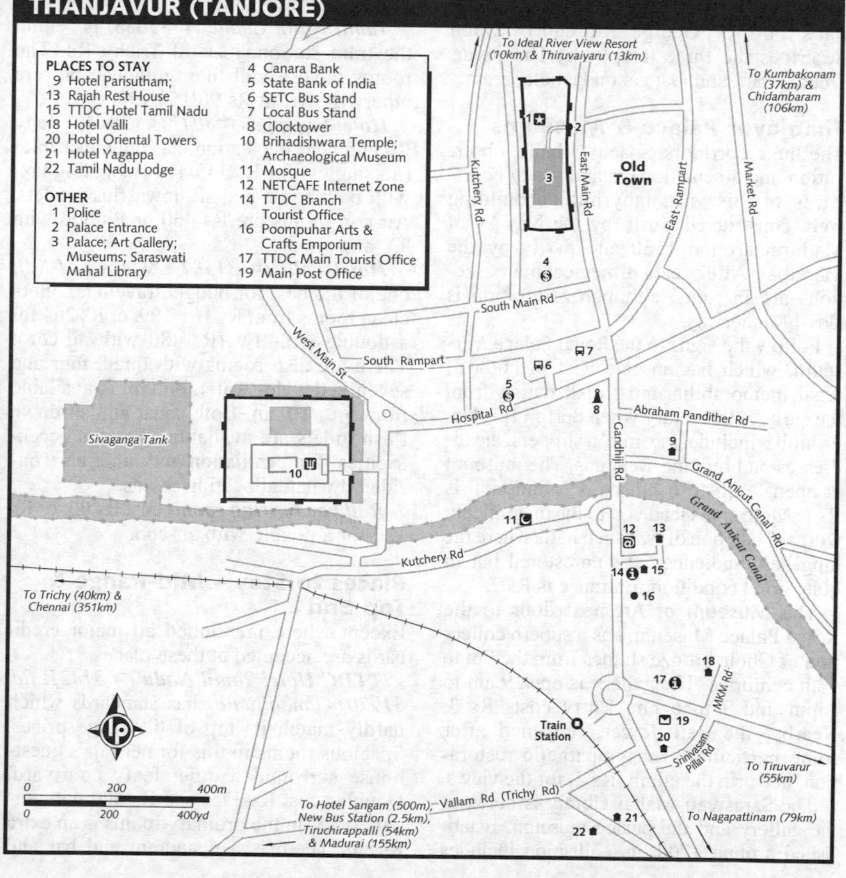

Unlike most South Indian temples where the gopurams are the highest towers, here it is the 13-storey tower above the sanctum at 66m that reaches further into the sky. Its impressive gilded top is the original. The sanctum contains a 4m-high lingam with a circumference of 7m.

The temple now comes under the jurisdiction of the Archaeological Survey but worship here has recommenced. It's open 6 am to 1 pm and 3 to 8 pm daily.

The **Archaeological Museum**, on the southern side of the courtyard, has some interesting sculptures and photographs that show the temple before restoration. Charts and maps detail the history of the Chola empire. Open 9.30 am to 1 pm and 3 to 7 pm daily, the museum sells an interesting booklet, *Chola Temples* by C Sivaramamurti for Rs 20 (it's also available at Chennai's Fort St George Museum), which describes the three temples at Thanjavur, Dharasuram and Gangakondacholapuram.

Thanjavur Palace & Museums

The huge corridors, spacious halls, observation and arsenal towers and shady courtyards of this vast, labyrinthine building were constructed partly by the Nayaks of Madurai around 1550 and partly by the Marathas. After years of neglect many sections are in ruins, although restoration is slowly underway.

Follow the signs to the **Royal Palace Museum**, which has an eclectic collection of regal memorabilia, most of it dating from the early 19th century when Serfoji II ruled. Exhibits include the raja's slippers, headdresses and hunting weapons. The museum is open 9 am to 6 pm daily; admission is Rs 1. More signs lead you to the magnificent **Durbar Hall**, one of two such halls where the king held audiences. It's unrestored but in quite good condition. Entrance is Rs 2.

The **Museum of Art** next door to the Royal Palace Museum, has a superb collection of Chola bronze statues from the 9th to 12th centuries. The gallery is open 9 am to 1 pm and 3 to 6 pm. Entry costs Rs 3. Nearby, the **Bell Tower**, reopened after some particularly unsympathetic restoration, is worth the climb (Rs 2) for the views.

The **Saraswati Mahal Library** is between the gallery and the palace museum. Established around 1700, its collection includes over 30,000 palm leaf and paper manuscripts in Indian and European languages. The library is closed to the public but you can visit the interesting **museum**, where exhibits range from the whole Ramayana written on palm leaf to explicit prints of prisoners under Chinese torture. Entry is free and it's open 10 am to 1 pm and 1.30 to 5.30 pm daily (except Wednesday and holidays).

Places to Stay – Budget

Rajah Rest House *(☎ 30515)*, down a quiet side street off Gandhiji Rd, is quite reasonable value and will be better value when maintenance is completed. The large, basic rooms, with bucket hot water, cost Rs 60 for single rooms with shared bathroom to 100/150/200 for singles/doubles/triples with private bathroom (both sit-down flush and squat toilets available).

Tamil Nadu Lodge *(☎ 31088)* is behind the train station, just off Trichy Rd. The rooms have a cell-like ambience but are otherwise OK at Rs 90/150/190.

Hotel Yagappa *(☎ 30421)*, just off Trichy Rd and near the station, has doubles/triples (no singles) for Rs 345/414 (including tax) with both squat and sit-down flush toilets. Air-con rooms are Rs 460 or Rs 600 with TV and phone.

Hotel Valli *(☎ 31584, 2948 MKM Rd)*, one of the best for budget travellers, offers clean rooms from Rs 165/199, or Rs 264 for a double with TV (Rs 480 with air-con). There are also rooms with three, four and seven beds. Hot water, on tap, is available from 5 to 10 am. Both squat and sit-down flush toilets are available. 'Foreign eccentricities' for ventilation and quiet are considered when allocating rooms.

Railway retiring rooms cost Rs 60, or Rs 120 for a double with air-con.

Places to Stay – Mid-Range & Top End

Except where mentioned all major credit cards are accepted at these places.

TTDC Hotel Tamil Nadu *(☎ 31421, fax 31970, Gandhiji Rd)* has standards which hardly match its top of the range prices. Spacious rooms in this former raja's guesthouse surround a quiet leafy courtyard. Doubles cost Rs 375, and Rs 600 with air-con. A TV in the ordinary rooms is an extra Rs 50. There is a restaurant and bar and

TAMIL NADU

cash only is accepted. A helpful branch of the tourist office is in the same grounds.

Hotel Parisutham *(☎ 31801, fax 30318, ⓔ hotel.parisutham@vsnl.com, 55 Grand Anicut Canal Rd)* retains its impeccable service and high standards. It has a large, pleasant swimming pool (which nonguests may use for US$15), manicured lawns, two restaurants and a bar. Single/double rooms, many with stocked fridges, are US$55/90 and US$120 for the 'honeymoon suite' (including breakfast).

Hotel Sangam *(☎ 39451, fax 36695, ⓔ hotelsangam@vsnl.com)* is a large, flashy new hotel on Trichy Rd with central air-con. Rooms (with bath and showers) cost US$45/88 (US$77/134 for full board). There's a pleasant pool (Rs 150 for nonguests), a hall to dance in, email facilities and a multicuisine restaurant with live veena music.

Hotel Oriental Towers *(☎ 30724, fax 30770, ⓔ hotelorientaltowers@vsnl.com, 2889 Srinivasam Pillai Rd)* has rooms with central air-con for US$37/47. It's a modern hotel that pays homage to an older style. It has a handy supermarket, a gym, sauna, spa and massage (Rs 150 for oil, Rs 250 for herbal) for both men and women. Nonguests may use the pool for Rs 100.

Ideal River View Resort *(☎ 50533, fax 51113, ⓔ ideal@md2.vsnl.net.in)* is set within peaceful gardens beside the river 10km north-west of the city. Its restaurant is excellent with much of the food fresh coming from the garden. Spacious rooms (cottages) with generously sized balconies cost Rs 950/1100 with Rs 250 for an extra person. There's a large pool, no TV and phone calls may be made from reception. Cash is preferred.

Places to Eat

For self-caterers there's a supermarket at Hotel Oriental Towers. There are numerous veg restaurants near the local bus stand and on Gandhiji Rd.

Golden Restaurant *(Hospital Rd)* does good vegetarian meals for Rs 25. ***Sathars*** *(Gandhiji Rd)* is a good veg (from Rs 20) and nonveg (from Rs 40) restaurant with great service and an extensive range of dishes. It's open until midnight.

Swagath *(Gandhiji Rd)*, near the roundabout, does nonveg food that's good value; thalis are Rs 15.

Hotel Yagappa has a large restaurant with reasonable food including ginger chicken for Rs 45. The bar is very pleasant; beers are Rs 55.

Hotel Sangam offers a wide selection in its multicuisine restaurant, with classical veena music.

There are two restaurants at Hotel Parisutham. The nonveg ***Les Repas*** serves Indian and Chinese dishes (around Rs 60), and ***Geetham*** offers veg food but apparently the food is now middle-of-the-road having been adjusted to suit Western tastes. The bar is a popular place for a late evening beer accompanied by complimentary peanuts.

Shopping

A stroll along Gandhiji Rd is a pleasant way to shop. Numerous places (including the ubiquitous Kashmiri emporiums) sell everything from quality crafts and readymade clothes to inexpensive kitsch. For fixed prices and hassle-free shopping, Poompuhar is the best bet.

Getting There & Away

Bus The city bus stands are for local and SETC buses. SETC has a computerised reservation office open 7.30 am to 9.30 pm. There are 24 buses a day to Chennai, the fastest and most expensive being the No 323FP Bye-Pass Rider (Rs 90, 7½ hours). Other buses that can be booked here include the daily No 851 to Tirupathi (Rs 100), No 725 to Ooty (Rs 90) and No 928 to Pondicherry (daily at midnight, 177km). Numerous buses pass on their way to Tiruchirappalli (Rs 14, 1½ hours) and Madurai.

The new bus station, 2.5km south of the centre, services local areas, such as Tiruchirappalli (Rs 12, 55km, every four minutes), Dindigul (Rs 30, 150km, nine daily) and Chidambaram (Rs 30, 127km, every 30 minutes).

Train To Chennai (351km), the overnight *6702-Rameswaram Express* departs at 8.25 pm, takes nine hours and costs Rs 431/128 in 1st/2nd class. For the same prices, the *Cholan Express* departs at 9.20 am. To Villupuram (for Pondicherry), the trip takes five hours and costs Rs 279/83. To Tiruchirappalli (1½ hours, 50km) the fare is Rs 173/22. It's one hour to Kumbakonam, and 2½ hours to Chidambaram.

AROUND THANJAVUR

About 13km north of Thanjavur, Thiruvaiyaru hosts the January international **music festival** in honour of the saint and composer, Thyagaraja. The saint's birthplace is at **Tiruvarur**, 55km east of Thanjavur. The Thyagararajaswami Temple here boasts the largest temple chariot in Tamil Nadu. The chariot is hauled through the streets during the 10-day car festival in April/May. Regular buses run from Thanjavur for Rs 2.

TIRUCHIRAPPALLI (TRICHY)

☎ 0431 • pop 770,800

Trichy's long history goes back to before the Christian era when it was a Chola citadel. During the 1st millennium AD, both the Pallavas and Pandyas took power many times before the Cholas regained control in the 10th century. When the Chola empire finally decayed, Trichy came into the realm of the Vijayanagar emperors of Hampi until their defeat in 1565 by the forces of the Deccan sultans. The town and its most famous landmark, the Rock Fort Temple, were built by the Nayaks of Madurai. Later in the 18th century Trichy witnessed much of the British-French struggle for supremacy in India.

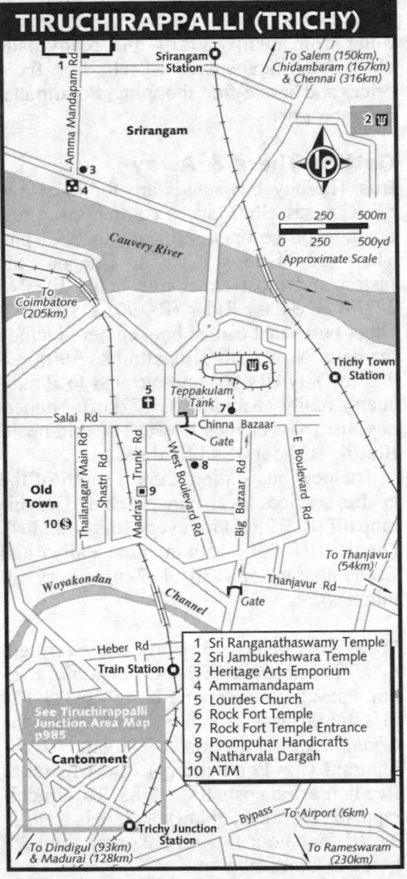

Orientation & Information

Trichy is scattered over a large area. Most of the hotels and restaurants, the bus station, train station, tourist office and main post office are within a few minutes walk of each other in the junction area. The Rock Fort Temple is 2.5km north of here, with the other temples a further 3km to 5km north again.

The tourist office (☎ 460136), 1 Williams Rd, with branch offices at the train station and airport, is open weekdays only. The staff are helpful and knowledgeable. The main post office on Dindigul Rd (State Bank Rd) is open 8 am to 7 pm Monday to Saturday and email may be accessed at Mas Media (Rs 60 per hour). Money can be changed at State Bank of India on Dindigul Rd or the very convenient ATM at HDFC Bank, 10th Cross, Thillai Nagar.

For medical attention visit the Seahorse Hospital (☎ 462660) or the Infant Jesus Hospital, which treats children (☎ 411663).

Rock Fort Temple

The spectacular Rock Fort Temple is perched 83m high on a massive rocky outcrop. This smooth rock was first hewn by the Pallavas who cut small cave temples into the southern face, but it was the Nayaks who made use of its naturally fortified position. There are two main temples: **Sri Thayumanaswamy Temple**, dedicated to Shiva, halfway to the top, and one at the summit dedicated to **Vinayaka** (Ganesh). It's a stiff climb to the top up the 437 stone-cut steps but well worth it. Non-Hindus are not allowed into either temple but occasionally (for a small fee) temple priests waive this regulation. It's open 6 am to 8 pm daily and entry is Rs 1.

Sri Ranganathaswamy Temple (Srirangam)

The superb temple complex at Srirangam, about 3km north of the Rock Fort, is

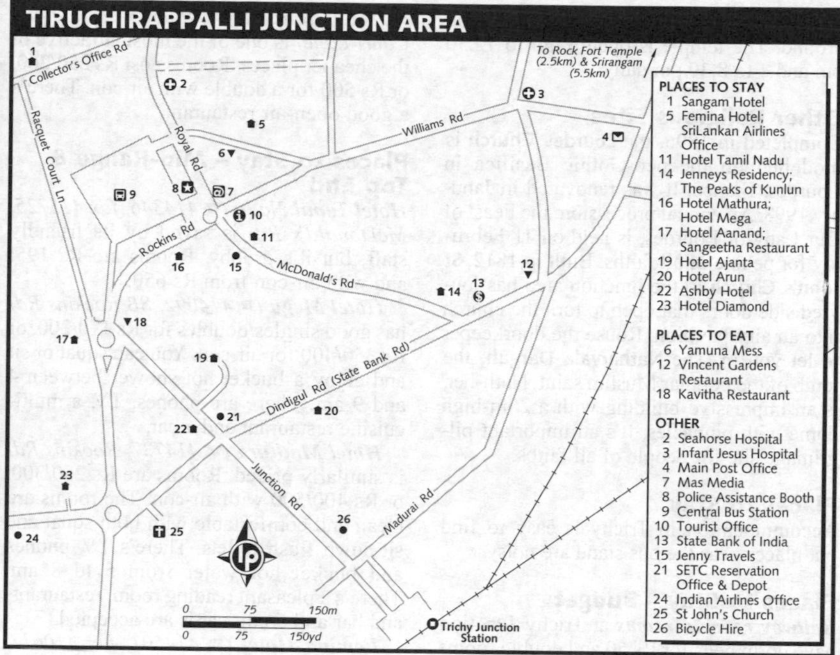

dedicated to Vishnu. Although mentioned in *sangam* poetry by the early academy of Tamil poets (see Madurai for more information on this academy), temple inscriptions date its existence from the 10th century. In the 12th century the philosopher, Ramanuja, became head of the temple school and his effective administrative practices continued until the 14th-century Muslim invasion. With the Vijayanagar victory the temple was restored to the structure that exists today. Many dynasties have had a hand in its construction, including the Cheras, Pandyas, Cholas, Hoysalas, Vijayanagars and Nayaks – and work continues. The largest gopuram, the main entrance, was completed in 1987, and now measures an astounding 73m.

At 60 hectares, the Srirangam complex with its seven concentric walled sections and 21 gopurams is probably the largest in India. Non-Hindus may go to the sixth wall but are not allowed into the gold-topped sanctum. You can buy the Rs 3 (camera Rs 20) ticket to climb the wall for a panoramic view of the entire complex. Avoid the greedy guides here (see the boxed text 'Beware of Temple Touts' earlier in this chapter) who'll impose hefty fees and lure you with bogus Lonely Planet recommendations. And avoid those wanting to take you shopping. Remember, if one of them 'guides' you to a shopping outlet the prices you pay will include a substantial commission for them.

A **Temple Chariot Festival** where statues of the deities are paraded aboard a fine chariot, is held here each January but the most important festival is the 21-day **Vaikunta Ekadasi** (Paradise Festival) in mid-December, when the celebrated Vaishnavaite text, Tiruvaimozhi, is recited before an image of Vishnu. There's a small **museum** containing sculptures, bronze figures and plaques. The area within the fourth wall is closed 10 pm to 6 am daily.

Sri Jambukeshwara Temple

The nearby Sri Jambukeshwara Temple, dedicated to Shiva and Parvati, was built around the same time as the Sri Ranganathaswamy Temple. Being one of the five temples honouring the elements – in this case, water – the temple is built around a partly immersed Shiva lingam. Non-Hindus may not enter the sanctum, but the rule may

TAMIL NADU

be waived. A helpful guide will show you around. The temple is open 6 am to 12.30 pm and 4 to 8.30 pm daily.

Other Religious Sites

Completed in 1896, the **Lourdes Church** is modelled on the neo-Gothic Basilica in Lourdes, France. It was renovated in January 1998. An annual procession, the Feast of Our Lady of Lourdes, is held on 11 February for people of all faiths. Built in 1812, **St John's Church** in the junction area has louvred side doors that open to turn the church into an airy pavilion. Rouse the doorkeeper to let you in. The **Natharvala Dargah**, the tomb of the popular Muslim saint, Nath-her, is an impressive building with a 20m-high dome with pinnacles. It's an important pilgrimage site for people of all faiths.

Places to Stay

Accommodation in Trichy is easy to find but places near the bus stand are noisy.

Places to Stay – Budget

Railway retiring rooms at Trichy Junction have dorm beds for Rs 50 and double rooms without/with air-con for Rs 150/350. ***Hotel Diamond*** (formerly Aristo; *☎ 415860, 2 Dindigul Rd)* has serious maintenance problems, yet it remains popular with visitors because it's friendly and has a quiet leafy garden and a laid-back atmosphere. There are both sit-down flush and squat toilets and some rooms have a TV. Singles/doubles cost Rs 130/195, quads are Rs 350, and air-con double cottages are Rs 450.

Hotel Arun *(☎ 461421, 24 Dindigul Rd)* is a good place set back from the road. Fairly clean rooms are Rs 160/185; air-con rooms are Rs 350/400. Rooms have sit-down flush or squat toilets, TV and phone. A thali in the restaurant costs Rs 15.

Ashby Hotel *(☎ 460652, 17A Junction Rd)* has crumbling, old-world atmosphere in a leafy garden. Spacious rooms are Rs 175/287, or Rs 460/630 with air-con (including tax). There's a pleasant bar and an outdoor restaurant.

Hotel Ajanta *(☎ 415501, Junction Rd)* has good rooms for Rs 165/210, or Rs 350/450 with air-con with either squat or sit-down flush toilets. A TV is Rs 40 extra and there's tap hot water from 5 to 8 am. There's also a good veg restaurant.

Hotel Aanand *(☎ 460545, 1 Racquet Court Lane)* is one of the most attractive of the cheaper places. Rooms cost Rs 250/260, or Rs 500 for a double with air-con. There's a good open-air restaurant.

Places to Stay – Mid-Range & Top End

Hotel Tamil Nadu *(☎ 414346, fax 415725, McDonald's Rd)* is saved by its friendly staff, but it's grubby. Rooms are Rs 195; and with air-con from Rs 650.

Hotel Mega *(☎ 414092, 8B Rockins Rd)* has good singles/doubles for Rs 170/200, or Rs 350/400 for air-con. You can squat or sit and enjoy a bucket hot shower between 4 and 9 am. There are phones, TV, a multi-cuisine restaurant and a bar.

Hotel Mathura *(☎ 414737, Rockins Rd)* is similarly priced. Rooms are Rs 250/300, or Rs 400/500 with air-con. The rooms are clean and comfortable with both squat and sit-down flush toilets. There's TV, phones and bucket hot water from 5 to 8 am. There's a pleasant reading room, restaurants and bar and credit cards are accepted.

Femina Hotel *(☎ 414501, fax 410615, e femina@md3.vsnl.net.in, 14C Williams Rd)* is a huge place offering rooms with TV and phone for Rs 225/400, or Rs 600/900 with air-con. The veg restaurant is better than the continental restaurant. There's a pool and major cards are accepted.

Jenneys Residency *(☎ 414414, fax 461451, 3/14 McDonald's Rd)* is enormous and luxurious, with the best rooms being on the 4th and 5th floors. For Indians, rooms cost Rs 1150/2500 and for foreigners it's US$30/100. The hotel has several restaurants, upmarket shops, a pool and a health club. Nonguests can use the pool for Rs 100 per day.

Sangam Hotel *(☎ 414700, Collector's Office Rd)* has all the facilities of a four-star hotel, including restaurants, a bar, pool and shopping arcade. Rooms are US$45/88.

Places to Eat

Many of the hotels have restaurants providing a variety of good foods.

Yamuna Mess, an open-air 'diner' on a gravel car park behind Guru Hotel, is a great place for cheap eats. In the evenings only it serves veg or nonveg dishes. There's mellow music and friendly service.

Sangeetha Restaurant *(1 Racquet Court Lane)*, at Hotel Aanand, is also a good place for dinner. In the open-air restaurant most dishes, including chilli *gobi fry* (cauliflower fried with spices) are Rs 25.

Vincent Gardens Restaurant *(Dindigul Rd)* is a plush place in a large garden setting. It has a multicuisine menu and mosquitos, but it gets good reports.

Kavitha Restaurant with excellent, elaborate thalis for Rs 25, has an air-con room.

The Peaks of Kunlun at Jenneys Residency has a not bad multicuisine menu and beer (not too cold) is Rs 70.

Shopping

It's fun to wander through the markets along Big Bazaar Rd. For crafts and gifts visit Poompuhar Handicrafts on West Boulevard Rd or Heritage Arts Emporium at 5 Amma Mandapam Rd, Srirangam, which is very popular especially for quality bronzes. There are also Heritage outlets at Jenneys Residency and Femina Hotel.

Getting There & Away

Air Indian Airlines (☎ 462233), 4A Dindigul Rd, flies daily (except Sunday) to Chennai for US$80. SriLankan Airlines (☎ 460844), at Femina Hotel, flies to Colombo on Wednesday, Thursday and Saturday.

Bus Most buses use the central bus station, with the former site on Junction Rd now housing a reservation office and depot. Services to most places are frequent and tickets are sold by the conductor as soon as the bus arrives. Services include Thanjavur (Rs 14, 1½ hours, 54km, every five minutes), Chidambaram (Rs 50, four hours, 150km, every 45 minutes), Coimbatore (Rs 90, seven hours, 244km, hourly) and Madurai (Rs 35, four hours, 128km, every 20 minutes).

Other SETC buses can be computer-booked in advance. For Chennai the fastest bus is the Bye-Pass Rider (Rs 75, 7½ hours). Other destinations include: Bangalore (10 daily, Rs 90), Coimbatore (every 30 minutes, Rs 38) and Tirupathi via Vellore (two daily, Rs 68, 9½ hours).

Private companies such as Jenny Travels, opposite Hotel Tamil Nadu, or KPN Travels, below Hotel Mathura, have super deluxe day/night services to Chennai for Rs 110/120 and Bangalore for Rs 130/150.

Train Trichy is on the main Chennai to Madurai and Chennai to Rameswaram lines and has a computerised booking system. Some trains run directly to/from Chennai while others go via Chidambaram and Thanjavur. The quickest trains to Chennai (337km, 5¼ hours) are the *Vaigai Express* and the *Pallavan Express*, which cost Rs 489/145 in 1st/2nd class. The fastest service to Madurai is also on the *Vaigai Express*, which leaves at 5.45 pm, takes 2¼ hours and costs Rs 242/46 in 1st/2nd class. The trip to Rameswaram (seven hours, 265km) costs Rs 352/67.

For Mamallapuram, take a Chennai train as far as Chengalpattu and a bus from there.

Getting Around

To/From the Airport The 7km ride into town is Rs 250 by taxi and Rs 100 by autorickshaw. Otherwise, take a No 7, 59, 58 or 63 bus to the airport (30 minutes).

Bus Trichy's local bus service is excellent. The No 1 (A or B) bus from the SETC bus station plies frequently between the train station, main post office, the Rock Fort Temple, the main entrance to Sri Ranganathaswamy Temple and close to Sri Jambukeshwara Temple.

Bicycle The town lends itself to cycling as it's dead flat. There are a couple of places on Junction Rd where you can hire bicycles for Rs 5 per hour. Note that the incredibly busy Big Bazaar Rd is a one-way road (heading north).

Southern Tamil Nadu

MADURAI

☎ 0452 • pop 1.23 million

Madurai is an animated city packed with pilgrims, beggars, businesspeople, bullock carts and underemployed rickshaw drivers. It's one of South India's oldest cities, and has been a centre of learning and pilgrimage for centuries.

Madurai's main attraction is the famous Sri Meenakshi Temple in the heart of the old town, a riotously baroque example of Dravidian architecture with gopurams covered from top to bottom in a breathtaking

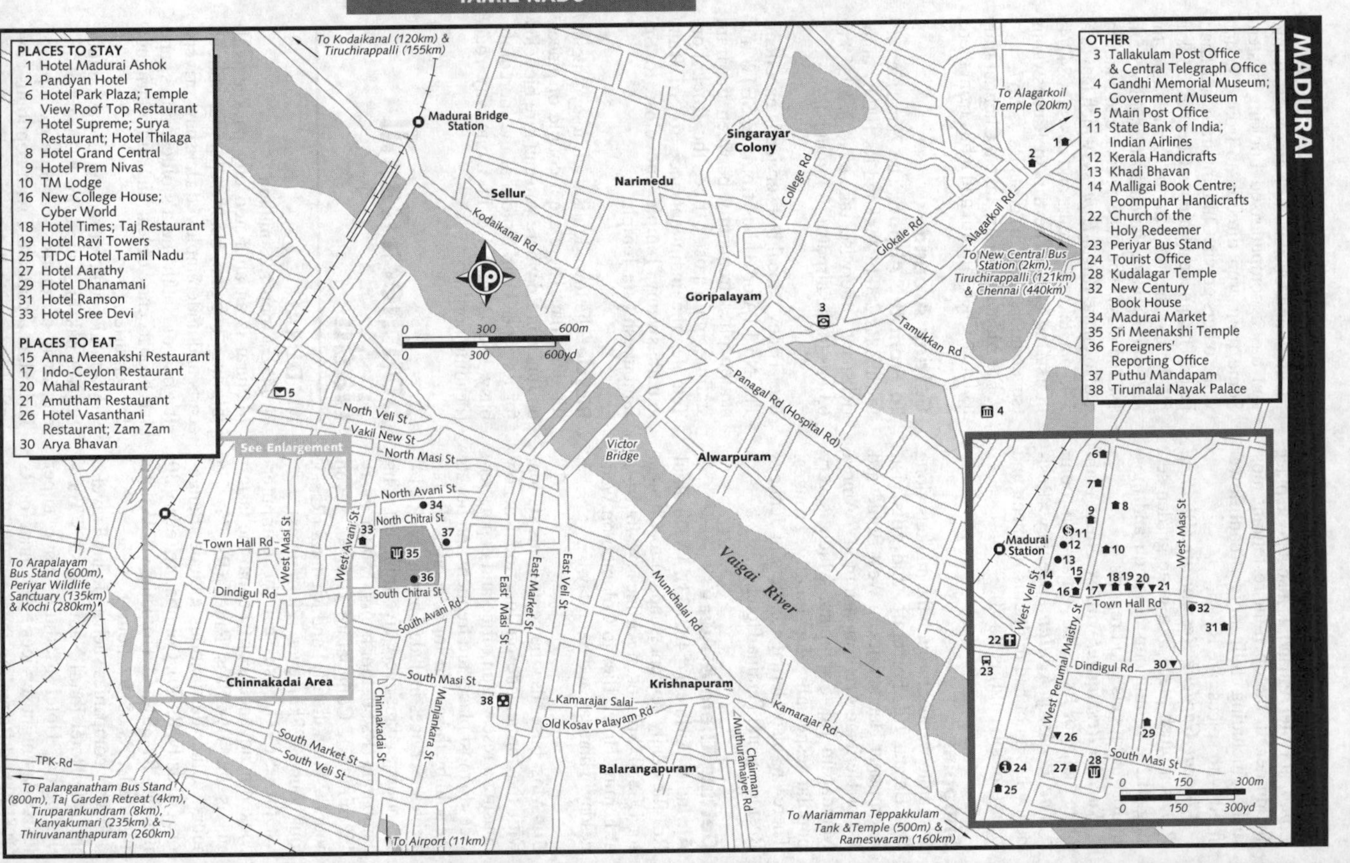
MADURAI
PLACES TO STAY
1 Hotel Madurai Ashok
2 Pandyan Hotel
6 Hotel Park Plaza; Temple View Roof Top Restaurant
7 Hotel Supreme; Surya Restaurant; Hotel Thilaga
8 Hotel Grand Central
9 Hotel Prem Nivas
10 TM Lodge
16 New College House; Cyber World
18 Hotel Times; Taj Restaurant
19 Hotel Ravi Towers
25 TTDC Hotel Tamil Nadu
27 Hotel Aarathy
29 Hotel Dhanamani
31 Hotel Ramson
33 Hotel Sree Devi
PLACES TO EAT
15 Anna Meenakshi Restaurant
17 Indo-Ceylon Restaurant
20 Mahal Restaurant
21 Amutham Restaurant
26 Hotel Vasanthani Restaurant; Zam Zam
30 Arya Bhavan
OTHER
3 Tallakulam Post Office & Central Telegraph Office
4 Gandhi Memorial Museum; Government Museum
5 Main Post Office
11 State Bank of India; Indian Airlines
12 Kerala Handicrafts
13 Khadi Bhavan
14 Malligai Book Centre; Poompuhar Handicrafts
22 Church of the Holy Redeemer
23 Periyar Bus Stand
24 Tourist Office
28 Kudalagar Temple
32 New Century Book House
34 Madurai Market
35 Sri Meenakshi Temple
36 Foreigners' Reporting Office
37 Puthu Mandapam
38 Tirumalai Nayak Palace
To Kodaikanal (120km) & Tiruchirappalli (155km)
To Alagarkoil Temple (20km)
To New Central Bus Station (2km), Tiruchirappalli (121km) & Chennai (440km)
To Arapalayam Bus Stand (600m), Periyar Wildlife Sanctuary (135km) & Kochi (280km)
To Palanganatham Bus Stand (800m), Taj Garden Retreat (4km), Tiruparankundram (8km), Kanyakumari (235km) & Thiruvananthapuram (260km)
To Airport (11km)
To Mariamman Teppakkulam Tank & Temple (500m) & Rameswaram (160km)
Madurai Bridge Station
Singarayar Colony
Narimedu
Sellur
Goripalayam
Alwarpuram
Krishnapuram
Balarangapuram
Chinnakadai Area
Victor Bridge
Vaigai River
See Enlargement
Kodaikanal Rd
College Rd
Glokale Rd
Alagarkoil Rd
Tamukkan Rd
Panagal Rd (Hospital Rd)
North Veli St
Vakil New St
North Masi St
North Avani St
North Chitrai St
West Avani St
West Masi St
Town Hall Rd
Dindigul Rd
South Chitrai St
South Avani Rd
East Masi St
East Market St
East Veli St
Munichalai Rd
South Masi St
Kamarajar Salai
Old Kosav Palayam Rd
Kamarajar Rd
Chinnakadai St
Manjankara St
South Market St
South Veli St
TPK Rd
Chairman Muthuramayer Rd
Madurai Station
West Veli St
West Perumal Maistry St
0 300 600m
0 300 600yd
0 150 300m
0 150 300yd

profusion of multicoloured images of gods, goddesses, animals and mythical figures. The temple seethes with activity from dawn to dusk, its many shrines attracting pilgrims and tourists from all over the world. It's estimated that 10,000 visitors may come here on any one day.

History

Tamil and Greek documents record the existence of Madurai from the 4th century BC. The city was known to the Greeks via Megasthenes, their ambassador to the court of Chandragupta Maurya. It was popular for trade, especially in spices. It was also the site of the *sangam* – the academy of Tamil poets, whose poems celebrate Madurai's many attributes. Over the centuries Madurai has come under the jurisdiction of the Cholas, the Pandyas, the Muslim invaders under Malik Kafur, the Hindu Vijayanagar kings and the Nayaks who ruled Madurai until 1781. During the reign of Tirumalai Nayak (1623–55), the bulk of the Meenakshi Temple was built, and Madurai became the cultural centre of the Tamil people, playing an important role in the development of the Tamil language.

Madurai then passed into the hands of the British East India Company. In 1840 the company razed the fort, which had previously surrounded the city, and filled in the moat. Four broad streets – the Veli streets – were constructed on top of this fill and to this day define the limits of the old city.

Orientation & Information

Most places, including the main post office, tourist office, mid-range and budget hotels, are near the temple. Street names can be a little confusing with alternatives frequently used. The Avani Streets are often referred to as Avani Moola and Dindingul Rd is also known as Nethaji Rd.

Tourist Offices The Madurai tourist office (☎ 734757), 180 West Veli St, is open 10 am to 5.45 pm weekdays. The staff are helpful and have brochures and maps. Seek their advice on the latest scams – they're interested to help and avert problems. Tourist counters are also at the train station (☎ 742888) and airport. For tourist complaints, the Foreigners' Reporting Office (☎ 744007) is at the Southern Tower, Sri Meenakshi Temple.

To cash travellers cheques go to State Bank of India on West Veli St.

Post & Communications The main post office is at the northern end of West Veli St and is open 7 am to 7.30 pm (10 am to 5 pm Sunday). The poste restante counter (No 8) is open 10 am to 5 pm daily. There are also numerous local/STD/ISD booths that offer excellent service.

Cyber World (☎ 742162) on the 2nd floor of College House is set up with Internet access at Rs 60 per hour, and there's an excellent service at the Hotel Supreme Complex.

Bookshops Malligai Book Centre, 11 West Veli St, has a good selection of books, maps and cassettes. The New Century Book House at 79–80 West Tower St is also well stocked.

Sri Meenakshi Temple

The Sri Meenakshi Temple was designed in 1560 by Vishwanatha Nayak and built during the reign of Tirumalai Nayak. But its history goes back 2000 years to the time when Madurai was a Pandyan capital. The temple complex occupies an area of six hectares. It has 12 towers, ranging in height from 45m to 50m, the tallest of which is the southern tower.

Also within the temple complex, housed in the 1000 pillared hall, is the **Temple Art**

Madurai Matters

There are a few annoyances in Madurai, but they can be avoided:

Beware of bogus film sellers, self-styled 'spiritual gurus', Romeos on bikes and temple touts. The film sellers have mastered the art of putting dud film into new cassettes. Avoiding them is easy – never buy film from street hawkers. The 'spiritual gurus' prey on the vulnerable, particularly Western women, seeking 'enlightenment'. It's easy to avoid them too. Seek your enlightenment through reputable teachers and ashrams. Avoid the sleek Tariqs, who want to whisk you away on their even sleeker bikes. As for the temple touts, they are particularly skilful in Madurai (see the boxed text 'Beware of Temple Touts' earlier in this chapter). And finally, once away from the temple environs, most annoyances will disappear and you'll be free to enjoy the local hospitality.

TAMIL NADU

Museum. It contains friezes, stone and brass images, as well as one of the best exhibits on Hindu deities. Entrance costs Rs 1 and it's open 7 am to 7 pm daily.

Allow plenty of time to see this temple. Early mornings or late evenings are the best times to avoid crowds. 'Temple guides' charge negotiable fees rarely below Rs 200. Haggle hard (refer to the boxed text 'Beware of Temple Touts' earlier in this chapter). The guides are usually a front for emporiums and tailor shops, so remember your 'guide fee' is payment for them to talk you into going shopping, where they'll receive handsome commissions on your purchases (and who pays for that?). Unless you want to shop, don't fall for the offer to take you up the tower where you can view the whole temple complex. Certainly you'll go up some steps – straight to the local emporium!

The temple usually opens 5 am to 12.30 pm and 4 to 9.30 pm. Entry is Rs 10 and Rs 30 for a permit to take photos. Cameras and videos are prohibited.

Madurai Market

Just north of the temple, before you get to North Avani St, is the Madurai Market. It's a labyrinth of bustling laneways strewn with aromatic herbs. Adjacent, in a nondescript cement building upstairs on the 1st floor, is the flower market. Vendors dexterously heap mountains of marigolds and jasmine onto scales for the temple flower sellers who buy their stock here.

Tirumalai Nayak Palace

About 1.5km south-east of the Meenakshi Temple, this Indo-Saracenic palace was built in 1636 by the ruler whose name it bears. Today, only the entrance gate, main hall and dance hall remain but these are well worth seeing. The rectangular courtyard, 75m by 52m, known as the Swargavilasa or Celestial Pavilion gives clues to the original grandeur of the building, regarded as one of the finest secular buildings in South India.

The palace was partially restored by Lord Napier, governor of Madras (1866–72). The entrance is on the far (eastern) side. It's open 9 am to 1 pm and 2 to 5 pm daily; entry costs Rs 1.

There's a daily sound-and-light show consisting of a few coloured lights and an audio presentation played at maximum volume and gross distortion – in English at 6.30 pm; Tamil at 8 pm. Tickets cost Rs 2 to 5.

The palace is a 20-minute walk from the Meenakshi Temple.

Museums

Housed in the old palace of the Rani Mangammal, the excellent **Gandhi Memorial Museum** is set in relaxing grounds and has a clear historical account of India's struggle for Independence. The Madurai **Government Museum** is in the same grounds, as is a small bookshop stocked with plenty of Gandhi reading matter. Both museums (free entry) open 10 am to 1 pm and 2 to 5.30 pm daily, although the latter closes Friday and the second Saturday of each month.

Mariamman Teppakkulam Tank

This tank, 5km east of the old city, covers an area almost equal to that of the Meenakshi Temple and is the site of the popular Teppam (Float) Festival, held in January/February. When it's empty (most of the year) it becomes a cricket ground for local kids. The tank was built by Tirumalai Nayak in 1646 and is connected to the Vaigai River by underground channels.

Special Events

Madurai celebrates many festivals. Times and dates are determined by temple astrologers so check with the temple or tourist office for details. Apart from **Teppam**, the main festivals celebrated are: **Pongal (Harvest Festival)**, **Avanimoolam** and **Navrati**.

Pongal – A Party on the Boil

Harvest is a time for celebration and for thanksgiving. It's the time of Pongal, a secular festival enjoyed by all. Pongal means boil, and as the rice boils over the new clay pots, it symbolises the prosperity and abundance a fruitful harvest brings. For many, the celebrations begin with temple rituals, followed by family gatherings. Later it's the animals who are honoured, especially cows, for their contribution to the harvest. Given the agricultural nature of Tamil Nadu, Pongal is an important festival especially in the villages.

If you are travelling during Pongal time (mid January), try to get out to a village where the true spirit of Pongal can be experienced.

TAMIL NADU

Madurai's main event is the 14-day **Chithrai Festival** (April/May), which celebrates the marriage of Meenakshi to Sundareshwara (Shiva). The deities are wheeled around the temple in massive chariots that form part of long colourful processions.

Places to Stay – Budget

In a pilgrim city of Madurai's size and importance, many of the cheap hotels are just flophouses that bear the scars of previous occupants' habits. The best places are mostly found along Town Hall and Dindigul Rds.

New College House *(☎ 742971, fax 741844, 2 Town Hall Rd)* is being spruced up. It's huge, but pleasant with singles/doubles at Rs 135/195 and air-con rooms are Rs 430. There's a business centre (Rs 30 per hour for email) and good veg restaurants.

Hotel Ravi Towers *(☎ 741961, 9 Town Hall Rd)* has good clean rooms for Rs 150/275. A TV costs Rs 50 extra. There are also good air-con rooms for Rs 350/500.

Hotel Ramson *(☎ 740407, 9 Permal Tank St)* looks expensive but isn't at Rs 100/150. In January the hotel is blasted with music from Pongal revellers.

Hotel Sree Devi *(☎ 747431, 20 West Avani St)* has clean rooms (no singles) starting at Rs 180, or Rs 500 with air-con. Avoid the room with no windows. There are both sit-down flush and squat toilets and hot water comes in a bucket any time. The rooftop room has a spectacular view of the temple and costs Rs 600, including tax.

Hotel Grand Central *(☎ 743940, fax 740656, 47 West Perumal Maistry St)* is another hotel that looks more expensive than it is. It's clean and friendly and has good-sized rooms for Rs 175/200 and air-con doubles for Rs 500. There's both squat and sit-down flush toilets, bucket hot water, phones and TV in every room.

Hotel Dhanamani *(☎ 742701, 20 Sunnambukara St)* has singles with shared bathroom for Rs 95, singles/doubles with bathroom for Rs 100/160, and good-value air-con doubles for Rs 300.

Hotel Times *(☎ 742651, 15–16 Town Hall Rd)* is a clean, friendly place and is excellent value with rooms for Rs 150/250 or Rs 500 for a deluxe double with air-con.

Railway retiring rooms at Madurai station are noisy and cost Rs 70/150; dorm beds (men only) are just Rs 25.

Places to Stay – Mid-Range

Hotel Aarathy *(☎ 537461, 9 Perumal Koil West Mada St)* has singles/doubles for Rs 250/370, or Rs 400/500 with air-con. They're comfortable and most have a small balcony with a great view over the temple. There's a pleasant open-air veg restaurant in the courtyard.

TTDC Hotel Tamil Nadu *(☎ 537461, fax 627945, West Veli St)* is good value with rooms from Rs 150/195, or Rs 260/400 with air-con and TV. There's also a bar and a good restaurant.

Hotel Prem Nivas *(☎ 742532, fax 743618, 102 West Perumal Maistry St)* is popular and has rooms for Rs 195/300 and air-con doubles at Rs 460. Facilities are excellent. There are both squat and sit-down flush toilets, TVs and phones and an air-con veg restaurant. Credit cards are accepted.

TM Lodge *(☎ 741651, 50 West Perumal Maistry St)* is a friendly place with clean linen and rooms for Rs 195/260. An air-con double with TV is Rs 375. The upper rooms are lighter and airier, and from the 5th floor up you can view the temple. There's squat and sit-down flush toilets, bucket hot water from 4 to 9 am and credit cards are accepted (not AmEx).

Hotel Supreme *(☎ 742637, 110 West Perumal Maistry St)* has got its act together. Double rooms (no singles) start at Rs 400, or Rs 730 with air-con. The rooms are dark but the facilities are good, with hot water morning and evening (or bucket anytime), squat and sit-down flush toilets, Internet, and credit cards accepted. There's a bar and an excellent rooftop veg restaurant.

Hotel Thilaga *(☎ 740762, 111 West Perumal Maistry St)* is clean and good value. Rooms with TV cost Rs 180/200. Air-con doubles are Rs 500.

Hotel Park Plaza *(☎ 742112, fax 743 654, 114 West Perumal Maistry St)* is similar to the Supreme, but somewhat overpriced for what it offers. It has comfortable rooms from Rs 775/1000 (including breakfast) with central air-con, TV and regular 'happy hours'. There's hot water morning and evening (bucket anytime) and a rooftop restaurant.

Places to Stay – Top End

Madurai's three top hotels are well out of the town centre.

Hotel Madurai Ashok *(☎ 537531, fax 537530, Alargakoil Rd)* has rooms starting from Rs 1350/2100. The pool is Rs 75 for nonguests.

Pandyan Hotel *(☎ 537090, fax 533424, ⓔ bhasker@md3.vsnl.net.in, Alargarkoil Rd)* has rooms for US$40/55. Fully air-con, it has a restaurant and bar. The manicured garden offers a respite from the city chaos but there's no pool.

Taj Garden Retreat *(☎ 601020)*, 4km south-west of town, ranks as Madurai's best hotel. Rooms start at US$110/120 a single/double for foreigners; Rs 3100/3450 for Indians. Facilities include all those of a luxury hotel including some unexpected ones – strong sewer smells.

Places to Eat

Indo-Ceylon Restaurant *(6 Town Hall Rd)* is popular, as is ***Amutham Restaurant***, near the corner of West Masi St.

New College House has good-value thalis in its dining hall. ***Arya Bhavan***, on the corner of West Masi St and Dindigul Rd, does titanic dosas.

Anna Meenakshi Restaurant is large, bright and serves good, vegetarian meals.

Hotel Vasanthani is good for cheap thalis and tiffin. ***Zam Zam***, nearby, is a popular shop for sweet or savoury snacks.

Taj Restaurant *(10 Town Hall Rd)* offers a varied cuisine including 'continentals', puddings and peach Melba! ***Mahal Restaurant*** *(Town Hall Rd)*, a few doors along from Taj Restaurant, is an excellent multicuisine restaurant that includes 'roast lamp'. Items from Rs 30 (none over Rs 60) are served in a comfortable air-con environment.

Surya Restaurant *(110 West Perumal Maistry St)*, on the roof of the Hotel Supreme, has a superb view and catches any breeze. It serves Indian, Chinese and continental veg food (5 pm to midnight). Most items are around Rs 40. It's also open for breakfast 6 to 11 am; for lunch, upmarket thalis are Rs 40.

Temple View Roof Top Restaurant, at Hotel Park Plaza, serves nonveg dishes with the same view as the Surya. Chicken garlic fry is Rs 40, the tandoori chicken is especially succulent and there are good-value veg dishes too.

Taj Garden Retreat is the place to go for a splurge. There are excellent a la carte meals in the multicuisine restaurant. On Saturday and Sunday evenings there's a deservedly popular buffet for Rs 300.

Shopping

Madurai, a textile centre from way back, teems with cloth stalls and tailors' shops. A great place for getting cottons and printed fabrics is Puthu Mandapam, the pillared former entrance hall at the eastern side to Sri Meenakshi Temple. Here you'll find tailors, all busily treadling away and capable of whipping up a good replica of whatever you're wearing in an hour or two.

Quality, designs and prices vary greatly. Touts are everywhere and their commissions will be added to the price of your garments.

If you want garments made, have your designs ready. It's also important to know a little about materials, quality and quantity required. As always, take your time, look around carefully and bargain hard.

The government shops are conveniently located together in West Veli St. There's Poompuhar, Khadi Bhavan and Kerala Handicrafts. Every tout, driver, 'temple guide' and tailor's brother will lead you to the Kashmiri shops in North Chitrai St, near the temple. Once again, remember who's paying their commissions.

Getting There & Away

Air Indian Airlines (☎ 741234) has an office on West Veli St. It has one flight daily to Chennai (US$90) and four flights a week to Mumbai (US$160).

Bus The Madurai bus system has been redesigned. All buses now arrive and depart from the new central bus station, 6km northeast of the old city. Officially it's Mattuthavani (Cow Auctioning Place), retaining its original name since renaming proved too politically difficult. However most people refer to it as the central, city or new bus station. It's a well-organised 24-hour operation. From here buses shuttle into the city every few minutes for just Rs 2. These's also rickshaw drivers who'll take you for Rs 25.

During heavy monsoon rain, the road to Kodaikanal sometimes gets washed away and the buses go via Palani, adding an hour or two to the journey.

Private bus companies offer superdeluxe video services to Chennai and Bangalore.

However, *beware*. Many agencies will sell you a ticket to virtually anywhere, but you'll find yourself dumped on a state bus having paid substantially more than required.

destination	daily departures	price (Rs)
Bangalore	6	141
Chennai	half hourly	113
Chidambaram	3	48
Coimbatore	35	36
Kanyakumari	20	50
Kodaikanal	15	25
Mysore	2	119
Palani	13	20
Pondicherry	2	85
Rameswaram	30	31
Thiruvananthapuram	2	97
Tiruapathi (via Vellore)	4	124
Tiruchendur	20	27

Train Madurai train station is on West Veli St. The following 'Major Trains from Madurai' table lists the more frequent trains leaving Madurai.

In addition to this schedule, there are train services from Madurai to Bangalore (two daily), Ernakulam (two daily), Kollam (two daily), Nagercoil (several daily), Trichy (seven daily), Villapuram (seven daily) and Chennai (six daily). There are also regular services to New Delhi and Kolkata (Calcutta).

Getting Around

The airport is 12km south of town and a taxi charges an extortionate Rs 250 to the town centre. Autorickshaws ask for around Rs 150 (even Rs 200). Alternatively, bus No 10A from the central bus station goes to the airport but don't rely on it being on schedule.

The Periyar bus stand in the old city is still in use for city travel, and it's from here you'll take buses to local sites such as the museums and tank. However things are in a state of flux. Check with your hotel or tourist office for current information.

Drivers will quote whatever they think you will pay. Take your time; haggle hard. Eventually they should settle on a reasonable rate. Madurai is small enough to get around on foot.

RAMESWARAM

☎ 04573 • pop 35,750

Known as the Varanasi of the South, Rameswaram is a major pilgrimage centre for both Shaivites and Vaishnavaites. It was here that Rama (an incarnation of Vishnu and hero of the Ramayana) offered thanks to Shiva. At the town's core is the Ramanathaswamy Temple, one of the most important temples in South India.

Rameswaram is on an island in the Gulf of Mannar, connected to the mainland at Mandapam by rail, and by one of India's greatest engineering wonders, the Indira Gandhi bridge, which was opened by Rajiv Gandhi in 1988.

The town lies on the island's eastern side. Although proximity to Sri Lanka results in a considerably high security presence due to the conflict between the LTTE (Tamil separatist movement) and government forces, Rameswaram still has a decidedly laid-back atmosphere.

Orientation & Information

Most hotels and restaurants are clustered around the Ramanathaswamy Temple. The bus stand, 2km to the west, is connected by shuttle bus to the town centre.

Major Trains from Madurai

destination	train No & name	departure time	distance (km)	duration (hrs)	fare (Rs) 2nd/1st class
Chennai	6718 *Pandian Exp*	7.25 pm	490	10½	166/562
	2636 *Vaigai Exp*	6.45 am		9¾	107/562
Coimbatore	6782 *Coimbatore-Quillon Exp*	6.40 am	229	5	61/321
Kanyakumari	6121 *Chennai-Kanniya Kumari Exp*	4.15 am	242	5¾	62/326
Rameswaram	6115 *Coimbatore-Rameswaram Exp*	5.40 am	164	5	48/252

TAMIL NADU

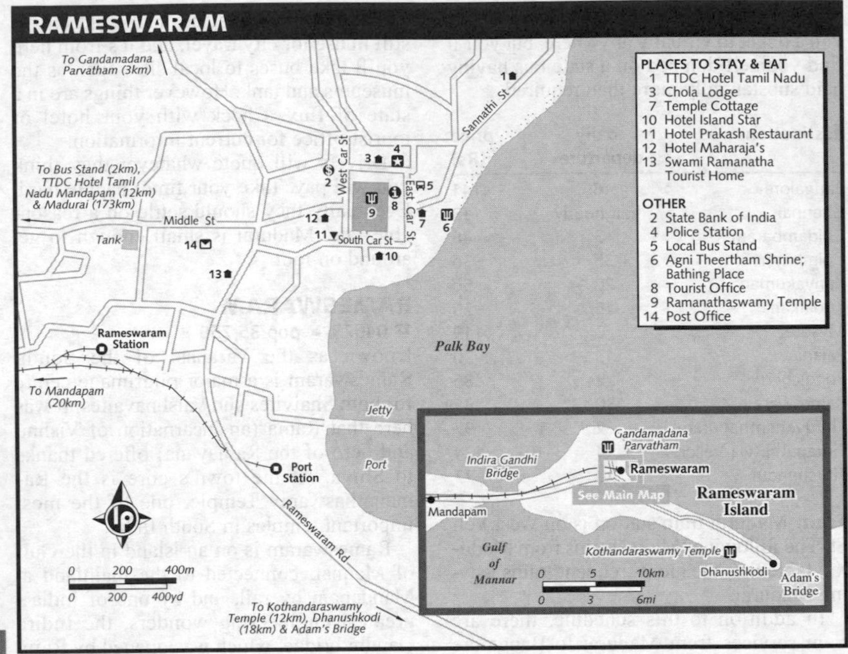

Staff at the tourist office (☎ 21371), East Car St, will recite the history and mythology of the island. The tourist counter at the train station has erratic times and is closed Sunday. The temple information centre sells booklets and organises official guides.

Money can be changed at State Bank of India on West Car St. Take a good book to read – it's a lengthy process.

Don't be rushed into taking a boat trip. There are no officially approved tourist boat operators. Touts hang around the TTDC Hotel Tamil Nadu, promising a one-hour 'luxury boat' trip with snorkel hire and a seafood meal for Rs 300. But this may mean a trip in a precarious fishing vessel with no snorkel equipment and where the only seafood is the flyblown leftovers of the morning catch! Check the boat before you make a deal, and then bargain hard. If boats venture too far they will be quickly spotted (and sometimes confiscated) by the military, which has the area under close surveillance.

Ramanathaswamy Temple

A fine example of late Dravidian architecture, this temple is most renowned for its four magnificent corridors lined with elaborately sculptured pillars. Spanning 1.2km, construction began in the 12th century AD. Later additions included a 53m-high gopuram. There are 22 *theerthams* (tanks) within the complex are believed by devotees to have particular powers. Only Hindus may enter the inner sanctum.

The temple is open 5 am to noon and 4 to 10 pm, but even when it's closed, it's possible to amble through the extensive corridors.

Kothandaraswamy Temple

About 12km south-east of town, this temple was the only structure to survive the 1964 cyclone that destroyed the rest of the village. Legend has it that Vibhishana, brother of Sita's kidnapper Ravana, surrendered to Rama at this spot.

Buses from the local bus stand on East Car St will bring you here. They continue 2km beyond the temple and then it's a 4km walk through fishing communities to **Dhanushkodi**. Local touts quote an exorbitant Rs 300 to show you around. There's little here now but a few ruined houses (which make good sun shelters) and a lovely bathing pool. The walk to the tip of the peninsula is hot but well worth it.

Other Attractions

Adam's Bridge refers to the chain of reefs, sandbanks and islets that almost connect Sri Lanka with India. According to legend, these are the stepping stones created and used by Hanuman to follow Ravana, in his bid to rescue Sita.

The **Gandamadana Parvatham**, 3km north-west of Rameswaram, is a shrine reputedly containing Rama's footprints. Pilgrims visit at sunrise and sunset (the shrine is closed 11.30 am to 3.30 pm).

Special Events

There are many small festivals in Rameswaram. The main ones are the **Car Festival** in February/March and **Thiru Kalyana** (Marriage Festival) in July/August. The first involves processions, the focus of which is a huge decorated chariot with idols of the deities installed. The second celebrates the celestial marriage of Shiva and Parvati. You can get all the details from the tourist office.

Places to Stay & Eat

Hotels, mainly geared towards pilgrims, are often completely booked out during festivals. There are no new hotels and existing ones are ageing quickly. Most of the following have both squat and sit-down flush toilets and there's bucket hot water in the morning. Near the temple loud music blasts out from 4.30 am daily.

Temple Cottage *(☎ 21223, Sannathi St)*, close to the temple, provides basic accommodation for pilgrims keen to wake at 4 am. Singles/doubles with bucket hot water are Rs 50/75.

Chola Lodge *(☎ 21307, North Car St)* offers doubles (no singles) for Rs 150. Family rooms (up to five beds) are Rs 300.

Swami Ramanatha Tourist Home *(☎ 21217)* has a good historical display and clean doubles for Rs 200. ***Hotel Maharaja's*** *(☎ 21271, 7 Middle St)* is a good choice. Clean, pleasant and renovated doubles with balcony cost Rs 250, or Rs 500 with air-con.

Hotel Island Star *(☎ 21472, South Car St)* is clean and friendly. Doubles/triples are Rs 195/275; a triple with air-con is Rs 650.

Railway retiring rooms are large and airy. Their distance from the temple makes them reasonably peaceful. Doubles/triples are Rs 95/150; dorm beds (men only) are Rs 25.

TTDC Hotel Tamil Nadu *(☎ 21277, Sannathi St)* faces the sea. Double/triple rooms are Rs 300/350 – Rs 650 for a double with air-con. There are also five- and six-bed rooms that are sometimes let as dorms at Rs 50 per bed. It has a popular restaurant offering reasonable food with painfully slow service. The bar is excellent and has some pleasant sea views.

TTDC Hotel Tamil Nadu Mandapam *(☎ 41512)* is 12km west of Rameswaram, over the bridge. If all the accommodation in Rameswaram is full, this is a good alternative, more for the sandy beach than the rooms. Basic doubles by the beach are Rs 300 in cement bunker-style cottages. A dorm bed is Rs 50.

A number of vegetarian restaurants (some pretty dismal) along West Car St serve thalis (Rs 10 to 15). ***Hotel Prakash Restaurant*** *(South Car St)* is open evenings only and has a wide range of good, cheap veg dishes.

Getting There & Away

Bus SETC buses run four times daily to Madurai (Rs 38, four hours) and Kanyakumari, and three times daily to Chennai (Rs 127, 13 hours). Local buses also go to Madurai more often, more slowly and more cheaply. Buses also go to Pondicherry and Thanjavur via Madurai.

Train There are two daily express trains to/from Chennai – the *Sethu Express* and the *Rameswaram Express*. The 666km trip, costing Rs 709/210 in 1st/2nd class, takes 17½ hours. Both take the direct route through Manamadurai and Trichy and therefore miss Madurai. The direct train from Madurai to Rameswaram (Rs 252/48/27 in 1st/2nd/3rd class, five hours, 164km) departs at 5.40 am and returns at 4.10 pm.

Getting Around

Town buses (Rs 1) travel between the temple and the bus stand from early morning until late at night. In town, the buses stop at the west gopuram and opposite the tourist office. Cycle- and autorickshaws are available at all hours; haggle hard!

Cycling is a good way to get around with many hire places charging just Rs 5 per hour.

KANYAKUMARI (CAPE COMORIN)

☎ 04652 • pop 18,900

Kanyakumari is the 'Land's End' of the Indian subcontinent. Here, the Bay of Bengal meets the Indian Ocean and the Arabian Sea. Chaitrapurnima (Tamil for the April full-moon day) is one of the best times to experience the sunset and moonrise over the ocean simultaneously.

Kanyakumari has great spiritual significance for Hindus. It's dedicated to the goddess Devi Kanya, an incarnation of Parvati. Pilgrims come here to visit the temple and bathe in the sacred waters.

For tourists Kanyakumari is a popular day trip from Kovalam in Kerala. However, it's best not to compare it with the Keralan beaches. It's essentially a pilgrimage town – a place where people fulfil their spiritual duties. Be aware that crowds flock to the town at weekends and during festivals. At such times you may queue for hours at popular sites.

Orientation & Information

The main temple is right on the point of Kanyakumari with all the facilities within 1km. The post office is on Main Rd and the tourist office, which is near the temple, is open 10 am to 5.30 pm weekdays. The train station is almost 1km north of the temple, while the bus stand is 500m to the west. You can change money at Canara Bank and State Bank of Travancore. Just near the temple there's a branch of the government emporium, Poompuhar.

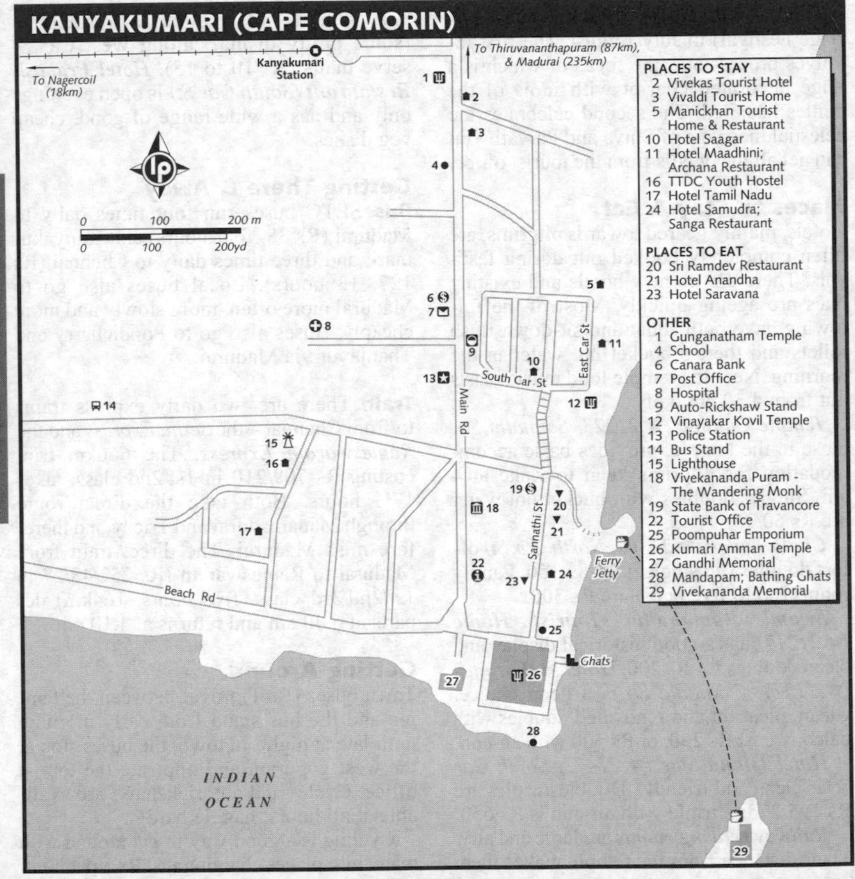

Kumari Amman Temple

According to legend, Devi (the goddess) single-handedly conquered demons and secured freedom for the world. Here at Kanyakumari, pilgrims give her thanks for the safety and liberty she attained for them.

In May/June there is a Car Festival where an idol of the deity is taken in procession, and in September/October the Navratri (Nine Nights) Festival, celebrates Devi's victory over the demons.

The temple is open 4.30 to 11.45 am and 5.30 to 8.30 pm daily. Men must remove their shirts, and everyone their shoes (as always). Cameras are taken and safeguarded until you return.

Gandhi Memorial

This striking memorial, resembling an Orissan temple, stored some of the Mahatma's ashes until they were immersed in the sea. Each year, on Gandhi's birthday (2 October), the sun's rays fall on the place where his ashes were kept. It's open 7 am to 12.30 pm and 3 to 7 pm daily.

Vivekananda Puram – the Wandering Monk

This museum details the extensive journey across India made by the Indian philosopher, Swami Vivekananda, who developed a synthesis between the tenets of Hinduism and concepts of social justice.

The Wandering Monk is open 8 am to noon and 4 to 8 pm daily. There's also a secure cloakroom available 6 am to 10 pm. Entry is Rs 2.

Vivekananda Memorial

This memorial is on two rocky islands about 400m offshore. Swami Vivekananda meditated here in 1892 before setting out as one of India's most important religious crusaders. The mandapam, built here in his memory in 1970, reflects architectural styles from all over India. The ferry to the island (every 30 minutes) costs Rs 8. It's a Rs 5 entry to the memorial, which is open 7 to 11 am and 2 to 5 pm.

Places to Stay

Although hotels are mushrooming in Kanyakumari, demand remains high. Some hotels have seasonal rates so you may find that during April and May and October to December, room prices are 100% up on what's quoted here. Few of the hotels here have single rooms.

Hotel Saagar *(☎ 71325, South Car St)* is a good place with doubles (no singles) starting from Rs 195 to 250.

TTDC Youth Hostel, at the entrance to Hotel Tamil Nadu, charges Rs 45 per dorm bed and is rarely full.

Railway retiring rooms include a six-bed dorm at Rs 20 per bed and singles/doubles for Rs 60/100.

Vivekas Tourist Hotel *(☎ 71192, Main Rd)* has clean, colourful rooms from Rs 195/250 a double/triple.

Manickhan Tourist Home *(☎ 71387)* has doubles for Rs 250, or Rs 320 for one with a sea view.

Vivaldi Tourist Home *(☎ 71972, Main Rd)* is clean and inexpensive at Rs 150/200 for doubles/triples. However, couples must be particularly slim to fit on the bed intended for two.

Hotel Maadhini *(☎ 71787, fax 71657, East Car St)* is a little upmarket with balconies virtually overhanging the village – fascinating for guests but probably a bit intrusive for villagers. The rooms are airy and clean. Doubles are Rs 400, or Rs 500/950 for ocean views without/with air-con.

Hotel Tamil Nadu *(☎ 71257)* has basic doubles for Rs 150 with shared bathroom, and much better doubles with private bathroom for Rs 400 (Rs 600 with air-con). Clean rooms, most with a balcony, have great views of the Gandhi Memorial to the east. Cottages and family rooms are also available.

Hotel Samudra *(☎ 71162)*, near the temple, has doubles from Rs 450 to 620, and a well-appointed air-con double with good views for Rs 990.

Places to Eat

Hotel Saravana, one of the town's most popular eateries, offers Chinese (of sorts) and South Indian cuisine from Rs 20. It has excellent dosas.

Hotel Anandha has a great ocean view and veg cuisine from Rs 25.

Sri Ramdev Restaurant offers a mean range of North Indian veg fare on its tiny open-air terrace.

Sanga Restaurant is an upmarket veg place in Hotel Samudra.

Archana Restaurant at Hotel Maadhini has good veg and nonveg meals (from Rs 40). The outdoor restaurant is open only 7 to 10 pm; for breakfast and lunch you'll be ushered to the indoor room, which has great ocean views.

The ***restaurant*** at Manickhan Tourist Home is perhaps the best in town with meals from Rs 60, but it's closed during low season.

Getting There & Away

Bus The bus stand is a dusty five-minute walk from the centre. It has timetables in Tamil and English, restaurants and waiting rooms. The reservation office is open 7 am to 9 pm.

SETC has buses to Madurai (Rs 75, six hours, 253km, hourly), Chennai (Rs 165, 16 hours, 679km, nine daily), Thiruvananthapuram (three hours, six daily) and Rameswaram (nine hours, seven daily).

Local buses go to Nagercoil, Padmanabhapuram (home to the palace of the former Travancore rulers – see under Around Thiruvanthapuram in the Kerala chapter for details), Thiruvananthapuram and Kovalam, among other places.

Train The daily *Nellai Express* departs for Chennai at 7.15 pm. It takes 16½ hours and tickets are Rs 762/225 for 1st/2nd class.

Trains journey to Thiruvananthapuram leaving Kanyakumari at 4.45 am, 6.35 am and 12.45 pm. The 87km trip takes two to three hours (Rs 173/30 in 1st/2nd class).

The *Kanyakumari Express* departs at 4.45 am daily and travels to Mumbai in 48 hours. The 2155km trip costs Rs 1525/410 in 1st/2nd class. This train will also take you to Thiruvananthapuram and Ernakulam (eight hours).

For the real long-haulers, the weekly *6317-Himsagar Express* runs all the way to Jammu Tawi (in Jammu and Kashmir), a distance of 3734km, in 74 hours. The longest single train ride in India, it leaves Kanyakumari at 12.45 pm on Friday and passes through Coimbatore (12 hours), Vijayawada (29 hours) and Delhi (60 hours).

KUTTRALAM (COURTALLAM)

☎ 04633

About 135km north-west of Kanyakumari, Kuttralam is popular for families who come to bathe at the waterfalls. Men wear sarongs; women full dress. Oil massages are available, but for men only.

In the high season, June to August, the place is impossibly crowded. In the low season the falls may dry up. Sadly, the scenic qualities are somewhat marred by litter.

Of the nine waterfalls, the only one in the village is the 60m-high **Main Falls**. Its sheer rock face is carved with old Hindu insignia, visible during the dry months of January and February. Other falls, mostly accessed by shuttle buses, are up to 8km away.

Kuttralam offers very basic lodging houses that aren't good value and are often full. Some people prefer to stay away from all the hype in Tenkasi, 5km north. ***Krishna Tourist Home*** *(☎ 23125)*, next to the Tenkasi bus stand, has doubles for Rs 250, or Rs 550 with air-con. ***Hotel Anandha Classic*** *(☎ 23303, 116–A/7 Courtallam Rd)* has a similar tariff and a reasonable veg restaurant.

Tenkasi is the closest train station to Kuttralam. However, the main line from Madurai to Kollam does not pass here. To get to Tenkasi, catch the train to Shencottah (Sengottai), from where there's one express daily to take you the remaining 6km to Tenkasi. Faster and more frequent buses also ply these routes.

The Western Ghats

The Western Ghats stretch about 1400km from north of Mumbai, across Maharashtra, Goa, Karnataka and Kerala, to the southernmost tip of Tamil Nadu. They are home to a number of tribal groups. The hills (with an average elevation of 915m) are covered with tropical and temperate evergreen forest, and mixed deciduous forest, and are the source of all major rivers in South India, including the Cauvery and Krishna. They also form a diverse biological and ecological haven with 27% of all India's flowering plants, 60% of all medicinal plants and an incredible array of endemic wildlife. While parts of the Ghats have suffered from development, naturalists regard this as one of the most important pristine forest and mountain areas left in Asia.

An integral part of the Western Ghats are the Nilgiri Hills, which provide opportunities for trekking and other outdoor activities.

KODAIKANAL

☎ 04542 • pop 31,200

Kodaikanal – better known as Kodai – is on the southern crest of the Palani Hills, about 120km north-west of Madurai at an altitude of 2100m. It is surrounded by wooded (not so thickly any more) slopes, waterfalls and precipitous rocky outcrops. The journey up and down is breathtaking.

Kodai is the only hill station in India set up by Americans. American missionaries established a school for European children here in the mid-1840s, the legacy of which is the Kodaikanal International School – one of the most prestigious private schools in the country.

The Kurinji shrub, unique to the Western Ghats, is found in Kodaikanal. This shrub has light, purple-blue coloured blossoms and flowers every 12 years.

Australian blue gums provide the eucalyptus oil sold in Kodai's street stalls and create numerous environmental problems. Such plantations together with rampant tourist development have resulted in local action to save Kodaikanal from further environmental damage. You'll notice the cleverly crafted paper carry bags – this is a no-go zone for plastic – an achievement of environmental groups.

Kodaikanal provides an escape from the heat and haze of the plains and the opportunity to hike in the quiet *sholas* (forests). April to June (the main season) or August to October are certainly the best times to visit. The mild temperatures here range from 11°

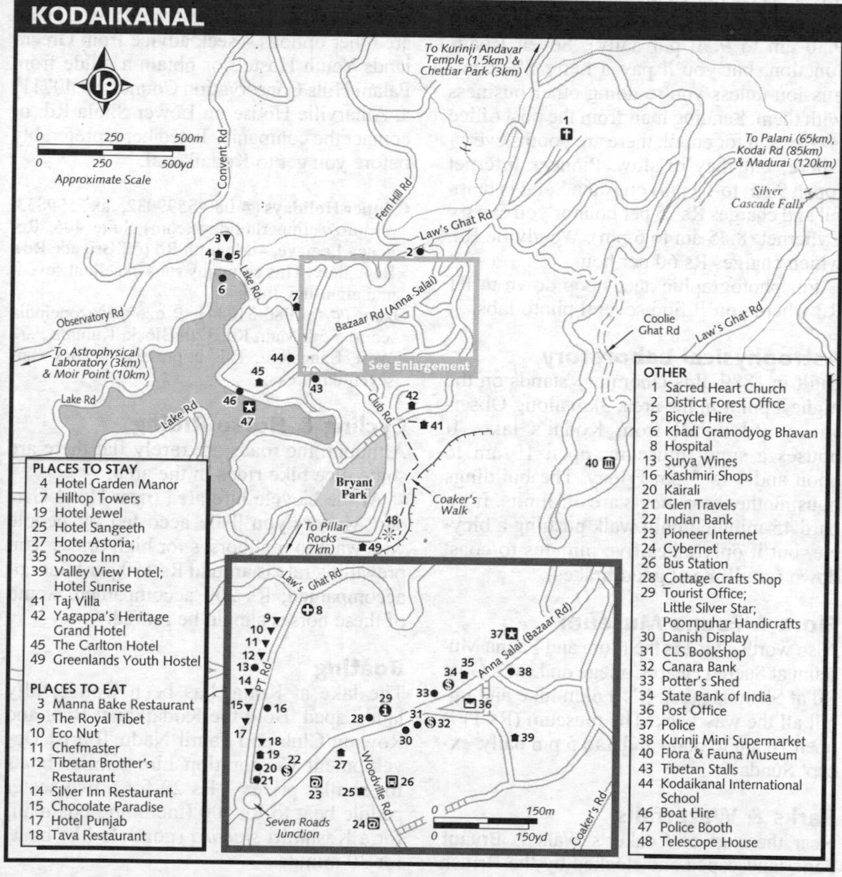

to 20°C in summer and 8° to 17°C in winter. Given the mountainous environment, heavy rain can occur at any time.

Orientation & Information

For a hill station, Kodai is remarkably compact. The main streets run from the Seven Roads Junction. Anna Salai (formerly Bazaar Rd) and Poet Theagarayar Rd (or PT Rd, formerly Hospital Rd) are where most of the action happens. The tourist office (☎ 41675) is often unstaffed. Try the CLS Bookshop on the other side of the road. The staff are helpful and knowledgeable.

State Bank of India is the best place to cash travellers cheques, between 10 am and 2 pm weekdays and Canara Bank gives cash advances on Visa cards. You can also cash travellers cheques and obtain cash advances on credit cards from Glen Travels (open 9.30 am to 9.30 pm daily), Seven Roads Junction, but you'll pay a hefty 8% commission unless you're doing other business with them. Sending mail from the post office is easy and for email, there are booths everywhere, but they're slow. Pioneer Internet (open 9 am to 10 pm) on Anna Salai is helpful and charges Rs 75 per hour or you can try Cybernet (8.45 am to 6 pm), Woodville Rd, which charges Rs 60 per hour.

For photographic needs pop down to PT Rd where you'll find several photo labs.

Astrophysical Laboratory

Built in 1889, this laboratory stands on the highest point in the area, 3km along Observatory Rd uphill from Kodai's lake. It houses a small museum, open 10 am to noon and 3 to 5 pm Friday. The buildings housing the instruments are off limits. It's a hard 45-minute uphill walk pushing a bicycle, but it only takes five minutes to coast down (you'll need good brakes).

Flora & Fauna Museum

Also worth a visit is the Flora and Fauna Museum at Sacred Heart College on Law's Ghat Rd at Shembaganur. It's a 6km hike and uphill all the way back. The museum (Rs 1) is open 10 am to noon and 3 to 5 pm daily, except Sunday.

Parks & Waterfalls

Near the start of Coaker's Walk is **Bryant Park**, landscaped and stocked by the British officer after whom it is named. At **Chettiar Park**, about 3km uphill from town and 1.5km past the Kurinji Andavar Temple, you may be able to see some Kurinji flowers. There are numerous waterfalls – the main one, **Silver Cascade**, is on the road up to Kodai.

Walking

The views along **Coaker's Walk**, which has an observatory with telescope (Telescope House, entry Rs 1), and from **Pillar Rocks**, a 7km hike (one way beginning near Bryant Park), are great. Greenlands Youth Hostel and Taj Villa also organise guided walks.

If you're interested in more serious trekking, the pamphlet, *Sholas For Survival*, available from the District Forest Office (DFO), describes 17 local treks, but estimates of time and difficulty are vague and most treks listed are in restricted areas. There are other options – seek advice from Greenlands Youth Hostel; or obtain a guide from Palani Hills Conservation Council (☎ 40711) at Amarville House on Lower Shola Rd; or contact the companies listed here, preferably before you get to Kodaikanal.

Clipper Holidays (☎ 080-5599032, fax 5599833, ⓔ info@clipperholidays.com) Suite 406, Regency Enclave, 4 Magrath Rd (off Brigade Rd), Bangalore. This company runs excellent seven- and eight-day treks.

Ozone (☎/fax 080-310441, ⓔ ozone@ozoneindia.com) 5 5th Main Rd, 12th Block, Kumara Park West, Bangalore. This impressive agency runs seven-day treks.

Cycling & Horse Riding

Although the roads are rarely flat there are some nice bike rides in the area.

At the bicycle hire area (near Hotel Garden Manor) you'll be accosted by people who want to rent horses for high prices. The prevailing rate is around Rs 150 per hour unaccompanied; Rs 200 accompanied. Some of these horses should be retired.

Boating

The lake at Kodai has been wonderfully landscaped. Both the Kodaikanal Boat and Rowing Club and Tamil Nadu Tourist Development Corporation hire similar boats for similar prices – Rs 20 for a two-seater peddle boat to Rs 100 (including boatman) for a Kashmiri *shikara* (gondola-like boat) for 30 minutes.

Places to Stay

Hotel prices jump by up to 300% during high season (1 April to 30 June) compared to those during the rest of the year. In some cases, this is nothing but a blatant rip-off, especially at the lower end of the market. During this season, it's worth staying in a mid-range hotel since their prices increase only marginally.

The majority of hotels here don't have single rooms and they're reluctant to give single occupancy prices in high season. Most hotels in Kodai have a 9 or 10 am checkout time in high season so don't get caught out. During the rest of the year it's usually, but not always, 24 hours.

And finally most hotels have carpet or some floor covering they call carpet. So in addition to the visual history, so common on many hotel walls, there's often an olfactory one, not guaranteed to stimulate the senses in a positive way.

Places to Stay – Budget

Greenlands Youth Hostel *(☎ 40899)* near Coaker's Walk, has the best views of any hotel in town. The dorms are a bit crowded with triple bunks arranged head to toe. Travellers' reports are ambiguous. Some claim the staff are rude. Others say they're fine, even charming. The management claim they're often required to intervene forcefully when guests disobey the rules (silence between 10 pm and 6 am, no drugs). A bed in the dorms (9 or 10 beds) costs Rs 60/70 in low/high season. There are also eight very pleasant double rooms (four have fireplaces) with private bathroom for Rs 235 to 290 in low season and Rs 290 to 360 in high season. There are both squat and sit-down flush toilets and there's hot water from 7 to 10 am (from tap to bucket only). Dorm residents pay Rs 5 for an additional bucket and additional blankets are Rs 5. People are welcome to pitch tents and use the facilities for the price of a dorm bed. Snacks are available.

Hotel Sunrise *(☎ 40358)* is a friendly place. There are doubles (no singles) for Rs 250. The view from the front is excellent, and the rooms have hot-water geysers that work from 6 am to 6 pm.

Yagappa's Heritage Grand Hotel *(☎ 41235, Noyce Rd)*, off Club Rd, is also friendly in a pleasant setting with a range of double rooms (single prices available) for Rs 300 and Rs 400 for a triple room. All rooms have hot-water geysers and there are both squat and sit-down flush toilets. Room heating is included in the tarriff. There's a TV and phone in all rooms. It has maintenance problems but sinks and linen are clean. Prices double during high season.

Places to Stay – Mid-Range

Taj Villa *(☎ 40940)*, off Club Rd in Coaker's Rd, is an old stone-built group of houses in its own spacious garden with sublime views from some rooms. Prices depend on the view. Pleasant double rooms here (no singles) cost from Rs 250 to 490 (low season), almost doubling in high season. Some rooms in the older house have fireplaces and all have hot-water geysers, direct dial phones and TV. There's a restaurant, Internet (Rs 80 per hour) and a handicraft shop (closed Sunday).

Snooze Inn *(☎ 40837, Anna Salai)* is friendly and well run with clean rooms, TV and phone. Economy doubles (no singles) cost Rs 250/500 in low/high season. Deluxe and family rooms are also available. Visa is accepted with advance notice.

Hotel Sangeeth *(☎ 40456)* is good value at Rs 200/450 for doubles with both squat and sit-down flush toilets, in low/high season. ***Hotel Astoria*** *(☎ 40524)* has ordinary doubles for Rs 350 and deluxe doubles for Rs 450 in low season and, in high season, they are Rs 650 and Rs 800, respectively. There's hot water from 4 pm to 11.30 am, TV and phone. Its restaurant is deservedly popular.

Hotel Jewel *(☎ 41029, PT Rd)* is good value at Rs 275 for ordinary doubles and Rs 300 for deluxe doubles in low season or Rs 450 and Rs 650 in high season. All the rooms are well furnished with wall-to-wall carpeting and TV.

Hilltop Towers *(☎ 40413, Club Rd)*, near the Kodai International School, is a pleasant place that's centrally located. The staff are keen and friendly and double rooms/suites cost Rs 490/990 in low/high season. All major credit cards are accepted.

Hotel Garden Manor *(☎ 40461, fax 42 187, ⓔ sealord@vsnl.com, Lake Rd)* lives up to its name. Set in very pleasant, terraced gardens overlooking the lake, it has spacious rooms from Rs 1000 to 1500 (low season) and Rs 1500 to 1900 (high season). All have hot-water geyser, direct dial phone

TAMIL NADU

and TV. Room heaters (the fireplaces are for show only) cost Rs 100 per day. Eat in the restaurant, your room or on the lawn.

Places to Stay – Top End

Valley View Hotel *(☎ 40181)* is a large modern hotel on Post Office Rd. The rooms are well appointed and those at the front have a wonderful view of the valley. It's a bargain during low season at Rs 400/600 for singles/doubles. High-season rates are Rs 1350/1650 but this includes all meals. There's a good veg restaurant.

The Carlton Hotel *(☎ 40071, Lake Rd)* is five star and Kodai's most prestigious hotel. Overlooking the lake, this hotel used to be a colonial-style wooden structure but was completely rebuilt a few years ago and is simply magnificent. Low-season rooms cost Rs 1800/3000 for singles/doubles with breakfast and dinner; in high season rooms cost Rs 2200/4000. There are also more-expensive suites and cottages. There's a children's playground, a gym, sauna, massage (Rs 480 per 30 minutes) and a boathouse (Rs 120 per hour for a boat). There's also an excellent restaurant and a bar.

Places to Eat

PT Rd is the best place for cheap restaurants and it's here that most of the travellers and students from the Kodai International School congregate. There's a whole range of different cuisines available. But breakfast comes late in PT Rd.

Tava Restaurant offers good veg food. ***Hotel Punjab*** does excellent tandoori food.

Silver Inn Restaurant is a good place for breakfasts (late) and also does pizzas and other Western dishes.

Tibetan Brothers Restaurant is a popular place serving Westernised Tibetan food.

The Royal Tibet serves veg and nonveg and is a popular place with budget travellers. Its noodle soups make a filling meal on a cool night. Just give the coffee a miss.

Chefmaster has continental, Chinese and Keralan dishes, and handmade chocolates.

Eco Nut has a wide range of health food – brown bread, cheese, essential oils etc. Try its 'nutri balls', which are a mixture of jaggery, peanuts, coconut and mung dhal.

Chocolate Paradise is a must for chocaholics. ***Little Silver Star*** is upstairs in the large building with the tourist office. It probably does the best tandoori chicken in Kodai – Rs 95 for half a chicken.

Manna Bake Restaurant on Bear Shola Falls Rd serves Western vegetarian food. The brown bread and apple crumble are legendary. It's open from 7.30 am until late. If you want dinner, order before 3 pm.

Of the hotels, ***Taj Villa*** has multicuisine fare that you can enjoy in the restaurant, your room or in the garden.

Hotel Astoria serves excellent veg food from North and South India. ***The Carlton Hotel*** puts on an excellent evening buffet from 7.30 to 10 pm for Rs 500 including tax. After eating you can relax in the bar.

If you're preparing your own meals, food items are available from the small shop, ***Kurinji Mini Market,*** just up from the post office. Kodai is a lush orchard area and, depending on the season, you'll find various fruits – pears, avocados, guavas, durians and grapefruit – in the street stalls around the bus stand. There are several wine shops. ***Surya Wines*** on PT Rd opens early.

Shopping

The many handicraft stores stock excellent crafts. The Cottage Crafts Shop on Anna Salai has all manner of bits and pieces. Run by Corsock, the Coordinating Council for Social Concerns in Kodai, this voluntary organisation sells goods crafted by development groups and uses the commission charged to help the needy. There's Poompuhar Handicrafts and just opposite there's Danish Display and the Potter's Shed with fine handicrafts and pots. On PT Rd you'll find Kairali and several Kashmiri shops, while on the northern part of Lake Rd there's a branch of Khadi Gramodyog Bhavan. The road leading south to the lake is sometimes lined with stalls run by Tibetans selling warm clothing, shawls and other fabrics – good stuff to keep you warm on chilly nights.

Getting There & Away

On arrival at Kodai you'll be overwhelmed by touts thrusting all kinds of offers for transport and accommodation your way. As always, resist the onslaught or you may find yourself settling for options that are not to your liking.

Bus The bus stand is well organised with information in several languages.

Bus Services from Kodaikanal Bus Stand

destination	frequency	fare (Rs)	duration (hrs)	distance (km)
Chennai	daily at 6.30 am	173	14	513
Dindigul	every 1½ hours	22	3	90
Kanyakumari	daily at 8.30 am	96	9	356
Madurai	hourly	26	3½	121
Palani	every 2 hours	15	3	65
Tiruchirappalli	1.30, 3.30 and 5.30 pm	45	5	197

There's also a KSRTC semideluxe bus to Bangalore for Rs 125 that leaves at 6 pm daily and takes 12 hours (480km).

Private buses run to Ooty (Rs 195, eight hours, twice daily), Coimbatore (Rs 175, five hours, twice daily), Madurai (Rs 100, three hours, twice daily), Chennai (Rs 300, 11 hours, once nightly) and Bangalore (Rs 300, 11 hours, once nightly). Inquire at hotels and travel agencies for times.

Avoid the private bus scams that promise the world to get you to Ernakulam. You'll pay superior prices for inferior services.

Train The nearest train stations are Palani to the north (on the Coimbatore-Madurai-Rameswaram line), and Kodai Road on the Madurai-Trichy-Chennai line to the east. Both are about three hours away by bus.

You can make train bookings at any of the many travel agencies in town.

Getting Around

Taxis are very expensive here compared with elsewhere even though half of them stand idle most of the day. The minimum charge is Rs 60 and daily charges are Rs 600. You won't be able to haggle – there's no competition and there's a powerful association of taxi drivers that determines rates. There are no rickshaws of any description.

The stall outside The Carlton Hotel rents mountain bikes for Rs 7/45 per hour/day. The bicycle stall (7 am to 7 pm) near Hotel Garden Manor has bicycles for Rs 10 per hour (ordinary and children's) and Rs 20 (with gears). The hills can present quite a problem but, as you'd be walking up them anyway, it's not that much extra hassle to push a bike and at least you can coast down. Check the brakes before attempting any steep descents.

INDIRA GANDHI WILDLIFE SANCTUARY (ANNAMALAI WILDLIFE SANCTUARY)

This is one of three wildlife sanctuaries in the Western Ghats along the Tamil Nadu/Kerala border. It covers almost 1000 sq km and is home to elephants, gaurs, tigers, panthers, spotted deer, wild boars, bears, porcupines

They Seek Him Here...

What do elephants, sandalwood trees and Indian film idols have in common? They have all fallen prey to Veerappan, the elusive bandit, and his gang of 30 who hide in the dense jungles of the Nilgiris. It's been a while since Veerappan poached any elephants – there aren't many left. But the precious sandalwood continues to be a lucrative trade, particularly with alleged assistance from numerous officials. And as for the film stars – when Veerappan kidnapped South Indian screen idol, Rajkumar, and kept him hostage for three months until November 2000, everyone agreed it was his most daring feat yet.

Mystery surrounds the circumstances of Rajkumar's release. Was a huge ransom paid? Does Veerappan have links to the LTTE (the Tamil Tigers fighting for a separate Tamil state)? Is Veerappan planning a career in politics? And why is it that politicians and some media seem to have easy access to this self-styled outlaw, yet veritable armies with state-of-the-art fire power have been unable to flush him from his jungle hideout? Two things remain certain – one is that his activities fuel the massive media industries, political rumour mongering and weapons dealing. The other is that whatever his fate, his name and his actions will continue to be a crucial part of South Indian folklore.

and civet cats. The Nilgiri tahr, commonly known as the ibex, may also be spotted, as may many birds. Six tribal groups engage in subsistence agriculture in the park – the Kadars, Malai, Malasars, Eravalars, Puliyars and Muthuvars.

Information

Visitors are not discouraged here, but limitations are placed on their entry; wildlife takes priority and at least 90% of the park is closed to visitors.

The reception centre and most lodges are at Topslip, about 35km south-west of Pollachi. Day visitors may proceed directly to Topslip. Entrance is Rs 5.

Unless you have accommodation you are only permitted in the park between 6 am and 6 pm. The infrequent buses make accessibility difficult. However, if you come by private vehicle you cannot use this in the park and you'll be restricted to the tours conducted in the departmental vans that run from 8 am to 1 pm and 3 to 5 pm. These tours take one hour, cover about 14km and cost Rs 30 per person. Along the route are two strategically placed domestic elephants. The bus will stop so you can have a better look and one of the elephants will perform various three-legged stunts and play a mouth organ. Sometimes there are elephant rides (Rs 100 per person per hour). In the little museum you'll see stuffed elephant legs, stuffed tigers and an elephant foetus preserved in formaldehyde!

Trekking in the park can be arranged at Topslip. However, you must be accompanied by a guide and the maximum length of trek is four hours for Rs 60 per person, including the cost of the guide.

The sanctuary can be visited at any time of year, but there are several factors to consider. It's best to come weekdays when there are staff to handle your inquiries and bookings. The time limitations for day and residential visitors mean you are unlikely to see many, if any, wild animals. The climate is cooler in January and February but you're more likely to see animals during the wet season in June and July and November and December. In March and April, with water shortages and fire risk, the sanctuary may be closed.

Once you get through the bureaucracy and arrive at the park, it's quiet, calm, cool and green. The staff are helpful and humorous. As they suggest, be content with the flora and the hope that, somewhere beyond it, wild animals may be living in sanctuary.

Places to Stay & Eat

Accommodation is available near Topslip and is usually limited to one night only, with a definite maximum of three nights. All accommodation *must* be booked in advance in Pollachi at the Wildlife Warden's Office (☎ 04259-25356) on Meenkarai Rd. The office is open 9 am to 5 pm weekdays (no booking possible on weekends or holidays). Sometimes there is a screening process, where prospective visitors are interviewed to determine their suitability. Interviews are conducted 10 am to noon. Since accommodation availability and cost are constantly under review, it's a good idea to phone first to get the lowdown.

The accommodation near Topslip consists of two dorms, a few suites, lodges and a small house.

Ambuli Illam, 2km from the reception centre, is the best. This has three 'suites' and costs Rs 50 per person. There's a canteen here, which is about the only place in the park where you'll get a decent meal. ***Hornbill House*** has four beds and costs Rs 350.

At Parambikulam, the very basic ***resthouse*** has no catering facilities and only a few 'meals' places nearby. For day visitors, although there is food and drink available, you may wish to bring your own.

Should you get stuck in Pollachi (a likely occurrence given the erratic hours of the Wildlife Warden's Office), you could stay at ***Sakthi Hotels*** *(☎ 04259-23060, Coimbatore Rd)* – the choice of the stars when they make their movies at Topslip. It offers doubles for Rs 250, or Rs 500 with air-con, and has a large (very noisy but very good) restaurant. A cheaper option on the same road, ***Ramesh Lodge***, has doubles for Rs 150 (no singles).

Getting There & Away

The sanctuary is located between Palani and Coimbatore. Regular buses from both places stop at the nearest large town, Pollachi, which is also on the Coimbatore to Dindigul train line. From Pollachi, buses leave the bus stand for Topslip at 6 am and 3.30 pm and return at 8.30 am and 6 pm. A taxi from Pollachi to the sanctuary is around Rs 600 one way.

COIMBATORE

☎ 0422 • pop 1.23 million

Coimbatore is a large business and industrial city and a hub of discussion and debate with many medical, educational, business and technology groups conducting seminars here. It's an organised, easy, friendly place and while it doesn't hold any particular attraction for tourists, it's a convenient overnight stop if you're heading up to Ooty or other Nilgiri hill stations.

Orientation & Information

The three main bus stands are close to each other (almost central) and 2km north of the train station. Low budget accommodation is generally in the bus stand area while more upmarket places are along Avanashi Rd (with numerous spelling options).

The main post office is open for poste restante collection from 10 am to 3 pm Monday to Saturday. An efficient fax and email facility is available from the cooperative staff at Best Business Centre (☎ 235538, fax 233894) in Kalingarayan St. Email facilities are also available throughout the city especially in the area around the bus stands. Blazenet on Nehru St, and Dishnet at HDFC Bank building, charge Rs 30 per hour.

Tamil Nadu tourist office (no phone) is officially open at the train station 10 am to 5.45 pm daily; unofficially it's a different matter so don't get there too early. But if you have to wait, it's worth it; you'll get lots of useful information.

You can change money (US dollars and pounds sterling) and travellers cheques at the State Bank of India as well as the HDFC Bank where there's a 24-hour ATM that accepts all major credit cards. And if you want to buy some warm clothing for the hills, drop in at the Tibetan market just down from Hotel Tamil Nadu.

Places to Stay – Budget

Hotel Sivakami *(☎ 210271, Dave & Co Lane)* is friendly and helpful and has basic singles/doubles for Rs 150/200. There are several other similar places on this relatively peaceful street opposite the train station.

Hotel Shree Shakti *(☎ 234225, 11/148 Sastri Rd)* is a large friendly hotel near the bus stand. It's fairly well maintained with rooms (both squat and sit-down flush

TAMIL NADU

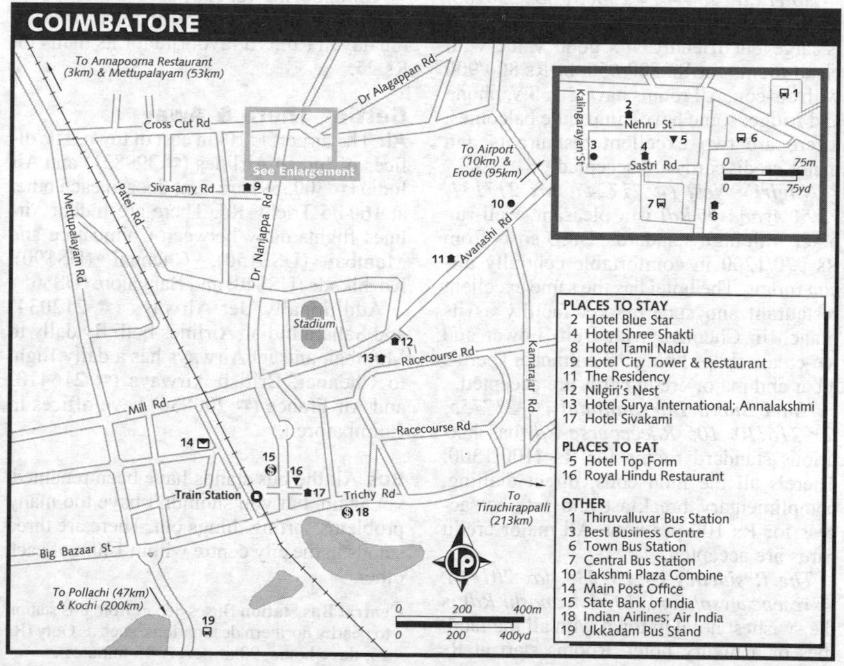

toilets) costing Rs 175/199. Hot water is available from 6.30 to 8.30 am.

Railway Retiring Rooms at the station include doubles for Rs 300, or Rs 400 with air-con. The dorm beds (men only) are Rs 70. There is an air-con suite for Rs 350. An electronic information board indicates which rooms are occupied.

Places to Stay – Mid-Range & Top End

Hotel Blue Star (☎ 230635, Nehru St) has well-appointed singles/doubles for Rs 250/350. The back rooms are quieter. There's a basement bar and both a veg and nonveg restaurant.

Hotel Tamil Nadu (☎ 302176, fax 303511, ⓔ tourism@kovai.tn.nic.in), conveniently located near the central bus stand, may need some physical maintenance but in the area of hospitality, it excels. Ordinary rooms are Rs 195/325, while air-con rooms are Rs 400/600. The water is hot but the taps are hotter, so take care! All rooms have phone, TV and erratic channel music, that will startle the daylights out of you until you discover the off-switch. There's a restaurant and bar.

Hotel City Tower (☎ 230681, fax 230103, ⓔ hcitytower@hotmail.com, Sivasamy Rd) is large but friendly. It's good value with clean rooms for Rs 500/650, or Rs 800/900 with air-con. All rooms have Star TV, phone and fridge; some have minuscule balconies. There are two excellent restaurants and major credit cards are accepted.

Nilgiri's Nest (☎ 217247, fax 217131, 739A Avanashi Rd) is a pleasant, well-run hotel with high standards. B&B costs from Rs 970/1200 in comfortable centrally air-con rooms. The hotel has the same excellent restaurant and supermarket facility as its branch in Chennai, with fruit, flower and ice-cream shops lining the entrance. There's a bar and major credit cards are accepted.

Hotel Surya International (☎ 217755, fax 216110, 105 Racecourse Rd) has luxurious standard rooms for Rs 1100/1300. There's all the mod cons, direct dialling, complimentary breakfast and Internet access for Rs 100 per hour. All major credit cards are accepted.

The Residency (☎ 201234, fax 201414, ⓔ rescbe@vsnl.com, 1076 Avanashi Rd) is the swishest hotel in town with all the facilities of a luxury hotel. Rooms start at Rs 1800/2000. The hotel also has a professional business centre offering an email and fax facility. The centre is available to nonguests for the same fee as guests. The lobby is worth exploring for its coffee shop with tantalising goodies and a reasonable bookstore.

Places to Eat

There are numerous places in the train station area serving thalis from around Rs 25.

Royal Hindu Restaurant (Nehru St) and *Hotel Top Form*, near the station, are both popular for their good veg meals.

Hotel City Towers has a very pleasant rooftop restaurant and is quite a good place for a splurge.

Annalakshmi, next to Hotel Surya International, is the top vegetarian restaurant. It's run by devotees of Swami Shatanand Saraswati, who established the educational trust, Shivanjali, for underprivileged children. It's an interesting place to eat and the food is very well prepared. There are set meals from Rs 250, and it's open for dinner from 6.45 to 9.45 pm daily and for lunch from noon to 3 pm Monday to Saturday. There's another branch in Chennai.

Annapoorna vegetarian restaurant, 3km north-west of the centre of town on Mettupalayan Rd, is a favourite for its thalis for Rs 25.

Getting There & Away

Air The airport is 10km east of town. The offices of Indian Airlines (☎ 399821) and Air India (☎ 300559) are next door to each other at 1604/5 Trichy Rd. There are Indian Airlines flights daily between Coimbatore and Mumbai (US$150), Chennai (US$90), Kozhikode (US$40) and Bangalore (US$65).

Additionally, Jet Airways (☎ 212034) and Sahara Indian Airlines both fly daily to Mumbai, and Jet Airways has a daily flight to Chennai. British Airways (☎ 216418) and Air France (☎ 200836) have offices in Coimbatore.

Bus All the bus stands have been renamed, yet again, but you shouldn't have too many problems sorting things out. There are three stands in the city centre within 100m of each other.

Central Bus Station Buses depart from this station to nearby northern destinations, such as Ooty (Rs 25, three hours, 90km, every 15 minutes).

Thiruvallur Bus Station State and interstate buses leave from here and bookings can be made at the reservation office (open 9 am to 9 pm) on Bay 1. There are 10 daily buses to Bangalore (Rs 95, nine hours, 312km) and three to Mysore (Rs 55, 205km).

Town Bus Station This services the entire city.

There's another bus station at Ukkadam south of the city and buses depart from here for nearby southern destinations including Pallani (every 20 minutes between 4 am and 11.30 pm), Pollachi (every three minutes from 6 am to 9 pm), Madurai (every 30 minutes from 5.30 am to 11.30 pm) and Dindigul (seven daily).

There are also numerous long-distance 'sightseeing video buses' operated by private companies that leave from all over town. Contact a travel agency for details.

Train Coimbatore is a major rail junction. For Ooty, catch the daily *Nilgiri Express* at 5.25 am; it connects with the miniature railway at Mettupalayam (arriving at 6.25 am) in time for the miniature departure at 7.10 am. The whole trip to Ooty and return takes 6½ hours and costs Rs 173/30 in 1st/2nd class.

There are numerous daily trains between Coimbatore and Chennai (494km), the fastest being the Kovai Express which departs at 1.40 pm, takes just over 6¼ hours and costs Rs 562/107 in 1st/2nd class. Other trains take up to nine hours.

The *Rameswaram Express* at 11.30 pm goes daily via Madurai (Rs 321/95 in 1st/2nd class, six hours, 229km) to Rameswaram (Rs 468/138, 11½ hours, 393km). The *Kanyakumari-Bangalore Express* runs daily to Bangalore (Rs 499/148, nine hours, 424km) and, in the other direction, to Kanyakumari (Rs 588/174, 12½ hours, 514km).

To the Kerala coast, the daily *West Coast Express* from Chennai Central goes to Kozhikode (Calicut; Rs 273/52, 4½ hours, 185km) and also on to Mangalore (Rs 489/145, nine hours, 407km).

Several trains go to Pollachi at 7.40 am and 12.30, 1.40, 6.30 and 11.30 pm. It's Rs 22 (2nd class).

Getting Around

For the airport take bus No 20 from the Town bus stand or Nos 10 or 16 from the train station (Rs 25). Many buses ply between the train station and the Town bus stand including bus Nos JJ, 24, 55 and 57 (Rs 1.50).

Autorickshaw drivers charge Rs 25 between bus and train stations, but you can purchase prepaid tickets at booths around the city that precludes the fun of negotiating.

NILGIRI HILLS

Coonoor

☎ 0423 • pop 48,000

At an altitude of 1850m, Coonoor is the first of the three Nilgiri hill stations – Udhagamandalam (Ooty), Kotagiri and Coonoor – that you come to when leaving behind the southern plains. Like Ooty, it's on the miniature train line from Mettupalayam.

Coonoor is now a bustling town where tenacious touts can be overwhelming. It's only after climbing up out of the busy market area that you'll get a sense of what hill stations were originally all about. For this reason, most of the better accommodation is in Upper Coonoor 1km to 2km up the hill.

Things to See & Do The 12-hectare **Sim's Park** in Upper Coonoor has over 1000 plant species, which include magnolia, tree ferns, pines and camellia. Opposite Sim's Park, the **Pasteur Institute** is renowned for its research on the treatment of rabies. **Dolphin's Nose** viewpoint, about 10km from town, exposes a vast panorama, which encompasses Catherine Falls. On the way to Dolphin's Nose you can stop off at **Lamb's Rock**. The site is named after the British captain who created a short path to this favourite picnic spot. The view extends to the town of Mettupalayam.

Upper Coonoor is the perfect place to relax and undertake a **yoga** course. Dr AR Hiruthayaraj ('Raj') is a qualified yoga teacher and natural therapist. He uses four techniques to increase relaxation and well-being – gentle exercise, posture, breathing exercises and meditation. He teaches young and old, beginners and the experienced for Rs 150 per hour, or Rs 2100 for a seven-day course. Numerous student/patient accounts (local and international) testify to the success of his techniques.

Places to Stay & Eat The ***YWCA Guesthouse*** *(☎ 34426)* in Upper Coonoor is the best budget option. Don't believe the touts, taxi and rickshaw drivers, who'll tell you it's full or overpriced. Phone first to check. This place continues to receive accolades from travellers, and deservedly so. Open to men and women, it's a handsome old colonial house with wooden terraces and views over Coonoor. You'll feel at home the minute you arrive. Spacious, clean singles/doubles with old-style furniture and both squat and sit-down flush toilets, cost Rs 200/400 (less in low season). The one-hour yoga class (Rs 120) is popular. To get there, take a town bus to Bedford; then it's a five-minute walk.

Vivek Tourist Home *(☎ 30658, Figure of '8' Rd)* is just around the corner from the YWCA. It's a large friendly place with small but OK rooms with phones from Rs 190/250, more for deluxe rooms with TV. There are squat and sit-down flush toilets and apart from the suites, hot water is available from 6.30 to 9.30 am.

Blue Hills *(☎ 30103, Mount Rd)* with its brown-and-grey striped walls with blue iridescent roof sets a fine pace. The rooms with squat and sit-down flush toilets, are small, comfortable and carpeted and range from Rs 300/400 to 500/700 (no singles) in low/high season. The nonveg restaurant overlooks a stunning view.

Taj Garden Retreat *(☎ 30021, fax 32775, Church Rd)*, on the hilltop, is an excellent hotel with a beautiful garden and a fine restaurant. The rooms are in cottages and cost from US$70/80 in low season, and from US$110/120 (doubles only with all meals) in high season. All facilities are available including email for Rs 100 per hour.

Ramachandra Restaurant *(32 Mount Rd)* has good veg and nonveg food from Rs 15.

Getting There & Away Coonoor is on the miniature train line between Mettupalayam (28km) and Ooty (18km) – see Getting There & Away under Ooty later. Buses to Kotagiri (Rs 8) leave every 15 minutes.

Kotagiri

☎ 0423 • pop 25,600

Kotagiri (Line of Houses of the Kotas) is a quiet village 28km east of Ooty. The oldest of the three Nilgiri hill stations, it's dusty and uninspiring but less frenetic than Ooty or Coonoor, and is surrounded by tea estates and tribal Kota settlements.

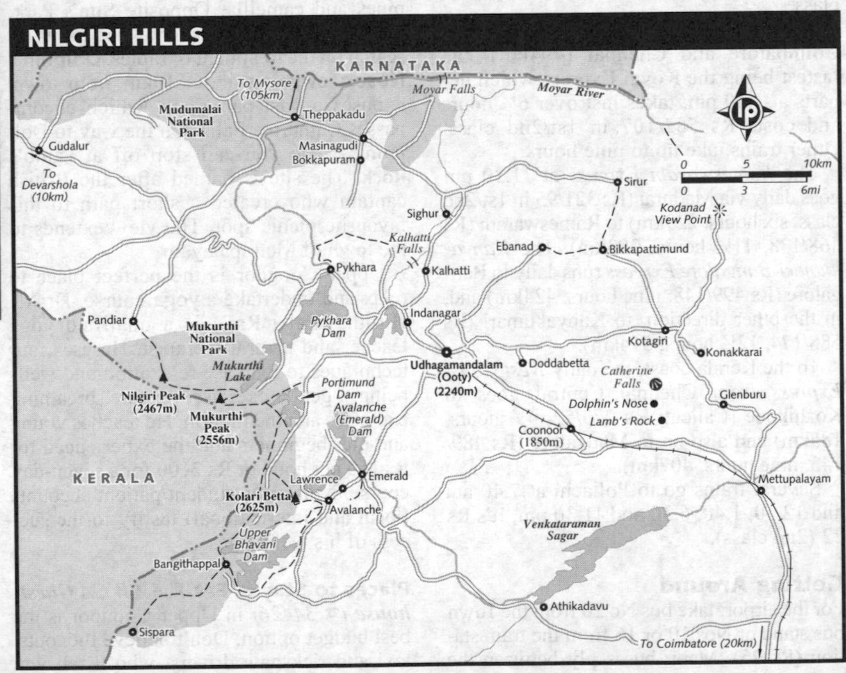

From Kotagiri you can visit **Catherine Falls**, 8km away near the Mettupalayam road (the last 3km is by foot only), **Elk Falls** (6km) and **Kodanad Viewpoint** (22km), where there's a panoramic view over the Coimbatore Plains and the Mysore Plateau. Buses and taxis (Rs 500 return to Ooty) will bring you here. Make sure you have enough cash; there's nowhere here to change money.

In town, a Women's Cooperative near Ramchand Square sells handicrafts such as traditional Toda embroidery. Part of the profit is put towards the preservation of Toda culture.

There are very basic lodges such as ***Majestic Lodge***, ***Blue Star*** and ***Hotel Ramesh Vihar***. Bring your own sheets. Double rooms start at Rs 130. Until accommodation improves, it's preferable to visit Kotagiri as a day trip from Ooty.

The vegetarian ***Kasturi Paradise Restaurant***, diagonally opposite the Women's Cooperative, is good value.

Getting There & Away Buses stop at the edge of town, about 1km from the centre. From there you walk or get a taxi. Buses journey to Ooty every 40 minutes (crossing one of Tamil Nadu's highest passes) and cost Rs 15. The trip takes almost two hours. Buses to Mettupalayam leave every 30 minutes and to Coonoor every 15 minutes.

Udhagamandalam (Ooty)

☎ 0423 • pop 89,000

Historically, this is the area of the Toda, the tribal people whose belief systems and practices centre on the buffalo. Today only about 1500 Toda remain, their cone-shaped shrines prominent throughout the hills.

In the early 19th century, the British established Ooty to serve as the summer headquarters of the Madras (now Chennai) government. Until about two decades ago, Ooty (altitude 2240m) resembled an unlikely combination of southern England and Australia; single-storey stone cottages, bijou-fenced flower gardens, leafy winding lanes, and tall eucalyptus stands.

Now tourist development has totally transformed Ooty, but it retains a certain appeal. Life is relaxed here and touting and haranguing is less prevalent than elsewhere. Just a few kilometres out of town you are in the peace of the hills with views and silence. You can find accommodation that takes advantage of this. You can even stay in a palace of a former Maharaja. The journey up to Ooty on the miniature train is stunning. Try to get a seat on the left side where you get the best chance to see the views. Ooty's a great place at any time; from April to June it's a welcome relief from the hot plains and in winter – October to March – it's crisp and clear and the best time to come. You'll need warm clothing as the overnight temperature occasionally drops to 0°C.

Orientation Ooty is spread over a large area among rolling hills and valleys. Between the lake and the racecourse are the train station and bus station. From either of these it's a 10-minute walk to the bazaar area and 20 minutes to Ooty's real centre, Charing Cross, the junction of Coonoor, Kelso and Commercial roads.

Information The tourist office (☎ 443977) has made an art form of uselessness. Euphemisms justify inaction. You might like to try the private tourist office near Charing Cross, which is enthusiastic and informative, if not always correct. There is a confusing array of forest departments in Ooty. They are all together (a regular blokes' club). It's here you'll need to come (heaven help you) if you want a permit to enter the surrounding forest areas, but permits are issued to serious researchers only.

You're most likely to visit the Wildlife Warden Office (WWO; ☎ 444098), which manages Mudumalai National Park (see later in this chapter for details), among other things. The warden is next door to the other blokes and you'll need to book with him if you wish to stay in the park. In the unlikely event that you get the opportunity, go for it. Details of accommodation are listed in the section on the park below.

The main post office is open 9 am to 5 pm Monday to Saturday. Email can be accessed at numerous places around town:

Global Net (☎ 447611) 29 Baffna Complex, Commercial Rd. Open 8.30 am to 11 pm daily. It charges Rs 50 per hour.

Heartbeat (and next door, The Garment Shop; ☎ 446098) 7 Charing Cross. Open 10 am to 8.30 pm daily, costing Rs 40 per hour.

Surf'n'Snack Commercial Rd (opposite Global Net). Open 9 am to 10 pm, costing Rs 50 per hour.

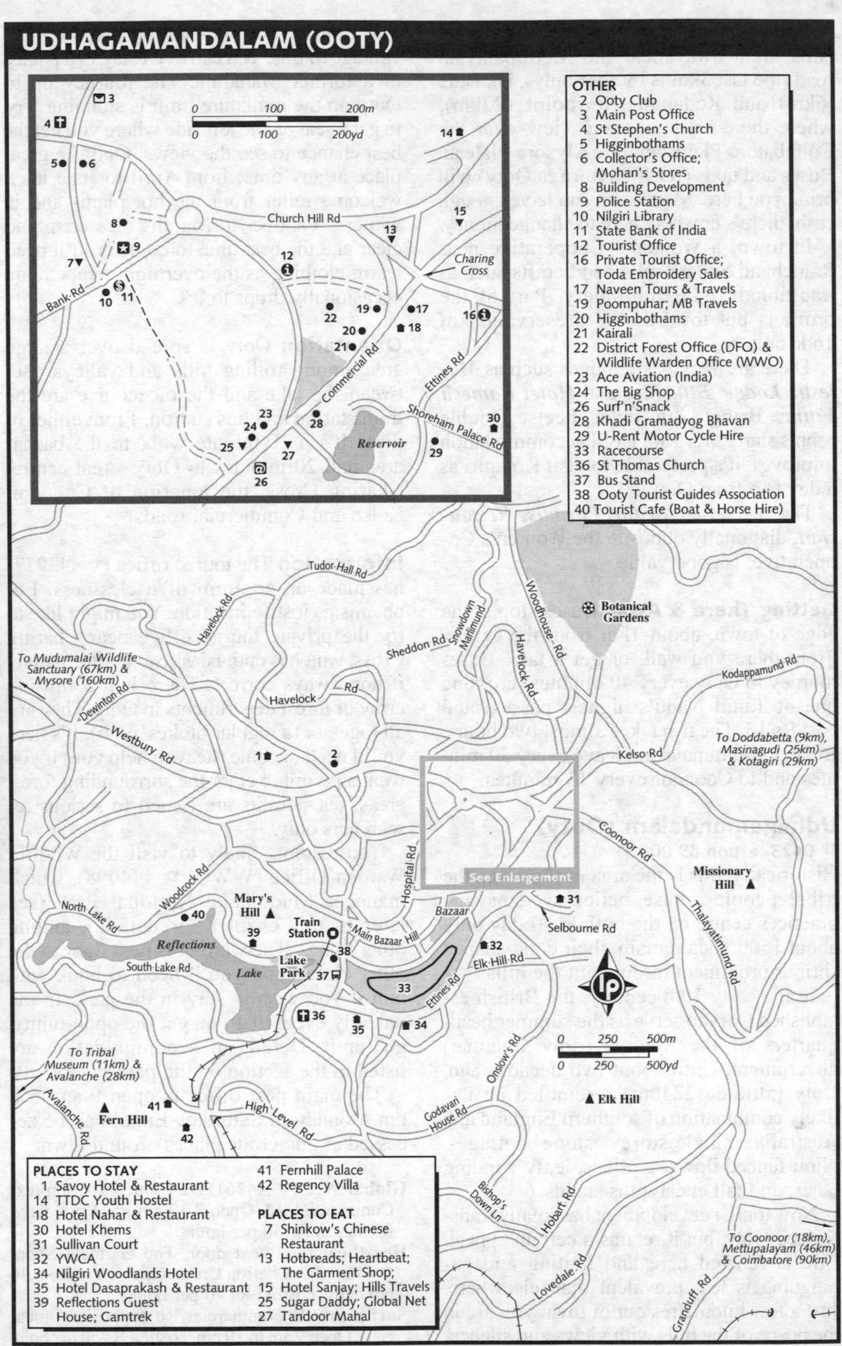
UDHAGAMANDALAM (OOTY)
0 100 200m
0 100 200yd
Church Hill Rd
Bank Rd
Charing Cross
Commercial Rd
Ettines Rd
Shoreham Palace Rd
Reservoir
Tudor Hall Rd
Havelock Rd
Sheddon Rd
Snowdown Marlimund
Woodhouse Rd
Botanical Gardens
Kodappamund Rd
To Mudumalai Wildlife Sanctuary (67km) & Mysore (160km)
Dewinton Rd
Havelock Rd
Westbury Rd
To Doddabetta (9km), Masinagudi (25km) & Kotagiri (29km)
Kelso Rd
Coonoor Rd
Hospital Rd
See Enlargement
Missionary Hill
Woodcock Rd
North Lake Rd
Mary's Hill
Train Station
Main Bazaar Hill
Bazaar
Selbourne Rd
Thalayatimund Rd
Reflections
Lake
Lake Park
South Lake Rd
Elk Hill Rd
Ettines Rd
0 250 500m
0 250 500yd
Onslow's Rd
To Tribal Museum (11km) & Avalanche (28km)
Elk Hill
Avalanche Rd
Fern Hill
High Level Rd
Godavari House Rd
Bishop's Down Ln
Hobart Rd
Lovedale Rd
Grandluff Rd
To Coonoor (18km), Mettupalayam (46km) & Coimbatore (90km)
OTHER
2 Ooty Club
3 Main Post Office
4 St Stephen's Church
5 Higginbothams
6 Collector's Office; Mohan's Stores
8 Building Development
9 Police Station
10 Nilgiri Library
11 State Bank of India
12 Tourist Office
16 Private Tourist Office; Toda Embroidery Sales
17 Naveen Tours & Travels
19 Poompuhar; MB Travels
20 Higginbothams
21 Kairali
22 District Forest Office (DFO) & Wildlife Warden Office (WWO)
23 Ace Aviation (India)
24 The Big Shop
26 Surf'n'Snack
28 Khadi Gramadyog Bhavan
29 U-Rent Motor Cycle Hire
33 Racecourse
36 St Thomas Church
37 Bus Stand
38 Ooty Tourist Guides Association
40 Tourist Cafe (Boat & Horse Hire)
PLACES TO STAY
1 Savoy Hotel & Restaurant
14 TTDC Youth Hostel
18 Hotel Nahar & Restaurant
30 Hotel Khems
31 Sullivan Court
32 YWCA
34 Nilgiri Woodlands Hotel
35 Hotel Dasaprakash & Restaurant
39 Reflections Guest House; Camtrek
41 Fernhill Palace
42 Regency Villa
PLACES TO EAT
7 Shinkow's Chinese Restaurant
13 Hotbreads; Heartbeat; The Garment Shop;
15 Hotel Sanjay; Hills Travels
25 Sugar Daddy; Global Net
27 Tandoor Mahal

You can change money at State Bank of India and also at The Big Shop (9.30 am to 9 pm daily), where you'll get a rate slightly less than the bank rate (about Rs 1 per US dollar) and you'll be charged Rs 20 commission, but it's very convenient and quick. Don't forget your encashment certificate.

Higginbothams with particularly knowledgeable staff, has two bookshops; one in Commercial Rd and the other just near the collector's office.

Nilgiri Library on Bank Rd (closed Friday) is a quaint little haven with a good collection of over 40,000 books, including rare titles on the Nilgiris and hill tribes. Temporary membership is Rs 20.

For police call ☎ 100; hospital ☎ 2212; fire ☎ 2999.

Tribal Research Centre Under the auspices of the Tribal Research Centre (TRC), this small but interesting museum has many

Hill Tribes of the Nilgiris

For centuries, the Nilgiris have been home to hill tribes who have lived together in relative peace and harmony. While retaining integrity in customs, dress, principal occupation and language, the tribes were interdependent economically, socially and culturally.

The Toda tribe lived on the western plateau in the area now called Ooty. Their social, economic and spiritual system centred on the buffalo. The produce derived from the buffalo (mainly milk and ghee) was integral to their diet and it was used as currency – in exchange for grain, tools, pots and even medical services. Most importantly, the dairy produce provided offerings to the gods as well as fuel for the funeral pyre. It was only at the ritual for human death that the strictly vegetarian Toda killed a buffalo. They killed not for food but to provide company for the deceased. Still today, the Toda believe that the soul of the dead buffalo accompanies the soul of a dead person to heaven and that the buffalo will continue to provide the valued dairy produce in heaven just as it did on earth. Other traditional customs that continue today include the division of labour; men care for the buffaloes and women embroider shawls used for ritual as well as practical purposes.

The Badaga migrated to the Nilgiri Hills in the wake of Muslim invasions in the north, and are thus not officially a tribal people. With knowledge of those outside the hills, they became effective representatives for the hill tribes. Their agricultural produce, particularly grain, added a further dimension to the hill diet, and they traded this for buffalo products from the Toda.

The Kotas lived in the Kotagiri area and were considered by other tribes to be lower in status. Artisans of leather goods and pots, the Kotas were also musicians. The Kotas still undertake ceremonies in which the gods are beseeched for rains and bountiful harvests. The Kurumbas inhabited the thick forests of the south. They gathered bamboo, honey and materials for housing, some of which they supplied to other tribes. They also engaged in a little agriculture, and at sowing and harvest times, they employed the Badaga to perform rituals entreating the gods for abundant yields. Kurumba witchcraft was respected and sought after by the other tribes.

The Irulus, also from the southern slopes, produced tools and gathered honey and other forest products that they converted into brooms and incense. They are devotees of Vishnu and often performed special rituals for other tribes. Some Irulus still practise these ancient rites at local shrines and temples.

British settlement in the Ooty area from the early 19th century impacted significantly on tribal life. Some tribes adapted quickly, especially the Badaga. Being cultivators, they continued their traditional pursuits in untraditional ways, they cultivated the cash crops (tea and coffee) of the new settlers, but they were no longer able to provide the grains that were essential to the economy of the other tribes. Eventually tribal systems, especially economic and cultural ones, began to collapse. Displaced tribes have been 'granted' land by the Indian government. But the cultivation of land is anathema to the Toda, who see themselves as caretakers of the soil – for them, to dig into the land is to desecrate it. To fulfil their traditional role and, at the same time, comply with government expectations, many have leased their land to others for cultivation. For this they have been labelled lazy and unwilling to work. Today many tribal people have assimilated almost to the point of invisibility. Some have fallen into destructive patterns associated with displacement and alienation. Others remain straddled across two cultures, maintaining vestiges of their traditions while embracing customs and beliefs of the dominant culture.

exhibits including models of homes of the various hill tribes. Each is carefully constructed and contains utensils and implements relevant to each tribe. There's also a small section devoted to the tribes of the Andamans. Upstairs an excellent photographic exhibition depicts aspects of tribal rituals. If you're lucky and have a Toda researchers guide you through the museum, you'll have a memorable experience. The museum is just beyond M Palada, 11km from Ooty on the way to Emerald. It's open 10 am to 5 pm weekdays (closed holidays). You must call in first at the TRC (on the way to the museum) to obtain permission for entry (free) to the museum. Photography is prohibited. To get here, catch an Emerald bus (several daily) to the TRC stop just after M Palada.

Botanical Gardens Established in 1848, these beautifully maintained gardens include numerous mature species as well as Italian and Japanese sections. There is also a fossilised tree trunk believed to be 20 million years old. At the eastern end of the gardens, there's a Toda *mund* (hill/village) where Toda people display aspects of their traditional culture to gawking tourists. Now a highly commercial show (described by one Toda activist as a human zoo), it is far removed from the reality of Toda life in the Nilgiri villages.

The gardens are open 8 am to 6.45 pm. Entry for adults/children is Rs 5/2.

St Stephen's Church Built in 1829, St Stephen's Church is the oldest in the Nilgiris. Its huge wooden beams came from the palace of Tipu Sultan in Srirangapatnam – hauled the 120km distance by a team of elephants. The attached cemetery contains the graves of many an Ooty pioneer, including John Sullivan, the founder of Ooty.

Walking Walking enables you to appreciate the natural beauty of Ooty. If you want to get out and about, off the beaten track, it's best to get a guide. Getting a reliable guide with good local knowledge is no mean feat (and there are many charlatans around ready to take you for a ride). To avoid this, try one of the following:

Camtrek (bookings should be made at the Reflections Guest House (☎ 443834) North Lake Rd, or Mohan's Stores (☎ 442736). Half- and full-day hikes into the forest with a well-versed guide for Rs 300 to 600 per person (depending on duration).

The Ooty Tourist Guides Association (☎ 445222) opposite the bus station. Walks mainly within the town area for about Rs 200 per day (negotiable).

YWCA (☎ 442218, Ettines Rd) Half-day hikes for about Rs 200.

Trekking For more serious hiking and overnight stays it's important that you organise things early (preferably before you get to Ooty). Make sure that your requirements are clearly understood. It's best to make your trekking plans with a reputable company or resort (see Bokkapuram under Places to Stay & Eat in the Mudumalai National Park section later in this chapter). The following companies organise trekking:

Camtrek (see details above)

Clipper Holidays (☎ 080-559 9032, fax 5599833, ⓔ info@clipperholidays.com) Suite 406, Regency Enclave, 4 Magrath Rd (off Brigade Rd), Bangalore. This company runs excellent seven- and eight-day treks.

Ozone (☎/fax 080-3310441, ⓔ ozone@ozoneindia.com) 5 5th Main, 12th Block, Kumara Park West, Bangalore. This impressive agency runs seven-day treks.

YHA Chennai Contact the YHA (☎ 412882), 2nd Ave, Indira Nagar, Chennai. It has about 20 camp sites throughout the Nilgiris. It can arrange treks from Rs 250 per person per day, including food, guide, and camping and cooking equipment.

Horse Riding Alone or with a guide, there are two choices. You can hire horses at the Tourist Cafe on the north side of the lake. The rides mostly consist of a short distance along bitumen. Choose your animal carefully; some of these horses have clearly seen better years. Prices are set, from Rs 30 for a short ride to Rs 150 for an hour. Even a photo will cost you – Rs 10. For more serious riding, book at Regency Villa. Each morning a pony man arrives with sturdy animals for a three-hour trek through rolling hills and into a Toda village. The ride is exhilarating (not for beginners) and costs Rs 150 per hour. However, the encounter with tribal people smacks of a beads and trinkets mentality.

Boating Rowboats can be rented from the Tourist Cafe (open 9 am to 6 pm) by the lake. High-season crowds can make boating somewhat tortuous. Prices start from Rs 50 for a two-seater pedal boat and up to Rs 250 for a 15-seater motor boat. There are dashing cars (Rs 20 for three minutes) and a minitrain (Rs 5 per ride) here too.

Paragliding If you want to get a different perspective on Ooty try paragliding, parascending or take a joy ride in a microlight. For experienced professionals there are also flying safaris. Contact Ace Aviation (India) (☎ 442313), which operates from Catwalk directly opposite Tandoor Mahal on Commercial Rd.

Horse Racing The season for the Ooty horse races begins on 14 April and lasts to about June. Some consider the racecourse tatty and the betting tame, but it is most entertaining.

Organised Tours The tourist office organises trips to Mudumalai National Park via the Pykhara Dam for Rs 200 (plus Rs 30 entrance to the park); and to Coonoor, taking in the Ooty botanical gardens, Doddabetta, Sim's Park and Dolphin's Nose for Rs 120. Naveen Tours & Travels (☎ 443747), near Hotel Nahar, and Hills Travels (☎ 442090), at Hotel Sanjay, are among several private operators which runs a range of tours.

MB Travels (☎ 442604, fax 444912) on Commercial Rd organises tours and airline reservations can also be arranged here.

Places to Stay Since Ooty is a sellers' market in the high season (1 April to 15 June), hoteliers double their prices, and these don't necessarily equate with quality. Note that checkout time is generally 9 am. In town, you'll be close to all amenities, noise and pollution. However, peace and tranquillity can be found just a few kilometres out.

Places to Stay – Budget The ***TTDC Youth Hostel*** *(☎ 443665, Charing Cross)* is not bad once you leave the flies at reception. Dorm beds (15 double bunks per room) cost Rs 125/175 in low/high season, and doubles are Rs 200/450. The linen and rooms are cleaner than at many other basic accommodation options. The dorm rate includes two meals (as you like) and hot water is available each morning (6 to 10 am). There's a restaurant and bar.

YWCA *(☎ 442218, Ettines Rd)* has many things to recommend it. Set in pleasant grounds it's close to the centre yet far enough away to enjoy the peace of the hills. Rooms are spacious, neat and clean. It costs Rs 66 for a dorm bed in low season and Rs 77 in high season, while singles/doubles cost Rs 214/286 (low season) to 214/390 (high season). There are several cottages for Rs 850 (low season) or Rs 1200 (high season). A few rooms have hot water only from 6.30 to 8.30 am. The remainder have constant hot water. Almost all rates are inclusive of tax. There's a library, a reading room and a music room with an open fireplace. Three-course multicuisine meals are available (Rs 70). This is a homey place well worth considering and whether you stay here or not, it's a good place to organise hiking.

Reflections Guest House *(☎ 443834, North Lake Rd)* is a delightful place with good views over the lake and doubles at Rs 200 (Rs 300 in high season). You can stay in the main home or in separate rooms further up the hill and hot water is available morning or night. This is a great place to experience a home-stay. Unfortunately it's had a review stating it was unsafe for women although it would seem that the contrary in fact is true and many women have testified to this. Good breakfasts and a range of snacks can be brought to your room or are served on the grassy terrace. The friendly owner, Mrs Dique, is a good source of information on the region's history. You can organise hiking and trekking from here.

Places to Stay – Mid-Range The ***Hotel Khems*** *(☎ 444188, Shoreham Palace Rd)* has reluctant management but helpful staff. The hotel is well appointed and good value. Standard/superior doubles with TV are clean and cost Rs 475/675 (low/high season). There's a multicuisine restaurant and major credit cards (not AmEx) are accepted.

Nilgiri Woodlands Hotel *(☎ 442551, fax 442530, Ettines Rd)* is a Raj-era hotel. Manicured gardens offer great views of Ooty. It needs some maintenance and the plumbing is due for retirement but it has alluring character. There are rooms in the main building, and a number of detached cottages. In low season, doubles cost Rs 400, cottages are Rs 750 and suites Rs 1100. In high season they range from Rs 500 to 1300. With taxes at 20% and a further service charge of 20%, prices become somewhat hefty. Numerous packages and plans are available and major credit cards (Visa preferred) are accepted.

Hotel Dasaprakash *(☎ 442434)*, on Ettienes Rd, is another long-established hotel, and reasonable value. Doubles range from Rs 300 to 500 in low season and Rs 450 to 700 in high season. Family rooms with six beds are Rs 420/600.

Hotel Nahar *(☎ 442173, fax 445173)* is a huge place at Charing Cross. Carpeted doubles with TV cost from Rs 900 to 1400 (low season), and 30% more in high season. Except for the odd bathroom, the rooms are attractive and well maintained. It's a 'teetotaller's paradise' and a there's multicuisine restaurant overlooking a pleasant garden.

Regency Villa *(☎ 443608, fax 443097)* is owned by the Maharaja of Mysore. Set within eight wooded hectares (along with Fernhill Palace) it is wonderfully atmospheric. There are potted plants, wicker chairs and faded photographs of the Ooty Hunt, a popular pastime of the Raj. Now as it gracefully languishes, it's the PR boys at work instead of the maintenance men. The best rooms are ultra spacious and have bay windows, fully tiled Victorian bathrooms and an open fire. Singles/doubles in the main building cost Rs 900/1200 in low season and Rs 1300/1600 in high season. The cottages are Rs 500/700 and Rs 800/900 in high season. There are all the services you could want – phone, TV, horse riding, golf, fishing and hiking in more ways than one – the hike in prices seems far too great for the standard offered. However the manager, Mr Kannan, maintains that he's 'flexible' so maybe you can negotiate a better deal.

Places to Stay – Top End The ***Savoy Hotel*** *(☎ 444142, fax 443318, 77 Sylks Rd)* is very comfortable. Part of the Taj Group, this place has doubles for US$85 in low season and US$130 in high season. It has manicured lawns, clipped hedges, rooms with bathtubs, wooden furnishings, working fireplaces, a 24-hour bar and an excellent multicuisine dining room.

Sullivan Court *(☎ 441416, fax 441417, ⓔ wgsull@md5.vsnl.net.in, 123 Selbourne Rd)* is one of the newest and plushest places in town with several restaurants, games rooms, children's play area, gym and massage (for men only). Rooms are Rs 1150/2000 and up to Rs 2600 (doubles only).

Fernhill Palace *(☎ 442555, fax 443097)* is still closed for renovations and still promising to open 'soon'. Owned by the Maharaja of Mysore, it was built in the days when expense was of no concern. When it finally reopens (supposedly April 2001) its facilities and prices will be top of the range and probably the best place to stay in Ooty.

Places to Eat Almost all places to stay have restaurants, and there are plenty of basic veg places on Commercial and Main Bazaar Rds.

The veg restaurant at ***Hotel Nahar*** has a garden outlook. There's also a popular snack bar serving ice cream and milkshakes.

Hotel Sanjay is a big, bustling place with generous servings of veg and nonveg fare.

Tandoor Mahal *(Commercial Rd)* has tasty veg dishes for around Rs 35 and nonveg meals for around Rs 50. The service is good, and beer is available (Rs 65).

Shinkow's Chinese Restaurant *(30 Commissioner's Rd)*, also known as the Zodiac Room, at has some really good food for around Rs 50 per main.

Hotel Dasaprakash is well known for its lunch thalis for Rs 30. People crowd in, sit in ashram-style rows and are fed huge quantities of delicious thali items.

Savoy Hotel is the place for a splurge. Buffet lunch or dinner costs Rs 300 (plus tax) for all you can eat. The dining room is particularly atmospheric with a roaring fire that takes the chill off the cool low-season nights.

Sugar Daddy on Commercial Rd is the place to take a break from Internet surfing.

Hot Breads has a gastronomical range including 20 varieties of bread, 50 types of pastry (croissants, strudel, eclairs) and 35 different pies (veg and nonveg).

Shopping The main places to shop are along Commercial Rd where you'll find several Kashmiri shops as well as the government outlets for Poompuhar, Kairali and Khadi Gramadyog Bhavan. Also have a look at The Big Shop. It has an exquisite range of gold and silver items, jewellery, statues and much more. You can buy tribal crafts at the Toda Embroidery Sales outlet.

Getting There & Away

Bus The state government-run bus companies all have reservation offices at the bus station, open 9 am to 5.30 pm daily. There are six buses daily to Mysore (Rs 55, five hours) and many continue to Bangalore (Rs 120, eight hours). There are buses every 10 minutes to Coimbatore (Rs 20, three hours), every 10 to 15 minutes to Mettupalayam (Rs 15, two hours), four buses to Chennai (Rs 120, 15 hours), and also direct services to Kanyakumari (14 hours), Thanjavur (10 hours) and Tirupathi (14 hours).

Most of the private companies are located at Charing Cross. They're a little more expensive than the state buses, but worth it.

To get to Mudumalai National Park (Rs 22, 2½ hours, 67km), take one of the Mysore buses or one of the small buses that go via the narrow and twisting Sighur Ghat road. Most of these rolling wrecks travel only as far as Masinagudi, from where there are buses every two hours to Theppakadu (at Mudumalai). Buses travelling via the park sometimes ask passengers for another Rs 30, which is the park entrance fee. Private bus services run to Mysore via Theppakadu for Rs 100.

Local buses leave hourly for Kotagiri (Rs 10, one to 1½ hours) and every 20 minutes to Coonoor (Rs 9, one hour). Buses to Doddabetta (Rs 12) depart about every 1½ hours.

Train The miniature train is the best way to get here with excellent scenery along the way. Departures and arrivals at Mettupalayam usually connect with those of the *Nilgiri Express*, which runs between Mettupalayam and Chennai. It departs Chennai Central at 8.15 pm and arrives in Mettupalayam at 6.20 am in time for the miniature train departure to Ooty at 7.10 am. The cost of the miniature train is Rs 114/22 in 1st/2nd class (five hours, 46km). If you're catching the miniature train from Ooty, and you want a seat, be at least 45 minutes early.

From Ooty the train leaves at 3 pm. The trip down takes about 3½ hours. During high season there may be an extra service in each direction, but check first to make sure.

Getting Around Plenty of autorickshaws hang around the bus station. In high season, the drivers quote outrageous fares. Taxis are also available.

You can hire a bicycle at the bazaar but many of the roads are steep so you'll end up pushing it uphill (great on the way down though!). Motorcycles can be hired from U-Rent (☎ 442128) at the Hotel Sapphire Buildings on Ettines Rd. A 100cc machine will set you back Rs 380 per 24-hour period (or Rs 75 first hour and Rs 50 thereafter), including insurance *and repairs* but excluding petrol. A deposit of Rs 550 is required plus your current international or home-country driving licence (a car licence will suffice). Helmets are not supplied. U-Rent is open 9 am to 7 pm daily.

Mudumalai National Park
☎ 0423

In the foothills of the Nilgiris, this 321 sq km park is part of the Nilgiri Biosphere Reserve (3000 sq km) that includes Bandipur and Wyanad in neighbouring Karnataka and Kerala states. The larger reserve's vegetation ranges from grasslands to semi-evergreen forests. In Mudumalai, the forest is home to chital (spotted deer), gaur, tiger, panther, wild boar and sloth bear. Otters and crocodiles inhabit the Moyar River. The park's wild elephant population supposedly numbers about 600; however, you're more likely to see their domesticated cousins as they carry out logging duties.

The best time to visit Mudumalai is between December and June although the park may be closed during the dry season, February to March. Heavy rain is common in October and November.

Orientation & Information The main service area in Mudumalai is Theppakadu, on the main road between Udhagamandalam (Ooty) and Mysore. Here you'll find the park's reception centre (☎ 56235), open 6.30 am to 6 pm daily. There is some very basic accommodation and an elephant camp here.

Entry fees to the park are Rs 5/2 for adults/children. Please note that alcohol is banned in the park.

Jeeps can be hired in Masinagudi for Rs 550 per half day.

Wildlife Tours It's not possible to hike in the park and tours are limited to the sanctuary's minibuses, jeeps and elephants. Private vehicles are not allowed. Minibus tours (morning and afternoon) cost Rs 25 per person for 45 minutes, and they go about 15km around the outskirts of the park. The one-hour elephant rides (Rs 140) can be booked in advance at the WWO in Ooty or direct at the Theppakadu reception centre.

Places to Stay & Eat All budgets are catered for – there are cheap bungalows inside the park at Theppakadu; mid-range hotels in Masinagudi (8km from Theppakadu) and expensive resorts in Bokkapuram (4km south of Masinagudi).

In the Park For accommodation in the park, book in advance with the WWO in Ooty (see Information under Ooty). There is a one-night maximum stay, but if business is slack, you can often stay another night or two.

Morgan Dormitory is clean and has two four-bed rooms for Rs 20 per person. Each room has a private bathroom with cold water only. ***Minivet*** is a pleasant dorm, similar and with the same prices as Morgan.

Sylvan Lodge is set along the Moyar River, in Theppakadu. Clean, small simple rooms are Rs 200/300 a single/double. Meals are Rs 25 extra. ***Theppakadu Log House***, next to Sylvan Lodge, is the nicest place in the park. Overlooking the river it has large carpeted wooden rooms for Rs 200/300. It's comfortable, well maintained and very good value. And there's a small restaurant and amiable kitchen staff.

Hotel Tamil Nadu (☎ *56249*) has OK rooms but its location is spoilt by loss of tree and grass cover as well as litter. Large family rooms (with three beds) cost Rs 350 while dorm beds are Rs 50 per person. There are squat and sit-down flush toilets. The restaurant is the best place for a meal or cold drink in Theppakadu.

Other places in the park are not well maintained and are best avoided.

Masinagudi There are several lodges on the main road in Masinagudi as well as the odd place for a meal. ***Hotel Dreamland*** (☎ *56127*) above the supermarket, looks better than the outside suggests. It has close-to-clean rooms with a small TV for Rs 250 a double. Prices are negotiable; the longer you stay the cheaper. You can share the upstairs open area with the drying chillies as you bask in the sun and enjoy the views.

Mountania Resthouse (☎ *56337*) is set in a dry patch back from the main road. A double room (no singles) costs Rs 420, and meals (for guests only) cost from Rs 30 to 40. There are squat and sit-down flush toilets and bucket hot water at any time. ***Green Park Resorts*** (☎ *56351, fax 56446, Singara Rd*) is 2km west of Masinagudi. It's not bad for the price but nowhere near the standard of the resorts described following. Cottages with tiny bedrooms, phone and TV, start at Rs 400 for a double to 1600 for an eight-bedder. Savour the decor – mauve and iridescent green with red geysers.

Bokkapuram This area is the site of many fine resorts. Most listed here are family-run businesses with a warm, homey atmosphere and are invariably of a high standard with breathtaking views. Many resorts provide a pick-up service from nearby towns (starting from Rs 500; less if they like you!) For those that don't pick-up, you'll need private transport. It's best to book rooms in advance. Each resort offers a range of services including:

- visits to Mudumalai National Park, including an elephant ride
- hikes with a guide (rates start from Rs 100 per person per hour)
- sightseeing tours
- fishing
- horse riding

If you have particular hiking requirements (overnight trekking, night walking, animal sighting etc) make it known at booking time to ensure that your needs can be met.

Costs shown here are for accommodation only. Meals are extra and usually start at around Rs 100.

Bamboo Banks (☎*/fax 56222*) is 1.5km from Masinagudi. One of the region's oldest private lodges, its owners, with a background in tea planting and hunting, are charged with lively stories and open to fascinating debate. It's pleasant and very comfortable with rooms and cottages for Rs 1800/2000 a single/double. There's an extensive menu including Indian and continental cuisine.

Forest Hills Guest House (☎ *56216*) is good value with spacious rooms from Rs 750/950/1250 for a single/double/triple. Follow the sign from Jungle Hut Guest House.

Jungle Hut Guest House (☎*/fax 56240*) in a grassy setting has very pleasant rooms for Rs 900/1000/1200. There's a small playground, and several farm animals – ducks, geese, pigs to interest children. You can fish from the duck ponds or paddle in the small swimming pool.

Jungle Retreat *(☎ 56470, fax 56469, e jungleretreat@yahoo.com)* almost next door, has a range of accommodation from camping to high-class resort style. It also has a tree house (Rs 600), but not during monsoon months (June to August). Rooms in stone cottages with warm red-tiled roofs and floors cost Rs 1000/1200 for a double/triple (no singles). Larger rooms have bars and fridges. You can stay in ecofriendly bamboo huts for Rs 600, or you can pitch a tent in the grounds and use the provided facilities for Rs 200 per person.

The Retreat also offers voluntary work for overseas visitors. Positions available include bar work, general hospitality and guides for walking tours. If you are interested you should send a detailed resume of your experience together with a covering letter outlining why you wish to undertake the work and what you might have to offer. Send these documents to The Manager, Jungle Retreat, Bokkapuram, Masinagudi PO, 643223, Nilgiri District, Tamil Nadu. Whatever you do, don't just turn up.

Belmont Retreat Guest House *(☎ 56253, fax 44242)* has simpler, but very pleasant, accommodation. Standard double rooms are Rs 500 to 700 with larger rooms at Rs 900.

Chitral Walk *(Jungle Trails Lodge; ☎ 56256)* has been recognised for a long time as one of the more ecofriendly places. Set within the jungle, rustic rooms cost Rs 800 a double.

Getting There & Away Buses from Ooty to Mysore, Bangalore or Hassan in Karnataka stop at Theppakadu.

An interesting short cut to or from Ooty (36km, 1½ hours) involves taking one of the small government buses that make the trip up (or down) the tortuous Sighur Ghat road. The bends are so tight and the gradient so steep that large buses simply can't use it. In fact, there's a sign warning that 'you will have to strain your vehicle much to reach Ooty'. The longer route via Gudalur is equally interesting but not quite as steep (2½ hours, 67km).

Buses run daily every two hours between Theppakadu and Masinagudi. A local taxi-jeep charges Rs 200 for the same trip.

Andaman & Nicobar Islands

In the Bay of Bengal, 1000km off the east coast of India, the Andaman and Nicobar Islands comprise around 500 mostly uninhabited tropical islands with unique fauna, lush forests, white sandy beaches and exquisite coral. For weary mainland travellers, the Andamans offer a welcome respite with plenty of opportunities to simply blob out or get physical and hike, snorkel or dive.

The islands form the peaks of a vast submerged mountain range that extends for almost 1000km between Myanmar (Burma) and Sumatra. The total land area is 8248 sq km with the majority being the Andamans at 6408 sq km. The highest point, Saddle Peak, at 732m, is on North Andaman. The Nicobar Islands begin 50km south of Little Andaman.

While geographically close to Myanmar, politically the Andaman and Nicobar Islands belong to the Union Territory of India.

Until the beginnings of colonial rule the Andamans were populated mainly by Andamanese, indigenous tribes of the Negrito peoples. Patterns of traditional life still remain among the Jarawa and Onge tribes who live in the interior regions of South Andaman. However, the majority of the 300,000 people on the Andamans are mainland settlers or their descendants who live in and around Port Blair, the capital on South Andaman.

The indigenous inhabitants of the Nicobars, the Nicobarese, probably descended from people of Malaysia and Myanmar. Their dialects belong to the Mon-Khmer group.

The islands are accessible by boat and plane from Chennai (Madras) and Kolkata (Calcutta; with an infrequent boat service from Visakhapatnam). Direct international charter flights are mooted for 2002. Despite significant travel restrictions (see Permits later in this chapter), there is still much that can be experienced on the islands.

Andaman & Nicobar Islands at a Glance

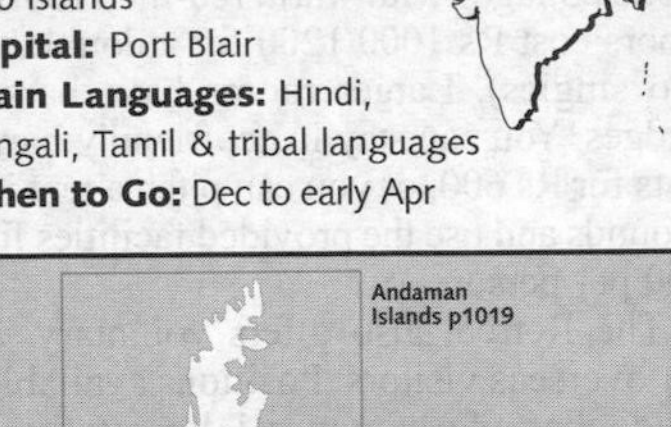

Population: 356,265
Area: 8248 sq km on about 500 islands
Capital: Port Blair
Main Languages: Hindi, Bengali, Tamil & tribal languages
When to Go: Dec to early Apr

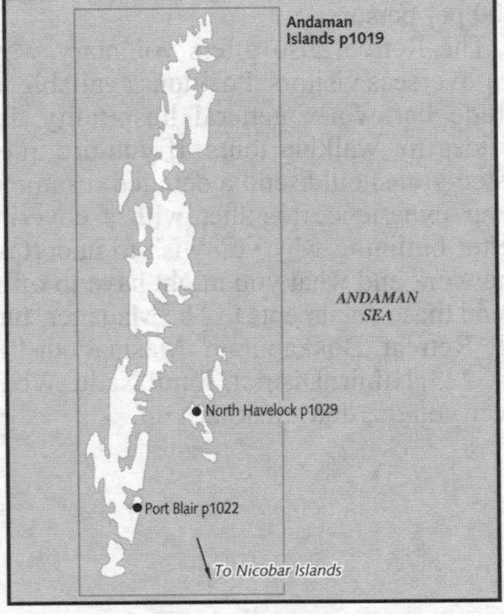

- Savour the seclusion of deserted beaches with white-powder sands
- Snorkel among superb coral reefs and vivid marine life
- Reflect on the triumph of the human spirit over brutality at the Cellular Jail – a sobering reminder of the history of Port Blair

History

It's not known when the first inhabitants arrived on the Andaman and Nicobar Islands. Their presence was documented in the 2nd century by Ptolemy, and later in the 7th century by Xuan Zang.

In the late 17th century, the islands were annexed by the Marathas whose empire consumed vast areas of India. Two centuries later the British used them as a penal colony, initially to detain 'regular criminals' from mainland India and later to incarcerate political dissidents – the freedom fighters for independence. For this purpose the British constructed the notorious Cellular Jail. Completed in 1908, it became a place of horrendous atrocities (see Cellular Jail National Memorial later in this chapter). During WWII, the islands were occupied by the Japanese, who were regarded

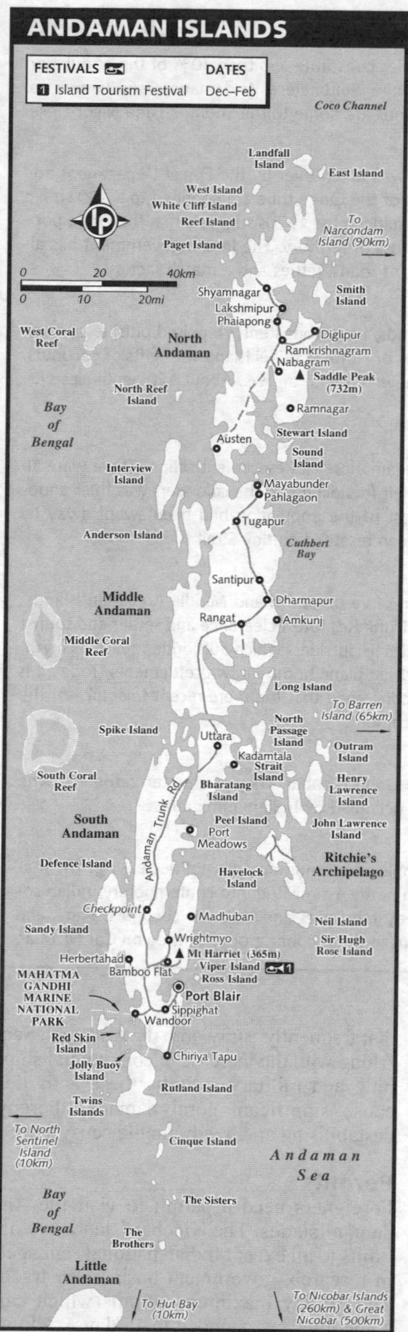

ambiguously by the islanders. Some initiated guerrilla activities against them while others regarded them as liberators from British colonialism. With Independence in 1947, the islands were incorporated into the Indian Union. Since then, massive migration from the mainland has inflated the island population from a few thousand to more than 300,000. Tribal land rights and environmental protection have at times been disregarded. The island administrators are mostly appointed from the mainland and their tour of duty is often viewed as a 'hardship' posting. Many are reluctant sojourners; others make a few nominal changes in the name of progress before returning home. Some of these 'inventive' schemes have included a velodrome (one of only four in India), a high-tech, rarely used swimming pool and the Andaman Grand Trunk Rd (dubbed the 'Road to Nowhere'), which cuts through tribal land and links destinations already well served by sea.

Climate

Sea breezes keep temperatures within the 23 to 31°C range and the humidity at around 80% all year. The south-west monsoons come to the islands between mid-May and June, and the north-east monsoons between November and December. The best time to visit is between December and early April. December and January are the high seasons.

Ecology & Environment

The isolation of the Andaman and Nicobar Islands has led to many endemic species of both flora and fauna. Of 62 identified mammals, 32 are unique to the islands. Among these are the Andaman wild pig, the crab-eating macaque, the masked palm civet and species of tree shrew and bats. Almost 50% of the islands' 250 bird species are endemic. Eagles, megapodes, swiftlets, doves, teals and hornbills inhabit the islands. The isolated beaches provide excellent breeding grounds for turtles. While dolphins are frequently sighted, the once abundant dugong has all but vanished, leaving scientists troubled and hunters lacking yet another food source.

Mangroves are an important aspect of the flora offering a natural protective barrier to both land and sea. Further inland the evergreen and moist deciduous forests contain

Island Indigenes

The Andaman and Nicobar Islands' indigenous peoples constitute less than 10% of the population and, in most cases, their numbers are falling. The Onge, Sentinelese, Andamanese and Jarawa are all resident in the Andaman Islands. The Nicobar Islands are home to the Shompen and Nicobarese.

Onge

Two-thirds of the Onges' island of Little Andaman was taken over by the Forest Department and 'settled' in 1977. The 100 or so remaining members of the Onge tribe are confined to a 100 sq km reserve at Dugong Creek. An anthropological study made in the 1970s suggests that the Onge population has declined due to demoralisation through loss of territory. The Indian government has allowed further development – including the building of roads, jetties and a match factory.

Sentinelese

The Sentinelese, unlike the other tribes in these islands, have consistently repulsed outside contact. Every few years, contact parties arrive on the beaches of North Sentinel Island with gifts of coconuts, bananas, pigs and red plastic buckets, only to be showered with arrows. About 120 Sentinelese remain, and North Sentinel Island is their territory.

Andamanese

Numbering only 30, it seems impossible that the Andamanese can escape extinction. There were almost 5000 Andamanese in the mid-19th century. Their friendliness to the colonisers was their undoing and, by the beginning of the 20th century, most of the population had been swept away by measles, syphilis and influenza epidemics. They've been resettled on tiny Strait Island.

Jarawa

The 250 remaining Jarawa occupy the 750 sq km reserve on South and Middle Andaman Islands. Their territory has been disrupted by the Andaman Trunk Rd, forest clearance and settler and tourist encroachment. Stories abound about Jarawa hostilities to outsiders which authorities quash as myth. In 1953 the chief commissioner requested an armed sea plane bomb Jarawa settlements. Today it is tourists that bombard the Jarawas. Authorities are concerned that the more recent tolerance of the Jarawa could result in further settler/tourist encroachment.

Shompen

Only about 200 Shompen remain in the forests on Great Nicobar. They are hunter-gatherers, who have resisted integration and shy away from areas occupied by Indian immigrants.

Nicobarese

The 30,000 Nicobarese are the only indigenous people whose numbers are not decreasing. The majority have converted to Christianity and have been partly assimilated into contemporary Indian society. Living in village units led by a headman, they farm pigs and cultivate coconuts, yams and bananas. The Nicobarese inhabit a number of islands in the Nicobar group, centred on Car Nicobar.

many important tree species, including the renowned padauk, a hardwood with light and dark colours occurring in the same tree.

Conflicts between development, cultural and environmental protection, defence strategies and plain greed define the social and political landscape of the islands. Indigenous land rights and conservation are under threat from increased population, unsustainable tourist development, poaching and defence activities.

The Indian navy attempts to patrol the gun runners, drug smugglers and coral poachers that frequently 'stray' into the Andaman Sea. Along with the increase in commercial shipping and military activity, these activities cause significant coral damage, thereby destabilising an already fragile ecosystem.

Permits

Foreigners need a permit to visit the Andaman Islands. The Nicobar Islands are off limits to all except Indian nationals engaged in research, government business or trade. The 30-day maximum permit (which can sometimes be extended to 45 days), allows foreigners to stay in the capital, Port Blair with short-term visits to other areas (see Around Port Blair and Other Islands later in this chapter for full details).

Obtaining visitor permits was once a logistical nightmare. Now it's an easy and painless process. Even the permit fee has now been waived. Air travellers simply fill out a form on arrival at the newly completed immigration hall at Port Blair airport. If you arrive with an unconfirmed return flight, you'll be given a permit for 10 to 15 days, but this can be extended to a 30-day stay.

Boat passengers can also apply for their permits on arrival at Port Blair. This is the easiest option although it's still possible to obtain a permit before your departure to the Andamans. You can apply to the Foreigners' Registration Office in either Chennai (☎ 8278210) or Kolkata (☎ 2473301); allow five hours – more if the application is submitted late in the day. You can also obtain a permit from any Indian embassy overseas, but this can often delay processing considerably. On arrival at Port Blair, ship passengers must immediately report to the deputy superintendent of police in Aberdeen Bazaar. If you fail to do this you could encounter problems when departing since it will be difficult to prove that you have not been here longer than 30 days.

As well as visitor permits, additional permits are required to visit some other islands. To obtain the required permits visit the Chief Wildlife Warden (CWW; ☎ 33549), Haddo Rd, Haddo. You'll need to make an application – a letter stating your case, name of boat and dates involved. Your case is apparently strengthened if you quote the date and file number of the Ministry of Home Affairs' document declaring the islands open to tourists (7 January 1966, File F. No 15011/4/94-F.1). The permit will be issued within the hour, but that's not the end of bureaucratic procedures. If you're intending to visit islands south of Mayabunder, you must present your permit to the Deputy Conservator of Forests (DCF), WL-I, Haddo (next door to the CWW). Visitors to islands north of Mayabunder should present their permit to the DCF, WL-II, Mayabunder, on arrival. Then the range officers come into the act, but all will be explained at the CWW when you make your application. All these offices open from 8.30 am to 4 pm weekdays with lunch from noon to 1 pm. The permits cost Rs 10 per person per day. Cameras are Rs 100 per day and diving will cost Rs 1000 per day (and that's just the permit). If you're Indian, then these costs are 50% lower.

Filming in the Andamans requires special permits from the Ministry for Home Affairs in Delhi and it costs Rs 1500 per day. If you join a group tour, the operators will organise the appropriate permits from the CWW.

Camping

While camping is permitted in various areas throughout the Andamans, it's important to observe good camping practices. Remember the island ecology is fragile and irresponsible behaviour can interfere with flora and the habitats of wildlife, especially turtles, which use the beach fronts to lay and hatch their eggs. See the boxed text 'Responsible Trekking' in the Facts for the Visitor chapter for ideas on safe ecological practices.

PORT BLAIR

☎ 03192

The capital sprawls around a harbour on the east coast of South Andaman. It's a laid-back place and if you've swallowed the hype on the islands you could well be disappointed on arrival – you need to venture beyond Port Blair to appreciate what the islands have to offer. You'll find it easy to obtain basic supplies such as bottled water and mosquito repellent. However, electricity and tap water are often restricted, the sewerage system is over-stretched and waste management doesn't exist. Port Blair is operating at capacity and further growth without appropriate infrastructure development will have disastrous consequences.

Even though 1000km east of the mainland, the Andamans still run on Indian time. This means that it can be dark by 5 pm and light by 4 am.

Orientation

Most of the hotels, the bus station, passenger dock (Phoenix Bay Jetty) and the offices of the Shipping Corporation of India (SCI) are in the central Aberdeen Bazaar area. The airport is 5km south of town, and the nearest beach is at Corbyn's Cove, 7km south of Aberdeen Bazaar.

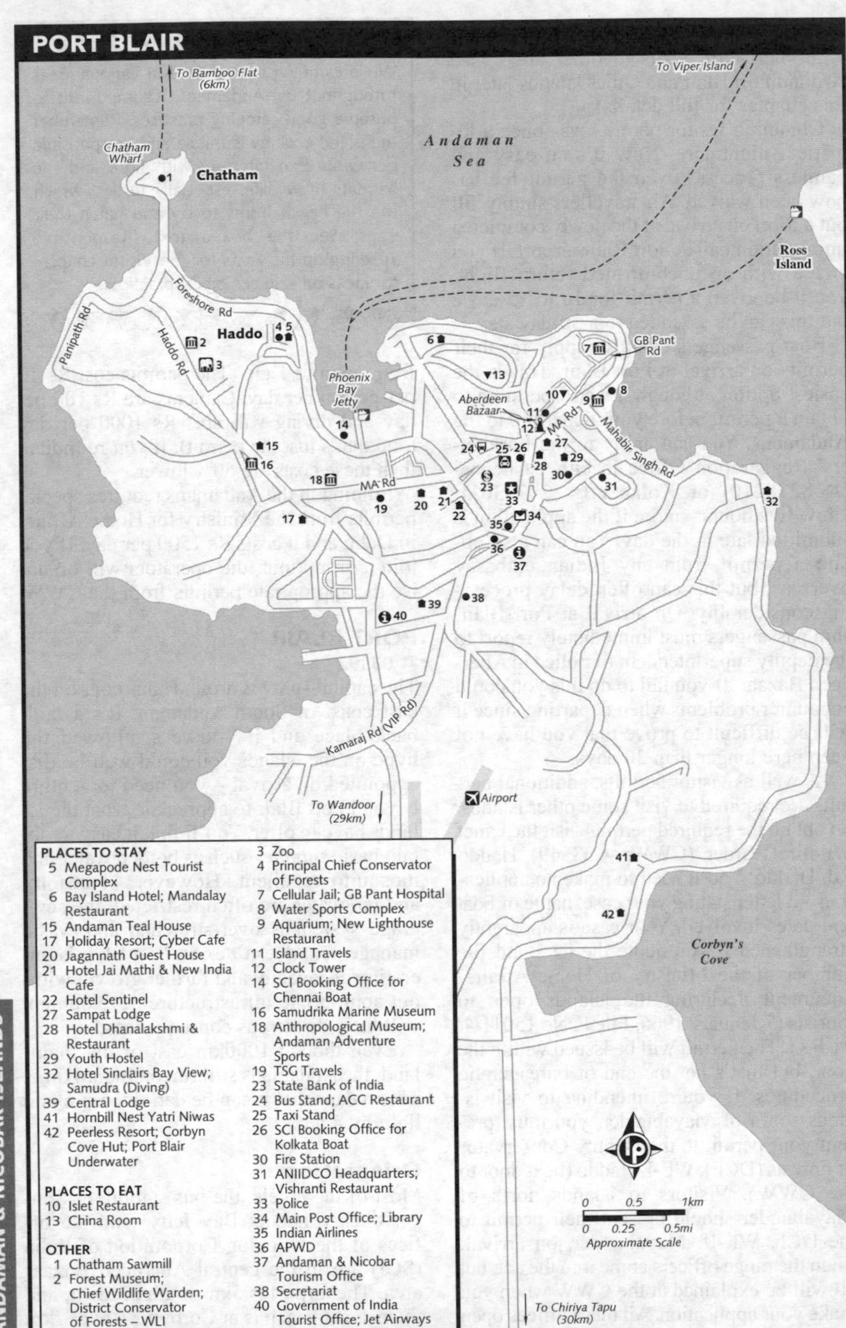
PORT BLAIR
To Bamboo Flat (6km)
To Viper Island
Andaman Sea
Chatham Wharf
Chatham
Ross Island
Foreshore Rd
Panipath Rd
Haddo Rd
Haddo
GB Pant Rd
Phoenix Bay Jetty
Aberdeen Bazaar
MA Rd
Mahabir Singh Rd
MA Rd
Kamaraj Rd (VIP Rd)
To Wandoor (29km)
Airport
Corbyn's Cove
To Chiriya Tapu (30km)
Approximate Scale
PLACES TO STAY
5 Megapode Nest Tourist Complex
6 Bay Island Hotel; Mandalay Restaurant
15 Andaman Teal House
17 Holiday Resort; Cyber Cafe
20 Jagannath Guest House
21 Hotel Jai Mathi & New India Cafe
22 Hotel Sentinel
27 Sampat Lodge
28 Hotel Dhanalakshmi & Restaurant
29 Youth Hostel
32 Hotel Sinclairs Bay View; Samudra (Diving)
39 Central Lodge
41 Hornbill Nest Yatri Niwas
42 Peerless Resort; Corbyn Cove Hut; Port Blair Underwater
PLACES TO EAT
10 Islet Restaurant
13 China Room
OTHER
1 Chatham Sawmill
2 Forest Museum; Chief Wildlife Warden; District Conservator of Forests – WLI
3 Zoo
4 Principal Chief Conservator of Forests
7 Cellular Jail; GB Pant Hospital
8 Water Sports Complex
9 Aquarium; New Lighthouse Restaurant
11 Island Travels
12 Clock Tower
14 SCI Booking Office for Chennai Boat
16 Samudrika Marine Museum
18 Anthropological Museum; Andaman Adventure Sports
19 TSG Travels
23 State Bank of India
24 Bus Stand; ACC Restaurant
25 Taxi Stand
26 SCI Booking Office for Kolkata Boat
30 Fire Station
31 ANIIDCO Headquarters; Vishranti Restaurant
33 Police
34 Main Post Office; Library
35 Indian Airlines
36 APWD
37 Andaman & Nicobar Tourism Office
38 Secretariat
40 Government of India Tourist Office; Jet Airways
ANDAMAN & NICOBAR ISLANDS

Information

Information on any subject is freely and readily available. Reliable information, however, is another thing. Whether you're seeking details as simple as ferry times, tour bookings or as complex as island permits you can ask six people (even experts) the same question and you're likely to get 10 different answers. You may think your mainland experience has prepared you well, but on these islands the mainland eccentricities can pale into insignificance.

Tourist Offices The Government of India tourist office (☎ 33006), 2nd floor, 189 Junglighat Main Rd, advises on which islands are accessible and how. It's open 8.30 am to 5 pm weekdays and can be found above Super Shoppe, about 1km from the centre of town.

The ultramodern Andaman & Nicobar (A&N) Tourism office (☎ 32694, fax 30933) is open from 8.30 am to 5.30 pm weekdays. Staff are friendly but be aware that printed schedules and prices they supply rarely reflect current reality.

The library, near the main post office, has a small collection of books on the history, geography, flora and fauna, and tribal people of the islands.

Money Travellers cheques and foreign currency can be converted at State Bank of India (open from 9 am to 1 pm weekdays). A similar (and much quicker) service is available at Island Travels (open from 2 to 4 pm daily, except Sunday). Some larger hotels have foreign exchange facilities, but few places accept credit cards.

Post & Communications The main post office is 750m south of Aberdeen Bazaar. The cheapest place to send and receive faxes is at the telegraph office (fax 21318) next door, which is open from 10 am to 5 pm Monday to Saturday. International telephone calls can be made from here, as well as from the numerous kiosks in Aberdeen Bazaar. There are several Internet cafes with the fastest being the Cyber Cafe at Holiday Resort for Rs 60 per hour.

Emergency The Aberdeen police station (☎ 33077, 32100) is near the main post office; for medical care go to the GB Pant Hospital (☎ 32102) next to the Cellular Jail.

Cellular Jail National Memorial

Built by the British over a period of 18 years from 1890, and preserved as a shrine to India's freedom fighters, the Cellular Jail is a major tourist attraction and a record of a significant moment in the island's history. Originally, seven wings radiated from a central tower, but only three remain. These remnants, however, give a fair impression of the 'hell on earth' that the prisoners endured.

Each evening (except Sunday) a sound and light show depicts the jail's brutal history, and it is well worth a visit. It's in Hindi at 6 pm, in English at 7.15 pm and costs Rs 10. The show is sporadic during the rainy season.

Museums

Samudrika Marine Museum Run by the Indian navy, this museum features displays of the history and geography of the islands. The museum is open from 9 am to noon and 2 to 5.30 pm Tuesday to Sunday; entry is Rs 10.

Anthropological Museum The small museum on MA Rd displays tools, clothing and photographs of the indigenous people of the islands. The captions are not informative and at times patronising, but apparently all this will change with the construction of a new museum close to the current site. There's a small but well-stocked library for researchers only. The museum is free and open from 10 am to 12.30 pm and 1.30 to 4 pm daily, except Sunday and holidays.

Zoo & Forest Museum Some of the 200 animal species unique to the islands can be seen at the small zoo. These include the Nicobar green imperial pigeon and Andaman pig, the staple diet of some tribal groups. The zoo's saltwater crocodile breeding program has been very successful and many have been returned to the wild. As with many zoos, the animals here seem jaded. The zoo is open from 8 am to 5 pm Tuesday to Sunday and entry is Rs 0.50.

Nearby is the small **Forest Museum**, which has a display of locally grown woods, including the famed padauk. The museum is open from 8 am to noon and 2.30 to 5 pm daily except Sunday; entry is free.

Aquarium This interesting aquarium and museum (formerly known as the Fisheries

Museum) displays some of the 350 species found in the Andaman Sea. It's open from 9 am to 1.30 pm and 2 to 5.30 pm daily (closed Monday and holidays).

Chatham Sawmill

This government operation on Chatham island, 5km north-west of Aberdeen Bazaar, is the largest wood processor in Asia. Commenced in 1836 by the British, the mill employs about 2000 people around the clock in three shifts. Most of the timber goes to the mainland.

The sawmill is open for visitors from 6.30 am to 2.30 pm daily except Sunday. Admission is free; and the guide will be more than happy to show you around 'for a small consideration'.

Water Sports Complex

At the water sports complex, near the aquarium, you can rent rowboats, windsurfing equipment and sailing dinghies. Water skiing costs Rs 75 for 15 minutes; windsurfing is Rs 50 for 30 minutes. You can rent snorkels here for Rs 25 per hour, but you can't take them anywhere else.

Snorkelling & Diving

The Andaman Islands offer great opportunities for snorkelling and diving. However, few visitors engage in diving and there's been little development of facilities for this activity.

Dive centres come and go, so before you venture out or part with any money, it's important to ascertain a centre's status, for example, whether it is registered with the Professional Association of Diving Instructors (PADI). This organisation ensures professional practices and standards. Prices of the dive companies vary depending on the location, number of participants and duration of the course. In national parks, there's an additional cost of Rs 1000 per person per day payable directly to the park. Generally, charges start at Rs 2500 for a couple of dives in the Port Blair area; Rs 3500 beyond (Wandoor etc). The PADI Open Water Certificate course (four to five days) will cost you around Rs 15,000, and the advanced PADI course is Rs 10,000. These courses lead to internationally recognised certification. Currently, there are three dive centres that are PADI registered:

Andaman Adventure Sports (☎/fax 03192-30295) MA Rd, Port Blair

Port Blair Underwater (☎ 03192-85389, 21358, fax 040-3392718 in Chennai) Peerless Resort, Corbyn's Cove

Samudra (☎ 03192-33159, 32937, fax 32038, e manavi_th@hotmail.com) Hotel Sinclairs Bay View, Port Blair

Organised Tours

In the bazaar numerous travel agencies offer even more numerous tours. Island Travels (☎ 32358), has a good reputation, and further afield you could try Andaman Teal House (☎ 32642). However, many tours will only operate once a minimum number of bookings has been made. This makes cancellations common, which can be very frustrating for travellers who are on a tight schedule. You may feel pressured to join one of these groups since independent travel is not encouraged and it can present problems with transport, accommodation and permits. However, since tours are rarely guaranteed, it's advisable to persist with your plans for independent travel especially if this is your preferred option.

Every afternoon at 3 pm, a boat leaves from the Phoenix Bay Jetty for a 1½-hour harbour cruise. The trip costs Rs 25 and stops briefly at Viper Island where the remains of the gallows tower, built by the British, still stand.

Special Events

A 10-day **Island Tourism Festival** is held in Port Blair some time between December and February each year. Dance groups are imported from surrounding islands and the mainland. The festival also gives local tourism operators an opportunity to showcase their products. One of the festival's more bizarre aspects is the Andaman dog show.

Places to Stay

Most budget and mid-range hotels don't levy additional taxes on their tariff. However, a 10% service charge applies to some top-end hotels. Checkout is usually 7 am.

Places to Stay – Budget

Youth Hostel (☎ 32459) has dorm beds for Rs 50 and doubles for Rs 80. (members receive a 50% discount). There are shared bathrooms with squat toilet and cold water only. There's a good restaurant for guests.

Central Lodge *(☎ 33632, Middle Point)* is a basic wooden building set back from the road. It's one of the most popular cheapies, with singles/doubles starting at Rs 60/90 with shared bathroom and Rs 120 for a double with private bathroom. You can camp in the garden for Rs 40.

Sampat Lodge *(☎ 30752, Aberdeen Bazaar)* is basic. Rooms are Rs 100/ 150 with shared bathroom, Rs 130/175 with private bathroom and Rs 200 with balcony. There are squat and sit-down flush toilets and bucket hot water is available from 7 am to 9 am.

Jagannath Guest House *(☎ 32148, MA Rd)* is a reasonable choice with singles/doubles/triples for Rs 200/300/450. There's cold water only and both squat and sit-down flush toilets. Run by a friendly manager, it's convenient for the bus stand and Phoenix Bay Jetty.

Hotel Jai Mathi *(☎ 30836, 78 MA Rd)* is another basic place with rooms for Rs 100/150/175. There are squat and sit-down flush toilets and bucket hot water is available in the morning.

Places to Stay – Mid-Range

Most of the places in the mid-range bracket can be bargained down if they're not full. All rooms have private bathroom and sit-down flush toilets unless stated otherwise.

Holiday Resort *(☎ 30516, fax 34231, Prem Nagar)* is cleaner than most and a good place to stay. Rooms are Rs 350/450, or Rs 600/800 with air-con. There is an attached bar and restaurant and the best Internet cafe in town.

Hotel Dhanalakshmi *(☎ 33953, fax 34964, Aberdeen Bazaar)* has basic rooms for Rs 300/500, or Rs 600/700 with air-con (the rooms at the back are the quietest). It also has a restaurant.

Hornbill Nest Yatri Niwas *(☎ 32018)* is run by A&N Tourism. It's about 1km north of Corbyn's Cove, but fails to take advantage of the magnificent sea views. Tired-looking and stuffy rooms with two/four/six beds are Rs 260/330/400. There's a basic restaurant, but some dishes need to be ordered in advance and service is painfully slow. Bookings must be made through the A&N Tourism office (see Tourist Offices earlier in this chapter for contact details).

Andaman Teal House *(☎ 34060)* is also run by the tourist office. Spacious doubles cost Rs 260, or Rs 450 with air-con. Bookings must be made through A&N Tourism.

Megapode Nest Tourist Complex *(☎ 32 207, fax 21227)* at Haddo on the hill above the bay, is probably the best value in the mid-range. Rooms, many with harbour views, are Rs 1000 for large air-con doubles and Rs 1400 for a generous Yurt-style air-con cottage. Breakfast is included, but you may wish it wasn't when you see the sad *idli* (South Indian rice dumpling) and soggy bread. The restaurant improves for lunch and dinner and it's always pleasant to sit in the garden and sip a cold beer. You may need it to help you cope with the discombobulated management. Major credit cards are accepted, but not American Express.

Places to Stay – Top End

Major credit cards are accepted at the following hotels.

Hotel Sinclairs Bay View *(☎ 32937, fax 31824)* has rooms with some spectacular views for Rs 1500/1800, or Rs 1900/2200 with air-con and breakfast. Although it's right on the coast there's no beach. It's a somewhat cavernous place with a good restaurant (though the service is excruciatingly slow). Bookings for accommodation can be made through the Chennai office (☎ 044-8526296, fax 8522506).

Peerless Resort *(☎ 33462, fax 33463)* at Corbyn's Cove is opposite the beach, although you can't see the beach from the resort. Standard air-con singles/doubles are small and overpriced at Rs 1850/2600; rooms in the air-con cottages are Rs 3000/3600. There's a bar, restaurant, foreign exchange facilities, boat hire and diving school.

Bay Island Hotel *(☎ 34101, fax 31555)*, with sea views, is the top hotel in Port Blair. The rooms, however, don't quite match the aesthetics of the lobby. They're rather small and way overpriced at Rs 4150/4950 – although this does include all meals. No singles are available in December and January. There's a restaurant, bar and a sea-water swimming pool.

Hotel Sentinel *(☎ 37914, fax 32425)* just behind the PWD, is new and grand, but it's already yearning for maintenance. Doubles start from Rs 1500, and Rs 2800 for air-con. Suites are available for Rs 4500. There's no beach and no view.

Places to Eat

There are numerous small restaurants in Aberdeen Bazaar and most hotels have restaurants. Good seafood is available but can be hard to find.

Vishranti Restaurant, to the side of the Aniidco building, with its perfectly arranged bamboo furniture, presents a detached air, but it's a friendly place with a varied menu of Indian and continental from Rs 40. Seafood is the speciality (Rs 350). There's a bar and you can eat in or outside.

Dhanalakshmi restaurant in the hotel of the same name, stays open late; Indian and Chinese dishes are around Rs 65.

New India Cafe, below Hotel Jai Mathi, does good basic and cheap meals, including thalis for Rs 25. It opens around 7 am for Indian or Western style breakfasts.

Islet Restaurant offers tasty inexpensive vegetarian and nonvegetarian dishes and has bay views. The narrow balcony is a good place to while away a warm night.

New Lighthouse Restaurant is a tower-like structure that is open to the sea breeze. Here you'll find probably the best fresh fish in town. Select your fish and your preferred style of cooking (lightly barbecued is best). This place is also good for an evening beer or breakfast – Indian or Western style.

China Room *(☎ 30759)* offers excellent meals in what is really the front room and garden of a private home. Some seafood dishes (steamed lobster or crab) require 24-hours notice.

Mandalay Restaurant at Bay Island Hotel offers reasonable, though rather tired looking, buffets. The open-air dining area catches the breeze and has bay views.

Corbyn Cove Hut on the beach at Peerless Resort is good for snacks and cold beer. It's a great place to watch the tide and cool down.

Shopping

You wouldn't come to the Andamans to shop. However, there are many things to be purchased, mainly in Aberdeen Bazaar in Port Blair. These include marine items, such as shells and corals. There are also photographs of tribal people, taken and sold illegally. Not only are the purchases of such items against the law, but they further the exploitation of the marine and cultural environment. Whatever you do, refrain from buying such items.

Getting There & Away

Air Jet Airways (☎ 36911) operates daily flights from Chennai (5.30 am) to Port Blair. Indian Airlines (☎ 33108) has four flights a week from Chennai to Port Blair and from Kolkata to Port Blair. These flights return to their city of origin on the same day. All flights take around two hours and cost around US$200 one way. Indian Airline tickets can be included on the discount two- or three-week flight pass. The 25% youth discount is also applicable on Indian Airlines.

Daily flights have ended the former difficulties of securing tickets and the new Port Blair passenger terminal ensures smooth and comfortable arrivals and departures.

Boat There are usually two to four sailings a month between Port Blair and Chennai or Kolkata on vessels operated by SCI (☎ 33347, fax 33778). Less-frequent (once every two months) services operate from Visakhapatnam (Andhra Pradesh). Contact SCI for the latest information on the erratic schedules. It's best to arrange return tickets when purchasing your outward ticket.

The length of the boat trip varies with the weather. On a good crossing it takes 60 hours to reach Port Blair from Chennai and 56 hours from Kolkata or Visakhapatnam.

The categories of accommodation include deluxe cabin (Rs 4140, two berth), 1st-class cabin (Rs 3420, usually two berth), 2nd-class A cabin (Rs 2700, four to six berth) and 2nd-class B (Rs 2070, similar to A, but smaller). Some ships have an air-con dorm for Rs 1449. If you can get a ticket for bunk class, it will cost Rs 1150. For residents of the Andaman or Nicobar Islands, fares are 40% cheaper. Food (thalis for breakfast, lunch and dinner) costs around Rs 120 per day. Almost everyone complains so you may wish to bring something (fruit in particular) to supplement this.

The SCI has the following office addresses:

Chennai (☎ 044-5226873) Rajaji Salai (opposite Customs House)
Kolkata (☎ 033-2842354) 1st floor, 13 Strand Rd
Port Blair (☎ 33347) Aberdeen Bazaar (opposite Hotel Dhanalakshmi); Bookings available just two days before departures.
Visakhapatnam (☎ 0891-565597, fax 566507) AV Bhanoji Row (within the port complex)

Getting Around

Port Blair has buses, taxis and autorickshaws. Meters are rarely used and it may be difficult to haggle with the taxi drivers. However, the autorickshaw drivers, more recent arrivals to the island, usually propose realistic rates. From the airport, the fare to Aberdeen Bazaar is around Rs 50 to 70 (less to Corbyn's Cove). The tourist office airport bus will take you to any bus station in Port Blair for Rs 25.

From the bus stand in Port Blair, there are regular departures to key destinations. To Wandoor there are four buses a day (Rs 7, 1½ hours). It's almost the same for Chiriya Tapu – four buses (Rs 8, 1½ hours). The bus to Diglipur leaves Port Blair at 5.30 am on Sunday, Friday and Wednesday. The journey is supposed to take eight hours (often it's much longer) and costs Rs 195 return. Daily buses for Rangat depart at 6 am, take six hours and cost Rs 60. There are also several private buses that generally run at more convenient times for similar prices.

It's best to have your own transport to explore parts of the island. You can hire bicycles in Aberdeen Bazaar for Rs 40 per day. Mopeds, scooters or motorcycles can be hired from TSG Travels (☎ 32894) for Rs 120 per day. A deposit of Rs 500 is required, but you'll be lucky to get helmets. Jagannath Guest House also has a few motorcycles for hire (Rs 150).

Private boats can be hired from tour operators, but charges are high – around Rs 10,000 per day.

AROUND PORT BLAIR

Viper Island

The moment you disembark on this tiny island you are confronted with a sign 'Way to the Gallows'. A path leads to the remains of the brick jail and the gallows built by the British in 1867. The stunning view from these gallows somehow accentuates the sheer horror of the place. The name Viper has nothing to do with snakes – it's the name of a 19th-century British trading ship that was wrecked nearby.

Unless you have access to a private boat, the best way to see Viper Island is to take the afternoon harbour cruise that departs from Phoenix Bay Jetty. Some of these boats only stop at the island for 15 minutes. If you want more time, negotiate with the captain.

Mt Harriet & Madhuban

Mt Harriet (365m) is across the inlet, north of Port Blair. There's a nature trail up to the top and, with Forest Department permits, it's possible to stay in the comfortable ***Forest Guest House***. (Permits are theoretically available from the Forest Department in Port Blair, but not many travellers are lucky enough to get one.)

To reach Mt Harriet, take the vehicle or passenger ferry from Chatham Wharf to Bamboo Flat (Rs 1.50, 10 minutes). From there, a road runs 7km along the coast and up to Mt Harriet. Jeep drivers, who charge an outrageous Rs 500 to take you to the top, insist that taxis can't make it to the top. They can, and a taxi costs only Rs 250. If you have time try walking up, but take plenty of water as there is none available en route.

To the north is Mt Harriet National Park and Madhuban, where elephants are sometimes trained for the logging camps. Madhuban is also accessible by boat; the tourist office and travel agencies organise occasional trips.

Ross Island

This eerie forlorn place was once the administrative headquarters for the British. Just 2km east of Port Blair, newspapers of the day called it the 'Paris of the East'. However, the manicured gardens and grand ballrooms were destroyed by an earthquake in 1941.

Six months later, after the Japanese entered WWII, the British transferred their headquarters to Port Blair.

Ferries to Ross Island depart Phoenix Bay Jetty at 8.30 and 10 am and 12.30 and 2 pm daily except Wednesday. From Ross Island, there are departures at 8.45 and 10.40 am and 12.40, 2.10 and 4.40 pm. The journey takes 20 minutes and a return ticket costs Rs 17, plus Rs 10 entry fee. Ross Island is controlled by the navy and visitors must sign in on arrival. The museum near the jetty displays the opulence and decadence of a bygone era.

Corbyn's Cove

Corbyn's Cove, 4km east of the airport and 7km south of the town, is the nearest beach to Port Blair. It's a long, though pleasant and easy, cliff-top stroll here from Port Blair. It's popular for swimming as well as lazing under the coconut trees – don't laze too long. Coconuts have a quaint habit of dropping, with some force, to the ground.

Nearby, **Snake Island** is surrounded by a coral reef. You can sometimes catch a ride to the island in a fishing boat, but swimming is not advised as the currents are particularly strong. If you do visit the island, watch out for snakes!

Sippighat Farm

On the road to Wandoor, 15km from Port Blair, research into spices such as cinnamon, pepper, nutmeg and cloves, is carried out at this government experimental farm. The staff here are particularly friendly and knowledgeable on local issues. The farm is open from 8 am to 5.30 pm daily except Sunday. Entry is free.

Wandoor

The Mahatma Gandhi National Marine Park at Wandoor covers 280 sq km and comprises 15 islands. The diverse scenery includes mangrove creeks, tropical rainforest and reefs supporting 50 types of coral. Boats leave from Wandoor village, 29km south-west of Port Blair, at around 10 am daily (except Monday) for visits to Jolly Buoy or Red Skin Islands. Although it's well worth seeing the coral (there are usually a few snorkels for hire – Rs 100), only a couple of hours are spent at the islands. On Jolly Buoy, for the best coral go to the left of the landing spot, not to the right as directed. Watch out for powerful currents.

The trip costs Rs 8 for a bus from Port Blair to Wandoor and Rs 125 by boat from Wandoor to Jolly Bouy. Private buses tend to make the boat connection more conveniently than the public services. At Wandoor jetty you'll need to buy an entry permit (Rs 10 per person; Rs 25 per camera) before you board the boat. You'll also need to supply your passport number. There are a number of good, sandy beaches at Wandoor and some excellent snorkelling, but you should take care not to walk on the coral exposed at low tide. Much of this reef has already been damaged.

Chiriya Tapu

Chiriya Tapu, 30km south of Port Blair, is a tiny fishing village with beaches and mangroves. It's possible to arrange boats from here to Cinque Island. There's a beach about 2km south of Chiriya Tapu that has some of the best snorkelling in the area. There are four buses a day to the village from Port Blair (Rs 8, 1½ hours).

OTHER ISLANDS

A&N Tourism has targeted half a dozen islands for development, but the tourist infrastructure is currently very limited and you shouldn't expect too much. These islands include Bharatang, North Passage, Narcondam, Interview, The Brothers, The Sisters and Barren Islands. No regular boats visit these places so you'll need to charter one and disembarkation is forbidden at Barren Island. To go to any of these islands you must have a permit from the CWW (see Permits earlier in this chapter).

Until the tourist complexes mooted for the islands are actually built, the only accommodation is in Andaman Public Works Department (APWD) or forest guesthouses (typically Rs 60 per bed in a double room). These should be reserved in advance in Port Blair, either at the APWD or the Chief Wildlife Warden (☎ 31371) in Haddo.

Some people bring tents or hammocks (made by tailors in Aberdeen Bazaar) and camp on the beaches. In Port Blair, you can rent two-person tents for Rs 40 per day from Andaman Teal House. If you do camp, make sure you carry your rubbish out with you (rather than bury it). Sadly all the islands opened to tourism now bear the scars, with mounds of rotting rubbish. Fires are not allowed so bring a stove and kerosene (available in Port Blair) with you.

Neil Island

Neil Island, 40km north-east of Port Blair, is populated by Bengali settlers. There's excellent snorkelling, but some of the coral has been damaged by explosives used for fishing. Beaches are numbered: No 1 Beach, a 40-minute walk west of the jetty and village, has been popular with campers, who set up hammocks under the trees. This is now banned. The snorkelling is best around the point at the far end of the beach, where you may also see very large fish. At low tide it's difficult getting over the coral into the water from the beach.

Places to Stay & Eat In the village there's a market, a few shops and a couple of basic restaurants serving *dosas* (filled pancakes), fried fish, vegetables and rice. The stalls and shops often run out of mineral water and soft drinks.

Hawabill Nest Yatri Niwas offers doubles with air-con for Rs 400 and deluxe doubles for Rs 800. There's also a four-bed room for Rs 300 or Rs 75 per bed. Reserve at the A&N Tourism office in Port Blair. ***APWD Guest House*** has two basic double rooms for Rs 60 per person.

Getting There & Away Ferries leave for Neil Island from Phoenix Bay in Port Blair at 6 am three to four times a week (Rs 12/17 for deck/upper class, three hours), continuing to Havelock. Occasionally they visit Havelock first.

Havelock Island

About 54km north-east of Port Blair, Havelock covers 100 sq km and is inhabited by Bengali settlers. There are picture-postcard, white-sand beaches, turquoise waters and good snorkelling. Although there are coral reefs, it's the marine life here – dolphins, turtles and very large fish – that make it interesting. So do the elephants that were brought to the island for work but now earn their keep from tourism. However, they're not always there.

Only the northern third of the island is settled, and each village is referred to by a number. Boats dock at the jetty at No 1; the main bazaar is 2km south at No 3.

Having your own transport is useful – bring a bicycle from Port Blair or rent one for Rs 40 per day in No 3 Village or from the *paan* (mixture of beetle nut and leaves for chewing) shop outside the entrance to Dolphin Yatri Niwas. A few scooters (Rs 180) are available from the Narayan paan store in No 3 Village. A local bus connects the villages on an hourly circuit and also runs out to No 7 Beach (the best beach on the island). A tourist bus meets the ferry.

Places to Stay & Eat You need to make a reservation in advance at the A&N Tourism office in Port Blair to stay in the Dolphin Yatri Niwas or the Tent Resorts. All the following places have cold water only.

Dolphin Yatri Niwas Complex offers pleasant accommodation in cottages beside a beautiful secluded beach, but there's no snorkelling here. It costs Rs 300 for an ordinary double, Rs 800 for a deluxe room and Rs 1500 for an air-con double. Good, but basic, meals are served in the restaurant.

There's a ***Tent Resort*** near No 5 Beach, and you can use the restaurant at the Dolphin Yatri Niwas. It's Rs 150 per double.

A&N Tourism's ***Tent Resort***, beside No 7 Beach, has eight roomy tents (twin beds) set up under the trees. They cost Rs 150 for a double and there's a maximum stay of four days. There's a couple of toilets but no washing facilities other than the wells. Basic fish thalis (Rs 30) and drinks (tea, coffee, soft drinks and mineral water) are available. Some people bring their own tents or hammocks and camp by the beach. The police come by occasionally to check that people aren't making fires or stripping off and indulging in 'hippie behaviour'. There's good snorkelling and the idyllic beach stretches for several kilometres. The sandflies make sunbathing impossible.

Jungle Resort *(☎ 37656, fax 37657)*, also at No 7 Beach, is the best on the island. Bamboo thatched hexagonal cottages are priced from Rs 3100 to 5100 for a four-bed room.

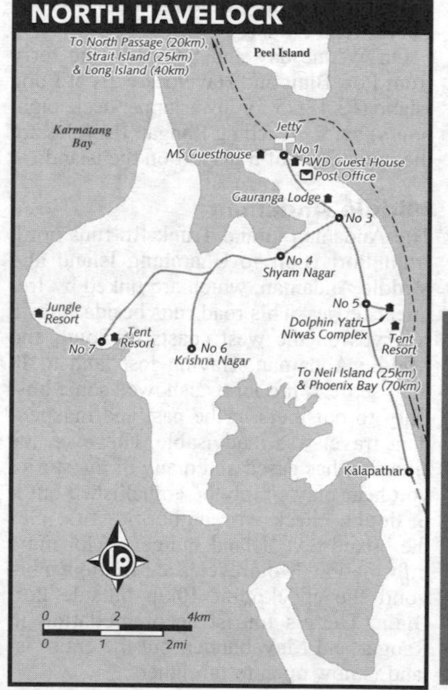

This includes meals that are simple but tastefully prepared. If the cottages stretch the budget too far you can stay in one of the popular huts for Rs 300 per night. These three-sided thatched dwellings provide shelter and a space to sleep and store your belongings. And you can still savour the offerings at the restaurant, including a beer.

MS Guest House, 500m west of the jetty, near No 1 Village, has rooms with private bathroom for Rs 150; Rs 50 for a dorm bed.

Gauranga Lodge is the green wooden building without a sign between villages Nos 1 and 3. It has doubles for Rs 75.

Getting There & Away Ferries depart at 6 am daily from Phoenix Bay in Port Blair. The four- to six-hour journey to Havelock costs Rs 12/17 on the lower/upper deck. Ferries return from Havelock to Port Blair the following day (usually about noon, depending on route and weather), except Sunday, which has a same-day return service.

Long Island

This little island off the south-east coast of Middle Andaman has one small village and several sandy beaches that are perfect for camping. The only accommodation is the ***Forest Rest House***.

On Wednesday and Saturday, the ferry from Port Blair and Havelock calls at Long Island (Rs 12/25 for lower/upper deck, eight hours) before reaching Rangat. Bicycles are the main form of transport on the island.

Middle Andaman

The Andaman Grand Trunk Rd runs north from Port Blair to Bharatang Island and Middle Andaman, which are linked by frequent ferries. This road runs beside Jarawa reserves on the west coasts of South and Middle Andaman. Having lost land to In dian settlers, the Jarawa showed some hostility to outsiders in the past and independent travel was inadvisable. However, the situation has eased and many of the stories you hear may simply be embellished but if in doubt, check with authorities first. See the boxed text 'Island Indigenes' for more information. Motorcycles are forbidden beyond the checkpoint 40km outside Port Blair. There's tourist accommodation in Rangat and Mayabunder, but the entire island is now open to foreigners.

You can get to **Rangat** from Port Blair via the Havelock, Neil or Long island ferries (Rs 17/38 for lower/upper deck, nine hours) or by bus (Rs 60, six hours). There are basic rooms at ***Hare Krishna Lodge*** (Rs 100/150), and ***PWD Guest House*** (Rs 100). A bus runs to Cuthbert Bay for A&N Tourism's ***Hawksbill Nest*** (Rs 80 per bed in a four-bed dorm, Rs 250/400 for nonair-con/air-con double). Bookings for Hawksbill Nest must be made at the A&N Tourism office in Port Blair.

Mayabunder, 71km north of Rangat, is linked by the daily bus from Port Blair (Rs 90, nine hours; Rs 190 for deluxe) and also by occasional ferries. There's an 18 bed ***APWD Guest House*** here. ***Swiftlet Nest*** at Karmatang Bay, 13km north-east of Mayabunder charges Rs 75 per bed in a four-bed dorm and Rs 250/400 for nonair-con/air-con doubles.

North Andaman

Diglipur is the only place on North Andaman where foreigners can stay. To get there you can catch either the weekly ferry from Port Blair, the daily ferry from Mayabunder or a bus that departs Port Blair at 5.30 am on Sunday, Wednesday and Friday. The bus fare is Rs 95 and the journey takes 17 hours. The 12-bed ***APWD Guest House*** and ***Turtle Resort*** cost Rs 400 for an air-con double. Bookings should be made through the APWD or A&N Tourism office.

Cinque Island

The uninhabited islands of North and South Cinque are part of the wildlife sanctuary south of Wandoor, just off Rutland Island. They are surrounded by coral reefs, and are among the most beautiful islands in the Andamans. Visiting boats usually anchor off South Cinque and passengers transfer via dinghy to the beach. The snorkelling here is first class; however, much of the coral close to the beach is dead and to see abundant marine life you need to swim out a few hundred metres.

Unless you are a VIP, only day visits are allowed. And unless you're going on one of the day trips occasionally organised by travel agencies, you need to get permission from the Forest Department. The islands are two hours by boat from Chiriya Tapu or 3½ hours from Wandoor. The advantage of departing from Wandoor is that you access the boat by a jetty. At Chiriya Tapu you join the boat via a dinghy. This is OK in the morning light, but when returning after dark it can be precarious.

Little Andaman

The 100 remaining members of the Onge tribe are confined to a reserve in the south of this island. As the northern part of Little Andaman has been settled, and was opened to foreigners in 1997, time has just about run out for the Onge.

Ferries land at Hut Bay on the east coast. Basic supplies are available in the village 2km to the north. Another 1km north is ***APWD Guest House***, which is the only accommodation (make reservations at the APWD in Port Blair). Just under 2km north of the guesthouse is the police station, where you must register on arrival, then it's about 15km north to the main beach at Butler Bay, where some people camp. The beach is good for swimming, but not for snorkelling.

The tribal reserve in the south is out of bounds to foreigners. Don't try to make contact with the Onge – you certainly won't help their cause by turning them into a tourist attraction.

Boats connect Port Blair with Hut Bay (Rs 18/38 for lower/upper deck, eight hours) once or twice a week.

Language

There is no one 'Indian' language as such. This is part of the reason why English is still widely spoken 50 years after the British left India and why it's still the official language of the judiciary.

Eighteen languages are recognised by the constitution, and these fall into two major groups: Indic, or Indo-Aryan, and Dravidian. Additionally, over 1600 minor languages and dialects were listed in the latest census. The scope for misunderstanding can be easily appreciated!

The Indic languages are a branch of the Indo-European group of languages (to which English belongs). The Indic languages were spoken by the Central Asian peoples who invaded what is now India. The Dravidian languages are native to south India, although they have been influenced by Sanskrit and Hindi over the years.

Most of India's languages have their own script, but written English can also be quite common; in some states, such as Gujarat, you'll hardly see a word of it, whereas in Himachal Pradesh virtually everything is in English. For a sample of the different scripts, look at a Rs 5 or larger banknote where 14 languages are represented. As well as Hindi and English there's a list of 12 other languages: from the top, they are Assamese, Bengali, Gujarati, Kannada, Kashmiri, Malayalam, Marathi, Oriya, Punjabi, Sanskrit, Tamil, Telugu and Urdu. (See the boxed text 'India's Official Languages' on the following page.)

Major efforts have been made to promote Hindi as the national language of India and to gradually phase out English. A stumbling block to this plan is that while Hindi is the predominant language in the north, it bears little relation to the Dravidian languages of the south; subsequently, very few people in the south speak Hindi. It is from here, particularly the state of Tamil Nadu, that the most vocal opposition to the adoption of Hindi comes, along with the strongest support for the retention of English.

For many educated Indians, English is virtually their first language, and for the large number of Indians who speak more than one language, English is often their second tongue. Thus it's very easy to get around India with English, but it's always good to know at least a little of the local language.

Strangely Familiar

Indian English is full of interesting everyday expressions. Where in New York you might get robbed by a mugger, in India it will be a *dacoit* who relieves you of your goods. Politicians in India may employ strong-arm heavies known as *goondas*. There is a plethora of Indian terms for strikes and lock-ins – Indians can have *bandhs*, *hartaals* and *gheraos*, for example. Then there are all those Indian servants – children get looked after by *ayahs*, your house and your *godown* (or warehouse) is guarded by a *chowkidar*, and when the toilet needs cleaning there is no way your *bearer* is going to do it.

It's surprising how many Indian terms have crept into English usage. We can sit on a veranda and drink chai, wear pyjamas or sandals and dungarees (which may well be khaki), shampoo our hair, visit the jungle, or worry about protecting our loot – they're all Indian words.

For definitions of everyday Indian terms, see the Glossary which follows this chapter.

Hindi

Hindi is written from left to right in Devanagari script. While the script may be unfamiliar, many of the grammatical features will be familiar to English speakers.

For a far more comprehensive guide to Hindi, get a copy of Lonely Planet's *Hindi & Urdu phrasebook*.

Pronunciation

Most of the sounds in Hindi correspond to the Roman letters used to represent them in the transliteration.

Vowels & Diphthongs

It's important to pay attention to the pronunciation of vowels and especially to their length. A stroke over a vowel (eg, **ā**, **ī**, **ū**)

India's Official Languages

Assamese State language of Assam, and spoken by nearly 60% of that state's population. Dates back to the 13th century.
Bengali Spoken by nearly 200 million people (mostly in what is now Bangladesh), and the state language of West Bengal. Developed as a language in the 13th century.
Gujarati State language of Gujarat, it is an Indic language.
Kannada State language of Karnataka, spoken by about 65% of that state's population.
Hindi The most important Indian language, although it is only spoken as a mother tongue by about 20% of the population, mainly in the area known as the Hindi-belt, the cow-belt or Bimaru, which includes Bihar, Madhya Pradesh, Rajasthan and Uttar Pradesh. This Indic language is the official language of the Indian government, the states already mentioned, plus Haryana and Himachal Pradesh.
Kashmiri Kashmiri speakers account for about 55% of the population of Jammu & Kashmir. It is an Indic language written in the Perso-Arabic script.
Konkani Konkani is a Dravidian language spoken by people in the Goa region.
Malayalam A Dravidian language, and the state language of Kerala.
Manipuri An Indic language of the north-east region.
Marathi An Indic language dating back to around the 13th century, Marathi is the state language of Maharashtra.
Nepali Nepali is the predominant language of Sikkim, where around 75% of the people are ethnic Nepalis.
Oriya An Indic language, it is the state language of Orissa where it is spoken by 87% of the population.
Punjabi Another Indic language, this is the state language of the Punjab. Although based on Devanagari (the same script as Hindi), it is written in a 16th-century script, known as Gurumukhi, which was created by the Sikh guru, Guru Angad.
Sanskrit One of the oldest languages in the world, and the language of classical India. All the Vedas and classical literature such as the Mahabharata and the Ramayana were written in this Indic language.
Sindhi A significant number of Sindhi speakers are found in what is now Pakistan, although the greater number are in India. In Pakistan, the language is written in a Perso-Arabic script, while in India it uses the Devanagari script.
Tamil An ancient Dravidian language at least 2000 years old, and the state language of Tamil Nadu. It is spoken by 65 million people.
Telugu The Dravidian language spoken by the largest number of people, it is the state language of Andhra Pradesh.
Urdu Urdu is the state language of Jammu & Kashmir. Along with Hindi, it evolved in early Delhi. While Hindi was largely adopted by the Hindu population, the Muslims embraced Urdu, and so the latter is written in the Perso-Arabic script and includes many Persian words.

indicates a longer vowel sound. The symbol ~ over a vowel (eg, ã̄, ĩ, ĩ̄, ũ, ũ̄,) indicates that it should be pronounced through the nose.

a as the 'u' in 'sun'
ā as in 'father'
e as in 'they'
i as in 'sit'
ī as the 'ee' in 'feet'
u as in 'put'
ū as the 'oo' in 'fool'
ai as the 'a' in 'care'
o as in 'both'
au as the 'aw' in 'saw'
o as in 'both'

Note that **ai** is pronounced as a diphthong when followed by **ya**, and **au** is pronounced as a diphthong when followed by **va**.

ai as the 'i' in 'high'
au as the 'ou' in 'ouch'

Consonants

Most consonants in the transliterations are pronounced as in English, with the following exceptions:

- **c** as the 'ch' in 'cheese'
- **g** always as in 'gun', never as in 'age'
- **ṭ** pronounced with the tongue further back than in English. Curl the tongue back towards the roof of the mouth.
- **ḍ** pronounced with the tongue curled back towards the roof of the mouth.
- **r** slightly trilled
- **ṛ** an 'r' with the tongue placed near the roof of the mouth and flapped quickly down, touching the roof as it moves.
- **q** as the 'k' in 'king', but pronounced further back
- **y** as in 'yak'
- **kh** similar to the 'ch' in Scottish *loch*
- **gh** like the 'g' in 'go' but pronounced further back in the throat

Aspirated consonats are pronounced with a breath of air, represented by an h after the consonant (except for **sh**, pronounced as in 'ship', and **kh** and **gh**).

Essentials

Hello.	*namaste/namskār*
Goodbye.	*namaste/namskār*
Yes.	*jī hā̃*
No.	*jī nahī̃*

'Please' is usually conveyed through the polite form of the imperative, or through other expressions. This book uses polite expressions and the polite forms of words.

Thank you.	*shukriyā/dhanyavād*
You're welcome.	*koī bāt nahī̃*
Excuse me/Sorry.	*kshamā kījiye*
How are you?	*āp kaise/ī haĩ?* (m/f)
Fine, and you?	*bas āp sunāiye* (m/f)
What's your name?	*āp kā shubh nām kyā hai?*

Language Difficulties

Do you speak English?	*kyā āp ko angrezī ātī hai?*
Does anyone here speak English?	*kyā kisī ko angrezī ātī hai?*
I understand.	*maĩ samjhā/ī*
I don't understand.	*maĩ nahī̃ samjhā/ī*

Signs – Hindi

प्रवेश/अन्दर	**Entrance**
निकार/बाहर	**Exit**
खुला	**Open**
बन्द	**Closed**
अन्दर आना [निषिा/मना] है	**No Entry**
धूम्रपान करना [निषिा/मना] है	**No Smoking**
निषिा	**Prohibited**
गर्म	**Hot**
ठंडा	**Cold**
शोचालय	**Toilets**

Please speak more slowly.	*dhīre dhīre boliye*
Please write it down.	*zarā likh ḍījiye*

Getting Around

How do we get to ...?	*... kaise jāte haĩ?*
When is the ... bus?	*... bas kab jāegī?*
first	*pehlā/pehlī*
next	*aglā/aglī*
last	*ākhirī*
What time does the ... leave?	*... kitne baje jāyegā/jāyegī?* (m/f)
What time does the ... arrive?	*... kitne baje pahũcegā/pahũcegī?* (m/f)
plane	*havāī jahāz* (m)
boat	*nāv* (f)
bus	*bas* (f)
train	*relgāṛī* (f)
I'd like a ... ticket.	*mujhe ek ... ṭikaṭ cāhiye*
one way	*ek-tarafā*
return	*do-tarafā*
1st class	*pratham shrēni*
2nd class	*dvitīy shrēni*

Accommodation

Where is the (best/cheapest) hotel?	*sab se (acchā/sastā) hoṭal kahā̃ hai?*
Please write the address.	*zarā us kā patā likh ḍījiye*
Do you have any rooms available?	*kyā koī kamrā khālī hai?*

How much for ...? ... *kā kirāyā kitnā hai?*
one night *ek din*
one week *ek hafte*

I'd like a ... *mujhe ... cāhiye*
single room *singal kamrā*
double room *ḍabal kamrā*
room with a bathroom *ghusalkhānevālā kamrā*

I'd like to share a dorm. *maĩ ḍorm mẽ ṭheharnā cāhtā/ī hũ* (m/f)
May I see it? *kyā maĩ kamrā dekh saktā/ī hũ* (m/f)
Is there any other room? *koī aur kamrā hai?*
Where's the bathroom? *ghusalkhānā kahã hai?*

bed *palang*
blanket *kambāl*
key *cābī*
shower *shāvar*
toilet paper *ṭailet pepar*
water (cold/hot) *pānī (ṭhandā/garam)*
with a window *khiṛkīvālā*

Around Town

Where's a/the ... ... *kahã hai?*
bank *baink*
consulate *kaũnsal*
embassy *dūtāvās*
Hindu temple *mandir*
mosque *masjid*
post office *ḍākkhānā*
public phone *sārvajanik fon*
public toilet *shaucālay*
Sikh temple *gurudvārā*
town square *cauk*

Is it far from/near here? *kyā voh yahã se dūr/nazdīk hai?*

Shopping

Where's the nearest ...? *sab se qarib ... kah hai?*
bookshop *kitāb kī dukān*
chemist/pharmacy *davāī kī dukān*
general store *dukān*
market *bāzār*
washerman *dhobī*

Where can I buy ...? *maĩ ... kah kharīd sakta hũ?*

I'd like to buy ... *mujhe ... kharidnā hai*
clothes *kapṛe*
colour film *rangin film*
handicrafts *hāth kī banī cīzẽ*
magazines *patrikāẽ*
newspaper (in English) *(angrezī kā) akhbār*
razor *ustarā*
soap *sābun*
toothpaste *manjan*
washing powder *kapṛre dhone kā sābun*
envelope *lifāfā*
paper *kāghaz*
stamp *ṭikaṭ*
map *naqshā*

big *baṛā*
small *choṭā*
more *aur*
a little *thoṛā*
too much/many *bahut/adhik*
enough *kāfi*

How much is this? *is kā dām kyā hai?*
I think it's too expensive. *yeh bahut mahẽgā/i hai* (m/f)
Can you lower the price? *is kā dām kam kījiye?*
Do you accept credit cards? *kyā āp vizā kārḍ vaghairah lete ha?*

Health

Where is a/the ...? ... *kahã hai?*
clinic *davākhānā*
doctor *ḍākṭar*
hospital *aspatāl*

I'm sick. *maĩ bīmār hũ*
antiseptic *ainṭīsepṭik*
antibiotics *ainṭībayoṭik*
asprin *(esprin) sirdard kī davā*
condoms *nirodhak*
contraceptives *garbnirodhak*
diarrhoea *dast*
medicine *davā*
nausea *ghin*
syringe *sūī*
tampons *ṭaimpon*

Time & Days

What time is it? *kitne baje haī?/ṭāim kyā hai?*

Emergencies – Hindi

Help!	*mada kījiye!*
Stop!	*ruko!*
Thief!	*cor!*
Call a doctor!	*ḍākṭar ko bulāo!*
Call an ambulance!	*embulains le ānā!*
Call the police!	*pulis ko bulāo!*
I'm lost.	*maĩ rāstā bhūl gayā/ gayī hũ* (f/m)
Where is the ...?	*... kahā̃ hai?*
police station	*thānā*
toilet	*ghusalkhānā*
I wish to contact my embassy/consulate.	*maĩ apne embassy ke sebāt katnā logõ cāhtā/cāhtī hũ* (f/m)

It's (ten) o'clock. *(das) baje haĩ*
half past two *ḍhāī baje haĩ*

When? *kab?*
today *āj*
tomorrow/yesterday *kal* (while *kal* is used for both, the meaning is made clear by context)
now *ab*

morning *saverā/subhā*
evening *shām*
night *rāt*
day *din*
week *haftā*
month *mahīnā*
year *sāl/baras*

Monday *somvār*
Tuesday *mangalvār*
Wednesday *budhvār*
Thursday *guruvār/brihaspativār*
Friday *shukravār*
Saturday *shanivār*
Sunday *itvār/ravivār*

Numbers

Whereas we count in tens, hundreds, thousands, millions and billions, the Indian numbering system goes tens, hundreds, thousands, hundred thousands, ten millions. A hundred thousand is a *lākh*, and 10 million is a *crore*. These two words are almost always used in place of their English equivalents.

Once into the thousands, large written numbers have commas every two places, not three.

1	*ek*
2	*do*
3	*tīn*
4	*cār*
5	*pā̃c*
6	*chai*
7	*sāt*
8	*āṭh*
9	*nau*
10	*das*
11	*gyārah*
12	*bara*
13	*terah*
14	*caudah*
15	*pandrah*
16	*solah*
17	*satrah*
18	*aṭṭhārah*
19	*unnīs*
20	*bīs*
21	*ikkīs*
22	*bāīs*
30	*tīs*
40	*cālīs*
50	*pacās*
60	*sāṭh*
70	*sattar*
80	*assī*
90	*nabbe/navve*
100	*sau*
1000	*hazār*
100,000 (written 1,00,000)	*ek lākh*
10 million (written 1,00,00,000)	*ek crore*

Food

breakfast *nāshtā*
lunch *din kā khānā*
dinner *rāt kā khānā*

fork *kā̃ṭā*
knife *churī*
glass *glās*
plate *pleṭ*

I'm a vegetarian.	*maĩ shākāhārī hũ*
food	*khānā*
bread	*roṭī*
fried bread	*parā̃ṭhā*
tandoori rounds	*nān or tandūrī roṭī*
Western-style bread	*ḍabal* (double) *roṭī*
butter	*makkhan*
cheese	*panīr*
chillies	*mirc*
(without chillies)	(*mirc ke binā*)
rice	*cāval*
fried rice	*pulāv*
salt	*namak*
spices	*masāle*
sugar	*cīnī*
yogurt	*dahī*

Vegetables

cabbage	*band gobhī*
lentils	*dāl*
peas	*maṭar*
potato	*ālū*
pumpkin	*kaddū*
spinach	*pālak*
tomato	*ṭamāṭar*
vegetable	*sabzī/sāg*

Fruit

apple	*seb*
apricot	*khubānī*
banana	*kelā*
fruit	*phal*
mandarin	*santarā*
mango	*ām*
orange	*nārangi*
peach	*ārū*

Meat & Poultry

beef	*gāy kā māns*
chicken	*murgh*
fish	*machlī*
goat	*bakrī kā māns*
meat	*māns/gosht*
mutton	*beṛ kā māns*

Drinks

coffee	*kāfi*
milk	*dūdh*
soft drink	*sauft ḍrink*
(cup of) tea	*cāy*
tea with milk	*dūdhvālī cāy*
tea with sugar	*cīnī ke sāth*
(boiled) water	(*ūblā*) *pānī*

Tamil

Tamil is the official language in the South Indian state of Tamil Nadu and the Union Territory of Pondicherry. In the 1991 census of India, Tamil speakers in Tamil Nadu alone numbered around 56 million; substantial numbers of Tamil speakers can also be found in Sri Lanka and Malaysia and significant minorities in Singapore, Fiji and Mauritius. There are around 71 million speakers worldwide.

Tamil is classed as a South Dravidian language, and is one of the major Dravidian languages of South India. The exact origins of the Dravidian family are unknown, but it is believed to have arrived in India's north-west around 4000 BC, gradually splitting into four branches with the passage of time. Tamil became isolated to India's south as the Indo-Aryan language varieties such as Hindi became more dominant in the north.

Along with Sanskrit, Tamil is deemed to be one of the two classical languages of India. It has a very rich historical tradition dating back more than 2000 years, since which time three forms have been distinguished: Old Tamil (200 BC to AD 700), Middle Tamil (AD 700 to AD 1600) and Modern Tamil (AD 1600 to the present).

Modern Tamil is diglossic in nature, which means it has two distinct forms: literary or classical (used mainly in writing and formal speech), and spoken (used in everyday conversation). The spoken form has a wide range of dialects, varying in social, cultural and regional dimensions. Irrespective of the differences, a common variety called Standard Spoken Tamil is widely used in mass media and by all Tamils in their day-to-day life.

Writing System & Transliteration

Tamil has its own alphabetic script which has not been included in this language guide. The transliteration system used here is intended as a simplified method for representing the sounds of Tamil using the Roman alphabet. As with all such systems it is not exact and should be seen only as an approximate guide to the pronunciation of the language.

Pronunciation

Vowels

Vowels are distinguished by length, and long vowels are represented in this guide by a macron (a stroke above the letter, eg, **ā**); pronounce them as you would short vowels but increase their duration.

Short		Long
a	as in 'father'	**ā**
e	as in 'met'	**ē**
i	as in 'bit'	**ī**
o	as in 'hot'	**ō**
u	as in 'boot'	**ū**

Vowel Combinations

ai as the word 'eye'
au as the 'ow' in 'how'

Consonants

Most consonants are similar to English. A few which could cause confusion are:

g as in 'go'
k as in 'kit'
ñ as the 'ni' in 'onion'
s as in 'sit'
zh as the 's' in 'pleasure'

Other consonants are a little more complicated because they represent sounds not found in English. The most common variants are 'retroflex' consonants, where the tongue is curled upwards and backwards so that the underside of the tip makes contact with the alveolar ridge (the ridge of tissue on the roof of the mouth a little behind the teeth). Retroflex consonants are represented in this guide by a dot below the letter (**ḷ**, **ṇ** and **ṭ**). If the lingual gymnastics prove too much you'll find that you can still make yourself understood by pronouncing the letter as you would in English.

Essentials

Hello.	*vaṇakkam*
Goodbye.	*pōyiṭṭu varukirēn*
Yes/No.	*ām/illai*
Please.	*tayavu seytu*
Thank you.	*nanri*
That's fine./You're welcome.	*nallatu varuka*
Excuse me./Sorry.	*mannikkavum*
Do you speak English?	*nīnkal ānkilam pēsuvīrkalā?*

Signs

Entrance
valli ullē வழி உள்ளே
Exit
valli veliyē வழி வெளியே
Open
tirantulladur திறந்துள்ளது
Closed
adekkappatulladur அடைக்கப்பட்டுள்ளது
Rooms Available
arekāl untu அறைகள் உண்டு
Full, No Vacancies
illē, ல்லை,
kāli illē காலி ல்லை
Information
tahavwel தகவல்
Prohibited
anumadī-illē அனுமதி இல்லை
Police Station
kāv'l nilayem காவல நிலையம்
Toilets
kālippadem மலசலகூடம்
Men *ān* ஆண்
Women *pen* பெண

How much is it?	*atu evvalavu?*
What's your name?	*unkal peyar enna?*
My name is ...	*en peyar ...*

Getting Around

Where is (a/the) ...?	*... enkē irukkiratu?*
Go straight ahead.	*nērāka sellavum*
Turn left/right.	*valatu/itatu pakkam tirumbavum*
near	*arukil*
far	*tūram*
When does the next ... leave/arrive?	*eppozhutu atutta ... varum/sellum?*
boat	*paṭaku*
bus (city)	*pēruntu (nakaram/ullūr)*
bus (intercity)	*pēruntu (veliyūr)*
tram	*trām*
train	*rayil*
I'd like a one-way/return ticket.	*enakku oru vazhi/iru vazhi ṭikkeṭ vēṇum*
1st/2nd class	*mutalām/irantām vakuppu*

Emergencies – Tamil

Help!	*utavi!*
Leave me alone!	*ennai taniyāka irukkavitu!*
Go away!	*tolaintu pō!*
Call a doctor!	*tāktarai kūppitavum!*
Call the police!	*pōlīsai kūppitavum!*
I'm lost.	*nān vazhi tavirittēn*

left luggage	*tavara vitta sāmān*
timetable	*kāla attavanai*
bus/trolley stop	*pēruntu nilayam*
train station	*rayil nilayam*

I'd like to hire ... *enakku ... vātakaikku vēnum*
- a car *kāra*
- a bicycle *saikkil*

Around Town

What time does it open/close?	*tirakkum/mūtum nēram enna?*
bank	*vangi*
chemist/pharmacy	*aruntukkataikkārar/ maruntakam*
... embassy	*... tūtarakam*
my hotel	*en unavu vituti*
market	*mārkkeṭ*
newsagency	*niyūs ējensi*
post office	*tabāl nilayam*
public telephone	*potu tolaipēsi*
stationers	*elutuporul vanikar*
tourist information office	*surrulā seyti totarpu aluvalakam*

Accommodation

Do you have any rooms available?	*araikal kitaikkumā?*
for one/two people	*oruvar/iruvarukku*
for one/two nights	*oru/irantu iravukal*
How much is it per night/per person?	*oru iravukku/oru nabarukku evallavu?*
Is breakfast included?	*kālai sirrunṭiyuṭan sērttā?*
hotel	*hōtal/vituti*
guesthouse	*viruntinar vituti*
youth hostel	*ilaiñar vituti*
camping ground	*tangumitam*

Useful Words

big	*periya*
small	*siriya*
bread	*roṭṭi*
butter	*vennai*
coffee	*kāppi*
egg	*muttai*
fruit	*pazham*
ice	*ais*
medicine	*maruntu*
milk	*pāl*
rice	*arisi*
sugar	*sakkarai*
tea	*tēnīr*
vegetables	*kāykarikal*
water	*nīr*

Time & Days

What time is it ?	*mani ettanai?*
day	*pakal*
night	*iravu*
week	*vāram*
month	*mātam*
today	*inru*
tomorrow	*nālai*
yesterday	*nērru*
morning	*kālai*
afternoon	*matiyam*
Monday	*tinkal*
Tuesday	*sevvāy*
Wednesday	*putan*
Thursday	*viyāzhan*
Friday	*velli*
Saturday	*sani*
Sunday	*ñāyiru*

Numbers

0	*būjyam*
1	*ondru*
2	*iranyu*
3	*mūnru*
4	*nānku*
5	*aintu*
6	*āru*
7	*ēzhu*
8	*ettu*
9	*onpatu*
10	*pattu*
100	*nūru*
1000	*āyiram*
2000	*irantāyiram*
100,000	*latsam*
one million	*pattu latsam*
ten million	*kōti*

Glossary

The glossary that follows is a sample of the words and terms you may come across during your Indian wanderings. For definitions of food and drink, see the separate 'Food & Drink' section at the end.

General

abbi – waterfall
Abhimani – eldest son of *Brahma*
Abhimanyu – son of *Arjuna*
acha – 'OK' or 'I understand'
acharya – revered teacher; originally a spiritual guide
Adivasi – tribal person
agarbathi – incense
Agasti – legendary Hindu sage, highly revered in the south as he is credited with introducing Hinduism and developing the Tamil language
Agni – major deity in the *Vedas*; mediator between men and the gods; also fire
ahimsa – discipline of nonviolence
AIR – All India Radio, the national broadcaster
air-cooled room – room in guesthouse, hotel or home, generally with a big, noisy water-filled fan built into the wall
Amir – Muslim nobleman
amrita – immortality
Ananda – *Buddha's* cousin and personal attendant
ananda – happiness
Ananta – snake on which *Vishnu* reclined
Andhaka – 1000-headed demon, killed by *Shiva*
angrezi – foreigner
anikut – dam
anna – 16th of a rupee; no longer legal tender but occasionally referred to in marketplaces
Annapurna – form of *Durga*; worshipped for her power to provide food
apsara – heavenly nymph
APSRTC – Andhra Pradesh State Road Transport Corporation
APTTDC – Andhra Pradesh Travel & Tourist Development Corporation
Aranyani – Hindu goddess of forests
Ardhanari – *Shiva* in half-male, half-female form
Arishta – *daitya* who, having taken the form of a bull, attacked *Krishna* and was killed by him
Arjuna – *Mahabharata* hero and military commander who married *Subhadra*, took up arms against and overcame all manner of demons, had the *Bhagavad Gita* related to him by *Krishna*, led Krishna's funeral ceremony at Dwarka and finally retired to the Himalaya
Aryan – Sanskrit word for 'noble'; refers to those who migrated from Persia and settled in northern India
ashram – spiritual community or retreat
ashrama – system; essentially there are three stages in life recognised under this system: brahmachari, grihastha and sanyasin but this kind of merit is only available to the upper three castes
attar – essential oil made from flowers and used as a base for perfumes
autorickshaw – small, noisy, three-wheeled, motorised contraption for transporting passengers, livestock etc for short distances; found throughout the country, they are cheaper than taxis
Avalokiteshvara – in *Mahayana* Buddhism, the *Bodhisattva* of compassion; called Kannon in Japan and Kuan Yin in China
avatar – incarnation of a deity, usually *Vishnu*
ayah – children's nurse or nanny
Ayurveda – the ancient and complex science of Indian herbal medicine and healing
azan – Muslim call to prayer

baba – religious master or father; term of respect
babu – a lower level clerical worker (derogatory)
bagh – garden
bahadur – brave or chivalrous; an honorific title
baksheesh – tip, bribe or donation
Balarama – brother of *Krishna*
bandar – monkey
bandh – general strike
banian – T-shirt or undervest
baniya – moneylender
banyan – Indian fig tree
baoli – see *baori*

baori – well, particularly a step-well with landings and galleries; in Gujarat it is more commonly referred to as a baoli
baradari – summer house
bazaar – market area; a market town is also called a bazaar
bearer – rather like a butler
beedi – see *bidi*
begum – Muslim woman of high rank
Bhadrakali – another name for *Durga*
Bhagavad Gita – Hindu Song of the Divine One; Krishna's lessons to *Arjuna*, the main thrust of which was to emphasise the philosophy of *bhakti*; Bhagavad Gita is part of the *Mahabharata*
Bhairava – the Terrible; refers to the eighth incarnation of *Shiva* in his demonic form
bhajan – devotional song
bhakti – surrendering to the gods; faith
bhang – dried leaves and flowering shoots of the marijuana plant
bhangra – Punjabi disco
Bharat – Hindi for India
Bharata – half-brother of *Rama*; ruled while Rama was in exile
bhavan – house; also spelt 'bhawan'
bheesti – see *bhisti*
bherra – big, important
Bhima – *Mahabharata* hero; he is the brother of *Hanuman* and renowned for his great strength
bhisti – water carrier
bhoga-mandapa – Orissan hall of offering
bhojanalya – basic restaurant or snack bar, also known as 'dhaba'
bidi – small, hand-rolled cigarette; really just a rolled-up leaf
bindi – forehead mark worn by women
BJP – Bharatiya Janata Party
black money – undeclared and untaxed money
Bodhi Tree – tree under which the *Buddha* sat when he attained enlightenment
Bodhisattva – literally 'one whose essence is perfected wisdom'; in *Early Buddhism*, Bodhisattva refers only to the *Buddha* during the period between his conceiving the intention to strive for Buddhahood and the moment he attained it; in *Mahayana* Buddhism, one who renounces *nirvana* in order to help others attain it
Bollywood – India's answer to Hollywood; the film industry of Mumbai (Bombay)
Brahma – Hindu god; worshipped as the creator in the *Trimurti*
brahmachari – chaste student stage of the *ashrama* system
Brahmanism – early form of Hinduism which evolved from Vedism (see *Vedas*); named after *Brahmin* priests and *Brahma*
Brahmin – member of the priest caste, the highest Hindu caste
BSTDC – Bihar State Tourist Development Corporation
Buddha – Awakened One; the originator of Buddhism; also regarded by Hindus as the ninth incarnation of *Vishnu*
Buddhism – see *Early Buddhism*
bugyal – high-altitude meadow
bund – embankment or dyke
burkha – one-piece garment used by Muslim women to cover them from head to toe
bustee – slum

cantonment – administrative and military area of a Raj-era town
caravanserai – traditional accommodation for camel caravans
caste – one's hereditary station in life
chaam – ritual masked dance performed by some Buddhist monks in *gompas* to celebrate the victory of good over evil and of Buddhism over pre-existing religions
chaitya – Sanskrit form of 'cetiya', meaning shrine or object of worship; has come to mean temple, and more specifically, a hall divided into a central nave and two side aisles by a line of columns, with a votive *stupa* at the end
chakra – focus of one's spiritual power; disc-like weapon of *Vishnu*
chalo, chalo, chalo – 'let's go, let's go, let's go'
Chamunda – form of *Durga*; a real terror, armed with a scimitar, noose and mace, and clothed in elephant hide, her mission was to kill the demons Chanda and Munda
chance list – waiting list on Indian Airlines flights
chandra – moon, or the moon as a god
Chandragupta – ruler of India in the 3rd century BC
chappals – sandals
Char Dham – four pilgrimage destinations of Badrinath, Kedarnath, Yamunotri and Gangotri
charas – resin of the marijuana plant; also referred to as 'hashish'
charbagh – formal Persian garden, divided into quarters (literally 'four gardens')

charpoy – Indian rope bed
chauri – fly whisk
chedi – see *chaitya*
chela – pupil or follower, as George Harrison was to Ravi Shankar
chhatri – cenotaph (literally 'umbrella')
chikan – embroidered cloth
chillum – pipe of a *hookah*; commonly used to describe the pipes used for smoking *ganja*
chinkara – gazelle
chital – spotted deer
chogyal – king
choli – sari blouse
chomos – Tibetan Buddhist nuns
chorten – Tibetan for *stupa*
choultry – pilgrim's resthouse; also called 'dharamsala'
chowk – town square, intersection or marketplace
chowkidar – night watchman, caretaker
chuba – dress worn by Tibetan women
Cong (I) – Congress Party of India; also known as Congress (I)
CPI – Communist Party of India
CPI (M) – Communist Party of India (Marxist)
crore – 10 million
cutcherry – office or building used for public business

dacoit – bandit (particularly armed bandit), outlaw
dagoba – see *stupa*
daitya – demon or giant who fought against the gods
dak – staging post, government-run accommodation
Dalit – preferred term for India's Untouchable caste; see also *Harijan*
Damodara – another name for *Krishna*
dargah – shrine or place of burial of a Muslim saint
darshan – offering or audience with someone; viewing of a deity
darwaza – gateway or door
Dasaratha – father of *Rama* in the *Ramayana*
Dattatreya – *Brahmin* saint who embodied the *Trimurti*
deul – temple sanctuary
devadasi – temple dancer
Devi – *Shiva's* wife
dhaba – see *bhojanalya*
dham – holiest pilgrimage places of India
dharamsala – pilgrim's resthouse
dharma – the word used by both Hindus and Buddhists to refer to their respective moral codes of behaviour
dharna – nonviolent protest
dhobi – person who washes clothes
dhobi ghat – place where clothes are washed
dholi – man-carried portable 'chairs'; you may still see some elderly tourists being carried in them
dhoti – like a *lungi*, but the cloth is then pulled up between the legs; worn by men
dhurrie – rug
Digambara – Sky-Clad; a Jain sect whose followers demonstrate their disdain for worldly goods by going naked
dikpala – temple guardian
Din-i-Ilahi – Akbar's philosophy asserting the common truth in all religions
diwan – principal officer in a princely state; royal court or council
Diwan-i-Am – hall of public audience
Diwan-i-Khas – hall of private audience
dowry – money and goods given by a bride's parents to their son-in-law's family; it's illegal but few arranged marriages (most marriages are arranged) can be made without it
Draupadi – wife of the five Pandava princes in the *Mahabharata*
Dravidian – member of one of the original races of India, pushed south by the Indo-Europeans and now mixed with them
dukhang – Tibetan prayer hall
dun – valley
dupatta – long scarf often worn with the *salwar* and *kameez*
durbar – royal court; also used to describe a government
Durga – the Inaccessible; a form of *Shiva*'s wife, *Devi*, a beautiful but fierce woman riding a tiger; a major goddess of the Shakti cult
dwarpal – doorkeeper; sculpture beside the doorways to Hindu or Buddhist shrines

Early Buddhism – any of the schools of Buddhism established directly after Buddha's death and before the advent of *Mahayana*; a modern form is the *Theravada* (Teaching of the Elders) practised in Sri Lanka and South-East Asia; early Buddhism differed from the *Mahayana* in that it did not teach the *Bodhisattva* ideal
elatalam – small hand-held cymbals

election symbols – identifying symbols for the various political parties, used to canvas illiterate voters
Emergency – period in the 1970s during which Indira Gandhi suspended many political rights
Eve-teasing – sexual harassment
export guru – *guru* whose followers are mainly Westerners

fakir – Muslim who has taken a vow of poverty; also applied to *sadhus* and other Hindu ascetics
filmee – music or other aspect of Indian movies
firman – royal order or grant

gabba – appliqued Kashmiri rug
gaddi – throne of a Hindu prince
Ganesh – Hindu god of good fortune; popular elephant-headed son of Shiva and Parvati he is also known as Ganpati and his vehicle is a rat-like creature
Ganga – Hindu goddess representing the sacred Ganges River; said to flow from the toe of *Vishnu*
ganga aarti – river worship ceremony
ganj – market
ganja – dried flowering tips of marijuana plant
gaon – village
garh – fort
gari – vehicle; 'motor gari' is a car and 'rail gari' is a train
Garuda – man-bird vehicle of *Vishnu*
gaur – Indian bison
Gayatri – sacred verse of *Rig-Veda* repeated mentally by *Brahmins* twice a day
geyser – hot-water heater usually found in bathrooms
ghat – steps or landing on a river, range of hills, or road up hills
ghazal – Urdu song derived from poetry; sad love theme
gherao – industrial action where the workers lock in their employers
giri – hill
Gita Govinda – erotic poem by Jayadeva relating *Krishna's* early life as *Govinda*
GITO – Government of India Tourist Office
GMVN – Garhwal Mandal Vikas Nigam, Garhwal tourist organisation
godmen – commercially minded gurus; see also *export guru*
godown – warehouse
gompa – Tibetan Buddhist monastery
Gonds – aboriginal Indian race, now mainly found in the jungles of central India
goonda – ruffian or tough; political parties sometimes employ them in gangs
Gopala – see *Govinda*
gopi – milkmaid; *Krishna* was fond of them
gopuram – soaring pyramidal gateway tower of Dravidian temples
Govinda – *Krishna* as a cowherd; also just cowherd
grihastha – householder stage of the *ashrama* system; followers discharge their duty to ancestors by having sons and making sacrifices to the gods
gufa – cave
gumbad – dome on a Muslim tomb or mosque
gurdwara – Sikh temple
guru – teacher or holy person; in Sanskrit literally 'goe' (darkness) and 'roe' (to dispel)
Guru Granth Sahib – Sikh holy book

haj – Muslim pilgrimage to Mecca
haji – Muslim who has made the *haj*
hammam – Turkish bath
Hanuman – Hindu monkey god, prominent in the *Ramayana*, and a follower of *Rama*
Hara – one of *Shiva's* names
Hari – another name for *Vishnu*
Harijan – name (no longer considered acceptable) given by Gandhi to India's *Untouchables*, meaning 'children of god'
hartaal – strike
hashish – see *charas*
hathi – elephant
haveli – traditional ornately decorated residences, particularly in reference to those found in Rajasthan and Gujarat
havildar – army officer
hijra – eunuch
Hinayana – see *Early Buddhism*
hindola – swing
Hiranyakasipu – *daitya* king killed by *Narasimha*
hookah – water pipe used for smoking *ganja*
howdah – seat for carrying people on an elephant's back
HPTDC – Himachal Pradesh Tourist Development Corporation
hypothecated – Indian equivalent of leased or mortgaged; you may see small signs on taxis or autorickshaws stating that the vehicle is 'hypothecated' to some bank or other

idgah – open enclosure to the west of a town where prayers are offered during the Muslim Eid al-Zuhara festival
ikat – fabric made with thread which is tie-dyed before weaving
imam – Muslim religious leader
imambara – tomb dedicated to a Shi'ia Muslim holy man
Indo-Saracenic – style of colonial architecture that integrated Western designs with Muslim, Hindu and Jain influences
Indra – most important and prestigious of the Vedic gods; god of rain, thunder, lightning and war
Ishwara – another name given to *Shiva*; lord

Jagadhatri – Mother of the World; another name for *Devi*
jagamohan – assembly hall
Jagannath – Lord of the Universe; a form of *Krishna*
Jalasayin – literally 'sleeping on the waters'; name for *Vishnu* as he sleeps on his couch over water during the monsoon
jali – carved marble lattice screen, also used to refer to the holes or spaces produced through carving timber
Janaka – father of *Sita*
janata – literally 'people'; the Janata Party is the People's Party
jataka – tale from *Buddha's* various lives
jauhar – ritual mass suicide by immolation, traditionally performed by *Rajput* women at times of military defeat to avoid being dishonoured by their captors
jawan – policeman or soldier
jheel – swampy area
jhuggi – shanty settlement; also called *bustee*
jhula – bridge
ji – honorific that can be added to the end of almost anything; thus 'Babaji', Memji, 'Gandhiji'
JKLF – Jammu & Kashmir Liberation Front
jooti – traditional pointy-toed shoe of Rajasthan
juggernaut – huge, extravagantly decorated temple 'car' dragged through the streets during Hindu festivals
jumkahs – earrings
jyoti linga – most important shrines to *Shiva*, of which there are 12

kabaddi – traditional game (like tag)
kachairri – see *cutcherry*
Kailasa – sacred Himalayan mountain; home of *Shiva*
Kali – the Black; terrible form of *Devi* commonly depicted with black skin, dripping with blood, surrounded by snakes and wearing a necklace of skulls
Kalki – White Horse; future (10th) incarnation of Vishnu which will appear at the end of Kali-Yug, when the world ceases to be; has been compared to *Maitreya* in Buddhist cosmology
Kama – Hindu god of love
kameez – woman's shirt-like tunic
Kanishka – important king of the Kushana empire who reigned in the early Christian era
Kanyakumari – Virgin Maiden; another name for *Durga*
kapali – sacred bowl made from a human skull
karma – Hindu-Buddhist principle of retributive justice for past deeds
karmachario – workers
Kartikiya – Hindu god of war, *Shiva's* son
kata – Tibetan prayer shawl, traditionally given to a *lama* when pilgrims are brought into his presence
kathputli – puppeteer; also known as 'putli wallah'
Kedarnath – name of *Shiva* and one of the 12 *jyoti linga*
khadi – homespun cloth; Mahatma Gandhi encouraged people to spin this rather than buy English cloth
Khalistan – Sikh secessionists' name for an independent Punjab
Khalsa – Sikh brotherhood
khan – Muslim honorific title
kho-kho – traditional game (like tag)
khur – Asiatic wild ass
kiang – wild ass found in Ladakh
kibla – direction in which Muslims face in prayer, often marked with a niche carved into the mosque wall
kirtan – Sikh hymn-singing
KMVN – Kumaon Mandal Vikas Nigam; Kumaon tourist organisation
koil – Hindu temple
kompu – C-shaped, metal trumpet
kos minar – milestone
kot – fort
kothi – residence, house or mansion
kotwali – police station
Krishna – Vishnu's eighth incarnation, often coloured blue; he revealed the *Bhagavad Gita* to *Arjuna*

Kshatriya – Hindu caste of soldiers or administrators; second in the caste hierarchy
kund – lake or tank; Toda village
kurta – long shirt with either short collar or no collar
Kusa – one of *Rama's* twin sons

Lakshmana – half-brother and aide of *Rama* in the *Ramayana*
Lakshmi – *Vishnu's* consort, Hindu goddess of wealth; she sprang forth from the ocean holding a lotus
lama – Tibetan-Buddhist priest or monk
lathi – large bamboo stick used by Indian police officers
Laxmi – see *Lakshmi*
lehanga – very full skirt with a waist cord
lhamo – Tibetan opera
lingam – phallic symbol; symbol of *Shiva*; plural linga
lok – people
Lok Dal – political party; one of the components of the Janata Party
Lok Sabha – lower house in the Indian parliament, (House of the People); comparable to the House of Representatives or House of Commons
loka – realm
Losar – Tibetan new year
lungi – worn by men, this loose, coloured garment (similar to a sarong) is pleated by the wearer at the waist to fit snugly

machaan – observation tower
madrasa – Islamic college
Mahabharata – Great Hindu Vedic epic poem of the Bharata dynasty; containing approximately 10,000 verses, describing the battle between the Pandavas and the Kauravas
Mahabodhi Society – founded in 1891 to encourage Buddhist studies
Mahadeva – Great God; *Shiva*
Mahadevi – Great Goddess; *Devi*
Mahakala – Great Time; *Shiva* and one of 12 *jyoti linga*
mahal – house or palace
maharaja – great king or princely ruler
maharana – see *maharaja*
maharao – see *maharaja*
maharawal – see *maharaja*
maharani – wife of a princely ruler or a ruler in her own right
mahatma – literally 'great soul'
Mahavir – last *tirthankar*

Mahayana – the 'greater-vehicle' of Buddhism; a later adaptation of the teaching which lays emphasis on the Bodhisattva ideal, teaching the renunciation of nirvana (ultimate peace and cessation of rebirth) in order to help other beings along the way to enlightenment
Mahayogi – Great Ascetic; *Shiva*
Maheshwara – Great Lord; *Shiva*
Mahisa – Hindu demon
mahout – elephant rider or master
Mahratta – see *Maratha*
maidan – open grassed area in a city or parade ground
Maitreya – future Buddha
Makara – mythical sea creature and *Varuna's* vehicle; crocodile
mali – gardener
mandal – shrine
mandala – circle; symbol used in Hindu and Buddhist art to symbolise the universe
mandapam – pillared pavilion in front of a temple
mandi – market
mandir – temple
mani stone – stone carved with the Tibetan-Buddhist mantra 'Om mani padme hum' or 'Hail to the jewel in the lotus'
mani walls – Tibetan stone walls with sacred inscriptions
mantra – sacred word or syllable used by Buddhists and Hindus to aid concentration; metrical psalms of praise found in the *Vedas*
Mara – the Buddhist personification of that which obstructs the cultivation of virtue, often depicted with hundreds of arms; also the god of death
Maratha – central Indian people who controlled much of India at various times and fought the *Mughals* and *Rajputs*
marg – major road
Maruts – Hindu storm gods
masjid – mosque
mata – mother
math – monastery
maund – unit of weight now largely superseded (about 20kg)
mehndi – henna; ornate henna patterns painted on women's hands and feet for important festivals and ceremonies (eg, marriage)
mela – fair
memsahib – married Western lady (from 'madam-sahib')
Meru – mythical mountain found in the centre of the earth; on it is *Swarga*

mihrab – prayer niche in the wall of a mosque indicating the direction of Mecca; see also *kibla*
mithuna – pairs of men and women; often seen in temple sculpture
Moghul – see *Mughal*
Mohini – *Vishnu* in his female incarnation
moksha – liberation from *samsara*
monsoon – rainy season
morcha – mob march or protest
MTDC – Maharashtra Tourism Development Corporation
mudra – ritual hand movements used in Hindu religious dancing; gesture of Buddha figure
muezzin – one who calls Muslims to prayer from the minaret
Mughal – Muslim dynasty of Indian emperors from Babur to Aurangzeb
mujtahid – divine
mullah – Muslim scholar, teacher or religious leader
mund – village
munshi – writer, secretary or teacher of languages

nadi – river
Naga – mythical serpent-like beings capable of changing into human form
namaz – Muslim prayers
Nanda – cowherd who raised *Krishna*
Nandi – bull, vehicle of *Shiva*
Narasimha – man-lion incarnation of *Vishnu*
Narayan – incarnation of *Vishnu* the creator
Narsingh – see *Narasimha*
natamandir – dancing hall
Nataraja – *Shiva* as the cosmic dancer
nautch – dance
nautch girls – dancing girls
nawab – Muslim ruling prince or powerful landowner
Naxalites – ultra-leftist political movement begun in Naxal Village, West Bengal, as a peasant rebellion characterised by extreme violence; it still exists in Uttar Pradesh, Bihar and Andhra Pradesh
Nilakantha – form of *Shiva*; his blue throat is a result of swallowing poison that would have destroyed the world
nilgai – antelope
nirvana – this is the ultimate aim of Buddhists and the final release from the cycle of existence
niwas – house, building
nizam – hereditary title of the rulers of Hyderabad
noth – the Lord (Jain)
NRI – Non-Resident Indian; of economic importance for modern India
nullah – ditch or small stream

Om – sacred invocation representing the absolute essence of the divine principle; for Buddhists, if repeated often enough with complete concentration, it should lead to a state of emptiness
Osho – Bhagwan Rajneesh, the guru who mixed Californian pop-psychology with Indian mysticism
OTDC – Orissa Tourism Development Corporation

pacha – green, pure
padma – lotus; another name for the Hindu goddess *Lakshmi*
padma – lotus
padyatra – 'foot journey' made by politicians to raise support at village level
pagoda – see *stupa*
palanquin – box-like enclosure carried on poles on four men's shoulders; the occupant sits inside on a seat
Pali – the language, related to Sanskrit, in which the Buddhist scriptures were recorded; scholars still refer to the original Pali texts
palia – memorial stone
palli – village
Panchatantra – series of traditional Hindu stories about the natural world, human behaviour and survival
panchayat – village council
pandal – marquee
pandit – expert or wise person; sometimes used to mean a bookworm
Parasurama – *Rama* with the axe; sixth incarnation of *Vishnu*
Parsi – adherent of the Zoroastrian faith; Persian
Parvati – another form of *Devi*
patachitra – Orissan cloth painting
PCO – public call office from where you can usually also make interstate and international telephone calls
peepul – fig tree, especially a bo tree
peon – lowest grade clerical worker
pietra dura – marble inlay work characteristic of the Taj Mahal
pinjrapol – animal hospital maintained by Jains

POK – Pakistan Occupied Kashmir
pradesh – state
pranayama – study of breath control
prasad – food offering used in religious ceremonies
puja – literally 'respect'; offering or prayers
pukka – proper; a Raj-era term
pukka sahib – proper European gentleman
punka – cloth fan, swung by pulling a cord
Puranas – set of 18 encyclopaedic Sanskrit stories, written in verse, relating to the three gods, dating from the 5th century AD
purdah – custom among some Muslims (also adopted by many Hindus, especially the Rajputs) of keeping women in seclusion
Purnima – full moon; considered to be an auspicious time
putli wallah – puppeteer; also known as 'kathputli'

Qawwali – Sufi devotional singing
qila – fort

Radha – favourite mistress of *Krishna* when he lived as a cowherd
raga – any of several conventional patterns of melody and rhythm that form the basis for freely interpreted compositions
railhead – station or town at the end of a railway line; termination point
raj – rule or sovereignty
raja, rana – king
rajkumar – prince
Rajput – Hindu warrior caste, former rulers of western India
Rajya Sabha – upper house in the Indian parliament (Council of States)
rakhi – amulet
Rama – seventh incarnation of *Vishnu*
Ramayana – the story of *Rama* and *Sita* and their conflict with *Ravana* is one of India's best-known legends, retold throughout almost all South-East Asia
rangoli – chalk design
rani – female ruler or wife of a king
ranns – deserts
rasta roko – roadblock set up for protest purposes
rath – temple chariot or car used in religious festivals
rathas – rock-cut *Dravidian* temples
Ravana – demon king of Lanka (modern-day Sri Lanka); he abducted *Sita*, and the titanic battle between him and *Rama* is told in the *Ramayana*
rawal – nobleman
rickshaw – small, two or three-wheeled passenger vehicle
Rig-Veda – original and longest of the four main *Vedas*, or holy Sanskrit texts
rishi – any poet, philosopher, saint or sage; originally a sage to whom the hymns of the *Vedas* were revealed
Road – railway town which serves as a communication point to a larger town off the line, eg, Mt Abu and Abu Road
rudraksh mala – strings of beads used in *puja*
Rukmani – wife of *Krishna*; died on his funeral pyre

sadar – main
sadhu – ascetic, holy person, one who is trying to achieve enlightenment; usually addressed as 'swamiji' or 'babaji'
sagar – lake, reservoir
sahib – respectful title applied to any gentleman
salai – road
salwar – loose trousers usually worn with a *kameez*
samadhi – in Hindusim, ecstatic state, sometimes defined as 'ecstasy, trance, communion with God'; in Buddhism, concentration; also a place where a holy man has been cremated, usually venerated as a shrine
sambalpuri – Orissan fabric
sambar – deer
samsara – Buddhists and Hindus alike believe earthly life is cyclical; you are born again and again, the quality of these rebirths being dependent upon your *karma* in previous lives
sangam – meeting of two rivers
sangha – community or order of Buddhist priests
Sankara – *Shiva* as the creator
sanyasin – like a *sadhu*; a wandering ascetic who has renounced all worldly things as part of the *ashrama* system
Saraswati – wife of Brahma, goddess of speech and learning; usually sits on a white swan, holding a *veena*
sardar – see *sirdar*
Sati – wife of *Shiva*; became a sati ('honourable woman') by immolating herself; although banned more than a century ago, the act of sati is still occasionally performed
satra – Hindu Vaishnavaite monastery and centre for art

satsang – discourse by a *swami* or *guru*
satyagraha – nonviolent protest involving a hunger strike, popularised by Mahatma Gandhi; from Sanskrit, literally meaning 'insistence on truth'
Scheduled Castes – official term used for the *Untouchables* or *Dalits*
sepoy – formerly an Indian solider in British service
serai – accommodation for travellers
shahada – Muslim declaration of faith ('there is no God but Allah; Mohammed is his prophet')
Shaivite – follower of *Shiva*
Shaivism – worship of *Shiva*
shakti – creative energies perceived as female deities; devotees follow the cult of Shaktism
Sheshnag – some believe that this snake is the one on which *Vishnu* reclines
shikara – gondola-like boat used on Srinagar's lakes in Kashmir
shikhar – hunting expedition
shirting – material from which shirts are made
Shiva – Destroyer; also the Creator, in which form he is worshipped as a *lingam*
shola – virgin forest
shree – see *shri*
shri – honorific; these days the Indian equivalent of Mr or Mrs
shruti – heard
Shudra – see *Sudra*
sikhara – Hindu temple-spire or temple
singh – literally 'lion'; a surname adopted by Rajputs and Sikhs
sirdar – leader or commander
Sita – The Hindu goddess of agriculture; more commonly associated with the *Ramayana*
sitar – Indian stringed instrument
Siva – see *Shiva*
Skanda – another name for *Kartikiya*
smriti – remembered
sonam – *karma* accumulated in successive reincarnations
sree – see *shri*
sri – see *shri*
stupa – Buddhist religious monument composed of a solid hemisphere topped by a spire, containing relics of the Buddha; also known as a 'dagoba' or 'pagoda'
Subhadra – *Krishna's* incestuous sister
Subrahmanya – another name for *Kartikiya*
Sudra – caste of labourers
Sufi – Muslim mystic
suiting – material from which suits are made
Sulh-i-Kul – peace for all
Surya – the sun; a major deity in the *Vedas*
sutra – string; list of rules expressed in verse
swami – title of respect meaning 'lord of the self'; given to initiated Hindu monks
swaraj – independence
Swarga – heaven of *Indra*
sweeper – lowest caste servant, performs the most menial of tasks
syce – groom

tabla – pair of drums
tal – lake
taluk – district
tandava – Hindu cosmic victory dance over *Mahisa*
tank – reservoir
tantric Buddhism – Tibetan Buddhism with strong sexual and occult overtones
tatty – woven grass screen soaked in water and hung outside windows to cool the air
tempo – noisy three-wheeler public transport vehicle; bigger than an autorickshaw
thakur – nobleman
thangka – rectangular Tibetan painting on cloth
theertham – temple tank
Theravada – orthodox form of Buddhism practiced in Sri Lanka and South-East Asia which is characterised by its adherence to the *Pali* canon; literally, dwelling
thiru – holy
thug – follower of Thuggee; ritual murderers centred in Madhya Pradesh in the last century
tikka – mark devout Hindus put on their foreheads
tilak – forehead mark worn by devout Hindu men
tirthankars – the 24 great Jain teachers
tonga – two-wheeled horse or pony carriage
topi – pith helmet; widely used during the Raj era
torana – architrave over a temple entrance
toy train – narrow-gauge railway
trekkers – jeeps
Trimurti – triple form; the Hindu triad of *Brahma*, *Shiva* and *Vishnu*
Tripitaka – classic *Theravada* Buddhist scriptures, divided into three categories, hence the name 'Three Baskets'
tripolia – triple gateway

Uma – *Shiva's* consort; light
Unesco – United Nations Educational, Scientific and Cultural Organization
Untouchable – lowest caste or 'casteless', for whom the most menial tasks are reserved; the name derives from the belief that higher castes risk defilement if they touch one; formerly known as *Harijan*, now *Dalit*
Upanishads – esoteric doctrine; ancient texts forming part of the *Vedas*; delving into weighty matters such as the nature of the universe and soul

Valmiki – author of the *Ramayana*
Vamana – fifth incarnation of *Vishnu*, as the dwarf
varku – sacred flute made from a thigh bone
varna – concept of caste
Varuna – supreme Vedic god
Vedas – Hindu sacred books; collection of hymns composed in pre-classical Sanskrit during the second millennium BC and divided into four books: *Rig-Veda*, Yajur-Veda, Sama-Veda and Atharva-Veda
veena – stringed instrument
vihara – Buddhist monastery, generally with central court or hall off which open residential cells, usually with a Buddha shrine at one end
vikram – large *tempo*
vimana – principal part of Hindu temple
vipassana – the insight meditation technique of *Theravada* Buddhism in which mind and body are closely examined as changing phenomena
Vishnu – third in the *Trimurti*; Vishnu is the Preserver and Restorer who so far has nine avatars: the fish Matsya; the tortoise Kurma; the wild boar Naraha; *Narasimha*; *Vamana*; *Parasurama*; *Rama*; *Krishna*; and *Buddha*

wallah – man; added onto almost anything, eg *dhobi*-wallah, taxi-wallah, Delhi-wallah
wavs – step-wells, northern India
wazir – chief minister
yagna – self-mortification
yakshi – maiden
yali – mythical lion creature
yantra – geometric plan thought to create energy
yatra – pilgrimage
yatri – tourist
yogini – female goddess attendants
yoni – female fertility symbol

zakat – charity or alms, the third 'pillar of Islam'; operates as a form of income tax
zamindar – landowner
zenana – area in an upper-class home where women are secluded; still part of some palaces in India

Food & Drink

The following are some of the more common food and drink terms you will come across in India. For more information see the special section 'Indian Cuisine'.

aloo tikka – mashed potato patty, often filled with vegetables or meat
appam – South Indian rice pancake
arak – liquor distilled from coconut milk, potatoes or rice
areca – see *betel*

barfi – fudge-like sweet made from milk
bati – baked ball of wholemeal flour
bebinca – Goan dish; layered 40-egg sweetmeat, rich with ghee and coconut milk
besan – chickpea flour
besan gate – spiced *besan* dough steamed and curried in gravy
betel – nut of the betel tree; the leaves and nut are mildly intoxicating and are chewed as a stimulant and digestive in a concoction called *paan*; the betel nut is also called areca nut
bhajia – vegetable fritter
bhang lassi – blend of *lassi* and bhang (a derivative of marijuana)
bhelpuri – thin, crisp fried rounds of dough mixed with puffed rice, fried lentil, lemon juice, chopped onion, herbs and chutney
biryani – fragrant steamed rice with meat or vegetables
bombil – fish that are dried in the sun and deep-fried to make Bombay Duck
bonda – mashed potato patty
boti – Punjabi dish; spicy bite-sized boneless lamb
chaat – snack
chai – tea (invariably very sweet)
chang – Tibetan rice or millet beer
chapati – unleavened Indian bread
chatni – chutney
cheiku – small brown fruit that looks like a potato, but is sweet

chicken cafreal – a dish originating in Goa; chicken pieces coated in a mildly spicy green paste
chikki – nut and *jaggery* toffee, renowned at Lonavla station, Maharashtra
chota – small, spirit drink measure (as in 'chota peg')
country liquor – locally produced liquor
curd – milk with acid or rennet added to solidify it

dahi – curd
dhaba – hole-in-the-wall restaurant or snack bar; boxed lunches delivered to office workers
dhal – curried lentil dish; a staple food of India
dhal makhani – black lentils and red kidney beans with cream and butter
dhansak – Parsi dish; meat, usually chicken, with curried lentils and rice
dosa – paper-thin pancakes made from lentil flour
dum pukht – steam-pressure cooking that uses a clay pot

falooda – rose-flavoured Muslim drink made with milk, cream, nuts and vermicelli
faluda – long chickpea-flour noodles
farsan – savoury nibbles
feni – Goan liquor distilled from coconut milk or cashews

ghanto tarkari – Orrisan dish of colocasia (leaves of the taro plant), yam, peas, potatoes, cauliflowers and brinjals spiced with gram and coconut slivers
ghee – clarified butter
gram – legumes
gulab jamun – deep-fried balls of dough soaked in rose-flavoured syrup
gyarhcee – famous Tibetan hotpot

haleen – pounded wheat with a mutton sauce
halwa – soft sweetmeat made with vegetables, cereals, lentils, nuts and fruit
harissa – wheat porridge with lamb
idli – South Indian spongy, round, fermented rice cake
IMFL – Indian Made Foreign Liquor; beer or spirits produced in India

jaggery – hard, brown sugar-like sweetener made from palm sap
jal jeera – refreshing drink made with limewater, cumin, mint and rock salt and sold in earthenware pots by street vendors and in restaurants
jhaal – Bengali dish; curry made with fish, mustard seeds and chillies

kakori kabab – Lucknow kabab speciality
katori – *thali* bowl/compartment
kachauri – Indian-style breakfast of *puris* and vegetables
khaja – popular Bihari puff-pastry sweet
khataie – biscuits, specialty of Fatehpur Sikri
kheer – North Indian rice pudding
khichdi – heavy rice dish sometimes made with lentils, potatoes and peanut
khoya – reduced milk
korma – curry-like braised dish
kulcha – charcoal-baked bread
kulfi – flavoured (often with pistachio) ice confection, very similar to ice cream
kumbh – pitcher

ladoo – sweetmeat ball made with *gram* flour and semolina
lassi – refreshing yogurt and iced-water drink

mahua – alcoholic drink distilled from the flower of the mahua tree
masala – mix (often spices)
masala dosa – South Indian dish; large lentil-flour crepe *(dosa)* stuffed with potatoes cooked with onions and curry leaves
masala soda – soft drink available at drink stalls
mattar paneer – peas and unfermented cheese in gravy
meen – Keralan fish curry cooked in earthenware pots and kept before serving with rice
milk badam – invigorating morning drink made with saffron and almonds
misthi dhoi – Bengali sweet; curd sweetened with *jaggery*
mitha – sweet, eg, *mitha paan*
mithai – sweets
molee – Keralan dish; fish pieces poached in coconut milk and spices
momo – Tibetan fried or steamed dumpling stuffed with vegetables or meat
Mughlai food – influenced by the Mughals, who ruled the north from the 16th to the 18th century

naan – flat bread
namkin – prepackaged savoury (often spicy) nibbles
nihari – rich goat's broth

paan – *betel* nut and leaves plus chewing additives such as lime
pakora – bite-size piece of vegetable dipped in chickpea-flour batter and deep-fried
palak paneer – unfermented cheese in spinach gravy
paneer – unfermented cheese
pappadam – thin, round crisp bread eaten with curries or as a snack
paratha – bread made with *ghee* and cooked on a hotplate
peitha – Agra sweet made from crystallised gourd
pilau – *see pulou*
pinda – funeral cake
poori – *see puri*
pulou – rice cooked in stock and flavoured with spices; known as 'pilau' in the West
puri – flat dough that puffs up when deep fried; also 'poori'

rabri – milky confectionery
raita – yogurt (usually mildly spiced and sometimes with shredded cucumber, pineapple etc) side dish
ras malai – milk and sugar-based sweet
rasam – South Indian dish; thin tamarind-flavoured vegetable broth
rasgulla – sweet little balls of cream cheese flavoured with rose-water
reshmi kabab – tender chicken kabab cooked in the *tandoor*
rogan josh – Kashmiri dish; fiery lamb curry
rumali roti – huge paper-thin *chapati*

saadha – plain, eg, saadha *paan*
saag – leafy greens
sabzi – vegetables
sambar – South Indian dish; dhal with cubed vegetables and puree
sattu – Orissan dish; roasted *gram* flour
sev – savoury nibbles
shami – wrapped (kabab)
sheekh – skewered (kabab)
soma – intoxicating drink derived from the juice of a plant
sonf – aniseed seeds; come with the bill after a meal and used as a digestive

tandoor – clay oven
tangri – Punjabi chicken drumsticks
tenga – Assamese fish stew
thali – traditional South Indian and Gujarati 'all-you-can-eat' meal
thugpa – Tibetan noodle soup
tiffin – snack or meal container often made of stainless steel
tikka – spiced, often marinated, chunks of chicken, *paneer*, lamb etc, which are sometimes skewered
toddy – alcoholic drink, tapped from palm trees
tongba – Himalayan millet beer
toran – Keralan dish; stir-fried green vegetables
tsampa – Tibetan staple of roast barley flour

vermicelli – thin rice noodles
vindaloo – Goan dish; fiery curry in a marinade of vinegar and garlic

Thanks

Many thanks to the travellers who used the last edition and wrote to us with helpful hints, useful advice and interesting anecdotes:

Oystein Aadland, Yonni Abitbol, A Michael & L Abraham, Dr Arun Abraham, PC Abraham, Patrick Abraham, Alexandr Abusinov, Sam Adam, Leon E Adelman, Kannan Adityan, N Adler, Jan Aengenvoort, Shabnam Arora Afsah, Christine Agnith, GS Agral, Ashish Agrawal, Rakesh Agrawal, Alana & Daine Aitken, Bill Aitken, Simon Aitken, Capt Ajay Sud, Elina Akujaervi, TAS Al-Damouk, Thomas Aldefeld, Laurie Alder, Mark Alder, Beverly Aldridge, TA Aldrin, Declan Alecner, R Alexander, Tim Alexander, Clasens Alexandre, Abira Ali, Cherie Allan, Keith Allan, Rachael Allan, Ann Allen, Sascha Allen, Allison Allgaier, Anders Allgulin, Lasse Almeback, Ana Almeida, Eliane Cavalcante de Almeida, Nora Alterman, Pablo Alvarez Lago, Maria Amelse, Efrat Amir, Ory Amitay, Mohit Anand, N Anantha Kumar, Nicholas Anchen, Moya Anchisi, Hakan Andekzen, Catherine Anderson, David Anderson, Gail Anderson, Paul Anderson, Ryan Anderson, Jonas Andersson, Beck Anderton, Szolnoki Andras, Patrick & Michele Andre, Andrej Andrejew, Lina Angelika Seifried, Bianco Anna, D Anthony, Giovannina M Anthony MD, Jordi Bosch I Anton, Nina Antonissen, L Antuin Caskey, Vito Anzelmi, Yvonne Apol, Christina Apostolidi, Herbert R Appell, Richard Appleton, Peter Apps, Yonat Arbel, Clare Arbuthnott, Nick & Sally Archer, Toby Archer, Anohea & Clara Architetto, Gino Arduini, Luis Arevalogarcia, Guido Arlt, D Armstrong, Leisa Armstrong, Matthew Armstrong, Robert Arnett, Catherine Arnold, Luke Arnold, Verity Arnold, Perri Arnold Jnr, Cathy Arnquist, P & L Arrowsmith, FA Ashcroft, Tony Ashcroft, Chen & Dorit Ashkenazi-Tzoref, Ulla Ashorn, Jane Aspinwall, Dan Asquiln, Jeanne van Asselt, Kristina Astrom, Michiel Aten, Nazir Athania, Dan Atkinson, Laura Atkinson, Mary Atkinson, Owen Atkinson, Aaron Auerbach, Elizabeth Augustine, Jan Auke Dijkstra, L Aurrekoetxea Ezkurdia, Andrew T Austin, Lochan Avinash, Gal Avneriu, M Avraham, Annelie Axelsson, Ronnie Aye Maung, Robert ES Ayurvedacharya, Yaell Azaryahu, Andres Azparre, A Baan, Fons Baars, Nancy Babb, Mats Backlund, Karina Backstrom, Sharon Baddeley, Martin Badley, Neelambar Badoni, K Bagram, Verena Bahler, Anthony Bailey, Bobbie Bailey, Horace Bailey, Sabina Bailey, Sue Bailey, David Bain, Stacey Bainbridge, Fiona Baker, llewellyn Baker, Mike Baker, Kimm Bakker, Jon Baldwin, Delyth Ball, Jemima Ball, Eve Ballenegger, Daniel Balogh, Simon Bamford, Dr BD Banerjee, Dr Sanjoy Banerjee, Imre Bangha, Mill Bank, Gerlinde Bankemper, Helen Banks, Dr Stephen S Bantz, Barbara Baracks, Marel Baran, James Barbar, Mary Barber, Anita Barewal, Aviram Barhuim, John Baring, Althea Barker, David Barker, Mike Barker, Rosie Barker, Arnold Barkhordarian, Lori Barkley, Jeff Barlow, Leonie Barner, Joshua Taylor Barnes, Christopher Barnett, Martin Barr, Douglas Barrett, Elizabeth Barrett, Greg Barrett, JC Barrett, Spencer Barrett, Julie Barrie, Giles Barroe, Claudia Bartasek, Christopher Barthel, Marc Barthelemy, Keith D Barton, Rebecca Bartow, Judy Baruth, Andy Baschong, Anton Baser, Bonnie Baskin, Claudio Bassetti, Elisabeth Batchelor, Kevin Bateman, Fiona Bates, Raouel Baueres Gpdeula, Larry Baumbach, Oliver Bayne, Dr Richard H Beal, Emma Beal, Chris Beall, Carrie Beam, Stephanie Beasley, Gerard Beaumont, Lucinda Beck, Bernd Becker, Dr Christine Becker, Dave Beedie, Doug & Sue Beedie, Petra Beerens, Jacob Beerkma, Asaf Begerano, Josee Belanger, Aseem Belcher, Anina Belhadj Corral, Andrew Bell, Jeff Bell, Michael Bell, Zoe Bell, Rune Bellesen, Jeevan Belliappa, Mara Benedict, Mathias Benesch, Ong Beng Wan, Cynthia Benjamin Copper, Alison Bennett, Andrew Bennett, Michele Bennett, Pat Bennett, Abigail Bentall, Lizzie Benzimra, Trond Berg, John Erik Berganus, Ami Berger, Regina Berger, Simon Berger, ME Van Der Bergh-Coumans, Marten Berglund, Heidi Bergsli, Erin Bernard, David Bernardini, Paul Bernet, Camilla Berntsson, Rufus Bertle, Dr Pradeep Bery, Marjan Besselink, Jessica Bessler, Paul Bett, Vanesssa Bettes, Debbie Beveridge, Hajra Bhamji, Rohith Bhandary, Jiwanand Bhanot, RN Bhargana, Ram Bhargava, Abhay Bharti, Kalyan Bhattacharjee, VP Bhavsar, R Bhogal, K Bhumeshwar, Avan Z Bhumgara, S Bhundia, Laurent Bianchi, Anna Bianco, Andrew Bickle, Veronica Bielinski, Patrik Bifeldt, Shannon Biggins, Colin J Biggs, Dr Andrew Biggs, Roger Biggs, Maria Bigler, I Bilsen, Inge Bilsen, Randi Bindra, Cheryl Binzen, Katoch Bipan, Geremy Birchard, Megan Bird, Barbel & Rolf Birk, DE Birmingham, Nick Bishop, Stephane Eric Bisson, Jamie Bixby, Penny Blackburn, Bob Blackham, James Blackstone, Ryan Blair, Geoffrey Blaisdell, M Blanc, Tatjana Blanchet, Mirjam Blom, Amanda Bloss, John Blunden, Patricia Blunt, Rachel Blythe, William

Boag, Johan Bockstael, Pamela Bode, Adrian Bohl, Harry Bohm, Eckhard Bokamper, L Boland, Frank Bolder, Patrick Bolster, Talia Boltin, Alan Boniface, Alistair Bool, Cathryn E Boomer, Michael Tan Koon Boon, Joop Boonen, Claire Booth, A Booth, David Bornstein, Elizabeth Borshard, Brett Bortzner, Bruno Bosch, Raffi & Marco Boss, Britt-Marie Bostrom, F Boucarut, Robert Bough, Nick Bourne, Pearl & Howard Bourne, Ellen Bouwer, Els Bouw-Rijlaarsdam, Jeffrey Bowe, Amanda Bowen, John Bower, Erroll Bowyer, C Boxall, Glen & Erika Boyd, Heather Boyd, Lisbeth Boye Schack, Thea Bracewell, Holly Brackenbury, Joel Bradley, Nick Bradley, Terence Alan Bradley, Anna Brady, Eric Brady, A Brager, Jutta Brandt, Caroline Brandtner, D Brannan, J Braun, Bill Bray, RN Breakfast, Sarah Breen, F Bregnard, Frank Breiting, John Breitweiss, Sarah & Ian Brenchley, Lynda Brenock, Jim Breret, Anthony Brevery, Jennifer Brewer, Emmanuel Bricoyne, Chele Bridger, Valerie Bridjanovic, Jasper Van Den Brink, John Brisby, David Britton, N Britton, L Britz, David Brodie, Joerg Broeker, Jean de Broima, Edwin Bronsteede, Sarah Bronzite, Lisa Brookshaw, Eric & Roel Brouwer, Ben & Kathie Brown, Christina Brown, Heather Brown, Jamie Brown, Jeff Brown, Joele Brown, Lucindia Brown, Mary Brown, Meg Brown, Nick Brown, Rhona Brown, Susan Brown, Tess Browne, Henry Browning, Simon Broyd, Tako Bruinsma, Bernhard Brummeir, Bernt Brun, Roberto Bruneri, Hakan Brusstrom, Michael Bruxner, PJ Bruyniks, Jim Bryant, Dr Stephen Bubert, Richard Buckland, Grant Buday, Robert Buerger, Eugene Buhler, Jean Bullard, Richard Bullock, Claire Bungay, Chaowalit Bunyaphusit, Stephanie Burch, H Burema, Brandon Burg, H Burgers, K Burgess, Patricia Burke, Steven Burke, AL Burnett, Jeannie Burnett, Nancy Burnett, Wendy & Lenny Burnett, Roger & Liz Burnley, Jane Burns, P Burns, El Burrell, Peter Burridge, Mark Burton, Pieter Buryland, D Busby, Gordon Buss, Peter Buszjager, John Butcher, Joyce Butcher, Wesley Butcher, Bob Butkus, Colin Butler, James Butler, Julian Butler, Sheridan Butler, Alan Butterworth, Karen & Graham Bygate, John Byram , Simon Byrom, John Bywell, Donna Cabell, Paul Caffrey, Charlotte Cain, Laura Cain, Staurt Caldwell, Lisa & Steve Caliga, T Callaghan, Rob Callen, Susanne Calundan, Justine O Calverley, Erika Calzaferri, Denis Cameron, Francesca Camisoli, Ursula Campbell, Sonja Candek, Naomi Canton, Sam Caplan, Shea Car, Jack Carbone, Ray Carey, Ryan & Daniel Carey, Hugo Cariss, M Carksun, Amanda Carlson, Erin R Carlson, Cor Caroli, Marianne Carpenter, Sue Carpenter, Grisel Carreira, Jennifer Carriage, Regina Carroll, Mike Carter, RJ Cartman, Radha Case, Matt Casey, George Casley, Joachim Caspar, Kim Casper, Eitan Caspi, Tom Cassidy, John Casson, Franck Castegnaro-Wurtz, Rowan Castle, Gregory Cathcart, Gail Cathro, Becca Catt, Catherine Causer, Luigi Cavaleri, Sandra Caville, Pat Celaya, Carrie Celloway, L Monica Cenqueira, Agnes Chague, Bratin Chakravorty, Martin Chalcraft, Emma Chamberlain, Martin Chamberlain, Belinda Chamley, KM Champs, Dweep I Chanana, David Chance, Shantanu Chand, Brenda Chandler, Hari Chandra, Jacquie Chang, Dianna Chapman, Anna Chapple, Gulzar Raisa Charania, Colin & Chris Charles, Keith Charlton, Dee Charlton, Guy & Liz Chasseloup, Robert Chatfield, C Chatham, Sanjit Chatterjee, T Chatterji, Dr JD Chaudhuri, Anjali Chauhan, UKS Chauhan, Karine Chavaux, Sundar Cheens, Irene Chen, Helen Cheng, Carlo Cheric, Mrs & Mr Cherouvim, Richard Cherrett, Michelle Chesnut, Leo Chessell, Andrea Cheung, Helen Chia, Pheobe Chick, Chris Chihrin, Louise Childs, Raffaele Chiodin, Yvonne Christ, Andrew Christensen, Douglas Christian, Mogens Christoffersen, Teufel Christoph, Lneka Chromcova, Judy Chung, Don Church, John Church, Paul Cina, Tim Clael, Tom Claes, Ellen Claesdotter, Jack Clancy, Elizabeth Claridge, Alan Clark, Alex Clark, Alexander Clark, Jennifer Clark, Mel Clark, Sarah Clark, Tony Clark, Bruce Clarke, Donna Clarke, L Clarke, Scott Clarke, Laurence Claude, Britter & Sascha Clausen, Lars Clausen, Soren Clausen, Gareth Clayton, Richard Clayton, Paula Clegg, Hans Clemensen, Jan Clement, Ramon Clemente, A Clemes, Mario Cleovoulou, Miler Clevet, Laurence Cliché, Marc Clissen, Murray Clodagh, Kevin Clogstoure, M & R Cobden, R Cochrane, Jennifer Coffin, Asaf Cohen, Ben Cohen, Irit Cohen, Orit Cohen, Ziv Cohen, Laurie Cohn, Rebecca Colclasire, Andrea Cole, Lesley J Cole, Zachary Cole, David Coleman, Shannon Coleman, C Colinet, Marina Collard, Johan Collier, John Collier, Jeanette Collins, Jon Collins, Lyn Collins, Shanine Collinson, Jenny Collis, Manuela Colpaert, Roberta Comini, Dave Compton, Alec Connah, Kathy L Conner, Iain Connor, Caroline Coode, Alex Cook, JA Cook, John Cook, Phillip Cook, Bergendy Cooke, David & Sarah Cooke, Stuart Cooke, Tom Coolidge, John Coombs, Chris Cooper, Helen Cooper, Francoise Cooperman, A Coppelmans, Paul Corallot, Ann Corcoran, John M Cord, Tui Cordemans, Dirk Cordes, Borja Cordoba Egia, Ana Cordoves, Jeffrey Cornia, Dominic Corrigan, Miles Cort, Marcos Carlos Costa, Juan I Costero, Jay Couch, Ally Couchman, Gerald Coulter, Diane Counsell, Adam Coupe, Monique Courson, C Covelli, Alistair Cowan, Kerrianne Cowley, Betty Cox, Dr Peter Cox, E & J Cox,

Joseph V Cox, Roy Cox, Ben Coyne, Gabrielle Cozzolius, Debbie Craft, Rob Craig, Michael R Crees, John & Marcia Crellin, Soonah & Michael Cribb, Michael Crim, Thomas L Crisman, Alma Cristina, Kate Cromb, George Cross, Howard W Crosthwaite, Wendy Crouch, Nic Crutchley, Dany Cuello, Bryan J Cuevas, Bob Cullen, Scott Culpepper, Maggi Culver, Lis & Stef Cumine, Simon Cumming, Wenche & John Cumming, Pauline Cummings, Carolyn Cunningham, John Cunningham, TA Cunningham, Caroline Cupitt, Clint Cure, Raphaelle Curis, Lucy Curry, D Curtis, Tomasz Czyzewski, Zoe D, Sophie Dackanbe, Catherine Daeues, Yigal Dafne, Rod Daldry, Jan Dale, Gregory Dale Smith, GM Dalladay, L Dallal, Paul Daly, Irene Dam, Hans en Mirjam Damen, M & H Damen, Peter Damm, Sameer Dandage, Dr S Dandapani, Mark Daniel, Lizz Daniels, Mr Daniels, Russell Danrich, Birgit Danz, Shai Dariti, Pamela Darling, Mrs G & Mr Darmon, Christopher & Victroia Darue, John Darwin, Ameyen Das, Prabal Das, Kavita Dass, Ayan Dasvarma, Hilary Date, Shreelata Datta, Ring-Tsshaw Daw Daulagupu, Rachael Davey, Peter David, Raja David, Ian Davidson, Allen Davies, Denis Davies, Jodie Davies, Karen Davies, Katy Davies, Lindsey Davies, Mr Davies, RJ Davies, Clive Davis, Des Davis, Erin Davis, Nick Davis, Harry Davis Jnr, Jan Dawson, C Day, Manish Dayal, Yigal Dayan, Manisha Dayaram, Altair de Almeida, Steven De Backer, Johanna de Bresser, Andrea de Capoa, Isabelle De Castro, Leo de Clercq, Corne de Graaf, Hein de Graaf, H De Greeve, Frank de Groot, Albert de Haas, Marjan De Jong, Thijs de Jong, Phil De Lange, Rosario de las Morenas, Jonathon de Mello, Sandro De Riu, Otto de Ruiter, Martes de Sa, Lynn De Snoo, Sebastian de Terssac, Martyn de Vrier, Laurens de Vries, Sarah Deakin, Dorothy Dean, Rob Dean, Bruce Deane, Tineke Debuyst, S & R DeCaroli, Joaclim Decker, Rita Deebest, Diane Defore, Santosh Dehadrai, Natasha Deighton, Alex Deissenbeck, Rina Delafield, Philippe Deling, Gus Della-Porta, Sonja Demuth, Laurens den Dulk, Tom Dennehy, CB Denning, Catherine Denny, Klaudia Deppisch, Susan Derby, Dorine Derks, Hugo Derlin, Alex Derom MD, Dr HB Desai, Utpal Desai, Marco Deterink, Giuliana Dettori, Andreas Deutscher, SW Devam Adityo, Josephine Deveaux, Yamuna Devi, Papan Devnani, Maria Deza, DH Baburao, D Dhaliwal, Narinder Dhami, PM Dharmalingam, Dhwana Dhondup, Rosemary Di Benedetto, John Diamandis, Paul Dickens, Deborah Dickey, Karin Diderich, Martin Didler, Magdalena Diehl, M Dilbury, Ann Ez El Din, Graham Dingwall, Giovanni Discenza, Wendy Dison, Andrew Dittfeld, Chris Ditzen, Michael Dixon, Steve & Cathy Dodge, Barb Dodson, Melanie Doehler, K Doherty, WK Dolphin, Cheryl Donald, Rob Donaldson, C Donnelly, TM Donohue, Francois Donovan, Kate Donovan, Peter Dooley, Rene Doosje, Gunter Doppler, Arne Dorando, Elisabeth Dordal, Cornelius Dorn, Vijay Doshi, Laurance Doucet, Michael Doud, Nell Doughrty, Daniele Dovesi, Peter Dowling, Lucinda Down, J Downs, D Doyle, Ellen Drake, Jenny Draper, ML Drayer, Matilda & Lawrence Dressman, Martina & Richard Drygas, Joseph D'Souza, Ronald & Gloria Duber, Helene Dubreuil, Benoit Dubuisson, Dave Dubyne, Amy Duckworth, Malcolm Ducret, George & Liz Duff, Emmett Duffy, Dr R Dufour, Jenny & Tim Duke, Monika Dukszta, Geoffrey Duncan, Laura Duncan, Meldrum Duncan, Rachel Duncan, Keely Dunhill, Jo & Mick Dunican, Steve Dunjee, Katherine Dunk, J Dunn, James Dunn, Hilary Dunne, Orla Dunne, Chris Dunning, Joan Dunphy, Silvia Durrsperger, Abhayjeet Dutt, Nandini Dutt, Diana Dwyer, Rachel Dwyer, Corey Dyer, J Dyer, Nicki Dyson, Ian Dyus, Robert Dzexhage, Ken Eaton, Iwona Eberle, Marion Eckert, Michael Eckert, David Edwardes, Mrs & Mr Edwards, Nick Edwards, RJ Edwards, Rachel Edwards, Nicky Efron, Nina Eg Hansen, Ilga Eger, Jack Egerton, Peter Ehrenkranz, Robert Eidschun, Gil Eiges, Russell Eisgrub, Leif & Kirsten Ekdahl, Eva Ekelund, Minna Eklof, Kabid Ekonomi, Rayomand E Elavia, Wilfried Elfner, Taye Elhadi, Joshua Eliezer, Alison Eliot, S Elisabeth Olsen, John Elk lll, Mary Ellen Friday-Leibheit, Ulf Ellervik, Jocelyn Elliot, Matthias Elliott, Benjamin Ellis, Bethany Ellis, Brian Ellis, Dave Ellis, Gideon Ellwood, Greg Elms, Tarek El-Sawy, Gill & John Ely, Carole Emmerson, Deborah Emmett, B Endicott, Angie Eng, E Engels, Isabelle & Dirk Engels, Simon Engemann, Jeremy Engineer, Chris England, Cynthia Enloe, Stewart Ennis, Rachel Enright, Livia Epps, Daniel Ericson, Linda Eriksson, Susan Erk, Karen Eryou, XC Escarra, Daniel Eschle, Offer Eshel, Marina Eskina, Catherine Essex, Pascal Esvan, Tagel Etgar, Konoura Etsuko, Alex Evanov, Caroline Evans, Janet Evans, Magnus Evans, Laurence Everard, Everlin Everz, Andrew Ewart, Tim Eyres, Belinguier Fabien, Cath Fagan, Jennifer Fahy, Marcus Fairs, Reg Fallah, Marianne Fallon, Musse Family, Linda Fane, Cindy Farina, Valerio Farinelli, Laura Farish, Eugenia Farkas, Yuval Farkash, Justin Farley, Steve Farrell, TT Farrell, Michael Fasman, Julie Faulk, Mark Fauver, Anne-Meike Fechter, Anja Feickert, Pia Feldman, Roland Felgentraeger, Andi Feller, Chris Felstead, Brian Fenn, John Fenner, Benedetto Ferci, Gary Ferguson, Una Ferguson, Mary Fernandez, Mauricio Fernandez, Emilic Ferrcia, Carol Ferris,

Sarah Ferris-Browne, Nick Fiddles, Terry & Wendy Fidgeon, Daniel & Anna Fieweger, Deborah Filcoff, H Filgate, JC Filmore, Gerald Fimberger, Andrew Fincham, Genia Findeisen, Ciara Finn, Rachel Fisher, Mark Fittal, David Flack, Steven Flanders, Emma Flatt, Caroline Fletcher, Mary Fletcher, Sharon Flier, Pedro Flombaum, Monique Floothuis, Greg Flynn, Lisa Flynn, Mark Follett, Tom Fontanna, Elizabeth Forbes, John & Bet Forbes, Tom Force, Anna K Ford, Quentin Ford, Yann Forget, Charlie Forman, Alberto Forneris, Helen Forrest, Dan Forrester, Barbara Forster, C Forster, Gordon Forster, Helena Forsyth, Nicole & Bibiana Foschetti, Paul Fossey, T Foster, Teresa Fowler, Jon Fox, Jack Foxall, Elizabeth Fox-Wolfe, Michael Foy, Elsa Frances, Luanne Frank, Boaz Franklin, Steve & Sue Frary, Paul Fraser, Judy Frater, Lucille Frauenstein, Steve Frayer, Hilary Frazer, C Freckmann, Charlesworth Frederick, Yvonne Freid, Margret Frenz, Lucia Fresa, Jose A Fribarren, M Friday, Idan Fridman, Frank Fried, Yvonne Fried, Matt Friedman, Bernd Friese, Kevin Friesen, Christopher Frost, Ben Fry, Elisabeth & Duncan Fry, Lorraine Fry, Salvador Fuensanta, Yvette Fulker, Dave Fuller, Sally Fuller, CG Gaanoo, Aitor G Gabilondo, Harun Gadatia, Dipesh Gadher, Yeela Gal, Tony Galanides, Michael Galea, Fergus Gallagher, Ian Galloway, Matt Galloway, Jon Galt, Jay Gandhi, Mahendra Gandhi, Vinod Gangadharan, Emily Garbutt, Julia Garcia, Maritza Adriana Garcia, G Gardner, George Gardner, Kate Gardner, Rebecca Garland, Bob Garner, Lucy Garrett, Hazel Garth, Prof Robert Gasser, Piotr Gaszynski, Robert Gatt, Stephanie Gavin-Brown, Michael Gawthorne, The Gebbett Family, Brian Gee, Kathy Gehman, Heike Geiselmann, Gerd Geissendorfer, Stuart Geltner, Henriuk Gemal, Vanessa Geneva Melter, Kym Gentry, Scott W Gentry, Stephen George, Sunil George, Toni Gerber, Andreas Gerner, Mandy Gerrard, Matt Gerry, Martine & Brian Gerth, Yasmine Ghandour, Madelene Ghattas, MA Ghattas, Aida Ghion, A Ghosh, Shami Ghosh, Joe Giamarese, Fara Giannina, Anne Giannini, Massimo Giannini, Iain Gibbs, Linda Gibbs, Julie Giblett, Freya Gibson, Lani Gibson, Jez Gidley, Mike Giles, Ruth Giles, Jason Gill, Paul Gill, Sophie Gill, M Gillett, Luke Gillian, Susan Gillman, Manu Gitai, Gesine Glaeser, R Glas, Dawn Glaser, Roy Glasner, Ian Gleave, Irene Glezos, Jeannie Glista, Melanie Glynn, Geoff Goats, David Godfrey, Diane Godfrey, Jean-Marie Godot, R & D Godrey, Mariana Goetz Quintana, Joachim Gohlicke, Ella Going, Hilary Goldberg, Jill Golden, Martin Golder, Lorne Goldman, Max Goldstein, Helmut Goller, Monica Gomez Santos, Dean Gomsalves, Eduardo Gonzalea, Kate Good, Savi & Nigel Goodall, Shankan Goodall, Julian Goode, Bryn Gooding, Allen Goodreds, KK Gopalakrishnan, Sharon Gorman, Patrick Gottsacker, Stephen Gough, John Goundry, Eric Govers, Raghuram Govindarajan, Mary Gow, Stephen Gow, L Gower, Rebecca Gowland, Anuj Goyal, Jennie Gozdz, Joanna Grabiak, Elizabeth Grace Burkhart, Erich Grader, Dean Gradon, An Robbrecht-De & Norbert Graef, Sabine Grafenstein, Breck A Graham, Brian & Jane Graham, Julian Graham, Dr DE Granger, Dr Travers Grant, Elizabeth Graves, Grant Graves, Laurie Graves, Hazel Gray, Lisa & Steve Gray, Peter Gray, Danielle Graysmark, Colin Green, David Green, Shira Green, Krischa Greenaway, Herman Greeven, Dr Hans-Joachim Gregor, Helen Gregory, Ursula Gregory, Luke Gregson, Clara Grein, G Gren-Eklund, Val Gretchev, Peter Gries, Catherine Griffiths, Peter Griffiths, Tom Grimm, Michael Grimmer, Mikael Grimmig, Jurek Grobosz, Nelleke & Jaques Groen, Nienke Groen, Chloe Groom, Richard Groom, David Grossblat, Danny Grossman, Richard Grove, Rebecca & Jamie Grover, Stephanie & Frank Gruson, Gster Guenero, Ashirvad Guesthouse, Agustin Guillen, Alexandra Gulemeester, Nerajana Gunetilleke, Abha Gupta, Stuart Gurner, Diana & David Gurney, Krishnan Guruswamy, Gote Gustafsson, Lena Gustavsson, Anna Guymolcs, Jacqueline Gygax, A & M Guymolcs, Jason Van Haard, Kim Haas, Baro Haauardsholm, Dr Joachim Hacker, P Hackett-Jones, John Hackney, J Hadlington, Brigitte Haehnle, Andrea Haennie Hoti, Annalisa Hainsome, L Haismanova, David Hall, Derek Hall, Eric Hall, Joanna Hall, Judy Hall, Ruth M Hall, Timothy Hall, Daniel Hallam, Maud Hallin, Larry Hallock, Michael Hallpike, Colin Hallward, Sheila Hally, Georgina Hambert, Remi Hamel, Thera Hamel, Louise Hamer-Keijser, Raphael Hamers, Stuart Hamilton, Allen Hammack, Kay Hammond, Mark Hammond, Davide Hanau, Annette Handley, Fiona Handley, Susanne Hangaard Jensen, Don Hanlon, Bhavani Hannon, Sheila Hannon, JL Hans, Brian Hansen, Lizette & Charlotte Hansen, Paul Hansen, Stine Moller Hansen, Emma Hanson, Premiata Haralalka, Dr Marcus Harbord, Anne Harding, Robert Harding, Maureen Hardinge, Paul Hardy, Dickon Hares, Zsout & Csaba Hargitai, Fran Harley, Assaf A Harlop, Abigail Harrap, Amy Harris, Maxine Harris, Simon Harris, Tim & Shirley Harris, MS K Harrison, Mark Harrison, Nicola Harrison, Katrin Hartmann, Michael Hartnett, Stacie Hartung, Michael Hartz, B Harvey, Jane Harvey, Dina Hashem, Kari & Larissa Hass, Taariq Hassan, AJ Hastak, Robert Hastie, James M Hastings, Jim Hastings, D Hatch,

James Hatcher, Stefanie Hatz, David Hatzkevich, Madri Haveli, Ted Haver, Rachel Hawkes, Paul Hawkie, Heather Hawkins, Joanne Hawkins, Natalie Hawkrigg, Judith Hayes, Vincent Hayes, Julia Haywood, Ian Hazel, WG Heap, Kevin & Trea Heapes, Ashley Heath, Barbara Heatherley, Alan Heathes, Keely Hegarty, Phyllis Hegeman, A Heim, Philip Heinemann, Petra Heitkamp, Andreas Heitman, Judith Heitman, Jensen Helge Vandel, Angus & Hanne Hellawell, Gudrun Heller, HH Hellin, Paul Hellings, Krystyna Hellstroem, Richard Hemingway, Dr Peggy Henderson, Kellie Henderson, Schuyler Henderson, Richard Henke, Michiel A Hensema, Sue Henshaw, Jason & Michelle Heppenstall, Ferdi Hepworth, Wayne Herd, Eva Herkenrath, David Herman, Itai Hermelin, Ingel Hernbdndez Mortin, Barbara Hersel, Johanna Hess, David Hewett, Sophie Hewlett, Alan & Pam Hey, Jenny Hicken, Lisa Hicks, Tracey Hicks, Claire Hickson, Rachel Higgens, Matt Hilburn, Debbie Hill, Sam Hill, Susanne Hill, Alsin Hillyer, Jacinta Hingston, Ella Hinman Young, Nina Hirst, Clare Hitchen, WS Hiyner, Casper Hjorth-Knudson, Tamara Hoad, Tony Hobbs, Geraldine Hobson, Martina Hodes, Phil Hoffer, Ursula Hoflin, P van der Hofstad, S Hofstede, SA & DE Holbrook, Peter Holdforth, Betse Holliday, Peter Holliger, Michael Holloway, A & C Holmes, Mark Holmes, Annelii Holmguist, Roland Holschuh, Jon Holton, Spencer Home, Anna Homs Torras, Sue Honeyford, Lode Hoo Gwendhoorn, Andrew Hood, Marti Hood, Michael Hope, Jeff Hopewell, Siobhan Hopkins, Martin Hopper, Jelka Hopster, Debbie Horbul, Bela Horvath, Douglas Hosdale, David Hothi, Marcelo Houacio Pozzo, Keiran Houghton, Hugo Houppermans, Eilish Hovengh, Jonathan Howard, Peter Howe, G Howell, Edward Hower, Emily Howie, Trudy Howson, Anne & Ken Hoy, Jiri Hruby, Peter Hruska, Gunther Hsue, Andrew Hubbard, Lee Hubbard, Heinrich Hubbert, Esther Huber, Robert Huber, Walter Huber, Mona Hubinette, John Hudson, Mike & Nadine Hudson, Becky Huges, David Hughes, Greeba Hughes, Heather Hughes, Paul Hughes-Smith, Roelof van der Hulst, Bram Hulzebos, Richard Humble, Blanche Hunt, Kelly Hunt, Bruce Hunter, Ed Hunter, JS Huntley, Risto Huoso, David Hupert, Ahmed Hussain, J Hutchinson, Jerry Hutt, Michael Huttner, A Huycke, Vicky Huyskens, Keith Hyams, Mair Hyman, Hussein Ibrahim, Rebecca Ilott, Pasi Ilvesmaki, Susan Immergut, C Van Immerseel, Trevor Ingham, Alfredo Ingino, Helel Ingram, Kati Inkinen, Irina Innes, Trina Innes, Gabriel Inoges, Merkis Irma Eeli, Vibhu-Irvin Fox, John Irvine, Rachel Irvine, Roland Ischanz, David Iser, Kevin Isfeld, Marko Istenic, Lara Iverson, Ben J, Friederike Jhnig, L Jaarsma, Markus Jaaskelainen, Abdeen Jabara, Anna Jablowska, Miki Jablowska, Angie Jackson, Claire & Paul Jackson, David Jackson, George Jackson, Graeme Jackson, Ian Jackson, Irene Jackson, Mark Jackson, Spencer Jackson, Gary Jacob, Paul Jacobs, AM Jacobsen, Astrid Jacobsen, TN Jacobson, Alain Jacquemin, Andre Jacques, Wolfgang Jaeger, Parela Jagger, Dr RK Jaggi, Justin Jagosh, Vivek Jain, Julia Jakubovics, Beigitta Jaleanssan, AA & Jr James, Andrew James, Betty W James, Helen James, Jeffy James, Nesta James, Robert James Olajos, Lynn Jamieson, Tarja Janhuen, MN Jani, Izabela Jankowska, Marjon Janmaat, Ton Janusch, Sonan Janzan Vertregt, Robert Janzic, Eila Jarvinen, Jan Jasiewicz, Liz Jason, Conny Jasperse, Jaishankar Jayaraman, Rajah Jayendran, Brendon Jaynes, Karen Jedema, Helen Jeffreys, PR Jeffreys-Powell, Dot Jellinek, T Jellings, Paul Jenkins, WE Jenkins, Satja Jennings, E Jensen, Jesper & Maria Jensen, Knud Erik Jensen, Eom Jeong-Moo, Judy Jere, Per Jerndal, Bernard Jervis, Jay Jessen, Attul Jetha, Darina Jevosova, S Jewitt, Sunil Ji Garg, Pau Chesa Jimenez, Mary Jo Kimbrough, Ella Jo Tarot, Cameron Joe, Didomizio Joel, Obin Joelle, Kjaer Johansen, Greta St John, Jopu John Tharappel, Andy Johnson, David Johnson, Dennis Johnson, Jo Johnson, Martha Johnson, Mary Johnson, Matt Johnson, Rebecca Johnson, Stephen Johnson, Tony Johnson, Ewa Johnsson, Craig Johnston, Frank & Elaine Johnston, Reggie & Don Johnston, Alok Johri, Andrew Jolly, Nagasha Jolob, Barry Jones, Ben Jones, Brian Jones, Craig Jones, Diana Jones, Frank Jones, Geoffrey Jones, Hilton Jones, Larry Jones, Mark Jones, DW & Mr Jones, Natalie Jones, Nick Jones, Owen Jones, Sally A Jones, Anita Joseph, Jacob Joseph, Dr Rohit Joshi, Mark Jowett, Amanda Joy Rubin, Anthony Jucha, Anne-Dorothee Jungblut, Erik Juul Pedersen, Katie Kabler, Sumeet Kachwaha, Zoyab A Kadi, Ahilan Kadirgamar, Bruno Kahn, Mr Kailash, T & J Kalaitzis, Melita M Kalama, Hans Kalma, NN Kalpa, Chandrakant Kalyanpur, Juray Kaman, Lindy Kandohla, Devendra Kandoi, Haemish Kane, Gerhard Kanne, C Kaplan, Stephanie Kaplan, Rajiv Kapoor, Ravi Kapur, Lisbeth van de Kar, George Karamanou, Cynthia Karena, Ylva Karlen, Jane Karlsson, Judith Karmen, Halina Karpowicz, Renko Karruppannan, D Karunanidhi, Anita Kashyap, Lindsay Kassof, Easan Katir, Hormuzd Katki, Alon Kaufman, Rupinderjit Kaur Dhami, Ketan Kavaria, Abby Kaye, Allyson Keane, Damien Kearns, Guy Kedar, Cheyne Keith, Christian Keller, Dr Joachim Keller, Laura Keller, Roy Kellett, Adam Kelley, Maurice Kellit, Brain Kelly, Chris Kelly, Iona Kelly, Liz Kelly, Rik Kelly, Lars

Kelstrup, Emma Kempton, Tim Kendall, Wee Keng Hor, Mattias Kenig, Clare Kenny, Megan Kenny, Julie Kepner, Miranda Kerklaan, Ladi Kern, John Kerr, Stephen Kerr, J Kerwick, VA Keshwala, Jorg Kessel, Anja Kessler, Philip Kestelman, CA Kesterton, M Ketterer, Eleanor Kettle, Xavier Keulen, Marghertia Keune, Yassaman Khalili, Rama Singh Khalsa, Anisa Khan, Demian Khan, Gazi Khan, Kavi Khanna, Priyanka Khanna, Dr Mahesh Tunk Khatri, Munindra Khaund, Muninidra Khaund, Dayalji Kheta, Mark Kidd, Guido Kies, H Kilday, Heather Kilday, Dave Kilsby, JL Kinder, Adi King, Catherine King, Ruth King, Stephen L King, Nanne Kingma, LA Kingsbury, Marie Kingsbury, Stefan Kintrup, S Kipakra, Ivan Kirac, Liz & Frank Kirk, Zena Kirkby, Hayley Kirkland, Andy Kirkwood, Sheila Kirwan, Petra & Steve Kitchman, Z Kittler, Tracey Kitzman, Rasheed Kizhisseri, Per Kjaer Johansen, N Kleerutunge, Leslie Klein, Borge & Jette Klemmensen, Esther Kleynen, Eddy Klijnen, Yechexkel Kling, Georg Klinghammer, Svenja Klotzbucher, Christoph Klug, Michael Knight, Tania Knight, Julia Knop, Martin Knoth, Oliver Knowles, Josef Koberl, Caroline Kobler, Michael Koester, Marianne Kohler, Helmut Kolb, Maria Kold Clemmensen, Iniva Konsas, Frits Koolschijn, Manfred Korell, Vimal Korstjens, Katarina Koskinen, Gerta Koster, Jan Koster, Mieke-Ien Koster, Rob Koster, Katerina Kotherova, Gerhard Kotschenruether, Stephanie Koutsaftis, Chris Koutsofrigas, Ursula Krahl, Tine Kratzer, Oliver Krause, Uli Krause, Pauline Krebbers, Charlie Kregel, M Kreiger, Stefan Krenn, Sebastian Kresow, Tim Krick, Michael Krieg, Vicky Krins, KP Krishan, Sue Krishnan, Jeroen Kroon, Michael & Nicole Kropf, Mike Krosin, Robert Krumm, Steve Krzystyniak, Rosie Kuhn, Judith Kuiperi, Anand Kumar, Arvind Kumar, Jayant Kumar, Piyush Kumar, Ram Kumar, Sanjay Kumar, VS Kumar, Michael Kunsmann, Nathan Kuppinger, Beksy Kurian, Peter Kurze, Igal Kutin, Anna Kwiecinska, Stephane La Branche, Paiva Laakso-Marsh, Daniela Labbe, Dr Rolf-Peter Lacher, Navroza Ladha, Stephanie Lafer, Raj Lalchandani, Gilbert Lamayo, Tracey Lamb, Digvijay Lamba, Ashlee Lambe, Miss Lammin, Baylor Lancaster, Mark Lancaster, Georges Landry, Kristine Lang, Veronique Langelier, Kim Langford, Romina Lanzani, Christy Lanzl, John Larmer, John Larner, Bjorn Larsen, Mads Larsen, Matthias Larson, Leyre Lasa, Stefan Lasagna, W De & S Lashmutt, Jodi Lathan, ML Lathia, Albert Latino, Winnie Lau, Anne Laudisoit, AC Lavenex, Fiona Law, Beth Lawrence, Gili Lazar, Jean le Tallec, Mark Leather, Adam Leavesley, Olaf Lechtenfeld, John Leckie, Alison Lecky, Lana Ledgerwood, Andrew Lee, Chonja Lee, Chris Lee, Denise Lee, Jackie & Fred Lee, Jonathan Lee, Ken Lee, Min Lee, Stewart Lee Allen, Alan Leedham, Marc Leest, Marie-Jose Leferink, Barbara Lehndorf, Andrew Leigh, Wendy Leighton, G Leiper, G Leitch, Jenni Leith, C Leland, Florian Lems, Timothy A Lenderking, Sarah Leonard, David Lepeska, Marie Lesaicherre, Mikel Letona, Meg Leug, Helen Leuschner, Tom Levine, David Levingston, Ron Levis, Boris Levit, Andrea Lewis, Stephen Lewis, G Liardet, Hermes Liberty, Paul Lichstein, R Lightbulb Winders, Mike Lilburn, Ylva Linn Liliegren, Eva-Maria Lill, Julia Lilley, Yvonne Lin, John & Heather Lindberg, Christian Lindquist, Lois Lindsay, Neal lindskoy, Katy Lindstrom, Amanda Ling, Michael Lingnau, Dr Hilde K Link, Heather Linson Lindberg, David Linton, Ian Lints, Corinna Lippe, D Litchfield, Cormal Little, Michael Livni, Jasper Lloyd, Malcolm Lloyd, Peggy & Kenneth Lloyd, Peter Lloyd, Del Llyod, J LM Elsberg, Dr James G Lochtefeld, Brian Locker, Ian Lockley, Bruce Lockyer, Edward Lockyer, Arvind Lodaya, Sophie Logan, Ellen & Jos Lommerse, Judy Loney, Michael Long, Vincent Lonjon, Myrna Looise, Manoela Lopez, Ramon Lopez, Richard Lorand, Colin Loth, Dolly Loth, Maria Lotriet, Kay Louise Cook, Ian Love, Chris Lovell, Marion Lowden, LG Lowe, Monica Lowenberg, Mark A Lucas-Phillips, Fernando & Forsberg Lucena, John Ludwig, E Luiken, Jo & Miche Luinthogen, Jim Lum, Nikita Lundin, Graham Lupp, Dr H Luthe, H Luthe, Raymond & Bodil Luthra, Terry Lynch, Susan Lynn, Roman Lysiah, Aileen A MacEwan, Andrew MacGregor, Rafael Macias-Giobbels, R & H MacIntosh, Selvaggia Macioti, Andrew Mack, John MacKay, Matt Mackay, Melissa MacKenzie, Judi & Colin Mackie, Dr J MacKinnon, Craig Mackintosh, Katie Macks, Dave Macmeekin, Donna MacRae, Adrianne MacWilliam, Emmanuel Madan, Chris Madden, Kathy Madson, Tom Maes, Chilik Magal, Eirik Magne Johansen, Jan Magnusson, Sarah Mahamed, Simone Maier, Larry J Maile, Geavauo Maio, Mirjam Malaika, Akhil Malaki, Elias Malamidis, Nischal Malarao, Zack Malcolmson, Douglas Malein, Aradhna Malik, Chris Malik, Jan Malik, Linda Malloy, Anita Mallya, Stefan Malmgren, Mei-See Man, Delian Manchev, Michelle Mandrekar, Michael Mann, Sarah Mann, Tom Manning, Francis Mansbridge, Yvonne Mansell, Jean Marc Dumont, Morgan Marckwald, Alex Marcovitch, Amy & Dan Marcus, Donna Marcus, Steve Marcus, Donna Marcus Leffel, Merau Marely, Anne Margarethe Sondersen, Dan Margolis, Jody Marie Blaylock, Lisa Marie Gonzales, Anne Marie Ligtenberg, Katrina Marino, Mike Marqusee, Cliff Marriott, Luis Marseleuno,

Anita Marshall, D Marshall, Deborah Marshall Warren, Robin Marston, Vicens Martf, Suteau Martial, Cristofre Martin, David Martin, E Martin, Hager Martin, Lisa Martin, T Martin, Paul & Tracey Martin, Bernado Martin Gomez, Jose Angel Martinez, Luis F Martinez, Isabelle Mas, Yubal Masalker, Vince Mash, Jane Masheder, Jane Mason, A Mast, RJ Mathers, Miguel Angel Diaz Matinez, Thomas Matros, Jan Matthe, Heather Matthews, R & Mr Matthews, Andreas Matthiess, Silke Matussek, Verity Maud, John Maude, Cera Maugey, Veri Mauro, Marjorie Maxwell, Mira Maymon, Clara Mazzi, Rebekah McCray, Neil McAllister, Jim & Lorraine McAndrew, Seema McArdle, Kellie McBride, Howard McCallum, Scott McCallum, Mary McCann, Eoin McCarney, Bernie & Anita McCarthy, Wendy McCarty, Frances McConnell, Mike McConnell, Pauline McConville, C McDermott, David & Jenny McDonald, Ruth McDonald, Anson McDougall, Rachel McEleney, Helen McElroy, Helen & Colette McGeough, Nick McGhee, David McGinniss, Caroline McGovern, Isabel McIntosh, Steve McIntosh, I McIntyre, Kevin McIntyre, Paul McKeagney, Dawn McKecmnie, Steve McKinnon, C McLain, Dana McLaughlin, Andrew McLellan, Liz McMillan, Tom McMillan, E McMurray, Kerry McPherson, Andrew McQuatt, Carolyn McQuire, Annie McStay, Helen Meade, Tony & Marion Meakin, Barbara Mears, Ony Meda, Andreas Medin Mortensen, Nicola Medlik, Linda Medoff, Nils Meester, Rita Meher, Ilka Mehlmann, Ritul Mehta, Rsihad Mehta, Eric Meijer, Sander Meijsen, Marvin & Helen Meistrich, Kristine Meldal, AP Melgrave, Susan Melick, Roberto Meliconi, Maux Meln, Emanuela Mencaglia Martignoni, Celina Mendore, Angelo Mercure, Anna Merimee, J Merino, Jacqueline Merino, Patrick Mertens, Dean van der Merwe, Wolfgang Messner, Jayne Metca, Jayne Metcalf, Dr Adolf Metzger, Etienne Meuleman, Simon Meurfis, Richard Meury, Grace Meyer, Simon Meyer, Solveig Jorgen Meyer, Sarah Michael, Aidan Michael Cunningham, Heather Michaud, Patricia Michaud, Karen Michel, Ivano Michelazzi, Elaine Michelson, Marcel Michiels, David Miclo, Francis Middel, David Middleton, Paul Middleton, Dr Kapil Midha, Rannveig Mietinen, Karen Miiler, Iron Mike, Karsten Mikkelsen, Peter Miletits, Tiffeny Millbourn, Andy Miller, Marc Miller, Phil Miller, Ron Miller, Danna Millett, Claire Millhouse, Katharine Mills, Michael Mills, Alex Milner, Richard Milton, Tom Milward, Ariel Minkman, Michal Miron, Kamal Mishra, Arvind Misra, Darshana Mistry, Anthea Mitchell, Claire Mitchell, Kaye Mitchell, Naomi Mitchell, Paul Mitchell, W Betty Moen, Audrea & Mark Moffat, Vik Moharir, Rugyer Mohn, Lissen Moller, Pascale Monard, Angus Moncur, Chantal Monkman, Lisa Montague, Philip Montanjees, Patina Monti, John Moon, David Moor, Tobias Moor, Adam Moore, Archie L Moore, Damian Moore, Dermot Moore, Gary Moore, Norman C Moore, Simon Moore, Seana Moorhead, Mr Moose, Floripes Moraes, Alex Moraitis, Ralph Morelot, Shawn Moren, Jose Moreno, Willie Moreschi, Jay & Graham Morgan, Martin Morgan, Tracey Morgan, Lawrence & Elliotte Morgan-Persad, Salli Morita, Kate Morley, Greg Morlow, Caroline Mornemont, Rachel Morrell, Dan Morris, Louise Morris, M Morris, Peter Morris, David Morse, Alan Mortimer, Tony Mortlock, Clemens Mosch, B & S Moseley, Doug Moseley, Bruria Moshe, Jennifer Moss, Davide Mosso, Jon Motchell, E Mounier, Dave Mountain, The Mountain Goat, Dr Anuradha Mouree, Suzanne Mrozik, Rita Mueller, Gerit Mueller-Hagen, Prachee mukherjee, Robin Mukherjee, Monica Mukherji, Rianda Mulder, Fabienne Mulders, Susan Mulholland, Yunus Mulla, Manuel Muller, Volker Muller, Uve Mullrich, Suchitra Mumford, Kian Mun, Joss Munro, Casper Munter, Renee Murnain, Joan Murphy, Michael Murphy, P Murphy, Ronald Murphy, W Murphy, Catriona Murray, JF Murray, JR Murray, Rosemary Murton, Dr Shailesh Murty, Francine Mury, Jim Mydosh, Dean Myerson, Jenni Myllynen, Ghulam Nabi Jetha, Muhammad Nadeem, D Naftalin, Alexandra Nagel, Angela Nair, Vinod Nair, Miss V Najran, Kaai Nakajima, Simon Nally, John Nankervis, Aravind Narasipur, Valerie Nash, Paul Nation, Kaveh Navaian, Petr Naxera, K Nazir, R Nazir, Antonin Kodet, Deborah Neal, Maya & Michael Negev, Robert Nelder, Adam Nelson, Saralie Nelson, Stephen Nelson, Claudius Nenninger, Daniela Nessi, C Netzest, John D Neumaier, Ute Neumaier, Adeel Neville, Susan & Paul Newby, Liz Newlands, Judy Newsome, Michelle Newton, Elaine Ng, Danell Nicholson, Pete Nicholson, Trevor Nicklette, Elke & Micheal Nied, Henriette Nielsen, Leif Nielsen, MS Nielsen, Camilla Nillson, Richard Nimmo, Rebekka Ninan, Dr Nitinkumar, Yoav Noam, Herman R Noback, Ellie Noij, Brian Nomi, Gabriella Nonino, Peter Norbury, Dr Andy Nordin, Torbjorn Nordin, Anders Nordstrom, Helen Normand, Jenny Norris, Ola North, Liz & Phil Norton, Tracy Norton, Martin Novak, Yoni Novick, Abe Nugent, Anssi & Voora Nurmi, Ellen Nursall, Massimo Nuvina, Erik Nyhus, Edo Nyland, Sue Oatley, Paul Oberndorfer, Mandeep Oberoi, S O'Brien, Irene O'Brien, Patricia O'-Caroll, JD van Oenen, Bettina Oertel, Maggie Offerhaus, Jim O'Hagan, Liora Oi-Nur, Quinn

Okamoto, Cynthia O'Keefe, Meike Okelmann, Jean-Remy & Gillian Olesen, Lisa Olier, Loretta & Graham Oliphant, Dr Charles Oliver, Elliot Olivestone, MH Olsthoorn, Mirjam Olsthoorn, Carole & Jean Olympio, Perry Omodei Zorini, Gary O'Neil, Daniel Ontell, Stefan Orani, Mirta Oregna, Joseph O'Reilly, Will O'Reilly, Kathleen O'Reily, Andrew Orme, Alexandra Ornston, Don Osborne, Lynn Osborne, Rebecca Osborne, Raymond Ostelo, Gerd Ostreicher, Surush Oswal, Oliver Ott, Mette Ottosen, Christian Overbeck, Eric Oving, Jenny & Chris Owen, Michael Owen Prior, Jenny Oxley, TR Oza, Naama Ozer, Juan Pablo Zuzunaga, Marion Pack, Christabel Padmore, Vece Paes, Sandra Pagano, Bradley Page, John Page, Mrs & Mr Page, Signi Page, Chris Paget, Vincent Pagliaro, Helen Pagliero, Yudi Palkova, Jeremy Pallot, Aline Palloure, Bryony Palmer, C Palmer, Caroline Pande, Alastair & Shona Pandelus, Navinder Pandher, Maninder Pannu, Pier Paolo Martini, Peggy Ann Paoloni, Michael Papantoniou, Benoit Paradis, Cathy Pardoe, Elizabeth Parker, Bryan Parkin, Penelope Parkin, Jo-Ann Parkinson, Kay Parkinson, Dave Parmar, Federico Parodi, Ange Parrish, Malcolm Part, David Pascoe, Jonathon Passmore, Michael Pastroff, Dhruv Patel, Dr Manubhai Patel, S Patel, Helen & Lee Paterson, Claire Patterson, Gary Patterson, Stephen Pattinson, Kate Pattison, Andrew Paull, Al Paulsen Petersen, Emma Pavey, Sharon Peake, Alan Pearce, CH Pearce, David Pearce, Mike Pearce, Sarah Pearce, C & D Pearlman, Dominic Pearson, Chris Peck, Ford Peck, Emily Peckham, Gitte Pedersen, Jannine Pedersen, Josh Pedersen, Lars Pedersen, Chris Peers, Claire Pellit, Renate Pelzl, Alison Pengelly, Alex Pennell, Merritt Pere, Eda Peredes, Janice Pereira, Adi & Nadev Peretz, Yves Perisse, Steve Perlman, Jennifer Perrin, Michael Perring, Sylvain Perron, Ben Perry, Jacqueline Perry, Janine Perry, Tomer Persico, Shawn Persinger, Andrew Pestel, Hans Peter Vetter, Ellie Peters, Jack Petersen, Lana Peth, Jan Petranek, Haavard Petterson, Gail Petticrew, Marie Philip, Andreas Philipp, Charlotte Phillips, Danny Phillips, Emma Phillips, Leland Phillips, Tony Phillips, Swanson Phung, Davide Piazza, Robin Pick, David & Pauline Pickles, Nick Picton, Anne-Marie Piedot, Shirley Pierce, Marele Pietsomis, Rochelle Pilsworth, Martin Pinke, John Pinnington, Carolyn M Pione, Gergio Pisano, Vikki Pitcher, Gregory Placonouns, Brigitte Plank, D Platt, Lynn Plautz, Montse Playa, Lidy van der Ploeg, Martin Plug, Robert Pocknell, Yvonne Poelen, Dr Bauke van der Pol, Stefan Polanyk, Sandra Polderman, Florence Polliand, J Pond, Nigel Pond, Samantha Pooley, Neil Popat, ARA Pope, Rishinoj A Porman, Renee Porte, Claudia Poser, S Posingis, Henry Posner, Volka Posselt, Hans-Joachim Possin, M Potrafke, Adam Potter, Martin Potter, Uta Potthast, Mhairi & Andy Potts, Shalak Powale, Matt Powell, Robert Powell, Susana Powell, Joel and Maria Teresa Prades, Atul Pradhan, Robin Prager, V Prakaasha, Ashwin Prasad, Gaya Prasad, Sanjay Prasad, N Prefontaine, Ian CH Prescott, Daryl Presswell, Andrea & Alan Preston, Dawn Price, Leslie Price, Martin Price, Matthew Price, EE & PJ Priest, Duncan Priestley, Nathan Prince, Pia Problemi, Helen Prosser, Huey Proudhon, Hilary Pugh, Charlotte Pulver, Dheeraj Pun, T & P Purgaric, Christa Purnell, Robert Purser, D Putney, Adi Putra, V & S Puttock, Minna Pyhala, Gareth Pyper, Andrew Quernmore, Floreida Quiaoit, Des & Kim Quilty, Meg Quinn, Tabish Qureshi, Anna R, Carla Rabolini, Michel Racine, Petra Raddatz, Jane & Mike Radford, Kieran Raftery, Rajen Raghavan, S Raghunath, Sohal Raghuvir Singh, Leonid Ragozin, Gurdev Rai, Ash Raichura, Esther Rainbow, Colleen Rains, Georg Raiser, Prakash A Raj, Sriram Rajagopal, Ganeve Rajkotia, Prabhat Raman, Juan Pablo Ramirez-Romero, Prithy Rampersad, Nicola Ramplin, Dr Riju C Ramrakha, Bruce Ramsay, John Rand, Kate Randell, Stuart Randell, Helen Ranger, Michael Ranson, MV Rarhe, Peter Ras, Jaliya Rasaputra, Babette Rasche, Solveg Rasmussen, Jamie Ratcliff, Jacqui Ratcliffe, Francisco Ratto, Joanne Rauscher, Tadeusz Rawa, Taj Rawait, Simon Rawson, M Rayappan, Rachle & Shelley Rayfield, Lior Razon, Della Reader, Paul Reardon, Joy Rebello, Jeff Redding, James Redfern, Janine & Graeme Redfern, Merkurious Redis, JF Reece, Alan Reed, Sue Rees, Anthea & Lynette Reid, David Reid, Douglas Reid, Edward Reilly, Trevor Reilly, Manja Rekhi, Michelle Renbaum, Peter Renee, Michael Rensford, Luke Requa, Kim Restivo, Claudia Reuter, Tony Revel, Michael Reynolds, Gina Rhodes, Simon Rhys Williams, Miriam Ribeiro, Tali Ricci, Heather Richards, Jay Richards, A Richardson, Andrew Richardson, JJC Richardson, Matt Richardson, MJ & A Richardson, Robert Richardson, Sue & David Richardson, Debbie Richards-Perakis, Yann Richet, Oren Ridenour, Barrie Ridout, Roger Ridsdill Smith, Ozarki Rie, Anton Rijsdijk, J Riley, John Riley, Sue Riley, Soren Rindal Nielsen, Laura-Maria Rinta, Catherine Ripou, Claudia Riquelme, Isabella Riva, Rami Rivlin, Alexandra Robak, Damien Robbins, Eric Robbins, Ann Roberts, Ben Roberts, Kailas Roberts, Linda Roberts, Lisa Roberts, Path Roberts, Simon Roberts, Fiona Robertson, John Robertson, Daniel Robinson, David Robinson,

Janet Robinson, Jean Robinson, Jimmy Robinson, Malcolm Robinson, Martin Robinson, JM Robinson, Nathan Robinson, Philip Robinson, Samuel Robinson Massey, Jackie Robson, Stephen Rock, Claudia Rodriguez, David Rodriguez, Griffin Rodriguez, Hector Rodriguez, Eb Roell, Tom Roelofs, Camilla & Soren Roesen, Andreas Rogall, Sonya Rogers, Lee Rogerson, Anne Rogiers, Anthony Romanidis, Robert Rome, Kalus Romer, Simonetta Roncaglia, Neils Ronnest, Yvonne Rooney, Michel & Anne Ropion, H Rose, Michael Rose, R Rose, Marvin Rosen, Stephen Rosenberg, Howard Rosenthal, John Rosley, Richard Rosow, David Ross, Duncan Ross, Sian Rosser, Christian Rosset, Enrico Rossi, Margareta Rossing, Mike Rothbart, Christoff & Marion Rothfuss, Kath & Harry Rothwell, Boaz Rottem, Helen Rouse, Elizabeth Rowe, Terry Rowe, Sanjoy Roy, Josiah Royce, Anja Roza, Yassi & Yifat Rubanenko, Jay Ruchamkin, Amy Rucinski, Dominik Ruckerl, Sue & Don Rudalevige, David Rudder, Emma Ruddock, Peter Ruebsamen, Francoise Ruffie, Marcilio Rufino, Wim Ruhe, Michael Ruland, Daniel Rule, Bruce Rumage, Annika & Goran Rumenius, Goran Rumenius, Susan Rummel, Simon Runnalls, Dell Russell, Lisa Ryan, Malin Rydeu, Andy & Ellyn Ryland, Watanabe Ryoko, Tanja Saarnio, Laura Sabbadin, O Sabbing, Eyal Sadeh, Lawrence Saez, Bijoy Sagar, Bert Sagebaum, Ravi Sahay, Sudhir Sahay, Wil Sahlman, Annamaria Sainaghi, Hiroko Sakamoto, Merja Salo, Sari Salonen, Neil Salt, Nicole Salzer, Katrien San Giorgi, Francis Sanctis, Greg Sandage, Donna Sanders, John Sanders, Mark Sanderson, Anna Sophie T Sandholdt, Adrian Sandhu, Brian Sands, Martin Sands, Frida Sandstrom, Dr B Sanjeev, Mala Sanmugartnam, RV Sansom, Shanker Sanyal, P Saraswat, Brihas Sarathy, Partha Sarathy Sarbadhikary, Dr Indrajit Sardar, Revd John Sargent, Sanjay Sarma, Eugenia Sarsanedas, Gregory Satir, Volker Sauer, Diana Saunders, Josh Saunders, Mark Saunders, Wendy Saunt, Sharma Saurabh, Anne Savage, Anthea Savage, Malcolm Savage, Nicholas Savage, DR Pereira Savid, Rebecca Say, Peter Saynt, Nicola Scatassi, R Schaafsma, Tbias Schade, Dr Walter Schaffer, Monika Scheiber, Bryan Scheideck, Stefan Schell, Stefan & Carmen Schiene, Markus Schilling, Marc Schipperheyn, U&S Schlippert, Becky & Loren Schmidt, Helmut Schmidt, Stevie Schmiedel, Sebastian Schmitz, Juergen Schneider, C Scholes, Eric Scholl, Ralp Schramm, Rosi & Hans Schreck, Rebecca Schroeder, Thomas Schrott, Eeva Schult, Olaf A Schulte, Pieter Schunselaar, C Schussler, Peter Schwarzkopf, Seth Schweitzer, Otto & Helene Schwelb, Greg Schwendinger, Anett Schwidrowski, Dede Schwidt-Pedersen, Anthony Scibberas, AT Scott, Anna Scott, Paul Scott, Rebecca Scott, A Scott Riach, Pam Scott-Hubbard, Antonio Scotti, Wendy Seaky, Lorne Sederoff, Ole See, Michelle Segal, Roland Seher, Seema Seiuastara, Frank Selbmann, E Septier, Deb Serginson, Baily Seshagiri, H Gae Sestero, Derek Severn, Eric Seymour, Jinesh Shah, S Shah, Pravin Shah, Sameer Shah, Yoram Shahak, Hasib Shakoor, Evelyne Shamier, Elizabeth Shanahan, Maria Shaneman, S Shankaran, Bhavani Shanker, Bob Shannahan, Dr Sharik, Hariash Sharma, Neeraj Sharma, Rajiv Sharma, S Sharma, Saurabh Sharma, Frank A Sharman, S Sharp, Andrew Sharpe, Jill Sharpe, Richard Sharpe, Ben Sharvy, S Shata, Amy Shavelson, Jennifer Shaw, Peter & Florence Shaw, Timothy Shaw, C Sheaf, Rajesh Shedde, Ajai Shekawat, Robyn Shelley, Denis Shelton, Rev Fr Baby Shepard, S Shepherd, Rajendra Shepherd, Rebecca Sheppard, Daniel Sher, Michele Sheridan, T Shering, Sham Shermiyas, Nicky Sherriff, Katie Shevlin, Tamar Shilgi, Dan Shingleton, A Short, Michael Shortland, Angie Showering, Donna Shrestha, Ian Shrier, Merav Shrira, Prakash Shukla, Victor Shum, Santanu Panigrahi, Ian Sid Crighton, Itay Sidat, Beth Sidaway, Annabelle Sidhu, Satnam Sidhu, Patrick Siefe, Bryan Siegfried, Esther Siegrist, Christopher Sigmond, Merrick J Silberman, Petr Silhanek, Barbara Siliquimi, Steve Silk, Don Silver, Arianna Silvestri, DR G Silvestro, A Sim, Natalia Simanovsky, Katrin Simanzik, EB Simonis-Warmersdam, Wilfried Simons, Clint Simpson, Jo & Brian Simpson, Peter Simpson, Trevor Simpson, Lynn Simson, Paul Sinclair, Ruth & Daniel Sinclair, AJ Singh, Ajai Singh, Anraj Singh, Davinder Singh, Deepa Singh, Gurcharan Singh, KB Singh, Krishna Singh, Megha Singh, Pushpraj Singh, Ramanpreet Singh, Sukhjit Singh Anand, Randheer Singh Geera, Alok Singhal, Michael Singleton, Debajyoti Sinha, Capt R Sircar, Alan Sirulnikoff, Goran Sjogren, John Skilton, Susan Skyrme, Rosemary Slack, Marco Slaghuis, Rosemary Slark, Michael Slattery, Nathalie van der Slikke, Michel Slinger, Kirsten Slots, Catherine Sluggett, Dylon Smallwood, Jane Smart, John Smart, Phil Smart, Petter Smeby, Barney Smedley, Alice Smith, Allan Smith, Allie & Ian Smith, Angela & John Smith, Cathy Smith, Fiona Smith, Frazer Smith, H Smith, Heather Smith, Helena Smith, J Smith, Jay Smith, L Smith, Lise Smith, Louise Smith, Pamela Smith, Perry EH Smith, Preston Smith, Rob Smith, Shanti Smith, Vanessa Smith Holburn, A Smithee, Wayne Smits, Joanna Snaith, Kaja Snedler, Michael Snell, Douglas Snyder, Alon Sobol, Dr Angela Sodan, Anders Soerensen, Sam Solomon, Peter Somani, Markus Sommer, Adam Sommerhause, Ore Somolu, Nikki Sones, Naveen Soni, Rald Soparkar,

Tal Soreq, Ann Sorrel, James Sorrell, Dirk Spaeth, David Spain, Jorg Spathelf, R Speakman, Jonathon Spear, Nick Spearing, Matthew Spears, Helen Speekley, Derek Speirs, Barbara Spencer, Paul Spencer, Richard Spencer, Stephen Spencer, A Spignesi, Ian Spiller, Graham Spoard, Linda & Tony Spooner, Frank Sporkert, Martin Springer, Stephanie Springgay, Dr RC Squires, Krishnan Sridharan, K Srivatsa, Florian Stadler, Peter H & Heike Stadler, Yvonne Stadler, Marilyn Staib, Jenny Stainbank, Tony Stanford, Thomas Stanke, William Stanley, Michelle Stanton, Julie Stapleton, Tara Star, Katherine Stark, Paul Starkey, K Starr, Lieve Stassen, Jorg Stauch, Gillian Steel, IVD Steel, James Steele, Craig Stehn, Jan Steibert, Ursula Steiger, Christian Steinmetz, Derek Stephen, Vanessa Stephen, Nichola Stephenson, Kendra & Simon Stepputat, Darlene & Greg Stevens, Jane Stevens, John Stevens, Michael Stevenson, Fiona Stewart, Jules Stewart, Jan Stiebert, Antje Stiebitz, Joanna Still, Willemke Stilma, Catherine Stock, Richard Stocker, James Stoddart, Franka Stoepler, Mirjam Stolwyk, Brian Stone, Cynthia Stone, Greg Stone, Cato Stonex, Emman Stott, M Stout, Raf Stout, Mark & Sue Strangeways, Leon Strauss, Domenik Strebel, Sue & Michael Streuli, Pamela Strivens, Debbie Strout, Sabrina Stryker, Gay Stuart, Julie Stuart-Smith, Dieter Stuckenberg, Brian Studd, Leticia Subira, KV Sudhakaran, Sam Suffit, Simona Sugoni, Ajit Sukhija, Nancy Sundberg, Eva Sunquist, Ritish Suri, Dany Surralles, Pete & Beth Sutch, Adam Sutcliffe, R Berge Svendsen, Robert Svoboda, Liam Swaffield, David Swait, D Swait, Peggy Swan, Jon Swannell, Brian Swanson, Rebecca Swanson, Royston Swarbrooke, Shirley Sweet, Barry & Wanda Syner, Risa Tabatznik, Anita Taheer, Alex Tait, Godfrey Talbot, Jack Talman, Ariel Talmor, Bacci Tamara, Yael Tamir, Alvin Tan, Kim Tan, Veronica Tani, Richard Tanner, Carole Tapp, Sarah Tarkenton, Zolton Tarodi, Tsegyal Tashi, David Taussig, David Tayar, Barb Taylor, Bronwyn Taylor, Chris Taylor, Crazy Dave Taylor, Hannah Taylor, James Taylor, Jeff Taylor, Lisa Taylor, Lorraine Taylor, Tansy Tazewell, Louise Teague, Mcdpower Nepal Team, AR Tebl, Amy Tees, Ronna Temkin, Jo Templey, Alexandra Terhorst, Beverly Terry, Dr James Terry, Folco Terzani, Frank Tesoriero, C Thacker, K Thavakumar, Claudia Theile, Gwendolyn Theresa Junod, Susan Theron, Aaron Thieme, Joanne Thirlwall, Dick Thoenes, Linda Thoerner, Bob Thomas, Mary & David Thomas, Sabina Thomas, Sarah Thomas, Eileen Thompson, Martin Thompson, Neil Thompson, Ted Thompson, Ashley Thomsen, Richard Thomson, D Thornber, J Thorne, Marg Thornell, Jessica Thornelor, Rick Thorngate, Jason Thornton, Sallie-Ann Thorp, A Throp, Premila Thurairatnam, David Thurlow, Elisabeth Thurn, Herby Thurn, Rob Thwaites, Kokeny Tibor, Maria Tiguerola, Clark Toes, Leon Toland, Celeste Tomkins, Stephen Tong, Linda Tony, Jan Toohey, Georgina Topp, Nana Torii, Stephanie Torrington, Suzanne Tourvillle, Christine Townend, Milton Townson, Ursula Trachsel, Luca Tramontin, Eliezer Traub, Noam Traub, Michael Travers, Stephen Travers, Jim Travis, Patrick Traynor, Sarah Treaddell, Tali Treibitz, Jean-Francois Tremblay, Duncan Trew, Frances Trim, Manu Trivedi, Allan Trojan, Rosanne Trottier, John & Telita Trower, Connie Tsang, Tatyana Tsinberg, Inbul Tubi, Ross Tucker, Stella M Tuft, Colin Tull, Wayne Tunnicliffe, Concetta Tuori, Tzuk Turbovich, Michael Turinski, Lindsay Turnball, Trish Turnbull, Bob & Ethel Turner, Jim Turner, Liz & Dick Turner, Daniel Tuslain, Jorge Tutor, Pauline Twigg, N Twomey, Chris Tyler, Justin Tynan, Gill Tyson, Peter Udsen, K Ujavari, Susanne Ulrich, BL Underwood, Christoper Univ, Sandra Unterweger, Grant Upson, Amy Urban, J Uzzeli, MS Vadiraja, Nick Vagg, Denis Vaillancourt, Jonathan Valdes, Pascal Valenduc, Cor & Jenny Valk, Saskia van der Valk, Sergi Valle Kattendahl, Hanneke Van Adrichem, Frans van Assendelft, Reni & Nadine van Brandenburg, Ton van Brienen, D Van Cappellen, Coony Van De Camp, Elly van den Brand, G van der Aa, Hennie van der Male, Jaap van Donkelaar, Maarten van Egmond, Wilna van Eyssen, Rene van Gent, Sietsche van Gunst, Jackie van Hal, Karel Van Hilst, Frank van Hulsentop, Pushpa Van Laeren, Ingrid van Loon, Leo van Riemsdyke, Pauline van Swaal, Jules Van Thieler, Anton van Veen, Mona Van Velson, Trudy van Wel, R Van Zeelst, Iris Vandemoortele, Chris Vanderoye, Sara Vanderstappen, Zinne Vandevelde, Francis Vanlangendonck, Marc Vannoverbeke, Tyrone Vargas, Rita Varghese Hicks, Ray VarnBuhler, Gwynneth Varner, Petr Vastl, Girish Vasudevan, Jerry van Veenendaal, Patrick & Regine Veldeman, Donald V Velsen, Mike Venamore, S Vengadesh, Gert Venghaus, Suvir Ventataraman, Paul Venturino, Eveline Vermeersch, Bart Vermeiren, Els & Andy Vermeulen, Stefan Vermuelen, Gil Vernik, Monique Verschuren, Sanderien Verstappen, Bart Versteijnen, Koen Vervacke, Daniel Vetter, Isabel Vietta, Rajneesh Vig, Klaus Viggers, M Vijaya, EK Vijayakumar, Jonathan Vince, A Vincent, David Vinkers, R Vinod, Narayan Vinodh, Arif Virani, Ann Virgin, Kewal Virk, Frank Visakay, Hans Visser, Mauro Vitale, Krishna Vittaldev, Carol A Vitty, Josephine Vliegen, Andreas Voigt, Arne Voigt, Marie & Paul Volkoff-Peschon, Fabian Von Beesten, Axel von Jentzkowski, Deborah von Kanel, Bob von Liski,

Jan & Leone Vorster, Claartje Vorstman, David Voss, Marloes Vrolijk, Yonathon Wachsmann, RC Wadkar, Joost Wagenar, Dirk Wagener, Christian Wagner, Aron Wahl, Frank Wahner, Ali Wale, Chris Walker, Fiona Walker, Nic Walker, Dean Wall, Sarah Wall, Miki Walleczek, Max Wallenberg, Carrie Waller, Brian Wallis, Courtney Walsh, Paul Walsh, Raymond Walsh, Birgit Walter, Maureen Walters, Megan Waltham, Gundula Walther, Mark Walton, Rik & Sally Walton, Bernd Wanderl, Sue Wang, JD Ward, Phillippa Ward, Simon Ward, Richard Wareham, Satish Warier, Dr Andrew Warmington, Andrew Warsap, Piotr Wasil, Duncan Watson, James Watson, Warren & Jan Watson, Zak Watson, Aaron Watt, Mark Watt, Jane Wayne, Paul Weaver, Cindy S Webb, Jill Webb, Lawrence Webb, Duncan Webster, Robert Webster, S Wedren, Tanya Wegner, Dr Peter Wehmeier, Werner Weick, Anne Weiler, Manuel Weiss, Mart Weiss, Vicki Weiss, Peter Weisshaupt, Patrick Wellaert, Des Wells, Juliet Wells, RE Wels, J Wemyss, David Wendland, Mark A Westgate, Carolyn Wetherby, Philippa Whalley, Philip Wharmby, Andrea Wheatley, Jonathan Wheatley, Natalie Wheatley, David Wheeler, E Wheeler, June Wheeler, Lisa Wheeler, Paul Whitby, Adeline White, Barry White, Kate White, Kathleen White, Laura White, Murdo White, Tony White, Claire Whitefield, David Whitehead, Yvonne Whiteman, Kerry Whitfield, M Whitfrew, Sharon Whitwham, Anthony Widdup, Glen Widing, Andrew Wigglesworth, Jackie Wigh, Stuart Wilber, Emma Wilde, Manfred Wilde, Mary Wilde, Susanne Wildi, Peter Wiles, Nicholas Wilkins, Pete Wilkins, Maria Wilkinson, Larissa Will, Helmi Willems, Pierre Willems, V Willems, A Williams, Amanda Williams, Anne Williams, Deborah Williams, G Williams, Ines Williams, Kathy Williams, Sandra Williams, Sarah Williams, Sylvia Williamson, David Willis, Russell Willmoth, Michelle Wilse, Anne Wilshin, Joy Wilson, Margaret Wilson, P Wilson, Stuart Wilson, Stuart C Wilson, Tim Wilson, Chritopher & Tanda Wilson-Clarke, Babs & Shane Wiltshire, Charles Windsor, Simon Winfried, Phil Wingfield, George Winiarski, Catherine Winter, Matthew B Winters, Lisa Winton, Pamela Winton, Cameron Wiseman, Joanna Wiseman, Jean-Philippe Wispelaere, Giles Witittarid, Marion & Chris Witt, Dr Ludwig Witzani, J & C Woesthuis, Kokoszka Wojciech, Christinsa & Monica Wojtaszewski, Meera Wolfe, Jeroen Wolfsen, Caroline Wols, Andy Wolton, Becki Wood, D Wood, Stella Wood, Stephen Wood, Kevin Woodcock, Chris Woodhouse, O Woodhouse, Wyn Woods, Simon Woolrych, Adrian Woolven, Julian Woonton, Stephen Wragg, Barrie Wraith, Becky Wright, David Wright, Dominic Wright, Lindsay Wright, Rcihard Wright, S Wright, Erik Wsppling, Mira Wuhr, Emanuel Wuthrich, Sandi Wy Lai, Sara Wyborn, Dick Wyckmans, Heidi & Andreas Wyder, M Wyszymska, Mark Yabsley, Keiji Yamaguchi, Renata Yang, Rebecca Yates, Melissa Yee, Elad Yom-Tov, A & S Yorkhire, David Youna, Alara Young, Megan Young, Sandy Young, Lynn Youngbar, Dave & Anna Youngs, Gill & John Yudkin, Takebayashi Yuri, Andreina Zagari, Faraz Zaidi, Krzysztof Zaleski, Justin Zaman, Alje Zandt, Esther Zaragoza, Jane Zaring, Tom Zarzecki, Kevin Zelko, M Zilberstain, Wolfgang Zilm, Bernard Zimmerman, David Ziringer, Mor Zohar, Marc U Zon, EMS PW Zuidgeest, Bostjan Zupancic, Norberto Zurita, Arno Zuudwuk, Elizabeth Zvonar

LONELY PLANET

You already know that Lonely Planet produces more than this one guidebook, but you might not be aware of the other products we have on this region. Here is a selection of titles that you may want to check out as well:

Indian Himalaya
ISBN 0 86442 688 7

Rajasthan
ISBN 0 86442 743 3

Healthy Travel Asia & India
ISBN 1 86450 051 4

North India
ISBN 1 86450 330 0

South India
ISBN 1 86450 161 8

Hindi & Urdu phrasebook
ISBN 0 86442 425 6

Trekking in the Indian Himalaya
ISBN 0 86442 357 8

Goa
ISBN 0 86442 681 X

World Food India
ISBN 1 86450 328 9

Istanbul to Kathmandu
ISBN 1 86450 214 2

Read this First: Asia & India
ISBN 1 86450 049 2

Delhi
ISBN 0 86442 675 5

Kerala
ISBN 0 86442 696 8

Mumbai (Bombay)
ISBN 0 86442 702 6

Sacred India
ISBN 1 86450 063 8

Available wherever books are sold

Guides by Region

Lonely Planet is known worldwide for publishing practical, reliable and no-nonsense travel information in our guides and on our Web site. The Lonely Planet list covers just about every accessible part of the world. Currently there are 16 series: Travel guides, Shoestring guides, Condensed guides, Phrasebooks, Read This First, Healthy Travel, Walking guides, Cycling guides, Watching Wildlife guides, Pisces Diving & Snorkeling guides, City Maps, Road Atlases, Out to Eat, World Food, Journeys travel literature and Pictorials.

AFRICA Africa on a shoestring • Cairo • Cairo City Map • Cape Town • Cape Town City Map • East Africa • Egypt • Egyptian Arabic phrasebook • Ethiopia, Eritrea & Djibouti • Ethiopian Amharic phrasebook • The Gambia & Senegal • Healthy Travel Africa • Kenya • Malawi • Morocco • Moroccan Arabic phrasebook • Mozambique • Read This First: Africa • South Africa, Lesotho & Swaziland • Southern Africa • Southern Africa Road Atlas • Swahili phrasebook • Tanzania, Zanzibar & Pemba • Trekking in East Africa • Tunisia • Watching Wildlife East Africa • Watching Wildlife Southern Africa • West Africa • World Food Morocco • Zimbabwe, Botswana & Namibia
Travel Literature: Mali Blues: Traveling to an African Beat • The Rainbird: A Central African Journey • Songs to an African Sunset: A Zimbabwean Story

AUSTRALIA & THE PACIFIC Auckland • Australia • Australian phrasebook • Australia Road Atlas • Cycling Australia • Cycling New Zealand • Fiji • Fijian phrasebook • Healthy Travel Australia, NZ & the Pacific • Islands of Australia's Great Barrier Reef • Melbourne • Melbourne City Map • Micronesia • New Caledonia • New South Wales • New Zealand • Northern Territory • Outback Australia • Out to Eat – Melbourne • Out to Eat – Sydney • Papua New Guinea • Pidgin phrasebook • Queensland • Rarotonga & the Cook Islands • Samoa • Solomon Islands • South Australia • South Pacific • South Pacific phrasebook • Sydney • Sydney City Map • Sydney Condensed • Tahiti & French Polynesia • Tasmania • Tonga • Tramping in New Zealand • Vanuatu • Victoria • Walking in Australia • Watching Wildlife Australia • Western Australia
Travel Literature: Islands in the Clouds: Travels in the Highlands of New Guinea • Kiwi Tracks: A New Zealand Journey • Sean & David's Long Drive

CENTRAL AMERICA & THE CARIBBEAN Bahamas, Turks & Caicos • Baja California • Belize, Guatemala & Yucatán • Bermuda • Central America on a shoestring • Costa Rica • Costa Rica Spanish phrasebook • Cuba • Dominican Republic & Haiti • Eastern Caribbean • Guatemala • Havana • Healthy Travel Central & South America • Jamaica • Mexico • Mexico City • Panama • Puerto Rico • Read This First: Central & South America • World Food Mexico • Yucatán
Travel Literature: Green Dreams: Travels in Central America

EUROPE Amsterdam • Amsterdam City Map • Amsterdam Condensed • Andalucía • Austria • Baltic States phrasebook • Barcelona • Barcelona City Map • Belgium & Luxembourg • Berlin • Berlin City Map • Britain • British phrasebook • Brussels, Bruges & Antwerp • Brussels City Map • Budapest • Budapest City Map • Canary Islands • Central Europe • Central Europe phrasebook • Copenhagen • Corfu & the Ionians • Corsica • Crete • Crete Condensed • Croatia • Cycling Britain • Cycling France • Cyprus • Czech & Slovak Republics • Denmark • Dublin • Dublin City Map • Eastern Europe • Eastern Europe phrasebook • Edinburgh • England • Estonia, Latvia & Lithuania • Europe on a shoestring • Europe phrasebook • Finland • Florence • France • Frankfurt Condensed • French phrasebook • Georgia, Armenia & Azerbaijan • Germany • German phrasebook • Greece • Greek Islands • Greek phrasebook • Hungary • Iceland, Greenland & the Faroe Islands • Ireland • Italian phrasebook • Italy • Krakow • Lisbon • The Loire • London • London City Map • London Condensed • Madrid • Malta • Mediterranean Europe • Mediterranean Europe phrasebook • Moscow • Munich • Netherlands • Normandy • Norway • Out to Eat – London • Out to Eat – Paris • Paris • Paris City Map • Paris Condensed • Poland • Polish phrasebook • Portugal • Portuguese phrasebook • Prague • Prague City Map • Provence & the Côte d'Azur • Read This First: Europe • Rhodes & the Dodecanese • Romania & Moldova • Rome • Rome City Map • Russia, Ukraine & Belarus • Russian phrasebook • Scandinavian & Baltic Europe • Scandinavian phrasebook • Scotland • Sicily • Slovenia • South-West France • Spain • Spanish phrasebook • St Petersburg • St Petersburg City Map • Sweden • Switzerland • Tuscany • Ukrainian phrasebook • Venice • Vienna • Walking in Britain • Walking in France • Walking in Ireland • Walking in Italy • Walking in Spain • Walking in Switzerland • Western Europe • World Food France • World Food Ireland • World Food Italy • World Food Spain
Travel Literature: After Yugoslavia • Love and War in the Apennines • The Olive Grove: Travels in Greece • On the Shores of the Mediterranean • Round Ireland in Low Gear • A Small Place in Italy

LONELY PLANET

Mail Order

Lonely Planet products are distributed worldwide. They are also available by mail order from Lonely Planet, so if you have difficulty finding a title please write to us. North and South American residents should write to 150 Linden St, Oakland, CA 94607, USA; European and African residents should write to 10a Spring Place, London NW5 3BH, UK; and residents of other countries to Locked Bag 1, Footscray, Victoria 3011, Australia.

INDIAN SUBCONTINENT & THE INDIAN OCEAN Bangladesh • Bengali phrasebook • Bhutan • Delhi • Goa • Healthy Travel Asia & India • Hindi & Urdu phrasebook • India • Indian Himalaya • Karakoram Highway • Kerala • Madagascar • Maldives • Mauritius, Réunion & Seychelles • Mumbai (Bombay) • Nepal • Nepali phrasebook • Pakistan • Rajasthan • Read This First: Asia & India • South India • Sri Lanka • Sri Lanka phrasebook • Tibet • Tibetan phrasebook • Trekking in the Indian Himalaya • Trekking in the Karakoram & Hindukush • Trekking in the Nepal Himalaya
Travel Literature: The Age of Kali: Indian Travels and Encounters • Hello Goodnight: A Life of Goa • In Rajasthan • Maverick in Madagascar • A Season in Heaven: True Tales from the Road to Kathmandu • Shopping for Buddhas • A Short Walk in the Hindu Kush • Slowly Down the Ganges

MIDDLE EAST & CENTRAL ASIA Bahrain, Kuwait & Qatar • Central Asia • Central Asia phrasebook • Dubai • Farsi (Persian) phrasebook • Hebrew phrasebook • Iran • Israel & the Palestinian Territories • Istanbul • Istanbul City Map • Istanbul to Cairo • Istanbul to Kathmandu • Jerusalem • Jerusalem City Map • Jordan • Lebanon • Middle East • Oman & the United Arab Emirates • Syria • Turkey • Turkish phrasebook • World Food Turkey • Yemen
Travel Literature: Black on Black: Iran Revisited • The Gates of Damascus • Kingdom of the Film Stars: Journey into Jordan

NORTH AMERICA Alaska • Boston • Boston City Map • Boston Condensed • British Columbia • California & Nevada • California Condensed • Canada • Chicago • Chicago City Map • Florida • Great Lakes • Hawaii • Hiking in Alaska • Hiking in the USA • Las Vegas • Los Angeles • Los Angeles City Map • Louisiana & the Deep South • Miami • Miami City Map • Montreal • New England • New Orleans • New York City • New York City City Map • New York City Condensed • New York, New Jersey & Pennsylvania • Oahu • Out to Eat – San Francisco • Pacific Northwest • Rocky Mountains • San Francisco • San Francisco City Map • Seattle • Southwest • Texas • Toronto • USA • USA phrasebook • Vancouver • Virginia & the Capital Region • Washington, DC • Washington, DC City Map • World Food New Orleans
Travel Literature: Caught Inside: A Surfer's Year on the California Coast • Drive Thru America

NORTH-EAST ASIA Beijing • Beijing City Map • Cantonese phrasebook • China • Hiking in Japan • Hong Kong • Hong Kong City Map • Hong Kong Condensed • Hong Kong, Macau & Guangzhou • Japan • Japanese phrasebook • Korea • Korean phrasebook • Kyoto • Mandarin phrasebook • Mongolia • Mongolian phrasebook • Seoul • Shanghai • South-West China • Taiwan • Tokyo • World Food Hong Kong
Travel Literature: In Xanadu: A Quest • Lost Japan

SOUTH AMERICA Argentina, Uruguay & Paraguay • Bolivia • Brazil • Brazilian phrasebook • Buenos Aires • Chile & Easter Island • Colombia • Ecuador & the Galapagos Islands • Healthy Travel Central & South America • Latin American Spanish phrasebook • Peru • Quechua phrasebook • Read This First: Central & South America • Rio de Janeiro • Rio de Janeiro City Map • Santiago de Chile • South America on a shoestring • Trekking in the Patagonian Andes • Venezuela
Travel Literature: Full Circle: A South American Journey

SOUTH-EAST ASIA Bali & Lombok • Bangkok • Bangkok City Map • Burmese phrasebook • Cambodia • Hanoi • Healthy Travel Asia & India • Hill Tribes phrasebook • Ho Chi Minh City • Indonesia • Indonesian phrasebook • Indonesia's Eastern Islands • Java • Lao phrasebook • Laos • Malay phrasebook • Malaysia, Singapore & Brunei • Myanmar (Burma) • Philippines • Pilipino (Tagalog) phrasebook • Read This First: Asia & India • Singapore • Singapore City Map • South-East Asia on a shoestring • South-East Asia phrasebook • Thailand • Thailand's Islands & Beaches • Thailand, Vietnam, Laos & Cambodia Road Atlas • Thai phrasebook • Vietnam • Vietnamese phrasebook • World Food Thailand • World Food Vietnam

ALSO AVAILABLE: Antarctica • The Arctic • The Blue Man: Tales of Travel, Love and Coffee • Brief Encounters: Stories of Love, Sex & Travel • Chasing Rickshaws • The Last Grain Race • Lonely Planet ... On the Edge: Adventurous Escapades from Around the World • Lonely Planet Unpacked • Not the Only Planet: Science Fiction Travel Stories • Sacred India • Travel Photography: A Guide to Taking Better Pictures • Travel with Children

Index

Abbreviations

A&C – Arts & Crafts
A&N – Andaman & Nicobar Islands
AP – Andhra Pradesh
B&J – Bihar & Jharkhand
Che – Chennai (Madras)
Del – Delhi
HP – Himachal Pradesh
J&K – Jammu & Kashmir
Kar – Karnataka
Ker – Kerala
Kol – Kolkata (Calcutta)
L&Z – Ladakh & Zanskar
MP&C – Madhya Pradesh & Chhatisgarh
Mah – Maharashtra
Mum – Mumbai (Bombay)
NER – North-Eastern Region
NP – National Park
Ori – Orissa
P&H – Punjab & Haryana
Raj – Rajasthan
Sik – Sikkim
TN – Tamil Nadu
UP&U – Uttar Pradesh & Uttaranchal
WB – West Bengal
WS – Wildlife Sanctuary

Text

Bold indicates maps.

C

Bold indicates maps.

L

M

Bold indicates maps.

N

O

P

Bold indicates maps.

Q

R

Bold indicates maps.

Boxed Text

Bold indicates maps.

MAP LEGEND

CITY ROUTES

Freeway — Freeway
Highway — Primary Road
Road — Secondary Road
Street — Street
Lane — Lane
Roadblocks
Unsealed Road
One-Way Street
Pedestrian Street
Stepped Street
Tunnel
Footbridge

REGIONAL ROUTES

Tollway, Freeway
Primary Road
Secondary Road
Minor Road

BOUNDARIES

International
State
Disputed
Fortified Wall

HYDROGRAPHY

River, Creek
Canal
Lake, Tank
Dry Lake, Salt Lake
Spring, Rapids
Waterfalls

TRANSPORT ROUTES & STATIONS

Train
Metro
Tramway
Bus Route
Monorail
Cable Car, Chairlift
Ferry
Path in Park
Walking Trail
Walking Tour

AREA FEATURES

Building
Park, Garden
National Park
Market
Beach
Campus
Cemetery
Urban

MAP SYMBOLS

CAPITAL — National Capital
CAPITAL — State Capital
City — City, Large Town
Town — Town
Village — Village
Place to Stay
Place to Eat
Point of Interest
Airfield, Airport
Bank
Bird Sanctuary
Border Crossing
Buddhist Temple
Bus Terminal, Stop
Camping Ground
Cathedral, Church
Cave
Cinema
Embassy, Consulate
Festival
Fountain
Gate
Ghat
Golf Course
Gompa
Hindu Temple
Hospital
Internet Cafe
Jain Temple
Lookout
Monument
Mosque
Mountain, Hill
Mountain Range
Museum, Gallery
Parking Area
Pass
Petrol/Gas Station
Police Station
Post Office
Pub, Bar
Ruins
Shopping Centre
Sikh Temple
Stately Home, Haveli
Stupa
Swimming Pool
Taxi
Transport (General)
Telephone
Temple
Theatre
Toilet
Tomb
Tourist Information
Zoo

Note: not all symbols displayed above appear in this book

LONELY PLANET OFFICES

Australia
Locked Bag 1, Footscray, Victoria 3011
☎ 03 8379 8000 fax 03 8379 8111
email: talk2us@lonelyplanet.com.au

USA
150 Linden St, Oakland, CA 94607
☎ 510 893 8555 TOLL FREE: 800 275 8555
fax 510 893 8572
email: info@lonelyplanet.com

UK
10a Spring Place, London NW5 3BH
☎ 020 7428 4800 fax 020 7428 4828
email: go@lonelyplanet.co.uk

France
1 rue du Dahomey, 75011 Paris
☎ 01 55 25 33 00 fax 01 55 25 33 01
email: bip@lonelyplanet.fr
www.lonelyplanet.fr

World Wide Web: www.lonelyplanet.com *or* AOL keyword: lp
Lonely Planet Images: lpi@lonelyplanet.com.au

India at a Glance

RICHARD I'ANSON

KAREN TRIST

Heroes and demons, saints and saviours, ascetics and seekers – India, despite being a secular state, is one of the world's richest sites of spiritual and religious heritage.

In one form or another, the mystical and the spiritual underpin the lives of Indians. Hinduism **(right)**, which is practised by approximately 82% of the population, often appears to outsiders as a complex mix of beliefs and deities.

Jainism was founded around 500 BC but most temples, such as the Digambara Temple **(top left)**, date from between AD 1000–1300.

Christianity is said to have arrived in South India with the apostle St Thomas in AD 52. India has about 19 million Christians, around three-quarters of whom are South Indian. Christian art, such as the beautiful mosaics in St Paul's Cathedral, Kolkata **(bottom)**, is highly decorative.

RICHARD I'ANSON

BILL WASSMAN

RICHARD I'ANSON

The four most holy places associated with Buddha are Lumbini (in Nepal), where he was born; Bodhgaya, where he attained enlightenment; Sarnath, where he first preached his message; and Kushinagar **(top)**, where he died.

Islam was introduced to northern India by invading armies and to the south by Arab traders. Today more than 12% of India's population is Muslim. Ideally, every Muslim should pray five times a day **(left)**.

There are some 18 million Sikhs in India, and most come from Punjab, where the Sikh religion was founded by Guru Nanak in the late 15th century. The most sacred of Sikh temples is the Hari Mandir (Golden Temple) in Amritsar, Punjab, to which many pilgrims travel **(bottom)**.

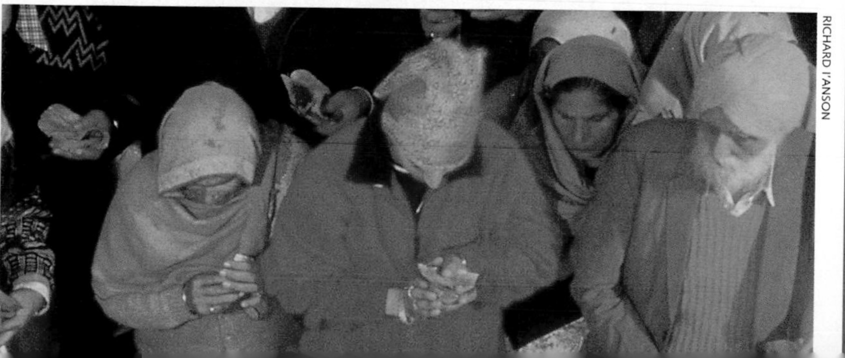
RICHARD I'ANSON

RICHARD I'ANSON

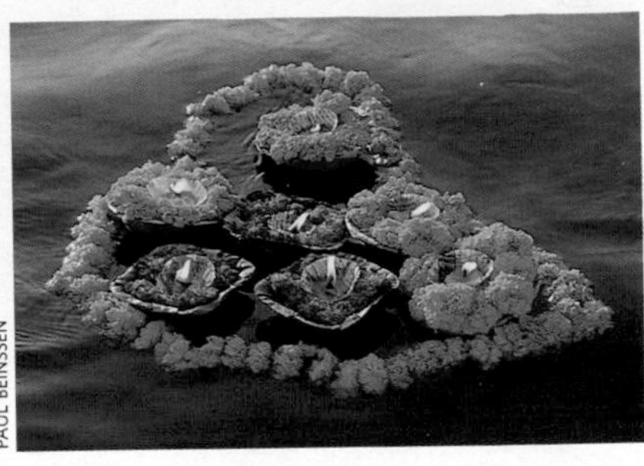
PAUL BEINSSEN

Of immense religious significance to Hindus is the holy Ganges, the repository for religious offerings both metaphorical and physical. Saffron-coloured marigolds float on the waters of the sacred Ganges **(top)**. The Kumbh Mela, held at the confluence of the Ganges and the Yamuna Rivers in Allahabad every 12 years **(left & title page)**, attracts many millions of pilgrims who come to take a holy dip. Dasawamedh Ghat fills to overflowing as devotees come to bathe and pray in Varanasi, Uttar Pradesh **(bottom)**.

RICHARD I'ANSON

HANNAH LEVY

Wherever you travel in India, from Himalayan gompas to the beaches of Goa, you're likely to encounter some kind of festival or celebration. Usually linked to religion, festivals often involve elaborate, colourful and riotous elements. They can be a time for jubilation, as shown in the main street of Orchha in Madhya Pradesh **(top)**; in the coloured water thrown with abandon to celebrate the end of winter during Holi **(right)**; and in the stick twirling of the Navaratri Festival in Gujarat **(bottom)**.

MICHELLE COXALL

PAUL BEINSSEN

JOHN MOCK

Despite India's many large cities, the nation is still overwhelmingly rural, with about three-quarters of the people living in the countryside. Poverty remains widespread and life can be difficult, especially for women, but times are changing. Inroads into male-dominated professions are being made and organisations such as the Self-Employed Women's Association (SEWA) in Gujarat offer hope and help through union membership. A young village girl watches intently **(top)** while a worker **(bottom)** sorts through produce from the turmeric harvest in Mattancherry, Kerala.

MARTIN HUGHES

CHRISTINE OSBORNE

MARK NEWMAN

CHRISTINE OSBORNE

Fishing has long been a traditional industry taking place in rivers, waterways and along India's coastline, such as here at Palolem Beach, Goa **(top)**. Agriculture employs over half of India's workforce and is highly protected and subsidised. A 'toddy tapper' **(bottom right)** collects palm sap from which a coconut wine is produced through fermentation. In rural India, many manual chores, such as collecting water, are carried out by women, who are also expected to keep house and raise the children **(bottom left)**.

CHRIS MELLOR

Commanding structures from an earlier imperial age are visible reminders of India's colonial past. One such structure is India Gate **(top)**, the 42m-high arch of triumph at the eastern end of Rajpath, Delhi. Officially known as the All India War Memorial, it bears the names of 85,000 Indian Army soldiers who died in the campaigns of WWI. The palatial Victoria Terminus **(bottom)** in Mumbai, completed in 1887 and now renamed Chhatrapati Shivaji Terminus or CST (in honour of the Maharashtrian hero), is a notable example of High Victorian architecture.

DAVID COLLINS

RICHARD I'ANSON

RICHARD I'ANSON

PAUL BEINSSEN

India's mind-boggling diversity leaves a lasting impression. With a heady mix of the sacred, materialistic and profane, the country is as vast as it is crowded, and as luxurious as it is squalid. Vendors compete for space at a Kolkata bazaar **(top)**; a cow wanders the busy streets of Old Delhi **(middle)**; and Bollywood blockbusters offer temporary escape from the rigours of daily life **(bottom)**.

CHRIS MELLOR

DAVID TIPLING

CHRIS MELLOR

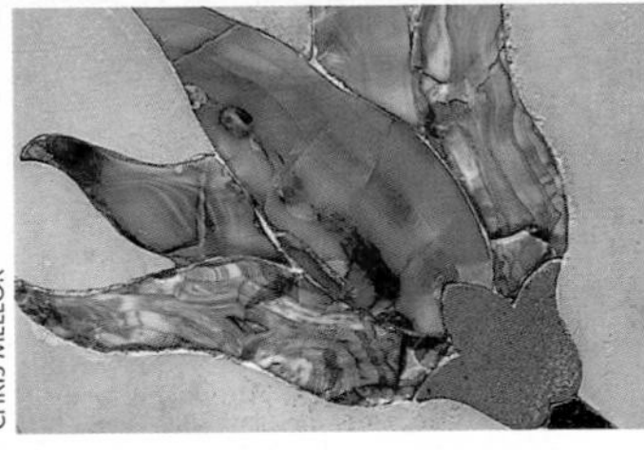

The Taj Mahal **(this page)** has been described as the most extravagant monument ever built in the name of love. Begun in 1631 on the death of Shah Jahan's second wife, Mumtaz Mahal, it was completed over 20 years later. The Taj is definitely worth more than a single visit as its appearance changes with the day's shifting light. Dawn is an especially magical time. The building is magnificent from a distance when reflected in the water-course, and is exquisite close up when the delicate marble inlay work, high-lighting flower themes and known as *pietra dura*, becomes apparent.

Shah Jahan (1627–58), the fifth of India's six great Mughal leaders, left an enduring mark on India's architecture. As well as the Taj Mahal, he created Old Delhi's Red Fort, which was completed in 1648. The fort's evocative red sandstone walls and mighty gates are a particularly impressive sight; these days the area outside the main gate **(top)** is constantly buzzing with tourists and hawkers. Completed in 1658, the Jama Masjid was another of Shah Jahan's great achievements. The largest mosque in India – the courtyard can hold 25,000 people – it has striking gateways **(bottom right)** and graceful domes **(middle left)**.

ALL PHOTOGRAPHS BY RICHARD I'ANSON

MARK KIRBY

TROY FLOWER

EDDIE GERALD

The Kandariya Mahadev **(facing page, top)** is the largest and most architecturally and artistically perfect of the temples of Khajuraho. Built by the Chandelas during their 100-year burst of artistic genius from 950 to 1050, the temples are famous for their erotic embellishments **(facing page, bottom)**.

Over the centuries, many empires have left their artistic mark on India; in the 7th century the Pallavas created the sublime Shore Temple at Tamil Nadu's Mamallapuram **(this page, top)**; the 9th century saw the creation of the Chaukhama Temple and Hindola Gate at Madhya Pradesh's Gyaraspur **(this page, middle)**; and in the 16th century the Vijayanagars built the Vittala Temple at Vijayanagar **(this page, bottom)**.

VIKRAMAJIT RAM

MARK DAFFEY

RICHARD I'ANSON

GARRY WEARE

Sages and mystics have travelled to India's north throughout the ages to draw inspiration from its soaring snow-clad peaks, deep valleys and life-giving rivers. Lamayuru Gompa in Ladakh **(top)**, perched atop an eroded crag, takes full advantage of its dramatic location. The Pin Parvati Pass **(bottom)** links the Kullu Valley and Spiti in Himachal Pradesh – at least for those few months of the year when it is not hidden beneath snow.

MARK HONAN

DENNIS JONES

Blessed with one of the world's richest natural heritages, India is the home to an extraordinary range of wildlife, including the colourful painted storks in Bhavnagar, Gujarat **(top)** and wild camels in rural Rajasthan **(middle)**. However, India's wildlife is struggling for its existence as the great forests are increasingly cleared for crops such as tea. Nepalese workers tend Darjeeling's Marybong Tea Gardens **(bottom)**.

MARTIN HUGHES

The tropical languor of South India is evident on the beaches of Goa and Kerala. Along Goa's 105km of coast, traditional fishing boats line the shore **(middle)** and sleepy villages nestle behind its dunes. Kerala, too, has many beautiful beaches, of which Kovalam and Varkala **(bottom)** are especially popular.

JOHN PENNOCK

ANDREW MARSHALL & LEANNE WALKER

PAUL BEINSSEN